WHO WAS WHO IN THE
CIVIL WAR

WHO WAS WHO IN THE CIVIL WAR

by

Stewart Sifakis

Facts On File Publications
New York • Oxford

PHOTO CREDITS

AC	Author's collection
B&L	Battles and Leaders of the Civil War
Harper's	"Harper's Weekly"
Leslie's	"Frank Leslie's Illustrated Newspaper"
LC	Library of Congress
NA	National Archives
NPS	National Park Service
SI	Smithsonian Institution

Who Was Who in the Civil War

First published in the United States of America by Facts On File, Inc.
460 Park Avenue South, New York, New York 10016.

Library of Congress Cataloging in Publication Data

Sifakis, Stewart.
Who was who in the Civil War.
1. United States—History—Civil War, 1861-1865—Biography. I. Title.
E467.S56 1986 973.7'092'2 84-1596
ISBN 0-8160-1055-2

Printed in the United States of America

10 9 8 7 6 5 4 3 2 1

CONTENTS

INTRODUCTION

It has been estimated that for every day since the end of the American Civil War one book, magazine or newspaper article has appeared dealing with some aspect of that fratricidal struggle. Why has interest been so extensive and enduring?

Most probably, because it was an all-American fight. Before and after the war the North and South were one common country. In fact, the war was the key factor in forming the two sections into a true nation. The relatively rapid cooling off of animosities is remarkable. Ex-Confederate generals, such as Joe Wheeler and M. Caldwell Butler, wore Federal blue as general officers in the Spanish-American War—alongside their former opponents. Other ex-Confederates were serving in the U.S. Congress as early as the 1870s. Well into the 20th century there were joint reunions of Union and Confederate veterans—most notably at Gettysburg, Pennsylvania.

In recent times it has been perfectly natural for Northerners to share in the admiration of the accomplishments of Robert E. Lee, "Stonewall" Jackson, Nathan B. Forrest or Jeb Stuart. The differences in nomenclature used to identify the Civil War—War of the Rebellion, War for Southern Independence, War of Secession, War of the Northern Aggression, and The Late Unpleasantness—have taken on an almost whimsical ring, while still identifying a speaker's attitude regarding the conflict.

But what of America's other wars? To a large extent, because of a matter of scale, they have not sparked the same level of interest as the Civil War. Great Britain did not use her full resources to oppose the American Revolution; and the American army itself was constantly dissolving and there were few Colonial successes to report. Furthermore, the Colonies themselves were not fully behind the Revolution. Modern estimates indicate that only one-third of the population of the 13 Colonies were for independence. Another third were either actively or pasively loyal to the crown. The balance just wanted to be left alone.

Like the Revolution, the War of 1812 sported few American battlefield successes and was fought with a lack of enthusiasm on both sides. The American army was composed mostly of short-term militia, and tended to melt away when the immediate danger had passed. In Europe the War was considered a sideshow in the conflict against Napoleon. Accordingly, Great Britain invested a minimum of her resources in the conflict on the western side of the Atlantic.

The Mexican War was fought against an enemy that most Americans felt was racially inferior and that it was only natural they should defeat easily. Actually, this conflict should be studied more closely by Civil War scholars since many of the senior Union and Confederate officers received their education in combat south of the Rio Grande.

The Spanish-American War, like the Mexican War, was fought against an "inferior" enemy and thus lacks the spark to kindle widespread interest. To a certain extent the same can be said of the various Indian wars.

World War I was for the United States only a brief conflict. While the European continent was convulsed in mutual genocide for years, Americans actively entered the conflict only in the final months.

World War II is the closest rival to the Civil War in the level of literature and public interest it has spawned. But it will probably never take over from the Civil War since America was only one of many actors in the global struggle.

The Korean War lacks interest on a wide scale since it ended in a draw. While the Vietnam War was an out and out debacle.

Another key factor in the continuing fascination with the War Between the States is its amazing cost. In four years of war over 600,000 lives were lost, North and South. To put this figure in perspective, when one puts America's losses in all of its other wars together, it is not until well into the Vietnam War that the losses in the Civil War are exceeded.

No large portion of the United States has ever felt the destruction wrought by a foreign, occupying power. Only the Confederacy has suffered such devastation and that at the hands of other Americans.

The Civil War marks a turning point in the history of the American republic. Not only did it forge a united nation but it also facilitated the Industrial Revolution that made the United

States a world power and leader by the early 20th century. New industries and inventions placed in operation during the Civil War, and expanded afterwards, prepared the nation for its role in the next century's world wars. Also, the release of so many men from the opposing armies, so soon after Appomattox, provided the manpower that led to the rapid conquest of the West and the establishment of a truly transcontinental power, with interests beyond both the Atlantic and Pacific oceans.

Furthermore, the Civil War was a war of innovation. The extensive use of longer-range rifles and artillery drastically altered battlefield tactics. Trench warfare became extensive. Railroads were used tactically and strategically for the first time; railroad artillery came into use. Aerial observation and fire-control of artillery came into being in the first years of the war. Telegraphic communications were used extensively. Land and water mines (they called them torpedoes) were devised, as were primitive hand grenades. Ironclad vessels fought each other for the first time. The first sinking of a warship by a submarine occurred. The first Congressional Medals of Honor were awarded. Breech-loading carbines, rifles and cannon were brought into battlefield use. Repeating carbines and rifles began to make their debut, and some primitive machine guns were developed. Both North and South introduced a national military draft for the first time in American history. The Union introduced the first federal income tax. And the war led to the first assassination of a president of the United States.

Many ask: If so much has been written on the Civil War, is there really a need for more? The answer is an emphatic yes. There are many aspects of the conflict that have been covered only superficially and require more in-depth research. But for such research a bedrock of reference works is essential. That is where *Who Was Who In The Civil War* comes in.

To date, there are encyclopedic biographies dealing collectively with Union generals, Confederate generals, West Point graduates, regular army officers, volunteer officers from certain states, field grade officers in Lee's army, medical officers, Confederate congressmen and civilian appointees in the regular army. Some of these were published in the last century and are hard to locate today. There is no one, current source available covering the full range of personalities who made—and fought—the Civil War.

In any collective biography the major difficulty is the establishment of selection criteria. For this work I have tried to include those persons who most affected the conflict. At the same time I have attempted to strike a reasonable balance betwwen North and South, military and civilian, and heroes and rogues.

Among the nearly 2,500 entries I have included those political leaders who had the most impact on prewar and wartime policy matters. Thus the presidential and vice presidential candidates in 1860 and 1864 are treated as well as several prewar U.S. presidents. For both the Northern and Southern congresses I have included most senators and those members of the lower houses who either served as committee chairmen or were particularly noted for their legislative activities, such as Justin S. Morrill and William P. Miles. All of the state governors, North and South—e.g., Andrew Curtin and Joe Brown—are covered.

Other political activists—such as secessionist Edmund Ruffin, abolitionist Frederick Douglass, Copperhead Clement L. Vallandigham and Southern Unionist John A. Gilmer—are included.

Of course, in dealing with any war most of the coverage is going to be devoted to the military. Accordingly, I have included all of those officers—583 Union and 425 Confederate—generally recognized as having attained one of the four (for the Confederates) or three (for the Union) grades of general. In addition I have treated most of those who were, then or later, generally referred to as having been general officers but for whom there is no official confirmation of their appointments, such as George P. Harrison, Jr. Militia officers who actually served at the front—like M. Jeff. Thompson for the Confederates and Robert Patterson for the Federals—are included. Also, those officers promoted to brigadier or major general by General E. Kirby Smith in the cut-off Trans-Mississippi Department—e.g., Alexander W. Terrell.

There is a far greater problem in selecting which officers below the grade of brigadier general rate inclusion. I rejected the expedient of simply taking the 1,367 officers of the Union army who achieved the rank of brigadier or major general only by brevet. (A "brevet" commission gives a military officer a higher nominal rank than that for which he is actually paid.) This rejection was based upon two considerations. First, the South did not have a system of brevet promotions. Thus meritorious officers, such as Edward Willis, did not receive appropriate recognition (when there was no vacancy for a brigadier general). Second, the whole system of brevets was so abused and politicized—especially by the mass issuance of brevets in March 1865—that many deserving officers never received them while others, whose services are rather obscure, did. Some of the latter served the entire war in obscure staff posts and only had the regular rank of captain but were brevetted through brigadier general. Others whose battlefield records were remarkable were not recognized. An excellent example of non-recognition is Colonel Edward E. Cross who was wounded three times in separate engagements before being mortally wounded while commanding a brigade at Gettysburg.

Instead, I have included those lower-ranking officers who led forces larger than a regiment for a lengthy period or in major actions. Thus Union Colonel Guy V. Henry is included. Also included are junior officers—like Bayard Wilkeson and John Pelham—who were particularly distinguished in leading smaller units. Officers and men who took part in important raids (Jesse C. McNeill) or won the Congressional Medal of Honor (Jacob Parrott) are treated.

Other combatants include: naval personnel, such as David D. Porter and Franklin Buchanan; scouts and spies, such as Longstreet's Harrison; and Marine Corps officers, such as John G. Reynolds and Lloyd J. Beall.

Among the noncombatants at the front were: the journalists, such as Samuel Wilkeson; the artist-correspondents, such as Alfred R. Waud; the surgeons, such as Jonathan Letterman; the nurses, such as Clara Barton; and members of the Christian and Sanitary commissions, such as Henry W. Bellows.

On the diplomatic front many ambassadors from North and South (Charles F. Adams and John Slidell) and from abroad (Henri Mercier) are included. Confederate purchasing agents abroad, such as James D. Bullock, also appear. Foreign leaders such as Napoleon III and Queen Victoria are treated. Foreign military observers such as Augusto Fogliardi also make their appearance.

In addition, all members of the Union and Confederate cabinets are covered.

This work concentrates on the characters' actions during the Civil War, giving researchers the basic career data of the participants. Thus pre- and postwar activities are only briefly sketched. Of course, when an individual played a role in bringing about secession and the war, much more attention is given to his prewar actions.

In the biographies of those military officers who led units larger than regiments it should be noted that armies and departments freqently operated as one organization with the same commander. Thus Robert E. Lee commanded the Department of Northern Virginia as well as the Army of Northern Virginia. Where confusion may occur both titles are given for clarity.

Another source of confusion is that Union officers may have as many as four different ranks. This resulted from the practice of regular army officers seeking advancement in the volunteer service (denoted by USV) while maintaining their regular army (USA) commissions. In addition an officer could win brevets in both services. A typical example is the case of George A. Custer. When he was killed by Indians in 1876 most Americans referred to him as a general. Technically, this was not the case. He was officially lieutenant colonel of the 7th Cavalry. However, he held a brevet as major general in the regular army. At the close of the Civil War he was only a captain of regulars but a major general of volunteers. In addition he held brevets at the latter grade in both services.

In the list of organizations led by an individual—especially in the case of Confederates—the dates of command are often only approximate due to the lack of adequate records. Those records in existence may indicate several different dates for an officer's assumption or relinquishment of command. These dates might be the actual date of physical assumption, the date on which he issues the order announcing his assumption of command, the date he was assigned by a local commander to duty, and/or the date that this was confirmed by the War Department. Due to the difficulties of travel it was not uncommon for an officer to take a matter of weeks in reporting to a new assignment. I have always tried to determine the date closest to actual assumption but this was freqently not possible. This has led to some overlapping of dates of assignment. Another cause of such overlapping are actual cases of duplicate assignments. Often an officer would command a field brigade and a geographical district simultaneously. Also, in times of limited activity a brigade commander would be in charge of the division while still retaining his normal command.

WHO WAS WHO IN THE CIVIL WAR

ABBOT, Henry Larcom (1831-1927)

A regular army engineer, Henry L. Abbot commanded the siege artillery of the Army of the Potomac during the siege of Petersburg. A native of Massachusetts and second in his class at West Point (1854), he was posted to the Topographical Engineers. His Civil War era assignments included: first lieutenant, Topographical Engineers (since July 1, 1857); captain, Topographical Engineers (June 18, 1862); colonel, 1st Connecticut Heavy Artillery (January 19, 1863); captain, Engineers (merger of the two engineering corps, March 3, 1863); commanding 3rd Brigade, Defenses South of the Potomac, 22nd Corps, Department of Washington (May 12-November 5, 1862); commanding 2nd Brigade, Defenses South of the Potomac, 22nd Corps, Department of Washington (November 5, 1863-March 1864); commanding 4th Brigade, Defenses South of the Potomac, 22nd Corps, Department of Washington (March 14-April 25, 1864 and July 16-August 2, 1865); commanding Siege Train, Army of the Potomac (1864-1865); and major, Engineers (November 11, 1865). At 1st Bull Run he was wounded and earned a brevet. On the Peninsula he won another brevet for Yorktown, then served as an aide to John G. Barnard. After service under Nathaniel P. Banks he took command of a regiment of volunteer heavy artillery in the Washington fortifications, where he was frequently in command of a brigade. He then moved to the Petersburg lines and directed the big guns. For the war he was brevetted major general of volunteers and brigadier general in the regular service. Mustered out of the former on September 25, 1865—with his regiment—he remained in the service until his 1895 retirement as a colonel of engineers.

ABBOTT, Joseph Carter (1825-1881)

A New Hampshire newspaper editor, Joseph C. Abbott entered the Union army upon the outbreak of the Civil War and rose to the rank of brevet brigadier general in the volunteer service. His assignments included: lieutenant colonel, 7th New Hampshire (December 13, 1861); colonel, 7th New Hampshire (November 17, 1863); commanding 2nd Brigade, 1st Division, 10th Corps, Army of the James (September 12-October 12, October 20-29 and November 4-18, 1864); commanding 2nd Brigade, 1st Division, 24th Corps, Army of the James (January 1-6, 1865); commanding Abbott's Brigade, Terry's Provisional Corps, Department of North Carolina (January 6-March 27, 1865); commanding 2nd Brigade, 1st Division, 10th Corps, Department of North Carolina (March 27-April 1, 1865); and commanding Abbott's Detached Brigade, District of Wilmington, Department of North Carolina (April 1-July 1, 1865). He served in Charleston Harbor and fought at Olustee before moving to Virginia where he took part in the operations against Richmond and Petersburg. During the 1864 presidential election, he went to New York City with his regiment to prevent trouble. Returning, he took part in the capture of Fort Fisher and the tail end of the Carolinas Campaign. Brevetted brigadier for Fort Fisher, he was mustered out with his regiment on July 17, 1865. Remaining in North Carolina, he returned to journalism and was a carpetbagger politician.

ABERCROMBIE, John Joseph (1798-1877)

Due to his advanced age John J. Abercrombie was relegated to garrison and administrative functions after an initial period in active field command. A native of Baltimore, he graduated from West Point in 1822 and served in the infantry throughout his career. He saw action in the Black Hawk and Seminole wars. In the latter he received a brevet, as he did for the Mexican War, during which he was wounded. A lieutenant colonel in the 2nd Infantry at the time of the secession crisis, his Civil War assignments included: colonel, 7th Infantry (February 25, 1861); commanding 2nd Brigade, Banks' Division, Army of the Potomac (August 17, 1861-March 13, 1862); brigadier general, USV (August 31, 1861); commanding 2nd Brigade, 1st Division, 5th Corps, Army of the Potomac (March 13-April 4, 1862); commanding 2nd Brigade, 1st Division, Department of the Shenandoah (April 4-30, 1862); commanding 2nd

Brigade, 2nd Division, 3rd Corps, Army of the Potomac (May 11-24, 1862); commanding 2nd Brigade, 1st Division, 4th Corps, Army of the Potomac (May 24-July 5, 1862); commanding the division (July 12-August 12, 1862); commanding division, Military District of Washington, Department of the Potomac (October 1862-February 2, 1863); and commanding division, 22nd Corps, Department of Washington (February 2-June 26, 1863). Serving in the failed campaign of General Patterson in the Shenandoah Valley early in the war, he was in overall field command at Falling Waters. After some further service in the Valley area, he was transferred to the Peninsula where he was wounded while commanding a brigade at Seven Pines. He saw further action in the last of the Seven Days-Malvern Hill. With the Army of the Potomac evacuated from the Peninsula and facing Lee in northern Virginia and Maryland, Abercrombie was assigned to a command in the capital's defenses. When his troops were ordered to join the field army in the Gettysburg Campaign he was deemed unfit for the rigors involved and was assigned to a series of boards and commissions. During the Overland Campaign of early 1864 he was in charge of forward supply depots and was involved in their defense against Confederate cavalry. He was mustered out of the volunteer service on June 24, 1864, but remained in the regular service until his June 12, 1865 retirement. Three months earlier he had been brevetted a brigadier in the regulars for his long career. He retired to New York with some time out for service on courts-martial.

ABERT, John James (1788-1863)

At the outbreak of the war Colonel John V. Abert was the chief topographical engineer and head of the Topographical Bureau. A graduate of West Point (1811), he held the office starting in 1834 and rose to the rank of colonel by 1838. After almost 40 years of service, he retired from the army on September 9, 1861, before the conflict began in earnest.

ADAMS, Charles Francis, Sr. (1807-1886)

As U.S. minister to Great Britain during the Civil War, John Quincy Adams' son, Charles Francis Adams, Sr., weathered some of the most difficult diplomatic crises between the two countries. Arriving in London during the first year of the war he soon become embroiled in the controversy over the seizure of the Confederate commissioners, Mason and Slidell, who were on board the British mail steamer *Trent*. With the crisis resolved, largely through the efforts of Prince Albert, and the diplomatic agents released, Adams became a watchdog over possible violations of British neutrality; he protested ship building and arms shipments for the Confederacy. He continued at the London post for three years after the close of the war. During the 1870s, he served as a member of the board of arbitrators in the case of the *Alabama* claims. (Duberman, Martin, *Charles Francis Adams*)

ADAMS, Charles Francis, Jr. (1835-1915)

The grandson of John Quincy Adams and the son of Diplomat Charles Francis Adams, Sr., Charles F. Adams, Jr., was a distinguished Civil War officer before he went on to his more famous postwar careers. His Union assignments included: first lieutenant, 1st Massachusetts Cavalry (December 28, 1861); captain, 1st Massachusetts Cavalry (December 1, 1862); lieutenant colonel, 5th Massachusetts Cavalry (Colored) (September 8, 1864); and colonel, 5th Massachusetts Cavalry (Colored) (March 14, 1865). His regiment saw action at Secessionville, South Mountain, Antietam, Shepherdstown, Fredericksburg, Kelly's Ford, Stoneman's Raid during the Chancellorsville Campaign, Brandy Station, Gettysburg, in the Bristoe and Mine Run campaigns, on the Kilpatrick-Dahlgren Raid, and at the Wilderness, Spotsylvania, North Anna, Yellow Tavern, Cold Harbor, and Petersburg. Near war's end he was brevetted brigadier general, USV, for the first three battles named. Seeking advancement, he transferred to a black cavalry regiment and was promoted to its command while guarding the prison camp at Point Lookout, Md. He served around Richmond in the final days of the war and was then sent to Texas. He resigned on August 1, 1865. He was subsequently active as an historian and economist and in railroading, exposing the scandalous financing of rail companies through his writings. (Adams, Charles Francis, Jr., *Autobiography*; and Kirkland, Edward C., *Charles Francis Adams, Jr. 1835-1915: The Patrician At Bay*)

ADAMS, Daniel Weisiger (1821-1872)

Wounded three times during the Civil War, Confederate General Daniel W. Adams spent the last several months of the war in district commands. The Kentucky lawyer had practiced in both Mississippi and Louisiana before the war. In a not-uncommon antebellum occurrence, he was acquitted of murder in the duelling death of a newspaper editor who Adams felt had slighted his father. At the outbreak of the secession crisis, Adams became part of a three-man board charged with preparing for war. His later assignments included: lieutenant colonel, 1st Louisiana Regulars (1861); colonel, 1st Louisiana Regulars (October 30, 1861); commanding 2nd Brigade, 2nd Corps, 2nd Grand Division, Army of the Mississippi (March 9-29, 1862); commanding 1st (Gladden's) Brigade, 2nd (Withers') Division, 2nd Corps, Army of the Mississippi (April 6, 1862); brigadier general, CSA (May 23, 1862); commanding 2nd Brigade, 2nd (Anderson's) Division, Left Wing, Army of the Mississippi (August 13-November 20, 1862); commanding 2nd Brigade, Anderson's-Breckinridge's Division, Hardee's Corps, Army of Tennessee (November 20-December 31, 1862 and early 1863-May 1863); commanding brigade, Breckinridge's Division, Department of the West (ca. May 31-July 1863); commanding brigade, Breckinridge's Division, Department of Mississippi and East Louisiana (July-August 25, 1863); commanding brigade, Breckinridge's Division, Hill's Corps, Army of Tennessee (August 28-September 20, 1863); commanding District of Central and North Alabama, Department of Alabama, Mississippi and East Louisiana (ca. August-September 24, 1864); commanding District of Central Alabama, Department of Alabama, Mississippi and East Louisiana (September 24, 1864-March 11, 1865); and commanding District of Alabama, Department of Alabama, Mississippi and East Louisiana (March 11-May 4, 1865). Initially stationed at Pensacola, he and his regiment were part of the Confederate buildup before Shiloh at Corinth, Miss. During the battle's first day he took command of the brigade when Adley H. Gladden was killed in front of the Hornet's Nest. Shortly thereafter Adams also fell with a wound that cost him an eye. Promoted to brigadier general, he returned to command a brigade at Perryville, and he was again wounded at Murfreesboro on the last day of 1862. Returning to duty early the next year, he led a brigade under Joseph E. Johnston during the siege of Jackson. Rejoining Bragg's army in northern Georgia, he was wounded for the third time on the second day at Chickamauga and was also taken prisoner. It appears that the Confederate authorities were reluctant to have him exchanged—possibly due to the number of wounds he had sustained—and he was not freed from his parole until the middle of 1864. At that time he was assigned to a series of district commands in Alabama and then spent the final days of the war in command of the entire state except for the Mobile area. He took part in the feeble defense against Wilson's raid through Alabama and Georgia. Included in Richard Taylor's surrender on May 4, 1865, he resumed his practice.

ADAMS, Henry Brooks (1838-1918)

While serving as an unofficial secretary to his father, Charles Francis Adams, Sr., minister to Great Britain, Henry Adams also served, secretly, as a correspondent for the *New York Times*. He had given up his law studies and accompanied his father in an unofficial capacity. But he also arranged to write anonymously for the *Times*. Utilizing his access to official secrets, he filed 35 reports with the paper until fear of discovery caused him to cease. Regretting that he could not serve his country in the field like his brother, Charles Francis, Jr., he took pride in his role during the crisis initiated by the American seizure of Confederate commissioners Mason and Slidell from the British mail steamer *Trent*. In his initial reports his anti-English bias showed greatly. He hoped the incident would bring about war between the two countries, thus possibly reuniting the United States. Reconsidering the matter he realized that such a war would be disastrous for his country and would not bring about the desired goal. He soon advised the return of the agents in order to smooth over the diplomatic difficulties. He continued to work for his father after the crisis. He was subsequently a prominent historian at Harvard and is noted for his *The Education of Henry Adams*. (Chalfant, Edward, *Both Sides of the Ocean: A Biography of Henry Adams*)

ADAMS, John (1825-1864)

In the suicidal Confederate attack at Franklin, John Adams became one of six generals to sustain a fatal wound in that battle. The native Tennesseean and West Pointer (1846) had won a brevet with the dragoons in the Mexican War. Following frontier duty he resigned as a captain in the 1st Dragoons on May 31, 1861. Joining the Confederacy, his assignments included: captain, Cavalry (May 27, 1861); colonel, Cavalry (May 1862); brigadier general, CSA (December 29, 1862); commanding 4th Military District, Department of Mississippi and East Louisiana (ca. January-June 1863); commanding Tilghman's (old) Brigade, Loring's Division, Department of the West (June-July 1863); commanding brigade, Loring's Division, Department of Mississippi and East Louisiana (July 1863-January 28, 1864); commanding brigade, Loring's Division, Department of Alabama, Mississippi and East Louisiana (January 28-May 1864); and commanding brigade, Loring's Division, Polk's (Army of Mississippi)-Stewart's Corps, Army of Tennessee (May-November 30, 1864). After service at Memphis he was promoted to command of the deceased Lloyd Tilghman's brigade during the operations around Vicksburg under Joseph E. Johnston. He took part in the defense of Jackson, Miss., and later faced Sherman's Meridian campaign. Going with Leonidas Polk to Mississippi, he served through the Atlanta Campaign and then went on the invasion of middle Tennessee. Once wounded at Franklin, he continued on until repeatedly struck on the very works of the enemy.

ADAMS, Robert Newton (1835-?)

A native Ohioan, Robert N. Adams enlisted in Miami University's "University Rifles" upon the outbreak of the war. His assignments included: private, company B, 20th Ohio (April 18, 1861); captain, 81st Ohio (August 30, 1861); lieutenant colonel, 81st Ohio (May 19, 1862); commanding 2nd Brigade, 2nd Division, 16th Corps, Army of the Tennessee (May 16-23 and August 2-September 18, 1864); colonel, 81st Ohio (August 12, 1864); and commanding 2nd Brigade, 4th Division, 15th Corps, Army of the Tennessee (October 5, 1864-April 26, 1865 and May 1, 1865). After serving as an enlisted man with his first regiment in western Virginia, he was mustered out upon the expiration of its term of service on August 18, 1861. As a company commander he fought in Missouri and at Shiloh. While he was a lieutenant colonel, the regiment fought at Corinth and against Forrest's cavalry. At times in command of the brigade, he fought in the Atlanta Campaign and was wounded at Jonesboro. He recovered to serve through the March to the Sea and the Carolinas Campaign. Brevetted brigadier for the war, he was mustered out with his regiment on July 13, 1865.

ADAMS, William Wirt (1819-1888)

Generally known simply as Wirt Adams, this Kentuckian refused Jefferson Davis' tender of a cabinet postal portfolio and instead rose to the rank of brigadier general in the Confederate cavalry. Adams had fought in Texas before becoming a Mississippi plantation owner, banker, and state legislator. His military assignments included: colonel, Adams' Mississippi Cavalry Regiment (October 15, 1861); brigadier general, CSA (September 25, 1863); commanding Logan's (old) Brigade, Jackson's Division, Lee's Cavalry Corps, Department of Mississippi and East Louisiana (ca. November 21, 1863-January 28, 1864); and commanding in the Department of Alabama, Mississippi, and East Louisiana: same brigade,

Jackson's Division, Lee's Corps (January 28-ca. May 4, 1864); cavalry division (May-August 1864); District North of Homochitto (August-November 6, 1864); District of Northern Mississippi, District of Mississippi and East Louisiana (November 6-mid November 1864); Northern Sub-District, District of Mississippi and East Louisiana (mid-November 1864-January 1865); Sub-District of Southwest Mississippi and East Louisiana, District of Mississippi and East Louisiana (January-February 3, 1865); also the district (January 31-February 3, 1865); District South Mississippi and East Louisiana, District of Mississippi and East Louisiana (February 3-18, 1865); and brigade, Chalmers' Division, Forrest's Cavalry corps (February 18-May 4, 1865). Before his promotion to brigadier general, he led his regiment at Iuka and Corinth and during Grant's drive into central Mississippi. He also tangled with Grierson's raiders and fought at Vicksburg and with Joseph E. Johnston at Jackson. Thereafter he held a number of district commands and ended the war with Nathan Bedford Forrest, facing Wilson's raid at Selma. After the war he was a public official until killed in a personal encounter with a journalist.

AGATE

See: *Reid, Whitelaw*

AINSWORTH, Fred Crayton (1852-1934)

Although not a veteran of the Civil War, Fred Ainsworth became very important to veterans as head of the Record and Pension Office; he was also responsible for the completion of the *Official Records*. The Vermonter served for almost 18 years as assistant surgeon and surgeon in the U.S. Army before being appointed chief of the Record and Pension Office of the War Department, with the rank of full colonel, on May 27, 1892. He had custody of the records of volunteer and militia soldiers who had served the country from the Revolution through the Civil War, including the records of Confederate troops. The principal purpose of the office was to rule on applications of veterans for pensions based on their military service. To this end, Ainsworth developed a system of card files for the various records. These card files contain the service records of individual soldiers and are now in the National Archives. In 1898 he took over direct control of the publication of the *Official Records* and completed the series. He was promoted brigadier general, USA, on March 2, 1899. (Mahan, Harold E., "The Arsenal of History," *CWH*, March 1983)

AKIN, Warren (1811-1877)

When many in the Confederate Congress became disillusioned with the leadership of Jefferson Davis in the latter stages of the war, Davis still had at least one hero-worshipping representative—Congressman Warren Akin of Georgia's 10th District. A native Georgian, Akin had been a lawyer, sometime Methodist minister, a trustee of Emory University, presidential elector in 1840, and a member of the Nashville convention of the Southern States in 1850. In 1859 he was defeated by Governor Joseph E. Brown when running as a Constitutional Unionist to become chief executive of Georgia. For the first two years of the Civil War he served in the lower house of the state legislature and, although a freshman, was given the position of speaker. In the fall elections in 1863 he was elected to the Second Congress on a platform of full support of the Davis Administration. The threatened 10th District appreciated this position after the peace resolutions of his predecessor, Augustus R. Wright. Taking his seat in May 1864, he was appointed to the Committee on Claims. Although his district was shortly overrun by Sherman's armies, his faith in Davis was never shaken and an interview with the president early in 1865 reconfirmed his position. Akin proposed an unsuccessful amendment to the law that had made Lee general in chief; he wanted to prevent any lessening of the President's powers. Following the collapse of the Confederacy, he resumed the practice of law. (Wiley, Bell I., ed., *Letters of Warren Akin*)

ALBERT, Prince (1819-1861)

Although Albert, the German Duke of Saxe-Coburg-Gotha, faced much resentment in England when he married Queen Victoria, he became a hard-working advisor to the queen and also earned a certain level of respect from the British. During the crisis created by the seizure of Confederate commissioners Mason and Slidell aboard the British mail steamer *Trent*, he served a moderating role, and may have averted war, between the United States and Great Britain. Despite suffering from an illness that made it difficult for him to hold a pen and that later claimed his life, he managed to muster enough strength to revise a draft ultimatum to the Lincoln administration penned by foreign secretary Lord John Russell. His moderating influence paved the way for the eventual release of the diplomats and a lessening of tensions. He died a few weeks after the crisis was resolved. (Warren, Gordon H., *Fountain of Discontent: The Trent Affair and Freedom of the Seas*)

ALCORN, James Lusk (1816-1894)

A plantation owner and lawyer, James Lusk Alcorn was an active Whig politician whose political associations earned him a position in the Mississippi military structure at the outbreak of the war. He served in the state legislature's lower and upper houses and failed in an attempt for a seat in congress. Attending the 1861 state convention he opposed secession but signed the ordinance in the end. In return the convention named him a brigadier general in the state army. By the fall of 1861 he was serving under General S.B. Buckner in Kentucky, and on October 2 he was assigned command of a district around Hopkinsville. In December and January he commanded, again in Kentucky, a force of three regiments of 60-day state troops known as the "Army of Mississippi." His troops were raw and were not counted on for much by the authorities. After leaving the service, he returned home to the Yazoo country of Mississippi. Here, during the Vicksburg Campaign, he provided information to Confederate military leaders about Union troop movements. After the war he served part of a term as governor before resigning to join the U.S. Senate in 1871; he had been refused his seat in 1865. He retired in 1877. (Pereyra, Lillian A., *James Lusk Alcorn, Persistent Whig*)

ALCOTT, Louisa May (1832-1888)

Most famous as the author of *Little Women* (1868-69), Louisa May Alcott's work in a Civil War hospital gained her the experience that provided material for some of her earliest work. While serving as a nurse at a Georgetown hospital in the nation's capital, she published in 1863 her *Hospital Sketches*, which had appeared earlier the same year in *Commonwealth*. The next year her first novel, *Moods*, appeared. Born in Pennsylvania, she was raised and died in Massachusetts where she did most of her writing. (Cheney, Ednah D., *Louisa May Alcott, Her Life, Letters, and Journals*)

Louisa May Alcott, *Little Women* author. (NA)

ALDEN, James (1810-1877)

Following the sinking of the monitor USS *Tecumseh* by a torpedo (mine) during the Battle of Mobile Bay, James Alden, commanding the USS *Brooklyn*, hesitated momentarily, allegedly prompting Admiral Farragut to order "Damn the torpedoes! Full speed ahead!" Born in Maine, he had served for decades at sea and on exploring expeditions. During the Civil War he commanded the USS *Richmond*, with the rank of commander, early in the conflict. At New Orleans his craft, armed with 22 guns, suffered a loss of two killed and four wounded. He again commanded the vessel in the successful passage of Port Hudson on the night of March 14-15, 1863. Promoted to the rank of captain, he commanded the *Brooklyn* at Mobile Bay and in the second attack on Fort Fisher, where it lost three wounded and two missing.

James Alden, hesitant captain of the USS *Brooklyn*. (*Leslie's*)

ALEXANDER II, Czar (1818-1881)

One of the Union's few staunch allies during the Civil War was Czar Alexander II of Russia. Despite the great difference in political systems, Russia had a certain kinship with the North because the Czar had abolished serfdom in his realm in 1861. The bond was even stronger because, unlike Queen Victoria and Napoleon III, he had refused to receive Confederate envoys at St. Petersburg. The Russian authorities also made clear their preferences by repeatedly congratulating the Union upon its military victories. Then, on September 11, 1863, the first of several Russian naval vessels entered New York harbor unannounced. Other craft visited San Francisco. Rumors spread of an all-out alliance between the two countries. Official Russian silence allowed this conviction to continue boosting Northern morale. It was not until the next century that the reasons for the visit were definitely established. Due to friction with Britain and France, Russia did not want to have its fleet trapped in its own icebound ports; the United States was a convenient place to winter over. Although Americans were grateful for the doubts placed in European diplomatic circles, many still had a distaste for Alexander's autocratic rule, and especially his suppression of Poland that same year. The Czar himself was eventually assassinated by terrorists. (Woldman, Albert A., *Lincoln and the Russians*)

The czar's frigate *Osliaba* at Alexandria, Virginia. (NA)

ALEXANDER, Edward Porter (1835-1910)

The most capable artillerist in the Army of Northern Virginia, E. Porter Alexander, was a West Point graduate, third in the 1857 class, with four years engineering experience. The second lieutenant resigned on May 1, 1861, to join the Confederacy where his assignments included: captain, Engineers (June 3, 1861); lieutenant colonel, Artillery (December 1861); colonel, Artillery (December 1862); commanding Lee's (old) Battalion, Reserve Artillery, 1st Corps, Army of Northern Virginia (November 7, 1862-July 1863); commanding artillery battalion, 1st Corps, same army (July-September 9, 1863); commanding artillery battalion, Longstreet's Corps, Army of Tennessee (September 19-November 5, 1863); commanding Artillery, Department of East Tennessee (November 5, 1863-April 7, 1864); brigadier general, CSA (February 26, 1864); and commanding Artillery, 1st Corps, Army of Northern Virginia (April 12-June 1864 and August 1864-April 9, 1865). Drawing upon his service with Albert J. Myer, he headed Beauregard's signal corps and at 1st Bull Run warned Colonel N.G. Evans (by signals) that his flank was about to be turned. As chief of ordnance after the battle he also was involved with signals, new weapons, engineering, reconnaissance, supply, training gun crews, and organizing a secret service. He witnessed the fighting at Gaines' Mill from a balloon and was transferred from ordnance duty to command an artillery battalion in time for Fredericksburg. His placement of the guns facilitated the easy repulse of the enemy. He fought again at Chancellorsville, and at Gettysburg he supervised the bombardment preceding Pickett's Charge, in effect supplanting Colonel J.B. Walton. Arriving too late for the battle of Chickamauga, he served as Longstreet's artillery chief in the Knoxville Campaign and back in Virginia, seeing action at Spotsylvania, Cold Harbor, and Petersburg. In June, he was wounded by a sharpshooter during the latter battle and was absent part of the summer. He then commanded the artillery on the north side of the James around Richmond for the remainder of the siege. After his surrender at Appomattox he was active in education and railroading and wrote a highly respected work, *Military Memoirs of a Confederate*. (Klein, Maury, *Edward Porter Alexander*)

ALEXANDER, Peter Wellington (1824-1886)

In at least one battle Southern reporter Peter W. Alexander crossed the vague line between reporter and military observer or scout. A native of Georgia, he had practiced law and journalism before the Civil War. His journalistic credits during the Civil War included the *Atlanta Confederacy*, *Columbus Sun*, and *Mobile Advertiser and Register*. Although he had been a staunch Unionist delegate to the state secessionist convention, he passed on information from his frontline observations to the Confederate high command at 1st Bull Run and was rewarded with the honorary title of colonel. Also present at Antietam, he became a friend and supporter of Confederate General Robert Toombs who resigned shortly after the battle because he felt he had been passed over for promotion. This may have contributed to Alexander's later writings, which were highly critical of the direction the government was taking, and his support for states' rights principles within the Confederacy. After the war he resumed the practice of law. (Andrews, J. Cutler, *The South Reports the Civil War*)

ALGER, Cyrus (1781-1856)

Although he died half a decade before the Civil War began, Cyrus Alger had a tremendous influence on how it was fought. Entering the iron foundry business, Alger eventually became an expert in artillery and much of his business's time was spent in filling government contracts. In 1834 his plant manufactured the first U.S.-made rifled cannon. Tackling the problems of the old-style wooden fuses for explosive shells, in the 1840s he invented a bronze model fuse that included several safety features. His innovation permitted the Navy to use its preferred method of firing, skipping the shell along the water and against its target, with a much lower percentage of duds when fuses were snuffed out by sea water. A safety plug allowed the already charged shells to be stacked on deck during an action. These improvements allowed for a much greater rate of fire, with the ability to actually roll shells into enemy coastal fortifications as was effected at Battery Wagner in Charleston Harbor. Alger never patented his process due to the War Department's fear that it would be appropriated by potential enemies. The Confederates immediately adopted it at the outbreak of the war.

ALLEN, E.J.

See: *Pinkerton, Allan*

ALLEN, Henry Watkins (1820-1866)

As Louisiana's last wartime governor, Henry W. Allen proved to be a highly effective leader. Born in Virginia, he fought in the war for the independence of Texas and then entered upon the practice of law. Following a journey to Europe he was elected to the Louisiana legislature and upon the outbreak of the Civil War joined the Confederate army. His assignments included: lieutenant colonel, 4th Louisiana (May 25, 1861); colonel, 4th Louisiana (March 1862); commanding 2nd Brigade, 2nd Division, District of the Mississippi, Department £2 (August 1862); and brigadier general, CSA (August 19, 1863). After service at Ship Island and Jackson, Mississippi, he was wounded in the face at Shiloh. In charge of a brigade, he was again wounded, this time in the leg, at Baton Rouge. During his lengthy recovery he was promoted to brigadier general and on November 2, 1863, he was elected governor of his adopted state. As the state's chief executive he organized exports to Mexico for needed goods. Leaving office on June 2, 1865, he went to Mexico where he ran an English-language newspaper until his death. (Dorsey, Sarah A., *Recollections of Henry Watkins Allen, Brigadier General Confederate States Army, Ex-Governor of Louisiana* and Cassidy, Vincent H., *Henry Watkins Allen of Louisiana*)

ALLEN, Robert (1811-1886)

Since he never held a Civil War field command Robert Allen is little remembered in history but his service as, in effect, the chief quartermaster for the entire western theater, was vital. Born in Ohio, he graduated from West Point in 1836 and was posted to the artillery. However, he transferred as a captain to the quartermaster's section in 1846 earning a brevet for his Mexican War service. His Civil War assignments included: major and quartermaster (May 17, 1861); colonel and addition al aide-de-camp (February 19, 1862); and brigadier general, USV (May 23, 2863). Early in the war he was the quartermaster chief for the Department of Missouri; his responsibilities continued to grow in the western theater of operations until, by the time of the Atlanta Campaign, he was in effect in the same position for the Military Division of the Mississippi. His supplies also reached troops in the Plains and in the Northwest. Mustered out of the volunteer service in 1866, he retired from the army in 1878 assistant quartermaster general; all of his books were found to be in perfect order after some 40 years in the department. In retirement he traveled widely abroad and died in Geneva.

ALLEN, Theodore (ca. 1838-1891)

A thorough scoundrel before the Civil War, Theodore Allen saw that he could make money from the misery of others during the conflict. He ran a saloon and was involved in gambling and prostitution in New York City, until the large bounties being offered to Army enlistees prompted him to become a broker. A typical ploy was to get a man drunk, take him to a local recruiting station and abscond with the bounty. Freshly arrived immigrants were often victims. Allen netted an estimated $100,000 during the war. Subsequently he resumed his other disreputable businesses and was involved in corrupt city politics. He was stabbed to death in 1891. (Murdock, Eugene Converse, *Patriotism Limited—1862-1865—The Civil War Draft and Bounty System*)

ALLEN, William Wirt (1835-1894)

William W. Allen may have been born in New York City, but he was raised to become an Alabama planter and eventually became a Confederate major general of cavalry. His assignments included: first lieutenant, Company A, 1st Alabama Cavalry (1861); major, 1st Alabama Cavalry (March 18, 1862); colonel, 1st Alabama Cavalry (ca. July 11, 1862); brigadier general CSA (February 26, 1864); commanding brigade, Kelly's Division,

Wheeler's Cavalry Corps, Army of Tennessee (spring 1864); commanding John T. Morgan's (old) Brigade, Martin's Division, Wheeler's Cavalry Corps, Army of Tennessee (ca. May-December 5, 1864); commanding division, Wheeler's Cavalry Corps, Army of Tennessee (ca. December 5, 1864-April 26, 1865); and major general, CSA (March 4, 1865). After serving as a subaltern in the Montgomery Mounted Rifles for a number of months he fought as a field officer at Shiloh and during the Corinth siege. Promoted to colonel, he was wounded at both Perryville and Murfreesboro. Not returning to field duty for a lengthy period, he was named brigadier general and assigned to a brigade under Joseph Wheeler. For the balance of the war he served under Wheeler as a brigade and division commander in the Atlanta, Savanah and Carolinas campaigns. After surrendering with Joseph E. Johnston, Allen engaged in planting and railroading, and also served as state adjutant general and as a U.S. marshal.

ALLISON, Alexander (?-?)

The lesser-known partner in the firm of Kurz and Allison, Alexander Allison had been a Chicago engraver when in 1880 he joined Kurz's lithograph business. Over the next two decades the firm produced scores of lithographs depicting various aspects of American life. However, their most famous work was a series of 36 chromolithographs of major Civil War battles. These somewhat less than realistic prints—showing perfectly uniformed men in well-dressed battle lines—are noted for their use of color, with as many as 10 being used in each print. Unfortunately the originals are now extremely rare. The firm closed its doors in 1903. (*Battles of the Civil War 1861-1865: The Complete Kurz & Allison Prints*)

ALLSMAN, Andrew

See: *Smith, Hiram*

ALVORD, Benjamin (1813-1884)

Although he served as a brigadier general of volunteers during the Civil War, Benjamin Alvord's primary problems were with the Nez Percé Indians and those white men who violated treaties to search for gold. A native of Vermont and a West Pointer (1833) he served in the infantry until transferred to the paymaster's office serving in the Department of Oregon. His Civil War assignments included: major and paymaster (since June 22, 1854); brigadier general, USV (April 15, 1862); and commanding District of Oregon, Department of the Pacific (April 1862-March 1865). For his administrative and diplomatic efforts on the coast he received brevets through that of brigadier in the regular service. Resigning from the volunteers on August 8, 1865, he reverted to his former rank as a paymaster and remained in the department until he retired as its chief in 1880. He was also known for his writing on mathematics and agriculture.

AMES, Adelbert (1835-1933)

When Adelbert Ames died in Florida on April 13, 1933, he was the last surviving general officer—other than by brevet—from either side. Originally a clipper seaman, he returned to shore to be appointed to West Point from his native Maine. Graduating in the class of May 1861, he was posted to the artillery and his Civil War assignments included: second lieutenant, 2nd Artillery (May 6, 1861); first lieutenant, 1st Artillery (May 14, 1861); colonel, 20th Maine (August 20, 1862); brigadier general, USV (May 20, 1863); commanding 2nd Brigade, 1st Division, 11th Corps, Army of the Potomac (May 24-July 1 and July 17-August 6, 1863); commanding the division (July 1-14, 1863); commanding 2nd Brigade, South End Folly Island, 10th Corps, Department of the South (August 16-November 27, 1863); commanding Forces Folly Island, Northern District, 10th Corps, Department of the South (January 15-23, 1864); commanding 2nd Brigade, Gordon's Division, same district, corps and department (January 23-28, 1864); commanding the division (January 28-February 25, 1864); commanding 1st Division, District of Florida, 10th Corps, Department of the South (February 25-April 25, 1864); commanding 3rd Division, 10th Corps, Army of the James (April 28-May 28, 1864); commanding 3rd Brigade, 3rd Division, 18th Corps, Army of the James (May 30-June 4, 1864); commanding the division (June 4-16, 1864); captain, 5th Artillery (June 11, 1864); commanding 2nd Division, 10th Corps, Army of the James (June 16-22, 1864); commanding 3rd Brigade, 2nd Division, 18th Corps, Army of the James (June 22-July 10, 1864); commanding the division (July 10-September 17, 1864); commanding 1st Division, 10th Corps, Army of the James (October 10-November 4 and November 18-December 3, 1864); commanding the corps (November 4-18, 1864); commanding 2nd Division, 24th Corps, Army of the James (December 3, 1864-January 6, 1865); commanding Ames' Division, Terry's Provisional Corps, Department of North Carolina (January 6-March 27, 1865); commanding 2nd Division, 10th Corps, same department (March 27-May 13, 1865); and commanding the corps (May 13-August 1, 1865). Badly wounded at 1st Bull Run he refused to be removed from his guns until too weak to sit on a caisson. For this he was brevetted captain and, in 1893, received the Congressional Medal of Honor. Returning to duty he directed his guns on the Peninsula, seeing action at Yorktown, Gaines' Mill and Malvern Hill and receiving another brevet for the latter. Returning to Maine he became colonel of a new regiment, which he led in the Maryland Campaign although it was not engaged at Antietam. He fought at Fredericksburg, and at Chancellorsville was detailed to General Meade's staff. Promoted to brigadier he was given a brigade in the 11th Corps, which he directed on the first day at Gettysburg, earning yet another brevet. Succeeding to division command he fought through the remainder of the battle. Transferred to the South Carolina coast, he took part in the operations against Charleston. Returning to Virginia in the spring of 1864 he served in brigade, division, and corps command during the operations against Richmond and Petersburg. His final service came in the capture of Fort Fisher. Brevetted to major general in both regular and volunteer service he was mustered out of the latter on April 30, 1866. As lieutenant colonel, 24th Infantry he continued in the regular army and was assigned to duty in Mississippi. In 1868 he was made military and then provisional governor. He left the army in 1870 when he took a seat in the U.S. Senate from Mississippi. Reelected governor in 1874 his administration was beset by race riots, official misconduct, and carpetbag rule. Faced with impeachment, he resigned in 1876 and moved via New York to Massachusetts where he engaged in the flour business. He served six months in the Spanish-American War as a brigadier of volunteers. (Ames, Blanche, *Adelbert Ames, 1835-1933, General, Senator, Governor*)

AMMEN, Jacob (1806-1894)

Virginia-born but Ohio-raised, Jacob Ammen served mostly in the rear areas of the war after an early period of combat. A West Pointer (1831) he had been posted to the artillery but during six years of service was an instructor at West Point for two tours. His civilian years were spent as a civil engineer and as a professor of mathematics at colleges in Indiana, Kentucky, and Mississippi. Returning to the army six days after the firing began at Fort Sumter, his assignments included: captain, 12th Ohio (April 18, 1861); lieutenant colonel, 12th Ohio (May 2, 1861); colonel, 24th Ohio (June 22, 1861); commanding 10th Brigade, Army of the Ohio (ca. November 9) (December 2, 1861); commanding 10th Brigade, 4th Division, Army of the Ohio (December 2, 1861-August 16, 1862); brigadier general, USV (July 16, 1862); commanding the division (August 16-23, 1862); and commanding 4th Division, 23rd Corps, Department of the Ohio (April 10, 1864-January 14, 1865). After initial service at the head of his regiment at Cheat Mountain and Greenbrier and of the brigade at Shiloh, he held various administrative posts in Ohio, Illinois, Tennessee, and Kentucky. In addition he served on a number of courts-martial. Given command of a division in the spring of 1864, he was left with it to protect the rear areas while three other divisions of the corps took part in the Atlanta Campaign. He resigned on January 4, 1865, to become a surveyor and civil engineer. A member of the board of visitors to his alma mater, he also took part in the canal explorations in Panama.

ANDERSON, Charles D. (1829-1901)

As the man who surrendered Fort Gaines in Mobile Bay, Charles D. Anderson came in for a great deal of criticism from his superiors. He dropped out of West Point after two years of study but eight years later was commissioned directly into the 4th Artillery. The South Carolina-born and Texas-raised first lieutenant resigned his commission on April 1, 1861, and offered his services to the Confederacy. Shortly after the Battle of Shiloh, on May 8, 1862, he was appointed colonel, 21st Alabama. A few months later the regiment was sent to the defense of Mobile where it served for the rest of the war. On August 7, 1864, he was commanding Fort Gaines, guarding the harbor. After a naval bombardment he raised the white flag. There were charges that his post was defended inadequately. The city itself held out until the very end of the war. He is sometimes confused with brigadier general Charles David Anderson of the Georgia Militia.

ANDERSON, Charles David (1827-1901)

Although wounded and forced to give up his commission, Charles David Anderson nevertheless found himself leading combat troops as the war ground on. His Confederate service included: captain, Company C, 6th Georgia (May 27, 1861); major, 6th Georgia (September 17, 1862); lieutenant colonel, 6th Georgia (May 15, 1863); colonel, 2nd Georgia Militia (early 1864); brigadier general, Georgia Militia (mid-summer 1864); and commanding 3rd Brigade, 1st Division, Georgia Militia (mid-summer-November 22, 1864). The 6th saw service at Yorktown, Williamsburg, Seven Pines, the Seven Days, Antietam, Fredericksburg, and Chancellorsville. The regiment subsequently went to South Carolina but he was forced by his wounds to resign on January 20, 1864. Commissioned into the state militia, he served during the latter stages of the Atlanta Campaign and was promoted to brigade command during the siege. With Hood's army off to Tennessee, the militia tried to delay Sherman's drive through Georgia. In the only major infantry action of the campaign, Anderson was wounded at Griswoldville. He served in the state legislature for the final months of the war. He is sometimes confused with Colonel Charles D. Anderson of the 21st Alabama who served mostly at Mobile and who surrendered Fort Gaines.

ANDERSON, George Burgwyn (1831-1862)

Although George B. Anderson effectively commanded a brigade for nine months, he was not recognized and promoted to brigadier until June 1862. The West Pointer (1852) had resigned his first lieutenant's commission in the 2nd Dragoons on April 25, 1861, to join the South. His assignments there included: colonel, 4th North Carolina (May 16, 1861); commanding Garrison at Manassas, 1st Corps, Army of the Potomac (October 14-22, 1861); commanding Garrison at Manassas, Potomac District, Department of Northern Virginia (October 22, 1861-March 25, 1862); commanding brigade, D.H. Hill's Division, same department (April 2-6, 1862); commanding Featherston's (old) Brigade, D.H. Hill's Division, Army of Northern Virginia (May-July 1 and July-September 17, 1862); and brigadier general, CSA (June 9, 1862). Until the evacuation of the Manassas lines he was in charge of the garrison and then of the brigade organized from it until relieved by General C.S. Winder. A few days later he was briefly back in command, but commanded only his regiment at Williamsburg. He directed the brigade at Seven Pines and a short time later was promoted to its permanent leadership. In the last of the Seven Days battles, Malvern Hill, he was wounded but returned in time to aid in the defense of the gaps in South Mountain during the Maryland invasion. Three days later, at Antietam, he was wounded in the foot. Carried back to North Carolina, he died on October 16 after amputation of the foot. (Freeman, Douglas S., *Lee's Lieutenants*)

ANDERSON, George Thomas (1824-1901)

Nicknamed "Tige," George T. Anderson was in command of a brigade for half a year before he received his Confederate general's wreath. A lieutenant of Georgia cavalry during the Mexican War, he received a captain's commission in the regular cavalry in 1855. He resigned three years later but when the Civil War broke out he went with his native Georgia. His assignments included: colonel, 11th Georgia (July 2, 1861); commanding S. Jones' Brigade, G.W. Smith's Division, Potomac District, Department of Northern Virginia (January 10-February 17, 1862); commanding D.R. Jones' Brigade, D.R. Jones' Division, Magruder's Command, same department (May-July 3, 1862); commanding D.R. Jones' Brigade, D.R. Jones' Division, 1st Corps, Army of Northern Virginia (July-October 27, 1862); commanding same brigade, Hood's-Field's Division, same corps and army (October 27, 1862-February 25, 1863; May-July 2, 1863; April 12, 1864-January 1865; and March-April 9, 1865); brigadier general, CSA (November 1, 1862); commanding brigade, Hood's Division, in the Department of Virginia and North Carolina (February 25-April 1, 1863) and in the Department of Southern Virginia (April 1-May 1863); commanding brigade, 1st Military District of South Carolina, Department of South Carolina, Georgia and Florida (September 1863); commanding brigade, Hood's Division, Longstreet's Corps, Army of Tennessee (October 5-November 5, 1863); and commanding brigade, Hood's-Field's Division, Department of East Tennessee (November 5, 1863-April 12, 1864). Too late for the fighting at 1st Bull Run, he saw action at Yorktown and, in command of the brigade, at the Seven Days, 2nd Bull Run, Turner's Gap, Antietam, and Fredericksburg. After service with Longstreet in southeastern Virginia he was wounded on the second day at Gettysburg. Recovering, he was detached to the Charleston area when Longstreet's Corps went to Georgia. He rejoined the corps after Chickamauga. After the Knoxville Campaign the corps rejoined Lee, and Anderson saw heavy action at the Wilderness, Spotsylvania, and Cold Harbor. After serving through the Richmond-Petersburg siege he surrendered with Lee at Appomattox. He was subsequently police chief in Atlanta and in Anniston, Alabama. (Freeman, Douglas S., *Lee's Lieutenants*)

ANDERSON, James Patton (1822-1872)

Briefly serving in the Provisional Confederate Congress, J. Patton Anderson resigned after only one session, joined the army and rose to the rank of major general. Born in Tennessee, he was a doctor in Mississippi when the Mexican War broke out. In that conflict he was lieutenant colonel of the 2nd Mississippi Rifles Battalion. He was then, successively, a Mississippi state legislator, U.S. marshal in Washington Territory, territorial delegate from the territory to Congress, and a resident of Florida. Attending the state secession convention, he was named to the Montgomery body and served on the committees on Military Affairs and Public Lands before resigning on April 8, 1861. During his brief tenure his main interest was in maritime matters. His military assignments included: colonel, 1st Florida (April 5, 1861); brigadier general, CSA (February 10, 1862); commanding brigade, Ruggles' Division, 2nd Corps, Army of the Mississippi (March 29-June 1862); commanding the division (June 1862); commanding brigade, 2nd Corps, Army of the Mississippi (June-July 1862); commanding division, Army of the Mississippi (July-August 15, 1862); commanding division, Left Wing, Army of the Mississippi (August 15-November 20, 1862); commanding division, Hardee's Corps, Army of Tennessee (November 20-December 1862); commanding brigade, Withers'-Hindman's Division, Polk's Corps, Army of Tennessee (December 1862-September 20, 1863); commanding Hindman's Division, Polk's-Breckinridge's-Hindman's Corps, Army of Tennessee (September 20, 1863-January 1864); major general, CSA (February 17, 1864); commanding District of Florida, Department of South Carolina, Georgia and Florida (March 4-August 3, 1864); commanding Hindman's (old) Division, Lee's Corps, Army of Tennessee (July 29-September 1, 1864); and commanding Taliaferro's (old) Division, Stewart's Corps, Army of Tennessee (April 9-26, 1865). His initial service came at Pensacola and then, promoted to brigadier general, as a brigade commander at Shiloh. He led a division at Perryville and a brigade again at Murfreesboro. On the second day at Chickamauga he succeeded the wounded Thomas C. Hindman in division command. Early in 1864 he was assigned to district command in Florida but was ordered to rejoin the Army of Tennessee during the Atlanta Campaign; he fought at Ezra Church and, until wounded, at Jonesboro. He did not rejoin the army until the Carolinas Campaign was virtually concluded. At that time he was given command of a division of troops drawn from the coastal defenses of South Carolina. Surrendering with Joseph E. Johnston at Durham Station, he became a tax official and ran a farming journal.

ANDERSON, Joseph Reid (1813-1892)

A Confederate brigadier early in the war, Joseph Anderson was more important in his civilian capacity as head of the Tredegar Works in Richmond, where he became the "Krupp of the Confederacy." In August 1861, the West Point graduate (1836) was made a major of artillery, after resigning from a year's service as a lieutenant of engineers and artillery. For two decades he had been the superintendent of the iron works; as a major he was assigned to continue his work there. However on September 3, 1861, he was appointed brigadier general, CSA, and assigned to field duty in North Carolina. His commands included: District of the Cape Fear, Department of North Carolina (October 5-March 19, 1862); the department (March 19-24, 1862); brigade, A.P. Hill's Division, Army of Northern Virginia (May 27-June 30 and early July 1862); and temporarily the division, Longstreet's Command, Army of Northern Virginia (July 13-19, 1862). After service in North Carolina, Anderson brought a brigade of Georgians to Virginia and took command of the force facing McDowell's command at Fredericksburg during April and May 1862. During the Seven Days he led his brigade at Beaver Dam Creek, Gaines' Mill and Frayser's Farm where he was wounded. Returning in July he took over command of A.P. Hill's Division while that officer was under arrest but resigned effective July 19, 1862, to return to the iron works. For almost three years, until the fall of Richmond, he provided arms for the men in the field. The federal government returned the confiscated plant to him in 1867 and he ran it until his death. (Dew, Charles B., *Ironmaker to the Confederacy: Joseph R. Anderson and the Tredegar Iron Works*)

ANDERSON, Richard Heron (1821-1879)

"Fighting Dick" Anderson served throughout the career of the Army of Northern Virginia only to be relieved of duty the day before the Appomattox surrender. A West Pointer (1842) from South Carolina, he was a veteran of the Mexican War and resigned a captaincy in the 2nd Dragoons on March 3, 1861, to join the South. His services included: major, Infantry (March 16, 1861); colonel, 1st South Carolina Regulars (early 1861); commanding Charleston Harbor (May 27-August 1861); brigadier general, CSA (July 19, 1861); commanding D.R. Jones' (old S.C.) Brigade, Longstreet's Division (in Potomac District until March), Department of Northern Virginia (February 15-May 31; June 1-29; and July 1-14, 1862); commanding the division (May 31-June 1 and June 29-July 1, 1862); major general, CSA (July 14, 1862); commanding Huger's (old) Division, 1st (3rd after May 30, 1863) Corps, Army of Northern Virginia (July 14-September 17, 1862 and November 1862-May 7, 1864); commanding 1st Corps, same army (May 7-October 19, 1864); lieutenant general, CSA (May 31, 1864); and commanding 4th Corps, same army (October 19, 1864-April 8, 1865). After commanding his regiment at the bombardment of Fort Sumter and, after Beauregard's departure, the Confederate forces in the harbor, he was transferred to western Florida where he was wounded in the October 9, 1861, attack at Santa Rosa Island. His connection with what was to become Lee's army began when he was assigned to a brigade on the Manassas lines on February 15, 1862. He led either a portion or all of the division at Williamsburg, Seven Pines, and during the latter stages of the Seven Days Battles. Promoted and given Huger's old command from Norfolk, he fought at 2nd Bull Run, Crampton's Gap, and was wounded at Antietam. Returning to duty he was lightly engaged at Fredericksburg but played a key role at Chancellorsville. With the reorganization of the army after Stonewall Jackson's death, his division was transferred to the newly created 3rd Corps. He fought at Gettysburg and the Wilderness after which he was given command of the wounded Longstreet's 1st Corps. He won the dramatic race from the Wilderness to Spotsylvania and went on to fight at North Anna, Cold Harbor, and near Richmond during the Petersburg operations. In the late summer of 1864 he was detached with part of his corps to reinforce Early in the Shenandoah but was soon recalled. Upon Longstreet's return he was given charge of a new corps, which he directed through the remainder of the siege. His command was virtually destroyed at Sayler's Creek and the day before Appomattox he was sent home by Lee since he had no command. After the war he was impoverished but declined a position in the Egyptian Khedive's army, preferring to stick with his Reconstruction-troubled state. (Walker, C. Irvine, *The Life of Lieutenant General R.H. Anderson*)

ANDERSON, Robert (1805-1871)

A pro-slavery Kentuckian but absolutely loyal to the Union, Robert Anderson was considered an ideal choice for commander in Charleston Harbor during the 1860 secession crisis. Having graduated from West Point (1825), he had risen to major, 1st Artillery, by the time of his assignment on November 15, 1860. Given little assistance by the Buchanan Administration, Anderson was greatly perturbed by having to choose between war and peace. He took matters into his own hands on December 26, following the secession of the state six days earlier, when he moved his two-company garrison from barely defensible Fort Moultrie to unfinished Fort Sumter in the middle of the harbor. After the unannounced relief ship *Star of the West* was fired upon by Carolinian gunners on January 9, 1861, Anderson, not wishing to start a war, withheld his fire. Later, after he had turned down an April surrender demand, Anderson was forced to return fire when the fort was bombarded on April 12-13. Forced to surrender, Anderson returned to the North with a sense of failure in not having prevented the war. He was appointed brigadier general, USA, on May 15, 1861, and commanded the Department of Kentucky (May 28-August 15, 1861), which was merged into the Department of the Cumberland (August 15-October 8, 1861), which he also commanded. When his health began to fail, he was relieved of field command and given duties at various posts in the North. He was retired from the regular army on October 27, 1863, and brevetted major general for Fort Sumter. After the recapture of Charleston, Anderson took part in a ceremony in which he reraised the same flag he had lowered exactly four years earlier. (Swanberg, W.A., *First Blood*)

Robert Anderson, Fort Sumter defender. (*Leslie's*)

ANDERSON, Robert Houstoun (1835-1888)

Despite the fact that his entire service in the old army was with the infantry, Georgia West Pointer (1857) Robert H. Anderson earned the three stars and wreath of a Confederate brigadier general with mounted troops. Serving in the Pacific Northwest, he resigned as a second lieutenant with the 9th Infantry on May 17, 1861, and tendered his services to the South. His assignments included: first lieutenant, Artillery (March 6, 1861); major and assistant adjutant general (September 1861); major, 1st Georgia Sharpshooters Battalion (June 20, 1862); colonel, 5th Georgia Cavalry (January 20, 1863); commanding Allen's (old) Brigade, Kelly's Division, Wheeler's Cavalry Corps, Army of Tennessee (ca. May-September 1864); brigadier general, CSA (July 20, 1864); and commanding brigade, Allen's Division, Wheeler's Cavalry Corps, Army of Tennessee (ca. January 2-April 26, 1865). His early service came as a staff officer with William H.T. Walker on the coast of South Carolina and Georgia before he transferred to a sharpshooters unit that continued to serve in the same area. Finally at the head of a mounted regiment, he joined the Army of Tennessee, seeing action through most of the Atlanta Campaign. He then participated, under Joseph Wheeler, in the efforts to stop Sherman during the March to the Sea and through the Carolinas. After the war he was the police chief of his native Savannah.

ANDERSON, Samuel Read (1804-1883)

Virginia-born and a former Kentucky resident, Tennesseean Samuel Anderson had been lieutenant colonel of the 1st Tennessee during the Mexican War and a bank cashier and postmaster in Nashville before being called upon to serve as one of the two state major generals on May 9, 1861. Exactly two months later, with the Tennessee troops transferred to Confederate service, Anderson accepted the rank of brigadier general for those forces. On August 5 he was assigned to command a brigade of Tennessee troops in western Virginia; as a part of Lee's Army of the Northwest, he took part in the first battle planned by that general. In this action at Cheat Mountain, Anderson led his men into position, as directed, behind the Union position. However, some of the other troops failed to complete their assignments and the attack fizzled out before it fairly got started. That winter Anderson's brigade accompanied the Army of the Northwest to join Stonewall Jackson's Romney Campaign. Although the expedition took the town, it failed to destroy the Union forces there. On February 24, 1862, Anderson was ordered to proceed with two of his regiments to Manassas and join Johnston's army. Anderson's brigade, reinforced by another regiment from Tennessee, was assigned to G.W. Smith's Division, Department of Northern Virginia. Anderson went with his brigade when the army was moved to the Peninsula, but on May 10, 1862, he resigned due to ill health. On November 19, 1864, Anderson was reappointed a brigadier general (to rank from November 7) and assigned to duty with the conscript bureau in Alabama where he was responsible for the Tennessee operations of that agency. He became a Nashville businessman after the war. (Freeman, Douglas S., *R. E. Lee*)

ANDERSON, William (1840-1864)

A graduate of the William C. Quantrill school of bushwhacking, "Bloody Bill" Anderson went off on his own hook to perpetrate some of the most brutal actions of the Civil War. When the Kansas City prison for women—which was being used to confine Southern sympathizers—collapsed, one of Anderson's sisters was killed and another crippled. With a band from Clay County, Missouri, Anderson joined up with Quantrill in time for the sacking of Lawrence, Kansas. Displaying an aptitude for cold-blooded killing, he became a first lieutenant in the guerrilla band early in 1864. A short time later he refused to serve under Quantrill after one of his men was shot for killing a farmer. Anderson and most of his men rode off for their own depradations north of the Missouri River and joined in Price's invasion of Missouri. That September 27 he perpetrated the infamous Centralia massacre in which he captured a train and killed the crew and 24 unarmed soldiers on furlough. Civilians trying to hide their valuables were also slain. When three companies of the 39th Missouri and a detachment of the 1st Iowa Cavalry set out in pursuit, they were ambushed. Out of 147 men, 116 were killed, two were wounded and six more were unaccounted for. A month later, on October 26, 1864, Anderson was killed in an assault on a militia company near Richmond, Missouri. He was decapitated and the trophy mounted on a telegraph pole. Anderson had a lasting impact on the West—he had given Jesse James his initiation in blood. (Hale, D.R., *They called Him Bloody Bill*)

ANDREW, John Albion (1818-1867)

One of the most effective of the Union war governors was John A. Andrew of Massachusetts. A native of Maine, he was practicing law in Boston when he became involved in the anti-slavery movement. He was an early organizer of the Free Soil Party and helped organize the state branch of the Republican Party. Elected governor in 1860, he served five terms beginning on January 2, 1861. Immediately organizing the militia for war, he provided some of the first volunteers to reach Washington after the firing on Fort Sumter. A believer in rights for blacks, he urged their recruitment for the army and led in the raising of the 54th Massachusetts, a colored unit. With the war won he did not seek renomination and left office on January 4, 1866. He practiced law until his death the next year. (Chandler, Henry, *The Life of John A. Andrew, Governor of Massachusetts, 1861-1865*)

ANDREWS, Christopher Columbus (1829-1922)

With no previous military experience Christopher C. Andrews rose from private to brevet major general. A native of New Hampshire he had attended Harvard and practiced law in

Massachusetts and Kansas before entering politics in Minnesota. After serving a term in the state senate he enlisted as a private in the Union army. His assignments included: captain, 3rd Minnesota (November 4, 1861); lieutenant colonel, 3rd Minnesota (December 1, 1862); colonel, 3rd Minnesota (August 9, 1863); brigadier general, USV (January 5, 1864); commanding 2nd Brigade, 2nd Division, 7th Corps, Department of Arkansas (May 19-June 16, 1864); commanding the division (June 16-December 1864); commanding 3rd Brigade, Reserve Corps, Department of the Gulf (December 1864-February 3, 1865); commanding 2nd Division, same corps and department (February 3-18, 1865); and commanding 2nd Division, 13th Corps, Department of the Gulf (February 18-July 20, 1865). Serving in middle Tennessee, he and his regiment were swept up near Murfreesboro by Nathan Bedford Forrest's cavalry on July 13, 1862. Exchanged in October, he served briefly against the Sioux in Minnesota before returning to Tennessee. He then fought at Vicksburg and, moving to the other side of the Mississippi, served in the Little Rock Expedition. The next year he was in charge of a brigade and then a division in Arkansas. In the final months of the war he participated in operations against Mobile, earning a brevet for Fort Blakely. Mustered out on January 15, 1866, he returned to politics and served as a diplomat to Norway, Sweden, and Brazil. He was also a newspaper editor and wrote *My Experience in Rebel Prisons* and *History of the Campaign of Mobile*.

ANDREWS, George Leonard (1828-1899)

Having graduated at the top of the 1847 West Point class, George L. Andrews reentered the military upon the outbreak of the Civil War and had a distinguished career, attaining the brevet rank of major general of volunteers. After eight years of service in the engineers he resigned to become a civil engineer in his native Massachusetts. His Civil War assignments included: lieutenant colonel, 2nd Massachusetts (May 25, 1861); colonel, 2nd Massachusetts (June 13, 1862); commanding 2nd Brigade, 1st Division, 12th Corps, Army of the Potomac (October 3-6, 1862); commanding 4th Brigade, 1st Division, 12th Corps, Army of the Potomac (October 6-26, 1862); brigadier general, USV (November 10, 1862); commanding Defenses of New Orleans, Department of the Gulf (ca. November 10-December 16, 1862); commanding 1st Brigade, 3rd Division, 19th Corps, Department of the Gulf (January 3-29 and February 12-March 5, 1863); chief of staff, Department of the Gulf (March 6-July 9, 1863); temporarily commanding 2nd Division, 19th Corps, Department of the Gulf (May 27-28, 1863); commanding District of Port Hudson 19th Corps, Department of the Gulf (July 9, 1863-April 23, 1864); commanding Corps d'Afrique, 19th Corps, Department of the Gulf (April 23-June 9, 1864); commanding Post of Port Hudson, District of (from September 12 Baton Rouge and) Port Hudson (in 19th corps until November 7), Department of the Gulf (August 6-December 26, 1864); commanding the district (December 26, 1864-February 9, 1865); provost marshal general, Department of the Gulf (February 27-June 6, 1865); and chief of staff, Military Division of West Mississippi (June 6-August 24, 1865). As a regimental officer he fought in the Shenandoah Valley, at Cedar Mountain and Antietam. Promoted to brigadier, he was dispatched to command at New Orleans. In Louisiana he also held brigade and division commands and was Banks' staff chief during the operations against Port Hudson. After its fall Andrews was made district and post commander of the river city. In 1864 he commanded the recruiting of black troops and the next year served as provost marshal of the forces operating against Mobile, for which he was brevetted. Mustered out on August 24, 1865, he spent a couple of years on a Mississippi plantation before returning to the North. From 1871 to 1892 he was a professor of French at West Point. He is sometimes confused with George Lippitt Andrews who as a regular army major briefly commanded a brigade of regulars in the 5th Corps.

ANDREWS, James J. (?-1862)

The man who led the famous railroad raid was also one of the most mysterious of Civil War personalities. It has been speculated that he was born Andreas Johan Kars in Finland and had been an officer in the Russian army before imigrating to America in 1850. The details of his life after he moved to Kentucky at the start of the conflict are somewhat less cloudy. After brief service in the State Guard, he entered the employ of General Buell as a spy posing as a quinine trafficker. His value to the general was dubious and he provided little timely intelligence. Andrews, in an effort to disrupt rebel communications, led a detail of 22 Ohio soldiers from General Sill's brigade and one civilian into Georgia dressed as civilians. Boarding a northbound Western and Atlantic train at Marietta, they disconnected the passenger coaches when the train stopped for breakfast on April 12, 1863 at Big Shanty. Climbing aboard the engine, *The General*, and three box cars, they started the run toward Chattanooga. Pursued by surprised railroad employees, Andrews and his men had little time to inflict significant damage to the line. After a chase of 87 miles, and running low on fuel, Andrews ordered the men to escape, each man for himself. All were eventually captured. Andrews was tried as a spy in Chattanooga and on June 7 was hanged in Atlanta, 10 days before his planned marriage. (O'Neill, Charles, *Wild Train: The Story of the Andrews Raiders*)

ANDREWS, Richard Snowden (1830-1903)

Baltimore architect turned artillery commander, R. Snowden Andrews was told that his abdominal wound from a shell was certain to prove fatal, but he defied the experts. Although born in the nation's capital, he decided to offer his services to the South but not until he had obtained technical information on the organizing of a battery from the U.S. government. His assignments included: captain, 1st Maryland Battery (May 29, 1861); major, Artillery (July 15, 1862); commanding Artillery Battalion, Jackson's (old) Division, Jackson's Command, Army of Northern Virginia (July-August 9, 1862); lieutenant colonel, Artillery (April 4, 1863); commanding Artillery Battalion, Early's Division, 2nd Corps, Army of Northern

Virginia (April 16-June 2, 1863); and commanding Artillery Battalion, Johnson's Division, 2nd Corps, Army of Northern Virginia (June 2-15, 1863). After serving in the blockade of the Potomac early in the war, he took part in the Seven Days Battles and was slightly wounded. Given command of a battalion, he distinguished himself at Cedar Mountain but was nearly cut in two by an enemy shell. Considered a hopeless case, he was left on the field with an old doctor friend who expected him to die. By the middle of October 1862 he was fit enough to perform ordnance duty. The next spring he rejoined Lee's army for Chancellorsville. In the early stages of the Gettysburg Campaign, he fought at 2nd Winchester and was again wounded the next day at Stephenson's Depot. In January 1864 he was dispatched to Europe to purchase much-needed ordnance supplies. He returned to Baltimore at the war's close. Despite his wounds, he died a natural death. (Wise, Jennings C., *The Long Arm of Lee*)

ANDREWS, Solomon (ca. 1806-1872)

Bureaucratic red-tape in the War Department proved the demise of many inventions. It was against this barrier that Dr. Solomon Andrews' aerodrome was crushed. A physician, Andrews served as a health official and three terms as mayor of Perth Amboy, N.J. However, he was also an inventor and had a tremendous interest in flying. Having experimented over the preceding dozen years, he contacted the Washington authorities with his plan for an airship superior to the observation balloons then in vogue, one that could possibly become a bomb-dropping warship. Following his initial August 1862 contact with the government, and some preliminary interest, but little real encouragement, the plan stalled. Reports of studies became lost in the labyrinth of the department, and petty regulations prevented prompt implementation of the plans. Fed up with the bureaucracy, he decided to go ahead on his own and in June 1863 made a successful flight in New Jersey. After some improvements and additional test flights, he met with President Lincoln who requested reports of the eyewitnesses to the tests. The reports never reached Lincoln's desk. In March 1865, with the war almost over anyway, Congress dropped all further consideration of the project. Trying to commercialize his invention, Andrews' company crashed in a postwar panic, and he returned to the health field for the remainder of his life.

ANDREWS, Timothy Patrick (?-1868)

Patrick Andrews spent most of his American military career in the Pay Department. He entered the service from the District of Columbia in 1822 as a major and paymaster. He continued in this department until his retirement, except for a year he served as colonel of the Regiment of Voltigeurs and Foot Riflemen specially raised for the Mexican War. At the time of the firing on Fort Sumter he was serving, with the rank of lieutenant colonel, as the deputy paymaster general. On December 11, 1862, he relieved Major C.H. Fry, an interim appointee, as paymaster general with rank of colonel. This appointment was back-dated to September 6, 1862, the date of death of the incumbent Colonel B.F. Larned. Andrews held this position until his retirement on November 29, 1864. During his tenure the troops were paid, although often late, on a far more regular basis than in the rebel army. Andrews was also a brevet brigadier general, USA, for the battle of Chapultepec in the Mexican War.

ANONYMOUS (?-1862)

While it is generally assumed that the Civil War was a man's fight, there were probably enough women disguised as men in order to fight, to have made up several companies. One apparent case was not discovered until 1934 when Mancil Milligan found several bones in his garden on the outskirts of the Shiloh National Battlefield Park. Subsequent investigations determined that it was the gravesite of nine Union soldiers who had been killed at Shiloh. Surprisingly, one of the bodies was a woman's. A minie ball was found next to her remains. Although her name cannot be discovered, she is the only female known to have been killed in the battle.

ANTHONY, Henry Bowen (1815-1884)

One of the first Republican senators, Rhode Island's Henry B. Anthony rose to be the Senate's president pro tempore in the postwar years. A native of the state, he was editor and part owner of the *Providence Journal* before being elected to the first of two one-year terms as governor in 1849. Not seeking reelection, he returned to journalism until his election, as a Republican, to the U.S. Senate in 1858. He was reelected four times and died in office. Serving from March 4, 1859, onwards, he became the state's senior senator during the Civil War. From 1869 to 1871 he served as the presiding officer of the Senate. In 1884 he refused election to that position on the grounds of ill health. He died later that year.

ANTHONY, Sister (1814-1897)

Born in Ireland, Mary O'Connell became known as the "Florence Nightingale of America" for her hospital work with Ohio soldiers during the Civil War. Educated in Massachusetts, she joined the American Sisters of Charity and, soon assigned to Cincinnati, Sister Anthony became involved in hospital work. She and her fellow sisters were in the camps and on the battlefields almost everywhere that there were Ohio troops throughout the war. She continued her medical work until her retirement in 1885, having worked in the 1877 outbreak of yellow fever in the Mississippi Valley.

ANTHONY, Susan Brownell (1820-1906)

Best known for her work on women's rights, Susan B. Anthony was an equally forceful worker on behalf of the often linked causes of abolition and temperance. The Massachusetts activist was brought up in a Quaker environment and began her career for reform in the anti-alcohol lobby. But ill-treatment she received at the hands of the all-male organizations prompted her and others to form the Woman's State Temperance Society of New York, an action that led to the conclusion that women needed the right to vote in order to be truly effective in the reform movements of the day. Equating the treatment of slaves in the South with that of women, she became a radical abolitionist. Lecturing widely, she denied the right of the law to interfere where she knew she was right. During the Civil War she aided the administration by being a cofounder of the Women's Loyal League. After the war she worked for Negro suffrage and tried to link it with the right to vote for white women. She gave up the so-called Bloomer costume in favor of more conventional dress since she found the former to be a distraction from the important issues of the day. She continued her activities until shortly before her death. (Harper, Ida H., *The Life and Work of Susan B. Anthony*)

APPLER, Jesse J. (?-?)

Ohioan Jesse J. Appler proved to be a man totally unfit to be a combat commander. On or about February 11, 1862, he became the colonel of the 53rd Ohio. In his first action, Shiloh, he allegedly called out to his men, "Retreat and save yourselves." He then proceeded to do just that. By the next month the 53rd had a new commanding officer. In fairness to Appler, it must be stated that he had been censured by General William T. Sherman on the day before the surprise attack for calling out the regiment when only a few picket shots were heard. It was the general who was surprised the most the next day.

ARCHER, James Jay (1817-1864)

A lawyer and Mexican War veteran, James Archer resigned his captain's commission in the regular army on March 14, 1861, to receive the same rank in the Confederate service two days later. Although a Marylander, Archer was appointed colonel, 5th Texas, a regiment organized in Richmond from independent companies, on October 2, 1861. He commanded his regiment, and sometimes the brigade, at the batteries at Evansport along the Potomac and on the Peninsula in the actions at Eltham's Landing and Seven Pines. He was promoted brigadier general, CSA, June 3, 1862, and given command of Hatton's old brigade of Alabama, Georgia, and Tennessee troops (that officer having been killed at Seven Pines). The Georgians were eventually transferred out and replaced by more Alabamians, but the brigade became known as the Tennessee Brigade. Archer's commands in the Army of Northern Virginia included: Tennessee Brigade, A.P. Hill's Division (June 3-July 1862); Tennessee Brigade, A.P. Hill's Division, Jackson's Corps (July 27, 1862-May 30, 1863); Tennessee Brigade, Heth's Division, A.P. Hill's Corps (May 30-July 1, 1863); and Archer's and Walker's Brigades, Heth's Division, A.P. Hill's Corps (August 19-October 24, 1864). Commanding his brigade, Archer took part in actions at Beaver Dam Creek, Gaines' Mill, Frayser's Farm, Cedar Mountain, 2nd Bull Run, the capture of Harpers Ferry, Antietam, Fredericksburg, and Chancellorsville. On the first day at Gettysburg he was picked up by an Irishman from the Union's Iron Brigade, becoming the first general captured from the Army of Northern Virginia since Lee took command. While imprisoned at Johnson's Island, Ohio, Archer let the Confederate War Department know through a paroled prisoner that the guards could be overwhelmed but the Southerners would have no way of getting off the island. On June 21, 1864, Archer was ordered sent to Charleston Harbor to be placed under Confederate fire in retaliation for southern treatment of prisoners. Later exchanged, Archer was ordered to the Army of Tennessee for duty on August 9, 1864, but he was redirected to the Army of Northern Virginia 10 days later. He was assigned command of his own as well as Walker's Brigades, which had been temporarily consolidated. Suffering from the effects of his imprisonment and the rigors of the Petersburg trenches, including the battle of Peebles' Farm, Archer died on October 24, 1864. (Freeman, Douglas S., *Lee's Lieutenants*)

James J. Archer, victim of Union prison camps. (NA)

ARMISTEAD, Lewis Addison (1817-1863)

Lewis A. Armistead nearly scuttled his military career when he broke a plate over the head of fellow cadet Jubal A. Early and was expelled from West Point. He was, however, commissioned directly into the infantry in 1839 and served in the Mexican War, being wounded at Chapultepec and earning two brevets. He resigned his captaincy on May 26, 1861, and headed back east to offer his services to the Confederacy. His assignments included: major, Infantry (from March 16, 1861); colonel, 57th

Virginia (September 23, 1861); brigadier general, CSA (April 1, 1862); commanding brigade, Department of Norfolk (ca. April 1-12, 1862); commanding brigade, Huger's Division, Department of Northern Virginia (April 12-July 1862); commanding brigade, Anderson's Division, 1st Corps, Army of Northern Virginia (July-September 17, 1862); and commanding brigade, Pickett's Division, in 1st Corps, Army of Northern Virginia (October 1862-February 25, 1863 and May-July 3, 1863), in the Department of Virginia and North Carolina (February 25-April 1, 1863), and in the Department of Southern Virginia (April 1-May 1863). After serving in western Virginia, he was given command of a brigade in the Norfolk area and later served with it on the Peninsula, seeing action at Seven Pines and in the Seven Days. He fought at 2nd Bull Run and Antietam, where he was wounded. After being lightly engaged at Fredericksburg, he went to southeastern Virginia, his home state, with Longstreet. Returning for the invasion of Pennsylvania, he fell mortally wounded among the guns of Cushing's Battery during Pickett's Charge at Gettysburg. He died two days later in Union hands. (Freeman, Douglas S., *Lee's Lieutenants*)

ARMSTRONG, Frank Crawford (1835-1909)

The only general officer in the Civil War who managed to fight on both sides, Frank C. Armstrong fought at 1st Bull Run before switching sides and becoming a Confederate brigadier general. Born in the Indian Territory—the son of an Indian agent—he received his appointment to the regular army from Texas and was named a second lieutenant in the 2nd Dragoons. His Civil War assignments, on both sides, included: first lieutenant, 2nd Dragoons (since March 9, 1859); captain, 2nd Dragoons (June 6, 1861); captain, 2nd Cavalry (designation change August 3, 1861—resignation accepted August 13); volunteer aide-de-camp (early August 1861); lieutenant and assistant adjutant general (1861); colonel, 3rd Louisiana (ca. May 26, 1862); acting brigadier general, CSA (July 7, 1862); commanding Cavalry Brigade, Price's Corps, Army of West Tennessee, Department £2 (September-October 1862); commanding brigade, Jackson's Division, Cavalry Corps, Department of Mississippi and East Louisiana (January-February 1863); commanding brigade, Forrest's Cavalry Division, Army of Tennessee (spring-September 1863); brigadier general, CSA (April 23, 1863, to rank from January 20); commanding division, Forrest's Cavalry Corps, Army of Tennessee (September-October 1863); commanding division, Wheeler's Cavalry Corps, Army of Tennessee (October 1863-March 5, 1864); commanding brigade, Jackson's Cavalry Division, Department of Alabama, Mississippi, and East Louisiana (spring-May 4, 1864); commanding brigade, Jackson's Cavalry Division, Polk's-Stewart's Corps (Army of Mississippi), Army of Tennessee (May 4-July 26, 1864); commanding brigade, Jackson's Cavalry Division, Army of Tennessee (July 26, 1864-February 18, 1865); and commanding brigade, Chalmers' Division, Forrest's Cavalry Corps, Department of Alabama, Mississippi, and East Louisiana (February 18-May 4, 1865). Having accepted a regular army captaincy in June he led the one company of his regiment present, K, at 1st Bull Run and performed well. However, the next month he served as a volunteer aide to Benjamin McCulloch at Wilson's Creek. Three days later his resignation from the old army was accepted without any recriminations for his having fought against it. He was still on McCulloch's staff when that general was killed at Pea Ridge. Soon thereafter he was elected colonel of the 3rd Louisiana in place of the promoted Louis Hebért. That summer he was given charge of all of Sterling Prince's cavalry as an acting brigadier, having served well in the Corinth siege. Formally promoted, he was given a brigade under Forrest and fought in the Tullahoma and Chickamauga campaigns. When Forrest was ordered to west Tennessee, Armstrong and his division were assigned to Wheeler's corps and served at Knoxville. After a brief stint back in Mississippi he returned to Georgia, leading a brigade throughout the Atlanta Campaign and into middle Tennessee with Hood. In the last months he led a brigade against Wilson's raid. Following the war he held numerous government posts.

ARMSTRONG, James (?-?)

A veteran of decades in the U.S. Navy, Commodore James Armstrong played a disgraceful role in the early stages of the Civil War. In charge of the navy yard at Pensacola, Florida, he was besieged by a large force of rebels who demanded his surrender. On January 12, 1861, he complied but not without resistance from his men. One seaman, William Conway, refused to obey an order to lower the national colors. The army commander at Forts McRae and Barrancas, Lieutenant Adam J. Slemmer, moved his command to nearby Fort Pickens, which was held by the Union throughout the war, but Armstrong failed to comply with Slemmer's request that in the case of a naval surrender the marine detachment be sent to reinforce Fort Pickens. While in captivity Armstrong was forced to turn over, unopened, dispatches from Washington to Florida officers. Soon released and sent north, he was courtmartialed and suspended from duty for five years, a part of that time without pay. The *New York Courier and Enquirer* on May 29, 1861, said that he "should have been driven from the Navy with disgrace."

ARMSTRONG, Sir William George (Baron Armstrong of Cragside) (1810-1900)

Most field artillery in the Civil War was of the muzzle-loading variety but some breechloaders, like that designed by Sir William George Armstrong, were tried by both sides. An English inventor of considerable renown, he became involved in military equipment during the Crimean War, when he designed submarine mines. In 1855 he developed a three-inch, 10-pound rifled breechloading cannon that was eventually adopted by the British military. Running a private company, he sold samples to the Union government during the Civil War and a few were run through the blockade to the Confederates. But, the technology being new, there were problems with the new ordnance. The breechblocks had a tendency not to fit in place properly. In 1863 he went out of business when the British army returned to the old-fashioned muzzleloaders. He kept on working and in 1880 developed an improved model that was adopted by the armed services. He continued his engineering pursuits until his death.

ARNOLD, Isaac Newton (1815-1884)

While serving as a Republican congressman from Illinois, Isaac N. Arnold also served on Colonel David Hunter's staff at 1st Bull Run. A New Yorker by birth, he practiced law there until moving to Chicago in 1836. Originally a Democrat, the slavery issue moved him into the Free Soil and later the Republican Party. Meanwhile he served in the state legislature and missed being elected its speaker. He was defeated for the U.S. Congress, as a member of the Republican Party, in 1858, but won two years later, serving from March 4, 1861, to March 3, 1865. Even while that body was in session he served in a military capacity. He did not seek reelection in 1864, but became a treasury auditor for a little more than a year before resuming his practice and beginning a writing career.

ARNOLD, Lewis Golding (1817-1871)

New Jerseyite Lewis G. Arnold had his career in both the regular army and the volunteers cut short by a stroke. A West Pointer (1837) and career artillery officer, he served in the Seminole and Mexican wars. In the latter he earned two brevets, being wounded at Vera Cruz and Churubusco. A captain in the 2nd Artillery since 1847 his Civil War assignments included: major, 1st Artillery (May 15, 1861); commanding Fort Pickens, Department of Florida (August 2, 1861-ca. February 22, 1862); brigadier general, USV (January 24, 1862); commanding Department of Florida (February 22-March 15, 1862); commanding District of Pensacola, Department of the South (April-August 8, 1862); commanding District of West Florida, Department of the Gulf (August 8-September 22, 1862); and commanding Defenses of New Orleans, Department of the Gulf (September 22-November 10, 1862). He received a brevet for commanding the threatened Fort Pickens, in Pensacola Harbor early in the war and commanded the department until it was merged into the Department of the South when he was given charge of a district. Transferred to New Orleans in the fall of 1862, he was reviewing his troops on November 10 when he was stricken by a stroke. Sent on sick leave, he was retired on February 8, 1864, when it was realized that his paralysis was permanent. He died seven years later.

ARNOLD, Richard (1828-1882)

Only a captain of regular artillery, Richard Arnold distinguished himself in numerous operations, earning the brevet rank of major general in both the volunteer and regular establishments while usually serving as a chief of artillery. A native of Rhode Island and a West Pointer (1850), he was serving as General Wool's aide-de-camp, with the rank of first lieutenant, 3rd Artillery, at the outbreak of the Civil War. His later assignments included: captain, 5th Artillery (May 14, 1861); chief of artillery, 1st Division, 1st Corps, Army of the Potomac (March-April 4, 1862); chief of artillery, 1st Division, Department of the Rappahannock (April 4-May 7, 1862); acting assistant inspector general, 6th Corps, Army of the Potomac (May-July 1862); brigadier general, USV (November 29, 1862); chief of Artillery, Department of the Gulf (November 1862-April 18, 1864 and June 25-September 1864); and commanding Cavalry Division, Department of the Gulf (April 18-June 25, 1864). At 1st Bull Run he was forced to abandon his guns during the rout of the Union forces. He then served as a divisional artillery chief in the Washington and Fredericksburg vicinity before serving as a corps inspector during the Peninsula Campaign, earning a brevet for Savage Station and also seeing action at Glendale and Malvern Hill. Promoted to brigadier of volunteers, he was sent to New Orleans to direct the artillery and participated in the siege and capture of Port Hudson. In the Red River Campaign he for a time directed the cavalry but soon returned to his regular branch, seeing his final action in the operations against Mobile. At the war's close he received a flurry of brevets but upon being mustered out of the volunteers on August 24, 1865, he reverted back to a captain of artillery. While still on active duty in New York he died, five days after his promotion to lieutenant colonel, 5th Artillery.

ARNOLD, Samuel Bland (1834-1906)

The last survivor of the eight conspirators tried in May and June 1865 for killing Lincoln, Samuel B. Arnold had actually withdrawn from the plot a month before the assassination. A school friend of John Wilkes Booth and fellow conspirator

Samuel Arnold, Lincoln kidnap conspirator. (NA)

Michael O'Laughlin, he had grown up in Baltimore before joining the Confederate army. After returning to Baltimore, when Booth told him of the plot to kidnap the president and smuggle him to Richmond, he thought his friend was mad. But although he thought there was little chance of success, he went along with the scheme until March 1865 when he informed Booth of his withdrawal until they should receive definite authority from Richmond. Arnold then secured a job as a supply clerk at Fortress Monroe. He was arrested there on April 17, 1865, and confined with the others aboard a monitor. Taken to the arsenal penitentiary, he sat through the one-sided trial presided over by General Lew Wallace. He admitted that he had been involved in the kidnapping caper, but denied any connection with the assassination. On June 30 he was found guilty and sentenced to life. Sent to Dry Tortugas, he survived a yellow fever epidemic and was pardoned in 1869 by Andrew Johnson.

ARNOLD, Samuel Greene (1821-1880)

With the August 15, 1862, resignation of Rhode Island Senator James F. Simmons, Republican Samuel G. Arnold was named to complete the few remaining months of his term in Washington. Arnold was a native of the state and a Harvard-educated lawyer and historian. He was elected lieutenant governor in 1852 and served at times as the acting chief executive of the state. He was in the number two spot again for two terms, at the outset of the Civil War and was instrumental in the raising of one of the state's first artillery batteries. On December 1, 1862, he took a seat in the U.S. Senate but left four months later at the conclusion of the 37th Congress. Returning to his research, he presided over the state historical society for the last dozen years of his life.

ARP, Bill

See: *Smith, Charles Henry*

ASBOTH, Alexander Sandor (1811-1868)

A native of Hungary, veteran of the Austrian army, and fellow refugee of Louis Kossuth, Alexander S. Asboth became a Union army general. He fled to the United States in 1851 via Turkey, and was a citizen by the outbreak of the Civil War. His assignments in the war included: brigadier general, USV by Frémont (September 3, 1861; not recognized by War Department in March 1862); chief of staff, Western Department (late 1861); commanding 5th Brigade, Army of Southwest Missouri, Department of the Missouri (February 1862); commanding 2nd Division, Army of Southwest Missouri (February-June 1, 1862); brigadier general, USV (March 21, 1862); commanding 5th Division, Army of the Mississippi (June 1-July 30, 1862); commanding District of Columbus, Kentucky (designation changed to 6th Division on March 31, 1863); 16th Corps, Army of the Tennessee (January 11-August 5, 1863); and commanding District of West Florida, Department of the Gulf (August 8, 1863-October 20, 1864 and February 15-July 1865). Called for by Frémont, he was given an appointment as brigadier of volunteers that was not recognized by Washington. But he served in a staff position and later in command of a brigade and division until he received an official appointment. Wounded at Pea Ridge, he later commanded in western Kentucky and then in western Florida. On October 2, 1864, he was wounded in a skirmish at Marianna, Florida, in the left arm and the cheek. The bullet remained in his face until he went to Paris after the war to have it removed. He resumed his duties for the final months of the war and, after being brevetted major general for the war, was mustered out on August 24, 1865. He died in Buenos Aires while serving as minister to Argentina and Uruguay.

ASHBY, Turner (1828-1862)

Although he was one of the South's early war heroes, as the ideal of a chivalrous cavalryman, Turner Ashby's control of his troopers, and his intelligence gathering, left much to be desired. Raising a company of cavalry at the time of John Brown's Raid, the Shenandoah Valley planter and politician arrived too late to take part in Brown's capture. Again reporting at Harpers Ferry, in early 1861, he offered his services to the Confederacy. His assignments included: captain, Virginia cavalry company (spring 1861); lieutenant colonel, 7th Virginia Cavalry (ca. June 25, 1861); colonel, 7th Virginia Cavalry (ca. October 1861); commanding cavalry, Valley District, Department of Northern Virginia (ca. October 1861-April 1862); commanding Cavalry, Jackson's Division, Valley District, Department of Northern Virginia (April 1862-June 2, 1862); brigadier general, CSA (May 23, 1862); and commanding Cavalry, Valley District, Department of Northern Virginia (June 2-6, 1862). Serving at Harpers Ferry, usually commanding a mixed force of cavalry and infantry, he quickly became known for his daring escapades, including his undercover intelligence gathering trip to Chambersburg, Pennsylvania. During the 1st Manassas Campaign he teamed up with Jeb Stuart to deceive Union General Patterson into believing that Johnston's army was still in the Shenandoah Valley. Remaining in the Valley, he joined Jackson in the fall of 1861 when that officer took over command of the Valley District. But by a misleading report of enemy strength he brought about the Confederate attack on Kernstown and the resulting defeat. Ashby rarely had all 21 of his companies under his immediate control, and those detached companies were often ill-led, causing demoralization in the ranks. Jackson tried to divide up Ashby's command but was forced to revoke the order when faced with the latter's resignation. Ashby went on to fight through the rest of the Valley Campaign and was promoted to brigadier general by the War Department without the recommendation of Jackson. On June 2 the district commander gave Ashby command of the full cavalry force of the enlarged Valley army. Four days later the newly-named general was killed in a minor action at Harrisonburg, Virginia. (Bushong, Millard K., *General Turner Ashby and Stonewall's Valley Campaign*)

ASHCRAFT, Thomas (1786-1866)

The Civil War left businessman-scientist Thomas Ashcraft a broken man and he died a year after the Confederacy's collapse.

General Asboth, his staff, and dog York at Pea Ridge. (*Leslie's*)

Born in North Carolina and South Carolina-raised, he lived in Georgia until he removed to Alabama as a farmer in 1836. There he also gained a reputation as something of an inventor, designing a threshing machine and a cotton press. Associated with the Selma Iron Works, he naturally came into the Confederate war effort. He served as a consultant for the War Department and gave it the plans for a torpedo—now called a mine—he had patented. He was also active in the manufacturing of material for uniforms for the field armies. He retired to Clay County, Alabama, after Appomattox.

ASHE, Thomas Samuel (1812-1887)

It was not until Lincoln made his April 1861 call for troops, including a quota from North Carolina, that Thomas S. Ashe, a lawyer, planter, and former legislator, changed from a Unionist to a secessionist. He attended the state's secession convention, and, the following November, was elected to the First Regular Confederate Congress, taking his seat in February 1862. A firm believer in the rights of persons and states, he made his principal legislative efforts in an attempt to constrict the powers of the national government. However he did support those war measures that he felt were essential. In 1863 the 7th District, in south-central North Carolina, rejected him in favor of a peace candidate. Out of office with the adjournment of the First Congress in February 1864, Ashe set his sights on the Senate seat of Edwin G. Read, whom he defeated in the December election. However, the South was defeated before he could take his seat. After the war he served two terms in the U.S. Congress and was a justice of the North Carolina supreme court.

ASHE, Thomas Samuel (ca. 1813-1862)

A North Carolina planter and attorney—who rarely practiced—Thomas S. Ashe had earned a reputation for building up the state's railroads and so served the Confederacy as director of rail transport, from Richmond to New Orleans. He had served in Congress for a number of years but did not let his secessionist sentiments interfere with his efforts to obtain internal improvments for his state. An opponent of rail lines from western North Carolina to South Carolina's Charleston, he was a prime mover in the construction of east-west communications within his own state. For the last eight years of his life he was president of the Wilmington and Weldon Railroad. Appointed major and later colonel in the Confederate army, he directed rail operations during the early part of the war. He was injured on September 14, 1862, when the hand-car he was using was struck by a train while he was en route to visit a wounded son. He died three days later. At the time he was trying to organize his own unit for the army.

ASHLEY, James Mitchell (1824-1896)

As a Democrat-turned-Republican member of Congress, Ohio Representative James M. Ashley proved to be one of the leading opponents of slavery in his five terms in Washington. Born in Pennsylvania, his views on the "peculiar institution" prompted the switch of parties. After taking his House seat in 1859, he tried to weaken slavery in the territories; during the Civil War, along with Lot M. Morrill, he drafted the legislation that eliminated slavery in the nation's capital. He was also an early leader in formulating Reconstruction policy and supported the effort to impeach Andrew Johnson. He also backed a constitutional amendment banning slavery. Defeated for reelection in 1868, he left office the following March and was promptly named governor of the Montana Territory. He was later engaged in railroading.

ASTOR, John Jacob (1822-1890)

Prominent New York capitalist and philanthropist John Jacob Astor, the third of that name, was most proud of his record of service in the Union army. A graduate of Harvard Law School, he left the management of the family fortune and on November 30, 1861, became a volunteer aide-de-camp, with the rank of colonel, on the staff of General McClellan. He served through the Peninsular Campaign and on July 11, 1862, shortly after the close of the Seven Days Battles, he returned to his estates. Near the close of the war he was brevetted brigadier of volunteers for his earlier service. After the war he confined himself to his estates and charities and only ventured into politics once, in a disreputable connection with the Tweed Ring.

ATHERTON, Charles Gordon (1804-1853)

In an unsuccessful attempt to avoid the sectional divisions being created by the slavery issue, New Hampshire Congressman Charles G. Atherton introduced the so-called "gag resolution," in effect prohibiting the discussion of the issue. A lawyer and state legislator, he had entered Congress in 1837 and the next year introduced these resolutions, which directed that all petitions concerning the "peculiar institution" be indefinitely tabled. Such rules were approved at each subsequent session until 1844. Instead of burying the issue, they exacerbated the situation. A member of the Committee on Ways and Means, he moved on to the Senate in 1843 where in the last two years of his term he was chairman of the Committee on Finance. After a two-year hiatus—engaged in the practice of law—he returned to the Senate in 1853 but died suddenly before the first session had even begun.

ATKINS, John DeWitt Clinton (1825-1908)

A native Tennesseean, John D.C. Atkins studied law and then immediately entered politics; he had already served in both houses of the state legislature and in the U.S. Congress when the Civil War began. Entering the military service, he was appointed lieutenant colonel, 5th Tennessee (May 20, 1861), before resigning his commission later in the year to become a representative to the Provisional Congress, where he served on the Committee on Military Affairs. In this position he began his policy of supporting almost anything to staff and equip the military forces. He carried this policy through into the First and Second Congresses in which he represented the 9th District in the northwestern corner of the state. In the First Congress he served on the Committee on Post Offices and Post Roads; in the Second on the Committees on Commerce, Foreign Affairs, and on Ordnance and Ordnance Stores. He was, despite his support for the military, a troublesome congressman for the administration. On domestic and foreign affairs matters he was frequently in opposition. After the overrunning of his home district by Union troops in early 1862, he wanted to launch an investigation into the conduct of General Albert S. Johnston in the disaster. Following Reconstruction he served a decade in the U.S. Congress and was commissioner of Indian affairs from 1885 to 1888. The remainder of his time was spent in farming.

ATKINS, Smith Dykins (1836-1913)

An Illinois lawyer, Smith D. Atkins commanded a regiment in Wilder's famous brigade of mounted infantry and on occasion was in command of a cavalry brigade. The native New Yorker's assignments included: captain, 11th Illinois (April 30, 1861); major, 11th Illinois (March 21, 1862); colonel, 92nd Illinois (September 4, 1862); commanding 2nd Brigade, Baird's Division, Army of Kentucky, Department of the Cumberland (February-June 8, 1863); commanding 1st Brigade, 1st Division, Reserve Corps, Army of the Cumberland (June 8-July 15, 1863); colonel, 92nd Illinois Mounted Infantry (change of designation July 22, 1863); commanding 3rd Brigade, 2nd Division, Cavalry Corps, Army of the Cumberland (January 28-February 20, 1864); commanding 3rd Brigade, 3rd Division, Cavalry Corps, Army of the Cumberland (May 13-23, 1864); and commanding 2nd Brigade, 3rd Division, Cavalry Corps, Military Division of the Mississippi (November 5, 1864-June 26, 1865). As a company officer, he fought at Forts Henry and Donelson, and as a field officer at Shiloh. Resigning his commission on April 17, 1862, to raise a new regiment, he again took the field in time for the Tullahoma Campaign. With his regiment mounted in the summer of 1863, he fought on the flanks at Chickamauga. He went on to fight in the Atlanta, Savannah, and Carolinas campaigns. Brevetted brigadier and major general, he was mustered out on June 21, 1865, and later served as a postmaster in Illinois and editor of the *Freeport Daily Journal*.

ATKINSON, Edmund Nathan (1834-1884)

Putting his Georgia Military Institute education to use for the Confederacy, Edmund Atkinson nevertheless wound up his Civil War career in the hands of the enemy for the second time. He entered the army of the Confederacy during the first year of the war and his assignments included: first lieutenant and adjutant, 26th Georgia (1861); colonel, 26th Georgia (May 9, 1862); commanding Lawton's Brigade, Ewell's Division, 2nd Corps, Army of Northern Virginia (fall 1862-December 13, 1862); and commanding Evans' Brigade, Gordon's Division, Valley District, Department of Northern Virginia (July 9-September 1864). At the regiment's reorganization in the spring of 1862, he was elected to command the regiment and he led it in the Seven Days Battles. He took over brigade command after Antietam, replacing the wounded General Lawton. In this position he was wounded and captured at Fredericksburg. Following his exchange, he led his regiment at Gettysburg, Mine Run, the Wilderness, Spotsylvania, and Cold Harbor. Taking part in Early's advance on Washington, he took over command of the brigade when General Clement A. Evans was wounded at Monocacy. Evans had been Atkinson's junior when he was promoted to general. Evans returned in September and Atkinson resumed command of his regiment for 3rd Winchester. At Fisher's Hill the latter was captured for a second time and this time was not released until three months after Lee's surrender.

ATWATER, Dorence (1845-1910)

If it weren't for Dorence Atwater and his foresight, the graves of 12,920 Union soldiers in the Andersonville National Cemetery would be marked, as so many others, merely as "Unknown." Although under age, Atwater joined the 1st Connecticut Cavalry Squadron on August 19, 1861. By October 1861, this unit had merged into Colonel Judson Kilpatrick's 2nd New York Cavalry and with it, over the next two years, Atwater participated in the fights at Cedar Mountain, 2nd Bull Run, Chantilly, South Mountain, Fredericksburg, on Stoneman's Raid, Brandy Station, and Gettysburg. While serving as a courier, he was captured on July 7, 1863, near Hagerstown, Maryland. After eight months imprisonment in Richmond he was transferred to the newly established Andersonville Prison. Arriving on March 23, 1864, he spent two months in the stockade before becoming ill and being sent to the prison hospital. Upon his recovery he was made clerk to the surgeon. With his desk next to that of the commandant, Captain Henry Wirz, he was charged with recording the deaths of fellow prisoners. Secretly duplicating the list, he took it with him when paroled in March 1865. Desiring to publish the list for the relief of the prisoners' families, he was opposed by the War Department, which had him arrested, court-martialed, dishonorably discharged, fined, and imprisoned at hard labor. However, he did succeed in having the graves marked, in an expedition led by Clara Barton. It was not until 1898 that his discharge was changed to honorable. Horace Greeley had already published the list, in 1866, and sold it for a little over cost, while Atwater since 1871 had been serving as U.S. consul in Tahiti. He became very popular there, married into the royal family and became wealthy in the pearl, gold, and steamship businesses. In the latter he was a partner of Robert Louis Stevenson who wrote about his friend in *Ebb Tide* (1894). In 1908 he returned to his home of Terryville, Connecticut, and visited the memorial to him dedicated the previous year. He died in California on his way back to Tahiti. Buried on the island, he was given a royal funeral and a monument was built in his honor.

ATZERODT, George A. (1835-1865)

The fact that he had lost the nerve to carry out his assignment, from John Wilkes Booth, to kill Vice President Andrew Johnson did not save George A. Atzerodt from hanging. Born in Germany, he immigrated to the United States and became a carriage maker in Port Tobacco, Maryland. During the Civil War he aided the Confederacy by smuggling mail and couriers and possibly some supplies across nearby Pope's Creek and the Potomac River. He became involved with Booth in unsuccessful attempts to kidnap Lincoln and spirit him off to Richmond. When the Confederate capital fell and the plan was changed to murder, Atzerodt remained an active conspirator. He was supposed to kill Andrew Johnson at the Kirkwood House while Lincoln was at Ford's Theater. After riding to Ford's, he saw the presidential carriage outside and headed for his assignment. But instead of carrying it out he went into a bar and waited until he got word that Booth had carried out his part of the plan. He then panicked and fled on his own. On April 20, 1865, a detachment from the 1st Delaware Cavalry captured him near Rockville, Maryland. He was confined aboard a monitor, then tried by the military commission under Lew Wallace. Sentenced to the gallows on June 30, 1865, he was hanged on July 7.

George Atzerodt failed to kill his target, Vice President Andrew Johnson. (NA)

AUGUR, Christopher Columbus (1821-1898)

During the first half of the Civil War New Yorker Christopher C. Augur had an active field career but in the latter part of the conflict he commanded the defenses of the capital. A West Pointer (1843) and Mexican War veteran, he was a captain in the 4th Infantry at the outbreak of the war. His later assignments included: major, 13th Infantry (May 14, 1861); brigadier general, USV (November 12, 1861); commanding 1st Brigade, McDowell's Division, Army ofthe Potomac (November 9, 1861-March 13, 1862); commanding 1st Brigade, 3rd Division, 1st Corps, Army of the Potomac (March 13-April 4, 1862); commanding 1st Brigade, 3rd Division, Department of the Rappahannock (April 4-June 26, 1862); commanding 1st Brigade, 1st Division, 3rd Corps, Army of Virginia (June 26-July 7, 1862); commanding 2nd Division, 2nd Corps, Army of Virginia (July 7-August 9, 1862) major general, USV (August 9, 1862); commanding 1st Division, 19th Corps, Department of the Gulf (January 12-July 15, 1863); lieutenant colonel, 12th Infantry (July 1, 1863); and commanding 22nd Corps and Department of Washington (October 13, 1863-June 7, 1865 and June 26, 1865-June 11, 1866). Assigned to a majority in one of the new regiments at the outbreak of the war, he was soon promoted to brigadier of volunteers and command of a brigade around Washington and Fredericksburg. Commanding a division at Cedar Mountain he was severely wounded but received a regular army brevet and promotion to major general of volunteers as compensation. During his recovery he served on the commission looking into the surrender of Harpers Ferry during the Antietam Campaign. During the siege of Port Hudson he was the second ranking officer and commanded one wing of the besieging forces. Once the city was taken he was sent east to command the Washington defenses, a post that he held until 1866. Mustered out of the volunteer service on September 1, 1866, he was a full lieutenant colonel and a brevet major general in the regular establishment. Until his retirement as a brigadier general in 1885 he held various departmental commands.

Washington defender Christopher Augur. (*Leslie's*)

AUTON, Lawrence W.

See: *Williams, William Orton*

AVERELL, William Woods (1832-1900)

A career cavalryman, William W. Averell is credited with having won the first sizable action against the Confederate cavalry; but he was also later relieved from duty by Sheridan for a lack of aggressiveness in the Shenandoah. The native New Yorker and West Pointer (1855) served in the Regiment of Mounted Riflemen, suffering a severe wound in an Indian fight along the Rio Puerco in New Mexico in 1858. He returned to duty in the latter stages of the secession crisis, but was still a second lieutenant upon the outbreak of the Civil War. His assignments included: first lieutenant, Mounted Riflemen (May 14, 1861); first lieutenant, 3rd Cavalry (change of designation August 3, 1861); colonel, 3rd Pennsylvania Cavalry (August 23, 1861); commanding 1st Brigade, Cavalry Division, Army of the Potomac (July-September 1862); captain, 3rd Cavalry (July 17, 1862); brigadier general, USV (September 26, 1862); commanding Cavalry Brigade, Centre Grand Division, Army of the

Cavalryman William W. Averell. (*Leslie's*)

Potomac (November 1862-January 1863); commanding 2nd Division, Cavalry Corps, Army of the Potomac (February 12-May 16, 1863); commanding 4th Separate Brigade, 8th Corps, Middle Department (May 23-June 26, 1863); commanding 4th Separate Brigade, Department of West Virginia (June 26-December 1863); commanding 4th Division, same department (December 1863-April 1864); and commanding 2nd Cavalry Division, same department (April 26-September 26, 1863). As a staff officer he fought at 1st Bull Run and soon thereafter was commissioned commander of a volunteer cavalry regiment. He led his men on the Peninsula and commanded a brigade at Antietam and Fredericksburg. During the Chancellorsville fighting he was briefly relieved from duty with his division by Hooker for a lack of fighting spirit. Ironically, only two months earlier he had bested the Southern cavalrymen at Kelly's Ford. For the next year he was engaged in mixed operations in western Virginia including Droop Mountain, the Salem Expedition, and Moorefield. Taking a cavalry division into the Shenandoah Valley, he fought at 3rd Winchester and Fisher's Hill but a few days later was relieved of duty by Sheridan for a lack of vigorous action. Nonetheless he received sufficient brevets in both services to achieve the rank of major general in both. He resigned both commissions on May 18, 1865, and after a stint as a diplomat in Canada became a highly successful—and profit-making—inventor.

AVERY, Clarke Mouton (1819-1864)

North Carolinian Clarke M. Avery spent almost half of his Confederate career as a prisoner of war. His assignments included: captain, Company C, 1st North Carolina Volunteers (April 25, 1861), lieutenant colonel, 33rd North Carolina (September 20, 1861); and colonel, 33rd North Carolina (January 17, 1862). After participating in the Battle of Big Bethel, his company was mustered out and he became the field officer of a new regiment. In the Confederate debacle in New Bern in March 1862 he was taken prisoner and not released until October 1863. Upon his release, he rejoined his regiment and commanded it until he was wounded at Spotsylvania on May 12, 1864. He lingered until June 18, but some accounts list him as having been killed at the Wilderness on May 6.

AVERY, Isaac Erwin (1828-1863)

A farmer and railroader, Isaac Avery was one of those able Confederate officers who did not live long enough to wear a general's wreath. He became captain of Company E, 6th North Carolina State Troops, when that regiment was organized on May 16, 1861. His later assignments included: lieutenant colonel, 6th North Carolina (June 1, 1862); colonel, 6th North Carolina (June 11, 1862): and commanding Hoke's North Carolina Brigade, Early's Division, Jackson's-Ewell's Second Corps, Army of Northern Virginia (May 4-July 2, 1863). During the Seven Days Battles he led his regiment at Gaines' Mill and Malvern Hill, where he was wounded. He returned to field duty in time to assume command of Hoke's Brigade after that officer was wounded at Chancellorsville. At the 2nd Battle of Winchester, Avery led the brigade but it was not actively engaged. On the first day at Gettysburg, the brigade advanced on the extreme left of the Confederate line of battle and in conjunction with Hays' Louisianans swung around Barlow's Knoll and smashed into Coster's Union Brigade, capturing two Napoleon cannons and driving them back into the town. The next evening the two brigades stormed East Cemetary Hill, but were driven back when support failed to arrive, resulting in the loss of many men, including Colonel Avery who was mortally wounded and died the next day. Avery's command was known for the high level of discipline and drill, and he had been recommended for promotion by Pender, Hood, Law, and Early.

AYER, Lewis Malone (1821-1895)

Although he demanded a vigorous prosecution of the war, if Lewis M. Ayer had had his conservative way on financial matters the Confederacy's military effort would have been scuttled. A South Carolina lawyer and militia general, Ayer was elected to the U.S. Congress in 1860 but instead attended the state's secession convention and urged the disruption of the Union. Elected to the First Confederate Congress, he took his seat in February 1862 and served on the committees on Quartermaster's and Commissary Departments and on Ordnance and Ordnance Stores. In the Second Congress he moved to the Committee on Commerce. He was also chairman of the Committee on the War Tax where his shortsightedness was apparent in proposals to cancel the tax in kind, on grounds of states' rights and constitutional questions. And yet he demanded that the war continue and opposed peace negotiations. After the war he was a cotton merchant; Baptist minister in Texas, Tennessee, and South Carolina; and a professor at a private military institute.

AYRES, Romeyn Beck (1825-1888)

A career army officer, Romeyn B. Ayres served the first part of the war in command of artillery until he transferred to the regular infantry in the Army of the Potomac. A West Pointer (1847), the New Yorker was immediately posted to the artillery and served in garrisons in both Mexico and the United States. By the outbreak of the Civil War he had been a first lieutenant in the 3rd Artillery for nearly a decade. His later assignments included: captain, 5th Artillery (May 14, 1865); chief of artillery, Smith's Division, Army of the Potomac (October 3, 1861-March 13, 1862); chief of artillery, 2nd Division, 4th Corps, Army of the Potomac (March 13-May 18, 1862); chief of artillery, 2nd Division, 6th Corps, Army of the Potomac (May 18-November 16, 1862); chief of artillery, 6th Corps, Army of the Potomac (November 16, 1862-April 4, 1863); brigadier general, USV (November 29, 1862); commanding 1st Brigade, 2nd Division, 5th Corps, Army of the Potomac (April 21-June 28, 1863 and June 6, 1864); commanding the division (June 28, 1863-March 24, 1864); commanding 4th Brigade, 1st Division, 5th Corps, Army of the Potomac (March 24-April

1864); commanding 1st Brigade, 1st Division, 5th Corps, Army of the Potomac (April-June 5, 1864); and commanding 2nd Division, 5th Corps, Army of the Potomac (June 6-December 22, 1864 and January 8-June 28, 1865). As an artillerist he fought at Yorktown, Williamsburg, the Seven Days, South Mountain, Antietam, and Fredericksburg. He led the regulars as a general at Chancellorsville and Gettysburg and was sent to New York to maintain order following the draft rioting. He then served in the Overland campaign and suffered a wound at Petersburg. At the close of the war he received brevets for Gettysburg, the Wilderness, Spotsylvania, Jericho Mills, Bethesda Church, Petersburg, Globe Tavern, the Weldon Railroad, Five Forks, and war service. Thus he became a brevet major general in both the regular and volunteer establishments. After the close of hostilities he commanded in the Shenandoah Valley until his April 30, 1866, mustering out of the volunteers. He was still on active duty—as colonel, 2nd Artillery—at the time of his death.

B

BABCOCK, Orville Elias (1835-1884)

Orville E. Babcock joined Grant's staff relatively late in the war and was later forced from his employ in Grant's White House administration by the Whiskey Ring investigations. Graduating third in his West Point class at the outbreak of the Civil War, his assignments included: brevet second lieutenant, Engineers (May 6, 1861); second lieutenant, Engineers (May 6, 1861); first lieutenant, Engineers (November 17, 1861); chief engineer, Left Grand Division, Army of the Potomac (November 16-December 18, 1862); lieutenant colonel and assistant inspector general (assigned January 1, 1863-March 28, 1864); assistant inspector general, 6th Corps, Army of the Potomac (January 1-February 6, 1863); assistant inspector general and chief engineer, 9th Corps, Army of the Potomac (February 6-March 19, 1863); assistant inspector general and chief engineer, 9th Corps, Army of the Ohio (March 19-April 10, 1863); chief engineer, District of Central Kentucky, Department of the Ohio (April 10-June 9, 1863); captain, Engineers (June 1, 1863); chief engineer, Army of the Ohio (January 23-March 20, 1864); lieutenant colonel and aide-de-camp (March 29, 1864); and colonel and aide-de-camp (July 25, 1866). Serving with the Engineer Battalion in the Peninsular campaign he earned a brevet at Yorktown and participated in the Seven Days. At Fredericksburg he was William B. Franklin's engineering chief. Assigned to inspector duty he accompanied the 9th Corps to the West and became acquainted with Grant during the Vicksburg Campaign. Back in Tennessee, he won a brevet for the operations at Knoxville and then joined Grant as an aide just prior to the Overland Campaign. He was again brevetted for the Wilderness and fought through to Appomattox. Staying with his chief after the war, and being brevetted brigadier general of regulars for his war service, he resigned his army commission when Grant was sworn in as president in 1869 and became Grant's personal secretary. Caught up in the Whiskey Ring frauds, he was forced out of the White House despite Grant's defense of him. He was appointed a lighthouse inspector by the president and drowned in 1884 while working at Mosquito Inlet, Florida. (McFeely, William S., *Grant: A Biography*)

BADEAU, Adam (1831-1895)

Badeau was Ulysses S. Grant's military secretary in the last year of the Civil War, but came into conflict with the general and his son over the authorship of Grant's memoirs (published in 1885-86) and the payment thereof. The native New Yorker's assignments included: captain and aide-de-camp, USV (April 29, 1862); lieutenant colonel and military secretary (March 29, 1864); and colonel and aide-de-camp (July 25, 1866). As a staff officer to General Thomas W. Sherman, he was wounded at Port Hudson. Recovering, he joined Grant's staff in time for the Overland, Petersburg and Appomattox campaigns and was brevetted brigadier. He claimed to have ghost written Grant's book but the record does not bear this out. He also wrote a three-volume account, *Military History of Ulysses S. Grant* and *Grant in Peace: From Appomattox to Mount McGregor*. Much of the latter work was based upon his service as a diplomat under Grant and his travels with the general. (McFeely, William S., *Grant: A Biography*)

BAGBY, Arthur Pendleton (1833-1921)

After the fall of Vicksburg, the Trans-Mississippi Department was cut off from regular communications with Richmond, and its commander, General E.K. Smith, was forced to resort to the appointment of general officers without complying with the legal requirement that the president make such appointments. One Texas officer, Arthur P. Bagby, received two such promotions. He had graduated from West Point in 1852 and served for one year in the 8th Infantry before resigning. The Alabama-born ex-officer offered his services to his adopted state of Texas upon the start of hostilities. His assignments in the Trans-Mississippi Department included: lieutenant colonel, 7th Texas Cavalry (1861); colonel, 7th Texas Cavalry (1862); commanding brigade, Green's Cavalry Division, District of

West Louisiana (ca. March 17-summer 1864); brigadier general, CSA by Smith (April 13 to rank from March 17, 1864); commanding 4th Texas Cavalry Brigade, 2nd Texas Cavalry Division, 1st Corps (summer 1864-early 1865); commanding cavalry division, 1st Corps (early 1865-May 26, 1865); and major general, CSA by Smith (May 16 to rank from May 10, 1865). His first service was in Sibley's New Mexico Campaign where he saw action at Valverde. He continued on the frontier until March 1864 when his command was ordered to western Louisiana to help stop Banks' Red River Campaign. For the rest of the war he served there and in Arkansas. After the department's surrender he resumed his law practice.

BAGBY, George William (1828-1883)

Briefly a Lynchburg physician, George W. Bagby, after dabbling in journalism with a few articles for the *Lynchburg Virginian*, served as the editor of the *Southern Literary Messenger* in Richmond during most of the Civil War. Joining the Confederate army, he was soon found to be unfit for the field and, after a stint on Beauregard's staff as a clerk, he returned to literary pursuits. From his Richmond post he served as a correspondent in the nation's capital for numerous Southern publications. Following his departure from the *Messenger* he was an associate editor for the *Richmond Whig* until the close of the war. After a journalistic career in New York came to an end due to failing eyesight, he returned to the Old Dominion to take up the lecture circuit on which he was highly popular. For almost a decade he was the state librarian and wrote numerous short works. (King, Joseph Leonard, *Dr. William Bagby, a Study of Virginian Literature, 1850-1880*)

BAILEY, Frederick Augustus Washington

See: *Douglass, Frederick*

BAILEY, Guilford Dudley (?-1862)

In the brutal Confederate attacks upon Casey's Division at Seven Pines the divisional artillery chief Guilford D. Bailey fell dead and one of his batteries was captured. The New Yorker was a career artillerist, having graduated from West Point in 1856. His assignments included: second lieutenant, 2nd Artillery (July 1, 1856); first lieutenant, 2nd Artillery (May 14, 1861); captain and commissary of subsistence (August 3, 1861); colonel, 1st New York Light Artillery (September 25, 1861); chief of artillery, Casey's Division, Army of the Potomac (December 1861-March 13, 1862); and chief of artillery, 2nd Division, 4th Corps, Army of the Potomac (March 13-May 31, 1862). After a brief stint as a staff officer he sought advancement in the volunteer service and raised a regiment of field artillery. With his 12 batteries divided among many commands he was given charge of Casey's guns and served on the Peninsula until the battle of Seven Pines. He was killed trying to maintain his batteries' position amidst the enemy assaults. A short time later his successor was also killed. (Nevins, Allan, ed., *A Diary of Battle: The Personal Journals of Colonel Charles S. Wainwright 1861-1865*)

BAILEY, Joseph (1825 or 1827-1867)

An Ohio-born Wisconsin civil engineer and lumberman, Joseph Bailey entered the Union army and became one of only 14 men to receive the Thanks of Congress for the Civil War—the only one who was not an army or corps commander at the time. His assignments included: captain, 4th Wisconsin (July 2, 1861); major, 4th Wisconsin (May 30, 1863); lieutenant colonel, 4th Wisconsin (July 15, 1863); lieutenant colonel, 4th Wisconsin Cavalry (change of designation August 22, 1863); colonel, 4th Wisconsin Cavalry (June 1, 1864); commanding Engineer Brigade, 19th Corps, Department of the Gulf (June 10-August 10, 1864); commanding District of West Florida, same department (October 20-November 25, 1864); brigadier general, USV (November 10, 1864); commanding District of Baton Rouge and Port Hudson, same department (December 3-28, 1864); commanding Cavalry Division, same department (December 28, 1864-February 9, 1865); commanding Northern District of Louisiana, same department (February 9-March 11, 1865); commanding Engineer Brigade, Military Division of West Mississippi (March 11-May 2, 1865); and brigadier general, USV (April 16, 1865 to rank from November 10, 1864, his original appointment having expired on March 4, 1865). After taking part in the capture of New Orleans, he soon became acting chief engineer of the city's defenses and as an engineer was distinguished in the capture of Port Hudson. On Banks' Red River Campaign he was the chief engineer; when the joint army-navy expedition failed and many of the vessels were left stranded by low water in an exposed position, it was Bailey who came to their rescue. Utilizing 3,000 troops he was able to construct a dam across the river, and through a spillway the craft made their escape downriver on May 12, 1864. For this he received a brevet as brigadier and was given the Thanks of Congress. Soon appointed a full brigadier general he held various commands and then directed the engineers in the campaign against Mobile for which he was brevetted major general. Resigning on July 7, 1865, he was shot and killed on March 21, 1867, while serving as a Missouri sheriff.

BAILEY, Theodorus (1805-1877)

A career naval officer, after joining the navy as a midshipman at the age of 13, Theodorus Bailey proved to be a capable senior officer during the Civil War. His prior services included cruises off Africa and in the Pacific and, during the Mexican War, off Lower California. He had been a captain for six years upon the outbreak of the war and served in that grade throughout. From May 2, 1861, he commanded the *Colorado* in the blockade of the Florida coast. In the New Orleans expedition he was in command of the first division of gunboats, and thus second in command to Farragut. It was Captain Bailey who accepted the surrender of the port city. From November 1862 until the spring of 1864 he successfully commanded the East Gulf Blockading Squadron, seizing 150 blockade runners. He finished out the war commanding the Portsmouth Navy Yard, then resigned in failing health in 1866, after making rear admiral earlier that year.

BAIRD, Absalom (1824-1905)

A career army officer, Absalom Baird emerged from the Civil War with brevets of general in both the regular and volunteer services and in 1896 received the Congressional Medal of Honor for the Battle of Jonesboro. A native of Pennsylvania and West Pointer (1849), he had seen service in the Florida Indian fighting. His Civil War assignments included: first lieutenant, 1st Artillery (since December 24, 1853); brevet captain and assistant adjutant general (May 11, 1861); captain and assistant adjutant general (August 3, 1861); major and assistant inspector general (November 12, 1861); inspector general and chief of staff, 4th Corps, Army of the Potomac (March-May 8, 1862); commanding 3rd Division, Army of Kentucky, Department of the Ohio (November 1862-February 1863); commanding division, Army of Kentucky, Department of the Cumberland (February-June 8, 1863); commanding 1st Division, Reserve Corps, Army of the Cumberland (June 8-August 11, 1863); commanding 1st Division, 14th Corps, Army of the Cumberland (August 23-September 21, 1863); and commanding 3rd Division, 14th Corps, Army of the Cumberland (October 10-25, 1863 and November 25, 1863-July 20, 1865). At first assigned to staff duty, he served with General Tyler at Blackburn's Ford and 1st Bull Run before taking a desk assignment. He was again called into the field for the Peninsula Campaign as Keyes' inspector and chief of staff. After action at Yorktown and Williamsburg he was given a brigadier's star and a brigade in the West. He took part in the capture of Cumberland Gap and the Perryville Campaign. He earned a brevet for his role in the fighting at Chickamauga and another for the lifting of the siege of Chattanooga. He took part in the Atlanta Campaign for which he was brevetted a brigadier in the regulars and major general in the volunteers. He was subsequently awarded the Medal of Honor for leading a brigade-level assault at Jonesboro shortly before Atlanta's fall. He later participated in the March to the Sea and the Carolinas Campaign. Mustered out of the volunteer service on September 1, 1866, he continued in the regular establishment until his 1888 retirement as inspector general with the rank of brigadier general. (Baird, John A., Jr., *Profile of a Hero: Absalom Baird, His family, and the American Military Tradition*)

BAKER, Alpheus (1828-1891)

Serving throughout the war in the western theater, Alpheus Baker of Alabama appears to have been a general without a command in the very final days of the Confederacy. The South Carolina-born attorney's military assignments included: private, Eufaula Rifles (January 1861); captain, Company B, 1st Alabama (January 1861); colonel, 1st Alabama, Tennessee and Mississippi or 4th Confederate (December 27, 1861); colonel, 54th Alabama (October 9, 1862); brigadier general, CSA (March 5, 1864); commanding Moore's (old) Brigade, Stewart's-Clayton's Division, Hood's-Lee's Corps, Army of Tennessee (March 19-September 1864); commanding some brigade, District of the Gulf, Department of Alabama, Mississippi and East Louisiana (September-October 1864); commanding brigade, Liddell's Division, District of the Gulf, Department of Alabama, Mississippi and East Louisiana (October 1864-early 1865); and commanding brigade, Clayton's Division, Lee's Corps, Army of Tennessee (March 16-April 9, 1865). The month before his company was disbanded upon the expiration of its one-year term of enlistment Baker was named colonel of a regiment composed of companies from three states. While commanding this he was captured at Island £10 and not exchanged until September 1862. The regiment was then reorganized, and Baker was transferred to an Alabama regiment with which he was wounded at Champion Hill while serving in William W. Loring's division (which was thereafter cut off from the rest of the army, which subsequently surrendered at Vicksburg). Promoted to brigadier general, he led a brigade through the Atlanta campaign—being wounded at Ezra Church—and then served several months near Mobile. Rejoining the main western army, he fought at Bentonville but in the subsequent reorganization and consolidation of brigades he appears to have become a supernumerary officer. In the postwar years he returned to his law practice.

BAKER, Cullen M. (1838-1869)

A deserter from both the Union and Confederate armies Cullen M. Baker became the head of a band of "Confederate" irregulars which terrorized much of Texas and Arkansas during and after the Civil War. Conscription into the Confederate army provided him with a refuge from an Arkansas murder case but he soon deserted, killed two Union soldiers and again found sanctuary by enlisting in the Northern army. He deserted again to join the irregulars—actually bandits preying on farmers—and continue the vicious ways he had practiced since at least 1855. With the war over he saw no reason to stop and by 1868 Arkansas Governor Clayton Powell, a former Union general, had put a $1000 reward on his head. Late that year he kidnapped a crippled teacher named Thomas Orr whom a girl had chosen over Baker, and hung him from a tree. Although Orr survived, this event destroyed the good reputation he had locally for fighting Union troops and black police. A posse caught up with him on January 7, 1869, and Orr shot and killed him.

BAKER, Edward Dickinson (1811-1861)

Probably only two things prevented Edward D. Baker from receiving censure for his role in the Union disaster at Ball's bluff—his death and his friendship with Abraham Lincoln who had named his second son after him. A London-born attorney, he was an active politician and veteran of the Black Hawk War of 1832 and the Mexican War, in which he commanded the 4th Illinois and later a brigade. He served in the Illinois legislature and represented it in Congress before moving to the West Coast. Shortly before the war he was named one of Oregon's senators. After working to save the Pacific states for the Union he received the following appointments: brigadier general, USV (May 17, 1861; declined); colonel, 71st Pennsylvania (June 22, 1861; also known as 1st California); major general, USV (September 21, 1861; neither accepted nor declined); and commanding 3rd Brigade, Stone's Division, Army of the Potomac (October 3-21,

1861). Under the law he was required to resign from the Senate if he accepted a generalship, and it is clear that he intended to decline the second appointment as well. His "California Volunteers" were, after much haggling, finally accepted by Governor Curtin of Pennsylvania. Ordered to make a demonstration along the Potomac in October 1861, he unwisely moved his entire brigade across and placed them atop Ball's Bluff. In the open they proved perfect targets for the Confederates in the woods. Baker was eventually shot down and his men driven down the steep bluff and into the river where many drowned. Bodies later washed up along Washington piers. With Baker dead, his division commander, General Stone, became the scapegoat for the fiasco. (Baltz, John, *Hon. Edward D. Baker*)

BAKER, James McNair (1821-1892)

In November 1861, after a closely contested election requiring 41 ballots, the Florida legislature appointed a former Unionist lawyer and judge to a two-year term in the Confederate Senate. He was James M. Baker, a transplanted North Carolinian. In 1863 he was unanimously reelected to a six-year term. He served on the Committees on Claims; Commerce (First Congress only); Engrossment and Enrollment (First Congress only); Naval Affairs; Post Offices and Post Roads; Public Buildings; and Public Lands, which he chaired during the Second Congress. Baker was primarily concerned with the administrative organization of the new nation. Although a supporter of the war policies, he felt that many of the measures taken were unduly affecting the economic life of much of the South. This view may have been influenced by the fact that throughout the war only a small portion of Florida was occupied or threatened by Union troops. Baker returned to the practice of law after the war, but was removed from the state supreme court during Reconstruction. Eventually receiving a judgeship, he held it for almost a decade until his retirement in 1890.

BAKER, John A. (?-?)

A resident of New Hanover County, North Carolina, John Baker's career during the Civil War made him *persona non grata* in the South after the war. The governor appointed Baker a first lieutenant in the "Wilmington Light Artillery," which was designated Company E, 1st North Carolina Artillery, on

Death of Lincoln's friend Edward Baker at Ball's Bluff, Virginia. (*Leslie's*)

May 16, 1861. He resigned that commission on April 9, 1862, and was promoted captain and aide-de-camp to General S.G. French. On September 3, 1862, he was again promoted, this time to colonel and given command of a group of independent cavalry companies that became the 3rd North Carolina Cavalry. Although his regiment was not serving together as a unit, Baker did take part in the fighting at White Hall, near Kingston, North Carolina, in mid-December 1862 and was slightly wounded there. After a year of service in North Carolina and southeastern Virginia, Baker and his regiment joined the Army of Northern Virginia on May 26, 1864. It was immediately involved in an almost daily series of cavalry fights on the Hanover Town Road, at Haw's Shop, Hanover Court House, Ashland, and near Meadows Bridge. During Grant's move from Cold Harbor to Petersburg, Baker and his men fought at White Oak Swamp, Malvern Hill and Harrison's Landing. In a fight along the Weldon Railroad, at Davis' Farm on June 21, 1864, Baker was captured. Part of the 600 rebel prisoners sent to Charleston Harbor to be placed under Southern fire in retaliation for Confederate treatment of Union captives, Baker did something that angered his fellow soldiers. When in September 1864, an exchange of prisoners seemed possible, Secretary of War James Seddon wrote that charges had been preferred against Colonel Baker and he did not wish there to be any furlough or indulgence shown him and that he should be sent to Richmond for appropriate measures. Seddon further wrote, "This last matter had best be preserved secret, as any intimation to him might probably cause him to remain with the enemy." The exchange never came off. In March 1865 Baker took the oath of allegiance to the U.S. government and was released on the 6th. Whatever the secret matter was, it was loathsome enough in the South that Baker fled to the West Indies and apparently never returned.

BAKER, Lafayette Curry (1826-1868)

A thoroughly unsavory character before the Civil War, Lafayette C. Baker remained that way for the duration and after. Born in New York, he appears to have lived in Michigan, New York, Philadelphia, and San Francisco during his prewar years. Some of his occupations included claim jumping and vigilantism. During the first months of the Civil War he served as a special agent for Commander-in-Chief Winfield Scott. Through connections with the secretaries of state and war, William H. Seward and Edwin M. Stanton, Baker became special agent of the Provost's branch in the War Department. Charged with rooting out corruption in the war effort, he was not of strong enough character to refrain from engaging in it himself. In order to give him the appropriate authority, he was granted military rank and his assignments included: colonel, 1st District of Columbia Cavalry (May 5, 1863); and brigadier general, USV (April 26, 1865). He rarely, if ever, actually commanded the regiment that had been raised for special service in and around Washington, although it did see some action under others against Mosby and near Richmond and Petersburg. Following the assassination of Lincoln his detectives fanned out across the countryside after the culprits. Two agents, his cousin Luther B. Baker and Everton J. Conger, brought back David Herold and the body of John Wilkes Booth with a cavalry detachment. For this Colonel Baker received $3,750 of the reward money. He was promoted to brigadier general from the date of the capture, and was mustered out on January 15, 1866. His working methods had been questionable to say the least. Arbitrary arrests were commonplace and charges were made without evidence, as happened when he was a witness in the impeachment proceedings against Andrew Johnson. His *History of the United States Secret Service* is of interest mainly for insights into his personality; otherwise it is highly unreliable. Over the years, alleged coded messages from Baker have surfaced indicating that the assassination was masterminded by Stanton and others. Even if they actually are Baker's work, one must still question the messages' veracity. Baker died (some say he was murdered to keep him quiet) in Philadelphia in 1868. (Mogelever, Jacob, *Death to Traitors: The Story of General Lafayette C. Baker, Lincoln's Forgotten Secret Service Chief*)

Detective chief Lafayette C. Baker. (*Leslie's*)

BAKER, Laurence Simmons (1830-1907)

A veteran of the Army of Northern Virginia's cavalry operations, Laurence S. Baker was wounded before he received formal notification of his promotion to brigadier and was never able to rejoin the unit. An 1851 graduate of West Point, he had served a decade in the Regiment of Mounted Rifles before resigning a first lieutenant's commission on May 10, 1861. His Confederate assignments included: lieutenant colonel, 1st North Carolina Cavalry (May 16, 1861); colonel, 1st North Carolina Cavalry (March 1, 1862); commanding Hampton's Brigade, Cavalry Division, Army of Northern Virginia (July 3-August 1, 1863); brigadier general, CSA (July 23, 1863); commanding 2nd Military District, Department of North Carolina (June 9, 1864-February 1865 but detached in Georgia November-December 1864); commanding 1st Brigade North Carolina Junior Reserves, Hoke's Division, Hardee's Corps (March-April 9, 1865); and commanding same brigade, Hoke's Division, Hardee's Corps, Army of Tennessee (April 1865). As a regimental commander he fought at the Seven Days, Antietam, Fredericksburg, and Gettysburg where he succeeded the wounded Hampton. Four weeks later he was himself wounded and after a long recovery was made a district commander in his native North Carolina. He was sent at the head of a brigade to aid in the unsuccessful defense of Savannah but then returned to his district. Commanding some reserves he fought at Bentonville but was absent at the time of the surrender. He was a farmer and a railroad employee after the war. (Freeman, Douglas S., *Lee's Lieutenants*)

BAKER, Luther B. (?-?)

Luther B. Baker was the junior detective supervising the cavalry detachment under Lieutenant Edward P. Doherty in the search for John Wilkes Booth and David Herold. He was a lieutenant in the War Department's Secret Service, headed by his cousin, Lafayette C. Baker. Under the direction of Colonel Everton J. Conger, he helped follow the trail of the assassins across the Rappahannock River at Port Conway. They finally caught up with their quarry at Richard H. Garrett's farm and captured Herold, but Booth either committed suicide or was killed by a soldier named Boston Corbett. Baker recrossed the river and headed off for Washington without waiting for the rest. He took Booth's body and two prisoners but managed to lose one, Willie Jett. All sorts of stories entwine the younger Baker with the activities of his cousin in some kind of coverup, but nothing has ever been conclusively proven.

BALDWIN, Philemon P. (?-1863)

In his second major battle as a brigade commander, Colonel Philemon P. Baldwin was killed in the Union rout at Chickamauga. His assignments included: lieutenant colonel, 6th Indiana (ca. September 20, 1861); colonel, 6th Indiana (ca. April 28, 1862); commanding 3rd Brigade, 2nd Division, Right Wing, 14th Corps, Army of the Cumberland (December 24, 1862-January 9, 1863); and commanding 3rd Brigade, 2nd Division, 20th Corps, Army of the Cumberland (January 9-27 and April 17-September 20, 1863). Fighting at Shiloh, he was in command of a brigade by the time of the battle of Murfreesboro. He led the brigade through Tennessee and into Georgia during the Tullahoma and Chickamauga campaigns. In the rout of the Union center and right on the second day of the latter battle he was struck and killed by enemy fire.

BALDWIN, William Edwin (1827-1864)

Having twice survived capture, Mississippi bookseller William E. Baldwin rose to the rank of brigadier general in the Confederate army only to die in a riding accident. The South Carolina native had entered the state militia in his adopted state. His assignments included: lieutenant, Columbus Riflemen (since 1849); captain, Company K, 14th Mississippi (spring 1861); colonel, 14th Mississippi (spring 1861); commanding 2nd Brigade, 2nd (Buckner's Division, Central Army of Kentucky, Department £2 (October 28, 1861-February 9, 1862); commanding 2nd Brigade, Buckner's Division, Fort Donelson, Central Army of Kentucky, Department £2 (February 9-16, 1862); brigadier general, CSA, (September 19, 1862); commanding Lee's (old) Brigade, Smith's Division, 2nd Military District, Department of Mississippi and East Louisiana (April 1863); commanding brigade, Smith's Division, Department of Mississippi and East Louisiana (April-July 4, 1863); commanding brigade, Forney's Division, Department of Mississippi and East Louisiana (November-December 1863); commanding brigade, Walker's Division, Hardee's Corps, Army of Tennessee (December 1863-January 1864); commanding brigade, Department of the Gulf (January-April 6, 1864); and commanding brigade, District of the Gulf, Department of Alabama, Mississippi and East Louisiana (April 6-February 19, 1864). After serving at Pensacola and in central Kentucky, he was captured while commanding a brigade at Fort Donelson. Exchanged in August 1862, he was captured again at Vicksburg when that place fell to Grant. Again freed from parole he led his brigade in Mississippi, northern Georgia and around Mobile. A fluke riding accident near Dog River Factory, Alabama, proved fatal on February 19, 1864.

BANKS, Nathaniel Prentiss (1816-1894)

Of the 14 Union officers who received the Thanks of Congress during the Civil War, Nathaniel P. Banks was the least entitled. Serving under five different party labels during his political career, he rose from a childhood job in a cotton mill in his native Massachusetts—which earned him the nickname "Bobbin Boy"—to become speaker of the state legislature's lower house, U.S. congressman and, just before the war, governor. As a political appointee, he was named a major general of volunteers. His field career was rather dismal but his appointment served its purpose in rallying support for the war effort. His assignments included: major general, USV (May 16, 1861); commanding division, Department of Annapolis (ca. May-June 11, 1861); commanding the department (June 11-July 19, 1861); commanding Department of the Shenandoah (July 25-August 17, 1861); commanding division, Military District of the Potomac (August 17-October 3, 1861); commanding division, Army of the Potomac (October 3, 1861-March 13, 1862); commanding 5th Corps, Army of the Potomac (March 13-April 4, 1862); again commanding Department of the Shenandoah (April 4-June 26, 1862); commanding 2nd Corps, Army of Virginia (June 26-September 4, 1862); commanding Military District of Washington, Army of

Political General Nathaniel P. Banks. (AC)

the Potomac (September 7-October 27, 1862); commanding 19th Corps, Department of the Gulf (December 16, 1862-August 20, 1863); commanding the department (December 17, 1862-September 23, 1864 and April 22-June 3, 1865). With no prior military experience, he was in divisional and departmental command near Washington early in the war. In the Shenandoah Valley he was routed by Stonewall Jackson and due to his tremendous loss of supplies was dubbed "Commissary Banks" by the Confederates. As part of Pope's army, he was again defeated at Cedar Mountain by Jackson and was at 2nd Bull Run. After a brief stint in the capital's defenses he went to New Orleans to replace Benjamin F. Butler. His operations against Port Hudson met with several bloody repulses but the place eventually fell after the surrender of Vicksburg made it untenable. For obvious political reasons, Congress awarded a resolution of thanks to one of its former members. Remaining in the Gulf area, he led the dismal Red River Campaign of 1864 and was then for a time without a command. With hostilities virtually over, he was returned to command but was mustered out on August 24, 1865. Continuing his political career, until 1890, he served in Congress, the state senate, and as a U.S. marshal. Congress awarded him a $1,200 annual pension. (Harrington, Fred Harvey, *Fighting Politician: Major General N.P. Banks*)

BARKER, Mrs. Stephen (?-?)

Following her husband, Chaplain Stephen Barker of the 13th Massachusetts, to Washington in July 1861, Mrs. Barker became a nurse. She served in one capacity or another throughout the Civil War. In 1864 she was a superintendent for the United States Sanitary Commission. In the war's final months she again accompanied her husband, this time on a fund-raising mission in New York. They both aided during the disbandment of the army in Washington.

BARKSDALE, Ethelbert (1824-1893)

One of Jefferson Davis' most influential supporters in the Confederate Congress was the representative from Mississippi's 6th District, Ethelbert Barksdale. A journalist, Barksdale was an editor by the time he was 21. He diffused his Democratic views through the pages of the *Yazoo City Democrat*, *Jackson Mississippian*, and the *Jackson Clarion*. A delegate to the 1860 Democratic convention and a supporter of John C. Breckinridge in the presidential race, Barksdale declared that he would become a secessionist if Lincoln were elected. Named to the First Confederate Congress, he soon became known as a powerful debater and an introducer of controversial bills supporting the Davis Administration. He even favored the institution of martial law. Having gained the support of Robert E. Lee in the final months of the war, Barksdale pushed through the bill to arm the slaves. Returning to journalism after the war, Barksdale was active in ending carpetbag rule in Mississippi. In the 1800s he served two terms in the U.S. Congress. Ethelbert's brother, General William Barksdale, was killed at Gettysburg.

BARKSDALE, William (1821-1863)

The brother of Confederate Congressman Ethelbert Barksdale, William Barksdale died as a Southern brigadier at Gettysburg. Born in Tennessee he moved to Mississippi to practice law and later edited the pro-slavery *Columbus Democrat*. After taking part in the Mexican War as an assistant commissary of subsistence for the volunteers with the rank of captain, he soon entered Congress as a states' rights representative. He resigned with the secession of his state and in March 1861 became quartermaster general of the state's forces. When he transferred to Confederate service his assignments included: colonel, 13th Mississippi (May 1861); commanding Griffith's (old) Brigade, Magruder's Division, Magruder's Command, Army of Northern Virginia (June 29-July 1862); commanding same brigade, McLaws' Division, 1st Corps, same army (July 1862-July 2, 1863); and brigadier general, CSA (August 12, 1862). He led his regiment at 1st Bull Run, Yorktown, and in the Seven Days. In the latter he succeeded to brigade command upon the death of General Richard Griffith at Savage Station. After service in the Maryland Campaign he particularly distinguished himself in the early stages at Fredericksburg. His brigade, along with other units, delayed the crossing of the Union troops by firing upon the engineers attempting to lay pontoon bridges. Despite artillery barrages that nearly leveled the town, Barksdale and his men fought on until forced out by a Union amphibious landing. His brigade was part of the force that defended Marye's Heights at Fredericksburg during the

Battle of Chancellorsville. He was mortally wounded in the attack on the second day at Gettysburg, and died the next day. (Freeman, Douglas S., *Lee's Lieutenants*)

Confederate General William Barksdale. (*Harpers*)

BARLOW, Francis Channing (1834-1896)

A Harvard graduate and New York lawyer with no military experience, Francis C. Barlow proved to be one of the more capable division commanders in the Army of the Potomac, but wounds and ill-health frequently kept him out of action. The New York native's assignments included: private, 12th New York Militia (April 19, 1861); first lieutenant, 12th New York Militia (May 1, 1861); lieutenant colonel, 61st New York (November 9, 1861); colonel, 61st New York (April 14, 1862); brigadier general, USV (September 19, 1862); commanding 2nd Brigade, 2nd Division, 11th Corps, Army of the Potomac (April 17-May 24, 1863); commanding 1st Division, 11th Corps, Army of the Potomac (May 24-July 1, 1863); commanding 1st Division, 2nd Corps, Army of the Potomac (March 25-July 29, 1864); commanding 2nd Division, 2nd Corps, Army of the Potomac (April 6-May 28, 1865); also commanding the corps (April 22-May 5, 1865); and major general, USV (May 25, 1865). After initial service, as an enlisted man and a company officer, with Patterson's army in the Shenandoah Valley he was mustered out on August 1, 1861. That fall he joined a new regiment as lieutenant colonel and was promoted to colonel by the time he led his regiment in the Peninsula Campaign. Wounded at Antietam, he did not return to duty until the spring of 1863, but he had in the meantime been made a brigadier and he commanded a brigade in the routed 11th Corps at Chancellorsville and a division on the first day at Gettysburg. Falling severely wounded he was provided with water by Confederate General John B. Gordon who also arranged for Barlow's wife—then serving as a nurse with the Union forces—to pass through the lines to his aid. Gordon assumed that Barlow was mortally hurt and the latter, in turn, heard of the death in 1864 of a James B. Gordon and assumed it to be his Gettysburg benefactor. Many years after the war the pair met in Washington and asked if each was related to the deceased officer they had briefly met. They became close friends until the time of Barlow's death. But earlier it took almost 10 months for Barlow to recover and return to duty. He led a division at the Wilderness and was distinguished in the assault on the Spotsylvania salient. He then fought at Cold Harbor. About a month after the investment of Petersburg he was granted an extended sick leave during which he traveled to Europe to regain his health. Returning to divisional command in the last days of the war, he was in reserve at Sayler's Creek but fought at Farmville and was at Appomattox. After hostilities had ceased he was promoted to major general—he had been brevetted to that rank the previous summer—and he resigned on November 16, 1865. Returning to the law he was a founder of the American Bar Association and entered Republican politics. He served as secretary of state for New York, U.S. marshal, and state attorney general. As such he investigated the disputed Tilden-Hayes election and prosecuted the notorious Tweed Ring. He was practicing law at the time of his death.

Division commander Francis C. Barlow. (*Leslie's*)

BARNARD, George N. (1819-1902)

In the photography business for 18 years when the Civil War started, George Barnard worked for Mathew Brady during the early years of the war. He was no stranger to photographic journalism, having taken two daguerreotypes of a mill fire in Oswego, New York, on July 5, 1853. These views might well be the very first news photos. Barnard's first Civil War photographs were taken in early 1862, on the old battlefield of 1st Bull Run. In late 1863, Barnard became an official photographer for the War Department and was assigned to the Military Division of the Mississippi. In this position, Barnard made his most important contribution to Civil War photography. His series of views of Sherman's campaigns against Atlanta, Savannah, and the Carolinas in 1864-65 is a landmark work. After the war, Barnard continued to be active as a journalistic photographer. (Barnard, George N., *Photographic Views of Sherman's Campaign*)

BARNARD, John Gross (1815-1882)

Since he served throughout the war in staff positions instead of in field command, John G. Barnard is little remembered in Civil War history. A Massachusetts native and number two graduate in his West Point class of 1833, he was routinely posted to the engineers. He served on all three coasts and in the Mexican War earned a brevet. His positions during the Civil War period included: major, Engineers (since December 13, 1858); chief engineer, Department of Washington (April-July 25, 1861); chief engineer, Military District of the Potomac (August 15, 1861-August 16, 1862); brigadier general, USV (September 23, 1861); chief engineer, Department of Washington (February 3, 1863-June 5, 1864); lieutenant colonel, Engineers (March 3, 1863); chief engineer, Grant's staff (June 5, 1864-April 1865); and colonel, Engineers (December 28, 1865). Initially charged with the construction of the Washington defenses, he took part in the 1st Bull Run campaign and served a year as the top engineer with McClellan's army. During this time he earned a regular army brevet to colonel and was made a brigadier of volunteers. Posted back to the nation's capital, he did not take the field again until he joined Grant's staff during the drive on Richmond. For the campaigns around Richmond and Petersburg, he was brevetted a regular brigadier, and for the war, a major general in both the regular and volunteer establishments. After the war he remained in the regular army and retired in 1881 as a colonel, after working on coastal defense and river management.

BARNES, James (1801-1869)

In his first major battle as a division commander, Massachusetts-born West Pointer (1829) James Barnes had his brigades divided between different parts of the line, lessening his impact on the crucial battle of Gettysburg. Posted to the artillery, he served as an instructor of tactics and French at his alma mater and in various garrison assignments until he resigned as a first lieutenant of the 4th Artillery in 1836. He spent the intervening years as an engineer for numerous railroads. Reentering the military, his Civil War services included: colonel, 18th Massachusetts (July 26, 1861); commanding 1st Brigade, 1st Division, 5th Corps, Army of the Potomac (July 10-December 26, 1862, February 1-May 5 and August 18-September 21, 1863); commanding Norfolk and Portsmouth, 18th Corps, Department of Virginia and North Carolina (October 1, 1863-January 8, 1864); and commanding District of St. Marys, same corps and department (July 2-7, 1864). He commanded his regiment in the Peninsula Campaign and was commanding the brigade by the time of Antietam and Fredericksburg. After a brief stint in division leadership he again directed his brigade at Chancellorsville. Just after that fight he was again charged with control of the division and fought at Aldie, Upperville, and Gettysburg, where one of his brigades was instrumental in the defense of Little Round Top. Wounded in this campaign, he never fully recovered for active field duty; he was relegated to quiet sectors, prison duty and court-martial service. Brevetted major general for war service, he was mustered out on January 15, 1866. Two years later he served on a board scrutinizing the Union Pacific.

BARNES, Joseph K. (1817-1883)

A Pennsylvania medical officer, Joseph Barnes became the surgeon general because of Secretary of War Stanton's dislike for Barnes' predecessor, General W.A. Hammond. Barnes, a medical graduate of the University of Pennsylvania, entered military service in 1840 as an assistant surgeon and had become a major and surgeon by the outbreak of the Civil War. His later assignments included: lieutenant colonel and medical inspector, USA (February 9, 1863); colonel and medical inspector general, USA (August 10, 1863); and brigadier general and surgeon general, USA (August 22, 1864). Recalled from the Pacific coast at the beginning of the war, the veteran of the Seminole and Mexican wars was assigned to duty in Washington. Assigned to inspection duties in 1863, he became acting surgeon general on September 3 when Hammond was sent on an extended inspection tour out of Stanton's way. After Hammond's dismissal from the service in August 1864, Barnes was promoted to brigadier general and given the complete charge of the post. Brevetted major general for his war service, Barnes retired a year before his death, having attended both Presidents Lincoln and Garfield in their last hours.

BARNEY, Joseph Nicholson (?-?)

A veteran of 16 years in the United States Navy, Lieutenant Joseph N. Barney resigned his commission in June 1861 in order to join the Confederacy. Commissioned a lieutenant in that service, he commanded the *Jamestown* during the battle between the *Monitor* and the *Virginia* in Hampton Roads in March 1862. The next month he took part in the successful capture of three Union transports under the guns of the *Monitor*. After taking part in the action at Drewry's Bluff he was named to the rank of commander and commanded the *Harriet Lane* after it was captured at Galveston at the beginning of 1863. He then briefly commanded the cruiser *Florida* off the coast of France in the winter of 1863-64 but was forced to relinquish command due to ill health.

Commandant James Barnes (standing at center with hand on belt) at Point Lookout prisoner of war camp. (NA)

BARNUM, Henry Alanson (1833-1892)

In the actions against Lookout Mountain on November 23, 1863, New Yorker Henry A. Barnum earned a Congressional Medal of Honor for continuing to lead his men despite being wounded, until wounded a second time. A lawyer active in the militia, he promptly entered the service upon the outbreak of the war and his assignments included: captain, 12th New York (May 13, 1861); major, 12th New York (November 1, 1861); colonel, 149th New York (September 17, 1862); commanding 3rd Brigade, 2nd Division, 20th Corps, Army of the Cumberland (September 9, 1864-June 1, 1865); and brigadier general, USV (May 31, 1865). At 1st Bull Run he kept his company in hand during the rout and went on to serve as a field officer on the Peninsula where the regiment fought at Yorktown and Hanover Court House. During the Seven Days he was seen to fall at Malvern Hill and the body of another officer was buried under his headstone. In reality he was only severely wounded and had been captured after the Union withdrawal. Exchanged, he was made colonel of a new regiment, but his old wound forced him to miss the fighting at Chancellorsville and the same wound caused him to leave the field on the second day at Gettysburg. Transferred with the 12th Corps to the aid of Chattanooga, he suffered two more wounds and earned his medal, which was awarded in 1889. Returning to duty during the Atlanta Campaign he was again wounded but served through the Savannah and Carolinas campaigns at the head of a brigade. Promoted to brigadier after the close of hostilities and brevetted major general for the war, he resigned on January 9, 1866. Active in veterans' organizations, he also held a number of government positions, including inspector of New York prisons.

BARNWELL, Robert Woodward (1801-1882)

A lifelong states' rights advocate, Robert W. Barnwell had a distinguished record before he began his career in the Confederate Congress. Born into the plantation society of South Carolina, Barnwell received his degree from Harvard summa cum laude. After serving in the state house, he served two terms in the U.S. Congress and was involved in the nullification crisis of 1832 on the side of his state. He spent half a dozen years as president of the South Carolina College. After nine years of retirement on his plantation, he succeeded to Calhoun's seat in the Senate but again went into retirement in 1853. He was a member of the South Carolina secession convention, a state commissioner to President Buchanan and temporary chairman of the Montgomery convention, which eventually became the Provisional Confederate Congress. Backing Davis for president, Barnwell turned down the state department portfolio and remained in the Congress. He was elected to a Senate seat for both regular congresses. Considered an ardent supporter of the Confederate president, Barnwell from the chair of the Committee on Finance actually often opposed the administration on fiscal matters. The Davis administration, however, usually got its way with Barnwell on military affairs. He opposed the establishment of the position of general in chief since it would weaken the executive's power. Financially ruined by the war, Barnwell was connected with the University of South Carolina until his death, except for a period of four years when he was removed by black and carpetbag rule.

BARRINGER, Rufus (1821-1895)

After serving for two years as captain, Rufus Barringer rose to brigadier in less than a year. A native North Carolina lawyer and politician, he had misgivings about secession but enlisted anyway. His assignments included: captain, Company F, 1st North Carolina Cavalry (May 16, 1861); major, 1st North Carolina Cavalry (May 16, 1861); major, 1st North Carolina Cavalry (August 26, 1863); lieutenant colonel, 1st North Carolina Cavalry (October 17, 1863); lieutenant colonel, 4th North Carolina Cavalry (temporarily assigned January 1864); brigadier general, CSA (June 1, 1864); and commanding Gordon's (old) Brigade, W.H.F. Lee's Division, Cavalry Corps, Army of Northern Virginia (June 4, 1864-April 3, 1865). As a company commander, he served at the Seven Days, Antietam, Fredericksburg, and Brandy Station, where he was severely wounded. After Gettysburg his rapid rise began. He served through the Bristoe and Mine Run campaigns and in January 1864 was transferred to the temporary command of the 4th North Carolina Cavalry. This unit was transferred out of the brigade and Barringer continued to serve with it in the Department of North Carolina and Southern Virginia until the death of General Gordon prompted his promotion and assignment to the old brigade. He led the unit through the Petersburg operations and in the Appomattox Campaign in which it was virtually destroyed. Barringer was captured at Namozine Church on April 3, 1865, and was not released until July. Active in Republican politics, he supported Reconstruction after the war.

BARRON, Samuel (1809-1888)

At the outbreak of the Civil War the chief of the Union navy's Bureau of Detail resigned his commission and offered his services to his native Virginia. A veteran of over 40 years at sea, Barron was commissioned commander CSN, on June 10, 1861. His first assignment was to take charge of all naval defenses on the coasts of Virginia and North Carolina. Arriving at Fort Hatteras a day after the bombardment of that position had begun, he was requested by the army commander to take over the general direction of the defense since the fort's armament was comprised of naval ordnance. However, the next day, August 29, Barron was forced to surrender the position to the overwhelming Union fleet. Exchanged after 11 months of confinement, he again commanded the naval forces in Virginia until sent to England as a captain, where he secured the *Stonewall* and *Georgia* for the Confederacy. Moving his Confederate operations to Paris, he continued procurement operations for the navy. Following the war, he went into retirement in Virginia. (Scharf, J. Thomas, *History of the Confederate States Navy*)

BARRY, John Decatur (1839-1867)

By the time that he got his temporary appointment as a Confederate brigadier John D. Barry had been wounded and, as his predecessor was ready to return to duty, his short-lived appointment was cancelled. After graduating from the University of North Carolina, Barry entered the service of his native North Carolina at the outbreak of the conflict. His assignments included: private, Company I, 8th North Carolina Volunteers (April 15, 1861); private, Company I, 18th North Carolina State Troops (a change of designation on November 14, 1861); captain, Company I, 18th North Carolina (April 24, 1862); major, 18th North Carolina (November 11, 1862); colonel, 18th North Carolina (May 27 to rank from May 3, 1863); commanding Lane's Brigade, Wilcox's Division, 3rd Corps, Army of Northern Virginia (June 2-July 2, 1864 and February-March 1865); and temporarily brigadier general, CSA (August 3, 1864). As he steadily rose in rank, his regiment saw action at the Seven Days, Cedar Mountain, 2nd Bull Run, Chantilly, Harpers Ferry, Antietam, Fredericksburg, and Chancellorsville. He led the regiment at Gettysburg, including Pickett's Charge. Directing his men through the Overland Campaign, he succeeded the wounded General Lane in command of the brigade, but he was wounded a month later on the Petersburg lines. His temporary brigadier's appointment came through while he was recuperating but was cancelled when Lane was able to return to duty first. Returning to his regiment in February 1865, as colonel, he was in temporary brigade command at the end of the month. Wounds or illness seem to have forced him from the field before the retreat to Appomattox; he returned from the war to run a Wilmington newspaper. In poor health, he died two years after the war.

BARRY, William Farquhar (1818-1879)

A career artillerist, New Yorker William F. Barry served as the artillery chief for one of the most unsuccessful Union generals, McClellan, and one of the most successful, Sherman. A West Pointer (1838), he had seen service in the artillery during the Seminole and Mexican wars as well as during the Kansas disturbance. His first Civil War action came at Fort Pickens as a recently appointed major in the new 5th Artillery. His Civil War-era assignments included: captain, 2nd Artillery (since July 1, 1852); major, 5th Artillery (May 14, 1861); chief of artillery, Department of Northeastern Virginia (July 1861); chief of artillery, Army of the Potomac (August 1861-summer 1862); brigadier general, USV (August 20, 1861); commanding Artillery Camp, Military District of Washington, Department of the Potomac (September 20, 1862-February 2, 1863); commanding Camp Barry, 22nd Corps, Department of Washington (March 3, 1863); chief of artillery, Military Division of the Mississippi (March 1864-May 1865); and colonel, 2nd Artillery (December 11, 1865). He was the chief artillerist at the 1st Bull Run disaster and during McClellan's unsuccessful Peninsula Campaign. After a year and a half in the defenses of the capital he was transferred west to direct Sherman's guns. He served through the Atlanta Campaign, the March to the Sea, and the Carolinas Campaign. He received brevets through major general in both the regulars and volunteers for the first and last campaigns and the war. Mustered out on January 15, 1866, he reverted to his regular army rank of colonel until his death on active duty.

BARRY, William Taylor Sullivan (1821-1868)

An extreme secessionist politician and plantation owner, William T.S. Barry took his fight for the South from the halls of political institutions to the battlefield and ended his Confederate career as a regimental commander. The Mississippi-born Barry was a Yale graduate, lawyer, state legislator, U.S. Congressman, and speaker in the Mississippi state house. He participated in the Southern walkout at the Democratic convention in Charleston. Barry then chaired the convention that took Mississippi out of the Union. Sent to the Provisional Confederate Congress, Barry was soon known for presenting extreme measures for consideration. For example, he favored the reopening of the African slave trade and wanted to constitutionally ban any Confederate state from abolishing slavery without the approval of the remainder. At the close of the Provisional Congress, Barry decided to enter the army. His assignments included: colonel, 35th Mississippi (spring 1862); commanding Sears' Brigade, French's Division, Army of Mississippi (May 1864); and commanding Sears' Brigade, French's Division, Stewart's Corps, Army of Tennessee (July-August 1864). He led his regiment at Corinth, Chickasaw Bluffs, and in the Vicksburg siege, where, in reply to an inquiry from his brigade commander, he stated that his men were in no condition to evacuate the city in the face of the enemy. Two days later the army surrendered. Paroled immediately, he was exchanged by the end of the year and served in the Atlanta Campaign, sometimes in command of a brigade, and suffered a wound. The regiment went on to the Tennessee invasion and then to Mobile where Barry was captured again. He returned to the legal profession for his few remaining years.

BARTLETT, Joseph Jackson (1834-1893)

With no prior military experience, New Yorker Joseph J. Bartlett served through all the principal engagements of the Army of the Potomac except 2nd Bull Run and Fredericksburg, rising at the same time from major to brevet major general. He gave up his law practice upon the outbreak of the war and his assignments included: major, 27th New York (May 21, 1861); colonel, 27th New York (September 21, 1861); commanding 2nd Brigade, 1st Division, 6th Corps, Army of the Potomac (May 18-November 1862, December 1862-July 1, 1863, July 2-4, 1863 and August 5-November 6, 1863); brigadier general, USV (October 4, 1862; expired March 4, 1863; reappointed March 30, 1863); commanding 3rd Division, 6th Corps, Army of the Potomac (July 4-August 4, 1863); commanding 1st Division, 5th Corps, Army of the Potomac (November 6-December 31, 1863, February 3-April 3, July 21-August 9, December 24, 1864-January 4, 1865 and April 1-25, 1865); commanding 3rd Brigade, 1st Division, 5th Corps, Army of the Potomac (April 3-July 20, August 9-17, October 1-December 23, 1864, January 6-27 and March 7-April 1, 1865); and commanding 2nd Division, 9th Corps, Army of the Potomac (April 25-May 3, 1865). His battle credits include 1st Bull Run, the Peninsula Campaign, Antietam, Chancellorsville, Gettysburg—where he was also in command of the 3rd Brigade, 3rd Division, 6th Corps on the third day—Mine Run Campaign (during which he had to flee Confederate cavalry in his underwear), the Wilderness, Spotssylvania, North Anna, Cold Harbor, Petersburg, and Appomattox. He received his brevet as a major general in 1864 for the campaign against Richmond and Petersburg. Mustered out on January 15, 1866, he was a diplomat to Sweden and Norway and served as deputy pension commissioner.

BARTLETT, William Francis (1840-1876)

Leaving his studies at Harvard to take part in the Civil War, William F. Bartlett ignored five wounds in order to build postwar friendship with the South. His assignments included: private, 4th Massachusetts Battalion (April 14, 1861); captain, 20th Massachusetts (August 8, 1861); colonel, 49th Massachusetts (November 19, 1862); colonel, 57th Massachusetts (April 9, 1864); brigadier general, USV (June 20, 1864); commanding 1st Brigade, 1st Division, 9th Corps, Army of the Potomac (July 23-30, 1864); and commanding the division (June 17-July 15, 1865). After brief service as an enlisted man he returned to class only to be commissioned as a captain. He fought in the disaster at Ball's Bluff and was one of only two regimental officers fit for duty after the action. As part of the 2nd Corps he led his company at Yorktown on the Peninsula where he was wounded in the leg, necessitating its amputation. He was mustered out on November 12, 1862, to take command of a new regiment of nine-month troops. He led this unit to New Orleans and in the assault on Port Hudson was twice more wounded. Mustered out with his regiment on September 1, 1863, he soon raised another regiment and rejoined the Army of the Potomac. He was wounded at the Wilderness and after fighting at Cold Harbor was given a general's star. Leading his brigade in the assault on the Crater at Petersburg on July 30, 1864, he was again wounded, had his cork leg torn off by a boulder after it had been riddled with bullets, and was finally forced to surrender. He was exchanged after two months in Libby Prison and returned to duty after the close of hostilities. He was finally mustered out on July 18, 1866. He remained for a time in Richmond in business with the Tredegar Iron Works and befriended many former foes. He returned to Massachusetts as a brevet major general for his war service and repeatedly rejected political office. He died at 36 in his wife's hometown, Pittsfield, Massachusetts.

BARTON, Clara (1821-1912)

"The Angel of the Battlefield," Clara Barton was not trained as a nurse but went on to found the American Red Cross in 1881. The Massachusetts native was a copyist in the patent office in Washington at the outbreak of the war and gained her first experience with the wounded when the casualties from the secessionist attack on the 6th Massachusetts were brought to the capital from Baltimore. Not connected with any of the nursing or relief agencies, she worked throughout the war as an independent, bringing medicines and supplies to the front lines. At Antietam her wagon followed the Union 2nd Corps onto the battlefield. A surgeon was killed while taking a drink from her and she even operated on one of the wounded, extracting a bullet from his cheek. Near the war's close she was assigned, by Lincoln, the duty of identifying missing soldiers. In this role she visited Andersonville and compiled a list of deceased prisoners. She later joined the International Red Cross and served with that organiation in the Franco-Prussian War. Returning to the United States, she founded the American branch and served as its president from 1882 to 1904. Under her leadership, the focus of the committee grew from warfare to include natural disasters. (Barton, William Eleazar, *The Life of Clara Barton, Founder of the American Red Cross* and Ross, Ishbel, *Angel of the Battlefield: The Life of Clara Barton*)

Clara Barton, "Angel of the Battlefield." (NA)

BARTON, Seth Maxwell (1829-1900)

Virginian Seth M. Barton had a great deal of difficulty in pleasing his divisional commanders in the latter half of the war. A West Pointer (1849), he was a veteran of a dozen years in the infantry when he resigned his captain's commission on June 11, 1861, to offer his services to the South. His assignments included: captain, Infantry (June 1861); lieutenant colonel, 3rd Arkansas (July 1861); brigadier general, CSA (March 11, 1862); commanding brigade, Department of East Tennessee (March-June 1862); commanding brigade, Stevenson's Division, same department (June-November 20, 1862); commanding brigade, Stevenson's Division, 2nd Military District, Department of Mississippi and East Louisiana (December 18, 1862-April 1863); commanding brigade, Stevenson's Division, same department (May-July 4, 1863); commanding Armistead's (old) Brigade, Department of North Carolina (October 4, 1863-February 1864); commanding same brigade (in Ransom's Division in May), Department of Richmond (February-May 11, 1864); commanding another brigade (in Lee's Division from March), Department of Richmond (September-December 1864 and January-April 2, 1865); and commanding brigade, Lee's Division, Army of Northern Virginia (April 2-6, 1865). After serving in the Cheat Mountain Campaign he was Stonewall Jackson's engineer during the Romney Campaign. Sent to East Tennessee, he commanded a brigade until Stevenson's Division was sent to Mississippi, where he was captured at Vicksburg. Exchanged on July 13, 1863, he was eventually given command of the late Lewis Armistead's Brigade, which was then serving with Pickett in North Carolina. In the January 1864 attack on New Bern he was accused of slowness in advancing, resulting in the Confederate failure. To avoid further conflict with Pickett, his brigade was transferred to Richmond. In May 1864 he came under General Ransom's control during the fighting at Drewry's Bluff and was again found wanting. He was relieved on May 11, 1864, but his request for a court of inquiry was never acted upon. Interestingly enough, the regimental commanders petitioned for his return to brigade command. Finally in September 1864, he was given command of another brigade with which he served until the fall of Richmond. In the retreat to Appomattox he was captured at Sayler's Creek on April 6, 1865. He was not released until July 1865. (Freeman, Douglas S., *Lee's Lieutenants*)

BARTOW, Francis Stebbins (1816-1861)

Although his only military experience was five years as a militia captain, lawyer Francis Bartow became Georgia's first martyr of the Civil War. As a Whig and later a member of the Know-Nothings, Bartow was a prominent local politician, although he had been defeated for a seat in Congress. As captain of the Oglethorpe Light Infantry, Bartow took part in the capture of

Francis S. Bartow, 1st Bull Run victim. (NA)

Fort McAllister at the time of the secession of Georgia. As a member of the secession convention he was named to the Confederate Provisional Congress where he chaired the Committee on Military Affairs. When the second session adjourned, Bartow's company volunteered for service for the term of the war. Bartow's assignments included: captain, Company B, 8th Georgia (May 21, 1861); colonel, 8th Georgia (June 1, 1861); and commanding 2nd Brigade, Army of the Shenandoah (June-July 21, 1861). After service in the Valley, Bartow led part of his brigade, along with the rest of Johnston's army, to join Beauregard along Bull Run. Here, on July 21, 1861, the partial brigade was part of the force that tried to stop the Union movement to turn the left flank. After fighting north of the Warrenton Turnpike, the remnants of his command were rallying on Henry House Hill when Bartow was killed. In Georgia he was popularly acclaimed a brigadier general, although never appointed to that rank, and was considered a martyr to the cause. (Freeman, Douglas S., *Lee's Lieutenants*)

BATCHELDER, Richard Napoleon (1832-1901)

While serving as a quartermaster, Richard N. Batchelder nonetheless earned the Congressional Medal of Honor for gallantry. The New Hampshire native's Civil War assignments included: first lieutenant and quartermaster, 1st New Hampshire (May 2, 1861); captain and assistant quartermaster, USV (August 3, 1861-June 8, 1865); assigned as lieutenant colonel and assistant quartermaster, USV (January 1, 1863-August 1, 1864); assigned as colonel and assistant quartermaster, USV (August 2, 1864-September 5, 1865); and captain and assistant quartermaster, USA (February 16, 1865). After the regiment for which he was quartermaster was mustered out at the expiration of its three-month term he was assigned to the supply department and served in it throughout the war. While serving as the chief quartermaster of the 2nd Corps in Virginia he particularly distinguished himself in the irregular warfare against Mosby between Catlett and Fairfax stations on October 13-15, 1863. In 1895 he was awarded the coveted medal for these actions. Remaining in the regular army after the war, he eventually became quartermaster general with the rank of brigadier. For the war, he had been brevetted to brigadier of volunteers and colonel of regulars. He retired in 1896.

BATE, William Brimage (1826-1905)

A division commander in the last year of the war, Tennesseean William B. Bate appears to have been without a command when the Confederate Army of Tennessee surrendered. In a varied prewar career he was a steamboatman, journalist, first lieutenant in the 3rd Tennessee during the Mexican War, lawyer, and state legislator. His Confederate assignments included: colonel, 2nd Tennessee (May 6, 1861); brigadier general, CSA (October 3, 1862); commanding Rains' (old) brigade, McCown's-Stewart's Division, Polk's Corps, Army of Tennessee (March 12-May 25, 1863); commanding brigade, Stewart's Division, Hardee's-Hill's-Breckinridge's Corps, Army of Tennessee (June 6-September 1 and October 1-November 12, 1863); commanding brigade, Stewart's Division, Buckner's Corps, Army of Tennessee (September 1-October 1, 1863); commanding Breckinridge's Division, Breckinridge's-Hindman's-Hood's Corps, Army of Tennessee (November 12, 1863-February 20, 1864); commanding division, Hardee's-Cheatham's Corps, Army of Tennessee (February 20-August 1864 and September 1864-April 9, 1865); and major general, CSA (February 23, 1864). In command of his regiment, which was sometimes designated the 2nd Confederate, he served in northern Virginia in the vicinity of Aquia Creek and was present at 1st Bull Run before being ordered to East Tennessee. Heading further west he was severely wounded at Shiloh and during his recovery was promoted to brigadier general. He recovered in time to command a brigade during the Tullahoma and Chickamauga compaigns. He led a division at Chattanooga and was promoted to major general just before the Atlanta Campaign. Leading his division he fought at Franklin and Nashville and then in the Carolinas. However, upon the April 9, 1865, reorganization and consolidation of the army he was left without a command. It does appear that he was included in the surrender at Durham Station. Having been wounded three times in the course of the war, he resumed his practice. During the war he had turned down the governorship but in 1882 he was elected and later served in the U.S. Senate.

BATES, Edward (1793-1869)

As a moderate, Lincoln's first attorney general had many differences with the more radical members of the cabinet—especially Salmon P. Chase, William H. Seward, and Edwin M. Stanton—and eventually resigned. Born in Virginia, he moved to St. Louis in 1814 and took up the practice of law two years later. In the late 1820s he served a term as a Whig congressman. He remained active in politics on a local level until propelled into national prominence two decades later. Although still a Whig as late as 1856, he opposed the Lecompton Constitution and the repeal of the Missouri Compromise line. Switching to the new Republican party, he quickly rose in its ranks and in 1860 stepped aside as a presidential contender in return for the choice of any cabinet post except secretary of state, which was reserved for Seward. Thus he became the first cabinet official ever appointed from west of the Mississippi. Concerned with individual rights, he soon came into conflict with Lincoln and several of the other secretaries. He continued to serve until his resignation on November 24, 1864. Returning to Missouri he fought the radical element that had taken over the state. At the time of his death the radicals were beginning to regain control. (Bates, Edward, *The Diary of Edward Bates* and Cain, Marvin R., *Lincoln's Attorney General: Edward Bates of Missouri*)

BATTLE, Cullen Andrews (1829-1905)

When General Lee found a newly appointed brigadier, E.A. O'Neal, failing the grade, he canceled his appointment and in his place Cullen A. Battle was promoted. A Georgia-born Alabama lawyer active in politics, he was a lieutenant colonel in a militia regiment even before the secession of his adopted state. His assignments for the Confederacy included: major, 3rd Alabama (April 28, 1861); lieutenant colonel, 3rd Alabama (July 31, 1861); colonel, 3rd Alabama (May 31, 1862); commanding Rodes' (old) Brigade, Rodes' Division, 2nd Corps, Army of Northern Virginia (July 1863-June 13, 1864); brigadier general, CSA (August 20, 1863); and commanding brigade, Rodes' Division, Valley District, Department of Northern Virginia (June 13-October 19, 1864). After service in the Norfolk area, the regiment moved to the Peninsula and Battle fought at Seven Pines. Missing the Seven Days Battles, he fought again in the Maryland Campaign at South Mountain and Antietam. After falling from his horse, he relinquished command of his regiment the day before Chancellorsville started. Briefly in command the next day, he suffered further damage when his horse jumped a ditch; Battle had to go off duty. Returning to duty just in time for the Gettysburg Campaign, he attached his regiment to Ramseur's Brigade when his own brigade, then under O'Neal, became disorganized on the first day of the battle. Later that month he replaced O'Neal and led the brigade at the Wilderness, Spotsylvania, and Cold Harbor. As part of Early's campaign, he fought at Monocacy and reached the suburbs of Washington. Back in the Valley, he was at 3rd Winchester and Fisher's Hill, and fell wounded at Cedar Creek. He was unable to return to duty before the close of hostilities. Returning to the law, he was refused a seat in congress and instead became mayor of New Bern. He was also a newspaper editor in New Bern, North Carolina. (Freeman, Douglas, S., *Lee's Lieutenants*)

BAXTER, DeWitt Clinton (?-1881)

A regimental commander in the Philadelphia Brigade—and frequently its commander—DeWitt C. Baxter was brevetted brigadier general at the war's end for his services at Gettysburg and the Wilderness. The Massachusetts native volunteered under Lincoln's first call for troops; his assignments included: lieutenant colonel, 19th Pennsylvania (April 27, 1861); colonel, 72nd Pennsylvania (August 10, 1861); commanding 2nd Brigade, 2nd Division, 2nd Corps, Army of the Potomac (July 30-August 27 and September 17-October 10, 1862, January 26-February 7, April 1-11 and September 2-October 22, 1863); commanding 1st Brigade, 2nd Division, 2nd Corps, Army of the Potomac (August 28-September 28 and October 22-December 10, 1863 and January 2-February 10, 1864), and commanding the division (December 10-21, 1863). As second in command of a three-months regiment, he served in the vicinity of Baltimore's famed Fort McHenry. The day after being mustered out most of the regiment reenlisted with Baxter at their head. Assigned to what was termed the Philadelphia Brigade, he went to the Peninsula where he fought at Seven Pines and in the Seven Days. At Antietam he succeeded to command of the brigade and was again in regimental command at Fredericksburg and Chancellorsville. On the second day at Gettysburg he was wounded but returned late that summer and was for a time in charge of two brigades. He served through the Bristoe and Mine Run campaigns and was briefly in command of the division. At the Wilderness he was in charge only of his own regiment and appears to have been wounded there. Not listed as at Cold Harbor or Petersburg, he was mustered out with his regiment on August 24, 1864.

BAXTER, Henry (1821-1873)

The highpoint of Henry Baxter's Civil War career came when he led his regiment across the Rappahannock River in pontoons to dislodge the Confederate sharpshooters taking shelter in the streets and buildings of Fredericksburg. A New York-born Michigan miller, he entered the army early in the war as a company commander. His assignments included: captain, Company C, 7th Michigan (August 22, 1861); lieutenant colonel, 7th Michigan (July 1, 1862); brigadier general, USV (March 12, 1863); commanding 2nd Brigade, 2nd Division, 1st Corps, Army of the Potomac (April 21-December 31, 1863 and February 2-March 24, 1864); commanding 2nd Brigade, 2nd Division, 5th Corps, Army of the Potomac (April-May 6, 1864); and commanding 2nd Brigade, 3rd Division, 5th Corps, Army of the Potomac (June 25-August 15, 1864 and August 29, 1864-June 29, 1865). Leading his company in the Seven Days, he received a severe abdominal wound but recovered to command the regiment at Fredericksburg. His actions there—he was again severely wounded—contributed to his appointment direct from lieutenant colonel to brigadier during his recovery. He led a brigade in the 1st Corps at Chancellorsville and Gettysburg and was wounded while leading a 5th Corps brigade at the Wilderness. He returned to duty for the operations against Richmond and Petersburg, which culminated in Lee's surrender and for which he was brevetted major general. Mustered out on August 24, 1865, he held appointive office and was minister to Honduras until the year before his death.

BAYARD, George Dashiell (1835-1862)

During the battle of Fredericksburg the cavalry of the Union Left Grand Division suffered only one fatality—the brigade's commander, General George Bayard. A graduate of West Point (1856), Bayard served on the frontier and in Kansas. His activities against the Indians included being wounded in the face by a poison arrow and, allegedly, starting an Indian uprising. At the time of the firing on Fort Sumter, he was a first lieutenant in the 1st, soon to be renamed the 4th, Cavalry. His later appointments were: captain, 4th Cavalry (August 20, 1861); colonel, 1st Pennsylvania Cavalry (September 14, 1861); and brigadier general, USV (April 28, 1862). He led the cavalry brigade in the following commands: Department of the Rappahannock (April 4-June 1862); Mountain Department (to June 26, 1862); 3rd Corps, Army of Virginia (June 26-September 12, 1862); Defenses of Washington (September 12-November 14, 1862); and Left Grand Division, Army of the Potomac (November 14-December 13, 1862). On November 26-27, 1862, he led his regiment to Dranesville, Virginia, and arrested six secessionist citizens. On the way back they were ambushed and his horse was killed. He fought at Harrisonburg and Port Republic in the Shenandoah Valley and commanded the brigade at Cedar Mountain and 2nd Bull Run. During the Antietam Campaign he directed a provisional cavalry division guarding the capital. On December 13, 1862, he was struck by shrapnel while standing near the grand division's headquarters. He died the next day. His command was hardly engaged in the battle. (Baynard, Samuel J., *The Life of George Dashiell Bayard*)

George D. Bayard, mortally wounded at Fredericksburg. (*Leslie's*)

BAYARD, James Asheton, Jr. (1799-1880)

A Peace Democrat in the U.S. Senate, James A. Bayard, Jr., was considered by many to be a traitor. The Delaware native had practiced law before becoming a district attorney in 1838. He was first elected to the Senate in 1851 as a Democrat and held his seat until he resigned on January 29, 1864, but remained active in the peace movement. During his first tenure in the Senate he reluctantly supported the Kansas-Nebraska Act and was a loyal backer of James Buchanan. He was also a leading force in the Democratic convention of 1860 in Charleston. During the secession crisis he felt that abolitionism was the cause of the secession feeling in the South. He even went so far as to propose the peaceful division of the United States along the lines of the Potomac and Ohio rivers. During the war he was critical of the more extreme measures of the Lincoln administration. After his resignation he resumed his law practice but was called upon to complete his own term when his successor, George R. Riddle, died in 1867. At the end of the term in 1869 Bayard again returned to his practice.

BAYLOR, George Wythe (ca. 1832-1916)

Failure to gain a promotion in the Confederate army was often considered grounds for personal violence among officers. Such was the case with George W. Baylor. Born into a military family on the frontier, Baylor had become a famed Indian fighter and secessionist by the outbreak of the Civil War. Joining the army early in 1861 he was commissioned lieutenant, 2nd Texas Cavalry, and took part in the Arizona Campaign before being detailed as aide-de-camp to General A.S. Johnston. Serving in the battle of Shiloh he lost his commander and joined Beauregard's staff. Given command of the 2nd Texas Cavalry, Arizona Brigade, with the rank of colonel, he distinguished himself in the battles of Mansfield and Pleasant Hill. Under consideration for promotion to a general's wreath, Baylor became disgusted with the failure of his division commander, John A. Wharton, to act in the matter. Then late in 1864 his regiment was dismounted and assigned to an infantry division. By this time the unit was back in Texas. Running into Wharton on a Houston street on April 6, 1865, Baylor had a heated discussion with his former commander. When the pair met again at General Magruder's headquarters a short while later, Wharton called Baylor a liar. A slap in the face followed. Baylor fired his pistol; the general fell dead. After the war Baylor served for two decades in the Texas Rangers and then in the state legislature. He regretted the death of Wharton, for which he was never tried, until his own death.

BAYLOR, John Robert (1822-1894)

One of the more varied of Confederate careers was that of John R. Baylor of Texas who served as a lieutenant colonel of cavalry, governor of the Arizona Territory, private soldier, and finally as congressman. Born in Kentucky, Baylor moved to Texas at the age of 17 and became an Indian fighter, but his hatred of the Indians led him into difficulties with the Richmond authorities during the Civil War. He served briefly in the state legislature until appointed as an Indian agent, but was then removed from this position because of his extreme views. However he urged and obtained the removal of Indians to the Indian Territory, now Oklahoma. In December 1860 he organized the famous "buffalo hunt" for rebel military operations. He was present at General Twiggs' surrender in May 1861. As lieutenant colonel, 2nd Texas Mounted Rifles, led a force of about 250 men from El Paso into the New Mexico Territory. On July 25, 1861, he won the battle of Mesilla and in the next two days took Fort Fillmore and captured 11 Union companies without firing a shot. On August 1, 1861, Baylor proclaimed himself governor of the provisional Confederate Territory of Arizona, the southern part of what is now Arizona and New Mexico. This action was formally recognized by the Confederate government on February 14, 1862. but his proposals to launch a war of extermination against the Indians forced his removal later in the year. While back in Texas, he participated in the capture of Galveston at the start of 1863. In the fall he was elected to the Second Confederate Congress from Texas' 5th District. In Richmond he supported extreme measures in the prosecution of the war but tried to restrict the powers of Jefferson Davis. He was a consistent opponent of a negotiated settlement of the conflict. Appropriately he served on the Committee on Indian Affairs and also on the Committee on Patents. Following the Confederacy's defeat, Baylor practiced law in San Antonio. (Thompson, Jerry Don, *Colonel John Robert Baylor: Texas Indian Fighter and Confederate Soldier*)

BAYLOR, William Smith Hanger (1831-1862)

The unusually high mortality rate among commanders of the famed Stonewall Brigade claimed William S.H. Baylor before he could be promoted to the appropriate rank of brigadier general. A lawyer and commonwealth attorney in his native Shenandoah Valley, he became captain of a militia company, the West August Guards, in the late 1850s. His Civil War assignments included: captain, Company L, 5th Virginia (April 1861); major, 5th Virginia (May 28, 1861); colonel, 5th Virginia (April 21, 1862); and commanding Stonewall Brigade, Jackson's (old) Division, Jackson's Corps, Army of Northern Virginia (ca. August 20-August 30, 1862). Serving with his regiment, and at times as Jackson's inspector general, he took part in the battles of 1st Bull Run and Kernstown. With the reorganization of the regiment in the spring of 1862 he was named its new commander with the support of all the regimental officers. His popularity with his fellow officers was to earn him yet another promotion, one he would not live to see. Distinguishing himself in the Valley Campaign of 1862, leading a charge on foot after his horse was shot out from under him at Winchester, he went on to further glory in the Seven Days battles. Moving north to face Pope's Union army, he fought at Cedar Mountain and upon the recommendation of all the field officers of the brigade he was placed in charge of Jackson's old command. In the defense of the railroad cut at 2nd Bull Run, Baylor distinguished himself for three days but in the final stages of the last day he picked up the fallen colors of the 33rd Virginia and led a counterattack. He was struck down by an enemy volley—and so denied a general's wreath. (Robertson, James I., Jr., *The Stonewall Brigade*)

BEAL, George Lafayette (1825-1896)

A Maine bookbinder, who in six years had risen to the rank of captain in the militia, George L. Beal is sometimes credited with being the first man to enlist in Maine for the Civil War. His assignments included: captain, Company G, 1st Maine (May 3, 1861); colonel, 10th Maine (October 26, 1861); colonel, 29th Maine (December 17, 1863); commanding 2nd Brigade, 1st Division, 19th Corps, Department of the Gulf (February 15-March 24, 1864); commanding 1st Brigade, 1st Division, 19th Corps, Department of the Gulf (April 18-July 5, 1864); commanding 1st Brigade, 1st Division, 19th Corps, Army of the Shenandoah (August 6-October 13, 1864 and December 13, 1864-March 20, 1865); and commanding 1st Brigade, Dwight's Division, 22nd Corps, Department of Washington (April-May 1865). His first company served its three months in Washington before being mustered out August 5, 1861. He reorganized many of the veterans into the 10th Maine and became its commander. He led it in the Shenandoah Valley, at Cedar Mountain, 2nd Bull Run—where it guarded the trains—and Antietam where he was wounded. With the regiment's term up, he was mustered out on May 8, 1863. Late that same year he raised a new unit, including men from the 10th and was sent to Louisiana where he commanded a brigade in the Red River Campaign. With the 19th Corps transferred to the Shenandoah Valley he fought at 3rd Winchester and Fisher's Hill. Mustered out on January 15, 1866, as a brigadier and brevet major general, he held appointive offices in Maine in the 1880s and 1890s.

BEALE, Richard Lee Turberville (1819-1893)

Throughout the war, Richard L.T. Beale followed W.H.F. Lee through the cavalry battles of the Army of Northern Virginia and up the ladder of command. A Virginia lawyer, he served one term each in the U.S. Congress and the state senate. His military assignments included: first lieutenant, Lee's Light Horse (May 1861); captain, Lee's Light Horse (July 1861); major, 9th Virginia Cavalry (January 1862); lieutenant colonel, 9th Virginia Cavalry (April 28, 1862); colonel, 9th Virginia Cavalry (October 18, 1862); commanding Chambliss' (old) Brigade, W.H.F. Lee's Division, Cavalry Corps, Army of Northern Virginia (October 1864-April 9, 1865); and brigadier general, CSA (February 6 to rank from January 6, 1865). After service along the Rappahannock, he moved to the Peninsula and saw action in the Seven Days. Later combat occurred at 2nd Bull Run, Antietam, Fredericksburg, and facing Stoneman's raid during the Chancellorsville Campaign. He led the regiment with Stuart around the Union army and at Gettysburg. Wounded in September 1863 he was out of action for several months but returned for the Overland and Petersburg campaigns. He succeeded to the command of the brigade, which had once been "Rooney" Lee's, in October during the siege. Not promoted until early the next year, he was one of only two cavalry generals who surrendered at Appomattox. He resumed the practice of law and sat in the congress of a reunited nation. (Freeman, Douglas S., *Lee's Lieutenants* and Beale, Richard Lee Turberville, *History of the Ninth Virginia Cavalry*)

BEALL, John Yates (1835-1865)

One of the greatest Confederate adventurers, John Y. Beall gave his life for his new country in the waning days of the Civil War. The Virginia native had studied law but never practiced and instead became a country gentleman. Early in the Civil War he enlisted in Company G, 2nd Virginia, as a private. With the Stonewall Brigade he fought at 1st Bull Run. On October 16, 1861, his infantry career came to an end with a bullet wound in the lung. He then turned to a scheme to release Confederate prisoners held at Johnson's Island, Ohio (in Lake Erie) from a Canadian base. Instead he was appointed an acting master in the Confederate navy and was assigned to raiding activities in Chesapeake Bay, at which he was highly successful. However on November 1, 1863, he and his band were captured and confined in Fort McHenry as pirates. Union hostages were named and Beall and his men were exchanged on May 5, 1864. He then went to Canada again and gained approval for his plan, now enlarged to encompass the capture of the only Union warship on the Great Lakes, the *USS Michigan*. Seizing the lake steamer *Philo Parsons*, he was closing in on his quarry when his crew mutinied due to the lack of a planned signal from shore (the agent there had been arrested as a spy). Beall then attempted to rescue prisoners being transported by rail in New York, but was captured on December 16, 1864, while attending to one of his party who had fallen asleep within a few hundred yards of the Canadian border. This man later testified against Beall, and the Confederate spy went to the gallows on February 24, 1865.

BEALL, Lloyd James (?-1887)

The one and only commandant of the Confederate Marine Corps was West Pointer (1830) Lloyd J. Beall. Born in Rhode Island, he had received his appointment to the military academy from Maryland. Initially posted to the infantry, he transferred to the dragoons and finally, in 1844, to the paymaster's department. On April 22, 1861, he resigned his commission as major and paymaster and joined the Confederate cause. Initially appointed an army colonel, he was transferred to the navy on May 23, 1861, and named colonel and commandant of the infant marine corps. It was only of regimental size, but was scattered from Virginia to Texas and served both ashore and afloat. Throughout the war Beall was forced to struggle with a shortage of funds and supplies that were slowed by the blockade. The corps was considered one of the best Confederate units in existence. After Appomattox Beall retired to his Richmond home where most of the corps' records that had survived the war were destroyed in a fire.

BEALL, William Nelson Rector (1825-1883)

Captured at Port Hudson, Kentucky-born West Pointer (1848) William N.R. Beall was paroled by the Union authorities to act as a Confederate agent in charge of supplying Southern prisoners of war. He had received his appointment to the military academy from Arkansas and upon his graduation was posted to the infantry. Transferred to the cavalry in 1855, virtually his entire service was on the western frontier. Resigning as a captain in the 1st Cavalry on August 20, 1861, his Confederate assignments included: captain, Cavalry (March 16, 1861); brigadier general, CSA (April 11, 1862); commanding 2nd District, Department of Southern Mississippi and East Louisiana (June 26-July 2, 1862); commanding 3rd Military District, Department of Mississippi and East Louisiana (October 21-December 27, 1862 and May 6-11, 1863); and commanding brigade, 3rd Military District, Department of Mississippi and East Louisiana (December 27, 1862-July 8, 1863). Following service in Arkansas and at Corinth,

William N.R. Beall, prisoner at Port Hudson. (NA)

Mississippi, he was assigned to duty at Port Hudson where he commanded a brigade until the city's surrender on July 8, 1863. Imprisoned on Johnson's Island, Ohio, he was freed and given an office in New York City in 1864. This arrangement came to an end on August 2, 1865, when he was formally released. After the war he was in business in St. Louis.

BEARDSLEE, George W. (?-?)

Inventor George W. Beardslee saw his telegraph system gain some acceptance early in the Civil War only to witness its eventually discardment. It was a portable system with a limited range of about 10 miles. Both the sender and receiver had identical alphabetical dials which would indicate the same letter on the receiver as sent by the sender. Approximately 30 pairs of sets were supplied, with wagons, poles, hand reels, and wire. They saw action during the Peninsula Campaign and were highly successful in providing communication across the Rappahannock River during the battle of Fredericksburg. They had served as part of A.J. Myer's Signal Corps until that body's telegraphic functions were absorbed into the Military Telegraph Service in late 1863. At that time the Beardslee Telegraph was scraped.

BEATTY, John (1828-1914)

When the Civil War began John Beatty and his brother William were engaged in the banking business. It was decided that John would go to war and William would remain in charge of the business. John's assignments included: lieutenant colonel, 3rd Ohio (April 27, 1861); colonel, 3rd Ohio (February 12, 1862); brigadier general, USV (November 29, 1862); commanding 2nd Brigade, 1st Division, Centre, 14th Corps, Army of the Cumberland (December 26, 1862-January 9, 1863); commanding 2nd Brigade, 1st Division, 14th Corps, Army of the Cumberland (January 9-April 17, 1863); commanding 1st Brigade, 2nd Division, 14 Corps, Army of the Cumberland (April 17-October 10, 1863); and commanding 2nd Brigade, 2nd Division, 14th Corps, Army of the Cumberland (November 10, 1863-February 1, 1864). He served at first in western Virginia under McClellan but was soon sent to Kentucky. He went with Mitchel to northern Alabama and later fought at Perrysville. Promoted to brigadier he compiled a creditable record as a solid brigade leader at Murfreesboro, in the Tullahoma Campaign, at Chickamauga and Chattanooga and in the relief of Knoxville. However, by the beginning of 1864 he felt that it was time for William to have a taste of the military life and on January 28 he resigned and returned to his banking. As a Republican he served three terms in Congress, was an unsuccessful bidder for the Ohio governorship and worked for the preservation of the Chickamauga and Chattanooga battlefields. (Beatty, John, *Memoirs of a Volunteer 1861-1863*)

BEATTY, Samuel (1820-1885)

An Ohio farmer and Mexican War veteran—as a first lieutenant in the 3rd Ohio—Samuel Beatty rose in the Civil War to become a highly competent brigade and division commander. The Pennsylvania-born officer's assignments included: captain, Company A, 19th Ohio (April 27, 1861); colonel, 19th Ohio (May 29, 1861); commanding 11th Brigade, 5th Division, Army of the Ohio (May 27-September 29, 1862); commanding 11th Brigade, 5th Division, 2nd Corps, Army of the Ohio (September 29-November 5, 1862); commanding 1st Brigade, 3rd Division, Left Wing, 14th Corps, Army of the Cumberland (November 5-December 31, 1862); brigadier general, USV (November 29, 1862); commanding the division (December 31, 1862-January 9, 1863); commanding 3rd Division, 21st Corps, Army of the Cumberland (April 11-October 9, 1863); commanding 3rd Brigade, 3rd Division, 4th Corps, Army of the Cumberland (October 10, 1863-February 7, 1864, April 16-May 23 and November 6-December 2, 1864 and March 20-June 7, 1865); commanding the division (December 2, 1864-January 31, 1865 and February 7-March 20, 1865); and commanding 2nd Brigade, 3rd Division, 4th Corps, Army of the Cumberland (June 7-August 1, 1865). He led his regiment at Shiloh and in the operations against Corinth. Directing a brigade, he fought at Perryville and Murfreesboro where he succeeded to divisional command. By now a brigadier, he led a brigade in the Tullahoma Campaign and at Chickamauga. At Chattanooga his command took part in the assault on Missionary Ridge. After the Atlanta Campaign his corps was sent back to Tennessee to halt Hood's invasion and he commanded a division at Nashville. Brevetted major general for his war service, he was mustered out on January 15, 1866, and returned to live out his years on his farm.

BEAUREGARD, Pierre Gustave Toutant (1818-1893)

The services of "The Hero of Fort Sumter," Pierre G.T. Beauregard, were not utilized to their fullest due to bad blood between the Confederate general and Jefferson Davis. The native Louisianan had graduated second in the 1838 class at West Point. There he had become a great admirer of Napoleon and was nicknamed "The Little Napoleon." Posted to the artillery, he was transferred to the engineers a week later. As a staff officer with Winfield Scott in Mexico he won two brevets and was wounded at both Churubusco and Chapultepec. In the interwar years he was engaged in clearing the Mississippi River of obstructions. In 1861 he served the shortest term ever—January 23-28—as superintendent at West Point. Southern leanings probably resulted in his prompt removal. On February 20, 1861, he resigned his captaincy in the engineers and offered his services to the South. His Confederate assignments included: brigadier general, CSA (March 1, 1861); commanding Charleston Harbor (March 3-May 27, 1861); commanding Alexandria Line (June 2-20, 1861); commanding Army of the Potomac (June 20-July 20, 1861); commanding 1st Corps, Army of the Potomac (July 20-October 22, 1861); general, CSA (August 31, 1861 to rank from July 21); commanding Potomac District, Department of Northern Virginia (October 22, 1861-January 29, 1862); commanding Army of the Mississippi (March 17-29 and April 6-May 7, 1862); second in command, Army of the Mississippi and Department £2 (March 29-April 6, 1862); commanding the department (April 6-June 17, 1862); commanding Department of South Carolina, Georgia and Florida (August 29, 1862-April 20, 1864); commanding Department of North Carolina and Southern Virginia (April 22-ca. September 23, 1864); commanding Military Division of the West (October 17, 1864-March 16, 1865); and second in command, Army of Tennessee (March 16-April 26, 1865). Placed in charge of the South Carolina troops in Charleston Harbor, he won the nearly bloodless victory at Fort Sumter. "The Little Creole" was hailed throughout the South. Ordered to Virginia, he commanded the forces opposite Washington and created the Confederate Army of the Potomac. Reinforced by Joseph E. Johnston and his Army of the Shenandoah, Beauregard was reduced to corps command under Johnston the day before 1st Bull Run. However, during the battle Beauregard, being familiar with the field, exercised tactical command while Johnston forwarded troops to the threatened left. Both officers later claimed that they could have taken the Union capital if they had been properly supplied with rations for their men. This was one of Beauregard's first conflicts with Davis. Nonetheless he was named a full general from the date of the battle and early in 1862 was sent to the West as Albert Sidney Johnston's second in command. Utilizing Napoleonic style, he drafted the attack orders for Shiloh and took command when Johnston was mortally wounded on the first day of the battle. On the evening of the first day he let victory slip through his fingers by calling off the attacks. Controversy over his decision has raged to this day. The next day he was driven from the field by Grant's and Buell's combined armies. He was eventually forced to evacuate Corinth, Mississippi—his supply base—in the face of Henry W. Halleck's overwhelming force. Shortly after that he went on sick leave without gaining Davis' permission; he was permanently relieved of his army and departmental commands on June 27, 1862, by special direction of the president. Two months later he returned to the scene of his earlier triumph as commander along the Southern coast from the North Carolina-South Carolina line to the tip of Florida. He held this command for over a year and a half and was engaged in the determined defense of Charleston against naval and ground forces. Ordered north, he took command in North Carolina and southern Virginia while Lee faced Grant in northern Virginia. Gradually the two forces were pushed together in an awkward command arrangement. Beauregard managed to bottle up Benjamin F. Butler in the Bermuda Hundred lines after defeating him at Drewry's Bluff. This was Beauregard's finest performance of the war. At this point he started making grandiose proposals for defeating both Butler and Grant and invading the North by taking a large part of Lee's army with him. This resulted in lengthy correspondence between the two commanders and the Richmond authorities. Beauregard also managed to thwart the early Union attempts to take Petersburg while Lee was still north of the James River. With the siege of the city under way, he continued to serve under Lee until September 1864 when he was assigned to overall command in the West with John B. Hood's Army of Tennessee and Richard Taylor's Department of Alabama, Mississippi and East

P.G.T. Beauregard, "The Little Napoleon." (NA)

Louisiana under him. With no forces under his immediate command he was powerless in trying to stop Sherman's March to the Sea. In the final days of the war he was again second in command to Joseph E. Johnston, this time in North Carolina. Following the capitulation he returned to New Orleans and refused high rank in the Egyptian and Rumanian armies. Engaged in railroading, his reputation was tarnished by his association with the Louisiana Lottery as a supervisor. For a time he was Louisiana's adjutant general, and he engaged in historical writing including his *A Commentary on the Campaign and Battle of Manassas*. (Williams, T. Harry, *P.G.T. Beauregard, Napoleon in Gray*)

BECKHAM, Robert Franklin (1837-1864)

In the battle of Franklin, General John B. Hood's chief of artillery, Robert F. Beckham, became one of the senior Confederate officers to lose his life in that disastrous fight. A West Pointer (1859) and sixth in his class, the Virginian resigned his commission as a brevet second lieutenant in the topographical engineers on May 3, 1861. His Confederate assignments included: lieutenant, Artillery (to date from March 16, 1861); captain, Jeff Davis Artillery (March 31, 1862; declined); major, Artillery (August 30, 1862); commanding Horse Artillery Battalion, Cavalry Division (Corps from September 9), Army of Northern Virginia (April 8, 1863-February 16, 1864); colonel, Artillery (early 1864); commanding Artillery, 2nd Corps, Army of Tennessee (July 24-November 30, 1864). Attached to the Culpeper (Virginia) Artillery, he commanded the battery at 1st Bull Run. On January 14, 1862, he was assigned to ordnance duty on the staff of General G.W. Smith. In this position he played a key role in the Battle of Seven Pines. He continued on staff duty until given command of the cavalry's artillery in the spring of 1863. He commanded the guns at Brandy Station and Gettysburg. Then in the winter of 1863-1864, he was promoted and transferred to the West. He commanded the artillery of Hood's Corps until that officer took over command of the Army of Tennessee. At that time Beckham became the army's chief artillerist. In these two positions he served throughout the Atlanta Campaign and later in the invasion of Tennessee. Mortally wounded at Franklin, he died on December 5, 1864. (Wise, Jennings C., *The Long Arm of Lee*)

BEE, Barnard Elliott (1824-1861)

The man who gave "Stonewall" Jackson his immortal nickname, was Barnard Bee, but it is not known for certain whether it was meant as a compliment or an insult. A native of South Carolina, Bee graduated from West Point in 1845 and served in the infantry in Mexico, being wounded at Cerro Gordo, and fought against Indians and bandits, until he resigned his captain's commission on March 3, 1861. Joining the Confederacy, his assignments included: major, Infantry (March 1861); colonel (spring 1861); brigadier general (June 17, 1861). Ordered to the Valley, Bee led his brigade, along with Johnston's army, to Beauregard's line on Bull Run. With the Union flank attack on July 21, Bee moved his men north of the Warrenton Turnpike and held back the Union force, in conjunction with Bartow's and Evans' commands, while reinforcements were sent to bolster the Confederate left. Falling back to Henry House Hill, Bee saw General T.J. Jackson's Virginia Brigade, a little to his rear, in line of battle and not yet engaged. Bee called out to his men, "There is Jackson, standing like a stone wall. Let us determine to die here, and we will conquer. Follow me." A dispute has arisen as to whether Bee was, in fact, knocking Jackson for not coming to his support. The answer will never be known since Bee fell mortally wounded moments later. He died the next day but Jackson and his brigade were thereafter known as "Stonewall." (Freeman, Douglas S., *Lee's Lieutenants*)

Barnard E. Bee, the man who nicknamed Jackson "Stonewall." (B&L)

BEE, Hamilton Prioleau (1822-1897)

Serving entirely beyond the Mississippi, Texas legislator Hamilton P. Bee consequently saw only limited action as a Confederate brigadier general. The South Carolina native—and brother of Barnard E. Bee—had moved with his family to Texas. During the Mexican War he served as a second lieutenant in both the Texas Rangers and Bell's regiment of Texas volunteers. His Civil War assignments included: brigadier general, Texas Militia (1861); brigadier general, CSA (March 6, 1862 to rank from the 4th); commanding Sub-District of the Rio Grande, Department of Texas (April 24-May 26, 1862); and commanding in the Trans-Mississippi Department: Sub-District of the Rio Grande (May 26, 1862-June 1863); Western Sub-District of Texas, District of Texas, New Mexico and Arizona (June 1863-March 16, 1864); also 1st Division, District of Texas, New Mexico and Arizona (December 15, 1863-March 16, 1864); brigade, Green's Cavalry Division, District of West Louisiana (March 16-spring 1864); division, Cavalry Corps (February-April 1864); and brigade, Maxey's Division, District of Texas, New Mexico and Arizona (April-May 26, 1865). Early in the war, from his station at Brownsville, Texas, he supervised smuggling operations via Mexico. His first major field service came during the Red River Campaign in which some of his superiors criticized him. In the final months of the war he was back in Texas serving with both infantry and cavalry. For a number of years he was in exile in Mexico.

BEECHER, Frederick H. (1841-1868)

Still wracked by wounds from the Civil War, Frederick H. Beecher, a nephew of Henry Ward Beecher, was seeking a transfer to a staff position when he was killed in the Indian fight that now bears his name. Born in New Orleans, he entered the Union army in the second year of the war and his assignments included: sergeant, Company B, 16th Maine (August 14, 1862); second lieutenant, Company B, 16th Maine (February 1, 1863); first lieutenant, Company B, 16th Maine (April 11, 1863); and second lieutenant, Veteran Reserve Corps (August 22, 1864). His regiment fought at Antietam and he was severely wounded at Fredericksburg. After being commissioned he fought at Chancellorsville and was again severely wounded at Gettysburg. On September 20, 1864, he resigned his commission, having previously been retired to the Veteran Reserve Corps. He was mustered out of that body on March 3, 1866, having been appointed to a lieutenancy in the regular army's 3rd Infantry. On September 17, 1868, he was serving with George A. Forsyth's command of frontiersmen when they were attacked along Kansas' Delaware Creek by a band of 600 Sioux and Cheyenne. In the first day's fighting many of the command fell, including Beecher. This was the same fight—Beecher's Island—in which Roman Nose was killed.

BEECHER, Henry Ward (1813-1887)

As a Congregationalist minister Henry Ward Beecher became one of the country's leading abolitionist speakers. His sister, Harriet Beecher Stowe, wrote *Uncle Tom's Cabin* (1892). The Connecticut native urged opposition to the Fugitive Slave Law but did not believe that the North had the right to instigate slave insurrections and labeled Harpers Ferry the act of a crazy old man. He supported the anti-slavery settlement of Kansas, and his name became attached, as "Beecher's Bibles," to the crates of arms smuggled into the territory. During the Civil War, while preaching at his church in Brooklyn, New York, he was highly critical of Lincoln for not declaring at the outset of war, the abolition of slavery to be a war aim. After the war he was condemned for his criticism of the Radical Republicans and their Reconstruction policies; he favored a quick return of the seceded states to the Union. (Hibben, Paxton, *Henry Ward Beecher: An American Portrait*)

BEEGER, Henry

See: *Bertram, Henry*

BEERS, Ethel Lynn (1827-1879)

Born Ethelinda Eliot, the New York daughter of a War of 1812 veteran started writing for numerous journals under the name of Ethel Lynn but adopted the surname of her husband to fill out her penname. During the first months of the war she adopted an oft-appearing newspaper dateline for her poem "The Picket Guard," which has become more famous as "All Quiet Along the Potomac." Although the South tried to claim it, with little basis, as one of their own, Beers is now considered the true author. Continuing her writings, she died, as per a premonition, on the day following the publication of her collected works, *All Quiet Along the Potomac and Other Poems*.

BEERS, Fannie A. (?-?)

Although born in the North, Fannie A. Beers served throughout the Civil War in Confederate hospitals, in both major theaters of the conflict. Marrying into a Louisiana family in the 1850s, she settled in New Orleans and was visiting her mother in New York when the war broke out. She refugeed to Richmond where she was persuaded to join the nursing staff, since her husband had already enlisted in the army. She later followed him to the western theater and at the close of the war chose to remain with her charges until the Union troops took over the hospital at Newnan, Georgia. In the late 1880s and early 1890s she published her *Memories*, which is the only known source on her life. It is full of anecdotes but very sketchy on her personal life.

BELKNAP, William Worth (1829-1890)

For this Iowa lawyer and politician, a distinguished Civil War military career was followed by his ignoble resignation as Grant's secretary of war. Born in New York he had set up his practice in Iowa before entering the army, where his services included: major, 15th Iowa (December 7, 1861); lieutenant colonel, 15th Iowa (August 20, 1862); colonel, 15th Iowa (June

Henry Ward Beecher, the man behind "Beecher's Bibles." (NA)

3, 1863); brigadier general, USV (July 30, 1864); commanding 3rd Brigade, 4th Division, 17th Corps, Army of the Tennessee (July 31-September 21, 1864 and October 31, 1864-May 29, 1865); commanding the division (September 20-October 31, 1864 and June 1-26 and July 9-27, 1865); and commanding the corps (July 19-August 1, 1865). As a regimental field officer he fought at Shiloh, Corinth, and in the Vicksburg and Meridian Campaigns. He led his regiment in the early stages of the Atlanta Campaign and, following the battles around the city in mid-summer, he was promoted to brigadier and given a brigade. This he directed during the siege and in the subsequent March to the Sea and through the Carolinas. During these later stages he frequently was in division command and for a time headed the corps after the close of hostilities. Mustered out with a brevet as major general on August 24, 1865, he returned to his adoptive state as a tax official until his 1869 appointment to President Grant's cabinet. He was impeached by a unanimous vote for "malfeasance" in 1876 for selling government positions and contracts—but was acquitted by a narrow vote. This was due to his prior resignation rather than any belief in his innocence. He resumed his law practice, this time in the nation's capital.

BELL, Caspar Wistar (1819-1898)

Due to the fact that his 3rd District in Missouri almost immediately fell into Union hands, Confederate Congressman Caspar W. Bell was never really elected to his position by his district's residents. A prominent lawyer with no political experience, he was named by the secessionist portion of the state legislature to represent them in Richmond. In the Provisional Congress he served on the Committees on Public Lands and on Territories. In the First Regular Congress his committee assignments were in the Medical Department, in Military Affairs, and as chairman of Patents. A close friend of Senator Henry Foote, Bell was not a friend of the Davis administration and constantly tried to limit the executive's power. He voted to override vetoes and was opposed to the suspension of the writ of habeas corpus, but he supported measures to further the Confederate cause in the military and financial fields. During his time in Richmond he wrote Missouri-related articles for the *Richmond Examiner*. In a May 1864 election among Missouri refugees and soldiers Bell lost his seat. Taking up his law practice again, he remained in Virginia until 1867, then returned home. Although referred to as a "general" after the war, he had in fact never been such. In early 1861 he had briefly served as an adjutant-general in the Missouri State Guard.

BELL, Henry Haywood (1808-1868)

A career naval officer, Henry H. Bell entered the service as a midshipman in 1823. He served against pirates in the waters around Cuba and then in the East India Squadron. During this latter period he took part in the reduction of the forts around Canton, China. His Civil War-era assignments included: commander, USN (since 1854); commodore, USN (1862); fleet captain, West Gulf Blockading Squadron (1862); commanding 2nd Division of Gunboats, West Gulf blockading Squadron (April 1862); and commanding East India Squadron (1865). During Farragut's assaults on Forts Jackson and St. Philip below New Orleans, Bell was in command of one of the three divisions of the fleet. He was present at the capture of the Crescent City. Three years after the Civil War he was accidentally drowned off Japan.

BELL, Hiram Parks (1827-1907)

Georgian Hiram P. Bell was never a supporter of secession, and so he became one of the most obstructionist members of the Second Confederate Congress. A teacher and lawyer, Bell entered politics as a Unionist delegate to the Georgia secession convention in 1861. But with secession a reality, he proceeded to Tennessee to urge that state to join in the movement. In October 1861 he was elected to the Georgia senate but resigned to become lieutenant colonel, 43rd Georgia. He fought and was wounded at Chickasaw Bayou in December 1862. During the siege of Vicksburg he was again wounded, this time severely enough to incapacitate him for further service; he resigned his commission. In October 1863 he was elected to the Second Regular Congress as the representative of the 9th District, in Georgia's northeastern corner. Bell later claimed that he took his seat in May 1864 with the determination to force the government to open peace negotiations. He served on the Committees on Elections, Patents, and Post Offices and Post Roads. He wanted to end the policy of impressment of supplies and eliminate the inequalities of existing tax policies. He tried to facilitate the payment of claims against the government. With only a month until the final adjournment of the Confederate Congress, Bell left Richmond to look after the safety of his family. Resuming his law practice, Bell was active in Democratic politics and served two terms in the U.S. Congress in the 1870s. Around the turn of the century he served in both houses of the Georgia legislature.

BELL, John (1797-1869)

In a forlorn attempt to prevent the Civil War he saw coming, Tennesseean John Bell ran for president in 1860 on the Constitutional Union ticket. A prominent Nashville attorney, he had served a term in the state senate and 14 years in Congress. Originally a Jacksonian, he split with them and became a leader of the Whig Party. He served a few weeks as Harrison's secretary of war in 1841 and then went into semi-retirement for six years. Elected to the U.S. Senate, he was recognized as a conservative Southerner. Himself a large slave owner, he had no love for the abolitionists but cautioned for moderation on the part of the South. He supported the right of petition, even on the sensitive issue that he would have preferred to see simply go away. He believed that Congress could, constitutionally, ban slavery in the territories but nevertheless thought it to be unwise policy. He voted against the admission of Kansas under the pro-slavery Lecompton Constitution. His actions were sharply criticized in the South but recognized in the North as those of moderation. With the death of the Whig Party Bell shifted around for some new alliance, even with moderate Republicans. In 1860 a group composed mostly of old Whigs nominated Bell for the presidency. Bell and his running mate, Edward Everett, ran on a platform of upholding the constitution, the union, and the laws. They carried only Tennessee, Kentucky, and Virginia. Once it became obvious that the North was going to use troops to preserve the Union, Bell reluctantly advised Tennessee to ally itself with the Confederacy to fight against suppression. A broken man, he lived through the fall of the Confederacy, his career over. (Parks, Joseph Howard, *John Bell of Tennessee*)

BELL, Tyree Harris (1815-1902)

When Kentucky planter Tyree H. Bell became a supernumerary officer he eventually was given command of a mounted brigade, under the famous Nathan Bedford Forrest, for the balance of the war. His assignments included: captain, Company G (later A), 12th Tennessee (June 4, 1861); lieutenant colonel, 12th Tennessee (June 1861); colonel, 12th Tennessee (May 1862); colonel, 12th and 22nd Tennessee Consolidated (June 17, 1862); commanding independent brigade, Forrest's Cavalry Corps, Department of Mississippi and East Louisiana (January 25-28, 1864); commanding independent brigade, Forrest's Cavalry Corps, Department of Alabama, Mississippi and East Louisiana (January 28-ca. February 1864); commanding brigade, Buford's Division, Forrest's Cavalry Corps, Department of Alabama, Mississippi and East Louisiana (ca. February 1864-May 4, 1865); and brigadier general, CSA (February 28, 1865). Entering the service at the head of the New Bern Blues, he was soon made a lieutenant colonel and commanded the regiment at Belmont and Shiloh. At the regiment's reorganization in May 1862 he was named colonel, but the unit was so depleted that it was permanently merged with the 22nd Tennessee. Bell retained command of the unit and led it in the operations about Corinth, Mississippi, and at Richmond, Kentucky. A field consolidation was then ordered on October 30, 1862, with the 47th Tennessee, and in the following spring Bell was determined to be an excess officer. Eventually given a mounted brigade, he fought at Fort Pillow, Brice's Crossroads, Tupelo, and against Andrew J. Smith in August 1864—all under Forrest. In addition he participated in a number of raids and took part as a brigadier general in the defense against Wilson's raid through Alabama and Georgia. In the postwar years he was a farmer in California.

BELLOWS, Henry Whitney (1814-1882)

A Boston native and New York clergyman, Henry W. Bellows was the moving force behind the establishment of the United States Sanitary Commission during the Civil War. Before the war he had been the editor of the *Christian Inquirer* and the founder of numerous clubs in New York. In April 1861 he unified a number of women's organizations as the Women's Central Association of Relief, which, when it was organized on a national basis, was known as the Sanitary Commission. He became the president of a group that was trying to fulfill the functions that the government failed to provide for its troops in the field. These included adequate nursing, proper diet, proper camp hygiene, and directories of sick and wounded for the folks at home. The Commission also provided a soldiers' home in the capital and several transient lodgings along railroad lines for soldiers returning to their units. After the war he pursued his religious and writing careers. (Chadwick, J.W., *Henry W. Bellows: His Life and Character*)

BELO, Alfred Horatio (1839-1901)

A former student at the University of North Carolina, Alfred Belo served in the Confederate infantry where he not only fought Yankees but also other Confederates, for the honor of the regiment. He was named captain, Company D, 21st North Carolina, on May 22, 1861, and fought at 1st Bull Run. In April 1862 he was defeated at the reorganization of the company and on November 1, 1862, he was made captain and assistant quartermaster, 55th North Carolina. Promoted to major, he was present at the action at Fort Huger during the siege of Suffolk by Longstreet's Confederates. On April 19, 1863, a force of Union troops attacked the garrison and captured some five guns and 137 men. There was much dispute over which of the defenders were responsible. Captains Terrell and Cussons, of General Law's staff, made a report which questioned the North Carolinians' bravery. Colonel Connally, the 55th's commander, after determining the source of the allegations, proposed to the officers of the regiment that they demand satisfaction and, if it were not given, challenge the offending officers to a duel, with each of the 55th's officers taking their turn until they were all dead or the Alabamians altered their statements. After Lieutenant Colonel Smith refused to take part on moral grounds, Major Belo joined Colonel Connally in making the challenge. Belo and Cussons accordingly faced each other with Mississippi rifles; at the first discharge Cussons' hat was hit. At the second Belo was nicked in the neck. While they were reloading the dispute was settled verbally between Connally and Terrell. Belo fought at Gettysburg, where he was severely wounded, and at the Wilderness, Spotsylvania, and Cold Harbor, where he was again wounded. He was made lieutenant colonel on July 3, 1863. After the war he joined a newspaper in Texas. (Freeman, Douglas S., *Lee's Lieutenants*)

BENBOW, Henry Laurens (1829-1907)

A South Carolina planter, Henry L. Benbow entered the Confederate army as a private and rose to the rank of colonel and temporary brigade command. His assignments included: private, Hampton Legion (1861); captain, Company I, 23rd South Carolina (November 15, 1861); colonel, 23rd South Carolina (April 16, 1862); and temporarily commanding Evans' Brigade, 1st Military District, Department of South Carolina, Georgia and Florida (summer and fall 1863). When one examines the service record of Colonel Benbow, it becomes obvious why the brigade became known as the "Tramp Brigade," since the unit served in most major theaters of the war. After service at 1st Bull Run, he received a commission in the 23rd on the South Carolina coast. Sent to join Lee in Virginia, he was wounded at 2nd Bull Run and missed the Maryland Campaign. He served again in the Charleston area before the brigade was dispatched to Mississippi in a futile effort to relieve besieged Vicksburg. He then took part in the defense of Charleston in the summer of 1863. At this point the brigade commander, Evans, was having constant problems with his superiors and the brigade was suffering. There were charges of lax discipline and near mutiny among the men. With Evans frequently suspended from command or assigned to other duties, Benbow was often left in command. A new brigade commander, Stephen Elliott, Jr., took Benbow and the 23rd to the defense of Petersburg. During the siege Benbow was wounded. At Five Forks he was again wounded and this time captured. He was not released until two months after Lee's surrender. He was a planter after the war.

BENEDICT, Augustus W. (?-?)

The decision of the Washington authorities to recruit black troops created a great demand on the army for white officers to command them. Many officers and men saw the chance for advancement by transferring to the new units. But the speed with which they were commissioned prevented a thorough check into their qualifications, and many were incompetent or, even worse, actually hated blacks. One of these was Augustus W. Benedict. His assignments included: lieutenant colonel, 4th Louisiana Native Guard (ca. February 10, 1863); and lieutenant colonel, 4th Infantry, Corps d'Afrique (change of designation June 6, 1863). With the black troops he fought at Port Hudson and then was assigned to garrison duty at Fort Jackson below New Orleans. Although highly respected by his regimental commander, Benedict gained a reputation for cruelty to his men. He once slashed a soldier with a sword for being improperly dressed, and he devised tortures for minor infractions of the rules. On December 9, 1863, he caught two privates sneaking out of the fort without orders. Without consulting the colonel, Benedict whipped the two in front of many onlookers. That evening a full mutiny broke out. Benedict was unable to come out of hiding until order was restored and the wild firing had ceased. There had been repeated cries of "Kill Colonel Benedict! Kill him!" The resulting court-martial sent several of the mutineers to terms at hard labor. Benedict's sentence was dismissal from the service.

BENEDICT, Lewis, Jr. (1817-1864)

Lewis Benedict, Jr., had been dead for almost a year when he was brevetted a Union brigadier general of volunteers in March 1865. The New York native had enlisted in Daniel E. Sickles' Excelsior Brigade early in the war and his assignments included: lieutenant colonel, 73rd New York (ca. September 13, 1861); colonel, 162nd New York (September 12, 1862); commanding 1st Brigade, 3rd Division, 19th Corps, Department of the Gulf (September 20, 1863-February 15, 1864); and commanding 3rd Brigade, 1st Division, 19th Corps, Department of the Gulf (March 29-April 9, 1864). Sent with the brigade to the Peninsula, he was captured at Williamsburg. Confined in Libby Prison, he was not exchanged until September 21, 1862. By that time he had been given the colonelcy of a new regiment, which he led to the Gulf coast. He took part in the operations against Port Hudson, for which he was later brevetted, and the campaign in Louisiana's Teche region. He then embarked on Nathaniel P. Banks' disastrous Red River Campaign and was killed on April 9, 1864, at Pleasant Hill.

BENHAM, Henry Washington (1813-1884)

A great success as an engineer at the outbreak of the Civil War, Henry W. Benham proved a failure as a leader of line troops and after some difficulties reverted to his original field. Having graduated at the top of his 1837 West Point class, he was routinely posted to the engineers and earned a brevet in the Mexican War. His Civil War assignments included: captain, Engineers (since May 24, 1848); major, Engineers (August 6, 1861); chief engineer, Department of the Ohio (May 14-July 22, 1861); brigadier general, USV (August 13, 1861; revoked August 7, 1862; revocation cancelled February 6, 1863); commanding brigade, Army of Occupation, West Virginia, Department of the Ohio (September-October 11, 1861); lieutenant colonel, Engineers (March 3, 1863); and commanding Engineer Brigade, Army of the Potomac (spring 1863-June 1865). Although an engineer, he directed with a small detachment the pursuit of the Confederate forces from Laurel Hill in western Virginia. This effort resulted in the death of the first general officer, North or South, during the war, General Robert Garnett, at Carrick's Ford. It also resulted in a regular army brevet and appointment as a volunteer brigadier. Given a line command, he fell into disfavor with his commander, William S. Rosecrans, and was soon sent to the coast of South Carolina and Georgia. After success at Fort Pulaski he led a disastrous operation at Secessionville, South Carolina. Removed from command, he was also relieved of his commission in the volunteers and posted to engineering duty in Massachusetts. Early in 1863 Lincoln reinstated Benham as a general officer and

Engineer Henry W. Benham. (*Leslie's*)

for the remainder of the war he directed the engineer troops of the Army of the Potomac. He received brevets through major general of both regulars and volunteers. Mustered out of the volunteers on January 15, 1866, he remained in the engineers until his retirement in 1882 as a colonel. His battle credits included Chancellorsville, Gettysburg, the Wilderness, Spotsylvania, Cold Harbor, Petersburg, and Appomattox.

BENJAMIN, Judah Philip (1811-1884)

Born in St. Croix, the Virgin Islands, Judah Benjamin resigned from the U.S. Senate in order to serve his state of Louisiana and the Confederacy. The lawyer and former state legislator was appointed attorney general in the provisional cabinet of Jefferson Davis, whom he had once challenged to a duel. On February 25, 1861, Benjamin entered upon the duties of the first of three portfolios he was to hold in the rebel nation. After a successful few months as attorney general, he took over the War Department from Leroy Walker, on September 17, 1861. Holding this position during the disastrous winter of 1861-62, he was blamed for the Confederate defeats in North Carolina, Kentucky, and Tennessee. The Congress called for his removal, and his friend Davis was forced to replace him. But on the same day, March 18, 1862, Davis appointed him secretary of state, a move that upset many of Davis' numerous critics. In this post Benjamin displayed the attributes that earned him the sobriquet "The Brains of the Confederacy." During his tenure he was instrumental in obtaining foreign loans for the government but failed as head of the diplomatic efforts to obtain recognition from European states. At the collapse of the Confederacy, Benjamin fled via Florida and in small boats to the West Indies and eventually reached England where he became Queen's Counsel. Upon his retirement in 1883, he was given a farewell banquet by the Bar of England. He died in Paris the next year. (Butler, Pierce, *Judah P. Benjamin*, and Meade, Robert D., *Judah P. Benjamin, Confederate Statesman*)

BENNETT, James Gordon (1795-1872)

Scottish-born journalist James Gordon Bennett became a late convert to the Lincoln administration, having at first favored allowing the South simply to go. Emigrating to the New World in his twenties he started out as a copyboy. After a stint with the *Charleston Courier*, he became connected with a number of New York papers. Then in May 1835 he founded the *New York Herald*, which soon had a reputation for sensationalism and a rising circulation. His editorials waged war on a number of prominent politicians, and he was considered to be pro-Southern in many of his positions. Utilizing a large pool of correspondents and the new technology of the telegraph, his sheet continued to grow in the 1840s and 1850s. Strangely, he backed Frémont for president in 1856 and then Douglas in 1860. He eventually came around in favor of a vigorous prosecution of the war and backed Lincoln for reelection in 1864. Resigning his publisher's position two years after the war, he continued to do some writing and maintained control over the editorial direction of the paper.

BENNING, Henry Lewis (1814-1875)

Nicknamed "Rock," Henry L. Benning proved to be one of the more capable brigadiers of Lee's army. A Georgia lawyer and justice of the state supreme court, he entered the military at the outbreak of the Civil War. His assignments included: colonel, 17th Georgia (August 15, 1861); commanding Toombs' Brigade, D.R. Jones' Division, 1st Corps, Army of Northern Virginia (July-August 30 and September 17-October 27, 1862); commanding same brigade, Hood's-Field's Division, same corps and army (October 27, 1862-February 25, 1863; May-September 9, 1863; April 12-May 6, 1864; October 1864-February 1865; and March-April 9, 1865); commanding brigade, Hood's Division, in the Department of Virginia and North Carolina (February 25-April 1, 1863) and in the Department of Southern Virginia (April 1-May 1863); brigadier general, CSA (April 23 to rank from January 17, 1863); commanding brigade, Hood's Division, Longstreet's Corps, Army of Tennessee (September 19-November 5, 1863); and commanding brigade, Hood's-Field's Division, Department of East Tennessee (November 5, 1863-April 12, 1864). After serving in the Seven Days he commanded the brigade in part of the fighting at 2nd Bull Run and Antietam. He became the permanent commander after Fredericksburg, when General Toombs resigned, and led the brigade through the rest of the war. He went with Longstreet to southeastern Virginia and saw action later at Gettysburg, Chickamauga, Knoxville and the Wilderness. In the latter he was severely wounded. Returning to duty in October he was present for most of the remainder of the Petersburg Campaign. Surrendered and paroled at Appomattox, he rebuilt his lucrative law practice. (Freeman, Douglas S., *Lee's Lieutenants*)

BENSON, Eugene (1839-1908)

A financially poor art student, New Yorker Eugene Benson supplemented his income by contributing articles to the *New York Evening Post*, signing as "Proteus." After completing his studies at the National Academy of Design, and with the secession crisis upon the country, he was dispatched to Charleston Harbor by *Frank Leslie's Illustrated Newspaper* and sent back his sketches of the attack on Fort Sumter. After continuing with the paper for a while, he went after the war to Europe to continue his studies. He worked in Europe for the rest of his life.

BENTEEN, Frederick William (1834-1898)

Frederick W. Benteen's role in saving Marcus A. Reno's column from the same fate as Custer at the Little Big Horn was preceded by a fighting career in the Civil War. Born in Virginia, he moved to St. Louis where he eventually enlisted in the Union army. His assignments included: first lieutenant, Bowen's Missouri Cavalry Battalion (September 1, 1861); captain, Bowen's Missouri Cavalry Battalion (October 1, 1861); captain, 9th Missouri Cavalry (October 1, 1862); captain, 10th Missouri Cavalry (December 4, 1862); major, 10th Missouri Cavalry (December 19, 1862); lieutenant colonel, 10th Missouri Cavalry (February 27, 1864); commanding 2nd Division,

Cavalry Corps, District of West Tennessee, Department of the Tennessee (October-November 1864); and colonel, 138th United States Colored Troops (July 15, 1865). Serving in a series of commands growing from the same original company, his battle credits included Wilson's Creek, Pea Ridge, Vicksburg, and Tupelo. Regular army brevets came his way in 1867 for Osage, Arkansas, and Columbus, Georgia. He was mustered out on June 30, 1865, took command of a black regiment and was again mustered out on January 6, 1866. Half a year later he was commissioned a captain in the new 7th Cavalry. As commander of Company H, he was frequently at odds with Custer. Again brevetted for Indian fighting, he played a key role in saving part of the regiment at the Little Big Horn and was brevetted for this in 1890. He retired as a major in 1888, having developed a drinking problem.

BENTON, Samuel *(1820-1864)*

A nephew of Thomas Hart Benton, Samuel Benton did not receive his commission as a brigadier general in the Confederate army until he had already been mortally wounded. Born in Tennessee, he was a lawyer and state legislator in Mississippi. After serving as a delegate to the state's secession convention he joined the army where his assignments included: captain, 9th Mississippi (1861); colonel, 37th Mississippi (April 19, 1862); colonel, 34th Mississippi (designation change ca. May 1864); commanding Walthall's (old) Brigade, Hindman's Division, Hood's Corps, Army of Tennessee (June-July 22, 1864); and brigadier general, CSA (July 26, 1864). After serving in the Tullahoma Campaign at the head of his regiment he missed the fighting at Chickamauga and Chattanooga. During the beginning of the Atlanta Campaign he was in charge of the 24th and 27th Mississippi regiments. On May 11, 1864, he returned to his own regiment but took charge of the brigade the next month. After fighting at Peach Tree Creek he took part in the Confederate attacks in the battle of Atlanta proper on July 22, 1864. There he was wounded in the foot and chest. The limb was amputated but he died in a hospital on July 28th. He had been promoted two days earlier.

BENTON, William Plummer (1828-1867)

A veteran, as an enlisted man, of the Mexican War, William P. Benton was an Indian lawyer and former judge when the Civil War prompted him to become one of the first enlistees. The Maryland-born soldier's assignments included: colonel, 8th Indiana (April 27, 1861; mustered out August 6, 1861; regiment reorganized September 5, 1861); brigadier general, USV (April 28, 1862); commanding 1st Division, Army of Southeast Missouri, Department of the Missouri (October 1862-March 28, 1863); commanding 1st Brigade, 14th Division, 13th Corps, Army of the Tennessee (March 28-May 31, 1863); commanding 1st Brigade and 1st Division, 13th Corps, Army of the Tennessee (July 28-August 7, 1863); commanding 1st Division, 13th Corps, Department of the Gulf (August 7-September 15, 1863 and November 25, 1863-February 8, 1864); commanding 2nd Brigade, 2nd Division, 13th Corps, Department of the Gulf (April 17-May 9, 1864); commanding District of Baton Rouge, Department of the Gulf (May 25-31 and June 13-October 3, 1864); commanding District of Baton Rouge and Port Hudson, Department of the Gulf (October 3-December 26, 1864); commanding 3rd Division, Reserve Corps, Department of the Gulf (February 3-18, 1865); and commanding 3rd Division, 13th Corps, Department of the Gulf (February 18-May 28 and June 3-July 20, 1865). During the regiment's first three-month enlistment he served in the campaign in western Virginia, seeing action at Rich Mountain. After reorganizing the regiment it and he were dispatched to Missouri and fought at Pea Ridge in Arkansas. As a brigadier he served in the Vicksburg Campaign during which he was slightly wounded at Jackson. Transferred to the Gulf coast he served in post and line duty in Louisiana until he took part in the operations against Mobile for which he received the brevet of major general. Mustered out on July 24, 1865, he briefly resumed the practice of law. Sent to New Orleans as a government agent in 1866, he died early the next year of yellow fever.

BERDAN, Hiram (ca. 1823-1893)

The guiding force behind the creation of the two regiments of United States Sharpshooters was New York inventor and crack rifleman Hiram Berdan. For a decade and a half before the war he had been the acknowledged top marksman in the country, and his inventions included a musket ball and a repeating rifle. In the summer and fall of 1861 he was involved in the recruiting of 18 companies, from eight states, which were formed into two regiments. His assignments included: colonel, 1st United States Sharpshooters (November 30, 1861); commanding 2nd Brigade, 3rd Division, 3rd Corps, Army of the Potomac (February 19-March 1863); commanding 3rd Brigade, 3rd Division, 3rd Corps, Army of the Potomac (March 13-June 20, 1863); and commanding 2nd Brigade, 1st Division, 3rd Corps, Army of the Potomac (July 2-7, 1863). His men, who had to pass rigorous marksmanship tests, were dressed in distinctive green uniforms and equipped with the most advanced long-range rifles equipped with telescopic sights. Even when assigned to a brigade, the regiments were usually detached for special assignments on the field of battle. They were frequently used for skirmish duty. Berdan fought at the Seven Days and 2nd Bull Run. In 1865 he was awarded the brevets of brigadier and major general for Chancellorsville and Gettysburg, at each of which he led a brigade. He resigned on January 2, 1864. He was considered by many to be a crack marksman but unfit for a command. Berdan subsequently invented numerous engines of war. (Stevens, C.A., *Berdan's United States Sharpshooters in the Army of the Potomac, 1861-1865*)

BERRY, Hiram Gregory (1824-1863)

Because he missed some of the most famous battles in Virginia, Hiram G. Berry is one of the less well-known of the major generals in the Army of the Potomac. A Maine native, he had risen to become a bank president and local politician by the outbreak of the Civil War. Having been active in the militia, he soon enlisted and his assignments included: colonel, 4th Maine

Union General Hiram G. Berry, killed at Chancellorsville. (*Leslie's*)

(June 15, 1861); commanding 3rd Brigade, 3rd Division, 3rd Corps, Army of the Potomac (March 13-August 5, 1862); brigadier general, USV (March 17, 1862); commanding 3rd Brigade, 1st Division, 3rd Corps, Army of the Potomac (September-October 1862 and November 1862-January 1863); major general, USV (November 29, 1862); and commanding 2nd Division, 3rd Corps, Army of the Potomac (February 8-May 3, 1863). He lead his raw troops in the flank attack at 1st Bull Run but then got caught up in the Union rout. By the time of the Peninsula Campaign he was in command of a brigade, which he led at Yorktown, Williamsburg, Seven Pines, and the Seven Days. Illness caused him to miss 2nd Bull Run, and the corps was not present at Antietam. He led a brigade at Fredericksburg, but in the meantime he had been promoted to major general and was given a division before Chancellorsville. Early on the morning of May 3, 1863, he was mortally wounded in the fighting following Jackson's famous attack late the previous day. He died in less than an hour. (Gould, Edward K., *Major General Hiram G. Berry: His Career as a Contractor, Bank President, Politician and Major General of Volunteers in the Civil War*)

BERRY, Nathaniel Springer (1796-1894)

Five-time unsuccessful Free-Soil candidate for New Hampshire's governorship, Nathaniel S. Berry was finally elected, as a Republican, in 1861. His prewar career included service in both houses of the state legislature, as a judge, justice of the peace, and militia officer—achieving the rank of lieutenant colonel. His early years had been spent as a Democrat but the slavery issue caused his rift with that party in 1840. During the Civil War he was an active supporter of the Lincoln administration and the war effort. It was Berry who advised the president of the governors' support after the Altoona Conference. At the end of his two terms in 1863 he retired to private life. (Hesseltine, William Best, *Lincoln and the War Governors*, and Waite, Otis F.R., *New Hampshire in the Great Rebellion*)

BERTRAM, Henry (?-1878)

A deserter from the regular army, Henry Bertram received a second chance during the Civil War and became a brigadier general of volunteers by brevet. The German native, whose real name was Henry Beeger, enlisted in 1846 as a private in Company D, 2nd Artillery, and rose to the rank of sergeant before his desertion in 1851. His Civil War assignments included: first lieutenant, 3rd Wisconsin (June 29, 1861); first lieutenant and adjutant, 3rd Wisconsin (August 26, 1861); captain, Company A, 3rd Wisconsin (October 1, 1861); lieutenant colonel, 20th Wisconsin (July 31, 1862); colonel, 20th Wisconsin (December 10, 1862); commanding 1st Brigade, 3rd Division, Army of the Frontier, Department of the Missouri (December 1862 and February-June 5, 1863); commanding 2nd Brigade, 2nd Division, 13th Corps, Department of the Gulf (January 10-March 12, 1864); commanding brigade, U.S. Forces Mobile Bay, Military Division of West Mississippi (August 17-31, 1864); commanding the forces (August 31-October 1864); and commanding 1st Brigade, 2nd Division, 13th Corps, Department of the Gulf (March 4-May 8, 1865). As a company commander, he fought at a skirmish on Bolivar Heights near Harpers Ferry. After that the regiment fought in the Shenandoah Valley before Bertram became a field officer in a new regiment. At Prairie Grove, while in temporary command of the brigade, he had a horse shot from under him. He then took part in the Vicksburg siege before moving to Texas, where his regiment was part of the force which crossed over into Mexico to protect the U.S. consul and the property of American citizens. His final service came in the lengthy operations against Mobile. Brevetted brigadier general for his war service, he was mustered out July 14, 1865, with his regiment.

BEST, Emory F. (ca. 1840-?)

Detailed with his regiment to guard an important position in Jackson's rear at the battle of Chancellorsville, Emory F. Best saved scarcely more than himself and the regimental colors. He had entered Confederate service in the war's first year and his assignments included: lieutenant, Company C, 23rd Georgia (August 31, 1861); major, 23rd Georgia (same date); lieutenant colonel, 23rd Georgia (August 16, 1862); and colonel, 23rd Georgia (November 25, 1862). After serving at Williamsburg and Seven Pines, he commanded the regiment in the Seven Days Battles. When his colonel was killed at Antietam, he took over command, only to fall severely wounded shortly thereafter. Taken prisoner at some time after this, he was exchanged in early December 1862. When Jackson made his famous flank march at Chancellorsville, Best and the 23rd were detached from Colquitt's Brigade and left at the Catharine Furnace to protect the column's rear. A Union attack on his position resulted in the capture of almost the entire unit. For this failure he was arrested and dismissed from the service by order of a court-martial on December 23, 1863.

BICKERDYKE, Mary Ann Ball (1817-1901)

Serving as a nurse in some 19 battles in the western theater of the war, the widow Mary Bickerdyke became known as "Mother Bickerdyke" to the grateful troops. Testimony to the value of her service can be found in Sherman's specific request of her for his corps and the general's later grant to her of a pass for the limits of his military division. The Sanitary Commission made her their agent in the field and she even rode at the head of her corps in the Grand Review in Washington at the war's close. The Ohio-born matron had studied some nursing before the war and was one of the most capable nurses in the field, looking after the enlisted men first. After the war she worked as a pension attorney securing benefits for her former patients. In 1886 she received a pension of her own from Congress.

BICKHAM, William Denison (1827-1894)

A reporter who got too close to his subject to be objective was William Bickham of the *Cincinnati Commercial*. When the Ohioan arrived in the camp of the newly renamed Army of the Cumberland in October 1862, he was immediately accepted by the army's new commander, Major General William S. Rosecrans, since the journalist's paper was a staunch supporter of the Lincoln administration. Rosecrans made Bickham a volunteer aide-de-camp with the rank of captain. In return Bickham became an image enhancer for the general. However, many of the officers and men of the army were displeased with what they considered Bickham's false reporting. Having witnessed the battle of Murfreesboro at the end of 1862 and the beginning of 1863, Bickham later published his account of the action, *Rosecrans' Campaign*. Shortly after the battle, and only three months after joining the army, he left to edit his new paper in Ohio, the *Dayton Journal*. This work filled the remaining three decades of his life.

BICKLEY, George Washington Layfayette (1823-1867)

A thorough scoundrel before the Civil War, George W.L. Bickley became a Copperhead but was never able to do the Union much harm. Having posed as a doctor and abandoned one wife and child and the child of a previous marriage, the Virginia-born schemer tried to regain control of an organization, the Knights of the Golden Circle, which he had formed before the war. Its original purpose, when established in 1857, was to launch a filibustering expedition into northern Mexico. With the outbreak of hostilities the southern wing of the organization faded away and "Major General" Bickley, being in the South at the time, lost control of the northern wing. After almost two years of trying to raise Confederate units, and apparently having worn out his welcome with the authorities, he escaped to the North. Requesting to return to his home in Cincinnati, he was tailed and arrested when he went to Indiana instead. Recognized as the founder of the secret Copperhead organization, he was confined from July 17, 1863, until October 14, 1865. His Knights continued to function throughout the war under a series of names and leaders. Bickley died shortly after the war.

BIDDLE, Champman (?-?)

Chapman Biddle played a major role in the opening stages of the Gettysburg fighting but he was wounded on the second day. The Pennsylvanian entered the service when Lincoln called for more men after the failure of the Peninsula Campaign. His assignments included: colonel, 121st Pennsylvania (ca. September 1862); and commanding 1st Brigade, 3rd Division, 1st Corps, Army of the Potomac (June 30-July 2, July 10-September 14 and October 14-December 28, 1863). His regiment was in Washington during the Maryland Campaign and was dispatched to reinforce the Army of the Potomac after the battle of Antietam. Assigned to the 1st Corps, he fought at Fredericksburg and Chancellorsville. Just before the battle of Gettysburg he took over command of the brigade and was heavily engaged west of town on the first day. The Union forces were forced back and he was wounded the next day on the new lines. He returned to command the brigade in the Bristoe and Mine Run campaigns but does not appear to have served after the end of 1863, although his regiment was not mustered out until June 2, 1865.

BIDWELL, Daniel Davidson (1819-1864)

A Buffalo, New York, police official and militia officer, Daniel D. Bidwell rose to the rank of brigadier general shortly before his death in battle. His assignments included: colonel, 49th New York (October 21, 1861); commanding 3rd Brigade, 2nd Division, 6th Corps, Army of the Potomac (May 28-June 10, 1863 and February-March 25 and May 6-July 8, 1864); commanding 3rd Brigade, 2nd Division, 6th Corps, Army of the Shenandoah (August 6-October 19, 1864); and brigadier general, USV (August 11, 1864). He led his regiment in the Seven Days but was not present during the Maryland Campaign. At Fredericksburg he directed the regiment on the left and served on that front during the fight at Chancellorsville. After fighting at Gettysburg he succeeded to brigade command during the battle of the Wilderness, having briefly held that position on two prior occasions. He led the larger unit through the rest of the Overland Campaign and after the fighting at Cold Harbor was recommended for a brigadier's star. The appointment came through two months later. By that time he had been transferred, with the corps, to the Shenandoah Valley. After participating in the fighting at 3rd Winchester and Fisher's Hill, he was fatally struck by a piece of shell in the early morning combat at Cedar Creek. He died later that day.

BIERCE, Ambrose Gwinnett (1842-1914?)

Raised in a large, impoverished Indiana family, Ambrose Bierce briefly worked as an apprentice for an abolitionist newspaper and studied at the Kentucky Military Institute before his Civil War service provided him with the material for his bitterly sarcastic short stories. His services in Company C, 9th Indiana, which he joined in April 1861, were the foundation for many of his later humorous works mocking the idiotic aspects of the military and society in general. His work was considered by contemporaries second only to that of Samuel Clemens. Rising from private to first lieutenant, Bierce served in West Virginia at the battles of Philippi, Girard Hill, Rich Mountain, and Carrick's Ford. With the regiment reenlisting in August, Bierce saw further service in the West at Shiloh, Corinth, Perryville, Stone's River, and Chickamauga. In Sherman's campaign for Atlanta, Bierce witnessed a suicidal attack by his brigade at Pickett's Mill merely to test the strength of the rebel works. Wounded in the head at Kennesaw Mountain on June 23, 1864, the returned to his brigade and was present at Franklin and Nashville. His service, especially at Shiloh and Pickett's Mill, led to morose post-war stories—"An Occurrence at Owl Creek Bridge," "Chickamauga," "The Coup De Grace," "One Officer, One Man," and "One of the Missing," in which a soldier trapped in a collapsed building dies of fright because his unloaded rifle is pointed at his head. In "A Son of the Gods," an officer sacrifices himself trying to determine if the enemy is present on a hill, only to have the skirmish line go forward anyway in a hopeless charge to avenge his fall. After the war, Bierce was a journalist for the Hearst newspapers in California and a humorist writer in London. He is presumed to have died while covering the Mexican civil war. (McWilliams, Carey, *Ambrose Bierce, A Biography*)

BIERSTADT, Albert (1830-1902)

Known primarily as a landscape artist, Albert Bierstadt did execute some works on Civil War themes but even in these the scenery is the main feature. Born in Solingen, Germany, he was brought to America as an infant. In his early twenties he studied art for four years back in Düsseldorf. Upon his return to the United States in 1857 he accompanied Frederick W. Lander on an expedition across the West. The scale of the scenery in that region caused him to execute his works on huge canvasses. His paintings now hang on both sides of the Atlantic, including the U.S. Capitol. In his Civil War works the soldiers tend to be incidental to the scene, as in "Attack on a Union Picket Post." He continued his landscapes after the war but also began to paint American wildlife. His oversize works now have lost some of their former popularity.

BIGELOW, John (1817-1911)

An anti-slavery editor of the *New York Evening Post* since 1848, John Bigelow was appointed consul to Paris in 1861 and served in France throughout the war. Born in New York, he had practiced law and served as a Sing Sing prison inspector. In 1856 he wrote a campaign biography, *Memoir of the Life and Public Services of John Charles Frémont*, having joined Frémont's Republicans after being for a time with the Free-Soilers. After traveling for a couple of years in Europe he was appointed to the consular post in which he worked successfully to prevent French intervention in the Civil War and prevent any growth of the crisis over the *Trent* affair. He advised Napoleon III not to get involved in Mexico and urged the United States to show restraint in the matter. In April 1865 he became minister to France, returning home the next year. He was a prolific writer after the war, his most important work being *France and the Confederate Navy, 1862-68: An International Episode*. (Bigelow, John, *Retrospections of an Active Life*, and Clapp, Margaret Antoinette, *Forgotten First Citizen: John Bigelow*)

BINGHAM, John Armor (1815-1900)

In a varied career before, during, and after the Civil War John A. Bingham had a large impact on the events of his day. The Pennsylvania native was admitted to the bar in Ohio in 1840 and served as district attorney before being elected to the House of Representatives as a Republican in 1854. He was defeated for reelection in 1862, his fourth term ending in the midst of the Civil War on March 3, 1863. During his last term he was one of the managers in the impeachment trial of Tennessee judge West H. Humphreys. The year after leaving Congress he was appointed to a military legal position by Abraham Lincoln. His official assignment was major and judge advocate, USV, and the appointment was dated January 12, 1864. He resigned this post on August 3, 1864, and became a solicitor with the court of Claims. He was reelected to Congress in 1864 and remained until 1873. In 1865 he was named a special judge advocate in the trial of the Lincoln conspirators and was noted for making loose accusations and trying to bait the witnesses into providing the right answers. In the impeachment trial of Andrew Johnson he was the chairman of the managers appearing before the Senate. Losing the nomination in 1872, he was named to a diplomatic post in Japan at the end of the term and remained there until 1885.

BINGHAM, Kinsley Scott (1808-1861)

The first man ever to head a ticket labeled "Republican," Kinsley S. Bingham died in the first year of a Republican presidency. Born in New York, he practiced law there before moving to Michigan and later becoming a farmer. He held a number of lesser offices until named to the state legislature upon the admission of the state to the Union. As a Democrat, he was a member of the House of Representatives in Washington from 1847-1851. Not seeking reelection, he returned to his agricultural pursuits until he ran for governor in 1854 and won. He was reelected two years later. He returned to Washington to serve as a Republican senator from 1859 until his death on October 5, 1861, between the first and second sessions of the 37th Congress.

BIRGE, Henry Warner (1825-1888)

Leaving his position on the Connecticut governor's staff, merchant Henry W. Birge raised the first three-year regiment from the state and served throughout the war, mostly along the Gulf coast. His assignments included: major, 4th Connecticut (May 23, 1861); colonel, 13th Connecticut (February 18,

Result of John A. Bingham's prosecution of the trial of the Lincoln conspirators: the hanging of Mary Surratt, Lewis Powell, David Herold, and George Atzerodt. (NA)

1862); commanding 3rd Brigade, 4th Division, 19th Corps, Department of the Gulf (January 3-July 10, 1863); commanding 1st Brigade, same division, corps, and department (August 10, 1863-January 25, 1864); also commanding District of La Fourche, Department of the Gulf (September 1863-May 4, 1864); brigadier general, USV (September 19, 1863); commanding 2nd Brigade, 2nd Division, 19th Corps, Department of the Gulf (February 15-April 30 and May 7-June 27, 1864); also commanding District of Baton Rouge, Department of the Gulf (May 2-25, 1864); commanding 1st Brigade, 2nd Division, 19th Corps, Department of the Gulf (July 2-5, 1864); commanding 1st Brigade, 2nd Division, 19th Corps, Army of the Shenandoah (August 6-October 19 and November 10-December 8, 1864 and December 28, 1864-January 6, 1865); commanding the division (October 19-November 10 and December 8-28, 1864); commanding 1st Brigade, Grover's Division, District of Savannah, Department of the South (January 6-February 12, 1865); commanding the division (February 12-March 26, 1865); commanding 1st Division, 10th Corps, Department of North Carolina (March 27-April 1865); commanding District of Savannah, Department of the South (June 5-26, 1865). After serving as a field officer in Patterson's army and the Washington defenses, Birge resigned on November 13, 1861, to organize a new regiment of which he became colonel. Joining Butler's expedition, he took part in the capture of New Orleans. After leading a brigade in the operations against Port Hudson he received his brigadier's star and spent the next several months in both field and district command. Following participation in the Red River Campaign he was transferred with much of the corps to the Shenandoah Valley where he fought at 3rd Winchester, Fisher's Hill, and Cedar Creek. Transferred to the South coast his brigade garrisoned Savannah and took part in the final stages of the Carolinas Campaign. Following that success, he was given command of the District of Savannah and received a brevet as major general before resigning on October 18, 1865. For a time he remained in the South engaged in a series of businesses before retiring to New York.

BIRNEY, David Bell (1825-1864)

Since he and his older brother, William, were sons of anti-slavery leader James G. Birney, it is no surprise that birth in Alabama had no effect upon the decision of David B. Birney to enter the Union army. His assignments included: lieutenant colonel, 23rd Pennsylvania (April 21, 1861); colonel, 23rd Pennsylvania (August 31, 1861); brigadier general, USV (February 17, 1862); commanding 2nd Brigade, Heintzelman's

Division, Army of the Potomac (February 19-March 13, 1862); commanding 2nd Brigade, 3rd Division, 3rd Corps, Army of the Potomac (March 13-May 30 and June 12-August 5, 1862); commanding 2nd Brigade, 1st Division, 3rd Corps, Army of the Potomac (August 5-September 1 and September 13-October 30, 1862); commanding the division (September 1-13, 1862, October 30, 1862-May 29, 1863, June 3-July 2, 1863, July 7, 1863-January 28, 1864 and February 17-March 24, 1864); major general, USV (May 20, 1863); commanding the corps (May 29-June 3 and July 2-7, 1863 and January 28-February 17, 1864); commanding 3rd Division, 2nd Corps, Army of the Potomac (March 25-June 18 and June 27-July 23, 1864); commanding the corps (June 18-27, 1864); commanding 10th Corps, Army of the James (July 23-October 10, 1864); and commanding the army (September 5-7, 1864). The Ohio-educated Philadelphia lawyer served with his three-months regiment in Patterson's army until mustered out on July 31, 1861. The next month the regiment reorganized for three years and he fought as a brigadier at Seven Pines. Cleared of charges of disobedience in that battle, he was restored to duty in time for the Seven Days. After fighting at 2nd Bull Run he replaced Kearny in command of the division when the latter was killed at Chantilly. Stationed around Washington, his command missed Antietam but he led it at Fredericksburg and Chancellorsville. He again managed to get out of trouble for his actions in the former. At Gettysburg he succeeded Sickles in corps command and the following spring when the corps was broken up he was transferred to a division of the 2nd Corps. Taking part in the Overland Campaign, he replaced Hancock during the early stages of the Petersburg operations when Hancock's Gettysburg wound broke out again. Following Hancock's return he was given command of another corps in the Army of the James. In October 1864 he went home suffering from malaria and died on the 18th. (Davis, Oliver Wilson, *Life of David Bell Birney, Major General United States Volunteers*)

BIRNEY, James Gillespie (1792-1857)

Although originally a slave-owner, Alabama and Kentucky lawyer James G. Birney was an anti-slavery leader, first working for laws protecting slaves, then favoring colonization, eventually working for the abolition of the institution through political means, and finally—after his death—providing his two sons as generals in the Union army. Having freed his slaves, he moved to Ohio, where he published the *Philanthropist* and was tried for violating the Fugitive Slave Act. He worked for the American Colonization Society and the American Anti-Slavery Society. He broke with William Lloyd Garrison on the question of political action. Carrying his views into that arena, he was the presidential candidate of the Liberty Party in both 1840 and 1844. He died four years before the Civil War began. (Birney, William, *James G. Birney and His Times*)

BIRNEY, William (1819-1907)

Son of anti-slavery leader James G. Birney and elder brother of General David B. Birney, William Birney earned steady promotion through his ability to organize black troops. Born in Alabama, he had been educated in Ohio where he became a lawyer. After serving as a journalist in Europe he returned to establish a paper in Philadelphia. His military assignments included: captain, 1st New Jersey (May 22, 1861); major, 4th New Jersey (September 27, 1861); colonel, 4th New Jersey (January 13, 1863); colonel, 2nd United States Colored Troops (May 22, 1863); commanding District of Florida, Department of the South (April 25-May 13, 1864); commanding District of Hilton Head, Department of the South (May 13-June 2, 1864); commanding 1st Brigade, 3rd Division, 10th Corps, Army of the James (September 1-October 5, 1864); commanding the Division (October 5-20 and October 29-December 3, 1864); and commanding 2nd Division, 25th Corps, Army of the James (December 3, 1864-February 21, 1865 and March 27-April 10, 1865). As a company commander he was in reserve at 1st Bull Run but soon earned the majority of a new regiment with which he served at Seven Pines, 2nd Bull Run, Antietam, and Fredericksburg. Promoted to colonel, he commanded at Chancellorsville. Following that action he volunteered to organize colored troops and was engaged in that duty for two years, earning promotion to brigadier. Beginning in the spring of 1864 he commanded on the coast and in the operations against Richmond and Petersburg. By the end of the war he was leading a division of black soldiers and had received the brevet of major general. He was mustered out of the service on August 24, 1865. After a stint in Florida he practiced law in the nation's capital.

BLACK KETTLE (ca. 1813-1868)

Formerly a great warrior of the Southern Cheyenne, Black Kettle, in late middle age, was a voice for peace with the white man during the Civil War. Despite continued incidents between his tribe and the soldiers of Colonel John M. Chivington, the Cheyenne chief continued to urge restraint on his younger warriors. After all, a large U.S. flag had been presented to him that spring by the Indian agent, who informed him that no soldier would fire if it was displayed. Then, on November 29, 1864, Chivington launched a surprise attack at Sand Creek, slaughtering 133 Indians, some say several hundred; very few of the dead were warriors. The U.S. flag, and a white one, could not help Black Kettle's people. In disbelief, the chief managed to escape, only to be killed in another massacre, this time at the hands of Custer's 7th Cavalry on the Washita, on November 27, 1868—almost exactly four years later. (Brown, Dee, *Bury My Heart at Wounded Knee*)

BLACKBURN, Luke Pryor (1816-1887)

One of the more shady episodes of the Civil War was the alleged plot of Dr. Luke Blackburn to infect the Union war machine with yellow fever. Before the war, Blackburn was well known for his work in the lower Mississippi Valley fighting the almost yearly outbreak of the dreaded disease. During the Civil War he served as a Confederate agent in Canada. When in the spring of 1864 yellow fever broke out in Bermuda, so the story goes, Blackburn was sent by the rebel government to gather infected clothing from the victims for shipment to the North. For his services aiding local doctors in the epidemic he was actually praised by the British authorities. But first word of the "plot" surfaced on April 14, 1865, and there was outrage both in the North and South. More detailed testimony was given by Godfrey Joseph Hyams, considered by many to be a less than totally reliable source. The Union informer had reported that at Blackburn's direction he had passed the infected trunks on to various parts of the North. One of these trunks was delivered to New Bern, North Carolina, where an epidemic broke out at the regimental hospital of the 9th Vermont. In October 1865 Blackburn was acquitted in a Canadian court, on the grounds that there was no evidence of the trunks having been in that country. There was no further action against him. Returning to medicine in Louisville, he became popular enough for the state to elect him governor. As for the plot itself, it may well have existed but modern knowledge shows that it could not have succeeded because yellow fever is transmitted by mosquitoes. Germ warfare would have to wait.

BLACKFORD, Eugene (1839-1908)

The effect of a continuous campaign over a long series of months upon a previously distinguished officer is exemplified by the case of Major Eugene Blackford of Alabama. He entered the army at the outbreak of the war and his assignments included: captain, Company K, 5th Alabama (May 15, 1861), and major, 5th Alabama (July 17, 1862). His unit served through 1st Bull Run, Williamsburg, Seven Pines, the Seven Days, Antietam, Fredericksburg, Chancellorsville, and Gettysburg. At least during the latter two engagements he commanded a specially organized battalion of sharpshooters drawn from the various units of Rodes', later O'Neal's, Brigade. In these actions he was praised by his superiors. But in the spring of 1864 Grant launched his relentless drive on Richmond. The 5th saw action at the Wilderness, Spotsylvania, North Anna, and Cold Harbor before being detached with Early to the Shenandoah Valley. A long series of actions followed including Monocacy, 3rd Winchester, Fisher's Hill, and Cedar Creek. In the latter action he failed to live up to the duties of an officer and was hauled before a court-martial, charged with misconduct in the face of the enemy. He was found guilty and dismissed from the service. However, he was reinstated in February 1865 upon the urging of senior and junior officers.

BLACKFORD, William Willis (1831-1905)

One of the few officers to leave Jeb Stuart's original staff, not as a result of enemy fire, was William W. Blackford, his engineer. An engineer by profession, he helped raise a company of cavalry at the beginning of the war. His assignments in the Confederate army included: lieutenant, 1st Virginia Cavalry (May 14, 1861); captain, Engineers (May 26, 1862); major, 1st Confederate Engineers (January 19, 1864); and lieutenant colonel, 1st Confederate Engineers (April 1, 1864). Reporting with his company to Harpers Ferry, he soon came to the attention of Jeb Stuart who detailed him as an aide in July 1861. He remained with Stuart, becoming his engineering officer, until January 1864 and saw action at 1st Bull Run, the Seven Days, Antietam, Fredericksburg, Chancellorsville, Brandy Station, and Gettysburg. With the formation of regular engineering units, he was promoted to major and assigned to the first such unit, ending his service with Stuart. Organizing the new unit, he took part in the Petersburg and Appomattox campaigns and surrendered at the latter place. Returning to civilian life, he wrote his famous memoirs. (Blackford, William W., *War Years With Jeb Stuart*)

BLACKWELL, Elizabeth (1821-1910)

The first female doctor of medicine graduated in the United States, Elizabeth Blackwell organized the consolidation of the women's relief organizations early in the Civil War; it was this group that eventually became the United States Sanitary Commission. Born in England, she immigrated to the United States as a child and fought against prejudice to graduate from the Geneva Medical School in New York in 1849. She subsequently studied in Europe and upon her return joined with her sister Emily, and Marie Zakrzewska, in founding what was to become the New York Infirmary and College for Women. Upon the outbreak of the Civil War she was greatly concerned with what the government was not doing for the troops. She organized a women's relief organization that was concerned with camp hygiene, diet, nursing, and special supplies. This organization was later merged into the Sanitary Commission. After the war she continued her medical work, trying to open the field further to women; she returned to England in 1869 to further the cause there. She was also an active writer on medical subjects.

BLACKWELL, Henry Brown (1825-1909)

English-born Henry B. Blackwell, one of the earliest proponents of equal suffrage for women and an opponent of slavery, managed to woo Lucy Stone—who had planned never to marry—and to make their marriage a truly liberated partnership. Emigrating to America in his youth, he admired the American system but wanted to improve it; his family was involved in the abolitionist movement and in protecting runaway slaves. Having begun his career in 1853 as a speaker for the women's rights movement, he soon met Lucy Stone and began a persistent campaign to gain her hand. Their 1855 marriage was preceded by a joint protest against the unfair marriage laws of the day. Afterwards they shared the platform for a couple of years, with Lucy Stone continuing, with her husband's blessing, to use her maiden name. The birth of a child converted the marriage, for a time, into a more conventional one. But Henry returned to the campaign trail for Lincoln in 1864 and soon persuaded Lucy to come out of retirement for the 1867 campaign for equal suffrage for blacks and women in Kansas. They continued their work for many years thereafter. He subsequently served as editor without pay for the *Woman's Journal* until his death. (Wheeler, Leslie, *Loving Warriors*)

BLACKWELL, Lucy Stone

See: *Stone, Lucy*

BLAIR, Austin (1818-1894)

The two gubernatorial terms of Michigan's Austin Blair virtually spanned the Civil War years. A native New Yorker, he took up the practice of law in Michigan in 1841 and later served as a county clerk, in both state houses, and as a prosecuting attorney. Active in the founding of the Republican Party, he was elected governor on Lincoln's ticket in 1860. Sworn in on January 2, 1861, he was promptly active in preparing for war and gave his full support to the war effort after the firing on Fort Sumter. His second term expired on January 4, 1865, and he later served three terms in Congress. An 1872 bid for the governorship failed. He then resumed his practice. (Moore, Charles, *History of Michigan*)

BLAIR, Francis Preston, Sr. (1791-1876)

An anti-slavery border state politician—who had taken a leading role in the founding of the Republican Party—Francis P. Blair, Sr., served Lincoln in a number of informal capacities during the Civil War. Allegedly, it was Blair who offered Robert E. Lee the command of the Union army at the very outset of the conflict. Late in 1864 he wrote Jefferson Davis about the possibility of a reconciliation between North and South. He gained Lincoln's permission to visit Richmond, and there the Maryland politician proposed a joint military venture against the French in Mexico in order to end the internal warfare. This proposal gained the acceptance of neither Davis nor Lincoln but did lay the groundwork for the Hampton Roads Conference early the next year. After the war—during which his Silver Springs home was destroyed by the Confederates—Blair found his moderate views unwelcome with the radical-dominated Republicans. He returned to the Democratic fold.

BLAIR, Francis Preston, Jr. (1821-1875)

A prominent Missouri lawyer and politician, Francis P. Blair, Jr., was instrumental in thwarting the secession attempts in his state; he later divided his Civil War years between the halls of Congress and the battlefield. Born in Kentucky, he had served as an enlisted man during the Mexican War. In 1857-59 he was a Free-Soil member of the House of Representatives but returned to Congress as a Republican from 1861-July 1862, when he resigned to accept a brigadier's star. His military assignments included: colonel, 1st Missouri (April 26, 1861); colonel, 1st Missouri Light Artillery (June 12, 1861); brigadier general, USV (August 7, 1862); major general, USV (to date from November 29, 1862); commanding 1st Brigade, 11th Division, 13th Corps, Army of the Tennessee (December 1862); commanding 1st Brigade, 4th Division, Yazoo Expedition, Department of the Tennessee (December 1862-January 4, 1863); commanding 1st Brigade, 4th Division, 2nd Corps, McClernand's Army of the Mississippi, Department of the Tennessee (January 4-12, 1863); commanding 1st Brigade, 1st Division, 15th Corps, Army of the Tennessee (January 12-April 1, 1863); commanding 2nd Division, 15th Corps, Army of the Tennessee (April 4-July 26, 1863); commanding the corps (October 29-December 11, 1863); commanding 17th Corps, Army of the Tennessee (April 23-September 22, 1864 and October 31, 1864-July 19, 1865). Before actually taking the field he sat in Congress and chaired the Committee on Military Defense. He fought at Chickasaw Bluff and took part in the capture of Arkansas Post before serving in the siege of Vicksburg. He went on to serve as a corps commander under his friend William T. Sherman at Chattanooga and in the Atlanta Campaign. Meanwhile he had served again in Congress from March 1863 until June 10, 1864, when he lost his seat to Samuel Knox who had contested his election. Blair went on to serve in the Savannah and Carolinas campaigns and resigned on November 1, 1865. The man who had masterminded the preservation of Missouri for the Union and raised seven regiments for the cause was all but broke by the end of the war. After an attempt at planting in Mississippi he returned to Missouri where he found himself forced into the Democratic Party by the policies of the Radical Republicans. He ran for vice president in 1868 and served briefly in the Senate, until he retired in ill health.

BLAIR, Montgomery (1813-1883)

A border-state Republican, Postmaster General Montgomery Blair was mistrusted by the Radical Republicans for his moderate influence in the Lincoln cabinet and was eventually forced to resign in order to ensure Radical support for Lincoln in the 1864 election. The Kentucky native had graduated from West Point in 1835 but resigned after less than a year as an artillery brevet second lieutenant. He settled in St. Louis as a lawyer and entered politics as a Democrat. He served a term as mayor and sat as a judge before moving to Maryland. As an attorney before the U.S. Supreme Court in 1856-57 he represented Dred Scott in his fight for freedom. His anti-slavery views were such that he switched over to the Republicans and upon Lincoln's election to the presidency became postmaster general. As a cabinet officer he opposed the abandonment of Fort Sumter and later came into conflict with the more radical members of the inner circle. He had offered to resign in 1862 and made it clear to Lincoln that he would do so whenever the president felt that the time had come. During the 1864 election campaign Lincoln asked and Blair did resign, on September 23, 1864. There is some speculation that this was in exchange for John C. Frémont's withdrawal from the race. In the Reconstruction period he supported Andrew Johnson and opposed the Radical Republicans. By the end of the decade he had switched back to the Democrats.

BLANCHARD, Albert Gallatin (1810-1891)

Massachusetts-born Confederate Albert G. Blanchard was not happy with his lot in the Southern military. A West Pointer (1829) and 11-year infantry veteran, he took time out from civilian pursuits to serve as a captain of volunteers and a major of regulars during the Mexican War. In peacetime he was in education, business, railroading, and engineering in New Orleans. His Civil War assignments included: colonel, 1st Louisiana (early 1861); commanding brigade, Department of Norfolk (May 1861-April 12, 1862); brigadier general, CSA (September 21, 1861); commanding 3rd Brigade, Huger's Division, Department of Northern Virginia (April 12-June 1862); and commanding brigade of South Carolina Reserves, McLaws' Division, Department of South Carolina, Georgia and Florida or Hardee's Corps (February-April 9, 1865). Following the fall of Norfolk, he led his brigade over to the Peninsula and was at Seven Pines, where the performance of the division was questionable. Sent to northern Louisiana on conscript duty a few days later, he was soon found to be incompetent by General Richard Taylor. He was blamed for allowing Grant's army to land on the Louisiana bank of the Mississippi, unchecked in the advance on Vicksburg. He had virtually no troops under his charge, still being on conscript duty. Asking for relief from this assignment to get back to the field, he was inactive until the War Department found work for him with the South Carolina Reserves, a brigade of which he led in the Carolinas Campaign until he apparently lost his post in the consolidating of Johnston's forces. He was a surveyor after the war.

BLAND, Elbert (ca. 1822-1863)

During the Civil War Elbert Bland faced hostile fire from both a fellow officer and the enemy, but it was the latter that proved fatal. A native South Carolinian, he had received his medical training in New York before being named as an assistant surgeon in the Palmetto (South Carolina) Regiment during the Mexican War. He then resumed his medical practice until the secession of his state. His Civil War assignments included: surgeon, 1st South Carolina, PACS (ca. January 7, 1861); first lieutenant, Company A, 7th South Carolina (early 1861); captain, Company A, 7th South Carolina (April 15, 1861); and lieutenant colonel, 7th South Carolina (May 14, 1862). After taking part in the battle of 1st Bull Run he became embroiled in a dispute with the regiment's major, Emmett Seibels. That winter it developed into a duel but neither party was killed. Seibels lost his election for colonel the following May but Bland became lieutenant colonel. Moving to the Peninsula, Bland saw action at Williamsburg and in the Seven Days Battles where he was wounded at Savage Station. He rejoined the regiment in time to command it at Fredericksburg where he was slightly wounded. He commanded the regiment at Chancellorsville and one wing of it at Gettysburg. Going west with Longstreet, he was killed on the second day of the Battle of Chickamauga while again in command of the 7th. (Dickert, D. Augustus, *History of Kershaw's Brigade*)

BLASDEL, Henry Goode (1825-1900)

An Indiana-born Nevada miner, Henry G. Blasdel became the first governor of his adopted state upon its admission to the Union in the midst of the Civil War. He had moved to California in 1852 and later into the Utah Territory—part of which became Nevada—to take up mining. In 1864 he was elected to a two-year term as governor and two years later to a four-year term. During his adminstration's first year he quelled a Shoshoni uprising by meeting with them, thus possibly preventing the necessity of detaching troops from the war against the Confederacy. He did not seek reelection, but left office in 1871 and returned to his mining interests. (Myles, Myrtle Tate, *Nevada's Governors*)

BLEDSOE, Albert Taylor (1809-1877)

At the end of the Civil War former Assistant Secretary of War for the Confederacy Albert T. Bledsoe was researching a constitutional defense of secession at the British Museum. The native Kentuckian was a total Southerner and never let his faith in the cause waver. He graduated from West Point in 1830 but, after two years of frontier duty as a brevet second lieutenant in the 7th Infantry, he submitted his resignation and became a college professor and lawyer. In 1856 he published a defense of Southern life entitled *An Essay on Liberty and Slavery*. In 1861 he was named the chief of the Bureau of War in the Confederate War Department and then became the assistant secretary of war. He held the latter post until October 1, 1862, and the next year he set sail for London to do his research. Returning to the re-United States in 1866, he found Jefferson Davis imprisoned and wrote *Is Davis a Traitor; Or, Was Secession a Constitutional Right*. It is sometimes credited with having halted an indictment for treason. The following year he began editing the quarterly *Southern Review* in Baltimore. Through that organ he continued to promote the South until his death.

BLENKER, Louis (1812-1863)

An exile from the 1848 revolutions in Germany, Louis (born Ludwig) Blenker had an unhappy career as a Civil War officer. Giving up his New York business at the outbreak of the war, he joined the army where his assignments included: colonel, 8th New York (April 23, 1861); commanding 1st Brigade, 5th Division, Department of Northeastern Virginia (June-August 17, 1861); brigadier general, USV (August 9, 1861); commanding brigade, Army of the Potomac (August 17-October 3, 1861); commanding 3rd Brigade, Hooker's Division, Army of the Potomac (October 3-December 1861); commanding division, Army of the Potomac (December 1861-March 13, 1862); commanding division, 2nd Corps, Army of the Potomac (March 13-31, 1862); and commanding division, Mountain Department (April 1-June 26, 1862). During the fighting at 1st Bull Run Blenker's brigade was held in reserve at Centerville under the drunken Colonel Dixon S. Miles but still performed creditably in covering the withdrawal. After serving in the Washington area his division was ordered to western Virginia to reinforce Frémont. The six week movement was an example of military foul-ups due to War Department bungling. After taking part in the unsuccessful operations against Stonewall Jackson, and fighting at Cross Keys, Blenker lost his command in the reorganization of June 26, 1862. Not receiving another assignment, he resigned on March 31, 1863. Seven months later he died of injuries suffered in an earlier fall off his horse.

Less-than-successful Union General Louis Blenker. (*Leslie's*)

BLUNT, James Gillpatrick (1826-1881)

A Maine-born Kansas doctor, James G. Blunt had long been active in the conflict over slavery in his adopted state. An ally of the martyred John Brown, he was involved with some irregular military units early in the war before being accepted into the national service. His assignments included: brigadier general, USV (April 8, 1862); commanding Department of Kansas (May 5-September 19, 1862); commanding 1st Division, Army of the Frontier, Department of the Missouri (October 12-December 31, 1862); major general, USV (November 29, 1862); commanding District of the Frontier, Department of the Missouri (June 9, 1863-January 6, 1864); commanding District of Upper Arkansas, Department of Kansas (July 25-December 22, 1864); and also commanding District of South Kansas, Department of Kansas (October 10, 1864-June 28, 1865). His battle credits in the Trans-Mississippi area include being in overall command at Old Fort Wayne and Cane Hill and serving at Prairie Grove, Honey Springs, and in the defense of Missouri during Price's 1864 invasion. He was mustered out on July 29, 1865, and resumed his Kansas medical practice until taking a job with the government in Washington. Before his death he was confined for insanity.

BOCOCK, Thomas Stanhope (1815-1891)

After he lost out to a compromise candidate for the speakership of the U.S. House of Representatives in the famous 1859-60 stalemate, Thomas S. Bocock of Virginia served as the speaker of the Confederate House of Representatives for over three years. After a career as a lawyer, Bocock began his 14 years in the U.S. Congress in 1847, being much of the time chairman of the Committee on Naval Affairs. Representing Virginia's 5th District, which was spared the depredations of the Union forces until the very end of the Civil War, Bocock served in the Provisional Congress and both of the regular congresses. Serving as speaker in the regular congresses, Bocock held himself aloof from debate as was the custom of the U.S. Congress. Nevertheless, the record does indicate that he generally supported the administration, but not until the end of the war was he willing to support the sacrifices that were really necessary for victory. Losing confidence in the cabinet, he led the Virginia delegation before Davis, expressing their disatisfaction. This resulted in Secretary of War Seddon's resignation. Following the war Bocock was active in law and Virginia politics.

BOGGS, William Robertson (1829-1911)

As a Confederate general, West Pointer (1853) William R. Boggs of Georgia never held a field command. For the first year after his graduation he was posted to the topographical engineers, then transferred to the ordnance service. Resigning as a first lieutenant on February 1, 1861, he joined the Confederacy and his assignments included: captain, Engineers (February 1861); chief of engineers and artillery, Pensacola (1861); chief engineer of Georgia (December 21, 1861); brigadier general, CSA (November 4, 1862); and chief of staff, Trans-Mississippi Department (ca. March 7, 1863-May 26, 1865). After serving as Bragg's artillery and engineering chief he resigned his Confederate commission on December 21, 1861, in order to accept the position of chief engineer with the state of Georgia. He held that position for about a year before reentering the Confederate service as a brigadier general. He then served the balance of the war as E. Kirby Smith's staff chief west of the Mississippi. After the war he was a civil engineer and professor. He also wrote his reminiscences. (Boggs, William Robertson, *Military Reminiscences of General William R. Boggs*)

BOHLEN, Henry (1810-1862)

German-born liquor merchant from Philadelphia, Henry Bohlen had the misfortune of serving under poor officers; it eventually cost him his life in a useless probing of the enemy's position. Based upon some alleged service in the Mexican War—he had come to America as a youth—Bohlen was able to raise and obtain the colonelcy of a local German regiment for the Union. His assignments included: colonel, 75th Pennsylvania (September 30, 1861); commanding 3rd Brigade, Blenker's Division, Army of the Potomac (December 1861-March 13, 1862); commanding 3rd Brigade, Blenker's Division, 2nd Corps, Army of the Potomac (March 13-31, 1862); commanding 3rd Brigade, Blenker's Division, Mountain Department (April 1-June 26, 1862); brigadier general, USV (April 28, 1862); and commanding 1st Brigade, 3rd Division, 1st Corps,

Army of Virginia (June 26-August 22, 1862). His command served in the vicinity of Washington until the spring of 1862 when it was transferred to western Virginia. Taking part in the campaign against Stonewall Jackson in the Shenandoah Valley, he fought at Cross Keys. When the Mountain Department was merged into Pope's Army of Virginia, Bohlen started on his last campaign, that of 2nd Bull Run. After covering the withdrawal from Cedar Mountain in early August 1862 he participated in the maneuvering in northern Virginia. On the 22nd he was ordered to make a reconnaissance across the Rappahannock at Freeman's Ford to determine the enemy's intentions. Useless and extremely hazardous—being in the face of Jackson's command—the order was undertaken, but Bohlen was cut down while trying to recross the stream.

BOMFORD, George (1780-1848)

Although he had been dead for over a dozen years, ordnance expert George Bomford had a great impact on the Civil War. Graduating at the head of his three-member 1805 West Point class, the native New Yorker served in the engineers, ordnance department and artillery. By 1811 he had put his knowledge to work and designed a large-caliber artillery piece that saw much service in the War of 1812. By 1860, with improvements made by Thomas J. Rodman, this had become the standard piece of seacoast artillery in the American arsenal. Generally referred to as a Columbiad, it came in various calibers; a rifled version was introduced during the Civil War.

BONDURANT, James William (?-?)

Although he had distinguished himself in some of the early actions of the war, and had earned promotions thereby, James W. Bondurant's later career is rather obscure. A native Virginian, he entered the Confederate service from Alabama. His assignments included: sergeant, Jeff Davis Artillery (July 23, 1861); lieutenant, Jeff Davis Artillery (January 28, 1862); captain, Jeff Davis Artillery (early 1862); major, Artillery (May 8, 1862); chief of artillery, Department of North Carolina (May-July, 1863); and chief of artillery, 2nd Corps, Army of Tennessee (July 1863-March 1864). In command of his battery he distinguished himself at Seven Pines and went on to fight with the Army of Northern Virginia in the Seven Days Battles and at Antietam and Fredericksburg. He joined his old division commander, D.H. Hill, in southern Virginia and North Carolina, serving as his artillery chief. When Hill was promoted and sent to the Army of Tennessee, Bondurant became head of his corps' artillery. He held this post under a series of commanders until early 1864. In September of that year he was assigned to duty at Andersonville, Georgia, and was apparently with Hill, back in the Carolinas, at the war's end.

BONHAM, Milledge Luke (1813-1890)

Although not a West Pointer, South Carolina lawyer Milledge Bonham did have some military experience commanding a company of volunteers in the Seminole War and a regular regiment in Mexico. After serving in the U.S. House of Representatives

Milledge L. Bonham, Confederate general, congressman, governor, and again general. (NA)

from 1857-60, Bonham was sent to Mississippi by the state legislature to obtain the cooperation of that state in the secession winter of 1860-61. As a major general of state volunteers, from February 1861, Bonham was placed in charge of Morris Island in Charleston Harbor on April 15, 1861, two days after the fall of Fort Sumter. His later assignments included: brigadier general, CSA (April 23, 1861); commanding Alexandria Line (May 21-31, 1861); commanding a South Carolina brigade, Alexandria Line (May 31-June 20, 1861); commanding same brigade, Army of the Potomac (June 20-October 22, 1861); and commanding same brigade, in Longstreet's Division (October 22-November 9, 1861) and in Van Dorn's Division (November 9, 1861-January 29, 1862), Potomac District, Department of Northern Virginia. Going to Virginia in May 1861, Bonham superseded Colonel Cocke in command of the Alexandria Line and was in general command of the area when the fight at Fairfax Court House took place. Superseded after 10 days by General Beauregard, he commanded his brigade at 1st Bull Run and until January 29, 1862, when, slighted over seniority matters, he resigned. Bonham won a seat in the Confederate House where he served on the Ways and Means Committee, then resigned on January 17, 1863, to become governor of his state. He served in that office for two years, until reappointed brigadier general, on February 16, 1865. He commanded a cavalry brigade under Johnston in the Carolinas Campaign. After the surrender he resumed the life of a lawyer and planter. (Freeman, Douglas S., *Lee's Lieutenants*)

BOOMER, George B. (?-1863)

In the second assault on Vicksburg—May 22, 1863—the Union lost an experienced brigade commander, George B. Boomer. Living in Missouri at the outbreak of the Civil War, he remained loyal to the Union and soon enlisted. His assignments included: colonel, 26th Missouri (ca. December 1861); commanding 3rd Brigade, 7th Division, Left Wing, 13th Corps, Army of the Tennessee (November 1-December 18, 1862); and commanding 3rd Brigade, 7th Division, 17th Corps, Army of the Tennessee (February 12-May 22, 1863). Following initial service in Missouri, he led his regiment in the capture of Island £10 and the subsequent advance on Corinth, Mississippi. Wounded at Iuka, he returned to duty in time to participate in the central Mississippi Campaign of Grant against Vicksburg. Then, as a brigade commander under James B. McPherson, Boomer took part in the successful investment of the city in the spring of 1863. During the second day of major assaults on the city he was killed near the Railroad Redoubt. Afterwards Grant settled down to a regular siege.

BOOTH, Edwin Thomas (1833-1893)

The assassination of President Lincoln sent the assassin's brother, Edwin T. Booth, into almost two years of retirement. The Maryland-born actor had made his stage debut in 1849 and by the time of the Civil War had overcome earlier difficulties and become an established actor and theater manager. Himself totally loyal to the Union, his career suffered from the connection with his brother, John Wilkes Booth, but upon Edwin's return to the stage early in 1866 he found that audiences judged him for his acting and not the actions of his late brother. His acting and managing career continued to 1891, alternating between successes and financial disasters. Ironically Booth had a long-standing dislike for actress Laura Keene who starred in *Our American Cousin* the night Lincoln was shot. (Winter, William, *Life and Art of Edwin Booth*)

BOOTH, John Wilkes (1838-1865)

When the fall of Richmond aborted his plan to kidnap Abraham Lincoln and take him to the Confederate capital for a prisoner exchange, noted actor John Wilkes Booth changed his plot to murder. Born into a Maryland stage family that included his father, Junius Brutus Booth, and his brother, Edwin Booth, he did not achieve the acting success that he thought he deserved. Although his family tended to support the Union, his sympathies were entirely with the South and, while he didn't enter the military service, he wanted to strike a blow for his "country." He apparently planned to kidnap the president-elect before the 1861 inauguration but failed when the travel plans were altered secretly. Late in the war he plotted with several others to capture Lincoln and spirit him off to Richmond. Several times the band went into action but for one reason or another never succeeded. With the collapse of the Confederacy, Booth realized that the kidnapping would serve no purpose. His new scheme called for simultaneous attacks on Lincoln, Andrew Johnson, cabinet members, and General Grant. On the night of

Actor-turned-assassin John Wilkes Booth. (NA)

April 14, 1865, Booth, having made arrangements earlier, entered the President's box at Ford's Theater and shot Lincoln in the back of the head. Major Henry Rathbone, who was a guest of the president, was wounded with a knife by the actor/assassin. Booth then jumped from the box but caught his leg in the decorative flags draped around the ledge and broke his leg landing on the stage. Despite attempts to stop him, notably that of Joseph B. Stewart, he managed to escape the theater. He crossed the Navy Yard Bridge after informing Sergeant Silas Cobb, the guard, who he was and that he had been unavoidably detained in the city. He met up with fellow conspirator David E. Herold who escorted him through his flight. He stopped at the farm of Dr. Samuel A. Mudd to have his leg set and then with the help of numerous people along the way, he made it to Virginia and across the Rappahannock River. But here his luck ran out and he was cornered at the farm of Richard H. Garrett near Port Royal. Trapped in the tobacco shed by a cavalry detachment under the direction of detectives Everton J. Conger and Luther B. Baker, he refused to surrender. The troopers were under the direct command of Lieutenant Edward P. Doherty. Herold surrendered but Booth remained stubborn. After the shed had been torched, a shot rang out and Booth fell mortally wounded. Whether it was suicide or a shot from Sergeant Boston Corbett has never been determined. The only other part of the conspiracy that was carried out was the attack on Secretary of State William H. Seward by Lewis T. Powell.

BOOTH, Lionel F. (1838-1864)

A Philadelphia clerk, Lionel Booth enlisted in the regular army in 1858 and entered upon a military career that was to end in one of the most controversial battles of the Civil War. Transferring to the volunteers in 1862, Booth was made quartermaster sergeant of the 1st Missouri Light Artillery. In mid-1863, Booth was appointed captain, Company A, 1st Alabama Siege Artillery (African Descent). Rising to major, he was given command of the 1st Battalion of the regiment. Booth was ordered to take his battalion to Fort Pillow, Tennessee, on March 28, 1864. There he took command of the garrison that comprised his battalion (the regimental designation had been changed on March 11 to the 6th United States Colored Heavy Artillery), a section of Battery D, 2nd United States Colored Light Artillery, and the 1st Battalion, 13th Tennessee Cavalry, a white regiment. On the morning of April 12, 1864, General Forrest's Confederate cavalry attacked with 1,500 men against the fort's 557. Booth refused to surrender as demanded and prepared to defend his post. Shortly after the commencement of the attack at about 9:00 A.M. Booth was struck and killed by a sharpshooter's bullet. The attack continued until mid-afternoon when the fort was forced to surrender. Enraged by the sight of armed blacks, the rebels continued their killing of black soldiers and their white officers, white soldiers and black civilians. Many argue that none were killed save those who refused to surrender. But there is ample evidence that a massacre did in fact occur. (Cimprich, John and Mainfort, Robert C., Jr., "Fort Pillow Revisited: New Evidence About an Old Controversy," *CWH*, December 1982)

BOREMAN, Arthur Ingraham (1823-1896)

In a unique case of secession from secession, Pennsylvania-born lawyer Arthur I. Boreman became the first governor of a new state, West Virginia. He had served three terms and an extra session ending in April 1861 in the Virginia legislature. A resident of Parkersburg in the western part of the state, he attended the state secession convention as a Unionist delegate. Dissatisfied with the results of that meeting, he presided over the Second Wheeling Convention, which, on June 19, 1861, named Francis H. Pierpont provisional governor of the "Restored Government of Virginia." From October of that year to June 1863 Boreman served as a judge. With the admission of West Virginia to the Union on June 20, 1863, he was sworn in as the state's first chief executive. Twice reelected, he served through the rest of the war and until his retirement in 1869, when he accepted a seat in the U.S. Senate. During his term such advancements were made for blacks as the creation of separate, free public schools—an amazing step for the day. After his single Senate term he practiced law and again served on the judicial bench.

BOTELER, Alexander Robinson (1815-1892)

As the representative of Virginia's 10th District to the Provisional and First Regular Confederate Congresses, Alexander R. Boteler lost about half of his district to the new state of West Virginia when it was recognized by the U.S. Congress. An opponent of secession, farmer Boteler served two years in Congress before the state of Virginia seceded early in his second term. He was then named to the Provisional Confederate Congress and was barely reelected in late 1861. During his term of service, Boteler proved to be a supporter of the Davis administration; he served on the Committees on Buildings; Flag and Seal; Indian Affairs; Ordnance and Ordnance Stores; Printing; and Rules and Officers. When Congress was not in session he served on the staff of Stonewall Jackson, becoming a sort of public, and congressional, relations officer. In this latter capacity he helped smooth over the Loring-Jackson feud and save Jackson's services for the South. Boteler failed to gain reelection to the Second Congress; he served as an aide to Jeb Stuart. Holding several political appointments in the post-war years, Boteler spent much of his time writing historical articles.

BOTTS, John Minor (1802-1869)

His long-known Unionist views made John Minor Botts a marked man when martial law was declared in the Richmond area. A Virginia lawyer and politician, he was a consistent opponent of John C. Calhoun and the disunionist Southern portion of the Democratic Party. He also opposed the abolitionists

Virginia Unionist John Minor Botts. (NA)

who were, in his view, giving the secessionists a weapon. Recognizing secession as an established fact, he tried to get the U.S. Constitution amended to accept it. Retiring to his farm he continued to speak out; the day after martial law was declared for the vicinity of the Confederate capital, March 1, 1862, he was arrested. His confinement lasted eight weeks, until a new secretary of war released him on parole. Moving to Culpeper County he was offered a nomination for the U.S. Senate from the wartime Unionist government. This he declined but after the war Botts was for a time presiding officer of the Republican Party in Virginia. He withdrew from politics for the last two years of his life.

BOTTS, Lawson (1825-1862)

When one looks at the pitiful remnant, 210 men, of the Stonewall Brigade when it surrendered at Appomattox, it becomes obvious that the unit had suffered tremendously during the conflict. The senior commanders were not exempt from the slaughter, as is evidenced by the case of Lawson Botts, one of the regimental commanders. A lawyer in Charlestown, now in West Virginia, he was appointed by the court to defend John Brown in his 1859 trial. During this time he also become captain of the Botts Greys, one of the many local companies raised following the raid on Harpers Ferry. With the outbreak of the Civil War the unit joined the Confederate army and Botts' assignments included: captain, Company G, 2nd Virginia (April 18, 1861): major, 2nd Virginia (June 12, 1861); lieutenant colonel, 2nd Virginia (September 11, 1861); and colonel, 2nd Virginia (to date from June 27, 1862). Having fought at 1st Bull Run, Kernstown, and the Shenandoah Valley Campaign, he took over command of the regiment upon the death of Colonel Allen at Gaines Mill and led it through the rest of the Seven Days Battles. After fighting at Cedar Mountain, Botts and the 2nd took part in the famed "stand up" fight with what later became known as the Iron Brigade, at Groveton—the start of 2nd Bull Run. During the conflict he was shot in the head but lingered about two weeks before dying on September 11, 1862. (Robertson, James I., Jr., *The Stonewall Brigade*)

BOUDINOT, Elias Cornelius (1835-1890)

Although only a non-voting representative to the Confederate Congress, Elias C. Boudinot was probably the most effective legislator his Indian constituency had in Richmond. Half-white and half-Cherokee, Boudinot had been a railroad engineer and Arkansas lawyer before the outbreak of the Civil War. He used his journalistic talents to further Democratic politics and attended the Arkansas secession convention. Returning home he served in the 1st Cherokee Mounted Rifles, seeing action at Oak Hills and Pea Ridge as a major. Appointed by his tribe, he took his seat in the First Regular Congress on October 9, 1862. He was made a non-voting member of the Committee on Indian Affairs. He frequently proposed and endorsed bills and amendments that would have an impact upon his people. Following the Confederacy's collapse, he was instrumental in regularizing Cherokee relations with the United States. Subsequently he practiced law in Arkansas and engaged in agricultural pursuits.

BOUTWELL, George Sewall (1818-1905)

George S. Boutwell was one of the founders of the Republican Party and one of the congressional leaders in the impeachment of Andrew Johnson. The Massachusetts native was a lawyer before entering politics as a Free-Soil Democrat. He served a term as governor in the early 1850s and later set about the organization of the state Republican Party. Elected to Congress in 1862, he served from March 4, 1863, until 1869. He chaired the important Joint Committee on Reconstruction and as a Radical opposed the lenient policies of Johnson towards the South. He was Secretary of the Treasury during Grant's first term and blocked the plans of Gould and Fisk to corner the gold market by selling off government holdings at the right time. He then sat for four years in the U.S. Senate. (Boutwell, George Sewall, *Reminiscences of Sixty Years in Public Affairs*)

BOWDEN, Lemuel Jackson (1815-1864)

After supporting the Constitutional Union ticket in 1860, Lemuel J. Bowden became a Republican and represented his native Virginia in the U.S. Senate during part of the Civil War. The native of Williamsburg was admitted to the bar in 1838 and sat in the House of Delegates from 1841 to 1846. After serving as an elector for John Bell in 1860, he joined the Republicans and served in the Senate from March 4, 1863, until his death during the second session of the 38th Congress on January 2, 1864.

BOWEN, James (1808-1886)

James Bowen spent his entire Civil War military career in staff assignments, until relieved from duty along with his chief. His assignments included: brigadier general, USV (October 11, 1862); and provost marshal, Department of the Gulf (ca. December 1862-ca. July 1864). A railroader and civic leader in New York—head of the first city board of police commissioners in 1855—he had been active in recruiting operations in his native city and was rewarded with a brigadier's star. Because of his age he was assigned to a desk job but still got caught up in Nathaniel P. Banks' disaster in the Red River Campaign of 1864. Relieved of duty shortly thereafter, he resigned on July 27, 1864, but received the brevet of major general the next year. After the war he resumed his civic activities.

BOWEN, John Stevens (1830-1863)

Appointed to a Confederate major generalcy during the Vicksburg siege, Georgian West Pointer (1853) John S. Bowen did not long survive the surrender. Serving mostly on the frontier with the Regiment of Mounted Riflemen after his graduation, he resigned as a second lieutenant in 1856 to become an architect in St. Louis. His Confederate assignments included: captain, Missouri State Guard (early 1861); colonel, 1st Missouri (June 11, 1861); commanding 4th Division, 1st Geographical Division, Department #2 (October 24-December 1861); commanding brigade, Central Army of Kentucky, Department #2 (January-February 1862); commanding brigade, 3rd (Pillow's) Division, Central Army of Kentucky, Department #2 (February-March 29, 1862); brigadier general, CSA (March 14, 1862); commanding brigade, Reserve Corps, Army of the Mississippi (March 29-April 6, 1862); commanding Green's (old) Brigade, Maury's Division, 2nd Military District, Department of Mississippi and East Louisiana (January 22-April 1863); commanding the division (April 17-April 1863); commanding division, Department of Mississippi and East Louisiana (April-July 4, 1863); and major general, CSA (May 25, 1863). After serving at Camp Jackson as Daniel M. Frost's chief of staff and being captured and released, he raised a volunteer regiment, which he took to central Kentucky. There he commanded at times a division or brigade and then moved to Corinth, Mississippi, for the pre-Shiloh buildup. Leading his brigade in that battle he was severely wounded. When he recovered he took over a brigade in the vicinity of Vicksburg and was soon promoted to brigadier general. During the Vicksburg Campaign he directed a division until the surrender on July 4, 1863. Paroled the same day, he died nine days later at Raymond, Mississippi, from the effects of the siege and while still a paroled prisoner of war.

BOWERMAN, Richard Neville (?-?)

Having served as an enlisted man in the famous 7th New York Militia in the early defense of Washington, Marylander Richard N. Bowerman eventually rose to the rank of brevet brigadier general. His wartime assignments included: corporal, Company G, 7th New York Militia (April 26, 1861); first lieutenant, 11th New York (July 11, 1861); captain, 11th New York (October 4, 1861); lieutenant colonel, 4th Maryland (August 1, 1862); colonel, 4th Maryland (April 3, 1863); commanding 3rd Brigade, 2nd Division, 5th Corps, Army of the Potomac (May 8-23, 1864); and commanding 2nd Brigade, 2nd Division, 5th Corps, Army of the Potomac (January 22-February 14 and March 31-April 1, 1865). With the capital secured, he was mustered out with his militia unit on June 3, 1861, and then joined the "Fire Zouaves" of the late Elmer E. Ellsworth as a first lieutenant. This unit served at 1st Bull Run and witnessed the fight between the *Monitor* and *Virginia* at Hampton Roads. Mustered out as a company commander on April 19, 1862, Bowerman became a field officer in a Maryland regiment that spent its early service in western Maryland and near Harpers Ferry. Following the Union victory at Gettysburg, he took his regiment to join the Army of the Potomac in the pursuit of Lee. Later in the year he served in the Bristoe and Mine Run operations. During the Overland Campaign he fought at the Wilderness and succeeded to command of the Maryland Brigade at Spotsylvania. Back in regimental command, he fought at Cold Harbor and took part in the siege of Petersburg. Again in charge of the brigade during the latter stages, he won his brevet as brigadier general for Five Forks. Mustered out with his regiment on May 31, 1865, he joined the regular army as lieutenant colonel, 31st Infantry, in 1866 but resigned after a year.

BOWLES, Pinckney Downie (1835-1920)

South Carolinian Pinckney D. Bowles entered the Confederate army from Alabama. His assignments included: captain, Company E, 4th Alabama (April 1, 1861); major, 4th Alabama (August 22, 1862); lieutenant colonel, 4th Alabama (September 30, 1862); colonel, 4th Alabama (October 3, 1862); and commanding Law's Brigade, Field's Division, 1st Corps, Army of Northern Virginia (ca. June 3-September 1864). Commanding his company, the "Conscript Guards," he participated in the Battle of 1st Bull Run and in the Seven Days. While he was a field-grade officer, the regiment fought at 2nd Bull Run, Antietam, Fredericksburg, in southeastern Virginia, Gettysburg, Chickamauga, Knoxville, and in the Wilderness Campaign. After the wounding of General E. M. Law at Cold Harbor, Bowles was in temporary brigade command until the general's recovery. Bowles was no longer with his regiment when it surrendered with Lee at Appomattox. He served for a time as a judge after the war.

BOYCE, William Waters (1818-1890)

William W. Boyce can certainly be said to have enjoyed a "safe district" in the Confederate Congress, in more ways than one. He was unopposed in his three races for his seat and the district itself was not occupied by Union forces until the final months of the war. Boyce, a native South Carolinian—lawyer, planter, and former state legislator—was completing his fourth term in the U.S. House of Representatives when his state seceded on December 20, 1860. He resigned the next day. His committee assignments included those on: Executive Departments (Provisional Congress); Postal Affairs (Provisional Congress); Ways and Means (First Congress); and Naval Affairs (First and Second Congresses). He chaired the Committee on Naval Affairs in the last congress. Having originally been a cooperationist before the war, Boyce favored the adoption of the U.S. Constitution with only a few changes. He favored incorporating the right of any state to secede and he succeeded in limiting the president to one six-year term. He wanted to remove the conduct of foreign policy from the hands of the executive and favored the creation of a general-in-chief to further limit Davis' authority on military matters. By 1864 Boyce was urging peace overtures be made. Wiped out by the war, he practiced law in the reunited nation's capital until his retirement.

BOYD, Belle (1843-1900)

One of the most famous of Confederate spies, Belle Boyd served the Confederate forces in the Shenandoah Valley. Born in Martinsburg—now part of West Virginia—she operated her spying operations from her father's hotel in Front Royal, providing valuable information to Generals Turner Ashby and "Stonewall" Jackson during the spring 1862 campaign in the

Valley. The latter general then made her a captain and honorary aide-de-camp on his staff. As such she was able to witness troops reviews. Betrayed by her lover, she was arrested on July 29, 1862, and held for a month in the Old Capitol Prison in Washington. Exchanged a month later, she was in exile with relatives for a time but was again arrested in June 1863 while on a visit to Martinsburg. On December 1, 1863, she was released, suffering from typhoid, and was then sent to Europe to regain her health. The blockade runner she attempted to return on was captured and she fell in love with the prize master, Samuel Hardinge, who later married her in England after being dropped from the navy's rolls for neglect of duty in allowing her to proceed to Canada and then England. Hardinge attempted to reach Richmond, was detained in Union hands, but died soon after his release. While in England Belle Boyd Hardinge had a stage career and published *Belle Boyd in Camp and Prison*. She died while touring the western United States. (Sigaud, Louis, A., *Belle Boyd, Confederate Spy*, and Scarborough, Ruth, *Belle Boyd: Siren of the South*)

Belle Boyd, effective Confederate spy. (NA)

BOYD, James William or Ward (ca. 1833-1865 or 1866)

A ruthless character, James W. Boyd has become in recent years a central point in Lincoln assassination theories. In 1977 a film and a book appeared, entitled *The Lincoln Conspiracy*, whose authors, David Balsiger and Charles E. Sellier, Jr., advanced the theory that several groups were involved in planning the kidnap or murder of Lincoln. All worked through John Wilkes Booth at one time or another. They included Confederate agents in Canada, Radical Republicans in Congress, northern cotton speculators, and New York financiers. At a time when Boyd was about to launch his own plan, having replaced Booth, the actor attacked at Ford's Theater. The most controversial part of this conspiracy theory is the claim that Boyd was killed at the Garrett farm in a case of mistaken identity while himself searching for Booth. The theory says that Booth in turn made good his own escape and there was a massive cover-up. There are major discrepancies in Boyd's career but he did serve in a Tennessee regiment, was cashiered, served as a Confederate secret agent, was captured, and offered to aid the U.S. War Department in western Tennessee. Enough evidence has now been found to show that Boyd actually was murdered on January 1, 1866, long after the shooting at the Garrett farm. Also the physical similarity of Boyd to Booth is not at all convincing. There was a 16-year difference in age, six inches in height, and eye and hair color differences.

BOYD, Thomas H.S. (?-?)

An accomplice of Union spy William Lloyd, Thomas Boyd actually carried his pass from President Lincoln when operating behind enemy lines. He had worked for Lloyd before the war, in the publishing of transportation guides for the South, and continued to work for him when Lloyd took on the added responsibilities of a spy. He joined his boss in Norfolk in midsummer 1861. The pair made observations along the coast and sent back a report to Washington. When his employer was imprisoned at various times, Boyd continued the work. The pair was able to observe the Richmond defenses with Lee's chief of artillery, General William Pendleton. That summer of 1862 Boyd brought the information to Lincoln who made him his second personal secret agent, after Lloyd, with a salary of $100 a month, plus whatever Lloyd was paying him. After several more missions back to Washington, Boyd was arrested and confined in Castle Thunder where he found that his contact with Union prisoners of war enabled him to send messages to Washington when they were exchanged. Following his release he resumed his courier and espionage activities until "forced" to flee Richmond on the same train as Jefferson Davis and his cabinet.

BOYLE, Jeremiah Tilford (1818-1871)

As military commander in Kentucky, Jeremiah T. Boyle was plagued with Confederate raiders—whom he appeared powerless to stop—and even earned the enmity of a large part of the civil population, by his heavy-handed methods. As a border-state lawyer and slave-owner who remained loyal to the Union, he fit into the Lincoln administration's scheme of placing such men in high military positions. His assignments included: brigadier general, USV (November 9, 1861); commanding 11th Brigade, Army of the Ohio (November-December 5, 1861); commanding 11th Brigade, 1st Division, Army of the Ohio (December 5, 1861-March 9, 1862); commanding 11th

Brigade, 5th Division, Army of the Ohio (March 9-May 27, 1862); commanding District of Louisville, Department of the Ohio (October-November 17, 1862); and commanding District of Western Kentucky, Department of the Ohio (November 17, 1862-April 4, 1863). After fighting at Shiloh, he was ordered by the War Department to report to Kentucky where he was in effect military governor until January 1864 when his high-handedness forced his removal. He also held some district commands in which he was principally noted for telegraphing for reinforcements whenever there was Confederate cavalry or guerrilla activity in his domain. He proved highly ineffective in countering such incursions. Removed and ordered to Knoxville, he resigned instead on January 26, 1864, and entered the land and railroad businesses at which he was much more adept.

BRADFORD, Augustus Williamson (1806-1881)

During the administration of Maryland Governor Augustus W. Bradford the state became a solid member of the Union. As a result his home was burned by invading Confederates. A native Maryland lawyer, he had begun his political career as a Whig but during the Civil War he became a Union party member. In 1861 he attended the Washington Peace Conference and that November was elected governor. Sworn in on January 8, 1862, he supported Lincoln, and the state abolished slavery in its 1864 constitution. His home had been destroyed by Early's troops earlier in the year. His term expired on January 10, 1866; he later served as surveyor of Baltimore's port and subsequently resumed his law practice. (Buchholz, Heinrich E., *Governors of Maryland: From the Revolution to the Year 1908*)

BRADFORD, William F. (ca. 1832-1864)

In October 1863 at Union City, Tennessee, William F. Bradford, a lawyer, began organizing a Union cavalry regiment, which would be nearly annihilated the next spring at Fort Pillow. By the end of the year Bradford had raised enough loyal Tennesseeans to have four companies mustered in as the 1st Battalion of the planned regiment. After serving briefly in Columbus, Kentucky, and Paducah, Kentucky, Bradford was directed to move his entire command to Fort Pillow, Tennessee, on February 2, 1864. There he continued his recruiting activities and raised a fifth company that was slated to muster at Memphis in early April. In late March the fort had been reinforced by the 1st Battalion, 6th United States Colored Heavy Artillery under Major Lionel F. Booth who took over command of the post. Major Bradford became the second in command. Also present in the fort was a section of Battery D, 2nd United States Colored Light Artillery. Then on April 12, 1864, General Forrest arrived at the fort with 1,500 of his Confederate cavalry and demanded the surrender of the fort. Major Booth refused. The attack began and Booth was killed shortly afterwards whereupon Major Bradford took over command. After another six hours of fighting the fort was overrun and surrendered. The rebels were outraged by the presence of armed blacks among the garrison and commenced an indiscriminate slaughter of blacks and whites. Bradford was captured. Two days later Major Bradford was led off by five men and shot near Brownsville, Tennessee. The Confederates said he was trying to escape. (Cimprich, John and Mainfort, Robert C., Jr., "Fort Pillow Revisited: New Evidence About an Old Controversy," *CWH*, December 1982)

BRADLEY, Amy M. (?-?)

Going to the front as a nurse with the 3rd Maine, Amy M. Bradley was present at 1st Bull Run and became an employee of the United States Sanitary Commission. The Maine native also served with the 5th Maine and in a brigade hospital. With the Commission she worked on the hospital ships *Elm City* and *Knickerbocker* during the Peninsula Campaign. That September she was placed in charge of the Washington Soldiers' Home and served as a relief agent at Camp Distribution nearby. She also arranged for the publication of the *Soldiers' Journal*, which was full of information on how to deal with the military bureaucracy.

BRADLEY, Luther Prentice (1822-1910)

A Chicago salesman and militia officer, Luther P. Bradley twice in the midst of battle succeeded fallen brigade commanders; he earned himself a lieutenant colonelcy in the postwar regular army. His assignments included: lieutenant colonel, 51st Illinois (November 6, 1861); colonel, 51st Illinois (October 15, 1862); commanding 3rd Brigade, 3rd Division, Right Wing, 14th Corps, Army of the Cumberland (December 31, 1862-January 9, 1863); commanding 3rd Brigade, 3rd Division, 20th Corps, Army of the Cumberland (January 9-September 28, 1863); commanding 3rd Brigade, 2nd Division, 4th Corps, Army of the Cumberland (June 27-December 16, 1864 and May 25-June 5, 1865); and brigadier general, USV (July 30, 1864). He fought with his regiment at Island #10 and led it at Murfreesboro where he succeeded his brigade commander who had been killed. After serving through the Tullahoma Campaign at the head of his brigade he fell wounded at Chickamauga, where he earned a postwar brevet in the regular army. When he returned to duty he directed his regiment in the early stages of the Atlanta Campaign—earning another brevet at Resaca—and again replaced a deceased brigade commander at Kennesaw Mountain. This time he was awarded a brigadier's star. Following the fall of Atlanta his corps was sent back into Tennessee to face Hood, during the course of which campaign he was again wounded. He did not return to duty until after the close of hostilities. In 1866 he entered the regular army from which he retired in 1886 as a colonel and brevet brigadier general.

BRADY, Mathew B. (ca. 1823-1896)

When we see the number of Civil War photographs bearing the name of Mathew B. Brady, we assume that he was the leading photographer of the war. In actuality he took few if, indeed, any of the estimated 3,500 pictures that bear his name. The native

Pioneering photographer Mathew B. Brady. (NA)

New Yorker had studied painting before being attracted to the photographic process of Louis J.M. Daguerre. He opened a portrait studio in New York during the 1840s, utilizing the improved daguerreotype. Eventually he also set up a studio in Washington, D.C., where he caught the images of some of the most famous people of the era. At the beginning of the Civil War he was determined to accompany the troops into the field and record the scenes of camps and battlefields utilizing the newer wet-plate process. However, by this time his eyesight was failing, and he probably took none of the images in the field. They were in fact taken by a large corps of assistants, most notably Alexander Gardner, Timothy O'Sullivan, and James F. Gibson. Many of his assistants resented the lack of credit and either joined other firms or set up their own. Brady, however, did accompany his teams into the field frequently, as is evidenced by the numerous exposures in which he is included. His postwar career was not very successful financially. Both the Library of Congress and the National Archives have extensive holdings of the work of his firm. (Horan, James D., *Mathew Brady: Historian With a Camera*)

BRAGG, Braxton (1817-1876)

Of the eight men who reached the rank of full general in the Confederate army Braxton Bragg was the most controversial. The North Carolinian West Pointer (1837) had earned a prewar reputation for strict discipline as well as a literal adherance to regulations. At one time, the story goes, he actually had a written dispute with himself while serving in the dual capacity of company commander and post quartermaster. His pre-Civil War career was highly distinguished. After seeing action against the Seminoles, he went on to win three brevets in the Mexican War, in which his battery of "flying artillery" revolutionized, in many respects, the battlefield use of that arm. In 1856 he resigned his captaincy—he was a lieutenant colonel by brevet—in the 3rd Artillery and became a Louisiana planter. His Confederate assignments included: colonel, Louisiana Militia (early 1861); major general, Louisiana Militia (early 1861); commanding Department of Louisiana (February 22-March 1861); brigadier general, CSA (March 7, 1861); commanding Pensacola, Florida (March 11-October 29, 1861); major general, CSA (September 12, 1861); commanding Department of Alabama and West Florida (October 14, 1861-February 28, 1862); also commanding Army of Pensacola (October 29-December 22, 1861); commanding Army of the Mississippi (March 6-17, May 7-July 5, August 15-September 28 and November 7-20, 1862); commanding 2nd Corps, Army of the Mississippi (March 29-June 30, 1862); general, CSA (April 12, 1862, to rank from the 6th); commanding Department £2 (June 17-October 24, 1862 and November 3, 1862-July 25, 1863); commanding Army of Tennessee (November 20, 1862-December 2, 1863); also commanding Department of Tennessee (August 6-December 2, 1863, except briefly in August); commanding Department of North Carolina (November 27, 1864-April 9, 1865, but under Joseph E. Johnston from March 6, 1865); and supervising Hoke's Division, Hardee's Corps, Army of Tennessee (April 9-26, 1865). Initially commanding in Louisiana, he was later in charge of the operations against Fort Pickens in Pensacola Harbor. Ordered to northern Mississippi in early 1862, he briefly commanded the forces gathering there for the attack on Grant at Shiloh. During the battle itself he directed a corps and was later rewarded with promotion to full general. As such he relieved Beauregard when he went on sick leave and was then given permanent command in the West. Having served during the Corinth siege, he led the army into Kentucky and commanded at Perryville, where he employed only a portion of his force. On the last day of 1862 he launched a vicious attack on the Union left at Murfreesboro but failed to carry through his success on the following days. Withdrawing from the area, he was driven into Georgia during Rosecrans' Tullahoma Campaign and subsequent operations. In September he won the one major Confederate victory in the West, at Chickamauga, but failed to follow up his success. Instead he laid siege to the Union army in Chattanooga and merely waited for Grant to break through his lines. In the meantime he had been engaged in a series of disputes with his subordinates—especially Leonides Polk, James Longstreet, and William J. Hardee—that severely injured the effectiveness of the Army of Tennessee. Several top officers left the army for other fields, and Longstreet and Simon B. Buckner were dispatched into East Tennessee. With the army thus weakened, Bragg was routed at Chattanooga and was shortly removed from command. Almost immediately he was appointed as an advisor to Jefferson Davis, his staunch supporter, and maintained an office in Richmond. Ineffective in the position of quasi-commander in chief, he was dispatched to North Carolina in the waning days of the war. The forces under his command remained inactive during the second attack on Fort Fisher, allowing it to fall. When Joseph E. Johnston assumed command of all forces in North Carolina on March 6, 1865, Bragg was soon relegated to supervision of Hoke's division from his old department. In that capacity he surrendered near Durham Station. For a time after the war he served as Alabama's engineer and then settled in Texas where he died. He was the brother of Confederate Attorney General Thomas Bragg. (McWhiney, Grady C., *Braxton Bragg and Confederate Defeat*)

BRAGG, Edward Stuyvesant (1827-1912)

As an officer of the famed Iron Brigade, New York-born Wisconsin lawyer Edward S. Bragg fought through most of the battles in the East and eventually rose to command the famous unit, after it had been decimated by battle casualties. His assignments included: captain, 6th Wisconsin (July 16, 1861); major, 6th Wisconsin (September 17, 1861); lieutenant colonel, 6th Wisconsin (June 21, 1862); colonel, 6th Wisconsin (March 24, 1863); commanding 3rd Brigade, 4th Division, 5th Corps, Army of the Potomac (May 6-June 6, 1864); commanding 1st Brigade, 4th Division, 5th Corps, Army of the Potomac (June 7-August 24, 1864); brigadier general, USV (June 25, 1864); commanding 3rd Brigade, 3rd Division, 5th Corps, Army of the Potomac (August 24-September 13, 1864); and commanding 1st Brigade, 3rd Division, 5th Corps, Army of the Potomac (September 13-December 22, 1864 and January 18-February 14, 1865). After service in the Washington and Fredericksburg areas he took part in the fighting at 2nd Bull Run. In the stand-up fire fight at Groveton at the outset of the battle the brigade earned its sobriquet. As a field officer he fought at Antietam and Fredericksburg then commanded the regiment at Chancellorsville. Missing Gettysburg due to illness, he led the remnants of the brigade—merged with other units—in the latter stages of the Overland Campaign. At the Wilderness through Cold Harbor he had directed a different brigade but took command of the Iron Brigade on June 7, 1864. He led the unit through most of the Petersburg siege. Mustered out on October 9, 1865, he became a Democratic congressman and served as a diplomat to Mexico, Cuba, and Hong Kong.

BRAGG, Thomas (1818-1872)

Resigning his U.S. Senate seat on March 8, 1861—and formally expelled from that body the following July 11—Thomas Bragg served the Confederacy as attorney general for four months and then was active in confronting the peace movement in his native North Carolina. A prominent lawyer, he had served in the state legislature and as a delegate to Democratic national conventions in the 1840s and 1850s before being elected governor in 1854. After serving two two-year terms he was named to the Senate, where he served until two-and-a-half months before the state's secession. Replacing Judah P. Benjamin in the cabinet on November 21, 1861, he was a close backer of Jefferson Davis and endorsed the establishment of a Confederate supreme court, which never came into existence. A strict legalist, he opposed the impressment of supplies for the army without full payment. Leaving the cabinet on March 18, 1862, he resumed his private practice but tried to thwart the calls for peace in North Carolina and tried to alleviate problems between Davis and Governor Zebulon Vance. Following the war he was active in efforts to bring the state back into the Union; a reluctant secessionist, he had never believed the South could establish its own country. (Patrick, Rembert W., *Jefferson Davis and His Cabinet*)

BRAMLETTE, Thomas E. (1817-1875)

Despite having served as a Union officer earlier in the war, Kentucky's last Civil War governor, Thomas E. Bramlette, was considered evenhanded in his treatment of returning veterans from both North and South. A native of the state, he had practiced law, served in the legislature, and been a commonwealth's attorney before becoming a judge in 1856. This post he resigned in order to raise the 3rd Kentucky of which he was made colonel on about October 8, 1861. After service in Kentucky and Tennessee he resigned the next year to take up his duties as a district attorney. On August 3, 1863, he was elected as a Union Democrat to the gubernatorial chair. He was sworn on the first of September. During his term he declined a congressional seat and the vice presidential slot on the 1864 Democratic ticket. Leaving office in 1867, he continued to practice and lost a race for the U.S. Senate. (Coulter, E. Merton, *The Civil War and Readjustment in Kentucky*)

BRANCH, Lawrence O'Bryan (1820-1862)

Early in the war North Carolinian Lawrence O'B. Branch fought in an independent capacity, but at the time of his death he was in charge of a brigade under Lee. A veteran of the Seminole War, he embarked on such civil pursuits as law, journalism, and politics. Upon the secession of his state, he resigned from Congress and joined the South. His assignments included: quartermaster and paymaster general, North Carolina Troops (May 20, 1861); colonel, 33rd North Carolina (September 1861); brigadier general, CSA (November 16, 1861); commanding District of the Pamlico, Department of North Carolina (November 16, 1861-March 18, 1862); commanding 2nd Brigade, same district and department (March 17-22, 1862); commanding 2nd Brigade, same department (March 22-May 1862); commanding separate brigade, Department of Northern Virginia (May 1862); and commanding brigade, A.P. Hill's Division (in 1st Corps from June 29 and in 2nd Corps from July 27), Army of Northern Virginia (May 27-September 17, 1862). Preferring the field, he gave up his staff position to take command of a regiment but was soon promoted to brigadier and given a district on the state's coast. He was defeated by Burnside's expedition at New Bern on March 14 and a few days later was superseded by General French and later General Holmes. Sent to Virginia in May, his brigade acted as a link between Johnston's army on the Peninsula and J.R.

Anderson's command facing McDowell near Fredericksburg. Merged into the newly created Light Division, he fought at Hanover Court House, the Seven Days, and under Jackson at Cedar Mountain, 2nd Bull Run, Chantilly, and Harpers Ferry. In Hill's charge to restore the Confederate right at Antietam, Branch played a leading role but was killed by a sharpshooter once the lines were stabilized. (Freeman, Douglas S., *Lee's Lieutenants*)

BRANDON, William Lindsay (1800 or 1802-1890)

The entire service of Mississippi planter William L. Brandon as a Confederate general was spent supervising the Bureau of Conscription in his native state. Along with some medical training and service in the state legislature, Brandon had been active in the militia when he joined the Confederacy. His assignments included: major general, Mississippi Militia (prewar); lieutenant colonel, 21st Mississippi (1861); colonel, 21st Mississippi (August 14, 1863); and brigadier general, CSA (June 18, 1864). Sent with his regiment to Virginia, he fought during the Seven Days and was severely wounded at Malvern Hill, where he lost a leg. Promoted to colonel in the summer of 1863, he returned to duty in time for the fighting at Chickamauga and Knoxville. Soon thereafter he was assigned to duty directing the draft and was promoted to brigadier general. He later retired to his plantation.

BRANNAN, John Milton (1819-1892)

A professionial soldier, John M. Brannan emerged from the Civil War with brevets of major general in both the volunteers and the regulars. The native of the nation's capital had entered West Point from Indiana. Graduating in 1841, he was posted to the artillery and saw action in Mexico where he was wounded and received a brevet. His Civil War assignments included: captain, 1st Artillery (since November 4, 1854); brigadier general, USV (September 28, 1861); commanding District of Key West, Department of the South (June-August 22, 1862); commanding Department of the South (August 22-September 13, 1862 and October 27, 1862-January 20, 1863); also commanding 10th Corps, Department of the South (September 3-17, 1862 and October 27, 1862-January 20, 1863); commanding U.S. Forces Beaufort, 10th Corps, Department of the South (September 17-October 1, 1862); commanding 1st Division, 21st Corps, Army of the Cumberland (April 13-May 10, 1863); commanding 3rd Division, 14th Corps, Army of the Cumberland (May 10-October 10, 1863); major, 1st Artillery (August 1, 1863); chief of artillery, Army and Department of the Cumberland (October 10, 1863-June 25, 1865). Initially serving on the Atlantic coast, he earned a brevet for the action at Jacksonville, Florida. Transferred to a divisional command in the western armies, he distinguished himself on the defensive in the disaster at Chickamauga. During the battles around Chattanooga and in the Atlanta Campaign he was the chief artillerist of the Army of the Cumberland. He subsequently went on an inspection tour of the department's artillery. Mustered out of the volunteer service on May 31, 1866, he remained in the regular army until his 1882 retirement as colonel, 4th Artillery.

Artillery specialist John M. Brannan. (*Leslie's*)

BRANTLEY, William Felix (1830-1870)

Having survived war wounds, Confederate General William F. Brantley died at the hands of an assassin five years after the close of hostilities. The Alabama-born Mississippi attorney sat in the state convention on secession before joining the army as captain of the Wigfall Rifles. His assignments included: captain, Company D, 15th Mississippi (1861); captain, Company D, 29th Mississippi (1862); colonel, 29th Mississippi (1862); commanding Walthall's-Benton's (old) Brigade, Hindman's-Anderson's-Johnson's-Hill's Division, Hood's-Lee's Corps, Army of Tennessee (July 22, 1864-April 26, 1865); and brigadier general, CSA (July 26, 1864). Wounded at Murfreesboro, he returned to command the regiment at Chickamauga and Chattanooga. During the Atlanta Campaign he commanded the consolidated 29th and 30th Mississippi until the Battle of Atlanta. In that action he succeeded the mortally wounded Samuel Benton in brigade command. Four days later he was named brigadier general. Accompanying Hood into middle Tennessee, he led his brigade at Franklin and Nashville and later in the Carolinas. After the surrender at Durham Station, he resumed his legal practice until killed by an unknown assailant near Winona, Mississippi.

BRAS COUPE (?-1837)

A talented Bamboula dancer named Squier, taught to shoot and given a taste of freedom by his master, escaped from slavery and became the scourge of New Orleans during the 1830s. Losing an arm to slave hunters in 1834, he was dubbed Bras Coupe. Raising a racially mixed gang of white renegades and runaway slaves, he raided outlying areas of the city, killing and robbing the inhabitants. Extraordinary qualities were attributed to Bras Coupe; bullets, for example, were said to bounce off his chest. His raids came to an end in 1837, when he was killed, apparently in his sleep, by a confidant. It was the actions of such rebel slaves as Squier that raised the Southern fears of a Northern abolitionist-sponsored insurrection.

BRATTON, John (1831-1898)

A South Carolina doctor, John Bratton rose through many grades to become a Confederate brigadier. His assignments included: private, 6th South Carolina (April 1861); second lieutenant, 6th South Carolina (July 1861); colonel, 6th South Carolina (April 1862); temporarily commanding Jenkins' Brigade, Pickett's Division, in the Department of Virginia and North Carolina (March-April 1, 1863); and in the Department of Southern Virginia (April 1-May 1863); commanding Jenkins' Brigade, Hood's Division, Longstreet's Corps, Army of Tennessee (September 19-November 5, 1863); commanding Jenkins' Brigade, Hood's Division, Department of East Tennessee (November 5, 1863-February 1864); commanding Jenkins' (old) Brigade, Field's Division, 1st Corps, Army of Northern of Northern Virginia (May 6, 1864-April 9, 1865); and brigadier general, CSA (May 6, 1864). After service in Charleston Harbor, he went to Virginia and was named colonel upon the reorganization of the regiment. He led it at Yorktown, Williamsburg, and Seven Pines where he was wounded and captured. Exchanged he resumed command and led the regiment at Fredericksburg and in southeastern Virginia where he was in temporary brigade command. Sent to Georgia and Tennessee, he again led the brigade at Wauhatchie and Knoxville. He directed his regiment at the Wilderness until General Jenkins was killed. Promoted to brigadier, Bratton led the unit through Spotsylvania, North Anna, Cold Harbor, Petersburg, and surrendered at Appomattox. After the war he was a farmer and was prominent in South Carolina politics. (Freeman, Douglas S., *Lee's Lieutenants*)

BRAYMAN, Mason (1813-1895)

Journalist and attorney Mason Brayman served as a brigadier in the Union army but spent most of his time in grade in post and district commands. The native New Yorker was residing in Illinois at the outbreak of the war and his military assignments included: major, 29th Illinois (August 19, 1861); colonel, 29th Illinois (April 19, 1861); brigadier general, USV (September 24, 1862); commanding 1st Brigade, 3rd Division, 16th Corps, Army of the Tennessee (March 18-May 28, 1863); commanding District of Cairo, Department of the Tennessee (March 19-April 24, 1864); commanding Post of Natchez, District of Vicksburg, Department of the Tennessee (July 9-November 28, 1864); and commanding Post of Natchez, District of Vicksburg, Department of Mississippi (November 28, 1864-February 26, 1865). As a regimental commander he fought at Fort Donelson and Shiloh before being promoted to brigadier and briefly commanding a brigade of infantry. Thereafter he held various post and district assignments in the Western theater. Brevetted major general for his war service, he was mustered out on August 24, 1865. Returning to his railroading and journalism interests, he later served as governor of Idaho.

BREATHED, James (1838-1870)

Marylander James Breathed is an example of the slowness of promotion faced by officers of artillery in the Confederate army and of their loyalty to their arm, refusing to seek advancement in the infantry or cavalry. Entering the army during the first summer of the war, he held the following assignments: private, Company B, 1st Virginia Cavalry (August 31, 1861); lieutenant, 1st Stuart Horse Artillery (March 23, 1862); captain, 1st Stuart Horse Artillery (to rank from August 9, 1862); major, artillery (February 27, 1864); commanding horse artillery battalion, in Cavalry Corps, Army of Northern Virginia and in Valley District, Department of Northern Virginia (March 1864-April 9, 1865). After service in the cavalry he joined with John Pelham to organize the first horse artillery battery to serve with Jeb Stuart. Serving as a subaltern, he took part in actions at Williamsburg, the Seven Days, 2nd Bull Run, and Antietam. Promoted to captain, he commanded the unit at Fredericksburg, Chancellorsville, and Gettysburg. In early 1864 he was promoted to field grade and was given command of a horse artillery battalion. In the Wilderness Campaign he distinguished himself by personally bringing off a gun with only two horses. Wounded at Yellow Tavern, he recovered to serve through the Shenandoah Valley Campaign of 1864 and returned to the Petersburg lines in time to take part in the retreat to Appomattox. At High Bridge he took part in hand to hand fighting. Following the surrender he resumed the practice of medicine in western Maryland. (Wise, Jennings C., *The Long Arm of Lee*)

BRECKINRIDGE, John Cabell (1821-1875)

The man who could have been president of the United States in 1861, John C. Breckinridge, fought for the neutrality of his native Kentucky but then joined the Confederacy, serving it as a general and cabinet member. He had served as a major in the 3rd Kentucky during the Mexican War but saw no action. Resuming his legal practice, he soon entered politics. He served in the state legislature and the U.S. Congress before being elected vice president on James Buchanan's ticket. The youngest man ever to hold that office, he was named to the U.S. Senate upon the completion of his term. However, in the meantime he had run as the 1860 candidate of the Southern faction of the split Democratic Party. In the four-way race he came in second in the electoral college with 72 votes but only third in the popular vote. Fighting to maintain Kentucky in the Union, he backed neutrality and retained his seat in the Senate.

However, on October 2, 1861, he felt sufficiently threatened by the military government in his state that he fled. He soon joined the Confederate army and his assignments included: brigadier general, CSA (November 2, 1861); commanding Kentucky Brigade, 2nd (Buckner's) Division, Army of Central Kentucky, Department #2 (ca. November 1861-February 1862); commanding Kentucky Brigade, Reserve, Army of Central Kentucky, Department #2 (February-March 29, 1862); commanding Reserve Corps, Army of the Mississippi (ca. March 29-June 23, 1862 and August-October 1862); major general, CSA (April 14, 1862); commanding Breckinridge's Command, District of the Mississippi, Department #2 (June 23-August 19, 1862); commanding Army of Middle Tennessee, Department #2 (October 28-November 7, 1862); commanding division, Polk's Corps, Army of the Mississippi (November 7-20, 1862); commanding division, Polk's Corps, Army of Tennessee (November 20-December 12, 1862); commanding division, Hardee's Corps, Army of Tennessee (December 12, 1862-January 1863 and early 1863-May 24, 1863); commanding division, Department of the West (May 31-July 1863); commanding division, Department of Mississippi and East Louisiana (July-August 25, 1863); commanding division, Hill's Corps, Army of Tennessee (August 28-November 8, 1863); commanding the corps (November 8-December 15, 1863); commanding division, Hindman's Corps, Army of Tennessee (December 15, 1863-February 15, 1864); commanding Department of Western Virginia (March 5-May 25, 1864); commanding division, Army of Northern Virginia (May-June 1864); commanding division, Valley District, Department of Northern Virginia (June-September 1864); again commanding Department of Western Virginia (September 17, 1864-February 4, 1865); also commanding Department of East Tennessee (September 27, 1864-February 4, 1865); and Secretary of War (February 6-April 1865). For his action in joining the enemy, he was expelled by the Senate on December 4, 1861. In the meantime he had become a brigadier general and was given charge of a brigade of Kentuckians later to be known as the Orphan Brigade. Serving in central Kentucky, he took charge of that army's reserve when the rest of Buckner's division was sent to reinforce Fort Donelson. Joining the army forming at Corinth, Mississippi, under Albert Sidney Johnston, he led the Reserve Corps at Shiloh and during the Union drive on Corinth. He was then dispatched with his command to Vicksburg and later directed the Confederate attack on Baton Rouge, which proved unsuccessful. Ordered to rejoin Bragg's army, his division failed to arrive in time to take part in the campaign to liberate his native state. Instead he was given command in middle Tennessee and then finally was incorporated into the newly named Army of Tennessee. His division made the disastrous attack, against Breckinridge's advice to Bragg, on the final day of fighting at Murfreesboro. Again sent to Mississippi the following spring, he served under Joseph E. Johnston in the attempt to relieve the pressure on Vicksburg and then took part in the unsuccessful defense of Jackson, Mississippi. Rejoining Bragg, he led his division at Chickamauga and a corps at Chattanooga. Transferred to Virginia, he was in departmental command when he won the

John C. Breckinridge, former vice president of the United States and Confederate general. (NA)

Battle of New Market in the Shenandoah Valley. He joined Lee in time for Cold Harbor and then took part in the defense of Lynchburg. Under Jubal A. Early he fought at Monocacy and on the outskirts of Washington. Returning to his department in the late summer of 1864, his authority was extended over eastern Tennessee as well. Jefferson Davis then appointed him war secretary and he served in this post until the Confederacy's fall. He had been an advisor during the surrender negotiations of his former commander, Joe Johnston. He then fled in an adventurous escape to Cuba and eventually to England and Canada. Not returning to his home until 1869, he practiced law until his death. (Davis, William C., *Breckinridge: Statesman, Soldier, Symbol*)

BRECKINRIDGE, Margaret E. (ca. 1832-1864)

In one of the endless number of cases of divided families in the Civil War, a cousin of Confederate General and Secretary of War John C. Breckinridge, Margaret E. Breckinridge, gave her life in the service of the United States Sanitary Commission. A New Jersey native, she ran a commission vessel along the Mississippi from St. Louis to Grant's army at Vicksburg. Before she could join the army in Virginia she died of typhoid fever on July 27, 1864.

BREESE, Randolph Kidder (1831-1881)

Entering the navy at the age of 15, Randolph K. Breese was a veteran of the Mexican War and voyages to Japan and South

America by the time of the Civil War. His Civil War assignments included: midshipman, USN (since 1846); lieutenant, USN (ca. 1861); commanding 3rd Division of Schooners, Mortar Division, West Gulf Blockading Squadron (April 1862); lieutenant commander, USN (1862); commanding *Black Hawk* (1862-63); and fleet captain, North Atlantic Blockading Squadron (1864-65). In the attack upon Forts Jackson and St. Philip below New Orleans he commanded six of the 19 mortar schooners under Commander David D. Porter. During the operations along the Mississippi, Breese was in command of Porter's flagship and later joined him as fleet captain on blockading duty. He died, with the rank of captain, on sick leave in 1881.

BREVARD, Theodore Washington (1835-1882)

Serving almost the entire Civil War in Florida, Theodore W. Brevard became the last formally appointed general in the Confederate army. The North Carolina-born lawyer was serving as Florida's adjutant and inspector general when the Civil War broke out. His Civil War assignments included: major, 1st Florida Partisan Rangers Battalion (September 2, 1862); lieutenant colonel, 2nd Florida Battalion (change of designation June 24, 1863); colonel, 11th Florida (June 11, 1864); brigadier general, CSA (March 22, 1865); and possibly commanding Florida Brigade, Mahone's Division, 3rd Corps, Army of Northern Virginia (briefly March-April 1865). Throughout the early part of the war he led his troops in the sparsely manned areas of Florida. Although it is frequently reported that he was present with his command at the one major battle, Olustee, on the soil of his adopted state, there is no record of either he or his men being in the action. Joining the Army of Northern Virginia at Cold Harbor, he became colonel of a new regiment created from part of his own battalion and all of another. This he led through the Petersburg siege until promoted to brigadier general in late March 1865. There are some claims that he commanded the brigade during the early stages of the Appomattox Campaign but nothing appears in the *Official Records* to confirm this. Thereafter he engaged in the practice of law.

BREWSTER, Charles (1836-1904)

A commissary of subsistence in the Civil War, Charles Brewster survived one of a seemingly endless series of retaliatory situations. Born in New York, he was a clerk before the war. His assignments included: captain and commissary of subsistence, USV (November 26, 1862); first lieutenant, 13th New York Cavalry (July 10, 1863); and captain and commissary of subsistence, USV (March 2, 1864). His original staff position expired when it failed to gain Senate approval and he served for a time as a line officer. Again a staff officer—with Custer—he was captured by John S. Mosby and forced, twice, to draw by lot to determine who would be executed in return for Custer's summary execution of some of Mosby's men. He drew right both times and later escaped. After service in New Orleans, he was mustered out on July 15, 1865, as a brevet major. Two years later he was commissioned in the new 7th Cavalry but resigned in 1870 under pressure for incompetence. For 30 years he tried to be reinstated but with no luck.

BREWSTER, William R. (?-1869)

It was almost six weeks after Colonel William R. Brewster was mustered out that he was brevetted a brigadier general for the operations against Richmond and Petersburg, which were still under way. The Connecticut native was living in New York at the outbreak of the Civil War and became a field officer in a three-months militia unit. His assignments included: major, 28th New York Militia (May 10, 1861); colonel, 73rd New York (September 13, 1861); commanding 2nd Brigade, 2nd Division, 3rd Corps, Army of the Potomac (May-July 11, 1863, August 10, 1863-January 1864, and February-March 24, 1864); commanding 2nd Brigade, 4th Division, 2nd Corps, Army of the Potomac (March 25-May 13, 1864); and commanding 4th Brigade, 3rd Division, 2nd Corps, Army of the Potomac (May 13-July 3, 1864). During the battle of 1st Bull Run, his regiment was guarding the Potomac River bridges and missed the fight. Mustered out on August 5, 1861, he became the head of a new unit, the fourth regiment of Daniel E. Sickles' Excelsior Brigade. This he led at Yorktown, Williamsburg, and Fredericksburg. In charge of the brigade, he fought at Gettysburg, the Wilderness, Spotsylvania, Cold Harbor, and in the early stages of the Petersburg siege. Mustered out on October 25, 1864, his brevet promotion was dated December 2, 1864.

BRICE, Benjamin William (ca. 1806-1892)

The last officer to hold the post of paymaster general during the Civil War was Benjamin Brice. Following his graduation from West Point (1829), Brice served for two-and-a-half years before resigning and becoming a lawyer, judge, and militia officer in Ohio. He served as a major in the pay department in the Mexican War. He again left civil life to accept the same position in 1852. On November 29, 1864, he was promoted to colonel and appointed paymaster general in place of the retired Colonel T.P. Andrews. He held the post for the rest of the war and received brevets through major general in the regular army. The appropriate grade for the paymaster general was increased to brigadier general in 1866 and Brice was promoted accordingly. He retired after six more years of service.

BRIDGFORD, David B. (?-?)

During the Civil War the equivalent of the modern day military police was the provost guard. It was in this line of work that David B. Bridgford spent most of the war. Of British descent, he was a merchant in New York City before the conflict, then migrated South. His assignments after going South included: captain, Company B, 1st Virginia Battalion Regulars (May 17, 1861); major, 1st Virginia Battalion Regulars (October 11, 1862); commanding Provost Guard, 2nd Corps, Army of Northern Virginia (fall 1862-June 4, 1863); and commanding Provost Guard, Army of Northern Virginia (June 4, 1863-April

9, 1865). He served at Cheat Mountain, Kernstown (commanding the battalion), McDowell, the Shenandoah Valley Campaign, the Seven Days, Cedar Mountain, and 2nd Bull Run. Promoted to battalion command he was soon detailed to provost duty for Jackson's Corps. As such he served at Fredericksburg. After Jackson's death he became provost marshal for the entire army, seeing action in the Petersburg and Appomattox campaigns. Following the surrender he returned to New York as a commission merchant and participated in a Cuban revolution.

BRIGGS, Henry Shaw (1824-1887)

An early war wound prevented Henry S. Briggs from exercising much field command during the Civil War. A Massachusetts lawyer he had long been active in the state militia. His Civil War assignments included: captain, 8th Massachusetts Militia (April 30, 1861); colonel, 10th Massachusetts (June 21, 1861); commanding 1st Brigade, 1st Division, 4th Corps, Army of the Potomac (March 13-May 1, 1862); brigadier general, USV (July 17, 1862); commanding 3rd Separate Brigade, 8th Corps, Middle Department (February 14-June 25, 1863); and commanding 1st Division, 1st Corps, Army of the Potomac (August 5-23, 1863). Taking part in the Peninsula Campaign, he was wounded at Seven Pines and during his recovery was promoted to brigadier. As such he returned to duty in command of a brigade guarding Maryland and, briefly, a division in the Army of the Potomac. Subsequently—his wounds making him incapable of further field service—he ran a camp for draftees at Alexandria, Virginia. Mustered out on December 4, 1865, he served as a judge and held other government posts in Massachusetts.

BRIGHT, Daniel (?-1863)

One of the most sensitive questions raised in occupied areas during the Civil War was who was a guerrilla and who was a duly authorized soldier empowered to raise troops in areas near to or even behind enemy lines. For Daniel Bright the legal question was moot. He had been a member of Company L, 62nd Georgia (Cavalry), which was partly made up of North Carolinians. According to Edward A. Wild and the Union authorities he was a deserter from his unit engaged in guerrilla activities. Caught up in General Wild's December 1863 raid in northeastern North Carolina, he was captured at his home, given a drumhead court-martial and promptly hanged from a beam in his house on the 18th of the month. His body was left dangling for 40 hours with a placard on his back that read, "This guerrilla hanged by order of Brigadier-General Wild." The Confederates were outraged and declared that Bright was on leave with an authorization from North Carolina's governor to raise a company in his home county. Confederate General George E. Pickett retaliated by hanging Private Samuel Jones, Company B, 5th United States Colored Troops, on January 12, 1864. A series of hostages were seized, including women, to guarantee treatment of captives as prisoners of war. The whole incident led to a lengthy series of communications between the two sides.

BRIGHT, Jesse David (1812-1875)

For having written to Jefferson Davis as "President of the Confederate States," Indiana Senator Jesse D. Bright was expelled from the Senate early in the Civil War. Born in New York, he had moved with his family in 1820 to Indiana where he was admitted to the bar in 1831. He opened a practice and served as a probate judge, U.S. marshal, state senator, and in 1843-45 as Lieutenant Governor. As a Democrat, he was sent to the U.S. Senate from 1845 until his expulsion. In the meantime he attended the Democratic convention of 1860 in Charleston as a manager of the administration faction. Following his expulsion on February 5, 1862, having three times served as president pro tempore, he attempted to gain reelection to his old seat in 1863 but lost to Thomas A. Hendricks. He then moved to Kentucky where he entered the coal business and sat in the state legislature before moving to Baltimore.

BRISBIN, James Sanks (1837-1892)

Active in the antislavery movement Pennsylvania teacher James S. Brisbin entered the Union army at the outbreak of the war and served briefly as a private before being commissioned into the regular army. His assignments included: second lieutenant, 1st Dragoons (April 26, 1861); second lieutenant, 1st Cavalry (change of designation August 3, 1861); captain, 6th Cavalry (August 5, 1861); colonel, 5th United States Colored Cavalry (March 1, 1864); and brigadier general, USV (May 1, 1865). Wounded at 1st Bull Run, he returned to duty with the army in Virginia as a company officer and was brevetted for his actions at Beverly Ford. In early 1864 he accepted promotion to the command of a black cavalry regiment. Detailed on staff duty for a time, he took part in the Red River Campaign during which he was wounded at Sabine Crossroads. He went to Kentucky to organize his regiment and earned another brevet for a fight at Marion in East Tennessee. With hostilities virtually at a close, he was promoted to brigadier and was mustered out of the volunteers as a brevet major general. He continued in the regular army until his death, having served in several white and black cavalry regiments until finally appointed colonel, 8th Cavalry.

BROCK, Sallie Ann (1828-1911)

Mary Boykin Chesnut was not the only woman to write of her experiences in war-torn Richmond. Her close rival was Sallie Ann Brock, who in 1867 published *Richmond During the War: Four Years of Personal Observation* by "A Richmond Lady." Although she did not have Boykin's access to the Confederate centers of power, Brock provided a much more representative view of the capital, albeit from a somewhat darker side. Born in Madison County, Virginia, she had moved to the state capital a couple of years prior to the war and was involved in all the standard tasks of the women of the Confederacy: providing clothes for the troops and caring for them when wounded. She recorded the plight of the refugees, the shortages imposed by a war-torn economy, the endless inflation and the problems, real and imagined, that the war brought to race relations in the Old Dominion. Moving North after the war, she wrote four more books under the pen-name "Virginia Madison."

BROCKENBROUGH, John Mercer (1830-1892)

A farmer and Virginia Military Institute alumnus, John Brockenbrough was one of those temporary Confederate brigade commanders who was found wanting. He was appointed colonel, 40th Virginia on May 25, 1861. He commanded Field's Virginia Brigade, A.P. Hill's Division, Jackson's Corps, Army of Northern Virginia (August 29, 1862-March 5, 1863 and May 2-30, 1863) and same brigade, Heth's Division, A.P. Hill's Corps (May 30-July 1863) but was never promoted to the appropriate grade of brigadier general. During the Seven Days he led his regiment at Mechanicsville, Gaines' Mill, Frayser's Farm and later at 2nd Bull Run, where he assumed command of the brigade upon the wounding of General Field. He led the brigade at Chantilly, the capture of Harpers Ferry, Antietam, and Fredericksburg before being relieved by the assignment of General Heth to command the brigade. Brockenbrough commanded the regiment until Heth took command of the division and Brockenbrough the brigade during the fight at Chancellorsville. At Gettysburg he led his brigade on the first day and took part in driving the enemy back through the town. For some unexplained reason he was not with his brigade when it took part in Pickett's Charge on the third day. Later in July 1863, he was relieved of brigade command and resumed command of the 40th Virginia, which he led at Bristoe Station and Mine Run. On January 21, 1864, Brockenbrough resigned his commission, probably at least in part because his lieutenant colonel, Henry H. Walker, had been promoted to brigadier general and given command of the brigade over him. (Freeman, Douglas S., *Lee's Lieutenants*)

BROCKENBROUGH, John White (1806-1877)

A prominent federal judge before the Civil War, John W. Brockenbrough was sent by his native state of Virginia, along with other commissioners, to Washington to seek a peaceful separation of the country. This having failed and active military operations having begun, Brockenbrough was named, in June 1861, to the Provisional Confederate Congress where he was appropriately assigned to the Committee on the Judiciary. Representing a district in what was to become West Virginia, he supported the administration in its military efforts and in the search for means to finance them. However, most of his congressional time was spent in the organization of the new government and especially in getting the court system functioning. With institution of the permanent constitution, Brockenbrough left the legislature to accept appointment as Confederate States judge for the Western District of Virginia, the same jurisdiction he had held in the federal service and which was to become the new state of West Virginia in 1863. Here again he was an active supporter of the administration. After the war he ran the Lexington Law School, which soon became part of Washington College, of which he had been a trustee since 1852. He was instrumental in obtaining the school's presidency for Robert E. Lee, which eventually resulted in the institution becoming Washington and Lee University.

BROOKE, John Mercer (1826-1904)

The man who proposed the conversion of the scuttled USS *Merrimac* into an ironclad vessel, John M. Brooke, was also the Confederacy's chief gun designer. The Florida native had entered the U.S. Navy as an enlisted man in 1841 and, after four years' service, was appointed to the Naval Academy. Following his 1847 graduation from Annapolis he served on the coastal survey and at the naval observatory. He also plotted the route to China. Resigning his commission is April 1861, he joined the Confederacy; he was named a lieutenant in the navy and joined the staff, as an acting aide, of Robert E. Lee. It was he who suggested to the secretary of the navy, Stephen R. Mallory, a fellow Floridian, that the *Merrimac* be converted into the *Virginia*. Brooke's design of a submerged bow was used on this revolutionary craft. In recognition of his status as a scientist of the sea in 1863, he was named a commander for the duration of the war and in the latter stages of the war was chief of the Office of Ordnance and Hydrography. This may seem to have been a strange combination but Brooke had also been active in designing artillery pieces for the South. Many of his ideas appear to have come from Robert Parrott, and his best known work was a three-inch 10-pounder rifle.

BROOKE, John Rutter (1838-1926)

Although his first command marched away from the front on the day before 1st Bull Run, Pennsylvanian John R. Brooke returned at the head of another regiment a few months later, fought through the war, and, joining the regular army in 1866, made it his career. His assignments included: captain, 4th Pennsylvania (April 20, 1861); colonel, 53rd Pennsylvania (November 7, 1861); commanding 3rd Brigade, 1st Division, 2nd Corps, Army of the Potomac (July 20-August 10 and September 6-October 6, 1862); commanding 3rd Brigade, 2nd Division, 2nd Corps, Army of the Potomac (December 29, 1862-March 20, 1863); commanding 4th Brigade, 1st Division, 2nd Corps, Army of the Potomac (April 13-May 20, June 12-August 29, and September 20-December 29, 1863 and March 25-June 3, 1864); brigadier general, USV (May 12, 1864); and commanding 2nd Provisional Division, Army of the Shenandoah (April-August 1865). Mustered out with his company on July 26, 1861, he raised a regiment and led it through the Peninsula Campaign. At Antietam he commanded a brigade but was back with his regiment at Fredericksburg. The following spring he assumed command of the brigade with which he was most closely associated. This he led at Chancellorsville before being wounded in the Wheatfield fight, on the second day at Gettysburg, when sent to the relief of the 3rd Corps. During his recovery he commanded a camp for convalescents in Pennsylvania in the winter of 1863-64. Returning to field duty in time for the Overland Campaign, he fought at the Wilderness and Spotsylvania before falling wounded in the assault at Cold Harbor on June 3. This wound forced him from the field for ten months during part of which—from September 1864 to the spring of 1865—he was assigned to court-martial duty. With the war almost over he was given a divisional command in the Shenandoah Valley. In 1866 he joined the regular army as a lieutenant colonel and the next year was brevetted through brigadier for the Civil War—he had previously been mustered out of the volunteer service as a brevet major general on February 1, 1866. After serving in the Spanish-American War he was forced—at the age of 64—to retire with the rank of major general. Living for another two dozen years, he was the next to last Union general to die.

BROOKE, Walker (1813-1869)

Although he had briefly served in the U.S. Senate, Walker Brooke was unsuccessful in two attempts to gain a seat in the Confederate Senate. Born in Virginia, Brooke was admitted to the bar in that state before relocating to Mississippi where he eventually served in both houses of the state legislature. After completing Henry Foote's term in the Senate in 1852-53, he resumed his law practice. In the Mississippi secession convention he was basically a Unionist, but voted for secession in the end when he saw the futility of opposition. However, he urged that the secession ordinance be submitted to the people for a popular vote. This effort having failed, he was named to the Provisional Confederate Congress and assigned to the Committee on the Executive Departments and was chairman of the Committee on Patents. A firm supporter of a strong central government, he was an early Davis supporter. Following election defeats, he held several minor appointments including services in the military courts system. The war had broken him, and Brooke ran a failing law practice until his death.

BROOKS, John Hampden (?-?)

By the fall of 1864 the Confederacy was desperately looking for ways to fill its ever-thinning ranks. One source of manpower was the prisoner of war camps where many Union prisoners were willing to do almost anything to escape horrible conditions. John H. Brooks was assigned the task of organizing these men. His Confederate record included: captain, Company G, 7th South Carolina (April 16, 1861); captain, Company H, 7th South Carolina Battalion (July 14, 1862); and acting major, Brooks' Battalion Confederate Regular Infantry (November 16, 1864). After serving with his original regiment in Virginia, he resigned his commission in order to raise a company of partisan rangers. With this unit he served in the defense of Charleston until the spring of 1864 when the battalion was sent to Virginia to defend the Richmond-Petersburg area. That October he was ordered to proceed to Florence, South Carolina, to raise a battalion from those Union prisoners who were not U.S. citizens and were willing to take the oath of allegiance to join the Confederate army. His command of six companies, commanded by detailed officers, was mustered in on November 17. However, as soon as the unit took the field near Savannah mass desertions began. Then on the night of December 15 a mutiny led by the non-commissioned officers was crushed before it had fairly begun. The leaders were shot and, upon Brooks' recommendation, the battalion was broken up and the men returned to prison. Their commander returned to his former company.

BROOKS, Noah (1830-1903)

Capitalizing on a long-term friendship with Abraham Lincoln, Noah Brooks was able to provide his California readers with a vivid picture of the Civil War from Washington. Born in Castine, Maine—he would later use the town's name as a pen name—he became a painter and dabbled in journalism before settling in Illinois, where he met the future president at an 1856 political rally. After joining the Free-Soil faction in Kansas he spent an unsuccessful year as a farmer before returning to Illinois and journalism. He eventually went to California and became co-editor of the *Marysville Daily Appeal*. He sold out in 1862 and went on a Washington assignment for the *Sacramento Union*, arriving that December. Reacquainting himself with Lincoln, he became a regular and popular figure at the White House. He penned some 258 reports to his paper based upon knowledge gathered in conversations with the president and others. He frequently visited the front and at least once came under enemy fire. He was in line to become Lincoln's private secretary in June in 1865 but the assassination of his friend intervened. Meanwhile he had also served as a part-time clerk for the House of Representatives. Andrew Johnson appointed him to a government post in San Francisco but by 1867 Brooks was back in his true profession. He continued writing until he retired back to Maine. (Brooks, Noah, *Mr. Lincoln's Washington* and *Washington in Lincoln's Time*)

BROOKS, Preston Smith (1819-1857)

Although he died almost four years before his home state of South Carolina seceded, Congressman Preston Brooks was an effective illustration of the violent feeling between the sections during the late ante-bellum period. A veteran of the Mexican War, Brooks was considered, even by some Republican friends, to be tolerant of interests other than his own—until May 19, 1856, when Massachusetts Senator Charles Sumner, an abolitionist Republican, began the two-day deliverance of his "Crime Against Kansas" speech. Part of the speech was a denunciation of South Carolina and one of her senators, Andrew P. Butler, a relative of Brooks. Brooks was outraged. On the 22nd he entered the chamber following an adjournment and, without offering Sumner time to make amends, he proceeded to mercilessly beat the senator with a gutta percha cane. Sumner, temporarily blinded, fell under his desk but rose, and the beating continued until the cane shattered. Others broke up the melee. While Brooks was being restrained, Lawrence Keitt, another South Carolina hothead, raced in with his cane raised, but Georgian Robert Toombs calmed Keitt and prevented a full-scale riot on the floor of the Senate. Brooks received praise from the South, and an expulsion resolution by the House failed to obtain the two-thirds required. He resigned anyway and was promptly reelected and presented with a cane with the motto "Hit him again." He was, however, fined $300 on an assault charge. He died a few months later from complications of a cold. (Donald, David, *Charles Sumner and the Coming of the Civil War*)

BROOKS, William Thomas Harbaugh (1821-1870)

When Ohio native William H.T. Brooks resigned both his volunteer and regular commissions and settled in Alabama he was well respected by his ex-Confederate neighbors. An 1841 graduate of West Point, he had been posted to the infantry where he saw action in both the Seminole and Mexican wars—earning two brevets in the latter. His Civil War assignments included: captain, 3rd Infantry (since November 10, 1851); brigadier general, USV (September 28, 1861); commanding 1st Brigade, Smith's Division, Army of the Potomac (October 3, 1861-March 13, 1862); major, 18th Infantry (March 12, 1862); commanding 2nd Brigade, 2nd Division, 4th Corps, Army of the Potomac (March 13-May 18, 1862); commanding 2nd Brigade, 2nd Division, 6th Corps, Army of the Potomac (May 18-October 18, 1862); commanding 1st Division, 6th Corps, Army of the Potomac (October 18, 1862-May 23, 1863); major general, USV (June 10, 1863; revoked April 18, 1864); commanding Department of the Monongahela (June 11, 1863-April 6, 1864); commanding 1st Division, 18th Corps, Army of the James (April 28-June 18, 1864); and commanding 10th Corps, Army of the James (June 21-July 18, 1864). He led his brigade in the Yorktown operations and in the Seven Days where he was wounded at Savage Station. He subsequently fought at South Mountain and was wounded a second time at Antietam. He directed a division at Fredericksburg and Chancellorsville and was then promoted to major general and placed in command of the Department of the Monongahela—with headquarters at Pittsburgh—during Lee's invasion of Pennsylvania. His command stretched into parts of that state, West Virginia, and Ohio. He left this post for active operations the following April, taking part in the fighting at Drewry's Bluff, Bermuda Hundred, and Cold Harbor. During the course of the operations against Petersburg and Richmond—now in command of a corps—he was forced to resign by ill health both his regular and volunteer appointments. He soon settled in Alabama, near Huntsville, and began farming. Six years later he died a much respected citizen of the community and region he had fought so long.

BROUGH, John (1811-1865)

A War Democrat, John Brough ran on the Republican or Union ticket and defeated the unofficial leader of the Copperhead or peace movement, Clement Vallandigham, for governor of Ohio. A local politician for a quarter of a century, Brough was also involved in journalism, having founded the *Cincinnati Enquirer*, and in railroading. The Ohio Democratic Party was deeply split by the Civil War, and he went with the faction that supported the Lincoln administration's war measures. Brough, then the state auditor, was tapped by the Republican or Union Party in 1863 to be their candidate for the governorship. His opponent, the arch-Copperhead Clement Vallandigham, was running an absentee campaign from Canada where he had ended up after being sent into the rebel lines by the order of the president and had not been warmly welcomed in the Confederacy. Vallandigham spent most of his time campaigning against the national authorities rather than against his opponent. With the war turning in favor of the Union, Brough received a 20 to one margin from Ohio soldiers and won the election with an unprecedented 100,000-vote margin. In the final stages of the war he was a staunch supporter of the government. He died in office on August 29, 1865, after hostilities had ended.

BROUN, William LeRoy (1827-1902)

There was great concern, whenever the Army of Northern Virginia got too far away from Richmond, that the capital would fall to a quick Union thrust. Therefore, emergency military units were formed, from the various government employees in the city, to be called upon when needed. William L. Broun, a native Virginian, was given command of one of these units. He was an ordnance officer and superintendent of the Richmond Arsenal. His employees were organized into a local defense unit on June 24, 1863, and he was made its lieutenant colonel. They were designated as the 5th Virginia Battalion, Local Defense Troops. After a year of this double duty he found that the military work was interfering with his work at the arsenal and on May 15, 1864, he submitted his resignation from the battalion. This was not accepted until August 11. He continued in his original post for the remainder of the war and served on a number of boards of review. He was subsequently a professor at several colleges and universities and a writer.

BROWN, Albert Gallatin (1813-1880)

His extreme views in the Confederate Senate and his post-war cooperationism have relegated Albert G. Brown to a less than popular place in Southern history. Emigrating from South Carolina to Mississippi as a child, Brown was admitted to the bar and became a militia general before launching his varied and lengthy political career. His service included the state legislature, where he was acting speaker for a time, two different periods of service in the U.S. House of Representatives, and governor of Mississippi. By the outbreak of the secession crisis, he had been serving in the U.S. Senate since 1853. With the secession of his state, he resigned his seat on January 12, 1861. Raising a company of infantry, Brown was commissioned captain, 18th Mississippi, early in 1861 and saw action at the Confederate victories at First Manassas and Ball's Bluff. Appointed to the Confederate Senate in November 1861, he left the army to take his seat at the convening of the First Confederate Congress in February 1862. His appointment being to

Senator Albert G. Brown, Davis opponent. (*Harper's*)

a four-year term, he served through the remainder of the war with assignment to the Committees on Naval Affairs and on Territories. Throughout his tenure he was chairman of the former. His primary concern for the new nation was the achievement of victory; he conceded that constitutional niceties might have to be sacrificed but could be corrected once independence had been secured. But he felt that these unlimited war powers rested with the legislative branch of the government and this led to an eventual break with Davis. He favored an expanded draft, the arming and emancipation of slaves, privateering, and increasing food production for the army at the expense of cotton planting. Feeling that a cooperationist attitude with the Northern authorities during Reconstruction would be more beneficial to the South than antagonism, he advised his fellow Southerners to in effect "shake hands." Labeled a submissionist, he retired to the life of a farmer for his remaining years. (Ranek, James B., *Albert Gallatin Brown, Radical Southern Nationalist*)

BROWN, Benjamin Gratz (1826-1885)

Both politically and militarily, B. Gratz Brown was one of the most important people responsible for keeping Missouri in the Union. Born in Kentucky, he began to practice law in St. Louis in 1849. Three years later he entered the state legislature and in 1854 became the chief editor of the *Missouri Democrat*. In 1857 he ran for governor and lost but remained active in politics. In 1860-61 he fought the influence of the slave owners in the state and on or about May 8, 1861, became colonel, 4th Missouri, United States Reserve Corps. Active in dispersing Confederate bands and guerrillas, he was mustered out with his unit on August 18, 1861, at the end of their three-month tour of duty. He continued to keep the Washington authorities informed on affairs in Missouri and on November 13, 1863, was elected as a Democrat to the U.S. Senate, replacing Waldo P. Johnson, who had been expelled. He served until March 3, 1867. In 1864 he was instrumental in organizing militia forces to aid Rosecrans' defense against Sterling Price's invasion. In 1871 he won the governorship but the next year was defeated as Horace Greeley's vice-presidential candidate. He then resumed his legal practice. (Peterson, Norma Lois, *Freedom and Franchise: The Political Career of B. Gratz Brown*)

BROWN, Egbert Benson (1816-1902)

A former mayor of Toledo, Ohio, St. Louis railroad man Egbert B. Brown was instrumental in the movement to keep Missouri in the Union. The native of New York entered the army during the first year of the war and his assignments included: lieutenant colonel, 7th Missouri (August 21, 1861); brigadier general, Missouri Militia (May 10, 1862); commanding District of Southwest Missouri, Department of the Missouri (June 5-September 24, 1862 and November 10, 1862-March 30, 1863); brigadier general, USV (November 29, 1862); commanding District of Central Missouri, Department of the Missouri (June 9-July 24 and September 3-November 3, 1864); and commanding District of Rolla, Department of the Missouri (December 31, 1864-March 6, 1865). He resigned his first commission on May 1, 1862, in order to accept advancement in the militia. Holding a number of district assignments, he was chiefly engaged in fighting the irregulars running rampant through much of the state. In the defense of Springfield on January 8, 1863, he was severely wounded in the shoulder; he lost the use of the arm and carried to his grave a bullet in the hip. During Price's invasion of the state—by this time he had been transferred to the federal volunteers with the same rank—Brown commanded a cavalry force at Westport where he apparently disobeyed General Alfred Pleasonton's order to charge. He was placed under arrest but the matter was soon dropped. Resigning his commission November 10, 1865, he worked as a pension agent and took up farming.

BROWN, Harvey (1796-1874)

Having already won three brevets in two wars, New Jersey careerofficer Harvey Brown received the brevet of regular army brigadier general for his defense of Fort Pickens in Pensacola Harbor during the first year of the Civil War. The West Pointer (1818) spent three years in the light artillery, five in the artillery and nine in the quartermaster's department before rejoining the artillery branch in 1835. He received his first brevet for fighting Seminoles and two more for the Mexican War. His Civil War-era assignments included: major, 2nd Artillery (since January 9, 1851); commanding Department of Florida (April 13, 1861-February 22, 1862); lieutenant colonel, 4th Artillery (April 28, 1861); colonel, 5th Artillery (May 14, 1861); brigadier general, USV (September 28, 1861; declined); commanding Defenses of New York Harbor, Department of the East (April 5, 1862-July 16, 1863); and commanding Fort Schuyler, Department of the East (July 16, 1863-June 29, 1864). While he sent part of his force to reinforce the beleaguered Fort Pickens, he directed the fight at Santa Rosa Island. He declined a brigadier generalship in the volunteer service, and was brevetted to that grade in the regular establishment on November 23, 1861. Assigned to New York Harbor, he won a brevet as major general for his role in suppressing the draft riots in July 1863. Although officially retired on August 1, 1863, he retained command of Fort Schuyler until the following summer.

BROWN, Isaac N. (?-?)

A veteran of 27 years in the U.S. Navy, Kentucky-born Isaac Brown, a Mexican War veteran, returned from a cruise to find his country divided. He quickly switched his allegiance to the South. Having given up a lieutenant's commission in the old navy, he was, on June 6, 1861, appointed lieutenant, CSN, and assigned to the army's Department of the West with instructions to assist in the construction of batteries for the defense of the Mississippi River. He later worked on a similar project along the Cumberland. The advance of Union forces put an end to this work as it did to his next assignment—supervising the construction of four ironclads at New Orleans. On May 26, 1862, he was given command of the ironclad *Arkansas*, which was then nearing completion. He sailed his new vessel down the Mississippi through the entire Union fleet and safely anchored under the guns of Vicksburg. The entire naval outlook on the river had changed. Brown was absent sick the next month when the vessel moved down to Baton Rouge to aid in a land attack on the Union force there. He never saw his vessel again. It was blown up by its own crew when its cranky engines broke down. Brown gathered the remnants of his crew and performed shore duty at Port Hudson and later along the Yazoo River, where he helped blow up the Union vessels *DeKalb* and *Cairo* by torpedoes. He took part in the defense of Fort Pemberton. Already promoted to commander on August 25, 1862, Brown was, following Vicksburg's fall, ordered to command the ironclad *Charleston* in Charleston Harbor. Here he remained until the fall of the city. The war ended before he could assume his next command, that of naval defenses west of the Mississippi. (Scharf, J. Thomas, *History of the Confederate States Navy*)

BROWN, John (1800-1859)

Martyr for freedom, inciter of slave insurrections, murderer—all were titles given to John Brown, one of the most controversial characters to come out of the sectional conflict of the 1850s. Born in Connecticut, he had engaged in numerous businesses in various locations, usually unsuccessfully. While residing in Richmond, Ohio, he was a part of the Underground Railroad. The dispute over Kansas attracted his attention and he moved there and helped establish a free state settlement at Osawatomie. Following the pro-slavery faction's sacking of Lawrence, Brown and six others—including four of his sons—raided along the Pottawatamie Creek in pro-slavery areas. In cold blood they murdered five men. Continuing his operations, he became the idol of some Eastern abolitionists, who then backed his plans to invade slave states and free the slaves. After arming them, he planned to set up a free state for blacks in the mountains of Virginia and Maryland. With a force of 21 men he took over the armory at Harpers Ferry, seizing hostages and killing six people. The next day Robert E. Lee and Jeb Stuart arrived with a detachment of marines. When the firehouse was stormed, ten of Brown's men and one marine were killed. Brown himself lost two sons and was taken prisoner after being knocked senseless. The October 1859 raid was finally over but its repercussions would further the movement toward secession and civil war. Following a trial in Charlestown, Virginia, Brown was hanged on December 2, 1859. To many in the North he became a martyr, even if many prominent abolitionists who had backed him secretly denied their involvement. (Oates, Stephen B., *To Purge This Land With Blood: A Biography of John Brown*)

Fanatical abolitionist John Brown. (NA)

BROWN, John Calvin (1827-1889)

Tennessee lawyer and minor politician John C. Brown rose to be one of the fighting division commanders of the Confederate Army of Tennessee. His assignments included: colonel, 3rd Tennessee (May 16, 1861); commanding 3rd Brigade, 2nd (Buckner's) Division, Central Army of Kentucky, Department #2 (October 28, 1861-February 11, 1862); commanding 3rd

Brigade, Buckner's Division, Fort Donelson, Central Army of Kentucky, Department #2 (February 11-16, 1862); brigadier general, CSA (August 30, 1862); commanding brigade, 2nd (Anderson's Division, Left Wing, Army of the Mississippi (September-October 8, 1862); commanding Breckinridge's Division, Hardee's Corps, Army of Tennessee (December 1862, January 16-22, 1863, and February 2-June 6, 1863); commanding brigade, Stewart's Division, Hill's-Breckinridge's Corps, Army of Tennessee (June 6-August and October 1-November 12, 1863); commanding the division (August 1863); commanding brigade, Stewart's Division, Buckner's Corps, Army of Tennessee (September 1863); commanding brigade, Stevenson's Division, Hardee's Corps, Army of Tennessee (November 12-23, 1863 and November 24, 1863-February 20, 1864); commanding the division (November 23-24, 1863); commanding brigade, Stevenson's Division, Hood's-Lee's Corps, Army of Tennessee (February 20-July 1864); commanding Hindman's Division, Hood's Corps, Army of Tennessee (early July 1864); commanding Stewart's Division, Hood's Corps, Army of Tennessee (July 1864); commanding Bate's Division, Hardee's-Cheatham's Corps, Army of Tennessee (August-November 30, 1864); major general, CSA (August 4, 1864); commanding division, Cheatham's Corps, Army of Tennessee (April 2-9, 1865); and commanding division, Hardee's Corps, Army of Tennessee (April 9-26, 1865). After commanding a brigade in central Kentucky he was sent with it to reinforce the garrison of Fort Donelson where he was captured. Exchanged on August 27, 1862, he was named a brigadier general and commanded a brigade at Perryville where he was wounded. Returning to duty, he commanded a brigade during the Tullahoma Campaign and was again wounded at Chickamauga. At Chattanooga he briefly commanded the division. During the Atlanta Campaign he led his brigade and then a succession of divisions whose leaders were temporarily or permanently absent. Finally taking charge of Bate's division, he served through the rest of the siege and then accompanied Hood into middle Tennessee. There he was wounded at Franklin and did not return to his division until the very final weeks of the war in North Carolina, where he surrendered with Joseph E. Johnston. After the war he resumed his political and legal careers. He served two terms as governor and then went into railroading.

BROWN, John Thompson (1835-1864)

It was generally recognized that J. Thompson Brown's undistinguished showing as the new chief of artillery for the 2nd Corps at Gettysburg was really the fault of the corps commander, Richard S. Ewell. Nonetheless, he was superseded in his position two months later. Joining the artillery service four days after the secession of his native Virginia, lawyer Brown held the following appointments: lieutenant, Richmond Howitzers (April 21, 1861); captain, 2nd Company, Richmond Howitzers (May 1861); major, 1st Virginia Artillery (September 1861); lieutenant colonel, 1st Virginia Artillery (spring 1862); colonel, 1st Virginia Artillery (June 2, 1862); commanding battalion, Reserve Artillery, Army of Northern Virginia (early 1862-mid December 1862); commanding battalion, Artillery Reserve, 2nd Corps, Army of Northern Virginia (mid December 1862-May 2, 1863); chief of artillery, 2nd Corps, Army of Northern Virginia (May 2-September 23, 1863); commanding artillery battalion, 2nd Corps, Army of Northern Virginia (September 23, 1863-spring 1864); and commanding artillery division, 2nd Corps, Army of Northern Virginia (spring-May 6, 1864). After service at the battle of Big Bethel, he commanded a battalion in the Peninsula Campaign and at Antietam, Fredericksburg, and Chancellorsville. At the latter he took over direction of the corps' artillery upon the wounding of Colonel Crutchfield. Instead of being kept in permanent charge, he was replaced by General Long who had been promoted from a position on Lee's staff. As a consolation he was later given charge of three battalions in the Overland Campaign. At the Wilderness he was killed by a sharpshooter while placing his guns. (Wise, Jennings C., *The Long Arm of Lee*)

BROWN, Joseph Emerson (1821-1894)

A country born from the states' rights movement, the Confederacy nevertheless had to fashion a centralized government to fight the war. One who refused to accept this was Georgia's governor, Joseph Brown. Born in South Carolina, Brown was raised in northern Georgia and attended Yale Law School. Admitted to the bar, he practiced until 1849 when he took a seat in the state legislature for one term. He served two years as a judge before being named as the surprise Democratic nominee for governor in 1857. Elected, he served for four two-year terms. Although pro-Union, he was known as an extreme states' rights man. On January 3, 1861, before the secession of the state, Georgia Militia, under Brown's direction, seized Fort Pulaski. Early in the conflict he was instrumental in raising troops in reply to calls by the Confederate administration. However, Davis' policy of appointing some field officers and later drafting men directly for the army, ignoring the state authorities, represented a violation of states' rights in Brown's eyes. In response to the Conscription Act he declared thousands of men to be necessary to his state's operations thus exempting them from the draft calls. He jealously guarded the Georgia Militia, withdrawing them from Confederate service whenever Georgia's borders were not threatened. He questioned taxation policies on literal readings of the Constitution. Throughout the war Davis and Brown exchanged long, angry letters arguing these points. Davis considered Brown to have been a major obstacle in the prosecution of the war. At the war's close he was arrested but shortly afterwards released. In June 1865 he resigned his office and turned to the Republicans, as the best way for the South to survive Reconstruction. Brown was despised by much of Georgia. In 1880, after returning to the Democrats, Brown was named to the U.S. Senate when former General John B. Gordon resigned. He was appointed by Governor Alfred Colquitt. The three men dominated Georgia politics for the next decade. Resigning in 1891, Brown died three years later. (Hill, Louise Biles, *Joseph E. Brown and the Confederacy*)

BROWN, Ridgely (1833-1864)

A farmer in his native Montgomery County, Maryland, Ridgely Brown had Southern sympathies, joined the Confederate army, and became a noted cavalryman before losing his life. Initially enlisting in a Virginia regiment, he later transferred to the Maryland Line. His assignments included: lieutenant, Company K, 1st Virginia Cavalry (1861); captain, Company A, Cavalry, Maryland Line (early 1862); major, 1st Maryland Cavalry Battalion (November 12, 1862); and lieutenant colonel, 1st Maryland Cavalry Battalion (August 20, 1863). Serving under Jeb Stuart, and later "Grumble" Jones, he was at 1st Bull Run. Transferred to the Maryland Line, he fought in the Shenandoah Valley Campaign and during the Seven Days on the Peninsula. He was wounded at Greenland Gap on April 25, 1863, but was able to serve in the advance of Richard S. Ewell's corps during the Gettysburg Campaign. When not with the main army he frequently participated in raids in West Virginia and western Maryland. While serving along the South Anna River he was shot in the head and killed on June 1, 1864.

BROWNE, Charles Farrar (1834-1867)

A professional humorist for the Cleveland *Plain Dealer*, Charles Browne took his pen-name, Artemus Ward, from the name of Revolutionary War General Artemas Ward, and became so popular during the Civil War that President Lincoln even recited his writings to cabinet meetings. Browne, an intimate friend of Samuel Clemens, styled his essays in the form of open letters signed "A. Ward, the showman." In his "Interview with President Lincoln," Ward condemned the horde of office-seekers who were descending upon the president-elect, declaring that he "hav no politics. Nary a one. I'm not in the bizniss." His advice on the division of the Union was that "if any State wants to secede, let 'em Sesesh!" When Abe asked about selecting the cabinet, A. Ward recommended, "Fill it up with Showmen, sir! Showmen is devoid of politics. They hain't gat any principles!" His career came to an end in England, where he was lecturing, when he died of tuberculosis at the age of 33. (Dudden, Arthur F., ed. *The Assault of Laughter* and Pullen, John J., *Comic Relief: The Life and Laughter of Artemus Ward, 1834-1867*)

BROWNE, Junius Henri (1833-1902)

Because of the animosity in the Southern states against the *New York Tribune*, reporter Junius H. Browne spent a year and a half in Confederate prisons. He had worked for several newspapers in Ohio before the war and then joined his lifelong friend Albert D. Richardson on Horace Greeley's paper. He covered Fremont's less-than-spectacular campaign in Missouri and then took part in the fighting at Fort Donelson while covering the battle. On the night of May 3, 1863—along with Richardson—he was captured in an attempt to run past the Vicksburg batteries on the steam tug *Sturgis*. The guns opened fire and scored a direct hit, sinking the vessel. They were soon captives but expected to be exchanged promptly. Instead they were shunted from one place of incarceration to another; after Grant's assumption of command there was even less chance of a release. Several attempts at escape failed. While the Confederacy exchanged other journalists—including one from the *New York World* who had been on the tug with Richardson and Browne—they were adamant in this case. The two escaped from Salisbury Prison in North Carolina on November 18, 1864, and began a cross-country trek to Knoxville, where Browne arrived on foot on January 14, 1865. Richardson had arrived there on horseback two days earlier. After the war Browne was a successful writer until his death.

BROWNE, William Montague (1823-1883)

In the waning days of the Confederacy, William M. Browne suffered the humiliation of having his appointment as a brigadier general rejected by an 18 to 2 vote in the Senate due to the animosity against Jefferson Davis, with whom he was so closely associated. The Dublin native had served in the Crimean War with the English army before settling in Washington where he was an editor with two political journals. Going over to the Confederacy, he obtained a staff position with the Confederate president and his assignments included: colonel, Cavalry (1861); and brigadier general, CSA (November 11, 1864). His request for field service turned down, he served most of the war in Richmond. When Robert M.T. Hunter left the post of secretary of state on February 17, 1862, Browne was appointed ad interim. This lasted until Judah P. Benjamin took over the portfolio on March 18, 1862. Browne then resumed his duties in the War Department's section dealing with organization until the fall of 1864. He was dispatched to Georgia to directly observe and report to Davis on Sherman's advance to the coast. At one point he commanded a brigade of local troops. Continuing in his reporting role during the Carolinas Campaign, he was included in Joseph E. Johnston's surrender. In the meantime he had been appointed and then rejected as a general officer. After the war he was a planter and educator. (Coulter, E. Merton, *William Montague Browne: Versatile Anglo-Irish American, 1823-1883*)

BROWNELL, Francis Edwin (?-1894)

Although the Congressional Medal of Honor was twice refused him and it was not finally awarded until 1877, Francis Brownell was the first soldier to earn it. His military service included: private, Company A, 11th New York (April 20-July 4, 1861); second lieutenant, 11th U.S. Infantry (to date from May 14, 1861); and first lieutenant, 11th U.S. Infantry (October 24, 1861). Enlisting shortly after Fort Sumter was fired upon, Brownell arrived with his unit in Washington in early May. On May 24 the regiment, known as the "Ellsworth Fire Zouaves," being composed mostly of New York City firemen, was ordered to sail down the Potomac and take Alexandria, Virginia. The small rebel force there fled with little opposition and the town was in Union hands. Colonel Ellsworth noticed a secessionist flag above the Marshall House and, with Private Brownell, proceeded to tear it down. While descending in the stairwell, they were accosted by the proprietor, James T. Jackson, with a shotgun. Although Brownell tried to deflect the piece, Jackson fired at point-blank range into the colonel's breast, killing him instantly. Brownell promptly shot the assailant in the forehead and then ran him through with a bayonet. The death of Ellsworth shook the country into a realization that men die in war. Shortly after this event Brownell was commissioned directly into the regular army and assigned to a newly organized regiment. He then served, apparently in staff positions, until he retired on November 4, 1863. Finally, 16 years after the event, and after his congressman had intervened in his behalf, Brownell received the medal for that day in Alexandria.

BROWNELL, Kady (1842-?)

The wife of an enlisted man, Kady Brownell accompanied her husband into the field and participated in a number of engagements. Born in Africa to a British soldier, she was not content with the life of a housewife. Accompanying her American husband, she attached herself to his regiment, the 1st Rhode Island, under Ambrose E. Burnside. She allegedly carried the colors at 1st Bull Run and also carried a rifle. But her normal routine entailed camp chores. When her husband was mustered out with the regiment on August 2, 1861, she returned to Rhode Island. However, later that year her husband reentered the service as a member of the 1st Battalion, 5th Rhode Island, which took part in the operations along the North Carolina coast under Burnside. Her husband was wounded in the battle of New Bern and she supervised his recuperation until he was discharged in the fall of 1863. Praised by Burnside, she disappeared from the pages of history.

BROWNING, Orville Hickman (1806-1881)

At a convention called to protest the Kansas-Nebraska Act, Orville H. Browning laid the groundwork for the national Republican Party. Born in Kentucky, he began practicing law in 1831, fought in the Black Hawk War of 1832, and sat in the state senate from 1836 to 1843. In the 1850s he was active in the organization of the new party and in 1860 helped gain the presidential nomination for Lincoln. Named to replace the deceased Stephen A. Douglas in the U.S. Senate, he took his seat on June 26, 1861. He was a staunch supporter of his president and was succeeded by William A. Richardson who had been elected to the unexpired term of the "Little Giant." He served as Andrew Johnson's interior secretary and for a time acted as attorney general. He remained loyal to Johnson throughout the impeachment proceedings and left office with him in 1869. Browning then resumed his legal pursuits. (Baxter, Maurice Glen, *Orville H. Browning, Lincoln's Friend and Critic*)

BROWNLOW, William Gannaway (1805-1877)

East Tennessee was a continuous thorn in the side of the Confederacy—its mountain people had little sympathy for the slave-holding class. One of the chief sources of this trouble was Parson William Brownlow. Converted to the Methodist faith, he served as a minister for a decade before, in 1839, founding the *Elizabethton Whig*, which eventually moved via Jonesboro to Knoxville. He kept all these communities in a virtually permanent state of political and religious uproar with his pro-Union, but pro-slavery, rhetoric. His extremist arguments, in support of the now defunct Whig Party, made him a victim of physical violence on at least one occasion. His anti-Confederate tirades were tolerated during the first few months of the war, but reports linking him to railroad bridge-burning, and a final vicious attack in *Brownlow's Knoxville Whig*, proved too much for the rebels. He was imprisoned on December 6, 1861, and on March 15, 1862, he was physically expelled from the Confederacy. He promptly published *Sketches of the Rise, Progress, and Decline of Secession; with a Narrative of Personal Adventures among the Rebels*, which sold 100,000 copies in three months. Greeted with open arms by the North, he accompanied the Union army upon its return to East Tennessee and reestablished the *Knoxville Whig and Rebel Ventilator*. Favoring harsh treatment of rebels, he succeeded Andrew Johnson as governor in 1865 and held that post until appointed to the Senate. Retiring in 1875 he resumed his vitriolic journalism until his death. (Coulter, Ellis Merton, *William G. Brownlow, Fighting Parson of the Southern Highlands*)

BRUCE, Eli Metcalfe (1828-1866)

One of the few Confederate congressmen who did not come from a legal or planting background, businessman Eli M. Bruce closed his Northern-based chain of meat packing houses and reopened them in the South at the outbreak of the Civil War. Becoming a major supplier to the Confederate armies, Bruce also became known for his charity towards Kentucky troops and in early 1862 he was elected to represent Kentucky's 9th District in the First Congress. With his district soon overrun by enemy forces, Bruce favored carrying the war into the North and the use of privateers to raid Union commerce. During this congress he served on the Committee on Military Affairs. A great believer in Jefferson Davis' military abilities, Bruce urged him to take personal command of the field armies. Reelected to the Second Congress by the exile vote, Bruce was, in recognition of his business knowledge, assigned to the Committee on Ways and Means. His ethics were questioned in his withdrawal from the Erlanger Loan but he was later cleared. Moving to New York at the war's close, Bruce ran the Southern Hotel where ex-Confederates were always welcome with or without money.

BRUCE, Horatio Washington (1830-1903)

One of the Davis administration's most consistent supporters in Congress was the representative from Kentucky's 7th District, Horatio W. Bruce. The Kentucky-born Bruce, without college training, was admitted to the bar at 21 and served one term in the state legislature. In November 1861 he served in the convention that claimed to have taken the state out of the Union. With the state "admitted" to the Confederacy, Bruce was rewarded for his secessionist vote in the convention by being elected to the First Confederate Congress in January 1862. With his district soon occupied by Union troops, Bruce adopted a policy of supporting all measures, military and economic, necessary to win the war. He supported conscription and wanted the War Department to do with its forces as it pleased. He rarely criticized government leaders, military or civilian, and felt peace overtures to be fruitless. On the flight from Richmond, Bruce accompanied Davis as far as Augusta. After the war he practiced law in Louisville, served as a judge and taught law.

BRYAN, Goode (1811-1865)

West Pointer (1834) Goode Bryan served less than a year before resigning from the regular army but continued to be active in militia affairs in Alabama and then back in his native Georgia. During the Mexican War he was major, 1st Alabama. The remainder of his time before the Civil War was spent in engineering, on his plantations, or in politics. A member of the Georgia secession convention, he entered the Confederate army where his assignments included: captain, 16th Georgia (early 1861); lieutenant colonel, 16th Georgia (July 1861); colonel, 16th Georgia (February 15, 1862); commanding Semmes' (old) Brigade, McLaws'-Kershaw's Division, 1st Corps, Army of Northern Virginia (July 2-September 9, 1863 and April 12-June 2, 1864); brigadier general, CSA (August 29, 1863); commanding same brigade, McLaws' Division, Longstreet's Corps, Army of Tennessee (September 19-November 5, 1863); and commanding brigade, McLaws'-Kershaw's Division, Department of East Tennessee (November 5, 1863-April 12, 1864). Serving in Cobb's-Wofford's Brigade, he fought at Yorktown, the Seven Days, Fredericksburg, and Gettysburg, where he was assigned to command the brigade of the mortally wounded General Semmes. Promoted to brigadier shortly afterwards, his brigade did not arrive in time to take part in the Chickamauga fighting, when Longstreet went west. He did fight during the Knoxville Campaign and back in Virginia at the Wilderness, Spotsylvania, and Cold Harbor. On June 2, 1864, during the latter engagement, he relinquished command to Colonel James P. Simms and resigned, citing ill health, on September 20. He then retired to his Georgia home. (Freeman, Douglas S., *Lee's Lieutenants*)

BRYANT, Julian (1836-1865)

Unlike many officers who accepted commissions in the black regiments, Julian Bryant was not interested in advancing himself. An Illinois native, from a family heavily involved in the Underground Railroad, he was firmly opposed to slavery. He was interested in art and was a professor at the outbreak of the Civil War. His assignments included: second lieutenant, Company E, 33rd Illinois (ca. September 3, 1861); major, 1st Mississippi African Descent (ca. May 16, 1863); lieutenant colonel, 51st United States Colored Troops (designation change March 11, 1864); and colonel, 46th United States Colored Troops (September 1864). Early in the war his party surprised a Confederate recruiting rendezvous; the prisoners were then escorted by freed slaves armed by the Union troops. Bryant went on to fight at Bayou Cache and served on the staff of General Charles Hovey at Chickasaw Bayou and Arkansas Post. In the spring of 1863 he became an officer with the black troops and eventually rose to a colonelcy. His troops fought well in the hand-to-hand combat at Milliken's Bend shortly after they were mustered in, but later, like most black units, they were relegated to construction and supply work. Bryant was outraged and used his uncle William Cullen Bryant's newspaper, the *New York Evening Post*, to vent his frustration at the unequal treatment of black and white soldiers. His campaign had some effect. Near the war's close Bryant was assigned to Texas, but on May 14, 1865, he drowned in a swimming accident in the Gulf of Mexico.

BUCHANAN, Franklin (1800-1874)

Although the Confederacy's senior admiral constantly desired action, Maryland-born Franklin Buchanan had only two days of combat during the war—and was wounded both times. Entering the U.S. Navy in 1815 as a 14-year-old midshipman, Buchanan saw service in the Mediterranean, against pirates in the Caribbean, was co-founder and first superintendent of the Naval Academy at Annapolis, in the Mexican War, on Perry's expedition to Japan and as commander of the Washington Navy Yard. With the firing on the 6th Massachusetts in Baltimore, Buchanan assumed that Maryland would secede and join the Confederacy. Therefore, on April 22, 1861, he resigned his command and his commission as captain. But when the state did not secede, he tried to cancel his resignation. This being refused, he maintained a four-month-long neutrality before finally offering his services to the Confederacy. On September 5 he was appointed captain, CSN, and chief of the Bureau of Orders and Details, where he was faced with a lack of commands, for a surplus of officers, and a lack of trained crews. Highly effective in this administrative post, he was nonetheless desirous of an active command. His wish was fulfilled when, on February 24, 1862, he was given charge of the Chesapeake Bay Squadron, with the just completed ironclad *Virginia* (or *Merrimack*) as his flagship. On March 8, 1862, he sailed his new command out of Norfolk, to attack the Union blockading fleet in Hampton Roads. His first target was the USS *Cumberland*, which he rammed and sank, losing in the process his ship's ram. Next turning his attention to the USS *Congress*, another wooden vessel, he gave her a series of broadsides that set her afire. The Union commander struck his flag, but when one of the *Virginia*'s escorts went to her relief, she was fired upon from shore by Union infantry. Enraged, Buchanan ordered the *Congress* destroyed and taking a rifle in hand himself opened fire on the stricken craft from an exposed position. He was struck in the thigh, taken below, and forced to relinquish command. He thus missed the next day's fight with the USS *Monitor*. Ironically, one of the Union officers aboard the *Congress* was his brother McKean Buchanan. Following a slow recovery from his wound and brief service on a court-martial, he was promoted to admiral, CSN, on August 21, 1862; in September he took over command of the Mobile defenses. After almost two years of work perfecting the defensive arrangements, he finally saw action again when Union Admiral Farragut entered the bay with his massive fleet. Aboard his flagship, the newly completed ironclad CSS *Tennessee*. Buchanan engaged the Union armada, repeatedly trying to ram Farragut's flagship, USS *Hartford*. With the rest of his fleet already gone and his flagship surrounded by the enemy, he suffered a broken leg from an iron splinter. Shortly after he turned over command, the *Tennessee* surrendered. Exchanged in March 1865, he was again captured in Mobile just after his resumption of command. After the war which served as a college president and in the insurance business until his retirement. (Lewis, Charles L., *Admiral Franklin Buchanan: Fearless Man of Action*)

BUCHANAN, James (1791-1868)

As president during the final stages of the sectional crisis, James Buchanan served an unhappy four years in the White House, with many of his fellow Northerners actually believing he was in league with the South. The Pennsylvania-born Buchanan graduated from Dickinson College, having once been dismissed, and was subsequently admitted to the bar in 1812. During the war with Britain he served briefly as a volunteer. As a Federalist, he served as a state assemblyman for two terms and in 1820 was elected to Congress. With the dissolution of his party he became a Democrat and continued in Congress until 1831. He next served as minister to Russia before returning to the United States, where he lost a race for the Senate. However, he was more successful the next year, 1834, and remained in the Senate until named as Polk's secretary of state in 1845. During this time he resolved the Oregon boundary dispute and avoided war with Britain. At the end of the Polk Administration, failing to get the party's nomination for president, he retired from public life but did work for the nomination in 1852. Missing out again, he was named minister to Britain in 1853 by President Pierce. By the time he returned in 1856, he had become acceptable to the Southern wing of the party by his involvement in the Ostend Manifesto, claiming an American right to wrest Cuba from Spain. After the election his administration tried to appease the South by such actions as supporting the pro-slavery Lecompton Constitution for Kansas. He presided over the division of his Democratic Party as the Republicans made gains in Congress. His cabinet was wracked by the Floyd scandals, and with the election of Lincoln and the secession of the Southern states it suffered numerous defections. As a lame duck, Buchanan determined not to do anything that would start the war, his job being to turn the government over to Lincoln and let him deal with the problem. He thus left Major Anderson, commanding in Charleston Harbor, in an unenviable position, without orders or even information on negotiations with the South Carolina and Confederate authorities. Buchanan refused, after one attempt, to reinforce or resupply Fort Sumter for fear of opening hostilities. With great relief, he turned over the whole situation to Lincoln and returned to Pennsylvania. He sided with the Union, and the war that followed was a great drain on his strength. He died three years after the war's close. (Klein, Philip Schriver, *President James Buchanan*)

BUCHANAN, Robert Christie (1811-1878)

Robert C. Buchanan was Grant's post commander, when the future commander-in-chief resigned in 1854, but only a colonel 10 years later, when Grant had become a lieutenant general. It must have been a bitter pill to swallow. Born in Maryland, the West Pointer (1830) was posted to the infantry upon graduation and saw service in the Black Hawk, Seminole, and Mexican wars. In the latter he earned two brevets. As a brevet lieutenant colonel, he was in command of Fort Humboldt in 1854 when Grant was stationed there. The latter despised his commander as a martinet, and it was at this time that he was allegedly drinking heavily. It may have been the threat of disciplinary action by Buchanan that prompted Grant to give up his captaincy. The older man remained in the army, and his Civil War-era assignments included: major, 4th Infantry (since February 3, 1855); lieutenant colonel, 4th Infantry (September 9, 1861); commanding 1st Brigade, 2nd Division, 5th Corps, Army of the Potomac (May 18, 1862-January 27, 1863); brigadier general, USV (November 29, 1862); and colonel, 1st Infantry (February 8, 1864). After service in the Washington defenses he commanded a brigade of regular troops on the Peninsula. During the Seven Days he earned brevets for Gaines' Mill and Malvern Hill. He also led his brigade at 2nd Bull Run, Antietam, and Fredericksburg, receiving the brevet of major general of regulars for the first and last. Just prior to the last battle he was promoted to brigadier of volunteers, but the Senate never acted upon the nomination and it expired on March 4, 1863. He then left the field to command Fort Delaware and serve on a number of boards. Promoted to a colonelcy, he worked with the Freedman's Bureau and commanded in Louisiana during Reconstruction. He retired in 1870.

BUCKALEW, Charles Rollin (1821-1899)

Early in the 38th Congress Senator Charles R. Buckalew took his seat on the Joint Committee on the Conduct of the War, replacing Benjamin F. Harding who had retired. Buckalew was a native Pennsylvanian who had been a prosecuting attorney before entering the state senate in 1850. In the 1850s he was a diplomat in Paraguay and Ecuador. Two years after his return he was elected to the U.S. Senate as a Democrat and served from March 4, 1863, to 1869, when he returned to the state senate. As a Democrat on the Radical Republican-controlled committee, he was not very active in its affairs. In 1872 he was defeated in a bid for the gubernatorial chair but again sat in Congress—the House of Representatives this time—from 1887 to 1891. He then resumed his private practice.

BUCKINGHAM, Catharinus Putnam (1808-1888)

The greatest service of Catharinus P. Buckingham in the Civil War was his delivery of the order that removed George B. McClellan from command of the Army of the Potomac. The West Pointer (1829) had returned to his native Ohio after only two years posted to the artillery—but actually detailed to topographical duty and later as an instructor at his alma mater—to become a professor at Kenyon College. In 1849 he became the owner of the Kokosing Iron Works in Knox County. It was from this position that he returned to the military in 1861. His assignments included: assistant adjutant general of Ohio (May 3-8, 1861); commissary general, Ohio (May 8-July 1, 1861); adjutant general, Ohio (July 1, 1861-April 2, 1862); and brigadier general, USV (July 16, 1862). After his service with the state volunteers he was assigned to special duty in the War Department. He only held this position for a brief time, resigning on February 11, 1863. But on November 7, 1862, a snowy night, he was sent from the capital to the headquarters of the Army of the Potomac with the orders assigning Ambrose E. Burnside to command in place of McClellan. Subsequently, he was in the grain elevator business in New York—unsuccessfully—and in Chicago. He also headed the Chicago Steel Works and wrote on mathematics.

BUCKINGHAM, William Alfred (1804-1875)

A Whig turned Republican, William A. Buckingham was the only Union governor to serve throughout the war, from South Carolina's secession to Appomattox. Before entering politics he had been engaged in surveying, education, dry-goods sales, carpet manufacturing, and rubber. In his adopted hometown of Norwich, Connecticut, he served as a council member and town treasurer before serving four terms as mayor. In 1858 he was elected to the first of his eight one-year terms as Connecticut's governor, taking up his duties later that same year. After urging the state to prepare for the coming war, he found that he had to borrow money in his own name in order to raise the troops called for by Lincoln in April 1861. With the aid of the legislature the state's quota was more than fulfilled. During the summer of 1863 he was successful in preventing the kind of draft rioting that rocked many other cities. Also in his term the 13th Amendment was passed. Refusing to accept renomination in 1866, he died while serving as the state's senator. (Buckingham, Samuel G., *The Life of William A. Buckingham, the War Governor of Connecticut*, and Niven, John, *Connecticut for the Union: The Role of the State in the Civil War*)

BUCKLAND, Ralph Pomeroy (1812-1892)

After over a year of active campaigning, Union General Ralph P. Buckland was relegated to the thankless job of duty in the District of Memphis protecting railroads and fending off Forrest's cavalry. Born in Massachusetts, he had been admitted to the bar in Ohio and served in the state legislature. Originally a Whig, he had been converted to Republicanism by the debate over slavery and eventually joined the Union army. His assignments included: colonel, 72nd Ohio (January 10, 1862); commanding 4th Brigade, 5th Division, Army of the Tennessee (March 1-May 15, 1862); commanding 5th Brigade, District of Memphis, 13th Corps, Army of the Tennessee (October 26-November 12, 1862); commanding 3rd Brigade, 1st Division, District of Memphis, Right Wing, 13th Corps, Army of the Tennessee (November 12-December 18, 1862); brigadier general, USV (November 29, 1862); commanding 3rd Brigade, 8th Division, 16th Corps, Army of the Tennessee (December 18, 1862-February 12, 1863); commanding 1st Brigade, 3rd Division, 15th Corps, Army of the Tennessee (April 3-June 22, September 10-October 15, and November 15-December 20, 1863); commanding the division (August 9-September 11, 1863); commanding 1st Brigade, 1st Division, 16th Corps, Army of the Tennessee (December 20, 1863-January 26, 1864); and commanding District of Memphis, District of West Tennessee, Army of the Tennessee (June 1864-January 6, 1865). Commanding one of Sherman's brigades during the initial onslaught at Shiloh, he earned the praise of his division commander for his steadfastness. He served in the advance on Corinth and in the operations against Vicksburg until June 22, 1863 when he went on leave. He subsequently served in western Tennessee and northern Mississippi, much of the time trying to catch Forrest. In the fall of 1864 he was elected to a seat in the U.S. Congress and on January 6 resigned his commission so that he could be sworn in on March 4, 1865. After serving two terms he returned to his law practice but reentered politics to support his former law partner Rutherford B. Hayes for the presidency. He was also in railroading and president of a soldiers' orphans home.

BUCKNER, Simon Bolivar (1823-1914)

The organizer of the Kentucky State Guard, which largely joined the Confederacy, Simon B. Buckner rose to the rank of lieutenant general during the war. The Kentucky West Pointer (1844) served with the infantry in Mexico, winning two brevets and suffering a wound at Churubusco. He then returned to his teaching post at his alma mater. Feeling that the mandatory presence at Sunday chapel was a violation of his rights, he quit that post and returned to infantry service in 1849. In 1852 he transferred to the commissary branch but resigned three years later to engage in the real estate business. In the remaining years before the Civil War he was adjutant general of the Illinois militia and directed the reorganization of his native state's armed forces. His Civil War assignments included: major general and inspector general, Kentucky State Guard (spring 1860); brigadier general, CSA (September 14, 1861); commanding Central Geographical Division of Kentucky, Department #2 (September 18-October 28, 1861); commanding 2nd Division, Central Army of Kentucky, Department #2 (October 28, 1861-February 11, 1862); commanding division, Fort Donelson, Central Army of Kentucky, Department #2 (February 11-16, 1862); commanding the fort (February 16, 1862); major general, CSA (August 16, 1862); commanding division, Left Wing, Army of the Mississippi (ca. September-November 20, 1862); commanding division, Hardee's Corps, Army of Tennessee (November 20-December 14, 1862); commanding District of the Gulf, Department #2 (December 14, 1862-April 27, 1863); commanding Department of East Tennessee (May 12-September 1863); commanding corps, Army of Tennessee (September 1863); commanding division,

Cheatham's Corps, Army of Tennessee (October-November 1863); commanding division, Department of East Tennessee (November 26-December 1863); again commanding the department (April 12-May 2, 1864); second in command, Trans-Mississippi Department (June-August 4, 1864); commanding District of West Louisiana, Trans-Mississippi Department (August 4, 1864-April 19, 1865); also commanding 1st Corps, Trans-Mississippi Department (September 1864-May 26, 1865); lieutenant general, CSA (September 20, 1864); commanding the department (April 19-22, 1865); and commanding District of Arkansas and West Louisiana, Trans-Mississippi Department (April 22-May 26, 1865). As the head of the state's military forces he attempted to preserve its precarious neutrality but in July 1861 the Unionist-controlled military board of the state ordered the State Guard, which they considered pro-secessionist, to turn in its arms. Buckner resigned on July 20th and two months later was named a Confederate brigadier general, neutrality having come to an end. Initially in command in central Kentucky, he later led a division from there to reinforce Fort Donelson. He directed the attempted breakout from the encircled post on February 15, 1862, but was called back by his superiors, John B. Floyd and Gideon J. Pillow. Both of them fled across the Cumberland River rather than surrender and left the task to Buckner. He was outraged by Grant's demand for unconditional surrender, but he was somewhat mollified by later developments. He had paid Grant's New York hotel bill when the future Union general was on his way home, having resigned from the army. Grant returned the favor in kind, knowing that Buckner would have difficulty obtaining funds as a prisoner—and put his purse at the disposal of the vanquished. Exchanged on August 27, 1862, Buckner was promoted to major general and led his division at Perryville before being ordered to take command along the Gulf coast. The next spring he took over the Department of East Tennessee. On July 25, 1863, this command was merged into the Department of Tennessee under Braxton Bragg but was retained for administrative purposes. Thus Buckner was reporting to both Bragg and Richmond. This awkward situation led to ill-feelings later on. During the buildup prior to the battle of Chickamauga Buckner reinforced Bragg and his command became a corps for the battle. When Jefferson Davis visited the army shortly thereafter Buckner was one of the leading critics of Bragg's generalship. For this reason Bragg shunted Buckner back off to East Tennessee just before Chattanooga. There he served under Longstreet during the siege of Knoxville. He then held a number of special assignments until again being placed in charge of the Department of East Tennessee in the spring of 1864. During this period he spent much of his time in Richmond where he became known as "Simon the Poet" for his penchant for writing poetry. Later that spring he was ordered to the virtually cut-off Trans-Mississippi as E. Kirby Smith's deputy. Not allowed to return to Kentucky for three years after the war, he resided for that period in New Orleans and then resurrected his fortune. After serving as a pallbearer at his old friend Grant's funeral he entered politics, serving a term as governor. In 1896 he ran for the vice presidency on John M. Palmer's Gold Democrats ticket. At the time of his death he was the only surviving Confederate officer over the rank of brigadier general. (Stickles, Arndt Mathias, *Simon Bolivar Buckner: Borderland Knight*)

BUDWIN, Florena (?-1865)

It has been estimated that there were enough women, disguised as men, serving in the Union and Confederate armies to have formed four companies. But only one woman is known to have died at the Confederate prison at Florence, South Carolina. Joining the Union army with her husband, Florena Budwin maintained her disguise throughout her service. Husband and wife were both captured and confined at the infamous Andersonville stockade. Here Mr. Budwin died either at the hands of guards or the Andersonville "Raiders." Florena's ordeal continued until Andersonville was threatened by Union forces and she was transferred to the South Carolina facility. Falling victim to an epidemic, her sex was discovered by a doctor. Special treatment, including a private room and special food supplies, failed to save her life and she died on January 25, 1865.

BUELL, Don Carlos (1818-1898)

A highly capable organizer and administrator, Don Carlos Buell lost his field command for failing to follow up the retreating Confederates after the battle of Perryville. But his friendship for the deposed McClellan may have contributed to his removal. The Ohio-born, Indiana-raised West Pointer (1841) had been posted to the infantry and seen service in the Seminole and Mexican wars. In the latter he was wounded at Churubusco and received two brevets. The outbreak of the Civil War found him on the West coast as the adjutant general of the Department of the Pacific. His Civil War-era assignments included: brevet captain and assistant adjutant general (since January 25, 1848); brevet major and assistant adjutant general (February 25, 1861); lieutenant colonel and assistant adjutant general (May 11, 1861); brigadier general, USV (May 17, 1861); commanding division, Army of the Potomac (October 3-November 9, 1861); commanding Department of the Ohio (November 15, 1861-March 11, 1862); commanding Army of the Ohio (November 15, 1861-October 24, 1862); major general, USV (March 21, 1862); and colonel and assistant adjutant general (July 17, 1862). Arriving in Washington in September 1861, he helped organize the Army of the Potomac under McClellan and briefly commanded a division. Transferred to Ohio, he was placed in command of the army for operations into East Tennessee. This represented a special desire of the president to liberate the mountain loyalists. But Buell had other ideas and, with the misgivings of both Lincoln and McClellan, moved against Nashville instead. His advance came simultaneously with Grant's against Forts Henry and Donelson. After taking the Tennessee capital—with little opposition—he moved to the support of Grant at Pittsburg Landing on the Tennessee. He arrived on the scene of the battle of Shiloh, with his leading divisions, late on the first day. Witnessing the fugitives from Grant's army cowering under the river bank, he believed that it

Don Carlos Buell, a friend of McClellan, shared his fellow general's slowness. (*Leslie's*)

was only his army that saved Grant from defeat. This point has long been debated. It must be remembered that the worst place from which to judge how a battle is going is the straggler-filled rear of an army. He took a notable part in the fighting of the second day. By this time his department had been absorbed into Halleck's—his army however maintained its name—and he commanded one of the three armies in the extremely slow advance on Corinth. He later led four divisions along the Memphis and Charleston Railroad towards Chattanooga while repairing the line. With his supply line destroyed by Rebel cavalry, his movement came to a halt. With Bragg's invasion of Kentucky, he was forced to fall back north to protect the line of the Ohio River. Dissatisfied with his progress, the authorities ordered him to turn over command to George H. Thomas on September 30, 1862, but the next day this order was revoked. On October 8 he fought the indecisive battle of Perryville, which halted a Confederate invasion that was already faltering. He failed, however, to follow up the retreating enemy and for this was relieved on October 24, 1862. For the next half year a military commission reviewed the facts but made no recommendation. Buell returned to Indianapolis, claiming that he had not advanced because of a lack of supplies. There he awaited orders that never came. He was mustered out of the volunteers on May 23, 1864. A few days later, on June 1, 1864, he resigned his regular commission as well. His friendship with the ousted McClellan was of no benefit to him. After the war he was in the Kentucky iron and coal industry.

BUELL, George Pearson (?-1883)

Entering the volunteer service in 1861, George P. Buell was brevetted brigadier general, for his role in directing the pontoon trains of the Army of the Cumberland, and then joined the regular army, remaining until his death. The Indiana native's assignments included: lieutenant colonel, 58th Indiana (December 17, 1861); colonel, 58th Indiana (June 24, 1862); and commanding in the Army of the Cumberland: 1st Brigade, 1st Division, Left Wing, 14th Corps (December 31, 1862-January 9, 1863); 1st Brigade, 1st Division, 21st Corps (June 10-July 25 and August 3-October 9, 1863); Pioneer Brigade (January-June 1864); Pontooneers (June-December 1864); 2nd Brigade, 1st Division, 14th Corps (January 17-March 28 and April 4-July 18, 1865); and the division (March 28-April 4 and June 17-27, 1865). He took part in the capture of Nashville but was too late to take part in the fight at Shiloh as part of Don C. Buell's army. Promoted to colonel, he commanded his regiment at Perryville and succeeded to brigade command at Murfreesboro. This brigade he led in the Tullahoma Campaign and at Chickamauga. At Chattanooga, where he apparently led a demi-brigade, he won a regular army brevet, which was awarded in 1867. With his regiment assigned to the pioneers, dealing mostly with pontoons, he served through the Atlanta Campaign and the March to the Sea. Brevetted brigadier general on January 12, 1865, for this service, he went on to command a brigade, and sometimes the division, during the Carolinas Campaign. Mustered out with his regiment on July 25, 1865, he joined the regulars the next year as lieutenant colonel, 29th Infantry. He died on active duty as colonel, 15th Infantry, with a brevet of brigadier general for the Civil War.

BUFORD, Abraham (1820-1884)

At some 320 pounds, Abraham Buford was apparently the heaviest Confederate general. The native Kentuckian and West Pointer (1841) had won a brevet as a dragoon officer during the Mexican War and served on the frontier before resigning in 1854 as a captain in the 1st Dragoons. In the years before the Civil War he was a noted breeder of horses and cattle. When the sectional conflict broke into open warfare he maintained his own neutrality almost a year longer than his state. He became one of the few recruits gained during Bragg's invasion of the state in the summer and fall of 1862. Buford's assignments included: brigadier general, CSA (September 2, 1862); commanding brigade, Cavalry Division, Army of Tennessee (ca. December 1862-January 1863); commanding brigade, Loring's Division, Department of Mississippi and East Louisiana (ca. April-May 16, 1863); commanding brigade, Loring's Division, Department of the West (May 16-July 1863); commanding brigade, Loring's Division, Department of Mississippi and East Louisiana (July 1863-January 28, 1864); commanding brigade, Loring's Division, Department of Alabama, Mississippi and

East Louisiana (January 28-March 2, 1864); commanding division, Forrest's Cavalry Corps, Department of Alabama, Mississippi and East Louisiana (February 18-May 4, 1865). Having finally made his decision, he covered the withdrawal from Kentucky and commanded a mounted brigade at Murfreesboro. Transferred to Mississippi, he was lightly engaged in actions against Grierson's raid and then took part in the early stages of the Vicksburg Campaign. Along with most of Loring's division, he was cut off from Pemberton's army after Champion Hill and joined the forces under Joseph E. Johnston. He took part in the defense of Jackson, Mississippi and in opposing Sherman's Meridian Campaign. Transferred to Forrest's cavalry, he fought in charge of a division at Brice's Crossroads, Tupelo, and during Andrew J. Smith's August 1864 invasion of Mississippi. Wounded at Lindville, Tennessee, on December 24, 1864, he was out of action for a time and was engaged in reorganizing the mounted forces under Richard Taylor when the end came. He then returned to horse raising but committed suicide after the deaths of his wife and son and financial losses.

BUFORD, Harry T.

See: *Velazquez, Loreta Janeta*

BUFORD, John (1826-1863)

Within six months of his having played a key role in the opening of the battle of Gettysburg, cavalryman John Buford was dead of typhoid fever. The Kentucky-born soldier had moved to Illinois before being appointed to West Point. Graduating in 1848 he was posted to the dragoons and saw some action along the frontier and in the expedition against the Mormons in Utah in 1857-1858. His Civil War-era assignments included: captain, 2nd Dragoons (since March 9, 1854); captain, 2nd Cavalry (change of designation August 3, 1861); major and assistant adjutant general (November 12, 1861); brigadier general, USV (July 27, 1862); commanding Cavalry Brigade, 2nd Corps, Army of Virginia (July 27-September 12, 1862); commanding Reserve Brigade, Cavalry Corps, Army of the Potomac (February 12-May 22, 1863); commanding the division (May 22-27, June 9-August 15, and September 15-November 21, 1863); and major general, USV (to rank from July 1, 1863). After staff duty in the Washington defenses he obtained a position on Pope's staff in northern Virginia. He was rewarded with a brigadier's star and command of a brigade of cavalry. While leading this at 2nd Bull Run he suffered a wound. The next spring he was commanding the Reserve Brigade, which was composed mainly of regular army units, and took part in

Gettysburg hero John Buford (seated) with his staff; Myles W. Keogh is second from the left. (NA)

Stoneman's raid during the Chancellorsville Campaign. He directed the division at Brandy Station, Aldie, Middleburg, and Upperville. It was two of his brigades that initiated the fighting at Gettysburg northwest of the town. He was able to hold off the Confederate assaults until the arrival of Union infantry and enabled Meade to make a stand south and east of the town on the next two days. He later served through the Bristoe Campaign, but just before the commencement of the Mine Run Campaign he was struck down by typhoid and had to relinquish his command on November 21, 1863. On his deathbed he received his commission as major general. He died on December 16, 1863.

BUFORD, Napoleon Bonaparte (1807-1883)

In spite of a truly military name, the half-brother of Gettysburg hero John Buford held the rank of major general for only a few months. Napoleon Bonaparte Buford was born into Kentucky's plantation society; the West Pointer (1827) served eight years in the artillery and as a professor at his alma mater. Following his 1835 resignation he settled in Illinois and engaged in banking, engineering, railroading, and iron. Financially ruined by the default of Southern bonds held by his bank, he entered the Union army where his assignments included: colonel, 27th Illinois (August 10, 1861); commanding Flotilla Brigade, Army of the Mississippi (April 24-26, 1862); commanding 1st Brigade, 3rd Division, Army of the Mississippi (April 26-June 25 and September 20-November 1, 1862); major general, USV (November 29, 1862); commanding District of Eastern Arkansas, 16th Corps, Army of the Tennessee (September 19, 1863-January 6, 1864); and commanding District of Eastern Arkansas, 7th Corps, Department of Arkansas (January 6-August 6, September 28-October 7, 1864, and October 10, 1864-March 9, 1865). He fought under Grant at Belmont, under Pope at Island #10, and under Rosecrans at Corinth. In each of the latter two he directed a brigade. He served in the very early stages of the Vicksburg Campaign but his appointment as a major general was not confirmed by the Senate and it expired on March 4, 1863. During the later part of the war he commanded in eastern Arkansas, with headquarters at Helena. On leave at the end of the war, he was brevetted major general and was mustered out on August 24, 1865; he was later a government appointee.

BULL BEAR (fl. 1860s-1870s)

Involved in the events leading up to the massacre at Sand Creek, Colorado, Bull Bear, a chief of the Cheyenne Dog Soldiers, had helped to assemble his people at that location at the behest of Major Edward Wynkoop of the 1st Colorado Cavalry. After the slaughter he was active in leading his braves in the fighting, and, although he signed the Treaty of Medicine Lodge in 1867, he fought at Beecher's Island the next year. He eventually returned to the reservation but left to join the Sioux in 1870-71 and during the Red River War of 1874-75. Although that was the last time he went on the war path, he never truly accepted the white man's rule. (Brown, Dee, *Bury My Heart At Wounded Knee*)

BULLOCH, James Dunwoody (1823-1901)

Never achieving his desire for a command of his own, James Bulloch fulfilled an even more important role for the Confederate navy—as purchasing agent in Europe providing many of the commerce raiders for a fledgling fleet. After 15 years in the U.S. Navy, rising to the rank of lieutenant, Bulloch resigned in 1854. Commanding the mail steamer *Bienville* at the outbreak of the Civil War, he refused to turn it over to the Confederate authorities when he offered his services, insisting on returning it to New York. Sent to Europe in May 1861 as a civilian purchasing agent for the rebel navy, he worked with the Fraser, Trenholm & Company financial office in Liverpool. Working in secrecy and through the loopholes in the British Neutrality Proclamation and the Foreign Enlistment Act, he contracted for numerous ships and naval stores. He ran the *Fingal*, laden with supplies, through the blockade at Savannah in late 1861. Returning to Europe with a commission as a commander, he looked forward to taking command of one of the commerce raiders under construction. But the "290," more famous as the *Alabama*, went to Raphael Semmes instead. Other vessels built in Britain included the *Florida* and *Shenandoah*. Working also in France Bulloch contracted for the ram *Stonewall*, which never reached the Confederacy. With the waning of Southern military fortunes, it became increasingly difficult to operate in Europe. Several vessels were seized in France and England when virtually completed. With the South's fall, Bulloch remained in England and became a naturalized citizen. He wrote *The Secret Service of the Confederate States in Europe* and was in the cotton trade.

BULLOCK, Robert (1828-1905)

A veteran of Seminole Indian fighting, North Carolina-born Floridian Robert Bullock rose to the rank of Confederate brigadier general before being wounded and put out of action during the Nashville Campaign. A teacher and court clerk before the war, his military assignments included: captain, Company H, 7th Florida (spring 1862); lieutenant colonel, 7th Florida (ca. April 26, 1862); colonel, 7th Florida (June 2, 1863); commanding Florida Brigade, Bate's Division, Hardee's-Cheatham's Corps, Army of Tennessee (ca. September 1-mid-December 1864); and brigadier general, CSA (November 29, 1864). His early war service came in East Tennessee in limited maneuvering and in fighting Unionist guerrillas in the area. Rising to command of the regiment, he led it to a junction with Braxton Bragg's main army and took part in the victory at Chickamauga. He missed Chattanooga but was advanced to brigade command during the Atlanta Campaign. He led the Floridian brigade at Franklin, and during the Nashville Campaign he fell severely wounded near Murfreesboro during a minor action. This ended his career in the field and the year after the close of hostilities he became an attorney. He was also active in politics and became a judge.

BURBANK, Sidney (ca. 1807-1882)

At a time when most regular army officers were taking commissions in the volunteers to further their careers, Sidney

Burbank remained in service with the small regular army. Burbank was a veteran infantryman, having graduated from West Point in 1829. He fought in the Seminole and frontier Indian wars and taught at his alma mater. His rank at the outbreak of the war was major in the 1st Infantry. His Civil War assignments included: lieutenant colonel, 13th Infantry (May 14, 1861); colonel, 2nd Infantry (September 16, 1862); and commanding 2nd Brigade (March-September 23, 1863) and 1st Brigade (September 23, 1863-January 1864), 2nd Division, 5th Corps, Army of the Potomac. His early service included Missouri in the summer of 1861 and commanding the defense of Cincinnati against Morgan's Raid in the summer of 1862. He continued as military commander of Cincinnati during the Perryville and Stones River campaigns. Sent East, he was given command of one of the two regular infantry brigades with the Army of the Potomac, which he led at Chancellorsville and in the "Valley of Death" on the second day at Gettysburg. Shortly after the last battle, the two brigades were ordered to New York City following the draft riots. That fall, the two brigades were consolidated and Burbank was given the command. Early in 1864, he was sent to Kentucky and Ohio where he was charged with enforcing the draft. He commanded the post at Newport Barracks, Kentucky, for the rest of the war. Brevetted brigadier general for Gettysburg, he remained in the regular army until 1870.

BURBRIDGE, Stephen Gano (1831-1894)

Kentucky plantation owner Stephen G. Burbridge was forced into exile from his native state for his support of the Union during the war. A lawyer with some training at the Kentucky Military Institute, he entered the army during the first summer of the war. His assignments included: colonel, 26th Kentucky (August 27, 1861); brigadier general, USV (June 9, 1862); commanding 1st Brigade, 1st Division, Army of Kentucky, Department of the Ohio (October-November 13, 1862); also commanding the division (October 1862); commanding 1st Brigade, 10th Division, 13th Corps, Army of the Tennessee (November-December 18, 1862); commanding 1st Brigade, 1st Division, Yazoo Expedition, Army of the Tennessee (December 18, 1862-January 4, 1863); commanding 1st Brigade, 1st Division, 1st Corps, Army of the Mississippi (January 4-12, 1863); commanding 1st Brigade, 10th Division, 13th Corps, Army of the Tennessee (January 12-July 28, 1863); commanding 1st Brigade, 4th Division, 13th Corps, Department of the Gulf (August 17-September 20, 1863); commanding the division (September 20-December 5, 1863); commanding District of Kentucky, 23rd Corps, Department of the Ohio (April 10, 1864-January 17, 1865); and commanding District of Kentucky, Department of the Cumberland (January 17-February 22, 1865). Although his regiment was present at Shiloh, it was under the command of the lieutenant colonel. He did command a brigade, however, at Chickasaw Bluffs and Arkansas Post as a brigadier. He served throughout the Vicksburg operations and in the early part of the campaign against Jackson, Mississippi. After a few months in the Department of the Gulf he was given a district command in his native state, succeeding the much-hated Jeremiah T. Boyle. Like his predecessor, he was despised by the local population for his harsh rule. Unlike Boyle, he was more capable in dealing with enemy cavalry raids. He earned a brevet major generalship for repulsing Morgan's raid in 1864. Nonetheless his arbitrary arrests and his system of retaliations forced his removal in the final months of the war. He resigned on December 1, 1865. After years of trying to live in Kentucky, he was forced to move his family and he died in New York.

BURDEN, Henry (1791-1871)

One of the major reasons why the Union cavalry was able to overwhelm its Confederate counterpart during the latter part of the Civil War was the ability to keep its mounts in serviceable condition. A leading contributor to this capability was Henry Burden. A Scottish-born inventor-genius, he came to America in 1819 and took out his first patent three years later. In 1834 he invented a horseshoe making machine and kept improving it over the next three decades. By the time of the Civil War his company was able to produce 600,000 shoes a year in 13 sizes, for horses and mules. When Confederates captured Union supplies, Burden's horseshoes were considered a special prize. He continued directing the operations of his company until his death.

BURGWYN, Henry King, Jr. (1841-1863)

An 1861 graduate of the Virginia Military Institute, Henry Burgwyn had the dubious distinction of commanding the regiment that suffered the highest numerical loss of any regiment in a single engagement. Burgwyn entered the Confederate service as lieutenant colonel of the 26th North Carolina on August 27, 1861, and was promoted to full colonel on August 19, 1862. His regiment saw service at New Bern in North Carolina and in the Seven Days with the Army of Northern Virginia. Sent back to eastern North Carolina and southeastern Virginia the regiment rejoined the army in time for the Gettysburg Campaign. On the first day of the battle, Burgwyn led his regiment until he was wounded in both lungs. He died shortly thereafter. The remnants of the command took part in the famed Pickett's Charge on the third day. In the two days of heavy fighting the regiment suffered 588 killed and wounded plus 120 prisoners out of somewhat over 800 engaged.

BURKS, Jesse Spinner (1823-1885)

During Stonewall Jackson's campaigns in late 1861 and early 1862 his brigade commanders were falling so rapidly, either from enemy fire or his own displeasure with them, that few of them ever reached the appropriate grade of brigadier general. Native Virginian Jesse S. Burks is one example of this attrition. Although he had graduated from the Virginia Military Institute in 1844, he was living the life of a farmer by the time of the outbreak of the war. Entering the military his assignments included: colonel, 42nd Virginia (July 1861); commanding 6th Brigade, Army of the Northwest (summer and fall 1861); and commanding Gilham's Old Brigade, Army of the Northwest and later in the Valley District, Department of Northern Virginia (January 20-March 23, 1862). Commanding a brigade he took part in Robert E. Lee's dismal Cheat Mountain Campaign and commanded another brigade during the winter at Romney, getting himself involved in the Loring-Jackson feud. At the battle of Kernstown, although in a supporting role, he fell wounded, after only two months in command. Never recovering sufficiently to take the field, he resigned on July 21, 1862. Returning to his farm, he served in the state legislature for a decade in the postwar years; he had also served one term 20 years earlier.

BURLING, George Childs (?-1885)

More than a year after his resignation from the Union army George C. Burling was awarded a brevet as a brigadier general, in the omnibus promotions of March 13, 1865, for his role in the defense of Sickles' salient at Gettysburg. The New Jersey native's assignments included: captain, 6th New Jersey (August 26, 1861); major, 6th New Jersey (March 18, 1862); lieutenant colonel, 6th New Jersey (May 7, 1862); colonel, 6th New Jersey (September 10, 1862); and commanding 3rd Brigade, 2nd Division, 3rd Corps, Army of the Potomac (June-August 29, 1863 and February-March 1864). On the Peninsula he fought at Yorktown and took over command of the regiment at Williamsburg. The regiment next saw action at Seven Pines and during the Seven Days. At 2nd Bull Run he again succeeded to command the regiment and was made its colonel the next month. In the Washington fortifications during the Maryland campaign, the corps was at Fredericksburg. Wounded at Chancellorsville, Burling returned to duty in time to command the 3rd Corps' primarily New Jersey brigade in the desperate fighting on the second day at Gettysburg. Following two periods in brigade command he submitted his resignation, effective on March 4, 1864.

BURLINGAME, Anson (1820-1870)

Born in New York and raised in Michigan, lawyer Anson Burlingame was a powerful orator before the war, being active in Free-Soil, Know-Nothing, and, finally, Republican politics. Following his graduation from Harvard Law School, he became connected with the abolition movement in Massachusetts and in 1855 gained a seat in the U.S. Congress. Defending Massachusetts and Senator Charles Sumner after Preston Brooks had attacked him on the floor of the Senate, he was challenged to a duel by the hot-headed South Carolinian. It never came off thanks to Burlingame's cool response to Brooks, diffusing the situation. Having stumped for the Republican ticket in 1860, he was rewarded with an appointment as minister to Austria. However, Austria named him *persona non grata* for his earlier support of Hungarian revolutionary Louis Kossuth; he was transferred to China. Serving from 1861 to 1867, he was successful in closing Chinese ports to Confederate vessels and also tried to create an air of cooperation between China and the Western powers. In return he was made China's envoy to the West in 1867. He was ever on guard against unfairness in relations between the two cultures.

BURNETT, Henry Cornelius (1825-1866)

Kentucky's Henry C. Burnett was one of Jefferson Davis' friends in the Confederate Senate. Born in Virginia, Burnett had settled in Kentucky as a child and was eventually admitted to the bar. A Democrat, he served four terms in the U.S. Congress before being expelled on December 3, 1861, for his outspoken secessionist sentiments. This was only to be expected, since the preceding month he had presided over the convention that claimed to have taken Kentucky out of the Union. Initially sent to Richmond to gain the state's admittance into the Confederacy, Burnett was appointed as a representative to the Provisional Congress. He was also appointed colonel, 8th Kentucky, on November 11, 1861, resigning on February 10, 1862. With the adoption of the permanent constitution, he was appointed to the Senate where he served for the remainder of the war. A general supporter of the administration's war effort, he did, however, want to give the states more control over exemptions from the draft. With his state behind enemy lines, Burnett was a major proponent of the use of partisan rangers.

Enlightened diplomat Anson Burlingame. (NA)

His committee assignments in the Senate included those on: Buildings; Claims; Commerce; Engrossment and Enrollment; Judiciary; Military Affairs; Naval Affairs; and Pay and Mileage. He repeatedly used his influence with the president in an effort to get the Confederate army to invade Kentucky. He returned to the practice of law after the peace but died before he was 41.

BURNETT, Henry Lawrence (1838-1916)

As an officer in the War Department's Bureau of Military Justice, Henry L. Burnett played a leading role in some of the primary constitutional questions raised by the Civil War. The Ohio native and lawyer had joined the Union army early in the conflict, but it was two years before he transferred from line to staff position. His assignments included: captain, 2nd Ohio Cavalry (August 23, 1861); and major and judge advocate, USV (August 10, 1863). With his cavalry unit, he served in Missouri, Kansas, and Kentucky. His regiment took part in the pursuit and capture of John Hunt Morgan and his Confederate raiders north of the Ohio River in the summer of 1863. His legal expertise was used in the military prosecution of the Knights of the Golden Circle and of the plotters in the scheme to free the Confederate prisoners at Camp Douglas at Chicago. He was also involved in the trial of the Lincoln assassination conspirators in 1865. Mustered out on December 1, 1865, he was brevetted through brigadier general for his legal services. Thereafter he was a lawyer, district attorney, and Republican organizer.

BURNETT, Theodore Legrand (1829-1917)

One of the more troublesome members of Kentucky's generally Davis-friendly congressioinal delegation was the 6th District's Theodore L. Burnett. A native of the state, Burnett spent most of the antebellum period in his private law practice, with time out for service in the Mexican War and as a county attorney. With the recognition of the state's secession by the Richmond authorities, he was appointed to the Provisional Congress, but he only attended its sessions for one day. He was, however, elected to represent the 6th District in the First Congress. Here he was assigned to the Committee on Claims and was named chairman of the Committee on Pay and Mileage. He demanded a hearing into the fall of Fort Donelson, which irritated the Davis administration. However, in the early years of the war he proved to be rather supportive of government policies. But by 1864 this had changed. No longer trusting Davis' military judgment, Burnett proposed that Congress name generals to high commands and frequently voted against giving the War Department additional powers. Ruined by the war, Burnett resumed his law practice and held minor elective office in Louisville.

BURNHAM, Hiram (ca. 1814-1864)

A Maine lumberman and local politician, Hiram Burnham rose to the rank of brigadier general shortly before his death in battle. His assignments included: lieutenant colonel, 6th Maine (July 15, 1861); colonel, 6th Maine (December 12, 1861); commanding Light Division, 6th Corps, Army of the Potomac (May 3-11, 1863); commanding 3rd Brigade, 1st Division, 6th Corps, Army of the Potomac (February-April 5, 1864); brigadier general, USV (April 26, 1864); commanding 2nd Brigade, 1st Division, 18th Corps, Army of the James (April 28-July 31 and September 27-29, 1864); and commanding the division (July 31-August 3, 1864). He led his regiment capably at Yorktown, Williamsburg, the Seven Days, Antietam, and Fredericksburg. At Chancellorsville he commanded the Light Division—in reality a large independent brigade—in the storming of Marye's Heights. He commanded his regiment in reserve at Gettysburg and participated in the campaigns in northern Virginia that fall. Promoted to brigadier in the spring of 1864, he was transferred to a brigade in Butler's army and served on the Bermuda Hundred lines. Sent to reinforce Grant at Cold Harbor, he took part in the Cold Harbor disaster. During service on the Richmond and Petersburg fronts, he was killed in action at Fort Harrison on September 29, 1864.

BURNS, John (ca. 1791-1872)

A veteran of the War of 1812, having fought in the battle of Lundy's Lane, John Burns was the only known Gettysburg civilian to participate in the battle. A former town constable and cobbler, he shouldered his antiquated musket and headed out to McPherson's Ridge on the first day of the battle. The commander of the 1st Corps, General Doubleday, wrote: "My thanks are specially due to a citizen of Gettysburg named John Burns, who, although over seventy years of age, shouldered his musket, and offered his services to Colonel Wistar, One hundred and fiftieth Pennsylvania Volunteers. Colonel Wistar advised him to fight in the woods, as there was more shelter there, but he preferred to join our line of skirmishers in the open fields. When the troops retired, he fought with the Iron Brigade. He was wounded in three places." Finally incapacitated, Burns was caught by the Confederates but escaped after he explained, according to one story, that he was out looking for his cow when he got caught up in the battle. Following Lincoln's famous speech, the President sought out the "Hero of Gettysburg" and they attended church together.

BURNS, William Wallace (1825-1892)

West Pointer (1847) William W. Burns served for a year and a half in line command before resigning his volunteer commission and returning to staff duty. The Ohio native had served his first few years after graduation in the infantry—seeing service in Mexico and against the Indians—before becoming a commissary officer. His Civil War assignments included: captain and commissary of subsistence (since November 3, 1858); chief commissary of subsistence, Department of the Ohio (March 24-October 1861); major and commissary of subsistence (August 3, 1861); brigadier general, USV (September 28, 1861); commanding 3rd Brigade, Stone's-Sedgwick's Division, Army of the Potomac (October 22, 1861-March 13, 1862); commanding 2nd Brigade, 2nd Division, 2nd Corps, Army of the Potomac (March 13-July 10 and October 10-November 12,

1862); commanding 1st Division, 9th Corps, Army of the Potomac (November 2, 1862-February 7, 1863); and chief commissary of subsistence, Department of the Northwest (September 1863-October 1865). Initially McClellan's commissary chief, he was made a brigadier and assigned to command Edward D. Baker's old brigade after his death at Ball's Bluff. He led this brigade at Seven Pines and in the Seven Days, where he was wounded at Savage Station. Awarded brevets for both Savage Station and Glendale, he went on sick leave for three months shortly after the close of the campaign. Returning in the fall, he was in command of a 9th Corps division at Fredericksburg and during the Mud March. He resigned his general's star on March 20, 1863, finishing the war as chief commissary for the department embracing Wisconsin, Iowa, Minnesota, Nebraska, and the Dakota Territory. Brevetted brigadier in the regular service for his war work he remained in the army until his 1889 retirement as a colonel and assistant commissary general.

BURNSIDE, Ambrose Everett (1824-1881)

If there is any mitigating circumstance in the failure of Ambrose E. Burnside as commander of the Army of the Potomac it is that he had twice previously refused the post, recognizing his own inexperience, and only accepted at the urging of others who said he had to obey the assignment order. An Indiana native and West Pointer (1847), he served six years in the regular artillery, including garrison duty in Mexico and being wounded in an 1849 fight with Apaches in New Mexico Territory. Resigning in 1853 to manufacture his breech-loading carbine, he settled in Rhode Island but failed to gain a government contract and had to assign his patent to creditors. During this period he was also a major general in the state militia. With the outbreak of the Civil War he raised a regiment and his assignments included: colonel, 1st Rhode Island (May 2, 1861); commanding 2nd Brigade, 2nd Division, Army of Northeastern Virginia (June-July 1861); brigadier general, USV (August 6, 1861); commanding North Carolina Expeditionary Corps (December 1861-April 1862); also commanding Department of North Carolina (January 13-July 10, 1862); major general, USV (March 18, 1862); commanding 9th Corps, Army of the Potomac (July 22-September 3, 1862, March 17-19, 1863, and April 13-August 14, 1864); commanding Left Wing, Army of the Potomac (September 1862); commanding Army of the Potomac (November 9, 1862-January 26, 1863); and commanding Department of the Ohio (March 25-December 11, 1863). After leading his brigade creditably in the flank attack at 1st Bull Run, he was mustered out with his three-months regiment on August 2, 1861. Four days later he was commissioned a brigadier general and organized an expedition against the North Carolina coast. For his successes at Roanoke Island and New Bern he was awarded a second star and was offered command of the main Union army following McClellan's failure on the Peninsula. Refusing this, he detached part of his corps to the aid of Pope in the 2nd Bull Run Campaign. Again offered command following that debacle, he again declined and was given

Ambrose Burnside, reluctant commander of the Army of the Potomac, with other officers. (AC)

charge of the 1st and 9th Corps during the Maryland operations. He fought at South Mountain and then at Antietam, where his two corps were placed on opposite ends of the Union battle line. He nonetheless remained in wing command over the 9th Corps—a cumbersome arrangement that may explain his slowness in attacking at the Stone Bridge. The delay allowed A.P. Hill's Confederate division to come up from Harpers Ferry and contain the Union breakthrough. With McClellan's removal he was assigned to the command of the army. He hesitated but was convinced that he had no alternative but to obey the order. His advance upon Fredericksburg was rapid but later delays, some not his fault, allowed Lee to concentrate along the heights and easily repulse the Union attacks. Upset by the failure of his plan, Burnside declared that he himself would lead an assault by his old corps. He was talked out of it but relations between the commander and his subordinates were strained. Accepting full blame, he offered to retire but this was refused. The next month he launched his ill-fated "Mud March," which bogged down before it was fairly underway. This time he asked that several officers be relieved of duty and court-martialed and also offered to resign. The latter was accepted; the former not. Lincoln was unwilling to lose him and assigned him to the Department of the Ohio. Here Burnside dealt with copperheads like Clement Vallandigham and Confederate raiders such as John Hunt Morgan. He advanced to Knoxville and was besieged there by Confederate General James Longstreet until a column under Sherman came to his relief. For his stand at Knoxville Burnside received the Thanks of Congress on January 28, 1864. Taking his freshly recruited 9th Corps back to Virginia, he fought directly under Grant—instead of being assigned to the Army of the Potomac because Meade was his junior—during the early part of the Overland Campaign. This cumbersome arrangement was soon rectified. He fought at the Wilderness and Spotsylvania where he did not shine, appearing reluctant to commit his troops after the Fredericksburg experience. After North Anna and Cold Harbor he took his place in the siege lines at Petersburg where he bungled the follow-up to the explosion of the mine. In reaction to this failure he was sent on leave and never recalled. He finally resigned on April 15, 1865, and later served as Rhode Island's governor for three years and as one of its senators until his death. Another of his legacies is the term "sideburns," which originated from his peculiar whiskers. (Poore, B.P., *The Life and Public Services of Ambrose E. Burnside*, and Woodbury, Augustus, *Major General Ambrose E. Burnside and the Ninth Army Corps*)

BURT, Erasmus R. (?-1861)

In one of the relatively small actions early in the war Erasmus R. Burt is credited with killing the enemy commander before himself falling victim to enemy fire. Active in Mississippi politics and government and in helping the handicapped before the war, he became captain of the Burt Rifles. His assignments included: captain, Company K, 18th Mississippi (April 22, 1861) and colonel, 18th Mississippi (June 7, 1861). After leading his men in some of the fringe operations at 1st Bull Run, he took an active part in the Battle of Ball's Bluff. Here, some accounts have him firing the pistol shot that killed the Union commander, Edward D. Baker. A short while later he was mortally wounded, dying after five days, on October 26, 1861.

BURTON, Henry Stanton (ca. 1816-1869)

Career artillerist Henry S. Burton emerged from the Civil War as a regular army brigadier general by brevet. The New York native had received his appointment to West Point from Vermont and was posted to the artillery upon his 1839 graduation. A veteran of both the Seminole and Mexican wars, he had also been a professor at West Point before the Civil War. His assignments in that conflict included: captain, 3rd Artillery (since September 22, 1847); major, 3rd Artillery (May 14, 1861); commanding Fort Delaware prisoner of war camp (June 1862-September 1863); lieutenant colonel, 4th Artillery (July 25, 1863); colonel, 5th Artillery (August 11, 1863); commanding Artillery Reserve, Army of the Potomac (January-May 16, 1864); inspector of artillery, Army of the Potomac (May 16-June 1864); commanding Artillery Brigade, 18th Corps, Army of the James (June-July 1864); and commanding Fort Richmond, New York (July-December 2, 1864). After a year and a quarter as prison commandant, he joined the field armies and directed the reserve guns of the Army of the Potomac in the Wilderness and until the unit was broken up at Spotsylvania. From then through Cold Harbor he was on inspection duty, then became a corps artillery chief during the early operations against Petersburg for which he was brevetted brigadier general. He served in New York Harbor and finished the war on boards and commissions. Remaining on active duty, he fulfilled similar functions until his death.

BURTON, James H. (?-?)

After running into trouble with the Confederate Congress in his role as an official in the ordnance department, Virginian James H. Burton went on to run an armory. Originally working for the Virginia state government, he transferred to the Confederate ordnance department under Josiah Gorgas. When push came to shove, he set up the Macon, Georgia, armory. He not only produced arms there, but also traveled to Europe to purchase ordnance machinery. In the final year of the war he was charged with inspecting the armories of the Confederacy.

BURTON, William (1789-1866)

As the governor of Delaware, a border slave state during the secession crisis, William Burton tried to use his influence to slow the movement toward war. A doctor and sheriff, he had once before tried for the governorship, in 1854, but failed. His luck was better four years later and he was inaugurated in January 1859. Although attempts to abolish slavery in the state failed during his term, he was active in raising funds and troops for the war effort. In fact, proportionally, the state sent more men to the Union army than any other. Leaving office on the expiration of his term, on January 20, 1863, he returned to medicine for the remaining three years of his life. (Conrad, Henry Clay, *History of the State of Delaware*)

BUSCHBECK, Adolphus (?-?)

It is a comment on the inconsistencies of the promotion and brevet systems in the Union army that the commander of the 11th Corps brigade, which did the best fighting in the rout at Chancellorsville, never received either reward, while both the division and corps commanders most responsible for the disaster were advanced. Early in the war Adolphus Buschbeck enlisted in the 27th Pennsylvania—which was attacked in the streets of Baltimore and was in reserve at 1st Bull Run—and by the spring of 1862 he was its colonel. His brigade and division commands included: 1st Brigade, 1st Division, 1st Corps, Army of Virginia (August 30-September 12, 1862); 1st Brigade, 2nd Division, 11th Corps, Army of the Potomac (October 27-November 27, 1862, December 1862-February 22, 1863, March 5-28, April 12-June 10, and July-September 25, 1863); the division (February 22-March 5 and March 28-April 12, 1863); 1st Brigade, 2nd Division, 11th Corps, Army of the Cumberland (September 25-November 28, 1863 and March 3-April 16, 1864); the division (November 28, 1863-March 3, 1864); and 2nd Brigade, 2nd Division, 20th Corps, Army of the Cumberland (April 14-May 22, 1864). He led his regiment in the fighting at Cross Keys in the Shenandoah Valley Campaign and succeeded to the command of the brigade at 2nd Bull Run. Following a stint in the Washington defenses and operations around Snicker's Gap he joined the Army of the Potomac and while in command of his brigade made one of the best stands in the face of Stonewall Jackson's surprise flank attack. Missing Gettysburg, he went west with the 11th and 12th Corps and fought at Chattanooga. The next year he performed creditably as a brigade commander in the Atlanta campaign until he and his regiment were mustered out on June 11, 1864. He was still a colonel.

BUSSEY, Cyrus (1833-1915)

Iowa Democratic politician turned soldier, Cyrus Bussey survived some early setbacks in his military career before becoming a brigadier general in the Union army. Born in Ohio and raised in Indiana, he had settled in Iowa in 1855, been elected to the state legislature, and was a delegate to the convention that nominated Stephen A. Douglas in 1860. His military assignments included: lieutenant colonel, Iowa Militia (1861); colonel, 3rd Iowa Cavalry (September 5, 1861); commanding 2nd Brigade, 3rd (Cavalry) Division, District of Eastern Arkansas, Department of the Missouri (December-December 22, 1862); commanding 2nd Brigade, 2nd Division, Cavalry, 13th Corps, Army of the Tennessee (February 8-April 3, 1863); commanding Cavalry Division, District of Eastern Arkansas, 13th Corps, Army of the Tennessee (April 3-May 1863); commanding 2nd Brigade, Cavalry Division, District of Eastern Arkansas, 13th Corps, Army of the Tennessee (May-June 1863); commanding Cavalry Brigade, Herron's Division, Army of the Tennessee (June-July 1863); commanding Cavalry 1st Division, 16th Corps (attached to 9th Corps), Army of the Tennessee (July 1863); commanding 1st (Cavalry) Division, Arkansas Expedition, Army of the Tennessee (November 3-December 1863); commanding 1st Brigade, 1st (Cavalry) Division, Arkansas Expedition, Army of the Tennessee (December 1863-January 6, 1864); brigadier general, USV (January 5, 1864); commanding 3rd Brigade, 1st Division, 7th Corps, Department of Arkansas (May 25-July 25, 1864); commanding the division (July 25-September 9, 1864); commanding 2nd Brigade, Cavalry Division, 7th Corps, Department of Arkansas (December 1, 1864-February 1, 1865); and commanding 3rd Division, 7th Corps, Department of Arkansas (February 6-August 1, 1865). In less than a month he raised his cavalry regiment under instructions from John C. Fremont. At Pea Ridge he panicked and his regiment had to be commanded by its lieutenant colonel. He had further problems at Bentonville and Village Creek. He then took part in the operations against Arkansas Post and was in command of a cavalry brigade, and occasionally a division, in eastern Arkansas before taking part in the siege of Vicksburg from the 11th of June. With his cavalry brigade he served in the operations against Jackson before returning to Arkansas with Steele's expedition. Promoted to brigadier, he finished the war in that theater. Mustered out on August 24, 1865, he was active in Louisiana politics—having become a Republican—and was in charge of the pension office. He died while practicing law in the nation's capital.

BUSTEED, Richard (1822-1898)

The fact that he was a vehement supporter of Stephen A. Douglas over Abraham Lincoln may explain why the brigadier general's commission of Richard Busteed was never submitted to the Senate and allowed to expire. A native of Ireland, he had worked in journalism before being admitted to the bar in New York. Early in the Civil War he raised a battery and offered it to the Union authorities. His assignments included: captain, Chicago (Ill.) Light Artillery (October 1, 1861); brigadier general USV (August 7, 1862); and commanding Independent Brigade, Yorktown, 7th Corps, Department of Virginia (December 15, 1862-April 1, 1863). His battery was disbanded and merged into the 1st New York Light Artillery on November 9, 1861; two days earlier Busteed had resigned. The following summer he was appointed a brigadier and the following winter and spring he commanded a brigade on the Peninsula. When his appointment expired on March 4, 1863, due to non-confirmation, he was relieved. That fall Lincoln appointed him a judge in Alabama but his duties, at first, were limited since most of the state was in Confederate control. During Reconstruction he struck Congress a blow by voiding the test oath for attorneys appearing before federal courts. Coming into the conflict with the Democrats as well, he resigned in 1874 and returned to private practice.

BUTLER, Andrew P. (1796-1857)

South Carolina Senator Andrew Butler may not have been alive when the Civil War really got started but he was, in some respects, a participant in one of the first physical actions of that war. Butler was respected by his legislative colleagues, and many Northern senators, including Stephen Douglas, were uneasy with the vehemence of attacks heaped upon him during

Union General Richard Busteed, absent from the heavy action, had time to pose with a drummer boy. (NA)

Senator Charles Sumner's two-day, 1856 speech, "Crime Against Kansas." Butler had been highly critical of Sumner, an abolitionist Republican, in recent months but this attack on the defender of slavery was too much for some to take. A relative of Butler, Congressman Preston Brooks, decided to take punitive action. On May 23, 1856, Brooks assaulted Sumner on the Senate floor with a cane. A full-fledged fight between the sections nearly erupted in the halls of Congress. On June 12 Butler supported Brooks' attack during a debate, and a move to expel Brooks failed to gain approval. Butler died almost exactly a year after the incident.

BUTLER, Benjamin Franklin (1818-1893)

The name of Benjamin F. Butler was one of the most-reviled in the South. Although a highly controversial, poltically appointed general, he won some early Union victories. A highly successful criminal attorney in Massachusetts—he had been born in New Hampshire—he entered the state legislature and served in both houses. At the Democratic convention of 1860, he walked out with the primarily Southern states' rights delegates after having staunchly backed Jefferson Davis for the presidency. At the Baltimore convention he supported John C. Breckinridge for that post. However, after secession he became a War Democrat and entered energetically upon his duties as a militia officer. His assignments included: brigadier general, Massachusetts Volunteers (April 17, 1861); commanding Department of Annapolis (April 27-May 15, 1861); major general, USV (May 16, 1861); commanding Department of Virginia (May 22-August 17, 1861); commanding Department of New England (October 1, 1861-February 20, 1862; commanding Department of the Gulf (March 20-December 17, 1862); commanding Department of Virginia and North Carolina (November 11, 1863-April 1864); also commanding 18th Corps, Department of Virginia and North Carolina (November 11, 1863-May 2, 1864); and commanding Army of the James (April-August 27, September 7-December 14, 1864, and December 24, 1864-January 8, 1865). After the 6th Massachusetts had been attacked in the streets of Baltimore and the railway bridges into that city had been destroyed, he lifted the blockade of Washington by moving the 8th Massachusetts by ship from Philadelphia to Annapolis and then funneling troops by rail into the capital. Lincoln rewarded the Democrat with the first commission as a major general of volunteers. His next exploit came on May 13, 1861, when he hoodwinked the pro-secessionists in Baltimore by suddenly seizing Fort Hill, which commanded the center of the city. Assigned to command the Department of Virginia, he saw a portion of his forces badly defeated at Big Bethel the next month but he did retain control of Fortress Monroe for the Union. In a controversial ruling he declared escaping slaves of secessionist masters to be "contraband," and thus subject to seizure and employment by the military. Already much despised in the Confederacy, his reputation was to grow worse the next year. In August 1861 he led the army portion of the successful combined operation against Hatteras Inlet in North Carolina and then commanded in New England while organizing another amphibious force for the move against New Orleans. The navy completed the capture on its own but Butler soon occupied the city and was faced with an extremely hostile public. He was roundly condemned after hanging William Mumford for tearing down a U.S. flag. There were false stories of his confiscating silver from churches and homes and he was dubbed "Spoons Butler." But his most lasting sobriquet, "Beast Butler," originated with his infamous "Woman Order." The women of the city had been dumping filthy water on officers, spitting on soldiers in church, and stepping off the curb to pull away their skirts in an exaggerated manner when an officer passed them. Part of the order read, "Hereafter when any female shall by word, gesture, or movement insult or show contempt for any officer or soldier of the United States she shall be regarded and held liable to be treated as a woman of the town plying her avocation." Although he also threatened soldiers who took advantage of the order with severe punishment, Butler was condemned throughout the South. Reports of financial scandal finally forced his removal from command in December 1862, and a few days later he was branded an outlaw by Jefferson Davis, for whom he had campaigned in 1860. Returning to field command a year later, he was bottled up at Bermuda Hundred while trying to cut the rail lines between Richmond and Petersburg. This failure was followed by others in the operations against the two cities under Grant and was capped by his dismal failure in the first attempt to take Fort Fisher. As the army commander of the joint operation, he was mostly responsible; shortly thereafter he was removed from command. Resigning on November 30, 1865, without ever receiving any further orders, he was elected to Congress the next year and, by now a Radical Republican, was a leader in the movement to remove Andrew Johnson from office for lenient treatment of ex-Confederates, especially Davis and Breckinridge. He served a total of five terms in Congress and one as governor. In 1884 he was the Greenback Party candidate for president. (West, Richard S., Jr., *Lincoln's Scapegoat General: A Life of Benjamin F. Butler, 1818-1893*; Trefousse, Hans L., *Ben Butler, the South Called Him Beast!*; Holzman, Robert S., *Stormy Ben Butler*; and Nash, Howard P., Jr., *Stormy Petrel: The Life and Times of General Benjamin F. Butler*)

BUTLER, Matthew Calbraith (1836-1909)

South Carolina lawyer and state legislator M.C. Butler followed Wade Hampton throughout the war. His assignments included: captain, Hampton (S.C.) Legion (early 1861); major, Hampton Legion (July 21, 1861); colonel, 2nd South Carolina Cavalry (August 1862); brigadier general, CSA (September 1, 1863); commanding brigade, Hampton's Division, Cavalry Corps, Army of Northern Virginia (early spring-summer 1864); commanding the division (summer 1864-January 19, 1865); major general, CSA (September 19, 1864); commanding cavalry division, Department of South Carolina, Georgia and Florida (January-February 1865); commanding division, Hampton's Cavalry Command (March-April 9, 1865); and commanding division, Hampton's Cavalry Command, Army of Tennessee (April 9-26, 1865). He fought with the legion at 1st Bull Run and on the Peninsula before being given command of a new cavalry regiment. He saw further action at Antietam and Fredericksburg and was severely wounded in the foot by a shell. While recovering from the amputation of the limb he was promoted to brigadier and assigned to a brigade. However, when it become apparent that he would be out of action for some time, Colonel P.M.B. Young was given charge in his stead. When in the spring of 1864 he did report for duty, he was given a brigade of three regiments just arrived from South Carolina and led them through the Overland Campaign and took over the division at Petersburg. At the beginning of 1865 he was sent with his division to South Carolina to reinforce the opposition to Sherman's drive. Failing in this he fought at Bentonville and surrendered with Johnston. After the war he was active in Democratic politics and sat as a senator in Washington for three terms. He was a major general of volunteers, in blue, during the war with Spain. He was also an officer of the Southern Historical Association. (Freeman, Douglas S., *Lee's Lieutenants*, and Brooks, U.R., *Butler and His Cavalry*)

BUTTERFIELD, Daniel (1831-1901)

Thoroughly hated by his fellow officers, Daniel Butterfield was wounded at Gettysburg and "fortunately for him and to the joy of all has gone home." A New York businessman with the American Express company, he had been active in the militia before the war. His assignments included: first sergeant, Clay Guards, District of Columbia Volunteers (April 16, 1861); colonel, 12th New York Militia (May 2, 1861); lieutenant colonel, 12th Infantry (May 14, 1861); commanding 8th Brigade, 3rd Division, Department of Pennsylvania (July 1861); brigadier general, USV (September 7, 1861); commanding 3rd Brigade, Porter's Division, Army of the Potomac (October 3, 1861-March 13, 1862); commanding 3rd Brigade, 1st Division, 3rd Corps, Army of the Potomac (March 13-May 18, 1862); commanding 3rd Brigade, 1st Division, 5th Corps, Army of the Potomac (May 18-August 30, 1862); also commanding 1st Brigade (August 30, 1862); commanding the division (November 1-16, 1862); commanding the corps (November 16-December 25, 1862); major general, USV (November 29, 1862); chief of staff, Army of the Potomac (January-July 3, 1863); colonel, 5th Infantry (July 1, 1863); chief of staff, 11th and 12th Corps, Army of the Cumberland (October 1863-April 14, 1864); and commanding 3rd Division, 20th Corps, Army of the Cumberland (April 14-June 29, 1864). Leading his regiment of militia—the first to cross the Long Bridge—into Virginia, he later commanded a brigade of Patterson's army. About this time he was given a commission in one of the new regular army regiments. In the Peninsula Campaign he earned a Congressional Medal of Honor—awarded in 1892—for the carrying of the flag of the 3rd Pennsylvania at Gaines' Mill. He was also wounded in this action. While the army was encamped at Harrison's Landing, he experimented with bugle calls, designing a special call for his brigade to be played before the regular calls to avoid confusion with those of other commands. He is also, somewhat questionably, credited with originating "Taps." His subsequent rise was rapid—commanding a brigade at 2nd Bull Run and a corps by Fredericksburg. When Hooker was given command of the army, Butterfield, by now a major general, was made his chief of staff. It was during this period that the army headquarters was termed "a combination of bar-room and brothel." Most officers considered the culprits to be Hooker, Daniel E. Sickles, and Butterfield. During the fighting at Chancellorsville, Butterfield was left behind at Falmouth to coordinate the actions of the two wings and communicate with Washington. With Meade's taking command of the army, a few days before Gettysburg, he reluctantly kept Butterfield as his staff chief, preferring not to replace him during active campaigning. The problem was finally solved when Butterfield was struck by a spent piece of shell on the third day of the battle. Returning to duty in the fall of 1863, he joined Hooker again at Chattanooga and was his chief of staff in the battle. With the formation of the 20th Corps he was given a division, which he commanded in the Atlanta Campaign. Illness forced him to leave the field before its conclusion. He later was given an assignment at Vicksburg and then was on recruiting duty in New York as a regular army colonel following his August 24, 1865, muster out of the volunteers. Resigning in 1870, he returned to his business interests and was active in veterans groups. Ironically he is buried at West Point, which he never attended, with one of the most ornate monuments. (Butterfield, Julia Lorriland, *A Biographical Memorial of General Daniel Butterfield*)

BYRNE, Richard (1832-1864)

The commanders of the famed Irish Brigade of the Union army frequently became casualties and Richard Byrne was no exception. His assignments included: colonel, 28th Massachusetts (ca. December 12, 1861); and commanding 2nd ("Irish") Brigade, 1st Division, 2nd Corps, Army of the Potomac (January 12-February 14, 1864). His regiment fought at Secessionville, 2nd Bull Run, South Mountain, and Antietam—he was not present at the latter three—before being assigned to the famous unit, which was principally composed of three New York regiments. He led the regiment at Fredericksburg, Chancellorsville, and Gettysburg. In the Overland Campaign he fought at the Wilderness and took over the brigade at Spotsylvania. In the assault on June 3, 1864, at Cold Harbor he fell mortally wounded. NOTE: His surname often appears as "Byrnes." (Conyngham, David Powers, *The Irish Brigade and Its Campaigns*)

C

CABELL, Henry Coalter (1820-1889)

It is a comment on the slowness of promotions in the Confederate artillery that Henry C. Cabell, although a colonel and battalion commander for most of the war, never made it to the rank of general. A Richmond lawyer, he raised an artillery company early in the conflict and his assignments included: captain, Richmond Fayette Artillery (April 25, 1861); lieutenant colonel, 1st Virginia Artillery (September 12, 1861); colonel, Artillery (July 4, 1862); chief of artillery, Magruder's Command, Department of Northern Virginia (April 12-June 1862); commanding Artillery Battalion, McLaws' Division, 1st Corps, Army of Northern Virginia (summer 1862-July 1863); commanding artillery battalion, 1st Corps, Army of Northern Virginia (July-September 1863 and May 1864-April 9, 1865); and commanding battalion, Artillery Reserve, Army of Northern Virginia (September 1863-May 1864). Initially serving on the Peninsula, he saw action on the Yorktown lines. He subsequently led his battalion at Antietam, Fredericksburg, Chancellorsville, and Gettysburg. When the corps went west with Longstreet, Cabell's Battalion was assigned to the army's reserve. With the return of Longstreet in the spring of 1864, Cabell served through the Wilderness and Petersburg campaigns, sometimes as acting corps chief of artillery. On the retreat to Appomattox, his battalion was assigned to General Walker's column bound for Lynchburg and thus was not present at the surrender. He resumed his private practice after the war. (Wise, Jennings, C., *The Long Arm of Lee*)

CABELL, William Lewis (1827-1911)

Having resigned from the old army at the outbreak of hostilities, Virginian West Pointer (1850) William L. Cabell has been credited with helping Beauregard and Joseph E. Johnston design the Confederate battleflag. Upon his graduation he was posted to the infantry for eight years before being transferred to the quartermaster's department. He resigned as a captain on April 20, 1861, and was almost immediately commissioned in the Southern army. His assignments included: major and assistant quartermaster (April 1861); chief quartermaster, Army of the Potomac (1861); chief quartermaster, Department of Northern Virginia (1862); commanding 1st Brigade, McCown's Division, Army of the West, Department #2 (spring-summer 1862); commanding cavalry brigade, Steele's Division, District of Arkansas, Trans-Mississippi Department (ca. February-late 1863); brigadier general, CSA (April 23, 1863 to rank from January 20); commanding brigade, Fagan's Cavalry Division, District of Arkansas, Trans-Mississippi Department (early 1864-September 18, 1864); commanding brigade, Fagan's Cavalry Division, Army of Missouri, Trans-Mississippi Department (September 18-October 25, 1864); and also commanding 1st (Arkansas) Cavalry Brigade, 1st (Arkansas) Cavalry Division, Cavalry Corps, Trans-Mississippi Department (September-October 25, 1864). After staff duty in northern Virginia he was transferred to the Trans-Mississippi and as an acting brigadier general was given charge of a mounted brigade, which he led across the Mississippi. He was wounded at Corinth and the Hatchie River. He returned to duty early in 1863 and continued to command a cavalry brigade in Arkansas until captured at Marais des Cygnes during Sterling Price's invasion of Missouri. Not exchanged until August 1865, he took up the practice of law, moved to Texas, entered railroading, was a U.S. marshal, and was connected with the Louisiana Lottery. He also served four terms as mayor of Dallas and was active in veterans' affairs. (Harvey, Paul, Jr., *Old Tige: General William L. Cabell, CSA*)

CADWALADER, George (1806-1879)

A Pennsylvania militia officer, George Cadwalader had been active as a brigadier general in the suppression of the 1844 Know-Nothing riots in Philadelphia. A native Pennsylvanian lawyer, he was appointed a brigadier of U.S. volunteers during the Mexican War and earned a brevet as major general for Chapultepec. His Civil War assignments included: major general, Pennsylvania Volunteers (April 19, 1861); commanding 1st Division, Department of Pennsylvania (April 27-May 15 and June 11-July 25, 1861); commanding Department of Annapolis (May 15-June 11, 1861); major general, USV (April 25, 1862); and commanding Department of Pennsylvania (December 1, 1864-June 27, 1865). Following the attack on Massachusetts troops in Baltimore, he was given command of the Annapolis area and then returned to Patterson's command as a division commander and second-in-command. He took part in the failed campaign to tie Joe Johnston down in the Shenandoah Valley while McDowell advanced on Manassas. Mustered out on July 19, 1861, he was appointed in the federal service the next year and served as a presidential advisor and on various boards dealing with military law and regulations. Late in the war he commanded at Philadelphia and commanded the Department of Pennsylvania in the last six months.

CADWALLADER, Sylvanus (?-?)

The 1955 publication of Sylvanus Cadwallader's memoirs started a new round of debate over Grant's drinking. A *Chicago Times* war correspondent, he was covering the Vicksburg Campaign when he claims to have been a principal in the events surrounding Grant's June 6 and 7, 1863, binge on board the steamer *Diligent*. The journalist claims that he witnessed the general leave the barroom in a drunken state and—fearing expulsion from the department—decided not to write the story and instead helped the army commander. He alleges that after two officers had refused to take care of their commander he took on the job himself, returning Grant to his quarters. The next morning Grant went for a drunken ride on a runaway horse and it was again Cadwallader who came to the rescue, calling for an ambulance. The reporter decided not to raise the issue with the general and was able to cover the rest of his campaigns. In recent years some historians have denied that Cadwallader was even present but only got his information—which he didn't put down on paper until the 1890s—from camp gossip. Both he and the 1955 editor came in for much vilification for the publication. (Cadwallader, Sylvanus, *Three Years with Grant*, edited by Benjamin P. Thomas)

CALDWELL, John Curtis (1833-1912)

A competent but not outstanding division commander, John C. Caldwell was displaced in the spring 1864 reorganization of the Army of the Potomac. He was a teacher and principal in Maine at the outbreak of the war. The native Vermonter's assignments included: colonel, 11th Maine (November 12, 1861); brigadier

Union division commander John C. Caldwell and staff. (AC)

general USV (April 28, 1862); commanding 1st Brigade, 1st Division, 2nd Corps, Army of the Potomac (June 4-December 13, 1862 and February 14-May 22, 1862); commanding the division (September 17, 1862, May 22-December 9, 1863, and January 15-March 24, 1864); and commanding the corps (August 26-September 2, December 16-29, 1863, and January 9-15, 1864). Commanding the regiment, he fought at Williamsburg and directed a division in the Seven Days. At Antietam he succeeded to division command briefly and was twice slightly wounded while in charge of the brigade at Fredericksburg. He led the brigade at Chancellorsville and the division at Gettysburg and in the Bristoe and Mine Run campaigns. Before Grant's Overland Campaign the Army of the Potomac was reduced from five to three corps and in the consolidations Caldwell lost his division. He spent the remainder of the war on a War Department board. He was part of the guard of honor, from the capital to Illinois, for Lincoln's funeral. Brevetted major general for his war service, he was mustered out on January 15, 1866, and took up the practice of law. For a time he was adjutant general of his adopted state and then was a diplomat in Chile, Uruguay, and Costa Rica.

CALEF, John Haskell (?-?)

When John Buford's Union cavalry opened the battle of Gettysburg the only battery of horse artillery present in support was John H. Calef's. The Massachusetts native graduated from West Point in the second year of the war and his assignments included: second lieutenant, 5th Artillery (June 17, 1862); second lieutenant, 2nd Artillery (October 6, 1862); first lieutenant, 2nd Artillery (November 4, 1863); and adjutant, 2nd Artillery (November 18, 1864-March 16, 1875). Eventually assigned to Captain John C. Tidball's Battery A, 2nd Artillery, he took command of the battery when Tidball took charge of a brigade of horse artillery in June 1863. On the first day at Gettysburg he placed his six three-inch rifles astride the Chambersburg Pike and supported the dismounted cavalrymen until relieved by James A. Hall's 2nd Maine Battery of the 1st Corps. Remaining with the battery he became its first lieutenant and was brevetted captain for the campaign from the Rapidan to Petersburg. In late 1864 he was appointed the regiment's adjutant and held that post for nearly a decade. Brevetted major for the war, he retired as lieutenant colonel, 3rd Artillery, in 1900.

CALHOUN, John Caldwell (1782-1850)

Although he died more than a decade before secession became a reality, the ideas on states' rights of John C. Calhoun make him the leading contender for the titles of father of secession and father of the Confederacy. A South Carolina lawyer, he was secretary of war under Monroe from 1817 to 1825 and vice president under John Quincy Adams and Andrew Jackson. In the latter administration he broke with the president over a protective tariff and developed his theory of nullification, which claimed that a state had the right to void any federal law that in its opinion violated the agreement made at the time of entry into the Union. If a compromise had not been achieved the Civil War might have been fought decades earlier, since Jackson was threatening the use of force. Calhoun later went to the U.S. Senate where he continued to focus on states' rights. "The Great Nullifier," as he was then known, earned another sobriquet for his outspoken defense of slavery: "The Napoleon of Slavery." After a brief return to his plantation he was Tyler's secretary of state in 1844-1845. Then returning to the Senate, he died in office. (Thomas, John L., *John C. Calhoun, A Profile*)

CALLAHAN, Samuel Benton (1833-1911)

Despite the fact that he was only one-eighth Creek, Samuel B. Callahan managed to serve in the Second Confederate Congress as a nonvoting representative for the Creek and Seminole nations. After working as a journalist in Texas, the Alabama-born Callahan moved to the Indian Territory and, based upon his mother's being one-quarter Creek, obtained Creek citizenship in 1858. He had been a commissioner to Washington but, being a slaveholder, felt that the Creeks should align themselves with the Confederacy. He served as captain, 1st Creek Cavalry. When the Creek and Seminole nations were given the right to alternately elect a nonvoting delegate to the Confederate Congress, Callahan was named to the position, taking his seat on May 30, 1864. Unable to vote, he took very little part in the activities of the legislature, but only considered matters relating to the Indians. After the war he resumed his ranching and farming operations and held various positions, often representing the Creeks, in the Indian Territory and later in Oklahoma, the state formed from the Indian Territory.

CAMERON, James (?-1861)

James Cameron, brother of the Union's secretary of war, died in the first major battle of the Civil War. He had been mustered in at the head of the "Highlanders," or 79th New York, on about May 29, 1861. Serving in William T. Sherman's brigade, he crossed Bull Run in support of the two divisions that had made the long circuit around the enemy flank. As the regiment moved forward it received a volley. A second volley then caught the regiment and Colonel Cameron fell mortally wounded. His brother Simon was one the spectators who had come out from Washington to view the contest.

CAMERON, Robert Alexander (1828-1894)

For a time a medical student, Robert A. Cameron gave up his studies to publish the *Valparaiso Republican* and later attended the 1860 Republican convention before entering the Union army. His assignments included: captain, 9th Indiana (April 23, 1861); lieutenant colonel, 19th Indiana (July 29, 1861); lieutenant colonel, 34th Indiana (November 3, 1861); colonel, 34th Indiana (June 15, 1862); brigadier general, USV (August 11, 1863); commanding 1st Brigade, 3rd Division, 13th Corps, Department of the Gulf (October 8-December 6, 1863, February 5-March 3, and May 24, 1864); commanding the corps (April 8-27, 1864); and commanding District of La Fourche, Department of the Gulf (June 9, 1864-June 1865).

With his original company he saw some service in western Virginia before taking a commission in a regiment serving along the Mississippi. He fought at New Madrid and Island #10 before being given command of the regiment. He served through the Vicksburg and Jackson campaigns. Promoted to brigadier, he led a division and corps during the Red River Campaign of 1864. He finished the war in command of a Louisiana district and was brevetted major general of volunteers for his war service. Resigning on June 22, 1865, he was active in the settlement of Colorado.

CAMERON, Simon (1799-1889)

In an age of political bosses, Simon Cameron was one of the most effective, controlling Pennsylvania politics for half a century. Cameron became a leading journalist in the state capital and, being a Democratic spokesman, he became the recipient of political patronage, serving as state printer and adjutant general of militia. Known thereafter as "General," he was accused of corruption in his handling of monies due the Winnebago Indians. During this period his businesses prospered through some questionable transactions. In 1845 he entered politics—replacing James Buchanan in the U.S. Senate—as a Democrat favoring a high tarriff. Losing his seat in 1849, he returned in 1857, as a Republican. A favorite-son candidate for the presidential nomination at the 1860 Republican national convention, he threw his support behind Lincoln when promised a cabinet post by the latter's campaign managers. Although disgusted by the deal, the newly-elected president named Cameron secretary of war. Cameron's administration of the department's contracts was full of corruption. This, in conjunction with military failures, forced his resignation in January 1862. He was immediately appointed minister to Russia where he was instrumental in gaining Russia's support of the Union cause. Within a year he was back in the United States, being defeated for a seat in the Senate, a race in which it was alleged that he had tried to bribe at least one legislator. Having supported emancipation of the slaves and favoring their enlistment, he supported Lincoln for reelection in 1864. After the war he resumed control of his Pennsylvania patronage machine and served in the Senate from 1867 to 1877, when he managed to pass his seat on to his son. Although he died in 1889, the political machine he had fashioned survived until 1921. (Bradley, Erwin Stanley, *Simon Cameron: Lincoln's Secretary of War, A Political Biography*)

CAMPBELL, Alexander William (1828-1893)

It was not until the final months of the war that Tennessee native Alexander W. Campbell received the wreath of a brigadier general around his three stars. The lawyer's Confederate assignments included: major and assistant inspector general, Provisional Army of Tennessee (ca. May 9, 1861); colonel, 33rd Tennessee (October 18, 1861); acting assistant inspector general, Forrest's Cavalry Corps, Department of Alabama, Mississippi and East Louisiana (February 18-ca. March 1865); brigadier general, CSA (March 1, 1865); and commanding brigade, Jackson's Division, Cavalry Corps, Department of Alabama, Mississippi and East Louisiana (ca. March-May 2, 1865). Following initial service in a staff position he was given charge of a regiment, which due to the lack of arms could not take the field until early 1862. At Shiloh he suffered a severe wound and following a lengthy recovery he found that he had not been reelected when his unit was reorganized on May 8, 1862. He served on Leonidas Polk's staff and then engaged in conscript and recruiting duties. While on the latter in July 1863 he was taken prisoner at Lexington, Tennessee. Apparently held for a year and a half before being exchanged, he served briefly as Nathan Bedford Forrest's inspector before taking charge of a mounted brigade until the Confederacy's demise. Returning to the legal profession, he lost a bid for the Democratic gubernatorial nomination in the postwar years.

CAMPBELL, Charles Thomas (1823-1895)

Partially disabled by seven wounds suffered in the Mexican and Civil wars, Charles T. Campbell finished the latter war in the relatively quiet command of the District of Wisconsin. During the former conflict he served as a first lieutenant, and later captain, of one of the extra regular army regiments created for that war. Mustered out after the peace treaty, he went into politics, serving in the state legislature. His Civil War assignments included: captain, Battery A, Pennsylvania Light Artillery (May 29, 1861); lieutenant colonel, 1st Pennsylvania Light Artillery (August 5, 1861); colonel, 1st Pennsylvania Light Artillery (September 13, 1861); colonel, 57th Pennsylvania (February 1862); brigadier general, USV (November 29, 1862); brigadier general, USV (reappointed March 13, 1863); and commanding District of Wisconsin, Department of the Northwest (ca. May 1863-ca. June 1865). After brief service as an artillery officer he accepted command of an infantry regiment, which he led at Yorktown, Williamsburg, and Seven Pines. In the latter he received three wounds but returned to duty in time for Fredericksburg where he was severely wounded in the liver and left for dead. Following his recovery he was found too incapacitated for active field duty and was sent to command in Wisconsin as a reappointed brigadier general—his original commission having expired on March 4, 1863, due to a lack of Senate confirmation. Mustered out on January 15, 1866, he was active in the settlement of South Dakota as an inspector of Indian agencies, operator of a stage line, and founder and mayor of Scotland, South Dakota.

CAMPBELL, John Archibald (1811-1889)

Although he had opposed secession, U.S. Supreme Court Justice John A. Campbell resigned to follow Alabama out of the Union and became the Confederacy's assistant secretary of war. The native of Georgia attended West Point for three years until the death of his father prompted his resignation. Taking up the practice of law, he spent two sessions in the Alabama legislature. A national reputation as a lawyer made him the choice of the other judges on the Supreme Court, and he was accordingly appointed to join them by Franklin Pierce on March 22, 1853, and then confirmed by a Senate voice vote three days later. In the *Dred Scott* case he ruled that since Scott was still a slave he was not a citizen and did not have the right to sue before a state or national court. Wishing to avoid war, he finally resigned on April 26, 1861, less than two weeks after Fort Sumter. Setting up a practice in New Orleans, he was appointed assistant secretary of war by Jefferson Davis on October 21, 1862. For the balance of the war his primary duties were related to the draft. In early 1865 he was one of three Confederate peace commissioners to meet with Lincoln and Secretary of State Seward in the Hampton Roads Peace Conference. At the close of the war he was confined for six months at Fort Pulaski. He then returned to the Crescent City and built a substantial practice. During the Tilden-Hayes presidential election dispute, he was one of Tilden's legal advisors. (Connor, Henry Groves, *John Archibald Campbell, Associate Justice of the United States Supreme Court*)

CAMPBELL, John Arthur (1823-1886)

The dreadful attrition rate in Stonewall Jackson's command during the campaigns of 1862 is exemplified by the case of John A. Campbell. He was the third commander of one of his brigades in a little over two months and he was destined to last two months himself. Having attended both the Virginia Military Institute and the state's secession convention put him in good stead to become an officer in the Confederate army. His assignments there included: colonel, 48th Virginia (September 1861); commanding 2nd Brigade, Valley District, Department of Northern Virginia (March 23-May 17, 1862); and commanding 2nd Brigade, Jackson's Division, Valley District, Department of Northern Virginia (May 17-25, 1862). Having commanded his regiment in the Cheat Mountain and Romney campaigns, he missed the battle of Kernstown but succeeded to the command of the brigade upon the wounding of Colonel Jesse S. Burks. Having led his new command at Front Royal, he moved on to Winchester where he was wounded at the side of Stonewall Jackson. Out of action until the fall, he resigned on October 16, 1862, out of resentment over the promotion of John R. Jones to brigadier general and Jones' assignment to command what Campbell felt was rightfully his brigade.

CAMPBELL, William Bowen (1807-1867)

As a part of Lincoln's policy of appointing loyal border state politicians to high military rank, William B. Campbell was named a brigadier general but appears to have held no commands. A volunteer veteran of both the Seminole and Mexican wars—as a captain and colonel, respectively—he had served in Congress and as the last Whig governor of Tennessee. An opponent of secession, he supported John Bell for the presidency in 1860. Spurning an offer of a Confederate military commission, he was named brigadier general, USV (June 30, 1862). However, he resigned this position on January 26, 1863, and, as a supporter of Andrew Johnson, tried to bring the state back into the Union. This support of the unpopular Johnson cost him his seat in Congress in 1865 when the Radical Republicans refused to seat him. He died two years later.

CANBY, Edward Richard Sprigg (1817-1873)

Although he commanded a military division and accepted the surrender of two of the four major Confederate armies, Edward R.S. Canby is not remembered with the Grants, Shermans, and Sheridans. The Kentucky-born and Indiana-educated West Pointer (1835) was posted to the infantry. He saw action in both the Seminole and Mexican wars—earning two brevets in the latter—and was involved in the "Trail of Tears" forced migration of the Cherokees, Choctaws, and Creeks to Arkansas. His Civil War-era assignments included: major, 10th Infantry (since March 3, 1855); colonel, 19th Infantry (May 14, 1861); commanding Department of New Mexico (June 16, 1861-September 18, 1862); brigadier general, USV (March 31, 1862); major general, USV (May 7, 1864); commanding Military Division of West Mississippi (May 11, 1864-May 1865); commanding Department of the Gulf (June 3-27, 1865); and brigadier general, USA (July 28, 1866). Serving in the Southwest at the outbreak of hostilities, he took command in New Mexico. Despite his defeat at Valverde—for which he was brevetted brigadier in the regular service—he was able to thwart Sibley's invasion of the territory. Relieved by James H. Carleton late in the second summer of the war, he served as an assistant adjutant general in Washington and went to New York City after the draft riots to enforce order. As a major general, he was given command of a military division comprising the Departments of the Gulf and Arkansas. His principal operations were against Mobile but, the fall of that city coming after

Edward R.S. Canby, Indian and Confederate fighter. (*Leslie's*)

Appomattox, he was robbed of the glory. During this command he was severely wounded by guerrillas. With the war winding down he accepted the surrenders of Richard Taylor and Edmund Kirby Smith. Brevetted to major general in the regular service for Mobile, he was mustered out of the volunteers on September 1, 1866. As a brigadier in the regular service he served in Washington and on Reconstruction duty in the South. In 1870 he went to the West Coast as commander of the Department of the Columbia and three years later was promoted to command the Division of the Pacific. During negotiations with the Modoc Indians in northern California on April 11, 1873, he was suddenly attacked by Captain Jack and several other Indians. His death led to further fighting. (Heyman, Max L., *Prudent Soldier: A Biography of Major General E.R.S. Canby, 1817-1873*)

CANDY, Charles (?-?)

A veteran of a decade's service in the regular army as an enlisted man, Charles Candy became an officer in the volunteer forces during the Civil War and two months after his mustering out was brevetted a brigadier general. The Kentucky native had served one five-year enlistment in the 1st Dragoons and another in the 1st Infantry. He completed his hitch on January 1, 1861, and soon entered the volunteer service. His assignments included: captain and assistant adjutant general, USV (September 21, 1861); colonel, 66th Ohio (December 17, 1861); commanding 1st Brigade, 2nd Division, 2nd Corps, Army of Virginia (August 9-September 12, 1862); commanding 1st Brigade, 2nd Division, 12th Corps, Army of the Potomac (September 12-17, September 18-October 26, December 30, 1862-February 1863, March-August 6, and September 6-25, 1863); commanding 1st Brigade, 2nd Division, 12th Corps, Army of the Cumberland (September 25-November 30, 1863 and February 18-April 14, 1864); commanding the division (February 9-18, 1864); and commanding 1st Brigade, 2nd Division, 20th Corps, Army of the Cumberland (April 14-August 4, 1864). Officially the adjutant on the staff of Frederick W. Lander, he temporarily joined the staff of Charles P. Stone, carrying messages from the field, during the disastrous fight at Ball's Bluff. Resigning his staff position on December 3, 1861, he was commissioned colonel of an Ohio regiment two weeks later. He served in the Shenandoah Valley Campaign of 1862 and, at Cedar Mountain, succeeded John W. Geary in command of the brigade. He led this command at 2nd Bull Run but was absent for Antietam. Still in a brigade leadership position, he fought at Chancellorsville and Gettysburg before being transferred, with the corps, to the West. As a brigade commander, he fought at Chattanooga and through most of the Atlanta campaign. He was mustered out of the army on January 14, 1865. Two months later he was awarded the rank of brigadier general by brevet—a rise from private to general officer's rank within a little more than four years.

CANNON, William (1809-1865)

In the little more than two years, of a four-year term, that William Cannon served as governor of Delaware he was in continual conflict with an unfriendly legislature. A Delaware merchant he had entered politics in 1844 as a Democratic member of the lower house of the state legislature. He went on to become state treasurer in 1851 and attended the Washington Peace Conference in 1861. Further trying to avoid the coming war, he supported the Crittenden Compromise but became a war supporter upon the firing on Fort Sumter. As a Union, or Republican, candidate he was elected to the governorship in the fall of 1862 and took his seat on January 20, 1863. There had been much unrest during the campaign over the arrest of "disloyal" citizens. The arrests were supported by the gubernatorial candidate but not the legislature. His calls for support of the war effort led the legislature to consider impeachment but it never came about. He aided in the raising of black troops and placed the state under martial law during Early's invasion of Maryland in 1864. Halfway through his term, he died on March 1, 1865, and a Democrat, Gove Saulsbury, succeeded him. (Conrad, Henry Clay, *History of the State of Delaware*)

CANTEY, James (1818-1874)

Plagued by illness, Confederate General James Cantey was frequently absent from his various commands. The South Carolina native had practiced law and sat in the state legislature before serving as a second lieutenant of South Carolina infantry during the Mexican War. Unlike many volunteer officers in that conflict he saw action and was wounded. The veteran of the Palmetto Regiment then settled in Alabama where he lived as a planter until the outbreak of the Civil War. His assignments included: colonel, 15th Alabama (July 27, 1861); brigadier general, CSA (January 8, 1863); commanding Eastern Division, Department of the Gulf (early 1863-summer 1863); commanding 1st Brigade, Western Division, Department of the Gulf (summer-August 1863); commanding Mobile, Department of the Gulf (August-September 1863); commanding 1st Brigade, Department of the Gulf (September 1863-April 6, 1864); commanding 1st Brigade, District of the Gulf, Department of Alabama, Mississippi and East Louisiana (April 6-April 1864); commanding brigade, Army of Mississippi, Department of Alabama, Mississippi and East Louisiana (April-May 19, 1864); commanding brigade, French's Division, Polk's Corps (or Army of Mississippi), Army of Tennessee (May 19-May 1864); and commanding division, Polk's-Stewart's Corps, Army of Tennessee (May-June 1864). He led his regiment in the Shenandoah Valley and during the Seven Days under Stonewall Jackson but was absent during the fights at Cedar Mountain, 2nd Bull Run, Antietam, and Fredericksburg. Promoted to brigadier general, he was ordered to Mobile where he served for somewhat over a year before joining the Army of Tennessee for the Atlanta Campaign in the early stages of which he was in charge of a brigade and then a division. However, after June 1864 he does not appear to have commanded his division in any major action although it was engaged at Franklin, Nashville, and in the Carolinas. Following the surrender he returned to his plantation.

C.A.P.

See: *Page, Charles Anderson*

CAPERS, Ellison (1837-1908)

South Carolina Military Academy graduate Ellison Capers rose to the rank of brigadier general in the Confederate service and subsequently wrote the South Carolina volume of *Confederate Military History*. The native South Carolinian and 1857 graduate became a professor at his alma mater, with the rank of second lieutenant, two years later. He was engaged in these educational pursuits during the lengthy secession crisis, then offered his services. His assignments included: major, 1st South Carolina Rifles (fall 1860); lieutenant colonel, 24th South Carolina (April 1, 1862); colonel, 24th South Carolina (January 1864); commanding Gist's Brigade, Cheatham's Division, Hardee's Corps, Army of Tennessee (August-September 1864); brigadier general, CSA (March 1, 1865); and commanding Gist's (old) Brigade, Bate's Division, Cheatham's Corps, Army of Tennessee (ca. March 1865). As a field officer he witnessed the bombardment of Fort Sumter and for a time served in northern Virginia before becoming second in command of a regiment enlisted for the war. With this unit he served mostly on the South Carolina coast—seeing action at Secessionville—until ordered to join Joseph E. Johnston in Mississippi in an attempt to relieve the pressure on Vicksburg. During these operations he was wounded at Jackson while commanding the regiment. Joining Bragg's army he succeeded to command again at Chickamauga and was again wounded. His regiment fought at Chattanooga and he was made its permanent commander early in 1864. During the Atlanta Campaign he commanded Gist's brigade for a time and later was wounded again at Franklin. Promoted to brigadier general, he led the brigade briefly in the Carolinas and apparently was captured at Bentonville. Following the war he rose to a high position in the Episcopal Church and also engaged in educational and veterans' affairs.

CAPERTON, Allen Taylor (1810-1876)

Originally a Unionist, Allen T. Caperton used his seat in the Confederate Senate to fight against those government policies that he felt were making the Confederacy's fight for independence a rich man's war and a poor man's fight. A lawyer and planter in western Virginia, Capterton had served for a decade in both houses of the state legislature before attending the Virginia secession convention where he opposed immediate secession—until Lincoln made a call for troops on Virginia to fight the rest of the South. With the death of Senator William B. Preston in November 1862, Caperton became one of five candidates for the vacant seat. After 20 ballots he took his seat on January 26, 1863. A personal animosity toward President Davis colored his voting record. From his position as chairman of the Committee on Accounts he fought for the maintenance of a strong internal economy, not willing to let it be sacrificed to the military effort. He fought Davis' policies on the land tax, the draft, the suspension of the writ of habeas corpus, foreign policy, and, albeit too late, the arming of the slaves. He was a constant critic of Davis' cabinet appointees. After the war he was instrumental in developing the resources of the new state of West Virginia, serving as its senator in the 1870s. He was also an official of the James River and Kanawha Canal.

CARLETON

See: *Coffin, Charles Carleton*

CARLETON, James Henry (1814-1873)

A regular army officer, who had been commissioned into the regular army following nonviolent militia service along the border between his native Maine and Canada, James Henry Carleton served throughout the Civil War on the West coast and in the Southwest, earning brevets as major general in both the regulars and volunteers. He had been named a second lieutenant in 1839 and was notably involved in explorations—including that of Stephen W. Kearny in the Rockies—and in the Mexican War, where he received a brevet. His Civil War-era assignments included: captain, 1st Dragoons (since February 16, 1847); captain, 1st Cavalry (change of designation August 3, 1861); major, 6th Cavalry (September 7, 1861); colonel, 1st California (August 19, 1861); commanding District of Southern California, Department of the Pacific (October 14, 1861-ca. April 13, 1862); commanding California Column (April 13-September 20, 1862); brigadier general, USV (April 28, 1862); and commanding Department of New Mexico (September 18, 1862-June 27, 1865). With the Confederate threat to Arizona and New Mexico, he was dispatched at the head of the California Column to the relief of the Union forces in that area. The march took five months and involved some fighting against hostile Indians. Just the news of the advance was sufficient to force the Rebels to withdraw back into Texas. For the remainder of the war he commanded the Department of New Mexico and was brevetted for his services. Mustered out of the volunteers on April 30, 1866, he died on active duty as lieutenant colonel of the 4th Cavalry. (Hunt, Aurora, *James A. Carleton, 1814-1873, Frontier Dragoon*)

CARLILE, John Snyder (1817-1878)

Refusing to accept defeat at the Virginia secession convention and in the referendum, John S. Carlile took the Unionist cause into the western counties of the state. A native of Winchester, in the Shenandoah Valley, he took up the practice of law in 1840 in what is now West Virginia. He sat in the state senate in 1847-1851 and was elected to Congress in 1854 as a member of the American Party. His term ended in 1857 and he returned to private practice. Again elected to Congress in 1860, he attended the state secession convention as a Unionist before taking his seat on March 4, 1861. He was one of the highest-ranking Virginia Unionists who refused to give in to secession and on July 9, 1861, was named to replace the withdrawn and expelled Robert M.T. Hunter in the U.S. Senate. Carlile took his seat four days later and held it until the term expired on March 3, 1865. In the meantime he had been highly active in the creation of the new state of West Virginia, and attended the convention that submitted the ordinance rejecting the actions of the Richmond convention.

CARLIN, William Passmore (1829-1903)

A highly capable brigade and division leader, William P. Carlin received every brevet he could earn. The Illinois native had been posted to the infantry following his 1850 graduation from West Point. Over the next decade he served against the Sioux, Cheyenne, and Mormons. His Civil War-era assignments included: first lieutenant, 6th Infantry (since March 3, 1855); captain, 6th Infantry (March 2, 1861); colonel, 38th Illinois (August 15, 1861); commanding 2nd Brigade, 4th Division, Army of the Mississippi (June 1-September 26, 1862); commanding 31st Brigade, 9th Division, Army of the Ohio (September 26-29, 1862); commanding 31st Brigade, 9th Division, 3rd Corps, Army of the Ohio (September 29-November 5, 1862); commanding 2nd Brigade, 1st Division, Right Wing, 14th Corps, Army of the Cumberland (November 5, 1862-January 9, 1863); brigadier general, USV (November 29, 1862); commanding 2nd Brigade, 1st Division, 20th Corps, Army of the Cumberland (January 9-February 15 and March 16-October 10, 1863); commanding 1st Brigade, 1st Division, 14th Corps, Army of the Cumberland (October 19-December 5, 1863, January 5-July 2, and August 3-17, 1864); major, 16th Infantry (February 8, 1864); commanding the division (August 17-November 2, 1864 and November 8, 1864-March 28, 1865). After initial service in Arkansas and Missouri, he performed creditably in brigade command at Perryville. He later served at Stones River, in the Tullahoma Campaign, and at Chickamauga. At Chattanooga his brigade was part of the command that broke through the Confederate lines on Missionary Ridge. He received a brevet for this action. Serving throughout the Atlanta Campaign, he emerged as a division commander, with another brevet for Jonesboro. He led his division on the March to the Sea and on into the Carolinas where he was again brevetted for Bentonville. Near the close of the war he was brevetted to major general in both services for the war. He then briefly commanded a division in West Virginia and was mustered out of the volunteers on August 24, 1865. Remaining in the regular service, he was finally retired in 1893 as colonel of the 4th Infantry. In the meantime he had served with the Freedmen's Bureau in Tennessee and in western commands.

CARNEGIE, Andrew (1835-1919)

The yet-to-be steel magnate Andrew Carnegie served the Union's war effort well in the field of transportation and communications. The Scottish-born future industrialist was an employee of the Pennsylvania Railroad at the outbreak of the Civil War. Going to Washington with the line's Pittsburgh Division superintendent, Thomas A. Scott, Carnegie became his assistant when Scott was named assistant secretary of war charged with overseeing the military's transportation needs. Carnegie rode on the engine of one of the first troop trains to arrive in the beleaguered capital. After the 1st Bull Run disaster, he organized the evacuation of the wounded and later worked in establishing a military telegraph network. Having succeeded Scott as superintendent, he left the line at the war's close to enter the iron business where he was to amass a fortune. In his later years he sought world peace—one idea being the simplification of the English language to make it a mode for common understanding.

CARNEY, Thomas (1824-1888)

One of the wealthiest men in his state, Kansas Governor Thomas Carney pledged his entire fortune as a guarantee for the repayment of state bonds he sold in New York to help the war effort. A native of Ohio, he had moved to Kansas in the late 1850s and amassed a substantial fortune from his mercantile ventures. As a Republican he served in the legislature immediately following Kansas' admission to the Union. Elected governor in November 1862 he took up his duties on January 12, 1863. He personally paid for a border patrol to prevent incursions by Confederate guerrillas and went to New York to sell bonds. He was elected to the U.S. Senate in early 1864, but the results were set aside since the vacancy was not to appear until over a year later. In the confusion over this technicality he was not renominated and left office early in 1865. Returning to his business interests, he was also active in railroading and banking and served as mayor of Leavenworth. (Crawford, Samuel J., *Kansas in the Sixties*)

CARR, Eugene Asa (1830-1910)

Despite a praiseworthy career in the Civil War—earning the Congressionial Medal of Honor and regular and volunteer brevets as major general—Eugene A. Carr is better remembered for his exploits against the Apaches, Cheyennes, and Sioux from whom he earned the sobriquet "War Eagle." A New York-born West Pointer (1850), he was posted to the mounted rifles and was wounded in an 1854 Indian fight at Fort Davis in Texas. His Civil War-era assignments included: captain, 1st Cavalry (since June 11, 1858); captain, Company I, 4th Cavalry (designation change August 3, 1861); colonel, 3rd Illinois Cavalry (August 16, 1861); commanding 3rd (Cavalry) Brigade, Army of Southwest Missouri, Department of the Missouri (January-February 1862); commanding 4th Division, Army of Southwest Missouri, Department of the Missouri (February-March 11, 1862); brigadier general, USV (March 7, 1862); commanding 4th Division, Army of Southwest Missouri, Department of the Mississippi (March 11-May 1862); commanding 2nd Division, Army of Southwest Missouri, Military District of the Missouri (June 5-September 19, 1862); major, 5th Cavalry (July 17, 1862); commanding 2nd Division, Army of Southwest Missouri, Department of the Missouri (September 19-October 7, 1862); commanding the army (October 7-November 13, 1862); commanding District of St. Louis, Department of the Missouri (November 13, 1862-February 23, 1863); commanding 2nd Division, Army of Southeast Missouri, Department of the Missouri (February-March 1863); commanding 14th Division, 13th Corps, Army of the Tennessee (March 28-July 28, 1863); commanding Left Wing, 16th Corps, Army of the Tennessee (September 3-October 15, 1863); commanding 2nd Division, Arkansas Expedition, Department of the Tennessee (November 30, 1863-January 6, 1864); commanding 2nd Division, 7th Corps, Department of Arkansas (January 6-February 13, 1864); commanding 1st (Cavalry) Division, 7th Corps, Department of Arkansas (February 13-May 11, 1864); commanding District of Little Rock, 7th Corps, Department of Arkansas (May 11-December 24, 1864); and commanding 3rd Division, 16th Corps, Department of the Gulf. (March 14-July 20, 1865). He was brevetted for the leadership of his company at the Wilson Creek defeat and six days later was given command of a volunteer regiment of cavalry. At Pea Ridge, while in charge of a brigade, he was thrice severely wounded but refused to leave his saddle and was treated there. In 1894 he was awarded the medal for his heroism. After additional service west of the Mississippi he crossed over for the Vicksburg Campaign where he earned a brevet for Big Black River Bridge. Sent back to Arkansas that fall, he was active in the capture of Little Rock and commanded for half a year in that district. His final wartime services came in the capture of Mobile. Brevetted to major general in both services, he was mustered out of the volunteers on January 15, 1866, and reverted to his majority in the regular army. For more than two decades he was active on the frontier against the Indians and was finally retired in 1893 as a full brigadier general. (King, James T., *War Eagle, A Life of General Eugene A. Carr*)

CARR, Joseph Bradford (1828-1895)

For some unexplained reason, Joseph B. Carr had a great deal of difficulty with Congress in the confirmation of his brigadier general's appointment; it eventually cost him the command of his division in the Army of the Potomac. The New York native was a tobacconist at the outbreak of the Civil War but had risen to the rank of colonel in the state militia. His federal assignments included: colonel, 2nd New York (May 14, 1861); commanding 3rd Brigade, 2nd Division, 3rd Corps, Army of the Potomac (June 1-6 and August 1862); brigadier general, USV (September 7, 1862); commanding 1st Brigade, 2nd Division, 3rd Corps, Army of the Potomac (September 16, 1862-January 12, 1863, February 8-May 3 and May 23-October 25, 1863); commanding the division (January 12-February 8, May 3-23, and July 9-10, 1863); brigadier general, USV (reappointed March 30, 1863); commanding 3rd Division, 3rd Corps, Army of the Potomac (October 5, 1863-March 24, 1864); commanding 4th Division, 2nd Corps, Army of the Potomac (March 25-May 2, 1864); commanding Defenses of Yorktown and Williamsburg, Army of the James (probably May-July 1864); commanding 3rd Division, 18th Corps, Army of the James (August 3-September 3, 1864); and commanding Separate Brigade, Army of the James (ca. October 1864-ca. June 1865). At the head of his regiment he fought at the Union defeat at Big Bethel and the next year in the Seven Days. In brigade command he fought at 2nd Bull Run and was promoted to brigadier the next month. He led a brigade at Fredericksburg and Chancellorsville, where he succeeded the mortally wounded Hiram G. Berry in division command. He was praised for his skill in the fighting to defend Sickles' advanced salient at Gettysburg. At the head of a division, he participated in the disappointing Bristoe and Mine Run campaigns. In the spring 1864 reorganization he was given a division in the 2nd Corps but before the opening of the Overland Campaign had to be relieved due to problems with his commission. His original appointment had expired on March 4, 1863, due to a lack of Senate confirmation. Reappointed later that same month, he was to rank from the original date but the Senate failed to confirm the earlier date. This made him junior to some of his brigade commanders and he had to be reassigned. He held several commands with the Army of the James but was usually in rear areas during the operations against Richmond and Petersburg. Brevetted major general for his war service, he was mustered out on August 24, 1865, but remained active in the state militia, becoming a major general. In the manufacturing business after the war in Troy, New York, he was active in Republican politics, including a failed bid for the lieutenant governorship.

CARRINGTON, Henry Beebee (1824-1912)

An abolitionist lawyer who had been active in recruiting troops first in Ohio and later in Indiana, Henry B. Carrington was later overruled by the Supreme Court for his methods in the suppression of the Copperhead Sons of Liberty. The Connecticut native had been charged with the reorganization of the Ohio militia by then-Governor and subsequently Secretary of the Treasury Salmon P. Chase in 1857. At the outbreak of the war he was able to forward nine state regiments to aid McClellan in western Virginia and was given the colonelcy of one of the new regular army infantry regiments. His assignments included: colonel, 18th Infantry (May 14, 1861); and brigadier general, USV (November 29, 1862). He continued in recruiting and organization in both Ohio and Indiana and then headed several military commissions that heavy-handedly suppressed both the secessionist and peace movements in the old Northwest. Many of his actions and the legality of his tribunals, since the area was not in rebellion, were overturned by the Supreme Court. He was mustered out of the volunteer service on August 24, 1865, and joined his regiment the next year on the frontier. While in command at Fort Phil Kearny in the Dakotas, he was tainted by his involvement in the notorious Fetterman Massacre. Neither Carrington nor Fetterman had much experience in this kind of warfare. He retired from the army in 1870 and was involved in negotiations with the Indians, lectured on the military art, and wrote several works, including *The Battles of the American Revolution*.

CARRINGTON, Isaac Howell (1827-1887)

When shortly after the close of the Civil War Major Isaac H. Carrington was arrested by the Federal authorities, he was able to prove, through a complete records file, that he was innocent of any wrongdoing in the disposition of monies belonging to prisoners of war. A native of Richmond, he was a lawyer when he accepted a commission as major, 38th Virginia, in June

1861. After service on the Manassas lines during the winter and later on the Peninsula, he failed to gain reelection in the spring reorganization. He was, however, kept in grade and in July 1863 was assigned to duty as a commissioner dealing with matters pertaining to prisoners of war. He later served as a provost marshal for the city of Richmond from February 1864 through the city's fall. During this time some funds taken from Union prisoners were deposited with him. He kept a complete file of the orders under which he made any disbursements from these monies. Thus any shortfall was due to his superiors. He was promptly released from arrest when this became clear. During the final stages of the war he attempted to find a route out of Richmond for the treasury funds of the dying nation. After the war he resided in Richmond and presumably practiced law.

CARROLL, Anna Ella (1815-1893)

In part because she has become wrapped up in the woman's movement, Anna Carroll is one of the more controversial female figures in the Civil War. Born into the famous Maryland family, she lived on her father's plantation for most of her life. In the 1850s she wrote a number of anti-Catholic tracts and was connected with the American or Know-Nothing Party. Having had an unusual interest in political matters since childhood, she became an accomplished propagandist. Maryland Governor Thomas Hicks believed that she was responsible for his 1856 election. With the outbreak of the Civil War and after freeing her slaves, she wrote a pamphlet defending the president's war-making powers. From this point on her career is surrounded by controversy, in part due to her tendency to exaggerate the importance of her works. During the first summer of the war she wrote a series of legally well-grounded papers on issues raised by the war. Her greatest claim was that of having originated the plan for the Union forces to advance up the Tennessee and Cumberland rivers rather than the Mississippi. The fact of the matter is that before she filed her November 30, 1861, report Grant had already occupied Paducah, Kentucky, at the mouth of the Tennessee (on September 6) indicating a possible move in that direction. Her "revolutionary" idea was also anticipated by the Confederates who attempted to block those avenues of advance with Forts Donelson and Henry. Lincoln himself declared her request for $50,000 for earlier tracts as "outrageous." Her post-war petitions for compensation from Congress for her work were never acted upon. Since that time there have been claims that she was an unofficial cabinet officer; even more fantastic claims as a strategic advisor have been made in her behalf. These and her responsibility for the battles of Fort Henry and Donelson are unfounded. However, she did play a significant role in justifying prosecution of the war and did have a good grasp of military strategy for which she has not received due credit due to her exaggerations. (Greenbie, Marjorie Barstow, *My Dear Lady, The Story of Anna Ella Carroll, The Great, Unrecognized Member of Lincoln's Cabinet*)

CARROLL, Samuel Sprigg (1832-1893)

Despite having commanded a brigade for two years—earning praise and brevets for some of the most important battles in the East—Samuel S. Carroll was not advanced to a brigadier general's star until he was virtually incapacitated by wounds for further field duty. A native of the nation's capital and a relatively recent (1856) graduate of West Point, he had been posted to the infantry and served on the frontier and as a quartermaster at West Point. His Civil War-era assignments included: second lieutenant, 10th Infantry (since October 1, 1856); first lieutenant, 10th Infantry (April 25, 1861); captain, 10th Infantry (November 1, 1861); colonel, 8th Ohio (December 7, 1861); commanding 4th Brigade, Shields' Division, Department of the Rappahannock (May 10-June 26, 1862); commanding 4th Brigade, 2nd Division, 3rd Corps, Army of Virginia (June 26-August 24, 1862); commanding 2nd Brigade, Whipple's Division, Military District of Washington, Department of the Potomac (September-November 1862); commanding 2nd Brigade, 3rd Division, 3rd Corps, Army of the Potomac (November 8, 1862-January 12, 1863); commanding 1st Brigade, 2nd Division, 2nd Corps, Army of the Potomac (March 25-May 13, 1864); brigadier general, USV (May 12, 1864); commanding Department of West Virginia (February 27-March 7, 1865); and commanding 4th Provisional Division, Army of the Shenandoah (April-July 1865). He accepted the colonelcy of a volunteer regiment from Ohio and served in western Virginia and fought at Kernstown. Assuming brigade command, he served through the Shenandoah Valley Campaign of 1862 and fought at Cedar Mountain. In the movements leading up to the battle of 2nd Bull Run, he was severely wounded while inspecting his pickets along the Rapidan River on August 24, 1862. Upon his recovery he was briefly assigned to the Washington fortifications before returning to the field in time to command a brigade in the 3rd Corps at Fredericksburg. The next month he requested that he and his regiment be transferred to the 2nd Corps. With the request granted, he commanded another brigade at Chancellorsville and Gettysburg, for both of which he earned regular army brevets. He fought at Bristoe Station and in the Mine Run Campaign. During the Overland Campaign he was wounded at the Wilderness on the first day but remained on duty, earning a brevet. A few days later at Spotsylvania he was severely wounded on the 13th when the division went forward to feel out Lee's new positions following the Union breakthrough the day before. He earned a brevet for this battle and received a brigadier's star effective from the date of the breakthrough. Following a lengthy recovery he served in relatively quiet sectors in West Virginia and the Shenandoah until the end of the war. Brevetted major general in both services for the war, he was mustered out of the volunteers on January 15, 1866. Continuing in the regular army and assigned mostly to staff duties, he served as lieutenant colonel, 21st Infantry, until disabilities caused by wounds forced him to retire with the advanced grade of major general. (Galway, Thomas, *The Valiant Hours*)

CARROLL, William Henry (ca. 1810-1868)

On the day before his division commander, George B. Crittenden, was arrested on charges of drunkenness, Confederate General William H. Carroll was himself arrested on that same charge plus those of incompetence and neglect of duty. A planter and postmaster before the war, the Tennessee native was also active in the state militia. His Confederate assignments included: brigadier general, Tennessee Militia (prewar); inspector general, Provisional Army of Tennessee (May 9, 1861); colonel, 1st East Tennessee Rifles (October 1861); brigadier general, CSA (October 26, 1861); commanding 2nd Brigade, District of East Tennessee, Department #2 (January-February 23, 1862); and commanding 1st Brigade, 2nd (Crittenden's) Division, Army of Central Kentucky, Department #2 (February 23-March 31, 1862). Following service in organizing the state forces he took command of a regiment from East Tennessee, which was later designated the 7th Tennessee, Provisional Army, and the 37th Tennessee. Within days he was named a Confederate brigadier general and eventually was given a brigade in East Tennessee. This he led at Mill Springs where he came in for his share of the criticism for the defeat there. While commanding his brigade under William J. Hardee he was relieved and placed under arrest on the above-mentioned charges. Following a court of inquiry he resigned on February 1, 1863, and joined his exile family in Canada. In the remaining five years of his life he never returned to the United States.

CARRUTH, Sumner (?-1892)

On his way to becoming a brevet brigadier general in the Union army, Massachusetts native Sumner Carruth suffered two wounds, was captured, and suffered from sunstroke. His assignments included: captain, 1st Massachsetts (May 23, 1861); major, 35th Massachusetts (August 21, 1862); colonel, 35th Massachusetts (May 1, 1863); commanding 2nd Brigade, 2nd Division, 9th Corps, Department of the Ohio (February 20-March 1864); and commanding in 9th Corps, Army of the Potomac: 2nd Brigade, 2nd Division (March-April 1864); 1st Brigade, 1st Division (April 25-May 6, 1864); and 1st Brigade, 2nd Division (January 23-February 11 and May 4-June 9, 1865). His first regiment fought at 1st Bull Run, Yorktown, Williamsburg, and Seven Pines where Carruth was wounded. After the regiment had fought through the Seven Days, he became a field officer in a new regiment. He was at South Mountain and sustained his second wound at Antietam. Returning to duty, he was captured at White Sulphur Springs on November 14, 1862, and thus missed Fredericksburg. Back on duty, he played a supporting role at Vicksburg in guarding against the advance of Joseph E. Johnston's relief force. After service in Kentucky and East Tennessee, he rejoined the Army of the Potomac. On the second day in the Wilderness he was felled by sunstroke while in command of a brigade. He later served at Petersburg and in the Appomattox Campaign, being brevetted for the former. Mustered out with his regiment on June 9, 1865, he returned to private life.

CARSON, Christopher Houston (1809-1868)

Better known as "Kit" Carson, Christopher H. Carson was oft troubled by the harsh treatment of the Indians that he was frequently ordered to carry out during the Civil War. Born in Kentucky, he had been raised mostly in Missouri until, at the age of 14, he jumped his apprenticeship as a saddler and launched his career as a mountain man. Traveling widely as a trapper, he came to know the Indians and at one time or another married into the Arapaho and Cheyenne nations. He was thrust into prominence as a guide to John C. Frémont's explorations in the 1840s. During the Mexican War he was the guide for Stephen W. Kearny's expedition to California and briefly served as an army lieutenant until his appointment was negated by the Senate. A rancher after that, he was an Indian agent at the outbreak of the Civil War, in which his assignments included: lieutenant colonel, 1st New Mexico (July 25, 1861); colonel, 1st New Mexico (September 20, 1861); colonel, 1st New Mexico Cavalry (May 31, 1862); and lieutenant colonel, 1st New Mexico Infantry and Cavalry Battalion (October 8, 1866). In early 1862 he took part in the battle of Valverde, which was important in driving the Confederates out of the Southwest. For this he was brevetted brigadier general in March 1865. The balance of his service was primarily against the Indians, where he tended to be much more humane than most of his superiors. He was highly successful in bringing in chiefs for talks and moving tribes to reservations, although they were sometimes met with treachery at the hands of other whites. Carson served against the Navajos, Mescalero Apaches, and Kiowas. His first regiment had been consolidated with the 2nd New Mexico and mounted shortly after the fight at Valverde, and in 1866 was reduced to a mixed unit of battalion size. The mountain man was thus reduced to a lieutenant colonelcy and was finally mustered out with this unit on November 23, 1867. He died the next year at Fort Lyon, Colorado. (Carter, Harvey Lewis, *Dear Old Kit: The Historical Christopher Carson*, and Kelly, Lawrence C., *Navajo Roundup: Selected Correspondence of Kit Carson's Expedition Against the Navajo, 1863-1865*)

CARSWELL, Reuben W. (1828-1886)

Worn out by campaigning in Virginia, Reuben W. Carswell returned to his native Georgia and fought in its defense as a militia general. His assignments included: lieutenant, Company C, 20th Georgia (June 14, 1861); captain, Company E, 48th Georgia (March 1862); lieutenant colonel, 48th Georgia (March 22, 1862); brigadier general, Georgia Militia (May 1864); and commanding 1st Brigade, 1st Division, Georgia Militia (May 1864-early 1865). After service on the Manassas line with his first company, Carswell became a field officer in a new regiment with which he saw action during the Seven Days. Next the unit fought at 2nd Bull Run and Antietam. At Chancellorsville he distinguished himself while in command of the regiment. Some time after this he left the unit and while in Georgia was made a general of militia. He commanded a brigade in the Atlanta Campaign. While opposing Sherman's March to the Sea, he resigned his commission in the 48th Georgia on November 12, 1864. He was also involved in the defense of Savannah.

CARTER, John Carpenter (1837-1864)

Serving through most of the battles of what was to become the Army of Tennessee, John C. Carter became one of six Confederate generals to be fatally struck during the suicidal attack at Franklin. The native of Georgia was a Memphis attorney when the war broke out; he soon enlisted in the Southern army where his assignments included: captain, Company B, 38th Tennessee (September 23, 1861); colonel, 38th Tennessee (May 1862); commanding Wright's (old) Brigade, Cheatham's Division, Hardee's Corps, Army of Tennessee (spring-September 1864); brigadier general, CSA (July 7, 1864); and commanding Maney's (old) Brigade, Brown's Division, Cheatham's Corps, Army of Tennessee (September-November 30, 1864). Leading his company at Shiloh, he seized the regimental colors and was later wounded. He returned in time to fight at Perryville and Murfreesboro and take part in the Tullahoma Campaign. At Chickamauga he led a field consolidation of the 38th Tennessee and Murray's 22nd Tennessee Battalion. Carter's regiment was detached at Charleston, Tennessee, during the fight at Chattanooga and was cut off from the army when Bragg's forces werre compelled to retire. Moving into East Tennessee they eventually rejoined the Army of Tennessee in time for the Atlanta Campaign during which Carter was named a brigadier general, having led a brigade throughout. After the fall of the city he was given charge of another brigade, which he led into middle Tennessee with Hood. In the assaults of November 30, 1864, at Franklin he fell mortally wounded. He died on December 10th, not far from the battlefield.

CARTER, Samuel Powhatan (1819-1891)

The loyalty of Tennessee naval officer Samuel P. Carter led the Washington authorities to detach him from the navy for special service ashore. He had entered the naval service in 1840 and served on both coasts and on the Great Lakes. At the request of Andrew Johnson and other loyal Tennesseeans, he was detached in July 1861 to try to develop Union support in East Tennessee. His Civil War-era assignments included: lieutenant, USN (since April 18, 1855); commanding 12th Brigade, Army of the Ohio (November-December 2, 1861); commanding 12th Brigade, 1st Division, Army of the Ohio (December 2-5, 1861); commanding 12th (Independent) Brigade, Army of the Ohio (December 5, 1861-March 26, 1862); commanding 24th Brigade, 7th Division, Army of the Ohio (March 26-November 10, 1862); brigadier general, USV (May 1, 1862); lieutenant commander, USN (July 16, 1862); commanding 1st Brigade, District of Central Kentucky, Department of the Ohio (March 18-June 24, 1863); commanding 1st Brigade, 1st Division, 23rd Corps, Army of the Ohio (August 6-September 10, 1863); commanding 2nd Division, District of Beaufort, Department of North Carolina (March 1-18, 1865); commanding Division, District of Beaufort, Department of North Carolina (March 18-April 2, 1865); commanding 3rd Division, 23rd Corps, Department of North Carolina (April 7-June 27, 1865); commander, USN (June 25, 1865); and commanding the corps (June 27-August 1, 1865). Participating in the Union victory at Mill Springs, he went on to serve in the vicinity of Cumberland Gap and in its capture. He continued to serve in Tennessee and Kentucky and led a cavalry raid into East Tennessee in December 1862, which was quite successful. With Burnside at Knoxville, he was transferred to the North Carolina coast, with the corps, in the war's final months. There, under Schofield, he directed a division cooperating with Sherman's forces. Brevetted major general for his war services, the man who had early in the war signed papers as "Lieutenant, U.S. Navy (on special duty)" was mustered out on January 15, 1866. Continuing in the navy until 1881, he was retired as a commodore and the next year was made a retired list rear admiral—making him the only man in American history to hold the ranks of brevet major general and rear admiral.

CARTER, Thomas Hill (1831-1908)

Educated at the Virginia Military Institute, Virginian Thomas H. Carter put his skills to good use as one of the senior artillerists in Lee's army. His assignments included: captain, King William Artillery (June 1, 1861); major, Artillery (to rank from December 12, 1862); commanding Artillery Brigade, D.H. Hill's-Rodes' Division, 2nd Corps, Army of Northern Virginia (early 1863-July 1863); lieutenant colonel, Artillery (March 2, 1863); commanding artillery battalion, 2nd Corps, Army of Northern Virginia (July1863-spring 1864); commanding artillery division, 2nd Corps, Army of Northern Virginia (spring 1864-September 2, 1864 and March-April 9, 1865); colonel, Artillery (February 27, 1864); chief of artillery, Valley District, Department of Northern Virginia (ca. September 2-late October 1864 and November 1864-January 1865); and commanding artillery battalion, Valley District, Department of Northern Virginia (late October-November 1864). Commanding his battery, he distinguished himself at Seven Pines and fought at the Seven Days, Antietam, and Fredericksburg. After being promoted, he commanded a battalion at Chancellorsville and Gettysburg. He directed a pair of artillery battalions through the Overland Campaign. After service on the Petersburg front, he was sent to join Early in the Valley and soon was serving as his artillery chief in the absence of General Long. He saw action at Cedar Creek, following which many of his guns were captured by Union cavalry. Returning east in the early part of 1865, he commanded a group of battalions on the Richmond front and finally surrendered at Appomattox. He was a doctor and farmer after the war. (Wise, Jennings. C., *The Long Arm of Lee*)

CARUTHERS, Robert Looney (1800-1882)

Due to the federal occupation of the state of Tennessee, Robert L. Caruthers was never able to take up his gubernatorial duties. A native Tennesseean, Caruthers had a distinguished antebellum career as lawyer, legislative clerk, judicial clerk, journalist, state's attorney, state legislator, educator, and congressman. At the outbreak of the Civil War, he had been serving on the Tennessee supreme court for nine years. Although a longtime secessionist, he attended the Washington peace convention. This having failed, he was appointed to represent Tennessee's 5th District in the Provisional Confederate Congress. Serving on the Committee on the Judiciary, he proved to be, when present, a supporter of the administration's program. He lost the race for the Senate of the First Regular Congress on the 32nd ballot in October 1861. For some reason he did not attend the sessions of the Provisional Congress in the first two months of 1862. In 1863 Caruthers was elected governor to succeed the also-exiled Isham G. Harris, who, however, continued to exercise the limited powers of an exiled governor when it was found impossible to inaugurate the new governor. Meanwhile, Andrew Johnson was serving as Union military governor in Nashville. Following the war, Caruthers became a law professor at Cumberland University.

CARY, Hetty (1836-1892)

To much of the Confederacy, Hetty Cary was the epitome of Southern womanhood, and it is perhaps appropriate that she suffered the fate of so many Southern women—widowhood. Born near Baltimore she belonged to an old Virginia family related to the Jeffersons and Randolphs. A firm supporter of secession she was eventually forced to either leave Baltimore or face imprisonment. After visiting the troops at Manassas Junction and a short stay in Charlottesville, she settled in Richmond with her sister, Jennie, and her cousin Constance. The trio immediately became part of the capital's social life, and Hetty was considered by many to be the most beautiful belle in the country. For the next three years she was involved in patriotic work and attracted the attention of many military figures. Finally, one of Lee's division commanders, General John Pegram, won her hand, and they were married on January 19, 1865, in a ceremony that was one of the highlights of a dismal winter. Joining her new husband's headquarters on the lines around Petersburg, she became very popular with his men. Three days after a triumphant review of the division, Pegram was killed in the battle of Hatcher's Run on February 5, 1865. No one had the heart to tell the widow, so his body was brought back to his quarters and she was brought down to see it. Exactly three weeks after the wedding the Pegrams were back at St. Paul's Church for the funeral. Returning to Baltimore after the war, Hetty Pegram was arrested, but General Grant ordered her release with an apology. She later taught and toured Europe and remarried in 1879.

CARY, Richard Milton (ca. 1824-1886)

When in the spring of 1862 the Confederate one-year regiments were reorganized, they were given the opportunity of electing new officers. This was very disruptive to the command structure and many commanders opposed it, including Richard M. Cary. A Richmond lawyer, he had been active in military affairs before the war and promptly entered the service when the war began. His assignments included: captain, 1st Virginia (early 1861); colonel, 30th Virginia (June 13, 1861); lieutenant, Artillery (June 4, 1862); captain, Artillery (March 26, 1863); and major, Artillery (September 10, 1863). After commanding his regiment in the Aquia District and the Department of North Carolina, he refused to stand for reelection on principle. He was elected over his protests but declined to serve. Thus a qualified regimental commander, who had penned an infantry drill manual, was lost to the service. Two months later, in June 1862, he accepted assignment as a lieutenant and was detailed to ordnance duty. Receiving two promotions, he continued in this duty for the remainder of the conflict. Settling in England after the war, he was in the tobacco and cotton business.

CASEY, Silas (1807-1882)

Perhaps career army officer Silas Casey's principal contribution to the Union war effort was the compilation of his *System of Infantry Tactics*—or more commonly *Casey's Tactics*—by which thousands of volunteer officers and men were trained. A Rhode Island-born West Pointer (1826), he had been posted to the infantry, was wounded at Chapultepec, and earned two brevets in Mexico. His Civil War assignments included: lieutenant colonel, 9th Infantry (since March 3, 1855); brigadier general, USV (August 31, 1861); colonel, 9th Infantry (October 9, 1861); commanding provisional brigade, Army of the Potomac (October-December 1861); commanding division, Army of the Potomac (December 1861-March 13, 1862); commanding 3rd Division, 4th Corps, Army of the Potomac (March 13-June 7, 1862); major general, USV (May 31, 1862); commanding 2nd Division, 4th Corps, Army of the Potomac (June 7-24, 1862); commanding provisional brigade, Military District of Washington, Department of the Potomac (August-October 1862); commanding division, Military District of Washington, Department of the Potomac (October 1862-February 2, 1863); and commanding division, 22nd Corps, Department of Washington (February 2-April 17, 1863). In 1862 the War Department adopted his manual for the training of volunteers. At Seven Pines he earned a brevet in what was his only major action of the war. He then commanded a brigade and a division in the Washington fortifications. From the spring of 1863 to the end of the war he headed a board which the examination of white officers for the command of black troops. During this time he wrote *Infantry Tactics for Colored Troops* and also served on the board that tried Fitz-John Porter for his role at 2nd Bull Run. Casey was brevetted a regular army major general at the end of the war and was mustered out of the volunteers on August 24, 1865. He retired from the army three years later.

CASHIER, Albert J. (1843-post 1914)

Among the 36, 312 names on the Vicksburg, Illinois Monument—the largest on the field—is that of Albert Cashier. In the Civil War record of this private soldier there appears nothing extraordinary. He enlisted in Company G, 95th Illinois, which was mustered into service on September 4, 1862. He was one of thousands who took part in the campaign that resulted in the fall of Vicksburg. He went to participate in the Red River Campaign and fought at Nashville. His final service came in the capture of Mobile. The regiment was mustered out on August 17, 1865, and Albert Cashier returned to private life. In 1899 he filed for a pension, requiring routine medical exams. Then in 1911 Albert Cashier was involved in an automobile accident and sent to the hospital, where it was discovered that Albert

Cashier was a woman. Her fellow veterans denied ever having suspected the fact. Her real name was Hodgers and she was born in Ireland.

CASTINE

See: *Brooks, Noah*

CATRON, John (ca. 1786-1865)

Supreme Court Associate Justice John Catron elected to remain on the bench when his adopted state, Tennessee, seceded. Born in Pennsylvania, he eventually settled in Tennessee. After serving in the War of 1812 he became a lawyer and businessman. In the 1820s and 1830s he sat on the state's highest court and then worked in political campaigns. He was rewarded by Andrew Jackson with one of two new seats on the Supreme Court, on the president's last day in office—March 3, 1837. Five days later he was confirmed by the Senate and began his 28 years of service. In the *Dred Scott* case he ruled for dismissal on the grounds that Scott was still a slave, despite his sojourn in free territory, and therefore not a citizen eligible to sue in the courts. Forced to leave Nashville early in the war, he died on May 30, 1865, before Reconstruction had brought before the Supreme Court many constitutional questions. (Fehrenbacher, Don E., *The Dred Scott Case: Its Significance in American Law and Politics*)

CATTERSON, Robert Francis (1835-1914)

On his way to becoming one of the last brigadier generals of the Civil War, Indiana native Robert F. Catterson held every rank, except major, from sergeant to brigadier. Giving up his brand new medical practice, he entered the Union army where his assignments included: first sergeant, 14th Indiana (June 7, 1861); second lieutenant, 14th Indiana (July 5, 1861); first lieutenant, 14th Indiana (March 15, 1862); captain, 14th Indiana (May 4, 1862); lieutenant colonel, 97th Indiana (October 18, 1862); colonel, 97th Indiana (November 25, 1862); commanding 2nd Brigade, 1st Division, 15th Corps, Army of the Tennessee (November 22, 1864-March 28, 1865 and April 4-July 26, 1865); and brigadier general, USV (May 31, 1865). His first unit served in western Virginia and fought at Kernstown, in the Shenandoah Valley Campaign of 1862, and at Antietam. Soon advancing to command of a new regiment he served at Memphis and from June 12, 1863, took part in the siege of Vicksburg. He then served in the Jackson Campaign and at Chattanooga before taking part in Sherman's operations against Atlanta. After that city's fall he went on the March to the Sea and participated in the Carolinas Campaign. During these two campaigns he was usually in command of the brigade. Mustered out on January 15, 1866, he was a failure in the cotton market, but then commanded the black Arkansas militia under Governor Powell Clayton against the Ku Klux Klan. After serving as Little Rock's mayor he was an unsuccessful farmer and farm equipment merchant before dying in the San Antonio veterans' hospital.

CAWTHORN, James (?-1861)

The battle of Wilson's Creek, although relatively small when compared to later engagements, was nonetheless devastating to the officer corps of the Missouri State Guard. Having joined up at the beginning of the conflict, Colonel James Cawthorn was commanding the 2nd (Cavalry) Brigade, 2nd Division during the early part of August 1861. At Wilson's Creek on the 10th he dismounted his troopers and held his position throughout the fight, mostly unsupported by infantry. His unit paid a price for this action—87 casualties, including their mortally wounded commander.

CEVER, Charles (?-?)

A veteran balloonist before the Civil War, Captain Charles Cever donated his skills to the Confederate cause. Working in Charleston, he accumulated silk frocks from the patriotic ladies of the city. Piecing them together, he constructed the second Confederate balloon. It was shipped, already inflated, to the Richmond area and placed on board the *Teaser*. Moving downriver on its first mission in the aerial service, the vessel ran aground and Cever's balloon was captured by the U.S.S. *Monitor* and U.S.S. *Maratanza*.

CHALMERS, James Ronald (1831-1898)

Following up his membership in the Mississippi secession convention, Virginia-born lawyer James R. Chalmers served as a brigadier general in both the Confederate infantry and cavalry. His assignments included: captain, Infantry (March 1861); colonel, 9th Mississippi (April 1861); brigadier general, CSA (February 13, 1862); commanding 2nd Brigade, 1st Corps, 2nd Grand Division, Army of the Mississippi (March 29-late June 1862); commanding 2nd Brigade, Reserve Corps, Army of the Mississippi (late June-July 2, 1862); commanding 2nd Brigade, Reserve Division, Army of the Mississippi (July 2-August 15, 1862); commanding 2nd Brigade, Withers' Division, Right Wing, Army of the Mississippi (August 15-November 20, 1862); commanding 2nd Brigade, Withers' Division, Polk's Corps, Army of Tennessee (November 20-December 31, 1862); commanding 5th Military District, Department of Mississippi and East Louisiana (April-summer 1863); commanding cavalry brigade, Department of Mississippi and East Louisiana (summer-October 18, 1863); commanding cavalry division, Department of Mississippi and East Louisiana (October 18-November 1863); commanding division, Lee's Cavalry Corps, Department of Mississippi and East Louisiana (November 1863-January 11, 1864); commanding division, Forrest's Cavalry Corps, Department of Mississippi and East Louisiana (January 11-28, 1864); and commanding division, Forrest's Cavalry Corps, Department of Alabama, Mississippi and East Louisiana (January 28, 1864-May 4, 1865). Initially stationed at Pensacola, he was promoted to brigadier general and was part of the Confederate buildup at Corinth, Mississippi, just before Shiloh. He led his brigade at that battle and during the Union drive on the Confederate base at Corinth. He was engaged against Philip H. Sheridan's cavalry at Booneville and then took part in Bragg's Kentucky Campaign. On the last day of the year he was severely wounded in the head at Murfreesboro in the fighting for the Round Forest. Upon his recovery he was assigned to district command in Mississippi. He led a cavalry brigade and then a division in the northern part of the state. Early in 1864 he joined Nathan Bedford Forrest's command and fought at Tupelo and faced Andrew J. Smith's August 1864 invasion of the state. He was also engaged on some of Forrest's raids. Cooperating with Hood's forces in middle Tennessee, he was present at Nashville, and he ended his Civil War career facing Wilson's raid through Alabama and Georgia. In the postwar years he served three terms in Congress and then resumed his legal practice.

CHAMBERLAIN, Joshua Lawrence (1828-1914)

A Bowdoin College professor, Joshua L. Chamberlain went to the Maine state capital to offer his services in 1862. Offered the colonelcy of a regiment, he declined, according to John J. Pullen in *The 20th Maine*, preferring to "start a little lower and learn the business first." He was made lieutenant colonel of the regiment on August 8. His later assignments were: colonel, 20th Maine (May 20, 1863); commanding 3rd Brigade, 1st Division, 5th Corps (August 26-November 19, 1863); 1st Brigade (June 6-18, 1864); brigadier general, USV (June 18, 1864); 1st Brigade (November 19, 1864-January 5, 1865); 1st Brigade (February 27-April 11, 1865); and brevetted major general, USV (March 29, 1865); 3rd Brigade (April 10-25, 1865). With the regiment Chamberlain took part in the battles of Antietam, Shepherdstown Ford, Fredericksburg (wounded), and Chancellorsville. At the battle of Gettysburg the regiment, now commanded by Chamberlain, held the extreme left flank on Little Round Top, a service for which he was later awarded the Congressional Medal of Honor. He also received a second wound. In November 1863 he was relieved from field service and sent to Washington suffering from malaria. He was given lighter duties. Resuming command of the regiment in May 1864, he led it in the battle of Cold Harbor. Assigned to brigade command in June, only to fall wounded 12 days later in the assault on Petersburg, he was promoted to brigadier general on the spot by General Grant, then carried to the rear, where a surgeon declared that he would certainly die from the wound. (The doctor was right. Fifty years later Chamberlain succumbed to its effects.) Rejoining the army in November, he was forced by his wound to return to Maine, but he came back again during the Petersburg siege during which he was wounded for the fourth time. He then took part in the Appomattox Campaign, about which he wrote *The Passing of the Armies*. He was given the honor of commanding the troops that formally accepted the surrender of the Confederate army. He later served as governor of Maine and president of Bowdoin. (Wallace, Willard M., *Soul of the Lion: A Biography of General Joshua L. Chamberlain*)

CHAMBERS, Alexander (1832-1888)

For some reason the U.S. Senate refused to confirm the nomination of Alexander Chambers to be a brigadier general of volunteers, and he reverted to his regular army rank of captain. A native New Yorker and West Pointer (1853), he had been posted to the infantry with which he had participated in the Third Seminole War. His Civil War-era assignments included: first lieutenant, 5th Infantry (since January 19, 1859); adjutant, 5th Infantry (June 9, 1857-August 7, 1861); captain, 18th Infantry (to rank from May 14, 1861); colonel, 16th Iowa (March 15, 1862); commanding 3rd Brigade, 6th Division, 17th Corps, Army of the Tennessee (June 6-July 30 and August 23-September 14, 1863); commanding the division (July 30-August 23 and September 3-14, 1863); and commanding 3rd Brigade, 1st Division, 17th Corps, Army of the Tennessee (October 10, 1863-April 20, 1864). Initially assigned to recruiting duty in Iowa, he was given command of a regiment of Iowa volunteers, which he led at Shiloh, where he was twice wounded and earned a brevet in the regular army. He then took part in the advance and seizure of Corinth. Again severely wounded at Iuka, he earned another brevet as he also did later, for his participation in the operations against Vicksburg. He then took part in Sherman's campaign against Jackson, Mississippi. During the Meridian Campaign, he earned a brevet for his brigade leadership at Champion Hills and Meridian. By this time he had been appointed a brigadier but the Senate's action cost him his star. He then rejoined his regular army regiment and finished the war in the vicinity of Chattanooga. Serving on the frontier, he died as colonel, 17th Infantry.

CHAMBERS, Henry Cousins (1823-1871)

Coming from the Southern plantation society and its acceptance of violence, Henry C. Chambers used a novel method to get himself elected to the First Regular Congress—he killed his opponent. The Alabama-born Chambers, after graduating from Princeton College, settled in Mississippi, enjoying the life of a substantial planter. At the outbreak of the war he was serving in the state legislature. In October 1861 he ran for the Confederate House from Mississippi's 4th District, along the Mississippi River. The race became heated, and Chambers provoked a duel with his opponent, William A. Lake. With rifles at 50 paces, Lake died. Chambers was unopposed in 1863. Taking his seat in February 1862, Chambers served on the Committees on Commerce; Enrolled Bills; Flag and Seal; and Military Affairs. He favored impressment as a means of supplying the army and opposed the idea of local defense, preferring stronger armies in the field. Thus he exhibited a strong centralist tendency. He did, however, oppose the arming of the slaves. He returned to farming after the war.

CHAMBLISS, John Randolph, Sr. (1809-1875)

Although a late convert to secession, in April 1861, John R. Chambliss proved to be an active supporter of the war for independence in his one term in the Confederate Congress. A Virginia native, Chambliss held numerous nonelective public offices and as a delegate to the Virginia constitutional conventions was at first a Unionist. Elected in November 1861 from southeastern Virginia's 2nd Ddistrict, he took his seat in the First Confederate Congress in February 1862. Here he served on the Committee on Naval Affairs. Initially opposed to the draft, he later worked to tighten up the list of exemptions. He favored giving the War Department a freer hand in determining army organization and was willing to allow the central government extensive control over the country's economy. He did, however, resist the extension of the suspension of the writ of habeas corpus. In 1863 he dropped out of the race for reelection. Impoverished after the war, he worked to improve the county's police and economic base. His son was Brigadier General John R. Chambliss, Jr.

CHAMBLISS, John Randolph, Jr. (1833-1864)

The son of Confederate congressman John R. Chambliss, Sr., West Pointer (1853) John R. Chambliss, Jr., remained in the mounted rifles for less than a year before resigning. Later, he left his Virginia plantation to join the Confederacy. He had long been active in the militia and as such was an aide to the governor. When he transferred to Confederate service his assignments included: colonel, 41st Virginia (July 1861); colonel, 13th Virginia Cavalry (July 1862); commanding W.H.F. Lee's Brigade, Cavalry Division, Army of Northern Virginia (June 9-September 9, 1863); commanding W.H.F. Lee's Brigade, F. Lee's Division, Cavalry Corps, same army (September 9, 1863-ca. April 23, 1864); brigadier general, CSA (December 19, 1863); and commanding brigade, W.H.F. Lee's Division, Cavalry Corps, same army (ca. April 23-August 16, 1864). After service in the infantry, near Norfolk and on the Peninsula, Chambliss was transferred to the head of a newly formed cavalry regiment. Initially this unit served along the Rappahannock River with other troops, all under his command. Becoming a part of the Army of Northern Virginia, it fought at Fredericksburg and opposed Stoneman's raid during the Chancellorsville Campaign. He succeeded the wounded "Rooney" Lee in brigade command at Brandy Station and led the unit at Aldie, Middleburg, Gettysburg, and in the Bristoe Campaign. Promoted to brigadier on a permanent basis and with the brigade shifted to "Rooney" Lee's newly created division, he fought through the Overland Campaign and was killed in fighting at Deep Bottom near Richmond on August 16, 1864. (Freeman, Douglas S., *Lee's Lieutenant*)

CHAMPLIN, Stephen Gardner (1827-1864)

By the time Stephen G. Champlin received his brigadier's star he was too incapacitated by wounds to serve in the field. A lawyer and judge in Michigan—he was born in New York—he entered the Union army at the beginning of the Civil War. His assignments included: major, 3rd Michigan (June 10, 1861); colonel, 3rd Michigan (October 22, 1861); and brigadier general, USV (November 29, 1862). In the war's first summer he attracted the attention of General McClellan for his performance in a skirmish at Bailey's Crossroads near Washington. At Seven Pines he was severely wounded but returned to duty before he had fully recovered. During the battle of 2nd Bull Run his wound broke out anew and he had to leave the field. Promoted to brigadier, he was assigned to duty recruiting volunteers at his home in Grand Rapids. On January 24, 1864, he died from the effects of his Seven Pines wound.

CHANAL, Francois-Victor-Adolphe de (?-?)

The interest of the Civil War to foreign military establishments is manifested, in the case of the French, by the 1864 visit of a team of observers headed by F.V.A. de Chanal. A lieutenant colonel in the French army, his commission was dispatched to the United States after a bit of difficulty over whether or not his team would be permitted to visit the Army of the Potomac in the field. With permission finally granted they joined the army around Petersburg in June. Frequent letters were sent to the war ministry describing military activities from various fronts, but mostly from the accounts of participants rather than by personal observation. An exception was a first person account of the battle of the Crater. He also studied the characters of the Union leaders and surprisingly enough was quite impressed with the political General Benjamin Butler who was despised by America's professional military men. After the war he wrote a short biography of General Meade. In August the commission left the army and visited war industries from New England to Missouri. At the year's close the commission returned home. In 1872 Chanal published a study of the war, *L'Armée américaine pendant la guerre de la Sécession.*

CHANDLER, Zachariah (1813-1879)

With the Union military situation stagnating in the summer of 1864 and the Republicans apparently about to enter the election divided, it appeared that Lincoln would not be reelected. But Michigan Senator Zachariah Chandler managed to strike a deal that reunited the party. A former Detroit mayor and organizer of the Republican Party, Chandler had entered the Senate in 1857. A vocal opponent of the pro-slavery Lecompton Constitution for Kansas, he believed that bloodshed might be good for the nation. Although a Radical Republican and member of the Committee on the Conduct of the War, he managed to stay on friendly terms with the more conservative Lincoln. In the summer of 1864 some radical elements of the party nominated a third ticket composed of former generals, John C. Frémont and John Cochrane, and it appeared that Lincoln would be defeated. Through the months of August and September Chandler shuttled between Frémont, Lincoln, and his fellow radicals trying to reunite the party. His original idea of both candidates standing aside having failed, he developed the formula whereby the challenger would withdraw and Lincoln was to dismiss his unpopular conservative postmaster general, Montgomery Blair. Although Frémont dropped out unilaterally, Chandler was able to hold the president to the deal. It assured a Republican victory. Continuing in the Senate, he favored harsh treatment of Jefferson Davis and later became Grant's secretary of the interior. Reelected to the Senate, he died shortly thereafter.

CHANNING, William Ellery (1780-1842)

A Massachusetts Unitarian clergyman, William E. Channing was one of the earlier opponents of slavery but was equally horrified by the thought of a civil war, which he did not live to see. A leader of the Unitarian movement he believed in reform but felt that the best way to rid mankind of its vices was to increase the quality of its life. Thus he did not believe in driving people into temperance. On the issue of slavery he appealed to the conscience of the South but fully realized that war between the states could erupt. He worked to make the external revolution peaceful. His writing on the institution included: *Slavery, The Abolitionist, Open Letter to Henry Clay,* and *Duty of the Free States*. On the issue of war and peace he condemned the War of 1812 and was a prime mover in the Massachusetts Peace Society. He recognized a limited right of self-defense for nations, as well as for individuals.

CHAPIN, Edward Payson (1831-1863)

Four months after his death in battle at Port Hudson, Edward P. Chapin was posthumously awarded a brigadier's star. A Buffalo lawyer, he was active in the militia of his native New York. His assignments included: captain, 44th New York (September 6, 1861); major, 44th New York (January 2, 1862); lieutenant colonel, 44th New York (July 4, 1862); colonel, 116th New York (September 5, 1862); commanding 1st Brigade, 1st Division, 19th Corps, Department of the Gulf (February 9-May 27, 1863); and brigadier general, USV (to rank from May 27, 1863). As a major, he fought at Yorktown and was severely wounded in the Seven Days. Resigning on the same day as his lieutenant colonelcy came through, he soon raised a new regiment and became its commander. With this command, he moved via Baltimore to the Department of the Gulf where he took part in the operations against Port Hudson, Louisiana. During the siege he was in brigade command, and he fell in the unsuccessful May 27 assault. His general's commission was made effective from that date.

CHAPLIN, Daniel (?-1864)

A Maine officer, Daniel Chaplin had the dubious honor of commanding the unit that set two battle-loss records, he himself contributing to them. He started his military career as a captain in the 2nd Maine on May 28, 1861. His subsequent assignments included: major, 2nd Maine (September 13, 1861); colonel, 18th Maine later converted to 1st Maine Heavy Artillery (August 21, 1862); and commanding 3rd Brigade (June 18-27, 1864) and 2nd Brigade (July 22-28, 1864), 3rd Division, 2nd Corps, Army of the Potomac. During his service with the 2nd Maine, it was engaged at 1st Bull Run and in the Peninsula Campaign. Made colonel of a new regiment in the summer of 1862, Chaplin was assigned to the Washington defenses and the unit was converted into a heavy artillery regiment. As such it had 12 instead of 10 companies, each of which was much larger than in the infantry. Sent to join the Army of the Potomac, following Grant's tremendous losses in the Wilderness, Chaplin led his large, green regiment, as infantry, in an assault at Spotsylvania where it lost 481 men. After further fighting at Cold Harbor, the 1st took part in the assault on Petersburg on June 18, 1864; out of some 900 engaged, 632 were lost, 210 of whom were killed or mortally wounded; a Union record for losses in a single battle. During this action Chaplin took command of the brigade as General Mott took the division and General Birney the corps after General Hancock's old wound broke out again. Commanding the regiment, Chaplin was mortally wounded and died three days later at Deep Bottom, on August 17, 1864. For this battle he was brevetted brigadier general. The regiment went on to lose, in less than a year of fighting, 423 killed and mortally wounded and 860 wounded out of a total enrollment of 2,202. This was the heaviest numerical loss of any regiment during the war. (Shaw, Horace E., *The First Maine Heavy Artillery, 1862-1865*)

CHAPMAN, Conrad Wise (1842-1910)

Although Conrad Chapman had left the Old Dominion when only six years old, he returned from his family's home in Rome to join the Virginia forces and become the Confederate artist of the Charleston defenses. Unable to get to Virginia from New York, Chapman ended up as a private in Company D, 3rd Kentucky, enlisting on September 30, 1861. He soon resumed his painting and his comrades began calling the accented eccentric "Old Rome." On the second day at Shiloh, Chapman was severely wounded in the head and upon his recovery joined Company A, 46th Virginia, by the request of General Henry A. Wise and the urging of Wise's close friend, Conrad's father, John G. Chapman. Conrad Chapman served in Virginia from September 1862 until the next year when Wise's Brigade was transferred to the Charleston defenses. Wise suggested that Chapman, who had become a professional artist, under his artist father's tutorship, be detailed to depict Charleston fortifications. Chapman began a comprehensive study, often under enemy fire, until March 1864, when he returned to Italy on furlough to visit his ill mother. Failing to rejoin his command before the collapse of the Confederacy, and having landed in Texas, Chapman joined those ex-Confederates who went to Mexico to join Maximilian. After the war he completed his sketches and continued to work, often in poverty, in Rome, Paris, London, New York, and Mexico before settling in Virginia, where he continued to work until his death.

CHAPMAN, George Henry (1832-1882)

A former midshipman in the U.S. Navy, George H. Chapman resigned as assistant clerk in the U.S. House of Representatives to enter the Union army in the fall of 1861. The Massachusetts-born, Indiana lawyer had served from 1847 to 1851 in the navy, including service during the Mexican War, and edited the *Indiana Republican* before entering the legal profession. His military assignments included: major, 3rd Indiana Cavalry (November 2, 1861); lieutenant colonel, 3rd Indiana Cavalry (October 25, 1862); colonel, 3rd Indiana Cavalry (March 12, 1863); commanding 1st Brigade, 1st Division, Cavalry Corps, Army of the Potomac (September 2-November 12, 1863 and December 21, 1863-March 24, 1865); commanding 2nd

Brigade, 3rd Division, Cavalry Corps, Army of the Potomac (April 20-August 6, 1864); brigadier general, USV (July 21, 1864); commanding 2nd Brigade, 3rd Division, Cavalry Corps, Army of the Shenandoah (August 6-September 19 and November 1-10, 1864); commanding 1st Brigade, 3rd Division, Cavalry Corps, Army of the Shenandoah (November 10, 1864-January 5, 1865 and January 30-February 25, 1865); commanding the division (January 5-30, 1865); also commanding 2nd Cavalry Division, Department of West Virginia (January 13-February 1865); serving with the Army of the Shenandoah); and commanding Cavalry Brigade, Army of the Shenandoah (March-ca. August 1865). As a field-grade officer, he fought at 2nd Bull Run, Antietam and Fredericksburg. He commanded the regiment during Stoneman's raid in the Chancellorsville Campaign and at Brandy Station and Upperville. He was heavily engaged as part of Buford's division in the opening stages of the fighting at Gettysburg. More action came his way at Falling Waters and during the Bristoe and Mine Run campaigns that fall. A brigade commander during the Overland Campaign, he was also involved in the early stages of the Petersburg siege. Promoted to brigadier, he went with Sheridan to the Shenandoah and was wounded at 3rd Winchester. Returning to duty with a brevet as a major general for that action, he was at times in command of two cavalry divisions. When Sheridan returned with two cavalry divisions to the Army of the Potomac, Chapman was left in charge of the one remaining cavalry brigade in the Valley. Before his January 7, 1866, resignation, he served on a number of boards. Returning to Indiana, he was a judge, state legislator, and involved in railroads.

CHAPMAN, William (?-1887)

Drunkenness on the field of battle may have had something to do with the relief from field command of William Chapman and his 1863 retirement from the regular army. The native Marylander and West Pointer (1831) had been posted to the infantry, with which he served in the Mexican War. South of the border he won two brevets and was wounded at Churubusco. His Civil War-era assignments included: captain, 5th Infantry (since June 8, 1845); major, 2nd Infantry (February 25, 1861); lieutenant colonel, 3rd Infantry (February 20, 1862); and commanding 2nd Brigade, 2nd Division, 5th Corps, Army of the Potomac (May 18-June 27 and June 29-September 1862). His regiment was at the siege of Yorktown and he was in charge of a brigade of regulars during the Seven Days. However, during that series of battles, he was seen to be drunk at Gaines' Mill and Malvern Hill. In the former case he was forced to relinquish the command for two days. He apparently redeemed himself at 2nd Bull Run where he won the brevet of colonel. But he disappeared from command sometime prior to the battle of Antietam and was retired on August 26, 1863. Nonetheless, the next year he was performing draft duty in Wisconsin.

CHAPMAN, William Henry (1840-1929)

As second-in-command to Confederate partisan leader John S. Mosby, William Henry Chapman was the man who arranged the meeting of that leader with Union General Hancock, which led to the disbandment—but not the surrender—of the partisans at the war's close. A native of Virginia, he lived in Fauquier County, which would become part of "Mosby's Confederacy." His Confederate assignments included: lieutenant, Monroe "Dixie" (Va.) Artillery (June 21, 1861); captain, Monroe "Dixie" (Va.) Artillery (December 8, 1861); captain, Company C, 43rd Virginia Cavalry Battalion (December 7, 1863); and lieutenant colonel, Mosby's (Va.) Cavalry Regiment (December 7, 1864). As an artillery battery commander, he fought at the Seven Days, 2nd Bull Run, and Antietam before his command was consolidated with other units in October 1862. Made a supernumerary by this action, he served as a recruiting officer until given charge of a company in Mosby's command. Operating behind Union lines, it was highly disruptive of Union communications. When the battalion was increased to a regiment, Chapman became its lieutenant colonel. He met with Hancock after Lee's surrender to arrange the Mosby meeting; Chapman himself was paroled at Winchester on April 22, 1865. After the war he worked for the revenue service in various cities. (Jones, Virgil Carrington, *Gray Ghosts and Rebel Raiders*)

CHARTRES, Robert d'Orleans, Duc de (?-?)

Along with his brother, the Comte de Paris, the Duc de Chartres accompanied his uncle, the Prince de Joinville, in a visit to the United States in 1861-62 to observe the Civil War. The duke refused any high position in the Union army and his assignments included: captain and additional aide-de-camp (September 24, 1861); and additional aide-de-camp, Army of the Potomac (September 24, 1861-July 15, 1862). He served on McClellan's staff during the creation of the Army of the Potomac and after many months of inaction around Washington went with the army to the Peninsula where he witnessed fighting at Yorktown, Williamsburg, Seven Pines, and the Seven Days. He resigned his commission on July 15, 1862, and left the country.

CHASE, John F. (?-?)

Twenty-three years after the event, Private John F. Chase of the 5th Maine Battery received his Congressional Medal of Honor for his devotion to duty at Chancellorsville. His artillery unit had already fought at Cedar Mountain, 2nd Bull Run, and Fredericksburg when it was called upon to go into battery in the face of Confederate attacks on May 3, 1863. As the company served in this exposed position, the men fell rapidly but somehow he remained unscathed despite his holding the dangerous No. 1 position. When the rest of his gun's crew had fallen he moved to the next piece and finally to a third that he succeeded in firing several times with only one comrade. Then that piece was disabled by an enemy shot and had to be removed with some aid from rescuing infantry. With this accomplished Chase and his companion returned to the position to rescue the wounded Lieutenant Edmund Kirby of the regular artillery who had been sent to direct the removal of guns after the fall of all the battery officers. The mission a success, Kirby promised that the pair would get the medal. True to his word he made the recommendation in a report filed before he died of his wound. Chase went on to the battle of Gettysburg where he was reported killed but was in reality severely wounded, losing an arm and an eye and receiving 48 additional wounds. Not realizing that Kirby had filed the report, he never requested the medal, thus accounting for its delay. (Mitchell, Joseph B., *The Badge of Gallantry*)

CHASE, Kate

See: *Sprague, Kate Chase*

CHASE, Salmon Portland (1808-1873)

His presidential ambitions went unfulfilled, but Salmon P. Chase provided the Union with important services as secretary of the treasury and chief justice of the Supreme Court during the Civil War years. Born in New Hampshire and raised in Ohio, he became an extreme anti-slavery politician. He took his religious fervor for abolition into his professional life, defending escaped slaves in the courts. He was nicknamed the "attorney general for runaway slaves." His prominence in the legal profession furthered his political activities, and he was one of the shining lights of the Liberty, and later the Free-Soil, parties. The latter party managed to obtain his appointment to the U.S. Senate in 1849. At the end of his term, he served two two-year terms as governor and was a contender for the Republican presidential nomination in 1860 but was considered too extreme for the young party. Chase was always bitter that the nomination had gone to the more conservative Lincoln. In 1861 he again took a seat in the Senate but resigned on March 6th, two days after he was named secretary of the treasury by his old rival. He almost immediately came into conflict with Secretary of State William H. Seward, and both soon submitted their resignations rather than serve with each other. Both resignations were rejected by Linicoln, but this was only the first of four resignation threats by Chase. During the course of the Civil War he did an exemplary job in financing the military effort and was a leader in the movement to make the greenback legal tender for the payment of all debts. He chafed under the slow movement toward freeing the slaves and felt that even the Emancipation Proclamation was too mild as well as being too late. He became involved with the anti-Lincoln faction and was the darling of the Radical Republicans in Congress, while Lincoln twice more rejected his resignations. In the so-called "Pomeroy Circular"—named for Senator Samuel C. Pomeroy of Kansas—which was leaked to the

Chief Justice Salmon P. Chase and his Supreme Court. Left to right: Justices Stephen J. Field, Samuel F. Miller, Nathan Clifford, Samuel Nelson, Salmon P. Chase, Robert C. Grier, Noah H. Swayne, and David Davis. (NA)

press, Chase was advanced as an alternative to Lincoln for the 1864 nomination, but Chase was apparently not directly involved. His fourth resignation, over a minor appointment, was accepted, somewhat to his surprise, on June 30, 1864. With the death of Roger B. Taney, Lincoln managed to move a rival aside by naming Chase to the chief justiceship on December 6, 1864. Lincoln also gained an ally in the court in support of the more controversial moves of the administration. Chase was confirmed the same day by a voice vote and proved to be a strong supporter of the war effort and of Radical Reconstruction. He supported the suspension of the writ of *habeas corpus* and dissented in the *Test Oath Cases* in 1867. He antagonized the Radicals by trying to maintain his constitutional prerogatives in the impeachment trial of Andrew Johnson, and his impartiality as presiding officer caused them to break with him. Becoming a Democrat, he reversed himself in 1870 on the matter of paper money being legal tender. Although mentioned from time to time for the presidency during his tenure, he never achieved his goal. (Donald, David, ed., *Inside Lincoln's Cabinet: The Civil War Diaries of Salmon P. Chase*)

CHEATHAM, Benjamin Franklin (1820-1886)

Serving throughout the Civil War in what would become the Confederate Army of Tennessee, Tennesseean Benjamin F. Cheatham proved himself to be a highly capable commander at brigade through corps level. A farmer, he had served as a captain in the 1st Tennessee and as the colonel of the 3rd Tennessee during the Mexican War. Active in the state militia during the interwar years, he was one of the state's senior officers during the period before it merged its forces into the Confederate army. His Civil War assignments included: major general, Tennessee Militia (prewar); brigadier general, Provisional Army of Tennessee (May 9, 1861); brigadier general, CSA (July 9, 1861); commanding 1st Brigade, 1st Geographical Division, Department #2 (September 7-October 24, 1861); commanding 2nd Division, 1st Geographical Division, Department #2 (October 24, 1861-March 9, 1862); major general, CSA (March 10, 1862); commanding 2nd Division, 1st Corps, Army of the Mississippi (March 29-July 2, 1862); commanding 1st Division, Army of the Mississippi (July 2-August 15, 1862); commanding division, Right Wing, Army of the Mississippi (August 15-November 20, 1862); commanding division, Polk's-Hardee's Corps, Army of Tennessee (November 20, 1862-October 23, 1863, January-July, and September-October 1864); commanding the corps (October 23-November 1863 and October 1864-April 9, 1865); and commanding division, Hardee's (new) Corps, Army of Tennessee (April 9-26, 1865). He led a division at Belmont and Shiloh, where he was wounded, and during the defense of Corinth, Mississippi. Having been promoted to major general before Shiloh, he fought as a division commander temporarily in charge of the wing at Perryville and later at Murfreesboro. After participating in the Tullahoma Campaign he fought in the Confederate victory at Chickamauga. Absent at Chattanooga—the one major action of the army that he missed—he returned for the Atlanta Campaign. When William J. Hardee left the army due to conflicts with Braxton Bragg, Cheatham took over the corps for the invasion of middle Tennessee. Just before the fight at Franklin the Confederates lost an opportunity to destroy a large portion of John M. Schofield's Union forces at Spring Hill. Instead of attacking, the enemy was allowed to slip by unmolested. Recriminations followed as Bragg focused on Cheatham, who retaliated in kind. Most historians believe that the facts are on Cheatham's side. In any event Cheatham went on to fight at Nashville and shortly thereafter Bragg asked to be relieved. Cheatham then went on to the Carolinas where in the April 9, 1865, reorganization and consolidation, he was reduced to command of a division. This he led until the surrender near Durham Station, North Carolina. He then returned to his farm and briefly entered politics as an unsuccessful congressionial candidate. He was later a prison official and postmaster.

CHESNUT, James, Jr. (1815-1885)

Although less well-known than his wife and her diary, James Chesnut, Jr., held several important posts in the Confederacy. A lawyer and former state legislator, he resigned a seat in the U.S. Congress on November 10, 1860, more than a month before the secession of his native South Carolina, to help move the state in that direction. At the secession convention he was one of the authors of the ordinance itself. Named to the Provisional Confederate Congress, he sat on the Committees on Naval Affairs and Territories. A product of the plantation society to which his father belonged, he advocated the legalization of the internationally prohibited African slave trade. During the recess between the first and second sessions he served, as an aide-de-camp to Beauregard, at the bombardment of Fort Sumter and later at 1st Bull Run. As a colonel, he served on the president's staff. The next year, as a member of his state's executive council, he was charged with the organization of the militia, but resigned this post to rejoin the chief executive. His later military assignments included: brigadier general, CSA (April 23, 1864); commanding brigade of reserves and militia, Department of South Carolina, Georgia and Florida (December 1864-January 1865); and commanding same brigade, McLaws' Division, same department (early January 1865). Sent to organize the reserve forces in his native state, he took a brigade to Georgia to participate in the Savannah Campaign but soon returned to his administrative duties. Following the South's collapse he was active in ending carpetbag rule.

CHESNUT, Mary Boykin (1823-1886)

Deservedly so, Mary Boykin Chesnut is the best known of Civil War diarists. Born into the South Carolina plantation aristocracy, as Mary Boykin Miller, she was married at 17 to a prominent lawyer and plantation owner, James Chesnut, Jr. Her husband's position in the Confederate government, as congressman, general and aide to Jefferson Davis, brought Mary into the inner social circles of the Confederacy, and she was active in politics. On February 15, 1861, she began her famous diary and continued it throughout the war. Her high connections in both the civilian and military sectors and her gossipy nature make for informative and interesting reading. She never got over the defeat of the South, and the couple lost much of their fortune in the war. She lived on for another two decades, trying to rebuild a part of their lives in the style of the antebellum period and revising her war diary. (Woodward, C. Van, *Mary Chesnut's Civil War*)

CHETLAIN, Augustus Louis (1824-1914)

Traveling in Europe on the profits from his former Galena, Illinois, businesses—Augustus L. Chetlain returned to the United States for the 1860 election campaign and then entered the Union army. The St. Louis-born businessman was recommended by Ulysses S. Grant for the captaincy of a local company before the future commander-in-chief had his own assignment. Chetlain's assignments included: captain, 12th Illinois (May 2, 1861); lieutenant colonel, 12th Illinois (May 3, 1861); colonel, 12th Illinois (April 27, 1862); brigadier general, USV (December 18, 1863); and commanding District of Memphis, District of West Tennessee, Department of the Tennessee (January 26, 1865). He was present at Fort Henry and commanded the regiment at Fort Donelson and Shiloh. He fought at the battle of Corinth and participated in Grant's unsuccessful early effort to get at Vicksburg through the heart of Mississippi. Promoted to brigadier general, he was given the assignment of raising colored troops in Kentucky and Tennessee. He briefly commanded at Memphis near the end of the war and was brevetted major general for war service after its close, then mustered out on January 15, 1866. After the war he was a tax official in Utah and a diplomat in Belgium. Returning to the United States, he went into banking and finance. He was active in charitable and veterans' affairs and wrote his *Recollections of Seventy Years*.

CHEVES, Langdon (1814-1863)

An engineering officer, Captain Langdon Cheves overcame the shortages of virtually everything in the Confederacy and constructed the first Southern balloon. Born and raised in Philadelphia, he went to college in South Carolina and for a time at the U.S. Military Academy. A lawyer, he married into the Southern plantation society. Becoming active in politics as a Democrat, he attended the secession convention of his adopted state. As an aide to General Thomas F. Drayton at Port Royal he took part in the defense of Forts Walker and Beauregard. For the next year and a half he worked on the fortifications on the coast, principally at Charleston and Savannah. While in the latter city he built a patchwork silk balloon that was sent to Virginia to observe the enemy's movements. On July 10, 1863, he was killed by a shell fragment from one of the monitors firing on Morris Island in Charleston Harbor.

CHEW, Robert Stanard (1828-1886)

A Fredericksburg physician turned field officer in Pickett's Division, Robert S. Chew may have survived the Civil War only because he was lucky enough to have served in the one brigade of the division that was not present at Gettysburg. His assignments included: captain, Company B, 30th Virginia (April 22, 1861); lieutenant colonel, 30th Virginia (April 19, 1862); colonel, 30th Virginia (November 5, 1864); and commanding Corse's Brigade, Pickett's Division, 1st Corps, Army of Northern Virginia (briefly in 1864). He served with his regiment in the Aquia District and the Department of North Carolina and during the Seven Days Battles. At Antietam he was in command of the regiment and was wounded. After service at Fredericksburg, the unit served in southeastern Virginia and was guarding Hanover Junction during the Gettysburg Campaign. Thus Chew missed the disastrous charge in which most of the division's field grade officers were cut down. He next served in western Virginia and back in the Department of North Carolina while most of the corps was off in Georgia and Tennessee with Longstreet. He took part in the initial defense of Petersburg before joining Lee at the North Anna and fighting at Cold Harbor. Returning to Petersburg, he took part in the siege of the town and part of the time was in command of the brigade. He surrendered with his regiment at Appomattox.

CHEW, Roger Preston (1843-1921)

Virginian Roger P. Chew raised and commanded the first Confederate horse artillery battery. After receiving some military education at the Virginia Military Institute just prior to the outbreak of the war, he held the following positions: captain, Ashby (Va.) Horse Artillery (September 1861); major, Artillery (February 27, 1864); executive officer Horse Artillery Battalion, Cavalry Corps, Army of Northern Virginia (March 19-April 29, 1864); commanding Horse Artillery, Cavalry Corps, Army of Northern Virginia (April 29, 1864-April 9, 1865); and lieutenant colonel, Artillery (February 18, 1865). His unit was raised with the intention that it should serve with Turner Ashby's cavalry in the Shenandoah Valley. Thus Chew saw action at Kernstown and in the Shenandoah Valley Campaign before the death of his commander. Joining Lee's army in 1862, he took part in the actions at 2nd Bull Run, Antietam, Fredericksburg, Chancellorsville, Gettysburg, and in the Bristoe and Mine Run campaigns. Promoted to chief of the cavalry's guns, he served through the Wilderness, Petersburg, and Appomattox campaigns before the surrender of the latter. In time Jeb Stuart, shortly before his death, came to the conclusion that Chew was a fitting successor to "The Gallant Pelham." After the war Chew returned to the Valley and served three terms in the state legislature. (Wise, Jennings C., *The Long Arm of Lee*)

CHILD, Lydia Maria Francis (1802-1880)

When Lydia Child began to write on abolitionist themes it cost her dearly in the declining sales of her other works and in the death of her bi-monthly magazine *Juvenile Miscellany*. Married to Boston lawyer David L. Child in 1828, she and her husband soon joined the abolitionist cause. It was her 1833 publication of *An Appeal in Favor of That Class of Americans Called Africans* that gave her prominence, not all in her favor. She became a regular attendee of anti-slavery meetings and even got mixed up in some of the resultant melees. Her request to tend to John Brown after his raid resulted in a series of letters with Governor Wise of Virginia and a Mrs. Mason. This correspondence was published in 1860 as *Correspondence Between Lydia Maria Child and Gov. Wise and Mrs. Mason of Virginia* and sold 300,000 copies. Dissatisfied with the relatively conservative prosecution of the war early on, she grew to respect Lincoln more and more as he himself became more vigorous in the fight against slavery. Her postwar activities were rather limited.

CHILTON, Robert Hall (1815-1879)

Frustrated in his ambitions for promotion, Virginia native Robert H. Chilton left Lee's staff and took a desk post in Richmond. The West Pointer (1837) had been posted to the dragoons with a brief stint in the quartermaster's branch. He saw frontier service and won a brevet in the Mexican War. In 1854 he transferred to the pay department and resigned his commission as a major on April 29, 1861. His Confederate assignments included: lieutenant colonel and assistant adjutant general, CSA (spring 1861); chief of staff, Army of Northern Virginia (June 4, 1862-April 1, 1864); and brigadier general, CSA (October 20, 1862). Joining Lee's staff days after Lee took over command of the Army of Northern Virginia, Chilton soon became its head. As such he served during the Seven Days and at 2nd Bull Run, Antietam, Fredericksburg, Chancellorsville, Gettysburg, and during the Bristoe and Mine Run campaigns. Named a brigadier general in the fall of 1862, he suffered a loss of rank when the Senate refused to confirm the appointment on April 11, 1863. Reverting to the rank of lieutenant colonel, he continued to serve for another year, but on April 1, 1864, his request for relief from field duty was granted and he spent the balance of the war in Richmond as an inspector. Settling in Georgia after Appomattox, he ran a manufacturing firm.

CHILTON, William Paris (1810-1871)

Serving through all three of the Confederate congresses, Alabama's 6th District representative, William P. Chilton, held an unusually high number of committee chairmanships and was considered one of the more hard working members of the legislative branch. Born in Kentucky, Chilton studied law in Tennessee and subsequently settled in Alabama. Active in Whig politics, he served in the state legislature and was unsuccessful in a bid for a seat in the U.S. House of Representatives. Appointed to the state's supreme court in 1847, he was its chief justice for the last four years of his tenure. He retired to private practice in 1856. At the beginning of the Civil War he was again in public office, having been elected to the state legislature's upper house in 1859. A convert to secessionism, he was named to the Provisional Congress and he remained in the legislature until the end of the Confederacy. Throughout the war he was chairman of the Committee on Post Offices and Post Roads. In the First Regular Congress he also chaired the Committee on the Quartermaster's and Commissary Departments and in the Second Congress the Committee on the Flag and Seal. Being very industrious, he was rewarded with additional committee appointments including the committees on: Buildings (Provisional Congress); Printing (Provisional Congress); Patents (Provisional Congress); the Judiciary (Second Congress); and Rules and Officers (Second Congress). His oratory attracted visitors to the galleries. A strong supporter of the war effort, he was accused of wanting to raise the black flag—fighting to the bitter end, with no prisoners. After the war he rebuilt his law practice and recouped much of his wartime losses.

CHIPMAN, Norton Parker (ca. 1838-1924)

As the prosecutor in the war crimes case against Andersonville's Henry Wirz, Norton P. Chipman spent much time supporting the unprecedented trial by a military commission. A native of Ohio, he was living in Iowa at the outbreak of the war. His military services included: major, 2nd Iowa (September 23, 1861); and colonel and additional aide-de-camp (April 17, 1862). Before being granted his staff appointment his regiment served in Missouri and at Fort Donelson and Shiloh. Assigned to the Bureau of Military Justice, he acted frequently as a judge advocate. By the time of the Wirz trial he had been brevetted a brigadier of volunteers for his bureau work. He managed to gain a conviction of Wirz before the commission despite contradictory evidence that was never reconciled. Twenty days after the execution of Wirz, Chipman was mustered out of the service, on November 30, 1865.

CHISOLM, John Julian (1830-1903)

At the outbreak of the war Charleston physician and surgeon, John J. Chisolm wrote the guide for untrained field surgeons, *Manual of Military Surgery*. A native of South Carolina, he received his medical education there as well as in London and Paris. At the outbreak of the war he was a professor at the South Carolina Medical College. As a military surgeon he was present at Fort Sumter and then went into the production of the necessary medicines for the war effort. After the war he returned to the field of medical education. (Cunningham, Horace Herndon, *Doctors in Gray*)

CHIVINGTON, John M. (1821-1894)

A minister turned soldier, John Chivington's name struck terror in the hearts of the Cheyenne Indians during the Civil War. After having served as major, 1st Colorado Infantry, in New Mexico during the early part of the war, the "Fighting Parson" was promoted colonel and the unit was converted into cavalry. On November 2, 1862, he was given command of the District of Colorado, where his principal role was to replace the regular army troops in defense against Indians. Over the protests of some of his officers, Chivington led parts of the 1st and 3rd Colorado Cavalry in a surprise attack on Black Kettle's Cheyenne camp on November 29, 1864. What was in fact a massacre—the "Battle of Sand Creek"—left at least 133 Indians dead and mutilated, with only 10 Coloradans dead, probably by their own reckless firing. Black Kettle had displayed an American flag and the white flag of surrender to no avail. Chivington claimed 500 to 600 Indians killed and boasted, "It may perhaps be unnecessary for me to state that I captured no prisoners." Most of the dead were women, children, and old men. Few braves were present. There was a congressional inquiry and a court-martial, but Chivington had relinquished his command on January 4, 1865, and resigned. After the war he served as a law officer in Denver. (Craig, Reginald S., *The Fighting Parson*)

CHRIST, Benjamin C. (ca. 1824-1869)

Pennsylvanian Benjamin C. Christ served in command of a brigade in the three major theaters of the war. His Civil War assignments included: lieutenant colonel, 5th Pennsylvania (April 21, 1861); colonel, 50th Pennsylvania (September 30, 1861); commanding 1st Brigade, 1st Division, 9th Corps, Army of the Potomac (August 3-September 1 and September 8-24, 1862); commanding the division (September 1-8, 1862); commanding 2nd Brigade, 1st Division, 9th Corps, Army of the Potomac (September 24-30 and October 8-26, 1862, December 15, 1862-January 1863, and February-March 19, 1863); commanding 2nd Brigade, 1st Division, 9th Corps, Department of the Ohio (March 19-June 5, 1863 and September 18, 1863-January 10, 1864); commanding 3rd Brigade, 2nd Division, 9th Corps, Department of the Ohio (June 5-mid-June 1863); commanding 3rd Brigade, 2nd Division, 9th Corps, Army of the Tennessee (June 14-August 18, 1863); commanding 2nd Brigade, 3rd Division, 9th Corps, Army of the Potomac (April 20-May 12 and May 30-June 17, 1864); commanding 1st Brigade, 3rd Division, 9th Corps, Army of the Potomac (August 28-September 13, 1864); and again commanding 1st Brigade, 1st Division, 9th Corps, Army of the Potomac (September 13-30, 1864). Until its muster out on July 25, 1861, his first regiment served at Annapolis, Washington, and Alexandria. As colonel of a new unit he survived a shipwreck on the Port Royal expedition late in 1861. After serving briefly in North Carolina, he served in brigade command at 2nd Bull Run although technically by then a part of the Army of the Potomac. He led a brigade at Antietam and Fredericksburg, having briefly commanded the division in the early part of the Maryland Campaign. Transferred to the Department of the Ohio with Burnside and the 9th Corps, he served for a time in East Tennessee before being sent with a detachment of the corps to reinforce Grant before Vicksburg. He took part in that campaign from mid-June until the fall of the river city and in the subsequent operations against Jackson. Returning to Virginia for the spring 1864 Overland Campaign, he was brevetted brigadier general for the fighting at the Ny River and the subsequent siege at Petersburg. The original term of his regiment having expired, he was mustered out on September 30, 1864.

CHRISTIAN, William A.

See: *Christian, William Henry*

CHRISTIAN, William Henry (?-1887)

Near the close of the Civil War there was a mass granting of brevet promotions. Unfortunately many of these were politically motivated and do not necessarily represent military merit. Such was the case of William Henry Christian. (NOTE: The *Official Records* gives a middle initial "A.") A veteran of the Mexican War, having risen from private to first sergeant in the 7th New York Volunteers, he was naturally considered for higher command in the Civil War. His assignments included: colonel, 26th New York (May 21, 1861); commanding 2nd Brigade, 2nd Division, 3rd Corps, Army of Virginia (August 30-September 12, 1862); and commanding 2nd Brigade, 2nd Division, 1st Corps, Army of the Potomac (September 12-18, 1862). After initial service in the vicinity of Washington and in the Shenandoah Valley, his regiment became part of Pope's army. He led the regiment at Cedar Mountain and succeeded to command of the brigade at 2nd Bull Run. His command soon was merged into McClellan's army and he directed it in the battle of South Mountain. However, a few days later at Antietam his incapacity for high command became apparent. After issuing a series of confusing orders he abandoned his men and fled the field, ducking and dodging Confederate shells. His men were livid and two days later, on September 19, 1862, Christian resigned. Nonetheless on March 13, 1865, he was brevetted brigadier general of volunteers.

CHRYSLER, Morgan Henry (1822-1890)

The next-to-last Civil War officer to receive the appointment of brigadier general of volunteers, Morgan H. Chrysler, was a New York farmer with no prior military experience at the outset. His assignments included: captain, 30th New York (June 1, 1861); major, 30th New York (March 11, 1862); lieutenant colonel, 30th New York (August 30, 1862); lieutenant colonel, 2nd New York Veteran Cavalry (September 8, 1863); colonel, 2nd New York Veteran Cavalry (December 13, 1863); commanding 4th Brigade, Cavalry Division, Department of the Gulf (August 6-September 22, 1864); commanding 1st Brigade, Lucas' Cavalry Division, District of West Florida, Department of the Gulf (March 25-April 14, 1865); commanding 3rd Brigade, 1st Division, Cavalry Corps, Military Division of West Mississippi (April 28-May 9, 1865); and brigadier general, USV (November 11, 1865). With his first regiment he fought at 2nd Bull Run, Antietam, and Chancellorsville. In the latter he commanded the regiment. Mustered out with his regiment on June 18, 1863, at the expiration of its term of service, he was instrumental in recruiting many of the discharged men into the new 2nd New York Veteran Cavalry. Commissioned lieutenant colonel in this new unit, he was soon its commanding officer and led it in the Red River Campaign in Louisiana. For much of the rest of the conflict he directed a brigade of cavalry and took part in the operations against Mobile. Already brevetted a brigadier general, he was granted the full rank well after the close of hostilities and brevetted major general for the war. Before his

January 15, 1866, mustering out he was military governor of the District of Northern Alabama. He then returned to his farming.

CHURCHILL, Sylvester (?-1862)

The health of Sylvester Churchill, inspector general of the U.S. Army for 20 years, was found to be too impaired for the rigors of the office in an expanded military establishment. Entering the military during the War of 1812 as an artillery company officer, he served for a time as a major and assistant inspector general. After the war he resumed his duties in the artillery, but in 1841 he was appointed colonel and inspector general. During the Mexican War he was brevetted brigadier general in the regular army for the battle of Buena Vista. He continued to head the department until the start of the Civil War, when he was retired on September 25, 1861. He died on December 7, 1862. (Churchill, Franklin H., *Sketch of the Life of Bvt. Brig. Gen. Sylvester Churchill, Inspector General U.S. Army*)

CHURCHILL, Thomas James (1824-1905)

Kentucky-born lawyer Thomas J. Churchill, serving most of the war west of the Mississippi River, rose to the rank of Confederate major general in its final months. After practicing in his native state he served as a first lieutenant of Kentucky cavalry during the Mexican War. Thereafter he was an Arkansas planter and was Little Rock's postmaster when secession came. His assignments included: colonel, 1st Arkansas Mounted Rifles (June 9, 1861); brigadier general, CSA (March 4, 1862); commanding cavalry brigade, Trans-Mississippi Division, Department #2 (ca. March-April 15, 1862); commanding 2nd Brigade, McCown's Division, Army of the West, Department #2 (April 15-June 27, 1862); commanding 2nd Brigade, McCown's Division, Department of East Tennessee (June 27-ca. September 1862); commanding division, Division of Arkansas, Trans-Mississippi Department (January-January 11, 1863); commanding brigade, Price's Division, District of Arkansas, Trans-Mississippi Department (ca. January-March 24, 1864); commanding 1st (Arkansas) Division, District of Arkansas, Trans-Mississippi Department (March 24-April 1, mid-April-early August, and August 4-late August 1864); commanding Detachment, District of Arkansas, District of West Louisiana, Trans-Mississippi (April 1-mid-April 1864); commanding District of Arkansas, Trans-Mississippi Department (August-August 4, 1864); commanding 1st (Arkansas) Division, 2nd Corps (or District of Arkansas), Trans-Mississippi Department (September 1864-May 26, 1865); and major general, CSA (March 18, 1865). He led his regiment at Wilson's Creek and Pea Ridge and was then promoted to brigadier general and assigned to command a cavalry brigade, which he led across the Mississippi to Corinth. There he took charge of an infantry brigade and took part in the siege of Corinth. Early that summer he was transferred with the rest of the division to East Tennessee and went on the invasion of Kentucky, fighting at Richmond. Shortly thereafter he was relieved and was commanding at Fort Hindman or Arkansas Post when he was forced to surrender to John. A. McClernand early in 1863. Following his release he led two divisions in the Red River Campaign and then one division at Jenkins' Ferry against Steele's drive against Camden, Arkansas. He finished out the war in division command in Arkansas.

CLANTON, James Holt (1827-1871)

Although he was killed six years after the end of the Civil War, Confederate General James H. Clanton was just as much a casualty of that conflict as those who fell on the field of battle. Born in Georgia, he entered upon the practice of law in Alabama. A state legislator, he was a Unionist until the last moment. In 1860 he backed the presidential bid of John Bell on the Constitutional Union ticket. Joining the Confederacy, his assignments included: captain, Company K, 1st Alabama Cavalry (1861); colonel, 1st Alabama Cavalry (March 18, 1862 to rank from December 3, 1861) brigadier general, CSA (November 16, 1863); commanding 2nd Brigade, Department of the Gulf (ca. November 1863-early 1864); aide-de-camp, Polk's Corps (Army of Mississippi), Army of Tennessee (spring 1864); commanding cavalry brigade, District of Central and Northern Alabama, Department of Alabama, Mississippi and East Louisiana (summer-September 24, 1864); commanding brigade, District of Central Alabama, Department of Alabama, Mississippi and East Louisiana (September 24-late November 1864); and commanding brigade, District of the Gulf, Department of Alabama, Mississippi and East Louisiana (early 1865-March 25, 1865). He led his regiment at Shiloh but the terrain gave the cavalry little opportunity for action. Later he took part in the defense of Corinth, Mississippi, and fought at Farmington and Booneville. Promoted to brigadier general, he led a brigade in various parts of Alabama. During the early stages of the Atlanta Campaign he was Leonidas Polk's aide and, after the corps commander's death, returned to his brigade. While serving in the District of the Gulf he was wounded at Bluff Spring, Florida, on March 25, 1865, and shortly thereafter he was taken prisoner. Released at the end of the war, he resumed his legal and political career until assassinated by an ex-Union officer "under the influence."

CLARK, Charles (1811-1877)

Invalided out of the army, Charles Clark became the last Confederate governor of Mississippi. A planter and politician on the state level, he had served during the Mexican War as colonel, 2nd Mississippi, but had not seen any action. Upon the secession of his adopted state—he was Ohio-born and Kentucky-educated—he entered its service and later that of the Confederacy. His assignments included: brigadier general, Army of Mississippi (early 1861); major general, Army of Mississippi (April 15, 1862); brigadier general, CSA (May 22, 1861); commanding Longstreet's (old) Brigade, Longstreet's Division in the 1st Corps, Army of the Potomac (October 14-22, 1861) and in the Potomac District, Department of Northern Virginia (October 22-November 2, 1861); commanding independent brigade, Central Army of Kentucky, Department #2, (November 1861-February 1862); commanding 1st Division, 1st Corps, Army of the Mississippi (March 12-April 6 and April

8-July 1862); and commanding 1st Division, Breckinridge's Command, District of the Mississippi (July-August 5, 1862). After initial service in Tennessee, Virginia, and Kentucky, he was wounded on the first day at Shiloh but returned to duty in a matter of days. Transferred farther south, he was wounded and captured in the unsuccessful attack on Baton Rouge. Exchanged in February 1863, he was so crippled that he had to use crutches for the rest of his years and resigned his commission on October 31. Earlier that month he had been elected governor and served through the Confederacy's collapse when he was removed by the Union authorities despite his urging compliance with the laws of the occupation. After his release from prison he resumed his law practice.

CLARK, Daniel (1809-1891)

During parts of the final year of the Civil War Daniel Clark served as the president pro tempore of the U.S. Senate. The native of New Hampshire had been admitted to the bar in 1837 and served in the state legislature in the 1840s and 1850s. In 1857 he was named to an unexpired term in the Senate. As a Republican, he was reelected once and served until July 27, 1866, when he resigned to accept a judgeship. At times in 1864 and 1865 he was the presiding officer of the Senate. He held the judicial position until his death.

CLARK, Henry Toole (1808-1874)

A non-elected governor of North Carolina, Henry T. Clark had a great deal of difficulty in gaining support in the face of the Confederate defeats along the coast in early 1862. A native of the state, he had been admitted to the bar but was never active in the profession. Instead he entered politics in 1840, winning the position of court clerk. Ten years later he was a state senator and was that body's speaker from 1858. With the death of Governor John W. Ellis on July 7, 1861, Clark succeeded to the gubernatorial post. An effective organizer, he established military districts within his domain and arranged for the overseas purchase of arms and equipment. Since his senate term had expired an attempt was made by William W. Holden to oust him from the state house. Declining reelection, he left office on September 8, 1862, at the expiration of Ellis' term and returned to his plantation. Not having been pardoned by the Union occupation, he was refused his seat in the state senate in 1865 when elected to that post. He then retired from politics. (Wheeler, John, *Reminiscences and Memoirs of North Carolina and North Carolinians*)

CLARK, John Bullock, Sr. (1802-1885)

Because of his personality, John B. Clark had frequent difficulties with other politicians but was able to keep coming back after elections. Born in Kentucky, Clark moved to Missouri and was admitted to the bar. He served as a judicial clerk, colonel in the Black Hawk War, militia officer and state legislator. At the outbreak of the Civil War he had been serving, since 1857, in the U.S. Congress. Having joined the Missouri State Guard as a brigadier general, he was expelled on July 13, 1861. He commanded the 3rd Division at Carthage and Wilson's Creek. In October 1861 he was named to the Provisional Confederate Congress and was assigned to the Committees on Foreign Affairs and Indian Affairs. When appointed to the Senate in the First Congress he drew a two-year term. Here he served on the equivalent committees plus those on: Post Offices and Post Roads; Printing; Public Lands; and Territories. He supported local defense units, partisan rangers, and the war effort in general. He was, however, sensitive to discrimination against Missouri and fought to end the draft in areas threatened by invasion or guerrillas. He antagonized Davis by trying to limit his powers of appointment in the army, preferring the seniority system. By the end of his term, Clark was in hot water with Missouri Governor Thomas Reynolds who believed that Clark was a drunkard, a liar, and immoral. Reynolds dropped his previous support for Clark and he failed to gain reelection to the Senate. He was, however, elected to the House by the exile vote of Missouri's occupied 3rd Division. Here he served on the Committees on Elections and Military Affairs. After the war he resumed his law practice. His son, John Bullock, Jr., was a Confederate brigadier.

CLARK, John Bullock, Jr. (1831-1885)

The son of Confederate Congressman John B. Clark, Sr., John B. Clark, Jr., rose to be a brigadier general. The Missouri native and graduate of Harvard Law School was practicing his profession upon the outbreak of the Civil War. His assignments included: lieutenant, Missouri State Guard (1861); captain, Missouri State Guard (1861); major, 1st Infantry, 3rd Division, Missouri State Guard (1861); colonel, 1st Infantry, 3rd Division, Missouri State Guard (1861); commanding 3rd Division, Missouri State Guard (March 1862); colonel, 9th Missouri (spring 1862); commanding brigade, Price's-Frost's Division, District of Arkansas, Trans-Mississippi Department (April-fall 1863); commanding Drayton's Brigade, Price's Division, District of Arkansas, Trans-Mississippi Department (January-February 1864); commanding brigade, Price's Division, District of Arkansas, Trans-Mississippi Department (March-March 24, 1864); brigadier general, CSA (March 6, 1864); and commanding in Trans-Mississippi Department: 1st Brigade, 1st (Missouri) Division, District of Arkansas (March 24-March and April-ca. September 18, 1864); 1st Brigade, 1st (Missouri) Division, Detachment, District of Arkansas, District of West Louisiana (March-April 1864); brigade, Marmaduke's Cavalry Division, Army of Missouri (September 18-December 18, 1864); also 2nd (Missouri) Cavalry Brigade, 1st (Missouri) Cavalry Division, Cavalry Corps (September 1864-early 1865); and Army of Missouri (temporarily December 1864). With the Missouri State Guard he fought at Carthage, and Wilson's Creek and at Pea Ridge led one of its divisions. Joining the Confederate volunteers, he continued to serve west of the Mississippi. He took part in the defense of Little Rock. The next year he fought in the Red River Campaign and at Jenkins' Ferry in the repulse of Steele's drive on Camden, Arkansas. That fall he led a cavalry brigade in Sterling Price's invasion of Missouri. A postwar lawyer, he also sat for five terms in the U.S. Congress.

CLARK, Meriwether Lewis (1809-1881)

The son of famed explorer William Clark, Meriwether Lewis Clark is sometimes mistakenly identified as a Confederate general. In fact he was never higher than a colonel in that service but was a brigadier in the Missouri State Guard early in the war. A native of Missouri and a West Pointer (1830), he had served three years in the regular army and commanded a volunteer artillery battalion in the Mexican War. Made a brigadier general in the Missouri State Guard, he commanded its 9th Military District in the latter part of 1861. Early the following year he served successively as chief of artillery for the Guard, Price's Division, and the Army of the West. On July 17, 1861, he was named the chief artillerist in Department #2. Having transferred to Confederate service, he rose in this period from major to colonel of artillery. In charge of Bragg's guns, he took part in the battle of Murfreesboro. In the summer of 1864 he was assigned to ordnance duty as an inspector. He held this post until the end of the war and was subsequently a faculty member at the Kentucky Military Institute.

CLARK, William T.

See: *Petersen, William A.*

CLARK, William Thomas (1831-1905)

Union Brigadier General William T. Clark followed up his Civil War military career as a carpetbagger in Texas. A native of Connecticut, he had practiced law in New York and Iowa before entering the military. His assignments included: first lieutenant and adjutant, 13th Iowa (November 2, 1861); captain and assistant adjutant general, USV (March 6, 1862); major and assistant adjutant general, USV (November 24, 1862); lieutenant colonel and assistant adjutant general, USV (assigned February 10, 1863-April 22, 1865); commanding 1st Brigade, 3rd Division, 15th Corps, Army of the Tennessee (January 26-April 26, 1865); commanding 2nd Brigade, 4th Division, 15th Corps, Army of the Tennessee (April 26-May 1, 1865); brigadier general, USV (May 31, 1865); and commanding 3rd Division, 25th Corps, Department of Texas (August 1-October 25, 1865 and December 20, 1865-January 8, 1866). After initial service in Missouri with his regiment he was appointed to staff duty and fought at Shiloh, Corinth, and through the Vicksburg Campaign. In the latter and in the later Atlanta Campaign he served as James B. McPherson's adjutant and received the brevet of brigadier general for the battle of Atlanta where his chief was killed. During the Carolinas Campaign he was given a line command as an acting brigadier general and was brevetted to major general of volunteers at the close of the war, as well as to the full rank of brigadier. Sent to Texas with Sheridan's forces, he proposed the acquisition of Matamoros to halt Maximilian's designs. Becoming connected with the black element after his February 1, 1866, mustering out, he was sent to the U.S. Congress in 1869 and was expelled following his disputed reelection two years later. Previously instrumental in the founding of a Galveston bank, he became a tax official until his death.

CLARK, Willis Gaylord (1827-1898)

As the co-editor of a Confederate newspaper, Willis G. Clark went to the front to cover the fighting for his readership. Born in New York, he studied in Illinois before becoming a lawyer in Mobile. His first journalism endeavor was editing the Democratic *Southern Magazine*. By the outbreak of the Civil War he was editing the *Mobile Daily Advertiser,* which soon merged with the *Mobile Register* of which he became co-editor. After his work as a war correspondent he was active in manufacturing and railroading. He also wrote *History of Education in Alabama*.

CLARKE, Henry Francis (ca. 1821-1887)

For his services as a commissary officer, Pennsylvania native Henry F. Clarke received the regular army brevet of major general. A West Pointer (1843), he had been initially posted to the artillery with which he fought in the Mexican War, earning a brevet and suffering a wound. Transferred to the subsistence department, he took part in the Seminole War. His Civil War assignments included: captain and commissary of subsistence (since January 12, 1857); chief commissary of subsistence, Department of Florida (April 13-May 31, 1861); chief-commissary of subsistence, Army of Northeastern Virginia (July 2-25, 1861); chief commissary of subsistence, Military Division of the Potomac (July 25-August 15, 1861); major and commissary of subsistence (August 3, 1861); chief commissary of subsistence, Army of the Potomac (August 15, 1861-January 8, 1864); colonel and additional aide-de-camp (September 28, 1861-May 31, 1866); and lieutenant colonel and assistant commissary general of subsistence (June 29, 1864). As the head of his department he was involved in the complicated decisions at Fort Pickens during the secession crisis and immediately following the firing upon Fort Sumter. Joining the main army in Virginia, he served as the subsistence chief in the campaigns of 1st Bull Run, the Peninsula, Antietam (brevetted), Fredericksburg, Chancellorsville, Gettysburg (brevetted brigadier general), Bristoe Station, and Mine Run. Leaving the Army of the Potomac, he was shortly named assistant commissary general and was assigned to duty in the Northeast. He retired with the rank of colonel in 1884.

CLARKE, Kate

See: *King, Kate*

CLARKE, Marcellus Jerome (ca. 1843-1865)

Newspaper publicity brought a minor Confederate guerrilla, Marcellus J. Clark, to the gallows near the end of the Civil War. The son of a prominent Kentucky family, he had entered the Confederate army in the first year of the conflict and had served under John Hunt Morgan. In September 1864 he began a career leading small independent bands against military targets. But like most guerrillas he was also something of a bandit. *Louisville Courier* editor George D. Prentice was, unfortunately for Clarke, engaged in a political feud with the Union commander in the area, Stephen G. Burbridge, and launched a journalistic campaign to embarrass the general. Since Clark was of slight stature, Prentice labelled him a mere woman that the Union forces could not deal with. Borrowing the name of a notorious black woman in the city, Prentice dubbed Clarke "Sue Mundy." His efforts against Burbridge may have had some effect since the general was removed and replaced by John M. Palmer. Meanwhile Clarke/Mundy continued his operations and in February 1865 worked with the notorious bushwhacker William C. Quantrill in a number of minor operations. On March 12, 1865, Clarke was captured by some of Palmer's men while tending a wounded associate. Following a perfunctory court-martial, Clarke was hanged three days later.

CLAUSEWITZ, Karl von (1780-1831)

At the time of the American Civil War Karl von Clausewitz's *Von Kriege* (*On War*) was gradually succeeding Antoine H. Jomini's *Summary of the Art of War* as the generally accepted theory of warfare. Born in Burg, Germany, he fought as a boy against the French at Mainz and at age 15 became a lieutenant. At age 21 he attended the Berlin war college and studied the theory and practice of war. Fighting throughout the Napoleonie Wars he emerged as a Prussian general. In 1818 he was placed in charge of the War College and began preparing his work. He studied the principles of leadership and felt that war was an extension of politics. The book was published posthumously but had only limited impact on the Civil War since an American English-language edition was not issued until the 20th century.

CLAY, Cassius Marcellus (1810-1903)

Appointed as Lincoln's minister to St. Petersburg, Kentucky Republican Cassius M. Clay delayed his departure for Russia in order to lead a miscellaneous force of volunteers in the defense of the capital before the arrival of regulars and volunteers from the Northern states. As a captain, he had commanded Company C, 1st Kentucky Cavalry, in Mexico, and was taken prisoner. As a long-time opponent of slavery he joined the Republicans upon the formation of the party. Considered for the vice presidency and the secretaryship of war, he was offered, as a consolation, a diplomatic post in Spain but refused. Accepting the second diplomatic offer, he was named to the Russian post on March 28, 1861. Delaying his sailing until the Capital was safe, his military assignments included: captain, Clay Battalion Washington Guards (April 1861); and major general, USV (April 11, 1862). With the city safe, he departed but returned to the United States in June 1862 to accept the major generalcy. But with slavery still being protected by the Union forces in occupied areas of the South, he soon announced his refusal to serve and on March 11, 1863, resigned to return to his duties in St. Petersburg. Returning from overseas in 1869, he broke with Grant in 1872 and backed the Democrat Tilden in 1876. Becoming paranoid in his final years, he armed his mansion with a cannon and was labeled a lunatic by the courts. (Robertson, James R., *A Kentuckian at the Court of the Tsars*)

CLAY, Clement Claiborne, Jr. (1816-1882)

Certainly one of the shining lights in the generally less-than-distinguished Confederate Congress was Alabama's Senator Clement C. Clay, Jr. Clay was a graduate of both the University of Alabama and the University of Virginia's law school. In his early years he worked as editor of the Huntsville *Democrat*, acquired a large plantation, and served as state legislator and as a county judge. In the meantime he practiced law. He was serving his second term in the U.S. Senate at the time of the secession crisis. On January 21, 1861, he was one of the five Southern senators, whose states had seceded, who made farewell speeches and then dramatically withdrew from the Senate chamber. Long a supporter of states' rights, Clay was offered the position of secretary of war by Jefferson Davis but declined in favor of Leroy P. Walker. Elected to the Senate of the First Regular Congress in November 1861, on the tenth ballot, he took his seat in February 1862 and drew a two-year term. He chaired the Committee on Commerce and also served on the committees on Indian Affairs and Military Affirs. A friend of Secretary of the

Confederate Senator Clement C. Clay, Jr. (*Harper's*)

Navy Stephen R. Mallory, who had left the U.S. Senate at the same time as Clay, he used his chairmanship of a special joint committee investigating the Navy Department for a whitewash protecting Mallory. A supporter of Davis' war effort, Clay did show much independence. He was well respected by both the pro- and anti-Davis forces for his non-dogmatic openness. Failing at reelection in November 1863, he left Congress in February 1864. Two months later he was sent to Canada to assist Jacob Thompson on a secret peace mission. Acknowledging failure, Clay returned South just in time for the final collapse of the Confederacy. Upon hearing that he was a suspect in the Lincoln murder, he surrendered to Union authorities and was confined at Fort Monroe for virtually a year without a trial. Restrictions upon his activities limited him to his law practice after the war. (Nuremberger, Ruth K., *The Clays of Alabama: A Planter-Lawyer-Politician Family*)

CLAYTON, Alexander Mosby (1801-1889)

Although he only served a few months in the Confederate Congress, Alexander M. Clayton played a major role in shaping the new nation. Born in Virginia, he had moved via Tennessee to Mississippi where he was a lawyer, judge, and planter. He was briefly, in 1853, U.S. consul to Havana. Lincoln's election converted Clayton into an immediate secessionist, and at the Mississippi convention he was instrumental in drawing up the ordinance that took the state out of the Union. Appointed to the Provisional Confederate Congress, he chaired the Committee on the Judiciary where he played a key role in securing the rights of the states within the new federal system. He was also instrumental in the creation of the new court system. Having supported Jefferson Davis for the presidency, he was rewarded by being named judge for the District of Mississippi, a post that he held until removed at the war's close. After the war Clayton served as a judge until removed in 1869 under Reconstruction by the U.S. Congress. Then he was a lawyer, planter, educator, banker, and was active in the railroad business.

CLAYTON, Henry DeLamar (1827-1889)

Georgia-born Alabama lawyer and state legislator Henry D. Clayton rose to division command in the Confederate Army of Tennessee but in the final reorganization appears to have become a supernumerary officer. His assignments included: colonel, 1st Alabama (March 27, 1861); colonel, 39th Alabama (May 15, 1862); commanding brigade, Stewart's Division, Hill's-Breckinridge's-Hindman's-Hood's Corps, Army of Tennessee (ca. April-September 1, 1863 and early 1864-July 7, 1864); brigadier general, CSA (April 22, 1863); commanding brigade, Stewart's Division, Buckner's Corps, Army of Tennessee (September 1-October 1, 1863); major general, CSA (July 7, 1864); and commanding Stewart's (old) Division, Hood's-Lee's Corps, Army of Tennessee (July 7, 1864-April 9, 1865). Initially stationed at Pensacola, he was relieved of command of his first regiment on January 18, 1862, upon the expiration of its original one-year term of enlistment. He then took command of a new regiment and led it in the Kentucky Campaign, although it was not present at Perryville, and at Murfreesboro where he was wounded. Returning to duty, he was promoted to brigadier general and commanded a brigade in the Tullahoma Campaign. Again wounded at Chickamauga, he returned in time to command the brigade in the Atlanta Campaign. During the campaign he was promoted to major general and took charge of Alexander P. Stewart's division when that officer took over Polk's Army of Mississippi. This division he led through the balance of the campaign and then went with Hood to middle Tennessee. The division was left south of the Duck River and thus missed the disastrous fight at Franklin but was present at Nashville where Clayton was praised for his role in covering the first part of the retreat. Moving on to the Carolinas, he led the division until the April 9, 1865, reorganization and consolidation of the Army of Tennessee. He appears to have been left without a command but remained with the army in some capacity since he was included in Joseph E. Johnston's surrender. After the war he returned to his plantation and resumed his legal practice, eventually becoming a judge.

CLAYTON, Philip (1815-1877)

A former U.S. treasury auditor, Philip Clayton quit his post as the Confederacy's assistant secretary of the treasury in a dispute with the secretary. A native Georgian lawyer and Democrat, he had also been a planter and journalist before taking the auditor's post. He then served as Buchanan's assistant treasury secretary and following secession took the same post in the Confederacy. Resenting the excessive demands of his boss, Christopher G. Memminger, he resigned in 1863. Washing his hands of the Confederacy, he became a Republican after the war and was a bank teller before becoming Grant's representative in Peru. He died there in 1877.

CLAYTON, Powell (1833-1914)

A Union brigadier general in the Civil War's Trans-Mississippi theater, Powell Clayton became the carpetbag governor of Arkansas and later, in the highly charged atmosphere of Reconstruction, faced impeachment and removal on charges of corruption and election fraud. Having received his education at a Pennsylvania military academy and in Delaware (in engineering) he became a civil engineer in Kansas in the mid-1850s. His military assignments included: captain, 1st Kansas (May 29, 1861); lieutenant colonel, 5th Kansas Cavalry (December 28, 1861); colonel, 5th Kansas Cavalry (March 7, 1862); commanding 2nd Brigade, Cavalry Division, District of Eastern Arkansas, Department of the Tennessee (April-May 1863); commanding Cavalry Brigade, 13th Division, 16th Corps, Army of the Tennessee (July 28-August 19, 1863); commanding independent cavalry brigade, Arkansas Expedition, Department of the Tennessee (August 4, 1863-January 6, 1864); commanding Independent Cavalry Brigade, 7th Corps, Department of Arkansas (January-September 15, 1864); also commanding Post of Pine Bluff, 7th Corps, Department of Arkansas (1864); brigadier general, USV (August 1, 1864); and commanding Separate Dismounted Cavalry Brigade, 7th Corps, Department of Arkansas (May 30-June 10 and July 12-August 1, 1865). With his first regiment he fought at Wilson's

Creek before transferring to the cavalry. There he was frequently in brigade command in eastern Arkansas and commanded the post at Pine Bluff when it was attacked in October 1863. At the war's close, he went into cotton planting near that post and in 1868 was elected as a carpetbag governor. In order to fight the Ku Klux Klan, he appointed former Union General Robert F. Catterson to command the state's black militia. In 1871 he fought off an impeachment challenge and won a seat in the U.S. Senate but was not reelected. Remaining powerful in the state's Republican Party, he was active in railroads, hotels, and served as ambassador to Mexico.

CLEBURNE, Patrick Ronayne (1828-1864)

The most popular Confederate division commander was the "Stonewall of the West"—Patrick R. Cleburne. Appropriately, the native of County Cork was born on St. Patrick's Day and became the only product of the Emerald Isle to become a Confederate major general. Failing the language requirements for a druggist's degree, he served with the British 41st Regiment of Foot as an officer for a number of years before purchasing his way out. Emigrating to America, he became a druggist and then a highly successful property attorney. He joined the Confederacy, and his military assignments included: captain, Company F, 1st Arkansas State Troops (early 1861); colonel, 1st Arkansas State Troops (early 1861); colonel, 15th Arkansas (designation change July 23, 1861); commanding 2nd Brigade, 1st (Hardee's) Division, Army of Central Kentucky, Department #2 (fall 1861-March 29, 1862); commanding 2nd Brigade, Hardee's Division, Army of the Mississippi (July 2-August 15, 1862); commanding 2nd Brigade, Buckner's Division, Left Wing, Army of the Mississippi (August 15-30, October-October 8, and October-November 20, 1862); commanding 2nd Brigade, Buckner's Division, Hardee's-Breckinridge's Corps, Army of Tennessee (November 20-December 1862); major general, CSA (December 20, 1862 to rank from the 13th); commanding the division (December 1862-November 30, 1863); commanding division, Hardee's (Polk's old)-Cheatham's Corps, Army of Tennessee (November 30, 1863-January 1864, January-August 31, and September 2-November 30, 1864); and commanding the corps (August 31-September 2, 1864). At the head of the Yell Rifles, he served in Arkansas before being named as commander of the state unit. Transferred with William J. Hardee to central Kentucky, he was promoted to brigadier general and fought at Shiloh and during the siege of Corinth. Taking part in the Kentucky Campaign, he was wounded at both Richmond and Perryville. Promoted to major general, he commanded a division at Murfreesboro, during the Tullahoma Campaign, and at Chickamauga. A favorite of Jefferson Davis, he is credited with covering the retreat from Chattanooga after his splendid defense of Tunnel Hill. That winter he and William H.T. Walker proposed that in order to reinforce the Confederate armies slavery would have to be abolished in a "reasonable time" and blacks be recruited for military service on the promise of their freedom. The proposal was rejected by the Richmond authorities and would not be passed by the Confederate Congress until a couple of months after Cleburne's death. Cleburne went on to command his division, and briefly the corps, through the Atlanta Campaign and then with Hood into middle Tennessee. At the battle of Franklin he became the senior of six Confederate generals to die in this fight, which did little more than commit mass suicide against the Union works. (Purdue, Howell and Elizabeth, *Pat Cleburne, Confederate General*)

CLEM, John Lincoln (1851-1937)

One of the youngest Union soldiers, John Lincoln Clem—he had just adopted his middle name—was turned down several times on account of his age but persevered and eventually became a regular army major general—in the next century. In June 1861 he tried to join up with a regiment, the 3rd Ohio, which was passing his Ohio home. Turned down, he tagged along with it secretly and then apparently attached himself to another unit. Considered too young to be mustered in, he was nevertheless appointed drummer, although proving to be a poor one, and was paid his wages through the donations of the company officers. He is alleged to have gone into the battle of Shiloh with this unit, had his drum smashed by an artillery round, and then picked up a gun. Over the years there appeared a play, poem, and song entitled "The Drummer Boy of Shiloh." There were several claimants to the title and a National Park Service study considered Clem to be a leading contender. The works themselves were highly romanticized and are certainly questionable as history. Clem was also known as "Johnny Shiloh." Clem is usually cited to have been with the 3rd Ohio, the 22nd Michigan, and the 22nd Wisconsin. However, the former was not at the battle and the latter two were not organized until four and five months later. Since his position was unofficial he could have been with yet another unit. On May 1, 1863, he was officially mustered in as a musician with Company C, 22nd Michigan and eventually rose to lance sergeant. At the battle of Chickamauga he did win the sobriquet as "the Drummer Boy of Chickamauga." There he went into action with a shortened rifle and when called upon to surrender by a Confederate colonel, he fired, wounding the officer and taking him prisoner. The next month he was captured while part of an escort for a supply train and during his two-month ordeal was shown off by his captors. Released before the end of the year, he served as a courier to George H. Thomas and was twice wounded during the Atlanta Campaign. He was mustered out on September 19, 1864, but was denied admittance to West Point due to the lack of adequate education. Nevertheless he was commissioned second lieutenant, 24th Infantry—a black unit—in 1871. He finally resigned, as a major general, in 1916.

CLEMENS, Samuel Langhorne (1835-1910)

Writing under the pen-name, Mark Twain, which he adapted from his days as a Mississippi River steamboat pilot, Sam Clemens is most remembered for his stories of boyhood in Hannibal, Missouri: *Tom Sawyer* (1876) and *Huckleberry Finn* (1884). He vented his bitterness toward the base condition of human civilization in many of his works—clearly in his account of his experiences as a citizen-soldier during the early

"Mark Twain," or Samuel Clemens, at center with George Alfred Townsend (left) and David Gray. (NA)

days of the Civil War in Missouri, when he served for less than a month in a Confederate company, the Marion Rangers. His short story entitled "The Private History of a Campaign that Failed" uses laughter to soften the horror of young men and boys going off to fight a war, the reasons for which were unclear in their minds. This tragicomic approach was a constant theme in his post war writings, especially in condemning American actions in the Philippines.

CLENDENIN, David Ramsay (?-1895)

Cavalryman David R. Clendenin played an important role in buying time for the defenders of the nation's capital during Early's raid. The Pennsylvania native was living in Illinois in 1861 and his assignments included: captain, 8th Illinois Cavalry (September 18, 1861); major, 8th Illinois Cavalry (September 18, 1861); and lieutenant colonel, 8th Illinois Cavalry (December 5, 1862). His regiment fought at Williamsburg, the Seven Days, South Mountain, Antietam, and Fredericksburg before he led it on Stoneman's raid during the Chancellorsville Campaign. He missed Gettysburg, being in the Washington defenses, and the Bristoe Campaign. He was back in command of his regiment for the Mine Run operations and was then engaged in operations against John S. Mosby in northern Virginia. When Jubal Early moved out of the Shenandoah Valley and began to threaten Washington Clendenin took command of a force of miscellaneous mounted troops under Lew Wallace and bought the city time at the battle of the Monocacy. He then helped man some of the city's fortifications near Fort Stevens. Brevetted brigadier general for the war, he was mustered out with his regiment on July 17, 1865. He became major of the regular army's 8th Cavalry two years later and remained in the service until his 1891 retirement as colonel, 2nd Cavalry.

CLIFFORD, Nathan (1803-1881)

The fears of many Northerners that Supreme Court Justice Nathan Clifford was a New Englander with Southern views were confirmed when he wrote the dissenting opinion in the highly important *Prize Cases* in 1863. The New Hampshire native had moved to Maine and opened a law practice, then became a Democratic politician. He sat in the state legislature, served as state attorney general, sat in Congress, and was U.S. attorney general under James K. Polk. He was sent to Mexico to negotiate a peace treaty and remained there for a time as a diplomat. He then returned to private practice until appointed to the Supreme Court by James Buchanan on December 9, 1857. Confirmation by the Senate followed on January 12, 1858, by a vote of 26 to 23. His opinion in the *Prize Cases*, supported by Chief Justice Roger B. Taney and two others, was that any vessel captured running the presidentially ordered blockade prior to July 13, 1861—the date Congress authorized such a move—were not legal prizes and had to be returned to their owners or compensated for. The close, five to four, vote created a demand for reform of the court and a tenth seat was created to guarantee support for the Union's war effort. In 1877 he chaired the commission that settled the disputed Tilden-Hayes presidential race in favor of the latter on strictly partisan lines—Clifford voting with the Democrats for Tilden. After an 1880 stroke left him unable to fulfill his duties he refused to resign but unsuccessfully attempted to survive until a Democratic president could name his successor. (Pfeffer, Leo, *This Honorable Court*)

CLINGMAN, Thomas Lanier (1812-1897)

North Carolina lawyer and politician Thomas L. Clingman spent most of his Confederate military service in the Carolinas and served only briefly under Lee in Virginia. He resigned his seat in the U.S. Senate on March 28, 1861 (he had previously sat in the lower house), to offer his services to his state. His assignments included: colonel, 25th North Carolina (August 15, 1861); brigadier general, CSA (May 17, 1862); commanding brigade, District of the Cape Fear, Department of North Carolina (November 20, 1862-February 1863); commanding brigade, 1st Military District of South Carolina, Department of South Carolina, Georgia and Florida (February-April 30, 1863); commanding brigade, Department of North Carolina (May-July 1863); commanding 2nd Subdivision, 1st Military District of South Carolina, Department of South Carolina, Georgia and Florida (July-August and September-October 1863); commanding brigade, same subdivision, district and department (August-September 1863); commanding brigade, same district and deparment (October-November 1863); commanding brigade, Department of North Carolina (December 1863-May 1864); commanding brigade, Hoke's Division, Department of North Carolina and Southern Virginia (May-June and June-August 19, 1864); and commanding brigade, Hoke's Division, Hardee's Corps, Army of Tennessee (ca. April 9-26, 1865). After initial service with his regiment in the Carolinas and southern Virginia he was promoted and eventually given a brigade at Wilmington, North Carolina. Traveling between Charleston and Petersburg, he and his brigade saw action at Goldsboro Bridge, Charleston, and New Bern. After fighting at Drewry's Bluff in May 1864, the division was sent to reinforce Lee at Cold Harbor, where Clingman was wounded. Soon returning to duty, he served in the early stages of the siege of Petersburg until wounded at the Weldon Railroad on August 19. Incapacitated for field duty, he did not return to his brigade until the final month of the war when it was serving under Joe Johnston in North Carolina. Surrendered at Greensboro, he returned to the law and took up surveying in the Alleghenies. (Freeman, Douglas S., *Lee's Lieutenants*)

Coastal defender Thomas L. Clingman. (NA)

CLITZ, Henry Boynton (ca. 1824-1888)

A West Pointer (1845), Henry B. Clitz was wounded early in the Civil War and then served as the commandant of cadets at his alma mater. A New Yorker by birth, he was appointed from Michigan and upon his graduation was posted to the infantry. Earning a brevet in Mexico, his Civil War-era assignments included: captain, 3rd Infantry (since December 6, 1858); major, 12th Infantry (May 14, 1861); Commandant of Cadets, United States Military Academy (1862-July 4, 1864); lieutenant colonel, 6th Infantry (November 4, 1863). As a major on the Peninsula he was brevetted for Gaines' Mill where he was wounded and captured. Confined at Libby Prison in Richmond, he was released on July 17, 1862, and soon thereafter returned to West Point. Then he was assigned to garrison duty in 1864. He retired from the regular army—having been brevetted brigadier general for the Civil War—as colonel, 10th Infantry in 1885. Three years later he apparently drowned.

CLUSERET, Gustave Paul (1823-1900)

In a career of military adventurism that spanned four continents, Gustave P. Cluseret mixed in much political activity. It almost cost him his life. Educated at the St. Cyr military academy in his native France, he served in the army during the 1848 uprisings in his own country, and in Algeria and the Crimea. He became a mercenary and commanded Garibaldi's French contingent before heading to the United States for the Civil War, where his assignments included: colonel and additional aide-de-camp (March 10, 1862); commanding Advance Brigade, Mountain Department (May-June 26, 1862); brigadier general, USV (October 14, 1862); and commanding 2nd Brigade, 2nd Division, 8th Corps, Middle Department (February 5-12, 1863). Initially serving on McClellan's staff, he was soon transferred to John C. Frémont's command in western Virginia. He led a brigade against Stonewall Jackson at Cross Keys in the Shenandoah Valley and received his brigadier's star a few months later. Then he started to run into trouble, was arrested for some unspecified reasons, and was generally considered a troublemaker by the War Department. He appears to have held only one later command assignment—and that briefly—before his resignation on March 2, 1863. During the 1864 election he was a journalistic backer of Frémont over Lincoln for the presidential nomination. In 1867 he returned to Europe where he meddled in the Irish problems of the English, and his arrest was sought. In his own country he was sentenced to death during the 1871 Commune but survived to serve in the Chamber of Deputies.

COBB, Amasa (1823-1905)

Two periods of service as a Union army colonel bracketed Amasa Cobb's congressional duties. A private in the Mexican War the Illinoisian moved to Wisconsin where he became a lawyer and served as the speaker of that state's lower house just prior to the Civil War. Based upon his experience and position, he entered the Union army where his assignments included: colonel 5th Wisconsin (July 12, 1861); commanding 1st Brigade, 2nd Division, 6th Corps, Army of the Potomac (September 17-25, 1862); colonel, 43rd Wisconsin (September 24, 1864); and commanding 3rd Brigade, 1st Sub-District, District of Middle Tennessee, Department of the Cumberland (April 23-June 17, 1865). In his first period of military service he was assigned to the Virginia front where he fought at Williamsburg, Golding's Farm (in the Seven Days), and Antietam. At the latter he assumed command of the brigade when Winfield S. Hancock was detached to command a division. For these three actions Cobb later received the brevet of brigadier general. Elected to Congress, he resigned his commission on December 25, 1862, and took his seat the following March. He sat four terms as a Republican. However, in the fall of 1864 he took leave from his legislative duties and returned to the field at the head of a new regiment. He served guarding the Nashville and Northwestern, and the Nashville and Chattanooga, railroads and at the close of the war was in command of a brigade performing garrison duty in central Tennessee. Mustered out on June 24, 1865, he returned to Congress and stayed until 1871, when he moved to Nebraska, where he practiced law, served as mayor of Lincoln, and rose to the chief justiceship of the state supreme court.

COBB, Howell (1815-1868)

A prominent Georgia Unionist, Howell Cobb served before the war as a lawyer, state legislator, solicitor general, U.S. congressman (including as Speaker of the House), governor, and secretary of the treasury. In February 1861 he was named the presiding officer of what became the Provisional Confederate Congress. He had advocated secession after Lincoln's election. A rival candidate for president at the Montgomery convention, he soon became known as an opponent of Davis. He left the congress to join the army, where his assignments included: colonel, 16th Georgia (July 15, 1861); brigadier general, CSA (February 12, 1862); commanding brigade, McLaws' Division, Department of the Peninsula (ca. February 12-April 12, 1862); commanding brigade, McLaws' Division, Magruder's Command, Department of Northern Virginia (April 12-June 1862); commanding brigade, Magruder's Division, Magruder's Command, Army of Northern Virginia (June-July 1862); commanding brigade, McLaws' Division, 1st Corps, same army (July-October 1862); commanding District of Middle Florida, Department of South Carolina, Georgia and Florida (November 11, 1862-ca. October 6, 1863); major general, CSA (September 9, 1863); commanding District of Northwest Georgia, Department of Tennessee (November 1863); commanding reserve forces in Georgia (December 1863-September 28, 1864); and commanding District of Georgia, Department of Tennessee and Georgia (September 28, 1864-March 27, 1865). After fighting at Yorktown, the Seven Days, and South Mountain, he was assigned to Florida and in the summer of 1863 served on a court investigating the disasters at Vicksburg, Port Hudson, and Jackson. He held various commands in Georgia and had to pacify the troublesome Governor Brown. He was involved in the operations to halt Wilson's raid through Alabama in the spring of 1865. Returning to the law after the war, he was active in opposition to the harsher aspects of Reconstruction until his death on a business trip to New York. (Montgomery, Horace, *Howell Cobb's Confederate Career*)

COBB, Silas T. (?-?)

The role of Sergeant Silas T. Cobb in the escape of John Wilkes Booth after the assassination of Lincoln, and Cobb's escape from punishment, have led to many suspicions and conspiracy theories. That April night the soldier was on guard duty at the western end of the Navy Yard Bridge across the Anacostia River. His orders were that no one was to cross without the password. However, Booth appeared at 10:30 or 11:00, as Cobb later testified, and explained that he lived in Maryland and had been unavoidably detained past the 9:00 P.M. deadline. He was allowed to cross. It must be remembered that the war was all but over and security was somewhat lax. But many claim that Secretary of War Edwin M. Stanton deliberately left this route open.

COBB, Thomas Reade Rootes (1823-1862)

The younger brother of Howell Cobb, Thomas R.R. Cobb, was a prominent Georgia lawyer before the Civil War who became an immediate secessionist upon the election of Lincoln. Named to the Provisional Confederate Congress, he served as chair of the Committee on Printing and was active in the establishment of the judicial system for the new nation. He left the Congress to raise a mixed force of infantry and cavalry. His military assignments included: colonel, Cobb's (Ga.) Legion (August 28, 1861); brigadier general, CSA (November 1, 1862); and commanding Howell Cobb's (old) Brigade, McLaws' Division, 1st Corps, Army of Northern Virginia (November 6-December 13, 1862). After service on the Peninsula, including action in the Yorktown operations and the Maryland Campaign, he was promoted and given charge of his brother's former command. In defense of the famed stone wall at Fredericksburg he was wounded in the thigh and bled to death in a short time. (McCash, William B., *Thomas R.R. Cobb: The Making of a Southern Nationalist*)

COBHAM, George Ashworth, Jr. (?-1864)

English-born George A. Cobham, Jr., gave his life for his adopted country and was rewarded with a posthumous brevet as a brigadier general of volunteers. His assignments included: lieutenant colonel, 111th Pennsylvania (January 28, 1862); colonel, 111th Pennsylvania (November 7, 1862); commanding 2nd Brigade, 2nd Division, 12th Corps, Army of the Potomac (May 7-July 2 and July 2-September 25, 1863); commanding 2nd Brigade, 2nd Division, 12th Corps, Army of the Cumberland (September 25-December 27, 1863 and March 9-April 14, 1864); and commanding 3rd Brigade, 2nd Division, 20th Corps, Army of the Cumberland (May 16-June 6, 1964). During the Shenandoah Valley Campaign of 1862 Cobham's regiment served as part of the garrison at Harpers Ferry. He appears not to have been with the unit in its subsequent campaigns until Chancellorsville. By that time he was its colonel. At Gettysburg he was in charge of the brigade except briefly on the second day when General Thomas L. Kane took over. Kane soon proved too ill to remain in command and Cobham was again in charge for the fighting on Culp's Hill the next day. Transferred to the West, he commanded the brigade in the Chattanooga and the early part of the Atlanta campaigns, seeing action at Wauhatchie, Lookout Mountain, Missionary Ridge, Ringgold, Mill Creek Gap, and Peach Tree Creek. In the latter action he was killed and he was then brevetted brigadier general for all his battles since Chancellorsville, to date from the day before his demise.

COBURN, Abner (1803-1885)

One of the largest landowners in Maine, Abner Coburn served a one-year term as governor. A native of the state, he had worked in the surveying and timber businesses and been engaged with railroads. His political career spanned the Federalist, Whig, and Republican parties. As a Whig he served in the state legislature and as an aide to several governors. He was a founder of the state branch of the Republican Party and a supporter of Lincoln. In 1862 he was elected governor and was inaugurated on January 7, 1863. During the course of the year he kept the state on a war footing despite some Union military reverses that provided ammunition to the opposition. Leaving office on January 6, 1864, he returned to his business interests and when he died left much of his money to churches and colleges. (Williams, Charles E., *Life of Abner Coburn, A Review of the Public and Private Career of the Late Ex-Governor of Maine*)

COBURN, John (1825-1908)

Despite having served primarily in reserve assignments, Indianian John Coburn earned a brevet brigadier generalship for his war service several months after having been mustered out. A lawyer, state legislator, and judge before the war he entered the army, where his assignments included: colonel, 33rd Indiana (September 16, 1861); commanding 27th Brigade, 7th Division, Army of the Ohio (March 26-April 12, 1862); commanding 1st Brigade, 3rd Division, Army of Kentucky, Department of the Ohio (October 1862-February 1863); commanding 1st Brigade, Baird's Division, Army of Kentucky, Department of the Cumberland (February-June 8, 1863); commanding 3rd Brigade, 1st Division, Reserve Corps, Army of the Cumberland (July 12-October 10, 1863); commanding Unattached Brigade, Department of the Cumberland (October 10-December 1863); commanding Coburn's Brigade, Post of Murfreesboro, Department of the Cumberland (December 1863-January 12, 1864); commanding 2nd Brigade, 1st Division, 11th Corps, Army of the Cumberland (January 12-March 25, 1864); and commanding 2nd Brigade, 3rd Division, 20th Corps, Army of the Cumberland (May 9-September 22, 1864). Early in the war he commanded his regiment in the capture of Cumberland Gap and then held various brigade commands, usually in the rear areas. During the Atlanta Campaign he led a brigade in the 20th Corps until he was mustered out of the service on September 20, 1864. After the war he was a judge, congressman, and member of the Montana supreme court.

COCHRANE, John (1813-1898)

Former two-term New York Congressman John Cochrane resigned his brigadier's commission in early 1863, claiming ill health. But it was more probably because of his problems with Congress, now dominated by the Republicans. A lawyer, he had served in Congress in the last four years of the secession crisis and was known for expressing his view that the North was in fact unfair to the South. Nonetheless he entered the Union army where his assignments included: colonel, 65th New York (June 11, 1861); commanding 3rd Brigade, 1st Division, 4th Corps, Army of the Potomac (July 5-September 26, 1862); brigadier general, USV (July 17, 1862); commanding 3rd Brigade, 3rd Division, 6th Corps, Army of the Potomac (September 26-October 1862); and commanding 1st Brigade, same division, corps and army (October 1862-March 1863). He was in command of his regiment at Seven Pines but not during the Seven Days. However, four days later he was given command of the brigade and later that month made brigadier. His division went to reinforce the Army of the Potomac in the Maryland Campaign but was too far in the rear to take part in the battle of Antietam. It was in the aftermath of Fredericksburg, in which the 6th Corps was not fully engaged, that Cochrane got into trouble. He became embroiled in the dispute of William B. Franklin and William F. Smith with their commander, Burnside. Franklin had already been relieved and Smith was about to be when Cochrane resigned. He then became New York's attorney general and was briefly on Frémont's ticket as a vice presidential candidate in the summer of 1864 before the slate's removal. Remaining in politics, he supported Lincoln in 1864 and Greeley in 1872 and was active in Tammany Hall and veterans affairs.

COCKE, Philip St. George (1809-1861)

Philip Cocke resigned from the regular army two years after graduating from West Point in 1832 to pursue the life of a planter and philanthropist—until he was called upon and appointed brigadier general of Virginia State Troops on April 21, 1861. Three days later he was assigned to command the Alexandria Line opposite Washington. He was transfered to Confederate service as colonel, 19th Virginia, on May 10 but retained command of the Alexandria Line until superseded by General Bonham on the 21st. On June 20, 1861, he was given command of a brigade in the Army of the Potomac, the newly organized successor to the Alexandria command. During the 1st Battle of Bull Run, Cooke had command of his own brigade plus Colonel Nathan Evans' demi-brigade. His knowledge of the battlefield was put to good use as he directed reinforcements to Evans' aid and finally, at the close of the battle, abandoned his sector of the line, which was then not seriously threatened, and took his own brigade to the main battle area. Promoted to brigadier general, CSA, on October 21, 1861, he shortly afterwards returned home, a man broken by the rigors of field service, and on the day after Christmas took his own life. (Freeman, Douglas S., *Lee's Lieutenants*)

COCKERILL, Joseph Randolph (1818-1875)

Until his resignation shortly before the start of the Atlanta Campaign, Virginia-born Joseph R. Cockerill fought through most of the important actions in the Western theater. He had a varied prewar career as lawyer, teacher, surveyor, Ohio legislator, and U.S. congressman. His Civil War assignments included: colonel, 70th Ohio (December 20, 1861); commanding 3rd Brigade, District of Memphis, 13th Corps, Department of the Tennessee (October 26-November 12, 1862); commanding 2nd Brigade, 1st Division, District of Memphis, 13th Corps, Department of the Tennessee (November 12-December 18, 1862); commanding 2nd Brigade, 1st Division, 17th Corps, Army of the Tennessee (December 18, 1862-January 20, 1863); commanding 2nd Brigade, 1st Division, 16th Corps, Army of the Tennessee (January 20-March 22, 1863); commanding 3rd Brigade, 1st Division, 16th Corps, Army of the Tennessee (March 22-July 28, 1863); and commanding 3rd Brigade, 4th Division, 15th Corps, Army of the Tennessee (July 28-August 20, 1863, September 20, 1863-January 27, 1864, and March 12-April 13, 1864). He led his regiment in the fighting at Shiloh and took part in the siege of Corinth. He then commanded a brigade in western Tennessee and northern Mississippi until ordered to the Vicksburg lines in early June 1863. Following the fall of that city, he accompanied Sherman to the relief of Chattanooga and then went to the aid of Burnside at Knoxville. Resigning on April 13, 1864, he was brevetted brigadier the following March. Afterwards he returned to the Ohio legislature.

COCKRELL, Francis Marion (1834-1915)

Starting the Civil War as a company commander in the Missouri State Guard, native Missourian lawyer Francis M. Cockrell rose to a brigadier generalship in the regular Confederate service and was in charge of a division when the end came. His assignments included: captain, 3rd Infantry, 1st Brigade, 2nd Division, Missouri State Guard (early 1861); captain, Company H, 2nd Missouri (January 15, 1862); lieutenant colonel, 2nd Missouri (May 1862); colonel, 2nd Missouri (June 29, 1862); commanding 1st (Missouri) Brigade, Bowen's Division, Department of Mississippi and East Louisiana (April 17-July 4, 1863); commanding brigade, French's Division, Polk's (Army of Mississippi)-Stewart's Corps, Army of Tennessee (May-July and August-November 30, 1864); and commanding French's Division, District of the Gulf, Department of Alabama, Mississippi and East Louisiana (March-April 12, 1865). With the Missouri State Guard, he fought at Carthage and Wilson's Creek. Early in 1862 he transferred to the Confederate service and fought at Pea Ridge. Crossing the Mississippi, he took part in the defense of Corinth and was then engaged in thwarting Grant's lengthy operations against Vicksburg. Finally captured, in command of the Missouri Brigade, upon the fall of the city, he was exchanged on September 12, 1863. In the meantime he had been promoted to brigadier general. A hand wound suffered in the siege did not prevent him from leading the brigade through most of the Atlanta Campaign. Accompanying Hood on his drive into middle Tennessee, Cockrell suffered three wounds at Franklin. During the final months of the war he commanded the division at Mobile. Following the surrender of the city on April 12, 1865, he was paroled and resumed his practice. Later he spent six terms in the U.S. Senate and sat on the Interstate Commerce Commission. (Anderson, Ephraim McD., Edwin C. Bearss, ed., *Memoirs: Historical and Personal; Including the Campaigns of the First Missouri Confederate Brigade*)

COEHOORN, Baron Menno van (1641-1704)

Although Baron Menno van Coehoorn had been dead for more than a century and a half, the mortar he designed proved very effective in some of the major siege operations of the Civil War. The Dutch fortifications expert had designed his 4.6-inch Coehoorn mortar in the 17th century. It was a highly portable weapon with a wide angle of fire and a range of 1,200 yards. The Union forces had both 17- and 24-pounder models in use, and they saw action in such sieges as Vicksburg and Petersburg and at Cold Harbor.

COFFEY, Titian J. (?-?)

In one of the shortest tenures as a cabinet official—albeit in an acting capacity—Titian J. Coffey served as U.S. attorney general for one week. Assistant attorney general during much of the Civil War, he took over the portfolio when Edward Bates resigned the office on November 24, 1864, in disgust over the actions of the more radical cabinet members, especially William H. Seward, Edwin M. Stanton, and Salmon P. Chase. On December 1, 1864, James Speed of Kentucky was permanently named to the position and Coffey returned to his former position.

COFFIN, Charles Carleton (1823-1896)

Many believe that the only journalist to cover the entire war was Charles Coffin of the *Boston Journal*—who used his middle name as a pen name. Briefly a farmer and surveyor, Coffin had been laid off for economic reasons by the *Journal* when the war started. In Washington at the time of the battle of 1st Bull Run, he covered the fight on his own hook and wired the story to Boston. He was promptly rehired. He went on to cover Fort Donelson, Antietam, the Charleston bombardment, Gettysburg, Grant's 1864 Virginia Campaign, briefly Atlanta, the capture of Richmond, and the ceremonial reraising of the U.S. flag at Fort Sumter. Frequently exposing himself in combat, he became known for his zeal in getting his copy to his editors before any of his competitors. He believed in "straight to the mark" reporting rather than the more common flowery variety and was known to make more judicious evaluations than his colleagues of the importance of various battles. His reputation from the Civil War years brought him some 2,000 postwar speaking engagements. (Coffin, Charles Carleton, *My Days and Nights on the Battlefield* and *Following the Flag* and *Marching to Victory*, and Griffis, William Elliott, *Charles Carleton Coffin, War Correspondent, Traveller, Author, Statesman*)

COLBAITH, Jeremiah Jones

See: *Wilson, Henry*

COLBERT, Wallace Bruce (1834-1865)

As the colonel of the 40th Mississippi, W. Bruce Colbert was in command of a brigade for a month early in the war but he never graduated to the position permanently. He became colonel upon the unit's organization in mid-1862 and fought at the battle of Iuka. Due to the death of division commander Little and the ascension of General Hébert to division level, Colbert commanded Hébert's (2nd) Brigade, Little's (1st) Division, Price's Corps, Army of West Tennessee, Department No. 2 (September 19-mid October 1862). At this higher level he fought at Corinth. He next took part in the Vicksburg Campaign and was captured with his command upon the river city's fall. Exchanged, he led his regiment in the Department of Alabama, Mississippi and East Louisiana until it accompanied General Polk to northern Georgia to help oppose Sherman's drive on Atlanta. He took part in the campaign until mid-June 1864. He rejoined the army of Tennessee for Hood's disastrous Tennessee Campaign, including fighting at Franklin and Nashville. This was his last service. He died in 1865.

COLEMAN, Henry Eaton (1837-1890)

During the Civil War Virginia born Henry E. Coleman was forced to leave his regiment on two occasions, first when he failed to gain reelection and second when he was wounded at Spotsylvania. In fact he was not even with his regiment when he achieved his greatest glory. Leaving his native North Carolina to serve the Confederacy, he held the following assignments: captain, Company B, 12th North Carolina (April 26, 1861); lieutenant colonel and volunteer aide-de-camp (early 1863); and colonel, 12th North Carolina (August 11, 1863 to rank from May 4, 1863). As with so many other qualified officers, he had attended the Virginia Military Institute, but he failed to gain reelection to his captaincy during the May 1862 reorganization of the regiment. Less than a year later he was serving on the staff of General Iverson, the 12th's brigade commander, and after distinguishing himself at Gettysburg he was commissioned colonel and assigned to his old regiment. He led this unit through the Bristoe and Mine Run campaigns and at the Wilderness. At Spotsylvania Court House, on May 12, 1864, he was wounded so severely that he was never able to rejoin his unit. While recovering from his injury, he took part in the defense of the Staunton River Bridge on June 25. He was cited for his gallant conduct in this action against Wilson's Union cavalry.

COLFAX, Schuyler (1823-1885)

Speaker of the House of Representatives in the latter part of the Civil War, Schuyler Colfax had his political career irreparably damaged by the Crédit Mobilier scandal while serving as Grant's first-term vice president. Born in New York City, he moved with his family to Indiana in 1836 and became an auditor. Entering the field of political journalism, he had an interest in the Whig newspaper for northern Indiana. As a member of that party he lost an 1850 bid for Congress but won four years later as a Republican. He served continuously from 1855 until he took office as Vice President on March 4, 1869. At the beginning of the first session of the 38th Congress, on December 7, 1863, he was elected to the speakership and held that office for the balance of his congressional career. He failed to gain the vice presidential renomination, in part due to revelations in the financial scandal. Although he was cleared of the charges it adversely affected his political aspirations. He thereafter limited himself to the lecture circuit. (Smith, Willard H., *Schuyler Colfax: The Changing Fortunes of a Political Idol*)

COLLAMER, Jacob (1792-1865)

Much of Jacob Collamer's political career focused on the sectional crisis which led to a civil war that he barely outlived. Born in New York, he was admitted to the Vermont bar in 1813 after serving in the War of 1812. In the 1820s he sat for four terms in the state legislature and served two years as a state attorney. From 1833 to 1842 he sat as a judge and then served three terms as a Whig representative in Congress from 1843 to 1849. In 1849-50 he was postmaster general in the cabinet of Zachary Taylor. For the next four years he was again a judge. During this time he was considered a moderate antislavery man and opposed Stephen A. Douglas on the right of outsiders, especially New Englanders, to support their Free-Soil friends in Kansas. Switching to the Republicans, he sat in the Senate from 1855 until his death on November 9, 1865. On the same day that

Schuyler Colfax, Speaker of the U.S. House of Representatives. (NA)

South Carolina seceded he was named to the Committee of Thirteen, which was supposed to seek a compromise to the sectional conflict. During the war itself Collamer repeatedly expressed a lack of confidence in Secretary of State William H. Seward and long doubted Lincoln's chances for reelection in 1864.

COLLINS, Napoleon (1814-1875)

A career naval officer, Napoleon Collins was in frequent hot water for his cavalier attitude toward international law. Having entered the U.S. Navy at the relatively old age of 20, he had seen combat action in the Mexican War and risen to the rank of lieutenant by the outbreak of the Civil War. On November 7, 1861, he was the skipper of the gunboat *Unadilla* in the battle of Port Royal. Promoted to commander in July 1862, he was captain of the *Octarara* in the West Indies Squadron when he seized a British vessel, the *Mont Blanc*, in the Bahamas. Although a prize court found some justification in his action, the vessel was returned and Collins was censured. Assigned to another craft, the *Wachusett*, he again got into trouble for violating international law. He was in the port of Bahia in neutral Brazil when on October 5, 1864, the C.S.S. *Florida* came into port. Two days later he rammed the raider at night and fired a couple of shots until the Confederates surrendered. He then proceeded to tow the prize out to sea, ignoring the pursuing and firing Brazilian gunboats. Upon landing in the United States, he was suspended from duty and ordered before a court-martial which sentenced him to dismissal. This was set aside, however, and he resumed active duty after the close of the war. Rising to rear admiral, he died in Peru still on duty. (Macartney, Clarence Edward, *Mr. Lincoln's Admirals*)

COLQUITT, Alfred Holt (1824-1894)

One of Lee's brigade commanders who failed the grade, Alfred H. Colquitt was traded, with his brigade, for another then serving in North Carolina but was back under Lee again a year later. His legal practice had been interrupted by the Mexican War in which he served as a paymaster of volunteers. Entering politics, he served his native Georgia in Congress and later in the state legislature. In the Civil War his assignments included: captain, Infantry (1861); colonel, 6th Georgia (May 27, 1861); commanding brigade, Department of the Peninsula (October 1861); commanding Rains' (old) Brigade, D.H. Hill's Division (in 1st Corps from June 29 and 2nd Corps from July 27), Army of Northern Virginia (June 18, 1862-May 20, 1863): brigadier general, CSA (September 1, 1862); commanding brigade, in the District of the Cape Fear in July); Department of North Carolina (May-July 1863); commanding 3rd Subdivision (Morris Island), 1st Military District of South Carolina, Department of South Carolina, Georgia and Florida (August 1863); commanding Western Division (or 2nd Sub-District), 7th Military District of South Carolina, same department (October 22, 1863-January 1864); commanding brigade, same district and department (January-February 1864); commanding brigade, District of (until February 23: East) Florida, same department (February-May 1864); commanding division, Department of North Carolina and Southern Virginia (mid-May 1864); commanding brigade, Hoke's Division, same Department (May-October 19, 1864); commanding brigade, Hoke's Division, Anderson's Corps, Army of Northern Virginia (October 19-December 20, 1864); commanding brigade, Hoke's Division, Department of North Carolina (December 1864-March 1865); commanding brigade, Hoke's Division, Hardee's Corps (March-April 9, 1865); and commanding brigade, same division and corps, Army of Tennessee (April 9-26, 1865). Sent to the Peninsula of Virginia in the first year of the war, Colquitt and his regiment fought at Yorktown, Williamsburg, and Seven Pines. He succeeded General Rains in brigade command for the Seven Days and later led it at Antietam. Promoted to the position permanently, he led the unit at Fredericksburg and Chancellorsville. At the latter he put in a poor performance during Jackson's attack on May 2. He halted his brigade because of the fear of enemy cavalry on his right. Although he redeemed himself somewhat the next day, his brigade was swapped for Junius Daniel's from the Department of North Carolina. After serving in the Carolinas, he led his brigade to Florida and took part in the victory at Olustee. Three months later he was back in Virginia, under Beauregard, and fought at Drewry's Bluff, temporarily in charge of a small division. Attached to Hoke's division, he soon joined Lee for Cold Harbor and took part in the first months of the siege of Petersburg. Sent in December 1864 to the Wilmington area, he later fought at Bentonville and surrendered with Johnston. After the war he spent a stormy term, full of charges of dishonesty, as governor and later sat in the U.S. Senate. (Freeman, Douglas S., *Lee's Lieutenants*)

COLQUITT, Peyton H. (1832-1863)

The brother of Confederate General Alfred H. Colquitt, Peyton H. Colquitt did not live long enough to reach that rank. The Georgian's assignments included: colonel, 46th Georgia (March 17, 1862); commanding 4th and 5th Military District of South Carolina, Department of South Carolina, Georgia and Florida (April-May 6, 1862); commanding Gist's Brigade, Department of the West (May-June 1863); and commanding Gist's Brigade, Walker's Division, Reserve Corps, Army of Tennessee (September-September 20, 1863). Assigned with his regiment to the Atlantic seaboard, he was for a time in command of two districts in South Carolina before being ordered to Mississippi in the spring of 1863. Serving under Joseph E. Johnston in the attempts to relieve Vicksburg, he led a brigade at the battle of Jackson and after the river city's fall in the defense of Jackson against Sherman. Part of the Confederate buildup in northern Georgia prior to Chickamauga, he led his brigade toward that bloody field. He became very impatient with the railroad engineers for delays, fearing that he would miss the battle. However, on the second day of the fight, September 20, he was killed in action.

COLSTON, Raleigh Edward (1825-1896)

Paris-born Raleigh E. Colston was found wanting by General Lee and was relegated to the less active areas of the war. Granted

U.S. citizenship, he was educated at the Virginia Military Institute and served there for a decade and a half as a French professor. His Civil War assignments included: colonel, 16th Virginia (May 1861); brigadier general, CSA (December 24, 1861); commanding 1st Brigade, Department of Norfolk (late 1861-early April 1862); commanding same brigade, McLaws' Division, Department of the Peninsula (early April-April 12, 1862); commanding brigade, McLaws' Division, Magruder's Command, Department of Northern Virginia (April 1862); commanding brigade, Longstreet's Division, same department (April-June 1862); commanding brigade, in Elzey's Command (December 20-late December 1862) and in French's Command (late December 1862-March 24, 1863), Department of Virginia and North Carolina; commanding Taliaferro's (old) Brigade, Jackson's (old) Division, 2nd Corps, Army of Northern Virginia (April and May 1863); commanding division (April-May 1863); commanding brigade, District of Georgia, Department of South Carolina, Georgia and Florida (October 20, 1863-April 16, 1864); commanding 1st Military District, Department of North Carolina and Southern Virginia (May 14, 1864-June 1, 1864); and commanding Post at Lynchburg, Virginia (June 4, 1864-April 1865). After serving around Norfolk, he moved to the Peninsula where he saw action at Williamsburg and Seven Pines. Sick for six months, he returned to command in the Richmond and Petersburg area before joining Lee's army. After a poor performance as a division leader at Chancellorsville he was shunted aside to less vital fields and after serving in Georgia finished the war at Lynchburg. A military educator after the war, he was paralyzed from the waist down in a camel accident while serving as a colonel in the Egyptian army. (Freeman, Douglas S., *Lee's Lieutenants*)

COLT, Samuel (1814-1862)

The inventor of the Union army's most popular revolver, Samuel Colt did not live to see the end of the Civil War. The Connecticut native had been interested in sidearms since the early 1830s. He received his first patent in 1836, but over the next few years he met with only limited success, even suffering a bankruptcy. The Mexican War changed this and by the outbreak of the Civil War his firm dominated the revolver market. His .36-caliber Navy and .44-caliber Army models were already widely distributed and the War Department's Ordnance Bureau purchased some 146,000 during the war. They were six-shooters that fired paper or linen cartridges—or loose powder and ball—by the action of old-fashioned percussion caps. Metallic cartridges would appear in Colts only after his death. He also designed a repeating rifle with a revolving barrel similar to that of a revolver that met with limited success in the war. It was briefly used by Hiram Berdan's 1st U.S. Sharpshooters. Although accurate at long range, it suffered from a defect that sometimes allowed more than one barrel to go off simultaneously, costing the marksman a hand or arm. After the regiment turned them in for Sharps rifles, the Colt Revolving Rifle saw little further service. Colt himself was authorized to raise the 1st Connecticut Revolving Rifles Regiment, but it was soon disbanded due to administrative problems.

COLTART, John Gordon (?-?)

In the final stages of the life of the Confederate Army of Tennessee the attrition among general officers was so great that John G. Coltart was commanding a division at Bentonville with the rank of colonel. His war assignments included: captain, Company E, 3rd (Coltart's) Battalion (April 2, 1861); lieutenant colonel, 3rd (Coltart's) Battalion (April 2, 1861); lieutenant colonel, 7th Alabama (May 18, 1861); colonel, 7th Alabama (January 1862); colonel, 26th (Coltart's) Alabama (April 3, 1862); commanding Deas' Brigade, Withers' Division, 1st Corps, Army of Tennessee (December 31, 1862-early 1863 and July-August 1863); colonel, 50th Alabama (June 6, 1863); commanding Deas' Brigade, Hindman's Division, 2nd Corps, Army of Tennessee (May-July 26 and July 28-August 1864); and commanding D.H. Hill's Division, 2nd Corps, Army of Tennessee (March 1865). His original unit was enlarged into a 12-months regiment, the 7th Alabama, with which he served in Pensacola and Tennessee. Upon its expiration of service he was given a new regiment, the 26th, later designated the 50th. A few days after taking command he was wounded on the first day at Shiloh. He recovered in time to fight at Murfreesboro where he took command of the brigade on the first day. He was at Chickamauga and Chattanooga as a regimental commander. In the Atlanta Campaign he was at times directing the brigade and was wounded. He went to Tennessee with Hood, seeing action at Franklin and Nashville. After those disasters, the remains of the army went to North Carolina trying to stop Sherman. His last service was as a division commander at Bentonville. This was two command levels above his appropriate rank due to heavy losses among generals. He does not appear to have been at the surrender in April.

COLVILL, William, Jr. (? - ?)

Having entered the Federal army as a captain in the 1st Minnesota at the beginning of the war, William Colvill, Jr., was later to have the distinction of leading the regiment that sustained the highest-percentage regimental loss in a single engagement during the war on either side. His commissions included: captain, 1st Minnesota (April 29, 1861); major, 1st Minnesota (August 28, 1862); lieutenant colonel, 1st Minnesota (September 26, 1862); colonel, 1st Minnesota (June 11, 1863); and colonel, 1st Minnesota Heavy Artillery (April 26, 1865). During the first two years of Colvill's service with the regiment, which was the first three-year unit mustered in, it served at 1st Bull Run, in the Peninsula Campaign, Antietam, Fredericksburg, and Chancellorsville, where as a lieutenant colonel, Colvill was in command of the regiment. On the second day at Gettysburg, during the later stages of Longstreet's assault on the Union lines, General Hancock ordered Colvill to take his regiment and stem the flight of the 3rd Corps. This proving impossible, Colvill ordered his men to charge the enemy. The unit took a position where it was fired upon from all sides until reinforcements came up. In this time the regiment lost 215 out of 262 soldiers, or 82 percent. Colvill, who had been under arrest for allowing his men to cross a stream on a log instead of wading it, redeemed himself, but suffered a wound in the action. With his term of service expired, Colvill was mustered out on May 5, 1864. At the very end of the war he was made colonel of the 1st Minnesota Heavy Artillery, which was stationed at Chattanooga. He was brevetted brigadier general of volunteers and resigned on July 13, 1865. (Imholte, John Quinn, *The First Volunteers, History of the Minnesota Volunteer Regiment, 1861-1865*)

COMMAGER, Henry Steele (ca. 1825-1867)

An Ohio Democratic politician, Henry Steele Commager became a brevet brigadier in the Union army and later passed his name down to a historian in the family. The Pennsylvania-born officer held the following commissions: second lieutenant, 67th Ohio (October 8, 1861); captain, 67th Ohio (November 10, 1861); major, 67th Ohio (August 8, 1862); lieutenant colonel, 67th Ohio (September 4, 1862); colonel, 184th Ohio (February 22, 1865); and brevet brigadier general, USV (February 27, 1865). Serving with the 67th, which fought in the Shenandoah Valley Campaign of 1862, on the North and South Carolina coasts, and in the operations against the railroad between Richmond and Petersburg, Commager was cited several times for distinguished service in official reports. During the siege operations against Richmond and Petersburg, he was sent back to Ohio to take command of a new regiment, the 184th, with which he served principally at Bridgeport, Alabama, protecting the Nashville and Chattanooga Railroad. After the war he served as a government bureaucrat.

COMSTOCK, Cyrus Ballou (ca. 1831-1910)

Having graduated first in his 1855 class at West Point, Massachusetts native Cyrus B. Comstock rose to the rank of brevet major general of volunteers while serving as an engineering and staff officer during the Civil War. In the prewar years he performed routine duties and was a lecturer at his alma mater. His Civil War-era assignments included: first lieutenant, Engineers (since July 1, 1860); assistant to the chief engineer, Army of the Potomac (spring-June 2, 1862); chief engineer, 2nd Corps, Army of the Potomac (June 2-July 3, 1862); chief engineer, Army of the Potomac (late 1862-March 30, 1863); captain, engineers (March 3, 1863); chief engineer, Army of the Tennessee (July 1-October 16, 1863); lieutenant colonel and assistant inspector general (November 19, 1863); assistant inspector general, Military Division of the Mississippi (November 19, 1863-March 20, 1864); lieutenant colonel and aide-de-camp (March 29, 1864); aide-de-camp, commander in chief (March 29, 1864-1866); chief engineer, Terry's Provisional Corps, Department of North Carolina (January 1865); chief engineer, Military Division of West Mississippi (spring 1865); major, Engineers (December 28, 1865); and colonel and aide-de-camp (July 25, 1866-May 3, 1870). Initially posted to the defenses of the capital, he then served on the Peninsula. At Antietam he served with the regular battalion of engineers. He was the army's engineering chief during the battle of Fredericksburg and was in the Chancellorsville Campaign. Transferred to the West, he was on Grant's staff at the fall of Vicksburg and the relief of Chattanooga. He then accompanied his chief to the eastern theater and won a brevet at the Wilderness. Serving through the rest of the Overland Campaign and much of the Petersburg siege, he was detached from Grant's staff for the operations against Fort Fisher and Mobile. For both of these he was brevetted. Emerging from the war as a brevet brigadier general of regulars and a brevet major general of volunteers, he continued on the staffs of Grant and Sherman, first as a lieutenant colonel and then colonel from 1866 to 1870. Then he reverted to his regular engineering rank and served until his 1895 retirement as a colonel.

CONGER, Everton J. (?-?)

Having served through much of the Civil War in the area of northern Virginia through which John Wilkes Booth and David Herold fled from their crimes, Everton J. Conger was a good choice to lead one of the most promising pursuit efforts. His earlier assignments had included: captain, 3rd (West) Virginia Cavalry (ca. December 1861); major, 1st District of Columbia Cavalry (1863); and lieutenant colonel, 1st District of Columbia Cavalry (1864). Under John C. Frémont, he had commanded a cavalry squadron at Cross Keys and elsewhere in the Shenandoah Valley. Made a field officer in a regiment raised for special service in and around Washington, he frequently operated against John S. Mosby. He commanded the regiment in Butler's operations along the James River and the subsequent siege operations against Richmond and Petersburg. Called back to Washington, he became a colonel in the Secret Service of the War Department, in which position he was given this assignment. Along with a detective lieutenant, Luther B. Baker, he supervised one of the many detachments of cavalry scouring the countryside for the Lincoln assassin. The actual cavalry detachment comprised 26 men from the 16th New York Cavalry and was under the immediate command of Lieutenant Edward P. Doherty. Picking up the trail, the 29-member detachment crossed the Rappahannock at Port Conway and caught up with a Confederate captain, Willie Jett, who had briefly accompanied Booth and Herold, in Bowling Green. Jett revealed to Conger that Booth was at the Richard H. Garrett farm. Returning the way they had come, the party caught Herold, but Booth was either shot by Boston Corbett or committed suicide. Conger's share of the reward money came to $15,000.

CONKLING, Roscoe (1829-1888)

As a result of Union military reverses, party zealot and Lincoln supporter Roscoe Conkling lost his seat in Congress in the 1862 elections but was able to regain it two years later. The New York native was a lawyer and had served as a district attorney in 1850. In 1858 he was the mayor of Utica and that year he was elected as a Republican to the U.S. House of Representatives. There he became involved in the dispute over issuing greenbacks as legal tender for all debts. After two terms he lost his bid for reelection and left office on March 3, 1863. He returned to his old seat on March 4, 1865, and was reelected in 1866. However he resigned on the first day of the 40th Congress in order to take a seat in the Senate. Twice reelected, he resigned in 1881 over an appointments dispute. Returning to his private practice, he declined an appointment to the Supreme Court the next year. (Chidsey, Donald Barr, *The Gentleman From New York: A Life of Roscoe Conkling*)

CONNALLY, John Kerr (1839-1904)

After attending the U.S. Naval Academy at Annapolis, John Connally entered the Confederate land forces and became an example of the problems caused by "honor" in the Southern military. A resident of Yadkin County, he was appointed captain, Company B, 21st North Carolina, on May 12, 1861. After seeing service at the battle of 1st Bull Run, Connally became colonel, 55th North Carolina, on May 19, 1862. During Longstreet's siege of Suffolk in April 1863, Connally's regiment was assigned the task of protecting the Confederate guns in Fort Huger. On the evening of the 19th a Union force attacked and captured five guns and 137 soldiers. There was negligence on the part of both Connally and General Law, both of whom tried to blame the other. Captains Terrell and Cussons of Law's staff reported that the 55th had acted in a cowardly manner. Connally demanded satisfaction and was joined by Major Belo in challenging the two staff officers to a duel. While Belo and Cussons fired two rounds at each other, Connally and Terrell settled the quarrel without violence, and all parties resumed the business of killing Yankees instead of each other. Joining the Army of Northern Virginia, Colonel Connally was wounded and captured at Gettysburg. He was not exchanged until March 1864. He fought in the Wilderness and at Spotsylvania, handicapped by the loss of one arm, and was again wounded at Cold Harbor and at Petersburg. He resigned on March 7, 1865, and became a lawyer. After nearly being killed in a collapse of part of the Virginia state capitol, he became a minister. (Freeman, Douglas S., *Lee's Lieutenants*)

CONNER, James (1829-1883)

It took two wounds in the same leg to permanently place James Conner out of commission for further field service. As a district attorney in his native South Carolina he had prosecuted both slave traders and a member of William Walker's Central American filibustering expedition. Nonetheless, he was an active secessionist and had pushed for the secession convention of which he was a member but did not vote on the ordinance itself. He declined appointment as a district attorney for the Confederacy preferring to enter the military. His assignments included: captain, Infantry Company A, Hampton's (S.C.) Legion (May 1861); major, Hampton's Legion (July 21, 1861); colonel, 22nd North Carolina (June 13, 1862); brigadier general, CSA (June 1, 1864); commanding McGowan's Brigade, Wilcox's Division, 3rd Corps, Army of Northern Virginia (June 4-summer 1864); and commanding Kershaw's (old) Brigade, Kershaw's Division, 1st Corps, Army of Northern Virginia (summer-October 13, 1864). At the head of the Washington Light Infantry, part of Hampton's Legion, he fought at 1st Bull Run and succeeded to its command upon the wounding of Colonel Wade Hampton. Promoted to major, he fought at Yorktown, West Point, and Seven Pines before being appointed colonel of a North Carolina regiment. At Mechanicsville, at the start of the Seven Days, he was wounded in the leg. Apparently not rejoining his regiment, he resigned on August 13, 1863, and became a member of the military court of the 2nd Corps in the fall of 1863. Appointed brigadier the following spring, he was given temporary charge of the wounded McGowan's Brigade. Upon the latter's return, Conner took command of Kershaw's old Brigade and led it to the Shenandoah Valley. In a small action near Fisher's Hill on October 13, 1864, he was again wounded in the same leg necessitating its amputation. This ended his field service. He was active in law and politics after Appomattox. (Moffett, Mary C., ed. *Letters of General James Conner, C.S.A.*)

CONNER, Zephaniah Turner (1811-1866)

Stonewall Jackson was known for his tendency to condemn subordinate officers, often on questionable grounds, but Zephaniah T. Conner was certainly deserving of the general's wrath. He had entered the Confederate army at the beginning of the war and his assignments included: private, Company A, 1st Georgia (May 15, 1861); lieutenant colonel, 12th Georgia (July 2, 1861); colonel, 12th Georgia (December 13, 1862); and commanding 1st Brigade, Army of the Northwest (ca. April-May 1862). After seeing action at Cheat Mountain, Romney, and McDowell he took part in the beginning stages of Jackson's Shenandoah Valley Campaign. When the Confederates scored a complete victory at Front Royal, capturing a large amount of supplies and some prisoners, it was the 12th Georgia which was detailed to guard the area while the rest of the army went on towards Winchester. But on May 30 Conner was faced with the advance of a Union column from the east. Losing his head, he took off for Winchester to report to Jackson. His regiment set fire to the captured supplies and withdrew after him. When Conner reported to Jackson that he had suffered no men killed or wounded, the general immediately placed him under arrest. The court-martial kept being delayed by the lack of officers for the court during a season of active campaigning. Finally, on about January 22, 1863, Conner resigned. He died a year after the war ended. (Freeman, Douglas, S., *Lee's Lieutenants*)

CONNESS, John (1821-1909)

The Civil War prompted many politicians to change their party affiliations and such was the case with California Senator John Conness. Born in County Galway, Ireland, he had immigrated to the United States in 1833 and gone west in the California gold rush. There he engaged in mining and became a merchant. In the mid 1850s and again in 1860-61 he sat in the state legislature. In 1861 he ran unsuccessfully for governor, then in 1863 was named to the U.S. Senate as a Douglas Democrat. During his one term, from March 4, 1863, to March 3, 1869, he switched to the Union Republicans. He then retired to Massachusetts.

CONNOR, Patrick Edward (1820-1891)

Union General Patrick E. Connor spent the Civil War dealing with Mormons and Indians rather than Confederates. A native of County Kerry, Ireland, he was raised in New York before entering the regular army as an enlisted man. He served against the Seminoles in Florida and moved to Texas after his discharge. During the Mexican War he was a lieutenant and captain of Texas volunteers and fought at Palo Alto, Resaca de la Palma, and Buena Vista. He was wounded at the latter. The Gold Rush drew him to California where he was living at the outbreak of the Civil War. He reenlisted and his assignments included: colonel, 3rd California (September 4, 1861); brigadier general, USV (March 30, 1863); and commanding District of Utah, Department of the Pacific (August 6, 1864-1865). Sent to Utah to maintain the lines of communication with the rest of the country, he became an opponent of the Mormon Church. With a limited force he was able to deal effectively with the various Indian tribes in his domain. On January 29, 1863, with only 300 men and two howitzers he defeated the Indians at Bear River, killing 224 of them. Only 68 of his men were killed or wounded. The Washington authorities rewarded him with the star of a brigadier. During the latter part of the war the Indians in his district were relatively peaceful but he continued to come into conflict with the Mormons. Brevetted major general for the war, he was mustered out on April 30, 1866. He settled in Utah and was a pioneer in journalism, mining, and transportation in Salt Lake City. (Colton, Ray C., *The Civil War in the Western Territories*)

CONNOR, Selden (1839-1917)

By the time Selden Connor received his brigadier general's commission, previous wounds would keep him from performing further field duty. A law student at the outbreak of the Civil War, he promptly entered the Union army from Vermont as an enlisted man before later accepting a commission in a unit from his native Maine. His assignments included: private, 1st Vermont (May 2, 1861); lieutenant colonel, 7th Maine (August 22, 1861); colonel, 19th Maine (January 11, 1864); commanding 1st Brigade, 2nd Division, 2nd Corps, Army of the Potomac (February 27-March 25, 1864); and brigadier general, USV (June 11, 1864). Five companies of his first regiment fought at Big Bethel before being mustered out on August 15, 1861. A week later he had a commission, and he fought with his regiment at Williamsburg and the Seven Days, but was not present at Antietam. During the Fredericksburg Campaign the regiment was recruiting in Maine. Returning to the army, he commanded the regiment at Chancellorsville—where it took part in the operations near Fredericksburg—and Gettysburg. In early 1864 he commanded a brigade until the spring reorganization returned him to his regiment. On the second day in the battle of the Wilderness he was particularly distinguished in the face of Longstreet's assault but suffered a crippling wound in the thigh. The next month he was made a general officer but was confined to administrative functions until he was mustered out on April 7, 1866. A fall then confined him to his home for two years. He was subsequently a tax official, governor of Maine, and pension agent.

CONRAD, Charles Magill (1804-1878)

One of the members of the Confederate Congress whose experiences typified those of Southern politicians in general, was Charles M. Conrad. Born in Virginia, Conrad moved to Louisiana with his family. He was in due course admitted to the bar in New Orleans and engaged in politics as a Jacksonian Democrat and later as a Whig. He developed a large plantation and was a successful duelist. He served in the state legislature and in both houses of the U.S. Congress, before becoming secretary of war under President Fillmore. In the mid and late 1850s he was highly successful in private practice but maintained an interest in politics, supporting the Constitutional Union ticket in 1860. He started his Confederate career as one of Louisiana's delegates to the Provisionial Congress. He remained in the legislative branch for the entire war. During his three terms representing the New Orleans district in Congress he served on the following committees: Executive Departments; Naval Affairs; Ordnance and Ordnance Stores; Public Buildings; and Ways and Means. While chairing the Committee on Naval Affairs, Conrad suggested the Navy Department's merger with the War Department in an effort to get rid of Secretary of the Navy Stephen R. Mallory. It is perhaps for this reason that Conrad was given a different committee assignment in the Second Congress. He felt that the conduct of the war should be left to the executive branch and the military, and he basically supported all war measures that Davis proposed. With his plantation confiscated, Conrad resumed the practice of law after Appomattox.

CONROW, Aaron H. (1824-1865)

Although he died after the end of hostilities, Missouri Congressman Aaron H. Conrow certainly was a casualty of the Civil War, dying in Mexico while trying to flee to England in order to avoid the uncertainties of defeat. Born north of the Ohio River, in Cincinnati, his family moved by way of Illinois to Missouri where he eventually became a lawyer and judge. His sympathies ultimately were with the South, so he became a secessionist and raised a company for the Missouri State Guard in which he was commissioned a colonel. With the alleged "secession" of Missouri Conrow was named to the Provisional Confederate Congress and remained in that body and the regular congresses throughout the war. A slow convert to the idea of total war, he soon became a supporter of the Davis administration. Representing the 4th Division in the northwestern corner of Missouri, which was in enemy hands for most of the war, Conrow was reelected by the exile vote. His committee assignments included those on: Finance; Post Offices and Post Roads; Public Buildings; and Quartermaster's and Commissary Departments. With the collapse of the Confederacy, Conrow accompanied General Mosby M. Parsons and two staff officers through Mexico in an effort to reach California and take ship for England. Attacked by Juarista troops on August 15, 1865, Conrow and the officers all perished.

CONWAY, William (?-?)

In the confusing days before Fort Sumter was fired upon, William Conway proved to be a hero. An ordinary seaman in the U.S. Navy, he was stationed at the Pensacola navy yard during the secession crisis when Commodore James Armstrong gave the order to turn the facility over to the rebels. Ordered to haul down the national colors by Lieutenant F.B. Renshaw, he defied the directive.

CONY, Samuel (1811-1870)

Originally a War Democrat, Samuel Cony was elected governor of Maine as a Republican. The Maine native had practiced law before entering the state legislature and serving on the council of the governor. He later served as a land agent and state treasurer. An abolitionist, he supported the early war effort wholeheartedly as a Democrat but soon found a better home in the Republican Party. Elected to the legislature in 1862, he won the gubernatorial race the next year and was inaugurated on January 6, 1864. He served a total of three terms. He was an energetic chief executive in providing troops and supplies. He retired to private practice on January 2, 1867. (Hebert, Richard A., *Modern Maine*)

COOK, George Smith (1819-1902)

Although overshadowed by Brady and other Northern photographers, George Cook was an outstanding artist who covered the war in Charleston Harbor. Moving to the South at the age of 14, the Connecticut-born Cook entered the field of photography and traveled throughout the South establishing daguerreotype studios. He settled in Charleston in 1849 and two years later, when Brady went overseas, Cook took over his gallery in New York and opened one of his own. He later set up shop in Chicago and Philadelphia. But with the coming of war, he concentrated his enterprises in Charleston. With an eye for history, he took the famous shot of Major Robert Anderson and his staff at Fort Sumter. Following the fort's fall, Cook continued to cover the war, in addition to his portrait business, photographing the fort after its fall and during the subsequent siege by the Union forces. He frequently exposed himself to enemy fire to acquire images. He scored a photographic first by capturing three monitors in action. On September 8, 1863, while exposing a view of Fort Sumter's interior, a Union shell exploded and he captured it on film—a rare occurrence. He remained financially solvent during the inflationary life of the Confederacy by requiring payment in gold. Cook remained active in photography, in New York, Richmond, and Charleston, until his death. (Kocher, A. Lawrence and Dearstyne, Howard, *Shadows in Silver*)

COOK, John (1825-1910)

After early fighting against the Confederates, Union General John Cook spent most of the Civil War serving against Indians and Copperheads. A native Illinois merchant and real estate speculator, he had held office as the mayor of Springfield and as a county sheriff. Joining the army upon the outbreak of hostilities, his assignments included: colonel, 7th Illinois (April 25, 1861); colonel, 7th Illinois (reorganized for three years July 25, 1861); commanding 4th Brigade, District of Southeast Missouri, Western Department (October 14-November 9, 1861); commanding 4th Brigade, District of Southeast Missouri, Department of the Missouri (November 9-December 23, 1861); commanding 4th Brigade, District of Cairo, Department of the Missouri (December 23, 1861-February 1, 1862); commanding 3rd Brigade, 2nd Division, District of Cairo, Department of the Missouri (February 1-17, 1862); commanding 3rd Brigade, 2nd Division, Army of the Tennessee (February 17-March 29, 1862); brigadier general, USV (March 21, 1862); and commanding District of Illinois, Northern Department (1864-65). He served under Grant in the operations against Forts Henry and Donelson and won a brigadier's star for the latter. Before the battle of Shiloh he was detached from Grant's command. He then fought the Sioux in the Minnesota area before returning to head the district composed of his native state. There he was primarily concerned with guarding prisoners and attempting to thwart the peace and Northwest separatist movements. On the day of his mustering out, August 24, 1865, he was brevetted major general for his war service. He was later a state legislator and an Indian agent.

COOK, Philip (1817-1894)

A Georgia attorney, Philip Cook rose from the ranks to the command of a brigade in Lee's army. His assignments included: private, Company I, 4th Georgia (May 1861); first lieutenant and adjutant, 4th Georgia (1861); lieutenant colonel, 4th Georgia (ca. August 15, 1862); colonel, 4th Georgia (November 1, 1862); commanding Doles' (old) Brigade, Rodes' Division, 2nd Corps, Army of Northern Virginia (June 2-13, 1864); commanding same brigade, Rodes'-Grimes' Division, Valley District, Department of Northern Virginia (June 13-December 1864); brigadier general, CSA (August 5, 1864); and commanding brigade, Grimes' Division, 2nd Corps, Army of Northern Virginia (December 1864-March 25, 1865). Having seen some action against the Seminoles, he was soon rewarded with the position of adjutant. After serving in the Norfolk area, the regiment moved to the Peninsula and fought at Seven Pines and in the Seven Days. As a field officer he served at Antietam and succeeded George Doles in command when that officer took charge of the brigade. He was wounded at Chancellorsville and did not return for several months. In the Overland Campaign he succeeded Doles in brigade command and was promoted to brigadier in August. He joined Early in the Valley and saw action at 3rd Winchester, Fisher's Hill, and Cedar Creek. Moving into the trenches at Petersburg in December, he was severely wounded in the assault on Fort Stedman on March 25. He was captured in a hospital upon the fall of the city and was not released until July. He was a lawyer, congressman, and member of the governor's cabinet after the war. (Thomas, Henry W., *A History of the Doles-Cook Brigade, Army of Northern Virginia*)

COOKE, James Wallace (?-1869)

Resigning from the old navy as a lieutenant on May 1, 1861, James W. Cooke rose through the ranks to become a captain in the Confederate navy. On May 4, 1861, he was appointed a lieutenant in the Virginia navy. Transferred with the same rank to the Confederate service, he was assigned to the batteries at Aquia Creek blockading the Potomac River. Sent to North Carolina shortly after the battle of 1st Manassas, Cooke was given command of a small one-gun steamer, the *Ellis*. During this period he placed obstructions in Albemarle Sound to delay the enemy. At the battle of Roanoke Island on February 8, 1862, Cooke kept his vessel fighting until he had fired off the last round of his ammunition and that of a disabled Confederate gunboat. Two days later, at Elizabeth City, Cooke was forced to order his ship abandoned. It was already surrounded and being boarded by men from two Union gunboats, but his orders to destroy the ship were not carried out. With a bullet wound in the arm and a bayonet cut in the leg, Cooke himself was taken prisoner. Paroled, he returned home until exchanged in September. On the 17th he was promoted to commander, CSN. Sent to the Roanoke River, he received instructions to construct the ironclad *Albemarle*. His efforts to obtain supplies earned him the nickname of the "Iron Captain." With his vessel completed, he joined in the successful April 1864 attack on Plymouth, North Carolina. For this battle and an action in the Roanoke River on May 5, Cooke was promoted to captain, CSN, and given command of all naval forces in the Plymouth area. He held this position until the area was abandoned at the close of the war. He then retired to his home in Portsmouth, Virginia. (Scharf, J. Thomas, *History of the Confederate States Navy*)

COOKE, Jay (1821-1905)

As the financial wizard of the Union war effort, Jay Cooke has been credited with doing as much to win the war as the armies in the field. Born in Ohio, he left school at the age of 14 and within eight years was a partner in a Philadelphia banking firm. By 1858 he was able to go into semi-retirement. Through his father and brother, he became a financial advisor to Lincoln's Secretary of the Treasury Salmon P. Chase, a fellow Ohioan. Throughout much of the war he was the sole agent for the sale of government bond issues to public and private investors. Although this monopoly arrangement was frequently criticized in Congress, Cooke's actions were defended by Chase and another Ohio friend, Senator John Sherman (eventually head of the Committee on Finance). Early in the war he was instrumental in negotiating loan guarantees from the banking sector. In about half a year his Jay Cooke and Company sold over $850 million in bonds. This money kept the army in the field. In the final stages of the war he used millions of dollars of his own and his company's money to stabilize the market, which, due to the actions of speculators, was facing a panic. After the war his banking house was involved in railroad financing but during a panic in the 1870s he lost most of his fortune. He subsequently regained much of his losses. (Oberholtzer, Ellis Paxson, *Jay Cooke: Financier of the Civil War*)

COOKE, John Esten (1830-1886)

An established writer before the Civil War, John Esten Cooke used his experiences as the milieu for his postwar works. In the antebellum period he had written to further the secessionist cause, often appearing in the *Southern Literary Messenger*. As a member of the elite Richmond Howitzers artillery company he was present at the capture of John Brown at Harpers Ferry. Early in the Civil War he joined the staff of his cousin's husband, Jeb Stuart, and served through most of the illustrious cavalryman's campaigns. Meanwhile his uncle, Philip St. George Cooke, had become a Union general and his cousin, John R. Cooke, a Confederate one. After Stuart's death in 1864, he served as an inspector of horse artillery. Following his surrender at Appomattox, he resumed his writing career with both novels and histories. His biographies include *The Life of Stonewall Jackson* and *The Life of R.E. Lee*. His historical novels include *Surry of Eagle's Nest* and *Wearing of the Gray*. When not writing he was involved in agricultural pursuits. (Beatty, John O., *John Esten Cooke, Virginian*)

COOKE, John Rogers (1833-1891)

Confederate Brigadier General John R. Cooke's own case is an example of a family divided by the Civil War. His father was Union General Philip St. George Cooke, his brother-in-law Confederate Major General Jeb Stuart, and his cousin John Esten Cooke was on Stuart's staff. He had held an infantry lieutenant's commission in the Old Army for almost six years when he resigned on May 30, 1861, to go with the South. His assignments included: first lieutenant, Infantry (1861); major, Artillery (February 1862); colonel, 27th Virginia (April 24, 1862); brigadier general, CSA (November 1, 1862); commanding Walker's (old) Brigade, Ransom's Division, 1st Corps, Army of Northern Virginia (November 6-December 13, 1862); commanding brigade, 3rd Military District of South Carolina, Department of South Carolina, Georgia and Florida (ca. January-April 23, 1863); commanding brigade, District of the Cape Fear, Department of North Carolina (April 26-May 1, 1863); commanding brigade, same department (May-July 1863); commanding brigade (in Ransom's Division from late July), Department of Richmond (July-August 1863); and commanding a brigade (assigned to Heth's Division ca. October 3), 3rd Corps, Army of Northern Virginia (September-October 14, 1863 and early 1864-April 9, 1865). After serving with General Holmes in Virginia and North Carolina he was elected colonel of a regiment that he led in the Seven Days and at the capture of Harpers Ferry. At Antietam he made a charge with one other regiment, which was commended, and was promoted to command the brigade six weeks later. Wounded at Fredericksburg, he went with his command to South Carolina, North Carolina, and finally to the Richmond vicinity during the Gettysburg Campaign. He rejoined Lee's army and was again wounded in the assault at Bristoe Station. He recovered in time for the Wilderness and led his men through Spotsylvania, Cold Harbor, Petersburg, and to the surrender at Appomattox. A Richmond merchant he helped found the Confederate Soldiers' Home. (Freeman, Douglas S., *Lee's Lieutenants*)

COOKE, Philip St. George (1809-1895)

Probably the most embarrassing moment in the Civil War career of Union General Philip St. George Cooke came during the Peninsula Campaign when his son-in-law, Confederate cavalry commander Jeb Stuart, rode around McClellan's army and Cooke was unable to intercept him with his own cavalry. A West Pointer (1827), he served in the infantry and the dragoons and was a veteran of the Black Hawk and Mexican wars and the expedition against the Mormons in Utah. Unlike his son, John R. Cooke, who went with his native Virginia and became a Confederate brigadier, Philip St. George Cooke remained loyal to the Union and his assignments included: colonel, 2nd Dragoons (since June 14, 1858); colonel, 2nd Cavalry (designation change August 3, 1861); brigadier general, USV (November 12, 1861); brigadier general, USA (November 28, 1861 to rank from the 12th); commanding Cavalry Reserve, Army of the Potomac (January-July 5, 1862); and commanding District of Baton Rouge, 19th Corps, Department of the Gulf (October 8, 1863-May 2, 1864). He commanded the brigade of cavalry that formed the reserve for the Army of the Potomac and retained command when it was increased to a division before the Peninsula Campaign. He fought at Yorktown, Williamsburg, and in the Seven Days. Following the conclusion of the campaign he was assigned to court-martial duty. He held a district command in Louisiana and finished the war superintending the Union's recruiting efforts. Brevetted major general in the regular services for the war, he remained in the army until his 1873 retirement, having served on administrative bodies and in departmental commands. (Cooke, P. St. George, *The Conquest of New Mexico and California*)

COOLEY, Samuel A. (?-?)

Capitalizing upon his occasional government contracts for his photographic work, Samuel A. Cooley adopted the titles "U.S. Photographer, Department of the South" and "Photographer Tenth Army Corps" to boost sales of his stereo images. He set up shop in Jacksonville, Florida, and Hilton Head, Folly Island, and Beaufort, South Carolina. His views included the full range of the war along the coast, from the blockading fleet to the camps, defenses, and hospitals on shore. His numerous views comprise a valuable historic glimpse. (Davis, William C., ed., *The Image of War 1861-1865*)

COON, Datus Ensign (1831-1893)

Engaged in journalism in Iowa in 1861, native New Yorker Datus E. Coon joined the Union cavalry and rose to brigade command. His assignments included: captain, 2nd Iowa Cavalry (August 31, 1861); major, 2nd Iowa Cavalry (September 14, 1861); colonel, 2nd Iowa Cavalry (May 5, 1864); commanding 2nd Brigade, 1st Division, Cavalry Corps, District of West Tennessee, Department of the Tennessee (June 1-November 27, 1864); and commanding 2nd Brigade, 5th Division, Cavalry Corps, Military Division of the Mississippi (November 27, 1864-June 1865). He fought at New Madrid, Island £10, during the advance on Corinth, Mississippi, and at Booneville as a field officer. Promoted to the colonelcy of the regiment, he led a brigade in the operations against Nathan Bedford Forrest at Tupelo and under Andrew J. Smith in August 1864. During Hood's invasion of middle Tennessee in the fall of that year, Coon led his brigade in the defense at Franklin and Nashville. Brevetted brigadier general for the war on March 8, 1865, he was mustered out with his regiment on September 19.

COOPER, Douglas Hancock (1815-1879)

A native Mississippian, Douglas H. Cooper was a veteran of the Mexican War, having served as a captain in the 1st Mississippi Rifles, and in 1853 was appointed as U.S. commissioner to the Choctaws, one of the Five Civilized Tribes, of the southeastern United States. Because of this connection with the Indians, he was appointed by the Confederacy as a representative to deal with the Five Tribes. Working with Albert Pike, he succeeded in getting portions of all five tribes to join with the South. On May 25, 1861, he was adopted into the Chickasaw tribe. Raising an Indian unit, he held the following assignments: colonel, 1st Choctaw and Chickasaw Mounted Rifles (1861); brigadier general, CSA (May 2, 1863); commanding District of Indian Territory, Trans-Mississippi Department (July 21, 1864-February 14 and February 21-May 1865); and also commanding Indian Division, Cavalry Corps, Trans-Mississippi Department (fall 1864-May 1865). Leading his mixed regiment, he took part in the pursuit of the Unionist Upper Creeks fleeing under Opothleyohola. He subsequently fought at Newtonia, having missed the action at Pea Ridge because the Indians refused to serve outside Indian Territory until they were paid. During Price's Missouri operations in 1864, Cooper commanded the Indian forces. By the end of the war he was in command of all the Indians serving in the Trans-Mississippi. After the peace he continued action against the U.S. government by pressing, and winning, claims for losses during the war for the Indians.

COOPER, James (1810-1863)

A border state politician who had worked hard to preserve the Union, James Cooper was rewarded by Abraham Lincoln with a brigadier general's commission. A Maryland native, he had studied law with Thaddeus Stevens in Gettysburg and served two terms in the U.S. House of Representatives as a Whig. He then served in the Pennsylvania legislature before returning to Washington as a senator. There he served on the committee that drafted the Compromise of 1850. In Maryland he was active in military affairs, and Lincoln named him in the first batch of brigadier generals of the volunteer service. His assignments included: brigadier general, USV (May 17, 1861); commanding a demi-brigade, Railroad Brigade, Middle Department (ca. May-June 1862); commanding 1st Brigade, Siegel's Division, Department of the Shenandoah (June 4-26, 1862); commanding 1st Brigade, 2nd Division, 2nd Corps, Army of Virginia (June 26-July 16, 1862); and also commanding the division (June 26-July 7, 1862). Initially assigned to recruiting duties in his native state, he was in command of an informal brigade at Harpers Ferry during the Shenandoah Valley Campaign of 1862. He then briefly commanded a brigade and a division under Pope. In the fall of 1862 he was sent to Ohio to command the prisoner of war camp at Camp Wallace near Columbus. He was soon transferred to the camp of instruction at Camp Chase, which, following Grant's victory at Fort Donelson, was also converted to contain captured Confederates. While on this duty Cooper died on March 28, 1863.

COOPER, John (1832-?)

For service in battle, and a humanitarian deed, Coxswain John Cooper, USN, became one of only three men to earn two Congressional Medals of Honor during the war. Serving on the *USS Brooklyn*, Cooper took part in the famed battle of Mobile Bay, in which Admiral Farragut allegedly "damned" the torpedoes and ordered his vessels forward. Following the iron monitors into the bay, the wooden vessels were lashed together in pairs, with the *Brooklyn* in the lead on the side facing Fort Morgan. Cooper continued firing his gun with precision and disregard for the fort's shells while his vessel hesitated for some time, under fire following the sinking of one of the monitors, the *Tecumseh*, by a torpedo. He kept up his fire during the subsequent fight with the Confederate ironclad *Tennessee*. For his bravery he was given a Medal of Honor. Cooper continued on duty along the Gulf Coast and following the capture of Mobile in April 1865 he was assigned to duty on shore as a quartermaster. While performing this duty, a fire broke out in the town and Cooper raced through exploding shells, ignited by the flames, to rescue a wounded sailor. He was awarded his second medal for this deed. (Mitchell, Joseph B., *The Badge of Gallantry*)

COOPER, Joseph Alexander (1823-1910)

A Tennessee Whig, Joseph A. Cooper remained loyal to the Union and earned a brevet as a major general of volunteers for his mililtary service. Born in Kentucky and raised in Tennessee, he served in a volunteer unit from the latter state as an enlisted man in the Mexican War. A farmer in the interwar years, he attended the Knoxville Unionist convention in 1861 and upon the outbreak of hostilities began recruiting for the Union. His assignments included: captain, Company A, 1st Tennessee (August 8, 1861); colonel, 6th Tennessee (May 18, 1862); commanding 3rd Brigade, 3rd Division, 23rd Corps, Army of the Ohio (June 1-4, 1863); commanding 3rd Brigade, 3rd Division, 12th Corps, Army of the Cumberland (March 7-April 14, 1864); commanding 1st Brigade, 2nd Division, 23rd Corps, Army of the Ohio (April 25-May 3, June 4-October 11, 1864, and November 11, 1864-February 2, 1865) brigadier general, USV (July 30, 1864); commanding the division (October 11-November 11, 1864 and January 14-February 2, 1865); commanding 1st Brigade, 2nd Division, 23rd Corps, Department of North Carolina (February 9-March 6, April 4-20 and 26-30, 1865); and commanding the division (April 20-26 and April 30-June 12, 1865). He led his company at Mills Springs and a new regiment, which he raised at the direction of the War Department, at Cumberland Gap. During the battle of Murfreesboro the regiment fought off Confederate cavalry while serving as guard for an ammunition train from Nashville. He commanded his regiment in the Chattanooga and Knoxville areas but was not engaged in either of the battles proper. Recognized as a capable officer, he was given a brigade—and later a brigadier's star—in time for the Atlanta Campaign. Facing Hood's invasion of Tennessee, he fought at Franklin and Nashville before being transferred with the corps to the North Carolina coast to join Sherman's operations. Mustered out on January 15, 1866, he returned to farming in Tennessee and Kansas, lost a bid for the Tennessee governorship, and was a tax official and active in church affairs.

COOPER, Samuel (1798-1876)

By the time of the Civil War, New Jersey-born West Pointer (1815) Samuel Cooper, having served mostly on staff assignments in the Seminole and Mexican wars, had become the adjutant general of the U.S. Army. Having married a Virginian, he resigned his position on March 7, 1861, and offered his services to the Confederacy. On March 16, 1861, the day after he arrived in Richmond, Jefferson Davis appointed him a brigadier general in the regular army of the Confederacy with the joint position of adjutant and inspector general. In this position, for which he was most qualified by his experience in the "Old Army," he was responsible for the organization of an army from scratch. On August 31, 1861, he was promoted to full general with rank from May 16. This made him the senior officer in the rebel military command. Although he is little remembered, he was largely responsible for having kept the Confederate forces in the field. He retained his position until the collapse of the rebel nation when he turned over the records of his department to the Washington authorities. Without this treasure, the *Official Records* would be much less reliable and valuable. After the war, Cooper took up farming near Alexandria, Virginia. However, by 1870 he was in such poor financial straits that General Lee raised $300 from ex-Confederates and added $100 himself for Cooper's relief.

COOPER, Wickliffe (1831-1867)

The distinguished army career of cavalryman Wickliffe Cooper ended from a cause that was common to the officer corps—alcoholism. Born in Kentucky, he enlisted early in the Civil War and his assignments included: sergeant, Company K, 20th Kentucky (November 15, 1861); second lieutenant, Company K, 20th Kentucky (January 24, 1862); lieutenant colonel, 4th Kentucky Cavalry (April 13, 1863); and colonel, 4th Kentucky Cavalry (May 29, 1863). He fought as a subaltern at Shiloh and during the Corinth siege. Captured at Richmond, Kentucky, he was exchanged and appointed second-in-command of a mounted regiment. As its permanent commander, he fought at Chickamauga, against Morgan, in the Atlanta Campaign—receiving a regular army brevet in 1867 for Resaca—and on Wilson's raid. During the latter he earned another 1867 brevet for Selma. Mustered out on August 21, 1865, he became a major in the 7th Cavalry the next year. While campaigning against Indians he ran out of alcohol and shot himself. Later Congress altered the record to indicate that he had "died by hand of person or persons unknown" so that his widow could obtain a pension.

COPELAND, Joseph Tarr (1813-1893)

Too old for the rigorous life of a cavalry commander, Joseph T. Copeland was relieved of command of his brigade in 1863 and assigned to recruiting and post duties. A Maine-born lawyer, he settled in Michigan where he eventually gained a seat on the state supreme court. He was living in retirement at the outbreak of the Civil War. His assignments included: lieutenant colonel, 1st Michigan Cavalry (August 22, 1861); colonel, 5th Michigan Cavalry (August 30, 1862); brigadier general, USV (November 29, 1862); commanding Provisional Cavalry Brigade, Casey's Division, Military District of Washington, Army of the Potomac (December 1862-February 1863); and commanding 1st Brigade, Cavalry Division, 22nd Corps, Department of Washington (March 2-June 26, 1863). He commanded a portion of his first unit when it was engaged at Kernstown in the Shenandoah Valley Campaign of 1862. Promoted to colonel and later brigadier general, he commanded a new regiment and a brigade in the Washington fortifications. In the June 1863 reorganization of the cavalry arm in the Army of the Potomac his Michigan cavalry brigade was given to newly promoted George A. Custer. Copeland was relegated to draft centers in Annapolis and Pittsburgh. He finished the war commanding the prisoner of war camp at Alton, Illinois, and resigned on November 8, 1865. He then returned to semi-retirement but was engaged in the hostelry trade.

CORBETT, Boston (1822-?)

One of the stranger stories to come out of the Lincoln assassination was that of Boston Corbett, the man who claimed to have shot John Wilkes Booth. In 1865 he was a sergeant in Company C, 16th New York Cavalry, who had spent five months in Andersonville prison. As part of one of the detachments under First Lieutenant Edward P. Doherty, sent out to find Booth, he and his comrades came upon the fugitive in the tobacco barn on Richard Garrett's Virginia farm. The barn was surrounded; David Herold surrendered but Booth remained. Orders were given that there be no gunfire and that the barn be set ablaze. Then a shot was fired and Booth was dragged out mortally wounded. Questions were asked and Corbett claimed to have fired against orders because he had higher instructions from the Almighty. The others laughed at him; they knew he had castrated himself before the war and was generally considered a strange soldier. He was arrested and taken before Secretary of War Stanton who decided to praise him instead and grant a reward of $1,653.85. He even issued a pistol to Corbett, since the autopsy indicated Booth had been struck by a pistol ball and Corbett only had a carbine. Although another theory is that Booth shot himself, Corbett nevertheless became the self-styled "Avenger of Blood." After a period on the lecture circuit he became the doorkeeper for the Kansas legislature until in 1886 he fired two revolvers in the hall, without killing anyone. Sent to an insane asylum, he escaped and vanished from view.

Boston Corbett, alleged killer of John Wilkes Booth. (NA)

CORBIN, William F. (?-1863)

A prominent Kentuckian, William F. Corbin had the misfortune to become the focal point in a dispute between the warring authorities over the status of recruiting officers found behind enemy lines. Under orders, he had entered Kentucky in search of Confederate recruits. On April 9, 1863, he and another officer, T.B. McGraw, were arrested while in civilian clothes and escorting enlistees to the Southern lines. The two were tried by court-martial and shot on May 15 at Johnson's Island. In retaliation, Richmond selected two captive captains, Henry W. Sawyer and John M. Flinn, for the gallows. General Burnside's position was that the two Confederates were considered to be spies since they were out of uniform and thus subject to the death penalty.

CORCORAN, Michael (1827-1863)

A New York militia officer, Michael Corcoran survived a long prison confinement, with threats of retaliatory treatment, only to die in a riding mishap. An Irish native, he fled that country after resigning as a police officer over British policy there. He held various clerical positions in New York and was active in the militia. His Civil War-era assignments included: colonel, 69th New York Militia (1859); colonel, 69th New York Militia (in federal service April 29, 1861); brigadier general, USV (July 21, 1861); commanding Division at Suffolk, 7th Corps, Department of Virginia (September 30, 1862-January 2, 1863); also commanding brigade, same division, corps and department (November 1862-April 9, 1863); commanding 1st Division, 7th Corps, Department of Virginia (April 9-July 11, 1863); commanding 1st Brigade, King's Division, 22nd Corps, Department of Washington (July 15-October 1863); and commanding the division (October-December 22, 1863). When Fort Sumter was fired on he was facing court-martial for refusing to call out his regiment in honor of the 1859 visit by England's Prince of Wales, the future Edward VII. The militia proceedings were dropped to allow him to volunteer for federal service. Wounded and captured at 1st Bull Run, he was not promptly paroled and exchanged. Instead, he was held until

Hostage Michael Corcoran. (*Leslie's*)

August 1862 as a hostage guaranteeing good treatment for Confederate privateers captured by the Washington authorities. Upon his release he was given a brigadier's star retroactively to the date of his capture. Serving in southeastern Virginia, he faced Longstreet at Suffolk in the spring of 1863 and was transferred to the Washington defenses after the Gettysburg Campaign had raised concerns for the city's safety. He was killed on December 22 when his horse fell near Fairfax Court House. Corcoran's body was returned to New York for burial.

CORLEY, James Lawrence (1828-1883)

Although he served on the staff of Robert E. Lee throughout his tenure as commander of the Army of Northern Virginia, Chief Quartermaster James L. Corley was not really a member of Lee's headquarters family. The South Carolina-born officer had graduated from West Point (1850) and served in the infantry before the war, part of the time as a regimental quartermaster. With the war already begun, he resigned his commission in the old army on May 4, 1861, and went South. His appointments included: captain and quartermaster (July 1861); lieutenant colonel, 60th Virginia (October 13, 1861); and chief quartermaster, Army of Northern Virginia (June 1862-April 9, 1865). After serving on the staff of General Garnett in western Virginia during the first summer of the war, he became second in command of the 60th Virginia. He served with this unit until his resignation on March 10, 1862. He took a position as judge advocate in the Department of South Carolina, Georgia, and Florida but, just prior to the Seven Days Battles, he returned to Virginia and was assigned to direct the Quartermaster's Department for Lee's army. Serving as head of a staff department, he was not strictly speaking a member of Lee's personal staff. After serving through all the army's campaigns he was given the task of reducing the amount of mules, horses, wagons, etc., for the transportation of the army on the dismal retreat to Appomattox. Settling in Norfolk after the war he was involved in the insurance business. He also served as an escort for his former chief during much of his Southern tour. (Freeman, Douglas S., *R.E. Lee*)

CORNING, Erastus (1794-1872)

As a leader of the Albany political machine, Erastus Corning was frequently critical of the policies of the Lincoln administration, especially arbitrary arrests and the suspension of the writ of *habeas corpus*. A native of Connecticut, he went into the iron business in New York. In the early 1840s he sat in the state senate and was an alderman in Albany. In the mid-1830s he was Albany's mayor. Elected as a Democrat to Congress in 1856 he lost his seat two years later. In 1860 he was again elected to the House and attended the Washington Peace Convention before taking his seat. Reelected in 1862, he resigned before the first session of the 38th Congress, on October 5, 1863. He remained critical of the Lincoln Administration and was active in postwar politics including attendance at a state constitutional convention in 1867.

CORSE, John Murray (1835-1893)

Although he never completed his West Point education, John M. Corse became the hero of Allatoona, one of the more dramatic Civil War actions. A Pittsburgh native, he was raised in Iowa and after leaving the military academy in 1855 became a lawyer and Democratic politician. His Civil War assignments included: major, 6th Iowa (July 13, 1861); lieutenant colonel, 6th Iowa (May 21, 1862); colonel, 6th Iowa (March 29, 1863); brigadier general, USV (August 11, 1863); commanding 4th Brigade, 4th Division, 15th Corps, Army of the Tennessee (August 27-September 1, 1863); commanding the division (September 1-October 16, 1863); commanding 2nd Brigade, 4th Division, 15th Corps, Army of the Tennessee (July 26-September 23, 1864); and commanding 4th Division, 15th Corps, Army of the Tennessee (September 23, 1864-July 24, 1865). As a member of John Pope's staff, he took part in the operations against New Madrid, Island #10, and Corinth. He was made a colonel in the meantime and rejoined his regiment to command it at Vicksburg and Jackson. Going in brigade command with Sherman to the relief of Chattanooga, he was wounded in action there. He then became Sherman's inspector during the early part of the Atlanta Campaign and was given a division during the fighting around the city itself. After the fall of the city he was assigned to garrison duty along the railroad and was attacked by Samuel G. French's division at Allatoona. Sherman could view the action from afar and was able to signal Corse to hold on. The October 5, 1864, action was the inspiration for the hymn "Hold the Fort, For We Are Coming." In the midst of his brilliant defense, he signaled that, "I am short of a cheekbone, and one ear, but am able to whip all hell yet." In fact he was only slightly wounded. The Confederates withdrew, and there were some 1,500 casualties out of about 4,000 engaged. Corse was brevetted a major general for the defense. He then led his division in the March to the Sea and the Carolinas Campaign. Mustered out on April 30, 1866, he refused a regular commission. After serving in Illinois as a tax official he moved into Massachusetts Democratic politics.

CORSE, Montgomery Dent (1816-1895)

A Virginia banker and veteran of the Mexican War, as a captain in the 1st Virginia, Montgomery D. Corse was skillfully prepared for the Civil War. In 1860 he organized the Old Dominion Rifles and became its captain. Following the secession of the state his assignments included: major, 6th Virginia Battalion (early 1861); colonel, 17th Virginia (spring 1861); commanding Kemper's Brigade, Kemper's Division, 1st Corps, Army of Northern Virginia (early August-August 30, 1862); brigadier general, CSA (November 1, 1862); temporarily commanding Garnett's brigade, Pickett's Division, same corps and army (November 6-26, 1862); commanding new brigade, same division, corps and army (November 26, 1862-February 25, 1863; May-September 23, 1863; and May 1864-April 6, 1865); commanding brigade, Pickett's Division, in the Department of Virginia and North Carolina (February 25-April 1, 1863) and in the Department of Southern Virginia (April 1-May 1863); commanding brigade Ransom's Division, Department of Western Virginia (September 1863-January 1864); and commanding brigade (in Hoke's Division in May), Department of North Carolina (January-May 1864). Corse commanded his regiment at Blackburn's Ford, 1st Bull Run, Yorktown, Williamsburg, Seven Pines, and in the Seven Days. At 2nd Bull Run he was in brigade command until wounded. The next month he was again wounded at both South Mountain and Antietam at the head of the regiment. A new brigade was created for him in November. After being lightly engaged at Fredericksburg he accompanied Longstreet to southeastern Virginia. During the Gettysburg Campaign he was detached from the division to guard vital Hanover Junction north of Richmond. The division was detached from the corps when Longstreet went to Georgia, with Corse's Brigade assigned to western Virginia. In January 1864 Corse and the brigade joined Pickett for the attack on New Bern, North Carolina. After seeing action at Drewry's Bluff the entire division rejoined Lee and fought at Cold Harbor and through the siege of Petersburg. After the disaster at Five Forks the retreat to Appomattox began and Corse was captured at Sayler's Creek on April 6, 1865. Following his July release he returned to banking in his native Alexandria. (Freeman, Douglas S., *Lee's Lieutenants*)

CORWIN, Thomas (1794-1865)

Shortly before the outbreak of the Civil War Thomas Corwin resigned from his House seat in Congress in order to become the U.S. minister to Mexico. Born in Kentucky, he moved with his parents to Ohio in 1798 and became an attorney in 1817. The next year he began a decade as a prosecuting attorney. Meanwhile he attended the state legislature's sessions of 1822, 1823, and 1829. He went to the U.S. House of Representatives in 1831 and remained until he resigned in 1840 to run for governor. Elected, he served from 1840 to 1842 but failed to gain reelection. In 1844 he presided over the state Whig convention and served as an elector for Henry Clay. The next year he took a seat in the Senate and held it until he resigned in 1850 to become Millard Fillmore's treasury secretary. Again elected to the House in 1858, he served as the chairman of the unsuccessful Committee of Thirty-three, which was charged with finding a solution to the sectional conflict. Shortly after Lincoln's inauguration he was named U.S. minister to Mexico and served through the troubling times of French involvement in that country. He resigned on September 1, 1864, and resumed the practice of law until his death.

COSBY, George Blake (1830-1909)

Transferring from the staff to the line in the middle of the Civil War, native Kentuckian George B. Cosby served throughout the western theater as commander of mounted troops. The West Pointer (1852) had been posted to the Regiment of Mounted Riflemen and with them was wounded fighting Indians at Lake Trinidad, Texas on May 9, 1854. The next year he was transferred to the cavalry, and he resigned as first lieutenant, 2nd Cavalry, on May 10, 1861. His Confederate assignments included: captain, Cavalry (ca. May 1861); major and assistant adjutant general (September 1861); colonel, Cavalry (1862); commanding brigade, Jackson's Division, Cavalry Corps, Department of Mississippi and East Louisiana (January 1863); commanding brigade, Martin's Division, Cavalry Corps, Department of Mississippi and East Louisiana (February-March 1863); brigadier general, CSA (April 23, 1863 to rank from January 20); commanding brigade, Jackson's Cavalry Division, Department of the West (June 9-July 1863); commanding brigade, Jackson's Cavalry Division, Department of Mississippi and East Louisiana (July-August 1863); commanding brigade, Jackson's Division, Lee's Cavalry Corps, Department of Mississippi and East Louisiana (August-December 24, 1863 and January-January 28, 1864); commanding brigade, Jackson's Division, Lee's Cavalry Corps, Department of Alabama, Mississippi and East Louisiana (January 28-February 1864); and commanding Hodge's (old) Brigade, Department of Western Virginia and East Tennessee (September 5, 1864-ca. April 1865). As a staff officer with Simon B. Buckner, he served in central Kentucky and was part of the force sent to reinforce Fort Donelson. As Buckner's staff chief he carried the first communications with Grant concerning a possible surrender. Not exchanged until August 27, 1862, he was promoted to a colonelcy. Early the next year he took command of a cavalry brigade and fought at Thompson's Station before being promoted to brigadier general. He took part in the unsuccessful defense of Jackson. Late in 1864 he was given command of another brigade in southwestern Virginia and eastern Tennessee, which he led until the end of the war. A postwar California farmer, he also was a public office holder. He committed suicide, allegedly due to his old wound (probably from Indian fighting).

COSTER, Charles Robert (?-1888)

Holding East Cemetery Hill on the first day at Gettysburg, Charles R. Coster was ordered forward with his brigade to stem the rout of the rest of the corps and accordingly suffered heavy losses. The native New Yorker's assignments included: private, Company K, 7th New York Militia (May 14, 1861); first lieutenant, 12th Infantry (May 14, 1861); captain, 12th Infantry (August 30, 1862); colonel, 134th New York (October 8, 1862); and commanding 1st Brigade, 2nd Division, 11th Corps, Army of the Potomac (June 10-July 1863). With the famed militia regiment, he was one of the first volunteers to reach Washington from the North at the outbreak of the war. However, on June 3, 1861, he left this unit to accept his regular army commission. With his newly organized outfit, he went to the Peninsula and took part in the operations at Yorktown. During the Seven Days he was wounded at Gaines' Mill. He returned to duty at the head of a volunteer regiment with which he took part in the infamous Mud March and was caught up in the rout of the corps at Chancellorsville. In his only major action in charge of a brigade—Gettysburg—he was again swept up in the corps' defeat. Shortly after the corps was transferred to Chattanooga he submitted his resignation, which became effective on November 12, 1863, from the volunteers and December 31, 1863, from the regular army. The machinery to administer the draft had been set up and he was named provost marshal of New York's 6th District on May 18, 1864. He was honorably discharged from this post on April 30, 1865, as the demobilization began.

COUCH, Darius Nash (1822-1897)

The senior Union corps commander at Chancellorsville, Darius N. Couch refused to serve any longer under Joseph Hooker and was permanently transferred out of the Army of the Potomac. A native New Yorker and West Pointer (1846), he spent eight years as an artillery lieutenant before resigning in 1855. His service had included a brevet for the Mexican War. Leaving the copper business, he reentered the military at the outbreak of the Civil War. His assignments included: colonel, 7th Massachusetts (June 15, 1861); brigadier general, USV (to rank from May 17, 1861); commanding brigade, Division of the Potomac (August-October 3, 1861); commanding 1st Brigade, Buell's-Keyes' Division, Army of the Potomac (October 3, 1861-March 13, 1862); commanding 1st Division, 4th Corps, Army of the Potomac (March 13-July 12 and August 12-September 26, 1862); major general, USV (July 4, 1862); commanding 3rd Division, 6th Corps, Army of the Potomac (June 26-October 18, 1862); commanding 2nd Corps, Army of the Potomac (October 7-December 26, 1862 and February 5-May 22, 1863); commanding Department of the Susquehanna (June 11, 1863-December 1, 1864); commanding 2nd Division, 23rd Corps, Army of the Ohio (December 8, 1864-January 14, 1865); and commanding 2nd Division, 23rd Corps, Department of North Carolina (February 9-28, April 8-20, and 26-30, 1865). By the time of the Peninsula Campaign he was in command of a division and fought at Yorktown, Williamsburg, Seven Pines, and the Seven Days. At the close of the campaign his resignation for health reasons was refused by the War Department and he was given the second star of a major general. During the Maryland Campaign his division was attached to the 6th Corps and fought at South Mountain but missed Antietam. At Fredericksburg his 2nd Corps made several doomed assaults against Marye's Heights. As Hooker's second-in-command at Chancellorsville, he became disgusted with that officer's timidity and the resulting failure of the campaign. He requested removal if Hooker were not replaced, and he was assigned to a command, principally militia, in Pennsylvania during the Gettysburg Campaign. After a year and a half in this position he was assigned to a division in middle Tennessee and fought at Nashville and later, from the coast, in the Carolinas Campaign. Resigning on May 26, 1865, he spent a few unsuccessful years as a Democratic officeholder in Massachusetts before moving to Connecticut in 1870. There he held several posts in the state's military hierarchy.

Refusal to serve under Joe Hooker cost Darius N. Couch his corps command. (*Leslie's*)

COURTNEY, Alfred Ranson (1833-1914)

For his failure to accompany two of his batteries to the field at Antietam, Alfred Ranson Courtney faced a court-martial for dereliction of duty and so requested a transfer out of the Army of Northern Virginia. He had entered the Confederate service early in 1861 and his assignments included: captain, Richmond

"Courtney" Artillery (July 8, 1861); major, Artillery (July 14, 1862); commanding Artillery Battalion, Ewell's Division, Jackson's Command, Army of Northern Virginia (July 14-fall 1862); commanding Artillery Battalion, Hindman's Division, 2nd Corps, Army of Tennessee (November 1863-February 1864); and commanding artillery battalion, 2nd Corps, Army of Tennessee (February-May 14, 1864 and summer-fall 1864). He led his battery in the Shenandoah and Peninsula campaigns before being promoted to command Ewell's artillery. In this capacity, he served through Cedar Mountain, 2nd Bull Run, and the capture of Harpers Ferry. Of the six batteries of his battalion only two were ordered into Maryland to join in the battle of Antietam. He chose to remain in Harpers Ferry with the majority of his command. For this action charges were preferred against him. Upon his own request he was assigned to staff duty in Richmond on April 20, 1863. Three months later he was directed to report to East Tennessee. Joining the Army of Tennessee, he fought at Chattanooga and in the early stages of the Atlanta Campaign. He was wounded at Resaca but returned to duty in time for the final unsuccessful battles for the city. He subsequently served at gathering up the fragments of the artillery after Hood's disastrous foray into Tennessee. A postwar lawyer, he served in the Virginia legislature and as an official of the masonic order.

COVODE, John (1808-1871)

During the first year of its existence, Representative John Covode was a member—albeit not a very active one—of the Joint Committee on the Conduct of the War. A farmer and businessman, he was elected to Congress in 1854 as a Whig from his native Pennsylvania and served from 1855 to March 3, 1863, in the House of Representatives. He was one of the original members of the joint committee but, although he had become a Republican upon the dissolution of the Whigs, he did not take a leading role in its witch hunts. He returned to Congress in 1867 and was serving in his second term when he died.

COWAN, Edgar (1815-1885)

Although a member of the Republican Party, Senator Edgar Cowan frequently was at odds with the party leadership. The native Pennsylvanian had been admitted to the bar in 1842 and in 1860 was an elector for the Lincoln-Hamlin ticket. As a Republican, he was elected to the Senate in 1861 and held his seat from March 4, 1861, to March 3, 1867, but lost a bid for reelection. During the course of the Civil War he was worried that the Emancipation Proclamation would lead to a large influx of freed blacks into his state, and pointed out that the states of New England would not be affected as greatly. As the conflict came to a close he disagreed with the party on the form of Reconstruction. In 1867 his nomination to a diplomatic post in Austria was rejected by the Senate. He then resumed his law practice.

COWDIN, Robert (1805-1874)

Boston lumberman and Massachusetts militia officer Robert Cowdin was appointed a brigadier general of volunteers but the Senate failed to confirm the commission. A native of Vermont, he was a colonel in the militia at the outbreak of hostilities and raised the state's first three-year regiment. His assignments included: colonel, 1st Massachusetts (May 25, 1861); commanding 1st Brigade, 2nd Division, 3rd Corps, Army of the Potomac (briefly in August 1862); brigadier general, USV (September 26, 1862); commanding 1st Brigade, Abercrombie's Division, Military District of Washington, Army of the Potomac (October 1862-February 2, 1863); and commanding 2nd Brigade, Abercrombie's Division, 22nd Corps, Department of Washington (February 2-March 31, 1863). At the head of his regiment he fought at 1st Bull Run and the next year on the Peninsula at Williamsburg and in the Seven Days. At 2nd Bull Run he succeeded to temporary command of the brigade. Promoted to brigadier the next month, he was posted to the Washington fortifications. On March 4, 1863, his commission expired when the Senate adjourned without confirming it. At the end of the month he was relieved of duty and returned home. After the war he was active in military affairs and local politics in Boston.

COX, Jacob Dolson (1828-1900)

Lawyer turned Union major general, Jacob D. Cox proved in the postwar years to be less of a friend to the freedmen than might have been expected. Born in Canada, he was taken by his American parents to New York and then Ohio. A graduate of Oberlin, he practiced law and as an Ohio abolitionist was active in the formation of the state's Republican Party. Shortly before the Civil War he served in the state senate. With the coming of the war he entered the army and his assignments included: brigadier general, Ohio Volunteers (April 23, 1861); brigadier general, USV (July 30, 1861 to rank from May 17, 1861); commanding Kanawha Brigade, Army of Occupation, West Virginia, Department of the Ohio (July-October 11, 1861); commanding District of the Kanawha, Department of West Virginia (October 11, 1861-March 11, 1862); commanding District of the Kanawha, Mountain Department (March 11-August 15, 1862; but department ceased to exist June 26, 1862); commanding Kanawha Division, 9th Corps, Army of the Potomac (September-October 1862); also commanding the corps (September 14-October 8, 1862); major general, USV (October 6, 1862); commanding District of Ohio, Department of the Ohio (April 16-late 1863); commanding 23rd Corps, Army of the Ohio (December 20, 1863-February 10, 1864, April 4-9, May 27-27, and September 14-October 22, 1864), commanding 3rd Division, 23rd Corps, Army of the Ohio (April 3-May 26 and May 27-September 16, 1864, October 21, 1864-January 13, 1865, and January 14-February 2, 1865); major general, USV (reappointed December 7, 1864); commanding 3rd Division, 23rd Corps, Department of North Carolina (February 9-25, 1865); commanding Cox's Provisional Corps, Department of North Carolina (February 25-March 31, 1865); commanding 23rd Corps, Department of North Carolina (March 31-June 17, 1865); and commanding the Department (June 17-27, 1865). Serving under McClellan, he took part in the occupation of western Virginia in the first year of the war. He remained on duty there until he took a division to join John Pope in northern Virginia but arrived too late for any more than two of his regiments to be engaged near the main battle at 2nd Bull Run. In the Maryland Campaign he succeeded Jesse L. Reno in command of the 9th Corps at South Mountain. He then returned to western Virginia and was in command of the District of Ohio in 1863. He commanded the 23rd Corps in East Tennessee and directed a division in the Atlanta Campaign. Sent back to Tennessee to fend off Hood's invasion, he fought well at Franklin and Nashville and later he wrote *The March to the Sea—Franklin and Nashville*. Transferred to the North Carolina coast he fought at Kingston during Sherman's Carolinas Campaign. Resigning on January 1, 1866—as a major general, although his first nomination had expired after the Senate failed to confirm it he served a term as Ohio's governor. During his tenure he favored forced segregation and opposed black voting rights. Initially he supported Andrew Johnson's Reconstruction policies and this contributed to his not being renominated. Breaking with Johnson he became a Grant partisan, although there had been little connection between the two during the war, and served as Grant's secretary of the interior in 1869-1870. He broke with Grant and resigned late in 1870. Resuming his law practice, he also sat in the House of Representatives and was involved in railroads and education. He was also a prolific writer on the war and an expert in the architecture of Gothic cathedrals. (Cox, Jacob Dolson, *Military Reminiscences of the Civil War*)

COX, Samuel, Jr. (?-?)

A strong Southern sympathizer during the Civil War, Samuel Cox, Jr., provided aid to the fleeing John Wilkes Booth and David Herold. At about midnight on April 15, 1865, the pair of fugitives appeared at the home of the wealthy Maryland planter. Following a conversation, which was whispered so that the fugitive's black guide, Oswald Swann, could not hear it, Cox ordered them from his house in a loud and clear manner. However, Swann later noticed the assassins returning to the house where they were given food and allowed to stay in the nearby woods. Cox then sent for his foster brother Thomas Jones to arrange for their further flight into Virginia. Strangely enough, Cox was never prosecuted for his role in the affair.

COX, Samuel Sullivan (1824-1889)

Although a friend of Copperhead Clement L. Vallandigham, Ohio Representative Samuel S. Cox supported the Union war effort while striving to preserve civil liberties. The Ohio native graduated from Brown University and was admitted to the bar in Ohio in 1849. In 1853-54 he was the publisher-editor of the *Columbus Statesman* and the next year served briefly as the secretary to the U.S. legation in Lima, Peru. In 1856 he was elected, as a Democrat, to the House of Representatives; he served from March 4, 1857 to March 3, 1865, having been defeated for reelection in 1864. Acknowledging that the South had legitimate grievances, he always was willing to vote men and money for the preservation of the Union—but nothing beyond that. He criticized his own section for lagging behind in its committment to the war effort. He favored the appointment of commissioners to meet with Southern officials to work for peace and reunion. In the field of civil liberties he opposed arbitrary arrests and argued against the expulsion of a congressman who favored recognizing the Confederacy. Because he saw a limited purpose to the war—the preservation of the Union—he opposed a bill for the creation of a Bureau of Emancipation and feared extending the powers of the national government. After his defeat he moved to New York City to resume the practice of law and won a House seat from that state in 1868. Reelected in 1870, he was defeated two years later. But in late 1873 he was named to fill an unexpired House term and won repeated reelections until he resigned in 1885 to again enter the foreign service. In the meantime he had been speaker of the House in 1876. In 1885-86 he was minister to Turkey. Resigning and returning to New York, he again was named to a House vacancy and was reelected in 1888. He died in office the next year. (Cox, Samuel Sullivan, *Eight Years in Congress from 1857 to 1865* and *Three Decades of Federal Legislation*)

COX, William Ruffin (1832-1919)

Suffering some 11 Civil War wounds, five at Chancellorsville, William R. Cox lived to be one of the last surviving general officers. A North Carolina lawyer and militia officer, he entered the service of the state even before its secession. His assignments included: major, 2nd North Carolina (May 8, 1861); lieutenant colonel, 2nd North Carolina (April 2, 1863, to rank from September 17, 1862); colonel, 2nd North Carolina (March 21, 1863); brigadier general, CSA (May 31, 1864); commanding Ramseur's (old) Brigade, Rodes'-Grimes' Division, 2nd Corps, Army of Northern Virginia (June 4-13 and December 1864-April 9, 1865); and commanding brigade, Rodes'-Grimes' Division, Valley District, Department of Northern Virginia (June 13-December 1864). After service near Fredericksburg, Virginia, and Wilmington, North Carolina, his regiment served at the Seven Days, South Mountain, Antietam, and Fredericksburg. In command of the unit at Chancellorsville he suffered multiple wounds on May 3 but was able to rejoin the regiment on August 1. He fought in the Bristoe Campaign and received two more wounds at Kelly's Ford. After Spotsylvania he was promoted to the temporary rank of brigadier and command of Ramseur's former command. He led this brigade for the remainder of the conflict including service with Early at Monocacy, on the outskirts of Washington, at 3rd Winchester, Fisher's Hill, and Cedar Creek. Directing his men in the trenches around Petersburg until its fall, he surrendered at Appomattox. A postwar politician he sat in congress for three terms. (Freeman, Douglas S., *Lee's Lieutenants*)

COZZENS, William Cole (1811-1876)

Following only two months in office as interim-governor of Rhode Island, William C. Cozzens was defeated in a bid for a full term. A native Newport merchant, he had amassed considerable wealth and served his city as mayor and in both houses of the state legislature. Originally a Whig he was a Democrat by the beginning of the Civil War. In 1863 he was named president of the state senate and when William Sprague resigned to become a U.S. senator, Cozzens automatically succeeded to the gubernatorial chair. Entering upon his duties on March 3, 1863, he faced an election in May. Defeated by Republican James Y. Smith, he left office.

CRAIG, Henry Knox (ca. 1791-1869)

At the beginning of the Civil War, the various staff departments were frequently headed by older career officers, many of whom had been in the service from the War of 1812 or even earlier. The Ordnance Department was a case in point. Colonel Henry Craig had entered the army as an artillery lieutenant in 1812 and transferred to the reestablished Ordnance Department in 1832, becoming its head in 1851. However, on April 23, 1861, only 10 days after the fall of Fort Sumter, Craig was replaced by lieutenant colonel James W. Ripley. A Mexican War veteran, having earned a brevet for Monterey, Craig remained in service until he retired on June 1, 1863. Near the close of the Civil War he was brevetted brigadier for his long service. He died four years later.

CRAIG, James (1817-1888)

The appointment of James Craig, a former Missouri Democratic congressman, to be a brigadier general was highly political. Born in Pennsylvania, Craig was raised in Ohio and admitted to the bar before moving to St. Joseph, Missouri. He was the commander of a company of mounted state volunteers in the Mexican War and then served, successively as a state attorney, state senator, and for two House terms as a U.S. congressman. Not renominated in 1860, he resumed his legal practice the next year. To help keep Missouri in the Union and guarantee the support of his political friends for the war effort, President Lincoln gave Craig the star of a brigadier general. His assignments included: brigadier general, USV (March 21, 1862); commanding District of Nebraska, Department of Kansas (June-October 11, 1862); commanding District of Nebraska, Department of the Missouri (October 11, 1862-June 4, 1863); and brigadier general, Missouri Enrolled Militia (May 19, 1864). His primary mission was to guard the Overland Mail route to the West. Resigning on May 5, 1863, he was relieved of duty the next month and returned home. The next year he served seven months as a militia general before resigning on January 2, 1865. His service during this period is vague. In the postwar years he was highly active in railroading.

CRANE, Stephen (1871-1900)

In an era when there were plenty of Civil War veterans around to criticize historical inaccuracies, Stephen Crane—born six years after the war's close—wrote one of the most accurate and extraordinary Civil War novels, *The Red Badge of Courage*. The New Jersey native and author of numerous short stories published the classic work in 1895. It is a penetrating account of the feelings of a young volunteer about to "see the elephant"—go into his first battle. The realistic depiction of the confusion of the battle—many historians speculate that it is Chancellorsville—is amazing for a non-participant. As a war correspondent, Crane covered fighting in Cuba, Greece, and Turkey. Faced with financial problems that he never overcame, he was also the victim of harassment by the New York City Police Department in his final years. This resulted from his testimony regarding an incident in which an officer, Charles Becker, viciously assaulted a prostitute for not paying him protection money. In return Crane was labeled a client of prostitutes and an opium smoker. When Crane returned to New York City in 1898, the campaign to smear him was renewed. In a later murder case, Becker went to the electric chair. Crane himself died of tuberculosis. (Stallman, R.W., *Stephen Crane: A Biography*)

CRANE, William T. (1832-1865)

William T. Crane was one of the least remembered special artists for the illustrated weeklies, perhaps because he barely outlived the Civil War. A native of New Hampshire, he was hired early in the war by *Frank Leslie's Illustrated Newspaper*. He primarily covered the military operations along the Southern coast. Most of his 244 sketches depicted scenes of military life and the operations against Charleston and Savannah. In 1864 he covered the Democratic convention in Chicago and visited with his pencils the site of the Canada-based Confederate raid on St. Albans, Vermont. His last works depicted the trial of the Lincoln assassination conspirators. He died in July 1865 while working in the nation's capital.

CRAPO, Henry Howland (1804-1869)

Michigan's second wartime governor, Henry H. Crapo was a staunch supporter of the Radical Republicans in Congress and a believer in congressional control of Reconstruction. A native of Massachusetts, he had held minor political offices there and served in the militia before moving to Michigan and entering the lumber business in 1858. As a Republican he was elected mayor of Flint in 1860 and served in the state senate in 1863-64. Late in the latter year he was elected governor and sworn in on January 4, 1865. He worked for the ratification of the constitutional amendment abolishing slavery and strongly opposed the policies of Andrew Johnson. After the expiration of his second term in 1869 he devoted his time to his lumber and railroad interests until his death later that year. (Lewis, Martin Demming, *Lumberman from Flint*)

CRAVEN, Tunus Augustus MacDonough (1813-1864)

Career naval officer Tunus A.M. Craven met his death in the confrontation of two revolutionary weapons of naval warfare—the monitor and the torpedo. His earlier naval career had included the editorship of the *U.S. Nautical Magazine* and duty in the seizure of California during the Mexican War. His Civil War assignments included: lieutenant, USN (since 1841); commander, USN (April 1861); and commanding *Tecumseh* (to August 5, 1864). Serving under Admiral Farragut in the battle of Mobile Bay he led his monitor at the head of the column of attack. As the column passed Forts Morganand Gaines and headed for the CSS *Tennessee* one or more torpedoes—known today as mines—exploded under the *Tecumseh*. Within a matter of minutes she went to the bottom with most of her crew. The rest of the Union fleet hesitated and it was at this moment that Farragut allegedly shouted, "Damn the torpedoes, full speed ahead." But Commander Craven had already gone to the bottom with his craft.

CRAWFORD, Martin Jenkins (1820-1883)

A moderate secessionist and a strong proponent of States' rights, Congressman Martin Crawford resigned his seat upon the secession of his native Georgia. In February he was appointed by Jefferson Davis as one of the three commissioners to the United States during the crisis over Forts Sumter and Pickens. When his commission failed, he returned to the South and entered the Provisional Congress where he served on the Accounts and the Commercial Affairs committees and was a supporter of Howell Cobb for the chief executive's position. Following the adjournment of the provisional body in February 1862, Crawford was appointed colonel, 3rd Georgia Cavalry, a newly organized regiment, on May 28. His military career was not a success. Near New Haven, Kentucky, Colonel Crawford and a large portion of his command was surprised while on outpost duty, and was captured without the Union cavalry having to fire a shot. After being paroled, Crawford was found guilty by a general court-martial and sentenced to "three months' suspension from rank and pay and to be reprimanded in orders by the general commanding." Before his suspension was over, Crawford resigned on March 13, 1863. He subsequently served as an unofficial aide to General Howell Cobb. After the war, he resumed his career as a lawyer and went on to become a judge on the state supreme court.

Martin J. Crawford, legislator turned cavalryman. (*Harper's*)

CRAWFORD, Samuel Johnson (1835-1913)

While sitting as Kansas' third—and youngest—governor Samuel J. Crawford received the brevet of brigadier general of volunteers for his earlier war service. The native of Indiana had settled in Kansas in 1859 to practice law and had become a Republican member of the legislature upon the admission of the state to the Union. He then took a leave to enter the Union army. His assignments included: captain, 12th Kansas (May 14, 1861); captain, 9th Kansas (change of designation February 4, 1862); captain, 2nd Kansas Cavalry (change of designation March 5, 1862); colonel, 2nd Kansas Colored Infantry (November 1, 1863); and colonel, 83rd United States Colored Troops (change of designation December 13, 1864) His service was mostly in Kansas, Missouri, Arkansas, and the Indian Territory. Nominated by the Republicans for the governorship, his campaign was interrupted by Price's 1864 invasion of Missouri and threatening of Kansas. Nonetheless Crawford was elected in November and took office early the next year. He then received his brevet. After selling bonds for the war effort he urged the passage of the antislavery constitutional amendments. As governor he urged the removal of the Indians from the state and he resigned on November 4, 1868—in his second term—to command the 19th Kansas Cavalry in operations against the Indians who had killed over 200 Kansans over the two previous years. One of his more nationally important acts as governor was the appointment of Edmund G. Ross to the late James H. Lane's U.S. Senate seat. Ross was the deciding vote in acquitting Andrew Johnson at his impeachment trial. He subsequently ran for numerous offices and practiced law. His *Kansas in the Sixties* appeared in 1911. (Plummer, Mark A., *Frontier Governor: Samuel J. Crawford of Kansas*)

CRAWFORD, Samuel Wylie (1829-1892)

A veteran of 10 years service as an assistant surgeon in Indian country, Samuel Crawford transferred to combat service after being given command of several guns during the bombardment of Fort Sumter. Following the surrender, the University of Pennsylvania Medical School graduate was formally assigned to the combat arm by promotion to the rank of major of the newly organized 14th Infantry on May 14, 1861. His later assignments included: brigadier general, USV (April 25, 1862); commanding 1st Brigade, 1st Division, in the Department of the Shenandoah (May 27-June 26, 1862), in 2nd Corps, Army of Virginia (June 26-September 4, 1862), and in 12th Corps, Army of the Potomac (September 12-17, 1862); com-

Samuel W. Crawford, surgeon turned combat commander, and his staff. (NA)

manding the division (September 4-12 and 17, 1862); commanding Pennsylvania Reserve Corps, 22nd Corps, Department of Washington (May 19-June 28, 1863); commanding 3rd Division (June 28-August 28, 1863; November 1, 1863-February 20, 1864; May 1-June 2, 1864; June 5, 1864-January 2, 1865; and January 27-June 28, 1865) and 2nd Division (June 2-5, 1864), 5th Corps, Army of the Potomac; lieutenant colonel, 2nd Infantry (February 17, 1864); and commanding temporarily 5th Corps, Army of the Potomac (October 7-15, 1863 and January 2-27, 1865). Assigned to duty in the Shenandoah Valley, Crawford later moved to join the Army of Virginia and fought at Cedar Mountain and 2nd Bull Run. At Antietam, he succeeded to command of the division and was wounded there. Returning to field duty, he commanded the Pennsylvania Reserves in the Defenses of Washington and at Gettysburg, the Wilderness, and Spotsylvania. He saw further action at Cold Harbor, Petersburg, and in the Appomattox Campaign. He received brevets through major general of both regulars and volunteers for Gettysburg, Five Forks, and the Wilderness through Petersburg. He was placed on the army's retired list in 1873.

CRENSHAW, William Graves (?-?)

A prominent Richmond businessman in the import-export field, William G. Crenshaw raised and equipped a Confederate artillery battery, but his talents were soon determined to be more useful in his own field. A native of the city, he was engaged in the running of his firm in 1861 when he raised the Richmond "Crenshaw" Artillery and became its captain. He led the unit during the Seven Days, at 2nd Bull Run, and Antietam. Missing Fredericksburg, he resigned in 1863 to accept an assignment to purchase supplies and naval vessels in England. Successful in this, he was however unable to achieve a second part of his assignment—to gain recognition and outright support from the London government. After the war he was highly successful in the mining field.

CREWS, Charles Constantine (?-?)

It is sometimes claimed that Colonel Charles C. Crews was promoted to brigadier general during the final days of the Confederate Army of Tennessee. However, despite his being in charge of a brigade for extended periods, there is no record of a formal appointment. His assignments included: captain, Company A, 2nd Georgia Cavalry (May 7, 1862); colonel, 2nd Georgia Cavalry (November 1, 1862), commanding brigade, Wharton's Division, Wheeler's Cavalry Corps, Army of Tennessee (summer-fall 1863); commanding brigade, Martin's Division, Wheeler's Cavalry Corps, Army of Tennessee (December 1863-February 29, 1864); and commanding brigade, Allen's Division, Wheeler's Cavalry Corps, Department of South Carolina, Georgia and Florida (September 1864-early 1865). During a raid in central Kentucky in the fall of 1862, he was captured but released in time to receive promotion to regimental command. After service in middle Tennessee he fought at Chickamauga, Knoxville, and in the Atlanta, Savannah, and Carolinas campaigns. He was wounded in the last-named campaign. By this time Wheeler's cavalry was serving with Johnston's army and he was mentioned as a colonel on April 15, 1865. The army surrendered on April 26. It is during this eleven-day period that it is claimed that he received promotion.

CRITTENDEN, George Bibb (1812-1880)

The son of the great compromiser of 1860, John J. Crittenden, George B. Crittenden's military career was greatly damaged by charges of drunkenness in the face of the enemy. The native Kentuckian and West Pointer (1832) had served in the Black Hawk War before resigning in 1833 while still a brevet second lieutenant of infantry. Relocating to Texas, he joined the army there and in 1843 was captured during the Mier invasion of Mexico. He escaped the fate of his compatriots when he drew the white bean and his life was spared. During the Mexican War, he was recommissioned as a captain in the Regiment of Mounted Riflemen and won a brevet. In 1848 he was cashiered from the Army but was reinstated the next year. By the time of his June 10, 1861, resignation he was the lieutenant colonel of the regiment. He offered his services to the Confederacy, and his assignments included: brigadier general, CSA (August 15, 1861); assigned command 4th Brigade, 2nd Division, Potomac District, Department of Northern Virginia (October 22, 1861); major general, CSA (November 9, 1861); commanding District of East Tennessee, Department #2 (December 8, 1861-February 23, 1862); commanding 2nd Division, Army of Central Kentucky, Department #2 (February 23-April 1,

1862); and commanding Departments of East Tennessee and Western Virginia (May 31-June 22, 1864). Appointed a brigadier general, he was assigned to a brigade in northern Virginia but the record is unclear whether or not he actually commanded one there. Promoted to major general, he was given command in East Tennessee. He lost the battle of Mill Springs in Kentucky early in 1862. Despite the fact that he was apparently drunk at the time much of the blame belongs to his subordinate, Felix K. Zollicoffer, who was killed in the action brought on by his own rashness. Nonetheless Crittenden came in for the bulk of the censure—much of it deserved—and was arrested for drunkenness on April 1, 1862. He resigned the following October 23rd. For much of the rest of the war he served on the staff of John S. Williams with the apparently unofficial rank of colonel. In the spring of 1864 he was briefly in departmental command in his old bailiwick. His brother Thomas L. Crittenden remained loyal to the Union and became a general officer. After the war George B. Crittenden served as Kentucky's state librarian.

CRITTENDEN, John Jordan (1787-1863)

John J. Crittenden's tireless efforts to maintain the Union capped a long and distinguished political career. The Kentucky native was admitted to the bar in 1807 and practiced until named attorney general for the Illinois Territory in 1809. He served for one year and then entered the Kentucky legislature. He served as a staff officer to the governor during the War of 1812. His subsequent political offices included: member of the state legislature (1811-17, 1825, and 1829-32); U.S. senator (1817-19 resigned, 1835-41, and 1842-48 resigned); U.S. district attorney (1827-29); U.S. Supreme Court nominee (not confirmed 1828); William Henry Harrison's attorney general (1841); governor (1848-50 resigned); and Millard Fillmore's attorney general (1850-53). Throughout this period he tried to resolve the sectional crisis and was elected to the Senate one last time in 1855. He sat from March 4, 1855, to March 3, 1861, and in the final months of 1860 and early 1861 pushed his compromise proposals whose primary feature was the extension of the Missouri Compromise line across the continent. But it was far too late for this to be acceptable to either side. The compromise failed as did his effort to get the constitutional amendment proposed by the Washington Peace Convention approved. Giving up on efforts to prevent the war, he tried to limit its purpose to restoration of the Union. He used his position as a Unionist member of the House of Representatives for this effort. He had been active in retaining Kentucky in the Union, but the divisions in the state were apparent in his own family, which provided a son to each side, as general officers. He left office on March 3, 1863, and was a candidate for reelection when he died on July 26 of that year. (Kirwan, Albert Dennis, *John J. Crittenden: The Struggle for the Union*)

CRITTENDEN, Thomas Leonidas (1819-1893)

The Union rout at Chickamauga virtually ended the Civil War career of Major General Thomas L. Crittenden. The son of the originator of the Crittenden Compromise of 1860, he was born in Kentucky and had a brother with the same rank in the Confederate army. A lawyer, he had served as a private in the state volunteers in 1836 and was the lieutenant colonel of the 3rd Kentucky during the Mexican War. In the interwar years he was a diplomat in Liverpool. Remaining loyal to the Union, he was in command of the loyal state's forces early in the war. His later assignments included: brigadier general, USV (September 27, 1861); commanding 5th Division, Army of the Ohio (December 2, 1861-September 29, 1862); major general, USV (July 17, 1862); commanding 2nd Corps, Army of the Ohio (September 29-November 5, 1862); commanding Left Wing, 14th Corps, Army of the Cumberland (November 5, 1862-January 9, 1863); commanding 21st Corps, Army of the Cumberland (January 9-February 19, March 19-July 15 and August 17-October 10, 1863); and commanding 1st Division, 9th Corps, Army of the Potomac (May 12-June 9, 1864). On the second day of Shiloh he commanded his division as part of Buell's force relieving the pressure on Grant. His corps was present at Perryville but saw little combat there. For his role in the battle of Murfreesboro, he was awarded the brevet of brigadier general in the regular service in 1867. He took part in the Tullahoma Campaign and the capture of Chattanooga, but then disaster struck at Chickamauga when he was swept from the field along with two-thirds of the army and the army commander, Rosecrans. The latter tried to blame the collapse of the second day on his subordinates, including Crittenden. The resulting inquiry in Nashville after much deliberation absolved the lesser officers of any guilt. But Crittenden briefly held only one other field command—with the Army of the Potomac—and fought at Spotsylvania and Cold Harbor. He resigned his

Union corps commander Thomas L. Crittenden. (*Leslie's*)

commission on December 13, 1864, but President Johnson appointed him to a regular army colonelcy upon the 1866 reorganization. He retired as the head of the 17th Infantry in 1881.

CRITTENDEN, Thomas Turpin (1825-1905)

Thomas T. Crittenden's military career was a victim of Nathan Bedford Forrest and his cavalry. The nephew of compromiser John J. Crittenden, this Alabama-born officer had cousins on opposite sides, each with the rank of major general. He settled in Missouri and interrupted his law practice to serve as a second lieutenant of Missouri volunteers during the Mexican War. By the outbreak of the Civil War he was living in Indiana as a lawyer. His assignments included: captain, 6th Indiana (April 19, 1861); colonel, 6th Indiana (April 27, 1861; three-months unit); colonel, 6th Indiana (September 20, 1861; three-years unit); brigadier general, USV (April 28, 1862); and commanding 3rd Brigade, 1st Division, 20th Corps, Army of the Cumberland (March 9-April 5, 1863). With his three-months regiment he fought at Philippi and Carrick's Ford before being mustered out on August 2, 1861. Reorganizing the regiment for a longer term, he was recommissioned and fought at Shiloh. Only one day after taking command of the post at Murfreesboro, he was surprised and captured with the garrison on July 13, 1862. He was severely criticized for his lack of preparations. Not exchanged until October, he briefly commanded a brigade under Rosecrans in early 1863. This appears to have been his only field service from his release to his May 5, 1863, resignation. He subsequently lived in the District of Columbia and California and was engaged in real estate.

CROCKER, John Simpson (?-1890)

Despite the fact that he had spent only two weeks in brigade command, New Yorker John S. Crocker was brevetted brigadier general six months after he had been mustered out of the service. His assignments included: colonel, 93rd New York (February 3, 1862); and commanding 2nd Brigade, 3rd Division, 2nd Corps, Army of the Potomac (May 5-18, 1864). His regiment fought on the Peninsula where he was evidently captured, since he was reported as exchanged on September 21, 1862. His regiment was part of the Army of the Potomac's provost guard detachment during the campaigns of Fredericksburg, Chancellorsville, and Gettysburg. However, during the latter battle his regiment was detached at Taneytown, Maryland. For the Overland Campaign the regiment was assigned to the 2nd Corps and Crocker led it in the Wilderness and succeeded to brigade command on the first day of the fight. He held this command until the battle of Spotsylvania where he relinquished command. Mustered out on September 7, 1864, he returned to New York.

CROCKER, Marcellus Monroe (1830-1865)

One of Grant's favorite division leaders, Marcellus M. Crocker succumbed to tuberculosis at the end of the war. The Indiana native attended West Point in 1847-49 but dropped out to take up the practice of law in Des Moines. When the Civil War began he gave up his practice. His military assignments included: captain, 2nd Iowa (May 27, 1861); major, 2nd Iowa (May 31, 1861); lieutenant colonel, 2nd Iowa (September 6, 1861); colonel, 13th Iowa (December 30, 1861); commanding 1st Brigade, 1st Division, Army of the Tennessee (February 23-March 15 and April 6, 1862); commanding 3rd Brigade, 6th Division, Army of the Tennessee (April 8-July 24, 1862); commanding 3rd Brigade, 6th Division, District of Corinth, Army of the Tennessee (July 24-November 1, 1862); commanding 3rd Brigade, 6th Division, Left Wing, 16th Corps, Army of the Tennessee (December 22, 1862-January 20, 1863); commanding 3rd Brigade, 6th Division, 17th Corps, Army of the Tennessee (May 2-16, 1863); commanding 4th Division, 13th Corps, Army of the Tennessee (August 7, 1863-May 27, 1864). He served with his first regiment in Missouri before being tapped to command a new regiment. At Shiloh he was briefly in command of a brigade and immediately afterwards he was given charge of a brigade of Iowa troops with which he was long associated. He fought at Corinth and was in command of a division during the Vicksburg Campaign, particularly distinguishing himself at Champion Hill. From the summer of 1863 to the spring of 1864 his division was engaged in operations and guard duty in Louisiana and Mississippi. During the movements of the corps to join Sherman's army in the Atlanta Campaign he was forced to relinquish command due to tuberculosis. He was then assigned to duty in the Department of New Mexico for health reasons but was sufficiently recovered by the end of the year to be ordered to report to Thomas' army at Nashville. But before he had reported, he was ordered to Washington. There was much speculation about Crocker's possibly being assigned to command in West Virginia. By the time he reached the nation's capital the war was nearing its conclusion and his health, having worsened, precluded active field command. He died in Washington on August 26, 1865.

CROOK, George (1828-1890)

Although he was better known for his Indian-fighting abilities, George Crook amassed a considerable record as a fighting general in the Civil War. A West Pointer (1852), Crook was wounded by a poison arrow in an Indian fight in California in 1857 and at the start of the war was a first lieutenant in the 4th Infantry. His later assignments included: captain, 4th Infantry (May 14, 1861); colonel, 36th Ohio (September 13, 1861); commanding 3rd Brigade, Kanawha District, Mountain Department (March 11-September 1862); brigadier general, USV (September 7, 1862); commanding 2nd Brigade, Kanawha Division, 9th Corps, Army of the Potomac (September-October 1862); commanding Kanawha Division, Department of the Ohio (October 1862-January 1863); commanding Crook's Brigade, Army of Kentucky, Department of the Cumberland (February-June 8, 1863); commanding 3rd Brigade, 4th Division, 14th Corps, Army of the Cumberland (June 8-July 28, 1863); commanding 2nd Division, Cavalry Corps, Army of the Cumberland (July 28, 1863-February 3, 1864); commanding 3rd Division, Department of West

George Crook, victim of McNeill's raiders. (*Leslie's*)

Virginia (February 11-April 1864); commanding 3rd Division, Department of West Virginia (February 11-April 1864); commanding 2nd Infantry Division, Department of West Virginia (April-July 22, 1864); also commanding 1st Infantry Division (July 3-22, 1864); commanding the department (August 8, 1864-February 22, 1865 and March 20-22, 1865); major general, USV (October 21, 1864); commanding 2nd Division, Cavalry Corps, Army of the Potomac (March 27-May 22, 1865); and commanding the corps (May 22-June 27, 1865). After service in West Virginia, Crook fought at South Mountain and Antietam. With his command sent west, he led it in the Tullahoma Campaign and later commanded a cavalry division at Chickamauga. Returning to the East, he commanded at the battle of Cloyd's Mountain and the Army of West Virginia, as the 8th Corps in Sheridan's Army of the Shenandoah, at 3rd Winchester, Fisher's Hill, and Cedar Creek. On the night of February 21-22, 1865, Confederate partisan leader Jesse McNeill led a small force of raiders into the town of Cumberland, Maryland, and routed Crook from his sleep for a long ride to Libby Prison. The owner of the hotel in which he was staying at the time was his future father-in-law and one of the raiders was his future brother-in-law. Exchanged on March 20, 1865, he soon joined the Army of the Potomac, commanding a cavalry division, and participated in the battle of Five Forks and in the pursuit of Lee to Appomattox. He was brevetted through grades in the regular army to major general for Lewisburg, Antietam, Farmington (Tennessee), West Virginia campaign of 1864, and Fisher's Hill. Mustered out of the volunteer service on January 15, 1866, he continued in the regular army, rising to the rank of major general. He died in 1890, after a highly successful career as an Indian fighter, and still on duty. In his last years he had become a champion of Indian rights.

CROOK, William H. (?-?)

A former policeman in the nation's capital, White House guard William H. Crook unfortunately was not on duty as Lincoln's bodyguard at Ford's Theater on April 14. That day of Lincoln's assassination he was assigned to the 8 A.M.-4 P.M. shift. However, his relief, John F. Parker, was some three hours late in reporting for duty so Crook was still at the White House at about the time the president set off for the show. Crook later noted that that night Lincoln had said "Good-bye, Crook," instead of the usual "Good night, Crook." Parker deserted his post and Crook always regretted not having been there himself. He later wrote his memoirs.

CROSS, Edward E. (1832-1863)

At the time of the firing on Fort Sumter, Edward Cross was holding a lieutenant colonel's commission in the Mexican army. Returning home to New Hampshire he organized a regiment for the Union cause. His assignments included: colonel, 5th New Hampshire (ca. October 22, 1861) and commanding 1st Brigade, 1st Division, 2nd Corps, Army of the Potomac (May 22-July 2, 1863). He led his regiment to the Peninsula and saw action at the siege of Yorktown and Seven Pines. Wounded at the latter, he missed the battle of the Seven Days but returned in time to be wounded again at Antietam. Recovering, he was wounded a third time at Fredericksburg. He came through the fight at Chancellorsville without a scratch, having commanded a demi-brigade during much of the action. Two weeks later he succeeded to command of the brigade and led it in the fighting

Colonel Edward E. Cross was repeatedly wounded. (*Leslie's*)

on the second day at Gettysburg. In the fighting in the woods near Devil's Den on the Union left he was again severely wounded. This time the wound proved to be fatal and he died late that night. (Child, William, *A History of the Fifth Regiment, New Hampshire Volunteers in the American Civil War*)

CROSSLAND, Edward (1827-1881)

A Kentucky farmer, lawyer, and politician, Edward Crossland served throughout the war in various theaters but did not earn his greatest distinction until his command was mounted and assigned to Forrest's Cavalry. His assignments included: captain, Company E. 1st Kentucky (April 23, 1861); major, 1st Kentucky (1861), lieutenant colonel, 1st Kentucky (1862); colonel, 7th Kentucky (May 20, 1862); commanding 3rd Brigade, Buford's Division, Forrest's Cavalry Corps, Department of Alabama, Mississippi and East Louisiana (May-July 14, 1864); and commanding independent brigade, Forrest's Cavalry Corps, Department of Alabama, Mississippi and East Louisiana (spring 1865). After seeing action at Dranesville, his original 12-months unit was mustered out in May 1862 and he was elected colonel of the veteran 7th. He led it at Baton Rouge, Corinth, Champion Hill, and Jackson. Having been cut off at Champion Hill with the rest of Loring's Division, he was not included in the capture of Vicksburg. On March 1, 1864, the regiment was mounted and joined the cavalry. Within a few days he was in command of the brigade and led it at Brice's Crossroads and Tupelo, where he was wounded, under Forrest. Returning to duty in August, he found that the brigade had been assigned to General H.B. Lyon. He resumed regimental command until early 1865 when he directed a separate brigade in opposing Wilson's Raid through Alabama. Crossland's command surrendered May 6, 1865, at Columbus, Mississippi.

CROWNINSHIELD, Casper (?-1897)

Serving mostly in northern Virginia and the Shenandoah Valley, Massachusetts native Casper Crowninshield won the brevet of brigadier general for the war. His assignments included: captain, 20th Massachusetts (August 18, 1861); captain, 1st Massachusetts Cavalry (November 28, 1861); major, 2nd Massachusetts Cavalry (January 31, 1863); lieutenant colonel, 2nd Massachusetts Cavalry (March 18, 1864); commanding Reserve Brigade, 1st Division, Cavalry Corps, Army of the Shenandoah (October 19-December 13, 1864, January 6-15, 18-26, and January 31-February 10, 1865); colonel, 2nd Massachusetts Cavalry (November 18, 1864); and commanding the division (January 26-31, 1865). As an infantry company commander he fought in the disaster at Ball's Bluff before transferring to the mounted arm. His new unit served at first on the South Carolina coast before moving to Virginia and Maryland. It fought at South Mountain and Crowninshield took command of it at Antietam. His unit fought at Fredericksburg and then in the vicinity of Washington, sometimes tangling with John S. Mosby and his partisan rangers. He took part in the defense of the city near Fort Stevens during Jubal A. Early's raid north of the Potomac. Joining Sheridan's cavalry, he fought at 3rd Winchester and succeeded to command of the brigade at Cedar Creek. Later he led his regiment in the final stages of the Petersburg Campaign and in the pursuit of Lee to Appomattox. Brevetted, he was mustered out on June 15, 1865.

CROXTON, John Thomas (1836-1874)

A Yale graduate and lawyer, John Croxton was one of only two persons to vote for Lincoln in his hometown of Paris, Kentucky in 1860. This move was so unpopular in the slave region that he went to the polls armed. During the period when the state was neutral, early in the war, Croxton was authorized by the Union authorities to raise troops. His assignments included: lieutenant colonel, 4th Kentucky (October 9, 1861); colonel, 4th Kentucky (May 9, 1862); commanding 2nd Brigade, 3rd Division, 14th Corps, Army of the Cumberland (August 15-September 20, 1863); commanding 1st Brigade, 1st Division, Cavalry Corps, Military Division of the Mississippi (October 29, 1864-June 26, 1865). With his regiment, Croxton took part in the battle of Mill Springs and the Perryville, Murfreesboro, and Tullahoma campaigns. Leading a brigade at Chickamauga, he was severely wounded on the second day. His wound reopened at Chattanooga and he was put out of action for several months. In the spring of 1864, the 4th, after its veteran furlough, was converted to mounted infantry. Croxton took part in the Atlanta and Franklin/Nashville campaigns. In the latter battle, Croxton's brigade played a conspicuous part in the rout of Hood's army. In the last months of the war Croxton led his brigade on a raid, in conjunction with Wilson's through Alabama, and captured Tuscaloosa and finally ended up in Macon. For Nashville and this raid he was brevetted major general of volunteers. After the war Croxton returned to law and became active in Republican politics and journalism. He died in La Paz, Bolivia, while serving as U.S. minister there. (Miller, Rex, *Croxton's Raid*)

CRUFT, Charles (1826-1883)

Having witnessed the battle of 1st Bull Run as a spectator, Charles Cruft returned to his native Indiana and raised a regiment for the Union army. A lawyer, he was formerly a school teacher, bank clerk, and railroad president. His military assignments colonel, 31st Indiana (September 20, 1861); commanding 13th Brigade, Army of the Ohio (November-December 2, 1861); commanding 13th Brigade, 5th Division, Army of the Ohio (December 2, 1861-February 14, 1862); commanding 1st Brigade, 3rd Division, District of Cairo, Department of the Missouri (February 14-17, 1862); commanding 3rd Brigade, 4th Division, Army of the Tennessee (February 17-April 5, 1862); brigadier general, USV (July 16, 1862); commanding 2nd Brigade, Army of Kentucky, Department of the Ohio (August 25-30, 1862); commanding 22nd Brigade, 4th Division, 2nd Corps, Army of the Ohio (September 29-November 5, 1862); commanding 1st Brigade, 2nd Division, Left Wing, 14th Corps, Army of the Cumberland (November 5, 1862-January 9, 1863); commanding 1st Brigade, 2nd Division, 21st Corps, Army of the Cumberland (January 9-March 21, April 21-July 15, and August 17-October 9, 1863); commanding the division (July

15-August 17, 1863); commanding 1st Division, 4th Corps, Army of the Cumberland (October 27-late November 1863 and February 13-March 14, 1864); commanding 1st Brigade, 1st Division, 4th Corps, Army of the Cumberland (January 15-February 13 and March 14-June 10, 1864); commanding Provisional Division, District of the Etowah, Department of the Cumberland (December 1864); commanding 2nd Separate Division, District of the Etowah, Department of the Cumberland (March 15-spring 1865); commanding 4th Division, District of East Tennessee, Department of the Cumberland (May 17-June 1865); and also commanding 1st Brigade, 4th Division, District of East Tennessee, Department of the Cumberland (June 1865). His first major action came as a brigade commander at Fort Donelson. He was later severely wounded twice on the first day at Shiloh. After recovering he was given command of a brigade in the Army of Kentucky and performed creditably at Richmond where nonetheless most of his command was captured during Bragg's invasion of Kentucky. Given a new command, he was present at Perryville but his brigade was not engaged. He saw further service at Murfreesboro, the Tullahoma Campaign, Chickamauga, and Chattanooga. He then participated in the Knoxville relief expedition under Sherman and the early portion of the Atlanta Campaign. Returning to Tennessee, he fought at Nashville in command of a division composed of miscellaneous detachments that were unable to join the army under Sherman on the March to the Sea. He finished the war in East Tennessee and was mustered out on August 24, 1865, and brevetted major general for his war service. In the postwar years he concentrated on the legal profession.

CRUIKSHANK, Marcus Henderson (1826-1881)

One of the most obstructionist of congressmen during the Second Confederate Congress was Alabama's 4th District representative, Marcus H. Cruikshank. A native Alabamian, Cruikshank practiced law and owned a small farming operation. On the political side, he was a half-owner of the *Alabama Reporter* and served for many years as the mayor of Talladega. A lifelong Whig he supported the Union and was an outspoken opponent of secession. Nonetheless, after running a saltworks during the early part of the war, he defeated Jabez L.M. Curry, the 4th District's incumbent, in the fall of 1863. Taking his seat in February 1864 he was named chairman of the Committee on Enrolled Bills and promptly became a thorn in the side of the Davis administration. He immediately moved to cancel the authorization to suspend the writ of habeas corpus and opposed virtually all war measures. Peace proposals always found favorable consideration with Cruikshank. He also served on the Committees on Ordnance and Ordnance Stores and on Printing. He followed the legal and journalistic professions after the war as well as helping the poor until his death in a riding accident.

CRUMP, William Wood (1819-1897)

An ardent secessionist and prominent attorney, William W. Crump served as the assistant secretary of the treasury in the Confederate government. A native Virginian he had been admitted to the bar in 1840 and after serving a year as a judge returned to private practice, preferring to work before a jury. During the war he worked to protect younger bureaucrats from military service. He was sitting in the state legislature when military rule was established after the war's close. Returning to his law practice, he worked on Jefferson Davis' defense and held no further public office excepting one term in the legislature. For the remaining years of his life he was a prominent defense attorney.

CRUTCHFIELD, Stapleton (1835-1865)

The battle of Chancellorsville deprived the Confederacy not only of Stonewall Jackson but also of Stapleton Crutchfield, one of the South's most able artillerists, who lost his leg in the battle, and a probable promotion to brigadier and further active service. Six years after graduating number one in his Virginia Military Institute class of 1855 he entered Confederate service. His assignments included: major, 9th Virginia (July 1861); major, 58th Virginia (October 1861); lieutenant colonel, 58th Virginia (early 1862); colonel, 16th Virginia (May 1862, declined); colonel, Artillery (May 5, 1862); chief of artillery, Valley District, Department of Northern Virginia (May 5-June 25, 1862); chief of artillery, 2nd Corps, Army of Northern Virginia (June 25, 1862-May 2, 1863); commanding Artillery Brigade, Department of Richmond (January 7-April 2, 1865); and commanding brigade, G.W.C. Lee's Division, attached to Army of Northern Virginia (April 2-6, 1865). After early service in the infantry on Crany Island and in western Virginia, he transferred to the artillery and served with Stonewall Jackson in the Shenandoah and at the Seven Days, Cedar Mountain, 2nd Bull Run, Antietam, Fredericksburg, and Chancellorsville. He was under active consideration for promotion to brigadier general but after losing his leg on the second day at Chancellorsville, he was incapacitated for further service in the field. Upon his recovery in March 1864, he was assigned to duty as an artillery inspector. In the following January he was given command of thc stationary artillery defenses of Richmond. With the fall of the city, his gun crews formed a brigade of infantry. Joining Lee's army in the retreat, he was decapitated by a cannonball at Sayler's Creek on April 6, three days before the surrender at Appomattox. (Wise, Jennings C., *The Long Arm of Lee*)

CULLUM, George Washington (1809-1892)

Best known in the field of Civil War history for his *Biographical Register of the Officers and Graduates of the United States Military Academy*, George W. Cullum was also one of the most senior staff officers in the Union army. Born in New York, he was admitted to West Point from Pennsylvania. Graduating in 1833, he was posted to the engineers and was assigned to coastal defense work. He also taught at his alma mater and was in charge of some of the construction there. His Civil War-era assignments included: captain, Engineers (since July 7, 1838); lieutenant colonel and aide-de-camp (April 9, 1861); aide-de-camp to commander-in-chief (April 9-November 1, 1861);

major, Engineers (August 6, 1861); colonel and additional aide-de-camp (August 6, 1861); brigadier general, USV (November 1, 1861); chief engineer and chief of staff, Department of the Missouri (November 19, 1861-March 11, 1862); chief engineer and chief of staff, Department of the Mississippi (March 11-July 11, 1862); chief of staff to commander-in-chief (July 11, 1862-March 12, 1864); lieutenant colonel, Engineers (March 3, 1863); chief of staff to the chief of staff of the Army (March 12-ca. September 8, 1864); and superintendent, U.S. Military Academy (September 8, 1864-August 28, 1866). In the first months of the war he was on the staff of Winfield Scott. Made a brigadier, he was sent west and served on Henry W. Halleck's staff as engineering officer and chief of staff. He held this position in St. Louis and during the slow advance on Corinth, Mississippi. He went with Halleck to Washington and served there even after Halleck had been superseded by Grant. In the summer of 1864 he took over as head of the military academy. Brevetted major general for his war service, he remained in the army until his 1874 retirement as a colonel. He had been mustered out of the volunteer service on September 1, 1866. He published his three-volume work in 1890, his will called for updates every decade.

West Point historian George W. Cullum. (*Leslie's*)

CULP, John Wesley (ca. 1838-1863)

Although born in Gettysburg, John Culp, better known by his middle name of Wesley, served in the Confederate army. Having worked for a number of years in Virginia, young Culp had politically become a Southerner. On April 20, 1861, he was enlisted in the Hamtranck Guards, officially Company B, 2nd Virginia, at Harpers Ferry. After initial service in the Shenandoah Valley, the company, from Shepherdstown, fought at the battle of 1st Bull Run. Early in 1862, Culp received a furlough but was captured by Union troops during his leave. He thus missed the Valley and Peninsula campaigns. Exchanged on August 5, 1862, he soon rejoined his regiment. The regiment, in the famed "Stonewall" Brigade, fought at Cedar Mountain, 2nd Bull Run, Antietam, Fredericksburg, and Chancellorsville. The next campaign, Lee's second invasion of the North, would take Culp to his hometown and to his death. Culp took part in the 2nd battle of Winchester on the way to Pennsylvania. Late on the second day of the battle of Gettysburg, Culp's division moved onto Culp's Hill, which was named for his family. In the fighting the next morning, as the Union forces retook the hill, Culp fell dead. His body was never identified and he lies with the unknown dead.

CUMMING, Alfred (1829-1910)

Promotion to brigadier general in the Confederate service brought Georgian West Pointer (1849) Alfred Cumming a transfer to the western theater. Upon his graduation he was posted to the infantry and served on the frontier. He took part in the Utah operations against the Mormons and served on the staff of David E. Twiggs for a time. Resigning as a captain in the 7th Infantry on January 19, 1861—the very day his native state seceded—he joined the Confederacy. His assignments included: major, Infantry (March 16, 1861); lieutenant colonel, Augusta Volunteer Battalion (spring 1861); lieutenant colonel, 10th Georgia (June 1861); colonel, 10th Georgia (September 25, 1861); commanding Wilcox's (Ala.) Brigade, Anderson's Division, Longstreet's Corps, Army of Northern Virginia (September 14-17, 1862); brigadier general, CSA (October 29, 1862); commanding 3rd Brigade, Stevenson's Division, Department of Mississippi and East Louisiana (April 15-July 4, 1863); commanding brigade, Stevenson's Division, Hill's-Breckinridge's Corps, Army of Tennessee (October 17-November 23, 1863); commanding brigade, Stevenson's Division, Hardee's Corps, Army of Tennessee (November 23, 1863-February 20, 1864); and commanding brigade, Stevenson's Division, Hood's-Lee's Corps, Army of Tennessee (February 20-August 31, 1864). Moving with his regiment to Virginia, he was stationed on the Peninsula and took part in the siege of Yorktown. During the Seven Days he was wounded at Malvern Hill but recovered in time to take part in the invasion of Maryland. He fought at Crampton's Pass on South Mountain and was again wounded at Antietam. During both actions he was detailed to command another brigade. The next month he was promoted to brigadier general and upon his recovery was sent to John C. Pemberton's army near Vicksburg. He commanded a brigade in the defense of that city until its fall and was exchanged in September 1863 in time to take part in the defeat at Chattanooga. He served throughout the Atlanta Campaign, at the head of his brigade, until severely wounded at Jonesboro. This ended his field career and after the war he became a farmer. In the late 1880s he was a U.S. military representative to Korea.

CUMMING, Kate (ca. 1833-?)

A nurse with the Army of Tennessee, Kate Cumming served from the battle of Shiloh through the final surrender. Born in Scotland, her family settled in Mobile, where her brother enlisted in the Confederate army. She then volunteered for hospital duty and treated the wounded following the battle of Shiloh. She was present through the campaigns in Mississippi, Tennessee, Kentucky, and Georgia. After serving in the Atlanta Campaign she completed the war in a hospital. In 1866 she published *A Journal of Hospital Life in the Confederate Army of Tennessee from the Battle of Shiloh to the End of the War.*

CUNNINGHAM, Richard H., Jr. (1834-1862)

The rate of attrition in the officers' ranks of Stonewall Jackson's command during the campaigns of 1862 was so great that Richard H. Cunningham, Jr., was commanding his regiment as a captain and his brigade as a lieutenant colonel. A merchant in Virginia's capital he had served in a local volunteer company long before the war. His unit volunteered for service a few days after the state's secession and his assignments included: first lieutenant, Company F, 21st Virginia (April 21, 1861); captain, Company F, 21st Virginia (May 1861); lieutenant colonel, 21st Virginia (April 21, 1862); and commanding 2nd Brigade, Jackson's Division, Jackson's Command, Army of Northern Virginia (June 26 and July 1-mid July 1862). After participating in the Cheat Mountain Campaign, he succeeded to command of the regiment, as a captain, during the Romney Campaign and became involved in the Loring-Jackson feud during the winter encampment there. Continuing in regimental command, he fought at Kernstown, McDowell, and in the Shenandoah Valley Campaign, where he was entrusted with escorting the prisoners captured at Front Royal and Winchester up the Valley. Moving to the defense of Richmond he commanded the brigade at Gaines' Mill while two grades short of the appropriate rank of brigadier. Relieved by Brigadier General John R. Jones, he resumed command of the 21st and led it through the rest of the Seven Days Battles before again taking over the brigade upon the wounding of Jones at Malvern Hill. Leaving an ambulance, where he had been for several days, to command his regiment at Cedar Mountain, he was killed while trying to rally his broken unit.

CURRIER, Nathaniel (1813-1888)

The senior partner in the famous lithographic firm Currier & Ives was Massachusetts-born Nathaniel Currier. As a youngster he was apprenticed to the first lithographic firm established in the United States. When one of the partners, John Pendleton, formed a new partnership and moved to Philadelphia Currier went along. In 1833 Currier moved to Pendleton's New York establishment and, following the completion of his apprenticeship, he went into business as a lithographer for himself. His first work appeared in late 1835, from which time his work represents a view of the history and customs of the emerging nation. His work continued to gain in popularity, being hung in many American homes, and in 1852 he went into business with another artist, J. Merritt Ives, who later became a partner. In 1857 their works began to carry the joint label that has since become so famous. Of course, with the coming of the Civil War, a considerable number of their prints dealt with war themes. Currier continued in the business until his 1880 retirement when he passed his share of the venture on to his son.

CURRY, Jabez Lamar Monroe (1825-1903)

Although he played an active role in the events of 1861-65, Jabez L.M. Curry's greatest service to the South was performed in the postwar period. Born in Georgia, Curry moved to Alabama and began the practice of law. After several terms in the state legislature, he was elected to the U.S. House of Representatives in 1856 where he remained until the secession of his state. An early secessionist, he was named to the Provisional Confederate Congress and served on the committees on: Comercial Affairs; Flag and Seal; and Postal Affairs. Running unopposed, he took his seat in the First Regular Congress. He chaired the Committee on Commerce and sat on the Committee on Elections. A consistent supporter of the war effort, he urged President Davis to take the field personally. As a lame duck, having been defeated for reelection in the 1863 elections, Curry was a driving force behind the call for additional sacrifices made by the First Congress as it adjourned. Having also lost a

Confederate Congressman Jabez L.M. Curry. (*Harper's*)

bid for a senatorship, Curry was appointed lieutenant colonel, 5th Alabama Cavalry, and commanded the regiment in central Alabama during the final stages of the war. His only previous military experience had been a brief stint in the Mexican War. Becoming a Baptist preacher, he became involved in education, establishing a public school system throughout most of the former Confederacy. His work was occasionally interrupted by diplomatic appointments, but he was active in education until his death. (Alderman, Edwin and Gordon, Armistead, *J.L.M. Curry: A Biography*)

CURTIN, Andrew Gregg (1817-1894)

Among the Union war governors, Andrew Curtin of Pennsylvania was one of the staunchest supporters of the administration as well as a great friend of the soldiers in the field. A lawyer and former Whig politician, Curtin became a Republican and in 1860 was elected to a three-year term as Pennsylvania's governor. Being elected to a second term in 1863, he was the commonwealth's chief executive for the entire Civil War. His inaugural address on January 15, 1861, set the tone for his administration—total support for Washington in the enforcement of the laws. Throwing himself into the organization of troops, he succeeded in having Pennsylvania provide the first volunteers to arrive in the nation's capital. Pennsylvania's response to Lincoln's first call for troops was so great that almost twice as many regiments as requested were provided. Finally the War Department refused to accept any more. So in May 1861 Curtin prodded the legislature to establish the Pennsylvania Reserve Corps—15 regiments of infantry, cavalry, and artillery—from the surplus recruits. Following the Union disaster at 1st Bull Run these troops were promptly turned over to the Federal authorities. With further Union reverses, he lobbied other governors to petition Lincoln to call for more troops in July 1862. He also helped arrange the Altoona conference in September 1862, which calmed the radical influences on the Northern governors and solidified support for Lincoln. During the Gettysburg invasion he organized the state's forces, which, although not engaged in the battle proper, were a factor in the campaign. For the soldiers he organized state-funded schools for their orphans and a Washington liaison office for their dealings with the central government. In 1864 he strongly supported the Lincoln reelection campaign. When his term expired in 1867 he became a contender for the vice presidency but instead became minister to Russia. Returning to the United States he served six years in the House of Representatives as a Democrat. (McClure, A.K., *The Life and Services of Andrew G. Curtin*)

CURTIN, John Irwin (?-?)

Serving with the widely traveled 9th Corps, Pennsylvania native John I. Curtin rose to the command of a division at the end of the war. His assignments included: captain, 45th Pennsylvania (September 9, 1861); major, 45th Pennsylvania (July 30, 1862); lieutenant colonel, 45th Pennsylvania (September 4, 1862); colonel, 45th Pennsylvania (April 13, 1863); commanding 1st Brigade, 2nd Division, 9th Corps, Army of the Potomac (May 6-June 18, 1864, August 21, 1864-January 23, 1865, February 11-May 4, and July 8-August 1, 1865); and commanding 3rd Division, 9th Corps, Army of the Potomac (May 3-July 8, 1865). After some initial service on the coast of South Carolina the regiment was transferred to Virginia in July 1862 and then took part in the fighting at South Mountain and Antietam, with Curtin in command at the latter. After fighting at Fredericksburg, the regiment was transferred to Kentucky. Joining Grant's army in Mississippi, Curtin took part in the operations to prevent Joseph E. Johnston from relieving the garrison of Vicksburg. Returning to Virginia in early 1864, he succeeded to brigade command at the Wilderness and retained command through Spotsylvania, Cold Harbor, and until wounded in the assaults at Petersburg. Later in the siege, he returned to command the brigade through Appomattox and led a division after the close of hostilities. Having been brevetted to brigadier general on October 14, 1864, he was mustered out with his regiment on July 17, 1865.

CURTIS, Benjamin Robbins (1809-1874)

In the infamous *Dred Scott* decision, Benjamin R. Curtis was one of only two justices—the other was John McLean—to vote to overturn the decision of the lower court and thus free the slave. A graduate of Harvard Law School, the Massachusetts native practiced his profession and sat in the state legislature. Through his support of Daniel Webster, Millard Fillmore's secretary of state, Curtis received the appointment to the highest court on December 11, 1851. In a voice vote on the 29th, the Senate confirmed the nomination. He frequently came into heated conflict with his fellow judges, especially Chief Justice Roger B. Taney, over issues touching upon slavery. The *Dred Scott* experience may have been the last straw since he resigned on September 30, 1857, after only five years of service. Strangely enough, during the Civil War he opposed the constitutionality of the Emancipation Proclamation and the suspension of the writ of *habeas corpus*. He interrupted his private practice to serve as Andrew Johnson's chief defense counsel at the 1868 impeachment proceedings. (Fehrenbacher, Don E., *The Dred Scott Case: Its Significance in American Law and Politics*)

CURTIS, Charles (?-1864)

As the leader of "Curtis' Raiders," one of the most feared of the numerous bandit gangs that plagued the prison population at Andersonville, Charles Curtis was a natural choice for the hangman's noose. Curtis was captured while serving with the 5th Rhode Island Heavy Artillery and sent to Andersonville. Here the gang he formed preyed upon their fellow prisoners, taking everything of value including clothing, blankets, and food. They responded violently to any sign of resistance. Finally, with the cooperation of the Confederate authorities, a prison police force was established within the compound. With assistance from prison guards, the police rounded up the criminal element and turned them over to the commandant, Major Henry Wirz, pending their trial. Curtis and five others, out of about 125 tried, were sentenced to death. Returned to the compound by Wirz along with lumber for the scaffold, Curtis made a break but was shortly dragged from the swamp in the middle of the camp. When asked for any final words, he replied that he just wanted to get it over with. As it turned out he died very slowly. (McElroy, John, *Andersonville: A Story of Rebel Military Prisons*)

CURTIS, Newton Martin (1835-1910)

With no prior military experience, Newton M. Curtis entered the Union army, where he was twice wounded, earning a promotion each time—and the Congressional Medal of Honor. A New York native, he had taught school and studied law before giving up farming to enlist. His assignments included: captain, Company G, 16th New York (May 15, 1861); lieutenant colonel, 142nd New York (October 22, 1862); colonel, 142nd New York (January 21, 1863); commanding 2nd Brigade, 3rd Division, 18th Corps, Army of the James (June 9-19, 1864); commanding 1st Brigade, 2nd Division, 10th Corps, Army of the James (June 21-September 17, October 4-29 and November 14-December 3, 1864); commanding 1st Brigade, 2nd Division, 24th Corps, Army of the James (December 3, 1864-January 6, 1865); commanding 1st Brigade, Ames' Division, Terry's Provisional Corps, Department of North Carolina (January 6-15, 1865); and brigadier general, USV (January 15, 1865). At the head of his company, he fought at 1st Bull Run and was severely wounded at West Point on the Peninsula. Recovering, he returned to the army as second-in-command of a new regiment. He was soon its commander and led it in operations in southeastern Virginia, North Carolina, the aftermath of the Gettysburg Campaign, and against Charleston. Returning to Virginia, he took part in Butler's campaign, which bogged down at Bermuda Hundred. He then fought at Cold Harbor and on the Richmond-Petersburg front. A participant in the abortive first attempt to take Fort Fisher—at the mouth of the Cape Fear River in North Carolina—he was among the first to enter the stockade in the second attempt the next month. He led each of the successive charges against the traverses and received four wounds in doing so. Promoted to brigadier general from the date of the action—he already held it by brevet for New Market Heights—he was mustered out on January 15, 1866. He received his medal in 1891. After the war he was a customs and treasury official and state and national legislator. He was a tireless fighter against capital punishment. In 1906 his history of his first unit appeared as *From Bull Run to Chancellorsville: The Story of the Sixteenth New York Infantry Together with Personal Reminiscences*.

CURTIS, Samuel Ryan (1805-1866)

Despite having commanded the Union army in one of its greatest victories west of the Mississippi, Samuel R. Curtis is little remembered in Civil War annals. Born in New York and raised in Ohio, he served the obligatory one year after his 1831 graduation from West Point. Resigning as a brevet second lieutenant in the 7th Infantry, he took up civil engineering in Ohio. He eventually shifted to the law. Active in the the militia, he was, first, adjutant general of Ohio and then colonel of the 3rd Ohio in the Mexican War. Moving to Iowa he took up the dual occupations of the law and, again, engineering. By the outbreak of the Civil War he was serving in his third term in Congress, having previously been the mayor of Keokuk. His military assignments included: colonel, 2nd Iowa (June 1, 1861); brigadier general, USV (ca. August 4, 1861 to rank from May 17); commanding Army of Southwest Missouri, in the Department of the Missouri (December 25, 1861-March 11, 1862); the Department of the Mississippi (March 11-June 5, 1862), and the Military District of the Missouri, Department of the Mississippi (June 5-August 29, 1862); major general, USV (March 21, 1862), commanding Department of the Missouri (September 24, 1862-March 24, 1863); commanding Department of Kansas (January 16, 1864-January 30, 1865); and commanding Department of the Northwest (February 13-June 27, 1865). At first commissioned a colonel of a volunteer regiment, he resigned from Congress on August 4, 1861, when he accepted his brigadier's commission. Serving in Missouri, he commanded at the victory at Pea Ridge in early March 1862. By the fall of that year he was in command of the department and had been a major general since March. But by the next spring he had to be removed because of difficulties with Governor William Gamble of Missouri. Eventually he was given charge of the Department of Kansas and took part in the repulse of Price's Missouri invasion in 1864. In the last months of the war he commanded in the Northwest. He was in charge of negotiations with several Indian tribes and assigned to inspecting railroads. Mustered out on April 30, 1866, he died within eight months.

Pea Ridge victor Samuel R. Curtis. (AC)

CUSHING, Alonzo Hersford (ca. 1841-1863)

Graduated from West Point at the very beginning of the war, Alonzo Cushing was to die at the "High Tide of the Confederacy." Assigned to Battery A, 4th U.S. Artillery, as a first lieutenant on June 24, 1861, Cushing left his battery in the defenses of Washington to take part in the battle of 1st Bull Run with Battery G, 2nd Artillery. In October 1861, Batteries A and C, 4th Artillery, were consolidated and Lieutenant Cushing joined the staff of his division and later corps commander, General E.V. Summner, as an aide-de-camp. In this position he served through the Peninsular and Maryland campaigns of 1862. When Sumner took command of the Right Grand Division of the Army of the Potomac on November 14, 1862, Cushing became his topographical engineer. As such he served at Fredericksburg for which he was brevetted captain. Upon Sumner's transfer to the West in early 1863, Cushing returned to his battery, which had been separated from Battery C on October 18, 1862, and commanded it at Chancellorsville where he earned a brevet as major. Two months later at Gettysburg, Cushing's guns were placed in the rear of a stone wall just to the right front of the famous copse of trees that was the focus of the Confederate bombardment and Pickett's Charge on the third day. During the final stages of the infantry assault, Cushing, although gravely wounded, stayed in command of his sole remaining gun. With Confederates over the wall, Cushing fell dead only a few paces from where rebel General Armistead fell. For his bravery Cushing was brevetted lieutenant colonel. (Haight, Theron W., *Three Wisconsin Cushings*).

CUSHING, WILLIAM B. (1842-1874)

Brother of the Union hero of the repulse of Pickett's Charge, Alonzo Cushing, William Cushing became a naval hero specializing in unconventional, commando-style attacks. The Wisconsin-born Cushing was attending the Naval Academy at the time of the secession crisis and withdrew from his course of study on March 23, 1861, in order to take a more active role in the war. His appointments included: master's mate, USN (May 1861); lieutenant, USN (July 16, 1862); and lieutenant commander, USN (October 27, 1864). Serving with the Union blockading forces, he became noted for his daring raids on Confederate shipping and shore facilities. On November 23, 1862, he took the tugboat *Ellis* into New River Inlet, North Carolina, to Jacksonville, where he captured two rebel schooners and returned with them to the fleet—having, however, lost the *Ellis* on a shoal. The following January with three cutters and 25 men he captured a Confederate earthwork on Little River. In an effort to seize rebel General Hébert, he led two boats and 20 men to Smithfield, North Carolina, but missed his prize who was away at the time. This February 1864 foray against the Cape Fear River defenses was followed in June by a 15-man, three-day reconnaissance mission to the area between Fort Fisher and Wilmington. Cushing's most famous exploit occurred on the night of October 27, 1864, when, again with 15 men, he took a spar torpedo and blew up the Confederate ram *Albemarle*. Cushing and one other man rejoined the fleet—the remainder having been killed or captured. Under heavy enemy fire, he took a small craft to reconnoiter the channel in close to Fort Fisher. After six hours he returned to his vessel, the USS *Monticello*, and in the ensuing attack on the fort led a contingent of sailors and marines. Remaining in the service after the war, he was promoted to full commander in 1872 and died two years later. (Roske, Ralph J. and Van Dorn, Charles, *Lincoln's Commando: The Biography of Commander W. B. Cushing U.S.N.*)

CUSHMAN, Pauline (1833-1893)

Using her career as an actress as a cover, Pauline Cushman served the United States as a spy. Born in New Orleans, she left her Michigan home to try out for the stage in New York but, failing to make the grade, she obtained an acting job in New Orleans. Marrying there, she lost all of her children in infancy and her husband died early in the Civil War. Resuming her stage career, she was offered $300 to propose a toast to the Confederacy on stage. After consulting the Louisville, Kentucky Union provost marshal, she complied with the request and thus launched her new career as a Union spy. Fired from the loyal theater company, she started to identify Southern sympathizers to the authorities while claiming she was looking for her rebel officer brother. Her "eviction" from Union lines provided her cover story. Her attractiveness gained her numerous invitations to accompany Confederate officers along their lines. After expressing the appropriate concerns over propriety, she accepted and gained valuable military intelligence for the Union army. When detained for questioning she panicked and made an unsuccessful attempt to escape. Upon her recapture her notes were discovered and she was eventually sentenced by General Bragg: "you'll be hanged—that's all." However, the sentence was delayed until she could recover her health. Because of this ill health she was left behind by the rebel forces and was rescued by Union forces at Shelbyville, Tennessee. Her usefulness to the Union at an end, she wrote accounts of her exploits, for which she had been named an honorary major. Eventually forgotten by the public she became a drug addict and committed suicide. In fitting contradiction to the failure of the government to provide her with a pension for her services, veterans of the Grand Army of Republic gave her a full military funeral in the veterans' section of the San Francisco city cemetery. (Sarmiento, F.L. *Life of Pauline Cushman*)

CUSSONS, John (1837-?)

An English-born Alabama journalist in the Southern army, John Cussons' most notable moment in the Civil War came when he suffered a wounded hat in an affair of honor with a fellow officer. Entering the Confederate army as a lieutenant in the 4th Alabama, the newspaper publisher served on the staffs of Generals Lee and Whiting and Colonel E.M. Law. With the latter officer he served at Thoroughfare Gap, 2nd Bull Run, and Antietam. Having been promoted to captain, Cussons was present at the action at Fort Huger—during Longstreet's half-hearted siege of Suffolk—on April 19 when some five guns and 137 men were captured by the enemy in a surprise attack. There was much recrimination among the various units involved, especially between officers of the 55th North Carolina and Law's Brigade. Cussons and fellow staff officer Captain Terrell filed a report that questioned the North Carolinians' bravery and Colonel Connally and Major Belo, of that regiment, challenged them to a duel. Thus Cussons and Belo found themselves facing one another over the sights of Mississippi rifles. In the first discharge Cussons' hat was hit. In the second round of fire, Belo suffered a nicked neck. Before a third round could be fired, word came that Terrell and Connally had resolved the dispute without violence and the matter was closed. Cussons was later captured at Gettysburg and confined at Forts McHenry and Delaware, Johnson's Island, and Point Lookout. After eight months he was exchanged and rejoined his division. He later served with Forrest's cavalry. He went into the hotel and printing businesses following the war. (Cussons, John, *A Glance at Current History*)

CUSTER, George Armstrong (1839-1876)

Although better known for his Indian fighting, George Custer compiled a creditable record as a cavalry leader in the latter part of the Civil War. Graduating at the bottom of his West Point (1861) class, he was commissioned a second lieutenant in the old 2nd Cavalry, later the 5th, on June 24, 1861. His Civil War assignments included: first lieutenant, 5th Cavalry (July 17, 1862); captain and additional aide-de-camp, USA (June 5,1862-March 31, 1863); brigadier general, USV (June 29, 1863); commanding 2nd Brigade, 3rd Division, Cavalry Corps, Army of the Potomac (June 28-July 15 and August 4-November 25, 1863 and December 20, 1863-January 7, 1864); temporarily commanding the division (July 15-August 4 and November 25-December 20, 1863); commanding 1st Brigade, 1st Division, Cavalry Corps, Army of the Potomac (March 25-August 6, 1864) and Army of the Shenandoah (August 6-September 26, 1864); temporarily commanding 2nd Cavalry Division, Army of West Virginia serving with the Army of the Shenandoah (September 26-30, 1864); commanding 3rd Division, Cavalry Corps, Army of the Shenandoah (September 30, 1864-January 5, 1865 and January 30-March 25, 1865) and Army of the Potomac (March 25-May 22, 1865); and major general, USV (April 15, 1865). Serving during the first two war years on the staffs of Generals McClellan and Pleasonton, Custer saw action in the Peninsular, Antietam, and Chancellorsville campaigns. Given his own star, he was assigned command of the Michigan cavalry brigade and, with it, took part in the Gettysburg, Bristoe, and Mine Run campaigns. At Gettysburg he remained with General Gregg east of town to face Jeb Stuart's threat to the Union rear, although he was previously ordered to the south. The combined Union force defeated Stuart. In Grant's Richmond drive in 1864, Custer participated in the fight at Yellow Tavern where Stuart was mortally wounded. Transferred to the Shenandoah Valley with his men, he played a major role in the defeat of Early's army at Winchester and Cedar Creek, commanding a division at the latter. Returning to the Army of the Potomac in early 1865, he fought at Five Forks; and in the Appomattox Campaign. His victories against the rebel cavalry came at a time when that force was a ghost of its former self. Custer was brevetted in the regulars through grades to major general for Gettysburg, Yellow Tavern, Winchester, Five Forks, and the Appomattox Campaign. In addition he was brevetted major general of volunteers for Winchester. Remaining in the army after the war he rose to lieutenant colonel, 7th Cavalry, and was killed in the massacre on the Little Big Horn. (Monaghan, Jan, *Custer: The Life of George Armstrong Custer*)

Future Indian fighter George A. Custer. (NA)

CUSTER, Thomas Ward (1845-1876)

The only soldier to win two Congressional Medals of Honor during the Civil War was the brother of General George A. Custer, Tom Custer. Although only a teenager, Custer enlisted as a private in Company H, 21st Ohio, on September 2, 1861. He saw action at Stones River, Chickamauga, Chattanooga, and in the Atlanta Campaign, before being mustered out of the service at the completion of his three-year term on October 10, 1864. Appointed second lieutenant in the 6th Michigan Cavalry, on November 8, 1864, Custer was promptly assigned to the staff of his brother in the Shenandoah Valley. He moved with Custer's Division to the lines around Petersburg and participated in the final victory at that place and in the campaign to Appomattox. On April 3, 1865, he captured a rebel flag in a fight at Namozine Church. Later that month he was given the Medal of Honor for this exploit. Three days after his first heroic display, he earned a second medal at the battle of Sayler's Creek. In this action, according to General Sheridan, "he leaped his horse over the enemy's works, being one of the first to enter them, and captured two stand of colors, having his horse shot under him and received a severe wound." In this charge, with the 2nd Ohio Cavalry, Custer was wounded in the face but after turning the captured colors over to his brother he wanted to return to the fray. General Custer had to place his younger brother under arrest to get him the needed medical attention. Lieutenant Custer was also honored by being brevetted through grades to major of volunteers and later to lieutenant colonel in the regulars. After the war he was commissioned directly into the regular army and soon joined his brother's regiment, the 7th Cavalry, with which he went to his death at the Little Big Horn. (Mitchell, Joseph B., *The Badge of Gallantry*)

CUTCHEON, Byron M. (1836-1908)

Not joining the Union army as a subaltern until the summer of 1862, New Hampshire-born Byron M. Cutcheon rose to a brevet brigadier generalship and earned the Congressional Medal of Honor before resigning a month before Appomattox. Graduating from college in 1861 he entered the army the next year, where his assignments included: second lieutenant, 20th Michigan (July 15, 1862); captain, 20th Michigan (August 16, 1862); major, 20th Michigan (October 14, 1862); lieutenant colonel, 20th Michigan (November 19, 1863); Colonel, 20th Michigan (January 8, 1864); commanding 2nd Brigade, 1st Division, 9th Corps, Army of the Potomac (October 16, 1864-March 10, 1865); and colonel, 27th Michigan (December 19, 1864). Joining the Army of the Potomac a few days after the battle of Antietam, he fought at Fredericksburg before going to Kentucky with the 9th Corps. There, on May 10, 1863, he led his regiment in a charge on an occupied house at Horseshoe Bend, and in 1891 he was awarded the medal for his gallantry. He took part in the fighting at Knoxville before returning to Virginia where he led his regiment through the Wilderness, Spotsylvania, and Petersburg, earning a brevet brigadier generalship. During the siege winter he directed a brigade. Resigning on March 6, 1865, he was a lawyer, congressman, writer, and educator after the war.

CUTLER, Lysander (1807-1866)

A frequent commander of the North's famed Iron Brigade, Lysander Cutler was eventually forced out of action by the effects of his wounds and the rigors of active field command. Born in Massachusetts, he had been highly successful as a teacher and businessman in Maine until ruined by the 1857 economic decline. Moving to Wisconsin, he was in the grain business at the outbreak of the war. He then enlisted and his assignments included: colonel, 6th Wisconsin (July 16, 1861); commanding 3rd Brigade, 3rd Division, 1st Corps, Army of the Potomac (March 13-April 4, 1862); commanding 3rd Brigade, 3rd Division, Department of the Rappahannock (April 4-June 26, 1862); commanding 4th ("Iron") Brigade, 1st Division, 1st Corps, Army of the Potomac (November 5-26 and December 13, 1862); brigadier general, USV (November 29, 1862); commanding 2nd Brigade, 1st Division, 1st Corps, Army of the Potomac (March 26-July 15, 1863); commanding the division (July 15-August 5 and September 23-November 13, 1863, November 13, 1863-January 14, 1864, and February 10-March 20, 1864); commanding 1st ("Iron") Brigade, 4th Division, 5th Corps, Army of the Potomac (March 25-May 6, 1864); commanding the division (May 6-August 24, 1864); and commanding draft rendezvous, Jackson, Michigan (September 1864-April 1865). Commanding one of the original regiments of what was to become famous as the "Iron Brigade," he was soon its leader. After lengthy service near Washington and in northern Virginia, he fought in the action of Groveton—part of 2nd Bull Run—in which the brigade earned its nickname. He was severely wounded in the leg in the battle. Returning to duty, he briefly commanded the brigade at Fredericksburg and was promoted to brigadier. Commanding another brigade, he fought at Chancellorsville and Gettysburg and shortly thereafter took over the division for the Bristoe and Mine Run campaigns. Transferred to the 5th Corps in the spring 1864 reorganization, he commanded the remnants of the Iron Brigade until he succeeded James S. Wadsworth at the head of the division when the latter was killed on the second day in the Wilderness. Due to heavy casualties the division was discontinued during the Petersburg siege and Cutler, worn out by the fighting at Spotsylvania, Cold Harbor, and Petersburg, was assigned to administrative duties in his home state. He was brevetted major general for the Overland and Petersburg campaigns and resigned on June 30, 1865. He died exactly 13 months later.

CUTSHAW, Wilfred Emory (1828-1907)

It was natural for Wilfred E. Cutshaw to have so much of his Civil War career connected with the Shenandoah Valley, since he had been born at Harpers Ferry. A graduate of the Virginia Military Institute, he was an instructor at another military academy when he joined the Confederacy, where his assignments included: lieutenant, Infantry (October 31, 1861); captain, Winchester (Va.) Artillery (March 1862); major, Artillery (February 27, 1864); commanding artillery battalion, 2nd Corps, Army of Northern Virginia (March 19-August 1864 and February-April 6, 1865); and commanding artillery battalion, Valley District, Department of Northern Virginia (August 1864-February 1865). During the first winter of the war, he commanded an improvised section of artillery, which was captured in an affair at Hanging Rock on January 7, 1862. Soon taking command of a new battery, he led it through the early stages of Jackson's Shenandoah Valley Campaign. Heavily engaged at 1st Winchester on May 25, the command lost all of its officers, including Cutshaw who was wounded and captured. Upon his exchange in April 1863, it was found that he was unfit for field service and he was assigned as acting commandant of cadets at VMI. Desiring a more active role, he obtained an assignment as inspector of artillery with the 2nd Corps in September. As such he served through the Bristoe and Mine Run campaigns. He led his newly assigned battalion at the Wilderness and Spotsylvania where he was wounded. He was detached from the Petersburg lines and sent with Kershaw to reinforce Early in the Valley in August 1864. There he took part in the action at Cedar Creek. His battalion having suffered heavily, especially in horses, it was returned to Richmond the following February and assigned to stationary guns. With the fall of the city, he joined in the retreat to Appomattox and was severely wounded, losing a leg, at Sayler's Creek. He later was a civil engineer in Richmond and a VMI professor.

CUTTS, Allen Sherrod (1827-ca. 1895)

A veteran of the Mexican War, as an enlisted artilleryman, Allen Cutts became one of the earliest artillery battalion commanders in the Army of Northern Virginia. Between the wars, Cutts was a planter in Americus, Georgia. At the outbreak of the Civil War he began organizing an artillery battery for Confederate service. His assignments included: captain, Sumter (Ga.) Flying Artillery (July 6, 1861); major, Artillery (May 22, 1862); commanding an artillery battalion, Reserve Artillery, Army of Northern Virginia (May 22, 1862-June 2, 1863); lieutenant colonel, Artillery (May 26, 1862); and commanding artillery battalion, 3rd Corps, Army of Northern Virginia (June 2, 1863-early 1865). Taking part in the battle of Dranesville, in command of his battery, Cutts was noticed by Jeb Stuart for bravery; he was seen to actually load the guns himself. Promoted the next spring, he was given command of a battalion that was known as the Sumter Battalion. He led his men in the Peninsular Campaign and at Antietam and Chancellorsville. In 1864 he fought from the Wilderness to Petersburg, where he had his greatest moment in the repulse of the Union attack on June 20. During much of the last campaign he was in charge of his own and Richardson's Battalions. He was often referred to as a full colonel but there is no official record of his promotion. After the war, Cutts was a state legislator, mayor, and law officer. (Wise, Jennings Cropper, *The Long Arm of Lee*)

D

DABNEY, Robert Lewis (1820-1898)

A Presbyterian minister, professor, and editor, Robert L. Dabney served on Stonewall Jackson's staff for only three months but nonetheless wrote a biography, *Life and Campaigns of Lieut.-Gen. Thomas J. Jackson*. The native Virginian became chaplain of the 18th Virginia upon the outbreak of the Civil War and in April 1862 reluctantly accepted the post of chief of staff for Jackson's Valley District. He was commissioned as a major and assistant adjutant general. Henry Kyd Douglas declares that while Dabney was a good staff officer in camp he was not up to the job in the field. After serving in the Shenandoah Valley Campaign and the Seven Days, he resigned in July 1862. Known for carrying an umbrella instead of a sword, he was once ridiculed by Jackson's "foot cavalry" when he was seen on the march with it opened against the weather. Resuming his religious pursuits, he never reconciled himself to the South's fall and proposed the emigration of the white populace. His Jackson biography had to be corrected on a number of points by a tactful General Lee. (Johnson, Thomas Cary, *Life and Letters of Robert Lewis Dabney*)

DAGUERRE, Louis Jacques Mandé (1787-1851)

Although he had been dead for a decade before the beginning of the Civil War France's Louis J.M. Daguerre played a leading role in the advancements in his art that made that conflict the first widely photographed war in history. Originally an opera scene painter, he tried to utilize sunlight to make permanent images on metal. By 1839 he had met with success and his daguerreotypes were a popular early form of photography that, along with further advances, made the work of many Civil War artists possible.

DAHLGREN, John Adolphus Bernard (1809-1870)

A Pennsylvania ordnance expert, John A.B. Dahlgren had been in the Navy since 1826. During the prewar years he had been nearly blinded when assigned to observe the solar eclipse of 1836. Serving as an ordnance officer he invented the 11-inch

John A.B. Dahlgren stands before his invention. (NA)

Dahlgren gun and developed a percussion lock. His Civil War assignments included: commander, USN (since 1855); captain, USN (July 16, 1862); chief, Bureau of Ordnance (July 18, 1862-63); rear admiral, USN (February 7, 1863); and commanding South Atlantic Blockading Squadaron (July 6, 1863-65). Following his ordnance duty in Washington he was given command for the operations against Charleston in which he was able to witness the effects of his invention. When Sherman arrived at Savannah from his March to the Sea, it was Dahlgren who opened communications between the general and Washington. After the war he continued in the service until his death at the Washington Navy Yard. His published works, all pre-war, included: *32 Pounder Practice for Ranges*, *The System of Boat Armaments in the United States Navy*, *Naval Percussion Locks and Primers*, and *Shells and Shell Guns*. Dahlgren's son Ulric died in a controversial cavalry raid on Richmond in 1864.

DAHLGREN, Ulric (1842-1864)

The death of the son of Union Admiral John A. Dahlgren, Ulric Dahlgren, in a raid on Richmond led to one of the more controversial incidents of the Civil War. The Pennsylvania native had become a lawyer in Philadelphia by the time he entered the Union army in 1862. His assignments included: captain and additional aide-de-camp (May 29, 1862); and colonel of cavalry, USV (July 20, 1863). He served successively on the staffs of Franz Sigel, Joseph Hooker, and George G. Meade and saw action at 2nd Bull Run, Chancellorsville, and other fields. During the aftermath of the battle of Gettysburg, he was wounded in the foot in a cavalry fight at Boonesboro, Maryland. Refusing to leave the field, he finally passed out from the loss of blood. This delay in medical treatment may have contributed to his loss of the leg below the knee. Equipped with a wooden leg, he was back in the field by early 1864. When Judson Kilpatrick approached the Washington authorities with a plan for a raid on the Confederate capital, Dahlgren was detailed to command a 500-man detachment, which would act independently in the later stages of the approach on the city. The scheme proved to be a dismal failure and Dahlgren himself was killed on March 2. On his body the Confederates claimed to have found papers which indicated that part of the plan—whether Dahlgren's, Kilpatrick's, or Washington's is not known—was to murder Jefferson Davis and other top officials and destroy the city. There were charges of forgery, hinging on a questionable signature. Protesting correspondence went back and forth between the two governments and their armies for some time. The matter is still debated today. (Jones, Virgil Carrington, *Eight Hours Before Richmond* and Dahlgren, J.A. *Memoir of Ulric Dahlgren*)

Controversial Ulric Dahlgren. (*Leslie's*)

DALY, Maria Lydig (1824-1894)

The wife of a New York City judge and a member of the established high society, Maria Lydig Daly was the closest the North came to a Mary Boykin Chesnut of its own. As she was a strongly pro-Union Democrat, her *Diary of a Union Lady, 1861-1865*, in a somewhat gossipy manner reminiscent of Chesnut's, levels sharp criticism on Lincoln and his Union generals, from McClellan to Grant. Lincoln was referred to as "Uncle Ape." The early Union defeats were a hard blow to the Dalys and Mrs. Daly dispensed her wrath freely on those responsible. It is strange that her diary is almost forgotten and Chesnut's is so well remembered.

DANA, Charles Anderson (1819-1897)

New Hampshire-born journalist Charles A. Dana gave up his calling fot a time in order to serve the Union cause. Buy the outbreak of the Civil War he was the managing editor of Horace Greeley's *New York Tribune*. In 1862 he resigned this post and joined the War Department as something of a troubleshooter. He was frequently in the field especially in the West, reporting on officers critical of Rosecrans and pro-Grant, and operations. On June 1, 1863, he was named major and assistant adjutant general, USV, but declined. Recognizing his abilities, Lincoln advanced him to assistant secretary of war on January 28, 1864, and Dana held that post until August 1, 1865. Returning to journalism after the war, he became publisher and editor of the *New York Sun*, which he turned into an important molder of public opinion. (Wilson, James Harrison, *The Life of Charles A. Dana*)

DANA, Napoleon Jackson Tecumseh (1822-1905)

Napoleon Jackson Tecumseh Dana, whose grandfather fought in the Revolution and his father in the War of 1812, earned a distinguished record in two wars. Born in Maine, he was a West Pointer (1842) and had been posted to the infantry. In Mexico he earned a brevet for Cerro Gordo where he was severely wounded and left for dead. He was recovered by a burial party a day and one half later. Later transferred to the Quartermaster's Department, he resigned in 1855 as a captain to become a banker. His Civil War assignments included: brigadier general, Minnesota Militia (prewar); colonel, 1st Minnesota (October 2, 1861); commanding 2nd Brigade, Stone's-Sedgwick's Division, Army of the Potomac (October 20, 1861-March 13, 1862); brigadier general, USV (February 3, 1862); commanding 3rd Brigade, 2nd Division, 2nd Corps, Army of the Potomac (March 13-August 5 and September 7-17, 1862); major general, USV (November 29, 1862); commanding 2nd Division, 13th Corps, Department of the Gulf (September 28, 1863-January 3, 1864); also commanding the corps (October 25, 1863-January 9, 1864); commanding 1st Division, 13th Corps, Department of the Gulf (March 11-April 3, 1864); commanding District of Vicksburg, Department of the Tennessee (August 14-November 28, 1864); also commanding 16th Corps, Army of the Tennessee (October 15-November 7, 1864); commanding District of Vicksburg, Department of Mississippi (November 28, 1864-May 14, 1865); and also commanding Department of Mississippi (December 8, 1864-May 14, 1865). With his regiment he was in a supporting position during the disaster at Ball's Bluff. Given a brigade, he was soon promoted to brigadier general and as such fought at Seven Pines and in the Seven Days. At Antietam he was severely wounded and unable to return to duty until July 1863 at which time he was assigned to Philadelphia. He then finished the war in relatively quiet sectors in Texas, Louisiana, and Mississippi. Resigning on May 27, 1865, he was active in trade with the Russians in Alaska, railroads, and was a pension official. By a special 1894 act of Congress, he was recommissioned as a captain and assistant quartermaster and placed on the retired list.

DANIEL, John Moncure (1825-1865)

As editor of the *Richmond Examiner*, John M. Daniel became increasingly critical of the Davis administration. Lacking an interest in the study of law, he gave it up to become a librarian and by 1847 was the editor of this new newspaper. In the 1850s he held a diplomatic post in Italy but was not very capable at the art of diplomacy. Returning home at the outbreak of the war, he served two stints in the army in staff positions and was slightly wounded in the summer of 1862. Returning to his paper, he developed intense dislikes for many of the figures in the Confederacy and even fought a duel with the Confederate treasurer in 1864 in which he was again wounded. Struck down by illness, he died a few days before his plant was destroyed in the fire upon the capture of Richmond. (Bagby, G.W., *John M. Daniel's Latch-key*)

DANIEL, Junius (1828-1864)

A West Pointer (1851), Junius Daniel spent most of his Confederate career in brigade command. The North Carolinian had resigned an infantry commission in 1858 to run a Louisiana plantation but returned to his native state upon the outbreak of the war. His assignments included: colonel, 14th North Carolina (June 3, 1861); colonel, 45th North Carolina (ca. April 14, 1862); commanding brigade, Holmes' Division (from the Department of North Carolina), Army of Northern Virginia (June-July 1862); commanding brigade, Department of North Carolina (July-August 1862); commanding brigade (in Elzey's Command from December 12 and in French's-D.H. Hill's Command from late December), Department of Virginia and North Carolina (August 1862-April 1, 1863); brigadier general, CSA (September 1, 1862); commanding brigade, Department of North Carolina (April 1-May 1863); and commanding brigade, Rodes' Division, 2nd Corps, Army of Northern Virginia (June 1863-May 12, 1864). Commanding his original regiment at Yorktown, he transferred to a new regiment upon the reorganization. He commanded a brigade in the Seven Days, seeing action at Malvern Hill. After service near Drewry's Bluff and in North Carolina, he was sent with his men to Lee's army, with which they suffered heavily on the first day at Gettysburg. He served through the autumn campaigns and in the Wilderness. At Spotsylvania on May 12, 1864, he was mortally wounded while trying to recapture the trenches at the Bloody Angle. He died the next day. (Freeman, Douglas, S., *Lee's Lieutenants*)

DANIEL, Peter V. (1784-1860)

In the highly controversial *Dred Scott* case, Supreme Court Justice Peter V. Daniel of Virginia took the most extreme position of the nine members of the court. His opinion clearly indicates that he was a bigot, even in his language, which his friends censured. Martin Van Buren appointed Daniel to the high court on February 26, 1841, despite a lack of formal legal training. Daniel ruled that Dred Scott's case should be dismissed since a black could never be a citizen, even if free, and therefore had no right to sue in either state or national courts. With the breakup of the Union only months away, he died on May 31, 1860. (Fehrenbacher, Don E., *The Dred Scott Case: Its Significance in American Law and Politics*)

DARGAN, Edmund Strother (1805-1879)

Being primarily self-educated, Edmund S. Dargan was a successful lawyer and former chief justice of the Alabama supreme court by the time of the secession crisis, during which he urged immediate disunion without the nicety of referring the ordinance to the people. Representing Alabama's 9th District, including Mobile, Dargan utilized his seat on the Committee on the Judiciary to busy himself with the judicial organization of the new nation. He also chaired the investigation of the Erlanger Loan. In order to win the war he was willing to bend and even violate the constitution until the emergency was past. In what can be cited as an example of the legislative behavior of the times, Dargan drew a knife on fellow representative Henry S. Foote. With his term in the First Congress coming to an end, Dargan declined to stand for reelection. He resumed his law practice.

DAVENPORT, Jean

See: *Lander, Jean Margaret Davenport*

DAVIDSON, Henry Brevard (1831-1899)

Transferring from the staff to the line, Tennessee West Pointer (1853) Henry B. Davidson became a brigadier general of Confederate cavalry. He had served in the Mexican War as a private and sergeant in Company K, 1st Tennessee, and his performance earned him his appointment to the academy. Upon his graduation he served on the frontier with the dragoons. On July 30, 1861, he was dropped from the rolls as captain, 1st Dragoons, when he did not report after his leave expired. In the meantime he had joined the Confederacy where his assignments included: major and assistant adjutant general (early 1861); colonel and assistant adjutant general (late 1862); commanding Post of Staunton, Virginia (late 1862); brigadier general, CSA (August 18, 1863); commanding brigade, Pegram's Division, Forrest's Cavalry Corps, Army of Tennessee (September-October 1863); commanding brigade, Wharton's Division, Wheelers' Cavalry Corps, Army of Tennessee (October 1863-early 1864); commanding Jackson's (old) Brigade, Lomax's Cavalry Division, Valley District, Army of Northern Virginia (fall 1864-January 1865); and commanding Cavalry Brigade, Valley District, Army of Northern Virginia (January-March 1865). His early service came in the West as a staff officer with John B. Floyd, Simon B. Buckner, Albert Sidney Johnston, and William W. Mackall. Captured at Island #10, he was not exchanged until August 27, 1862. Promoted to colonel, he was assigned to post duty for a time and then was advanced to brigadier general. Commanding a mounted brigade, he fought at Chickamauga and then was transferred back to Virginia. Commanding a cavalry brigade in the Shenandoah Valley, he fought at Cedar Creek and at Waynesboro. Then he apparently joined Joseph E. Johnston in North Carolina and was included in Johnston's surrender. A civil engineer in California after the war, he was also engaged in railroading and held minor state office.

DAVIDSON, John Wynn (1824-1881)

Union General John W. Davidson survived Indian fighting and the Civil War, only to be killed by the fall of his horse. A native Virginian and West Pointer (1845), he was posted to the dragoons and was wounded in a fight with a band of Apaches at Cienequilla, New Mexico, on March 30, 1854. At the outbreak of the Civil War he was serving in California and remained with the Union when his state seceded. His Civil War-era assignments included: captain, 1st Dragoons (since January 20, 1855); captain, 1st Cavalry (change of designation August 3, 1861); major, 2nd Cavalry (November 14, 1861); commanding 2nd Brigade, Smith's Division, Army of the Potomac (October 26, 1861-March 13, 1862); brigadier general, USV (February 3, 1862); commanding 3rd Brigade, 2nd Division, 4th Corps, Army of the Potomac (March 13-May 18, 1862); commanding 3rd Brigade, 2nd Division, 6th Corps, Army of the Potomac (May 18-July 1862); commanding District of St. Louis, Military District of the Missouri, Department of the Mississippi (August 6-September 19, 1862); commanding District of St. Louis, Department of the Missouri (September 19-November 13, 1862); commanding Army of Southeast Missouri, Department of the Missouri (October 1862-February 23, 1863); also commanding District of Southeast Missouri, Department of the Missouri (November 13-February 23, 1863); again commanding District of St. Louis, Department of the Missouri (February 23-June 6, 1863); commanding 1st Cavalry Division, District of Southeast Missouri. Department of the Missouri (June 6-August 10, 1863); commanding 1st (Cavalry) Division, Arkansas Expedition, Army of the Tennessee (August 10-November 3, 1863 and December 1863-January 6, 1864); and commanding Post of Natchez, District of Vicksburg, Department of Mississippi (February 26-May 1865). Heading east, he took command of a brigade near Washington—he was soon given a general's star and led it in the 4th and then the 6th Corps on the Peninsula. During the Seven Days he earned regular army brevets for Gaines' Mill and Golding's Farm. Transferred to Missouri that summer, he commanded at St. Louis and southeastern Missouri. He participated in the operations that resulted in the capture of Little Rock and received a brevet as brigadier in the regular army. He finished the war in charge at Natchez and was brevetted major general in both services for his war record. Mustered out of the volunteers on January 15, 1866, he remained on active duty, serving for a time as second-in-command of the 10th Cavalry, a black unit. Eventually he took command of the 2nd Cavalry and died after his horse fell upon him at Fort Custer.

DAVIDSON, Thomas J. (?-1862)

During the defense of Fort Donelson Confederate brigade commander Thomas J. Davidson had to be relieved due to illness but this did not save him from capture, imprisonment, and death as a prisoner. In 1861 he became a colonel of a regiment that was variously designated as the 2nd and 3rd Mississippi. While serving in Kentucky, on November 19, 1861 the designation was officially changed to the 23rd. Sent to the aid of the beleaguered fort, he commanded a brigade, Johnson's Division, Fort Donelson, Department No. 2 (February 9-15, 1862). On the morning of the planned breakout attempt Davidson was so ill that he had neglected to give the order for his troops to move to the jumpoff point. General Bushrod Johnson saw the problem and relieved him of duty. But the timing of the attack was ruined and the move failed. With the fall of the fort, Davidson became a prisoner and was sent to Fort Warren in Boston Harbor. The Union authorities were anxious to exchange him quickly, perhaps because they knew his situation was serious and he might die before they could get one of their colonels back for him. On April 29, 1862, he died.

DAVIES, Henry Eugene (1836-1894)

By the end of the war in Virginia, New Yorker Henry E. Davies was a prominent cavalry leader in that theater. He had been a practicing attorney in New York City in 1861 when he enlisted in the Union infantry. His assignments included: captain, 5th New York (May 9, 1861); major, 2nd New York Cavalry (August 1, 1861); lieutenant colonel, 2nd New York Cavalry

(December 6, 1862); colonel, 2nd New York Cavalry (June 16, 1863); commanding 1st Brigade, 3rd Division, Cavalry Corps, Army of the Potomac (July 15-25, 1863, August 22, 1863-February 12, 1864, and April 12-30, 1864); brigadier general, USV (September 16, 1863); commanding 1st Brigade, 2nd Division, Cavalry Corps, Army of the Potomac (April 17-July 30, September 13-15, and September 25-December 22, 1864, January 12-19, and March 27-May 22, 1865); commanding the division (September 15-25, 1864, December 22, 1864-January 19, 1865, and March 14-27, 1865); and major general USV (May 4, 1865). With his first company he fought at Big Bethel before transferring to the mounted force that summer. His regiment had originally been slated to become the seventh regiment of cavalry in the regular army but this would have exceeded Congressional authorization. After service near Washington and in northern Virginia he fought at 2nd Bull Run and commanded the regiment at Fredericksburg and on Stoneman's raid during the Chancellorsville Campaign. In the Gettysburg Campaign the regiment was badly cut up at Aldie but missed the main battles being at Westminister, Maryland, with its brigade. That summer Davies had his first experience in brigade command and received a brigadier's star. He served in the Bristoe and Mine Run operations that fall and the next spring he served in the Overland Campaign, taking part in most of the important cavalry raids of that and the later Petersburg fighting. Wounded at Hatcher's Run in February 1865, he was back in the saddle for the Appomattox surrender. Having already been brevetted major general for Vaughn Road, he was given the full rank almost a month after Lee's surrender. Following garrison duty in Alabama he resigned on January 1, 1866, and returned to private practice. He was a city administrator and assistant district attorney and wrote a biography, *General Sheridan*.

DAVIES, Thomas Alfred (1809-1899)

A West Pointer (1829) and uncle of Henry E. Davis, Thomas A. Davies served in a variety of positions in the Civil War before becoming a brevet major general of volunteers. Posted to the infantry, he had served on the frontier for two years before resigning as a brevet second lieutenant in 1831 to become a civil engineer in New York. At the outbreak of the Civil War he gave up his mercantile interests to enter the Union army. His assignments included: colonel, 16th New York (May 15, 1861); commanding 2nd Brigade, 5th Division, Army of Northeastern Virginia (June-August 1861); brigadier general, USV (March 7, 1862); commanding 2nd Division, Army of the Tennessee (April 18-June 2, 1862); commanding 1st Division, Army of the Tennessee (June 2-10, 1862); commanding 2nd Division, District of Corinth, Army of the Tennessee (August 5-September 24, 1862); commanding 3rd Division, Army of the Tennessee (September 24-October 1862); commanding 4th Division, Army of the Tennessee (October 5-30, 1862); commanding District of Columbus (Ken.), 13th Corps, Department of the Tennessee (November 1-December 18, 1862); commanding District of Columbus (Ken.), 16th Corps, Department of the Tennessee (December 18, 1862-January 11, 1863); commanding District of Rolla, Department of the Missouri (March 13, March 25, 1864); commanding District of North Kansas, Department of Kansas (June 25, 1864-April 4, 1865); and commanding District of Wisconsin, Department of the Northwest (spring-summer 1865). In his only action in the Eastern theater he commanded a brigade in reserve near Centreville and covered the retreat of the troops from 1st Bull Run while his division commander, Dixon S. Miles, was drunk. Made a brigadier he was sent to the West where he commanded a division in the advance on Corinth, Mississippi, in the spring of 1862 and fought in the battle there the following October. For the remainder of the war he was in district command in Kentucky, Missouri, Kansas, and Wisconsin. He engaged in a varied postwar writing career following his mustering out on August 24, 1865.

DAVIS, Benjamin Franklin "Grimes" (ca. 1832-1863)

During a dramatic escape from beleaguered Harpers Ferry, Benjamin F. "Grimes" Davis was able to capitalize on his Southern accent to capture James Longstreet's reserve ammunition train. The Alabama-born West Pointer (1854) and wounded veteran of Indian fighting in the infantry and dragoons along the Gila River in New Mexico, had remained loyal to the Union. His Civil War-period assignments included: first lieutenant, 1st Dragoons (January 9, 1860); captain, 1st Dragoons (July 30, 1861); captain, 1st Cavalry (change of designation on August 3, 1861); lieutenant colonel, 1st California Cavalry (August 19, 1861, resigned November 1, 1861); colonel, 8th New York Cavalry (June 25, 1862); commanding 5th Brigade, Cavalry Division, Army of the Potomac (September-November 1862); commanding 1st Brigade, 1st Division, Cavalry Corps, Army of the Potomac (February 16-May 27 and June 6-9, 1863); and commanding the division (May 27-June 6, 1863). Briefly serving in the California volunteers, he resigned that commission when his regular army regiment was ordered to the East. He fought in the siege of Yorktown and at Williamsburg before being assigned to command a New York regiment in the early summer of 1862. Serving in the vicinity of Harpers Ferry, the regiment was entrapped at that place during the Antietam Campaign. Davis urged upon his commander that all the cavalry at the doomed post be allowed to cut their way out. It was reluctantly agreed to and the attempt was made on the night of September 14, 1862. After a series of minor collisions with Confederate pickets, the 8th managed to stumble upon the enemy wagons and Davis was able, the darkness concealing the color of his uniform, to order the train into his column. Many of the teamsters did not know they were prisoners until daylight. He was brevetted for his action. Joining the Army of the Potomac, Davis commanded a brigade at Antietam and his regiment at Fredericksburg. During the Chancellorsville Campaign he took part in Stoneman's Raid. The next month he was killed, commanding a brigade, in the great cavalry battle at Brandy Station. (Murfin, James V., *The Gleam of Bayonets*)

DAVIS, Charles Henry (1807-1877)

During the course of a fighting Civil War naval career, Charles H. Davis was involved in some major victories, especially on the Mississippi. A native of Massachusetts, he had entered the navy in 1824 and in 30 years had risen to the rank of commander. His Civil War assignments included: commander, USN (since 1854); captain, USN (November 1861); fleet captain, South Atlantic Blockading Squadron (November 1861); executive officer, Bureau of Detail (early 1862); chief, Bureau of Detail (early 1862); commanding Upper Mississippi Gunboat Flotilla (May-October 1, 1862); chief, Bureau of Navigation (late 1862-64); rear admiral, USN (February 1863); and superintendent, U.S. Naval Observatory (1864-66). In the first fall of the war he took part in the battle of Port Royal Sound, which gained the Union a coaling and repair station on the South Carolina coast. The next spring he took command on the upper Mississippi River and scored major victories at Plum Run Bend and Memphis, capturing the latter city as a Union base for further operations. He then took part in the early operations against Vicksburg and along the Yazoo River in Mississippi. Replaced by David D. Porter, he became the head of the Bureau of Navigation in Washington until named to head the Naval Observatory. By this time he had risen to the rank of rear admiral. In 1863 he had been one of the founders of the National Academy of Sciences. He continued in the Navy until his death. His works include: *The Coast Survey of the United States and Narrative of the North Pole Expedition of the USS Polaris*. (Davis, Charles Henry, *Life of Charles Henry Davis, Rear Admiral, 1807-1877*)

DAVIS, David (1815-1886)

A longtime friend of Abraham Lincoln, David Davis was named to the Supreme Court vacancy created when John A. Campbell resigned to join the Confederacy. A Maryland-born lawyer, he had set up his practice in Illinois and was elected to the state legislature and then as a circuit judge. The former Whig joined the Republican Party in the 1850s, became associated with Lincoln, and in 1860 was his campaign manager. Lincoln appointed him to the bench December 1, 1862, and Davis was confirmed by a voice vote in the Senate one week later. He proved to be an unwavering Unionist in the court, especially in the *Prize Cases*, but became alienated from the Republicans in the postwar years. Dabbling in presidential politics, he resigned in 1877 to enter the Senate. Becoming its president pro tempore, he would have succeeded to the presidency if Chester A. Arthur had died, there being no vice president at the time. At the end of his term in 1883 he retired from political life. (Pfeffer, Leo, *This Honorable Court*)

DAVIS, Edmund Jackson (1827-1883)

Defeated in a bid for a seat in the Texas secession convention—presumably as a Unionist—Edmund J. Davis just escaped being hanged by Confederates in Mexico, where he organized a loyal Texas regiment. Born in Florida, he was raised in Texas where he became a lawyer and judge. Dissatisfied with secession, he went off to Mexico where he was involved in political intrigues relating to the war and raised a regiment of cavalry from men of similar views. His military assignments included: colonel, 1st Texas Cavalry (October 26, 1862); commanding 4th Brigade, Cavalry Division, Department of the Gulf (April 18-August 6, 1864); commanding 1st Separate Cavalry Brigade, Department of the Gulf (October-December 1864); brigadier general, USV (November 10, 1864); commanding Cavalry Brigade, District of Baton Rouge and Port Hudson. Department of the Gulf (February 15-27, 1865); commanding District of Morganza (Tex.), Military Division of West Mississippi (February 27-March 3, 1865); and commanding District of Baton Rouge and Port Hudson, Department of the Gulf (March 11-18, 1865). He served throughout his term in Louisiana and Texas, including the operations against Morganza. He was mustered out on August 24, 1865, and proposed harsh treatment for ex-Confederates. He favored their disenfranchisement, full black voting rights, and the dismantling of Texas into three smaller states. He attended the state conventions in 1866 and 1869, presiding over the latter, and served a term as a Reconstruction governor. Deposed by white supremacists, he resumed private practice. Although apparently untainted himself, his administration was an example of the corruption in many carpetbagger governments. He tried to remain in office through force but was refused aid by President Grant.

DAVIS, Garrett (1801-1872)

Opposed to secession, Kentucky Unionist Garrett Davis remained loyal and served his country in the Senate during most of the Civil War. Admitted to the bar in his native state in 1823, he entered the state legislature a decade later. Beginning in 1839, he served four consecutive terms in the House of Representatives as a Whig before refusing to seek reelection in order to resume his practice and take up farming. He declined the 1856 vice-presidential nomination of the American Party and in 1860 as an opponent of secession supported the Constitutional Union ticket of John Bell. When John C. Breckinridge was expelled from the Senate for having joined the Confederate army Davis was named as a Whig to succeed him. As a Democrat, he was reelected in 1867 and served from December 10, 1861, until his death on September 22, 1872.

DAVIS, George (1820-1896)

Although he had long been an opponent of secession, George Davis wound up serving in both the legislative and executive branches of the Confederate government. Active in Whig politics, lawyer Davis did not, however, run for public office. He did attend the Washington Peace Conference whose recommendations he criticized as dishonorable for the South. With the secession of his native North Carolina, he was named to an at-large seat in the Provisional Confederate Congress. After 25 ballots in September 1861 he was appointed to the Senate of the First Regular Congress, but it turned out to be only a two-year term. In the First Congress he chaired the Committee on Claims and also served on those on Buildings,

Finance, and Naval Affairs. Becoming a strong nationalist, even favoring appellate jurisdiction over state courts for the proposed supreme court, Davis became unpopular with much of the North Carolina delegation. The same feeling permeated the state legislature and he failed to be reelected in the summer of 1863. While serving as a lame duck, he was tapped by Jefferson Davis to serve as attorney general. He was confirmed by the Senate on January 2, 1864, and, with only six weeks to go in his term, he resigned his seat to take up his new duties. Here his nationalist tendencies became even more pronounced as he sided with the central government opinions against the individual states. Fleeing Richmond at the war's close and heading for Europe, Davis was captured at Key West and imprisoned until New Year's Day 1866. He resumed his law practice and was successful enough at it to decline an 1878 offer of the chief justice's seat on the state supreme court, for financial considerations.

DAVIS, George (1839-1926)

Commanding a small force that was presumed lost by his superiors, George Davis managed to bring his men off the field at Monocacy and in the effort earn himself a Congressional Medal of Honor. A native Vermonter, he had served in the 1st Vermont as an enlisted man and fought in the battle of Big Bethel before being mustered out in the summer of 1861. After getting married he reenlisted in the 10th Vermont and was soon made second lieutenant of Company D. His regiment served in the Washington vicinity before joining the Army of the Potomac and fighting through Grant's Overland Campaign. Then, with Early threatening Washington the 6th Corps was detached from the siege lines at Petersburg and sent to the capital's aid. The 10th moved into western Maryland and at Monocacy Davis commanded an advance force that was left behind when the Union forces withdrew. But he managed to extradite most of the command and be the last man to cross the river on the ties of the railroad bridge while under heavy enemy fire. (In 1892 he received the Medal of Honor for his role in this important Union delaying action.) He then fought in the Shenandoah Valley Campaign but was severely injured on the Petersburg front when a log cabin collapsed on him. He was soon mustered out of service.

DAVIS, Hasbrouck (1827-1870)

Assisting Benjamin F. "Grimes" Davis, Hasbrouck Davis took part in one of the outstanding adventures of the Civil War. The Massachusetts-born Illinois lawyer's military assignments included: lieutenant colonel, 12th Illinois Cavalry (November 18, 1861); colonel, 12th Illinois Cavalry (January 5, 1864); and commanding 2nd Brigade, Cavalry Division, District of West Tennessee, Department of the Tennessee (February-April 1865). Serving in western Virginia in 1862, he was trapped in Harpers Ferry with his regiment when Stonewall Jackson besieged the town. The two Davises determined to make a breakout attempt with the mounted forces of the garrison in order to avoid capitulation. With the reluctant permission of the post commander, Colonel Dixon S. Miles, the pair led the cavalry out on the night of September 14, 1862. Not only were they successful in guiding their men out but they also captured James Longstreet's 97-wagon reserve ammunition train and brought it into the Union lines. Davis later led his regiment in western Maryland and on Stoneman's Raid during the Chancellorsville Campaign. Subsequently transferred to the Gulf, he took part in a raid through Arkansas and ended up commanding a brigade in the District of West Tennessee. Brevetted brigadier general for the war, he resigned on August 1, 1865. Five years later he disappeared at sea.

DAVIS, Henry Winter (1817-1865)

Bucking the wishes of the Maryland legislature, Congressman Henry W. Davis voted with the Republicans upon the organization of Congress in January 1860. A lawyer and former Whig, he had entered the national legislature in 1855 as a leader of the American or Know-Nothing Party. Until his 1860 vote he had tried to remain neutral on the slavery issue but that vote cost him his reelection. Over the next two years he was a harsh critic of the Lincoln administration for its arbitrary arrests. A powerful speaker, he was able to woo audiences and in 1862 he won back his old seat and became the chairman of the Committee on Foreign Relations. He also became one of the principal leaders of the Radical Republicans and continued his harsh attacks on the president of his own party. In the fight over a reconstruction plan he, believing that all the power was vested in the legislative branch, urged a much harsher plan than Lincoln's. He cosponsored the Wade-Davis Bill, which Lincoln pocket vetoed. In the 1864 elections he was defeated, but he continued to attack Lincoln and his successor Andrew Johnson until his death in December 1865. (Steiner, Bernard C., *The Life of Henry Winter Davis*)

DAVIS, James Lucius (1813-1871)

A graduate of West Point (1833) and a veteran of three years in the 4th Artillery, Virginian J. Lucius Davis was well qualified to write a cavalry manual for the Confederate army. With the outbreak of war, he returned to the military where his assignments include: colonel, 46th Virginia (June 24, 1861); lieutenant colonel, 8th Virginia Cavalry Battalion (early 1862); colonel, 10th Virginia Cavalry (officially September 24, 1862, although he appears to have acted as such since the spring); and commanding Chambliss' Brigade, W.H.F. Lee's Division, Cavalry Corps, Army of Northern Virginia (August 16-October 1864). After initial service with the infantry in western Virginia, he transferred to the cavalry, seeing action at Williamsburg, the Seven Days, Fredericksburg, and Gettysburg. During the retreat from the latter he was wounded and captured at Hagerstown, on July 6, 1863. Declared exchanged on March 10, 1864, he commanded the regiment during the siege of Petersburg. He commanded Chambliss' Brigade for about two months after that officer was killed. He appears to have been absent from October 1864 until his resignation on February 2, 1865. He retired to Buckingham County, Virginia, after the war.

DAVIS, Jefferson (1808-1889)

The only president of the Confederacy, Jefferson Davis proved to be something less than the revolutionary leader necessary to lead a fledgling nation to independence; he himself would have preferred to serve as a military leader. Born in Kentucky, he was graduated from West Point in 1828 and was posted to the Pacific Northwest. There he served with the infantry until 1833 when he transferred to the dragoons. Two years later he resigned as a first lieutenant when he eloped with the daughter of his commander, Zachary Taylor. Thereafter a Mississippi planter, he lost his wife shortly after the wedding and then married Varina Howell. Elected as a Democrat to Congress he served in the House of Representatives from 1845 to 1847. During the Mexican War he compiled an enviable record as colonel of the 1st Mississippi Rifles. Wounded at Buena Vista, he turned down a commission as a brigadier general. He then won a seat in the U.S. Senate, which he held until named Franklin Pierce's war secretary in 1853. He held this post for the full tenure of the Pierce presidency and then won reelection to the Senate. A staunch supporter of states' rights, he backed his state's secession and made a powerful speech on the floor of the Senate when he and four other senators withdrew from that body on January 21, 1861. Almost immediately named commander of the state military forces with the rank of major general—in recognition of his Mexican War service—he became a compromise candidate for the provisional presidency of the Confederacy and was so elected on February 9, 1861. Inaugurated nine days later in Montgomery, Alabama, he was elected as regular president for a six-year term on November 6, 1861, and was reinaugurated on Washington's Birthday in Richmond. His interest in the military defense of his country soon became apparent; his early war secretaries served as little more than clerks as he himself supervised the affairs of the department. He made frequent forays into the field, arriving at 1st Bull Run just as the fight was ending, and was later under fire at Seven Pines where he placed Robert E. Lee in command of what became the Army of Northern Virginia. Later he toured the western theater where he supported his old friend Braxton Bragg against the criticisms of his subordinates. His handling of the high command was extremely controversial. There were long-standing feuds with Beauregard and Joseph E. Johnston. His defense of certain non-performing generals, such as Bragg and Pemberton, irritated many in the South. On the political front his autocratic ways fostered a large and well-organized anti-Davis faction in the Confederate Congress, especially in the Senate. His attempts to manage the war effectively by placing more power in the hands of the central government were often thwarted by the states' rights philosophy that had led to its very founding. It is quite apparent that he is more popular in the South today than he was during his tenure. Upon the fall of Richmond he fled south with the remnants of his government and was finally captured near Irwinville, Georgia, on May 10, 1865. He was sent off to prison at Fort Monroe, faced with charges of treason. Never brought to trial, he was finally released on bail after two years of confinement. Always contentious, he wrote his autobiography entitled *The Rise and Fall of the Confederate Government*. In this 1881 work he refought the war, including his views of those feuds with officers like Beauregard and Johnston who received much of the blame for the Confederacy's demise. He lived out his remaining years in Mississippi, never seeking to have his citizenship restored. In spite of this, it was restored during the presidency of Jimmy Carter. (Eaton, Clement, *Jefferson Davis*)

President Jefferson Davis. (*Leslie's*)

DAVIS, Jefferson Columbus (1828-1879)

Of all the general officers serving the Union cause during the Civil War, Jefferson C. Davis had the most inappropriate name. An enlisted man in the volunteers during the Mexican War, he was commissioned directly into the 1st Artillery as a second lieutenant in 1848. By the time of the secession crisis he was a first lieutenant in Charleston Harbor. After the capitulation of Fort Sumter, Davis was promoted to captain, 1st Artillery, on May 14, 1861. His later commands included: colonel, 22nd Indiana (August 1, 1861); brigadier general, USV (dated from December 18, 1861); commanding 3rd Division, Army of Southwest Missouri, Department of the Missouri (February-April 1862); commanding 4th Division, Army of the Mississippi (April 24-August 12, 1862); commanding 1st Division, in Right Wing, 14th Corps (November 5, 1862-January 9, 1863) and in 20th Corps (January 9-October 9, 1863), Army of the Cumberland; commanding 2nd Division, 14th Corps, Army of the Cumberland (October 10, 1863-August 22, 1864); and commanding the corps (August 22, 1864-August 1, 1865). After being appointed colonel by his friend, Governor Morton of Indiana, he fought at Booneville,

Missouri and led a division at Pea Ridge. While on sick leave, Davis volunteered his services in defense of Cincinnati and Louisville during the Perryville Campaign. After a series of altercations with General William Nelson, his superior, he killed him in cold blood. Due to the crisis a board of inquiry could not be impaneled and no charges were ever pressed. Through the influence of Governor Morton he was given a new command and fought at Stones' River, Chickamauga, and in the Atlanta, Savannah, and Carolinas campaigns as a division and corps commander. He was never made a major general except by brevets for Pea Ridge, Resaca, Rome, Kennesaw Mountain, and Jonesboro. Remaining in the regular army until his death, he served against the Modocs and in Alaska. (Fry, James B., *Killed by a Brother Soldier*)

DAVIS, Joseph (ca. 1858-1864)

Both Presidents Lincoln and Davis lost a son during their tenures in their respective White Houses. At mid-day on April 30, 1864, little Joe Davis was playing with the other children of the White House, when his mother went to take lunch to the president. While in the presence of the family nurse, the five-year old fell off the gallery railing and struck his head on the brick floor of the garden. The parents raced to his side but he was dead within a few minutes. The bereaved father soon had to deal with the double crisis of the advances of Grant into the Wilderness and Sherman towards Atlanta—while the executive mansion was in a state of mourning.

DAVIS, Joseph Robert (1825-1896)

When the Confederate Senate received the nomination of Joseph R. Davis to be a brigadier general it was rejected and the president was charged with nepotism. A few days later, after some bargaining, the nephew of Jefferson Davis was finally confirmed. The former Mississippi state senator and lawyer had entered the army at the head of a local company and his assignments included: captain, 10th Mississippi (spring 1861); lieutenant colonel, 10th Mississippi (April 1861); colonel and aide-de-camp to President Davis (August 31, 1861); brigadier general, CSA (September 15, 1862); commanding brigade (in French's Command from early 1863), Department of Virginia and North Carolina (fall 1862-April 1, 1863); commanding brigade, Department of Southern Virginia (April 1-May 1863); commanding brigade, Heth's Division, 3rd Corps, Army of Northern Virginia (May 30-July and August 1863-April 9, 1865). After brief service in the Pensacola area, he joined the staff of his uncle and was assigned to several fact-finding missions. Following the delay in his confirmation he was given a brigade, which he led in the Richmond area and in southeastern Virginia. Sent to reinforce Lee's army, he fought at Gettysburg where he allowed two of his regiments to be decimated in the railroad cut on the first day. He also led the brigade in Pickett's Charge two days later. Later the same month he was taken ill and Lee considered breaking up the brigade but felt that he could not because it was the president's nephew. Davis fought through the rest of the campaigns of the army including the Wilderness, Spotsylvania, Cold Harbor, Petersburg and the surrender at Appomattox. He practiced law for the next three decades. (Freeman, Douglas S., *Lee's Lieutenants*)

DAVIS, Reuben (1813-1890)

Although he shared the same family name and the same home state as the Confederate president, Mississippi's Senator Reuben Davis was one of that body's most vehemently anti-administration members. Davis was born in Tennessee and raised in Alabama before moving to Mississippi to study and practice medicine. He later switched to the law. He served as a district attorney and a judge before serving as colonel, 2nd Mississippi, in the Mexican War. After serving in the state legislature, Davis took a seat in the U.S. Congress and was there when his state seceded. Believing disunion to be a disaster but inevitable, he was considered by many to be a fire-eater. With the outbreak of the war, he saw some limited service in Kentucky as a brigadier general of state troops. In the fall elections he was named as the representative of the 2nd District to the First Regular Congress. Opposed to the war effort, Davis fought against the draft, and attempted to abolish the House's Committee on Military Affairs, but when this failed he resigned from the committee. Defeated as an anti-war candidate for governor in 1863, he resigned from Congress before the final session of the First Congress and rendered the Confederacy no further service. After the war Davis was a highly successful defense attorney and was a supporter of harsh treatment of freed blacks. (Davis, Reuben, *Recollections of Mississippi and Mississippians*)

Ruben Davis, one of Jefferson Davis' harshest critics. (*Harper's*)

DAVIS, Samuel (1842-1863)

Convicted Confederate spy Samuel Davis went to the gallows rather than provide the information demanded by the Union authorities. The 21-year-old had been caught by some of Grenville M. Dodge's command with maps and papers describing the Federal dispositions and likely plans. The capture had taken place near Pulaski, Tennessee, and he was taken into the town for court-martial. Convicted and sentenced to hang, he was offered a commutation of his sentence if he would reveal information about enemy spying activities. What the Union was most interested in was the identity of a Captain E. Coleman, Braxton Bragg's fictitious chief of scouts. Coleman was actually Captain Henry Shaw, but Davis refused to reveal this. In fact, Shaw witnessed the November 27, 1863, hanging from his cell in the same jail that had held Davis. (Whitley, Edythe Johns Rucker, *Sam Davis: Confederate Hero*)

DAVIS, Varina Howell (1826-1906)

The second wife of Jefferson Davis, Varina Howell became the butt of much of Richmond's gossip during the Civil War years. Born in Mississippi she had met the future Confederate president in 1844 and married him the next year. During his years in the U.S. Senate she managed the family plantation. When he was inaugurated in Montgomery, she was not present, but she soon arrived and moved with the Confederate capital to Richmond. As the country's first lady, she was roundly criticized for the almost royal manner in which the new nation's White House was run. She clashed with the wives of many prominent Southern leaders but was informed on Richmond matters. After the war she lived for a time in England when her husband was released from custody. She then helped with his memoirs and wrote her own *Memoir of Jefferson Davis*. After his death she retired in New York. (Ross, Ishbel, *First Lady of the South* and Randall, Ruth P., *I Varina: A Biography of the Girl Who Married Jefferson Davis and Became the First Lady of the South*)

DAVIS, William George Mackey (1812-1898)

After donating $50,000 to the Confederate cause, William G.M. Davis resigned his brigadier general's commission to become something of a profiteer. The Virginia native had sailed the high seas before settling in Florida where he engaged in the cotton brokerage business and practiced law. He was engaged in these pursuits when the Civil War broke out and he offered his services. His assignments included: colonel, 1st Florida Cavalry (January 1, 1862); commanding 2nd Brigade, 2nd (Heth's) Division, Department of East Tennessee (ca. July 3-ca. October 31,1862); commanding 1st Brigade, 3rd (Heth's) Division, Department of East Tennessee (ca. October 31-December 1862); brigadier general, CSA (November 4, 1862); commanding 1st Brigade, District, Department of East Tennessee (December 1862-early 1863); and commanding the department (spring-April 25, 1863). In command of a mounted regiment, he spent the first couple of months of his service in eastern Florida before being sent to East Tennessee in March 1862. There the regiment served dismounted and Davis soon found himself in brigade command. His remaining service being in that department, he was promoted to brigadier general and for a time commanded it. Resigning on May 6, 1863, he engaged in directing blockade-running operations. Once restrictions were lifted after the close of the conflict he resumed his legal career.

DAWKINS, James Baird (1820-1883)

By the time he was elected to the U.S. House of Representatives in 1860, James B. Dawkins was a devout secessionist and never took his seat because of the rapid development of the crisis. Instead, the South Carolina-born and-educated lawyer and planter served on the committee of the Florida convention, which drew up the document that took the state out of the Union. In November 1861 he was elected to represent the eastern half of Florida in the First Regular Confederate Congress, where he served on the committees on: Elections; Naval Affairs; and Quartermaster's & Commissary departments. Dawkins concerned himself primarily with matters relating directly to his home state, including the urging of construction of a military railroad for Florida. Elected to a judgeship in the Suwanee district, he resigned his congressional seat on December 8, 1862. His judicial appointment lasted until the Confederacy's fall. Following Reconstruction, during which he was banned from politics, he again served as a judge until his death.

DAY, Hannibal (ca. 1804-1891)

Foregoing the volunteers, and easy promotion, Hannibal Day remained in command of regular troops throughout the war and at one point commanded a brigade of them in battle. A West Pointer (1823) and veteran infantryman, Day saw service on the frontier and in the Seminole and Mexican wars. A major in the 2nd Infantry at the time of South Carolina's secession, his later assignments included: lieutenant colonel, 2nd Infantry (February 25, 1861); colonel, 6th Infantry (June 7, 1862); commanding 1st Brigade, 2nd Division, 5th Corps, Army of the Potomac (June 28-August 22, 1863); and commanding Fort Hamilton, City and Harbor of New York, Department of the East (August 1863-June 8, 1864). During the first two years of the war, Day served in Washington and on recruiting duty in Boston. Joining the Army of the Potomac, he commanded one of the two regular army brigades and led it in the "Valley of Death" on the second day at Gettysburg. He retired from active field duty on August 1, 1863, commanded at Fort Hamilton until late spring 1864, and then served on commissions and courts-martials until his 1869 retirement. Near the close of the war he was brevetted brigadier general in the regular army.

DAYTON, William Lewis (1807-1864)

Although he did not speak French or have a background in diplomacy, William L. Dayton, U.S. minister to France, was highly successful in his dealings with Napoleon III. A New Jersey lawyer he had served on the state supreme court and in the U.S. Senate where he verbally attacked the Mexican War but supported most war measures. He feared the creation of more slave states from the annexation of Texas, sensing that this would hurt the Whig Party's protectionist policies. He was also an opponent of the Compromise of 1850 and in particular the Fugitive Slave Act. After his reelection defeat he served as New Jersey's attorney general and was Frémont's running mate in 1856. With the advent of a Republican administration in 1861 the former Whig was named to the Paris post. Here he developed good relations with the emperor and was able to forestall his tendency toward intervention in the American Civil War. His other successes included the closing of French ports to Confederate craft, smoothing over the *Trent* affair, the French ban on construction of naval vessels for the South, and France's internment of the *Rappahannock*. His was also a leading role in the French decision to force the famed Confederate raider *Alabama* out of the harbor at Cherbourg to face the *Kearsarge* in June 1864. On December 1, 1864, Dayton died suddenly of apoplexy.

DEARING, James (1840-1865)

Finding the promotion potential of the artillery too limited, Virginian James Dearing transferred to the cavalry—and was destined to be the last general officer of the Army of Northern Virginia to be fatally shot. He was three-quarters of the way through his studies at West Point when they were interrupted by the outbreak of war; he resigned, on April 22, 1861, to go with his state. First commissioned in the state forces as a lieutenant of artillery, he served at 1st Bull Run attached to the Washington Artillery of New Orleans. His later assignments included: captain, Lynchburg (Va.) Artillery (1861); major, Artillery (early 1863); commanding Artillery Battalion, Pickett's Divison, Department of Southern Virginia (April 16-May 1863); commanding Artillery Battalion, Pickett's Division, 1st Corps, Army of Northern Virginia (May-July 1863); lieutenant colonel, Artillery (ca. July 1863); commanding artillery battalion, same corps and army (July-September 1863); commanding artillery battalion, Department of North Carolina (fall 1863-January 1864); colonel, 8th Confederate Cavalry (January 13, 1864); brigadier general, CSA (April 29, 1864); commanding Cavalry Brigade, Whiting's Division, Department of North Carolina and Southern Virginia (mid-May 1864); commanding Cavalry Brigade, same department (May-September 1864); commanding independent brigade, Cavalry Corps, Army of Northern Virginia (September-November 1864); commanding brigade, W.H.F. Lee's Division, same corps and army (November 1864-March 1865); and commanding brigade, Rosser's Division, same corps and army (March-April 6, 1865). Commanding his guns he fought with Pickett's Brigade and later his division at Yorktown, Williamsburg, Seven Pines, and Fredericksburg. He was given command of a battalion under Pickett and served in southeastern Virginia and at Gettysburg. Again serving south of Richmond, he was assigned to command the army's horse artillery but apparently never joined, having previously been named colonel of a cavalry regiment. He was promoted to brigadier and given a brigade when his regiment was disbanded in April 1864. He then served through the Petersburg Campaign, eventually being incorporated into the cavalry with Lee's army. In the fighting at High Bridge during the retreat to Appomattox, he engaged in a close-range pistol duel with Union General Theodore Read. Read was killed and Dearing was wounded. On April 23, the wound proved fatal. By that time Lee's army was no more. (Freeman, Douglas S., *Lee's Lieutenants* and Wise, Jennings C., *The Long Arm of Lee*)

DEARING, St. Clair (1833-?)

It was not until less than a month before Appomattox that the Confederate government finally decided to recruit black soldiers. One of the officers detailed to this serice was a native Georgian, St. Clair Dearing. Commissioned directly into the regular army in 1855, he had served in the infantry and artillery. He resigned as second lieutenant, 2nd Artillery, on February 7, 1861. His Confederate assignments included: lieutenant colonel, 25th North Carolina (August 15, 1861) and second lieutenant, Cavalry, CSA (December 6, 1864 to rank from November 16, 1864). After serving with his regiment in North Carolina he claims that he declined reelection out of "petulance," but other records indicate he was under charges for excessive drinking. After this April 1862 departure he served on the staffs of General Ripley, during the April 1863 bombardment of Fort Sumter, and General Gist, supervising slaves detailed to work on fortifications. These services were as a volunteer. After petitioning Jefferson Davis for any commission, he was appointed a lieutenant and when final congressional approval was given he was sent to Georgia to recruit slaves into the army. The war ended before they could take the field.

DEAS, Zachariah Cantey (1819-1882)

A wealthy Alabama cotton broker, Zachariah C. Deas raised his regiment at his own expense and rose to the rank of Confederate brigadier general. Although born in South Carolina he had made his fortune in Alabama. A veteran, as an enlisted man, of the Mexican War, he immediately threw himself into the Confederate cause and raised a regiment of which he became colonel. His assignments included: colonel, 22nd Alabama (October 25, 1861); commanding Gladden's Brigade, 2nd (Withers') Division, 2nd Corps, Army of the Mississippi (April 6, 1862); brigadier general CSA (December 13, 1862); and commanding in the Army of Tennessee: Gardner's (old) Alabama Brigade, Withers'-Hindman's Division, Polk's Corps (December 14, 1862-November 1863); brigade, Hindman's-Anderson's-Johnson's-Hill's Division, Breckinridge's-Hindman's-Hood's-Lee's Corps (November 1863-January 1864, January-May 1864, and August 1864-ca. March 1865); and the division (January 1864). On the first day at Shiloh his brigade commander Adley H. Gladden was mortally wounded and his successor, Daniel W. Adams, also fell wounded. At this point Deas took charge but also was hit. Upon his recovery he took part in the Kentucky Campaign but was not present at Perryville. Appointed brigadier general, he also appears to have been absent at the time of Murfreesboro. However, he served in the Tullahoma Campaign and fought at Chickamauga and Chattanooga. He led his brigade during parts of the Atlanta Campaign and then went on Hood's invasion of middle Tennessee. After fighting at Franklin and Nashville he moved on to the Carolinas where he served until illness forced him to relinquish command in the final months of the war. After the war he joined the New York Stock Exchange.

DeBOW, James Dunwoody Brownson (1820-1867)

As the editor of *DeBow's Review* James D.B. DeBow played a very important restraining role in the sectional crisis but eventually did embrace secession. Failing as a lawyer—as an orphan he had struggled through his education—he found his niche writing for the *Southern Quarterly Review* on philosophical and political topics. The first of his reviews, which appeared under varying titles, appeared in 1846 but was soon forced to close down for financial reasons. But he eventually got the publication on its feet. Being primarily an economic journal, it tried to remain above the politics that were tearing the country apart. This was difficult because the native Charlestonian was an admirer of John C. Calhoun. DeBow did, however, maintain a more national perspective. In the 1850s he was head of the Census bureau and in 1854 he published *Statistical View of the United States*. A Breckinridge backer in 1860, he suppported the secession movement after the election of Lincoln and during the war itself was an adherent of Jefferson Davis. Continuing to publish the *Review*, he was enthusiastic about the prospects for the new nation and also served in the Treasury Department, working on foreign loans to be backed by cotton. He died shortly after the fall of the South, having continued in journalism and railroading. (Skipper, Otis Clark, *J.D.B. DeBow, Magazinist of the South*)

DeBRAY, Xavier Blanchard (1819-1895)

Cut off from Richmond by the fall of Vicksburg, Trans-Mississippi Department commander E. Kirby Smith was forced to promote deserving officers like Xavier B. DeBray without the formalities of presidential appointment and senate confirmation. A native of France, DeBray had been educated at the French military school, St. Cyr, and had served as a diplomat. Settling in Texas in 1852, he became the governor's aide-de-camp upon the outbreak of war. His later assignments in the Trans-Mississippi Department included: major, 2nd Texas (August 1861); lieutenant colonel, DeBray's (Tex.) Cavalry Battalion (1861); colonel, 26th Texas Cavalry (December 5, 1861); commanding 2nd Brigade, 2nd Division, District of Texas, New Mexico and Arizona (June 25-November 11, 1863); commanding brigade, District of Texas, New Mexico and Arizona (November 11-December 15, 1863); commanding cavalry brigade, 2nd Division, District of Texas, New Mexico and Arizona (December 1863); brigadier general, CSA, by Smith (April 13, 1864); commanding 6th Texas Cavalry Brigade, 2nd Texas Cavalry Division, 1st Corps (ca. April 13, 1864-early 1865); and commanding brigade, Bee's Division, Cavalry Corps (early 1865-May 1865). With his regiment he took part in the fight at Galveston during his stationing in Texas. In the spring of 1864 he was sent as part of the reinforcements to the District of West Louisiana to face Banks during the Red River Campaign. It was during this operation that he was promoted to brigadier by Smith. He finished out the war in Louisiana and served as a translator back in Texas.

De FONTAINE, Felix Gregory (1834-1896)

A prewar reporter, Felix G. De Fontaine moved to Columbia, South Carolina, shortly before the war and as founder and editor of the *Daily South Carolinian* became an ardent Southern apologist, although he had been born in Boston. Maintaining his connections with the *New York Herald*, in February 1861 he wrote a defense of the actions of the South, which was later published in book form as *A History of American Abolitionism Together with a History of the Southern Confederacy*. His friendship with Beauregard enabled him to write the first report of the bombardment of Fort Sumter to appear in the Northern papers. He later went to the Virginia front, apparently with the honorary rank of major, with the 1st South Carolina as a military correspondent. Signing most of his writings as "Personne," he produced much Southern propaganda until his press was destroyed in the fire following the Union occupation of Columbia. After the war he wrote to keep Southerners active in the defense of their values, but soon moved to New York where he was editor for the *Telegram* and then the *Herald*. He held the latter post for the remainder of his life.

DEGATAGA

See: *Watie, Stand*

DEITZLER, George Washington (1826-1884)

Long active in the tragedy of "Bleeding Kansas," George W. Deitzler became a Union brigadier general and narrowly missed becoming another casualty in Quantrill's sacking of Lawrence in 1863. Born in Pennsylvania, he had lived in Illinois and California before settling in Lawrence, Kansas, where he was in the land and farming businesses. In the fight over whether Kansas would be admitted to the Union as a slave or free state, he was an active organizer and publicist for the Free-Soil faction. On a visit to the Boston Emigrant Aid Society he acquired some rifles, nicknamed "Beecher's Bibles." For his role in the Wakarusa War he was threatened with trial for treason. Serving in both branches of the territorial legislature, he was for a time the presiding officer of the lower body. Upon the outbreak of the war he began recruiting and his later assignments included: colonel, 1st Kansas (June 5, 1861); commanding 1st Brigade, 6th Division, Left Wing, 13th Corps, Army of the Tennessee (November 1-December 18, 1862); commanding 1st Brigade, 6th Division, Left Wing, 16th Corps, Army of the Tennessee (December 22, 1862-January 20, 1863); brigadier general,

USV (April 4, 1863 to rank from November 29, 1862); major general, Kansas Militia (ca. October 1864); and commanding Kansas Militia (ca. October 1864). He was severely wounded while commanding his regiment at Wilson's Creek. Although he never recovered fully, he was able to command a brigade near Corinth and in the early operations against Vicksburg. Shortly after being appointed a brigadier he had to relinquish command on April 22, 1863, and go on sick leave. While at home he survived the bloody Lawrence raid by hiding in a gulch. A few days later, on August 27, 1863, he resigned. He commanded the Kansas militia during Price's invasion of Missouri and performed creditably at the battle of Westport and in the pursuit of the retreating Confederates. For several years after the war he was active in the growth of his state and its railroads but moved to California in 1872. He died in a carriage accident while on a visit to Arizona. (Monaghan, Jay, *Civil War on the Western Border 1854-1865*)

DELAFIELD, Richard (1798-1873)

One of the senior engineering officers at the beginning of war was West Pointer (1818) Richard Delafield who rose to chief of Engineers during the conflict. Having entered the military academy during the War of 1812, the New Yorker graduated first in his class and spent his entire career in the engineers. By the time of the secession crisis he had risen to the rank of major in the corps and was serving as superintendent at his alma mater. In the initial stages of the conflict he took charge of the New York Harbor defenses and aided the governor in organizing the state's volunteer forces for the front. During the war he was promoted as follows: lieutenant colonel, Corps of Engineers (August 6, 1861); colonel, Corps of Engineers (June 1, 1863); and brigadier general, USA, and chief of Engineers (May 18, 1864 to rank from April 22, 1864). After his service in New York Harbor he was ordered to Washington to take over command of the corps upon the death of General J.G. Totten. For his services during the war, Delafield was brevetted major general in the regular establishment. He continued as engineering chief after the war until he retired under a 45-year retirement policy in 1866. Keeping active in engineering in civilian life, he served on a number of commissions concerned with coastal matters. He was also a Smithsonian Institution regent before his death in 1873.

de LAGNEL, Julius Adolph (1827-1912)

For somes unexplained reason Julius A. de Lagnel turned down a commission as a Confederate brigadier general early in the war and completed his service in the ordnance branch. The New Jersey native received a direct commission into the regular army from Virginia in 1847. He served as a subaltern in the 2nd Artillery until he resigned as a first lieutenant on May 17, 1861, in order to join the South. His Confederate assignments included: captain, artillery (March 16, 1861); chief of artillery, Army of the Northwest (June-July 11, 1861); brigadier general, CSA (July 31, 1862 to rank from April 18, 1862); and lieutenant colonel, Ordnance (1862). With Robert S. Garnett he was sent to western Virginia during the first spring of the war. When the forces of George B. McClellan advanced into the area de Lagnel was stationed at Rich Mountain with a small force—numbering a few companies and only one gun—with which to face the column under William S. Rosecrans. In the subsequent battle the confederates made a heroic stand but were eventually forced from their positions by the force of numbers. Falling severely wounded, their chief secreted himself until he could make his getaway. By the time that he had recovered in a mountain cabin the enemy was between him and the Confederate lines. Captured in an attempt to join them, he was not exchanged until December 20, 1861. The next summer he was promoted to brigadier general but declined on July 31, 1862. As an ordnance officer, he served frequently on inspection duty. Engaged in shipping after the war, he eventually settled in the reunited nation's capital.

DELANEY, Patrick (?-1864)

Although his real name is not known for certain, there was in the early summer of 1864 a gang of "Raiders" operating in Andersonville Prison under the leadership of Patrick Delaney, allegedly of the 83rd Pennsylvania. These cutthroats terrorized the rest of the prison population with sneak thievery, armed robbery, beating, and an occasional killing. Finally the prisoners themselves put an end to this reign of terror by organizing their own police force and turning over their arrestees to the Confederate commandant, Major Henry Wirz, for safekeeping. Under the terms of Wirz's General Order No. 57, a prisoners' court tried the offenders. Of the 125 tried, six were felt deserving of the death sentence. Delaney was among them. In his final speech before hanging, he declared his preference for execution over continued existence in the starvation conditions of the camp. With his means of subsistance—stealing—cut off, he felt he could no longer go on. He further stated that his family would be saved the knowledge of his fate since his name was not Delaney. On the scaffold he was fortunate to be one of the two condemned to die relatively easily. (McElroy, John, *Andersonville: A Story of Rebel Military Prisons*)

De LEON, Edwin (1818-1891)

One of the few high ranking Confederate officials of the Jewish faith, Edwin De Leon resigned his U.S. consular post in Egypt to join his native South. Born in South Carolina, he studied law and had a journalistic career that included the editorship of the *Savannah Republican*, the *Columbia Telegraph*, and *The Southern Press* in Washington, before becoming a diplomat in 1854. Returning to North America, he was appointed as a Confederate agent in Europe and was primarily concerned with propaganda. He was based in Paris and came into conflict with John Slidell. By February 1864 he had become so disillusioned with the idea of French aid or recognition that he publicly denounced that government, effectively ending his usefulness. He did not return to the United States until 14 years after Appomattox, having lived in both Europe and Egypt. He had spent most of his own wealth in the service of the Confederacy. In his later years he introduced the telephone to Egypt and wrote *The Kedive's Egypt*, *Under the Stars and Crescent*, and *Thirty Years of Life in Three Continents*.

DENNIS, Elias Smith (1812-1894)

Although he compiled a creditable Civil War record, Elias S. Dennis is one of the less-remembered brigade commanders. Born in New York, he moved to Illinois, becoming a miller and member of both houses of the legislature. He was also a peace officer in Kansas during the turbulent 1850s. His Civil War assignments included: lieutenant colonel, 30th Illinois (August 28, 1861); colonel, 30th Illinois (May 1, 1862); brigadier general, USV (November 29, 1862); commanding 2nd Brigade, 3rd Division, 17th Corps, Army of the Tennessee (April 13-May 11, 1863); commanding District of Northeast Louisiana, Army of the Tennessee (May 11-July 31, 1863); commanding 1st Division, 15th corps, Army of the Tennessee (July 28-September 1, 1863); commanding 1st Division, 17th Corps, Army of the Tennessee (October 23, 1863-late summer 1864); commanding 2nd Division, 19th Corps, Department of the Gulf (late summer-November 7, 1864); commanding 2nd Brigade, Reserve Corps, Department of the Gulf (December 5, 1864-February 3, 1865); commanding 2nd Brigade, 1st Division, Reserve Corps, Department of the Gulf (February 3-18, 1865); commanding 2nd Brigade, 1st Division, 13th Corps, Department of the Gulf (February 18-May 25, 1865); and commanding the division (May 25-July 20, 1865). He took part in the capture of Forts Henry and Donelson. Made part of the garrison of the latter, he missed Shiloh but was promoted to brigade command shortly thereafter. He served in the early operations against Vicksburg and the beginning of the campaign proper before taking charge across the river in Louisiana supporting the siege operations. He served the rest of the war in the Mississippi Valley and along the Gulf coast where he earned a brevet as major general of volunteers for his role in the capture of Mobile. Mustered out on August 24, 1865, he settled in Louisiana, becoming a sheriff and planter. In 1886 he retired back to Illinois.

DENNISON, William (1815-1882)

As Ohio's first war governor, William Dennison actually exceeded his authority in his efforts to surpass the troop quotas called for by the Washington government. A native of the state, he had practiced law and served one term in the state legislature. A leading Whig, he was one of the first to join the Republican Party in 1856. Three years later he was elected to the gubernatorial chair on that ticket. Taking office in 1860, he proved to be a rather unpopular chief executive even before being thrust into the Civil War. In suppport of the war effort he instituted virtual state control over telegraph, express and rail lines. Funds were sometimes expended in the war effort that had not been legally appropriated. But his efforts were vital to the war in that theater. He directed McClellan to take state forces into the loyalist areas of western Virginia in order to provide an

William Dennison, Ohio's war governor and Lincoln's postmaster general. (NA)

added measure of security for Ohio. Denied renomination in 1861, he resumed private practice and advised Governor David Tod. Then in 1864 he chaired the Republican national convention and notified Lincoln of his renomination. On September 24, 1864, he was named postmaster general, replacing Montgomery Blair who had been asked to resign by Lincoln. He resigned in 1866 when he found he could not support Andrew Johnson's policies and returned to his legal, banking, and railroad interests. (Reid, Whitelaw, *Ohio in the War*)

DENT, Frederick Tracy (1820-1892)

West Point (1843) classmate and brother-in-law of U.S. Grant, Frederick T. Dent spent the first half of the Civil War on the West Coast before transferring to the active front and eventually joining Grant's staff. A veteran of the Mexican War—earning two brevets and being severely wounded at Molino del Rey—Dent also saw some Indian fighting and was a captain in the 9th Infantry at the outbreak of hostilities; he remained in the San Francisco area for the first two years of the war. His later assignments included: major, 4th Infantry (March 9, 1863); lieutenant colonel and aide-de-camp (March 29, 1864); and brigadier general, USV (April 5, 1865). He briefly commanded his new regiment in the Army of the Potomac before being sent to New York City to prevent further draft rioting. With Grant's appointment to supreme command Dent was named to his staff and served through the Overland, Petersburg, and Appomattox campaigns. During this time he earned four brevets including that of brigadier in the regular army. Mustered out of the volunteer service on April 30, 1866, he remained in the army serving as an aide to Grant and later to Sherman. However, under Sherman he was detailed to the White House as Grant's military secretary. After 40 years of service Dent retired in 1883 as colonel, 3rd Artillery.

DENVER, James William (1817-1892)

Virginia native James W. Denver served in a number of capacities during his life, including that of brigadier general of volunteers in the Civil War. A student of civil engineering, he had tried his hand at surveying, teaching, law, and journalism before he served a year as a regular army company commander in the Mexican War. Drawn by California gold, he served in that state's senate for a time and fought a fatal duel with a critical editor. President Buchanan appointed him to territorial posts in Kansas and Colorado. Denver is named for him, but after failing to win a senate seat from California he returned to his boyhood home of Ohio. Called back to the military at the outbreak of the Civil War, he was appointed to inspection duty in Kansas. His later assignments included: brigadier general, USV (August 14, 1861); commanding 3rd Brigade, 5th Division, Army of West Tennessee (May 12-July 21, 1862); commanding 2nd Brigade, 5th Division, District of Memphis, Department of the Mississippi (July 21-October 26, 1862); commanding 2nd Brigade, same district, 13th Corps, Army of the Tennessee (October 25-November 12, 1862); commanding 1st Division, same district, corps and army (November 12-December 18, 1862); commanding 1st Division, 17th Corps, Army of the Tennessee (December 18, 1862-January 19, 1863); and commanding 1st Division, 16th Corps, same army (January 19-March 22, 1863). He took part in the taking of Corinth in the spring of 1862 and spent most of the rest of his military service assigned to guard duty along the supply lines in northern Mississippi and western Tennessee. His resignation was accepted to take effect from March 5, 1863. He was a lawyer and politician after the war.

De RUSSY, Gustavus Adolphus (1818-1891)

The Mexican War enabled Gustavus A. De Russy to resume the military career that his drinking had interrupted at West Point. The native New Yorker who came from a military family was permitted to resign in 1838, after three years at the military academy, rather than face disciplinary actions. Commissioned directly into the regular artillery in 1847, he won two brevets in Mexico and remained in the army until his retirement in 1882 as colonel, 3rd Artillery. His Civil War-era assignments included: captain, 4th Artillery (since August 17, 1857); commanding Reserve Artillery, 3rd Corps, Army of the Potomac (June-July 1862); colonel, 4th New York Heavy Artillery (March 17, 1863); brigadier general, USV (May 23, 1863); and commanding Defenses South of the Potomac, 22nd Corps, Department of Washington (May 25, 1863-August 20, 1865). Serving on the Peninsula, he earned brevets for Seven Pines and the Seven Days fight at Malvern Hill. He commanded the artillery on the left at Fredericksburg and then entered the volunteer service at the head of a New York regiment of heavy artillery. Assigned to the Washington fortifications, he was almost immediately promoted to brigadier general of volunteers and assigned to command on the south side of the Potomac. He served in the defenses for the remainder of the conflict and was brevetted brigadier in the regular establishment for his work. At the end of his military service he settled in Michigan.

DESHLER, James (1833-1863)

Within two months of receiving his promotion to brigadier general in the Confederate service, Alabamian West Pointer (1854) James Deshler was dead. Initially posted to the artillery, he transferred to the infantry in 1855. Before being dropped on July 15, 1861, as a first lieutenant in the 10th Infantry—for failing to return following a leave—he had seen action against the Sioux and on the expedition against the Mormons in Utah. His Confederate assignments included: captain, Artillery (1861); colonel, Artillery (early 1862); chief of artillery, Department of North Carolina (spring 1862); commanding Artillery, Holmes' Division, Army of Northern Virginia (June-July 1862); commanding brigade, Churchill's Division, District of Arkansas, Trans-Mississippi Department (January-January 11, 1863); brigadier general, CSA (July 28, 1863); commanding Artillery Reserve, Army of Tennessee (ca. July-August 13, 1863); and commanding brigade, Cleburne's Division, Hill's Corps, Army of Tennessee (August 13-September 20, 1863). Sent to western Virginia, he served as Henry R. Jackson's adjutant during the campaigning there late in 1861 and was severely wounded on December 13 at Allegheny Summit. Promoted to colonel, he was dispatched to North Carolina where he became Theophilus H. Holmes' chief gunner. As such he served through the Seven Days and was later sent to the West. Commanding a brigade at Arkansas Post he was taken prisoner and upon his exchange was named a brigadier general. After leading the Army of Tennessee's reserve guns for a time he took charge of an infantry brigade and on the second day at Chickamauga he was killed by the explosion of a shell.

de TROBRIAND, Philippe Régis Dénis de Keredern (1816-1897)

Following the consolidation of his own 3rd Corps into the 2nd in early 1864, Philippe Regis de Trobriand, a native of Tours, France, became the defender of the defunct unit's reputation. Becoming a United States citizen following his marriage to an heiress, the poet, novelist, lawyer, and duelist was active in militia affairs. Entering the Union army, he held the following assignments: colonel, 55th New York (August 28, 1861); commanding 3rd Brigade, 1st Division, 3rd Corps, Army of the Potomac (October-November 1862 and June 3-November 22, 1863); colonel, 38th New York (55th merged into this unit December 21, 1862); commanding 2nd Brigade, 1st Division, 3rd Corps, Army of the Potomac (January 26-February 15,

March-April, and May 29-June 3, 1863); brigadier general, USV (January 5, 1864); commanding 1st Brigade, 3rd Division, 2nd Corps, Army of the Potomac (July 12-October 8, 1864, October 21, 1864, January 2, 1865, January 25-February 15-March 2, April 6, and May 16-June 28, 1865) and commanding the division (October 8-21, 1864, February 15-March 2, April 6-May 16, and June 9-20, 1865). In regimental, brigade, and divisional command he proved to be a distinguished citizen soldier. He led his first regiment at Williamsburg and Fredericksburg before it was merged into another decimated unit. This he commanded at Chancellorsville before it was mustered out. He remained to fight at Gettysburg and in the Bristoe and Mine Run campaigns before himself being mustered out on November 21, 1863. Six weeks later he was commissioned a brigadier general and returned to command old 3rd Corps troops in the 2nd Corps. There he complained that corps commander Hancock preferred the two divisions of the old 2nd Corps to the one from the old 3rd. He fought through the late Petersburg and Appomattox campaigns—in both brigade and divisional command—earning a brevet as a major general of volunteers for the latter. Mustered out on January 15, 1866, he accepted a regular army colonelcy later that year. He served on the frontier and on Reconstruction duty until his 1879 retirement. He divided his remaining years between Louisiana and New York, having succeeded his father as a baron in 1874. His account of the war appeared in English as *Four Years with the Army of Potomac*. (Post, Marie Caroline, *The Life and Memories of Comte Régis de Trobriand*)

DEVENS, Charles, Jr. (1820-1891)

As a U.S. marshal, Charles Devens, Jr., came into conflict with the Fugitive Slave Act—a fitting prelude to his Civil War role as a brevet major general in the Union army. A native of Massachusetts, he was a graduate of Harvard Law School and served as a state senator. By law he was required, in his official capacity, to return a fugitive slave. When he attempted to buy one instead and set him free, the owner refused. A militia officer, he joined the Union army upon Lincoln's first call for 75,000 men. His assignments included: brigadier general, Massachusetts Militia (prewar); major, 3rd Massachusetts Rifle Battalion (April 19, 1861); colonel, 15th Massachusetts (July 24, 1861); brigadier general, USV (April 15, 1862); commanding 3rd Brigade, 1st Division, 4th Corps, Army of the Potomac (May 1-31, 1862); commanding 1st Brigade, 1st Division, 4th Corps, Army of the Potomac (July 26-September 26, 1862); commanding 1st Brigade, 3rd Division, 6th Corps, Army of the Potomac (September 26-October 1862); commanding 2nd Brigade, 3rd Division, 6th Corps, Army of the Potomac (October-December 1862 and February-April 1863); commanding the division (December 1862-February 1863); commanding 1st Division, 11th corps, Army of the Potomac (April 20-May 2, 1863); commanding 3rd brigade, 1st Division, 18th Corps, Army of the James (May 26-30, 1864); commanding 3rd Division, 18th Corps, Army of the James (May 30-June 4, 1864); commanding 1st Division, 18th Corps, Army of the James (October 29-December 3, 1864); commanding 3rd Division, 24th Corps, Army of the James (December 3, 1864-July 10, 1865); and also commanding the corps (January 2-15, 1865). With his 90-day battalion, he served at Baltimore's Fort McHenry until its July 20, 1861, mustering out. After an interlude of only four days he was in command of a newly organized regiment, which he led at the Ball's Bluff disaster where a button stopped a Confederate bullet from killing him. Promoted to brigadier the next fall, he was wounded at Seven Pines. Returning to duty after the close of the Peninsula Campaign, in which he had fought at Yorktown and Williamsburg as well as Seven Pines, he was not engaged at Antietam as his division was too far to the rear. He commanded his brigade at Fredericksburg and was soon in charge of the division. Commanding a division of the 11th corps at Chancellorsville, he was caught up in the disaster on the Union right flank. His division was all but destroyed and he was himself severely wounded, but the collapse did not hurt his career. Returning to duty a year later, he commanded a division in Butler's army and fought at Cold Harbor where rheumatism forced him to relinquish command. In the fall of 1864 he returned and commanded a division through the rest of the Petersburg and Appomattox campaigns. For the operations leading up to the fall of Richmond he was brevetted major general and after Lee's surrender served in command of the occupation of Charleston until his muster out on June 2, 1866. In the postwar years he had a distinguished legal career. He was a Massachusetts supreme court justice and attorney general under President Rutherford B. Hayes. (Walker, Francis A., *Major General Charles Devens*)

DEVEREUX, Arthur Forrester (?-?)

Only half a year after coming out of the repulse of Pickett's Charge with four Confederate battle flags, Arthur F. Devereux resigned a colonelcy in the Union army. The Massachusetts native had been a student at West Point for a time and then entered the volunteers at the beginning of the Civil War. His assignments included: captain, 8th Massachusetts (May 18, 1861); lieutenant colonel, 19th Massachusetts (August 3, 1861); colonel, 19th Massachussetts (May 1, 1863); and commanding 2nd Brigade, 2nd Division, 2nd Corps, Army of the Potomac (October 22, 1863-January 8, 1864). As a company officer, he served with his first regiment in Maryland before transferring to a field grade position in a new regiment. This unit served at Yorktown and Seven Pines and he succeeded to its command during the Seven Days. He fought later at South Mountain and again took charge of the regiment at Antietam. The regiment fought at Fredericksburg and he was once more in command at Chancellorsville. Facing Pickett's Charge at Gettysburg, he commanded the regiment and ended up in possession of four stands of colors. He subsequently commanded a brigade in the Mine Run operations and resigned on February 27, 1864. In the omnibus bill of March 13, 1865, he was brevetted brigadier general for his war service.

DEVIN, Thomas Casimer (1822-1878)

One of the heroes of the opening of the battle of Gettysburg, Thomas C. Devin joined the regular army after the Civil War and served until his death. A New York born house painter, he had risen in the officers rank of the New York militia. His Civil War assignments included: lieutenant colonel, 1st New York Militia (prewar); captain, 1st New York Cavalry (July 19, 1861); colonel, 6th New York Cavalry (November 18, 1861); commanding 2nd Brigade, Cavalry Division, Right Grand Division, Army of the Potomac (December 13, 1862-January 1863); commanding 2nd Brigade, Pleasanton's Cavalry Division, Army of the Potomac (January-February 16, 1863); commanding 2nd Brigade, 1st Division, Cavalry Corps, Army of the Potomac (February 16-June 6, 1863, June 9, 1863-January 3, 1864, and January 25-August 6, 1864); commanding the division (June 6-9, 1863); commanding 2nd Brigade, 1st Division, Cavalry Corps, Army of the Shenandoah (August 30-November 13 and November 28-December 31, 1864); brigadier general, USV (October 19, 1864); commanding the division (November 13-28, 1864, December 31, 1864-January 15, 1865, and February 10-March 25, 1865); and again commanding 1st Division, Cavalry Corps, Army of the Potomac (March 25-May 28, 1865). Following brief service as a company commander in his first unit, he was mustered out on October 19, 1861, to accept a colonelcy of a new regiment. This he commanded at Antietam and at Fredericksburg he succeeded to brigade command. He fought at Chancellorsville in command of the only mounted brigade with the main army. After service at Brandy Station his troops were among the first engaged at Gettysburg. He served in the Bristoe and Mine Run operations and early the next year rode in the Kilpatrick-Dahlgren raid on Richmond. He fought through the Overland Campaign and the beginnings of the Petersburg operations. Transferred to the Shenandoah Valley in the summer of 1864, he fought at 3rd Winchester and was slightly wounded at Crooked Run. At Fisher's Hill he earned an 1867 brevet in the regular army. His volunteer brigadier's star came for his actions at Cedar Creek. Returning to the Petersburg front, he fought at Five Forks and Sayler's Creek. For the latter he was brevetted to brigadier in the regular army in 1867. He was present at the surrender of Lee's army. Brevetted major general of volunteers and mustered out on January 15, 1866, he was commissioned in the regular establishment six months later as a lieutenant colonel. He died while on sick leave as colonel, 3rd Cavalry.

DEVINE, Thomas Jefferson (1820-1890)

A Texas judge and secessionist, Thomas J. Devine was a special trade negotiator with the Mexican authorities. Born in Halifax, Nova Scotia, he reached maturity in Florida and studied law in Mississippi and Kentucky before emigrating to the Lone Star state in 1843. Practicing law in San Antonio, he served a year as attorney for the city and in 1851 became a district judge. Still a judge, he attended the secessionist convention and worked hard to gain possession of federal property and to assure the removal of national forces from the state. That same year he was appointed to the state supreme court. He went to Mexico City in 1863 and upon his return, at the war's close, he was arrested and indicted for treason but not tried. After practicing law he was again named to the supreme bench in 1873. Resigning in 1875, he ran unsuccessfully for the governor's chair three years later. (Johnson, Sidney Smith, *Texans Who Wore the Gray*)

DEWEY, George (1837-1917)

Best remembered for his victory at Manila Bay in the Spanish-American War, George Dewey gained his first naval combat experience in the Civil War. A native Vermonter, he had entered Annapolis as a midshipman in 1854, graduating four years later with assignment to the *Wabash* in the Mediterranean. His Civil War assignments included: lieutenant, USN (April 1861); executive officer, *Mississippi* (mid-1861-March 14, 1863); executive officer, *Monongahela* (1863); and executive officer, *Colorado* (1864-65). Despite his youth he was given the number two post on one of the most powerful Union vessels in the first year of the conflict. Taking part in the operations against New Orleans early in 1862, he directed the *Mississippi* in the passage of Forts Jackson and St. Philip while the captain, Melancton Smith, who didn't trust his eyes sufficiently for the nighttime operation, directed the guns. After the fall of the city Dewey continued to serve on the river until early 1863 when the vessel was run aground while trying to pass the batteries at Port Hudson. He was particularly commended for his actions in the futile effort to save the craft. Next posted to Farragut's flagship, the *Monongahela*, he had the opportunity to study under America's first admiral. After service in the James River he took part in the bombardments and capture of Fort Fisher a few months before the war's close. He remained in the service until his death, earning promotions and lasting fame, and even toyed with the idea of running for president. (Dewey, George, *Autobiography of George Dewey*)

DEWEY, Joel Allen (1840-1873)

The last Union brigadier general of volunteers appointed in the Civil War era was Joel A. Dewey. Born in Vermont, he was studying at Oberlin when he entered the Union Army. His assignments included: second lieutenant, 58th Ohio (October 10, 1861); captain, 43rd Ohio (January 12, 1862); lieutenant colonel, 3rd Alabama Colored Infantry (February 14, 1862); lieutenant colonel, 111th United States Colored Infantry (June 25, 1864); colonel, 111th United States Colored Infantry (April 29, 1865); and brigadier general, USV (November 20, 1865). His first unit was still in the process of organizing at Camp Chase when he transferred to the 43rd Ohio as a company commander. This unit fought at Island #10, took part in the advance on Corinth, and fought at Iuka and Corinth. It was stationed at Memphis when Dewey transferred to the command of black troops. His regiment was stationed at Pulaski, Tennessee, when its designation was changed from an Alabama organization to that of the United States Colored Troops. The regiment served there and as guards for the Nashville and Northwestern Railroad and later in Middle Tennessee. Since apparently he was never in command of a brigade, it is hard to explain his promotion to the rank of brigadier general. Mustered out on January 31, 1865, he turned down a position in the regular establishment and studied law in New York. Practicing in Tennessee, he was serving as a district attorney general when he died of a heart attack in a courthouse in Knoxville.

DIBRELL, George Gibbs (1822-1888)

Although not promoted to Confederate brigadier until the war was virtually over, Tennessee farmer and merchant George G. Dibrell was frequently in command of a brigade in the early years of the war. A Unionist at the secessionist convention, he nonetheless joined the Confederate army. His assignments included: lieutenant colonel, 25th Tennessee (August 10, 1861); colonel, 13th (unofficially 8th) Tennessee Cavalry (September 1862); commanding brigade, Forrest's Cavalry Division, Army of Tennessee (August-September 1863); commanding brigade, Armstrong's Division, Forrest's Cavalry Corps, Army of Tennessee (September-October 1863); commanding brigade, Armstrong's Division, Wheeler's Cavalry Corps, Army of Tennessee (October-November 1863); commanding brigade, Armstrong's Division, Martin's Detachment of Wheeler's Cavalry Corps, Department of East Tennessee (November-December 1863); commanding division, Cavalry, Department of East Tennessee (February-March 1864); commanding brigade, Kelly's-Humes' Division, Wheeler's Cavalry Corps, Army of Tennessee (April-late 1864); commanding brigade, Humes' Division, Wheeler's Cavalry Corps, Department of South Carolina, Georgia and Florida (late 1864-March 1865); brigadier general, CSA (January 28, 1865 to rank from July 26, 1864); and commanding brigade, Humes' Division, Wheeler's Cavalry Corps, Army of Tennessee (March-April 26, 1865). With his initial regiment he fought at Mill Springs but failed to gain reelection on May 10, 1862. He then became commander of a mounted regiment, which was originally organized as partisan rangers but quickly converted to normal cavalry. This he led on Nathan Bedford Forrest's first raid in western Tennessee during the winter of 1862-63. The following summer he took charge of a brigade and fought at Chickamauga and Knoxville. He served through the Atlanta Campaign in brigade command but during its latter stages was cut off from the main army while on a raid in east Tennessee. Before he could rejoin it he commanded his few troops in the fight at Saltville, Virginia. Rejoining Wheeler he participated in the opposition to Sherman's March to the Sea and fought in the Carolinas campaign, seeing action at Averysboro and Bentonville. Surrended with Joseph E. Johnston, his final years were spent in a series of enterprises that included finance, mercantile, rail, and mining ventures. He also sat for five terms in the U.S. House of Representatives.

DICKISON, John J. (?-?)

With most of the Florida troops ordered out of the state for service with the Armies of Northern Virginia and Tennessee, there was ample opportunity for small-unit commanders like John J. Dickison, still in the state, to gain more distinction than equally-ranked Floridians elsewhere. His Confederate assignments included: first lieutenant, Marion (Fla.) Light Artillery (December 12, 1861); captain, Lee (Fla.) Dragoons (August 21, 1862); and captain, Company H, 2nd Florida Cavalry (December 4, 1862). Upon the reorganization of the artillery unit in the spring of 1862, he decided that he preferred the cavalry service and was granted authority to raise a company. At first independent, the company was assigned to the 2nd Florida Cavalry but rarely served with more than a few of its sister companies. Operating independently in Palatka and the St. Johns River region, he proved the bane of Union detachments and supply trains. One typical foray occurred in February 1865 when he attacked a portion of the 17th Connecticut, which was guarding 10 wagons. Although outnumbered two to one he captured the train and killed or captured the entire escort. Dickison himself mortally wounded the 17th's commander. Events elsewhere ended the war for Dickison. (Dickison, John J., "Florida," *Confederate Military History*, Vol. XI)

DILL, Benjamin Franklin (?-ca. 1866)

Along with co-editor John R. McClanahan, Benjamin Dill led the *Memphis Appeal* in one of the most outstanding odysseys of journalism. Having directed the paper for a decade, supporting the candidacy of Stephen A. Douglas and the preservation of the Union, Dill finally threw his wholehearted support behind the Confederacy. His editorial line never wavered during a three-year series of relocations due to military defeats. The refugee paper published in Grenada, Jackson, and Meridian, Mississippi, Atlanta, and lastly in Montgomery, Dill was the last editor to close up shop in Atlanta before Sherman took the city. Finally, in April 1865, Dill's, and his paper's luck ran out. They were captured with most of the equipment and staff, at Columbus, Georgia. Although McClanahan managed to smuggle the press to Macon, commander of the Union cavalry was still ecstatic at the capture of their long-sought quarry. The fight against equipment and supply shortages was over. On November 5, 1865, with the press brought back from Macon, Dill published the first edition of the *Appeal* in its old home. He died shortly after. The paper later became the *Memphis Commercial Appeal*. (Baker, Thomas Harrison, *The Memphis Commercial Appeal*)

DILLARD, R.K. (?-?)

Thoroughly acquainted with the area along the James River in Virginia, a civilian, R.K. Dillard, took part in the most devastating Confederate sabotage attacks. In late July 1864 Dillard was hired by John Maxwell, a secret agent belonging to "Captain Z. McDaniel's Company, Secret Service," as a guide and accomplice in the detonation of an invention of Maxwell's, a "horological" device or time bomb. On the 26th the pair left Richmond and soon decided on the immense Union supply center at City Point as their target. On August 9, 1864, Dillard remained about half a mile outside the base while Maxwell managed to get the explosives planted on a Union ordnance boat. The resulting explosion caused two million dollars in damage and 169 casualties. Rejoining Maxwell, Dillard slipped back out of the Union lines. For several days the two continued their spying operations on the river. The records are silent on Dillard's further activities. (Stern, Philip Van Doren, *Secret Missions of the Civil War*)

DILWORTH, Caleb James (?-1900)

Entering the Union army after Lincoln's summer 1862 call for more troops, Ohio-born Illinois resident Caleb J. Dilworth rose to brigade command and was brevetted brigadier general for the battle of Atlanta. His assignments included: lieutenant colonel, 85th Illinois (August 27, 1862); colonel, 85th Illinois (June 26, 1863); commanding 3rd Brigade, 2nd Division, 14th Corps, Army of the Cumberland (June 27-September 1, 1864); and commanding 2nd Brigade, 1st Separate Division, District of the Etowah, Department of the Cumberland (March 7-June 1, 1865). His regiment was at Perryville but was guarding the trains during the battle of Murfreesboro. He led his regiment during the Tullahoma Campaign and, as part of the Reserve Corps, at Chickamauga played a key role on the second day. After fighting at Chattanooga he entered upon the drive on Atlanta. At Kennesaw Mountain he took part in the futile charges ordered by Sherman. The brigade commander Daniel McCook was mortally wounded and his successor was also struck. Dilworth took over and held the command for over two months until he was apparently wounded at Jonesboro. In the meantime he had won his brevet in the battle of Atlanta proper. Upon his return to duty, he commanded a brigade in Tennessee and was then mustered out with his regiment on June 5, 1865.

DIMICK, Justin (ca. 1800-1871)

In a military career spanning half a century, Justin Dimick rose from a cadet during the War of 1812 to the rank of brevet brigadier general. The Connecticut native had received his appointment to West Point from Vermont and graduated in 1819. He served two years in the light artillery before being assigned to the artillery branch. He won a brevet for his Seminole fighting. For a time he taught infantry tactics at his alma mater and also served on the frontier. During the war with Mexico he was wounded at Chapultepec and won two more brevets. At the outbreak of the Civil War he was commanding at Fortress Monroe on the tip of Virginia's Peninsula. His wartime assignments included: lieutenant colonel, 2nd Artillery (since October 5, 1857); commanding Fortress Monroe (1860-61); colonel, 1st Artillery (October 26, 1861); and commanding Fort Warren prison camp (1861-January 1, 1864). He was in charge of fitting out the Fort Sumter relief expedition and was then assigned to Boston Harbor and placed in charge of the prisoner of war camp at Fort Warren, which held some of the more important civilian and military prisoners. Although he was officially retired on August 1, 1863, he retained command of the prison until the beginning of the next year. On March 13, 1865, he was brevetted brigadier general for his long career.

DIVEN, Charles Worth (?-1889)

The high point in the Civil War career of Mexican War veteran Charles W. Diven came at Fort Stedman on the Petersburg lines. He had served earlier in the war as an enlisted man in a volunteer unit from his native Pennsylvania. The lawyer's military assignments included: captain, 12th Pennsylvania Cavalry (June 25, 1861); major, 12th Pennsylvania Cavalry (April 19, 1864); colonel, 200th Pennsylvania (September 3, 1864); and commanding 1st Brigade, 3rd Division, 9th Corps, Army of the Potomac (December 15, 1864-February 11, 1865 and March 7-April 3, 1865). After service in the vicinity of the nation's capital the regiment took part in the battle of Antietam. Serving in the Shenandoah Valley the next year he got caught up in the defeat at 2nd Winchester. Mustered out on June 11, 1864, to engage in recruiting, he returned to the field as a colonel that fall. After brief service with the Army of the James facing Richmond his unit was transferred to the Army of the Potomac and the Petersburg trenches. He was in brigade command when Lee tried to break Grant's stranglehold on the city at Fort Stedman. The attack was a surprise to the first Union line but Diven and his brigade are given much credit for the repulse of the Confederates. Diven himself was wounded in the action. Brevetted brigadier general for Petersburg, he was honorably discharged on May 18, 1865. Resuming his law practice, he also engaged in railroading.

DIVERS, Bridget (?-?)

When in the summer of 1861 the 1st Michigan Cavalry was formed, Bridget Divers followed her husband into the unit as a vivandière—or a combination cook, nurse and laundrywoman who usually served with troops of foreign extraction. She found military life so much to her liking that she remained with the regular army after the war. An apparent native of Ireland, she did not shrink in times of danger and frequently had horses shot out from under her, was surrounded by the enemy, or rallied the regiment. Becoming an employee of the United States Sanitary Commission, she was attached to the Michigan Cavalry Brigade, which gained fame under George A. Custer. Remaining in the field even after the wounding of her husband, she was at Cedar Creek. Not wishing to leave the army after Appomattox, she became a laundress for the regulars on the frontier. By this time she was known variously as Irish Bridget and Michigan Bridget.

DIX, Dorothea Lynde (1802-1887)

For more than two decades before the Civil War reformer Dorothea Lynde Dix was a leader in the movement to improve the lot of prisoners, the insane, and the mentally ill. With the coming of the war she took time out from these pursuits to offer her services as a nurse. On May 29, 1861, Secretary of War Simon Cameron appointed her as the superintendent of the nursing corps. She had to fight the prejudice of the day—that women were not fit to be nurses. Her system for the use of nurses reflects this view. Appointees had to be plain-looking and over 30 years of age. Unadorned black or brown dresses without hoops were to be uniform. Following many threats to her authority during the course of the war, she returned to her earlier reform movements. (Marshall, Helen, E., *Dorothea Dix, Forgotten Samaritan*)

DIX, John Adams (1798-1879)

A veteran of the War of 1812, John A. Dix was called back into service for the Civil War. Born in New Hampshire, he had entered the army as ensign, 14th Infantry, during the War of 1812 and emerged as a second lieutenant of artillery. He remained in the regular army until his 1828 retirement as captain, 3rd Artillery. He was admitted to the bar in the nation's capital and managed his father-in-law's affairs before becoming influential in New York State politics and railroading. He served in the Senate and his antislavery views led him to switch from the Democratic to the Republican Party in 1859. As Buchanan's last treasury secretary, his order to New Orleans that "If anyone attempts to haul down the American flag, shoot him on the spot," has gone down in history. Reentering the military, his assignments included: major general USV (May 16, 1861); commanding Department of Maryland (July 19-25, 1861); commanding Department of Pennsylvania (July 25-August 24, 1861); commanding division, Baltimore, Division and Department of the Potomac (August 24, 1861-March 22, 1862); commanding Middle Department (March 22-June 9, 1862); commanding Department of Virginia (June 17, 1862-July 15, 1863); also commanding 7th Corps, Department of Virginia (July 22, 1862-July 16, 1863); and commanding Department of the East (July 18, 1863-June 27, 1865). The senior officer in the volunteer service throughout the war, he was considered too old for active field command and was assigned to departmental posts. At first he commanded the old Department of Annapolis—then Maryland—which was merged into that of Pennsylvania. Merged into the Division of the Potomac after 1st Bull Run, he was given charge of the division guarding Baltimore. He then commanded the forces operating from Fortress Monroe in eastern Virginia. After the draft riots he was given command of the Department of the East with headquarters in New York City. He held this post until the end of the war and resigned on November 30, 1865. He was subsequently a diplomat in France and a governor of his adopted state, New York. (Dix, Morgan, comp., *Memoirs of John Adams Dix*)

"Shoot him on the spot" John A. Dix. (*Leslie's*)

DIXON, George E. (?-1864)

An army officer, Lieutenant George E. Dixon, gave his life in command of the first successful sinking of a vessel by a submarine. While serving with the 21st Alabama in the defenses of Mobile, Dixon was witness to some of the early trials of the *H.L. Hunley*, a submersible craft. In command of one trial, his crew of nine remained submerged for two hours and 35 minutes. Dixon maintained interest in the vessel despite its sinking in Mobile and at least three times in Charleston, with heavy loss of life including that of its inventor, Horace L. Hunley. With the loss of at least 33 lives, General Beauregard stopped further trials until Dixon requested permission to try again. But there was a condition imposed that required the vessel to remain only partially submerged. On February 17, 1864, Dixon, with eight men operating the crank propulsion system, made for the blockading fleet. The submarine's spar torpedo was detonated under the USS *Housatonic*, which quickly went to the bottom with the loss of five lives. But the *Hunley* was missing. The Confederate authorities long hoped that the crew had been captured or drifted out to sea and would yet return. It was not until after the war that the wreck was located next to the first victim of a submarine.

DIXON, James (1814-1873)

A moderate Republican senator from Connecticut, James Dixon was feared by many Radical Republicans for his influence over Lincoln. He had been admitted to the bar in his native state in 1834 and was speaker of the state legislature's lower house in 1837. He was also a member of that body the next year and in 1844. Also in 1844 he was elected to Congress as a Whig and served two terms. In 1854, back in the state legislature, he declined the nomination for governor and lost a bid for a Senate seat. Two years later he won the latter post as a Republican and was reelected once, serving from 1857 to 1869. Having joined the Democrats, he failed in his bid for a third term in 1868. He also lost a race for a seat in the House of Representatives the same year. Associated with William H. Seward, Montgomery

Blair, and Thurlow Weed during the Civil War years, he was despised by such radicals as Zachariah Chandler. In 1869 Dixon declined an appointment as minister to Russia and instead took to traveling and writing.

DOCKERY, Oliver Hart (1830-1906)

As the Civil War progressed, there was a growing Unionist sentiment in North Carolina, and it even affected some of the early volunteers like Oliver H. Dockery. A Wake Forest plantation owner, he entered the Confederate army in the first fall of the war and his assignments included: captain, Company E, 38th North Carolina (October 30, 1861) and lieutenant colonel, 38th North Carolina (January 17, 1862). After serving in North Carolina during the first winter of the war, he was defeated during the April 1862 reorganization elections. Gradually he became a Unionist and even claimed that he had really removed himself from the race because of a desire to support the federal government. After the war he became a scalawag serving in the Reconstruction state legislature and failed in a bid to become governor. He also represented his district in the U.S. Congress.

DOCKERY, Thomas Pleasant (1833-1898)

All of Thomas P. Dockery's service as a Confederate general was spent in the western theater. Born in North Carolina, he had been raised in Tennessee and Arkansas. His Civil War assignments included: colonel, 5th Arkansas State Troops (summer 1861); colonel, 19th Arkansas (May 12, 1862); commanding Middle Sub-District of Arkansas, District of Arkansas, Trans-Mississippi Department (late 1862); commanding Green's (old) Brigade, Bowen's Division, Department of Mississippi and East Louisiana (June 27-July 4, 1863); brigadier general, CSA (August 10, 1863); and commanding brigade, Fagan's Cavalry Division, District of Arkansas, Trans-Mississippi Department (April 1864). In command of a regiment of state troops he fought at Wilson's Creek and the next spring became colonel of a regiment of Arkansas troops in Confederate service. Crossing the Mississippi he took part in the defense of Corinth and that fall fought in the battle there. During the siege of Vicksburg he succeeded Martin E. Green, who had been killed, in brigade command. Captured upon the fall of the city, he was paroled the same day and later exchanged. In the spring of 1864 he commanded a cavalry brigade at Jenkin's Ferry, an action in the effort to drive back Steele's campaign in support of Nathaniel P. Banks in Louisiana. In the postwar years he was a civil engineer in Texas.

DODD, David Owen (1846-1864)

Given a last-minute reprieve from his scheduled execution as a Confederate spy, if he would reveal the names of his accomplices, Arkansan David O. Dodd refused to betray a trust and instead went to the gallows. Born in Texas, he was only 17 at the time of his hanging. With the capture of Little Rock, the family home, Dodd's father returned secretly to smuggle the family to Mississippi. However, the elder Dodd left behind some unfinished business and sent his son back to tie up the loose ends. It is not known how he also came to be given a spying assignment, but on his return journey to the Confederate lines young Dodd was taken in for questioning by Union pickets. In his possession they found a small pocket notebook that included a page in Morse Code (young Dodd had previously worked as a telegraph operator). Deciphered, the message proved to be a report on the strength of Union forces in the Little Rock area. Tried on the last day of 1863, he was found guilty and sentenced to hang. At the last moment Union General Frederick Steele offered Dodd his life in return for the names of those who had aided him in gathering the intelligence. The reply, "I can die, but I cannot betray the trust of a friend," were his last words. The bungled hanging took eight minutes. There is speculation that the "friend" was his girlfriend, Mary Dodge, who was quickly sent to her former Vermont home by special government transport.

DODGE, Charles Cleveland (1841-1910)

Due to problems with his superiors and a feeling of having been passed over in command appointments, Union Brigadier General Charles C. Dodge resigned his commission on June 12, 1863. A native of New Jersey, he entered the army in the war's first year at age 20. His assignments included: captain, 1st New York Mounted Rifles (December 10, 1861); major, 1st New York Mounted Rifles (January 3, 1862); lieutenant colonel, 1st New York Mounted Rifles (July 1, 1862); colonel, 1st New York Mounted Rifles (August 13, 1862); and brigadier general, USV (November 29, 1862). As a company and field grade officer, he served in southeastern Virginia and fought in the Suffolk Campaign against James Longstreet. While he served in the Department of Virginia's Division at Suffolk, neither the divisional leader, John J. Peck, nor the department head, John A. Dix, wanted Dodge to head the division's cavalry. Resenting the appointment of fellow Colonel Samuel P. Spear to the post, he quit the army. Nonetheless he volunteered his services during the draft rioting in New York City and was accepted. He was subsequently with his family's Phelps Dodge Corporation and in canal construction.

DODGE, Grenville Mellen (1831-1916)

In addition to some active combat roles, Grenville M. Dodge spent much of the Civil War in garrison duty and appropriately, considering his prewar career in railroad engineering, in repairing and guarding railroads. The Massachusetts native and civil engineer entered the military at the beginning of the Civil War and held the following assignments: colonel, 4th Iowa (July 6, 1861); commanding 1st Brigade, Army of Southwest Missouri, Department of the Missouri (January-February 1862); commanding 1st Brigade, 4th Division, same army and department (February-May 1862); brigadier general, USV (March 21, 1862); commanding District of Mississippi, Department of the Tennessee (September 29-October 5, 1862); commanding 4th Division, District of Jackson, Army of West Tennessee (October 5-30, 1862); commanding 4th Division, Right

Wing, 13th Corps, Army of the Tennessee (October 30-November 11, 1862); commanding District of Corinth, 13th Corps (November 11-December 18, 1862); 17th Corps (December 18, 1862-January 20, 1863), and 16th Corps (January 20-March 18, 1863), Army of the Tennessee (March 18-August 12, 1863); commanding Left Wing, same corps and army (July 7-August and October 15, 1863-August 19, 1864); major general, USV (June 7, 1864); and commanding Department of the Missouri (December 9, 1864-July 1865). Wounded in the battle of Pea Ridge, he returned to perform garrison duty in Tennessee and Mississippi and rebuild railroads during the Chattanooga Campaign. He was in command of that portion of the corps that fought through the Atlanta Campaign and became embroiled in a dispute with General Thomas W. Sweeny, one of his subordinates, which had originated in the District of Corinth and finally came to a climax during the campaign in Georgia. Dodge survived Sweeny's physical assault but received a head wound on August 19, 1864, during the siege. When he returned to duty he was given command west of the Mississippi and served there till the close of the war. Resigning on May 30, 1866, he became one of the principal movers in the construction of America's railroads and served a term as a congressman. (Perkins, J.R., *Trails, Rails and War; the Life of General G.M. Dodge.*)

DOHERTY, Edward P. (?-1897)

As commander of the cavalry detachment that captured the mortally wounded John Wilkes Booth, 1st Lieutenant Edward P. Doherty received as a reward promotion to captain, and $5,250—and later secured a regular army commission. The Canada native was residing in New York at the outbreak of the Civil War and promptly joined a militia regiment. His assignments included: private, Company A, 71st New York Militia (April 20, 1861); first lieutenant, 16th New York Cavalry (September 12, 1863); captain, 16th New York Cavalry (April 23, 1865); captain, 3rd New York Provisional Cavalry (June 23, 1865); second lieutenant, 5th Cavalry (April 19, 1866); and first lieutenant, 5th Cavalry (March 1, 1867). His regiment fought at 1st Bull Run in Burnside's Brigade before being mustered out on August 9, 1861. Two years later he joined a new cavalry regiment, which performed its entire service in the Washington defenses. However, Doherty was praised for his role in an 1864 scout to the Rapidan. Then on April 24, 1865, he was ordered to report, with a detail of 25 enlisted men, to the Washington offices of Lafayette C. Baker in order to search for Lincoln's assassin. Two days later they caught up with Booth and David Herold on the Virginia farm of Richard H. Garrett. Herold gave himself up, but Booth refused to come out and either shot himself or was shot by Sergeant Boston Corbett after the tobacco shed had been set on fire. Taking their prisoner and the assassin's corpse back to the capital, Doherty and his men received their rewards. Doherty's regiment was merged with the 13th New York Cavalry to form the 3rd New York Provisional Cavalry, which was mustered out on September 21, 1865. Seven months later he joined the regular cavalry and served until mustered out in late 1870.

DOLES, George Pierce (1830-1864)

A Georgia businessman, George P. Doles had been active in the militia before the war and was captain of the Baldwin Blues, which enlisted shortly after the fall of Fort Sumter. Doles led them and his later assignments included: captain, Company H, 4th Georgia (April 1861); colonel, 4th Georgia (April 26, 1861); commanding brigade D.H. Hill's-Rodes' Division, 2nd Corps, Army of Northern Virginia (September 17, 1862-June 2, 1864); and brigadier general, CSA (November 1, 1862). After serving in the Norfolk area, Doles led his regiment to the Peninsula where they saw action at Seven Pines and in the Seven Days. Having distinguished himself in the defense along South Mountain, he succeeded to command of the brigade when General R.S. Ripley was wounded at Antietam. Promoted to brigadier six weeks later and given permanent charge of the brigade, he led it at Fredericksburg, Chancellorsville, Gettysburg, and the Wilderness. At Spotsylvania, despite his vigilance, a large number of his men and a battery were captured when Union troops under Emory Upton made a sudden assault on his lines on May 10. Doles fought through the rest of the battle and the actions at the North Anna. Countering Grant's next side step toward Richmond, Doles was killed by a sniper at Bethesda Church while checking his lines on June 2, 1864. (Thomas, Henry W., *A History of the Doles-Cook Brigade, Army of Northern Virginia*)

DONEHOGAWA

See: *Parker, Ely Samuel*

DONELSON, Daniel Smith (1801-1863)

Five days after his death the man who had given his name to the Cumberland River fort, Daniel S. Donelson, was promoted to major general, apparently when the authorities in Richmond were not yet aware of his demise. The Tennessee native and West Pointer (1825) had served less than a year when he resigned as a second lieutenant in the 3rd Artillery. A planter and politician, he was the speaker of the lower house of the state legislature at the outbreak of the Civil War. In the meantime he had been active in the militia and his assignments included: brigadier general, Tennessee Militia (prewar); adjutant general, Provisional Army of Tennessee (May 9, 1861); brigadier general CSA (July 9, 1861); commanding 3rd Brigade, Army of Northwestern Virginia (summer-December 16, 1861); commanding brigade, Department of South Carolina and Georgia (December 1861-spring 1862); commanding 1st Brigade, 2nd (Cheatham's) Division, 1st Corps, Army of the Mississippi (spring-July 2, 1862); commanding 1st Brigade, Cheatham's Division, Army of the Mississippi (July 2-August 15, 1862); commanding 1st Brigade, Cheatham's Division, Right Wing, Army of the Mississippi (August 15-November 20, 1862); temporarily commanding the division (October 8, 1862); commanding 1st Brigade, Cheatham's Division, Polk's Corps, Army of Tennessee (November 20, 1862-January 17, 1863); commanding Department of East Tennessee (January 17-April 17, 1863); and major general, CSA (April 22, 1863 to rank from January 17). While serving the state forces he determined the location for Fort Donelson and, following his commission in the Confederate service, he led a brigade under Lee in the Rich Mountain Campaign in western Virginia. Late in the year his brigade was transferred to the South Carolina coast and in the spring joined Bragg's army in Mississippi. For the balance of his life Donelson was to serve under Bragg and to earn his respect. Taking part in the Kentucky Campaign in the fall of 1862, he was in temporary command of a division at Perryville. He resumed command of his brigade and led it at Murfreesboro. Shortly after that action he was assigned to command in East Tennessee with a recommendation for promotion to major general. However, on April 17, 1863, he died of disease at Montvale Springs, Tennessee. Five days later he was confirmed at the higher grade by the Confederate Senate, back-dated to his assumption of departmental command.

DOOLITTLE, Charles Camp (1832-1903)

As a colonel, Charles C. Doolittle played a key role in the defeat of Hood's invasion of Tennessee in late 1864. Born in Vermont, he was raised in Canada and New York. He was an employee of a glassworks when the Civil War came and he enlisted. His assignments included: first lieutenant, 4th Michigan (June 30, 1861); captain, 4th Michigan (August 20, 1861); colonel, 18th Michigan (August 13, 1862); commanding 3rd Brigade, 1st Division, Army of Kentucky, Department of the Ohio (October 1862); commanding 3rd Brigade, District of Central Kentucky, Department of the Ohio (January-April 1863); commanding 3rd Brigade, 2nd Division, Reserve Corps, Army of the Cumberland (June 8-August 10, 1863); commanding 1st Brigade, 3rd Division, 23rd Corps, Army of the Ohio (December 14, 1864-January 13, 1865); commanding the division (January 13-14, 1865); brigadier general, USV (January 27, 1865); and commanding 1st Brigade, 3rd Division, 4th Corps, Army of the Cumberland (May 15-June 2, 1865). His first regiment served with the Army of the Potomac fighting at Yorktown and the Seven Days, having already seen action at 1st Bull run. He then transferred to a new unit that was assigned to duty in Kentucky opposing the raids of Confederate cavalry under John Pegram and Joseph Wheeler. For a time the regiment was part of the provost guard at Nashville. Sent into the field, he played a prominent role at Decatur, Alabama, diverting Hood to a crossing of the Tennessee at Tuscumbia. This delay was crucial in the defeat of the Confederate invasion of Tennessee. At Nashville he commanded a brigade and the next month was made a brigadier general. For his war service he was brevetted major general was mustered out on November 30, 1865. He was a bank cashier in Ohio after the war.

DOOLITTLE, James Rood (1815-1897)

During the 1850s James R. Doolittle left the Democratic Party because of its failure to maintain the Missouri Compromise, but by the winter of 1860-61 he felt that it was too late to extend the line to the Pacific, as proposed in the Crittenden Compromise. He had been admitted to the bar in his native New York in 1837 and served three years as a district attorney before moving to Wisconsin in 1851. There he served three years as a judge before resigning to become a Republican senator. Reelected once, he served from 1857 to 1869. As a member of the Senate's Committee of Thirteen he voted against that portion of Crittenden's proposal calling for the extension of the line of the Missouri Compromise and so permanently delineating free and slave territory. Returning to the Democratic fold, he lost a race for governor in 1871 and set up his practice in Chicago where he became a law professor of the University of Chicago.

D'ORLEANS, Louis Philippe Albert

See: *Paris, Louis Philippe Albert d'Orleans, Comte de*

D'ORLEANS, Robert

See: *Chartres, Robert d'Orleans, Duc de*

DORTCH, William Theophilus (1824-1889)

A wealthy North Carolina lawyer and planter, William T. Dortch was serving as the speaker of the state legislature's lower houses during the secession crisis. Although professing an attachment to the Union, Dortch actually worked with the immediate secessionists during the crisis winter. He did not, however, attend the state's secession convention. In late 1861, a deadlocked state legislature named Dortch as a compromise appointee to the Senate of the First Regular Confederate Congress. He was assigned to the committees on: Accounts; Commerce; Naval Affairs; and Engrossment and Enrollment, being chairman of the latter. He often served as a liaison between the central government and North Carolina's touchy governor Zebulon Vance. While working to strengthen the war effort, Dortch did try to protect local rights from excessive measures being used indiscriminately. His was one of the few North Carolina legislative voices to oppose peace negotiations. After the war Dortch rebuilt his law practice and his plantation, served in the state legislature, was a railroad director, and supervised the revision of the state's laws.

DOUBLEDAY, Abner (1819-1893)

A career artillerist, West Pointer (1842) Abner Doubleday fired the first Union shot in response to the Confederate attack on Fort Sumter but later in the war was found wanting and removed from field command. Following the surrender of the fort, where as captain, Company E, 1st Artillery, he was the senior company commander, he was made a major in the newly organized 17th Infantry on May 14, 1861. His later assignments included: brigadier general, USV (February 3, 1862); commanding an independent brigade in the Department of the Rappahannock (May-June 26, 1862); commanding 2nd Brigade, 1st Division, in the 3rd Corps, Army of Virginia (June 26-August 30, 1862); and in the 1st Corps, Army of the Potomac (September 12-14 and December 22-28, 1862 and January 4-18, 1863); commanding the division (August 30-September 12 and September 14-December 22, 1862 and January 2-4, 1863); major general, USV (November 29, 1862); commanding 3rd Division, 1st

Corps, Army of the Potomac (January 18-February 3, February 5-June 30, and July 2-11, 1863); and commanding the corps (July 1-2, 1863). Given command of a brigade, Doubleday took part in the fights at 2nd Bull Run and South Mountain. In both actions he assumed divisional command and he continued in that capacity at Antietam and Fredericksburg. Commanding another division at Chancellorsville and Gettysburg, he took over the corps upon the death of General Reynolds on the first day of the latter battle. The next day he was relieved by General Newton, his junior, and returned to his division. Nine days later, he was relieved of field duty. For the rest of the war he served in Washington except for a stint in Buffalo trying to prevent trouble during the draft. He was brevetted major general in the regular army for Antietam, Gettysburg, and the war. His alleged invention of baseball has been refuted. He remained in the army until 1873. During the war he became so known for his deliberate and slow-moving actions that he was dubbed "Old Forty-eight Hours" because he seemed to act as if there were that many hours in a day. He wrote *Reminiscences of Forts Sumter and Moultrie in 1860-1861* and *Chancellorsville and Gettysburg.*

DOUGLAS, Henry Kyd (1838-1903)

A veteran of the campaigns in the Shenandoah Valley and with the Army of Northern Virginia, Henry Kyd Douglas had served on the staffs of Generals Jackson, Edward Johnson, Gordon, and Early before being assigned to the command of a brigade at the close of the war. Time ran out before he could be commissioned a brigadier general. He had studied law before returning to his hometown of Shepherdstown, Virginia, to enlist in the Confederate army. His assignments included: private, Company B, 2nd Virginia (April 1861); corporal, Company B, 2nd Virginia (1861); sergeant, Company B, 2nd Virginia (1861); second lieutenant, Company B, 2nd Virginia (August 1861); assistant inspector general, Valley District, Department of Northern Virginia (spring-June 1862); assistant inspector general, Jackson's Command, Army of Northern Virginia (June-November 11, 1862); captain, Company B, 2nd Virginia (ca. November 11, 1862); major and assistant adjutant general (May 1863); assistant adjutant general, Johnson's Division, 2nd Corps, Army of Northern Virginia (May-July 1863 and May 1864); assistant adjutant general, Gordon's Division, 2nd Corps, Army of Northern Virginia (May 1864); assistant adjutant general, Early's Division, 2nd Corps, Army of Northern Virginia (May 1864); assistant adjutant general, 2nd Corps, Army of Northern Virginia (May-June 1864); assistant adjutant general, Valley District, Department of Northern Virginia (June-December 1864); assistant adjutant general, 2nd Corps, Army of Northern Virginia (December 1864-March 1865); and commanding Walker's (old) Brigade, Ramseur's (old) Division, 2nd Corps, Army of Northern Virginia (March-April 1865). As an enlisted man he served at Harpers Ferry and fought at 1st Bull Run. Promoted to a lieutenancy, he joined Stonewall Jackson's staff in the spring of 1862 and served at Kernstown and during the Shenandoah Valley Campaign of 1862. He then fought at Cedar Mountain, 2nd Bull Run, Harpers Ferry, and Antietam before being given the captaincy of his old company. As such he fought at Fredericksburg and Chancellorsville. He then joined Johnson's staff as adjutant until his wounding and capture at Gettysburg. Not released until March 1864 he served successively on the staffs of Johnson, Gordon, and Early. He took part in the Overland, Shenandoah Valley, and Petersburg campaigns. Shortly before the Appomattox Campaign he was assigned to command of a Virginia brigade with the unfulfilled intention that he be made a brigadier general. During this campaign he suffered the last two of his six wartime wounds. Arrested after the surrender, he was a witness at the trial of the Lincoln conspirators through his acquaintance with some suspects. Long after the war he wrote a lively account of his war experiences, *I Rode With Stonewall.*

DOUGLAS, Stephen Arnold (1813-1861)

Although he had twice already been a serious contender for the Democratic nomination for president, in 1852 and 1856, Stephen Douglas finally received the nod in 1860, only to suffer the division of his party and defeat at the hands of the new Republican Party. Born in Vermont, he moved to Illinois where he was instrumental in the organization of the Democratic Party and practiced law for a year before entering the state legislature and later becoming a state supreme court judge. Elected to Congress in 1842, he moved to the Senate in 1847. In both houses, as chairman of the Committee on Territories, he supported expansion, a transcontinental railroad, the Mexican War, and a free land policy. Although he wished slavery would disappear, he steadfastly maintained that it was the right of the people in a given territory to decide whether or not they wanted to admit the institution. This popular sovereignty theory was not satisfactory to either side. In 1858 Douglas debated another Illinois lawyer, Abraham Lincoln, for his Senate seat. Douglas won, but the series of debates raised Lincoln to national prominence. Douglas' introduction of the Kansas-Nebraska Bill, which nullified the Missouri Compromise provision prohibiting slavery in the Louisiana Purchase territories, and support of the earlier Compromise of 1850, linked him too closely with the South for many Northerners. Appalled by the pro-slavery Lecompton Constitution for Kansas, which did not have the support of the majority and therefore was in violation of his principle of popular sovereignty, Douglas enunciated his Freeport Doctrine, declaring that the populace could enact local ordinances unfriendly to slavery. This earned him the enmity of many Southern Democrats, and in 1858 they engineered his removal from the chairmanship of the Committee on Territories. Finally achieving his goal of the Democratic presidential nomination in 1860, his position was undercut by the dissatisfied Southerners who bolted and nominated John C. Breckinridge. With the party divided, and in a four-way race, Lincoln was elected. Returning to the Senate from the campaign trail, Douglas tried to arrange a compromise even after a number of states had seceded. Once Fort Sumter had been fired upon and war had begun, he rallied to the support of the administration and urged the same patriotic spirit from Illinois Democrats. Thoroughly defeated by the failures of his policies, he died in Chicago on June 3, 1861, before the war had begun in earnest. He may have preferred it that way. (Johannsen, Robert W., *Stephen A. Douglas*)

DOUGLASS, Frederick (1817-1895)

Although his experiences as a Maryland slave were relatively fortunate—he was taught to read and write by his mistress—Frederick Augustus Washington Bailey made good his escape and, changing his name to Frederick Douglass, became one of the leading champions of his race in the antebellum period. Three years after his 1838 journey to freedom, Douglass, living in New Bedford, Massachusetts, made an address before the Massachusetts Anti-Slavery Society. In the audience was the abolitionist William Lloyd Garrison who hired him as one of the society's speakers. Douglass eventually broke with Garrison over the latter's steadfast belief in non-resistance and opposition to working in the political parties. Another strain with the Garrisonians was over Douglass' allowing, while in Britain, a group of friends to purchase his freedom from slavery so that he would not have to fear arrest as a fugitive. This was felt by many to be tacit recognition of the institution. In 1847 Douglass founded *The North Star* in Rochester, New York, to further the progress of the Negro. Having known John Brown for a decade, he was sympathetic to his planned raid on Harpers Ferry but thought it impractical. Following the raid Douglass fled to Canada and Europe. Returning to the United States, he tried to convince the Lincoln administration to make the Civil War a war on slavery and to enlist freed blacks in the military. With the eventual acceptance of both causes, Douglass launched into the raising of black regiments for the Union army, a task at which he was highly successful. After the war he was allied with the Radical Republicans and remained loyal to Grant in the party split of 1872. As a reward, he served in a number of governmental posts including: federal marshal of the District of Columbia, recorder of deeds, and minister to Haiti. He continued to lobby for the improvement of conditions for the freed slaves until his death. (Huggins, Nathan Irwin, *Slave and Citizen: The Life of Frederick Douglass*)

Frederick Douglass, escaped slave and abolitionist. (NA)

DOUGLASS, Joseph Beeler (?-?)

As an officer of the Missouri enrolled militia, Kentucky-born Joseph B. Douglas dealt with guerrillas and Confederate incursions into the state, especially that of Sterling Price in 1864. His assignments included: colonel, 1st Missouri Provisional Enrolled Militia (1861); brigadier general, Missouri Enrolled Militia (September 1, 1864); commanding 8th Military District, Missouri Enrolled Militia (late 1863-early 1865); also commanding 9th Military District, Missouri Enrolled Militia (December 1863). He was mustered out on March 12, 1865.

DOUGLASS, Marcellus (1830-1862)

Although his military service was relatively brief, Marcellus Douglass did manage to serve in three theaters of operation. Following attendance at the Georgia secession convention he entered the Confederate army. His assignments included: captain, Company E, 13th Georgia (June 19, 1861); lieutenant colonel, 13th Georgia (July 8, 1861); colonel, 13th Georgia (February 1, 1862); and commanding Lawton's Brigade, Ewell's Division, Jackson's Corps, Army of Northern Virginia (August 28-September 17, 1862). He served in the Kanawha Valley, in what is now West Virginia, in the latter part of 1861 before his unit was recalled to protect the Georgia coast. Then in June 1862 when Robert E. Lee was trying to scratch together enough men for the defense of Richmond, the 13th, as part of Lawton's brigade, returned to Virginia. As a part of Jackson's Division they fought through the Seven Days with Douglass at their head. Serving in Ewell's Division, Douglass fought at 2nd Bull Run and assumed command of the brigade when Lawton took over the division from the wounded Ewell. He held this position through the rest of the battle and during the Maryland invasion, including participation in the capture of Harpers Ferry. At Antietam he was struck down by enemy fire, dying before he could earn a permanent promotion.

DOUTY, Jacob (?-?)

A lieutenant in the 48th Pennsylvania, a regiment made up in large part of miners, Jacob Douty accompanied Lieutenant Colonel Pleasants and Sergeant Henry Reese into the mine tunnel at Petersburg early on the morning of July 30, 1864. In the 510-foot tunnel Pleasants lit the fuse to the four tons of powder that would blow up that portion of the Confederate lines known as Elliott's Salient. The three men scampered out of the shaft at 3:15 A.M. An hour later nothing had happened. Douty and Reese went back in to examine the fuse. It had gone out at a splicing point. Reese went for a knife to fix it while the lieutenant waited. Finally the fuse was relit, the two men raced for safety, and at 4:44 the powder exploded, killing and wounding some 278 South Carolinians. But Jacob Douty's courage was not rewarded with a Union victory; instead, through Union bungling and deft Confederate countermoves, the follow-up assault became a debacle and the siege of Petersburg was destined to continue for another eight months. (Pleasants, Henry, Jr., *The Tragedy of the Crater*)

DOW, Neal (1804-1897)

For his role in the Civil War Neal Dow was ousted from the Quaker Church. A businessman, he served as mayor of his native Portland, Maine, and was largely responsible for the state becoming dry in 1884. His military assignments included: colonel, 13th Maine (November 23, 1861); brigadier general, USV (April 28, 1862); commanding District of West Florida, Department of the Gulf (October 2, 1862-January 24, 1863); and commanding 1st Brigade, 2nd Division, 19th Corps, Department of the Gulf (February 26-May 27, 1863). In the movement on New Orleans he survived a shipping mishap off the North Carolina coast and was not present for the capture of the Crescent City. Promoted to brigadier shortly after the fall of Pensacola, he commanded there for a number of months. Taking part in the operations against Port Hudson he was twice severely wounded in the failed assault on May 27, 1863. During his convalescence he fell into enemy hands and was confined in Libby Prison until the next winter, when he was finally exchanged for Robert E. Lee's son, W.H.F. "Rooney" Lee. He never regained his health and resigned effective November 30, 1864. Resuming his anti-alcohol campaign after the war, he ran as a prohibitionist candidate for President in 1880.

DOWLING, Richard W. (ca. 1848-1867)

A native of County Galway, Ireland, Dick Dowling commanded the only Confederate soldiers to receive a medal for valor. Entering the Confederate service, he was appointed a first lieutenant in the Davis Guards on August 13, 1861. His first service was along the Rio Grande. In October 1862, the company became Company F, 1st Texas Heavy Artillery. On January 1, 1863, Dowling saw his first action in the attack on Galveston Island. Sent to Sabine Pass, Dowling and his men were placed upon two steamers, the *Uncle Ben* and the *Josiah H. Bell*, and sent out to attack the Union blockaders, two of which, the *Morning Light* and *Velocity*, were captured on January 21. Returning to shore he continued to serve in the defenses of the pass until September 8, 1863, when a Union expedition up the Sabine River was stopped by Dowling and 42 others—with only six guns—from their mud earthwork, Fort Griffin. The first wave of the Union fleet was composed of four gunboats and seven transports carrying the first of some 4,000 trooops. After an artillery duel, the *Clifton* and *Sachem* surrendered, with about 200 prisoners, and the other two Union gunboats withdrew. The garrison received the thanks of the Confederate congress for stopping the invasion of southeastern Texas. Dowling continued with his company until July 28, 1864, when he was reported sick, but was paroled at Houston as a major on June 21, 1865. He died of yellow fever two years later in Houston where he was involved in the local gaslight company, real estate, and oil speculation. (Tolbert, Frank X., *Dick Dowling at Sabine Pass*)

DOWNER, William S. (?-?)

As the Civil War progressed, the Confederate capital became subject to Union cavalry raids, often without many regular line troops to defend it. As a result the Local Defense Troops were established utilizing the manpower employed by the various government agencies. Among those placed in these units were the workmen under William S. Downer at the Richmond Armory. He had been the superintendent of the armory since 1861 and when the 1st Virginia Local Defense Troops Battalion, or the "Armory Battalion," was organized in mid-1863 he was made its major and first commander. However, he was relieved on August 6, 1863, so that he could devote his full energies to the armory. He held this post for most of the war.

DOWNEY, John G. (1826-1894)

After serving only five days as lieutenant governor of California Democrat John G. Downey moved into the top executive position in the state on January 14, 1860, when his predecessor became a senator. A native of Ireland, he had immigrated to the West Coast during the Gold Rush and become a rancher. During his term of office there was talk of an independent Pacific Republic in the event of the breakup of the Union. However Union clubs sprang up throughout the state and the idea died. Downey left office upon the expiration of his term on January 10, 1862, and was an unsuccessful candidate for governor later that year. In the race for the newly authorized four-year term he was defeated by Frederick F. Low. He subsequently returned to ranching. (Hittell, Theodore, H., *History of California*)

DRAKE, Joseph (?-1878)

Capture of Fort Donelson ended the Confederate military career of Colonel Joseph Drake of the 4th Mississippi. Named to head the regiment in 1861, he commanded it at Fort Henry, and, after the initial bombardment by the Union fleet, he was ordered to move it over to Fort Donelson. There he was given command of a brigade in Johnson's Division (February 9-16, 1862). With the surrender of the fort, he was confined at Fort Warren in Boston Harbor. Exchanged on August 27, 1862, he was not reelected upon the reorganization of the regiment.

DRAYTON, Percival (1812-1865)

Despite being a native of South Carolina, the first state to secede, and having as a brother Confederate Brigadier General

Union Navy Captain Percival Drayton. (NA)

Thomas F. Drayton, Percival Drayton remained loyal to the Union and continued to serve in the Navy. His Civil War assignments included: commander, USN (since 1855); commanding *Pocahontas* (November 1861); captain, USN (1862); commanding *Passaic* (1862); fleet captain, West Gulf Blockading Squadron (1863-64); commanding *Hartford* (August 1864); and chief, Bureau of Navigation (1865). Commanding the first craft, he took part in the fight at Port Royal Sound and was subsequently promoted to captain and given command of a monitor. Transferring to Farragut's fleet, he was the commander of the admiral's flagship and also his fleet captain. In this capacity he took part in the battle of Mobile Bay. The next year he was transferred to a desk assignment in Washington where he died on August 4, 1865.

DRAYTON, Thomas Fenwick (1808-1891)

In order to dispose of a failed brigadier, Thomas F. Drayton, General Lee used the expedient of breaking up his brigade and leaving him without a command. He had graduated from West Point (1828) in the same class as Jefferson Davis and served eight years in the infantry before retiring to his South Carolina plantation. Although active in railroading and politics, as a state legislator, Drayton kept up his military interests through the local militia. Offering his services to the South, they included: brigadier general, CSA (September 25, 1861); commanding 3rd Military District, Department of South Carolina (September-November 1861); commanding 5th Military District of South Carolina, Department of South Carolina and Georgia (December 1861-early 1862); commanding 6th (known as 4th after May 28) Military District of South Carolina, Department of South Carolina, Georgia and Florida (early 1862-July 1862); commanding brigade, D.R. Jones' Division, 1st Corps, Army of Northern Virginia (August-September 1862); commanding brigade, McLaws' Division, same corps and army (September-November 26, 1862); commanding brigade, Price's Division, District of Arkansas, Trans-Mississippi Department (ca. August 26, 1863-January 11, 1864 and March 1864); commanding the division (January 11-March 1864 and March 16-April 1864); commanding Western Sub-District of Texas, District of Texas, New Mexico and Arizona, Trans-Mississippi Department (June 26-fall 1864); commanding Central Sub-District of Texas, same district and department (fall 1864-March 8, 1865); and also commanding 3rd Texas Cavalry Division, 3rd Corps, Trans-Mississippi Department (September 1864-March 8, 1865). Assigned to duty in South Carolina, he led the unsuccessful defense of Port Royal in November 1861. He joined Lee's army in August 1862 and promptly displayed an incapacity for command by failing to launch his brigade into the attack at 2nd Bull Run on time. After further poor showings at South Mountain and Antietam, his regiments were divided among three other brigadiers. Assigned to court duty, he returned to the field in Arkansas and later in Texas. The war ended while he was sitting on the court investigating the 1864 Missouri expedition of General Price. He was in insurance and farming after the war. (Freeman, Douglas S., *Lee's Lieutenants*)

DRED SCOTT

See: *Scott, Dred*

DREW, John (?-?)

Cherokee chief John Drew organized a regiment, the 1st Cherokee Mounted Rifles, when his nation seceded from the United States and allied itself with the Confederacy at the beheft of Albert Pike. He was commissioned colonel on October 4, 1861. Serving initially in the Indian Territory, today Oklahoma, his command proved of dubious value. In pursuit of loyal Creeks, who were fleeing to Union-controlled areas under their chief Opothleyohola, Drew's braves refused to attack when it was discovered that there were some Cherokees among them. Drew and his command formed part of Pike's Brigade at Pea Ridge but, having become dissatisfied with Confederate service and coming under Union artillery fire, they tried to defect to the enemy. Fighting broke out between them and Stand Watie's regiment of Cherokee Confederates. During the night following the first day's battle the regiment dispersed and headed home. Then in June 1862 a Union force of whites and Indians entered the Cherokee country and many of Drew's men joined the Union army, becoming part of the 3rd Indian Home Guard. Drew was humiliated by this defection and the following year was reported as negotiating his surrender with only some 40 followers. (Monaghan, Jay, *Civil War on the Western Border, 1854-1865*)

DROUYN De L'HUYS, Édouard (?-?)

When French Emperor Napoleon III found that his desire for intervention in the sectional conflict in America was not being furthered by his foreign minister, Édouard Thouvenel, he replaced the man on October 15, 1862, with Édouard Drouyn de L'Huys. Thought to be more conservative, and thus more amenable to an interventionist policy, the latter was entering the third of his four stints in ministerial posts. However, when he examined the situation he realized that the abstentionist policy of his predecessor was the prudent one for France. With the empire already involved in adventures in Italy and Mexico, he feared that further commitments across the Atlantic would be unwise, especially in the face of Bismarck's German threat. Thus he rode out the war across the ocean, keeping the country from becoming embroiled in the American conflict. (D'Harcourt, Bernard, *Diplomatie et diplomates, les quatre ministères de M. Drouyn de L'Huys*)

DUANE, James Chatham (1824-1897)

One of the top engineering officers in the Union army, James C. Duane became involved in a controversy over the parole and exchange of prisoners of war. The New Yorker had graduated third in his 1848 class at West Point and been posted to the engineers. In this capacity, he worked on river clearance and coastal defenses, taught at his alma mater, and went on the expedition against the Mormons in Utah. His Civil War-era assignments included: first lieutenant, Engineers (since July 1, 1855); captain, Engineers (August 6, 1861); and major, Engineers (March 3, 1864). In April 1861 he was in charge of the company of sappers and miners aboard the steamer *Atlantic* on the relief expedition to Fort Pickens in Pensacola Harbor. He took command of the Engineers Battalion before the Peninsula Campaign and was instrumental in laying bridges once it was under way. He then served as McClellen's chief engineer during the Maryland Campaign and upon his relief was dispatched to the Southern coast for the operations against Charleston. Recalled to the Army of Potomac in June 1863, he was captured by Jeb Stuart's cavalry in Maryland on the 28th. He was almost immediately paroled but the conditions were not considered binding by the U.S. authorities. This resulted in much correspondence. Duane later served with the Army of the Potomac in the campaign from the Rapidan River to the final surrender at Appomattox. He was brevetted through brigadier general for his services in this lengthy campaign. He remained in the regular army until his resignation as brigadier general and chief engineer in 1888.

DUBOSE, Dudley McIver (1834-1883)

A Georgia lawyer, Dudley M. DuBose rose rapidly in rank in the Confederate army. His assignments included: lieutenant, 15th Georgia (1861); captain, 15th Georgia (1862); colonel, 15th Georgia (1862); colonel, 15th Georgia (January 1863); brigadier general, CSA (November 16, 1864); and commanding Wofford's (old) Brigade, Kershaw's Division, 1st Corps, Army of Northern Virginia (December 5, 1864-April 6, 1865). As a junior officer he served in the Peninsular and 2nd Manassas campaigns. He fought at Antietam on the staff of his father-in-law, Brigadier General Robert Toombs. Promoted to the colonelcy of his regiment, he took part in the campaign under Longstreet in southeastern Virginia in early 1863. He rejoined the Army of Northern Virginia in time for Gettysburg where he was especially distinguished in extricating his command from virtual encirclement. Going west with Longstreet, he was wounded at Chickamauga but returned to duty for the Knoxville Campaign. Back in Virginia, his command fought through the Overland Campaign, at Richmond and Petersburg and in the Shenandoah. In the retreat from the trenches around Richmond, DuBose was captured at Sayler's Creek three days before Appomattox. He was not released until July after which he resumed the practice of law and served one term in the U.S. Congress.

DUDLEY, Nathan Augustus Monroe (1825-1910)

While engaged in commercial activities Nathan A.M. Dudley maintained an active interest in the militia of his native Massachusetts and, upon the enlargement of the regular army in 1855, he became a first lieutenant. His Civil War assignments included: first lieutenant, 10th Infantry (since March 3, 1855); captain, 10th Infantry (May 7, 1861); colonel, 30th Massachusetts (March 1, 1862); commanding 3rd Brigade, 1st division, 19th Corps, Department of the Gulf (January 12-July 10, 1863); commanding 1st Brigade, 1st Division, 19th Corps, Department of the Gulf (July 11-24, 1863); commanding 4th Brigade, Cavalry Division, Department of the Gulf (December 1863-April 18, 1864); commanding 1st Brigade, Cavalry Division, Department of the Gulf (June 30-July 3, 1864); major, 15th Infantry (September 13, 1864); commanding 3rd Brigade, 1st Division, 19th Corps, Army of the Shenandoah (October 26-November 1, 1864); commanding 1st Brigade, 1st Division, 19th Corps, Army of the Shenandoah (November 1-December 13, 1864); and commanding 2nd Brigade, 1st Sub-District, District of Middle Tennessee, Department of the Cumberland (March 1865-mid-1865). Transferring to the volunteer service, he took part in the capture of New Orleans. Continuing operations along the Mississippi, he took part in campaigning against Vicksburg, in defense of Baton Rouge and in the capture of Port Hudson. He earned regular army brevets for each of the latter two. He went with the 19th Corps of Virginia but apparently missed the major battles of the Shenandoah Valley Campaign. Brevetted brigadier of volunteers in early 1865 he commanded in central Tennessee and was mustered out of the volunteers on February 16, 1865. Reverting to his regular army rank of major, he remained in the service until his 1889 retirement as colonel, 1st Cavalry.

DUFFIÉ, Alfred Napoleon Alexander (1835-1880)

In many ways French career military man Alfred N.A. Duffié was too flashy for the American military. The Parisian was a graduate of St. Cyr and had served in Algiers, Senegal, the Crimea, and against the Austrians. In the United States for his health at the outbreak of the Civil War, he resigned his French commission and joined the Union army. Nicknamed "Nattie," his assignments included: captain, 2nd New York Cavalry (August 9, 1861); major, 2nd New York Cavalry (October 5, 1861); colonel, 1st Rhode Island Cavalry (July 6, 1862); commanding 1st Brigade, 2nd Division, Cavalry Corps, Army of the Potomac (February 16-26, 1863); commanding the division (May 16-June 11, 1863); brigadier general, USV (June 23, 1863); commanding 3rd Brigade, 3rd Division, Department of West Virginia (December 1863-April 26, 1864); commanding 1st Brigade, 2nd Cavalry Division, Department of West Virginia (April 26-June 6, 1864); and commanding 1st Cavalry Division, Department of West Virginia (June 9-October 20, 1864). His first regiment had originally been intended for the regular army but there was no statutory authorization for a seventh cavalry regiment. He led a new regiment at Cedar Mountain, 2nd Bull Run, and Kelly's Ford and a division at Brandy Station. Rewarded for these actions with a brigadier's star, he was sent to western Virginia and took part in numerous raids and in protecting the railroads. In the winter of 1863-64 he commanded a mixed brigade of infantry, cavalry, and artillery. However, a lack of discipline within his commands led him into conflicts with his superiors, Benjamin F. Kelley and Sheridan. Finally, on October 20, 1864, after having led his division in the Lynchburg Expedition, he was relieved of his command at Cumberland, Maryland. A few days later he foolishly rode ahead of a wagon train with only a small escort and was captured by Mosby's rangers. Sheridan was so outraged that he urged Duffié's immediate dismissal. Paroled in February 1865, he was exchanged two months later. However, he received no further commands before being mustered out on August 24, 1865. Later he served as U.S. consul in Cadiz, Spain, until his death.

DUKE, Basil C. (1815-?)

A border state physician, Basil C. Duke had sought to preserve the Union by supporting John Bell for the presidency in 1860, but once the Lower South had seceded he joined the Confederacy, despite the fact that Kentucky remained in the Union. He had received his medical training in Baltimore. His military assignments included: private, 5th Kentucky (1861); surgeon, 5th Kentucky (late 1861); and medical director, District of Abingdon, Department of Southwestern Virginia (ca. May 1862-May 1863). Serving in the mountain area of southwestern Virginia, eastern Kentucky, and east Tennessee, he was under the command of General Humphrey Marshall. Apparently he was recommended for a brigadier generalship. Following the war and settlement in Memphis, the former Whig became a democrat and resumed his private practice. (Cunningham, Horace Herndon, *Doctors in Gray*)

DUKE, Basil Wilson (1838-1916)

Kentuckian Basil W. Duke, brother-in-law of John H. Morgan, succeeded the fallen raider in command of the brigade, was promoted to Confederate brigadier general, and remained in the service until well after the flight of the government from Richmond had begun. Practicing law in St. Louis at the outbreak of the Civil War, he was a staunch secessionist and eventually returned to his native state and sought to raise a company. However, he ended up enlisting as a private in Morgan's Lexington Rifles. His assignments included: private, Morgan's Cavalry Company (1861); first lieutenant, Company A, Morgan's Kentucky Cavalry Squadron (October 1861), first lieutenant and acting adjutant, Morgan's Kentucky Cavalry Squadron (October 1861), lieutenant colonel, 2nd Kentucky Cavalry (June 1862); colonel, 2nd Kentucky Cavalry (December 7, 1862); commanding Morgan's Brigade, Department of Western Virginia and East Tennessee (September 4, 1864-April 10, 1865); brigadier general, CSA (September 15, 1864); and commanding brigade, Jefferson Davis' Escort (April-May 8, 1865). Wounded on the first day at Shiloh, he returned to take part in the Kentucky Campaign and join in on some of Morgan's famous raids. In the summer of 1863 he took part in the raid north of the Ohio river and was captured at Buffington Island, Ohio. Not exchanged until August 3, 1864, he rejoined Morgan just before he was killed, then took over the remnants of Morgan's command for the balance of the war. Promoted to brigadier general, he took most of the brigade to join Jefferson Davis when Lee surrendered and Richmond fell. For a time he escorted the remaining treasury of the Confederacy and then set off as a decoy to lure Union cavalry away from Davis' trail. In the postwar years he resumed his practice, sat in the legislature, and entered journalism. In matters relating to the war he served as as commissioner for the park at Shiloh and engaged in historical writing. (Duke, Basil Wilson, *Reminiscences of General Basil W. Duke, C.S.A.* and *Morgan's Cavalry*)

DUMONT, Ebenezer (1814-1871)

A native Indiana lawyer and state legislator, Ebenezer Dumont was a veteran of the state volunteers in the Mexican War as both a company and field grade officer. His Civil War assignments included: colonel, 7th Indiana (April 27, 1861); colonel, 7th Indiana (recommissioned in the three-year unit); brigadier general, USV (to rank from September 3, 1861); commanding 17th Brigade, Army of the Ohio (early December 1861); commanding 17th Brigade, 3rd Division, Army of the Ohio (December 22, 1861-March 21, 1862); commanding 12th Division, Army of the Ohio (September-November 5, 1862); and commanding 5th Division, Center, 14th Corps, Army of the Cumberland (November 5-December 11, 1862). In the first months of the war he served in western Virginia fighting in the Laurel Hill, Carrick's Ford, and Greenbrier operations. He then served in Kentucky opposing the raids of John Hunt Morgan. His division was not present at Perryville to face Bragg and E. Kirby Smith's invasion of the state. Two months after relinquishing command for medical reasons he resigned from the service. In the fall of 1862 he had been elected to the U.S. Congress from the Indianapolis area and so he took his seat at the beginning of the 38th Congress. He sat in the succeeding congress but did not seek election to the 40th. He died before he could become Grant's appointee as governor of the Idaho Territory.

DUNCAN, Johnson Kelly (1827-1862)

Residence in the South overrode Johnson K. Duncan's northern birth and led him into the Confederate army and up to the rank of brigadier general before his death. The native Pennsylvanian and West Pointer (1949) served on the frontier and in Florida before resigning in 1855 to engage in civil engineering in Louisiana. His Confederate assignments included: major, Artillery (ca. March 1861); colonel, Artillery (1861); commanding Coast Defenses, Department #1 (1861-April 28, 1862); brigadier general, CSA (January 7, 1862); commanding 4th Brigade, Reserve (Withers') Division, Right Wing, Army of the Mississippi (August-October 12, 1862); commanding the division (October 12-November 10, 1862); and chief of staff, Department #2 (November-December 18, 1862). In the early stages of the war he was placed in charge of the fortifications along the lower Mississippi (Forts Jackson and St. Philip). Taking overall charge of the defenses of the coasts of Alabama, Mississippi, and Louisiana, he was promoted to brigadier general early in 1862. With the majority of his organized units ordered north to Corinth, Mississippi, in the pre-Shiloh Confederate buildup there, he was left with inadequate means for defending the approaches to New Orleans. Obliged to surrender on April 28, 1862, he was declared exchanged on August 27, 1862, and was then given charge of an infantry brigade during the operations in Kentucky. After briefly commanding a division he became Bragg's staff chief but died of typhoid fever in Knoxville on December 18, 1862.

DUNGAN, Robert H. (1834-1903)

By the time that Robert H. Dungan took over the command of the old 2nd Brigade of Jackson's original division it had been reduced to the size of a single regiment, and it was soon consolidated into one. An educator before the war, Dungan entered the Confederate army and his assigments included: lieutenant, Company A, 48th Virginia (May 18, 1861); captain, Company A, 48th Virginia (April 21, 1862); lieutenant colonel, 48th Virginia (October 16, 1862); colonel, 48th Virginia (late 1863 to date from May 3, 1863); commanding Jones' 2nd Brigade, Johnson's Division, 2nd Corps, Army of Northern Virginia (July 2-3, 1863 and May 5-14, 1864); and commanding 21st, 25th, 42nd, 44th, 48th and 50th Virginia consolidated (May 14-late October 1864). As a company officer, he took part in the Cheat Mountain and Romney campaigns and fought at Kernstown and Cedar Mountain. In each of the latter two he was wounded. He returned to duty in time to be promoted and then suffer a third wound at Chancellorsville. On the second day at Gettysburg he succeeded to brigade command but was relieved the next day. He then served in the Bristoe and Mine Run campaigns and at the Wildnerness he took over the brigade again when General J.M. Jones was killed. After suffering heavily at Spotsylvania on May 12, the brigade was consolidated into a single regiment. Dungan commanded this field organization through Early's Shenandoah Valley Campaign seeing action at Monocacy, 3rd Winchester, Fisher's Hill, and Cedar Creek. He later commanded the remnants of the 48th at Petersburg and surrendered the command at Appomattox.

DUNLOP, George

See: *Peter, Walter*

DUNN, Ambrose C. (1835 or 1840-post 1907)

Twice thrown out of the Confederate army, Georgian Ambrose C. Dunn managed to get reinstated each time. His assignments included: captain, Company A, 60th Georgia (August 21, 1861); and lieutenant colonel, 37th Virginia Cavalry Battalion (August 2, 1862). His command of a Georgia infantry company lasted less than three months before he was ousted by order of a court-martial on November 20, 1861. Going to western Virginia he raised a battalion of partisan rangers and became their commander. This time he lasted 15 months before he was dismissed on charges of disobedience of orders brought by then-Colonel William L. Jackson. Eight months later he was back in command, having been reinstated, and led his command at Monocacy, the burning of Chambersburg, 3rd Winchester, Fisher's Hill, and Cedar Creek. With the war coming to a close, Dunn resigned on March 31, 1865. After the war he moved to New York City.

DUNOVANT, John (1825-1864)

Appointed to the temporary rank of brigadier in the Confederate cavalry, John Dunovant held the post for a little over a month before he was felled by enemy fire. He had served as an enlisted man in the Palmetto regiment during the war with Mexico and gained a regular army captaincy upon the 1855 expansion of the military. Resigning that commission nine days after the secession of his native South Carolina, he was present at the firing on Fort Sumter as a major in his state's forces. His later assignments included: colonel, 1st South Carolina Regulars (July 22, 1861); colonel, 5th South Carolina Cavalry (ca. Janaury 18, 1863); brigadier general, CSA (August 22, 1864); and commanding Butler's (old) Brigade, Hampton's-Butler's Division, Cavalry Corps, Army of Northern Virginia (August 22-October 1, 1864). He was charged with drunkenness while serving in the Charleston area in June 1862 and was dismissed on November 7. However, two months later he was appointed to the colonelcy of a new cavalry regiment with which he served for over a year in his native state before being sent to Virginia.

After serving through the Overland Campaign and the early portion of the Petersburg siege, he was advanced to the temporary grade of brigadier and given charge of Butler's brigade while that officer led the division. On October 1 he was killed in action along the Vaughan Road near Petersburg.

DU PONT, Henry (1812-1889)

A member of Delaware's famous chemical company family, Henry Du Pont served a dual role in the Civil War—as a manufacturer of gunpowder and as a state militia officer whose actions were crucial in keeping the border state in the Union. A West Pointer (1833), he had served a year in the artillery before resigning to take a position in the family business. During the Mexican War the company provided much of the army's gunpowder. Du Pont was a member of the Republican Party in his state and kept up his interest in military affairs by being active in the militia. By the time of the Civil War he was a major general in that body and demanded that each member take the oath of allegiance. His order was vetoed by the governor but Du Pont received the support of the Union army in keeping the state in the Union. For the remainder of the war Du Pont made sure that his company provided the Union armies with the gunpowder they needed. He continued in the business until his death.

DU PONT, Henry Algernon (1838-1926)

A son of a founder of the Delaware chemical dynasty, Henry A. Du Pont graduated at the top of the West Point Class of 1861. His assignments included: brevet second lieutenant, Engineers (May 6, 1861); second lieutenant, Engineers (May 6, 1861); first lieutenant, 5th Artillery (May 14, 1861); adjutant, 5th Artillery (July 6, 1861); assigned command of Battery B, 5th Artillery (ca. June 30, 1863); captain, Battery B, 5th Artillery (March 24, 1864); and commanding Artillery Brigade, Army of West Virginia (ca. June 1864-May 1865). After his brief stint in the engineers, Du Pont was assigned to a newly organized regular artillery regiment and was soon made its adjutant. He served at the regimental headquarters at Fort Hamilton, New York, until given command of a battery that was sent to aid in the repulse of the Confederate invasion of Pennsylvania. Du Pont's unit served in the Departments of the Susquehanna and West Virginia. Taking part in Franz Sigel's Shenandoah Valley Campaign, Du Pont was engaged in the battle of New Market and was instrumental in organizing the retreat. Soon thereafter he was given command of the artillery brigade, with which he served when Sigel's army became part of Sheridan's command in the Valley. Fighting at 3rd Winchester, Fisher's Hill, and Cedar Creek, Du Pont earned a brevet as major for the first two battles and a brevet as lieutenant colonel and a Medal of Honor for the last. Continuing in command of his brigade in the Valley and West Virginia until the end of the war, he remained in the army until 1875. After his resignation, he joined his family's industrial empire and served for two terms in the Senate. (Du Pont, Henry A. *The Campaign of 1864 in the Valley of Virginia and the Expedition to Lynchburg*)

DU PONT, Samuel Francis (1803-1865)

An early naval hero of the Civil War, Samuel F. Du Pont went into virtual retirement after his failure at Charleston in the spring of 1863. He had entered the Navy in 1815 as a midshipman and had risen to the rank of captain and was commandant of the Philadelphia Navy Yard by the outbreak of the Civil War. He was tapped to head the commission that worked out the plan of naval operations at the start of the conflict. His wartime assignments included: captain, USN (since 1855); commanding South Atlantic Blockading Squadron (September 1861-July 5, 1863); and rear admiral, USN (July 16, 1862). The veteran of cruises to Europe, the Mediterranean, the West Indies, South America, the Far East, and along the Pacific coast in the

Union Admiral Samuel F. Du Pont. (*Leslie's*)

Mexican War, was given command of the operations along the Southern coast in the fall of 1861. He scored a major victory at the battle of Port Royal Sound. He continued to score successes along the coast until he was ordered to attack Charleston in April 1863. Not convinced that the Navy Department knew what it was doing, he reluctantly followed orders and was defeated. He offered to resign if he had lost the confidence of the administration and was replaced three months later. His health weakened, he worked on some boards before his death in June 1865. (Du Pont, Henry A., *Rear Admiral Samuel Francis Du Pont*)

DUPRÉ, Lucius Jacques (1822-1869)

A native Louisiana lawyer and judge, Lucius J. Dupré, began his Confederate career by enlisting in the 18th Louisiana, but in November 1861 he won an uncontested election to represent the state's 4th District in the First Congress. He served on the committees on: Indian Affairs; Judiciary; and Printing, chairing the latter in the Second Congress. A believer in a strong military effort, he repeatedly called for the reconquest of New Orleans. But his financially conservative views led him to demand economy from the commanders in the field. He felt that the Davis administration should be given a free hand by Congress to direct the purely military aspects of the war. With the South's fall he resumed his legal pursuits.

DURBEC, F.E. (fl. 1861-1866)

The Union navy's blockade of Charleston was probably responsible for the breakup of the photographic partnership of F.E. Durbec and James M. Osborn. The pair had been running a "Photographic Mart" at 223 King Street before the war. Shortly after the surrender of Fort Sumter the two artists took their stereo camera to the fort and the surrounding batteries to capture the historic scene. The resulting extensive record of the sites was impressive considering the relative novelty of war photography. Unfortunately their inability to obtain quantities of chemicals and other supplies prevented the wide distribution of their work and discouraged them from other endeavors in the field. By the end of the war they had dissolved their partnership.

DURYÉE, Abram (1815-1890)

Petty considerations of rank and status cost both sides numerous officers during the Civil War. Such was the case for Abram Duryée. A wealthy importer in his native New York City, he had been highly active in the state militia for over a quarter of a century when he resigned in 1859. In the meantime he had risen to the rank of colonel and been wounded in the 1849 Astor Place riots—the ridiculous outgrowth of a feud between an American and a British actor. Reentering the army in 1861, his assignments included: colonel 5th New York (May 14, 1861); brigadier general, USV (August 31, 1861); commanding 2nd Brigade, Ord's Division, Department of the Rappahannock (May 16-June 10, 1862); commanding 1st Brigade, Ord's Division, Department of the Rappanhannock (June 10-26, 1862); commanding 1st Brigade, 2nd Division, 3rd Corps, Army of Virginia (June 26-September 12, 1862); and commanding 1st Brigade, 2nd Division, 1st Corps, Army of the Potomac (September 12-October 5, 1862). Initially commanding his regiment—which was known as Duryée's Zouaves, for its fancy uniforms—he served in the Washington area and was soon named a brigadier general. In the next year he served in northern Virginia and Maryland but felt slighted upon his return from leave to find a junior in charge of a division and his own brigade dispersed. He resigned on January 5, 1863, and held no further commands in the war. Nonetheless, in the omnibus promotions of March 13, 1865, he was made a brevet major general for the battles at Cedar Mountain, Rappahannock Station, Thoroughfare Gap, Groveton, Chantilly—the latter two were part of 2nd Bull Run—South Mountain, and Antietam. In the postwar years he held several city appointments including that of police commissioner.

DUVAL, Isaac Hardin (1824-1902)

A native of that part of Virginia that stayed with the Union and became West Virginia, Isaac H. Duval had been a frontiersman and prominent explorer in the American West, Mexico, Central and South America. Back at home he became a businessman in 1853. The coming of the war brought him into uniform and his assignments included: major, 1st (West) Virginia (June 1, 1861); major, 1st West Virginia (October 29, 1861); colonel, 9th West Virginia (September 19, 1862); commanding 2nd Infantry Division, Department of West Virginia (July 22-October 19, 1864 and December 24, 1864-January 1865); brigadier general, USV (September 24, 1864); and commanding 1st Infantry Division, Department of West Virginia (January-February 25, 1865). Most of his service was in his native region and in the Shenandoah Valley. He fought well at Cloyd's Mountain and served through the Lynchburg expedition of David Hunter. As a division commander under Sheridan, he fought at 3rd Winchester and Fisher's Hill and was awarded with a brigadier generalcy a few days later. Near the war's conclusion he was brevetted major general and was mustered out on January 15, 1866. His postwar political offices included seats in both houses of the state legislature, and in the U.S. House of Representatives; he was also a tax official and West Virginia's adjutant general.

DWIGHT, William (1831-1888)

Discharged from West Point in 1853 for poor grades, William Dwight received a second chance at the outbreak of the Civil War only to get into trouble again in its last year. Following his expulsion he had been in the manufacturing business until his appointment as the second-in-command of the first regiment of what was to become Daniel E. Sickles' Excelsior Brigade—(Sickles was the regiment's first commander). Dwight's assignments included: lieutenant colonel, 70th New York (June 29, 1861); colonel, 70th New York (July 1, 1861); brigadier general, USV (November 29, 1861); commanding 1st Brigade, 4th Division, 19th Corps, Department of the Gulf (February 12-May 30, 1863); commanding 2nd Division, 19th

Corps, Department of the Gulf (May 30-June 18, 1863); commanding 3rd Division, 19th Corps, Department of the Gulf (July 6-August 15, 1863); commanding 1st Brigade, 1st Division, 19th Corps, Department of the Gulf (February 20-25 and March 25-April 18, 1864); chief of staff, Department of the Gulf (spring 1864); commanding 1st Division, 19th Corps, Department of the Gulf (July 1-5, 1864); commanding 1st Division, 19th Corps, Army of the Shenandoah (August 6-October 5, 1864, October 19, 1864-January 25, 1865, and March 1-20, 1865); commanding division, 22nd Corps, Department of Washington (April-May 1865). Thrice wounded at Williamsburg, he was left on the field and presumed dead. Taken up by the enemy he was exchanged and upon his recovery was given a brigadier's star. Sent to the Gulf coast, he distinguished himself in the seizure of Port Hudson following his fighting at Bayou Teche and Irish Bend. After an apparent absence of several months, he commanded a brigade in the early part of the Red River Campaign. He then acted as Bank's staff chief, and there were charges that he was involved in the speculation over seized Confederate cotton. Transferred to the Virginia theater, he was stationed in the Shenandoah Valley, seeing action as a division commander at 3rd Winchester, Fisher's Hill, and Cedar Creek. He conflicted with other commanders over their roles in the former battle and spent a period under arrest on charges that he had sought a safe position for his battle-time lunch. At the end of the war he was placed in command of a division in the Washington fortifications and was mustered out on January 5, 1866. Moving to the Old Northwest, he became active in railroading.

DYER, Alexander Brydie (1815-1874)

By far the youngest man to serve as chief of Ordnance in the Union army during the Civil War was Virginia-born Alexander Dyer. An 1837 graduate of West Point, Dyer had served in the artillery in the Second Seminole War before being transferred to the Ordnance Department in 1838. After service in the Mexican War he rose to the rank of captain by the time of the firing on Fort Sumter. He also invented a three-inch shell, called the Dyer shell, which utilized the flame from the propulsion charge to ignite the fuse. He was given charge of the Springfield Armory in August 1861 and there produced 1,000 rifles a day. Promoted to major on March 3, 1863, he continued in command of the armory until he was promoted to brigadier general, USA, and assigned as chief of Ordnance on September 12, 1864. Near the close of the conflict, he was brevetted major general and continued in his post until he died on active duty on May 20, 1874. His enlightened approach to his department, especially toward breech-loading and repeating weapons, was dampened by the return to a peace-time establishment.

DYER, Frederick Henry (1849-1917)

Under the assumed name of Frederick H. Metzger—in order to conceal his true age—Frederick H. Dyer enlisted in the Union army as a musician and in his later years secluded himself from his family to produce one of the most useful compilations on the Civil War, *A Compendium of the War of the Rebellion*. The Connecticut native enlisted in Company H, 7th Connecticut, on September 29, 1863. As a musician he was probably in action only to recover the wounded but his regiment was present at Olustee, Swift Creek, Chesterfield Station, Drewry's Bluff, Port Walthall Junction, Bermuda Hundred, Deep Bottom, Chaffin's Farm, New Market Heights, Darbytown Road, New Market Road, and Fort Fisher. In addition, the regiment was stationed in New York City to prevent election day violence in 1864. Dyer was mustered out with his unit on July 20, 1865. Settling in Philadelphia, he went into business manufacturing and marketing patriotic escutcheons for veterans. He was later in the printing business. Throughout the postwar years he compiled statistical information on the war and the units involved. Eventually the idea for the *Compendium* developed and in 1903 he moved away from his family to maintain a rigorous schedule for five years of research and writing. The book appeared in 1909 and 1910. He then returned to his family. (NOTE: See the Bibliography for a descripton of the information included in this work.)

E

EADS, James Buchanan (1820-1887)

Summoned out of semi-retirement by President Lincoln, noted riverine engineer James B. Eads offered to construct seven armored gunboats within 65 days—a remarkable feat which he completed in 45. He had long been involved in the dragging of the western rivers and had invented an early diving-bell. The native Indianan's vessels were highly effective in the opening of the western rivers during the war. Subsequently he built additional gunboats and provided further innovations in naval equipment until failing health slowed his work. After the war he was active in bridge building and river clearing. (How, Louis, *James B. Eads*)

EARLY, Jubal Anderson (1816-1894)

Always an irascible officer, Jubal A. Early suffered overwhelming defeats in the Shenandoah Valley and went on after the conflict to wage a literary war with a fellow Confederate corps commander. A West Pointer (1837) from Virginia, Early had served one year in the artillery, and later in the Mexican War as a major of volunteers, before taking up law. Also involved in politics, he served in the legislature. Although he voted against secession at the convention, he entered the military where his assignments included: colonel, 24th Virginia (early 1861); commanding 6th Brigade (in 1st Corps from July 20), Army of the Potomac (June 20-October 22, 1861); brigadier general, CSA (July 21, 1861);

One of James B. Eads' gunboats, USS *St. Louis*, later the *Baron de Kalb*. (NA)

commanding brigade, Van Dorn's-D.H. Hill's Division (in Potomac District until March), Department of Northern Virginia (October 22, 1861-May 5, 1862); commanding Elzey's Brigade, Ewell's Division, 2nd Corps, Army of Northern Virginia (July 1-September 17, 1862); commanding the division (September 17, 1862-November 1863; ca. December 4-15, 1863; February-May 7; and May 21-27, 1864); major general, CSA (April 23 to rank from January 17, 1863); commanding the corps (November-ca. December 4, 1863 and May 27-June 13, 1864); commanding Valley District, Department of Northern Virginia (December 15, 1863-February 1864 and June 13, 1864-March 29, 1865); commanding 3rd Corps, Army of Northern Virginia (May 7-21, 1864); and lieutenant general, CSA (May 31, 1864). Leading a brigade at 1st Bull Run and Williamsburg, he was wounded at the latter. Returning to duty, he was given another command on the day of Malvern Hill. At Cedar Mountain and 2nd Bull Run he directed this unit and continued until he succeeded to division level at Antietam. He went on to Fredericksburg, Chancellorsville, and Gettysburg and commanded the corps in the Mine Run operations. Detached, he commanded in the Shenandoah during the winter of 1863-64. After the battle of the Wilderness he took over temporary control of Hill's Corps during the operations at Spotsylvania. He directed his division at the North Anna and took over Ewell's Corps before Cold Harbor. A couple of weeks later this command was sent back to the Valley and Early invaded Maryland, fighting at Monocacy and on the outskirts of Washington. Falling back to Virginia, he dispatched part off his cavalry to burn Chambersburg, Pennsylvania, in retaliation for Union devastation. In September and October he was defeated in a series of disasters at the hands of Sheridan. The reverses at 3rd Winchester, Fisher's Hill, and Cedar Creek ended his power in the Valley and the old 2nd Corps and was recalled to Lee in December. However, Early remained with a small force that was destroyed at Waynesborough the following March. Lee then removed him, explaining that he was forced to by public reaction and the fact that he could not defend his subordinate without revealing how weak the Confederacy was. Early fled to Mexico but soon returned to practice law. He was connected with the Louisiana Lottery and was president of the Southern Historical Society. Becoming a defender of Lee, he feuded with Republican convert James Longstreet until his death. (Bushong, Millard K., *Old Jube*)

EATON, Amos Beebe (1806-1877)

The field of advancement for regular army staff officers was greatly widened by the Civil War. New Yorker Amos Eaton was a case in point. Graduating from West Point (1826) near the bottom of his class, he served initially in the infantry. In 1838, during the Second Seminole War, Eaton was assigned to commissary duties as a captain. Serving as Taylor's chief commissary officer in Mexico and on the Pacific coast, Eaton was still a captain and brevet major for Buena Vista, at the outbreak of the war. His Civil War appointments included: major and commissary of subsistence (May 9, 1861); lieutenant colonel and assistant commissary general of subsistence (September 29, 1861); colonel and assistant commissary general of subsistence (February 9, 1863); and brigadier general, USA, and commissary general of subsistence (June 29, 1864). From the time of the death of George Gibson, the commissary general for 43 years, Eaton served as the number two man in the department. With the death of General Taylor, Gibson's replacement, Eaton was assigned to head it. In 1865 Eaton was brevetted major general in the regular army for services, supplying the armies, and handling large sums for the government. After 45 years of service General Eaton was retired in 1874. After touring Europe he died in 1877.

EATON, John, Jr. (1829-?)

Starting the war as a chaplain, New Hampshire native John Eaton, Jr., was brevetted a brigadier general of volunteers for his services with the escaped slaves who threatened to paralyze Grant's army. His assignments included: chaplain, 27th Ohio (August 15, 1861); colonel, 9th Louisiana African Descent (October 10, 1863); and colonel, 63rd United States Colored Troops (designation change March 11, 1864). His first unit fought in Missouri and then Mississippi. But much of the time Eaton was assigned to duty with the freedmen in the Memphis area. His success in this field brought wider responsibilities at the hands of Grant who had him appointed to the command of a black regiment in order to give him the proper authority. Many of his innovations were later adopted into the Freedmen's Bureau, and he became its commissioner in the capital's vicinity. Brevetted in March 1865, he was discharged on December 18, 1865. He was then involved in civilian and military education.

ECHOLS, John (1823-1896)

Virginia lawyer and state legislator John Echols served as a Confederate general officer mostly in western Virginia and the Shenandoah Valley. His assignments included: lieutenant colonel, 27th Virginia (May 30, 1861); colonel, 27th Virginia (October 14, 1861); brigadier general, CSA (April 16, 1862); commanding Department of Southwestern Virginia (October 16-November 19, 1862); commanding brigade, Department of Western Virginia (November 19, 1862-May 1864); commanding brigade, Breckinridge's Division, Army of Northern Virginia (May-June 1864); commanding brigade, Breckinridge's Division, Valley District, Army of Northern Virginia (June-July 9, 1964); commanding the division (July 9, 1864); and commanding Department of Western Tennessee (January-February and March 29-April 1865). He commanded his regiment, in what became the Stonewall Brigade, at 1st Bull Run and was later wounded at Kernstown in the Valley. Promoted to brigadier general, he was assigned to western Virginia where he remained until the spring of 1864. At that time he took part in the victory at New Market over Franz Sigel and then went to Lee's army, seeing action at Cold Harbor. Heading west he took part in the defense of Lynchburg and served for a time in the Valley again before taking command in southwestern Virginia. Engaged in business after the war he was a leading force in the rebuilding of the commonwealth's railroads.

ECKERT, Thomas Thompson (1825-1910)

Working in the War Department's telegraph office, Thomas Eckert was destined to come in close contact with President Lincoln. Appointed a major and additional aide-de-camp on April 7, 1862, Eckert was assigned to the staff of General McClellan and served as head of the Army of the Potomac's telegraphic organization during the Peninsula Campaign. On July 17, 1862, he was commissioned a captain and assistant quartermaster general. The following September he was transferred to the War Department in Washington where he was placed in charge of the telegraph office that was in touch with the field armies. He devised a means of laying telegraph wire using reels mounted on the backs of mules with the wire and then mounted on lances or trees. During important military operations Lincoln would often spend long hours with Eckert awaiting news from the front. Becoming quite close to Lincoln, entertaining the President by breaking pokers over his arm, he was asked to accompany Lincoln to Ford's Theater. Secretary of War Stanton, fearing trouble, said Eckert had too much work to do that evening. Stanton later sent Eckert home, leading to speculation that Stanton was involved in a conspiracy. Later that night Eckert visited the dying president in the Petersen House. Shortly before the end of the war, Eckert was brevetted through grades to brigadier general of volunteers. Continuing in the Army until 1867, he served as assistant secretary of war for seven months in 1866-67. In private life he became head of a commercial telegraph company and later a judge in Texas. (Bishop, Jim, *The Day Lincoln Was Shot*)

ECTOR, Matthew Duncan (1822-1879)

The loss of a leg in the Atlanta Campaign put an end to the active military career of Georgia-born Confederate General Matthew D. Ector. The lawyer and Texas legislator enlisted first as a private and then became a staff officer with Joseph L. Hogg. As such he was present for part of the Corinth siege and was then named to a colonelcy. His later assignments included: colonel, 14th Texas Cavalry (May 1862); brigadier general, CSA (August 23, 1862); commanding brigade, McCown's Division, Department of East Tennessee (fall-December 1862); commanding brigade, McCown's Division attached to Hardee's Corps, Army of Tennessee (December 1862-January 1863); commanding brigade, McCown's Division, Smith's Corps, Army of Tennessee (January-March 1863); commanding brigade, McCown's Division, Polk's Corps, Army of Tennessee (March-ca. May 1863); commanding brigade, Walker's Division, Department of the West (May 19-July 1863); commanding brigade, Walker's Division, Department of Mississippi and East Louisiana (July-August 25, 1863); commanding brigade, Walker's Division, Hill's Corps, Army of Tennessee (August 28-September 1863); commanding brigade, Walker's Division, Reserve Corps, Army of Tennessee (September 1863); commanding brigade, Walker's Division, Polk's Corps, Army of Tennessee (September-September 22, 1863); commanding brigade, French's Division, Department of Mississippi and East Louisiana (September 22, 1863-January 28, 1864); commanding brigade, French's Division, Department of Alabama, Mississippi and East Louisiana (January 28-May 4, 1864); commanding brigade, French's Division, Polk's (Army of Mississippi)-Stewart's Corps, Army of Tennessee (May 4-July 22, 1864); and commanding brigade, French's Division, District of the Gulf, Department of Alabama, Mississippi and East Louisiana (spring 1865). Transferred from the Corinth area to East Tennessee, Ector led a brigade there and at Richmond, Kentucky. Attached to Bragg's army, he fought at Murfreesboro and in the attempt under Joseph E. Johnston to relieve Vicksburg. Returning to Bragg, he fought at Chickamauga and a few days later was ordered back to Mississippi. In the spring of 1864 he accompanied Leonidas Polk to northern Georgia and served through the Atlanta Campaign until wounded outside the city. The loss of a leg kept him out of action for some time. In the meantime his brigade had fought in middle Tennessee with Hood before being dispatched to Mobile where he apparently rejoined it in the war's final days. Postwar he was a lawyer and judge.

EDMONDS, Sarah Emma (1841-1898)

It has been estimated that the equivalent of several companies of women fought in disguise with the armies of the United and Confederate States. One of them was Sarah Edmonds, alias Private Franklin Thompson of Company F, 2nd Michigan Infantry. She was already a veteran at wearing male clothing by the time of the Civil War. At the age of six she was working her family's Canadian farm dressed as a boy to fill her father's need for sons. Running away from an arranged marriage, she immigrated to the United States and became Bible seller Franklin Thompson. Later working for a Michigan publisher she enlisted in the first state unit raised to serve for three years. However she failed her first physical, not for being a woman but for being too short. Her second attempt, on May 14, 1861, was more successful. After undergoing training she was named a field nurse, and as such she was heavily engaged during the battle of 1st Bull Run. Spurred into action by the death in the Peninsula Campaign of a childhood friend in her company, who didn't know her true identity, Edmonds left nursing and volunteered for duty as a spy. An expert in disguise, she was able to pass for male or female, black or white. She was apparently present at the battle of Antietam, where she claimed to have buried another female soldier. After her regiment moved to Kentucky in early 1863, she came down with malaria. Fearing the discovery of her secret, on April 22, she deserted to protect it. She resumed her female identity and her nursing, as a Christian Commission worker, until the war ended. It was not until 1884 that Edmonds, now married, revealed her secret by attending a regimental reunion without her disguise. She was urged to file for a veteran's pension and she took her case to Congress—but with more interest in having the charge of desertion removed from her record. She achieved both goals and lived out her life as the only female member of the Grand Army of the Republic. (Dannett, Sylvia, *She Rode With Generals*)

EDWARD, Prince of Wales (1841-1910)

To a large degree it was the visit of Edward, Prince of Wales, to the United States that brought about the brief era of good feeling between the United States and Great Britain immediately preceding the Civil War. Since the Crimean War it had been proposed that Queen Victoria visit her North American colony, Canada, but it had been considered too risky to expose the monarch to the rigors of the crossing. However, she promised that when her eldest son, Edward, was old enough he would be sent to represent her on a royal visit. When President Buchanan learned of the planned summer 1860 trip, he asked that it be extended to the crown's former colonies to the south. In a triumphant tour Edward contributed to a growing spirit of goodwill between the two nations. Returning home, Edward tended to confine himself to dealing with European diplomatic problems, especially with concern over the 1864 attack of Bismarck upon his father-in-law, Christian IX of Denmark. He was little involved with the deteriorating Atlantic relations, strained by the *Trent* affair and other aspects of the Civil War. As King Edward VII, he ruled Britain for the last nine years of his life. (St. Aubyn, Giles, *Edward VII: Prince and King*)

EDWARDS, J.D. (ca. 1831-?)

New Hampshire-born J.D. Edwards has been called the "Photographer of the Confederacy" for his early war work. Little is known of him before or after the war but he had apparently opened his New Orleans business by 1860 or shortly before. With the outbreak of war he packed his equipment and headed for the front at Pensacola. There he took an amazing series of images of the camps, guns, men, and fortifications under the command of Braxton Bragg. In a May 14, 1861, newspaper advertisement he offered some 39 views for sale. However, it is now apparent that he probably exposed about twice as many images. Some of his views were pirated as woodcuts in *Harper's Weekly*. He also took images around Mobile and, it is suspected, also in New Orleans. However, after early 1862 he disappears from the field—possibly due to the lack of photographic supplies—although there are statements that he was later in the Confederate secret service.

EDWARDS, John (1815-1894)

Union General John Edwards spent most of his Civil War service in the vicinity of Fort Smith, Arkansas. The Kentucky-born lawyer had lived in Indiana, California, and Iowa before the war. He served in the state legislatures of Indiana and Iowa and had been a justice of the peace in California where he had gone during the Gold Rush. He also dabbled in journalism as the founder of the *Patriot*. His military assignments included: lieutenant colonel and aide-de-camp to Governor Samuel J. Kirkwood (May 21, 1861); colonel, 18th Iowa (August 8, 1862); commanding 2nd Brigade, District of the Frontier, Department of the Missouri (December 1863-January 6, 1864); commanding 2nd Brigade, District of the Frontier, 7th Corps, Department of Arkansas (January 6-March 21, 1864); commanding 1st Brigade, District of the Frontier, 7th Corps, Department of Arkansas (March 21-December 3, 1864); brigadier general, USV (September 26, 1864); commanding 1st Brigade, Frontier Division, 7th Corps, Department of Arkansas (January 16-February 1, 1865); commanding 1st Brigade, 3rd Division, 7th Corps, Department of Arkansas (February 16-May 7, 1865); and commanding 2nd Brigade, 2nd Division, 7th Corps, Department of Arkansas (May 7-June 18, 1865). Until his appointment to regimental command Edwards served on the staff of Iowa's governor. In 1863 the regiment was assigned to Springfield, Missouri and the next year Edwards took charge of the post at Fort Smith. He took part in the Camden expedition as a brigade commander and that fall was named a brigadier general. He then returned to the vicinity of Fort Smith until the end of the war. Mustered out on January 15, 1866, he settled at Fort Smith and in 1870 was elected as a Liberal Republican to the House of Representatives, but the election was contested and he was ousted. He then practiced law in the nation's capital.

EDWARDS, Oliver (1835-1904)

Massachusetts native Oliver Edwards rose from an adjutancy to the rank of brevet major general in the Union army. He was engaged in the foundry business at the outbreak of the Civil War, but returned from Illinois to his native state in order to enlist. His assignments included: first lieutenant and adjutant, 10th Massachusetts (June 21, 1861); aide-de-camp, 1st Division, 4th Corps, Army of the Potomac (spring 1862); colonel, 37th Massachusetts (September 4, 1862); commanding 4th Brigade, 2nd Division, 6th Corps, Army of the Potomac (January 29-March 26 and May 9-July 6, 1864); commanding 3rd Brigade, 1st Division, 6th Corps, Army of the Shenandoah (August 6-September 19, and September 21-October 31, 1864); commanding the division (September 19-21, 1864); commanding 3rd Brigade, 1st Division, 6th Corps, Army of the Potomac (March 17-June 21, 1865); and brigadier general, USV (May 19, 1865). He was tapped early as a staff officer with Darius N. Couch and was particularly distinguished in the Peninsula fighting at Yorktown, Williamsburg, Seven Pines, and during the Seven Days. Rewarded with the colonelcy of a new regiment, he rejoined the army in time to fight at Fredericksburg, Chancellorsville and Gettysburg. His regiment was then detached to restore order after draft riots in New York City. He returned for the Mine Run Campaign and during the Overland Campaign succeeded to brigade command at Spotsylvania. He retained command through Cold Harbor and the early stages at Petersburg. Taking his brigade to the Shenandoah Valley, he took command of the division at 3rd Winchester. For this and Spotsylvania he was brevetted brigadier general. In brigade command, he fought at Fisher's Hill and Cedar Creek before returning to the Petersburg front. During the final assault the city surrendered to him. During the pursuit his command captured Generals Custis Lee and Richard

S. Ewell at Sayler's Creek. Brevetted major general for this, he received the full rank of brigadier general after the fighting was over. Mustered out January 15, 1866, he returned to his business interests and became something of an inventor.

EGAN, Thomas Wilberforce (1834-1887)

Well after Thomas W. Egan's regiment had been consolidated with five other regiments and he was placed in command, he was incapacitated by wounds for active field service. Joining the "Mozart Regiment," the New Yorker's assignments included: lieutenant colonel, 40th New York (July 1, 1861); colonel, 40th New York (June 5, 1862); commanding 1st Brigade, 1st Division, 3rd Corps, Army of the Potomac (temporarily May 4, 1863); commanding 3rd Brigade, 1st Division, 3rd Corps, Army of the Potomac (November 22-December 30, 1863 and February-March 24, 1864); commanding 1st Brigade, 3rd Division, 2nd Corps, Army of the Potomac (March 24-April 20 and May 12-June 16, 1864); commanding 1st Brigade, 2nd division, 2nd Corps, Army of the Potomac (August 27-September 4, and September 25-November 14, 1864); commanding the division (September 4-25 and October 8-29, 1864); brigadier general, USV (September 3, 1864); and commanding 3rd Provisional Division, Army of the Shenandoah (April-July 1865). He fought at Yorktown and commanded the regiment at Seven Pines. A few days later he was made its permanent leader and he led them in the Seven Days. Supporting Pope's army, he fought at 2nd Bull Run but was defending Washington during the Maryland Campaign. At Chancellorsville he briefly commanded the brigade. After serving the Bristoe and Mine Run operations he entered the Wilderness under Grant and at Spotsylvania succeeded to brigade command when J.H. Hobart Ward was relieved. He led the brigade at Cold Harbor until wounded at Petersburg on June 16, 1864. Back on duty two months later, he was again wounded during the siege on November 14, 1864. By this time he had been brevetted major general for the Boydton Plank Road on October 27, 1864. He returned to serve under Winfield S. Hancock in organizing the 1st Veteran Volunteer Corps and in the Shenandoah Valley at the end of the war. He was mustered out on January 15, 1866, and for about a decade and a half served as a custom's official.

ELLET, Alfred Washington (1820-1895)

The brother of Charles Ellet, Jr., the engineer and designer of the ram fleet on the Mississippi, Alfred W. Ellet was frequently in conflict with the naval commanders on the Mississippi. Like his brother he was born in Pennsylvania and was working as a civil engineer in Illinois at the outbreak of the Civil War. His Union army assignments included: captain, 59th Illinois (August 20, 1861); lieutenant colonel and additional aide-de-camp (April 28, 1862); and brigadier general, USV (November 1, 1862). After a brief period of service as an infantry company commander he was tapped to become second-in-command to his brother who was in charge of the small fleet of unarmed rams on the Mississippi River. He took part in the battle of Memphis—one of the few fleet actions in the Civil War—and succeeded to command of the fleet when his brother was mortally wounded. Promoted to brigadier general, he was also given charge of the Mississippi Marine Brigade. It was an awkward arrangement as the fleet and the brigade were "in" the army but subject to orders from naval commanders on the western rivers. This led to a lengthy series of inter-service rivalries. After part of his forces had run the batteries at Vicksburg his command was sent to support Rosecrans' forces along the Tennessee. With the river relatively free for navigation—except for the ever-present guerrillas—Ellet resigned effective December 31, 1864, while stationed at New Orleans, and returned to private life. He later moved to Kansas and engaged in railroading.

ELLET, Charles, Jr., (1810-1862)

Early in 1862 civil engineer Charles Ellet, Jr., an expert in bridges, locks, and dams, sold Secretary of War Edwin M. Stanton on the idea of a group of unarmed, speedy rams for service on the western rivers. The native of Pennsylvania had been working in Illinois for a number of years and was thoroughly familiar with navigation problems on the Mississippi and other waterways. The month after getting the go-ahead from the War Department he was commissioned as an additional aide-de-camp with the rank of colonel on April 28, 1862, and was assigned to command the fleet of rams. On June 6, 1862, he led his flotilla in a highly successful fight against the Confederate forces afloat at Memphis and virtually destroyed the enemy. The one casualty aboard the ram fleet was Ellet himself. He died of his wounds on June 21, 1862, and was succeeded in command by his brother, Alfred W. Ellet.

ELLET, Charles Rivers (ca. 1843-?)

Son of the originator of the Mississippi ram fleet, Charles Ellet, Jr., Charles R. Ellet was a medical cadet at the beginning of the war but rose to command the infantry regiment of the Mississippi Marine Brigade, which operated in conjunction with the fleet. When the decision was made to create the brigade in about December 1862 young Ellet was commissioned a colonel. Early the next year, in February, he suffered a reverse when he led the ram *Queen of the West* up the Red River without waiting for his support, the gunboat *Indianola*. His vessel was sunk by enemy artillery fire and his crew fled on foot. When the *Indianola* came up it was set upon by Confederate craft including the refloated *Queen* and was lost too. Commander Porter, the naval commander in the area, was not impressed by the incident and the army-navy rivalry was exacerbated (the fleet was controlled by the War Department). Ellet's next adventure came when he directed the ram *Switzerland* in the run past the Vicksburg batteries the following month. Although the craft was severly damaged, repairs only required a few days. However, instead of Ellet continuing in command and joining Admiral Farragut, his cousin John A. Ellet was given the command. Charles R. Ellet was assigned to infantry duty with the brigade and went to the relief of Rosecrans' army along the Tennessee River.

ELLET, John A. (?-?)

As a member of the "family fleet" of rams in the West, John A. Ellet came into conflict with the naval commanders on the Mississippi and was threatened at one point with arrest and court-martial for insubordination. A nephew of both the inventor and engineer Charles Ellet, Jr., and General Alfred W. Ellet, he was commissioned a lieutenant colonel in about December 1862 and was assigned to duty with the Mississippi Marine Brigade as second-in-command to his cousin Charles R. Ellet. He commanded the ram *Lancaster* in the run past the Vicksburg batteries in March 1863. His vessel was sunk during the passage but he took over command of the *Switzerland* from his cousin after it had been repaired following its ordeal. By joining Admiral Farragut's fleet below the river city he avoided charges about to be pressed by Porter, the commander of the naval forces on the upper river. Porter had issued an order to Ellet, and the latter had insisted on first communicating with his uncle the general whom he considered to be his superior. With the ram fleet and the marine brigade part of the army there was an extremely awkward command system on the river. Once below Vicksburg, Lieutenant Colonel Ellet strictly obeyed his instructions not to do anything without Farragut's permission. There was no further trouble between the services in that sector.

ELLIOTT, Joel H. (1840-1868)

With the cry, "Here goes for a brevet or a coffin," the career of Joel H. Elliott came to an end. An Indiana native, he enlisted during the war's first year and his assignments included: private, Company C, 2nd Indiana Cavalry (September 13, 1861); second lieutenant, 7th Indiana Cavalry (June 25, 1863); and captain, 7th Indiana Cavalry (October 23, 1863). He fought at Shiloh and was Alexander D. McCook's orderly at Perryville and Murfreesboro. Becoming a company commander, he fought during much of the rest of the war against Nathan Bedford Forrest in Mississippi. Before being mustered out on February 18, 1866, he had suffered two wounds. The next year he became the junior major of the 7th Cavalry and was in command of the regiment for much of the time. Chasing after Cheyennes at the Washita massacre, he was killed on November 27, 1868.

ELLIOTT, John Milton (1820-1879)

Born in Virginia and raised in Kentucky, John Milton Elliott had practiced law and served in both the state legislature and the U.S. House of Representatives before launching his career in the Confederate Congress—a career that would be as long as the life of that body itself. While serving again in the state legislature, Elliott was tapped by the provisional pro-Southern government of Kentucky to serve in the Provisional Confederate Congress. Taking his seat, he soon became identified as an ardent supporter of both the Davis administration and the war effort. Reelected to both of the regular congresses he was appointed to the committees on: Indian Affairs; Post Offices and Post Roads; and Enrolled Bills, of which he was chairman in the First Congress. Once the issue of local defense troops was moot in relation to Kentucky, Elliott was willing to grant almost anything to the army. Ater the war he served as a lawyer and judge. While serving on the state's highest court, on March 26, 1879, Elliott was struck down by a shotgun blast fired by an irate litigant in a land case.

ELLIOTT, Stephen, Jr. (1830-1866)

South Carolina plantation owner and state legislator Stephen Elliott, Jr., served most of the war in his native state. His assignments included: captain, Company A, 11th South Carolina (early 1861); major and lieutenant colonel, Artillery (1863); colonel, Holcombe (S.C.) Legion (early 1864); brigadier general, CSA (May 24, 1864); commanding brigade, Johnson's Division Department of North Carolina and Southern Virginia (May-July 30, 1864); commanding brigade, Taliaferro's Division, Department of South Carolina, Georgia and Florida and Hardee's Corps (January ?-April 9, 1865); and commanding brigade, Anderson's division, Stewart's Corps, Army of Tennessee (April 1865). At the head of the Beaufort Artillery, he reported to the state authorities and the company soon became part of an infantry regiment. Elliott attached himself to another unit to take part in the bombardment of Fort Sumter. During the next three years he served as the chief of artillery for various districts in the state and for a time commanded in the rubble known as Fort Sumter. During the early part of the war he had fought at Port Royal and had earned a reputation as a daring raider. Transferred to Virginia in the spring of 1864, heading a legion, he was soon promoted brigadier and assigned a brigade on the Petersburg lines. Part of his brigade was blown up at the Crater on July 30, and he himself was wounded while organizing a counterattack. After a lengthy recovery he directed a brigade of former Charleston defenders in North Carolina, suffering another wound and eventually surrendering with Johnston. He died of his wounds and debilitation from the war a few months later. (Freeman, Douglas S., *Lee's Lieutenants*)

ELLIOTT, Washington Lafayette (1825-1888)

Having sailed aboard his father's naval vessel as a child it must have been hard for Washington L. Elliott to resign from West Point because of poor grades in philosophy, but the coming of the Mexican War gave him a second chance. After resigning in 1844, he was commissioned directly into the Regiment of Mounted Rifles in 1846 and served in Mexico and on the frontier. He also performed recruiting duties. His Civil War assignments included: captain, Mounted Rifles (since July 20, 1854); captain, 3rd Cavalry (designation change August 3, 1861); colonel, 2nd Iowa Cavalry (September 14, 1861); major, 1st Cavalry (November 5, 1861); commanding 2nd Brigade, Cavalry Division, Army of the Mississippi (April 24-June 1, 1862); brigadier general, USV (June 11, 1862); commanding the division (July 30-August 11, 1862); chief of Cavalry, Army of Virginia (August 1862); commanding Department of the

Northwest (November 28, 1862-February 18, 1863); comanding 1st brigade, 2nd Division, 8th Corps, Middle Department (February-June 26, 1863); commanding Elliott's Command, 8th Corps, Middle Department (June 26-July 10, 1863); commanding 3rd Division, 3rd Corps, Army of the Potomac (July 10-October 5, 1863) commanding 1st Division, Cavalry Corps, Army of the Cumberland (October 12-November 20, 1863); commanding the corps (November 20, 1863-August 19, 1864); and commanding 2nd Division, 4th Corps, Army of the Cumberland (December 2, 1864-June 24, 1865). Initially serving in the West, he took command of a volunteer mounted regiment that he led at New Madrid and Island #10 where he earned a brevet. The native Pennsylvanian then led the first raid against the Mobile and Ohio Railroad and was named a brigadier general of volunteers. For the raid and his role in the advance on Corinth, Mississippi, he was brevetted again. Following his chief, John Pope, to Virginia, he was wounded at 2nd Bull Run while serving as chief of cavalry. Upon his recovery he briefly relieved his old commander at the head of the Department of the Northwest and then held various posts in the Middle Department. During the Gettysburg Campaign he supported the Army of the Potomac and was merged into it shortly after the battle. That fall he was again in charge of a cavalry unit during the relief of Knoxville and later during the Atlanta Campaign. Returning to Tennessee, he was brevetted brigadier general of regulars and major general of volunteers for Nashville. Brevetted a regular major general for the war, he was mustered out of the volunteers on March 1, 1866, but remained in the Army until his 1879 retirement as colonel, 3rd Cavalry. He was subsequently a San Francisco banker.

ELLIS, John Willis (1820-1861)

The death of North Carolina Governor John W. Ellis on July 7, 1861, from overwork deprived the Confederacy of a loyal supporter at the head of that state. A North Carolina native, he practiced law before entering politics as a Democrat. He served in the legislature in the 1840s and was also a militia officer. During the late 1840s and 1850s he served as a judge. A moderate on secession, he was elected governor in 1858 and was reelected two years later. Following John Brown's raid on Harpers Ferry he became a believer in military preparedness and reorganized the militia. He favored the calling of a convention of the Southern states but his proposal was defeated by a popular vote. Trying to avoid hostilities, he returned two forts to federal authorities after they had been seized by the citizenry during the secession crisis. The firing on Fort Sumter galvanized him into action and he called for 30,000 troops. He called the legislature back into session, and they in turn established the secession convention that took the state out of the Union. On a trip to Red Sulpher Springs, now in West Virginia, he died from the complications arising from stress. (Boykin, James, *North Carolina in 1861*)

ELLSWORTH, Ephraim Elmer (1837-1861)

A personal friend of Abraham Lincoln, Colonel Elmer Ellsworth became the first martyr for the Union, and the country's grief over his fall was destined to be repeated thousands of times on both sides. A New York-born Chicago lawyer, Ellsworth became a close friend of the future president and accompanied him to the nation's capital for the inauguration. Although he had failed to obtain an appointment to West Point, he maintained an interest in military affairs and had commanded a premier drill unit in Chicago and on tour. With the firing on Fort Sumter, Ellsworth returned to New York City and, principally from the fire department, raised the 11th New York or "Ellsworth's Fire Zouaves." With the organization completed, and Ellsworth as colonel, it moved to Washington on April 29, 1861. In the movement of the Union forces to the Virginia shore of the Potomac on May 24, the 11th was assigned the duty of sailing down the river to Alexandria and capturing that city in conjunction with a land force. With the rebels abandoning the town with minimal resistance, the place was occupied. In the early hours of the occupation, Colonel Ellsworth noticed a Confederate banner flying from the Marshall House. Entering the hotel, Ellsworth demanded of the proprietor, James T. Jackson, what flag it was, but he pretended to be a mere boarder. Ellsworth then went to the roof and seized the emblem, but while descending the stairs was accosted by the owner with a shotgun. Ellsworth died instantly and his body was laid in state at the White House. (Randall, Ruth Painter, *Colonel Elmer Ellsworth: A Biography of Lincoln's Friend and First Hero of the Civil War*)

E. Elmer Ellsworth, an early Union martyr. (*Leslie's*)

ELLSWORTH, George A. (1834-1899)

Canadian-born telegrapher George A. Ellsworth became a major asset to Confederate raider John Hunt Morgan's command. Working in Texas at the outbreak of hostilities, he enlisted in a local regiment but was not allowed to go to the front, his services being considered too valuable at home. But he eventually made his way to Mobile where he joined up with Morgan. On the cavalryman's July 1862 raid into Kentucky, Ellsworth's value became apparent when he began to tap enemy communications, gathering valuable information. When the Confederates found an intact, abandoned telegraph station, he was able to provide the frantic Union forces with faulty information as to Morgan's whereabouts. Subsequently he served with Morgan until the latter's capture, then on Simon Buckner's staff, and was wounded at Chickamauga. Briefly he was an agent in Kentucky but fled to Canada, his native country, in April 1864. After the war he was in and out of trouble with the law but continued to find jobs in the United States in his old trade.

ELZEY, Arnold (1816-1871)

A career soldier, Arnold Elzey had dropped the family name of Jones about the time he graduated from West Pont in 1837. Having served in the artillery for nearly a quarter century, earning a brevet in Mexico, Captain Elzey resigned on April 25, 1861, to offer his services to the South—despite the fact that his native Maryland never joined the Confederacy. His assignments included: major, Artillery (spring 1861); colonel, 1st Maryland (1861); commanding brigade, 2nd Corps, Army of the Potomac (July 21-October 22, 1861); brigadier general, CSA (July 21, 1861); commanding brigade, E.K. Smith's-Ewell's Division, Potomac District (Valley District after April), Department of Northern Virginia (October 22, 1861-June 8, 1862); commanding brigade, Ewell's Division, Jackson's Command, Army of Northern Virginia (June 26-27, 1862); major general, CSA (December 4, 1862); commanding Elzey's Command, Department of Virginia and North Carolina (December 12, 1862-April 1, 1863); commanding Department of Richmond (April 1, 1863-April 25, 1864); and chief of artillery, Army of Tennessee (September 8, 1864-February 17, 1865). He succeeded to brigade command at 1st Bull Run and continued in charge until wounded at Port Republic at the end of the Shenandoah Valley Campaign. His wound being slight, he soon returned to duty but was severely wounded in the head at Gaines' Mill, his first action in the Seven Days. Unfit for active field duty he was given charge of the captal's defenses. In April 1864 he was sent to Staunton, Virginia to work on the long-delayed organization of the Maryland Line. That fall and winter he was artillery chief under Hood but was apparently not in the Franklin-Nashville Campaign. After his parole he retired to a Maryland farm.

EMILY (?-1863)

A girl from Brooklyn, known to history only as Emily, became one of the combatant casualties of the battle of Chickamauga. When, in early 1863, her parents saw her desire to enlist in the Union army, they thought her mentally disturbed and so sent her off to an aunt in Michigan to forget the notion. Escaping from her confinement, she disguised herself and joined the army as a drummer. She allegedly served through the Tullahoma and Chickamauga campaigns in a Michigan regiment in Van Cleve's Division. However, there were no units from that state in that division at that time. In any event on the second day of the battle she was wounded in the side. It was at this time that her true sex was revealed. Told the wound was fatal she wrote her father: "Forgive your dying daughter. I have but a few moments to live. My native soil drinks my blood. I expected to deliver my country, but the Fates would not have it so. I am content to die. Pray, pa, forgive me. Tell ma to kiss my daguerreotype. Emily."

EMMETT, Daniel Decatur (1815-1904)

If he had known in advance that his song "Dixie" would become an unofficial national anthem of the Confederacy, Ohio Unionist Daniel Emmett would probably have never written it. Although he had no formal musical education, Emmett early developed a talent for music. During the Black Hawk War he served as a fifer and drummer in the 6th Infantry until his father had him discharged as a minor. However, he had mastered the drum sufficiently to write the army's first manual for drummers, *Emmett's Standard Drummer*. He then joined a series of small circuses until he formed possibly the first blackface minstrel show. He did all the writing and costume designing for the show himself. While working for another minstrel show (his own had gone broke on a English tour) as a songwriter and performer, Emmett wrote "I Wish I was in Dixie's Land," which was copyrighted in 1860. The next year it was played at the inauguration of Jefferson Davis, and was enthusiastically adopted by the troops. Throughout the war he continued to write for the New York minstrel company. But none of his works achieved the fame of "Dixie." A fan of General McClellan, Emmett wrote, "Mac Will Win the Union Back." Maybe if he had been right it would have become famous. After the war and until his retirement in 1888 he worked as a theater manager and conductor. Eventually his song, which Lincoln had declared to be captured property at the war's close, became a force for reuniting the country. (Galbreath, Charles Burleigh, *Daniel Decatur Emmet*)

EMORY, William Hemsley (1811-1887)

Although he had long been in command of a corps, William H. Emory did not receive his second star until well after the close of hostilities. The native Marylander and West Pointer (1831) had been posted to the artillery before resigning as a second lieutenant in 1836. Two years later he was recommissioned as a first lieutenant in the topographical engineers. During the war with Mexico he earned two brevets and a further one for his work in establishing the new U.S.-imposed boundary with Mexico. In 1855 he transferred to the mounted arm and his Civil War-era assignments included: major, 1st Cavalry (since May 26, 1855); lieutenant colonel, 1st Cavalry (January 31, 1861); lieutenant colonel, 3rd Cavalry (May 14, 1861); lieutenant colonel, 6th Cavalry (designation change August 3, 1861); commanding brigade, Cavalry Reserves, Army of the Potomac (March 13-July 5, 1862); brigadier general, USV (March 17, 1862); commanding 1st Brigade, 2nd Division, 4th Corps, Army of the Potomac (July 6-August 10, 1862); commanding 3rd Division, 19th Corps, Department of the Gulf (January 3-May 2 and September 4-17, 1863); commanding Defenses of New Orleans, 19th Corps, Department of the Gulf (May 21-August 25, 1863); also commanding 4th Division, 19th Corps, Department of the Gulf (July 30-August 25, 1863); colonel, 5th Cavalry (October 27, 1863); commanding 1st Division, 19th Corps, Department Gulf (December 13, 1863-May 2, 1864); commanding the corps (May 2-July 2, 1864); commanding 19th Corps, Army of the Shenandoah (August 6-December 8, 1864 and December 28, 1864-March 20, 1865); commanding Department of West Virginia (temporarily April 1865); and major general, USV (September 25, 1865). He was highly successful in withdrawing his men from the Indian Territory—now Oklahoma—at the outbreak of the war but resigned his commission on May 9, 1861. However, five days later he was commissioned at the same grade in the newly authorized 3rd, later 6th Cavalry. As such he commanded a brigade of the Cavalry Reserve near Washington. As a newly commissioned brigadier general of volunteers he led his brigade to the Peninsula where it saw service at Yorktown, Willamsburg, and Hanover Court House. For the latter he was brevetted. During the Seven Days he was in charge of a specially organized mixed command. His next field service came in the Red River Campaign when he succeeded to command of the 19th Corps. Taking a detachment of his command to reinforce Grant before Petersburg, he was diverted to the Shenandoah Valley. There he fought at 3rd Winchester and earned the regular army brevets of brigadier and major general for Fisher's Hill and Cedar Creek. As of July 23, 1864, he had already been brevetted to major general in the volunteer service. At the end of the war he briefly succeeded Winfield S. Hancock in western Virginia. Five months later he was awarded his second star. Mustered out of the volunteers on January 15, 1866, he remained in the regular establishment until his retirement in 1876 with the advanced rank of brigadier general. His prewar years had been highlighted by his scientific writings, especially *Notes of a Military Reconnaissance from Fort Leavenworth in Missouri, to San Diego in California*.

ERICSSON, John (1803-1889)

After service in his native Sweden's army and navy, where he became noted for his inventive abilities, John Ericsson took a year's leave of absence in 1826, from which he never returned, to demonstrate his caloric engine in England. Eventually allowed to resign from the army, thus extraditing himself from legal difficulties, Ericsson remained in England until 1839, earning 30 patents. His failures to interest the Admiralty in his screw propeller wrecked his personal finances and landed him in debtor's prison. In late 1839 he went to Washington but there too he failed to convince the authorities. However, following Harrison's death and John Tyler's succession to the Presidency, Ericsson was given the green light to design the U.S. Navy's first steam-powered vessel, the USS *Princeton*, completed in 1844. It was also the first vessel with its vital machinery located below the waterline. However, Ericsson's reputation became tarnished that same year when, during a demonstration on the Potomac, a 12-inch gun exploded. Among the fatalities were the Secretaries of State and the Navy and the head of the Navy's Bureau of Construction and Equipment. It didn't seem to matter that the gun, nicknamed "Peacemaker," had been designed by Captain Robert Field Stockton and not by Ericsson. The Swede failed to get his due compensation. Not until the Civil War did he work for the U.S. government again. Then on September 3, 1861, he submitted his design for an ironclad to the Department of the Navy. After much hesitation the plan was accepted on October 4, with the vessel to be completed in 100 days. Fighting against supply shortages, specification changes, and problems inherent in any vessel incorporating so many revolutionary technologies—including armor plating, screw propellers, revolving turret, and machinery placed below the waterline, he managed to launch the USS *Monitor* on January 30, 1862. With its successful showing in the fight with the CSS *Virginia*, Ericsson went to work on the 10 member *Passaic* class, USS *Dictator*, USS *Puritan*, and the nine-member *Canonicus* class. He also did the preliminary work on the later, unsuccessful 20-member *Casco* class, which project was directed by his superintendent, Chief Engineer Alban Stimers. Following the war he sold his vessels to several nations and continued his work on solar energy, ordnance, and torpedoes. (Church, William C., *The Life of John Ericsson* and White, Ruth, *Yankee from Sweden*)

ESHLEMAN, Benjamin Franklin (1830-1909)

A member of the famed Washington Artillery of New Orleans, Benjamin F. Eshleman rose to command the unit in the latter stages of the Civil War. He was a student at West Point when the war began but resigned to offer his services to the South despite the fact that he had been born in Pennsylvania. His assignments included: captain, 4th Company, Washington Artillery Battalion (May 26, 1861); major, Washington Artillery Battalion (March 26, 1862); commanding Washington Artillery Battalion, Reserve Artillery, 1st Corps, Army of Northern Virginia (June 4-July 1863); commanding Washington Artillery Battalion, 1st Corps, Army of Northern Virginia (July-September 1863); commanding Washington Artillery Battalion, Department of North Carolina (September 1863-May 1864); lieutenant colonel, Washington Artillery Battalion (February 22, 1864); commanding another artillery battalion, Department of North Carolina and Southern Virginia (May 1864); and commanding Washington Artillery Battalion, 3rd Corps, Army of Northern Virginia (June 1864-April 9, 1865). Severely wounded at Blackburn's Ford, he missed the battle of 1st Bull Run three days later. He returned to command his battery at 2nd Bull Run, Antietam, Fredericksburg, and Chancellorsville, sometimes commanding the battalion. Following the last action he was promoted to major, to date from the previous spring. After leading the battalion in action at Gettysburg, he was left with his command in the Department of North Carolina while the corps went to Georgia and East Tennessee. The new lieutenant colonel was given command of a new artillery battalion, which he led in the defense of Petersburg, before resuming direction of the Louisiana unit in order to join Lee in time for Cold Harbor. He served through the Petersburg Campaign and during the retreat he was assigned to the column under General Walker bound for Lynchburg and thus was not present at the surrender. He returned to New Orleans and was active in business affairs as a merchant. (Owen, William M., *In Camp and Battle With the Washington Artillery of New Orleans*)

ESTE, George Peabody

See: *Estey, George Peabody*

ESTEY, George Peabody (1829-1881)

New Hampshire native George P. Estey (sometimes Este) practiced law in Illinois and Ohio before entering the Union army and rising to the rank of brigadier general. His assignments included: lieutenant colonel, 14th Ohio (three-months unit April 24, 1861); lieutenant colonel, 14th Ohio (three-years unit August 16, 1861); colonel, 14th Ohio (November 20, 1862); commanding 3rd Brigade, 3rd Division, 14th Corps, Army of the Cumberland (April 1-October 25, 1864 and November 16, 1864-March 29, 1865); commanding the division (October 25-November 25, 1864); and brigadier general, USV (June 25, 1865). He served in western Virginia with his original unit until it was mustered out on August 13, 1861. Three days later he was recommissioned in the reorganized three-years regiment. This unit fought at Mill Springs and with Estey in command at Perryville. He then led it through the Tullahoma Campaign but missed both Chickamauga and Chattanooga. During the Atlanta Campaign he commanded a brigade and was slighty wounded at Jonesboro. He participated in the March to the Sea, part of the time in charge of the division, and was brevetted brigadier general for the war to date from December 9, 1864. Following service in the Carolinas Campaign he was promoted to the full rank after the close of hostilities. Resigning on December 4, 1865, he practiced law in Washington, D.C., until his death.

ETHERIDGE, Anna (?-?)

Not shirking the front lines in her treatment of the wounded, Anna Etheridge was herself slightly wounded in the hand and earned the Kearny Cross for bravery in action. A Wisconsin native, she cut short a visit to Detroit to join the 2nd Michigan as a nurse and was on the field of 1st Bull Run. With the 3rd and later the 5th Michigan she served with the Army of the Potomac throughout the war, and General Philip Kearny wanted to make her a sergeant major before his death. Instead she became one of the first recipients of the Kearny Cross devised by his successor, David Birney. During the Petersburg siege she was assigned to the hospital in the rear of City Point. By this time she had received many bullet holes in her clothing. Affectionately, she was called "Gentle Anna" and "Michigan Annie" by the troops. She was a government clerk after the war.

EUSTIS, Henry Lawrence (1819-1885)

Henry L. Eustis who came from a military family was forced out of the Army for reasons of ill health apparently caused by an addiction to opium. The native of Massachusetts graduated from Harvard before accepting an appointment to West Point. Graduating first in his 1842 class he was posted to the engineers. Resigning in 1849, he taught engineering at Harvard until the Civil War. Volunteering for the war, his assignments included: colonel 10th Massachusetts (August 21, 1862); commanding 2nd Brigade, 3rd Division, 6th Corps, Army of the Potomac (late December 1862-January 1863 and May 3, 1863-January 29, 1864); brigadier general, USV (September 12, 1863); commanding 2nd Division, 6th Corps, Army of the Potomac (February 21-March 25, 1864); commanding 4th Brigade, 2nd Division, 6th Corps, Army of the Potomac (March 26-May 9, 1864); and commanding 3rd Brigade, 1st Division, 6th Corps, Army of the Potomac (May 9-June 12, 1864). Answering the summer of 1862 call for troops, he took command of a volunteer regiment that was too far to the rear to fight at Antietam. After fighting at Fredericksburg he succeeded to brigade command at Chancellorsville. In reserve at Gettysburg, he served through the Bristoe and Mine Run campaigns. After serving through the Overland Campaign he resigned on June 27, 1864, citing health reasons. However, there is some evidence that he was addicted to opium and that he was threatened with charges of neglect of duty unless he submitted his resignation. He spent the remainder of his life at Harvard.

EVANS, Augusta Jane (1835-1900)

A novelist of some note who had received recognition for her second novel *Beulah* shortly before the Civil War, Augusta Jane Evans threw herself wholeheartedly into the Confederate cause. During the conflict itself she was a nurse in a hospital in Mobile, where she had been raised, and an advisor to Confederate Congressman J.L.M. Curry. The Georgia-born author wrote another novel, *Macaria*, in 1863, predicting dire consequences in the emancipation of the slaves. It was popular in both the South and North, and some Union commanders such as George H. Thomas banned the book because of its adverse affect on morale. Highly critical of the Davis regime, she wrote numerous articles favoring Beauregard over Bragg for command in the West. She continued her career until her sudden death. (Fidler, William Percy, *Augusta Jane Evans Wilson, 1835-1900*)

EVANS, Clement Anselm (1833-1911)

A Georgia lawyer and politician, Clement A. Evans became a division commander in the last months of the war. His assignments included: major, 31st Georgia (November 19, 1861); colonel, 31st Georgia (May 13, 1862); commanding

Lawton's-Gordon's Brigade, Ewell's-Early's Division, 2nd Corps, Army of Northern Virginia (September-October and December 13, 1862-ca. April 11, 1863 and May 8-21, 1864); commanding brigade, Gordon's Division, Valley District, Department of Northern Virginia (June 13-July 9 and late summer-December 1864); and commanding Gordon's Division, 2nd Corps, Army of Northern Virginia (December 1864-April 9, 1865). Wounded in the Seven Days Battles, he was back on duty in time to succeed to command of the brigade at Fredericksburg. Replaced by General Gordon, he commanded the 31st at Gettysburg and the Wilderness. When Gordon was raised to division command, Evans took over the brigade and a few days later was transferred with Gordon to the remnants of Johnson's Division after Spotsylvania. Evans fought at Cold Harbor and then accompanied the corps to the Valley. In the invasion of Maryland he was wounded at Monocacy but returned in time to fight at 3rd Winchester, Fisher's Hill, and Cedar Creek. Returning to Lee's army, he directed the division in the Petersburg trenches and surrendered at Appomattox. Becoming a minister after the war, he wrote *Military History of Georgia* and edited *Confederate Military History*, a 13-volume work.

EVANS, Nathan George (1824-1868)

Of all the Confederacy's early heroes, one of the most troublesome was South Carolinian Nathan G. Evans. A West Pointer (1848), he was a veteran of 13 years in the mounted service when he resigned his captaincy on February 27, 1861. Not receiving immediate appointment in the Confederate service, he entered that of his state and his assignments included: major, S.C. Army (ca. March 1861); captain, Cavalry (May 21, 1861); major and colonel, Cavalry (July 1861); commanding a 7th Brigade, 1st Corps, Army of the Potomac (ca. July 21-25, 1861); commanding a new 7th Brigade, 1st Corps, Army of the Potomac (July 25-October 22, 1861); brigadier general, CSA (October 21, 1861); commanding 4th Brigade, 4th Division, Potomac District, Department of Northern Virginia (October 22-November 24, 1861); commanding 3rd (called 2nd after June) Military District of South Carolina, Department of South Carolina, Georgia and Florida (December 18, 1861-July 1862); commanding independent brigade (in McLaws' Division from late September), 1st Corps, Army of Northern Virginia (August-November 6, 1862); commanding brigade, Department of Virginia and North Carolina (November 6, 1862-April 1, 1863); commanding brigade, Department of North Carolina (April 1-11, 1863); commanding subdivision, 1st Military District of South Carolina, Department of South Carolina, Georgia and Florida (April 11-May 15, 1863); commanding brigade, Loring's Division (May-June 1863), Breckinridge's Division (June 1863), and French's Division (June 21-August 4, 1863), Department of the West; commanding 2nd Subdivision, 1st Military District of South Carolina, Department of South Carolina, Georgia and Florida (August-October 5, 1863); and commanding the district (March 21-April 1864). As a staff officer, he witnessed the attack on Fort Sumter before going to Virginia where he became a hero of 1st Bull Run, slowing a surprise Union flank attack. He was in general command at the Ball's Bluff victory and later at Secessionville in South Carolina. With a new brigade in Virginia, he fought at 2nd Bull Run. Also in control of Hood's Division, he placed that officer under arrest in a dispute over some captured ambulances. Hood was later freed by Lee at Antietam. After that battle Evans was transferred to North Carolina where he got into a dispute with his regimental commanders. He placed one of them under arrest and, in retaliation, another brought him up on charges of drunkenness. Eventuallythey were both acquitted. Evans' brigade served in South Carolina and Mississippi during the Vicksburg Campaign where he got in a scrape over disobediance and, although acquitted, was kept off duty by Beauregard until March 1864. The next month he was injured in a fall from his horse and never returned to command his "Tramp Brigade," so named because of its travels. Evans recovered but he was passed over for assignment to duty. After the war he claimed to have undergone a moral reformation. (Freeman, Douglas S., *Lee's Lieutenants*)

EVARTS, William Maxwell (1818-1901)

Having represented the United States in the trial and dispute over privateers early in the Civil War (See: Smith, Walter W.), William M. Evarts became a diplomat in Europe. Active in the Union defense committees movement, he was dispatched to England in 1863 and remained for about a year. As the chief defense attorney in the impeachment trial of Andrew Johnson he has been credited with a skillful presentation in a highly political atmosphere. (Barrows, Chester Leonard, *William M. Evarts, Lawyer, Diplomat, Statesman*)

EVERETT, Edward (1794-1865)

Although he gave the principal address at the dedication of the national cemetery at Gettysburg, Edward Everett was overshadowed by the brief but poignant speech by a relatively last minute invitee, Abraham Lincoln. The Massachusetts native was educated at Harvard and in Europe. He taught for a time at Harvard and edited the *North American Review*. In the pre-Civil War years he had sat in both houses of the national legislature, served as Massachusetts' chief executive and headed the State Department under Millard Fillmore. A Unionist, he resigned when he felt that he had deserted his principles by not voting on the Kansas-Nebraska Act. In 1860 he ran as John Bell's running mate in the presidential canvass on the Constitutional Union ticket. Thereafter he made repeated speeches in favor of the war effort and was given the honor of the main address at Gettysburg. However, his two-hour oration has been all but forgotten. Everett died the year the war ended.

EWELL, Richard Stoddert (1817-1872)

As Stonewall Jackson's successor, the gallant Richard S. Ewell proved to be a disappointment and the argument as to why is still around today. Some claim it was the loss of a leg, others that it was the influence of the "Widow Brown" who he married during his recovery. But the fact of the matter is that he was ill-prepared by Jackson for the loose style of command practiced by Lee. A West Pointer (1840) and veteran of two decades as a company officer, he never quite made the adjustment to commanding large-scale units. He once went out foraging for his division and returned—with a single steer—as if he was still commanding a company of dragoons. Resigning his captaincy on May 7, 1861, to serve the South, he held the following assignments: colonel, Cavalry (1861); brigadier general, CSA (June 17, 1861); commanding brigade (in 1st Corps after July 20), Army of the Potomac (June 20-October 22, 1861); commanding brigade, Longstreet's Division, Potomac District, Department of Northern Virginia (October 22, 1861-February 21, 1862); major general, CSA (January 23, 1862); commanding E.K. Smith's (old) Division, same district and department (February 21-May 17, 1862); commanding same division, Valley District, same department (May 17-June 26, 1862); commanding division, 2nd Corps, Army of Northern Virginia (June 26-August 28, 1862); commanding the corps (May 30, 1863-May 27, 1864); lieutenant general, CSA (May 23, 1863); and commanding Department of Richmond (June 13, 1864-April 6, 1865). After serving at 1st Bull Run he commanded a division under Jackson in the Shenandoah Valley Campaign where he complained bitterly about being left in the dark about plans. Jackson's style of leadership was to prove the undoing of Ewell once Jackson was gone. Ewell fought through the Seven Days and at Cedar Mountain before being severely wounded and losing a leg at Groveton, in the beginning of the battle of 2nd Bull Run. After a long recovery, he returned to duty in May 1863 and was promoted to command part of Jackson's old corps. At 2nd Winchester he won a stunning victory and for a moment it looked like a second Stonewall had come. But at Gettysburg he failed to take advantage of the situation on the evening of the first day when given discretionary orders by Lee. He required exact instructions, unlike his predecessor. After serving through the fall campaigns he fought at the Wilderness where the same problem developed. At Spotsylvania one of his divisions was all but destroyed. After the actions along the North Anna he was forced to temporarily relinquish command due to illness but Lee made it permanent. He was given command in Richmond and was captured at Sayler's Creek on April 6, 1865, during the retreat to Appomattox. After his release from Fort Warren in July "Old Baldy" retired to a farm in Tennessee. (Hamlin, Percy Gatling, *"Old Bald Head"*)

"Old Baldy" Richard S. Ewell. (*Leslie's*)

EWEN, John (?-?)

A native New Yorker and brigadier general in that state's National Guard, John Ewen was accepted into the U.S. service—despite War Department policy against accepting officers above the rank of colonel—due to the crisis posed by the Pennsylvania invasion by the Army of Northern Virginia. Moving with his three regiments to the war zone, his command designated the 4th Brigade, 1st (Smith's) Division, Department of the Susquehanna. This force operated on the flanks of the enemy but was not directly involved in the fighting at Gettysburg. With the victory won Ewen and his men were mustered out on July 20, 1863, and returned home. They had been in the service since June 18, barely more than a month.

EWING, Charles (1835-1883)

One of three Sherman brothers-in-law to become Union generals in the Civil War, Charles Ewing spent the second half of that conflict on Sherman's staff. The native Ohioan had grown up in the same household with the famous general and practiced law before accepting a commission in one of the newly authorized regular army infantry regiments at the outbreak of the war. His assignments included: captain, 13th Infantry (May 14, 1861); lieutenant colonel and assistant adjutant general (June 22, 1863); and brigadier general, USV (March 8, 1865). He spent the first year of the war organizing the new unit and did not join the forces in the field until the fall of 1862. Taking part in the operations against Vicksburg, with the regiment's 1st Battalion, he took temporary charge of it during the first assault at the city itself until wounded while carrying the flag. Brevetted for this he was further rewarded with promotion to lieutenant colonel and assignment to Sherman's staff. As an inspector, he took part in the Chattanooga and Meridian campaigns and was brevetted for the Atlanta Campaign. He continued with Sherman on the March to the Sea and through the Carolinas. Late in the war he was promoted to brigadier general of volunteers and was brevetted colonel of regulars. Resigning on December 1, 1865, from the volunteers, he served two more years in the regulars until he resigned to practice law in the nation's capital.

EWING, Hugh Boyle (1826-1905)

Although he had dropped out of West Point in 1848 because of poor grades in engineering, Hugh B. Ewing, like his two brothers, became a Union general in the Civil War. After taking part in the gold rush in California, he became a lawyer in Missouri and Kansas before returning to his native Ohio. Upon the outbreak of the Civil War he offered his services to Governor William Dennison. His assignments included: brigade inspector, Ohio Volunteers (May 6, 1861); colonel, 30th Ohio (August 20, 1861); commanding 1st Brigade, Kanawha Division, 9th Corps, Army of the Potomac (September 17-October 1862); brigadier general USV (November 29, 1862); commanding 3rd Brigade, 2nd Division, 15th Corps, Army of the Tennessee (January 9-July 21, 1863); commanding 1st Division, 16th Corps, Army of the Tennessee (July 20-28, 1863); commanding 4th Division, 15th Corps, Army of the Tennessee (July 28-September 1, 1863 and October 16, 1863-February 8, 1864); commanding 2nd Division, District of Kentucky, 23rd Corps, Department of the Ohio (April 7, 1864-January 17, 1865); and commanding 2nd Division, Department of Kentucky (February-spring 1865). Initially he served on the staffs of McClellan and Rosecrans in western Virginia before being named to a colonelcy. He took this regiment to reinforce the Army of the Potomac and fought at South Mountain and in the capture of Burnside's Bridge at Antietam. Transferred to the West and named brigadier general, he led a brigade through the Vicksburg Campaign and then went to the relief of Chattanooga. There, under Sherman, who had grown up in the Ewing home, he led his division in the assaults on Tunnel Hill and suffered severely. Early the following year he was assigned to command the post at Louisville, Kentucky. He spent most of the rest of the war in that state. He was ordered to join Sherman in the Carolinas but the war ended before he could launch his planned expedition along the Roanoke River.

EWING, Thomas, Jr. (1829-1896)

Brother-in-law of William T. Sherman and brother of Charles and Hugh B. Ewing, Thomas Ewing, Jr., gave up his position as the first chief justice of Kansas' supreme court in order to join the Union army. The Ohio-born lawyer had been active in the Free-Soil movement in his adopted state. His military assignments included: colonel, 11th Kansas (September 15, 1862); brigadier general, USV (March 13, 1863); and commanding in the Department of Missouri: 1st Division, Army of the Frontier (April 26-June 5, 1863); District of the Border (June 9, 1963-January 1864); District of St. Louis (March 25-November 21, 1864 and December 9, 1864-April 5, 1865); and District of Rolla (November 21-December 9, 1864). He led his regiment, which was subsequently converted to cavalry, at Cane Hill and Prairie Grove before being named a brigadier general in early 1863. He was then assigned to command along the troublesome border between Missouri and Kansas and in his frustration issued his infamous General Order No. 11 depopulating four Missouri counties in a fruitless effort to curb guerrilla activity. Transferred to St. Louis, he took part in the efforts to halt Sterling Price's 1864 invasion of the state. Brevetted for Pilot Knob, he resigned on February 23, 1965, and resumed the practice of law. He also served two terms in Congress as a Democrat.

F

FAGAN, James Fleming (1828-1893)

An early Arkansas Confederate, Kentucky-born lawyer and Mexican War veteran—as a second lieutenant in Yell's Arkansas Regiment—James F. Fagan rose to a major generalcy in charge of a mounted division. His assignments included: colonel, 1st Arkansas (May 8, 1861); brigadier general CSA (September 12, 1862); commanding brigade, Frost's Division, 1st Corps, Trans-Mississippi Department (December 1862-January 1863); commanding brigade, Hindman's-Price's Division, District of Arkansas, Trans-Mississippi Department (January-July 23 and August 17-late 1863); commanding Price's Division, District of Arkansas, Trans-Mississippi Department (July 23-August 17, 1863); commanding cavalry division, District of Arkansas, Trans-Mississippi Department (late 1863-September 18, 1864); major general, CSA (April 25, 1864); and commanding in Trans-Mississippi Department: cavalry division, Army of Missouri (September 18-late 1864); also 1st (Arkansas) Cavalry Division, Cavalry Corps (September 1864-early 1865); and Cavalry, District of Arkansas (February 1-spring 1865). He led his regiment at Shiloh and during the defense of Corinth, Mississippi. Promoted to brigadier general and transferred west of the Mississippi, he fought at the head of a brigade at Prairie Grove, Helena, and Little Rock. During the repulse of Steel's Arkansas expedition in April 1864 Fagan led a mounted division at Jenkins' Ferry and that fall went on Sterling Price's invasion of Missouri. Surrendering on June 14, 1865, he was a postwar farmer, U.S. marshal, and minor goverment official.

FAIRBANKS, Erastus (1792-1864)

Based upon a pledge made in the 1860 election campaign, Vermont governor Erastus Fairbanks refused to seek reelection in 1861. The Massachusetts-born merchant and manufacturer had been active in canals and railroads and served in the state legislature before becoming governor in 1852 in an election that had to be determined in the legislature since no candidate had achieved a majority. Three years later he was defeated in a similar election in which his plurality was ignored by the legislators. With the formation of the Republican Party he switched from the Whigs and was elected overwhelmingly as governor in 1860. His primary concern in this term was the recruitment and equipping of volunteers. As promised he left office during the first year of the Civil War and died before it closed, on November 20, 1864.

FAIRCHILD, Lucius (1831-1896)

Born in Ohio but raised in Wisconsin, Lucius Fairchild fought with the famed Iron Brigade. Only five days after Fort Sumter had been fired upon, the Democrat-turned-Republican officeholder enlisted in the Union army. His assignments included: private, 1st Wisconsin (April 17, 1861); captain, 1st Wisconsin (May 17, 1861); captain, 16th U.S. Infantry (August 5, 1861); lieutenant colonel, 2nd Wisconsin (August 20, 1861); colonel, 2nd Wisconsin (September 1, 1862); and brigadier general, USV (October 19, 1863). During the 1st Bull Run Campaign, Fairchild saw action at Falling Waters and was mustered out at the end of his regiment's term of service on August 17, 1861. Although appointed a captain in the regular army he continued in the volunteer service, becoming lieutenant colonel of a Wisconsin regiment. In the fight at Groveton on August 28, 1862, which was in fact the opening of the battle of 2nd Bull Run, Fairchild assumed command of the regiment upon the death of the colonel, Edgar O'Connor. This fight was a stand-up battle between the brigade, which hereafter was known as the Iron Brigade, and two of Stonewall Jackson's division. The fire fight continued for an hour and a half before sunset brought it to a close. After serving in command of his regiment at South Mountain, Fredericksburg, and Chancellorsville, Fairchild led his men in the fighting along Willoughby Run west of Gettysburg on July 1, 1863. During the fighting in the woods he was severely wounded and his arm had to be amputated. Although promoted to brigadier, he saw no further service because of his wound and resigned both his regular and volunteer commission on November 2, 1863. His regiment went on to compile the highest percentage of casualties of any Union regiment in the war, 62%. After the war Fairchild became governor of his state and served in diplomatic posts, but was most noted for his postwar bitterness towards the South. (Ross, Sam, *The Empty Sleeve: A Biography of Lucius Fairchild*)

FARNSWORTH, Elon John (1837-1863)

Elon Farnsworth was an officer who experienced a meteoric rise to a general's star only to be killed five days later in a suicidal charge. A civilian veteran of the Mormon expedition, Farnsworth was appointed first lieutenant and adjutant of his uncle's regiment, the 8th Illinois Cavalry, on September 18, 1861. Having been promoted captain on December 25, 1861, he attended services on February 9, 1862, at Saint Paul's Church in Alexandria, Virginia. When Reverend J.R. Stewart refused to read the required prayer for the U.S. President, Farnsworth ordered him arrested. The preacher was subsequently released. Farnsworth served in all his regiment's campaigns. During the Chancellorsville Campaign, he participated in Stoneman's Raid and on the retreat saved the horse artillery's ammunition chests by floating them over a river. On June 28, 1863, Farnsworth was jumped from captain to brigadier and given command of the 1st Brigade, 3rd Division, Cavalry Corps, Army of the Potomac. The reason for this unusually rapid advancement, other than his staff association with General Pleasonton, the new cavalry chief, does not appear in the records. After several days of chasing rebel cavalry, Farnsworth was ordered to charge the Confederate right flank at Gettysburg on July 3. Questioning his division commander, General Kilpatrick, about the wisdom of this move of cavalry against infantry behind stone walls, Farnsworth had his own bravery challenged. Making the doomed charge with the 1st West Virginia Cavalry, he was struck by five bullets and killed. Farnsworth had been right!

FARNSWORTH, John Franklin (1820-1897)

Abolitionist-Representative John F. Farnsworth spent a two year congressional term as a Union officer after he was denied renomination. Born in Canada, he studied law in Michigan and entered practice in Illinois. Originally a Democrat, he served his first two terms in Congress from 1857 to 1861. At the end of his second term he raised a cavalry regiment for the Union army. His assignments included: colonel, 8th Illinois Cavalry (September 18, 1861); commanding 2nd brigade, Pleasonton's Cavalry Division, Army of the Potomac (September-November 1862); commanding 1st Brigade, Pleasonton's Cavalry Division, Right Grand Division, Army of the Potomac (November 1862-January 1863); and brigadier general, USV (November 29, 1862). He led his regiment on the Peninsula at Yorktown, and during the Seven Days. His brigade was only lightly engaged during the Maryland Campaign. Promoted to brigadier general, he led another brigade at Fredericksburg. He had already been elected to Congress, and he resigned to begin his third term on March 4, 1863. He quickly became associated with the Radical Republicans and their policies. A supporter of Lincoln's Emancipation Proclamation and the 13th Amendment, he was also a believer in congressional control of Reconstruction. He supported all the radical measures in Congress. After the war he supported the impeachment of Andrew Johnson. He lost the elections of 1872 and 1874 and returned to practicing law in Chicago. His nephew Elon J. Farnsworth was killed at Gettysburg.

FARNUM, John Egbert (1824-1870)

One of the best examples of the thesis that many Union soldiers served, not to free the slaves, but to preserve the Union is the case of J. Egbert Farnum. The native of New Jersey had served as an overland express rider and been to Nicaragua as a filibusterer under William Walker. In the years immediately preceding the Civil War he was the supercargo aboard the *Wanderer*, America's last slaving ship. Landing his captives in Georgia, he was arrested in early 1859. Tried by Georgia prosecutor Henry R. Jackson, he was acquitted. Nonetheless, upon the outbreak of the Civil War, the New York City resident entered the Union army and his assignments included: major, 70th New York (June 27, 1861); lieutenant colonel, 70th New York (June 29, 1861); colonel, 70th New York (January 14, 1863); commanding 2nd ("Excelsior") Brigade, 2nd Division, 3rd Corps, Army of the Potomac (February, May 3-May, and July 24-August 10, 1863); and colonel, 11th Veteran Reserve Corps (July 26, 1864). His high rank at the start of the war was due to his service in the Mexican War as a noncommissioned officer in the Pennsylvania volunteers. He was wounded at Williamsburg on the Peninsula but returned to command the regiment at Fredericksburg. Promoted to colonel, he took over the brigade at Chancellorsville and fought at Gettysburg. He was mustered out with his regiment on July 7, 1864, to date from the first. Late that same month he was appointed to a colonelcy in the Veteran Reserve Corps serving in the Department of Washington. Early in 1866 he was brevetted brigadier general for his war service and on June 30 he was mustered out. Ironically, his prosecutor, Jackson, became a Confederate general.

FARRAGUT, David Glasgow (1801-1870)

Best remembered for allegedly crying at Mobile Bay, "Damn the torpedoes, full speed ahead," David G. Farragut—like his land-based colleague U.S. Grant—was the first officer to hold the top two grades in his service during the Civil War era. Born into a military family in Tennessee he was virtually adopted by his father's fellow naval officer, David Porter. At the age of nine Farragut entered the navy as a midshipman and was destined to spend the rest of his career in the service. He served as a prize master in the War of 1812 when only 12 years of age and then served in the Caribbean and Mediterranean. His Civil War-era assignments included: captain, USN (since 1855); commanding West Gulf Blockading Squadron (1862-1864); rear admiral, USN (July 16, 1862); vice admiral, USN (December 23, 1864); and admiral, USN (July 25, 1866). His initial assignment during the war was to a board to examine officers for retirement but he was then placed in command of the expedition to capture New Orleans. He ran the batteries of Forts Jackson and St. Philip, below the city, and forced the capitulation of the Crescent City. For this action he received the Thanks of Congress and the promotion to rear admiral. He was unsuccessful in operations against Vicksburg but did accomplish the capture of Galveston, Corpus Christi, and Sabine Pass in Texas. He then took part in the operations against Port Hudson and following its capture returned to a hero's welcome in New York. Returning to the Southern coast, he commanded the naval forces in the battle of Mobile Bay where he is said to have

"Damn the torpedoes" David G. Farragut. (*Leslie's*)

issued his immortal words following the sinking of the monitor *Tecumseh* by torpedoes—today known as mines. Returning to New York again, he was granted $50,000 for a home there. He was one of the first to enter Richmond upon its fall and in 1866 became the first man to hold the rank of admiral in the U.S. service. After the war he commanded the European Squadron and died of a heart attack while on an inspection tour in Portsmouth, New Hampshire. (Lewis, Charles, *David Glasgow Farragut* and Martin, Christopher, *Damn the Torpedoes: the Story of America's First Admiral, David Glasgow Farragut*)

FARRAR, Bernard Gains (?-?)

In a varied Civil War career, Brevet Brigadier General Bernard G. Farrar held several staff assignments, a brigade command at Vicksburg and Jackson, and command of a regiment of black troops. The Missouri native's assignments included: major and aide-de-camp, Missouri State Troops (May 12, 1861); colonel and aide-de-camp, Missouri State Troops (December 4, 1861); provost marshal, Military District of the Missouri (July-September 1862); colonel, 30th Missouri (October 29, 1862); superintendent of contraband and Confederate property in St. Louis (November 1862-June 1863); commanding 1st Brigade, 1st Division, 15th Corps, Army of the Tennessee (June 13-July 28, 1863); colonel, 2nd Mississippi Heavy Artillery African Descent (January 21, 1864); colonel, 5th United States Heavy Artillery Colored Troops (change of designation March 11, 1864); and colonel, 6th United States Heavy Artillery Colored Troops (change of designation April 26, 1864). As a Missouri officer he served as Halleck's aide and then on provost duty. He served in command of his regiment for only four weeks before being assigned to duty in St. Louis dealing with escaped slaves. He was recalled to his regiment in June 1863 so that he could command a brigade, which he did through the remainder of the Vicksburg and Jackson campaigns. He then organized a black regiment, which he commanded in the Natchez area. Two months after being brevetted for his war service he resigned on May 8, 1865.

FARWELL, Nathan Allen (1812-1893)

A cousin of Owen, and the martyred Elijah, Lovejoy, Nathan A. Farwell served during the last session of the 38th Congress as a senator from Maine. The Maine native had studied law but was not admitted to the bar and never practiced. Instead he became a manufacturer and ship builder. Eventually he became an accomplished seaman and a successful trader before entering the insurance business. He began his political career by serving in the state senate in 1853 and 1854. He was elected to the lower house in 1860 and the next two years was in the state senate again, the latter as presiding officer. He was serving in the lower chamber once more when he was named to succeed U.S. Senator William P. Fessenden, who had resigned to replace Salmon P. Chase as secretary to the treasury. As a Republican, he sat from October 27, 1864, until the end of the session on March 3, 1865. He returned to the insurance business rather than run for reelection.

FAULKNER, W.W. (?-?)

The Union forces in the West seemed to have a great deal of difficulty in controlling one partisan leader, W.W. Faulkner. Commanding as a captain an irregular band of Confederate cavalry in northern Mississippi and western Tennessee, he had led a raid on Island #10 in the Mississippi River on October 17, 1862. In this attack he and a number of his command were taken prisoner. At first the Union authorities refused to consider them as regular Confederate soldiers subject to the normal procedures for exchange. Confederate General Pemberton eventually got them to agree to an exchange but it was already too late. On November 15, 1862, less than a month after his capture, Faulkner escaped while being transferred from Alton, Illinois, to Johnson's Island, Ohio. What made it even worse for the Union authorities was that he had publicly boasted of his planned break ahead of time and subsequently sent a letter to one of his fellow prisoners while on the run. He later became colonel, 12th Kentucky Cavalry, and served under Nathan Bedford Forrest. At the battle of Tupelo in July 1864 he led a charge and kept going after being wounded. He was finally stopped by a second wound. During Forrest's operations against A.J. Smith's second Mississippi invasion in August 1864, he commanded the 3rd Brigade, Buford's Division, Forrest's Cavalry Corps, Department of Alabama, Mississippi, and East Louisiana. His final action of the Civil War was in opposing Wilson's raid through Alabama.

FAUNTLEROY, Thomas Turner (1795-1883)

A veteran of two and a half decades in the regular army, Thomas T. Fauntleroy was not pleased with the treatment he received at the hands of the Virginia and Confederate authorities and resigned his commission as a brigadier general in the state forces. A native of Virginia, he had served as a lieutenant in the War of 1812 and entered the regular service in 1836 as a major of dragoons. On May 13, 1861, he resigned his commission as colonel, 1st Dragoons, and was soon thereafter appointed a brigadier in the provisional army of Virginia. On May 19 he was given command of the forces in and around Richmond. Tendered a brigadier generalship in the Confederate army with assignment to command of the militia serving with General J.E. Johnston near Harpers Ferry on July 9, 1861, he declined. After much of his command was taken from his jurisdiction he requested to be relieved of duty on August 17. The formal order was issued on the 30th. (Freeman, Douglas S., *Lee's Lieutenants*)

FEATHERSTON, Winfield Scott (1820-1891)

A Tennessee-born youth, Winfield Scott Featherston had fought in the Creek War before becoming a Mississippi lawyer. He took time out from his practice to sit for two terms in Congress in the late 40s and early 50s. Once the Civil War began, his services included: colonel, 17th Mississippi (spring 1861); brigadier general CSA (from March 4, 1862); commanding brigade, D.H. Hill's Division, Department of Northern Virginia (April 6-May 1862); commanding a different brigade, Longstreet's Division, Army of Northern Virginia (June 1862); commanding brigade, Wilcox's Division, 1st Corps, same army (August-September 1862); commanding brigade, Anderson's Division, same corps and army (November 1862-January 19, 1863); commanding brigade, Loring's Division (in 2nd Military District until April), Department of Mississippi and East Louisiana (ca. February-June 1863 and August 1863-January 28, 1864); commanding brigade, Loring's Division, Department of Alabama, Mississippi and East Louisiana (January 28-May 4, 1864); commanding brigade, Loring's Division, Army of Mississippi (May 4-June 14 and July 7-26, 1864); commanding the division (June 14-July 7, 1864); commanding brigade, Loring's Division, Stewart's Corps, Army of Tennessee (July 26-28 and September-December 1864 and early April-April 26, 1865); and commanding the division (July 28-September 1864). Sent to Virginia, he took part in the victories at 1st Bull Run and Ball's Bluff and the following spring was given a brigade composed of the old Manassas garrison. He fought at Yorktown and Williamsburg and was wounded at Glendale on June 30, 1862, during the Seven Days. He fought at 2nd Bull Run commanding several brigades on the field. Sick at the time of Antietam, he was slated to be replaced by Carnot Posey but returned to duty, upsetting Lee's plan. After the victory at Fredericksburg Featherston requested—there may have been some hints—transfer to his threatened state. Assigned to a brigade under Loring, he fought at Champion Hill; he and the division were cut off from Vicksburg, joining the forces under J.E. Johnston. He later was engaged in the Atlanta Campaign, at times in charge of the division, and in Hood's invasion of Tennessee. He appears to have been off duty for a time following Franklin and Nashville but assumed command of a brigade in Johnston's reorganized army in the final weeks of the war in North Carolina; he surrendered at Greensboro. As a lawyer and politician he campaigned against the carpetbaggers and served in the legislature. (Freeman, Douglas S., *Lee's Lieutenants*)

FEE, John Gregg (1816-1901)

Disinherited by his slave-owning parents, victimized by mob violence, and driven from his home state, John G. Fee continued his abolitionist crusade. The Kentucky-born youth prepared for the ministry and then attended Lane Theological Seminary, which turned him into an abolitionist. After failing to convert his parents to the cause, he was disowned by them. Ignoring mob attacks, he became an abolitionist preacher, founding Berea Union Church and what later became Berea College. He was a frequent speaker, often working as a fundraiser for the school and church. But after John Brown's attack on Harpers Ferry, Fee was driven from the state. Returning with the Union troops in 1863 he worked with the Union black troops at Camp Nelson. He continued to a lessening degree to work for the college and church after the war.

FENTON, Reuben Eaton (1819-1885)

As New York's Republican governor, Reuben E. Fenton was highly concerned with the social aspects of wartime that affect the soldiers and their families. A native New York logger and merchant he had been active in the founding of the state party and served four terms in the U.S. House of Representatives before resigning to take up his duties as governor. In Congress during the early years of the Civil War he was a strong supporter of the Lincoln administration. As a Union candidate he was elected governor on November 8, 1864, and was sworn in on the following New Years Day. A state agency was set up during his term for the care of the wounded and sick troops. Provisions were also made for the disabled veterans and the widows and orphans. Soldiers in the field were guaranteed the vote by a constitutional amendment. After the war he served a second term and in 1869 went on to the U.S. Senate. Active in banking, he represented the United States in Paris at the International Monetary Conference in 1878. (Alexander, D.S., *A Political History of the State of New York*)

FERGUSON, Champ (?-1865)

On October 25, 1865, Confederate guerrilla Champ Ferguson was hanged in front of a detachment of United States Colored Troops for his role in the massacre of black prisoners after the fight at Saltville, Virginia the previous year. From the mountainous region of East Tennessee, he had raised a company of irregulars, which at times served with conventional troops, most notably under Joseph Wheeler. When Union forces tried to seize the vital salt works at Saltville, he took part in the October 2, 1864, battle there. The next day he proved to be one of the leaders in the massacre of wounded and captured blacks and their white officers. Confederate General John Breckinridge had him arrested and reported the incident to the authorities. Ferguson had already developed an unsavory reputation and was seized surreptitiously by federal forces. Tried for the murders of 53 persons, including 14 at Saltville, he was sentenced to the gallows. There is some evidence that a Confederate general was also involved in the massacre, and it is speculated that it was Felix H. Robertson who ironically lived to be the last living ex-general of the Confederacy. (Sensing, Thurman, *Champ Ferguson, Confederate Guerilla*)

FERGUSON, Samuel Wragg (1834-1917)

When, in August 1864, there was talk of promoting Samuel W. Ferguson to major general, Confederate cavalryman Joseph Wheeler protested so forcefully that not only was the promotion not made but Ferguson appears not to have held a significant command thereafter. The South Carolinian West Pointer (1857) had taken part in the expedition against the Mormons before resigning on March 1, 1861, as a second lieutenant with the 1st Dragoons. His Confederate assignments included: brigadier general, CSA (July 23, 1863); commanding cavalry brigade, Department of Mississippi and East Louisiana (late August 1863-January 1864); commanding brigade, Jackson's Division, Lee's Cavalry Corps, Department of Mississippi and East Louisiana (January-January 28, 1864); commanding brigade, Jackson's Division, Lee's Cavalry Corps, Department of Alabama, Mississippi and East Louisiana (January 28-May 4, 1864); commanding brigade, Jackson's Cavalry Division, Polk's-Stewart's (Army of Mississippi) Corps, Army of Tennessee (May 4-July 26, 1864); and commanding brigade, Jackson's Cavalry Division, Army of Tennessee (July 26-late August 1864). Initially he performed staff duty, mostly with Beauregard, before transferring to the line midway through the conflict. He commanded at first an independent brigade in Mississippi and as part of William H. Jackson's division took part in the Atlanta Campaign. It was during the siege of that city that dispute over discipline within the brigade and Ferguson's often insubordinate attitude came to the fore. Relegated to minor duties for the balance of the war, he later took up the practice of law and was a minor officeholder in Mississippi.

FERRERO, Edward (1831-1899)

Union General Edward Ferrero's pre-Civil War military experience came from his service in the New York militia and as a dance instructor for the cadets at the United States Military Academy. Born in Spain, he was raised in New York and followed his Italian-born father's career as a dance teacher. Joining the army, his assignments included: lieutenant colonel, New York Militia (prewar); colonel, 51st New York (October 14, 1861); commanding 2nd Brigade, 2nd Division, Department of North Carolina (April 2-July 6, 1862); commanding 2nd Brigade, 2nd Division, 9th Corps, Army of the Potomac (July 22, 1862-February 7, 1863 and March 6-19, 1863); brigadier general, USV (September 10, 1862); commanding the division (February 7-March 6, 1863); commanding 2nd Brigade, 2nd Division, 9th Corps, Department of the Ohio (March 19-April and June 5-14, 1863); brigadier general, USV (reappointed May 6, 1863); commanding 2nd Brigade, 2nd Division, 9th Corps, Army of the Tennessee (June 14-August 18, 1863); commanding 1st Division, 9th Corps, Department of the Ohio (August 18, 1863-March 14, 1864); commanding 1st Division, 9th Corps, Army of the Potomac (March 14-April 19, 1864); commanding 4th Division, 9th Corps, Army of the Potomac (April 18-July 21 and July 29-September 13, 1864); commanding 3rd Division, 9th Corps, Army of the Potomac (September 13-October 9 and October 25-December 15, 1864); commanding Defenses of Bermuda Hundred, Army of the James (December 4, 1864-February 17, 1865); and commanding Infantry Division, Defenses of Bermuda Hundred, Army of the James (February 17-April 1865). He led his regiment to the North Carolina coast under Ambrose E. Burnside and fought at Roanoke Island and New Bern. He led a brigade of the Army of the Potomac at 2nd Bull run and as a brigadier general at Antietam and Fredericksburg. Although the Senate failed to confirm his promotion and it expired on March 4, 1863, he was reappointed two months later. He went west with the corps that March and in the summer fought at Vicksburg, mainly facing Joseph E. Johnston's threatened relief of the city. Moving back to East Tennessee, he led the division at Knoxville but was criticized for his failed leadership during an assault there. Returning to Virginia, he commanded the division of colored troops in the Overland Campaign but was mostly assigned to guarding the trains. At Petersburg, his division was initially chosen to spearhead the charge after the explosion of the mine on July 30, 1864. At the last minute this was changed for fear a repulse would leave the military open to charges of needlessly sacrificing black lives. In the botched assault, Ferrero and his fellow division commander, James H. Ledlie, remained in a bombproof drinking rum. The resulting confusion among the brigades kept them milling around the Crater instead of advancing farther. They were slaughtered where they stood. Despite a harsh ruling from a court of inquiry, Ferrero retained his command until the end of the war and was brevetted major general on December 2, 1864. During the final months of the war he was in charge at Bermuda Hundred. Mustered out on August 24, 1865, he returned to the teaching of dancing.

Edward Ferrero, dance instructor turned general. (*Leslie's*)

FERRY, Orris Sanford (1823-1875)

Yale graduate, lawyer, and judge Orris S. Ferry interrupted his political career to enter the Union army. The Connecticut politician served in the state senate and won the second of his three bids for a seat in the U.S. Congress. His Civil War assignments included: colonel, 5th Connecticut (July 23, 1861); brigadier general, USV (March 17, 1862); commanding 2nd Brigade, Shield's Division, Department of the Rappahannock (May 10-June 26, 1862); commanding 3rd Brigade, 2nd Division, 4th Corps, Army of the Potomac (July 5-September 26, 1862); commanding brigade, Division at Suffolk, 7th Corps, Department of Virginia (September 23-December 26, 1862); commanding 3rd Division, 18th Corps, Department of North Carolina (January 6-February 1863); commanding 2nd Division (detachment 18th Corps), St. Helena Island, 10th Corps, Department of the South (February-March 6, 1863); commanding 1st Division (detachment 18th Corps), St. Helena Island, 10th Corps, Department of the South (March 5-Arpil 17, 1863); commanding U.S. Forces, Seabrook Island, 10th Corps, Department of the South (April 16-May 11, 1863); commanding 3rd Division, 10th Corps, Army of the James (June 19-August 27, 1864); commanding Juniata District, Department of the Susquehanna (September 6-December 1, 1864); commanding Juniata District, Department of Pennsylvania (December 1-16, 1864); and commanding District of Philadelphia (December 16, 1864-ca. June 5, 1865). Before his regiment saw any major action he was named a brigadier general and fought in the Shenandoah Valley. Sent to the Peninsula just after the close of the Seven Days, he served there in southeastern Virginia until the end of the year. He later served in North Carolina and on the South Carolina coast. Returning to Virginia, he fought in the Richmond-Petersburg area for over two months before being ordered to central Pennsylvania. In the final months of the war he commanded at Philadelphia. Brevetted major general on May 23, 1865, he resigned on June 15, 1865. Resuming his political career, he was named to the U.S. Senate as a Radical Republican. His sponsors were soon disillusioned with his moderate voting record, but he was brought back into line during the impeachment trial of Andrew Johnson. He died while serving a second term.

FESSENDEN, Francis (1839-1906)

There is little in the military career of Francis Fessenden to explain his phenomenal rise in rank, but he was the son of William P. Fessenden, a U.S. senator from Maine, who was also Lincoln's secretary of the treasury. The Maine native was a lawyer when he was commissioned in one of the regular army's newly authorized infantry regiments, probably in deference to his father. His assignments included: captain, 19th Infantry (May 14, 1861); colonel, 25th Maine (September 29, 1862); commanding 1st Brigade, Casey's Division, 22nd Corps, Department of Washington (February 2-April 17, 1863); commanding 1st Brigade, Abercrombie's Division, 22nd Corps, Department of Washington (April 17-June 28, 1863); colonel, 30th Main (January 11, 1864); commanding 3rd Brigade, 1st Division, 19th Corps, Department of the Gulf (February 15-March 29 and April 9-22, 1864: brigadier general, USV (May 10, 1864); commanding 1st Brigade, 2nd Infantry Division, Department of West Virginia (May 1865); commanding 1st Infantry Division, Department of West Virginia (May 1865); and major general, USV (November 9, 1865). As a regular officer, he was engaged in recruiting and garrison duties. Taking the field with his regiment, he was wounded on the second day at Shiloh. Upon his recovery he took command of a new nine-months volunteer regiment. Stationed in the Washington defenses, he spent five months in charge of a brigade. Mustered out with his troops just after Gettysburg, he reverted to his regular army rank until named colonel of yet another new volunteer regiment, the 30th Maine. With this unit he went to the Gulf coast and in the Red River Campaign fought at Pleasant Hill and lost his right leg at Monett's Bluff. As at Shiloh, he received a regular army brevet for his wound. When he returned to duty he was a brigadier general, assigned mostly to guarding supply trains and bases in the Shenandoah Valley. Ater the close of hostilities he was one of the military judges who tried Andersonville commandant Henry Wirz. Brevetted brigadier and major general for the war in the regular service, he was given the full rank of major general of volunteers in November 1865 and mustered out of that service on September 1, 1866. He refused a lieutenant colonelcy in the peacetime regular establishment in 1866 and was retired with the advanced rank of brigadier general—due to wounds and the loss of his leg—on November 1, 1866. He resumed the practice of law and later was the mayor of Portland. His older brother, also a Union general, was James Deering Fessenden.

FESSENDEN, James Deering (1833-1882)

Like his younger brother, Francis, James D. Fessenden seems to have benefited in his military career from the fact that his father was a prominent senator and for a time Lincoln's treasury secretary. The Maine native was a lawyer at the outbreak of the Civil War. His assignments included: captain, Company D, 2nd United States Sharpshooters (November 2, 1861); colonel and additional aide-de-camp (July 16, 1862); brigadier general, USV (August 8, 1864); commanding 2nd Brigade, 1st Division, 19th Corps, Army of the Shenandoah (October 26-November 1, 1864); commanding 3rd brigade, 1st Division, 19th Corps, Army of the Shenandoah (November 1, 1864-March 20, 1865); commanding 3rd Brigade, 1st Provisional Division, Army of the Shenandoah (March 20-April 1865); and commanding 3rd Brigade, Dwight's Division, 22nd Corps, Department of Washington (April-May 1865). After serving with his company in northern Virginia, he was appointed to the staff of David Hunter on the coast of South Carolina where he was involved in recruiting the first regiment—later abolished by Washington—of black troops. He took part in the bombardment of the forts in and around Charleston in the summer of 1863 and then went west to serve on Hooker's staff as an aide during the Chattanooga and Atlanta campaigns. Promoted to brigadier general in the summer of 1864, he was assigned to duty in the Shenandoah Valley but does not appear to have been present at any of the major engagements. Brevetted major general for the war, he was mustered out on January 15, 1866. He resumed his private practice and sat in the state legislature.

FESSENDEN, William Pitt (1806-1869)

William P. Fessenden reluctantly agreed to replace Salmon P. Chase as secretary of the treasury but resigned within a year to return to the Senate. The New Hampshire-born Maine attorney had served as a Whig in the state legislature, in Congress and at three of his party's national conventions. When the Whigs broke up in the 1850s he was a U.S. Senator in the party's anti-slavery wing, and helped organize the Republican Party. In 1861 he attended the unsuccessful Washington Peace Convention. Two of his sons were Union army generals. On July 1, 1864, he resigned his seat in the Senate, which he had held since 1854, in order to accept the cabinet position. There he proved highly adept at issuing government war bonds. Reelected to the Senate, he resigned his cabinet post and took his seat on March 4, 1865. He was the chairman of the Radical-oriented Joint Committee on Reconstruction, but during the impeachment crisis he proved to be somewhat conservative. He died during his term. (Fessenden, Francis, *Life and Public Services of William Pitt Fessenden* and Jellison, Charles, *Fessenden of Maine*)

FIELD, Charles William (1828-1892)

A devastating wound at 2nd bull Run kept Kentucky-born career soldier Charles W. Field out of active service for a year and a half but he returned to command a division for the final battles. A West Pointer (1849), he had spent a dozen years in the mounted service when he resigned his captaincy on May 30, 1861. His assignments for the Confederacy included: captain, Cavalry (spring 1861); colonel, 6th Virginia Cavalry (summer 1861); brigadier general, CSA (March 9, 1862); commanding brigade, Aquia District, Department of Northern Virginia (March 27-May 27, 1862); commanding brigade, A.P. Hill's Division (in 1st Corps from June 29 and 2nd Corps from July 27), Army of Northern Virginia (May 27-August 29, 1862); and commanding Hood's (old) Division, 1st Corps, same army (April 1864-January 1865 and March-April 9, 1865). Initially serving in Jeb Stuart's cavalry, he was promoted and transferred to command a brigade of Virginia troops near Fredericksburg. He served with the forces facing McDowell's overland advance in connection with the Peninsula Campaign. Assigned to Hill's Light Division, he fought at the Seven Days and later with Jackson at Cedar Mountain and 2nd Bull Run. Wounded at the latter, he was incapacitated for months. After serving for a time in Richmond on conscript duty, he was assigned to take charge of Hood's former command, then in East Tennessee with Longstreet, in February 1864 but does not appear to have joined it until about the time that it reached Virginia in April. He fought through the Overland and Petersburg campaigns and surrendered with Lee. He was in private business after the war and was a colonel of engineers in Egypt. Returning to the United States, he worked as a government engineer. (Freeman, Douglas S., *Lee's Lieutenants*)

FIELD, Richard Stockton (1803-1870)

Appointed to a vacancy in the U.S. Senate by New Jersey's governor, Richard S. Field determined not to run for the position himself and was named a district judge by Lincoln in 1863. The New Jersey native had practiced law since 1825 and sat in the state legislature in 1837. In 1838-41 he was state attorney general and was later a law professor at Princeton. He was named to replace the deceased John R. Thomson in the Senate and took his seat on November 21, 1862, as a Republican. When James W. Wall was elected by the legislature, Field relinquished his seat on January 14, 1863. One week later he was named to a judicial post in New Jersey and held it until his death.

FIELD, Stephen Johnson (1816-1899)

The closeness of the decision in the controversial *Prize Cases*, five to four, prompted the expansion of the Supreme Court to ten seats. Abraham Lincoln appointed Stephen J. Field to the new seat. Born in Connecticut, he had practiced law in New

York before resettling in California, where he held local office and served in the state legislature. He sat on the Supreme Court in California from 1857 until his appointment to the Supreme Court. As expected he was an ardent supporter of the Union. He was in the Democratic minority on the electoral commission that voted along party lines to certify Hayes as president in 1877. He failed to gain the chief justiceship in 1888 and toyed with the idea of a presidential race. He was persuaded to resign due to ill health in 1897 after 34 years on the bench. (Swisher, Carl Brent, *Stephen J. Field, Craftsman of the Law*)

FILLMORE, Millard (1800-1874)

Being one of the five living ex-presidents in 1861 did not save Millard Fillmore from being labeled a traitor in the press. Always sensitive to the wrongs of both the North and South—he had supported the Compromise of 1850 during his term, an action which dashed his hopes for reelection—he felt the war was unnecessary. Caught up in the moment after the firing on Fort Sumter, he was active in encouraging Union enlistments. But as the war dragged on he became more and more critical of the Republican administration and confined his support to aiding the sick and wounded. Then in February 1864 he lashed out in a speech against the "partisan prejudice, petty jealousies, malignant envy and intriguing ambition" that was running the war that was bound to end in a military dictatorship. In that moment his popularity virtually disappeared. While he was away from home, a mob attacked his residence when it did not display the required mourning for Lincoln. Nonetheless he was part of the escort for the Lincoln funeral through his Buffalo home. (Rayback, Robert J., *Millard Fillmore*)

FINEGAN, Joseph (1814-1885)

An Irish-born Florida planter and mill operator, Joseph Finegan spent most of the war commanding the small and widely scattered forces in that state. A member of the secession convention, he supervised the state's military affairs under Governor Milton until he entered the Confederate service. His assignments included: brigadier general, CSA (April 5, 1862); commanding Department of East and Middle Florida (April 18-October 7, 1862); commanding District of Middle and Eastern Florida, Department of South Carolina, Georgia and Florida (October 7-November 4, 1862); commanding District of East Florida, same department (November 4, 1862-February 23, 1864); also temporarily commanding District of Middle Florida, same department (August 7-November 11, 1863); and commanding Florida Brigade, Anderson's-Mahone's Division, 3rd Corps, Army of Northern Virginia (May 28, 1864-March 20, 1865). The high point of his Florida service came in February 1864, when he defeated a Union expedition at Olustee. Sent with some Florida reenforcements to the Army of Northern Virginia in May 1864, he was given charge of the enlarged Florida Brigade under Lee. He fought at Cold Harbor and in the trenches at Petersburg. In the late winter of 1864-65 he was ordered back to Florida but there is no record of his arriving before the close of hostilities. A state legislator immediately after the war, he was for a while in the cotton trade in Savannah before returning to Florida.

FINLEY, Clement Alexander (ca. 1797-1879)

Although he was newly appointed to his position, Surgeon General Clement Finley was the chief medical officer of the Union army during the first year of conflict. Beginning his military career as a surgeon's mate in 1818, Finley had been a major and surgeon since 1832. He was a veteran of the Black Hawk and Mexican wars, and upon the death of Colonel Thomas Lawson, the surgeon general, on May 15, 1861, he was promoted colonel and assigned to duty according to the seniority system. During his year in this post, the size of the department grew dramatically as the needs of the volunteer regiments were met. However, Finley was retired on April 14, 1862, before the heaviest fighting of the war got started. Near the end of the war he was brevetted brigadier general in the regular army.

FINLEY, Jesse Johnson (1812-1904)

Giving up a Confederate judgeship, Tennessee native Jesse J. Finley enlisted as a private and rose to the rank of brigadier general. A lawyer, he had also been active in politics in Tennessee, Arkansas, and Florida. A judge at the outbreak of the Civil War, he continued in the same position under the Confederate government until early 1862. At that time—having been a company commander in Seminole fighting—he decided to rejoin the military. His assignments included: private, Company D, 6th Florida (March 1862); captain, Company D, 6th Florida (March 1862); colonel, 6th Florida (April 14, 1862); brigadier general, CSA (November 16, 1863); commanding Florida Brigade, Breckinridge's-Bate's Division, Breckinridge's Corps, Army of Tennessee (November 1863-January 1864); and commanding Florida Brigade, Bate's Division, Hardee's Corps, Army of Tennessee (February-September 1, 1864). His unit served in Florida until June 1862 when it was ordered to East Tennessee. After taking part in the Kentucky Campaign that fall, Finley returned to East Tennessee until ordered to join Bragg's army shortly before Chickamauga. He led his regiment on that field and was rewarded with the rank of brigadier general and assigned to command the newly constituted Florida Brigade. This he led at Chattanooga and during the Atlanta Campaign. During the latter he was severly wounded at Resaca and Jonesboro. The second wound incapacitated him for field service and he finished the war in administrative assignments. He was a U.S. congressman after the war.

FISER, John Calvin (1838-1876)

A highly popular officer with his command, John C. Fiser proved to be one of the heroes of the battle of Fredericksburg. A native of Tennessee, he had been raised in Mississippi. He entered the Confederate service at the war's commencement and his assignments included: lieutenant, Company H, 17th Mississippi (May 27, 1861); first lieutenant and adjutant, 17th Mississippi (June 7, 1861); lieutenant colonel, 17th Mississippi (April 26, 1862); colonel, 17th Mississippi (February 26, 1864); colonel, Provisional Army (mid-1864); and commanding brigade, McLaw's Division, Department of South Carolina, Georgia and Florida (December 24, 1864-ca. April 9, 1865). As regimental adjutant, he fought at 1st Bull Run and Ball's Bluff before being promoted to field officer. During the Seven Days Battles, he succeeded to command of the regiment when the colonel was wounded at Malvern Hill. He continued in command at Antietam and at Fredericksburg he directed a detachment of Barksdale's Brigade in the town itself. This command held up the Union crossing of the river for several hours by delaying the placement of pontoon bridges. Although hit by a falling wall when Union gunners opened up, he retained command. He subsequently was wounded at Gettysburg after again assuming regimental command, fought at Chickamauga, and took part in the siege of Knoxville. Here he led the 17th at the head of one of the assaulting columns at Fort Sanders. It cost him his right arm. Promoted to colonel that winter, he was unable to perform his duties and resigned on June 12, 1864. Soon thereafter he was appointed a colonel in the Provisional Army and joined his old division commander, McLaws, on the coast. He was later given a brigade, composed mostly of Georgia Reserves, and opposed Sherman during the Carolinas Campaign. After the war he settled in Memphis as a merchant.

FISHER, Benjamin Franklin (?-?)

A volunteer officer in the Civil War, Benjamin Fisher rose to become head of one of the regular army bureaus, the Signal Corps. His military assignments included: first lieutenant, 3rd Pennsylvania Reserves (June 18, 1861); captain, 3rd Pennsylvania Reserves (July 8, 1862); major, Signal Corps (March 3, 1863); and colonel and chief signal officer (December 3, 1864). As early as February 1862, Fisher was serving as an acting signal officer with the Army of the Potomac and was active in the Peninsula, Antietam, Fredericksburg, and Chancellorsville campaigns in that capacity. In the early stages of the Gettysburg Campaign, he was captured while on a reconnaissance near Aldie, Virginia on June 17, 1863. Confined in Libby Prison he was exchanged in time to serve as the chief signal officer with the Army of the Potomac. In this post he participated in the Wilderness through Petersburg Campaign and in the siege of Petersburg. He was appointed Chief Signal Officer in December and was thus stationed in Washington for the rest of the war. He was brevetted brigadier general for his war service and was mustered out on July 28, 1866.

FISK, Clinton Bowen (1828-1890)

After serving as a Union general and an assistant commissioner of the Freedmen's Bureau, Clinton B. Fisk continued his work for the ex-slaves with the founding of Fisk University. Born in New York and raised in Michigan, he was wiped out by the 1857 financial disaster and was a St. Louis insurance broker at the outbreak of the Civil War. His military assignments included: colonel, 33rd Missouri (September 5, 1862); brigadier general, USV (November 24, 1862); commanding 13th Division, 13th Corps, Army of Tennessee (January 22-February 8, 1863); commanding 2nd Brigade, 13th Division, 13th Corps, Army of the Tennessee (February 8-June 10, 1863); commanding District of Southeastern Missouri, Department of the Missouri (July 20-November 30, 1863); commanding District of St. Louis, Department of the Missouri (November 30, 1863-March 25, 1864); and commanding District of Northern Missouri, Department of the Missouri (June 10, 1864-May 24, 1865). It is sometimes claimed that he took part in the seizure of Camp Jackson early in 1861. The majority of his recorded services came in the Missouri-Arkansas area and he fought against such Confederate raiders as Sterling Price, John S. Marmaduke, and Joe Shelby. Brevetted major general for the war, he was mustered out on September 1, 1866, after Andrew Johnson had supported his efforts in the Freedmen's Bureau by saying "Fisk ain't a fool, he won't hang everybody." He went to New York and returned to banking. He was an Indian commissioner for the last 16 years of his life and ran for governor of New Jersey in 1886 and president in 1888, both times on the Prohibition ticket.

FLAGG, Benjamin (?-?)

Together with William Glaze of South Carolina, Massachusetts musket manufacturer Benjamin Flagg was awarded on April 15, 1851, contract with the state of South Carolina—which a decade later would fire on Fort Sumter—to provide 9,000 firearms and 2,000 swords and sabers. Flagg's Milbury, Massachusetts plant provided the equipment to make 1842 model muskets and pistols. The work itself was done at Glaze's Palmetto Iron Works in Columbia, South Carolina.

FLANAGIN, Harris (1817-1874)

New Jersey-born Arkansas lawyer Harris Flanagin left the field as a Confederate colonel to become governor of his adopted state following a special election. He had taught school in Pennsylvania before relocating to Arkansas where he was admitted to the bar. A former state Legislator, he gave up his practice to enter the Confederate army. His assignments included: captain, Company E, 2nd Arkansas Mounted Rifles (July 29, 1861); and colonel, 2nd Arkansas Mounted Rifles (May 8, 1862). He fought at Wilson's Creek, and Pea Ridge before being transferred to the east side of the Mississippi. While still in the field he was elected to the governorship in a special election and resigned on November 8, to take up his duties on November 15, 1862. During his term much of the state fell under Union control and he was effectively removed from office on April 18, 1864. He resumed the practice of law and attended the 1874 state constitutional convention.

FLANDERS, Benjamin Franklin (1816-1896)

New Hampshire native Benjamin F. Flanders remained loyal to the Union and became an official when his adopted city of New Orleans was captured by Union forces in early 1862. Although he had studied law he never practiced and instead became editor of the *New Orleans Tropic* in 1845, two years after his arrival in the Crescent City. In the prewar years he was a minor officeholder and was active in railroading. On July 20, 1862, Benjamin F. Butler appointed Flanders city treasurer, and he held the post until near the end of the year. He became captain, Company C, 5th Louisiana African Descent, on July 13, 1863, but was mustered out less than a month later, on August 12, when the unit failed to complete its organization. In the meantime, he had served as a Unionist in the House of Representatives in Washington, from December 3, 1862, to March 3, 1863. He then became a special agent of the Treasury Department for the area covering western Florida and all of Louisiana, Texas, Mississippi, and Alabama. After losing a bid for the governship in 1864, he went into banking until reappointed to the Treasury Department two years later. During Reconstruction he served as military governor of Louisiana in 1867-68 and mayor of New Orleans in 1870-72. The next year he was named assistant treasurer of the United States and held the post until 1882.

FLETCHER, Thomas (1819-1900)

A native of Arkansas, Thomas Fletcher held the governorship of that state for only 11 days. A teacher and farmer, he was serving as sheriff of Pulaski county upon the outbreak of the Civil War. In 1862 he became the president of the new state senate orgainzation under the pro-Confederate constitution. When Governor Henry M. Rector was in effect forced from office by the new document on November 4, 1862—for his uncooperative attitude toward the Richmond authorities—Fletcher automatically assumed the governorship temporarily. He promptly called new elections and served until November 15 when Harris Flanagin was able to take office. After the war he farmed, practiced law, and served again as sheriff and later as a U.S. marshal.

FLETCHER, Thomas Clement (1827-1899)

A Missouri Unionist, Thomas C. Fletcher served in regimental command for much of the Civil War before being elected to the governorship in 1864. A lawyer, he had been involved in the formation of the Republican Party and attended the 1860 convention. For the first part of the war he served as the state's provost marshal and then took a line command. His assignments included: colonel, 31st Missouri (October 7, 1862); and colonel, 47th Missouri (September 17, 1864). He led his regiment in the Vicksburg Campaign and at Pilot Knob before resigning on June 16, 1864. With his second regiment he served in his native state. Ten days after being elected governor he resigned his commission, on November 18, 1864. Sworn in on January 2, 1865, he oversaw the adjustment of the state in a totally slave-free nation. Two months after his inauguration he received the brevet of brigadier general in the volunteers for his war service. He left office in 1869 and resumed his legal pursuits.

FLINN, John M. (?-?)

A veteran of the battle of Murfreesboro, Captain John M. Flinn, Company F, 51st Indiana, was a prisoner at Libby Prison when he was selected by lot to hang. Two Confederate captains had been executed by the Union authorities in Kentucky. They had been recruiting behind Union lines and convicted as spies. Flinn was unlucky enough to be the second name drawn. He and Captain Henry W. Sawyer were placed in close confinement while Washington was informed of their impending doom—with a warning that more executions would follow if the North did not treat recruiting officers as regular prisoners of war. The Union War Department wasted no time. Following Lincoln's directions, General W.H.F. Lee, son of Robert E. Lee, and another officer were placed in close confinement as hostages for Flinn and Sawyer. After months of threats and counterthreats all four men were exchanged.

FLOURNOY, Thomas Stanhope (1811-1883)

By the time of the Civil War the cavalry charge had pretty much become a thing of the past and those that were made were frequently made out of desperation and were disastrous. An exception on both counts was the charge of Thomas S. Flournoy and his 6th Virginia Cavalry at Front Royal, Virginia. With no apparent previous military experience the native Virginian had entered the Confederate army as a captain, on August 19, 1861. On November 20, 1861, his unit was assigned to the 6th Virginia Cavalry as Company G. Rising to colonel by the time of the Shenandoah Valley Campaign of 1862, he commanded all the cavalry of Ewell's Division at the battle of Front Royal. After first cutting the railroad into the town, to prevent reenforcements, he led part of his regiment across the Shenandoah River and charged upon the Union 1st Maryland which had been driven from its positions by the Confederate infantry. Although outnumbered by about four to one, the pursuing cavalry managed to gather in most of the Union force as prisoners. Flournoy continued the pursuit into the night. Jackson praised the cavalry's actions. Remaining in the Valley when Jackson moved to Richmond, the 6th became part of the Laurel Brigade and joined the army for the battle of 2nd Bull Run. It was detailed to gather up abandoned weapons on the field and did not rejoin the Army of Northern Virginia until after the battle of Antietam. Less than a month later, on October 15, 1862, Flournoy resigned. After the war he resided in Halifax County, Virginia.

FLOYD, John Buchanan (1806-1863)

One of the greatest rogues ever to serve in high position in both the U.S. and Confederate governments must have been John B.

Floyd. A native Virginian lawyer and politician, he became James Buchanan's war secretary in 1857. During his tenure he became embroiled in a controversy over the misuse—possibly for personal purpose—of funds earmarked for the Indians. He survived this and other disputes. But when Buchanan refused to order Robert Anderson's garrison back from Fort Sumter to Fort Moultrie, Floyd resigned on December 29, 1860. Raising a brigade for the Confederacy, his assignments included: brigadier general, CSA (May 32, 1861); commanding Army of the Kanawha (August 12, 1861-January 1862); commanding division, Army of Central Kentucky, Department #2 (January-February 13. 1862); commanding Fort Donelson, Army of Central Kentucky, Department #2 (February 13-15, 1862); and major general, Virginia State Line (May 17, 1862). Commanding an independent force in western Virginia, he displayed a singular inability to cooperate with his fellow commanders in the region. Sent west with his command, he took command of Fort Donelson from Gideon J. Pillow. With the post besieged, he launched a breakout attempt but lost his nerve and recalled the troops at the moment an escape could have been made. That night he relinquished command and turned it over to Pillow who did the same, passing it on to Simon B. Buckner. Floyd then commandeered some river steamers and ferried his own division across the Cumberland River, abandoning the rest of the troops. Jefferson Davis relieved Floyd of his commission on March 11, 1862, without any formal hearing. The displaced general was then appointed to a state military post two months later but his health failed and he died on August 26, 1863.

FOGG, George Gilman (1813-1881)

After serving as the secretary of Lincoln's campaign committee in 1860, George G. Fogg was diplomatic representative to Switzerland during the Civil War. A former journalist, he had been active in the Free-Soil Party. When that organization broke up he became associated with Lincoln as one of the founders of the national Republican Party.

FOGG, Isabella (?-?)

In her work for the United States Sanitary Commission, Isabella Fogg was hospitalized for exhaustion and maimed for life in an accident. A Maine native she followed her son into the Union army in 1861. After serving as a nurse in Annapolis and Washington for a Maine regiment, she joined the commission and served aboard its hospital vessel *Elm City* during the Peninsula Campaign. Going ashore during the Seven Days, she set up the Savage Station field hospital, which was subsequently captured by the Confederates. Resting at home until after Antietam, she was present at Fredericksburg, Chancellorsville, Gettysburg, Mine Run, and the Overland Campaign. She once had to nurse her own wounded son and soon thereafter collapsed. Hospitalized near the end of the war, she was injured in a fall in January 1865, ending her work.

FOGLIARDI, Augusto (1818-ca. 1900)

The Civil War was of great interest to foreign governments and the Swiss Federal Council dispatched Augusto Fogliardi in 1863 as its observer. A former lawyer and politician, Fogliardi served in Italian fighting before rising to the grade of colonel, the highest peacetime rank in Switzerland, and command of a division. He was also the inspector general of sharpshooters. Being a native of the canton of Ticino, his reports to the Federal Council were in Italian. Arriving in the United States in February 1863 he visited New York and Washington, including dinner with Secretaries of State and War, Seward and Stanton, before joining the Army of the Potomac just prior to the battle of Chancellorsville. An admirer of General Hooker, he felt that there were problems with the Union army that could adversely affect Hooker's plans. He was highly critical of the Union cavalry, felt the artillery was not deliberate enough in firing, was concerned about a lack of staff work, was upset by the mustering out of troops whose time had expired, and was unalterably opposed to the paroling of prisoners. He was greatly impressed by the infantry, which had historically been the backbone of the Swiss military, and the sharpshooters, many of whom were Swiss. He witnessed the last day of the battle of Gettysburg and was critical of General Lee's apparent lack of planning. Moving west, he joined the Army of the Cumberland for Chickamauga. A supporter of the Union cause, he predicted that the strength of the United States would soon be felt in Europe. He returned home and in 1867 resigned his commission.

FOOTE, Andrew Hull (1806-1863)

Due to his unity of mind with General Grant early in the war, Andrew Foote would probably have served a much greater role in the naval prosecution of the war had he lived long enough. The Connecticut-born Foote had briefly attended West Point before entering the navy as a midshipman in 1822. His sea service led him to the four corners of the globe, fighting pirates off Sumatra, Chinese near Canton, and the African slave trade. At the outbreak of the Civil War he was commanding the Brooklyn Navy Yard when, as a commodore, he was given command of the naval forces on the upper Mississippi. Quickly adapting to the confines of river warfare, he amassed a substantial hodge-podge fleet of improvised vessels. Known as the "Gunboat Commodore," his strategic views coincided with those of the area's army commander, General Grant, and the two worked well in joint operations. In February 1862 the two commanders launched operations against Forts Henry and Donelson on the Tennessee and Cumberland rivers. Although the attack on the first fort was to be a combined operation, Foote was able to induce the work to surrender before the army arrived. At Fort Donelson, a few days later, the land forces prematurely opened the action but Foote promptly joined in and was repulsed, being himself wounded by splinters of wood in his foot. However, the rebel commander credited the navy with making the surrender mandatory. Foote later took part in the operations against Island #10 but, his wound not having

Andrew H. Foote's bombardment of Island #10. (AC)

healed he was forced to seek shore duty. Given the Thanks of Congress for his action in the Western waters, he was promoted to rear admiral on June 16, 1862. On the 20th he was made chief of the Bureau of Equipment and Recruiting. At his own urging, he was appointed to command the South Atlantic Blockading Squadron on June 4, 1863, although he knew he did not have long to live. While on his way to assume command he died on June 26, a victim of Bright's Disease. (Hoppin, James Mason, *Life of Andrew Hull Foote, Rear Admiral, United States Navy*)

FOOTE, Henry Stuart (1804-1880)

A violent-tempered man, Henry Foote was a perpetual opponent of Jefferson Davis in both the U.S. and Confederate Congresses. Born in Virginia, Foote had practiced law in Richmond before moving to Alabama and then Mississippi. Having served in the state legislature, he was, in 1847, named to the Senate where, in an effort to reconcile the two sections of the country, he supported the Compromise of 1850, the only member of the Mississippi congressional delegation to do so. This conciliatory nature brought him into confrontation with his fellow Mississippi senator, Davis; it had already resulted in a fistfight between the two on Christmas Day 1847. The two faced each other in the 1851 gubernatorial election and Foote won the seat for a two-year term. His Unionist policies being unpopular, he spent the following four years in California. Returning, he soon moved to Nashville. Following the secession of Tennessee, he was elected to the Confederate 1st and 2nd congresses, from the 5th District. He continued to serve, although his district was soon behind Union lines. He served on the Quartermaster's and Commissary Department Committee and was chairman of the Foreign Affairs Committee in the 1st Congress. From his first entry into the House, in February 1862, he was a vocal opponent of the rebel president. Long in favor of negotiating a return to the Union, he resigned from the Foreign Affairs Committee on December 20, 1864, and headed for Washington to try to open negotiations. He was captured but, soon released, he tried again. Getting to the Union lines, he was met coolly as Lincoln was about to attend the Hampton Roads Conference. Foote was held in custody until he sailed for Europe. Returning six weeks later, in violation of State Department orders, he was promptly arrested. Again directed to leave the country, he went to Canada until things calmed down following Lincoln's assassination. After the war he served as superintendent of the mint in New Orleans before returning home to Nashville. (Foote, Henry S., *Casket of Reminiscences*)

FOOT, Solomon (1802-1866)

Native Vermont lawyer Solomon Foot served several tours of duty as the president pro tempore of the U.S. Senate during the 37th and 38th congresses. After being admitted to the bar in

1831, he began practice in Rutland and entered the state legislature in 1833, serving as speaker from 1836 to 1838. During the mid-1840s he served two terms as Whig member of the House of Representatives. In 1851 he entered the Senate and became a Republican upon the break-up of the Whigs. He held his seat until his death in 1866 and president pro tempore until April 26, 1864, when New Hampshire's Daniel Clark was given the honor.

FORBES, Edwin (1839-1895)

Accompanying the Army of the Potomac from 1861 to 1864 Edwin Forbes was probably the best of the artist-correspondents working for *Frank Leslie's Illustrated Newspaper*. The New York-born Forbes was originally an animal painter who had begun the study of art at the age of 18. In 1876 his copperplate etchings were published as *Life Studies of the Great Army* and the originals were purchased by General Sherman. In later years he produced hundreds of sketches for various books, drawing mostly on his wartime experiences. He published his remaining works in *Thirty Years After, An Artist's Story of the Great War*. For his work he received honors in the United States, France, and Great Britian. During his last few years, he was forced to work with the left hand because of paralysis. (Dawson, William Forrest, *A Civil War Artist at the Front: Edwin Forbes' Life Studies of the Great Army*)

FORCE, Manning Ferguson (1824-1899)

Harvard Graduate Manning F. Force who had once considered going to West Point, interrupted a promising career to serve in the Union army and later won the Congressional Medal of Honor. Born in the nation's capital, he set up his practice in Ohio. His military assignments included: major, 20th Ohio (August 26, 1861); lieutenant colonel, 20th Ohio (September 11, 1861); colonel, 20th Ohio (May 1, 1862); commanding 2nd Brigade, 3rd Division, 17th Corps, Army of the Tennessee (June 3-November 17, 1863); brigadier general, USV (August 11, 1863); and commanding in the 17th Corps, Army of the Tennessee: 1st Brigade, 3rd Division (November 17, 1863-March 6, 1864, May 2-July 22, 1864, and October 1864-January 15, 1865); the division (January 15-April 3, 1865); and 1st Division (April 5-August 1, 1865). Fighting at Fort Donelson, he went on to command the regiment at Shiloh and during the advance on Corinth. During the siege of Vicksburg he was advanced to brigade command and following his participation in the capture of Jackson, Mississippi, he was named brigadier general. After Sherman's Meridian Campaign he joined the main army in Georgia on June 8, 1864, when the Atlanta Campaign was well under way. He fought through to the outskirts of the city where he received a severe face wound in the battle of Atlanta proper. He returned to duty in the fall, having been brevetted major general for his wounds in time to lead a brigade on the March to the Sea and a division through the Carolinas. Mustered out on January 15, 1866, he resumed his practice and went on to become a judge. He also wrote on historical and legal subjects. In 1892 he was awarded the nation's highest decoration for the battle of Atlanta. His final years were spent in charge of the Soldiers' and Sailors' Home in Sandusky, Ohio.

FORD, Antonia (ca. 1838-1871)

From her home within the Union lines surrounding Washington, Antonia Ford was able to provide the Confederates with much valuable information about the Union forces in and around Fairfax, Virginia, and she spent many months in the Old Capitol Prison for her efforts. Early in the war she rode to warn the Southerners of a ruse that the federals were planning for an upcoming battle. As a reward Jeb Stuart granted her a whimsical commission as a major and aide-de-camp. She carefully studied troop positions around Fairfax and pumped the officers quartered in her father's home for more information. This she provided to Mosby who used it to plan his raids. Following the raid in which General Edwin H. Stoughton was captured, she was investigated and four days later arrested. Confined for many months, she became the object of a campaign to gain her freedom. In poor health she was finally released and before the end of the war married the Union officer who had been instrumental in obtaining her release. Her early death was, by many Southerners, blamed upon her poor diet in the prison. (Jones, Virgil Carrington, *Gray Ghosts and Rebel Raiders*)

FORD, John T. (1829-1894)

A theater owner in Baltimore and Richmond, John Ford may well have wished that he had never expanded his activities to Washington. A native of Baltimore, Ford left his antebellum affairs in Washington to his two brothers but made frequent visits there and to Richmond. For two years before the war he was acting mayor of his native city. But with the war and the influx of people to the nation's capital, Ford decided to build a new theater, the Anthenaeum, which soon burned down. His next new theater has borne his name ever since the assassination of Abraham Lincoln. Attending the theater on April 14, 1865, the President was shot by John Wilkes Booth. In the hysteria that followed, Ford was thrown in jail as a possible conspirator and held for 39 days in the Old Capitol Prison. Released, he faced the confiscation of his theater by the government. Naturally unwilling to accept such a loss, he forced the government to pay $100,000 for his property. He continued in show business and eventually became the sole American producer for Gilbert and Sullivan. A year before his death, Ford heard of another tragedy at his former property—a wall had collapsed killing 28 employees of the War Department, mostly women and girls. (Leech, Margaret, *Reveille in Washington*)

FORNEY, John Horace (1829-1902)

Resigning from the old army 12 days after the secession of his adopted state, Alabama, North Carolina-born West Pointer (1852) John H. Forney rose to the rank of major general in the Confederate service while performing duty in most of the major theaters of the war. After frontier duty and participation in the campaign against the Mormons in Utah he resigned as a first lieutenant in the 10th Infantry on January 23, 1861. His Confederate assignments included: colonel, Alabama Artillery (early 1861); captain, Infantry (March 16, 1861); colonel, 10th Alabama (June 4, 1861); commanding 5th Brigade, Army of the Shenandoah (July 21-October 1861); also commanding detachment (still in Shenandoah Valley), Army of the Shenandoah (July 21-July 1861); brigadier general, CSA (March 10, 1862); commanding Department of Alabama and West Florida (April 28-June 27, 1862); commanding District of the Gulf, Department #2 (July 2-December 8, 1862); major general, CSA (October 27, 1862); commanding division, 2nd Military District, Department of Mississippi and East Louisiana (early 1863-April 17, 1863); commanding Maury's (old) Division, 2nd Military District, Department of Mississippi and East Louisiana (April 17-April 1863); commanding division, Department of Mississippi and East Louisiana (April-July 4, 1863 and fall 1863-February 1864); and commanding 1st (Texas) Division, 1st Corps (or District of West Louisiana), Trans-Mississippi Department (September 1864-ca. May 26, 1865). Although it is frequently stated that he fought at 1st Bull Run, in fact on that very day he took command of the Army of the Shenandoah's 5th Brigade and other forces from that army that were still in the Shenandoah Valley. However, fighting at Dranesville that December he was wounded. Promoted to brigadier general that winter, he was assigned to command along the Gulf coast for most of 1862. As a major general he was transferred to Mississippi where he commanded a division at Vicksburg. Following his exchange he again took charge of the division until early 1864. Transferred to the Trans-Mississippi West he led a division in western Louisiana for the balance of the war. Returning to Alabama, he became a planter and civil engineer.

FORNEY, William Henry (1823-1894)

North Carolina-born lawyer William Forney was a Mexican War veteran when he became captain of a company in the 10th Alabama in June 1861. He accompanied his regiment to Virginia where it served in the 5th Brigade, Army of the Shenandoah. Colonel John Forney, the regimental commander and William Forney's brother, took command of this brigade on July 21, 1861. In August William Forney was promoted to major. Joining Johnston's army, later known as the Army of Northern Virginia, the regiment was engaged at Dranesville on December 20, 1861, where Forney was wounded. On March 17, 1862, he was promoted to lieutenant colonel. At Williamsburg he was wounded and later captured in the hospital. After four months in prison he rejoined his regiment, having been made its colonel as of June 27. He led his men at Fredericksburg, Chancellorsville, and at Gettysburg where on the second day he was again wounded and captured. Imprisoned for over a year, he did not rejoin his command until November 1864 when he, as senior colonel, took command of the brigade in Mahone's Division, A.P. Hill's Corps, Army of Northern Virginia. The previous commander, General Sanders, had been killed some three months earlier, and the brigade had been without a regular commander ever since. Forney commanded the brigade through the rest of the Petersburg siege, finally achieving the rank of brigadier general on February 15, 1865. On April 9 he surrendered the remnant of his brigade at Appomattox. After the war he resumed his law practice and served as member of congress for 18 years. (Freeman, Douglas S., *Lee's Lieutenants*)

FORNO, Henry (1797-1866)

Although he survived a war wound that many considered to be fatal, Henry Forno did not long outlast the war, dying in a railroad accident less than a year later. He was born in Louisiana when it belonged to the Spanish and was a veteran of the Mexican War, having served in the infantry and the artillery. In the decade before the Civil War he was chief of police in New Orleans. Reentering military service, this time for the Confederacy, his assignments included: lieutenant colonel, 5th Louisiana (May 10, 1861); colonel 5th Louisiana (July 31, 1862); and commanding Taylor's (old) Brigade, Ewell's Division, Jackson's Corps, Army of Northern Virginia (ca. August 8-29, 1862). He served through the battles at Yorktown, the Seven Days, Cedar Mountain, and 2nd Bull Run. Severely wounded at the latter, he was feared by some to be mortally hurt. He eventually recovered and served as commander of the post garrison at Andersonville in late 1864. He was subsequently on recruiting duty. (Freeman, Douglas S., *Lee's Lieutenants*)

FORREST, French (1796-1866)

Already 65 by the outbreak of the Civil War, French Forrest failed to measure up as the commander of the Confederacy's James River Squadron. The Maryland native was a veteran of five decades in the navy including the War of 1812 battle of Lake Erie and service at Alvarado and Vera Cruz during the Mexican War. He joined the Southern war effort in 1861, and his assignments included: captain, Virginia Navy (1861); commanding Norfolk Navy Yard (ca. April 25, 1861-ca. May 9, 1862); captain, CSN (1861); chief, Office of Orders and Detail (1862-63); and commanding James River Squadron (1863-ca. May 1864). When the Union fleet abandoned Norfolk, Forrest was dispatched by the Virginia authorities to take charge of the naval equipment and stores there. During the famous fights of the *Virginia* and *Monitor* in Hampton Roads he was aboard the tugboat *Harmony*. After the fall of Norfolk he was made a bureau chief in the Navy Deaprtment and then took charge of the small flotilla on the James. During 1863 the squadron's poor behavior was blamed on Forrest who was relieved by John K. Mitchell in early 1864. While Forrest's name had appeared on the naval register of January 1, 1864, it was missing from that of June 1, and it must be assumed that he had been dropped from the rolls. In any event he barely outlived the war.

FORREST, Nathan Bedford (1821-1877)

With no formal military training, Nathan Bedford Forrest became one of the leading cavalry figures of the Civil War. The native Tennessean had amassed a fortune, which he estimated at $1,500,000, as a slave trader and plantation owner before enlisting in the Confederate army as a private in Josiah H. White's cavalry company on June 14, 1861. Tapped by the governor, he then raised a mounted battalion at his own expense. His assignments included: lieutenant colonel, Forrest's Tennessee Cavalry Battalion (October 1861); colonel, 3rd Tennessee Cavalry (March 1862); brigadier general, CSA (July 21, 1862); commanding cavalry brigade, Army of the Mississippi (summer-November 20, 1862); commanding cavalry brigade, Army of Tennessee (November 20, 1862-summer 1863); commanding cavalry division, Army of Tennessee (summer 1863); commanding cavalry corps, Army of Tennessee (ca. August-September 29, 1863); commanding West Tennessee, (probably in) Department of Mississippi and East Louisiana (November 14, 1863-January 11, 1864); major general, CSA (December 4, 1863); commanding cavalry corps, Department of Mississippi and East Louisiana (January 11-28, 1864); commanding District of Mississippi and East Louisiana, Department of Alabama, Mississippi and East Louisiana (January 27-May 4, 1865); also commanding cavalry corps, Department of Alabama, Mississippi and East Louisiana (January 28-May 4, 1865); and lieutenant general, CSA (February 28, 1865). When the mass Confederate breakout attempt at Fort Donelson failed, Forrest led most of his own men, and some other troops, through the besieging lines and then directed the rear guard during the retreat from Nashville. At Shiloh there was little opportunity for the effective use of the mounted troops and his command again formed the rear guard on the retreat. The day after the close of the battle Forrest was wounded. After serving during the Corinth siege he was promoted to brigadier general, and he raised a brigade with which he captured Murfreesboro, its garrison and supplies. In December 1862 and January 1863 he led another raid, this time in west Tennessee, which contributed to the abandonment of Grant's campaign in central Mississippi; the other determining factor was Van Dorn's Holly Springs raid. Joining up with Joseph Wheeler, Forrest took part in the unsuccessful attack on Fort Donelson which resulted in Forrest swearing he would never serve under Wheeler again. His next success came with the capture of the Union raiding column under Abel D. Streight in the spring of 1863. On June 14, 1863, he was shot by a disgruntled subordinate, Andrew W. Gould, whom Forrest then mortally wounded with his penknife. Recovering, he commanded a division that summer and then a corps at Chickamauga. Having had a number of disputes with army commander Braxton Bragg, Forrest was humiliated by being placed under Wheeler again. His request for transfer to west Tennessee was granted and he was dispatched there with a pitifully small force. Recruiting in that area, he soon had a force large enough to give Union commanders headaches. Sherman kept ordering his Memphis commanders to catch him. When Forrest captured Fort Pillow a controversy developed over reports of a massacre of the largely black garrison. Apparently a massacre did occur as there are numerous Confederate firsthand accounts of it. He defeated Samuel D. Sturgis at Brice's Crossroads and under Stephen D. Lee fought Andrew J. Smith at Tupelo. He again faced Smith during August 1864 and then provided the cavalry force for Hood's invasion of middle Tennessee that fall. Finally the force of numbers began to tell when he proved incapable of stopping Wilson's raid through Alabama and Georgia in the final months of the war. His diminished command was included in Richard Taylor's surrender. Wiped out financially by the war, he resumed planting and became engaged in railroading. Joining the Ku Klux Klan shortly after the war, he was apparently one of its early leaders. Forrest once summed up his military theory as "Get there first with the most men." (Wyeth, John, *Life of Nathan Bedford Forrest* and Henry, Robert Selph, *"First with the Most" Forrest*)

FORSYTH, Alexander John (fl. 1805)

It took some three decades for the percussion cap invented by Reverend Alexander J. Forsyth to be adopted for use on military weapons. The Scottish cleric had developed his improvement over the flintlock firing system in 1805 but it took a long time for the small metal caps to gain acceptance and supersede the flint. Even at the outbreak of the Civil War the conversion was not complete. Many regiments, especially Confederate, still went into the field with flintlocks or with flintlocks poorly altered and adapted to the percussion system.

FORSYTH, George Alexander (1837-1915)

Starting the war as a private in the Chicago Dragoons (April 19-August 18, 1861), George Forsyth rose through the ranks. His later assignments in the 8th Illinois Cavalry were was follows: first lieutenant (September 18, 1861); captain (February 12, 1862); and major (September 1, 1863). Serving in the Eastern Theater, Forsyth was cited for distinguished service in the Antietam Campaign and at Brandy Station. Serving through the campaign to Petersburg, he led 300 of his men on a raid to Guinea Station on May 18, 1864. Going to the Shenandoah Valley as part of Sheridan's command, Forsyth took part in the battles of 3rd Winchester and Cedar Creek, for which he was brevetted colonel. He led his men in the final battles at Dinwiddie Court House and Five Forks. Brevetted brigadier general, USV, March 13, 1865, for his war service he was mustered out on February 1, 1866. A few months later he entered the regular army, rising to rank of lieutenant colonel, 4th Cavalry, and serving for several years as military secretary to General Sheridan. He was brevetted, in the regular army, colonel and brigadier general for Five Forks and Beecher's Island, where in 1868 his band of frontiersmen were under siege for six days. He retired in 1890. (Forsyth, George Alexander, *Thrilling Days in Army Life*)

FORSYTH, James William (1835-1906)

The military career of Ohio native James W. Forsyth stretched from before the Civil War through the massacre at Wounded Knee. Graduating from West Point in 1856, he was posted with the infantry in the Washington Territory and served there until 1861. His wartime assignments included: second lieutenant, 9th Infantry (since July 1, 1856); first lieutenant,

9th Infantry (March 15, 1861); first lieutenant, 18th Infantry (May 14, 1861); captain, 18th Infantry (October 24, 1861); major and assistant adjutant general, USV (April 7, 1864); lieutenant colonel and assistant inspector general (April 19, 1864); and brigadier general USV (May 19, 1965). He was on McClellen's staff during the Peninsula and Maryland campaigns. He fought with his regiment at Chickamauga and then returned to staff duty in the East. He was the inspector and then the chief of staff of the Army of the Potomac's Cavalry Corps during the last year of the war. Promoted to brigadier general after hostilities had ceased, he was mustered out on January 15, 1866. Later that year he was promoted to major in the regular army in one of the two new black mounted regiments. Rejoining Philip H. Sheridan, he was his aide-de-camp and military secretary from 1869 to 1878. As colonel of Custer's old 7th Cavalry, he led the massacre of Indians at Wounded Knee in 1890 but was cleared by a court of inquiry. He retired as a major general in 1897.

FORSYTH, John (1812-1879)

The mayor of Mobile, John Forsyth was chosen by Jefferson Davis to be one of the peace commissioners sent to Washington to negotiate the turning over of Forts Sumter and Pickens to the new Confederacy. Convinced of the hopelessness of his endeavors, Forsyth, a Douglas supporter in 1860, threw his full efforts into the secessionist movement. As editor of the Mobile *Register*, Forsyth was able to provide propaganda for the rebel nation. Forsyth was instrumental in the planning of the defense of the city from the Union fleet, carrying on an extensive correspondence with the Richmond authorities. Having served as mayor throughout the war, he used his paper as a critical voice against the postwar policies of Andrew Johnson's administration. (Swanberg, W.A., *First Blood*)

FOSTER, John Gray (1823-1874)

Having earned two brevets in the Mexican War, West Pointer (1846) and career engineer Captain John Foster was in charge of the engineering operations in Charleston Harbor at the outbreak of the war. For his actions on the night of December 26, 1860, when he helped to move the garrison of Fort Moultrie into unfinished Fort Sumter, he was brevetted major. During the siege of the fort, Foster refused to allow his engineering officers to double as line officers to aide Major Robert Anderson's overworked artillery officers. Following the capitulation and brief service in Washington and Maryland, Foster was named brigadier general, USV, on October 23, 1861. His commands included: 1st Brigade, Burnside's North Carolina Expedition (December 20, 1861-April 2, 1862); 1st Division, Department of North Carolina (April 2-July 6, 1862); and the Departments of North Carolina (July 6, 1862-July 18, 1863); Virginia and North Carolina (July 18-Novmeber 11, 1863), the Ohio (December 9, 1863-February 9, 1864), and the South (May 26, 1864-February 9, 1865). During Burnside's expedition to the coast of North Carolina, Foster participated in the victories at Roanoke Island, New Bern and

Union department commander John G. Foster. (*Leslie's*)

Fort Macon and later succeeded that officer in command of the department. In early 1863, Foster took a detachment of his 18th Corps to St. Helena Island in South Carolina to support operations there. That summer Foster's command was united with the Department of Virginia and he took over the enlarged command. Taking part in operations around Knoxville in the fall, he again succeeded Burnside in departmental command on December 9. Injured in the fall of his horse, Foster was out of action for several months, but he was given charge of operations against Charleston in May 1864. A major general of volunteers, since July 18, 1862, Foster reverted to the rank of major of engineers after the war and remained in the regular service until his death. He received brevets in the regular army to major general.

FOSTER, Lafayette Sabine (1806-1880)

Although he opposed the idea of the Senate investigating military failures, Lafayette S. Foster voted with the 33 to three majority to establish the Joint Committee on the Conduct of the War. The Connecticut native had graduated from Brown University and taught school before being admitted to the bar in Maryland in 1830. The next year he moved his practice to Connecticut and edited the *Norwich Republican*. From the late 1830s to the mid 1850s he served in the state legislature and was eventually its speaker. He lost two races for governor and was mayor of Norwich. As a Republican he was elected to the U.S. Senate and held his seat from 1855 to 1867, until defeated for reelection in 1866. During his last two years in that body—including the last months of the Civil War—he was the president pro tempore. In December 1861 debate over the establishment of an investigative body after the disasters at 1st Bull Run and Ball's Bluff, he said, "in heaven's name do not let us make it worse by tampering, for worse we shall make it, and only worse." But nonetheless he voted for its creation. None of its later members had the least bit of military experience. After leaving the Senate he taught law at Yale and again served as speaker of the state house. For the final six years before his retirement in 1876 he was an associate justice on the state supreme court. He lost an 1874 bid for a congressional seat as a Democrat.

FOSTER, Robert Sanford (1834-1903)

Indiana tinner Robert S. Foster rose to the rank of brevet major general of volunteers during the Civil War. His assignments included: captain, 11th Indiana (April 22, 1861); major, 13th Indiana (June 19, 1861) lieutenant colonel, 13th Indiana (October 28, 1861); colonel, 13th Indiana (April 30, 1862); commanding provisional brigade, Division at Suffolk, 7th Corps, Department of Virginia (September 23, 1862-April 9, 1863); commanding 2nd Brigade, 1st Division, 7th Corps, Department of Virginia (April 9-July 7, 1863); brigadier general, USV (June 12, 1863); commanding 1st Brigade, U.S. Forces North End of Folly Island, 10th Corps, Department of the South (August 16-December 16, 1863); commanding U.S. Forces North End of Folly Island, 10th Corps, Department of the South (December 16, 1863-January 15, 1864); commanding Vodges' Division, Northern District, 10th Corps, Department of the South (January 15-February 25, 1864); commanding 1st Brigade, 2nd Division, District of Florida, 10th Corps, Department of the South (February 25-28, 1864); commanding the division (February 28-April 25, 1864); commanding 1st Division, 10th Corps, Army of the James (April 28-May 4, June 14-21, and July 18-23, 1864); chief of staff, 10th Corps, Army of the James (spring 1864); commanding 3rd Brigade, 1st Division, 10th Corps, Army of the James (June 23-July 18 and July 23-August 23, 1864); commanding 2nd Division, 10th Corps, Army of the James (August 23-December 3, 1864); and commanding 1st Division, 24th Corps, Army of the James (December 6, 1864-January 1, 1865, February 2-May 2, and July 8-August 1, 1865). He was a company officer in a three-months regiment in western Virginia before accepting an appointment as a field officer in a three-year regiment. He took part in the fighting at Romney and Rich Mountain and then commanded his regiment at Kernstown and Port Republic. Transferred to southeastern Virginia, his regiment faced James Longstreet and then moved farther south to take part in operations against Charleston. After nine months on that front, he joined Benjamin F. Butler and fought at Bermuda Hundred. He then took part in the operations against Richmond and Petersburg and was particularly distinguished in the attack on Fort Gregg on April 2, 1865. Two days earlier he had been brevetted a major general of volunteers for his field services. He resigned on September 25, 1865, having served in the trial of the Lincoln conspirators, and held minor governmental and business posts for the rest of his life.

FOWLE, Elida Rumsey (ca. 1841-?)

When Union hospital worker Elida Rumsey married co-worker John Fowle, her reputation was so great that the cermony, at Lincoln's suggestion, was held before a joint session of Congress on the floor of the House of Representatives. Disqualified on account of age from joining Dorothea Dix's nursing corps, she independently visited hospitals singing to the sick and wounded. With Fowle as a campanion, she raised funds for a soldiers' library and clubhouse on a concert tour. Following 2nd Bull Run the pair was involved in nursing the wounded.

FOX, Gustavus Vasa (1821-1883)

The United States' first assistant secretary of the navy was a former naval officer with 18 years experience, including the Mexican War. Gustavus V. Fox had left the service in 1856, but was called from his woolen business in his native Massachusetts to advise General Winfield Scott on the Fort Sumter crisis; the former lieutenant served in a civilian capacity. He was a key planner in the relief expedition, having actually visited Major Anderson in the bastion, but was plagued with problems and was only able to pick up the garrison after the capitulation. After a stint as the Navy Department's chief clerk he became Gideon Welles' official assistant on August 1, 1861. He was to hold the post until 1866. Actually he was in essence a chief of staff but many critics thought he was maneuvering for Welles' position. He became a convert to the new technology represented by the monitors and became an active booster of the craft. He was active in the planning of the operation that resulted in the capture of New Orleans. To show his confidence in the seaworthiness of the armored vessels he went along on the first oceanic crossing to Russia after the close of the war. He subsequently returned to his business interests. (MacCartney, Clarence Edward, *Mr. Lincoln's Admirals*)

FRANKLIN, William Buel (1823-1903)

Graduating number one at West Point (1843), Pennsylvanian William B. Franklin had his military career demolished by the Civil War. Posted to the Topographical Engineers, his prewar services included: captain, Topographical Engineers (since July 1, 1857); colonel, 12th Infantry (May 14, 1861); brigadier general, USV (May 17, 1861); commanding 1st Brigade, 3rd Division, Army of Northeastern Virginia (June-August 17, 1861); commanding brigade, Division of the Potomac (August 17-October 3, 1861); commanding division, Army of the Potomac (October 3, 1861- March 13, 1862); commanding 1st Division, 1st Corps, Army of the Potomac (March 13-April 4, 1862); commanding 1st Division, Department of the Rappahannock (April 4-May 18, 1862); commanding 6th Corps, Army of the Potomac (May 18-November 16, 1862); commanding 6th Corps, Army of the Potomac (May 18-November 16, 1862); major general, USV (July 4, 1862); commanding Left Grand Division, Army of the Potomac (November 16, 1862-Janaury 25, 1863); and commanding 19th Corps, Department of the Gulf (August 20, 1863-May 2, 1864). As a brigadier he led his men creditably in the Union defeat at 1st Bull Run and that fall was given a division. After service around Washington and Fredericksburg he was given command of the new 6th Corps on the Peninsula. He led the corps in the Seven Days, earning a regular brevet to brigadier. He commanded at Crampton's Gap during the forcing of South Mountain in the Maryland Campaign and led his corps at Antietam. With Burnside promoted to army command and the resultant reorganization, Franklin was given command of a grand division. In the battle of Fredericksburg he directed the assault on the Confederate right. One of his divisions—Meade's—was able to break through the enemy lines but was not supported by the remainder of Franklin's two corps. Burnside blamed him for the failure of the entire battle. The situation was not helped when a week after the fight Franklin, together with William F. Smith, submitted a letter to Washington declaring the campaign hopeless and outlining their own ideas for a new campaign. Burnside insisted upon Franklin's removal—as well as those of several other officers—or his own. On January 25, 1863, both were relieved. After a period of inactivity Franklin was sent to Louisiana to command the 19th Corps. He took part in the operations at Sabine Pass and in the Red River Campaign of 1864. Although wounded at Sabine Crossroads, during the latter campaign, he remained in the field until the end of the campaign. Returning North to recover, he was captured on July 11, 1864, by Gilmor's partisans when his Baltimore and Ohio Railroad train was stopped. However, he made his escape that night. While awaiting orders for the remainder of the war, he performed routine administrative duties. Although brevetted major general in the regular army for the war, it was obvious that he was not popular with the authorities. He resigned his volunteer commission on November 10, 1865, and four months later, on March 15, 1866, his regular one too. A civil engineer after the war, he directed the Colt's Fire Arms Manufacturing Company for over two decades and held several government appointments. (*General William B. Franklin and the Operations of the Left Wing at the Battle of Fredericksburg December 13, 1862*)

FRAZER, John Wesley (1827-1906)

The fall of Cumberland Gap into the hands of the Union Army under Burnside in late 1863 unfairly cost John W. Frazer his reputation as a Confederate general. This unfairness was recognized by Jefferson Davis but not until 1883. The Tennessee-born West Pointer (1849) was posted to the infantry with which he performed frontier and routine garrison duties until his March 15, 1861, resignation as a captain in the 9th Infantry. His Confederate assignments included: captain, Infantry (March 1861); lieutenant colonel, 8th Alabama (June 11, 1861); colonel, 28th Alabama (March 1862); brigadier general, CSA (May 19, 1863); and commanding brigade, Department of East Tennessee (May-September 9, 1863). With his first regiment—the first to enlist for the war—he served in Virginia until he accepted the colonelcy of a new unit. This he led in the defense of Corinth, Mississippi, at Munfordville and Murfreesboro. Promoted to brigadier general, he was ordered to East Tennessee and was eventually stationed at Cumberland Gap. With a small force, and his supports called into northern Georgia in the buildup for Chickamauga, he was faced with an impossible dilemma when Burnside's forces approached the gap. Most of his troops were untried and untrusted; rather than sacrifice his command he surrendered on September 9, 1863. There was a public outcry throughout the South against this "cowardly" action and the Confederate Senate rejected his nomination as brigadier general on February 16, 1864. Frazer himself was not released from Fort Warren, Boston Harbor, until the summer of 1865. Afterwards he was an Arkansas planter and New York City businessman. It was 20 years before Davis' mollifying comments were printed in his memoirs.

FRÉMONT, John Charles (1813-1890)

The Civil War proved to be the high watermark in the outstanding career of John C. Frémont. Expelled from Charleston College, the native Georgian taught mathematics aboard the USS *Natchez* before being commissioned a second lieutenant in the prestigious Corps of Topographical Engineers—a rare honor for a nongraduate of West Point—in 1838. Nicknamed the "Pathfinder" for his western explorations, he played a key role in securing California for the United States during the Mexican War. However, he was hauled before a Washington court martial on charges of mutiny when he disobeyed the orders of Stephen W. Kearny, who had been sent to California to establish a local government. He was convicted and allowed to resign in 1848 rather than face the humiliation of being dismissed. Settling in California, he made a fortune from the gold found on his property and was sent to the U.S. Senate for a special one-year term upon the admission of the state to the Union. In 1856 he became the first presidential candidate of the New Republican Party, but lost to Democrat James Buchanan in the Electoral College by a vote of 174-114. The popular vote was Buchanan 1,927,995 and Frémont 1,391,555. Largely for political reasons Abraham Lincoln appointed him to the highest rank in the army upon the outbreak of the Civil War. His assignments included: major general, USA (July 3, 1861, to rank from May 14, 1861); commanding Western Department (July 25-November 2, 1861); commanding Mountain Department (March 29-June 26, 1862); and commanding 1st Corps, Army of Virginia (June 26-28, 1862). Sent to command in the West, he was quickly involved in the troubled affairs of the state of Missouri. After the battle of Wilson's Creek he was criticized for failing to provide support to his subordinate and predecessor, Nathaniel Lyon, who was killed in the action. Then on August 30, 1861, he declared martial law throughout Missouri and took the unprecedented step of issuing his own emancipation proclamation. He refused to honor Lincoln's request for a more moderate policy, and the president felt himself forced to revoke the order directly from Washington. Outraged by the revocation Jessie Benton Frémont, the general's wife and daughter of former Senator Thomas Hart Benton, raced to the White House and had a heated conversation with Lincoln. After orders relieving Frémont had repeatedly been either postponed or not delivered he was finally relieved in November 1861 when a disguised staff officer bypassed his

Troublesome Union General John C. Frémont. (AC)

guards and handed the order directly to him. He was given a second chance and put in command of the Mountain Department, and charged with catching the troublesome Stonewall Jackson in the Shenandoah Valley. He proved singularly unsuccessful and was defeated at Cross Keys. When all the forces operating in northern Virginia were organized into the Army of Virginia under John Pope, Frémont refused to serve under him as a corps commander and was relieved. Although he held no further commands he did not resign until June 4, 1864. A few days earlier he had been nominated for the presidency by a small faction of Radical Republicans as an alternative choice to Lincoln. He withdrew in September 1864, claiming that he was trying to avoid the election of George B. McClellan, but there is evidence that a deal was made, through the good offices of Senator Zachariah Chandler, whereby Frémont would step aside in return for the removal of Postmaster General Montgomery Blair from the cabinet. His investments in California meanwhile evaporated and he later served as Arizona's territorial governor for about a decade. He was placed upon the army's retired list as a major general in 1889. (Nevins, Allan, *Frémont, the West's Greatest Adventurer* and *Frémont the Pathfinder*)

FRENCH, Samuel Gibbs (1818-1910)

Despite his Northern birth Samuel G. French joined the Confederate army and rose to the rank of major general. The New Jersey native and West Pointer (1843) won two brevets and was wounded at Buena Vista while serving as an artillery officer in Mexico. Transferring to the quartermaster department in 1848, he resigned as a captain eight years later. He spent the next five years managing his Mississippi plantation—he had married into a prominent family there—and answered his new country's call. His assignments included: chief of ordnance, Mississippi forces (early 1861); major, Artillery (April 1861); brigadier general CSA (October 23, 1861); commanding Evansport, Department of Fredericksburg (November 14-22, 1861); commanding 1st Brigade, Aquia District, Department of Northern Virginia (November 22, 1861-February 1862); commanding Department of North Carolina and Southern Virginia (February 17-26, 1862); commanding District of the Pamlico, Department of North Carolina (March 18-20, 1862); commanding District of the Cape Fear, Department of North Carolina (ca. March 20-ca. September 1862); commanding French's Command (North Carolina), Department of North Carolina and Southern Virginia (ca. September 1862-April 1, 1863); major general, CSA (October 22, 1862, to rank from August 31); commanding division, Department of the West (June-July 1863); commanding division, Department of Mississippi and East Louisiana (July 1863-January 28, 1864); commanding division, Department of Alabama, Mississippi and East Louisiana (January 28-May 4, 1864); commanding division, Polk's Louisiana (January 28-May 4, 1864); commanding division, Polk's (Army of Mississippi)-Stewart's Corps, Army of Tennessee (May 4-mid-December 1864); and commanding division, District of the Gulf, Department of Alabama, Mississippi and East Louisiana (spring 1865). In the early part of the war he served in various fringe commands in Virginia and North Carolina before being dispatched to command a division under Joseph E. Johnston in Mississippi. As such he took part in the unsuccessful attempt to free the garrison of Vicksburg. He later faced Sherman's movements against Jackson and Meridian before accompanying Leonidas Polk to northern Georgia for the Atlanta Campaign. Following the fall of that city he was ordered northward by Hood to cut Sherman's communication lines. He commanded the unsuccessful attack on Allatoona, which was defended by troops under John M. Corse. Later he went with Hood into middle Tennessee and commanded his division at Franklin. Just before the battle of Nashville he was forced to relinquish command due to a severe eye infection. Returning to duty, his unit was soon transferred to the Mobile area and he finished the war there. He then returned to his plantation. (French, Samuel G., *Two Wars: An Autobiography*)

FRENCH, William Henry (1815-1881)

The Union setback at Mine Run marked William H. French as a surplus corps commander when the Army of the Potomac was reduced from five to three corps the following spring. The Maryland native had received his appointment to West Point from the District of Columbia. Graduating in 1837, he was posted to the artillery and saw early action against the Seminoles and, as Franklin Pierce's aide, won two brevets in Mexico. His Civil War-era assignments included: captain, 1st Artillery (since September 22, 1848); brigadier general, USV (September 28, 1861); major, 2nd Artillery (October 26,

1862); commanding 3rd Brigade, Sumner's Division, Army of the Potomac (November 25, 1861-March 13, 1862); commanding 3rd Brigade, 1st Division, 2nd Corps, Army of the Potomac (March 13-July 20 and August 10-September 6, 1862); commanding 3rd Division, 2nd Corps, Army of the Potomac (September 10-December 20, 1862 and January 10-June 28, 1863); major general, USV (November 29, 1862); commanding French's Command, 8th Corps, Middle Department (late June-July 7, 1863); commanding 3rd Corps, Army of the Potomac (July 7, 1863-January 28, 1864 and February 17-March 24, 1864); lieutenant colonel, 2nd Artillery (February 8, 1864); and chief of artillery, Middle Department (January 5-July 1865). Stationed at Eagle Pass, Texas, at the outbreak of the war, he ignored David E. Twigg's treacherous surrender and marched his command to the coast where it could be transferred to Key West. He remained there until his promotion and then led his brigade from the Washington defenses to the Peninsula. He fought at Yorktown and was brevetted for Seven Pines. After serving through the Seven Days he went north for the Maryland Campaign and took command of a division shortly before South Mountain and Antietam. At Fredericksburg his division took part in the futile assaults against Marye's Heights. For his role in the Chancellorsville fighting he was brevetted brigadier general in the regular army. He was already a full major general in the volunteers. Just before the battle of Gettysburg he was given charge of an improvised division in the Middle Department assigned to assist the Army of the Potomac. Shortly after the battle this command was assigned to that army's 3rd Corps and through seniority he became a corps commander. After the Bristoe Campaign his career was severely damaged by the charges of Meade that French had been slow in moving up his command at Mine Run and thus had prompted the plan's aborting. French in turn blamed an unnamed division commander. When the army was reorganized a few months later he lost his command and on May 6, 1865, he was mustered out of the volunteer service. Reverting to his regular army lieutenant colonelcy, he was stationed for a time at Fort McHenry and later served as Lew Wallace's chief artillerist. In the postwar years he served for a time on the West Coast and was retired in 1880 as colonel, 4th Artillery, having been brevetted major general for the war.

FREY, Emil (1838-1922)

It is generally stated that only six members of the Union army became president, but there was a seventh, Emil Frey, who in 1894 became president of the Swiss Confederation. The Civil War broke out while he was touring the American Midwest. Caught up in the war fever, he enlisted in the Union army. His assignments included: sergeant, Company E, 24th Illinois (July 8, 1861); second lieutenant, Company H, 24th Illinois (August 29, 1861); first lieutenant, Company H, 24th Illinois (January 1, 1862); and captain, Company H, 82nd Illinois (September 1862). After serving in Kentucky, Tennessee and Alabama, he was commissioned to command his own company in a newly raised regiment that was sent to the Virginia front. With this command he fought at Chancellorsville where his corps was routed by Stonewall Jackson's famous flank attack. On the first day at Gettysburg the corps was again defeated north of town and in the confused fighting young Frey was taken prisoner. Sent to Libby Prison, he was chosen by lot, along with four other officers, to serve as hostages for the fair treatment of some Rebel prisoners. This lasted for 77 days. Not paroled until January 14, 1865, he rejoined his regiment, which had in the meantime been transferred to the Western armies. He took part in the final campaign in the Carolinas. Brevetted major for his war service, he was mustered out on June 9, 1865. Returning to Switzerland he became a journalist and entered politics. In the 1880s he served five years as minister to the United States and as minister of war. In 1894 he became the president of the Federal Assembly, the only known case of a Civil War soldier becoming the head of a foreign government.

FRITCHIE, Barbara (1766-1862)

A 95-year-old resident of Frederick, Maryland, has come down through Civil War mythology as the Barbara Fritchie who waved a Union flag at Confederate troops passing her home and shouted at Stonewall Jackson, "Shoot if you must this old gray head, but spare your country's flag." In fact Barbara Fritchie did wave a flag at troops during the Antietam Campaign but it was on September 10 and not September 6, 1862, and the troops were part of the Union's 9th Corps. There is plenty of testimony that Fritchie and Jackson never saw each other. It further appears that there was a Mrs. Mary S. Quantrill who waved several flags at the enemy in Frederick on the 6th. Nonetheless through John G. Whittier's poem, "Barbara Frietchie," the wrong person has received the credit. Fritchie died the following December while celebrating her 96th birthday. (Quynn, Dorothy Louise, *Barbara Frietschie*)

FROST, Daniel Marsh (1823-1900)

The only Confederate general to be dropped from the army's rolls was New York native Daniel M. Frost for, in effect, desertion. The West Pointer (1844) had been posted initially to the artillery but transferred to the Regiment of Mounted Riflemen in 1846. During the Mexican War he won one brevet and then served on the frontier and a tour of duty in Europe before resigning as a first lieutenant in 1853. He then went into business in St. Louis and sat in the state legislature. Having been in the militia for a number of years, he joined the Southern faction in 1861. His Southern assignments included: brigadier general, Missouri Militia (prewar); brigadier general, Missouri State Guard (early 1861); commanding 7th and 9th Divisions, Missouri State Guard, Trans-Mississippi District, Department #2 (March 1862); commanding Artillery Brigade, Price's Division, Trans-Mississippi District, Department #2 (March 17-April 15, 1862); commanding Artillery Brigade, Army of the West, Department #2 (April 15-April 1862); inspector general, Army of the West, Department #2 (May 8-26, 1862); commanding division, 1st Corps, Trans-Mississippi Department (late 1862-January 1863); brigadier general, CSA

(October 10, 1862, to rank from March 3); commanding brigade, Hindman's Division, District of Arkansas, Trans-Mississippi Department (January-March 2 and March 30-May 1863); commanding the division (March 2-30, 1863); and commanding division, District of Arkansas, Trans-Mississippi Department (May-fall 1863). It was his command at Camp Jackson that Nathaniel Lyon seized in order to protect the arsenal in St. Louis. At Pea Ridge he commanded two tiny divisions of the State Guard and then took command of an artillery brigade, which he took across the Mississippi. During the siege of Corinth he served as an inspector and then recrossed the river. At Prairie Grove he led a division, having been named a brigadier general in the Confederate service. He continued in Arkansas until he joined his wife and family in Canada where they had gone to flee the Union occupation of St. Louis. Not having tendered his resignation, he was simply dropped on December 9, 1863. After the war he returned to the St. Louis area and engaged in farming.

FRY, Birkett Davenport (1822-1891)

Wounded four times during the Civil War, Virginian Birkett D. Fry rose to the rank of Confederate brigadier general but is largely forgotten because he spent so little time in command. A graduate of the Virginia Military Institute, he flunked out of the 1866 class at West Point for a deficiency in mathematics. The Mexican War, however gave him another chance as he was commissioned directly into the Regiment of Voltigeurs—which was raised especially for that conflict—as a first lieutenant. During a part of the war he served as the unit's adjutant. Mustered out in 1848, he settled in California. In the late 1850s he accompanied William Walker's filibustering expedition to Nicaragua. Managing a cotton mill in Alabama at the outbreak of the Civil War, he joined the Confederacy. His assignments included: colonel, 13th Alabama (July 19, 1861); commanding Archer's Brigade, A.P. Hill's Division, 2nd Corps, Army of Northern Virginia (May 3, 1863); commanding Archer's brigade, Heth's Division, 3rd Corps, Army of Northern Virginia (July 1-3, 1863); commanding Barton's Brigade, Ransom's Division, Department of North Carolina and Southern Virginia (May 1864); and brigadier general, CSA (May 24, 1864). With his regiment he fought on the Peninsula, seeing action at Yorktown, Williamsburg, Seven Pines (wounded), and the Seven Days. He fought at Antietam and was wounded a second time. At Chancellorsville he took over the brigade when James J. Archer took over the division but soon fell wounded again. When Archer was captured on the first day at Gettysburg, Fry again took over. During Pickett's Charge on the third day Fry was wounded a fourth time and captured. Not exchanged until April 1864, he fought under Beauregard at Drewry's Bluff and was rewarded with promotion to brigadier general. In the fall of 1864 he was dispatched to Augusta, Georgia, to command in that area in the face of Sherman's March to the Sea. After three years in Cuban exile he returned to the cotton business in Alabama. (Freeman, Douglas S., *Lee's Lieutenants*)

FRY, Cary Harrison (ca. 1817-1873)

Graduating from West Point in 1834, Cary Fry resigned from military service two years later to take up medicine. But he was destined to return to the military twice and serve briefly as acting Paymaster General during the Civil War. Giving up his Louisville practice he served as major, 2nd Kentucky, during the Mexican War. Mustered out, he returned to his patients, but in 1833 he accepted an appointment as major in the Pay Department. He served throughout the Civil War in this grade and temporarily relieved Colonel B.F. Larned as Paymaster General when that officer was ill. With the death of Larned on September 6, 1862, a new departmental head was needed. On December 11, 1862, Colonel T.P. Andrews was given the post and Fry resumed his former duties for the rest of the war. In 1866 he became deputy paymaster general with the rank of lieutenant colonel. From 1865-67 Fry was brevetted lieutenant colonel, colonel, and brigadier general in the regular army for his services during the war. He died while on duty in San Francisco in 1873.

FRY, James Barnet (1827-1894)

A West Pointer (1847) and Mexican War veteran, James Fry became the army's first provost marshal general in 1863. Assigned first to the artillery, the Illinois-born Fry had served as an artillery instructor at his alma mater and was a brevet captain and assistant adjutant general by the time of the firing on Fort Sumter. His later appointments included: captain and assistant adjutant general, USA (August 3, 1861); colonel and additional aide-de-camp, USA (November 14, 1861); major and assistant adjutant General, USA (April 22, 1862); lieutenant colonel and assistant adjutant general, USA (December 31, 1862); colonel and provost marshal general, USA (March 17, 1863); and brigadier general and provost marshal general USA (April 21, 1864). During the 1st Bull Run Campaign he served as chief of staff to General McDowell, and later, serving in the same position to General Buell, he saw action at Shiloh, Corinth, and Perryville. He then returned to Washington to serve in the Adjutant General's Department. Appointed provost marshal general, he was responsible for apprehending deserters, enforcing the draft, and enlisting volunteers. The creation of this bureau replaced the previous system of having separate provost marshals with the armies, each acting without central direction. Under Fry's direction the bureau managed to arrest 76,526 deserters of the total of about 200,000 cases during the entire war. The per capita enlistment costs were cut by more than two-thirds by the operations of Fry's staff. When Fry's position was eliminated in 1866, he reverted to his grade in the Adjutant General's department where he served until his retirement in 1881.

FRY, Speed Smith (1817-1892)

Lawyer and county judge Speed S. Fry was a captain of Kentucky volunteers during the Mexican War. Appointed a colonel of the Unionist state militia during the secession crisis, Fry raised the

4th Kentucky and became its first colonel on October 9, 1861. At the battle of Mill Springs, while examining the situation on his regiment's flank, Fry came upon an officer in a raincoat with no insignia of rank or army. This officer directed Fry not to fire on friendly troops and Fry turned to give the order to cease. While in the process he was fired upon, and his horse was wounded. Realizing his mistake, Fry and the rest of the soldier fired on the mystery officer and killed him. It was rebel General F.K. Zollicoffer. Fry's later assignments included: brigadier general, USV (March 21, 1862); commanding 2nd Brigade, 1st Division, Army of the Ohio (March 22-September 29, 1862); commanding 2nd Brigade, 1st Division, 3rd Corps, Army of the Ohio (September 29-October 18, 1862); commanding 3rd Division, Center, Army of the Cumberland (November 5, 1862-Janaury 9, 1863); and commanding District of Northern Central Kentucky, 1st Division, 23rd Corps, Department of the Ohio (August 1863-January 1864). Fry's career as a general was not creditable. At both Shiloh and Stones' River he failed to bring his men into action and he was relegated to post duty. In January 1864, he was ordered, with some of his force from Camp Nelson, to join the army in the field, but his advance was severely criticized for being too slow. Ordered to resume command of the post at Camp Nelson, he was criticized for frequent absences from his station but was not relieved until March 24, 1865, and was mustered out on August 24, 1865. After the war he was a tax official.

FÜGER, Frederick (?-?)

Born in Germany, Frederick Füger was one of the few regular army enlisted men to become an officer, without transferring to the volunteers, during the Civil War. Having served in Battery A, 4th Artillery, since 1856 and in all enlisted grades through first sergeant, Frederick Füger was to have his moment of glory at Gettysburg. His battery saw action in the Peninsula Campaign and at Antietam, Fredericksburg, and Chancellorsville. Holding the position to the right of the famed clump of trees on Cemetery Ridge, on the third day at Gettysburg the battery faced Pickett's Charge. During the fierce fighting the two lieutenants serving with the unit that day, Alonzo Cushing and Joseph S. Milne of the 1st Rhode Island Light Artillery, were struck down. Füger took command on the one remaining gun and continued firing until ordered to retire. For his behavior he was especially cited in the reports of Generals Hancock and Webb and recommended for a commission. Still a first sergeant, he commanded a section in the fight at Sulphur Springs during the Bristoe Campaign and again distinguished himself. He was promoted to second lieutenant, 4th Artillery, on October 31, 1863, taking command of the battery now in the horse artillery until the spring of 1864. Subsequently his battery fought in the campaign of Petersburg and was sent to the Washington defenses in June 1864. He received brevets to first lieutenant for Yellow Tavern and captain for Dinwiddie Court House. In 1897 he was awarded the Congressional Medal of Honor for Gettysburg. Continuing in the regular army until 1900, he rose to be a major in his old regiment.

FULKERSON, Samuel Vance (1822-1862)

Although a favorite of Stonewall Jackson, Samuel V. Fulkerson did not live long enough to receive his rightful promotion to a brigadier generalship. A native of Virginia, he served in a Tennessee regiment as adjutant during the Mexican War. A lawyer and judge at the outbreak of the Civil War, he reentered military service where his assignments included: colonel, 37th Virginia (May 28, 1861); commanding 3rd Brigade, Jackson's Division, Valley District, Department of Northern Virginia (ca. February-April 13, 1862 and May 1862); and commanding the same brigade, Jackson's Division, Jackson's Corps, Army of Northern Virginia (June 27, 1862). He commanded the regiment in the Cheat Mountain and Romney campaigns and got involved in the Loring-Jackson feud near the latter place. He then took part in the Shenandoah Valley Campaign, sometimes commanding the brigade. Again in brigade command he was killed at the battle of Gaines' Mill during the Seven Days.

FULLER, John Wallace (1827-1891)

The highlight of John W. Fuller's military career came when he bested the famous Nathan Bedford Forrest at the end of 1862. Born in Great Britain, he was brought to America as a child and eventually settled in Ohio where he became a publisher, militia officer, and public official. His military assignments included: colonel, 27th Ohio (August 17, 1861); commanding 1st Brigade, 2nd Division, Army of the Mississippi (September 10-October 26, 1862); commanding 1st Brigade, 8th Division, Left Wing, 13th Corps, Army of the Tennessee (November 1-December 18, 1862); commanding 1st Brigade, 8th Division, Left Wing, 16th Corps, Army of the Tennessee (December 18, 1862-March 18, 1863); commanding 4th Brigade, 2nd Division, District of Corinth, 16th Corps, Army of the Tennessee (March 18-May 2, 1863); commanding 3rd Brigade, 5th Division, District of Memphis, 16th Corps, Army of the Tennessee (May 1-July 25 and August 25-November 14, 1863); commanding brigade, 2nd Division, 16th Corps, Army of the Tennessee (November 11, 1863-January 2, 1864 and February 2-March 10, 1864); brigadier general, USV (January 5, 1864); commanding 1st Brigade, 4th Division, 16th Corps, Army of the Tennessee (March 10-July 17 and August 4-19, 1864); commanding the division (July 17-August 4 and August 19-September 23, 1864); commanding 1st Division, 17th Corps, Army of the Tennessee (September 22-October 23, 1864); and commanding 1st Brigade, 1st Division, 17th Corps, Army of the Tennessee (November 7-December 24, 1864 and January 25-June 24, 1865). After training recruits in western Virginia he led his regiment at Island #10 and in the advance on Corinth, Mississippi. As a brigade commander he fought at Iuka and Corinth. His greatest moment came at Parker's Store (or Crossroads) on the last day of 1862. Forrest was returning from raiding Grant's supply lines when he was caught in a crossfire from Fuller's command. Forrest lost much equipment and 300 men as prisoners. Fuller was stationed near Memphis during Grant's operations against Vicksburg but rejoined frontline troops in the Atlanta Campaign as a brigadier general.

He went on to participate in the March to the Sea and through the Carolinas. Brevetted major general for the war, he resigned on August 15, 1865. After the war he was in the footwear business and held public office.

FULLER, William A. (ca. 1836-1905)

The conductor of the train pulled by *The General*, which was hijacked by Union raiders under James J. Andrews, became the Confederate hero of the raid. With the Western and Atlantic train making a scheduled breakfast stop at Big Shanty, Georgia, William A. Fuller was astonished to see the engine and three box cars leaving the station without him and the rest of his crew. Thinking deserters from a nearby Confederate camp were responsible for the theft, Fuller and a handful of other railroad employees gave chase—on foot! Soon picking up a pushcart, they continued the pursuit at a faster pace. Derailed by a track torn up by the raiders, Fuller continued on foot until he picked up the first of three pursuit engines. Changing trains several times and sometimes running backwards, the pursuers easily pushed aside any obstructions laid by the fugitives. Finally, after about 87 miles, the raiders were forced by a lack of fuel to abandon *The General* and were soon captured by the alerted authorities. Fuller's pursuit prevented the raiders from inflicting any serious damage to the line. With the excitement of April 12, 1862, over, Fuller resumed his duties with the road and in 1864 was made a captain of Georgia Local Defense Troops assigned to protecting the railroad. With the impending fall of Atlanta, it was Fuller who was responsible for the removal of most of the railroads engines to safer areas. (O'Neill, Charles, *Wild Train: The Story of the Andrews Raiders*)

FULTON, John S. (1828-1864)

In a little over two years of active service John S. Fulton took part in military operations in several major theaters of the Civil War. His Confederate assignments included: private, Company G or K, 44th Tennessee (March 27, 1862); captain, Company F, 44th Consolidated Tennessee (April 18, 1862); major, 44th Consolidated Tennessee (April 19, 1862); colonel, 44th Consolidated Tennessee (May 15, 1862); temporarily commanding Johnson's Brigade, Johnson's Provisional Division, Army of Tennessee (September 19-20, 1863); colonel, 25th and 44th Tennessee Consolidated (October 1863); commanding Johnson's Brigade, Buckner's-Johnson's Division, Department of East Tennessee (November 26, 1863-April 1864); commanding same brigade, Hoke's Division, Department of North Carolina and Southern Virginia (May 1864); and commanding same brigade, Johnson's Division, Department of North Carolina and Southern Virginia (ca. May 21-June 30, 1864). Following the heavy losses suffered at Shiloh, he became captain of his company, but a few days later the 44th was merged with the 55th (McKoin's) Tennessee. He became, in quick succession, captain of a consolidated company, major and colonel. Commanding the new regiment, he fought at Perryville and Murfreesboro. At Chickamauga he commanded the brigade. Having again suffered severe casualties, the regiment was "temporarily" united the 25th Tennessee. Still in command of the brigade, Fulton fought at Knoxville and, after moving to Virginia, at Port Walthall Junction, Swift Creek, and Drewry's Bluff. Taking position in the Petersburg trenches, he was struck by shell fragment on the last day of June 1864. He died four days later.

FUNSTEN, David (1819-1866)

Having provided his initial service to the Confederacy in the army, David Funsten became an innovative legislator in the field of military affairs. A native Virginian, he had served one term in the state legislature before the war. His army assignments included: captain, 11th Virginia (early 1861); lieutenant colonel, 11th Virginia (May 16, 1861); and colonel, 11th Virginia May 23, 1862). He saw action at 1st Manassas and Seven Pines, where he was severely wounded. His wound eventually forced his resignation on September 24, 1863. Running for the 9th Congressional District's seat, which had been vacated by William Smith, Funsten won election to both the unexpired portion of the term in the First Congress and for the Second. Taking his seat at the commencement of the next session on December 7, 1863, Funsten was assigned to the Committees on Naval Affairs and on Flag and Seal, as well as numerous special bodies. An extreme proponent of all-out warfare, he favored the drafting of whites and even blacks, heavy taxes, impressments, military control of railroads and minerals, and the suspension of the writ of habeas corpus on the slightest of pretexts. Drawing on his military experiences, he initiated legislation that consolidated decimated field units and provided for limited service by invalided soldiers. Returning to his home near Alexandria, Virginia, he died of pneumonia, a complication from his war wound, less than a year after Lee's surrender.

FURY, Bridget (1837-1872?)

Born Delia Swift in Cincinnati, Bridget Fury was a notorious prostitute, pickpocket, and mugger in that city by the age of 13. Moving to New Orleans—teaming up for a time with Mary Jane Jackson—she continued to ply her trade, earning her more famous name, and becoming one of the South's most notorious female Civil War criminals. For a time a part of a women's street gang that terrified even sailors, she was sent to prison in 1858 for murdering a man. Her life sentence was canceled when the Union forces occupied the city in 1862 and the military governor, General George F. Shepley, issued a blanket pardon emptying the jails. For a time she operated a brothel but spent more time in jail for robbery and finally ended up in the gutter.

G

GALWAY

See: *Wilkie, Franc Bangs*

GALLOWAY, Edward (?-1861)

Private Edward Galloway, 1st U.S. Artillery, was one of only two men to die at Fort Sumter, although he did not receive his fatal wound in combat. After the surrender of the fort, General Beauregard permitted the departing Union garrison to fire an artillery salute to the flag as it was lowered. At about the midway point of the planned 100-gun honors, the scene suddenly turned to one of horror. A barbette gun discharged prematurely and killed Private Daniel Hough. Sparks from the gun then ignited some loose artillery rounds next to the piece. In the resulting explosions five men standing nearby were wounded. The two most severely wounded were transferred to Charleston. One of them was Private Galloway. Five days after the tragedy he died while his comrades were on their way to a heroes' welcome in New York.

GAMBLE, Hamilton Rowan (1798-1864)

The secession crisis of 1861 prompted Hamilton R. Gamble to return from Pennsylvania to Missouri where he had lived for four decades. A native of Virginia, he had practiced law in Virginia and Tennessee before transferring his business to the Missouri Territory. Besides practicing in St. Louis he served as a court clerk, prosecuting attorney, secretary of state, state legislator, and as president of the state supreme judicial body. Having moved to Pennsylvania in 1858, he returned to Missouri and was a delegate to the state convention in 1861. With Governor Claiborne F. Jackson having joined the Confederacy, Gamble was named by the convention as provisional governor. He took up his duties in June. As a Unionist, he ruled over a divided state and in effect shared power with Jackson's exiled government. But Gamble held the state in the Union and a loyalty oath was required of officials and voters. Slavery was abolished in his term. Gamble died in office on January 31, 1864. (Davis, Walter B. and Drurrie, Daniel S., *History of Missouri*)

GAMBLE, William (1818-1866)

A Seminole War veteran, William Gamble survived the Civil War only to die the next year of cholera while on active duty. The native of County Tyrone, Ireland, was about 20 years old when he settled in the United States. From 1839 to 1843 he was an enlisted man in the regular army's 1st Dragoons in which he rose to sergeant major. At the outbreak of the Civil War he was a civil engineer in Chicago. His military assignments included: lieutenant colonel, 8th Illinois Cavalry (September 18, 1861); colonel, 8th Illinois Cavalry (December 5, 1862); commanding 1st Brigade, Cavalry Division, Army of the Potomac (January-February 1863); commanding 1st Brigade, 1st Division, Cavalry Corps, Army of the Potomac (May 27-June 6, June 9-September 2, and November 12-December 21, 1863); commanding Cavalry Division, Camp Stoneman, 22nd Corps, Department of Washington (May 2-November 1864); commanding 1st Separate Brigade, 22nd Corps, Department of Washington (November 1864-June 22, 1865); brigadier general, USV (September 25, 1865); and major, 8th Cavalry (July 28, 1866). Serving with his regiment in the Peninsula Campaign, he was wounded at Malvern Hill—the last of the Seven Days. He returned to command the regiment at Fredericksburg and was in charge of a brigade at Gettysburg where his men opened the battle. Following service in the Mine Run Campaign he was assigned to the Washington fortifications and after a period directing the cavalry of that department he took charge of a mixed brigade, which was frequently engaged against John S. Mosby. On December 14, 1864, he was brevetted brigadier general and, with his regiment, was mustered out on July 15, 1865. Two months later he was recommissioned with the full rank of brigadier. Again mustered out on March 13, 1866, he was made a major in the new 8th Cavalry four months later. While his regiment was in transit to the Pacific coast, he died of cholera in Nicaragua on December 20, 1866.

GANO, Richard Montgomery (1830-1913)

A veteran of Texas Indian fighting, Richard M. Gano got his early Civil War cavalry training under John Hunt Morgan. The Kentucky-born doctor had sat in the Texas legislature before the Civil War. His Confederate assignments included: captain, Texas Cavalry Squadron (1861); captain, Company A, 7th Kentucky Cavalry (May 6, 1862); colonel, 7th Kentucky Cavalry (September 2, 1862); commanding brigade, Maxey's Cavalry Division, District of Arkansas, Trans-Mississippi Department (April 1864); commanding 5th (Texas) Cavalry Brigade, 2nd (Texas-Maxey's) Cavalry Division, 1st Corps (or District of West Louisiana), Trans-Mississippi Department (September 1864-ca. March 1865); and brigadier general, CSA (March 17, 1865). He took part in a number of Morgan's raids and was given command of a regiment during the Kentucky Campaign. Transferred to the far side of the Mississippi, he commanded a mounted brigade during the repulse of Steele's drive on Camden, Arkansas, in the spring of 1864. During these operations he was wounded but returned to duty to command the brigade again and receive promotion to brigadier general in the final months of the war. He then became a minister in the Christian Church for the remainder of his life. He was also active in veterans' affairs.

GARDNER, Alexander (?-?)

Formerly Mathew B. Brady's Washington, D.C. branch manager, Alexander Gardner succeeded in establishing his own photographic firm midway through the Civil War. A pioneer of the wet-plate process, he had been imported from his native Scotland by Brady when that artist was switching over from the daguerreotype in 1856. Within two years he was in charge of the Washington office and upon the outbreak of the Civil War was frequently sent into the field with the masses of Brady's assistants. Brady unfortunately had a poor relationship with his employees, especially due to his failure to give his artists credit for their work. Early in 1863 Gardner left the firm and set up his own business. He scored a major coup when he lured away two of Brady's top assistants—James F. Gibson and Timothy O'Sullivan. Together the trio did an outstanding job as the first photographers to reach the field at Gettysburg. His brother James was also a member of the firm.

GARDNER, Franklin (1823-1873)

During the Civil War Jefferson Davis came in for much criticism for his predilection of appointing Northern-born officers to important commands—where they were frequently unsuccessful. Such is the case of New York City-born Franklin Gardner who surrendered the last major Confederate post on the Mississippi River. The West Pointer (1843) had received his appointment from Iowa and was then posted to the infantry. He won two brevets in Mexico, fought the Seminoles, was stationed on the frontier, and campaigned against the Mormons. With the secession crisis reaching its peak, he abandoned his post and was dropped as a captain in the 10th Infantry on May 7, 1861. Joining the Confederacy, his assignments included: lieutenant colonel, Infantry (March 16, 1861); commanding Cavalry Brigade, 2nd Grand Division, Army of the Mississippi (March 25-29, 1862); brigadier general, CSA (April 11, 1862); commanding Cavalry, 2nd Division, 2nd Corps, Army of the Mississippi (ca. May-late June 1862); commanding 1st Brigade, Reserve Corps, Army of the Mississippi (late June-July 2, 1862); commanding 1st Brigade, Reserve (Withers') Division (Right Wing from August 15), Army of the Mississippi (July 2-November 20, 1862); commanding 1st brigade, Withers' Division, Polk's Corps, Army of Tennessee (November 20-December 1862); major general, CSA (December 13, 1862); commanding 3rd Military District (or District of Eastern Louisiana), Department of Mississippi and East Louisiana (December 28, 1862-May 6, 1863 and May 6-July 8, 1863); also temporarily commanding District of the Gulf, Department of Mississippi and East Louisiana (April 27, 1863); commanding District of the Gulf, Department of Alabama, Mississippi and East Louisana (early September 1864); commanding the department (September 1864); and commanding District of Mississippi and East Louisiana, Department of Alabama, Mississippi and East Louisiana (October 4, 1864-May 4, 1865). Early in the war he served in Tennessee and Mississippi. During the battle of Shiloh he was in charge of the cavalry in the rear, but due to the terrain his command played little part in the fight. He commanded a brigade—which was not present at Perryville—during the Kentucky Campaign in the fall of 1862. Promoted to major general, he was ordered to the Mississippi Valley with principal responsibility for Port Hudson, which next to Vicksburg was the most important Confederate stronghold on the river. The fall of Vicksburg on July 4, 1863, virtually made Port Hudson untenable and Gardner surrendered the post on the 8th, having repulsed several determined Union assaults during the seven weeks of siege. Not exchanged until August 1864, his promotion to major general was not confirmed by the Senate until two months earlier due to the anti-Davis sentiment in that body. He spent the balance of the war in district command and took part in no further major battles. Surrendered under the terms of Richard Taylor's capitulation, he lived out his years as a planter in Louisiana.

GARDNER, William Montgomery (1824-1901)

Resigning his regular army commission on the date of his native Georgia's secession, William M. Gardner rose to the rank of brigadier general in the Confederate service. The West Pointer (1846) had been posted to the infantry with which he was wounded on two consecutive days in Mexico. For this he was brevetted. The interwar years were spent mostly on the frontier and by the time of his resignation on January 19, 1861, he was a captain in the 2nd Infantry. His Confederate assignments included: major, Infantry (March 16, 1861); lieutenant colonel, 8th Georgia (ca. June 1861); colonel, 8th Georgia (August 21, 1861 to rank from July 21); brigadier general, CSA (November 14, 1861); commanding District of Middle Florida, Department of South Carolina, Georgia and Florida (November 11, 1863-February 23, 1864); and commanding Post of Richmond, Department of Richmond (January-April 2, 1865). Badly wounded at 1st Bull Run, he was promoted to colonel and brigadier general during his lengthy recovery. Late in 1863 he finally returned to duty as a district commander in Florida. Although most sources state that he fought at Olustee there is no evidence of this in the *Official Records*. Shortly thereafter he was placed in charge of all prisoners of war camps east of the Mississippi River except in Alabama and Georgia. During the final months of the conflict he commanded the post at Richmond. After Appomattox he returned quietly to his home.

GARESCHÉ, Julius Peter (?-1862)

After 21 years in the regular army, Julius P. Garesché did not survive his first battle. He was born in Cuba, and received his West Point appointment from Delaware, graduating in 1841. Posted to the artillery, he served with it until his assignment to the adjutant's branch in the mid 1850s. His Civil War assignments included: brevet captain and assistant adjutant general (since November 9, 1855); brevet major and assistant adjutant general (May 14, 1861); major and assistant adjutant general (August 3, 1861); lieutenant colonel and assistant adjutant general (July 17, 1862); and assistant adjutant general and chief of staff, Army of the Cumberland (November 13-December 31, 1862). In the early days of the war he organized volunteers in the nation's capital and then worked in the adjutant's department until assigned to the staff of William S. Rosecrans in Tennessee. As his chief of staff, he renewed a friendship that stretched back to West Point days. Garesché had been a major influence in Rosecrans' conversion to Catholicism. On the first day of the fighting at Murfreesboro—on the last day of 1862—he was riding at his chief's side when he was decapitated by a cannonball. Rosecrans was splattered in blood but had no time to stop and look back after his friend in the face of the heavy Confederate attacks. Garesché was buried on the field that night. (Garesché, Louis, *Biography of Lieutenant Colonel Julius P. Garesché*)

GARFIELD, James Abram (1831-1881)

James A. Garfield survived the Civil War as a Union major general, but was felled by an assassin's bullet just months after being sworn in as the 20th President of the United States. The Ohio native struggled through early life after the death of his father and taught school before entering politics as a Republican. In 1859 he was elected to the upper house of the state legislature and practicing law when he began recruiting for the Union army. His wartime assignments included: lieutenant colonel, 42nd Ohio (August 21, 1861); colonel, 42nd Ohio (November 27, 1861); commanding 18th Brigade, Army of the Ohio (December 17, 1861-March 26, 1862); brigadier general, USV (January 11, 1862); commanding 20th Brigade, 6th Division, Army of the Ohio (April 5-July 10, 1862); chief of staff, Army of the Cumberland (January-October 1863); and major general, USV (September 19, 1863). Following his highly successful recruiting activities he moved into Kentucky where he was engaged in a pair of minor victories at Middle Creek and Pound Gap in the fighting against Humphrey Marshall. Rewarded with the star of a brigadier general, he arrived on the field of Shiloh too late on the second day for his brigade to be of much service. He then took part in Halleck's painfully slow advance on Corinth before being taken ill in the summer of 1862. The following November he was named to the commission that cashiered Fitz-John Porter, a decision in which he heartily concurred. Returning to the field, he became Rosecrans' staff chief and took part in the operations during the Tullahoma Campaign and the capture of Chattanooga. His greatest moment of the war came late on the second day at Chickamauga when his chief and two-thirds of the Union army had already been driven from the field. Caught up in the rout himself, he volunteered to return and ascertain the cause of the firing that was still coming from the battlefield. There he helped the "Rock of Chickamauga"—George H. Thomas—to perfect his defensive line. Garfield had learned his military lessons well during the war but failed to learn the requirements of military etiquette. He was long felt to be a spy sent by Washington to report on Rosecrans and was in fact harshly critical of his chief in letters sent out of the ordinary channels. Within a month after the battle he was headed back to Washington with a second star. On December 5, 1863, he

Future president James A. Garfield. (*Leslie's*)

resigned his commission to take the seat in Congress to which he had been elected the previous year. During his nine terms in the House of Representatives he became involved in the Crédit Mobilier scandal and was a member of the commission that settled the Tilden-Hayes election dispute of 1876-77. He was elected to the Senate in 1880, but declined to take his seat, as he was subsequently elected president. Within four months of his inauguaration he was shot in a Washington railroad station on July 2, 1881, by a disgruntled office seeker, Charles J. Guiteau. Removal of the bullet was deemed impossible but Garfield lingered on for some 11 weeks before dying at Elberon, New Jersey—to which he had been removed a couple of weeks earlier—on September 19. (Taylor, John M., *Garfield of Ohio: The Available Man*; Peskin, Allan, *Garfield*; and Williams, Frederick D., *The Wild Life of the Army, Civil War Letters of James A. Garfield*)

GARIBALDI, Giuseppe (1807-1882)

For many years before the Civil War, the activities of Giuseppe Garibaldi in fighting for liberty in Latin America and his native Italy had attracted the attention of the American public. In fact, when the war started both sides wanted to claim a connection with him. The 39th New York adopted the name of the "Garibaldi Guard" and in Louisiana there was a Confederate "Garibaldi Legion." In semi-retirement at the outbreak of the war, he got involved in a long correspondence with the author of an article full of praise for the Italian. It developed into a possibility that Garibaldi would be willing to fight for the North. Eventually Secretary of State Seward became involved in the discussions, but Garibaldi was reluctant to commit himself until the war became one against slavery. With Lincoln's approval, Garibaldi was offered a major generalcy. The disaster at 1st Bull Run had already occurred, but the freedom fighter balked at the offer. He still had the problem over slavery and a major general's stars were not necessarily equal to the position of commander in chief, which he desired. The negotiations broke down and Garibaldi went to fight against the papal states and for France in the Franco-Prussian War. (Ridley, Jasper, *Garibaldi*)

GARLAND, Augustus Hill (1832-1899)

The youngest member of the Confederate Congress, Augustus H. Garland was a late convert to the secessionist cause, not committing himself to the idea until the call for troops made by Lincoln following the fall of Fort Sumter. The Tennessee-born and Arkansas-raised Garland was a successful lawyer by this time and took an active role in the Arkansas secession convention. He was promptly sent to Montgomery as an at-large delegate to the Provisional Congress. In a disputed election in November 1861, Garland won reelection as representative for the 3rd District in the southeastern corner of the state. Defeated in an attempt to gain election to the senate in 1862, he continued to serve in the House, into the Second Congress, before taking a seat in the Senate on November 8, 1864, upon the death of the incumbent. Although a staunch supporter of the Davis administration's war policies and favoring an extended draft, Garland became known as one of the most articulate opponents of the suspension of the writ of habeas corpus and of martial law. After the war, he played a key role in the overturning of the "iron-clad oath," required by Congress before a lawyer could argue a case before the U.S. Supreme Court. He later served as governor, senator, and as Cleveland's attorney general. He died, fittingly, while presenting arguments before the Supreme Court. (Newberry, Farrar, *A Life of Mr. Garland of Arkansas*)

GARLAND, Samuel, Jr. (1830-1862)

A graduate of the Virginia Military Institute, Samuel Garland, Jr., was a practicing attorney but active in military affairs at the outbreak of the Civil War. He promptly joined the Virginia forces and his assignments included: captain, Company G, 11th Virginia (April 24, 1861); colonel, 11th Virginia (April 1861); brigadier general, CSA (May 23, 1862); and commanding Early's (old) Brigade, D.H. Hill's Division, Army of Northern Virginia (May 24-September 14, 1862). He fought at 1st Bull Run, Dranesville, and was wounded at Williamsburg but remained on duty. Later that month he was promoted and transferred to command the wounded General J.A. Early's Brigade. He led this unit at Seven Pines, in the Seven Days, and on the fringes of the 2nd Bull Run Campaign. In the invasion of Maryland, he was assigned to hold Fox's Gap in South Mountain on September 14, 1862. In its defense he fell mortally wounded, dying later that day. (Freeman, Douglas S., *Lee's Lieutenants*)

GARNETT, John Jameson (1839-1902)

One of the artillery battalion commanders of the Army of Northern Virginia who failed to make the grade was John J. Garnett. He was scheduled to graduate from West Point in the spring of 1861 when the outbreak of hostilities interrupted his studies. Joining the Confederacy immediately, he received the following assignments: lieutenant, Artillery (March 16, 1861); lieutenant, 3rd Company, Washington (La.) Artillery Battalion (June 20, 1861); major, Artillery (June 16, 1862); chief of artillery, D.R. Jones' Division, Magruder's Command, Army of Northern Virginia (June 16-July 1862); inspector of ordnance and artillery, 1st Corps, Army of Northern Virginia (November 14, 1862-early 1863); commanding Artillery Battalion, Anderson's Division, 1st Corps, Army of Northern Virginia (early 1863-June 2, 1863); commanding Artillery Battalion, Heth's Division, 3rd Corps, Army of Northern Virginia (June 2-July 1863); commanding artillery battalion, 3rd Corps, Army of Northern Virginia (July 1863-February 18, 1864); and commanding Post at Hicksford, 1st Military District, Department of North Carolina and Southern Virginia (summer-November 30, 1864). He was initially assigned to duty with the Washington Artillery of New Orleans with which he served at 1st Bull Run. He was a divisional artillery chief during the Seven Days, 2nd Bull Run, and Antietam. He was an inspector during the battle of Fredericksburg but was again in charge of a battalion at Chancellorsville and Gettysburg. His performance not being up to the standards required, he was suspended from duty on February 18, 1864, and relieved of duty with the army six weeks later. The army's chief artillerist, General Pendleton, had felt him better qualified for conscript duty than field command. He was assigned to post duty and finished the war as artillery inspector with the Army of Tennessee. (Wise, Jennings C., *The Long Arm of Lee*)

GARNETT, Richard Brooke (1817-1863)

Like his cousin, Robert S. Garnett, Richard B. Garnett rose to be a Confederate brigadier and lost his life in the war. Graduating from West Point in 1841, he spent two decades in the old army before resigning as captain, 6th Infantry on May 17, 1861. The veteran of the Seminole and Utah campaigns received the following assignments: major, Artillery (May 1861); brigadier general, CSA (November 14, 1861); commanding Stonewall Brigade, Valley District, Department of Northern Virginia (November 1861-April 1, 1862); commanding Pickett's Brigade, Jones' Division, 1st Corps, Army of Northern Virginia (September 5-late September 1862); commanding brigade, Pickett's Division, same corps and army (September 1862-February 25, 1863 and May-July 3, 1863); and commanding brigade, Pickett's Division, in the Department of Virginia and North Carolina (February 25-April 1, 1863) and in the Department of Southern Virginia (April 1-May 1863). Given command of the famed Stonewall Brigade, he commanded it in the Romney Campaign and at Kernstown where he withdrew it when his ammunition was exhausted, much to the displeasure of Jackson. He was placed under arrest on April 1, but the requirements of active campaigning prevented completion of the court-martial. Ordered back to duty on September 5, 1862, he led Pickett's old command at Antietam, Fredericksburg, in southeastern Virginia, and at Gettysburg. In Pickett's Charge on the third day he was killed and buried in a mass grave. Less than two months earlier he had served as pallbearer for his accuser, Stonewall Jackson. (Robertson, James I., Jr., *The Stonewall Brigade*)

GARNETT, Robert Selden (1819-1861)

The first general officer to die in action during the Civil War was Confederate Robert S. Garnett. The Virginian and West Pointer (1841) was a veteran of the infantry, artillery, and cavalry, and had received two brevets for the Mexican War. He resigned as major, 9th Infantry, on April 30, 1861, and entered the service of his state as adjutant general of Virginia troops. Working on the staff of Robert E. Lee, he became more of a chief of staff than any other officer was to become during the conflict. Transferred to Confederate service his assignments included: brigadier general, CSA (June 6, 1861) and commanding Army of the Northwest (June 8-July 13, 1861). Departing Richmond, he took command in what is now West Virginia. Covering a withdrawal in the face of Union forces under General Rosecrans, he was killed at Carrick's Ford on July 13. His cousin, General Richard Brooke Garnett was destined to die two years later in Pickett's Charge. (Freeman, Douglas S., *R.E. Lee*)

GARNETT, Thomas Stuart (1825-1863)

On both occasions when Virginian Thomas S. Garnett took over command of his brigade he soon fell victim to enemy fire. A former student at the Virginia Military Institute, he had served as a first lieutenant in the 1st Virginia during the Mexican War. When the Civil War began he gave up his medical practice and entered the Confederate army where his assignments included: captain, Company C, 9th Virginia Cavalry (May 1861); lieutenant colonel, 48th Virginia (mid 1861); commanding J.R. Jones' (2nd) Brigade, Jackson's (old) Division, Jackson's Corps, Army of Northern Virginia (summer 1862-August 9, 1862 and May 2-3, 1863); and colonel 48th Virginia (October 16, 1862). After initial service with his company, Lee's Light Horse, he was promoted to field officer with the 48th Virginia. With this command he served through the Cheat Mountain and Romney campaigns and fought at Kernstown and part of the 1862 Shenandoah Valley Campaign. At Cedar Mountain he commanded the brigade and was wounded but did not relinquish command until the fight was concluded. He returned, with the rank of colonel, and led his regiment at Chancellorsville. When on the night of May 2, General Jones left the field he took over the brigade. The next day he was mortally wounded, living until the following morning. (Freeman, Douglas S., *Lee's Lieutenants*)

GARRARD, Israel (?-?)

Although he had taken part in some of the major mounted operations of the Civil War, Israel Garrard did not receive his brevet promotion to brigadier general until several weeks after the close of hostilities—on June 20, 1865. The Ohio native's assignments included: colonel, 7th Ohio Cavalry (September 18, 1862); commanding 1st Brigade, 2nd Division, Cavalry Corps, Department of the Ohio (November 1863-January 1864); commanding the division (January-April 1864); commanding 1st Brigade, 1st Division, Cavalry Corps, Department of the Ohio (April 8-10, 1864); commanding 1st Brigade, Cavalry, District of Kentucky, 23rd Corps, Department of the Ohio (April-July 1864); commanding 1st Brigade, Cavalry Division, 23rd Corps, Army of the Ohio (July 27-August 11, 1864); commanding the division (August 11-November 1, 1864); and commanding 2nd Brigade, 4th Division, Cavalry Corps, Military Division of the Mississippi (December 1864-February 10, 1865). His unit served in Kentucky and East Tennessee and took part in the pursuit and capture of John Hunt Morgan on his raid north of the Ohio River. Garrard led a brigade at Knoxville and then joined Sherman's army late in the campaign against Atlanta. During the final stages of the siege, after George Stoneman's disastrous raid, he led the cavalry of John M. Schofield's Army of the Ohio. He then took part in the repulse of John B. Hood's invasion of middle Tennessee. His final exploit came as a brigade leader on Wilson's raid through

Finding the body of the first Confederate general to die in action, Robert S. Garnett. (*Leslie's*)

Alabama and Georgia. Two weeks after being brevetted he was mustered out on July 4, 1865, with his regiment.

GARRARD, Kenner (1827-1879)

A career cavalryman, Kenner Garrard served ably in command of both infantry and mounted troops and emerged from the Civil War with the regular army brevet of major general. The Kentucky native and West Pointer (1851) served briefly in the artillery before transferring to the cavalry. He was serving on the frontier during the secession crisis. His Civil War assignments included: first lieutenant, 2nd Cavalry (since March 3, 1855); captain, 2nd Cavalry (February 27, 1861); captain, 5th Cavalry (change of designation August 3, 1861); colonel, 146th New York (September 23, 1862); commanding 3rd Brigade, 2nd Division, 5th Corps, Army of the Potomac (July 2-December 7, 1863); brigadier general USV (July 23, 1863); major, 3rd cavalry (November 2, 1863); chief of Cavalry Bureau (December 1863-January 1864); commanding 2nd Division, Cavalry Corps, Army of the Cumberland (February 3-October 29, 1864); commanding 2nd Division, Cavalry Corps, Military Division of the Mississippi (October 29-November 16, 1864); commanding 2nd Division, Detachment Army of the Tennessee, Department of the Cumberland (December 7, 1864-February 18, 1865); and commanding 2nd Division, 16th Corps, Department of the Gulf (February 18-July 20, 1865). When Texas was seceding he was taken prisoner, along with other troops, at San Antonio on April 23, 1861. Although freed early, he was not formally exchanged until August 27, 1862, and the next month took command of a volunteer infantry regiment, which he led at Fredericksburg and Chancellorsville. In the fighting on Little Round Top on the second day at Gettysburg he succeeded to command of the brigade when General Stephen H. Weed was killed. Retaining command he soon received his star and a regular army brevet. Following service in the Bristoe and Mine Run campaigns he served briefly in charge of the War Department's mounted bureau before returning to the field in charge of a division of cavalry in the western theater. During the Atlanta Campaign he earned another brevet for the three-day raid he led on Covington, Georgia, but he failed to impress Sherman and his division was not taken on the March to the Sea. Instead he eventually found himself in command of an infantry division of the Army of the Tennessee, unofficially called the 16th Corps, that joined Thomas at Nashville. In the decisive defeat of Hood there he earned a brevet as regular brigadier general and another as volunteer major general. His division was transferred to the Gulf coast for the operations against Mobile, where he finished the war. He then received for his war services that last brevet he could earn, that of regular major general. Mustered out of the volunteer service on August 24, 1865, he reverted to the rank of major—to which he had risen during the war—before resigning on November 9, 1866. He was in the Cincinnati real estate business after his retirement.

GARRARD, Theophilus Toulmin (1812-1902)

Kentucky legislator Theophilus T. Garrard remained loyal to the Union and became a brigadier general. His military experience had come from his service as a company commander in one of the regular army infantry regiments raised especially for the Mexican War. His Civil War assignments included: colonel, 7th Kentucky (September 22, 1861); brigadier general, USV (November 29, 1862); commanding 1st Brigade, 9th Division, 13th Corps, Army of the Tennessee (February 4-May 19, 1863); commanding District of Somerset, Kentucky, 1st Division, 23rd Corps, Department of the Ohio (August 1863-January 1864); and commanding District of the Clinch, Department of the Ohio (January-April 1864). From the first action in Kentucky, Wild Cat Mountain, until Richmond he led his regiment and sometimes others as well. In the winter of 1862-1863 he served on the staff of Samuel P. Carter and was promoted to brigadier general. Leading a brigade under John A. McClernand, he fought through the campaign to Vicksburg. On the day of the first assault on the city proper, he was relieved and ordered to Arkansas. He was soon transferred back to his native state where he held a couple of district-level commands. He may have displeased his superiors or been suffering from ill health since he was mustered out on April 4, 1864. He returned to his farm and ran a salt business.

GARRETT, Richard H. (?-?)

The Virginia farm of Richard H. Garrett was the scene of one of the last episodes of the Civil War—the death of John Wilkes Booth. On the 24th of April 1865 John Wilkes Booth was left at the farm, between Port Conway and Bowling Green, by Willie Jett. The next day he was rejoined by Davis Herold who had been guiding him on his escape. They came to believe that federal cavalry were pursuing them and asked Mr. Garrett for horses to take them to the next railroad station. When he became suspicious and refused, the two conspirators asked to sleep in the tobacco shed. When the cavalry arrived in the early hours of April 26 Garrett refused to reveal that the pair were on the farm and in hiding. The shed was surrounded and Herold came out to surrender. The barn was then set ablaze and Booth was shot either by Boston Corbett, one of the soldiers, or by himself. Dragged from the flaming structure fatally wounded, Booth died on Garrett's porch.

GARRETT, Thomas (1789-1871)

Credited with having aided in the escape of around 2,700 slaves over the years, Pennsylvania-born Quaker Thomas Garrett managed to avoid prosecution until 1848. After rescuing a free black woman kidnapped from his father's home, he joined the Pennsylvania Abolition Society. Moving to Delaware in the early 1820s, he repeatedly had been warned about his activities in that slave state, and Maryland put a $10,000 reward on his head for his work with the underground railroad. Convicted in 1848, he was financially wiped out by the fine. Upon the passing of the Fifteenth Amendment in 1870 the blacks of Wilmington drew him through the streets in an open carriage as part of the celebrations. The next year they mourned his passing.

GARRISON, William Lloyd (1805-1879)

As a proponent of the nonviolent abolishment of slavery, editor-publisher William Lloyd Garrison was a leader in the crusade for over three decades. The Massachusetts native had been recruited by Benjamin Lundy in the late 1820s and in 1831 founded the abolitionist newspaper, *The Liberator*. He remained at its head until 1866 when the victory had been achieved. In 1833 he was one of the founders of the American Anti-Slavery Society. Not backing the Lincoln administration's war effort until the issuance of the Emancipation Proclamation, he saw his goal achieved with the fall of the Confederacy. Continuing his reform work, he was involved in the prohibition and women's suffrage movements and in pushing for a more humane policy toward the Indians. (Thomas, John L., *The Liberator, William Lloyd Garrison* and Merrill, Walter McIntosh, *Against Wind and Tide, A Biography of William Lloyd Garrison*)

Abolitionist William Lloyd Garrison. (NA)

GARROTT, Isham Warren (1816-1863)

Although appointed a brigadier general in the Confederate army, Isham Garrott never knew it. At the time of the secession movement, Garrott had been a lawyer and local politician in Mobile. He was sent by Alabama's governor to the state of his birth, North Carolina, to induce it to join the Confederate cause. His military assignments included: lieutenant colonel, 20th Alabama (September 9, 1861); colonel, 20th Alabama (October 8, 1861); temporarily commanding Tracy's old Brigade, Stevenson's Division, Department of Mississippi and East Louisiana (May 1-mid May 1863); and brigadier general (May 28, 1863). After his initial service in the Army of Mobile, Colonel Garrott and the 20th were sent to the Department of East Tennessee early in 1862. Here he saw action at Cumberland Gap in June; in December, the 20th along with the rest of Stevenson's Division, was ordered to Mississippi and took part in the defense at Chickasaw Bluff over the New Year holiday. Garrott then led his men in the battle of Port Gibson, the first fight in Grant's victorious drive on Vicksburg. When General E.D. Tracy was killed, Garrott took over temporary command of the brigade until he was superseded by General S.D. Lee. He again led his regiment at Champion's Hill and in the siege of Vicksburg. On June 17, 1863, while on the skirmish line, Garrott was killed by a sharpshooter's bullet. Word had not yet been received that he had been named brigadier general to rank from May 28, 1863.

GARTRELL, Lucius Jeremiah (1821-1891)

An early and extreme states' righter and secessionist, Lucius J. Gartrell carried his convictions into the field and into the halls of the Confederate Congress. A native Georgian, Gartrell had been a lawyer, former judge, former state legislator, and former Whig by 1861, when he was serving as a Democratic member of the U.S. House of Representatives. With the secession of Georgia, he resigned his seat and in May 1861 was commissioned colonel, 7th Georgia. With this command he fought at 1st Manassas where his son was killed and where Colonel and Congressman Francis S. Bartow died in his arms. Elected in November 1861 to be Georgia's 8th District representative in the First Regular Confederate Congress, he resigned his commission on February 13, 1862, in order to take his seat. During his term in Congress, Gartrell chaired the Committee on the Judiciary. Supporting the Davis administration he favored abolishing exemptions from conscription, nationalizing some vital industries, suspending the writ of habeas corpus, and government price regulation. He even went so far as to support the Davis administration before the less than friendly Georgia legislature. It may have been his unpopular views that prompted his decision not to seek reelection. Instead he was commissioned brigadier general, CSA, on August 22, 1864 and assigned to duty in Georgia, where his assignments included: the organization of the Georgia Reserves, a portion of which he commanded in the Savannah Campaign until wounded on December 9 near Coosawhatchie. He was a lawyer and unsuccessful politician after the war.

Confederate legislator Lucius J. Gartrell. (*Harper's*)

GARY, Martin Witherspoon (1831-1881)

A South Carolina defense attorney and state legislator, Martin W. Gary served from 1st Bull Run to Appomattox. His mother's home was the scene of one of the last Confederate cabinet meetings. His assignments included: captain, Company B, Infantry Battalion, Hampton (S.C.) Legion (June 12, 1861); lieutenant colonel, Hampton Legion (ca. April 1862); colonel, Hampton Legion (late 1862); brigadier general, CSA (May 19, 1964); commanding Cavalry Brigade, Department of Richmond (ca. May 19-December 1864 and January 1865); and commanding brigade, F. Lee's Cavalry Division, Cavalry Corps, Army of Northern Virginia (January-April 9, 1865). With the legion's infantry he fought at 1st Bull Run, at the head of his company, the Watson Guards. As a field officer he fought at Seven Pines, the Seven Days, 2nd Bull Run, Antietam, and Fredericksburg. The unit served with Longstreet, in southeastern Virginia in early 1863 and during the Gettysburg Campaign was in the vicinity of Richmond. Rejoining Longstreet, the command was too late for Chickamauga but served in East Tennessee before being sent to South Carolina to secure horses in early 1864. As mounted infantry the legion went to the Richmond front in May 1864. Promoted to brigadier, Gary led the mounted defenders of the capital until his command was absorbed into the cavalry of Lee's army early in 1865. He continued to serve near the city until its fall when he was the last general officer to leave. At Appomattox he cut his way out and joined President Davis in North Carolina and escorted him in part of his flight, with the stop at his mother's residence. After the war he was part of the powerful Hampton-Butler faction but eventually broke with them, leading to his defeat in two bids for a senatorship. He had previously served in the state legislature. (Freeman, Douglas S., *Lee's Lieutenants*)

GATES, Elijah (ca. 1829-?)

A Missouri farmer, Elijah Gates served with the Missouri Brigade of the western armies up until the battle of Franklin and was often in command. His Confederate assignments included: lieutenant colonel, 1st Cavalry, 5th Division, Missouri State Guard (early 1861); colonel, 1st Missouri Cavalry (December 31, 1861); commanding 1st Brigade, 1st Division, Army of the West, Department No. 2 (June-July 1862); commanding 1st Brigade, 1st Division, Price's Corps (Army of the West), Army of West Tennessee, Department No. 2 (July-October 1, 1862); commanding 1st Brigade, 1st Division, Price's Corps, Department of Mississippi and East Louisiana (October 1862); and commanding Cockrell's Brigade, French's Division, Stewart's Corps, Army of Tennessee (July-August 1864). After leading his regiment at Pea Ridge, he went with the rest of the Army of the West to the east bank of the Mississippi to join in the attack at Shiloh but arrived too late. At this time the regiment was dismounted and served for the remainder of the war as infantry. After serving in the siege of Corinth in the spring of 1862, he commanded the brigade at Iuka and Corinth. During the Vicksburg Campaign he was captured at Big Black River Bridge but escaped two days later and rejoined his command for the siege. Captured and exchanged, he joined Johnston's army in the Atlanta Campaign and was wounded on June 20, 1864, at Lattimer's Mills. During the latter part of the campaign and the beginning of the siege he commanded the brigade. On August 23, 1864, he suffered another wound during the siege. Following Atlanta's fall he accompanied Hood northward seeing action at Allatoona. In the invasion of Tennessee he took part in the futile charge at Franklin. He returned from the repulse with his horse's reins in his teeth, having been wounded in both arms. His left arm had to be amputated, ending his military service. (Anderson, Ephraim McD., *Memoirs: Historical and Personal: Including the Campaigns of the First Missouri Confederate Brigade* 2nd ed.—Notes and Foreword by Edwin C. Bearss)

GATH

See: *Townsend, George Alfred*

GATLIN, Richard Caswell (1809-1896)

Veteran infantryman and West Pointer (1832), Richard Gatlin became the Confederate scapegoat for the fall of New Bern in early 1862. A veteran of the Black Hawk, Seminole and Mexican wars and the Mormon Expedition, Gatlin was a major in the 5th Infantry when hostilities began. Captured and paroled by Arkansas forces, he soon resigned his commission and returned to his native state North Carolina and became adjutant general of the state militia. His Confederate assignments included: colonel (ca. June 22, 1861); commanding Southern Department, Coast Defenses (June 22-August 20, 1861); brigadier general, CSA (July 8, 1861); and commanding Department of North Carolina (August 20, 1861-March 19, 1862). Commanding in North Carolina he was responsible for the defense of that state in the face of general Burnside's expedition against the coast. After a string of defeats, General J.R. Anderson relieved him, the day after the Union capture of New Bern. After relinquishing command on March 29, 1862, Gatlin served for the rest of the war as adjutant and inspector general of North Carolina and resigned his Confederate commission on September 8, 1862. The explanation for his removal from command was officially listed as "ill health." Moving to Arkansas after the war, Gatlin was a farmer until his death.

GATLING, Richard Jordan (1818-1903)

This North Carolina doctor—he had studied medicine only to treat himself following a bout with smallpox—living in the North is credited with manufacturing the first practical machine gun. An inventor of some note, Richard J. Gatling had primarily engaged in the design and manufacture of farming implements before the Civil War. His rapid-fire gun, capable of firing 250 rounds a minute, was not accepted by the War Department until 1865, too late to see official active service. However, some had previously been placed upon gunboats and two saw some action with Butler at Petersburg. In addition, General Hancock ordered a dozen for his prestigious First Veteran Volunteer Corps but his unit never saw action. Subsequently Gatling perfected his gun and sold the rights to the Colt Fire Arms Company. President of the American Association of Inventors and Manufacturers for six years, he was working on a motorized plow when he died.

GAUL, Gilbert (1855-1919)

Although of Northern birth and too young to have participated in the Civil War, Gilbert Gaul became one of the outstanding artists in the depiction of the "Lost Cause." Receiving his artistic training at the National Academy of Design in New York, he developed an early interest in things military and subsequently spent most of his creative time in depicting the Civil War, and frequently the Confederate side of it. He traveled widely, researching army life, an experience that greatly enhanced the realism of his work. Many of his works, including "With Fate Against Them" and "Waiting for the Dawn," show a strong sympathy for the Confederate soldier and his tribulations. Some of his other famous works include: "Sergeant Hart Nailing the Colors to the Flagstaff of Fort Sumter," "General Thomas' Bivouac," and "Between the Lines During a Truce." Many of Gaul's works were reproduced in the Century Magazine's publication, *Battles and Leaders*.

GAY, Sydney Howard (1814-1888)

Massachusetts lawyer Sydney H. Gay gave up the practice of law because he felt he could not take an oath to uphold a constitu-

"With Fate Against Them" by Gilbert Gaul. (*B&L*)

tion that protected the institution of slavery, and so joined the abolitionists. He lectured for a time for the American Anti-Slavery Society and edited the *American Anti-Slavery Standard*. After 14 years, in which time he was an agent of the underground railroad, he left to join the *New York Tribune* in 1857. As managing editor from 1862 to 1865 he kept the paper running as a pro-war paper despite owner Horace Greeley's attacks on the Lincoln adminstration. After the war he served on the staff of the *Chicago Tribune* and the *New York Evening Post* and wrote a sympathetic biography, *James Madison*. He was still writing at the time of his death.

GEARY, John White (1819-1873)

Although he was only 53 at the time of his death, John W. Geary had had an active military and civil career, including Mexican War hero, San Francisco's first mayor, Kansas Territory governor, Civil War general, Pennsylvania governor, and potential presidential candidate. A lawyer and civil engineer from western Pennsylvania, he had served with the Allegheny Portage Railroad before his service in Mexico, when he rose to the command of a regiment and received five wounds in the storming of Chapultepec. He served as mayor in San Francisco in 1850-51 and for six months, not very successfully, in Bleeding Kansas. His Civil War assignments included: colonel, 28th Pennsylvania (June 28, 1861); commanding independent brigade, Department of the Shenandoah (April-June 1862); brigadier general, USV (April 25, 1862); commanding separate brigade, department of the Rappahannock (May-June 26, 1862); commanding 2nd Brigade, 1st Division, 2nd Corps, Army of Virginia (June 26-July 16, 1862); commanding 1st Brigade, 2nd Division, 2nd Corps, Army of Virginia (July 16-August 9, 1862); commanding 2nd Division, 12th Corps, Army of the Potomac (October 15, 1862-September 25, 1863); commanding 2nd Division, 12th Corps, Army of the Cumberland (September 25, 1863-January 27, 1864 and February 18-April 18, 1864); and commanding 2nd Division, 20th Corps, Army of the Cumberland (April 14, 1864-June 1, 1865). Wounded at Bolivar Heights near Harpers Ferry, he was captured at Leesburg in March 1862 but was soon exchanged and promoted to brigadier. Serving in the Shenandoah and then in northern Virginia he was seriously wounded twice at Cedar Mountain. Returning to duty in October, he led a division at Chancellorsville where he was struck in the chest by a cannonball. Regaining conciousness he was able to talk only in whispers for weeks. At Gettysburg he commanded his men on Culp's Hill and that fall accompanied the 11th and 12th Corps to the relief of Chattanooga, storming Lookout Mountain. In the earlier fighting at Wauhatchie his son had died in his arms. The rest of the war was for him one of revenge, and he enjoyed the burning in the Atlanta and Savannah campaigns. After serving as the latter city's military governor he went on the final campaign in the Carolinas. Mustered out on January 15, 1866, he had received a brevet major generalship with the unusual citation, "for fitness to command and promptness to execute." Returning to civil life, he was elected governor the same year and served two terms. He was briefly considered for the presidential nomination by the National Labor Reform Party but ended up supporting Grant's reelection in 1872. During his Pennsylvania years Geary supported the 40-hour week, Negro rights, and mine safety. Eighteen days after leaving office he died suddenly while facing charges in a claims scandal. (Tinkcom, Harry M., *John White Geary, Citizen of the World*)

GEE, John Henry (1819-1876)

Unlike his fellow prison camp commander, Henry Wirz, John H. Gee was acquitted in his war crimes trial. A physician before the war, he entered the Confederate army. His assignments included: captain, Company G, 1st Florida (April 5, 1861); major, 4th Florida Battalion (May 2, 1863); major, 11th Florida (June 11, 1864); and commanding post at Salisbury, North Carolina (August 24, 1864-April 1865). After initial service in Florida, he was sent to reinforce the Army of Northern Virginia in the spring of 1864. His battalion was merged into a new regiment, and he was soon thereafter assigned to command the prison camp at Salisbury. The prison had a good reputation for being spacious for a mixed population of prisoners of war, deserters, and convicts, but later it became overcrowded. On November 25 a mass escape attempt was made and had to be contained in part by the use of artillery. There were casualties on both sides. Gee was arrested in November 1865 and charged with ordering these and other "murders." There were also the usual charges of cruel conditions. After a trial that lasted over five months, he was acquitted and released in August 1866. He died fighting a fire in Florida where he had returned to practice medicine.

GENTRY, Meredith Poindexter (1809-1866)

After a distinguished career in the U.S. Congress, Meredith P. Gentry sank into virtual obscurity during his term in the Confederate Congress. To a large extent the North Carolina-born Gentry was a self-educated man, and although he had been admitted to the bar in Tennessee, he rarely practiced. Instead he built-up his plantation and devoted his interest to politics. After three years in the state legislature, he was sent to the U.S. Congress where he remained, on and off, for 12 years. Here he was noted for his opposition to the Mexican War, his moderation on the issue of slavery, and his oppositon to secession. Having retired to his plantation in 1855, he was finally convinced of the propriety of secession with the firing in Charleston Harbor. Elected to the First Regular Confederate Congress in November 1861 from Tennessee's 6th District, he failed in a bid to become the House's speaker. He is said to have made only one speech in Richmond and became known as one disenchanted with the idea of secesssion itself and with the war effort. He stopped attending the congressional meetings on October 13, 1862, but had been frequently absent from the deliberations previously. Taken into Federal custody at home in 1864, he died on his impoverished farm two years later.

GEORGE, Mrs. E.E. (?-1865)

In her role as a United States Sanitary Commission nurse, Mrs. E.E. George gave her life in caring for the sick and wounded in the Western armies. An Indiana resident, she was one of the older field operatives of the commission. Her first assignment came in January 1863 when she was attached to a Memphis hospital where she primarily dealt with soldiers from her own state. She was then attached to the 15th Corps in the Atlanta Campaign and later served in the Franklin-Nashville Campaign. She was struck down by typhoid fever in 1865 when she was receiving the released prisoners from Andersonville and other camps in Wilmington, North Carolina.

GETTY, George Washington (1819-1901)

With promotion potential in his own branch exceedingly slow, career artillerist George W. Getty became a brigadier general of volunteers and commanded infantry for the balance of the Civil War. The Washington, D.C. native and West Pointer (1840) had seen action in Mexico, where he earned a brevet, and during two tours against the Seminoles. He had also served on the frontier. His Civil war-era assignments included: captain, 4th Artillery (since November 4, 1853); captain, 5th Artillery (May 14, 1861); lieutenant colonel and additional aide-de-camp (September 28, 1861); chief of artillery, Hooker's Division, Army of Potomac (fall 1861); commanding 2nd Brigade, Artillery Reserve (attached to 5th Corps), Army of the Potomac (May-September 1862); chief of artillery, 9th Corps, Army of the Potomac (September 1862); brigadier general, USV (September 25, 1862); commanding 3rd Division, 9th Corps, Army of the Potomac (October 4, 1862-March 2, 1863); commanding 2nd Division, 7th Corps, Department of Virginia (March 21-August 1, 1863); also commanding the department (July 15-20, 1863) and the corps (July 20-August 1, 1863); commanding division, 18th Corps, Department of Virginia and North Carolina (August 1-12, 1863); major 5th Artillery (August 1, 1863); commanding division, District of Virginia, 18th Corps, Department of Virginia and North Carolina (August 12-September 23, 1863); commanding division, U.S. Forces Norfolk and Portsmouth, 18th Corps, Department of Virginia and North Carolina (September 23, 1863-Janaury 14, 1864); acting inspector general, Army of the Potomac (early 1864); commanding 2nd Division, 6th Corps, Army of the Potomac (March 25-May 6 and June 28-July 8, 1864); commanding 2nd Division, 6th Corps, Army of the Shenandoah (August 6-October 19-December 6, 1864); commanding the corps (October 19, 1864); again commanding 2nd Division, 6th Corps, Army of the Potomac (December 6, 1864-January 16, 1865 and February 11, 1865). Originally stationed at Fortress Monroe, he later commanded the guns of Hooker's Division along the lower Potomac in the fall of 1861. During the Peninsula Campaign, he directed a brigade of reserve artillery as a staff lieutenant colonel. He was Burnside's chief artillerist at Antietam and within days was named a brigadier general. He led a division at Fredericksburg and later in southeastern Virginia where he earned a regular army brevet for his role in the repulse of James Longstreet's attempt to capture Suffolk. Involved in diversionary actions during the Gettysburg Campaign, he acted as chief inspector in the Army of the Potomac in early 1864 and was given charge of a 6th Corps division for the Overland Campaign. He was severely wounded on the second day at the Wilderness. Returning to duty late the next month, with a brevet for his wounding, he took part in the early siege operations against Richmond before being ordered north to face Jubal Early's threat. Under Sheridan in the Shenandoah, as major general of volunteers, he earned a brevet for 3rd Winchester and Fisher's Hill and briefly led the corps at Cedar Creek. Returning to the Petersburg front, he was brevetted brigadier in the regular service for the assault which captured Petersburg. He took part in the Appomattox Campaign and was brevetted major general for the war. Mustered out of the volunteers on October 9, 1866, he remained in the regular army artillery until his 1883 retirement as a colonel. In the meantime he had directed the artillery school at Fortress Monroe and was one of the commissioners who reversed the findings in the Fitz-John Porter case.

GHOLSON, Samuel Jameson (1808-1883)

Having spent most of the Civil War as a Mississippi state officer, Kentucky-born Samuel J. Gholson served only briefly as a Confederate brigadier general. A lawyer in both Alabama and Mississippi, he sat in the latter's state legislature and represented it in Congress. He was a district judge upon the outbreak of hostilities when he entered the army as captain of the Monroe Volunteers. His assignments included: captain, Company I, 14th Mississippi (1861); major general, Mississippi State Troops (April 1863); brigadier general, CSA (May 6, 1864); commanding brigade, Forrest's Cavalry Corps, Department of Alabama, Mississippi and East Louisiana (May-June 1864); and commanding brigade, Adams' Cavalry Division, Department of Alabama, Mississippi and East Louisiana (June-August 1864). As a company commander, he was wounded and captured at Fort Donelson. He then appears to have carried messages and seen service in East Tennessee until appointed to a major generalcy in the state forces when Vicksburg was being threatened. He had a brush with a portion of Grierson's raiders. Gholson also came into conflict with the regular Confederate officers in his area. The next spring he became a Confederate brigadier general and led a brigade of cavalry in Mississippi and Alabama. A wound at Egypt, Mississippi, on December 27, 1864—which cost him an arm—appears to have put him out of the war. Following the peace he was again a state legislator.

GHOLSON, Thomas Saunders (1808-1868)

Having no prior legislative experience, Virginia Congressman Thomas S. Gholson did not become a leader in the Second Confederate Congress but nonetheless became known as a proponent of a vigorous war effort. A native of Virginia, Gholson was a lawyer who had been prominent in civic improvements in his adopted home of Petersburg. By the time of the outbreak of the Civil War he was serving as a circuit judge, a position he continued to hold under the Confederate regime. Then in 1863 he defeated the incumbent in a race for the 4th District's seat in the Second Congress. Here he naturally served on the committee on the Judiciary. Considering any infringements to the new constitution to be only temporary emergency measures, he threw his entire effort behind the military effort. About the only thing he would not grant the Davis administration was the recruiting of slaves. He favored wartime nationalization of many industries and wanted to grant the War Department full powers over all state forces. He also felt that the writ of habeas corpus was dispensable. Following the fall of Richmond, Gholson fled to England and went into the cotton and tobacco business.

GIBBON, John (1827-1896)

Although he had three brothers fighting for the Confederacy, Mexican and Seminole wars veteran John Gibbon remained loyal to the Union. Philadelphia-born, he had been raised in North Carolina. A West Pointer (1847), his Civil War assignments included: captain, 4th Artillery (since November 2, 1859); chief of artillery, McDowell's Division, Army of the Potomac (October 29, 1861-March 13, 1862); chief of artillery, 1st Corps, Army of the Potomac (March 13-April 4, 1862); chief of artillery, Department of the Rappahannock (April 4-ca. May 2, 1862); brigadier general, USV (May 2, 1862); commanding 4th Brigade, 1st Division, 3rd Corps, Army of Virginia (June 26-September 12, 1862); commanding 4th Brigade, 1st Division, 1st Corps, Army of the Potomac (September 12-November 5, 1862); commanding 2nd Division, 1st Corps, Army of the Potomac (November 5-December 13, 1862); commanding 2nd Division, 2nd Corps, Army of the Potomac (April 11-July 1, 1863, July 2-3, 1863, December 21, 1863-July 31, 1864, August 22-September 4, September 25-October 8, and October 29-December 23, 1864); commanding the corps (July 1-2, 1863); major general, USV (June 7, 1864); commanding 18th Corps, Army of the James (September 4-22, 1864); and commanding 24th Corps, Army of the James (January 15-April 27 and May 17-July 8, 1865). After serving several months as McDowell's chief artillerist Gibbon was granted a brigadier's star and assigned to the only all-Western brigade serving with the armies in Virginia. This brigade was already noted for its distinctive black hats and was accordingly dubbed "The Black Hat Brigade." In their first fight at Groveton—actually the beginning of 2nd Bull Run—the brigade had a stand-up close-range fight of several hours duration with Stonewall Jackson's command. They had become the famed "Iron Brigade." Gibbon led the brigade at Antietam and was wounded at Fredericksburg while commanding a division. He returned to fight at Chancellorsville and was again seriously wounded at Gettysburg on the final day. He had briefly commanded the corps during a part of the battle. Recovering, he was assigned to recruiting duty and returned for the spring 1864 campaign, seeing action at the Wilderness, Spotsylvania, North Anna, Cold Harbor, and the early

Petersburg fighting. Promoted to major general, he commanded a corps in the final stages of the war. Having received brevets in the army through major general, he was mustered out of the volunteer establishment on January 15, 1866. Remaining on active duty he served mainly against the Indians. He participated in the Little Big Horn Campaign, rescued Custer's survivors, and was wounded the next year at Big Hole Basin, Montana. Retiring as a brigadier general in 1891, he was active in veterans' affairs. His *Artillerist's Manual* wa a key tool in the training of the volunteer batteries for the Civil War. (Gibbon, John, *Personal Recollections of the Civil War*)

GIBBS, Addison C. (1825-1886)

Switching from the Democrats to the Union-Republican ticket in 1862, Addison C. Gibbs became the active war governor of Oregon. A New York native, he was admitted to the bar in that state before heading to California in search of gold. Moving to Oregon he was in the land business and served in the 1853 Rogue River Indian War. He then practiced law and was elected as a Democrat to the territorial legislature. He was serving there when he switched his allegiance. Inaugurated as governor on September 10, 1852, he became a firm supporter of the Lincoln administration's war policies. Failing in a bid for a U.S. Senate seat in 1866, he left office and later served as a prosecuting and district attorney. He then resumed his private practice and died while in England on land business.

GIBBS, Alfred (1823-1868)

The Civil War career of Alfred Gibbs got off to a slow start but he finished the war as a brevet major general of both regulars and volunteers. The native New Yorker and West Pointer (1846) had served with the Regiment of Mounted Rifles in Mexico, where he was wounded and earned two brevets and on the frontier, where he was again wounded in Apache fighting. His Civil War assignments included: first lieutenant, Mounted Rifles (since May 31, 1853); captain, Mounted Rifles (May 13, 1861); captain, 3rd Cavalry (destination change August 3, 1861); commanding 2nd Provisional Brigade, Division at Suffolk, 7th Corps, Department of Virginia (December 5, 1862-January 21 1863); colonel, 130th New York (September 6, 1862); colonel, 19th New York Cavalry (designation change August 11, 1863); commanding Reserve Brigade, 1st Division, Cavalry Corps, Army of the Potomac (August 12-September 12, 1863, November 21, 1863-April 10, 1864, and May 7-25, 1864); colonel, 1st New York Dragoons (designation change September 10, 1863); commanding Reserve Brigade, 1st Division, Cavalry Corps, Army of the Shenandoah (August 6-September 8, December 13-31, 1864, January 15-18, and February 10-March 25, 1865); brigadier general, USV (October 19, 1864); commanding the division (February 3-10, 1865); and again commanding Reserve Brigade, 1st Division, Cavalry Corps, Army of the Potomac (March 25-May 25, 1865). Captured by Texan troops on July 27, 1861, at San Augustine Springs, he was paroled but not exchanged until August 7, 1862. Almost immediately thereafter he was commissioned colonel of a volunteer infantry unit which he led to southeastern Virginia. Converting his regiment into mounted troops, he joined the Army of the Potomac's Cavalry Corps in time for the Bristoe Campaign. During the Overland Campaign he won a brevet for Trevilian Station. After serving in the early operations against Petersburg, he was transferred to the Shenandoah for Sheridan's campaign. Brevetted for 3rd Winchester, he also fought at Cedar Creek. Returning to the Petersburg front, he again was brevetted for Five Forks and also fought at Sayler's Creek and Appomattox. For his war service he was awarded every brevet he could receive and was mustered out of the volunteer service on February 1, 1866, as a brigadier general, since the date of Cedar Creek. In 1866 he was transferred to the newly created 7th Cavalry as major and took a leading role in its organization. He died suddenly of "congestion of the brain" on December 26, 1868.

GIBBS, George Cooper (1822-1873)

Although the colonel of an infantry regiment, Floridian George C. Gibbs spent most of the Civil War guarding prisoners of war. His Confederate assignments included: captain, Infantry (May 20, 1861); major, Infantry (1861); and colonel, 42nd North Carolina (April 22, 1862). By the first summer of the war he was commanding the prison guard forces in Richmond. Then on January 11, 1862, he was ordered to Salisbury, North Carolina, to take command of the prison at that place. He was also given authority to raise three or four companies to serve as guards. Shortly thereafter he was authorized to raise a regiment for service in the field. He recruited the guard companies into this regiment. Moving his unit to Virginia, he was soon in command of the prison at Lynchburg. On January 7, 1864, he resigned his regimental commission but continued in prison work. On June 2, 1864, he wsa transferred to command the post at Andersonville, with the infamous prison a part of his jurisdiction. He was respected by the prisoners at Salisbury and Macon as a fair jailer. He was later a witness at the trial of Major Henry Wirz.

GIBSON, George (?-1861)

An example of the slow rate of promotions in the regular army, especially for staff officers, is George Gibson, the commissary general at the start of the Civil War. The Pennsylvania-born Gibson entered the military in 1808 as an infantry captain and served during the War of 1812 as an infantry field officer. Discharged in 1815, in the general reduction of the army after that war, Gibson was recommissioned in 1816 as a colonel and quartermaster general of the army's Southern Division. Two years later he was transferred to become the commissary general of the entire army, with the same rank. He held this position for over four decades. He was brevetted brigadier general in 1826 for 10 years' service as a colonel and brevetted major general for the Mexican War. Gibson died a few months after the outbreak of the Civil War.

GIBSON, James F. (?-?)

Poor relations with his employees cost Mathew Brady one of his top assistants, James F. Gibson, in early 1863. Having worked for Brady since early in the war, Gibson, like many others in the firm, felt that he was being cheated out of the credit for his work when photographs were simply listed as "Brady's." Thus when Alexander Gardner left Brady and set up his own firm, Gibson went along. Some of his best work was done on the Gettysburg battlefield.

GIBSON, Randall Lee (1832-1892)

Kentucky-born Yale graduate Randall L. Gibson had had a distinguished prewar career as a lawyer and diplomat in Madrid before entering the Confederate army and rising to brigadier general. He had been raised in his family's home state, Louisiana, and upon the secession crisis coming to a peak he became an aide to the governor, Thomas O. Moore. His later military assignments included: captain, 1st Louisiana Artillery (March 1861); colonel, 13th Louisiana (September 16, 1861); commanding 1st Brigade, 1st (Ruggles') Division, 2nd Corps, Army of the Mississippi (ca. March 29-April 1862); commanding Adams' Brigade, 1st (Breckinridge's) Division, Hardee's Corps, Army of Tennessee (December 31, 1862-early 1863); commanding Adams' Brigade, Breckinridge's Division, Hill's-Breckinridge's Corps, Army of Tennessee (September 20-November 12, 1863); commanding Adams' Brigade, Stewart's-Clayton's Division, Breckinridge's-Hindman's-Hood's-Lee's Corps, Army of Tennessee (November 12, 1863-early 1865); brigadier general, CSA (January 11, 1864); and commanding Louisiana Brigade, District of the Gulf, Department of Alabama, Mississippi and East Louisiana (early 1865-April 8, 1865). He led a brigade at Shiloh and then the regiment during the Corinth siege and at Perryville. At Murfreesboro he was in charge of the consolidated 13th and 20th Louisiana and succeeded the wounded Daniel W. Adams in brigade command. At Chickamauga he was again at the head of the paired regiments when called upon, the second day, to take over brigade leadership from the wounded and captured Adams. He retained command, thereafter fighting at Chattanooga and then being promoted to brigadier general. As such he served throughout the Atlanta Campaign. During the battle of Franklin his division was still south of the Duck River so it did not take part in the action. He did however fight at Nashville and early the next year was sent with his brigade to the Gulf coast. There he directed the unsuccessful defense of Spanish Fort near Mobile. After the war he returned to his law practice and served in both houses of the national legislature.

GIDDINGS, Joshua Reed (1795-1864)

The U.S. consul to Canada during the Civil War, Joshua R. Giddings can best be remembered as an abolitionist and friend of and influence on Abraham Lincoln. Born in Pennsylvania, he was raised in New York and Ohio. He was a lawyer and former state legislator when first elected to Congress in 1838. Four years later he resigned after being censured for his antislavery proposals, only to be vindicated by a prompt reelection by his constituents the same year. He opposed both the Texas annexation and the Mexican War as a plot to expand slavery. With the continuing shift in party alignments, he was first a Whig, then a Free-Soiler, and finally a Republican. Ill health ended his congressional career in 1859. In the meantime he had been a companion in Washington to Abraham Lincoln and was later active in the Republican convention of 1860. Upon his inauguration Lincoln dispatched Giddings to the Canadian post. He died in Montreal in 1864. (Julian, George W., *The Life of Joshua R. Giddings*)

GIFT, George W. (1833-1879)

Lieutenant George W. Gift of Tennessee was one of the Confederacy's more unorthodox naval officers. A graduate of Annapolis in 1848, he had resigned from the navy in 1852 to enter the banking business in California. Returning East at the outbreak of the war, he entered the Confederate army but on March 18, 1862, was transferred to the navy as a lieutenant. Assigned to the C.S.S. *Arkansas*, then under construction, he commanded two of the ironclad's guns during its run through the Union fleet on the Mississippi, from the Yazoo to Vicksburg. After the *Arkansas'* destruction at Baton Rouge in August 1862, Gift performed shore duty for a time. In February 1864 he was in command of one portion of John Taylor Wood's expedition, which destroyed the *Underwriter*. Having served as executive officer with the *Chattahoochee* on the Appalachicola River, until that vessel accidentally blew up there on May 27, 1863, Gift was placed in command of it when it was reraised. Returning from the *Underwriter* raid in North Carolina, Gift and his officers devised a plan to attempt with small boats, the seizure of the two Union blockaders guarding the mouth of the river. The expedition was a disaster, with all but one of the seven craft lost. Gift's boat was driven 15 miles across the sound to St. George's Island. He was forced to turn over command due to illness on the way to the island. After two days of near starvation, eating alligators, the crew returned to the mainland. With the abandonment of the river, the *Chattahoochee* was destroyed. After the war Gift returned to California and edited the *Napa City Reporter*. (Scharf, J. Thomas, *History of the Confederate Navy*)

GILBERT, Charles Champion (1822-1903)

A poor performance as a corps commander at Perryville cost Charles C. Gilbert his brigadier general's commission. The Ohio native and West Pointer (1846) had been posted to the infantry and fought at Vera Cruz during the Mexican War. His remaining prewar service included frontier duty and a professorship at his alma mater. His Civil War assignments included: captain, 1st Infantry (since December 8, 1855); acting inspector general, Department of the Cumberland (1861); acting inspector general, Army of the Ohio (November 9, 1861-September 1862); acting major general, USV (per Buell September 1, 1862); commanding Army of Kentucky, Department of the Ohio (September 11-27, 1862); brigadier general, USV (September 9, 1862); commanding 3rd Corps, Army of the Ohio (September 29-ca. October 23, 1862); commanding 10th Division, 1st Corps, Army of the Ohio (October 23-November 5, 1862); and major, 19th Infantry (July 2, 1863). He commanded his company at Wilson's Creek and was severely wounded. He later served as Buell's inspector and won a brevet for the Shiloh Campaign, although he himself was not at the fight. Present at Richmond, Kentucky, where he won another brevet, he was named by Buell as an acting major general subject to the approval of the president. He was then placed in command of the Army of Kentucky which had been under the command of the wounded William Nelson. Washington responded with a commission as a brigadier general, but Gilbert was still acting at the higher grade at Perryville where he failed to live up to expectations. Although he won a brevet for the battle, he was strongly criticized by the panel investigating the campaign. Because of this the Senate failed to confirm his appointment and he reverted to his regular army captaincy on March 4, 1863. Promoted to major a few months later, he held administrative posts for the balance of the war. Remaining in the service after 1865, he rose to Colonel, 17th Infantry, and after serving mostly in the West was retired in 1886.

GILBERT, James Isham (1823-1884)

James I. Gilbert did not see action until relatively late in the war, from which he emerged as a Union brevet major general. The Kentucky-born businessman had been engaged in the lumber, livery, real estate, and general store businesses. At the outbreak of the war he lived in Lansing, Iowa, which he had helped to found a decade before. His military assignments included: colonel, 27th Iowa (October 3, 1862); commanding 3rd Brigade, 3rd Division, 16th Corps, Army of the Tennessee (July 19-August 14, 1863); commanding brigade, 5th Division, 16th Corps, Army of the Tennessee (November 22, 1863-January 25, 1864); commanding 2nd Brigade, 3rd Division, 16th Corps, Army of the Tennessee (June 11-September 25 and October 15-December 5, 1864); commanding 2nd Brigade, 2nd Division, Detachment Army of the Tennessee, Department of the Cumberland (December 5, 1864-February 18, 1865); brigadier general, USV (February 9, 1865); and commanding 2nd brigade, 2nd Division, 16th Corps, Department of the Gulf (February 18-June 22, 1865). His regiment spent its first period of service on the Indian frontier in Minnesota before being ordered to western Tennessee in November 1862. He took part in the expedition to take Arkansas' capital, Little Rock, and the Meridian Campaign. His first major fighting came in the Red River Campaign of Nathaniel P. Banks. During this 1864 operation he fought at Fort DeRussy and Pleasant Hill. He took part in the defeat of Nathan Bedford Forrest at Tupelo. The detachment of the 16th Corps to which he belonged was then transferred to Tennessee where he fought in the battle of Nashville. Transferred to the forces attacking Mobile, he was promoted to brigadier general and later won a brevet as major general for the capture of the city. Mustered out on August 24, 1865, he returned to the lumber business and lost money on investments in mining operations.

GILHAM, William (1818-1872)

The fact that William Gilham was ordered away from the field to resume his duties on the faculty of the Virginia Miliary Institute, seems to indicate that he was more in demand to train future officers—than to fight a war himself. But it may in fact be more truthful to conclude that the order resulted from a dispute with his superior, Stonewall Jackson. An Indianan, Gilham had graduated fifth in his 1840 class at West Point. The Civil War found him serving as an instructor and commandant of cadets at VMI. Having authored a drill manual, his first service to the Confederacy was as drill master at Camp Lee at Richmond. His later assignments included: colonel, 21st Virginia (July 1861); and commanding brigade, Army of the Northwest (July 1861-January 20, 1862). He led his brigade in Robert E. Lee's failure at Cheat Mountain and continued campaigning in western Virginia into the winter. He got involved in the Loring-Jackson feud over the stationing of the former's command at Romney under dismal conditions. The latter pressed charges against Gilham for neglect of duty. It was at about this time on January 20, 1862, that he was relieved of brigade command and ordered back to the school. Here he devoted his full time to his courses and dropped the position of commandant. The postwar economic crunch at the academy forced him to become a chemist for a private firm. (Wise, Jennings C., *The Military History of the Virginia Military Institute from 1839 to 1865*)

GILLEM, Alvan Cullem (1830-1875)

A Tennesseean who remained loyal to the Union, General Alvan C. Gillem was considered by the Radical Republicans to be too soft on the South during Reconstruction. A West Pointer (1851), he had been posted to the artillery and seen service in Florida and on the Texas frontier. His Civil War-era assignments included: first lieutenant, 1st Artillery (since March 3, 1855); captain, 1st Artillery (May 14, 1861); captain and assistant quartermaster (July 12, 1861); colonel, 10th Tennessee (May 13, 1862); brigadier general, USV (August 17, 1863); commanding 4th Division, Cavalry Corps, Army of the Cumberland (April 1-August 16, 1864); commanding Cavalry Division, District of East Tennessee, Department of the Cumberland, (March 17-July 1865). As George H. Thomas's quartermaster, he fought at Mill Springs and won a regular army brevet. He held the same position on Don C. Buell's staff at Shiloh and in the advance on Corinth, Mississippi. Taking command of a volunteer regiment, he served in Tennessee and Kentucky and took part in a number of raids. Much of the time he was provost marshal at the Tennessee capital and in June 1863 he was named state adjutant general by Andrew Johnson. Advanced to a brigadier generalship two months later, he later commanded the cavalry division of the Army of the Cumberland, which did not embark on the Atlanta Campaign. Afterwards he helped reorganize the state government and in the final months of the war he took part in Stoneman's raid into North Carolina. Having already been brevetted in the regular service for a fight at Marion, Virginia, on December 16, 1864, and brigadier general of regulars for the war, he was brevetted major general for the capture of Salisbury, North Carolina. Promoted to major general of volunteers months after the close of hostilities, he was mustered out on September 1, 1866. Remaining in the regular army, he got into trouble with the

Radical Republicans in Congress over his lenient treatment of the ex-rebels as commander of the occupation of Mississippi and Arkansas. Following service on the Texas frontier he made his last campaign against the Modocs under Captain Jack. Shortly thereafter he died while serving as colonel, 1st Calvalry.

GILLMORE, Quincy Adams (1825-1888)

Putting his engineering training to good use, Quincy A. Gillmore won accolades for his plan to reduce Fort Pulaski at the mouth of the Savannah River. The Ohio native had graduated at the head of the 1849 class at West Point and was accordingly appointed to the engineers. Before the Civil War he worked on fortifications and taught at his alma mater. His wartime assignments included: first lieutenant, Engineers (since July 1, 1856); captain, Engineers (August 6, 1861); chief engineer, South Carolina Expeditionary Corps (1861-62); brigadier general USV (April 28, 1862); commanding 2nd Division, Army of Kentucky, Department of the Ohio (October 14, 1862-January 25, 1863); commanding District of Central Kentucky, Department of the Ohio (January 25-April 10, 1863); major, Engineers (June 1, 1863); commanding 10th Corps, Department of the South (June 12, 1863-April 17, 1864); also commanding the department (June 12, 1863-May 1, 1864); major general, USV (July 10, 1863); commanding 10th Corps, Army of the James (May 4-June 14, 1864); commanding 19th Corps, Department of Washington (July 11-13, 1864); and again commanding Department of the South (February 9-June 26, 1865). As a staff engineer he took part in the capture of Port Royal and later took the leading role in the successful move against Fort Pulaski. Rewarded with a volunteer brigadier general's star, he commanded for several months in Kentucky before returning to coastal operations. He directed the siege operations against Charleston until he accompanied most of his troops to join the Army of the James in the spring of 1864. He took part in the Bermuda Hundred fighting and then briefly commanded the 19th Corps against Jubal Early's raid on Washington until he was injured by the fall of his horse. In the final months of the war he resumed command in the field that had seen his most famous exploits. He had been given his second star during the Charleston operations and been brevetted through regular army major general for Fort Pulaski, Somerset, Kentucky, Battery Wagner, and the bombardment of Fort Sumter. Resigning his generalship on December 5, 1865, he reverted to his rank as an engineering major and rose to the grade of colonel before his death on active duty. In the meantime he had written widely on his specialty.

GILMER, Jeremy Francis (1818-1883)

A North Carolinian by birth, Jermey Gilmer was the premier engineer in the service of the Confederacy. Graduating fourth at West Point in 1839, Gilmer's entire antebellum service was in the engineers; he was serving as a captain when he resigned on June 29, 1861. His Confederate assignments included: lieutenant colonel, Engineers (September 1861); chief engineer, Department No. 2 (September 1861-April 7, 1862); chief engineer, Department of Northern Virginia (August 4-September 25, 1862); chief of Engineer Bureau (September 25, 1862-August 17, 1863); colonel, Engineers (October 4, 1862); chief engineer, Department of South Carolina, Georgia and Florida (August 17-31, 1863); major general, CSA (August 25, 1863); second in command of the department (August 31, 1863-May 25, 1864); and chief of Engineer Bureau (June 1864-April 1865). Serving under General A.S. Johnston in Kentucky and Tennessee, Gilmer saw action at Forts Henry and Donelson, escaping capture at the latter, and at Shiloh where Johnston was killed on the first day and Gilmer was wounded on the second. Returning to duty, Gilmer was assigned to Lee's command but spent most of his time working on the defenses near Richmond. He then headed the bureau at the War Department until sent to South Carolina. Much of the time he was in charge of the Savannah defenses and also worked on the Atlanta fortifications. He again served, for the last year of the war, as head of the Engineer Bureau in Richmond. For 16 years before his death, Gilmer was the head of the Savannah Gaslight Company.

GILMER, John Adams (1805-1868)

A congressman from the Piedmont region of North Carolina, John Gilmer often voted against some of his more radical colleagues from the rest of the South. In 1858, he opposed the admission of Kansas as a slave state under the Lecompton Constitution. Following the election of Lincoln, Gilmer still maintained hopes for peace, despite the secessionist movement. During the winter of 1860-61, Gilmer personally paid for and franked an estimated 100,000 pieces of Unionist mail to North Carolina, with more going to the rest of the Upper South. Lincoln offered the position of Secretary of the Interior to Gilmer in a move to prevent the states of the Upper South from joining those of the Lower South. While waiting for the Inaugural Address, he urged Lincoln to be conciliatory and grant the South its meaningless and "foolish abstraction of Congressional protection to slavery in the Territories." The failure to get a truly conciliatory message from the incoming president and the makeup of the rest of the blatantly pro-Union cabinet led Gilmer to refuse the appointment. After Fort Sumter, he declared, "All hope is now extinguished." Serving in local posts for the first years of the Confederacy, Gilmer was elected to the Second Confederate Congress, which convened on May 2, 1864. He chaired the House Elections Committee and served on the Ways and Means Committee. Gilmer was a vocal opponent of Jefferson Davis and supported higher taxes and less impressment of supplies (some of his own whiskey had been impressed). After the war he returned to his law practice. He died on May 14, 1868. (Croft, Daniel W., "A Reluctant Unionist: John A. Gilmer and Lincoln's Cabinet," *CWH*, September 1978)

GILMER, John Alexander, Jr. (1838-1892)

The son of prominent North Carolina Unionist John Adams Gilmer, John Alexander Gilmer adopted "Jr." to distinguish them. Not in tune with his father's sentiments, he joined the Confederacy at the outbreak of the Civil War. His assignments included: second lieutenant, Company B, 27th North Carolina

(April 20, 1861); first lieutenant and adjutant, 27th North Carolina (November 18, 1861); major, 27th North Carolina (January 6, 1862); lieutenant colonel, 27th North Carolina (November 1, 1862); and colonel, 27th North Carolina (December 5, 1862). He commanded the regiment in the disaster at New Bern and then fought at the Seven Days, Harpers Ferry, Antietam, and Fredericksburg. Wounded at the latter, he rejoined the regiment and led it in South Carolina, North Carolina, and in the Department of Richmond. With the brigade ordered to rejoin the Army of Northern Virginia it took part in the charge at Bristoe Station. For a second time Gilmer was struck in the leg. Upon his recovery, he was assigned, on June 8, 1864, to command the post and prisoner of war camp at Salisbury, North Carolina. Relieved on August 24, 1864, he was directed to rejoin his regiment. Apparently he was still unfit for field service since he never reported to his command. Finally, on January 11, 1865, he was retired to the Invalid Corps. After the war he served in the North Carolina legislature and on its supreme court.

GILMOR, Harry W. (1838-1883)

With a turf between those of other partisan leaders—John S. Mosby to the east and John H. McNiel to the west—Harry Gilmor was an effective scout and raider in the Shenandoah Valley and western Maryland. A native Baltimorean, (he dropped his middle initial), he had lived in Wisconsin and the Nebraska Territory before the war. His Civil War assignments included: private, Company G, 7th Virginia Cavalry (August 31, 1861); captain, Company F, 12th Virginia Cavalry (March 27, 1862); and major, 2nd Maryland Cavalry Battalion (May 27, 1863). Beginning his service under Turner Ashby, he became one of Ashby's company commanders in time for the Shenandoah Valley Campaign. In the aftermath of the Maryland Campaign, he was captured while on a raiding mission in western Maryland during September 1862. Exchanged five months later, he was soon commanding a battalion of Marylanders who, despite being labeled as regular cavalry, were frequently engaged in irregular warfare. In the Gettysburg Campaign he led his battalion in advance of Ewell's Corps in Pennsylvania. He continued to be a bane to federal commanders during the 1864 Shenandoah Valley Campaign. Finally on February 4, 1865, he was captured in bed in Moorefield, West Virginia by Major Harry Young of Sheridan's staff with a command dressed in Confederate uniforms. Confined in Boston Harbor, he was not released until July 24, 1865, but had meanwhile compiled a series of historical sketches of his career, which were later developed into a book, ghostwritten by Francis H. Smith, and published as *Four Years in the Saddle*. In 1874-79 Gilmor served as Baltimore's police commissioner. (Jones, Virgil Carrington, *Gray Ghosts and Rebel Raiders*)

Partisan Harry Gilmor. (NA)

GILMORE, Joseph Albree (1811-1867)

As New Hampshire's last wartime governor, Joseph A. Gilmore was active in raising troops for the army, including such measures as having the state borrow money to pay the enlistment bounties. The Vermont native had moved to New Hampshire and entered the grocery and then the railroad businesses before becoming active in politics as a Whig. But he entered the state senate as a Republican and during the early part of the war was its presiding officer. In an election that had to be carried over into the legislature, he was elected governor in 1863 and took up his duties later that year. In 1864 he provided for furloughs and free transportation for soldiers to return home for the elections. On constitutional grounds, he opposed absentee voting in the field. Reelected, he served until 1865 and supported the passage of the 13th Amendment. (Hesseltine, William Best, *Lincoln and the War Governors* and Waite, Otis F.R., *New Hampshire in the Great Rebellion*)

GILTNER, Harry Liter (?-?)

While the two principal armies of the Confederacy were usually kept relatively close to the authorized level of general officers, many of the fringe commands were not so fortunate, with colonels like Henry L. Giltner commanding brigades for a year or more. His assignments included: captain, Kentucky cavalry company (September 10, 1862); colonel, 4th Kentucky Cavalry (October 5, 1862); commanding Williams' Cavalry Brigade, Department of Southwestern Virginia (November-December 1863); commanding cavalry brigade, Department of East Tennessee (February-May 23, 1864); and commanding cavalry brigade, Department of Western Virginia and East Tennessee (May 23, 1864-April 1865). Serving in western Virginia and eastern Tennessee, Giltner led his regiment in frequent operations against Union raiders and in protecting railroads and salt works. Joining Longstreet, he commanded the brigade during the siege of Knoxville. In December 1864 he directed the initial defense of Saltville against the Union cavalry. Although his role in protecting the supplies and supply lines for the major armies was vital, it was not considered crucial enough for his promotion to brigadier. He commanded his brigade in the region until after Lee's surrender.

GIRARDEY, Victor Jean Baptiste (1837-1864)

Thirteen days was the length of time that Victor J.B. Girardey held his appointment as a brigadier after being promoted four grades from staff captain to general officer. Born in France and raised as an orphan in Georgia and Louisiana, he entered the Confederate military early in the war. His assignments included: first lieutenant and aide-de-camp (October 12, 1861); captain and assistant adjutant general (January 1862); brigadier general, CSA (August 3 to date from July 30, 1864); and commanding Wright's Brigade, Mahone's Division, 3rd Corps, Army of Northern Virginia (August 3-16, 1864). On the staff of General A.R. Wright he fought through the Seven Days, Chancellorsville, and Gettysburg. At Manassas Gap that summer he directed the operations of half the brigade. He was at the Wilderness and Spotsylvania before being transferred to the staff of General Mahone on May 21, 1864. He so impressed General Lee during the battle of the Crater in bringing up two brigades to plug the gap, that he was shortly after promoted four grades and given command of Wright's Brigade. He died on August 16 while repulsing a Union assault at Fussell's Mill near Richmond. (Freeman, Douglas S., *Lee's Lieutenants*)

GIST, States Rights (1831-1864)

With a given name such as his there could be little doubt of which side his parents wanted States Rights Gist to fight on, and so he ended up giving his life as a Confederate brigadier general. The South Carolina native graduated from Harvard Law School and was practicing his profession in his native state when the secession movement reached crisis proportions. Realizing this, he entered the militia and his Civil War-era assignments included: brigadier general, South Carolina Militia (1859); adjutant and inspector general, South Carolina Army (1861); colonel and volunteer aide-de-camp (July 1861); brigadier general, CSA (March 20, 1862); commanding James Island, Department of South Carolina, Georgia and Florida (May-June, July-September 25, 1862, and October 17, 1862-May 1863); commanding James Island, 1st Military District of South Carolina, Department of South Carolina, Georgia and Florida (June-July 1862); commanding the district (September 25-October 17, 1862); commanding brigade, Department of the West (May-June 1863); commanding brigade, Walker's Division, Department of the West (June-July 1863); commanding brigade, Walker's Division, Department of Mississippi and East Louisiana (July-August 25, 1863); commanding brigade, Walker's Division, Hill's Corps, Army of Tennessee (August 28-September 1863); commanding Walker's Division, Reserve Corps, Army of Tennessee (mid-September 1863); commanding brigade, Walker's Division, Polk's Corps, Army of Tennessee (September-September 26, 1863); commanding brigade, Walker's Division, Longstreet's Corps, Army of Tennessee (September 26-November 12, 1863); commanding brigade, Walker's Division, Hardee's Corps, Army of Tennessee (November 12-November 1863 and November 1863-July 24, 1864); commanding the division (late November 1863); and commanding brigade Cheatham's-Brown's Division, Hardee's-Cheatham's Corps, Army of Tennessee (July 24-November 30, 1864). As a state officer, he was present at the reduction of Fort Sumter and then went to Virginia as a volunteer aide to Barnard E. Bee. There Bee was killed at 1st Bull Run, all the field officers of the 4th Alabama being put hors de combat Gist took command of it. After the battle he returned to his state post until appointed a brigadier general in the Confederate service. For over a year he served on the South Carolina coast until ordered to Mississippi with a brigade in May 1863. There he joined Joseph E. Johnston in his attempt to relieve the garrison of Vicksburg and after the fall of the river city defended Jackson, Mississippi, for a time. As part of William H.T. Walker's division, he joined Bragg's army and led the division at Chickamauga while Walker exercised temporary corps command. At Chattanooga Gist was again in charge of the division. He served throughout the Atlanta Campaign—being transferred to Cheatham's division when Walker's was broken up following his death—and then accompanied Hood into middle Tennessee. In the suicidal assault at Franklin on November 30, 1864, Gist became one of six generals to be fatally struck. He died instantly.

GLADDEN, Adley Hogan (1810-1862)

Adley Gladden was destined to die in his first major battle as a Southern officer. His Confederate services included: colonel, 1st Louisiana Regulars (early 1861); brigadier general, CSA (September 30, 1861); commanding 1st Brigade, Army of Pensacola (late September 1861-January 27, 1862); temporarily commanding the army (from October 22, 1861); commanding brigade, Army of Mobile (January 27-March 1862); commanding 2nd Corps, 2nd Grand Division, Army of the Mississippi (March 9-29, 1862); and commanding 1st Brigade, 2nd Division, 2nd Corps, Army of the Mississippi (March 29-April 6, 1862). After serving on the Florida coast, and under the Union bombardment in late November 1861, and at Mobile, Adley Gladden was ordered the following March to Corinth in northern Mississippi to oppose forces under General Grant gathering along the Tennessee River. After briefly commanding a "corps," in reality only a division, he was given command of a brigade of troops brought up from the Gulf coast and led it in the surprise attack on the Union army at Shiloh on April 6, 1862. At about 8:00 A.M., while overrunning the federal camps, Gladden was hit by a cannon projectile and mortally wounded. He lingered, back in Corinth, until April 12.

GLASSEL, William T. (? -1879)

If any man can be said to have been enlisted for Confederate service by the U.S. government it was Lieutenant William T.

Glassel, USN. The North Carolinian had returned aboard the U.S.S. *Hartford* from a lengthy voyage to China in mid-1862 and was promptly confronted with a demand that he take a new oath of allegiance or be imprisoned. He felt the oath conflicted with the original one he took upon entering the service and he refused. On August 5, 1862, he was sent into imprisonment at Fort Warren in Boston Harbor. Exchanged eight months later as a prisoner of war and delivered into the Confederate lines, he was promptly appointed lieutenant, CSN, to date from his original confinement and he was assigned to duty with the *Chicora* in Charleston Harbor. He took part in the attempt to raise the blockade on January 31, 1863, and was involved in the employment of spar torpedoes. Following the collapse of the Confederacy he settled in California. (Scharf, J. Thomas, *History of the Confederate States Navy*)

GLAZE, William (?-?)

Almost a decade before secession, and foreshadowing its role as the first state to secede from the Union, South Carolina had become the only Southern state to begin in-state manufacture of weapons to prepare for war. On April 15, 1851, it issued a contract to William Glaze of South Carolina and Benjamin Flagg of Massachusetts, calling for the production of 9,000 firearms—rifles, muskets and pistols—and 2,000 swords and sabers. Glaze was the proprietor of the Palmetto Iron Works of Columbia and he converted it to the manufacture of what became known as Palmetto Arms. Continuing in its new military role during the Civil War, Glaze's plant switched to the production of munitions and was severely damaged when Sherman took the city in 1865.

GLEASON, Newell (?-1886)

Serving through most of the major battles in the western theater, from Perryville through the surrender of Johnston's army, Vermont native Newell Gleason rose to brigade command during the last year of the war. Enlisting in Indiana, his assignments included: lieutenant colonel, 87th Indiana (August 28, 1862); colonel, 87th Indiana (March 22, 1863); and commanding 2nd Brigade, 3rd Division, 14th Corps, Army of the Cumberland (June 27, 1864-January 21, 1865 and April 3-June 9, 1865). His regiment fought at Perryville but was guarding the fords of the Cumberland River at the time of Murfreesboro. Gleason led the unit through the Tullahoma Campaign and fought at Chickamauga and Chattanooga. With the army in front of Kenesaw Mountain during the Atlanta Campaign, the brigade commander, Colonel Ferdinand Van Derveer, became ill, and Gleason took over from him for the balance of the campaign and the subsequent March to the Sea. He also commanded the brigade during part of the Carolinas Campaign. Brevetted brigadier general for the war, he was mustered out June 10, 1865, with his regiment.

GODWIN, Archibald Campbell (1831-1864)

A rancher and miner in California, Archibald C. Godwin returned to his native Virginia in 1861 and became a captain, later major and provost marshal of Richmond. Transferred to Salisbury, North Carolina, he continued in charge of prisoners. He then raised a regiment and transferred to the line where his assignments included: colonel, 57th North Carolina (July 17, 1862); Commanding Hoke's Brigade, Early's Division, 2nd Corps, Army of Northern Virginia (July 2-November 7, 1863); brigadier general, CSA (August 5, 1864); and commanding Hoke's (old) Brigade, Ramseur's Division, Valley District, Department of Northern Virginia (August 5-September 18, 1864). His first action came at Fredericksburg, and he went on to fight in the Fredericksburg portion of the battle of Chancellorsville. At Gettysburg he succeeded to brigade command and led a brigade until captured at Rappahannock Bridge on November 7, 1863. Exchanged in 1864, he was promoted to brigadier and relieved temporary Brigadier William G. Lewis in command of Hoke's Brigade. The next month he was killed at 3rd Winchester. At both Libby and Salisbury he was remembered for his cruelty toward the captives, and there was some discussion of trying him after the war (until it was discovered that he was already dead).

GOGGIN, James Monroe (1820-1889)

For some unexplained reason James M. Goggin's appointment as brigadier was canceled shortly after its issuance and he reverted to his position as a staff oficer. The Virginia-born former West Point student had not graduated from the military academy but had served briefly in the army of the Republic of Texas and served the postal department in California before he settled in Memphis, where he was a businessman when the war began. He returned to his native state to enlist and his assignments included: major, 32nd Virginia (July 1, 1861); major and assistant adjutant general (spring 1862); and brigadier general, CSA (December 4, 1864). Serving on the Peninsula, he soon held a position on Lafayette McLaws' staff. He was distinguished at Yorktown and Williamsburg but lost his commission when all the field officers of the regiment failed to gain reappointment at the May 21, 1862, reorganization. McLaws, however, had him appointed to a formal staff position. Sometimes as inspector but mostly as adjutant, Goggin was with his chief at the Seven Days, Harpers Ferry, South Mountain, Antietam, Fredericksburg, Chancellorsville, and Knoxville. At the latter he advised Longstreet on the futility of continuing the attack on Fort Sanders. He fought through the Overland Campaign on Kershaw's staff and went to the Shenandoah Valley where he commanded Conner's, formerly Kershaw's own, Brigade at Cedar Creek. In December 1864 he was appointed brigadier, probably intended for the same brigade. However this was revoked, possibly because he was a Virginian designated to direct South Carolinians. Back on Kershaw's staff he served through part of the Petersburg operations and was captured at Sayler's Creek on the retreat. He resided in Texas after his release.

GOLDSBOROUGH, Louis Malesherbes (1805-1877)

One of the less aggressive Union naval commanders was Louis Goldsborough. He entered the navy as a midshipman in 1816 and served as commander of a company of volunteers during the Seminole War before returning to the navy in 1841. He was a veteran of the Mexican War and superintendent at Annapolis for four years. At the outbreak of the Civil War, he was serving off the coast of Brazil as a captain. In September 1861, he was given command of the North Atlantic Blockading Squadron, responsible for that portion of the coast north of the North Carolina-South Carolina border. He led the naval portion of General Burnside's expedition to the North Carolina coast and defeated the small Confederate flotilla off Roanoke Island. During the Peninsula Campaign he was criticized for lack of cooperation with McClellan's Army of the Potomac. His performance in the capture of Norfolk was less than shining and he failed in the attempt to pass Drewry's Bluff and attack Richmond with part of his fleet. He was promoted to rear admiral in July 1862, but the James River Flotilla was made a special command separate from his control. At his own request he was relieved of his duties and assigned to administrative tasks for the balance of the war. For three years following the war he was at sea, but returned to Washington in 1868 for his last five years in the service.

GOOCH, Daniel W. (?-?)

As one of four House members of the Joint Committee on the Conduct of the War, Daniel W. Gooch was a critic of the Lincoln administration and its military leaders. The representative from Massachusetts sat upon the committee throughout its existence. Along with Chairman Benjamin F. Wade and members Zachariah Chandler—both of the Senate—and George W. Julian of the House, he was a thorn in the side of the administration's war effort. The committee ruined many a military career with investigations of numerous Union defeats. Ironically, none of the committee's members had any military experience. Gooch and his colleagues also investigated other matters, such as the Fort Pillow massacre.

GOODE, John, Jr. (1829-1909)

One of the closest friends of the Davis administration in the Virginia congressional delegation was John Goode, Jr., of the 6th District. A native Virginian, Goode was a practicing attorney and active in politics before the Civil War. Favoring secession in the event of Lincoln's election, he attended the convention that eventually took Virginia out of the Union. Serving in the 2nd Virginia Cavalry and on the staff of Colonel Jubal A. Early, he saw action at 1st Manassas. Without campaigning he was elected to represent his district in the First Regular Congress in November 1861. Taking his seat the following February, he served on the committees on: Enrolled Bills; Indian Affairs; and the Medical Department. Following his reelection, again without any campaigning, he served on the committees on Printing and Commerce. A convert to the need for conscription, he favored its rigid enforcement and the supplying of the army through impressments. A Davis confidant, he broke with the president on the issue of freeing the slaves, although he would accept their being armed for the nation's defense. Resuming the practice of law after the war, he continued to be active in politics into the 20th century, serving in the U.S. Congress and as U.S. solicitor general. (Goode, John, *Recollections of a Lifetime*)

GOODE, John Thomas (1835-1916)

Despite the fact that his command was designated as a heavy artillery regiment, John Thomas Goode was usually leading infantry. A native Virginian, he had attended the Virginia Military Institute before being commissioned directly into the regular army in 1855. He saw service against the Seminoles, in the Kansas troubles, and during the Mormon expedition. After tendering his services to the state of Virginia he was dismissed from the old army on July 3, 1861. His Confederate assignments included: captain, Artillery (March 16, 1861); major, Artillery (October 1861); lieutenant colonel, Artillery (April 1862); colonel, 4th Virginia Heavy Artillery (May 12, 1862); colonel, 34th Virginia (early 1864); commanding Wise's Brigade, Johnson's Division, Department of North Carolina and Southern Virginia (ca. June 1-ca. October 17, 1864); and commanding Wise's Brigade, Johnson's Division, 4th Corps, Army of Northern Virginia (ca. October 17-December 1864). After serving as chief of artillery during the siege of Yorktown, he was given command of an artillery regiment. Lacking a sufficient number of artillery pieces in the defenses of Richmond, he had his men equipped with rifles. It was not until 1864 that this change was officially recognized and the unit was given an infantry designation. His unit was sent to Charleston in September 1863 and did not return to Virginia until the following spring. Assigned to the Petersburg-Richmond lines Goode led his regiment and then the brigade at Stony Creek, Port Walthall Junction, the Petersburg assaults, and the battle of the Crater. The next spring he was in command of the regiment at Hatcher's Run, Boydton Plank Road, Sayler's Creek, and at the Appomattox surrender. After the war he served a term in the state legislature.

GOODING, Oliver Paul (ca. 1839-1909)

A late graduate of West Point (1858), Indiana native Oliver P. Gooding emerged from the Civil War as a brevet major general of volunteers. Posted to the infantry, he had participated in the campaign against the Mormons before the outbreak of the sectional conflict. His Civil War assignments included: second lieutenant, 10th Infantry (since February 5, 1859); first lieutenant, 10th Infantry (May 7, 1861); colonel, 31st Massachusetts (February 18, 1862); captain, 10th Infantry (June 27, 1862); and commanding in the Department of the Gulf: 3rd Brigade, 3rd Division, 19th Corps (January 24-July 11, 1863); 2nd Brigade, 1st Division, 19th Corps (July 11-August 15 and October 20-November 20, 1863); District of Baton Rouge (September 1-October 19, 1863); 5th Brigade, Cavalry Division (February 24-June 4, 1864); 1st Brigade, Cavalry Division (September 24-October 27, 1864); and the division (October 27-November 11, 1864). He spent the first year of the war in the capital before being given command of a volunteer regiment from Massachusetts, which he led in the capture of New Orleans. Remaining on duty in the Department of the Gulf, he fought at Camp Bisland and in the reduction of Port Hudson. After serving in the Teche Campaign his regiment was mounted and sometimes referred to as the 6th Massachusetts Cavalry, although it was usually labeled the 31st Massachusetts Mounted Infantry. Having earlier commanded infantry brigades, he now directed similar mounted forces. He served in the Red River Campaign and was mustered out of the volunteers on November 26, 1864, when the non-reenlisting members of his unit were discharged and the regiment was reduced, in effect, to a battalion. Until his March 20, 1865, resignation from the regular establishment he was employed on inspection duty. That same month he was brevetted brigadier general for the war and major general for Port Hudson and the Red River Campaign. A St. Louis attorney, he later headed the city's police.

GOODWIN, Ichabod (1794-1882)

When, upon the firing on Fort Sumter, the New Hampshire legislature was not in session, Governor Ichabod Goodwin unilaterally went out and borrowed funds to raise troops for the Union army. A sailing and shore merchant, he had entered politics in his adoped state as a Whig. The Maine native later joined the Republicans and in his second bid—the first had been as a Whig—he was elected to the gubernatorial chair. After two terms, in which his financial arrangements for the war were given legislative approval, he was renominated and left office late in 1861. He returned to his business pursuits. (Hesseltine, William Best, *Lincoln and the War Governors* and Waite, Otis F.R., *New Hampshire in the Great Rebellion*)

GORDON, B. Frank (?-?)

By the time that B. Frank Gordon was appointed a brigadier general by General E. Kirby Smith, the president of the dying Confederacy was already a prisoner. Gordon's assignments included: adjutant, 1st Brigade, 2nd Division, Missouri State Guard (1861); major, 5th Missouri Cavalry (1862); lieutenant colonel, 5th Missouri Cavalry (1862); commanding Shelby's Brigade, Marmaduke's Division, District of Arkansas, Trans-Mississippi Department (August 1863); colonel, 5th Missouri Cavalry (ca. December 15, 1863); commanding 1st Missouri Cavalry Brigade, 1st Missouri Cavalry Division, Cavalry Corps, Trans-Mississippi Department (October 25, 1864-May 1865); and brigadier general, CSA, by Smith (May 16, 1865). With the Missouri State Guard he served in the battle of Wilson's Creek before becoming an officer in Shelby's cavalry regiment. While Shelby commanded a brigade, Gordon led the regiment at Newtonia, Helena, and Little Rock. During a part of the latter action he was in temporary command of the brigade. He joined Price's expedition to reclaim Missouri for the South and took command of the brigade after the division commander, J.S. Marmaduke, was captured. With the war virtually over, Smith promoted Gordon to the wreathed stars of a general in recognition of his months in charge of a brigade. Ten days later the department was surrendered.

GORDON, George Henry (1823-1886)

Massachusetts West Pointer (1846) George H. Gordon served in several regions during the Civil War and was brevetted major general of volunteers. As a subaltern in the Regiment of Mounted Rifles, he had twice been wounded and was brevetted in Mexico. Resigning as a first lieutenant in 1854, he became a lawyer in his native state. He joined the volunteers in 1861, and his assignments included: colonel, 2nd Massachusetts (May 25, 1861); commanding 1st Brigade, Bank's Division, Division of the Potomac (August 28-October 3, 1861); commanding 1st Brigade, Bank's Division, Army of the Potomac (March 13, 1862); commanding 3rd Brigade, 1st Division, 5th Corps, Army of the Potomac (March 13-April 4, 1862); commanding 3rd Brigade, 1st Division, Department of the Shenandoah (April 4-May 27 and June 18-26, 1862); brigadier general, USV (June 9, 1862); commanding 3rd Brigade, 1st Division, 2nd Corps, Army of Virginia (June 26-September 12, 1862); commanding 3rd Brigade, 1st Division, 12th Corps, Army of the Potomac (September 12-17 and October 20, 1862-early 1863); commanding the division (September 17-October 20, 1862); commanding 2nd Division, 4th Corps, Department of Virginia (May 4-July 15, 1863); commanding 1st Division, 11th Corps, Army of the Potomac (July 17-August 6, 1863); commanding U.S. Forces South End of Folly Island, 10th Corps, Department of South (August 16-October 24, 1863 and November 28, 1863-January 15, 1864); commanding division 10th Corps, Department of the South (January 15-28, 1864); commanding District of Florida, Department of the South (May 13-June 2, 1864); commanding U.S. Forces White River, Military Division of West Mississippi (July 19-late July 1864); commanding U.S. Forces Mobile Bay, Military Division of West Mississippi (August 1-31, 1864); chief of staff, District of New York, Department of the East (November 1864); and commanding District of Eastern Virginia, Department of Virginia (February 11-ca. June 1865). Serving under Nathaniel P. Banks, he took part in the campaign against Stonewall Jackson in the Shenandoah Valley. Joining John Pope's army, he fought at Cedar Mountain and 2nd Bull Run before serving in Maryland—at South Mountain and Antietam—under McClellan. After service along the upper Potomac near Williamsport and Harpers Ferry he was transferred to southeastern Virginia and took part in the repulse of James Longstreet at Suffolk. He was briefly back with the Army of the Potomac during the Pennsylvania Campaign and then commanded forces operating against Charleston. After serving for a short time in Florida, he transferred to the West and led a force from Arkansas to take part in the operations against Mobile. After helping to maintain the peace during the 1864 presidential elections in New York he finished the war in district command in Virginia. Mustered out on August 24, 1865, he settled in Boston as an attorney and was active in military history circles.

GORDON, George Washington (1836-1911)

In the battle that cost the Army of Tennessee six general officers killed or mortally wounded, the Confederacy also lost the services of Brigadier General George W. Gordon, who was wounded and captured. The native Tennesseean and graduate of Nashville's Western Military Institute was working as a surveyor when the Civil War began. His Confederate assignments included: drillmaster, 11th Tennessee (June 1861); captain, Company I, 11th Tennessee (1861); lieutenant colonel, 11th Tennessee (1862); colonel, 11th Tennessee (December 1862); brigadier general, CSA (August 15, 1864); and commanding Vaughan's Brigade, Cheatham's-Brown's Division, Hardee's-Cheatham's Corps, Army of Tennessee (September-November 30, 1864). Initially serving in East Tennessee he gradually rose to command of the regiment, which had been James E. Rains', and was wounded at its head at Murfreesboro. He later fought at Chickamauga but missed Chattanooga. Serving in the Atlanta Campaign, he was promoted to brigadier general and shortly after the city's fall took command of a Tennessee brigade. This he led at Franklin in the futile assaults and was wounded and captured. Confined in Boston Harbor's Fort Warren, he was not released until July 1865. After the war he was active in veterans' affairs and took up the practice of law. After holding a series of minor public offices he was elected to Congress. During much of the postwar period he was also a planter.

GORDON, James Byron (1822-1864)

It was the death of Confederate General James Byron Gordon that led Union General Francis C. Barlow to believe that his benefactor at Gettysburg, in reality John Brown Gordon, had been killed in the war. Like Barlow's Gordon, James Gordon had no prior military experience but served throughout his career as a cavalry officer. A farmer, businessman, and state legislator, he had served briefly as an enlisted man and officer in an infantry company. His later assignments included: major, 1st North Carolina Cavalry (May 16, 1861); colonel, 1st North Carolina Cavalry (July 23, 1863); commanding Baker's (intended) Brigade, Hampton's Division, Cavalry Corps, Army of Northern Virginia (September 9, 1863-ca. April 23, 1864); brigadier general, CSA (September 28, 1863); and commanding brigade, W.H.F. Lee's Divison, same corps and army (ca. April 23-May 12, 1864). As a regimental officer, he served through the major campaigns of the army including the Seven Days, Antietam, Fredericksburg, and Gettysburg. With the September 1863 reorganization of the cavalry, an all-North Carolina brigade was created for General L.S. Baker who had been wounded the month before. For a time Gordon commanded the unit as a colonel but was promoted to brigadier when it became apparent that Baker would not be fit for field duty for a long period. Gordon led his fellow North Carolinians through the Bristoe, Mine Run, and Overland campaigns. He fought at Yellow Tavern, where Stuart was mortally wounded, and himself fell with a mortal hurt the next day, May 12, fighting Sheridan's raid at Meadow Bridge. He died six days later. (Cowles, William H., *The Life and Services of James B. Gordon* and Freeman, Douglas S., *Lee's Lieutenants*)

GORDON, John Brown (1832-1904)

A civilian turned soldier, John B. Gordon became a trusted corps commander under Lee in the final days of the Confederacy. Involved in the coal industry in his native Georgia, Gordon raised the Racoon Roughs for the Southern cause. His assignments included: captain, Company I, 6th Alabama (May 1861); major, 6th Alabama (ca. May 14, 1861); colonel, 6th Alabama (April 28, 1862); commanding Rodes' brigade, D.H. Hill's Division, Department of the Virginia (May 31-June and July 1862); brigadier general, CSA (November 1, 1862; not confirmed and reappointed May 7, 1863); commanding Lawton's (old) Brigade, Early's Division, 2nd Corps, Army of Northern Virginia (April 11, 1863-May 8, 1864); commanding the division (May 8-21, 1864); major general, CSA (May 14, 1864); commanding Johnson's (old) Division, same corps

Civilian General John B. Gordon. (NA)

and army (May 21-June 13, 1864); commanding same division, Valley District, Department of Northern Virginia (June 13-December 1864); and commanding 2nd Corps, Army of Northern Virginia (December 1864-April 9, 1865). Having fought at 1st Bull Run, he was elected colonel upon the regiment's reorganization and led it at Williamsburg. At Seven Pines he distinguished himself when he assumed command of the brigade. He fought through the Seven Days, part of the time in brigade command. He led the regiment at Antietam where he was wounded in the head and lived to relate how a hole in his cap from a bullet earlier in the day saved him from drowning in his own blood, which had accumulated in it. Recovering, he was given command of a Georgia brigade with which he fought at Chancellorsville and Gettysburg. At the latter he aided a wounded Union general, Francis C. Barlow, whom he met, decades later, each thinking the other had died in the war. They were friends until Barlow's death. Gordon received Lee's praise for planning a successful attack on the Union right at the Wilderness, and two days later Lee juggled a number of commands so that Gordon could lead Early's Division. At Spotsylvania, Gordon earned permanent promotion to major general and was soon given the remnants of Johnson's former division plus his own Georgia brigade. This unit he led at Cold Harbor and in the Shenandoah Valley Campaign during which he was sometimes in charge of an informal corps. He saw action at Monocacy, on the outskirts of Washington, at 3rd Winchester, Fisher's Hill, and Cedar Creek. Rejoining Lee in the trenches at Petersburg, he directed the corps and planned the attack on Fort Stedman. At Appomattox his men made the last charge of the Army of Northern Virginia. It is often claimed that he was a lieutenant general, but Gordon himself is silent on the matter in his *Reminiscences of the Civil War* in which he recounts each of his other promotions. He went on to a distinguished career in politics, serving as governor and senator and was active in veterans' affairs. (Tankersley, Allen P., *John B. Gordon: A Study in Gallantry*)

GORDON, Nathaniel (?-1862)

When Nathaniel Gordon was captured and charged with violating the United States Slave Trade Act, he was little concerned, since no one had ever been convicted and sentenced under the act. He had been involved in the trade at least since 1857; then on August 8, 1860, his vessel, the *Erie* was seized by the USS *Mohican* just outside the mouth of the Congo River. On board the American officers found some 800 or 900 captives who were eventually landed in Liberia instead of being returned up the river to their homes. Returned to the United States, Gordon was convicted (on a second attempt) of piracy, subjecting him to the death sentence. President Lincoln resisted all requests for pardon or commutation of the sentence, feeling an example was needed. After a suicide attempt, Gordon went to the hangman on February 20, 1862. His timing had been off; with the country now in a civil war, he might have met a different fate.

GORGAS, Josiah (1818-1883)

Taking advantage of the fact that his entire service in the U.S. Army was in the ordnance branch, the Confederacy utilized Josiah Gorgas as its chief ordnance officer throughout the war. The Pennsylvanian West Pointer (1841) had risen to the rank of captain before he resigned on April 3, 1861. Five days later he was commissisoned in the Confederate service and his assignments included: major, Ordnance (April 8, 1861); chief, Bureau of Ordnance (April 8, 1861-April 1865); lieutenant colonel, Ordnance (from March 16, 1861); colonel, Ordnance (1863); and brigadier general, CSA (November 10, 1864). His task was an extremely difficult one; given the Union blockade of Confederate ports and the lack of materials for weapons and ammunition at home. He was amazingly successful in keeping the armies in the field relatively well supplied. Recognizing that his best source of munitions was abroad, he organized a small fleet of blockade runners on his own authority. Jospeh E. Johnston was a great admirer of Gorgas. After Appomattox Gorgas was engaged in the iron business and then in education. (Gorgas, Josiah, *Civil War Diary*)

GORMAN, Willis Arnold (1816-1876)

Willis A. Gorman twice interrupted his legal and political careers to serve his country as an officer. The Kentucky native had been admitted to the Indiana bar and was a member of the state legislature. He fought as a major of volunteers in Mexico, rose to colonel, and soon after was elected to Congress. He was named territorial governor of Minnesota and stayed there after his term expired practicing law. His Civil War assignments in-

Less-than-successful General Willis A. Gorman. (*Leslie's*)

cluded: colonel, 1st Minnesota (April 29, 1861); commanding 1st Brigade, Stone's-Sedgwick's Division, Army of the Potomac (October 3, 1861-March 13, 1862); brigadier general, USV (September 7, 1861); commanding 1st Brigade, 2nd Division, 2nd Corps, Army of the Potomac (March 13-October 29, 1862 but not late June and early July); commanding Army of Southwest Missouri, Department of the Missouri (November 13-December 13, 1862); commanding District of Eastern Arkansas, Department of the Missouri (December 13-22, 1862); commanding District of East Arkansas, 13th Corps, Army of the Tennessee (December 22, 1862-February 8, 1863); also commanding 12th Division (part of the District of Eastern Arkansas), 13th Corps, Army of the Tennessee (January 22-February 8, 1863); and commanding Post of Helena, District of Eastern Arkansas, 13th Corps, Army of the Tennessee (spring 1863). Praised for his regimental leadership at 1st Bull Run, he was given a brigade that he directed in a supporting role during the fight at Ball's Bluff. Promoted to brigadier general effective from the previous month, he led his men to the Peninsula and saw action at Yorktown and Seven Pines but missed the Seven Days. After fighting at Antietam he was sent west of the Mississippi. During the operations against Vicksburg he was promoted from district to post command by Grant. He was mustered out on May 4, 1864, and returned to his practice.

GOULD, Andrew Wills (1840-1863)

The officer corps of the Confederate army was very sensitive about what they considered slights to their honor and hindrances to their careers. The June 13, 1863, affair at Columbia, Tennessee, between General Nathan Bedford Forrest and a young artillery lieutenant, Andrew Wills Gould, is a typical example. At the outbreak of the war Gould, a graduate of Cumberland University, was attending the military school of the University of Nashville. Leaving school he joined his cousin Colonel Alonzo Napier's Tennessee Cavalry Battalion. The command captured two artillery pieces from a Union transport and Gould was placed in charge. After serving with Forrest in west Tennessee, Gould's section was assigned on December 23, 1862, to Morton's Tennessee Battery. Gould became a first lieutenant in the new unit. The commander of Forrest's other battery had been killed on April 10, 1863, and it was widely rumored that Gould would get the command, but first came operations against Streight's Raid. On April 30, in the fight at Sand Mountain, Gould was forced to abandon his guns, which had been serving on the skirmish line. Word of his gallant action in spiking the pieces unaided in the face of enemy did not reach Forrest, only the loss of the section. Forrest was outraged and questioned Gould's courage. The vacant battery command was given to another lieutenant in May. Back in Columbia Gould went to confront Forrest and, not being satisfied with an order transferring Gould to Bragg's army, started to draw his pistol, which went off before he had fully raised it. The ball hit Forrest in the hip. Forrest opened a penknife with his teeth and stabbed the subordinate in the ribs. Gould fled across the street to a tailor shop where a doctor began to treat him. Forrest burst in with two borrowed pistols, intent upon killing the man who had, according to preliminary diagnosis, mortally wounded him. Forrest fired but hit a staff officer instead and Gould again fled. Forrest's rage subsided when informed that his wound was not serious, and he directed that Gould be well treated. On the other hand, Gould was fatally injured and he died a few days later. It has been alleged that the general forgave his dying lieutenant in a bedside visit. But this meeting has been denied by many then-present in Columbia.

GOVAN, Daniel Chevilette (1829-1911)

As a Confederate officer, North Carolina-born Daniel C. Govan rose from command of a company to that of a brigade and received the three stars and the wreath of a general officer. A veteran of the 1849 gold rush, he was an Arkansas planter when the war came. His assignments included: captain, Company F, 2nd Arkansas (June 5, 1861); lieutenant colonel, 2nd Arkansas (June 1861); colonel, 2nd Arkansas (January 6, 1862); commanding Liddell's Brigade, Liddell's Division, Reserve Corps, Army of Tennessee (September 1863); commanding Liddell's-Govan's Brigade, Cleburne's Division, Hardee's- Cheatham's Corps, Army of Tennessee (November 1863-September 1, 1864 and ca. October-December 16, 1864); brigadier general, CSA (December 29, 1863); and commanding brigade, Brown's Division, Hardee's Corps, Army of Tennessee (April 9-26, 1865). He led his regiment at Shiloh and it fought at Perryville. After fighting at Murfreesboro he commanded a brigade at Chickamauga and Chattanooga. Rewarded with the rank of brigadier general, he led Liddell's old brigade through the Atlanta Campaign until he was captured at Jonesboro. Exchanged on September 20, 1863, he resumed command and led his men at Franklin and Nashville. For a time thereafter he appears not to have been on duty but reappears as a brigade commander in the final stages of the Carolinas Campaign. Surrendered at Durham Station, he returned to planting and served for a time as an Indian agent.

GRACIE, Archibald, Jr. (1832-1864)

Heidelberg educated, a West Point graduate and an Indian fighter, New York City-native Archibald Gracie, Jr., resigned from the regular army in 1856 to join his father's mercantile business in Mobile. In 1860, he was appointed to the captaincy of the Washington Light Infantry, a Mobile militia company. His military assignments included: captain, Company E, 3rd Alabama (April 18, 1861); major, 11th Alabama (July 12, 1861); colonel, 43rd Alabama (May 7, 1862); brigadier general (November 4, 1862); commanding brigade, Department and Army of East Tennessee, sometimes in the field as part of the Army of Tennessee (ca. October 31, 1862-April 1864); commanding brigade, Department of Richmond and of North Carolina and Southern Virginia (ca. May 10-October 1864); and commanding brigade, Johnson's Division, Anderson's Corps, Army of Northern Virginia (October-December 2, 1864). Before Alabama seceded, Gracie took part, under the governor's orders, in the seizure of the Mount Vernon Arsenal on

January 4, 1860. His militia company later became part of the 3rd Alabama, but a few months later he was promoted to major and transferred to the 11th Alabama, which took part in the 1st battle of Bull Run, July 21, 1861. In the spring of 1862, he raised and was given command of the 43rd Alabama. Serving in the Department of East Tennessee, Gracie was promoted to brigadier general and given command of a brigade that served principally in Cumberland Gap. The forces in East Tennessee were sent to northern Georgia in the summer of 1863 to join the Army of Tennessee. At the battle of Chickamauga, Gracie's Brigade experienced its baptism of fire when on the second day it attacked the federals on Snodgrass Hill for over an hour. The brigade suffered heavily in the unsuccesful effort. In November the command returned to East Tennessee to aid Longstreet in his campaign against Burnside at Knoxville. At Bean's Station on December 4, 1863, Gracie suffered a severe flesh wound. Returning to duty in early 1864, he led his brigade to Richmond in early May where it played a key role in driving back Butler at Drewry's Bluff and bottling him up, for which Gracie was recommended for promotion. Subsequently the brigade was moved to the trenches just east of Petersburg, where Gracie was credited with "ceaseless energy." During the siege operations in November, General Lee stood upon the parapet of Gracie's works exposing himself to Union fire. Silently, in a famous incident, Gracie joined him and placed himself between his commander and the enemy. A few weeks later, on December 2, 1864, Gracie was killed in the trenches by a piece of shell (Freeman, Douglas., *R.E. Lee*)

GRAHAM, Charles Kinnaird (1824-1889)

When the Civil War broke out, Mexican war naval veteran Charles K. Graham was both a lawyer and engineer. The New York native helped plan that city's Central Park and then worked at the Brooklyn Navy Yard. At the start of the war he enlisted in a regiment that was largely composed of fellow navy yard workers and became part of the Excelsior Brigade of General Daniel E. Sickles. His assignments included: colonel, 74th New York (May 26, 1861); colonel, 74th New York (reappointment May 26, 1862, following April 10 resignation); brigadier general, USV (November 29, 1862); commanding 2nd Brigade, 2nd Division, 3rd Corps, Army of the Potomac (February-March 1863); commanding 1st Brigade, 1st Division, 3rd Corps, Army of the Potomac (March-May 14 and June 20-July 2, 1863, except briefly on May 4, 1863); also commanding 3rd Division, 3rd Corps, Army of the Potomac (May 3-June 20 and July 2, 1863); commanding Naval Brigade, Army of the James (April 28, 1864-February 17, 1865); and commanding Infantry Division, Defenses of Bermuda Hundred, Army of the James (February 17-March 19, 1865). On the Peninsula he was at Yorktown, Seven Pines and Seven Days. For health reasons he was then assigned to recruiting duty in New York. Returning to duty in the field early in 1863, he led a brigade at Chancellorsville and succeeded to temporary command of the division there. In the debacle at the Peach Orchard on the second day at Gettysburg he again took cover command of the division and was soon wounded and captured. Exchanged in September, he was assigned to duty with the Army of the James the next spring. His subsequent services were primarily in the inactive areas. Brevetted major general for the war, he was mustered out on August 24, 1865. Returning to engineering he was concerned for over a decade with maritime affairs in New York Harbor.

GRAHAM, Lawrence Pike (1815-1905)

Native Virginian Lawrence P. Graham remained loyal to the Union but had his active field career terminated by ill health. The only one of four brothers who did not attend West Point, he was commissioned directly into the dragoons in 1837. He saw action against the Seminoles in Florida and earned a brevet in the Mexican War. His Civil War-era assignments included: major, 2nd Dragoons (since June 14, 1858); major, 2nd Cavalry (designation change August 3, 1861); brigadier general, USV (August 31, 1861); lieutenant colonel, 5th Cavalry (October 1, 1861); commanding brigade, Division of the Potomac (September-October 3, 1861); commanding 2nd Brigade, Buell's-Keyes' Division, Army of the Potomac (October 3, 1861-March 13, 1862); commanding 2nd brigade, 1st Division, 4th Corps, Army of the Potomac (March 13-May 19, 1862); and colonel, 4th Cavalry (May 9, 1864). After serving in part of the operations against Yorktown he was forced to relinquish command for health reasons. For the rest of the war his service was limited to cavalry training at Annapolis and service on courts-martial and retirement boards. Brevetted brigadier general in the regular service for the war, he was mustered out of the volunteers on August 24, 1865. After five more years of service in the regular army he was retired and later became noted for his studies of Shakespeare.

GRAHAM, William Alexander (1804-1875)

If any Confederate congressional election race can be considered a rebuke to a perceived movement toward military rule in the new nation, it was the North Carolina victory of William A. Graham over the incumbent Senator George Davis. Graham had had a distinguished career in politics before the Civil War, serving as: state legislator (including the speakership); governor; secretary of the navy; and unsuccessful vice-presidential candidate in 1852. During the secession crisis he opposed taking the drastic step, was prominent in the Constitutional Union movement, and attended the Washington Peace Conference. While he was attending the North Carolina convention as a unionist, Lincoln's call for troops moved Graham into the secessionists' camp. In the election campaign for the Senate seat of George Davis for the Second Congress, Graham prevailed. Serving on the committees on Finance and Naval Affairs, he quickly became known for his opposition to the administration. He condemned an effective draft without exemption, arming the slaves, suspension of the writ of habeas corpus, and most presidential vetoes and legislative requests. By the end of the war he was calling for each Confederate state to make a separate peace with the enemy. After the war he held a respected position in the eyes of his fellow North Carolinians.

GRANBURY, Hiram Bronson (1831-1864)

Starting the war as a captain, Hiram Granbury rose to comand the Texas brigade of Cleburne's Division and died in the assault at Franklin, Tennessee. The local politician from Texas raised the Waco Guards and became its first captain. His later assignments included: major, 7th Texas (November 1861); colonel, 7th Texas (August 29, 1862); commanding Smith's old Brigade, Cleburne's Division, Hardee's-Cheatham's Corps, Army of Tennessee (November 25, 1863-November 30, 1864); and brigadier general (February 29, 1864). Sent to Kentucky, Granbury's regiment later moved into Fort Donelson, where he was captured on Feburary 16, 1862. Imprisoned at Fort Warren in Boston Harbor, he was allowed to visit Baltimore on parole to attend his wife while she was undergoing an operation. He was exchanged on August 27, 1862, for two lieutenants and almost immediately promoted to colonel. But the 7th Texas was not exchanged until November and was then consolidated with the 49th and 55th Tennessee regiments under Colonel J.E. Bailey. This left Granbury without a command until January 1863 when the unit was again independent. He led the regiment at Raymond and Jackson in the Vicksburg Campaign as part of Johnston's command and went to the Army of Tennessee in time for Chickamauga where he was wounded. At Chattanooga, Granbury assumed command of the brigade upon the wounding of General J.A. Smith and led it until Smith resumed command after the Atlanta Campaign had started. Granbury, having been promoted to brigadier, was again in command by the end of the campaign. He led his men in Hood's invasion of Tennessee, where, in the desparate Confederate attacks on the Union positions at Franklin, he was one of six rebel generals killed. He died almost within the Union positions.

GRANGER, Gordon (1822-1876)

Gordon Granger, with two brevets in the Mexican War and extensive frontier service, rose to rank of major general of volunteers during the Civil War. The native New Yorker and West Pointer (1845) had been posted first to the infantry and then to the mounted riflemen. His Civil War-era assignments included: first lieutenant, Regiment of Mounted Riflemen (since May 24, 1852); lieutenant colonel, Ohio Volunteers (ca. April 23, 1861); captain, Regiment of Mounted Riflemen (May 5, 1861); captain, 3rd cavalry (designation change August 3, 1861); colonel, 2nd Michigan Cavalry (September 2, 1861); commanding Cavalry Division, Army of the Mississippi (March 4-July 30, 1862); brigadier general, USV (March 26, 1862); commanding 5th Division, Army of the Mississippi (July 30-September 4, 1862); major general, USV (September 17, 1862); commanding District of Central Kentucky, Department of the Ohio (November 17, 1862-January 25, 1863); commanding Army of Kentucky, Department of the Cumberland (February-June 8, 1863); commanding Reserve Corps, Army of the Cumberland (June 8-October 9, 1863); commanding 4th Corps, Army of the Cumberland (October 10, 1863-April 10, 1864); commanding District of Southern Alabama, Department of the Gulf (December 1864-February 18, 1865); and

Union corps commander Gordon Granger. (*Leslie's*)

commanding 13th Corps, Department of the Gulf (February 18-July 20, 1865). In the early months of the war he served on McClellan's staff in western Virginia. Brevetted in the regular army for his service on the staff of Samuel D. Sturgis at Wilson's Creek, he became the commander of a volunteer cavalry regiment the next month. He directed the Army of the Mississippi mounted troops at Island #10 and on the advance to Corinth. In the meantime promoted to brigadier general, he commanded an infantry division for a time and then the Army of Kentucky. At Chickamauga he led the Reserve Corps, part of which played a major role in preventing a complete rout of the Union forces. Brevetted for this, he won a similar reward for Chattanooga. After taking part in the relief of besieged Knoxville, he was transferred to the Gulf. There he was brevetted brigadier general for the capture of Mobile and major general for the capture of Forts Gaines and Morgan. Mustered out of the volunteer service on January 15, 1866, he remained in the regular army, serving at Memphis and on the frontier. He died while on active duty as colonel, 15th Infantry.

GRANGER, Robert Seaman (1816-1894)

Although he had not been engaged in any of the major actions of the Civil War, Ohio native Robert S. Granger emerged from the conflict as a brevet major general and full brigadier general of volunteers. The West Pointer (1838) had been posted to the infantry and seen service against the Seminoles and in the Mexican War. He had also taught at his alma mater before the war. At the outbreak of the Civil War, he was stationed in Texas and was forced to surrender at Saluria in April 1861. Not exchanged until August 1862, his assignments included: captain, 1st Infantry (since September 8, 1847); major, 5th Infantry (September 9, 1861); brigadier general, Kentucky Volunteers (ca. September 1862); brigadier general, USV (October 20, 1862); commanding 1st Division, 14th Corps, Army of the Cumberland (January 17-March 29, 1863); commanding 3rd Brigade, 1st Division, 14th Corps, Army of the Cumberland (April 17-May 6, 1863); commanding District of Nashville, Army of the Cumberland (June 2-November 10, 1863); also commanding 3rd Division, Reserve Corps, Army of the Cumberland (June 8-October 9, 1863); commanding Post of Nashville, District of Nashville, Army of the Cumberland (November 1863-June 1864); also commanding 1st Brigade, District of Nashville, Army of the Cumberland (January 1864); also commanding 1st Brigade, 3rd Division, 12th Corps, Army of the Cumberland (January 2-April 14, 1864); commanding District of North Alabama, Department of the Cumberland (June 2, 1864-September 10, 1865). Finally exchanged after more than a year of administrative work, he was named a Kentucky brigadier general and later won a brevet in the U.S. volunteers for a small action at Lawrenceburg, Kentucky, on October 9, 1862. He was named to the same grade in the national service the next month. For the rest of the war he held a variety of district, post, brigade, and division commands, mostly in Kentucky, Tennessee, and Alabama. While in these positions he frequently had to deal with the raids of Joseph Wheeler, Philip D. Roddey, and Nathan Bedford Forrest. His greatest contribution to the war effort for which he was brevetted brigadier general in the regular establishment, came during John B. Hood's advance into Tennessee in late 1864. Granger also distinguished himself in the defense of Decatur, Alabama. Brevetted major general in both services, he was mustered out of the volunteers on August 24, 1865. Remaining in the army, he served in the Occupation of the South and on recruiting duty until his 1873 retirement as colonel, 21st Infantry.

GRANT, Hiram Ulysses

See: *Grant, Ulysses Simpson*

GRANT, Lewis Addison (1828-1918)

Serving with the famed 1st Vermont Brigade, Lewis A. Grant compiled an enviable record—suffering three wounds in the process—that included a brevet as major general and a Congressional Medal of Honor. The native Vermonter was practicing law in 1861 when he entered the Union army. His assignments included: major, 5th Vermont (August 15, 1861); lieutenant colonel, 5th Vermont (September 25, 1861); colonel, 5th Vermont (September 16, 1861); commanding 2nd Brigade, 2nd Division, 6th Corps, Army of the Potomac (February-December 1863, January-July 8, 1864, December 6-26, 1864, and February 11-20, March 7-April 2, and April 2-June 28, 1865); brigadier general, USV (to rank from April 27, 1864); commanding 2nd Brigade, 2nd Division, 6th Corps, Army of the Shenandoah (August 6-September 18, October 3-19, 1864); commanding the division (August 16-October 19, 1864); and commanding 2nd Division, 6th Corps, Army of the Potomac (January 16-February 11, 1865). He fought well in the Peninsula Campaign, commanding the regiment at Williamsburg and the Seven Days. He was made its colonel on the day before Antietam. At Fredericksburg he was wounded. During the Chancellorsville Campaign he was again on the Fredericksburg field and stormed the Confederate works, earning a Congressional Medal of Honor—awarded in 1893—for the action in which his men had captured three enemy flags. He was again wounded in the action. He commanded his brigade in reserve at Gettysburg and through the Bristoe and Mine Run campaigns. Promoted to brigadier general shortly before the Overland Campaign, he fought at the Wilderness, Spotsylvania, Cold Harbor, and Petersburg before being sent to the aid of Washington during Early's invasion of Maryland. At times during the succeeding Shenandoah Valley Campaign he was in charge of the division and at times in charge of the Vermonters. He fought at 3rd Winchester, Fisher's Hill, and Cedar Creek. He was brevetted major general for several of his 1864 battles. Returning to the Petersburg front he again briefly commanded the division. Back in command of his old brigade, he was wounded in the final assaults on Petersburg but returned to duty later that day. He was present at Appomattox. Declining a regular army commission, he was mustered out of the volunteer service on August 24, 1865. After the war he lived in Vermont, Illinois, Iowa, and Minnesota. He was assistant secretary of war for three years during the term of Benjamin Harrison.

GRANT, Ulysses Simpson (1822-1885)

The best evidence of the changes that had occurred in warfare from Jomini to Clausewitz can be found in the campaigns of Robert E. Lee and Ulysses S. Grant. The latter was born Hiram Ulysses Grant in Ohio but through confusion at West Point he became Ulysses Simpson Grant. Appointed to the military academy, he found it distasteful and hoped that Congress would abolish the institution, freeing him. He excelled only in horsemanship—for that he had displayed a capability early in life—and graduated in 1843, 21st out of 39 graduates. Posted to the 4th Infantry, since there were no vacancies in the dragoons, he served as regimental quartermaster during most of the Mexican War. Nonetheless he frequently led a company in combat under Zachary Taylor in northern Mexico. He came to greatly admire his chief but was transferred with his regiment to Winfield Scott's army operating from the coast. He received brevets for Molino del Rey and Chapultepec. With the resumption of peace he was for a time stationed in Mexico, a country which he came to admire greatly, and then was posted to the West coast. Separated from his wife, he tried numerous business ventures to raise enough capital to bring her to the coast but proved singularly unsuccessful. On July 31, 1854, he resigned his captaincy amid rumors of heavy drinking and warnings of possible disciplinary action by his post commander. His return

Grant at his field headquarters. (NA)

to civilian life proved unsuccessful. Farming on his father-in-law's land was a failure, as was the real estate business and attempts to gain engineering and clerk posts in St. Louis. He finally became a clerk in a family leather goods store in Galena, which was run by his two younger brothers. Before he had been there long the Civil War broke out. Offering his services to the War Department and to General George B. McClellan in Ohio, he met with no success in gaining an appointment. After organizing and mustering state volunteers and with the aid of local Congressman Elihu B. Washburne, he got his second military career off to a start. His assignments included: colonel, 21st Illinois (June 17, 1861); brigadier general, USV (July 31, 1861, to rank from May 17); commanding District of Ironton, Western Department (August 8-21, 1861); commanding U.S. Forces Jefferson City, Western Department (August 21-28, 1861); commanding Post of Cape Girardeau, Western Deparatment (August 30-September 1, 1861); commanding District of Southeast Missouri, Western Department (September 1-November 9, 1861); commanding District of Southeast Missouri, Department of the Missouri (November 9-December 23, 1861); commanding District of Cairo, Department of the Missouri (December 23, 1861-February 21, 1862); major general, USV (February 16, 1862); commanding District of West Tennessee, Department of the Missouri (February 21-March 11, 1862); commanding District of West Tennessee, Department of the Mississippi (March 11-April 29 and June 10-October 16, 1862); second-in-command, Department of the Mississippi (April 29-June 10, 1862); commanding Army and Department of the Tennessee (October 16, 1862-October 24, 1863); also commanding 13th Corps, Army of the Tennessee (October 24-December 18, 1862); major general, USV (July 4, 1863); commanding Military Division of the Mississippi (October 18, 1863-March 18, 1864); lieutenant general, USA (March 2, 1864); commander-in-chief, United States Army (March 12, 1864-March 4, 1869); general, USA (July 25, 1866); secretary of war ad interim (August 17, 1867-January 14, 1868); and President of the United States (March 4, 1869-March 4, 1877). When Kentucky's fragile neutrality was falling apart, Grant moved quickly from his Cairo, Illinois base to take Paducah, Kentucky at the mouth of the Tennessee River. His subsequent action at Belmont, Missouri, turned into a defeat following early success. In a joint operation with the navy his land forces arrived too late to take part in the capture of Fort Henry but at neighboring Fort Donelson a major engagement was fought by the ground forces, defeating a Confederate breakout attempt. When asked for terms his reply earned him the nickname "Unconditional Surrender" Grant. He got in hot water with his superior, Henry W. Halleck, over reports not being filed and his unauthorized trip to Nashville. Ordered to remain at Fort Henry while his forces advanced up the Tennessee, he was restored to field command upon the injury of General Charles F. Smith. Surprised by the Confederate attack at Shiloh—William T. Sherman was in charge on the field at the time—Grant recovered to score a major victory on the second day. Again in trouble with Halleck, he was demoted to second-in-command of Halleck's field army in the slow advance on Corinth, Mississippi. Subsequently restored to command, he was thwarted in his attempt to reach Vicksburg by following the railroads through central Mississippi when his supply base at Holly Spring was destroyed by Confederate cavalry. Over the next months he tried various routes to get at the river city but didn't launch his final thrust until late April 1863. In a brilliant manner he shifted his troops south of the city and advanced on Jackson to defeat Joseph E. Johnston before scoring two victories over Pemberton—at Champion's Hill and Big Black River Bridge—and finally besieging Vicksburg. With the July 4, 1863, capitulation of the city he was awarded a major generalcy in the regular army. His return was complete. After some minor operations in Mississippi he was given charge of all the armies in the West and raised the siege of Chattanooga and sent Sherman to raise that of Knoxville. That winter he was appointed to the re-created grade of lieutenant general and given command of all the Union armies. He also received the thanks of Congress. Making his headquarters with George G. Meade's Army of the Potomac, he hammered away at Lee—the devout follower of Jomini—in his Overland Campaign. Despite heavy losses at the Wilderness, Spotsylvania, and Cold Harbor, Grant kept going. His attack at the latter was one of two movements he wished he had never ordered (the other was at Vicksburg). Swinging south of Richmond he besieged Petersburg and after a 10-month siege took both cities. Pursuing Lee to Appomattox, he had virtually ended the war. Meanwhile, the other armies under his direction had torn the Confederacy apart. In the postwar reorganization of the army he was promoted to full general and oversaw the military portion of

Reconstruction and the reduction of the army. During Andrew Johnson's fight with the Radical Republicans in Congress Grant was in an awkward position. He was ordered to replace the suspended Edwin M. Stanton as secretary of war, in violation of the Tenure of Office Act. He weathered the storm and became the party's nominee for president in 1868. Elected, he served two terms during which—although he personally remained untainted—there were many scandals, especially in relation to the Whiskey Tax and the appointment of Indian agents. Despite his interest in creating a peace with the Indians, Custer's Massacre occurred during his tenure. Also the freedmen lost much ground during his term, as the white supremacists regained control in the Southern states. During his term the problems with England evolving from the Civil War were resolved and an attempt to gain Santo Domingo for the United States failed. Thwarted for a third term, he embarked on a two-year tour around the world, which took on the appearance of a political campaign. Denied renomination in 1880, he was involved in a number of unsuccesssful ventures, the worst of which—in the brokerage firm of Grant & Ward—wiped him out. He then wrote his excellent *Personal Memoirs of U.S. Grant*, while dying of cancer of the throat. His family realized profits of almost $450,000. Shortly before his death on July 23, 1885, he had been placed on the retired list with the rank of general in order to ease his financial situation. (Lewis, Lloyd, *Captain Sam Grant*; Catton, Bruce, *Grant Moves South* and *Grant Takes Command*; and McFeely, William S., *Grant: A Biography*)

GRAY, Henry (1816-1892)

By the time that South Carolina native Henry Gray was officially named a brigadier general he was representing western Louisiana in the Confederate Congress. Before the Civil War he was a lawyer and politician in Mississippi and Louisiana. Upon the outbreak of the conflict he enlisted in a regiment from the former state. His later assignments included: colonel, 28th Louisiana (ca. May 17, 1862); brigadier general, CSA (per E.K. Smith, April 15, 1864); commanding brigade, Mouton's-Polignac's Division, District of West Louisiana, Trans-Mississippi Department (ca. April-October 1864); and brigadier general, CSA (March 18, 1865, to rank from the 17th). In 1862 his regiment was stationed at Vicksburg and defended it from the early Union attempts to take it. He was then dispatched to western Louisiana and took part in the Teche Campaign of 1863, being wounded in the battle there. During the Red River Campaign he led a brigade at Mansfield and Pleasant Hill. On October 17, 1864, he was elected, without his knowledge, to represent Louisiana's 5th District in the Second Confederate Congress. Taking his seat on December 28, 1864, he was assigned to the Judiciary Committee. He was a noted opponent of peace overtures. During the final session he was confirmed as a brigadier general, a position he had held informally under E.K. Smith for almost a year. Following a term in the state senate he retired from politics.

GRAYSON, John Breckinridge (1806-1861)

Although a brigadier general in the Confederate army, John Grayson did not get a chance to serve his country in combat. Graduated from West Point (1826), Grayson served in the artillery and as commissary during the Seminole and Mexican wars. At the outbreak of the Civil War he resigned his major's commission and on May 25, 1861, was named brigader general of state forces by the governor of North Carolina. On August 15, 1861, he was transferred to Confederate service with the same rank and six days later was assigned to command of the Department of Middle and Eastern Florida. Suffering from a lung ailment, he was relieved by the War Department on October 10, 1861, and succumbed to the disease 11 days later.

GREBLE, John Trout (ca. 1834-1861)

A graduate of West Point in 1854, Pennsylvanian John Greble rose to the rank of first lieutenant in the regular artillery before becoming the first regular army officer to die in the war. Stationed at Fort Monroe, Virginia, Greble and a detachment of his Company B, 2nd U.S. Artillery, accompanied the 2,500-man expedition to Big Bethel under General Ebenezer Pierce on June 9, 1861. The next morning, after a confusing night march, the federal troops launched a feeble attack against a 1,200-man Confederate force under Colonel John Magruder. Driven back in about an hour, the Union command lost 76 men, including Lieutenant Greble, who fell dead next to his gun after firing about a dozen rounds. He was posthumously brevetted captain, major, and lieutenant colonel from the date of this action (Lossing, Benson, J., *Memoir of Lieutenant Colonel John T. Greble of the United States Army*)

GREELEY, Horace (1811-1872)

Within one month in 1872 the founder of the *New York Tribune* lost his wife, a presidential bid, his paper, his mind, and his life. The New Hampshire native founded the paper in 1841 and within five years it was considered the best in the city and one of the top journals of the day. During the 1850s he used it to express his antislavery views. He opposed Lincoln for president but supported him during the Civil War. As an abolitionist he argued with Democrats and conservative Republicans alike. In 1864 he backed the movement to supplant Lincoln as the candidate but ended up backing his reelection. In the latter stages of the war he favored a negotiated peace and engaged in some questionable political dabbling of his own. With the war won, he pushed for the 14th and 15th Amendments to the Constitution. He was critical of the lenient treatment that the South received at the hands of Andrew Johnson but ironically was a cosigner of Jefferson Davis' bail bond. This latter act cost the *Tribune* thousands of subscribers. Critical of the Grant administration and its corruption, and himself known as a reformer in many fields, he was a leading force behind the Liberal Republican movement in 1872. Agreeing to become its standard bearer, he was thoroughly trounced by Grant in what was, even for its day, a dirty campaign. A few

Recovery of the body of John T. Greble, the first regular army officer to die in the Civil War. (*Leslie's*)

days earlier his wife had died, and he now found he had lost his editorship. His mind snapped and he died on November 29, 1872. (Fahrney, Ralph Ray, *Horace Greeley and the Tribune in the Civil War* and Van Deusen, Glyndon Garlock, *Horace Greeley, Nineteenth Century Crusader*)

GREEN, Martin Edwin (1815-1863)

Two days after being slightly wounded, Confederate General Martin E. Green was fatally struck at Vicksburg. The Virginia native had settled in Missouri in the 1830s and was running a sawmill at the outbreak of the Civil War. Siding with the South, his assignments included: colonel, Green's Cavalry Regiment, Missouri State Guard (1861); brigadier general, Missouri State Guard (ca. September 1861); commanding 2nd Division, Missouri State Guard (ca. September 1861-ca. March 17, 1862); commanding 4th Brigade, Trans-Mississippi District, Department #2 (ca. March 17-April 15, 1862); commanding 3rd Brigade, Price's Division, Army of the West, Department #2 (April-May 1862); commanding 3rd Brigade, 1st (Little's) Division, Army of the West, Department #2 (June-October 4, 1862); brigadier general, CSA (July 21, 1862); commanding the division (October 4-20, 1862); commanding 2nd Brigade, Bowen's Division, Price's Corps (or Army of the West), Army of West Tennessee, Department of Mississippi and East Louisiana (October 20-22, 1862); commanding 1st Brigade, Bowen's Division, Price's Corps (or Army of the West), Department of Mississippi and East Louisiana (October 22, 1862-early 1863); and commanding brigade, Forney's-Bowne's Division (in 2nd Military District during April), Department of Mississippi and East Louisiana (April-June 27, 1863). Raising a cavalry regiment he took part in the capture of Lexington, Missouri, and was soon thereafter promoted to brigadier general in the Missouri State Guard. As such he commanded a division at Pea Ridge and that summer was named to the same rank in the Confederate service. He fought at Iuka and succeeded to command of Little's Division at Corinth when Louis Hébert reported himself as too ill to command. He led a brigade in opposing Grant's campaign in central Mississippi and then commanded it during the beginning of the Vicksburg Campaign fighting at Port Gibson. Falling back with the rest of Pemberton's command into the city's defenses, he was wounded during the siege on June 25, 1863. Two days later he was killed when he exposed himself to a sharpshooter.

GREEN, Thomas (1814-1864)

Virginia native and a veteran of the Texas independence movement and the Mexican War, Thomas Green gave his life for the Confederacy. After studying law in Tennessee, he moved in 1835 to what would later become the Lone Star Republic and served in its army. He commanded a company of the 1st Texas Rifles in Mexico and was a court clerk at the time of the state's secession from the Union. Joining the Confederate army, his assignments included: colonel, 5th Texas Cavalry (August 1861); brigadier general, CSA (May 20, 1863); commanding cavalry brigade, District of Western Louisiana, Trans-Mississippi Department (late 1863); commanding Cavalry Division, District of Western Louisiana, Trans-Mississippi Department (November 1863 and March 16-April 12, 1864); and commanding cavalry brigade, District of Texas, New Mexico and Arizona, Trans-Mississippi Department (early 1864). Early in 1862 he took part in Henry H. Sibley's campaign in the New Mexico Territory and fought at Valverde. Returning to Texas after the unsuccessful conclusion of the operation, he played a leading role in the fight at Galveston on the first day of 1863. Promoted to brigadier general he served under Richard Taylor in western Lousiana and during the Red

River Campaign fought at Mansfield and Pleasant Hill. In an attack on the Union gunboats at Blair's Landing he was killed by a shell on April 12, 1864. (Nunn, W. Curtis, Ed., *Ten More Texans in Gray*)

GREENE, George Sears (1801-1899)

When the Civil War ended, 63-year-old George S. Greene was one of the oldest generals serving with an active field army, although a severe face wound had kept him from the field for almost a year and a half. Graduating number two in the West Point class of 1823, he was posted to the artillery and taught at the academy. After 13 years, interspersed with New England garrison duty, he resigned to enter civil engineering. At the beginning of 1862 he quit work on a reservoir in New York to enter the volunteer service. His assignments included: colonel, 60th New York (January 18, 1862); brigadier general, USV (April 28, 1862); commanding 3rd Brigade, 1st Division, Department of the Shenandoah (May 27-June 18, 1862); commanding 3rd Brigade, 2nd Division, 2nd Corps, Army of Virginia (August 1-9, 1862); commanding the division (August 9-September 12, 1862); commanding 2nd Division, 12th Corps, Army of the Potomac (September 12-October 15, 1862); commanding 3rd Brigade, 2nd Division, 12th Corps, Army of the Potomac (ca. October 15, 1862-September 25, 1863); commanding 3rd Brigade, 2nd Division, 12th Corps, Army of the Cumberland (September 25-October 29, 1863); and commanding 3rd Brigade, 3rd Division, 14th Corps, Army of the Cumberland (April 9-June 6, 1865). Within months of his enlistment he was a brigadier general commanding a brigade in the Shenandoah Valley. At Cedar Mountain he succeeded to command of the division when Christopher C. Augur was wounded and Henry Prince captured. He continued to lead the division at 2nd Bull Run and Antietam and was back in charge of his brigade at Chancellorsville. He was particularly distinguished on Culp's Hill at Gettysburg and then went west with the rest of the corps. In the early stages of the effort to relieve Chattanooga he was severely wounded in the face, at Wauhatchie on October 29, 1863. Following an operation in May 1864 he was assigned to administrative and court-martial duties. Finally fit enough to take the field, he joined Sherman for the conclusion of the Carolinas Campaign. Brevetted major general for the war, he was mustered out on April 30, 1866, and returned to engineering. A founder and president of the American Society of Civil Engineers, he worked in New York, Washington, Detroit, Troy, and Yonkers. His work included water and sewer systems, streets, and elevated railways. When he died, he was the oldest living graduate of West Point. His son, Samuel Dana Greene, was an officer aboard the USS *Monitor*.

GREENE, Samuel Dana (1840-1884)

A late graduate of Annapolis (1859), Marylander Samuel D. Greene commanded the *Monitor* in the latter part of its action against the *Virginia*. His wartime assignments included: lieutenant, USN (1861); executive officer, *Monitor* (1862); temporarily commanding *Monitor* (from March 9, 1862); executive officer, *Florida* (1863-64); and lieutenant commander, USN (1865). Volunteering for duty aboard the experimental ironclad *Monitor*, he took part in history's first battle between ironclad vessels and succeeded to its command upon the wounding of its captain. Greene was criticized in some circles for allowing the escape of the *Virginia*, but in fact his assignment was to protect the wooden fleet and this he accomplished. Following the sinking of the vessel in late 1862 he was assigned to the *Florida* and eventually rose to the grade of lieutenant commander. Following the war he remained in the navy until his suicide while serving as executive officer at the Portsmouth Navy Yard.

GREENHOW, Rose O'Neal (1817-1864)

One of the most effective female Confederate spies, Rose O'Neal Greenhow continued her activities even during her imprisonment. Born in Port Tobacco, Maryland, she had become a Washington belle and friend of politicians as diverse as James Buchanan and John C. Calhoun. A staunch Southerner, she backed Calhoun's call for a separation of the states. By the time of the Civil War she was a widow and one of the most traveled women in the capital. Working for the Confederate espionage system, she was able to supply much information gleaned from her admirers. She is credited with providing Richmond with the intelligence of McDowell's advance in time to provide for the uniting of Johnston and Beauregard for the victory at 1st Bull Run. Imprisoned in her own home in August 1861, she continued to send messages south. The following January she was transferred to the Old Capitol Prison and for five months—despite tightening security—managed to continue some clandestine activities. Finally in May she was sent into the Confederate lines along with her young daughter, Rose, who had also been confined. In August 1863 she was sent to England and France to plead the Confederacy's cause. From abroad she published *My Imprisonment and the First Year of Abolition Rule at Washington*. Returning aboard the *Condor*—her mission a failure—she was at her own request placed in a small craft in order to land when they arrived off Wilmington, North Carolina, on October 1, 1864, in the midst of a raging storm. Her vessel swamped and the weight of the gold she was carrying for the cause forced her under. She was given a military funeral and her grave is decorated on Confederate Memorial Day. (Ross, Ishbel, *Rebel Rose: Life of Rose O'Neal Greenhow, Confederate Spy*)

GREGG, David McMurtrie (1833-1916)

The resignation of the distinguished Union cavalry commander David McM. Gregg is one of the mysteries of the Civil War. A Pennsylvanian and West Pointer (1855), he had seen frontier service with the dragoons before the Civil War. His assignments included: second lieutenant, 1st Dragoons (since September 4, 1855); first lieutenant, 1st Dragoons (March 21, 1861); first lieutenant and adjutant, 1st Dragoons (April 12, 1861); captain, 3rd Cavalry (May 14, 1861); captain, 6th Cavalry (designation change August 3, 1861); colonel, 8th Pennsylvania Cavalry (January 24, 1862); commanding 2nd Brigade, Cavalry Division, Army of the Potomac (July 7-16, 1862); commanding 2nd Brigade, Pleasonton's Cavalry Division, Right Grand Division, Army of the Potomac (November-December 13, 1862); brigadier general, USV (November 29, 1862); commanding Cavalry Brigade, Left Grand Division, Army of the Potomac (December 13, 1862-February 5, 1863); commanding Cavalry Brigade, Army of the Potomac (February 5-12, 1863); commanding 3rd Division, Cavalry Corps, Army of the Potomac (February 12-June 11, 1863); commanding 2nd Division, Cavalry Corps, Army of the Potomac (Jusne 11-August 24, September 4-December 25, 1863, January 5-22, February 12-March 25, April 4-August 2, August 6-September 15, September 25-December 22, 1864, and January 19-February 8, 1865); and commanding the corps (January 22-February 12, March 25-April 4, and August 2-6, 1864). Coming east from California, he was made colonel of a volunteer regiment from his own state and led it at Yorktown, Seven Pines, and in the Seven Days. At Fredericksburg he was transferred from command of a brigade under Alfred Pleasonton—Gregg was now a brigadier general—to direct the brigade of George D. Bayard who had been killed. After the breakup of the grand divisions he led his unattached brigade for a few days before becoming a division commander in the newly created Cavalry Corps. A modest man, he was overshadowed by some of the more flamboyant horsemen but compiled a superb combat record. In his new post, he took part in Stoneman's raid during the Chancellorsville Campaign and fought at Aldie and Upperville. On the final day at Gettysburg he thwarted Jeb Stuart's planned attack on the Union rear but much of the credit went instead to brigade commander George A. Custer who was temporarily assigned to Gregg's sector. In 1907 Gregg published his account of the action, *The Second Cavalry Division of the Army of the Potomac in the Gettysburg Campaign*. He then went on to fight in the Bristoe, Mine Run, and Overland campaigns. When the 1st and 3rd divisions were sent to Sheridan in the Shenandoah Valley, Gregg commanded the only mounted division with the Army of the Potomac on the Petersburg-Richmond front—the other division present was part of the Army of the James. During the Petersburg operations he was brevetted major general of volunteers on August 1, 1864, especially for actions at Charles City Road. For some inexplicable reason this highly capable commander resigned from both the regular and volunteer services on February 3, 1865. Sheridan later expressed his regrets at Gregg's decision. Becoming a farmer, he served briefly in Prague as a diplomat under Grant.

GREGG, John (1828-1864)

A native of Alabama, lawyer John Gregg had emigrated to Texas a decade before the Civil War and served as a judge and as a member of the secession convention. Named to the Provisional Confederate Congress, he was admitted on February 15, 1861, and served on the committee on Accounts; Claims; and Military Affairs. He left the capital to raise a regiment for the war effort. His military assignments included: colonel, 7th Texas (September 1861); brigadier general, CSA (August 29, 1862); commanding brigade, 3rd Military District, Department of Mississippi and East Louisiana (late 1862-May 1863); commanding brigade (in Walker's Division from June), Department of the West (May-July 1863); commanding brigade, Walker's Division, in Department of Mississippi and East Louisiana (July-September 1863) and in Reserve Corps, Army of Tennessee (September 1863); and commanding Texas Brigade, Field's Division, in Department of East Tennessee (January 11-April 12, 1864) and in 1st Corps, Army of Northern Viriginia (April 12-October 7, 1864). Captured at Fort Donelson he was exchanged and promoted. Assigned to command a brigade in eastern Louisiana, he was detached to fight at Chickasaw Bluffs in December 1862. He returned to Louisiana until May 1863 when he again went to Mississippi and joined Johnston in his attempt to save Pemberton at Vicksburg; he was wounded on the first day at Chickamauga. Upon recovering he was assigned to the Texas Brigade and led it at the Wilderness, Spotsylvania, Cold Harbor, and around Richmond and Petersburg. He was killed on the Darbytown Road on October 7, 1864. (Freeman, Douglas S., *Lee's Lieutenants*)

GREGG, John Irvin (?-1892)

When Lee's army surrendered at Appomattox, Colonel J. Irvin Gregg of the Union cavalry was freed—after three days of captivity. During the Mexican War the native Pennsylvanian had served as an enlisted man and officer in the state volunteers and then joined the regular army as an officer for the balance of the conflict. Returning to civilian life when peace was declared, he was again commissioned when the regular establishment was expanded at the outbreak of the Civil War. His assignments included: captain, 3rd Cavalry (May 14, 1861); captain, 6th Cavalry (designation change August 3, 1861); colonel, 16th Pennsylvania Cavalry (November 14, 1862); commanding 2nd brigade, 2nd Division, Cavalry Corps, Army of the Potomac (May 13-June 14, August 12-24, 1863, September 4, 1863-August 2, 1864, August 6-16, 1864, November 10, 1864-February 9, 1865, and February 17-April 7, 1865); commanding 3rd Brigade, 2nd Division, Cavalry Corps, Army of the Potomac (June 14-August 17, 1863); and commanding the division (August 24-September 4, 1863, March 25-April 4, August 2-6, 1864, and February 9-March 14, 1865). With his regular regiment, he commanded a squadron at Williamsburg and fought through the Seven Days. Taking command of a newly formed volunteer mounted regiment, he earned a brevet at Kelly's Ford. In charge of a brigade, he fought at Brandy Station, Middleburg, and Upperville. With his brigade in the division of his distant relative David McM. Gregg, he was engaged at Gettysburg and participated in the Bristoe and Mine Run campaigns. During this time he earned another brevet for Sulpher Springs on October 12, 1863. Taking part in the cavalry operations during the Overland Campaign, he remained on the Richmond-Petersburg front throughout the siege. He was wounded at both Deep Bottom and Hatcher's Run and earned a brevet for the former. In the final operations against Lee's army he fought at Dinwiddie Court House, Five Forks, and Sayler's Creek. The day after the last action, April 7, 1865, he was captured in the action at Farmville. But with the imminent demise of the Army of Northern Virginia it was only a matter of time before he would be liberated. Having been brevetted brigadier general for actions on the Brock Turnpike and Trevilian Station, he received a like promotion to major general of volunteers for his war service. Mustered out on August 11, 1865, with his regiment, he remained in the regular service as captain and brevet brigadier general for the war. The next summer he was named colonel of the newly created 8th Cavalry and was retired at that grade in 1879.

GREGG, Maxcy (1814-1862)

Although a regular army major in the Mexican War, South Carolina lawyer and amateur scientist Maxcy Gregg did not see any action there. A longtime proponent of states' rights, he was a member of the state secession convention. His military assignments included: colonel, 1st South Carolina, Provisional Army (January 1861); brigadier general (December 18, 1861); commanding brigade, Department of South Carolina, Georgia, and Florida (early 1862); commanding same brigade, J.R. Anderson's Command (April-May 27, 1862) and A.P. Hill's Division (May 27-July 1862), Department and Army of Northern Virginia; and commanding brigade, A.P. Hill's Division, Jackson's Corps, Army of Northern Virginia (July-December 13, 1862). After observing the capitulation of Fort Sumter, Gregg took his regiment to Virginia where on June 17 it attacked a train full of Ohio troops at Vienna. After reorganizing his regiment in the summer Gregg returned to Virginia during the fall until promoted and ordered back to South Carolina in December. Given a brigade he led it at Beaver Dam Creek, Gaines' Mill, at Frayser's Farm during the Seven Days Battles, and at Cedar Mountain. Known for carrying a scimitar, instead of a sword, Gregg led the brigade at 2nd Bull Run where it held the extreme left of Jackson's line and Gregg was wounded. Taking part in the capture of Harpers Ferry, the brigade arrived just in time to drive back the final Union advance at Antietam. At Fredericksburg his men were placed behind a supposedly impenetrable gap in the line. Surprised by the breakthrough of Meade's Union Division, Gregg was trying to rally his men when he was killed. (Caldwell, J.F.J., *The History of a Brigade of South Carolinians*)

GREGG, William (1800-1867)

A leading advocate of Southern industry, Virginia-born William Gregg was recognized before the Civil War as the leader in cotton manufacturing. Having completed his apprenticeship in Kentucky, he eventually established the Graniteville Manufacturing Company in South Carolina. Arguing for more internal manufacturing of cotton, he also urged the South to prepare financially for secession. In 1845 he wrote *Essays on Domestic Industry*. Before the war he served two years in the state legislature but was unsuccessful in an attempt to gain election to the upper house in 1858. Having bought new equipment before the outbreak of hostilities, the manufacturer was able to keep his enterprise running throughout the war. Through his articles in *DeBow's Review* and his signing of South Carolina's secession document, he played an important role in bringing about the war for which he had prepared. He rebuilt his plant after the war but died soon thereafter from exposure while repairing a mill dam. (Mitchell, Broadus, *William Gregg, Factory Master of the Old South*)

GREER, Elkanah Brackin (1825-1877)

Having served under Jefferson Davis in the 1st Mississippi Rifles during the Mexican War, Tennessee native Elkanah B. Greer received a commission of brigadier general from the Confederate president. A Texas farmer and businessman, he had been a leader in the pro-expansion of slavery Knights of the Golden Circle. This group would later become a band of Southern sympathizers in the North during the Civil War. Joining the Confederate army, his assignments included: colonel, 3rd Texas Cavalry (July 1, 1861); brigadier general CSA (October 8, 1862); chief, Bureau of Conscription, Trans-Mississippi Department (October 8, 1862-May 26, 1865); also commanding Texas Reserve Forces (1864); and also commanding Reserve Corps, Trans-Mississippi Department (March 27-May 26, 1865). At the head of his regiment—then known as the South Kansas-Texas Mounted Regiment—he fought at Wilson's Creek. Slightly wounded at Pea Ridge, he was promoted to brigadier general the next fall and assigned to conscript duty. In the final stages of the war he was also in charge of the reserve forces in Texas. After the war he resettled in Texas and later moved to Arkansas.

GRENFELL, George St. Leger (1807-1868?)

Not, strictly speaking, a soldier of fortune, since he had recently inherited funds adequate enough to enable him to serve the Confederacy without pay, George St. Leger Grenfell was certianly a military adventurer. Born in England, he was denied his father's permission to join the French army. He subsequently served as a French Foreigh Legion officer, with various Arab chieftains, against Mediterranean pirates, as a British officer, with the Turks in the Crimean War, against the Sepoy Mutiny, and with Garibaldi in both South America and Italy before heading to America in early 1862 to join the Confederacy. Although lacking a commission, he served as Morgan's adjutant for half a year before a dispute with the general led to his departure. From November 1862 until the following spring he was a cavalry inspector with the Army of Tennessee. In May 1863 he was appointed a lieutenant colonel of cavalry, legitimatizing his position on General Wheeler's staff. But Grenfell got himself arrested in June for aiding a slave to escape. Bailed out by General Bragg, he went east and, in September 1863, joined Jeb Stuart's cavalry in Virginia. This lasted until January when he rejoined Morgan for two months before leaving the South. Taking the amnesty oath in Washington he went "hunting" in Illinois. Here he got caught up in the conspiracy to free the prisoners at Camp Douglas and stage an uprising in the Northwest. The depth of his involvement is a matter of dispute. He was arrested on November 6, 1864, and convicted, early the next year, primarily on the testimony of ex-Confederate captain John Shanks with whom Grenfell had had a dispute in 1862. Of all the conspirators, Grenfell received the harshest sentence—death. His sentence was commuted to life imprisonment on Dry Tortugas. Being the last conspirator in confinement and despairing of being released, Grenfell on March 7, 1868, fled the island prison, with three other prisoners and a bribed guard. None of the five was ever seen again, apparently drowning in the rough seas. (Starr, Stephen Z., *Colonel Grenfell's Wars: The Life Of A Soldier Of Fortune*)

GRESHAM, Walter Quintin (1832-1895)

The battle of Peachtree Creek brought an effective end to the field career of Union General Walter Q. Gresham. The native Indianan lawyer and state legislator was a moderate Republican who had been at odds with Governor Oliver P. Morton over the distribution of patronage jobs. Thus Gresham was initially turned down when he applied for a commission and was forced to raise his own company, which was mustered into the 38th Indiana. His assignments included: lieutenant colonel, 38th Indiana (September 18, 1861); colonel, 53rd Indiana (March 10, 1862); brigadier general, USV (August 11, 1863); commanding 3rd Brigade, 4th Division, 17th Corps, Army of the Tennessee (August 26, 1863-May 27, 1864); and commanding

Union General Walter Q. Gresham. (*Leslie's*)

the division (May 27-July 20, 1864). Not haaving seen any major action with his first unit he was colonel of a new regiment the following March. This unit took part in the advance on Corinth, Mississippi. Gresham led the regiment in Grant's attempt to get at Vicksburg through central Mississippi and was present in the later stages of the siege of the city itself. Named a brigadier general that summer, he took part in Sherman's Meridian Campaign. By June 8, 1864, when the 17th Corps joined the main army under Sherman on its drive against Atlanta, Gresham was in command of the division. As the Union forces were closing in on the city, he was wounded in the knee at Peachtree Creek. Holding no further commands, he was brevetted major general for the war and mustered out on April 30, 1866. Unsuccessfully running for political office in later years, he was Chester A. Arthur's postmaster general. By prohibiting the Louisiana state lottery from the mails he severely injured that corrupt organization. He also served as secretary of the treasury and judge and died as the less than outstanding secretary of state for Grover Cleveland. He was a long-shot presidential contender in 1884, 1888, and 1892. (Gresham, Matilda, *Life of Walter Quintin Gresham 1832-1895*)

GRIER, Robert Cooper (1794-1870)

In 1863 Supreme Court Associate Justice Robert C. Grier gave the majority opinion in the vital *Prize Cases*. A Pennsylvania lawyer, he served for 13 years as the presiding judge of a county court and on August 3, 1846, was named to the highest court in the land by President James K. Polk. He was confirmed on a voice vote the next day to the seat, which had been vacant for two years. In the *Dred Scott* case he favored dismissal on the grounds that the appellant was still a slave and therefore not a citizen eligible to bring a case before a state or national court. However, he also felt that the lower court should be upheld on the merits of the case. In the case over the legitimacy of the Union blockade he argued that the Civil War was both a war and an insurrection and thus ships running it were subject to seizure as prizes. His argument carried by a vote of five to four. At the suggestion of his colleagues, he resigned on January 31, 1870, upon the grounds of ill health and after 23 years on the bench. (Fehrenbacher, Don E., *The Dred Scott Case: Its Significance in American Law and Politics*)

GRIERSON, Benjamin Henry (1826-1911)

One of the greatest, and militarily most important cavalry raids of the Civil War was the raid of Benjamin H. Grierson and his brigade through the length of Mississippi in the spring of 1863. The Pittsburgh-born Illinois music teacher and merchant entered the Union army early in the war as a volunteer without pay. His assignments included: captain and volunteer aide-de-camp (May 8, 1861); major, 6th Illinois Cavalry (October 24, 1861); colonel, 6th Illinois Cavalry (April 12, 1862); commanding 3rd Brigade (assigned to District of Memphis), Cavalry Division, 13th Corps, Army of Tennessee (November-December 18, 1862); commanding 1st Brigade, Cavalry Divi-

Famed cavalry raider Benjamin H. Grierson. (*Leslie's*)

sion, 16th Corps, Army of the Tennessee (December 18, 1862-March 31, 1863); commanding 1st Brigade, 1st Cavalry Division, 16th Corps, Army of the Tennessee (March 31-June 9, 1863); commanding Cavalry Brigade, 19th Corps, Department of the Gulf (May-July 1863); brigadier general, USV (June 3, 1863); commanding 1st Division, 16th Corps, Army of the Tennessee (July 24-September 24, 1863, October 24, 1863-April 27, 1864, and May 11-June 20, 1864); commanding Cavalry Corps, District of West Tennessee, Army of the Tennessee (June-November 1864); commanding 4th Division, Cavalry Corps, Military Division of the Mississippi (November 9-December 13, 1864); commanding Cavalry Division, District of West Tennessee, Army of the Tennessee (December 1864-March 1865); commanding Cavalry Corps, Military Division of West Mississippi (March-May 1865); and major general, USV (March 19, 1866, to rank from May 27, 1865). At first he served as a staff member to Benjamin M. Prentiss in Illinois and Missouri and then was made a battalion commander in a mounted regiment. With this unit, of which he soon became colonel, he served in Tennessee and northern Mississippi in some minor affairs and participated in Grant's campaign against Vicksburg by a route through central Mississippi. The purpose of his famous 800-mile ride from La Grange, Tennessee, to Baton Rouge, Louisiana, was to distract attention from Grant's planned crossing of the Mississippi River below Vicksburg. With three regiments, 6th and 7th Illinois Cavalry and 2nd Iowa Cavalry, and Battery K, 1st Illinois Light Artillery, he made the raid in the period from April 17 to May 2, 1863. In the operation he fought numerous skirmishes and a more significant action at Wall's Brigade. With a loss of three killed, seven wounded, nine missing, and seven left behind sick or tending the wounded, the command killed or wounded an estimated 100 and paroled an additional 500. Also, 1,000 horses and mules were captured, 50 or more miles of rail and telegraph lines were destroyed, 3,000 stands of arms were destroyed as well as large quantities of other government supplies. The month after arriving in Baton Rouge Grierson was appointed a brigadier general. Returning from the Gulf, he again commanded mounted troops in Sherman's Meridian Campaign and fought against Nathan Bedford Forrest at Brice's Cross Roads, Tupelo, and during Andrew J. Smith's invasion of Mississippi. In 1864 he made a second major Mississippi raid and then went on to the operations against Mobile. In March 1866 he received the next to last appointment as a major general in the Civil War era—he had been brevetted to that grade on February 10, 1865—but it was backdated to May 1865. Mustered out of the volunteer service on April 30, 1866, he soon received the colonelcy of one of the two newly created regiments of black troopers. For nearly a quarter century he commanded the 10th Cavalry in the Southwest until his appointment in 1890 as a brigadier general in the regular army. He retired that same year. In 1867 he had received the brevets in the regular establishment of brigadier and major general for his two Mississippi raids. His first raid provided the basis for the movie "The Horse Soldiers."

GRIFFEN, John (?-1884)

In the mid-1850s New York native John Griffen developed the first wrought iron cannon, and it became one of the standard guns of the Union army, especially the horse artillery, due to its light weight and easy maneuverability. Discussions with army officers in Philadelphia led Griffen, Superintendent of the Safe Harbor Iron Works of Lancaster, Pennsylvania, to team up with the Reeves' Phoenix Iron Company. His early prototypes managed to surpass the army's testing procedures more than a hundred times over. The coming of the Civil War brought a flood of orders for what was designated a three-inch ordnance rifle. More than 1,400 were manufactured and delivered to the Union forces at prices ranging from $320 to $350 each. One of these guns, with the Union horse artillery, fired the first artillery shot of the battle of Gettysburg. Griffen stayed as superintendent of the Phoenix works until his death, continuing his prewar career as an inventor of note.

GRIFFIN, Charles (1825-1867)

Native Ohioan and West Pointer (1847) Charles Griffin survived a reputation as a troublemaker to rise from a battery commander to leader of an infantry corps in the final days of the war in Virginia. Posted to the artillery after his graduation, he served in Mexico and on the frontier before returning to his alma mater in 1860 as an artillery instructor. Upon the outbreak of hostilities he organized the "West Point Battery," which later became Battery D of the newly authorized 5th Artillery. His wartime assignments include: first lieutenant, 2nd Artillery (since June 30, 1849); captain, 2nd Artillery (April 25, 1861); captain, 5th Artillery (May 14, 1861); brigadier general, USV (June 9, 1862); commanding 2nd brigade, 1st Division, 5th Corps, Army of the Potomac (June 26-October 30 and November 1-16, 1862); commanding the division (October 30-November 1, November 16-December 26, 1862, February 1-May 5, July 21-October 24, 1863, April 3-July 21, August 9-December 24, 1864, and January 4-April 1, 1865); commanding the corps (January 26-February 1 and April 1-June 28, 1865); and major general, USV (April 2, 1865). With his battery of four 10-pound Parrotts and two 12-pound Howitzers he fought on Henry House Hill at 1st Bull Run as part of David Hunter's division. Although he lost all of his guns except one of the Parrotts, he was brevetted for his role in the battle. Taking his battery to the Peninsula, he was named a brigadier general during the midst of the campaign and took charge of a 5th Corps brigade for the Seven Days. He remained with this corps until the end of the war. Although not actively engaged at 2nd Bull Run he got caught up in the controversy over Fitz-John Porter's role in the battle. Despite his support for Porter, Griffin survived and was able to remain in command. As a division commander he fought at Fredericksburg and Chancellorsville but was ill during the Pennsylvania Campaign. Although he arrived on the field of Gettysburg on the third day, he was unable to assume command. He served in the Bristoe Campaign and rejoined the division for the Overland Campaign, during which he earned a brevet for the Wilderness, and also fought at Spotsylvania and Cold Harbor. During the Petersburg operations he was again brevetted for the Weldon Railroad. At Five Forks he took charge of the corps when Gouverneur K. Warren was removed, having incurred the displeasure of Sheridan. For his role in the crushing attack that led to the fall of Richmond and Petersburg he was brevetted a regular army brigadier. Having been brevetted major general of volunteers on August 1, 1864, he was given full rank on April 2, 1865, the day he participated in the final assault on Petersburg. Taking part in the final campaign, he was named one of the commissioners assigned by Grant to organize the surrender of Lee's army. This is somewhat ironic since Grant had often considered Griffin to be insubordinate. For his war service, Griffin was brevetted major general of regulars and was mustered out of the volunteers on January 15, 1866. That same year he was advanced to colonel, 35th Infantry, and placed in charge in Texas. He died of yellow fever in Galveston on September 15, 1867.

GRIFFIN, Simon Goodell (1824-1902)

A state legislator before the Civil War, Simon G. Griffin found that his military career did not aide him in a quest for a seat in Congress—as it had countless others—and he ended up serving in the state body. He had been born in New Hampshire and entered upon the practice of law the year before hostilities broke out. Enlisting as a company commander early in the war, his assignments included: captain, 2nd New Hampshire (June 1, 1861); lieutenant colonel, 6th New Hampshire (November 28, 1861); colonel, 6th New Hampshire (April 22, 1862); commanding 1st Brigade, 2nd Division, 9th Corps, Army of the Potomac (February-March 1863); commanding 1st Brigade, 2nd Division, 9th Corps, Army of the Ohio (May 21-June 14 and August 18-30, 1863); commanding 1st Brigade, 2nd Division, Army of the Tennessee (June 14-August 18, 1863); commanding 2nd Division, 9th Corps, Army of the Ohio (August 25-October 1863); commanding 2nd Brigade, 2nd Division, 9th Corps, Army of the Potomac (May 1-December 22, 1864, February 25-April 2, and April 22-May 3, 1865); brigadier general, USV (May 12, 1864); and commanding the division (April 2-May 1, 1864, December 22, 1864-January 1865, April 2-22 and May 3-August 1, 1865). After fighting in Burnside's brigade at 1st Bull Run he resigned his captaincy on October 31, 1861, in order to become second-in-command of a new regiment. While serving on the North Carolina coast he was promoted to colonel and as such commanded the regiment at 2nd Bull Run, Antietam, and Fredericksburg. Transferred with the corps to the West, he served in Kentucky, during the Vicksburg and Jackson sieges, and back with the Army of the Ohio, much of the time in brigade command. He then reorganized the regiments from his native state for a return to Virginia campaigning. In the course of the Overland Campaign, he was awarded a brigadier general's star and went on to command a division during part of the Petersburg Campaign. He was brevetted major general for his role in the final assaults and capture of the city. Mustered out on August 24, 1865, he was engaged in railroading and land speculation in occupied Texas and manufacturing back in New Hampshire. Despite three terms in the state legislature, he lost two bids for Congress.

GRIFFITH, Richard (1814-1862)

Jefferson Davis' adjutant during the Mexican War, Richard Griffith, became a Confederate brigadier and, in late 1861, a focal point in the feud between Davis and General Joseph E. Johnston. After serving in the 1st Mississippi Rifles in Mexico, Griffith, a former Vicksburg teacher, became a banker in Jackson and was the state's treasurer at the time of its secession. As the first colonel of the 12th Mississippi, he went to Virginia and arrived at Manassas a few days after 1st Bull Run. His later assignments included: brigadier general (November 2, 1861); commanding Clark's old Brigade, First Corps, Army of the Potomac (November 2-9, 1861); commanding a Mississippi Brigade, Forces at Leesburg, Potomac District, Department of Northern Virginia (November 9, 1861-early 1862); commanding same brigade, D.H. Hill's Divison, Department of Northern Virginia (early 1862-April 18, 1862); and commanding same brigade, Magruder's Division, Department of Northern Virginia (April 18-June 29, 1862). While serving around Leesburg, it was decided in Richmond that Mississippi regiments should be assigned to the brigades of Griffith and General W.H.C. Whiting. Johnston, however, felt that it was not advisable to reorganize in the face of the enemy. This dispute continued for months. In the end, Griffith led his brigade to the Peninsula, and in the battle of Savage Station on June 29, 1862, during McClellan's retreat from in front of Richmond,

Griffith was mortally wounded. He died in Richmond that evening. (Freeman, Douglas S., *Lee's Lieutenants*)

GRIGSBY, Andrew Jackson (1819-1895)

Profanity may have been the root cause of Virginian Andrew Jackson Grigsby's leaving the Confederate army. A Shenandoah Valley farmer, he had seen service in a Missouri unit during the Mexican War. Based upon this experience he was quickly commissioned in the Southern army. His assignments included: major, 27th Virginia (June 12, 1861); lieutenant colonel, 27th Virginia (October 14, 1861); colonel, 27th Virginia (May 28, 1862); commanding Stonewall Brigade, Jackson's (old) Division, Jackson's Corps, Army of Northern Virginia (August 30-September 17, 1862); and commanding the division (from September 17, 1862). After serving at 1st Bull Run, Kernstown, and in the early part of Shenandoah Valley Campaign of 1862, he was promoted to command of the regiment. Following the close of the campaign, the 27th moved to the Richmond area and took part in the Seven Days Battles where Grigsby was wounded at Malvern Hill. Missing the fighting at Cedar Mountain, he rejoined the army in time for 2nd Bull Run where he was slightly wounded at Groveton on August 28, 1862. Two days later he assumed command of the Stonewall Brigade upon the death of Colonel W.S.H. Baylor. He suffered a third wound later that day but remained in command for the rest of the battles. After serving at the capture of Harpers Ferry, Grigsby commanded the brigade at Antietam and succeeded to the direction of the division. Knowing that Stonewall Jackson was going to appoint a staff officer to the permanent command of the brigade, Grigsby resigned on November 19, 1862. Legend has it that the pious Jackson refused to promote a man who swore so much. But Jackson had other concerns. The 27th had an extremely high casualty rate and he feared that this was due to its commanders. He was also worried about a lack of discipline in the regiment and Grigsby's failure to deal promptly with a mutiny. Grigsby was also a leader in the conspiracy of silence against a previous brigade commander. (Robertson, James, I., Jr., *The Stonewall Brigade*)

GRIMES, Bryan (1828-1880)

North Carolina planter Bryan Grimes survived Civil War injuries only to be assassinated a decade and a half after the war's close. His Confederate assignments included: major, 4th North Carolina (May 16, 1861); lieutenant colonel, 4th North Carolina (May 1, 1862); colonel, 4th North Carolina (June 19, 1862); commanding Ramseur's Brigade, D.H. Hill's Division, 2nd Corps, Army of Northern Virginia (December 1862); brigadier general, CSA (May 19, 1864); commanding Daniel's (old) Brigade, Rodes' Division, same corps and army (June 4-13, 1864); commanding brigade, Rodes' Division, Valley District, Department of Northern Virginia (June 13-September 19 and September 20-October 19, 1864); commanding the division (September 19-20 and October 19-December 1864); commanding division, 2nd Corps, Army of Northern Virginia (December 1864-April 9, 1865); major general, CSA (February 15, 1865). He served with his regiment at Yorktown and Williamsburg and commanded it at Seven Pines and South Mountain. Kicked by a horse in the latter, he was out of action for several months but returned to lead the brigade at Fredericksburg. He led the 4th at Chancellorsville, suffering another wound, Gettysburg, the Wilderness, and Spotsylvania. He was promoted and transferred to command the brigade of deceased General J. Daniel, which he led from Cold Harbor to the outskirts of Washington. At 3rd Winchester he succeeded to the command of Rodes' Division when Rodes was killed. Replaced by General Ramseur the next day, he led his brigade at Fisher's Hill. When Ramseur was killed at Cedar Creek, Grimes took over the division and led it from Petersburg to Appomattox. He was the last major general assigned to Lee's army. He ran his plantation until his assassination in a deportation case. (Freeman, Douglas S., *Lee's Lieutenants*)

GRIMES, James Wilson (1816-1872)

Republican Senator James W. Grimes took the lead in expanding the scope of what was to be the Joint Committee on the Conduct of the War. Born in New Hampshire, he took up the practice of law in what became the state of Iowa. Entering politics, he served in the territorial legislature and was the state's governor from 1854 to 1858. The next year he took his senate seat and held it until his resignation on December 6, 1869. When Senator Zachariah Chandler proposed an investigative panel to examine the causes of the Union defeats at 1st Bull Run and Ball's Bluff, and James H. Lane added Wilson's Creek and Lexington, Grimes suggested that Big Bethel and Belmont be included as well. He then proposed that the committee be empowered to investigate all failures of the Union military. In a final revision, he initiated the idea of a joint committee with the power to investigate the conduct of the war, not just its failures. This committee became a thorn in the side of the Lincoln administration and cost many generals their reputations. It is interesting to note that Grimes had been a member of the Washington Peace Conference earlier that year in a futile effort to prevent hostilities.

GRIMKÉ, Angelina Emily (1805-1879)

Despite being born into a wealthy, aristocratic Charleston, South Carolina, family, Angelina E. Grimké and her sister Sarah rebelled at Southern society. Although initially influenced by her older sister, by the age of 30 she was far more radical in her opposition to slavery and at the formalism of the Espiscopal Church. Having experimented with Presbyterianism, Angelina moved to Philadelphia and became a Quaker but found that they were too restricting in regard to her wish to end slavery. An 1835 letter she wrote to William Lloyd Garrison speaking out against slavery was published in the *Liberator*. This started her on a public campaign. The next year she wrote *Appeal to the Christian Women of the South*, making her *persona non grata* in her native city. She was active on the lecture circuit until her health declined after her marriage to fellow abolitionist Theodore Weld in 1838. She spent the rest of her life teaching in New Jersey and Massachusetts but kept an active interest in the cause. (Birney, Catherine H., *The Grimké Sisters: Sarah and Angelina Grimké*)

GRIMKÉ, Sarah Moore (1792-1873)

Like her sister Angelina, Sarah M. Grimké was a devout abolitionist, shocking the senses of 1830s America by taking to the lecture platform, an almost unheard-of action for women. Born into a wealthy Charleston family, she found herself becoming disenchanted with Southern society, especially the Episcopal Church and the institution of slavery. Having been introduced to Quakers on a trip to Philadelphia, she eventually moved there and joined the Friends. Both sisters soon found the Quakers too confining for their political beliefs. Although she had greatly influenced her sister in their earlier years, by the 1830s Sarah was the more conservative. For several years she was active in the abolition and women's rights movements until she started teaching in Massachusetts. (Birney, Catherine H., *The Grimké Sisters: Sarah and Angelina Grimké*)

GRINNELL, Josiah Bushnell (1821-1891)

An early abolitionist, Josiah B. Grinnell is credited with delivering the first antislavery sermon in the nation's capital. A native of Vermont, he was forced to leave his Washington church after the sermon and took a pastorate in New York. A failing voice prompted him to take his friend Horace Greeley's advice and go West. Settling in Iowa, he helped found the town of Grinnell, Grinnell College, and the Iowa Republican Party. He continued to speak out against slavery and was a delegate to the party's convention in 1860. From 1863 to 1867 he was a congressman from Iowa and a strong backer of Lincoln. Defeated for governor in the latter year, his career in the party came to an end when he supported Greeley over Grant in 1872. He resumed his practice of law and was active in railroading, education, and agriculture. (Grinnell, Josiah Bushnell, *Men and Events of Forty Years*)

GROSE, William (1812-1900)

Ohio-born Indiana lawyer and judge William Grose served in brigade and higher command for over two years before being named a brigadier general. His assignments included: colonel, 36th Indiana (October 23, 1861); commanding 19th Brigade, 4th Division, Army of the Ohio (June 2-July 10, 1862); commanding 10th Brigade, 4th Division, Army of the Ohio (August 16-September 29, 1862); commanding 10th Brigade, 4th Division, 2nd Corps, Army of the Ohio (September 29-November 5, 1862); commanding 3rd Brigade, 2nd Division, Left Wing, 14th Corps, Army of the Cumberland (November 5, 1862-January 9, 1863); commanding 3rd Brigade, 2nd Division, 21st Corps, Army of the Cumberland (January 9-March 12 and April 14-October 9, 1863); commanding 3rd Brigade, 1st Division, 4th Corps, Army of the Cumberland (October 10-December 31, 1863, January 31-July 27, August 5-September 5, 1864, November 29, 1864-February 16, 1865, March 16-31 and May 9-June 7, 1865); commanding the division (July 27-August 5, 1864 and February 16-March 16, 1865); brigadier general, USV (July 30, 1864); and commanding 2nd Brigade, 2nd Division, 4th Corps, Army of the Cumberland (October 10-November 29, 1864). Unlike most units of Buell's relieving force, Grose's regiment fought on both days at Shiloh. His brigade was not engaged at Perryville but fought at Murfreesboro and at Chickamauga, Chattanooga, and before Atlanta where, after assuming temporary division command, he was named a brigadier general. Fighting against Hood at Franklin and Nashville he was brevetted, somewhat belatedly, major general on August 13, 1865. Resigning on December 31, the Democrat turned Republican served as tax official and state commissioner on the board charged with the supervision of mental care. In 1891 he published his history of his old regiment, *The Story of the Marches, Battles and Incidents of the Thirty-Sixth Regiment Indiana Volunteer Infantry.*

GROVER, Cuvier (1828-1885)

Serving in New Mexico at the outbreak of the Civil War, Cuvier Grover refused to surrender and managed to safely withdraw his command. A West Pointer (1850) from Maine, he had been posted to the artillery before transferring to the infantry in the 1855 enlargement of the regular establishment. His Civil War-era assignments included: captain, 10th Infantry (since September 17, 1858); brigadier general, USV (April 14, 1862); commanding 1st Brigade, 2nd Division, 3rd Corps, Army of the Potomac (April 27-September 16, 1862); commanding the division (briefly in August 1862); commanding brigade, Military District of Washington, Army of the Potomac (October-November 1862); commanding U.S. Forces Baton Rouge (also styled a division), Department of the Gulf (December 16, 1862-January 3, 1863); commanding 4th Division, 19th Corps, Department of the Gulf (January 3-July 30, 1883); major, 3rd Infantry (August 31, 1863); commanding 3rd Division, 19th Corps, Department of the Gulf (October 2, 1863-January 12, 1864); commanding 2nd Division, 19th Corps, Department of the Gulf (February 15-June 18 and June 25-July 5, 1864); commanding 2nd Division, 19th Corps, Army of the Shenandoah (August 6-October 19, November 10-December 8, 1864, and December 28, 1864-January 6, 1865); commanding the corps (December 8-28, 1864); commanding division, Department of the South (January 6-February 12, 1865); and commanding District of Savannah, Department of the South (February 12-June 5, 1865). The veteran of western railroad explorations and the Mormon expedition was on leave from November 1861 to April 1862 when he was named a brigadier general in the volunteer service. On the Peninsula he led a brigade at Yorktown and was brevetted for Williamsburg and Seven Pines. After fighting at the Seven Days he joined Pope's army for 2nd Bull Run where he succeeded to direction of the division. Sent to the Gulf coast, he was active in the campaigns against Port Hudson and along the Red River. In the summer of 1864 his division was sent to reinforce the Army of the Potomac but was diverted to the Shenandoah Valley where

Union division commander Cuvier Grover. (*Leslie's*)

he fought at 3rd Winchester and was brevetted major general of volunteers for Fisher's Hill. Wounded at Cedar Creek, he was brevetted brigadier general in the regulars. After commanding at Savannah in the final months of the war he was mustered out of the volunteers on August 24, 1865. Having been brevetted major general for his war service, he remained in the army until his death while serving as colonel, 1st Cavalry.

GROW, Galusha Aaron (1823-1907)

The speaker of the U.S. House of Representatives during the first half of the Civil War was Pennsylvania Republican Galusha A. Grow. Originally a native of Connecticut, he had moved to Pennsylvania in 1834 and 13 years later was admitted to the practice of law. Beginning in 1853 he served three terms in Congress as a Free-Soil Democrat. His three subsequent congressional House terms were as a Republican. In 1857 he lost a bid to become that body's speaker but was successful four years later. He served as such from July 4, 1861, until he left Congress at the end of his sixth term, on March 3, 1863, to enter business. His interests included railroading, oil, coal, and lumber. However, he did keep up his activity in politics, attending three Republican national conventions as a delegate. In 1894-1903 he again sat in Congress but declined renomination in 1902. During the Civil War years he guided the Homestead Act through the House.

GUILD, Lafayette (?-?)

From the Seven Days to the trenches of Petersburg the medical needs of the Army of Northern Virginia were met by Surgeon Lafayette Guild, the army's medical director. He joined Lee's departmental staff in the spring of 1862. Throughout the war he fought against supply and transportation problems in an effort to provide the best treatment possible to wounded and ill Confederates. He is truly one of the unsung heroes of the Civil War.

GURLEY, Frank B. (?-1920)

The legitimate killing of Union General Robert L. McCook on August 5, 1862, brought Frank B. Gurley seemingly endless trouble. A member of Forrest's cavalry, he had been detailed to organize a company for the yet to be organized 4th Alabama Cavalry. At the time of the incident Gurley had succeeded in raising most of his company, and it was with this force together with another company that he attacked an ambulance and its escort. In riding past the ambulance, in pursuit of the escort, he fired at the man whipping the horses to higher speed. He wounded McCook in the abdomen. Returning later he heard of who he had shot and talked with the mortally wounded officer. Despite the rag-tag appearance of his attackers, McCook apparently believed them to be legitimate soldiers and never said anything to the contrary before he died the next day. But the North did not look at it that way. Although Gurley had a commission to raise troops from Forrest it was not legal since only Jefferson Davis, under Confederate law, could issue such authority. This meant Gurley was a guerrilla. Furthermore, Union accounts claimed that McCook had been shot—murdered—while lying in the vehicle. Gurley was officially mustered in as captain, Company C, 4th (Russell's) Alabama Cavalry, on November 23, 1862, and rejoined Forrest. After fighting at Chickamauga illness forced him to take a leave at home. He was captured there in October 1863 and almost immediately placed on trial. On January 11, 1864, he was found guilty and sentenced to the gallows. He was fortunate to have his case repeatedly delayed, and in January 1865, apparently by mistake, he was exchanged. After the close of the war Gurley thought his troubles were over, but he was wrong. Late in 1865 a nationwide search for the "murderer" of McCook was launched. He was arrested at his Madison County, Alabama, home on November 28, 1865, and was again scheduled for the hangman, but proceedings were suspended by Andrew Johnson two days later. He was finally released in April 1866. After that he hosted annual reunions for his regiment.

GWIN, William (?-?)

With the rank of lieutenant commander in the Union navy, William Gwin commanded various vessels in some of the major actions on the western rivers in the early stages of the Civil War. Commanding the USS *Tyler*, armed with one 32-pounder and six eight-inch guns, he fought at Forts Henry and Donelson, Shiloh, and in the action with the CSS *Arkansas* on July 15, 1862. At Shiloh his craft was one of only two gunboats in action. That summer he transferred to the command of the USS *Mound City* for the August raid up the Yazoo River. This vessel was equipped with one howitzer and 13 guns. In December 1862 he directed the USS *Benton*, 16 guns, on the Yazoo River.

H

HACKLEMAN, Pleasant Adam (1814-1862)

A brigadier for five months, Pleasant Hackleman died in his first battle as general. By the time of the Civil War, Hackleman had earned a distinguished career as a lawyer, judge, county clerk, and Republican congressional candidate. He participated in the failed peace conference at the start of the war. He was appointed colonel, 16th Indiana, on May 20, 1861, and led his regiment to Virginia in July. Serving in western Maryland and the Shenandoah Valley, the regiment saw little fighting. With the approach of the expiration of the 16th's time, Hackleman was appointed brigadier general, USV, on April 18, 1862. Ordered to the Department of the Tennessee on May 7, 1862, his commands included: 1st Brigade, 2nd Division, District of Corinth (September 1-24, 1862); and 1st Brigade, 2nd Division, Army of West Tennessee (September 24-October 3, 1862). On the first day of the battle of Corinth, Hackleman, while trying to rally the troops in the face of the Confederate assaults, was mortally wounded and he died that night.

HAGOOD, Johnson (1829-1898)

Despite becoming a lawyer during the antebellum period, Johnson Hagood never forgot his military education at the South Carolina Military Academy, the Citadel, and served in the state militia. By the outbreak of the war he was a brigadier but soon transferred to the volunteers. His assignments included: colonel, 1st South Carolina Volunteers (January 8, 1861); brigadier general, CSA (July 12, 1862); commanding 2nd Military District of South Carolina, Department of South Carolina, Georgia and Florida (July 19, 1862-June 1863); commanding brigade, 1st Subdivision, 1st Military District of South Carolina, same department (September-October 22, 1863); commanding Eastern Division (or 1st Sub-District), 7th Military District of South Carolina, same department (October 22, 1863-January 1864); commanding brigade, same district and department (January-April 1864); commanding brigade, Hoke's Division, Department of North Carolina and Southern Virginia (May-October 19, 1864); commanding brigade, Hoke's Division, Anderson's Corps, Army of Northern Virginia (October 19-December 20, 1864); commanding brigade, Hoke's Division, Department of North Carolina (December 1864-March 1965); commanding brigade, Hoke's Division, Hardee's Corps (March-April 9, 1865); and commanding brigade, same division and corps, Army of Tennessee (April 1865). After service in Charleston Harbor during the firing on Fort Sumter, Hagood took his regiment to Manassas, but it returned to South Carolina to reorganize prior to going into Confederate service. Hagood remained behind and as a volunteer private in Kershaw's 2nd South Carolina fought at 1st Bull Run. He led the reorganized unit at Secessionville and soon thereafter received a commission as brigadier. For almost two years he was stationed in his native state but in the spring of 1864 he was sent to the Petersburg area and fought at Port Walthall Junction, Drewry's Bluff, joined Lee at Cold Harbor, and then served through the first months of the Petersburg siege. In December 1864 the division was sent to North Carolina and after fighting at Bentonville was surrendered as a part of J. E. Johnston's army. Hagood had been sent a short time before to South Carolina to recruit for his unit. He played an active role in the wresting of power from the Reconstruction forces and eventually was elected governor. (Hagood, Johnson, *Memoirs of the War of Secession*)

HAHN, Michael (1830-1886)

The first elected Unionist governor of Louisiana—in the occupied areas of the state—was Bavarian native Michael Hahn. Raised in New Orleans, he practiced law in the Crescent City until its occupation by Union forces. An opponent of slavery, he was elected as a Unionist to the Thirty-seventh Congress, taking his House seat on December 3, 1862. At the expiration of his term the following March, he took up journalism in Louisiana. As the candidate of the Union Free Trade Party, he was elected governor of the Union-controlled portions of the state on February 22, 1864. He was sworn in on March 4 and favored the granting of suffrage to the freed slaves. Named to the U.S. Senate, he resigned on March 3, 1865, to present his credentials, but, the climate having changed with Lincoln's death, he was never seated. He then edited the *New Orleans Daily Republican*, served in the state house, superintended the U.S. Mint there, sat as a judge, and died while serving as a Republican in the Forty-ninth Congress. (Fortier, Alcee, *A History of Louisiana*)

HALE, John Parker (1806-1873)

The first member of the U.S. Senate to be named to it as an antislavery candidate was John P. Hale of New Hampshire. Admitted to the bar in his native state in 1830, he entered the state legislature two years later. Andrew Jackson appointed Hale a U.S. attorney in 1834 but he was removed by John Tyler in 1841. As a Democratic member of the House of Representatives, 1843-45, he bucked the instructions of the state legislature in order to vote against the annexation of Texas. In 1846 he returned to the state legislature as its speaker and the next year returned to Washington as senator. In 1848 he withdrew as the presidential candidate of the Liberty Party. In the following presidential canvass he was the Free-Soil candidate. He returned to the Senate in 1855 to fill a vacancy and held the seat until March 3, 1865, when he was named to head the diplomatic mission in Madrid until 1869.

HALL, Cyrus (ca. 1825-1878)

An Illinois hotel owner, Cyrus Hall served through three years of the Civil War only to lose his commission—temporarily—when his unit was consolidated due to casualties and the expiration of terms of enlistment. He had served as both an enlisted man and officer during the Mexican War. His Civil war assignments included: captain, Company B, 14th Illinois (May 25, 1861); major, 7th Illinois Cavalry (September 21, 1861); colonel, 14th Illinois (February 1, 1862); commanding 2nd Brigade, 4th Division, Right Wing, 13th Corps, Army of the Tennessee (November 1-December 18, 1862); commanding 2nd Brigade, 4th Division, 17th Corps, Army of the Tennessee (December 18, 1862-January 20, 1863 and August 7, 1863-March 16, 1864); commanding 2nd Brigade, 4th Division, 16th Corps, Army of the Tennessee (January 20-March 22 and April 22-July 28, 1963); commanding 2nd Brigade, 4th Division, 13th Corps, Army of the Tennessee (July 28-August 7, 1863); colonel, 144th Illinois (October 21, 1864); and colonel, 14th Illinois (March 13, 1865). Originally an infantry company commander, he was soon promoted to command of a cavalry battalion, before returning to his original regiment as its colonel. He led the regiment at Shiloh, in the Corinth siege, and at the battle of the Hatchie. He was given charge of a brigade in the 4th Division, which successively served in the 13th, 17th, 16th, 13th, and 17th corps. This he lead through the Vicksburg and Jackson campaigns. On May 25, 1864, he was mustered out when it became apparent that the 14th and 15th Illinois regiments would have to be consolidated into one battalion. That fall he became colonel of a one-year regiment, which was stationed at St. Louis. Resigning this commission on March 7, 1865, he was recommissioned in his old regiment just before the close of the fighting, when the two regiments were reconstituted. He was finally mustered out of the service on September 16, 1865.

HALL, James Abram (?-1893)

Maine artillerist James A. Hall played a crucial role in the defense of the 1st Corps' position on the first day at Gettysburg. His assignments included: first lieutenant, 2nd Maine Battery (November 20, 1861); captain, 2nd Maine Battery (May 22, 1862); major, 1st Maine Light Artillery Battalion (July 19, 1863); commanding Camp Barry, 22nd Corps, Department of Washington (late 1863, July 9-August 9, September 22-October 12, October 26-November 1, 1864 and April 7-May 7, 1865); lieutenant colonel, 1st Maine Light Artillery Battalion (September 9, 1864); and colonel, 2nd United States Veteran Volunteers (August 15, 1865). After service in his own state and in Washington, he commanded his battery at 2nd Bull Run. He directed the six three-inch Rifles at Fredericksburg and Chancellorsville. Then, when the 1st Corps relieved John Buford's cavalry along the Chambersburg Pike, Hall's battery relieved John H. Calef's horse battery astride the road and held its position through much of the heavy fighting. Shortly thereafter Hall was made the major of the grouping of Maine's previously independent batteries. As such he was assigned to the Washington defenses and was generally in command of the artillery at Camp Barry in the capital itself. Brevetted brigadier general for his war service, he finished the war there and was mustered out on July 22, 1865. The next month he was commissioned in the veteran volunteers and was finally mustered out on March 1, 1866.

HALL, Maria M.C. (?-?)

Turned down for nursing service by Dorothea Dix—who considered her too young and pretty for the corps—Maria M.C. Hall wrangled a position on her own at the Patent Office hospital for Indiana troops. Starting her nursing in July 1861, she went to the Peninsula the next spring and joined the United States Sanitary Commission, serving on one of the hospital boats. Later field work included the Maryland Campaign. She left the field in the summer of 1863 and became the administrator for an Annapolis hospital.

HALL, Norman Jonathan (ca. 1837-1867)

The youngest officer in the garrison, Michigan West Pointer (1858) Norman J. Hall was serving as acting assistant quartermaster and acting assistant commissary of subsistence for Fort Sumter at the outbreak of hostilities. As a second lieutenant in Company H, 1st Artillery, he was in charge of the evacuation of the soldiers' dependents when the crisis arose. After the surrender, Hall was in charge of the detail that fired the salute to the flag as it was lowered. His later assignments included: first lieutenant, 5th Artillery (May 14, 1861); colonel, 7th Michigan (July 14, 1862); commanding 3rd Brigade, 2nd Division, 2nd Corps, Army of the Potomac

(September 17-December 15, 1862 and March 20-July 18, 1863); and captain, 5th Artillery (August 1, 1863). Hall served in the Peninsula Campaign as adjutant general on the staff of Brigadier General Barnard, the Army of the Potomac's Chief of Engineers. Transferring to the volunteers, he was appointed to command the 7th Michigan, which had also seen service in the Peninsula Campaign. He led the regiment at Antietam until he relieved his wounded brigade commander, General Dana. He then led the brigade in the assault on the stone wall on Marye's Heights at Fredericksburg and at Chancellorsville. At Gettysburg his brigade held the position to the left front of the copse of trees, famed as the "High Water Mark of the Confederacy." During Pickett's Charge, the brigade was driven back into the trees but aided in the final repulse of the Confederates. Hall left the volunteers and returned to the regulars on June 4, 1864, and retired from the military on February 22, 1865. He earned brevets in the regular army as captain for Antietam, major for Fredericksburg, and lieutenant colonel for Gettysburg.

HALL, Robert M. (?-1874)

An enlisted man in the regular army at the beginning of the Civil War, Robert M. Hall, a native of Scotland, served through much of the conflict as a staff officer and rose in the war's final months to the command of a brigade of black troops. Starting as a private in 1848, he was first sergeant of Company M, 1st Artillery, on November 13, 1861, when he embarked on his duties as an officer. His assignments included: second lieutenant, 1st Artillery (October 24, 1861); first lieutenant, 1st Artillery (February 20, 1862); colonel, 38th United States Colored Troops (December 31, 1864); commanding 1st Brigade, 1st Division, 25th Corps, Department of Texas (September 22-October 5, 1865); and commanding 2nd Brigade, 1st Division, 25th Corps, Department of Texas (October 5-December 8, 1865). Early in the war he served on the staffs of Truman Seymour, John P. Hatch, and William Birney in the Department of the South, much of the time in Florida. He won regular army brevets for Bermuda Hundred and the Darbytown Road and was given charge of a regiment of Virginia blacks at the end of 1864. After taking part in the occupation of Richmond he was sent to join Sheridan in Texas and commanded a brigade there. Brevetted brigadier general of volunteers for the war, he was finally mustered out of that service on January 25, 1867, with his regiment. Remaining in the regular army, he died while on active duty as the regimental quartermaster of the 1st Artillery.

HALL, William Preble (1820-1882)

While serving as Missouri's lieutenant governor, William P. Hall also held the rank of brigadier general in the state militia. A native of Virginia, he had moved to Missouri and taken up the practice of law before serving as an enlisted man in the state volunteers during the Mexican War. In the interwar period he served three terms in the House and was defeated in a bid for the Senate. When the three top executive offices in the state were declared vacant by the state convention—the incumbents having joined the Confederacy—Hall was named lieutenant governor and took up his duties in June 1861. Meanwhile he was active in military affairs and his assignments included: brigadier general, Missouri Militia (ca. 1861); commanding District of Northwest Missouri, Military District of the Missouri (August 25-September 24, 1862); and commanding District of Northwest Missouri, Department of the Missouri (September 24, 1862-April 10, 1863). With the January 31, 1864, death of Governor Hamilton R. Gamble, Hall was sworn in as the new chief executive. During his administration Price's invasion of the state was turned back and the divided state began to recover from the effects of civil warfare. Gamble's unexpired term ran out on January 2, 1865, and Hall left office to farm and resume his law practice. (McElroy, John, *The Struggle for Missouri*)

HALLECK, Henry Wager (1815-1872)

The Civil War career of the much-maligned Union commander in chief and chief of staff, Henry W. Halleck, was summarized by Secretary of the Navy Gideon Welles as he "originates nothing, anticipates nothing, . . . takes no responsibility, plans nothing, suggests nothing, is good for nothing." This harsh assessment was shared by many but is really unfair. The New York native and West Pointer (1839) had been posted to the engineers and earned a brevet in Mexico. He also worked on fortifications, taught at the academy, and studied the French military. His writings included: *Report on the Means of National Defense*, *Elements of Military Art and Science*, and a translation of Henri Jomini's *Vie Politique et Militaire de Napoleon*. Due to his scholarly pursuits he became known as "Old Brains," but this sobriquet became derogatory during the Civil War. Resigning as a captain in 1854, he became highly successful in the San Francisco law profession and helped frame the state's constitution. He maintained his interest in martial affairs through the militia and was recommended by Winfield Scott for a high post at the outset of the Civil War. His assignments included: major general, USA (August 19, 1861); commanding Department of the Missouri (November 19, 1861-March 11, 1862); commanding Department of the Mississippi (March 13-September 19, 1862); commander in chief (July 11, 1862-March 12, 1864); chief of staff (March 12, 1864-ca. April 16, 1865); commanding Department of Virginia and Army of the James (April 16-June 28, 1865); and commanding Military Division of the James (April 19-June 27, 1865). Succeeding John C. Frémont at St. Louis, he straightened out the mess that had been left behind. After Grant, his subordinate, had captured Forts Henry and Donelson, Halleck was rewarded with command of all the forces in the West. His enlarged command won victories at Pea Ridge, Island #10, and Shiloh. Taking immediate command of his three united field armies after the latter battle, he proved to be an incapable field commander in his only campaign. The advance on Corinth, Mississippi, was so slow that the Confederates were able to withdraw at their leisure; Halleck was advancing at a rate of about one mile per day and then entrenching. Made commander in chief shortly thereafter, he displayed tremendous administrative abilities, but many of his subordinates complained that he never gave adequate indications of what he wanted them to do or kept them informed of what other field leaders were doing. Halleck was also noted for a tendency to blame others for failures and was deeply resented by most top generals. When Grant took over as commander in chief, Halleck became the army's staff head and proved highly capable, if unpopular. At the end of the war he commanded in Virginia and later on the Pacific. He died while heading the Division of the South at Louisville, Kentucky. (Ambrose, Stephen E., *Halleck: Lincoln's Chief of Staff*)

HALPINE, Charles Graham (1829-1868)

A humorist writer before the Civil War, Charles G. Halpine is best remembered for his humorous articles, under the name of "Private Miles O'Reilly," written during the war while he served on David Hunter's staff. A native of Ireland and a graduate of Trinity College in Dublin, he had briefly studied both medicine and law before immigrating to the United States. Settling at first in Boston, he gained a reputation as a satirist for the *Boston Post* and as coeditor of the humorous weekly, the *Carpet-Bag*. He soon moved to New York where he contributed to the *Herald* and *Tribune* and became an editor with the *Times*, for which paper he covered the Washington scene and Walker's Nicaragua filibustering expedition. Long active in political matters, even in Ireland, he served for a time as Stephen Douglas' private secretary. He entered the military upon the outbreak of the Civil War, where his assignments included: private, Company D, 69th New York Militia (April 20, 1861); major and assistant adjutant general, USV (September 5, 1861); and temporarily assigned as lieutenant colonel and assistant adjutant general, USV (November 8, 1862-July 1, 1863). After a brief stint as an enlisted man—including the battle of 1st Bull Run—he was mustered out with his regiment on August 3, 1861. He shortly received a position on General Hunter's staff. Throughout his military career he wrote humorous articles for the nation's press under the penname "Private Miles O'Reilly." A collection of his works was published in 1864 as *The Life and Adventures, Songs, Services, and Speeches of Private Miles O'Reilly*. Like Hunter, his chief, Halpine favored the enlistment of black troops and wrote the famous poem, "Sambo's Right to be Kilt," to influence public opinion. He also drafted Hunter's order to raise the first such unit. Halpine received a brevet for his actions at Piedmont in 1864 and two more, to brigadier, for his war service. However, failing eyesight caused him to resign on July 31, 1864. For the four remaining years of his life he continued his versatile writing and was active in trying to reform New York's Tammany Hall. He died by an accidental overdose of chloroform as a result of his use of opiates to cure insomnia. (Hanchett, William, *Irish: Charles S. Halpine in Civil War America*)

Charles Halpine as "Private Miles O'Reilly." (NA)

HAMBLIN, Joseph Eldridge (1828-1870)

Taking part in all of the campaigns of the armies of the Potomac and the Shenandoah, New York insurance broker Joseph E. Hamblin rose from regimental adjutant to brigade commander during the Civil War. The Massachusetts native had been active in the 7th New York Militia from 1851 to 1861, except for four years when he lived in St. Louis. He accompanied the unit to Washington at the outbreak of the war and then became the adjutant of Duryée's Zouaves. His assignments included: first lieutenant and adjutant, 5th New York (May 14, 1861); captain, 5th New York (September 8, 1861); major, 65th New York (November 4, 1861); lieutenant colonel, 65th New York (July 20, 1862); colonel, 65th New York (May 26, 1863); commanding 1st Brigade, 3rd Division, 6th Corps, Army of the Potomac (December 30, 1863-January 10, 1864); commanding 4th Brigade, 1st Division, 6th Corps, Army of the Potomac (June 20-July 6, 1864); commanding 2nd Brigade, 1st Division, 6th Corps, Army of the Shenandoah (September 19-October 19, 1864); commanding 3rd Brigade, 1st Division, 6th Corps, Army of the Potomac (January 31-March 17, 1865); commanding 2nd Brigade, 1st Division, 6th Corps, Army of the Potomac (March 17-June 28, 1865); and brigadier general, USV (May 19, 1865). As regimental adjutant he fought at Big Bethel and then in the defenses at Baltimore. Named major of the "1st U.S. Chasseurs," or 65th New York, he served in the capital's defenses and then went to the Peninsula where he fought at Yorktown, Williamsburg, Seven Pines, and in Seven Days. At Antietam he was the regiment's lieutenant colonel but the unit was too far to the rear to take part in the action. He fought at Fredericksburg and succeeded to regimental command at Chancellorsville. Named permanently to the post, he fought at Gettysburg and took part in the Bristoe and Mine Run campaigns. During the Overland Campaign he fought at the Wilderness, Spotsylvania, and Cold Harbor. In the early stages of the Petersburg fighting he succeeded to command of the brigade. Going to the Shenandoah Valley under Sheridan, he again took over a brigade at 3rd Winchester. This he led at Fisher's Hill and until his wounding at Cedar Creek. For this last battle he was brevetted brigadier general. Returning to the Petersburg lines, he again led a brigade at Hatcher's Run and won another brevet, as major general, at Saylor's Creek during the Appomattox Campaign. Promoted to a full brigadier generalship after the close of hostilities, he was mustered out on January 15, 1866, and returned to the brokering of insurance in New York. Rejoining the state national guard, he became its adjutant general and chief of staff three years before his death. (Hamblin, Deborah, *Brevet Major General Joseph Eldridge Hamblin 1861-1865*)

HAMBRIGHT, Henry Augustus (?-1893)

Mexican War veteran (as a first sergeant of Pennsylvania volunteers) Henry A. Hambright served in the western theater and won the brevet of brigadier general on June 7, 1865, for the war. The Pennsylvania native's assignments included: captain, 1st Pennsylvania (April 20, 1861); captain, 11th Infantry (May 14, 1861); colonel, 79th Pennsylvania (October 18, 1861); and commanding in the 14th Corps, Army of the Cumberland: 3rd Brigade, 1st Division, Center (November 5-December 20, 1862); 3rd Brigade, 1st Division (March 9-April 17, 1863); 2nd Brigade, 1st Division (April 17-21, June 15-July 30, and September 28-October 9, 1863); again 3rd Brigade, 1st Division (January 12-March 23, September 12-November 18, 1864 and March 28-June 6, 1865); and 1st Brigade, 1st Division (June 8-July 18, 1865). After serving as a company commander under Robert Patterson and receiving a regular army commission, he was mustered out with his regiment on July 26, 1861. Three months later he took charge of a volunteer regiment and led it at Perryville and Murfreesboro, for which he was brevetted. During the Tullahoma Campaign he commanded a brigade but at Chickamauga he was again in charge of his regiment. Brevetted for that battle, he went on to win another in the Atlanta Campaign. Becoming ill during the March to the Sea, he relinquished command of a brigade. He rejoined this unit during the Carolinas Campaign and was mustered out of the volunteer service on July 20, 1865. Remaining in the regular establishment, he retired in 1879 as major, 19th Infantry.

HAMILTON, Andrew Jackson (1815-1875)

Texas Unionist Andrew Jackson Hamilton was forced to flee the South and became a Union brigadier general. Born in Alabama, he practiced law there before moving to Texas and becoming the state attorney general. In Congress during the secession crisis, he refused to leave until the end of his term, unlike the rest of the delegation. Then, sitting in the state legislature, he worked against secession but after it came about fled via Mexico. Lincoln then made him a brigadier general of volunteers, on November 14, 1862, and installed him as the military governor of Texas. The Senate failed to ratify his commission and it expired on March 4, 1863. However, Lincoln reappointed him on September 18, 1863. Never holding a field command, he spent most of the war in New Orleans at the head of a kind of government in exile. Following the collapse of the Confederacy he was appointed provisional governor in June 1865, and he resigned his commission on June 9, 1865, to take up his duties. Highly successful in reorganizing the state governmental machinery, he favored a moderate form of Reconstruction. Opposed to disenfranchisement on a wholesale basis, he was backed for the governorship by local whites in 1869 but was defeated. Thereafter he was little involved in politics.

HAMILTON, Charles Smith (1822-1891)

An ambitious officer, Charles Hamilton was not above using political pressure to gain advancement. A West Pointer (1843) and Mexican War veteran wounded at Molino del Ray, Hamilton had returned to civil life in 1853 as a farmer and flour manufacturer. He served for six days as colonel, 3rd Wisconsin, before being appointed in the first batch of volunteer brigadier generals on May 17, 1861. His later assignments included: commanding 3rd Brigade, Banks' Division, Army of the Potomac (October 8, 1861-March 13, 1862); commanding 3rd Division, 3rd Corps, Army of the Potomac (March 13-April 30, 1862); commanding 3rd Division, Army of the Mississippi (June 18-October 1862); major general, USV (September 19, 1862); commanding 3rd Division, Army of West Tennessee (October 24-30, 1862); commanding Left Wing, 13th Corps (November 1-December 18, 1862); and Left Wing, 16th Corps (December 22, 1862-April 1, 1863); Army of the Tennessee; and also temporarily commanding 16th Corps, Army of the Tennessee (January 10-February 5, 1863). During the siege of Yorktown when McClellan removed Hamilton from command of his division, tremendous political pressure was brought to bear on the commander of the Army of the Potomac. He stood firm however, and Hamilton was dispatched to Pope's Army of the Mississippi. After a creditable showing at the battle of Iuka, Hamilton, on the first day at Corinth, failed to take advantage of an exposed Confederate flank. He made up for this mistake, at least in part due to vague orders, the next day with a flank attack. That winter Hamilton started lobbying for command of the 17th Corps and privately wrote his senator that Grant, who had apparently pushed for his promotion to major general, was, in fact, a drunkard. Grant complained to Washington of Hamilton's maneuvering to take over McPherson's Corps, although he did not know of the drunkard charge. In April 1863, Hamilton, under pressure, submitted his resignation, which was accepted on the 13th. He returned to Wisconsin and resumed his manufacturing career and was subsequently appointed U.S. marshal by President Grant. (Catton, Bruce, *Grant Moves South*)

HAMILTON, Schuyler (1822-1903)

Being unfit for duty, Schuyler Hamilton realized that his appointment as a Union major general could not be sent to the Senate for confirmation under the law, and he therefore submitted his resignation. The New York City native and West Pointer (1841) had been posted to the infantry, with which he served in the Mexican War, earned two brevets, and suffered a lance wound in the lung that was to give him trouble for the balance of his life. After the war and until his 1855 resignation as a first lieutenant in the 1st Infantry he was an aide to Winfield Scott. He gave up farming in 1861 in order to put on a uniform again. His assignments included: private, 7th New York Militia (April 19, 1862); lieutenant colonel and military secretary to Scott (May 9, 1861); colonel and additional aide-de-camp (August 7, 1861); brigadier general, USV (November 12, 1861); commanding in the Army of the Mississippi: 1st Division (February 23-March 4, 1862); 2nd Division (March 4-April 24, 1862); and 3rd Division (April 24-May 29, 1862); and major general, USV (September 17, 1862). Following a brief tour in the famous New York militia unit he served as Scott's military secretary until the latter's retirement in November 1861. At that time Hamilton was named brigadier general and sent to the West. Under John Pope, he took part in the actions at New Madrid and Island #10. As a part of Halleck's forces, he led a division in the advance on Corinth. Shortly thereafter he was attacked by malaria and forced to relinquish his command. Named major general in September, he resigned on February 27, 1863, as unfit for duty. His health ruined by long and arduous service, he was unsuccessful in attempts to be placed on the retired list.

HAMLIN, Cyrus (1839-1867)

Despite entering the army relatively late in the war, Cyrus Hamlin, the son of Lincoln's first vice president, nevertheless rose to the rank of brigadier general while serving with black troops. A lawyer at the outbreak of the war, he continued to practice until the spring of 1862. His assignments included: captain and additional aide-de-camp (April 3, 1862); commissary of subsistence, Mountain Department (spring 1862); colonel, 8th Corps d'Afrique (February 12, 1863); commanding 2nd brigade, 1st Division, Corps d'Afrique, Department of the Gulf (September 22, 1863-April 23, 1864); colonel, 80th United States Colored Troops (designation change April 4, 1864); commanding 1st Division, Corps d'Afrique, Department of the Gulf (April 23-June 9, 1864); commanding 3rd Division, United States Colored Troops, Department of the Gulf (October 1864); brigadier general, USV (December 13, 1864); and commanding Post of Port Hudson, Northern District of Louisiana, Department of the Gulf (February 13-July 1865). After serving on Fremont's staff in the Shenandoah he volunteered for service with black troops and was active in their recruitment in Louisiana. He was present at Port Hudson and later commanded a brigade and then a division of ex-slaves. Brevetted major general for the war, he was mustered out on January 15, 1866. As a carpetbag lawyer in New Orleans he died of yellow fever the next year.

HAMLIN, Hannibal (1809-1891)

When it appeared that the Republicans were headed for defeat in 1864, it was found that Lincoln's first vice president, Hannibal Hamlin, was expendable. Born and raised in Maine, he had been admitted to the bar in 1833 and became a Democratic politician serving in the state legislature, including three years as the speaker of the lower house. After one unsuccessful attempt, he entered the U.S. House of Representatives in 1843 where the "Carthaginian of Maine," as he was known, became a leader of the Free-Soil faction of the party. In line with district tradition, he left the House after two terms and served briefly back in the legislature before being named to the Senate in 1848. While he believed that the central government did not have the right to abolish existing slavery, he vehemently opposed any attempts to spread the institution into new territories. Thus Democratic support for the Kansas-Nebraska Bill brought him into conflict with the party. On June 12, 1856, he bolted the party and resigned his seat. The Republicans elected him governor and after a matter of weeks he was back in the Senate as a Republican. Despite instructions to his friends not to manipulate a place on the presidential ticket in 1860, he was nominated for the number two spot. Not meeting Lincoln until after the election, he found himself relegated to the political limbo represented by his office. Although friendly with Lincoln, he tended to more radical views and his advice was generally welcomed but rarely acted upon. Distressed by his position, Hamlin was pleased when, on June 18, 1862, Lincoln requested that he postpone a planned trip home to Maine in order to accompany him to the presidential retreat at the Soldiers' Home. After dinner the president showed him the draft of the Emancipation Proclamation. He was the first to see the document that he had long been urging. Hamlin was honored when most of his wording suggestions were approved. The main point of dispute, however, was the timing of the document's issuance. Hamlin wanted it immediately, but Lincoln wanted it to follow a Union military victory. Hamlin later acknowledged that the president had been right. Returning to his relative obscurity as presiding officer of the Senate, where he abolished the Senate's bar, he continued in the expectation of being renamed as Lincoln's running mate. Although Lincoln declared a hands-off policy, leaving the matter in the hands of the convention, he apparently maneuvered behind the scenes for Andrew Johnson. Returning home early in 1865, Hamlin was bitter against everyone but the president, whom he did not believe to be involved. He altered that opinion in 1889. During the war Hamlin also had a military career, as a private in Company A, Maine Coast Guards, and actually served in the ranks during a two-month encampment. Appropriately, two of his sons served in command of black troops, a policy he had long favored. After the war he served as collector at Boston, again as a senator, and as minister to Spain. During the last period he traveled extensively through Europe. (Hunt, H. Draper, *Hannibal Hamlin of Maine*)

HAMMOND, William Alexander (1828-1900)

At the beginning of the Civil War, former army Assistant Surgeon William Hammond gave up a lucrative practice and a professorship at the University of Maryland to rejoin the medical corps. A graduate of New York University's Medical College, Hammond had served from 1849-1860 with the army on the frontier before resigning to go into teaching and private practice. Reenlisting on May 28, 1861, he was responsible for establishing military hospitals in Maryland. Becoming popular with General McClellan, and the Sanitary Commission, he was named surgeon general with the rank of brigadier general on April 25, 1862, in place of the retired Colonel C.A. Finley. Bringing new life into the department, Hammond oversaw the medical service as it provided the best care for the wounded ever seen in any war to that time. He eliminated the excessive red tape of a peacetime staff department and supervised the establishment of the system of ambulance corps for the armies in the field. Coming into conflict over his methods with Secretary of War Stanton, Hammond was, on September 3, 1863, sent on inspection duties leaving the Washington office in the hands of Colonel J.K. Barnes. He was later court-martialed and dismissed from the service for alleged irregularities in the distribution of liquor contracts, though this charge was subsequently removed. He returned to civil life and was successful in private practice and research.

HAMPTON, Wade (1818-1902)

One of the largest plantation and slave owners in the South, Wade Hampton, with no military training, rose to the second highest rank in the Confederate army. Organizing and equipping a legion of infantry, cavalry, and artillery in his home state of South Carolina, he offered it to the government. His assignments included: colonel, Hampton's (S.C.) Legion (July 1861); commanding brigade, Whiting's-Smith's Division (known as Forces Near Dumfries in Potomac District until March), Department of Northern Virginia (fall 1861-May 31, 1862); brigadier general, CSA (May 23, 1862); commanding 3rd Brigade, Jackson's (old) Division, Jackson's Command, Army of Northern Virginia (June 28-July 1862); commanding brigade, Cavalry Division, same army (July 28, 1862-July 3, 1863); major general, CSA (September 3, 1863); commanding division, Cavalry Corps, same army (December 1863-August 11, 1864); commanding Cavalry Corps, same army (August 11, 1864-January 19, 1865); commanding Cavalry, Johnston's Command (February-April 9, 1865); lieutenant general, CSA (February 15, 1865); and commanding Cavalry, Army of Tennessee (April 9-26, 1865). He distinguished himself and was slightly wounded leading his infantry at 1st Bull Run. Commanding a brigade he was wounded at Seven Pines but returned in time to command a different brigade in the latter part of Seven Days. Transferring to the cavalry, with which he was to become famous, he fought at Antietam and took part in Stuart's ride around McClellan's army in Maryland. He was at Fredericksburg and made a series of raids that winter. He was wounded in the cavalry fight at Gettysburg and, when he returned to duty late that year, he had already been given a division and a major generalcy. He fought at the Wilderness, but after Stuart's death he was not given charge of the cavalry, despite the fact that he was the senior division commander. Instead, Lee had the three cavalry divisions report directly to him. Hampton fought at Trevilian Station and on the flanks of the siege lines at Petersburg. In August he was finally given overall command of the mounted troops. In September 1864 he staged a brilliant raid, bringing in 2,500 head of cattle for the hungry Confederates. On one occasion he is reported to have released a bathing federal soldier he came across but he kept his clothes. True to the soldier's word to name a son for the Confederate, Hampton met a Northern youngster years later, while he was serving in the Senate, who identified himself as the naked soldier's son and said that he had been named in honor of the Confederate cavalryman. Early in 1865, Hampton was detached from Lee's army to recruit his old division and was then promoted and assigned to command Wheeler's Cavalry Corps and his own former division under M.C. Butler. Thus in charge of all Johnston's cavalry, he fought at Bentonville and surrendered with Johnston. He reentered politics and after Reconstruction dominated South Carolina for many years, serving as governor and senator. (Wellman, Manly Wade, *Giant in Gray: A Biography of Wade Hampton of South Carolina*)

HANCOCK, Winfield Scott (1824-1886)

Although named for America's top military hero of the day, Winfield Scott Hancock was not originally intended for a military career; nevertheless he was destined to become one of the best corps commanders in the Union army. An 1844 graduate of West Point, he had served in the infantry during the Mexican War and earned a brevet before transferring to the quartermaster's department. His Civil War assignments included: captain and assistant quartermaster (since November 7, 1855); brigadier general, USV (September 23, 1861); commanding 3rd Brigade, Smith's Division, Army of the Potomac (October 3, 1861-March 13, 1862); commanding 1st Brigade, 2nd Division, 4th (6th after May 18) Corps, Army of the Potomac (March 13-September 17, 1862); commanding 1st Division, 2nd Corps, Army of the Potomac (September 17, 1862-January 24, 1863 and February 20-May 22, 1863); major general, USV (November 29, 1862); commanding the corps (May 22-July 1, and July 2-3, 1863 and March 24-June 18 and July 27-November 26, 1864); major and quartermaster (November 30, 1863); brigadier general, USA (August 12, 1864); commanding 1st Veteran Volunteer Corps (November 27, 1864-February 27, 1865); commanding Middle Military Division (February 27-June 27, 1865); also commanding Department of West Virginia (February 28-March 1, March 7-20, and March 22-June 27, 1865); major general, USA (July 26, 1866). Fearing that he would be left to sit in

Winfield Scott Hancock (seated) with his division commanders. Left to right: Francis C. Barlow, David B. Birney, and John Gibbon. (AC)

California—where he had been instrumental in frustrating the plans of local secessionists—while the war raged elsewhere, he was ordered East for quartermaster duties but arrived to a brigadier's star. Taking his brigade to the Peninsula, he led a critical flank attack at Williamsburg and earned the sobriquet "Superb." He continued to distinguish himself during the rest of the dismal campaign. During the battle of Antietam, Israel B. Richardson was killed and Hancock was sent to command his division in the 2nd Corps—thus beginning an historic association. At Fredericksburg his division took part in the costly assaults on Marye's Heights and at Chancellorsville he skillfully covered the Union withdrawal. With corps commander Couch's request for transfer accepted, Hancock stepped up to the 2nd Corps leadership. With the fall of John F. Reynolds early on the first day at Gettysburg, Meade dispatched Hancock to take over that wing of the army and decide whether the battle should be fought there or not. This was a high honor since Oliver O. Howard, a senior officer, was already on the field. Belatedly he received the Thanks of Congress for this action. On the second and third days of the battle Hancock directed the Union center until wounded by a nail and by wood fragments—possibly from his saddle—driven into his thigh by enemy fire. A long recovery followed during which he performed some recruiting duty. Returning in time for the Overland Campaign, he fought well at the Wilderness and was brevetted major general in the regular army for his crashing through the Confederate salient at Spotsylvania. At Cold Harbor his troops were slaughtered in a futile assault ordered by Grant. Arriving on the Petersburg front, he deferred command to the corps commander on the field—because of a lack of knowledge of the situation—who failed to launch a final assault, which could very well have ended the war 10 months earlier. Shortly afterwards Hancock's old wound broke open and he had to leave the army for a time. Returning, he was humiliated by the defeat at Reams' Station and in November was forced to give up field command; he began recruiting the 1st Veteran Volunteer Corps. Results were poor and early in 1865 he took over command in Washington, D.C., Maryland, West Virginia, and the Shenandoah Valley. Following the Confederacy's collapse he came into conflict with Grant who objected to his lenient treatment of the South. He was mustered out of the volunteer service on July 26, 1866, the same day that he received the appointment of major general in the regular establishment. Remaining in the army, he held various departmental commands and was a potential Democratic candidate for the presidency in 1868. In 1880 he was the nominee but was narrowly defeated by James Garfield. He died, still on active duty. (Tucker, Glenn, *Hancock: The Superb*)

HANGER, James E. (1843-1919)

A college sophomore, Jim Hager left school to join Captain Franklin Sterrett's Virginia company, the Churchville Cavalry, in the spring of 1861. On June 3 his company was present when the battle of Philippi, or more aptly the "Philippi Races," occurred. Among the few Confederate casualties was Private Hanger who had been struck in the leg by a cannonball and captured. His leg amputated, he was exchanged and returned home to work secretly for several months designing and constructing a homemade artificial limb out of barrel staves. His whittling became popularly known and he started to make these "Hanger Limbs" for other unfortunate Confederates. He eventually received a commission from the state government to manufacture even more. His enterprise became J.E. Hanger Comapny, still in business today.

HANNON, Moses Wright (1827-?)

General Joseph Wheeler claims that one of his brigade commanders, Moses W. Hannon, received a promotion to brigadier general in the final stages of the war, but there is no official record of this. Hannon's assignments included: lieutenant colonel, 1st Alabama Cavalry (ca. December 3, 1861); colonel, 53rd Alabama Partisan Rangers (November 5, 1862); commanding brigade, Hume's Division, Cavalry Corps, Army of Tennessee (April-May 1864); commanding brigade, Kelly's Division, Cavalry Corps, Army of Tennessee (May-fall 1864 and April 9-26, 1865); commanding brigade, Kelly's Division, Wheeler's Cavalry Corps, Department of South Carolina, Georgia and Florida (fall 1864-April 9, 1865). The Georgia-born merchant entered the Confederate army upon the outbreak of the war and, after his initial regiment served at Shiloh, he raised a regiment of partisans, which at first served under General Roddey in northern Alabama. Joining Wheeler, he fought at Chickamauga and commanded a small brigade in the Atlanta Campaign, after he was detached from Roddey's command. This may have had something to do with his resignation the previous December, which had been revoked in January. He served in the delaying actions against Sherman in the Savannah and Carolinas campaigns. His command was ordered disbanded on January 2, 1865, but the order appears never to have been carried out. He was praised by Wheeler for his service in the final campaigns and after the war he was a merchant in Alabama and Louisiana and a planter in Texas.

HANSON, Roger Weightman (1827-1863)

When Roger W. Hanson received the order to make a suicidal attack in his first, and last, battle as a Confederate brigadier general, he reportedly wanted to go to army headquarters and kill Braxton Bragg. Following service as the first lieutenant of an independent company of volunteers from his native Kentucky during the Mexican War, he was admitted to the bar. In the late 1850s he lost a bid for the U.S. Congress and, as a conservative on secession, backed John Bell for president in 1860; he then favored the neutrality of his state during the early stages of the war. Finally won over to secession, his assignments included: colonel, Kentucky State Guard (August 19, 1861) colonel, 2nd Kentucky (September 3, 1861); commanding 1st (Kentucky) Brigade, Army of Middle Tennessee, Department #2 (ca. September-November 20, 1862); commanding 4th (Kentucky) Brigade, 1st (Breckinridge's) Division, Hardee's Corps, Army of Tennessee (November 20, 1862-January 2, 1863); and brigadier general, CSA (December 13, 1862). Following initial service in central Kentucky, he was detached with his regiment to join the garrison at Fort Donelson where he was captured. Exchanged for Michael Corcoran on August 27, 1862, he took command of the Kentucky Brigade. Known for his strict discipline he was "Old Flintlock" to his men. In the antebellum period he had been wounded in the leg during a duel. Never recovering full use of the leg, he was also nicknamed "Bench Leg." Promoted to brigadier general he led the Orphan Brigade at Murfreesboro. There on January 2, 1863, Breckinridge's division was ordered to assault the Union left. Breckinridge and his brigade commanders realized it was futile but obeyed orders. Hanson was mortally wounded and died on the 4th. (Davis, William C., *The Orphan Brigade*)

HARBIN, Thomas (?-?)

Like his brother-in-law Thomas Jones on the Maryland side of the Potomac River, Thomas Harbin ran a Confederate signal station on the Virginia shore, reporting on Union naval movements. He was called upon to aid in the escape of John Wilkes Booth and David Herold. When the fugitive pair finally managed to cross the river on April 22, 1865, Harbin met them and turned them over to a guide who took them to the home of Dr. Richard H. Stewart. There is also some evidence that Harbin had been part of the original plan to kidnap Lincoln and smuggle him South to Richmond for a prisoner exchange.

HARDEE, William Joseph (1815-1873)

Problems with Braxton Bragg affected only slightly the outstanding record of the premier lieutenant general to serve in the Confederate Army of Tennessee. By the time that this Georgian West Pointer (1838) resigned as lieutenant colonel, 1st Cavalry, on January 31, 1861, he was one of the most distinguished and well-known officers in the old army. Serving in the Seminole and Mexican conflicts, he won two brevets in the latter and was wounded at La Rosia, Mexico. He returned to his alma mater as a tactics instructor and served as commandant of cadets. His textbook *Rifle and Light Infantry Tactics*, or more familiarly *Hardee's Tactics*, became the standard textbook and was widely used by both sides during the Civil War. Joining the Confederacy, his assignments included: colonel, Cavalry (March 16, 1861); brigadier general, CSA (June 16, 1861); commanding Upper District of Arkansas, Department #2 (July 22-October 1861); major general, CSA (October 7, 1861); commanding 1st Division, Central Army of Kentucky, Department #2 (October 28-December 5, December 18-December 1861, and February 23-March 29, 1862); commanding the army (December 5-18, 1861 and December 1861-February 23, 1862); commanding 3rd Corps, Army of the Mississippi (March 29-July 5, 1862); commanding the army (July 5-August 15, 1862); commanding Left Wing, Army of the Mississippi (August 15-November 20, 1862); lieutenant general, CSA (October 10, 1862); commanding 2nd Corps, Army of Tennessee (November 20, 1862-July 14, 1863); commanding Army of the Department of Mississippi and East Louisiana (July 14-November 1863); commanding 1st (Polk's old) Corps, Army of Tennessee (November-December 2, 1863, December 22-January 1864, early 1864-August 31, and September 2-October 5, 1864); commanding the army (December 2-22, 1863); commanding his own and Lee's corps, Army of Tennessee (August 31-September 2, 1864); commanding Department of South Carolina, Georgia and Florida (October 5, 1864-February 16, 1865); commanding Hardee's Corps, cooperating with Joseph E. Johnston's forces (February 16-April 9, 1865); and commanding corps, Army of Tennessee (April 9-26, 1865). As a brigadier general, he served in Arkansas and was then promoted to major general and assigned to central Kentucky. He commanded one of the corps in the Confederate attacks at Shiloh where he was wounded. He led his corps during the defense of Corinth, Mississippi, and after leading the Army of Mississippi into Kentucky under Bragg, he commanded the left at Perryville. One of the original lieutenant generals allowed under Confederate law, he led an official corps at Murfreesboro and during the Tullahoma Campaign. In order to get away from the despised army commander, Bragg, he took an assignment in Mississippi under Joseph E. Johnston but after taking part in the minor operations there was recalled to the Army of Tennessee to take over Leonidas Polk's corps at Chattanooga and during the Atlanta Campaign. During the final stages of the latter, i.e., at Jonesboro, he was in charge of two corps in the Confederate attacks. Disenchanted with Hood's leadership, he accepted transfer to command of the Atlantic coast and served there for the balance of the war. He was unable to stop Sherman's March to the Sea but successfully evacuated Savannah at the last minute. Forced to abandon Charleston as Sherman's command bypassed it, he continued to withdraw into North Carolina with his "corps" drawn from the coastal defenders. Joining Johnston's forces, his last fight was at Bentonville. It was also the last for his only son who was killed there. In the final reorganization and consolidation of the Army of Tennessee he retained corps command. His new corps comprised two divisions of Army of Tennessee men who had previously served under him and one from the Department of North Carolina. This force he surrendered along with Johnston's command on April 26, 1865. "Old Reliable" refused command of the army just after the disaster at Chattanooga but seems to have found his appropriate position as a top corps leader. After the war he settled on an Alabama plantation. (Hughes, Nathaniel C., *General William J. Hardee: Old Reliable*)

HARDEMAN, William Polk (1816-1898)

This veteran of the War for Texan Independence and the Mexican War saw his entire Confederate service west of the Mississippi, and eventually rose to the rank of brigadier general. William P. Hardeman's assignments included: captain, 4th Texas cavalry (1861); lieutenant colonel, 4th Texas Cavalry (1862); colonel, 4th Texas Cavalry (late 1862); commanding 3rd (Texas) Cavalry Brigade, 1st (Texas) Cavalry Division, 2nd Corps (or District of Arkansas), Trans-Mississippi Department (September 1864-March 1865); brigadier general, CSA (March 18, 1865); and commanding brigade, Bee's Division, Cavalry Corps, Trans-Mississippi Department (March-May 26, 1865). Taking part in the operations in New Mexico, he fought at Valverde. He then held various assignments in Texas while rising to command of his regiment by late 1862. He led it in the Red River Campaign and in the last eight months of the war was in command of a mounted brigade in Arkansas and Texas. Having been promoted to brigadier general two months before the surrender, he was a planter and minor office holder. During the war he had been known to his troops as "Gotch."

HARDIE, James Allen (1823-1876)

Probably the greatest service of staff officer James A. Hardie was carrying the order to the Army of the Potomac that relieved Joseph Hooker and placed George G. Meade in command just before Gettysburg. The New York City native and West Pointer (1843) was appointed to the artillery. During the Mexican War he served at San Francisco as the major of the 1st New York. His Civil War assignments included: captain, 3rd Artillery (since October 5, 1857); captain, 5th Artillery (May 14, 1861); lieutenant colonel and additional aide-de-camp (September 28, 1861-March 24, 1864); brigadier general, USV (November 29, 1862); major and assistant adjutant general, USA (February 9, 1863); and colonel and inspector general, USA (March 24, 1864). At the outbreak of hostilities he was the adjutant for the Department of Oregon but came east to serve as McClellan's adjutant on the Peninsula and as judge advocate during the fall of 1862. He was then named brigadier general and was placed by Burnside on the staff of William B. Franklin as something of a spy. For some reason that is not apparent in the records his appointment as a brigadier general was revoked on January 22, 1863. This was possibly due to the relief of Burnside. As a major in the adjutant general's branch, he carried the Hooker-Meade relief order from Washington. In 1864 he transferred to the inspector general's branch and served there for the balance of the war. He was brevetted brigadier general for the war and major general for his services in the inspector's department. He died on active service.

HARDIN, Martin Davis (1837-1923)

As a Union general, Martin D. Hardin seems to have been a magnet for bullets. The Illinois native, whose father had been killed in Mexico, was appointed to the artillery after his graduation from West Point in 1859. His Civil War assignments included: second lieutenant, 3rd Artillery (since January 2, 1860); first lieutenant, 3rd Artillery (May 14, 1861); lieutenant colonel, 12th Pennsylvania Reserves (July 8, 1862); colonel, 12th Pennsylvania Reserves (September 1, 1862); commanding 3rd Brigade, 3rd Division, 1st Corps, Army of the Potomac (December 30, 1862-January 10, 1863); commanding 3rd Brigade, 3rd Division, 5th Corps, Army of the Potomac (September 18-December 4, 1863); commanding 1st Brigade, 3rd Division, 5th Corps, Army of the Potomac (May 18-25, 1864); brigadier general, USV (July 2, 1864); and commanding Defenses North of the Potomac, 22nd Corps, Department of Washington (July 8, 1864-August 2, 1865). On the Peninsula he was aide-de-camp to Henry J. Hunt, the commander of the army's reserve artillery. Made second-in-command of one of the regiments of the Pennsylvania reserves, he led them at Groveton and 2nd Bull Run, earning brevets and suffering wounds at each. Made colonel a few days later, he missed Fredericksburg on account of his wounds. The unit itself was not at Chancellorsville but he commanded them at Gettysburg. In brigade command, he participated in the Bristoe and Mine Run campaigns. On December 14, 1863, he was wounded by guerrillas near Catlett's Station in northern Virginia. This wound cost him his left arm. Returning to duty during the Overland Campaign, he took command of a brigade of the Reserves at Spotsylvania but a week later fell wounded again at the North Anna River. Promoted to brigadier general that summer, he finished the war in command of the Washington defenses on the north side of the Potomac. He had been mustered out with his regiment on June 11, 1864, but had been recommissioned during Jubal Early's raid on the capital. He was brevetted brigadier general in the regular establishment for the war and was mustered out of the volunteers on January 15, 1866. Promoted to major of the 28th Infantry that year, he was retired in 1870 with the advanced grade of brigadier general due to his wounds and the loss of the arm. In the postwar years he practiced law and wrote on military history. Also active in veterans' affairs, it is ironic that when he died after World War I he was all but forgotten.

HARDING, Abner Clark (1807-1874)

In his only significant military action of the war, Abner C. Harding managed to administer a bloody repulse to Confederate cavalrymen Joe Wheeler and Nathan Bedford Forrest and was rewarded with the star of a brigadier general. The Connecticut native became an Illinois lawyer and politician, moving through a series of party affiliations to become a Republican. His Civil War services included: colonel, 83rd Illinois (August 21, 1862); and brigadier general, USV (March 13, 1863). His regiment was initially assigned to routine guard duty before being assigned as part of the garrison of Fort Donelson, which had been captured in February 1862. Taking command of the post early in 1863, he was called upon to surrender by the enemy cavalry. Refusing, he invited the Confederates to attack and on February 3, 1863, they did. The results was disastrous for the troopers and they were forced to withdraw. Harding was promoted and Forrest swore he would never serve under Wheeler again. Failing eyesight forced Harding to resign on June 3, 1863. However, the next year he was elected as a Republican congressman and served two terms from March 4, 1865, to 1869. Not seeking reelection in 1868, he went into railroading and banking.

HARDING, Benjamin Franklin (1823-1899)

When Joseph A. Wright left the U.S. Senate to become the U.S. commissioner to the Hamburg Expedition of 1863, Benjamin F. Harding took over his seat on the infamous Joint Committee on the Conduct of the War. Born in Pennsylvania, Harding practiced law in Illinois and California before settling in Oregon in 1850. Almost immediately entering politics, he rose to the speakership of the territorial legislature. He also served as U.S. district attorney and territorial secretary. On September 12, 1862, he was named to replace Senator Edward D. Baker who had been killed at Ball's Bluff. He took his seat on December 1 and held it until he retired at the conclusion of the incomplete term on March 3, 1865. In his brief tenure on the committee he did not take an active role in its investigations. He then retired to his farm.

HARDINGE, Belle Boyd

See: *Boyd, Belle*

HARKER, Charles Garrison (1835-1864)

Sherman's blunder in ordering the June 27, 1864, attack on Kennesaw Mountain cost the life of a promising young officer, Charles G. Harker. Posted to the infantry on the frontier after his 1858 graduation from West Point, the New Jersey native transferred to the volunteers during the first year of the Civil War. His assignments included: second lieutenant, 9th Infantry (since August 15, 1858); first lieutenant, 15th Infantry (May 14, 1861); captain, 15th Infantry (October 24, 1861); colonel, 65th Ohio (November 11, 1861); commanding 20th Brigade, 6th Division, Army of the Ohio (July 10-September 29, 1862); commanding 20th Brigade, 6th Division, 2nd Corps, Army of the Ohio (September 29-November 5, 1862); commanding 3rd Brigade, 1st Division, Left Wing, 14th Corps, Army of the Cumberland (November 5, 1862-January 9, 1863); commanding 3rd Brigade, 1st Division, 21st Corps, Army of the Cumberland (January 9-February 17 and March 17-October 9, 1863); commanding 3rd Brigade, 2nd Division, 4th Corps, Army of the Cumberland (October 10, 1863-June 27, 1864); and brigadier general, USV (April 10, 1864, to rank from September 20, 1863). After organizing Ohio troops he took charge of a volunteer regiment, which he led under Buell at Shiloh. Commanding a brigade, he was not engaged at Perryville but did fight at Murfreesboro and took part in the Tullahoma Campaign. On the second day at Chickamauga he won his brigadier general's star for his defensive fighting on Snodgrass Hill. Then at Chattanooga he led his brigade in the assault on Missionary Ridge. Having finally gotten his star, he directed his brigade through the Atlanta Campaign until cut down in the futile assault. He died a few hours later.

HARLAN, James (1820-1899)

A convert to the Republican Party, James Harlan served in the Senate throughout the Civil War and was secretary of the interior during the early Reconstruction period. Born in Illinois, he had moved with his family to Indiana in 1824 and 21 years later settled in Iowa where he entered upon the practice of law in 1848. He had served as a university president for two years when he took a seat in the Senate as a Whig on December 31, 1855. However, after much haggling his credentials were rejected and his seat was declared vacant on January 12, 1857. He was then reelected to the vacancy as a Republican and served continually until his May 15, 1865, resignation in order to become Andrew Johnson's interior secretary. Resigning the cabinet post on July 27, 1866, he returned to the Senate for one more term the next year. He subsequently served as a judge. (Brigham, Johnson, *James Harlan*)

HARLAND, Edward (1832-1915)

After participating in some of the major battles early in the Civil War, lawyer and Connecticut native Edward Harland spent the balance of the war on the coasts of Virginia and North Carolina. His assignments included: captain, Company D, 3rd Connecticut (May 11, 1861); colonel, 8th Connecticut (October 5, 1861); commanding 2nd Brigade, 3rd Division, 9th Corps, Army of the Potomac (July 22, 1862-March 2, 1863); commanding 2nd Brigade, 2nd Division, 7th Corps, Department of Virginia (March 21-July 31, 1863); brigadier general, USV (April 4, 1863, to rank from November 29, 1862); commanding 2nd Brigade, Getty's Division, 18th Corps, Department of Virginia and North Carolina (July 15-August 12, 1863); commanding 2nd Brigade, Getty's Division, District of Virginia, 18th Corps, Department of Virginia (August 12-September 23, 1863); commanding 2nd Brigade, Getty's Division, U.S. Forces Norfolk and Portsmouth, 18th Corps, Department of Virginia and North Carolina (September 23-December 29, 1863); commanding Sub-District of the Pamlico, District of North Carolina, Department of Virginia and North Carolina (March 13-May 2, 1864); commanding Defenses of New Bern, District of North Carolina, Department of Virginia and North Carolina (July 27, 1864-January 31, 1865); commanding Sub-District of New Bern, Department of Virginia and North Carolina (January 31-February 9, 1865); and commanding 1st Division, District of Beaufort, Department of North Carolina (March 1-18, 1865). As a commander of a company of three-months volunteers, he fought at 1st Bull Run before being mustered out on August 12, 1861. At the head of a three-year regiment, he accompanied Burnside to the coast of North Carolina and saw action at Roanoke Island and New Bern. Joining the Army of the Potomac, he fought at South Mountain,

Antietam, and Fredericksburg in charge of the brigade. After that disaster his brigade was transferred to the coastal area of Virginia and he finished out the war in various districts there and in North Carolina. Resigning on June 22, 1865, he resumed the practice of law and entered politics. He sat in both houses of the state legislature and was also a judge, banker, and public official.

HARNDEN, Henry (?-1900)

The fact that he was involved in the capture of the fleeing Confederate president, Jefferson Davis, may have helped Henry Harnden receive the brevet of brigadier general of volunteers despite the fact that by 1865 he had only become a lieutenant colonel. The Massachusetts-born Wisconsin resident's assignments included: captain, 1st Wisconsin Cavalry (January 1, 1862); major, 1st Wisconsin Cavalry (June 8, 1864); and lieutenant colonel, 1st Wisconsin Cavalry (January 6, 1865). Following initial service in Missouri and Arkansas his regiment took part in the Tullahoma Campaign and the fighting at Chickamauga. While commanding the regiment in the Atlanta Campaign he was wounded at Dallas and later met the same fate during Wilson's Raid through Alabama and Georgia. It was during these mopping-up operations that his command came upon the trail of Davis who was nonetheless captured by other units. Brevetted for his war service, he was mustered out with his regiment on July 19, 1865.

HARNEY, William Selby (1800-1889)

One of the only four general officers of the line at the outbreak of the Civil War, William S. Harney was removed from his departmental command due to doubts about his fidelity to the Union. A native of Tennessee, he had been commissioned into the regular army from Louisiana in 1818. He earned brevets in both the Seminole and Mexican wars and later fought Indians on the plains. While in command of the Department of Oregon he came into conflict with the British and had to be removed. His Civil War-era assignments included: brigadier general, USA (since June 14, 1868); and commanding Department of the West (November 17, 1860-April 21, 1861 and May 8-31, 1861). Married into a St. Louis family and surrounded by secessionist friends, he was watched closely by Nathaniel Lyons and Francis P. Blair, Jr., in the period of uncertainty about Missouri's possible secession. The Washington authorities were also leery of him and by mid-May he had already been once relieved and reinstated. At that time Lincoln gave Blair discretionary power to remove Harney should it become necessary. Then on the 21st Harney signed a pact with the Missouri State Guard's (the pro-secessionist militia) General Sterling Price, declaring that U.S. forces would not act against that body so long as it did not take action against federal authority. Ten days later Blair removed him from duty. Not given another post, Harney was retired on August 1, 1863. Near the end of the conflict he was, however, brevetted major general for his war services. He spent his retirement in Mississippi. (Snead, Thomas L., *The Fight for Missouri* and Reavis, Logan Uriah, *The Life and Military Services of General William Selby Harney*)

HARPER, Fletcher (1806-1877)

Although he was the youngest and the last to join Harper & Brothers, in 1825, Fletcher Harper is the most important member of the family in Civil War journalism. Born in New York, he was apprenticed before joining his brothers (it was never stated which was "Harper" and which were the "Brothers"). Fletcher managed his brother James' creation, *Harper's New Monthly Magazine* in the 1850s before founding *Harper's Weekly* in 1857. It was this illustrated journal that was the nationwide competition to *Frank Leslie's Illustrated Newspaper*. Both provided the public with relatively current on-the-scene sketches of important Civil War events. In the postwar years he founded *Harper's Bazaar* and was active in gaining British serializations for his journals. This entailed many trips to England. His papers had a major political impact.

HARRIS, Clara (?-?)

Having witnessed the murder of Abraham Lincoln, Clara Harris also met a violent death, years later. The daughter of New York's senator and her fiancé, Major Henry R. Rathbone, had been asked by the President to attend the theater with the first couple as stand-ins for the Grants. When John Wilkes Booth entered the box at Ford's Theater, Lincoln was mortally wounded and Rathbone received a severe knife wound. Miss Harris later married Rathbone and the couple moved to Germany following his discharge from the army in 1870. He lost his mind there and murdered her. He lived, until 1911, in an insane asylum.

William S. Harney, the relieved commander of the Department of the West. (*Leslie's*)

Clara Harris, witness to the Lincoln killing. (NA)

HARRIS, David Bullock (1814-1864)

Engineering officer David B. Harris is another example of the South's penchant for postwar grade inflation. A West Pointer (1833), Harris served two years in the regular artillery before resigning to become a civil engineer in his native Virginia. A planter by the outbreak of the Civil War, he offered his services to the state and held the following appointments: captain, Virginia Engineers; major, Engineers; lieutenant colonel, Engineers; and colonel, Engineers. He played a distinguished role at the battle of 1st Bull Run. On the staff of General Beauregard he worked on the fortifications at Columbus, Kentucky, Island #10, Fort Pillow, Vicksburg, Charleston, Drewry's Bluff, and Petersburg. He was Beauregard's chief engineer when the latter commanded the Department of South Carolina, Georgia, and Florida and later of North Carolina and Southern Virginia. Returning to Charleston in the fall of 1864, he succumbed to yellow fever on October 10. There is no record of his holding any rank above that of colonel, although several postwar accounts credit him with being a brigadier general, but they cite no date of appointment.

HARRIS, Elisha (1824-1884)

When, on June 12, 1861, Elisha Harris became a member of the United States Sanitary Commission he was the only professional sanitarian in the organization. Born in Vermont he became a doctor in New York. In 1855 he was named superintendent of the Staten Island quarantine station. He also directed the construction of a floating hospital. Joining with Henry Bellows in 1861, he urged that the commission work for prevention as well as the relief of disease in the army. In 1863 his work prompted him to write *Hints for the Control and Prevention of Infectious Diseases in Camps, Transports, and Hospitals*. He designed a railroad hospital car and at the close of the war he co-edited *Sanitary Memoirs of the War of the Rebellion*. He continued to be a pioneer in the field and was named one of the original commissioners of the New York State Board of Health.

HARRIS, Eliza (?-1867)

Serving with the Union army from 1st Bull Run to Gettysburg, Pennsylvania-born Eliza Harris was a capable field worker for the United States Sanitary Commission. Not only did she cook and care for the sick and injured but she also wrote articles for various Pennsylvania newspapers, which served as a fundraising tool for the commission. After Gettysburg she went to Tennessee and Georgia until forced by ill-health to return to the capital to recover. She later served back in Virginia, at Fredericksburg, and helped care for the living skeletons returning from Andersonville.

HARRIS, Ira (1802-1875)

The father of Clara Harris—who was in Lincoln's box at Ford's Theater when he was assassinated—Ira Harris served throughout the Civil War as a Republican senator. The New York native entered upon the practice of law in 1832 and served in the lower house of the state legislature in 1845 and 1846. The next year he moved to the upper house and became a law professor. From 1847 until 1859 he sat on the state supreme court. During the peak of the secession crisis he was elected to the Senate for a six-year term but failed to gain reelection and upon leaving office in 1867 became a professor at Albany Law School. He was honored early in the Civil War by the naming of a regiment of New York cavalry as the "Ira Harris Guard." Harris taught law until his death.

HARRIS, Isham Green (1818-1897)

Following the election of Abraham Lincoln, Tennessee's Isham G. Harris, governor since 1857, was the foremost voice calling for secession. As a native Democratic lawyer he served two terms in Congress before rejecting renomination in order to return to his private Memphis practice. Called back into politics, he was elected governor in 1857 and reelected two and four years later. When called upon by Washington for troops he replied, "Tennessee will not furnish a single man for the purpose of coercion, but 50,000 if necessary for the defense of our rights and those of our Southern brothers." With the secession of the state, he turned over twice that number to the Confederacy. With the capture of Forts Henry and Donelson and the imminent fall of Nashville, he tried to move the state government to Memphis, but he was soon driven from the state and Andrew Johnson was installed as military governor. He then served on the staffs of Generals Albert S. Johnston, Pierre G.T.

Beauregard, Braxton Bragg, Joseph E. Johnston, and John B. Hood. All of this service was as a volunteer. With a price of $5,000 on his head for treason he fled to Mexico and England. Following over two years of exile he returned to his Memphis practice and served in the U.S. Senate from 1878 until his death. (Connelly, Thomas Lawrence, *Army of the Heartland*)

HARRIS, John V. (?-?)

With the federal drive on Vicksburg, it became necessary for some Mississippi state forces to join in the campaign. These forces were officially known as Mississippi State Troops (the governor called them "Minute Men") and were under command of state Brigadier General John V. Harris. They were called into service in the fall of 1862 and the brigade of one regiment and one battalion was assigned to the 1st Military District, Department of Mississippi and East Louisiana. In the final campaign for the river fortress, Harris and his men were attached to Vaughn's Brigade, Smith's Division, Department of Mississippi and East Louisiana. Harris was included among the prisoners after the siege but was declared exchanged on July 16, 1863. On August 26, 1863, he was ordered to pay off and muster out the paroled men in his command. This ended his active service. Harris is sometimes erroneously listed as a Confederate general officer when in fact he was only in the state service.

HARRIS, Nathaniel Harrison (1834-1900)

A Vicksburg lawyer, Nathaniel H. Harris entered the Southern military at the head of the Warren Rifles on May 8, 1861. His later assignments included: captain, Company C, 19th Mississippi (June 1, 1861); major, 19th Mississippi (May 5, 1862); lieutenant colonel, 19th Mississippi (November 24, 1862); colonel, 19th Mississippi (April 2, 1863); commanding Posey's (old) Brigade, Anderson's-Mahone's Division, 3rd Corps, Army of Northern Virginia (October 14, 1863-April 9, 1865). He served in the Shenandoah, northern Virginia, and then on the Peninsula where he saw action at Williamsburg. The regiment went on to fight at Seven Pines, the Seven Days, 2nd Bull Run, Antietam, and Fredericksburg. Attrition among the field officers resulted in his promotion through grades to the colonelcy. He directed the 19th at Chancellorsville and Gettysburg. At Bristoe Station he succeeded the wounded Carnot Posey in command of the brigade, and when Posey's wound proved fatal Harris was promoted to brigadier general. He served through the Overland Campaign and in the siege lines at Petersburg. His troops held Forts Gregg and Whitworth during the final collapse of the defenses of the city. His surrender came at Appomattox a week later. A lawyer and businessman postwar, he eventually made his home in California and died on a business trip to England. (Harris, W.M., *From the Diary of General Nat. H. Harris*)

HARRIS, Thomas Maley (1817-1906)

Born in that part of Virginia that became West Virginia, Thomas M. Harris remained loyal to the Union and rose to become a brevet major general of volunteers. A doctor by training, he entered upon recruiting duty late in 1861 and his later assignments included: lieutenant colonel, 10th West Virginia (March 17, 1862); colonel, 10th West Virginia (May 20, 1862); commanding 1st Brigade, 3rd Division, Department of West Virginia (July 1864); commanding 3rd Brigade, 1st Infantry Division, Department of West Virginia (August-September 19, 1864); commanding the division (September 19-December 24, 1864); commanding Independent Division, 24th Corps, Army of the James (December 24, 1864-March 25, 1865 and April 27-July 10, 1865); and commanding 3rd Brigade, Independent Division, 24th Corps, Army of the James (March 25-April 27, 1865); brigadier general, USV (March 29, 1865); commanding 1st Independent Brigade, 24th Corps, Army of the James (July 10-August 1865). Most of his early service was in the guerrilla fighting in western Virginia. In spring of 1864 he fought at Cloyd's Mountain. Under Sheridan, he succeeded to the command of a division at 3rd Winchester and led it at Fisher's Hill and Cedar Creek. For the latter battle he was brevetted brigadier general and next spring he was given the full rank. For the final assault on Petersburg he was brevetted major general and then took part in the Appomattox Campaign. Mustered out on April 30, 1866, he returned to the practice of medicine and wrote *Assassination of Lincoln*. He also served as a state legislator, state adjutant general, and pension agent. (Matheny, H.E., *Major General Thomas Maley Harris . . . A Member of the Military Commission That Tried the President Abraham Lincoln Assassination Conspirators . . . And a Roster of the Tenth West Virginia Volunteer Infantry Regiment, 1861-1865*)

HARRISON, Benjamin (1833-1901)

One of six Union officers to become president, Benjamin Harrison achieved the grade of brigadier general by brevet only. A lawyer and Republican politician before the war, his assignments included: second lieutenant, 70th Indiana (July 14, 1862); captain, 70th Indiana (July 22, 1862); colonel, 70th Indiana (August 7, 1862); commanding 2nd Brigade, 3rd Division, Reserve Corps, Army of the Cumberland (August 5-October 9, 1863); commanding 1st Brigade, 1st Division, 11th Corps, Army of the Cumberland (January 12-April 16, 1864); commanding 1st Brigade, 3rd Division, 20th Corps, Army of the Cumberland (May 15, June 29-September 23, 1864, and April 19-June 1, 1865); and commanding 1st Brigade, Provisional Division, Army of the Cumberland (December 1864). Rising quickly to command of his regiment, he was soon disliked by his men for his strict sense of discipline. The regiment's early service was spent mostly in routine garrison and guard duty. He did however serve in the Atlanta Campaign, part of the time in charge of a brigade. When the army under Sherman began the March to the Sea, Harrison took charge of a brigade in Tennessee, composed of men who could not rejoin their proper units, and fought at Nashville. Early the next year he was brevetted brigadier general for his ability to command a brigade. In the latter stages of the Carolinas Campaign he rejoined Sherman and again led a brigade. Mustered out with

Future president Benjamin Harrison. (*Leslie's*)

his regiment on June 8, 1865, he resumed his political career. After sitting in the U.S. Senate, he ran for the presidency in 1888 on a Republican reform platform and won. He was defeated for reelection partially due to the defection of many reformers. (Sievers, Harry J., *Benjamin Harrison*)

HARRISON, George Paul, Jr. (1841-1922)

It may have been that, since he commanded in a relative backwater of the war, George P. Harrison, Jr., never received the rank of brigadier general proper for the various brigade-size units he led in the last half of the Civil War. Born in Georgia, he was a student at the Georgia Military Institute when he took part in the seizure of Fort Pulaski even before the state seceded. He then enlisted and his assignments included: second lieutenant, 1st Georgia Regulars (January 1861); first lieutenant and adjutant, 1st Georgia Regulars (ca. May 1861); colonel, 5th Georgia State Troops (April 1862); colonel, 32nd Georgia (late 1862); commanding 2nd Brigade, District of East Florida, Department of South Carolina, Georgia and Florida (February 1864); commanding brigade, McLaws' Division, Department of South Carolina, Georgia and Florida or Hardee's Corps (December 28, 1864-April 9, 1865); and commanding brigade, Walthall's Division, Stewart's Corps, Army of Tennessee (April 9-26, 1865). Following his enlistment he was detailed back to the military school to complete his studies and serve as commandant of cadets. Graduating at the top of his class, he rejoined his regiment and served with it in western Virginia. Returning to Georgia, he commanded a regiment of state troops for six months before recruiting the 32nd Georgia. With this regiment he fought at Pocotaligo, Coosawhatchie, and at Charleston, including the defense of Battery Wagner. He was twice wounded in the defense of the city where secession had been born. Sent to the defense of Florida he commanded one of the two brigades in the Confederate victory at Olustee and was again wounded. Shortly thereafter he was assigned to command the prison camp at Florence, South Carolina. Serving there for most of 1864, he became known for his fair treatment of his charges. As a reward his family was guarded and fed by Union troops when they occupied Savannah. Returning to field duty before the end of the year, he commanded a brigade in the composite forces facing Sherman's march through the Carolinas. After seeing action at Bentonville, he was surrendered with the rest of Joe Johnston's command. He subsequently became a lawyer in Alabama, served in the state legislature and the U.S. Congress.

HARRISON, Henry Thomas (ca. 1832-post 1900)

Long a mystery who was known to history simply as "Harrison," Henry T. Harrison was an effective spy for the South. His most famous coup came after spying in Washington, when he reported back to his chief, James Longstreet, near Chambersburg, Pennsylvania, on June 28, 1863. He brought the first news that the Confederates received of George G. Meade's relief of Joseph Hooker in command of the Army of the Potomac. He also reported that that army had crossed its namesake river. With this information passed along to Lee the stage was set for the battle of Gettysburg. In 1970 historian James Bakeless claimed to have identified the mysterious Harrison as a Richmond actor, James Harrison. However, in the mid-1980s James O. Hall, working through the National Archives and other sources, positively identified the spy as one Henry Thomas Harrison. This Harrison had been one of the original Mississippi Scouts serving with the Confederate army in northern Virginia during the first year of the war. In 1862 he became a special agent with Secretary of War James A. Seddon. The following spring he served with Longstreet in southeastern Virginia and then went on his Washington information hunt. In the fall of 1863 he appears to have been paid off for his services due to the security risks of his heavy drinking. But within a couple of months, while Longstreet was serving in East Tennessee, he was sought out by his old chief for further work. He could not be located. After the war he allegedly went to Mexico to aid Maximilian and later disappeared in the Montana Territory until 1900, when he again vanished into oblivion. (Hall, James O., "The Spy Harrison," *Civil War Times Illustrated*, February 1986)

HARRISON, James Edward (1815-1875)

Serving throughout the war in the Trans-Mississippi West, James E. Harrison rose to the rank of brigadier general in the Confederate army. The native South Carolinian had served in the Alabama state senate before moving on to Texas where he was charged with negotiating with the Indians in the pre-Civil

War years. His Confederate assignments included: lieutenant colonel, 15th Texas (ca. May 20, 1862); commanding cavalry brigade, District of West Louisiana, Trans-Mississippi Department (fall 1863); colonel, 15th Texas (1864); brigadier general, CSA (November 22, 1864); commanding brigade, District of Texas, New Mexico and Arizona, Trans-Mississippi Department (March-April 7, 1865); and commanding 1st Brigade, Maxey's Division, District of Texas, New Mexico and Arizona, Trans-Mississippi Department (April 7-May 26, 1865). Before being named a brigadier general he served in the Teche and Red River campaigns, his principal field service. Returning home to Texas after the surrender of E. Kirby Smith's department, he was active in education.

HARRISON, Thomas (1823-1891)

Having served as an enlisted man in Jefferson Davis' 1st Mississippi Rifles in Mexico, Thomas Harrison received a commission as brigadier general from the Confederate president. Born in Alabama, he was raised in Mississippi. Taking up the practice of law in Texas before the Mexican War, he returned to it after his first round of military service. Sitting in the state legislature, he was also active in the militia. His Confederate assignments included: captain, 8th Texas Cavalry (1861); major, 8th Texas Cavalry (early 1862); colonel, 8th Texas Cavalry (November 18, 1862); commanding brigade, Wharton's Division, Wheeler's Cavalry Corps, Army of Tennessee (July-November 1863); commanding brigade, Wharton's Division, Martin's detachment of Wheeler's Cavalry Corps, Department of East Tennessee (November-December 1863); commanding brigade, Armstrong's Division, Martin's detachment of Wheeler's Cavalry Corps, Department of East Tennessee (December 1863-February 1864); commanding brigade, Humes' Division, Wheeler's Cavalry Corps, Army of Tennessee (February-fall 1864 and February-April 26, 1865); commanding brigade, Humes' Division, Wheeler's Cavalry Corps, Department of South Carolina, Georgia and Florida (fall 1864-February 16, 1865); and brigadier general, CSA (January 14, 1865). He was a field officer in the Texas Rangers by the time of Shiloh and went on to the Corinth and Perryville operations. He commanded the regiment at Murfreesboro and during the Tullahoma Campaign. Leading a brigade at Chickamauga, Knoxville, and during the Atlanta and Savannah campaigns, he was not, however, named a brigadier general until the beginning of the Carolinas Campaign. Following the surrender in North Carolina he was a judge and politician. His older brother was a general in the Trans-Mississippi region.

HARROW, William (1822-1872)

There is little doubt that the troublesome nature and repeated resignations of Union General William Harrow contributed to his not being listed in the omnibus brevet promotions near the end of the war. Born in Kentucky, he was a lawyer in Illinois and was living in Indiana at the outbreak of the Civil War. His military assignments included: captain, Knox County Invincibles (April 1861); captain, 14th Indiana (May 1861); major, 14th Indiana (June 7, 1861); lieutenant colonel, 14th Indiana (Feburary 14, 1862); colonel, 14th Indiana (April 26, 1862); colonel, 14th Indiana (reappointed August 23, 1862); brigadier general, USV (April 4, 1863, to rank from November 29, 1862); commanding 1st Brigade, 2nd Division, 2nd Corps, Army of the Potomac (June 8-July 1 and July 2-4, 1863); commanding the division (July 1-2 and July 4-August 15, 1863); and commanding 4th Division, 15th Corps, Army of the Tennessee (February 8-September 14, 1864). As a field-grade officer he served in the early fighting in western Virginia and commanded the regiment at Kernstown and in the Shenandoah Valley Campaign. Having resigned on July 29, 1862, he was reappointed in time to lose half his men in the bitter fighting at Antietam. Promoted to brigadier general the following spring he led a 2nd Corps brigade at Gettysburg—and at times the division—and was directly in the line of Pickett's Charge. When later that summer he was relieved of his new division command he resigned his commission, but Lincoln ordered it revoked on October 5, 1863. Early the next year he was assigned to command a division in the Army of the Tennessee and fought throughout the Atlanta Campaign. Shortly thereafter his command was broken up and no one seemed to want to find a place for him. After being shunted around for a number of months in search of a command he resigned effective April 20, 1865. He was apparently too much of a troublemaker to be popular with his potential superiors. He practiced law for a time and engaged in Radical Republican politics. Breaking with that faction, he was campaigning for Horace Greeley when he lost his life in a railroad wreck.

HART, Charley

See: *Quantrill, William Clarke*

HART, Peter (?-?)

Having been a sergeant in Captain Robert Anderson's company of the 3rd U.S. Artillery in the Mexican War, Peter Hart became one of the heroes of the fight at Fort Sumter at the beginning of the Civil War. Hart had left the army and was a member of the New York City Police Department when Mrs. Anderson tracked down her husband's trusted former orderly. She asked him if he would be willing to join her husband's command at the beleaguered fort. The former artilleryman was excited by the chance to take part in the events unfolding in Charleston Harbor. Quitting the police force, he journeyed with Mrs. Anderson to South Carolina where the authorities, in the strange twilight period between secession and open hostilities, told him that he would not be allowed to go the the fort as a soldier but would be permitted to go as a laborer. Thus, he joined Captain Foster's working party as a carpenter. Volunteering to remain in the fort when the attack appeared imminent, Hart was instrumental in directing the other loyal workers in dousing the flames in the wooden barracks, which had been ignited by Confederate fire. When on the second day of the bombardment the garrison flag fell, it was Peter Hart who nailed it to a spar that he attached to a gun carriage. With the

Gilbert Gaul's "Seargeant Hart Nailing the Colors to the Flagstaff of Fort Sumter." (*Drumbeat of a Nation*)

fall of the fort Hart returned to New York. In April 1865, Hart was again in Fort Sumter with now-General Anderson and holding the same flag that had been lowered exactly four years earlier. That day the war was nearly over. That same night Lincoln was assassinated. (Swanberg, W.A., *First Blood*)

HARTRANFT, John Frederick (1830-1889)

Although his regiment had marched to the rear for mustering out on the day before 1st Bull Run, John F. Hartranft remained and in 1886 was awarded the Congressional Medal of Honor for his action. The Pennsylvanian had practiced engineering and then law while gaining some military experience in the militia. Volunteering, his assignments included: colonel, 4th Pennsylvania (April 20, 1861); colonel, 51st Pennsylvania (November 16, 1861); commanding 2nd Brigade, 2nd Division, 9th Corps, Army of the Potomac (February-March 1863); commanding 2nd Brigade, 2nd Division, 9th Corps, Department of the Ohio (April-May 1863); commanding the division (May 21-June 5, 1863 and November 16, 1863-January 26, 1864); commanding 1st Brigade, 3rd Division, 9th Corps, Army of the Potomac (April 20-August 28, 1864); brigadier general, USV (May 12, 1864); and commanding in the 9th Corps, Army of the Potomac: 1st Division (August 28-September 1, 1864); 3rd Division (September 2-13, 1864); 2nd Brigade, 1st Division (September 30-October 9, 1864); 3rd Division (October 9-25, 1864); 1st Brigade, 1st Division (October 25-November 28, 1864); Provisional Brigade (November 28-December 15, 1864); and 3rd Division (December 15, 1864-May 3, 1865). Despite the pleas of Hartranft and army commander Irvin McDowell, the 4th Pennsylvania insisted on leaving the front exactly when its three-month enlistment had expired. The imminence of battle would not get them to extend their commitment. The colonel joined the staff of William B. Franklin and won his medal. Raising a new regiment, Hartranft was back in the field under Burnside in the operations along the North Carolina coast. He fought at Roanoke Island and New Bern before returning to Virginia. His regiment reinforced Pope in northern Virginia and fought at 2nd Bull Run. Moving into Maryland, Hartranft fought at South Mountain and Antietam. After the battle of Fredericksburg the corps was transferred to the Ohio Valley and after some service in Kentucky he led his regiment in the Vicksburg siege. Returning to the Department of the Ohio, he commanded a division at Knoxville. The corps then rejoined the Army of the Potomac and he led a brigade in the Overland Campaign. Particularly distinguished at Spotsylvania, his brigadier general's commission was dated from that action. He went on to serve in the operations against Petersburg and Richmond. He was brevetted major general for his successful defense in the Fort Stedman fighting—Lee's last offensive. He continued to lead his division in the Appomattox Campaign. He was noted for his consideration for the defendants in the Lincoln conspiracy trial, expecially Mary Surratt, while serving as the provost marshal at the proceedings. Mustered out on January 15, 1866, he held various governmental posts in Pennsylvania and was a two-term governor.

HARTRIDGE, Julian (1829-1879)

One of the best orators in the Confederate Congress, Julian Hartridge generally used his skills to the benefit of the Davis administration. Born in South Carolina, Hartridge received his education in Georgia and later took up the practice of law in Savannah. He subsequently served a term in the state legislature and attended the Democratic convention in 1860. With Lincoln's election, he embraced secession. With war at hand, he was commissioned lieutenant, Chatham (Ga.) Artillery, and saw service in coastal defense. He won an easy election to the First Regular Congress during the first year of the war and took his seat in February 1862 where he served on the committees on: Commerce; Ordnance and Ordnance Stores; and Ways and Means. His reelection to the Second Congress was a closer contest but he was made chairman of the Committee on Commerce, dropping his other two committee assignments. Although highly critical of some administration appointees, especially Secretaries Mallory and Memminger and General Bragg, Hartridge generally backed the Davis regime. He usually supported the national interest over those of the states. However, he broke with the administration on the issues of the suspension of the writ of habeas corpus and arming the slaves. Rebuilding his financial status through his legal practice, he reentered politics after Reconstruction, eventually serving in the U.S. Congress, a position he held at the time of his death.

HARTSUFF, George Lucas (1830-1874)

New Yorker George L. Hartsuff survived a Civil War wound only to die a dozen years later from the effects of a wound suffered in 1855 at the hands of the Seminoles in Florida. He had received his West Point appointment from Michigan and upon his 1852 graduation was posted to the artillery. He suffered two wounds at Fort Myers, Florida three years later. His Civil War assignments included: first lieutenant, 2nd Artillery (since March 8, 1855); brevet captain and assistant adjutant general (March 22, 1861); chief of staff, Department of the Ohio (July-September 21, 1861); captain and assistant adjutant general (August 3, 1861); chief of staff, Department of Western Virginia (October 11, 1861-March 11, 1862); chief of staff, Mountain Department (March 11-29, 1862); brigadier general, USV (April 15, 1862); commanding 2nd Brigade, 1st Division, Department of the Shenandoah (April 30-May 10, 1862); commanding 3rd Brigade, Ord's Division, Department of the Rappahannock (June 10-26, 1862); commanding 3rd Brigade, 2nd Division, 3rd Corps, Army of Virginia (June 26-August 29 and September 2-12, 1862); major and assistant adjutant general (July 17, 1862); commanding 3rd Brigade, 2nd Division, 1st Corps, Army of the Potomac (September 12-17, 1862); major general, USV (November 29, 1862); captain, 2nd Artillery (May 23, 1863-June 15, 1864); commanding 23rd Corps, Department of the Ohio (May 28-September 24, 1863); lieutenant colonel and assistant adjutant general (June 1, 1864); and commanding Defenses of Bermuda Hundred, Army of the James (March 19-April 16, 1865). After serving in the successful defense of Fort Pickens in Pensacola Harbor, Florida, he became Rosecrans' staff chief in western Virginia and was highly esteemed by that officer. He was then given a brigadier general's commission in the volunteers and assigned to a brigade in the Shenandoah Valley. Joining Pope's army, he fought at Cedar Mountain but was ill at Alexandria at the time of 2nd Bull Run. Back with his brigade, he became part of the Army of the Potomac and was so severely wounded at Antietam that he was relegated to boards and commissions after the expiration of his sick leave. In the spring and summer of 1863 he led the 23rd Corps in Kentucky and East Tennessee. However, his health again gave way and he then performed court-martial duty. In the last days of the Petersburg operations and during the Appomattox Campaign he commanded at Bermuda Hundred and was brevetted for his efforts. He had previously been brevetted for Antietam. Having already been made a full major general of volunteers in 1862, he was brevetted to that grade for the war in the regular service. Mustered out of the former, he was retired with the advanced grade of major general on account of his wounds in 1871. Three years later he died of pneumonia caused by one of his old Seminole wounds.

HARVEY, Cordelia Adelaide Perrine (?-?)

The widow of a Wisconsin governor, Cordelia Harvey worked for the Wisconsin troops. A native of New York she had married Louis P. Harvey in 1847. He had been elected governor of Wisconsin in 1861 and, on a relief expedition for the Wisconsin troops after Shiloh, had drowned in the Tennessee River. Cordelia took over this relief role that same spring and became affiliated with the United States Sanitary Commission. After the war she was the superintendent of soldiers' orphans' home in Wisconsin for many years. (McLenegan, Annie Susan, *The Harvey Play: A Pageant in Memory of Governor Louis Powell Harvey and His Wife, Cordelia A.P. Harvey*)

HARVEY, Louis Powell (1820-1862)

The recently inaugurated governor of Wisconsin, Louis P. Harvey, lost his life in an accident, while bringing aid to the wounded soldiers of his state after the battle of Shiloh. He had been born in Connecticut and raised in Ohio. He later taught in Kentucky before settling in Wisconsin as a journalist. He entered politics in 1853 as a state senator. Switching from the Whigs to the Republicans, he became the secretary of state for Wisconsin. In 1861 he was elected governor on the Union and Republican tickets. His service was mostly taken up by the war effort, including the forwarding of troops to the front. Upon the news reaching Madison that Wisconsin troops had suffered severely at Shiloh he headed to the scene at the head of a relief expedition. Boarding a vessel he accidentally slipped into the Tennessee River; his body was discovered some 60-odd miles downstream, due to the heavy current. Ironically, in 1847 he had opposed the creation of the office of lieutenant governor because governors rarely died in office. He was Wisconsin's first governor to die during his term. (McLenegan, Annie Susan, *The Harvey Play: A Pageant in Memory of Governor Louis Powell Harvey and His Wife, Cordelia A.P. Harvey*)

HASCALL, Milo Smith (1829-1904)

As was often the case in the Union army, unfulfilled ambition for higher rank may have cost the government the services of a capable man, in this case division commander. Native New Yorker, Milo S. Hascall resigned from the regular army only a year after his graduation from West Point in 1852. A second lieutenant in the 2nd Artillery stationed on the New England coast at the time, he found promotion potential minimal in the peacetime establishment and sought his fortune elsewhere. Becoming an attorney he was also active in railroading in the 1850s. He offered his services at the outbreak of the Civil War and his assignments included: captain and aide-de-camp, Indiana Volunteers (spring 1861); colonel, 17th Indiana (June 12, 1861); commanding 15th Brigade, Army of the Ohio (November-December 2, 1861); commanding 15th Brigade, 4th Division, Army of the Ohio (December 2, 1861-March 9, 1862); commanding 15th Brigade, 6th Division, Army of the Ohio (March 9-September 29, 1862); brigadier general, USV (April 25, 1862); commanding 15th Brigade, 6th Division, 2nd Corps, Army of the Ohio (September 29-November 5, 1862); commanding 1st Brigade, 1st Division, Left Wing, 14th Corps, Army of the Cumberland (November 5-December 31, 1862); commanding the division (December 31, 1862-January 9, 1863); commanding 1st Division, 21st Corps, Army of the Cumberland (January 9-February 19, 1863); commanding District of Indiana, Department of the Ohio (early 1863); and commanding in the 23rd Corps, Army of the Ohio: 3rd Division (August 6, 1863-March 12, 1864); 1st Brigade, 2nd Division (March-April 16, 1864); 2nd Brigade, 2nd Division (April 16-May 16, 1864); 2nd Brigade, 3rd Division (May 16-18, 1864); and 2nd Division (May 18-October 11, 1864). His initial assignment was as an aide on the staff of Indiana volunteers Brigadier General Thomas A. Morris, in western Virginia. As such he directed a regiment at Philippi and within a matter of days had a regiment of his own. He then led a brigade in Kentucky and Tennessee. Although his command did not arrive on the battlefield of Shiloh until the day after the fight ended, he was named a brigadier general later in the month. Again at Perryville his brigade, like most of the corps, was not engaged. At Murfreesboro he succeeded the wounded Thomas J. Wood in charge of the division. After a stint of district command in his adopted state he served under Burnside in the defense of Knoxville. As part of John M. Schofield's Army of the Ohio—in reality only a corps with attached cavalry—he fought through the Atlanta Campaign and was recommended by his chief for a second star. This had not been acted upon when the next month he resigned, on October 27, 1864. He was subsequently in the banking and real estate businesses in Indiana and Illinois.

HASKELL, Frank Aretas (1828-1864)

Although he did not survive the Civil War, Frank Haskell wrote one of the classic battle accounts of that conflict. A graduate of Dartmouth College, Haskell was commissioned a first lieutenant in Company I, 6th Wisconsin, on June 20, 1961. He served as regimental adjutant until tapped to be an aide-de-camp to General John Gibbon, the brigade commander. After its first fight at Groveton, Virginia, it was dubbed the "Iron Brigade." Haskell served with Gibbon at 2nd Bull Run, South Mountain, and Antietam and continued on his staff when Gibbon was given command of a division in the Second Corps. He saw further action at Fredericksburg, Chancellorsville, and Gettysburg, where the division held that portion of the Union lines that repulsed Pickett's Charge. After the battle he wrote an account of the defense, which subsequently appeared as *The Battle of Gettysburg*. While Gibbon was recovering from the effects of his Gettysburg wound, Haskell served temporarily on the corps staff. In February 1864 Haskell was rewarded for his service by being appointed colonel of a new regiment, the 36th Wisconsin. After completing its organization, it joined the Army of the Potomac as a part of Gibbon's Division. In its first battle, Cold Harbor, it took part in the futile Union charge. In the first few minutes, Colonel H.B. McKean, the brigade commander, was killed and Haskell took over. After the attack stalled, Haskell was shot in the brain while standing behind his prone firing line. Gibbon said, "I have lost my best friend, and one of the best soldiers in the Army of the Potomac has fallen!" (Byrne, Frank L. and Weaver, Andrew., eds., *Haskell of Gettysburg*)

HASKELL, John Cheves (1841-1906)

Although he did not join the artillery of the Army of Northern Virginia until the second half of the war, John Cheves Haskell soon became one of the more distinguished of its battalion commanders. He entered the Confederate army at the outbreak of the conflict and his assignments included: lieutenant, Company A, 1st South Carolina Artillery (May 18, 1861); major and commissary (December 21, 1861); major, Artillery (April 13, 1863); executive officer, Henry's Artillery Battalion, Hood's Division, 1st Corps, Army of Northern Virginia (June-July 1863); executive officer, Henry's Artillery Battalion, 1st Corps, Army of Northern Virginia (July-September 1863); commanding artillery battalion, 1st Corps, Army of Northern Virginia (September 1863-April 9, 1865); and lieutenant colonel, Artillery (February 18, 1865). After serving on the South Carolina coast, he joined G.W. Smith's, and later D.R. Jones', staff in Virginia. He was wounded, losing his right arm, at Gaines' Mill during the Seven Days Battles. Recovering, he served in the artillery in the Department of North Carolina in the spring of 1863 before joining Lee. He was second in command of Hood's artillery at Gettysburg. When Major Henry was transferred, Haskell took over the battalion. During the absence of the 1st Corps in Georgia and Tennessee the battalion served in the army reserve and temporarily with the 3rd Corps. When the corps returned in the spring of 1864, Haskell and his guns rejoined it. Haskell served through the Overland Campaign and in the defense of Petersburg where he was especially distinguished. He surrendered at Appomattox. After the

Confederate artillerist John C. Haskell. (NA)

war he was a lawyer and legislator in South Carolina and a plantation owner in Mississippi. (Wise, Jennings C., *The Long Arm of Lee* and Haskell, John, *The Haskell Memoirs*)

HASKIN, Joseph Abel (1818-1874)

Virtually all of the Civil War career of Union General Joseph A. Haskin was spent in the Washington fortifications. The New York native and West Pointer (1839) had been posted to the artillery and lost his left arm at Chapultepec in Mexico, where he won two brevets. His interwar assignments included three years in the quartermaster's department and recruiting duty, followed by a period of garrison duty. His Civil War-era assignments included: captain, 1st Artillery (since February 22, 1851); major, 3rd Artillery (February 20, 1862); lieutenant colonel and additional aide-de-camp (June 26, 1862); commanding Defenses North of the Potomac, Military District of Washington, Department of the Potomac (August 1862-February 2, 1863); commanding Defenses North of the Potomac, 22nd Corps, Department of Washington (February 2, 1863-July 8, 1864); chief of artillery, 22nd Corps, Department of Washington (July 26, 1864-April 10, 1866); and brigadier general, USV (August 4, 1864). On January 10, 1861, Haskin was summoned by the governor of Louisiana, Thomas O. Moore, to surrender the U.S. arsenal at Baton Rouge. Facing a force of 600 men, he had no choice but to comply. During the first year of hostilities he was in command at Fort Washington just outside the capital. The following June he was given the staff rank of lieutenant colonel and soon was given charge of the fortifications north of the river. He held this post for two years and participated in the repulse of Jubal Early's forces in July 1864. From that month until a year after the war had ended he was the capital's chief artillerist, in the meantime having been made a brigadier general of volunteers. Mustered out of the volunteers on April 30, 1866, he commanded forts in Boston and New York harbors until his 1870 retirement as lieutenant colonel, 1st Artillery, on account of disabilities.

HATCH, Edward (1832-1889)

Vermont-born Iowa lumberman Edward Hatch entered the Union army early in the Civil War, compiled an enviable record, and then remained in the regular army until his death. His assignments included: captain, 2nd Iowa Cavalry (August 12, 1861); major, 2nd Iowa Cavalry (September 5, 1861); lieutenant colonel, 2nd Iowa Cavalry (December 11, 1861); colonel, 2nd Iowa Cavalry (June 13, 1862); commanding 1st Brigade, Cavalry Division, Army of the Mississippi (August 11-November 1, 1862); commanding 2nd Brigade (assigned to Right Wing), Cavalry Division, 13th Corps, Army of the Tennessee (November 26-December 18, 1862); commanding 2nd Brigade, 1st Cavalry Division, 16th Corps, Army of the Tennessee (June 9-August 20, 1863); commanding 3rd Brigade, 1st Cavalry Division, 16th Corps, Army of the Tennessee (August 20-November 30, 1863); also commanding the division (September 24-October 24, 1863); brigadier general, USV (April 27, 1864); commanding 1st Division, Cavalry Corps, District of West Tennessee, Army of the Tennessee (June-November 1864); and commanding 5th Division, Cavalry Corps, Military Division of the Mississippi (November 9, 1864-January 18, 1865). Beginning as a company commander, he finished the war in charge of a division. His regiment fought at Island #10 and participated in the advance on Corinth, Mississippi. Having led his regiment at Iuka and Corinth, he took part in Benjamin H. Grierson's famous raid through Mississippi (to distract attention from Grant's movement against Vicksburg) and then returned to western Tennessee from which he was engaged in raiding northern Alabama. In December 1863 he was wounded in a minor action at Moscow, Tennessee, and spent several months recovering. Returning to duty as a brigadier general, he commanded the St. Louis cavalry depot until ready for the field. Under Andrew J. Smith he took part in operations against Nathan Bedford Forrest in the summer of 1864. During Hood's invasion of Tennessee he won a brevet as brigadier general in the regular army for Franklin—issued in 1867—and the brevets of major general in both the regulars and volunteers for Nashville. Mustered out of the latter in January 15, 1866, he was commissioned colonel of one of the two newly created black cavalry regiments in the regular establishment. Serving mostly on the Indian frontier, he held this post until his death nearly 23 years later.

HATCH, John Porter (1822-1901)

West Pointer (1845) John P. Hatch had already earned two brevets during the Mexican War when he earned the Congressional Medal of Honor for fighting the Confederacy. The New Yorker had originally been posted to the infantry but the next year was transferred to the newly organized Regiment of Mounted Rifles. Following the fighting below the border he served on the frontier. His Civil War-era assignments included: captain, Mounted Rifles (since October 13, 1860); captain, 3rd cavalry (designation change August 3, 1861); brigadier general, USV (September 28, 1861); commanding Cavalry Brigade, 5th Corps, Army of the Potomac (March 28-April 4, 1862); commanding Cavalry Brigade, Department of the Shenandoah (April 4-June 26, 1862); commanding Cavalry Brigade, 2nd Corps, Army of Virginia (June 26-July 27, 1862); commanding 1st Brigade, 1st Division, 3rd Corps, Army of Virginia (July 27-August 28, 1862); commanding the division (August 28-30, 1862); commanding 1st Brigade, 1st Division, 1st Corps, Army of the Potomac (September 12-14, 1862); commanding the division (September 14, 1862); major, 4th Cavalry (October 27, 1863); commanding District of Florida, 10th Corps, Department of the South (March 24-April 25, 1864); commanding the department (May 1-26, 1864); commanding District of Hilton Head, Department of the South (June 2-August 1, 1864); commanding District of Florida, Department of the South (August 4-October 26, 1864); commanding 1st Separate Brigade, Department of the South (November 14-28, 1864 and January 23-February 26, 1865); and also commanding Coast Division, Department of the South (November 1864-March 1865). He led the Union cavalry under Nathaniel P. Banks in the Shenandoah Valley and as part of

Pope's army earned a brevet for 2nd Bull Run where he succeeded to division command. Again at South Mountain, during the Maryland Campaign, he took over the division but was soon wounded in the costly assaults. He was awarded his medal for this exploit in 1893. After a lengthy recovery and court-martial and cavalry rendezvous duty he rejoined the forces in the field in the Department of the South. He operated along the fringes of Sherman's army during the Carolinas Campaign. Brevetted major general, he was mustered out of the former on January 15, 1866. Remaining in the service, he returned to the frontier and was active in campaigning against the Indians until his 1886 retirement as colonel, 2nd Cavalry.

HATTON, Robert Hopkins (1826-1862)

A lawyer and Know-Nothing congressman from Tennessee, Robert Hatton was made colonel of the 7th Tennessee on May 26, 1861. After a brief stint in East Tennessee, the regiment was mustered into Confederate service in July, then sent to western Virginia where it served in General S.R. Anderson's Brigade under Loring and Lee at Cheat Mountain and under Jackson in the unsuccessful Romney Campaign that winter. On February 24, 1862, the 7th and 14th Tennessee regiments were sent to Johnston's army at Manassas and organized with another regiment into a new brigade for General Anderson. On May 10, 1862, General Anderson resigned due to ill health and Colonel Hatton was commissioned a brigadier general on May 23, 1862, and given comand of the Tennessee Brigade. By this time the brigade was serving on the Peninsula and was a part of General G.W. Smith's Division, Department of Northern Virginia. On May 31, during the battle of Seven Pines, Hatton was shot in the head and killed north of Fair Oaks Station. (Drake, James Vaulx, *Life of General Robert Hatton*)

Confederate General Robert H. Hatton, killed at Seven Pines. (NA)

HAUPT, Herman (1817-1905)

One of the moving forces in the revolutionary use of railroads for military purposes, Herman Haupt never accepted his commission as brigadier general. The Philadelphia native had graduated from West Point in 1835 but resigned within a matter of months in order to enter civil engineering. He was responsible for the design and construction of some of the most difficult stretches of rail lines in the Northeast. In 1851 he published his *General Theory of Bridge Construction*. Called upon to serve the Union cause, his assignments included: colonel and additional aide-de-camp (April 27, 1862); and brigadier general, USV (September 5, 1862). Initially on the staff of Irvin McDowell, he was charged with the supervision of construction and transportation on the military railroads. A contentious person, he did not want any interference in his domain and was frequently in conflict with field commanders. The necessities of military operations forced him to make many innovations in order to quickly repair damaged or destroyed lines and bridges. Lincoln himself marveled at some of his "bean-pole bridges." On September 5, 1863, he finally declined his appointment as brigadier general and resumed his work in the private sector. For his remaining years he continued to write treatises on the science of railroading. It is perhaps fitting that he died of a heart attack on a train. (Ward, James A., *That Man Haupt* and Haupt, Herman, *Reminiscences of General Herman Haupt*)

HAWES, James Morrison (1824-1889)

Considering the amount of military training and experience that James M. Hawes had acquired prior to the Civil War, it is surprising that he saw only limited action as a Confederate brigadier general. The native Kentuckian and West Pointer (1845) had furthered his education in France at the Saumur cavalry school for two years. He also taught at his alma mater. In the field he won a brevet in the Mexican War and served on the frontier and in troubled Kansas. Resigning on May 9, 1861, as a captain in the 2nd Dragoons, he joined the Confederacy. His assignments included: captain, Cavalry (May 1861); major, Cavalry (June 16, 1861); colonel, 2nd Kentucky Cavalry (June 26, 1861); brigadier general, CSA (March 14, 1862, to rank from the 5th); commanding brigade, Reserve Corps, Army of the Mississippi (April 26-late June 1862); and commanding in the Trans-Mississippi Department: brigade, District of Arkansas (October 1862-63); brigade, Walker's Division, District of West Louisiana (November 1863); cavalry brigade, Green's Division, District of West Louisiana (March 16-March 1864); 1st Sub-District, District of Texas, New Mexico and Arizona (April-December 1864); also 5th (Texas) Brigade, 2nd (Texas) Division, 3rd Corps (or District of Texas, New Mexico

Railroad specialist Herman Haupt, with one of his inventions, an experimental pontoon for examining the underside of bridges. (NA)

and Arizona) (September 1864-spring 1865); and Defenses of Galveston, District of Texas, New Mexico and Arizona (December 1864-April 1865). After commanding the cavalry under Albert S. Johnston until Shiloh, he asked to be relieved and was placed in charge of an infantry brigade. Transferring west of the Mississippi, his principal action came at Milliken's Bend. He finished the war in the Galveston area and then went into the hardware business in Kentucky.

HAWES, Richard (1797-1877)

With the state of Kentucky divided in its loyalties, Richard Hawes became the unrecognized governor of the pro-Southern faction. A native of Virginia and veteran of the Black Hawk War, he was a lawyer and Whig member of the Kentucky legislature and the U.S. Congress. Joining the Democratic Party in 1856, he backed John C. Breckinridge in the 1860 presidential race and then supported the state's neutrality during the secession crisis and the early part of the Civil War. Believing that this stance had to be upheld by force, he became major, 5th Kentucky, and eventually became part of the Confederate army and served at Shiloh. In May 1862, following the death of George W. Johnson at Shiloh, he became the provisional governor of the state in exile. It was not until Bragg's invasion of Kentucky that he could be sworn in at the capitol in Frankfort on October 4, 1862. After the battle of Perryville, he was forced to flee with the Confederate army. He continued in his role in exile and returned again to the state before being forced finally to leave in 1864. Returning after the war, he resumed his private practice and became a judge. (Clift, G. Glenn, *Governors of Kentucky*)

HAWKINS, John Parker (1830-1914)

It was not until the middle of 1863 that Indianapolis native and West Pointer (1852) John P. Hawkins switched from the staff to the line as a Union brigadier general. Upon his graduation he had been assigned to the infantry and served mostly on the frontier. His Civil War-era assignments included: first lieutenant and regimental quartermaster, 2nd Infantry (since

October 1, 1858); lieutenant colonel and commissary of subsistence (August 3, 1861); lieutenant colonel and commissary of subsistence (November 1, 1862); brigadier general, USV (April 13, 1863); commanding District of Northeastern Louisiana, Army of the Tennessee (August 17, 1863-February 7, 1864); commanding 1st Division, U.S. Colored Troops, District of Vicksburg, Department of the Tennessee (March-November 28, 1864); also commanding 4th Division, 16th Corps, Army of the Tennessee (October 11-November 7, 1864); commanding 1st Division, U.S. Colored Troops, District of Vicksburg, Department of Mississippi (November 28, 1864-February 1865); and commanding 1st Division, U.S. Colored Troops, District of West Florida, Department of the Gulf (March-June 1865). He initially served as a quartermaster near Washington and then transferred to the commissary department and took up duties in St. Louis. He was thereafter a commissary officer with the District of Southwest Missouri, Department of the Missouri, District of West Tennessee, 13th Corps, and Army of the Tennessee. Ill for three months in the spring and summer of 1863, he returned to duty as a brigadier general of volunteers and commanded (mostly black troops) in Louisiana. He then led a black division in the occupation forces at Vicksburg and in the later movements against Mobile, for which he was brevetted. Brevetted major general in both the regulars and volunteers for the war, he was mustered out of the latter on February 1, 1866. Remaining in the regular army until he reached the mandatory retirement age in 1894, he continued to serve in the commissary department and for the last two years of his service he was the commissary general with the staff rank of brigadier general.

HAWKINS, Rush Christopher (1831-1920)

In two years of service at the head of a colorful regiment of New York Zouaves, Rush C. Hawkins was frequently in hot water but earned a brevet as brigadier at the war's close. A veteran of the Mexican War, he raised a regiment known as Hawkins' Zouaves at the outbreak of the Civil War. His assignments included: colonel, 9th New York (May 4, 1861); commanding Hatteras Inlet, N.C., Department of Virginia (fall 1861); commanding 4th Brigade, 3rd Division, Department of North Carolina (April 2-July 6, 1862); commanding 1st Brigade, 3rd Division, 9th Corps, Army of the Potomac (July 22-August 3, 1862, early December 1862-January 1863, and February-March 2, 1863); and commanding 1st Brigade, 2nd Division, 7th Corps, Department of Virginia (April 9-May 8, 1863). Criticized for some minor setbacks while in command at Hatteras Inlet, he was replaced by Brigadier General Thomas Williams. Hawkins soon came into conflict with his superiors over the latter's severe regime. He even went so far as to take his case to Lincoln but was careful at the same time, to point out the military value of the Inlet in order to bolster his position. The president was so impressed he had the young colonel address the cabinet. Facing arrest by Williams, he was unable to return until Burnside arrived to take overall command. Hawkins then took part in the fighting at Roanoke Island and later joined the Army of the Potomac, leading a brigade at Fredericksburg where he ran into trouble with Burnside over the disastrous assaults. After brief service in Southeastern Virginia he was mustered out with his regiment on May 20, 1863. Brevetted brigadier near the war's end, he went on to amass a fortune in real estate and other investments and was a noted collector of 15th- and 16th-century printed materials, second only to the British Museum. (Graham, Matthew J., *The Ninth Regiment New York Volunteers (Hawkins Zouaves)*)

Colonel Rush C. Hawkins of Hawkins' Zouaves. (NA)

HAWLEY, Harriet Ward Foote (?-1886)

The wife of Union General Joseph R. Hawley, Harriet W.F. Hawley, joined his field command in 1862 as a nurse. Leaving her Connecticut home, she took up her medical duties at Beaufort, North Carolina. She also served in Florida and South Carolina before being assigned to Washington when her husband's command was assigned to the Army of the James in April 1864. Returning to North Carolina in March 1865, she finished the war in Wilmington, treating the former inmates of Andersonville.

HAWLEY, Joseph Roswell (1826-1905)

A North Carolinian by birth, Joseph R. Hawley nonetheless became a leader in the antislavery movement and a Union general. He had moved to his father's home state, Connecticut, at the age of 11 and become a lawyer. Active in the Free-Soil Party he was one of the founders of the state's Republican Party. He was also editor of the *Hartford Evening Press*. One of the first to volunteer, his assignments included: captain, 1st Connecticut (April 22, 1861); colonel, 7th Connecticut (June 20, 1862); commanding 3rd Brigade, U.S. Forces Morris Island, 10th Corps, Department of the South (September 19-October 19, 1863); commanding U.S. Forces St. Helena Island, 10th Corps, Department of the South (December 1863-February 5, 1864); commanding brigade, District of Florida, 10th Corps, Department of the South (February 16-29, 1864); commanding 2nd Brigade, 1st Division, District of Florida, 10th Corps, Department of the South (February 25-April 25, 1864); commanding 3rd Brigade, 1st Division, 10th Corps, Army of the James (April 28-May 2, 1864); commanding 2nd Brigade, 1st Division, 10th Corps, Army of the James (May 2-September 12, October 12-20, October 29-November 4, and November 18-December 3, 1864); brigadier general, USV (September 13, 1864); commanding 3rd Division, 10th Corps, Army of the James (October 20-29, 1864); commanding 2nd Brigade, 1st Division, 24th Corps, Army of the James (December 3, 1864-January 1, 1865); commanding the division (January 1-February 2, 1865); and commanding District of Wilmington, 10th Corps, Department of North Carolina (March 1-June 23, 1865). He led his company at 1st Bull Run before it was mustered out on July 31, 1861. Six weeks later he became second in command of a new regiment and accompanied it to the southern coast. He took part in the operations against Port Royal, Fort Pulaski, and Charleston. He then led a brigade to Florida and took part in the defeat at Olustee. Transferred with the 10th Corps to Virginia, he led his brigade and frequently a division at Bermuda Hundred and in the fighting for Richmond and Petersburg. He finished the war in command at Wilmington, North Carolina, and was brevetted for his war service on September 28, 1865. Mustered out on January 15, 1866, he entered politics and was his state's chief executive and represented it in both houses of Congress. His wife was a Union army nurse.

HAWTHORN, Alexander Travis (1825-1899)

After having been twice defeated for reelection to the colonelcy of two different regiments, Alexander T. Hawthorn was named a Confederate brigadier general. The Alabama native was practicing law in Arkansas in 1861. Joining the army, his assignments included: lieutenant colonel, 6th Arkansas (June 7, 1861); colonel, 6th Arkansas (October 15, 1861); colonel, Hawthorn's Arkansas Regiment (November 4, 1862); brigadier general, CSA (February 18, 1864); commanding brigade, Arkansas (Churchill's) Division, District of Arkansas, Trans-Mississippi Department (ca. February-September 1864); and commanding 4th (Arkansas) Brigade, 1st (Arkansas) Division, 2nd Corps (or District of Arkansas), Trans-Mississippi Department (September 1864-May 26, 1865). After leading his regiment at Shiloh he was defeated for reelection at the reorganization on May 14, 1862, but that fall he took command of a new regiment. This he led at Helena and Little Rock but on January 5, 1864, he was again defeated for continuance as colonel. The next month he was named a brigadier general, and he led a brigade in Arkansas for the balance of the war, seeing action at Jenkins' Ferry facing Steele's expedition against Camden. After nearly a decade in Brazil he became an Atlanta businessman and then a Baptist minister in Texas.

HAY, John Milton (1838-1905)

Although he later served as an ambassador and secretary of state, John Hay is best remembered as the personal secretary of Abraham Lincoln and, with John Nicolay, as his biographer. Born in Indiana, Hay became a friend, while studying law in Springfield, of Lincoln and became his assistant personal secretary at the beginning of his presidency. During the latter part of 1863 he served as a volunteer aide-de-camp in South Carolina on the staff of General Q.A. Gillmore. Early in 1864, he was sent, as a major and assistant adjutant general (from January 12, 1864) to Florida in order to enlist support for the Union among the population. Although his mission was not very successful he was brevetted lieutenant colonel and colonel of volunteers at the close of the war. His intimate connection with Lincoln led him and John Nicolay to write a 10-volume biography of their former employer. After the war he served in the foreign service in Paris, Vienna, and Madrid. After a stint in journalism, he rejoined the State Department and was secretary from 1898 to 1905 under McKinley and Roosevelt. He died in office in 1905. (Nicolay, John G. and Hay, John, *Abraham Lincoln: A History* and Kushner, Howard I. and Sherrill, Anne Hummel, *John Milton Hay: The Union of Poetry and Politics*)

HAYES, Joseph (1835-1912)

Maine-born banker, engineer, and real estate broker Joseph Hayes returned to command a brigade—after long being held in the hands of the enemy—only a few days before Appomattox. He was in the real estate business in Boston when he enlisted for the war. His assignments included: major, 18th Massachusetts (August 24, 1861); lieutenant colonel, 18th Massachusetts (August 25, 1862); colonel, 18th Massachusetts (March 1, 1863); commanding 1st Brigade, 1st Division, 5th Corps, Army of the Potomac (October 1-November 19, 1863); commanding 3rd Brigade, 1st Division, 5th Corps, Army of the Potomac (November 19, 1863-April 3, 1864); brigadier general, USV (May 12, 1864); and commanding 1st Brigade, 2nd Division, 5th Corps, Army of the Potomac (June 20-August 19, 1864 and April 3-June 28, 1865). On the Peninsula his regiment fought at Yorktown and in the Seven Days. At 2nd Bull Run he commanded his regiment under Fitz-John Porter. He ably led it through the battles of Antietam, Fredericksburg, Chancellorsville, and Gettysburg. During the Bristoe and Mine Run operations he led a brigade. After the spring 1864 reorganization he again took charge of his regiment and on the first day at the Wilderness received a severe skull wound that gave some trouble for the rest of his days. In return he was named a brigadier general and was again given a brigade when he returned to duty the next month. In the Petersburg operations he fell into enemy hands in the fight for the Weldon Railroad. On parole, he was assigned to oversee the distribution of supplies to Union prisoners in the South. Exchanged in about February 1865, he resumed command of his brigade in the midst of the Appomattox Campaign. Brevetted major general for the war, he was mustered out on August 24, 1865, and was later active in mining in both the United States and Latin America.

HAYES, Rutherford Birchard (1822-1893)

One of six Civil War soldiers to become president of the United States, Rutherford B. Hayes emerged as a brevet major general of volunteers but most of his service was in the lesser theaters of operations. The Ohio lawyer was active in politics first as a Whig and later as a Republican, although not of the "Black" Republican type. Throwing himself into the war effort, his assignments included: major, 23rd Ohio (June 27, 1861); lieutenant colonel, 23rd Ohio (October 24, 1861), colonel, 23rd Ohio (October 24, 1862); commanding 1st Brigade, 3rd Division, 8th Corps, Middle Department (March 17-June 26, 1863); commanding 1st Brigade, Scammon's Division, Department of West Virginia (June 28-December 1863); commanding 1st Brigade, 2nd Infantry Division, Department of West Virginia (April-October 19, 1864 and December 24, 1864-January 1865); brigadier general, USV (October 19, 1864); commanding the division (October 19-December 24, 1864); commanding 1st Brigade, 1st Infantry Division, Department of West Virginia (January-February 25, 1865); and commanding the division (February 25-April 1865). Initially he served in western Virginia but joined the Army of the Potomac during

Future president Rutherford B. Hayes. (*Leslie's*)

the Maryland Campaign, where he was severely wounded at South Mountain. He then returned to western Virginia and took part in the defense against Morgan's raid. In the spring of 1864 he fought at Cloyd's Mountain and in the Lynchburg expedition. Under Sheridan, he was engaged at 3rd Winchester, Fisher's Hill, and Cedar Creek where he assumed command of the division. Brevetted major general for western Virginia, Fisher's Hill, and Cedar Creek, he resigned on June 8, 1865. He had been promoted to brigadier general to date from the last-named action. Taking the seat in the House of Representatives to which he had been elected the previous fall, he was reelected the next year and then ran successfully for two terms as Ohio's governor. He was again elected to the gubernatorial chair in 1875 and launched his presidential campaign from that post. In the 1876 contest, which the Democrats considered stolen, Hayes was elected over Samuel J. Tilden by one electoral vote when Florida's and Louisiana's electoral votes were switched by the election boards to Hayes' column. A commission confirmed the results only two days before the inauguration. But part of the deal had been the promise to remove troops from the South. In his one term—he did not seek reelection—he was a champion of civil service reform but lost much of his party's support because of his lenient treatment of the South. (Barnard, Harry, *Rutherford B. Hayes and His America*)

HAYMAN, Samuel Brincklé (1820-1895)

Despite being recommended for a brigadier generalship by Daniel E. Sickles, Samuel B. Hayman was mustered out of the volunteer service upon the expiration of his regiment's two-year term of enlistment and reverted to his regular army rank of major. The Pennsylvanian West Pointer (1842) had served in the Mexican War in the infantry. His Civil War assignments included: Captain, 7th Infantry (since March 3, 1855); colonel, 37th New York (September 28, 1861); commanding 1st Brigade, 1st Division, 3rd Corps, Army of the Potomac (December 30, 1862-February 1863); major, 10th Infantry (January 21, 1863); and commanding 3rd Brigade, 1st Division, 3rd Corps, Army of the Potomac (February-June 3, 1863). With his volunteer regiment, he fought at Yorktown, Williamsburg, Seven Pines, and during the Seven Days. In 1865 he was brevetted for Seven Pines. He then fought at 2nd Bull Run and Fredericksburg and commanded a brigade at Chancellorsville. Winning another brevet for the latter, he did not receive the recommended promotion and was mustered out with his regiment on June 22, 1863. During the Gettysburg and Bristoe campaigns he served as commissary of musters on the staff of General William H. French who in the latter campaign commanded the 3rd Corps. On the second day in the Wilderness he was wounded while directing the three companies of his regular regiment present. Upon his recovery, he continued in the regular establishment until his 1872 retirement as lieutenant colonel, 17th Infantry.

HAYNES, Landon Carter (1816-1875)

In the prewar years, Landon C. Haynes was one of the staunchest secessionists in East Tennessee, an area heavily pro-Union in sentiment. A native of his region, Haynes was a preacher, lawyer, and farmer before becoming active in politics. He later served in both houses of the state legislature (including the speakership of the lower chamber) and as a presidential elector before being named to a six-year term in the Confederate Congress. Taking his seat in February 1862 he was appointed to the committees on: the Judiciary; Patents; Post Offices and Post Roads; Printing; and (in the Second Congress) Commerce. His fiscal and economic conservatism proved to be a thorn in the side of the war effort. However, he did support the Davis administration on the purely military aspects. His excessive states' rights views, which views had really launched the secession movement and the Confederacy, were to prove the Confederacy's demise by denying it the means to achieve its independence. Uncomfortable with the Unionist dominance in East Tennessee, Haynes moved to Memphis shortly after the war's end and resumed the practice of law.

HAYNIE, Isham Nicholas (1824-1868)

At the same time that his appointment as brigadier general expired, due to the failure of the U.S. Senate to confirm it, Isham N. Haynie submitted his resignation, citing the illness of his wife. Born in Tennessee and raised in Illinois, he became a lawyer and served as a lieutenant of Illinois volunteers in the Mexican War. In the interwar years he sat in the legislature and was named to a judgeship. His Civil War assignments included: colonel, 48th Illinois (November 10, 1861); commanding 3rd Brigade, 1st Division, District of Cairo, Department of the Missouri (briefly February 1862); brigadier general, USV (November 29, 1862); and commanding 1st Brigade, 3rd Division, 17th Corps, Army of the Tennessee (January 25-April 23, 1863). He temporarily commanded a brigade at Fort Donelson and was wounded at Shiloh. Upon his recovery he was given a brigade preparing for the Vicksburg Campaign. With the expiration of his commission on March 4, 1863, he was relieved on April 23, 1863. Resuming the practice of law in Illinois, he was state adjutant general for a number of years.

HAYS, Alexander (1819-1864)

A regular army officer who had resigned to enter business, Pennsylvanian Alexander Hays reentered the service—both in the regulars and volunteers—upon the outbreak of hostilities. A West Pointer (1844), he had been assigned to the infantry, with which he earned a brevet in the Mexican War. He resigned as a second lieutenant in 1848, then failed in the iron business before going to California in search of gold. He returned to his native state and was engaged in bridge construction in 1861. His wartime assignments included: major, 12th Pennsylvania (April 25, 1861); captain, 16th Infantry (May 14, 1861); colonel, 63rd Pennsylvania (October 9, 1861); brigadier general, USV (September 29, 1862); commanding 3rd Brigade, Casey's Division, 22nd Corps, Department of Washington (February 2-April 17, 1863); commanding 3rd Brigade, Abercrombie's Division, 22nd Corps, Department of Washington (April 17-June 26, 1863); commanding 3rd Division, 2nd Corps, Army of the Potomac (June 28-August 15 and September 6-December 14, 1863 and January 4-February 10, 1864); and commanding 2nd Brigade, 3rd Division, 2nd Corps, Army of the Potomac (March 25-May 5, 1864). His initial service was with Patterson's army before his three months regiment was mustered out on August 5, 1861. In the meantime he had been commissioned a captain in one of the newly authorized regiments for the regular army. However, he raised a new volunteer regiment, which he led at Williamsburg, Seven Pines, and in the Seven Days. During the latter he earned two brevets. Severely wounded at 2nd Bull Run, he did not return to duty until early the following year. By then he wore a brigadier's star and was assigned to the Washington fortifications. Rejoining the Army of the Potomac, he earned another brevet for his leading of a 2nd Corps division at Gettysburg. In the reorganization of March 1864 he was reduced—by reasons of seniority—to the command of a brigade. On the first day at the Wilderness he was killed in the early morning fighting. From his West Point days he was a close friend of Grant and Winfield S. Hancock.

HAYS, Harry Thompson (1820-1876)

A New Orleans lawyer and politician, Harry T. Hays had been born in Tennessee and raised in Mississippi and had some military experience from the Mexican War, where he served as a first lieutenant and regimental quartermaster in the 5th Louisiana. With the outbreak of the Civil War he reentered the military and his assignments included: colonel, 7th Louisiana (1861); brigadier general, CSA (July 25, 1862); commanding 1st Louisiana Brigade, Ewell's-Early's Division, 2nd Corps, Army of Northern Virginia (September 17, 1862-December 15, 1863 and February-May 18, 1864); commanding the division (December 15, 1863-February 1864); commanding his and Stafford's brigades, Johnson's Division, same corps and army (May 8-10, 1864); and major general, CSA, by E.K. Smith (May 10, 1865). After fighting at 1st Bull Run he was in the Shenandoah Valley Campaign until wounded at Port Republic. Promoted to brigadier while recovering, he returned to duty on the day of the battle of Antietam. He went on to Fredericksburg, Chancellorsville, and Gettysburg. At times he was in command of the division during the absence of General Early but directed only his brigade at the Wilderness and both Louisiana brigades at Spotsylvania, being severely wounded on May 10, 1864. On July 9 he was ordered to the Trans-Mississippi Department to round up absentees from western units serving east of the Mississippi. He was engaged in this work until the fall of the Confederacy and was promoted extra-legally by General E.K. Smith to the rank of major general only weeks before his surrender. Subsequently he resumed his law practice and was briefly sheriff in New Orleans. (Freeman, Douglas S., *Lee's Lieutenants*)

HAYS, William (1819-1875)

Caught sleeping too late on one of the last mornings of the war, William Hays was relieved of his command and thus missed the final part of the Appomattox Campaign. Although a Southerner—Virginia-born, with a West Point appointment from Tennessee—he remained loyal. Following his 1840 graduation he had been posted to the artillery and seen action in both the Mexican and Seminole wars. In the former he earned two brevets and was wounded at Molino del Rey. His Civil War-era assignments included: captain, 2nd Artillery (since October 8, 1853); lieutenant colonel and additional aide-de-camp (September 28, 1861); commanding Artillery, Stoneman's Command, Army of the Potomac (May 1862); commanding 1st Brigade (Horse Artillery), Artillery Reserve, (attached to) 5th Corps, Army of the Potomac (May 18-September 1862); commanding Artillery Reserve, (attached to) 5th Corps, Army of the Potomac (September 1862); commanding Artillery Reserve, Army of the Potomac (September 1862-ca. February 1863); brigadier general, USV (November 29, 1862); commanding 2nd Brigade, 3rd Division, 2nd Corps, Army of the Potomac (February 12-May 3, 1863); commanding 2nd Corps, Army of the Potomac (July 3-August 16, 1863); major, 5th Artillery (August 1, 1863); provost marshal general, Southern District of New York (November 1863-February 1865); and commanding 2nd Division, 2nd Corps, Army of the Potomac (February 25-April 6, 1865). Serving with the horse artillery, he fought at Williamsburg and the Seven Days on the Peninsula and earned a brevet as lieutenant colonel for the campaign. He commanded the army's artillery reserve at both Antietam and Fredericksburg before being given a brigadier's star and an infantry brigade. On May 3, 1863, he was captured at Chancellorsville but returned to the army at the close of the battle of Gettysburg when he was placed in command of Hancock's corps. He subsequently served in New York enforcing the draft but rejoined the army in the final months. He was found asleep at 6:30 A.M. on April 6, 1865. The rest of the army had moved out in its continuing pursuit of Lee towards Appomattox, but Hays' division was not in motion. He was promptly relieved of duty. He had previously been brevetted to brigadier in the regular service but for the 10 remaining years of his army career he was not to receive another promotion, either normal or by brevet. Mustered out of the volunteers on January 15, 1866, he died on active duty in Boston Harbor.

HAZARD, John Gardner (?-1897)

Beginning as a first lieutenant in a volunteer battery, John G. Hazard rose to the command of the 2nd Corps' guns in the latter part of the war and achieved the rank of brevet brigadier general. A Rhode Island native, he was commissioned in the first summer of the war. His assignments included: first lieutenant, 1st Rhode Island Light Artillery (August 25, 1861); captain, Battery B, 1st Rhode Island Light Artillery (August 18, 1862); commanding Artillery Brigade, 2nd Corps, Army of the Potomac (May-October 1863 and late 1864-May 1865); major, 1st Rhode Island Light Artillery (April 19, 1864); executive officer, Artillery Brigade, 2nd Corps, Army of the Potomac (spring-summer 1864); and colonel, 5th United States Veteran Volunteers (July 14, 1865). Serving as a subaltern in the early part of the war, he directed his guns at Antietam and Fredericksburg. At Gettysburg he commanded all of the cannon belonging to the 2nd Corps and thus played a leading role in the repulse of Pickett's Charge. He was in the Bristoe and Mine Run campaigns. During the Overland Campaign he won a brevet at Cold Harbor. Later and again in charge of the 2nd Corps batteries, he fought at Petersburg and Appomattox. Early that summer he took charge of an infantry regiment destined for assignment to the Veteran Volunteer Corps, which never came into being due to the cessation of hostilities. Already brevetted through brigadier general for the war, he served with this regiment in the District of Columbia, Rhode Island, and New York before being mustered out on March 5, 1866.

HAZEN, William Babcock (1830-1887)

By the outbreak of the Civil War—in which he was destined to distinguish himself—William B. Hazen had already suffered a wound and earned a regular army brevet during Indian fighting in Texas in 1859. Born in Vermont, he was raised in Ohio before receiving his appointment to West Point. Graduating in 1855, he was posted to the infantry and his pre-war service was performed on the Pacific coast and in Texas. His wartime assignments included: second lieutenant, 8th Infantry (since September 4, 1855); first lieutenant, 8th Infantry (April 1, 1861); captain, 8th Infantry (May 14, 1861); colonel, 41st Ohio (October 29, 1861); commanding 19th Brigade, Army of the Ohio (January 3, 1862); commanding 19th Brigade, 4th Division, Army of the Ohio (January 3-June 2, 1862 and July 10-September 29, 1862); commanding 19th Brigade, 4th Division, 2nd Corps, Army of the Ohio (September 29-November 5, 1862); commanding 2nd Brigade, 2nd Division, Left Wing, 14th Corps, Army of the Cumberland (November 5, 1862-January 9, 1863); commanding 2nd Brigade, 2nd Division, 21st Corps, Army of the Cumberland (January 9-September 3 and September 13-October 9, 1863); brigadier general, USV (April 30, 1863, to rank from November 29, 1862); commanding 2nd Brigade, 3rd Division, 4th Corps, Army of the Cumberland (October 10, 1863-March 17, 1864 and April 17-August 17, 1864); commanding 2nd Division, 15th Corps, Army of the Tennessee (August 17, 1864-May 18, 1865); major general, USV (April 1865 to rank from December 13, 1864); and commanding the corps (May 28-August 1, 1865). Transferring to the volunteers, he fought under Buell at Shiloh but was not engaged at Perryville. With Rosecrans he participated in the Tullahoma Campaign after having fought at Murfreesboro, and went on to win a brevet for Chickamauga. He took part in the battles around Chattanooga, winning another regular army brevet, and took part in Sherman's expedition to relieve Knoxville. By now a brigadier general, he led a brigade in the Atlanta Campaign and during the siege proper was advanced to divisional command. However, he did not become a major general until the virtual end of the war. In the meantime he went on the March to the Sea—winning the brevet of brigadier of regulars for the capture of Fort McAllister—on through the Carolinas. After the close of the war he was in charge of the corps and was brevetted major general for his wartime services. Mustered out of the volunteers on January 15, 1866, he continued in the army until his death while on duty as a full brigadier general and chief signal officer. In the meantime he served on the frontier, was active in rooting out corruption, and was an observer during the Franco-Prussian War. (Hazen, William Babcock, *A Narrative of Military Service*)

HAZLETT, Charles Edward (ca. 1838-1863)

A graduate of West Point (1861), Charles Hazlett played an important role in the fighting on Little Round Top on the second day at Gettysburg. The Ohioan was appointed second lieutenant in the 2nd U.S. Cavalry on May 6, 1861, only to be promoted to first lieutenant and assigned to Battery D, 5th Artillery, eight days later. Serving with Griffin's famous battery, Hazlett participated in the battle of 1st Bull Run, where the command was devastated, and in two fights at Lewinsville, Virginia, near Washington, on September 11 and 25, 1861. In the spring of 1862, the battery took part in the Peninsula Campaign, with Hazlett seeing action at Hanover Court House and in the Seven Days. Hazlett commanded the battery with distinction at 2nd Bull Run, Antietam, Fredericksburg, and Chancellorsville before going to Pennsylvania to help stop Lee's invasion. With the rebels driving on the Union left flank at Gettysburg, Hazlett's battery was ordered up Little Round Top, a rocky, wooded, roadless hill. The army's chief of artillery, General Hunt, said of the climb, "Under ordinary circumstances it would have been considered an impossible feat, but the eagerness of the men" was equal to the task. Although the six 10-pounder Parrotts could not be depressed enough to fire on the nearby Confederates, the friendly fire of the guns was a welcome sound to the infantry protecting the summit. While bending over the mortally wounded General Weed, to get his last message, Hazlett was killed by sharpshooters picking off Union officers from Devil's Den.

HÉBERT, Louis (1820-1901)

Twice a prisoner, West Pointer (1845) Louis Hébert rose to the rank of brigadier general in the Confederate army. Posted to the engineers, the native Louisianan resigned as a brevet second lieutenant the year after his graduation. While engaged in the sugar business he also kept up his interest in military affairs through the state militia. In the antebellum period he was a civil engineer and served in the state legislature. Offering his services to the Confederacy, his assignments included: colonel, 3rd Louisiana (May 11, 1861); commanding 2nd Brigade, McCulloch's Division, Department #2 (late 1861-March 8, 1862); commanding 2nd Brigade, 1st Division, District of Trans-Mississippi, Department #2 (March-April 1862); commanding 2nd Brigade, Price's Division, Army of the West, Department #2 (April-September 1862); brigadier general, CSA (May 26, 1862); commanding 2nd Brigade, 1st Division, Price's Corps (or Army of the West), Army of West Tennessee, Department #2 (September-October 4, 1862); commanding 1st Brigade, Bowen's Division, Price's Corps (or Army of the West), Army of West Tennessee, Department of Mississippi and East Louisiana (October 20-22, 1862); commanding brigade, Maury's Division, Price's Corps (or Army of the West), Army of West Tennessee, Department of Mississippi and East Louisiana (October 22-late 1862); commanding brigade, Maury's-Forney's Division, 2nd Military District, Department of Mississippi and East Louisiana (April-July 4, 1863); commanding Heavy Artillery, District of the Cape Fear (ca. February-April 18, 1864); commanding Heavy Artillery, District of the Cape Fear, Department of North Carolina (April 18-May 19, 1864); and commanding Defenses Mouth of the Cape Fear, 3rd Military District, Department of North Carolina and Southern Virginia (May 19, 1864-January 15, 1865). His regiment fought well at Wilson's Creek but the next spring much of it including Hébert was captured at Pea Ridge. Exchanged on March 20, 1862, he resumed command of a brigade and led it at Iuka and Corinth until illness forced him to relinquish command. Transferred to the Vicksburg area, he was again captured. Paroled on July 4, 1863, he was exchanged on the 13th. Thereafter he was concerned with artillery and engineering matters near Fort Fisher. After the war he was engaged in education and journalism. (Tunnard, W.H., *A Southern Record: The History of the Third Regiment Louisiana Infantry*)

HÉBERT, Paul Octave (1818-1880)

Serving throughout the war in the trans-Mississippi region, Paul O. Hébert took part in only one major action, Milliken's Bend, during the Civil War. The Louisiana West Pointer (1840) had served five years before resigning as a second lieutenant of engineers. Donning the uniform again for the Mexican War, he served as lieutenant colonel of the 3rd and 14th Infantry, winning a brevet before being mustered out in 1848. In the early 1850s he served as his state's governor. His Confederate assignments included: colonel, 1st Louisiana Artillery (early 1861); commanding Department of Louisiana (April 16-17, 1861); brigadier general, CSA (August 17, 1861); temporarily commanding Trans-Mississippi Department (spring 1862); commanding District of West Louisiana and Texas, Trans-Mississippi Department (fall-December 1862); commanding 6th (Texas) Brigade, 2nd (Texas) Division, 3rd Corps, Trans-Mississippi Department (fall 1864-May 26, 1865); also commanding Eastern Sub-District of Texas, District of Texas, New Mexico and Arizona, Trans-Mississippi Department (January 1865); and temporarily commanding 2nd (Texas) Division, 3rd Corps, Trans-Mississippi Department (February 1865). During the Vicksburg Campaign he attempted to relieve the pressure on Vicksburg from the Louisiana side of the Mississippi River but this failed. Much of his service was performed even farther west in Texas. Included in the surrender of E. Kirby Smith, he returned to his native state and again engaged in politics.

HECKMAN, Charles Adam (1822-1896)

The Civil War career of railroad conductor Charles A. Heckman was not very successful. The Pennsylvania native had given up a clerkship in a hardware store to join the regular army—as a private and later sergeant of the Regiment of Voltiguers—during the Mexican War. In the interwar years he resided in New Jersey but received his first commission back in

Pennsylvania. His assignments included: captain, 1st Pennsylvania (April 20, 1861); lieutenant colonel, 9th New Jersey (October 8, 1861); colonel, 9th New Jersey (February 10, 1862); commanding 1st Brigade, 3rd Division, Department of North Carolina (April 2-July 6, 1862); brigadier general, USV (November 29, 1862); commanding brigade, Department of North Carolina (December 10, 1862-January 2, 1863); commanding 1st Brigade, 2nd Division, 18th Corps, Department of North Carolina (January 2-March 6 and April 16-May 10, 1863); commanding the division (March 6-April 16, 1863); also commanding 1st Brigade, 1st Division, St. Helena Island (detachment 18th Corps), 10th Corps, Department of the South (January-March 6, 1863) and 2nd Division, St. Helena Island (detachment 18th Corps), 10th Corps, Department of the South (March 6-April 16, 1863); commanding District of Beaufort, 18th Corps, Department of North Carolina (May 2-25 and May 29-July 21, 1863); commanding Defenses of New Bern, District of North Carolina, 18th Corps, Department of Virginia and North Carolina (August 1-14, 1863); commanding Sub District of Beaufort, District of North Carolina, 18th Corps, Department of Virginia and North Carolina (August 14-October 11, 1863); commanding Newport News, 18th Corps, Department of Virginia and North Carolina (October 18, 1863-January 14, 1864); commanding Getty's (old) Division, U.S. Forces Norfolk and Portsmouth, 18th Corps, Department of Virginia and North Carolina (January 14-April 28, 1864); commanding 1st Brigade, 2nd Division, 18th Corps, Army of the James (April 26-May 16, 1864); commanding the division (September 17-December 3, 1864); also commanding the corps (September 29-October 1, 1864); commanding 3rd Division, 25th Corps, Army of the James (December 3-30, 1864); and commanding the corps (January 1-February 2, 1865). His first company served under Patterson in the Shenandoah Valley in July 1861 before being mustered out on the 27th. As a lieutenant colonel, he commanded his New Jersey regiment at Roanoke Island and New Bern, being wounded at the latter. He was again wounded at Young's Crossroads on July 26, 1862. By this time a colonel, he spent most of the rest of the war in brigade, or higher, command in southeastern Virginia and North and South Carolina. Made a brigadier general in the fall of 1862, he took part in some of the operations against Charleston before joining Butler's army in the spring of 1864. Wounded at Port Walthall Junction, he was captured on May 16, 1864, at Drewry's Bluff after having withstood several enemy assaults. Blame for the defeat rested largely upon Heckman and Isaac J. Wistar. Held for four months, he was placed under the fire of Union guns at Charleston. Exchanged in September 1864, he commanded a division and then the corps at Fort Harrison where his performance was below par. However, he retained command until early 1865 and was relieved by Grant on March 23. Resigning on May 25, 1865, he returned to the Jersey Central Railroad.

HEG, Hans Christian (ca. 1829-1863)

Acting upon his Viking heritage, Hans C. Heg raised a regiment of Norsemen for the Union army and became a capable citizen-soldier. Born in Lier, Norway, he had emigrated to Wisconsin in his youth. Following a stint in the California gold fields he returned to Wisconsin and became the state's prison commissioner. He resigned this post to enter the army at the head of a thousand Danes, Swedes, and Norwegians. His assignments included: colonel, 15th Wisconsin (ca. February 14, 1862); commanding 2nd Brigade, 1st Division, 20th Corps, Army of the Cumberland (February 15-March 16, 1863); and commanding 3rd Brigade, 1st Division, 20th Corps, Army of the Cumberland (May 15-September 19, 1863). At the head of the regiment he fought at Island #10, Perryville, and Murfreesboro. During the Tullahoma Campaign he was commanding a brigade. On the first day at Chickamauga, in the heavy fighting on the Union right, Heg was shot in the bowels while directing his brigade in the defense. He continued to rally his men and then after riding a quarter-mile was felled by the loss of blood. He died at dusk.

HEIMAN, Adolphus (?-1862)

Native Prussian Adolphus Heiman spent most of his Confederate career at Fort Henry on the Tennessee River, but led most of its garrison over to Fort Donelson before the attack on the latter work. Coming to America, he had served as adjutant of the 1st Tennessee during the Mexican War. Upon the outbreak of the Civil War he was named colonel of the 10th Tennessee in May 1861. This unit was organized in the state army at Fort Henry and was active in the fort's construction. A subsidiary work was constructed on the opposite bank, in Kentucky, and named after him. For much of 1861 he was in command of the two fortifications. On February 5, 1862, Heiman was ordered to lead the garrison, except the heavy artillery, to Fort Donelson since Fort Henry was flooded and indefensible. His superior, General Tilghman, remained behind with the heavy guns. At Donelson, Heiman commanded a brigade in Johnson's Division (February 9-16, 1862). After a defense of several days that post also fell to the enemy. Heiman was imprisoned until paroled with the regiment the following September. The unit was reorganized in October but Heiman died from the effects of his incarceration the next month, at about the time that his command was declared exchanged. (Hamilton, James, *The Battle of Fort Donelson*)

HEINTZELMAN, Samuel Peter (1805-1880)

McClellan had been reluctant to form his army into corps until such time as he could test his division commanders in the field to determine those most capable for higher command. But the Washington authorities insisted and he was forced to appoint corps commanders largely on the basis of seniority. One of the failures of this system was Samuel P. Heintzelman. The Pennsylvania native was a West Pointer (1826) who had served in the infantry and quartermaster's department and earned a brevet in Mexico. His Civil War-era assignments included: major, 1st Infantry (since March 3, 1855); colonel, 17th Infantry (May 14, 1861); brigadier general, USV (May 17, 1861); commanding 3rd Division, Army of Northeastern Virginia

(June-August 17, 1861); commanding brigade, Division of the Potomac (August 17-October 3, 1861); commanding division, Army of the Potomac (October 3, 1861-March 13, 1862); commanding 3rd Corps, Army of the Potomac (March 13-October 30, 1862); major general, USV (May 5, 1862); commanding Military District of Washington, Army of the Potomac (October 27, 1862-February 2, 1863); commanding 22nd Corps, Department of Washington (February 2-October 13, 1863); commanding the department (February 2-October 14, 1863); and commanding Northern Department (January 20-October 1, 1864). Taking part in the occupation of Alexandria, he was later slightly wounded at 1st Bull Run where he led his division in the wide flanking movement. Under McClellan, he commanded a brigade, division, and finally a corps. On the Peninsula he proved to be overly cautious at Yorktown—having an unfortunate influence on the normally timid McClellan—but particularly distinguished himself at Williamsburg where he earned an 1865 brevet as major general in the regular army. His full commission at that grade in the volunteer service was dated from this action. His leadership at Seven Pines earned him the regular army brevet of brigadier general. He went on to serve in the Seven Days and at 2nd Bull Run. Following the latter defeat his corps was assigned to the Washington fortifications during the Antietam Campaign and he eventually took charge of the defenses. Late in 1863 he took command of the Northern Department—Michigan, Ohio, Indiana, and Illinois. In the final half year of the war he was detailed to court-martial duty. Mustered out of the volunteer service on August 24, 1865, he continued to serve as a regular army colonel until his retirement in 1869 with the advanced grade of major general.

HEISKELL, Joseph Brown (1823-1913)

A veteran of the state legislature in his native Tennessee, Joseph B. Heiskell became a secessionist only upon the call for troops by Lincoln following the firing on Fort Sumter. Although he was elected to the Provisional Confederate Congress, he voluntarily never took his seat because the candidate for his East Tennessee district running for the U.S. House of Representatives had drawn twice as many votes on the same day. While he did not serve, his opponent was imprisoned by the Confederates! Reelected in the November 1861 elections, Heiskell finally took his place in the Confederate Congress the next February. He was assigned to the Committee on the Judiciary. Reelected to the Second Congress in 1863 he served on the committees on: Claims; Elections; and Patents. His primary concern during his tenure was with those citizens living in enemy-occupied territories. He favored a vigorous war effort, especially when it held out the prospect of recovery of lost areas. While visiting his home in 1864 he was captured by Union forces and not released until after the close of the war. After the war he moved to Memphis, where pro-Confederate sympathies provided a more friendly home than East Tennessee. He resumed the practice of law, served as state attorney general, and as state reporter, compiled *Heiskell's Reports* for eight years.

HELM, Benjamin Hardin (1831-1863)

In an example of how the Civil War tore families apart, the U.S. White House went into mourning when Confederate General Benjamin H. Helm was mortally wounded at Chickamauga. The Kentucky native and West Pointer (1851) resigned the next year as a second lieutenant in the 2nd Dragoons in order to practice law. Marrying the half-sister of Mary Todd Lincoln in 1856, he formed a close friendship with the future Civil War president. When the secession crisis came to a head Lincoln offered Helm the position of paymaster with the rank of major. This was refused after a few days' deliberation. Joining the Confederacy, Helm's assignments included: colonel, 1st Kentucky Cavalry (October 19, 1861); brigadier general, CSA (March 14, 1862); commanding 3rd Brigade, Reserve Corps, Army of the Mississippi (spring-June 1862); commanding 2nd Brigade, 1st Division, Breckinridge's Command, District of the Mississippi, Department #2 (July-August 5, 1862); commanding Kentucky Brigade, Breckinridge's Division, Hardee's Corps, Army of Tennessee (January 31-May 1863); commanding Kentucky Brigade, Breckinridge's Division, Department of the West (May-August 1863); and commanding Kentucky Brigade, Breckinridge's Division, D.H. Hill's Corps, Army of Tennessee (August-September 20, 1863). Raising a regiment of mounted troops, Helm served in Mississippi before being promoted to brigadier general. He was then given charge of a brigade under John C. Breckinridge, which he led in the Confederate attack on Baton Rouge. In the operations against that city he was injured by the fall of his horse. Not returning to duty immediately, he spent some time serving along the Gulf coast. He then took command of the Kentucky Brigade, again under Breckinridge, and led it in the expedition to relieve the pressure on Vicksburg. With Rosecrans' advance through middle Tennessee, the brigade and its division rejoined Bragg just before Chickamuaga. In the Confederate attacks on the second day of that battle Helm fell mortally wounded. He died on the next day, September 21, 1863. (Davis, William C., *The Orphan Brigade* and McMurtry, R. Gerald, *Ben Hardin Helm: "Rebel Brother-In-Law of Abraham Lincoln"*)

HELPER, Hinton Rowan (1829-1909)

Not even *Uncle Tom's Cabin* garnered more Southern wrath than the 1857 publication, *The Impending Crisis of the South: How To Meet It*, and its author, Hinton Helper—all the more so because Helper was one of their own. Orphaned at an early age, Helper was an indentured servant in antebellum North Carolina before absconding with money from his employer, going to New York, and then joining the California Gold Rush. Returning to New York broke, he observed that the North was far advanced over the South in culture, trade, and society in general. Blaming this situation on the relatively small slaveholding class, he became a practical abolitionist, not from any compassion for the blacks but rather as a means to rectify the regional imbalance. His book, which had been rejected by several major publishing houses in fear of losing the Southern market, projected this thesis in a highly incendiary and somewhat less than purely factual manner. Reaction was immediate and harsh. It became illegal through most of the South to read or even possess a copy; the speaker of the House of Representatives, John Sherman, lost his post for his endorsement; and men were hanged in Arkansas for supporting Helper's thesis. In the 1860 elections the Republicans used excerpts as campaign literature. Although the book had a wide distribution, it brought Helper little financial reward, and he was penniless when appointed consul in Argentina where he served throughout the Civil War. In the postwar period he had little success, went insane, and finally committed suicide. (Bailey, Hugh C., *Hinton Rowan Helper, Abolitionist Racist*)

HENAGAN, John Williford (1822-1865)

A dependable Confederate officer, John W. Henagan fell victim to the advanced technology of the Union forces. A native South Carolinian, he had served in that state's legislature and as a sheriff. Capitalizing on his experience in the militia, where he had risen to the rank of brigadier general, he offered his services to the South. His assignments included: lieutenant colonel, 8th South Carolina (April 13, 1861); colonel, 8th South Carolina (May 14, 1862); and commanding Kershaw's Brigade, Kershaw's Division, 1st Corps, Army of Northern Virginia (April-May 1864). He saw early action at 1st Bull Run, Williamsburg, and the Seven Days before being wounded at South Mountain. Returning, he commanded the regiment at Chancellorsville, Gettysburg, Chickamauga, and Knoxville. At the Wilderness and Spotsylvania he led the brigade and in both instances spearheaded the corps' advance. He subsequently fought at Cold Harbor and Petersburg before being sent to the Shenandoah Valley to reenforce General Early. In a small action near Winchester on September 13, 1864, Union General John B. McIntosh led his cavalry brigade, armed with repeating rifles, across the Opequon on a reconnaissance. The prize was nearly the entire 8th South Carolina, including Colonel Henagan. Confined at Johnson's Island, Henagan died on April 26, 1865, the same day the remnant of the 8th laid down their arms. (Dickert, D. Augustus, *History of Kershaw's Brigade*)

HENDERSON, John Brooks (1826-1913)

The expulsion of Missouri Senator Trusten Polk on January 10, 1862, opened the way for Douglas Democrat John B. Henderson to take a seat in Washington. A native of Virginia, he had moved with his family to Missouri in 1832 and 16 years later entered into the practice of law. The same year he began an eight-year career in the state legislature. At the 1860 Democratic national convention he was a delegate for Stephen A. Douglas and served as an elector in the general election. Loyal to the Union, he worked in the state convention to retain the state as a member of the Union. With the war underway he became a brigadier general in the Missouri militia and was serving as such when named to the Senate. He took his seat on January 29, 1862, and was reelected the next year. His term ran out on March 3, 1869, and he subsequently served as a prosecutor in the Whiskey Ring scandals and as an Indian commissioner.

HENDRICKS, Thomas Andrews (1819-1885)

In a political career spanning almost 40 years, Thomas A. Hendricks rose from the state legislature to become Grover Cleveland's vice president. Born in Ohio, he moved to Indiana where he took up the practice of law in 1843. Five years later he served a term in the lower house of the legislature and in 1849 moved on to the state senate. Beginning in 1851 he was twice a Democratic member of the U.S. House of Representatives but failed to gain reelection to a third term. He was then named commissioner of the General Land Office and headed that agency until 1859. In 1860 he lost a bid for the gubernatorial chair as a Democrat and resumed the practice of law. Elected to the Senate he served one full term from 1863 to 1869. Three years later he became governor. In the disputed Tilden-Hayes election of 1876 he was the Democrat Tilden's running mate. In 1884 he was successful in his second bid for the vice presidency but only served eight months until his death.

HENNINGSEN, Charles Frederick (1815-1877)

A military adventurer of some note, Charles F. Henningsen had only a brief career in the Confederate army. The native of Brussels, Belgium, had served the Carlists in Spain and fought with Kossuth in Hungary before immigrating to the United States in the early 1850s. He became a noted author, recounting his adventures, and was involved in the expansionist plots of William Walker in Central America. Offering his services to the South, he was commissioned colonel, 59th Virginia, on August 1, 1861. Serving under General Wise, he took part in the campaigns in western Virginia, North Carolina, and on the Peninsula. Much of the time he directed the artillery of Wise's Legion. When the regiment was reorganized under the Conscript Act in November 1862 he was relieved of his command. He subsequently lived in Washington, D.C.

HENRY, B. Tyler (?-?)

For his work in developing the famous Henry Rifle, the Winchester firearms company to this day places an "H" in honor of B. Tyler Henry on all its rim-fire cartridges. While working as plant superintendent for Oliver Winchester's New Haven Arms Company, Henry patented his invention. It was a rim-fire 15-round rifle, which unfortunately for Henry and Winchester was considered too fragile for military service by the U.S. War Department. Only 1,731 were purchased by the general government but thousands of others were bought by state governments and private citizens. Nonetheless the Spencer became the preferred weapon in the field of repeating firearms.

HENRY, Guy Vernor (ca. 1839-1899)

In a career that spanned the Civil and Spanish-American wars Guy V. Henry rose to the rank of major general of volunteers and brigadier general of regulars. Born in the Indian Territory—which is now Oklahoma—he was graduated from

West Point (May 1861) at the very outset of the Civil War. His assignments included: second lieutenant, 1st Artillery (May 6, 1861); first lieutenant, 1st Artillery (May 14, 1861); colonel, 40th Massachusetts (November 9, 1863); commanding brigade, District of Hilton Head, 10th Corps, Department of the South (January 18-February 6, 1864); commanding Light Brigade, District of Florida, 10th Corps, Department of the South (February 16-April 25, 1864); commanding 1st Brigade, 2nd Division, 10th Corps, Army of the James (April 28-May 2, 1864); commanding 3rd Brigade, 1st Division, 18th Corps, Army of the James (May 30-August 12, 1864); commanding 3rd Brigade, 3rd Division, 24th Corps, Army of the James (December 3, 1864-January 29, 1865); and captain, 1st Artillery (December 1, 1865). While serving with his battery along the South Carolina coast he received a regular army brevet for an affair at the Pocotaligo River. Taking a volunteer commission, he commanded a mounted brigade at the defeat at Olustee in Florida before being assigned to Butler's army in Virginia. There he earned a Congressional Medal of Honor—awarded in 1893—for his leadership of a brigade in the bloody assault at Cold Harbor. Two more brevets were received for the fighting around Petersburg. Brevetted brigadier general in the volunteers for the war, he was mustered out on June 30, 1865, with his regiment. Retaining his regular army commission, he was soon transferred to the cavalry. In subsequent Indian fighting he was wounded at the Rosebud River in 1876, a few days before Custer's command was massacred. He was brevetted brigadier in the regular service for this action. During the Spanish-American War he was a full brigadier of regulars and a major general of volunteers. Meanwhile, as a supplement to Cullum's compilation of West Point graduates, he wrote *Military Record of Civilian Appointments in the United States Army*. He died on active duty in 1899.

HENSON, Josiah (1789-1883)

Himself an escaped slave, Josiah Henson like Frederick Douglass became a leader in the antislavery movement. He took his family from bondage to freedom in Canada and from there launched his crusade to help his less fortunate brethren. He lectured in North America and England. Many in the abolitionist movement believed that to a large extent he was the basis for "Uncle Tom" in Harriet Beecher Stowe's explosive novel *Uncle Tom's Cabin*, of which Charles Sumner said that if it "had not been written Abraham Lincoln could not have been elected President of the United States."

HERBERT, Arthur (1829-1919)

By the time Arthur Herbert got to command a brigade there were only three days left in its life. A native of Alexandria, Virginia, he was a barber at the outbreak of the war when he helped raise a local company. His Confederate assignments included: lieutenant, Company G, 6th Virginia Battalion (early 1861); captain, Company H, 17th Virginia (April 17, 1861); major, 17th Virginia (April 27, 1862); lieutenant colonel, 17th Virginia (November 1, 1862); colonel, 17th Virginia (July 8, 1864); and commanding Corse's Brigade, Pickett's Division, 1st Corps, Army of Northern Virginia (April 6-9, 1865). He saw action at Blackburn's Ford, 1st Bull Run, Yorktown, Williamsburg, Seven Pines, the Seven Days, and 2nd Bull Run. In the latter battle he succeeded to command of the regiment upon the wounding of the lieutenant colonel. Again, at Antietam, he moved up to regimental command, this time when Colonel M.D. Corse was injured. After being only lightly engaged at Fredericksburg, the division took part in Longstreet's campaign, in southeastern Virginia, missing the battle of Chancellorsville. During the Gettysburg Campaign, the brigade, now under Corse, was left in Virginia to guard Hanover Junction. In the fall and winter of 1863-64 the brigade was again detached from the army, with Herbert and the 17th serving in southern Virginia. Rejoining the army in May 1864, he fought at North Anna, Cold Harbor, Petersburg, Five Forks, and Sayler's Creek. In the last action, he took over the brigade after General Corse was captured. Three days later he surrendered the command at Appomattox. Returning to Alexandria, he was active in banking.

HERBERT, Caleb Claiborne (ca. 1814-1867)

Confederate congressmen from the Trans-Mississippi area were generally advocates of states' rights within the new nation, demanding that their region not be stripped of troops. One of the most vehement of these radicals was Caleb C. Herbert of Texas' 2nd District. Born in Virginia, Herbert had moved to Texas where he became a wealthy farmer. In the immediate prewar years he served in the state legislature's upper house where he furthered the movement toward secession. Winning election to the First Regular Congress in November 1861, he served on the committees on Ordnance and Ordnance Stores; and Post Offices and Post Roads. As chairman of a special committee investigating the treatment of Union prisoners, Herbert wrote a minority report condemning the management of Castle Thunder. Considering the draft to be class discrimination and a drain upon the defenses of the Texas frontier, he even threatened the secession of the state from the Confederacy. He rejected all administration proposals, especially those threatening his constituents' cotton crop. Winning by a narrow margin in his 1863 reelection campaign, he served on the committees on Claims and Commerce. With the impending doom of the Confederacy, Herbert supported the Davis administration's foreign policy and opposed peace negotiations. After the war he was twice refused admittance to the U.S. Congress and two years after the war was shot and killed, apparently a case of the "wrong man."

HERNDON, William Henry (1818-1891)

A staunchly antislavery Illinois lawyer, William H. Herndon took advantage of his friendship and law partnership with Abraham Lincoln to press his views. It is an open question as to how much influence can really be credited to Herndon. He joined Lincoln's law firm in about 1844 and almost immediately began working on the older man's political career. The partnership was not dissolved in 1860 and after Lincoln's death Herndon continued his practice. At the same time, he traveled widely through Lincoln country, gathering information for his later book *Herndon's Lincoln: The True Story of a Great Life*, written with Jesse W. Weik. (Newton, Joseph Fort, *Lincoln and Herndon* and Donald, David, *Lincoln's Herndon: A Biography*)

HEROLD, David E. (1842-1865)

On the flight from Ford's Theater, it was an unemployed druggist's clerk, David E. Herold, who was the almost constant companion of John Wilkes Booth. He went to the gallows for it. Meeting Booth through his acquaintance with John Surratt, he had become involved in the plan to capture Lincoln and spirit him off to Richmond where he would be exchanged for Confederate prisoners of war. Apparently at least one attempt was made. When the plan was changed to assassination following Appomattox, Herold was assigned to aid Lewis Paine to make his escape through Maryland after killing Secretary of State William H. Seward. Herold had grown up in the area and was thoroughly familiar with the roads and terrain. In advance of the planned murders he placed guns in the Maryland countryside to facilitate the plotters' getaway. In the actual event Herold hooked up with Booth on the far side of the Anacostia River, having passed Silas T. Cobb, the sentry on the Navy Yard Bridge. From there their route took them to Dr. Samuel A. Mudd, then across the Potomac and eventually to the tobacco shed on the Richard H. Garrett farm near Port Royal, Virginia. When surrounded by Union cavalrymen, Herold begged to be allowed to come out and surrender and did so, being cursed by Booth. With Booth in a maimed condition, Herold had already shown extreme loyalty in staying with him this far; he had always been going off to get aid for his friend. Following Booth's death Herold was taken to Washington and tried by a military court. He went to the hangman on July 7, 1865.

David Herold on wanted poster. (AC)

HERRON, Francis Jay (1837-1902)

Already offering his militia company to President-elect Lincoln in January 1861, Iowa banker Francis Jay Herron served throughout the Civil War and won the Congressional Medal of Honor. The Pittsburgh native's assignments included: captian, "Governor's Grays" (prewar); captain, 1st Iowa (May 14, 1861); lieutenant colonel, 9th Iowa (September 24, 1861); brigadier general, USV (July 16, 1862); commanding 3rd Division, Army of the Frontier, Department of the Missouri (October 12, 1862-February 1863); major general, USV (March 10, 1863, to rank from November 29, 1862); commanding the army (March 30-June 5, 1863); commanding division, Army of the Tennessee (June 11-July 28, 1863); commanding 2nd Division, 13th Corps, Army of the Tennessee (July 28-August 7, 1863); commanding 2nd Division, 13th Corps, Department of the Gulf (August 7-September 28, 1863 and January 3-June 11, 1864); also commanding U.S. Forces in Texas, Military Division of West Mississippi (May 1-June 9, 1864); commanding District of Port Hudson, 19th Corps, Department of the Gulf (August 6-September 12, 1864): commanding District of Baton Rouge and Port Hudson, 19th Corps, Department of the Gulf (September 12-October 3, 1864); and commanding Northern District of Louisiana, Department of the Gulf (February 9-July 1865). Having led his three-months company at Wilson's Creek, he was mustered out on August 20, 1861. As a lieutenant colonel, he was wounded and captured at Pea Ridge while leading the regiment. In 1893 he received the coveted medal for this. Exchanged on March 20, 1862, he received a more immediate reward in the form of a brigadier general's star. After fighting at Prairie Grove, he led his division to the Vicksburg front where he held the Union left from mid-June until the surrender of the city. Transferred to the Department of the Gulf shortly thereafter, he served out the war in Louisiana and Texas. After a stint negotiating with the Indians, he resigned effective June 7, 1865, and he entered upon the practice of law in occupied Louisiana, holding several offices in the Reconstruction government. In the late 1870s he moved to New York and engaged in manufacturing but may also have practiced law.

HETH, Henry (1825-1899)

Graduating at the very bottom of his 1847 class at West Point, Henry Heth served 14 years on frontier duty before resigning his infantry captaincy on April 25, 1861, to serve his native Virginia. His assignments included: captain, Infantry (spring 1861); colonel, 45th Virginia (1861); brigadier general, CSA (January 6, 1862); commanding District of Lewisburg (February 6-May 8, 1862); commanding division, Department of East Tennessee (July 3-December 1862); commanding the District, same department (December 1862); commanding the department (January 1863); commanding Field's (old) Brigade, A.P. Hill's Division, 2nd Corps, Army of Northern Virginia (March 5-May 2, and late May 1863); major general, CSA (May 24, 1863); commanding the division (May 2-3, 1863) commanding division, 3rd Corps, same army (May 30-July 1 and July 1863-February 1865 and March-April 9, 1865); and commanding the corps (February-March 1865). His initial service came in the Kanawha Valley and the Lewisburg area of western Virginia. He joined Kirby Smith in East Tennessee in the summer of 1862 and commanded a division and briefly the department. At the request of Robert E. Lee, who called the brigadier by his first name, allegedly the only case of Lee doing this with his generals, Heth was transferred to the Army of Northern Virginia. Commanding a Virginia brigade he fought at Chancellorsville and was in command of the division until wounded. Returning to duty he was soon promoted (an October 1862 appointment as major general had not been confirmed), and given a division in the new 3rd Corps. On the first day at Gettysburg he was wounded but recovered to fight at Falling Waters, Bristoe Station, and Mine Run before the end of the year. The next spring and summer he guided his men through the Overland Campaign and supervised them in the trenches around Petersburg, often sallying forth to defeat Union attempts to cut the railroads and highways into the beleaguered city. Briefly in corps command during the final winter of the conflict, he surrendered with his chief at Appomattox. He was involved in insurance after the peace. (Morrison, James L., ed., *The Memoirs of Henry Heth*)

Henry Heth, whose division opened the battle of Gettysburg. (NA)

HEYWARD, William Cruger (1808-1863)

West Pointer (1830) and ex-brevet second lieutenant in the 3rd Infantry, William C. Heyward was living on his plantation in South Carolina when the Civil War prompted him to reenter the military, which he had left in 1832. In July 1861 he was named colonel, 11th South Carolina. This unit was sometimes referred to as the 9th. On the morning of November 7, 1861, he was placed in command of Fort Walker at Port Royal. The Union fleet attacked within a few hours and when he was about out of ammunition, he ordered the fort's evacuation. The following spring he was not reelected to the colonelcy and he was accordingly dropped in May. He retired to his plantation where he died on September 1, 1863, a couple of months after most of his slaves were lost to Union raiders.

HICKENLOOPER, Andrew (1837-1904)

An Ohio civil engineer, Andrew Hickenlooper proved so adept at military engineering duties that he was one of the heroes of the victory at Vicksburg, earning a gold medal for his efforts. Joining the artillery at the outbreak of the Civil War, his assignments included: captain, 5th Ohio Battery (August 31, 1861); chief of artillery, 6th Division, District of West Tennessee, Department of Tennessee (spring-summer 1862); chief of Artillery, 6th Division, District of Corinth, Department of the Tennessee (July-October 1862); chief of Ordnance and Artillery, Right Wing, 13th Corps, Army of the Tennessee (October-December 1862); chief engineer, 17th Corps, Army of the Tennessee (ca. December 1862-March 1864); chief engineer, Army of the Tennessee (ca. March-July 1864); judge advocate and assistant chief of Artillery, Army of the Tennessee (July-September 1864); lieutenant colonel and assistant inspector general (September 14, 1864-May 13, 1865); assistant inspector general, 17th Corps, Army of the Tennessee (September 14, 1864-May 13, 1865); and commanding 3rd Brigade, 4th Division, 17th Corps, Army of the Tennessee (June 16-August 1, 1865). After directing his battery at Shiloh he was a divisional artillery chief at Corinth. His greatest glory came in the siege of Vicksburg as a corps chief engineer where he was responsible for the progress of the parallels. The board of honor for the corps awarded him a gold medal for the campaign. During the advance on Vicksburg he had constructed a bridge over the Big Black River from cotton bales. He served the remainder of the war in a number of staff positions and was brevetted brigadier near its close. He finished his service in command of an infantry brigade after the cessation of hostilities. Mustered out on July 31, 1865, he entered the gaslight business, writing a number of technical books on gas and electricity. He also wrote an account of Shiloh and entered politics, rising to be Ohio's lieutenant governor.

HICKOK, James Butler (1837-1876)

The famed gunfighter/lawman "Wild Bill" Hickok once claimed to have killed 50 Confederates with 50 shots from a special rifle. This is hogwash and in fact his career in the war itself is shrouded in mystery. James B. Hickok was born in Illinois and at 18 went west. He was allegedly involved in the Kansas fighting of the late 1850s. His reputation as a gunslinger began in Nebraska in 1861 when he killed three men, apparently in cold blood. What can be documented is a series of questionable killings that earned him his nickname. There is no direct evidence that he ever took part in the Civil War, but it is likely that he might have been drawn to the guerilla conflicts in Missouri. After the war his trail switched from lawman to gunman to army scout until his death in a saloon in Deadwood. He was shot in the back. (Rose, Joseph G., *They Called Him Wild Bill: The Life and Adventures of James Butler Hickok*)

"Wild Bill Hickok," noted western killer and alleged Civil War participant. (NA)

HICKS, Thomas Holliday (1798-1865)

In a political career that spanned the Democratic, Whig, American, and Republican parties, Thomas H. Hicks was Maryland's governor during the uncertain days of the secession crisis. A native of the state, he had served as a sheriff, state legislator, and member of the governor's council. In 1857—on the American ticket—he was elected to the gubernatorial chair and was inaugurated on January 18, 1858. A self-proclaimed Unionist, he let the state drift while public opinion was sharply divided. He tried to avoid any action that might upset one faction or the other. Forced to act by the April 19, 1861, secessionist riot and attack on Massachusetts troops, he called on the federal government to route its troops around the city. He acquiesced in the burning of bridges in the vicinity in order to force compliance on the part of the government. Calling a special session of the legislature, he was powerless in preventing the arrest of pro-Southern members by the national government in September 1861. On January 8, 1862, his term expired and on December 29 he was named to fill the unexpired term of deceased Senator James A. Pearce. Elected to a full term, he died in office on February 14, 1865. (Buchholz, Heinrich, E., *Governors of Maryland: From the Revolution to the Year 1908*)

HIGGINS, Edward (1821-1875)

Being twice captured while commanding river defenses, Confederate artillerist Edward Higgins rose to the rank of brigadier general. Born in Virginia, he had spent nearly two decades in the navy before resigning as a lieutenant in 1854 and entering the mail steamer business on his own hook. Residing in New Orleans at the outbreak of the war, he offered his services and his assignments included: captain, 1st Louisiana Artillery (April 1861); lieutenant colonel, 21st Louisiana (February 1862); colonel, Artillery (post April 1862); commanding River Batteries, Vicksburg, Department of Mississippi and East Louisiana (winter-July 4, 1863); brigadier general, CSA (October 29, 1863); commanding 3rd Brigade, Department of the Gulf (fall 1863-early 1864); and commanding brigade, District of the Gulf, Department of Alabama, Mississippi and East Louisiana (spring-fall 1864). His initial service came as an aide to David E. Twiggs on the Louisiana coast and then in command of Forts Jackson and St. Philip. When the Union fleet passed his outposts on the way to New Orleans and captured the city he faced mutinies by the garrisons and was forced to surrender. Eventually exchanged, he was promoted to colonel and commanded the batteries commanding the river at Vicksburg. When that city fell he again became a prisoner of war and was not exchanged until October 27, 1863. Two days later he was named a brigadier general and he spent most of the balance of the war on the Gulf coast. However, he disappears from the records in the fall of 1864. In the postwar years he engaged in various business enterprises on both the East and West coasts.

HIGGINSON, Thomas Wentworth (1823-1911)

A prominent abolitionist—who had been forced to relinquish his pastorate due to his views and who believed in fighting the return of fugitive slaves—became the commander of the first regiment of black troops accepted officially into the Union army. A Massachusetts-born reformer he worked for abolition, temperance, and the vote for women. He was linked to John Brown, and some have charged that he helped organize the Harpers Ferry raid. Having helped raise a regiment in the fall of 1862 he was a company commander in it when offered the colonelcy of the 1st South Carolina Colored Infantry. This unit was redesignated the 33rd United States Colored Troops on February 8, 1864, and he commanded it in minor operations along the South Carolina coast. Suffering from a wound in May 1864 he was forced to resign. After the war he wrote several works, including *Army Life in a Black Regiment*. (Higginson, Mary Potter, *Thomas Wentworth Higginson, The Story of His Life*; Wells, Anna Mary, *Dear Preceptor: The Life and Times of Thomas Wentworth Higginson*; and Meyer, Howard, *Colonel of the Black Regiment, Life of Thomas W. Higginson*)

HILGARD, Ferdinand Heinrich Gustav

See: *Villard, Henry*

HILL, Adams Sherman (1833-1910)

In his first experience as a war correspondent, at Blackburn's Ford during the 1st Bull Run Campaign, Harvard graduate Adams S. Hill fled from the field but kept his journalism career intact. He soon rose to head the *New York Tribune's* office in the nation's capital. However, conflicts with Horace Greeley prompted him to resign in December 1863. Along with Henry Villard, he challenged the domination of the Associated Press by setting up the unsuccessful Independent News Room Service. Upon its failure he held numerous journalistic posts and in 1872 returned to his alma mater as a professor and later as head of the English department. (Starr, Louis M., *Bohemian Brigade*)

HILL, Ambrose Powell (1825-1865)

Known for his red battle shirt and his hard-hitting attacks at the head of the famed Light Division, Ambrose P. Hill proved to be an example of the Peter principle. A West Pointer (1847) and veteran artilleryman, he resigned as a first lieutenant on March 1, 1861, and joined the South, where his services included: colonel, 13th Virginia (spring 1861); brigadier general, CSA (February 26, 1862); commanding brigade, Longstreet's Division, Department of Northern Virginia (ca. February 26-May 27, 1862); major general, CSA (May 26, 1862); commanding Light Division (in 1st Corps from June 29 and 2nd Corps from July 27, 1862), Army of Northern Virginia (May 27, 1862-May 2, 1863); commanding 2nd Corps, Army of Northern Virginia (May 2 and 6-30, 1863); lieutenant general, CSA (May 24, 1863); and commanding 3rd Corps, Army of Northern Virginia (May 30, 1863-May 7, 1864 and May 21, 1864-April 2, 1865). In reserve at 1st Bull Run, he fought at Yorktown and Williamsburg before being given command of a division. On the day he assumed command he directed the fight at Hanover Court House. He then took part in the Seven Days, distinguishing himself. After fighting at Cedar Mountain, 2nd Bull Run, and the capture of Harpers Ferry, he launched powerful

A.P. Hill, Confederate corps commander killed in the final days of the war. (NA)

counterattacks at the right moment at both Antietam and Fredericksburg. At Chancellorsville he was on Jackson's famed march around the Union left flank. When Jackson was wounded, Hill took command of the corps but was wounded carrying his chief to the rear. At the end of the month he was given command of the new 3rd Corps, which he led to Gettysburg where, suffering from a now unidentifiable illness, he put in a lackluster performance. He was responsible for the disaster at Bristoe Station that fall and, again ill, was virtually circumvented at the Wilderness when Lee in effect took over command of the corps. He relinquished command temporarily after the battle and missed Spotsylvania but returned for the North Anna and Cold Harbor. Taking part in the siege of Petersburg, he was again ill during part of the winter of 1864-65. With the lines around the city collapsing on April 2, 1865, he was shot and killed in an encounter with a stray group of federal soldiers. Interestingly enough, both Stonewall Jackson and Lee called for Hill and his division in their dying delirium. It must have been the old Hill they were recalling. (Hassler, William W., *A.P. Hill: Lee's Forgotten General* and Schenck, Martin, *Up Came Hill: The Story of the Light Division and of its Leaders*)

HILL, Benjamin Harvey (1823-1882)

One of the politicians most adept at flowing with the times was Georgia's Benjamin H. Hill, who at one time or another served under just about every political banner of the mid- and late-19th century. Initially an opponent of secession, the plantation owner and lawyer had been active in Whig politics before becoming a Know-Nothing upon the breakup of the Whigs. In the 1860 election he backed the Constitutional Union ticket, but with the election of Lincoln he determined that secession was inevitable and signed the document taking Georgia out of the Union, rather than cause division in his state. Having served in both houses of the state legislature, he was named to the Provisional Confederate Congress where he was active in the organization of the new government. With the adoption of the regular constitution he was named to the Senate for both of the regular congresses. His congressional service included appointments to the following committees: Claims; the Judiciary; Naval Affairs; Patents; Postal Affairs; and Printing. From his position chairing the Committee on the Judiciary, he tried to establish a Confederate supreme court but this was never accomplished. A general supporter of the president, he opposed the creation of the position of general in chief (for Robert E. Lee), fearing that it would weaken Davis' authority. Although he would sometimes oppose administration requests, once they were enacted he would act as liaison to Georgia in support of the administration's policy. Confined for three months after the war, Hill soon reentered politics, eventually accepting the harsh Reconstruction policies of the Radical Republicans. Five years later, the resulting furor in Georgia over his acceptance of the political realities having died down, he was elected to the U.S. House of Representatives and later the Senate, where he fought for southern rights. He died in office. (Pearce, Haywood Jefferson, *Benjamin H. Hill, Secession and Reconstruction* and Hill, Benjamin Harvey, Jr., *Senator Benjamin H. Hill of Georgia*)

HILL, Benjamin Jefferson (1825-1880)

Native Tennessee merchant Benjamin J. Hill spent most of the war serving with the infantry, but once he was promoted to be a Confederate brigadier general he was transferred to the mounted arm. His assignments included: colonel, 5th Tennessee, Provisional Army (September 11, 1861); colonel, 35th Tennessee (designation change November 1861); commanding Cleburne's Brigade, Buckner's Division, Left Wing, Army of the Mississippi (August 30 and October 1862); provost marshal general, Army of Tennessee (late 1863-August 24, 1864); and brigadier general, CSA (November 30, 1864). He led his regiment at Shiloh and during the Corinth siege. During the Kentucky Campaign he commanded the brigade at Richmond and succeeded to the command again when Patrick R. Cleburne was wounded at Perryville. He led his regiment at Murfreesboro and Chickamauga and at Chattanooga he directed the consolidated 35th and 48th Tennessee. During most of the Atlanta Campaign he served as provost marshal and then resumed command of his regiment. This he led at Franklin and he was then promoted to brigadier general. Transferred to the cavalry, he eventually surrendered to Henry M. Judah on May 16, 1865. He was a lawyer postwar.

HILL, Charles W. (?-1881)

Although he only served in the federal service for a little over a year and a half, Charles W. Hill was brevetted brigadier and major general for his war service. The Vermont native had been active in the Ohio militia before the Civil War and his assignments included: brigadier general, Ohio Militia (1861); commanding brigade, Army of Occupation, West Virginia, Department of the Ohio (July 1861); adjutant general, Ohio (1862-63) and colonel, 128th Ohio (December 25, 1863). After initially commanding an Ohio brigade in western Virginia in the first summer of the war he became the state's adjutant general and then was in charge of various prison camps. At the end of 1863 he was named to head a new regiment, which spent its entire tour in the state mostly guarding prisoners of war. Having received his brevets, Hill was mustered out of the national service.

HILL, Daniel Harvey (1821-1889)

Criticism of his army commander, Braxton Bragg, to Jefferson Davis cost South Carolinian West Pointer (1842) Daniel H. Hill his corps command and his promotion to lieutenant general in the Confederate army. Posted to the artillery, he had won two brevets in the Mexican War before resigning as a first lieutenant in the 4th Artillery in 1849. Active in education until the outbreak of the Civil War, he was superintendent of the North Carolina Military Institute in 1861. His Southern assignments included: colonel, 1st North Carolina Volunteers (May 11, 1861); commanding Department of the Peninsula (May 31-June 1861); brigadier general, CSA (July 10, 1861); commanding Department of Fredericksburg (July 17-July 1861); commanding District of the Pamlico, Department of North Carolina (ca. October 4-November 16, 1861); commanding 1st Brigade, 3rd (Longstreet's) Division, Potomac District, Department of Northern Virginia (November 16, 1861-January 1862); commanding Forces at Leesburg, Potomac District, Department of Northern Virginia (January-March 1862); major general, CSA (March 26, 1862); commanding 4th (Van Dorn's old) Division, Department of Northern Virginia (March-July 17, 1862); commanding Department of North Carolina (July 17-August 1862 and April 1-July 1, 1863); commanding division, Jackson's Corps, Army of Northern Virginia (August 1862-April 1, 1863); temporarily commanding Valley District, Army of Northern Virginia (September 6, 1862); lieutenant general, CSA (July 11, 1863); commanding 2nd (Hardee's old) Corps, Army of Tennessee (July 24-November 8, 1863); volunteer aide-de-camp, Department of North Carolina and Southern Virginia (May 5-18 and May 21-ca. June 1864); commanding division, Department of North Carolina and Southern Virginia (May 18-21, 1864); commanding District of Georgia, Department of South Carolina, Georgia and Florida (January 21-ca. March 1865); commanding division, Lee's Corps, Army of Tennessee (ca. March and late March-April 26, 1865); and commanding the corps (late March 1865). Commanding a regiment of six-months volunteers, he played a leading role in the Confederate victory at Big Bethel. Promoted to brigadier general, he served for a time in northern Virginia and then returned to the Peninsula as a division leader with the rank of major general. He saw action at Yorktown, Williamsburg, Seven Pines, and during the Seven Days. Left in southeastern

Virginia during the 2nd Bull Run Campaign, he rejoined Lee's army for the Maryland Campaign, performing well at both South Mountain and Antietam. His last battle with the Army of Northern Virginia came at Fredericksburg. He then returned to command the Department of North Carolina until named a lieutenant general and ordered to Bragg's army. He took over Hardee's old corps, leading it at Chickamauga. Disgusted with Bragg's failure to reap the benefits of the victory he made his view known to the president, who still supported his friend. Hill was relieved of corps command and Davis refused to submit his nomination as lieutenant general to the Senate. Thus he reverted to a major generalcy on October 15, 1863. His next action came as a volunteer on Beauregard's staff at Drewry's Bluff and Petersburg. He was in command of a provisional division for a couple of days. Ordered to the Atlantic coast he finished out the war with Joseph E. Johnston's army in the Carolinas as a division commander. After the surrender he returned to education and engaged in literary and historical writing. (Bridges, Leonard Hal, *Lee's Maverick General, Daniel Harvey Hill*)

HILLIARD, Henry Washington (1808-1892)

Although he only commanded it for about half a year, Henry W. Hilliard raised one of the larger commands of the Civil War. Born in North Carolina, he moved to Alabama and was a lawyer, state and national legislator, and diplomat before the war. An opponent of secession, he nonetheless went along with his adopted state. On April 24, 1862, he was commissioned a colonel and authorized to raise a legion for Confederate service. When it was complete in June its 3,000 men were divided into a cavalry battalion, three battalions of infantry, and one of artillery, which served mostly as infantry. His principal service was in East Tennessee during the latter part of 1862. However, on December 1, 1862, he resigned. After Reconstruction he served as U.S. minister to Brazil. (Hilliard, Henry Washington, *Politics and Pen Pictures at Home and Abroad*)

HILLYER, William Silliman (1831-1874)

Having befriended Ulysses S. Grant in his less than happy years in St. Louis, William S. Hillyer was rewarded by a staff position with the newly appointed brigadier. When Grant had been looking for work, Hillyer suggested him for the post of county engineer but Grant had lost out on political grounds. The Kentucky-born Missouri resident accepted Grant's appointment and his assignments included: captain and volunteer aide-de-camp (September 8, 1861); and colonel and additional aide-de-camp (May 3, 1862). As Grant's aide, he fought at Belmont, Fort Henry, Fort Donelson, Shiloh, in the advance on Corinth, and in the Vicksburg Campaign. In the midst of the latter he resigned on May 15, 1863. Near the close of the war he was brevetted brigadier general for his war service.

HILTON, Robert Benjamin (1821-1894)

Born Robert B. Smith in Virginia, Hilton changed his name and moved to Florida where he worked his way up in the journalism profession to the editorship of the *Tallahassee Floridian*. He later moved to Georgia, where he had previously worked, and became editor and owner of the *Savannah Georgian*. He divided his time between his journalism pursuits and the practice of law. Having supported secession as far back as 1850, it is not surprising that Hilton never took his seat in the U.S. Congress, following his election in the fall of 1860. Instead, he received a commission as captain, 1st Florida, with which he served at Pensacola. In November 1861 he won election to be the western 2nd District's representative to the First Regular Confederate Congress, and he was reelected in 1863. Within a month of taking his seat he proposed limiting the planting of cotton in favor of foodstuffs for the military. He generally supported the war effort, although he tried to prevent the War Department from draining away Florida's military defenders for other fronts. During his two terms in Congress Hilton served on the committees on: Elections; Military Affairs; Patents; Post Offices and Post Roads; and Territories and Public Lands. Wiped out by the war, Hilton resumed his legal and journalistic pursuits, eventually becoming a judge.

HINCKS, Edward Winslow

See: *Hinks, Edward Winslow*

HINDMAN, Thomas Carmichael (1828-1868)

Surviving a Civil War wound, which put him out of action for the balance of the war, Thomas C. Hindman died at the hands of an unknown assassin four years later. Born in Tennessee, he had seen heavy action as a second lieutenant in the 2nd Mississippi during the Mexican War and then took up the practice of law in Arkansas. For a time a state legislator, he was about to begin his second term in Congress when his state seceded. Instead, he rejoined the military—this time the Southern—and his assignments included: colonel, 2nd Arkansas (spring 1861); brigadier general, CSA (September 28, 1861); commanding 1st Brigade, 1st Hardee's Division, Central Army of Kentucky, Department #2 (October 28, 1861-March 29, 1862); commanding 1st Brigade, 3rd Corps, Army of the Mississippi (March 29-April 1862); also commanding 3rd Brigade, 3rd Corps, Army of the Mississippi (April 6-7, 1862); major general, CSA (April 18, 1862); commanding Trans-Mississippi District, Department #2 (May 31-July 30, 1862); commanding District of Arkansas, Trans-Mississippi Department (August 20-September 26, 1862); commanding 1st Corps, Trans-Mississippi Department (fall 1862-early 1863); commanding Wither's (old) Division, Polk's Corps, Army of Tennessee (August 13-September 20, 1863); commanding division, Breckinridge's-Hindman's-Hood's Corps, Army of Tennessee (December 1863 and February 25-June 27, 1864); and commanding the corps (December 15, 1863-February 25, 1864). Following service in central Kentucky he commanded two brigades at Shiloh and was rewarded with promotion to major general. Transferred west of the Mississippi, he was in command in the Confederate defeat at Prairie Grove. In 1863 he asked to be relieved of duty in Arkansas and in the summer was posted back to what had become the Army of Tennessee. He was wounded at Chickamauga while leading a division but recovered and after briefly commanding the corps led his division in the Atlanta Campaign until severely wounded in the face, and partially blinded at Kennesaw Mountain on June 27, 1864. Incapable of performing further field duty, he went to Mexico for three years after the surrender and then resumed his practice in Arkansas. His killing was probably related to the throes of Reconstruction.

HINKS, Edward Winslow (1830-1894)

Massachusetts politician Edward W. Hinks is best remembered in Civil War history for commanding the first division-sized unit of black troops in a major action. The Maine native had taken up the printing trade before settling in Boston, where he eventually became a member of the legislature and an ally of Benjamin F. Butler. Upon entering the army at the outbreak of the Civil War he dropped the "c" from his surname, "Hincks." Commissioned directly into the regular service, he soon joined the volunteers as well. His assignments included: second lieutenant, 2nd Cavalry (April 26, 1861); lieutenant colonel, 8th Massachusetts Militia (April 30, 1861); colonel, 8th Massachusetts Militia (May 16, 1861); colonel, 19th Massachusetts (August 3, 1861); brigadier general, USV (November 29, 1862); commanding Point Lookout prisoner of war camp (March-April 1864); commanding Hinks' Division, U.S. Colored Troops, Army of the James (April 20-June 19, 1864); and commanding 3rd Division, 18th Corps, Army of the James (June 19-July 1, 1864). Resigning his regular commission on June 4, 1861, he served with his ninety-day militia unit in the vicinity of Washington until being mustered out on August 1, 1861. Two days later he was commissioned colonel of a three-year regiment. With this unit he was in a supporting position during the Union disaster at Ball's Bluff. Moving to the Peninsula, he fought at Yorktown and Seven Pines and was wounded at Glendale during the Seven Days. Recovering, he was again twice wounded at Antietam. For this battle he received an 1867 regular army brevet. Returning to limited duty, he performed court-martial and recruiting duties and briefly was in charge of a Maryland prison camp. Back in the field he led his division of black troops in the initial assaults on Petersburg. Soon thereafter he returned to recruiting and aided in the administration of the draft. Brevetted major general for his war service, he resigned on June 30, 1865. The next year he was commissioned lieutenant colonel in the regular army. Brevetted in 1867 for the Petersburg assaults, he retired in 1870 as a colonel. Thereafter he was employed in the care of disabled volunteers.

HITCHCOCK, Ethan Allen (1798-1870)

Too old for active field duty, the grandson of Ethan Allen, Ethan A. Hitchcock, donned his uniform again and served throughout the Civil War as a staff officer. The native Vermonter had graduated from West Point in 1817 and been posted first to the artillery and then the infantry. He saw Indian fighting in Florida and in the Pacific Northwest. During the Mexican War he served as Winfield Scott's inspector general and earned two brevets, one as brigadier general. Following a dispute with Secretary of War Jefferson Davis, over sick leave, he resigned his colonel's commission in 1855. Once turned down for service early in the Civil War, he finally accepted, and his assignments included: major general, USV (February 10, 1862); commissioner for Exchange of War Prisoners (November 15, 1862-November 3, 1865); and commissary general of Prisoners (November 3, 1865-66). His position required extensive correspondence with the Confederate authorities in smoothing over various disputes. Mustered out on October 1, 1867, he retired in the South.

HITZ, Ann (?-?)

The wife of the Swiss consul in Washington, Ann Hitz became known as "Mother Hitz" for the attention she provided for German-speaking Union soldiers. With her husband, John, their home was converted into an aid center and she visited the area hospitals, helping those soldiers who spoke little or no English.

HITZ, John (?-?)

The consul in Washington from the Swiss Confederation, John Hitz proved to be something of a Good Samaritan during the Civil War. Avoiding any questions of neutrality, he and his wife, Ann, converted their home into an open house for German-speaking Union soldiers. His diplomatic commitments limited his activities at home but his wife went beyond the house. They were fondly remembered by many a soldier.

HOBART-HAMPDEN, Augustus Charles (1822-1886)

Resigning a Royal Navy commission, Augustus C. Hobart-Hampden sought the immense profits possible in the trade with the Confederate States by successfully running the Union blockade. Before the war he had operated against the African slave trade. Aboard the *Don* in 1863 he began his dangerous career as a blockade runner. Using a series of aliases, he always made it through safely. After the war he published his account, *Never Caught*. After rejoining the Queen's fleet, he again quit to serve in the Turkish navy and earned the title of "Hobart Pasha."

HOBSON, Edward Henry (1825-1901)

In one of the strange reversals of fate that occur in war, Union General Edward H. Hobson, having participated in the capture of John Hunt Morgan during his raid north of the Ohio River, found himself a prisoner of the same raider and became embroiled in a dispute over parole. The native Kentucky merchant and banker had seen service as a lieutenant of volunteers in Mexico, fighting at Buena Vista. At the outbreak of the Civil War he engaged in recruiting and his later assignments included: colonel, 13th Kentucky (January 1, 1862); brigadier general, USV (April 1863, to rank from November 29, 1862); commanding 2nd Brigade, 3rd Division, 23rd Corps, Department of the Ohio (June 24-August 6, 1863); commanding 2nd Brigade, 4th Division, 23rd Corps, Department of the Ohio (August 6-21, 1863); commanding District of South Central Kentucky, 1st Division, 23rd Corps, Department of the Ohio (October 1863-January 1864); commanding District of Southwest Kentucky, 1st Division, 23rd Corps, Department of the Ohio (January-April 1, 1864); commanding District of Kentucky (or 5th Division), 23rd Corps, Department of the Ohio (April 1-10, 1864); commanding 1st Division, District of Kentucky, 23rd Corps, Department of the Ohio (April 10-June 11, June-July 6, 1864, and December 29, 1864-January 17, 1865); commanding 1st Brigade, 1st Division, District of Kentucky, 23rd Corps, Department of the Ohio (July 6-October 15, 1864); and commanding 1st Division, Department of Kentucky (February-August 1865). He commanded his regiment under Buell at Shiloh and then, although not present at Perryville, returned to Kentucky. During Morgan's raid through Indiana and Ohio in the summer of 1863 Hobson—now a brigadier general—led his men in the pursuit. He fought in the action at Buffington's Island and took part in the capture of Morgan at New Lisbon, Ohio. Hobson then returned to district and garrison duty. Morgan, having made good his escape, again raided into Kentucky in June 1864. Hobson was again sent in pursuit and on the 11th, after a lengthy fight, was forced to surrender to Morgan at Cynthiana. In an informal parole, Hobson and some of his officers were sent under escort to negotiate an exchange but if this failed they were to return to Morgan. But before they could accomplish this the Confederate was defeated and forced to parole his prisoners. This left Hobson and the others in limbo and the Union authorities ordered them back on duty and censured Hobson entering into a questionable and unorthodox agreement. After this Hobson returned to his usual duty in Kentucky for the balance of the war. Mustered out, without a brevet, on August 24, 1865, he engaged in railroading and became a Radical Republican. He died at a reunion of the Grand Army of the Republic.

HODGE, George Baird (1828-1892)

Although he had been a member of the Confederate House of Representatives, George B. Hodge had the disappointment of twice seeing his nomination as a brigadier general rejected by the Senate. The native Kentuckian and lawyer had graduated from Annapolis in 1845 and served five years before resigning as a passed midshipman. Taking up the practice of law, he also entered politics and lost an 1852 bid for a congressional seat. Having sat in the state legislature in the late 1850s, he backed his fellow Kentuckian, John C. Breckinridge, for the presidency in 1860. Briefly serving as a Confederate private, he was appointed to the Provisional Confederate Congress where he held no committee assignments. In the elections for the First Regular Confederate Congress he was elected from Kentucky's 8th District, located just across the Ohio River from Cincinnati. In that Congress he sat on the committees on Naval Affairs and Ordnance and Ordnance Stores. However, he was frequently absent in the field as a staff officer to Breckinridge. As such he fought at Shiloh. His military assignments included: captain (1861); major (May 6, 1862); colonel and assistant adjutant general (May 6, 1863); commanding brigade, Armstrong's Division (detached in Department of East Tennessee), Wheeler's Cavalry Corps, Army of Tennessee (November 1863-early 1864); reappointed brigadier general, CSA (August 4, 1864); commanding District of Southwest Mississippi and East Louisiana, Department of Alabama, Mississippi and East Louisiana (ca. August 25, 1864-February 3, 1865); and commanding District of South Mississippi and East Louisiana, District of Mississippi and East Louisiana, Department of Alabama, Mississippi and East Louisiana (March 14-May 4, 1865). Having been promoted from captain through colonel on staff duty, he transferred to the line as a brigadier general of cavalry. Leading a brigade of Wheeler's cavalry he fought in East Tennessee during the Knoxville Campaign, before having his appointment rejected on February 17, 1864. Reappointed six months later, he held district command in Mississippi and Louisiana, and his appointment was again turned down on February 8, 1865. Nonetheless he was paroled as a brigadier general when Richard Taylor's department surrendered. Thereafter he practiced law and sat in the state legislature.

HOFFMAN, William (ca. 1808-1884)

Himself a prisoner of war during the first year of the conflict, career officer William Hoffman later served as the Union's commissary general of prisoners. A native of New York and West Pointer (1829), he had served in the regular infantry for more than three decades by the outbreak of the Civil War. In the meantime he had earned two brevets in Mexico—as well as being wounded at Churubusco—and fought the Seminoles and western Indians. His wartime assignments included: lieutenant colonel, 8th Infantry (since October 17, 1860); colonel, 3rd Infantry (April 25, 1862); and commissary general of Prisoners (1862-November 3, 1865). With the secession of Texas and the surrender by David E. Twiggs, Hoffman became a prisoner at San Antonio on April 23, 1861. He was not exchanged until August 27, 1862, and then entered upon his administrative duties for the balance of the conflict. He was brevetted brigadier general for his war service and major general for supervision of the prisoners. At the time of his 1870 retirement he was a colonel but without an assignment.

HOFMANN, John William (?-1902)

Although J. William Hofmann never made it to the full rank of brigadier general he spent much of the war exercising brigade command. A Pennsylvania native he entered the Union army under Lincoln's first call for men and his assignments included: captain, 23rd Pennsylvania (April 21, 1861); lieutenant colonel, 56th Pennsylvania (October 1, 1861), commanding 2nd Brigade, 1st Division, 3rd Corps, Army of Virginia (August 30-September 12, 1862); commanding 2nd Brigade,

1st Division, 1st Corps, Army of the Potomac (September 17-November 9, 1862 and January 14-February 10, 1864); colonel, 56th Pennsylvania (January 8, 1863); commanding 2nd Brigade, 4th Division, 5th Corps, Army of the Potomac (May 22-August 24, 1864); commanding 3rd Brigade, 2nd Division, 5th Corps, Army of the Potomac (August 24-September 14, 1864); and commanding 3rd Brigade, 3rd Division, 5th Corps, Army of the Potomac (September 13, 1864-January 24, 1865 and February 10-15, 1865). After serving as a company commander under Patterson he was mustered out on July 31, 1861. With a new three-year regiment he went to the front as its executve officer. In his first major action, 2nd Bull Run, he succeeded to regimental command upon the wounding of the colonel. At Antietam, although only a lieutenant colonel, he commanded his brigade. He led his regiment on the left at Fredericksburg and played a minor role at Chancellorsville. On the first day of Gettysburg he led his regiment in the heavy fighting west of town. He went on to serve at the Wilderness, Spotsylvania, Cold Harbor, and Petersburg—much of the time in brigade command—and earned a brevet brigadiership for it. He was mustered out of the service on March 7, 1865, a little over a month before Appomattox.

HOGE, Jane (?-?)

A co-founder—along with Mary Livermore—of the Chicago chapter of the United Sates Sanitary Commission, Mrs. A.H. Hoge made numerous lectures in highly successful attempts to raise funds. She ran the first commission fair, raising $80,000 in Chicago. Other fairs soon followed. Once the funds were raised she frequently went into the field to supervise the distribution to the troops of the supplies that had been purchased. The Pennsylvania native continued her efforts until the war's close.

HOGG, Joseph Lewis (1806-1862)

Lawyer, planter, politician, and Mexican War veteran Joseph Hogg voted for the secession of his adopted state of Texas at its convention on February 1, 1861. Appointed colonel of Texas troops shortly thereafter, Hogg was active in raising troops for the field. Appointed brigadier general in Confederate service, February 14, 1862, Hogg was sent to Arkansas and assigned to command a brigade of Arkansas and Texas troops. This brigade subsequently became part of McCown's Division, Army of the West. On March 22, 1862, the Army of the West was ordered to Corinth, Mississippi, to join the army of General A.S. Johnston. However, the command failed to join before the battle of Shiloh and Hogg's Brigade was in Memphis on April 23. It did reach Corinth by the end of April. However, on May 16, before he could lead his men into battle, Joseph Hogg died of dysentery, which was ravaging the army then under Beauregard.

HOKE, Robert Frederick (1837-1912)

When serving in a semi-independent fashion Robert F. Hoke proved to be a capable division leader but it later turned out that he lacked the ability to coordinate with others. Having been educated at the Kentucky Military Institute, the North Carolinian left the family cotton and iron businesses to join the Confederate military. His assignments included: second lieutenant, 1st North Carolina (spring 1861); major, 33rd North Carolina (ca. September 20, 1861); major, 33rd North Carolina (ca. September 20, 1861); lieutenant colonel, 33rd North Carolina (ca. January 17, 1962); colonel, 21st North Carolina (fall 1862, to rank from August 5); commanding Trimble's (old) Brigade, Ewell's-Early's Division, 2nd Corps, Army of Northern Virginia (fall 1862-May 4, 1863); brigadier general, CSA (April 23, to rank from January 17, 1863); commanding brigade, Department of North Carolina (January-April 1864); major general, CSA (April 20, 1864); commanding division, Department of North Carolina and Southern Virginia (May-October 19, 1864); commanding division, 4th Corps, Army of Northern Virginia (October 19-December 20, 1864); commanding division, Department of North Carolina (December 20, 1864-ca. March 25, 1865); commanding division, Hardee's Corps from Department of South Carolina, Georgia and Florida (ca. March 25-April 9, 1865); and commanding division, Hardee's Corps, Army of Tennessee (April 9-26, 1865). As a company officer he fought at Big Bethel and became a field officer in the 33rd after the 1st was mustered out. After the colonel was captured at New Bern, he led the regiment at Hanover Court House, the Seven Days, Cedar Mountain, 2nd Bull Run, and Antietam. Transferred to the 21st as colonel, he directed a brigade at Fredericksburg and until wounded at Chancellorsville. Upon his recovery he was detached to deal with deserters in western North Carolina. He joined Pickett for the action against New Bern and played a leading role in the capture of Plymouth. By now a major general and division commander, he took part in the fighting at Bermuda Hundred and Cold Harbor where he displayed a lack of cooperation in joint operations. After serving several months in the Petersburg trenches, his division was transferred to the defenses of Wilmington, North Carolina, in December 1864. Following the fall of that port, the division joined the composite forces trying to halt Sherman in the Carolinas. After seeing action at Bentonville, Hoke surrendered as part of Johnston's army. After the war he returned to the iron business. (Freeman, Douglas S., *Lee's Lieutenants*)

HOLBROOK, Frederick (1813-1909)

Under the gubernatorial supervision of Frederick Holbrook, Vermont became the first Northern state to establish hospitals for its state volunteers. A native of Connecticut, he had settled in Vermont where he took up farming and became a leading advocate for the advancement of agricultural science and policy. As a republican, he served in the legislature and then ran for governor in 1861. He was elected to two one-year terms. A former militia officer, he offered to raise volunteer units subject to the reimbursement of the state by the Washington authorities. Lincoln sought his advice on recruiting and other war matters. He retired to private life in 1863.

HOLCOMBE, James Philemon (1820-1873)

Although he had never previously had any desire to become really active in politics, James P. Holcombe became prominent in Virginia politics during the crisis winter of 1860-61 because of his strong secessionist views. Lacking real interest in the actual practice of law, Holcombe had become a legal authority, authoring several law texts and teaching at the University of Virginia's law school. In the decade before the Civil War he penned several defenses of slavery and justifications for secession. In November 1861 he was elected to the First Regular Confederate Congress from the 7th District. Naturally he was assigned to the Committee on the Judiciary. He proved to be one of Virginia's more flexible representatives in his willingness to accept questionable constitutional measures during the emergency of the war. He supported heavy, but equalized, taxation, punishment of speculators and military control over the means of production whenever necessary. Originally an opponent of conscription, he eventually accepted it as a necessary evil. Declining reelection, Holcombe was sent in February 1864 to Nova Scotia where he defended some unauthorized Confederate privateers. Afterwards he worked with the Confederate agents in Canada and upon his return to Richmond urged active operations to foster war weariness in the North and to attempt to provoke the northwestern states to secede into their own confederacy. After the war Holcombe was active in literary and educational pursuits.

HOLDEN, William Woods (1818-1892)

A North Carolina journalist and would-be politician, William W. Holden traversed the spectrum of beliefs on Civil War issues. Admitted to the bar in 1841, he became a Democrat in order to become the editor of the *North Carolina Standard* in Raleigh. He became an ardent supporter of secession and served a term in the legislature. However, his efforts to gain the governorship and a senatorship met with defeat. In 1860 he attended the Democratic conventions in Charleston and Baltimore and switched his allegiance from Douglas to Breckinridge. Inexplicably he was a Union delegate to the secession convention but then backed the disruption of the Union. Continuing his editorship, he came into opposition with the war party and the Davis administration and favored peace. His presses were wrecked for his sentiments. He ran as a peace candidate for governor in 1864 but lost to Zebulon Vance. He was the fonder of the "Heroes of America," also known as the "Red Strings," as a secret society working for an end to the war. Andrew Johnson appointed him provisional governor on May 29, 1865, and instructed him to call a state convention to abolish slavery and void secession. In the election later that year he was defeated for a regular term, and a diplomatic assignment to San Salvador was not confirmed by the Senate. His editorials took up a decidedly Radical Republican slant and he became an organizer of the party in the state. As a party member, he was elected governor in 1868 and served until 1870, overseeing a corrupt regime. The state legislature impeached and removed him from office in 1870. He moved to Washington and edited the *Daily Chronicle* and held a diplomatic post in Peru before splitting with the party over black voting rights, which he had formerly backed, and other issues. (Folk, Edgar, *W.W. Holden, Political Journalist*)

HOLLAND, Milton M. (1844-1910)

One of only 16 blacks to win the Congressional Medal of Honor for gallantry in the Civil War, Milton M. Holland won the honor by taking command of a company after all of its white officers had been made hors de combat. Sent to Ohio by his Texas owner, he was educated in a black-owned academy. From the beginning of the war he served as a servant to a Union officer and then enlisted in the 5th United States Colored Troops, which was raised in Ohio. Made first sergeant of Company C, he experienced the usual routine of construction and garrison assignments given to black troops until joining Benjamin F. Butler's Army of the James. Butler had faith in the fighting qualities of black units and during the operations against Richmond and Petersburg, he was not afraid to use them. Promoted to regimental sergeant major, Holland assumed command of his former company at the battle of New Market Heights on September 29, 1864. His unit then went on to fight at Fort Fisher and in support of Sherman's army during the Carolinas Campaign. The regiment was mustered out on September 20, 1865. Holland later became a government employee and founded an insurance company in the nation's capital.

HOLLIDAY, Frederick William Mackey (1828-1899)

Utilizing his record as an early secessionist and as a regimental commander in the famed Stonewall Brigade, Frederick W.M. Holliday managed to defeat incumbent Virginia 10th District Representative Alexander R. Boteler in the race for the Second Confederate Congress. A native Virginian, Holliday was a commonwealth attorney at the outbreak of the Civil War when he entered the military service. His grades included: captain, 33rd Virginia (May 10, 1861); major, 33rd Virginia (April 22, 1861); and colonel, 33rd Virginia (February 1, 1863). During this period of service the regiment saw action at 1st Manassas, during the Shenandoah Valley Campaign of 1862, and in the Seven Days Battles around Richmond. At Cedar Mountain on August 9, 1862, a preliminary action in the Manassas Campaign, Holliday was severely wounded, losing an arm. His wound forced him resign on March 21, 1864. The previous year he had defeated Boteler and taken his seat in February 1864. In Congress he served on the committees on: Claims; and Quartermaster's and Commissary Departments. His primary interest in legislative matters was in relation to military affairs. Working to improve organization, supplies, and pay, he also tried to find useful employment for disabled soldiers in the war effort. Returning to the law and his farm after the war, he served a term as governor during which he halted the movement to cancel the debt incurred during the war.

HOLLINS, George Nichols (1799-1878)

Dressed as a woman, Captain George N. Hollins, CSN, scored his first victory for the Confederacy. The veteran of action against the Barbary pirates, the War of 1812, and in Nicaragua had resigned his captain's commission in order to join the Confederacy. In the early hours of June 29, 1861, disguised as a women, Hollins seized the Chesapeake Bay steamer *St. Nicholas*. From July 10-31, 1861, he was in command of the naval defense along the James River. He then took over the naval station at New Orleans trying to keep the port open despite the Union blockade. With pressure growing on the upper Mississippi, Hollins moved his small fleet north. Returning to threatened New Orleans in April 1862, he was assigned to the court of inquiry investigating the scuttling of the *Virginia* before the fall of the city. For the remainder of the war Hollins served on numerous boards and courts. Paroled, he became a court officer in Baltimore after the war. (Scharf, J. Thomas, *History of the Confederate States Navy*)

HOLMES, Oliver Wendell, Jr. (1841-1935)

Wounded three times during the Civil War, future supreme court justice Oliver Wendell Holmes, Jr., is said to have passed on his battle wisdom to President Lincoln during the fight at Fort Stevens outside Washington. The Massachusetts lawyer enlisted in April 1861, just prior to his graduation from Harvard, and was commissioned a second lieutenant. He fought in the Union disaster at Ball's Bluff with the 20th Massachusetts and was wounded at Antietam so severely that he was left for dead. However he recovered from his neck wound in time to fight at Fredericksburg. Rising to captain by the time that he was mustered out, his exact words to Lincoln are variously reported. But in effect he said that only a fool would put his head above the breastworks and risk getting it shot off. Following his discharge, he returned to Harvard and graduated from the law school in 1866. Becoming prominent in this profession, he taught at his alma mater and became a justice of the state supreme court and in 1909 an associate justice of the U.S. Supreme Court—where he served for some 30 years and compiled a remarkable record. (Holmes, Oliver Wendell, Jr., Mark DeWolfe Howe, ed., *Touched With Fire, Civil War Letters and Diary of Oliver Wendell Holmes, Jr., 1861-1864* and Howe, Mark DeWolfe, *Justice Oliver Wendell Holmes*)

HOLMES, Theophilus Hunter (1804-1880)

A case of partial deafness did not help Theophilus H. Holmes repeat his distinguished Mexican War career for the South. The North Carolinian West Pointer (1829) had won a brevet south of the border and fought the Seminoles and Navajos before resigning on April 22, 1861, as major, 8th Infantry. Joining the Confederacy, his assignments included: brigadier general, CSA (June 5, 1861); commanding Department of Fredericksburg (June 5-October 22, 1861); major general, CSA (October 7, 1861); commanding Aquia District, Department of Northern Virginia (October 22, 1861-March 23, 1862); commanding Department of North Carolina (March 25-July 17, 1862); com-

Oliver Wendell Holmes, future Supreme Court justice. (NA)

manding Trans-Mississippi Department (July 30, 1862-March 18, 1863); lieutenant general, CSA (October 10, 1862); commanding District of Arkansas, Trans-Mississippi Department (May 18-July 24, 1863 and September 25, 1863-March 16, 1864); and commanding Reserve Forces of North Carolina (April 18, 1864-Arpil 1865). Placed in command along the Rappahannock in Virginia, he took a small brigade of two regiments to join Beauregard at 1st Bull Run but did not get into the action. He continued to command in that area as a major general until ordered to command in North Carolina. He led a division to join Robert E. Lee in June 1862 for the Seven Days but performed poorly. Due to his deafness, at times he did not even know if there was a fight in progress. In Lee's general housecleaning the next month Holmes was displaced but his friend Jefferson Davis found him a place west of the Mississippi. There he was in overall charge, as a lieutenant general, during the defeat at Prairie Grove. Even Holmes deemed himself too old to command the vast department and was pleased when E. Kirby Smith arrived to succeed him. Retaining command in Arkansas, he directed the unsuccessful attack on Helena. This was designed to relieve the pressure on Vicksburg, which coincidentally fell on the same day. Smith soon felt that Holmes was too old and slow for even his more limited district command

and so informed the Richmond authorities. An incensed Holmes resigned. Davis then put him in charge of organizing the reserves in North Carolina, a duty he performed for the remaining year of the war. After the war he was a small-scale farmer in his native state. (Freeman, Douglas S., *Lee's Lieutenants*)

HOLT, Joseph (1807-1894)

On September 3, 1862, Joseph Holt became the judge advocate general of the American army. Before the war he was a Democratic politician in Kentucky as well as a lawyer, newspaper editor, patent commissioner, postmaster general, and secretary of war under President Buchanan. In the latter position, Holt was deeply involved in the crisis of Forts Sumter and Pickens until the incoming Lincoln administration took over the problem. Subsequently he was a key figure in preventing the secession of his native Kentucky and in ending its neutrality in favor of the Union. Lincoln appointed him the chief of military justice with the rank of colonel in the fall of 1862. In this position, with the unusual conditions of civil war, Holt was empowered to make arrests outside the armed forces and this without writ of *habeas corpus*. His policies were extremely popular with the Radical Republicans in Congress. He was responsible for the trial of General Fitz-John Porter for his role at 2nd Bull Run, Andersonville commandant Henry Wirz, copperhead Clement Vallandigham, and the Lincoln assassination conspirators. Holt seemed to care more about political considerations than justice and has since been shown to have suppressed evidence. Many of his witnesses were later found to have perjured themselves. He also prevented President Andrew Johnson from seeing the recommendation for clemency written on behalf of Mary Surratt, written by the military commission that tried the Lincoln conspirators. She was executed although Johnson probably would have pardoned her if he had seen the plea. Losing favor with a more conservative Congress, Holt was forced to change his ways and eventually resigned in 1875. He had been appointed brigadier general, USA on June 22, 1864, and was brevetted major general for his war service.

HOLTZCLAW, James Thadeus (1833-1893)

His brother's death caused James T. Holtzclaw to skip the West Point education he had been selected for, but the Civil War still brought him the three stars and wreath of a Confederate general. Born when his parents were on a visit to Georgia, he was raised in Alabama and practicing law there in 1861. His Confederate assignments included: lieutenant, Montgomery True Blues (1861); major, 18th Alabama (September 1861); colonel, 18th Alabama (May 10, 1862); commanding Clayton's Brigade, Stewart's Division, Breckinridge's Corps, Army of Tennessee (November 1863); brigadier general, CSA (July 7, 1864); commanding Clayton's (old) Brigade, Clayton's Division, Hood's-Lee's Corps, Army of Tennessee (July 7-September 1864 and ca. October 1864-January 26, 1865); and commanding brigade, District of the Gulf, Department of Alabama, Mississippi and East Louisiana (ca. January-May 4, 1865). As a field officer he was wounded at Shiloh and was elected colonel during the regiment's reorganization the following month. Wounded again at Chickamauga, he was in charge of the brigade at Chattanooga two months later. During the Atlanta Campaign he led the regiment until promoted and given permanent command of Henry D. Clayton's brigade when that officer took over Alexander P. Stewart's division. During the fight at Franklin the division was still south of the Duck River and thus missed the action. However Holtzclaw did fight at Nashville and played a leading role in covering the retreat. Early the next year he and his brigade were transferred to the Gulf and he was surrendered with the rest of Richard Taylor's forces on May 4, 1865. Resuming his practice he was active in Democratic circles.

HOMER, Winslow (1836-1910)

Although he had been apprenticed to a lithographer in Boston, the Civil War and country artist Winslow Homer was primarily self-taught in his trade. As a free-lance artist he had already developed a reputation by the outbreak of the Civil War when he joined *Harper's Weekly* as a special correspondent. Covering the routine of army life his works frequently appeared in the weekly editions of the paper and depicted the boredom and frustations of life in the field. Working from his field sketches he finished his paintings in a New York studio and in 1864, he was elected an associate of the National Academy. The next year he was advanced to be an academician. Some of his most famous works include: "Defiance: Inviting a Shot Before Petersburg, Va., 1864," "Prisoners From the Front," "A Rainy Day in Camp," and "Pitching Horseshoes." Leaving the field of journalism at the close of the war, Homer concentrated on the depiction of country life.

HOOD, John Bell (1831-1879)

A premier example of the Peter principle is the case of John B. Hood who excelled as a brigade and division leader, was uncooperative as a corps commander, and was an unqualified disaster at the head of an army, which he all but destroyed. A Kentucky-born West Pointer (1853), he became associated with Texas while with the 2nd Cavalry. Resigning the first lieutenant's commission on April 16, 1861, he joined the South. His assignments included: first lieutenant, Cavalry (spring 1861); colonel, 4th Texas (October 1, 1861); commanding Texas Brigade, Whiting's Division (known as Forces Near Dumfries and in the Potomac District until March and the Valley District in June), Department of Northern Virginia (February 20-June 1862); brigadier general, CSA (March 3, 1862); commanding Texas Brigade, Whiting's Division, 2nd Corps, Army of Northern Virginia (June 26-July 1862); commanding the division, 1st Corps, same army (July-August 30, 1862; September 14, 1862-February 25, 1863; and May-July 2, 1863); major general, CSA (October 10, 1862); commanding division in the Department of Virginia and North Carolina (February 25-April 1, 1863); in the Department of Southern Virginia (April 1-May 1863); temporarily commanding the corps (September 20, 1863); lieutenant general, CSA (February 1, 1864); commanding 2nd Corps, Army of Tennessee

John Bell Hood, a success as a division commander, proved a dismal failure as head of the Army of Tennessee. (NA)

(February 28-July 18, 1864); temporary rank of general, CSA, and commanding the army (July 18, 1864-January 23, 1865); and also commanding Department of Tennessee and Georgia (August 15, 1864-January 25, 1865). He organized cavalry on the Peninsula and was distinguished at the small action at West Point and saw later action at Seven Pines and Seven Days. He delivered a powerful attack at 2nd Bull Run but was arrested by General Nathan G. Evans after a dispute over some captured ambulances. Allowed to accompany his division, in arrest, he was released by Lee on the morning of South Mountain. After distinguishing himself at Antietam he was promoted to major general and fought at Fredericksburg. After service in southeastern Virginia he led his division at Gettysburg where he suffered a crippling wound in his arm. He resumed command as Longstreet was headed for Georgia and while commanding the corps at Chickamauga—Longstreet was directing a wing—was wounded in the leg. Recovering in Richmond from the amputation, he received a promotion and was permanently assigned to the Army of Tennessee. It was at this time that Hood underwent a change. He had a great deal of difficulty in coordinating with the other corps commanders during the Atlanta Campaign, especially General Hardee. With the army having fallen back to the outskirts of Atlanta, Hood was appointed a temporary general and replaced Joe Johnston. In a series of disastrous attacks over the next several days he failed to drive Sherman from the city. After a siege he was forced to evacuate and that fall resorted to attacking Union supply lines to force Sherman north. This failing, he launched a move into middle Tennessee, hoping that a threat to the Ohio Valley might dislodge the enemy from Georgia. After a missed opportunity at Spring Hill, he threw his infantry into a bloody frontal attack at Franklin that decimated them. Besieging the Union forces in Nashville, he attacked in mid-December 1864 and his army was annihilated. Retreating into the deep South with the fragments of the army he relinquished his command and his temporary commission in January 1865. After the war he settled in New Orleans and was a prosperous merchant until an 1878 financial crisis. He died the next year in a yellow fever epidemic. His memoirs are entitled *Advance and Retreat.* (McMurry, Richard M., *John Bell Hood and the War for Southern Independence*)

HOOKER, Joseph (1814-1879)

One of the most immodest and immoral of the high Union commanders, "Fighting Joe" Hooker frequently felt slighted by his superiors and requested to be relieved of duty. The Massachusetts native and West Pointer (1837) had been posted to the artillery but was serving as a staff officer when he won three brevets in Mexico. Unfortunately for his later career he testified against Winfield Scott before a court of inquiry on the Mexican War. After a two-year leave he resigned on February 21, 1863, to settle in California where he was in the farming and land businesses. At the outset of the Civil War he became a colonel of the state militia but soon offered his services to Washington where his anti-Scott testimony came back to haunt him. As a civilian he witnessed the disaster at 1st Bull Run and wrote to Lincoln complaining of the mismanagement and advancing his own claim to a commission. Accepted, his assignments included: brigadier general, USV (August 3, 1861, to rank from May 17); commanding brigade, Division of the Potomac (August-October 3, 1861); commanding division, Army of the Potomac (October 3, 1861-March 13, 1862); commanding 2nd Division, 3rd Corps, Army of the Potomac (March 13-September 5, 1862); major general, USV (May 5, 1862); commanding 3rd Corps, Army of Virginia (September 6-12, 1862); commanding 1st Corps, Army of the Potomac (September 12-17, 1862); brigadier general, USA (September 20, 1862); commanding 5th Corps, Army of the Potomac (November 10-16, 1862); commanding Center Grand Division, Army of the Potomac (November 16, 1862-January 26, 1863); commanding Department and Army of the Potomac (January 26-June 28, 1863); commanding 11th and 12th Corps, Army of the Cumberland (September 25-April 14, 1863); commanding 20th Corps, Army of the Cumberland (April 14-July 28, 1864); and commanding Northern Department (October 1, 1864-June 27, 1865). After leading a brigade and then a division around Washington he went with McClellan's army to the Peninsula, earning a reputation for looking after his men during the siege operations at Yorktown. His other reputation as a heavy user of alcohol was not so enviable. He was particularly distinguished at Williamsburg and although he felt slighted by his commander's report he was

"Fighting Joe" Hooker. (AC)

named a major general of volunteers from the date of the action. Further fighting for Hooker came at Seven Pines and throughout the Seven Days. Following its close he scored a minor success in the retaking of Malvern Hill from the Confederates. Transferred to Pope with his division, he took part in the defeat at 2nd Bull Run. Given command of a corps for the Maryland Campaign, he fought at South Mountain and was wounded in the foot early in the morning fighting at Antietam. Three days later he was named a regular army brigadier general. Returning to duty, he briefly commanded the 5th Corps before being given charge of the Center Grand Division when Burnside reorganized his army into these two-corps formations. After the defeat at Fredericksburg and the disastrous Mud March, Burnside was relieved. In a letter to the Army of the Potomac's new commander, Hooker, Lincoln praised the general's fighting abilities but strongly questioned Hooker's previous criticism of commanders and feared that this might come back to haunt the new chief. Lincoln was also critical of the general's loose talk on the need for a military dictatorship to win the war. Once in charge, Hooker's headquarters were roundly criticized by many as a combination of bar and brothel. When he launched his campaign against Lee, Hooker swore off liquor. This may have hurt more than it helped. After a brilliantly executed maneuver around Lee's flank and the crossing of two rivers, Hooker lost his nerve and withdrew his forces back into the Wilderness to await reinforcements from John Sedgewick's command coming from Fredericksburg. Here he felt convinced that Lee was in retreat but was surprised by Jackson's flank attack, which routed Oliver O. Howard's 11th Corps. To make matters worse Hooker was dazed by the effects of a shell striking a pillar on the porch of his headquarters. He lost control of the army and ordered a withdrawal. Kept in command, he led the army northward in the early part of the Gettysburg Campaign until he resigned on June 28, 1863, over control of the garrison at Harpers Ferry. On January 28, 1864, he received the Thanks of Congress for the beginnings of the campaign. With the Union defeat at Chickamauga, he was given charge of the Army of the Potomac's 11th and 12th Corps and sent to the relief of the Army of the Cumberland at Chattanooga. In the battles around that place in November 1863 he did well in keeping open the supply lines and in the taking of Lookout Mountain. However, in Grant's report his actions were overshadowed by the less distinguished role of Sherman. The next spring the two corps were merged into the new 20th Corps with Hooker at their head. He fought through the Atlanta Campaign but when McPherson was killed before the city and Howard received command of the Army of the Tennessee, he asked to be relieved. This was granted and he finished the war in the quiet sector of Michigan, Ohio, Indiana, and Illinois. Brevetted major general in the regular army for Chattanooga, he was mustered out of the volunteers on September 1, 1866, and two years later was retired with the increased rank of major general. Always popular with his men, he lacked the confidence of his subordinate officers and was quarrelsome with his superiors. His nickname, which he never liked, resulted from the deletion of a dash in a journalistic dispatch that was discussing the Peninsula Campaign and "Fighting" was thereafter linked to his name. Popular legend has it that his name was permanently attached to prostitutes from his Civil War actions in rounding them up in one area of Washington. (Herbert, Walter H., *Fighting Joe Hooker*)

HOTCHKISS, Charles Truman (?-?)

New York-born Illinois resident Charles T. Hotchkiss rose from private to the command of a Union brigade. His assignments included: private, Company F, 11th Illinois (April 23, 1861); first lieutenant and adjutant, 11th Illinois (May 2, 1861); captain, 11th Illinois (July 30, 1861); lieutenant colonel, 89th Illinois (August 25, 1862); colonel, 89th Illinois (February 24, 1863); and commanding 1st Brigade, 3rd Division, 4th Corps, Army of the Cumberland (March 11-April 20, August 25-September 15, 1864, and March 15-May 15, 1865). He was rapidly promoted to regimental adjutant and then company commander before the regiment fought at Fort Donelson. At Shiloh he served as the adjutant of the brigade and during the advance on Corinth was John A. McClernand's adjutant for the Reserve. Becoming a field officer in a new regiment that summer, he commanded the regiment at Murfreesboro. He served in the Tullahoma Campaign but missed Chickamauga and Chattanooga. During the siege of Atlanta he succeeded to brigade command. His regiment was present at Franklin but he appears to have missed the fight at Nashville. Brevetted brigadier general for the war, he was mustered out on June 10, 1865, with his regiment.

HOTCHKISS, Jedediah (1828-1899)

A transplanted New Yorker, Jedediah Hotchkiss became the most famous of Confederate topographers. After a tour of Virginia in the late 1840s he settled there and founded an academy. In 1861 he gave up teaching and offered his services as a map maker to General Garnett in western Virginia. After serving at Rich Mountain and mapping out General Lee's planned campaign in the mountains, he fell ill with typhoid fever. In March 1862 he joined Stonewall Jackson in the Shenandoah Valley as a captain and chief topographical engineer of the Valley District. Often personally directing troop movements he took part in the actions of the Valley Campaign and at Cedar Mountain, Chantilly, Harpers Ferry, Antietam, and Fredericksburg. At Chancellorsville he found the route by which Jackson was able to launch his surprise flank attack on the Union 11th Corps. After the death of his chief he served the next two commanders of the corps, Generals Ewell and Early, but was frequently assigned to work for Lee's headquarters. In this dual role he served at Gettysburg and in the Mine Run and Wilderness campaigns. Accompanying Early to the Shenandoah, he served through the campaigns there until after the disaster at Waynesborough. He gave himself up upon notification of Lee's surrender. By now a major, he was arrested but General Grant had him released and returned his maps. Grant even paid for the right to copy some of them for his own reports. Most of the Confederate maps in the atlas of the *Official Records* were drawn by Hotchkiss. After the war he was energetic in trying to develop the economy of his adopted state. Also involved in veterans' affairs, he authored the Virginia volume of *Confederate Military History*. (Hotchkiss, Jedediah, *Make Me A Map of the Valley*)

HOTZE, Henry (1833-1887)

A prewar journalist and diplomat, Henry Hotze was sent to Europe and became one of the Confederacy's leading propagandists. A native of Zurich, Switzerland, he had emigrated to the United States and settled in Mobile. He soon became an editor for the *Mobile Register* and served at a Belgian diplomatic post in 1858-59. At the outbreak of the Civil War he enlisted in the Mobile Cadets, which served in the harbor defenses. Sent to Europe in August 1861 on a purchasing mission, within three months he had become a commercial agent posted to London. He edited the Confederate propaganda organ the *Index* in London for over three years and worked hard to gain European recognition and support. He was also active on the propaganda front in France working with Edwin De Leon. In a move to gain diplomatic capital he favored the arming of the slaves in return for their freedom. After the Confederacy's collapse he remained as a journalist in Europe, dying in Zug, Switzerland. (Cullop, Charles P., *Confederate Propaganda in Europe*)

HOUGH, Daniel (?-1861)

Surviving the bombardment of Fort Sumter, Private Daniel Hough, Company E, 1st U.S. Artillery, was accidentally killed in a salute to the colors, becoming the first fatality of the Civil War. Following the capitulation of the fort to Confederate authorities, it was decided to permit the garrison to fire a hundred gun salute to the American flag before departing for the North. When the discharge of the guns was about half over, Hough was placing another round in the muzzle of one of the barbette guns when a spark, which had not been sponged out, ignited it. The premature discharge tore off Hough's right arm and he died almost instantly. The first of over 600,000 dead had paid the supreme sacrifice—by accident. (Swanberg, W.A., *First Blood*)

HOUGHTALING, Charles (?-1883)

Serving through most of the war as an artillery commander, Charles Houghtaling received the brevet of brigadier general for the war. The New York-born Illinois resident's assignments included: captain, 10th Illinois (April 29, 1861); captain, Battery C, 1st Illinois Light Artillery (July 30, 1861); major, 1st Illinois Light Artillery (February 22, 1863); commanding Artillery Brigade, 14th Corps, Army of the Cumberland (July 24, 1864-June 1865); and colonel, 1st Illinois Light Artillery (August 20, 1864). Following brief service as an infantry company commander he transferred to the artillery branch and led his battery at Island #10 and during the Corinth siege. He also fought at Murfreesboro. Promoted to major, he served in various capacities as an artillery officer and in the midst of the Atlanta Campaign took command of the artillery of the 14th Corps. Promoted to colonel, he led this unit through the balance of the war seeing action during the March to the Sea and the Carolinas Campaign. Mustered out with his former battery, he was brevetted brigadier for the war.

HOUGHTON G.H. (?-?)

A Vermont landscape photographer, G.H. Houghton recognized the Civil War as a fertile ground for the relatively new art of photography and proved to be one of the art's more daring practitioners in his coverage of troops from his native state. He visited the Vermont Brigade in the Army of the Potomac on two or more occasions in 1862 and 1863. Not limiting his views to soldiers in the safety of the camps, he took his equipment daringly close to the actual front lines. Back home there was a tremendous market for his unusually-large-format prints. Returning to Brattleboro, he resumed his more orthodox photographic pursuits. (Davis, William C., ed., *The Image of War 1861-1865*)

HOUSTON, Sam (1793-1863)

The "Father of Texas," Sam Houston was a military hero in the Texas fight for independence from Mexico and in 1836 became the first president of the Republic of Texas. When Texas joined the Union in 1856, he became a U.S. Senator for the next 14

Sam Houston, ousted loyalist governor of Texas. (NA)

years. His staunch Unionist principles put him at odds with most state leaders, and the secessionist-minded Texas legislature elected his successor two years before his term was to expire. However, Houston's personal popularity continued and he surprised his political foes by being elected governor in 1859. A case of the wrong man at the wrong time, Houston could not stem the flow of events as the forces for Civil War multiplied. When secessionist forces carried the day in 1861, Houston tried to resist by insisting that Texas had reverted back to independent status. He refused to support the Confederacy. His office was declared vacant and Lt. Gov. Edward Clark succeeded him. Houston spent the last two years of his life in retirement on his farm.

HOVEY, Alvin Peterson (1821-1891)

When in the midst of the Atlanta Campaign Union General Alvin P. Hovey went on leave, his commander, William T. Sherman, thought he was off seeking advancement and broke up his division. Hovey never returned to his command. A native Indiana lawyer and politician, he lost a bid for Congress in 1858. Enlisting early in the Civil War, his credentials as a volunteer in the Mexican War marked him for a colonelcy. His assignments included: colonel, 24th Indiana (July 31, 1861); brigadier general, USV (April 28, 1862); commanding 2nd Division, District of Eastern Arkansas, Department of the Missouri (December 1862); commanding 1st Brigade, 12th Division, 13th Corps, Army of the Tennessee (January 22-February 8, 1863); commanding the division (February 8-July 26, 1863); also commanding 4th Division, 16th Corps, Army of the Tennessee (July 12-23, 1863); commanding 1st Division, 23rd Corps, Army of the Ohio (April 10-June 9, 1864); and commanding District of Indiana, Department of the Ohio (summer 1864-65). After initial service in Missouri he won his brigadier general's star for his fighting ability on the second at Shiloh in Lew Wallace's division. He led a division throughout the Vicksburg Campaign and during the subsequent advance on Jackson, he was given charge of a second division when its commander, Jacob Lauman, failed to live up to expectations. In the former campaign Hovey won the praise of Grant for his role in the fight at Champion Hill. After a tour of recruiting duty in Indiana he returned to command a division in the drive on Atlanta. Going on leave, he was again assigned to recruiting duty and finished the war in district command north of the Ohio. Brevetted major general for his war service on July 4, 1864, he resigned on October 7, 1865. His postwar career included the practice of law, five years as a diplomat in Peru, two terms as congressman and a partial term—he died in office—as governor.

HOVEY, Charles Edward (1827-1897)

Apparently there was not enough merit in the military career of Illinois educator Charles E. Hovey to warrant the Senate's confirmation of his commission as a brigadier general of volunteers. The Vermont native had risen in teaching circles as he moved from there to Massachusetts and then Illinois. Upon the outbreak of the Civil War he organized a regiment of students and professors and his assignments included: colonel, 33rd Illinois (August 15, 1861); brigadier general, USV (September 5, 1862); commanding 1st Brigade, 2nd Division, District of Eastern Arkansas, Department of the Missouri (December 1862); commanding 2nd Brigade, 11th Division, 13th Corps, Army of the Tennessee (December 1862); commanding 2nd Brigade, 4th Division Yazoo Expedition, Army of the Tennessee (December 18, 1862-January 4, 1863); commanding 2nd Brigade, 1st Division, 2nd Corps, Army of the Mississippi (January 4-12, 1863); and commanding 2nd Brigade, 1st Division, 15th Corps, Army of the Tennessee (January 12-May 22, 1863). He led his regiment in Missouri before being named a brigadier general. At Arkansas Post he refused to relinquish command after his arm had been mangled and won a brevet as major general for it. He then took part in operations against Vicksburg, but his appointment as a general officer expired on March 4, 1863, when the Senate had failed to confirm it. He gave up brigade command on May 22, 1863, and left the service. He later moved to Washington where he was a pension lawyer.

HOWARD, Jacob Merritt (1805-1871)

The death of Michigan Senator Kinsley S. Bingham on October 5, 1861, led to the election in his place of the state's attorney general, Jacob M. Howard. Born in Vermont, he had moved to Michigan in 1832 and the next year began the practice of law. In 1838 he was elected to the state legislature. As a Whig he served one term in the U.S. House of Representatives but was not a candidate for reelection in 1842. A dozen years later he wrote much of what became the first platform for the Republicans. In 1855 he was named the state's attorney general and held the post until named to the Senate. Taking his seat on January 17, 1862, he was reelected in 1865 and served until 1871. Within a month of leaving office he died.

HOWARD, Joseph, Jr. (1833-1908)

By manipulating war news *Brooklyn Eagle* city editor Joseph Howard, Jr., was able to net many thousands of dollars on the gold market. At the outbreak of the Civil War Howard had been a reporter for the *New York Times*. It was he who created the story of Lincoln sneaking through Baltimore to his inauguration "in a Scotch cap and long military cloak." Covering the front he had earned a regular byline for his special copy. Moving to the Brooklyn paper he came up with an idea to make a fast buck. Working with a reporter, Francis A. Mallison, he designed a phony presidential proclamation on imitation Associated Press paper and had it distributed by a young boy to the various New York papers. After recounting various setbacks, the document called for a day of fasting and prayer and announced a call for 400,000 more troops. Most of the papers doubted the authenticity of the dispatch and checked on it before publication. But two, the *World* and the *Journal of Commerce*, were too pressed by deadlines and ran the news on May 18, 1864. As Howard knew it would, the news had an electrifying effect on the markets. The price of gold shot up 10 percent. Of course, he had bought large amounts of the precious metal on margin using several names. When Washington heard the news it was outraged and the two papers were seized—as was a telegraph company suspected of transmitting the phony news—and many of their employees were incarcerated. Neither Stanton nor Lincoln realized that they too were victims. Two days later the two journalists were arrested—Howard had predicted the market shake-up to one too many persons—and Howard confessed, clearing the papers of blame. But the damage was done. The administration was accused of turning into a dictatorship—and this during an election campaign. The two papers were free to print their condemnation of the unconstitutional actions and they did. Meanwhile, the two schemers sat in Fort Lafayette. Finally, after three months Howard's father, an elder in Henry Ward Beecher's church, persuaded the minister to intercede in the case. Lincoln agreed to the release but probably not out of compassion. When the hoax had occurred he had a similar proclamation calling for 300,000 men in his desk. The reaction persuaded him to wait for two months before issuing the call. After the war Howard worked for numerous papers in New York and went on the lecture circuit.

HOWARD, Oliver Otis (1830-1909)

Known for abolitionist sentiments while he was attending West Point, Oliver O. Howard survived several military setbacks to become an army commander and later, as head of the Freedmen's Bureau, a champion of the ex-slave. Already a graduate of Bowdoin College, the Maine native graduated from the military academy in 1854 fourth in his class and was assigned to the Ordnance Department. During much of the time prior to the outbreak of the Civil War he was a mathematics instructor at his alma mater. His wartime assignments included: first lieutenant, Ordnance (since July 1, 1857); colonel, 3rd Maine (June 4, 1861); commanding 3rd Brigade, 3rd Division, Army of Northeastern Virginia (June-August 17, 1861); commanding brigade, Division of the Potomac (August 17-October 3, 1861); brigadier general, USV (September 3, 1861); commanding 1st Brigade, Sumner's Division, Army of the Potomac (November 25, 1861-March 13, 1862); commanding 1st Brigade, 1st Division, 2nd Corps, Army of the Potomac (March 13-June 1, 1862); commanding 2nd Brigade, 2nd Division, 2nd Corps, Army of the Potomac (August 27-September 17, 1862); commanding the division (September 17, 1862-January 26, 1863 and February 7-April 1, 1863); major general, USV (November 29, 1862); commanding the corps (January 26-February 5, 1863); commanding 11th Corps, Army of the Potomac (April 2-September 25, 1863), commanding 11th Corps, Army of the Cumberland (September 25, 1863-January 21, 1864 and February 25-April 18, 1864); commanding 4th Corps, Army of the Cumberland (April 10-July 27, 1864); commanding Department and Army of the Tennessee (July 27, 1864-May 19, 1865); and brigadier general, USA (December 21, 1864). His brigade was routed at 1st Bull Run along with most of the rest of McDowell's army. Given a brigadier's star, he took command of a brigade around Washington, which eventually went to the Peninsula. Howard fought at Yorktown and on the second day at Seven Pines, he fell severely wounded—his right arm had to be amputated. Returning to duty in late summer, he succeeded the wounded John Sedgwick in divisional command at Antietam. His division took part in the bloody assaults on Marye's Heights at Fredericksburg. After having briefly commanded the 2nd Corps, he was assigned in place of Franz Sigel in charge of the largely German 11th Corps. Holding the Union right at Chancellorsville, he did not take adequate precautions to secure his own right, believing Hooker's claim that Lee was retreating. Instead, Stonewall Jackson marched around the exposed flank and routed the corps. On the first day at Gettysburg he took over command of the field when John F. Reynolds was killed. His own corps was again routed and fled to Cemetery Hill. Here he was relieved of overall command by Winfield S. Hancock, Meade's specially designated representative, and returned to command of his corps. This greatly upset Howard since Hancock was his junior in rank. Nonetheless Howard received the Thanks of Congress for his role in the battle. In September 1863 the 11th and 12th corps were transferred to Tennessee and Howard fought at Chattanooga. When the two corps were consolidated the next spring Howard was transferred to command the 4th Corps, which he led through the Atlanta Campaign. Following the death of James B. McPherson at the battle of Atlanta, Sherman picked Howard to take over the Army of the Tennessee; this was to the displeasure of John A. Logan who thought that he would get the post. Howard served through the rest of the operations against the city and then commanded the army—as Sherman's right wing—in the Savannah and Carolinas campaigns. A major general of volunteers since just prior to Fredericksburg, he was now recommissioned in the regular army with the rank of brigadier general. (He had resigned his ordnance lieutenancy on June 7, 1861, because of difficulties in obtaining leave to take charge of the volunteer regiment from his native state). In 1893 he received the Congressional Medal of Honor for leading the 61st New York in a charge at Seven Pines and suffering the two wounds that cost him his arm. On May 12, 1865, he became the first commissioner of the Freedmen's Bureau and, although unable to stop corruption and mismanagement, he did much of value for his charges. He survived a court of inquiry in 1874. He founded the black Howard University in the nation's capital and was its president from 1869-1874. Still in the army, he commanded in the West and was superintendent at West Point. He retired in 1894 as a full major general; he had held that rank by brevet since 1864 for the Battle of Ezra Church in the Atlanta Campaign. A religious man, he caused much controversy by trying to integrate a church. Following his retirement he was active in education and historical writing although he never wrote on the war. (Carpenter, John A., *Sword and Olive Branch: Oliver Otis Howard*)

HOWE, Albion Parris (1818-1897)

Not considered one of the Army of the Potomac's top divisional leaders, Albion P. Howe was shunted aside even before the March 1864 reorganization. A Maine West Pointer (1841), he became a career artillerist, earning a brevet for the Mexican War and seeing much duty on the frontier and in the East. He taught at West Point and was at Harpers Ferry with a battery shortly after John Brown's raid. His Civil War-era assignments included: captain, 4th Artillery (since March 2, 1855); brigadier general, USV (June 11, 1862); commanding 1st Brigade, 1st Division, 4th Corps, Army of the Potomac (June 23-July 5, 1862); commanding 2nd Brigade, 1st Division, 4th Corps, Army of the Potomac (July 5-September 26, 1862); commanding 2nd Brigade, 3rd Division, 6th Corps, Army of the Potomac (September 26-October 1862); commanding 3rd Brigade, 3rd Division, 6th Corps, Army of the Potomac (October-November 16, 1862); commanding the division (November 16, 1862-January 4, 1864); major, 4th Artillery (August 11, 1863); commanding Light Artillery Camp, 22nd Corps, Department of Washington (March 3-July 9, August 9-September 22, and October 12-26, 1864, November 1, 1864-April 7, 1865, and May 7-July 20, 1865); and commanding Reserve Division, Department of West Virginia (July 8-August 6, 1864). Initially he remained with the artillery, serving with McClellan in western Virginia before going to the Peninsula as a brigadier general in charge of a brigade of infantry. With this unit he fought in the Seven Days, earning a brevet for Malvern Hill. In the Maryland Campaign his division was attached to the 6th Corps but was too far to the rear to get into action at Antietam. Only lightly engaged at Fredericksburg, he again fought—in command of a division—on the same field during the Chancellorsville Campaign and took part in the storming of Marye's Heights. He won another brevet for his assault. At Gettysburg the division was again in reserve but he won another brevet that fall for Rappanhannock Station and served in the Mine Run Campaign. Apparently Meade or John Sedgwick wanted his removal and he gave up command of the division at the beginning of the year. In March he took over the artillery depot in Washington. He was thus out of the field for the rest of the war with the exception of a month in the Department of West Virginia during Early's incursion into Maryland. Nonetheless he received brevets through major general in both the volunteers and the regulars for his war service. Mustered out of the former on January 15, 1866—he had served as a guard of honor for the Lincoln funeral—he remained in the regular army until his 1882 retirement as colonel, 4th Artillery.

HOWE, Julia Ward (1819-1910)

The wife of Samuel Gridley Howe, Julia Ward Howe became most famous for writing the "Battle Hymm of the Republic." The New York native had long served as a hostess for Boston reformers. She was active in the peace, abolition, and woman suffrage movements. Leaving her Boston home, she visited a Union army camp near Washington in the fall of 1861, and this prompted her to write her famous work, which first appeared in February 1862 and by that spring was highly popular with the troops. (Richards, Laura Elizabeth, *Julia Ward Howe 1819-1910*)

HOWE, Samuel Gridley (1801-1876)

A lifelong reformer, Samuel Gridley Howe had a reputation for always helping those in need both in the United States and Europe. A native of Boston he graduated from Harvard as an M.D. He spent six years in Greece as a fleet surgeon, friend of Florence Nightingale, guerrilla fighter, and worker for reconstruction after the fighting with the Turks. Returning to the United States he was active in helping the blind, deaf, retarded, and insane. Seeking to aid Polish refugees, he spent six weeks in a Prussian prison. It was not until relatively late that he turned to the antislavery movement, co-editing with his wife, Julia Ward Howe, the antislavery periodical *The Commonwealth*. He served in a group sworn to prevent the return of escaped slaves and was defeated in a bid for Congress as a Conscience Whig. He next worked for the Free-Soilers in Kansas and was connected with John Brown. After the Harpers Ferry raid he fled to Canada, denying prior knowledge. With the Civil War he became one of the New England directors of the United States Sanitary Commission, with which he served throughout the war. He was again in Greece after the war, aiding the Cretan uprising during 1866-1867. Often overshadowed by his wife, he nonetheless had a distinguished career of helping others. (Sanborn, F.B., *Dr. S.G. Howe, The Philanthropist* and Schwartz, Harold, *Samuel Gridley Howe, Social Reformer, 1801-1876*)

HOWE, Timothy Otis (1816-1883)

In a political career lasting almost four decades, Timothy O. Howe rose from the state legislature to a cabinet portfolio. Born in Maine, he entered upon the practice of law in 1839. In 1845 he served a term in the Maine legislature and then moved to Wisconsin, becoming a judge in 1850. In his five years of judicial work, he spent some time on the state supreme court. A Union Republican, he was elected to the Senate in 1860 and served three full six-year terms before being defeated for reelection. After leaving office in 1879, he served for a time as a commissioner negotiating the purchase of Indian lands and in 1881 went to Paris as a delegate to the International Monetary Conference. Returning to the United States, he became Chester A. Arthur's postmaster general the next year and held the post until his death.

HOWELL, Joshua Blackwood (1806-1864)

Having long held important commands on the South Carolina coast and in Virginia as a colonel, Joshua B. Howell was only to receive his brigadier general's commission posthumously. The New Jersey native had been a lawyer in Pennsylvania and a Douglas Democrat in 1860. Joining the army, his assignments included: brigadier general, Pennsylvania Militia (prewar) colonel, 85th Pennsylvania (November 12, 1861); commanding 2nd Brigade, 3rd Division, 18th Corps, Department of North Carolina (January 6-February 1863); also commanding 2nd Brigade, 2nd Division, Detachment 18th Corps, St. Helena Island, 10th Corps, Department of the South (January-April 1863); commanding 2nd Brigade, U.S. Forces Folly Island, 10th Corps, Department of the South (June-July 19, 1863); commanding 2nd Brigade, U.S. Forces Morris Island, 10th Corps, Department of the South (July 19-September 19, 1863); commanding 3rd Brigade, South End Folly Island, 10th Corps, Department of the South (October-December 28, 1863); commanding brigade, District of Hilton Head, 10th Corps, Department of the South (December 28, 1863-February 6, 1864); commanding the district (February 5-April 26, 1864); commanding 1st Brigade, 1st Division, 10th Corps, Army of the James (May 2-June 11, June 14-July 28, and August 18-September 1, 1864); commanding the division (June 11-14, 1864); commanding 3rd Division, 10th Corps, Army of the James (September 1-13, 1864); and brigadier general, USV (April 1865 to rank from September 12, 1864). At the head of his regiment he went to the Peninsula where he saw action at Yorktown, Williamsburg, Seven Pines, and during the Seven Days. Transferred to North Carolina, he fought at Goldsboro and, after briefly commanding a brigade, set off to take part in the operations against Charleston. He took part in the siege operations on the various islands and the following spring was transferred back to Virginia as a brigade commander. Serving under Benjamin F. Butler at Bermuda Hundred, he was particularly distinguished leading a charge on May 20, 1864. He continued to serve in front of Richmond and Petersburg for the next several months until his horse fell, severely injuring him on September 12, 1864. The next day he was relieved of command of the division, which he was temporarily leading (still as a colonel), and on the 14th he died. The following spring he was posthumously promoted to brigader general to rank from the date of his injury.

HUBBARD, David (1792-1874)

A wounded veteran of the battle of New Orleans, David Hubbard served the Confederacy as its commissioner of Indian affairs in the latter part of the Civil War. A lawyer and Democrat, he was in the manufacturing and railroad businesses and employed slave labor. He served two nonconsecutive terms in the U.S. Congress from Alabama, supported John C. Breckinridge in 1860, and favored secession. In 1863 he took over the troubling job of dealing with the Indians and preventing their defection to the Union. He met with mixed success. Impoverished by the war, he ran a tannery in Tennessee.

HUDSON, Frederic (1819-1875)

Massachusetts native Frederic Hudson entered the journalistic profession in New York City when he joined the staff of the *New York Herald* in 1836. Over the next 30 years he rose to be its managing editor. In addition to his editorship he was, for a quarter of a century, the president of the Associated Press of which he was one of the organizers. Retiring the year after the Civil War ended, he wrote *Journalism in the United States from 1690 to 1872*. However, after 1866 he refused all journalistic offers. (Starr, Louis M., *Bohemian Brigade*)

HUFF, John A. (ca. 1816-1864)

Formerly the best marksman in Berdan's crack 1st United States Sharpshooters, John A. Huff of Company E, 5th Michigan Cavalry, fired the shot that mortally wounded Jeb Stuart. After having served as a marksman through most of the Army of the Potomac's campaigns he transferred to the mounted arm before the beginning of the Overland Campaign. In the fighting at Yellow Tavern on May 11, 1864, he charged with his regiment, pursuing fleeing Confederates, and rode right past the famed cavalry leader. Dismounted in the charge, he was returning to the Union lines on foot when he again passed Stuart and a small band of rebels. He then fired and ran on. On the 28th of the same month Huff was himself mortally wounded in another cavalry action at Haw's Shop.

HUGER, Benjamin (1805-1877)

Having spent most of his tour in the old army in staff positions, South Carolinian West Pointer (1825) Benjamin Huger proved to be another early failure as a Confederate general. Initially posted to the artillery upon his graduation, he transferred to the ordnance branch in 1832 and won three brevets in Mexico on Winfield Scott's staff. Resigning as a captain on April 22, 1861, he joined the Confederacy and his assignments included: commanding Department of Norfolk (May 26, 1861-April 12, 1862); brigadier general, CSA (June 17, 1861); major general, CSA (October 7, 1861); commanding Department of Norfolk under the Department of Northern Virginia (April 12-May 1862); and commanding division, Department of Northern Virginia (May-July 12, 1862). Assigned to command at Norfolk, he came in for his share of the blame for the loss of Roanoke Island, North Carolina, which was part of his department. His command was placed under that of Joseph E. Johnston on April 12, 1862, and the next month the Confederate withdrawal from the Yorktown lines compelled him to abandon the port city and also resulted in the scuttling of the *Virginia*. Joining Johnston's forces with what was now styled a division he fought at Seven Pines and later, under Lee, in the Seven Days. He performed poorly in the latter campaign and fell victim to Lee's weeding out process the next month. For the balance of the war the major general performed routine inspection duty for ordnance and artillery mostly west of the Mississippi. His postwar years were spent as a farmer. (Rhoades, Jeffrey, *Scapegoat General: The Story of Major General Benjamin Huger, C.S.A.*)

HUGER, Frank (1837-1897)

Virginian Frank Huger was one of those relatively recent graduates of West Point (1860) who resigned their commissions to serve the South and whose military skills brought them rapid advancement. Resigning from the 10th Infantry on May 21, 1861, he launched his Confederate career, which included the following assignments: captain, Norfolk (Va.) Artillery (June 1861); major, Artillery (March 2, 1863); executive officer, Alexander's Battalion, Reserve Artillery, 1st Corps, Army of Northern Virginia (April 16-July 1863); executive officer, Alexander's Artillery Battalion, 1st Corps, Army of Northern Virginia (July-September 1863); executive officer, Alexander's Artillery Battalion, Longstreet's Corps, Army of Tennessee (September-November 1863); commanding Alexander's-Huger's Artillery Battalion, Department of East Tennessee (November 1863-April 1864); lieutenant colonel, Artillery (February 27, 1864); commanding artillery battalion, 1st Corps, Army of Northern Virginia (April 1864-April 6, 1865); and colonel, Artillery (February 18, 1865). After initial service in the Norfolk area, including duty as an aide-de-camp to his father, General Benjamin Huger, he led his battery in the Seven Days and at Fredericksburg. He served under E. Porter Alexander at Chancellorsville and Gettysburg but arrived too late at Chickamauga when the battalion accompanied Longstreet to Georgia. He led the battalion in the Knoxville Campaign and was named to its permanent command in early 1864. Back with Lee's army, he fought at the Wilderness, Spotsylvania, Cold Harbor, and in the siege of Petersburg. During the retreat to Appomattox he was captured in the rear guard action at Sayler's Creek on April 6, 1865. He was active in railroading after the war. (Wise, Jennings C., *The Long Arm of Lee*)

HUGER, Thomas B. (?-1862)

In the rather dismal performance of the Southern naval forces on the Mississippi at New Orleans, the skipper of the gunboat *McRae*, Lieutenant Thomas B. Huger, was one of the shining stars. But he also lost his life. A veteran of a quarter-century in the U.S. Navy, Huger resigned his commission as first lieutenant of the U.S.S. *Iroquois* upon the secession of South Carolina, his native state. After early service in the ordnance department and commanding shore batteries at Charleston, Huger was given command of the 7-gun *McRae* at New Orleans. When on April 24, 1862, Farragut's Union fleet passed Forts Jackson and St. Philip below the city they were met by a ragtag Confederate fleet. It was past Confederate Navy vessels, part Louisiana State vessels and part the southern division of the River Defense Fleet, former riverboats commanded by steamboatmen under the loose direction of the War Department. The net result was a confused action in which many vessels declined to take part, especially parts of the River Defense Fleet. Huger's *McRae* was an exception however. Engaging his vessel in the unequal contest, he fell mortally wounded and was succeeded in command by Lieutenant Charles W. Read. Huger died the next day. (Scharf, J. Thomas, *History of the Confederate States Navy*)

HUGHS, John M. (ca. 1832-?)

Rising from company officer to acting brigade commander, John M. Hughs was finally found wanting. A native of Tennessee he entered the Confederate service from Overton County. His assignments included: lieutenant, Company D, 25th Tennessee (August 1, 1862); major, 25th Tennessee (summer 1862); colonel, 25th Tennessee (July 21, 1862); and commanding Johnson's Brigade, Department of Richmond (August 1864-January 1865). He saw action at Mill Springs, Perryville, and Murfreesboro, commanding the regiment at the latter two engagements. Having suffered a wound at Murfreesboro, he rejoined his command but was detached in August 1863 to conscript duty. Cut off for a time, he rejoined the Army of Tennessee in Georgia but found that his regiment had been transferred to Virginia. After the battle of Chickamauga, where it had suffered heavily, it had been consolidated with another unit and he was now a supernumerary. Therefore he was given various forces over the next few months with which he raided Union garrisons in Kentucky and Tennessee. With the death of Colonel John S. Fulton of the consolidated regiment, Hughs was sent to Virginia where he took over command of the brigade in the defenses of Richmond. He was relieved in January 1865 when the brigade was consolidated with Archer's old Brigade and was found to be incompetent by an examining board. He resigned on March 17, 1865, citing the reduced state of his old regiment.

HUMES, William Young Conn (1830-1882)

Although he did not transfer from the staff to the line until late in 1863, William Y.C. Humes rose to the rank of brigadier general in the Confederate cavalry and the command of a mounted division. The Virginia native had graduated one place from the top of the 1851 class at the Virginia Military Institute before becoming a Tennessee lawyer. His military assignments included: lieutenant, Artillery (April 1861); lieutenant, Bankhead's Tennessee Battery (May 13, 1861); captain, Artillery (June 1861); brigadier general, CSA (November 16, 1863); chief of Artillery, Wheeler's Cavalry Corps, Army of Tennessee (March-November 1863); commanding brigade, Armstrong's Division, Martin's detachment, Wheeler's Cavalry Corps, Department of East Tennessee (November 1863); commanding brigade, Kelly's Division, Wheeler's Cavalry Corps, Army of Tennessee (January-ca. March 5, 1864); commanding division, Wheeler's Cavalry Corps, Army of Tennessee (ca. March 5-late 1864); commanding division, Wheeler's Cavalry Corps, Department of South Carolina, Georgia and Florida (late 1864-February 16, 1865); and commanding division, Wheeler's Cavalry Corps, Army of Tennessee (spring-April 26, 1865). Serving as a staff artillerist he was captured at Island #10 and subsequently exchanged. As chief of artillery to Wheeler, he attracted the general's attention and won the rank of brigadier general commanding brigades at Chickamauga and Knoxville. He had quickly risen to division command in time for the Atlanta Campaign and went on to serve opposing the March to the Sea of William T. Sherman and Sherman's drive through the Carolinas. Included in Joseph E. Johnston's surrender, he returned to his practice.

HUMISTON, Amos (1830-1863)

It was not the fact Amos Humiston was killed in action that was unusual but rather the the manner of his death that earned national attention and led to the establishment of the Soldiers' Orphans' Home in Gettysburg. An upstate New York harness maker, Humiston had made sure that his family would be taken care of during his absence before enlisting in response to Lincoln's summer 1862 call for more volunteers. Joining Company C, 154th New York, in July, he was mustered in as corporal on September 24. The next January 25 he was promoted to sergeant; after service in the Washington defenses, the regiment joined the Army of the Potomac. He got caught up in the rout of the 11th Corps at Chancellorsville in May. On the first day at Gettysburg, his brigade was sent forward to try to stem another rout of the corps. Instead, Sergeant Humiston found himself retreating through the confusing streets of town. Mortally wounded, he was found several days later by the burial details on Statton Street. In his hands was an ambrotype of his three children, Franklin, age 8, Alice 6, and Frederick, 4. But there was no identification on the body. A Philadelphia physician heard about the case and decided to try to locate the family and inform them of Amos' fate. Through the distribution of copies of the photo, the family was eventually located. The search had generated so much publicity that the doctor continued the sale of the photos and a newspaper ran a poetry contest. With the proceeds of the sales an orphanage was opened in 1866 with Mrs. Humiston as the first matron. Amos was buried nearby in the National Cemetery. (Dunkelman, Mark H., and Winey, Michael J., *The Hardtack Regiment*)

HUMPHREY, William T.

See: *Smith, Hiram*

HUMPHREYS, Andrew Atkinson (1810-1883)

A career military officer, Pennsylvanian Andrew A. Humphreys had a distinguished Civil War career in both line and staff assignments, rising to major general of volunteers and retiring from the postwar army as a brigadier general and chief of engineers. A West Pointer (1831), he had originally been posted to the artillery before being transferred to the topographical engineers seven years later. As such he was assigned to survey and bridge construction duties. The year the Civil War began he published *Report upon the Physics and Hydraulics of the Mississippi River*. His wartime assignments included: captain, Topographical Engineers (since May 31, 1848); major, Topographical Engineers (August 6, 1861); attached to the staff, Army of the Potomac (December 1, 1861-March 5, 1862); colonel and additional aide-de-camp (March 5, 1862); chief topographical engineer, Army of the Potomac (March 5-September 12, 1862); brigadier general, USV (April 28, 1862); commanding 3rd Division, 5th Corps, Army of the Potomac (September 12, 1862-January 27, 1863 and February 12-May 25, 1863); temporarily commanding the corps (February 23-28, 1863); lieutenant colonel, engineers (March 3, 1863); commanding 2nd Division, 3rd Corps, Army of the Potomac (May 23-July 9, 1863); major general, USV (July 8, 1863); chief of staff, Army of the Potomac (July 9, 1863-November 25, 1864); and commanding 2nd Corps, Army of the Potomac (November 26, February 15, 1865 and February 25-April 22, May 5-June 9, and June 20-28, 1865). As McClellan's topographical chief he served through Yorktown, Williamsburg, and the Seven Days. Just before the battle of Antietam he was given charge of a newly raised division of nine-months troops, which were held in reserve during the battle. He later earned a brevet for his leadership of these troops at Fredericksburg. After leading them at Chancellorsville he was given a division in the 3rd Corps when the nine months term had expired. With his new command Humphreys earned another brevet for his actions on the second day at Gettysburg. A few days later he was promoted major general and assigned as Meade's chief of staff. Holding this post for well over a year, he was present during the Bristoe, Mine Run, Overland, and Petersburg campaigns. When Winfield S. Hancock was forced by his old Gettysburg wound to relinquish command of the 2nd Corps Humphreys was tapped by Grant for the post that he held through the end of the war. He directed the corps through the remainder of the Petersburg operations and in the Appomattox Campaign, earning another brevet—to major general in the regulars—for Sayler's Creek. He was mustered out of the volunteers on September 1, 1866, but had the previous month been appointed chief engineer with the regular rank of brigadier general. He retired in 1879. He wrote *From Gettysburg to the Rapidan* and *The Virginia Campaign of 1864 and 1865*. Active in engineering circles, he was a member or honorary member of various engineering and philosophical societies in Europe and the United States. (Humphreys, Henry Hollingsworth, *Andrew Atkinson Humphreys: A Biography*)

HUMPHREYS, Benjamin Grubb (1808-1882)

Despite having been expelled from West Point in 1827 over a Christmas Eve riot the previous year, Benjamin G. Humphreys rose to the rank of brigadier during the Civil War. A planter and state legislator before the war, he promptly entered the military in 1861. His assignments included: captain, 21st Mississippi

(May 18, 1861); colonel, 21st Mississippi (September 11, 1861); commanding Barksdale's (old) Brigade, McLaws'-Kershaw's Division, 1st Corps, Army of Northern Virginia (July 2-September 9, 1863 and April 12-September 13, 1864); brigadier general, CSA (August 14, 1863); commanding same brigade, McLaws' Division, Longstreet's Corps, Army of Tennessee (September 19-November 5, 1863); commanding brigade, McLaws'-Kershaw's Division, Department of East Tennessee (November 5, 1863-April 12, 1864); and commanding District South of Homochitto, Department of Alabama, Mississippi and East Louisiana (spring 1865). He led his regiment at Yorktown, the Seven Days, Antietam, Fredericksburg, Chancellorsville, and Gettysburg. In the latter he succeeded to brigade command upon the mortal wounding of General William Barksdale on the second day. Promoted to brigadier, he led the unit west to Chickamauga and Knoxville. Returning to Virginia, he led the brigade at the Wilderness, Spotsylvania, Cold Harbor, and in the defense of Richmond and Petersburg. Sent to reinforce Early in the Shenandoah in the late summer of 1864, he was wounded at Berryville on September 13. Upon his recovery he was assigned to command in southern Mississipi and eastern Louisiana. He was governor of his native Mississippi during much of Reconstruction and later retired to his plantation. (Freeman, Douglas S., *Lee's Lieutenants*)

HUNLEY, Horace L. (?-1863)

Although he would not live to see the day, Horace L. Hunley was the inventor of the first submarine to sink an enemy vessel. Hunley had made two previous attempts to create a submersible fighting craft during the Civil War before his third effort, although it cannot be called completely successful, scored its victory. The first attempt, the *Pioneer*, had to be destroyed when Union forces occupied its home port of New Orleans. Hunley moved on to Mobile, where his second effort failed with the swamping of his invention in rough weather during an attempt to attack the blockaders. Hunley financed the third venture himself and the craft was dubbed the *H.L. Hunley* in his honor. Manned by a crew of nine, the vessel was operated by hand cranks and could be propelled under water. However, when submerged the vessel lacked light and fresh air. Nonetheless, it could remain below the surface for as along as two hours and 35 minutes. The vessel also had an unfortunate tendency to sink quickly to the bottom. The first disaster in Mobile drowned the entire crew. After moving to Charleston, two more accidents occurred, killing 15 more crew members. Hunley then took charge of a volunteer crew and made several successful dives. Then on October 15, 1863, the *Hunley* failed to resurface. Hunley and his second in command had suffocated and the remainder of the crew drowned. In February 1864 Hunley's dream came true when his invention, under the command of Lieutenant George E. Dixon, sank the USS *Housatonic*—but was itself lost with all hands.

HUNT, Henry Jackson (1819-1889)

While he frequently came into conflict with army and corps commanders over the organization and use of his artillery arm, Henry J. Hunt was the driving force in welding the Army of the Potomac's artillery into a superb organization. Born in Michigan, he entered West Point from Ohio after having been orphaned. Upon his 1839 graduation, he was posted to the artillery and in the Mexican War suffered one wound and earned two brevets. In one instance he charged with a field piece right into the face of the enemy's works and at pointblank range demolished a Mexican gun. Along with William F. Barry and William H. French, he sat on a board that completely revised the theories of field artillery tactics. It proved to be the basis of much of the army's artillery practice in the Civil War. His Civil War assignments included: captain, 2nd Artillery (since September 28, 1852); major, 5th Artillery (May 14, 1861); colonel, and additional aide-de-camp (September 28, 1861); commanding Artillery Reserve, Army of the Potomac (to May 18, 1862); commanding Artillery Reserve, (attached to) 5th Corps, Army of the Potomac (May 18-September 1862); brigadier general, USV (September 15, 1862); chief of Artillery, Army of the Potomac (September 1862-May 1865); and lieutenant colonel, 3rd Artillery (August 1, 1863). At the head of Battery M, 2nd United States Artillery, he proved one of the heroes in the Union disaster at 1st Bull Run. With his four guns he covered the withdrawal of the green army from an exposed position at Blackburn's Ford. He was soon appointed to a staff position and given charge of organizing the batteries in the Washington fortifications. By the time of the Peninsula Campaign he was commanding the artillery reserve and at Malvern Hill he proved the effectiveness of his batteries. One-hundred guns ripped into the charging Confederate infantry and played a major role in their defeat. In the midst of the Maryland campaign McClellan made Hunt his chief artillerist. As a newly promoted brigadier, he again proved his worth at Antietam. At Fredericksburg he massed some 147 guns to cover the river crossing. This is one reason Lee did not counterattack after the Union repulse. Feuding with the army's next commander—Joseph Hooker—Hunt was relegated to primarily administrative functions with little control over the guns. As a result the artillery branch put in a poor showing at Chancellorsville and Hunt was restored. On the third day at Gettysburg Hunt came into conflict with Winfield S. Hancock over how the guns should be used in facing Pickett's Charge. The artillerist wanted to save his ammunition for the assault and the infantrymen wanted the guns to reply to the Confederate bombardment and encourage the Union infantry. As it turned out the artillery tore tremendous gaps in the advancing Confederate ranks. Hunt also feuded with army commander George G. Meade but worked well under Grant who placed the artillerist in charge of the Petersburg siege operations after the Overland Campaign. Having already been brevetted major general in the volunteers for Gettysburg, he was given the same honor in the regular establishment for his wartime services. Mustered out of the volunteer service on April 30, 1866, he remained in the army until his retirement as colonel, 5th Artillery in 1883. His lenient treatment of the South during Reconstruction led to criticism by the Radical Republicans. The acknowledged expert in his branch, he wrote a series of articles on Gettysburg for *Battles and Leaders of the Civil*

War. In retirement he was governor of the Soldiers' Home in the nation's capital. (Downey, Fairfax, *The Guns at Gettysburg* and Longacre, Edward G., *The Man Behind the Guns: A Biography of General Henry J. Hunt*)

HUNT, Lewis Cass (1824-1886)

Career infantryman Lewis C. Hunt switched to the volunteer service during the Civil War and rose to the grade of brigadier general. The Wisconsin native received his West Point appointment from Missouri and upon his 1847 graduation was assigned to the 4th Infantry. He served in Mexico, on the Pacific Northwest, and in an American-British invasion of San Juan in 1859. His Civil War assignments included: captain, 4th Infantry (since May 23, 1855); colonel, 92nd New York (May 2, 1862); brigadier general, USV (December 24, 1862, to rank from November 29); commanding 1st Brigade, 1st Division, Department of North Carolina (December 28, 1862-January 2, 1863); commanding 1st Brigade, 4th Division, 18th Corps, Department of North Carolina (January 2-March 12 and April 13-May 3, 1863); major, 14th Infantry (June 8, 1863); and commanding Defenses of New York Harbor, Department of the East (July 1864-January 1866). As a regular army company commander he took part in the operations against Yorktown before accepting the colonelcy of a volunteer regiment. Within a month he was severely wounded at Seven Pines and was out of action until late in the year. Returning as a brigadier general, he won a brevet for leading his brigade at Kinston—he had already won one for his wounding—and fought at Whitehall and Goldwater. Promoted to major in the regular army, he was assigned to command the draft rendezvous at New Haven, Connecticut, from June 1863 to March 1864 when he was sent on special assignment to Kansas and Missouri. In June 1864 he was assigned to command in New York Harbor and held that post until he was mustered out of the volunteer service on January 15, 1866. Brevetted colonel and brigadier general in the regular service for the war, he died on active duty as colonel, 14th Infantry.

HUNTER, Charles (?-?)

Career naval officer Charles Hunter paid the price for violating the rights of neutral nations, and his case is still cited today as a warning to young officers. As a commander in the Union navy during the Civil War, he was attached to the West Gulf Blockading Squadron in charge of the USS *Montgomery*. Sailing his vessel out of the harbor of Havana, Cuba, he spotted the blockade-runner *Blanche* making its way toward the harbor entrance close to shore. The captain of the runner, spotting the Union vessel, ran his craft ashore and raised both the British and Spanish colors. The vessel was registered in the former and an official of the latter was on board. Hunter sent a boarding party aboard and over the protests of the Spanish harbor master started an inspection of the ship. Soon a fire was discovered—who set it is still a mystery—and the vessel was abandoned. Both Britain and Spain lodged formal protests with the State Department and an investigation was launched. Hunter was hauled before a court-martial and found guilty on February 16, 1863. The October 7, 1862, incident had violated the rights of two nations which the United States did not want to offend. Although the panel recommended that the sentence—dismissal from the service—be mitigated, Lincoln feld obligated, for foreign policy reasons, to have it carried out. Thus on June 19, 1863, Hunter's naval career came to an end.

HUNTER, David (1802-1886)

Having befriended Lincoln, David Hunter accompanied the president-elect on part of his inaugural journey, became one of his more controversial generals (thoroughly hated in the South), accompanied Lincoln's body back to Illinois, and then tried his assassination plotters. A native of the District of Columbia, he received his West Point appointment from Illinois. Graduating in 1822, he served in the infantry and dragoons before resigning as a captain in 1836 to enter the Chicago real estate business. Five years later he rejoined the army as a paymaster; he served in Mexico and then in Kansas where he corresponded with Lincoln on the secession movement. His Civil War-era assignments included: major and paymaster (since March 14, 1842); colonel, 3rd Cavalry (May 14, 1861); brigadier general, USV (May 17, 1861); commanding 2nd Division, Army of Northeastern Virginia (June-July 21, 1861); colonel, 6th Cavalry (change of designation August 3, 1861); major general, USV (August 13, 1861); commanding brigade, Division of the Potomac (August-October 1861); commanding Western Department (November 2-9, 1861); commanding Department of Kansas (November 20, 1861-March 11, 1862); commanding Department of the South (March 31-August 22, 1862 and January 20-June 12, 1863); also commanding 10th Corps, Department of the South (January 20-June 12, 1863); and commanding Department of West Virginia (May 21-August 9, 1864). While on crowd control duty with Lincoln's inaugural tour he suffered a dislocated collarbone at Buffalo, New York. Transferring to the line, he was soon a brigadier and lead one of the two divisions on the flank march at 1st Bull Run but was wounded early in the action. Recovering he was briefly in command of a brigade before being sent to Missouri as a major general. He found himself in an awkward position with the department commander, John C. Frémont, who feared Hunter as a rival. In fact he did shortly succeed to the command. But the department was dismantled within a few days and he was relegated to the Department of Kansas where he became a chronic complainer on the smallness of his command and the heavy detachments sent to join Grant and Canby. Transferring to the Southern coast, he got the credit for the completion of the reduction of Fort Pulaski. However, his operations against Charleston failed, most notably at Secessionville. In the meantime he had roused the ire of Confederates by his "abolition" of slavery in the department and his formation of the 1st South Carolina Colored Infantry. Washington quickly disavowed his policies. While on leave to improve his position in the fall of 1862 he was detailed to a board of inquiry on the surrender of Harpers Ferry and then was made the presiding officer at the Fitz-John Porter court-martial. Returning to the coast, he failed in another attempt on Charleston and was removed from command on what was called

David Hunter, despised Union commander in the Shenandoah Valley, faced a death penalty if captured. (*Leslie's*)

a temporary basis. For almost a year he was either at home or on some assignment for the War Department. During this time he did witness the Chattanooga fighting and made a good impression on Grant, who the next spring named him to replace Franz Sigel after the latter's failure at New Market in the Shenandoah Valley. Off to a good start, Hunter earned a regular brevet to brigadier for his victory at Piedmont. He then proceeded with the policy of massive burning in the district. The South condemned him—he was already threatened with death if captured—for his burnings, especially that of former Virginia Governor John Letcher's residence and the Virginia Military Institute, certainly a legitimate target. Approaching Lynchburg, he found that the town had been reinforced by men from Lee's army at Petersburg and withdrew without applying much pressure. After a defeat at Liberty in the retreat, he moved into West Virginia and out of the war, burning as he went. He then offered to step down and was replaced by Philip H. Sheridan. After the sad funeral trip to Illinois and the trial of the conspirators he mustered out of the volunteers on January 15, 1866. Brevetted major general for the war, he retired completely on July 31, 1866.

HUNTER, Robert Mercer Taliaferro (1809-1887)

In a forlorn attempt to salvage the Confederacy Confederate Senator Robert M.T. Hunter—and two other commissioners, Alexander Stephens and John A. Campbell—met with Lincoln and Seward in the Hampton Roads Peace Conference in February 1865. A Calhoun states' righter and Democratic lawyer, Hunter came from one of the first families of Virginia. He began his political career as an independent in the state legislature in 1834 and three years later he entered the U.S. House of Representatives as a Whig. In his second term he served as its speaker and continued to be reelected, but not as a speaker, until defeated in 1842. He returned to Congress in 1845 as a Calhoun Democrat. His U.S. Senate career began in 1847. From then until the Civil War he proved to be a moderate secessionist willing to compromise to preserve the Union. Having backed Breckinridge in 1860, he nonetheless remained in the Senate well after Lincoln's inauguration, hoping for a settlement. He finally withdrew on March 28, 1861, and was expelled on July 11, 1861. On May 10 he was admitted as a member of the Virginia delegation to the Provisional Confederate Congress where he served on the Committee on Finance. With the resignation of Secretary of State Robert Toombs, Hunter was given the portfolio on July 25, 1861. Resigning on February 17, 1862, he took his seat as one of Virginia's representatives in the Confederate Senate where he served on his old committee for the remainder of the war. During the First Confederate Congress he also sat on the Committee on Foreign Affairs. His policy positions were a mix of support for the war effort and restrictions on the power of the central government and the president. After the failure of the February 3, 1865, conference and the fall of the Confederacy he spent several months confined in Fort Pulaski. With his estate looted during the war and its aftermath, he served as Virginia's treasurer and as a port collector. (Simms, Henry Harrison, *Life of Robert M.T. Hunter*)

HUNTER, William Wallace (1803-?)

With nearly four decades of service in the old navy, including capture by and escape from pirates in the West Indies, it was natural that when Commander William W. Hunter resigned his commission he was appointed captain, CSN, immediately. Assigned to duty in New Orleans, he was given responsibility for the protection of the Louisiana and Texas coasts. Highly successful here, he was transferred to Virginia where he supervised the batteries at the mouth of the Rappahannock River for four months. After service in Richmond, he became the last commander of the Savannah River Squadron. With his fleet of nine craft, he cooperated with Lieutenant General William Hardee in the defense of Savannah against Sherman's armies. At the fall of the city, Hunter was able to save two of his gunboats by running them up the river to August. He and the remnants of his command were included in the surrender of General Joe Johnston. (Scharf, J. Thomas, *History of the Confederate States Navy*)

HUNTON, Eppa (1822 or 1823-1908)

Fighting bouts of illness, Eppa Hunton, who had distinguished himself early in the war, rose to brigadier general in the Confederate army. An attorney and militia brigadier, he was a member of the secession convention of his native Virginia and soon thereafter entered the army. His assignments included: colonel, 8th Virginia (spring 1861); commanding Pickett's Brigade, Longstreet's Division, Army of Northern Virginia (June 27-30, 1862); commanding Pickett's Brigade, Kemper's Division, 1st Corps, same army (August-September 5, 1862); brigadier general, CSA (August 9, 1863); commanding Garnett's (old) Brigade, Pickett's Division same corps and army (August 15-September 23, 1863; May 1864-January 1865; and March-April 6, 1865); and commanding brigade, Department of Richmond (September 23, 1863-May 19, 1864). He distinguished himself at 1st Bull Run and, despite being ill, at Ball's Bluff. Again fighting illness, he took over brigade command at Gaines' Mill but was forced to leave the field by exhaustion three days later at Glendale. He led the brigade at 2nd Bull Run and the regiment at South Mountain and Antietam. Wounded in Pickett's Charge at Gettysburg, he recovered to be promoted and given command of the brigade, replacing deceased General Richard B. Garnett. After services in the defenses of Richmond, he rejoined the reconstituted Pickett's Division and fought with Lee at Cold Harbor and along the Richmond and Petersburg siege lines. After the debacle at Five Forks, he took part in the retreat toward Appomattox until he was captured at Sayler's Creek on April 6, 1865. He returned to the law after his release and sat in both houses of congress. (Hunton, Eppa, *Autobiography of Eppa Hunton*)

HURLBUT, Stephen Augustus (1815-1882)

Only one Union general had been born in South Carolina and he, Stephen A. Hurlbut, became noted for corrupt practices while serving in occupied areas of the South and elsewhere during the postwar years. A lawyer in his native Charleston, he served as a regiment adjutant in the fighting against the Seminoles. The 30-year-old Hurlbut moved to Illinois in 1845 and became a prominent Republican politician and state legislature who was rewarded with a commission as a brigadier general at the outbreak of the Civil War. His assignments included: brigadier general, USV (June 14, 1861, to rank from May 17); commanding 4th Division, Army of the Tennessee (February 17-April 6 and April 6-July 1862); commanding 4th Division, District of Memphis, Army of the Tennessee (July-September 24, 1862); major general, USV (September 17, 1862); commanding 4th Division, District of Jackson, Army of the Tennessee (September 24-October 5, 1862); commanding 3rd Division, Army of the Tennessee (October 5-26, 1862); commanding District of Jackson, 13th Corps, Army of the Tennessee (October 26-November 19, 1862); commanding District of Memphis, 13th Corps, Army of the Tennessee (November 25-December 22, 1862); commanding 16th Corps, Army of the Tennessee (December 22, 1862-January 10, 1863 and February 5, 1863-April 17, 1864); and commanding Department of the Gulf (September 23, 1864-April 22, 1865). Following service in his adopted state he led one of Grant's divisions at Shiloh and in the subsequent advance on Corinth, Mississippi. As commander of the widely dispersed 16th Corps, he was in charge of the base camp at Memphis during the operations against Vicksburg and later against the Confederate cavalryman Nathan Bedford Forrest. While commanding on the Gulf coast he was charged with corruption but instead of a trial he was mustered out, honorably, on June 20, 1865. Resuming his political career, he was Grant's representative in Columbia and Garfield's in Peru. At the latter post he was again cited for mismanagement and corruption. In the meantime, active in veterans' circles, he was the Grand Army of the Republic's first president. His political career seems to have withstood all charges, including that of drunkenness. He died at his diplomatic post in Lima, Peru.

HUSBAND, Mary Morris (?-?)

A Pennsylvanian, Mary M. Husband worked throughout the war—and beyond—for the United States Sanitary Commission. Her career began with hospital work in Philadelphia; nursing on the hospital boats on the James and York rivers during the Peninsular Campaign followed. Further field hospital service and Washington duty kept her busy for the remainder of the war. With the surrender of the Confederate armies she began work with the returning Union veterans.

HUSE, Caleb (1831-1905)

Although he had been born in Massachusetts, Caleb Huse became the chief, and for much of the war, the only purchaser abroad of supplies for the Confederate army. After graduating from West Point in 1851 and serving there as a professor for a number of years, Huse was a first lieutenant of the 1st Artillery by late 1859 when he was granted a six-months leave of absence for a tour of Europe. On this trip he obtained the knowledge of European armament industries that would serve him so wll in the Civil War. Returning to the United States in May 1860, he accepted an appointment, with the rank of colonel in the state forces, as commandant of cadets at the University of Alabama under a special arrangement whereby he was given an additional year's leave from the army after which he was to resign if he liked his new post. In February 1861, with conflict looming, his leave was revoked and he resigned on the 25th. In April he was appointed a captain, and soon promoted to major, in the Confederate army and assigned to the duty of purchasing ordnance supplies in Europe. After much difficulty traveling through the North with almost no funds, he made his way to England on May 10. Here he entered upon his work at which he was very successful. He managed to wrest the full production of the London Armory Company away from U.S. agents for the length of the war. He astounded many by his purchase from the Austrian government of 10 fully equipped artillery batteries and 100,000 rifles. A critic of the contract system for running the blockade, whereby contractors made huge profits, Huse was often in conflict with Confederate diplomats. Charges of corruption were leveled at him but disproved and Jefferson

Davis gave him complete independence from political officers in Europe. Working through the Liverpool financial firm of Fraser, Trenholm & Company, in reality a branch of the Charleston firm John Fraser & Company, he continued his purchasing until the close of the war. Returning to the United States in 1868, he launched a number of unsuccessful business enterprises before establishing a successful prep school for West Point. (Huse, Caleb, *The Supplies for the Confederate Army*)

HYAMS, Godfrey Joseph (?-?)

The Civil War was full of shady characters operating in Canada for both sides. One of the more untrustworthy was Godfrey Hymans. Living in Arkansas early in the war he was evicted by the Union occupation forces who also appropriated his property. He moved to St. Louis but soon went to Canada to offer his services to the Confederacy. Meeting Dr. Luke Blackburn at the end of 1863, he was offered $60,000, and more fame than General Lee, if he would hold himself ready for a special assignment from Blackburn. He agreed, according to his own account, but denied interest in acquiring wealth from his service. This seems strange since earlier in the war he had sold lists of Confederate sympathizers to Union authorities. Later, he provided damaging testimony against Confederate agents and the famed St. Albans raiders. In May 1864 he was directed by a letter from Blackburn to proceed to Halifax for a meeting. In the July 18 meeting Hyams was directed take some trunks, filled with infected clothing from yellow fever victims in Havana, and distribute them throughout the North in places likely to reach the forces in the field. They were sent to Washington, New York, Philadelphia and Norfolk and Hyams was convinced that one trunk reached New Bern, North Carolina, because an epidemic broke out there shortly afterwards. In fact he was not responsible for the 2,000-plus deaths because yellow fever, it is now known, can only be transmitted by a mosquito. With the plot revealed in April 1865, Hyams testified to his own involvement. Not enough proof ever existed to convict either Hyams or Blackburn in the germ warfare plot.

I

IMBODEN, John Daniel (1823-1895)

The commander of a group of partisan rangers, John D. Imboden was relieved of duty when it was found that his men, while capable as raiders, were not effective as regular cavalry. A former state legislator, he had failed in a bid to attend the secession convention but raised a battery upon the withdrawal of his native Virginia from the Union. His assignments included: captain, Staunton Artillery (April 1861); colonel, 1st Virginia Partisan Rangers later known as 62nd Virginia Mounted Infantry (ca. July 1862); brigadier general, CSA (January 28, 1863); commanding Northwestern Brigade, Department of Northern Virginia (ca. January 28-July 28, 1863); commanding Valley District same department (July 28-December 15, 1863 and early 1864-June 1864); commanding Northwestern Brigade, same district and department (December 15, 1863-early 1864); and commanding brigade, Ransoms-Lomax's Cavalry Division, same district and department (June-December 6, 1864). After participating in the occupation of Harpers Ferry he directed his guns at 1st Bull Run. The next summer he organized a regiment of partisans to serve in the Valley and the western part of the state. Promoted to the command of a brigade reporting directly to Lee he was active in raiding operations. He covered the advance in Pennsylvania in June 1863 but angered Lee when the brigade went off to rest at Hancock, Maryland, without informing him. Following the defeat at Gettysburg Imboden was charged with escorting the wagon train including the ambulances to the Potomac. Placed in command in the Valley, he served under Breckinridge in the New Market victory the next spring. In June Early took over the district and Imboden led his brigade in the advance via Monocacy to the outskirts of Washington. Back in the Shenandoah proper, he fought at 3rd Winchester, Fisher's Hill, and Cedar Creek. Following a bout with typhoid, he was relieved of his command. Ransom had recommended his replacement as early as August 1864 for inefficiency. Imboden finished out the war guarding prisoners at Aiken, South Carolina. A businessman and lawyer after the surrender, he wrote several articles for the *Century Magazine's Battles and Leaders* series. (Freeman, Douglas S., *Lee's Lieutenants*)

John D. Imboden, escort of the ambulances from Gettysburg. (NA)

INGALLS, Rufus (1818-1893)

With all the command changes in the Union army in Virginia, Rufus Ingalls remained the chief quartermaster throughout the war. A Maine West Pointer (1843), he was originally posted to the riflemen—a temporary designation for the dragoons—and

Quartermaster Rufus Ingalls at City Point. (NA)

received a brevet for his Mexican War role in New Mexico. A short time later he transferred to the supply department. His Civil War-era assignments included: captain and assistant quartermaster (since January 12, 1848); lieutenant colonel and additional aide-de-camp (September 28, 1861); chief quartermaster, Army of the Potomac (late 1861-June 16, 1864); major and quartermaster (January 12, 1862); brigadier general, USV (May 23, 1863); and chief quartermaster, Armies of the Potomac and the James (June 16, 1864-May 9, 1865). Named to McClellan's staff, he was soon engaged in quartermaster duties and served through all the campaigns of the Army of the Potomac under its successive leaders—Burnside, Hooker, and Meade. All were pleased with his work and when Grant took command in Virginia he tapped Ingalls to perform the functions of his department for all the forces operating against Richmond. Near the war's conclusion he received brevets of major general in both services. Mustered out of the volunteers on September 1, 1866, he remained in the regular service but reverted back to the rank of colonel and assistant quartermaster general. As such he served in the Divisions of the Pacific and the Missouri and in New York City. With the rank of brigadier general he became the quartermaster general in 1882. He retired the next year.

INGRAHAM, Duncan N. (1802-1891)

Having entered the U.S. Navy at the age of ten, South Carolinian Duncan N. Ingraham was, by the outbreak of the Civil War, a veteran of almost half a century of naval service including the War of 1812, the Mexican War, command of the Philadelphia Navy Yard, a diplomatic incident with Austrian warships over a naturalized U.S. citizen, and duty as chief of the Bureau of Ordnance and Hydrography. When his state seceded, Ingraham was commanding the U.S.S. *Richmond* in the Mediterranean. He promptly returned home and resigned his commission. On March 26, 1861, he was appointed captain, CSN, and following some duty on a board studying the problems of building a navy from scratch was assigned to duty at Pensacola. Then on November 16, 1861, he was ordered to Charleston Harbor and given command of the naval defenses of South Carolina. One of his first accomplishments in his new command was the supervision of the construction of the *Palmetto State*, an armored ram. On the night of January 30, 1863, Ingraham sailed out of the harbor aboard the *Palmetto State*, accompanied by another ironclad, the *Chicora*. The next day they "lifted" the Union blockade of Charleston. In the attack, the blockading vessels, *Mercedita* and *Keystone State* were severely damaged and the former barely avoided sinking. Other blockaders were less severely damaged and the rest of the fleet was driven off. Later that day the Confederate authorities declared the blockade lifted and even had foreign consuls verify the fact. However, it was not recognized by other nations. The blockade resumed. In March 1863, Ingraham was relieved of sea duty, being thought to be too old, but retained command of the shore station. (Scharf, J. Thomas, *History of the Confederate States Navy*)

IRISH BRIDGET

See: *Divers, Bridget*

IVERSON, Alfred, Jr. (1829-1911)

Although he had originally urged the promotion of Alfred Iverson, Jr., General Lee found it necessary to quietly get rid of him. A second lieutenant of Georgia volunteers in the Mexican War, Iverson had received a commission as a first lieutenant directly into the 1st Cavalry in 1855. He resigned on March 21, 1861, to go with the South and his assignments included: captain, PACS (spring 1861); colonel, 20th North Carolina (August 20, 1861); brigadier general, CSA (November 1, 1862); commanding Garland's (old) Brigade, D.H. Hill's-Rodes' Division, 2nd Corps, Army of Northern Virginia (November 6, 1862-July 1, 1863); commanding 2nd Louisiana Brigade, Johnson's Division, same corps and army (July 21-October 6, 1863); commanding brigade, Martin's Division, Wheeler's Cavalry Corps, Army of Tennessee (February 29-fall 1864); commanding division, Wheeler's Cavalry Corps, Department of South Carolina, Georgia and Florida (fall 1864-February 1865); and commanding Cavalry Division, District of Georgia and South Carolina, same department (February-March 25, 1865). Wounded at Gaines' Mill during the Seven Days Battles, he returned to fight at South Mountain and Antietam. Promoted and given command of the brigade, he fought at Fredericksburg and Chancellorsville. In the latter his performance was less than shining. In the heavy fighting on the first day at Gettysburg he suffered a breakdown when he saw what looked like his whole brigade surrendering. He had to be relieved by his assistant adjutant general and later in the day General S.D. Ramseur took command of the brigade as well as his own. Three weeks later Iverson was placed in charge of a brigade of Louisiana troops but in October Lee got his way and sent the Georgian to his native state to work with the reserve forces. In early 1864, Iverson took command of a cavalry brigade under Wheeler and fought throughout the Atlanta Campaign including the capture of raider Stoneman. He directed a division during the Savannah Campaign and part of the Carolinas Campaign. In late March he was ordered to leave his division and report to Wade Hampton in North Carolina, but it apprears that he never made it as he was paroled at his home in Georgia in May. He became a Florida citrus farmer after the Confederacy's collapse. (Freeman, Douglas S., *Lee's Lieutenants*)

IVES, James Merritt (1824-1895)

Married to the sister-in-law of lithographer Nathaniel Currier, J. Merritt Ives joined Currier's successful house in 1852 as a clerk. Having long shown an interest in art, and an aptitude as well, he was given more and more responsibility until he was made a partner in 1857 and was in effect managing the company. He also drew a small number of the highly popular Currier & Ives series. During the war many of the lithographs covered military themes. Ives himself served as captain, 23rd New York National Guard, during June and July 1863, seeing duty in Pennsylvania during the Gettysburg Campaign. The native New Yorker continued in business after Currier's 1880 retirement, working with the latter's son. His connection with the popular series of lithographs covering virtually all aspects of American life came to an end with his death. His son took over, and the firm came to an end shortly after the turn of the century.

J

JACKMAN, Sidney D. (?-?)

Missourian Sidney D. Jackman was one of the final batch of general officers appointed extralegally by General E. Kirby Smith in his Trans-Mississippi Department. Early in the war Jackman had proved a nuisance to the Union occupation forces in Missouri at the head of small groups of irregulars. In 1863 he raised a regiment which was designated the 7th Missouri Infantry, but sometimes designated as the 14th or 16th, and became its colonel. He subsequently commanded a cavalry regiment in the District of Arkansas and the District of Indian Territory. During Price's invasion of Missouri he commanded a brigade in Shelby's Division, Army of Missouri. In recognition of his service at brigade level, Smith promoted him in orders to brigadier general on May 16, 1865. However this could not be made official since President Davis was a prisoner and the senate was no longer in session.

JACKSON, Alfred Eugene (1807-1889)

Age may have been a major factor in bringing to an end the active field career of Confederate General Alfred E. Jackson. A farmer, manufacturer and merchant from Tennessee, he entered the Confederate service in the quartermaster's branch. His assignments included: major and assistant quartermaster (1861); major and paymaster (1862); brigadier general, CSA (October 29, 1862); commanding brigade, Department of East Tennessee (March-fall 1863); reappointed brigadier general, CSA (April 22, 1863, to rank from February 9); commanding brigade, Department of Southwestern Virginia and East Tennessee (January 1864); commanding brigade, Ransom's Division, Department of East Tennessee (January-February 1864); commanding brigade, Department of East Tennessee (February-March 1864); and commanding brigade, Buckner's Division, Department of East Tennessee (spring 1864). As a quartermaster he served on the staff of Felix K. Zollicoffer until his death at Mill Springs. Transferring to the pay branch he served until he received his first appointment as a brigadier general, which was canceled. Reappointed the next spring, he led a brigade in East Tennessee and southwestern Virginia until 1864. At times his command was composed principally of William H. Thomas' Legion of North Carolinian mountaineers and Cherokee Indians. On November 23, 1864, he was reported as unfit for field duty and appears to have finished the war in staff assignments. After the war he was engaged in farming for a time.

JACKSON, Claiborne Fox (1806-1862)

After leading a rump session of the Missouri state legislature into exile, Governor Claiborne F. Jackson was effectively removed from office by federal authorities. A former cashier in the state bank, he had served several terms in the state legislature, including holding the speakership. After several candidacies he was finally elected governor by the proslavery faction of the state in 1860. The Kentucky-born politician entered upon his new duties on January 3, 1861, and was promptly embroiled in the secession crisis. Advocating separation from the Union, he was active in preparing the state for war. Mobilizing the Missouri State Guard, he also called for 50,000 volunteers to resist federal coercion. In May 1861 he authorized General Sterling Price to negotiate a settlement with Union General William S. Harney, but his purpose was by this time merely to gain time for further war preparations. Forced by military operations from the state capital, he was effectively replaced by Hamilton R. Gamble on July 31, 1861. That November he headed a portion of the legislature in a meeting in Neosho that resulted in the issuance of a secession ordinance. He was active in pressing for Confederate aid in support of the exiled Rebel government of his state. He died on December 6, 1862. (Snead, Thomas L., *The Fight for Missouri*)

JACKSON, Conrad Feger (1813-1862)

Long associated with the Pennsylvania militia, Conrad F. Jackson is thought to have served in the Mexican War and to have been engaged in railroading in his native state before becoming an officer in the Pennsylvania Reserves Division during the Civil War. His assignments included: colonel, 9th Pennsylvania Reserves (July 27, 1861); commanding 3rd Brigade, 3rd Division, 5th Corps, Army of the Potomac (June 30-August 26, 1862); brigadier general, USV (July 17, 1862); commanding 3rd Brigade, 3rd Division, 3rd Corps, Army of Virginia (August 26-30, 1862); and commanding 3rd Brigade, 3rd Division, 1st Corps, Army of the Potomac (October 2-December 13, 1862). When his unit was finally accepted by the national authorities he was assigned to the Washington area and took part in the fight at Dranesville. Transferred to the Peninsula, he fought in the Seven Days and succeeded to command of the brigade when Truman Seymour moved up to direct the division after George A. McCall was captured at Glendale. Promoted to brigadier general the next month, he was forced to leave the field of 2nd Bull Run due to illness. He apparently missed the fighting at South Mountain and Antietam but returned to command the next month. At Fredericksburg his horse was shot from under him and shortly afterwards he was killed while directing his men from a position along the Richmond, Fredericksburg and Potomac Railroad.

JACKSON, Henry Rootes (1820-1898)

It is ironic that a leading Savannah lawyer who had prosecuted the owners and crew of the slaver *Wanderer* in 1859, Henry R. Jackson, became a Confederate brigadier general, while one of the principal defendants in the case, John E. Farnum, became a brevet brigadier general in the Union army. A Democrat, the native Georgian attended both the divided party's conventions in 1860, backed Breckinridge, and attended his native state's secession convention. His Confederate military assignments included: brigadier general, CSA (June 4, 1861); commanding Army of the Northwest (July 14-20, 1861); commanding brigade, Army of the Northwest (July 20-November 22, 1861); commanding 1st Division, Army of the Northwest (November 22-December 2, 1861); major general, Georgia State Troops (December 1861); reappointed brigadier general, CSA (September 23, 1863); and commanding Stevens' (old) Brigade, Bate's-Brown's-Bate's Division, Hardee's-Cheatham's Corps, Army of Tennessee (July 29-September and October-December 16, 1864). During the first year of the war he served in western Virginia, taking part in Robert E. Lee's dismal Cheat Mountain operations. Resigning on December 2, 1861, he took a position with the state forces until they were absorbed into the Confederate army. Recommissioned in that service, he held a number of positions before taking charge of the deceased Clement H. Stevens' brigade during the battles around Atlanta. He led the brigade through the rest of that campaign and at Franklin and Nashville. At the latter he was captured and not released until July 1865. Following his confinement in Boston Harbor's Fort Warren he resumed his distinguished practice and served as a diplomat in Mexico.

JACKSON, James Streshly (1823-1862)

In the 1860 elections in which Lincoln was chosen president, James S. Jackson was elected as a Unionist congressman from Kentucky. After serving briefly as an enlisted man and third lieutenant in a volunteer regiment in the Mexican War, he had resigned his commission when faced with a court-martial for participating in a duel with a fellow officer. He left the Congress and on December 13, 1861, was made colonel of the 3rd Kentucky Cavalry. His later assignments included: brigadier general, USV (July 16, 1862); commanding 10th Division, Army of the Ohio (mid-September 1862-September 29, 1862); and commanding 10th Division, 1st Corps, Army of the Ohio (September 20-October 8, 1862). Jackson's regiment was engaged in active operations in Kentucky while still organizing in the fall of 1861. Moving into Tennessee, Jackson led his regiment at Shiloh but it was not actively engaged. During the advance on and siege of Corinth, Jackson was in command of all the cavalry in the Army of the Ohio. Promoted to brigadier, he was sent, in late August 1862, to Lexington, Kentucky, to help organize the forces gathered there to oppose Bragg's invasion. Given command of a division of these troops the next month, he led it at the battle of Perryville on October 8. While standing by the divisional artillery, he was killed. The division suffered the heaviest losses of any division in the battle, including its commander and its two brigade commanders.

JACKSON, James T. (?-1861)

An Alexandria, Virginia, hotel owner, James T. Jackson became the South's first martyr to the cause of secession. Despite the dangerous proximity of the town to the Union buildup of volunteers in the capital, Jackson insisted upon flying a banner proclaiming his support for the new Confederacy. Then, on May 24, 1861, it happened. Union forces occupied the town. One unit of the invading force was the 11th New York or "Ellsworth's Fire Zouaves." Late that day, Colonel Ellsworth spied the secession flag floating over Jackson's establishment, the Marshall House. Awakened by the commotion of the federals in his hotel, Jackson denied any knowledge of the flag, claiming to be a boarder. He then went for his shotgun and confronted the Union colonel as he descended with his trophy. Firing at close range, he killed Ellsworth. Union private Francis E. Brownell then shot the rebel in the head and ran him through with his bayonet. From this wasteful incident each side could claim a martyr.

JACKSON, James W. (ca. 1832-?)

The case of Colonel James W. Jackson shows that not all of the officers of the Army of Northern Virginia were heroes. He entered Confederate service in the second year of the war and his assignments included: captain, Company I, 47th Alabama (May 20, 1862); lieutenant colonel, 47th Alabama (May 22, 1862): colonel, 47th Alabama (August 11, 1862); and commanding Taliaferro's Brigade, Jackson's (old) Division, Jackson's Corps, Army of Northern Virginia (September 17, 1862). After seeing action at 2nd Bull Run he took part in the Maryland Campaign, briefly commanding the brigade at Antietam until he was wounded. He rejoined the regiment in time for Gettysburg, but, as Major James M. Campbell put it in his battle report, was "left behind." After praising the 21

Confederate martyr James Jackson. (*Leslie's*)

officers taking part in the attack on Little Round Top, the major made it clear that "The colonel and adjutant are not included in this number." A week later, on July 10, 1863, Jackson resigned.

JACKSON, John King (1828-1866)

Confederate Brigadier General John K. Jackson barely survived the Civil War. A practicing attorney in Augusta, Georgia, he was active in military matters well before the sectional conflict burst into war. His assignments in the Confederate service included: captain, Oglethorpe Infantry (prewar); lieutenant colonel, Augusta City Battalion (1861); colonel, 5th Georgia (May 1861); brigadier general, CSA (January 14, 1862); commanding 3rd Brigade, 2nd (Withers') Division, 2nd Corps, Army of the Mississippi (March 29-July 2, 1862); commanding 3rd Brigade, Reserve (Withers') Division, Army of the Mississippi (July 2-August 15, 1862); commanding 3rd Brigade, Withers' Division, Right Wing, Army of the Mississippi (August 15-November 20, 1862); commanding brigade, Withers' Division, Polk's Corps, Army of Tennessee (November 20-December 1862); commanding independent brigade, Hardee's-Hill's Corps, Army of Tennessee (December 1862-August 23, 1863); commanding brigade, Cheatham's Division, Polk's-Hardee's Corps, Army of Tennessee (August 23, 1863-February 20, 1864); commanding brigade, Walker's Division, Hardee's Corps, Army of Tennessee (February 20-July 3, 1864); and commanding District of Florida, Department of South Carolina, Georgia and Florida (July-September 29, 1864). Following initial service at Pensacola he was promoted to brigadier general and commanded a brigade at Shiloh and in the delaying action back towards Corinth. He led his brigade into Kentucky with Bragg but did not fight at Perryville. His command was made independent from any division late in the year but fought at Murfreesboro attached to Breckinridge's division. He continued in an independent status in the Tullahoma Campaign and a month before Chickamauga was assigned to Benjamin F. Cheatham's division. Missing Chattanooga, he fought through the Atlanta Campaign until ordered to the Georgia coast in July 1864. He served through parts of the Savannah Campaign and then held administrative and supply positions in the Carolinas Campaign. Before dying of pneumonia in February 1866 he briefly resumed his legal career.

JACKSON, Mary Jane (1836-?)

Known as "Bricktop," one of New Orleans' most notorious and vicious street criminals, Mary Jane Jackson was freed from prison as a result of the Civil War. A prostitute by the age of 13, she had been thrown out of several whorehouses because of her violent streak which kept the other girls in a state of fear. By 1861 she had killed at least three men and then got into a fight with her lover, John Miller, who also ended up dead. Sent to prison for 10 years, she was confined in the Parish Prison when the Union forces captured the city. A Union general, George F. Shepley, was appointed military governor and one of his early acts was the issuance of a blanket pardon virtually emptying the jails, enraging the citizenry, especially in Jackson's case. Following her release, she apparently left the city.

JACKSON, Nathaniel James (1818-1892)

An unfortunate accident cost the Union army the field services of General Nathaniel J. Jackson for over a year in the middle of the war. Running a mill in Maine upon the outbreak of hostilities, the native of Massachusetts had promptly raised a regiment of three-months volunteers. His assignments included: colonel, 1st Maine (May 3, 1861); colonel, 5th Maine (September 3, 1861); brigadier general, USV (September 24, 1862); commanding 2nd Brigade, 1st Division, 12th Corps, Army of the Potomac (March 21-29, 1863); commanding 2nd Brigade, 2nd Division, 12th Corps, Army of the Potomac (October 28-December 22, 1862 and January 3-March 21, 1863); and commanding 1st Division, 20th Corps, Army of the Cumberland (November 11, 1864-April 2, 1865). His first regiment spent its entire tour in the Washington defenses and was mustered out on August 5, 1861. The next month Jackson was back in the service at the head of a new three-years regiment, which he led during the Seven Days, where he was wounded at Gaines' Mill. For this action he was brevetted major general in 1865. Recovering, he fought at South Mountain and Antietam before being named a brigadier general a week later. Assigned to the 12th Corps, he missed Fredericksburg and, shortly before the battle of Chancellorsville, he suffered an accident which incapacitated him for field duty for a lengthy period. Recovering sufficiently, he commanded draft rendezvous at various points in New York City until September 20, 1864, when he was ordered to join Sherman. He then led a division in the Savannah and Carolinas campaigns. In the final days of the war he was relieved as a supernumerary officer and was mustered out on August 24, 1865, and retired to private life.

JACKSON, Richard Henry (1830-1892)

Native of County Westmeath, Ireland, Richard H. Jackson won a regular army commission, after almost a decade as an enlisted man, and emerged from the Civil War as a brevet major general of volunteers and a brevet brigadier general of regulars. Immigrating to the United States, he soon enlisted as a private in Company L, 4th Artillery, in 1851. Fighting against the Seminoles in Florida and on the frontier, he had risen to the rank of first sergeant by the time that he was accepted by an examining board for a commission. His Civil War-era assignments included: brevet second lieutenant, 4th Artillery (since September 13, 1859); second lieutenant, 1st Artillery (July 13, 1860); first lieutenant, 1st Artillery (May 14, 1861); captain, 1st Artillery (February 20, 1862); lieutenant colonel and assistant inspector general (April 15, 1863); commanding 2nd Division, 25th Corps, Army of the James (April 10-November 4, 1865); and brigadier general, USV (May 19, 1865). Early in the war he served at Fort Pickens in Pensacola Harbor. Serving most of the war in the Department of the South with the rank of lieutenant colonel in the inspector's branch, he commanded the artillery in the attacks on Battery Wagner and during the siege operations against Charleston in the summer of 1863. Transferred with the 10th Corps to Virginia, he was brevetted for his behavior at Drewry's Bluff and later for New Market Heights while serving as chief of artillery of the corps. For the overall campaigning of 1864 he was brevetted brigadier general of volunteers and was advanced to the full grade following the close of hostilities. He continued on the Richmond-Petersburg front and the day after Lee's surrender at Appomattox he was given charge of a division of black troops. Receiving a final brevet in both the regulars and volunteers in 1865, he was mustered out of the latter on February 1, 1866. Continuing in the regular army, he died as lieutenant colonel, 4th Artillery, while still on active duty in Georgia.

JACKSON, Thomas Jonathan (1824-1863)

Next to Robert E. Lee himself, Thomas J. Jackson is the most revered of all Confederate commanders. A graduate of West Point (1846), he had served in the artillery in the Mexican War, earning two brevets, before resigning to accept a professorship at the Virginia Military Institute. Thought strange by the cadets, he earned "Tom Fool Jackson" and "Old Blue Light" as nicknames. Upon the outbreak of the Civil War he was commissioned a colonel in the Virginia forces and dispatched to Harpers Ferry where he was active in organizing the raw recruits until relieved by Joe Johnston. His later assignments included: commanding 1st Brigade, Army of the Shenandoah (May-July 20, 1861); brigadier general, CSA (June 17, 1861); commanding 1st Brigade, 2nd Corps, Army of the Potomac (July 20-October 1861); major general, CSA (October 7, 1861); commanding Valley District, Department of Northern Virginia (November 4, 1861-June 26, 1862); commanding 2nd Corps, Army of Northern Virginia (June 26, 1862-May 2, 1863); and lieutenant general, CSA (October 10, 1862). Leaving Harpers Ferry, his brigade moved with Johnston to join Beauregard at Manassas. In the fight at 1st Bull Run they were so distinguished that both the brigade and its commander were dubbed "Stonewall" by General Barnard Bee. (However, Bee may have been complaining that Jackson was not coming to his support). The 1st Brigade was the only Confederate brigade to have its nickname become its official designation. That fall Jackson was given command of the Valley with a promotion to major general. That winter he launched a dismal campaign into the western part of the state that resulted in a long feud with

"Stonewall" Jackson. (NA)

General William Loring and caused Jackson to submit his resignation, which he was talked out of. In March he launched an attack on what he thought was a Union rear guard at Kernstown. Faulty intelligence from his cavalry chief, Turner Ashby, led to a defeat. A religious man, Jackson always regretted having fought on a Sunday. But the defeat had the desired result, halting reinforcements being sent to McClellan's army from the Valley. In May Jackson defeated Frémont's advance at McDowell and later that month launched a brilliant campaign that kept several Union commanders in the area off balance. He won victories at Front Royal, 1st Winchester, Cross Keys, and Port Republic. He then joined Lee in the defense of Richmond but displayed a lack of vigor during the Seven Days. Detached from Lee, he swung off to the north to face John Pope's army and after a slipshod battle at Cedar Mountain, slipped behind Pope and captured his Manassas Junction supply base. He then hid along an incomplete branch railroad and awaited Lee and Longstreet. Attacked before they arrived, he held on until Longstreet could launch a devastating attack which brought a second Bull Run victory. In the invasion of Maryland, Jackson was detached to capture Harpers Ferry and was afterwards distinguished at Antietam with Lee. He was promoted after this and given command of the now-official 2nd Corps. It had been known as a wing or command before this. He was disappointed with the victory at Fredericksburg because it could not be followed up. In his greatest day he led his corps around the Union right flank at Chancellorsville and routed the 11th Corps. Reconnoitering that night, he was returning to his own lines when he was mortally wounded by some of his own men. Following the amputation of his arm, he died eight days later. A superb commander, he had several faults. Personnel problems haunted him, as in the feuds with Loring and with Garnett after Kernstown. His choices for promotion were often not first rate. He did not give his subordinates enough latitude, which denied them the training for higher positions under Lee's loose command style. This was especially devastating in the case of his immediate successor, Richard Ewell. Although he was sometimes balky when in a subordinate position, Jackson was supreme on his own hook. (Henderson, G.F.R., *Stonewall Jackson and the American Civil War*; Vandiver, Frank E., *Mighty Stonewall*; and Chambers, Lenoir, *Stonewall Jackson*)

JACKSON, William A. (?-?)

One of the most highly placed of all Union spies was a black man serving as the personal coachman of Confederate President Jefferson Davis. In this capacity he was able to learn many of the military and diplomatic plans of the Confederacy and relay them through the lines to the Union authorities. He was never detected and is one of the true unsung heroes of the Civil War.

JACKSON, William Hicks (1835-1903)

Known to his troopers as "Red," Tennesseean William H. Jackson became one of the hard-hitting Confederate cavalry division commanders in the West. The West Pointer (1856) had been posted to the Regiment of Mounted Riflemen with which he served until his resignation as a second lieutenant on May 16, 1861. His Confederate assignments included: captain, Artillery (1861); captain, Jackson's Tennessee Heavy Artillery Company (July 1861); captain, Company D, 1st Tennessee Light Artillery (August 12, 1861); colonel, 7th (AKA 1st) Tennessee Cavalry (April 1, 1862); brigadier general, CSA (December 29, 1862); commanding 1st Division, Cavalry Corps, Department of Mississippi and East Louisiana (late 1862-early 1863); commanding Cavalry Division, Department of the West (June 9-July 1863); commanding Cavalry Division, Department of Mississippi and East Louisiana (July-August 1863); commanding division, Lee's Cavalry Corps, Department of Mississippi and East Louisiana (August 1863-January 28, 1864); commanding division, Lee's Cavalry Corps, Department of Alabama, Mississippi and East Louisiana (January 28-May 4, 1864); commanding Cavalry Division, Polk's (Army of Mississippi)-Stewart's Corps, Army of Tennessee (May 4-July 26, 1864); commanding cavalry division, Army of Tennessee (July 26, 1864-ca. February 1865); and commanding division, Forrest's Cavalry Corps, Department of Alabama, Mississippi and East Louisiana (ca. February-May 4, 1865). When his battery could not make it across the Mississippi in time to take part in the fight at Belmont Jackson joined Gideon J. Pillow's staff as a volunteer and was wounded. Upon his recovery he became a colonel of a Tennessee mounted regiment. With this unit he took part in Earl Van Dorn's raid on Holly Springs. He was rewarded with promotion to brigadier general and later led a division under Joseph E. Johnston on the fringes of the Vicksburg Campaign. He fought at Jackson and during the

Meridian Campaign. Accompanying Leonidas Polk to northern Georgia, he took part in the Atlanta Campaign and then went with Hood on the campaign into middle Tennessee. Joining Forrest's forces, he tried to defend against Wilson's raid through the deep South and was included in Richard Taylor's surrender. Thereafter he engaged in horse breeding and agricultural pursuits.

JACKSON, William Lowther (1825-1890)

In order to prevent confusion with his more famous second cousin, William L. Jackson became known as "Mudwall" Jackson. A lawyer, judge, and former lieutenant governor in his native Virginia, he entered the Confederate army as a private but was soon commissioned as an officer. His assignments included: lieutenant colonel, 31st Virginia (June 1861); colonel, 19th Virginia Cavalry (April 11, 1863); commanding cavalry brigade, Department of Western Virginia and East Tennessee (December 1863-January 1864); commanding cavalry brigade, Department of Western Virginia (January-June 1864); commanding brigade, Ransom's Cavalry Division, Valley District, Department of Northern Virginia (summer 1864); commanding brigade, Lomax's Cavalry Division, Valley District, Department of Northern Virginia (September-October and November-December 1864) and brigadier general, CSA (December 19, 1864). Following service in western Virginia, he joined his cousin's staff as a volunteer aide, seeing action in the Shenandoah Valley, during the Seven Days, and at 2nd Bull Run and Antietam. Raising a mounted regiment he became its colonel and served in Virginia and Tennessee. He participated in the defense of Lynchburg and then went on Jubal A. Early's drive on Washington, fighting at Monocacy. Back in the Valley he fought at 3rd Winchester, Fisher's Hill, and Cedar Creek. Disbanding his command on April 15, 1865, rather than surrender, he ended his military career as a brigadier general and fled to Mexico. Eventually settling in Kentucky, he resumed his practice and was again named to the judicial bench.

JAMES, Charles Tillinghast (1805-1862)

Noted for his work with steam-powered cotton mills, Charles T. James became interested in the production of firearms with the coming of the Civil War. This interest led to his death. A native of Rhode Island, he had been a carpenter and a mechanic before becoming involved in the starting of 23 steam mills, mostly in New England. In the 1850s he served one term in the U.S. Senate but suffered financially in that time. After declining to run for reelection, he turned his attention to the manufacture of weapons (having been a major general in the state militia). He developed a rifled cannon, an improved bullet, and an explosive projectile. In the midst of an experiment, on October 16, 1862, a shell exploded while he was working on it. He died the next day of his wounds.

JAMES, Frank (1843-1915)

The elder brother of the more famous Western outlaw Jesse James, Frank James received his training in brigandage under the noted Confederate guerrilla William Quantrill. Frank took part in the bloody massacre at Lawrence, Kansas; after the breakup of the gang due to dissension among the leaders he remained loyal to Quantrill and went with him to Kentucky, from James' native Missouri, where Quantrill was killed at the very end of the war. By this time brother Jesse had joined the irregulars, and in 1866 the two Jameses linked up with the four criminal Younger Brothers and continued their violent ways. Robbing banks, fairs, and the hated railroads, they were seen by many as the stuff of legend since they were, in many Southern eyes, still fighting Northern (business) oppression. The Jameses were forced into three years of semi-retirement following the disastrous 1876 Northfield, Minnesota, bank raid. After his brother's murder in 1882—the gang had been reconstituted three years earlier—Frank James turned in his guns at the governor's office and stood trial in both Missouri and Alabama. However, the legend made it impossible to constitute a jury that would convict him. Following his release he was a farmer and held a number of odd jobs, but to many he was always a hero, his ruthlessness ignored.

JAMES, Jesse (1847-1882)

With his older brother, Frank, already a longtime member of the bloody gang of Confederate guerrillas under William C. Quantrill, Jesse James joined the irregulars in 1864, when he was only 17. By this time Quantrill's band had dissolved, and Jesse joined that remnant now under Quantrill's former

Noted outlaw Jesse James, with his brother Frank and two of the Youngers. (LC)

lieutenant, "Bloody Bill" Anderson. That year they attacked the railroad station at Centralia, Missouri, and killed several unarmed Union soldiers on furlough. They also killed some passengers who hid their valuables. When Union troops followed, they were ambushed and slaughtered, with Jesse noted for his brutality. With the death of Anderson, Jesse joined brother Frank in Quantrill's reconstituted gang and resumed pillaging, this time in Kentucky. In 1866, with the war over and Quantrill dead, the Jameses joined the Youngers to continue their depredations. Their robberies of banks and the despised railroads made them heroes to many, who saw them as fighting Northern business aggression. An unfounded legend developed that Jesse was America's Robin Hood. The fact is that he never helped the poor and was nothing more than a brutal bandit. The James-Younger gang operated until the disaster of the 1876 Northfield, Minnesota, bank robbery. With the band decimated the Jameses went into three years of semi-retirement. In 1879 Jesse formed a new gang but three years later he was betrayed and assassinated by one of his new recruits, Bob Ford, on April 3, 1882.

JAMESON, Charles Davis (1827-1862)

Even general officers were not immune to the numerous diseases which were prevalent in Civil War camps: Charles D. Jameson succumbed to disease rather than enemy fire. In the prewar years he was a leader in the lumber, shipping, and manufacturing businesses in his native Maine. Active in the militia, he volunteered for the Union army early in the war and his assignments included: colonel, Maine Militia (prewar); colonel, 2nd Maine (May 28, 1861); brigadier general, USV (September 3, 1861); commanding 3rd Brigade, Heintzelman's Division, Army of the Potomac (October 3, 1861-March 13, 1862); and commanding 1st Brigade, 3rd Division, 3rd Corps, Army of the Potomac (March 13-June 12, 1862). At 1st Bull Run he helped cover the retreat and was rewarded with the star of a brigadier. He led his brigade to the Peninsula where it was he who discovered that the enemy had evacuated their works at Yorktown. He then fought at Williamsburg and was particularly distinguished at Seven Pines. Shortly thereafter he was forced by ill health to relinquish command. On November 6, 1862, he died aboard a steamboat en route home. The cause of his death is variously stated as tuberculosis or typhoid fever.

JEMISON, Robert, Jr. (1802-1871)

A long-standing political opponent of William L. Yancey, Robert Jemison, Jr., nonetheless succeeded him in the Confederate Congress and became part of the faction which sought peace. Born in Georgia, he was an Alabama planter and Whig politician before the war. From 1837 to 1863 he served in both houses of the state legislature, with only a few interruptions. Much of the time he was chairman of the Committee on Ways and Means and became an expert in financial and banking matters. He attended the secession convention as the leader of the Unionists and roundly condemned Yancey's call for immediate separation from the Washington government. He replaced the deceased Yancey in the Confederate Senate on December 28, 1863, and served on the Committee on Finance in both the First and Second Congresses. His other assignments included the committees on Claims (First Congress); Naval Affairs (First Congress); and Post Offices & Post Roads (Second Congress). His loyalty came into question with his departing speech in the state senate as he expressed his desire for a just peace settlement. In Richmond he failed to vote for the sacrifices that were necessary for a military victory and favored local defense rather than moves to increase the main field armies. After June 1864 he ceased to attend any sessions and looked after his personal business interests. Retired from politics after the war, he was involved in railroading.

JENKINS, Albert Gallatin (1830-1864)

Accomplished as raiders in their own region, the western Virginia cavalry brigade of Albert G. Jenkins was found to be less than effective when serving as regular cavalry under Lee. A lawyer, Jenkins had been representing his district in the western part of Virginia in the U.S. Congress when the secession crisis came. Resigning his seat he organized a cavalry company with which he gained a reputation as an independent raider. Although made a lieutenant colonel in the 8th Virginia Cavalry in about January 1862, he had also been elected to the First Confederate Congress and left to take his seat in February. He served only briefly in the legislative body but did serve on the Committees on Printing and Territories and Public Lands. Resigning on August 5, he accepted another field appointment.

Albert G. Jenkins, loser at Cloyd's Mountain, also lost his life. (NA)

His assignments included: brigadier general, CSA (August 5, 1862); commanding cavalry brigade, Department of Western Virginia (August 1862-spring 1863); commanding brigade, Cavalry Division, Army of Northern Virginia (spring-July 2, 1863); and commanding cavalry brigade, Department of Western Virginia (fall 1863-May 9, 1864). His early activities as a general were in raids in western Virginia and one into Ohio. He was attached to Lee's army during the Gettysburg Campaign and was wounded during the main battle, when many of his men deserted rather than serve away from home. He apparently resumed command in the fall when the brigade was back in its proper department. This is not certain, since the brigade was operating in widely scattered detachments over much of the following months. However, on May 9, 1864, he was the senior officer on the field at Cloyd's Mountain where he was severely wounded in the arm and captured. Following amputation of his arm he died on May 21. (Freeman, Douglas S., *Lee's Lieutenants*)

JENKINS, Micah (1835-1864)

A graduate of the South Carolina Military Academy, Micah Jenkins spent the prewar years affiliated with the King's Mountain Military School. Offering his services to the South, they included: colonel, 5th South Carolina (April 13, 1861); colonel, Palmetto (S.C.) Sharpshooters (April 1862); temporarily commanding R.H. Anderson's Brigade, Longstreet's Division, Department of Northern Virginia (May 5; May 31-June 1; and June 29-July 1, 1862); commanding Anderson's (old) Brigade, Longstreet's Division, 1st Corps, Army of Northern Virginia (July 14-August 1862); brigadier general, CSA (July 22, 1862); commanding brigade, Kemper's Division, same corps and army (August 1862); commanding brigade, Pickett's Division, same corps and army (ca. November 1862-February 25, 1863); commanding brigade, Pickett's Division, in the Department of Virginia and North Carolina (February 25-April 1, 1863) and in the Department of Southern Virginia (April 1-May 1863); commanding brigade, in the Department of North Carolina (May-July 1863) and in Ransom's Division, Department of Richmond (July-September 1863); commanding brigade, Hood's Division, Longstreet's Corps, Army of Tennessee (September 1863); commanding the division (September-November 1863); commanding division, Department of East Tennessee (November 1863-February 1864); commanding brigade, Hood's (old) Division, same department (February-April 12, 1864); and commanding brigade, Field's Division, 1st Corps, Army of Northern Virginia (April 12-May 6, 1864). After leading his regiment at 1st Bull Run he commanded a brigade on a temporary basis at Williamsburg, Seven Pines, and in the latter stages of the Seven Days. Given permanent command of the brigade, he led it and was wounded at 2nd Bull Run. He returned in time for Fredericksburg but was only lightly engaged. After serving with Longstreet in southeastern Virginia, his brigade was detached from its division and remained in the area until it was attached to Hood's Division during the movement to Georgia. Arriving too late for Chickamauga, he directed the division at Wauhatchie and Knoxville, where the division's effectiveness was lessened by the dispute between Jenkins and General Law. Returning to Virginia, he led the brigade in the second day's fighting at the Wilderness until he was mortally wounded, at the same time that Longstreet was hit, by Confederate troops. He died after babbling in his delirium for the troops to move forward. His wound being in the brain he never knew he was hit. (Freeman, Douglas S., Lee's Lieutenants)

JENNISON, Charles R. (?-?)

Taking a lesson from his experiences in "Bleeding Kansas," Charles R. Jennison carried that vicious brand of civil war into Missouri at the head of a regiment which became known as "Jennisons's Jayhawkers." He had been a relatively late free-state arrival in the territory but soon became a leader of the movement under James H. Lane and others. His Civil War assignments included: colonel, 7th Kansas Cavalry (ca. October 28, 1861); and colonel, 15th Kansas Cavalry (ca. fall 1863). Early in the war he was involved in raids into Missouri, from which raids had been launched in the previous decade. His command became known for horse stealing and disregard for private property. In many parts of the North he was extremely popular because of his exploits and his belief in the ruthless prosecution of the war. This was especially the case following the sacking of Lawrence, Kansas, by the guerrilla band of William C. Quantrill. At that time a Chicago mob called for Jennison to be let loose in Missouri in order to safeguard the loyal citizens of Kansas. Despite his harsh methods, Jennison was a valuable asset in fundraising and recruiting. For a time he was assigned to the raising of black troops. His principal major battle was at Westport while facing Price's 1864 invasion of Missouri. (Starr, S., *Jennison's Jayhawkers*)

JETT, Willie (?-?)

When Confederate Captain Willie Jett was on his way home from the war, he and two other ex-Confederate officers met John Wilkes Booth and David Herold at the Port Conway ferry across the Rappahannock River. Told of their identities, he agreed to help them and left Booth at the farm of Richard H. Garrett without informing Garrett that Booth was Lincoln's assassin. Jett then rode on to visit his girl in Bowling Green. Meanwhile, the Union cavalry detachment under Lieutenant Edward P. Doherty found out at the ferry that Booth had crossed with Jett and that Jett would probably head to his girl's house. The cavalry caught Jett in Bowling Green and demanded to know where Booth was. Jett was then taken back to Garrett's and witnessed the scene there as a prisoner. Detective L.B. Baker took charge of him, and Booth's corpse, and rode ahead of the main body. Apparently Jett made good his escape. Unpopular in his home area over his role in the affair, he eventually died in a Maryland mental facility.

JOHNSON, Adam Rankin (1834-1922)

For his ingenious capture of Newburgh, Indiana, on July 18, 1862, Kentuckian Adam R. Johnson won the nickname

"Stovepipe." Having settled in Texas in the prewar years, he worked as a surveyor and mail contractor and also engaged in various Indian fights. He started his Civil War career as a scout under Nathan Bedford Forrest, escaping with him from Fort Donelson. He then fought as an irregular in his native state. Capturing the Union town of Newburgh in the summer of 1862 with only 12 men and parts of stovepipes on the running gear of a wagon to resemble a cannon, he was promoted to the colonelcy of a partisan rangers unit. His later assignments included: colonel, 10th Kentucky Partisan Rangers (August 1862); brigadier general, CSA (September 6, 1864, to rank from June 1); and commanding Department of Western Kentucky (September 6-26, 1864). On August 21, 1864, in a fight at Grubbs Crossroads in Kentucky, he was severely wounded. Both of this eyes were totally blinded. He spent the rest of his life in Texas, remaining active in civic affairs despite his disability. He was also at work in historical writing. (Johnson, Adam Rankin, *The Partisan Rangers*)

JOHNSON, Andrew (1808-1875)

The only U.S. senator from a seceded state to retain his seat, Andrew Johnson was rewarded with the posts of brigadier general of volunteers and military governor of Tennessee before being tapped as Lincoln's 1864 running mate on the Union—or Republican and War Democratic—ticket and succeeding to the presidency (with the threat of impeachment). Born in North Carolina, he had moved to Tennessee as a tailor and allegedly was taught to read and write by his wife. A Jacksonian Democrat, he started his political career as an alderman and mayor in Greeneville in the late 1820s and 1830s. In the latter half of the 1830s he served in the state house and in the next decade in the state senate. He sat in Congress for five terms, from 1843 to 1853, then ran for governor—the Whigs having redistricted him into an unfriendly district. Elected and reelected governor, he served from 1853-1857 and greatly advanced public education in the state through tax legislation. He was elected to the U.S. Senate in 1857 and remained in his seat throughout the secession crisis. No friend of the abolitionists, he was nonetheless an opponent of the slaveowner's power. Recognized as a loyalist from East Tennessee, he was noticed by Lincoln and seen as a useful tool in the region. Accordingly, his Civil War-era posts included: brigadier general, USV (March 4, 1862); military governor of Tennessee (March 4, 1862-March 3, 1865); vice president (March 4-April 15, 1865); and president (April 15, 1865-March 4, 1869). As military governor he tried to institute civil government—in effect an early attempt at establishing Reconstruction policy. As a Southern Unionist, Johnson was felt to add regional balance to the Union ticket and, as a Democrat, to also add party balance. Elected in the November 1864 election, he appeared at the inauguration in an intoxicated condition. Some claim that this was the result of his having suffered from typhoid during the winter. Nonetheless his rambling inauguration oration was not an auspicious beginning to his term. With the assassination of Lincoln, Johnson was sworn in as president on April 15, 1865. At first he simply tried to follow what he thought had been Lincoln's plans for Reconstruction. In his early months he was active in granting pardons and reestablishing state governments in the South. This went along fine until the reconvening of Congress in December. The Radical Republicans couldn't stomach a Democrat—even a War Democrat—in the White House, and the war over Reconstruction was on. The executive and legislative branches fought for control and Johnson continued to lose ground, defiantly refusing to enforce the laws passed by Congress. Finally he deliberately suspended Secretary of War Edwin M. Stanton from office in violation of the Tenure of Office Act of 1867. Early in 1868 he was impeached by the House of Representatives, and in a lengthy trial before the Senate the only president ever so tried was acquitted by a vote of 35 for conviction and 19 against. The Radicals were one vote short of the required two-thirds. He was powerless for the remaining year of his presidency. A subsequent Senate bid in 1871 and a congressional bid in 1873 failed. However, on his third try, in 1875, he returned to the Senate but died that July. (Stryker, Lloyd Paul *Andrew Johnson: A Study in Courage*)

JOHNSON, Bradley Tyler (1829-1903)

Despite his state remaining in the Union, Maryland lawyer Bradley T. Johnson rose to the rank of Confederate brigadier general and took part in the burning of Chambersburg, Pennsylvania, late in the war. He had backed John C. Breckinridge at both Democratic conventions in 1860 and in the general election. His military assignments included: major, 1st Maryland Battalion (1861); colonel, 1st Maryland (early 1862); commanding J.R. Jones' Brigade, Jackson's Division, Jackson's Corps, Army of Northern Virginia (late August-September 17, 1862); brigadier general, CSA (June 28, 1864); and commanding brigade, Ransom's-Lomax's Cavalry Division, Valley District, Department of Northern Virginia (summer-November 1864). He fought at 1st Bull Run and commanded his regiment in the Shenandoah Valley and during the Seven Days. He led a brigade, as colonel, at 2nd Bull Run and until wounded at Antietam. Promoted to brigadier general in the early summer of 1864, he led a mounted brigade at Monocacy and to the very gates of Washington. He then took part in the ransoming attempt at Chambersburg, in retaliation for the destruction in the Shenandoah Valley, and subsequent burning. Returning to Virginia, he fought against Sheridan at 3rd Winchester, Fisher's Hill, and Cedar Creek. The heavy losses in the Valley cavalry necessitated a consolidation and Johnson became supernumerary in November 1864. Ordered to North Carolina, he commanded the prison at Salisbury for the balance of the conflict. In his later years he resumed his legal practice and sat in the Virginia legislature. He also wrote biographies of George Washington and Joseph E. Johnston. (Freeman, Douglas S., *Lee's Lieutenants*)

JOHNSON, Bushrod Rust (1817-1880)

After spending a lifetime in the military, Ohio-born Bushrod R. Johnson found himself without a command when Lee's army surrendered. A West Pointer (1840) and veteran of the Seminole and Mexican wars, he resigned in 1847 to teach at military achools in Kentucky and Tennessee. Active in the militia, he sided with the South in the secession crisis. His assignments included: colonel and chief engineer, Provisional Army of Tennessee (June 28, 1861); brigadier general, CSA (January 24, 1862); commanding, Fort Donelson, Department No. 2 (February 7-9, 1862); commanding division, Fort Donelson, Central Army of Kentucky, Department No. 2 (February 9-16, 1862); commanding brigade, 2nd Division, 1st Corps, Army of the Mississippi (March-April 6, 1862); commanding 3rd Brigade, Buckner's Division, Left Wing, Army of the Mississippi (ca. September 1862-November 20, 1862); commanding 3rd Brigade, Buckner's-Cleburne's Division, Hardee's Corps, Army of Tennessee (November 20, 1862-May 20, 1863); commanding brigade, Stewart's Division, Hardee's-Hill's-Breckinridge's Corps, Army of Tennessee (May 20-November 1863); commanding provisional division (temporarily in September 1863), commanding Buckner's Division, Department of East Tennessee (November 26, 1863-April 1864); commanding brigade (part of the time in Hoke's Division), Department of North Carolina and Southern Virginia (May 1864); major general, CSA (May 21, 1864); commanding division, same department (May-October 19, 1864); and commanding division, Anderson's Corps, Army of Northern Virginia (October 19, 1864-April 8, 1865). He escaped the debacle at Fort Donelson by slipping through enemy lines after the capitulation and was assigned to command a brigade which he led at Shiloh until wounded. He rejoined the army for the Kentucky Campaign, leading his brigade at Perryville and later at Murfreesboro. At Chickamauga he directed a provisional division and later led Buckner's Division to aid Longstreet in the Knoxville Campaign. Transferred to Virginia in the spring of 1864, he fought at Drewry's Bluff and in the early defense of Petersburg. His new division held a portion of the trenches once Lee's army arrived and it was part of his command that was blown up when Grant set off the mine explosion on July 30. In the retreat to Appomattox his division was badly cut up at Sayler's Creek and two days later he was relieved of duty by Lee. He was still with the army the next day when the surrender came. Johnson returned to the field of education. (Cummings, Charles M., *Yankee Quaker, Confederate General: The Curious Career of Bushrod Rust Johnson*)

JOHNSON, Edward (1816-1873)

Twice captured during 1864, Confederate Major General Edward Johnson finished the Civil War as a prisoner of war. The Virginia-born and Kentucky-raised West Pointer (1838) had been posted to the infantry with which he saw action in the Seminole War, on the frontier, and during the Mexican War. In the latter conflict he won two brevets. Resigning as a captain in the 6th Infantry on June 10, 1861, he joined the Southern forces. His assignments included: colonel, 12th Georgia (June 15, 1861); commanding brigade, 1st Division, Army of the Northwest (November 22-December 1861); brigadier general, CSA (December 13, 1861); commanding Army of the Northwest (spring 1862); major general, CSA (February 28, 1863); commanding division, 2nd Corps, Army of Northern Virginia (May 8, 1863-May 12, 1864); and commanding Hindman's-Anderson's (old) Division, Lee's Corps, Army of Tennessee (September 1-December 16, 1864). Sent into western Virginia, he commanded his regiment under Lee during the Cheat Mountain Campaign, and then a brigade. Taking his army to join Stonewall Jackson, he was severely wounded, as a brigadier general, at McDowell on May 8, 1862. By the time he returned to field duty he was a major general and was placed in command of a division. This he led on Culp's Hill at Gettysburg and during the Bristoe and Mine Run operations. During Grant's Overland Campaign he fought in the Wilderness and then held the angle of the Confederate lines at Spotsylvania. When the line was broken he was taken prisoner along with much of his division. Exchanged in the summer of 1864, he was ordered to the Army of Tennessee and given charge of a division. This he led in the final stages of the defense of Atlanta and then took it into middle Tennessee under Hood. After fighting at Franklin he was captured in the Confederate rout at Nashville. Due to a new exchange policy, whereby release was determined by the date of capture, the requests of Robert E. Lee to have him exchanged were rejected by the Confederate War Department. Not released until July 1865, "Old Allegheny" became a farmer (Freeman, Douglas S., *Lee's Lieutenants*)

JOHNSON, George W. (1811-1862)

Having been forced to flee Kentucky with the Confederate forces in early 1862, George W. Johnson became the only Civil War governor to die of wounds received in action. A native of the state, he was a lawyer and large-scale planter. A Democrat and former state legislator, he strongly supported John C. Breckinridge for the presidency in 1860 and backed the secession of the state, which never came about. He became the first governor of the provisional Confederate government of the state in 1861 and joined the military forces of Albert Sidney Johnston at Bowling Green where he served as an advisor. After the fall of Forts Henry and Donelson, the Confederates at Bowling Green were forced to withdraw from the state and Johnson went with them. On the first day at Shiloh he was a volunteer aide to General Breckinridge and had his horse shot out from under him. That night he enlisted as private, 1st Kentucky. He fell mortally wounded on the second day and died on April 9. (Clift, G. Glenn, *Governors of Kentucky*)

JOHNSON, Herschel Vespasian (1812-1880)

A Southern Democrat seeking a compromise between the sections, Herschel V. Johnson was the running mate of Stephen A. Douglas in 1860. Reluctantly going with his state, he represented Georgia in the Confederate Senate where he took typical states' rights positions. A native Georgian lawyer, he served his state as a U.S. senator, judge, and governor. His quest for moderation brought him to support the Compromise of 1850 and the Kansas-Nebraska Act. He was deeply troubled by the excessive violence on both sides in the fighting in Kansas. After his defeat for the vice presidency he attended the state secession convention where he tried to achieve unified action on the part of the Southern states rather than individual secession. When Robert A. Toombs refused a senate seat, Johnson was named in his place and was admitted to the First Confederate Congress on January 19, 1863. He won reelection to the Second Congress and served during both congresses on the Committee on Naval Affairs. During the First Congress he also sat on the committees on: Finance; Foreign Affairs; and Post Offices and Post Roads. He favored a heavy income tax but opposed other tax increases and generally failed to make the hard decisions necessary to win the war. He was active in seeking a peaceful settlement and eventually favored reunion if slavery could be guaranteed. After the Confederacy's fall he presided over the state constitutional convention and was elected to the U.S. Senate but was denied admission. He then returned to his practice and was named a judge in 1873. (Flippen, Percy Scott, *Herschel V. Johnson of Georgia*)

JOHNSON, Jonathan Eastman (1824-1906)

An established genre painter, Eastman Johnson traveled widely to observe at first hand the inspiration for his scenes. Born in Maine, he early showed an aptitude for drawing with crayons and soon took an apprenticeship in Boston. A portrait painter early on, he worked in New England and Washington, where he did black and white drawings of famous men in the Capitol itself. He studied for many years in Germany, Italy, France, and the Netherlands. Returning to the United States, he opened a studio in New York in 1858, having in the meantime become a genre painter. He traveled through the South to gain close knowledge of Negro life for his work. He also executed several works upon the Civil War. The most famous of these is "The Wounded Drummer Boy" which it is believed that he did from personal observation at Antietam. He was still painting into the next century.

JOHNSON, Reverdy (1796-1876)

Having served as an attorney for the slaveholder in the *Dred Scott* case, former U.S. Attorney General Reverdy Johnson first justified the possible secession of the South but then denounced it as treason, when it had come to pass and his own state appeared on the brink of withdrawing from the Union. A native Marylander, he entered the legal profession in 1816 and became one of the leaders of the field in his state. He served as the state's deputy attorney general in 1816-1817 and four years later entered the state senate. After eight years in that body he resigned to return to private practice. As a Whig, he took a seat in the U.S. Senate in 1845 and held it until he submitted his resignation in order to become Zachary Taylor's attorney general in 1849. He left that post the next year and a decade later was back in the state senate. He was a member of the Washington Peace Convention in early 1861. As a Democrat, he took a seat in the Senate again on March 4, 1863. In order to become the chief diplomat to Great Britain, Johnson resigned from the Senate in 1868 and served for a year abroad. He then returned to private pursuits. (Steiner, Bernard Christian, *Life of Reverdy Johnson*)

JOHNSON, Richard W (1827-1897)

A veteran of a decade on the frontier, Richard W Johnson emerged from the Civil War with every brevet he could earn. The Kentucky native and West Pointer (1849) had served with the infantry until transferred to the mounted arm in the 1855 expansion of the army. His Civil War assignments included: captain, 2nd Cavalry (since December 1, 1856); captain, 5th Cavalry (designation change August 3, 1861); brigadier general, USV (October 11, 1861); commanding 3rd Brigade, McCook's Command, Department of the Cumberland (October-November 9, 1861); commanding 6th Brigade, Army of the Ohio (November 9-December 2, 1861); commanding 6th Brigade, 2nd Division, Army of the Ohio (December 2, 1861-July 24, 1862 but not early April); major, 4th Cavalry (July 17, 1862); commanding 2nd Division, Right Wing, 14th Corps, Army of the Cumberland (December 1862-January 9, 1863); commanding 2nd Division, 20th Corps, Army of the Cumberland (January 9-19, and February 20-September 19, 1863); commanding 1st Division, 14th Corps, Army of the Cumberland (November 17, 1863-May 27, 1864, June 6-13, July 13-August 7, and November 2-8, 1864); commanding the corps (August 7-22, 1864); commanding Cavalry Corps, Army of the Cumberland (August 19-October 29, 1864); commanding 6th Division, Cavalry Corps, Military Division of the Mississippi (November 17, 1864-July 1865); and commanding 2nd Sub-District, District of Middle Tennessee, Department of the Cumberland (July-September 1865). Serving under Buell in Kentucky and Tennessee, he took part in the capture of Nashville but was absent ill at the time of the battle of Shiloh. Returning to duty he was captured by John Hunt Morgan's cavalry when he himself was attempting to catch the elusive Confederate. He was exchanged in December 1862 in time for the fighting at Murfreesboro and in charge of a division which he led in the Tullahoma Campaign and at Chickamauga, where he earned a regular army brevet. A similar reward was his for Chattanooga. Leading his division in the Atlanta Campaign, he was wounded at New Hope Church in late May. Returning to duty, he briefly commanded the corps before taking charge of the army's mounted arm. As a division commander, he served under the cavalryman James H. Wilson in the Nashville fighting for which he was brevetted brigadier general in the regular service and major general of volunteers. At the war's conclusion he was brevetted major general in the regular establishment and on January 15, 1866, was mustered out of the volunteers. He then reverted to his regular rank of major, 4th Cavalry, but was retired on account of his wounds in 1867 as a major general. Eight years later this was reduced to that of a brigadier generalship. A professor of military science at the universities of Missouri and Minnesota, he was an unsuccessful Democratic candidate for governor in the latter state. It should be noted that he had no middle name. (Johnson, Richard W, *A Soldier's Reminiscences in Peace and War*)

JOHNSON, Robert Ward (1814-1879)

As Arkansas' congressional representative for most of the Civil War, Robert W. Johnson proved to be a strong supporter of the Davis administration except for the fact that he wanted Western troops kept in the Trans-Mississippi Department. Born in Kentucky, he moved to Arkansas where he practiced law and served as a prosecutor. He went to Congress and then became a senator. He did not seek reelection in 1860 and left office at the peak of the secession crisis. Despite his connections with the slave powers he favored compromise and supported the Kansas-Nebraska Act. The election of Lincoln, however, converted him into an immediate secessionist. The state secession convention named him to the Provisional Confederate Congress, and he subsequently won a seat in the Confederate Senate. He took his seat in Montgomery on May 18, 1861, only two days before the decision to move the capital to Richmond. He was given a seat on the Committee on Indian Affairs and in both regular congresses he chaired it. Throughout his service he also sat on the Committee on Military Affairs. His other assignments included the committees on: Accounts (First Congress); Naval Affairs (First Congress); Public Lands (Second Congress); and Rules (Second Congress). He pursued a liberal policy toward the Indians and favored an independent status for the western Confederate states. He proposed that cabinet officers be reconfirmed every two years—a distinct limitation on the executive power. Missing the final session, he wanted to flee to Mexico but instead sought a pardon in Washington, which was granted. He ran a marginal law practice with Albert Pike in Washington after the war and failed in a bid for a U.S. Senate seat. (Thomas, Davis Yancey, *Arkansas in War and Reconstruction, 1861-1874*)

JOHNSON, Waldo Porter (1817-1885)

A friend of Jefferson Davis, Waldo P. Johnson nonetheless became highly critical of two of his cabinet members and a number of Western generals. Born in what is now West Virginia, he established a law practice in Missouri and served as a private in the Mexican War before taking a seat in the state legislature. He later served as a judge and continued his private practice. With the coming of the secession crisis he attended the Washington Peace Conference and was elected as a Democrat to the U.S. Senate. Taking his seat on March 17, 1861, he was expelled from that body on January 10, 1862, for having joined the Confederate army. His military assignments included: major, 1st Missouri Battalion (1861); and lieutenant colonel, 4th Missouri (1861 or early 1862). Twice wounded at the battle of Pea Ridge, he worked to transfer the Missouri troops into Confederate service. With the death of Missouri Senator Robert L.Y. Peyton, the governor named Johnson to fill the unexpired term. He was admitted on December 24, 1863, and was seated on the Committee on Claims in the First Confederate Congress. In the next he also sat on the committees on: Engrossment and Enrollment, Foreign Relations, and Indian Affairs. He favored heavy taxation to fund the war effort but was highly critical of Davis appointments, especially those of cabinet secretaries Benjamin and Memminger and of General Braxton Bragg. He wanted the war switched from Davis' hands to those of Generals Lee, Beauregard, and Joseph E. Johnston. After the Confederacy's collapse he spent a year in Canadian exile before returning to his Missouri practice.

JOHNSON, William A. (?-?)

Since the brigade which William A. Johnson commanded during the spring and summer campaigns of 1864 was not officially sanctioned by the War Department, he was not considered for promotion to brigadier general. His Confederate assignments included: major, 4th (Roddey's) Alabama Cavalry (October 21, 1862); lieutenant colonel, 4th (Roddey's) Alabama Cavalry (April 23, 1863); colonel, 4th (Roddey's) Alabama Cavalry (August 3, 1863); and commanding brigade, Roddey's Cavalry Division, Department of Alabama, Mississippi and East Louisiana (April-September 24, 1864). He served at first in Mississippi and northern Alabama but joined Wheeler's cavalry for the victory at Chickamauga shortly after his promotion to regimental command. Returning to northern Alabama, he was given command of an unofficial brigade in the spring of 1864 when General Roddey decided to divide his brigade into two brigades. Johnson led one to reinforce Forrest's cavalry in Mississippi, seeing action at Brice's Crossroads and Tupelo. Rejoining Roddey, his brigade was merged with the other brigade and Roddey became commander of the District of Northern Alabama on September 24, 1864. Three days later Johnson was wounded at Pulaski, Tennessee, and it is unclear whether he ever rejoined the regiment.

JOHNSTON, Albert Sidney (1803-1862)

At the beginning of the Civil War it was almost universally agreed that the finest soldier, North or South, was Albert Sidney Johnston. But his Civil War career was a definite disappointment to the Confederacy. The Kentucky-born Johnston was appointed to West Point from Louisiana and graduated eighth in the class of 1826. After eight years of service he resigned to care for his terminally ill wife. A failure at farming, he went to Texas and joined the revolutionary forces as a private. He rose to the forces' chief command as senior brigadier the next year. He served as secretary of war in the Republic of Texas and commanded the 1st Texas Rifles in the Mexican War. Reentering the regular army in 1849 as a major and paymaster, he became colonel, 2nd (old) Cavalry, in 1855. For his services in the 1857 campaign against the Mormons in Utah he was brevetted brigadier general. He resigned his commission on April 10, 1861, but did not quit his post on the West Coast until his successor arrived. Relieved, he began the long trek to Richmond overland. Meeting with Jefferson Davis, he entered Confederate service where his assignments included: general, CSA (August 30, 1861, to date from May 30, 1861); commanding Department No. 2 (September 15, 1861-April 6, 1862); and in immediate command of the Central Army of Kentucky, Department No. 2 (October 28-December 5, 1861 and February 23- March 29, 1862). As the second ranking general in the Southern army he was given command of the western theater of operations. Establishing a line of defense in Kentucky from the Mississippi River to the Appalachians, he held it until it was broken at Mill Springs in January and at Forts Henry and Donelson in February 1862. Abandoning Kentucky and most of Tennessee, he fell back into northern Mississippi where he concentrated his previously scattered forces. In early April he moved against Grant's army at Shiloh. In what was basically a surprise attack, he drove the enemy back. While directing frontline operations he was wounded in the leg. Not considering his wound serious, he bled to death. Grant, writing in his memoirs, considered Johnston as having failed to live up to earlier expectations. (Roland, Charles P., *Albert Sidney Johnston: Soldier of Three Republics*)

JOHNSTON, George Doherty (1832-1910)

Alabama lawyer and politician George D. Johnston entered the Confederate army and rose to the rank of brigadier general, serving mostly in the western theater. The North Carolina-born officer's assignments included: second lieutenant, Company G, 4th Alabama (May 7, 1861); major, 25th Alabama (January 1862); lieutenant colonel, 25th Alabama (April 6, 1862); colonel, 25th Alabama (September 14, 1863) brigadier general, CSA (July 26, 1864); commanding Deas' Brigade, Hindman's Division, Lee's Corps, Army of Tennessee (July 26-28, 1864); commanding Quarles' Brigade, Walthall's Division, Stewart's Corps, Army of Tennessee (fall 1864-late March 1865); and commanding the division (late March-ca. April 9, 1865). Commissioned in the Marion Light Infantry, he fought at 1st Bull Run before being promoted to field officer in a new regiment in the West. He succeeded to command of the unit at Shiloh and then served in the Corinth, Murfreesboro, and Tullahoma campaigns. Made colonel a few days before Chickamauga, he led the regiment there and at Chattanooga. During the Atlanta Campaign he received the three wreathed stars of a brigadier general and two days after being given charge of a brigade was wounded at Ezra Church. Returning to duty that fall, he took command of another brigade but did not command it at Franklin. In charge at Nashville, he later fought at Bentonville during the Carolinas Campaign and soon thereafter rose to command the division. When the army was reorganized about April 9, 1865, he became supernumerary and was en route to the Department of Alabama, Mississippi and East Louisiana when the Confederacy collapsed. Resuming his practice, he was also involved in military education and held national appointive office.

JOHNSTON, Joseph Eggleston (1807-1891)

Petty considerations over rank and military etiquette and wounds cost the Confederacy, for lengthy periods, the services of one of its most effective, top commanders, Joseph E. Johnston. The Virginia native and West Pointer (1829), rated by many as more capable than Lee, was the highest-ranking regular army officer to resign and join the Confederacy. With the staff rank of brigadier general, he had been the national army's quartermaster general for almost a year when he quit on April 22, 1861. His earlier career had included eight years in the artillery before he was transferred to the topographical engineers in 1838, when he rejoined the army a year after his resignation. During the Mexican War he won two brevets and was wounded at both Cerro Gordo and Chapultepec. He had also been brevetted for earlier service against the Seminoles in Florida. Having been appointed quartermaster general on June 28, 1860, he remained in the service until after the secession of his native state. His Virginia and Confederate assignments included: major general, Virginia Volunteers (April 1861); brigadier general, CSA (May 14, 1861); commanding Army of the Shenandoah (June 30-July 20, 1861); commanding Army of the Potomac (July 20-October 22, 1861); general, CSA (August 31, 1861, to rank from July 21); commanding Department of Northern Virginia (October 22, 1861-May 31, 1862); commanding Department of the West (December 4, 1862-December 1863); commanding Army of Tennessee (December 27, 1863-July 18, 1864); commanding Army of Tennessee and Department of Tennessee and Georgia (February 25-April 26, 1865); also commanding Department of South Carolina, Georgia and Florida (February 25-April 26, 1865); and also commanding Department of North Carolina (March 16-April 26, 1865). Initially commissioned in the Virginia forces, he relieved Thomas J.—later "Stonewall"—Jackson in command at Harpers Ferry and continued the organization of the Army of the Shenandoah. When the Virginia forces were absorbed into the Confederate army he was reduced to a brigadier generalship. When the Union army under Irvin McDowell moved out of Washington and Alexandria to attack Pierre G.T. Beauregard at Manassas, Johnston managed to totally fool Pennsylvania General Robert Patterson with a small force in the Shenandoah Valley and move the bulk of his forces to Beauregard's support. During the battle of 1st Bull Run, Johnston, although senior to Beauregard, left the general direction of the battle to the junior officer due to a lack of familiarity with the terrain. Johnston was basically engaged in forwarding freshly arrived Valley troops to the threatened sectors. The two generals shared the glory and were critical of supply problems which they felt prevented a march on Washington. The next month Johnston became one of five men advanced to the grade of full general—all Confederate generals wore the same insignia of rank, three stars in a wreath—but was not pleased with the relative ranking of the five. He felt that since he was the senior officer to leave the "Old" service and join the Confederacy he sould not be ranked behind Samuel Cooper, Albert Sidney Johnston, and Robert E. Lee. Only Beauregard was placed behind Johnston on the list. This led to much bad blood between Johnston and Jefferson Davis. There would be more. With his increased rank, Johnston was given command of the Department of Northern Virginia and became engaged in what was virtually a phony war with the Washington-based army of George B. McClellan. Throughout the winter of 1861-62 he maintained his position at Manassas Junction and then withdrew just as McClellan's superior force advanced. In the meantime he had engaged in a dispute with his president over a policy of brigading troops from the same state together. Johnston argued that a reorganization could not with

Joseph E. Johnston, a capable Confederate army commander, was handicapped by his feud with President Davis. (NA)

propriety be carried out in the face of an active enemy. When he withdrew his army from the line of Bull Run he reinforced John B. Magruder on the Peninsula east of Richmond and took command there. With McClellan again facing him, he held Yorktown for a month before pulling back just before his opponent again advanced. His forces fought a rearguard action at Williamsburg and were then encamped on the very outskirts of the new nation's capital. In an effort to drive McClellan off, Johnston launched an attack south of the Chickahominy River at the end of May 1862. The battle of Seven Pines, or Fair Oaks, turned out to be a confusion of errors in the confusing terrain. For years afterwards there was acrimonious debate among various Confederate generals over who was to blame for the limited success. On the first day of the battle Johnston reexhibited his tendency to attract enemy bullets and was succeeded the next day by Robert E. Lee who was to lead the Army of Northern Virginia for the balance of the war. Upon his recovery he was given charge of a largely supervisory command entitled the Department of the West. He was in charge of Braxton Bragg's Army of Tennessee and John C. Pemberton's Department of Mississippi and East Louisiana. With few troops under his immediate command he proved powerless in attempting to relieve the besieged garrison of Vicksburg under Pemberton. Following the river city's fall, he made a feeble attempt to hold Jackson, Mississippi, against the advance of William T. Sherman. Following Bragg's disastrous defeat at Chattanooga, Johnston was given immediate command of his army and the next spring and summer directed a masterful delaying campaign against Sherman during his advance on Atlanta. However, his continued withdrawals raised the ire of Jefferson Davis, and he was relieved in front of the city. His successor, John B. Hood, then began his destruction of the Army of Tennessee with reckless tactics. With Sherman having marched clear through Georgia and begun his drive through the Carolinas, a clamor arose in the Confederate Congress for Johnston's resumption of command. Davis finally relented in early 1865 and the general took eventual command of three departments. Unfortunately for the Confederacy his forces were heavy on generals but weak on men. He could do little but hope for a linkup with Lee's army so that they could turn on either Grant or Sherman and then on the other. It never came off and he surrendered his forces following some difficulties over terms, bordering on the political, on April 26, 1865, at the Bennett House near Durham Station, North Carolina. He had been one of the most effective Confederate commanders when he was not hampered by directives from the president. Following the war he sat in Congress and was a federal railroad commissioner. Engaged in much debate over the causes of the Confederate defeat, he wrote his *Narrative of Military Operations* which was highly critical of Davis and many of his fellow generals. In an example of the civil relationships between former wartime opponents, Johnston died of a cold caught while attending the funeral of his arch-opponent, Sherman. (Govan, Gilbert E. and Livingood, James W., *A Different Valor: The Story of General Joseph E. Johnston*)

JOHNSTON, Robert Daniel (1837-1919)

A North Carolina lawyer with some militia experience, Robert D. Johnston entered Confederate service early in the war and rose to be a brigadier. His assignments included: captain, Company K, 23rd North Carolina (July 15, 1861); lieutenant colonel, 23rd North Carolina (April 16, 1862); brigadier general, CSA (September 1, 1863); commanding Iverson's (old) Brigade, Rodes' Division, 2nd Corps, Army of Northern Virginia (September 8, 1863-May 8, 1864); commanding same brigade, Early's Division, same corps and army (May 8-12, 1864); commanding brigade, Ramseur's-Pegram's Division, Valley District, Department of Northern Virginia (August-December 1864); commanding brigade, Pegram's Division, 2nd Corps, Army of Northern Virginia (December 1864-February 1865); and commanding the division (February-March 1865). He saw action at Williamsburg and succeeded to command of the regiment at Seven Pines where he was wounded. He returned to duty in time to fight at South Mountain and Antietam and at Chancellorsville he was placed in command of the 12th North Carolina when that unit had lost all of its field officers. Back with his own regiment he was again wounded at Gettysburg but recovered to accept promotion and charge of the brigade. He fought at the Wilderness and, in a different division, at Spotsylvania, suffering a third wound. Returning to duty in August he served through Early's Valley Campaign, fighting at 3rd Winchester, Fisher's Hill, and Cedar Creek before moving to the Petersburg trenches. After briefly leading the division, he was detached to round up deserters. With the war ending while he was on this duty, he resumed his law practice in his native state and later became a banker in Alabama. (Freeman, Douglas S., *Lee's Lieutenants*)

JOHNSTON, William Preston (1831-1899)

The son of General Albert Sidney Johnston, William Preston Johnston became one of the leading participants in the controversy over the battle of Shiloh. A Louisville lawyer, he had some military training at the Western Military Institute. His Confederate assignments included: major, 2nd Kentucky (early 1861); lieutenant colonel, 1st Kentucky (ca. July 3, 1861); and colonel and aide-de-camp to Jefferson Davis (May 1862). He saw action at Dranesville with the second unit and upon its muster-out in the spring of 1862, he joined the president's staff. After being present at Seven Pines, he was sent to Mississippi to report upon the situation in the western theater where his father had lost Kentucky and most of Tennessee and, at Shiloh, his life. The younger Johnston reported that the Confederates had been on the verge of victory when his father had been mortally wounded and his successor, General Beauregard, had muffed the opportunity. This lost opportunity thesis was further stated in his *The Life of Albert Sidney Johnston*, published in 1878, and in an article for the *Century Magazine*. Continuing on Davis' staff, Johnston saw action in the vicinity of Richmond whenever it was threatened. Fleeing with his chief, he was captured in Georgia and jailed. He resided in Canada briefly after regaining his liberty and then became a professor and university president. (Shaw, Arthur Marvin, *William Preston Johnston: A Transitional Figure of the Confederacy*)

JOHNSTON, Willie (1850-?)

Following his father into the Union army, Willie Johnston was the youngest person in the Civil War to earn the Congressional Medal of Honor. Born in New York, he was living in Vermont when his father enlisted in Company D, 3rd Vermont, in the summer of 1861. Young Willie joined the company as a musician shortly thereafter. In the fighting during the Seven Days, when not more than 12 years old, he so distinguished himself that he was awarded the medal in 1863. (Mitchell, Joseph B., *The Badge of Gallantry*)

JOINVILLE, Prince de (1818-?)

Along with two of his nephews—the Comte de Paris and the Duc de Chartres—the Prince de Joinville travelled to the United States to witness the Civil War. The son of French King Louis-Philippe, he was a vice admiral at the time of the monarchy's fall. Arriving in the United States in 1861, he attached himself to the staff of General McClellan, without rank. As an unofficial member of the general's headquarters family he witnessed the organization of the Army of the Potomac and its long period of inactivity during the winter of 1861-62. Accompanying the army to the Peninsula, he served through the campaign and won the praise of McClellan for his services on the field. During his stay in America he practiced his watercoloring hobby, depicting scenes of camp and battle. He returned to Europe later that year, but did write a useful account of the campaign. (Joinville, Prince de, *The Army of the Potomac: Its Organization, Its Commander and Its Campaign*)

JOMINI, Baron Antoine Henri (1779-1869)

On both sides of the Atlantic in the mid-1800s the works on the theory of war by Baron Antoine H. Jomini were considered the leading authorities in the field. His principal work was published in French and translated as *Summary of the Art of War*. The historian and theorist of the Napoleonic Wars was challenged in his preeminence in Europe by the German General Karl von Clausewitz and his *Vom Kriege* (*On War*). But on the other side of the ocean there was no English-language version available before the Civil War and Clausewitz had little impact on the combatants. Jomini however was read by many of the cadets at West Point. It is interesting to note that Grant claimed never to have read anything by him.

JONES, Arnold Elzey

See: *Elzey, Arnold*

JONES, Catesby ap Roger (1821-1877)

Having supervised the armament of the CSS *Virginia*—the armored version of the USS *Merrimac*—former U.S. naval officer Catesby ap R. Jones commanded her in the historic encounter with the USS *Monitor*. The Virginia native had entered the U.S. Navy in 1836 as a midshipman and was a passed midshipman during the Mexican War, during which he was assigned to the Pacific Squadron but did not see any action. Promoted to lieutenant in 1849, he served with John A. Dahlgren on ordnance projects during the 1850s. Resigning in 1861, his Confederate assignments included: captain, Virginia Navy (1861); lieutenant, CSN (1861); executive officer CSS *Virginia* (March 1862); commanding CSS *Virginia* (March 8-9, 1862); commanding CSS *Chattahoochie* (1862); and commander, CSN (1863). After aiding in the construction of the revolutionary vessel, he was its second in command when it sailed out into Hampton Roads to engage the wooden Union fleet. On March 8, 1862, it put two Union warships out of action and was threatening a third. Meanwhile the ship's skipper, Franklin Buchanan, was wounded and Jones took over. The next day the *Monitor* appeared and the first battle between iron-clad vessels was under way. Although a draw, Jones withdrew and the *Virginia* rarely ventured out of its port again. Jones later commanded another vessel and then directed the naval foundry and ordnance works at Selma, Alabama. Promoted to commander in 1863, he appears to have left the service in the first six months of 1864. Engaged in business in the postwar years, he died in a quarrel with one J.S. Harral who shot him dead.

JONES, David Rumph (1825-1863)

It was heart disease and not enemy action that deprived the Confederacy of a capable, but not brilliant, division leader, David

R. Jones. The South Carolinian was a West Pointer (1846) and Mexican War veteran when he resigned as a brevet staff captain on February 15, 1861, to serve the South. His assignments included: major, CSA (early 1861); brigadier general, CSA (June 17, 1861); commanding 3rd Brigade (in 1st Corps after July 20), Army of the Potomac (June 20-October 22, 1861); commanding a different brigade, Longstreet's Division, Potomac District, Department of Northern Virginia (October 22, 1861-February 17, 1862); commanding S. Jones' (old) Brigade, G.W. Smith's Division, in Potomac District until March), Department of Northern Virginia (February 17-April 1862); major general, CSA (April 5, to rank from March 10, 1862); commanding division, Magruder's Command, same department (April-July 3, 1862); and commanding division, 1st Corps, Army of Northern Virginia (July 3-October 1862). After serving as Beauregard's chief of staff during the bombardment of Fort Sumter he was given command of a Virginia brigade which he led at 1st Bull Run. He then commanded a South Carolina and later a Georgia brigade before leading a division on the Peninsula. There he fought in the Seven Days. In the 2nd Bull Run campaign he distinguished himself when Longstreet forced his way through Thoroughfare Gap in order to join Jackson. He saw further action at 2nd Bull Run and played a key role guarding a gap in South Mountain. He resisted Burnside's attack on the Confederate right at Antietam and joined A.P. Hill in driving the enemy back. Shortly afterwards heart trouble forced him to give up his command. He died the following January 15. (Freeman, Douglas S., *Lee's Lieutenants*)

JONES, George Washington (1806-1884)

As the chairman of the Committee on Rules and Officers of the House in the First Regular Confederate Congress, George W. Jones was one of Tennessee's top states' righters in the congressional delegation. A native of Virginia he had worked as a saddler, justice of the peace, state legislator, and court clerk before the Civil War. Named to the Washington Peace Conference in 1861, he failed to attend and worked instead for the secession of his adopted Tennessee. In November 1861 he was elected to represent the 7th District in the Confederate Congress, where he also served on the Committee on Ways & Means. He worked to keep the control of the army in the hands of the states, granting the president only the right to select his own cabinet officers and direct foreign policy. He did not seek reelecton to his seat and in 1870 attended the state constitutional convention.

JONES, Hilary Pollard (1833-1913)

Opinion upon the military merits of artillerist Hilary P. Jones was divided when he received a promotion over the strenuous objections of Stonewall Jackson and his artillery chief, Stapleton Crutchfield. A teacher at the outbreak of the war, he entered the Confederate army, where his assignments included: lieutenant, Morris (Va.) Artillery (August 1861); captain, Morris (Va.) Artillery (February 1862); major, Artillery (May 28, 1862); commanding battalion, Reserve Artillery, Army of Northern Virginia (June 1862-fall 1862); commanding Artillery Battalion, D.H. Hill's Division, 2nd Corps, Army of Northern Virginia (fall 1862-January 1863); commanding Artillery Battalion, Jackson's (old) Division, 2nd Corps, Army of Northern Virginia (January-June 2, 1863); lieutenant colonel, Artillery (March 2, 1863); commanding Artillery Battalion, Early's Division, 2nd Corps, Army of Northern Virginia (June 2-July 1863); commanding artillery battalion, 2nd Corps, Army of Northern Virginia (July 1863-March 19, 1864); colonel, Artillery (February 27, 1864); commanding artillery battalion, 1st Corps, Army of Northern Virginia (March 19-early May 1864); commanding Artillery, Department of North Carolina and Southern Virginia (early May-October 1864); and commanding Artillery, Anderson's Corps, Army of Northern Virginia (October 1864-April 9, 1865). As a battalion commander, he saw service at the Seven Days, Antietam, and Fredericksburg. Before Chancellorsville he was promoted upon the recommendation of the army's chief artillerist, General William Pendleton, despite the objections of the corps commander and chief of artillery. He then fought at Chancellorsville, 2nd Winchester, where he distinguished himself, and Gettysburg before being transferred to the Petersburg area. As Beauregard's chief of artillery he directed operations at Drewry's Bluff and the initial attacks on Petersburg. When Beauregard's command was absorbed into the Army of Northern Virginia, he directed the guns of the new corps. In this capacity he served throughout the rest of the siege and in the retreat to Appomattox where he was surrendered. He resumed his role as an educator after the war. (Wise, Jennings C., *The Long Arm of Lee*)

JONES, John Beauchamp (1810-1866)

Athough he served for a time in the Local Defense Troops, units composed of government and other vital workers in Richmond who were only called out when the city was seriously threatened, Baltimore-born John Jones is better known for his diary chronicling the homefront and military affairs as viewed them from the Confederate capital. Having previously worked as a editor for the *Southern Monitor*, a proslavery Philadelphia weekly, Jones offered his services to the new government early in 1861 and was given a clerkship in the rebel War Department. Serving under all six Secretaries of War, Jones was well placed, in his passport office, to gain intimate knowledge of the military and civil affairs of the Confederacy. His diary is full of the ups and downs of the Southern peoples' hopes, the spiraling inflation and profitering that wreaked havoc on the home front. Jones recounts the bread riots of 1863 and the repeated scares of enemy raids, and provides evaluations of military and civil leaders. While his diary was going to press in early 1866, Jones died. (Jones, John B., *A Rebel War Clerk's Diary*)

JONES, John Marshall (1820-1864)

On May 21, 1863, there occurred in the Army of Northern Virginia one of the most confusing command changes in Confederate history. John M. Jones was assigned to the command of a brigade which up until a couple of weeks earlier had been directed by General John Robert Jones. John M. was a graduate of West Point (1841) and had resigned his commission as captain, 7th Infantry, on May 27, 1861, in order to offer his services to his native Virginia. His assignments included: captain, CSA (spring 1861); lieutenant colonel, CSA (ca. September 1861); brigadier general, CSA (from May 15, 1863); and commanding brigade, Trimble's-Johnson's Division, 2nd Corps, Army of Northern Virginia (May 21-July 2, 1863 and August 1863-May 5, 1864). From September 1861 he served as adjutant general, and sometimes also as inspector general, for Generals Ewell and Early. In this capacity he saw action at Front Royal, Winchester, Cross Keys, Port Republic, the Seven Days, Cedar Mountain, 2nd Bull Run, Fredericksburg, and Chancellorsville. Promoted to brigadier, he took over the brigade formerly belonging to John R. Jones whose courage had become a matter of question. In the assault on Culp's Hill on the evening of the second day at Gettysburg, he was severely wounded. He returned to command for the Bristoe and Mine Run campaigns. He was wounded in the head in a skirmish in the latter campaign but returned to duty within a few days. Then, on the first day of battle at the Wilderness, he was killed while trying to rally his brigade in the face of a Union onslaught. (Freeman, Douglas S., *Lee's Lieutentants*)

JONES, John Robert (1827-1901)

Stonewall Jackson had a tendency to name new generals for brigades from outside the units which they were to direct. This policy led to much friction in the officer corps; often, as in the case of John R. Jones, Jackson's choices were not top-notch. A native Virginian and graduate of the Virginia Military Institute, Jones had been active in military affairs in Florida and Maryland before returning to the Shenandoah Valley where he raised the Rockingham Confederates at the outbreak of the Civil War. His unit was assigned to what became the Stonewall Brigade and his assignments included: captain, Company I, 33rd Virginia (July 1861); lieutenant colonel, 33rd Virginia (early 1862); brigadier general, CSA (June 23, 1863); commanding 2nd Brigade, Jackson's (old) Division, Jackson's Corps, Army of Northern Virginia (ca. June 27-July 1, 1862 and December 12, 1862-May 2, 1863); and commanding the division (September 7-17 and September 18-December 12, 1862). He served at 1st Bull Run and in the Shenandoah Valley before being tapped to command the 2nd Brigade. His appointment led to the resignation of a former brigade commander, Colonel John A. Campbell. Joining the command during the Seven Days, he led it at White Oak Swamp and Malvern Hill, where he was wounded. Rejoining the army in Maryland he took command of Jackson's (old) Division for the operations against Harpers Ferry. At Antietam he was stunned, although not hit by, a bursting shell and forced to relinquish command. Sent to the Valley to gather stragglers, he resumed command of the division until the day before Fredericksburg. He was praised by his superiors for the manner in which he handled his brigade there, but charges of cowardice were also leveled at him by subordinates. He apparently sheltered himself behind a tree. In his next action, Chancellorsville, he left the field complaining of an ulcerated leg. Never allowed to resume command, he also had the humiliation of not receiving confirmation of his appointment. Seized by Union troops in Tennessee on July 4, 1863, he was imprisoned for the duration with no desire on the part of the Richmond authorities to effect his exchange. After his release he was a businessman and minor office holder in Harrisonburg, Virginia. (Freeman, Douglas S., *Lee's Lieutenants*)

JONES, Joseph (1833-1896)

A medical professor before the Civil War, Joseph Jones served in the latter part of the war as a surgeon at the Andersonville prisoner of war compound in his native Georgia. He received his training in South Carolina, New Jersey, and Pennsylvania. He was a professor of medicine at several Georgia colleges when in 1861 he joined the Confederate army as a surgeon. In 1864 he was assigned to Andersonville and out of necessity became a specialist in the treatment of gangrene. Despite his training and efforts the high mortality rate continued at the camp. Moving to New Orleans after the war, he was again involved in education and was active in historical circles, writing his three-volume *Medical and Surgical Memoirs*.

JONES, Patrick Henry (1830-1900)

Born in Ireland, Patrick Henry Jones came to the United States at the age of 10 and became a Buffalo newspaper editor and lawyer before entering the military in the Civil War. His assignments included: second lieutenant, 37th New York (June 7, 1861); first lieutenant and adjutant, 37th New York (November 4, 1861); major, 37th New York (January 21, 1862); colonel, 154th New York (October 8, 1862); commanding 1st Brigade, 2nd Division, 11th Corps, Army of the Cumberland (January 30-February 25, 1864); commanding 2nd Brigade, 2nd Division, 20th Corps, Armies of the Cumberland and Georgia (June 7-August 8, 1864; September 17, 1864-January 19, 1865; and March 30-June 1, 1865); and brigadier general USV (April 18, 1865, to rank from December 6, 1864). With the 37th New York, he fought at Yorktown, Williamsburg, Seven Pines, Malvern Hill, 2nd Bull Run, and Chantilly. Given command of a new regiment in the fall of 1862, he was wounded and captured while commanding it against Stonewall Jackson's flank attack at Chancellorsville. Although paroled almost immediately, he was not formally exchanged until October. He rejoined his regiment which was sent to help relieve besieged Chattanooga. His regiment was only lightly engaged in the resulting battle. During the Atlanta campaign he was temporarily incapacitated by injuries received at Rocky Face Ridge but later commanded the brigade for much of the rest of the campaign. He went on to command the brigade in the Savannah Campaign and part of the Carolinas Campaign. Resigning at the end of the war, he resumed the practice of law and held several appointive offices. (Drunkelman, Mark H. and Winey, Michael J., *The Hardtack Regiment*)

JONES, Robert McDonald (1808-1872)

A Choctaw Indian and large plantation owner—with an estimated 500 slaves—Robert M. Jones was for economic reasons very inclined to the Confederacy. He was the principal negotiator for his tribe in its dealings with Albert Pike, the Confederate Indian commissioner. He signed the treaty of alliance and was named as the non-voting representative of both his own tribe and the Chickasaws in the Confederate Congress. He was admitted on January 17, 1863, but held no committee assignments. When his term expired he was supposed to have made way for a representative from the Chickasaws, but they had already returned to their allegiance with the Union. So Jones continued in office for a second term. Before his admission to Congress he had raised a battalion of Choctaws for Confederate service at his own expense. He represented the tribe in negotiations in Washington after the Confederacy's collapse. He then returned to his devastated plantation.

JONES, Samuel (?-1864)

A private in Company B, 5th United States Colored Troops, Samuel Jones got caught up in the dispute between Union and Confederate officers over the question of whether certain parties were guerrillas or legitimate recruiting officers operating in contested territory. He lost his life as a result. His unit had been raised in Ohio and he had been captured during Edward A. Wild's raid into northeastern North Carolina in December 1863. (See also: Bright, Daniel)

JONES, Samuel (1819-1887)

West Pointer (1841) and veteran of two decades in the artillery, Samuel Jones served the Confederacy in most of the major theaters. He resigned his commission as captain on April 27, 1861, to change his allegiance. His assignments included: colonel, Artillery (early 1861); brigadier general, CSA (July 21, 1861); commanding brigade, 2nd Corps, Army of the Potomac (summer-fall 1861); commanding brigade, G.W. Smith's Division, Potomac District, Department of Northern Virginia (October 22, 1861-January 10, 1862); commanding Army of Pensacola, Department of Alabama and West Florida (January 27-March 3, 1862); commanding the department (March 3-24 and April 2-28, 1862); major general, CSA (March 10, 1862); commanding 1st Division, Army of the West, Department No. 2 (May-June 1862); commanding Hindman's (old) Division, 2nd Corps, Army of the Mississippi, Department No. 2 (June 1862); commanding the corps (June-July 1862); commanding District of Middle Tennessee, Department No. 2 (September 27-November 4, 1862); commanding Department of Western Virginia (December 10, 1862-March 5, 1864); commanding Department of South Carolina, Georgia and Florida (April 20-October 5, 1864); commanding District of South Carolina (also called a division), same department (October 17-December 1864); and commanding District of Florida, same department (February 2-May 1865). After serving as Beauregard's chief artillerist at 1st Bull Run and commanding a brigade in northern Virginia he was assigned to the Gulf coast. He next served in northern Mississippi and middle Tennessee before being assigned to command in western Virginia. Here he guarded supply sources and lines and quibbled with Lee over certain regiments and to whom they belonged. Sent to the southern coast, he apparently initiated the keeping of prisoners within the range of the guns bombarding Charleston. This led to a series of retaliations to no purpose. He finished the war in Florida. After the war he was a farmer and government clerk. (Jones, Samuel, *The Siege of Charleston*)

JONES, Thomas (ca. 1821-1895)

At the behest of his foster brother, Samuel Cox, Jr., Thomas Jones provided the boat that ferried John Wilkes Booth and David Herold across the Potomac River in their flight from Washington. During the Civil War, being of Southern leanings, he had been in charge of a signal station along the river which reported the movements of federal shipping. He was introduced to Booth in a thicket near his foster brother's home and agreed to help. His first assignments were in gathering information on the public reaction to the assassination. In addition to bringing back newspapers he gathered local opinion. He himself believed the assassination to have been a great act, but later felt that it had badly hurt the South. Never prosecuted for his role in the escape, he did however lose his subsequent job in the Washington Navy Yard for political reasons.

JONES, William Edmondson (1824-1864)

Former regular army officer William E. "Grumble" Jones lived up to his nickname in his feud with his superior, Jeb Stuart, and the latter had the subordinate court-martialed for disrespect. A West Pointer (1848), Jones had served almost a decade in the mounted riflemen until he resigned to manage his estate in southwestern Virginia. His Confederate assignments included: captain, Washington Mounted Rifles (spring 1861); major, Virginia Volunteers (May 1861); colonel, 1st Virginia Cavalry (September 24, 1861); colonel, 7th Virginia Cavalry (ca. June 1862); brigadier general, CSA (September 19, 1862); commanding Laurel Brigade, Cavalry Division, Army of Northern Virginia (November 8, 1862-September 9, 1863 but detached in the Valley District fall 1862-spring 1863); also commanding Valley District, Department of Northern Virginia (December 29, 1862-May 1863); commanding brigade, Hampton's Division, Cavalry Corps, Army of Northern Virginia (September 9-October 9, 1863); commanding cavalry brigade, Ransom's Division, Department of Western Virginia (October 1863-February 1864 but detached with Longstreet in East Tennessee in November and December); commanding brigade, Cavalry, Department of East Tennessee (February-March and April-May 1864); commanding division, Cavalry Corps, same department (March-April 1864); commanding cavalry brigade, Department of Western Virginia (May 1864 and June 1-5, 1864); and temporarily commanding the department (May 25-31, 1864). After serving in western Virginia, he succeeded Jeb Stuart in command of the 1st Virginia Cavalry, but his strict old army discipline cost him his chance of reelection at the spring 1862 reorganization. However, he was soon given charge of a portion of Ashby's cavalry and fought at Cedar Mountain and 2nd Bull Run. Promoted to brigadier, he led the Laurel Brigade in the Valley and on a raid to Beverly in western Virginia. He joined Lee's army for the Gettysburg Campaign but did not shine. His feud with Stuart coming to the fore, he was deprived of his command and sent to southwestern Virginia to organize cavalry. He directed a brigade there and in the Knoxville campaign. After a brief stint in departmental command he was in overall command in the fighting at Piedmont on June 5, 1864, and was killed. (Freeman, Douglas S., *Lee's Lieutenants* and McDonald, William N., *A History of the Laurel Brigade*)

JORDAN, Thomas (1819-1895)

Although a Confederate brigadier, Thomas Jordan rarely commanded troops in the field. An 1840 graduate of West Point, where he had roomed with William Sherman, he served in the infantry and as a quartermaster until he resigned his captaincy on May 21, 1861. His assignments for the Confederacy included: colonel and assistant adjutant general (early 1861); brigadier general, CSA (April 14, 1862); and commanding 3rd Military District of South Carolina, Department of South Carolina, Georgia and Florida (May 1864). On the staff of Beauregard, the Virginian served at 1st Bull Run, Shiloh, and in the Corinth siege. In the summer of 1862 he was on Bragg's staff but soon rejoined his old chief on the Southern coast. Here he participated in the defense of Charleston. He briefly commanded a district in May 1864 but mostly performed vital staff work. However, his connection with Beauregard did not make him a favorite of the president and his circle. When Richmond was threatened late in September 1864, he tendered his services as he was temporarily in the city, but the offer went unanswered. For a time he edited the *Memphis Appeal* after the war and in 1869 joined the revolutionaries in Cuba. With the revolt's collapse he returned to the United States and resumed writing. Several of his articles appear in *Battles and Leaders*.

JUAREZ, Benito (1806-1872)

In 1861, at the outbreak of the American Civil War, the president of Mexico, Benito Juarez, announced a two-year moratorium on the payment of Mexico's national debt. This prompted a joint military operation by the British, Spanish, and French. After her allies had departed, France maintained a presence and eventually forced Juarez out and placed Archduke Maximilian of Austria on an imperial throne. Juarez, the former president, became the leader of the republican revolutionary forces and received aid from the United States, which feared possible French intervention on behalf of the Confederacy. Juarez in return prohibited trade with the South. After the Civil War in the United States, the French withdrew their troops and Maximilian soon fell, being executed in 1867. Juarez again became president and held office until his death.

JUDAH, Henry Moses (1821-1866)

His handling of troops in the field was not up to the level expected of a brigadier general, so Henry M. Judah was relegated to the rear areas of the war. The Maryland-born son of a Connecticut minister received his West Point appointment from New York and upon his 1843 graduation was posted to the infantry. He served on the West Coast and won two brevets in the Mexican War. His Civil War-era assignments included: captain, 4th Infantry (since September 29, 1853); colonel, 4th California (September 6, 1861); brigadier general, USV (March 21, 1862); acting inspector general, Army of the Tennessee (April 12-July 16, 1862); also commanding 1st Division, Army of the Tennessee (May 3-14, 1862); major, 4th Infantry (June 30, 1862); acting inspector general, Department of the Ohio (October 10, 1862-February 25, 1863); commanding 3rd Division, 23rd Corps, Department of the Ohio (June 24-August 6, 1863); commanding 2nd Division, 23rd Corps, Army of the Ohio (January 26-May 18, 1864); commanding 1st Brigade, 2nd Separate Division, District of the Etowah, Department of the Cumberland (March 15-September 1865); and also commanding the division (temporarily March 1865). Serving as an inspector with Grant's army, he also commanded a division during a part of the advance on Corinth, Mississippi. After a few months in command of training camps in Kentucky he became the inspector for the Department of the Ohio. In command of a division, he took part in the pursuit of John Hunt Morgan during his raid north of the Ohio. He was apparently found wanting and he was thereafter given commands in Kentucky and Tennessee, well behind the lines, or administrative duties, for the balance of the war. His division of the Army of the Ohio was one that was not taken along on the Atlanta Campaign. Mustered out of the volunteer service on August 24, 1865, he reverted to his regular army grade of major, 4th Infantry. Having been brevetted to colonel in that service for the war, he was assigned to command at Plattsburgh, New York, where he died on January 14, 1866.

JULIAN, George Washington (1817-1899)

As a Radical Republican on the Joint Committee on the Conduct of the War, George W. Julian believed that the Union defeats early in the war were due to the Democratic generals at the head of the major field forces. The native Indianan lawyer entered the state legislature in 1845 and served one term, 1849-51, in Congress as a free-soil representative. He lost his bid for reelection and the next year was the party's candidate for vice president. Joining the Republicans by 1856, he served in the House of Representatives from 1861 to 1871. As one of four House members on the committee—there were three from the Senate—he was one of its driving forces. His speeches in and out of the committee room could be rather blunt. In 1863 he declared, "Democratic polity, in the year of 1861, gave us as commanders of our three great military departments McClellan, Halleck, and Buell, whose military administrations have so terribly cursed the country while it impressed upon our volunteer forces in the field such officers as Fitz-John Porter, General Nelson, General Stone, and many more whose sympathy with the rebels were well known throughout the country." This was just an example of the partisanship pervading the panel. In the late 1890s he spent four years as New

Mexico's surveyor general. (Riddleberger, Patrick W., *George Washington Julian, Radical Republican*)

JUMPER, John (?-?)

A pure-blood Seminole, John Jumper was a chief of the old treaty faction of the tribe, part of the Five Civilized Tribes, dating back to the removal west of the Mississippi River. Having adopted many of the white Southerner's ways, he urged many of his fellow tribesmen to agree to the treaty with the Confederacy being negotiated by Albert Pike. When a sizeable portion of the nation agreed, Jumper organized the 1st Seminole Battalion on September 21, 1861, and became first its major and later its lieutenant colonel. In 1864 the battalion was increased to a regiment with Jumper as colonel. In November and December 1861, Jumper and his men took part in the pursuit of Opothleyohola of the Upper Creeks who was leading his people and some non-Confederate Cherokees and Seminoles to Kansas and Union protection. The remainder of his Civil War service was in the Indian Territory and along the borders of Kansas, Missouri, and Arkansas. (Monoghan, Jay, *Civil War on the Western Border, 1854-1865*)

K

KANE, Thomas Leiper (1822-1883)

Morally opposed to the Fugitive Slave Act, Thomas L. Kane resigned his post as a U.S. commissioner and found himself in jail for contempt of court—sent there by his own father. The Philadelphia native had been educated in the United States and in Paris and had become a dedicated abolitionist. The requirement that he aid in the return of escaped slaves prompted Kane to submit his resignation which was construed by his father, a judge, as an insult to the court. Freed by an order of the Supreme Court, he joined the Underground Railroad and was associated with the Mormons. During the Utah Expedition of 1858 he was instrumental in avoiding armed conflict with the army. Returning to Pennsylvania, he raised a regiment for the Civil War and became its second-in-command at his own request due to his lack of military experience. His assignments included: lieutenant colonel, 13th Pennsylvania Reserves (June 21, 1861); brigadier general, USV (September 7, 1862); commanding 2nd Brigade, 1st Division, 12th Corps, Army of the Potomac (October 6, 1862-March 21, 1863); and commanding 2nd Brigade, 2nd Division, 12th Corps, Army of the Potomac (March 21-May 7 and July 2, 1863). In his first significant action—at the head of his unit which was also known as the "Bucktails" or 1st Pennsylvania Rifles—he was slightly wounded at Dranesville. Participating in the Shenandoah Valley Campaign he was wounded and captured at Harrisonburg on June 6, 1862. Exchanged on August 16, 1862, he took command of a 12th Corps brigade in October and the previous month was awarded a brigadier's star. His corps was not at Fredericksburg but he fought at Chancellorsville. A few days after that fight he was forced to relinquish command due to pneumonia. He did return to the field on the second day at Gettysburg—allegedly from a Baltimore hospital bed—but was forced to again give up his command later the same day. His resignation, for health reasons, was accepted on November 7, 1863. In the omnibus brevet promotions bill of March 13, 1865, he was brevetted major general for his efforts at Gettysburg. Retiring to the town he had founded before the war—Kane, Pennsylvania—and later to his birthplace, he was active in business, writing, and charitable work.

KARGÉ, Joseph (?-1892)

One of the numerous refugees from the 1848 uprising's in Europe, Joseph Kargé immigrated to the United States a decade before the Civil War; he rose to the rank of brevet brigadier general, having raised and trained two regiments of volunteer cavalry for the conflict. A young officer in the Prussian Royal Horse Guard, he had been arrested for his role in the liberal revolutionary movement. By 1851, he had fled to the United States where he ran a private school. With the coming of the Civil War, he offered his services and his assignments included: lieutenant colonel, Halsted's Horse (October 18, 1861); lieutenant colonel, 1st New Jersey Cavalry (change of designation February 19, 1862); colonel, 2nd New Jersey Cavalry (September 25, 1863); commanding 1st Brigade, 1st Cavalry Division, 16th Corps, Army of the Tennessee (April 27-May 11, 1864); commanding 1st Brigade, 2nd Division, Cavalry Corps, District of West Tennessee, Army of the Tennessee (June-July and August 17-November 1864); commanding 2nd Brigade, 4th Division, Cavalry Corps, Military Division of the Mississippi (November 9-December 1864); commanding 1st Brigade, 1st Division, Cavalry Corps, Military Division of West Mississippi (March 15-April 14, 1865); and commanding 2nd Brigade, 1st Division, Cavalry Corps, Department of the Gulf (April 17-June 1, 1865). His initial regiment was raised by special order of the War Department and it was not designated a New Jersey outfit until early 1862. During the Shenandoah Valley Campaign Kargé assumed command of the regiment upon the capture of Colonel Percy Wyndham. Continuing at the head of the unit until his resignation on December 22, 1862, he fought at Cedar Mountain, 2nd Bull Run—where he was wounded—and Fredericksburg. He took several months in raising a new regiment and was named its commander late the next year. Sent to West Tennessee, he was frequently in brigade command there and in Mississippi in operations against Nathan Bedford Forrest. He saw action at Okolona and Brice's Crossroads. Taking part in a number of Benjamin H. Grierson's lesser-known mounted raids, he finished the war in the actions against Fort Blakely near Mobile. Mustered out with his regiment on November 1, 1865, he was brevetted for his war service. Two years later he was a cavalry first lieutenant in the regular army but was soon transferred to the infantry. Mustered out at the beginning at 1871, he became a Princeton language professor. (Kajencki, Francis C., *Star On Many a Battlefield*)

KAUTZ, August Valentine (1828-1895)

Pre-Civil War infantry officer August V. Kautz became a cavalryman during the conflict but proved somewhat unsuccessful and completed the war as, again, an infantry commander. Born in Pforzheim, Baden, he was taken as an infant to Ohio. Serving as a private in the 1st Ohio during the Mexican War, he won an appointment to West Point in 1848. Graduating four years later he was posted to the infantry. Seeing some heavy Indian fighting on the Pacific coast, he was wounded in Oregon in 1855 and again the next year in Washington. His Civil War assignments included: first lieutenant, 4th Infantry (since December 4, 1855); captain, 3rd Cavalry (May 14, 1861); captain, 6th Cavalry (designation change August 3, 1861); colonel, 2nd Ohio Cavalry (September 2, 1862); commanding Cavalry Brigade, District of Central Kentucky, Department of the Ohio (April-June 1863); commanding 3rd (Cavalry) Brigade, 1st Division, 23rd Corps, Department of the Ohio (June 24-August 6, 1863); chief of cavalry, Department of the Ohio (November-December 1863); commanding Cavalry Division, Army of the James (April 28-October 23, 1864 and November 5, 1864-March 11, 1865); brigadier general, USV (May 7, 1864); and commanding 1st Division, 25th Corps, Army of the James (March 27-May 4, 1865). With his regular army mounted unit he took part in the operations on Virginia's Peninsula and after the Seven Days was named to command a volunteer cavalry regiment. He then served on the Kansas-Missouri border and at Camp Chase, Ohio. In a skirmish at Monticello, Kentucky, on June 9, 1863, he won a regular army brevet and then went on to face John Hunt Morgan's raid north of the Ohio. Transferred to the East, he became the cavalry commander for the Army of the James and took part in the operations against Richmond and Petersburg. Taking part in the numerous raids against enemy lines of communications, he failed to score any major successes. Nonetheless he was awarded three brevets during the campaign including that of major general of volunteers on October 28, 1864. However just before the final offensive it was decided to give him command of a black infantry division instead. His troops were among the first to occupy the Confederate capital. Brevetted both brigadier and major general for the war in the regular army, he was mustered out of the volunteers on January 15, 1866. In the meantime he had been one of the commissioners at the trial of the Lincoln conspirators. Remaining in the army, he rose to brigadier general while serving mostly on the frontier and finally retired in 1892.

KEAN, Robert Garlick Hill (1828-1898)

For the final three years of the Confederacy's life Virginia lawyer Robert G.H. Kean served as the head of the War Department's Bureau of War. A longtime backer of states' rights, he became an early believer in secession and, when the Civil War came, promptly enlisted. When his father-in-law George W. Randolph was promoted to brigadier general, Kean joined his staff as assistant adjutant general. He then followed his relative into the War Department and succeeded Albert T. Bledsoe in the Bureau of War. Holding the post until the fall of the would-be nation, he served under several secretaries of war and then returned to his practice. (Younger, Edward, ed., *Inside the Confederate Government: The Diary of Robert Garlick Hill Kean*)

KEARNY, Philip (1815-1862)

Honored in death by both sides, a combat veteran on three continents, Philip Kearny was one of the abler Union officers early in the Civil War. His wealthy New York City family denied him a military career, and he became a lawyer until the death of his grandfather made him a millionaire. He then secured a commission as a lieutenant of dragoons and was dispatched to study at France's Saumur cavalry school. He volunteered for Algerian service with the Chasseurs d'Afrique and earned France's Legion of Honor. He then served as a staff officer with U.S. generals-in-chief Alexander Macomb and Winfield Scott. Leading his company in Mexico, he lost his left arm at Churubusco. Brevetted major for that conflict, he resigned as a captain in 1851—having seen some service in the meantime against Indians in the Far West—and again headed for Europe. With Napoleon III's army he fought in Italy and was particularly distinguished at Magenta and Solferino. After fighting in the Crimea he returned to the United States for the Civil War. His assignments included: brigadier general, USV (August 7, 1861, to rank from May 17); commanding brigade, Division of the Potomac (August 17-October 3, 1861); commanding 1st Brigade, Franklin's Division, Army of the Potomac (October 3, 1861-March 13, 1862); commanding 1st Brigade, 1st Division, 1st Corps, Army of the Potomac (March 13-April 4, 1862); commanding 1st Brigade, 1st Division, Department of the Rappahannock (April 4-ca. 30, 1862); commanding 3rd Division, 3rd Corps, Army of the Potomac (April 30-August 5, 1862); major general, USV (July 4, 1862); and commanding 1st Division, 3rd Corps, Army of the Potomac (August 5-September 1, 1862). Given charge of a brigade of New Jersey troops, he served initially in northern Virginia before taking over a division on the Peninsula late in the operations against Yorktown. He fought ably at Williamsburg, Seven Pines, and during the Seven Days and was rewarded with a second star just after the close of the campaign. While in division command he devised the so-called Kearny patch to identify the men of his division. After his death this was expanded into the system of corps badges which eventually covered most of the Union forces. With the failure of the Peninsula Campaign, his division, along with other Army of the Potomac units, was sent to reinforce John Pope in northern Virginia. He fought at 2nd Bull Run and in the rear guard action at Chantilly. In the latter action he rode into the enemy lines and fled when called upon to surrender. A volley from the 55th Virginia ended his military adventures. The enemy division commander, Ambrose P. Hill, expressed regrets at the manner of his death and Lee later sent Kearny's horse and equipment to the widow. In his honor a medal and cross were devised for the officers and men, respectively, of the division who distinguished themselves. (Werstein, Irving, *Kearny the Magnificent*)

KEENAN, Peter (?-1863)

At a crucial point in the fighting at Chancellorsville a Union cavalry officer Peter Keenan, was ordered to make a suicidal charge to gain time for the Northern line to stabilize. He died in the attempt. His earlier assignments included: captain, 8th Pennsylvania Cavalry (ca. late 1861); and major, 8th Pennsylvania Cavalry (late 1862). His regiment fought at Yorktown, Seven Pines, the Seven Days, Antietam—where he commanded it—and Fredericksburg. Then came the fatal day when it served as part of the small brigade of cavalry that was left with the main army while the rest of the corps took part in Stoneman's raid. In the latter stages of Stonewall Jackson's attack on the federal right, General Alfred Pleasonton, the division commander who was also left behind, noticed a Southern force advancing on Hazel Grove. The grove was a point which would command the Union center. Pleasonton saw Keenan's command approaching and ordered a last-ditch charge. The major complied—he and many of his men being killed—while the general rounded up 20 artillery pieces to stop the Confederates. (Stackpole, Edward J., *Chancellorsville: Lee's Greatest Battle*)

KEENE, John (?-1865)

A resident of Memphis at the outbreak of the Civil War, John Keene was a criminal wanted by both sides, but it was a miners' court which finally got him. Enlisting in the Confederate navy, he fled after striking his captain on the head with a marlinespike. On his way back to Memphis, he killed one or two men. Back in Union-controlled Memphis, he was safe from Confederate authorities, but he soon got on the wrong side of the occupation forces by killing another man. Under the name Bob Black, he headed a band of cutthroats who pillaged the countryside and kept troops busy hunting them. Caught and confined, he made good his escape and became a fence in St. Paul, Minnesota. When the heat got too much for him he headed to Utah but soon had to flee to Montana where his association with the Innocents bandit gang earned him a notice to leave or face lynching. Instead, he shot a sleeping enemy. Within an hour of his sentencing by the miners he was swinging from a nearby tree.

KEENE, Laura (1826-1873)

Under the stage-name of Laura Keene an English actress really had only one connection with the Civil War: She starred in the show which lured Abraham Lincoln to the scene of his murder. She had made her American debut in 1852 and was a pioneer as a woman manager until 1863. It was one of her more popular performances as the female lead in *Our American Cousin* which had drawn the president to Ford's Theater in April 1865. Her career was already in decline but she continued to work as a playwright, editor, actor, and lecturer until her sudden death, said to have been from overwork. (Creahan, John, *The Life of Laura Keene*)

KEIFER, Joseph Warren (1836-1932)

Only a general officer by brevet during the Civil War, Ohio lawyer J. Warren Keifer attained the full rank of major general of volunteers during the Spanish-American War. His Civil War assignments included: major, 3rd Ohio (April 27, 1861); lieutenant colonel, 3rd Ohio (February 12, 1862); colonel, 110th Ohio (September 30, 1862); commanding 2nd Brigade, 3rd Division, 3rd Corps, Army of the Potomac (July 10-August 14, 1863 and September 14, 1863-March 24, 1864); commanding 2nd Brigade, 3rd Division, 6th Corps, Army of the Shenandoah (August 26-October 16 and October 19-December 6, 1864); commanding the division (October 16-19, 1864) and commanding 2nd Brigade, 3rd Division, 6th Corps, Army of the Potomac (December 6-29, 1864 and February 8-June 28, 1865). After initial service in the West Virginia fighting of 1861, he took part in the campaigning in Kentucky, Tennessee, and Alabama. Taking command of a new regiment, he fought at 2nd Winchester and then the regiment moved to Washington. Joining the Army of the Potomac just after Gettysburg, the regiment was detached to cope with the New York draft riots before returning for the Bristoe and Mine Run campaigns. During the Overland Campaign it fought at the Wilderness, Spotsylvania, North Anna, and Cold Harbor. After a period in the trenches before Petersburg, Keifer commanded a brigade in the Shenandoah Valley Campaign where he earned a brevet as brigadier for 3rd Winchester, Fisher's Hill, and Cedar Creek. Returning to the main front, he was awarded another brevet for the Appomattox Campaign. Mustered out on June 12, 1865, he was a banker, legislator, and congressman and was back in uniform for the war with Spain.

KEIM, William High (1813-1862)

A Pennsylvania politician with a lifelong career in the state militia, William H. Keim died, apparently of dysentery, before he could really demonstrate any military merit. He was a former mayor of Reading and a former congressman, serving as surveyor general of the state when he was called up for military service. His assignments included: major general, Pennsylvania Volunteers (April 20, 1861); commanding 2nd Division, Department of Pennsylvania (April 27-July 21, 1861); brigadier general, USV (December 20, 1861); commanding 2nd Brigade, Casey's Division, Army of the Potomac (December 1861-March 13, 1862); and commanding 2nd Brigade, 3rd Division, 4th Corps, Army of the Potomac (March 13-May 18, 1862). His initial service was unspectacular when as second in command of General Patterson's campaign in the

Shenandoah Valley he was part of the failure to stop Joe Johnston from reinforcing Beauregard for the fight at 1st Bull Run. A few days later, July 21, 1861, he was mustered out upon the expiration of the three-months term of enlistment of the Pennsylvania volunteers. However, in December he received an appointment in the national volunteers and commanded a brigade at Yorktown and Williamsburg. By the time he wrote his report of the latter he was already seriously ill and he died on May 18, 1862 while in Harrisburg, Pennsylvania.

KEITT, Lawrence Massillon (1824-1864)

A longtime supporter of states' rights, even to the extent of South Carolina seceding alone, Lawrence Keitt had served in the U.S. House of Representatives until the South Carolina Secession convention, of which he was a member, voted the state out of the Union. During the first year of the new nation he was a member of the Confederate Provisional Congress, serving on the Foreign Affairs, Indian Affairs and Rules committees. In this body he was a frequent critic of Jefferson Davis and is said to have despised him; he supported Howell Cobb for the presidency. He was also instrumental in the drafting of the Confederate Constitution. He favored an early attack on Fort Sumter. With the Provisional Congress coming to an end, Keitt was elected colonel, 20th South Carolina, on January 11, 1862. With this unit he served on the South Carolina coast, mostly in Charleston Harbor, until ordered to Virginia in mid-May 1864. Arriving on the South Anna River, the 20th was assigned to Kershaw's (old) Brigade, Kershaw's Division, First Corps, Army of Northern Virginia, about May 28. With Kershaw commanding the division, Keitt was the senior officer present in the brigade, the other regiments having suffered heavily in three years of arduous service. Four days later the inexperienced combat officer led the brigade in the battle of Cold Harbor. Kershaw's and Hoke's divisions were to make a major attack but Keitt, needlessly mounted, failed to keep his command in order and the entire effort collapsed. In trying to rally his regiment before the confusion spread to other units, Keitt fell mortally wounded. (Dickert, D. Augustus, *History of Kershaw's Brigade*)

KELL, John McIntosh (1823-1900)

A veteran of 17 years in the old navy, John M. Kell joined the Southern navy and served mostly under Raphael Semmes on commerce raiders. The Georgia-born graduate of Annapolis had served in the Mexican War and sailed to Paraguay and Japan. He resigned his lieutenant's commission at the outbreak of the war, and his Confederate assignments included: lieutenant, CSN (early 1861); executive officer, CSS *Sumter* (April 18, 1861-early 1862); executive officer, CSS *Alabama* (August 24, 1862-1864); commanding CSS *Richmond* (early 1864); and commander, CSN (1864). He took part in the famous cruises of the *Sumter* and *Alabama* as a first lieutenant and then was placed in charge of the ironclad *Richmond* in the James River. In this latter capacity he took part in the operations near Drewry's Bluff. After the fall of the Confederacy he took up farming in his native state. In the year of his death he published his memoirs, *Recollections of a Naval Life*, one of the prime sources of information on Confederate commerce raiders. (Delaney, Norman C., *John McIntosh Kell of the Raider* Alabama)

KELLEY, Benjamin Franklin (1807-1891)

In charge of protecting the Baltimore and Ohio Railroad from rebel raiders, Benjamin Kelley instead ended up as a rebel prisoner. Kelley had been an employee of the railroad for 10 years before the war, when he raised the 1st Virginia, a loyal regiment. Appointed its colonel, on May 22, 1861, he led it in the Union victory at Philippi, where he was wounded. Returning to duty, he was promoted brigadier general, USV, to rank from May 17, 1861, as part of the first group of brigadiers in the volunteer service. His commands included: Kelley's Command, Army of Occupation—West Virginia, Department of the Ohio (May-August 1861); Railroad District, in the Department of West Virginia (October 11, 1861-March 11, 1862), in the Mountain Department (March 11-June 26, 1862), in the 8th Corps, Middle Department (July 22-September 20, 1862), and in the Department of the Ohio (September 20, 1862-January 5, 1863); Defenses Upper Potomac, 8th Corps, Middle Department (January 5-March 27, 1863); 1st Division, 8th Corps, Middle Department (March 27-June 26, 1863); Department of West Virginia (June 26, 1863-March 10, 1864); and Forces West of Sleepy Creek, Department of West Virginia (April 1864-February 21, 1865). After recovering from his wound, Kelley was responsible for the protection of the rail line for most of the war. He was engaged with portions of his command at Cumberland, Moorefield, and New Creek. He was brevetted major general on August 5, 1864. On the night of February 21-22, 1865, Confederate Lieutenant Jesse McNeill with 62 partisan rangers rode into Cumberland, Maryland, Kelley's headquarters, and captured him and his superior, General George Crook. After a brief stay in Libby Prison, he was exchanged in March and resigned on June 1, 1865. After the war, he was a political appointee in numerous posts.

KELLY, John Herbert (1840-1864)

Resigning from West Point upon the outbreak of the secession crisis, Alabamian John H. Kelly became the youngest Confederate general upon his appointment in late 1863. He had been enrolled in the class of June 1861 when he withdrew on December 29, 1860. Joining the South, his assignments included: second lieutenant, Artillery (early 1861); captain and assistant adjutant general (October 5, 1861); major, 9th Arkansas Battalion (September 23, 1861); colonel, 8th Arkansas (May 7, 1862); commanding brigade, Preston's Division, Buckner's Corps, Army of Tennessee (September 1863); commanding division, Wheeler's Cavalry Corps, Army of Tennessee (October 1863-September 2, 1864); and brigadier general, CSA (November 16, 1863). He initially served on William J. Hardee's staff in Arkansas and then accompanied him to central Kentucky as a battalion commander. He fought at Shiloh and his battalion was shortly thereafter merged into an existing regiment and he became its colonel. As such he took part in the operations around Corinth, and fought at Perryville. Wounded at Murfreesboro, he returned to lead a brigade at Chickamauga and soon won promotion to brigadier general. Assigned to Wheeler's cavalry, he directed a mounted division throughout the Atlanta Campaign and then went on a raid into Tennessee. Mortally wounded near Franklin, apparently on September 2, 1864, he died two days later.

KELLY, Patrick (?-1864)

A native of Ireland, Patrick Kelly died at the head of the Union army's Irish Brigade. His assignments included: captain, 69th New York Militia (May 9, 1861); captain, 16th Infantry (October 26, 1861); lieutenant colonel, 88th New York (September 14, 1861); colonel, 88th New York (October 20, 1862); and commanding 2nd ("Irish") Brigade, 1st Division, 2nd Corps, Army of the Potomac (December 20, 1862-February 18, 1863, May 8, 1863-January 12, 1864, and June 3-16, 1864). After fighting as a company commander at 1st Bull Run he was mustered out with his militia regiment on August 3, 1861. Commissioned at the same rank in one of the regular army's new infantry regiments, he earned a brevet of major for his role at Shiloh. Shortly thereafter he accepted a previously tendered appointment as the second-in-command of one of the regiments of the Irish Brigade. Joining his regiment, he led it at Seven Pines and Antietam before being made colonel. He then fought at Fredericksburg and Chancellorsville. He then led the decimated brigade in the actions at Gettysburg, Bristoe Station, and in the Mine Run Campaign. He again led his regiment in the Overland Campaign, succeeding to command of the brigade during the disastrous assault at Cold Harbor. Two weeks later, on June 16, 1864, he fell in one of the early assaults at Petersburg. (Conyngham, David Powers, *The Irish Brigade and Its Campaigns*)

KEMPER, James Lawson (1823-1895)

A Virginia lawyer with a meager experience in military matters, gained as a regimental quartermaster and an assistant quartermaster of volunteers in the Mexican War, James L. Kemper had served as chairman of the military affairs committee in the Virginia legislature before the Civil War. When he entered the Confederate army his assignments included: colonel, 7th Virginia (May 2, 1861); commanding A.P. Hill's (old) Brigade, Longstreet's Division (in the 1st Corps from June 29), Army of Northern Virginia (May 27-July 1862); brigadier general, CSA (June 3, 1862); commanding division, 1st Corps, same army (August-September 1862); commanding brigade, Jones' Division, same corps and army (September-October 1862); commanding brigade, Pickett's Division, in 1st Corps, Army of Northern Virginia (October 1862-February 25 and May-July 3, 1863), in the Department of Virginia and North Carolina (February 25-April 1, 1863), and in the Department of Southern Virginia (April 1-May 1863); and major general, CSA (September 19, 1864). After fighting at 1st Bull Run, Yorktown, and Williamsburg, he took over Hill's former command. He fought through the Seven Days Battles and then commanded a temporary division, formed from half of Longstreet's

James L. Kemper, a survivor of Pickett's Charge. (NA)

old command, at 2nd Bull Run. This force was merged into Jones' Division before Antietam and later became part of Pickett's Divison. Lightly engaged at Fredericksburg, he participated in the southeastern Virginia campaign under Longstreet. At Gettysburg he was severely wounded and captured in Pickett's Charge. Exchanged in September 1863, he returned to duty in May 1864 and was assigned to organize the reserve forces of Virginia. He finished the war in this post and resumed his legal and political careers, becoming governor in 1874. (Freeman, Douglas S., *Lee's Lieutenants*)

KENEALY, Jim (?-?)

At the head of his band of counterfeiters, Big Jim Kenealy devised a plan in 1876 to steal the body of the martyred president, Abraham Lincoln. Once the casket was in their possession, they would contact the authorities with a ransom demand. When they got their money they would unearth the coffin from its hiding place and return it. They never got that far. Their group had been infiltrated by a Secret Service informer working on counterfeiting matters, and the Secret Service was notified. Agents arrived just as the plotters were about to remove the casket. Fleeing, they were all caught within 10 days. Big Jim then informed the authorities that there was no law against stealing a corpse, no matter whose it was. The prosecutors knew he was right but countered by charging them with the attempted theft of the casket. Each got the maximum sentence of one year for their plot. This event and several other similar attempts resulted in the casket being moved from one hiding place to another 17 times from 1865-1901.

KENLY, John Reese (1818-1891)

During the Shenandoah Valley Campaign of 1862, Baltimorean John R. Kenly became a victim of one Stonewall Jackson's surprise maneuvers and lightning-quick marches. Admitted to the state bar, he had also been active in the militia and served as a captain and later major of Maryland and District of Columbia volunteers in Mexico. In the interwar years he returned to his practice but again donned a uniform in 1861. His assignments included: colonel, 1st Maryland (June 11, 1861); brigadier general, USV (August 22, 1862); commanding Maryland Brigade, 8th Corps, Middle Department (September 17, 1862-January 5, 1863); commanding Maryland Brigade, Defenses of the Upper Potomac, 8th Corps, Middle Department (January 5-February 1863); also commanding 3rd Division, 1st Corps, Army of the Potomac (January 11-18, 1863); commanding 1st Brigade, 1st Division, 8th Corps, Middle Department (March 27-June 26, 1863); commanding brigade, French's Command, 8th Corps, Middle Department (June 26-July 11, 1863); again commanding 3rd Division, 1st Corps, Army of the Potomac (July 11, 1863-March 24, 1864) commanding District of Delaware, 8th Corps, Middle Department (April 2-May 5, 1864); commanding 3rd Separate Brigade, 8th Corps, Middle Department (May 16-July 20, 1864); commanding brigade, Reserve Division, Department of West Virginia (ca. August 15-ca. October 1864); commanding 1st Separate Brigade, 8th Corps, Middle Department (November 18-December 20, 1864 and June 5-July 31, 1865); commanding District of the Eastern Shore, 8th Corps, Middle Department (December 13, 1864-March 24, 1865); and commanding District of Delaware and the Eastern Shore, 8th Corps, Middle Department (March 24-June 5, 1865). With his loyal Marylanders and some supporting cavalry and artillery, he was in charge of guarding the railroad at Front Royal. Jackson swiftly moved his men through New Market Gap and up the Luray Valley and attacked the post. Most of Kenly's command was captured and their leader fell wounded and was made a prisoner. A week after being exchanged on August 15, 1862, he was given the star of a Union brigadier general and following his return to duty he was placed in charge of a brigade of troops from his native state that moved from the Baltimore defenses to the aid of the Army of the Potomac during the Antietam Campaign. It then moved to Harpers Ferry where Kenly was briefly also in command of a division of the Army of the Potomac. Remaining in the Middle Department during the Fredericksburg and Chancellorsville campaigns, he again rejoined the main army just after the battle of Gettysburg—during which the command had operated against Lee's lines of communications. He remained in charge of a division in the operations in the Bristoe and Mine Run campaigns but lost his command in the spring 1864 reorganization when the 1st Corps ceased to exist. Commanding in Delaware, he pursued Early back to the Shenandoah but, due to his failures there, was again relegated to district command. Brevetted major general for his war service, he was mustered out on August 24, 1865, and retired to his home.

KENNEDY, Anthony (1810-1892)

Although he came from a slaveholding border state and spent three decades of his life in Virginia, Anthony Kennedy was a Unionist. The native Marylander had moved to Virginia in 1821 and became a lawyer and farmer. He served in that state's legislature from 1839 to 1843 and the next year lost a bid for a congressional seat as a Whig. Serving as a magistrate for a decade, he declined a diplomatic post in Cuba in 1850 and the next year returned to his native state. He entered Maryland's legislature in 1856 and the following year was named as a Unionist to the U.S. Senate. His term expired on March 3, 1863, and he did not seek reelection, instead returning to his farm.

KENNEDY, John Doby (1840-1896)

Despite being wounded six times and struck by 15 spent balls, John D. Kennedy managed to survive the Civil War. A young lawyer at the outbreak of hostilities, the South Carolina native entered the Confederate army where his assignments included: captain, Company E, 2nd South Carolina (January 8, 1861); colonel, 2nd South Carolina (May 13, 1862); commanding Kershaw's (old) Brigade, Kershaw's Division, 1st Corps, Army of Northern Virginia (October 1864-January 3, 1865); commanding same brigade, McLaws' Division, Department of South Carolina, Georgia and Florida (January-April 9, 1865); and commanding same brigade, Walthall's Division, Stewart's Corps, Army of Tennessee (April 9-26, 1865). After witnessing the bombardment of Fort Sumter from Morris Island, he went with his company, the Camden Volunteers, to Virginia. There he took part in the fights at 1st Bull Run, Yorktown, Seven Pines, and the Seven Days. After the battle of Savage Station in the latter he was incapacitated. Returning to duty, he was wounded at Antietam but recovered to fight at Fredericksburg and Chancellorsville. He was also wounded at Gettysburg, on the second day, and at Knoxville. Returning to Virginia, he fought at Petersburg and was present during a portion of the Shenandoah Valley Campaign under Early. In early January 1865 the brigade, which he had been commanding since October, for which he received promotion to brigadier in December, was ordered to the Carolinas to help stop Sherman. He fought at Bentonville and was surrendered with Johnston's army. A lawyer and state legislator after the war, he also served as consul general in Shanghai. (Dickert, D. Augustus, *History of Kershaw's Brigade*)

KENNEDY, Robert Cobb (1835-1865)

For his role in the attempt to burn New York City on November 25, 1864, Robert C. Kennedy paid with his life. Born in Georgia, he was raised in Alabama and Louisiana. A member of the West Point class of 1858, he was expelled in 1856 for poor grades and conduct. Running his father's plantation at the outbreak of the Civil War, he joined Company G, 1st Louisiana, on April 30, 1861, and soon became its captain. Wounded at Shiloh, he later served on the staff of General Jospeh Wheeler and while on an errand was captured near Trenton, Georgia, on

October 16, 1863. After nearly a year's captivity at Johnson's Island, Ohio, he made good his escape on the night of October 4, 1864, and made his way to Canada. His escape went unnoticed for some two weeks due to a ruse by his fellow prisoners. Sent by Jacob Thompson, Captain Kennedy and seven others set off for New York with the intention of setting the city aflame on election day. However, Union precautions prompted a delay until the 25th. The fires set in several hotels and P.T. Barnum's Museum proved highly ineffective, and the conspirators returned to Canada. Kennedy later took part in the failed raid to free captured Confederate generals being transferred by train near Buffalo, New York. It was in this misadventure that John Yates Beall was captured. Kennedy himself determined to return to the Confederacy and, with a companion, set off on December 28, 1864. He was captured near Detroit—his companion made good his escape—and was sent to New York for trial, by a military commission headed by General Fitz-Henry Warren, as a spy. Convicted, he was hanged at Fort Lafayette on the following May 25th. (Brandt, Nat, *The Man Who Tried to Burn New York*)

KENNER, Duncan Farrar (1813-1887)

One of the great ironies of the Civil War was the plan of Confederate Congressman Duncan F. Kenner to abolish slavery in order to gain European recognition for the Confederacy—which to a large degree had been established because of slavery. Having studied law, but not practiced, the native Louisianan had become a successful plantation owner and horse breeder. He served in both houses of the state legislature and upon the formation of the Confederacy was named to the Provisional Congress where he served on the committee on Finance and Patents. During both regular congresses he served as chairman of the Committee on Ways and Means, where he favored higher taxes. Realizing that foreign recognition was vital to the survival of his country, he reasoned that the abolition of slavery would achieve that end. Approaching Jefferson Davis, he was, with misgivings, dispatched to Europe to discuss the subject. However, by that time interest in the Confederacy had waned in the face of military failures. His trip via New York in disguise had been for naught. After the war he returned to his devastated plantation, served in the legislature, and was active in supplanting the Radical Republican government in the state. His agricultural operations became even more profitable without slavery and he was active in horse racing. Defeated for the U.S. Senate in 1878, he was on President Arthur's tariff commission four years later.

KEOGH, Myles W. (1842-1876)

One of the most well-remembered of the officers killed at the Little Big Horn, Myles W. Keogh also had a distinguished—albeit mostly forgotten—career as a staff officer in the Civil War. The Irish native had resigned a commission which he had secured in the Italian army, to go to America to join the Union army. His assignments included: captain and additional aide-de-camp, USV (April 9, 1862); aide-de-camp, 2nd Division, Department of the Shenandoah (April-May 1862); aide-de-camp, Shield's Division, Department of the Rappahannock (May-June 1862); aide-de-camp, Army of Virginia (June-September 1862); aide-de-camp, Army of the Potomac (September 1862); aide-de-camp, Reserve Brigade, Cavalry Corps, Army of the Potomac (May 1863); aide-de-camp, 1st Division, Cavalry Corps, Army of the Potomac (May 1863-early 1864); major and aide-de-camp, USV (April 7, 1864); aide-de-camp, Cavalry Division, 23rd Corps, Army of the Ohio (May-July 31, 1864); aide-de-camp, Army of the Ohio (November-December 1864); aide-de-camp to George Stoneman (December 1864-March 1865); and aide-de-camp, District of East Tennessee, Department of the Cumberland (March 9-April 1865). As James Shields' aide he fought in the Shenandoah Valley, especially at Port Republic. As Pope's staff officer he was at 2nd Bull Run and went on to Antietam with McClellan. Moving to the mounted arm the next year, he was on John Buford's staff at Aldie, Beverly Ford, Culpeper, Brandy Station, Gettysburg, Bristoe Station, and Mine Run. Moving to the western theater, he was captured on July 31, 1864, in Stoneman's raid during the Atlanta Campaign. Paroled in September or October, he was at Franklin and Nashville and at the end of the war he participated in Stoneman's raid into North Carolina. Before his September 1, 1866, muster out of the volunteer service he received a second lieutenancy in the 4th Cavalry. But before he could report this was changed to a captaincy in the newly organized 7th Cavalry. The next year he was brevetted major and lieutenant colonel for Gettysburg and Dallas, Georgia. In command of the Seventh's I Troop, he was killed with Custer.

KERSHAW, Joseph Brevard (1822-1894)

A solid brigade and division commander in Lee's army, Joseph B. Kershaw is a fine example of the citizen turned soldier who proves capable despite a tendency to sound off about his abilities. He had served as a first lieutenant of South Carolina troops in the Mexican War, much of the time wracked with fever, before returning to his law career and entering politics. A member of the secession convention in his native South Carolina, he raised a militia regiment which went into state and then Confederate service. His assignments included: colonel, 2nd South Carolina (February 2, 1861); commanding Bonham's (old) Brigade, Van Dorn's (old) Division, Potomac District, Department of Northern Virginia (January 29-April 12, 1862); brigadier general, CSA (February 13, 1862); commanding brigade, McLaw's Divison, Magruder's Command, Army of Northern Virginia (April 12-July 1862); commanding brigade, McLaws' Division, 1st Corps, Army of Northern Virginia (July 1862-September 9, 1863); commanding brigade, McLaws' Division, Longstreet's Corps, Army of Tennessee (September 19-November 5, 1863); commanding the division (September 20, 1863); commanding brigade, McLaws' Division, Department of East Tennessee (November 5-December 17, 1863); commanding the division (December 17, 1863-January and February-April 12, 1864); commanding Division, 1st Corps, Army of Northern Virginia (April 12, 1864-April 6, 1865); and major general, CSA (June 2, to date from May 18, 1864). He was present with the regiment on Morris Island during the bombardment of Fort Sumter. Moving to Virginia, he played a key role at 1st Bull Run but annoyed General Beauregard by not filing a report with him and instead writing an article for a South Carolina newspaper in which it appeared that he won the battle himself. Beauregard later referred to him as "that militia idiot." Despite Beauregard's views, Kershaw went on to command a brigade at Williamsburg, Savage Station in the Seven Days, Antietam, Fredericksburg, Chancellorsville, and Gettysburg. He was especially distinguished at Fredericksburg. Going west with Longstreet, he commanded that portion of the division which arrived in time to fight at Chickamauga. He took part in the Knoxville Campaign and succeeded to division command when McLaws was relieved. Returning to Virginia he was still a brigadier but in charge of the division at the Wilderness where he led a crucial assault on the second day. He also helped save the life of General Longstreet by yelling "Friends!" when he had been wounded by fellow Confederates. He went on to fight at Spotsylvania, Cold Harbor, and around Richmond and Petersburg. Promoted, he led the division to the Shenandoah in late summer and fought at Cedar Creek. Returning to the lines at Richmond, he was captured at Sayler's Creek during the retreat to Appomattox. He was released in July, and later served as a lawyer, state senator, judge, and postmaster in South Carolina. (Dickert, D. Augustus, *History of Kershaw's Brigade*)

KETCHAM, John Henry (1832-1906)

New York politician John H. Ketcham interrupted his political career to enter the Union army after Lincoln's summer 1862 call for more men. During the first year of the war the New York native had sat as a state senator but then raised a regiment. His assignments included: colonel, 150th New York (October 11, 1862); and brigadier general, USV (April 1, 1865). His unit spent several months in the Baltimore defenses before being sent to reinforce the Army of the Potomac in Pennsylvania where it fought on Culp's Hill at Gettysburg. Sent to the West with the 11th and 12th corps, Ketcham was guarding the rail supply lines into Chattanooga during the battles there. As a part of the new 20th Corps, he led his regiment through the Atlanta Campaign, falling wounded before that city. Returning to command during the March to the Sea he was again wounded. On December 6, 1864, he was brevetted brigadier general for his services thus far in the war. In the omnibus promotions of March 13, 1865, he was named brevet major general of volunteers. This was unusual since he had never commanded more than his own regiment. On April 1, 1865, he was promoted to the full rank of brigadier but resigned on December 2, 1865, to take a seat in Congress. He died while serving in his 17th nonconsecutive term.

KETCHUM, William Scott (1813-1871)

Emerging from the Civil War with the rank of brigadier general of volunteers and brevet major general in the regular establishment, William S. Ketchum never served in a combat leadership role. The Connecticut native and West Pointer (1834) had been posted to the infantry but also acquired seven years of experience in the quartermaster's department before the war. His wartime assignments included: major, 4th Infantry (since June 5, 1860); lieutenant colonel, 10th Infantry (November 1, 1861); acting inspector general, Department of the Missouri (March-June 1862); brigadier general, USV (February 3, 1862); and colonel, 11th Infantry (May 6, 1864). His services included recruiting duty in Pennsylvania and administrative duties. He was also given special assignments by the War Department and the quartermaster's branch. On February 1, 1863, he received the brevet of colonel for his services in Missouri and near the end of the conflict was brevetted brigadier and major general for his war service and his special services for the War Department respectively. Mustered out of the volunteers on April 30, 1866, he reverted to his rank as colonel, 11th Infantry, to which he had been promoted during the war in place of the resigned Erasmus D. Keyes. While unassigned in 1870 he was retired. The next year he died, apparently murdered by his boarding house landlady. She was acquitted, but the case received extensive coverage in the newspapers and medical journals of the day.

KEWEN, Edward J.C. (?-?)

The 1862 arrest of secessionist Edward J.C. Kewen in California is a ludicrous example of suppression in that state far off from Civil War combat. A native of Mississippi he had settled in the Los Angeles area and on September 3, 1862, was elected as a pro-Southern Democrat to the California assembly. However, the defeated Union candidate contested the results on October 6, charging the victor had spoken out in favor of the rebellion. The very next day Kewen found himself under arrest and on his way to Alcatraz. The incident was one of many which occurred in the fall of 1862. At that time the war was going badly for the North and the War Department had issued a series of orders which authorized the suppression of newspapers and the military confinement of dangerous secessionists. On the West Coast this was taken to the extreme. While the secessionists had been a power in California in the 1850s, by this time most of them had gone east to join the Confederates and many of the others were swept out of office. The remaining secessionist activity was actually confined mostly to the drunken firing of guns accompanied by cheers for Jeff Davis and various Confederate generals. Finally, on October 24, 1862, department commander Wright ordered Kewen's release upon payment of a $5,000 bond and the taking of the oath of allegiance. If anything, Kewen's political standing was enhanced by the unnecessary incarceration.

KEYES, Erasmus Darwin (1810-1895)

As a Union army general, Erasmus D. Keyes spent most of the Civil War on the Peninsula of Virginia. The Massachusetts native had received his appointment to West Point from Maine and was graduated in 1832. Posted to the artillery, he was an instructor at the academy and served two tours as an adjutant on the staff of Winfield Scott, but was not in Mexico. His Civil War-era assignments included: major, 1st Artillery (since October 12, 1858); lieutenant colonel and military secretary to

Winfield Scott (January 1, 1860-April 19, 1861); colonel, 11th Infantry (May 14, 1861); commanding 1st Brigade, 1st Division, Army of Northeastern Virginia (June-August 17, 1861); brigadier general, USV (August 1861, to rank from May 17); commanding brigade, Division of the Potomac (August 17-October 3, 1861); commanding 1st Brigade, McDowell's Division, Army of the Potomac (October 3-November 9, 1861); commanding Buell's (old) Division, Army of the Potomac (November 9, 1861-March 13, 1862); commanding 4th Corps, Army of the Potomac (March 13-summer 1862); major General, USV (May 5, 1862); commanding 4th Corps, Department of Virginia (summer 1862-August 1, 1863); commanding Yorktown, 7th Corps, Department of Virginia (ca. December 1862-ca. April 1863); and commanding Division at Suffolk, 7th Corps, Department of Virginia (April 6-August 14, 1863). After leaving Scott's staff he was active in forwarding New York troops to the front and was named to command one of the newly authorized regular army regiments. As such he commanded a brigade in the defeat at 1st Bull Run. When Don C. Buell was promoted and sent to the West, Keyes was transferred to the command of his division. When the Army of the Potomac was organized into corps he was assigned to direct the 4th Corps. Accompanying McClellan to the Peninsula, he participated in the Yorktown operations and earned a regular army brevet as a brigadier general at Seven Pines, where his corps received the brunt of the Confederate assault. After fighting through the Seven Days his corps was left on the Peninsula when the Army of the Potomac was moved out. Eventually it became part of the Department of Virginia, but during much of this time it was only a paper organization with most of its troops assigned elsewhere. It was not formally abolished until August 1, 1863. In the meantime Keyes also held commands in the 7th Corps. During Lee's invasion of Pennsylvania the forces on the Peninsula were supposed to put pressure on Richmond to prevent the sending of reinforcements. In these operations Keyes was roundly criticized by his department commander, John A. Dix. From the summer of 1863 he was assigned to administrative work until he resigned from both the regular and volunteer services on May 6, 1864. Settling in California, he was successful in the wine, mine, and banking businesses. (Keyes, Erasmus D., *Fifty Years Observation of Men and Events, Civil and Military*)

KEYES, Wade, Jr. (1821-?)

A noted Alabama attorney, Wade Keyes, Jr., served throughout the life of the Confederacy as its assistant attorney general and at one point briefly headed the Justice Department. He had practiced his profession in Kentucky, Florida, and Alabama and had written a couple of legal treatises. Appointed to the number two legal position in the new government, he quickly became its guiding force, citing many U.S. precedents in support of government positions in the unprecedented war. When Thomas H. Watts left the cabinet late in 1863 to take up his duties as governor of Alabama, Keyes became acting attorney general until George Davis was appointed to the post. After the war Keyes returned to Alabama and resumed his practice.

KICKING BIRD (?-1875)

The principal voice for peace within his tribe, Kiowa chief Kicking Bird may have paid for his beliefs with his life. During the Civil War he was already known as peaceful but nonetheless the Indian agent Jesse H. Leavenworth reported him as leading some of the depradations occurring in 1865 following the Sand Creek massacre. Kicking Bird was a signer of the 1867 Treaty of Medicine Lodge and thereafter was staunchly for peace. In the Red River War of 1874-75 he managed to get his people back to the agency, where they were then imprisoned. The military decided that 26 Kiowas must be sent to confinement in Florida. They insisted that Kicking Bird make the selections of those to be so punished. Reluctantly, he did. Upon their departure one of the chained Indians accused Kicking Bird of being a big man with the whites and threatened to make sure that he did not live long. Two days later, on May 5, 1875, Kicking Bird died suddenly after drinking a cup of coffee—probably poisoned. (Brown, Dee, *Bury My Heart At Wounded Knee*)

KIERNAN, James Lawlor (1837-1869)

The history of one Civil War general, James L. Kiernan, is shrouded by lack of information in official records. Born in County Galway, Ireland, he attended Dublin's Trinity College before coming to America and earning a medical degree in New York. His first Civil War service apparently came as an assistant surgeon with the 69th New York Militia at 1st Bull Run. His next appears with the following assignments: surgeon, 6th Missouri Cavalry (March 1, 1862); brigadier general, USV (August 1, 1863); and commanding Post of Milliken's Bend, District of Northeastern Louisiana, Department of the Gulf (August-November 10, 1863). His cavalry regiment served at Pea Ridge, Prairie Grove, and Chickasaw Bayou. In the early stages of the Vicksburg Campaign proper he was wounded and captured at Port Gibson but soon made his escape. He resigned shortly thereafter on May 24, 1863, but soon was named a brigadier general and assigned to duty in command of black troops in Louisiana. Going on sick leave on November 10, 1863, it appears that he did not return to duty before his February 3, 1864 resignation, which cited health reasons. After the war he served as a diplomat in China and an examining surgeon for the Bureau of Pensions.

KILPATRICK, [Hugh] Judson (1836-1881)

For his rough handling of his cavalrymen and horses, Judson Kilpatrick created many enemies on his own side in the Civil War and earned the nickname "Kill-Cavalry." The New Jersey native had been born Hugh Judson Kilpatrick but dropped his first name upon entering West Point. Graduating in May 1861, his military assignments included: second lieutenant, 1st Artillery (May 6, 1861); captain, 5th New York (May 9, 1861); first lieutenant, 1st Artillery (May 14, 1861); lieutenant colonel, 2nd New York Cavalry (September 25, 1861); lieutenant colonel and additional aide-de-camp (January 29, 1862); colonel, 2nd New York Cavalry (December 6, 1862);

commanding 1st Brigade, 3rd Division, Cavalry Corps, Army of the Potomac (February 16-May 13 and June 7-14, 1863); brigadier general, USV (June 13, 1863); commanding 2nd Brigade, 2nd Division, Cavalry Corps, Army of the Potomac (June 14-28, 1863); commanding 3rd Division, Cavalry Corps, Army of the Potomac (June 28-July 15 and August 4-November 25, 1863 and December 20, 1863-April 13, 1864); commanding 3rd Division, Cavalry Corps, Army of the Cumberland (April 26-May 13 and July 23-October 29, 1864); commanding 3rd Division, Cavalry Corps, Military Division of the Mississippi (October 29, 1864-June 26, 1865); captain, 1st Artillery (November 30, 1864); and major general, USV (June 18, 1865). Serving as a company commander at Big Bethel, he became the first regular army officer—although serving with volunteers—to be wounded in the Civil War. While recuperating he landed himself a field officer's commission in the cavalry; after a brief stint (ending on March 21, 1862) as a staff officer, he took part in numerous skirmishes in northern Virginia. He fought at 2nd Bull Run and took part in Stoneman's unsuccessful raid during the Chancellorsville Campaign. In the early stages of the Gettysburg Campaign he was engaged at Brandy Station, Aldie, Middleburg, and Upperville. Just prior to the battle itself he was given charge of a division and on the third day of the battle he ordered a reckless charge by one of his brigade commanders, Farnsworth, on the Confederate right. Farnsworth was killed and Kilpatrick was on the way to earning his nickname. The next setback came in the Kilpatrick-Dahlgren raid on Richmond. The latter lost his life, and Kilpatrick was transferred to Sherman's army. He directed a cavalry division in the Atlanta Campaign until wounded at Resaca. Returning to duty he was present for the fall of the city and his division was the only cavalry to accompany Sherman on the March to the Sea and into the Carolinas. During the last weeks of the war he was forced to flee from his quarters without his pants but with a lady friend when Confederate cavalry raided his camp. He was known to be something of a ladies' man. Following Johnston's surrender he was promoted to major general. He had already been brevetted through to that rank in both the regulars and volunteers for the actions at Aldie, Gettysburg, Resaca, Fayetteville, and in the Carolinas Campaign. He resigned his regular commission on December 1, 1865, and his volunteer one on the first day of the next year. He was twice minister to Chile and a one-time congressional candidate. Kilpatrick died at his post in Santiago. (Moore, James, *Kilpatrick and Our Cavalry*)

"Kill-Cavalry" Judson Kilpatrick. (*Leslie's*)

KIMBALL, Nathan (1822-1898)

Indiana native Nathan Kimball twice interrupted his practice of medicine to serve his country in the military. He was company commander during the Mexican War and fought well at Buena Vista where the remainder of his regiment fled in disorder. He returned to private practice until the Civil War, when his assignments included: colonel, 14th Indiana (June 7, 1861); commanding 1st Brigade, Landers' Division, Department of West Virginia (January-March 13, 1862); also commanding the division (March 3-6, 1862); commanding 1st Brigade, 2nd Division, 5th Corps, Army of the Potomac (March 13-April 4, 1862); also commanding the division (March 22-23, 1862); commanding 1st Brigade, 2nd Division, Department of the Shenandoah (April 4-May 10, 1862); brigadier general, USV (April 15, 1862); commanding 1st Brigade, Shield's Division, Department of the Rappahannock (May 10-June 26, 1862); commanding brigade (unattached; June 26-July 4, 1862); commanding unattached brigade, 2nd Corps, Army of the Potomac (July 4-September 10, 1862); commanding 1st Brigade, 3rd Division, 2nd Corps, Army of the Potomac (September 10-December 13, 1862); commanding 3rd Division, 16th Corps, Army of the Tennessee (March-May 28, 1863); commanding Provisional Division, 16th Corps, Army of the Tennessee (May 28-July 29, 1863); commanding division, District of Eastern Arkansas, 16th Corps, Army of the Tennessee (July 29-August 4, 1863); commanding 3rd Division, Arkansas Expedition, 16th Corps, Army of the Tennessee (August 4-September 13, 1863); commanding 2nd Division, Arkansas Expedition, 16th Corps, Army of the Tennessee (September 13-November 30, 1863); commanding 2nd Division, 7th Corps, Department of Arkansas (February 13-April 25, 1864); commanding 1st Brigade, 2nd Division, 4th Corps, Army of the Cumberland (May 22-August 4, 1864); and commanding 1st Division, 4th Corps, Army of the Cumberland (August 5-September 19, 1864, November 28, 1864-February 16, 1865, and March 13-August 1, 1865). In charge of his regiment he fought at Cheat Mountain and Greenbrier. At Kernstown he succeeded to command of the field upon the wounding of James Shields. He went to fight at Port Republic in a subordinate position. Going to reinforce the Army of the Potomac on the Peninsula after the Seven Days, his brigade became part of the 2nd Corps and fought at Antietam. In the assaults on Marye's Heights at

Fredericksburg he was badly wounded. Returning to duty, he led a provisional division during the latter part of the Vicksburg siege operations and then went to Arkansas where he took part in the Little Rock expedition. In the spring of 1864 he was assigned command of a brigade in the campaign against Atlanta and finished the campaign in charge of a different division. Sent to face Hood in Tennessee, he fought at Franklin and Nashville. Late in the conflict he was brevetted major general and was mustered out on August 24, 1865. Thereafter he was state treasurer and served in the state legislature. Also active in veterans' affairs, he was appointed surveyor general in Utah by Grant and resided there until his death.

KINCAID, George Washington (ca. 1813-?)

The creator of Iowa's "Graybeards" Regiment, George W. Kincaid proved to be something less than a popular commander. An early settler of the state, he approached Governor Samuel J. Kirkwood late in 1862 with the idea of raising a regiment of men, over the age of 45 but for garrison duty, that would serve as an inspiration for increased enlistments by younger men. Kincaid got his permission and was mustered in as colonel, 37th Iowa, on December 15, 1862. The regiment was primarily used to guard prisoners of war at Rock Island and Camp Morton. Disease and discharge took their toll on the unit but it also suffered two combat deaths while serving as a guard aboard Memphis and Charleston supply trains. Kincaid's high sense of discipline was resented by the old men, who considered themselves true volunteers. To make matters worse, when the regiment was mustered out on May 24, 1865, the War Department ruled that members were not eligible to receive the remaining $75 of the usual $100 enlistment bounty. In addition a mistaken advance payment of $25 would be deducted from their final pay. Apparently Kincaid had been informed of this before the unit was even mustered into service but concealed the fact from the recruits. A howl was raised and eventually Congress voted them their money in 1866.

KING, John Haskell (1820-1888)

For most of the Civil War John H. King was in command of regular troops but emerged with the brevets of major general in both the regulars and the volunteers. The New York native was commissioned directly into the army from Michigan in 1837 and served in both the Seminole and Mexican wars. He safely brought his command out of Texas at the beginning of the Civil War, during which his assignments included: captain, 1st Infantry (since October 31, 1846); major, 15th Infantry (May 14, 1861); brigadier general, USV (April 1863, to rank from November 29, 1862); commanding 3rd Brigade, 1st Division, 14th Corps, Army of the Cumberland (May 6-July 26 and August 24-October 10, 1863); lieutenant colonel, 14th Infantry (June 1, 1863); commanding the division (July 26-August 23, 1863, May 29-June 6, June 13-July 13, and August 7-17, 1864); commanding 2nd Brigade, 1st Division, 14th Corps, Army of the Cumberland (October 9-13, 1863, November 15, 1863-June 13, 1864, and July 13-August 7, 1864); commanding Regular Brigade, Post of Chattanooga, Army of the Cumberland (September-November 1863); commanding 1st Brigade, 1st Separate Division, District of the Etowah, Army of the Cumberland (November 12, 1864-August 1865); and colonel, 9th Infantry (July 30, 1865). At Shiloh he led a battalion composed of various companies from the 15th and 16th Infantry. After serving in the advance on Corinth, Mississippi, he was wounded at Murfreesboro while leading the 1st Battalion of his own regiment. Returning to duty as a brigadier general of volunteers he won a brevet for commanding the regular brigade at Chickamauga. At times in charge of the division he participated in the Atlanta Campaign and was brevetted regular brigadier general for Ruff's Station. He finished the war in post and district assignments and was brevetted major general in both services for the war. Mustered out of the volunteers on January 15, 1866, he reverted to the regular grade of colonel of infantry and served mostly on the frontier until his 1882 retirement.

KING, Kate (1842-?)

The mistress of Missouri bushwhacker William C. Quantrill, Kate King (sometimes rendered Clarke) used the money gained from his will to open a posh St. Louis brothel. She had been kidnapped by the Confederate guerrillas—in actuality nothing more than bandits—early in the war. She was frequently with Quantrill and upon his death came into half of his loot from the war. A chance reference to Quantrill as a mere butcher led to the demise of one of her clients by the outraged madam. She recruited many of her clients from the ranks of the former guerrillas. Following her marriage she disappeared from history.

KING, Preston (1806-1865)

Switching his allegiance from the Democrats to the Republicans in the mid-1850s, Preston King sat in the U.S. Senate during the first half of the Civil War. The native New Yorker was a lawyer and the founder of the *St. Lawrence Republican*. After a stint as a postmaster he entered the state legislature in 1835 and served until 1838. In the 1840s and 1850s he served four nonconsecutive terms in Congress as a Democrat. Leaving the House of Representatives in 1853, he soon joined the Republicans and took a seat in the Senate in 1857. Not seeking reelection, he left office on March 3, 1863, and resumed his private practice. However, he maintained his interest in politics, attending the Republican convention of 1864 and serving as an elector for the Lincoln-Johnson ticket. In the summer of 1865 he was rewarded with the appointment as port collector for New York Harbor; three months later he drowned when he fell from a ferry.

KING, Rufus (1814-1876)

Although he was the first commander of what was to become famous as the "Iron Brigade" Rufus King did not have as distinguished a career as the brigade itself. The native of New York City and West Pointer (1833) had resigned after three years as a brevet second lieutenant in the engineers to enter civil engineering. Before the Civil War he also edited a number of newspapers. Volunteering his services, he was in the first batch of brigadier generals of volunteers to be named in the Civil War. His assignments included: brigadier general, USV (May 17, 1861); commanding 3rd Brigade, McDowell's Division, Army of the Potomac (October 3, 1861-March 13, 1862); commanding 3rd Division, 1st Corps, Army of the Potomac (March 13-April 4, 1862); commanding 3rd Division, Department of the Rappahannock (April 4-June 26, 1862); commanding 1st Division, 3rd Corps, Army of Virginia (June 26-August 28, 1862); commanding 1st Division, 1st Corps, Army of the Potomac (September 12-14, 1862); commanding King's Independent Brigade, Yorktown, 7th Corps, Department of Virginia (April 1-May 1863); commanding King's Independent Brigade, 4th Corps, Department of Virginia (May-June 17, 1863); commanding 1st Division, 4th Corps, Department of Virginia (June 17-July 15, 1863); and commanding division, 22nd Corps, Department of Washington (July 15-October 1863). After training the future "Iron Brigade" he led a division in northern Virginia. During the 2nd Bull Run Campaign, he withdrew from Gainesville prematurely, forcing Ricketts' division to abandon Thoroughfare Gap, thus allowing Longstreet's command to join Jackson's on the main battlefield. At the opening of the battle proper, part of the division—including his old brigade—was assailed by Jackson's men at Groveton and performed heroically. But there were reports that King himself had been intoxicated. Whatever the cause, he was shunted off to southeastern Virginia within weeks. He was reprimanded for his failure at Gainesville but then sat on the panel which kicked Fitz-John Porter out of the Army. After briefly commanding a division in the Washington fortifications he resigned on October 20, 1863, citing health reasons. Having given up an appointment as a diplomat to the Vatican in 1861 in order to take the field, he was reappointed and was instrumental in the capture of John H. Surratt, one of the Lincoln assassination conspirators. He was later a customs official.

Rufus King, allegedly drunken general. (*Leslie's*)

KING, Wilburn Hill (1839-1910)

Although his appointment as a brigadier general was never recognized by the Richmond authorities, Wilburn H. King served in that grade for the final year of the war in the Trans-Mississippi. His assignments in the Trans-Mississippi Department included: major and quartermaster, CSA (October 15, 1861) major, lieutenant colonel and colonel, 18th Texas; brigadier general, CSA by Smith (April 16, to rank from April 8, 1864); commanding brigade, Walker's Division, District of West Louisiana (spring-July 17, 1864); commanding Walker's Division, District of West Louisiana (July 17-September 2, 1864); commanding 4th Texas Brigade, Polignac's Division, 1st Corps (September 1864-February 27, 1865); and commanding brigade, Forney's Division, 1st Corps (February 27-May 1865). Most of his service was in western Louisiana, including action at Bayou Bourbeau in November 1863 and in the Red River Campaign. He was appointed a brigadier in orders by General E. Kirby Smith in the spring of 1864 and held brigade and higher commands for the rest of the war but was never legally promoted.

KIRBY, Edmund (1840-1863)

Coming from a military family that was to be divided during the Civil War, Edmund Kirby was promoted from first lieutenant to brigadier general, especially at the president's direction and enabling the young man's widowed mother to receive a substantially increased pension. The New Yorker had entered West Point in 1856 and graduated in the class of May 1861. His assignments included: second lieutenant, Battery I, 1st Artillery (May 6, 1861); first lieutenant, Battery I, 1st Artillery (May 14, 1861); and brigadier general, USV (May 28, 1863). He served at 1st Bull Run and commanded his battery in the 2nd Corps at Yorktown, Seven Pines, Seven Days, and Fredericksburg. At Chancellorsville he was detached from his own battery and given charge of the 5th Maine Battery which had lost all of its officers in the fighting through May 3. Arriving at the scene to remove the exposed guns, he almost immediately fell wounded with a fractured thigh. Insisting that the guns be removed first, he had two men come back for him later. He wrote his report of the fight from the ambulance and recommended them both for the Medal of Honor. When Lincoln visited him in the hospital he was already known to be dying. The wound had become infected and the leg's amputation didn't save him. Kirby told Lincoln that his only concern over his impending death was the loss of support for his widowed mother and his sisters. The president had the dying young man commissioned a brigadier general of volunteers. He died on the date of the promotion, May 28, 1863. (See also: Chase, John F.)

KIRBY-SMITH, Edmund

See: *Smith, Edmund Kirby*

KIRK, Edward Needles (1828-1863)

It was almost seven months after he had been injured that Union General Edward N. Kirk succumbed to his Murfreesboro wound. The Ohio-born Illinois lawyer entered the Union army at the beginning of the Civil War and his assignments included: colonel, 34th Illinois (September 7, 1861); commanding 5th Brigade, 2nd Division, Army of the Ohio (January 8-April 7 and June 20-September 29, 1862); commanding 5th Brigade, 2nd Division, 1st Corps, Army of the Ohio (September 29-November 5, 1862); commanding 2nd Brigade, 2nd Division, Right Wing, 14th Corps, Army of the Cumberland (November 5-December 31, 1862); and brigadier general, USV (November 29, 1862). After service in Kentucky he was wounded on the second day at Shiloh while commanding a brigade in his first major battle. Returning to duty two and a half months later, he took part in the Kentucky campaign in the summer and fall of 1862, but his division was not present at Perryville. At Murfreesboro, his next major action, he fell severely wounded in the early morning attack on the Union right on the first day of battle, December 31, 1862. The recently promoted brigadier general was taken to his home, where he died in July 1863—various accounts giving the date of death as the 21st, 23rd, and 29th.

KIRKLAND, Richard R. (1841-1863)

Following the disastrous charges of the Union forces against the stone wall at Fredericksburg, the victorious Confederates were forced to remain under cover and to listen to the piteous cries of their fallen foes. This proved to be too much for Richard Kirkland, a sergeant in the 2nd South Carolina. A veteran of all the regiment's battles since 1st Bull Run, he pleaded with his brigade commander for permission to leave the safety of the Sunken Road and carry water to the suffering Federals. His request granted, he asked, as an after-thought, to be allowed to wave a white handkerchief. This was refused. Still, he jumped over the wall and into the face of almost certain death, but no shots were fired for the hour and half during which he succored the enemy's wounded. Ten months later, "The Hero-Sergeant of Fredericksburg" fell at Chickamauga. (Kershaw, C.D., comp., *Richard Kirkland, CSA*)

KIRKLAND, William Whedbee (1833-1915)

It happened twice: When William W. Kirkland returned to duty after being wounded he found that he had been supplanted in his command and had to be assigned to other duties. He had attended West Point for a while but instead entered the Marine Corps, resigning his commission the year before the war. His Confederate assignments included: colonel, 11th North Carolina Volunteers (July 3, 1861); colonel, 21st North Carolina (designation change on November 14, 1861); reappointed colonel, 21st North Carolina (April 21, 1863); brigadier general, CSA (August 29, 1863); commanding Pettigrew's (old) Brigade, Heth's Division, 3rd Corps, Army of Northern Virginia (September 7-October 14, 1863 and early 1864-June 2, 1864); commanding Martin's (old) brigade, Hoke's Division, Department of North Carolina and Southern Virginia (August 19-October 19, 1864); commanding brigade, Hoke's Division, Anderson's Corps, Army of Northern Virginia (October 19-December 1864); commanding brigade, Hoke's Division, Department of North Carolina (December 1864-March 1865); commanding brigade, Hoke's Division, Hardee's Corps (in Army of Tennessee from April 9) (March-April 26, 1865). He fought at 1st Bull Run but failed to gain reelection at the spring 1862 reorganization. However, when the victor declined appointment, Kirkland was appointed acting colonel. Wounded in Jackson's Valley Campaign at 1st Winchester, he recovered to serve as chief of staff to Patrick Cleburne, seeing action at Murfreesboro. During his convalescence a permanent colonel for the 21st had been named and that is what forced him to look for other duty. When the new man was promoted, Kirkland was reappointed to his old regiment. After fighting at Gettysburg he was promoted and transferred to the command of another brigade. Wounded in a futile attack at Bristoe Station, he returned to fight at the Wilderness and Spotsylvania. Again wounded at Cold Harbor, he returned to find his brigade had gone to William MacRae. In August 1864 he was assigned to another North Carolina brigade and served at Petersburg and Richmond before being sent to North Carolina. He served near Fort Fisher and then fought at Bentonville, finally surrendering with Johnston at Greensboro. (Freeman, Douglas S., *Lee's Lieutenants*)

KIRKWOOD, Samuel Jordan (1813-1894)

As long as Republican Samuel J. Kirkwood was governor of Iowa there was no draft in the state. A native of Maryland, he had been an attorney before moving to Iowa City in 1855. The flour- and saw-miller had originally been a Democrat, but the Kansas-Nebraska Act galvanized him into the free-soil and later the Republican parties. A founder of the state branch of the latter, he served as a state senator and successfully ran for governor in 1859. In his second term he was active in recruiting for the preservation of the Union. Not seeking a third term, he left office in 1864; that fall the state had to resort to the draft. He twice served as a U.S. senator and, reluctantly, took a third gubernatorial term. He was later Garfield's secretary of the interior. (Clark, Dan E., *Samuel J. Kirkwood*)

KITCHING, John Howard (1840-1865)

When Grant's Overland Campaign in 1864 began to create a manpower problem, several heavy artillery regiments were converted to infantry service and New Yorker John H. Kitching was placed in command of a brigade of two such regiments. His assignments included: captain, 2nd New York Heavy Artillery (September 18, 1861); lieutenant colonel, 135th New York (September 6, 1862); lieutenant colonel, 6th New York Heavy Artillery (change of designation October 3, 1862); colonel, 6th New York Heavy Artillery (April 26, 1863); commanding Independent Brigade, 5th Corps, Army of the Potomac (May-June 6, 1864); commanding 3rd Brigade, 2nd Division, 5th Corps, Army of the Potomac (June 6-August 1864); commanding 1st Brigade, Defenses North of the Potomac, 22nd Corps, Department of Washington (mid-August-September 17, 1864); and commanding Provisional Division, 6th Corps, Army of the Shenandoah (September 27-October 19, 1864). With his first regiment he served in the defenses of Washington until he resigned on July 6, 1862, to seek promotion. His next regiment was converted from infantry to heavy artillery and garrisoned Baltimore, Harpers Ferry, and Washington. With the defeat of Lee at Gettysburg, Kitching and his regiment joined the Army of the Potomac with which the regiment served—as ammunition train guards—through the Bristoe and Mine Run campaigns. Reconverted to infantry, the command took part in the Overland Campaign to Richmond for which Kitching was brevetted brigadier. After a time back in the Washington fortifications, Kitching was given a temporary division in the Shenandoah Valley. At Cedar Creek he was mortally wounded, not dying until January 10, 1865.

KNEFLER, Frederick (?-1901)

As chief of the Pension Bureau in the late 1870s, Frederick Knefler was in effect continuing his Civil War military career. Born in Hungary, he was residing in Indiana at the outbreak of the Civil War and promptly offered his services. His assignments included: first lieutenant, 11th Indiana (April 24, 1861); captain, 11th Indiana (June 5, 1861); captain, 11th Indiana (three-years regiment, August 31, 1861); captain and assistant adjutant general, USV (October 21, 1861); major and assistant adjutant general, USV (May 16, 1862); colonel, 79th Indiana (September 28, 1862); commanding 1st Brigade, 3rd Division, 21st Corps, Army of the Cumberland (February 12-April 11, 1863); and commanding 3rd Brigade, 3rd Division, 4th Corps, Army of the Cumberland (March 20-April 16, May 23-November 6, 1864, ca. November 30, 1864, and December 2, 1864-February 21, 1865). With his initial three-months regiment he served under Robert Patterson before being mustered out on August 10, 1861. Remustered at the end of the month, he was stationed at Paducah, Kentucky when assigned to staff duty. In the fall of 1862 he took command of a new regiment of volunteers and led it at Perryville, Murfreesboro, during the Tullahoma Campaign and Chickamauga. At Chattanooga he took part in the assaults on Missionary Ridge. During the Atlanta Campaign he took charge of the brigade and directed it against John B. Hood at Franklin and Nashville. Brevetted brigadier general for the war, he was mustered out on June 7, 1865, with his regiment.

KNIPE, Jospeh Farmer (1823-1901)

An enlisted man during the Mexican War, Joseph F. Knipe became a brigadier general in the Union army during the Civil War. The Pennsylvania native had also taken part in the U.S. Army's disgraceful role in the 1842 suppression of Rhode Island's Dorr Rebellion, which had been trying to achieve universal suffrage. After his 1847 discharge from the army and until the Civil War, he was a railroad employee. His Civil War assignments included: colonel, 46th Pennsylvania (October 31, 1861); commanding 1st Brigade, 1st Division, 2nd Corps, Army of Virginia (September 4-12, 1862); commanding 1st Brigade, 1st Division, 12th Corps, Army of the Potomac (September 17, 1862-May 18, 1863, July 26-August 31, and September 13-25, 1863); brigadier general, USV (November 29, 1862); commanding 1st Brigade, 1st Division, Department of the Susquehanna (June-July 1863); commanding the division (August 31-September 13, 1863); commanding 1st Brigade, 1st Division, 12th Corps, Army of the Cumberland (September 25-December 22, 1863, January 30-February 2, and March 5-April 14, 1864); commanding the division (December 22, 1863-January 30, 1864); commanding 1st Brigade, 1st Division, 20th Corps, Army of the Cumberland (April 14-July 3, July 17-28, and August 28-September 21, 1864); commanding the division (July 28-August 27, 1864); commanding 7th Division, Cavalry Corps, Military Division of the Mississippi (November 16, 1864-January 3, 1865 and February 3-19, 1865); commanding 2nd Brigade, 1st Division, Cavalry Corps, Military Divison of West Mississippi (April 14-17, 1865); also commanding division (March-May 17, 1865); commanding 1st Brigade, 2nd Division, Cavalry Corps, Military Division of West Mississippi (May 15-17, 1865); commanding 1st Brigade, 2nd Division, Cavalry Corps, Department of the Gulf (May 17-June 12, 1865); and commanding 1st Division, Cavalry Corps, Department of the Gulf (June 1865). As a regimental commander, he fought against Jackson in the Shenandoah Valley and was wounded at Cedar Mountain. Back in the field for the Maryland Campaign, he succeeded to brigade command at Antietam. After fighting at Chancellorsville he was in charge of a militia brigade in Pennsylvania during the Gettysburg Campaign. Transferred to the West in the fall of 1863, his men were guarding supply lines during the Chattanooga fighting, but he served throughout the movement against Atlanta at times in divisional command. Joining the mounted arm, he played a leading role in the pursuit of Hood's army after Nashville. Mustered out on August 24, 1865, following service on the Gulf coast, he spent his remaining years as a minor governmental official.

KNOBELOCH, Margaret Anna Parker (1833-1916)

Born in the North and raised in the South, Margaret A.P. Knobeloch was driven by compassion to approach the U.S. War Department with an unusual request. She wanted to distribute aid to Confederate prisoners of war from funds provided by Southerners living in Europe. The Philadelphia native had married a German immigrant, John Knobeloch, in Charleston, South Carolina, and the couple had moved to Philadelphia upon the outbreak of the Civil War. John returned to Germany in order to avoid the draft but Margaret remained. In the summer of 1862 she approached Secretary of War Edwin M. Stanton with her proposal, utilizing her connections in the South and in Europe. Informal permission was granted and she began her work in the hospitals of her native city and in nearby Fort Delaware. She kept her work up until the end of the war. In subsequent years she wrote of her experiences in relief work.

KOLTES, John A. (?-1862)

In the second Union disaster at Bull Run, Pennsylvanian John A. Koltes sacrificed his life. His military assignments included: colonel, 73rd Pennsylvania (ca. September 19, 1861); commanding 2nd Brigade, Blenker's Division, Mountain Department (May 1862); and commanding 1st Brigade, 2nd Division, 1st Corps, Army of Virginia (June 26-August 30, 1862). Following initial service in the Washington vicinity and along the upper Potomac, he moved as part of the forces opposing Stonewall Jackson in the Shenandoah Valley. While in temporary command of a brigade he fought at Cross Keys. Transferred into John Pope's Army of Virginia, he was leading his brigade in the assaults upon the Confederate positions when he fell.

KOSSUTH, Louis (1802-1894)

For a number of years just after the Mexican War Louis Kossuth and his failed 1848-49 Hungarian uprising attracted the interest of the public. Upon the collapse of his revolution, Kossuth had fled to Turkey, and in 1851 he received a hero's welcome upon a visit to the United States. Seeking to gain support for his cause, he was also courted by the abolitionists for their cause. When he announced his neutrality upon the slavery question, interest quickly faded. While he gained sympathy from Secretary of State Daniel Webster, Webster was quick to state—for Austrian consumption—that it was his personal opinion not official policy. In the summer of 1851 Kossuth sailed away, his mission a failure. He lived out his years in exile in Italy but had a lasting impact on America, with at least one Confederate unit being called the "Kossuth Hunters." (Spencer, Donald S., *Louis Kossuth and Young America: A Study of Sectionalism and Foreign Policy, 1848-1852*)

KRZYZANOWSKI, Wladimir (1824-1887)

A Polish emigré from the revolution of 1846, Wladimir Krzyzanowski failed to have his appointment as brigadier general confirmed by the Senate; fellow refugee Carl Schurz retorted facetiously that it was because no one in Congress could pronounce the name. Settling in New York in 1846 he had taken up engineering and was so engaged when, upon the outbreak of the Civil War, he organized a regiment made up mostly of Germans and Poles. His assignments included: colonel, 58th New York (October 22, 1861); commanding 2nd Brigade, 3rd Division, 1st Corps, Army of Virginia (June 26-September 12, 1862); commanding 2nd Brigade, 3rd Division, 11th Corps, Army of the Potomac (September 12, 1862-September 25, 1863); brigadier general, USV (November 29, 1862); commanding 2nd Brigade, 3rd Division, 11th Corps, Army of the Cumberland (September 25, 1863-January 8, 1864 and March 7-April 16, 1864); commanding Post of Bridgeport (Alabama), Department of the Cumberland (ca.

Kurz and Allison print of the battle of Pea Ridge. (NPS)

April-ca. July 1864); commanding 3rd Brigade, Defenses of Nashville and Chattanooga Railroad, Department of the Cumberland (July 1864-February 1865); and commanding Post of Stevenson, District of North Alabama, Department of the Cumberland (March-July 1865). Serving under Frémont in the Shenandoah, he led his regiment at Cross Keys and later commanded a brigade at 2nd Bull Run. Following that defeat, he served in the Washington defenses with his brigade and was promoted to brigadier, but this expired on March 4, 1863, due to a lack of confirmation and he reverted back to the colonelcy of his regiment but retained command of the brigade. Joining the Army of the Potomac in time for the battle of Chancellorsville, he was swept up in the rout of the corps when Stonewall Jackson struck its exposed flank. At Gettysburg the corps was again routed on the first day and Krzyzanowski was forced to flee with his men. Transferred with the corps to Chattanooga, he fought in the battles around that place but lost his command when the 11th and 12th Corps were consolidated to create the new 20th Corps. For the rest of the war he was assigned to guarding the Nashville and Chattanooga Railroad. Brevetted brigadier general on March 2, he was mustered out with his regiment on October 1, 1865. Holding several minor government offices after the war, he died while serving as a special treasury agent in the New York custom house.

KURZ, Louis (?-1921)

A native of Salzburg, Austria, Louis Kurz came to the United States as an artist in 1848. His most famous work is a set of 36 lithographs of famous Civil War battles, produced from 1880 on with Alexander Allison. At first he lived in Milwaukee but then he moved to Chicago where he became acquainted with Abraham Lincoln. An early sketch was "Mr. Lincoln, Residence and Horse." During the Civil War Kurz apparently served as first lieutenant, Company G, 1st United Sharpshooters, a Wisconsin company. But by 1863 he was being sent by Lincoln to visit battle sites and submit sketches. At some point in the 1860s he became a lithographer and became known as the "father of Chicago art" for his cofounding of the Chicago Academy of Design. After the Civil War Kurz was primarily involved in scenic design. In 1880 he formed a partnership with a Chicago engraver, Alexander Allison. The Kurz and Allison firm put out an amazing series of chromolithographs depicting the major battles and often utilizing as many as 10 colors in the complicated process. However, they are not really very accurate; for example, the troops always appear in perfect uniform and usually in perfectly formed lines of battle. The firm closed its doors in 1903 after Kurz's retirement. (*Battles of the Civil War 1861-1865: The Complete Kurz & Allison Prints*)

L

LA GRANGE, Oscar Hugh (?-?)

Serving during most of the Civil War in the mounted arm, Oscar H. La Grange rose to brigade command, and spent four months as a prisoner on the way. The New Yorker entered the Union army in Wisconsin and his assignments included: captain, 4th Wisconsin (July 2, 1861); major, 1st Wisconsin Cavalry (December 10, 1861); lieutenant colonel, 1st Wisconsin Cavalry (June 12, 1862); colonel, 1st Wisconsin Cavalry (February 5, 1863); commanding 2nd Brigade, 1st Division, Cavalry Corps, Army of the Cumberland (September 9-October 12, 1863, November 20, 1863-April 1, 1864, and April 20-May 9, 1864); and commanding 2nd Brigade, 1st Division, Cavalry Corps, Military Division of the Mississippi (October 29, 1864-June 26, 1865). Following brief service as an infantry company commander stationed in Baltimore he became a field officer in a mounted regiment. While rising to command of the regiment, he served against guerrillas in Missouri and then took part in the Tullahoma Campaign. He also fought at Chickamauga in charge of a brigade before embarking upon the Atlanta Campaign. Early in this operation he was captured on May 9, 1864. Exchanged on September 12, 1864, he was detached with his brigade in western Kentucky during the Nashville Campaign. His final exploit of the war came with the raid through Alabama and Georgia of James H. Wilson. Brevetted brigadier general for the war, he was mustered out with his regiment on July 19, 1865.

LAIBOLDT, Bernard (?-?)

For some unexplained reason Bernard Laiboldt did not receive a brevet for his heroic defense of Dalton, Georgia against Joseph Wheeler's Confederate cavalry. The Missourian's assignments included: lieutenant colonel, 2nd Missouri (ca. September 10, 1861); commanding 2nd Brigade, 5th Division, Army of the Mississippi (June 1-September 4, 1862); commanding 35th Brigade, 11th Division, Army of the Ohio (September 4-29, 1862); commanding 35th Brigade, 11th Division, 3rd Corps, Army of the Ohio (September 29-October 8, 1862); commanding 2nd Brigade, 3rd Division, Right Wing, 14th Corps, Army of the Cumberland (December 31, 1862-January 9, 1863); colonel, 2nd Missouri (ca. January 1863); and commanding 2nd Brigade, 3rd Division, 20th Corps, Army of the Cumberland (January 9-February 2 and March 3-October 9, 1863). Serving initially in his home state, Laiboldt commanded the regiment at Pea Ridge and then moved east of the Mississippi where he took part in the advance on Corinth. Joining the Army of the Ohio, he commanded a brigade at Perryville and succeeded to brigade direction again at Murfreesboro. He led the brigade in the Tullahoma Campaign and at Chickamauga. At Chattanooga he directed a demi-brigade in the assault on Missionary Ridge under Sheridan. Taking part in the first part of the Atlanta Campaign, his regiment was detached to guard Dalton, where, on August 14, 1864, Wheeler demanded his surrender. Despite the fact that he had only his own regiment and some small detachments, he refused and managed to beat off two attacks. His regiment was mustered out on October 1, 1864.

LAIRD, John (1805-1874)

One of the first to construct ships of iron and the first to build one with guns was Englishman John Laird. He had been constructing vessels for several decades, and selling throughout the British Empire and to the United States, when the American Civil War came. That same year he retired from his firm and became a member of Parliament. The company continued under his sons and constructed the *Alabama* for the Confederacy. Later in the war two rams were contracted for by the South under the cover of being intended for the Egyptian government. After prolonged pressure from Washington, the Laird rams were seized by the British authorities on September 5, 1863. While in Parliament and until his death, John Laird continued to play a role in maritime affairs.

LAMAR, Gazaway Bugg (1798-1874)

A Georgia-born banker in New York, Gazaway B. Lamar provided his first service to the Confederacy in November 1860 by purchasing and shipping 10,000 muskets to Georgia. In 1834 he had introduced iron steamships to America, only to see his first wife and six of his seven children drowned in the sinking of one of his vessels, the *Pulaski*. In the early months of the Civil War he remained in New York as a Confederate intelligence and postal agent. Moving to Savannah to head the Bank of Commerce, he was chairman of the 1861 banking convention in Atlanta. Seeking ways to weaken the blockade, he negotiated with former New York mayor Fernando Wood to bribe the appropriate persons to allow his blockade runners through. Lamar was sharply criticized in the South when this became public knowledge. He took the Union loyalty oath upon the seizure of Savannah to try to save his property. Soon thereafter he was arrested for a bribery plot. Following his release in late 1865 he returned to New York.

LAMAR, Lucius Quintus Cincinnatus (1825-1893)

For L.Q.C. Lamar the Civil War was just one episode in a varied career. A lawyer and educator he had developed an interest in Democratic politics, become a defender of states' rights, and served in the Georgia legislature. Moving to Mississippi, he was elected to the U.S. House of Representatives. Originally opposed to individual state action, he assisted in the drafting of Mississippi's secession ordinance. Entering the military, he held the following appointments: lieutenant colonel, 19th Mississippi (June 11, 1861); and colonel, 19th Mississippi (May 5, 1862). Seeing action at Williamsburg, he succeeded to regimental command when the colonel was killed, but suffering from vertigo, he resigned on November 24, 1862. He then served as a special commissioner to England, France, and Russia. Never confirmed by the Senate, he returned home in late 1863 and became a vocal supporter of the president. On December 3, 1864, he reentered the military service as a judge on the court of the 3rd Corps, Army of Northern Viriginia. As such he received a parole at Appomattox. He later served as representative, senator, secretary of the interior, and as a justice on the Supreme Court. (Cate, Wirt Armistead, *Lucius Q.C. Lamar*)

LAMB, William (1835-1909)

It was not until the final few weeks of his Confederate career that William Lamb saw heavy action. A Norfolk publisher, he entered the army the day after Virginia's secession. His assignments included: captain, Company C, 6th Virginia (April 18, 1861); major and quartermaster, CSA (September 24, 1861); colonel, 2nd North Carolina Artillery (May 14, 1862); and commanding Fort Fisher, North Carolina (July 4, 1862-January 15, 1865). After only brief service in the Norfolk area he resigned his company command on August 6, 1861. Given a staff appointment the next month he was ordered to Wilmington, North Carolina. He resigned this position to accept a new appointment following his election as colonel of an artillery unit. His unit was for a long time a fluid paper organization for the various batteries serving in the District of the Cape Fear. Lamb was given command of Fort Fisher below Wilmington and had little to do with the regiment until its organization was stabilized and most of its companies were assigned to the fort late in the war. On December 24-25, 1864, the garrision beat off the first Union assault on the fort. On January 15, 1865, a joint army-navy expedition against the fort was more successful. With Union troops, sailors, and marines already over the wall, Lamb fell wounded. The fort soon surrendered and Lamb was held as a prisoner until after the war's close.

LAMON, Ward Hill (1828-1893)

Despite the fact that he was staunchly anti-abolitionist, Lincoln's former law partner Ward Hill Lamon frequently served as his bodyguard. Having become a Republican, he campaigned actively for his friend, accompanied the president-elect on the journey to Washington, and took part in altering the travel itinerary when there were reports that there would be an assassination attempt in Baltimore. Following his inaugura-

Confederate diplomat L.Q.C. Lamar. (*Harper's*)

tion Lincoln dispatched Lamon to Charleston to discuss the situation with South Carolina Gorvernor Pickens and Fort Sumter's commander, Major Anderson. The mission was doomed to failure since both parties assumed he carried news of the decision to evacuate the fort. He didn't and was forced to report the explosive situation to his chief. On April 6, 1861, Lamon was appointed the District of Columbia's marshal. He held this post throughout the war although he did try to organize a loyal Virginia command in the first year of the conflict. Lamon frequently slept next to the president's room when there were fears of assassination. Despite his obvious loyalty to his boss, Lamon was the target of Senate attacks for his anti-abolitionist views. He was in Richmond when Lincoln was shot and always regretted that fact. Quitting his post in June 1865, he resumed the practice of law and in 1872 published volume one of *The Life of Abraham Lincoln from His Birth to His Inauguration as President*. It received such poor public acceptance that volume two never appeared.

LANDER, Frederick West (1821-1862)

Two weeks after requesting to be relieved of duty—a plea which went unanswered—Frederick W. Lander died of pneumonia after 20 hours of morphine treatment. A distinguished explorer, having taken part in some five transcontinental railroad surveys, the Massachusetts-born engineer was sent to Texas in 1861 to offer aid to Governor Sam Houston if the latter felt it appropriate. The mission a failure, he returned north to be appointed in the first batch of volunteer generals in the Civil War. His assignments included: brigadier general, USV (May 17, 1861); commanding 2nd Brigade, Stone's Division, Army of the Potomac (October 3-29, 1861); and commanding Lander's Division, Department of West Virginia (January 5-March 2, 1862). His initial service was as an aide to McClellan during the latter's campaign in western Virginia. Commanding a brigade at Edwards' Ferry the day after the Union disaster at nearby Ball's Bluff, Lander was severely wounded in the leg. Returning to duty in early 1862 he was given a division with which he defended Hancock, Maryland on January 5. In his report of the fight at Bloomery Gap—in which he had led a charge—he requested relief due to ill health. While moving to the aid of Banks in the Shenandoah Valley, he was struck by what was termed a "congestive chill." It proved fatal on March 2, 1862. His English-born actress wife served later as a Union army nurse.

LANDER, Jean Margaret Davenport (1829-1903)

The widow of a Union general, Jean M.D. Lander served from 1862 as a Union army nurse for the remainder of the war. Born in Staffordshire, England, she was considered a child prodigy at acting, performing Shakespeare at the age of eight. On her second American tour she decided to settle here, but continued to have a distinguished career, returning on tour to England and also visiting Germany and the Netherlands. In 1860 she married the explorer Frederick West Lander. He died in early 1862 and she joined the nursing corps at Port Royal, South Carolina, until her return to the stage on February 6, 1865. She retired from acting in 1877.

LANDRAM, William Jennings (?-1895)

A native Kentuckian and veteran of the Mexican War battle at Buena Vista, as a private in the 1st Kentucky Cavalry, William J. Landram quit his circuit clerkship to accept a colonelcy in the forces under General William Nelson. His first assignment in the summer of 1861 was the organization of Nelson's command, especially his cavalry. He then took command of one of the infantry regiments. His assignments included: colonel, 19th Kentucky (January 2, 1862); commanding 2nd Brigade, 1st Division, Army of Kentucky, Department of the Ohio (October-November 13, 1862); commanding 2nd Brigade, 10th Division, Left Wing, 13th Corps, Army of the Tennessee (November 13-December 18, 1862); commanding 2nd Brigade, 1st Division, Yazoo Expedition, Army of the Tennessee (December 18, 1862-January 4, 1863); commanding 2nd Brigade, 1st Division, 1st Corps, Army of the Mississippi (January 4-12, 1863); commanding 2nd Brigade, 10th Division, 13th Corps, Army of the Tennessee (January 12-February 9 and March 9-August 17, 1863); commanding 2nd Brigade, 4th Division, 13th Corps, Department of the Gulf (August 17-24 and October 6-November 21, 1863); commanding 1st Brigade, 4th Division, 13th Corps, Department of the Gulf (November 21-December 5, 1863 and January 9-March 15, 1864); commanding the division (December 5, 1863-January 4, 1864 and March 15-May 29, 1864); and commanding 2nd Brigade, Cavalry Division, Department of the Gulf (August 18-September 24, 1864). In command of his regiment, he served at Cumberland Gap before being transferred farther west to Grant's command. He took part in the Yazoo Expedition and the capture of Arkansas Post while leading a brigade. Continuing in brigade command, he served through the Vicksburg and Jackson campaigns before being sent, with the corps, to the Department of the Gulf. There he directed a division—while still only a colonel—in the Red River Campaign of 1864. He subsequently led a cavalry brigade for a few weeks. On January 26, 1865, he was mustered out with his regiment, its term of enlistment having expired. About seven weeks later he was brevetted brigiader general for his war service.

LANE, Henry Smith (1811-1881)

After serving only two days as governor of Indiana, Henry S. Lane resigned to become one of his state's U.S. senators. Born in Kentucky, he had practiced law there before taking his practice to Indiana. Before the Mexican War he served in the state legislature and the U.S. Congress, later becoming a major and then a lieutenant colonel of state volunteers in the fighting below the border. He was subsequently a leader in the founding of the Indiana Republican Party and chaired the 1856 national convention. He was also at the Chicago convention in 1860. Later that same year he was elected governor, taking his seat on January 14, 1861. Two days later he resigned and went to

Washington. In the Senate he was a backer of the policies of the administration. After completing his term he became a government commissioner.

LANE, James Henry (1814-1886)

Actually a political opportunist, one of the free-state leaders in Kansas during the 1850s was future Senator Jim Lane. A lawyer and former colonel of the 5th Indiana Volunteers during the Mexican War, Lane, in 1854 a member of Congress from Indiana, voted in favor of Stephen Douglas' Kansas-Nebraska Bill. Since this act nullified the 1820 Missouri Compromise and opened the territory to slavery, it was very unpopular with Lane's Indiana constituents. Not seeking reelection, he moved to Kansas and, seeing how the wind was blowing, he soon joined the free-state faction. Becoming a leader in the territory's antislavery movement, Lane presided at the Topeka Convention and took the resulting constitution to Washington in an effort to gain statehood. The mission rejected, he challenged Douglas, chairman of the Senate's Committee on Territories, to a duel—which challenge was ignored. Returning to what was now "Bleeding Kansas," Lane advocated direct attacks on the institution of slavery in neighboring Missouri and was associated with John Brown. Leading an "army" of several hundred FreeStaters, he skirmished with bands of Missouri "Border Ruffians." It was the influx of antislavery settlers that eventually gained Kansas admittance to the Union as a free state, but Lane claimed that he had saved the state. In 1861 this reputation achieved for him his cherished goal of becoming a senator, and his effective use of patronage made him the power in the new state. He forged a special relationship with President Lincoln by organizing a force of some 50 Kansas politicians into a military unit and offering it to protect the vulnerable capital at the beginning of the Civil War. Subsequently he organized an irregular force, known as "Jayhawkers," which raided into Missouri, freeing slaves, looting, and pillaging. He organized some of the earliest black regiments and urged Lincoln to make the conflict one against slavery. However, by 1863, Lane had begun to lose his hold in Kansas. He barely survived Quantrill's bloody sacking of Lawrence on August 21, 1863, and lost his home to the flames. During this period he almost despaired of being reelected in 1864, but his role in the repulse of Price's Missouri Raid in that election year gained him the victory. Following Lincoln's death, Lane supported Andrew Johnson's policies against the Radical Republicans and was roundly criticized by his constituents. After one unsuccessful attempt at suicide, he succeeded on July 1, 1866.

LANE, James Henry (1833-1907)

A graduate and former professor at the Virginia Military Institute, James Henry Lane was teaching at the North Carolina Military Institute when the war began. Leading the cadet corps to war, he held the following assignments: major, 1st North Carolina Volunteers (May 11, 1861); lieutenant colonel, 1st North Carolina Volunteers (September 3, 1861); colonel, 28th North Carolina (September 21, 1861); commanding Branch's (old) Brigade, A.P. Hill's Division, 2nd Corps, Army of Northern Virginia (September 17, 1862-May 30, 1863); brigadier general, CSA (November 1, 1862); commanding brigade, Pender's-Wilcox's Division, 3rd Corps, same army (May 30-July 2; July 3; mid-July 1863-February 1865; and March-April 9, 1865); and commanding the division (July 2-3; July 3-mid July 1863; and February-March 1865). He fought from Big Bethel to Appomattox in Virginia. After the small actions at the former and Hanover Court House, he was twice wounded during the Seven Days, at Frayser's Farm and the next day at Malvern Hill. Still on duty, he moved north with Jackson and participated in operations at Cedar Mountain, 2nd Bull Run, Harpers Ferry, and Antietam where he succeeded the slain General L. O'B. Branch. Lane led his brigade at Fredericksburg and Chancellorsville and was in temporary command of the division on the second day at Gettysburg. Relieved the next day, before Pickett's Charge, he returned from the famed assault again in charge of the division since his replacement had fallen. The Virginian led his North Carolinians through the Overland and Petersburg operations and surrendered with Lee at Appomattox. (Freeman, Douglas S., *Lee's Lieutenants*)

LANE, Joseph (1801-1881)

Running for the vice presidency on the ticket of John C. Breckinridge effectively ended the political career of Joseph Lane. The North Carolina native had engaged in trade in Indiana and sat in the state legislature. During the Mexican War he entered the military as colonel of the 2nd Indiana but within a month was named a brigadier general of volunteers. During the course of the war he won the brevet of major general and was mustered out in the summer of 1848. From 1848-1850 he was territorial governor of Oregon and then became its House of Representives delegate. In 1859 he became one of the new state's two senators. Noted for his proslavery and secession views he was chosen by the Southern faction of the Democratic party as its vice presidential nominee. After the defeat he remained a Southern partisan but lost most of his political clout.

LANE, Walter Paye (1817-1892)

Definitely an adventurer, Walter P. Lane rose to the rank of brigadier general in the final days of the Confederacy. The native of County Cork had been brought to the United States by his parents in 1821. They settled in Ohio but Lane eventually went off to Texas and, joining the forces of Sam Houston, fought at San Jacinto. He then served on a Texas privateer in the Gulf of Mexico and fought Indians until the Mexican War. During that conflict he served as a first lieutenant in the Texas Rifles and then as major of a battalion of Texas mounted volunteers. Some of his quieter activities included teaching and mining, with mixed success, in the United States and Peru. Joining the Confederacy, his assignments included: lieutenant colonel, 3rd Texas Cavalry (early 1861); colonel, 1st Texas Partisan Rangers (ca. 1864); brigadier general, CSA (March 17, 1865); and commanding brigade, Steele's Division, Cavalry Corps, Trans-Mississippi Department (March-May 26, 1865). He fought at Wilson's Creek and on December 26, 1861, against the Creeks at Chustenahlah. He also participated in the defense of Corinth,

Mississippi. Given command of a regiment of partisan rangers, he served in Louisiana until wounded at Mansfield during the Red River Campaign. Returning to duty in western Louisiana, he was eventually promoted to brigadier general and in the final months of the war led a mounted brigade. Returning to Texas, he engaged in mercantile pursuits and was active in veterans' affairs. (Lane, Walter Paye, *The Adventures and Recollections of Walter P. Lane.*)

LANG, David (1838-1917)

Rising from the enlisted ranks, David Lang became the temporary commander of the Florida Brigade shortly before Appomattox. A native Georgian, he graduated from Georgia Military Institute before moving to Florida and becoming a surveyer. Entering the Confederate army his assignments included: private, Company H, 1st Florida (early 1861); sergeant, Company H, 1st Florida (April 1862); captain, Company C, 8th Florida (May 10, 1862); colonel, 8th Florida (October 2, 1862); commanding Perry's Brigade, Anderson's Division, 3rd Corps, Army of Northern Virginia (spring 1863-fall 1863); and commanding Finegan's Brigade, Mahone's Division, 3rd Corps, Army of Northern Virginia (early 1865-April 9, 1865). After serving his 12-month enlistment, he raised his own company and was soon sent with it to Virginia. He saw action at 2nd Bull Run, Antietam, and Fredericksburg where he was severely wounded in the head while commanding the regiment. He recovered in time to command the brigade at Gettysburg. He then led his regiment at the Wilderness, Spotsylvania Court House, Cold Harbor, and Petersburg. Again in command of the brigade, he led it through the final stages of the Petersburg siege and the Appomattox Campaign. After the surrender, he served in civil and military appointive positions in the state of Florida. (Freeman, Douglas S., *Lee's Lieutenants*)

LANGBEIN, J.C. Julius (1845-?)

When J.C. Julius Langbein enlisted as a musician in Company B, 9th New York, in the spring of 1861 he was only 15 years old, but before he was 17, he would earn a congressional Medal of Honor. When he went off to war one of his officers had promised the German-born youth's mother to watch Langbein. In a role reversal it was the drummer—nicknamed "Jennie" for his girlish features—who aided in the rescue of the wounded officer. For this action in the April 19, 1862, battle of Camden, North Carolina, Langbein was honored with the award. (Mitchell, Joseph B., *The Badge of Gallantry*)

LANIER, Sidney (1842-1881)

A firm believer in the myth of the "Old South" as fostered by the novels of Sir Walter Scott, poet Sidney Lanier supported the secession of his home state of Georgia. He enlisted in June 1861 in the Macon County Volunteers, which became Company I, 4th Georgia, and reported to Virginia. On March 9, 1862, he witnessed the battle between the *Monitor* and the *Merrimac.* His next action was defending Drewy's Bluff, Virginia, against the *Monitor* and other Union vessels on May 15, 1862. Transferring to the Signal Corps, Lanier served on the staff of Major General S.G. French. In May 1863, he visited the battlefield of Chancellorsville, thus inspiring the 1865 poem, "The Dying Words of Jackson." He was subsequently captured while serving on a blockade-runner and confined principally at Point Lookout, Maryland. Although he rarely wrote about the war, his novel *Tiger-Lilies* dealt with prison life. Released four months later, his health was permanently impaired and he died of tuberculosis at the age of 39. His unhappiness with Northern reconstruction policies led to his condemnatory, and sometimes racist poems: "Laughter in the Senate," The Raven Days," "Civil Rights," "Betrayal," and "The Ship of the Earth." (Parks, Ed Winfield, *Sidney Lanier: The Man, The Poet, The Critic*)

LARNED, Benjamin Franklin (?-1862)

At the outbreak of the Civil War many of the staff departments were headed by men who had held their staff posts for several decades in the small, regular establishment. One of these men was Benjamin Larned, who had served in the Pay Department for four and a half decades. Entering the army during the War of 1812 as an ensign in the 21st Infantry, he rose to first lieutenant and served as a regimental paymaster. He also received a brevet as captain for the defense of Fort Erie in Upper Canada. Transferred from the infantry to the Pay Department, he became a deputy paymaster in 1847, as a lieutenant colonel. In 1854 he became paymaster general with the rank of full colonel. He held this post until July 15, 1862, when he was temporarily relieved due to ill health.

LATHAM, George R. (?-?)

In what he himself described as his "first disaster in over three years' active service," the military career of George R. Latham was brought to a close. A native Virginian, he had entered the Union army where his assignments included: captain, 2nd West Virginia (May 25, 1861); colonel, 2nd West Virginia (May 24, 1862); colonel, 2nd West Virginia Mounted Infantry (designation change spring 1863); colonel, 5th West Virginia Cavalry (designation change January 26, 1864); and colonel, 6th West Virginia Cavalry (consolidation of 5th and 6th, December 14, 1864). His regiment served at McDowell and in the Shenandoah Valley Campaign of 1862 and he commanded the regiment at 2nd Bull Run. With the command mounted, he served on raids in western Virginia and in opposing Confederate raiders and guerrillas. While in command at New Creek, West Virignia, he was surprised by the sudden appearance of enemy cavalry under General Thomas L. Rosser. Since the Confederate column was thought to be a returning Union patrol, it was able to pass the pickets and capture the town without a shot. The result was the destruction of much Baltimore and Ohio Railroad property. Latham placed the blame upon himself and was promptly arrested for trial by court-martial. Eventually he was sentenced to dismissal, but this was cancelled and he was able to request an honorable discharge. This came through on March 9, 1865. Nonetheless, he was brevetted brigadier general for the war four days later. (Jones, Virgil Carrington, *Gray Ghosts and Rebel Raiders*)

LATHAM, Milton Slocum (1827-1882)

Having immigrated to California via the slaveholding South, Milton S. Latham represented his state in the U.S. Senate during the first part of the Civil War. Born in Ohio, he had taught school in Alabama before moving to California during the gold rush and becoming an attorney. After serving as a court clerk he was named district attorney for Sacramento. In the mid-1850s he served one term as a Democratic congressman but declined to seek reelection. He was then named as San Francisco's port collector. Elected to the gubernatorial chair in 1859, he resigned after only two days in office due to his election to the Senate in place of the deceased David C. Broderick. The unexpired term lasted only until March 3, 1863, when he returned to California and engaged in the legal and banking businesses. He spent his final three years in New York City.

LATIMER, Joseph White (1843-1863)

Interrupting his studies at the Virginia Military Institute, young Joseph W. Latimer became one of the most promising artillery field officers in the Army of Northern Virginia. His assignments included: first lieutenant, Richmond Courtney Artillery (September 15, 1861); captain, Richmond Courtney Artillery (ca. July 14, 1862); commanding Courtney's Artillery Battalion, Ewell's Division, 2nd Corps, Army of Northern Virginia (fall 1862-ca. March 2, 1863); major, Artillery (March 2, 1863); commanding Andrew's Artillery Battalion, Ewell's-Early's Division, 2nd Corps, Army of Northern Virginia (ca. March 2-ca. April 4, 1863); and commanding Andrew's Artillery Battalion, Johnson's Division, 2nd Corps, Army of Northern Virginia (June 15-July 2, 1863). After having served as a cadet drillmaster for the Richmond Hampden Artillery in the spring and summer of 1861, he received a commission in a new battery with which he saw action in the Shenandoah Valley Campaign, the Seven Days, Cedar Mountain, 2nd Bull Run, and Harpers Ferry. He especially distinguished himself at 1st Winchester, in the Valley, and at Cedar Mountain. Remaining at Harpers Ferry, his battery did not see action at Antietam, but Latimer took over battalion command soon thereafter when his superior, Major A.R. Courtney, was brought up on charges for his behavior there. He commanded the battalion at Fredericksburg and the next winter received promotion to major and assignment as executive officer in Andrews' Battalion. He commanded part of the unit at 2nd Winchester and took over the battalion when Andrews was wounded at Stephenson's Depot the next day. On the second day at Gettysburg, he was fatally wounded while withdrawing his battalion from an unequal artillery duel supporting the attack on Culp's and Cemetery Hills. He died on August 1. (Wise, Jennings C., *The Long Arm of Lee*)

LAUMAN, Jacob Gartner (1813-1867)

When one of his brigades lost more than half its members in a bungled assault, division commander Jacob G. Lauman was relieved of duty and sent home to await orders—which never came. Born in Maryland, he was a businessman in Iowa when the Civil War broke out. His military assignments included: colonel, 7th Iowa (July 11, 1861); commanding 4th Brigade, 2nd Division, Military District of Cairo, Department of the Missouri (February 1-17, 1862); commanding 1st Brigade, 2nd Division, Army of the Tennessee (February 17-April 5, 1862); brigadier general, USV (March 21, 1862); commanding 3rd Brigade, 4th Division, Army of the Tennessee (April 5-6, 1862); commanding the division (April 6, 1862); commanding 1st Brigade, 4th Division, Army of the Tennessee (April 6-7, 1862); commanding 1st Brigade, 4th Division, District of Memphis, Army of the Tennessee (July-September 24, 1862); commanding 1st Brigade, 4th Division, District of Jackson, Army of the Tennessee (September 24-October 26, 1862); commanding Reserve (6th) Brigade, District of Memphis, 13th Corps, Army of the Tennessee (November 23-December 9, 1862); commanding 4th Division, Right Wing, 13th Corps, Army of the Tennessee (December 9-18, 1862); commanding 4th Division, 17th Corps, Army of the Tennessee (December 18, 1862-January 20, 1863); and commanding 4th Division, 16th Corps, Army of the Tennessee (January 20-July 12, 1863). Seeing early action at Belmont, he was severely wounded. Recovering in time to command a brigade in the Henry-Donelson Campaign, he was particularly distinguished at the latter place, earning himself a brigadier's star. He fought well at Shiloh and then commanded around Memphis and Jackson in western Tennessee. Sent to reinforce Grant's army near Vicksburg, his division arrived between the 13th and 20th of May and was temporarily attached to Sherman's 15th Corps until June 12. He fought through the remainder of the siege and was attached to Ord's 13th Corps for the subsequent campaign against Jackson. In the July 12, 1863, assaults outside Jackson, one of his brigades—under Colonel Isaac C. Pugh—was thrown forward against Confederate fortifications despite the protests of the brigade commander. It was deciminated and when Lauman was slow in regrouping the survivors, Ord summarily relieved him from command. This was upheld by Sherman and Grant, and Lauman was sent back to Iowa to await orders. At the end of the war he was still waiting. Nonetheless he was brevetted major general for his war services. Resigning on August 24, 1865, he had only two more years to live. Assistant Secretary of War Dana summed him up thus, "[He] got his promotion by bravery on the field and Iowa political influence. His is totally unfit to command—a very good man but a very poor general."

LAW, Evander McIvor (1836-1920)

A distinguished brigade commander, E. McIvor Law became embroiled in a dispute with another brigadier which virtually destroyed the efficiency of Hood's former division. A graduate of the South Carolina Military Academy, he became involved with a number of such academies in his native South Carolina and in Alabama. With the outbreak of hostilities he raised a company and joined the Confederacy where his assignments included: captain, Company B, 4th Alabama (spring 1861); lieutenant colonel, 4th Alabama (May 1861); colonel, 4th Alabama (October 28, 1861); commanding Whiting's Brigade, Smith's-Whiting's Division (in the Valley District in June),

Department of Northern Virginia (May-June 1862); commanding same brigade, Whiting's Division, 2nd Corps, Army of Northern Virginia (June 26-July 1862); commanding brigade, Whiting's-Hood's-Field's Division, 1st Corps, Army of Northern Virginia (July 1862-February 25, 1863; May-July 2, 1863; and April-June 3, 1864); brigadier general, CSA (October 3, 1862); commanding brigade, Hood's Division, in the Department of Virginia and North Carolina (February 25-April 1, 1863) and in the Department of Southern Virginia (April 1-May 1863); commanding Hood's Division, 1st Corps, Army of Northern Virginia (July 2-September 1863); commanding brigade, Hood's Division, Longstreet's Corps, Army of Tennessee (September-November 5, 1863); temporarily commanding the division (September 20, 1863); commanding brigade, Hood's-Field's Division, Department of East Tennessee (November 5-December 19, 1863); and commanding brigade, Butler's Division, Hampton's Cavalry Command with Johnston's army (March-April 1865). After being severely wounded at 1st Bull Run, he was promoted to regimental command. Leading the brigade he fought at Seven Pines, the Seven Days, 2nd Bull Run, and Antietam before being promoted to brigadier general. After fighting at Fredericksburg he served in southeastern Virginia with Longstreet and then returned to Lee's army. At Gettysburg he succeeded to divisional command upon the wounding of General Hood. Going west, he led the division temporarily at Chickamauga while Hood led the corps. Hood was wounded again but Law was relieved by Micah Jenkins who was senior brigadier in the division but had long been detached with his brigade. During the battle of Wauhatchie and in the East Tennessee Campaign there were charges of a lack of cooperation. Eventually Law took his resignation to Richmond, having taken it back from Longstreet. He was talked out of it, but Longstreet filed charges against Law for stealing the document. He was reinstated by the War Department in time for the Wilderness, and he fought later at Spotsylvania and North Anna before being badly wounded at Cold Harbor. Returning to duty in the final months of the war, he commanded a cavalry brigade in North Carolina and fought at Bentonville. After the war he was active in education, journalism, and veterans' affairs. (Freeman, Douglas S., *Lee's Lieutenants*)

LAWLER, Michael Kelly (1814-1882)

Known for his strict discipline—which early in the war caused him to be brought up on charges—County Kildare native Michael K. Lawler fought for his adopted land in two wars. Brought to the United States in 1816, he became a farmer when he reached maturity and also maintained an interest in the militia. During the Mexican War he was a company commander in the 3rd Illinois and later directed an independent mounted company. His Civil War assignments included: colonel, 18th Illinois (June 30, 1861); commanding Post of Jackson, District of Jackson, Army of the Tennessee (July-November 1862); brigadier general, USV (November 29, 1862); commanding 1st Brigade, District of Jackson, Left Wing, 16th Corps, Army of the Tennessee (December 18, 1862-March 18, 1863); commanding 2nd Brigade, 3rd Division, 16th Corps, Army of the Tennessee (March 18-April 22, 1863); commanding 2nd Brigade, 14th Division, 13th Corps, Army of the Tennessee (May 2-July 28, 1863); commanding 4th Division, 13th Corps, Department of the Gulf (August 17-September 20, 1863); commanding 3rd Brigade, 1st Division, 13th Corps, Department of the Gulf (September 23-October 19, October 26-December 23, 1863, and February 28-March 10, 1864); commanding the division (October 19-26, 1863 and May 23-June 11, 1864); commanding 2nd Brigade, 1st Division, 13th Corps, Department of the Gulf (March 10-April 27 and May 9-23, 1864); commanding District of Morganza, Department of the Gulf (July 5-November 23, 1864); temporarily commanding 19th Corps, Department of the Gulf (July 6-7, 1864); commanding 1st Brigade, Reserve Corps, Department of the Gulf (December 5, 1864-February 3, 1865); commanding 1st Brigade, 1st Division, Reserve Corps, Department of the Gulf (February 3-4, 1865); and commanding District of Baton Rouge and Port Hudson, Department of the Gulf (March 23-May 30, 1865). Taking his regiment into the field, he was wounded at Fort Donelson and thus missed Shiloh and the subsequent operations. Returning to duty, he took part in the movements against Vicksburg and Jackson. Afterwards his corps was transferred to the Department of the Gulf where he finished out the war. Brevetted major general for his war service, he remained in the South for a while, in the horse trade, before returning to farming in Illinois.

LAWSON, Thomas (ca. 1781-1861)

The surgeon general at the beginning of the war, Thomas Lawson had held his office for 24 years but did not live long enough to have an impact on the expansion of his department during the war. Lawson, a Virginian, began his service as a surgeon's mate in the navy in 1809. He transferred to the army during the War of 1812 and became surgeon general with the rank of colonel in 1836. He served in the war with Mexico and was brevetted brigadier general for his meritorious conduct in that conflict. However, he died a month after the fall of Fort Sumter, on May 15, 1861.

LAWTON, Alexander Robert (1818-1896)

South Carolina-born Alexander R. Lawton's service with the Army of Northern Virginia was brief, and he finished out the war in a thankless military job—quartermaster general. A West Pointer (1839), he served only a year in the artillery before resigning to attend Harvard Law School. Settling in Savannah to practice, he entered politics, serving in both state houses. Also involved in railroads and the militia, he seized Fort Pulaski, as colonel of the 1st Georgia, even before the state seceded. His later assignments included: brigadier general, CSA (April 13, 1861); commanding District of Savannah (April 17-October 26, 1861); commanding Department of Georgia (October 26-November 5, 1861); commanding District of Georgia, Department of South Carolina, Georgia and Florida (May 28-June 1862); commanding brigade, Jackson's Division, in the Valley District, Department of Northern Virginia (June

1862) and in Jackson's Command, Army of Northern Virginia (June 26-mid-August 1862); commanding brigade, Ewell's Division, Jackson's Command, Army of Northern Virginia (mid-August-August 28, 1862); commanding the division (August 28-September 17, 1862); and quartermaster general, CSA (August 10, 1863-April 1865). After serving on the coast he was sent to Virginia where he arrived too late to participate in the Valley Campaign but fought in the Seven Days. His brigade was left guarding the trains during the fighting at Cedar Mountain so that a junior officer, General Winder, could lead the division. Transferred to Ewell's Division, he fought at 2nd Bull Run, taking over the division until he was wounded at Antietam. After a long recovery he was assigned to the staff department. Active in law and politics after the war, he served as U.S. minister to Austria. (Freeman, Douglas S., *Lee's Lieutenants*)

LAWTON, Hattie (?-?)

Already one of the Pinkerton detective organization's most experienced operatives at the outbreak of the Civil War, Hattie Lawton went on to become the agency's best female agent. Because Baltimore was a secessionist trouble spot during the early part of the war, she was assigned there and worked with Timothy Webster gathering information on the Southern activities. In January 1862 she accompanied Webster on a mission to Richmond. Webster, however, became ill and Lawton had to take care of him. The illness caused them to be out of touch with Pinkerton for several weeks, and he sent two more agents, Pryce Lewis and John Scully, after them to bring back the intelligence reports and lend any assistance necessary. They found the couple in a Richmond hotel room and, while there, were visited by a Confederate officer who directed them to report to General Winder. While at Winder's office they were recognized by a man who had been their prisoner earlier in the conflict. Identified, Scully spilled the entire story. Lawton was sentenced to a year in prison and tried desperately to get the death sentence against Webster commuted. She even had an unsuccessful interview with Mrs. Davis. She was released in 1863 but her effectiveness had been destroyed by her arrest. (Horan, James D., *The Pinkertons: The Detective Dynasty That Made History*)

LEADBETTER, Danville (1811-1866)

A career engineer, Danville Leadbetter was highly respected by some of the top Confederate commanders but came in for much criticism from a fellow engineer, E. Porter Alexander. The Maine native and West Pointer (1836) had shifted back and forth a couple of times between the artillery and engineers in his first two years after graduation. From then until his resignation as a captain in 1857 he served in the latter. Having for a time been stationed in Mobile, he spent the remaining antebellum years as Alabama's chief engineer. Adopting Southern political beliefs, he entered the Confederate service and his assignments included: lieutenant colonel, Alabama Troops (1861); major, Engineers, CSA (summer 1861); acting chief, Engineer Bureau (August 3-November 11, 1861); brigadier general, CSA (March 6, 1862, to rank from February 27); commanding Leadbetter's Command, District of East Tennessee, Department #2 (early 1862); and chief engineer, Army of Tennessee (1863-64). His earliest service came in constructing the defenses at Mobile. Throughout the war he kept returning to this post for further engineering work. During the first summer of the war he was in temporary charge of the War Department's engineering branch. Promoted to brigadier general, he held brief command of line troops at Chattanooga and Knoxville. When Bragg besieged the former city, Leadbetter designed the lines on Missionary Ridge and Lookout Mountain. It was at Knoxville that he came into conflict with Alexander over the advice given to the operation's commander, James Longstreet. Apparently his work was not of the best—there were especially grievous faults in the works at Chattanooga. After the war Leadbetter went via Mexico to Canada where he died.

LEALE, Charles A. (ca. 1842-?)

It was only a matter of days after having been commissioned as an army assistant surgeon that Charles A. Leale became the first person to reach the side of Abraham Lincoln at Ford's Theater. The native New Yorker had completed his year-long medical cadetship on February 17, 1865, and was commissioned in the volunteer service on April 8. When the assassination occurred he happened to be attending the show. Racing to the box, his entry was blocked by the post Booth had used to secure the door. The injured Henry Rathbone managed to open the door. When Leale reached the president he found no pulse and stretched him out on the floor. Having been joined by Dr. Charles Taft, he administered artificial respiration and the pair detected a pulse. Leale was present in the Peterson house when Lincoln expired the next morning. Brevetted captain, Leale was mustered out on January 20, 1866.

LEAVENWORTH, Jesse Henry (1807-1885)

As a commander on the Civil War's far western frontier, Jesse H. Leavenworth got into trouble for exceeding his authority and was removed from command. Born in Vermont, he was a West Pointer (1830) who resigned as an infantry second lieutenant in 1836 to enter civil engineering. He was engaged in this profession in Chicago for a number of years before moving to Colorado. On February 17, 1862, he became colonel, 2nd Colorado, and served in keeping the lines of communication with California open. For raising another unit without proper authority he was dishonorably discharged on September 26, 1863, but this was later changed to honorable. However, the next month his regiment was consolidated with the 3rd Colorado to form the 2nd Colorado Cavalry. In 1864 he became the Indian agent for the Kiowas and Comanches but was soon found—by both sides—to be incompetent and probably corrupt. He resigned this post in 1868 and moved east.

LEDLIE, James Hewett (1832-1882)

General U.S. Grant best summed up the military career of James H. Ledlie when he wrote, ". . . besides being otherwise inefficient, [he] proved also to possess disqualification [cowardice] less common among soldiers." A native New Yorker, he was able to gain advancement through political lobbying, and his fellow officers appear to have covered up his failing, possibly to protect their own reputations. A civil and railroad engineer, he became a field officer at the outbreak of the Civil War. His assignments included: major, 19th New York (May 22, 1861); lieutenant colonel, 19th New York (September 28, 1861); lieutenant colonel, 3rd New York Light Artillery (changed of designation December 11, 1861); colonel, 3rd New York Light Artillery (December 23, 1861); commanding Artillery Brigade, Department of North Carolina (December 4, 1862-January 2, 1863); brigadier general, USV (December 24, 1862, expired March 4, 1863); commanding Artillery Brigade, 18th Corps, Department of North Carolina (January 2-May 1863); commanding Artillery, Defenses of New Bern, 18th Corps, Department of North Carolina (May-August 1863); brigadier general, USV (reappointed October 27, 1863); commanding 1st Brigade, 1st Division, 9th Corps, Army of the Potomac (May 12-June 9, 1864); and commanding the division (June 9-August 6, 1864). After seeing only limited action he obtained permission to convert his regiment into a light artillery unit and spent several months recruiting and training it. Sent to the North Carolina coast, he was placed in charge of the department's artillery. He seems to have seen limited action there and not all of it was viewed in the best of lights. For example, at the battle of Whitehall he was praised by his superior, but others claimed that he had wounded many Union infantrymen with his fire. For some vague reason, he was promoted to brigadier but it was not approved by Congress. He was reappointed later and confirmed. Meanwhile, he continued to serve in North Carolina. Joining the Army of the Potomac during the battle of Spotsylvania, he was assigned to the command of the 9th Corps brigade. His performance at North Anna appears to have been substandard, but nonetheless he succeeded to the command of the division following Cold Harbor. Taking his place in the siege lines before Petersburg, his division was chosen by lot to lead the assault following the explosion of the mine. While his command bungled forward, he remained secure in a bombproof, drinking rum and issuing orders from his sanctuary. On August 6, 1864, he was sent on 20-day sick leave and it was extended for four months. Returning on December 8, he was sent home the next day to await orders which never came. He resigned on January 23, 1865. One relieved subordinate declared that his "removal from command was a heavy loss to the enemy." After the war he was successful in engineering and railroading.

James H. Ledlie, inhabitant of a bombproof.

LEE, Albert Lindley (1834-1907)

Giving up a seat on the Kansas Supreme Court, New York-born attorney Albert L. Lee rose from major to brigadier general in the Civil War. His assignments included: major, 7th Kansas Cavalry (October 29, 1861); colonel, 7th Kansas Cavalry (May 17, 1862); commanding 2nd Brigade, Cavalry Division, Army of the Mississippi (September 4-November 1, 1862); commanding 1st Brigade (assigned to the Left Wing), Cavalry Division, 13th Corps, Army of the Tennessee (November 26-December 18, 1862); commanding 2nd Brigade, Cavalry Division, 16th Corps, Army of the Tennessee (December 18, 1862-March 1863); brigadier general, USV (April 1863, to rank from November 29, 1862); acting chief of staff, 13th Corps, Army of the Tennessee (spring 1863); commanding 9th Division, 13th Corps, Army of the Tennessee (May 17-19, 1863); commanding 1st Brigade, 9th Division, 13th Corps, Army of the Tennessee (May 19, 1863); commanding 12th Division, 13th Corps, Army of the Tennessee (July 26-18, 1863); commanding 3rd Division, 13th Corps, Army of the Tennessee (July 28-August 7, 1863); commanding 3rd Division, 13th Corps, Department of the Gulf (August 7-September 13, 1863); commanding Cavalry Division, Department of the Gulf (September 14, 1863-April 18, 1864 and August 18-October 27, 1864); and commanding 1st Brigade, 3rd Division, 19th Corps, Department of the Gulf (June 27-August 16, 1864). Initially serving in Kansas and Missouri, he commanded a brigade at Corinth and during Grant's campaign in central Mississippi. During the Vicksburg Campaign he was John A. McClernand's staff chief until tapped to replace the wounded Peter J. Osterhaus in charge of a division at Big Black River Bridge. Two days later, while directing a brigade in the first assault on the city proper, he suffered wounds in the face and head. Returning to duty that summer, he briefly directed an infantry division on the Gulf coast and then led the cavalry division in the disastrous Red River Campaign. In trouble with this superiors, he soon found himself without a command and resigned effective May 4, 1865. He then engaged in business on both sides of the Atlantic.

LEE, Charles Cochrane (1834-1862)

Although he was well qualified, having graduated fourth in his 1856 class at West Point, and having served as an instuctor at the Charlotte Military Academy after his resignation from the regular army in 1859, Charles Lee was deprived of his general's wreath by an early death. The former ordnance second lieutenant was appointed lieutenant colonel, 1st North Carolina Volunteers, on May 11, 1861. Lee participated in the small, early Confederate victory in the battle of Big Bethel on June 10. On September 1, 1861, he was promoted to colonel of the regiment, then dubbed the "Bethel Regiment," and served until it was discharged at the end of its term of service. On November 20 he was made colonel of a new unit, the 37th North Carolina. After participating in the battle of New Berne on March 15, 1862, the regiment moved to Virginia as part of General Branch's Brigade which was made part of General A.P. Hill's Division. Lee took part in the battle of Hanover Court House on May 27. In the Seven Days Battles Branch's Brigade was held in reserve at Beaver Dam Creek but was engaged at Gaines' Mill and Frayser's Farm. In the latter battle, Colonel Lee was killed leading a charge.

LEE, Edwin Gray (1836-1870)

The least-known of the Confederate Generals Lee, Edwin G. Lee finished out the war as a Southern agent in Canada. A second cousin of *the* General Lee, Edwin was a lawyer in what is now West Virginia and was a son-in-law of General William N. Pendleton. Lee gave up his practice to join the Confederacy as an officer in the Hamtranck Guards, a company he had been associated with since John Brown's raid. His assignments included: second lieutenant, Company B, 2nd Virginia (1861); first lieutenant and adjutant, 2nd Virginia (1861); lieutenant colonel, 33rd Virginia (ca. April 22, 1862); colonel, 33rd Virginia (to date from August 28, 1862); and brigadier general, CSA (September 23, 1864). As part of the Stonewall Brigade he served at Harpers Ferry and 1st Bull Run on Jackson's staff. He then served through the Shenandoah Valley Campaign and the Seven Days. After Cedar Mountain and 2nd Bull Run he was promoted to colonel. Shortly after Antietam, he was captured while visiting his ill father but was freed in time to fight at Fredericksburg. Upon his doctor's advice he resigned that winter. Later in 1863 he was reappointed but assigned to less arduous duty, although he did see action at Drewry's Bluff and Bermuda Hundred in May 1864. The next month he was ordered to Staunton to organize the reserve forces in the Valley District and a few months later was promoted to brigadier. The appointment was rejected by the Senate in February but by then he was already on a mission to Canada. By the time he had set up shop as successor to Jacob Thompson and Clement Clay the war was ending. He remained in Canada until early 1866, dispensing funds to needy Confederates in exile. Returning, he was a witness at the trial of John Surratt whom he had known in Montreal. He had also looked after the interests of the St. Albans raiders while they were in a Canadian prison. The next few years were spent in an unsuccessful attempt to improve his long-failing health.

LEE, Fitzhugh (1835-1905)

The nephew of two of the Confederacy's top generals, R.E. Lee and Samuel Cooper, Fitzhugh Lee himself held the rank of major general in both a gray and blue uniform. A West Pointer (1856) and a wounded veteran of Texas Indian fighting, Lee resigned a first lieutenancy in the 2nd Cavalry on May 21, 1861, to go with his native Virginia. His assignments included: first lieutenant, Cavalry (1861); lieutenant colonel, 1st Virginia Cavalry (August 1861); colonel, 1st Virginia Cavalry (April 1862); brigadier general, CSA (July 24, 1862); commanding brigade, Cavalry Division, Army of Northern Virginia (July 28, 1862-September 9, 1863); major general, CSA (August 3, 1863); commanding division, Cavalry Corps, same army (September 9, 1863-August 1864 and January-March 1865); commanding cavalry division, Valley District, Department of Northern Virginia (August-September 19, 1864); and commanding Cavalry Corps, Army of Northern Virginia (March-April 11, 1865). He served at 1st Bull Run as a staff officer and the next month was named a field officer in the 1st Virginia Cavalry. Promoted to colonel in the spring 1862 reorganization, he led the regiment in Stuart's first ride around McClellan's army and served through the Seven Days. Promoted and given a brigade, he fought at 2nd Bull Run, South Mountain, Antietam, in the December 1862 raids, at Kelly's Ford, and with the main army at Chancellorsville. After participating in Stuart's wide swing around the Union army in the Pennsylvania Campaign, he fought in the cavalry action on the third day at Gettysburg. Back in Virginia he was given charge of a newly organized division. At Spotsylvania he held off the Union forces until Lee's infantry arrived on the field. After serving on the Petersburg-Richmond lines, he was sent to the aid of Early in the Valley but was soon wounded out of action at 3rd Winchester. Not returning to duty until the beginning of the next year he found his division by that time back from the Shenandoah, and led the cavalry on the Richmond front. In the final month of the war he headed the mounted corps and cut his way out of the Appomattox encirclement with a portion of his command but surrendered two days after Lee. A farmer after the war, he became governor of the state and was a diplomat in Cuba just before the war with Spain. Donning the blue, he was a major general of volunteers and soon thereafter was placed on the retired list of the regular army at the same grade. (Freeman, Douglas S., *Lee's Lieutenants*)

LEE, George Washington Custis (1832-1913)

Robert E. Lee's eldest son, George W.C. Lee, chaffed in his position as an aide-de-camp to Jefferson Davis, desiring instead a field position. Having been graduated at the head of his 1854 class at West Point, he had accordingly been assigned to the engineers. He had resigned his first lieutenant's commission on May 2, 1861, to follow his father into the service of their native Virginia. His assignments included: captain, Engineers (July 1, 1861); colonel, Cavalry, and aide-de-camp (August 31, 1861); brigadier general, CSA (June 25, 1863); commanding Local

Defense Troops Brigade, Department of Richmond (October 1864-January 1865); major general, CSA (to rank from October 20, 1864); commanding division, Department of Richmond (March-April 2, 1865); and commanding separate division, Army of Northern Virginia (April 2-6, 1865). Initially assigned to the designing of the capital's defenses, Lee was tapped by the president as an aide. In addition he finally got a troop assignment with the organization of the government workers into the Local Defense Troops. Whenever these units were called into active duty he would command. The remainder of his time would be spent serving the chief executive. During the Richmond-Petersburg operations he was regularly at the head of his brigade. In the final month, he directed a division of Local Defense units, reserves, regular line troops, and landlocked sailors and marines. In the retreat to Appomattox he was with his father's army and was captured at Sayler's Creek. Quickly paroled to tend to his ill mother, he eventually succeeded his father as president of Washington College. (Freeman, Douglas S., *R.E. Lee*)

LEE, John Fitzgerald (ca. 1813-1884)

When in 1849 the position of judge advocate of the army was re-created, John Lee was brevetted major and assigned to the position. A graduate of West Point (1834), Lee had served in the artillery and ordnance branches and had risen to a captaincy. During the Seminole War he had been brevetted a captain for gallant conduct. As judge advocate in the early stages of the Civil War, Lee was responsible not only for military justice but also for implementing the policy of the administration in placing civilians under military arrest. After a little over a year of this duty he resigned on September 4, 1862.

LEE, Mary W. (?-?)

When at the outbreak of the Civil War it became apparent that Philadelphia was going to be a transportation center for the Union volunteers going to the front, English-born Mary W. Lee decided to make the soldiers' journey as comfortable as possible by setting up the Union Refreshment Saloon. At first merely a stove and coffeepot, it grew into an operation which treated some four million troops to meals, medical treatment, quarters, and cleaning facilities. Joining the United States Sanitary Commission, she served as a nurse in field hospitals during the Peninsula Campaign and the subsequent operations of the Army of the Potomac until Lee's surrender.

LEE, Robert Edward (1807-1870)

The idol of the South to this day, Virginian Robert E. Lee had some difficulty in adjusting to the new form of warfare that unfolded with the Civil War, but this did not prevent him from keeping the Union armies in Virginia at bay for almost three years. The son of Revolutionary War hero "Light Horse" Harry Lee—who fell into disrepute in his later years—attended West Point and graduated second in his class. During his four years at the military academy he did not earn a single demerit and served as the cadet corps' adjutant. Upon his 1829 graduation he was posted to the engineers. Before the Mexican War he served on engineering projects in Georgia, Virginia, and New York. During the war he served on the staffs of John Wool and Winfield Scott. Particularly distinguishing himself scouting for and guiding troops, he won three brevets and was slightly wounded at Chapultepec. Following a stint in Baltimore Harbor he became superintendent of the military academy in 1852. When the mounted arm was expanded in 1855, Lee accepted the lieutenant colonelcy of the 2nd Cavalry in order to escape from the painfully slow promotion in the engineers. Ordered to western Texas, he served with his regiment until the 1857 death of his father-in-law forced him to ask for a series of leaves to settle the estate. In 1859 he was called upon to lead a force of marines, to join with the militia on the scene, to put an end to John Brown's Harpers Ferry Raid. Thereafter he served again in Texas until summoned to Washington in 1861 by Winfield Scott who tried to retain Lee in the U.S. service. But the Virginian rejected the command of the Union's field forces on the day after Virginia seceded. He then accepted an invitation to visit Governor John Letcher in Virginia. His resignation as colonel, 1st Cavalry—to which he had recently been promoted—was accepted on April 25, 1861. His Southern assignments included: major general, Virginia's land and naval forces (April 23, 1861); commanding Virginia forces (April 23-July 1861); brigadier general, CSA (May 14, 1861); general, CSA (from June 14, 1861); commanding Department of Northwestern Virginia (late July-October 1861); commanding Department of South Carolina, Georgia and Florida (November 8, 1861-March 3, 1862); and commanding Army of Northern Virginia (June 1, 1862-April 9, 1865). In charge of Virginia's fledgling military might, he was mainly involved in organizational matters. As a Confederate brigadier general, and later full general, he was in charge of supervising all Southern forces in Virginia. In the first summer of the war he was given his first field command in western Virginia. His Cheat Mountain Campaign was a disappointing fizzle largely due to the failings of his superiors. His entire tenure in the region was unpleasant, dealing with the bickering of his subordinates—William W. Loring, John B. Floyd, and Henry A. Wise. After this he became known throughout the South as "Granny Lee." His debut in field command had not been promising, but Jefferson Davis appointed him to command along the Southern Coast. Early in 1862 he was recalled to Richmond and made an advisor to the president. From this position he had some influence over military operations, especially those of Stonewall Jackson in the Shenandoah Valley. When Joseph E. Johnston launched his attack at Seven Pines, Davis and Lee were taken by surprise and rode out to the field. In the confusion of the fight Johnston was badly wounded, and that night Davis instructed Lee to take command of what he renamed the Army of Northern Virginia. He fought the second day of the battle but the initiative had already been lost the previous day. Later in the month, in a daring move, he left a small force in front of Richmond and crossed the Chickahominy to strike the one Union corps north of the river. In what was to be called the Seven Days Battles the individual fights—Beaver Dam Creek, Gaines' Mill, Savage Station, Glendale, White Oak Swamp, and Malvern Hill—were

Robert E. Lee, Confederate commander-in-chief at war's end. (NA)

all tactical defeats for the Confederates. But Lee had achieved the strategic goal of removing McClellan's army from the very gates of Richmond. This created a new opinion of Lee in the South. He gradually became "Uncle Robert" and "Marse Robert." With McClellan neutralized, a new threat developed under John Pope in northern Virginia. At first Lee detached Jackson and then followed with Longstreet's command. Winning at 2nd Bull Run, he moved on into Maryland but suffered the misfortune of having a copy of his orders detailing the disposition of his divided forces fall into the hands of the enemy. McClellan moved with unusual speed and Lee was forced to fight a delaying action along South Mountain while waiting for Jackson to complete the capture of Harpers Ferry and rejoin him. He masterfully fought McClellan to a standstill at Antietam and two days later recrossed the Potomac. Near the end of the year he won an easy victory over Burnside at Fredericksburg and then trounced Hooker in his most creditable victory at Chancellorsville, where he had detached Jackson with most of the army on a lengthy flank march while he remained with only two divisions in the immediate front of the Union army. Launching his second invasion of the North, he lost at Gettysburg. On the third day of the battle he displayed one of his major faults when—as at Malvern Hill and on other fields—he ordered a massed infantry assault across a wide plain, not recognizing that the rifle, which had come into use since the Mexican War, put the charging troops under fire for too long a period. Another problem was his issuance of general orders to be executed by his subordinates. Returning to Virginia he commanded in the inconclusive Bristoe and Mine Run campaigns. From the Wilderness to Petersburg he fought a retiring campaign against Grant in which he made full use of entrenchments, becoming known as "Ace of Spades" Lee. Finally forced into a siege, he held on to Richmond and Petersburg for nearly 10 months before beginning his retreat to Appomattox, where he was forced to surrender. On January 23, 1865, he had been named as commander in chief of the Confederate armies but he found himself too burdened in Virginia to give more than general directives to the other theaters. Later in 1865 he became president of Washington College (now Washington and Lee University) in Lexington, Virginia, and his reputation revitalized the school after the war. He died of heart disease which had plagued him since the spring of 1863. Somehow, his application for restoration of citizenship was mislaid, and it was not until the 1970's that it was found and granted. (Freeman, Douglas S., *R.E. Lee* and Connelly, Thomas L., *The Marble Man: Robert E. Lee and His Image in America Society*)

LEE, Samuel Phillips (1812-1897)

A distant relative of the famous Confederate general, Samuel Phillips Lee remained true to his oath taken upon his 1827 entrance into the U.S. Navy. The Virginian's early career was spent cruising all over the world. Something of a troublesome officer, he was suspended from duty as first lieutenant of the *Peacock* by Commodore Charles Wilkes during an 1830s Pacific cruise. During the early part of his naval career he fought two duels and while on a Mississippi steamboat he killed a passenger. Transferred in 1841 to the Coast Survey, he was back afloat during the Mexican War as commander of the *Washington*. Following a stint on hydrographic duty, he was a commander in charge of the *Vandalia* at the outbreak of the Civil War. While at Cape Town, South Africa—en route to the East India Squadron—he heard of the firing on Fort Sumter, returned his vessel to the United States on this own authority and joined the blockading fleet. His Civil War assignments included: commander, USN (1850s); commanding *Vandalia* (1861-early 1862); commanding *Oneida* (early 1862-July 1862); captain, USN (July 1862); acting rear admiral, USN (July 1862); commanding North Atlantic Blockading Squadron (July 1862-October 12, 1864); and commanding Mississippi Squadron (October 12, 1864-ca. May 1865). Highly successful on blackade duty, he received a record $100,000-plus in prize money. During his more than two years in command of his squadron his fleet grew from 48 to more than 100 craft. However, his cooperative efforts with the army proved less than successful and in late 1864 he was transferred to command on the western waters. During Hood's invasion of Tennessee Lee cooperated well with the army under George H. Thomas. After the war he served on various boards and on post duty. Named a full rear admiral in 1870, he retired three years later. He was subsequently a Maryland farmer. (Cornish, Dudley Taylor and Laas, Virginia Jeans, *Lincoln's Lee: The Life of Samuel Phillips Lee, United States Navy, 1812-1897*)

LEE, Stephen Dill (1833-1908)

One of the Confederacy's most capable lieutenant generals, Stephen D. Lee has been overshadowed by the likes of Stonewall Jackson and James Longstreet. The native South Carolinian and West Pointer (1854) had seen service with the artillery against the Seminoles and on the frontier before resigning as a first lieutenant with the 4th Artillery on February 20, 1861. His Confederate assignments included: captain and aide-de-camp, South Carolina Army (spring 1861); captain, Artillery, Hampton (S.C.) Legion (1861); major, Artillery (November 1861); lieutenant colonel, Artillery (June 1862); chief of Artillery, Magruder's Command, Army of Northern Virginia (June 17-July 1862); temporarily commanding 4th Virginia Cavalry (July 1862); colonel, Artillery (ca. July 1862); commanding battalion, Artillery, Longstreet's Corps, Army of Northern Virginia (ca. July-November 1862); brigadier general, CSA (November 6, 1862); commanding Provisional Division, 2nd Military District, Department of Mississippi and East Louisiana (December 1862-January 1863); commanding brigade, Smith's Division, 2nd Military District, Department of Mississippi and East Louisiana (January-April 1863); chief of Artillery, Department of Mississippi and East Louisiana (May-July 4, 1863) major general, CSA (August 3, 1863); commanding cavalry corps, Department of Mississippi and East Louisiana (August 1863-January 28, 1864); commanding cavalry corps, Department of Alabama, Mississippi and East Louisiana (January 28-May 9, 1864); commanding the department (May 9-July 26, 1864); lieutenant general, CSA (June 23, 1864); and commanding Hood's (old) Corps, Army of Tennessee (July 26-December 1864 and late March-April 26, 1865). Highly commended by Beauregard for his staff services at Fort Sumter, he went to Virginia with the Hampton Legion and was engaged in closing the Potomac to Union shipping. Transferred to the Peninsula, he fought at Seven Pines and became Magruder's artillery chief for the Seven Days. Briefly in command of a cavalry regiment in the summer of 1862, he led an artillery battalion under Longstreet at 2nd Bull Run and played a vital role in repulsing the Union assaults and paving the way for Longstreet's steamroller attack. After fighting at Antietam, he was named a brigadier general and ordered to Mississippi where he played a leading role in the repulse of Sherman's attacks at Chickasaw Bayou at the end of 1862. For a time he commanded an infantry brigade at and near Vicksburg, and during the siege of the city itself he was Pemberton's chief artillerist. Paroled and exchanged by July 13, 1863, he was promoted to major general and assigned to command the cavalry in Mississippi and eastern Louisiana. As such he greatly hampered Sherman's Meridian expedition the next year. For a time in charge of the department, he was named a lieutenant general—the youngest in the Confederacy—and was soon engaged against Andrew J. Smith at Tupelo. Ordered to Georgia, he took over Hood's former corps and led it through the balance of the Atlanta Campaign. He continued under Hood into middle Tennessee. He fought at Franklin and at Nashville where his corps was forced to retreat when the others did. Covering the retrograde movement, Lee was wounded. He rejoined the army in the Carolinas in the final days of the war and was surrendered with Joseph E. Johnston. Besides being active in veterans' affairs after the war he was a farmer, legislator, and college president. (Hattaway, Herman, *General Stephen D. Lee*)

LEE, Sydney Smith (1805-1869)

Brother of General Robert E. Lee, father of Major General Fitzhugh Lee, and uncle of Major General W.H.F. Lee, Captain Sydney Smith Lee, CSN, is little remembered in Civil War history. Born in New Jersey, while his Virginia congressman father was attending a session of Congress in Philadelphia, Lee was raised in Virginia. At the age of 14 Lee entered the navy and saw action during the Mexican War. His later services included: command of the Philadelphia Navy Yard, commandant at Annapolis, commanding the U.S.S. *Mississippi* on Perry's Japan mission, and chief of the Bureau of Coast Survey. With the secession of Virginia, he resigned his captain's commission and received one of like grade from the Confederacy. He was assigned initially to duty at the Norfolk Navy Yard until its evacuation. Next assigned to command at Drewry's Bluff, he arrived during the Union naval attack. Declining to relieve his predecessor during the action, Lee gave him all the assistance possible in the Confederate victory. Subsequently, he served on several courts-martial, as an examiner in the Confederate States Naval Academy, and as chief of the Bureau of Orders and Detail. Following the war he retired to live out his final four years in Virginia. (Scharf, J. Thomas, *History of the Confederate States Navy*)

LEE, William Henry Fitzhugh (1837-1891)

The eldest and most famous of Robert E. Lee's sons, "Rooney" Lee was a Harvard graduate and regular army veteran when he entered the cavalry service of the South in which he was to rise to division leadership. In the period from 1857 to 1859 he had served as a second lieutenant of infantry but resigned to run a family plantation. His Civil War assignments included: captain and major, Cavalry (May 1861); lieutenant colonel, 9th Virginia Cavalry (January 1862); colonel, 9th Virginia Cavalry (ca. April 28, 1862); brigadier general, CSA (to rank from September 15, 1862); commanding brigade, Cavalry Division, Army of Northern Virginia (November 10, 1862-June 9, 1863); major general, CSA (April 23, 1864); and commanding division, Cavalry Corps, same army (ca. April 23, 1864-April 9, 1865). After service as Loring's cavalry chief in western Virginia, Lee was sent to the Aquia District to organize the cavalry along the Rappahannock River. He was upped from lieutenant colonel to colonel upon the reorganization of the 9th Virginia Cavalry for the war and led it in Stuart's ride around McClellan on the Peninsula and during the Seven Days, 2nd Bull Run, and Antietam. Promoted and given charge of a newly formed brigade, he fought at Fredericksburg and in opposing Stoneman's raid during the Chancellorsville Campaign. The next month he was wounded in the great cavalry battle at Brandy Station. While recuperating at home he was captured and got caught up in the retaliation for the Confederate threat to hang two Union captains. Kept in close confinement under threat of death, he was finally exchanged in March 1864 only to find that his wife had died during his incarceration. A new division of cavalry was formed for him and he was promoted to a major generalcy. He led his division through the Overland and Petersburg campaigns. After Appomattox, he was a farmer, he sat in the state senate and in the U.S. Congress, and he served as president of the state agricultural society. (Freeman, Douglas, S., *R. E. Lee* and *Lee's Lieutenants*)

LEE, William Raymond (ca. 1804-1891)

Captured early in the Civil War, Massachusetts native William R. Lee got himself caught up in the controversy over whether privateers were pirates or subject to treatment as regular prisoners of war. He had for a time attended West Point in the class of 1829 but dropped out prior to the completion of his studies. The engineer and railroader's assignments included: colonel, 20th Massachusetts (July 21, 1861); and commanding 3rd Brigade, 2nd Division, 2nd Corps, Army of the Potomac (December 15-29, 1862). Captured in the Union disaster at Ball's Bluff, he was held as a hostage for the good treatment of the captured crewmembers of the Confederate privateer *Savannah*. Eventually the U.S. courts ruled that the crews were in fact prisoners of war and, in turn, the conditions under which Lee and other officers were held improved. Exchanged in April 1862, he rejoined his regiment and was wounded at Nelson's Farm on the Peninsula. He nonetheless fought at Seven Pines and during the Seven Days. He also played a distinguished role in the battle of Antietam where his regiment got caught up in the virtual ambush of Sedgwick's division in the West Woods. He returned to command his brigade while it was still on the Fredericksburg side of the Rappahannock River after the disastrous Union defeat there. However, on December 17, 1862, his resignation became effective and he relinquished command on the 29th. In 1865 he was brevetted brigadier general for the war, especially for Antietam.

LEGGETT, Mortimer Dormer (1821-1896)

A friend of George B. McClellan, New York-born Ohio lawyer Mortimer D. Leggett spent the first part of the Civil War serving as McClellan's volunteer aide-de-camp in western Virginia before formally enlisting late in the first year. Also an educator in the prewar years, he was noted for his innovativeness. His military assignments included: lieutenant colonel, 78th Ohio (December 18, 1861); colonel, 78th Ohio (January 21, 1862); commanding 2nd Brigade, 3rd Division, Right Wing, 13th Corps, Army of the Tennessee (November 1-December 18, 1862); commanding 2nd Brigade, 3rd Division, 17th Corps, Army of the Tennessee (December 18, 1862-April 13, 1863 and May 11-June 3, 1863); brigadier general, USV (April 15, 1863, to rank from November 29, 1862); commanding 1st Brigade, 3rd Division, 17th Corps, Army of the Tennessee (June 3-November 17, 1863); commanding the division (November 17, 1863-March 6, 1864, April 6-August 23, 1864, September 22, 1864-January 15, 1864, and April 3-August 1, 1865); commanding the corps (October 10-24, 1864 and May 8, 1865); and major general, USV (August 21, 1865). Only lightly engaged at Fort Donelson and Shiloh, his regiment went on to take part in the advance on Corinth, Mississippi. During the Vicksburg operations he commanded two different brigades as a brigadier general. Under Sherman he successfully led a division through the Atlanta, Savannah, and Carolinas campaigns and gave his name to a feature of the battlefield at Atlanta—Leggett's Hill—because of his stern defense of the position in the face of Hood's assaults. Having been brevetted major general from September 1, 1864, he was given the full rank after the close of hostilities. Resigning on September 23, 1865. he returned to the law, served as patent commissioner, and was active in the new field of electricity.

LE MAT, J.A.F. (?-?)

Popular with many of the top Confederate generals were the revolvers designed by J.A.F. Le Mat. Born in France, the New Orleans doctor sometimes referred to himself as "Colonel." His weapon was of an eight shot design with an extra lower barrel which was capable of firing a charge of buckshot. A few hundred were manufactured in the Crescent City immediately prior to the Civil War, but with the outbreak of the conflict Le Mat found it too difficult to continue manufacturing and sailed for France. Later he produced his sidearms in Britain and Belgium. In all some 3,000 made it through to the Confederacy, where they were carried by the likes of Jeb Stuart and Beauregard.

LEOPOLD I, King of Belgium (1790-1865)

Like Queen Victoria of Britain and Emperor Napoleon III of France, King Leopold I of Belgium was lobbied by Confederate agents for his recognition of the fledgling nation. By the outbreak of the Civil War Leopold had been on his throne for three decades. While toying with the Southern agents, he, like his fellow monarchs, never acceded to the pleas of such Confederate diplomats as, principally, Ambrose D. Mann. He died the same year the American war ended.

LESLIE, Frank (1821-1880)

A pioneer in the field, Frank Leslie published an illustrated weekly newspaper that was, for the first time, able to present pictures of events as soon as they were reported. Born in England, he had declined to enter his father's glove-making business, preferring to pursue his wood-carving and engraving interests. After working for the *Illustrated London News* under the name Frank Leslie (he had been named Henry at birth), he immigrated to the United States. There he worked for a number of publications and became the head of the engraving department of the *Illustrated News*. Here he scored a major coup by producing a two-page illustration, that would normally have taken four months, in only three days. His method was to divide the drawing into 34 parts and assign an engraver to each. After starting several papers of his own, he launched *Frank Leslie's Illustrated Newspaper* on December 15, 1855. During the Civil War his paper was one of the two national pictorial weeklies dispatching swarms of artist-correspondents to the armies. There was also a German edition, *Illustrierte Zeitung*. He ran several papers in the post war years but died in bankruptcy.

LETCHER, John (1813-1884)

To the Confederacy John Letcher was the opposite of Joseph Brown of Georgia—a cooperative governor. Born in the Shenandoah Valley, he became a lawyer and editor of the *Lexington Valley Star*, a Democratic organ. A champion of his section of the state against the historic domination of the Tidewater, he was propelled to a seat in Congress in 1851. Although a states' righter he opposed the extreme doctrines of John C. Calhoun. He kept his seat in Congress until 1859 when he ran for and was elected to a four-year term as Virginia's governor. Taking office at the start of 1860, he supported Douglas for president and urged a convention of the states to attempt to iron out the nation's difficulties. At the same time, as a precaution, he strengthened Virginia's military position. His planned convention was not called by the state legislature until a year after he took office; by this time it was too late, Lincoln having been elected and several states having seceded. He delayed calling a state convention, which might take the state out of the Union, until January 1861. Thanks in large part to his efforts, the convention had a large cooperationist element and refused to secede in February and March. With the firing on Fort Sumter and Lincoln's call for troops from Virginia, Letcher promptly refused and in a matter of days Virginia was out of the Union. Letcher supervised the organization of the Virginia land and naval forces and their eventual incorporation into the Confederate service. One of his chief accomplishments was the appointment of such officers as Lee and Jackson. During the war he opposed many of Jefferson Davis' war measures, especially the draft and impressment of supplies for the army, but went along with them until the victory could be won. Only then would he challenge them in court to prevent the Confederacy from becoming too centralized, as had happened in the United States, and infringing upon states' rights. His constant collaboration with the Confederate authorities in unpopular measures did not sit well with his constituency. He did oppose the central government on such matters as the treatment of Union officers who incited slave revolts and Union soldiers from western Virginia. He wanted to be more severe but gave in to fears of retaliation. In order to continue his political career after the conclusion of his term, he ran, in 1863, for a seat in the Second Confederate Congress but was defeated. He returned home in early 1864, and his home was burned by federal forces in June. Impoverished by his service to the state, he resumed his law practice. He was imprisoned for six weeks at the end of the war and served briefly in the state legislature before his death. (Boney, Francis Nash, *The Life of John Letcher, Virginia's Civil War Governor*)

LETTERMAN, Jonathan (1824-1872)

An organizational genius, Jonathan Letterman became the father of modern battlefield care for the wounded. A graduate of Philadelphia's Jefferson Medical College, Letterman joined the regular army in 1849 as an assistant surgeon with the rank of captain. His medical service in Florida, Minnesota, and New Mexico did not prepare him for the large scale of medical operations necessitated by the Civil War. But he measured up. Promoted to full surgeon and major on April 16, 1862, he was appointed medical director of the Army of the Potomac, then licking its wounds at Harrison's Landing following the Seven Days, and assumed his new post on July 4, 1862. Granted wide powers by General McClellan, he proceeded to evacuate the worst cases to general hospitals in Northern cities. For service on the battlefield he established an ambulance corps, whose detailed line soldiers were the only persons authorized to remove the wounded and to bring the casualties to the newly established division hospitals close to the front line. His system was proven effective at Antietam where the field was cleared of wounded within 24 hours. Under his direction, sanitary conditions throughout the army were improved and the soldiers' diet bettered. His system was in use throughout the Union armies by 1863, and he relinquished his post the following January. He resigned from the army on December 22, 1864, and entered business and practiced medicine in California until his early death.

LEVENTHORPE, Collett (1815-1889)

A veteran of the British army's 14th Regiment of Foot, Collett Leventhorpe lent his military talents to the Confederacy but for some reason refused to accept a brigadier generalship in the final months of the Civil War. The Devonshire officer eventually settled in North Carolina. His Confederate assignments included: colonel, 34th North Carolina (November 1861); colonel, 11th North Carolina (April 2, 1862); brigadier general, North Carolina State Troops (1864); and brigadier general, CSA (February 18, 1865). He commanded one regiment from his adopted state until taking charge of what was nicknamed the "Bethel Regiment" in the spring of 1862. With this unit he served in North Carolina until joining the Army of Northern Virginia for the invasion of Pennsylvania. He was wounded on the first day at Gettysburg and was taken prisoner on July 5, 1863. Following his recovery he was confined at Fort McHenry and Point Lookout before being exchanged on or about March 10, 1864. On the 27th of April he resigned his colonelcy, citing his Gettysburg wounds. However, that same year Governor Zebulon Vance named him a state brigadier and he was assigned to duty guarding the railroad to Petersburg. The next winter, however, he declined a Confederate appointment on March 6, 1865. After the war he retired to North Carolina.

LEWIS, David Peter (ca. 1820-1884)

A confirmed Unionist, but one-time Confederate congressman and judge, David P. Lewis quit the Confederacy and after the war was the scalawag governor of Alabama. A native of Virginia, he had practiced law and run a plantation in Alabama. A Democrat and Unionist, he voted against secession but nonetheless signed the ordinance. Named to the Provisional Confederate Congress, he was admitted on February 8, 1861, but resigned on April 29 after the close of the first session, claiming inconvenience in his further attendance. During his brief tenure he served on the committees on Indian Affairs and Patents. Alabama Governor John G. Shorter appointed him a judge, but he soon fled to Union-controlled Nashville where he remained for the balance of the war. Returning to Alabama in 1865, he resumed his practice and joined the Radical Republicans in Reconstruction. From 1872 to 1874 he served as governor and became thoroughly hated by the ex-Confederate population. He was forced into private life by the return of white supremacist rule.

LEWIS, James Taylor (1819-1904)

A Democrat running on the Union ticket, James T. Lewis was the last war governor of Wisconsin. A New Yorker by birth, he taught and studied law there before taking up his practice in Wisconsin. He served as a district attorney and judge and then sat in both houses of the legislature. In the mid-1850s he served a term as lieutenant governor. He was elected secretary of state in 1861 on the Republican ticket and two years later governor on the Union label. Once in the gubernatorial chair he was active in providing funds for the war effort. He visited the troops in the field and established medical facilities for the sick and wounded at home. A prime mover in the founding of a soldiers' orphans home, he also took measures to aid the families of those in the service. He oversaw the legislature's ratification of the 13th Amendment and supervised a referendum which defeated black suffrage. Refusing renomination, he left office in 1866 to continue in the legal profession and take up farming.

LEWIS, John Wood (1801-1865)

A successful Georgia businessman and farmer, John W. Lewis was appointed to the Confederate Senate by Governor Joseph E. Brown—whom Lewis had earlier loaned the money to attend Yale Law School. Born in South Carolina, Lewis practiced medicine and sat in the state legislature there before becoming a Baptist preacher and moving to Georgia where he also proved effective as a railroad superintendent, an appointment from Brown. When Robert Toombs rejected election to the Confederate Senate, Lewis was appointed. He sat on the committees on: Finance; and Post Offices and Post Roads. Allied with Brown, he proved to be an ardent states' righter doing much to hinder the central government in its ability to wage war. He opposed the draft and the establishment of a Confederate supreme court and was part of the anti-Bragg faction—he supported P.G.T. Beauregard for command in the West. Not seeking reelection to a full six-year term, he finished the war looking after Georgia's share in the salt mines at Saltville, Virginia.

LEWIS, Joseph Horace (1824-1904)

As commander of the famed Kentucky, or Orphan, Brigade, Joseph H. Lewis finished the Civil War as part of the escort for the fleeing Jefferson Davis and his party. The native Kentuckian was a lawyer and state legislator before the war. His Confederate assignments included: colonel, 6th Kentucky (November 1, 1861); commanding Helm's Brigade, Breckinridge's-Bate's Division, Hill's-Breckinridge's-Hindman's Corps, Army of Tennessee (September 20, 1863-February 28, 1864); brigadier general, CSA (September 30, 1863) commanding Kentucky Brigade, Bate's-Brown's Division, Hardee's Corps, Army of Tennessee (February 28-September 4, 1864); commanding brigade, Iverson's Division, Wheeler's Cavalry Corps, Army of Tennessee (September 4-late 1864); commanding brigade, Iverson's Division, Wheeler's Cavalry Corps, Department of South Carolina, Georgia and Florida (late 1864-March 1865); and commanding brigade, Iverson's Cavalry Division, Military District of South Carolina and Georgia, Department of South Carolina, Georgia and Florida (March-May 9, 1865). He led his regiment at Shiloh, Murfreesboro, and during the Tullahoma Campaign. On the second day at Chickamauga he succeeded the deceased Benjamin H. Helm in command of the Kentucky Brigade and was promoted to brigadier general at the end of the month. He led the brigade at Chattanooga and throughout the Atlanta Campaign at the conclusion of which the brigade was mounted. Serving out the balance of the war as cavalry, the brigade, under Lewis' direction, fought in the Savannah Campaign and in May 1865 was part of Davis' escort. Surrendering when the president was captured in Georgia, Lewis resumed his practice and again entered politics as a state legislator and U.S. congressman. He later spent nearly two decades as a judge. (Davis, William C., *The Orphan Brigade: The Kentucky Confederates Who Couldn't Go Home*)

LEWIS, Levin M. (?-?)

Serving in the Trans-Mississippi, Levin M. Lewis received an extralegal promotion to brigadier after most of the Confederate armies had surrendered. His service included: colonel, 3rd Missouri, 5th Division, Missouri State Guard (early 1861); lieutenant colonel, 7th Missouri; colonel, 16th Missouri; and brigadier general, CSA, by General E. Kirby Smith (May 16, 1865). During the first year of the war he served in the state forces. Transferring to Confederate service, he became second in command of the 7th Missouri which became the 16th when he took over as colonel. His service was principally in the District of Arkansas but he was part of the detachment sent to the District of West Louisiana to face N.P. Banks' Red River Campaign in the spring of 1864. In the final days of the war he commanded a brigade and was rewarded with a promotion to brigadier 10 days before the surrender of the Trans-Mississippi Department.

LEWIS, Pryce (ca. 1835-?)

One of Allan Pinkerton's best undercover agents during the first year of the Civil War was Pryce Lewis. A former bookseller in England, he had joined the detective agency in the 1850s and was conducting a murder investigation in Jackson, Mississippi, in early 1861. Completing the case, he returned to the North in June. But he had brought with him, without instructions, much information of military importance. He joined

Pinkerton's secret military intelligence organization and conducted a highly successful expedition into western Virginia, posing as an English nobleman, and contributed to the Union capture of Charleston, Virginia. He next took part in the disruption of Rose O'Neal Greenhow's spying activities in Washington. When the espionage team of Timothy Webster and Mrs. Hattie Lawton failed to report to Pinkerton during January and February 1862, Lewis and John Scully were sent after them to Richmond. Lewis was to continue on to Chattanooga while Scully returned the Webster-Lawton reports to Washington. In Richmond the pair were recognized by a man they had held as a prisoner the previous year. Arrested, Lewis denied everything but Scully, who had a weakness for the bottle, began to talk. As a result Webster was hanged, Lawton imprisoned for a year, and the rescue pair sentenced to the gallows. However, Lewis claimed the protection of the British crown since neither he nor Scully had become U.S. citizens. After a series of delays they were exchanged in 1863 but were shunned by the War Department and Pinkerton for having sent Webster to his doom. Lewis became a bailiff at the Old Capitol Prison in Washington. (Horan, James D., *The Pinkertons: The Detective Dynasty That Made History*)

LEWIS, William Gaston (1835-1901)

Educated at a military school, former North Carolina educator William G. Lewis gave up a railroading job to enter the Confederate military where he was twice assigned to duty as a temporary brigadier general. His assignments included: ensign, 1st North Carolina (April 21, 1861); major, 33rd North Carolina, (January 17, 1862); lieutenant colonel, 43rd North Carolina (April 25, 1862); commanding Hoke's (old) Brigade, Ransom's Division, Department of North Carolina and Southern Virginia (May 1864); temporary brigadier general, CSA (May 31, 1864); commanding same brigade, Early's-Ramseur's-Pegram's Division, 2nd Corps, Army of Northern Virginia (May-June 1864 and December 1864-April 7, 1865); and commanding brigade, Ramseur's-Pegram's Division, Valley District, Department of Northern Virginia (June-August 5 and November-December 1864). Serving with his first regiment, he fought at Big Bethel before it was mustered out in the fall of 1861. He soon became a field grade officer in the 33rd North Carolina but remained only a few months before transferring to the 43rd. However, he did see action at New Bern. In his new unit, he served in the Seven Days, in the Department of North Carolina, and at 2nd Winchester before succeeding to regimental leadership upon the capture of the colonel at Gettysburg. After serving at Bristoe Station and in the Mine Run Campaign, his regiment was temporarily detached to serve with Hoke's Brigade in North Carolina. Fighting at Plymouth, he earned temporary promotion to brigadier and the command of Hoke's brigade which he led back to Lee's army for the fighting at the North Anna and Cold Harbor and with Early at Monocacy. In August 1864 he was relieved of brigade command upon the return of newly promoted General A.C. Godwin. Following the latter's death he again served as a general through the Petersburg siege and in the retreat to Appomattox until wounded and captured at Farmville on April 7, 1865. He engaged in civil engineering for over three decades. (Freeman, Douglas S., *Lee's Lieutenants*)

LEYDEN, Austin (?-1900)

Pennsylvania-born Atlanta manufacturer Austin Leyden served with his artillery battalion throughout most of the war but mostly in the less- chronicled theaters. He entered his adopted state's service at the outbreak of hostilities and his assignments included: lieutenant, Company F, 1st Georgia (March 18, 1861); major, 9th Georgia Artillery Battalion (April 1862); commanding Artillery Battalion, Preston's Division, Buckner's Corps, Army of Tennessee (August 6-late September 1863); commanding artillery battalion, Longstreet's Corps, Army of Tennessee (September-November 1863); and commanding artillery battalion, Department of East Tennessee (November 1863-April 1864). On November 5, 1861, he resigned his infantry commission in order to raise an artillery unit with which he served in Georgia, southwest Virginia, and East Tennessee. When the forces in the Department of East Tennessee were organized into a corps and assigned to the Army of Tennessee, Leyden took part in the Chickamauga Campaign and the beginning of the Chattanooga siege. Accompanying Longstreet back into East Tennessee, he took part in the unsuccessful Knoxville siege. Moving into Virginia, he was in charge of a reserve artillery camp at Staunton in the summer of 1864. By that fall the battalion had been assigned to the fortifications around the capital where it served until the city's fall. Leyden returned to Atlanta after Appomattox and was active in local politics and as an inventor.

LIDDELL, St. John Richardson (1815-1870)

Resigning in 1838 after only one year at West Point, St. John R. Liddell settled on a Louisiana plantation until the Civil War gave him a second chance for a military career—in the Southern service. The Mississippi native's assignments included: colonel and volunteer aide-de-camp (1861); commanding 1st Brigade, 3rd Corps, Army of the Mississippi (June-July 5, 1862); commanding brigade, Buckner's Division, Army of the Mississippi (July 5-August 15, 1862); brigadier general, CSA (July 17, 1862); commanding brigade, Buckner's Division, Left Wing, Army of the Mississippi (August 15-November 20, 1862); commanding brigade, Buckner's-Cleburne's Division, Hardee's-Breckinridge's Corps, Army of Tennessee (November 20, 1862-September 1863 and September 22-November 30, 1863); commanding division, Reserve Corps, Army of Tennessee (September 1863); commanding brigade, Cleburne's Division, Hardee's (new) Corps, Army of Tennessee (November 30-December 2, 1863); commanding Sub-District of North Louisiana, District of West Louisiana, Trans-Mississippi Department (spring 1864); and commanding in the Department of Alabama, Mississippi and East Louisiana: District of Southwest Mississippi and East Louisiana (August 2-25, 1864); brigade, District of the Gulf (August-October 1864); and division, District of the Gulf (October 1864-April 9, 1865). He held a staff position in central Kentucky with William J.

Hardee early in the war and then served as a special messenger to Richmond for Albert S. Johnston. For a few weeks he commanded a brigade in Mississippi before being named a brigadier general. He led a brigade at Perryville, Murfreesboro, and during the Tullahoma Campaign. At Chickamauga he led a division in William H.T. Walker's Reserve Corps. Back with his regular brigade, he fought at Chattanooga and the next year led a sub-district in Louisiana during the Red River Campaign. Transferring back to the east of the Mississippi, he led a brigade and division around Mobile during the final stages of the war. Captured at the fall of Fort Blakely, he returned to his plantation upon his release and was killed by a fellow planter five years later. (Hughes, Nathaniel C., ed., Liddell, St. John Richardson, *Liddell's Record*)

LIEBER, Francis (1800-1872)

During and after the Civil War Francis Lieber became known as a pioneer in the field of military law, primarily through his contributions to General Order No. 100, which adapted the Rules of War to the Civil War. A native of Berlin, he had served in the Prussian forces against Napoleon in 1815, being wounded, and in the Greek war for independence in 1822. Returning home, he continued his education despite governmental restrictions and an arrest for his liberal views. Finally fleeing to England he later moved to the United States. By the time of the Civil War he was already widely respected for his legal works, including *Manual of Political Ethics*, *Legal and Political Hermeneutics*, and *On Civil Liberty and Self-Government*. A Columbia College professor in New York at the outbreak of the war, he was frequently consulted by the War Department on legal matters relating to an internal, civil war. In *Guerrilla Parties Considered with Reference to the Laws and Usages of War* he declared that guerrillas and partisan rangers should be treated as prisoners of war but not ordinary bushwhackers and brigands. Many of his decisions were published in orders as *Instructions for the Government of Armies in the Field*. Germany later adopted this document for its own use. After the war Lieber was a professor of law and was a custodian of captured Confederate papers. He himself had three sons in the Civil War—one Confederate and two Union. (Harley, Lewis R., *Francis Lieber: His Life and Political Philosophy* and Freidel, Frank Burt, *Francis Lieber, Nineteenth-century Liberal*)

LIGHTBURN, Joseph Andrew Jackson (1824-1901)

A veteran of a five-year enlistment in the regular army, 1846 to 1851, Joseph A.J. Lightburn was active in the movement to keep the western counties of Virginia loyal to the Union; he subsequently became a Union general. Lightburn had been born in Pennsylvania but had moved with his family to Virginia before beginning his army enlistment and rising to the rank of sergeant. His Civil War assignments included: colonel, 4th West Virginia (August 14, 1861); commanding 4th Brigade, District of the Kanawha, Mountain Department (March 11-August 15, 1862); commanding the district (August 15-September 1862); commanding District of the Kanawha, Department of the Ohio (September 1862-early 1863); brigadier general, USV (March 14, 1863); commanding 2nd Brigade, 2nd Division, 15th Corps, Army of the Tennessee (May 23-July 26, 1863, October 19, 1863-January 12, 1864, February 12-July 22, July 27-August 5, and August 17-24, 1864); commanding the division (July 26-September 10, 1863, July 22-27, and August 5-17, 1864); and commanding 2nd Infantry Division, Department of West Virginia (January-May 1865). Having been defeated for a West Point cadetship by his neighbor, the future Stonewall Jackson, Lightburn finally received a commission as colonel of a volunteer regiment in 1861. After extensive service in the Kanawha Valley of western Virginia he was advanced to a brigadier generalship and assigned to a brigade in Grant's army operating against Vicksburg. After that city's fall he participated in the capture of Jackson, Mississippi. In the relief of Chattanooga he fought in the attacks on the north end of Missionary Ridge. He led his brigade through the advance on Atlanta and in the battle proper advanced to command of the division. Back in brigade command during the siege of the city, he was wounded in the head on August 24, 1864. Not returning to the field until the beginning of the next year, he directed a division in West Virginia and the lower Shenandoah Valley. Resigning on June 22, 1865, he became a Baptist preacher two years later.

LIGHTFOOT, Charles Edward (1834-1878)

Starting out in the Confederate infantry, Charles Edward Lightfoot ended up serving for most of the war in the artillery defenses of the capital. A graduate of the Virginia Military Institute, he was teaching at the Hillsboro Military Academy in North Carolina at the outbreak of the war. His service included: major, 6th North Carolina (May 16, 1861); lieutenant colonel, 6th North Carolina (July 11, 1861); colonel, 22nd North Carolina (March 29, 1862); lieutenant colonel, Artillery (August 18, 1862); commanding Light Artillery Battalion, Richmond Defenses, Department of Richmond (ca. April 1, 1863-ca. April 2, 1865); and commanding artillery battalion, 2nd Corps, Army of Northern Virginia (ca. April 2-9, 1865). With his first regiment he served at the battle of 1st Bull Run and was praised by his superiors. Elected to command another regiment, he was captured at Seven Pines on May 31, 1862. Upon his exchange on August 5, 1862, he found that he had been defeated for reelection upon the reorganization of the regiment on June 13. However, within two weeks he was given an appointment in the artillery. He eventually commanded an artillery battalion defending Richmond until the fall of that city. He then took command of a battalion in the retreat to Appomattox. Settling back in his native Culpeper County, Virginia, he served on the faculty of the Bethel Military Academy.

LILLEY, Robert Doak (1836-1886)

Appointed under the act authorizing Jefferson Davis to appoint temporary general officers, Robert D. Lilley did not last long in active field command. A native Virginian and a survey equipment salesman, he raised the Augusta Lee Rifles for the Confederate army. His assignments included: captain, Company C (D from May 1862), 25th Virginia (ca. May 1861); major, 25th Virginia (January 28, 1863); lieutenant colonel, 25th Virginia (August 20, 1863); brigadier general, CSA (May 31, 1864); commanding Pegram's Brigade, Early's-Ramseur's Division, 2nd Corps, Army of Northern Virginia (June 4-13, 1864); commanding Pegram's Brigade, Ramseur's Division, Valley District, Department of Northern Virginia (June 13-July 20, 1864); and commanding reserve forces, same district and department (November 28, 1864-April 1865). His company and regiment fought at Rich Mountain, Greenbrier River, Allegheny, McDowell, in the Shenandoah Valley Campaign, the Seven Days, at Cedar Mountain, 2nd Bull Run, Antietam (commanding the regiment), Fredericksburg, Gettysburg, Mine Run, and the Wilderness. At Spotsylvania his regiment was so mauled that it was consolidated with the other regiments of the brigade. Lilley was soon promoted to temporary brigadier and placed in charge of the wounded General Pegram's Brigade. After fighting at Cold Harbor he went with Early to the Shenandoah and fought at Monocacy and on the outskirts of Washington. While scouting near Winchester, Virginia, on July 20, 1864, he received three wounds and was captured. When federals left the area a few days later they left Lilley, who recovered to finish the war in command of the reserve forces in the Valley. After the war he was employed by Washington College. (Freeman, Douglas S., *Lee's Lieutenants*)

LILLY, Eli (1838-1898)

Having opened a pharmacy the year before the Civil War, Eli Lilly took time out to serve in the Union infantry, artillery, and cavalry before returning to the business which he built into today's Eli Lilly and Company. Born in Baltimore his family had moved via Kentucky to Indiana. Active in religious circles he was a proponent of abolition and temperance. Having been a sergeant in the militia since 1858, he enlisted early in the war. His assignments included: second lieutenant, Company E, 21st Indiana (ca. July 24, 1861); captain, 18th Indiana Battery (August 6, 1862); major, 9th Indiana Cavalry (ca. April 1864); and lieutenant colonel, 9th Indiana Cavalry (1864 or 1865). With his infantry company he was sent to Baltimore where he watched the coastal and field batteries practice. Desiring to command a battery of his own, he resigned on December 9, 1861. Ironically the 21st was converted to heavy artillery in February 1863. The next summer he completed the organization of his battery, which he led—as part of Wilder's Brigade of mounted infantry—in Tennessee and Georgia, including Hoover's Gap, Chickamauga, the Knoxville relief expedition, and Mossy Creek. Seeking advancement, he transferred to the cavalry and served at Nashville and in Mississippi. Mustered out, he returned to build his pharmaceutical empire. He was active in veterans' affairs, helping to organize reunions. (Rowell, John W., *Yankee Artillerymen: Through the Civil War with Eli Lilly's Indiana Battery*)

LINCOLN, Abraham (1809-1865)

As president during the Civil War, Abraham Lincoln was forced to more radical views by the times. Born in humble surroundings in Kentucky and raised there and in Indiana, he rarely discussed his background, being embarrassed by it. Following some odd jobs and a basically self-taught education, he served in the Illinois legislature and was admitted to the bar in 1836. He served in the U.S. Congress from 1847 to 1849, where he opposed the war with Mexico. With the demise of the Whigs, he became a Republican and in 1858 tried to unseat Senator Stephen A. Douglas, a longtime rival. The high point of the unsuccessful bid was a series of debates which propelled Lincoln to national prominence, although he lost the race. During the debates, Lincoln hit hard at Douglas' introduction of the Kansas-Nebraska Bill, which allowed the area to possibly become a slave territory, and Douglas' doctrine of popular sovereignty. Following a series of speaking engagements throughout the North, Lincoln was a serious contender for the Republican presidential nomination in 1860. His campaign managers struck a deal, which he subsequently found distasteful, with Pennsylvania's political boss Simon Cameron whereby he gained the nomination—and, if elected, would name Cameron secretary of war. Lincoln was elected and some Southern states, feeling their power was gone, seceded before he was inaugurated. Despite a conciliatory address, the movement continued and Fort Sumter was fired upon. Lincoln called for 75,000 volunteers and much of the Upper South joined the Confederacy. The war weighed heavily upon the president and he was said to have aged greatly. He lost a son to disease during the conflict, and gained a sense of the suffering being visited upon thousands of families. The times forced the radicalization

Abraham Lincoln, the "Great Emancipator." (*Leslie's*)

of the basically conservative president. In the 1858 debates with Douglas he had denied the equality of the blacks except in their right to freedom and the fruits of their labors and was a supporter of their colonization in Africa or the Caribbean. He also felt that the federal government could only limit the spread of the dreaded institution of slavery, not abolish it in those states where it already existed. The war changed all this, and he took actions that many considered dictatorial. After resisting for many months, he issued the Emancipation Proclamation following the narrow Union victory at Antietam. His Gettysburg Address declared the blacks' equality, and, dropping his colonization ideas, he finally decided to enlist former slaves into the Union army. There is even some evidence that his announced plans for the lenient treatment of the conquered South would have been radicalized had he lived. In 1864 Lincoln won reelection (despite a brief Fremont challenge, supported by radicals who soon withdrew) over the Democratic challenger, George McClellan. Lincoln was the only sitting president ever to be under fire—off Norfolk in 1862 and at Fort Stevens in 1864 during Early's raid on Washington. After a visit to the captured Confederate capital, he attended the play "Our American Cousin" at Ford's Theatre in Washington on April 14, 1865. Shot by John Wilkes Booth, he died the next day—and became the first American president to be assassinated.

LINCOLN, Mary Todd (1818-1882)

A temperamental woman, Mary Lincoln never got over the personal tragedies of her life. Born into the Kentucky aristocracy she married Abraham Lincoln after an on-again-off-again courtship in 1842. Not only was her husband assassinated at the war's close but she also lost one son, Edward Baker, before the war and another, William Wallace, in 1862. The husband of her half-sister, Confederate General Benjamin Helm, was killed at the Battle of Chickamauga. The loss of the idolized Willie deeply disturbed her and she refused to enter the rooms in which he had died and been embalmed. She even held at least one seance in the White House to try to make contact with his departed soul. After the assassination of her husband, money problems led her to scandalously sell part of her jewelry and wardrobe. She was always harshly treated by the press for her temperamental behavior, and the 1871 loss of a third son, Thomas or "Tad," only served to deepen her depression. In 1875, her sole remaining son, Robert Todd, had her committed as insane. After a suicide attempt, she recovered sufficiently to be released the following year. Following extensive travel abroad, she spent her final months at the home of her sister, wearing mourning clothes. (Randall, Ruth Painter, *Mary Lincoln: Biography of a Marriage*)

LINCOLN, Robert Todd (1843-1926)

The eldest of Abraham Lincoln's sons, Robert Todd Lincoln, was also the last surviving son. Having entered Harvard in 1859, Lincoln, at the request of his mother, continued his studies during the war. After graduating in 1864, he studied for four months at the Harvard Law School. However, with a draft in effect, the newspapers were sharply critical of the Lincolns for keeping their son out of the army. At the president's request, General Grant appointed the law student to his staff with the rank of captain and assistant adjutant general of volunteers on February 11, 1865. In this capacity Lincoln particpated in the final stages of the Petersburg siege and returned to Washington in time to refuse to accompany his parents to Ford's Theater. He never forgave himself for this. Following his resignation, on June 10, 1865, he returned to Illinois with his widowed mother and completed his law studies. In 1875 he felt obligated to have his mother committed as insane. He served from 1881 to 1885, in the Garfield and Arthur administrations, as secretary of war. He did not capitalize upon his name by running for office and was afterwards appointed as minister to Great Britain. He was later in the railroad business and eventually rose to be president of the Pullman Company. He retired in 1911 and went into semi-seclusion until his death.

LINCOLN, William Wallace (1850-1862)

Young Willie Lincoln was a joy to his parents and thus his death a year into the war was a great tragedy to the White House family. According to Attorney General Edward Bates, the Lincolns idolized their thoughtful and imaginative third child who used to make up fanciful timetables for trains to Illinois. Going riding in the rain, the child became ill, an event that cast a dark cloud over a previously scheduled White House ball and filled his father with dread of the outcome. On February 20, 1862, Willie died of typhoid. At the same time that battle casualty lists were bringing grief to many households, the President had his own casualty. Mary Lincoln never again entered the death-filled Guest Room nor the Green Room where the child was embalmed. In order to get in touch with her lost son, the first lady held at least one seance in the Executive Mansion, and many say that the tragedy contributed to her psychological problems. (Sandburg, Carl, *Abraham Lincoln: The Prairie Years and The War Years*)

LINEBAUGH, John H. (?-ca. 1865)

One striking victim of the historic conflict between the press and the military was John Linebaugh. Using the pen-name "Shadow," Linebaugh was the special correspondent for the *Memphis-Grenada-Jackson-Meridian-Atlanta-Montgomery Appeal* in Chattanooga. While reporting for the refugee paper, he became very critical of General Braxton Bragg's apparent lack of willingness to fight the Union forces. Finally, in September 1863, the commander of the Army of Tennessee, who had retired from middle Tennessee into northern Georgia, abandoning Chattanooga, placed the reporter under arrest for excessive criticism. The *Appeal* struck back in behalf of its correspondent, who was being held without a trial, and obtained his release in early October. The paper blasted Bragg's actions as a "civil offense." Resuming his reportorial duties, Linebaugh was accidentally drowned in the Alabama River during one of the paper's many flights from capture.

LITTLE, Lewis Henry (1817-1862)

Baltimore native Lewis Henry Little resigned his regular army captaincy in the 7th Infantry on May 7, 1861, and ended up giving his life to the Confederate cause. He had been commissioned directly into the old army in 1839 and had won a brevet in Mexico. His Confederate assignments included: major, Artillery (ca. May 1861); colonel and assistant adjutant general (1861); commanding 1st Brigade, Missouri State Guard (Confederate volunteers), Trans-Mississippi District (Army of the West), Department #2 (ca. February-March 17, 1862); commanding 1st Brigade, 1st Division, Trans-Mississippi District (Army of the West), Department #2 (March 17-April 1862); brigadier general, CSA (April 12, 1862); commanding 1st Brigade, Price's Division, Army of the West, Department #2 (April-June 1862); commanding the division (June-September 1862); and commanding 1st Division, Price's Corps (Army of the West), Army of West Tennessee, Department #2 (September-September 19, 1862). Attracting the attention of Sterling Price of the Missouri State Guard, on whose staff he was serving, he was given charge of a brigade which he led at Pea Ridge. Promoted to brigadier general, he led his command across the Mississippi and took part in the operations around Corinth. Then, on September 19, 1862, he was instantly killed by a bullet in the head while meeting with Price and other officers during the battle of Iuka.

LITTLE ROBE (fl. 1860s-1870s)

It was the massacre at Sand Creek which prompted Little Robe to move from being a proponent of peace with the whites, into the war camp. One of the leading Cheyenne chiefs, he had long urged accommodation with the advancing whites. In this he was allied with Black Kettle. He had been reported as killed at Sand Creek in 1864, so Coloradons were surprised to hear that he was alive and well and stirring up trouble in the war camp in early 1865. He fought actively for the next two years but then signed the Treaty of Medicine Lodge in 1867. The next year he again went on the war path but surrendered shortly after the battle of the Washita. Placed on a reservation, he again counseled peace. By this time he was the principal chief of the Cheyennes—succeeding Black Kettle who had been killed in the massacre on the Washita. Twice, in 1871 and 1873, he toured the East—meeting President Grant on the latter trip. The next year he stayed on the reservation when the Red River War broke out. (Brown, Dee, *Bury My Heart At Wounded Knee*)

LITTLE SIX

See: *Shakopee*

LIVERMORE, Mary Ashton Rice (1820-1905)

The wife of a Chicago clergyman and publisher, Mary A.R. Livermore was one of the Chicago area founders of the United States Sanitary Commission and became one of its national directors. Massachusetts-born, she was a teacher before she married the Universalist minister in 1845. After he preached for a while in New England, they settled in Chicago where he edited the *New Covenant*. She also worked as an editor and covered the 1860 Republican convention. Active in various reform movements before the war, she became upset with some of the failings of the national government in providing for the troops in the field. In 1862 she, with others, helped found the Commission in the Chicago area and later traveled widely in the Midwest helping organize other chapters. In December 1862 she was made a national director. She later wrote an account of her experiences, *My Story of the War: A Woman's Narrative of Four Years Personal Experience*. After the Civil War she worked for women's suffrage as a means to further her other reform goals.

LIVERMORE, Thomas Leonard (1844-1918)

Although he had been born in Illinois, Thomas L. Livermore became the most famous writer on New Hampshire's Civil War history and also authored one of the top statistical studies on that conflict, North and South. Having applied to West Point, he went to Washington in 1861 to speed up his appointment but got caught up in the war fever raging there and enlisted in a New Hampshire unit. His assignments included: private, 1st New Hampshire (spring 1861); lieutenant, 5th New Hampshire (ca. October 22, 1861); captain, 5th New Hampshire (1863); chief of Ambulance Corps, 2nd Corps, Army of the Potomac (fall 1863); major, 5th New Hampshire (1864); acting assistant inspector general, 2nd Corps, Army of the Potomac (1864-spring 1865); and colonel, 18th New Hampshire (mid 1865). He took part in Patterson's campaign in the Shenandoah in July 1861 before being mustered out on August 9, 1861. Soon becoming a line officer in a new unit, he was highly commended by his regimental commander, Edward E. Cross, at Antietam. The regiment also fought on the Peninsula and at Fredericksburg, Chancellorsville, and Gettysburg. As a captain, he directed the 2nd Corps' ambulances at Bristoe Station. The following year, he became acting assistant inspector general on the staff of Winfield Hancock and was advanced to major. Continuing under Andrew A. Humphreys in the same position, he took part in the Petersburg and Appomattox campaigns. With hostilities at a close he was named to head the 18th New Hampshire, of which he wrote *History of the Eighteenth New Hampshire Volunteers, 1864-5*. Mustered out on July 29, 1865, he became a lawyer and was engaged in the mining and milling businesses. Entering the historical writing field, he wrote several articles. His statistical work was *Numbers and Losses in the Civil War in America, 1861-65*. His memoirs, *Days and Events, 1860-1866*, appeared two years after his death. (See also: Bibliography)

LLOYD, John M. (?-1892)

One of the key witnesses against Mary E. Surratt, John M. Lloyd did much to send her to the gallows but later declared that he had been coerced into giving testimony. When the widowed

Mrs. Surratt moved into Washington, Lloyd had rented the tavern at Surrattsville in Maryland. It was here that the guns to be used in the escape of the assassins were stored for convenient use. At the conspirators' trial Lloyd claimed that it was Mrs. Surratt who brought the message from Booth telling Lloyd to have the guns handy for imminent use. Lloyd's testimony should have been somewhat suspect because he was noted for his heavy drinking and lapses of memory. He was, however, supported in his claims by a boarder at the Surratt house in the city, Louis J. Weichmann. Lloyd later claimed that he was threatened with death in the event that he did not testify against Mrs. Surratt.

LLOYD, William Alvin (?-?)

One of the more reckless of Union spies, William Lloyd actually carried his espionage contract with him into the Confederacy. As a publisher of maps and timetables for railroads and river transportation in the South, Lloyd had an ideal cover as a spy. Approaching President Lincoln, he received an assignment to report back any knowledge of military matters. In exchange he received a promise of $200 per month and, more important, the required pass through Union lines that was absolutely necessary to his business. Without setting up a communications system with Washington, he was off to the South, with his assistant, Thomas H.S. Boyd, soon to follow. He visited Nashville, Grand Gulf, Chattanooga, and Memphis before his wife and maid joined him. In Grand Gulf he was briefly arrested, on suspicion, but soon released. Continuing on his way he visited New Orleans before proceeding to Richmond where he became friendly with government officials, including the city's provost marshal, General John H. Winder, upon whom he and Boyd showered gifts. After observing enemy positions at Norfolk and Portsmouth, Virginia, they sent their first message north. Moving on to Savannah, he was arrested late in 1861. The Confederates did not find his pass from Lincoln. In mid-1862 the authorities, thinking he was a reporter, released him on parole. He soon gained valuable information about the Confederate defenses of Richmond from Lee's chief of artillery, General William Pendleton. Suspicion again aroused, he ended up in Libby Prison briefly. Freed, he continued his operations for the rest of the war, even leaving Richmond on the same train as Jefferson Davis and his cabinet. He landed in jail several more times but was never tried. Since Lloyd was forced to destroy his contract with Lincoln, the government refused to make good the payments due on the contract for the four years of the war. His expenses were paid, however, but his health had been severely damaged in his adventures and he died shortly after the war. Suits by his wife for the money were denied by the Supreme Court.

LOAN, Benjamin F. (?-?)

A general officer only in the Missouri Militia, Benjamin F. Loan was principally engaged in fighting an irregular war against Confederate guerrillas and bushwhackers. Born in Kentucky, he had moved to Missouri sometime before the Civil War. His assignments included: brigadier general, Missouri Militia (in U.S. service November 27, 1861-June 8, 1863); commanding District of Northwest Missouri, Department of the Mississippi (March 12-June 5, 1862); commanding District of Northwest Missouri, Military District of the Missouri, Department of the Mississippi (June 5-August 25, 1862); and commanding District of Central Missouri, Department of the Missouri (October 12, 1862-June 9, 1863). His first district command was composed entirely of Missouri Enrolled Militia assigned to clear out the northwestern part of the state which was still infested with guerrillas. After commanding in central Missouri, he was honorably discharged from the federal service on June 8, 1863.

LOCKE, David Ross (1833-1888)

Editor and publisher of the Findlay (Ohio) *Jeffersonian*, David Locke enjoyed a broad circulation of his bitter attacks on the Southern cause. Using the vitriolic letters of the fictitious Petroleum Vesuvius Nasby, a pro-Southern Ohio Democrat and Copperhead, Locke ridiculed the secession movement in an account of the secession of "Wingert's Corners, Ohio." Nasby justified the drastic move on the grounds that the state had not established the capital there and "never appointed any citizen of the place to any office where theft was possible." With the declining fortunes of the rebel cause, Nasby in "Waileth and Cusseth" cursed virtually everyone who he felt had let down the Confederacy. Locke's satire was so popular with Lincoln that the president kept a full set of the "letters" close at hand in his office. Grant's secretary of the treasury, George S. Boutwell, credited "the Army and Navy, the Republican Party, and the letters of Petroleum V. Nasby" with the defeat of the South. Nasby continued to provide a commentary upon the issues of the day into the 1880s, when Locke died. (Dudden, Arthur P., ed., *The Assault of Laughter*)

LOCKWOOD, Henry Hayes (1814-1899)

West Pointer (1836) Henry H. Lockwood taught at Annapolis, was a naval officer in the Mexican War, returned to the army for the Civil War, and then returned to the naval academy. The Delaware native had resigned as a second lieutenant of artillery, after campaigning against the Seminoles, a year after his graduation. Engaged in farming, he was named a mathematics faculty member at Annapolis. Aboard the USS *United States* he served off the California coast in the Mexican War. The interwar years again saw him as a professor. However, upon the outbreak of the Civil War he returned to the army. His assignments included: colonel, 1st Delaware (May 25, 1861); brigadier general, USV (August 8, 1861); commanding District of the Eastern Shore, Middle Department (ca. March-July 22, 1862); commanding District of the Eastern Shore, 8th Corps, Middle Department (July 22, 1862-January 5, 1863); commanding 1st Separate Brigade, 8th Corps, Middle Department (January 5-February 4, February 14-June 26, October 28-December 18, 1863, and March 12-24, 1864); commanding Independent Brigade, 12th Corps, Army of the Potomac (July 2-5, 1863); commanding 2nd Brigade, 1st Division, 12th Corps, Army of the Potomac (July 5-15, 1863); commanding Maryland Heights Division, Department of West Virginia (July 15-

September 18, 1863); commanding 8th Corps, Middle Department and the department (December 5, 1863-March 22, 1864); commanding 3rd Separate Brigade, 8th Corps, Middle Department (March 24-May 9 and July 20, 1864-July 31, 1865); and commanding 2nd Division, 5th Corps, Army of the Potomac (May 9-June 2, 1864). Most of his wartime service was on the eastern shore of Maryland and Virginia. But during the Gettysburg Campaign he led a brigade to reinforce the Army of the Potomac and, being assigned to the 12th Corps, fought on Culp's Hill. After brief service near Harpers Ferry, he returned to his old post and for a time commanded the corps and the department. Early in the Overland Campaign he was sent with reinforcements for Grant and briefly commanded a division at Cold Harbor until relieved by Grant's order and sent back to Maryland. There he led a provisional force in the defense of Washington against Early's raid. He then finished the war in Maryland and was mustered out on August 24, 1865. He returned to the naval academy and later served at the Washington Naval Observatory.

LOGAN, George Washington (1815-1889)

The disatisfaction with the war in North Carolina led to the formation of the "Red Strings" and their election of George W. Logan as a peace candidate to the Second Confederate Congress. A lawyer and former Whig, he never accepted secession and held no position of importance in the first years of the war. Elected as an antiwar congressman, he served on the committees on: Printing; and Ordnance and Ordnance Supplies. Reflecting his 10th District constituents' views, he proposed the repeal of the tax-in-kind and fought arbitrary impressments. On conscription he favored a wide range of exemptions. Turning Republican at the close of the war he served as a superior court judge. Considered too friendly to the freed slaves in his decisions, he required military protection from the Ku Klux Klan to hold his court sessions. In 1874 he retired to private life and was engaged in the real estate business.

LOGAN, John Alexander (1826-1886)

William T. Sherman considered nonprofessional soldier John A. Logan to be "perfect in combat," but when Logan was denied an army command Logan considered it a conspiracy among the West Pointers. A native Illinois lawyer and prominant Democratic politician, Logan proved his loyalty to the Union when he spoke to Ulysses S. Grant's 21st Illinois on the question of their reenlistment. Grant was not sure what Logan would say, but he wanted the Democratic congressman to appear before the largely Democratic regiment. With a mixture of humor and patriotism, Logan got most of the regiment to reenlist. The next month, while still a sitting congressman, he followed the Union army onto the field of 1st Bull Run and, joining a Michigan regiment, actually fired at the enemy before concentrating on helping the wounded. He then entered the army officially but without giving up his seat in Washington. His assignments included: colonel, 31st Illinois (September 18, 1861); brigadier general, USV (March 21, 1862); commanding 1st Brigade, 1st Division, Army of the Tennessee (April 19-July 1862); commanding 1st Brigade, 1st Division, District of Jackson, Army of the Tennessee (July-September and September-November 1862); commanding the district (September 1862); commanding 3rd Division, Right Wing, 13th Corps, Army of the Tennessee (November 1-December 18, 1862); major general, USV (November 29, 1862); commanding 3rd Division, 17th Corps, Army of the Tennessee (December 18, 1862-July 20, 1863); commanding 15th Corps, Army of the Tennessee (December 11, 1863-July 22, 1864, July 27-September 23, 1864, and January 8-May 23, 1865); and commanding the army (July 22-27, 1864 and May 19-August 1, 1865). The Mexican War veteran—as a second lieutenant of Illinois volunteers—fought well at Belmont where he had a horse shot out from under him. He missed Shiloh due to a wound suffered at Fort Donelson and had to resign his congressional seat on April 2, 1862, because of his acceptance of a brigadier generalship. He recovered to take part in the slow operations against Corinth, Mississippi, and then led a division through the Vicksburg Campaign. He was also distinguished in the Atlanta Campaign, especially at Dallas. After the fall of McPherson he took over command of the Army of the Tennessee. However, Sherman did not trust his performance in non-combat situations (regulations, etc.) and placed another West Pointer, Oliver O. Howard, in command. Logan was thereafter prejudiced against graduates of the military academy. He returned to his 15th Corps for the fall of Atlanta. He then went on leave to campaign for Lincoln in Illinois, having previously renounced his threat to take the Midwestern troops home if black troops were recruited for the army. While Logan

Union General John A. Logan, "perfect in combat." (*Leslie's*)

was in Washington after the election, Grant sent him to Nashville with instructions to take over command from Thomas if he had not yet attacked Hood. While en route at Louisville, Logan heard of Thomas' crushing victory and aborted his mission. He rejoined Sherman at Savannah, instead, and served through the Carolinas Campaign. He was given the honor of commanding the Army of the Tennessee in the Grand Review in Washington. In part this may have been in reward for his role in preventing the rioting of his troops upon the news of Lincoln's murder. Becoming a Republican after resigning his commission on August 17, 1865, and declining a regular army brigadier generalship, he was elected to Congress and served on the committee which voted the articles of impeachment against Andrew Johnson. Active in veterans' affairs, he wrote *The Volunteer Soldier of America* in praise of the volunteers over the West Pointers. In 1884 he ran for vice president with James G. Blaine and was favored by many for the top spot on the 1888 ticket, but he died before the movement could gather force. (Jones, James P., *"Black Jack". John A. Logan and the Civil War in Southern Illinois* and *John A. Logan: Stalwart Republican From Illinois*)

LOGAN, Thomas Muldrop (1840-1914)

A recent South Carolina College graduate, Thomas M. Logan fought throughout the war and was one of the last men in the cavalry to become a general officer. After witnessing the bombardment of Fort Sumter he joined the Confederate army. His assignments included: first lieutenant, Company A, Hampton (S.C.) Legion (early 1961); captain, Company A, Hampton Legion (ca. July 21, 1861); major, Hampton Legion (1862); lieutenant colonel, Hampton Legion (1862); colonel, Hampton Legion (ca. May 19, 1864); brigadier general, CSA (February 15, 1865); and commanding brigade, Butler's Cavalry Division, Hampton's Cavalry Command (February-April 9, 1865); and commanding brigade, Butler's Division, Hampton's Cavalry Command, Army of Tennessee (April 9-26, 1865). He fought at 1st Bull Run and on the Peninsula until wounded at Gaines' Mill during the Seven Days. The legion went on to fight at Antietam, Fredericksburg, in southeastern Virginia, Chickamauga, and Knoxville. Having steadily risen in rank he was with the unit when it was converted into mounted infantry in early 1864 and succeeded to command it that spring. Serving with the cavalry of the Department of Richmond, he was wounded during the Richmond-Petersburg operations. Two months before the war ended he was promoted to brigadier and was transferred to his native state to join Hampton and Butler in trying to stop Sherman. Commanding a brigade, he fought at Bentonville and surrendered what was left of the division at Greensboro with Joe Johnston. He was a lawyer and highly successful railroader after the conflict.

LOMAX, Lunsford Lindsay (1835-1913)

Born to a Virginia army officer in Rhode Island, Lunsford L. Lomax followed his father's lead and opted for a career in the military. An 1856 graduate of West Point, he served in the cavalry until his April 25, 1861, resignation as first lieutenant. Originally a captain and assistant adjutant general in the state forces, he transferred to those of the Confederacy as an inspector. Serving on the staffs of Ben McCulloch, J.E. Johnston, and Earl Van Dorn, he rose from captain to lieutenant colonel. His later assignments included: colonel, 11th Virginia Cavalry (ca. February 15, 1863); brigadier general, CSA (July 23, 1863); commanding brigade, F. Lee's Division, Cavalry Corps, Army of Northern Virginia (September 9, 1863-August 10, 1864); major general, CSA (August 10, 1864); commanding Ransom's (old) Cavalry Division, Valley District, Department of Northern Virginia (August 10, 1864-April 1865); and also the district (from March 29, 1865). After serving with his new regiment in the Shenandoah Valley he fought at Brandy Station and Gettysburg. Promoted and given a brigade, he served through the Overland Campaign and in the early operations at Petersburg. Taking over Ransom's Cavalry Division in the Valley, he fought under Early at 3rd Winchester and Fisher's Hill. The day after the latter he was temporarily captured at Woodstock but escaped within hours. He then fought at Cedar Creek and took part in a number of raids in the western part of the state. In the last days he was in charge of the district and following Lee's surrender he made his way to Johnston's army in North Carolina and commanded some fragments from the former's army. He was surrendered at Greensboro and subsequently was a farmer and educator. Lomax worked on the *Official Records* for six years and sat on the commission for the Gettysburg park. (Freeman, Douglas S., *Lee's Lieutenants*)

LONG, Armistead Lindsay (1825-1891)

Veteran artilleryman Armistead L. Long was promoted from a staff position with Lee to the command of the 2nd Corps' Artillery. The native Virginian and West Pointer (1850) resigned his first lieutenant's commission and a position as aide-de-camp to his father-in-law, General Edwin V. Sumner, on June 10, 1861. For the South his assignments included: major, PACS (1861); colonel, PACS (ca. March 1861); brigadier general, CSA (September 21, 1863) and commanding Artillery, 2nd Corps, Army of Northern Virginia (September 23, 1863-April 9, 1865, with frequent absences). In western Virginia he served as W.W. Loring's artillery chief and inspector before being transferred to the southern coast as chief of artillery and ordnance for Lee and Pemberton. When Lee became the advisor to the president he made Long his military secretary, with the rank of colonel. In this position Long served in all of Lee's campaigns through Gettysburg. In the fall of 1863 he was promoted and given charge of the 2nd Corps' guns. He led them at the Wilderness, Spotsylvania, and Cold Harbor. At times in charge of the Valley District's artillery during Early's campaign there, he was often off duty due to illness. Returning to the main army, he surrendered with it at Appomattox. A civil engineer after the war for five years, he subsequently wrote *Memoirs of Robert E. Lee* despite being completely blind. President Grant appointed Long's wife postmistress of Charlottesville. (Freeman, Douglas S., *R.E. Lee* and Wise, Jennings C., *The Long Arm of R.E. Lee*)

LONG, Eli (1837-1903)

In the final days of the Civil War Union General Eli Long received a wound which left him partially paralyzed for the rest of his life. The Kentucky native had attended the Frankfort military academy and been commissioned directly into the regular army in 1856. Following frontier duty in the prewar years, his assignments included: second lieutenant, 1st Cavalry (since June 27, 1856); first lieutenant, 1st Calvalry (January 1, 1861); captain, 1st Cavalry (May 24, 1861); captain, 4th Cavalry (designation change August 3, 1861); Colonel, 4th Ohio Cavalry (February 23, 1863); commanding 2nd Brigade, 2nd Division, Cavalry Corps, Army of the Cumberland (March 1863-August 20, 1864); brigadier general, USV (August 18, 1864); and commanding 2nd Division, Cavalry Corps, Military Division of the Mississippi (November 16, 1864-April 2, 1865). Leading Company K of his regular regiment he won a brevet for an affair at Farmington on October 7, 1862, and was wounded on the first day at Murfreesboro. He then took the field as commander of a demoralized mounted volunteer regiment and soon whipped it back into shape. He led a brigade during the Tullahoma Campaign and at Chickamauga and Chattanooga. Winning a brevet for his role in the relief of Knoxville, he then took part in the Atlanta Campaign. On the March to the Sea he was brevetted for Lovejoy's Station, and then went on Wilson's raid through Alabama and Georgia at the head of a division. Wounded in the taking of Selma, he was brevetted a regular army brigadier general for it. Already named a brigadier of volunteers the previous summer, he was brevetted major general for the war in both services. Mustered out of the volunteers on January 15, 1866, he served in New Jersey until retired in 1867 with the advanced grade of major general due to his wounds. This grade was reduced by law to brigadier general in 1875. He then took up the practice of law until his death following an operation.

LONG, Stephen Harriman (1784-1864)

New Hampshire-born engineer Stephen Long was the last commander of the Corps of Topographical Engineers, the mapmakers of the army. Entering the army as an engineering lieutenant in the War of 1812, he was transferred to the Topographical Bureau when it was set up as a separate entity. On September 9, 1861, he was promoted to colonel and made commander of the corps in place of the retired Colonel J.J. Abert. Long held this position, dispatching officers to serve with the armies in the field, until the corps was merged into the larger Corps of Engineers on March 3, 1863. Serving in the larger bureau for only three months, he retired on June 1, 1863. He died the next year on September 4.

LONGSTREET, James (1821-1904)

Corps commander James Longstreet made three mistakes that have denied him his deserved place in Southern posterity: He argued with Lee at Gettysburg, he was right, and he became a Republican. Born in South Carolina, he entered West Point from Alabama, graduated in 1842, and was wounded at Chapultepec in Mexico. With two brevets and the staff rank of major he resigned his commission on June 1, 1861, and joined the Confederacy. His assignments included: brigadier general, CSA (June 17, 1861); commanding brigade (in 1st Corps after July 20), Army of the Potomac (July 2-October 7, 1861); major general, CSA (October 7, 1861); commanding division, 1st Corps, Army of the Potomac (October 14-22, 1861); commanding division (in Potomac District until March 1862), Department of Northern Virginia (October 22, 1861-July 1862); commanding 1st Corps, Army of Northern Virginia (July 1862-February 25, 1863; May-September 9, 1863; April 12-May 6, 1864; and October 19, 1864-April 9, 1865); lieutenant general, CSA (October 9, 1862); commanding Department of Virginia and North Carolina (February 25-May 1863); commanding his corps, Army of Tennessee (September 19-November 5, 1863); and commanding Department of East Tennessee (November 5, 1863-April 12, 1864). Commanding a brigade, he fought at Blackburn's Ford and 1st Bull Run before moving up to divisional leadership for the Peninsula Campaign. There he saw further action at Yorktown, Williamsburg, Seven Pines, and the Seven Days. In the final days of the latter he also directed A.P. Hill's men. Commanding what was variously styled a "wing," "command," or "corps," the latter not being legally recognized until October 1862, he proved to be a capable subordinate to Lee at 2nd Bull Run, where he delivered a crushing attack, South Mountain, Antietam, and Fredericksburg. By now promoted to be the Confederacy's senior lieutenant general, he led an independent expedition into southeastern Virginia where he displayed a lack

James Longstreet, Lee's "war horse." (NA)

of ability on his own. Rejoining Lee, he opposed attacking at Gettysburg in favor of maneuvering Meade out of his position. Longstreet, who had come to believe in the strategic offense and the tactical defense, was proven right when the Confederate attacks on the second and third days were repulsed. Detached to reinforce Bragg in Georgia, he commanded a wing of the army on the second day at Chickamauga. In the dispute over the follow-up of the victory he was critical of Bragg and was soon detached to operate in East Tennessee. Here again he showed an incapacity for independent operations, especially in the siege of Knoxville. Rejoining Lee at the Wilderness, he was severely wounded, in the confusion, by Confederate troops. He resumed command in October during the Petersburg operations and commanded on the north side of the James. Lee's "Old War Horse" remained with his chief through the surrender at Appomattox. After the war he befriended Grant and became a Republican. He served as Grant's minister to Turkey and as a railroad commissioner. Criticized by many former Confederates, he struck back with his book, *From Manassas to Appomattox*. He outlived most of his high-ranking postwar detractors. (Eckenrode, H.J. and Conrad, Bryan, *James Longstreet, Lee's War Horse* and Sanger, Donald and Hay, Thomas, *James Longstreet*)

LOOMIS, John Q. (?-?)

Heavy casualties in the brigade to which he was attached twice brought John Q. Loomis to its temporary command, but he was never given permanent charge, in part because he also became a victim of enemy fire. His Confederate assignments included: lieutenant colonel, 1st Alabama Battalion (September 17, 1861); colonel, 25th Alabama (January 28, 1862); commanding Gladden's Brigade, Withers' Division, 2nd Corps, Army of the Mississippi (ca. April 8-23, 1862); and commanding Gardner's Brigade, Withers' Division, Polk's Corps, Army of Tennessee (December 1862). After initial service in the Mobile area his battalion was merged with another and he was given command of the resulting regiment. He led his command at Shiloh until superficially wounded late on the first day. Returning shortly after the battle, he took over direction of the brigade until General Gardner was assigned to replace the deceased Gladden. Loomis fought at Farmington and Bridge Creek and took part in the Kentucky Campaign but was not actively engaged. In December he again took command of the brigade and on the last day of the year was struck by a falling tree limb during the battle of Murfreesboro. He does not appear to have rejoined the regiment and resigned on September 14, 1863.

LORING, William Wing (1818-1886)

A one-armed veteran of the Mexican War, William W. Loring became one of the more troublesome of Confederate generals, frequently engaging in disputes with his superiors. The North Carolina native had been raised in Florida and served as a second lieutenant of state volunteers in the fighting against the Seminoles. He then practiced law and became a state legislator before being commissioned directly into the regular army for the Mexican War. As a captain of the Mounted Riflemen, he won two brevets in that conflict, being wounded at both Churubusco and Chapultepec and losing an arm at the latter. By the time of his May 13, 1861, resignation he was his regiment's colonel. His Confederate assignments included: brigadier general, CSA (May 20, 1861); commanding Army of the Northwest (July 20-August 3, 1861 and October 1861-February 9, 1862); commanding brigade, Army of the Northwest (August 3-October 1861); major general, CSA (February 17, 1862); commanding Department of Southwestern Virginia (May 8-October 16, 1862); commanding division, 2nd Military District, Department of Mississippi and East Louisiana (ca. January-April 1863); commanding division, Department of Mississippi and East Louisiana (April-May 16, 1863); commanding division, Department of the West (May 16-July 1863); commanding division, Department of Mississippi and East Louisiana (July 1863-January 28, 1864); commanding division, Department of Alabama, Mississippi and East Louisiana (January 28-May 4, 1864); commanding division, Polk's (Army of Mississippi)-Stewart's Corps, Army of Tennessee (May 4-June 14, June 14-July 28, 1864, September 1864-ca. March 1865, and April 9-26, 1865); and temporarily commanding the corps (June 14, 1864). While serving under Robert E. Lee in the first summer of the war, he took part in the disappointments of the campaign in western Virginia. That winter his command was placed under the overall command of Stonewall Jackson. Following the Romney Campaign, Loring opposed the stationing of his men in the exposed town during the bitter winter and obtained orders from Secretary of War Judah P. Benjamin to move to Winchester. Outraged, Jackson threatened to resign and was eventually upheld in his views of military etiquette. On February 9, 1862, Loring was removed from his post but a few days later was appeased with promotion to major general. After departmental command in southwestern Virginia, he was named to command a division in Mississippi. Frequently in conflict with department commander John C. Pemberton, he fought in the Vicksburg Campaign until cut off from the rest of Pemberton's force at Champion Hill. The two generals blamed each other for the defeat there. Loring then joined the forces under Joseph E. Johnston and took part in the defense of Jackson, Mississippi, and the Meridian Campaign. By now he was known to his men as "Old Blizzards" because of his battle cry "Give them blizzards, boys!" Transferred to Georgia, he fought in the Atlanta Campaign. When Leonidas Polk was killed at Pine Mountain, Loring briefly took charge of the corps but was succeeded the same day by Alexander P. Stewart. Returning to divisional command, he was wounded at Ezra Church and was out of action until after the fall of Atlanta. He then fought at Franklin, Nashville, and in the Carolinas. From 1869 to 1879 he was a division commander in Egypt and upon his return was called "Pasha Loring." (Loring, William Wing, *A Confederate Soldier in Egypt*)

LOVEJOY, Elijah Parish (1802-1837)

The early abolitionists faced the constant threat of mob violence and Elijah P. Lovejoy became a martyr in the cause. A native of Maine he had preached in Philadelphia and become involved in the Presbyterian campaign against slavery. For two years he edited the *St. Louis Observer* before his views made it wise to relocate to Alton, Illinois. Repeatedly his press was smashed or thrown into the river, but friends kept sending new ones and the *Alton Observer* continued to be published. In 1837 he worked to establish an Illinois chapter of the American Anti-Slavery Society. The local citizens were outraged by his activities and his press was again destroyed. On November 7, 1837, another press arrived from Ohio. That night a mob attacked the warehouse where it was being stored. The armed defenders were not able to hold them off and the building was burned and the press destroyed. In the conflict Lovejoy fell dead from a gunshot. The next day the mob returned for the murdered man's corpse and dragged it through town in triumph. (Lovejoy, Joseph C. and Owen, *Memoir of the Reverend Elijah P. Lovejoy*)

LOVEJOY, Owen (1811-1864)

After the death of his martyred brother, Elijah, Owen Lovejoy became one of the leading abolitionists in Illinois. A native of Maine, he had studied law but never practiced, instead following his older brother into the clergy. During the hectic days of 1837 in Alton, Illinois, Owen remained by his brother and, kneeling next to his body, swore never to give up the abolitionist cause. Violating a state law prohibiting abolitionist meetings, he continued to speak out across the state. In 1854 he sat in the state legislature and was active in the organization of the Republican Party in Illinois. He urged Lincoln to take the leadership position in the state organization but was unsuccessful in this. Elected to Congress in 1856 he sat there until his death and was one of the most violent opponents of slavery in that body. However, upon the election of his friend Lincoln he toned himself down and supported Lincoln's more conservative war and reconstruction programs. He was given the honor of introducing the bill abolishing slavery in the territories. Lovejoy died on March 25, 1864, before he could see the total abolition of the peculiar institution. (Magdol, Edward, *Owen Lovejoy, Abolitionist in Congress*)

LOVELL, Charles Swain (?-1871)

Rising from the ranks of the regular army, Massachusetts native Charles S. Lovell rose to the grade of brevet brigadier general in the regular army during the Civil War. Enlisting in 1830, he served as private through sergeant major of the 2nd Artillery. In 1837 he was commissioned as a second lieutenant in the 6th Infantry. He saw service on the frontier and during the Mexican War. His Civil War assignments included: captain, 6th Infantry (since June 18, 1846); major, 10th Infantry (May 14, 1861); commanding 2nd Brigade, 2nd Division, 5th Corps, Army of the Potomac (June 27-29, ca. September 17, October-November 1862, and December 14, 1862-January 1863); lieutenant colonel, 18th Infantry (January 21, 1863); and colonel, 14th Infantry (February 16, 1865). During the Seven Days he won brevets for Gaines' Mill and Malvern Hill. At 2nd Bull Run he commanded the three companies of his regiment present. While in command of a regular brigade at Antietam he won the brevet of brigadier general and went on to succeed to brigade command again at Fredericksburg. Promoted to major, and later to lieutenant colonel, he served as provost marshal in Wisconsin from April 1863 through the end of the war, with much of his work relating to the enforcement of the draft. He continued in the regular army until his 1870 retirement.

LOVELL, Mansfield (1822-1884)

With a greatly insufficient force Mansfield Lovell was charged with the defense of the Confederacy's largest port, New Orleans, and its fall became his own. The native of the nation's capital and a West Pointer (1842) had served as an artillery officer during the Mexican War, winning a brevet and being wounded at Chapultepec. Resigning from the army as first lieutenant, 4th Artillery, in 1854, he was New York City street commissioner Gustavus W. Smith's deputy at the outbreak of the Civil War. Heading south, his assignments included: major general, CSA (October 7, 1861); commanding Department #1 (October 18, 1861-June 25, 1862); commanding 1st Division, District of the Mississippi, Department #2 (September 8-October 16, 1862); and commanding corps, Army of West Tennessee, Department #2 (October 16-December 7, 1862). Relieving David E. Twiggs from command in Texas and Louisiana, his major chore was the defense of the Crescent City. With most of his organized units called to Corinth, Mississippi, for the buildup prior to the battle of Shiloh, Lovell was left with only a handful of green troops. When the city fell in April 1862 he was blamed for the loss, but the next year a court of inquiry he had asked for absolved him of blame. In the meantime he led a division at the battle of Corinth and for a time a corps facing Grant's attempt to get at Vicksburg through central Mississippi. Relieved of duty he awaited orders until March 1865 when he was directed to join Joseph E. Johnston's forces in North Carolina. He was included in Johnston's surrender before he could be given a command. As a civil engineer he was John Newton's assistant in removing obstructions in New York's East River at Hell Gate.

LOW, Frederick Ferdinand (1828-1894)

It was with much difficulty that California Congressman Federick F. Low was finally able to take his seat in the 37th Congress. A Maine native, he had participated unsuccessfully in the California Gold Rush and then become a merchant and banker. In 1861 he was elected to Congress but was refused his House seat because the results of the census did not authorize the state to have that many seats. He finally took his seat on June 3, 1862, under the provisions of a special act of Congress. Not a candidate for reelection, he left office upon the expiration of the term on March 3, 1863. That summer he was elected to his first four-year term as governor and was inaugurated on December 10, 1863. A Union Republican, he aided in recruiting for the Union army and in relief for the victims of the conflict. After his term he was a diplomat in China and then returned to banking in San Francisco. (Hittell, Theodore H., *History of California*)

Professor Lowe's observation balloon "Intrepid" at Fair Oaks. (NA)

LOWE, Thaddeus Sobieski Coulincourt (1832-1913)

Until the Union high command inexplicably abandoned the program, Thaddeus S.C. Lowe was the driving force behind the balloon corps. A native of New Hampshire, he had entered the field in 1856. In a test flight he travelled 900 miles in nine hours on April 20, 1861. Landing in agitated South Carolina, he was promptly arrested as a Yankee spy. He was released the next day, but not until after there had been much talk of a hanging. Two months later a demonstration so impressed Lincoln that Lowe was assigned to duty as a civilian with what later became the Army of the Potomac. He missed 1st Bull Run due to a manpower shortage, but in subsequent months proved the worth of his corps—it soon amounted to seven balloons—by locating enemy positions and troop movements in the Washington vicinity. On the Peninsula he provided information which prevented a total surprise of the Union army at Fair Oaks. He was even able to direct artillery fire by means of a telegraph line from his basket. Administrative problems plagued the corps, and it was repeatedly transferred from one bureau to another. He soon resigned in disgust and, much to the relief of the Confederates, the corps had come to an end by the middle of 1863. (Hoehling, Mary, *Thaddeus Lowe: America's One-Man Air Corps*)

LOWE, William Warren (1831-1898)

The adjutant of Robert E. Lee's cavalry regiment in the prewar years, William W. Lowe won the Union army brevets of brigadier general in both the regulars and the volunteers. The Indiana native had received his West Point appointment from Iowa and had been posted first to the dragoons upon his 1853 graduation and to the cavalry two years later. Having seen frontier duty before the war, his Civil War assignments included: first lieutenant and adjutant, 2nd Cavalry (since May 31, 1855); captain, 2nd Cavalry (May 9 1861); captain, 5th Cavalry (designation change August 3, 1861); colonel, Curtis Horse (January 1, 1862); colonel, 5th Iowa Cavalry (designation change June 1862); commanding 3rd Brigade, 2nd Division, Cavalry Corps, Army of the Cumberland (August 5-November 8, 1863); commanding 1st Brigade, 2nd Division, Cavalry Corps, Army of the Cumberland (January 24-April 1, 1864); commanding 1st Brigade, 3rd Division, Cavalry Corps, Army of the Cumberland (April 2-May 21, 1864); also commanding the division (April 2-17 and May 21-July 23, 1864); and commanding 2nd Brigade, 6th Division, Cavalry Corps, Military Division of the Mississippi (November 17-December 9, 1864 and January 1-February 1865). Named to command a regiment composed of companies from Nebraska, Minnesota, Iowa, and Missouri, which was later designated as an Iowa unit, he served mostly in routine garrison duty near Forts Henry and Donelson until 1863. He won regular army brevets for an October 9, 1863, action near Chickamauga and one near Huntsville, Albabama, on December 15, 1863. During the Atlanta Campaign he commanded a brigade and then a division. He was mustered out of the volunteer service on January 24, 1865, and resigned from the regular army in 1869 as major of the 6th Calvalry. He was subsequently involved in railroading and mining.

LOWELL, Charles Russell, Jr. (1835-1864)

Already once wounded in the battle, Harvard graduate Charles R. Lowell, Jr. suffered a second and mortal wound at Cedar Creek. In the Maryland iron business in 1861—following years of overseas travel—the Boston native joined the regular army. His assignments included: captain, 3rd Cavalry (May 14, 1861); captain, 6th Cavalry (designation change August 3, 1861); colonel, 2nd Massachusetts Cavalry (May 10, 1863); commanding Independent Cavalry Brigade, 22nd Corps, Department of Washington (August 1, 1863-February 1864 and April-July 1864); commanding 3rd Brigade, 1st Division, Cavalry Corps, Army of the Shenandoah (August 9-September 8, 1864); commanding Reserve Brigade, 1st Division, Cavalry Corps, Army of the Shenandoah (September 8-October 19, 1864); and brigadier general, USV (posthumously to rank from October 19, 1864). After serving on the Peninsula with his regiment he joined the staff of General McClellan for the Maryland Campaign. In the spring of 1863 he took command of a newly recruited volunteer cavalry regiment from his native state and was assigned to the Washington defenses. He was active in defending the capital against Jubal A. Early in July 1864 and then took the field as a brigade commander in the Valley. He was distinguished at 3rd Winchester and Tom's Brook, but at Cedar Creek he sustained two wounds, the second of which proved mortal the next day, October 20. He was posthumously promoted brigadier general from the date of his wounding.

LOWREY, Mark Perrin (1828-1885)

Leaving the Baptist ministry in Mississippi in order to join the Confederate army, Tennessee-born Mark P. Lowrey resigned his brigadier general's commission shortly before the fledgling nation's demise. A veteran of the Mexican War as a member of the 2nd Mississippi, his Civil War assignments included: colonel, 4th Mississippi State Troops (fall 1861); colonel, 32nd Mississippi (April 3, 1862); brigadier general, CSA (October 4, 1863); commanding brigade, Cleburne's Division, Hill's-Breckinridge's Corps, Army of Tennessee (October-November 1863); commanding brigade, Cleburne's Division, Hardee's-Cheatham's Corps, Army of Tennessee (November 1863-August 31, 1864 and September 2, 1864-ca. March 14, 1865); and temporarily commanding the division (August 31-September 2, 1864). After commanding his first 60-days unit, he took charge of a regular volunteer unit which, although participating in the Kentucky, Murfreesboro, and Chickamauga campaigns, was not present in the main battles. Given command of a brigade, with the rank of brigadier general, he fought at Chattanooga. During the Atlanta Campaign he was briefly in command of the division at the battle of Jonesboro. He later fought at Franklin and Nashville and in the early stages of the Carolinas Campaign before resigning on March 14, 1865. Thereafter he was engaged in religious and educational matters.

LOWRY, Robert (1830-1910)

South Carolina-born merchant and lawyer Robert Lowry rose to the rank of brigadier general during the final months of the Confederacy. Enlisting in the Rankin Grays, his assignments included: private, Company I, 6th Mississippi (1861); major, 6th Mississippi (August 1861); colonel, 6th Mississippi (May 23, 1862); commanding John Adams' (old) Brigade, Loring's Division, Stewart's Corps, Army of Tennessee (November 30, 1864-March 1865 and April 9-26, 1865). As a field officer, he was twice wounded at Shiloh before being advanced to command of his regiment. This he led at Corinth and in the Vicksburg Campaign. During the latter he was serving in Loring's division and after the battle at Champion Hill was cut off from the rest of John C. Pemberton's army. The division then joined the forces under Joseph E. Johnston in a feeble, unsuccessful attempt to lift the siege of the city. Again joining Johnston in northern Georgia in May 1864, Lowry led his regiment through the Atlanta Campaign and then accompanied John B. Hood into middle Tennessee. When John Adams was killed at Franklin, Lowry took over the brigade and let it at Nashville. Early the next year he was advanced to brigadier general and led his brigade in the Carolinas Campaign, seeing action at Bentonville, before being included in the surrender to Johnston's forces. Thereafter he was active in politics and veterans' organizations. In the 1880s he served two four-year terms as governor of his adopted state.

LUBBOCK, Francis Richard (1815-1905)

During his two years as governor of Texas, South Carolina-born Francis R. Lubbock was primarily concerned with the raising of state funds to support the war. Having turned down a West Point appointment, he engaged in several business ventures before moving to Texas in 1836 where he was a druggist. As a militiaman, he fought Indians and Mexicans. Under the Texas Republic he was clerk of the House of Representatives, comptroller of the treasury, and a district clerk before being elected lieutenant governor of the state in 1857. He attended the Democratic national convention in 1860 and the next year was elected governor. Taking office three days later (November 7, 1861), he found the state's financial situation in a mess and attempted to remedy it. One method was the exportation of cotton through Mexico in order to bypass the Union blockade along the coast. Not seeking reelection, he left the governor's mansion on November 5, 1863, and joined the army. His assignments included: lieutenant colonel, PACS (late 1863); and colonel and aide-de-camp (1864). His entire service was on the staff of Jefferson Davis in Richmond. He fled South with his chief after the fall of Richmond and was then imprisoned for a time. He later returned to Texas as a rancher and served as a tax official. (Lubbock, Percy, *Six Decades in Texas: The Memoirs of Francis R. Lubbock*)

LUCAS, Thomas John (1826-1908)

Native Indianan watchmaker and Mexican War veteran—as a second lieutenant in the 4th Indiana—Thomas J. Lucas rose to the command of a mounted division late in the Civil War. His assignments included: lieutenant colonel, 16th Indiana (May 20, 1861); colonel, 16th Indiana (May 6, 1862); colonel, 16th Indiana (three-years unit May 27, 1862); commanding 1st

Brigade, 4th Division, 13th Corps, Department of the Gulf (September 20-October 7, 1863); commanding 1st Brigade, Cavalry Division, Department of the Gulf (November 3, 1863-April 9, 1864); brigadier general, USV (November 10, 1864); commanding Separate Cavalry Brigade, District of West Florida, Department of the Gulf (February 8-March 28, 1865); commanding Cavalry Division, District of West Florida, Department of the Gulf (March 28-April 14, 1865); and commanding 3rd Brigade, 1st Division, Cavalry Corps, Military Division of West Mississippi (April 14-28 and May 9-July 1865). His initial one-year regiment served in western Maryland and in the early stages of the Shenandoah Valley Campaign of 1862 before being mustered out on May 23, 1862. Four days later a new regiment was formed for three years, and Lucas became its colonel. Much of the unit was captured in the disaster at Richmond, Kentucky, but was soon exchanged and reorganized for the operations against Vicksburg during which Lucas suffered three wounds. Transferred to the Gulf, he led a mounted brigade in the Red River Campaign and was promoted to brigadier general in November 1864. The next year he commanded the mounted forces in the campaign against Mobile and was brevetted major general for it. Following duty in New Orleans, he was mustered out on January 15, 1866, and was a tax official, postmaster, and unsuccessful Republican politician in the postwar years.

LUCAS, William (?-?)

A black living on the plantation of Dr. Richard H. Stewart, William Lucas was the driver of the team which took John Wilkes Booth and David Herold from Stewart's plantation to Port Conway, a ferry crossing point on the Rappahannock River. It was also Lucas who carried the insulting note and the money back to Dr. Stewart. He himself received $10 for his services.

LUDLOW, William Handy (?-1890)

As the Union's exchange agent at Fortress Monroe, Virginia, William H. Ludlow often engaged in delicate negotiations with his Confederate counterpart, Robert Ould. The native New Yorker had entered the army shortly after 1st Bull Run and his assignments included: private, Company B, 73rd New York (July 27, 1861); second lieutenant, Company B, 73rd New York (September 29, 1861); major and additional aide-de-camp (November 18, 1861); and lieutenant colonel and assistant inspector general (assigned August 20, 1862-April 4, 1864). Initially he served in Daniel Sickles' Excelsior Brigade before being named to a staff position as an aide. In the second year of the war he was made an inspector and assigned to duty exchanging prisoners. Over a year and a half's time he supervised the transfer of thousands of captives, although sometimes his negotiations bogged down, as in the case of the *New York Tribune* correspondents Albert D. Richardson and Junius H. Browne. Shortly after Grant became commander-in-chief the cartel organizing the exchanges was dropped as too great a benefit to the manpower-starved Confederate armies. Ludlow returned to other staff duties as an aide for the rest of the war. Brevetted a brigadier general of volunteers for his services, he was mustered out on July 20, 1866.

LUNDY, Benjamin (1789-1839)

A founder of the Union Humane Society, an antislavery organization, in 1815, Benjamin Lundy was one of the earliest abolitionists. A native of New Jersey, he had been introduced to the peculiar institution on a trip to Virginia. After settling in Ohio, Lundy for a number of years published *The Genius of Universal Emancipation*. Interested in the colonization solution, he traveled widely in search of a suitable location. He also traveled as a lecturer and was a vigorous opponent of the annexation of Texas, providing John Quincy Adams with much of the information with which to oppose the scheme. For a time he published *The National Enquirer* in Philadelphia. He died while working on the *Genius* in Illinois, long before his goal was even in sight. (Earle, Thomas, *The Life, Travels and Opinions of Benjamin Lundy*)

LYLE, Peter (?-1879)

By the time Peter Lyle was awarded the brevet rank of brigadier general on March 13, 1865, he had been out of the service for more than three months. The native Pennsylvanian entered the Union army under Lincoln's first call for volunteers. His assignments included: colonel, 19th Pennsylvania (April 27, 1861); colonel, 90th Pennsylvania (March 10, 1862); commanding 2nd Brigade, 2nd Division, 1st Corps, Army of the Potomac (September 17, 1862 and September 18, 1862-April 21, 1863); commanding 1st Brigade, 2nd Division, 1st Corps, Army of the Potomac (July 3 and July 5-December 11, 1863); commanding 1st Brigade, 2nd Division, 5th Corps, Army of the Potomac (May 6-June 5, 1864); and commanding 1st Brigade, 3rd Division, 5th Corps, Army of the Potomac (June 6-August 27, 1864). His initial three-months regiment served near Baltimore's Fort McHenry until its muster out on August 29, 1861. In charge of a new unit, he fought at Cedar Mountain and 2nd Bull Run. At Antietam he succeeded to command of the brigade and soon fell wounded. Returning to duty the next day, he led the brigade at Fredericksburg and the regiment at Chancellorsville. Following the heavy loss of officers in his division on the first day at Gettysburg he was assigned to command another one of its brigades. In this capacity he served through the Bristoe and Mine Run campaigns. At the Wilderness he again succeeded to brigade command and fought at Spotsylvania, Cold Harbor, and Petersburg. On November 26, 1864, the remnants of his unit were merged into the 11th Pennsylvania and he was mustered out of the service. He later received his brevet for gallantry in battle.

LYMAN, Theodore (1833-1897)

A Harvard graduate and naturalist, Theodore Lyman served as a volunteer aide-de-camp to the Army of the Potomac's commander, George G. Meade, during the last 20 months of the

Civil War. Having met Meade, then an engineering officer, in Florida in 1856 while on a scientific expedition, Lyman became one of Meade's staff officers upon Lyman's return from Europe in the summer of 1863. Entering upon his duties, with the rank of lieutenant colonel, on September 2, 1863, Lyman participated in the Bristoe and Mine Run campaigns later that year. Following the arrival next spring of General Grant, in command of all the Union armies, Lyman continued with Meade's staff and served through the Wilderness, Spotsylvania, North Anna, Cold Harbor, and Petersburg. After Lee's surrender at Appomattox, Lyman was discharged on April 20, 1865. During his military service, Lyman wrote a series of letters to his wife, later published in book form, which provide a frank view of the Union army. After the war, he became a prominent zoologist and naturalist and served a term in the House of Representatives. (Agassiz, George R., ed., *Meade's Headquarters 1863-1865: Letters of Colonel Theodore Lyman From The Wilderness to Appomattox*)

LYNCH, William Francis (1801-1865)

A navy veteran since 1819, William F. Lynch had had a distinguished career when he resigned in 1861 to go with his native Virginia. His service included cruises to Brazil, China, in the West Indies, and around the world. In 1848 he made an historic exploration of the Jordan River and the Dead Sea. During the Mexican War he was at sea in the Gulf of Mexico. Early in 1861 he was named a captain in the Virginia naval forces and then on June 10 he was commissioned captain, CSN. As such he commanded the Aquia Creek batteries during their bombardment early in the war and then was sent to North Carolina where he commanded the mismatched Confederate fleet in the fighting at Roanoke Island and Elizabeth City. In the latter engagement he lost all his vessels. From March to October 1862 he served on the Mississippi near Vicksburg and then returned to North Carolina in charge of all naval operations on the coast of that state. He was at Smithville at the time of the fall of Fort Fisher. Settling in Baltimore he barely outlived the war, dying on October 17, 1865. (Scharf, J. Thomas, *History of the Confederate States Navy*)

LYNDE, Isaac (?-1886)

For his role in the early days of the Civil War in the Southwest, Vermonter Isaac Lynde was dropped from the army rolls. A graduate of West Point (1827), he had been appointed major, 7th Infantry, on October 18, 1855. He was commanding at Fort Fillmore in the New Mexico Territory during the war's first months and attacked a 250-man Texan force under John R. Baylor at Mesilla on July 21, 1861. The next day he abandoned the fort and withdrew. He was forced to surrender the 500 men of his 10 companies at San Augustine Springs on the 27th. Returning to Washington, he was dismissed on November 25, 1861, and did not serve during the rest of the Civil War. The authorities considered him responsible for the opening up of the territory to Confederate forces. However, a year after the close of hostilities he was recommissioned as a major and was placed on the retired list the same day.

LYON, Francis Strother (1800-1882)

Having earned a reputation as a financial expert in the liquidation of Alabama's state bank in the 1840s and 1850s, Francis S. Lyon served as the chairman of the Confederate House of Representatives' Committee on Ways and Means in the Second Regular Congress. A North Carolinian by birth, he was a lawyer and served in the upper house of the Alabama legislature. While in private practice he had become a secession Democrat and took part in the walkout at the Charleston convention in 1860. He was returned to the legislature in 1861 and late that year was elected to the First Regular Confederate Congress where he sat on the Committee on Ways and Means. He chaired the committee in the next congress. His votes in Richmond indicate that he strongly favored a powerful national government supporting higher taxes and in effect the nationalization of the railroads. He lost heavily in his private investment in the cotton loan and his large plantation was devastated during the war. Returning to private practice after the war, he was active in the reclaiming of the state government for the white supremacists and served a term in the state senate.

LYON, Hylan Benton (1836-1907)

In his Confederate career Kentucky native and West Pointer (1856) Hylan B. Lyon served in all three branches of the service. Upon his graduation, he had been posted to the artillery and served on the frontier before resigning on April 30, 1861, as a first lieutenant in the 3rd Artillery in order to join the Confederacy. His assignments there included: first lieutenant, Artillery (ca. April 1861); captain, Cobb's (Ken.) Battery (late 1861); lieutenant colonel, 8th Kentucky (February 3, 1862); colonel, 8th Kentucky (September 1862); commanding brigade, Buford's Division, Forrest's Cavalry Corps, Department of Alabama, Mississippi and East Louisiana (early June 1864) and August-September 1864); brigadier general, CSA (June 14, 1864); commanding Infantry Division, Forrest's Cavalry Corps, Department of Alabama, Mississippi and East Louisiana (improvised organization July 1864); and commanding Department of Western Kentucky (September 26, 1864-spring 1865). After serving as an artillery officer he was captured at Fort Donelson while commanding an infantry regiment. Not exchanged until September 1862—having been imprisoned on Johnson's Island, Ohio—he was promoted to the permanent command of the regiment, which was converted to mounted infantry during the Vicksburg operations. Cut off from the city with William W. Loring after Champion Hill, he joined Joseph E. Johnston for the defense of Jackson, Mississippi. Following a period of detached service with Joseph Wheeler in East Tennessee, he returned to Mississippi, fighting at Brice's Crossroads. Promoted to brigadier general, he led the dismounted troopers of the infantry division under Forrest at Tupelo. In the final months of the war he commanded in western Kentucky. After a year in Mexico he took up farming in his native state.

LYON, Nathaniel (1818-1861)

One of the leading forces in the preservation of Missouri for the Union was an obscure infantry captain, Nathaniel Lyon. The Connecticut West Pointer (1841) was posted to the infantry with which he saw action against the Seminoles in Florida. During the Mexican War he was brevetted and received a wound at Chapultepec. After serving in Kansas during the troubles there, he was commander of the St. Louis arsenal at the peak of the secessionist agitation in Missouri. His Civil War assignments included: captain, 2nd Infantry (since June 11, 1851); brigadier general, 1st Brigade, Missouri Volunteers (May 12, 1861); brigadier general, USV (May 17, 1861); commanding Department of the West (May 31-July 3, 1861); and commanding District and Army of Southwest Missouri, Western Department (July-August 10, 1861). He angered St. Louis's pro-Southern elements when he refused to remove his troops from certain public buildings. On May 10, 1861, he seized the pro-Confederate militia gathered at nearby Camp Jackson, and fighting broke out in the streets when he marched the prisoners through the city. Two days later he became a brigadier general of state volunteers and on the 17th was awarded the same grade in the national volunteers. At the end of the month he succeeded William S. Harney in command of the Department of the West. On June 11, 1861, he attended, with Francis P. Blair, Jr., a meeting with pro-Confederate Governor Claiborne Jackson and Sterling Price to avoid violence. The demand that the governor control the movements of federal troops in return for peace could not be tolerated and Lyon responded that, "This means war!" In July the old Department of the West became part of the newly created Western Department. Lyon then took charge of the Army of Southwest Missouri and after much maneuvering attacked the enemy at Wilson's Creek. In the confused fighting of raw troops Lyon fell dead. Many believed that he had been abandoned by the department commander, John C. Frémont. On December 24, 1861, more than four months after his death, Lyon received the Thanks of Congress for his role in saving

Death of Nathaniel Lyon at Wilson's Creek. (*Leslie's*)

Missouri for the cause. (Woodward, Ashbel, *Life of General Nathaniel Lyon*)

LYON, William Penn (1822-1913)

Despite coming from a Quaker family, Wisconsin lawyer and state legislator Willaim P. Lyon answered Lincoln's summer 1862 call and went into the field at the head of a Wisconsin regiment. Ironically, his unit was destined to serve most of its term in guard and garrison duty, losing only five men killed or mortally wounded. His assignments included: colonel, 13th Wisconsin (September 26, 1862); and commanding 1st Brigade, 3rd Division, Reserve Corps, Army of the Cumberland (June 8-July 10, 1863). After spending much of the war in the vicinity of Fort Donelson, Tennessee, he was mustered out on September 11, 1865. The following month he was brevetted brigadier. He subsequently became a judge and eventually was named the chief judge of his state's supreme court.

LYONS, James (1801-1882)

The defeat of Virginia Congressman James Lyons' bid for reelection in 1863 was considered a rebuke to the Davis administration. A Whig-turned-Democrat lawyer, he was an early (1856) proponent of secession. In the 1861 congressional election he was defeated by former president John Tyler. But Tyler died before the beginning of the Regular Congress and Lyons won in a special election. Once in office he chaired the Committee on Public Buildings and sat on the Committee on Commerce. A Davis friend, he was one of the administration's staunchest supporters and fought against local interests which were tearing the states' rights-based Confederacy apart. In retaliation for the Emancipation Proclamation he favored the raising of the black flag and the payment of rewards to blacks who killed the enemy. In the fall of 1863 he was defeated by Williams C. Wickham and retired to private practice. He later served as Jefferson Davis' defense counsel.

LYONS, Richard Bickerton Pemell, Lord (1817-1887)

A veteran of 20 years in the British diplomatic corps, Lord Lyons assumed his duties as his country's minister to the United States in 1859 during the peak of the sectional crisis. He favored a neutral stance and warned his government not to allow either side to have a pretext for demanding British support in the war. He greatly feared Union Secretary of State Seward's desire to provoke a foreign conflict to reunite the United States. Following the *Trent* crisis, he was embarassed at the permission granted by Seward for British troops and supplies to cross Maine to get to Canada when blocked by ice from going directly. The troops had originally been intended to intimidate the United States during the crisis. Believing himself to be seriously ill, Lyons resigned his post in February 1865 but went on to serve the crown for another two decades. (Newton, T.W.L., *Lord Lyons: A Record of British Diplomacy*)

LYTLE, William Haines (1826-1863)

Best remembered for his poetry, especially "Anthony and Cleopatra," William H. Lytle died at Chickamauga as a Union brigadier general. The Ohio native was a lawyer and politician before the Civil War. His military experience came from service as a company commander in the 2nd Ohio during the Mexican War. Reentering the service in 1861, his assignments included: major general, Ohio Militia (since 1857); colonel, 10th Ohio (May 3, 1861); commanding 17th Brigade, 3rd Division, Army of the Ohio (December 2-22, 1861, March 21-August 19, and August 23-September 29, 1862); commanding 17th Brigade, 3rd Division, 1st Corps, Army of the Ohio (September 29-October 18, 1862); and brigadier general, USV (November 29, 1862); and commanding 1st Brigade, 3rd Division, 20th Corps, Army of the Cumberland (April 12-September 20, 1863). In his first significant action he was wounded at Carnifax Ferry while commanding his regiment. Upon his recovery he was posted to Bardstown, Kentucky, for recruiting duties. Taking the field again as a brigade commander, he was severely wounded at Perryville and taken prisoner. By the time that he was exchanged on February 4, 1863, he had been appointed a brigadier general. He took part in the Tullahoma Campaign and went on to Chickamauga. On the second day there he was killed while resisting the onslaught of James Longstreet's hordes. (Tucker, Glenn, *Chickamauga: Bloody Battle in the West*)

Lord Lyons, British minister to Washington. (NA)

M

MABRY, Hinchie Parham (1829-1885)

Whenever he was superseded by a senior colonel, Hinchie P. Mabry received the thanks of his superiors, but he never received promotion to brigadier. His Confederate assignments included: captain, Company G, 3rd Texas Cavalry (June 13, 1861); lieutenant colonel, 3rd Texas Cavalry (May 8, 1862); colonel, 3rd Texas Cavalry (October 8, 1862); commanding Whitfield's (old) Brigade, Jackson's Division, Lee's Cavalry Corps, Department of Mississippi and East Louisiana (fall-December 16, 1863); and commanding in the Department of Alabama, Mississippi and East Louisiana the following: brigade, Adams' Cavalry Division (ca. March 28-August 1864); brigade, District North of Homochitto (August-November 6, 1864); brigade, Northern Sub-District, District of Mississippi and East Louisiana (November 6, 1864-March 3, 1865); and Ross' Cavalry Brigade, District of Mississippi, East Louisiana and West Tennessee (March-May 4, 1865). He raised the "Dead Shot Rangers" which was assigned to the South Kansas-Texas Mounted Regiment and later designated as Company G, 3rd Texas Cavalry. He fought at Wilson's Creek, suffering a slight wound in the hand, and in the pursuit of the loyal Indians under Opothleyohola. After fighting at Pea Ridge, his regiment was dismounted and sent east of the Mississippi where he was wounded and captured at Iuka. Exchanged in October 1862, and with his regiment remounted, he served the rest of the war in the cavalry. He was on the fringes of the Vicksburg Campaign and was detached from Wirt Adams' command to join Forrest at Tupelo and in opposing A.J. Smith's August 1864 invasion of Mississippi. His brigade was broken up in early 1865 and he rejoined his regiment. Within a short time he was again an acting brigade commander. He was included in Richard Taylor's surrender in May 1865.

McANERNEY, John, Jr. (1838-1928)

A clerk in the Confederate post office in Richmond, John McAnerney, Jr., was serving as a captain of local defense troops when he earned great distinction in the repulse of the Kilpatrick-Dahlgren raid on Richmond. A native of Rhode Island, he was living in New Orleans when the Civil War began and entered the Confederate service. His assignments included: sergeant, Company F, 3rd Alabama (1861); captain, Company B, 3rd Virginia Battalion, Local Defense Troops (June 18, 1863); lieutenant colonel, 3rd Virginia Battalion, Local Defense Troops (April 20, 1864); and colonel, 3rd Virginia, Local Defense Troops (September 23, 1864). After serving as an enlisted man, he received a clerkship at the Richmond post office and became the commander of the company made up of the department's employees which was to be used only when the capital was directly threatened. In repulsing the February 1864 cavalry raid on the city, he was wounded while distinguishing himself. As the war progressed his regiment spent more and more time in the trenches. He was there for at least three months straight at the end of 1864. After the war he was in the railroad equipment and banking businesses in New York City.

MacARTHUR, Arthur, Jr. (1845-1912)

After a distinguished career in the Civil and Spanish-American wars, Arthur MacArthur, Jr., did not simply fade away. He fathered one of the 20th century's most controversial generals, Douglas MacArthur. The Massachusetts-born lad had joined the 24th Wisconsin and was made its adjutant on August 4, 1862. Young MacArthur saw action at Perryville, Stones River, Chickamauga, and Chattanooga. At Stones River, he was cited by his brigade commander for having "behaved with great coolness and presence of mind, ever ready to obey my commands." In the storming of Missionary Ridge on November 25, 1863, part of the battle of Chattanooga, he seized the regimental colors from the exhausted color sergeant and, moving in front of the regiment, called upon the men to follow as he planted the flag on the enemy's works. In 1890 he received the Congressional Medal of Honor for his deed. He was promoted to major on January 25, 1864, and to lieutenant colonel on May 18, 1865. He saw further action in the Atlanta Campaign and at the battle of Franklin. Mustered out of the army in June 1865, he returned the next year to make it a career. During the war with Spain he served as a brigadier and major general of volunteers and after the war he held the same ranks in the regular army. During the Civil War he received brevets as: lieutenant colonel for Perryville, Stones River, Chattanooga, and Dandridge; and colonel for the Atlanta Campaign and Franklin.

McARTHUR, John (1826-1906)

Scottish-born Chicago iron works manager John McArthur was already the captain of a militia company, the Chicago Highland Guards, by the time the war in which he was to rise to brevet major general had begun. His assignments included: colonel, 12th Illinois (May 3, 1861); colonel, 12th Illinois (reorganized for three years, August 1, 1861); commanding 1st Brigade, 2nd Division, District of Cairo, Department of the Missouri (February 1-17, 1862); commanding 2nd Brigade, 2nd Division, Army of the Tennessee (February 17-April 9, 1862); brigadier general, USV (March 21, 1862); commanding the division (April 9-14, 1862); commanding 1st Brigade, 6th Division, Army of the Tennessee (May 23-July 24, 1862); commanding 1st Brigade, 6th Division, District of Corinth, Army of the Tennessee (July 24-September 21 and October 3-6, 1862); commanding the division (September 21-October 3 and October 6-November 1, 1862); commanding 6th Division, Left Wing, 13th Corps, Army of the Tennessee (November 1-December 18, 1862); commanding 6th Division, Left Wing, 16th Corps, Army of the Tennessee (December 22, 1862-January 20, 1863); commanding 6th Division, 17th Corps, Army of the Tennessee (January 20-July 30, 1863); commanding 1st Division, 17th Corps, Army of the Tennessee (September 28-October 23, 1863); commanding Post of Vicksburg, District of Vicksburg, Department of the Tennessee (April-September 27, 1864); commanding 1st Division, 16th Corps, Army of the Tennessee (November 3-December 5, 1864); commanding 1st Division, Detachment Army of the Tennessee, Army of the Cumberland (December 5, 1864-February 18, 1865); and commanding 1st Division, 16th Corps, Department of the Gulf (February 18-July 20, 1865). Named colonel of a three-month regiment, he managed to reenlist it for a full three-year term during the first summer of the war. He led a brigade at Fort Donelson and was wounded at Shiloh in the foot. He then briefly commanded a division but was again in brigade command during the Corinth, Mississippi operations. Not present at Iuka or Corinth, he took part in the Vicksburg Campaign. Brevetted major general for Nashville, he next participated in the operations against Mobile before being mustered out on August 24, 1865. After the war he was singularly unsuccessful in business and official matters.

MACAULEY, Daniel (?-1894)

After serving mostly in the western theater, New York-born Daniel Macauley won his brevet in the Shenandoah Valley. Enlisting in an Indiana unit, his assignments included: first lieutenant and adjutant, 11th Indiana (April 25, 1861); first lieutenant and adjutant, 11th Indiana (three-years unit, August 31, 1861); major, 11th Indiana (April 21, 1862); lieutenant colonel, 11th Indiana (September 4, 1862); colonel, 11th Indiana (March 10, 1863); commanding 1st Brigade, 3rd Division, 13th Corps, Department of the Gulf (December 6, 1863-February 5, 1864); commanding 3rd Brigade, 2nd Division, 19th Corps, Army of the Shenandoah, (September 21-October 19, 1864); and commanding 2nd Separate Brigade, 8th Corps, Middle Department (January 31-April 19, 1865). His three-months unit served under Robert Patterson before being mustered out on August 4, 1861. Reorganized later in the month, it went on to serve at Paducah, Kentucky, and fought at Fort Donelson, Shiloh (under Lew Wallace) and in the advance on Corinth. At Vicksburg, Macauley was wounded but recovered to serve in the Department of the Gulf and then be transferred to Virginia. He succeeded to brigade command at Fisher's Hill and was brevetted brigadier general for Cedar Creek. With the war over, he was mustered out on July 26, 1865.

McBRIDE, James H. (?-?)

A brigadier general in the Missouri State Guard, James H. McBride does not appear to have ever received a commission in the Confederate army. From the time of its formation, he commanded the Guard's 7th Division, seeing action at Wilson's Creek and in the siege of Lexington. In February 1862 he resigned his command and thus was not in the battle of Pea Ridge. However, his resignation does not appear to have been acted upon right away since he still appears as commanding a brigade as late as September 1862. At this point he disappears from the military records.

McCABE, Joseph E. (?-?)

In the final days of the Civil War, General Robert E. Lee was hampered by a group of Union scout-spies, not the least important of which was Sergeant Joseph E. McCabe. Attached to the band of scouts headed by Major Harry Young, McCabe had served the Union forces under Philip H. Sheridan well in the Shenandoah Valley in 1864 and early 1865. He then accompanied Sheridan when he joined the Army of the Potomac before Petersburg. On the night before the battle of Five Forks, McCabe and a band of other scouts—probably in Confederate uniforms—operated behind George E. Pickett's lines, cutting telegraph wires to separate him from Lee. This hindered rapid communications during the battle, which resulted in the evacuation of both Petersburg and Richmond. During the retreat to Appomattox he frequently assumed the identity of a Confederate soldier to gain information on the positions of Lee's supply trains, relaying the information to Sheridan who was then able to attack. He was involved in the capture of the four trains filled with rations intended for the Army of Northern Virginia at Appomattox Station just prior to the surrender. Ironically it was these rations which were later used to feed the surrendered Confederates. McCabe had done his job well, and Lee probably never knew the damage he had wrought.

McCALL, George Archibald (1802-1868)

When the Civil War began Governor Andrew G. Curtin of Pennsylvania organized more than the state's quota of regiments, and the War Department would not accept all of them. So Curtin organized the Pennsylvania Reserve Corps—12 infantry regiments and one each of rifles, cavalry, and light artillery—with West Pointer (1822) George A. McCall at its head. The native Philadelphian had been posted to the infantry upon graduation and served in the Seminole and Mexican wars and in frontier Indian fighting before transferring in 1850 to the inspector general's department. In the meantime he had earned two brevets in the fight against Mexico. In 1853 he retired as one of the army's two inspector generals, with the rank of colonel. However, 1861 brought him back into the service despite his advanced age. His assignments included: major general, Pennsylvania Volunteers (May 15, 1861); brigadier general, USV (ca. July 23, 1861, to rank from May 17, 1861); commanding Pennsylvania Reserves Division, Army of the Potomac (October 3, 1861 March 13, 1862); com manding 2nd Division, 1st Corps, Army of the Potomac (March 13, April 4, 1862); commanding 2nd Division, Department of the Rappahannock (April 4-June 12, 1862); and commanding 3rd Division, 5th Corps, Army of the Potomac (June 18-30, 1862). When the Reserves were finally accepted into federal service in July 1861, his Pennsylvania commission lapsed on the 23rd and he was appointed in the national volunteers. Part of his command fought at Dranesville, and after further service in northern Virginia the division joined the Army of the Potomac on the Peninsula in time for the Seven Days. At Beaver Dam Creek his division formed the bulk of the Union defenders and mowed down the assaulting enemy. The next day his men were heavily engaged at Gaines' Mill and then took part in the army's change of base. During the fighting at Glendale on June 30, 1862, he rode into the 47th Virginia while scouting his position and was captured. He was declared exchanged for Simon B. Buckner on August 18, 1862, and then went on an indefinite sick leave. Without returning to duty, he resigned on March 31, 1863.

McCALMONT, Alfred Brunson (1825-?)

Native Pennsylvanian Alfred B. McCalmont won his brevet as a Union brigadier general in one of the last episodes of the Civil War. His assignments included: lieutenant colonel, 142nd Pennsylvania (September 1, 1862); commanding 1st Brigade, 3rd Division, 1st Corps, Army of the Potomac (September 14-October 14, 1863); colonel, 208th Pennsylvania (September 12, 1864); and commanding 1st Brigade, 3rd Division, 9th Corps, Army of the Potomac (February 11-25 and April 3-June 1, 1865). Answering Lincoln's summer 1862 call for more men, the unit fought at Fredericksburg and Chancellorsville. At Gettysburg McCalmont succeeded to command of the regiment and went on to lead it during the Bristoe and Mine Run operations. In 1864 he took command of a new regiment which was assigned to the Petersburg trenches. When Lee made his breakout attempt at Fort Stedman, McCalmont won a brevet for his role in stabilizing the lines. His corps remained in the Petersburg vicinity during the Appomattox Campaign, and McCalmont was mustered out with his regiment on June 1, 1865.

McCAULEY, Charles Stewart (1793-1869)

The one significant action taken by career naval officer Charles S. McCauley during the Civil War was his last. He had been appointed a midshipman in 1809 and served through the War of 1812 as a lieutenant. During the Mexican War he was in charge of the Washington Navy Yard and later commanded the Pacific Squadron and the South Atlantic Squadron. The year 1861 found him in command of the Gosport Navy Yard in Norfolk, Virginia, with the rank of captain. On the night of April 20, 1861, only a week after Fort Sumter, he felt that the yard was under the threat of imminent attack. He therefore ordered the scuttling of several vessels in the docks—one of which was later raised to become the Confederate ironclad *Virginia*—and the burning of the shops and stores. The destruction was incomplete and the South benefitted greatly from the prize. Censured by the Navy Department for his actions, he was retired the next year. Five years later he was promoted, on the retired list, to the grade of commodore.

McCAUSLAND, John (1836-1927)

The next-to-last Confederate general to die, John McCausland spent most of his postwar years trying to justify his 1864 burning of Chambersburg, Pennsylvania. A graduate of the Virginia Military Institute, he had served as a professor at his alma mater during the intervening years before the Civil War. Despite being from the Unionist, western part of Virginia, he decided to join the majority of the state and not really the Confederacy proper. He had had some military field experience at the John Brown hanging. His Civil War assignments included: colonel, 36th Virginia (early 1861); commanding brigade, Floyd's Division, Army of Central Kentucky, Department No. 2 (January-February 1862); commanding brigade, Department of Southwestern Virginia (May 8-November 25, 1862); commanding brigade, Department of Western Virginia (November 25, 1862-May 1864); brigadier general, CSA (May 18, 1864); commanding brigade, Ransom's-Lomax's Cavalry Division, Valley District, Department of Northern Virginia (June 1864-March 1865); and commanding brigade, Rosser's Division, Cavalry Corps, Army of Northern Virginia (March-April 9, 1865). During the first year of the war he served under Generals Wise and Floyd in the western part of the state. At the beginning of 1862 the command was moved into Kentucky where McCausland directed a brigade. Part of the defending force at Fort Donelson, he managed to ferry his small brigade out of the capitulating fortification. For the next two years he was stationed in western Virginia protecting the Virginia and Tennessee Railroad and the local saltworks. After the battle of Cloyd's Mountain, in which he succeeded to overall command upon the death of General A.G. Jenkins, he was promoted to brigadier. He blamed his connection with the Donelson disaster for not having received the general's wreath earlier. Assuming command of part of Jenkins' old cavalry, he went with Early to the outskirts of the Union capital, fighting well at Monocacy on the way. After returning to the Valley, he was sent by Early to demand $100,000 in gold from the residents of Chambersburg. If not paid he was to fire the town. He did. Afterwards he served through the Valley Campaign, fighting at 3rd Winchester, Fisher's Hill, and Cedar Creek. Joining Lee before Petersburg in March 1865, he cut his way out rather than surrender his brigade at Appomattox. A few days later he disbanded his men. Returning home to what was now West Virginia, he had difficulties with his Unionist neighbors. He soon went into exile and spent several years in Canada, Europe, and Mexico. He was formally charged with arson in Pennsylvania, but President Grant intervened on his behalf. He increasingly felt mistreated by his neighbors and the press, who he felt never presented his case properly, and became something of a recluse on his farm until his death. (Freeman, Douglas, S., *Lee's Lieutenants*)

McCAW, James Brown (1823-1906)

When Richmond periodically turned into one large hospital after many of the battles of the Army of Northern Virginia, Dr. James McCaw was the director of its largest hospital—the largest in the Confederacy. A native of Richmond, McCaw received his medical training at the University of the City of New York. Returning to his home town he was a physician of some note before joining the Confederate army as a surgeon. He was assigned to the post of chief surgeon at Chimborazo Hospital on the outskirts of Richmond on October 9, 1861. He was responsible for a number of innovations in the operation of the hospital, including effective use of the hospital fund to purchase special food stuffs, purchase of cows, rental of farm and pasture land, and the purchase of two canal boats to transport supplies. However, he was in frequent conflict with the Quartermaster's and Commissary Departments which stuck to the absolute letter of the army's regulations, often bringing to naught McCaw's efforts. During the Peninsula Campaign his hospital was filled to well over its capacity of 3,000 but muddled through. The surgical staff, although always shorthanded, managed to perform some innovative operations, preventing the loss of limbs by many a Confederate. During the latter part of the war, McCaw was also editor of the *Confederate States Medical Journal*. Based on very incomplete figures, it has been claimed that Chimborazo had a very low mortality rate. While this is questionable, the hospital was one of the most efficient of its time. McCaw returned to civilian practice after Richmond's fall and was also a college professor.

McCLANAHAN, John R. (18 ?-ca. 1865)

A case of journalistic persistence in the face of adversity is that of the *Memphis Appeal* and its coeditors, Benjamin F. Dill and John R. McClanahan. They had succeeded to their positions in 1851 upon the death of Henry Van Pelt. Editorially, the paper was not originally a secessionist organ, and it stuck to the candidacy of Democrat Stephen A. Douglas despite the breakaway of the Southern part of the party. Finally giving up on the preservation of the Union, McClanahan and his associates threw the paper into complete support for the Confederacy. With the military fortunes of the South on the decline in early 1862, the paper and its staff fled the city just before it fell to Union forces. Setting up shop in Grenada, Mississippi, McClanahan started a three-year career as a refugee journalist. With successive Union advances, the paper subsequently published in Jackson and Meridian, Mississippi, Atlanta, and, finally, Montgomery, Alabama. Offering half-price subscriptions to soldiers in the field, McClanahan and Dill were able to keep the paper thriving, and even survived a strike. The paper was not very popular with the Union army, whose grasp it eluded in several narrow escapes, particularly at Jackson and Atlanta. With the surrender at Appomattox and Wilson's cavalry closing in on its last refuge, the *Appeal* staff fled again but was surrounded and captured at Columbus, Georgia. McClanahan managed to smuggle the press away, but Dill and the other equipment were not so lucky. Returning to Memphis, McClanahan's own luck ran out and he died in a fall from a hotel. (Baker, Thomas Harrison, *The Memphis Commercial Appeal*)

McCLELLAN, George Brinton (1826-1885)

A brilliant engineer and highly capable organizer, George B. McClellan just wasn't an army commander. In that position he proved the weakness of West Point in its early years; the academy was simply geared to the production of engineers and company officers for a small, pre-Civil War regular army. The Philadelphia native had entered the academy from the University of Pennsylvania and graduated in 1846 in the second position of his class. Accordingly he was assigned to the engineers. He earned two brevets under Winfield Scott in Mexico and later served at his alma mater. The slow promotions in the regular army prompted him to take a captaincy in the cavalry in the 1855 expansion of the service. He was dispatched to study European armies and filed an extensive report centering on the Crimean War siege operations at Sebastopol. This experience would later influence his decisions on the Virginia Peninsula. During the rest of his year overseas he travelled widely and altered the Prussian and Hungarian cavalry saddles into the "McClellan Saddle" that was used until the army abolished its mounted arm. He resigned his commission on January 16, 1857, and entered railroad engineering. He worked for the Illinois Central—as chief engineer and vice president—and just before the Civil War became a division president for the Ohio & Mississippi. Despite his success in the private field he was happy to reenter the military in 1862. His assignments included: major general, Ohio Volunteers (April 23, 1861); commanding Ohio Militia (April 23-May 13, 1861); commanding Army of Occupation, West Virginia, Department of the Ohio and the department (May 13-July 23, 1861); major general, USA (May 14, 1861); commanding Military Division of the Potomac (July 25-August 15, 1861); commanding Army and Department of the Potomac (August 15, 1861-November 9, 1862); and commander-in-chief, USA (November 5, 1861-March 11, 1862). Initially appointed by Ohio's Governor William Dennison, he was soon made second

McClellan receiving a visit from the President following the battle of Antietam. (AC)

only to Scott by a former attorney for the Illinois Central—Abraham Lincoln. Letting his rapid rise from retired captain to major general go to his head, he issued comical denials of any desire to become a dictator. By then he had won some minor victories in western Virginia, receiving the Thanks of Congress on July 16, 1861, although much of the credit belonged to his subordinates there and in Kentucky. He was called to take charge at Washington after the disaster at 1st Bull Run, but his behavior toward Scott and the civil authorities was unpardonable. Now called "The Young Napoleon," he actively worked for Scott's retirement and was named in his place. His engineering and organizational skills shined bright in the creation of the Army of the Potomac, a mighty machine. But he did not advance and refused to divulge his plans to the civilians over him. He even refused to see the president on one occasion. In December 1861 he was downed by typhoid and this prolonged the delays. By the time he did advance on Manassas, Joseph E. Johnston's army had withdrawn. McClellan then planned an advance on Richmond by way of the Peninsula between the James and York Rivers. It was a good plan despite Lincoln's fears for Washington. But McClellan did not have the ability to direct it. The movement started well but—remembering Sebastopol—he began siege operations at Yorktown which allowed Johnston to move in reinforcements. When Johnston withdrew McClellan followed, fighting at Williamsburg, to within sight of the Confederate capital. He then stopped. He was constantly overestimating the strength of the enemy facing him. It was these constant delays which prompted Lincoln to suspend him from command of all the armies on March 11, 1862, so that he could concentrate on the Army of the Potomac and Richmond. He survived the Confederate counterattack at Seven Pines, principally through confusion in the Confederate army and the actions of his own subordinates. When Lee attacked him in the Seven Days in late June he failed to take the opportunity to strike at Richmond along the weakly defended south side of the Chickahominy River. Instead he panicked and ordered a dangerous change of base from the York to the James River in the facing of Lee's attacks. Most of the battles fought in the movement were Union successes but the overall outcome of the campaign was negative as a result of McClellan's weaknesses. Safely entrenched at Harrison's Landing he began condemning the War Department, Lincoln, and Stanton, blaming them for the defeat. Finally it was decided in Washington to abandon the campaign and transfer most of McClellan's men to John Pope's army in northern Virginia. There were charges that McClellan—now called by the press "Mac the Unready" and "The Little Corporal of Unsought Fields"—was especially slow in cooperating. With Pope defeated at 2nd Bull Run and his men streaming back to the Washington fortifications, McClellan was restored to active command of his reconstituted army and was welcomed by his men who affectionately called him "Little Mac." In the Maryland Campaign he advanced to confront Lee in the western part of the state and moved uncharacteristically fast when some of his command found a copy of Lee's orders for the movement of his troops. Lee fought several delaying actions along South Mountain in order to reconcentrate his army. His caution returning, McClellan slowed down, and Lee was able to get most of his men in line at Antietam. McClellan attacked piecemeal and his attacks failed to crush Lee who was heavily outnumbered with his back to the Potomac River. Lincoln was extremely upset by the escape of Lee and his army but nonetheless used the "victory" to issue the Emancipation Proclamation. Continuing his dilatory tactics, McClellan resorted to constant demands for more men and called for massive reequipping and fresh mounts for his cavalry. Then for the second time Jeb Stuart's cavalry rode completely around the Army of the Potomac. Under orders from the War Department, McClellan relinquished command on November 9, 1862, and repaired to his Trenton, New Jersey, home to await new directives—destined never to arrive. The Democratic candidate for president in 1864, he was hampered by the party's plank calling for an end to the war, which was labelled a failure. He himself denounced the plank and was for the rigorous pursuit of victory. At first it appeared that he would defeat Lincoln, but Union victories in the field diminished the public's war weariness. Winning in only three states, he resigned from the army on election day. Active in state politics, he served as New Jersey's governor in the late 1870's and early 1880's. (McClellan, George Brinton, *McClellan's Own Story*; Hassler, Warren W., Jr., *General George B. McClellan: Shield of the Union*; and Myers, William Starr, *General George Brinton McClellan: A Study in Personality*)

McCLELLAN, Henry Brainerd (1840-1904)

One of the most well-known memoirs dealing with the life of Jeb Stuart was written by his one-time adjutant, Henry B. McClellan. Joining the 3rd Virginia Cavalry, he had become a first lieutenant and adjutant and served through most of Jeb Stuart's early campaigns. On June 1, 1863, he was announced in orders as a member of the cavalryman's staff as a major and assistant adjutant general. In this position he played a key role in the fighting on Fleetwood Hill at Brandy Station a few days later. He took part in Stuart's ride around the Army of the Potomac during the Gettysburg Campaign. After serving in the fall campaigns, he continued with his chief in the Wilderness Campaign until the fall of Stuart at Yellow Tavern. With the death of his commander, he joined General Lee's staff as an aide for the next several months. After the war he was active in veterans' affairs and wrote his memoirs. (McClellan, Henry Brainerd, *The Life and Campaigns of Maj. Gen. J. E. B. Stuart*)

McCLERNAND, John Alexander (1812-1900)

Political appointee John A. McClernand carried on his political career in the military and became a thorn in the sides of Grant, Sherman, and other West Pointers. However, he did add tremendous weight to the Union war effort through his recruiting abilities. Born in Kentucky, he moved with his family to Illinois where he became a lawyer. Beginning in 1836 he served seven years in the state legislature and quickly became noted for his oratory. An opponent of abolitionists, he was considered a moderate on the idea of secession and was highly popular in the southern part of the state, which closely associated itself with the slave-owning state across the Ohio River. As a Jacksonian Democrat he took a seat in the U.S. House of Representatives in 1843 and, joining the faction of Stephen A. Douglas, was reelected four times. Again in Congress in 1861, he was considered by Lincoln as an ally in the maintenance of midwestern support for the Union. Up until this time McClernand had no military experience other than two months of service as a private in the Illinois volunteers during the Black Hawk War in the summer of 1832. At the time of the firing upon Fort Sumter he was in Illinois and took a leading part in the occupation of Cairo and the cutting off of supplies moving south. Lincoln—also a veteran of the Black Hawk War—nominated him to a brigadier generalship in order to spur support for the war effort throughout the Midwest. McClernand's assignments included: brigadier general, USV (August 1861 to rank from May 17); commanding 1st Brigade, District of Southeast Missouri, Western Department (October 14-November 9, 1861); commanding 1st Brigade, District of Southeast Missouri, Department of the Missouri (November 9-December 23, 1861); commanding 1st Brigade, District of Cairo, Department of the Missouri (December 23, 1861-February 1, 1862); commanding 1st Division, District of Cairo, Department of the Missouri (February 1-17, 1862); commanding 1st Division, Army of the Tennessee (February 17-May 3 and June 10-July 1862); major general, USV (March 21, 1862); commanding 1st Division, District of Jackson, Army of the Tennessee and the district (July-September 1862); commanding Army of the Mississippi, Department of the Tennessee (January 4-12, 1863); commanding 13th Corps, Army of the Tennessee (January 31-June 19, 1863); and commanding 13th Corps, Department of the Gulf (February 20-March 15, 1864). One of his earliest contributions to the Union war effort was his role in getting the 21st Illinois (Grant's regiment) to reenlist for three years. As a brigadier, he was given charge of a brigade under Grant and was stationed at Cairo. Having resigned from Congress on October 28, 1861, in order to take to the field, he fought well at the minor Union setback at Belmont, Missouri. In a couple of months he was given charge of a division and took part in the advance against Fort Henry on the Tennessee River, but the infantry arrived too late to assist the naval forces in its capture. Marching overland to the Cumberland River, the army moved against Fort Donelson where McClernand launched a premature attack and was criticized by Grant for his recklessness. Following the fall of the fort McClernand led his division back to the Tennessee where he fought well on the first day at Shiloh. After taking part in Halleck's slow advance on Corinth, Mississippi, and serving in district command in Tennessee, McClernand was sent home to raise troops in Illinois, Indiana, and Iowa. Highly successful, he forwarded troops to Memphis for planned operations against Vicksburg which he himself would lead. This was to the disgust of both Halleck and Grant but had been arranged by Lincoln and Stanton. To forestall McClernand taking command of the expedition, Grant sent Sherman to Memphis and authorized him to make the movement down the Mississippi. This failed miserably at Chickasaw Bayou, and shortly thereafter an angry McClernand arrived to take command. He led an expedition up the Red River and captured Fort Hindman, or Arkansas Post. Grant characterized this operation as "a wild goose chase" until he found out that Sherman had suggested it and it proved to be of some benefit. Nonetheless McClernand was reduced to corps command and he fought through the beginning of the Vicksburg Campaign. Much of the time he spent praising the achievements of his corps in congratulatory orders and disparaging achievements of the others; he had no use for West Pointers like Sherman and McPherson. The final straw came when the assaults against the fortress city were made on May 22, 1863. The first round of attacks had failed, but McClernand claimed that he had gained a foothold and that if the other corps supported him he could exploit the breakthrough. The result was a second round of bloody repulses. What made matters worse was the fact that McClernand supplied newspapers back home with his congratulatory orders to his men condemning the efforts of the other corps—without going through military channels. Grant relieved him on June 19, 1863, and sent him home to await orders. Early the next year he briefly commanded the corps again on the Gulf coast but saw little action and contracted malaria. He resigned his commission for health reasons on November 30, 1864. His military career had been most productive in recruiting assignments but, despite some battlefield abilities, he was a liability in the field. Returning to his private practice, he later became a judge and was active in politics.

McCOMB, William (1828-1918)

Pennsylvania-born manufacturer William McComb entered Confederate service from his adopted state of Tennessee. He was elected a second lieutenant in the 14th Tennessee in May 1861. His later positions included: major, 14th Tennessee (ca. April 26, 1862); lieutenant colonel, 14th Tennessee (ca. August 15, 1862); colonel, 14th Tennessee (September 2, 1861); brigadier general, CSA (January 20, 1865); and commanding brigade, Heth's Division, A. P. Hill's Corps, Army of Northern Virginia (January 20-April 9, 1865). After service in the Cheat Mountain and Peninsula campaigns, McComb took part in the battles of Cedar Mountain, 2nd Bull Run, and Antietam where he was seriously wounded. Returning to the army he led the regiment at Chancellorsville where he was again severely wounded. Participating in the campaign from the Wilderness to Petersburg, McComb took part in the siege at the latter place and temporarily commanded Archer's Brigade during the battle of Poplar Spring Church. During the siege winter McComb was given his general's wreath and assigned to command a new brigade formed from the Tennessee regiments of Archer's and Bushrod Johnson's brigades. Leading this brigade, McComb took part in the remainder of the siege and finally surrendered at Appomattox Court House. After the war he settled in Virginia and became a farmer for nearly half a century. (Freeman, Douglas S., *Lee's Lieutenants*)

McCONNELL, Henry Kumler (?-1889)

Although he spent much of the Civil War in garrison duty, New York-born Ohio resident Henry K. McConnell still won the brevet of brigadier general for the war. His assignments included: second lieutenant, 71st Ohio (October 4, 1861); captain, 71st Ohio (November 14, 1861); colonel, 71st Ohio (June 7, 1863); and commanding 2nd Brigade, 3rd Division, 4th Corps, Army of the Cumberland (December 26, 1864-June 7, 1865). His regiment fought at Shiloh and then was in various posts until July 1864 when ordered to join Sherman before Atlanta. McConnell took part in the siege of the city and was then sent back to Tennessee to deal with Hood's invasion of the state. The regiment fought at Franklin and Nashville, but McConnell was not with them at the latter. Late in the war he commanded a brigade and was mustered out with his unit on November 30, 1865.

McCOOK, Alexander McDowell (1831-1903)

The Union debacle at Chickamauga effectively ended the field career of Alexander McD. McCook. The Ohio native was a member of a family which provided numerous officers to the Union army during the Civil War. A West Pointer (1852), he was posted to the infantry after taking an extra year to complete his studies. Having served on the frontier, he was a professor at his alma mater upon the outbreak of hostilities. His wartime assignments included: first lieutenant, 3rd Infantry (since December 6, 1858); colonel, 1st Ohio (April 16, 1861); captain, 3rd Infantry (May 14, 1861); brigadier general, USV (September 3, 1861); commanding Division at Nolin, Ken., Department of the Cumberland (October-November 9, 1861); commanding Division at Nolin, Ken., Department of the Ohio (November 9-December 2, 1861); commanding 2nd Division, Army of the Ohio (December 2, 1861-September 29, 1862); major general, USV (July 17, 1862); commanding 1st Corps, Army of the Ohio (September 29-October 24, 1862); commanding Right Wing, 14th Corps, Army of the Cumberland (October 24, 1862-January 9, 1863); commanding 20th Corps, Army of the Cumberland (January 9-October 9, 1863); and commanding District of Eastern Arkansas, 7th Corps, Department of Arkansas (March 9-May 25, 1865). For his role in leading his volunteer regiment at 1st Bull Run, he was brevetted major in the regular army. Mustered out with his three-months unit on August 16, 1861, he was given a brigadier's star the next month and assigned to duty in Kentucky. He took part in the capture of Nashville, for which he earned another brevet, and received a similar reward for the battle of Shiloh where he served under Don C. Buell in reinforcing Grant. After participating in the slow advance on Corinth, Mississippi, he took part in Buell's advance against Chattanooga and then moved to the defense of the Ohio River line. Fighting at Perryville, he was later brevetted brigadier general in the regulars for his actions, in the omnibus promotion bill of March 13, 1865. By now a major general of volunteers he led his corps at Stone's River and in the Tulllahoma Campaign. At

Chickamauga he got caught up in the rout of two-thirds of the Union army and fled along with its commander, Rosecrans. The latter tried to place the blame for the debacle on McCook and Thomas L. Crittenden. They were, however, both cleared. Nonetheless, McCook's reputation was so damaged he was never again trusted with a major field command. In the final months of the conflict he commanded a district in Arkansas and resigned from the volunteers on October 21, 1865. Although a major general by brevet in the regular army he failed to gain advancement from his captaincy in the 1866 expansion of the military. The next year however he became lieutenant colonel, 26th Infantry and, in 1895, he retired as a major general, having served a number of years as a staff officer with William T. Sherman. Daniel McCook, Jr., and Robert L. McCook were his brothers and Edward M. McCook was a cousin.

McCOOK, Anson George (1835-1917)

Ohio lawyer Anson G. McCook was one of 17 close members of his family to serve the Union during the Civil War and emerged with the brevet of brigadier general for it. His assignments included: captain, 2nd Ohio (April 17, 1861); major, 2nd Ohio (August 6, 1861); lieutenant colonel, 2nd Ohio (January 1, 1863); colonel, 2nd Ohio (January 20, 1863); commanding 1st Brigade, 1st Division, 14th Corps, Army of the Cumberland (July 2-27, 1864); colonel, 194th Ohio (March 1865); and commanding 1st Brigade, 3rd Provisional Division, Army of the Shenandoah (ca. April-August 1865). He fought at 1st Bull Run, where a cousin in the same regiment was killed, before being mustered out with his three-months unit on July 31, 1861. Recommissioned a week later as a major, he served under Ormsby M. Mitchel in Tennessee and northern Alabama. The unit went on to fight at Perryville and McCook went on to succeed to its command at Murfreesboro. He took part in the Tullahoma Campaign and fought at Chattanooga. During the Atlanta Campaign he took charge of the brigade but a few weeks later, on July 27, 1864, was ordered to Chattanooga with his regiment. There, most of the unit was mustered out and the remainder was merged into the new 18th Ohio Veteran Infantry. McCook himself was mustered out and he later organized a new regiment which he led in the Shenandoah Valley in 1865, for a time commanding a brigade. Brevetted, he was honorably discharged on October 21, 1865, and resumed his law practice. He also served as a Republican congressman and edited what later became the *New York Law Journal*.

McCOOK, Daniel (1798-1863)

Sending 10 sons into the Union army—three of whom were killed—Daniel McCook himself gave his life in the attempt to capture John Hunt Morgan during his raid north of the Ohio River. Considered too old for active field duty, the native Pennsylvanian and Illinois resident was commissioned as an additional paymaster of volunteers on March 24, 1862. The next year he was mortally wounded on July 19 near Buffington Island, Ohio, in an attempt to stop Morgan. He died two days later. His brother and five nephews also served in the Union army and navy.

McCOOK, Daniel, Jr. (1834-1864)

Sherman's blunder in ordering the assaults on Kennesaw Mountain during the Atlanta Campaign cost the life of an experienced brigade leader, Daniel McCook, Jr. One of three Ohio brothers to become Union generals—the others were Alexander McD. and Robert L.—Daniel had practiced law in Kansas with Thomas Ewing and William T. Sherman. Enlisting early in the war, his assignments included: captain, 1st Kansas (May 31, 1861); captain and assistant adjutant general, USV (November 9, 1861); colonel, 52nd Ohio (July 15, 1862); commanding 36th Brigade, 11th Division, Army of the Ohio (September-September 29, 1862); commanding 36th Brigade, 11th Division, 3rd Corps, Army of the Ohio (September 29-November 5, 1862); commanding 2nd Brigade, 4th Division, Center, 14th Corps, Army of the Cumberland (November 5, 1862-January 9, 1863); commanding 2nd Brigade, 4th Division, 14th Corps, Army of the Cumberland (January 9-June 8, 1863); commanding 2nd Brigade, 2nd Division, Reserve Corps, Army of the Cumberland (June 8-October 9, 1863); commanding 3rd Brigade, 2nd Division, 14th Corps, Army of the Cumberland (October 10-December 16, 1863 and February 15-June 27, 1864); and brigadier general, USV (July 16, 1864). As a company commander, he fought at Wilson's Creek before transferring to the staff. Although arriving too late for the fighting at Shiloh, he was the divisional chief of staff to George H. Thomas in the campaign and was later given charge of a volunteer regiment from his native state. As a brigade commander, he fought at Perryville but missed Murfreesboro since the division to which he was attached was assigned to guard the supply trains. He did however lead a brigade in the Tullahoma Campaign and at Chickamauga and Chattanooga. He then led his brigade throughout the Atlanta Campaign until the army reached the Confederate positions at Kennesaw Mountain. Sherman then ordered a fruitless charge on the 27th of June. McCook's brigade was assigned the lead and McCook knew that it was a desperate effort but gallantly went forward. He fell mortally wounded in front of the enemy's works and was taken back to Ohio to die. Promoted to brigadier general on July 16, 1864, he died the next day.

McCOOK, Edward Moody (1833-1909)

One of the fighting McCooks of Ohio—there were 17 of them in the Union army and navy, four of whom became generals—Edward M. McCook gave up his law practice in order to enter the regular army. His assignments included: second lieutenant, 1st Cavalry (May 8, 1861); second lieutenant, 4th Cavalry (designation change August 3, 1861); major, 2nd Indiana Cavalry (September 29, 1861); lieutenant colonel, 2nd Indiana Cavalry (February 11, 1862); colonel, 2nd Indiana Cavalry (April 30, 1862); first lieutenant, 4th Cavalry (July 17, 1862); commanding 1st Brigade, Cavalry Division, Army of the Ohio (September 5-November 5, 1862); commanding 2nd Brigade, 1st Division, Cavalry Corps, Army of the Cumberland (January 9-September 9 and October 12-November 20, 1863);

commanding the division (September 9-October 12, 1863) brigadier general, USV (April 27, 1864); and commanding 1st Division, Cavalry Corps, Military Division of the Mississippi (October 29, 1864-June 26, 1865). Having been commissioned directly into the regular establishment, he transferred to the volunteers in September 1861. Although his regiment was not actively engaged at Shiloh, as part of Buell's Army of the Ohio, he was brevetted for the fight. In the Perryville Campaign he won another brevet for his commanding a brigade. Missing Murfreesboro, he led a brigade through the Tullahoma Campaign and a division at Chickamauga where he won his third brevet in the regular service. Again brevetted for operations in eastern Tennessee, he then took his division on the movement toward Atlanta. In conjunction with George Stoneman, he launched a raid against the city's rail supply lines but suffered heavy losses in making his way back to the Union lines. His final exploit of the war came in Wilson's raid through Alabama and Georgia. For the capture of Selma on this raid he was brevetted a fifth time. Having been promoted to brigadier general of volunteers in the spring of 1864, he was brevetted major general for the war and brigadier general of regulars as well. Mustered out of the volunteers on January 15, 1866, he resigned from the army on May 9, 1866. For the next decade he served as a diplomat to Hawaii and territorial governor of Colorado. His business interest, which included telephone companies in Europe, made him a wealthy man.

McCOOK, Robert Latimer (1827-1862)

When Union General Robert L. McCook received his mortal wound, he accepted it as an act of war, but many Northerners considered it an act of murder and sought the execution of the perpetrator, Frank B. Gurley. The Ohio-born lawyer came from a family that was destined to provide 17 soldiers and sailors to the Union cause. His assignments included: colonel, 9th Ohio (May 8, 1861); commanding brigade, Army of Occupation—West Virginia, Department of the Ohio (July 1861); commanding 3rd Brigade, Army of Occupation—West Virginia (July-September 1861); commanding 2nd Brigade, District of the Kanawha, Department of West Virginia (October 11-November 1861); commanding 3rd Brigade, Army of the Ohio (November-December 2, 1861); commanding 3rd Brigade, 1st Division, Army of the Ohio (December 2, 1861-August 6, 1862); and brigadier general, USV (March 21, 1862). He served under both McClellan and Rosecrans in western Virginia, seeing action at Carnifax Ferry in charge of a brigade. Wounded at Mill Springs in early 1862, he then led his brigade in Halleck's painfully slow "drive" on Corinth, Mississippi. While following General Buell's advance along the Memphis and Charleston Railroad he was confined to an ambulance by illness. Near Decherd, Tennessee, on August 5, 1862, while scouting with a small escort he was overtaken by a band of what appeared to be irregulars and he was shot by Gurley as he tried to whip the ambulance's team into going faster. He died the next day but not without talking with Gurley, who was destined to have years of trouble over a legitimate act of war.

McCOOK, Roderick Sheldon (1839-1886)

Of the 17 McCooks from Ohio to serve the Union cause only one, Roderick S. McCook, was a naval officer. A graduate of Annapolis (1859), he was a midshipman when the war broke out. On June 5, 1861, he was serving aboard the USS *Minnesota*, the flagship of the Atlantic Blockading Squadron, when he was made the prize master of the first Confederate privateer to be captured—the *Savannah*. The treatment that the crew received raised a number of legal questions about the legality of letters of marque that had not been settled this early in the war. Early the next year McCook commanded a battery of six naval howitzers in the attack on New Bern. Continuing on blockade duty, he took part in the attacks on Fort Fisher in the last months of the war. Suffering from ill-health, he spent most of his remaining years in the service, until his 1885 retirement, performing lighthouse duty.

McCOWN, John Porter (1815-1879)

As a Confederate major general, West Pointer (1840) John P. McCown had a troubled career. Posted to the artillery, he had seen service in the Seminole War, on the frontier, during the Mexican War—winning a brevet—and on the expedition against the Mormons. Resigning his captaincy in the 4th Artillery on May 17, 1861, he offered his services to his native Tennessee. His Southern assignments included: lieutenant colonel, Artillery (1861); colonel, Tennessee Corps of Artillery (May 17, 1861); commanding 2nd Brigade, 1st Geographical Division, Department #2 (September 7-October 24, 1861); brigadier general, CSA (October 12, 1861); commanding 3rd Division, 1st Geographical Division, Department #2 (October 24, 1861-February 1862); commanding McCown's Command, 1st Geographical Division, Department #2 (February-April 1862); major general, CSA (March 10, 1862); commanding division, Army of the West, Department #2 (April-July 1862); also commanding the army (June 20-27 and July 20, 1862); commanding division, Department of East Tennessee (summer-December 1862); commanding the department (September 1-19 and September 27-October 1862); commanding division, attached to Hardee's Corps, Army of Tennessee (December 1862-January 1863); and commanding division, Smith's Corps, Army of Tennessee (February-March 1863). Initially in charge of the state's artillery, he commanded a brigade and then a division at Columbus, Kentucky. He did not however cross the Mississippi for the fight at Belmont. Commanding at New Madrid and Island #10, he came in for severe criticism for his handling of the defense and withdrawal from the latter. By now a major general he led a division in the Corinth siege before being transferred to East Tennessee. On the invasion of Kentucky he fought at Richmond and then, attached to Bragg's army, fought at Murfreesboro. He then ran into trouble with the army commander who brought charges against him for disobedience of orders. Court-martialed on March 16, 1863, McCown was sentenced to six months' suspension from duty without pay. Afterwards he held only minor posts for the balance of the war. He was a teacher and farmer postwar.

McCULLAGH, Joseph Burbridge (1842-1896)

Writing under the name of "Mack," Joseph B. McCullagh found a wide audience for his journalistic reports from the Western theater of the war. A native of Dublin, he had worked his way to America on a ship at age 11 and eventually become an apprentice printer. His first reporting assignment was for the *St. Louis Democrat* in 1859. After a stint in Frémont's bodyguard he became a war correspondent for the *Cincinnati Daily Gazette* and in the Henry-Donelson Campaign he served as a volunteer secretary to Commodore Foote. He was lucky to have survived the fight at Fort Donelson when the USS *St. Louis* was hit 65 times. After his paper refused to publish his account of the Union disaster on the first day of Shiloh, he quit, only to be immediately picked up by the *Cincinnati Commercial* at double salary. After the Vicksburg Campaign he became that paper's Washington correspondent. Also working for the Associated Press of New York, he was noted for his interviews with prominent persons, including Alexander Stephens and Andrew Johnson. After the war he edited several papers, finally the *St. Louis Globe-Democrat*. He died in an accidental fall from his window during an illness.

McCULLOCH, Ben (1811-1862)

By the outbreak of the Civil War, Ben McCulloch had already served in two wars—the War for Texas Independence and the Mexican War. The Tennesseean had gone to Texas for the first struggle and had settled there as a surveyor and later as a U.S. marshal. With Texas' secession he offered his services to the state and his subsequent assignments included: colonel, Texas State Troops (February 1861); brigadier general, CSA (May 11, 1861); commanding all Confederate forces in the Indian Territory (May 11-summer 1861); commanding all Confederate forces in Arkansas (summer 1861); commanding division, Department #2 (September 2, 1861-January 9, 1862); and commanding division, District of the Trans-Mississippi, Department #2 (January 9-March 7, 1862). Commanding state troops he accepted the surrender of regular army units in Texas during the first month of Texas' new status. Promoted to a general's wreath, although he never wore a uniform, he commanded a force sent to the Indian Territory (now Oklahoma) and moved with it into Arkansas and later into Missouri. Assuming command of Price's Missouri State Guard and N.B. Pearce's Arkansas state forces as well, he won a victory at Wilson's Creek, but bickering among the commanders prevented exploitation of the success. Returning to Arkansas, he commanded his division, under Earl Van Dorn, at Pea Ridge until he was almost instantly killed by a bullet in the chest on March 7, 1862. (Nunn, W. Curtis, ed., *Ten More Texans in Gray*)

Ben McCulloch, victor at Wilson's Creek, was later killed at Pea Ridge. (*Leslie's*)

McCULLOCH, Henry Eustace (1816-1895)

The younger brother of Ben McCulloch, Henry E. McCulloch also became a Confederate general, but his service was confined to the area west of the Mississippi River. Born in Tennessee, he had moved to Texas in 1837. For a time he served as a sheriff and during the Mexican War was a company commander in the 1st Texas Rifles, Bell's Regiment and Smith's Battalion. In the interwar years he was a state legislator and U.S. marshal. His Confederate assignments included: colonel, 1st Texas Mounted Rifles (April 15, 1861); commanding Department of Texas (September 4-18, 1861); commanding Military Sub-District of the Rio Grande, Department of Texas (February 25-April 24, 1862); brigadier general, CSA (March 14, 1862); and commanding in the Trans-Mississippi Department: Eastern Sub-District of Texas, District of Texas, New Mexico and Arizona (August 15-29, 1863); Northern Sub-District of Texas, District of Texas, New Mexico and Arizona (August 29, 1863-May 26, 1865); and also 8th (Texas) Cavalry Brigade, 3rd (Texas) Cavalry Division, 3rd Corps (or District of Texas, New Mexico and Arizona) (September 1864-May 26, 1865). Serving mostly in Texas he held various sub-district commands and in the final months of the war he also commanded a paper organization cavalry brigade. His one major action came in Louisiana during the Vicksburg Campaign when he took part in the attack on Milliken's Bend. Following the department's surrender on May 26, 1865, he returned to his farm for the balance of his life.

McCULLOCH, Hugh (1808-1895)

Little more than a month before his assassination Abraham Lincoln appointed Indiana banker Hugh McCulloch as his third treasury secretary. The Maine native had practiced law in Boston before relocating to Indiana and entering the banking profession. Favoring the gold standard, he did accept the post of comptroller of currency in March 1863 and was in charge of the new system of a national paper currency. He held this post for some two years and when William P. Fessenden returned to the U.S. Senate, McCulloch was named to succeed him, on March 6, 1865. Remaining on under Andrew Johnson, he finally gave up his portfolio when Grant was inaugurated in 1869. Returning to his banking interests, he favored the resumption of the gold standard. He again served as secretary of the treasury in the final five months of Chester A. Arthur's presidency, October 1884 to March 1885.

Hugh McCulloch, Lincoln's last treasury secretary. (NA)

McCULLOCH, Robert (1820-1905)

Known as "Black Bob," Colonel Robert McCulloch was in command of a brigade of cavalry for the latter half of the war but without receiving promotion to the appropriate rank. His Confederate assignments included: captain, 1st Cavalry, 6th Division, Missouri State Guard (May 12, 1861); lieutenant colonel, 1st Cavalry, 6th Division, Missouri State Guard (June 1861); colonel, 1st Cavalry, 6th Division, Missouri State Guard (October 1, 1861); commanding 6th Division, Missouri State Guard (December 28, 1861-March 4, 1862); lieutenant colonel, 4th Missouri Cavalry Battalion (April 27, 1862); colonel, 2nd Missouri Cavalry (August 1862); and in the Department of Mississippi and East Louisiana: commanding brigade, Jackson's Division, Van Dorn's Cavalry Corps (November 7, 1862-January 1863); commanding 1st Brigade, 5th Military District (May 30-June 1863); commanding brigade, Chalmers' Cavalry Division (October 18-November 1863); commanding brigade, Chalmers' Division, Lee's Cavalry Corps (November 1863-January 11, 1864); commanding brigade, Chalmers' Division, Forrest's Cavalry Corps (January 11-28, 1864); and commanding brigade, Chalmers' Division, Forrest's Cavalry Corps, Department of Alabama, Mississippi and East Louisiana (January 28-ca. August 4 and late August 1864-May 1865). With the state forces, he saw action at Boonville, Carthage, Wilson's Creek, Dry Wood, Lexington, and Pea Ridge. Transferring to Confederate service, he raised a cavalry battalion which was later increased to a regiment and was sent across the Mississippi. Serving initially dismounted, it fought at Corinth during the siege. Remounted, McCulloch and his men fought at Iuka, Corinth, Okolona, and Tupelo. He was wounded at each of the latter two. His brigade, which he had been leading under Forrest, was detached to the District of the Gulf from September 1864 to February 6, 1865. The command's horses suffered severely at Mobile and the command was sent to northern Mississippi to recuperate and gather up deserters. They finished the war in this service.

McDANIEL, Zedekiah (?-?)

One of the more mysterious of Civil War soldiers was Captain Zedekiah McDaniel, the commander of a Confederate secret service company. A Kentuckian, McDaniel worked with the torpedo service. He was responsible for the sinking of the Union gunboat *Cairo* in the Yazoo River of Mississippi on December 12, 1862. His expenses were paid by the War Department as engineering services. On February 29, 1864, he was authorized to recruit a secret service company of up to 50 men. The unit was designated as "Captain Z. McDaniel's Company, Secret Service." A shadowy organization, it appears to have operated in various theaters. One of McDaniel's agents, John Maxwell, with a civilian companion on August 9, 1864, detonated an "horological" torpedo, or time bomb, at the immense Union supply base at City Point, Virginia, where Grant maintained his headquarters. An estimated total of 169 soldiers and civilian dock workers were killed or wounded. Some $2 million was lost to the Union cause and, although General Grant survived unscathed, some members of his headquarters were among the casualties. On March 28, 1865, McDaniel was ordered to the Mississippi Valley to report to General Henry Gray. Following the Union capture of the Confederate War Department's records, Maxwell's report to McDaniel of the City Point sabotage was found. Based on this evidence General Halleck ordered McDaniel's arrest on June 3, 1865, but here the record ends and McDaniel vanishes into obscurity. (Stern, Philip Van Doren, *Secret Missions of the Civil War*)

McDOUGAL, David Stockton (1809-1882)

A career naval officer, David S. McDougal fought his one major Civil War action against the Japanese. After entering the navy as a midshipman in 1828, he served in the West Indies, and while stationed at Pensacola, he saved a sailor from shark-infested waters. During the war with Mexico he was a lieutenant at Vera Cruz aboard the *Mississippi*. At the beginning of the Civil War he was given command of the *Wyoming* and directed to search for Confederate raiders, especially the *Alabama*. He once got within 25 miles of his quarry before it made good its escape. After cruising the South American coast he set off for the Far East. Having heard of the firing upon an American vessel by the Japanese in the Straits of Shimonoseki, he set sail for the relief of the beleaguered foreigners who were being threatened with expulsion. Once in the straits, on July 16, 1863, he attacked with his single vessel. In the hour-long fight several Japanese vessels were sunk and some shore batteries were destroyed. McDougal lost 11 men killed and wounded. His actions were approved at Washington, and an international fleet later forced better terms from the Japanese. Returning to the United States the next year, he was commandant at Mare Island for the rest of the war. Remaining in the navy, he became a rear admiral in 1873.

McDOUGALL, James Alexander (1817-1867)

California immigrant James A. McDougall represented his adopted state in Washington throughout the Civil War and the early part of Reconstruction. Born in New York, he had entered the practice of law in Illinois in 1837. Drifting to the West coast, he became California's attorney general during 1850 and 1851. In the mid 1850s he served one term as a Democratic member of the U.S. House of Representatives but did not seek renomination. He again went to Washington and took a seat—in the Senate this time—on March 4, 1861. In 1864 he was a delegate to the Democratic national convention which nominated McClellan to oppose Lincoln. Not seeking reelection, he left office in March 1867 and died four months later.

McDOWELL, Irvin (1818-1885)

Civil War actions at Bull Run twice almost brought the military career of Irvin McDowell to an inglorious end. The Ohio native had been raised and educated in France before returning to the United States to attend West Point where he graduated in 1838 and was posted to the artillery. He spent four years as a tactics instructor before serving on John E. Wool's staff during the Mexican War and being brevetted for Buena Vista. During the interwar years he served in the adjutant general's department. His Civil War-era assignments included: first lieutenant, 1st Artillery (since October 7, 1842); brevet major and assistant adjutant general (since March 31, 1856); brigadier general, USA (May 14, 1862); commanding Army and Department of Northeastern Virginia (May 27-July 25, 1861); commanding Army and Department of Northeastern Virginia, Division of the Potomac (July 25-August 17, 1861); commanding division, Division of the Potomac (October 3, 1861-March 13, 1862); commanding 1st Corps, Army of the Potomac (March 13-April 4, 1862); major general, USV (March 14, 1862); commanding Department of the Rappahannock (April 4-June 26, 1862); commanding 3rd Corps, Army of Virginia (June 26-September 5, 1862); and commanding Department of the Pacific (July 1, 1864-June 27, 1865). While serving in Washington he became acquainted with Secretary of the Treasury Chase who proved to be instrumental in obtaining his promotion to regular army brigadier and assignment to command of the troops around the capital. Political pressure made it necessary for McDowell to advance on Manassas before his troops were ready. He sent part of his force against Blackburn's Ford along Bull Run and then a few days later made his main attack. While his plan had merit, it was too much for the raw volunteers to accomplish. Four days after the rout McClellan was placed over McDowell, who a few months later was relegated to the command of a division. When the Army of the Potomac was organized into corps he became head of the 1st Corps which was left behind to guard the approaches to Washington when McClellan moved to the Peninsula. His command was redesignated the Department of the Rappahannock and was supposed to march overland to join McClellan but the activities of Stonewall Jackson in the Shenandoah Valley precluded this. When John Pope was brought east to command the newly constituted Army of Virginia—the previously independent commands of McDowell, John C. Frémont, and Nathaniel P. Banks—McDowell was given a corps. Although his actions at Cedar Mountain earned him the regular army brevet of major general in 1865—he already had his second star in the volunteer service—he was blamed in part for the disaster

Irvin McDowell, loser at 1st Bull Run. (*Leslie's*)

at 2nd Bull Run. Requesting a court of inquiry, he was eventually cleared of culpability possibly as a reward for his testimony against Fitz-John Porter. Nonetheless he was not given another combat command and it was not until the last year of the war that he was put in charge of the Pacific Coast. Mustered out of the volunteers on September 1, 1866, he became a major general in the regular establishment six years later and retired in 1882.

McGILVERY, Freeman (?-1864)

A hero of the second day at Gettysburg, Maine artillerist Freeman McGilvery gave his name to a fort on the Richmond front near where he was mortally wounded. His assignments included: captain, 6th Maine Battery (ca. January 1, 1862); major, 1st Maine Light Artillery Battalion (ca. December 24, 1862); commanding 1st Volunteer Brigade, Artillery Reserve, Army of the Potomac (May 16-ca. December 1863); lieutenant colonel, 1st Maine Light Artillery Battalion (June 1863); commanding Ammunition Park, Army of the Potomac (spring-August 12, 1864); and commanding Artillery Brigade, 10th Corps, Army of the James (August 13-16, 1864). As a battery commander he fought at Cedar Mountain, 2nd Bull Run, and Antietam. At Gettysburg he directed one of the five reserve artillery brigades and assembled a line of guns—unsupported by infantry—to secure the Cemetery Ridge position following Daniel E. Sickles' rout in the Peach Orchard area. In the Overland Campaign and the beginning of the Petersburg operations he was charged with the management of the army's reserve ammunition train. In August he was named to command the 10th Corps' artillery and three days later was wounded at Deep Bottom on the 16th. On September 2 he died from the effects of the chloroform administered during the amputation of his finger.

McGINNIS, George Francis (1826-1910)

Although he achieved the rank of brigadier general of volunteers, George F. McGinnis was relegated to a series of minor commands after his promotion, possibly due to his connections with two unpopular officers, John A. McClernand and Lew Wallace. The Boston-born Indiana hatter had served as a company officer of the 2nd Ohio during the Mexican War. Upon the outbreak of the Civil War he gave up his business and enlisted in Wallace's regiment. His assignments included: private, Company K, 11th Indiana (April 15, 1861); captain, Company K, 11th Indiana (April 16, 1861); lieutenant colonel, 11th Indiana (April 25, 1861); lieutenant colonel, 11th Indiana (three-years unit August 31, 1861); colonel, 11th Indiana (September 3, 1861); commanding 3rd Brigade, 2nd Division, District of Eastern Arkansas, Department of the Missouri (December 1862); commanding 3rd Brigade, 12th Division, 13th Corps, Army of the Tennessee (January 22-February 20, 1863); commanding 1st Brigade, 12th Division, 13th Corps, Army of the Tennessee (February 20-July 14, 1863); brigadier general, USV (April 4, 1863, to rank from November 29, 1862); and commanding in the Department of the Gulf: 1st Brigade, 3rd Division, 13th Corps (August 7-September 13, 1863); the division (September 13, 1863-March 3, 1864 and May 24-June 11, 1864); 2nd Division, 19th Corps (June 18-25, 1864); 3rd Division, 19th Corps (August 25-November 7, 1864); 3rd Brigade, 3rd Division, 19th Corps (November 6-December 5, 1864); 3rd Brigade, Reserve Corps (December 5-10, 1864); and U.S. Forces Mouth of White River (December 1864-May 30, 1865). Quickly rising to become Wallace's second in command, McGinnis served in the western Virginia operations of 1861 before being mustered out at the end of his regiment's three-months enlistment on August 4, 1861. Four weeks later he was recommissioned in the reorganized three-years regiment. A few days later he became its colonel and led it at Fort Donelson, Shiloh, and during the advance on Corinth, Mississippi. As a brigade commander, he took part in the Yazoo Pass expedition and later in the campaign against Vicksburg, having been named a brigadier general. After the fall of the city, he was transferred with the corps to the Gulf and he finished out the war in minor assignments. Mustered out on August 24, 1865, he did not receive a brevet major generalship. After the war he held various state and local offices.

McGLASHAN, Peter Alexander Selkirk (1831-1908)

The incompleteness of Confederate records often makes it difficult to determine who was a general officer and who was not. Such is the case of Peter A.S. McGlashan who some claim was made a brigadier general in the last days of the war but never received the actual commission. A native of Edinburgh, Scotland, he had come to America in time to take part in the California Gold Rush. An adventurer, he also went to Nicaragua with William Walker's expansionist scheme. When he entered the Confederate army in the war's second year, his assignments included: first lieutenant, Company E, 50th Georgia (March 4, 1862); captain, Company E, 50th Georgia (October 1, 1862); colonel, 50th Georgia (July 31, 1863); and commanding Bryan's (old) Brigade, Kershaw's Division, 1st Corps, Army of Northern Virginia (February-March 1865). After service on the Georgia coast, his regiment was sent to join Lee in Virginia and saw action at 2nd Bull Run, Antietam, Fredericksburg, Chancellorsville, and Gettysburg. Going west with Longstreet in September 1863, his unit arrived too late to take part in the fighting at Chickamauga. Moving to East Tennessee he commanded the regiment at Knoxville and returned with it to Virginia for the Wilderness and Petersburg campaigns. During these actions he was wounded and did not return until February 1865 when he took over command of Bryan's Brigade. By the time of the fall of Richmond and Petersburg he was back in command of the 50th and led it at Sayler's Creek where he was captured. He was not released until July 25. Active in politics and veterans' affairs, he served as mayor of Thomasville, Georgia.

McGOWAN, Samuel (1819-1897)

A quartermaster of volunteers during the Mexican War, South Carolinian Samuel McGowan had served in the state legislature and was a militia major general at the outbreak of the war. Becoming a brigadier general of state troops, he commanded a brigade at the attack on Fort Sumter. Serving as a volunteer aide to General Bonham he was present at 1st Bull Run. His later positions included: lieutenant colonel (ca. September 9, 1861) and colonel (ca. April 11, 1862), 14th South Carolina; brigadier general, CSA (April 23, 1863, to date from January 17); commanding Maxcy Gregg's old Brigade, A.P. Hill's Division, Jackson's Corps, Army of Northern Virginia (January 19-May 3, 1863); and commanding same brigade, Wilcox's Division, Hill's Corps, Army of Northern Virginia (early 1864-April 9, 1865). After service on the South Carolina coast McGowan accompanied the brigade to Virginia in the spring of 1862. He led his regiment in the Seven Days Battles at Beaver Dam Creek, Gaines' Mill, and Frayser's Farm. He remained in the field despite being wounded at Gaines' Mill. Fighting at Cedar Mountain he was later wounded at 2nd Bull Run. Returning to his command after the battle of Antietam, he took part in the battle of Fredericksburg. He was then promoted to replace the slain General Gregg in command of the brigade. Wounded again at Chancellorsville, he was out of action for the rest of 1863. He then fought at the Wilderness and was wounded at Spotsylvania. Resuming command of his brigade he led it through the siege at Petersburg and in the Appomattox Campaign. After the surrender he resumed his political career, serving in the state legislature, having been refused a seat in Congress, and as a judge on the state supreme court. (Caldwell, J.F.J., *The History of a Brigade of South Carolinians*)

McGRAW, T.G. (?-1863)

The manpower shortage in the South caused the Richmond authorities to authorize their recruiting officers to operate in territory under Union control. This was hazardous duty, with many officers like T.G. McGraw being caught. He was arrested in Pendleton County, Kentucky, on April 9, 1863, along with William F. Corbin. They were charged with being Confederates out of uniform taking enlistees to the Southern forces. Found guilty, they were taken to Johnson's Island, Ohio, and on May 15 were shot by a firing squad. This led to a series of threatened retaliatory killings. The Richmond authorities refused to accept the Union position that recruiting behind enemy lines was a form of espionage.

McGREGOR, John Dunn (?-1878)

Although Dyer lists native New Yorker John D. McGregor as having been killed while commanding a brigade at Chancellorsville, he actually survived the battle and was later brevetted brigadier general of volunteers. His assignments included: lieutenant colonel, 4th New York (May 15, 1861); colonel, 4th New York (July 9, 1862); and commanding 3rd Brigade, 3rd Division, 2nd Corps, Army of the Potomac (January 5-February 24 and April 27-May 2, 1863). His two-years unit saw little action in Maryland and Virginia until the battle of Antietam where McGregor commanded the regiment. Wounded at Fredericksburg, he recovered in time to lead a brigade at Chancellorsville. However, he was forced to leave the field due to ill health, and he was mustered out with his regiment a few weeks later on May 25, 1863. It was almost two years before his brevet for war service was issued.

McGUIRE, Hunter Holmes (1835-1900)

A secessionist medical professor, Virginian Hunter H. McGuire served as the medical director for the troops under Stonewall Jackson and Richard S. Ewell. Born in Winchester, he had received his training in Virginia and Pennsylvania and taught in Louisiana. His military assignments included: major and surgeon, CSA (May 1861); medical director, Valley District, Department of Northern Virginia (spring 1862); medical director, 2nd Corps, Army of Northern Virginia (June 1862-June 1864): and medical director, Army of the Valley District, Department of Northern Virginia (1864). He was instrumental in the organization of the ambulance corps and a system of reserve hospitals. Captured in March 1865, he was held until the end of the war. Subsequently he was active in medical education. (Cunningham, Horace Herndon, *Doctors in Gray*)

McINTOSH, Chilly (?-?)

The elder brother of Daniel N. McIntosh, Chilly McIntosh was also a chief of the Creek Indians and played a leading role in the aligning of the nation with the Confederacy. He took part in the bloody pursuit of the fleeing Upper Creeks under Opothleyohola, who wanted to remain loyal to the Union. Early in 1862 he raised the 1st Creek Cavalry Battalion and became its lieutenant colonel. This unit was subsequently increased to a regiment and designated the 2nd Creek Cavalry with McIntosh as colonel. He served through the remainder of the war in the Indian Territory and in raids into Kansas. (Monaghan, Jay, *Civil War on the Western Border, 1854-1865*)

McINTOSH, Daniel N. (?-?)

After being instrumental in getting his tribe to join with the Confederacy, mixed-blood chief Daniel N. McIntosh of the Creeks raised and commanded the 1st Creek Mounted Rifles. His commission was dated August 19, 1861. In November and December of that year he led his regiment in pursuit of the fleeing band of Upper Creeks under Opothleyohola. Unlike Drew's regiment of Cherokees—some of that tribe were also fleeing toward Kansas—McIntosh's men had no qualms about killing members of their own tribe. Early the following year the treaty with the Confederacy was violated by the whites when they ordered the regiment out of the Indian Territory to serve in Arkansas. Here serving under General Albert Pike, who had negotiated with the Indians, McIntosh's command fought at Pea Ridge. Following the capture of three enemy cannons, of which the Indians were greatly afraid, they celebrated by scalping a disputed number of the enemy. Subsequently returned to the Indian Territory, McIntosh finished out the war there. (Monaghan, Jay, *Civil War on the Western Border, 1854-1865*)

McINTOSH, David Gregg (1836-1916)

Without any prior artillery experience, South Carolinian David Gregg McIntosh received relatively rapid promotion in the artillery of the Army of Northern Virginia. While practicing law he had also been an officer in a local volunteer company which offered its services soon after the state's secession. His assignments included: captain, Company D, 1st South Carolina (July 29, 1861); captain, Pee Dee (S.C.) Artillery (March 1862); major, Artillery (March 2, 1863); commanding artillery battalion, Reserve Artillery, 2nd Corps, Army of Northern Virginia (April 16-June 2, 1863); commanding artillery battalion, Reserve Artillery, 3rd Corps, Army of Northern Virginia (June 2-July 1863); commanding artillery battalion, 3rd Corps, Army of Northern Virginia (July 1863-March 1865); lieutenant colonel, Artillery (February 27, 1864); and colonel, Artillery (February 18, 1865). He saw action with his infantry company at Vienna. With his company converted to a light artillery battery, he fought in the Seven Days Battles, 2nd Bull Run, Harpers Ferry, Antietam, and Fredericksburg. Promoted to battalion commander, he led his enlarged command at Gettysburg and in the Bristoe, Mine Run, and Wilderness campaigns. Taking part in the defense of Petersburg he was slightly wounded at the Crater. He was again wounded at the battle of the Weldon Railroad a couple of weeks later. He was present with his battalion until shortly before the Appomattox Campaign. After the war he settled in Towson, Maryland, and resumed the practice of law, becoming head of the state bar association. (Wise, Jennings C., *The Long Arm of Lee*)

McINTOSH, James McQueen (1828-1862)

The brother of Union General John B. McIntosh, James M. McIntosh gave his life for the Confederacy at the same rank. The Florida-born West Pointer (1849) was, by virtue of his standing at the bottom of his class, posted first to the infantry, but in 1855 he transferred to the cavalry when the mounted branch was expanded. Most of his service was spent on the frontier before resigning as a captain in the 1st Cavalry on May 7, 1861. His Confederate assignments included: captain, cavalry (May 1861); colonel, 2nd Arkansas Mounted Rifles (July 29, 1861); commanding 1st Brigade, McCulloch's Division, Department #2 (late 1861-March 1862); brigadier general, CSA (January 24, 1862); and commanding Cavalry Brigade, McCulloch's Division, Trans-Mississippi District (or Army of the West), Department #2 (March-March 7, 1862). Taking charge of a mounted Arkansas regiment, he was soon in command of a brigade and as brigadier general he directed Ben McCulloch's mounted troops at Pea Ridge. There, while he was leading his regiment, a bullet pierced his heart on March 7, 1862.

McINTOSH, John Baillie (1829-1888)

A naval veteran of the Mexican War, John B. McIntosh was prompted to join the Union army when his brother, James McQ. McIntosh joined the Confederacy (eventually becoming a brigadier general). A New Jersey businessman at the outbreak of the Civil War, the loyal McIntosh was commissioned directly into the regular army. His assignments included: second lieutenant, 2nd Cavalry (June 8, 1861); second lieutenant, 5th Cavalry (change of designation August 3, 1861); first lieutenant, 5th Cavalry (June 27, 1862); colonel, 3rd Pennsylvania Cavalry (November 15, 1862); commanding 2nd Brigade, 2nd Division, Cavalry Corps, Army of the Potomac (February 17-May 13, 1863); commanding 1st Brigade, 2nd Division, Cavalry Corps, Army of the Potomac (June 11-October 1, 1863); captain, 5th Cavalry (December 7, 1863); commanding Cavalry Division, 22nd Corps, Department of Washington (January 9-May 2, 1864); commanding 1st Brigade, 3rd Division, Cavalry Corps, Army of the Potomac (May 5-August 6, 1864); brigadier general, USV (July 21, 1864); and commanding 1st Brigade, 3rd Division, Cavalry Corps, Army of the Shenandoah (August 6-September 19, 1864). With his regular army unit he fought at the Seven Days—earning a brevet for White Oak Swamp, South Mountain, and Antietam before taking charge of a volunteer regiment. In command of a brigade, he was at Kelly's Ford and took part in Stoneman's raid during the Chancellorsville Campaign. After leading his brigade at Gettysburg he was injured in the fall of his horse that autumn. He was temporarily assigned to command the cavalry of the Washington defenses but rejoined the Army of the Potomac in time for the Overland Campaign. During that campaign he received his third brevet—the second had come for Gettysburg—at Ashland on June 1, 1864. After participating in the early part of the Petersburg operations he was transferred to the Shenandoah Valley with his command. At 3rd Winchester he was severely wounded, losing a leg and ending his active field service during the war. Brevetted major general of volunteers for 3rd Winchester, he was mustered out of that service on April 30, 1866. In the expansion of the regular establishment later that year McIntosh became an infantry lieutenant colonel and was retired four years later with the increased rank of brigadier general. He had achieved that grade by brevet for 3rd Winchester.

MACK

See: *McCullagh, Joseph Burbridge*

MACKALL, William Whann (1817-1891)

The Civil War was the first war in which William W. Mackall served without being wounded. The Maryland West Pointer (1837) had served with the artillery in Florida against the Seminoles. During this tour he was ambushed and wounded at River Inlet on February 11, 1839. During the Mexican War he won two brevets and was wounded at Chapultepec. After transferring to the adjutant's branch in 1846, he later declined an appointment as a lieutenant colonel, offered on May 11, 1861, and instead resigned as a brevet major on July 3. His Confederate assignments included: lieutenant colonel and assistant adjutant general (ca. July 1861); brigadier general, CSA (March 6, 1862, to rank from February 27); commanding District of the Gulf, Department #2 (December 8-14, 1862); chief of staff, Army of Tennessee (April-fall 1863 and January-July 17,

1864); and commanding Hébert's (old) Brigade, Forney's Division, Department of Mississippi and East Louisiana (November 1863-January 1864). After serving as Albert Sidney Johnston's adjutant, he was promoted to brigadier general and was captured at Island #10 while serving as second in command. Exchanged on or about August 27, 1862, he held minor posts until he became Bragg's staff chief. After the victory at Chickamauga he asked to be relieved of staff duty and for a time commanded a brigade of paroled and exchanged prisoners from Vicksburg. Shortly after Joseph E. Johnston took over the Army of Tennessee, Mackall resumed his old staff post and held it until John B. Hood superseded Johnston. At that time Mackall again asked to be relieved and held no more assignments for the balance of the war. Thereafter he was a Virginia farmer.

McKAY, Charlotte (?-?)

In answer to her personal losses, Massachusetts native Charlotte McKay decided to help others. The deaths of both her husband and sole child prompted her to join the Union army as a nurse. She was posted to a hospital in Frederick, Maryland, on March 24, 1862, and served there in the aftermath of the Antietam fighting. The battle of Fredericksburg led to her reassignment to Washington and then Falmouth with the 3rd Corps. She was rewarded with the Kearny Cross for her services. She was later at Chancellorsville and in the Pennsylvania Campaign. In 1864 she was the dietitian for the hospital of the Army of the Potomac's Cavalry Corps. At the war's close she devoted her time to caring for the ex-slaves in Virginia.

McKAY Henry K. (?-?)

Although he held the rank of brigadier general during the Civil War, it appears that Henry K. McKay's only military experience was with the Georgia militia. Officers in this force were elected by the rank and file. In May 1864 he was elected lieutenant colonel, 1st Georgia Militia Battalion, and at some point during the siege of Atlanta he was elected brigadier and assigned to command the new 4th Brigade. He took part in the defense of the city and served with the forces vainly trying to slow down Sherman's advance to the coast. In this latter effort he fought in the dismal defeat at Griswoldville. His last service appears to have been in the unsuccessful defense of Savannah.

McKEAN, Thomas Jefferson (1810-1870)

For native Pennsylvanian Thomas J. McKean the Civil War was his third conflict. A West Pointer (1831), he had been posted to the infantry and assigned to garrison duty until he resigned in 1834 as second lieutenant, 4th Infantry. He interrupted his work as a civil engineer to serve against the Seminoles in Florida as a first lieutenant and adjutant of a Pennsylvania volunteer regiment. When the Mexican War broke out he offered his services but was not commissioned. Instead, he enlisted in one of the regular army regiments created for that war and served as a private and sergeant major of the 15th Infantry. Wounded at Churubusco, he was mustered out with the peace and returned to private life. Again offering his services in 1861, this time he received a commission. His assignments included: additional paymaster, USV (June 1, 1861); brigadier general, USV (November 21, 1861); commanding Jefferson City, District of Central Missouri, Department of the Missouri (December 1861-March 1862); commanding 6th Division, Army of the Tennessee (April 10-30 and June 10-15, 1862); commanding 6th Division, District of Corinth, Army of the Tennessee (July 24-September 21 and October 3-6, 1862); commanding 4th Division, Right Wing, 13th Corps, Army of the Tennessee (November 11-December 9, 1862); commanding District of Northern Missouri, Department of the Missouri (January 29-June 4, 1863); commanding District of Nebraska, Department of Kansas (June 4, 1863-January 1864); commanding District of South Kansas, Department of Kansas (June 25-September 1, 1864); chief of Cavalry, Department of the Gulf (ca. October 1864); commanding District of West Florida, Department of the Gulf (November 25, 1864-February 15, 1865); commanding District of Morganza, Military Division of West Mississippi (March 3-29, 1865); and commanding District of Southwest Missouri, Department of the Missouri (June 19-July 10, 1865). Too old for active service in the field, his only major action came as a division commander at Corinth in the fall of 1862. The rest of the time was spent in district commands in Missouri, Nebraska, Kansas, Florida, and Louisiana. One exception was when he briefly served as chief of cavalry in the Department of the Gulf in the fall of 1864. Brevetted major general for the war, he was mustered out on August 24, 1865, and was thereafter active in Republican politics.

MACKENZIE, Ranald Slidell (1840-1889)

Graduating from West Point in the second year of the Civil War, Ranald S. Mackenzie had risen to become a brevet major general of volunteers and a brevet brigadier general in the regular army by the end of the conflict and went on to become a distinguished Indian fighter. Born in New York, he was a nephew of Confederate diplomat John Slidell and received his appointment from New Jersey. He graduated at the head of his class and was accordingly assigned to the engineers. His assignments included: second lieutenant, Engineers (June 17, 1862); first lieutenant, Engineers (March 3, 1863); captain, Engineers (November 6, 1863); colonel, 2nd Connecticut Heavy Artillery (July 10, 1864); brigadier general, USV (October 19, 1864); commanding 2nd Brigade, 1st Division, 6th Corps, Army of the Shenandoah (November 3-December 6, 1864); commanding 2nd Brigade, 1st Division, 6th Corps, Army of the Potomac (December 6, 1864-January 23, 1865 and February 6-March 17, 1865); and commanding Cavalry Division, Army of the James (March 20-May 9, 1865). As the assistant engineer for the 9th Corps, he was wounded at 2nd Bull Run but recovered in time to direct bridging operations during the Maryland Campaign. He was Edwin V. Sumner's engineering officer at Fredericksburg and later won brevets for Chancellorsville and Gettysburg. He served with the engineer battalion during the Overland Campaign and in the early operations against Petersburg. Wounded during the latter, he won another brevet. Given charge of a volunteer heavy artillery regiment, he served briefly in the Washington fortifications and then went to the Shenandoah Valley. Fighting at 3rd Winchester and Fisher's Hill, he was brevetted for Cedar Creek where he suffered yet another wound. Promoted to brigadier general to date from the last battle, he commanded a brigade in the Shenandoah and again on the Petersburg front. Just before the final offensive he was named to lead the Army of the James' mounted troopers, replacing August V. Kautz. He fought at Five Forks and in the pursuit to Appomattox. Receiving brevets in both services for the war he was mustered out of the volunteers on January 15, 1866. The next year he was transferred to a colonelcy in the infantry and later in the cavalry. Having been wounded six times in the Civil War, he was again struck in Indian fighting in 1871 at the Brazos River, Texas, while serving as colonel, 4th Cavalry. Two years later he violated Mexican sovereignty, under verbal orders from Sheridan, while searching for hostiles who had been raiding into the United States. In 1875 he landed on his head when thrown from a wagon and was dazed for a length of time. In 1882 he became a brigadier general but two years later was retired when his mind started to give way from the affects of the accident and his multiple wounds. He died at the home of his sister in New York.

McKINLEY, William (1843-1901)

Surviving the Civil War, Ohioan William McKinley fell to an assassin's bullet while serving as the 24th president of the United States. His Civil War assignments, in the 23rd Ohio, included: private (June 23, 1861); commissary sergeant (April 15, 1862); second lieutenant (September 23, 1862); first lieutenant (February 7, 1863); and captain (July 25, 1864). This unit also carried Rutherford B. Hayes on its rolls. Serving mostly in western Virginia, the unit fought at South Mountain and Antietam and later in Sheridan's campaign in the Shenandoah Valley. McKinley was brevetted major for his service in western Virginia and the Valley and was mustered out with his regiment on July 26, 1865. Admitted to the bar two years later, he entered politics in 1871. As a Republican and backer of Hayes, he rose rapidly in committee assignments in Congress. Finally in 1896 he was elected to the highest office in the land, largely due to his role in furthering protective tariffs. While attending the Pan-American Exposition in Buffalo, New York, he was struck by the second bullet fired—the first bounced off a button—by an anarchist, Leon Czolgosz, on September 6, 1901. On the 14th McKinley became the third president to die at the hands of an assassin. Many believe that it was poor medical attention that consequently elevated Theodore Roosevelt to the presidency.

McKINSTRY, Justus (1814-1897)

While there may well have been other crooks in the uniform of a Union general, New York-born Justus McKinstry was the only one convicted and dismissed during the Civil War. A West Pointer (1838), he had had a distinguished career during the Mexican War when, while serving as a quartermaster, he took command of a company of volunteers and earned a brevet as major. His Civil War positions included: captain and assistant quartermaster (since March 3, 1847); major and quartermaster (August 3, 1861); and brigadier general, USV (September 2, 1861, but never confirmed by the Senate, thus expiring on July 17, 1862). Serving as the chief quartermaster in Frémont's Department of the West, he was granted the authority to suspend the normal military purchasing regulations. The temptations must have become too great. He was soon refusing to deal with any suppliers that were unwilling to line his pockets or aid in cheating the army out of untold thousands of dollars. The bubble burst when he took command of an infantry division in the march on Springfield. Investigations began and he was soon under arrest, then cashiered on January 28, 1863. Unsuccessful at trying to clear himself he nonetheless had a successful post-army career as a New York stockbroker and Missouri land agent. All in all he was a rogue all the way through, but many others benefitted from his schemes, especially one dealer, Child, Pratt & Fox, whose profits on $800,000 business with the army came to $280,000. (Longacre, Edward G., "A Profile of Justus McKinstry," *CWTI* July 1978)

McLAREN, Robert Neill (1828-1886)

The Civil War career of Union Brevet Brigadier General Robert N. McLaren was confined to Indian fighting and it is doubtful if he ever saw an armed Confederate. The New York native's assignments included: second lieutenant, 6th Minnesota (August 1, 1862); captain, 6th Minnesota (August 18, 1862); major, 6th Minnesota (August 22, 1862); and colonel, 2nd Minnesota Cavalry (January 14, 1864). During most of the war he was stationed at or near Fort Snelling and much of the time was in command of the post. It was during his tenure that the two Sioux chiefs Medicine Bottle and Shakopee were captured in Canada, in violation of international law, and by treachery. In early 1864 they were tried and hanged. Mustered out with his regiment on November 17, 1865, McLaren was brevetted for his war service nearly a month later, on December 14.

McLAUGHLEN, Napoleon Bonaparte (1823-1887)

Having served for nearly a decade as an enlisted man in the regular army's 2nd Dragoons, Napoleon B. McLaughlen was commissioned in that service at the outbreak of the Civil War and rose to the rank of brevet brigadier general in both the regulars and volunteers. The Vermonter had entered the army in New York and his wartime assignments included: second lieutenant, 1st Cavalry (March 27, 1861); first lieutenant, 1st Cavalry (May 3, 1861); first lieutenant, 4th Cavalry (designation change August 3, 1861); captain, 4th Cavalry (July 17, 1862); colonel, 1st Massachusetts (October 1, 1862); colonel, 57th Massachusetts (September 14, 1864); commanding 3rd Brigade, 1st Division, 9th Corps, Army of the Potomac (September 15-December 30, 1864, February 2-25, March 7-25, and May 11-August 1, 1865); and commanding the division (December 30, 1864-February 2, 1865, February 25-

March 7, and July 15-August 1, 1865). Promoted to the colonelcy of a volunteer regiment, he fought at Fredericksburg and won a brevet for Chancellorsville. A similar reward came his way for Gettysburg. Following service maintaining order in New York, he and his regiment rejoined the army in time for the Mine Run operations. He then fought during the beginning of the Overland Campaign but was mustered out upon the expiration of his unit's enlistment on May 28, 1864. He then took charge of a new regiment which joined the 9th Corps before Petersburg. He was brevetted brigadier general of volunteers for Poplar Grove Church. Continuing in the siege operations, he was captured when Lee tried to break the Union lines at Fort Stedman. Brevetted for this, he was confined in Libby Prison until the fall of Richmond. Brevetted brigadier general in the regular establishment for the war, he was mustered out of the volunteer service on August 10, 1865, and remained in the army until his 1882 retirement as major, 10th Cavalry.

McLAWS, Lafayette (1821-1897)

A division commander early in the war, Lafayette McLaws proved capable but not brilliant enough to warrant further advancement. A graduate of West Point in 1842, he had been serving as a captain of infantry for almost 10 years when he resigned his commission to join the South on March 23, 1861. The native Georgian's assignments included: major, Infantry (May 1861); colonel, 10th Georgia (June 17, 1861); brigadier general, CSA (September 25, 1861); commanding 1st brigade, Department of the Peninsula (October 3-November 10, 1861); commanding 2nd Division, Department of the Peninsula (November 10, 1861-April 12, 1862); commanding division, Magruder's Command, Department of Northern Virginia (April 12-July 1862); major general, CSA (May 23, 1862); commanding division, 1st Corps, Army of Northern Virginia (July 1862-September 9, 1863); commanding division, Longstreet's Corps, Army of Tennessee (September 19-November 5, 1863); commanding division, Department of East Tennessee (November 5-December 17, 1863); commanding District of Georgia and 3rd Military District of South Carolina, Department of South Carolina, Georgia and Florida (May 25-July 1864); and commanding division, same department (July 1864-April 9, 1865). Serving on the Peninsula during the first year of his service, he saw action during the Seven Days. In the Maryland Campaign he fought at Harpers Ferry and Antietam and later at Fredericksburg, Chancellorsville, and Gettysburg. He did not reach Chickamauga in time to serve with the part of the division which arrived from Virginia but took part in the Knoxville Campaign. Longstreet became displeased with his cooperation and preparations for the assault at Fort Sanders and at Bean's Station. On December 17, 1863, he was relieved of command, and Longstreet brought charges against him for the Fort Sanders incident. A court found him guilty of some charges on May 4, 1864, but Jefferson Davis disapproved the findings on the 7th and ordered him back to duty with his division, now back in Virginia. It was thought better, however, to assign him other duty, and he was sent to the Southern coast where he fought at Bentonville during the Carolinas Campaign against Sherman. Following the surrender he was in insurance, a tax collector, and a postmaster. (Freeman, Douglas S., *Lee's Lieutenants*)

MACLAY, Robert Plunket (ca. 1820-1903)

Relatively little is known about the Confederate career of Robert P. Maclay despite the fact that he was a West Pointer (1840) and was appointed brigadier general extralegally by General E. Kirby Smith. He had resigned his commission as captain, 8th Infantry, on December 31, 1860, to retire to a Louisiana plantation. The veteran of the Seminole and Mexican wars—during the latter he was wounded at Resaca de la Palma—held the following assignments for the South: major, Artillery; brigadier general, CSA, by Smith (May 13, to rank from April 30, 1864); commanding brigade, District of West Louisiana, Trans-Mississippi Department (spring and summer 1864); and commanding 3rd Texas Brigade, 1st Texas Division, 1st Corps, Trans-Mississippi Department (September 1864-January 1865). He appears to have been assigned to command of a brigade from a staff position with General J.G. Walker. This move seems to have created dissension within the brigade to which he was named, and when a leave of absence was about to expire, Smith felt obliged to grant a 60-day extension on January 31, 1865. Smith feared that Maclay's promotion, which had not been legally made by the president, would be challenged. He felt the added time would delay a test until an appointment was forthcoming from Richmond. It never came and Maclay does not appear to have rejoined the brigade.

McLEAN, James Robert (1823-1870)

The Confederate congressional career of James R. McLean was spent mostly in defending the reputation of his native North Carolina as a loyal part of the Confederacy. A lawyer and planter, he served in the state legislature and became a proponent of secession. Elected from the state's 6th District to the First Regular Confederate Congress, he served on the committees on Claims and Foreign Affairs. Generally a supporter of the war effort, he did however have some disagreements with the administration. Matters of health prompted him not to seek reelection in 1863. Entering the state reserves, his assignments included: major, Camp Stokes Light Duty Battalion (1864); and major, 7th North Carolina Senior Reserves (1864). His regiment served in the defenses of Wilmington, then took part in the operations against Sherman's invading forces, and later fought at Bentonville. After the war he tried to recoup his prewar fortune but died before he could accomplish this.

McLEAN, John (1785-1861)

A perennial aspirant for the presidency, John McLean instead spent 32 years as a Supreme Court justice and was one of the two dissenting votes in the *Dred Scott* case. Born in New Jersey, he was raised in Virginia and Kentucky, but mostly in Ohio. Admitted to the bar, he dabbled in political journalism and served two terms in Congress, where he supported the War of 1812. He then became a judge on Ohio's highest court. His later offices included commissioner of the General Land Office and postmaster general. On March 6, 1829, Andrew Jackson appointed him to the Supreme Court. He was confirmed by a voice vote the next day. Even during his tenure, he sought the presidency, but he died on April 4, 1861, before he could achieve his goal and less than two weeks before the firing on Fort Sumter. (Nevins, Allan, *The Ordeal of the Union* and Fehrenbacher, Don. E., *The Dred Scott Case: Its Significance in American Law and Politics*)

McLEAN, Nathaniel Collins (1815-1905)

At least twice Nathaniel C. McLean was charged by his superiors with battlefield failures. The Ohio native had given up his Cincinnati law practice in 1861 to join the Union army. His assignments included: colonel, 75th Ohio (September 18, 1861); commanding 2nd Brigade, 1st Division, 1st Corps, Army of Virginia (June 26-September 12, 1862), commanding 2nd Brigade, 1st Division, 11th Corps, Army of the Potomac (September 12, 1861-January 10, 1863, February 5-March 10, and April 20-May 2, 1863); brigadier general, USV (November 29, 1862); commanding the division (January 10-February 5, March 10-April 20, and May 2-24, 1863); provost marshal general, Department of the Ohio (May 1863-ca. May 1864); commanding 1st Brigade, 2nd Division, 23rd Corps, Army of the Ohio (May 3-June 4, 1864); commanding 3rd Brigade, 3rd Division, 23rd Corps, Army of the Ohio (June 4-17, 1864); commanding 1st Division, District of Kentucky, 23rd Corps, Department of the Ohio (July 6-December 29, 1864); commanding 3rd Brigade, 2nd Division, 23rd Corps, Department of North Carolina (February 9-28, 1865); and commanding the division (February 28-April 4, 1865). Leading his regiment, he fought at McDowell and Cross Keys in the Shenandoah Valley. As part of Pope's army, he led a brigade at 2nd Bull Run and was named a brigadier general that fall. His corps rejoined the main army for Chancellorsville where he succeeded the wounded Charles Devens in divisional command. His corps commander Oliver O. Howard was upset with his inability to reorganize his troops promptly after Stonewall Jackson's flank attack. Within weeks he was shunted off to the Ohio Valley in a staff position. It was a year before he again held a field command. He led a brigade in the Atlanta Campaign but again ran afoul of Howard for failures at New Hope Church. McLean once more found himself relegated to a rear area. Transferred to North Carolina, he served in part of Sherman's Carolinas Campaign but resigned on April 20, 1865, and returned to his law practice.

McLEAN, Wilmer (?-?)

Despite the fact that he was an elderly noncombatant, Wilmer McLean seems to have been incapable of remaining out of the war's path. At the outbreak of the conflict he was maintaining his acreage, "Yorkshire," in Prince William County, Virginia. Unfortunately for McLean, his estate bordered on Bull Run. With the formation of the Confederate Army of the Potomac and its positioning along the creek, troops began to construct defensive works on his fields. Then, on July 18, 1861, General Beauregard took over the house as his headquarters. During the battle of Blackburn's Ford, McLean aided the general with his knowledge of the area. Three days later, during the battle of 1st Bull Run, a shell ripped into his home while Beauregard was breakfasting. That was enough for McLean. He moved his family to an estate in Appomattox County. Here he was far removed from the war—for three and a half years. Then, on the morning of April 9, 1865, he was stopped by two mounted men, one in blue and one in gray. They were looking for a place to hold a meeting between Grant and Lee. After the first place McLean showed them was rejected, he took the officers to his own home, and it was here that agreement for the surrender of the Army of Northern Virginia was made. (Hanson, Joseph Mills, *Bull Run Remembers*)

McMILLAN, James Winning (1825-1903)

After serving as an enlisted man in both the 4th Illinois and 3rd Louisiana Battalions during the Mexican War, James W. McMillan was later brevetted major general at the close of the Civil War. Born in Kentucky, he was an Indiana businessman at the outbreak of the Civil War. Raising a regiment, his assignments included: colonel, 21st Indiana (July 24, 1861); colonel, 1st Indiana Heavy Artillery (designation change February 1863); brigadier general, USV (April 4, 1863, to rank from November 29, 1862); commanding 2nd Brigade, 3rd Division, 19th Corps, Department of the Gulf (August 15-29, October 4-November 2, 1863, and December 3, 1863-January 12, 1864); commanding the division (August 29-September 4, September 17-October 2, 1863, and January 12-February 15, 1864); commanding 2nd Brigade, 1st Division, 19th Corps, Department of the Gulf (March 24-May 29 and June 20-July 5, 1864); also commanding the division (May 2-June 24, 1864); commanding 2nd Brigade, 1st Division, 19th Corps, Army of the Shenandoah (August 6-October 15, October 24-26, 1864, and December 3, 1864-January 25, 1865); commanding the division (October 15-24, 1864 and January 25-March 1, 1865); and commanding 1st Provisional Division, Army of the Shenandoah (March 1-April 1865). After serving in the Baltimore defenses he was present at the capture of New Orleans. However he missed the fighting at Baton Rouge later that year. The next year his regiment was converted to heavy artillery and he was shortly thereafter promoted to brigadier general. Holding a series of brigade and division commands, he served in the Red River Campaign, fighting at Mansfield, Pleasant Hill, and Monett's Ferry. Transferred with parts of the 19th Corps to Virginia, he commanded his brigade at 3rd Winchester and Fisher's Hill. In charge of the division, he performed heroically in the early stages of the Union surprise at Cedar Creek. He finished the war in the Valley, which had by that time become a backwater, and he resigned on May 15, 1865. After the war he was a pension official.

McMILLEN, William Linn (1829-1902)

Transferring from the medical to the infantry service, Ohioan William L. McMillen compiled a distinguished career and earned brevets through major general. A physician, he had had military medical experience from his service with the Russians

The second Wilmer McLean house at Appomattox, where Lee surrendered to Grant. (NA)

during the Crimean War. His Civil War assignments included: surgeon, 1st Ohio (April 17, 1861); colonel, 95th Ohio (August 16, 1862); commanding 1st Brigade, 3rd Division, 15th Corps, Army of the Tennessee (June 22-August 3 and October 15-November 15, 1863); commanding 1st Brigade, 1st Division, 16th Corps, Army of the Tennessee (January 26-December 5, 1864); commanding 1st Brigade, 1st Division, Detachment of the Army of the Tennessee, Department of the Cumberland (December 5, 1864-January 19, 1865); and commanding 1st Brigade, 1st Division, 16th Corps, Department of the Gulf (February 18-July 20, 1865). His first regiment fought at 1st Bull Run before being mustered out at the expiration of its term of enlistment on August 16, 1861. He was then Ohio's surgeon general. Transferring to the line, he commanded a newly organized regiment, most of which was captured at Richmond, Kentucky. Following a period of reorganization and guard duty in Indiana, the regiment joined Grant's operations against Vicksburg where, during the latter part of the siege, McMillen led a brigade. Also in brigade leadership, he took part in the Jackson Campaign. Operations against Forrest's cavalry followed and McMillen commanded an improvised division at Brice's Crossroads and a brigade at Tupelo and in A.J. Smith's second invasion of Mississippi. After brief service in Arkansas and Missouri against Sterling Price, he commanded his brigade at Nashville, earning his first brevet. After that victory he took part in the capture of Mobile and was then brevetted major general for the war. Mustered out on August 14, 1865, he settled in Louisiana and took up planting. Sitting for a time in the state legislature, he was denied a seat in the U.S. Senate in the Reconstruction years.

McMULLEN, LaFayette (1805-1880)

Representing Virginia's 13th District (the southwest corner of the state), LaFayette McMullen became a peace man in the Second Confederate Congress but wanted terms that would not be construed as submission. A native of the state, he had sat in the state legislature and in Congress. In 1856 he predicted that a Republican victory for president would terminate the Union. The next year he was named to the governorship of the Territory of Washington by fellow Democrat James Buchanan. After one year he returned to a Virginia farm. On his second bid he won a seat in the Confederate House of Representatives where he chaired the Committee on Public Buildings. He also sat on the committees on: Post Offices and Post Roads; and Territories and Public Lands. Generally a supporter of the war effort, he favored price controls and wanted taxes concentrated away from small farmers who predominated in his district. Despite his desire for an end to the war, he felt that congressmen who were absent from Richmond were deserters and proposed their arrest at the last meeting of Congress. After the collapse he returned to agriculture and was engaged in banking and railroading enterprises until a rail accident ended his life. He had made one last entry into politics in 1878, when he was soundly defeated for the governorship.

McNAIR, Evander (1820-1902)

Having served as a noncommissioned officer under Jefferson Davis in Mexico, North Carolina native Evander McNair rose to a brigadier generalship under Davis' presidency. A Mississippi merchant at the outbreak of the Mexican War, he had served as first sergeant of Company E, 1st Mississippi Rifles. In the mid-1850s he moved his business to Arkansas. Donning the gray, his assignments in the Civil War included: lieutenant colonel, McNair's Arkansas Battalion (1861); colonel, 4th Arkansas (August 17, 1861); commanding Infantry Brigade, McCulloch's Division, Trans-Mississippi District, Department #2 (March 1862); commanding brigade, 2nd (McCown's) Division, Department of East Tennessee (ca. October 31-December 1862); brigadier general, CSA (November 4, 1862); commanding brigade, McCown's Division, attached to Hardee's Corps, Army of Tennessee (December 1862); commanding brigade, McCown's Division, Smith's Corps, Army of Tennessee (January-March 1863); commanding brigade, McCown's Division, Polk's Corps, Army of Tennessee (March-May 1863); commanding brigade, Walker's Division, Department of the West (May 19-June 1863); commanding brigade, French's Division, Department of the West (June-July 1863); commanding brigade, French's Division, Department of Mississippi and East Louisiana (July-September 1863); commanding brigade, Johnson's Provisional Division, Army of Tennessee (mid-September 1863); and commanding 2nd (Arkansas) Brigade, 1st (Arkansas) Division, 2nd Corps (or District of Arkansas), Trans-Mississippi Department (September 23, 1864-ca. May 26, 1865). After fighting at Wilson's Creek his battalion was increased to regimental size and he was advanced to its colonelcy. At Pea Ridge he succeeded to brigade command when Louis Hébert was captured. Transferred to the east side of the Mississippi he was engaged in the operations around Corinth, before being sent to East Tennessee. Taking part in the Kentucky Campaign, he fought at Richmond and was soon named a brigadier general. He fought at Murfreesboro and the following May was sent to Mississippi to aid in the relief expedition for Vicksburg. After that failure he fought around Jackson, Mississippi, and then went to Georgia where he was wounded at Chickamauga. Upon his recovery he was dispatched to the west of the Mississippi where he commanded a brigade in Arkansas. He is said to have taken part in Sterling Price's invasion of Missouri, but there is no record of this. He was, however, during the final months of the war on the board of inquiry looking into the expedition. He subsequently lived in Louisiana and Mississippi.

McNEIL, John (1813-1891)

Canadian-born hatter John NcNeil spent most of the Civil War in Missouri dealing with guerrillas and bushwhackers. Leaving Nova Scotia, he had learned his trade in Boston and then went into business in St. Louis. He also ran an insurance business and was a state legislator. Enlisting early in the war, his assignments included: colonel, 3rd Missouri United States Reserve Corps (May 8, 1861); commanding District of Northern Missouri, Department of Missouri (June 5, 1862-January 29, 1863); colonel, 2nd Missouri Militia Cavalry (June 30, 1862); brigadier general, USV (November 29, 1862); commanding District of Southwest Missouri, Department of the Missouri (July 15-October 15, 1863); commanding District of La Fourche, Department of the Gulf (May 4-June 9, 1864); commanding Post of Port Hudson, District of Port Hudson, Department of the Gulf (June 9-August 6, 1864); also commanding the district (June 9-August 6, 1864); commanding District of Rolla, Department of the Missouri (August 23-September 5, 1864); and commanding District of Central Missouri, Department of the Missouri (February 27-April 22, 1865). With his first regiment he won a minor victory at Fulton on July 17, 1861, before being mustered out exactly one month later upon the expiration of the three-months term of his regiment. The next year he became the commander of a militia cavalry regiment and embarked upon a series of district commands in his adopted state and Louisiana. His frustrating duties in dealing with irregulars in a state with divided loyalties were interrupted by Sterling Price's invasion of the state in 1864. However, at the battle of Westport he earned the displeasure of the department commander, William S. Rosecrans, and was relieved. In the final months of the war he was again in district command until his resignation was accepted, effective April 12, 1865. He was brevetted major general for the war on the same date. In the postwar years he held a series of local and national appointive offices.

McNEILL, Jesse C. (ca. 1842-?)

During most of the Civil War Jesse McNeill served as first lieutenant in his father's company of partisan rangers but after his father's death he became famous for his exploit in raiding Cumberland, Maryland. While assisting his father, John Hanson McNeill, to raise a new company in Missouri, young McNeill was captured but escaped within a few days and went to Virginia where his father had been born. After his father joined him, McNeill was elected first lieutenant in his father's new Virginia company and participated in raids on Union forces and their supply lines, especially the Baltimore and Ohio Railroad. With his father's death in October 1864, McNeill took over command. In memory of his father, he decided to get revenge upon General B.F. Kelley who had been responsible for the arrest of his mother, brother, and sister. Leading his 62 men into the town of Cumberland, in the midst of large Union forces, he came out with Kelley, and General George Crook, another officer, and two privates as prisoners. This exploit muted criticism of the irregular cavalry as ineffective and possibly saved the unit from being broken up. McNeill was praised in orders by General Lee and promoted to captain. But by the time of the February 21-22, 1865, affair the war was nearly over and it was merely a bright spot in the dismal prospects of the Confederacy. (Jones, Virgil Carrington, *Gray Ghosts and Rebel Raiders*)

McNEILL, John Hanson (1815-1864)

One of the more effective partisan leaders in the western portion of Virginia was John McNeill. Born in what is now West Virginia, McNeill later moved to Kentucky and finally to Missouri where, after being a Unionist during the secession crisis, he raised a company of cavalry as part of the Missouri State Guard. He led his company in combat at Booneville, Carthage, Wilson's Creek, and Lexington. He was wounded in the last action. With the December 1861 expiration of the time of his company, McNeill returned home to raise a new unit. During this time he was captured but escaped on June 15, 1862. Making his way back to West Virginia, he was granted authority to raise a company of partisan rangers. He became captain of this new command in about September 1862. Although officially designated Company E, 18th Virginia Cavalry, McNeill's men served mainly as an independent unit. He led his men in numerous raids, especially against the Baltimore and Ohio Railroad. During this time he developed a personal grudge againt General B.F. Kelley, the Union defender of the line, but he did not live long enough to get revenge for Kelley's treatment of his wife. That would be up to his son Jesse. In the fall of 1864, his command joined Early's command in the Shenandoah Valley where, in an attack at Mt. Jackson on October 3, he was mortally wounded by one of his own men, apparently by accident. (Jones, Virgil Carrington, *Gray Ghosts and Rebel Raiders*)

McPHERSON, James Birdseye (1828-1864)

When Union General James B. McPherson was killed before Atlanta he became the only federal department commander to die in battle. The Ohio native had graduated at the head of the 1853 West Point class and had accordingly been assigned to the engineers. He then taught at the academy and worked on both the Atlantic and Pacific coasts on various engineering projects. With the coming of the Civil War he rose rapidly in rank and eventually switched from staff to line duty. His assignments included: first lieutenant, Engineers (since December 13, 1858); captain, Engineers (August 6, 1861); lieutenant colonel and additional aide-de-camp (November 12, 1861); aide-de-camp, Department of the Missouri (1861-62); chief engineer, District of Cairo, Department of the Missouri (February 1862); chief engineer, Army of the Tennessee (February-October 4, 1862); colonel and additional aide-de-camp (May 1, 1862); brigadier general, USV (May 15, 1862); commanding Engineer Brigade, Army of the Tennessee (June 4-October 4, 1862); major general, USV (October 8, 1862); commanding Right Wing, Army of the Tennessee (November 1-December 18, 1862); commanding 17th Corps, Army of the Tennessee (December 18, 1862-April 23, 1864); brigadier general, USA (August 1, 1863); and commanding Department and Army of the Tennessee (March 26-July 22, 1864). At first an aide to Henry W. Halleck, he joined Grant, as Grant's engineering chief, in time for Forts Henry and Donelson. He went on to Shiloh and the advance on Corinth, Mississippi. He was present at Iuka and was then placed in charge of rail transportation in western Tennessee and northern Mississippi. In October he was advanced from brigadier to major general and next month he transferred to the line. He commanded one wing of Grant's drive into central Mississippi, its objective the seizing of Vicksburg and the opening of the Mississippi River. With the reorganization of the army, he took charge of the new 17th Corps and led it with some distinction throughout the remaining operations against the river city. Following Vicksburg's fall he was rewarded with a regular army promotion to brigadier general. Early in 1864 he took part in Sherman's Meridian Campaign before transferring to Chattanooga as commander of the Army of the Tennessee, which did not operate as an independent force but rather as one of the three components of Sherman's Military Division of the Mississippi. In the early stages of the Atlanta Campaign his slowness wasted an excellent opportunity to crush Joseph E. Johnston's army at Snake Creek Gap. Thereafter Sherman kept a closer eye on his subordinate. With the Union army on the outskirts of the city itself,

James B. McPherson, killed in the battle of Atlanta. (*Leslie's*)

McPherson's classmate John B. Hood, who had succeeded Johnston, made one of his sorties which threatened to crush the Army of the Tennessee's flank. The resulting battle of Atlanta was the last for McPherson. Trying to cross a no-man's-land with one staff officer—he was returning to his army from Sherman's headquarters—he ran into a squad of enemy skirmishers and was shot down. (Whaley, Elizabeth J., *Forgotten Hero: General James B. McPherson*)

McQUEEN, John (1804-1867)

One of South Carolina's most ardent secessionists, John McQueen lost his seat in the Confederate Congress to an anti-Davis candidate. A native of North Carolina, he had taken up the practice of law in South Carolina and subsequently become a planter and a major general in the militia. In 1849 he took a seat in the U.S. House of Representatives where he sat until his resignation, with the rest of the delegation, on the day after the state's secession. He then served as his state's commissioner to urge Texas to secede. Unopposed for his bid to sit in the First Regular Confederate Congress, he chaired the Committee on Accounts and also served on the Committee on Foreign Affairs. On matters of taxation and the draft, he was an opponent of Confederate nationalism. However, on matters of foreign relations, peace negotiations, and presidential appointments he was a staunch supporter of the Davis administration, and this support cost him his reelection from the state's northeastern 1st District. After the Confederacy's fall he retired to private pursuits. (Cauthen, Charles Edward, *South Carolina Goes to War, 1861-1865*)

McRAE, Colin John (1812-1877)

One of the Gulf coast's most prominent businessmen, Colin J. McRae served the Confederacy as its chief financial agent in Europe and got caught up in the disastrous Erlanger Loan. Born in North Carolina, he came to settle in Mobile, Alabama, via Mississippi—including a term in the Mississippi legislature. His enterprises included coastal shipping, railroads, land, slaves, and the commission trade. With the secession of Alabama, the Democrat was named to the Provisional Confederate Congress where he sat on the committees on Buildings, Engrossment, Finance, and Naval Affairs. Naturally, on military matters he was most concerned with the defense of Mobile and keeping the port open. Thus he favored state control over large numbers of troops. He worked toward the eventual approval of privateering. Not seeking reelection, he went into the arms and munitions business with an arsenal at Selma, Alabama. His European assignment began in 1863 when he negotiated the unfavorable terms of the cotton loan. Nonetheless his record of financial dealings was about the best that could be expected for the failing South. Finally cleared of liabilities in England, for the Confederate debts, in 1867, he never returned to the United States. Instead, he settled in Belize, British Honduras. Buying some land, he resumed some of his former business activities for the remaining decade of his life. (Davis, Charles Shepard, *Colin J. McRae: Confederate Financial Agent*)

McRAE, Dandridge (1829-1899)

Before his 1864 resignation as a Confederate brigadier general, Alabama-born Arkansas lawyer Dandridge McRae had commanded a battalion, two regiments and a brigade. At the outbreak of the Civil War he was the inspector general of his adopted state. His later assignments included: lieutenant colonel, 3rd Arkansas Battalion (July 15, 1861); colonel, 21st (McRae's) Arkansas (December 3, 1861); colonel, 28th (McRae's) Arkansas (June 1862); brigadier general, CSA (November 5, 1862); and commanding brigade, Hindman's-Price's Division, District of Arkansas, Trans-Mississippi Department (January 1863-early 1864). He led his battalion at Wilson's Creek and his first regiment at Pea Ridge. However, on May 20, 1862, he declined reelection to its colonelcy. The next month he took command of a new unit with which he served mostly in Arkansas until named brigadier general that fall. Leading a brigade he fought at Helena and Little Rock. Commanding in northeastern Arkansas in the spring of 1864, he resigned and returned to his home and practice. He also held minor state offices in the postwar years.

McRAE, Duncan Kirkland (1820-1888)

Petty jealousies over rank cost the Confederacy some of its experienced officers. Such was the case with Colonel Duncan K. McRae. A state legislator in his native North Carolina and a diplomat to France before the war, he entered the Confederate army shortly after the state's secession. His assignments included: colonel, 5th North Carolina (May 16, 1861) and commanding Garland's Brigade, D.H. Hill's Division, Jackson's Command, Army of Northern Virginia (September 14-ca. November 6, 1862). After serving at Yorktown, he displayed his inexperience when he led a gallant but futile charge upon a Union battery at Williamsburg. He fought at Seven Pines until overtaken by exhaustion. During the Seven Days he led the regiment through the early battles, but then the unit was detailed to guard prisoners and gather abandoned equipment. Rejoining Lee's army in Maryland, the division was assigned to guarding the passes through South Mountain. When General Garland was killed at Fox's Gap, McRae took over brigade command and also received a wound. He remained in command however and suffered another wound at Antietam. Still retaining command after that action, he submitted his resignation on November 13, 1862, only a week after his junior, Colonel Alfred Iverson, was promoted to brigadier and given permanent command of the brigade. The resignation was accepted on December 12. He represented the Richmond government in Europe in regards to a cotton deal and subsequently returned to North Carolina as a newspaper editor during the final months of the conflict.

MacRAE, William (1834-1882)

A North Carolina civil engineer, William MacRae entered the service of the South at the head of the Monroe Light Infantry. His later assignments included: captain, Company B, 15th North Carolina (June 11, 1861); lieutenant colonel, 15th North Carolina (May 2, 1862); commanding Cobb's Brigade,

McLaws' Division, 1st Corps, Army of Northern Virginia (briefly in September 1862); colonel, 15th North Carolina (February 27, 1863); temporary brigadier general, CSA (June 22, 1864); commanding Kirkland's Brigade, Heth's Division, 3rd Corps, Army of Northern Virginia (June 27, 1864-April 9, 1865); and permanent brigadier general, CSA (November 4, 1864). His regiment was initially sent to the Peninsula and fought at Yorktown and the Seven Days before moving north to 2nd Bull Run and into Maryland. At Antietam MacRae succeeded to command of the brigade after it had suffered extreme losses. He was promoted to colonel after Fredericksburg, and his regiment was sent to North Carolina and southern Virginia. During the Gettysburg Campaign it was stationed at Hanover Junction just north of Richmond. Rejoining Lee's army, MacRae took part in the futile charge at Bristoe Station. In the Overland Campaign, he led the regiment at the Wilderness, Spotsylvania, and Cold Harbor. With the wounding of General Kirkland of the other North Carolina brigade in the division, MacRae was given temporary rank as a brigadier and transferred to its direction. He led the unit through the Petersburg operations and to the surrender at Appomattox. During the siege his promotion had been made permanent. He was a railroad superintendent in his remaining years. (Freeman, Douglas S., *Lee's Lieutenants*)

MACWILLIE, Marcus H. (?-?)

Nothing is known about the Arizona Territory delegate to the Confederate Congress, Marcus H. Macwillie, before the Civil War—except that he had been a lawyer in Mesilla, New Mexico Territory—nor after its close. He worked for the secession of the southern half of the territory to become the Confederacy's Arizona Territory. Confederate forces from Texas invaded the area in the summer of 1861 and in August John R. Baylor established a military government with Macwillie as attorney general. Then in a disputed election, Macwillie was elected as the territory's delegate to the First Regular Confederate Congress. Replacing the provisional representative Granville H. Oury, he was seated on March 11, 1862. Not entitled to sit on any committees, he seems to have taken little part in legislation other than to favor the extermination of the Indians in the territory and to support his friend Baylor. Reelected to the Second Congress, he vanished into oblivion after the South's fall.

MACHEN, Willis Benson (1810-1893)

As the representative of Kentucky's 1st District in both of the regular Confederate congresses, Willis B. Machen was, with some limitations, a staunch supporter of the Davis regime. A native Kentucky farmer he had served in both state houses before the Civil War. In the Confederate Congress he served on the committees on: Accounts (First Congress); Ways and Means (First Congress); and Quartermaster's and Commissary Departments (Second Congress). He opposed military destruction of private property in retreat, impressment without payment, and governmental control of railroads. Also part of the anti-Bragg faction, he nonetheless usually supported presidential appointees. At the close of the war he returned to his farm but served a couple of months as a Democratic U.S. Senator.

MAFFITT, John Newland (1819-1886)

The first commander of the famed Confederate commerce raider *Florida*, John N. Maffitt, was forced to relinquish command of his vessel because of the effects of yellow fever contracted in the service of the Confederacy. Born at sea, it was natural for Maffitt to enter the old navy at the age of 13. He fought against the slave trade and worked for the U.S. Coastal Survey before the Civil War. Educated in North Carolina, he resigned his lieutenant's commission on April 28, 1861. Appointed a lieutenant in the Confederate Navy on May 2, he served at Hilton Head. Promoted to captain in January 1862, he ran the blockade with a cargo of cotton to England aboard the *Cecile*. Here he took command of the steamer *Oreto*, which was soon to become the first of the British-built Confederate raiders, the *Florida*. Despite problems with the British and Spanish authorities and a yellow fever epidemic, Maffitt managed to bring his undermanned craft into Mobile to complete its outfitting. On the night of January 15, 1863, the *Florida* finally broke out onto the high seas to become a terror to Union merchant vessels. After seven months of raiding, Maffitt put his vessel into dock at Brest, France, on August 23. Weakened by the fever and the rigors of the voyage, he asked to be relieved. His record included about 55 prizes, but with a couple of brief exceptions he held no further commands. After the war he retired to his farm. (Boykin, Edward C., *Sea Devil of the Confederacy: The Story of the Florida and Her Captain, John Newland Maffitt*)

MAGEVNEY, Michael, Jr. (?-?)

Michael Magevney, Jr., commanded a regiment which greatly confused the Union authorities as to the number of regiments Tennessee had provided the Confederacy. His command, the 154th Tennessee Senior Infantry, was formed from a fraternal order of an old militia unit which kept its former numeric designation and received permission to append "Senior" to its name in order to indicate that it was in fact an older unit than those with lower numbers. But since no other Tennessee unit had a number higher than the 80s, the Union Command was befuddled. Magevney's assignments included: captain, Company C, 154th Tennessee (May 14, 1861); lieutenant colonel, 154th Tennessee (1862); colonel, 154th Tennessee (to date from August 30, 1862); and commanding Vaughan's Brigade, Cheatham's Division, Hardee's Corps, Army of Tennessee (July 4-September 1864). He fought at Belmont commanding his company, the Jackson Guards, and at Shiloh. At Richmond, Kentucky, during the Perryville Campaign he succeeded to regimental command upon the death of the colonel. After leading his men at Murfreesboro, he became a supernumery in March 1863 when the regiment was consolidated with the 13th Tennessee. Returning from detached service, he commanded the consolidated unit in the Atlanta Campaign and took over the brigade upon the wounding of General Vaughan. He retained this command through the siege until General G.W. Gordon was assigned. Again in command of the 13th and 154th, Magevney took part in the Tennessee Campaign and was captured at Nashville, ending his Civil War career.

MAGOFFIN, Beriah (1815-1885)

A proslavery governor of Kentucky, Beriah Magoffin attempted to keep his state neutral at the beginning of the Civil War. The native Kentuckian had practiced law in Mississippi and Kentucky, served as a judge, been a state legislator, and served as a delegate to several Democratic conventions. An unsuccessful 1855 candidate for lieutenant governor, he was elected to the top spot four years later. Looking for a secession compromise, he supported the Crittenden proposals but insisted on a rigid enforcement of the Fugitive Slave Law. He called for a state convention but was turned down by the legislature. In response to Lincoln's call for 75,000 volunteers following the firing on Fort Sumter, he declared that the state would "furnish no troops for the wicked purpose of subduing her sister Southern states." In May he issued a proclamation of neutrality for the state and this awkward situation lasted until September 1861. With a Unionist legislature overriding his vetoes, he resigned on August 18, 1862, and returned to his law practice and his farm. Reconciled to the defeat of slavery, he urged the ratification of the 13th Amendment and the granting of civil rights to the freedmen. He later sat in the legislature and was in the real estate market. (Coulter, E. Merton, *The Civil War and Readjustment in Kentucky*)

MAGRATH, Andrew Gordon (1813-1893)

Taking office as South Carolina's last Confederate governor on December 18, 1864, Andrew G. Magrath was almost immediately faced with Sherman's invasion of the state and the resultant disruption of civil government. A native Charlestonian lawyer and Democrat, he served two terms in the state legislature and was a U.S. district judge at the outbreak of the Civil War. He had been Governor Picken's secretary of state during the secession winter in which he attended the convention which dissolved the Union. With the formation of the Confederacy he was named Confederate district judge for South Carolina. Since some of his rulings were counter to a strong central Confederate government, he became unpopular with Jefferson Davis. In 1864 he left the bench to take up his duties as governor—to which post he had been elected by a secret, closed session of the legislature. Within months the capital was occupied and his effectiveness was diminished. With the fall of Richmond he called on the other Southern governors to continue the fight. Arrested by the Union forces on May 28, 1865, he spent seven months behind bars. Following his release he resumed his practice. (Wallace, David D., *History of South Carolina*)

MAGRUDER, John Bankhead (1807-1871)

The life style of Confederate General John B. Magruder, which earned him the nickname of "Prince John," did not do much for his popularity with his troops. The Virginian West Pointer (1830) had spent a year with the infantry before securing a transfer to the artillery. He won two brevets during the Mexican War, being wounded at Chapultepec. Also a veteran of Seminole fighting and frontier service, he spent most of the interwar years in various garrison assignments where he earned a reputation as a *bon vivant*. On April 20, 1861, he gave up this life when he resigned his captaincy in the 1st Artillery and offered his services to the South. His assignments included: colonel, Virginia Volunteers (May 16, 1861); commanding Department of the Peninsula (May 21, 1861-April 12, 1862); brigadier general, CSA (June 17, 1861); major general, CSA (October 7, 1861); commanding Magruder's Command, Department of Northern Virginia (April 12-July 3, 1862); commanding District of Texas, Trans-Mississippi Department (November-December 1862); commanding District of Texas, New Mexico and Arizona, Trans-Mississippi Department (December 1862-August 4, 1864 and March 31-May 26, 1865); commanding District of Arkansas, Trans-Mississippi Department (August 4, 1864-January 29, 1865, February 1-15, and ca. February-March 31, 1865); also commanding 2nd Corps (or District of Arkansas), Trans-Mississippi Department (September 1864-January 29, 1865, February 1-15, and ca. February-March 31, 1865); and also commanding 3rd Corps (or District of Texas, New Mexico and Arizona), Trans-Mississippi Department (March 31-May 26, 1865). Assigned to command on the Peninsula, he won the early fight at Big Bethel and soon rose to the rank of major general. The next spring he performed

South Carolina Governor Andrew G. Magrath. (*Harper's*)

admirably in fortifying Yorktown and delaying McClellan's advance on Richmond until Joseph E. Johnston could arrive with reinforcements from northern Virginia. Magruder's command was absorbed into what became the Army of Northern Virginia. In May 1862 it was determined to place him in charge of the Trans-Mississippi West but this was put in abeyance until after the Seven Days. During that series of battles he did not enhance his reputation. He did hold most of McClellan's army in check while the initial flank attack on the other side of the Chickahominy was being launched. He failed at Savage Station, Glendale, and Malvern Hill in the later stages of the campaign. At his own request he was then reordered to the West, but charges of drunkenness and cowardice forced his recall before he could take command. Eventually cleared, he took command of only the Texas district in November 1862. At the beginning of the next year he scored a major success in Galveston Harbor, driving off portions of the blockading fleet. He spent the rest of the war in district command in Texas and Arkansas and then fled to Mexico. With a band of fellow ex-Confederates he offered his services to Emperor Maximilian but, turned down, set up a colony at Cordoba. Magruder returned to the United States as a lecturer in 1867 but failed to earn the kind of living he was used to. He died in relative poverty.

"Prince John" Magruder. (NA)

MAHAN, Alfred Thayer (1840-1914)

The son of West Point professor Dennis Hart Mahan, Alfred Thayer Mahan built on his Civil War and later experiences to become one of the world's leading historians of naval matters. Born at his father's alma mater, he did not attend it, but chose instead, to study at Annapolis where he was graduated in 1859. During the Civil War he performed blockade duty. Remaining on active duty thereafter, he had risen to the rank of captain by 1886 when he became president of the Naval War College. After retiring in 1896, he returned to duty for the Spanish-American War in a planning capacity. In the meantime his works included: *The Influence of Seapower Upon History, 1660-1783* and *The Influence of Seapower Upon the French Revolution and Empire, 1783-1812*, and subsquently his memoirs, *From Sail to Steam*. (Seager, Robert, *Alfred Thayer Mahan, The Man and His Letters*)

MAHAN, Dennis Hart (1802-1871)

West Point professor Dennis Hart Mahan had a great deal of influence not only over the training of regular army officers prior to the Civil War but also over the thousands of volunteer officers called from civilian life with no military education. The native New Yorker received his appointment to the military academy from Virginia and was graduated at the head of his class in 1824. He was accordingly posted to the prestigious engineers. The War Department then sent him to the French military engineering school at Metz. He resigned as a first lieutenant in 1832 and that year became a full professor at his alma mater. Among his written works were *Advanced-Guard* and *Out-Post*. The latter was used on both sides during the Civil War. His teaching spanned the Mexican and Civil wars and he was one of the organizers of the Virginia Military Institute. He drowned in the Hudson River in 1871.

MAHONE, William (1826-1895)

Mediocre in his two years as a brigade commander, William Mahone excelled once promoted to division command—in a reverse of the Peter Principle. A graduate of the Virginia Military Institute, he was active prewar in education and railroading in his native Virginia. His assignments for the Confederacy included: colonel, 6th Virginia (1861); commanding 2nd Brigade, Department of Norfolk (by October 2, 1861-April 12, 1862); brigadier general, CSA (November 16, 1861); commanding brigade, Huger's-Anderson's Division (in 1st Corps from July 1862 and 3rd Corps from May 30, 1863), Army of Northern Virginia (April 12-August 30 and fall 1862-May 7, 1864); commanding the division (May 7, 1864-April 9, 1865); and major general, CSA (July 30, 1864). Following the Union evacuation of the Gosport Navy Yard at Norfolk, Virginia forces under Mahone occupied it. When the South abandoned the city, he fought against the federal flotilla at Drewry's Bluff and then moved to the Peninsula. There he saw action at Seven Pines and Malvern Hill. In Longstreet's assault at 2nd Bull Run he suffered a severe wound. When his wife was told by the governor that it was only a flesh wound she knew it

Hardhitting "Little Billy" Mahone. (NA)

was serious, as she exclaimed, "the General hasn't any flesh!" Mahone weighed less than 100 pounds. He returned to duty for Fredericksburg and Chancellorsville. At Gettysburg he displayed a reluctance to commit his brigade. His record had not been outstanding to this time. Following the Wilderness, where some of his men accidentally wounded General Longstreet, he succeeded to division command when Anderson was transferred to command Longstreet's men. He fought through Spotsylvania and Cold Harbor and took his place in the Petersburg trenches. Following the explosion of the Union mine on July 30, he became the hero of the battle of the Crater. In brilliant fashion he led two of his brigades up to the edge of the gaping hole and kept up a merciless fire on the troops, white and black, milling about within until they surrendered. For this he was upped to major general. He continued to distinguish himself during the remainder of the siege and in the retreat to the Appomattox surrender. Returning to the railroads in peacetime he soon entered politics and lost much of his popularity, since he dominated the state's Republican Party affiliate. (Blake, N.M., *William Mahone of Virginia, Soldier and Political Insurgent*)

MAJOR, James Patrick (1836-1877)

On his way to becoming a Confederate brigadier general, Missourian West Pointer (1856) James P. Major served mostly west of the Mississippi River. Upon his graduation he was posted to the cavalry and participated in Indian fighting in Texas. Resigning as a second lieutenant in the 2nd Cavalry on March 21, 1861, he offered his services to his native state. His assignments included: lieutenant, Cavalry (ca. March 1861); lieutenant colonel, 1st Cavalry, 3rd Division, Missouri State Guard (1861); colonel, Cavalry Regiment, 3rd Division, Missouri State Guard (1862); chief of Artillery, District of the Mississippi, Department #2 (summer 1862); brigadier general, CSA (July 21, 1863); and commanding in the Trans-Mississippi Department: brigade, District of West Louisiana (summer 1863-March 1864); brigade, Green's-Wharton's Cavalry Division, District of West Louisiana (March-summer 1864); and 2nd (Texas) Cavalry Brigade, 1st (Texas) Cavalry Division, 2nd Corps (or District of Arkansas) (September 1864-May 26, 1865). He led a mounted battalion of the Missouri State Guard at Wilson's Creek. Crossing the Mississippi in 1862, he was Earl Van Dorn's artillery chief in the defense of Vicksburg. Promoted to brigadier general, he commanded a brigade during the Red River Campaign and later in Arkansas. Following a period of residence in France, he returned as a planter to Louisiana and Texas.

MALLET, John William (1832-1912)

This Irish-born chemist came to America in 1853 and eventually became the head of the Richmond ordnance labs. Educated in his field in Ireland and Germany, Mallet served the Alabama geological survey and taught at the state university in the 1850s. Enlisting in an Alabama unit early in the war, he became a staff officer to Robert E. Rodes. In 1862 he was given the rank of colonel of artillery and assigned to the labs where he fought against shortages to aid the Southern military effort. After the war he taught at several Southern universities, dying in retirement in Virginia.

MALLISON, Francis A. (?-?)

A reporter for the *Brooklyn Eagle*, Francis A. Mallison was recruited by city editor Joseph Howard, Jr., to aid in the manipulation of war news in order to make a fast buck on the gold market. On May 17, 1864, the pair drafted a series of documents that purported to be Associated Press dispatches of a presidential proclamation. The document related the stalemated military situation and called for a day of prayer and fasting and called for 400,000 more men. In the early hours of the next day a young boy delivered the copies to the various New York papers. Most were suspicious, but two, the *World* and the *Journal of Commerce*, were too pressed by deadlines to check and went ahead with the story. As a result the price of gold shot up 10 percent; of course, the pair had foreseen this by buying large quantities of the commodity on margin. An outraged Lincoln ordered the seizure of the papers and the arrest of their employees, not realizing that they too were victims. Two days later Howard was caught and the next day Mallison was sent to Fort Lafayette. Three months later they were freed through the intercession of Henry Ward Beecher. Ironically, the embarrassed Lincoln had been about to issue a similar proclamation of his own when the storm broke, prompting him to delay it for two months.

MALLORY, Stephen Russell (1813-1873)

Secretary of the Navy Stephen R. Mallory was one of only two Confederate cabinet members to serve throughout the war in one post. Born in Trinidad, he was raised in Florida where he became familiar with naval matters. Not old enough to vote, and with only about three years of formal schooling, he was appointed customs inspector at Key West. Studying law, he was given a judgeship. During the Seminole War he served in the militia. Elected to the U.S. senate in 1851, he served for almost 10 years on the Committee on Naval Affairs, most of the time as chairman. A reluctant secessionist, he resigned in early 1861 and strived, during the lull between secession and war, to prevent the outbreak of war at Fort Pickens in Pensacola Harbor. On February 21, 1861, he was named head of the navy department by Jefferson Davis, who, not being well-informed on naval matters, left the department's running almost entirely to Mallory—who faced the problem of organizing from scratch. He made some mistakes, such as refusing to accept jurisdiction over the River Defense Fleet and leaving it in a command limbo which contributed to the defeats at New Orleans and Memphis. But he was eager to accept new technologies to counterbalance the Union's superiority, even travelling to England in his search. He remained with Davis in the flight from Richmond until shortly before they were both captured in Georgia. He was paroled in March 1866 and returned to his Florida law practice. (Durkin, Joseph T., *Stephen R. Mallory: Confederate Naval Chief*)

MALLOY, Adam Gale (?-?)

Serving briefly in what was to become the Iron Brigade, Irish native Adam G. Malloy won his brevet as brigadier general of volunteers for his war service in the western theater. His assignments included: captain, 6th Wisconsin (July 16, 1861); lieutenant colonel, 17th Wisconsin (March 3, 1862); colonel, 17th Wisconsin (December 1, 1862); commanding 2nd Brigade, 1st Division, 17th Corps, Army of the Tennessee (November 15, 1863-March 10, 1864); commanding 3rd Brigade, 3rd Division, 17th Corps, Army of the Tennessee (May 1-September 22, 1864); commanding 2nd Brigade (Army of the Tennessee), Provisional Division, Provisional Detachment, Department of the Cumberland (December 1864); and commanding 1st Brigade, 2nd Division, Sub-District of Beaufort, Department of North Carolina (March 1-18, 1865). Briefly serving in the nation's capital, he was mustered out on February 2, 1862, and a month later became a field officer. His new unit took part in the advance on Corinth, Mississippi, and he led it at the battle there. The unit then took part in Grant's central Mississippi Campaign and Malloy won an 1867 brevet in the regular army for Vicksburg. Joining Sherman's army in the Atlanta Campaign on June 8, 1864, he led a brigade at Kennesaw Mountain and won another brevet. A similar reward came for the battle of Atlanta proper and again for Nashville, in both of which he was in brigade command. His final service came in North Carolina supporting Sherman's drive through the state. Mustered out with his regiment on July 14, 1865, he was commissioned a first lieutenant of infantry the next year and served until he was discharged at his own request in 1870.

MALTBY, Jasper Adalmorn (1826-1867)

After the fall of Vicksburg Union General Jasper A. Maltby spent most of the balance of the Civil War in the vicinity of the captured city and settled there after the war. The Ohio-born Illinois gunsmith had served in the Mexican War as a private in one of the regular army infantry regiments created especially for that conflict. The private was severely wounded at Chapultepec. Living in Grant's hometown at the outbreak of the war, he enlisted near the end of 1861. His assignments included: lieutenant colonel, 45th Illinois (December 26, 1861); colonel, 45th Illinois (March 5, 1863); brigadier general, USV (August 4, 1863); commanding 3rd Brigade, 3rd Division, 17th Corps, Army of the Tennessee (September 8, 1863-May 1, 1864); also commanding the division (March 6-April 6, 1864); commanding brigade, District of Vicksburg, Department of the Tennessee (May-November 28, 1864); and commanding District of Vicksburg, Department of Mississippi (November 28, 1864-June 1865). Wounded at Fort Donelson, Maltby returned to command the regiment in the Vicksburg Campaign as colonel. Distinguished in that operation, he was promoted to brigadier general a month after the fall of the city and given a brigade which was assigned to garrison duty in the vicinity. It is somewhat strange that a newly appointed brigadier not be given a chance to command in the field, but that is what happened, intentionally or not, to Maltby. Without the normal brevet as major general, he was mustered out on January 15, 1866, and settled in Vicksburg as a merchant until his death the next year, having served briefly as the town's occupation mayor.

MANEY, George Earl (1826-1901)

Tennessee lawyer and Mexican War veteran—as a first lieutenant in the 3rd Dragoons—George E. Maney rose to the command of a Confederate division. Giving up his Nashville practice, his assignments included: captain, Company A, 11th Tennessee (May 1861); colonel, 1st Tennessee (May 9, 1861); commanding 2nd Brigade, 2nd (Cheatham's) Division, 1st (Polk's) Corps, Army of the Mississippi (April 6-July 2, 1862); brigadier general, CSA (April 16, 1862); commanding 2nd Brigade, Cheatham's Division, Army of the Mississippi (July 2-August 15, 1862); commanding 3rd Brigade, Cheatham's Division, Right Wing, Army of the Mississippi (August 15-November 20, 1862); commanding brigade, Cheatham's Division, Polk's-Cheatham's Corps, Army of Tennessee (November 20, 1862-November 12, 1863); commanding brigade, Walker's Division, Hardee's Corps, Army of Tennessee (November 12-25, 1863); commanding brigade, Cheatham's Division, Hardee's Corps, Army of Tennessee (May-early July 1864); and commanding the division (July-August 31, 1864). Sent with his regiment to western Virginia, he participated in the fizzle at Rich Mountain under Robert E. Lee and then served for a time under Stonewall Jackson before being ordered to Mississippi. Taking command of a brigade, he led it at Shiloh and was promoted to brigadier general a few days later. He then took part in the defense of Corinth, Mississippi, and fought at Perryville during the Kentucky Campaign. After seeing further action at Murfreesboro, during the Tullahoma Campaign, and at Chickamauga, he was wounded at Chattanooga. He returned to duty at the beginning of the Atlanta Campaign and took charge of Cheatham's division that summer. However, he appears to have been relieved during the action at Jonesboro. This was apparently his last command and after the war he was engaged in railroading, Republican politics, and as a diplomat in Latin America—in Colombia, Bolivia, Paraguay, and Uruguay.

MANGAS COLORADAS (1795?-1863)

What happened to Apache chief Mangas Coloradas early in 1863 is still an open question, but most now believe that he was murdered by California Volunteers. The official army version is that he was killed trying to escape. In the late 1840s he had professed to be a friend of the whites while he despised the Mexicans. But in 1861 he joined with Cochise in his war against the whites in Arizona. In July 1862 he was wounded in a fight with a detachment of the California Column at Apache Pass. Taken to Mexico for recovery, he was later captured near Pinos Altos, New Mexico. Taken to Fort McLane he was awaiting the arrival of General Joseph R. West. While asleep West had two men assigned to guard the chief. Others later reported hearing the general instruct the guards that he did not want to find the Apache alive in the morning. Apparently what happened was that the guards began to torture him with red-hot bayonets. When he objected they bayonetted him and then emptied their revolvers into him. In any case he was dead by morning. (Brown, Dee, *Bury My Heart at Wounded Knee*)

MANIGAULT, Arthur Middleton (1824-1886)

South Carolina businessman and Mexican War veteran—as a first lieutenant in the Palmetto Regiment—Arthur M. Manigault reentered the military in 1860 and rose to the rank of brigadier general in the Confederate service. His assignments included: captain, North Santee Mounted Rifles (December 1860); lieutenant colonel and adjutant and inspector general (April 1861); colonel, 10th South Carolina (May 31, 1861); commanding 1st Military District of South Carolina, Department of South Carolina, Georgia and Florida (December 10, 1861-May 28, 1862); commanding 4th Brigade, Reserve Corps, Army of the Mississippi (June-July 2, 1862); commanding 4th Brigade, Withers' Division, Army of the Mississippi (July 2-August 15, 1862); commanding 4th Brigade, Withers' Division, Right Wing, Army of the Mississippi (August 15-November 20, 1862); commanding brigade, Withers'-Hindman's Division, Polk's-Cheatham's-Breckinridge's-Hardee's Corps, Army of Tennessee (November 20, 1862-January 1864); brigadier general, CSA (April 26, 1863); and commanding brigade, Hindman's-Anderson's-Johnson's Division, Hindman's-Hood's-Lee's Corps, Army of Tennessee (January-November 30, 1864). After commanding a militia company he joined Beauregard's staff in Charleston Harbor and took part in the bombardment of Fort Sumter. Shortly thereafter he took command of a regiment. For a time he was in district command in his native state before joining Beauregard's army at Corinth. He later fought at Murfreesboro as a brigade commander and was advanced to brigadier general in time for the Tullahoma Campaign. Fighting at Chickamauga and Chattanooga, he was slightly wounded at Resaca during the Atlanta Campaign. A head wound at Franklin ended his active field career. A postwar planter, he served as his state's adjutant and inspector general. (Tower, R. Lockwood, ed., *A Carolinian Goes to War: The Civil War Narrative of Arthur Middleton Manigault, Brigadier General, CSA*)

MANN, Ambrose Dudley (1796-1889)

The Confederate diplomatic career of Ambrose D. Mann was far from a success. Born in Virginia, he had attended West Point until his resignation shortly before his graduation. Following admission to the bar, he served as a diplomat in Germany, Hungary, and Switzerland. In the mid-1850s he was assistant secretary of state. A staunch Southerner, he urged that the South be made commercially independent. With secession he was appointed a commissioner to Great Britain on March 16, 1861, but despite his efforts to gain recognition and a meeting with Lord Russell he and his fellow commissioners failed. He subsequently attempted to get the friendly King Leopold of Belgium to use his influence with Queen Victoria and Napoleon III in behalf of the South. Again he was unsuccessful. His efforts with the press in both Britain and Belgium were more favorable. On September 24, 1863, he was named special agent to the Vatican and was successful in enlisting the support of the Pope in opposing the Union army's efforts to recruit Catholics in Europe, primarily Irish and German. However, this appears to have had little impact on Union manpower. Settling in Paris after Appomattox, he worked as a journalist until his death.

MANNING, Vanney Hartrog (1839-1892)

It took a year's imprisonment to put an end to Vanney H. Manning's fighting career in the Civil War. He had been born in North Carolina and educated in Tennessee before settling in Arkansas. Entering the Confederate army, he received the following assignments: captain, Company K, 3rd Arkansas (June 20, 1861); major, 3rd Arkansas (July 9, 1861); colonel, 3rd Arkansas (March 11, 1862); commanding Walker's Brigade, Holmes' Division, Army of Northern Virginia (early July 1862); commanding same brigade, Walker's Division, Longstreet's Command, Army of Northern Virginia (August 1862-September 17, 1862); and commanding Texas Brigade, Hood's Division, Longstreet's Corps, Army of Tennessee (temporarily from September 20, 1863). Following some initial difficulty in getting his company accepted into Confederate service, he took part in the Cheat Mountain and Romney campaigns before being transferred to the Rappahannock line and then to Southside Virginia. Taking part in the Seven Days he succeeded to temporary brigade command. Wounded at

Antietam, where he distinguished himself, he returned in time for a relatively inactive role at Fredericksburg. After taking part in Longstreet's Suffolk Campaign he was again wounded on the third day at Gettysburg. Moving west with the corps, he fought at Chickamauga, where he again took over command of a brigade, and at Knoxville. The corps rejoined Lee and on the second day at the Wilderness Manning was severely wounded and left upon the field. He was captured and confined until July 24, 1865. During a part of his confinement he was exposed to Confederate fire by order of the Union authorities. He was a lawyer and U.S. congressman after the war.

MANSFIELD, Joseph King Fenno (1803-1862)

Graduating second in the West Point Class of 1822, Connecticut-born Joseph Mansfield, a veteran of the Mexican War during which he earned three brevets, had risen to become the inspector general of the U.S. Army, with the rank of colonel, by the start of the war. Shortly after the fall of Fort Sumter, he was given command of the Department of Washington, on April 28, 1861. Promoted to brigadier general, USA, on May 14, he held this command until it was merged into the Department of the Potomac which was placed under the command of General George B. McClellan. While in charge in the capital, he directed the occupation of that part of Virginia immediately across the river. He later served on the Virginia coast holding various assignments at Fort Monroe, Suffolk, and Newport News. While on duty at the latter point he witnessed the duel between the *Montior* and the *Virginia*. After General Pope's defeat at 2nd Bull Run, McClellan placed Mansfield in charge of the 12th Corps on September 15, 1862. He thus became the oldest general officer in the Army of the Potomac. Two days later, in the battle of Antietam, while rallying his wavering men he was mortally wounded, dying the next day. On March 12, 1863, Mansfield was posthumously promoted major general, USV, to rank from July 18, 1862. (Gould, John Mead, *Joseph King Fenno Mansfield, Brigadier General of the U.S. Army*)

MANSON, Mahlon Dickerson (1820-1895)

The explosion of an enemy shell at Resaca put an end to the military career of General Mahlon D. Manson. Born in Ohio, he had been an Indiana druggist at the outbreak of the Civil War and also a veteran, as a company commander in the 5th Indiana, of the Mexican War. He was commissioned again within days of the firing upon Fort Sumter, and his assignments included: captain, 10th Indiana (April 17, 1861); major, 10th Indiana (April 25, 1861); colonel, 10th Indiana (May 10, 1861); colonel, 10th Indiana (reorganized September 18, 1861); commanding 2nd Brigade, Army of the Ohio (November-December 2, 1861); commanding 2nd Brigade, 1st Division, Army of the Ohio (December 2, 1861-March 22, 1862); brigadier general, USV (March 24, 1862); commanding 22nd Brigade, 4th Division, Army of the Ohio (May 30-August 16, 1862); commanding 1st Brigade, Army of Kentucky, Department of the Ohio (August 25-30, 1862); commanding 1st Brigade, 3rd Division, 23rd Corps, Army of the Ohio (June 24-August 6, 1863); commanding 2nd Division, 23rd Corps, Army of the Ohio (August 6-21, 1863); commanding the corps (September 24-December 20, 1863); again commanding 2nd Division, 23rd Corps, Army of the Ohio (December 24, 1863-January 26, 1864); and commanding 2nd Brigade, 3rd Division, 23rd Corps, Army of the Ohio (April 7-May 14, 1864). After fighting at Rich Mountain he was mustered out with his regiment at the end of their term of enlistment on August 6, 1861, but he reorganized the unit in about six weeks. He commanded a brigade at Mill Springs. During the invasion of Kentucky by Bragg and Kirby Smith, Manson was wounded and captured in the Union rout at Richmond. Not exchanged until December 1862, he returned to the field to face the depredations of the Confederate cavalry raider John Pegram. At Knoxville he commanded the corps. Taking part in the Atlanta Campaign he was so severely wounded that he was unable to return to duty and resigned on December 21, 1864. A Democrat, he served one term in Congress and held several state and national positions in the postwar years.

MARCY, Randolph Barnes (1812-1887)

Although twice appointed a brigadier during the Civil War, Randolph Marcy did not have an appointment at that grade

Union General J.K.F. Mansfield, mortally wounded at Antietam. (*Leslie's*)

approved by the Senate until 1878. An 1832 graduate of the military academy, he had served in the infantry, including the Mexican War and the Mormon expedition, until he joined the Pay Department as a major in 1859. On August 9, 1861, Marcy was appointed the senior colonel in the Inspector General's Department and its titular head. He served in the field with his son-in-law George McClellan's Army of the Potomac during the Peninsula and Antietam campaigns. After McClellan's removal, Marcy served in Washington and in several of the field departments on inspection duty. On September 23, 1861, and also September 13, 1862, he was appointed brigadier general, USV, but the Senate refused to confirm him, possibly due to his relationship to the unpopular McClellan. The appointments expired on July 17, 1862, and March 4, 1863, respectively. Continuing in the military after the war, he was named inspector general as a brigadier in the regular army in 1878. Late in the Civil War he had been brevetted to this rank, and that of major general of volunteers, for his service. He retired in 1881.

MARKS, Samuel F. (?-?)

One of the older regimental commanders in the Confederate army at the beginning of the Civil War, Samuel F. Marks had commanded the 3rd Louisiana during the Mexican War. His assignments in the Civil War included: colonel, 11th Louisiana (August 9, 1861); commanding 1st Brigade, 3rd Division, 1st Geographical Division, Department No. 2 (October 24, 1861-February 1862); and commanding brigade, McCown's Command, 1st Geographical Division, Department No. 2 (February-March 1862). When Grant made his attack on Belmont, Missouri, Marks led his small brigade across the Mississippi from Columbus, Kentucky, to take part in the Union general's defeat. After service at Island #10, he was wounded early on the first day of the battle of Shiloh. This effectively ended his military service.

MARMADUKE, John Sappington (1833-1887)

At the time of his promotion to major general Missourian West Pointer (1857) John S. Marmaduke was confined in Boston Harbor's Fort Warren and would not be released until well after the fall of the Confederacy. Posted to the infantry, he had been a veteran of frontier service and the expedition against the Mormons in Utah when he resigned on April 17, 1861, as a second lieutenant in the 7th Infantry. His Confederate assignments included: first lieutenant, Infantry (ca. April 1861); colonel, Missouri State Guard (1861); lieutenant colonel, 1st Arkansas Battalion (summer 1861); colonel, 18th (Marmaduke's) Arkansas (fall 1861); colonel, 3rd Confederate (designation change January 31, 1862); brigadier general, CSA (November 15, 1862); commanding 4th (Cavalry) Division, 1st Corps, Trans-Mississippi Department (ca. November 1862-January 1863); commanding cavalry division, District of Arkansas, Trans-Mississippi Department (January 1863-September 18, 1864); commanding cavalry division, Army of Missouri, Trans-Mississippi Department (September 18-October 25, 1864); also commanding 1st (Missouri) Cavalry Division, Cavalry Corps, Trans-Mississippi Department (September-October 25, 1864); and major general, CSA (March 18, 1865, to rank from the 17th). With the Missouri State Guard he fought at Booneville and then took command of an Arkansas Battalion which was subsequently increased to regimental size. The unit was later designated as a "Confederate" unit and as such fought at Shiloh and during the Corinth siege. Resigning his colonelcy on September 12, 1862, Marmaduke was named a brigadier general two months later. He led his mounted division at Prairie Grove, Helena, Little Rock, and Jenkins' Ferry. He then joined Sterling Price for the invasion of Missouri and was captured during the rearguard action at Marais des Cygnes on October 25, 1864. Not released until July 1865, he never served at the higher rank. An insurance man after the war, he eventually won the gubernatorial chair, having once been defeated as a Democrat and having held other state offices.

MARR, John Quincy (1825-1861)

In a little remembered action at Fairfax Court House, Virginia, John Q. Marr was the only fatality, becoming the first martyr of the Confederacy to die in combat. A graduate and former faculty member of the Virginia Military Institute, he had been enjoying the advantages of planter society in his native county of Fauquier, when the secession crisis broke into war. He immediately took the field with the Warrenton Rifles, which he had raised after John Brown's Raid. Colonel Richard S. Ewell stationed Captain Marr's company at Fairfax, C.H., and on June 1, 1861, at about 3:00 A.M., Company B, 2nd U.S. Cavalry, passed through town firing a few shots. After a defense was prepared and the federals driven off, it was noticed that Marr was missing. He was dead from a wound in the chest.

MARSH, George Perkins (1801-1882)

America's minister to Italy during the Civil War years is also considered the first ecologist. A native of Vermont, he was a keen observer of nature and noted the affects of man upon the planet's ecological systems. A graduate of Dartmouth, he was not particularly successful at law or business. He spent eight years in the U.S. Congress and, capitalizing upon his knowledge of 20 languages, was appointed minister to Turkey in the late 1840s. With the election of Lincoln, he was appointed to the post in Italy which he held until his death two decades later. His wide travels convinced him of the finiteness of the Earth's resources, and in May 1864 he published his *Man and Nature*. It was a full century earlier than the ecology movement of the 1960s and after.

MARSHALL, Henry (1805-1864)

A native of South Carolina and ardent believer in states' rights, Henry Marshall was an extremely wealthy Louisiana planter at the onset of the secession crisis. At the time he sat in the state's upper legislative house and was a delegate to the secession convention. Elected to the Provisional Confederate Congress, he chaired the Committee on Public Lands and sat on those on

Charge of Company B, 2nd United States Cavalry, during which John Q. Marr became the first Confederate combat fatality. (*Leslie's*)

Claims and Territories. In the first Regular Congress he was on the committees on: Patents; Quartermaster's and Commissary Departments; and Territories and Public Lands. With a portion of his wealth he equipped a regiment for his cousin, Colonel (later Brigadier General) Maxcy Gregg. His states' rights views worked to the detriment of the Davis administration's efforts to organize a centralized government to win the war. Not seeking reelection, he retired to his plantation where he died on July 13, 1864, before the Confederacy's demise. (Bragg, Jefferson Davis, *Louisiana in the Confederacy*)

MARSHALL, Humphrey (1812-1872)

One of the leaders of the neutrality movement in Kentucky, Humphrey Marshall in the end joined the Confederacy as a brigadier general but failed to attain military distinction. The Kentucky-born West Pointer (1832) had served a year with the mounted rangers and dragoons before resigning as a brevet second lieutenant. Practicing law at the outbreak of the Mexican War, he became colonel of the 1st Kentucky Cavalry and unlike many volunteers saw heavy action south of the border. From then until the Civil War he served almost continuously in the House of Representatives, interrupted by a year as a diplomat to China. During the secession crisis he backed John C. Breckinridge for the presidency. When his native state's neutrality was finally violated in the fall of 1861, he cast his lot with the South. His assignments included: brigadier general, CSA (October 30, 1861); commanding 1st Brigade, Army of Eastern Kentucky (early 1862); commanding District of Abingdon (May 2-8, 1862); commanding District of Abingdon, Department of Southwestern Virginia (May 8, 1862-May 9, 1863); and brigadier general, CSA (reappointed June 20, 1862, to rank from October 30, 1861). He served mostly in western Virginia and in Kentucky. He was involved in Bragg's campaign in Kentucky in the fall of 1862 but was not at the battle of Perryville itself. For unexplained reasons he resigned his commission on June 16, 1862, but was reinstated four days later. He resigned a second time on June 17, 1863, and early the next year was elected to the Second Confederate Congress. Taking his seat on May 2, 1864, he was a member of the Committee on Military Affairs. With his district occupied by Union forces he was a backer of the president and believed in extreme measures for maintaining the army's strength. He also favored government control over railroads and the use of slaves in the army. However, he opposed Davis on many tax issues and the question of suspending the writ of habeas corpus. After the war he resumed his law practice.

MARSTON, Gilman (1811-1890)

Like many of his fellow politicians, Gilman Marston interrupted his career to serve in the Union army. The New Hampshire native graduated from Harvard Law School and practiced his profession until his election to the state legislature in 1845. He was elected to Congress in 1858 and continued in that body during the first two years of the war but was usually absent in the field. His military assignments included: colonel, 2nd New Hampshire (June 10, 1861); brigadier general, USV (November 29, 1862); commanding Point Lookout prison camp (summer 1863); commanding District of St. Mary's, 18th Corps, Department of Virginia and North Carolina (December 1, 1863-April 28, 1864); commanding 1st Brigade, 1st Division, 18th Corps, Army of the James (May 1-June 18, 1864); commanding the division (June 18-20, September 3-15, and September 29-October 29, 1864); and commanding 1st Brigade, 3rd Division, 10th Corps, Army of the James (June 19-August 27, 1864). He was wounded while leading his regiment in Burnside's brigade at 1st Bull Run. On the Peninsula he fought at Yorktown, Williamsburg, Seven Pines, and during the Seven Days. After leading his regiment at Fredericksburg he was promoted to brigadier general and assigned to duty at Washington. After the Union victory at Gettysburg he set up the prison camp at Point Lookout and was soon given command of the district. In the spring of 1864 he was given a brigade under Butler and fought at Cold Harbor and Petersburg. Despite his political connections he did not receive a brevet promotion in the omnibus bill of March 1865. Resigning on April 20, 1865, he returned to his practice and then, as a Republican, to Congress.

MARTIN, James Green (1819-1878)

"Old One Wing"—he had lost an arm at Churubusco in the Mexican War—James G. Martin was popular with his men because of his bravery. Once they even tossed the West Pointer (1840) in the air on the Petersburg front. He resigned his captaincy on June 14, 1861, to tender his services to his native North Carolina. His assignments included: adjutant general, North Carolina State Troops (September 20, 1861); major general, North Carolina Militia (September 28, 1861); brigadier general, CSA (June 2, to rank from May 15, 1862); commanding brigade, Department of North Carolina (June 19-July 25, 1862); reappointed brigadier general, CSA (August 11, to rank from May 15, 1862); commanding District of North Carolina, same department (August 18-September 1862); commanding brigade, same department (May-October 1863); commanding brigade, District of the Cape Fear (October 1863-April 1864); commanding brigade, Whiting's Division, Department of North Carolina and Southern Virginia (mid-May 1864); commanding brigade, Hoke's Division, same department (May-June 28, 1864); and commanding District of Western North Carolina, Department of East Tennessee (late 1864-April 1865). A brilliant organizer, he was to a large degree responsible for North Carolina providing, some claim, the largest number and best equipped troops of any Southern state in the first year of the war. He resigned his first commission in the Confederate service because the duties conflicted with his state job. However, Lee had him reappointed from the original date and assigned to North Carolina so that he could handle both jobs. By April of 1863 Martin was looking for a more active role, and he received command of a brigade with which he served for a year in the Kinston and Wilmington areas. Sent to Virginia he assisted in bottling up Butler at Bermuda Hundred and was involved in the early fighting at Petersburg. His health soon broke down and he was forced to retire from active field service. For a while he guarded the Richmond and Danville and the Southside railroads and later in 1864 he was given command of the western part of his own state. He held this post until the close of hostilities. After the war he was admitted to the bar and practiced for his remaining years.

MARTIN, John D. (?-1862)

When his regiment was broken up, Colonel John D. Martin was kept in grade and assigned to command of a new brigade. His Confederate assignments included: colonel, 25th Mississippi (1861); commanding 1st Brigade, 4th Division, 1st Geographical Division, Department No. 2 (October 24-November 1861); colonel, 2nd Confederate (January 31, 1862); commanding Bowen's Brigade, Reserve Corps, Army of the Mississippi, Department No. 2 (April 6-May 8, 1862), and commanding 4th Brigade, Price's Corps, Army of West Tennessee, Department No. 2 (summer-October 3, 1862). He briefly led a brigade in western Kentucky during the first fall of the war and was in command of the regiment at Shiloh. Here, upon the wounding of the brigade commander, Martin took command of the brigade on the first day and led it through the rest of the battle. Since his regiment was made up of companies from different states, it had been designated as a "Confederate" regiment. However, on May 8, 1862, it was broken up and the companies assigned to units from their respective states. That summer Martin was given command of another brigade which he led at Iuka and Corinth. At the latter he was mortally wounded on the first day.

MARTIN, William Thompson (1823-1910)

Promotion to Confederate brigadier general brought Kentucky native William T. Martin a transfer to the western theater and service under Joseph Wheeler. A Unionist lawyer in Mississippi at the outbreak of the war, he threw in with the Confederates, raising a company. His assignments included: captain, Adams County Cavalry Company (spring 1861); major, Jeff Davis Legion (1861); lieutenant colonel, Jeff Davis Legion (February 13, 1862); brigadier general, CSA (December 2, 1862); commanding division, Wheeler's Cavalry Corps, Army of Tennessee (March 16-November 1863 and February-fall 1864); major general, CSA (November 10, 1863); commanding detachment Wheeler's Cavalry Corps, Department of East Tennessee (November 1863-February 1864); and commanding District of Mississippi and East Louisiana, Department of Alabama, Mississippi and East Louisiana (January 15-30, 1865). As a field officer in the Jeff Davis Legion, which was composed of companies from Alabama, Georgia, and Mississippi, he fought at Yorktown and Williamsburg. He took part in Jeb Stuart's ride around McClellan in June 1862 and commanded the legion and the 4th Virginia Cavalry during the Seven Days. After fighting at South Mountain and Antietam he was promoted to brigadier general and was eventually given command of a mounted division under Wheeler. With this command he took part in the Tullahoma and Chickamauga campaigns. Promoted to major general, he led that portion of the cavalry corps which went to East Tennessee for the Knoxville operations. Rejoining the main army, he led his division through the Atlanta Campaign and later briefly held a district command in Mississippi. As a Democrat, he served for over a decade in the state legislature and was also active in railroading and education.

MARTINDALE, John Henry (1815-1881)

Having survived a court of inquiry, John H. Martindale saw his military career ended by ill health. The native New Yorker and West Pointer (1835) was disappointed when only the top two members of his class were posted to the engineers—he was number three. The next year he finished a leave of absence and resigned before ever reporting to his assignment with the dragoons. He was involved in railroading before being admitted to the bar. In 1861 the ex-brevet second lieutenant was awarded a brigadier general's star in the volunteers. His assignments included: brigadier general, USV (August 9, 1861); commanding 2nd Brigade, Porter's Division, Army of the Potomac (October 3, 1861-March 13, 1862); commanding 1st Brigade, 1st Division, 3rd Corps, Army of the Potomac (March 13-May 18, 1862); commanding 1st Brigade, 1st Division, 5th Corps, Army of the Potomac (May 18-July 10, 1862); commanding District of Washington, 22nd Corps, Department of Washington (February 2-September 16, 1863 and October 1, 1863-May 2, 1864); commanding 2nd Division, 18th Corps, Army of the James (May 20-July 10, 1864); and commanding the corps (July 10-21, 1864). He led his brigade to the Peninsula and saw action at Yorktown. He then took part in the Seven Days fighting but was charged with having proposed surrender rather than withdrawal after Malvern Hill. His corps commander, Fitz-John Porter, had him relieved and brought before a court of inquiry. Cleared in October 1862, he was later brevetted major general for Malvern Hill and his other war services. After spending over a year in the Washington defenses he led a division at Bermuda Hundred, Cold Harbor, and Petersburg and was briefly in charge of the corps before ill health prompted his relief and later his resignation, which was accepted on September 13, 1864. Returning to his practice, he became New York's attorney general and was an official in the care of disabled veterans. He died when on a visit to the French Riviera for health reasons.

MASON, A.P. (?-?)

From 1862 until 1865 A.P. Mason rose from captain to full colonel while serving on the staffs of several of the South's top generals. He joined the staff of General Joseph E. Johnston early in 1862 and served with that officer on the Peninsula until the general was wounded at Seven Pines on May 31, 1862. The next day, when Robert E. Lee took over what was to become known as the Army of Northern Virginia, Mason was the only one of Johnston's staff officers to elect to remain. He retained his position as assistant adjutant general with Lee until the spring of 1863. He participated in the Seven Days, 2nd Bull Run, Antietam, and Fredericksburg campaigns. He rejoined Johnston in the western theater and participated in the Vicksburg and Atlanta campaigns. When Johnston was relieved by General John B. Hood, Mason remained as assistant adjutant general of the Army of Tennessee. After the fall of Atlanta and the disastrous Tennessee invasion, he served under Lieutenant General Richard Taylor until Johnston returned to duty opposing Sherman in North Carolina. Here he finished out the war as a colonel. He was apparently named colonel of the 2nd Mississippi Cavalry at some time in the war, but this was either not accepted by him or was never confirmed.

MASON, Charles (1804-1882)

The one man to graduate ahead of Robert E. Lee in the 1829 class at West Point, Charles Mason, did not serve in the military in the Civil War. He was instead a copperhead. The native New Yorker had resigned his commission in the engineers after only two years to become a patent lawyer and moved to Wisconsin. He served as a member of the supreme court of Iowa Territory until Iowa became a state and was active in Democratic politics. After toying with the idea of obtaining a commission he continued his law pracitce in Washington and wrote letters on the Washington scene for the *Dubuque Herald*. Signing as "X," he opposed most of the war measures enacted by the Lincoln administration. However, he did not bemoan Stephen Douglas' defeat in 1860, believing it to be justified retribution for Douglas' role in dividing the Democratic Party. Privately, Mason wrote that he favored reunion but with an unhumiliated Confederacy returning to the fold. He favored a period of independence for the South after which reunification could be achieved. Fearing that the measures necessary for Union victory would lead to a despotism, he was saddened by Northern victories. An opponent of slavery, he believed that states had the right to maintain the institution if they chose. Although he opposed the war effort he was not disloyal and was not in touch with the Confederates. After the war he helped to drive a wedge between Andrew Johnson and the Radical Republicans.

MASON, James Murray (1798-1871)

The seizure of Confederate emissary James M. Mason and his colleague John Slidell from the British mail-steamer *Trent* probably did the Confederacy more good on the foreign affairs front than did Mason's activities in England following his release. Born in the nation's capital, he became a lawyer in Winchester, Virginia, before launching his political career. A state legislator, he was a states' righter and supporter of John C. Calhoun. He served in both houses of the national legislature, including 10 years as the chairman of the Senate Committee on Foreign Affairs. He gave up his seat on March 28, 1861—before Virginia's secession—and was formally expelled on July 11. Two weeks later, on July 24, he was admitted to the Confederacy's Provisional Congress where he may have sat on the Committee on Foreign Affairs before being tapped by Jefferson Davis to serve on a diplomatic mission to Great Britain. On the way his vessel was stopped by the USS *San Jacinto* under the command of Charles Wilkes on November 8, 1861. The violation of international law in the captives' removal to Boston brought the United States and Britain to the brink of war, but the United States backed down and released the captives. Mason tried to curry favor with the English upper classes, but his prediction that the cotton weapon would force recognition of the Confederacy proved faulty. Upon the Confederacy's collapse, he settled briefly in Canada before returning to Virginia. (Mason, Virginia, *The Public Life and Diplomatic Correspondence of James M. Mason, with Some Personal History by His Daughter*)

Diplomat James M. Mason of the *Trent* affair. (NA)

MASON, John Sanford (1824-1897)

The battle of Fredericksburg effectively ended the field career of Union General John W. Mason before he had even received his commission. The Ohio native and West Pointer (1847) had served with the artillery on garrison duty in Mexico and on routine frontier assignments. His Civil War-era assignments included: first lieutenant, 3rd Artillery (since September 7, 1850); captain, 11th Infantry (May 14, 1861); colonel, 4th Ohio (October 3, 1861); commanding 1st Brigade, 3rd Division, 2nd Corps, Army of the Potomac (December 13, 1862); brigadier general, USV (to rank from November 29, 1862); and major, 17th Infantry (October 14, 1864). Transferring to the volunteers in the first autumn of the war, he led his regiment in western Virginia and during the Shenandoah Valley Campaign fought at 1st Winchester and Port Republic. Brevetted for Antietam, for the first time he succeeded to command of the brigade during the assaults on Marye's Heights at Fredericksburg. He then fell severely wounded. Having been named a brigadier general to rank from weeks before the battle, he was unable to return to even limited duty until the following April, when he was assigned to recruiting duties in Ohio. He later performed similar functions in California and Nevada. Mustered out of the volunteers on April 30, 1866, he reverted to his regular rank of major with brevets through brigadier general for the war. He finally retired in 1888 as colonel, 9th Infantry, having served much of the time on the frontier.

MATHEWS, Joseph Ard (?-1872)

For his role commanding a brigade of Union troops during Lee's last offensive—Fort Stedman—Joseph A. Mathews won the brevet of brigadier general. The Pennsylvania native's assignments included: major, 46th Pennsylvania (September 27, 1861); colonel, 128th Pennsylvania (November 1, 1862); colonel, 205th Pennsylvania (September 2, 1864); and commanding in the 3rd Division, 9th Corps, Army of the Potomac: 1st Brigade (November 26-December 15, 1864); and 2nd Brigade (December 15, 1864-February 1, 1865 and February 21-June 2, 1865). His first unit served initially in the Shenandoah Valley, seeing action at 1st Winchester, and then joined Pope's army in northern Virginia with which Mathews was wounded at Cedar Mountain. He was then named to the colonelcy of a nine-months regiment in the same brigade. With this he was captured at Chancellorsville, and shortly thereafter his unit was mustered out on May 19, 1863, upon the expiration of its term of enlistment. Over a year later he again took the field at the head of a new regiment which was assigned to the 9th Corps before Petersburg. Taking part in the thwarting of Lee's breakout attempt he was brevetted and was then mustered out for the final time on June 2, 1865, with his regiment.

MATTHIES, Charles Leopold (1824-1868)

In the aftermath of the revolutions in Europe in 1848, Prussian army veteran Charles L. Matthies came to America and later offered his services to the Union cause as early as January 9, 1861. Born in that part of Prussia which is now Poland, he had arrived in America in 1849 and become an Iowa liquor salesman. Entering the army early in the war, his assignments included: captain, 1st Iowa (May 14, 1861); lieutenant colonel, 5th Iowa (July 23, 1861); colonel, 5th Iowa (May 23, 1862); commanding 3rd Brigade, 7th Division, 16th Corps, Army of the Tennessee (December 22, 1862-January 20, 1863); commanding 3rd Brigade, 7th Division, 17th Corps, Army of the Tennessee (January 20-February 12, June 2-July 27, and August 28-September 14, 1863); commanding 2nd Brigade, 7th Division, 17th Corps, Army of the Tennessee (February 12-April 24, 1863); brigadier general, USV (April 4, 1863, to rank from November 29, 1862); commanding 3rd Brigade, 3rd Division, 15th Corps, Army of the Tennessee (May 2-June 1, 1863 and March 14-May 15, 1864); and commanding 3rd Brigade, 2nd Division, 17th Corps, Army of the Tennessee (September 14-November 25, 1863). After brief service as a company commander he became a field officer in a new regiment with which he fought at Island #10. During the advance on Corinth, Mississippi, he was advanced to a colonelcy and led his regiment at Iuka and Corinth that fall. He then served in the Vicksburg Campaign and went to the relief of the Army of the Cumberland at Chattanooga where he was severely wounded in the head. He returned to duty for two months before his resignation was accepted, effective May 14, 1864. In his remaining years he sat in the state legislature's upper house.

MATTHIES, Karl Leopold

See: *Matthies, Charles Leopold*

MAURY, Dabney Herndon (1822-1900)

A nephew of the famed oceanographer Matthew Fontaine Maury, Virginian West Pointer (1846) Dabney H. Maury spent the last two years of the Civil War as a Confederate major general commanding the defenses of Mobile. Posted initially to the Regiment of Mounted Rifleman, he had served briefly the next year with the artillery and then rejoined his former unit. During the Mexican War he won a brevet and was wounded at Cerro Gordo. In the interwar years he taught at his alma mater and in 1860 transferred to the adjutant's office. On June 25, 1861, he was dismissed as a brevet captain for having "expressed treasonable designs." Joining the Confederacy, his assignments included: captain, Cavalry (1861); colonel and assistant adjutant general (1862); brigadier general, CSA (March 12, 1862); commanding Army of the West, Department #2 (June 27-July 3, 1862); commanding division, Price's (Army of the West) Corps, Army of West Tennessee, Department #2 (fall 1862); major general, CSA (November 4, 1862); commanding Provisional Division, 2nd Military District, Department of Mississippi and East Louisiana (December 1862-January 1863) commanding division, 2nd Military District, Department of Mississippi and East Louisiana (January-April 15, 1863); commanding Department of East Tennessee (April 25-May 12, 1863); commanding District of the Gulf, Department #2 (May-July 25, 1863); commanding Department of the Gulf (July 25, 1863-April 6, 1864); and commanding District of the Gulf, Department of Alabama, Mississippi and East Louisiana (April 6, 1864-May 4, 1865). Fighting at Pea Ridge as Earl Van Dorn's chief of staff, he won promotion to brigadier general and led a division at Corinth. At the end of the year he played a leading role in the defense of Vicksburg at Chickasaw Bayou. After serving for a few more months as a division commander at Vicksburg he was placed in command of the Department of East Tennessee, but the next month was transferred to Mobile where he spent the balance of the war. In designing the defensive works for the city and harbor he displayed great talent and only lost the city at the very end of the war. Financially ruined by the war, he became a teacher in the former Confederate capital. Interested in historical matters, he wrote widely and founded the Southern Historical Society. A man of principle he refused to be associated with the Louisiana Lottery, although he could have used the money. During a New Orleans yellow fever outbreak he risked his own health while working as a volunteer nurse. He also served as a diplomat in Colombia. (Maury, Dabney Herndon, *Recollections of a Virginian*)

MAURY, Matthew Fontaine (1806-1873)

In actuality the founder of the science of oceanography, Matthew F. Maury has been called the "Pathfinder of the Seas." Born near Fredericksburg, Virginia, he was raised in Tennessee before becoming a midshipman in the U.S. Navy at the age of 19. Having already published his *A New Theoretical and Practical Treatise on Navigation*, he was lamed in an accident and devoted the remainder of his prewar years to studying the sea and publishing his findings. His works included: *Wind and Current Chart of the North Atlantic*, *Abstract Log for the Use of American Navigators*, *A Scheme for Rebuilding Southern Commerce*, *Sailing Directions*, and, most famously, *The Physical Geography of the Sea*. Following his adopted state out of the Union, he resigned his commander's commission in 1861. On June 10, 1861, he was appointed a commander in the Confederate navy. Following court-martial duty he became chief of river and harbor defenses and was charged with mining the James River approaches to Richmond. After inventing the electric torpedo, or mine, he was sent to Europe to further his research in this new field. During his stay abroad he was also engaged in preparing commerce raiders for service on the high seas. Following the Confederacy's fall he joined the cabinet of Emperor Maximilian in Mexico and then returned to England. His final years were spent as a professor of meteorology. (Williams, Frances Leigh, *Matthew Fontaine Maury, Scientist of the Sea* and Corbin, Diana Fontaine Maury, *A Life of Matthew Fontaine Maury*)

MAXEY, Samuel Bell (1825-1895)

Giving up a state senate seat in Texas, Kentucky-born lawyer and West Pointer (1846) Samuel B. Maxey was named a major general by E. Kirby Smith, but this was never recognized by the Richmond authorities. He had won a brevet in Mexico before resigning in 1849 as a second lieutenant in the 7th Infantry in order to study law. His Confederate assignments included: colonel, 9th Texas (1861); brigadier general, CSA (March 7, 1862, to rank from the 4th); commanding Detached Brigade, 1st Corps, Army of the Mississippi (ca. May-July 1862); commanding brigade, 1st (Cheatham's) Division, Army of the Mississippi (July-August 15, 1862); commanding brigade, District of East Louisiana, Department of Mississippi and East Louisiana (late 1862-early May 1863); commanding brigade, attached to Loring's Division, Department of the West (May-June 1863); commanding brigade, French's Division, Department of the West (June-July 1863); commanding brigade, French's Division, Department of Mississippi and East Louisiana (July-ca. December 11, 1863); commanding Indian Territory, Trans-Mississippi Department (December 11, 1863-ca. April 1864); commanding cavalry division, District of Arkansas, Trans-Mississippi Department (ca. April-summer 1864); major general, CSA (by E. Kirby Smith, April 18, 1864); commanding 2nd (Texas) Cavalry Division, 1st Corps (or District of West Louisiana), Trans-Mississippi Department (summer 1864-February 14, 1865); commanding District of the Indian Territory, Trans-Mississippi Department (February

14-21, 1865); and commanding division, District of Texas, New Mexico and Arizona, Trans-Mississippi Department (April 7-May 26, 1865). As a brigadier general, he commanded a brigade around Corinth, Mississippi, and then in East Tennessee before being ordered to Port Hudson, Louisiana. With the pressure building on Vicksburg, he led his brigade northward to join Joseph E. Johnston at Jackson. Following the fall of Vicksburg he took part in the defense of Jackson. Late in the year he was ordered back across the Mississippi to reorganize the troops in the Indian Territory. Rewarded for this by Smith with a promotion, he was given a division first in Arkansas and then in Louisiana. Early in 1865 he returned briefly to the Indian Territory but finished the war commanding a division in his adopted state. After the war he was an attorney and U.S. senator. (Horton, Louise, *Samuel Bell Maxey: A Biography*)

MAXIMILIAN, Archduke (1832-1867)

In 1864 Archduke Maximilian of Austria was made emperor of Mexico by Napoleon III—and the French army then occupying the capital of Mexico City. His presence and that of the French military raised fears in the North that France might intervene in the Civil War or try to take advantage of it. These concerns affected military strategy, causing the postponement of Grant's plans to move on Mobile, so that a campaign could be launched into Texas. After the fall of the Confederacy, General Sheridan was dispatched with a sizable army to guard the line of the Rio Grande. However, once the French forces were withdrawn, the archduke was overthrown and executed.

MAXWELL, Augustus Emmett (1820-1902)

Georgia-born and Alabama-raised Florida lawyer and Democrat, Augustus E. Maxwell proved to be one of the staunchest supporters of the Davis administration—and especially of Secretary of the Navy Stephen R. Mallory—in the Confederate Senate. He had practiced law in Alabama for two years before moving to Florida where he served as attorney general, secretary of state, state legislator, and U.S. congressman. Elected to the Confederate Senate in November 1861, he was chairman of the Committee on Patents and also served on the Committees on: Commerce; Engrossment and Enrollment; Foreign Affairs (First Congress); Indian Affairs (Second Congress); and Naval Affairs (First Congress). He chaired a special investigatory committee to check on naval matters and Mallory came out of it looking good. Maxwell proved willing to support strong measures to win the war, wanting to draft speculators and concentrate on food production. After the Confederacy's fall, Maxwell served on the state supreme court before returning to private practice with Mallory. He later presided over the court and again returned to his practice.

MAXWELL, John (?-?)

The most successful confederate saboteur was John Maxwell of the shadowy organization known as "Captain Z. McDaniel's Company, Secret Service." The company was authorized by the War Department on February 29, 1864, and Maxwell would have joined some time after that date. Apparently members of company worked as individuals or in small teams in the torpedo service. Maxwell himself had devised a "horological" device, or time bomb. Under Captain McDaniel's orders, he left Richmond on July 26, 1864, headed for the Union supply depot at City Point. He was accompanied by a civilian accomplice, R.K. Dillard. Approaching the wharves, he and Maxwell went forward with a package which he induced a Negro dock worker to take upon a nearby ordnance boat, explaining that it was the captain's orders. An hour later, at just before noon on August 9, 1864, there was a tremendous explosion. Two million dollars in damage was done. Some 169 soldiers and civilians were dead or wounded. Supply buildings and 180 feet of wharf were demolished. Grant's nearby headquarters were showered with explosives and debris. The general was unharmed but some of his orderlies and staff officers were not so lucky. Maxwell and Dillard slipped back out of the Union lines and resumed spying activities along the river. The explosion was originally ruled an accident by the Union authorities until Maxwell's report was discovered in the captured rebel archives. He survived the war and in 1872, during Grant's presidency, he visited Grant's secretary and former staff officer, Horace Porter, in an unsuccessful effort to obtain patents on some of his inventions. He even described his adventure at City Point. (Stern, Philip Van Doren, *Secret Missions of the Civil War*)

MAYNARD, Edward (1813-1891)

His inability to pursue a military career—he was forced by ill health to drop out of West Point in his first year—did not prevent Edward Maynard from keeping up his interest in military matters. He studied dentistry, settled in Washington, D.C., and became one of the premier researchers in the field, first theorizing on the existence of dental fevers as early as 1836. But at the same time he tinkered with weapons, developing the Maynard Tape Primer which was a safe method for automatically feeding caps into a breech-loading firearm. He later designed his own breech-loading carbine, which was highly popular in both the military and sporting fields. He also developed a system for the conversion of old style muzzleloaders into more modern breechloaders. For his work in dentistry and weaponry he received awards and honors, both abroad—in Russia, Prussia, and Sweden—and at home.

MAYO, Robert Murphy (1836-1896)

When Robert M. Mayo offered his services to the South, his status as a graduate and faculty member of the Virginia Military Institute indicated that much could be expected from him, but he never made it to general officer, perhaps due to a fondness for the bottle. The native Virginian's assignments included: major, 47th Virginia (May 8, 1861); colonel, 47th Virginia (May 1, 1862); commanding Heth's (old) Brigade, Heth's Division, 3rd Corps, Army of Northern Virginia (July 3-19, 1863); commanding Walker's and Archer's brigades, Heth's Division, 3rd Corps, Army of Northern Virginia (May 9-August 19, 1864 and October 24, 1864-January 20, 1865); and commanding

Walker's (old) Brigade, Department of Richmond (January 20-February 1865). As a field officer he served at Mathias Point and in the siege at Yorktown. Promoted to command the regiment, he led it at Seven Pines, the Seven Days, 2nd Bull Run, Fredericksburg, and Chancellorsville. A wound received at 2nd Bull Run prevented him from taking part in the Maryland invasion. At Gettysburg he led the brigade, for some unexplained reason, in Pickett's Charge. Back in command of the regiment he served through the Bristoe, Mine Run, and Wilderness campaigns. Upon the wounding of General H.H. Walker at Spotsylvania, he took over command of that brigade and soon of Archer's as well. He then served at Cold Harbor and in the defense of Petersburg. In January 1865 the Virginia regiments of Walker's old command were transferred to the Department of Richmond where Mayo was soon replaced. One of the reasons he was never made a general may have been a July 8, 1863, incident in which he was charged and convicted of being drunk on duty. After the war he served in the state legislature and briefly in the U.S. Congress. (Freeman, Douglas S., *Lee's Lieutenants*)

MEADE, George Gordon (1815-1872)

The victor of Gettysburg, George G. Meade does not rank with the great captains of the Civil War in part because of his eclipse in the last year of the conflict by the presence of Grant with his army, and a journalistic conspiracy of silence. Born of American parents in Cadiz, Spain—where his father had run into financial and legal difficulties as a result of the Napoleonic Wars—he was appointed to West Point from Pennsylvania. Graduating in 1835, he served a year in the artillery before resigning to become a civil engineer. After some difficulty in finding employment he reentered the army in 1842 and earned a brevet in Mexico. His Civil War assignments included: captain, Topographical Engineers (since May 19, 1856); brigadier general, USV (August 31, 1861); commanding 2nd Brigade, McCall's Division, Army of the Potomac (October 3, 1861-March 13, 1862); commanding 2nd Brigade, 2nd Division, 1st Corps, Army of the Potomac (March 13-April 4, 1862); commanding 2nd Brigade, 2nd Division, Department of the

Gettysburg victor George G. Meade at his field headquarters. (NA)

Rappahannock (April 4-June 12, 1862); commanding 2nd Brigade, 3rd Division, 5th Corps, Army of the Potomac (June 18-30, 1862); major, Topographical Engineers (June 18, 1862); commanding 1st Brigade, 3rd Division, 3rd Corps, Army of Virginia (August 26-September 12, 1862); commanding 3rd Division, 1st Corps, Army of the Potomac (September 12-17 and September 29-December 25, 1862); commanding the corps (September 17-29, 1862); major general, USV (November 29, 1862); commanding 5th Corps, Army of the Potomac (December 25, 1862-January 26, 1863 and February 5-16 and February 28-June 28, 1863); commanding Center Grand Division, Army of the Potomac (January 1863); commanding Army of the Potomac (June 28, 1863-December 30, 1864 and January 11-June 27, 1865); brigadier general, USA (July 3, 1863); and major general, USA (August 18, 1864). Serving on a survey of the Great Lakes at the outbreak of the Civil War, he received a volunteer brigadier's star in the first summer of the war and was assigned to the division of Pennsylvania Reserves. After training and service near Washington and in northern Virginia, the command joined the Army of the Potomac on the Peninsula. During the Seven Days he fought at Beaver Dam Creek and Gaines' Mill before falling wounded at Glendale. He led his brigade at 2nd Bull Run, following his recovery, and the division at South Mountain and Antietam. At the latter he succeeded the wounded Hooker in command of the 1st Corps and received his second star before Fredericksburg. In that action his division broke through the Confederate right but was thrown back after his supports failed to arrive. Transferred to the direction of the 5th Corps, he briefly commanded the Center Grand Division after the Mud March until that cumbersome organization was disbanded. At Chancellorsville he led his corps well but was held back by Hooker's timidity. With the invasion of Pennsylvania, Meade was chosen to relieve Hooker in army command only three days before Gettysburg. Originally planning to fight farther to the rear along Pipe Creek, he dispatched General Winfield S. Hancock to Gettysburg—following the death of General John F. Reynolds—to determine if it would be an acceptable battlefield. Accepting that officer's opinion, he ordered a continued concentration there. During the next two days he masterfully shifted his troops from one threatened sector to another. He received the thanks of Congress and an appointment as a brigadier in the regulars. However, he soon came in for criticism for allowing Lee to escape to Virginia without another battle. His handling of the Bristoe and Mine Run campaigns was not shining. In the spring of 1864 newly-appointed General-in-Chief U.S. Grant set up his headquarters with Meade's army. This cumbersome arrangement worked out surprisingly well. However, since Meade was known for his temper and had come into conflict with a number of correspondents, there was an agreement not to mention him in dispatches except in reference to setbacks. He fought through the Overland and Petersburg campaigns, earning Grant's respect and being considered for command in the Shenandoah. At Grant's request he was advanced to major general in the regular army. He served in the Appomattox Campaign but feltslighted by the reports which seemed to give all the credit to Grant and Sheridan. Mustered out of the volunteer service, he continued in the regular army, performing Reconstruction duty in the South, and died while in command of the Division of the Atlantic. (Cleaves, Freeman, *Meade of Gettysburg*)

MEADE, Richard Kidder (ca. 1836-1862)

Virginia-born West Pointer (1857) Richard Meade's divided loyalties led him to fight for both the Union and the Confederacy. A second lieutenant in the engineers, Meade found himself a newly assigned engineer in charge at Castle Pinckney in Charleston Harbor when South Carolina seceded on December 20, 1860. A few days later he joined Major Robert Anderson's two companies of artillery in the move to uncompleted Fort Sumter. When the *Star of the West* made its attempt to reprovision the garrison on January 9, 1861, Meade urged Anderson not to fire on the batteries that were in action against the vessel because, "It will bring civil war on us." The guns remained silent. When the South Carolinians made their later demand for the surrender of the fort itself, Meade, remembering his oath and his debt for his military training, voted against complying. During the bombardment of the fort, Meade was busy directing the manufacture of cartridge bags from clothing, sheets, and paper. After the surrender of the fort Meade went with the garrison to New York but then resigned, returned to his native state, and became a captain of engineers in Confederate service. In this capacity, he worked on the Confederate works on the Peninsula, at Drewry's Bluff, and in North Carolina where he was engaged in the battle of New Bern. In the spring of 1862, he was promoted to major and died of disease on July 31, 1862. (Swanberg, W.A., *First Blood*)

MEAGHER, Thomas Francis (1823-1867)

With his fierce Irish nationalism, Thomas F. Meagher managed to get himself into difficulties on both sides of the Atlantic. Born in County Waterford, Ireland, he opposed British rule and was exiled to Tasmania in 1849. He fled to the United States in 1852, eventually settling in New York, where he was active in the Irish independence movement. Raising an Irish Zouave company in 1861, he joined the Union army, where his assignments included: major, 69th New York Militia (ca. April 20, 1861); brigadier general, USV (February 3, 1862); commanding 2nd ("Irish") Brigade, Sumner's Division (November 25, 1861-March 13, 1862); and commanding 2nd ("Irish") Brigade, 1st Division, 2nd Corps, Army of the Potomac (March 13-June 28, June 29-July 16, August 8-September 17, September 18-December 20, 1862, and February 18-May 8, 1863). He served as a field officer at 1st Bull Run before being mustered out with his militia regiment on August 3, 1861. That winter he organized the Irish Brigade which was assigned to Sumner's Division. Early the following year his commission as a brigadier came through. He led the Irishmen in the fighting at Seven Pines and during most of the Seven Days. At Antietam he was injured in the fall of his wounded horse but was able to return to duty the following day. At Fredericksburg his command was slaughtered in the assaults on Marye's Heights. Meanwhile he had become embroiled in army politics. Himself

Irish Brigade commander Thomas F. Meagher. (NA)

a Democrat, he was highly critical of political—read "Republican"—generals. This may have contributed to the later refusal by the authorities to grant him permission to recruit for his own ranks. After the battle of Chancellorsville he resigned on May 14, 1863, in protest over this refusal and the proposal that the regiments of his brigade be distributed among other commands. His resignation was rejected on December 23, 1863, and he returned to duty, holding minor commands in the Western theater. He finally resigned on May 15, 1865. After serving over a year as acting governor of Montana he fell off a boat on the Missouri River and drowned. He had been drinking. (Conyngham, David Powers, *The Irish Brigade and Its Campaigns* and Cavanagh, Michael, *Memoirs of General Thomas Francis Meagher*)

MEDARY, Samuel (1801-1864)

Ohio Copperhead Samuel Medary paid the price for his antiwar views in the sacking of his *Crisis* newspaper office by a "mob" which was in fact part of the 2nd Ohio Cavalry. Born into a Pennsylvania Quaker family, he became an agitator, edited a number of periodicals, and served in the state legislature. In the late 1850s he was territorial governor first of Minnesota and then of troubled Kansas. There he backed the questionable Lecompton Constitution and tried to capture John Brown. In fact he had long supported the positions of the South. He was expansionist in outlook with regards to Texas, Mexico, Cuba, and Oregon. Some claim that he even originated the cry, "Fifty-four Forty or Fight." Early in 1861 he founded the *Columbus Crisis* in which he declared that only the states of a united confederacy could abolish the institution of slavery. Having been a prewar Democrat, he backed Vallandigham and later McClellan. Finally, on the night of March 5, 1863, some 50 or 75 Union cavalrymen invaded his premises destroying and carrying off his equipment. When he died in late 1864, he was under charges of treason.

MEDICINE BOTTLE (?-1864)

Through a violation of international law Santee Sioux chief Medicine Bottle lost his life on the gallows for his part in the Sioux uprising of 1862 in Minnesota. He had led one of the war parties under Little Crow in the attacks on New Ulm and Fort Ridgely. When it became apparent that the Indians did not have enough strength to win against the increasing concentration of troops, Medicine Bottle fled to Canada where he assumed himself to be safe. This was not the case, however, as a Minnesota cavalry battalion under Major Edwin A.C. Hatch approached the international frontier in December 1864. Hatch dispatched a lieutenant across the line. This officer, working with an American and two Canadians, drugged the alcohol they gave to Medicine Bottle and another Santee leader, Shakopee. When they fell asleep they were bound, placed on a dogsled, and spirited across the border. Tried on flimsy evidence, the pair was hanged in early 1864. (Brown, Dee, *Bury My Heart At Wounded Knee*)

MEIGS, John Rodgers (ca. 1842-1864)

The only son of Quartermaster General Montgomery Meigs, John Meigs suffered a controversial death. Entering West Point in 1859, he was on furlough in Washington in the summer of 1861 and accompanied the army in its march to the 1st Battle of Bull Run where he served as a volunteer aide to Colonel I.B. Richardson. Returning to the academy he was graduated at the top of his class in 1863. Appointed a first lieutenant in the engineers he served in West Virginia and the Shenandoah Valley, including staff duty with Generals B.F. Kelley and R.C. Schenck. In July 1863 he was in command of a detachment that was manning some "railroad monitors," or armored trains. He was named chief engineer on General Sheridan's staff when that officer came to the valley. Becoming popular with his new commander, he fought at the battles of 3rd Winchester and Fisher's Hill, earning brevets for each action. On October 3, 1864, Meigs was killed near Dayton, Virginia, in a fight with three rebel scouts. Sheridan claimed that they were in Union uniforms and Meigs had already been captured when killed. General Early claimed after the war that the scouts were in their own uniforms and that Meigs was offering resistance. Sheridan, in his outrage, burned numerous houses in the area in retaliation. (Weigley, Russell F., *Quartermaster General of the Union Army: A Biography of Montgomery Meigs*)

MEIGS, Montgomery Cunningham (1816-1892)

Replacing General Joseph E. Johnston, who went over to the Confederacy, West Pointer (1836) Montgomery Meigs served as

Quartermaster General Montgomery C. Meigs. (NA)

quartermaster general of the Union Army throughout the war. Graduating fifth in his class, Meigs had served for a year in the artillery before transferring to the engineers. During the antebellum period he was in charge of construction of the House and Senate wings and the dome for the nation's capitol, as well as the Potomac Aqueduct. By the time of the firing on Fort Sumter, Meigs was serving as a captain. His later appointments included: colonel, 11th Infantry (May 14, 1861); and brigadier general, USA, and quartermaster general (May 15, 1861). He served as head of the department until 1882, providing the armies in the field with all kinds of supplies except those with which they ate or fought. His responsibilities also included transportation by railroad, wagon, and ship of both the army and its supplies. His department also oversaw the operations of the Military Telegraph Corps. He was brevetted major general in the regular army on July 5, 1864. In the postwar period he designed the Pension Office Building in Washington. After the war he was bitter toward friends who had fought for the Confederacy having lost his son in the Shenandoah Valley fighting and believing him to have been murdered after his capture. Meigs died 10 years after his retirement from the army. (Weigley, Russell F., *Quartermaster General of the Union Army: A Biography of Montgomery Meigs*)

MEMMINGER, Christopher Gustavus (1803-1888)

As the Confederacy's first secretary of the treasury, Christopher G. Memminger faced a hopeless situation aggravated by poor relations with Congress. A native of Wurttemberg, in Germany, Memminger's father had been killed in the duke's army, and he was soon an orphan in South Carolina where his widowed mother had brought him. Comfortably adopted, he studied law and became a leader in education. Despite his hatred for the abolitionists he didn't favor secession until Harpers Ferry was attacked by John Brown. He signed South Carolina's secession ordinance and became chairman of the Provisional Confederate Congress' Committee on Commercial Affairs. Under the provisional constitution he was able to keep his congressional seat when he became a member of the cabinet on February 21, 1861. For three and a half years he struggled with the dismal financial situation of the South. Despite unfriendly meddling with his plans by Congress, he retained the faith of Jefferson Davis of whom he was an unwavering follower. He opposed the embargo of cotton shipments to force foreign recognition, realizing that Southern credit would evaporate. Blamed for the mess by many in and out of the Congress—which he had left at the end of the Provisional Government—he resigned on June 15, 1864. In 1867 he was pardoned; he resumed his law practice and favored the establishment of educational opportunities for the freedmen. (Capers, Henry D., *The Life and Times of C.G. Memminger*)

MENDENHALL, Elizabeth (?-?)

A capable organizer for the United States Sanitary Commission, Elizabeth Mendenhall was able to raise a quarter of a million dollars in January 1864 to aid the Union troops in the field. She had begun her war work early in 1862 in a hospital in her native Cincinnati. Having joined the commission she was the driving force behind the Great Western Sanitary Fair that raised so much for the aid of the Union soldier.

MENDENHALL, John (?-1892)

In a typical example of the vagaries of the system of brevet promotions, artillerist John Mendenhall did not receive one for his greatest wartime service—at Stone's River—but did for two other actions. The Indianan had graduated from West Point in 1851 and had briefly been assigned to the dragoons before transferring to the artillery the following year. His wartime assignments included: first lieutenant, 4th Artillery (since March 12, 1856); captain, 4th Artillery (July 3, 1861); chief of Artillery and Topographical Engineer, Left Wing, 14th Corps, Army of the Cumberland (ca. November 5, 1862-January 9, 1863); chief of Artillery and Topographical Engineer, 21st Corps, Army of the Cumberland (January 9-October 10, 1863); major and judge advocate, USV (March 17, 1863); assistant to chief of Artillery, Army of the Cumberland (fall 1863); chief of Artillery and judge advocate, 4th Corps, Army of the Cumberland (November 19, 1863-February 27, 1864); lieutenant colonel and assistant inspector general (February 27-September 26, 1864); assistant inspector general, Army of the Cumberland (February 27-September 26, 1864); inspector of Artillery, Department of the Cumberland (late 1864-February 12, 1865); and commanding Light Artillery Reserve, Department of the Cumberland (February 12-July 1865). As part of

Buell's army, he commanded Batteries H and M, 4th Artillery, at Shiloh and in the advance on Corinth. In the former he earned a brevet as major. On January 2, 1863, at Murfreesboro, he gathered 58 artillery pieces and played a major role in the repulse of John C. Breckinridge's attack. He earned another brevet for his service on Thomas L. Crittenden's staff at Chickamauga and then served in staff positions through the Chattanooga and Atlanta campaigns. Back in Tennessee, he fought at Nashville and finished the war in charge of the department's reserve artillery. Mustered out of the volunteer service on October 23, 1865, he was brevetted colonel for his war service. Remaining in the regular establishment, he died as colonel, 2nd Artillery.

MENDELL, George Henry (?-1902)

Serving the Union's Army of the Potomac was the regular establishment's only engineering battalion, and it was much of the time under the command of George H. Mendell. A Pennsylvanian and West Pointer (1852), he had served in the topographical engineers before the war. His wartime assignments included: first lieutenant, Topographical Engineers (since July 1, 1856); captain, Topographical Engineers (September 28, 1861); captain, Engineers (consolidation of the two engineering branches March 3, 1863); and major, Engineers (August 15, 1864). As a topographical engineer, he served the early part of the war on staff assignments. Transferred to the engineers, he was soon in charge of the four-company battalion which served with the Army of the Potomac in the Gettysburg Campaign. However, being at Taneytown, Maryland, the battalion missed the main battle. Mendell did command the battalion through the Wilderness, Spotsylvania, Cold Harbor, and the beginning of the siege at Petersburg. For this series of actions he wasbrevetted lieutenant colonel and, for the war, colonel. He remained in the army until his 1895 retirement as a full colonel of engineers.

MERCER, Hugh Weedon (1808-1877)

Poor health forced Confederate Brigadier General Hugh W. Mercer—grandson of Revolutionary War General Hugh Mercer who was mortally wounded at Princeton—from the field. The Virginian West Pointer (1828) had served for seven years before resigning in 1835 as a first lieutenant in the 2nd Artillery. A bank cashier at the outbreak of the Civil War, he joined the Confederacy and his assignments included: colonel, 1st Georgia (early 1861); brigadier general, CSA (October 29, 1861); commanding brigade, District of Georgia, Department of South Carolina and Georgia (early 1862-May 28, 1862); commanding 2nd Military District of South Carolina, Department of South Carolina, Georgia and Florida (May 28, 1862); commanding 1st Military District of South Carolina, Department of South Carolina, Georgia and Florida (May 28-June 1862); commanding District of Georgia, Department of South Carolina, Georgia and Florida (June 1862-April 26, 1864); commanding brigade, Walker's Division, Hardee's Corps, Army of Tennessee (May-July 22, 1864); and commanding the division (July 22-24, 1864). Most of his early war service came in the Savannah area, with a brief stint in South Carolina. Just before the start of the Atlanta Campaign he took command of a brigade in the Army of Tennessee. When the division commander, William H.T. Walker, was killed at the battle of Atlanta, Mercer took over the larger unit. But this was broken up two days later and about this time Mercer's health broke. He soon returned to Savannah for the balance of the war and with his field career at an end. He was in banking and trade in Savannah and Baltimore after the war before moving to Baden Baden, Germany, in the early 1870s.

MERCIER, (Édouard) Henri (1816-1886)

A career foreign service officer, and the French ambassador to the United States during the first portion of the Civil War, Henri Mercier was frequently considered to be pro-Southern. He had been born in Baltimore when his father was stationed there as consul for Louis XVIII but received his education in France and Switzerland. He managed to survive the transitions in French government from monarchy to republic to monarchy while serving in diplomatic missions to Dresden, Athens, and Stockholm. He took up his Washington duties in July 1860, at the peak of the sectional crisis. Closely attuned to the policies of Napoleon III, he favored French mediation efforts and joint recognition, with Great Britain, of the Confederacy. He also proposed a common market for the United and Confederate States which would have allowed commercial unity while providing the necessary political separation. Despite his leanings toward the South—he even visited Richmond in 1862—he developed a respectful and friendly relationship with Secretary of State Seward. Seward even congratulated Mercier on a later appointment. The Frenchman had long desired a transfer and finally got it in December 1863 after it became apparent that a mediation effort would not be acceptable to Washington. He left as the problem over Mexico was developing and later served in Madrid until the collapse of France in the Franco-Prussian War. (Carroll, Daniel B., *Henri Mercier and the American Civil War*)

MEREDITH, Solomon (1810-1875)

Already one of the older field commanders, Solomon Meredith was forced by two wounds to serve in more quiet posts and district assignments late in the war. A native of North Carolina, he spent his adult life in Indiana where he was highly respected as a state legislator and law officer. Appointed to a regimental command at the outbreak of the Civil War, his assignments included: colonel, 19th Indiana (July 29, 1861); brigadier general, USV (October 6, 1863); commanding 4th ("Iron") Brigade, 1st Division, 1st Corps, Army of the Potomac (November 26-December 13, 1862 and March 1-June 16, 1863); commanding the division (February 27-March 1 and November 13, 1863); commanding 1st ("Iron") Brigade, 1st Division, 1st Corps, Army of the Potomac (June 16-July 2, 1863); commanding District of Western Kentucky, Department of the Ohio (September 11, 1864-February 10, 1865); and commanding District of Western Kentucky, Department of Kentucky (February 10-May 21, 1865). His regiment was

Part of the diplomatic corps on an outing in New York. Henri Mercier is fifth from the right while Secretary of State William H. Seward sits, hat in hand. British envoy Lord Lyons stands next to Mercier and directly behind Seward. (NA)

assigned to the only all-Midwestern brigade in the Army of the Potomac. While serving with Pope's army of Virginia, Meredith saw his first large action. In the fighting in which the brigade earned its nickname as the "Iron Brigade," Groveton, he fell severely wounded. When he returned to duty he wore the star of a brigadier general and took charge of the brigade. He led it at Fredericksburg and was later briefly in command of the division. His brigade had a limited role at Chancellorsville, but on the first day at Gettysburg it was heavily engaged in the early fighting west of the town. In the conflict he was again wounded and relinquished command early the next day. In November he commanded the division for a day, but he was soon sent to command the post at Cairo, Illinois. He finished the war in Paducah, commanding in western Kentucky. Brevetted major general for his war services, he was mustered out on May 22, 1865, and was for a couple of years the Montana territorial surveyor general.

Gettysburg veteran Solomon Meredith. (NA)

MEREDITH, Sullivan Amory (1816-1874)

Severely wounded at 2nd Bull Run, Philadelphia native Sullivan A. Meredith was appointed a brigadier general in the Union army three months later but never again served in the field. The businessman had sailed to China twice before joining the army. His assignments included: colonel, 10th Pennsylvania (April 26, 1861); colonel, 56th Pennsylvania

(March 6, 1862); and brigadier general, USV (November 29, 1862). With his initial three-months regiment he served under Patterson in the lower Shenandoah Valley before being mustered out on August 1, 1861. Taking command of a three-years unit in early 1862, he was stationed around Washington and in northern Virginia until his unit became part of John Pope's Army of Virginia. Having missed the battle of Cedar Mountain, he was wounded at the head of his men at 2nd Bull Run. Recovering sufficiently for limited duty, he was stationed at Fortress Monroe as an exchange agent from July 1863 until January 1864 when he was relieved by Benjamin F. Butler. Sent to Missouri to report to William S. Rosecrans, he was not given a command there either, and he spent the rest of the war awaiting orders. He was mustered out on August 24, 1865, without the customary brevet of major general for the war. He then settled in Buffalo and engaged in the drug business.

MERRITT, Wesley (1834-1910)

Within five years of graduating from West Point (1860) Wesley Merritt was a major general of volunteers. Posted to the dragoons, the New York City-born and Illinois-raised soldier served in Utah until the outbreak of the Civil War. His assignments included: brevet second lieutenant, 2nd Dragoons (July 1, 1860); second lieutenant, 2nd Dragoons (January 28, 1861); first lieutenant, 2nd Dragoons (May 13, 1861); adjutant, 2nd Dragoons (July 1, 1861); first lieutenant, 2nd Cavalry (change of designation August 3, 1861); adjutant, 2nd Cavalry (August 3, 1861-January 1, 1862); aide-de-camp, Cavalry Reserve, Army of the Potomac (February-July 5, 1862); captain, 2nd Cavalry (April 5, 1862); Mustering and Ordnance Officer, Cavalry Corps, Army of the Potomac (April-May 1863); commanding Reserve Brigade, 1st Division, Cavalry Corps, Army of the Potomac (June 28-August 12, September 12-November 21, 1863, April 10-May 7, and May 25-August 6, 1864); brigadier general, USV (June 29, 1863); commanding the division (August 15-September 15, 1863, November 21, 1863-April 10, 1864, and May 7-25, 1864); commanding 1st Division, Cavalry Corps, Army of the Shenandoah (August 6-November 13, November 28-December 31, 1864, and January 15-26, 1865); commanding the corps (January 26-March 25, 1865); commanding Cavalry Corps, Army of the Potomac (March 25-May 22, 1865); and major general, USV (April 1, 1865). Returning to the East from Utah, he served as an aide to Philip St. George Cooke during the Peninsula Campaign. Again a staff officer, he led a 50-man detachment on a bridge-destroying mission during the raid of General George Stoneman during the Chancellorsville Campaign. His phenomenal rise was highlighted by his promotion from captain to brigadier general of volunteers just before the battle of Gettysburg. There he commanded the Reserve Cavalry Brigade on the southern flank and earned a regular army brevet. He participated in the Bristoe and Mine Run campaigns, at times in charge of a division. Early in the Overland Campaign he succeeded to command of the division and earned brevets at Yellow Tavern and Haw's Shop. Again commanding the Reserve Brigade, he fought at Cold Harbor and in the early stages of the Petersburg siege. Transferred to the Shenandoah Valley, he commanded the division and won the brevet of major general of volunteers for 3rd Winchester and Fisher's Hill and also fought at Cedar Creek. Succeeding to corps command he followed Sheridan back to the Petersburg lines and won the brevet of brigadier general in the regular army for Five Forks. The regular brevet of major general followed for the Appomattox Campaign during which he had received his second star in the volunteer service. Mustered out of the volunteers on February 1, 1866, he continued in the regular establishment principally in Indian operations and as commandant at the military academy. By the time of the Spanish-American War he was a full, regular army major general and received the surrender of Manila along with Admiral Dewey. (Alberts, Don E., *Brandy Station to Manila Bay: A Biography of Wesley Merritt*)

MERSY, August (?-1866)

Serving throughout the Civil War with the Army of the Tennessee, German native August Mersy emerged with the brevet of brigadier general for the war. His assignments included: captain, 9th Illinois (April 25, 1861); lieutenant colonel, 9th Illinois (April 26, 1861); lieutenant colonel, 9th Illinois (three-years unit July 26, 1861); colonel, 9th Illinois (September 5, 1861); and commanding in the Army of the Tennessee: 2nd Brigade, 2nd Division, District of Corinth (October 3-24, 1862); 2nd Brigade, District of Corinth, 13th Corps (October 24-December 18, 1862); 2nd Brigade, District of Corinth, 17th Corps (December 18, 1862-January 20, 1863); 2nd Brigade, District of Corinth, 16th Corps (January 20-March 20, 1863); 2nd Brigade, 2nd Division, Left Wing, 16th Corps (March 18-August 12, 1863, September 12, 1863-April 22, 1864, and May 23-July 24, 1864); also the wing (August 7-September 9, 1863); and the division (August 12-September 12, 1863). His initial three-months unit was mustered out on July 24, 1861, but was reorganized two days later. The unit fought at Fort Donelson and Shiloh with Mersy as colonel. It then proceeded to the slow advance on Corinth, Mississippi, and at the battle there the next fall he succeeded to command of the brigade. Following participation in Grant's unsuccessful drive on Vicksburg via central Mississippi, the regiment was mounted on March 15, 1863. Taking part in the Atlanta Campaign, Mersy was in charge of a brigade during much of the operation, but on August 20, 1864, he was mustered out of the service. He received his brevet early the next year.

MERVINE, William (1791-1868)

A career naval officer, Pennsylvanian William Mervine served the first part of the Civil War in command of the blockade along the Gulf coast. After entering the navy in 1809 as a midshipman, he had fought along the Great Lakes in the War of 1812, rising to the rank of lieutenant, and was appointed a captain in 1841. He was given command of the Gulf Blockading Squadron in the first year of the Civil War, the next year was promoted to commodore, and the year after the war's close was named a rear admiral. He died two years later.

METZER, Frederick H.

See: *Dyer, Frederick Henry*

MICHIE, Peter Smith (1839-1901)

Although he didn't graduate from West Point until the Civil War was half over, Scottish-born Peter S. Michie still managed to emerge from the conflict with the regular army brevet of brigadier general. Having settled as a child in Ohio, he received his appointment from that state and was number two in the 1863 class at the military academy. Accordingly he was posted to the engineers and his assignments included: first lieutenant, Engineers (June 11, 1863); lieutenant colonel and assistant adjutant general (March 23-June 6, 1865); and captain, Engineers (November 23, 1865). His early service came in the operations against Charleston and in Florida. Joining Butler's command in Virginia, he was soon placed in charge of the Dutch Gap Canal. This was an attempt to outflank Confederate obstructions and gunboats on the James River. Utilizing mostly black troops for the digging, the project was not completed in time to affect the security of Richmond, the city having already fallen. Nonetheless Michie was brevetted brigadier general for his work in front of Richmond and Petersburg in 1864. After the war he performed routine engineering duties until 1871 when he became a professor in philosophy at his alma mater. He served for the three decades until his death. Also engaging in the writing of military history, he authored biographies of Emory Upton and George McClellan and a collective work on coastal defenders. He also wrote on scientific subjects.

MICHIGAN BRIDGET

See: *Divers, Bridget*

MILES, Dixon Stansbury (?-1862)

If he had survived the Union capitulation of Harpers Ferry in the fall of 1862, professional soldier Dixon S. Miles would probably have been tried for his role in the disaster and probably would not have gotten off as easily as in his previous court of inquiry. He had graduated from West Point in 1824 and been posted to the infantry where he earned two brevets during the Mexican War. His Civil War-era assignments included: colonel, 2nd Infantry (since January 19, 1859); commanding 4th Brigade, 1st Division, Department of Pennsylvania (July 1861); commanding 5th Division, Army of Northeastern Virginia (July 1861); commanding Railroad Brigade, Middle Department (March 22-July 22, 1862); and commanding Railroad Brigade, 8th Corps, Middle Department (July 22-September 15, 1862). After a brief period of service with Patterson's army he took part in the advance on Manassas. His own division was left in a supporting position at Centerville during the battle of 1st Bull Run, but he attempted to exercise control over Colonel I.B. Richardson's Brigade of another division. Richardson later reported Miles to have been drunk at the time, and a subsequent court of inquiry found the charge justified but considered further proceedings to be detrimental to the army. So in March 1862 Miles was posted to duty along the Baltimore and Ohio Railroad. Stationed at Harpers Ferry, he was slated to be superseded by General Julius White, but at the same time Stonewall Jackson was advancing upon the post. White deferred assuming command due to Miles' having a greater knowledge of the vicinity. Miles made a rather poor disposition of his 12,000 troops which, in effect, left them in a trap. Miles himself was mortally wounded as the surrender was being arranged. If he had lived he probably would have been arrested. As it was, White was arrested but later cleared.

Dixon S. Miles, loser of Harpers Ferry. (NA)

MILES, Nelson Appleton (1834-1925)

With no formal military training Nelson A. Miles entered the Union army during the Civil War and rose to be the U.S. Army's commander in chief by the Spanish-American War. The Massachusetts native had received some education in military matters from a retired French colonel while working as a store clerk in Boston. His Civil War assignments included: first lieutenant, 22nd Massachusetts (September 9, 1861); aide-de-camp, 1st Brigade, 1st Division, 2nd Corps, Army of the Potomac (May-June 1862); lieutenant colonel, 61st New York (May 31, 1862); colonel, 61st New York (September 30, 1862); commanding 1st Brigade, 1st Division, 2nd Corps, Army of the Potomac (July 4-19, July 28-December 25, 1863, and

March 25-July 29, 1864); brigadier general, USV (May 12, 1864); commanding the division (July 29, 1864-February 15, 1865 and February 25-May 20, 1865); commanding the corps (February 17-25, 1865); and major general, USV (October 21, 1865). Serving on Oliver O. Howard's staff on the Peninsula, he fought at Yorktown and was wounded at Seven Pines. Named to a lieutenant colonelcy in a New York regiment, he went on to fight in the Seven Days. At Antietam he succeeded the wounded Francis C. Barlow in charge of both his own and the 64th New York regiments. Named a full colonel, he commanded the two regiments at Fredericksburg and was again wounded. Wounded a third time at Chancellorsville—he was to receive a regular army brevet for this in 1867—he did not return to duty until the day after Gettysburg when he took charge of the brigade. This he led in the Bristoe and Mine Run campaigns. After fighting at the Wilderness he won another 1867 brevet for the Union breakthrough at the "Bloody Angle" of Spotsylvania. From the date of this action, May 12, 1864, he was named a brigadier general of volunteers. He then fought at Cold Harbor and during the Petersburg siege operations. During the latter he was particularly distinguished at Ream's Station, for which he was brevetted major general of volunteers. At times in charge of the division, and briefly of the corps, he served to the end of the siege and in the subsequent Appomattox Campaign. In charge of Fortress Monroe at the close of the war, he served as the jailer of Jefferson Davis, and has been criticized for the harshness of the confinement but appears to have been acting under War Department directives. Since he had determined upon a military career, he apparently did not wish to question orders. In the 1866 expansion of the regular service he was named to command the new 40th Infantry, a black regiment, and was mustered out of the volunteers on September 1, 1866, as a major general. Rising steadily in rank, he became commander in chief in 1895 and a lieutenant general five years later. Much of his service was on the western frontier, and he was involved in the shameful treatment of Geronimo after his surrender. In 1892 he was awarded the Congressional Medal of Honor for his actions at Chancellorsville. During the war with Spain he was mostly involved in organizational matters but did personally lead the U.S. forces into Puerto Rico. Coming into conflict with President Theodore Roosevelt, he was retired in 1903. He then served as head of numerous veterans' organizations and became something of a historical and military writer; his *Personal Recollections* had already appeared in 1897. (Johnson, Virginia Weisel, *The Unregimented General: A Biography of Nelson A. Miles*)

MILES, William Porcher (1822-1899)

While serving as South Carolina's 2nd District congressman and chairman of the Committee on Military Affairs, William P. Miles was a steady supporter of Jefferson Davis, only questioning—late in the war—his commitment to the defense of Charleston. A native of the first state to secede, he practiced law for a time before entering education and politics. He served in Congress from 1857 until just before his state seceded. As chairman of the Committee on Foreign Relations, he was a member of the secession convention and signed the document which took South Carolina out of the Union. He sat in the Provisional and both regular congresses. During the crisis in Charleston Harbor, he was sent by Beauregard to arrange Fort Sumter's submission. During the Provisional Congress he sat on the committees on: Commercial Affairs; Flag and Seal; Military Affairs; and Printing. During the regular congresses he chaired the Committee on Military Affairs but gave up the rest of his committee assignments. On war matters he was an unwavering supporter of the president and of an all-out effort, despite being a member of the pro-Beauregard anti-Bragg faction. He did oppose the suspension of the writ of habeas corpus and other Davis-proposed issues less connected with his specialty. After the war he was president of the University of South Carolina and ran his father-in-law's Louisiana sugar plantation.

MILLER, Abram O. (?-?)

As a regimental commander and sometime brigade commander of John T. Wilder's brigade of mounted infantry, Ohio native Abram O. Miller took part in some of the principal mounted operations of the war and was brevetted brigadier general for his services. His assignments included: first lieutenant, 10th Indiana (April 25, 1861); captain, 10th Indiana (June 23, 1861); captain, 10th Indiana (three-years unit September 18, 1861); major, 10th Indiana (September 18, 1861); lieutenant colonel, 10th Indiana (April 5, 1862); colonel, 72nd Indiana (August 24, 1862); commanding 40th Brigade, 12th Division, Army of the Ohio (September-November 5, 1862); commanding 2nd Brigade, 5th Division, Center, 14th Corps, Army of the Cumberland (November 5, 1862-January 9, 1863); commanding 1st Brigade, 4th Division, 14th Corps, Army of the Cumberland (July 10-August 10, 1863); commanding 3rd Brigade, 2nd Division, Cavalry Corps, Army of the Cumberland (December 25, 1863-January 28, 1864 and June 14-October 29, 1864); commanding 3rd Brigade, 2nd Division, Cavalry Corps, Military Division of the Mississippi (October 29-November 6, 1864); and commanding 1st Brigade, 2nd Division, Cavalry Corps, Military Division of the Mississippi (November 6, 1864-April 2, 1865). After brief service in western Virginia his three-months unit was mustered out on August 6, 1861, but was reorganized the next month. By the time that it fought at Mill Springs, Miller was a field officer. After serving in the advance on Corinth, Mississippi, he transferred to the command of a new regiment with which he was engaged in operations against John Hunt Morgan during the Murfreesboro fighting. The regiment was mounted along with the rest of its brigade on March 17, 1863, and Miller led it in the Tullahoma Campaign and at Chickamauga. In the midst of the Atlanta Campaign he took charge of the brigade. In the final days of the war he was wounded during Wilson's raid in Alabama and Georgia. He was mustered out on June 26, 1865.

MILLER, James M. (1816-1865)

One of the most horrid aspects of warfare occurs when a commander feels that he must resort to retaliatory executions. James M. Miller was the first victim of one such order. At the age of 48 he was captured while serving in the 3rd South Carolina Reserves Battalion opposing Sherman's march through that state. Atrocities had been occurring for previous several days, and Sherman had announced that for every Union soldier murdered he would execute one prisoner of war. On February 28, 1865, Private Robert M. Woodruff of the 30th Illinois was found with a crushed skull. On March 2 some prisoners were forced to draw lots. An hour later Miller, a father of nine, was dead. It later turned out that the Union soldier had been killed by a slave while the soldier was looting the plantation of the slave's master.

MILLER, John Franklin (1831-1913)

It is somewhat ironic that after having fought as a Union brevet major general to free the slaves, Senator John F. Miller was a leading proponent of the exclusion laws and other anti-Chinese measures. A native Indiana lawyer and state legislator, he took the field in 1861 at the head of a regiment of volunteers. His assignments included: colonel, 29th Indiana (August 27, 1861); commanding 7th Independent Brigade, Army of the Ohio (September 14-November 5, 1862); commanding 3rd Brigade, 2nd Division, Center, 14th Corps, Army of the Cumberland (November 5, 1862-January 9, 1863); commanding 3rd Brigade, 2nd Division, 14th Corps, Army of the Cumberland (January 9-June 9, 1863); brigadier general, USV (April 10, 1864, to rank from January 5); commanding Post of Nashville, District of Nashville, Department of the Cumberland (June 1864-March 1865) and commanding Post of Nashville, District of Middle Tennessee, Department of the Cumberland (March-July 1865). It is sometimes stated that he fought at Shiloh on the second day, but the 29th Indiana is listed as having been commanded by its lieutenant colonel. He did, however, fight at Murfreesboro where he sustained his first wound while in command of a brigade. On June 24, 1863, he was again wounded at Liberty Gap, Tennessee. This injury seems to have kept him from active service for a year and even then he had to be assigned to post duty. Stationed at Nashville, having been named a brigadier general during his recuperation, he took part in the battle there and won the brevet of major general. Resigning on September 25, 1865, and having once practiced law in California, he returned to the West Coast and engaged in the Alaskan fur trade. His last six years were spent in the U.S. Senate.

MILLER, Samuel Freeman (1816-1890)

The death of Supreme Court Justice Peter V. Daniel created the vacancy which made Samuel F. Miller the second Lincoln appointee to the bench and the first ever from west of the Mississippi River—despite his lack of judicial experience. The Kentucky-born doctor-turned-lawyer freed his slaves and moved to Iowa when he realized that his hopes for gradual emancipation would not be forthcoming in Kentucky. In Iowa he was one of the founders of the state Republican Party and held minor political offices. His work was rewarded by the judicial appointment on July 16, 1862, and confirmed the same day by a voice vote in the Senate. During the Civil War he was a staunch supporter of the Union cause and supported the narrow majority in the *Prize Cases*. In the Tilden-Hayes dispute in 1876-77 he voted with the Republican majority in supporting the latter for the presidency. At the time of his death he had been on the bench for 28 years. (Fairman, Charles, *Mr. Justice Miller and the Supreme Court 1862-1890*)

MILLER, Stephen (1816-1881)

After presiding over the mass hanging of 38 Sioux Indians, Pennsylvania native Stephen Miller was promoted to brigadier and later elected governor of Minnesota. A former journalist, he had moved to Minnesota in 1858 and become a merchant. As a Republican he attended the 1860 nominating convention before entering the Union army. His assignments included: lieutenant colonel, 1st Minnesota (April 29, 1861); colonel, 7th Minnesota (August 24, 1862); commanding District of Minnesota, Department of the Northwest (June-September 1863); and brigadier general, USV (October 26, 1863). He fought at 1st Bull Run, Seven Pines, and—in command of the regiment—the Seven Days. With the 1862 Sioux uprising in Minnesota he was given command of a regiment raised to confront the threat. On December 26, 1862, he directed the hanging, ordered by Lincoln, of 38 braves at Mankato. (One Indian had been pardoned at the last minute.) Shortly after being promoted to brigadier he was elected governor and took the oath on January 11, 1864. He resigned his commission seven days later. He was active in recruitment and caring for the victims of war. Not seeking another term, he left office on January 8, 1866, and was active in railroading. He also sat in the state legislature in the 1870s. (Baker, James H., *Lives of the Governors of Minnesota*)

MILLER, William (1820-1909)

Florida attorney and Mexican War veteran William Miller was operating a saw mill at the outbreak of the Civil War. The New York-born Confederate's assignments included: lieutenant colonel, 3rd (also known as 1st) Florida Battalion (early 1862); colonel, 1st Florida (August 15, 1862); commanding Brown's Brigade, Anderson's Division, Left Wing, Army of the Mississippi (October 8-fall 1862); brigadier general, CSA (August 2, 1864); commanding Reserve Forces, Florida (September 8, 1864-April 26, 1865); and also commanding District of Florida (or Miller's Brigade), Department of South Carolina, George and Florida (September 29, 1864-April 26, 1865). His battalion joined the main army in Mississippi shortly after the battle of Shiloh and was merged into the old 1st Florida. Rising to colonel, Miller led this unit at Perryville and succeeded the wounded John C. Brown in brigade command. At Murfreesboro he was in charge of the consolidated 1st and 3rd Florida and was wounded during Breckinridge's doomed assault on January 2, 1863. Following a lengthy recovery he was placed in charge of the conscription operations in Alabama and Florida. Promoted to brigadier general, he was placed in command of the Florida reserve forces and shortly thereafter of the District of Florida. Included in Johnston's surrender, he returned to his milling business and was a state legislator.

MILROY, Robert Huston (1816-1890)

The time spent in the Shenandoah Valley by Union General Robert H. Milroy was less than a happy experience, as he suffered defeats at the hands of Stonewall Jackson and Richard S. Ewell. Trained at a private military academy, he commanded a company of the 1st Indiana in the Mexican War and then entered upon the practice of law. The Indiana native served for a time as a judge before entering the Union army upon the outbreak of the Civil War as the commander of a three-months regiment. His assignments included: captain, 9th Indiana (April 23, 1861); colonel, 9th Indiana (April 27, 1861; three months unit); colonel, 9th Indiana (August 27, 1861; three-years unit); brigadier general, USV (September 3, 1861); commanding Cheat Mountain District, Mountain Department (March 11-April 19, 1862); commanding independent brigade, Mountain Department (April 19-June 26, 1862); commanding Independent Brigade, 1st Corps, Army of Virginia (June 26-September 12, 1862); major general, USV (November 29, 1862); commanding Division at Winchester, Defenses of the Upper Potomac, 8th Corps, Middle Department (January-February 1863); commanding 2nd Division, 8th Corps, Middle Department (February-June 26, 1863); commanding Defenses of Nashville and Chattanooga Railroad, Department of the Cumberland (July 1864-March 1865); and commanding 1st Sub-District, District of Middle Tennessee, Department of the Cumberland (March-July 1865). When his regiment was mustered out upon the expiration of its term on July 29, 1861, he promptly reorganized it for a term of three years and remained at its head. Following service in western Virginia, he led one of the two Union brigades engaged at McDowell against the forces of Stonewall Jackson and then unsuccessfully moved against Jackson in the Shenandoah Valley proper. With his command merged into the Army of Virginia he fought at 2nd Bull Run. Commanding in the lower Shenandoah Valley, he was soundly defeated by elements of Richard S. Ewell's Corps at 2nd Winchester during the Confederate advance into Pennsylvania. A court of inquiry later cleared Milroy of any blame for his miserable performance. However, he spent 10 months without a command and then was only assigned to garrison duties in Tennessee, where his duties did pick up somewhat during Hood's invasion of middle Tennessee. Resigning his commission on July 26, 1865, he was involved in the canal business and served as an Indian agent.

Robert H. Milroy, repeated loser in the Shenandoah Valley. (*Leslie's*)

MILTON, John (1807-1865)

Although elected to the Florida governorship in October 1860, John Milton did not take office until the state was a part of the Confederacy—a nation he would not outlive. Born in Georgia, he had practiced law in Georgia, Alabama, and Louisiana and served as a captain of Alabama volunteers in the Seminole War before moving to a Florida plantation in 1846. Three years later he was elected to the state senate. Taking his seat as a Democratic governor on October 7, 1861, he was quickly involved in war work. He favored paper money and the banning of alcohol during the war. He actively supported the formation of infantry and artillery units but was opposed to the use of cavalry in the rough terrain of the state. Noted for cooperating with the central government, he was committed to the Confederate cause and just before the fall of Richmond he committed suicide, on April 1, 1865. (David, William W., *The Civil War and Reconstruction in Florida*)

MINIÉ, Claude Étienne (?-?)

It was the perfection of the Minié ball, actually a conical bullet with a hollowed out base, by Claude É. Minié in 1848 that converted the rifle into a truly effective combat weapon. A captain in the Chasseurs d'Orleans of the French army, Minié realized the need to develop a method for speedily loading rifles. A normal bullet had to be laboriously hammered home. Captain Minié designed an oblong projectile that was slightly smaller than the diameter of the barrel and thus could be dropped into the piece. Upon firing, the exploding gases entered the hollowed out portion, expanding the bullet to accept the rifle grooves. Seven years later the U.S. Army adopted the principle, and the increased range of rifles, without a decline in the rate of fire, eventually required a major shift in battlefield tactics.

MINOR, Robert Dabney (1827-1891)

A veteran of the U.S. Navy, Robert D. Minor held positions in both the Confederate naval and land forces. The Fredericksburg, Virginia, native resigned his commission and headed south where he was appointed almost immediately as a naval lieutenant. Assigned to the CSS *Virginia* early in 1862, he led the detachment which burned the USS *Congress* during the attack on the wooden blockaders in Hampton Roads. He subsequently became superintendent of the Naval Ordnance Works in Richmond. When the workers in his plant were organized into an infantry battalion for local defense he accordingly became major, 4th Virginia Battalion, Local Defense Troops, on June 30, 1863. This unit was usually referred to as the "Naval Battalion." When ordered to duty in North Carolina he resigned his army commission on February 13, 1864. Later in the year he commanded a small fleet in the Chowan River and then finished out the war with the James River Squadron. After the war he maintained his interest in maritime affairs. His papers are in the collection of the Virginia Historical Society.

MINTY, Robert Horatio George (1831-1906)

For his services in command of the Sabre Brigade during much of the Civil War Robert H.G. Minty should have been promoted to full brigadier general; instead he was only rewarded with brevets as brigadier and major general. Born in Ireland to a British officer, he served four years in the British army until he immigrated to Michigan in 1853. Drawing on his military experience he joined the Union army where his assignments included: major, 2nd Michigan Cavalry (September 2, 1861); lieutenant colonel, 3rd Michigan Cavalry (September 7, 1861); colonel, 4th Michigan Cavalry (July 31, 1862); commanding 1st Brigade, Cavalry Division, Army of the Cumberland (November 5, 1862-January 9, 1863); commanding 1st Brigade, 1st Division, Cavalry Corps, Army of the Cumberland (January 9-March 1863); commanding 1st Brigade, 2nd Division, Cavalry Corps, Army of the Cumberland (March-December 1863 and April 1-September 29, 1864); commanding 2nd Brigade, 2nd Division, Cavalry Corps, Military Division of the Mississippi (November 16, 1864-April 2, 1865); and commanding the division (April 2-June 26, 1865). Staying with his first unit for only five days before receiving a promotion, he served with the 3rd Michigan Cavalry at Island #10 and in the siege of Corinth. Taking command of the 4th Michigan Cavalry, he was soon in command of a brigade which he led at Murfreesboro. At Chickamauga he commanded his brigade on the Union right and covered the retreat of Thomas' men after most of the army had fled the field. He participated in the Chattanooga and Knoxville campaigns in the next few months and returned to command his men in the Atlanta Campaign before being ordered back to Tennessee to refit. There his brigade fought at Nashville, and later it took part in Wilson's raid through Alabama and Georgia and in the capture of Jefferson Davis. Brevetted to major general of volunteers, he was mustered out on August 15, 1865, having declined a commission in the regular army. Compared by Wilson to the famous French cavalryman, Murat, Minty instead went into railroading. (Vale, J.G., *Minty and the Cavalry*)

MITCHEL, Charles Burton (1815-1864)

As Arkansas' Confederate senator, Charles B. Mitchel proved to be regional in his outlook on legislative issues. The Tennessee native had practiced medicine in Arkansas for a quarter of a century and served in the state legislature. Defeated for a congressional seat in 1860, he was then named to the U.S. Senate and attended the special session of that body in March 1861. Before the first regular session was held, he had joined the Confederacy with his state and was expelled by a resolution of July 11, 1861. Elected to the Confederate Senate, he chaired the Committee on Accounts in the First Congress and also sat on the committees on: Engrossment and Enrollment; and Post Offices and Post Roads. In the Second Congress he chaired the last committee and also served on the Committee on Territories. Interested primarily in the affairs of the Trans-Mississippi Department, he favored E. Kirby Smith over Thomas C. Hindman for the regional command. Between sessions he died at his Little Rock home on September 20, 1864.

MITCHEL, Ormsby MacKnight (1809-1862)

Within months of having his resignation rejected, noted astronomer and Union General Ormsby McK. Mitchel was dead from yellow fever. The Kentucky-born youth had obtained his appointment to West Point from Ohio and upon his graduation in 1829 was posted to the artillery. But most of his time until his 1832 resignation as a second lieutenant was spent as an instructor of mathemtics at the military academy. He then taught astronomy at Cincinnati College and helped found the Naval and Harvard observatories. He also headed smaller observatories in New York and Ohio. With the coming of the Civil War he was tapped by Lincoln for military service. His assignments included: brigadier general, USV (August 9, 1861); commanding Department of the Ohio (September 21-November 15, 1861);

Ormsby M. Mitchel, astronomer and general. (AC)

commanding 3rd Division, Army of the Ohio (December 2, 1861-July 2, 1862); major general, USV (April 11, 1862); and commanding 10th Corps, Department of the South and the department (September 17-October 27, 1862). His initial command was soon merged into that of Don C. Buell. Commanding a division in Buell's Army of the Ohio, as a brigadier general, he moved from the vicinity of Nashville into northern Alabama. It was a group of his men who made the famous railroad raid under civilian James J. Andrews in April 1862. Promoted to major general that same month, Mitchel soon ran into difficulties with Buell over discipline in Mitchel's division. His request to be allowed to resign was denied by the War Department and in September 1862 he was sent to command on the coast of South Carolina, Georgia, and Florida. However, suffering from yellow fever, he was forced to relinquish command on October 27. He died three days later. (Headley, Rev. P.C., *Old Stars: The Life and Military Career of Major General Ormsby M. Mitchel* and Mitchel, F.A., *Ormsby MacKnight Mitchel: Astronomer and General, A Biographical Narrative*)

MITCHELL, John Grant (1838-1894)

Native Ohioan lawyer John G. Mitchell joined the Union army at the beginning of the Civil War and was only 26 when he became a brigadier general and brevet major general. His assignments included: first lieutenant and adjutant, 3rd Ohio (July 30, 1861); captain, Company C, 3rd Ohio (December 21, 1861); lieutenant colonel, 113th Ohio (September 2, 1862); colonel, 113th Ohio (May 6, 1863); commanding 2nd Brigade, 1st Division, Reserve Corps, Army of the Cumberland (September 9-October 9, 1863); commanding 2nd Brigade, 2nd Division, 14th Corps, Army of the Cumberland (October-November 10, 1863, February 1-September 26, 1864, and February 7-June 20, 1865); commanding 2nd Brigade, Provisional Division, Army of the Cumberland (late 1864-early 1865); and brigadier general, USV (January 12, 1865). In western Virginia he served as Colonel John Beatty's adjutant and took part in Ormsby M. Mitchel's drive into northern Alabama in early 1862. Helping to raise a new regiment, he became its second in command but by the time that it took part in the Tullahoma Campaign he was its colonel. At Chickamauga he led a brigade under James B. Steedman which arrived late on the second day of the battle and played a leading role in aiding George H. Thomas to hold onto his delaying position at Horseshoe Ridge. He led a detachment of the brigade to the battlefield at Wauhatchie but arrived too late for the fight. He and his command were only lightly engaged at Chattanooga, principally in the pursuit of Bragg's army. During the Atlanta Campaign he directed his men in the disastrous charge at Kennesaw Mountain on June 27, 1864. At Nashville he directed a brigade composed of detachments from Sherman's army which were unable to rejoin him during the March to the Sea. Back in charge of his regular brigade during the Carolinas Campaign, he was brevetted for his role at Averysboro and Bentonville. Resigning on July 3, 1865, he took up the practice of law in his native state and held minor local office. Late in life he served as Ohio's pension commissioner.

MITCHELL, John K. (?-?)

Surviving a court of inquiry into his role in the fall of New Orleans, John K. Mitchell went on to a desk job and then again took command of a river borne flotilla and received a promotion to captain. During the operations along the lower Mississippi River—below Forts Jackson and St. Philip—in the spring of 1862 Mitchell was hampered by a divided command of the forces afloat. He himself commanded the Confederate States vessels while the army controlled the River Defense Fleet. In addition, two vessels belonged to the state of Louisiana. Thus, with the rank of commander, and aboard the flagship CSS *Louisiana*, he commanded only six armed vessels directly. Following the dispersal of the fleet and the eventual fall of the Crescent City, a court of inquiry was called to look into the actions of Mitchell. Cleared, he later served as chief of the Bureau of Orders and Detail. Then in 1864 he led the James River Squadron in the defense of Richmond with a subsequent promotion to captain.

MITCHELL, Robert Byington (1823-1882)

Wounds caused Union General Robert B. Mitchell to give up command of the Army of the Cumberland's mounted arm and switch to court-martial duty and district command. The Ohio-born lawyer had fought in the Mexican War as a first lieutenant in the 2nd Ohio before settling in Kansas where he sided with the Free-Soilers. Having served in a number of political offices as a Democrat, he joined the army upon the outbreak of hostilities. His assignments included: colonel, 2nd Kansas (May 23, 1861); brigadier general, USV (April 8, 1862); commanding 1st Brigade, 4th Division, Army of the Mississippi (April 24-August 12, 1862); commanding the division (August 12-September 26, 1862); commanding 9th Division, Army of the Ohio (September 26-29, 1862); commanding 9th Division, 3rd Corps, Army of the Ohio (September 29-November 5, 1862); commanding 4th Division, Center, 14th Corps, Army of the Cumberland (November 5, 1862-January 9, 1863); commanding 1st Division, Cavalry Corps, Army of the Cumberland (March-September 9, 1863); commanding the corps (September 29-November 9, 1863); commanding District of Nebraska, Department of Kansas (January-April 11, 1865); and commanding District of North Kansas, Department of Kansas (April 11-June 28, 1865). At the head of his volunteer infantry regiment he was severely wounded at Wilson's Creek. Upon his recovery he wore the star of a brigadier general and led a brigade at Perryville. His division was not present at Murfreesboro, and he directed a mounted division during the Tullahoma Campaign. In the late summer of 1863 he was advanced to command of all the cavalry with the army, and his forces fought on the flanks at Chickamauga. However by November 1863 he was on leave due to ill-health and wounds. Assigned to court-martial duty, he commanded districts in the far West during the last months of the war. Mustered out on January 15, 1866, that year he became the territorial governor of New Mexico. A notable failure in this post, he resigned in 1869 and lost a bid for Congress in 1872.

MONTGOMERY, James Ed (c. 1817-?)

Displeased with the level of effectiveness of the Confederate navy in protecting the Mississippi River, Kentucky steamboatman James Ed Montgomery cajoled the Confederate Congress into adopting his defense plans. One million dollars was to be spent purchasing 14 vessels and converting them into rams carrying only one gun apiece and protected by cotton bales. The vessels were to be commanded by rivermen and not by naval officers. The Navy Department expressed no interest in the plan. So the River Defense Fleet was made part of the War Department. This division of authority led to a miserable showing of the naval forces at New Orleans and the loss of the entire lower division of the River Defense Fleet, six vessels, most of them being deserted by their inexperienced crews and officers. Montgomery, with the eight vessels of the upper division, fought the Union fleet at the battle of Plum Run Bend. Despite the steamboatmen's inability to cooperate among themselves, they won a victory, sinking the *Mound City* and *Cincinnati* on May 10, 1862. Navy officers scoffed at the ragtag fleet, controlled by the army and officered by men who had no idea of how to fight a naval action. They felt that they should direct the vessels. Montgomery's next battle proved to be his last. On June 6, 1862, in the battle of Memphis, Montgomery lost all his vessels except the *Van Dorn*, which fled, to the Union gunboats and Colonel Ellet's rams. His flagship, the *Little Rebel*, was run aground by a Union ram and he fled into the Arkansas woods. Escaping capture, Montgomery later turned up in Mobile.

MONTGOMERY, Milton (?-1897)

Serving throughout the war in the Department of the Tennessee, Ohio native Milton Montgomery won the brevet of brigadier general of volunteers for the March to the Sea and the Carolinas Campaign. His assignments included: colonel, 25th Wisconsin (September 14, 1862); and commanding in the Department or Army of the Tennessee: 3rd Brigade, Kimball's Provisional Division, 16th Corps (May 28-August 10, 1863); 3rd Brigade, Kimball's Division, District of Eastern Arkansas, 16th Corps (July 29-August 6, 1863); the district (August 3-September 19, 1863); 1st Brigade, 4th Division, 16th Corps (January 24-March 10, 1864); and 2nd Brigade, 1st Division, 17th Corps (January 29-March 10, 1864); and 2nd Brigade, 1st Division, 17th Corps (January 29-March 28 and May 20-June 7, 1865). His unit served in Missouri, Tennessee, and Louisiana before joining the besieging forces at Vicksburg on June 3, 1863. After the city's fall he was sent to eastern Arkansas where he for a time exercised district command. Serving under Sherman, he took part in the Meridian Campaign as a brigade commander. Wounded and captured at Decatur on July 19, 1864, during the Atlanta Campaign, he returned to lead a brigade in the Carolinas. He was mustered out on June 7, 1865.

MONTGOMERY, William Reading (1801-1871)

Having been dismissed from the regular army in 1855, New Jersey native William R. Montgomery received a second chance in the Civil War but served mainly in administrative posts. The West Pointer (1825) had been posted to the infantry and served through the disturbances on the border with Canada and the Seminole and Mexican wars. In the latter he won two brevets, having been wounded on both sides of the Rio Grande, namely at Resaca de la Palma and Molino del Rey. While stationed in Kansas during the troubles, he was dismissed for having misappropriated some government land for a town site that was apparently planned as a free-soil community. The proslavery faction may have had a hand in his ouster. Returning to his native state, he again offered his services to the country. His assignments included: colonel, 1st New Jersey (May 21, 1861); and brigadier general, USV (August 9, 1861, to rank from May 17, 1861). His highest regular army rank having been major, 2nd Infantry, he was made a regimental commander in the volunteer service and led his three-year unit in the campaign of 1st Bull Run. However, the division to which he was assigned missed the fight when it was detailed to guard the areas around Arlington Heights and Fairfax Court House. The next month he was named a brigadier general but saw no further field service. For almost three whole years he performed duties at Arlington, Annapolis, Philadelphia, and Memphis, and then resigned on April 4, 1864. He retired in Pennsylvania.

MOODY, Young Marshall (1822-1866)

Surviving four years of war, Confederate Brigadier General Young M. Moody went on a business trip to New Orleans the very next year—and succumbed to yellow fever. The Alabamian had given up a judicial clerkship to lead a company to war in 1861. His assignments included: captain, Company A, 11th Alabama (June 11, 1861); lieutenant colonel, 43rd Alabama (May 15, 1862); colonel, 43rd Alabama (November 4, 1862); commanding Gracie's (old) Brigade, Johnson's Division, Anderson's Corps, Army of Northern Virginia (December 2, 1864-April 9, 1865); and brigadier general, CSA (March 4, 1865). He served in northern Virginia with his original company but returned to the Mobile area to assist in the raising of the 43rd Alabama of which he became the second-ranking officer. This unit served in eastern Tennessee and Kentucky but its first heavy action came at Chickamauga where Moody distinguished himself at its head. He then served under Longstreet in East Tennessee and in the spring of 1864 moved to Virginia. Wounded at Drewry's Bluff in May, he returned to command his regiment in the Petersburg trenches. When Archibald Gracie was killed by a sharpshooter in December, Moody succeeded him (for the second time since Gracie had been the 43rd's first colonel). Four months later Moody was promoted officially to brigadier, but with only a month to go in the war. Following his parole at Appomattox, Moody was a Mobile businessman until his ill-fated excursion to Louisiana. (Freeman, Douglas S., *Lee's Lieutenants*)

MOORE, Andrew Barry (1807-1873)

Upon its secession on January 11, 1861, the state of Alabama was already in a good position for defense due to the actions of its governor, Andrew B. Moore. A South Carolina-born lawyer, he had entered the Alabama legislature in 1839 and served two years as the speaker of the lower house. In the 1850s he was a judge and was elected governor in 1857. A staunch Democrat, he was a long-time advocate of secession. On December 24, 1860, he ordered the seizure of all army depots in the state, gaining valuable supplies for the Confederate cause. He also offered troops to South Carolina before his own state's secession. Further aid was sent to Florida for the capture of Pensacola. With a constitutional provision barring another term, he left office on December 2, 1861. He then became an aide to Governor John G. Shorter and, later, to Governor Thomas H. Watts. At the close of the war he was arrested by Union authorities but soon was released due to his poor health. Until his death he practiced law. (Denman, Clarence P., *The Secession Movement in Alabama*)

MOORE, Henry P. (?-?)

Concord, New Hampshire, photographer Henry P. Moore saw a potential market for his work by following a hometown unit to the war zone. In 1862 and 1863 he was at Hilton Head, South Carolina, with the 3rd New Hampshire, taking images of the soldiers, their camps and duties. The pictures were sold both to the troops and to families and friends back in New England. With the regiment moving on to more active operations against Charleston, Moore returned home to routine photographic work. (Davis, William C., ed., *The Image of War 1861-1865*)

MOORE, John Creed (1824-1910)

Native Tennesseean West Pointer (1849) John C. Moore served the Confederacy well until his February 3, 1864, resignation as a brigadier general. As an artillery officer, he fought the Seminoles in Florida and served on the frontier before resigning as a first lieutenant in the 2nd Artillery in 1855. A college professor at the outbreak of the Civil War, he offered his services to the Confederacy. His assignments included: captain, Artillery (April 1861); colonel, Artillery (1862); commanding District of Galveston, Department of Texas (October 2-December 7, 1861); colonel, 2nd Texas (January 1862); commanding District of Houston, Department of Texas (January 3-February 25, 1862); commanding Sub-District of Houston, Department of Texas (February 25-ca. March 1862); commanding 4th Brigade, Cheatham's-Ruggles' Division, 2nd Corps, Army of the Mississippi (April-June 1862); brigadier general, CSA (May 26, 1862); commanding brigade, Maury's Division, Army of the West, Department #2 (June-October 19, 1862); commanding brigade, Maury's-Forney's Division, 2nd Military District, Department of Mississippi and East Louisiana (October 21, 1862-April 1863); commanding brigade, Forney's Division, Department of Mississippi and East Louisiana (April-July 4, 1863); and commanding brigade, Cheatham's Division, Hardee's Corps, Army of Tennessee (November-December 1863). While in district command in Texas he raised an infantry regiment with which he joined Albert Sidney Johnston's army in northern Mississippi. He fought on both days at Shiloh and on the second was placed in command of an informal demi-brigade. During the defense of Corinth, Mississippi, he was advanced to brigadier general. He led a brigade in the battle there that fall and later in the Vicksburg Campaign. Captured when that city fell, he was paroled the same day and was exchanged on September 12, 1863. Taking charge of a brigade under Bragg at Chattanooga, he fought in the battle there, although he was already under orders to report to Mobile. He reported there in December but resigned in two months and returned to Texas. He was a postwar writer and teacher.

MOORE, John Wheeler (1833-1906)

North Carolinian John W. Moore has earned himself an important page in the history of the Civil War, not so much for his rather uneventful role in the conflict as for his postwar writings. His Confederate service included: captain and assistant commissary of Subsistence, 2nd North Carolina Cavalry (June 18, 1861); and major, 3rd North Carolina Light Artillery Battalion (February 24, 1862). He served in the supply department with the cavalry regiment on the North Carolina coast until transferred to the artillery in early 1862. The battalion was soon ordered to Richmond and remained to camp there until it reinforced the Army of Northern Virginia in late September 1862 after the battle of Antietam. But, the horses being in such poor condition, it was ordered back to the capital. During the battle of Fredericksburg Moore was stationed along the North Anna River to guard the railroad bridge against a cavalry raid. Subsequent service took the battalion to various points in North Carolina, mostly in the District of the Cape Fear. Near the close of the war he led the command at Bentonville and was surrendered as part of Joe Johnston's army. After the war he wrote several histories and novels. His most important work was *Roster of North Carolina Troops in the War Between the States*.

MOORE, Patrick Theodore (1821-1883)

Knocked out of action early in the war, County Galway native Patrick T. Moore spent the balance of the Civil War primarily in staff and administrative assignments. His family moved to Canada in his mid-teens and then to Boston where his father was a British diplomat. In 1850 he relocated to Richmond where he served in the militia while engaged in mercantile pursuits. Joining the Confederacy, his assignments included: colonel, 1st Virginia (May 1861); brigadier general, CSA (September 30, 1864); and commanding 1st Brigade, Virginia Reserves, Department of Richmond (December 1864-April 1865). While most accounts report him as being wounded at the head of his regiment at 1st Bull Run he was in fact wounded three days earlier at Blackburn's Ford along the same creek. Unable to lead his men, he served on Joseph E. Johnston's staff on the Peninsula, seeing action at Seven Pines. When Johnston was wounded there, Moore joined James Longstreet's staff for the Seven Days. From the summer of 1862 until the fall of 1864 he was engaged primarily on court-martial duty. Promoted to brigadier general, he assisted James L. Kemper in organizing the Virginia Reserves. He commanded a brigade of these during the final months of the war at Richmond, but it did not take part in the retreat to Appomattox. Thereafter he was in the insurance business.

MOORE, Samuel Preston (1813-1889)

Given the circumstance of a constantly low stock of supplies, the Confederacy's surgeon general, Samuel Moore, did an amazing job in keeping the medical services operating. Receiving his medical education in his native state of South Carolina, Moore had accepted an appointment in 1835 as a regular army assistant surgeon with the rank of captain and served in the Mexican War, being promoted to surgeon and major in 1849. Resigning this commission in 1861, he briefly practiced in Arkansas before being named to the top medical post that June. He organized the system of general hospitals to replace the existing confusing situation of each state having its own hospitals in the field. He also established the *Confederate States Medical Journal*. His methods of improvising medicines and other supplies saved many Confederate lives. Following the war he practiced in Richmond.

MOORE, Thomas Overton (1804-1876)

A firm believer in the power of cotton diplomacy, Louisiana Governor Thomas O. Moore banned the export of that staple on October 3, 1861, in the hope that a shortage would prompt the foreign recognition of the Confederacy. Born in North Carolina, he became a Louisiana sugar planter and served in both houses of the legislature before being elected as a Democrat to the gubernatorial chair in November 1860. Inaugurated in January 1861, he recommended the state convention which took the state out of the Union. He promptly began the organization of supply depots and packing houses to supply an army in the field. He called for an additional 5,000 volunteers over the number requested by Jefferson Davis. With the fall of New Orleans, he moved the state government from Baton Rouge to Opelousas and had to share control of the state with Union military governor George F. Shepley, who ruled in the occupied areas. Moore banned trade with the enemy and halted the export of the cotton crop. His term ended on January 25, 1864, and he fled to Cuba upon the fall of the Confederacy to avoid the arrest which had been ordered by the state senate. A year later he returned, fully pardoned, to his plantation. (Gayarre, Charles, *History of Louisiana* and Bragg, Jefferson Davis, *Louisiana in the Confederacy*)

MORELL, George Webb (1815-1883)

The highly politicized case against Fitz-John Porter also irreparably damaged the military career of New York West Pointer (1835) George W. Morell. Resigning after two years in the engineers, he had briefly engaged in railroading before taking up the practice of law. Reentering the military, his assignments included: colonel and quartermaster, New York Volunteers (May 16-July 25, 1861); brigadier general, USV (August 9, 1861); commanding 1st Brigade, Porter's Division, Army of the Potomac (October 3, 1861-March 13, 1862); commanding 2nd Brigade, 1st Division, 3rd Corps, Army of the Potomac (March 13-May 18, 1862); commanding the division (May 18-October 30, 1862); and major general, USV (July 4, 1862; expired March 4, 1863). During the first months of the war he was on the staff of Charles W. Sandford, the commander of the New York militia. Appointed a brigadier general in the national volunteer service, he led a brigade under Fitz-John Porter to the Peninsula and fought at Yorktown. By the time of the Seven Days he was in charge of a division which fought well at Gaines' Mill and Malvern Hill. The battle of 2nd Bull Run was the turning point in his military career. After serving in reserve at Antietam he was a witness in the case against Porter and proved to be unfriendly toward the government's position in his testimony. He had been awarded a second star at the close of the Peninsula Campaign but, due to his support of the politically unpopular Porter, it was not confirmed and he held no further field commands. He did serve near Washington and after a lengthy period awaiting orders was in charge of the Indianapolis draft rendezvous before his December 15, 1864, muster out. He was a farmer and active in church affairs thereafter.

MORGAN, Charles Hale (1834-1875)

Career officer Charles H. Morgan served through most of the Civil War as a staff officer and received the star of a brigadier general of volunteers well after the end of the active campaigning of the Army of the Potomac. The native New Yorker and West Pointer (1857) had been posted to the artillery and seen service against the Mormons in 1859. His Civil War-era assignments included: second lieutenant, 4th Artillery (since September 10, 1857); first lieutenant, 4th Artillery (April 1, 1861); captain, 4th Artillery (August 5, 1862); lieutenant colonel, and assistant inspector general (January 1, 1863); and brigadier general, USV (May 21, 1865). He commanded his battery at Yorktown on the Peninsula and was promoted to captain that summer. Following an illness he served as chief of artillery for the 2nd Corps during the post-Antietam period. At Fredericksburg he directed that corps' reserve artillery and at Chancellorsville served both as its artillery chief and inspector. Shortly thereafter he was promoted to a staff lieutenant colonelcy and served as the corps chief of staff under Winfield S. Hancock at Gettysburg—where he won a brevet—and beyond. He won further brevets for Bristoe Station, the Wilderness, Spotsylvania, and the campaign before Richmond. The latter was as a brigadier general of volunteers on December 2, 1864. Continuing through the Petersburg and Appomattox campaigns, he was promoted to the full volunteer rank of brigadier general more than a month after Lee's surrender. He remained on Hancock's staff until he was mustered out on January 15, 1866. Remaining in the regular army, he died at Alcatraz while still on active duty as major, 4th Artillery.

MORGAN, Edwin Denison (1811-1883)

In order to enhance his civil powers, President Lincoln had New York Republican Governor Edwin D. Morgan commissioned a major general of volunteers and placed him in military command in that state. A highly successful merchant, the

Massachusetts native had held a number of political offices before the Civil War, including a seat on the Hartford City Council, and as a New York City assistant alderman, a state senator, and immigration commissioner. He also chaired the national conventions for his party in 1856 and 1860, and later, in 1864, 1872, and 1876. First elected governor in 1858, he was reelected two years later. His second term was dominated by the war effort in which he was extremely active. As a reward he was given military rank and his assignments included: major general, USV (September 28, 1861); and commanding Department of New York (October 26, 1861-January 3, 1863). Initially calling for 25,000 volunteers, he eventually provided the Washington authorities with many times that number. He declined renomination for a third term and left office on January 1, 1863. He resigned his commission at the same time. For a time he was charged by the legislature with the supervision of the harbor defense at New York City. Later that same year he was named to the U.S. Senate and served, supporting the war measures, for the rest of the conflict. He was defeated for reelection and later in bids for the governorship and again for the Senate. He twice declined the position of secretary of the treasury, in 1865 and 1881. (Rawley, James A., *Edwin D. Morgan, 1811-1883; Merchant in Politics*)

George W. Morgan, captor of Cumberland Gap. (*Leslie's*)

MORGAN, George Washington (1820-1893)

Already a brevet brigadier general of regulars in 1861, George W. Morgan would resign his commission as a volunteer officer at the same grade in part because of the use of blacks as soldiers. Before attending West Point (class of 1845) he had already served as a captain in the army of the Republic of Texas. Poor grades at the academy had prompted his resignation in 1843, but three years later he took the field as commander of the 2nd Ohio. He was soon named colonel of the 15th Infantry, one of the regular army regiments raised for the war with Mexico. Wounded at Churubusco, he was brevetted brigadier general for that action and Contreras. He then spent the interwar years as a lawyer and farmer. From 1856 until the outbreak of the war he was a diplomat, first in Marseilles and then in Lisbon. Returning to the United States, he entered the army and his assignments included: brigadier general, USV (November 12, 1861); commanding 7th Division, Army of the Ohio (March 26-October 10, 1862); commanding Cumberland Division, Department of the Ohio (October 10-November 1862); commanding 9th Division, Right Wing, 13th Corps, Army of the Tennessee (November-December 18, 1862); commanding 3rd Division, Yazoo Expedition, Army of the Tennessee (December 18, 1862-January 4, 1863); commanding 1st Corps, Army of the Mississippi (January 4-12, 1863); and commanding 13th Corps, Army of the Tennessee (January 12-31, 1863). His greatest accomplishment was the seizure of vitally strategic Cumberland Gap in June 1862. At Chickasaw Bayou he led a division and was roundly criticized by Sherman. He then commanded half of the forces which captured Arkansas Post. His problems with Sherman, his health, and his opposition to changing the purpose of the war from preserving the Union to the abolition of slavery prompted him to submit his resignation, which was accepted effective June 8, 1863. The next year he was a backer of the presidential bid of McClellan and later sat for three terms as a Democrat in Congress in opposition to the Radicals.

MORGAN, James Dada (1810-1896)

As a youth, Boston native James D. Morgan survived a mutiny at sea and two weeks adrift in a lifeboat; he later became a Union general. A merchant and militiaman in Illinois, he was involved in the Mormon conflict there and in the Mexican War served as a company commander in the 1st Illinois. His Civil War assignments included: lieutenant colonel, 10th Illinois (April 29, 1861); colonel, 10th Illinois (July 29, 1861); commanding 4th Brigade, 1st Division, District of Cairo, Department of the Missouri (February 10, 1862); commanding 1st Brigade, 4th Division, Army of the Mississippi (March 4-April 24, 1862); commanding 2nd Brigade, 1st Division, Army of the Mississippi (April 24-May 1, June 27-July 17, and August 15-September 29, 1862); also commanding the division (July 15-August 15 and August 30-31, 1862); brigadier general, USV (July 17, 1862); commanding 2nd Brigade, 13th Division, Army of the Ohio (September-November 5, 1862); and commanding in the Army of the Cumberland: 1st Brigade, 4th Division, Center, 14th Corps (November 5, 1862-January 9, 1863); the division (January 9-May 5, 1863); 2nd Division, Reserve Corps (June 8-October 8, 1863); 1st Brigade, 2nd Division, 14th Corps (November 12, 1863-August 22, 1864); and the division (August 22, 1864-June 23, 1865). Initially second-in-command of his regiment, Morgan became its colonel when it was reorganized for three years. He commanded a brigade at Island #10 and the regiment in the advance on

Corinth, Mississippi. His next major action did not come until the battle of Chattanooga in November 1863, where he was in brigade command having been promoted to brigadier general in the summer of 1862. During the course of the Atlanta Campaign he succeeded to command of the division and held it for the balance of the war. Having participated in the Savannah and Carolinas campaigns, he was brevetted major general for Bentonville and was mustered out on August 24, 1865. After the war he returned to his business interests and entered banking. He was also active in veterans' affairs.

MORGAN, John Hunt (1825-1864)

One of the leading Confederate raiders, John Hunt Morgan found it difficult to comply with the constraints placed upon his activities by his superiors. Born in Alabama, he had served in the Mexican War as a first lieutenant with the 1st Kentucky. Unlike many volunteer officers he did see action in that conflict. A Lexington merchant between the wars, he raised the Lexington Rifles in 1857. Even though his state never did secede, he did join the Confederacy and his assignments included: captain, Morgan's Kentucky Cavalry Squadron (1861); colonel, 2nd Kentucky Cavalry (to rank from April 4, 1862); commanding cavalry brigade, Army of Tennessee (November 20, 1862-February 25, 1863); brigadier general, CSA (December 11, 1862); commanding brigade, Wheeler's Cavalry Division, Army of Tennessee (February 25-March 16, 1863); commanding division, Wheeler's Cavalry Corps, Army of Tennessee (March 16-July 26, 1863); commanding cavalry brigade, Department of East Tennessee (early 1864-May 2, 1864); commanding cavalry brigade, Department of Southwestern Virginia (May 2-June 22, 1864); and commanding Departments of East Tennessee and Southwestern Virginia (June 22-August 30, 1864). He led his squadron in central Kentucky and at Shiloh and was then promoted to colonel. He led his regiment during the Corinth siege and then took two regiments on a raid through Kentucky from July 4, to August 1, 1862. This raid, together with that of Nathan Bedford Forrest, greatly hampered the advance of Don C. Buell on Chattanooga. In October 1862 shortly after the collapse of the Southern campaign in Kentucky, he led his brigade on another raid through his adopted state. During the Murfreesboro Campaign he led a mounted division into Kentucky, from December 21, 1862, through January 1, 1863, against Rosecrans' supply lines. Having been promoted to brigadier general, he also received the thanks of the Confederate Congress for his exploits. Following the Tullahoma Campaign he again received permission to enter Kentucky. On this raid from July 2 to 26, 1863, he violated Bragg's instructions not to cross the Ohio River. Crossing over into Indiana, he moved into Ohio, skirting Cincinnati which went into a panic. Pursued by cavalry and militia, he was finally captured near New Lisbon, Ohio, on July 26th after most of his command had been taken prisoner. Confined in the Ohio State Penitentiary, he escaped on November 26, 1863. Placed in command in East Tennessee and southwestern Virginia the next year, he was surprised and killed at Greeneville, Tennessee, on September 4, 1864. (Holland, Cecil Fletcher, *Morgan and His Raiders, A Biography of the Confederate General*; Noel, Lois, *John Hunt Morgan*; and Swiggert, Howard, *Rebel Raider: A Life of John Hunt Morgan*)

Confederate raider John Hunt Morgan. (*Leslie's*)

MORGAN, John Tyler (1824-1907)

In an effort which proved to be too little too late, Confederate Brigadier General John T. Morgan was recruiting black troops when the end came for the fledgling nation. The Tennessee-born Alabama lawyer attended his adopted state's secession convention and then enlisted in the Cahaba Rifles. His assignments included: private, 5th Alabama (May 5, 1861); major, 5th Alabama (ca. May 11, 1861); lieutenant colonel, 5th Alabama (ca. November 20, 1861); colonel, 51st Alabama Partisan Rangers (September 2, 1862); brigadier general, CSA (June 6, 1863); commanding brigade, Martin's Division, Wheeler's Cavalry Corps, Army of Tennessee (summer-November 1863 and February-ca. June 1864); reappointed brigadier general, CSA (November 17, 1863, to rank from the 16th); and commanding Martin's Division, Martin's detachment of Wheeler's Cavalry Corps, Department of East Tennessee (November 1863-February 1864). He served at 1st Bull Run as a field officer with his first unit and then resigned in 1862 to raise a regiment of partisan rangers. As a colonel, he led it at Murfreesboro and during the Tullahoma Campaign. Named a brigadier general with the idea that he would command Robert E. Rodes' old brigade in the Army of Northern Virginia, Morgan declined the appointment on July 14, 1863. Given command of a cavalry brigade under Joseph Wheeler, he was reappointed four months later. He commanded the division in the operations against Knoxville and was back in charge of his brigade during the early portion of the Atlanta Campaign. Recruiting in Mississippi at the close of the war, he resumed his practice and was a leader in the movement to end black rule in Alabama. He spent his last three decades in the U.S. Senate.

MORRILL, Justin Smith (1810-1898)

In a congressional career lasting more than 43 years, Justin S. Morrill authored and pushed through to passage two highly significant pieces of legislation, both signed into law during the Civil War years: the Morrill Tariff Act of 1861 and the Morrill Educational Land Grant Bill of 1862. A native of Vermont, he had engaged in mercantile pursuits, there and in Maine, and in farming before being elected to Congress as a Whig in 1854. Taking his seat the next year, he was repeatedly reelected to the House until 1866 when, having already switched to the Republicans, he was elected to the Senate. He sat there until his death. His tariff bill was signed into law on March 2, 1861, and his most important piece of legislation on July 2, 1862. The latter provided that each state be given, for each senator and representative, 30,000 acres to fund agricultural and mechanical schools. The effects of this act are still apparent today. (Parker, William Belmont, *The Life and Public Services of Justin Smith Morrill*)

MORRILL, Lot Myrick (1813-1883)

Originally a Democrat, Lot M. Morrill broke with that party over its concessions to the slave states and became a Republican and a supporter of Lincoln. A Maine native, he had been a lawyer before becoming a member of the lower house of the state legislature. Opposed to the expansion of slavery, he allied himself with the Republicans to gain a seat in the upper house in 1856. The next year, as a full Republican, he was elected governor, and was sworn in on January 6, 1858. He supported the state's prohibition law. After having supported Lincoln he was named to fill Hannibal Hamlin's unexpired Senate term; Morrill's gubernatorial term had expired on January 2, 1861. He took his new seat on January 17, 1861, and served throughout the Civil War. In an attempt to avert that war, he was a delegate to the Washington Peace Conference in 1861. He favored the emancipation of slaves and giving them the vote and felt that Reconstruction should be controlled by Congress. He voted for the conviction of Andrew Johnson during his impeachment trial. His full term—he had been reelected—expired in 1869 but later that same year he succeeded the deceased William P. Fessenden and was again elected in 1870. Resigning six years later, he was secretary of the treasury under Grant. (Herbert, Richard A., *Modern Maine*)

MORRIS, Thomas Armstrong (1811-1904)

Later in the war it became unusual to accept state officers with higher rank than that of colonel into the national service, but Brigadier General Thomas A. Morris was taken early, with his Indiana brigade. An 1834 graduate of West Point, he had only served two years in the artillery as a lieutenant before resigning to work in railroading and engineering until the outbreak of the Civil War. He was appointed brigadier general, Indiana Volunteers, on April 27, 1861, and after some organizational work commanded Indiana Brigade, Army of Occupation, West Virginia, Department of the Ohio (June-July 1861). He fought at Philippi and helped drive the Confederates from Laurel Hill to Carrick's Ford—where their commander Robert Garnett became the first general officer fatality of the war. With the expiration of his brigade's term of service Morris was mustered out on July 27, 1861. Probably due to McClellan's animosity he did not receive a reappointment in the national volunteers until the fall of 1862. At that time he elected to remain in private life.

MORRIS, William Hopkins (1827-1900)

A West Pointer (1851) who had resigned as a second lieutenant of infantry in 1854, New York City native William H. Morris reentered the military in 1861 and rose to the rank of brevet major general of volunteers. In his civilian years he had gone into journalism as an assistant to his father, the editor of the *New York Home Journal*. In the meantime he also invented a repeating carbine and published several works in trying to sell it to the War Department. With the firing on Fort Sumter he reentered the service and his assignments included: captain and assistant adjutant general, USV (August 20, 1861); assistant adjutant general, 3rd Brigade, Buell's-Keyes' Division, Army of the Potomac (October 3, 1861-March 13, 1862); assistant adjutant general, 1st Brigade, 1st Division, 4th Corps, Army of the Potomac (March 13-June 23, 1862); assistant adjutant general, 2nd Division, 4th Corps, Army of the Potomac and Department of Virginia (June 24-September 1, 1862); colonel, 135th New York (September 2, 1862); colonel, 6th New York Heavy Artillery (designation change October 3, 1862); brigadier general, USV (March 16, 1863, to rank from November 29, 1862); commanding 2nd Brigade, 1st Division, 8th Corps, Middle Department (March 27-June 26, 1863); commanding 3rd Provisional Brigade, French's Division, 8th Corps, Middle Department (June 26-July 10, 1863); commanding 1st Brigade, 3rd Division, 3rd Corps, Army of the Potomac (July 10, 1863-March 24, 1864); and commanding 1st Brigade, 3rd Division, 6th Corps, Army of the Potomac (March 25-May 9, 1864). As a staff officer under John J. Peck, he fought on the Peninsula until his September 1, 1862, resignation. The next day he was commissioned colonel of an infantry regiment which was converted to a heavy artillery unit the next month. With this command he was stationed in the Baltimore defenses until sent to Maryland Heights as a brigadier general, where he was stationed during the Gettysburg Campaign. Incorporated into the Army of the Potomac, he led a brigade in the Bristoe and Mine Run operations. Retaining command after the spring 1864 reorganization, he fought at the Wilderness and on May 9, 1864, his active field career came to an end when he was severely wounded at Spotsylvania. Until his August 24, 1865, muster out of the service he was engaged on numerous commissions. He then continued his military writing and became a brevet major general in his state's national guard organization.

MORRIS, William S. (?-?)

The telegraph was an innovation in warfare during the Civil War, and it was William S. Morris who was the key to its use by the Confederacy. A Georgia physician and businessman before the war, he owned a large share of the American Telegraph Company at the outbreak of the Civil War. He was named to head the military telegraph operations by Confederate Postmaster General John Reagan and was the prime mover in establishing its potential for warfare in the South. He served throughout the war and then returned to private business.

MORTON, Jackson (1794-1874)

When his old political foe, Stephen R. Mallory, was named to the cabinet without the customary consultation with the Florida delegation, Jackson Morton developed a lasting dislike for Jefferson Davis. The Virginia native had established himself as a Florida merchant, lumberman, and plantation owner. Politically a Whig he served in the state's legislative and constitutional bodies before serving a term in the U.S. Senate. He tried to delay secession by making it a cooperative venture with neighboring Alabama. He was admitted to the Provisional Confederate Congress on February 6, 1861, and became chairman of the Committee on Indian Affairs. He also sat on the committees on: Commercial Affairs; and Flag and Seal. His principal activities appear to have been to protect the Florida coastline and limit the president's appointive powers in the wake of the Mallory affair. Failing in a bid for the Senate in the First Regular Congress in November 1861, he retired from public life at the conclusion of the Provisional Congress. (Davis, William W., *The Civil War and Reconstruction in Florida*)

MORTON, James St. Clair (1829-1864)

Perhaps in order to return to the kind of engineering work that he preferred, James St. Clair Morton voluntarily gave up his volunteer brigadier generalship and reverted to his regular army grade as a major of engineers. The Philadelphia native had graduated second in his West Point class of 1851. Accordingly, he had been assigned to the engineers where he performed well on a large number of construction projects up and down the Atlantic coast. He stayed with this kind of work until the war was over a year old. His assignments included: first lieutenant, Engineers (since July 1, 1856); captain, Engineers (August 6, 1861); chief engineer, Army of the Ohio (June 9-October 27, 1862); chief engineer, Army of the Cumberland (October 27, 1862-August 22, 1863 and September 17-November 14, 1863); commanding Pioneer Brigade, Army of the Cumberland (December 1862-January 1864); brigadier general, USV (April 4, 1863, to rank from November 29, 1862); major, Engineers (July 3, 1863); assistant to the chief engineer, USA (January-May 16, 1864); and chief engineer, 9th Corps, Army of the Potomac (May 16-June 17, 1864). He served as engineering chief to both Buell and Rosecrans. He saw action at Perryville under the former and under the latter won a brevet for commanding the pioneer brigade at Murfreesboro. He won another brevet at Chickamauga where he was also wounded. Having been made a brigadier general of volunteers the previous spring, he was mustered out at his own request on November 7, 1863. As a regular officer, he then worked on the Nashville defenses and did a stint in Washington. Becoming Burnside's chief engineer he fought at the North Anna, Totopotomy, Cold Harbor, and in the advance on Petersburg. It was here, on June 17, 1864, that he was killed while planning the day's assaults. He was brevetted brigadier general in the regular army from the date of his death.

MORTON, Oliver Perry (1823-1877)

Despite an unfriendly legislature, Indiana Governor Oliver P. Morton was one of the most effective Northern governors in support of the Union war effort. A native of the state, he had studied law before becoming a judge. A founder of the state's Republican Party, he was an unsuccessful gubernatorial candidate in 1856. In 1860 he was successful in a bid for the number two spot and two days after being inaugurated he succeeded Governor Henry S. Lane who had resigned to take a seat in the U.S. Senate. Taking up his duties on January 16, 1861, he was soon busied by the war effort. At one point the state legislature did not provide funding for the troops, and Morton had to borrow over $1 million for pay and equipment. Reelected in 1864, he resigned three years later to become a senator. He died during his second term. (Foulke, William D., *Life of Oliver P. Morton*)

Indiana Governor Oliver P. Morton. (NA)

MOSBY, John Singleton (1833-1916)

It has been claimed by some that the activities of partisan ranger bands in northern and western Virginia, especially those of John S. Mosby, may have prevented a Union victory in the summer or fall of 1864. A Virginian with a penchant for violence, Mosby had been practicing law at the outbreak of the war. His assignments included: private, 1st Virginia Cavalry (1861); first lieutenant, 1st Virginia Cavalry (February 1862); captain, PACS (March 15, 1863); major, PACS (March 26, 1863); major, 43rd Virginia Cavalry Battalion (June 10, 1863); lieutenant colonel, 43rd Virginia Cavalry Battalion (January 21, 1864); and colonel, Mosby's (Va.) Cavalry Regiment (December 7, 1864). Originally an enlisted man and officer in the 1st Virginia Cavalry, he came into conflict with that unit's colonel, "Grumble Jones," and joined Jeb Stuart's staff as a scout. During the Peninsula Campaign he paved the way for Stuart's famous ride around McClellan. After a brief period of captivity in July 1862 he rejoined Stuart and was rewarded with the authority to raise a band of partisans for service in the Loudoun Valley in northern Virginia. Originally a battalion, his command was raised to a regiment in the last months of the war. In the meantime he managed to wreak havoc among the Union supply lines, forcing field commanders to detach large numbers of troops to guard their communications. His forays took him within the lines guarding Washington, with Mosby himself often doing the advance scouting in disguise. Early in 1863, with 29 men, he rode into Fairfax Court House and roused Union General Edwin H. Stoughton from bed with a slap on the rear end. Following the capture of Generals Crook and Kelley by McNeil's partisans, Mosby complimented them, stating that he would have to ride into Washington and bring out Abraham Lincoln to top their success. On another occasion he came near capturing the train on which Grant was travelling. The disruption of supply lines and the constant disappearance of couriers frustrated army, and lesser-group, commanders to such a degree that some took to the summary execution of guerrillas, i.e. partisan rangers. George Custer executed six of Mosby's men in 1864, and the partisan chief retaliated with seven of Custer's. A note attached to one of the bodies stated that Mosby would treat all further captives as prisoners of war unless Custer committed some new act of cruelty. The killings stopped. With the surrender of Lee, Mosby simply disbanded his command on April 20, 1865, rather than formally surrender. While the partisans were certainly a nuisance to federal commanders, it is an open question as to how effective they were in prolonging the conflict. Many Southerners were very critical of the partisans, only some Southerners excepting Mosby's command. Not pardoned until 1866, Mosby practiced law and befriended Grant. For supporting Grant, a Republican, in the 1868 and 1872 elections, he earned the emnity of many Southerners. He received an appointment as U.S. consul in Hong Kong and other government posts. (Jones, Virgil Carrington, *Ranger Mosby*)

John Singleton Mosby, master Confederate raider. (NA)

MOSLER, Henry (1841-1920)

Having studied woodcarving and drawing until the outbreak of the Civil War, New Yorker Henry Mosler became an artist/correspondent for *Harper's Weekly*. Joining "Bull" Nelson's staff in Kentucky, he portrayed numerous generals for his journal and in 1863 went to Europe to continue his studies. Settling in Paris after residing for a time in Germany and France, he eventually won the Legion of Honor for his work. (Starr, Louis M., *Bohemian Brigade*)

MOTT, Gershom (1822-1884)

Following two failures in the early stages of the Overland Campaign, division commander Gershom Mott, lost his command and was demoted to brigade command. A New Jersey businessman, he had served a year as a second lieutenant in the regular army during the Mexican War, although he never left the United States. His Civil War assignments included: lieutenant colonel, 5th New Jersey (August 17, 1861); colonel, 6th New Jersey (May 7, 1862); brigadier general, USV (September 7, 1862); commanding 3rd Brigade, 2nd Division, 3rd Corps, Army of the Potomac (February 25-May 3, 1863, August 29, 1863-February 16, 1864, and ca. March 1-24, 1864); commanding 1st Brigade, 4th Division, 2nd Corps, Army of the Potomac (March 25-May 2, 1864); commanding the division (May 2-13, 1864); commanding 3rd Brigade, 3rd Division, 2nd Corps, Army of the Potomac (May 13-June 18 and June 27-July 23, 1864); commanding the division (June 18-27 and July 23-October 8, 1864, October 21, 1864-February 15, 1865, and March 2-April 6, May 16-June 9, and June 20-28, 1865); commanding the corps (February 15-17 and

June 9-20, 1865); and major general, USV (May 26, 1865). He fought at Williamsburg and the Seven Days on the Peninsula before being wounded at 2nd Bull Run in command of his regiment. During his recovery he was given a brigadier's star and upon returning to duty shortly after Fredericksburg took over a 3rd Corps brigade. This he led at Chancellorsville where he again fell wounded. During the Mine Run Campaign he was back in command. In the spring of 1864 the 3rd Corps was broken up and his brigade went to the 2nd Corps as part of the 4th Division. By the time of the Wilderness Mott was in charge of the division. A few days later on the second day of the battle his division broke. This was the first black mark against him. A few days later, at Spotsylvania, it was felt that his division did not give sufficient support to Upton's May 10 attack. Three days later the division was consolidated into a brigade and assigned to another division. Mott went on to serve in this reduced capacity through the combat at the North Anna and Cold Harbor before regaining divisional command during the Petersburg fighting. Although he took part in the Appomattox Campaign, he was not present at the surrender. He had received the brevet of major general in the summer of 1864 and achieved the full rank after the close of hostilities. Resigning on February 20, 1866, he became a railroad employee and held state appointments including the direction of the New Jersey National Guard.

MOUTON, Jean Jacques Alfred Alexander (1829-1864)

Confederate division commander Jean J.A.A. Mouton gave his life in the defeat of Nathanial P. Banks at Mansfield, which brought to an end the Union advance in the Red River Campaign. Better known as Alfred Mouton, the Louisiana Acadian had graduated from West Point in 1850 but was allowed to resign as a brevet second lieutenant with the 7th Infantry less than three months later since the Mexican War was over and a retrenchment was taking place in the regular army. A railroading engineer for the next decade, he also rose to the rank of brigadier general in the militia of his native state. His Confederate assignments included: brigadier general, Louisiana Militia (prewar); colonel, 18th Louisiana (October 5, 1861); brigadier general, CSA (April 16, 1862); and commanding in the District of West Louisiana, Trans-Mississippi Department: Sub-District of Lafourche (October 1862); brigade (October 1862-November 1863); and 2nd Division (November 1863-April 8, 1864). On the second day at Shiloh he was severely wounded while leading his regiment. Promoted to brigadier general that same month, he was assigned to western Louisiana upon his recovery. He led a brigade and then a division under Richard Taylor and was part of the force gathered to confront Banks in April 1864. On the 8th he was instantly killed while leading a charge. (Arceneaux, William, *The Acadian General*)

MOWER, Joseph Anthony (1827-1870)

A favorite of William T. Sherman, Joseph A. Mower rose to the command of a corps in the final days of the Civil War. Having been a carpenter for a while, he had entered the regular army's small engineer battalion during the Mexican War; he served in Company A as a private and artificer. Mustered out at the close of the conflict, he was commissioned directly into the army as a second lieutenant in the 1st Infantry upon the expansion of the regular establishment in 1855. With the coming of the Civil War, his assignments included: first lieutenant, 1st Infantry (since March 13, 1857); captain, 9th Infantry (September 9, 1861); colonel, 11th Missouri (May 3, 1862); commanding 2nd Brigade, 2nd Division, Army of the Mississippi (August 9-October 26, 1862); commanding 2nd Brigade, 8th Division, 16th Corps, Army of the Tennessee (December 18, 1862-April 3, 1863); brigadier general, USV (March 16, 1863, to rank from November 29, 1862); commanding 2nd Brigade, 3rd Division, 15th Corps, Army of the Tennessee (April 3-July 4 and September 15-December 20, 1863); commanding 2nd Brigade, 1st Division, 16th Corps, Army of the Tennessee (December 20, 1863-March 7, 1864), commanding the division (March 7-October 11, 1864); also commanding 1st and 3rd divisions, 16th Corps, Detachment Army of the Tennessee, Department of the Gulf (March-June 1864); major general, USV (August 12, 1864); commanding 17th Corps, Army of the Tennessee (October 24-31, 1864); commanding 1st Division, 17th Corps, Army of the Tennessee (October 31, 1864-April 5, 1865); and commanding 20th Corps, Army of Georgia (April 2-June 9, 1865). After service in Missouri, he was given command of a volunteer regiment from that state and led it during the advance on Corinth, Mississippi. In the process, he won a regular army brevet for an action at Farmington. Winning yet another brevet at Iuka, he went on to the battle of Corinth where he briefly fell, wounded, into the hands of the enemy but made good his escape when they retired from the field. Promoted to brigadier general, he led his brigade throughout the Vicksburg Campaign and won a brevet for the movement against, and first capture of, Jackson, Mississippi, in May 1863. Early the next year he took part in Sherman's Meridian expedition and then commanded that part of the 16th Corps which went on Banks' Red River Campaign. He was brevetted brigadier general of regulars for the capture of Fort DeRussy, Louisiana, and was then recalled to the main army by Sherman. He was on the March to the Sea and in the Carolinas Campaign he won the brevet of major general of regulars for effecting the crossing of the Salkehatchie River. A major general of volunteers since the summer of 1864, he commanded a corps in the final stages of the war and was mustered out on February 1, 1866. Remaining in the regular army, he was placed in command of black regiments and died in New Orleans of pneumonia while serving as colonel, 25th Infantry.

MUDD, Samuel A. (1833-1883)

Then as now the case of Dr. Samuel A. Mudd in the Lincoln assassination plot has been a subject of much debate. The Maryland physician had not practiced medicine for years and was running a farm near Bryantown. At about 4:00 A.M. on April 15, 1865, two men—John Wilkes Booth and David E. Herold—came to his door. The former was injured in the leg and Dr. Mudd invited them in and set the broken limb. Although it has been shown that Mudd had met Booth on at least two occasions, he later claimed that he did not recognize the Lincoln assassin because he was wearing a phony beard. Whatever the case, detectives soon arrested the doctor and hustled him off to join the other conspirators. Largely through the testimony of Louis J. Weichmann, he was found guilty of involvement in the conspiracy and was sentenced to life imprisonment. President Andrew Johnson determined that those conspirators not sentenced to death should be sent to Fort Jefferson in Dry Tortugas, Florida—a hellhole for guards as well as prisoners. The place suffered from frequent yellow fever outbreaks and one of Mudd's fellow prisoners, Michael O'Laughlin (convicted in the Lincoln Plot), succumbed to the epidemic. Ironically, after having been treated inhumanely by the prison staff, Dr. Mudd volunteered to treat guards, officials, and prisoners alike after the army surgeons had died in 1867. News of this got out and there was a campaign to gain Mudd's freedom, spurred on by his wife. One of Johnson's last acts as president was the release of Mudd and his fellow conspiracy convicts, Edward Spangler and Samuel Arnold. Dr. Mudd lived out his life in Maryland and has been the subject of controversy ever since. Led by members of his family, there have been repeated movements to gain a pardon. While these movements have gained the support of many political leaders, including former president Jimmy Carter, there are also a number of experts on the assassination who believe that Mudd was involved in the plots to kidnap the president, if not also the murder scheme. (Mudd, Nettie, *Life of Samuel A. Mudd*)

MULHOLLAND, St. Clair Augustin (?-?)

As commander of the one Pennsylvania regiment in the famed Irish Brigade of the Army of the Potomac, St. Clair A. Mulholland won lasting fame and a Congressional Medal of Honor for his actions in covering the withdrawal of the Union Army at Chancellorsville. His assignments included: lieutenant colonel, 116th Pennsylvania (June 26, 1862); major, 116th Pennsylvania (February 27, 1863); colonel, 116th Pennsylvania (May 3, 1864); and commanding 4th Brigade, 1st Division, 2nd Corps, Army of the Potomac (October 7-December 30, 1864, and May 20-June 3, 1865). In his first major battle, Fredericksburg, he was wounded in the assault on Marye's Heights. Just over two months later, on February 24, 1863, he was mustered out so that he could be remustered at a lower rank, the decimated regiment having been reduced to a battalion of four companies. With the decision to withdraw the army across the river after Chancellorsville, Mulholland volunteered to command the 400-man picket line left to cover the retreat. It was considered tantamount to certain capture. Amazingly, his force kept up their fire all night, and, with the exception of 12 men, made it across the river themselves the next morning. In 1895 he received his medal. He later fought at Gettysburg and in May 1864 was wounded three times at the Wilderness, Spotsylvania, and Totopotomy Creek. With the regiment transferred to another brigade, he served through the Petersburg and Appomattox campaigns, at times commanding the brigade. He earned brevets through that of major general of volunteers for his war service and the Boydton Plank Road. (Conyngham, David Powers, *The Irish Brigade and Its Campaigns*)

MULLEN, Patrick (?-?)

Although the Congressional Medal of Honor was awarded much more often in the Civil War than in more recent wars—1,524 were given for exploits during the conflict—only Boatswains Mate Patrick Mullen, USN, and two other men received two each. Serving with the Potomac Flotilla aboard the USS *Don*, a captured blockade runner, Mullen took part in numerous expeditions into the creeks along the Virginia and Maryland sides of the lower Potomac to break up the illegal trade and mail across the river. In one such episode, Mullen commanded a small boat expedition up Mattox Creek. His command was surprised by a Confederate force. During the action Mullen was forced to lie on his back in his boat in order to fire his cannon. Despite the uncomfortable position he was able to force the enemy to retire. He received his first medal for this adventure. His second medal was earned on May 1, 1865, when he saved an officer who had fallen overboard. (Mitchell, Joseph B., *The Badge of Gallantry*)

MULLIGAN, James Adelbert (1830-1864)

An Irish politician in Chicago, James Mulligan raised the "Irish Brigade," officially the 23rd Illinois, and became its colonel on June 18, 1861. Serving in Missouri he commanded an improvised force of about 3,500 in the defense of Lexington, which

James A. Mulligan, surrenderor of Lexington, Missouri. (NA)

was besieged by Missouri Confederates. Forced to capitulate on September 20, 1861, Mulligan was exchanged, but his regiment had been mustered out by order of General Frémont. However, by order of General McClellan the regiment was reassembled and assigned to duty guarding rebel prisoners at Camp Douglas in Chicago and Mulligan was made camp commandant. Although his authorization had been revoked, Mulligan went ahead and enlisted into the Union army 228 prisoners who had taken the oath of allegiance. Transferred with his regiment to West Virginia, his higher commands included: 5th Brigade, 1st Division, 8th Corps, Middle Department (March 27-June 28, 1863); and in the Department of West Virginia: Mulligan's Separate Brigade (June 28-December 1863); 2nd Division (December 1863-April 1864); and 3rd Division (early July-July 23, 1864). Mortally wounded at the 2nd battle of Kernstown on July 23, 1864, he died three days later. He was porthumously brevetted brigadier general, USV, for that battle.

MUMFORD, William B. (ca. 1820-1862)

One of the actions of Benjamin F. Butler in New Orleans that earned him the nickname of "Beast Butler" was the hanging of William B. Mumford. When the New Orleans gambler had spied a U.S. flag flying over the Mint, he climbed to the roof and tore it down. It was still prior to the official surrender of the Crescent City and the flag had been raised without Farragut's knowledge. Thus it could not properly be considered an act of treason. Nonetheless Butler had him arrested and tried on that charge. On June 7, 1862, Mumford was hanged in front of the U.S. Mint. In retaliation Jefferson Davis declared Butler to be a common felon deserving of capital punishment and ordered that any Confederate officer capturing the Union general immediately execute him by hanging. He further ordered that no Union officers be paroled before being formally exchanged.

MUNDY, Sue

See: *Clarke, Marcellus Jerome*

MUNFORD, Thomas Taylor (1831-1918)

Despite the recommendations of most of his superiors, Thomas T. Munford never appears to have made it to the rank of general. A native of Virginia and a graduate of the Virginia Military Institute, he was a planter before the Civil War. His Confederate assignments included: lieutenant colonel, 2nd Virginia Cavalry (May 8, 1861); colonel, 2nd Virginia Cavalry (April 25, 1862); commanding Cavalry Brigade, Valley District, Department of Northern Virginia (June 6-26, 1862); commanding Cavalry, Jackson's Command, Army of Northern Virginia (June 26-July 1862); commanding Robertson's Brigade, Cavalry Division, Army of Northern Virginia (early September-ca. November 10, 1862); commanding Wickham's (old) Brigade, Fitz Lee's Division, Cavalry Corps, Army of Northern Virginia (ca. November 9, 1864-March 1865); and commanding the division (March-April 9, 1865). After distinguished service at 1st Bull Run, he commanded the regiment in the Shenandoah Valley until the death of General Ashby, when he took over brigade command. Accompanying Jackson to Richmond, he took part in the Seven Days and later at 2nd Bull Run, where he was twice wounded. He commanded the brigade at Crampton's Gap and Antietam. Again leading his regiment, he fought at Fredericksburg, Brandy Station, Gettysburg, the Wilderness, and in the Shenandoah Valley Campaign of 1864. Upon the resignation of his brigade commander, he took over command but remained a colonel. Back on the Petersburg lines and in the retreat to Appomattox, he commanded Fitzhugh Lee's division. Although he had been recommended for promotion all the way up the chain of command and actually used the title of general in the final days of the war, the Richmond authorities never acted. He led most of his men out of the trap at Appomattox but disbanded his men soon thereafter. After the war he maintained his residence in Lynchburg and ran planting operations there and in Alabama. He also continued a wartime feud with General Thomas L. Rosser. In 1861 he had been several grades ahead of Rosser and yet in 1864 he had to serve under the general while still a colonel. The Confederate disaster at the battle of Five Forks and the relative responsibility of each party kept the fires burning until 1910 when Rosser died. (Freeman, Douglas S., *Lee's Lieutenants*)

MUNN, A. (?-1864)

Being one of the more notorious of the dreaded "Raiders" who had terrorized the prison pen at Andersonville, a sailor, A. Munn, met his fate at the hands of his fellow prisoners. At the end of June 1864 some 125 of the culprits were turned over to the Confederate commandant, Major Henry Wirz, for safekeeping. In compliance with Wirz's General Orders No. 57 a prisoners' court was convened to try those charged with a variety of crimes from thievery to murder. The sentences included: sitting in the stocks, wearing a ball and chain, being strung up by the thumbs, and running the gantlet. However, six were considered to have earned the death penalty. Among this number was Munn. Before being hanged on July 11, 1864, Munn declared that he had come to Andersonville an honest man who had fallen in with bad company, and the need to survive in the starvation environment had launched him upon his four months of crime. He regretted having been born because of the impact the news of his prison activities would have on his mother and sisters. He was fortunate to be one of the two to be executed—and die quickly. (McElroy, John, *Andersonville: A Story of Rebel Military Prisons*)

MURDAUGH, William H. (?-?)

A veteran of almost two decades of service to the old navy, Virginian William H. Murdaugh is an example of how some Southern officers were treated by the U.S. Navy Department. Although intending to resign his lieutenant's commission in the event that his native state seceded, he loyally followed orders to land a force of troops in Fort Pickens in violation of an agreement with the Confederate forces at Pensacola. When, on April 25, 1861, Murdaugh received notice of the secession of Virginia, he submitted his resignation to his captain. The captain refused to allow Murdaugh to quit the vessel until Washington had accepted the resignation. So for six weeks Murdaugh performed faithful but distasteful service. He was then retroactively dismissed from the service. In June he was assigned to duty obstructing the James River for the Southern navy. Sent to North Carolina, he was wounded at Fort Hatteras in August. Assigned to ordnance duty at Norfolk, he witnessed the fight at Hampton Roads from aboard the tug *Harmony*. Setting up ordnance operations at Charlotte, North Carolina, Murdaugh remained there until ordered to the command of the *Beaufort* in the James River Squadron. Shortly thereafter he was sent to Europe to purchase ordnance supplies. He was praised for his tact and judgment by his superior, Commander Bulloch. Before he could be assigned to an ironclad built in Europe the war came to an end. (Scharf, J. Thomas, *History of the Confederate States Navy*)

MURPHY, Isaac (1802-1882)

The only man in Arkansas' secession convention to vote against the secession of Arkansas, later joined the Union army and served as his state's Union governor during the last year and a half of the Civil War. Moving to Arkansas, Murphy had worked as a teacher, lawyer, and surveyor, and his service in the state legislature was split by four years in the California Gold Rush. At the secession convention in 1861 he was the sole member to vote no. He then allegedly served as major of the 1st Arkansas in the Union army. With the capture of Little Rock in September 1863 the Confederate state government was virtually dissolved. On January 20, 1864, Murphy was appointed provisional governor and was inaugurated as the elected governor on April 18, 1864. Following the end of his administration in 1868, he resumed the practice of law.

MURPHY, Robert C. (?-?)

Earl Van Dorn's raid on the Union supply base at Holly Springs, Mississippi, not only ended Grant's Central Mississippi Campaign (against Vicksburg) but also destroyed the career of Robert C. Murphy. The Wisconsinite's assignments included: colonel, 8th Wisconsin (ca. September 3, 1861); and commanding 2nd Brigade, 2nd Division, Army of the Mississippi (May 29-June 18, 1862). He had led his regiment in Missouri, mostly protecting railroads, but missed the fighting at Island #10. Crossing the Mississippi River, he took part in Halleck's painfully slow advance on Corinth as a brigade commander. Again absent for the battles of Iuka and Corinth, he was assigned to guarding the rail lines supporting Grant's overland advance against Vicksburg. Stationed at Holly Springs, he failed to take adequate defensive precautions; his men were surprised in their camps by the Confederate cavalry, and some 1,500 were paroled. On January 8, 1863, it was decreed that Murphy be dismissed from the service for his failure. This action was backdated to December 20, 1862, the date of the debacle.

MURPHY, Robinson B. (1849-?)

After twice being caught by his father while running away to join the Union army, in 1861 and 1862, 13-year-old Robinson B. Murphy finally was allowed to enlist with his father—and went on to earn the Congressional Medal of Honor. Serving as a musician in Company A, 127th Illinois, Murphy participated in the Vicksburg and Chattanooga campaigns. By the time of the battle of Atlanta he was serving on the brigade commander's staff—presumably as a courier—and then on July 28, 1864, the youth earned his medal by volunteering to lead two regiments to the critical point during a Confederate assault. In the effort his horse was shot out from under him, and 26 years later he was given his medal. (Mitchell, Joseph B., *The Badge of Gallantry*)

MURRAH, Pendleton (1824-1865)

The last Confederate governor of Texas, Pendleton Murrah was forced to flee to Mexico during the confusion rampant in the state following the death of the Confederacy. Born in South Carolina, he had been a lawyer in Alabama before moving to Texas where he was also in the legal business. Defeated for a congressional seat in the mid-1850s, he won a seat in the legislature in 1857. A Democrat, he took a favorable view of secession and served in the Quartermaster's Department in Texas early in the war. In 1863 he was elected governor and three days later—November 5—was sworn in. The increasingly harsh measures of the Richmond authorities in trying to preserve the Confederate States brought Murrah into conflict with their representatives, especially the military. He resented impressments and the draft which was robbing the state of manpower to maintain law and order and guard the frontier. Trying to maintain order after the final collapse, he worked for the state's early reentry into the Union. He called a constitutional convention but was labelled a traitor by the Union authorities and was forced to flee before it could be held as scheduled on June 11, 1865. He was succeeded by the lieutenant governor, Fletcher S. Stockdale. Within two months Murrah was dead in Mexico. (DeShields, James T., *They Sat in High Places: The Presidents and Governors of Texas, 1835-1939*)

MURRAY, Eli Huston (1844-1896)

A loyal native of Kentucky, Eli H. Murray served in the mounted branch throughout the Civil War and emerged with the brevet of brigadier general of volunteers. His assignments included: major, 3rd Kentucky Cavalry (November 12, 1861); colonel, 3rd Kentucky Cavalry (October 9, 1862); commanding 3rd Brigade, 3rd Division, Cavalry Corps, Army of the Cumberland (April 2-May 13, May 23-August 18, and August 22-October 29, 1864); commanding the division (April 17-26 and May 13-21, 1864); commanding 3rd Brigade, 3rd Division, Cavalry Corps, Military Division of the Mississippi (October 29-November 10, 1864); and commanding 1st Brigade, 3rd Division, Cavalry Corps, Military Division of the Mississippi (November 10, 1864-January 20, 1865). Although his regiment came on the field at Shiloh with Buell's reinforcements, it was not actively engaged. Murray then commanded the regiment at Murfreesboro and in the pursuit of John Hunt Morgan during the raid north of the Ohio River. During the Atlanta and Savannah campaigns he commanded a mounted brigade and at times a division. Brevetted for the war, he was mustered out with his regiment on July 15, 1865. Engaged in journalism, he also served as territorial governor of Utah. Ironically, the state was admitted to the Union the year he died.

MYER, Albert James (1827-1880)

At the outbreak of the Civil War, Albert Myer was the entire Signal Corps of the U.S. Army. A graduate of the Buffalo Medical College, Myer developed an interest in visible codes for communication by deaf-and-dumb patients. After becoming an assistant surgeon in the regular army in 1854, he worked with E.P. Alexander, later a rebel general, and they developed the wigwag method of signalling with flags and torches. Having tested the system in campaigning against the Indians, Myer was appointed major and signal officer on June 27, 1860. At the battle of 1st Bull Run he failed in an attempt to use a balloon in conjunction with his system. With a team of detailed line officers his corps was present during McClellan's Peninsula and Antietam campaigns. He was promoted to colonel and chief signal officer on March 3, 1863, but he reverted to the rank of major when his commission was revoked on July 21, 1864. Because of a conflict between the corps and the Military Telegraph Service, both dealing in part with telegraphy, Myer was relieved and ordered to duty in the West on November 10, 1863. At the October 5, 1864, fight at Allatoona, Georgia, Myer's men were responsible for the sending of a relief column, requested by signal, to the rescue of the beleaguered post. Myer went on to serve in the operations against Mobile. For his war service he was brevetted: lieutenant colonel for Hanover Court House, colonel for Malvern Hill, and brigadier general for Allatoona. Continuing after the war in the corps, he again became its chief and died as a brigadier general in 1880 on active duty.

Albert J. Myer used signal towers similar to this one. (NA)

MYERS, Abraham Charles (1811-1889)

South Carolinian by birth and Louisianan by adoption, Abraham Myers had a long record of service in the Quartermaster's Department when he resigned on January 28, 1861, and offered his services to the Confederacy. On March 25, he was appointed the first Quartermaster General, with the rank of lieutenant colonel. The West Pointer's (1833) duties included the supply of the armies in the field with everything that was not either eaten or fired by the troops. His efforts to keep the field forces clothed, shod, and mobile with thousands of wagons and teams was a losing battle. Naturally, he was a prime target for the wrath of the soldiers, possibly more so because he was Jewish. Promoted colonel on February 15, 1862, he had to compete with other supply departments for the limited resources of the South. Superseded by General Lawton, Myers resigned from the army on August 10, 1863. At least in part, his removal was not due to his failures, but rather to the activities of his gossipy wife in criticizing Mrs. Davis and describing her as a squaw. Myers, bitter toward Davis, lived for the rest of the war in poor circumstances in Georgia. He died in Washington in 1889.

MYERS, John B. (?-?)

Even the postwar authorities in Ohio wanted to forget that John B. Myers' 13th Ohio Battery had ever existed—they never mention it in their official military histories. Myers' battery was mustered into service on February 15, 1862, and, upon reporting at Pittsburg Landing on April 4, was assigned to the 4th Division under General Stephen A. Hurlbut. Two days later the bloody fight at Shiloh opened. The division was ordered forward to support Prentiss' hard-pressed division, but it took repeated prodding from staff officers to get the guns of this battery into position. They had just gotten into position when, as the division commander reported, "A single shot from the enemy's batteries struck . . . [in the battery], when officers and men, with a common impulse of disgraceful cowardice, abandoned the entire battery, horses, caissons, and guns, and fled, and I saw them no more until Tuesday [two days later]." Hurlbut believed that Myers had been cowering under the banks of the Tennessee for the rest of the two-day fight. When the department commander, Henry W. Halleck, received this report he ordered Myers to be mustered out and the battery disbanded. This was done on April 20, 1862, and the men were transferred to the 7th, 10th, and 14th Ohio batteries. In defense of Myers it must be pointed out that his command was not properly trained when placed in the field. For a time at least, Myers attempted to bring journalistic and political pressure to bear on the military authorities, even enlisting the state's lieutenant governor, but it appears that he never received another commission, and the 13th Ohio Battery is all but forgotten.

N

NAGLE, James (1822-1866)

Although he had resigned his brigadier's commission for reasons of ill health, Pennsylvanian James Nagle twice led emergency units when Confederates invaded the North. A housepainter and paperhanger but with militia experience, he had commanded a company of volunteers in Mexico. His Civil War assignments included: colonel, 6th Pennsylvania (April 22, 1861); colonel, 48th Pennsylvania (October 1, 1861); commanding 1st Brigade, 2nd Division, Department of North Carolina (April 2-July 6, 1862); commanding 1st Brigade, 2nd Division, 9th Corps, Army of the Potomac (July 22, 1862-February 1863 and March-March 19, 1863); brigadier general, USV (September 10, 1862); brigadier general, USV (reappointed March 13, 1863); commanding 1st Brigade, 2nd Division, 9th Corps, Department of the Ohio (March 19-May 21, 1863); colonel, 39th Pennsylvania Militia (July 1, 1863); and colonel, 194th Pennsylvania (July 24, 1864). With his 90-day regiment, he took part in Patterson's unsuccessful effort to hold Joseph E. Johnston in the Shenandoah Valley during the 1st Bull Run Campaign. Mustered out on July 26, 1861, he soon raised a new regiment, which he took to the North Carolina coast. Leading a brigade, he fought at 2nd Bull Run and took part in the capture of Burnside's Bridge at Antietam. Promoted to brigadier general, he fought at Fredericksburg and then accompanied the 9th Corps to Kentucky. The Senate having failed to confirm his appointment, it expired on March 4, 1863, but he was reappointed nine days later. However, on May 9, 1863, he resigned. When Lee invaded Pennsylvania, Nagle led a militia unit until mustered out on August 2, 1863. When Early raided Maryland, Nagle led a 100-days regiment in the Baltimore defenses. Finally mustered out on November 5, 1864, he died less than two years later.

NAGLEE, Henry Morris (1815-1886)

Without serving the customary year following his 1835 graduation from West Point, Pennsylvania native Henry M. Naglee resigned to become a civil engineer—but still fought in the Mexican and Civil wars. Following his brief service in the infantry he had settled in New York to practice his profession. During the Mexican War he was a company commander in the New York volunteers in California and Lower California. Remaining on the West Coast, he was involved in banking until the Civil War when he was named second-in-command of one of the newly authorized infantry regiments. However, he resigned before his unit could be formed to accept a commission in the volunteers. His assignments included: lieutenant colonel, 16th Infantry (May 14, 1861); commanding 1st Brigade, Casey's Division, Army of the Potomac (December 1861-March 13, 1862); brigadier general, USV (February 4, 1862); commanding 1st Brigade, 3rd Division, 4th Corps, Army of the Potomac (April 27-June 7, 1862); commanding 1st Brigade, 2nd Division, 4th Corps, Army of the Potomac (June 7-July 6, 1862); commanding brigade, Department of North Carolina (December 1862-January 2, 1863); commanding 2nd Division, 18th Corps, Department of North Carolina (January 2-February and April 16-May 10, 1863); commanding 1st Division, Detachment 18th Corps, St. Helena Island, 10th Corps, Department of the South (February-March 5, 1863); temporarily commanding the detachment (February 1863); commanding 7th Corps, Department of Virginia (July 16-20, 1863); and commanding District of Virginia, Department of Virginia and North Carolina (August 21-September 23, 1863). Having resigned from the regular army on January 10, 1862, he led a brigade of volunteers to the Peninsula where he fought at Yorktown, Williamsburg, Seven Pines, and during the Seven Days. With the departure of the Army of the Potomac, Naglee remained in the vicinity and served in North and South Carolina. In the summer of 1863 he was commanding the District of Virginia when he came into conflict with Governor Francis H. Pierpont. The latter wanted the oath of allegiance to be broadened to include loyalty to his "Restored Government of Virginia." Because of Naglee's reluctance to comply he was removed and ordered to report to Grant for further orders which were never issued. He was then mustered out on April 4, 1864, and returned to California where he engaged in the banking and wine industries. (Schell, Mary L., *The Life of Brig. Gen. Henry M. Naglee Consisting of a Correspondence on Love, War and Politics*)

NAPOLEON, Louis (1808-1873)

French Emperor Napoleon III wanted to recognize the Confederacy early in the war and offered an effort to mediate the conflict but wished that Britain and Russia would go along with the proposal. Not gaining such an agreement, he never went ahead with the idea, but the North always feared his possible actions in the New World. Having granted the South the status of a belligerent, he criticized the North for the seizure of Mason and Slidell from the British steamer *Trent* and refused suggestions that he mediate that dispute. Expansionist in his policies, he had his forces remain in Mexico after a joint operation with the British and Spanish to force repayment of debts. He established Archduke Maximilian of Austria on a throne in Mexico City. Lincoln's fears of the French designs in Mexico prompted him to postpone Grant's projected movement against Mobile, after the fall of Vicksburg and Port Hudson. Instead, he ordered a large portion of the forces sent to Texas. The South often toyed with the idea of an alliance with Napoleon, and there were even suggestions that the Confederacy become a French protectorate. Napoleon was deposed after the Franco-Prussian War of 1870-71.

NASBY, Petroleum Vesuvius

See: *Locke, David Ross*

NAST, Thomas (1840-1902)

German-born Thomas Nast was probably the most effective satirical cartoonist during the Civil War and Reconstruction periods. Emigrating to the United States as a child, he had developed an interest in art and by the age of 15 was drawing for *Frank Leslie's Illustrated Newspaper*. By 1857 he had expanded his mere depictions to include satirical content with his coverage of a police scandal in New York. Sent in 1860 to Europe, he covered England and Garibaldi's campaigns in Italy. Returning at the beginning of the Civil War, he at first worked for the *New York Illustrated News*, then briefly for *Leslie's*, and for most of the conflict for *Harper's Weekly*. He made his way to the capital and put his wit to work in support of the Union cause. He was so effective that Lincoln called him "our best recruiting sergeant." During the war he also contributed to *Le Monde Illustré*. Subsequently, his attacks centered upon the corrupt Tweed Ring in New York. He tried his hand at his own paper after the war and died while serving as consul in Ecuador. (Paine, A.B., *Thomas Nast: His Period and His Pictures*)

NEELY, James Jackson (1827-?)

A grudge over being superseded in command of a brigade of cavalry led to James J. Neely being cashiered from the Confederate army and charged with inciting a mutiny. A native of Tennessee, he joined the Confederate army where his service included: captain, Company B, 6th Tennessee Cavalry Battalion (ca. June 1861); colonel, 14th Tennessee Cavalry (July 1, 1863); and commanding Richardson's Brigade, Chalmers' Division, Forrest's Cavalry Corps, Department of Alabama, Mississippi and East Louisiana (May 10-August 30, 1864). With his original company, the "Hardeman Avengers," he took part in the battle of Belmont. In April 1862 the battalion was merged with other companies to form a regiment. However, in the consolidation he became a supernumerary without a command. In the spring of the next year he was granted authority to raise a regiment behind Union lines in West Tennessee. He completed the assignment in August and took part in numerous raids in the enemy's country. Ordered to northern Mississippi, he joined the regular cavalry forces operating there and fought under Forrest at Okolona and against A.J. Smith the next year. In the spring of 1864 he assumed command of the brigade but was relieved by Colonel E. W. Rucker in late August. Resenting the outsider taking over the command, the regimental commanders refused to obey Rucker's orders and even wrote him requesting that he not take command. They were arrested and suspended from command. That is, all except Neely who was kicked out of the army on October 18, 1864.

NEFF, John Francis (1834-1862)

The famed Stonewall Brigade often suffered from dissension among its officer corps. This was the case for one regimental commander, John Neff, and the brigade commander, General Charles S. Winder. Neff, born into a Shenandoah Valley Dunkard-sect family, felt it necessary to slip away from home, with $200 of his father's money, after being refused permission to attend the Virginia Military Institute. Eventually gaining admission, he graduated in 1858 and then studied law and was admitted to the bar. With the outbreak of the war he went to Richmond and was ordered to Harpers Ferry to help drill the volunteers. With the formation of the 33rd Virginia in July 1861 he was appointed a first lieutenant and regimental adjutant. With the brigade under General Thomas J. Jackson, the regiment moved to Manassas Junction and took part in the battle of 1st Bull Run, earning the sobriquet "Stonewall." Several months later the command returned to the Valley, fought at Kernstown, and on April 22, 1862, the regiment was reorganized with Neff as its colonel. He led the regiment through the Valley Campaign (1st Winchester and Port Republic) and the Seven Days (Gaines' Mill, White Oak Swamp, and Malvern Hill). After a brief rest the command moved to Gordonsville where Neff was highly critical of Winder's harsh treatment of some of the men. Word got back to Winder, and Neff, repeating the offending remarks to Winder's face, was placed under arrest. Despite his disqualification, Neff led his men at Cedar Mountain where Winder was killed. The charges dropped, Neff resumed formal command and was killed less than three weeks later at Groveton, the opening of the battle of 2nd Bull Run. Had he lived, his calm demeanor in battle would have probably earned him a promotion and the leadership of the Stonewall Brigade, which never kept a commander for very long. (Robertson, James I., Jr., *The Stonewall Brigade*)

NEGLEY, James Scott (1826-1901)

When Chickamauga ended the active field career of Union general James S. Negley, he felt that he was a victim of the prejudice of West Pointers against civilian officers. The Pennsylvania native had spent a year and a half as a private in the 1st Pennsylvania during the Mexican War and in the interwar years maintained an interest in the militia while becoming a noted horticulturalist. His Civil War assignments included: brigadier general, Pennsylvania Militia (prewar); brigadier general, Pennsylvania Volunteers (April 19, 1861); commanding 5th Brigade, 2nd Division, Department of Pennsylvania (June-July 1861); brigadier general, USV (February 6, 1862, to rank from October 1, 1861); commanding 4th Brigade, McCook's Command, Department of the Cumberland (October-November 1861); commanding 7th Brigade, Army of the Ohio (November-December 2, 1861); commanding 7th Brigade, 2nd Division, Army of the Ohio (December 2, 1861-March 15, 1862); commanding 7th Independent Brigade, Army of the Ohio (March 15-September 14, 1862); commanding 8th Division, Army of the Ohio (September 14-November 5, 1862); commanding 2nd Division, Center, 14th Corps, Army of the Cumberland (November 5, 1862-January 9, 1863); major general, USV (November 29, 1862); and commanding 2nd Division, 14th Corps, Army of the Cumberland (January 9-October 10, 1863). After supervising recruiting in his native area around Pittsburgh, he took the field under Robert Patterson until he was mustered out on July 20, 1861. Back in service that fall, he was given a brigade in Kentucky and served there and in the advance on Nashville. With Bragg's movement into Kentucky, Negley remained in Tennessee guarding Nashville while Buell went in pursuit. Thus Negley missed the fighting at Perryville but capably directed his division at Murfreesboro. Promoted to major general, he served through the Tullahoma Campaign and then on to Chickamauga. There on the second day of the battle he was caught up in the rout of nearly two-thirds of the Army of the Cumberland. Not long afterwards he was relieved of duty and was charged with cowardice and deserting his men. Cleared by a court of inquiry, he spent the balance of his time in uniform awaiting orders which never came. Finally realizing the writing on the wall, he resigned on January 19, 1865. A four-term congressman from Pittsburgh, the Republican was also active in railroading.

The career of James S. Negley was another victim of Chickamauga. (*Leslie's*)

NEILL, Thomas Hewson (1826-1885)

A career officer, Thomas H. Neill served for much of the Civil War in staff assignments and thus is one of the lesser-known brigadier generals in the Union army. The Pennsylvanian West Pointer (1847) was posted to the infantry but missed the Mexican War, instead performing frontier duty and being an instructor at his alma mater. His Civil War assignments included: captain, 5th Infantry (since April 1, 1857); assistant adjutant general, 1st Division, Department of Pennsylvania (summer 1861); colonel, 23rd Pennsylvania (February 17, 1862); commanding 3rd Brigade, 2nd Division, 6th Corps, Army of the Potomac (December 13, 1862-May 28, 1863, June 10, 1863-January 4, 1864, and March 25-May 6, 1864); brigadier general, USV (April 15, 1863, to rank from November 29, 1862); major, 11th Infantry (August 26, 1863); commanding the division (January 4-February 21 and May 7-June 21, 1864); and acting inspector general, Middle Military Division (September-December 1864). After serving on George Cadwalader's staff in the first summer of the war, he was commissioned a colonel in the volunteer service from his native state and led his regiment to the Peninsula and the fighting at Yorktown, Williamsburg, Seven Pines, and in the Seven Days. In the latter he earned a brevet for Malvern Hill. His division being too far in the rear, he did not get into action at Antietam but succeeded to brigade command at Fredericksburg. Again at Chancellorsville he received a brevet for the actions at Marye's Heights and Salem Church. His promotion to brigadier had come through shortly before this battle but had been backdated to November 29, 1862. At Gettysburg his brigade had a limited role. He then participated in the Bristoe and Mine Run campaigns. In the Overland Campaign, he succeeded the wounded George W. Getty in divisional command and held the post through Spotsylvania—where he was again brevetted—Cold Harbor, and the beginnings of the Petersburg Campaign. That summer he served in a staff position with the 18th Corps before joining Sheridan in the Shenandoah Valley, again as a staff officer, seeing action at Cedar Creek. After December 1864 his role is not apparent in the records. Mustered out of the volunteer service as a brevet major general on August 24, 1865, he retained his regular army commission until his 1883 retirement as colonel, 8th Cavalry. He had been brevetted brigadier general in that service for the war. Before his retirement he spent four years at his alma mater, as the commandant of cadets, and in Texas.

NELSON, Allison (1822-1862)

For Allison Nelson the Civil War was but another in a series of adventures. The Georgia-born local politician had always been more interested in things military. He took part in the Mexican War as captain of an independent Georgia company, the Cuban independence movement as a general, and in the agony of "Bleeding Kansas." Having moved to Texas in 1856 and favoring secession at the Texas convention, he helped raise the 10th Texas. Becoming the regiment's first colonel, he was stationed initially at Galveston and along the coast. Moving his regiment to Arkansas in June 1862, his later commands included: commanding a brigade, Trans-Mississippi Department (late June-August 20, 1862); commanding a brigade and a division, District of Arkansas, Trans-Mississippi Department (August 20-September 28, 1862); brigadier general (September 12, 1862); and commanding 1st Brigade, 2nd Division, Trans-Mississippi Department and the division (September 28-October 11, 1862). After seeing only limited campaigning he died of fever on October 11, 1862. His most important contribution was in stemming organized desertion by the strict punishment of ringleaders.

NELSON, Samuel (1792-1873)

One of the less controversial jurists to sit upon the Supreme Court during the Civil War era, New York Samuel Nelson spent nearly half a century as a judge. A lawyer and politician, he became a circuit judge in 1823 and joined the state supreme court in 1831; he became the latter's presiding judge in 1837. Then, after two other appointees had been rejected by the Senate, President John Tyler named Nelson to a Supreme Court vacancy on February 4, 1845. Ten days later he was confirmed by a voice vote. In the highly controversial *Dred Scott* case he ruled that Scott had the right to sue in the courts but favored upholding the lower court's ruling against him on the merits of the specific case. This was the least extreme of the majority opinions. He sat throughout the Civil War and in 1871 was a member of the commission which settled the claims against Great Britain for damages resulting from the *Alabama* and other British-built Confederate raiders. He resigned from the bench for health reasons on November 28, 1872. (Fehrenbacher, Don E., *The Dred Scott Case: Its Significance in American Law and Politics*)

NELSON, William (1824-1862)

A naval officer, Kentuckian William Nelson joined the land forces for the Civil War only to be murdered by one of his fellow officers. As a 20-year veteran of the U.S. Navy, Nelson had risen to the rank of lieutenant by the start of hostilities. Reporting to Lincoln that there was strong Union sentiment in his home state, Nelson was made a recruiting officer there, and he established Camp Dick Robinson as a depot. Made a brigadier general of volunteers on September 16, 1861, his later assignments included: commanding 4th Division, Army of the Ohio, in the Department of the Ohio (December 2, 1861-March 11, 1862) and in the Department of the Mississippi (March 11-August 16, 1862); lieutenant commander, USN (July 16, 1862); major general, USV (July 17, 1862); and commanding Army of Kentucky, Department of the Ohio (August 19-September 29, 1862). As a part of Buell's reinforcing army, Nelson led his division across the Tennessee River at Pittsburg Landing to find masses of defeated Union soldiers cowering under the bluffs late on the first day at Grant's battle of Shiloh. That evening he helped stabilize the position and took part in the counterattack the next day. After the advance on Corinth, he returned to Kentucky to oppose Bragg's invasion. Arriving late in the day at the battle of Richmond, Kentucky, he took command but was badly defeated by Kirby Smith and was slightly wounded. While organizing the defense of Louisville, Nelson had several altercations with General Jefferson C. Davis, who was a volunteer assisting him. On September 29, 1862, in a hotel, Davis shot Nelson at close range with a borrowed pistol, and Nelson died a few minutes later. Davis was soon released from arrest because officers couldn't be spared to form a court-martial. (Fry, James B., *Killed by a Brother Soldier*)

NESMITH, James Willis (1820-1885)

An early settler of the Oregon Territory, James W. Nesmith served it in the field against Indians, as a judge, and in Washington. Born in Canada to parents on a visit there from Maine, he moved to New Hampshire in the late 1820s, to Ohio in 1838, and finally to the West Coast in 1843. He was admitted to the bar but never practiced law. Instead he was a farmer and rancher before becoming a judge two years after his arrival. In the various Indian wars of the 1840s and 1850s, he served as a captain and colonel of volunteers. He was a U.S. marshal for two years and briefly was the superintendent for Indian Affairs for the territories of Washington and Oregon. He went to Washington as a Democratic senator and took his seat on March 4, 1861. Having lost a reelection bid he left office in 1867, and his appointment to a diplomatic post in Austria was not confirmed. In the 1870s he again served one term in Congress, this time in the House, but did not seek reelection.

NEWSOM, Ella King (ca. 1830s-post 1913)

A wealthy Arkansas widow, Ella K. Newsom became "The Florence Nightingale of the Southern Army." The Mississippi-born widow of a doctor, she joined the Confederate army as a nurse upon the outbreak of the war and afterwards served in hospitals at Memphis, Nashville, Chattanooga, Bowling Green, Atlanta, Corinth (Mississippi), and Abingdon (Virginia). Much of her time was spent in the training of other nurses. After the war she was married for a time to an ex-Confederate Arkansas officer. While working for the Washington pension office she wrote *Reminiscences of War*

Time. She died in the nation's capital. (Richard, J. Fraise, *The Florence Nightingale of the Southern Army*)

NEWTON, John (1823-1895)

Highly competent, Virginian John Newton nonetheless lost his second star due to his problems with Congress. Graduating number two from West Point (1842), he was posted to the Engineers and performed routine engineering duty, instructed at the academy, and was chief engineer during the 1858 expedition against the Mormons. His Civil War-era assignments included: captain, Engineers (since July 1, 1856); chief engineer, Department of Pennsylvania (May 29-July 23, 1861); chief engineer, Department of the Shenandoah (July 23-August 17, 1861); major, Engineers (August 6, 1861); brigadier general, USV (September 23, 1861); commanding 3rd Brigade, Franklin's Division, Army of the Potomac (October 3, 1861-March 13, 1862); commanding 3rd Brigade, 1st Division, 1st Corps, Army of the Potomac (March 13-April 4, 1862); commanding 3rd Brigade, 1st Division, Department of the Rappahannock (April 4-May 18, 1862); commanding 3rd Brigade, 1st Division, 6th Corps, Army of the Potomac (May 18-September 21, 1862); commanding the division (October 15-18, 1862); commanding 3rd Division, 6th Corps, Army of the Potomac (October 18-late December 1862 and February-July 1, 1863); major general, USV (March 30, 1863); commanding 1st Corps, Army of the Potomac (July 2, 1863-March 24, 1864); commanding 2nd Division, 4th Corps, Army of the Cumberland (April 16-September 30, 1864); brigadier general, USV (reappointed April 18, 1864); commanding District of Key West and Tortugas, Department of the Gulf (October 15, 1864-July 1865); and lieutenant colonel, Engineers (December 28, 1865). Early in the war he continued his engineering duties, including as chief of that branch for the forces engaged at Falling Waters. Promoted to brigadier of volunteers during the first fall of the war, he commanded a brigade in the vicinity of Washington and Fredericksburg before leading it in action at the Seven Days, South Mountain, and Antietam. In the latter he received his first regular army brevet. At Fredericksburg his division was only slightly engaged, but he soon became involved in a dispute with army commander Burnside. A number of officers were displaced, but for Newton the penalty was the later revocation of his major general's commission. But as a major general he distinguished himself in the assault on Marye's Heights during the battle of Chancellorsville. At Gettysburg Meade tapped him to command the 1st Corps after the fall of John F. Reynolds. He continued in command of that unit—through the Bristoe and Mine Run campaigns—until the spring 1864 reorganization displaced him. Sent to the West, as a brigadier again as of April 18, 1864, he commanded a division throughout the Atlanta Campaign, being brevetted brigadier in the regular army for Peach Tree Creek. After the fall of the city he commanded for the rest of the war at Key West. Brevetted major general in both the volunteers and the regulars, he was mustered out of the former on January 31, 1866. In 1886 he retired from the regular establishment as brigadier general and chief engineer of the army. Subsequently he was in railroading and public works.

NICHOLLS, Francis Reddin Tillou (1834-1912)

In a rather limited combat career Francis R.T. Nicholls suffered two amputations and was retired to post and conscript duty. A West Pointer (1855), he had served one year in the artillery before resigning to study law. Giving up his practice, he raised the Phoenix Guards and offered them to the Confederacy. His assignments included: captain, Company K, 8th Louisiana (spring 1861); lieutenant colonel, 8th Louisiana (June 9, 1861); colonel, 15th Louisiana (June 24, 1862); brigadier general, CSA (October 14, 1862); commanding 2nd Louisiana Brigade, Jackson's (old) Division, 2nd Corps, Army of Northern Virginia (January 16-May 2, 1863); and commanding post at Lynchburg, Va. (August 11, 1863-June 1864). He fought at 1st Bull Run and joined Jackson for the Shenandoah Valley Campaign in which he was captured and lost his left arm at 1st Winchester. During his convalescence after an exchange he was transferred to a new regiment and twice promoted. Finally returning to duty in January 1863, he led a brigade at Chancellorsville until again wounded, this time in the foot by a shell. Amputation completed the projectile's work. Three months later he was assigned to post duty at Lynchburg, holding the position until June 1864. The next month he was ordered to the Trans-Mississippi Department to head the volunteer and conscript service. He finished the war there. Back in Louisiana he served two separate terms as governor, supressed the Louisiana Lottery, and headed the state supreme court. (Freeman, Douglas S., *Lee's Lieutenants*).

NICHOLSON, Alfred Osborn Pope (1808-1876)

In a manner highly typical of the nineteenth century, Alfred O.P. Nicholson mixed the fields of law, politics, and journalism in his career. The native Tennessean was admitted to the bar in 1831 and the next year became the editor of the *Columbia (Tenn.) Western Mercury*. Sent to the state legislature in 1833, he gave up his editorship two years later. He remained in the legislative post until named to fill a vacancy in the U.S. Senate in 1839. He took his seat as a Democrat in 1840 and held it until 1842 when his appointment lapsed. The next year he was elected to the upper house of the state legislature and served there until 1845. From 1844 until 1846 he edited the *Nashville Union* and then went into banking. Having turned down a cabinet post in 1853, he became the editor of the *Washington Union* until 1856. He was again named to the U.S. Senate and served from 1859 until March 3, 1861. He did not return for the next congress and was formally expelled by a resolution on July 11, 1861. After the war he was the chief justice of the Tennessee Supreme Court from 1870 until his death.

NICKERSON, Franklin Stillman (1826-1917)

Native Maine lawyer and customs official Franklin S. Nickerson was among the last Union generals to die just as the United

States was about to enter World War I. His assignments included: major, 4th Maine (June 5, 1861); lieutenant colonel, 4th Maine (September 9, 1861); colonel, 14th Maine (November 25, 1861); commanding 3rd Brigade, 2nd Division, 19th Corps, Department of the Gulf (January 13-August 10, 1863); brigadier general, USV (March 16, 1863, to rank from November 29, 1862); also commanding the division (May 28-30, 1863); commanding 1st Brigade, 3rd Division, 19th Corps, Department of the Gulf (July 10-August 15 and August 29-September 20, 1863); commanding the division (August 15-29, 1863); and commanding 1st Brigade, 2nd Division, 19th Corps, Department of the Gulf (February 15-June 29, 1864). He was a field officer at 1st Bull Run where he distinguished himself. Promoted to the colonelcy of a new regiment, he sailed with it to New Orleans and commanded the left wing at the battle of Baton Rouge. Promoted to brigadier general in early 1863, he led a brigade and briefly the division at Port Hudson. His brigade played a minor role in the Red River Campaign in the spring of 1864. After the summer of 1864 he held no further command assignments and he resigned on May 13, 1865, and resumed the practice of law.

NICODEMUS, William Joseph Leonard (ca. 1835-1879)

With the removal of Colonel A.J. Myer as chief signal officer on November 10, 1863, Lieutenant Colonel William Nicodemus took over that position. A West Pointer (1858), Nicodemus had served on the frontier and was, by the time of Fort Sumter, a second lieutenant in the 5th Infantry. His later assignments included: first lieutenant, 11th Infantry (May 14, 1861); captain, 12th Infantry (October 24, 1861); colonel, 4th Maryland (October 11-November 17, 1862); major, Signal Corps (September 18, 1863, to rank from March 3, 1863); and lieutenant colonel, Signal Corps (June 30, 1864, to rank from March 3, 1863). After Nicodemus transferred to the Signal Corps, eventually becoming its head, he was removed from his post just over a year later, on December 26, 1864. He was dismissed from the army for having published documents without the permission of the secretary of war. He was restored to duty in the corps on March 31, 1865, but under a new chief, Colonel B.F. Fisher. He was mustered out of the Signal Corps in August and resumed his captaincy in the 12th Infantry. He was brevetted major for the battle of Valverde, New Mexico, and continued in the regular army until 1870.

NICOLAY, John George (1832-1901)

A German-born newspaper editor in Springfield, Illinois, John Nicolay became associated, as a Republican, with Abraham Lincoln and was asked to become the president-elect's personal secretary. Living in the White House, Nicolay was more of a chief of staff than a secretary and became intimately acquainted with the president. After the war he was with the foreign service in Paris and was the marshal at the U.S. Supreme Court. He also collaborated with his old assistant from the White House, John Hay, in a 10-volume biography of the martyred president, published in 1890. (Nicolay, John G. and Hay, John, *Abraham Lincoln: A History* and Sandburg, Carl, *Abraham Lincoln: The Prairie Years and The War Years*)

NISBET, Eugenius Aristides (1803-1871)

As the culmination of a political career which spanned the Whig, Know-Nothing, and Democratic parties, Eugenius A. Nisbet chaired the convention committee which drafted Georgia's secession ordinance. The Georgia native had practiced law, served in both houses of the state legislture, served a term in the U.S. Congress, and been an associate justice of the state supreme court before returning to private practice in 1853. Always a states' righter, he nonetheless supported Stephen A. Douglas in the 1860 election and was elected to the secession convention as a staunch Unionist. Named to the Provisional Confederate Congress after his shift to secession, he sat on the committees on: Foreign Affairs; and Territories. He backed Alexander H. Stephens for vice president and favored a single eight-year presidential term. Although generally a supporter of the central government, he wished to maintain state control over volunteers. For reasons of health he resigned on December 10, 1861, and returned to private life.

NORTHROP, Lucius Bellinger (1811-1894)

One of the most hated men in any army is the commissary, and Lucius B. Northrop was no exception. Born in Charleston, South Carolina, he had graduated from West Point in 1831 and been posted to the infantry but two years later secured his transfer to the dragoons. Severely wounded fighting the Seminoles in Florida, he went on an apparently permanent sick leave. (Actually, the knee wound was inflicted by his own pistol when it accidentally discharged). He studied at the Jefferson Medical College in Philadelphia and then entered upon private practice in Charleston. In 1848 he was dropped from the army rolls for practicing his profession but was reinstated at the behest of his old army comrade, Jefferson Davis, who then sat in the U.S. Senate. On January 8, 1861, he resigned his commission as a captain in the 1st Dragoons and joined the South. There his assignments included: lieutenant colonel and acting commissary general of Subsistence (March 27, 1861); colonel and commissary general of Subsistence (June 21, 1861, to rank from March 16); and Brigadier General, CSA (November 26, 1864). He almost immediately ran into problems with field commanders when, after 1st Bull Run, Joseph E. Johnston and Beauregard blamed their inability to follow up the victory with a drive on Washington on the commissary department. Northrop was forced to deal with an inadequate transportation system and did the best anyone probably could. But that was not good enough for the Confederate cause, and he was too dedicated to red tape to come up with the miracles required. Lee was also displeased with Northrop but did not insist upon his removal until early 1865. In the meantime Northrop had survived a number of congressional investigations, and his friend Davis was even afraid to submit his appointment of Northrop to brigadier general to the Senate for confirmation. In the end even Davis despaired of the wisdom of retaining

Northrop and the latter was finally relieved on February 16, 1865. After the fall of the Confederacy, he was arrested by the Federals, on June 30, 1865, on the charge of having deliberately starved Union war prisoners. The charges were never pressed and he was released in October. He then retired to a Virginia farm. (Dufour, Charles L., *Nine Men in Gray*)

NORTON, Lemuel B. (?-1871)

Entering the volunteer army in 1861, Pennsylvanian Lemuel B. Norton became a signal officer and remained in the army until his death a decade later. His assignments included: first lieutenant, 10th Pennsylvania Reserves (July 21, 1861); captain, 10th Pennsylvania Reserves (May 1, 1863); captain, Signal Corps (March 3, 1863); chief signal officer, Army of the Potomac (1863-65); chief signal officer, Army of the James (1864-65); and chief signal officer, Department of the Susquehanna (1864). His regiment served in the Seven Days, 2nd Bull Run, Antietam, and Fredericksburg before he relinquished his line commission on June 27, 1863, having been made an officer in the Signal Corps. He had been detailed to such duty for some time. He received a brevet for commanding the corps at Gettysburg and another for the Overland and Richmond-Petersburg campaigns. In the 1866 army reorganization he was commissioned a second lieutenant in the 30th Infantry. Mustered out as a signal officer on May 7, 1867, he joined the regiment and died while serving as a first lieutenant in the 1st Artillery.

NUGENT, Robert (?-1901)

An officer of the famed Irish Brigade, Robert Nugent lost his home in the New York draft riots in July 1863. The native of Ireland had been a War Democrat when he entered the Union army. His assignments included: lieutenant colonel, 69th New York Militia (April 20, 1861); captain, 13th Infantry (August 5, 1861); colonel, 69th New York (November 1, 1861); commanding 2nd ("Irish") Brigade, 1st Division, 2nd Corps, Army of the Potomac (June 28-29 and July 16-August 8, 1862, November 5, 1864-January 29, 1865, and February 17-June 28, 1865); acting assistant provost marshal general, Southern Division of New York (April-October 1863); and colonel, 69th New York (recommissioned October 30, 1864). After serving at 1st Bull Run he was mustered out with his militia regiment on August 3, 1861. Two days later he was commissioned a captain in one of the new regular army infantry regiments. That fall he took the field at the head of one of the Irish Brigade regiments. He fought at Seven Pines and during the Seven Days earned a brevet at Gaines' Mill and briefly commanded the brigade. He was later brevetted in the regular army for Fredericksburg where the command wasdecimated. With the 69th reduced to a battalion of only two companies Nugent was detached to serve as a draft official in New York City. He was instrumental in calming the disturbances, but his home was destroyed by the rioters. On November 28, 1863, he was mustered out of the volunteer service. However, late in the war he was recommissioned and he served through the Petersburg and Appomattox campaigns, being brevetted a regular army colonel for the former. Finally mustered out of the volunteers on June 30, 1865, he remained in the army until his retirement as major, 24th Infantry—one of the black regiments—in 1879. (Conyngham, David Powers, *The Irish Brigade and Its Campaigns*)

NYE, James Warren (1815-1876)

Upon the admission of Nevada to the Union, James W. Nye became the state's junior senator in Washington. Born in New York, he was a lawyer and anti-slavery politician. In 1839 he had served as a district attorney and from 1840 to 1848 was a judge. In 1846 he ran for Congress on the Anti-Slavery ticket but was defeated. After leaving the bench he resumed his private practice for almost a decade. In 1857 he was tapped to become the first president of the newly formed Metropolitan Board of Police in New York City. Holding the post until 1860, he presided over the conflict with the rival Municipal Police, which was deemed to be highly corrupt; there were actual battles between the two forces. Upon his inauguration, Lincoln chose Nye to be the governor of Washoe (later Nevada) Territory. When the state was admitted to the Union on October 15, 1864, Nye was elected to a senatorship and took his seat on December 16. Drawing lots for the length of his term, it was determined that it would end in 1867, at which time he gained a full six-year term. He died three years after leaving office, back in New York.

O

OATES, William Calvin (1833-1910)

It was not until the Spanish-American War that William C. Oates got to wear the stars of a general. A native of Alabama, he had entered the Confederate army where his assignments included: captain, Company G, 15th Alabama (July 1861); colonel, 15th Alabama (April 28, 1863); major, 15th Alabama (in 1864, to date from April 28, 1863); and lieutenant colonel, 15th Alabama (December 7, 1864). With his company he served in the Shenandoah Valley Campaign, the Seven Days, Cedar Mountain, Antietam, and Fredericksburg. While taking part in Longstreet's campaign in southeastern Virginia he was named colonel, but it was never confirmed and he officially became a major from that date at some time in early 1864. He became a bitter enemy of the man who became colonel in his stead, Alexander A. Lowther, and charged him with incompetence and cowardice. In the meantime, he had commanded the regiment at Gettysburg where he led his command to the top of Big Round Top. Realizing that this point was the key to the Union's southern flank, he wanted to hold the position and bring up some artillery. His orders were to advance against Little Round Top and this was confirmed by a staff officer. Advancing down the hill and up the next, he took part in the attack on the 20th Maine. He never forgot the lost opportunity, when he actually saw the enemy supply trains in their rear. Oates went on to command the 15th at Chickamauga and Knoxville. He served in his reduced capacity through the rest of the war in Virginia. After the war he was a governor and congressman and in the war with Spain donned the blue uniform of a U.S. brigadier general. He wrote an excellent war memoir. (Oates, William C., *The War Between the Union and the Confederacy and Its Lost Opportunities*)

O'BRIEN, J.H. (?-1863)

The colonel of a New York regiment in the New York City Draft Riots, J.H. O'Brien was tortured at the hands of an irate mob. During the course of the three days of heavy fighting he fell into the hands of rioters and was dragged through the cobblestoned streets at the end of a rope. Given the last rites by a Catholic priest, who quickly made his departure, the officer was repeatedly slashed and stoned. After a respite, laying in the street, he was finally killed in his own backyard.

Like this policeman, Colonel J.H. O'Brien lost his life in the New York City draft riots. (NA)

O'CONNELL, Mary

See: *Anthony, Sister*

O'CONNOR, Edgar (ca. 1833-1862)

An 1854 graduate of West Point, Edgar O'Connor was the only regimental commander of the "Iron Brigade" to be killed in the encounter at Groveton, Virginia. Having served four years as a subaltern in the 7th Infantry, O'Connor had resigned from the army in 1858. Returning to the military, he was named colonel of the 2nd Wisconsin on August 2, 1861. After a year serving in northern Virginia, the brigade, including the 2nd Wisconsin, was struck by two divisions under Stonewall Jackson while marching along the Warrenton Turnpike. Wheeling off the road, the four regiments formed a battle line, reinforced by two regiments from another brigade, and, facing the rebel line at close range, exchanged fire with it. The fight lasted an hour and a half until night brought a close to the action. Thus, on August 28, 1862, the Iron Brigade was born. But Edgar O'Connor was dead on the field.

O'CONNOR, John (fl. 1861-1865)

Military justice in the Civil War was unevenly administered, as is demonstrated by the case of bounty jumper John O'Connor. By his own count he had enlisted, collected a bounty, and deserted 32 times before being caught. Tried in Albany, New York, by a military court-martial in March 1865, he received a four-year prison term. This is almost unbelievably mild. At the same time, true soldiers who had tired of the army and deserted, or just fallen asleep on picket duty, were being executed.

ODELL, Moses Fowler (1818-1866)

The entire period of Moses F. Odell's two terms in Congress was embraced by the Civil War, and perhaps his most important committee assignment was to the Joint Committee on the Conduct of the War. Employed by the customs department since 1845, the New York native entered politics by winning, as a Democrat, a seat in the U.S. House of Representatives in 1860. His two terms ran from March 4, 1861, to March 3, 1865. Since the joint investigating committee was controlled by the Radical Republicans, Odell did not take a leading role in its proceedings. At the end of his second term he was named an agent of the navy at New York City and held the post until his death.

OGLESBY, Richard James (1824-1899)

An original member of the Republican Party, Richard Oglesby resigned his major general's commission to run successfully for the governorship of his adopted state, Illinois. Born in Kentucky, he had practiced law in Illinois before serving as a lieutenant of Illinois troops in the Mexican War and taking part in the California Gold Rush. Returning to practice law in Illinois, he joined the fledgling Republican Party and failed in an 1858 bid for a seat in Congress. He resigned a seat in the state senate to join the Union Army. His assignments included: colonel, 8th Illinois (April 25, 1861); colonel, 8th Illinois (reorganized July 25, 1861); commanding 2nd Brigade, Military District of Cairo, Department of the Missouri (October 14, 1861-February 1, 1862); commanding 1st Brigade, 1st Division, Military District of Cairo, Department of the Missouri (February 1-17, 1862); commanding 1st Brigade, 1st Division, Army of the Tennessee (February 17-23, 1862); brigadier general, USV (March 21, 1862); commanding 3rd Brigade, 1st Division, Army of the Tennessee (April 13-15, 1862); commanding 2nd Brigade, 2nd Division, Army of the Tennessee (April 15-July 1862); commanding 2nd Brigade, 2nd Division, District of Corinth, Army of the Tennessee (July-October 3, 1862); major general, USV (November 29, 1862); and commanding Left Wing, 16th Corps, Army of the Tennessee (April 1-July 7, 1863). Upon the expiration of his unit's original three-months term he was able to reenlist the regiment and lead a brigade at Forts Henry and Donelson. After participating in the advance upon Corinth, Mississippi, he was stationed there for some months before being severely wounded on the first day of the battle there. When he returned to duty the following spring, he had a second star. For a time he commanded the part of the 16th Corps still in western Tennessee and northern Mississippi. He resigned his commission on May 26, 1864, to run as the Republican candidate for governor and was successful. Inaugurated on January 16, 1865, he oversaw the ratification of the Civil War-era constitutional amendments and the repeal of anti-black legislation. Ineligible for reelection, he practiced law until again elected governor in 1872. He served only a few days in 1873 before resigning to take a seat in the U.S. Senate. Serving only one term, he was again inaugurated as governor in 1885. He finally retired in 1889. (Davidson, Alexander and Stuve, Bernard, *A Complete History of Illinois from 1673 to 1873*)

Richard J. Oglesby, Union general and Illinois governor. (*Leslie's*)

O'LAUGHLIN, Michael (1840-1867)

He was only one of the four Lincoln assassination conspirators sent to Dry Tortugas not to benefit from Andrew Johnson's 1869 releases; Michael O'Laughlin had died there in a yellow fever epidemic two years earlier. Like Samuel B. Arnold, he had been a childhood friend of John Wilkes Booth in Baltimore and had been in the Confederate army for a time. He was working as a clerk in Baltimore when he was summoned by Booth. When he heard the plan to kidnap Lincoln and cart him off to Richmond for a possible prisoner exchange, he was shocked. However, the well-known magnetism of the actor won him over and he was involved in the planning and attempts. But when the plan turned to murder, O'Laughlin did not play an active role, but neither did he report what he knew. After hearing of the assassination he turned himself in on April 17, 1865, in Baltimore. Tried with seven other plotters, in a proceeding in which there was little if any concern for the rights of the defendants; he was found guilty on June 30, 1865, and was sentenced to life imprisonment. During the epidemic at Dry Tortugas in which Dr. Samuel A. Mudd so distinguished himself, O'Laughlin succumbed.

Michael O'Laughlin, Lincoln conspirator. (NA)

OLD ABE (1861-1881)

Stolen from his nest by a young Indian in Wisconsin, Old Abe served through most of the Civil War as the mascot of the 8th Wisconsin Infantry and became the Union's war eagle. The eagle was given to Company C, the color company of the regiment, by a farmer in 1861 and soon went to the front in Missouri where it was introduced to war, riding on a specially designed perch next to the regimental standards. Often breaking free, the bird would soar over the battle lines and swoop down against enemy positions. The eagle would then return to its post next to the colors. Despite deliberate enemy attempts to shoot him down, he survived the fighting at Island #10, Farmington, Iuka, Corinth, and Vicksburg. Although the regiment was serving in the Red River Campaign and not in the operations against Atlanta, Old Abe is depicted in the Atlanta Cyclorama circling over the battle lines. The bird was considered a patriot and was known to salute by spreading its wings, flapping, and issuing a special scream. Recipients of these salutes included General Grant and the colors of passing regiments. On September 26, 1864, Old Abe returned to Wisconsin with the non-reenlisting veterans and was given to the state. Over the succeeding years pictures of the war eagle and some of his old feathers were sold for charitable enterprises. The loyal bird would even allow his fellow veterans of the 8th to hug him. In 1881 he died from the inhalation of toxic fumes in a capitol fire. His remains were stuffed and finally destroyed in another capitol blaze in 1904. (Nelson, C.P., *Abe—The War Eagle*)

OLDEN, Charles Smith (1799-1876)

Due to its state constitution, New Jersey lost a Republican governor, Charles S. Olden, because he could not succeed himself, and the state fell into Democratic hands. Olden had been engaged in several businesses in his native New Jersey, Pennsylvania, and Louisiana before returning to Princeton as a farmer. After a brief time in banking he entered the state senate and in 1859 was elected governor. He was sworn in on January 17, 1860, and was soon embroiled in preparations for war. He was active in supporting the military effort until forced to retire at the end of his term on January 20, 1863. He subsequently held a number of judicial and governmental appointments. (Kull, Irving S., *New Jersey: A History*)

OLDHAM, Williamson Simpson (1813-1868)

A deeply disappointed secessionist, Williamson S. Oldham refused to take the oath of allegiance upon his return to his adopted Texas from Canada. A Tennessee native, he was a teacher and lawyer before moving to Arkansas where he served as speaker of the lower house of the legislature and as a state supreme court justice. Defeated in bids for both houses of the national legislature he moved to Texas in 1849. A Democrat, he edited the *Texas State Gazette* and became an ardent secessionist. He attended the secession convention and sat in the Confederate Congress from March 2, 1861, to the end of the Confederacy. During the Provisional Congress he sat on the Committees on: Engrossment; Judiciary; Naval Affairs; and Territories. Named to the Senate, his committee assignments included those on: Claims (Second Congress); Commerce (both congresses; chairman in Second Congress); Finance (Second Congress); Indian Affairs; Judiciary (Second Congress); Naval Affairs (First Congress); and Post Offices and Post Roads (chairman in both congresses). A firm believer in states' rights, he wanted many limitations on the national administration but in some fields was willing to grant predominate power to the Richmond authorities. He favored the fight against inflation, heavy taxes, and the recruiting of black troops. He also fought for better protection for his state. When the end came he fled via Mexico to Canada and became a photographer and wrote *The Last Days of the Confederacy*. He returned to Texas in 1866, embittered, and soon died of typhoid fever.

OLIVER, John Morrison (1828-1872)

New York-born Michigan druggist John M. Oliver rose from the rank of first lieutenant to that of brigadier general during the Civil War. His assignments included: first lieutenant, 4th Michigan (June 20, 1861); captain, 4th Michigan (September 25, 1861); Colonel, 15th Michigan (March 13, 1862); commanding 1st Brigade, 6th Division, Army of the Tennessee (temporarily April 1862); commanding 2nd Brigade, 6th Division, Army of the Tennessee (April 20-July 24, 1862); commanding 2nd Brigade, 6th Division, District of Corinth, Army of the Tennessee (July 24-November 1, 1862); commanding 2nd Brigade, 4th Division, 15th Corps, Army of the Tennessee (August 5-October 25, 1863); commanding 3rd Brigade, 4th Division, 15th Corps, Army of the Tennessee (May 6-August 4, 1864); commanding 1st Brigade, 4th Division, 15th Corps, Army of the Tennessee (August 4-September 14, 1864); commanding 3rd Brigade, 2nd Division, 15th Corps, Army of the Tennessee (November 2, 1864-May 18, 1865); brigadier general, USV (January 12, 1865); and commanding the division (May 18-August 1, 1865). As a subaltern in his initial regiment, he took part in the campaign of 1st Bull Run but was not present at the main battle, as the regiment was detached at Fairfax Courthouse during the advance. Named to the colonelcy of a new regiment, he led it in an unassigned capacity at Shiloh with part of Buell's army although it belonged properly to Grant's. He led a brigade both in the advance on Corinth, Mississippi, and in the subsequent battle there. Again as a regimental commander, he fought at Vicksburg and in the recapture of Jackson. In brigade command he fought through the Atlanta, Savannah, and Carolinas campaigns and was rewarded with the star of a brigadier general in early 1865. Brevetted major general for the war, he was mustered out on August 24, 1865. He earned his living as a lawyer and later as a postal official in Little Rock, before retiring to the nation's capital.

OLIVER, Paul Ambrose (1830-1912)

While serving as a staff officer, Paul A. Oliver won the Congressional Medal of Honor for preventing Union troops from firing upon each other. Born aboard a vessel in the English Channel, he was raised with a military training in Germany before becoming a merchant in the United States in 1849. His military assignments included: second lieutenant, 12th New York (October 29, 1861); first lieutenant, 12th New York (May 17, 1862); captain, 12th New York (April 22, 1864); and captain, 5th New York Veteran (June 1, 1864). His regiment fought at 1st Bull Run, on the Peninsula, at 2nd Bull Run—for which Oliver was commended by his regimental commander—Antietam, Fredericksburg, and Chancellorsville. After the last battle the regiment was reduced to a battalion of two companies and was assigned to provost guard duty with the 5th Corps. As such it fought at Gettysburg and in the Overland Campaign. Oliver was then transferred with the remnants of his battalion to a veteran regiment. During much of the war Oliver performed staff duty and eventually became detached from his command. Thus he fought in the western theater where he won his medal—awarded in 1892—for Resaca; on March 8, 1865, he was also brevetted brigadier general for this action. Resigning on May 6, 1865, he settled in Pennsylvania where he engaged in the manufacture of explosives. He is often given credit for developing dynamite. He was eventually bought out by the Du Pont firm of Delaware.

OLMSTEAD, Charles Hart (1837-1926)

Although he served through some of the heavy campaigns of the Army of Tennessee in the last year of the war, Charles H. Olmstead was fortunate enough to be on detached service during the disasters under Hood in Tennessee. His assignments included: major, 1st Georgia (1861); colonel, 1st Georgia (December 26, 1861); commanding Mercer's-Smith's Brigade, Cleburne's Division, 1st Corps, Army of Tennessee (August-fall and November 30, 1864-early 1865); and colonel, 1st Georgia Consolidated (April 9, 1865). Initially serving in the Savannah area, he surrendered Fort Pulaski after a two-day bombardment. Exchanged, he continued to serve on the Georgia coast until sent to the defense of Charleston in the summer of 1863. He then returned to the Savannah region until ordered to report to the Army of Tennessee on May 24, 1864. He served through the remainder of the Atlanta Campaign and during the siege took over command of the brigade. Relinquishing command to newly assigned General J.A. Smith after the fall of the city, he led his regiment into Tennessee with Hood. Smith took over the division after General Cleburne had been killed at Franklin and Olmstead was again in command of the brigade, which had been detached guarding a supply train during the fight. The brigade was again absent when the army was all but destroyed at Nashville. The army was then sent to North Carolina in the spring of 1865 to stop Sherman and on April 9, 1865, Olmstead took command of the 1st Georgia Consolidated which was composed of the old 1st, 57th, and 63rd regiments. He surrendered the command as a part of Johnston's army a few weeks later.

OLMSTED, Frederick Law (1822-1903)

Frederick Law Olmsted, the chief architect and superintendent of New York City's Central Park, took a leave of absence in 1861 to aid in the Union war effort. A Connecticut-born Yale student, he had studied engineering and then traveled widely. He wrote of his travels and joined the park and its operation in 1857. Granted his leave, he became the secretary general of the United States Sanitary Commission, a forerunner of the Red Cross, which concerned itself with providing for the troops what the government failed to provide. He was highly successful in his organizing work until ill health forced him to retire in 1863. He then superintended John C. Frémont's California estate until his return to the park in 1865. For the rest of his life he worked as a landscape architect. (Stevenson, Elizabeth, *Park Maker: A Life of Frederick Law Olmsted*)

O'NEAL, Edward Asbury (1818-1890)

A poor performance at Gettysburg caused the appointment of Edward A. O'Neal as a brigadier general to be revoked. A lawyer and secessionist politician in his native Alabama, he entered the Confederate army at the head of the Calhoun Guards. His later assignments included: captain, Company I, 9th Alabama (June 1861); lieutenant colonel, 9th Alabama (October 21, 1861); colonel, 26th Alabama (April 2, 1862); commanding Rodes' (old) Brigade, D.H. Hill's-Rodes' Division, 2nd Corps, Army of Northern Virginia (ca. January 14-May 3 and June-July 1863); brigadier general, CSA (June 6, 1863; revoked); and commanding Cantey's Brigade, Walthall's Division, Polk's-Lee's Corps (known as Army of Mississippi until July), Army of Tennessee (ca. June-fall 1864). On the Peninsula he fought at Yorktown and Seven Pines where he suffered a wound. Back on duty he fought in the Seven Days only to be hit again at South Mountain. In command of the brigade, he was wounded yet again at Chancellorsville. By the time of the battle of Gettysburg, General Lee had already received O'Neal's appointment to brigadier general but had not yet delivered it to him. Then disaster struck the recipient on the first day of the battle. He proved unable to control his five Alabama regiments which became scattered. Then Lee sent the commission back to the War Department, and President Davis canceled the appointment and recalled the request for Senate confirmation. Cullen A. Battle was assigned in his stead. In early 1864, O'Neal and the 26th were sent to Georgia and he commanded a brigade in the Atlanta Campaign. That fall he was relieved and he served out the war gathering up deserters in northern Alabama. A post-war lawyer he reentered politics and served two terms as governor. (Freeman, Douglas S., *Lee's Lieutenants*)

OPDYCKE, Emerson (1830-1884)

In a gallant display of initiative, Colonel Emerson Opdycke saved the day at the battle of Franklin and was later brevetted major general for it. The Ohio-born merchant had twice gone in search of gold to California but was back at home when the Civil War broke out. An abolitionist at heart, he enlisted early in the conflict and his assignments included: first lieutenant, 41st Ohio (August 26, 1861); captain, 41st Ohio (January 9, 1862); lieutenant colonel, 125th Ohio (October 1, 1862); colonel, 125th Ohio (January 14, 1863); commanding 1st Brigade, 2nd Division, 4th Corps, Army of the Cumberland (August 4, 1864-February 15, 1865 and March 15-June 7, 1865); commanding the division (June 24-July 11, 1865); and brigadier general, USV (July 26, 1865). With his initial unit he fought as a company commander at Shiloh and then resigned on September 17, 1862, to engage in recruiting a new regiment. As its lieutenant colonel, he aided in its training and was named its colonel before it took part in the Tullahoma Campaign. He led it at Chickamauga and stood with George H. Thomas on Horseshoe Ridge on the second day. At Chattanooga he was in charge of a demi-brigade in the charge up Missionary Ridge. During the Atlanta Campaign he was severely wounded at Resaca but was able to take command of a brigade within a few months. He was leading this unit, when, at Franklin, he was posted in reserve. When the Confederates forced back the two brigades of George D. Wagner—in his unauthorized stand beyond the Union works—and managed to break through the Union fortifications (since the Union troops couldn't fire into their retreating comrades), Opdycke acted without orders. He advanced and threw back the enemy. He later fought at Nashville and then served in East Tennessee and in Texas. While in the latter state he was named a brigadier general in the summer of 1865 but resigned on January 1, 1866. Settling in New York, he was again a merchant until he mortally wounded himself while cleaning a pistol.

OPDYKE, George (1805-1880)

During the draft riots of July 1863 New York City Mayor George Opdyke stood firm in his support of the federal Enrollment Act, twice vetoing bills passed by the city council authorizing the city to pay the $300 exemption fee for draftees. Having become a millionaire in clothing and dry goods, Opdyke entered politics and in 1854 became an early Republican. After a term in the state assembly he served as mayor in 1862 and 1863. During the riots his powers were relatively limited since the police were under the control of a state commission. However, he was able to gain the commission's cooperation as well as the aid of federal troops and marines to restore order. He also issued proclamations to citizens to help maintain order. With calm restored, he vetoed an ordinance authorizing the expenditure of $2,500,000 to pay commuta-

George Opdyke, mayor of New York City during the draft riots, tried to halt such actions as the burning of the Second Avenue Armory. (AC)

tion. He opposed the bill because it tended to appease the mob and nullify a federal law. A similar bill was also vetoed. Opdyke did however favor the payment of commutation for police, firemen, and militia, and did sign a bill which added a fourth category--the indigent. Nonetheless his support of the draft was a shining example. During the riots his property had been a target. He remained active in political, especially economic, affairs for the rest of his life.

OPOTHLEYOHOLA (ca. 1781-?)

Although himself a slave holder, the chief of the Upper Creek, Opothleyohola, remained loyal to the Union despite the entreaties of Confederate agent Albert Pike and of the other leaders of the Five Civilized Tribes. Originally, the Creeks and Seminoles, both relatively small tribes, felt safe from the pro-Confederate Chickawaws and Chocktaws since the Cherokee were neutral. But in August 1861 the Cherokee signed a treaty with Pike. Realizing his position was now untenable, Opothleyohola in November led his people and some loyal Seminoles and Cherokees toward the Kansas border and the protection of the Union authorities. Attacked by Confederate Indians and Texas Cavalry, they suffered an estimated 700 casualties before reaching Kansas. Many of his men later enlisted in the Union's Indian Home Guard regiments rather than remain on the destitute reservations of other Indian tribes.

Opothleyohola, loyalist sub-chief of the Upper Creeks. (SI)

(Monaghan, Jay, *Civil War on the Western Border, 1854-1865*)

ORD, Edward Otho Cresap (1818-1883)

At least twice, Edward O.C. Ord was Grant's choice to succeed a troublesome subordinate. The Maryland native had received his West Point appointment from the nation's capital and upon his graduation in 1839 was posted to the artillery. His pre-Civil War service included fighting Seminoles, Mexican War duty in California, Indian fighting in the Northwest, and the aftermath of John Brown's Harpers Ferry raid. In California again at the outbreak of the Civil War his assignments included: captain, 3rd Artillery (since September 7, 1850); brigadier general, USV (September 14, 1861); commanding 3rd Brigade, McCall's Division, Army of the Potomac (October 3, 1861-March 13, 1862); major, 4th Artillery (November 21, 1861); commanding 3rd Brigade, 2nd Division, 1st Corps, Army of the Potomac (March 13-April 4, 1862); commanding 3rd Brigade, 2nd Division, Department of the Rappahannock (April 4-May 16, 1862); major general, USV (May 2, 1862); commanding division, Department of the Rappahannock (May 26-June 10, 1862); commanding 2nd Division, Army of the Tennessee (June-August 5, 1862); commanding 2nd Division, District of Corinth, Army of the Tennessee (August 5, 1862); commanding 3rd Division, Army of the Tennessee (September 24-October 5, 1862); commanding 13th Corps, Army of the Tennessee (June 19-July 28, 1863); commanding 13th Corps, Department of the Gulf (September 15-October 29, 1863 and January 9-February 20, 1864); commanding 18th Corps, Army of the James (July 21-September 4 and September 22-29, 1864); commanding the army (August 27-September 5, December 14-24, 1864, and January 8-May 1865); and also commanding 24th Corps, Army of the James (December 3-6, 1864). Ordered to the East as a brigadier general, he won one of the North's earliest victories at Dranesville, Virginia, while commanding a brigade of the Pennsylvania Reserves. While serving in northern Virginia, he rose to divisional command and received his second star. Soon thereafter he joined the forces in western Tennessee and northern Mississippi. Not actually present at either Iuka or Corinth, he received a regular army brevet for the former action in which he played a supporting role. After the latter he led his division in pursuit of the fleeing enemy and engaged them at the Hatchie. In the action he fell wounded and was out of service for a number of months. Returning to duty, he was tapped by Grant to take over the 13th Corps from the oft-troublesome John A. McClernand. He led the corps during the balance of the Vicksburg siege and accompanied Sherman in his capture of Jackson. Ord then took his corps to join Banks along the Gulf. Returning to Virginia, he was briefly in the Shenandoah Valley before being assigned to a corps in the Army of the James. Again wounded in the storming of Fort Harrison outside Richmond, he returned to duty in December 1864 and was then tapped, again by Grant, to replace Butler in charge of that army. As such he played a leading role in the final operations against Richmond and Petersburg and to Appomattox. Having been brevetted brigadier and major general in the regular army for the two battles in which he had been wounded, he was mustered out of the volunteer service on September 1, 1866. He reverted to his grade as brigadier general in the regulars, to which he had been appointed on July 26, 1866. In 1881 he was retired with the advanced grade of major general. He died of yellow fever in Cuba two years later. (Cresap, Bernard, *Appomattox Commander: The Story of E.O.C. Ord*)

Edward O.C. Ord, Appomattox commander of the Army of the James. (*Leslie's*)

O'REILLY, Miles

See: *Halpine, Charles Graham*

ORME, William Ward (1832-1866)

A friend and associate of Abraham Lincoln from the legal circuit in Illinois, William W. Orme was forced out of the Union army not by wounds but by tuberculosis, which was to kill him the year after the Civil War ended. The District of Columbia native's assignments included: colonel, 94th Illinois (August 20, 1862); commanding 2nd Brigade, 3rd Division, Army of the Frontier, Department of the Missouri (October 12-December 1862 and April 10-June 5, 1863); brigadier general, USV (March 13, 1863, to rank from November 29, 1862); commanding 2nd Brigade, Herron's Division, Army of the Tennessee (June 11-July 28, 1863); commanding 2nd Brigade, 2nd Division, 13th Corps, Army of the Tennessee (July 28-August 7, 1863); and commanding 2nd Brigade, 2nd Division, 13th Corps, Department of the Gulf (August 7-25, 1863). Leading a brigade at Prairie Grove, he was particularly distinguished and was soon advanced to a brigadier generalship. He accompanied Francis J. Herron's command to the Vicksburg siege lines where, from mid-June, it held the southern end of the Union position. Transferred to the Department of the Gulf shortly after the fall of the city, he was forced to relinquish command due to the health problems he developed while in Mississippi and Louisiana. Assigned to duty inspecting prisoner of war camps, he was later in charge of one, Camp Douglas, while in command of the Chicago area. Even this duty proved too much for his condition and he resigned on April 26, 1864. He was an agent of the Treasury Department at Memphis until his November 1865 resignation. Within a year he was dead.

O'RORKE, Patrick Henry (ca. 1836-1863)

Patrick O'Rorke, an Irish-born graduate of West Point (1861), played an important role in the defense of Little Round Top on the second day at Gettysburg. Appointed second lieutenant of engineers on June 24, 1861, his later assignments included: colonel, 140th New York (September 19, 1862); commanding 3rd Brigade, 2nd Division, 5th Corps, Army of the Potomac (December 1862-January 1863 and February 5-June 6, 1863); and first lieutenant, Corps of Engineers in the regular army (March 3, 1863). Serving as an engineer on the staff of General Tyler, O'Rorke participated in the battle of 1st Bull Run. Accompanying General T.W. Sherman's South Carolina expedition, O'Rorke participated in the actions at Port Royal Sound on that officer's staff. Remaining in the Department of the South he took part in the capture of Fort Pulaski. Switching to the volunteers, he was made colonel of a new regiment, the 140th New York, with which he participated in the fighting at Fredericksburg and Chancellorsville. At the latter place he commanded the brigade, which was the only volunteer brigade in the division. Again in command of only his regiment, the brigade being under General Weed, O'Rorke was on the way to bolster the lines of Sickles' 3rd Corps when his former brigade commander General Warren, now chief engineer of the army, directed him to the crest of Little Round Top. While the remainder of the brigade continued on its way, O'Rorke led the regiment up the wooded and rocky hill. Without waiting to realign his men O'Rorke led them in a charge down the south slope, driving the enemy back. He fell dead, a hero, in this charge. He was brevetted in the regular army: captain for Port Royal, major for Fredericksburg, lieutenant colonel for Chancellorsville, and colonel for Little Round Top.

ORR, James Lawrence (1822-1873)

The dilemma of the Confederacy, with its need for a strong central government in order to win it's independence and its inability to achieve that independence because of its own birth from a states' rights philosophy, is demonstrated in the Confederate career of James L. Orr. A native South Carolina lawyer, he had also edited the *Anderson Gazette* for two years before serving in the state legislature. He then served for five terms in the U.S. Congress--the last of which, 1857 to 1859, he served as speaker of the house--and was a supporter of Stephen A. Douglas. A Democrat, he was nonetheless a moderate on the question of secession and opposed the theory of nullification as it had been presented by John C. Calhoun. A believer in states' rights, he attended the 1851 Southern convention in Charleston and the Democratic conventions in 1856 and 1860. In December 1860 he attended the state secession convention and was sent to Washington, with two other commissioners, to negotiate the surrender of the national forts and other property in Charleston Harbor. After the fall of Fort Sumter he organized a regiment and was commissioned colonel, 1st South Carolina Rifles (July 20, 1861). He served with the regiment in the harbor area until February 1, 1862, when he resigned, having been elected to the Senate in the First Regular Confederate Congress. He was specially seated in the Provisional Congress on February 17, 1862, the day of its final adjournment. The next day he was formally seated in the Senate where he served for the remainder of the war. He was chairman of the Committee on Foreign Affairs throughout and of the Committee on Rules in the Second Congress. He also served on the First Congress committees on Commerce, Flag and Seal, and Pay and Mileage and the Second Congress committees on Finance and Printing. Initially supporting the required war measures, his states' rights philosophy caused him to revolt at increasing infringements on that philosophy. He opposed the draft and demanded full payment for impressed goods. He was a member of the group opposed to Jefferson Davis' friend General Braxton Bragg and opposed the suspension of the writ of habeas corpus. Late in the war he was the leader of the Senate peace block. The states' righters were denying the Confederacy the means to gain its independence. With the collapse of the Confederacy he went to Andrew Johnson to set up a provisional government for the state. Successful, he was elected governor in October 1865 and proved to be a moderate. He served until 1868 and then was a circuit judge. Becoming a Republican and a supporter of Grant's anti-KKK measures, he was named minister to Russia in late 1872. He died within a matter of months at St. Petersburg. (Leembuis, Roger, *James L. Orr and the Sectional Conflict*)

ORTON, Lawrence W.

See: *Williams, William Orton*

OSBORN, James M. (fl. 1861)

The high prices caused by the Union blockade ensured the virtual anonymity of Charleston photographer James M. Osborn despite his excellent work. Together with his partner, F.E. Durbec, he was operating "Osborn & Durbec's Photographic Mart" at 223 King Street at the outbreak of the Civil War. Within days of the firing upon Fort Sumter the pair took their stereo camera to the scene of the action and compiled an extraordinary record of the fort and the batteries which had compelled its submission. However, the blockade which was soon in place prevented them from acquiring the supplies they needed to market their prints in any large quantities. This may have led to the disruption of their partnership before the close of the war, but not before they had made a valuable contribution to the photographic coverage of the conflict.

OSBORN, Thomas Ogden (1832-1904)

By the time that Thomas O. Osborn received his commission as a brigadier general, hostilities had virtually ceased. The Ohio native had studied law in Indiana under Lew Wallace before setting up his own practice in Chicago. Recruiting for the Union army, he was soon commissioned and his assignments included: lieutenant colonel, 39th Illinois (October 11, 1861); colonel, 39th Illinois (January 1, 1862); commanding 3rd Brigade, 2nd Division, Detachment 18th Corps, St. Helena Island, 10th Corps, Department of the South (January-April 1863); commanding 2nd Brigade, Morris Island, 10th Corps, Department of the South (September 19-October 12, 1863); commanding 1st Brigade, 1st Division, 24th Corps, Army of the James (December 12, 1864-May 2, 1865 and July 8-25, 1865); brigadier general, USV (May 1, 1865); and commanding the division (May 2-July 8, 1865). After service in western Virginia he fought at Kernstown and in the Shenandoah Valley Campaign of 1862. Subsequently he was engaged in operations in southeastern Virginia and North Carolina before moving farther south, against Charleston. There he held a couple of brigade commands. Sent to join Benjamin F. Butler, he fought at Bermuda Hundred and lost the use of an arm at Drewry's Bluff. In the latter stages of the Petersburg siege and during the Appomattox Campaign he led a brigade. He was brevetted brigadier general of volunteers for his war service on March 10, 1865, and major general for his actions in the storming of Fort Gregg during the final assault on Petersburg. Following Lee's surrender he received the star of a full brigadier and resigned on September 28, 1865. He worked briefly as a lawyer and county treasurer and held minor governmental posts before becoming a highly successful diplomat in South America.

OSBORN, Thomas W. (1836-1896)

For some inexplicable reason, the rapid increase in Thomas W. Osborn's responsibilities—from battery commander to artillery chief for an army—was not matched by a commensurate rise in rank. The New Jersey-born New Yorker was studying law when the defeat at 1st Bull Run prompted him to enlist. His assignments included: captain, Battery D, 1st New York Light Artillery (ca. September 6, 1861); commanding Artillery, 2nd Division, 3rd Corps, Army of the Potomac (May 1863); major, 1st New York Light Artillery (spring 1863); commanding Artillery Brigade, 11th Corps, Army of the Potomac (May-September 25, 1863); commanding Artillery Brigade, 11th Corps, Army of the Cumberland (September 25, 1863-ca. April 13, 1864); chief of Artillery, 4th Corps, Army of the Cumberland (April 13-July 26, 1864); commanding Artillery Brigade, 4th Corps, Army of the Cumberland (July 26-ca. September 27, 1864); chief of Artillery, Army and Department of the Tennessee (ca. September 27, 1864-May 1865); and assistant commissioner, Freedmen's Bureau for Alabama (May

18, 1865). As a battery commander, he fought his guns on the Peninsula at Yorktown, Williamsburg, Seven Pines and during the Seven Days. He was at Fredericksburg, and at Chancellorsville he directed the guns of Berry's division. By the time of Gettysburg he was directing the 11th Corp's batteries—the command being for the first time designated a brigade. Going west with the corps, he fought at Chattanooga. When in the spring of 1864 the 11th and 12th corps were consolidated into the 20th, Osborn and his corps commander and close friend, Oliver O. Howard, were transferred to the 4th. For the balance of the war Osborn served as Howard's artillery chief, first at the corps level and later at the departmental level. As such he served throughout the Atlanta Campaign and on the March to the Sea. He took especial pleasure from the destruction that was wrought upon South Carolina, which state he blamed for the war, calling it the "meanest patch of country." His last fighting came in North Carolina at Averasboro and Bentonville. Following the surrender of the Confederate army under Joe Johnston he followed his friend Howard into the Freedmen's Bureau, serving in Alabama. Throughout the war he maintained a detailed diary. (Harwell, Richard and Racine, Philip, eds., *The Fiery Trail: A Union Officer's Account of Sherman's Last Campaigns*)

OSTERHAUS, Peter Joseph (1823-1917)

One of numerous Europeans to flee the continent in the aftermath of the 1848 uprisings and end up in the Union army, Peter J. Osterhaus was one of the best of the generals. The Koblenz native had settled in St. Louis, via Illinois, and there enlisted in the army. His assignments included: major, Osterhaus' Missouri Battalion (April 27, 1861); colonel, 12th Missouri (December 19, 1861); commanding 2nd Brigade, Army of Southwest Missouri, Department of the Missouri (January-February 1862); commanding 1st Brigade, 1st Division, Army of Southwest Missouri, Department of the Missouri (February-March 11, 1862); temporarily commanding the division (March 6-8, 1862); commanding 1st Brigade, 1st Division, Army of Southwest Missouri, Department of the Mississippi (March 11-May 1862); commanding 3rd Division, Army of Southwest Missouri, Department of the Mississippi (May-September 19, 1862); brigadier general, USV (June 9, 1862); commanding 3rd Brigade, Army of Southwest Missouri, Department of the Missouri (September 19-December 1862); 1st Brigade, 1st Division, District of Eastern Arkansas, Department of the Missouri (December 1862); commanding 9th Division, 13th Corps, Army of the Tennessee (January 4-May 17 and May 19-July 28, 1863); commanding 1st Division, 15th Corps, Army of the Tennessee (September 1, 1863-January 4, 1864, February 6-July 15, and August 19-September 23, 1864); major general, USV (July 23, 1864); commanding the corps (September 23, 1864-January 8, 1865); and chief of staff, Military Division of West Mississippi (January 8-May 27, 1865). He took part in Nathaniel Lyon's seizure of Camp Jackson and led his battalion, which at times was considered a part of the 2nd Missouri, at Wilson's Creek. At Pea Ridge he was in temporary command of the division as a colonel. As a brigadier general he took part in the operations in Arkansas and then joined Grant's campaign against Vicksburg. There he was wounded at Big Black River Bridge but returned to duty two days later. He then served through the balance of the siege and took part in the capture of Jackson, Mississippi. Accompanying Sherman, he took part in the relief of Chattanooga and fought well there. In the midst of the Atlanta Campaign he became a major general and went on, with some absences, to march to the sea at Savannah in corps command. After the city's fall he participated in the early stages of the Carolinas Campaign but was soon sent to the Gulf coast as Canby's staff chief during the operations against Mobile. Mustered out on January 15, 1866, he was a U.S. diplomat at Lyon, France, and Mannheim, Germany. He was still collecting a pension while living in Duisburg, Germany, a few months before the United States entered World War I.

O'SULLIVAN, Timothy (? ?)

Now considered one of the best battlefield photographers to have emerged from the Civil War, Timothy O'Sullivan was something of a prize when Alexander Gardner stole him from Mathew Brady's firm. O'Sullivan had worked for Brady almost from the beginning of the war but became disenchanted with Brady's policy of not crediting individual artists for their work. Instead, all images were listed simply as "Brady's." Finally, in the spring of 1863 he joined Gardner's firm. Some of his most famous work was done on the field of Gettysburg. After the war he continued in field photography, including work in Central America. (Horan, James David, *Timothy O'Sullivan, America's Forgotten Photographer*)

OULD, Robert (1820-1881)

A prominent attorney in his native District of Columbia, Robert Ould was a Southern partisan and left his post as U.S. district attorney to join the Confederacy. During the first three months of 1862 he was the assistant secretary of war but later that year became the chief of the Bureau of Exchange of Prisoners. It was in this post that he made his mark in the history of the Confederacy. Paying great attention to details, he represented the Richmond authorities in their dealings with Washington over the formal parole and exchange of prisoners of war. Thousands of officers and men on both sides benefitted from this cartel until its collapse in early 1864. Ould subsequently held a judicial post in the military. At the war's close he was confined for eight weeks until cleared of charges that he had misappropriated the funds of captured Federal prisoners. After his release he resumed the practice of law, this time in Richmond.

OURY, Granville Henderson (1825-1891)

In a disputed election, Granville H. Oury lost his seat as Arizona Territory's nonvoting delegate to the Confederate Congress and spent the remainder of the war in the military. Born in

Virginia, he had become a Missouri lawyer before moving to Texas and participating in the California gold rush. In 1856 he moved to Tucson, New Mexico Territory, and five years later was sent to Richmond by a convention of voters to represent them before the Confederate Congress and push for a new territory, Arizona, to be formed from the southern half of the then-New Mexico Territory. This was done and he was admitted as a nonvoting delegate to the Provisional Congress on January 18, 1862. Meanwhile, the military governor, John R. Baylor, called an election in which Oury's supporters refused to take part on the grounds of insufficient notice, with the result that Marcus H. Macwillie was elected. Leaving Richmond, Oury joined the army where his assignments included: captain, Herbert's (Ariz.) Cavalry Battalion (1862); and colonel (ca. 1863). In the latter part of the war he served as a staff officer to General Henry H. Sibley. After the war he served in the new Arizona's Territorial legislature and as its congressional delegate—again nonvoting.

OWEN, Joshua Thomas (1821-1887)

The Union disaster at Cold Harbor cost Joshua T. Owen his command, and he was soon thereafter mustered out of the volunteer service. The native of Wales had immigrated to the United States at the age of nine but nonetheless was known as "Paddy"—a poor sense of geography was common at the time. Settling in Philadelphia, he taught for a time and then practiced law and sat in the legislature. Also active in the militia, he volunteered for service and soon raised a 90-day regiment. His assignments included: colonel, 24th Pennsylvania (May 8, 1861); colonel, 69th Pennsylvania (August 18, 1861); commanding 2nd ("Philadelphia") Brigade, 2nd Division, 2nd Corps, Army of the Potomac (July 10-30, September 17, November 12, 1862-January 26, 1863, February 7-April 1, April 11-June 28, 1863, and April 25-June 12, 1864); brigadier general, USV (from November 29, 1862); commanding the division (January 26-February 7 and April 1-11, 1863); brigadier general, USV (reappointed March 30, 1863); commanding 3rd Brigade, 3rd Division, 2nd Corps, Army of the Potomac (August 15-December 14, 1863 and January 4-February 10, 1864); and commanding the division (August 15-September 6, 1863, December 14, 1863-January 4, 1864, and February 10-March 25, 1864). After serving with his first regiment under Patterson he was mustered out on August 10, 1861. Eight days later he was mustered in at the head of a new three-year regiment. It is frequently claimed that he fought in all of the Army of the Potomac's battles from Seven Pines to Cold Harbor. However, he was under arrest during the battle of Gettysburg, and his Philadelphia Brigade was given to Alexander S. Webb. His record, however, does show that he took part in the operations against Yorktown and fought at Seven Pines and during the Seven Days on the Peninsula. He briefly succeeded to brigade command at Antietam. Given a brigadier's star, he led the brigade at Fredericksburg, but the Senate failed to confirm his appointment and it expired on March 4, 1863. Reappointed later that month, he fought at Chancellorsville but got into trouble on the march into Pennsylvania. Restored to command, he took part in the Bristoe and Mine Run operations. Serving in the Overland Campaign, he was removed from his post for having failed to support the brigade on his flank at Cold Harbor. The charges, pressed by his division commander, John Gibbon, were dropped when he was mustered out on July 18, 1864. Presumably he had requested this action. Resuming his practice, he founded a law journal, the *New York Daily Register*, for which he worked for the balance of his life.

OWEN, William Miller (1840-1893)

The historian of the famed Washington Artillery of New Orleans, William Miller Owen was for much of the war the unit's adjutant. A native of Ohio, he had relocated to Louisiana three years before the outbreak of the conflict. His assignments included: first lieutenant and adjutant, Washington (La.) Artillery Battalion (May 26, 1861); major, Artillery (August 10, 1863); executive officer, King's Artillery Battalion, Departments of Western Virginia and East Tennessee (1863-64); commanding Artillery Battalion, Colquitt's Division, Department of North Carolina and Southern Virginia (May-June 1864); commanding Gibbes' Artillery Battalion, 3rd Corps, Army of Northern Virginia (July 20, 1864-spring 1865); lieutenant colonel, Artillery (early 1865); and commanding McIntosh's Artillery Battalion, 3rd Corps, Army of Northern Virginia (spring-April 9, 1865). As a battalion staff officer, he served at 1st Bull Run, Yorktown, the Seven Days, 2nd Bull Run, Antietam, and on Marye's Heights at both Fredericksburg and Chancellorsville. After serving at Gettysburg, he was promoted to major and transferred to duty with King's Battalion in southwestern Virginia. The next spring he returned east and commanded a battalion in the hastily gathered forces defending Petersburg. His command was soon absorbed into the Army of Northern Virginia. Despite a wound received at the Crater he commanded a battalion through most of the siege and was in command of a different battalion during the final campaign to Appomattox. He returned to Louisiana after the war and wrote his memoirs. (Owen, William Miller, *In Camp and Battle with the Washington Artillery of New Orleans*)

OWENS, James Byeram (1816-1889)

As one of Florida's representatives to the Provisional Confederate Congress, James B. Owens proved to be a doctrinaire states' righter and an opponent of Jefferson Davis. He had been a Baptist minister in his native South Carolina before moving to Florida where he became a wealthy cotton and citrus planter, and was something of a pioneer in the latter field. A signer of the secession ordinance, he was chairman of the Committee on Accounts and also sat on the Committee on Naval Affairs in Congress. He refused to grant the central government much in the way of emergency powers. Not seeking election to the First Regular Congress, he returned to his plantation and did some preaching. Having nothing further to do with the conflict and with this area virtually untouched by the war, he was able to reestablish his lifestyle, with many of his former slaves working for him.

P

PAGE, Charles Anderson (1838-1873)

A clerk with the *New York Tribune* at the outbreak of the Civil War, Charles A. Page had become one of that paper's top correspondents by the time of Appomattox. He had edited a weekly journal in Iowa before coming to New York. The Illinois native was then sent to the Peninsula to cover the Army of the Potomac's campaign againt Richmond in the spring of 1862. Since there were restrictions on the presence of reporters in the army's camps, he served as a hospital worker in the 2nd Bull Run Campaign. By 1863, he had been granted a byline, C.A.P., and was back covering the Army of the Potomac during the Gettysburg Campaign. Highly respected by Horace Greeley, he nonetheless left the *Tribune* in 1865 to become a diplomat to Switzerland where he eventually took up residence. He died in London. (Starr, Louis M., *Bohemian Brigade*)

PAGE, Richard Lucian (1807-1901)

Due to the Confederacy's policy of issuing army ranks to naval officers serving with troops defending land positions, Richard L. Page was an officer in both branches of the service. Resigning his commander's commission in the old navy, in which he had served since 1824, Page became an aide-de-camp to Virginia's Governor Letcher. He was charged with organizing the state navy. His later assignments included: commander, CSN (June 10, 1862); captain, CSN (spring 1862); brigadier general, CSA (March 1, 1864); and commanding Page's Brigade, District of the Gulf, Department of Alabama, Mississippi, and East Louisiana (March 1-August 23, 1864). After working on the fortifications of the James and Nansemond Rivers, Page was assigned to ordnance duty at the Norfolk Navy Yard until it was abandoned. During the *Virginia*'s battles in Hampton Roads, he served a gun in the Sewell's Point battery. After the abandonment of Norfolk, he transferred his ordnance operations to Charlotte, North Carolina, where he remained in charge until early 1864, except for one brief period in command at Savannah during which he saw action at Port Royal. On March 1, 1864, he was appointed to a brigadier general's rank in the army so that he could command the outer defenses of Mobile Bay. With headquarters in Fort Morgan, he worked on strengthening the defenses until he surrendered after two days of attack by the Union Fleet. He was not released from captivity until July 24, 1865. Settling in Norfolk, he was public school superintendent there for eight years.

PAINE, Charles Jackson (1833-1916)

A lawyer from a prominent Boston family, Charles J. Paine rose to the rank of brevet major general while commanding black troops. His Civil War assignments included: captain, 22nd Massachusetts (October 5, 1861); major, 30th Massachusetts (January 16, 1862); colonel, 2nd Louisiana (October 23, 1862); commanding 1st Brigade, 1st Division, 19th Corps, Department of the Gulf (May 27-July 11, 1863); commanding 3rd Brigade, Cavalry Division, Department of the Gulf (November 3, 1863-January 20, 1864); brigadier general, USV (July 4, 1864); commanding 3rd Division, 18th Corps, Army of the James (August 3-October 14, 1864); commanding 1st Division, 25th Corps, Army of the James (December 3-31, 1864); commanding 3rd Division, 25th Corps, Army of the James (December 31, 1864-January 6, 1865); commanding division, Terry's Provisional Corps, Department of North Carolina (January 6-March 27, 1865); and commanding 3rd Division, 10th Corps, Department of North Carolina (March 27-July 6, 1865). His early war service is rather obscure, but his initial regiment was stationed near Washington during the time he was a member of it. He apparently went to the Gulf coast with the 30th Massachusetts. Mustered out on March 27, 1862, he became colonel of a Louisiana unit seven months later. At Port Hudson he succeeded to the command of a brigade and that fall his regiment was mounted. After commanding a cavalry brigade he was honorably discharged on March 8, 1864, and joined Butler's staff. Promoted to brigadier general, he took command of a black division in Virginia and fought at Drewry's Bluff, New Market Heights, and in general along the

Richmond-Petersburg lines. Leading his division, he took part in both attacks on Fort Fisher. His final campaigning came in supporting Sherman in North Carolina. Brevetted major general for the war, he was mustered out on January 15, 1866. Active in railroading, he was also involved in monetary reform and yachting.

PAINE, Eleazer Arthur (1815-1882)

The field service of Union General Eleazer A. Paine appears to have been unsatisfactory since he was soon shunted off to guard duty in the rear areas of the war. A West Pointer (1839), he had served briefly in a staff position during the Seminole War before resigning in 1840 to study law. He practiced in his native Ohio and served as a militia brigadier general until 1848 when he moved to Illinois. His Civil War assignments included: colonel, 9th Illinois (July 26, 1861); brigadier general, USV (September 3, 1861); commanding 3rd Brigade, 1st Division, Military District of Cairo, Department of the Missouri (February 1, 1862); commanding 4th Division, Army of the Mississippi (March 4-April 24, 1862); commanding 1st Division, Army of the Mississippi (April 24-July 15 and August 15-30, 1862); commanding guards, Louisville and Nashville Railroad, Department of the Ohio (November 1862-May 1864); and commanding District of Western Kentucky, Department of the Ohio (August 7-September 11, 1864). He fought at Island #10 and took part in the operations against Corinth following Shiloh. That summer he was removed from field command and spent a year and a half commanding railroad guards. He then briefly held a district command and resigned from the army on April 5, 1865, having awaited assignment for over six months. He resumed the practice of law until his death.

PAINE, Halbert Eleazer (1826-1905)

Without any prior military training, Halbert E. Paine became one of the more controversial Union officers. A native of Ohio, he had practiced law there before moving to Wisconsin where he formed a partnership with Carl Schurz. His military assignments included: colonel, 4th Wisconsin (July 2, 1861); commanding 2nd Brigade, Department of the Gulf (August-December 16, 1862); commanding 2nd Brigade, Grover's Division, Department of the Gulf (December 16, 1862-January 1863); commanding 2nd Brigade, 3rd Division, 19th Corps, Department of the Gulf (January 3-June 14, 1863); brigadier general, USV (March 13, 1863); and also commanding the division (May 2-June 14, 1863). His first controversial act came while moving his regiment to the front; he turned down a cattle train for his men and commandeered a better form of transport. After brief service in the vicinity of Washington he took part in the capture of New Orleans. When his brigade commander, General Thomas Williams, ordered him to return fugitive slaves Paine refused and was placed under arrest. In return he filed lengthy charges against his superior. After Williams' death in the battle of Baton Rouge, Paine took over the brigade and both sets of charges were dropped. The next spring he was promoted to brigadier and commanded a brigade and a division at Port Hudson. He lost a leg in one of the assaults and was brevetted major general. He had previously refused General Butler's order to destroy Baton Rouge upon its evacuation. During Early's raid on Washington Paine commanded a portion of the defenses and later served in Illinois. Resigning on May 15, 1865, he served three terms as a Radical Republican congressman and was appointed patent commissioner by Schurz. He introduced typewriters to the government bureaucracy and authorized the acceptance of drawn plans with patent applications instead of models. Between these appointments he practiced law in the capital.

PAINE, Lewis

See: *Powell, Lewis Thornton*

PALMER, Innis Newton (1824-1900)

A career officer in the mounted arm, Innis N. Palmer commanded the only Union cavalry on the field of 1st Bull Run. The native New Yorker and West Pointer (1846) had been posted to the Regiment of Mounted Rifles and fought in Mexico. Wounded at Chapultepec, he earned two brevets during that war and, remaining in the service, was transferred to the cavalry in the 1850's and continued to perform frontier duty. His Civil War-era assignments included: captain, 2nd Cavalry (since March 3, 1855); major, 2nd Cavalry (April 25, 1861); major, 5th Cavalry (change of designation August 3, 1861); brigadier general, USV (September 23, 1861); commanding 3rd Brigade, Casey's Division, Army of the Potomac (December 1861-March 13, 1862); commanding 3rd Brigade, 3rd Division, 4th Corps, Army of the Potomac (March 13-June 7, 1862); 1st Brigade, 1st Division, 4th Corps, Army of the Potomac (June 7-July 26, 1862); commanding 1st Division, 18th Corps, Department of North Carolina (January 30-May 23, 1863); commanding 18th Corps, Department of Virginia and North Carolina (July 18-August 18, 1863); commanding Defenses of New Bern, District of North Carolina, Department of Virginia and North Carolina (August 14-October 7, 1863 and November 7, 1863-January 15, 1864); lieutenant colonel, 2nd Cavalry (September 23, 1863); commanding District of North Carolina, Department of Virginia and North Carolina (January 4-February 5, 1864 and April 28, 1864-January 31, 1865); commanding Department of North Carolina (January 31-February 9, 1865); commanding Sub-District of New Bern, Department of North Carolina (February 9-June 27, 1865); commanding Sub-District of Beaufort, Department of North Carolina (February 25-March 1, 1865); and commanding 1st Division, District of Beaufort, Department of North Carolina (March 1-18, 1865. At 1st Bull Run he commanded a provisional battalion of seven mounted regular companies drawn from three different regiments. He was brevetted for leading the only cavalry on the field. Two months later he was given a brigadier general's star and led a brigade to the Peninsula where he saw action at Yorktown, Williamsburg, Seven Pines, and during the Seven Days. Following several months on recruiting duty in New Jersey and Delaware he returned to the field in North Carolina. Brevetted major general, he was mustered out of the volunteers on January 15, 1866. He was also brevetted through brigadier general in the regulars and remained on active duty—mostly on the frontier—until 1876. After three years of sick leave he retired as colonel, 2nd Cavalry, and settled in Washington, D.C.

PALMER, John B. (?-?)

The consolidation of regiments due to heavy casualties resulted in Colonel John B. Palmer being detached from his command as a supernumerary and assigned elsewhere. His Confederate assignments included: lieutenant colonel, 5th North Carolina Partisan Rangers Battalion (1862); colonel, 58th North Carolina (July 29, 1862); commanding brigade, Department of East Tennessee (fall 1862-ca. May 19, 1863); commanding District of Western North Carolina, Department of East Tennessee (November 18, 1863-December 1864); and commanding brigade, District of Western North Carolina, Department of East Tennessee (December 1864-May 10, 1865). After his battalion was increased to regimental size, he served initially in eastern Tennessee. His command became part of the Southern buildup for the victory at Chickamauga where he was wounded on the second day. On November 18, 1863, he was assigned to command the District of Western North Carolina but he may not have left the Army of Tennessee until after the defeat at Chattanooga. Shortly after his detachment from his regiment it was consolidated with the 60th North Carolina. In the mountains of North Carolina he was responsible for rounding up deserters and draft evaders and fighting off Union raids. He continued on this duty until he was included in the surrender of his successor as district commander, on May 10, 1865.

PALMER, John McCauley (1817-1900)

A dispute over rank between himself and John M. Schofield, led John M. Palmer to ask for relief from Sherman's army during the siege operations before Atlanta. He got it and finished the war in command in Kentucky. He had been born in that state but his father, being opposed to slavery, had moved to Illinois when his son was 14. There Palmer became an attorney and entered politics first as a Democrat but later was a founder of the state Republican Party. In the late 1850s he lost a bid for Congress but was a delegate to the 1860 party convention. Joining the Union army early, his assignments included: colonel, 14th Illinois (May 25, 1861); brigadier general, USV (December 20, 1861); commanding 2nd Division, Army of the Mississippi (February 23-March 4, 1862); commanding 3rd Division, Army of the Mississippi (March 4-April 24, 1862); commanding 1st Brigade, 1st Division, Army of the Mississippi (April 24-August 10, 1862); commanding the division (August 31-September 29, 1862); commanding 13th Division, Army of the Ohio (September 29-November 5, 1862); commanding 2nd Division, Left Wing, 14th Corps, Army of the Cumberland (December 10, 1862-January 9, 1863); commanding 2nd Division, 21st Corps, Army of the Cumberland (January 9-July 15 and August 17-October 9, 1863); major general, USV (March 16, 1863, to rank from November 29, 1862); commanding the corps (July 15-August 17, 1863); commanding 1st Division, 4th Corps, Army of the Cumberland (October 10-27, 1863); commanding 14th Corps, Army of the Cumberland (October 28, 1863-August 7, 1864); and commanding Department of Kentucky (February 18-June 27, 1865). Leading a division, he fought at Island #10 and directed a brigade in the advance on Corinth, Mississippi. Again in charge of a division, he fought at Murfreesboro and was named a major general before the Tullahoma Campaign. He led a division at Chickamauga and a corps at Chattanooga and the early stages of the Atlanta Campaign. He was relieved at his own request after the dispute over relative rank on August 7, 1864, while Sherman's forces were in front of Atlanta. The balance of the war was spent in departmental command in Kentucky. Mustered out on September 1, 1866, he returned to politics and served as Illinois' Republican governor in the late 1860s and early 1870s. Drifting back into the Democratic Party, he lost another bid for the gubernatorial chair but did go to the U.S. Senate. In 1896 he lost a bid for the presidency at the head of a faction of his party. (Palmer, George Thomas, *A Conscientious Turncoat: The Story of John M. Palmer 1817-1900*)

PALMER, Joseph Benjamin (1825-1890)

Despite being a prewar Unionist, Tennessee lawyer, and politician, Joseph B. Palmer entered the Confederate army and rose to the rank of brigadier general. His prewar career had included service in the state legislature and as mayor of Murfreesboro. His military assignments included: captain, Company C, 18th Tennessee (May 1861); colonel, 18th Tennessee (June 11, 1861); commanding 2nd Brigade, Army of Middle Tennessee, Department #2 (October 28-November 7, 1862); commanding 2nd Brigade, Breckinridge's Division, Right Wing, Army of the Mississippi (November 7-20, 1862); commanding 2nd Brigade, Breckinridge's Division, Polk's Corps, Army of Tennessee (November 20, 1862-January 2, 1863); commanding Western District of North Carolina, Department of East Tennessee (November 18-December 4, 1863); commanding Brown's (old) Brigade, Stevenson's Division, Hood's-Lee's Corps, Army of Tennessee (early July-September 1864); commanding Brown's and Reynolds' Brigades (consolidated), Stevenson's Division, Lee's Corps, Army of Tennessee (September 1864-April 9, 1865); brigadier general, CSA (November 15, 1864); and commanding brigade, Cheatham's Division, Hardee's Corps, Army of Tennessee (April 9-26, 1865). Captured at Fort Donelson, he was confined in Boston Harbor's Fort Warren until his exchange on September 26, 1862. Commanding a brigade, he fought at Murfreesboro until relieved by Gideon J. Pillow on the last day of the fight. Leading his regiment that same day in the disastrous assault of Breckinridge's division on the Union left, Palmer suffered three wounds. Returning to duty in the spring, he resumed command of the regiment for the Tullahoma Campaign. Still in regimental command at Chickamauga he sustained another wound. Recovering, he served for a time in North Carolina and then took command of a brigade during the Atlanta Campaign. Wounded at Jonesboro, he remained to lead two consolidated brigades in the Franklin-Nashville Campaign. Detached during both battles, his brigade did take part in covering the retreat from the latter. Moving back to North Carolina, Palmer led his command in the Carolinas Campaign against Sherman. In the final reorganization he was given charge of a brigade composed of the remnants of 38 Tennessee regiments and two battalions which were consolidated into four regiments. Surrendered at Durham Station, he resumed his law practice but stayed aloof from politics.

PALMERSTON, Henry John Temple, 3rd Viscount (1784-1865)

A veteran of over a half century in British politics, Lord Palmerston served as prime minister throughout the American Civil War. Although personally inclined toward the South, he enforced the Queen's neutrality proclamations, opposing moves in Parliament to get involved in the struggle. During the *Trent* affair his government presented an ultimatum, softened somewhat by Prince Albert, to the United States demanding the release of Confederate diplomats Mason and Slidell. To back up his demands he dispatched a naval squadron with 8,000 troops and munitions to Canada. It is also reported that immediately following the seizure he actually discussed joint military operations with Confederate operatives. However, once the dust had settled he returned to his policy of maintaining a general neutrality. He died the year the war ended. (Ridley, Jasper, *Lord Palmerston*)

PARDEE, Ario, Jr. (?-1901)

The son of a Pennsylvania philanthropist who partially equipped his son's regiment, Ario Pardee, Jr., served in both major theaters of the Civil War and was brevetted brigadier general for Peach Tree Creek. The native Pennsylvanian's assignments included: captain, 28th Pennsylvania (June 28, 1861); major, 28th Pennsylvania (November 1, 1861): lieutenant colonel, 147th Pennsylvania (October 10, 1862); commanding 1st Brigade, 2nd Division, 12th Corps, Army of the Cumberland (January 18-February 18, 1864); colonel, 147th Pennsylvania (March 19, 1864); and commanding 1st Brigade, 2nd Division, 20th Corps, Army of the Cumberland (August 4-September 27, 1864, October 28, 1864-April 11, 1865, and May 10-June 1, 1865). His regiment fought at 2nd Bull Run and he commanded it at Antietam, and another at Chancellorsville and Gettysburg's Culp's Hill before being transferred to the West with the rest of the 11th and 12th corps. There he fought at Chattanooga and succeeded to brigade command during the siege of Atlanta. He led his brigade on the March to the Sea and on January 12, 1865, received his brevet for the Atlanta Campaign's battle of Peach Tree Creek. He then held brigade command during parts of the campaign in the Carolinas. He resigned on June 13, 1865.

PARHAM, William Allen (?-?)

Severely injured at the Battle of Malvern Hill, Colonel William A. Parham was, successively, forced out of field service, forced to retire from the army, and finally died from the effects of the wound after the close of the war. His Confederate assignments included: lieutenant, Company A, 41st Virginia (May 24, 1861); captain, Company A, 41st Virginia (early 1862); lieutenant colonel, 41st Virginia (May 3, 1862); colonel, 41st Virginia (July 25, 1862); and commanding Mahone's Brigade, Anderson's Division, Longstreet's Corps, Army of Northern Virginia (August-September 1862). Originally stationed at Norfolk, he moved to the Peninsula when the former was abandoned. He saw action at Seven Pines and during the Seven Days, being severely wounded in the last action at Malvern Hill. He recovered in time to receive a promotion and to be in temporary command of the brigade at South Mountain. Here he made a gallant defense at Crampton's Gap. He also led the brigade at Antietam and the regiment at Chancellorsville and Gettysburg. However, by the fall of 1864 his wound was giving him so much trouble that he was assigned to provost duty along the Blackwater River and soon thereafter was made post commandant at Hicksford. Finally he retired from the service on March 31, 1865, and eventually succumbed to his wound.

PARIS, Louis Philippe Albert d'Orleans, Comte de (?-1894)

The Comte de Paris, an exiled member of the French monarchy, accompanied his brother the Duc de Chartres and their uncle, the Prince de Joinville, on a visit to the United States to witness the Civil War. His assignments included: captain and additional aide-de-camp (September 24, 1861); and additional aide-de-camp, Army of the Potomac (September 24, 1861-July 15, 1862). Refusing any higher rank, he joined McClellan's staff and studiously observed the organization of the principal Union army. The count accompanied the army the following spring to the Peninsula and observed the actions at Yorktown, Williamsburg, Seven Pines, and the Seven Days. Resigning on July 15, 1862, he returned to Europe. In his *History of the Civil War in America*, originally published in French, he was harshly critical of the improvised nature of the volunteer army's organization and the election of its officers.

PARKE, John Grubb (1827-1900)

A career engineering officer, John G. Parke proved to be a top line commander in the Civil War. The native Pennsylvanian had graduated second in his 1849 class at West Point and had accordingly been assigned to the topographical engineers. Most of his prewar work was along the boundary with Canada. His wartime assignments included: first lieutenant, Topographical Engineers (since July 1, 1856); captain, Topographical Engineers (September 9, 1861); brigadier general, USV (November 23, 1861); commanding 3rd Brigade, North Carolina Expedition (December 1861-April 2, 1862); commanding 3rd Division, Department of North Carolina (April 2-July 6, 1862); commanding 3rd Division, 9th Corps, Army of the Potomac (July 22-September 3 and September 17-October 4, 1862); major general, USV (August 20, 1862, to rank from July 18); chief of staff, 9th Corps, Army of the

Potomac (September 1862); chief of staff, Army of the Potomac (November 7, 1862-January 25, 1863); captain, Engineers (merger of two branches March 3, 1863); commanding 9th Corps, Army of the Ohio (March 19-April 11 and June 5-14, 1863); commanding 9th Corps, Army of the Tennessee (June 14-August 18, 1863); again commanding 9th Corps, Army of the Ohio (August 18-25, 1863, and January 26-March 16, 1864); chief of staff, Army of the Ohio (late 1863); chief of staff, 9th Corps, Army of the Potomac (spring-summer 1864); major, Engineers (June 17, 1864); commanding 9th Corps, Army of the Potomac (August 14-December 31, 1863, January 12-24, February 2-June 17, and July 2-August 1, 1865); commanding the army (December 30, 1864-January 11, 1865); commanding District of Alexandria, 22nd Corps, Department of Washington (April 26-June 5, 1865); and commanding the corps and department (June 7-26, 1865). Most of his Civil War service was under the aegis of Ambrose E. Burnside. Transferring to the line, he was made a brigadier general and given a brigade in Burnside's expedition against the North Carolina coast. He fought in this campaign at Roanoke Island, New Bern, and Fort Macon. For the latter he was brevetted in the regular army. With Burnside's new 9th Corps he went to Virginia as a major general but missed 2nd Bull Run. However, during the Maryland Campaign he was Burnside's staff chief at South Mountain and took over the division at Antietam when Isaac P. Rodman was killed. He was again Burnside's chief of staff at Fredericksburg and then accompanied the 9th Corps to the West. There he commanded it in Kentucky, at Vicksburg, the Jackson siege, and back in Kentucky while Burnside exercised departmental command. He was brevetted for Jackson and the defense of Knoxville where he was again staff head. Returning to Virginia, he was again on Burnside's staff throughout the Overland Campaign and succeeded to corps command when Burnside was relieved after the failure of the Mine attack at Petersburg. He temporarily commanded the Army of the Potomac during Meade's winter leave. He played a leading role in the repulse of the enemy assault on Fort Stedman and won the brevet of major general in the regular army. After the fall of Petersburg and temporary occupation duty there, he took his corps to the vicinity of Washington and also commanded parts of its defenses. Mustered out of the volunteers on January 15, 1866, he continued as an engineering officer until his 1889 retirement as colonel and assistant chief of engineers. During his final two years in service he was West Point's superintendent.

PARKER, Ely Samuel (1828-1895)

A full-blooded Seneca Indian, Ely S. Parker—or Donehogawa—fought against discrimination to become a Union officer and the first Indian commissioner of Indian affairs. Born in New York, he studied law but was not allowed to practice on the grounds of a lack of citizenship. He then took up civil engineering and met Ulysses S. Grant in Galena, Illinois. Initially denied a commission, his military assignments included: captain and assistant adjutant general, USV (May 25, 1863); chief engineer, 7th Division, 17th Corps, Army of the Tennessee (1863); lieutenant colonel and military secretary (August 30, 1864); second lieutenant, 2nd Cavalry (March 22, 1866); and colonel and aide-de-camp (July 25, 1866). Initially assigned as an engineer, he became reacquainted with Grant during the Vicksburg operations. He then served at Chattanooga and during the siege of Petersburg joined Grant's staff. There he was often derogatorily called "The Indian." At Appomattox he recorded the surrender meeting. General Lee is said to have called Parker the one "real American" present. According to the story, the reply was "Now we are *all* Americans." Continuing on the general's staff until the beginning of Grant's presidency, Parker was brevetted brigadier in both the volunteers and the regulars for the war. He served as Indian commissioner under Grant and then retired to private business. (Parker, Arthur C., *The Life of Ely S. Parker*)

PARKER, Joel (1816-1888)

Despite the changeover from a Republican to a Democratic governor when Joel Parker was sworn in on January 20, 1863, New Jersey remained committed to the war effort. A native New Jersey lawyer, he had served in the legislature and as a prosecutor. A major general of the state militia in 1861, he was nonetheless opposed to war until the firing on Fort Sumter. In the fall of 1862 he was elected to the gubernatorial chair. Following his inauguration the state continued to work for a Union victory. His term expired, he left office in 1866 but again served as governor from 1872 to 1875. His name was placed in nomination at the Democratic conventions of 1868 and 1876. From 1880 until his death he sat on the state supreme court. (Kull, Irving S., *New Jersey: A History*)

PARKER, John Frederick (ca. 1831-?)

In modern times a police officer with the record of John F. Parker would probably not be assigned to guard the president. Unfortunately, that was not the case at Ford's Theater. The Virginia native had served in a three-months unit early in the Civil War. He then joined the Metropolitan Police force and promptly got himself into a series of scrapes with higher-ups. He faced disciplinary boards on 14 occasions during the war, sometimes being acquitted and sometimes reprimanded or fined. Nonetheless, he received the appointment to the White House bodyguard detail—which was not universally sought after. But there was one advantage for a man of his age: As Lincoln's bodyguard, he could obtain an exemption from the draft. On the day of the assassination he was more than three hours late for the beginning of his 4 P.M. to midnight shift. He then relieved William H. Crook and walked to the theater in order to be there when the presidential party arrived. At one point he left his post outside the box and went into the neighboring saloon where John Wilkes Booth was also drinking. He again left the box to get a view of the play, and it was then that Booth entered and shot Lincoln. Parker did not report to the station house until the next morning and never filed a report. Amazingly, no charges were ever pressed against him, and he remained on the force until 1868.

PARKER, Theodore (1810-1860)

A Unitarian preacher from Massachusetts, Theodore Parker became extremely active in the abolitionist cause. In 1848 after a trip abroad he published *A Letter to the People of the United States Touching the Matter of Slavery*. He was active in aiding fugitive slaves to escape and even took part in some efforts to rescue runaways being taken back South. For one such episode he was indicted, but the case was dropped. He secretly backed John Brown's raid on Harpers Ferry although he felt it would probably fail. Even in failure he thought it would speed up the inevitable conflict over slavery. He was not opposed to the breakup of the Union if it would eliminate the "peculiar institution" in the United States. In 1859 he went abroad for medical reasons and died the next spring in Florence. (Chadwick, J.W., *Theodore Parker, Preacher and Reformer*)

PARKER, William Harwar (1826-1896)

Graduating first in his class at Annapolis in 1848, New York City native William H. Parker later organized and superintended the Confederate States Naval Academy. In the prewar years he had served afloat during the Mexican War and as an instructor at his alma mater before resigning as a lieutenant in 1861. His Confederate assignments included: lieutenant commander, CSN (1861); commanding CSS *Beaufort* (February 1862); executive officer, *Palmetto State* (winter 1862-63); captain, CSN (1863); and Superintendent, Confederate State Naval Academy (1863-65). He fought at Roanoke Island and in South Carolina waters before organizing the naval school. During the retreat from Richmond he escorted the national archives and the remaining treasures of the Confederacy. In the postwar years he was a mail steamer captain and served as a diplomat to Korea. He also wrote a number of technical works.

PARROTT, Jacob (ca. 1844-?)

The youngest member of the group of Union raiders who stole the rebel engine, *The General*, Jacob Parrott was the first soldier to receive the Congressional Medal of Honor. Serving as a private in Company K, 33rd Ohio, Parrott was detailed to accompany civilian James J. Andrews and 22 others on the raid against rebel communications. The group boarded the northbound train hauled by the engine *The General* at Marietta, Georgia, on April 12, 1862. Stopping at Big Shanty for breakfast, the train was temporarily abandoned, giving the raiders their chance. Uncoupling the rest of the train, the raiders fled in the engine and three boxcars. After a run of 87 miles toward Chattanooga, in which they were unable to inflect any serious damage on the road, they were forced to flee the train, being low on fuel and closely pursued. Parrott was captured shortly after the raiders split up, and the remainder were also caught eventually. Parrott was flogged more than 100 times by his captors for his part in the engine-stealing adventure. Confined in Chattanooga and Atlanta, Parrott escaped the fate of eight of his comrades who were hanged, and was exchanged on March 17, 1863. Eight days later, he and the five other exchanged men were presented their medals by Secretary of War Stanton. Promoted to a lieutenancy, Parrott rejoined his unit and participated in actions at Chickamauga, Chattanooga, the Atlanta Campaign, the March to the Sea, and the Carolinas Campaign. (O'Neill, Charles, *Wild Train: The Story of the Andrews Raid*)

PARROTT, Robert Parker (1804-1877)

As superintendent of the West Point Foundry, Robert P. Parrott was in a position to provide valuable service to the Union cause. The native of New Hampshire and West Pointer (1824) had served a dozen years in the artillery and ordnance branches before resigning in 1836 to take over the foundry position. Following developments in the ordnance field, he was able to find time for his own experiments. Interested in rifled guns, he developed one with a wrought-iron hoop welded into a solid ring and cooled onto the breech of the piece. These weapons were manufactured at cost for the Union armies in 10-, 20-, 30-, 100-, 200- and 300-pound models. The lighter models were widely used in the field by both armies, the Confederates having captured many during the early part of the war. The heavier models were used in coastal and fixed positions or altered for naval use. However, many artillerists preferred the three-inch Ordnance Rifle which was less likely to burst from rapid firing. Two years after the close of the war he retired from the foundry. During the conflict he had also developed a popular projectile for his Parrott rifles.

PARSONS, Lewis Baldwin (1818-1907)

Little-remembered as a Civil War general, Lewis B. Parsons provided valuable services to the Union war effort while in charge of rail and river transport. Born in New York, he was a graduate of both Yale and the Harvard Law School. After briefly practicing in Illinois he had become the president of the Ohio and Mississippi Railroad. Upon the outbreak of the Civil War he served as a volunteer aide to Frank Blair. As such he took part in the seizure of the pro-Southern Missouri State Guard camp at Camp Jackson near St. Louis. Recognizing that his expertise in railroad matters would be helpful, the War Department appointed him to a staff position a short time later. His assignments included: captain and assistant quartermaster, USV (October 31, 1861); chief of rail and river transportation, Department of the Missouri (December 1861-March 11, 1862); colonel and additional aide-de-camp (February 19, 1862); chief of rail and river transportation, Department of the Mississippi and later the western theater (March 11, 1862-August 1864); colonel and quartermaster (August 2, 1864); chief of rail and river transportation, U.S. Armies (August 1864-April 1866); and brigadier general, USV (May 11, 1865). Serving in the West his authority stretched from Pittsburgh to the Plains and south to New Orleans. In the summer of 1864 he was promoted to the same position in Washington for all the armies in the field. One of his greatest achievements was the transfer of the Army of the Ohio from Tennessee to the North Carolina coast near the close of the war. Remaining on duty until mustered out on April 30, 1866, he supervised the demobilization of the volunteer forces. Having been made a brigadier general shortly after the close of hostilities, he was brevetted major general on the date of his muster out. Following a two-year vacation in Europe he returned to railroading and entered banking as well. He was also active in Democratic circles.

PARSONS, Mosby Monroe (1822-1865)

A lawyer, Mexican War veteran, and Missouri politician, Mosby M. Parsons survived some heavy fighting in the Civil War only to die a few months later in Mexico's internal conflict. The Virginia-born politician had offered his services to his adopted state and his assignments included: brigadier general, Missouri State Guard (spring 1861); commanding 6th Division, Missouri State Guard (spring 1861-April 9, 1862); commanding Missouri State Guard (April 9-summer 1862); commanding brigade, District of Arkansas, Trans-Mississippi Department (summer and fall 1862); brigadier general, CSA (November 5, 1865); commanding brigade, Hindman's-Price's Division, District of Arkansas, Trans-Mississippi Department (winter 1862-63-March 24, 1864); commanding the division (March 24, 1864-January 29, 1865 and February 1-15 and to May 26, 1865); and commanding the district (January 29-February 1 and briefly from February 15, 1865). While in the command of state troops he fought at Carthage and Wilson's Creek but missed the fighting at Pea Ridge. Moving to the east side of the Mississippi he arrived too late for the battle of Shiloh and three months later was ordered to take his men who had not joined Confederate service back to Arkansas. Commissioned into the Confederate army shortly thereafter, he held a series of commands in the Trans-Mississippi Department, seeing action at Helena and near Little Rock. Sent in early 1864 to western Louisiana he helped repulse Banks' Red River Campaign before returning to Arkansas to face Steele's Union column. Later that year he took part in Price's invasion of Missouri. Following the department's surrender he went to Mexico. Accounts differ on his motives, some saying he intended to join one side or the other and others claiming he was trying to flee to Europe, and differ as to who was responsible for his death—near the village of China about August 15, 1865.

PATE, Henry Clay (1832-1864)

During the battle of Yellow Tavern, Henry C. Pate and Jeb Stuart ended their longstanding feud. Within a matter of hours both had suffered mortal wounds. Pate was a native Virginian who had moved to Missouri by way of Kentucky and Ohio. Living close to the Kansas border, he led a Missouri militia force against John Brown in 1856. By the outbreak of the Civil War he was back in Virginia editing the *Petersburg Bulletin*. Enlisting in the Confederate army, he received the following assignments: captain, Petersburg Rangers (June 5, 1861); lieutenant colonel, 2nd Virginia Cavalry Battalion (May 1862); lieutenant colonel, 5th Virginia Cavalry (June 24, 1862); and colonel, 5th Virginia Cavalry (September 28, 1863). After seeing service during the Seven Days, 2nd Bull Run, Antietam, and Fredericksburg, he was hauled before a court-martial in March 1863. It was from this hearing that Jeb Stuart and John Pelham set out for Kelly's Ford where Pelham was killed. Pate soon rejoined his regiment and took part in countering Stoneman's Raid during the Chancellorsville Campaign and at Gettysburg. Receiving a promotion to colonel, he led the regiment in the Bristoe and Mine Run campaigns and at the Wilderness. Then on May 11, 1864, at Yellow Tavern, Stuart directed that Pate make a desperate stand against the Union cavalry. He promised to hold them off. Stuart complimented his attitude and Pate offered his hand. With the two reconciled, Pate rode to his assignment which he accomplished at the cost of his life. Stuart was mortally wounded later in the fight. From his death bed he told a staff officer of the reconciliation and praised Pate's services, stopping now and then from the pain of his mortal wound. (Freeman, Douglas S., *Lee's Lieutenants*)

PATRICK, Marsena Rudolph (1811-1888)

After a relatively short stint in command of a combat brigade, Marsena R. Patrick became, in effect, the Army of the Potomac's police chief. Born in New York, he had run away from home and held odd jobs before entering West Point. Graduating in 1835, he was posted to the infantry and earned a brevet in Mexico while serving as General Wool's commissary. Also a veteran of Seminole Indian fighting, he resigned his captaincy in the 2nd Infantry to become a farmer in New York. He was involved in the state's agricultural society before again donning the blue at the outbreak of the Civil War. His assignments included: brigadier general and inspector general, New York Volunteers (May 16, 1861-February 9, 1862); brigadier general, USV (March 17, 1862); commanding 2nd Brigade, 3rd Division, 1st Corps, Army of the Potomac (March 17-April 4, 1862); commanding 2nd Brigade, King's Division, Department of the Rappahannock (April 4-June 26, 1862); commanding 3rd Brigade, 1st Division, 3rd Corps, Army of Virginia (June 26-September 12, 1862); commanding 3rd Brigade, 1st Division, 1st Corps, Army of the Potomac (September 12-October 6, 1862); and provost marshal general, Army of the Potomac (October 6, 1862-May 1865). After serving on McClellan's staff as inspector of New York troops he was given a brigade which he led at 2nd Bull Run, South Mountain, and Antietam. His strict discipline made him unpopular with his men, but this same attribute was to prove appropriate for his next post. As provost marshal he was charged with maintaining march discipline, guarding prisoners (both enemy and friends), directing executions and other punishments, and protecting private property. Additionally he became involved in some aspects of espionage. His imposing presence was an asset in his work and during the final campaigns against Richmond he was the provost marshal for all the attacking forces. Brevetted major general for his war services, he was made military commander of the captured capital but was removed for what was deemed excessive kindness to the population. His position as a lifelong Democrat did not help him with the Radical Republicans. A McClellan man, he came into conflict with Stanton and resigned on June 12, 1865. He returned to scientific farming and dabbled in postwar politics. (Sparks, David S., ed., *Inside Lincoln's Army: The Diary of Marsena Rudolph Patrick, Provost Marshal General, Army of the Potomac*)

PATTERSON, Francis Engle (1821-1862)

The son of Mexican War veteran and Pennsylvania Civil War General Robert Patterson, Francis E. Patterson, died under clouded circumstances in the second year of the Civil War. A Pennsylvania native, he had also fought in the Mexican War, as an artillery lieutenant in the regular army, and remained in the service until his resignation from the infantry in 1857. Leaving his business interests, he rejoined the military upon the outbreak of the Civil War and his assignments included: colonel, 17th Pennsylvania (April 25, 1861); brigadier general, USV (April 11, 1862); and commanding 3rd Brigade, 2nd Division, 3rd Corps, Army of the Potomac (May 3-31 and June 6-November 22, 1862, but not late June-early July). Until his August 2, 1861, muster out he served under his father along the Potomac. Commissioned a brigadier, he fought at Williamsburg and Seven Pines. At the latter he was taken ill and forced to leave the field. He was also absent during the Seven Days and 2nd Bull Run. During the operations subsequent to the Maryland Campaign—during which his corps was defending Washington—he was charged by Daniel E. Sickles, his division commander, with having withdrawn his command without orders upon the false information that the enemy was at Warrenton Junction. With the dispute still raging he was found dead in his tent, from the apparently accidental discharge of his own sidearm, on November 22, 1862.

PATTERSON, Josiah (1837-1903)

Because he commanded an unofficial brigade, Colonel Josiah Patterson was not considered to be eligible for promotion. His Confederate assignments included: first lieutenant, 1st Alabama Cavalry (September 1861); captain, 1st Alabama Cavalry (1862); colonel, 5th Alabama Cavalry (December 1862); and commanding brigade, Roddey's Cavalry Division, Department of Alabama, Mississippi and East Louisiana (April-September 24, 1864). The Alabama lawyer adapted quickly to military life, distinguishing himself in the battle of Shiloh for which he was promoted to captain. Detached from his company, he saw action at Iuka and Corinth before being given command of a newly organized regiment which he led under General P.D. Roddey in Northern Alabama. A part of the buildup in northern Georgia, Roddey and Patterson participated in the victory at Chickamauga. Serving back in northern Alabama, Patterson was given a brigade when Roddey divided his command. Joining Forrest in Mississippi, he fought at Tupelo. Again joining with Forrest, Roddey and Patterson were active in the campaign to stop Wilson's Raid through Alabama in the final months of the war. Although much of his command surrendered at Selma, Patterson was still at liberty with a sizable force in late April 1865 when he declared his opposition to the idea of a guerrilla war.

PATTERSON, Robert (1792-1881)

Having served in various military capacities, Robert Patterson's career was ruined by the Civil War. His prewar service had included the War of 1812 as a colonel of Pennsylvania militia and a regular army commission as a captain, and the Mexican War as a major general of volunteers. During the years of peace, he served in the state militia where for many years he was a major general. At the beginning of the Civil War, the Irish-born mill and plantation owner was tapped by his old friend General Winfield Scott to command the Department of Pennsylvania, including that state, Delaware, and part of Maryland, with the rank of major general of Pennsylvania volunteers. His commission was dated April 15, 1861, and he assumed command a few days later. At first he faced Confederates under Colonel Thomas J. Jackson at Harpers Ferry, but Jackson was soon replaced by General J.E. Johnston. Patterson, who had never before held an independent command, devised a plan to capture the stronghold and move into Virginia. After initial success Patterson withdrew to the Maryland side of the Potomac when called upon to send his regulars to Washington. With the planned advance of McDowell on the rebels at Manassas, Patterson was directed to occupy Johnston's forces in the Shenandoah Valley to prevent their joining Beauregard at Manassas. Patterson was totally duped by Johnston who moved most of his command to take part in the victory at 1st Bull Run on July 21, 1861. On the 25th Patterson was relieved of his command and was mustered out of service two days later. His request for a court of inquiry was never acted upon and he returned to civil life. (Patterson, Robert, *A Narrative of the Campaign in the Valley of the Shenandoah, in 1861*)

General Robert Patterson of the Pennsylvania militia. (*Leslie's*)

PATTON, George Smith (1833-1864)

Following graduation from the Virginia Military Institute in 1852, the grandfather of the famous World War II General

George S. Patton III, George S. Patton became a lawyer and captain of a local militia company which entered Confederate service. Patton's assignments included: captain, Company H, 22nd Virginia (May 22, 1961); lieutenant colonel, 22nd Virginia (July 1861); colonel, 22nd Virginia (January 1863, to rank from November 23, 1861); and in 1863-64 frequently commanding a brigade, Department of Western Virginia, which sometimes served with the Army of Northern Virginia or in the Valley District. In his first engagement, at Scary Creek, Patton was wounded and captured but shortly exchanged. Serving mainly in western Virginia and the Shenandoah Valley, he saw further action in the Kanawha Valley in September 1862, on Imboden's June 1863 expedition, combating Averell's August 1863 raid, and during the Lewisburg Expedition in November 1863. Moving to the Shenandoah, he participated in the Confederate victory at New Market and then joined the Army of Northern Virginia at the battle of Cold Harbor where he commanded Echols' Brigade. Moving to Lynchburg, Patton then participated in General Early's invasion of Maryland in July 1864. After being driven back from the outskirts of Washington, Patton's brigade faced Sheridan's advance on Winchester and in the third battle at that place Colonel Patton was severely wounded in the leg. Refusing an amputation, he died a few days later from loss of blood.

PATTON, John Mercer, Jr. (1826-1898)

This ancestor of World War II's General Patton, John M. Patton, Jr., did not have a career as glorious as those of his two brothers or of his great nephew, but he did survive the Civil War. A graduate of the Virginia Military Institute and a Richmond lawyer, he entered the Confederate service where his assignments included: lieutenant colonel, 21st Virginia (ca. June 1861); and colonel, 21st Virginia (April 21, 1862). After leading the regiment at the battle of Kernstown, he was elected colonel of the regiment at the spring 1862 reorganization of the unit and led it through part of Stonewall Jackson's Shenandoah Valley Campaign. Having missed the Seven Days Battles due to ill health, he resigned on August 8, 1862. He was a leading postwar legal authority.

PATTON, Waller Tazewell (1835-1863)

Brother of George Smith Patton, Waller Patton graduated from the Virginia Military Institute and was serving as a Latin instructor at that school at the outbreak of the Civil War. A lawyer in his community, Patton became captain of a local militia company and took it to Harpers Ferry when the state seceded. His later commissions included: major, 7th Virginia (July 1, 1861); lieutenant colonel, 7th Virginia (April 27, 1862); and colonel, 7th Virginia (June 3, 1863). Patton saw action at 1st Bull Run, Williamsburg, Seven Pines, the Seven Days, and at 2nd Bull Run where he was severely wounded. Returning to his regiment in the spring of 1863, he commanded it in the Suffolk and Gettysburg campaigns. Exactly one month after being promoted to the three stars of a colonel, Patton took part in Pickett's famous charge at Gettysburg, as a part of General Kemper's brigade. He was struck down by Union artillery fire as he approached the stone wall in front of the Yankee lines. With his lower jaw nearly removed, Patton lingered until July 21, 1863, in extreme agony. His great-nephew was General George S. Patton, III, of World War II fame.

PAUL, Gabriel René (1813-1886)

When the advance of the Union forces upon his city forced *Chattanooga Daily Rebel* editor Franc M. Paul to move his paper to Georgia and later Alabama, it was dubbed "The Chattanooga Rebel-on-Wheels." The North Carolina native had been serving as the clerk of the Tennessee state senate when Federal forces occupied the capital. He then moved to Chattanooga where, on August 1, 1862, he published the first issue of his paper. It enjoyed a wide circulation in the Confederate Army of Tennessee and the vicinity. Unfortunately the editorial line of the paper was noted for its harsh criticism of that army's commander, Braxton Bragg. At least twice the paper was banned from his lines, and Paul was forced to demand the resignation of his editor, Henry Watterson, late in 1863. With the fall of the city Paul took his equipment to Marietta and later to Atlanta. But further Union advances forced its removal to Selma, Alabama, where the press and equipment were finally destroyed by Union forces in April 1865. From the rubble, Paul was able to publish a series of one-page flyers for a few days following his release after being captured while serving in the militia defending the town. (Andrews, J. Cutler, *The South Reports the Civil War*)

PAUL, Gabriel René (1813-1886)

An experienced regular army officer, Gabriel Paul may have owed some credit for his brigadier general's star to his wife's lobbying visit to President Lincoln. Paul, a West Pointer (1834), had been a captain in the 7th Infantry at the start of the conflict. His assignments during the war included: major, 8th Infantry (April 22, 1861); colonel, 4th New Mexico (December 9, 1861-May 31, 1862); lieutenant colonel, 8th Infantry (April 25, 1862); brigadier general, USV (September 5, 1862, appointment expired by lack of Senate confirmation March 4, 1863); commanding 3rd Brigade, 1st Division, 1st Corps, Army of the Potomac (October 14, 1861-February 17, 1863, March 9-29, and April 20-June 16, 1863); temporarily commanding the division (December 22-27, 1862 and March 1-9, 1863); reappointed brigadier general, USV (April 18, 1863); commanding 1st Brigade, 2nd Division, 1st Corps, Army of the Potomac (June 17-July 1, 1863), and colonel, 14th Infantry (September 13, 1864). During the Confederate invasion of New Mexico in the spring of 1862, Paul was in command of Fort Union which supported the troops in the field. With the expiration of the term of the 4th New Mexico he reverted to his regular army rank which had recently been increased to lieutenant colonel. In August 1862, his wife visited Lincoln urging a promotion for her husband, although Paul's service in New Mexico and earlier in the Seminole and Mexican wars and against the Indians in the Southwest, had in truth earned him a generalship. Being absent with "severe domestic affliction," he missed Fredericksburg but led his brigade at Chancellorsville.

Blinded Union General Gabriel R. Paul. (NA)

Given a new brigade, his original one having been mustered out, he led it on the first day at Gettysburg until wounded in the eyes on Oak Ridge. Although he was initially reported by Meade to Washington as having been killed, Paul recovered to perform some light administrative duties until he retired on February 16, 1865. He was advanced on the retired list to brigadier general, USA, after the war and in 1870 Congress authorized him full pay. He had previously been brevetted brigadier general in the regular army for Gettysburg.

PAULDING, Hiram (1797-1878)

The man who led the evacuation of the Gosport Navy Yard at Norfolk, Hiram Paulding, spent most of the war in charge of the New York Navy Yard. He had been appointed a midshipman in 1811 and was a veteran of the War of 1812. His sailings included voyages to China and Germany and the capture of William Walker and his filibustering expedition to Nicaragua. His Civil War-era assignments included: captain, USN (since ca. 1844); chief, Bureau of Detail (1861); commandant, New York Navy Yard (1861-65); and rear admiral, USN (1865). His most important Civil War service was the salvaging of several vessels from the Norfolk naval base before the yard's commander ordered the destruction of those craft that could not be removed. Following his 1865 retirement he served as head of the U.S. Naval Asylum in Philadelphia. In 1831 he published *Journal of a Cruise of the United States Schooner Dolphin* of which he had been first lieutenant. (Meade, Rebecca Paulding, *Life of Hiram Paulding*)

PAXTON, Elisha Franklin (1828-1863)

The promotion of E. Frank Paxton from a staff position and over the heads of the regimental commanders of the Stonewall Brigade prompted one of their number, A.J. Grigsby, to resign in disgust. A graduate of Yale, he had practiced law until 1859 when eye problems forced him to give it up. At the outbreak of the war he joined the Rockbridge Rifles. His assignments included: first lieutenant, Company B, 5th Virginia (April 1861); major, 27th Virginia (October 14, 1861); major and assistant adjutant general (spring 1862); brigadier general, CSA (November 1, 1862); and commanding Stonewall Brigade, Jackson's (old) Division, 2nd Corps, Army of Northern Virginia (November 6, 1862-May 3, 1863). He fought at 1st Bull Run and was promoted to major in October. Having served through the Romney Campaign, he failed to gain reelection in the May 1862 reorganization of the regiment. He then was named to Jackson's staff and remained with him through the fall when he was promoted three grades to command his old brigade. He fought at Fredericksburg and was present at Chancellorsville when Jackson made his famous attack. However, the brigade did not take part, being assigned to guard a flank. The next day he led the brigade into action and soon fell dead. (Paxton, Dick, ed., *Civil War Letters of General Frank "Bull" Paxton*)

PAYNE, Lewis

See: *Powell, Lewis Thornton*

PAYNE, William Henry Fitzhugh (1830-1904)

Virginia lawyer turned cavalry general, Willaim H.F. Payne appears to have had a great deal of difficulty in remaining out of Union hands. After serving in the ranks in the occupation of Harpers Ferry he began his career as an officer. His assignments included: captain, Black Horse Cavalry (April 26, 1861); major, 4th Virginia Cavalry (September 27, 1861); lieutenant colonel, 4th Virginia Cavalry (August 1862); lieutenant colonel, 2nd North Carolina Cavalry (temporarily assigned September 1862 and June 1863); colonel, 4th Virginia Cavalry (September 1, 1863); brigadier general, CSA (November 1, 1864); commanding Lomax's (old) Brigade, F. Lee's-Rosser's Cavalry Division, Valley District, Department of Northern Virginia (August 1864-January 1865); and commanding brigade, F. Lee's Division, Cavalry Corps, Army of Northern Virginia (January-April 1, 1865). It was his company at 1st Bull Run which placed such fear in the hearts of the fleeing Union troops. While serving on the Peninsula, he was wounded at Williamsburg and taken prisoner. He was declared exchanged, after confinement on Johnson's Island, Ohio, in August 1862 and rejoined his regiment. But around the time of the battle of Antietam he was given temporary charge of a North Carolina regiment. He saw action at Antietam, Fredericksburg, and in facing Stoneman's column during the Chancellorsville Campaign. After having returned to his regiment he fought at Brandy Station where the North Carolina regiment lost its colonel. Payne was again placed at their head and during the ride around the Army of the Potomac in the Gettysburg Campaign he was again wounded and captured at Hanover. This time he was confined for about a year. He returned to take over Lomax's Brigade in the Valley and fought at 3rd Winchester and Cedar Creek. Joining Lee's army at Petersburg early in 1865, he was wounded a third time at Five Forks. Cut off from the army at the time of the surrender, he was captured later in northern Virginia while on his way to turn himself in. At the time he was laid up by his wound. He was not ordered paroled and released until June. A lawyer after the war, he sat for one term in the lower house of the state legislature. (Freeman, Douglas S., *Lee's Lieutenants*)

PEABODY, Everett (1831-1862)

The surprise Confederate attack on the Union forces at Shiloh was not a surprise to all of the Northern officers. One of the alert ones was Everett Peabody. A native of Massachusetts, he had graduated from Harvard and become an engineer on the western railroads. Entering the army at the outbreak of the Civil War, his assignments included: colonel, 13th Missouri (June 1861); colonel, 25th Missouri (September 1861); and commanding 1st Brigade, 6th Division, Army of the Tennessee (March 26-April 6, 1862). After serving in the Department of Missouri, where the unit underwent a change of designation, the regiment moved to join Grant's army at Pittsburg Landing where Peabody was given command of a brigade. Early on the morning of April 6, 1862, fearing that the enemy was nearby, he sent out a three-company patrol to check the area to his front and right.

Everett Peabody, alert Union brigade commander at Shiloh. (*Leslie's*)

They struck an enemy battalion and the battle of Shiloh was on. Later in the day, after his superiors finally agreed with him that the Confederates were there, his division commander, General B. M. Prentiss, blamed him for having initiated a battle. However, no charges could ever be pressed since Peabody, while rallying his men and already suffering from four wounds, was shot in the head and instantly killed. He had in fact contributed greatly to the Union army's ability to survive that day and go on to win on the next.

PEARCE, James Alfred (1804-1862)

With the breakup of the Whig Party—largely over the issue of slavery—Senator James A. Pearce won his final race as a Democrat. Born in Virginia, he had taken up the practice of law in Maryland in 1824. The next year he became a Louisiana planter but after three years he returned to Maryland and the law. In 1831 he served in the state legislature and in the 1830s and 1840s he was a Whig in the House of Representatives in three out of four consecutive congresses, having lost one bid for reelection. At the end of his third term he moved up to the Senate and was repeatedly reelected—in 1861 as a Democrat. He served from 1843 until his death on December 20, 1862.

PEARCE, Nicholas Bartlett (ca. 1816-1894)

West Pointer (1850) and frontier veteran Nicholas Bartlett, a farmer and merchant at the outbreak of the war, was made a brigadier general in the Arkansas state forces and assigned to command the western part of the state. Assuming command at Fort Smith on May 20, Pearce organized his forces which he led into southwestern Missouri in the summer of 1861. Joining forces with Price's Missouri State Guard and McCulloch's Confederate troops, Pearce's Arkansans took part in the Southern victory at Wilson's Creek after being surprised at the start of the battle. At the beginning of September 1861, the troops under Pearce's command unanimously voted not to enter Confederate service, because they would be transferred to the command of General Hardee instead of remaining under General McCulloch, their victorious leader at Wilson's Creek. Pearce promptly marched them back to Arkansas and disbanded them, a move for which he was severely criticized and his potential general's appointment in the Confederate army was scuttled. Pearce was appointed a major in the commissary department of the rebel army and assigned as chief commissary for the Indian Territory and western Arkansas on December 20, 1861. He served in various locations in the Trans-Mississippi Department and at one point in 1862 was post commandant at Fort Smith. There were also accusations that he was too closely linked with speculators who were making large profits while he was chief commissary of the District of Texas, New Mexico and Arizona.

PEARSON, Richmond Mumford (1805-1878)

As chief justice of North Carolina's supreme judicial body, Richmond M. Pearson exemplified the difficulties faced in administering the national draft in a country founded on the basis of states' rights. A native of the state, he had begun the practice of law in 1826 and after several terms in the state legislature began his judicial career in 1836. A dozen years later he was named to the state supreme court and in 1858 became its presiding officer. An opponent of secession, his opinions releasing numerous individuals from military service greatly annoyed the Richmond authorities. He was destined to remain a thorn in their side through the end of the war. In the reorganization of the state under Reconstruction he was continued in office until his death. He became a Republican and supporter of Governor William W. Holden three years after the close of the war. (Mitchell, Memory F., *Legal Aspects of Conscription and Exemption in North Carolina 1861-1865*)

PECK, John James (1821-1878)

Interrupting his business career, West Pointer (1843) John J. Peck reentered the military for the Civil War. Upon his graduation he had been posted to the artillery with which he served for a decade, earning two brevets in Mexico before resigning as a first lieutenant to enter business in his native New York. He was involved in railroading, banking, and education before the war. In politics he twice lost elections to Congress but was a delegate to the 1856 and 1860 Democratic conventions. His military assignments included: brigadier general, USV (August 9, 1861), commanding 3rd Brigade, Buell's-Keyes' Division, Army of the Potomac (October 3, 1861-March 13, 1862); commanding 1st Brigade, 1st Division, 4th Corps, Army of the Potomac (March 13-June 23, 1862); commanding 2nd Division, 4th Corps, Army of the Potomac (June 24-September 1862); major general, USV (July 4, 1862); commanding Division at Suffolk, 7th Corps, Department of Virginia (September 1862, January 2-April 6, and April 14-August 1, 1863); commanding District of North Carolina, Department of Virginia and North Carolina (August 14, 1863-January 4, 1864 and February 5-April 28, 1864); second-in-command, Department of the East (July 5, 1864-April 10, 1865 and late April-June 1865); and commanding the department (April 10-late April 1865). On the Peninsula he led his brigade at Yorktown, Williamsburg, and Seven Pines. Taking charge of a division just before the Seven Days, he was rewarded with a second star at the close of the campaign. Serving in southeastern Virginia after the withdrawal of the Army of the Potomac from the Peninsula, he was wounded in his successful defense of Suffolk against James Longstreet. He then spent eight relatively quiet months in North Carolina. In the summer of 1864 he was sent to New York where his duties included preventing draft violence, securing the Canadian border from Confederate raids, ensuring the peace during the presidential elections, and the funeral procession of Lincoln. Mustered out on August 24, 1865, he spent the remainder of his life in the insurance business.

Deputy department commander John J. Peck. (*Leslie's*)

PECK, William Raine (1818-1871)

Serving with the Louisiana troops in the Army of Northern Virginia, Louisiana planter William R. Peck rose to the rank of brigadier general in the final months of the war. The Tennessee-born soldier's assignments included: private, 9th Louisiana (July 7, 1861); lieutenant colonel, 9th Louisiana (ca. July 4, 1863); colonel, 9th Louisiana (October 8, 1863); commanding Consolidated Louisiana Brigade, Gordon's Division, 2nd Corps, Army of Northern Virginia (January-February 1865); and brigadier general, CSA (February 18, 1865). Rising through the grades from private to colonel of his regiment, he was present during most of the campaigns of the unit, which included the Shenandoah Valley Campaign of 1862, the Seven Days, 2nd Bull Run, Antietam, Fredericksburg, Chancellorsville, and Gettysburg. He commanded the regiment in the Bristoe and Mine Run operations. The regiment then served in opposing Grant's Overland Campaign until sent to the Shenandoah Valley to threaten Washington. During the fight at Monocacy he was in charge of half of the Consolidated Louisiana Brigade. He served later in the Shenandoah Valley under Jubal A. Early. Returning to the main army, he took command of the brigade in the Petersburg trenches and was promoted to brigadier general. He apparently went on leave before the final debacle at Appomattox and was paroled in Mississippi. Thereafter he resumed the now-altered life of a planter.

PEGRAM, John (1832-1865)

Marrying one of the belles of the Confederacy, General John Pegram's wedded life is symptomatic of the collapse of the South. Three weeks after his wedding, which was the social high point of the dismal last winter of the war in Richmond, the guests were back in the same church for his funeral. A Virginia-born West Pointer (1854), he had resigned as a first lieutenant of dragoons on May 10, 1861, to join the South. His assignments included: lieutenant colonel, PACS (early 1861); colonel, PACS (ca. April 1862); commanding cavalry brigade, Department of East Tennessee (ca. October 31, 1862-August 1863); brigadier general, CSA (November 7, 1862); commanding division, Forrest's Cavalry Corps, Army of Tennessee (August-September 1863); commanding Smith's (old) Brigade, Early's Division, 2nd Corps, Army of Northern Virginia (October 11, 1863-May 5, 1864); commanding brigade, Early's-Ramseur's Division, Valley District, Department of Northern Virginia (July-September 20, 1864); commanding the division (September 20-December 1864); and commanding division, 2nd Corps, Army of Northern Virginia (December 1864-February 6, 1865). Serving under General Garnett, he was captured at Rich Mountain early in the war. Upon his exchange he went west and was Beauregard's and Bragg's chief engineer and chief of staff to E.K. Smith before being given a cavalry brigade with which he was detached to serve at Murfreesboro. He later led the command in a raid into Kentucky and joined Forrest in command of the cavalry from the Department of East Tennessee for Chickamauga. Transferred to Virginia for reasons of the heart, he led an infantry brigade at Mine Run and was wounded at the Wilderness. Returning to duty while the unit was in the Shenandoah, he fought at 3rd Winchester and the next day took over command of the division when General Ramseur transferred to the deceased Rodes' Division. Although never promoted to major general, Pegram led the division at Fisher's Hill, Cedar Creek, and in the Petersburg trenches until killed at Hatcher's Run shortly after his marriage to Hetty Cary. (Freeman, Douglas, S., *Lee's Lieutenants*)

PEGRAM, William Johnson (1841-1865)

After serving throughout the entire Civil War and rising from private to colonel, artillerist Willie Pegram was killed a few days before Lee's surrender. His Confederate assignments included: private, 21st Virginia (April 1861); lieutenant, Richmond "Purcell" Artillery (May 1861); captain, Richmond "Purcell" Artillery (April 1862); major, Artillery (from March 2, 1863); executive officer, Walker's Artillery Battalion, A.P. Hill's Division, 2nd Corps, Army of Northern Virginia (April 16-June 2, 1863); executive officer, Walker's Battalion, Reserve Artillery, 3rd Corps, Army of Northern Virginia (June 2-4, 1863); commanding battalion, Reserve Artillery, 3rd Corps, Army of Northern Virginia (June 4-July 1863); and commanding same battalion, 3rd Corps, Army of Northern Virginia (July 1863-April 1, 1865). After seeing some initial service along the Potomac, he commanded his battery at the Seven Days, Cedar Mountain, 2nd Bull Run, Harpers Ferry, Antietam, and Fredericksburg. At Antietam he suffered his first wound. Promoted to major, he served as second in command of A.P. Hill's artillery at Chancellorsville. When R. Lindsay Walker moved up to command of the new 3rd Corps' artillery, Pegram took over the battalion. He served through the remaining campaigns of the Army of Northern Virginia, rising rapidly to the rank of colonel despite the normally slow promotions common in the artillery. Less than two months after the death of his brother, General John Pegram, Willie Pegram was himself killed at the battle of Five Forks. His loss was mourned throughout the army, which itself had only about a week of life left. (Freeman, Douglas S., *Lee's Lieutenants* and Wise, Jennings, C., *The Long Arm of Lee*)

Confederate artillerist Willie Pegram. (NA)

PEGUES, Christopher Claudius (1823-1862)

Lee's first action in command of the Army of Northern Virginia, the Seven Days Battles, cost the Confederacy many regimental commanders who, had they survived, might well have grown into solid brigade commanders. One of these was a native of South Carolina, Christopher C. Pegues. By the time of the secession crisis he was a lawyer in Alabama, and he entered the military two days before Fort Sumter was fired upon. His assignments included: captain Company G, 5th Alabama (April 10, 1861); and colonel, 5th Alabama (April 27, 1862). After service at 1st Bull Run and on the Manassas and Yorktown lines, he was elected to command the regiment upon its reorganization in the spring of 1862. He then served through the actions at Williamsburg and Seven Pines. In his first action during the Seven Days, Gaines' Mill, he fell mortally wounded. He died on July 15.

PEIRCE, Ebenezer Weaver (?-?)

A brigadier general in the Massachusetts militia, Ebenezer W. Peirce was accepted into the Federal service shortly after the firing upon Fort Sumter. His assignments included: brigadier general, Massachusetts Militia (in U.S. service April 22, 1861); commanding Camp Hamilton, Department of Virginia (ca. April-July 1861); colonel, 29th Massachusetts (December 31, 1861); commanding 2nd Brigade, 1st Division, 9th Corps, Department of the Ohio (August 18-September 18, 1863 and January 10-March 16, 1864); and commanding 2nd Brigade, 1st Division, 9th Corps, Army of the Potomac (June 4-17, 1864). Taking several regiments from his native state to Fortress Monroe—at the tip of the Peninsula between the James and York rivers—he reported to Benjamin F. Butler who placed him in charge of nearby Camp Hamilton. From this base, Peirce advanced against Big Bethel and was repulsed. He was mustered out of the national service on July 22, 1861, upon the expiration of his three-month term. By the end of the year he had raised a volunteer regiment for three years. He was commissioned its colonel. Back on the Peninsula he was wounded during the Seven Days but later fought at Knoxville, Cold Harbor, and Petersburg. Although he occasionally led a brigade, he was never able to equal his militia rank in the volunteer service. He was honorably discharged on November 8, 1864.

PELHAM, John (1838-1863)

Although "The Gallant Pelham" served the entire war with the artillery, he was destined to fall while moonlighting in a cavalry charge. A native Alabamian, he withdrew from West Point upon the outbreak of hostilities and joined the Confederate army. His assignments included: lieutenant, Wise (Va.) Artillery (early 1861); captain, Stuart Horse Artillery (March 23, 1862); major, Artillery (August 9, 1862); lieutenant colonel, Artillery (April 4, 1863, to rank from March 2); and commanding Horse Artillery Battalion, Cavalry Division, Army of Northern Virginia (August 1862-March 17, 1863). After fighting at 1st Bull Run, he became the captain of the first horse artillery battery that served with Jeb Stuart, becoming close friends with the general. Commanding his unit, he saw action at Yorktown and during the Seven Days. Promoted, he commanded all of Stuart's horse batteries at 2nd Bull Run and Antietam. At Fredericksburg he held up the advance of a Union division against the Confederate right with only two guns. With only one gun left, he continued to shift positions despite the fact that 24 enemy guns were now concentrating their fire on him. Disobeying repeated orders to withdraw, he only did so upon running out of ammunition. General Lee observed and said, "It is glorious to see such courage in one so young!" Known as the "Boy Major," he heard of an impending action at Kelly's Ford on March 17, 1863. Away from his battalion at the time, he joined the fray with the cavalry. He fell victim to a shell fragment while directing a column past a fence. Thought to be dead, he was thrown over a horse and led from the field. Quite a while later he was lowered to the ground and found to be still alive. He died shortly thereafter. Some believed that prompt attention might have saved his life. (Hassler, William Woods, *Colonel John Pelham, Lee's Boy Artillerist*)

PEMBER, Phoebe Yates (1823-1913)

While serving as the chief matron of Chimborazo Hospital's second division, Phoebe Yates Pember gathered the material for *A Southern Woman's Story*, the best first person account of Confederate hospitals. Born into a wealthy Jewish Charleston family, she was widowed during the early months of the war when her husband died of tuberculosis. Through her friendship with the wife of the Confederate Secretary of War George W. Randolph, she was offered the hospital post in late 1862. Her account relates the activities of the next two and a half years with a mixture of realism and humor. She recounts the sufferings and the spirit of the wounded, criticizes many of the surgeons, and bemoans the shortages of supplies. Her combativeness appears in her efforts to define her status, especially in dealing with the thorny question of the rationed whiskey for which she was held accountable. Her fall 1864 trip to visit her refugeed family in Georgia provides glimpses of the difficulties of travel. But it is the stories of individual patients which provide the most interesting reading. After the fall of Richmond she remained with her charges until the transition to Federal control was completed. She devoted the rest of her life to travel.

PEMBERTON, John Clifford (1814-1881)

In an unusual case of self-sacrifice for the Civil War officer corps, Northern-born John C. Pemberton resigned his lieutenant general's commission in order to serve as a private when it became obvious that his loss of Vicksburg made him unacceptable with the army and the South for high command. The Philadelphian West Pointer (1837) had served his entire old army tour with the artillery. He saw service in the Seminole War, Mexican War (winning two brevets) on the frontier, and on the Utah expedition against the Mormons. Having married a Virginian, he resigned as a captain in the 4th Artillery on April 29, 1861, and joined that state's forces. His Southern assignments included: lieutenant colonel, Virginia Volunteers (April 28, 1861); colonel, Virginia Volunteers (May 8, 1861); major, Artillery (June 15, 1861); brigadier general, CSA (June 17, 1861); commanding brigade, Department of Norfolk (summer-November 1861); commanding 4th Military District of South Carolina, Department of South Carolina, Georgia and Florida (December 10, 1861-March 4, 1862); major general, CSA (January 14, 1862); commanding the department (March 4-September 24, 1862); lieutenant general, CSA (October 13, 1862); commanding Department of Mississippi and East Louisiana (October 17, 1862-July 4, 1863); lieutenant colonel, Artillery (May 1864); and commanding Richmond Defenses, Department of Richmond (May 1864-February 1865). Following service at Norfolk he commanded along the Atlantic coast. Promoted to lieutenant general, he was sent to Mississippi with the assignment to guard Vicksburg and Port Hudson. When Grant crossed the river below Vicksburg, Pemberton sent portions of his command. After fighting at Port Gibson, Raymond, Jackson, Champion Hill, and Big Black River Bridge, Pemberton was forced back into the Vicksburg defenses and was compelled to undergo a siege. With his command starving, he determined to surrender on the Fourth of July in the hopes of gaining a more favorable agreement. This coupled with his Northern birth led to charges of treason in the press and among the public. Once declared exchanged, it became obvious that it would be difficult to find a place for Pemberton at his high rank. The possibility of a corps command with the Army of Tennessee evaporated when even Jefferson Davis realized that he would not be acceptable to the soldiers. Finally on May 18, 1864, he resigned and offered to serve as a private. However, Davis would not allow that and recommissioned him as a lieutenant colonel of artillery. For nine months he commanded the artillery defenses of the Confederate capital and then went on inspection duty. Having loyally served his adopted country, he lived on a Virginia farm after the war. (Pemberton, John C., III, *Pemberton: Defender of Vicksburg*)

PENDER, William Dorsey (1834-1863)

A career soldier, North Carolinian William Dorsey Pender gave his life to the Confederacy. A West Pointer (1854), he had served the intervening years, mostly on the West Coast, in the artillery and dragoons before resigning on March 21, 1861. His Southern assignments included: captain, Artillery (spring 1861); colonel, 3rd North Carolina Volunteers (May 16, 1861); colonel, 6th North Carolina (August 17, 1861); brigadier general, CSA (June 3, 1862); commanding brigade, A.P. Hill's Division, (in 1st Corps June 29 and in 2nd Corps from July 27), Army of Northern Virginia (June-December 13, 1862 and early 1863-May 3, 1863); commanding the division (May 3, 1863); major general, CSA (May 27, 1863); and commanding division, 3rd Corps, Army of Northern Virginia (May 30-July 2, 1863). Having distinguished himself at Seven Pines he was promoted to brigadier a few days later and assigned to Hill's Light Division. With that famous command he fought through the Seven Days, suffering a wound at Malvern Hill, and Cedar Mountain, 2nd Bull Run, Harpers Ferry, and Antietam. Wounded at Fredericksburg, he returned for Chancellorsville and was in command of the division when wounded. Promoted to major general, he was assigned to command a division of four of the six brigades from Hill's former command and attached to Hill's new 3rd Corps. The North Carolinian led this unit on the first day at Gettysburg and on the second was hit by a shell fragment. Following the amputation of his leg back in Virginia he died on July 18. (Freeman, Douglas S., *Lee's Lieutenants*)

PENDLETON, George Hunt (1825-1889)

The Civil War, and his vice presidential candidacy on the Democratic ticket with McClellan, severely damaged the political career of George H. Pendleton. Born in Cincinnati, he had been educated there and at the University of Heidelberg before taking up the practice of law in his hometown in 1847. Seven years later he took a seat in the state senate and held it for two years. In 1854 he had lost a bid for a House seat as a Democrat but was successful two years later. He served four terms before being defeated for reelection in 1864 and leaving office on March 3, 1865, as the war was coming to a close. Early in the Civil War he became notorious as a copperhead and for his suggestion that Lincoln let the erring states go in peace and friendship. At the 1864 Democratic convention the peace faction managed to get him nominated to the number two spot on the ticket by a unanimous vote. Whereas the presidential candidate, McClellan, did not recognize the defeatist planks of the party's platform, George H. Pendleton continued to speak out in opposition to the war and support the party position. With the Democratic ticket handily defeated in the electoral college the nation registered itself as behind the vigorous prosecution of the war. After the war Pendleton was defeated for a congressional seat in 1866 and the governship in 1869. For the next decade he engaged in railroading. In 1879 he was elected to a term in the Senate but failed to gain renomination. He left office in 1885, whereupon he was appointed minister to Germany. While serving in this post he died in Brussels, Belgium.

PENDLETON, William Nelson (1809-1883)

An accomplished administrator, William N. Pendleton was less than effective as a battlefield tactician while serving as chief artillerist in Lee's army. The Virginian was a West Pointer (1830) who had resigned, after three years in the artillery and as a faculty member at his alma mater, to become an educator and Episcopal minister. He reentered the military upon the secession of his state. His assignments included: captain, Rockbridge Artillery (May 1, 1861); colonel, Artillery (July 13, 1861); chief of Artillery, Army of the Shenandoah (July 1861); chief of Artillery, Army of the Potomac (July-October 22, 1861); chief of Artillery, Department (later Army) of Northern Virginia (October 22, 1861-April 9, 1865); and brigadier general, CSA (March 26, 1862). Not forgetting his religious training in his first battle, he shouted "May the Lord have mercy on their poor souls—Fire!" as his four guns, "Matthew," "Mark," "Luke," and "John" roared into action. As Johnston's artillery chief he fought at 1st Bull Run and served on the Peninsula. Under Lee, he failed to mass his guns before the assault at Malvern Hill. Another failure came at the end of the Maryland invasion when he reported, incorrectly, that the entire reserve artillery of the army has been captured; only four pieces had been lost. However, his administrative talents proved his value. He developed the system of artillery battalions assigned to the infantry divisions which allowed for a more rapid concentration of firepower. His skill was also apparent to Lee in the supplying, officering, and equipping of the long arm. Following the Chancellorsville reorganization, the last reserve battalions were assigned to the corps and he was confined to administrative work. In March 1864 President Davis dispatched Pendleton to Johnston's Army of Tennessee to report on its internal artillery organization and suggest improvements. His recommendations did the impossible in pleasing the ever-feuding Davis and Johnston. Rejoining Lee he served for the remainder of the war as nominal chief artillerist. At one point

Davis considered naming Pendleton to an infantry corps command in the West, but Lee refused to endorse the idea. After the war he returned to his preaching in Lexington and was closely linked with Lee during his years at Washington College. There was a striking facial resemblance between them. (Wise, Jennings C., *The Long Arm of Lee* and Freeman, Douglas S., *R.E. Lee*)

PENNINGTON, Alexander Cummings McWhorter (1838-1917)

An 1860 graduate of West Point, New Jersey native Alexander C.M. Pennington found promotion in the regular artillery too slow—even in wartime—and transferred to the volunteer cavalry for advancement. His Civil War-era assignments included: brevet second lieutenant, 2nd Artillery (July 1, 1860); second lieutenant, 2nd Artillery (February 1, 1861); first lieutenant, Battery M, 2nd Artillery (May 14, 1861); captain, 1st Artillery (March 30, 1864); colonel, 3rd New Jersey Cavalry (October 1, 1864); commanding 1st Brigade, 3rd Division, Cavalry Corps, Army of the Shenandoah (October 7-November 10, 1864 and February 25-March 25, 1865); and commanding 1st Brigade, 3rd Division, Cavalry Corps, Army of the Potomac (March 25-May 29, 1865). The battery to which he was chiefly assigned served for much of the war as a horse battery attached to the cavalry. This battery fought at 1st Bull Run, Yorktown, Williamsburg, the Seven Days, and Antietam. Pennington commanded the guns at Fredericksburg and was apparently in a subordinate post at Chancellorsville. At Brandy Station and Gettysburg—in the latter serving with Custer—he won regular army brevets. Despite promotion to a captaincy in early 1864 he opted to accept command of a cavalry regiment from his own state. Commanding a brigade, he won a brevet at Cedar Creek and fought at Five Forks and in the Appomattox Campaign. Mustered out of the volunteers on August 1, 1865, he held brevets as a colonel of regulars and brigadier of volunteers. Remaining in the service, he was retired in 1899 as a full brigadier general, having also served as brigadier of volunteers in the Spanish-American War.

PENNYPACKER, Galusha (1844-1916)

The youngest man ever to become a general officer in the United States Army—unable even to vote for the president who signed his commission—Galusha Pennypacker was appropriately born in George Washington's old Valley Forge headquarters. After having toyed with journalism he was studying law at the time of the firing on Fort Sumter. Joining the army, his assignments included: private, Company A, 9th Pennsylvania (April 1861); first lieutenant, Company A, 9th Pennsylvania (April 1861; declined); quartermaster sergeant, 9th Pennsylvania (April 22, 1861); captain, Company A, 97th Pennsylvania (August 22, 1861); major, 97th Pennsylvania (October 7, 1861); lieutenant colonel, 97th Pennsylvania (April 3, 1864); colonel, 97th Pennsylvania (August 15, 1864); commanding 2nd Brigade, 2nd Division, 10th Corps, Army of the James (September 14-December 3, 1864); commanding 2nd Brigade, 2nd Division, 24th Corps, Army of the James (December 3, 1864-January 6, 1865); commanding 2nd Brigade, Ames' Division, Terry's Provisional Corps, Department of North Carolina (January 6-15, 1865); and brigadier general, USV (February 18, 1865). Turning down a lieutenancy due to his youth, he served as a quartermaster sergeant with his first unit, in Patterson's army, before being mustered out on July 29, 1861. Recruiting many of his comrades, he became a company commander and was soon made a field officer. Serving on the Southern coast, he fought at Secessionville and in the operations against Charleston, including the assault on Battery Wagner. Much of the remainder of his time was taken up by court-martial duties. Joining Butler's army, he fought at Swift Creek, Drewry's Bluff, Chester Station, and Green Plains. Wounded three times at the latter, he returned to duty following a three-month convalescence and was soon commissioned colonel. The next month he was given a brigade and led it in the operations against Petersburg and Richmond. He saw action at Chaffin's Bluff, Fort Harrison, New Market Heights, and Fort Gilmer. At the latter his horse was killed and he was himself wounded. Never relinquishing command, he fought at the Darbytown Road before taking part in the unsuccessful first movement against Fort Fisher in North Carolina. In the second, successful, attempt he was severely wounded when mounting the parapet. The 97th's flag was the first to be planted on the fort's walls. Pennypacker was brevetted brigadier and granted the Medal of Honor for this action and the next month was given the full rank. He was soon brevetted major general for his war service. Not returning to duty due to his wounds, he resigned on April 30, 1866. A few months later he entered the regular army as a colonel and the next year was brevetted brigadier and major general in that service for Fort Fisher and the war. He retired in 1883 as colonel, 16th Infantry, having served in the South and on the frontier. Active in veterans' affairs he died in his hometown of Philadelphia. (Price, Isaiah, *History of the Ninety-Seventh Regiment Pennsylvania Volunteers*)

PENROSE, William Henry (1832-1903)

The son of a regular army officer, William H. Penrose obtained a commission in that body upon the outbreak of the Civil War and rose to the rank of brigadier general of volunteers. Born in New York, he had been practicing engineering in 1861 when he received his appointment. His assignments included: second lieutenant, 3rd Infantry (April 13, 1861); first lieutenant, 3rd Infantry (May 14, 1861); first lieutenant and adjutant, 3rd Infantry (March 1-April 18, 1863); colonel, 15th New Jersey (April 18, 1863); commanding 1st Brigade, 1st Division, 6th Corps, Army of the Potomac (May 3, May 4-June 27, 1863 and May 9-July 8, 1864); captain, 3rd Infantry (September 11, 1863); commanding 1st Brigade, 1st Division, 6th Corps, Army of the Shenandoah (August 6-September 18 and September 20-October 19, 1864); again commanding 1st Brigade, 1st Division, 6th Corps, Army of the Potomac (February 26-June 28, 1865); and brigadier general, USV (June 27, 1865). With his regular regiment he fought on the Peninsula and at 2nd Bull Run. At Fredericksburg he was in command of two of its companies, B and G, and the following spring was named colonel of a volunteer regiment. Twice at Chancellorsville he moved up to brigade command and received a brevet for his actions there. He won another brevet for Gettysburg and then took part in the Bristoe and Mine Run campaigns. During the Overland Campaign he was brevetted for the Wilderness and again rose to brigade command at Spotsylvania. He fought at Cold Harbor and in the early stages of the Petersburg siege before being sent to the Shenandoah Valley. There he led his regiment at 3rd Winchester and the New Jersey brigade at Fisher's Hill and Cedar Creek where he was wounded and brevetted. Returning to duty early the next year, he led the brigade in the final stages at Petersburg and in the pursuit to Appomattox. He was brevetted brigadier general in the regular army for the war and was named to that rank in full in the volunteer service after the close of hostilities. He was also brevetted major general of volunteers for Cedar Creek. Mustered out of that service on January 15, 1866, he reverted to his regular army rank of captain and remained in the service until his 1896 retirement as colonel, 16th Infantry.

PERKINS, John, Jr. (1819-1885)

Confederate Congressman John Perkins, Jr., was planning beyond victory and the permanent establishment of the new nation when he called for the creation of a tariff specifically adverse to the United States after the war. The Mississippi native and former lawyer had been a marginal Louisiana cotton planter, a judge, and a U.S. congressman before the Civil War. He chaired the state's secession convention and then was named to the Provisional Congress. Remaining throughout the life of the Confederacy, he rose to be the chairman of the Committee on Rules and Officers; he had sat on that panel in the previous Confederate congress as well. Representing Louisiana's northeastern 6th District, his constituents were fully under Union control by the end of 1864. He also sat on the committees on: Commerce (Second Congress); Foreign Affairs; Military Affairs (Provisional Congress); Printing (Provisional Congress); and Ways and Means (First Congress). Although often linked with the Davis administration, he opposed the draft, blacks in the army, and many presidential appointees. Viewing a negotiated settlement to be possible, he based economic planning on that premise. After the war he went into exile in Mexico and Europe until 1878; a venture in the cultivation of coffee in Spain failed, and he then returned to Louisiana.

PERRIN, Abner Monroe (1827-1864)

Having served as a regular army first lieutenant in the Mexican War, Abner Perrin was made a captain in the 14th South Carolina in the summer of 1861. His later assignments, mostly in the Army of Northern Virginia, included: colonel, 14th South Carolina (February 20, 1863); commanding McGowan's Brigade, A.P. Hill's Division, Jackson's Corps (May 3, 1863); commanding same brigade, Pender's-Wilcox's Division, A.P. Hill's Corps (May 30, 1863-early 1864); brigadier general, CSA (September 10, 1863); and commanding Wilcox's old Brigade, Anderson's Division, Hill's Corps (early 1864-May 12, 1864). After service on the South Carolina coast, including its first fight at Port Royal Ferry on New Year's Day 1862, the regiment was ordered to Virginia in the spring. Serving in Maxcy Gregg's Brigade of A.P. Hill's Division, Perrin participated with his regiment in the fighting in the Seven Days, Cedar Mountain, 2nd Bull Run, the capture of Harpers Ferry, Antietam, and Fredericksburg. Promoted to colonel he led the regiment in Jackson's famous flank attack on the Union 11th Corps at Chancellorsville until, following the wounding of McGowan and Colonel Edwards, he took over command of the brigade. Perrin directed the brigade during all three days at Gettysburg. Perrin's promotion to brigadier general over the more senior Colonel D.H. Hamilton caused that officer's resignation in disgust two months later. Perrin continued in temporary command of the brigade, during the Bristoe and Mine Run campaigns, until McGowan's return when Perrin was given command of Wilcox's Alabama Brigade which had been without a general since that officer had been given a division. Perrin led this brigade at the Wilderness and in the fighting at Spotsylvania Court House where he led a counterattack against the Union breakthrough at the Bloody Angle on May 12, when he was struck by seven bullets and fell dead. (Freeman, Douglas S., *Lee's Lieutenants*)

PERRY, Edward Aylesworth (1831-1889)

Born and raised in New England, Edward A. Perry taught school and practiced law in Alabama and Florida before the war in which he was to rise to brigade command. At the head of the Rifle Rangers he entered the Confederate service where his assignments included: captain, Company A, 2nd Florida (July 13, 1861); colonel, 2nd Florida (May 11, 1862); brigadier general, CSA (August 28, 1862); and commanding Florida Brigade, Anderson's-Mahone's Division, 1st (after May 30, 1863, 3rd) Corps, Army of Northern Virginia (November 10, 1862-May 1864). After fighting at Williamsburg he was elected colonel to replace Colonel Ward who had been killed. He led his men at Seven Pines and was severely wounded at Frayser's Farm during the Seven Days. Promoted during his absence, he commanded the Florida troops of Lee's army at Fredericksburg and Chancellorsville. Felled by typhoid he was out of action for an undetermined period of time, including the Gettysburg Campaign. He was back on duty by the time of the Wilderness but was wounded there. Later that month his three regiments were merged into another brigade of Florida troops recently arrived. Upon his recovery, he was ordered, on September 28, 1864, to duty with the Alabama reserve forces. The war ended while he was performing these duties. A postwar lawyer, he was active in politics and served a term as governor of Florida. (Freeman, Douglas S., *Lee's Lieutenants*)

PERRY, Madison Stark (1814-1865)

As a South Carolina-born governor of Florida, Madison S. Perry steered his state into becoming the third state to secede from the Union. A plantation owner in Florida, he entered politics as a Democratic member of the lower state house in 1849 and the next year moved on to the upper house. In October 1856 he was elected governor but did not take his seat until the following October. A leading force in the secession crisis within the state, he recommended a state convention as early as November 27, 1860, and with legislative approval called for an election of delegates on December 22. By January 10, 1861, the secession ordinance had passed and he affixed his signature the next day. During the next few months he was busy in preparing the state for war. His term expired and he left office on October 7, 1861. He was commissioned colonel, 7th Florida (1862), and served in East Tennessee. Ill-health forced his resignation the next year and he returned to his plantation where he died the month before Lee's surrender. (David, William W., *The Civil War and Reconstruction in Florida*)

PERRY, William Flank (1823-1901)

By the time that William F. Perry received his well-deserved promotion to brigadier he had already been in command of the wounded General Law's Brigade for some eight months. Born in Georgia and self-educated he had been a non-practicing attorney active in public education in his adopted Alabama. Enlisting as a private in the 44th Alabama in early 1862, he rose rapidly in the Confederate army. His assignments included: major, 44th Alabama (May 1862); lieutenant colonel, 44th Alabama (September 1, 1862); colonel, 44th Alabama (September 17, 1862); commanding Law's Brigade, Hood's-Field's Division, Department of East Tennessee (December 19, 1863-April 1864); commanding Law's Brigade, Field's Division, 1st Corps, Army of Northern Virginia (June 3, 1864-April 9, 1865); and brigadier general, CSA (February 21, 1865). He served in the Seven Days and at 2nd Bull Run before receiving the colonelcy upon the death of the regimental commander at Antietam. After service with Longstreet around Suffolk, Virginia, he fought at Little Round Top at Gettysburg. Ordered west with Longstreet, he saw action in the victory at Chickamauga and around Knoxville. As a result of the Law-Jenkins feud, he was in brigade command that winter. He commanded the regiment at the Wilderness, Spotsylvania, and the North Anna. Upon the wounding of General Law at Cold Harbor, he again assumed charge of the brigade, a position he held until the surrender at Appomattox. It was not until the winter of the Petersburg and Richmond siege that he received the general's wreath. He was an Alabama planter and Kentucky educator after the war. (Freeman, Douglas S., *Lee's Lieutenants*)

PETER, Walter G. (?-1863)

Although he was hung as a spy, Walter G. Peter was probably on some other kind of secret mission. A lieutenant in the Confederate army, he accompanied his cousin, William Orton Williams, on a mission behind enemy lines on June 8, 1863. Posing as Union inspectors they visited Fort Granger where Peter was identified as one "Major George Dunlop," After showing their papers and borrowing some money, they were quickly on their way. Suspicions having arisen, they were brought back and their true identities were revealed. A 3:00 A.M. a court-martial was convened. Found guilty, they were executed the same morning. It now appears that Williams was on a mission to Europe and Peter was escorting him at least to Canada.

PETERS, William Elisha (1829-1906)

Virginia-born and Berlin-educated William E. Peters was arrested for refusing to make war on civilians. He had entered the Confederate army in the war's first year. His assignments included: lieutenant colonel, 45th Virginia (November 14, 1861); colonel, 45th Virginia (January 6, 1862); colonel, 2nd Virginia State Line (fall 1862); and colonel, 21st Virginia Cavalry (August 31, 1863). After service in western Virginia and East Tennessee, he failed to gain reelection at the Spring 1862 reorganization of the 45th. Given command of a mixed infantry and cavalry regiment of the Virginia State Line, he served in western Virginia and Kentucky. With his regiment transferred to Confederate service as a cavalry unit, he served in those areas and in the Knoxville Campaign. Later serving in the Shenandoah Valley he joined McCausland's raid on Chambersburg, Pennsylvania. When the general revealed his orders to burn the city in the event of non-payment of tribute, Peters refused to comply, threatening to break his sword in two or in effect resign in protest on the spot. He was immediately placed under arrest. Following the burning he was restored to duty. He later served in the Valley under General Early. After the war he was a university professor.

PETERSEN, William A. (?-1871)

Washington tailor William A. Petersen rented out rooms in his 10th Street home. It was here that Abraham Lincoln died. When it was determined that Lincoln should be removed from Ford's Theater, a procession carried him across the street, but the first house tried was locked, with no one at home. They moved on to number 453 but Petersen informed the party that the house was full. However, when told that it was for the wounded president he led the party to a room behind the staircase on the first floor. The current occupant, Private William T. Clark, 13th Massachusetts, immediately vacated the room. Ironically, John Wilkes Booth had once slept in this very bed when it was rented by a friend. The Petersen home became host to many of the top officials of the government during the night, and the next morning Lincoln died there. The building is now run by the National Park Service.

PETIGRU, James Louis (1789-1863)

A prominent and longtime lawyer in South Carolina, James L. Petrigru was an ultra-Unionist in a land given over to rabid secessionists. Despite such statements as "South Carolina is too small to be a republic, and too large to be an insane asylum," he continued to be respected in the community. Years before, he had been the tutor of Robert Barnwell Rhett, the latter-day "Father of Secession." Throughout the decades of secessionist agitation the two men maintained their mutual respect and friendship. When the dreaded event came, Petigru said, "I have seen the last happy day of my life." Upon Petigru's death Rhett had nothing but praise for his friend, in a Charleston then being bombarded in a war that Petigru had tried so hard to prevent. (Carson, James Petigru, ed., *Life, Letters and Speeches of James Louis Petigru*)

PETTIGREW, James Johnston (1828-1863)

Lacking combat experience, J. Johnston Pettigrew was loath to accept a brigadier generalship and actually sent the commission back to the Confederate War Department. The North Carolinian had taught at the Washington Naval Observatory and studied law in the United States and Germany. Practicing in Charleston, he was involved in the militia and became an officer. His military assignments included: colonel, 1st South Carolina Rifles (November 1860); private, Hampton (S.C.) Legion (1861); colonel, 12th North Carolina Volunteers (July 11, 1861); colonel, 22nd North Carolina (designation change on November 14, 1861); brigadier general, CSA (February 26, 1862); commanding French's (old) Brigade, Aquia District, Department of Northern Virginia (March 12-mid April 1862); commanding brigade, Whiting's-G.W. Smith's Division, same department (April-May 31, 1862); commanding Martin's (old) Brigade, Department of North Carolina (September 1862-February and April 1-May, 1863); commanding brigade, Hill's Command, Department of Virginia and North Carolina (February-April 1, 1863); commanding brigade, Heth's Division, 3rd Corps, Army of Northern Virginia (May 30-July 1 and July-July 14, 1863); and commanding the division (July 1-mid July 1863). After commanding his rifles at Fort Sumter, he went to Virginia as a private but was appointed to the colonelcy of the North Carolina regiment before 1st Bull Run. He served that winter in the Fredericksburg area and the next spring moved to the Peninsula. After the Yorktown siege he was wounded and captured at Seven Pines. Exchanged in late August 1862, he commanded a brigade in southern Virginia and North Carolina until May 1863 when it was ordered to Lee's army. At Gettysburg he succeeded the wounded Heth in charge of the division and led it in Pickett's Charge two days later. During the retreat he was mortally wounded on July 14 at Falling Waters while commanding his brigade. Carried back to Virginia, he died three days later. (Freeman, Douglas S., *Lee's Lieutenants*)

PETTUS, Edmund Winston (1821-1907)

Serving throughout the Civil War in the western theater, Alabama-born lawyer and judge Edmund W. Pettus rose to brigade command and the rank of brigadier general in the Confederate service. His assignments included: major, 20th Alabama (September 16, 1861); lieutenant colonel, 20th Alabama (October 8, 1861); colonel, 20th Alabama (May 28, 1863); brigadier general, CSA (September 18, 1863); commanding brigade, Breckinridge's Division, Breckinridge's Corps, Army of Tennessee (November 3-12, 1863); commanding brigade, Stevenson's Division, Hardee's Corps, Army of Tennessee (November 12, 1863-February 20, 1864); and commanding brigade, Stevenson's Division, Hood's-Lee's Corps, Army of Tennessee (February 20, 1864-January 1865 and April 9-26, 1865). Stationed in East Tennessee during the early part of the war, he did take part in E. Kirby Smith's drive into Kentucky in the summer and fall of 1862. He was then transferred with Stevenson's division to the Vicksburg area in late 1862. He was briefly captured at Port Gibson, during the early stages of the Vicksburg Campaign proper but, escaping, rejoined his command. He fought at Champion Hill and rose to regimental command during the siege of the city. Paroled upon the surrender of Vicksburg, he was exchanged on September 12, 1863, and was promoted to brigadier general six days later. Commanding a brigade, he fought at Chattanooga and throughout the Atlanta Campaign. His command was not engaged at Franklin but did fight at Nashville. Wounded during the Carolinas Campaign, he was back in brigade command at the final surrender of Joseph E. Johnston's forces. Resuming his law practice, he also became active in Democratic politics and died during his second term in the U.S. Senate.

PETTUS, John Jones (1813-1867)

After previously serving as Mississippi's governor for five days, John J. Pettus was again in that position at the time of the state's secession, which he had been active in achieving. A native of Tennessee, he had settled in Mississippi and become active in Democratic politics. He served in both houses of the state legislature before succeeding Governor Henry S. Foote in 1854, since Pettus was then president of the state senate. The term expired in less than a week. He was elected in his own right in October 1859 and took up his duties the next month. After the secession of the state he was reelected to a second term. He was active in supporting the Confederacy and in preparing the defense of the state. However, he had to move the capital from Jackson to Meridian and finally to Macon. His second term expired on November 16, 1863, and after the war he moved to Arkansas. (Dubay, Robert W., *John Jones Pettus, Mississippi Fire-Eater: His Life and Times 1813-1867*)

PEYTON, Robert Ludwell Yates (1822-1863)

Virginia-born and Ohio-raised lawyer Robert L.Y. Peyton survived a number of battles only to die while representing the rival, secessionist government of Missouri in the Confederate Senate. At the outset of the war he was in the state senate and served as colonel, 3rd Cavalry, 8th Division, Missouri State Guard. Under Price he fought at Carthage, Wilson's Creek, Big Dry Wood, and Lexington. Named to the Confederate Senate for the First Regular Congress, he arrived early enough to be seated on January 22, 1862, in the Provisional Congress. He was not, however, assigned any committee duties. Once in the Senate he served on the committees on: Claims; Commerce; Engrossment and Enrollment; Indian Affairs; and Post Offices and Post Roads. He was a supporter of strong war measures but was protective of local interests on most matters. He died of malaria in Alabama on September 3, 1863, either while returning home or as a result of the Vicksburg siege.

PHELAN, James (1821-1873)

Mississippi's Confederate Senator James Phelan may well have written off his reelection chances when he proposed the government's impressment of all cotton—to build up the Confederacy's foreign credit—and the death penalty for violations. The Alabama native had been, successively, an editor, state printer, lawyer, and, in 1860, state senator. Named to the First Regular Confederate Congress in the fall of 1861, he only received a two-year term. He sat on the committees on: Engrossment and Enrollment; Indian Affairs; Judiciary; and Printing. He was critical of the system of military exemptions which favored the upper classes and the use of substitutes in the army. In an 1863 rematch he was defeated for a full six-year term by John W.C. Watson. After finishing the war as a judge advocate in the army he was a Memphis attorney.

PHELPS, Charles Edward (1833-1908)

At first in disagreement with the prosecution of the Civil War, Vermont-born Maryland militia officer Charles E. Phelps finally entered the Union army in the second year of the war, winning a brevet to brigadier general and the Congressional Medal of Honor. Having taken part in the crushing of the Know-Nothing movement in his adopted state, he resigned from the militia in 1861. His assignments included: major, Maryland Militia (1858); lieutenant colonel, 7th Maryland (August 20, 1862); commanding 2nd Brigade, 3rd Division, 1st Corps, Army of the Potomac (December 28, 1863-January 20, 1864); colonel, 7th Maryland (April 13, 1864); and commanding 3rd Brigade, 2nd Division, 5th Corps, Army of the Potomac (May 8, 1864). Answering Lincoln's summer 1862 call for more troops, he became a field officer and served the early part of his tour in western Virginia and western Maryland. The regiment joined the Army of the Potomac shortly after Gettysburg and took part in the Bristoe and Mine Run operations. Phelps commanded the regiment in the latter. Promoted to colonel, he led his regiment into the Wilderness and succeeded to brigade command at Spotsylvania where he was promptly wounded and captured. Custer's cavalry recaptured him a few days later before he could be shipped off to a prisoner of war camp. In 1898 Phelps received his medal for this exploit. He appears not to have returned to duty after this incident and was honorably discharged on September 9, 1864. A professor, scientist, and writer after the war, he also sat as a judge and in the U.S. Congress.

PHELPS, John Smith (1814-1886)

The appointment of Missouri Democratic politician John S. Phelps to a brigadier generalship in the Union army was not really in recognition of military genius but rather to cloak him with the appropriate authority to serve as military governor of Arkansas. Born in Connecticut, he had practiced law there for two years before settling in Missouri. Quickly building his practice, he entered politics three years later as a member of the state legislature. In 1844 he won the first of nine consecutive House terms as a Democrat before deciding not to run in 1862. Upon the outbreak of the Civil War he began recruiting back in Springfield, and his record included: lieutenant colonel, Phelps' (Mo.) Regiment (October 2, 1861); colonel, Phelps' (Mo.) Regiment (December 19, 1861); and brigadier general, USV (November 19, 1862, to rank from July 19). At the head of his six-months volunteers, he was wounded at Pea Ridge before being mustered out with the regiment on May 13, 1862. Two months later Lincoln named him military governor of Arkansas and in November he was named brigadier general to give him the military authority necessary. He held this post until early 1863. His commission expired on March 4, 1863, due to the failure of the Senate to confirm the nomination. On the previous day he had left the House at the end of his term. Resuming his law practice, he was defeated for the Missouri governorship in 1868 but was successful eight years later. After a highly accomplished term of four years he again resumed his private practice until his death.

PHELPS, John Wolcott (1813-1885)

Abolitionist Vermonter John W. Phelps resigned his commission as a Union brigadier general on August 21, 1862, because he was ahead of the times in his recruitment of blacks as soldiers. The West Pointer (1836) had been posted to the artillery and saw action in the Seminole War and along the troubled border with Canada. During the Mexican War he declined a brevet. This unusual happening may have been due to the fact that the war was not popular in his part of the country, as it was considered to be a Southern move to gain slave territories. He resigned as captain in the 4th Artillery in 1859 and then campaigned against slavery. At the outbreak of the Civil War he was named commander of his native state's first regiment, a three-months unit. His assignments included: colonel, 1st Vermont (May 9, 1861); brigadier general, USV (August 9, 1861, to rank from May 17, 1861); commanding Ship Island Expedition (December 1861-March 1862); and commanding 1st Brigade, Department of the Gulf. He led the force from Fortress Monroe which captured Newport News and was then given charge of the expedition which seized Ship Island, Mississippi, which became the jumping-off point for the capture of New Orleans. Under Benjamin F. Butler, he took part in that capture and then, while performing garrison duty, he embarked on the first recruitment of black soldiers. Branded an outlaw by the Confederacy, he endured the humiliation of having the administration revoke his actions—so he resigned. Active in educational and historical groups, he also resumed his crusade against the Masons. He was the Anti-Mason candidate for president in 1880. (Cecil, Hampden Cutts Howard, *Life and Public Services of General John Wolcott Phelps*)

PHELPS, Mary Whitney (?-?)

The Maine-born wife of Missouri's Union General John S. Phelps, Mary W. Phelps converted her Springfield home into a field hospital and was rewarded with a grant of $20,000 from Congress for the care she gave to the body of General Nathanial Lyon who was killed at Wilson's Creek. With the proceeds she promptly established an orphanage for the unfortunate children of both sides in divided Missouri.

PHELPS, S. Ledyard (?-?)

With the rank of lieutenant commander in the Union navy, S. Ledyard Phelps commanded various vessels on the western rivers. At Fort Henry he commanded the 2nd Division of Foote's flotilla as well as his own USS *Conestoga*, armed with four 32-pounders. He again commanded this craft on the Cumberland River in the attacks on Fort Donelson. During the fights at Island #10, Fort Pillow, Memphis, and in the early Vicksburg operations he directed the 16-gun flagship *Benton*. In January 1863 he commanded the USS *Lexington* on the Cumberland River, with one howitzer and seven guns. During the Red River Campaign he was in charge of the eight-gun *Eastport*.

PHELPS, Walter, Jr. (?-1878)

Almost two years after being mustered out of the Union army, upon the expiration of his regiment's term, New York native Walter Phelps, Jr., was brevetted brigadier general for his service. His assignments included: colonel, 22nd New York (June 6, 1861); and commanding 1st Brigade, 1st Division, 1st Corps, Army of the Potomac (September 14, 1862-March 20, 1863 and April 9-May 30, 1863). Serving initially near Washington and in northern Virginia, his regiment became part of the Army of Virginia under Pope in the summer of 1862. His division was not engaged at Cedar Mountain but fought at 2nd Bull Run. At South Mountain he succeeded to brigade command when John P. Hatch took over the division. Continuing in brigade leadership, he fought at Antietam, Fredericksburg, and Chancellorsville before his two-months regiment was mustered out on June 19, 1863, ending his military career.

PHIFER, Charles W. (?-?)

Appointed by General Earl Van Dorn, Charles W. Phifer served as a brigadier general for five months before he was rejected by President Davis. A native of Tennessee, he had entered the regular army from Mississippi in 1855 as a lieutenant of cavalry. He resigned his commission on April 1, 1861, to offer his services to the South. His assignments included: first lieutenant, Cavalry (April 1861); major, 6th (sometimes called 1st) Arkansas Cavalry Battalion (ca. June 1861); acting brigadier by Van Dorn (May 25, 1862); commanding 3rd Brigade, 3rd Division, Army of the West, Department No. 2 (June-summer 1862); and commanding brigade, Maury's Division, Price's Corps, Army of West Tennessee, Department No. 2 (summer-October 16, 1862). He was initially assigned to recruiting duty in New Orleans until he took command of a battalion of cavalry composed of companies from Louisiana and Arkansas. He led this unit in central Kentucky and northern Mississippi until it was merged into a new regiment on May 15, 1862. Shortly thereafter he was appointed a brigadier, extralegally, and assigned to command a brigade of dismounted cavalry in Price's Army of the West. He led the brigade at Corinth but a couple of weeks later, on October 16, 1862, was relieved of duty due to the fact that Jefferson Davis refused to appoint him officially. He later served, with the rank of major, on the staff of Colonel A.W. Reynolds as an assistant adjutant general and was captured at Vicksburg.

PHILLIPS, Eugenia Levy (1819-?)

The sister of Chimborazo Hospital matron Phoebe Yates Pember and wife of former Alabama congressman Philip Phillips, Eugenia Levy Phillips became a target of what many would term Ben Butler's tyranny in New Orleans. An open Rebel sympathizer in the occupied city, she was charged with laughing as the funeral procession of a Union officer passed her home. Allegedly, she was at a children's party in her residence and was not laughing at the events outside. Giving this explanation, she refused to apologize and Butler banished her to Ship Island, which at that time was a yellow fever station in the Gulf of Mexico, as "a vulgar woman of the town." Told that she would only be allowed to communicate with Butler and her own maid she retorted, "It has one advantage over the city, sir; you will not be there." She further stated that "It is fortunate that neither the fever nor General Butler is contagious." The incident received international attention.

PHILLIPS, Pleasant J. (ca. 1824-1876)

A longtime militia officer, Georgian Pleasant J. Phillips spent very little time in the Confederate army, and most of his combat action was while serving with the state forces. His assignments included: colonel, 31st Georgia (November 19, 1861); brigadier general, Georgia Militia; and commanding 2nd Brigade, 1st Division, Georgia Militia serving with the Army of Tennessee and in the Department of South Carolina, Georgia and Florida. With his first command he went to Virginia but resigned on May 13, 1862, even before Robert E. Lee took over command of what was to be the Army of Northern Virginia. Returning to the militia, he commanded a brigade in the Atlanta Campaign and remained behind when Hood headed his army to Tennessee and disaster. In Georgia he commanded the forces in the wasteful battle of Griswoldville while opposing Sherman's march through the state. He served in later operations against Sherman while the latter was still in Georgia.

PHILLIPS, Wendell (1811-1884)

It was the 1837 murder of abolitionist Elijah Lovejoy that galvanized wealthy Massachusetts lawyer Wendell Phillips into becoming an extreme opponent of slavery even condemning the constitution for allowing it. Lecturing widely, Phillips opposed all compromise and demanded immediate emancipation. One of the leaders of the movement, he differed with William Lloyd Garrison on the issue of non-resistance. Considering Lincoln far too conservative, he later found that he was able to support the administration—after the issuance of the Emancipation Proclamation. At the close of the war he became president of the American Anti-Slavery Society and continued his efforts to aid the freedmen. A total reformer, he backed the women's rights movement, favored prison reform, and wanted to ban alcohol. He was a candidate for governor on an anti-capitalist ticket. (Bartlett, Irving H., *Wendell Phillips, Brahmin Radical* and

Sherwin, Oscar, *Prophet of Liberty: The Life and Times of Wendell Phillips*)

PHILLIPS, William (1824-1908)

A Georgia attorney, William Phillips became the organizer and first commander of one of the handful of Confederate "legions," a mixed force of infantry, cavalry, and sometimes artillery, to serve throughout the war. Having attended the University of Georgia, the North Carolina-born lawyer was a respected member of the Marietta community. Thus, although he had no military training, it is no surprise that his friend, Governor Joseph Brown, placed him in charge of the recruiting and training of the area's volunteer forces. On August 2, 1861, he was appointed colonel of a portion of the recruits which became known as Phillips' Georgia Legion. Moving to western Virginia, the command took part in the campaigning in the Kanawha Valley, where Phillips was wounded and lost an eye. In December 1861, the legion was transferred to the Department of South Carolina, Georgia and Florida where it was assigned to duty protecting the rail lines near Hardeeville, South Carolina. Ordered to reinforce the Army of Northern Virginia in late 1862, the infantry and cavalry battalions (the artillery having previously been detached) were separated and assigned to different brigades. While the cavalry served on the right, the infantry battalion fought on Marye's Heights at Fredericksburg. On February 13, 1863, Phillips was forced to resign due to "paralysis." However, later in the war he served as major of a local unit, the 9th Georgia Cavalry Battalion, State Guard. He subsequently resumed his Marietta law practice.

PIATT, Abraham Sanders (1821-1908)

It was a back injury, suffered in the fall of his horse at the battle of Fredericksburg, which apparently ended the military career of Abraham—sometimes styled Abram—S. Piatt. The native Ohioan was a lifelong farmer and dabbled in journalism. The Civil War prompted him to volunteer and his assignments included: colonel, 13th Ohio (April 20, 1861); colonel, 34th Ohio (September 2, 1861); brigadier general, USV (April 28, 1862); commanding brigade, Whipple's Division, Military District of Washington, Department of the Potomac (August and September-November 8, 1862); commanding brigade, Sturgis' Reserve Corps, Army of Virginia (August-September 1862); and commanding 1st Brigade, 3rd Division, 3rd Corps, Army of the Potomac (November 8-December 14, 1862 and January-February 1863). His first regiment served solely in its own state until its muster out on August 25, 1861. He then raised a zouave regiment which he took to western Virginia before becoming a brigadier general. Commanding a brigade in the Washington fortifications, his command became part of Samuel D. Sturgis' provisional force which went to the aid of Pope's Army of Virginia at 2nd Bull Run. During the Maryland campaign he was back in the defenses but joined the Army of the Potomac for Fredericksburg where he was injured when his horse fell on him. Relinquishing command, he returned the next month but his resignation was accepted on February 17, 1863. Returning to his farm, he became active in political movements to benefit the farmers. In 1879 he was almost elected governor by the Greenback-Labor Party.

PICKENS, Francis Wilkinson (1805-1869)

At the beginning of the war the governor of the first seceding state, South Carolina, was Francis Pickens. Although admitted to the bar, he had never practiced law and, having inherited great wealth, he spent his time on his plantation or in politics. After a term in the state legislature, he was elected to Congress in 1834. A Democrat, he supported Calhoun's nullification policies during his tenure in Washington. In 1844 he left Washington to become a state senator. A secessionist at heart, he did support efforts to settle the sectional dispute. He attended the 1850 Nashville convention. He was appointed minister to Russia in 1858 and returned to become governor in December 1860 just as the secession crisis was coming to a head. It was under Pickens' direction that the preliminary efforts were made to force the capitulation of the Fort Sumter garrison before Confederate authorities took over. Early in the war he was responsible for organizing the state forces; he preferred enlistments "for the war" rather than for 12 months. Privately, he was critical of Southern generals for their lack of dash. With no military experience he was a behind-the-lines commander. In 1862 he retired to his plantation and after the war he favored compliance with federal reconstruction policies. (Cauthen, Charles Edward, *South Carolina Goes to War, 1861-1865*)

South Carolina Governor Francis W. Pickens. (*Harper's*)

PICKETT, George Edward (1825-1875)

The "leader" of the famous doomed charge at Gettysburg, George E. Pickett, never forgave Lee ("that old man . . . had my division massacred") for it. Graduating at the bottom of the 1846 West Point class, he earned two brevets for fighting Indians and Mexicans. He resigned an infantry captaincy on June 25, 1861, to join the Confederacy where his assignments included: major, Artillery, and colonel, PACS (summer 1861); commanding on lower Rappahannock, in the Department of Fredericksburg (September 23-October 22, 1861) and in the Aquia District, Department of Northern Virginia (October 22, 1861-February 28, 1862); brigadier general, CSA (February 13, to rank from January 14, 1862); commanding Cocke's (old) Brigade, Longstreet's Division, same department (February 28-June 27, 1862); commanding division, 1st Corps, Army of Northern Virginia (late September 1862-February 25, 1863, May-September 23, 1863, and May 1864-April 8, 1865); major general, CSA (October 10, 1862); commanding division, Department of Virginia and North Carolina (February 25-April 1, 1863); commanding division, Department of Southern Virginia (April 1-May 1863): and commanding department of North Carolina (September 26, 1863-May 19, 1864). After serving on the Rappahannock, he joined the main army for actions at Williamsburg, Seven Pines, and Gaines' Mill. Wounded at the latter he returned to a division and a major generalcy after Antietam. Only lightly engaged at Fredericksburg, he next served in Longstreet's campaign in southeastern Virginia. At Gettysburg he became linked with the futile charge on the third day despite commanding only a third of the troops. When Longstreet went west, Pickett was sent to North Carolina where he directed operations against New Bern. He distinguished himself in the defense of Drewry's Bluff and then rejoined Lee for Cold Harbor. During the siege of Petersburg and Richmond his men were often used as a mobile reserve, seeing action throughout the lines. As such they were defeated by Sheridan at Five Forks, necessitating the evacuation. Pickett was relieved by Lee the day before the surrender and ordered home to await orders, his division having been all but destroyed at Five Forks and at Sayler's Creek. However, he surrendered with the army the next day. A postwar meeting with the dying Lee was an icy affair as reported by witness John S. Mosby to whom Pickett made the massacre comment. (Pickett, LaSalle Corbell, *Pickett and His Men* and Freeman, Douglas S., *Lee's Lieutenants*)

PICKETT, John T. (ca. 1820s-1890s)

The most important Civil War role played by Confederate diplomat John T. Pickett was his postwar sale to the U.S. government of the largest batch of Confederate diplomatic papers. A native of Kentucky, he had been educated there and briefly at West Point before studying law. A filibusterer and adventurer, he took part in the Cuban operations of Lopez and served in the Hungarian army. A diplomat at the outbreak of the Civil War, he resigned to join the Confederacy and served two stints as a diplomat in Mexico. In between he served as a staff officer to John C. Breckinridge. Returning to Washington at the close of the war, he netted $75,000 from the sale of the "Pickett Papers."

PIERCE, Byron Root (1829-1924)

On his way to becoming a brigadier general and brevet major general, Michigan dentist Byron R. Pierce fought in most of the battles of the Army of the Potomac. He had been in the wool business in his native New York before moving to Grand Rapids in 1856. Enlisting early in the Civil War, his assignments included: captain, Company K, 3rd Michigan (June 10, 1861); major, 3rd Michigan (October 28, 1861); lieutenant colonel, 3rd Michigan (July 25, 1862); colonel, 3rd Michigan (January 1, 1863); commanding 3rd Brigade, 1st Division, 3rd Corps, Army of the Potomac (December 30, 1863-January 1864); commanding 2nd Brigade, 3rd Division, 2nd Corps, Army of the Potomac (May 23-29, 1864); commanding 1st Brigade, 2nd Division, 2nd Corps, Army of the Potomac (June 3-22, 1864); brigadier general, USV (June 7, 1864); again commanding 2nd Brigade, 3rd Division, 2nd Corps, Army of the Potomac (June 24-July 22, 1864, August 26, 1864-January 25, 1865, and February 15-June 28, 1865). His regiment fought at 1st Bull Run, Yorktown, Williamsburg, and Seven Pines. He succeeded to regimental command both during the Seven Days and at 2nd Bull Run. Missing Fredericksburg, he became the unit's permanent commander at the beginning of 1863. Having already suffered one wound, he was again wounded at Chancellorsville and on the second day at Gettysburg. The latter would cost him his leg. He took part in the Bristoe and Mine Run operations and rose to brigade command and a brigadier generalship during the Overland Campaign. Serving throughout the Petersburg siege, he joined the pursuit of Lee and was brevetted major general for Sayler's Creek. After Appomattox he was mustered out on August 24, 1865, and was a postal employee. Active in veterans' affairs, he directed the Michigan Soldiers' Home and subsequently was a successful hosteler.

PIERCE, Franklin (1804-1869)

One of the five living ex-presidents in 1861 Franklin Pierce actually believed that he would be arrested for his opposition to the prosecution of the war. The New Hampshire native had succeeded to the presidency upon the death of Zachary Taylor in 1850 and during the next three years was noted for his Southern leanings. Calling the war "suicidal madness," he was known for his antiwar stance from the very beginning. In December 1861 he actually received a communication from the State Department inquiring whether he was "a member of a secret league, the object of which is to overthrow the Government." In a Fourth of July speech in 1863 he was harshly critical of the Republicans and the war and expressed his fear that he would be a victim "of unconstitutional, arbitrary, irresponsible power." At about the same time a letter of his to Jefferson Davis written in 1860 came to light. Being a very friendly letter it lost for Pierce much of his dwindling respect in the North. He survived the war by four years. (Nichols, Roy F., *Franklin Pierce: Young Hickory of the Granite Hills*)

PIERPOINT, Francis Harrison

See: *Pierpont, Francis Harrison*

PIERPONT, Francis Harrison (1814-1899)

With the vast divergence of opinion—principally along geographic lines—on the issue of secession in the Old Dominion, Francis H. Pierpont became the governor of the "Restored Government of Virginia" in 1861. Born in what was to become West Virginia, he had been an antislavery lawyer who for a time worked on legal matters for the Baltimore and Ohio Railroad. He was also involved in the coal business. Following the secession of Virginia in April, a loyalist convention was called and held at Wheeling. There, on June 19, 1861, he was unanimously chosen as the provisional head of a new state government. On June 20, 1863, the western counties of the state were admitted to the Union as "West Virginia," with Arthur I. Boreman as governor. Pierpont moved his "restored" state offices to Alexandria and continued to act as the Union governor of Virginia. He was reelected to this position that December but was not officially recognized by Washington until May 9, 1865. Continuing in office after the war, he failed in a bid to push through the 14th Amendment in the legislature. Under Reconstruction he was displaced on April 16, 1868, and later served in the West Virginia legislature and as a tax official. NOTE: His name is sometimes spelled Pierpoint. (Ambler, Charles Henry, *Francis H. Pierpoint, Union War Governor of Virginia and Father of West Virginia*)

PIERSON, Scipio Francis (?-?)

Artillery battalion commander S.F. Pierson seems to be one of those early officers in the Army of Northern Virginia who did not survive the shakedown period. His Confederate assignments included: lieutenant, Orleans (La.) Artillery (April 9, 1861); major, Artillery (March 27, 1862); chief of artillery, D.H. Hill's Division, Army of Northern Virginia (March-July 1862); commanding Artillery Battalion, D.H. Hill's Division, 1st Corps, Army of Northern Virginia (July-September 1862); and commanding Artillery Battalion, D.H. Hill's Division, 2nd Corps, Army of Northern Virginia (September-fall 1862). After serving with his battery, as heavy artillery, on the Peninsula in Virginia, he was promoted to battalion level and fought at Seven Pines, the Seven Days, and Antietam. Relieved from duty with the army he was sent to Europe in 1863 to purchase ordnance. Returning in the middle of 1864 he was assigned to duty with the Virginia Reserves on July 21 but four days later was ordered to report to General E. Kirby Smith in Texas. He served out the war in the Trans-Mississippi Department.

PIKE, Albert (1809-1891)

A prominent Arkansas lawyer, Albert Pike had earned a position of trust in representing the Creeks, one of the Five Civilized Tribes, in a victorious lawsuit before the war. A native Bostonian, he was opposed to secession but went along with the South because of his friends and extensive property and became the Confederate commissioner to the Indians. Using large cash subsidies and gifts he eventually brought over to the Confederate side portions of the Creeks, Chickasaws, Choctaws, Cherokees, and Seminoles. A former captain of Arkansas volunteers in the Mexican War, he was appointed brigadier general, CSA, on August 15, 1861, and on November 22, 1861, he was given command of the newly created Department of Indian Territory. He led a brigade of Indians at Pea Ridge the following winter where they proved of dubious value. He came into conflict with his superiors and charged that the Indians had been promised that they would only be used in their home territory. On July 12, 1862, he submitted his resignation which was accepted on November 5. He returned home and resumed his activities as a teacher, journalist, writer, poet, and Freemason. After the war he was indicted but never tried. Living in Memphis and Washington after the war he became something of a legal scholar. (Duncan, Robert Lipscomb, *Reluctant General, The Life and Times of Albert Pike*)

Albert Pike, commander of Confederate Indians. (NA)

PIKE, Edward C. (?-?)

With the state of Missouri divided in its loyalties, it was subjected to intense guerrilla warfare. In response the Missouri

Enrolled Militia was established. This force would only be called out in an emergency and was divided into districts. Missouri resident Edward C. Pike was one of those who joined this force and his assignments included: lieutenant general, 7th Missouri Enrolled Militia (September 23, 1861); colonel, 7th Missouri Enrolled Militia (January 13, 1864); brigadier general, Missouri Enrolled Militia (March 29, 1864); and commanding 1st Military District, Missouri Enrolled Militia (spring-late 1864). At times he would be ordered to supply some of his regiments to replace regular volunteers in garrisons while they went to face Confederate invasions. He was thus involved in repelling Price's 1864 invasion of the state. He was mustered out on January 13, 1865.

PILE, William Anderson (1829-1889)

Switching from the chaplain's corps to the line, William A. Pile rose to a brigadier generalship in charge of a brigade of black troops. Born in Indiana, he was raised in St. Louis and became a Methodist Episcopal minister. Joining the Union army, his assignments included: chaplain, 1st Missouri Light Artillery (June 12, 1861); captain, Battery I, 1st Missouri Light Artillery (March 1, 1862); lieutenant colonel, 33rd Missouri (September 5, 1862); colonel, 33rd Missouri (December 23, 1862); brigadier general, USV (December 26, 1863); commanding Post of Port Hudson, District of Baton Rouge and Port Hudson, Department of the Gulf (December 26, 1864-February 13, 1865); and commanding 1st Brigade, 1st Division, United States Colored Troops, District of West Florida, Department of the Gulf (February 19-April 25, 1865). Three of the regiment's batteries were at Fort Donelson and apparently Pile was too. Made a battery commander, it is stated that he was at Shiloh; however, the records indicate that it was under the command of Lieutenant Charles H. Thurber. He was, however, in the Corinth, Mississippi, operations which followed. As an infantry commander he fought at Devall's Bluff and took part in the Yazoo River expedition. Named a brigadier general, he took up recruiting duties in St. Louis and was not particularly concerned to whom—loyal or secessionist—the slaves he inducted belonged. After serving in a post command, he led a black brigade at Mobile. For the attack on Fort Blakely he was brevetted major general and was mustered out on August 24, 1865. His later career included one term as a Radical Republican congressman; he was also territorial governor of New Mexico and a diplomat in Venezuela.

PILLOW, Gideon Johnson (1806-1878)

One of the most reprehensible men ever to wear the three stars and wreath of a Confederate general was certainly Gideon J. Pillow. The Tennessee native lawyer had been appointed a brigadier general of volunteers by his former law partner, President James K. Polk, during the Mexican War. His performance south of the border was less than outstanding, but he had friends in high places. He was twice wounded in that war and was rewarded with promotion to major general. Mustered out at the conclusion of the peace treaty, he resumed his legal career and engaged in national politics as a conservative on secession. However, when push came to shove, he followed his state out of the Union. His Tennessee and Confederate assignments included: major general, Provisional Army of Tennessee (May 9, 1861); brigadier general, CSA (July 9, 1861); commanding 1st Geographical Division, Department #2 (September 7-late September 1861); commanding 1st Division, 1st Geographical Division, Department #2 (October 24, 1861-February 1862); commanding Fort Donelson, Army of Central Kentucky, Department #2 (ca. February 9-13 and 15, 1862); commanding 2nd Brigade, 1st (Breckinridge's) Division, Hardee's Corps, Army of Tennessee (January 2, 1863); and Commissary General of Prisoners (February 14-April 1865). Named the senior major general in the Tennessee forces, he took a leading role in their organization and was then named a brigadier general in the Confederate service. Serving at Columbus, Kentucky, he fought across the Mississippi at Belmont and several months later took command at Fort Donelson on the Cumberland River. While the post was being invested he was superseded by John B. Floyd. Following an unsuccessful breakout attempt Floyd turned over command again to Pillow who followed his chief's lead and also fled the post, leaving the surrender to Simon B. Buckner. He was then relieved of field duty and was eventually assigned to conscript duty in his native state. He was very briefly in the field again when he was given charge of a brigade during the battle of Murfreesboro on January 2, 1863. When Breckinridge's division made its futile assault on the Union left it was reported that Pillow hid behind a tree rather than lead his men foward into the holocaust. In any event he never again held field command. After performing conscript duties for almost two years he was placed in charge of the Union prisoners in the final months of the war. Bankrupted by the war, he managed to scrape together a living by returning to his law practice.

PINKERTON, Allan (1819-1884)

The Civil War career of pioneer detective Allan Pinkerton can be summed up as: highly efficient in the gathering of information for the Union military but a disastrous failure in analyzing the data. A Scottish native, he had fled his native land at the age of 23 following his involvement in the Chartist movement to improve the lot of the ghetto worker. While working as a cooper in Illinois he displayed great ability as an amateur in the capture of a counterfeiting ring. Eventually establishing his own agency in Chicago, he brought many innovations to the field of law enforcement. An abolitionist, he worked on the Underground Railroad—including work with John Brown—and was soon providing the services of his agency to the Illinois Central Railroad, the same line for which Abraham Lincoln provided legal services. When Lincoln went to Washington, Pinkerton escorted him and discovered the Baltimore plot to kill or kidnap the president-elect. The travel plans were altered and Lincoln arrived safely in the capital. But many detractors claimed that the detective had fabricated the plot to enhance the reputation of his agency. Remaining in Washington for a time, Pinkerton tried to formalize his relationship with the Union cause but soon left to join McClellan's Department of the Ohio as its chief of the secret service. In this capacity he proved highly successful in his own spying expedition into the seceded states. Accompanying McClellan to Washington, and later to the Peninsula, he was charged with the gathering of information concerning the strength and disposition of the enemy's forces. Gathering much of his information from escaping slaves, he proved totally inept at consolidating the numerous reports. The result was that he overestimated the enemy strength by as much as two or three times the actual number. Known by his code name of Major E.J. Allen, he seems to have supplied McClellan's need to feel that he was outnumbered enabling him to call continuously for more men and supplies. Pinkerton continued to serve his chief during the Maryland Campaign and following the battle of Antietam he posed for a photograph with his two former colleagues from the Illinois Central—Lincoln and McClellan. When his chief was removed from command, Pinkerton returned to his agency in Chicago and confined his military work to investigating frauds in the army supply departments and among the government contractors. Following the war he continued to build his agency and became associated with the interests of the "big money." He was hated through much of the South for his role in the killing of Jesse James' eight-year-old half-brother and the wounding of Jesse's mother in a bombing of the family home. His actions against the Younger Brothers did not help his reputation in the region. In the North he was also hated by the labor movement for his union-busting activities and support of the railroads and major industrial corporations. His nickname, "The Eye," eventually came to identify all members of his profession. (Horan, James D., *The Pinkertons: The Detective Dynasty That Made History*)

PITCHER, Thomas Gamble (1824-1895)

Wounded severely at Cedar Mountain, his one major action of the war, Thomas G. Pitcher spent the balance of the war enforcing the draft. The native Indianan and West Pointer (1845) had been posted to the infantry with which he won a Mexican War brevet. His Civil War-era assignments included: captain, 8th Infantry (since October 19, 1858); brigadier general, USV (March 20, 1863, to rank from November 29, 1862); and major, 16th Infantry (September 19, 1863). Stationed in Texas at the outbreak of the war, he was brought east and was for a time at Harpers Ferry commanding a battalion composed of companies of his own 8th and the 12th regular infantry regiments. He led this force in John Pope's campaign in northern Virginia and fell severely wounded at Cedar Mountain. Following his return to duty on January 10, 1863, he performed commissary duties until June 1863 when he was sent to Vermont to enforce conscription. That same month his enrolling agents were driven from the town of Rutland by an angry mob. Once peace was restored, Pitcher was transferred to the same post in Indiana and finished the war there. Mustered out of the volunteer service on April 30, 1866, he was brevetted through brigadier general in the regular army. In 1878 he retired as colonel, 1st Infantry. For five years, 1866 to 1871, he was the superintendent of his alma mater.

Allan Pinkerton (seated, with pipe), McClellan's secret service chief. (NA)

PLEASANTS, Henry (1833-1880)

Born in South America, Henry Pleasants was raised in Pennsylvania where he became an engineer, a profession which helped out his later military career. The former chief engineer for the Pittsburgh and Connellsville Railroad had become a mining engineer in the coal districts of Pennsylvania by 1857 and had developed a new method for deep shaft mining. With the outbreak of the Civil War he entered military service where his appointments included: second lieutenant, 6th Pennsylvania (April 22, 1861); captain, Company C, 48th Pennsylvania (August 10, 1861); lieutenant colonel, 48th Pennsylvania (September 21, 1862); provost marshal general, 23rd Corps, Department of the Ohio (July 23-December 21, 1863); and commanding 1st Brigade, 2nd Division, 9th Corps, Army of the Potomac (June 18-July 25, 1864). After brief service in the Department of the Shenandoah, Pleasants and the 6th Pennsylvania were mustered out on July 26, 1861. Reentering the service Pleasants served with his new regiment in North Carolina at New Bern and in Virginia at 2nd Bull Run and Chantilly before moving into Maryland, fighting at South Mountain and Antietam. After fighting at Fredericksburg the regiment went west where Pleasants served on detached duty. Returning east to participate in Grant's drive on Richmond, Pleasants commanded the regiment at the Wilderness, Spotsylvania, Cold Harbor, and Petersburg. Endorsing an idea of some of his men, Pleasants was given authority to begin a mine, from under the Union siege lines to Elliott's Salient on the rebel lines at Petersburg. The regiment dug from June 25 to July 23, 1864, when some four tons of powder were placed under the Confederate works. After several delays the mine was finally exploded early on the morning of July 30. Some 278 rebels were killed, wounded or buried. Due to confusion in the Union assault and quick reaction on the part of the Southerners the advantage was not exploited and it became a bloody disaster. Pleasants, after serving through several months more of the siege, was mustered out on December 18, 1864, with the expiration of his term of service. He was subsequently brevetted brigadier general for the mine, returning to the Pennsylvania coal country as an engineer and later as a law officer he took part in the breaking up of the "Mollie Maguires." (Pleasants, Henry, Jr., *The Tragedy of the Crater*)

PLEASONTON, Alfred (1824-1897)

Thought by many to be a *beau sabreur*—the very ideal of a cavalryman—Alfred Pleasonton nonetheless proved ineffective at intelligence gathering and was eventually exiled to the Department of the Missouri for the balance of the war. A West Pointer (1844) from the nation's capital, he had been posted to the dragoons and had served in Mexico and against the Seminoles in Florida. In the former conflict he earned a brevet. His Civil War-era assignments included: captain, 2nd Dragoons (since March 3, 1855); captain, 2nd Cavalry (change of designation August 3, 1861); major, 2nd cavalry (February 15, 1862); brigadier general, USV (July 16, 1862); commanding 2nd Brigade, Cavalry Division, Army of the Potomac (July 16-September 1862); commanding cavalry division, Army of the Potomac (September-November 1862 and January-February 12, 1863); commanding Cavalry Division, Right Grand Division, Army of the Potomac (November 1862-January 1863); commanding 1st Division, Cavalry Corps, Army of the Potomac (February 12-May 22, 1863); commanding the corps (May 22, 1863-January 22, 1864 and February 12-March 25, 1864); major general, USV (June 22, 1863); commanding District of Central Missouri, Department of the Missouri (July 24-September 3, 1864); commanding District of St. Louis, Department of the Missouri (November 21-December 9, 1864); and commanding District of Wisconsin, Department of the Northwest (1865). After initial recruiting duty in Delaware, he commanded his regiment in Utah where he feared he would be left out of the war. His regiment was, however, transferred to Washington in the fall of 1861 and he attracted McClellan's notice the next year while commanding the regiment at army headquarters on the Peninsula. Following his service during the Seven Days he was made a brigadier and given a brigade in the newly organized cavalry division. By the battle of Antietam he commanded the army's cavalry and had earned a brevet for the unimpressive role of guarding the artillery and a little skirmishing along the center. His role in the aftermath of the campaign was even less auspicious. His reports of enemy activity were so unreliable—due to his failure to break Jeb Stuart's screen—that he earned the nickname, "Knight of Romance," for the deluge of paper he sent to army headquarters. He also failed to catch Jeb Stuart's cavalry in its second ride around McClellan's army. At Fredericksburg he commanded the cavalry division attached to the Right Grand Division. At Chancellorsville, the corps commander George Stoneman, in an effort to slight Pleasonton, left him with only one brigade to accompany the main army while he himself would get the glory

Alfred Pleasonton, sacked commander of the Army of the Potomac's cavalry. (*Leslie's*)

in a major raid. The raid failed while Pleasonton earned laurels for his ordering the suicidal charge of the 8th Pennsylvania cavalry to buy time for the cavalryman to gather up a number of guns to hold a vital position, Hazel Grove, in front of Jackson's assault. While his role was overrated, he was nonetheless named to replace Stoneman. His command did fairly well against Stuart at Brandy Station, Aldie, Middleburg, and Upperville, with the Union cavalry beginning to hold its own against the Rebels. At Gettysburg he for some reason served more as a chief of cavalry at headquarters than as a corps leader. He failed to replace Buford's division on the left, which almost led to disaster on July 2. In the campaign as a whole he again failed as an intelligence gatherer. Early the following year he opposed the Kilpatrick-Dahlgren Raid—rightly—but earned the emnity of its administration backers. In the March 1864 reorganization under Grant he was replaced by Philip H. Sheridan and later sent to Missouri where he performed creditably against Price's invasion, but he received little more credit than a brevet. His role was critical at both Westport and Marais des Cygnes. Mustered out of the volunteers on January 15, 1866, he was a major general by brevet in the regular army but only a major in line rank. Disgusted by his future potential in the army, he resigned on January 1, 1868, and held numerous minor governmental appointments and entered railroading.

PLUMMER, Joseph Bennett (1816-1862)

Probably Joseph B. Plummer should not have returned to the field so soon after being wounded, since he died of complications caused by exposure. The Massachusetts West Pointer (1841) had been posted to the infantry and performed routine garrison and frontier duties until the Civil War. His wartime assignments included: captain, 1st Infantry (since May 1, 1852); colonel, 11th Missouri (September 25, 1861); commanding 2nd Brigade, 1st Division, Army of the Mississippi (February 23-March 4, 1862); commanding 5th Division, Army of the Mississippi (March 4-April 24, 1862); brigadier general, USA (March 11, 1862, to rank from October 22, 1862); and commanding in the Army of the Mississippi: 1st Brigade, 3rd Division (April 24-26, 1862); 2nd Brigade, 2nd Division (April 26-May 29, 1862); and 3rd Division (May 29-June 18, 1862); and major, 8th Infantry (April 25, 1862). While in command of four companies of regulars, he was wounded at Wilson's Creek. The next month he was named to a volunteer colonelcy and by October was back in the field when the regiment fought at Fredericksto wn. The next day he was named a brigadier general, and he commanded a division at New Madrid and Island #10. He led a brigade and briefly a division in the slow advance on Corinth, Mississippi. But this proved too much for him and he had to be relieved in June. On August 9, 1862, he died in camp.

POAGUE, William Thomas (1835-1914)

One of the most effective of the Army of Northern Virginia's battalion level artillery commanders, William Thomas Poague saw heavy fighting in all the campaigns of that army. A native of Virginia, he was practicing law in Missouri when the secession crisis came to a head. He returned to the state of his birth in order to be of service to it. As soon as the state seceded, he entered the military where his assignments included: second lieutenant, Rockbridge (Va.) Artillery (April 1861); first lieutenant, Rockbridge (Va.) Artillery (1861); captain, Rockbridge (Va.) Artillery (April 22, 1862); major, Artillery (March 2, 1863); executive officer, McIntosh's Artillery Battalion, Reserve Artillery, 2nd Corps, Army of Northern Virginia (April 16-June 2, 1863); commanding Artillery Battalion, Pender's Division, 3rd Corps, Army of Northern Virginia (June 2-July 1863); commanding artillery battalion, 3rd Corps, Army of Northern Virginia (July 1863-April 9, 1865); and lieutenant colonel, Artillery (February 27, 1864). As a battery officer he fought at 1st Bull Run, Romney, Kernstown, McDowell, in the Shenandoah Valley Campaign of 1862, the Seven Days, Cedar Mountain, 2nd Bull Run, Harpers Ferry, Antietam, and Fredericksburg. Then came the well-deserved promotion to field grade. He served as deputy to McIntosh at Chancellorsville, but with the creation of a third corps, he was assigned to command a new battalion before Gettysburg. After that battle he went on to fight at Mine Run, the Wilderness, Spotsylvania, the North Anna, and Cold Harbor. In the latter he was twice wounded. He took part in the defense of Petersburg and finally surrendered at Appomattox. After the war he was a farmer, teacher, state legislator, and treasurer of the Virginia Military Institute. (Poague, William T., *Gunner With Stonewall, Reminiscences of William T. Poague*)

POE, Orlando Metcalfe (1832-1895)

Due to the failure of the Senate to confirm his appointment as brigadier general of volunteers, Orlando M. Poe finished the war in his regular army capacity as an engineering officer. The Ohio native and West Pointer (1856) had been posted to the topographical engineers and was surveying the Great Lakes when the Civil War broke out. His assignments included: first lieutenant, Topographical Engineers (since July 1, 1860); colonel, 2nd Michigan (September 16, 1861); commanding 3rd Brigade, 1st Division, 3rd Corps, Army of the Potomac (August 5-September 1862); commanding 1st Brigade, 1st Division, 9th Corps, Army of the Potomac (November 15-December 15, 1862 and February 11-March 19, 1863); brigadier general, USV (from November 29, 1862); first lieutenant, Engineers (merger of the two engineering branches March 3, 1863); captain, Engineers (March 3, 1863); commanding 1st Brigade, 1st Division, 9th Corps, Department of the Ohio (March 19-April 11, 1863); chief engineer, Department of the Ohio (spring-December 1863); assistant engineer, Military Division of the Mississippi (December 1863-April 1864); and chief engineer, Military Division of the Mississippi (April 1864-June 1865). As an engineer he served under McClellan in western Virginia and at Washington. Named to command of a volunteer regiment, he fought at 2nd Bull Run and Fredericksburg while directing a brigade. He accompanied the 9th Corps when it was transferred to the West but soon thereafter his brigadier general's appointment expired, on

March 4, 1863, when the Senate failed to confirm it. He reverted to a captaincy in the regular engineers and served under Burnside and Sherman as such for the balance of the war. He received brevets for Knoxville, Atlanta, Savannah, and the Carolinas Campaign. Remaining in the service, he attained the rank of colonel in his branch before his demise from a service-related injury. In the meantime he had served for a number of years as Sherman's aide; he had been his chief engineer for the last year of the Civil War.

POLIGNAC, Camille Armand Jules Marie, Prince de (1832-1913)

The only person still owing allegiance to a foreign power to rise to the rank of major general in the service of either the Union or the Confederacy was French Prince de Polignac who served the South. He was a veteran of six years with the French army in the 3rd Chasseurs, 4th Hussars, and 4th Chasseurs before resigning as a lieutenant in 1859. Sailing for America in 1861 he secured a commission through his acquaintance with Pierre G.T. Beauregard. His assignments included: lieutenant colonel, Infantry (July 16, 1861); brigadier general, CSA (January 10, 1863); commanding brigade, District of West Louisiana, Trans-Mississippi Department (summer-November 1863); commanding brigade, 2nd (Mouton's) Division, District of West Louisiana, Trans-Mississippi Department (November 1863-April 8, 1864); commanding the division (April 8, 1864-February 1865); and major general, CSA (June 13, 1864, to rank from April 8). Assigned to inspection duty with Beauregard, he found himself chafing for action and advancement. After taking part in the Corinth siege, he fought at Richmond, Kentucky, before being named a brigadier general early in 1863. Transferred to western Louisiana, he was given a brigade which he led into the Red River Campaign. At Mansfield or Sabine Crossroads on April 8, 1864, the division commander, Jean J.A.A. Mouton, was killed and Prince de Polignac took over the unit with a subsequent promotion to major general. He served through the rest of the campaign and in March 1865 he sailed to France, through the blockade, on a diplomatic mission which proved to be too late. Remaining in Europe, he became a mathematician and economist.

POLK, Leonidas (1806-1864)

Soldier-turned-bishop Leonidas Polk finally complied with the request of his friend Jefferson Davis, reentered the military as a Confederate general, and gave his life to the cause. The North Carolina native and West Pointer (1827) had served only a few months in the artillery before his resignation as a brevet second lieutenant was accepted. Becoming an Episcopal minister, he rose to become Missionary Bishop of the Southwest in 1838 and Bishop of Louisiana three years later. Finally agreeing to join the Confederate army, his assignments included: major general, CSA (June 25, 1861); commanding Department #2 (July 13-September 15, 1861 and October 24-November 3, 1862); commanding 1st Geographical Division, Department #2 (September 15, 1861-March 5, 1862) commanding 1st Grand Division, Army of the Mississippi (March 5-29, 1862); commanding 1st Corps, Army of the Mississippi (March 29-July 2, 1862); second in command, Department #2 (July 2-October 24, 1862); also commanding Right Wing, Army of the Mississippi (August 15-September 28, 1862); commanding Army of the Mississippi (September 28-November 20, 1862); lieutenant general, CSA (October 10, 1862); commanding corps, Army of Tennessee (November 20, 1862-October 23, 1863); commanding the army (August and December 23-27, 1863); commanding Department of Mississippi and East Louisiana (December 23, 1863-January 28, 1864); commanding Department of Alabama, Mississippi and East Louisiana (January 28-May 4, 1864); and commanding corps (or "Army of Mississippi"), Army of Tennessee (May 4-June 14, 1864). Davis assigned Polk the duty of fortifying the Mississippi Valley, and the general occupied Columbus, Kentucky, ending that state's neutrality. From that post he ferried troops across the river to repulse Grant at Belmont. He commanded a corps under Albert Sidney Johnston at Shiloh and under Beauregard in the defense of Corinth. At Perryville he was in charge of the Army of the Mississippi while Braxton Bragg headed the department. He fought at Murfreesboro and during the Tullahoma Campaign. At Chickamauga he came in for much criticism from Bragg for his slow performance on the second day while in command of the army's right. In fact there had long been trouble between the two officers, Polk having urged Davis to remove Bragg. Bragg retaliated by relieving his subordinate and ordering a court-martial. Davis reversed this move and then sent Polk to Mississippi. At the beginning of the Atlanta Campaign Polk led a corps, styled an "army" to join Joseph E. Johnston in northern Georgia. While consulting with Johnston and William J. Hardee at Pine Mountain he was struck by an artillery round and intantly killed on June 14, 1864. He was not considered to be one of the shining lights of the Confederacy's high command. (Parks, Joseph H., *General Leonidas Polk, C.S.A.*)

POLK, Lucius Eugene (1833-1892)

The nephew of the "Bishop General"—Leonidas Polk—Lucius E. Polk also received the three stars and wreath of a Confederate general but later proved to be an opponent of the Ku Klux Klan. The North Carolina-born and Tennessee-raised officer had been a planter in Arkansas in 1861. Joining Patrick R. Cleburne's Yell Rifles, his assignments included: private, Company F, 1st Arkansas State Troops (1861); second lieutenant, Company B, 1st Arkansas (July 23, 1861); second lieutenant, Company C, 15th Arkansas (designation change December 31, 1861); colonel, 15th Arkansas (April 12, 1862); brigadier general, CSA (December 13, 1862); commanding Cleburne's (old) brigade, Cleburne's Division, Hardee's-Hill's-Breckinridge's Corps, Army of Tennessee (December 1862-November 1863); and commanding brigade, Cleburne's Division, Hardee's Corps, Army of Tennessee (November 1863-June 27, 1864). Serving mostly under Cleburne, he was in central Kentucky and was wounded in the face at Shiloh. Named colonel a week later, he was again wounded at Richmond, Kentucky, but went on to fight at Perryville. Promoted to brigadier general, he led his brigade at Murfreesboro, during the Tullahoma Campaign, at

Chickamauga, and Chattanooga. During the Atlanta Campaign he was severely wounded at Kennesaw Mountain on June 27, 1864, so that he was unable to again take the field. His brigade was accordingly broken up the next month. Active in Democratic politics, he sat in the state legislature. When one of his black employees was being whipped by the K.K.K., Polk, in an act of bravery uncommon at that place and time, faced them down.

POLLARD, Edward Alfred (1831-1872)

Law school graduate and journalist Edward Pollard became editor of the *Richmond Examiner* in 1861 just as the war was beginning. During his tenure with the newspaper in the Confederate capital he was one of the harshest journalist critics of Jefferson Davis. His commentary on the progress of the war gave the *Examiner* a shrill voice that made it one of the more interesting papers in the city. In installments from 1862 to 1866, Pollard wrote his *Southern History of the War*. In 1866 he published *The Lost Cause*. The thrust of both books was to point out the failures of the Confederate President which led to the collapse of the fledgling nation. He also lamented the fact that the Confederate Congress did not measure up to the standards needed for a revolutionary cause. Although Pollard left the *Examiner* in 1867, he continued in the journalism profession until his death in 1872, and is more remembered for his anti-Davis rhetoric than as a journalist-historian.

POMEROY, Samuel Clarke (1816-1891)

One of the first senators from the new state of Kansas—the other was James H. Lane—Samuel C. Pomeroy is best remember in Civil War history for his authorship of the so-called "Pomeroy Circular" which advanced Secretary of the Treasury Salmon P. Chase as a more radical alternative to the candidacy of Abraham Lincoln in 1864. The movement failed and Chase later resigned but was eventually appointed to the chief justiceship of the Supreme Court. Pomeroy was reelected to the Senate in 1866 but was defeated in 1872. He was born in Massachusetts and had been involved with the New England Emigrant Aid Company while serving in the state legislature in his native state. Moving to Kansas in 1854 and attending the free-state convention in Lawrence in 1859. He attended the Republican national conventions of 1856 and 1860 before being himself named to the U.S. Senate.

POND, Preston, Jr. (?-?)

A brigade commander at Shiloh, Preston Pond, Jr., appears to have had a great deal of difficulty in serving the Confederacy. On September 29, 1861, he was mustered in as colonel of the 16th Louisiana. Joining in the Confederate buildup of forces in northern Mississippi in early 1862, he commanded the 3rd Brigade, Ruggles' 1st Division, 2nd Grand Division or Corps, Army of the Mississippi (March 9-May 8, 1862). Leading this brigade at Shiloh, he did not receive the order at the end of the first day to retire slightly. The next morning he found his command in an untenable position. After extricating the brigade he received too many orders and his brigade kept going from one area to another in the confusion. When the regiment was reorganized the next month he was not reelected to the colonelcy. Retiring to his home near Clinton, Louisiana, he sent letters of advice to the War Department. In August 1862 he appears to have commanded an irregular unit known as the 1st Louisiana Partisan Rangers during the fighting at Baton Rouge. As late as mid-1864 he still wished to take the field again but in a letter to the governor he stated that President Davis would consider it to be undue favoritism. There is no record of his receiving another command.

POOK, Samuel M. (?-?)

A riverboat designer before the war, Samuel M. Pook was charged by the Union government with the design and construction of a series of ironclad gunboats, for service on the western waters, which were destined to prove, despite several defects, to be the backbone of the river navy. Working with the army, Pook designed a series of vessels, clad with 2-1/2 inches of armor, which became nicknamed the "Pook turtles." Each carried a battery of 10 eight-inch guns and were of shallow enough draft to be effective on the rivers. Named for river cities, they were seven in number: *Cairo*, *Carondelet*, *Cincinnati*, *Louisville*, *Mound City*, *Pittsburg*, and *St. Louis*. Their first action was at Fort Henry where they were severely battered. At Fort Donelson they proved unsuccessful. By the end of the war three of the heavy and underpowered craft had been sunk. The *Cairo* had struck a torpedo near Vicksburg.

POPE, John (1822-1892)

The only army commander operating against the Army of Northern Virginia to earn the personal animosity of Robert E. Lee was John Pope. The Kentucky native had spent his entire career in the military service. Receiving an appointment to West Point from Illinois, he was graduated in 1842 and was posted to the topographical engineers. Performing creditably, he was considered a top soldier. The Mexican War brought him two brevets and he continued to rise regularly in rank. His Civil War-era assignments were somewhat less happy and included: captain, Topographical Engineers (since July 1, 1856); brigadier general, USV (June 14, 1861, to rank from May 17); commanding District of North Missouri, Western Department (July 29-October 1861); commanding 2nd Division, Army of Southwest Missouri, Western Department (October-November 9, 1861); commanding 2nd Division, Army of Southwest Missouri, Department of the Missouri (November 9-December 1861); commanding District of Central Missouri, Department of the Missouri (December 1861-February 18, 1862); commanding Army of the Mississippi (February 23-June 26, 1862); major general, USV (March 21, 1862); commanding Army of Virginia (June 26-September 2 1862); brigadier general, USA (July 14, 1862); and commanding Department of the Northwest (September 16-November 28, 1862 and February 13, 1863-February 13, 1865). Having served in the escort of Lincoln to the Washington inaugural ceremonies, Pope was named to be a brigadier of volunteers and performed organizational duties in Illinois before serving under Frémont in the Western Department. His capabilities being displayed in Missouri, he was eventually given charge of the operations along the Mississippi River. In early 1862 he scored major successes at New Madrid and Island #10 and the advance on Memphis. He then led one of the three field armies serving under Henry W. Halleck in a painfully slow advance on Corinth, Mississippi. In the meantime he had been awarded a second star in the volunteer service and was marked for advancement. With the scattered forces in northern Virginia unable to contain Stonewall Jackson's small mobile command in the Shenandoah Valley and thus unable to advance on Richmond from the North, Pope was called east. Three departments were merged into his newly formed Army of Virginia. His former commander, Frémont, refused to be one of his corps commanders and was relieved. Pope was then advanced to a brigadier generalship in the regular establishment. Not taking command of his scattered forces in the field until late July, he lost the faith of his men when he made an address praising the western armies and disparaging the efforts of the eastern forces up to that time. In bombastic fashion he declared his headquarters would be in the saddle. This led to a quip that he didn't know his headquarters from his hindquarters. His proposals on how to deal with the secessionist population raised the ire of his opponents, especially Lee. Part of Pope's command was defeated at Cedar Mountain. Later that month his command and parts of McClellan's Army of the Potomac fought at 2nd Bull Run. Pope had no idea of the true situation on the field and was routed. Blaming the defeat upon his subordinates, he came into conflict with those officers who were McClellan partisans. He charged Fitz-John Porter with disobedience of orders in failing to launch an attack which was in fact impossible. Nonetheless Porter was cashiered, but Pope also lost his command on September 2, 1862, and the Army of Virginia was merged into the Army of the Potomac 10 days later. While there was recognition of a lack of support from McClellan and his officers, Lincoln felt he had little choice but to give the consolidated command to McClellan in the face of the Confederate invasion of Maryland. Pope then spent most of the balance of the war commanding the Department of the Northwest and dealing with the Sioux uprising. He performed his job ably and in 1865 was brevetted a regular army major general for Island #10. Mustered out of the volunteers on September 1, 1866, he held departmental commands in the regular army, mostly in the West, until his 1886 retirement. Four years later he was named a full major general. (Ropes, John C., *The Army Under Pope* and Ellis, Richard N., *General Pope and U.S. Indian Policy*)

Bombastic General John Pope. (AC)

PORCHER, Francis Peyre (1825-1895)

A Confederate surgeon, Francis P. Porcher wrote one of the leading medical manuals prepared by the Confederate government. A native of South Carolina, he had recieved his medical training in South Carolina and France. Until the Civil War he was in private practice and medical education. Early in the Civil War he became the surgeon for the state's Holcombe Legion and served at Norfolk and Petersburg. In 1863 his *Resources of the Southern Fields and Forests* was published by the Surgeon General's Department. He then returned to the classroom and edited the *Charleston Medical Journal and Review.*

PORTER, Andrew (1820-1872)

Although he attended West Point for only half a year, in 1836 and 1837, Pennsylvanian Andrew Porter rose to become a Union brigadier during the Civil War. He had been commissioned a first lieutenant in the Mounted Riflemen, a regiment raised at the beginning of the Mexican War. In the 15 years before the beginning of sectional hostilities, Porter rose to a captaincy and earned two brevets for combat action south of the border. On May 14, 1861, he was assigned to the newly authorized 16th Infantry as its colonel and commander. His commands during the war included: 1st Brigade, 2nd Division, Army of Northeastern Virginia (May 28-July 21, 1861); the division (July 21-30, 1861); and provost guard, Army of the Potomac (October 3, 1861-August 8, 1862). He led his brigade in the Union flank movement at 1st Bull Run and took over command of the division upon the wounding of General David Hunter. On July 30, 1861, he was detailed as provost marshal in the nation's capital. He was appointed brigadier general, USV, on August 6, to rank from May 17, 1861. Taking the post of provost marshal with the Army of the Potomac he participated in the Peninsular Campaign. For the next two years he served in enforcing the draft and in Washington but was frequently on sick leave. He resigned from the volunteers and regular army on April 4 and 20, 1864, respectively. Moving to Paris, he died there in 1872.

PORTER, David Dixon (1813-1891)

Coming from a naval family, David D. Porter became one of the best Union naval officers in cooperating with the army. Beginning his sailing career at the age of 11, he fought pirates and was an officer in the Mexican Navy before joining the U.S. Navy in 1829. With the exception of six years, he was in the service until the outbreak of the Civil War, seeing action in the war with Mexico. On April 22, 1861, he was promoted to commander and soon took up his duties blockading the Gulf coast. He also participated in the pursuit of the raider CSS *Sumter*. During the operations against New Orleans he commanded the mortar flotilla which forced the capitulation of Forts Jackson and St. Philip. after taking part in the bombardment of Vicksburg, Porter was given command of the Mississippi Squadron with which he proved his ability to coordinate his operations with those of Grant's army. He commanded the naval portion of the attack on Arkansas Post in January 1863 and ran his command past the Vicksburg batteries in conjunction with Grant's movements. In July 1863, following the capture of the river fortress of Vicksburg, Porter's acting rank as rear admiral, which he had held since taking command of the river squadron in September 1862, was made permanent. Coordinating with Banks' land forces, Porter commanded the naval forces in the disastrous Red River Campaign. Given command of the North Atlantic Blockading Squadron on October 12, 1864, he took part in both the unsuccessful and successful attacks on Fort Fisher, receiving his third Thanks of Congress for the capture. His final war service was in the James River. He was commandant at Annapolis after the war and in 1870 he became the navy's senior officer. (West, Richard S., *The Second Admiral; A Life of David Dixon Porter, 1813-1891*)

PORTER, Fitz-John (1822-1901)

In one of the greatest miscarriages of military justice during the Civil War, Fitz-John Porter was cashiered for failing to obey an order which a later inquiry determined was impossible of execution. A cousin of David D. Porter, the New Hampshire native had received an appointment to West Point from New York. Graduating in 1845, he was posted to the artillery. Wounded at Chapultepec, he earned two brevets in Mexico and transferred to the adjutant general's department in the 1850s. He was Albert Sidney Johnston's adjutant during the operations against the Mormons. His Civil War-era assignments included: first lieutenant, 4th Artillery (since May 29, 1847); brevet captain and assistant adjutant general (since June 27, 1856); colonel, 15th Infantry (May 14, 1861); chief of staff, Department of Pennsylvania (summer 1861); brigadier general, USV (August 7, 1861, to rank from May 17); commanding division, Army of the Potomac (October 3 1861-March 13, 1862); commanding 1st Division, 3rd Corps, Army of the Potomac (March 13-May 18, 1862); commanding 5th Corps (a provisional organization until July 22), Army of the Potomac (May 18-November 10, 1862); and major general, USV (July 4, 1862). Following initial service as a staff officer under Robert Patterson he began his long-lasting and damaging friendship with McClellan. He led a division to the Peninsula and saw action in the operations against Yorktown. When McClellan created two provisional corps he appointed Porter to the command of one of them. At Beaver Dam Creek and Gaines' Mill—at the start of the Seven Days—he displayed excellent generalship in the defensive fighting. Again at Malvern Hill he played a leading role in covering the withdrawal of the army. For this series of battles he was awarded a second star and was brevetted regular army brigadier. His command was sent to reinforce Pope in northern Virginia—an assignment for which he made no secret of his displeasure. At 2nd Bull Run he was ordered to attack the flank and rear of Stonewall Jackson's command. But no attack was launched because the order was based upon faulty information and the indications that Longstreet was then present on the field. An 1878 inquiry under John M. Schofield found that Porter was right in not committing his men to a doomed assault which Longstreet would have crushed. It further found that Porter's actions probably saved the Army of Virginia from an even greater disaster. However, these findings came too late to save his military career. After serving in reserve under his friend McClellan at Antietam he was relieved of command on November 10, 1862, and placed under arrest. In the trial for disloyalty, disobediance of orders, and misconduct in the face of the enemy he was damaged by his friendship for the now-deposed McClellan and his own anti-Pope statements. There was a political atmosphere to the court which was composed of Stanton appointees, most of whom received promotions,

Fitz-John Porter, unjustly cashiered general. (*Leslie's*)

brevets, or higher commands for their service on the panel. Porter was found guilty on January 10, 1863, and sentenced to be cashiered from the army. Eleven days later the sentence was carried out, and Porter spent much of the remainder of his life trying to get his name cleared. The 1878 Schofield board was a first step and, following its recommendations, President Chester A. Arthur remitted the sentence four years later. By a special act of Congress in 1886 he was recommissioned an infantry colonel, to rank from May 14, 1861, but back pay was denied him. Two days later, with his battle largely won, Porter was retired at his own request. In the postwar years he was involved in mining, construction, and the mercantile businesses. He refused an appointment in the Egyptian army and served as New York City's police, fire, and public works commissioners. NOTE: His 1862-63 trial is fully reported in the *Official Records*, Series I, Volume XII, Part II, Supplement (Eisenschiml, Otto, *The Celebrated Case of Fitz-John Porter*)

PORTER, George Camp (?-1919)

Upon the secession of Tennessee, George C. Porter raised the "Haywood Blues," and entered the service of the state. His later assignments included: captain, Company A, 6th Tennessee (May 1861); major, 6th Tennessee (May 23, 1861); colonel, 6th Tennessee (May 6, 1862); and commanding Maney's Brigade, Cheatham's Division, 1st Corps, Army of Tennessee (early 1864-May 1864 and July 22-fall 1864). He was at Columbus, Kentucky, while the battle of Belmont took place across the Mississippi. After fighting at Shiloh, he was elected colonel upon the reorganization of the regiment. He led the regiment at Perryville in the Kentucky Campaign, after which the regiment was consolidated with the 9th Tennessee. Porter assumed command after Murfreesboro and led the consolidated unit at Chickamauga and Chattanooga. At times during the Atlanta Campaign he was in command of the brigade. He left the regiment after Franklin and appears to have never returned.

PORTER, Horace (1837-1921)

West Pointer (1860) Horace Porter is best known as a staff officer and biographer of General Grant. Serving in the ordnance department, Porter had been a brevet second lieutenant at the beginning of the war. His later assignments included: second lieutenant, Ordnance Department (April 22, 1861); first lieutenant, Ordnance Department (June 7, 1861); captain, Ordnance Department (March 3, 1863); and lieutenant colonel and aide-de-camp (April 4, 1864). After service as an ordnance officer on the South Carolina coast, Porter was made chief of Ordnance, Army of the Potomac, during the latter part of the Peninsula Campaign. During late 1862 he served as ordnance chief for the Department of the Ohio and in 1863 in the same position with the Army of the Cumberland. While in the latter post, Porter on the second day of the battle of Chickamauga rallied fugitives from the broken line and held some important ground, allowing batteries and wagon trains to leave the field during the disastrous retreat. For his actions he was awarded the Congressional Medal of Honor in 1902. During the Chattanooga Campaign, Porter came to the attention of General Grant and served on his staff, as an aide, from the spring of 1864 until the close of the war. He received regular army brevets to captain for Fort Pulaski, major for the Wilderness, lieutenant colonel for New Market Heights, and colonel and brigadier general for the war. Porter continued as an aide to Generals Grant and Sherman until 1873, when he resigned to become a railroad man. His *Campaigning With Grant* was published in 1897. (Mende, Elsie Porter, *An American Soldier and Diplomat Horace Porter*)

PORTER, Jonathan R. (ca. 1838-1923)

Although he did not take part in the actual theft of the rebel engine *The General*, Jonathan Porter was a member of James J. Andrews' original 24-member expedition and was twice in the hands of the Confederate authorities, facing a possible execution. A private in Company G, 21st Ohio, Porter had been chosen to take part in the raid to upset Confederate communications. In civilian clothes, the members of the raiding force made their way to Marietta, Georgia, in pairs. However, on the fateful morning of April 12, 1862, Porter and his companion overslept in their hotel room and failed to make the appointed rendezvous. After some initial hesitation, they determined to follow the prearranged contingency plan and enlist in the rebel army to avoid suspicion. But the authorities were soon tipped off and the two were arrested. After being confined in Chattanooga and Atlanta with the other raiders, all of whom were captured (and eight of their number hanged), the remaining raiders escaped. Eight of the 14 made it to the Union lines after their October 16, 1862 break. Porter made it to Corinth, Mississippi, after a month on the run, and was given the Medal of Honor for his exploits. Rejoining his unit, he was again captured at the battle of Chickamauga and recognized as one of the train thieves. Confined in Richmond and Danville, he made numerous escape attempts. Finally, on June 29, 1864, while being transferred to Andersonville, he escaped from the train and made his way to join Sherman's forces near Atlanta. Rejoining his regiment, he fought through the March to the Sea and the Carolinas Campaign. He was mustered out of the service on March 31, 1865. At the age of 85 he was the last of the raiders to die. (O'Neill, Charles, *Wild Train: The Story of the Andrews Raid*)

PORTER, William David (1809-1864)

Commodore William D. Porter's naval and Civil War careers can best be summed up by his nickname, "Dirty Bill." Son of the War of 1812's hero, Commodore David Porter, William Porter entered the navy as a midshipman at the age of 14. During the prewar years he invented a less than successful exploding shell and adjusted lighthouse deployments along the coast. On the debit side he was court-martialed for a long list of charges and in 1855 was placed on the retired list. Reinstated in 1859, the outbreak of the Civil War found him in command of the USS *St. Mary's* in the Pacific. Born in New Orleans, Porter went so far as to divorce his Southern-born second wife in order to prove his fidelity to the Union. On October 4, 1861, he was ordered to Paducah, Kentucky, to take command of the USS *New Era* which he soon renamed the *Essex*, the name being that of his father's old command. While fitting out his new vessel, Porter became embroiled in a controversy with the army over some stolen barges. Chafing for action, Porter tried to use inflammatory language to get the opposing fleet to engage in combat. Porter got his wish for action at Fort Henry, where a rebel shot through the *Essex*'s boiler, forcing him and many of his men overboard. His craft was sent to St. Louis for repairs, and Dirty Bill virtually rebuilt it—at the enormous cost of $91,000. Joining the naval forces on the Mississippi in July 1862, he was engaged in actions against Vicksburg, Port Hudson, and the ram CSS *Arkansas*. Following the battle of Baton Rouge he engaged the ram, and when it was scuttled by its own crew claimed that the *Essex*'s guns had set her afire. This claim was denied, bringing to the fore his long-standing resentments of fellow officers, including Commodore C.H. Davis, his own brother, Admiral David Porter, and his foster brother, Admiral David Farragut. He was promoted to commodore, to date from July 16, 1862, but in September, when he received the commission, Dirty Bill was ordered to New York to answer charges made by Davis and to explain an extraordinary letter to Secretary of the Navy Gideon Welles, attacking the department. For the next year he served on various commissions and saw no further action. Still angry about his treatment, he died on May 1, 1864. Welles described Porter as "a courageous, daring, troublesome, reckless officer."

"Dirty Bill" Porter. (NA)

PORTERFIELD, George Alexander (1822-1919)

A graduate of the Virginia Military Institute and a veteran of the Mexican War, George A. Porterfield was appointed colonel of Virginia Volunteers and assigned to staff duty at Harpers Ferry on April 24, 1861. Sent to western Virginia in early May to raise troops there, he destroyed two bridges on the Baltimore and Ohio Railroad before retiring to Philippi. In one of the Confederacy's first military defeats, Porterfield and his 800 men were surprised and routed by a part of McClellan's command on June 3. The victory was celebrated in the North as "The Philippi Races," and in disgrace Porterfield was superseded by Brigadier General Robert S. Garnett. A subsequent Court of Inquiry praised his actions during the fighting itself but censured him for a "want of forethought and vigilance." He was relegated to staff positions until May 1862, when he was not reelected colonel of the 25th Virginia under the Reorganization Act. The next month he was captured and paroled by the Federals, ending his military career. He was a successful Charlestown banker after the war.

POSEY, Carnot (1813-1863)

Mississippi lawyer and planter Carnot Posey was promoted to brigadier to succeed an ill officer only to find himself without a command when that general resumed his post even before Posey reported. Posey had been wounded at Buena Vista during the Mexican War while serving as a first lieutenant in Jefferson Davis' 1st Mississippi Rifles. He entered the Southern army at the head of the Wilkinson Rifles and his later assignments included: captain, Company K, 16th Mississippi (spring 1861); colonel, 16th Mississippi (June 1861); commanding Featherston's Brigade, Wilcox's Division, 1st Corps, Army of Northern Virginia (August 30 and September-November 1862); brigadier general, CSA (November 1, 1862); and commanding Featherston's (old) Brigade, Anderson's Division, 1st (3rd after May 30) Corps, same army (January 19-October 14, 1863). His regiment was not at 1st Bull Run and Ball's Bluff, as commonly indicated, but he did see action under Ewell in Jackson's Valley Campaign where he was wounded. After being engaged in the Seven Days, he directed the brigade during part of 2nd Bull Run and at Antietam. Promoted to brigadier, he was displaced by Featherston's return and was without a brigade until that officer, at his own request but probably with some hints, transferred to Mississippi. Posey then led the brigade at Chancellorsville and Gettysburg. In covering the assault at Bristoe Station on October 14, 1863, he was struck by an artillery projectile. The wound was not assumed to be mortal but he died on November 13, from infection. (Freeman, Douglas S., *Lee's Lieutenants*)

POST, Philip Sidney (1833-1895)

Although he never received the commission of a brigadier general, New York native Philip S. Post spent much of the Civil War in brigade command and won the Congressional Medal of Honor at Nashville. His assignments included: second lieutenant, 59th Illinois (July 17, 1861); first lieutenant and adjutant, 59th Illinois (July 21, 1861); major, 59th Illinois (January 17, 1862); colonel, 59th Illinois (March 20, 1862); and commanding in the Army of the Cumberland: 1st Brigade, 1st Division, Right Wing, 14th Corps (November 5, 1862-January 9, 1863); 1st Brigade, 1st Division, 20th Corps (January 9-October 9, 1863); 3rd Brigade, 1st Division, 4th Corps (July 27-August 5, 1864); 2nd Brigade, 3rd Division, 4th Corps (August 19-December 6, 1864); and also the division (September 2-6, 1864). As a field officer, he fell wounded at Pea Ridge but returned to duty in time to fight at Murfreesboro in charge of a brigade. Taking part in the Tullahoma Campaign, his brigade missed the battle of Chickamauga when it was assigned to duty guarding supply trains. Post himself was absent at the time of Chattanooga but did serve through the Atlanta Campaign, even, as a colonel, being in charge of the division for a few days. Sent back with the corps to Tennessee to face Hood's invasion, he led his brigade well on both days of the fighting at Nashville. On the second day, while leading his command in an attack against heavy fire on Overton Hill, he had his arm smashed by grapeshot. This ended his field duty but earned him the brevet of brigadier general and, in 1893, the Medal of Honor. He was mustered out with his regiment on December 8, 1865, and was later a lawyer, a journalist, a diplomat in Austria, and a Republican congressman.

POTTER, Edward Elmer (1823-1889)

Serving mostly on the Southern coast during the Civil War, Union General Edward E. Potter won a brevet as major general for his war service. The New York City native was a lawyer and farmer before the conflict. His assignments included: captain and commissary of Subsistence, USV (February 3, 1862); lieutenant colonel, 1st North Carolina (October 1, 1862); brigadier general, USV (December 24, 1862, to rank from November 29); commanding U.S. Forces Norfolk and Portsmouth, Department of Virginia and North Carolina (September 23-October 1, 1863); commanding 3rd Separate Brigade, Department of the South (November 14-28, 1864); commanding 1st Brigade, Coast Division, Department of the South (November 28, 1864-January 23, 1865); and commanding 2nd Separate Brigade, Department of the South (January 23-May 13, 1865). During Burnside's expedition against the coast of North Carolina, Potter served as commissary with John G. Foster's brigade. Detailed to raise a regiment of loyal North Carolinians, he soon was promoted to brigadier general. Much of the time Potter served on the staff of General Foster in various capacities, and Potter accompanied him to the Department of the Ohio for a tour of duty there. At other times he served in the operations against Charleston and later, as a field commander, in the Carolinas Campaign. He resigned on July 24, 1865, and returned to New York.

POTTER, Joseph Haydn (1822-1892)

The fact that he was twice a prisoner of war during the Civil War did not prevent New Hampshire native Joseph H. Potter from rising to the rank of brigadier general at its close. The West Pointer (1843) had been posted to the infantry and had been wounded at Monterey and won a brevet during the Mexican War. His Civil War-era assignments included: captain, 7th Infantry (since January 9, 1856); colonel, 12th New Hampshire (September 22, 1862); commanding 2nd Brigade, 3rd Division, 3rd Corps, Army of the Potomac (January 12-February 19, 1863); major, 19th Infantry (July 4, 1863); assistant provost marshal general, Department of the Ohio (1864); commanding Provisional Division, Army of the James (October-December 1864); commanding 2nd Brigade, 3rd Division, 24th Corps, Army of the James (December 3, 1864-January 17, 1865); chief of staff, 24th Corps, Army of the James (January-ca. August 1, 1865); and brigadier general, USV (May 1, 1865). Stationed in Texas during the secession crisis, he was surrendered to the state authorities on July 27, 1861, and, although paroled, was not formally exchanged until August 7, 1862. He was then named to command a volunteer regiment from his native state. He won brevets for Fredericksburg and Chancellorsville. In the latter he was wounded and captured. Exchanged in the fall of 1863, he served in the Department of the Ohio in a staff position and then joined the Army of the James in front of Petersburg and Richmond. He served the final months of the war as a corps chief of staff and was brevetted brigadier general for the Petersburg to Appomattox Campaign. With the war all but over in Virginia, he was named to the full rank and was mustered out of the volunteer service on January 15, 1866. Remaining in the regular army, he served on the frontier until his 1886 retirement as a brigadier general.

POTTER, Robert Brown (1829-1887)

Coming from a religious family, Robert B. Potter rose from the rank of militia private to the grade of major general of volunteers. The New York native had given up his law practice at the outbreak of the Civil War and his assignments included: private, New York Militia (1861); lieutenant, New York Militia (1861); major, 51st New York (October 14, 1861); lieutenant colonel, 51st New York (November 1, 1861); colonel, 51st New York (September 10, 1862); brigadier general, USV (March 13, 1863); commanding 2nd Division, 9th Corps, Department of the Ohio (June 5-14 and August 18-25, 1863); commanding 2nd Division, 9th Corps, Army of the Tennessee (June 14-August 18, 1863); commanding 9th Corps, Army of the Ohio (August 25, 1863-January 17, 1864); commanding 2nd Division, 9th Corps, Army of the Potomac (May 1-December 22, 1864 and January-April 2, 1865); and major general, USV (September 29, 1865). As a field officer, he went on Burnside's expedition to the North Carolina coast, fighting at Roanoke Island and being wounded at New Bern. He commanded the regiment at 2nd Bull Run and was promoted to its permanent command just before South Mountain and Antietam. At the latter his unit was one of two regiments which finally succeeded in storming Burnside's Bridge. After

Fredericksburg he went west as a brigadier general and division commander and at Vicksburg was part of the force posted to watch out for Joseph E. Johnston's relieving force. He took part in the recapture of Jackson, Mississippi, and then returned to Kentucky and East Tennessee. He led the corps at Knoxville and then returned to Virginia as one of its four division commanders. Serving through the Overland and Petersburg campaigns, he was wounded during the final assaults on the latter place. Brevetted major general for the early stages of the latter campaigning on August 1, 1864, he was mustered out with the full grade on January 15, 1866. For a number of years he was a railroad employee and then spent four years in England.

POTTS, Benjamin Franklin (1836-1887)

A Douglas Democrat before the Civil War, in which he served as a brigadier general in the Union army, Benjamin F. Potts later became a Republican territorial governor. The native Ohio lawyer had attended both Democratic national conventions in 1860 before raising a volunteer company following the firing on Fort Sumter. His assignments included: captain, 32nd Ohio (August 20, 1861); lieutenant colonel, 32nd Ohio (November 21, 1862); colonel, 32nd Ohio (December 28, 1862); commanding 2nd Brigade, 3rd Division, 17th Corps, Army of the Tennessee (November 17, 1863-March 6, 1864); commanding 1st Brigade, 4th Division, 17th Corps, Army of the Tennessee (July 18, 1864-June 26, 1865 and July 9-23, 1865); brigadier general, USV (January 12, 1865); and commanding the division (June 26-July 9, 1865). As a company commander he served in western Virginia and fought under Frémont at McDowell and Cross Keys. During the Vicksburg Campaign he fought as a regimental commander under John A. Logan and James B. McPherson. He led a brigade during Sherman's Meridian Campaign and again succeeded to brigade command during the battles before Atlanta. Still in charge of the brigade, he participated in the March to the Sea and was promoted to brigadier general early in 1865. He then served throughout the Carolinas Campaign and was brevetted major general for the war. Mustered out on January 15, 1866, he returned to his practice and soon reentered politics. After service in the state legislature he was Montana's territorial governor from 1870 until removed in 1883. He then took up ranching and served in the territorial legislature.

Union division commander Robert B. Potter (hatless) and photographer Mathew Brady (far right). (NA)

POWEL, Samuel (1821-1902)

In the summer of 1861, Samuel Powel raised a company for the Confederate army. In his brief career, he held the following assignments: captain, Company A, 29th Tennessee (summer 1861); colonel, 29th Tennessee (September 30, 1861); commanding 3rd Brigade, Anderson's Division, Left Wing, Army of the Mississippi (fall-November 20, 1862); and commanding 3rd Brigade, Anderson's Division, Hardee's Corps, Army of Tennessee (November 1862). In his first battle, Mill Springs, Powel suffered a severe wound. During the battle of Shiloh, the regiment was stationed at Iuka, Mississippi. Powel and his command then joined the Army of the Mississippi and by the fall of 1862 he was in command of the brigade, replacing General Marmaduke. He led the brigade at Perryville where it suffered heavily. Powel resigned near the end of November 1862.

POWELL, Lazarus Whitehead (1812-1867)

The one six-year senatorial term of former Kentucky governor Lazarus W. Powell spanned most of the Civil War, when the loyalties of the state's citizens were sharply divided. A native of the state, Powell had begun the practice of law in 1835 and the next year entered the legislature. He resumed his law practice and kept up his interest in politics by serving as an elector for the Democrats in 1844. He was governor from 1851 to 1855 and four years later took a seat in the U.S. Senate. With the secession crisis and Kentucky's original stand of neutrality, Powell remained loyal to the Union and retained his seat in Washington. Not a candidate for reelection, he returned to his private practice at the end of his term, on March 3, 1865.

POWELL, Lewis Thornton (1844-1865)

When John Wilkes Booth was making his attack on Lincoln at Ford's Theater, Lewis T. Powell was making the only other attack—on Secretary of State William H. Seward. Known to his fellow conspirators as Lewis Paine, or Payne, he was a large-framed Floridian who had been captured at Gettysburg, made good his escape, and served for a time with John S. Mosby. As a Confederate courier, he was known as Wood, and was so introduced to his fellow plotters in the beginning. Because of his size it was assumed that he would be able to overpower Lincoln in the original kidnapping scheme. When the plan was changed to assassination his assigned target was Seward. The secretary was bedridden from a carriage accident. Powell smashed the skull of Frederick Seward with his pistol butt and forced his way into the bedroom where, after wounding others, he set upon the cabinet official. Stabbed several times around the face and neck, Seward was at first thought to be dead but his neck brace had saved him. Powell fled from the scene but lost his way and was not able to join in the general flight. He was arrested on April 17, 1865, when he arrived at the Surratt boardinghouse. During the trial he professed the innocence of Mary Surratt. Found guilty on June 30, 1865, he was hanged on July 7. His bravery impressed Christian Rath, the hangman.

Lewis Powell, Seward's would-be assassin. (NA)

POWELL, William Henry (1825-1904)

Having dealt for nearly three years with guerrilla activities, Union General William H. Powell had earned a reputation in 1864 for his summary execution of suspected partisans; it may have been the official reaction which prompted his resignation. The Welshman had been in the Ohio iron business at the outbreak of the war. His military assignments included: captain, 2nd West Virginia Cavalry (November 8, 1861); major, 2nd West Virginia Cavalry (June 25, 1862); lieutenant colonel, 2nd West Virginia Cavalry (October 25, 1862); colonel, 2nd West Virginia Cavalry (May 18, 1863); commanding 3rd Brigade, 2nd Cavalry Division, Department of West Virginia (June 10-July 1864); commanding 2nd Brigade, 2nd Cavalry Division, Department of West Virginia (August-September 26, 1864); commanding the division (September 30, 1864-January 13, 1865); and brigadier general, USV (October 19, 1864). His early service was in West Virginia making and opposing raids. On November 26, 1862, he led a detachment of only 20 men and, without loss, surprised and captured a 500-man camp in Sinking Creek Valley. In 1890 this action was recognized by the awarding of the Congressional Medal of Honor. He was wounded and captured in a charge at Wytheville, Virginia, on July 18, 1863. Released from Libby Prison and exchanged in February 1864, his command soon joined the forces in the Shenandoah Valley, taking part in the unsuccessful Lynchburg expedition. By now commanding a brigade, he returned to the Valley under Sheridan and following the fighting at 3rd Winchester and Fisher's Hill was given charge of Averell's division. It was in this capacity that he fought at Cedar Creek, earning a brigadier's star, and became notorious for promptly hanging suspected guerrillas. His resignation for unknown reasons was accepted on January 5, 1865, and he left his division eight days later. Brevetted major general two months later, he returned to the iron business and was active in veterans and Republican groups and was a government appointee. (Jones, Virgil Carrington, *Gray Ghosts and Rebel Raiders*)

POWER, John Logan (1834-1901)

As the editor of the *Jackson* (Miss.) *Daily News*, John L. Power was an active supporter of the Confederacy. A native of Ireland, he had been raised in poverty in the United States and became a printer on a number of New Orleans newspapers. Moving to Jackson, Mississippi, he became co-owner of the *Mississippian* in 1855. A year before the state's secession he commenced the publication of the *News*. He was the official reporter of the proceedings at the state secession convention. Active in support of the war effort, he was rewarded in 1864 with the clerkship of the lower house of the state legislature. At the same time he was made superintendent of the state's military records. After Appomattox he ran the *Jackson Mississippi Standard* and served as state printer and secretary of state.

PRATT, Calvin Edward (1828-1896)

Putting his militia experience to use, Calvin E. Pratt raised a regiment for the Union army and rose to the rank of brigadier general before his resignation was accepted to date from April 25, 1863. The Massachusetts-born lawyer had been living in Brooklyn, New York, upon the outbreak of hostilities and spent much of his own money equipping his regiment. His assignments included: colonel, 31st New York (May 14, 1861); brigadier general, USV (September 13, 1862); commanding 1st Brigade, 2nd Division, 6th Corps, Army of the Potomac (September 25, 1862-January 26, 1863); and commanding Light Division, 6th Corps, Army of the Potomac (January 26-April 28, 1863). Part of Dixon S. Miles' division in reserve at Centerville during the battle of 1st Bull Run, Pratt helped to cover the withdrawal of the Union forces. Leading his regiment on the Peninsula, he was wounded at Mechanicsville during the Seven Days. Named a brigadier general of volunteers, he led a brigade on the left at Fredericksburg. In command of the Light Division—in actuality a brigade—he took part in the early stages of the Chancellorsville Campaign before being informed that his resignation had been accepted by Washington. He then resumed his law practice and served as a tax official and judge.

PRENTICE, George D. (?-?)

A prominent Kentucky Unionist, George D. Prentice turned his newspaper into a "noosepaper" for guerrilla Marcellus J. Clarke in a political feud with the Union commander in the Louisville area, Stephen G. Burbridge. Angered by Burbridge's political activities in behalf of the Republican Party, Prentice decided to launch a campaign against the general in his *Louisville Courier* over his inability to effectively deal with the guerrilla warfare that was being waged throughout the state in the later part of the Civil War. He picked a minor guerrilla leader who was small enough to be confused for a woman and developed a major military problem for Burbridge. He renamed the bandit Sue Mundy after a disreputable black woman of the city and charged that Burbridge could not deal with him or her. He quipped that his paper would be a "noosepaper" for the young Confederate and it turned out to be so when Clarke-Mundy was captured and hanged by Burbridge's successor John M. Palmer in March 1865.

PRENTISS, Benjamin Mayberry (1819-1901)

For the Union setbacks on the first day at Shiloh a scapegoat had to be found and, despite his tenacious defense at the Hornet's Nest, Benjamin M. Prentiss was the man chosen. He was relegated to the war's backwaters for the balance of his service. The Virginia native had lived for a time in Missouri before settling in Illinois where he served in the militia during the conflict over the presence of the Mormons in the state. During the Mexican War he was regimental adjutant and then a company commander in the 1st Illinois. Becoming a lawyer and Republican politician, he lost a bid for Congress in 1860. A militia officer at the outbreak of the Civil War, he enlisted and his assignments included: captain, 10th Illinois (April 29, 1861); colonel, 10th Illinois (April 29, 1861); brigadier general, USV (August 9, 1861, to rank from May 17); commanding 6th Division, Army of the Tennessee (March 26-April 6, 1862); commanding District of Eastern Arkansas, Army of the Tennessee (February 8-April 3, 1863); major general, USV (March 13, 1863 to rank from November 29, 1862); commanding District of Eastern Arkansas, 13th Corps, Army of the Tennessee (July 1863); and commanding District of Eastern Arkansas, 16th Corps, Army of the Tennessee (July 29-August 3, 1863). As a division commander, he made a desperate stand on the first day at Shiloh until captured late in the day with much of his remaining force. In actuality he had bought valuable time for Grant to stabilize his line nearer the river. Exchanged in October 1862, Prentiss was assigned to the court-martial of Fitz-John Porter after which he was exiled to eastern Arkansas. Much of the time he was in charge at Helena and there he repulsed a Confederate attack that was aimed at relieving the pressure upon Vicksburg. Citing health reasons, but probably feeling himself cast aside despite making major general, he resigned on October 28, 1863, and returned to the practice of law in Illinois and Missouri. He also served as a pension agent and postmaster.

PRESTON, John Smith (1809-1881)

A leading secessionist in his adopted South Carolina, John S. Preston became a Confederate general but saw only limited action. The Virginia native had practiced law there and in South Carolina. He also was a Louisiana planter for a time. He attended the Charleston convention of 1860 and with South Carolina already out of the Union was sent the next year to Virginia to urge his native state to follow suit. Joining the military his assignments included: lieutenant colonel and assistant adjutant general (August 31, 1861); commanding prisoner of war camp, Columbia, S.C. (January 28, 1862-July 30, 1863); colonel and assistant adjutant general (April 23, 1863); superintendent, Bureau of Conscription (July 30, 1863-March 17, 1865); and brigadier general, CSA (June 10, 1864). After serving on Beauregard's staff at Fort Sumter and 1st Bull Run he was placed in charge of a prison camp until named to the Conscription Bureau. While engaged in the neverending search for more men he was promoted to brigadier general. He held the post until the bureau was abolished in the final months of the war. After three years in England after the collapse of the Confederacy, he continued to speak out on the justification for succession.

PRESTON, William (1816-1887)

Harvard-educated lawyer William Preston served his native Kentucky before and after the Civil War, in which he rose to the rank of Confederate brigadier general. During the Mexican War he had held the position of lieutenant colonel in the 4th Kentucky and in the interwar period sat in both houses of the state legislature and in the U.S. Congress. In the years just before the Civil War, he was James Buchanan's representative in Spain. During the secession crisis he urged his state to withdraw from the Union but was unsuccessful. Joining the Confederate army, his assignments included: colonel (September 1861); brigadier general, CSA (April 14, 1862); commanding 2nd (Kentucky) Brigade, Reserve Corps, Army of the Mississippi (May-June 1862); commanding 3rd Brigade, Breckinridge's Division, Hardee's Corps, Army of Tennessee (December 1862-May 9, 1863); commanding the division (January 1863); commanding District of Abingdon, Department of Western Virginia (May 9, 1863-January 7, 1864); also commanding Department of East Tennessee (June 26-July 4, 1863); and commanding division, Buckner's Corps, Army of Tennessee (September 1864). At Shiloh he served on the staff of Albert Sidney Johnston and was promoted to brigadier general later in the month. He took part in the Siege of Corinth, Mississippi, and at the end of the year led a brigade at Murfreesboro. After service in western Virginia and East Tennessee he led a division from there to reinforce Bragg before Chickamauga. On January 7, 1864, he was named as minister to the court of Maximilian but found it impossible to reach Mexico City. Returning to the Confederacy, he was in the Trans-Mississippi Department at the close of the war. He did not return to Kentucky until 1866, having traveled via Mexico, England, and Canada. He then resumed his political career as a Democrat sitting in the state legislature.

PRESTON, William Ballard (1805-1862)

A veteran of both houses of the state legislature and of the U.S. Congress—as an antislavery Whig—William B. Preston was a long-standing opponent of secession. The Virginia native had practiced law before his entry into politics and served as Zachary Taylor's secretary of the navy. It was not until Lincoln's call for 75,000, after the firing on Fort Sumter, that Preston became a secessionist. At that time, in a move to gain support from former Unionists, he was tapped to present the ordinance of secession to the state convention—unexpected for a man who had favored the admission of California as a free state. Named to the Provisional Confederate Congress from his western Virginia district, he was admitted on July 20, 1861, and sat on the Committee on Military Affairs. Named to the Senate in the First Regular Congress he sat on the corresponding committee and on those on: Flag and Seal; and Foreign Affairs. He wanted strict limits on the national government's war-making ability that would favor state and local control. He also wanted to keep the economy free from government regulations. Between the second and third congressional sessions, he died at his Montgomery County home on November 16, 1862.

PREVOST, Charles Mallet (1818-1887)

In less than a month after transferring from a staff position to the command of a volunteer regiment, Charles M. Prevost was severely wounded in one of the great debacles of the Civil War. The Maryland-born soldier had entered the service from Pennsylvania. His assignments included: captain and assistant adjutant general, USV (May 1, 1862); colonel, 118th Pennsylvania (August 28, 1862); commanding Harrisburg, Department of the Susquehanna (summer 1863); colonel, 16th Veteran Reserve Corps (September 29, 1863); and commanding Camp Butler, District of Illinois, Northern Department (late 1864-spring 1865). As a staff officer he served with Francis E. Patterson in Virginia before resigning on August 16, 1862, to become colonel of the "Corn Exchange Regiment." This unit was assigned to the 5th Corps just prior to Antietam and was held in reserve. After Lee's army had recrossed the Potomac, the 118th took part in the pursuit at Shepherdstown Ford and advanced too far. When the Confederates under Ambrose P. Hill counterattacked Prevost grabbed the regimental colors and tried to control his green troops. The colonel fell wounded and the regiment suffered one-third casualties in the debacle. Prevost recovered to command his unit at Chancellorsville but his wound continued to trouble him and during the Gettysburg Campaign he was in command of detachments of the Invalid Corps at Harrisburg. Commissioned a colonel in the Veteran Reserve Corps (wounded and sick soldiers on limited duty) he served the rest of the war at Harrisburg and in Illinois. Honorably discharged on June 30, 1866, he was brevetted brigadier general for his war service.

PRICE, Sterling (1809-1867)

As the leader of the Missouri State Guard, Virginia-born Sterling Price became one of the principal forces in Confederate Missouri at the beginning of the Civil War. A lawyer and farmer in his adopted state, he had gradually entered politics as a state legislator and U.S. congressman. During the Mexican War he was colonel of the 2nd Missouri and a brigadier general of volunteers. In the interwar years he served as governor and, as the secession crisis approached, he opposed separation but gradually altered his views. Accepting command of the Missouri State Guard, his assignments included: major general, Missouri State Guard (May 1861); commanding Missouri State Guard (May 1861-March 17, 1862); major general, CSA (March 6, 1862); commanding 1st Division, Trans-Mississippi District, Department #2 (March 17-April 1862); commanding division, Army of the West, Department #2 (April-May 1862); commanding the army (July 3-September 26, 1862); also commanding District of the Tennessee, Department #2 (July 1862); commanding corps (Army of the West), Army of West Tennessee, Department #2 (October-December 1862); commanding corps, Department of Mississippi and East

Louisiana (ca. December 1862-February 27, 1863); commanding division, District of Arkansas, Trans-Mississippi Department (March 30-July 24, 1863 and September 25, 1863-March 16, 1864); commanding the district (July 24-September 25, 1863 and March 16-early August 1864); commanding Army of Missouri, Trans-Mississippi Department (September 18-December 1864); and also commanding Cavalry Corps, Trans-Mississippi Department (September 1864-early 1865). Meeting in June 1861 with Francis P. Blair and Nathaniel Lyon at the Planter's Hotel in St. Louis, he felt himself pushed into the

Sterling Price (center), Missouri State Guard commander, with fellow exiles in Mexico after the war. Clockwise from Price: Cadmus M. Wilcox, John B. Magruder, William P. Hardeman, and Thomas C. Hindman. (NA)

Confederate camp. Leading the Missouri State Guard under Ben McCulloch, he fought at Wilson's Creek and then captured the Union garrison at Lexington. Unable to cooperate with McCulloch, he agreed to the idea of both of them serving under Earl Van Dorn and in such a setup fought in the Southern defeat at Pea Ridge. Appointed to a major generalcy in the regular Confederate forces from the date of the opening of the battle, he worked to transfer his men to that service. Transferred to the east of the Mississippi River, his forces arrived too late for the battle of Shiloh but took part in the defense of Corinth, Mississippi. He lost the fight at Iuka and again under Van Dorn took part in the unsuccessful attacks on Corinth. He maneuvered against Grant during that officer's drive into central Mississippi and then transferred back west of the Mississippi where he led the unsuccessful attack on Helena in an effort to relieve the pressure on Vicksburg which, ironically, fell the same day. Commanding the District of Arkansas, he failed to hold Little Rock but the next year campaigned successfully against Steele's drive on Camden, taking part in the victory at Jenkins' Ferry. Placed in charge of a large force of cavalry, he was dispatched on a raid into Missouri in the late summer and fall of 1864. Deterred from an attack on St. Louis by Union reinforcements, he moved to the West and was finally defeated at Westport. After fighting a rear-guard action at Marais des Cygnes, Kansas, he continued his retreat back into Arkansas by a roundabout route. While the campaign had thrown a fright into the Union high command, which felt this to be a dormant sector, it had not achieved any significant lasting result and had decimated Price's command. In the final months of the war there was a Confederate inquiry into the causes of the failure. At the war's close he moved into Mexico where he remained until the fall of Maximilian. The final year of his life was spent in St. Louis. To the end he had been popular with his Missourians who dubbed him "Old Pap." (Castel, Albert, *General Sterling Price and the Civil War in the West* and Stalhope, Robert E., *Sterling Price, Portrait of a Southerner*)

PRINCE, Henry (1811-1892)

When Henry Prince committed suicide in 1892 he was in one sense a casualty of the Civil War since he was suffering from earlier wounds which had been aggravated by hard service in that conflict and by four months imprisonment. The Maine native and West Pointer (1835) had been posted to the infantry. He was wounded in the Seminole War and again during the Mexican War in which he also won two brevets. The interwar years saw him take several lengthy leaves of absence for his health and transfer to the paymaster's department. His Civil War services included: major and paymaster (since May 23, 1855); brigadier general, USV (April 28, 1862); commanding 2nd Brigade, 2nd Division, 2nd Corps, Army of Virginia (July 16-August 9, 1862); commanding the division (August 9, 1862); commanding 5th Division, 18th Corps, Department of North Carolina (January 11-April 22, 1863); commanding District of Pamlico, 18th Corps, Department of North Carolina (April 22-June 20, 1863); commanding 2nd Division, 3rd Corps, Army of the Potomac (July 10, 1863-March 24, 1864); commanding 3rd Division, 6th Corps, Army of the Potomac (March 25-April 4, 1864); commanding District of Cairo, Department of the Tennessee (April 24-June 1864); and commanding District of Columbus, 16th Corps, Army of the Tennessee (ca. June-August 7, 1864). He served in the staff department until his appointment to a brigadier generalship in the volunteers in the spring of 1862. He was shortly thereafter assigned to command of a brigade in Pope's army. In the fighting at Cedar Mountain he succeeded to the command of the division upon the wounding of Christopher C. Augur. He was then captured and not released until December 1862. Sent to North Carolina, he held divisional and district commands before joining the Army of the Potomac just after Gettysburg. He led a 3rd Corps division in the Bristoe Campaign but was slow in moving up his command at Mine Run. Nonetheless he survived the March 1864 reorganization and consolidation and briefly commanded a division of the enlarged 6th Corps. This did not last long however and he was shunted off to the West where he held district and garrison commands for the balance of the war. Mustered out of the volunteers, he rejoined the paymaster's department and rose to lieutenant colonel and deputy paymaster general before his 1879 retirement. He was in London when he killed himself.

PRYOR, Roger Atkinson (1828-1919)

Twice Roger A. Pryor found himself a brigadier without a brigade and finished out the war, in effect, as a private. He had had a distinguished career before the war as a lawyer, journalist, and politician. He resigned from the U.S. Congress on March 3, 1861, and witnessed the shelling of Fort Sumter. On July 24, 1861, he took a seat in the Provisional Congress and was later reelected to the First Regular Congress. During both congresses he served on the Committee on Military Affairs but resigned on April 5, 1862, to devote his full energies to his military career. His assignments included: colonel, 3rd Virginia (1861); brigadier general, CSA (April 16, 1862); commanding brigade, Longstreet's Division (in 1st Corps from July), Army of Northern Virginia (May-August 1862), commanding brigade, Wilcox's Division, same corps and army (August-early September 1862); commanding brigade, Anderson's Division, same corps and army (September 1862); commanding the division (September 17, 1862); commanding brigade, Pickett's Division, same corps and army (September-November 10, 1862); and commanding brigade, Department of Virginia and North Carolina (December 1862-March 1863). He led his men at Williamsburg, Seven Pines, the Seven Days, and 2nd Bull Run. At Antietam he succeeded to division command. Apparently having displeased both Lee and Longstreet, he was sent to southern Virginia and his brigade was divided up. With Longstreet sent to command in this area later, the process was repeated in March with Pryor's new command being broken up. In disgust, he resigned and served after that as a special courier with the cavalry until captured on November 27, 1864, near Petersburg. Not released until near the war's close, he moved to New York as a journalist and lawyer, eventually becoming a judge. (Holzman, Robert, *Adapt or Perish, The Life of General Roger Pryor, C.S.A.*)

PUGH, Isaac C. (ca. 1822-1874)

When he protested against a further advance, Isaac C. Pugh was ordered ahead by his division commander, General Jacob G. Lauman. The results were casualties of more than half those engaged and the relief of the division leader. An Illinois lawyer, Pugh had served as a captain of Illinois troops in the Mexican War and entered the Union army at the same rank in 1861. His assignments included: captain, 8th Illinois (April 25, 1861); colonel, 41st Illinois (August 5, 1861); commanding 1st Brigade, 4th Division, Army of the Tennessee (April 6, 1862); commanding 1st Brigade, 4th Division, Right Wing, 13th Corps, Army of the Tennessee (November 1-December 18, 1862); commanding 1st Brigade, 4th Division, 17th Corps, Army of the Tennessee (December 18, 1862-January 20, 1863 and August 7-October 24, 1863); commanding 1st Brigade, 4th Division, 16th Corps, Army of the Tennessee (January 20-July 28, 1863); commanding 1st Brigade, 4th Division, 13th Corps, Army of the Tennessee (July 28-August 7, 1863); and commanding 2nd Brigade, 4th Division, 17th Corps, Army of the Tennessee (July 5-19, 1864). He commanded his regiment at Fort Heiman—opposite Fort Henry—and Fort Donelson and commanded a brigade at Shiloh when its commander was wounded. He served in the siege of Vicksburg and it was in the subsequent drive on Jackson that his command made its futile attack. His final service came in the Atlanta Campaign. He was mustered out on August 20, 1864, and the next March he was brevetted a brigadier.

Q

QUANTRILL, Mary S. (?-?)

The myth of Barbara Fritchie's having flaunted a Union flag in the face of Stonewall Jackson and his men finds a basis in fact in the actions of Mrs. Mary S. Quantrill. A resident of Frederick, Maryland, and a relative of the noted Missouri bushwhacker William C. Quantrill, she, in fact, with her daughter waved several flags at the passing Confederates on September 6, 1862, during the Antietam Campaign. But the credit went instead, in John G. Whittier's poem, to Barbara Fritchie who only waved her flag at Union troops several days later.

QUANTRILL, William Clarke (1837-1865)

While there are other contenders for the title of "The Bloodiest Man in American History"—Civil War leaders "Bloody Bill" Anderson and John M. Chivington quickly come to mind—William C. Quantrill earned his share of the sobriquet for his depredations in the Trans-Mississippi area. An Ohio native, he had earned a prewar reputation as an outlaw while living under the name of Charley Hart in Kansas. After some regular service at Wilson Creek he became a guerrilla leader and was soon branded an outlaw by the Union authorities. His band attracted some of the most notorious names in Missouri's Civil War, and Wild West, history—including Anderson, the Youngers, and Frank James. Officially made a captain in the Confederate army, he claimed a shadowy commission as colonel. In August 1862 he took Independence, but his most famous exploit came the next year when he returned to Lawrence, Kansas, destroying much of the community and killing all the male inhabitants he could find—about 150, young and old. In 1864 his command broke up when he quarreled with his principal lieutenants, but he soon organized another, smaller group, which now included Jesse James, and moved his operations to Kentucky. He continued his pillaging, which most Rebel leaders considered counterproductive, until May 10, 1865, when he was paralyzed by a Union bullet at Bloomfield. He died a prisoner on June 6. (Castel, Albert E., *William Clarke Quantrill: His Life and Times*)

QUARLES, William Andrew (1825-1893)

Captured for the second time at Franklin, William A. Quarles ended his career as a Confederate brigadier general. The Virginia-born Tennessee lawyer and judge had also been involved in politics, railroading, and banking before the outbreak of sectional warfare. His Confederate assignments included: colonel, 42nd Tennessee (November 28, 1861); brigadier general, CSA (August 25, 1863); commanding brigade, Department of the Gulf (fall 1863); commanding brigade, Breckinridge's Division, Breckinridge's-Hindman's Corps, Army of Tennessee (December 1863-early 1864); commanding brigade, Department of Mississippi and East Louisiana (early 1864); commanding brigade, District of the Gulf (April 6-May 1864); and commanding brigade, Cantey's-Walthall's Division, Polk's (Army of Mississippi)-Stewart's Corps, Army of Tennessee (May-November 30, 1864). Leading his regiment, he was taken prisoner at Fort Donelson. Exchanged on September 21, 1862, he for a time commanded a consolidated regiment composed of the remnants of five Tennessee regiments and a battalion which had been captured at Fort Donelson. With this unit he served at Port Hudson. Promoted to brigadier general, he led a brigade through the Atlanta Campaign and then embarked on Hood's ill-fated invasion of middle Tennessee. Wounded at Franklin, he was taken prisoner and not released until May 25, 1865. Thereafter he practiced law and later sat in the state legislature.

QUINBY, Isaac Ferdinand (1821-1891)

With the outbreak of the Civil War, Isaac F. Quinby gave up his professorship at the University of Rochester, New York, to return to the military. The New Jersey native had taught at West Point following his 1843 graduation. In 1852, following some frontier duty, he resigned as a first lieutenant of artillery and joined the New York faculty. His Civil War assignments included: colonel, 13th New York (May 14, 1861); brigadier general, USV (March 17, 1862); commanding 6th Division, Army of the Tennessee (mid-1862); commanding District of Corinth, Army of the Tennessee (mid-1862); commanding District of the Mississippi, Army of the Tennessee (ca. May-September 24, 1862); commanding 4th Division, Army of the Tennessee (September 24-29, 1862); commanding 3rd Division, Army of the Mississippi (October 26-November 2, 1862); commanding District of Corinth, 13th Corps, Army of the Tennessee (October 30-November 11, 1862); commanding 7th Division, Left Wing, 13th Corps, Army of the Tennessee (November 1-December 18, 1862); commanding 7th Division, Left Wing, 16th Corps, Army of the Tennessee (December 22, 1862-January 20, 1863); commanding 7th Division, 17th Corps, Army of the Tennessee (January 20-April 14 and May 16-June 3, 1863); and provost marshal, 28th District of New York (1865). He served under Sherman in the defeat at 1st Bull Run and resigned from the command of his regiment on August 4, 1861, in order to return to his academic pursuits. The next March he was appointed a brigadier of volunteers and sent to the western theater. There he was involved in the operations against Corinth, Mississippi, and later in the attempt to reach Vicksburg via the Yazoo Pass. In the eventually successful campaign against the river city, he fought off illness to fight at Champion Hill and Big Black River Bridge. He also participated in the doomed assaults against Vicksburg itself in May 1863 but early the next month was forced to relinquish his command. Resigning on December 31, 1863, he returned to his classroom but did serve in enforcing the draft in New York in the latter stages of the war. During Grant's two presidential terms he was a U.S. marshal in New York.

QUINTARD, Charles Todd (1824-1898)

Despite his Northern birth, Charles T. Quintard became one of the more popular of Confederate regimental chaplains. A native of Connecticut, he had studied law in New York and taken up practice in Georgia. In the 1850s he became a medical professor in Tennessee where he eventually joined the ministry as an Episcopalian rector. His long residence in the South affected his political views and in 1861 he was appointed the chaplain of the 1st Tennessee. As such he was present at Cheat Mountain, Perryville, Murfreesboro, Chickamauga, Chattanooga, the Atlanta Campaign, and Franklin and Nashville. During much of his service he also doubled as a regimental surgeon, for which the men were highly grateful. Settling in Nashville after the war, he became the second bishop of the state and helped refound the University of the South. (Noll, Arthur Howard, *Doctor Quintard*)

QUINTERO, Juan (?-?)

Juan Quintero was a native of Havana, Cuba, and served the Confederacy well as a diplomat to its Southern neighbor, Mexico. A U.S. citizen since 1853, he had been a lawyer, apparently in New Orleans. Offering his services to the Confederate government, he was dispatched to Mexico where he befriended the Vidaurri government and ensured the neutrality of Juarez in the American Civil War. He was also involved in the smuggling of cotton southwards, out of the Confederacy. He was a government official in Texas after the war.

R

RAINS, Gabriel James (1803-1881)

A tinkerer at heart rather than a field commander, Gabriel J. Rains was involved in a line of war work that raised grave questions about the ethical conduct of military operations among his fellow Confederates—as well as the enemy. Graduating in 1827 from West Point, he had risen to the rank of lieutenant colonel, 5th Infantry, by the time his native North Carolina withdrew from the Union. Pre-secession he had been wounded while fighting Seminoles near Fort King, Florida, and had gained a reputation for experimenting with explosives. Resigning on July 31, 1861, he entered the Southern army and his assignments included: brigadier general, CSA (September 23, 1861); commanding division, Department of the Peninsula (October 3, 1861-April 12, 1862); and commanding brigade, D.H. Hill's Division, Army of Northern Virginia (April 12-June 16, 1862). Following long service in the defenses of Yorktown, his forces were merged into D.H. Hill's Division. He fought at Williamsburg but was roundly criticized by Hill for his failures in the fighting at Seven Pines on May 31. On June 18, Rains was removed from field duty and received an appointment better fitted to his capabilities. He was to direct the submarine defenses of the James and Appomattox Rivers. His use of hidden explosive devices caused a debate within the Confederate hierarchy, and in December 1862 he was assigned as chief of the Bureau of Conscription. But from May 25, 1863, he was back at work, placing his weapons around Richmond, Mobile, and Charleston. After the war he briefly held a government clerkship. (Freeman, Douglas S., *Lee's Lieutenants*)

RAINS, George Washington (1817-1898)

The brother of the Confederate general—Gabriel J. Rains—who was so deeply involved in the development of mine warfare, George W. Rains rose to the rank of colonel in the ordnance department while in charge of the powder works at Augusta, Georgia. The North Carolinian had received his West Point appointment from Alabama. Upon his 1842 graduation, he was posted to the engineers but the next year transferred to the artillery. He won two brevets in Mexico and then fought the Seminoles in Florida. Resigning as a captain in the 4th Artillery in 1856, he spent the next five years in the iron business in New York. Joining the Confederacy, his assignments included: major, Artillery (July 10, 1861); lieutenant colonel, Artillery (May 22, 1862); and colonel, Artillery (July 12, 1863). Working under Josiah Gorgas, he was assigned to the Augusta works and was responsible for providing the Confederate armies with some 2,750,000 pounds of gunpowder. In addition he was in charge of the post there until it was threatened by Sherman's Union forces. During the war he published a manual entitled *Notes on Making Saltpetre from the Earth of the Caves*. Following the war he engaged in business in New York and was a college professor. He also authored *History of the Confederate States Powder Works*.

RAINS, James Edwards (1833-1862)

Tennessee lawyer, journalist, and district attorney, James E. Rains gave his life for the Confederacy—a brigadier general for less than two months. His Confederate assignments included: captain, Company A, 11th Tennessee (May 2, 1861); colonel, 11th Tennessee (May 10, 1861); commanding Cumberland Gap, District of East Tennessee, Department #2 (January-ca. March 1862); commanding 2nd Brigade, 1st (Stevenson's) Division, Department of East Tennessee (ca. March-June and July-December 1862); brigadier general, CSA (November 4, 1862); and commanding 2nd Brigade, McCown's Division (detached from Department of East Tennessee), Hardee's Corps, Army of Tennessee (December-December 31, 1862). Originally the head of the Hermitage Guards, he rose to regimental command and was stationed in East Tennessee. For a time he commanded at Cumberland Gap and then took part in driving the Union forces under George W. Morgan from the region during the Kentucky Campaign. Rewarded with promotion to brigadier general, he commanded a brigade at Murfreesboro and led his men on the extreme Confederate left during the initial assaults on the first day of the battle—the last day of the year. In these attacks he was killed.

RAINS, James S. (?-?)

An active politician before the war, James S. Rains was made a brigadier general in the Missouri State Guard at the beginning of the Civil War but appears to have preferred to remain in state service when most of his command was enlisted in the Confederate army. At Dug Springs he commanded the Guard's 8th Division. Commanding the 2nd Division, he fought at Wilson's Creek before resuming command of his own division in the actions at Lexington and Pea Ridge. Returning to Missouri when most of his command was absorbed into the Confederate army, he remained active in recruiting for the Southern army and commanded small forces when General Price invaded Missouri in 1864.

RALLINGS, George (fl. 1863)

A bloody chapter in the history of New York City—the Draft Riots—would have been even more bloody if it had not been for the actions of George Rallings. A city police officer, he got wind of the mob's plan on the first day of the disorders—July 13, 1863—to sack the Negro Orphanage located at Fifth Avenue and 43rd Street. Racing to the scene, he was able to evacuate about 260 children of ex-slaves. As a result of his actions only one little girl was killed by a blow from an axe. The building itself was burned to the ground.

George Rallings, hero of the draft riots, saved many black children who otherwise would have suffered the fate of this freedman. (AC)

RAMSAY, George Douglas (1802-1882)

Although he had entered the military during the War of 1812, George Ramsay proved to be one of the more modern officers in the very conservative Ordnance Department. Graduating from West Point in 1820, Ramsay had served in the artillery until transferred to the Ordnance Department in 1835 as a captain. He still held this position at the time of the firing on Fort Sumter. His later promotions in the department were: major (April 22, 1861); lieutenant colonel (August 3, 1861); colonel (June 1, 1863); and brigadier general, USA (September 15, 1863). During the early part of the war he was in charge of the Washington Arsenal and later was responsible for artillery ordnance operations. On September 15, 1863, he was named chief of Ordnance in place of the unimaginative General J.W. Ripley. During his year in this position Ramsay almost doubled the number of breech-loading rifles purchased for the army and introduced some 33,652 repeating rifles and carbines. He retired on September 12, 1864. After his retirement he was an inspector of arsenals. He was brevetted major general in the regulars near the close of the war.

RAMSEUR, Stephen Dodson (1837-1864)

Three days after receiving word that he was a father, West Pointer (1860) Stephen D. Ramseur was mortally wounded; he died surrounded by former fellow cadets from the other side. He had served less than a year in the artillery when he resigned on April 6, 1861, to aid the South. His assignments included: first lieutenant, Artillery (to rank from March 16, 1861); captain, Battery A, 1st North Carolina Artillery (April 16, 1861); major, 1st North Carolina Artillery (May 8, 1861); colonel, 49th North Carolina (April 12, 1862); brigadier general, CSA (November 1, 1862); commanding G.B. Anderson's (old) Brigade, Rodes' Division, 2nd Corps, Army of Northern Virginia (April 1863-June 4, 1864); commanding the division (May 2, 1863); also commanding Iverson's (old) Brigade (July 1-September 8, 1863); major general, CSA (June 1, 1864); commanding Early's (old) Division, same corps and army (June 4-13, 1864); commanding same division, Valley District, Department of Northern Virginia (June 13-September 20, 1864); and commanding Rodes' (old) Division, same district and department (September 20-October 19, 1864). After serving in the artillery in North Carolina and on the Peninsula, he was elected to command an infantry regiment. Leading his men he fell wounded at Malvern Hill, the last of the Seven Days Battles. During his long recovery, he was promoted and assigned to command a brigade in the fall of 1862. Taking up his assignment the next spring, he distinguished himself in a charge on May 3 at Chancellorsville. Wounded in the battle he remained on duty. At Gettysburg he led the brigade and that of Iverson, after that general suffered a breakdown on the first day. During a leave that fall, he was married. During the battle of the Wilderness, his brigade was not engaged but at Spotsylvania it played a leading role in plugging the holes in the Southern lines on May 12. Three weeks later he was rewarded with promotion to major general and command of Early's Division. Taking charge at Cold Harbor, he then went on the raid through the Shenandoah Valley to Monocacy and the outskirts of Washington. Retiring into the Valley, his division was routed on July 20 in a small action at Winchester. He was severely censured for his failures in the independent action. He went on to fight at 3rd Winchester and was then transferred to the division of the deceased General Rodes. He fought at Fisher's Hill and in the early defeat of two Union corps at Cedar Creek. In the Union counterattack he fell mortally wounded. Visited by friends from the military academy still in the old service, he died the next day in the hands of the enemy. (Freeman, Douglas S., *Lee's Lieutenants*)

RAMSEY, Alexander (1815-1903)

The first territorial governor of Minnesota and a defeated candidate for governor in 1857, Alexander Ramsey won his second bid in 1859. A Pennsylvania native, he had practiced law and represented that state in Congress from 1843 to 1847, before being named Minnesota's territorial governor by President Zachary Taylor in 1849. Leaving that post in 1853, he was mayor of St. Paul two years later. The Whig-turned-Republican lost a bid for the governorship in 1857 but won two years later. Sworn in on January 2, 1860, he tried to reduce the scope of the state and local governments, but this had to be halted due to the Civil War. The first state head to offer Washington troops, he was active in recruitment. Having been named to the Senate, he resigned the gubernatorial chair on July 10, 1863. He served until 1875. From 1879 to 1881 he was Hayes' secretary of war and later served on the Edmunds Commission dealing with the Mormon problem in Utah. Retiring in 1886, he later served two stints as president of the state historical society. (Baker, James H., *Lives of the Governors of Minnesota*)

RANDAL, Horace (1831-1864)

Horace Randal, one of E. Kirby Smith's extralegal appointees as a general, did not live long enough to find out if Richmond would approve of Smith's action. Graduating from West Point in 1854, he had served in both the infantry and the dragoons before resigning his second lieutenant's commission on February 27, 1861. Offering his services to the Confederacy he was soon commissioned colonel, 28th Texas Cavalry. When this regiment reached Arkansas it was dismounted and served the entire war as infantry. His entire service being in the Trans-Mississippi Department, he held the following commands: brigade, District of West Louisiana (spring-fall 1863); brigade, Walker's Division, District of West Louisiana (early 1864); and a brigade, Walker's Division, District of Arkansas (April 1864). Serving in Louisiana, he fought at Milliken's Bend during the Vicksburg Campaign and at Mansfield in the Red River Campaign. For the latter action, General Smith promoted him to brigadier general on April 13, 1864, to rank from the day of the battle. A November 1863 request to Jefferson Davis for Randal's promotion had received no action, so Smith acted on his own, claiming his distance from the government required this unorthodox action. On April 30, 1864, Randal was mortally wounded in the battle of Jenkins' Ferry, Arkansas, in the action against Union General Steele's expedition.

RANDALL, Alexander Williams (1819-1872)

An early abolitionist, Alexander W. Randall was Wisconsin's loyal governor during the first part of the Civil War but had his hopes for a generalship dashed by the Lincoln administration. A New Yorker by birth, he had briefly practiced law there before moving his practice to Wisconsin in 1840. His political career spanned several offices and parties. He began as a Whig, became a Democrat in Wisconsin, joined the Free-Soil party in support of Martin Van Buren, sat in the state legislature as an independent Democrat, and finally found a home with the Republicans. He served as a postmaster, district attorney, and was an unsuccessful candidate for attorney general. At the time of his first gubernatorial triumph in 1857, he was serving as a judge. Sworn in the next year, he rooted out corruption at home and condemned the morality of slavery. Assuming the Southern states would secede, he called for military preparedness and favored the severe chastisement of the Rebels. Following Fort Sumter's fall, Wisconsin was called upon for one regiment of volunteers. Randall promptly forwarded four. He continued to furnish troops until his second term expired in early 1862. Instead of his hoped-for general's star he was sent to the Vatican as U.S. minister. Returning within a year, his military ambitions were again denied by his appointment as assistant postmaster general. Under Andrew Johnson, he became postmaster general and remained in office until 1869 when—with anti-Johnson sentiment high in his adopted state—he returned to New York and the legal profession.

RANDALL, James Ryder (1839-1908)

The first clash of arms—between Massachusetts troops and pro-Southern citizens of Baltimore—of the Civil War in Maryland resulted in James R. Randall writing the memorable lyrics for "Maryland, My Maryland." The resident of that city, then a college professor in Louisiana, was mourning the death of a former classmate in the melee. Believing the South the aggrieved party, he tried to enlist in the army but was turned down for medical reasons. Meanwhile his poem gained popularity after his reading of it before his English class and its publication in the *New Orleans Delta*. The Cary sisters further popularized it by putting it to the tune "Lauriger Horatius." But it achieved its immortality when it was put to the music of "Tannenbaum, O Tannenbaum." Following the battle of Antietam and the failure of the campaign in western Maryland—where Southern sentiment was weak—many Confederate soldiers did not want to hear the song again. After the war Randall was active in journalism and continued to write poetry. (Andrews, M.P., *The Poems of James Ryder Randall*)

RANDOLPH, George Wythe (1818-1867)

Tuberculosis deprived the Confederacy of the services of Virginia lawyer George W. Randolph who had served it as a general and cabinet officer early in the Civil War. The Virginia native had served six years at sea by the time he was 19 and two years later resigned as a midshipman to enter upon the practice of law. He was engaged in this profession in Richmond when John Brown's Harpers Ferry raid occurred. As a response he founded the Richmond Howitzers which were absorbed into the Confederate army shortly after Virginia formed its military bonds with the Confederacy. His assignments included: major, Richmond Howitzers (spring 1861); colonel, 1st Virginia Artillery (September 1861); commanding Artillery, Department of the Peninsula (fall 1861-early 1862); and brigadier general, CSA (February 12, 1862). Two companies from his three-company battalion joined John B. Magruder and fought at Big Bethel in one of the earliest actions of the war. As colonel of an artillery regiment, he continued to serve on the Peninsula and took command of that arm under Magruder. Promoted to brigadier general in February 1862, he was named secretary of war the next month, on March 18, 1862. He served in this position only until November 15, 1862, and then with his illness diagnosed he set off for France in a doomed attempt to regain his health. While still overseas, he resigned his general's commission on December 18, 1864; he returned to his native state shortly after the fall of the Confederacy. He died less than two years after Appomattox.

RANSOM, Matthew Whitaker (1826-1904)

When his younger brother Robert was promoted to other duties, Matthew W. Ransom, a lawyer and state legislator in his native North Carolina, was made a brigadier to succeed him. Before the secession of the state Ransom had served as a commissioner to the fledgling Confederacy. Entering the army as a private early in the war, his later assignments included: lieutenant colonel, 1st North Carolina State Troops (May 16, 1861); colonel, 35th North Carolina (April 21, 1862); brigadier general, CSA (June 13, 1863); commanding R. Ransom's Brigade, Department of North Carolina (June-July and October 1863-May 1864); commanding brigade, R. Ransom's Division, Department of Richmond (July-September 1863); commanding brigade, Colquitt's Division, Department of North Carolina and Southern Virginia (mid-1864); commanding brigade, Johnson's Division, Anderson's Corps, Army of Northern Virginia (October-December 1864 and February-April 9, 1865). Sent to join Lee's army on the Peninsula, the elder Ransom was twice wounded at Malvern Hill during the Seven Days. He returned to command the regiment at Antietam before being transferred back to North Carolina. During the course of the next year he fought at Plymouth and Weldon and at Suffolk in southeastern Virginia and rose to brigade level. In May of 1864 he was wounded during the fighting at Drewry's Bluff and did not rejoin his unit until his command had been absorbed into Lee's army. He served through parts of the Petersburg siege and surrendered at Appomattox at the head of a unit shattered at Five Forks and Sayler's Creek. Law, politics, and farming filled his later years. (Freeman, Douglas S., *Lee's Lieutenants*)

Confederate brigade commander Matthew W. Ransom. (NA)

RANSOM, Robert, Jr. (1828-1892)

The younger brother of M.W. Ransom, Robert Ransom, Jr., rose one grade higher in the Confederate service until felled by illness. The North Carolinian was a West Pointer (1850) and veteran of a decade in the mounted service when he resigned from the Old Army on January 31, 1861. His Southern assignments included: captain, Cavalry (spring 1861); colonel, 1st North Carolina Cavalry (October 13, 1861); brigadier general, CSA (March 1, 1862); commanding brigade, Department of North Carolina (April-July 1862); commanding brigade, Walker's-Ransom's Division, 1st Corps, Army of Northern Virginia (August 1862-January 3, 1863); also commanding the division (November 7, 1862-January 3, 1863); commanding brigade, Department of Virginia and North Carolina (January-April 1, 1863); commanding brigade, Department of North Carolina (April 1-May 1863); major general, CSA (May 26, 1863); commanding division, Department of Richmond (July 1863); commanding division, Department of West Virginia and East Tennessee (October 1863-January 1864); temporarily commanding the department (January 1864); commanding Cavalry, Department of East Tennessee (March-April 1864); commanding Department of Richmond (April 25-June 13, 1864); and commanding Cavalry Division, Valley District, Department of Northern Virginia (June-August 10, 1864). Serving with his cavalry regiment in Northern Virginia, he commanded the forces in the skirmish at Vienna on November 26, 1861, before being returned to North Carolina. Soon promoted to brigadier he fought at the Seven

Days attached to Huger's Division although his brigade properly belonged to Holmes'. In the Maryland invasion, he led his North Carolinians at the capture of Harpers Ferry and in the action at Antietam. In the victory at Fredericksburg he commanded the division on Marye's Heights. The next month his command was sent back to North Carolina and he was soon promoted. He then performed duty at Richmond and in western Virginia and East Tennessee. Returning to Richmond, he led a field division under Beauregard in the defense at Drewry's Bluff in May 1864. Sent to command the cavalry in the Valley, he participated in the raid on Washington, including action at Monocacy. Too ill for active duty, he was relieved on August 10, 1864. After military court duty and the end of the war, he became a civil engineer. (Freeman, Douglas S., *Lee's Lieutenants*)

RANSOM, Thomas Edward Greenfield (1834-1864)

The cumulative impact of four wounds, without proper recovery time, was fatal to a promising young officer, Thomas E.G. Ransom. Born in Vermont, the son of an officer killed in Mexico, he had settled in Illinois where he worked as an engineer and in the real estate business. Enlisting in the Union army, his assignments included: captain, 11th Illinois (April 24, 1861); major, 11th Illinois (June 4, 1861); lieutenant colonel, 11th Illinois (July 30, 1861); colonel, 11th Illinois (February 15, 1862); commanding 2nd Brigade, 6th Division, Left Wing, 16th Corps, Army of the Tennessee (December 22, 1862-January 20, 1863); commanding 2nd Brigade, 6th Division, 17th Corps, Army of the Tennessee (January 20-September 14, 1863); brigadier general, USV (April 15, 1863, to rank from November 29, 1862); commanding 3rd Brigade, 2nd Division, 13th Corps, Department of the Gulf (December 3, 1863-January 4, 1864); commanding 4th Division, 13th Corps, Department of the Gulf (January 4-March 15, 1864); commanding the corps (March 15-April 8, 1864); commanding 4th Division, 16th Corps, Army of the Tennessee (August 4-19, 1864); commanding Left Wing, 16th Corps, Army of the Tennessee (August 19-September 23, 1864); commanding 1st Division, 17th Corps, Army of the Tennessee (September 22, 1864); and commanding the corps (September 22-October 10, 1864). He suffered his first wound in an August 1861 fight at Charlestown, Missouri, but refused to leave the field. The story was similar at Fort Donelson where he returned to duty only hours after he had been hit. As in the previous battle he was commanding the regiment at Shiloh when he was struck a third time. During the advance on Corinth, he was chief of staff to John A. McClernand and later commanded a brigade in the Vicksburg Campaign. Transferred to the Department of the Gulf, he took part in operations along the Texas coast before entering upon the Red River Campaign. At Sabine Crossroads a leg wound forced him from the field while in command of the 13th Corps. Joining Sherman's forces operating against Atlanta upon his recovery, he took part in the siege of the city and particularly distinguished himself at Jonesboro, for which he was posthumously brevetted major general. He was assigned to the forces sent to pursue Hood's army into Alabama and while returning to Sherman he was forced to relinquish command of the 17th Corps. On October 29, 1864, he died at Rome in northern Georgia.

Union division commander Thomas E.G. Ransom. (*Leslie's*)

RATH, Christian (?-?)

Something of a soldier of fortune, Christian Rath was assigned to the arsenal prison as hangman even before the trial of the Lincoln conspirators was concluded. He had served as a captain in the 17th Michigan during the war and had been recommended for services before Petersburg in 1864 and 1865. He soon set to work making everything ready and by July 7, 1865, he was prepared. Rath himself tied the knots on the four ropes with seven for each of the men and only five on that of Mary Surratt. The captain also put the hoods over the victims' heads and made sure the ropes were in the correct position. His work had been thoroughly done since it was apparently a "clean" hanging.

RATHBONE, Henry Reed (?-1911)

It was the cry of "Stop that man!" shouted by the wounded Henry R. Rathbone that alerted the audience in Ford's Theater that the shot they had heard was not a part of the play. The New York native had been commissioned directly into the regular army when it was expanded early in the Civil War. His assignments included: captain, 12th Infantry (May 14, 1861); and major and assistant adjutant general, USV (March 13, 1865). At Antietam he was an acting field officer and at Fredericksburg led his regiment's Company C. He was brevetted for the Overland Campaign. Similar rewards came for his service in the provost marshal's office and, as colonel, for

Henry R. Rathbone, companion of Lincoln at Ford's Theater. (NA)

recruiting duty. Stationed on administrative duties in Washington in 1865 he was asked by Lincoln to bring his fiancée Clara Harris and accompany the first couple to the theater in place of several cancelations. When John Wilkes Booth burst into the presidential box and shot Lincoln, Rathbone lunged for him but received a severe slash across his forearm. He still shouted his alert and was able to free the obstruction of the door to admit Dr. Charles A. Leale. He resigned his volunteer commission on July 8, 1867, but remained in the army until the end of 1870 when he was honorably discharged at his own request as an unassigned major. Having married Clara Harris, he moved to Germany where he went insane and murdered her. He lived out his life in an asylum.

RAUM, Green Berry (1829-1909)

By the time that Illinois lawyer Green B. Raum received his commission as a Union brigadier general of volunteers he had already given up active field command. As a Douglas Democrat, he had attended the national convention as an alternate and then enlisted in the army during the same month as the firing on Fort Sumter. His assignments included: major, 56th Illinois (September 28, 1861); lieutenant colonel, 56th Illinois (June 26, 1862); colonel, 56th Illinois (August 31, 1862); commanding 2nd Brigade, 7th Division, 17th Corps, Army of the Tennessee (June 10-August 12, 1863); commanding 2nd Brigade, 2nd Division, 17th Corps, Army of the Tennessee (October 2-November 25, 1863); commanding 2nd Brigade, 3rd Division, 15th Corps, Army of the Tennessee (February 10, 1864-January 29, 1865); and brigadier general, USV (February 15, 1865). While he was serving as a field officer the regiment fought during the advance on Corinth, Mississippi, and during the battle there a few months later he was in charge of the unit. He took part in the central Mississippi campaign of Grant against Vicksburg and during the Vicksburg siege he took over the brigade. At Chattanooga he was severely wounded while leading his brigade in the charge up Missionary Ridge. Returning to field duty early the next year, his brigade was left behind during the Atlanta Campaign in order to secure Sherman's communications. However, he did take part in the March to the Sea. On January 29, 1865, he went on leave and never joined the army in the field again. Apparently he was involved in Winfield S. Hancock's fruitless efforts to recruit the Veteran Volunteer Corps in the final stages of the war, having been promoted to brigadier general in February 1865. Resigning on May 6, 1865, he became involved in railroading, sat in Congress as a Republican, was commissioner of internal revenue, practiced law, and was commissioner of the Pension Bureau. Criticized for possible corruption in the latter post, he returned to Illinois and the practice of law in Chicago.

RAWLINS, John Aaron (1831-1869)

Described by Grant as "most nearly indispensable," John A. Rawlins served his chief throughout the Civil War and until his death. Many claimed that his role was to prevent Grant from drinking too much. A lawyer in Grant's prewar home of Galena, Illinois, Rawlins was a Douglas Democrat in the 1860 election but strongly supported the war when it came. When Grant was promoted to a brigadiership Rawlins was asked to serve as a lieutenant and aide-de-camp; this was soon raised to captain and assistant adjutant general. His military assignments included: captain and assistant adjutant general, USV (August 30, 1861); major and assistant adjutant general, USV (May 14, 1862); lieutenant colonel and assistant adjutant general, USV (November 1, 1862); brigadier general, USV (August 11, 1863); brigadier general and chief of staff, USA (March 3, 1865); and secretary of war (March 11-September 6, 1869). Joining Grant's headquarters on September 14, 1861, he fought at Belmont, Forts Henry and Donelson, Shiloh, and in the long campaigns against Vicksburg. When Grant was given overall command in the West, Rawlins went to Chattanooga; Grant's next promotion took his staff chief to Virginia and the Overland, Petersburg, and Appomattox campaigns. Near the end of the war a new office was created for Rawlins, that of brigadier and chief of staff to the commander-in-chief. This was the last regular army brigadier's star awarded during the war. How much of Rawlins' service was mere staff work, military advice, or the self-appointed duty against alcohol has been a matter of debate for decades. When Grant became president, Rawlins resigned from the army to become secretary of war but died six months later of tuberculosis. (McFeely, WIlliam S., *Grant: A Biography* and Wilson, James Harrison, *The Life of John A. Rawlins*)

READ, Charles William (1840-1892)

Having earned the sobriquet of "Savez" for the one word of French he had mastered on his way to graduating at the bottom of the 1860 class at Annapolis, no one would have thought that the Mississippian Charles W. Read would develop into one of the Civil War's more daring naval commanders. Joining the Southern forces in 1861, he was assigned to duty in August, assisting in the construction of batteries along the Potomac River near Quantico Creek. Following this service he was transferred to the West and with the rank of lieutenant served as the executive officer aboard the *McRae*, part of Commander George N. Hollins' fleet on the upper Mississippi, where he participated in operations around Island #10. Moving downriver, the fleet made a poor showing in the naval actions below New Orleans. One of the few exceptions was the behavior of Lieutenant Read who took command of the *McRae* when her commander, Lieutenant Thomas B. Huger, was mortally wounded. Involved in the preparation of the ram CSS *Arkansas*, Read served as a lieutenant aboard her during her summer of spreading consternation among the Union's Mississippi fleet. However, faulty engines caused her to break down on the way to join the Confederate land attack on Baton Rouge. Shortly thereafter she was destroyed by her crew when attacked. Next serving aboard the commerce raider CSS. *Florida*, from November 4, 1862, Read suggested in May 1863 that the captured brig *Clarence* be converted into a raider as well and he himself placed in command. His request granted, he found his new command sluggish and spent the next few weeks in fruitless search of prey. Then on June 6 he secured his first prize and his luck turned and he captured several more vessels. On June 12 Read transferred his crew aboard the *Tacony*, one of three vessels taken that day. The *Clarence* was burned. His new command made its first capture that very afternoon and his subsequent cruise, capturing 14 more vessels, led to a massive search by the Union navy. But Read burned the *Tacony* on June 25 and took over the captured *Archer*. The next night the *Archer* entered the harbor at Portland, Maine, in an effort to seize the revenue cutter *Caleb Cushing*. However, the cutter's new commander, arriving to assume command, reported the unexpected sailing of his vessel and soon a scratch fleet was in pursuit of the Confederates. After running out of ammunition Read abandoned the vessel and he and his men became prisoners. After 16 months of imprisonment, Read was exchanged. Made a lieutenant commander, Read took part in one more adventure, the attempted escape of the ram *Webb* from the Red River to the Gulf of Mexico as a cruiser. The effort was made following Lee's surrender and Read was forced to run his vessel ashore below New Orleans where he was captured. After the war he was a harbor master in New Orleans. (Read, Charles W., "Reminiscences of the C.S. Navy," *Southern Historical Society Papers*, Vol. I. No. 5. May 1876)

READ, Theodore (?-1865)

With only a few days to go in the life of Lee's Army of Northern Virginia, Union Brevet Brigadier General Theodore Read gave his life in pursuit of it. Born in Ohio, he had entered the Union army from Illinois and his assignments included: captain and assistant adjutant general, USV (October 24, 1861); major and assistant adjutant general, USV (July 25, 1864); and lieutenant colonel and assistant adjutant general (February 17-April 6, 1865). Having served in staff positions throughout the war, he had suffered several wounds and had lost an arm. On September 29, 1864, he was brevetted brigadier general for gallantry before the enemy. During the Appomattox Campaign, he was an adjutant on the staff of the commander of the Army of the James, Edward O.C. Ord. In an attempt to burn one of Lee's escape routes, High Bridge, on April 6, 1865, he took command of a small mounted detachment. In the ensuing cavalry skirmish Read fell with a fatal wound. Some reports indicate that it was at the hands of Confederate General James Dearing, who also died in the encounter.

READE, Edwin Godwin (1812-1894)

A former Know-Nothing congressman and Unionist, Edwin G. Reade was appointed by Governor Zebulon Vance to complete the Confederate Senate term of the resigned George Davis. He quickly became identified with the growing North Carolina peace movement. A native North Carolina lawyer, he had served only one term in the U.S. legislature where his most notable act was to be the only Southerner to vote for the censure of Congressman Lawrence M. Keitt in the Brooks-Sumner beatings. In 1861 Reade turned down both a Lincoln offer of a cabinet position and a seat at the state secession convention. Elected to a judgeship, he was named to the Senate on January 22, 1864, before he could be sworn into the judicial post. He was soon threatening separate peace negotiations on the part of his state and was a thorn in the Davis administration's side. As a peace candidate, he was defeated for reelection and so retired to private practice. During Reconstruction he supported Andrew Johnson and chaired the convention held at the end of the war. As a Republican, he sat on the state supreme court until he went into banking. (Hamilton, Joseph Gregoire de Roulhac, *Reconstruction in North Carolina*)

REAGAN, John Henninger (1818-1905)

As the Confederacy's only postmaster general, John Reagan struggled to keep his department functioning in the black as mandated by the constitution. Born in Tennessee, Reagan moved to Texas when 21 and became an Indian fighter, farmer, lawyer, judge, and state legislator. With the secession crisis in Texas, he was a participant in the state convention as a moderate and, giving up his seat in congress which he had held since 1857, was appointed to the Provisional Confederate Congress. Before receiving any committee assignments, he was appointed to the cabinet on March 6, 1861. Realizing the difficulties of the post, he twice turned it down, not wanting to become a martyr, before finally accepting. He had flattered Jefferson Davis by opposing his naming as president, preferring to place Davis in military command. Becoming a close and trusted advisor, he remained with his chief until the final capture. Through a combination of high rates, consolidation of post offices, low pay, and equipment and supplies taken from the

U.S. Post Office, Reagan was able to keep the department running, albeit slowly, without being a drain on the treasury. During the final days of the Confederacy he advised Davis on acceptable peace terms. Captured with Davis in Georgia, Reagan spent several months imprisoned in Boston Harbor during which he wrote his fellow Texans advising compliance with reconstruction. After a period of enmity from his constituents for this, he was elected to the U.S. House of Representatives and later served in the Senate and on the state railroad commission. (Procter, Benjamin H., *Not Without Honor, the Life of John H. Reagan*)

REAM, Vinnie (1847-1914)

Born on the Wisconsin frontier, young Vinnie Ream became the first woman to be commissioned by the U.S. Congress to do a sculpture. Her subject: the martyred Lincoln. Displaying an early talent for music, she had been sent to school in Missouri where her artist abilities also appeared. With the outbreak of the war, Ream's family moved to Washington where her surveyor father became employed as a mapmaker. In order to make ends meet, Vinnie Ream went to work as the first female clerk with the Post Office. Washington's public buildings rekindled her interest in sculpture, and she soon became an assistant to the master sculptor Clark Mills. Becoming an apprentice in 1863, she set her mind on sculpting the president. By December 1864 her wish had come true; Lincoln couldn't resist sitting for a poor struggling sculptress. Following Lincoln's death and a stiff competition for the commission for a life-size, full-length statue in marble, the bill awarding her the $10,000 contract went before the Senate on July 27, 1866. The bill passed after a debate over the granting of such a commission to an unknown who had lobbied so strongly for it. Despite some political difficulties during the Johnson impeachment crisis, Ream completed her work in 1870 and, well received, it was placed in the Capitol's Statuary Hall. She married some years later, and her husband, following Victorian ideas about working women, put an end to her career. In her final years, however, he did relent and she sculpted until her death.

RECTOR, Henry Massey (1816-1899)

A reluctant secessionist, Henry M. Rector was forced out of the Arkansas governorship for his opposition to the central Confederate government. Born in Kentucky, he had relocated to Arkansas where he was, successively, a bank teller, farmer, U.S. marshal, state legislator, and surveyor. He had been admitted to the bar in 1854 and again sat in the legislature before becoming a judge. Inaugurated as governor in 1860, he refused Lincoln's call for 75,000 volunteers and pushed the state toward secession. But he soon came into conflict with the Confederate authorities and began to prevent state troops from leaving the state. When a new state constitution was approved, it effectively eliminated him from office and he resigned on November 4, 1862. A postwar planter, he attended two constitutional conventions but never again held public office.

REDWOOD, Allen Christian (1844-1922)

After a career in the Confederate army—being thrice wounded and twice captured—Allen C. Redwood went on to become one of the premier artists in depicting the Southern soldier, earning the praise of former General Bradley Johnson as "the best drawer of the Confederate soldier who has ever lived." His military service included: private, Middlesex Southrons (July 24, 1861); private, Company C, 55th Virginia (September 1861); detailed to Commissary Department (December 1862); sergeant major, Commissary Department (March 1, 1863); rejoined company (April 1863); and private, Company C, 1st Maryland Cavalry (January 12, 1864). He saw action at Mechanicsville (slightly wounded by a shell), 2nd Bull Run (captured and paroled the next month), Chancellorsville (wounded by a shell), and Gettysburg (wounded in Pickett's Charge). Transferring to the cavalry, he took part in the drive to the outskirts of Washington and in the Valley Campaign of 1864. He later served on the staff of General Lomax as a clerk and courier. While trying to locate a remount in southeastern Virginia he was captured two days before Lee's surrender. Released in July, the Virginia-born, New York-educated veteran converted his prewar art hobby into a career. His concentration was upon the Southern soldier in battle and camp. Many of his realistic works were produced especially for numerous soldiers' reminiscences. His crowning achievement was his illustration of *Battles and Leaders*, originally published serially by the *Century Magazine*. Many of the scenes he sketched were first-hand accounts. He died in North Carolina more than a half century after the war.

REESE, Henry (?-?)

By the time of the siege of Petersburg, Pennsylvania coal miner Henry Reese was a sergeant in the 48th Pennsylvania, a regiment principally made up of coal miners from the Schuylkill region. When the regimental commander, Lieutenant Colonel Henry Pleasants, started digging his 510-foot tunnel under the Confederate works, Reese was made the mine boss. With the shaft completed in late July, the explosion of the four tons of powder was set for the early morning of the 30th. Reese accompanied Pleasants and Lieutenant Jacob Douty into the tunnel and ignited the fuse at about 3:15 A.M. After waiting about an hour, Reese and Douty went back in to see what had gone wrong. Their investigation indicated that the fuse had gone out at a splicing point and Reese went back out of the tunnel on all fours to get a knife to repair the damage. Finally they refired the fuse and raced out just in time to see Elliott's Salient blown up and with it 278 South Carolinians. The Pennsylvanians' efforts came to naught when the attack which was to exploit the advantage was bungled. (Pleasants, Henry, Jr., *The Tragedy of the Crater*)

REID, Hugh Thompson (1811-1874)

The interest of Hugh T. Reid in the recruitment of black troops did not stem from any belief in the equality of the races but rather from the opinion that every black who got shot would be saving a white soldier. The Indiana-born Iowa lawyer, who was

"The Washington Artillery on Marye's Hill Firing Upon the Union Columns Forming for the Assault" by Allen C. Redwood. (*B&L*)

also engaged in railroading, had entered the Union army shortly after the fall of Fort Donelson and his assignments included: colonel, 15th Iowa (February 22, 1862); commanding 3rd Brigade, 6th Division, District of Corinth, Army of the Tennessee (temporarily October 1862); commanding 3rd Brigade, 6th Division, Left Wing, 13th Corps, Army of the Tennessee (November 1-12, 1862); brigadier general, USV (April 9, 1863, to date from March 13); commanding 1st Brigade, 6th Division, 17th Corps, Army of the Tennessee (April 22-August 1, 1863); and commanding District of Cairo, Department of the Tennessee (January 25-March 19, 1864). At Shiloh he was severely wounded but returned to take part in the advance on Corinth, Mississippi. Ill at the beginning of the battle there, he did manage to rejoin his regiment in the later fighting. Before the beginning of the Vicksburg Campaign he was made a brigadier general and led a brigade throughout the siege and at times commanded black troops in Louisiana. After being placed in charge at Cairo, Illinois, and Columbus, Kentucky, he resigned effective April 4, 1864, and returned to railroading.

REID, Whitelaw (1837-1912)

An Ohio journalist, Whitelaw Reid became one of the leading war correspondents of his time. A previous supporter of Frémont, Reid switched his allegiance to Lincoln following the debates with Douglas. During the 1860 election campaign he left his post on the *Zenia News* and took a position on the local Republican campaign staff. After briefly serving with other papers at the beginning of the conflict he went to Washington as war correspondent for the *Cincinnati Gazette*. Signing his field reports as "Agate," he covered the West Virginia Campaign of 1861, Shiloh, and Gettysburg; he also served as Rosecrans' aide and was critical of McClellan's timidity. When not in the field he covered the political infighting at Washington, and in 1863 he became the House of Representatives' librarian. He was one of the first three journalists to enter Richmond after its fall and covered the Lincoln funeral. Following an unsuccessful attempt at cotton planting in the Deep South he returned to journalism. In 1868 he published a state history entitled *Ohio in the War* and then joined the *New York Tribune*, succeeding Greeley four years later. To a large extent he was responsible for that paper's excellent coverage of the Franco-Prussian War. In the latter part of the century he served as a special diplomat and was one of the commissioners to settle the war with Spain. (Cortissoz, Royal, *The Life of Whitelaw Reid*)

REILLY, James William (1828-1905)

Not entering the service until the war was already over a year old, Ohio lawyer and legislator James W. Reilly rose to the rank of brigadier general of volunteers in the Union army. His assignments included: colonel, 104th Ohio (August 30, 1862); commanding 2nd Brigade, 1st Division, 23rd Corps, Department of the Ohio (June 30-July 5, 1863); commanding 1st Brigade, 3rd Division, 23rd Corps, Army of the Ohio (October 21-December 14, 1863, January 6-16, April 3-May 26, May 27-September 22, and October 22-December 14, 1864); commanding the division (March 12-April 3, May 26-27, and September 16-October 21, 1864); brigadier general, USV (July 30, 1864); and commanding 3rd Division, 23rd Corps, Department of North Carolina (February 25-April 7, 1865). His initial service came in Kentucky before he took part in the capture and subsequent siege of Knoxville under Ambrose E. Burnside. During the Atlanta Campaign he succeeded temporarily to division command but most of the time was directing the brigade. He fought at Franklin but was forced to relinquish command the day before the battle of Nashville for some reason. Having been named a brigadier general the previous summer, he took part in the fringe operations of Sherman's march through the Carolinas after the 23rd Corps had been transferred to the coast of North Carolina. Resigning on April 20, 1865, he did not receive the brevet of major general that was commonplace, possibly because the enemy army in North Carolina had not yet surrendered. He then resumed his legal career and entered banking.

REMINGTON, Frederic (1861-1909)

Although his painting career was after the Civil War and he is best known for his works dealing with the American West, Frederic Remington did execute a number of works depicting the sectional conflict. A native of New York he had travelled widely gathering material for his work—even being deported from Russia. But the West was his primary artistic interest. He became known for his action scenes and his ability to faithfully portray man and horse. His characters included Indians, cowboys, and soldiers. He covered the war with Spain but for some of his military works he dug back into recent history to depict the Civil War. He died suddenly of appendicitis. (Vail, R.W.G., *Frederic Remington, Chronicler of the Vanished West*)

RENAULT, Jesse Lee

See: *Reno, Jesse Lee*

RENO, Jesse Lee (1823-1862)

Jesse Reno, born Renault, served in the Ordnance Department, earned two brevets in the Mexican War, and was for a time a professor of mathematics at his alma mater, West Point, from which he graduated in 1846. A captain at the start of the conflict, his later assignments included: brigadier general, USV (November 12, 1861); commanding 2nd Brigade, in the North Carolina Expeditionary Corps (December 1861-January 7, 1862) and in the Department of North Carolina (January 7-April 2, 1862); major general, USV (July 18, 1862); commanding 2nd Division, 9th Corps, Army of the Potomac (July 22-September 3, 1862); and commanding the corps (September 3-14, 1862). At the outbreak of the war he was serving as an ordnance officer in Missouri until promoted to brigadier. Assigned to Burnside's North Carolina expedition, he commanded his brigade at Roanoke Island and New Bern and a division at South Mills. With his command sent to Virginia, Reno served in temporary command of the corps as well as his division at 2nd Bull Run and Chantilly. Following McClellan's accidental discovery of intelligence revealing Lee's divided army, Reno led the corps in an attack on Fox's Gap in the Antietam Campaign, in an attempt to get between the parts of the rebel force. He died in the attacks which were held off by a small Confederate force in the September 14, 1862, battle of South Mountain.

Jesse L. Reno, South Mountain victim. (*Leslie's*)

RENO, Marcus Albert (1835-1889)

After a Civil War career that had shown some promise for the future, Marcus A. Reno lost his commission as a result of the disaster at the Little Big Horn in 1876. The Illinois native's military career had started with his appointment to West Point, from which he graduated in 1857. His Civil War assignments included: second lieutenant, 1st Dragoons (since June 14, 1858); first lieutenant, 1st Dragoons (April 25, 1861); first lieutenant, 1st Cavalry (designation change August 3, 1861); captain, 1st Cavalry (November 12, 1861); and colonel, 12th Pennsylvania Cavalry (January 1, 1865). He fought on the Peninsula, and at Antietam and Fredericksburg. Wounded at Kelly's Ford, he was brevetted for the action. During the Gettysburg Campaign he was William F. Smith's chief of staff. He commanded his regiment during the Bristoe and Mine Run campaigns and won another regular army brevet for Cedar Creek and later was Alfred T.A. Torbert's chief of staff. At the beginning of the following year he was given command of a volunteer cavalry regiment in the Shenandoah Valley. Brevetted brigadier general of volunteers for the war, he was mustered out of that service with his regiment on July 20, 1865. Also brevetted colonel in the regular establishment, he gained promotion to major in the new 7th Cavalry in 1868. In the same battle in which Custer lost his life Reno commanded another battalion of three companies but panicked temporarily when attacked by overwhelming numbers of Indians. To a large extent Captain Frederick W. Benteen was in actual charge of the two columns which survived the battle. Reno was hauled before a court of inquiry but was not dismissed from the service until 1880.

REVERE, Joseph Warren (1812-1880)

A grandson of Revolutionary War hero Paul Revere, Joseph W. Revere did not achieve that same level of distinction in the Civil War. On the contrary, he was forced to resign his commission. The Boston native had entered the navy as a midshipman in 1828 and risen to be a lieutenant by 1841. Resigning in 1850, he became a colonel of artillery in the Mexican army and suffered a wound in a local rebellion. Settling in New Jersey, he again entered the service but this time with the land forces after his offer to the navy was not promptly accepted. His assignments included: colonel, 7th New Jersey (September 19, 1861); brigadier general, USV (October 25, 1862); commanding 3rd Brigade, 2nd Division, 3rd Corps, Army of the Potomac (November 22-December 25, 1862); commanding 2nd Brigade, 2nd Division, 3rd Corps, Army of the Potomac (December 24, 1862-February 1863 and March-May 3, 1863); and commanding the division (temporarily May 3, 1863). As a regimental commander, he fought during the Seven Days and at 2nd Bull Run before being named a brigadier general. At Fredericksburg his brigade was not engaged but did sustain a handful of casualties. At Chancellorsville he succeeded temporarily to the command of the division when Hiram G. Berry was killed on May 3, 1863. Claiming that his command was widely scattered and disorganized, he withdrew it three miles toward United States Ford. Since he had done this without orders he was relieved and convicted by a court-martial. The sentence, dismissal from the service, was revoked by Lincoln in return for his resignation which was accepted on August 10, 1863. He then travelled widely and wrote memoirs of his experiences.

REVERE, Paul Joseph (1832-1863)

Grandson of Revolutionary War hero Paul Revere, Paul J. Revere survived two wounds and being held hostage by the Richmond authorities only to succumb to yet another wound at Gettysburg. The Massachusetts native had entered the Union army shortly before the fight at 1st Bull Run and his assignments included: major, 20th Massachusetts (July 19, 1861); lieutenant colonel and assistant adjutant general (August 20, 1862); assistant inspector general, 2nd Corps, Army of the Potomac (September 4-November 14, 1862); assistant adjutant general, Right Grand Division, Army of the Potomac (November 14, 1862-February 5, 1863); and colonel, 20th Massachusetts (April 14, 1863). Wounded and captured at Ball's Bluff, he was named as a hostage to guarantee the treatment of Walter W. Smith and other privateers as prisoners of war. Finally exchanged and recovered, he became Edwin V. Sumner's inspector but was again hit at Antietam. Recovering, he was named to command the 20th Massachusetts which he led to Gettysburg where he fell mortally wounded on the second day. Two days later he died and was posthumously brevetted brigadier general to rank from the date of his wounding.

REYNOLDS, Alexander Welch (1816-1876)

A veteran of Seminole fighting, Virginia West Pointer (1838) Alexander W. Reynolds served as a Confederate brigadier general and later joined the Egyptian army. Posted to the infantry upon his graduation, he had transferred to the quartermaster's branch in 1847 but was dismissed in 1855 in a dispute over his accounts. Reinstated three years later, he was dropped, as a captain, on October 4, 1861, having joined the Confederacy seven months earlier. His assignments in the latter service included: captain, Infantry (March 1861); colonel, 50th Virginia (July 10, 1861); commanding brigade, Department of East Tennessee (May-July 3, 1862); commanding brigade, 1st (Stevenson's) Division, Department of East Tennessee (July 3-October 31, 1862); commanding brigade, Heth's Division, Department of East Tennessee (October 31-December 1862); commanding 4th Brigade, Stevenson's Division, 2nd Military District, Department of Mississippi and East Louisiana (December 1862-April 1863); commanding 4th Brigade, Stevenson's Division, Department of Mississippi and East Louisiana (April-July 4, 1863); brigadier general, CSA (September 14, 1863); commanding brigade, Buckner's Division, Army of Tennessee (October-November 30, 1863); commanding brigade, Stevenson's Division, Hardee's Corps, Army of Tennessee (November 30, 1863-February 20, 1864); and commanding brigade, Stevenson's Division, Hood's Corps, Army of Tennessee (February 20-May 27, 1864). Following service as a regimental commander in western Virginia and at Cumberland Gap he was transferred with Stevenson's division to Mississippi where he took part in the unsuccessful defense of Vicksburg. Paroled on the day of the river city's surrender, he was formally exchanged in September 1863 in time to fight in command of a brigade, with the increased rank of brigadier general, at Chattanooga. He led his brigade in the early stages of the Atlanta Campaign. Wounded at New Hope Church, his active field career was ended. In Egypt he served with the rank of colonel on the staff of William W. Loring, and he died there.

REYNOLDS, Belle (?-?)

With the coming of the Civil War Massachusetts-born Belle Reynolds attached herself to her husband's regiment, the 17th Illinois, as a nurse and served throughout his enlistment. During the first winter she served in Missouri, and then the regiment took part in the fighting at Fort Henry, Fort Donelson, and Shiloh. Present during the Vicksburg Campaign, she was quartered with General John A. McClernand's wife (Lieutenant Reynolds was the general's aide-de-camp at the time). The regiment was stationed in Vicksburg until May 1864. The next month Mrs. Reynolds went home to Illinois upon the expiration of her husband's regiment's term of enlistment.

REYNOLDS, Daniel Harris (1832-1902)

Rising from the rank of captain to a brigadier generalship, Ohio-born Arkansas lawyer Daniel H. Reynolds fought across the breadth of the map for the Confederacy. His assignments included: captain, Company A, 1st Arkansas Mounted Rifles (June 14, 1861); major, 1st Arkansas Mounted Rifles (April 14, 1862); lieutenant colonel, 1st Arkansas Mounted Rifles (May 1, 1862); colonel, 1st Arkansas Mounted Rifles (September 20, 1863); brigadier general, CSA (March 5, 1864); commanding brigade, Department of the Gulf (April 1-6, 1864); commanding brigade, District of the Gulf, Department of Alabama, Mississippi and East Louisiana (April 6-May 1864); and commanding brigade, Cantey's-Walthall's Division, Polk's (Army of Mississippi)-Stewart's Corps, Army of Tennessee (May 1864-March 19, 1865). He fought at Wilson's Creek and Pea Ridge before his regiment was transferred east of the Mississippi. He served in the Kentucky and Tullahoma campaigns. Promoted to the unit's colonelcy following Chickamauga, he soon became part of the Mobile garrison where he led a brigade as a brigadier general. Joining the main western army in Georgia, he served throughout the Atlanta Campaign and then embarked on Hood's disastrous invasion of middle Tennessee. He took part in the assault at Franklin and the defeat at Nashville. During the Carolinas Campaign he was wounded at Bentonville, losing a leg, and was effectively put out of the war. He subsequently practiced law and sat in the Arkansas legislature. It should be noted that during much of the conflict his original regiment served dismounted as infantry.

REYNOLDS, Jim (?-1864) and John (?-1871)

As the heads of a band of allegedly Confederate irregulars in Colorado, Jim and John Reynolds ended up on the wrong side of Colonel John M. Chivington of subsequent Sand Creek fame. Suspected of being highwaymen in 1863, and being from Texas, it was considered expedient to simply place the brothers in the local internment center for southern sympathizers in Denver. Making their escape to Texas, the pair returned to Colorado at the head of a band of Confederate irregulars who allegedly were to turn over their loot to the Confederacy. Until the spring of 1864 the gang was highly successful, supposedly burying much of the loot for the cause. Then the gang got into a gunfight in which one man was killed. Jim and four others were captured while John and one other got away. The five were tried in a civilian court and sentenced to life imprisonment. Reacting to fears that sympathizers might stage a breakout attempt, Chivington stepped in and tried the prisoners as conspirators against the United States, sentencing them to hang. Sending them to Leavenworth, Kansas, for review of the case, Chivington entrusted them to Captain George Cree of the Colorado Cavalry. A few days after his departure on August 19, 1864, the captain returned, reporting the prisoners shot while attempting to escape. However, their bodies were soon found tied to trees and full of bullet holes. Cree claimed that he merely followed Chivington's verbal orders, but no one believed him—until after the Sand Creek massacre. Meanwhile John Reynolds returned in 1871, allegedly to look for the buried treasure. Instead he committed a few more holdups until mortally wounded.

REYNOLDS, John Fulton (1820-1863)

One of the most highly esteemed of Union corps commanders, John F. Reynolds was destined to fall in the defense of his native state. The Pennsylvanian West Pointer (1841) had been posted to the artillery with which he won two Mexican War brevets. In the interwar period he was an instructor and commandant of cadets at his alma mater and upon the outbreak of the Civil War was made second in command of one of the newly authorized regular army infantry regiments. His assignments included: captain, 3rd Artillery (since March 3, 1855); lieutenant colonel, 14th Infantry (May 14, 1861); brigadier general, USV (August 20, 1861); commanding 1st Brigade, McCall's Division, Army of the Potomac (October 3, 1861-March 13, 1862); commanding 1st Brigade, 2nd Division, 1st Corps, Army of the Potomac (March 13-April 4, 1862); commanding 1st Brigade, 2nd Division, Department of the Rappahannock (April 4-June 12, 1862); commanding 1st Brigade, 3rd Division, 5th Corps, Army of the Potomac (June 18-27, 1862); commanding 3rd Division, 3rd Corps, Army of Virginia (August 26-September 12, 1862); commanding Pennsylvania Militia (September 13-ca. 29, 1862); commanding 1st Corps, Army of the Potomac (September 29, 1862-January 2, 1863, January 4-March 1, and March 9-July 1, 1863); major general, USV (November 29, 1862); colonel, 5th Infantry (June 1 1863); and commanding Left Wing (1st, 3rd, and 11th Corps), Army of the Potomac (June 30-July 1, 1863). He was assigned to the command of a brigade of the Pennsylvania Reserves which he trained in the Washington area. After service in northern Virginia, the division was moved to the Peninsula where during the Seven Days it made a stout defense at Beaver Dam Creek. The next day the command was again engaged at Gaines' Mill and following the close of the action Reynolds fell asleep after being cut off from his troops. Captured the next morning, he was exchanged on August 13, 1862, in time to command the Pennsylvania Reserves in the defeat at 2nd Bull Run. At the request of Pennsylvania's Governor Andrew G. Curtin,

John F. Reynolds, making a decision to fight at Gettysburg, gave his life there. (*Leslie's*)

Reynolds was detached and assigned to organize the state militia during the panic occasioned by Lee's invasion of Maryland. He thus missed the fighting at Antietam but returned to command the corps at Fredericksburg where one of his divisions, under George G. Meade, made the only breach in the Confederate lines, albeit temporary. His corps played only a minor role at Chancellorsville, and he became disgusted with Hooker's leadership. By now a major general and senior corps commander, he heard rumors of his pending appointment to command of the Army of the Potomac. He rushed to Washington and in a meeting with Lincoln declared that he would not accept the post unless the usual strings from the capital were severed. Thus Meade ended up in command of the army and Reynolds was in charge of three corps on the first day at Gettysburg. With his command heavily outnumbered on the field, he realized that he had to reinforce the position being held by John Buford's troopers. While placing the first of his infantry in line he was instantly killed by a Confederate shot. Accounts vary as to whether it was a stray bullet or one from a sharpshooter. As the ambulance carrying his body passed by the troops advancing to the victory—which he had done so much to make possible—it cast a pall of sadness over the regiments. (Roland, Charles P., *Toward Gettysburg: A Biography of John F. Reynolds No. 186*)

REYNOLDS, John G. (?-1865)

The American Civil War was not a high point in the history of the U.S. Marine Corps; and John G. Reynolds, in fact, played a leading role in many of its setbacks. A veteran of 37 years in the corps, Reynolds was a major with a good reputation earned in the Mexican War and a bad one earned as a heavy drinker. At 1st Bull Run he led a battalion of 348 raw recruits. After defending Griffin's Battery against the 33rd Virginia and reforming his men three times, Reynolds was swept up in the rout of the Union army. This was the first time that part of the corps had turned its back on the enemy. Given command of an amphibious battalion, he distinguished himself in the saving of most of his command when their transport sank in a fall storm. He was the last to leave the vessel. But early in 1862 operations against Fernandina and St. Augustine, Florida, proved dismal failures. In a squabble over who would succeed to the commandant's post he ended up facing a court-martial, charged with drunkenness at Fernandina. Although he was acquitted, it was a year before he was again given a combat assignment. Wishing to avoid another failure at Charleston he soon transferred to Washington. With the death of Commandant Harris, Secretary of the Navy Welles handpicked a successor on June 10, 1864, and ordered all senior officers retired on account of age. Thus the career of Lieutenant Colonel Reynolds (he had been promoted during the war) came to an end. He died a few months after the close of hostilities. (Pierce, Philip, *The Compact History of the United States Marine Corps*)

REYNOLDS, Joseph Jones (1822-1899)

Having compiled a distinguished record in the Civil War, Joseph J. Reynolds had his military career shattered in an action against the Indians. The Kentucky native had received his appointment to West Point from Indiana. Graduating in 1843, he was posted to the artillery. He served on the frontier and on the faculty of his alma mater until his 1857 resignation as second lieutenant, 3rd Artillery. Until the outbreak of the Civil War he taught engineering at St. Louis' Washington

Rescue operations in which John G. Reynolds' battalion of marines was saved from the *Governor* on November 2, 1861. (*Leslie's*)

University. Reentering the service, his assignments included: colonel, 10th Indiana (April 25, 1861); brigadier general, USV (June 14, 1861, to rank from May 17, 1861); commanding Cheat Mountain District, Army of Occupation—West Virginia, Department of the Ohio (September-October 11, 1861); brigadier general, USV (reappointed September 17, 1862); commanding 5th Division, Center, 14th Corps, Army of the Cumberland (November 11, 1862-January 9, 1863); major general, USV (November 29, 1862); commanding 5th Division, 14th Corps, Army of the Cumberland (November 11, 1862-January 9, 1863); major general, USV (November 29, 1862); commanding 5th Division, 14th Corps, Army of the Cumberland (June 8-October 9, 1863); commanding 4th Division, 14th Corps, Army of the Cumberland (June 8-October 9, 1863); chief of staff, Army of the Cumberland (October 10-ca. December 1863); commanding 4th Division, 19th Corps, Department of the Gulf (January 25-February 15, 1864); commanding District of Morganza, Military Division of West Mississippi (June 16-July 5, 1864); commanding 19th Corps, Department of the Gulf (July 7-November 7, 1864); commanding Reserve Corps, Department of the Gulf (December 5, 1864-January 12, 1865); and commanding 7th Corps, Department of Arkansas and the department (December 22, 1864-August 1, 1865). Early in the war he was named a brigadier general and assigned to command a district in western Virginia. However, on January 23, 1862, he had his resignation accepted due to the death of his brother and business partner. Having gotten his affairs in order he was recommissioned in September and led a division in the Tullahoma Campaign. Winning a brevet in the regular army as brigadier general, at Chickamauga, he became Thomas' chief of staff the next month. Ordered to the Gulf, he spent most of 1864 there and was involved in the operations against Mobile. He was then assigned to command in Arkansas during the final months of the war. Having been named a major general of volunteers in late 1862, he was mustered out of that service on September 1, 1866. By that time he had reentered the regular establishment as a colonel. Until his 1877 retirement he commanded the 26th and 25th Infantry and the 3rd Cavalry. In 1867 he had received the brevet of major general for his role on Thomas' staff at Chattanooga. The Powder River Expedition of 1876 proved to be the end of his career. He withdrew after having successfully attacked an Indian village. His retreat was, for no apparent reason, precipitous, and he left behind his dead and a wounded soldier who was later tortured to death. A court-martial was held and Reynolds resigned the next year.

REYNOLDS, Thomas C. (1821-1887)

A native of South Carolina, Missouri Lieutenant Governor Thomas C. Reynolds was an outspoken secessionist. After studying at Heidelberg, he had served as a diplomat in Spain. Settling in St. Louis in the early 1850s, he soon became embroiled in the violent politics of the day, including a duel with B. Gratz Brown. Entering the state's number two office at the beginning of 1861, he was active in the preparations for war. Out of state when the capital was abandoned, he sought the aid of the Confederate government in the liberation of his state and later joined Governor Claiborne F. Jackson in a government in exile which declared Missouri to be out of the Union and part of the Confederacy. With the December 1862 death of Jackson, Reynolds took over the governor's chair with the backing of Confederate Missouri troops. But with the state under Union control and with a new Union governor, he was unable to exercise most of his duties. He served as a volunteer aide in the 1864 invasion of the state by General Sterling Price. Fleeing the United States at the war's conclusion, he served Emperor Maximilian in Mexico. Returning three years later, he was subsequently elected to the state legislature and in 1887 committed suicide. (Snead, Thomas L., *The Fight for Missouri*)

REYNOLDS, William (1815-1879)

With the outbreak of the Civil War former naval officer William Reynolds—the brother of General John F. Reynolds who was killed at Gettysburg—was called back from retirement. The Pennsylvanian had entered the navy as a midshipman in 1833 and taken part in a cruise to the Antarctic in 1838. Due to failing health he was retired as a lieutenant in 1855. Two years later, however, he was sent to Hawaii as a naval storekeeper. In 1862 he was reactivated with the increased rank of commander and assigned to command the recently captured base at Port Royal, South Carolina. Here he was instrumental in keeping the ships for the coastal blockade in fighting condition. He held the command through the end of the war and then remained in the service until finally retired in 1877 as a rear admiral.

RHETT, Robert Barnwell (1800-1876)

Lawyer, plantation owner, but, most importantly, politician Robert Barnwell Rhett was one of the earliest secession advocates in South Carolina. A supporter of Nullification during the Jackson Administration, he spent decades working for an independent South. In 1860, he drafted South Carolina's Ordinance of Secession and the next year took part in the writing of the Confederate Constitution, gaining for himself the title of the "Father of Secession." He was considered too extreme for the presidency, though. As owner-editor of the *Charleston Mercury* he became a harsh critic of the Davis administration. By 1863, his brand of fire-eater secessionism had been sufficiently discredited so that he was defeated in a race for a seat in the Confederate Congress. After the war he refused to apply for a pardon. He died in 1876, with his dream of a new nation crushed. (White, Laura A., *Robert Barnwell Rhett: Father of Secession*)

RHETT, Thomas Smith (1827-1893)

A West Pointer (1848), Thomas S. Rhett of South Carolina had resigned his commission as a first lieutenant in the 2nd Artillery in 1855 and then left his job as a Baltimore bank clerk to offer his services to the South. His assignments included: captain, Artillery (November 19, 1861); colonel, Artillery (May 10, 1862); commanding the artillery defenses of Richmond (August 30, 1862-April 1, 1863); and commanding Richmond

Defenses, Department of Richmond (April 1-October 28, 1863). After service in South Carolina training artillery batteries in 1861 he was assigned to duty with the Ordnance Department in Richmond. Placed in command of the guns defending the capital, he directed them until the fall of 1863 when he was ordered to Europe to purchase arms. His principal activities were in France. Ordered back across the Atlantic on October 16, 1864, he finished out the war in the Ordnance Department. After the surrender he resettled in Baltimore.

RHIND, Alexander Colden (1821-1897)

Naval veteran of the Mexican War, Alexander C. Rhind had entered the navy in 1838 and later attended the naval school in Philadelphia. The New Yorker's Civil War assignments included: lieutenant, USN (since 1854); commanding *Crusader* (1861); commanding *Seneca* (1862); lieutenant commander, USN (1862); commanding *Keokuk* (1862-63); commanding *Paul Jones* (1863); commanding *Wabash* (1863); and commander, USN (1863). The first year of the war he served on blockade duty in the South Atlantic Blockading Squadron. He later commanded the monitor *Keokuk*. In 1863 he took part in the attack on Fort Wagner and the various bombardments of Charleston. Remaining in the service after the war he served as a lighthouse inspector and rose to the rank of rear admiral.

RICE, Americus Vespucius (1835-1904)

Severely wounded in the June 27, 1864, assault on Kennesaw Mountain, Americus V. Rice did not return to active duty until the Civil War was over—but then, as a brigadier general of volunteers. The native Ohioan law student had given up his studies to enter the Union army and his assignments included: captain, 21st Ohio (April 27, 1861); captain, 57th Ohio (September 2, 1861); lieutenant colonel, 57th Ohio (February 8, 1862); colonel, 57th Ohio (May 24, 1863); brigadier general, USV (May 31, 1865); and commanding 3rd Brigade, 2nd Division, 15th Corps, Army of the Tennessee (June 23, August 1, 1865). With his initial three-months company, he served in western Virginia before being mustered out on August 12, 1861. Recommissioned within a month, he soon became a field-grade officer and commanded the new regiment at Shiloh. The unit went on to serve during the Corinth siege and at Chickasaw Bayou. The next month he took part in the successful capture of Fort Hindman or Arkansas Post. In the midst of the siege of Vicksburg he was advanced to the colonelcy. Wounded during the Atlanta Campaign at Kennesaw Mountain, he did not return to duty until he took charge of a brigade in June 1865. Mustered out on January 15, 1866, he entered banking. He also served as a Democratic congressman and as a pension and census agent.

RICE, Elliott Warren (1835-1887)

The younger brother of Samuel A. Rice—who would die in the Civil War—Elliott W. Rice himself suffered some seven wounds on his way to becoming a Union brevet major general. The Pennsylvania native had been practicing law in Iowa in 1861 when he enlisted. His assignments included: sergeant, Company C, 7th Iowa (July 24, 1861); major, 7th Iowa (August 30, 1861); colonel, 7th Iowa (April 7, 1862); commanding 1st Brigade, 2nd Division, 16th Corps, Army of the Tennessee (March 4-September 23, 1864); brigadier general, USV (June 20, 1864); also commanding the division (July 25-26, 1864); and commanding 1st Brigade, 4th Division, 15th Corps, Army of the Tennessee (October 14, 1864-August 1, 1865). When the colonel and lieutenant colonel of his regiment fell at Belmont he briefly took charge of it until he himself fell wounded. He was too incapacitated to take an active role in the fighting at Fort Donelson but did see action at Shiloh. Promoted to permanent command of the unit from the date of this battle, he took part in the advance to Corinth, Mississippi, and fought in the battle there the following October. Assigned to duty guarding rail lines for a lengthy period, he returned to the field army in time for the Atlanta Campaign in the midst of which he was named a brigadier general of volunteers. He went on to the Savannah and Carolinas campaigns. Brevetted major general for the war, he was mustered out on August 24, 1865. But he took home one of the bullets that had wounded him—it was never removed from his body. He practiced law for the balance of his life.

RICE, Henry Mower (1817-1894)

An early settler in Minnesota, Henry M. Rice was instrumental in opening up much of the territory to settlement, and upon the admission of the state to the Union he became one of its first two senators. Born in Vermont, he had lived in Michigan, Iowa, and Wisconsin before finally settling in the territory in 1839. There he was the post sutler for the army at Fort Atkinson and engaged in the fur trade. These experiences enabled him to successfully negotiate treaties in 1847 with the Winnebagos and the Chippewas and to persuade the Sioux to agree to the treaty of 1851. From 1853 to 1857 he served as the territorial delegate to Congress but did not seek reelection. Through most of the 1850s he was a regent of the University of Minnesota. As a Democrat, he was sent to the Senate upon the granting of statehood and served from 1858 until March 3, 1863, when his term expired—he had not stood for reelection. He lost an 1865 bid for the gubernatorial chair. Later he headed the state's historical society and was involved in public works. For half a dozen years he was a county treasurer and in the late 1880s was again negotiating treaties with the Indians.

RICE, James Clay (1829-1864)

A hero of the fighting on Gettysburg's Little Round Top, James C. Rice died of wounds less than a year later. The Massachusetts native and Yale graduate had taught school and was involved in Mississippi journalism before taking up the practice of law in New York. Upon the outbreak of the Civil War he left his profession to join the Garibaldi Guards. His assignments included: first lieutenant, 39th New York (May 10, 1861); captain, 39th New York (August 1861); lieutenant colonel, 44th New York (September 13, 1861); colonel, 44th New York (July 4, 1862); commanding 3rd Brigade, 1st Division, 5th

Corps, Army of the Potomac (August 30, 1862 and July 2-August 26, 1863); brigadier general, USV (August 17, 1863); commanding 1st Division, 1st Corps, Army of the Potomac (August 23-September 23, 1863, January 14-February 10, and March 20-24, 1864); commanding 2nd Brigade, 1st Division, 1st Corps, Army of the Potomac (September 23-24, 1863, October 5, 1863-January 14, 1864, and February 10-March 24, 1864); and commanding 2nd Brigade, 4th Division, 5th Corps, Army of the Potomac (March 25-May 10, 1864). After brief service with the Garibaldi Guards—including being in reserve at 1st Bull Run—he became second in command of a newly organized regiment. As such he commanded the regiment during the Seven Days and was made its permanent leader a few days later. He succeeded briefly to brigade command at 2nd Bull Run but did not again hold such a post until almost a year later. Meantime he fought at Chancellorsville. On the second day at Gettysburg his small regiment, along with the three others in the brigade, were raced to the crest of Little Round Top on the Union left flank. There they were responsible for preventing the enemy from turning the flank. In the midst of the fighting the brigade commander, Colonel Strong Vincent, was killed and Rice succeeded him. A few weeks after the battle he was rewarded with the star of a brigadier and was assigned to the 1st Corps. He served in the Bristoe and Mine Run campaigns that fall and was transferred back to the enlarged 5th Corps in the March 1864 reorganization. He led his brigade through the Wilderness fighting. A few days later, on May 10, 1864, at Spotsylvania he was so severely wounded in the leg that it required amputation. He survived the surgery only a matter of hours.

RICE, Samuel Allen (1828-1864)

Serving in the lesser known theater of the war west of the Mississippi, Samuel A. Rice gave his life in the retreat of an unsuccessful expedition. The New York native was the elder brother of Elliott W. Rice and had set up a law practice in Iowa before the war and held a number of political offices, including state attorney general. Not entering the service until the second year of the war, his assignments included: colonel, 33rd Iowa (October 1, 1862); commanding 2nd Brigade, 13th Division, 13th Corps, Army of the Tennessee (June 10-July 28, 1863); commanding 2nd Brigade, 3rd Division Arkansas Expedition, Army of the Tennessee (October 3-November 12, 1863); commanding 2nd Brigade, 13th Division, 16th Corps, Army of the Tennessee (July 28-August 10, 1863); brigadier general, USV (August 4, 1863); commanding 3rd Division, Arkansas Expedition, Army of the Tennessee (August and September 13-October 8, 1863); commanding 2nd Brigade, 3rd Division, 7th Corps, Department of Arkansas (February 1-March 12, 1864); and commanding 1st Brigade, 3rd Division, 7th Corps, Department of Arkansas (March 12-April 30, 1864). Serving mostly in Missouri and Arkansas, he was however involved in the Yazoo Pass affair east of the Mississippi. He commanded a brigade in the defense of Helena, Arkansas, when it was attacked to relieve the pressure on Vicksburg which surrendered the same day. He took part in the capture of Little Rock, the state capital, and then went on Frederick Steele's unfortunate Camden expedition in support of Banks' Red River Campaign. With the movement a failure, the command fought at Jenkins' Ferry on the last day of April 1864, and Rice's spur was struck by a bullet which drove parts of it into his ankle. He died on July 6.

RICHARDSON, Albert Deane (1833-1869)

Journalist Albert D. Richardson survived many dangerous Civil War adventures only to die in a love triangle four years later. A native of Massachusetts he had worked for several papers in Pittsburgh and Cincinnati before moving his family to Kansas where he covered the troubles there for the *Boston Journal*. Based upon his trip to Pike's Peak with Horace Greeley and the resulting friendship, he volunteered to serve in New Orleans during the secession crisis as a secret correspondent for the latter's *New York Tribune*. Narrowly avoiding a noose, he returned North to become that paper's chief war correspondent. After initially covering the fighting in Virginia, he went to cover the operations against Vicksburg. On May 3, 1863, he and two other journalists were captured while attempting to pass the fortified city on a tug. With one of his companions he made good his escape 19 months later from the prison at Salisbury, North Carolina, on December 18, 1864, and managed to reach the Union lines 400 miles away at Strawberry Plains in East Tennessee. Based upon his war experiences he published *The Secret Service, the Field, the Dungeon, and the Escape* in 1865. During the 1868 election he wrote a campaign biography, *Personal History of Ulysses S. Grant*. The next year he became engaged to marry a woman as soon as her divorce became final. Then on November 25 the outraged husband walked into the *Tribune* office and shot Richardson at his desk. But Richardson was married—a second time, his first wife had died while he was in prison—while on his deathbed. The ceremony was performed by Henry Ward Beecher. (Vinton, J.A., *The Richardson Memorial*)

RICHARDSON, Israel Bush (1815-1862)

While commanding a division in his third war Israel B. Richardson lost his life. The native Vermonter had graduated from West Point in 1841. Posted to the infantry, he had fought the Seminoles in Florida and earned two brevets in Mexico. In 1855 he gave up his commission as captain, 3rd Infantry, and settled on a Michigan farm. "Fighting Dick" reentered the military upon the outbreak of the Civil War and his assignments included: colonel 2nd Michigan (May 21, 1861); commanding 4th Brigade, 1st Division, Army of Northeastern Virginia (June-August 17, 1861); brigadier general, USV (August 9, 1861, to rank from May 17); commanding brigade, Division of the Potomac (August 17-October 3, 1861); commanding 1st Brigade, Heintzelman's Division, Army of the Potomac (October 3, 1861-March 13, 1862); commanding 1st Division, 2nd Corps, Army of the Potomac (March 13-July 17 and August 15-September 17, 1862); and major general, USV (July 5, 1862 to rank from July 4). His brigade of Daniel Tyler's division was involved in limited action at 1st Bull Run and in covering the withdrawal. With the star of a brigadier he led a brigade around Washington and then took a division to the Peninsula where he saw action at Yorktown, Seven Pines, and the Seven Days. Awarded a second star at the close of the campaign, he took part in the Maryland Campaign. At Antietam he attacked the enemy center and was wounded while supervising his artillery. At first it was not considered a dangerous wound but on November 3 he died while still at the Pry House, McClellan's headquarters.

RICHARDSON, Robert Winkler (1820-1870)

Questions of recruiting authority, discipline, and effectiveness prompted Jefferson Davis to request that the nomination of Robert W. Richardson as a Confederate brigadier general be returned by the Senate, despite the fact that Richardson had actually been confirmed at that rank. A North Carolina-born Tennessee lawyer, he had served in a minor military capacity in the early part of the Civil War before receiving permission to raise units behind enemy lines. In the meantime he had fought at Shiloh and in the defense of Corinth, Mississippi. His later assignments included: colonel, 12th Tennessee Cavalry (February 14, 1863); brigadier general, CSA (December 3, 1863, to rank from the first); commanding brigade, Chalmers' Cavalry Division, Department of Mississippi and East Louisiana (October 18-December 1863); commanding brigade, Forrest's Cavalry Corps, Department of Mississippi and East Louisiana (January 25-28, 1864); and commanding brigade, Chalmers' Division, Forrest's Cavalry Corps, Department of Alabama, Mississippi and East Louisiana (January 28-March 20, 1864). His regiment was also known as the 1st Tennessee Partisan Rangers and served in western Tennessee. Richardson was then authorized to raise more units in occupied areas and was named a brigadier general. But after a series of recruiting controversies and battlefield misfortunes he was ordered to join Nathan Bedford Forrest. On February 9, 1864, his nomination was returned to the president and he performed little service thereafter. Engaged in railroading after the war, he was murdered for obscure reasons five years after the Confederacy's fall.

RICHARDSON, William Alexander (1811-1875)

Twice William A. Richardson succeeded to the congressional seats of Stephen A. Douglas. The Kentucky-born teacher had begun the practice of law in 1831 in Illinois and three years later entered upon a two-year stint as a state's attorney. In the legislature in 1836-1838 and 1844-1846, he was that body's speaker in 1844. In the interim he was in the state senate from 1838 to 1842 and served as a Democratic elector in 1844. When Douglas resigned, Richardson was named to replace him in Congress, and he served from 1847 to August 25, 1856, when he resigned. During the Mexican War he was a captain and major of the Illinois Volunteers. He attended as a delegate and Douglas man the Charleston convention of his party in 1860 and secured another election, to the House of Representatives. He served from March 4, 1861, until his resignation on January 29, 1863, in order to succeed the deceased Douglas in the Senate the next day. Not a candidate for reelection, he left office on March 3, 1865, and later was involved in journalism.

RICKETTS, James Brewerton (1817-1887)

Career artillerist James B. Ricketts spent three lengthy periods during the Civil War recovering from battlefield injuries. The New York City native and West Pointer (1839) had fought in Mexico and become a battery commander in the 1850s. His Civil War assignments included: captain, 1st Artillery (since August 3, 1852); brigadier general, USV (April 30, 1862, to rank from July 21, 1861); commanding 1st Brigade, Ord's Division, Department of the Rappahannock (May 16-June 10, 1862); commanding the division (June 10-26, 1862); commanding 2nd Division, 3rd Corps, Army of Virginia (June 26-September 12, 1862); also commanding the corps (September 5-6, 1862); commanding 2nd Division, 1st Corps, Army of the Potomac (September 12-October 4, 1862); major, 1st Artillery (June 1, 1863); commanding 3rd Division, 6th Corps, Army of the Potomac (April 4-July 8, 1864); also commanding the corps (April 6-13, 1864); commanding 3rd Division, 6th Corps, Army of the Shenandoah (August 6-October 16, 1864); commanding the corps (October 16-19, 1864); and again commanding 3rd Division, 6th Corps, Army of the Potomac (April 16-June 28, 1865). At 1st Bull Run he directed his six 10-pound Parrotts on Henry House Hill—in conjunction with Charles Griffin's battery—and was four times severely wounded. He and all his guns of Battery I, 1st Artillery, were captured by the enemy. Confined in a Richmond hospital, he was not exchanged until January 1862 when he was freed for Julius A. de Lagnel. Continuing his long convalescence, he was named a brigadier general of volunteers in April with the date of the commission ranking from 1st Bull Run. He commanded a brigade and then a division in northern Virginia and fought at Cedar Mountain, Thoroughfare Gap, and 2nd Bull Run. At Antietam he was badly injured when the second horse to be shot out from under him that day fell upon him. Not yet fit for field duty, he was a member of the court which forced Fitz-John Porter out of the army. Rejoining the Army of the Potomac for the Overland Campaign, he fought at the Wilderness and Spotsylvania and was brevetted for Cold Harbor. He was involved in the early operations against Petersburg before going to the aid of Washington during Early's raid. At Monocacy his division joined Lew Wallace in buying time for the capital. On August 1, 1864, he was brevetted major general of volunteers for his services to date and then joined Sheridan's command in the Shenandoah. He fought at 3rd Winchester and Fisher's Hill. During Sheridan's temporary absence, Ricketts commanded the 6th Corps while Horatio G. Wright directed the army at Cedar Creek. During the battle he was permanently disabled by a chest wound. It is sometimes claimed that he was present during the latter part of the Appomattox Campaign but he was not reassigned to command of the division until April 16, 1865, when he relieved Truman Seymour. Mustered out of the volunteers on April 30, 1866, he remained in the regular army with the brevet of major general for the war. Due to his extensive wounds he was retired in 1867 with the advanced grade of major general. Even in retirement he continued on court-martial duty for two years.

RICKSON, W.

See: *Sullivan, Cary*

RIDDLE, George Read (1817-1867)

A former member of the House of Representatives, Delaware native George R. Riddle served his state as a senator during the last year of the Civil War. He had engaged in railroad and canal engineering before being admitted to the bar in 1848. The next year he was part of the commission which retraced the Mason-Dixon Line. In 1849 and 1850 he was deputy attorney general and continued his political interests by serving as a delegate to several Democratic national conventions. A member of the House from 1851 to 1855, he failed to gain reelection in 1854 and returned to his practice. With the resignation of Senator James A. Bayard in January 1864, Riddle was named in his place and served until his death in 1867.

RION, James Henry (1828-1866)

The case of James H. Rion demonstrates the poor state of command that existed under Brigadier General Nathan G. Evans during his service in South Carolina. Rion, a native of Canada, was a colonel of the South Carolina militia at the outbreak of the Civil War. His war assignments included: colonel, 6th South Carolina (early 1861); captain, Company B, 7th South Carolina Battalion (November 13, 1861); major, 7th South Carolina Battalion (March 5, 1863); temporarily commanding 22nd South Carolina (early 1863); and lieutenant colonel, 7th South Carolina Battalion (June 24, 1864). He led part of his regiment to Charleston Harbor just after the fall of Fort Sumter but failed to gain reelection to his post when the command went into Confederate service that summer. Organizing the Lyle Rifles, he became their captain but was placed under arrest on February 5, 1862, along with all three of his lieutenants for refusing to obey Evans' orders. He was finally released on May 21, 1862. He fought at Battery Wagner and through much of the siege of Charleston until the spring of 1864 when his command moved to Virginia. Here the unit was engaged at Bermuda Hundred and during the sieges of Richmond and Petersburg. Moving to North Carolina, it was engaged in the defense of Wilmington and surrendered with Johnston's army. Rion went back to the practice of law.

RIPLEY, Edward Hastings (1839-1915)

A college student at the outbreak of the war, Edward H. Ripley, despite a rather limited combat record, was named to command the garrison of the captured Confederate capital immediately after its fall. A native of Vermont, he had answered Lincoln's summer 1862 call for men and joined the army where his assignments included: captain, Company B, 9th Vermont (July 9, 1862); major, 9th Vermont (March 20, 1863); lieutenant colonel, 9th Vermont (May 19, 1863); colonel, 9th Vermont (June 1, 1863); commanding 2nd Brigade, 2nd Division, 18th Corps, Army of the James (September 19-December 3, 1864); and commanding 1st Brigade, 3rd Division, 24th Corps, Army of the James (March 22-April 16 and May 5-June 13, 1865). Assigned to the garrison of Harpers Ferry, he was captured when Stonewall Jackson captured the place in September 1862. Paroled immediately, he and his regiment were sent to Camp Douglas, Illinois—a prisoner of war camp—where there was little distinction between them and the Rebel prisoners. Exchanged in January 1863, he served in southeastern Virginia, on the Peninsula, and in North Carolina. Finally moving into a more active sector, he took part in the operations against Richmond, including the actions at Fort Harrison and Darbytown Road. As of August 1, 1864, he was brevetted brigadier and was in command of a brigade in the above two actions. With the Confederate evacuation of the capital, Ripley's brigade was among the first infantry to enter the city. With the City Hall as his headquarters, he was placed in charge of the city's garrison. He was responsible for fighting the raging fires and the looting, and rounding up stragglers. He was mustered out on June 13, 1865, and was later active in hotels, railroads, and steamships, and served in the state legislature. (Ripley, Edward Hastings, *Vermont General: The Unusual War Experiences of Edward Hastings Ripley*)

RIPLEY, James Wolfe (1794-1870)

At the outbreak of the Civil War, the U.S. Ordnance Department's senior positions were filled with many officers who had been born in the last century and were resistant to change and modernization of military weaponry. A prime example was James Ripley. Entering West Point during the War of 1812, Ripley and his classmates were raced through their studies to be commissioned in only one year. He served in the artillery during that war and until 1832, when he was transferred to the newly independent Ordnance Department as a captain. Serving during the war with Mexico and earning a brevet, Ripley was a lieutenant colonel at the start of the Civil War. Returning from a foreign inspection trip upon the outbreak of hostilities, he was named chief of Ordnance with the rank of colonel on April 23, 1861, replacing the 70-year-old Colonel H.K. Craig. On July 2 he was brevetted brigadier general and given the full rank on August 3, 1861. Responsible for the testing and purchasing of arms, Ripley was often stubbornly resistant to change. Out of over 700,000 rifles purchased in his first 14 months in office only 8,271 were breechloaders. These were not totally new weapons; the Prussian army had already adopted them by the outbreak of the war. Ripley was also reluctant to purchase similar advancements in artillery. Finally Lincoln and Stanton forced him out in favor of a more enlightened officer, George D. Ramsay, on September 15, 1863. Near the close of the conflict he was brevetted major general in the regular establishment.

RIPLEY, Roswell Sabine (1823-1887)

West Pointer (1843) and 10-year artilleryman Roswell S. Ripley became a brigadier general during the first year of the war but never rose any higher, in part due to an inability to get along with his superiors. An Ohio native, he had resigned his commission, having earned two brevets in Mexico, in 1853 to become a businessman in his wife's state, South Carolina. He cast his lot with the South, his services including: lieutenant colonel, 1st South Carolina Artillery Battalion Regulars (January 1861); brigadier general, CSA (August 15, 1861); commanding Department of South Carolina (August 21-November 5, 1861); commanding 2nd Military District of South Carolina, Department of South Carolina, Georgia and Florida (December 10, 1861-May 28, 1862); commanding brigade, D.H. Hill's Division (in 2nd Corps in September), Army of Northern Virginia (June-September 17, 1862); commanding the division (August 1862); commanding 1st Military District of South Carolina, Department of South Carolina, Georgia and Florida (October 17, 1862-October 17, 1864); commanding Sub-district No. 2, District of South Carolina, same department (October 17-late 1864); also commanding brigade, same department (July-late 1864); and commanding Brown's Division, Cheatham's Corps, Army of Tennessee (March 19-April 9, 1865). During the bombardment of Fort Sumter Ripley commanded some artillery on Sullivan's Island. After some more service on the coast, and having problems with the departmental commander, he transferred to Lee's army for the Seven Days. Severely wounded at Antietam, he was again assigned to Charleston where he served until the last few months of the war. After Bentonville he commanded Brown's Division but lost his post during the reorganization of Johnston's forces on April 9, 1865. After the South's collapse he was in business in England, Charleston, and New York.

RIVES, Alfred Landon (1830-1903)

Colonel Alfred L. Rives served for almost half of the war as chief of the Confederate War Department's Engineer Bureau, but only in an acting capacity. After receiving his engineering training at the Virginia Military Institute, the University of Virginia, and in France, he had been active in railroad engineering before the war. He had also been secretary of the interior under Franklin Pierce. Entering the Confederate engineers, he served successively at the ranks of captain, lieutenant colonel, and colonel. He was acting chief of the bureau at three periods during the war: November 13, 1861-September 24, 1862; August 18, 1863-March 1864; and April-June 1864. His position in Richmond naturally led him to work closely with the Army of Northern Virginia. Resuming his railroad engineering career, he was active in the United States and Panama. (Nichols, James L., *Confederate Engineers*)

ROANE, John Selden (1817-1867)

Mexican War veteran John S. Roane spent his entire service as a Confederate brigadier general in the Trans-Mississippi West. As second in command of Yell's Arkansas Regiment in the fighting south of the Rio Grande, he succeeded to its colonelcy upon the death of his superior. The Tennessee native had entered politics in his adopted state, sitting in the legislature and serving as Arkansas' governor. Opposed to secession he did not join the Confederate service until almost a year after the firing on Fort Sumter. His assignments included: brigadier general, CSA (March 20, 1862); commanding Trans-Mississippi District, Department #2 (May 11-31, 1862); commanding brigade, Shoup's Division, 1st Corps, Trans-Mississippi Department (December 1862); and commanding 1st (Arkansas) Brigade, 1st (Arkansas) Division, 2nd Corps (or District of Arkansas), Trans-Mississippi Department (September 1864-May 26, 1865). He briefly commanded all Southern forces in Arkansas but was soon succeeded by Thomas C. Hindman. He led a brigade at Prairie Grove and in the final half year of the war but spent most of his career in post and special assignments throughout the Trans-Mississippi West. He lived less than two years longer than the Confederacy.

ROBERTS, Benjamin Stone (1810-1875)

"Exiled" to Minnesota because of too close an association with the unpopular John Pope, Benjamin S. Roberts spent part of the Civil War there, fighting the Sioux. The Vermonter and West Pointer (1835) had resigned as a first lieutenant of dragoons in 1839 to enter railroading. He was employed in the construction of the Moscow-St. Petersburg (now Leningrad) railroad and then took up the practice of law. Reentering the service for the Mexican War, he was made a first lieutenant in the Regiment of Mounted Riflemen and won two brevets during the war. Remaining in the military, he served on the frontier until the Civil War when his assignments included: captain, Regiment of Mounted Riflemen (since February 16, 1847); major, Regiment of Mounted Riflemen (May 14, 1861); major, 3rd Cavalry (designation change August 3, 1861); colonel, 5th New Mexico (December 9, 1861); brigadier general, USV (June 16, 1862); inspector general and chief of Cavalry, Army of Virginia (summer 1862); inspector general, Department of the Northwest (late 1862); commanding 4th Separate Brigade, 8th Corps, Middle Department (March 11-May 23, 1863); also commanding 3rd Division, 8th Corps, Middle Department (March 11-16, 1863); commanding 1st Division, 19th Corps, Department of the Gulf (June 25-July 1, 1864); commanding the corps (July 2-6, 1864); commanding Cavalry Division, Department of the Gulf (November 11-December 28, 1864); commanding District of West Tennessee, Army of the Tennessee (February 3-March 4, 1856); and commanding Cavalry Division, District of West Tennessee, Army of the Tennessee (May 15-July 14, 1865). Commanding a volunteer regiment in New Mexico, he won a brevet at Valverde and fought at Glorietta Pass. Mustered out of the volunteer service on May 31, 1862, he was quickly named a brigadier general and joined the staff of John Pope in Virginia. For Cedar Mountain he was brevetted brigadier general in the regular service and, for it and 2nd Bull Run, major general of volunteers. However, having pressed the charges against Fitz-John Porter—for his role in the latter battle—Roberts was sent to Minnesota with his chief, Pope. Part of the anti-McClellan faction, he was recalled for a time to the Washington area but was then shunted off to the Gulf. Finishing the war in western Tennessee, he was mustered out of the volunteer service on January 15, 1866, and reverted to his regular rank of major. He retired in 1870 as lieutenant colonel, 3rd Cavalry.

ROBERTS, George W. (?-1862)

In a rare honor for the midst of a savage battle, Union Colonel George W. Roberts received a formal burial by his foes. The Illinois soldier's assignments had included: colonel, 42nd Illinois (ca. July 22, 1861); commanding 1st Brigade, 1st Division, Army of the Mississippi (August 10-September 29, 1862); commanding 1st Brigade, 13th Division, army of the Ohio (September 29-November 5, 1862); and commanding 3rd Brigade, 3rd Division, Right Wing, 14th Corps, Army of the Cumberland (November 5-December 31 , 1862). His regiment served in Missouri, at the capture of Island #10, and during the advance on Corinth, Mississippi. Having been in brigade command for over four months, he went into the battle of Murfreesboro. With the Union right surprised, Roberts was able to hold his brigade in line of battle for a longer period of time than most others and later made a counterattack which slowed the enemy advance. But soon he was fatally shot and his position was overrun by the enemy. That New Year's Eve the Confederates occupying the area known as the Cedars buried him with honors, acknowledging his fighting ability.

ROBERTS, William Paul (1841-1910)

Holding every lower commissioned rank but two, William P. Roberts rose to be the Confederacy's youngest general officer. Enlisting at the beginning of the war, he held the following assignments: third lieutenant, 2nd North Carolina Cavalry (August 30, 1861); first lieutenant, 2nd North Carolina Cavalry (September 13, 1862); captain, Company C, 2nd North Carolina Cavalry (November 19, 1863); major, 2nd North Carolina Cavalry (February 18, 1863); colonel, 2nd North Carolina Cavalry (August 19, to rank from June 23, 1864); brigadier general, CSA (February 23, to rank from February 21, 1865); and commanding Dearing's (old) Brigade, W.H.F. Lee's Division, Cavalry Corps, Army of Northern Virginia (March-April 9, 1865). The regiment, with Roberts as a junior officer, served at New Bern, Fredericksburg, Brandy Station, Gettysburg, and in the Overland Campaign. At Black and Whites on June 23, 1864, the colonel was killed and Roberts succeeded to command the regiment. He served through the Petersburg siege, including distinguished action at Ream's Station. When General Dearing was assigned to a different brigade in March 1865, Roberts, who had recently been promoted, was transferred to replace him. At Five Forks his command, only one regiment and a battalion, was decimated and he surrendered with the fragments at Appomattox a week later. After the war he served as a legislator in his native North Carolina and was state auditor for eight years. (Freeman, Douglas S., *Lee's Lieutenants)*

ROBERTSON, Beverly Holcombe (1826-1910)

Somehow Beverly H. Robertson never fit into the cavalry command of Jeb Stuart, having irritated that officer as early as October 1861. A West Pointer (1849), he had been dismissed as a captain, 5th Cavalry (late 2nd Dragoons), on August 8, 1861, for having accepted an appointment from the Confederate War Department. His Southern assignments included: captain and assistant adjutant general (1861); colonel, 4th Virginia Cavalry (November 19, 1861); brigadier general, CSA (June 9, 1862); commanding Cavalry Brigade, Valley District, Department of Northern Virginia (June-August 1862); commanding brigade, Cavalry Division, Army of Northern Virginia (August-September 5, 1862); commanding Cavalry Brigade, Department of North Carolina (October 1862-May 1863); commanding brigade, Cavalry Division, Army of Northern Virginia (May-August 1863); commanding 2nd Military District of South Carolina, Department of South Carolina, Georgia and Florida (October 15, 1863-October 17, 1864); commanding 4th Sub-District of South Carolina, District of South Carolina, same department (October 17-late 1864); and also commanding brigade, same department (from July 1864). After initial service under Stuart in northern Virginia and on the Peninsula he was transferred to the command of Ashby's old cavalry in the Valley after the close of the campaign there. He joined Jackson at Cedar Mountain and was at 2nd Bull Run under Stuart. A few days later he was dispatched to organize the cavalry in North Carolina. In May 1863 he rejoined Lee and Stuart with two North Carolina regiments from his new brigade. Left with Lee during Stuart's ride around the Union army in the Gettysburg Campaign, he put in a poor performance, not complying promptly enough with Lee's orders to join him in Pennsylvania. In August he was again transferred out of Stuart's command and spent a year or more commanding a district in South Carolina. There is no record of his service after November 20, 1864. He was in the insurance business in the reunited nation's capital after the war. (Freeman, Douglas S., *Lee's Lieutenants)*

ROBERTSON, Felix Huston (1839-1928)

Starting the Civil War as a staff officer, native Texan Felix H. Robertson transferred to the artillery and finally the cavalry, as a Confederate brigadier general, before his field career was ended by wounds. Appointed to West Point in 1857, he had resigned on January 29, 1861, within months of his planned graduation, to offer his services to the South. His assignments there included: second lieutenant, Artillery (March 9, 1861); captain and assistant adjutant general (October 1861); captain, Robertson's Florida Battery (January 1, 1862); major, Artillery (July 1, 1863); commanding Reserve Artillery, Army of Tennessee (September-November 1863); commanding battalion, Reserve Artillery, Army of Tennessee (November 1863-April 3, 1864); lieutenant colonel, Artillery (January 1864); commanding Artillery, Wheeler's Cavalry Corps, Army of Tennessee (April 3-July 1864); commanding battalion, Artillery, Wheeler's Cavalry Corps, Army of Tennessee (July-August 6, 1864); brigadier general, CSA (July 26, 1864); chief of staff, Wheeler's Cavalry Corps, Army of Tennessee (summer 1864); and commanding brigade, Wheeler's Cavalry Division, Army of Tennessee (fall 1864). He served at Fort Sumter and then as a staff officer with Adley H. Gladden at Pensacola before taking command of an artillery battery which he led at Shiloh and Murfreesboro. After serving in the Tullahoma Campaign he became an artillery field officer. He led a reserve battalion at

Chickamauga and Chattanooga and Wheeler's artillery in the early part of the Atlanta Campaign. After a stint as the cavalry chieftain's staff chief he was promoted to brigadier general and assigned command of a mounted brigade. Opposing Sherman's March to the Sea, he was wounded on November 29, 1864, at Buckhead Creek, Georgia. Removed from active field duty, his nomination as brigadier general was rejected by the Senate on February 29, 1865. However, he was assigned the task of surrendering the city of Macon and was paroled at his highest rank. After the war he returned to his home state and became a practicing attorney. At the time of his death he was the sole surviving Confederate general officer.

ROBERTSON, James Madison (?-1891)

Because of his long affiliation with the Cavalry Corps of the Army of the Potomac, New Hampshire artillerist James M. Robertson was given the honor of heading his brigade in the march of the corps in the Grand Review, although it no longer belonged to the corps. After 10 years' service as an enlisted man in the 2nd Artillery, including service in the Mexican War, he was commissioned a month after that conflict's conclusion. As an officer, he fought in the Seminole War of 1855 to 1858. His Civil War assignments included: first lieutenant, 2nd Artillery (since September 28, 1852); captain, 2nd Artillery (May 14, 1861); commanding Horse Artillery Brigade, Cavalry Corps, Army of the Potomac (February-June 1863); commanding 1st Horse Artillery Brigade, Cavalry Corps, Army of the Potomac (June 1863-August 1864); commanding Horse Artillery Reserve, Army of the Shenandoah (January-April 1865); and commanding Horse Artillery Brigade, 22nd Corps, Department of Washington (April-June 1865). After service at Fort Pickens he took command of his battery, which soon became a horse battery. In charge of the consolidated Batteries B and L, he commanded his six three-inch Rifles at Williamsburg and during the Seven Days. In the latter he was brevetted for Gaines' Mill. During the Maryland Campaign the battery's armament was six Napoleons. After commanding his battery at Fredericksburg, he took over a brigade of horse artillery for Stoneman's raid during the Chancellorsville Campaign. After fighting at Brandy Station, he received a brevet for Gettysburg. He was again brevetted—this time as a brigadier general—for the Overland Campaign and the early stages of fighting at Petersburg. He had previously been brevetted especially for the campaign's fight at Cold Harbor. From August 1864 until January 1865 he was stationed in St. Louis, assigned to the inspection of horses for the government. In the last months of the war he commanded the horse artillery in the relatively quiet sectors of the Shenandoah and Washington. Remaining in the service after the Grand Review, he retired as major, 3rd Artillery, in 1879.

ROBERTSON, Jerome Bonaparte (1815-1891)

John B. Hood's successor in command of the famed Texas Brigade, Jerome B. Robertson, was found to be a poor officer. A Kentucky native and physician, he had relocated to Texas in the 1830s where he had gained some military experience in serving the republic and as an Indian fighter. Also active in politics he sat in both houses of the state legislature and in the secession convention. For the Confederacy, his assignments included: captain, 5th Texas (1861); lieutenant colonel, 5th Texas (November 1861); colonel, 5th Texas (June 1, 1862); brigadier general, CSA (November 1, 1862); and commanding Texas Brigade, Hood's Division, in 1st Corps, Army of Northern Virginia (November 6, 1862-February 25 and May-September 9, 1863), in Department of Virginia and North Carolina (February 25-April 1, 1863), in Department of Southern Virginia (April 1-May 1863), in Longstreet's Corps, Army of Tennessee (September 19-October 1863), and in Department of East Tennessee (November 1863-January 26, 1864). He saw early action at West Point, Seven Pines, and in the Seven Days. At 2nd Bull Run he was wounded and at South Mountain he had to be taken from the field after collapsing from exhaustion and the effects of the recent wound. Promoted, he led the Texans at Fredericksburg, in southeastern Virginia, and at Gettysburg where he was slightly wounded. Sent west he fought at Chickamauga but was removed as incompetent by Longstreet after the battle of Wauhatchie. Reinstated by Bragg, he was again relieved after Bean's Station. Never tried, he was sent to command the reserve forces of Texas in June 1864 and finished the war there. After the war he practiced medicine, was a state official, and was in railroading. (Freeman, Douglas S., *Lee's Lieutenants*)

ROBINSON, Charles (1818-1894)

Kansas' first state governor, Charles Robinson, had been a leader in bringing it into the Union as a free state. A Massachusetts native, he had practiced medicine before taking part in the California Gold Rush. Remaining in California for a number of years, he was a restaurateur, newspaper editor, and state legislator. As a leader of the squatter riots in 1850, he was severely wounded. He returned to Massachusetts and edited a paper before going to Kansas with a group of New Englanders. Soon involved in the slave vs. free debate, he helped organize the Free State Party and became its extralegal governor in 1855. As a Republican—and a founder of that organization—he was elected governor in December 1859 but was not inaugurated until February 9, 1861, upon the admission of Kansas to the Union. He fought James H. Lane for control of the party in the state. He was then impeached by the legislature for his handling of the sale of state bonds, but was acquitted. Refused renomination, he left office on January 12, 1863. He was subsequently active in various reform movements and ran for public office as an Independent, Democrat, Independent Reform, and Independent Greenback candidate. He was successful only for the state legislature and lost twice for governor and once for congressman. (Wilson, Don W., *Governor Charles Robinson of Kansas* and Blackmar, Frank Wilson, *Charles Robinson, the First Free-State Governor of Kansas*)

ROBINSON, George Foster (?-?)

For his actions on the bloody Washington night of April 14, 1865, Private George F. Robinson of Company B, 8th Maine, was awarded a gold medal by a joint resolution of Congress in 1871. The Maine native had enlisted on August 15, 1863, and after that time his regiment served on the South Carolina coast, at Bermuda Hundred, Cold Harbor, and in the operations against Petersburg and Richmond. By the night of Lincoln's murder, he had been detailed as a nurse for Secretary of State William H. Seward who had been severely injured in a carriage accident. On that fatal night he opened the door to the secretary's room to find the would-be assassin Lewis Paine who promptly cut him with a knife in the forehead. Recovering, he assisted in grabbing Paine after Paine had inflicted several wounds upon the statesman. But Paine caught Robinson around the neck and then knocked him down with a blow to the head, making good his escape. After receiving his medal Robinson in 1879 became a major and paymaster in the regular army; he had been discharged from the volunteers on May 19, 1865. He finally retired in 1896. (Weichmann, Louis J., *A True History of the Assassination of Abraham Lincoln and of the Conspiracy of 1865*)

ROBINSON, James Fisher (1800-1882)

With no lieutenant governor, it was the speaker of the Kentucky Senate, James F. Robinson, who completed the term of the retiring Governor Beriah Magoffin in 1862. A native of the state, he had been a farmer and lawyer before entering the legislature as a Whig in 1851. Returning to office in 1861 as a Democrat and moderate conservative, he was elected speaker on September 2. Two days after being reelected speaker he was inaugurated governor on August 18, 1862. He faced a Confederate invasion that summer and came into conflict with the Lincoln administration. He opposed the arbitrary military arrests and other interference in the state's internal affairs. With his state so sharply divided, he opposed the recruiting of troops for the Union army. Although the Emancipation Proclamation was not in effect in Kentucky—the document only affected states in rebellion—he thought it an insult to Kentucky's loyalty. Not seeking reelection, he retired to his practice and his farm. After the war he was in education and banking. (Coulter, E. Merton, *The Civil War and Readjustment in Kentucky*)

ROBINSON, James Sidney (1827-1892)

Four days after the surrender of Fort Sumter the editor of the *Kenton* (Ohio) *Republican* enlisted as a private in the Union army and within four years was a brigadier general of volunteers. The Ohio native's assignments included: private, Company G, 4th Ohio (April 17, 1861); first lieutenant, Company G, 4th Ohio (April 18, 1861); captain, Company G, 4th Ohio (May 4, 1861); major, 82nd Ohio (December 31, 1861); lieutenant colonel, 82nd Ohio (April 9, 1862); colonel, 82nd Ohio (August 29, 1862); commanding 1st Brigade, 3rd Division, 11th Corps, Army of the Cumberland (March 13-April 16, 1864); commanding 3rd Brigade, 1st Division, 20th Corps, Army of the Cumberland (May 2-July 24, 1864 and September 27, 1864-June 7, 1865); and brigadier general, USV (January 12, 1865). As a company commander, he fought at Rich Mountain before his initial three-months regiment was mustered out on July 24, 1861. Five months later he was commissioned as a field officer in a new regiment which fought under John C. Frémont at McDowell and Cross Keys in the Shenandoah Valley. After the unit's colonel was killed at 2nd Bull Run Robinson was advanced to the colonelcy. At Chancellorsville his regiment was caught up in the rout of the 11th Corps, and again disaster struck on the first day at Gettysburg when Robinson was wounded and the corps was again routed. Rejoining his unit early the next year in the West—where it had been transferred with the 11th and 12th corps—he commanded a brigade of the new 20th Corps during the Atlanta Campaign and during the March to the Sea. Brevetted brigadier general on December 9, 1864, for the war to date, he was named to the full rank early the next year. He than led his brigade throughout the Carolinas Campaign and was brevetted major general for the war. Mustered out on August 31, 1865, he directed rail and telegraph lines in his native state and represented it in Congress. He also served as its secretary of state.

ROBINSON, John Cleveland (1817-1897)

In the initial confusion at the outbreak of civil war, New York-born John C. Robinson was one regular army officer who knew how to react. For a breach of regulations he had been expelled from West Point in 1838 during his third year. After briefly studying law he was nonetheless commissioned directly into the regular army as a second lieutenant in the 5th Infantry. He served in the Mexican War but suspected the Mormon expedition of the late 1850s was really a move to occupy the regular army and thus make secession easier. His Civil War assignments included: captain, 5th Infantry (since August 12, 1850); colonel, 1st Michigan (September 1, 1861); major, 2nd Infantry (February 20, 1862); brigadier general, USV (April 28, 1862); commanding brigade, Department of Virginia (May 8-28, 1862); commanding 2nd Brigade, 3rd Division, 3rd Corps, Army of the Potomac (June 9-12, 1862); commanding 1st Brigade, 3rd Division, 3rd Corps, Army of the Potomac (June 12-August 5, 1862); commanding 1st Brigade, 1st Division, 3rd Corps, Army of the Potomac (August 5-December 30, 1862); commanding 2nd Division, 1st Corps, Army of the Potomac (December 30, 1862-March 24, 1864, except briefly in February 1863); and commanding 2nd Division, 5th Corps, Army of the Potomac (April-May 8, 1864). When the 6th Massachusetts was attacked in the streets of Baltimore, he secretly prepared his men at Fort McHenry for a siege by the prosecessionist citizens and then persuaded the the local officials to leave his post alone. Sent on recruiting duty, he became a colonel of volunteers and then a brigadier in command of some of the first troops stationed on the Peninsula. He fought in the Seven Days and 2nd Bull Run but his corps was around Washington at the time of Antietam. Commanding his brigade, he fought at Fredericksburg before transferring to the command of a 1st Corps division. It was not heavily engaged at Chancellorsville but held Oak Ridge—on the corps' right—on the first day of Gettysburg. He held, even after the 11th Corps had been driven back. In fact the two corps had never linked up and had a half mile gap. For his tenacious defense he was brevetted lieutenant colonel in the regular army. His next brevet came for the Wilderness where he led a 5th Corps division. At Laurel Hill, in the initial fighting at Spotsylvania, he was ordered to assault the enemy's position, and he did so with his leading brigade, the others not being up yet. A Confederate bullet in the knee cost him his leg and his field command. In 1894 he received the Congressional Medal of Honor for this action at Laurel Hill. He was also brevetted brigadier general in the regular army for the same action. Upon his recovery he was relegated to commissions and district commands. At the close of hostilities he headed the North Carolina branch of the Freedmen's Bureau. Brevetted major general in both services, he was mustered out of the volunteers on September 1, 1866. After the war he was the commander of the 43rd Infantry and in 1870 was placed upon the retired list as a major general—a fitting honor. A one-time lieutenant governor of his native New York, he headed at different times both the Society of the Army of the Potomac and the Grand Army of the Republic.

ROBINSON, Milton Stapp (?-1892)

It was almost a year after Union officer Milton S. Robinson had resigned that he received his brevet as a brigadier general of volunteers. The Indiana native's assignments included: lieutenant colonel, 47th Indiana (December 13, 1861); colonel, 75th Indiana (October 29, 1862); and commanding 2nd Brigade, 4th Division, 14th Corps, Army of the Cumberland (July 8-August 2 and September 20-October 9, 1863). He commanded his first regiment at the capture of Island #10 and then served in Memphis and Arkansas. Taking charge of a new regiment, he was engaged in pursuing the raider John Hunt Morgan during the winter of 1862-63. He then took part in the Tullahoma Campaign and when his brigade commander was killed at Chickamauga on the second day he took over the post. After fighting at Chattanooga he resigned on March 29, 1864, a month before the opening of the Atlanta Campaign.

ROCHELLE, James Henry (?-?)

In almost two decades in the old navy, James H. Rochelle had seen action in the Mexican War and risen from master to lieutenant before he resigned his commission on April 17, 1861, while serving aboard the USS *Cumberland*. Finally allowed to leave his vessel before the acceptance of his resignation, he was appointed a lieutenant in the Virginia service on May 2, 1861. On the 29th he was assigned to command the *Teaser*. Transferred to the Confederate Navy on June 6, he commanded the *Jackson* on the Mississippi River until the 27th. He was then appointed executive officer of the *Patrick Henry* back at Richmond, with which he took part in the fight at Hampton Roads in March 1862, and the subsequent defense of Drewry's Bluff. He was shortly given command of the *Nansemond*, a gunboat in the James River which he commanded until September 6, 1863, with the exception of a brief period in command of the blockade runner *Stono* which was destroyed on June 5, 1863. Relinquishing command of the *Nansemond*, Rochelle was next engaged in the assembly of guard boats in Charleston Harbor. From April 24, 1864, to the fall of Charleston he commanded the ironclad *Palmetto State*. He later took part in the defense of Wilmington, North Carolina, and as commander served in the final stages of the war as commandant of cadets and executive officer at the South's naval school. During the retreat of the Treasury Department from Richmond he guarded the specie shipments. For a time after the war he was employed by the Peruvian Hydrographical Society. (Scharf, J. Thomas, *History of the Confederate States Navy*)

RODDEY, Philip Dale (1826-1897)

In his scouting and raiding operations—mostly in northern Alabama—Alabama tailor, sheriff, and riverman Philip D. Roddey proved highly successful and rose to the command of a Confederate cavalry division. His assignments included: captain, Roddey's Alabama Cavalry Company (spring 1861); colonel, 4th (Roddey's) Alabama Cavalry (October 1, 1862); commanding brigade, 2nd Division, Cavalry Corps, Department of Mississippi and East Louisiana (January-February 1863); commanding brigade, Martin's Division, Cavalry Corps, Department of Mississippi and East Louisiana (February-April 1863); commanding District of Northern Alabama, Department of Tennessee (July 1863); brigadier general, CSA (August 3, 1863); commanding cavalry brigade, Army of Tennessee (August 1863); commanding brigade, Martin's Division, Wheeler's Cavalry Corps, Army of Tennessee (September 1863); commanding cavalry brigade, Army of Tennessee (October 1863-July 1864); commanding cavalry division, Department of Alabama, Mississippi and East Louisiana (July 1864); and commanding District of North Alabama (also called Roddey's Brigade), Department of Alabama, Mississippi and East Louisiana (September 24, 1864-May 4, 1865). He served as Bragg's escort at Shiloh and then led forces in northern Alabama where he raised several regiments. Sometimes cooperating with larger forces in Georgia, Tennessee, and Mississippi, he usually operated independently in his home region. He did however fight at Tupelo. His command was engaged in the unsuccessful resistance to Wilson's raid through Alabama in the final days of the war. He was later a New York City businessman.

RODES, Robert Emmett (1829-1864)

Distinguishing himself early in the war, Virginian Robert E. Rodes had risen to be the senior division commander in Stonewall's old 2nd Corps by the time of his death at 3rd Winchester. A Virginia Military Institute student and professor, Rodes had been a railroad engineer at the commencement of the war. At the head of the Warrior Guards, he joined the Southern war effort. His assignments included: captain, Company H, 5th Alabama (May 1861); colonel, 5th Alabama (May 11, 1861); brigadier general, CSA (October 21, 1861); commanding Ewell's (old) Brigade, Van Dorn's-D.H. Hill's Division (in Potomac District until March), Department of Northern Virginia (October 22, 1861-May 31 and June 1862); commanding brigade, D.H. Hill's Division (in 2nd Corps from September), Army of Northern Virginia (ca.

August 1862-January 14, 1863); commanding the division (January 14-May 2 and May 3, 1863-June 13, 1864); major general, CSA (May 7, 1863); temporarily commanding the corps (May 2, 1863); and commanding division, Valley District, Department of Northern Virginia (June 13-September 19, 1864). Basically not engaged at 1st Bull Run, Rodes was promoted to brigade command three months later and led the unit at Yorktown and Williamsburg. At Seven Pines the brigadier led his men in a series of attacks and continued at their head even though himself wounded. He relinquished command that evening but was soon back on duty and fought at Gaines' Mill in the Seven Days. He was still suffering from his wound and had to again give up his post before the fight at Malvern Hill. Next action for Rodes came at South Mountain and Antietam where he was slightly injured. The brigade was not directly engaged at Fredericksburg but the next month he replaced Hill in charge of the division when that officer was sent to North Carolina. At Chancellorsville Rodes earned his promotion to major general and briefly led the corps on the evening of May 2, following the wounding of Generals Jackson and A.P. Hill. Heavily engaged on the first day at Gettysburg, he went on to serve at Kelly's Ford, the Wilderness, Spotsylvania, and Cold Harbor. Accompanying Early to the Valley, he was at Monocacy, in the suburbs of Washington, and at 2nd Kernstown. In covering the Confederate withdrawal at 3rd Winchester he was hit by a shell fragment. He was dead in minutes. (Freeman, Douglas S., *Lee's Lieutenants)*

RODGERS, John (1812-1882)

Having entered the navy as a midshipman in 1828, Marylander John Rodgers scored his greatest Civil War success in the capture of the Confederate ironclad *Atlanta*. He had served in the Seminole War and later in the Pacific. His Civil War-era assignments included: commander, USN (since 1855); commanding *Flag* (1861); commanding naval forces on the Western Rivers (May 16-August 26, 1861); aide to Du Pont (November 1861); commanding *Galena* (1862); captain, USN (1862); commanding *Weehawken* (1863); commodore, USN (1863); and commanding *Dictator* (1864). Following brief service in the west, he served as an aide to Du Pont during the action at Port Royal Sound. He then commanded the monitor *Weehawken* with which he captured the *Atlanta* on June 17, 1863. He lost his vessel in later operations against Charleston. Promoted to commodore, he was given another vessel. After the war he rose to the rank of rear admiral. (Johnson, Robert Erwin, *Rear Admiral John Rodgers 1812-1882*)

RODMAN, Isaac Peace (1822-1862)

Although a Quaker, Isaac Rodman, a businessman and local politician, entered the Union army at the beginning of the Civil War. His military assignments included: captain, 2nd Rhode Island (June 6, 1861); colonel, 4th Rhode Island (October 30, 1861); brigadier general, USV (April 28, 1862); and commanding 3rd Division, 9th Corps, Army of the Potomac (September 3-17, 1862). Serving as a company commander, Rodman fought at 1st Bull Run where his regiment suffered heavily. He resigned his captaincy on October 25 to become colonel of a new regiment which he led in an expedition, in early November, into southern Maryland, a pro-Southern area. Sent to the coast of North Carolina as part of General Burnside's expedition, Rodman saw action at Roanoke Island, New Bern, and Fort Macon and came to the favorable attention of his commander who recommended him for promotion. Burnside also made Rodman the military governor of the area around Beaufort, North Carolina. Rodman soon contracted typhoid and was sent home to Rhode Island to recover. After several months he returned to the army and was given command of a division in Burnside's Corps for the Maryland Campaign. After fighting at South Mountain, Rodman led his men across Snavely's Ford on Antietam Creek and came in on the right flank of the rebels defending the crossing at Burnside's Bridge just as other troops forced their way across the bridge. In the later fighting, as his men were driving on the town of Sharpsburg, Rodman's line was struck by A.P. Hill's famed Light Division which had just arrived on the field. While bringing up his old regiment to stabilize the line, Rodman fell wounded. He died on September 30.

RODMAN, Thomas Jefferson (1815-1871)

Indiana-born West Pointer (1841) Thomas Rodman performed his Civil War service in the ordnance department where he worked on methods to improve siege and coastal artillery. At the outbreak of the war, he had been serving in the department as a captain. He was promoted to the rank of major on June 1, 1863, and to lieutenant colonel after the war. His most important contribution to the field came in 1861 when he perfected a method by which large-caliber smoothbore guns could be cast with iron cooled by a water-filled hollow core. With the inside of the barrel cooling first the outer part compressed upon the inner, reinforcing it. The result was a gun that was less likely to burst during firing. This system was used on the large Columbiad guns made after 1861 in eight-, 10-, 13-, 15-, and even 20-inch varieties. The 15-inch caliber was the most common and only a few of the larger caliber were manufactured. These guns were primarily used in seacoast fortifications. He also found a system, utilizing larger grains, of producing more efficient black powder. Most of his Civil War work was performed at the Watertown Arsenal, which he commanded. For his work during the war he was brevetted lieutenant colonel, colonel, and brigadier general in the regular army on March 13, 1865. He remained in the department, commanding the Rock Island Arsenal, until his death in 1871.

ROGERS, William P. (?-1862)

The colonel of the 2nd Texas, William Rogers, entered the service of the Confederacy as lieutenant colonel of the 2nd in October 1861 and served initially in his home state. The regiment left Houston on March 12 and arrived at Corinth, Mississippi, on April 1, 1862, in time to participate in the Confederate successes on the first day at Shiloh. On the second day he led the regiment while Colonel J.C. Moore commanded an informal brigade. After the ultimate defeat, the rebels retired to

A 15-inch Rodman gun in the defenses of Alexandria, Virginia (NA)

and were eventually driven out of their base at Corinth. About May 26, 1862, Rogers became colonel when Moore was promoted brigadier general. During the September fight at Iuka, Rogers led his men in skirmishing, away from the battlefield, to prevent a Union column from aiding the forces in the main battle. At Corinth, after the Confederates had driven the Union forces back to the outskirts of town on the first day, Rogers led the regiment in an assault on Battery Robinett. Just as his command entered the work, and he had grabbed a Union flag, an enemy flanking column appeared. In the resulting volley, Rogers fell dead with 11 wounds.

ROMAN NOSE (?-1868)

Having for years maintained an uneasy truce with the white man, Sauts, or Roman Nose to the whites, a Northern Cheyenne warrior of the Crooked Lance band, was stirred to action by Chivington's massacre at Sand Creek, Colorado, in November 1864. At Valley Station on January 7, his braves killed 18 members of a company of Chivington's 1st Colorado Cavalry and then moved on to attack Julesburg. Driven off, Roman Nose continued depredations along the stage line, including the massacre on January 28 of some ranchers who had been members of the 3rd Colorado Cavalry and participants in the Sand Creek massacre (some of whom had scalps and other trophies from that affair). Following the end of the Cheyenne-Arapaho War later in 1865, Roman Nose continued on the war path until he was killed in the fight at Beecher's Island on September 17, 1868. (Brown, Dee, *Bury My Heart at Wounded Knee*)

RONALD, Charles A. (1827-1898)

A Virginia lawyer and Mexican War veteran, Charles A. Ronald entered the Confederate army as soon as his state seceded and rose to the command of one of the regiments of the prestigious Stonewall Brigade. His assignments included: captain, Company E, 4th Virginia (April 18, 1861); colonel, 4th Virginia (April 23, 1862); and commanding Stonewall Brigade, Jackson's (old) Division, Jackson's Corps, Army of Northern Virginia (August 7-8 and 9, 1862). Leading his company, the Montgomery Highlanders, he fought at 1st Bull Run and in the early stages of the Shenandoah Valley Campaign of 1862 before being promoted to regimental command upon the spring reorganization of the unit. He then commanded the 4th through the rest of the current campaign and in the Seven Days battles around Richmond. Taking part in the campaign against Union General Pope, he was in temporary command of the brigade at Cedar Mountain where his men broke in the face of the enemy. Missing the remainder of the campaign and the invasion of Maryland, Ronald was severely wounded in the thigh by a piece of shell in a skirmish at Kearneysville, West Virginia, on October 16, 1862. The wound and complications forced his resignation on September 11, 1863. With the Confederacy about to collapse in March 1865, he petitioned the War Department to be recommissioned at his old grade. It was too late for any action to be taken. (Robertson, James I., Jr., *The Stonewall Brigade*)

ROOSEVELT, George W. (1843-?)

The third cousin of future president Franklin D. Roosevelt, George W. Roosevelt won a Congressional Medal of Honor for two different exploits involving a flag. Enlisting at the age of 17, in the spring of 1861, he soon became first sergeant of Company K, 26th Pennsylvania. At 2nd Bull Run he recaptured his regiment's colors from the enemy. Then, in the battle of Gettysburg he took the flag of a Confederate regiment from its bearer but was wounded while trying to make off with it. As a result of this wound he lost his left leg. In the 1890s he served as U.S. consul in Brussels. (Mitchell, Joseph B., *The Badge of Gallantry*)

ROOT, Adrian Rowe (?-1899)

On the first day at Gettysburg Adrian R. Root became the third commander of his brigade to fall wounded that day. A New Yorker by birth, he had enlisted in the Union army shortly after the outbreak of the war. His assignments included: lieutenant colonel, 21st New York (May 20, 1861); colonel, 94th New York (May 2, 1862); commanding 1st Brigade, 2nd Division, 1st Corps, Army of the Potomac (November 15, 1862-May 11, 1863 and July 1, 1863); and commanding 3rd Brigade, 3rd Division, 5th Corps, Army of the Potomac (May 13-June 28, 1865). His first regiment served in northern Virginia but saw no major action before his transfer to the new regiment. He then fought at Cedar Mountain and was wounded at 2nd Bull Run. Returning to the command of the brigade, he led it at Fredericksburg and Chancellorsville. He was the third officer to lead his brigade at Gettysburg and fell wounded on the first day. A long recovery followed but he returned in time for the Grand Review and commanded the brigade after the close of hostilities. He was brevetted both brigadier and major general of volunteers for his war service and was mustered out on July 18, 1865, with his regiment.

ROOT, George Frederick (1820-1895)

Although involved in the music profession for over two decades, when the Civil War began George Root had only written one song that had received even the least bit of notice. But things were to change for the organist, choirmaster, singing teacher, and music teacher instructor who had recently moved to Chicago. Root already had under his baton employment by the Rutgers Female Academy and the Union Theological Seminary, but his fame was to come for a different kind of music. Following the Union losses in early 1862, President Lincoln called for 300,000 more troops in the summer. An idea for a song was born in Root's mind. The result was the patriotically stirring "We'll Rally 'Round the Flag, Boys." When the song was first sung at a war rally the crowd joined in with the chorus on the fourth stanza. That same year Root wrote two popular sentimental songs, "The Vacant Chair" and "Just Before the Battle, Mother." In 1864 Root wrote a song of encouragement for imprisoned soldiers called "The Prisoner's Hope" but better known as "Tramp! Tramp! Tramp! the Boys are Marching." After the war Root returned to his instruction but continued to receive the accolades of old veterans.

ROSE, Thomas Ellwood (1830-1907)

Although he was the guiding force behind the great breakout of Union prisoners from the Confederacy's Libby Prison, Pennsylvania native Thomas E. Rose was one of 50 escapees who did not make it to the Union lines. An engineer before the Civil War, his military assignments included: private, Company I, 12th Pennsylvania (April 25, 1861); captain, 77th Pennsylvania (October 28, 1861); colonel, 77th Pennsylvania (February 1, 1863); commanding 2nd Brigade, 2nd Division, 20th Corps, Army of the Cumberland (May 18-June 18, 1863); and commanding 1st Brigade, 1st Division, 4th Corps, Army of the Cumberland (June 12-August 15, 1865). As a private he served under Robert Patterson until his regiment was mustered out on August 5, 1861. Later commissioned a company commander, he moved on to the western theater where his regiment fought at Shiloh, in the advance on Corinth, and at Murfreesboro. In the latter he succeeded to regimental command and a month later was promoted to a colonelcy. He took part in the Tullahoma Campaign and won a brevet for Liberty Gap. Fighting at Chickamauga, he was captured and sent to the Richmond prison. Following several attempts to escape by overpowering the guards, he worked with one other prisoner in an effort to build a tunnel. They soon found that more help was required, and so eventually, 109s officer made the escape attempt on the night of February 9, 1864. Of this number, two drowned, 48 (including Rose) were recaptured, and 59 made it to freedom. Rose was exchanged on July 6, 1864, and fought at Franklin and Nashville. He later led a brigade in Texas before being mustered out with his regiment on December 6, 1865. The next year, having been brevetted brigadier general in the volunteers for the war on July 22, 1865, he was commissioned a captain in the regular army and served until his retirement as major, 18th Infantry, in 1894.

ROSECRANS, William Starke (1819-1898)

The military successes of William S. Rosecrans were overshadowed by others and were insufficient to protect him from the wrath of his superiors—with whom he had difficulties in dealing—when he met with a major defeat at Chickamauga. Born in Ohio he had been graduated from West Point in 1842 and, ranking fifth in his class, was posted to the engineers. After a series of routine assignments and faced with the ever-slow peacetime promotions, he resigned as a first lieutenant in 1854. Entering the business field, he was severely burned in 1859 in an accident at his kerosene plant in Cincinnati. With none of his business ventures being really profitable, he reentered the military service at the outbreak of the Civil War. His

Notorious Libby Prison, from which Thomas E. Rose engineered a mass escape. (AC)

assignments included: volunteer aide-de camp, Ohio Volunteers (April 23, 1861); colonel, Engineers, Ohio Volunteers (April 23, 1861); commanding brigade, Army of Occupation—West Virginia, Department of the Ohio (May-July 23, 1861); colonel, 23rd Ohio (June 12, 1861); brigadier general, USA (June 17, 1861, to rank from May 16); commanding Army of Occupation—West Virginia, Department of the Ohio (July 23-October 11, 1861); also commanding the department (July 23-September 21, 1861); commanding Department of Western Virginia (October 11, 1861-March 11, 1862); commanding Mountain Department (March 14-29, 1862); commanding Right Wing, Army of the Mississippi (May-June 1862); commanding the army (June 26-October 24, 1862); also commanding District of Corinth, Army of the Tennessee (July-September 24, 1862); also commanding 3rd Division, Army of the Tennessee (September 24-October 20, 1862); major general, USV (September 17, 1862; reappointed October 25, to rank from March 21, 1862); commanding 14th Corps, Army of the Cumberland (October 24, 1862-January 9, 1863); commanding Army and Department of the Cumberland (October 30, 1862-October 20, 1863); and commanding Department of the Missouri (January 30-December 9, 1864). Shortly after the fall of Fort Sumter Rosecrans was assigned to the staff of George B. McClellan and took part in the early campaigning in western Virginia. He scored a minor victory at Rich Mountain but the credit went instead to his superior, McClellan, who had failed to carry out his part of the operation. When McClellan went to Washington, Rosecrans took over command in the region and fought at Carinfax Ferry and Gauley River Bridge. After being superceded by John C. Frémont he was assigned to guide Louis Blenker's division on its new assignment in West Virginia. A brigadier general from the early stages of the war, he was sent to the West at his own request and served under John Pope in the advance on Corinth. He commanded the only Union forces to get into action at Iuka, under a plan that had been approved by his new superior, Grant. He also fought at Corinth and then was named to succeed Don C. Buell in charge of the Army of the Ohio, which was renamed the Army of the Cumberland. A heavy drinker and profuse swearer, he was extremely popular with his men who dubbed him "Old Rosey." After much prodding he advanced from Nashville to near Murfreesboro where he was set upon by Braxton Bragg's Army of Tennessee. Hard pressed at first, he managed to hold on and score a victory for the Union cause. Lincoln expressed his gratefulness for the battle and his faith in the general and Rosecrans received the Thanks of Congress. His next achievement is little remembered but of vital importance. In a campaign that produced no major battle he maneuvered the Confederates out of middle Tennessee and into northern Georgia. Known as the Tullahoma Campaign, it and its aftermath was one of the most important moves of the war since it forced Bragg back to his base at Chattanooga and set the stage for the capture of that city, which was accomplished in September 1863. Rosecrans then spread his forces out in pursuit of the "fleeing" enemy who turned, reinforced, and attacked him along Chickamauga Creek. The first day's battle gave the advantage to neither side but on the next day Rosecrans mistakenly believed that there was a gap in the defensive line and ordered Thomas J. Wood's division to fill it. This created a real gap which the Confederates under James Longstreet promptly exploited. The result was that Rosecrans and almost

William S. Rosecrans, unfortunate loser at Chickamauga. (AC)

two-thirds of his army found themselves fleeing from the field toward Chattanooga. However, a stand was made by mixed forces under George H. Thomas, who would succeed Rosecrans in army command. Relieved by Grant the next month, Rosecrans was shunted off to the troublesome Department of the Missouri where his limited forces had difficulty in dealing with Sterling Price's invasion of the state. He was suddenly relieved in December 1864 and spent the balance of his career on leave or awaiting orders which never came. Mustered out of the volunteers on January 15, 1866, he was brevetted major general in the regular service for his victory at Murfreesboro but resigned in disgust at his treatment, on March 28, 1867. Settling in California, he became the chairman of the Military Affairs Committee of the U.S. House of Representatives; but this was not until after he had repeatedly turned down nominations for congress. He was so noted for this that he became known as the "Great Decliner." For the second time he was removed from a position by Grant, when he was ambassador to Mexico. He got even with his old chief while in Congress by opposing Grant's attempts to collect back pay. Rosecrans won a certain degree of recognition in 1889 when he was placed on the retired list as a brigadier general. (Lamers, William M., *The Edge of Glory: A Biography of General William S. Rosecrans*)

ROSS, Anna Maria (ca. 1811-1863)

Like Mary W. Lee and her Union Refreshment Saloon, Anna Maria Ross established, on the Philadelphia riverside, the aid station called Cooper's Shop Saloon. Serving soldiers going to and coming from the front, her saloon provided quarters, food, clothing, and the necessary medical treatment. Her December 1863 death was a loss to thousands of Union soldiers.

ROSS, John (1790-1866)

Although only one-eighth Cherokee, John Ross was the principal chief of the tribe both before and after its forced transplantation from Georgia to what is now Oklahoma. A well-educated planter, he dreamed of statehood for the Cherokee Nation under the U.S. Constitution. He was able to maintain a state of neutrality at the outbreak of the Civil War but after the Confederate victory at Wilson's Creek, the pressure became too great and he entered into an alliance with the Confederacy. However, much of the tribe refused to agree to the treaty and joined with the Upper Creeks under Opothleyohola in a flight to Union-occupied Kansas. Ross took part in the bloody pursuit. He also took part in the battle of Pea Ridge in March 1862. In June 1862 a Union force of loyal Indians and whites invaded the Cherokee country and Ross gave up without a fight, with many of his people switching sides to join with the Union. The split in the nation widened as Colonel Stand Watie's regiment remained with the Confederacy and eventually burned Ross' home in retaliation for his defection. Ross died a year after the war ended, while on a mission to Washington. (Eaton, Rachel C., *John Ross and the Cherokee Indians*)

Cherokee chief John Ross switched sides in the midst of the Civil War. (SI)

ROSS, Lawrence Sullivan (1838-1898)

Financially ruined by his service as a Confederate brigadier general, Iowa native and noted Indian fighter Lawrence S. Ross returned to his adopted Texas where he became one of the state's most popular private citizens. Raised on the Texas frontier he had fought against the Comanches, killing chief Peta Necona, and becoming a captain in the Texas Rangers. His Civil War assignments included: private, 6th Texas Cavalry (1861); major, 6th Texas Cavalry (September 1861); colonel, 6th Texas Cavalry (May 14, 1862); commanding brigade, Jackson's Cavalry Division, Department of Mississippi and East Louisiana (September 1863-May 1864); brigadier general, CSA (December 21, 1863); commanding brigade, Jackson's Cavalry Division, Polk's (Army of Mississippi)-Stewart's Corps, Army of Tennessee (May-July 26, 1864); commanding brigade, Jackson's Cavalry Division, Army of Tennessee (July 26-31, 1864 and August 1864-February 13, 1865); and commanding brigade, Jackson's Division, Forrest's Cavalry Corps, Department of Alabama, Mississippi and East Louisiana (February 13-May 4, 1865). He led his regiment dismounted at Corinth before it was reconverted into cavalry. After taking part in the efforts to relieve the pressure on Vicksburg he was promoted to brigadier general and led his brigade through the Atlanta and Franklin-Nashville campaigns. In the final months of the war he served under Nathan Bedford Forrest. He was subsequently a farmer, sheriff, state legislator, governor, and president of Texas A. & M. (Benner, Judith Ann, *Sul Ross: Soldier, Statesman, Educator*)

ROSS, Leonard Fulton (1823-1901)

After the fall of Vicksburg, Union General Leonard F. Ross, thinking the war about over, resigned his commission in order to return to private pursuits. The Illinois native had been a judge and Democratic politician. In the Mexican War he served as a private and first lieutenant in the 4th Illinois. Practicing law at the time of the firing upon Fort Sumter, he promptly became a regimental commander in the Union army. His assignments included: colonel, 17th Illinois (May 25, 1861); commanding 3rd Brigade, 1st Division, Army of the Tennessee (February 17-April 1 and April 15-July 1862); brigadier general, USV (April 25, 1862); also commanding the division (May 14-June 2, 1862); commanding 2nd Division, District of Corinth, Army of the Tennessee (October 24-November 1, 1862); commanding 8th Division, Left Wing, 13th Corps, Army of the Tennessee (November 11-December 18, 1862); and commanding 13th Division, 13th Corps, Army of the Tennessee (February 8-May 23, 1863). He fought at Frederickstown, Missouri, and commanded a brigade at Fort Donelson. Although he missed Shiloh he was named a brigadier general later that month. As such he led a division in Grant's unsuccessful overland movement against Vicksburg. He also participated in the Yazoo Pass expedition. His final service came when he was stationed at Helena, Arkansas, during the final operations against the river city. Thinking the war to be over, he resigned on July 22, 1863. He entered the livestock business and remained active in politics—but now as a Republican.

ROSSER, Thomas Lafayette (1836-1910)

Resigning from the United States Military Academy on April 22, 1861, only two weeks before graduation, Thomas L. Rosser was nonetheless able to don the stars of a general in both the Confederate and U.S. armies. A native of Virginia and a former resident of Texas, he joined the Confederacy where his assignments included: first lieutenant, Washington (La.) Artillery Battalion (May 1861); captain, Washington (La.) Artillery Battalion (summer 1861); lieutenant colonel, Artillery (June 1862); colonel, 5th Virginia Cavalry (ca. June 25, 1862); brigadier general, CSA (September 28, 1863); commanding Laurel Brigade, Hampton's-Butler's Division, Cavalry Corps, Army of Northern Virginia (October 1863-October 5, 1864); commanding same brigade, F. Lee's Division, Army of the Valley District, Department of Northern Virginia (October 1864); commanding the division (October 1864-January 1865); major general, CSA (November 1, 1864); and commanding his own division, in the Valley District (January-March 1865) and in the Army of Northern Virginia (March-May 2, 1865). Serving in the artillery initially as an instructor, he commanded a battery at Blackburn's Ford, 1st Bull Run, and Yorktown. Transferred to the cavalry, he commanded a regiment at the Seven Days (wounded at Mechanicsville), 2nd Bull Run, South Mountain, Antietam, Kelly's Ford (wounded), Chancellorsville, and Gettysburg. Promoted to brigade command, he fought in the campaign from the Rapidan to the James, before being sent to the Shenandoah Valley in the fall of 1864. Here he quickly became known as the "Saviour of the Valley." However, he was bested by his old classmate and friend, George Custer, at Woodstock. He later fought at Cedar Creek in temporary divisional command. In the next few months Rosser led three successful raids into West Virginia. Returning to the Petersburg front in March 1865 he was hosting a shad-bake for Pickett and Fitzhugh Lee when their lines were broken at Five Forks. Retreating with the army, he fought his way out with much of his command but was himself captured a month later. Active in farming and railroading after the war, he again donned a blue uniform as a brigadier general for the Spanish-American War and for a time commanded a training camp on the old battlefield of Chickamauga. (Bushong, Millard K., *Fightin' Tom Rosser, C.S.A.*)

ROTHERMEL, Peter Frederick (1817-1895)

When the state of Pennsylvania was looking for an artist to commemorate the battle of Gettysburg it chose Peter Rothermel for the job. Having studied in Philadelphia and Europe and served as director of the Pennsylvania Academy of Art, the Pennsylvania-born Rothermel had already become known for his depiction of such historical events as "De Soto Discovering the Mississippi" and "Patrick Henry before the Virginia House of Burgesses." Receiving the commission, which had been suggested by Governor Curtin, he chose the moment when Pickett's Charge was being turned back on Cemetery Ridge as the focus of his main work. General Meade praised the finished work, with the one critical comment that he himself should not have been included in the work as he was not present at that moment. However, the display of the painting for a fee by Rothermel was a matter of controversy. He also did four smaller paintings to accompany "Pickett's Charge," the largest painting on a single canvas in the United States. Two were on the Pennsylvania Reserves in the Wheatfield, and one each, for Reynolds' death on the first day and the fight for Culp's Hill. His commission for the series amounted to $25,000 and his work is now on display in Harrisburg.

ROUSSEAU, Lovell Harrison (1818-1869)

Leaving the volunteer service at the end of the Civil War, Lovell H. Rousseau engaged in a highly controversial congressional career before being named a regular army general and formally accepting "Seward's Folly": Alaska. The Kentucky native had received his military training as a company commander in an Indiana regiment during the Mexican War. Having sat in both houses of that state's legislature, he was practicing law in his native state at the outbreak of the Civil War. His assignments included: colonel, 3rd Kentucky (September 9, 1861); brigadier general, USV (October 1, 1861); commanding 1st Brigade, McCook's Division, Army of the Cumberland (October-November 1861); commanding 4th Brigade, Army of the Ohio (November-December 2, 1861); commanding 4th Brigade, 2nd Division, Army of the Ohio (December 2, 1861-July 11, 1862); commanding 3rd Division, Army of the Ohio (July 11-September 29, 1862); commanding 3rd Division, 1st Corps, Army of the Ohio (September 29-November 5, 1862); major general, USV (October 22, 1862, to rank from October 8); commanding 1st Division, Center, 14th Corps, Army of the Cumberland (November 5, 1862-January 9, 1863); commanding 1st Division, 14th Corps, Army of the Cumberland (January 9-17, March 29-July 26, and September 21-November 17, 1863); commanding District of Nashville, Department of the Cumberland (November 10, 1863-July 3, 1865); also commanding in the district: 3rd Division, 12th

Rothermel's painting of Pickett's Charge. (AC)

Corps (January 2-April 14, 1864) and 4th Division, 20th Corps (April 14, 1864-65); and commanding District of Middle Tennessee, Department of the Cumberland (March-summer 1865). During the period of Kentucky's "neutrality" Rousseau raised volunteers there in a somewhat undercover manner. Thus he was not officially mustered into the service until the late summer of 1861. Promoted to a brigadier generalship shortly thereafter, he led a brigade in Buell's relief force on the second day at Shiloh. His division fought at both Perryville and Murfreesboro and through the Tullahoma Campaign. Rousseau was, however, absent during the bloody fighting at Chickamauga. Thereafter he commanded the garrison forces around Nashville as a major general. On November 10, 1865, he resigned to take a seat in Congress as a Radical Republican. However, he quickly became a supporter of the more conservative Andrew Johnson. Censured by the House of Representatives for his caning of Radical Congressman Josiah B. Grinnell—reminiscent of the antebellum Brooks-Sumner affair—he resigned and was reelected. At this juncture—1867—Johnson rewarded Rousseau with a regular army commission as a brigadier general. He was also brevetted major general for his war service and was dispatched to take possession of Alaska from the Russians. He died in New Orleans while in charge of the occupation of Louisiana.

ROWAN, Stephen Clegg (1808-1890)

A native of Ireland, Stephen C. Rowan is credited with having directed the firing of the first shot from a naval vessel in the Civil War. After immigrating to the United States in 1818, he joined the navy and served in the Mediterranean, off Brazil, and in the Pacific. During the Mexican War he participated in the recapture of Los Angeles and was subsequently assigned to shore duty. His Civil War assignments included: commander, USN (since 1855); commanding *Pawnee* (early 1861); commanding Naval Division, North Atlantic Blockading Squadron (February-March 1862); captain, USN (1862); commodore, USN (1862); commanding *New Ironsides* (1863); and commanding naval forces in North Carolina sounds (1864). In trying to end the blockade of the Potomac River, which was cutting off Washington, he ordered his guns for the first time to fire on the Confederate batteries at Aquia Creek. Early the next year he fought at Roanoke Island, Cable's Point, and New Bern. In 1863 he was engaged in the actions in Charleston Harbor and the next year moved to overall command in North Carolina waters. The year after the war ended he was promoted to rear admiral and he finally retired in 1889 as a vice admiral.

ROWLEY, Thomas Algeo (1808-1892)

While in command of Doubleday's division at Gettysburg, Mexican War veteran Thomas A. Rowley was under the influence of alcohol and was guilty of conduct "unbecoming of an officer and a gentleman"—so found the court-martial which tried him. The Pittsburgh native had been a captain of volunteers in the 1840s and was a court clerk shortly before the outbreak of the Civil War. Enlisting under Lincoln's first call for troops, his assignments included: colonel, 13th Pennsylvania (April 25, 1861); colonel, 102nd Pennsylvania (August 6, 1861); commanding 3rd Brigade, 3rd Division, 6th Corps, Army of the Potomac (November-December 15, 1862); brigadier general, USV (November 29, 1862); commanding 1st Brigade, 3rd Division, 1st Corps, Army of the Potomac (March 28-June 30 and July 2-10, 1863); commanding the division (June 30-July 2, 1863); and commanding District of the Monongahela, Department of the Susquehanna (late 1864). With his three-months regiment he served in Patterson's army before it was mustered out on August 6, 1861. On the same day the majority of the regiment reenlisted, again with Rowley at their head, but with a new unit number. At their head he fought at Williamsburg, Seven Pines, and the Seven Days. In the second-named of the Peninsula Campaign actions Rowley was wounded. During McClellan's shift to the aid of Pope in northern Virginia, Rowley's men were detached and assigned to the support of some artillery at Chantilly but were not actively engaged. This action was really the end of 2nd Bull Run. The 4th Corps division in which the 102nd served was detached from the corps and served with the 6th Corps in the Maryland Campaign but was not close enough to the front for the fighting at Antietam. Shortly after the battle the division was permanently attached to the 6th Corps. At Fredericksburg Rowley led his brigade on the left, but two days later—the same day that the army completed its withdrawal across the Rappahannock—he was replaced by Frank Wheaton. Both had been made brigadier generals to rank from November 29, 1862, but Wheaton was well ahead of Rowley on the list of promotions and thus ranked him. By March 1863 Rowley was commanding a 1st Corps brigade and fought at Chancellorsville although the corps' role was limited. On the day before Gettysburg he took command of the division when Abner Doubleday took charge of the corps, replacing John F. Reynolds who was directing the army's left wing. The three-day battle proved to be Rowley's undoing. Doubleday having been replaced by John Newton, Rowley was back in brigade command on the second and third days. A week after the battle's close he was shunted off to draft duty in Maine and was subsequently sentenced by the court-martial to be cashiered for his poor behavior at Gettysburg. Secretary of War Edwin M. Stanton overturned the decision, and Rowley reported to Grant in Virginia who promptly returned him to the adjutant general for new orders. Grant's position was that the feeling against Rowley in the Army of the Potomac was too great to make him an effective leader. He was then relegated to district command in his home town and his resignation took effect on December 29, 1864. He was a Pittsburgh lawyer and peace officer after the war. Not surprisingly, his name did not appear on the list of brevet promotions issued on March 13, 1865.

RUCKER, Daniel Henry (1812-1910)

Career army officer Daniel H. Rucker served throughout the Civil War in command of the Quartermaster's Depot in Washington, D.C., and emerged from the conflict with the brevets of major general in both the volunteers and the regular establishment. The New Jersey native had been commissioned directly from Michigan as a second lieutenant in the 1st

Dragoons in 1837. Winning a brevet in the Mexican War, he transferred to the quartermaster's department in 1849. His Civil War-era assignments included: captain and assistant quartermaster (since August 23, 1849); major and quartermaster (August 3, 1861); colonel and additional aide-de-camp (September 28, 1861); and brigadier general, USV (May 23, 1863). Throughout the war he served under Quartermaster General Montgomery Meigs and was named a brigadier general of volunteers in the spring of 1863. Stationed in Washington until 1867, he was mustered out of the volunteers on September 1, 1866, and was named colonel and assistant quartermaster general the same year. He held this position until he was promoted to the staff rank of brigadier general and placed in charge of the quartermaster's department in 1882. Ten days later he was retired. He then settled in the nation's capital.

RUCKER, Edmund Winchester (1835-?)

A self-educated surveyor and engineer, Edmund W. Rucker started his Confederate service in that field before transferring to the cavalry. His assignments included: private and second lieutenant, Pickett's (Tenn.) Company Sappers and Miners (May 1861); captain, Stewart Invincibles (Tenn.) Heavy Artillery Company (fall 1861); captain, Company E, 1st Tennessee Heavy Artillery (May 10, 1862); major, 16th Tennessee Cavalry Battalion (October 1862); colonel, Cavalry (February 1863); colonel, Rucker's Legion (ca. June 1, 1863); and commanding in Forrest's Cavalry Corps, Department of Alabama, Mississippi and East Louisiana: 6th Brigade, Buford's Division (spring 1864); 6th Brigade, Chalmers' Division (June-July 14, 1864); and 1st Brigade, Chalmer's Division (September 1864-February 13, 1865). After serving in the engineers at Columbus, Kentucky, he was given command of a group of Illinoisans who wanted to join the Confederacy. Serving as heavy artillery, he commanded them at Island #10 and escaped with part of his unit upon the fall of the place. After some service at Fort Pillow, he was transferred to the cavalry in East Tennessee and was assigned to rounding up conscripts, a duty which he detested. He also took part in Pegram's Kentucky raid. He led a field organization of the 12th and 16th Cavalry Battalions, known as Rucker's Legion, from June 1863 to February 1864, including fighting at Chickamauga. At Forrest's request he was transferred to Mississippi and given command of a brigade, which he led at Brice's Crossroads and Tupelo until wounded. Returning to duty, he was given command of another brigade, causing great dissatisfaction among the regimental commanders. One of them, James J. Neely, was cashiered for disobedience of orders. With Chalmers' Division, he was temporarily assigned to duty with the Army of Tennessee and fought at Nashville. In the February 1865 reorganization of Forrest's cavalry, Rucker lost his brigade.

RUFF, Solon Zackery (1837-1863)

A graduate and former faculty member of the Georgia Military Institute, Solon Z. Ruff had a promising career in the Confederate army until he was cut down in the disastrous assault on Fort Sanders at Knoxville. His assignments included: lieutenant colonel, 18th Georgia (April 25, 1861); colonel, 18th Georgia (fall 1863, to rank from January 17, 1863); and commanding Wofford's Brigade, McLaws' Division, Longstreet's Corps, Department of East Tennessee (early November-November 29, 1863). Initially assigned to the Texas Brigade, Ruff and the 18th saw action at Seven Pines, in the Seven Days, 2nd Bull Run, and Antietam. In all but the first-named battle Ruff was in command of the regiment. In the fall of 1862 the 18th was transferred to Cobb's, later Wofford's, Brigade and Ruff continued in regimental command at Fredericksburg, in the Suffolk Campaign, and at Gettysburg. The brigade arriving too late, he missed the battle of Chickamauga when Longstreet went west. Shortly after this, Ruff finally received his colonel's commission, backdated to the start of the year. In the Knoxville Campaign he was in temporary command of the brigade until he was killed on November 29, 1863, directing its assault on Fort Sanders.

RUFFIN, Edmund (1794-1865)

Having argued so long and so hard for the establishment of the Confederacy, Edmund Ruffin was unable to bear the thought of

Edmund Ruffin, secession fanatic and suicide. (NA)

living in a reunited nation. Born into the Virginia plantation society, Ruffin had attended William and Mary. Entering the life of a gentleman farmer, he was dissatisfied and became what can best be described as a scientific farmer, the preeminent leader of Virginia agriculture, urging others to follow his system of crop rotation and the use of marl as fertilizer. As editor of the *Farmer's Register* and president of the Virginia Agricultural Society, he was able to foster a recovery of the industry in the Upper South. Retired from farming in 1856, he visited throughout the South and wrote articles for various publications, urging and campaigning for the region's secession and the formation of an independent country. He also wrote *Slavery and Free Labor Described and Compared.* He was present at the hanging of John Brown, whose raid added fuel to his arguments. He also attended three state secession conventions and, disgusted with the failure of Virginia to take the final step, went to South Carolina where he was given the honor, as a member of the Palmetto Guards, to fire one of the first shots at Fort Sumter (the 1812 veteran claimed it was the first). At 1st Bull Run it has been alleged that he fired the artillery shot which blocked the Cub Run Bridge, leading to the Union rout and abandonment of much of its equipment. Too old for military service, he retired from the field but continued to write in his diary which he had started in 1856. With the collapse of the South he committed suicide on June 15, 1865, rather than live under the American flag. (Mitchell, Betty L., *Edmund Ruffin: A Biography*)

RUGER, Thomas Howard (1833-1907)

West Pointer (1854) Thomas H. Ruger rejoined the army for the Civil War and remained in the service until he was retired on account of age. Graduating third in his class, he had been posted to the engineers but served for less than a year before resigning to practice law in Wisconsin. The native New Yorker volunteered upon the outbreak of the Civil War and his assignments included: lieutenant colonel, 3rd Wisconsin (June 29, 1861); colonel, 3rd Wisconsin (September 1, 1861); commanding 3rd Brigade, 1st Division, 12th Corps, Army of the Potomac (September 17-October 20, 1862, February-July 1, July 4-August 16, and September 16-25, 1863); commanding 1st Brigade, 2nd Division, 12th Corps, Army of the Potomac (October 26-December 30, 1862); brigadier general, USV (November 29, 1862); commanding 1st Division, 12th Corps, Army of the Potomac (July 1-4, 1863); commanding 3rd Brigade, 1st Division, 12th Corps, Army of the Cumberland (September 25, 1863-April 14, 1864); commanding 2nd Brigade, 1st Division, 20th Corps, Army of the Cumberland (April 14-September 17 and October 17-November 5, 1864); commanding 2nd Division, 23rd Corps, Department of the Ohio (November 11-December 8, 1864); commanding 1st Division, Cox's Provisional Corps, Department of North Carolina (February 25-March 18, 1865); commanding 1st Division, 23rd Corps, Department of North Carolina (March 18-June 17, 1865); commanding the corps (June 17-27, 1865); and commanding the department (June 27-July 17, 1865). Leading his regiment he fought in the Shenandoah Valley, at Cedar Mountain and Antietam, where he was wounded while exercising temporary brigade command. Recovering, he was given a brigadier's star and led his brigade at Chancellorsville. In 1867 he was brevetted brigadier general in the regular army for his role at Gettysburg where he was in temporary command of the division when Alpheus S. Williams led the corps while Henry W. Slocum exercised command of the army's right wing. In August he enforced order in New York following the draft riots. Transferred to the West, he led his brigade in guarding the supply lines during the battle of Chattanooga. The division was assigned this duty because Slocum refused to serve under Hooker, and the corps sent only one division into the fight so that Slocum could have his way. Retaining brigade command in the merger of the 11th and 12th corps the following spring, Ruger fought through the Atlanta Campaign and later faced Hood's invasion of Tennessee at Franklin. For this battle he was brevetted major general of volunteers. Missing the battle of Nashville, he was transferred to the North Carolina coast along with most of the 23rd Corps and joined Sherman for the surrender of Johnston's army. Continuing on duty in that state until his September 1, 1866, muster out, he became colonel of one of the newly created regular army infantry regiments. Eventually rising to the rank of major general, he served as commandant at his alma mater (1871-76), as commander of the Department of the South (1876-78), and on the frontier as commander of the District of Montana (1878-85). He finally retired in 1895.

RUGGLES, Daniel (1810-1897)

Although a Confederate brigadier general, Daniel Ruggles fought in only one major action and appears to have displeased his superiors to such an extent that he could not get another command. The Massachusetts-born West Pointer (1833) had served in the Seminole War with the infantry and won two brevets in Mexico. Marriage into a Virginia family linked him with the South and he resigned as a captain in the 5th Infantry on May 7, 1861. His Confederate assignments included: brigadier general, Virginia Volunteers (April 1861); commanding Department of Fredericksburg (April 22-June 5, 1861); brigadier general, CSA (August 9, 1861); commanding District of North Alabama, Department of Alabama and West Florida (February 23-ca. February 1862); commanding 1st Corps, 2nd Grand Division, Army of the Mississippi (March 5-29, 1862); commanding 1st Division, 2nd Corps, Army of the Mississippi (March 29-April 1862); commanding 1st District, Department of Southern Mississippi and East Louisiana (June 26-July 2, 1862); and temporarily commanding District of Mississippi, Department #2 (September 5-October 3, 1862). As a Virginia officer he commanded along the Rappahannock in the early months of the war before being named a Confederate brigadier general. Ordered to New Orleans, he proved too ill for a time to command troops. Eventually he commanded a brigade at Shiloh where he is credited with gathering a large number of guns to fire on the Union position at the Hornet's Nest. However, he lost that command the same month and then held minor district-level commands. In the final days of the Confederacy he was appointed commissary general of prisoners. He was subsequently a Virginia resident, Texas planter, and member of the West Point board of visitors.

RUMSEY, Elida

See: *Fowle, Elida Rumsey*

RUNYON, Theodore (?-1896)

A militia general from his native state of New Jersey, Theodore Runyon served the Union cause only during the campaign of 1st Bull Run, and even there he was in reserve. His assignments included: brigadier general, New Jersey Militia (April 30, 1861); and commanding 4th (Reserve) Division, Army of Northeastern Virginia (June-July 31, 1861). He arrived with his militia regiments at Washington in May 1861 and was soon joined by some volunteer regiments from New York and New Jersey. Upon the advance on Manassas the division was left to guard the area between Alexandria and Fairfax Court House and did not take part in the fighting. However, following the defeat Runyon's command held the fortifications until the other divisions could be reconcentrated and placed in line. On July 31, 1861, Runyon was mustered out with his militia regiments and appears no more in Civil War annals.

RUSH, Richard Henry (?-1893)

Englishman Richard H. Rush commanded the only regiment of Union lancers to see active field service in the Civil War. A West Pointer (1846), he had been posted to the artillery until his 1854 resignation as a first lieutenant. Upon the outbreak of the Civil War he raised his regiment in Philadelphia and his assignments included: colonel, 6th Pennsylvania Cavalry (July 27, 1861); commanding 3rd Brigade, Pleasonton's Cavalry Division, Army of the Potomac (September-November 1862); colonel, 1st Veteran Reserve Corps (ca. October 1863); and commanding 1st Brigade, Veteran Reserve Corps, District of Washington, 22nd Corps, Department of Washington (March 23-May 21, 1864). At first the regiment was utilized as if it were regular cavalry, despite its unique equipment. Rush led his unit to the Peninsula and saw action at Yorktown and during the Seven Days. During the Maryland Campaign he commanded a brigade, but once the unit was back in Virginia the cumbersome lances were found to limit its usefulness as regular cavalry and it was assigned to special duties more fitting to its equipment. At Fredericksburg the unit served as escort to William B. Franklin, commanding the Left Grand Division. Rush does not appear to have commanded the regiment after April 1863, and that spring the unit was reequipped as normal cavalry. Later that year he was transferred to the Veteran Reserve Corps and the next spring commanded a brigade in the Washington fortifications. He resigned on July 1, 1864.

RUSSELL, Alfred A. (?-?)

Although he was not in many of the great battles of the western theater, Alfred A. Russell did see a great deal of action on the fringes of the larger campaigns, on raids and in fighting enemy raids. His Confederate services included: major, 7th Alabama (May 18, 1861); lieutenant colonel, 15th Tennessee Cavalry Battalion (1862); colonel, 4th (Russell's) Alabama Cavalry

Some of Rush's Lancers on guard duty the day after Antietam. (*Leslie's*)

(November 23, 1862); commanding brigade, Martin's Division, Wheeler's Cavalry Corps, Army of Tennessee (July-fall 1863); and commanding Morgan's Brigade, Martin's Division, Wheeler's Cavalry Corps, Army of Tennessee (December 1863-February 1864). His first regiment was only a 12-months unit, but he did see action with it in the bombardment of Pensacola in October 1861. Following its muster out, he was given command of a cavalry battalion which was soon raised to a regiment. With this unit he took part in Forrest's December 1862 West Tennessee raid. He then fought at Chickamauga and took part in Wheeler's Sequatchie raid. He was with the Army of Tennessee throughout the Atlanta Campaign, after having been with Longstreet in East Tennessee. He took part in the defeat of Stoneman's raid. When Hood invaded Tennessee in the fall of 1864 Russell served in the Tennessee Valley, joining up with General Roddey and later with Forrest. He took part in the unsuccessful defense against Wilson's raid through Alabama and surrendered with Forrest. He survived two wartime wounds.

RUSSELL, Andrew J. (1838-?)

Relatively unknown in Civil War history, in part because many of his photographs have been credited to others and in part for his more famous postwar work, Andrew Russell was the only official army photographer in the war. Born in Vermont, it is believed that Russell worked for a time in Brady's New York studios before the war. On August 19, 1862, he was commissioned captain of Company F, 141st New York. In February 1863, he was detailed from his command by General Herman Haupt, the Union military railroad chief, to serve as an official photographer. The idea was for Russell to photograph railroad installations and innovations, the prints to accompany Haupt's reports and directions for construction crews. However, Russell did not limit himself to railroads; in his free time he made images of various fortifications around Washington. With Haupt he was present during the Chancellorsville Campaign and here made some of his most memorable exposures, including one of a demolished Confederate caisson and one of the abandoned enemy lines, full of impedimenta and rebel dead. After Haupt's resignation, Russell usually accompanied the Army of the Potomac in its campaigns until near the end of the conflict, when he was mustered out following a dispute over reimbursement of expenses and ownership of the negatives. Russell went on to become a photographer for the Union Pacific.

Andrew J. Russell's view of the destruction on Marye's Heights, during the Chancellorsville fighting, with Herman Haupt leaning on the tree stump. (NA)

RUSSELL, David Allen (1820-1864)

In honor of his role in the successful attack at Rappahannock Station, David A. Russell was given the privilege of taking the eight captured battle flags to Washington. The native New Yorker had been posted to the infantry in view of his poor class standing at West Point (1845), but he distinguished himself in Mexico and earned a brevet. His Civil War assignments included: captain, 4th Infantry (since June 22, 1854); colonel, 7th Massachusetts (February 18, 1862); major, 8th Infantry (August 9, 1862); brigadier general, USV (November 29, 1862); commanding 3rd Brigade, 1st Division, 6th Corps, Army of the Potomac (December 10, 1862-February 23, 1863, March 15-November 20, and December 5-16, 1863, and April 5-May 9, 1864); commanding the division (December 16, 1863-March 25, 1864 and May 9-July 8, 1864); commanding 2nd Brigade, 3rd Division, 6th Corps, Army of the Potomac (March 25-April 7, 1864); and commanding 1st Division, 6th Corps, Army of the Shenandoah (August 6-September 19, 1864). With his regular army unit, he was in the Washington defenses until given command of a volunteer regiment. He earned a brevet for the Peninsula Campaign where he saw action at Yorktown, Williamsburg, Seven Pines, and in the Seven Days. His division was too far in the rear to have taken an active part in the fighting at Antietam, but he soon received a brigadier's star and a brigade in the 6th Corps. This was only lightly engaged at Fredericksburg, but he led his men in the storming of Marye's Heights the following May during the Chancellorsville Campaign. The brigade was in reserve at Gettysburg but took part in the fall campaigns where Russell spearheaded the attack at Rappahannock Station and was wounded. Brevetted brigadier general in the regular army for the Wilderness, he fought through the rest of the Overland Campaign and into the Petersburg Campaign. Sent to Washington to help repulse Jubal Early, he became a division commander in Sheridan's army in the Valley. In the fighting at 3rd Winchester, he remained in command despite a chest wound. Then a piece of shell struck his heart, killing him instantly. Posthumously he was awarded the last two brevets that he could receive, those of major general in both services for 3rd Winchester.

RUSSELL, Lord John (1792-1878)

The British foreign secretary during the Civil War, Lord Russell was quick to explain that the granting of belligerent status to both sides during the conflict was not to be followed by recognition of the Confederate States. Nevertheless, in retaliation the United States refused to accept the Declaration of Paris on the rights of neutrals in time of war, due to the clause outlawing privateers if private property was not respected. Russell was outraged, since the United States had pushed for neutral's rights ever since the Revolution. In 1862 Russell almost came to the point of offering mediation services to resolve the crisis. His neutrality pleased neither side. He failed to stop the sailing of the vessel which became the Confederate raider *Alabama*, a lack of decision which in 1872 cost Britain £3,000,000 in settlements, but, in contrast, he was also considered rude to the Confederate commissioner Mason when approached on British recognition. After the war he succeeded Palmerston as prime minister. (Walpole, Spencer, *The Life of John Russell*)

RUSSELL, Robert Milton (1826-1894)

A West Pointer (1848) and veteran of two years in the infantry of the old army, Robert M. Russell commanded a Confederate brigade in the early part of the Civil War but commanded only his own regiment for most of the conflict. The native Tennessean held the following positions: colonel, 12th Tennessee (May 1861); commanding 3rd Brigade, 1st Geographical Division, Department No. 2 (September 7-October 24, 1861); commanding 2nd Brigade, 1st Division, 1st Geographical Division, Department No. 2 (October 24, 1861-March 5, 1862); commanding 3rd Brigade, 1st Grand Division, Army of the Mississippi, Department No. 2 (March 5-29, 1862); commanding 1st Brigade, 1st Division, 1st Corps, Army of the Mississippi, Department No. 2 (March 29-May 1862); colonel, 20th (sometimes called 15th) Tennessee Cavalry (February 5, 1864); and colonel, 19th and 20th Consolidated Tennessee Cavalry (February 13, 1865). He led an infantry brigade at Belmont, where he was among the first engaged, and at Shiloh before he failed to gain reelection at the May 1862 reorganization of the regiment. A year and a half later he was given command of a cavalry regiment which was formed from various units raised behind enemy lines. Serving under Nathan Bedford Forrest, he saw action at Okolona, Paducah, Fort Pillow, Brice's Crossroads, and Tupelo. Wounded at the latter, he returned to participate in Hood's Tennessee Campaign. After being given command of the consolidated regiment he helped oppose Wilson's raid through Alabama. He was surrendered with Forrest at Gainesville.

RUSSELL, William Howard (1820-1907)

An experienced war correspondent, having covered the Crimean War, Englishman William Russell was dispatched to America by the London *Times* to report the unfolding events in America early in 1861. After a month reporting from Washington, he headed south, arriving in Charleston after the fall of Fort Sumter. Russell then toured the South, making perceptive appraisals of the abilities of many of the not-yet-famous leaders he encountered. Returning to Washington, he covered the 1st Battle of Bull Run from a close-up position, having crossed the stream itself just in time to be caught up in the rout of the Union forces. His unflattering reports were not well received on the western side of the Atlantic. The Americans resorted to calling him "Bombast" and "London Stout" Russell. The recipient of many threats, Russell was warned not to appear in public unarmed. In fact he was nearly killed by an unappreciative sentry. The reaction to "Bull Run" Russell was just as harsh in official circles. Being refused permission to accompany the Army of the Potomac to the Peninsula in early 1862, he returned to England. He later reported from the fields of the Franco-Prussian and Zulu Wars. (Russell, William Howard, *My Diary North and South* and Atkins, John Black, *The Life of Sir William Howard Russell*)

RUST, Albert (1818-1870)

Born in Virginia, Arkansas Congressman Albert Rust was a reluctant secessionist when he resigned his seat to join his state. With the admission of Arkansas to the Confederacy he was named as a representative to the Provisional Congress, where he served on the Postal Affairs Committee through February 17, 1862. However, in the spring and early summer of 1861 Rust raised the 3rd Arkansas and was named its colonel on July 5, 1861. Sent to western Virginia, Rust's regiment was assigned to General H.R. Jackson's Brigade in General Loring's Army of the Northwest. Taking part in General Lee's Cheat Mountain Campaign, Rust discovered a route to outflank the Union forces. Given command of this movement, which would signal the start of the action, Rust for some reason failed to act and the attack never materialized. Subsequently Rust was commended for his actions during the Romney Campaign and was promoted to brigadier general on March 6, 1862, to rank from two days earlier. Transferred back to Arkansas he was directed on March 13 to gather up scattered Confederate forces and reinforce General Van Dorn. With the organization complete he was given command of the brigade on April 8 and directed later that month to move to Corinth, Mississippi. He commanded this brigade as part of Jones' Division, Army of the West (April 29-May 27, 1862), before being ordered back to the Trans-Mississippi District. His later commands included: 4th Brigade, Breckinridge's-Lovell's Division, District of the Mississippi (September 8-October 1862); commanding brigade, Department of Mississippi and East Louisiana (October 1862-early 1863); and commanding same brigade, District of East Louisiana, Department of Mississippi and East Louisiana (early 1863-April 15, 1863). On October 3 and 4, 1862, he took part in the battle of Corinth. Transferred again to the Trans-Mississippi in April 1863, he was shifted frequently from one post to another. He was ordered to the District of Texas, New Mexico and Arizona on January 19, 1864. By March 16, 1865, the commander of the Trans-Mississippi Department, General E.K. Smith, reported that Rust was "without command and not on duty." It appears that he was removed from duty for unionist sentiments and his criticism of the rebel government. After the war he returned to the U.S. Congress and eventually became a Republican in 1869. He died the next year.

RUTH, Samuel (1818-1872)

As the Northern-born superintendent of transportation for the vital Richmond, Fredericksburg and Potomac Railroad, Samuel Ruth was in an advantageous position to obtain military information, and that is exactly what he did as one of the most effective of Union spies. Ruth was a Pennsylvania mechanic who had moved to Virginia in 1839 and eventually rose to his important position with the rail line. During the early years of the war it has been claimed that he deliberately hampered Confederate military operations by slowing the movement of troops and food supplies. More than once General Lee requested that Ruth be superseded by a military transportation expert but this was never acted upon. However, there is no question that in 1864 and 1865 he was actually a Union agent. During this period he reported on supplies and guards along his line, blockade runners' supplies transferred to rail lines, troops detached from Lee's army to North Carolina, the size of rebel forces in the Shenandoah Valley and southwestern Virginia, the supply crisis and attempts to remedy it, and that an attack was planned at Petersburg on Fort Stedman. Unfortunately this last report was not acted upon. Living in Richmond, he also served as part of the underground aiding escaped prisoners and deserters to reach the Union lines. This last activity caused his arrest on January 23, 1865, but no one in authority could believe the charges against such a respected citizen, and he was released nine days later. The *Richmond Whig* was outraged by the arrest. After the war he continued in his position and served as a revenue collector. Repeated requests for compensation netted him only $500, while General George Sharpe believed he deserved $40,000 or more.

RUTHERFORD, Friend Smith (1820-1864)

Since he had died a week before being commissioned, Friend S. Rutherford is sometimes not listed as a Union general. The New York native was practicing law in Illinois at the outbreak of the war. His military assignments included: captain and commissary of Subsistence, USV (June 30, 1862); colonel, 97th Illinois (September 16, 1862); and brigadier general, USV (June 27, 1864). He resigned his supply duties on September 2, 1862, in order to accept an infantry colonelcy. He led his regiment at Arkansas Post and in the Vicksburg Campaign but was absent at the time of the advance on Jackson in July 1863. The regiment then took part in the operations in western Louisiana and served through the winter and early spring as provost guard in New Orleans. Rutherford resigned his commission on June 15, 1864, due to ill-health brought on by exposure. Five days later he was dead. This was probably unknown in Washington when he was appointed brigadier general a week later.

RYAN, Abram Joseph (1838-1886)

A Catholic priest and chaplain in the Confederate army, who lost a brother in battle, became one of the most famous poets of the "Lost Cause." Born in Hagerstown, Maryland, and ordained into the priesthood in 1856, Ryan was a mystical character who appeared and disappeared throughout the conflict. Unreconciled to the collapse of the South, he wrote a series of poems that achieved great popularity throughout the old Confederacy. His works included: "Land without Ruins," "The Sword of Robert E. Lee," "March of the Deathless Dead," and his most famous "The Conquered Banner." About 15 years after the war, he retired to a monastery. Following his death, Southern children contributed to a monument over his grave. (Weaver, Gordon, ed., *Selected Poems of Father Ryan*)

RYAN, Jonathan George (?-?)

Lincoln's assassination sparked a wave of terror which transcended all bounds imposed by the Constitution, and one of its unfortunate victims was Confederate Captain Jonathan Ryan. Canadian-born Ryan was traveling through the South from late 1859 until the Civil War began. The Toronto printer finally caught the war fever and joined an Arkansas regiment in early 1862. Initially he was detailed as a clerk in the medical service but joined his regiment for the battle of Corinth, where he was wounded and captured. He made good his escape while recuperating from his wounds. After serving again with his unit, he was directed to raise a company which served in the Volunteer and Conscript Bureau rounding up draft dodgers. Early in 1864 the company became Company B, 12th Mississippi Cavalry, and Ryan was detailed in charge of a horse depot at Talladega, Alabama. In September he was demoted to second lieutenant in Captain Johnson's Company of special service troops operating along the Mississippi River, often behind Union lines. At the close of the year he was directed to raise a similar company of his own and was restored to the rank of captain. However, he never raised the unit, being on sick leave for most of the remainder of the war. On May 4, 1865, General Richard Taylor surrendered his department, which included Ryan, who was paroled on May 12 upon condition that he not again serve the Confederacy until exchanged. However, Ryan's troubles started with an angry letter to the editor of a Jackson, Mississippi, newspaper praising the assassination of Lincoln. He penned the letter on April 26, 1865, before he was surrendered. In the crazy times following the president's death facts such as these were often ignored. On the basis of an anonymous letter, Ryan was arrested on July 22, 1865, in Memphis, where he was trying to make arrangements to get home to Canada. He was held four months without a trial or even being told why he was being confined, much of the time with ball and chain. Letters from Union officers, stating that Ryan had written the letter to the editor prior to his parole, were of no avail. On November 5, 1865, following a letter to President Johnson and imprisonment in Memphis, Washington, and Vicksburg, Ryan was freed without an explanation of the cause of his incarceration. Becoming a lawyer in Chicago, he petitioned the authorities for 20 years before finding out that it was his letter to the editor that had caused him so much trouble. He never received his personal belongings seized at the time of his arrest. During his imprisonment, the press wondered about the mysterious prisoner, speculating that it was John Surratt. But it was just an unfortunate soldier who was a little too free with his pen.

RYAN, Thomas (?-1864)

One of the top bounty jumpers during the Civil War, Thomas Ryan finally paid the price. He was credited with having enlisted 30 times, collecting the bounty, and deserting to repeat the process. It was a lucrative business if you got away with it. Caught by the military authorities in 1864, he was tried by court-martial and sentenced to appear before a firing squad. President Lincoln—who was noted for commuting death sentences—did not intervene in this case and the sentence was carried out late in the year.

S

SAFFORD, Mary J. (?-?)

An unfortunate spinal injury ended the career of the "Angel of Cairo," Mary J. Safford. As a young nurse for the United States Sanitary Commission, she had begun her duties at the Union post at the junction of the Ohio and Mississippi rivers which was under the command of Ulysses S. Grant. Her work earned her the affectionate sobriquet. In the aftermath of the battle of Shiloh she had suffered a back injury and this was further complicated by overwork. Fortunately she had a wealthy brother who could afford to send her to Paris for medical care. But her nursing career in the Civil War was at an end.

ST. JOHN, Isaac Munroe (1827-1880)

Early in the Civil War it became apparent that the South was desperately lacking in the raw materials to manufacture gunpowder, and therefore Isaac M. St. John was named superintendent of the newly created Niter (soon to be Niter and Mining) Bureau in the Confederate War Department. A native of Georgia, he was raised in New York and studied law but instead took journalism and then civil engineering in Baltimore. His Civil War military assignments included: private, Fort Hill (S.C.) Guards (1861); private, Engineers (1861); captain, Engineers (February 1862); major, Artillery (ca. May 1862); superintendent, Niter (and Mining) Bureau (ca. May 1862-February 16, 1865); lieutenant colonel, Artillery (May 28, 1863); colonel, Artillery (June 15, 1864); brigadier general, CSA (February 16, 1865); and commissary general of Subsistence (February 16-April 1865). He first served as an engineering officer under Magruder on the Peninsula. As the bureau's superintendent he oversaw the necessarily improvised methods to produce the required raw materials. After his successful performance in this field he was named to replace the highly unpopular Commissary General Lucius B. Northrop near the end of the war. In this post he was responsible for some major innovations, but they came too late.

SALLIE (?-1865)

When the veterans of the 11th Pennsylvania erected a monument on the field of Gettysburg they placed a likeness of one of their fallen comrades, facing in the direction from which the enemy had come on the first day of the battle. It was Sallie—their dog mascot. She had marched north with the regiment from the Fredericksburg front to face Lee's invasion. During the hectic fighting on the first day at Gettysburg she became separated from the command which then fell back to the other side of town. Returning to the unit's original position, she remained with the dead and wounded who had been left behind. Following the Union victory she was found there in a weakened condition. Brought back to health she served in the Overland Campaign, being wounded in May 1864. Her neck wound soon healed and she continued to campaign with the regiment. Then in February 1865 while the unit was going into action at Hatcher's Run—with Sallie in the line of battle—she was killed by a bullet in the head.

SALM-SALM, Agnes Elisabeth Winona Leclerq Joy, Princess (1840-1912)

The location of her birth is not clear—various sources list Maryland, Vermont, and Quebec—but her service tending to the needs of the sick in her husband's regiment is clear. In the summer of 1862 she married the Prussian Prince Felix Salm-Salm, a nobleman and soldier-of-fortune. She accompanied his regiment in the field, and her service in one hospital earned her an honorary captain's commission from the governor of Illinois. After the Civil War she accompanied her husband to Mexico where he became a top aide to Maximilian. When they were captured, she pleaded for Maximilian's life. Although she was unsuccessful, Maximilian awarded her with the Grand Cordon of the Order of San Carlos. The Austrian emperor, Maximilian's brother, granted her a pension. Following her husband back to Europe, she served in hospitals during the Franco-Prussian War and earned the Prussian Medal of Honor. After the death of her husband during that war she settled down in Germany, dying in Karlsruhe in 1912. Her book, *Ten Years of My Life*, appeared in English in 1876.

SALM-SALM, Felix Constantin Alexander Johann Nepomuk, Prince (1828-1870)

The younger son of a reigning Prussian nobleman, Prince Felix Salm-Salm appears to have constantly been looking for a war. Decorated for his role in the Schleswig-Holstein War, having served in the Prussian cavalry, he briefly served in the Austrian army before heading to America to join the Union army. For a time he served on General Blenker's staff and his later assignments included: colonel, 8th New York (October 21, 1862); colonel, 68th New York (June 8, 1864); and commanding 2nd Brigade, 2nd Separate Division, District of the Etowah, Department of the Cumberland (March 15-June 20, 1865). With his first regiment he served in the Fredericksburg Campaign but was not engaged in the battle proper, and the unit was mustered out on April 23, 1863, prior to Chancellorsville. Over a year later he gained command of another regiment which was primarily assigned to guarding supply lines. However, he was engaged at Nashville where he earned a brevet brigadier generalship. Mustered out on November 30, 1865, he became Maximilian's chief staff aide in Mexico. Captured with his chief, he was allowed to return to Europe where he became a major in the Prussian Grenadier Guards. In the Franco-Prussian War battle of Gravelotte on August 18, 1870, he was killed.

SALOMON, Edward (1828-1909)

The Democratic running mate of Wisconsin's Republican governor, Louis P. Harvey, Edward Salomon moved up to the number one spot on April 19, 1862, when in the aftermath of the battle of Shiloh Harvey accidentally drowned during a relief mission. Salomon had moved to Wisconsin in the wake of the 1848 revolution in his native Prussia and taken up the practice of law. At the outbreak of the Civil War he was also on the regents board at the University of Wisconsin. Despite his party affiliation, he backed the Lincoln ticket in 1860 and was rewarded the next year with the Republican nomination for lieutenant governor. Elected, he was sworn early in 1862 but was soon advanced to the top post. There he was an active executive in the recruitment of the volunteers and was quick in taking action against riots over the draft. He also had to fear that the Sioux uprising in Minnesota might spread across the Mississippi to the tribes still in Wisconsin. Wishing to serve another term, he was denied the Republican nomination in 1863 and left office early the following year. After an unsuccessful bid in 1869 for the U.S. Senate he moved to New York and went into private practice. For his wife's health he moved to Frankfort-am-Main in Germany in 1894 and remained there after her death.

SALOMON, Friedrich (1826-1897)

One of four brothers who fled Prussia following the revolutions of 1848, Friedrich Salomon saw only limited action in the Civil War but still emerged as a brevet major general in the Union army. A former lieutenant in the Prussian army he was a student in 1848 when he got caught up with the wrong side in the uprisings. Settling in Wisconsin, where his brother Edward S. Salomon was destined to become a Civil War governor—his other two brothers became brevet brigadier generals—he engaged in civil engineering before entering the Union army. His assignments included: captain, 5th Missouri (May 19, 1861); colonel, 9th Wisconsin (November 26, 1861); brigadier general, USV (June 16, 1862); commanding 1st Brigade, Department of Kansas (August 24-October 12, 1862); commanding 1st Brigade, 1st Division, Army of the Frontier, Department of the Missouri (October-December 1862); commanding District of Eastern Arkansas, Department of the Missouri (December 1862); commanding 1st Brigade, 13th Division (in District of Eastern Arkansas), 13th Corps, Army of the Tennessee (February 8-May 25, 1863); commanding the division (May 25-July 20, 1863), commanding 1st Brigade, 13th Division, District of Eastern Arkansas, 16th Corps, Army of the Tennessee (July 28-August 10, 1863); commanding 3rd Division, Arkansas Expedition, Army of the Tennessee (October 8, 1863-January 6, 1864); commanding 3rd Division, 7th Corps, Department of Arkansas (January 6-May 11, 1864); and commanding 1st Division, 7th Corps, Department of Arkansas (May 11-July 25, 1864 and September 25, 1864-August 1, 1865). As a company commander he fought at Wilson's Creek before being mustered out with his three-months unit on August 14, 1861. Named colonel of a regiment from his adopted state, he served exclusively west of the Mississippi. His greatest accomplishments came while commanding a division in the defense of Helena, Arkansas, in the summer of 1863 and the following spring, when he covered the withdrawal of Frederick Steele's column at Jenkins' Ferry. Having been made a brigadier general in 1862, he finished out the war in Arkansas and was brevetted major general for his services. Mustered out on August 24, 1865, he was a surveyor until his death.

SANBORN, Franklin Benjamin (1831-1917)

After failing to persuade John Brown to drop his designs upon Harpers Ferry, Franklin B. Sanborn determined to lend him all the support he could. Sanborn had been influenced by Theodore Parker in the antislavery cause and moved from his native New Hampshire to Concord, Massachusetts. He became the secretary of the Massachusetts Free Soil Association and made Brown's acquaintance in 1857. When the raid failed, he was ordered arrested by the Senate for refusing to go to Washington to give his testimony. After twice fleeing to Canada he was arrested in early 1860 but was freed by the actions of the state courts and a mob. During the latter years of the Civil War he was editor of the *Boston Commonwealth* and served on the state board of charities. In the postwar years he was active in journalism and charitable work. His writings included: *The Life and Letters of John Brown; Dr. S.G. Howe, the Philanthropist; Ralph Waldo Emerson*; and *The Life of Henry David Thoreau*. (Sanborn, Franklin Benjamin, *Recollections of Seventy Years*)

SANBORN, John Benjamin (1826-1904)

The quartermaster general of the state of Minnesota upon the outbreak of the Civil War, John B. Sanborn entered the Federal volunteer service and rose to the rank of brevet major general. The New Hampshire lawyer had settled in St. Paul in 1854. His military assignments included: quartermaster general, Minnesota (prewar); quartermaster and adjutant general, Minnesota (April 1861); colonel, 4th Minnesota (December 23, 1861); commanding 1st Brigade, 3rd Division, Army of the Mississippi (June 25-September 20, 1862); commanding 1st Brigade, 7th Division, Left Wing, 13th Corps, Army of the Tennessee (November 1-December 18, 1862); commanding 1st Brigade, 7th Division, 17th Corps, Army of the Tennessee (February 5-April 12 and May 2-August 21, 1863); commanding the division (April 14-May 2, 1863); brigadier general, USV (August 4, 1863); commanding District of Southwest Missouri, Department of the Missouri (October 15, 1863-December 9, 1864 and January 9-June 10, 1865); and commanding District of the Upper Arkansas, Department of Kansas (July 1, 1865). Having aided in the organization of volunteer troops, he finally took command of an infantry regiment late in 1861. This unit took part in the advance on Corinth, Mississippi. Sanborn led a brigade at Iuka and the regiment at Corinth. Based upon his leadership of a brigade during the Vicksburg Campaign he was promoted to a brigadier generalship in August 1863. Assigned to district command in Missouri, he took part in the repulse of Sterling Price's 1864 invasion of the state. Brevetted major general on February 10, 1865, he served against the Indians until his muster out on April 30, 1866. He was later a practicing attorney and state legislator.

SANDERS, Christopher Columbus (1840-1908)

Georgian Christopher Columbus Sanders graduated from the Georgia Military Institute in the spring of 1861 and immediately entered the service of the Confederacy. His assignments included: lieutenant colonel, 24th Georgia (August 30, 1861); commanding Cobb's Brigade, McLaws' Division, Longstreet's Command, Army of Northern Virginia (September 17, 1862); colonel, 24th Georgia (January 9, 1864); and commanding DuBose's Brigade, Kershaw's Division, 1st Corps, Army of Northern Virginia (October-December 1864). As a field-grade officer he saw action at Yorktown, in the Seven Days, and at South Mountain. At Antietam he was in temporary command of the brigade and directed its actions until forced to leave the field, exhausted. He had been unwell for a time. The regiment then fought at Fredericksburg and Chancellorsville before taking part in the invasion of Pennsylvania. He led the regiment at Gettysburg. Going west, the brigade arrived too late for Chickamauga, and Sanders was not present during the operations against Knoxville. He did, however, participate in the Overland and Petersburg campaigns back in Virginia. After service in the Shenandoah, the 24th returned to the siege lines at Petersburg, with Sanders commanding the brigade during the latter part of 1864. Taking part in the Appomattox retreat, he was captured at Sayler's Creek. Paroled in July 1865, he became active in the banking business after the war.

SANDERS, John Caldwell Calhoun (1840-1864)

A student at the Alabama state university, John Sanders left his classes to join the Confederate army and was elected captain of the Confederate Guards, or Company E, 11th Alabama, on June 11, 1861. Ordered to Virginia the 11th was assigned to Colonel Forney's 5th Brigade, Army of the Shenandoah, on July 21, 1861. At this time most of the army had left for Manassas and was engaged in the battle of 1st Bull Run but the brigade was still in the Valley. Eventually the brigade, now under General C.M. Wilcox, joined Johnston's army. Captain Sanders led his company in its first action at Seven Pines May 31 and June 1, 1862, on the Peninsula. During the Seven Days Battle Sanders saw action at Gaines' Mill and Frayser's Farm where he was wounded. He rejoined his company on August 11, 1862, and assumed command of the regiment as the senior officer present. In this position he saw action at 2nd Bull Run and Antietam where he was again wounded. Having been promoted to major in the late summer he was promoted to colonel of his regiment to date from September 11, 1862, shortly after Antietam. Sanders led his regiment at Fredericksburg, Chancellorsville, and Gettysburg where on the second day he was severely wounded. With General Wilcox promoted to command a division, Sanders took over the brigade on August 15, 1863. He commanded the brigade in R.H. Anderson's Division, A.P. Hill's Corps, Army of Northern Virginia, in the Bristoe and Mine Run campaigns. In early 1864, he resumed command of his regiment when General Perrin was assigned to command of the brigade. Sanders saw action at the Wilderness and Spotsylvania where Perrin was killed. Sanders again took command and was promoted brigadier general on a temporary basis from May 31, 1864. He commanded the brigade at Cold Harbor and Petersburg, including the fight at the Crater. On August 21, 1864, Sanders was killed in the battle of Globe Tavern, near Petersburg. (Freeman, Douglas S., *Lee's Lieutenants*)

SANDERS, William Price (1833-1863)

Ten days after the death of William P. Sanders, a fort in the defenses of Knoxville named in his honor withstood a Confederate assault and stalemated the Southern effort to take the city. The Kentucky native had been raised in Mississippi and through political connections obtained and preserved his cadetship at West Point. Graduating in 1856, he was posted to the dragoons and took part in the Mormon expedition. His later assignments included: second lieutenant, 2nd Dragoons (since May 27, 1857); first lieutenant, 2nd Dragoons (May 10, 1861); captain, 3rd Cavalry (May 14, 1861); captain, 6th Cavalry (designation change August 3, 1861); colonel, 5th Kentucky Cavalry (March 4, 1863); brigadier general, USV (October 18,

1863); chief of Cavalry, Department of the Ohio (October-November 3, 1863); and commanding 1st Division, Cavalry Corps, Department of the Ohio (November 3-18, 1863). He served in the operations against Yorktown with his regiment and commanded the 5th Squadron—Companies A and M—at Williamsburg. He then fought through the Seven Days and commanded the regiment at Antietam. The next winter he was named to command the 5th Kentucky Cavalry with which he took part in operations against John Hunt Morgan's raids. Awarded a brigadier's star, he became the chief of mounted forces in the Department of the Ohio in October 1863 but the next month was reduced to a divisional command. He took part in the preliminary operations of the Knoxville Campaign, including Campbell's Station, but was mortally wounded on the 18th in front of Fort Loudon which was renamed in his honor. He died the next day.

SANDORD, Charles W. (?-?)

Although his direct military service for the national government lasted little more than three months, Charles W. Sanford performed valuable behind the scenes duties throughout the war. A major general in the militia of his native New York, he had been mustered into the Federal service on April 19, 1861. In July of that year, he led the 3rd Division, Department of Pennsylvania, under Robert Patterson. Thus he was part of the force which proved incapable of tying down the forces of Joseph E. Johnston in the Shenandoah Valley and preventing the junction of enemy forces at 1st Bull Run. Mustered out on July 25, 1861, Sandford continued in his state position, directing the militia and forwarding troops to the front as needed. One of his principal services came in June 1863 when he sent troops to Harrisburg and Baltimore during the Gettysburg Campaign. The next month he was involved in controlling the New York City draft riots.

SANFORD, Edward Sewall (?-1882)

With the government's realization that the telegraph would play an important military role, the president of American Telegraph, Edward Sanford, was given responsibility for military telegrams and ciphers used in connection with dispatches. While the telegraph in the nation's capital had been taken over by the military authorities within a few days of Fort Sumter, it was not until February 25, 1862, that all lines were placed under the control of the War Department. At this time Sanford was assigned to work with Western Union's general superintendent, Anson Stager, who was appointed superintendent of the U.S. Military Telegraph Corps. Sanford was appointed a colonel and additional aide-de-camp on February 26, 1862. He continued in his military post until 1867, although the corps was disbanded at the close of the war. He was brevetted brigadier general for his service. He returned to civilian life after his military retirement.

SANFORD, Martin L.

See: *Smith, Morgan Lewis*

SARSFIELD, John (?-1864)

As the leader of one of the numerous gangs of "Raiders" who terrorized their fellow inmates at Andersonville, John Sarsfield met an end which pleased many of his former victims. When the lawless situation in the prison camp had become so intolerable, the inmates, with the approval of the commandant, Major Henry Wirz, established a camp police force. At the end of June and beginning of July 1864, about 125 of the most notorious raiders were arrested, removed from the compound, and tried by a prisoners' court. Sarsfield, being one of the ringleaders, was dealt with severely. He and five others were sentenced to hang. Returned to the control of the prisoners on July 11, along with lumber for a scaffold, Sarsfield of the 144th New York met his end. In his final words he blamed the effects of harsh imprisonment and evil associates for turning him to the criminal life. Of the six, he died the hardest, drawing his knees almost up to his chin before expiring. (McElroy, John, *Andersonville: A Story of Rebel Military Prisons*)

SAULSBURY, Gove (1815-1881)

The elevation of Democrat Gove Saulsbury to the Delaware governorship upon the death of his Republican predecessor doomed each of the Civil War-era constitutional amendments to defeat in the border slave state. A Delaware doctor for 20 years, he was elected as a Democrat to the state senate in 1862 and the next session rose to be its speaker. Under the state constitution, there being no lieutenant governor, he succeeded Unionist William Cannon in the gubernatorial seat upon the latter's death on March 1, 1865. An outspoken critic of Reconstruction, he opposed the amendments abolishing slavery and each of them was defeated by the state legislature. Elected to a full term in 1866, he served until 1871. Although he did not hold further office, he was a delegate to the 1876 and 1880 Democratic conventions. (Conrad, Henry Clay, *History of the State of Delaware*)

SAULSBURY, Willard (1820-1892)

A Delaware Democrat, Willard Saulsbury served as a senator throughout the Civil War and much of Reconstruction. Trained in the legal profession, he had been the state's attorney general from 1850 to 1855 and attended the Democratic national convention the next year. He began the first of two senate terms in 1859 but left office in 1871, having failed to gain reelection. In the meantime he had attended the Democratic convention of 1864 which nominated McClellan for the presidency. After leaving Congress he resumed his legal practice and was state chancellor from 1874 until his death.

SAVAGE, John Houston (1815-1904)

Colonel John H. Savage was able to bluff himself into the single-handed capture of an entire Union company. During the Mexican War he had served as major, 14th Infantry, and lieutenant colonel, 11th Infantry, both of which were regular army regiments raised especially for the war. Entering the Confederate service, he held the following assignments: colonel, 16th Tennessee (June 1861), and commanding Donelson's Brigade, Cheatham's Division, Right Wing, Army of the Mississippi. His regiment was sent to western Virginia in the late summer of 1861 and it was here that Savage made his capture. Accompanied only by a guide on September 21, 1861, he suddenly came upon an enemy company with both parties being greatly surprised. Calling upon them to surrender, he warned that his men would open fire. They gave up to a force that was not there. He then participated in the Cheat Mountain fizzle before the regiment was transferred to South Carolina. After the winter on the coast, the regiment went to northern Mississippi and took part in the defense of Corinth. In command of the brigade, he fought at Munfordville and Perryville during the Kentucky Campaign. Falling back into Tennessee, he resumed command of the 16th which he led at Murfreesboro. He resigned his commission on February 20, 1863. (Head, Thomas A., *Campaigns and Battles of the Sixteenth Tennessee Volunteers*)

SAWYER, Henry Washington (?-?)

Captured in the action at Brandy Station, Henry W. Sawyer got caught up in the circle of retaliations practiced by both sides in the Civil War. He was serving as captain, Company K, 1st New Jersey Cavalry, when he fell wounded at the great cavalry battle. He had previously been wounded at Fairfax Court House on October 31, 1862, but this time he was not so lucky. Left on the field he was captured and confined at Libby Prison in Richmond. In the early part of July 1863, less than a month after his capture, the Confederate authorities decided to execute two prisoners with the rank of captain in reprisal for the shooting of two captains in Kentucky by General Burnside. The two rebels had been recruiting units behind Union lines and were deemed to be spies by the Union forces. In the drawing by lot among the Federal captains in the prison, Sawyer's name was drawn first. He and the other unlucky officer, John M. Flinn, were placed in close confinement until the executions could take place. The Richmond authorities notified Washington of the action and declared that should more recruiting officers be executed as spies, more prisoners would die. Washington then ordered that General W.H.F. Lee, Robert E. Lee's son, be placed in irons along with another officer. Richmond was informed that they would receive treatment equal to Sawyer and Flinn. Finally, in February 1864 the stalemate was resolved by the exchange of the officers involved. Sawyer returned to duty and was promoted to major. He served principally with the dismounted Union cavalry near Washington for the rest of the war but did see action at Cool Spring, West Virginia.

SAXTON, Rufus (1824-1908)

Although he had little combat duty in major theaters of the Civil War, Massachusetts native Rufus Saxton was awarded the Congressional Medal of Honor in 1893. The West Pointer (1849) had been posted to the artillery and seen service against the Seminoles, taught at the academy, and been an observer in Europe. His Civil War assignments included: first lieutenant, 4th Artillery (since March 2, 1855); captain and assistant quartermaster (May 13, 1861); chief quartermaster, Army of Southwest Missouri, Department of the West (spring-summer 1861); chief quartermaster, Army of Occupation-West Virginia, Department of the Ohio (1861); chief quartermaster, South Carolina Expeditionary Corps (fall 1861-March 15, 1862); brigadier general, USV (April 15, 1862); commanding Harpers Ferry, Department of the Shenandoah (May-June 1862); commanding U.S. Forces Beaufort, 10th Corps, Department of the South (February 19-June 14, 1863 and July 6, 1863-April 17, 1864); commanding District of Beaufort, Department of the South (April 25-September 1, 1864); commanding Northern District, Department of the South (September 1-October 3, 1864); and commanding 2nd Separate Brigade, Department of the South (October 26, 1864-January 23, 1865). Commanding an artillery detachment under Nathaniel Lyon, he took part in the dispersal of the Missouri State Guard at Camp Jackson and then transferred to the quartermaster's department. As such he served on the staffs of Lyon, McClellan, and Thomas W. Sherman. After taking part in the latter's operations along the South Carolina coast, he was promoted to brigadier general of volunteers and was placed in charge of the defenses of Harpers Ferry during the Shenandoah Valley Campaign of 1862. He successfully defended the place against an attack in late May and more than three decades later was rewarded with the medal. Assigned to special service in the Department of the South he was principally engaged in the recruiting and training of ex-slaves for the army. He did however hold a series of district commands during much of this period. He was brevetted major general of volunteers and brigadier general of regulars for his wartime services and was mustered out of the volunteers on January 15, 1866, after having served as assistant commissioner of the Freedmen's Bureau in Florida, Georgia, and South Carolina. Remaining in the regular army's quartermaster service, he retired in 1888 as colonel and assistant quartermaster general.

SCALES, Alfred Moore (1827-1892)

The Confederate career of Alfred M. Scales seems to march in step with that of William D. Pender, with Scales succeeding Pender in the chain of command and the pair even riding in the same ambulance in the retreat from Gettysburg. Only Scales lived. Prewar he had been a lawyer and state legislator and sat one term in the U.S. House of Representatives. Entering the Southern military as a private, his later assignments included: captain, Company H, 3rd North Carolina Volunteers (May 27, 1861); colonel, 3rd North Carolina Volunteers (October 12, 1861); colonel, 13th North Carolina (designation change on November 14, 1861); commanding Pender's Brigade, A.P. Hill's Division, 2nd Corps, Army of Northern Virginia (December 13, 1862); brigadier general, CSA (June 13, 1863); and commanding Pender's (old) Brigade, Pender's-Wilcox's Division, 3rd Corps, same army (June 20-July 1 and August 1863-February 1865). After service in the Norfolk area, his regiment, formerly Pender's, was transferred to the Peninsula where it saw action at Yorktown, Williamsburg, Seven Pines, and in the Seven Days. At Fredericksburg he succeeded Pender in brigade command for an unspecified period. Returning from a Chancellorsville wound, he was given permanent charge of the brigade but suffered another wound on the first day at Gettysburg. Rejoining his unit, he saw further action in the Overland and Petersburg campaigns but was on sick leave at the time of Lee's surrender. He returned to the legal and political professions, as congressman and governor, and also went into banking. (Freeman, Douglas S., *Lee's Lieutenants*)

SCAMMON, Eliakim Parker (1816-1894)

Having been dismissed from the regular army, Eliakim P. Scammon received a second chance at a military career with the coming of the Civil War. The Maine native had graduated from West Point in 1837 and been posted to the artillery. However, the next year he was transferred to the topographical engineers and served at his alma mater and in Florida and Mexican War fighting. Serving on the frontier he got into trouble and was dismissed for disobeying orders in 1856. Before the Civil War he was a teacher but again donned the blue early in that conflict. His assignments included: colonel, 23rd Ohio (June 27, 1861); commanding brigade, Army of Occupation, West Virginia, Department of the Ohio (September-October 11, 1861); commanding 3rd Brigade, District of the Kanawha, Department of Western Virginia (October 11, 1861-March 11, 1862); commanding 1st Brigade, District of the Kanawha, Mountain Department (March 11-ca. June 26, 1862); commanding 1st Provisional Brigade, Kanawha Division, Army of Virginia (ca. June 26, 1862-early September 1862); commanding 1st Brigade, Kanawha Division, 9th Corps, Army of the Potomac (early September-September 17, 1862); commanding the division (September 17-October 1862); commanding 1st Brigade, Kanawha Division, Department of the Ohio (October 1862-March 1863); brigadier general, USV (October 15, 1862); commanding 3rd Division, 8th Corps, Middle Department (March 27-June 26, 1863); commanding division, Department of West Virginia (June 28-December 1863); commanding 3rd Division, Department of West Virginia (December 1863-February 3, 1864); commanding 1st Separate Brigade, Department of the South (October 3-26, 1864); commanding 3rd Separate Brigade, Department of the South (November 1-14, 1864); and commanding 4th Separate Brigade, Department of the South (November 14, 1864-April 7, 1865). He led his volunteer regiment in western Virginia and was part of the force sent to reinforce Pope in northern Virginia in August 1862. He participated in some of the fringe actions at 2nd Bull Run and became part of the 9th Corps in the Maryland Campaign where he was particularly distinguished at South Mountain. At Antietam he succeeded to divisional command and was returned to West Virginia the following month. On February 3, 1864, he was captured by partisan rangers raiding on river traffic. Exchanged on August 3, 1864, he was given a command on the South Carolina coast. He was again briefly taken prisoner there on October 26, 1864. The final months of the war he spent in command in Florida. Mustered out on August 24, 1865, he served as a diplomat, government engineer, and college professor.

SCHAEFER, Frederick (?-1862)

On the last day of 1862, Union Colonel Frederick Schaefer gave his life while commanding a brigade at the battle of Murfreesboro. The Missourian's assignments included: colonel, 2nd Missouri (1861); commanding 1st Brigade, 2nd Division, Army of the Southwest Missouri, Department of the Missouri (February-June 1862); commanding 35th Brigade, 11th Division, 3rd Corps, Army of the Ohio (October 8-November 5, 1862); and commanding 2nd Brigade, 3rd Division, Right Wing, 14th Corps, Army of the Cumberland (November 5-December 31, 1862). He led a brigade at Pea Ridge and in the slow advance on Corinth, Mississippi before taking part in the pursuit of Bragg into Kentucky. Not at the battle of Perryville, he took part in Rosecrans' advance from Nashville and got caught up in the rout of the Union right on the first day at Murfreesboro during the Confederate assaults. Here he was shot and killed.

SCHARF, John Thomas (1843-1898)

As a midshipman in the Confederate navy, J. Thomas Scharf took part in some of the more daring exploits of the war. A native of Maryland, he left his father's lumber business to enter the Confederate service and apparently served originally in the army. As a naval officer, he took part in the February 1864 raid led by John Taylor Wood which destroyed the USS *Underwriter*. Shortly after that success he served in the failed expedition of Lieutenant George W. Gift to destroy two Union blockaders guarding the mouth of the Appalachicola River. He succeeded Gift in command of the one surviving boat, which was sailed 15 miles to St. George's Island where the crew ate alligators to survive. After his rescue he returned to his previous duty station, the Charleston Naval Station. In December 1864 he served on the *Sampson* on the Savannah River. Near the close of the war he was captured on a mission to Canada. His varied postwar career included the lumber business, law, journalism, and service as an immigration official in New York. Throughout this time he devoted much time to historical writing, mostly on his native state. His works include *History of Maryland* and *History of the Confederate States Navy*.

SCHENCK, Robert Cumming (1809-1890)

One of Lincoln's many political appointees as a general officer, Robert C. Schenck was incapacitated for further field service by a severe wound at 2nd Bull Run. In the prewar years he had practiced law, served in the state legislature of his native Ohio, spent eight years in the U.S. Congress, and been a diplomat to Brazil. Having worked for Lincoln's election, he was rewarded with the star of a brigadier general. His assignments included: brigadier general, USV (June 5, 1861, to rank from May 17); commanding 2nd Brigade, 1st Division, Army of Northeastern Virginia (June-August 1861); commanding 1st Brigade, District of the Kanawha, Department of West Virginia (October 1861-March 11, 1862); commanding District of the Cumberland, Mountain Department (March 11-April 1862); commanding independent brigade, Mountain Department

(April-June 26, 1862); commanding 1st Division, 1st Corps, Army of Virginia (June 26-August 30, 1862); also commanding the corps (June 28-30 and July 7-12, 1862); major general, USV (August 30, 1862); commanding 8th Corps, Middle Department (December 22, 1862-March 12, 1863, March 22-August 10, August 31-September 22, and October 10-December 5, 1863); and also commanding the department (December 22, 1862-August 10, 1863, August 31-September 28, and October 10-December 5, 1863). After fighting at 1st Bull Run he was transferred to western Virginia and then moved against Jackson in the Shenandoah Valley. He was in overall charge at the battle of McDowell and then served under John C. Frémont in the Valley proper. With his command merged into Pope's Army of Virginia, he led a division at 2nd Bull Run where he was severely wounded and incapacitated for further field service on August 30, 1862. From that date he was promoted to major general and he served the remainder of his military career in the Maryland area. Elected during his recovery to the 38th Congress, he resigned on December 5, 1863 to take his House seat in that body's first session two days later. He was named chairman of the Committee on Military Affairs. Remaining in Congress for four terms—he eventually served as chairman of the Committee on Ways and Means—he was defeated in 1870 and the next year was sent to the Court of St. James as a diplomat. He had previously served on the commission which settled the so-called Alabama Claims. While serving as a diplomat in London he became involved in the sale and promotion of stock in the Emma Mine in Utah. When this was exposed as a fraud he resigned in 1876 and resumed the practice of law. In his final years he became noted as an expert in draw poker.

SCHIMMELFENNIG, Alexander (1824-1865)

Poor Alexander Schimmelfennig is best remembered in Civil War history for his two-and-a-half-day stay in a Gettysburg pigsty. A veteran Prussian engineering officer of the Schleswig-Holstein War, he opposed that same army in the 1848 uprising in the Palatinate. Fleeing first to Switzerland and then to England, he settled in Washington in 1853 where he became an engineer with the War Department. With the coming of the Civil War his assignments included: colonel, 74th Pennsylvania (September 30, 1861); commanding 1st Brigade, 3rd Division, 1st Corps, Army of Virginia (August 22-September 12, 1862); commanding 1st Brigade, 3rd Division, 11th Corps, Army of the Potomac (September 12, 1862-January 19, 1863, and February 5-March 5, April 2-July 1, and July 4-13, 1863); brigadier general, USV (November 29, 1862); commanding the division (January 19-February 5, March 5-April 2, and July 1, 1863); commanding 1st Division, 11th Corps, Army of the Potomac (July 14-17, 1863); commanding 1st Brigade, same division, corps, and army (July 17-August 6, 1863); commanding 1st Brigade, South End Folly Island, 10th Corps, Department of the South (August 16-October 24, 1863); commanding, in effect, the division (October 24-November 28, 1863); commanding Northern District, same corps, and department (February 1864); commanding Gordon's Division, same district, corps and department (February 25-April 25, 1864); commanding Northern District, Department of the South (April 25-September 1, 1864); and commanding 1st Separate Brigade, Department of the South (November 28, 1864-January 23, 1865 and February 26-April 8, 1865). Suffering from a fall and smallpox, he did not serve in the field until the 2nd Bull Run Campaign when he succeeded General Henry Bohlen in command of the brigade after the latter's death at Freeman's Ford. After he led the brigade in the main battle, it was absorbed into the Army of the Potomac but missed Antietam and Fredericksburg. At Chancellorsville his brigade was caught up in the corps' rout when Jackson delivered his surprise flank attack. The Prussian was a vocal supporter of the primarily German 11th Corps' reputation. But on the first day at Gettysburg the corps, with Schimmelfennig temporarily in division command, was forced back through the town. In the confusion he was struck in the head by a rifle butt while climbing a fence blocking his escape. He then crawled into a pigsty where he was fed secretly by the woman of the house while the town was occupied by the Confederates. After their withdrawal he emerged to rejoin his command. Actively seeking transfer, he found the entire division being sent to operate against Charleston. There he held various commands but suffered several bouts with malaria. Near the very end of the war he went on sick leave when he developed tuberculosis. He died while seeking treatment in September 1865. There is an unverified story that Lincoln had made him a general because he needed another German commander for political reasons (probably the case) and particularly liked his name (probably not the case).

SCHOEPF, Albin Francisco (1822-1886)

Claiming reasons of health, Union General Albin F. Schoepf resigned his field command and completed the war as one of the more respected prison commandants at Fort Delaware. Born in that part of Austria-Hungary that became Poland, he had become a captain in the Austrian army before joining the Hungarian revolutionaries in 1848. For his role in Kossuth's unsuccessful revolt he was exiled. Going via Syria to Turkey, he was involved in training the Ottoman army before immigrating to America. As a hotel porter, he was tapped by Joseph Holt, commissioner of patents, to take a clerkship. With Holt in the War Department, Schoepf was destined for a high position. His assignments included: brigadier general, USV (September 30, 1861); commanding 1st Brigade, Army of the Ohio (November-December 2, 1861); commanding 1st Brigade, 1st Division, Army of the Ohio (December 2, 1861-September 29, 1862); commanding 1st Division, 3rd Corps, Army of the Ohio (September 29-ca. October 17, 1862); and commanding Fort Delaware prisoner of war camp (April 23, 1863-January 1, 1866). In eastern Kentucky he had alternate successes and failures in operations against Felix K. Zollicoffer in late 1861. Early the following year he led the pursuit after the Confederate disaster at Mill Springs. Commanding a division, he fought at Perryville but the failure of the Union army to administer a crushing defeat on Bragg led to endless recriminations, and this may have led to Schoepf's request for relief from command. The next spring he took over a prison and over the next two and a half years became known for trying to do all that he dared to alleviate the conditions of his charges. He was often at odds with Secretary of War Stanton and did not receive a brevet at the close of hostilities. Mustered out on January 15, 1866, he later rose to chief examiner of the patent office.

SCHOFIELD, John McAllister (1831-1906)

Considering the fact that he went on to become the commander in chief of the U.S. Army, it is surprising that John M. Schofield is one of the lesser-known Civil War major generals. Born in New York, he had worked as a surveyor and teacher before securing a West Point appointment. Graduating in 1853, he was posted to the artillery and served in Florida and back at his alma mater. His Civil War-era assignments included: first lieutenant, 1st Artillery (since March 3, 1855); major, 1st Missouri (April 26, 1861); assistant adjutant general, Department of the West (spring-August 1861); captain, 1st Artillery (May 14, 1861); major, 1st Missouri Light Artillery (change of designation June 26, 1861); brigadier general, USV (November 21, 1861); commanding District of St. Louis, Department of the Missouri and the Missouri Militia (November 21, 1861-April 10, 1862); commanding Military District of the Missouri, Department of the Mississippi (June 5-September 24, 1862); commanding District of Southwest Missouri, Department of the Missouri (September 24-November 10, 1862 and March 30-May 24, 1863); also commanding Army of the Frontier, Department of the Missouri (October 12, 1862-March 30, 1863); major general, USV (November 29, 1862; expired March 4, 1863); reverted to brigadier general, USV (March 4, 1863); commanding 3rd Division, 14th Corps, Army of the Cumberland (April 17-May 10, 1863); major general, USV (reappointed May 12, 1863, to date from November 29, 1862); commanding Department of the Missouri (May 24, 1863-January 30, 1864); commanding Department of the Ohio (February 9-November 8, 1864); also commanding 23rd Corps, Department of the Ohio (April 9-May 26 and May 27-September 14, 1864, and October 22, 1864-February 2, 1865); brigadier general, USA (November 30, 1864); commanding 23rd Corps, Department of North Carolina (February 9-March 31, 1865); and also commanding the department (February 9-June 17 and July 17, 1865). As a staff officer to General Nathaniel Lyon he took part in the capture of Camp Jackson and in the battle of Wilson's Creek. Following that disaster, in which he earned a Medal of Honor, he converted his volunteer regiment into an artillery unit and directed the Missouri militia as a brigadier. He was also engaged at Fredericktown. For a time he commanded in southwestern Missouri and northeastern Arkansas. His major general's appointment was bottled up in committee by some petty grievances over his policies in the strife-torn state. Reverting to brigadier, he commanded a division briefly in Tennessee before being named to head the Department of Missouri. In this post he faced difficulties resulting from the divided loyalties in the state. Eventually he had to be replaced and was sent to the Department of the Ohio. He took part of his forces to join Sherman for the Atlanta Campaign. Following that city's fall his "army," in reality only a corps with an attached cavalry division, was sent back to middle Tennessee to cope with Hood's invasion. He was in charge during the controversial affair at Spring Hill when Hood failed to take advantage of Schofield's awkward location. During the course of this campaign Schofield earned a reputation, possibly undeserved, for plotting to obtain overall command in the area from George H. Thomas. Although he gave up the field, Schofield administered a severe defeat to Hood's Army of Tennessee at Franklin, and as a reward he was jumped from captain to brigadier in the regular army. He also fought creditably in the crushing victory at Nashville. Sent to North Carolina with his corps, he operated on the fringes of the final stages of the Carolinas Campaign. During Reconstruction he commanded in Virginia and was mustered out of the volunteer service on September 1, 1866. Remaining in the army, he rose to major and later lieutenant general and served as secretary of war in 1868 and 1869. He regretted the country's Indian policy, even while he served as commander in chief from 1888 to 1895. Retiring in the latter year, he died in Florida. (McDonough, James L., *Schofield: Union General in the Civil War and Reconstruction.*)

SCHRIVER, Edmund (1812-1899)

A West Pointer (1833) who had left the army after 13 years to enter railroading, Edmund Schriver reentered the army in 1861

Future commander in chief John M. Schofield. (*Leslie's*)

as second-in-command of one of the newly organized regular army regiments but spent most of the war in staff assignments. The Pennsylvania veteran of the Seminole War had given up a post on the staff of New York's governor to join the conflict. His assignments included: lieutenant colonel, 11th Infantry (May 14, 1861); chief of staff, 1st Corps, Army of the Potomac (March 15-April 4, 1862); chief of staff, Department of the Rappahannock (April 4-June 26, 1862); colonel and additional aide-de-camp (May 18, 1862); chief of staff, 3rd Corps, Army of Virginia (June 26-September 12, 1862); chief of staff, 1st Corps, Army of the Potomac (September 12, 1862-January 1863); inspector general, Army of the Potomac (ca. January 1863-June 1865); and colonel and inspector general (March 13, 1863). He served as McDowell's and Hooker's staff chief at 2nd Bull Run, Antietam, and Fredericksburg. With Hooker's assumption of command of the Army of the Potomac, Schriver became that army's inspector and on March 13, 1863, this was formalized by his appointment in that department. This action voided his commissions in the 11th Infantry and as an aide. When Meade replaced Hooker, Schriver remained at his post until the close of hostilities. During the war he was brevetted both brigadier and major general in the regular army. He remained on active duty until his 1881 retirement.

SCHURZ, Carl (1829-1906)

A refugee from the European uprisings of 1848, Carl Schurz was one of those political generals appointed by Lincoln to attract the support of the German community. He was born near Köln and was educated at the University of Bonn. He had served as a company officer in the uprising against the Prussian government and then fled via Switzerland to France. Expelled from the latter, he went to England for a year before turning to the United States. As a farmer he settled in Wisconsin but soon became active in politics of the antislavery type. At first he backed John C. Frémont but by 1860 he was a Lincoln man. For his work in the campaign, he was named minister to Spain in July 1861, but he was more interested with events in America and returned in January 1862 to seek a commission in the army. At first Lincoln was not cooperative but he finally consented, in part, to please the Germans. His military assignments included: brigadier general, USV (April 15, 1862); commanding 3rd Division, 1st Corps, Army of Virginia (June 26-September 12, 1862); commanding 3rd Division, 11th Corps, Army of the Potomac (September 12, 1862-January 19, 1863, February 5-March 5, and April 2-September 25, 1863); commanding the corps (January 19-February 5, March 5-April 2, and July 1, 1863); major general, USV (March 14, 1863); commanding 3rd Division, 11th Corps, Army of the Cumberland (September 25, 1863-January 21, 1864); commanding the corps (January 21-February 25, 1864); on recruiting duty for the 1st Veteran Volunteer Corps (February 18-April 1, 1865); and chief of staff, Army of Georgia, Military Division of the Mississippi (April-May 1865). He joined Frémont's forces in the Shenandoah following the close of the campaign but fought at 2nd Bull Run. He led his division at Chancellorsville and was caught up in the rout of the 11th Corps. At Gettysburg he was in command of the corps briefly on the first day while Oliver O. Howard was in charge of the field. Again the corps was routed. Sent west with the corps, he led his division at Chattanooga, but due to problems with Hooker he was soon relegated to a rear echelon. Giving up his command early in 1864, Schurz stumped the campaign trail on behalf of the Union ticket. Following Lincoln's reelection, Schurz returned to duty and was assigned to assist Winfield S. Hancock in the creation of the 1st Veteran Volunteer Corps, of which it was expected he would command a division. During the last month of the war he served as Henry W. Slocum's chief of staff in the Carolinas. Resigning on May 6, 1865, he resumed his writings on political issues and was active in political campaigns. He himself sat one term in the Senate and was Grant's interior secretary. A true 1848 liberal, he opposed imperialism, favored a civil service system, and favored full and equal rights for whites and blacks. He kept up his literary and political pursuits right until his death. (Schurz, Carl, *The Reminiscences of Carl Schurz*)

SCOTT, Dred (ca. 1800-1858)

Although he lost his Supreme Court fight for his freedom from slavery, Dred Scott furthered the movement toward the abolition of the "peculiar institution." Born into slavery in Virginia at about the turn of the century, he had been moved with his owner to Alabama and then Missouri before being sold in 1833 to an army assistant surgeon from Pennsylvania, John Emerson, who took him into the free areas of Illinois, Iowa, and Minnesota before returning to Missouri. Following the doctor's death he twice attempted to purchase his freedom but was refused by the widow. In 1846 Scott launched his legal battle in the Missouri courts, citing his family's travels in free territory as justification for his freedom. The decision of the Supreme Court was finally tendered in 1857. It stated that slaves were not citizens of the United States or Missouri and thus could not sue in the courts, that he was still a slave due to his being returned to Missouri, and that the Missouri Compromise—which prohibited slavery in certain territories—was unconstitutional. The following year Scott and his family achieved their freedom through a private manumission. The freed slave had only a year to live and died before he could realize the impact of his case upon history. The outrage against the decision furthered the cause of the Republicans and contributed to the election of Lincoln in 1860. (Fehrenbacher, Don E., *The Dred Scott Case: Its Significance in American Law & Politics*)

SCOTT, John S. (?-?)

A brigade and district commander during much of the war, John S. Scott never received promotion to brigadier general, perhaps because he earned the displeasure of General Forrest. His assignments for the Confederacy included: colonel, 1st Louisiana Cavalry (May 4, 1861); commanding 3rd Cavalry Brigade, Department of East Tennessee (October 31-December 1862); commanding 2nd Cavalry Brigade, Department of East Tennessee (spring-August 6, 1863); commanding brigade, Pegram's Division, Forrest's Cavalry Corps, Army of Tennessee (August 6-October 1863); and in the Department of Alabama,

Mississippi and East Louisiana: commanding District of Southwest Mississippi and East Louisiana (April 5-June 1864); commanding brigade, Adams' Cavalry Division (June-August 1864); commanding Cavalry Brigade, District South of Homochitto (August-October 6, 1864); and commanding brigade, Forrest's Cavalry Corps (early 1865). After service in central Kentucky he served under Forrest in East Tennessee. After the battle of Murfreesboro, Scott led his regiment in Pegram's raid into Kentucky in the spring of 1863. The forces in East Tennessee joined Bragg's army for the Chickamauga Campaign during which Scott commanded the brigade. Sent to Mississippi in early 1864, he commanded a district and later a brigade serving in the southern part of the state and in eastern Louisiana. It was during this time that Forrest expressed displeasure with Scott's performance in controlling deserters and conscripts in his vicinity. He even suggested dismounting the command. In the final days of the war Scott was ordered to join Forrest with his brigade to face Wilson's raid in Alabama and was surrendered with him.

SCOTT, Julian [A.] (ca. 1847-?)

As most Congressional Medals of Honor were awarded for something involving a flag—capturing, carrying or saving one—Julian Scott, who received his middle initial as a clerical error at enlistment, is somewhat of an exception. He was only 15 at the time of his enlistment in the 3rd Vermont as a musician in July of 1861. With his regiment serving on the Peninsula he was the only musician present with the unit when it made a charge at Lee's Mill on April 16, 1862, during the Yorktown siege. Unlike the common misconception, musicians did not usually play in battle. Instead, the drummers became the stretcher bearers. Scott particularly distinguished himself in that he "crossed the creek under a terrific fire of musketry several times to assist in bringing off the wounded." He was sixteen at the time he earned his medal. He later served in the Seven Days where he was slightly wounded at White Oak Swamp and later at Drewry's Bluff. After the regiment saw action at Antietam and Fredericksburg Scott was mustered out in April 1863. He studied art for a year and then joined the staff of General William F. Smith where he sketched the life of the common soldier. (Mitchell, Joseph B., *The Badge of Gallantry*)

SCOTT, Robert Kingston (1826-1900)

The distinguished Civil War career of Robert K. Scott was marred by his postwar activities. The Pennsylvania native had sought gold in California, Mexico, and South America before taking up the practice of medicine in Ohio. He was a company commander of Pennsylvania volunteers during the Mexican War and again donned the blue uniform for the Civil War. His assignments included: lieutenant colonel, 68th Ohio (November 30, 1861); colonel, 68th Ohio (July 12, 1862); commanding 2nd Brigade, 3rd Division, 17th Corps, Army of the Tennessee (March 6-July 24, September 30-December 27, 1864, and March 28-August 1, 1865); and brigadier general, USV (April 21, 1865, to rank from January 12). Following garrison duty he led his regiment during part of the Vicksburg Campaign. In the Atlanta Campaign he was in charge of a brigade until the battle of Atlanta. Resuming leadership of the brigade, he participated in the March to the Sea and the campaign in the Carolinas. Near the war's close he was promoted to brigadier general to date from early 1865, having already been brevetted to that grade on January 26, 1865. Brevetted major general as well on December 5, 1865, he directed the Freedmen's Bureau in South Carolina until 1868 when he became South Carolina's Reconstruction governor. Resigning his commission on July 6, 1868, he fell into the system of corruption so common in the postwar South. With the end of carpetbag government in the state, Scott fled to Ohio in 1877, fearing prosecution for a fraudulent bond issue. On Christmas Day three years later he killed a man for allegedly making his son drunk. Scott claimed it was accidental and got off free.

SCOTT, Robert Nicholson (1837-1887)

Robert N. Scott earned his place as one of the most important Civil War historians for his work on the massive, 128-volume *The War of the Rebellion: A Compilation of the Official Records of the Union and Confederate Armies.* Born in Tennessee and raised in Louisiana, Scott joined the regular army directly from civilian life as a second lieutenant in the 4th Infantry in 1857 and served as a post adjutant in California. His later assignments included: first lieutenant, 4th Infantry (May 14, 1861); regimental adjutant (July 1-September 25, 1861); captain, 4th Infantry (September 25, 1861); major and assistant adjutant general, USV (September 28, 1864); lieutenant colonel and assistant adjutant general, USV (July 5, 1865); captain, 16th Infantry (January 29, 1870); captain, 3rd Artillery (December 31, 1870); major, 3rd Artillery (March 20, 1879); and lieutenant colonel, 3rd Artillery (March 22, 1885). Scott served on Colonel Buchanan's staff during the Peninsula Campaign where he was wounded at the battle of Gaines' Mill. After his recovery, Scott served on the staffs of Generals Casey and Halleck. He was brevetted major for Gaines' Mill and lieutenant colonel for work in organizing the Union volunteers. In 1878, he was chosen to head the War Records Office, in the War Department, which was charged with the compilation and publication of the significant records of the war. Scott was responsible for setting up the criteria and system for the inclusion of documents. Much of his time was taken up in locating and organizing the masses of paper. Scott made a firm ruling that no postwar memoirs could be included, in order to preserve the historical integrity of the work. To locate records in private Southern collections and obtain them he arranged for the appointment of former Confederate General Marcus J. Wright, who was indefatigable in his efforts. Scott, working long hours and with his health impaired, died in 1887. Although only 26 volumes of the *Official Records* had been published by the time of his death, his name was still listed in those volumes published through 1891 in recognition of his work in compiling the information. (Mahan, Harold E., "The Arsenal of History," *CWH*, March 1983)

SCOTT, Thomas Alexander (1823-1881)

By the outbreak of the Civil War Thomas A. Scott had become vice president of the Pennsylvania Railroad and as such arranged a secret route for President-elect Lincoln to follow to Washington and so foil the rumored assassination attempt en route. On August 3, 1861, the U.S. Congress created the new position of assistant secretary of war and Scott was named to fill it. His principal duties were to coordinate the connections and schedules of the various railroads for military purposes. After about a year of such service, frequently in the Western theater, he resigned and returned to the Pennsylvania Railroad. However, in the fall of 1863 he was instrumental in the transfer of the 11th and 12th corps from the Army of the Potomac to that of the Cumberland following the defeat at Chickamauga. General Halleck had expected this transfer from Virginia to Tennessee to take months; in fact, Scott accomplished it in 11 1/2 days. After the war, Scott became president of the Union Pacific and eventually, of the Pennsylvania Railroad. (Kamm, Samuel R., *Civil War Career of Thomas A. Scott*)

SCOTT, Thomas Moore (1829-1876)

Until severely wounded at Franklin in late 1864, Georgia-born Louisiana farmer Thomas M. Scott served as a Confederate regimental and brigade commander in some of the most important actions of the western theater. His assignments included: colonel, 12th Louisiana (August 13, 1861); commanding Buford's (old) Brigade, Loring's Division, Department of Alabama, Mississippi and East Louisiana (early March-May 1864); brigadier general, CSA (May 10, 1864); and commanding brigade, Loring's Division, Polk's (Army of the Mississippi)-Stewart's Corps, Army of Tennessee (May-November 20, 1864). His regiment was apparently present at Columbus, Kentucky, during the battle of Belmont but did not cross the river. He fought at Island #10 and then was stationed for a time at Fort Pillow and Port Hudson. During the Vicksburg Campaign he served in Loring's division and was cut off with it after the fight at Champion Hill. Joining Joseph E. Johnston's forces trying to lift the siege against the river city, he was later engaged in the Jackson and Meridian campaigns. He led a brigade, as a newly appointed brigadier general, in the Atlanta Campaign and then accompanied Hood into middle Tennessee. There he was severely wounded by a shell at Franklin and held no further field positions. He returned to planting in Louisiana.

SCOTT, William Campbell (1809-1865)

A prominent Virginia lawyer and state legislator, William C. Scott was already active in the state militia by the outbreak of the Civil War. His assignments for the South included: colonel, 112th Virginia Militia (early 1861); brigadier general, Virginia Militia (early 1861); colonel, 44th Virginia (June 14, 1861); commanding 2nd Brigade, Army of the Northwest (early May-May 17, 1862); and commanding 2nd Brigade, Ewell's Division, Valley District, Department of Northern Virginia (May 17-June 4 and June 8-9, 1862). He saw action at Rich Mountain and in the Cheat Mountain and Romney campaigns, and he commanded a brigade at McDowell and in the Shenandoah Valley Campaign. Relieved of command of the brigade for four days during the latter, he was again in charge at the campaign's close. With his health failing, he was apparently absent from any further actions with the regiment. On January 14, 1863, he resigned. Returning home to Powhatan County, he died on the day Lee surrendered.

SCOTT, Winfield (1786-1866)

Known as "Old Fuss and Feathers" for his devotion to military regulations, Winfield Scott had been America's first soldier for two decades at the beginning of the Civil War. The Virginian had practiced law briefly until he received a commission as a captain of artillery in 1808, when trouble with Great Britain prompted an expansion of the military establishment. Chaffing under overage superiors, he was frequently in trouble, being suspended for a year just prior to the War of 1812. During that conflict he redeemed himself by distinguished actions in generally dismal operations on the Canadian front. Captured at Queenston Heights and wounded at Lundy's Lane, he emerged from the war with a reputation second only to Andrew Jackson's. In the succeeding years he negotiated the end of the

"Old Fuss and Feathers" Winfield Scott. (AC)

Black Hawk War, showed a strong hand during the Nullification Crisis with South Carolina, fought the Seminoles and Creeks, smoothed out problems along the Canadian border, and aided in the removal of the Cherokees and Winnebagoes. In this quarter of a century he proved himself an able soldier and an effective diplomat. After some political problems early in the Mexican War, he led the expedition from Vera Cruz to Mexico City. Since 1841 he had been commander in chief of the army and he subsequently received the Thanks of Congress and a gold medal for the Mexican War, having previously received one for the War of 1812. In 1852 he was the Whig nominee for president but was badly beaten. By the time of the Civil War he was greatly overweight and could not mount a horse. He was simply too old for active field command and offered it to Robert E. Lee, who declined. Unlike his fellow Virginian, Scott remained loyal to the Union. Directing operations from the capital, he came in for criticism for his role in the 1st Bull Run Campaign when his subordinate Robert Patterson failed to hold Joe Johnston's army in the Shenandoah, contributing to the disaster. With McClellan called to the Washington front, Scott found himself in an untenable position, with the younger officer reporting directly to the president. Finally, after much machination by McClellan, Scott retired on November 1, 1861; Lincoln insisted upon his retaining full rank and pay. Despite his retirement, it was Scott's Anaconda Plan that provided the major aspects of Union victory: the holding of the Mississippi Valley and the blockade. For his remaining years Scott kept an active interest in the war effort and sent a copy of his *Memoirs* to Grant, with the inscription, "From the oldest general to the greatest general." Appropriately he died at West Point—which he had not attended—and was buried there. (Elliot, Charles Winslow, *Winfield Scott: The Soldier and the Man*)

SCRIBNER, Benjamin Franklin (?-1900)

It was only a matter of weeks after he had received the brevet of brigadier general of volunteers before Benjamin F. Scribner resigned his commission. The Indiana native had taken the field as a regimental commander late in the first summer of the war. His assignments included: colonel, 38th Indiana (September 18, 1861); and commanding in the 14th Corps, Army of the Cumberland: 1st Brigade, 1st Division, Center (November 5, 1862-January 9, 1863); 1st Brigade, 1st Division (January 9-October 19, 1863 and December 5, 1863-January 5, 1864); and 3rd Brigade, 1st Division (May 3-July 5, 1864). He led his regiment at Perryville and a brigade through the Tullahoma Campaign. Having directed it at Chickamauga, he was present at Chattanooga where he was possibly in charge of an informal demi-brigade. During the Atlanta Campaign he received his brevet for the war-to-date on August 8, 1864. On the 21st his resignation became effective. He later wrote the regimental history. (Scribner, Benjamin Franklin, *How Soldiers Were Made*)

SCULLY, John (?-?)

A Pinkerton agent, John Scully panicked when arrested and began to talk, sending one man to the gallows and a woman to prison for a year—and almost sending two more, including himself, to the hangman. In the first year of the war (he had joined the firm in the 1850s), he worked with Pinkerton in cracking Rose O'Neal Greenhow's spy ring in Washington, and as courier for Timothy Webster and Mrs. Hattie Lawton while they were working in Baltimore. When in February 1862 Pinkerton had not received any reports from the same team operating in Richmond, he sent Scully and Pryce Lewis after them. Scully was to bring back their intelligence reports. While visiting Webster in his sick bed, they were recognized by a former prisoner of theirs. Tried as spies they were both sentenced to hang. But Scully panicked and spilled all he knew about the foursome. Webster was exposed as a double agent and was also sentenced to the gallows. But Lewis acted quickly and since they were both British subjects (Scully was Irish) and not American citizens, contacted the consul and demanded the protection of the crown. The execution of the pair was delayed and they were released in 1863. Scully, shunned by both the War Department and Pinkerton for his role in the death of Webster, went on to become a guard in Chicago until he faded from view. (Horan, James D., *The Pinkertons: The Detective Dynasty That Made History*)

SCURRY, William Read (1821-1864)

A highly competent Confederate officer, as shown by his performance at Glorieta Pass, the Tennessee-born Mexican War veteran William R. Scurry gave his life for the South later in the Civil War. During the earlier part of the war he had fought as a private in the 2nd Texas Mounted Volunteers. In the late 1850s he had been a boundary commissioner and upon the outbreak of the Civil War joined the Confederate army. His assignments included: lieutenant colonel, 4th Texas Cavalry (1861); brigadier general, CSA (September 12, 1862); commanding Eastern Sub-District of Texas, District of Texas, New Mexico and Arizona, Trans-Mississippi Department (February 13-June 10, and ca. August-September 17, 1863); and commanding brigade, 1st (Walker's) Division, District of West Louisiana, Trans-Mississippi Department (fall 1863-April 30, 1864). Accompanying Henry H. Sibley into the New Mexico-Arizona area, he fought at Valverde. At Glorieta pass he directed the forces in the pass itself—and was highly successful. Only the capture and destruction of the Confederate supply train by a Union flanking column under John M. Chivington forced the Southerners to withdraw from the territory. The balance of Scurry's service came in the Trans-Mississippi West. He fought at Galveston and in the Red River Campaign. Moving north to face Steele's drive on Camden, Arkansas, he was mortally wounded at Jenkins' Ferry and bled to death on the field.

SEARS, Claudius Wistar (1817-1891)

Marriage into a Texas family overrode the northern birth and military academy appointment of Claudius W. Sears and led him to a Confederate brigadier generalship. The Massachusetts-born West Pointer (1841) had received his appointment from New York. He served only a year before resigning as a second lieutenant in the 8th Infantry. A college professor before the war, he was a school president in 1861 when he offered his military services to the Confederacy. His assignments included: captain, Company G, 17th Mississippi (spring 1861); colonel, 46th Mississippi (December 11, 1862); brigadier general, CSA (March 1, 1864); and commanding brigade, French's Division, Polk's (Army of Mississippi)-Stewart's Corps, Army of Tennessee (May-December 15, 1864). Named to command the Magnolia Guards early in the war, he became part of the 17th Mississippi. Before his promotion to colonel of a new regiment this unit fought at 1st Bull Run, Ball's Bluff, Yorktown, Seven Pines, in the Seven Days, and at Antietam. His new regiment fought at Chickasaw Bayou against Sherman in the defense of Vicksburg, and Sears was captured while commanding at Vicksburg. Paroled on the day of the surrender, he was eventually exchanged. Despite illness, he served through most of the Atlanta Campaign. Heading north, he fought at Allatoona, Franklin and Nashville. In the latter he was wounded and a few days later was taken captive. Having lost a leg, he was paroled until June 23, 1865. He served as a college professor until two years before his death.

SEBASTIAN, William King (1812-1865)

Expelled from the U.S. Senate after his state had seceded, William K. Sebastian became the focus of a plan late in the Civil War to bring Arkansas back into the Union. Born in Tennessee, he had become a cotton planter in Arkansas and, becoming a lawyer, was a state judge. In 1846 and 1847 he presided over the state senate and the next year was named to the U.S. Senate as a Democrat. Reelected in both 1853 and 1859, he was sitting in that body when the state seceded. After he failed to show up for the session beginning July 4, 1861, he was expelled a week later. The readmittance plan simply called for him to return to his seat as if nothing had ever happened, and that this would signify that at least one state was back in the Union. Nothing came of it and Sebastian—who had been practicing law in Helena, Arkansas, and Memphis, Tennessee—died on May 20, 1865. In 1877 the Senate revoked the expulsion order and authorized the payment of his back salary to his children.

SEDDON, James Alexander (1815-1880)

The longest-lasting of the Confederate secretaries of war, James A. Seddon was nonetheless highly criticized by both the Confederate Congress and the public for his unquestioning support of Jefferson Davis. A native Virginia lawyer, he had served two nonconsecutive terms in the U.S. Congress. He came out of retirement during the secession winter to attend the Washington Peace Conference. After one unsuccessful bid for a seat in the Provisional Confederate Congress, he was seated on July 20, 1861, but was given no committee assignments. He did not seek reelection but later changed his mind and ran for a vacant seat in April 1862, finishing third. On November 21, 1862, Jefferson Davis, seeking a loyal supporter for his cabinet, appointed Seddon secretary of war in place of the resigned George W. Randolph. Once in office he was virtually a total yes-man—and was condemned for it. His complicity in the removal of Joseph E. Johnston in front of Atlanta lowered his stock in the eyes of the public as well as the already hostile Congress. Faced with a demand from the Virginia congressional delegation for a cabinet reshuffle, Davis accepted Seddon's resignation on February 6, 1865, but not without a harsh condemnation of the legislative branch. Following a brief internment at the end of the war, Seddon returned to his retirement.

SEDGWICK, John (1813-1864)

Affectionately called "Uncle John" Sedgwick by his troops, he became the third and final corps commander in the Army of the Potomac to be killed in action. The Connecticut-born West Pointer (1837) had an unusually active prewar career. Originally posted to the artillery, he fought in the Seminole War, was involved in the Trail of Tears episode, and earned two brevets in the Mexican War. Upon the expansion of the regular establishment in 1855 he transferred to the mounted arm. In this branch he served in "Bleeding Kansas," on the Mormon Expedition, and in further Indian fighting. During the secession crisis he was twice in a matter of weeks promoted to replace Robert E. Lee, once when that officer was himself promoted and once when Lee resigned. Sedgwick's Civil War assignments included: major, 1st Cavalry (since March 3, 1855); lieutenant colonel, 2nd Cavalry (March 16, 1861); colonel, 1st Cavalry (April 25, 1861); colonel, 4th Cavalry (change of designation August 3, 1861); brigadier general, USV (August 31, 1861); commanding 2nd Brigade, Heintzelman's Division, Army of the Potomac (October 3, 1861-February 9, 1862); commanding Stone's (old) Division, Army of the Potomac (February 9-

"Uncle John" Sedgwick. (NA)

March 13, 1862); commanding 2nd Division, 2nd Corps, Army of the Potomac (March 13-September 17, 1862); major general, USV (July 4, 1862); commanding 2nd Corps, Army of the Potomac (December 26, 1862-January 26, 1863); commanding 9th Corps, Army of the Potomac (January 16-February 5, 1863); and commanding 6th Corps, Army of the Potomac (February 4 1863-April 6, 1864 and April 13-May 9, 1865). Initially in charge of a brigade in the fall of 1861, Sedgwick took over a division when General Charles P. Stone was placed under arrest. This he led to the Peninsula where he fought at Yorktown and Seven Pines. During the Seven Days he was wounded at Frayser's Farm. On the nation's birthday he received the second star of a major general and continued in division command until Antietam where his division marched into a trap, being struck on three sides. Sedgwick himself suffered three wounds and was out of action until after Fredericksburg when he returned to lead first the 2nd Corps, then the 9th, and finally the 6th. In the Chancellorsville Campaign he commanded Hooker's force at Fredericksburg. He broke through Marye's Heights in an effort to relieve the pressure on his chief but was stopped at Salem Church and was forced to withdraw north of the river. At Gettysburg his corps was in reserve, but he scored a signal success at Rappahannock Bridge that fall. One of the top corps commanders with the army, he retained command when the five corps were reduced to three. He led his men into the tangled fighting of the Wilderness and then on to Spotsylvania. While placing his corps artillery he was shot by a Confederate sharpshooter in the head. Ironically he had just declared that they couldn't fire accurately at that distance. He died almost immediately. (Winslow, Richard Elliott, *General John Sedgwick: The Story of a Union Corps Commander*)

SEIBELS, Emmett (1821-1899)

One in the seemingly endless stream of duels between Confederate officers was that between Major Emmett Seibels and Captain Elbert Bland of the 7th South Carolina. Seibels had been a lawyer before the war and his later military assignments included: major, 7th South Carolina (April 15, 1861) and lieutenant colonel, 7th South Carolina (May 9, 1862). Having enlisted shortly after the firing on Fort Sumter, he took part in the battle of 1st Bull Run. That winter he became embroiled in a dispute with one of the company commanders, Bland. The result was a duel in which neither party was fatally hurt. It is, however, interesting to note that in the elections held upon the May 1862 reorganization of the regiment, while Bland won a lieutenant colonelcy, Seibels failed in his attempt to become a colonel. After the duel both officers went on to fight at the battle of Williamsburg. Displaced in the elections, Seibels tried for the rest of the war to gain another appointment but failed. He did serve for a while as a volunteer aide to General M.C. Butler.

SELFRIDGE, Thomas Oliver (1804-1902)

By the time of the Civil War, Thomas O. Selfridge had already been incapacitated by wounds received on active sea duty. The native Bostonian had entered the navy as a midshipman in 1818 and risen in rank, slowly but steadily. During the Mexican War he was wounded at Guaymas. The necessities of the service early in the Civil War forced him to return to the sea in charge of the *Mississippi* in the Gulf of Mexico. He subsequently commanded the Mare Island Navy Yard in San Francisco, when he was no longer capable of active service. A captain during the war, he was retired in April 1866, with a promotion to rear admiral three months later. (Selfridge, Thomas O., *Memoirs of Thomas O. Selfridge, Jr., Rear Admiral, USN*)

SELLERS, Alfred Jacob (1836-?)

A native Pennsylvanian, Alfred J. Sellers entered the Union army at the beginning of the Civil War and compiled an impressive record, including brevets for South Mountain and Antietam and the Congressional Medal of Honor for Gettysburg. His assignments included: captain, Company D, 19th Pennsylvania (April 27, 1861); major, 90th Pennsylvania (February 26, 1862); and captain and assistant quartermaster, USV (July 2, 1864). His first company was mustered out on August 29, 1861, before he could see any action. The next year, however, he fought at Cedar Mountain, 2nd Bull Run, South Mountain, Antietam, and Fredericksburg. At Antietam he commanded a skirmish line which brought in 125 prisoners the day after the battle and at Fredericksburg he received a leg wound. He recovered to fight at Chancellorsville and Gettysburg where he took command of the regiment and changed its front in the immediate face of the enemy. This latter action earned him the medal in 1894. Shortly after this battle he was detailed to draft duty, bringing a detachment of draftees to the Army of the Potomac despite an uprising in which the ringleader was killed. After serving in the Mine Run Campaign he was mustered out on February 29, 1864. That summer he was assigned to quartermaster duty in the Shenandoah Valley and volunteered on General Dwight's staff during the fighting at Cedar Creek. He was finally mustered out on October 31, 1865, after turning down an appointment in the regular army. (Mitchell, Joseph B., *The Badge of Gallantry*)

SEMMES, Paul Jones (1815-1863)

For a decade and a half Georgia banker and plantation owner Paul J. Semmes had been an officer in the militia of Columbus, Georgia. Upon the outbreak of the Civil War he put this experience to use for the Confederacy. his assignments included: colonel, 2nd Georgia (ca. June 1, 1861); brigadier general, CSA (to rank from March 11, 1862); commanding McLaws' (old) Brigade, McLaws' Division, Magruder's Command, Department of Northern Virginia (early May-July 1862); and commanding brigade, McLaws' Division, 1st Corps, Army of Northern Virginia (July 1862-July 2, 1863). After serving at Yorktown, he was given command of a brigade which he was to command for the remainder of his career. He led it at Williamsburg and in the Seven Days on the Peninsula. In the Maryland Campaign he fought at Crampton's Gap on South Mountain and at Antietam. He was on Marye's Heights at Fredericksburg and at Salem Church at Chancellorsville. In the

Confederate attack on the Union left on the second day at Gettysburg he fell mortally wounded. Carried back with the retreating army, he died on the 10th at Martinsburg, in what had officially become West Virginia three weeks earlier. (Freeman, Douglas S., *Lee's Lieutenants*)

SEMMES, Raphael (1809-1877)

The second-ranking Confederate naval officer, Marylander Raphael Semmes, along with his most famous command, CSS *Alabama*, became the most renowned of the Southern commerce raiders. Having entered the Old Navy in 1826, Semmes had risen to the rank of commander by the time of the secession crisis. In between assignments he had also studied law and been admitted to the bar in 1834. His Mexican War command, the brig *Somers*, sank off Vera Cruz, and Semmes and 38 of his crew went down with her. Semmes and two others were rescued by the *Somers'* sole lifeboat, returning after landing its first load. A court of inquiry praised Semmes' actions during the crisis. He later served as a naval observer/adviser on the march to Mexico City. In the interwar period Semmes frequently made use of his legal skills in defending other officers against the "system." Having come to consider Mobile his home, Semmes resigned his commission on February 15, 1861, just over a month after Alabama's secession. Offering his services to Jefferson Davis, he was sent north to obtain naval supplies before the outbreak of actual hostilities. After much success he returned south and on April 4, 1861, found a commission as commander, CSN, awaiting him in Montgomery. For two weeks he served as chief of the Lighthouse Bureau, before gaining permission to convert a former packet steamer, the *Havana*, into a commerce raider. This first of the Confederate raiders, renamed the *Sumter*, hit the open seas on June 30, 1861. Three days later Semmes made his first capture. After cruising on both sides of the Atlantic and capturing some 18 prizes, the *Sumter*, in desperate need of repairs, was blockaded at Gibraltar by three Union vessels, including the USS *Kearsarge*. Leaving the vessel there (it was sold in December 1862), Semmes started on his return to the Confederacy but was promoted to captain and ordered to England to take command of the *290*, soon to become infamous as the *Alabama*. From September 1862 to June 1864, Semmes sailed his new command from the Atlantic to the China Sea, taking some 69 prizes including the Union gunboat *Hatteras* which he sank in a naval battle in the Gulf of Mexico. Finally, on June 11, 1864, the *Alabama* put into Cherbourg, France, for much-needed repairs. But soon her old nemesis, the *Kearsarge*, set up a blockade outside the harbor. Semmes decided to fight and after an hour's conflict and with his vessel sinking, on June 19 was forced to strike his colors. Picked up by the *Deerhound*, an English yacht, he and several of his officers were feted in England before returning to the Confederacy. At home he was promoted to rear admiral and in February 1865 was given command of the James River Squadron. With the fall of the Confederate capital, he was forced to destroy his vessels and form his men into an infantry unit. He finally surrendered with Johnston's army, signing his parole as rear admiral and brigadier general. He had been appointed to the army grade by Jefferson Davis after he scuttled his fleet, but with the fall of the country it could not be confirmed by the Senate. In December 1865 he was imprisoned for four months while the Union authorities tried to find a way to try him for treason and piracy. Returning to Mobile, he was elected to a judgeship, but the authorities removed him from office. He was also driven from employment in education and journalism. Resuming the practice of law, he later published *Memoirs of Service Afloat, During the War Between the States*. During the periods between his numerous captures, Semmes was noted for passing the time by walking the decks, supervising the crew, and at the same time engaging in an endless battle with his unruly mustache. His crew dubbed him "Old Beeswax." (Roberts, W.A., *Semmes of the Alabama*)

SEMMES, Thomas Jenkins (1824-1899)

The cousin of the famed commander of the CSS *Alabama*, Raphael Semmes, Thomas J. Semmes served the Confederacy as a senator from Louisiana. The native of the nation's capital had practiced law first in Washington and then in New Orleans. He was a one-term state legislator and, as district attorney, prosecuted filibuster William Walker. At the outbreak of the Civil War he was serving as the state's attorney general. Elected to the Confederate Senate, he was admitted on February 19, 1862. In the First Regular Congress he sat on the committees on: Finance; Flag and Seal; and Judiciary. In the next Congress he substituted the Committee on Rules for that on the Flag and Seal. In his support for the war effort he had a mixed record. For example, he supported conscription but opposed the suspension of the writ of habeas corpus and its uncontrolled use. A defender of the president's right to make military appointments, he was part of the Beauregard-bloc but a critic of Joseph E. Johnston. In a pragmatic manner, he favored the recruiting of slaves to preserve a part of the "peculiar institution." After the war he retired to private practice and legal instruction. Except for his leadership role in the 1879 constitutional convention he withdrew from the political arena.

SERRELL, Edward Wellman (1826-1906)

A U.S. citizen born in England, Edward W. Serrell put his experience as a civil engineer to work for the Union army and developed many inventions to solve problems in warfare along the coast. His Civil War assignments included: lieutenant colonel, 1st New York Engineers (October 10, 1861); colonel, 1st New York Engineers (February 14, 1862); chief engineer, 10th Corps, Department of the South (1863-April 1864); chief engineer, Army of the James (May 1864-February 1865); and also chief of staff, Army of the James (1864). In all, he was in some 126 engagements in Georgia, South Carolina, and Virginia. He was involved in the siege operations against Fort Pulaski, Charleston, Petersburg, and Richmond. He was present at the taking of Battery Wagner and later emplaced the Swamp Angel batteries which bombarded the city of Charleston. Mustered out on February 15, 1865, he was brevetted brigadier general of volunteers the following month. Returning to civilian life he was active in engineering for railroads and canals.

SEWARD, Frederick William (1830-1915)

Acting secretary of state at the time of the attack upon his father during the Lincoln assassination, Frederick W. Seward was also seriously injured that bloody night. For a time he had served as his father's secretary and then on the staff of the *Albany Evening Journal*. In the Lincoln administration he served as assistant secretary of state, again under his father. He took an active role in the diplomatic affairs of the United States during the war and was present for the signing of the Emancipation Proclamation. With his father injured in a carriage accident in the spring of 1865, he attended Lincoln's final cabinet meeting in his place. That night when Lewis Paine broke into the Sewards' Washington home to kill the secretary of state, Frederick encountered him but, being severely wounded in the assault, failed to prevent Paine from reaching the secretary's sick bed. After the war the younger Seward was active in diplomatic affairs and as a New York politician. He again served as assistant secretary in the late 1870s. (Seward, Frederick William, *Reminiscences of a War-Time Statesman and Diplomat*)

SEWARD, William Henry (1801-1872)

Himself a contender for the 1860 Republican presidential nomination, New York lawyer William H. Seward assumed that his position as Lincoln's secretary of state would make him the prime force in the administration, but Lincoln quickly put him in his place. As a Whig, he had been in the state legislature and served as governor from 1839 to 1842. He joined the Republicans in 1856, but his extreme opposition to slavery was a prime cause of his 1856 and 1860 failures to gain the presidential nomination. In return for support of Lincoln he was promised the state portfolio. In the first months of the war he proposed a war with European powers in order to reunite the states and hinted at the president turning over most of his powers to himself. Lincoln deftly deflected his maneuverings and, following Seward's meddling in the reinforcement plans for Fort Sumter, Seward became an effective foreign minister. He successfully handled the explosive *Trent* affair by returning the Confederate emmisaries Mason and Slidell. For the balance of the war he sought to prevent foreign intervention and stop the flow of arms and vessels to the South. While suffering from a carriage accident he was attacked in his bed by Lewis Paine on the night of the Lincoln assassination. He survived multiple knife wounds, probably due to the neck brace he was wearing. He remained in the cabinet of Andrew Johnson during which time he successfully negotiated the purchase of "Seward's Folly"—Alaska—from the Russians. The "folly" was to prove a major coup. During his tenure Seward had to deal with other matters than those relating to the Civil War, most notably the French presence in Mexico. An advocate of mild treatment of the South, he supported Johnson throughout his term and left the State Department when Grant was inaugurated president. Retiring from public life, he made a world tour. (Lothrop,

Secretary of State William H. Seward. (AC)

Thornton Kirkland, *William Henry Seward*; Van Deusen, Glyndon Garlock, *William Henry Seward*; and Ferns, Norman B., *Desperate Diplomacy: William H. Seward's Foreign Policy, 1861*)

SEWARD, William Henry, Jr. (1839-1920)

The son of Lincoln's secretary of state, William H. Seward, Jr., did not see any major action until the last year of the war but nonetheless rose to the rank of brigadier general. When his father was in the Senate, the native New Yorker served as his private secretary. Involved in banking at the outbreak of the Civil War, he was active in recruiting until he received his own commission. His assignments included: lieutenant colonel, 138th New York (August 22, 1862); lieutenant colonel, 9th New York Heavy Artillery (designation change December 9, 1862); colonel, 9th New York Heavy Artillery (June 10, 1864); brigadier general, USV (September 13, 1864); commanding 1st Brigade, 3rd Division, Department of West Virginia (January-April 1865); and also commanding Reserve Division, Department of West Virginia (February 21-27, 1865). His regiment was assigned to the defenses of the capital and was converted into a heavy artillery unit. In the spring of 1863 young Seward was dispatched to Louisiana with a confidential message from Lincoln to Nathaniel P. Banks. With Grant's heavy losses in the Wilderness and at Spotsylvania, Seward and his regiment were sent to him as infantry. Seward fought at the North Anna and Cold Harbor before being promoted to the colonelcy of the regiment. Part of the force sent to delay Jubal A. Early's drive on Washington, he was slightly wounded in the arm at Monocacy. He also suffered a broken leg when his horse fell. Promoted to brigadier general during his recuperation, he returned to duty in West Virginia in the final months of the war. Resigning on June 1, 1865, he returned to banking and was also active in political, charitable, veterans', and historical organizations.

SEYMOUR, Horatio (1810-1886)

Despite his own opposition to conscription, New York Governor Horatio Seymour declared New York City to be in a state of insurrection during the July 1863 draft rioting and called for a return to order. A New York native with some military education, he had been a lawyer and military secretary to Governor Marcy before the war. He served in the legislature and as Utica's mayor in the 1840s. As a Democrat, he served as the speaker of the state assembly and was defeated for governor in 1850. Winning in 1852, he was defeated for reelection two years later in part due to his veto of a prohibitionist bill. Taking up farming, he was retired from politics for a number of years but the Civil War again brought him to the fore. An initial proponent of compromise, he supported the war effort once the war began and contributed his own money to enlistment drives. Late in 1862 he was elected to a second term in the gubernatorial chair and was inaugurated early the next year. An opponent of the excesses of the war as he saw them—the draft, arbitrary military arrests, and the Emancipation Proclamation—he supported the war effort within that context. His term ended on January 1, 1865, following his defeat by the Republican Reuben E. Fenton. In 1868 he was the Democratic nominee for president but was defeated by Grant. That was the end of his political career. (Mitchell, Stewart, *Horatio Seymour of New York*)

SEYMOUR, Isaac Gurdon (1804-1862)

Receiving his first chance to direct a brigade in combat, Isaac G. Seymour lost his life after only one day in temporary command. A one-time mayor of Macon, Georgia, he had served in the early Indian wars and in Mexico as a lieutenant colonel of Georgia volunteers. At the outbreak of the Civil War he was editing the *New Orleans Bulletin*. His Confederate assignments included: colonel, 6th Louisiana (June 4, 1861); and commanding Taylor's Brigade, Ewell's Division, Jackson's Command, Army of Northern Virginia (June 26-27, 1862). He led his regiment at 1st Bull Run and in Jackson's Valley Campaign. Moving to the defense of Richmond, he took over brigade command when General Richard Taylor became too ill to remain on duty the day before the battle of Gaines' Mill. In the struggle the next day, Seymour was shot and killed. The demoralized Louisiana brigade broke shortly afterwards. The publication of an obituary for Seymour in occupied New Orleans angered General Benjamin F. Butler who sent Seymour's son to jail.

SEYMOUR, Truman (1824-1891)

A veteran artillerist, having won two brevets in the Mexican War, West Pointer (1846) Truman Seymour was commanding Company H, 1st Artillery, at the time of the bombardment of Fort Sumter. Following his capture and release, Captain Seymour was transferred to the newly authorized 5th Artillery and assigned to the Washington defenses. His later assignments included: brigadier general, USV (April 28, 1862); commanding 3rd Brigade, 2nd Division, Department of the Rappahannock (May 16-June 12, 1862); commanding 3rd Brigade, 3rd Division, 5th Corps, Army of the Potomac (June 18-30, 1862); commanding the division (June 30-August 26, 1862); commanding 1st Brigade, 3rd Division, in the 3rd Corps, Army of Virginia (August 26-September 12, 1862) and in the 1st Corps, Army of the Potomac (September 12-17 and September 29-November 14, 1862); and commanding the division (September 17-29, 1862). In the 10th Corps, Department of the South, he commanded: Port Royal Island (December 26, 1862-February 9, 1863); 2nd Division (July 6-19, 1863); Morris Island (October 18-November 10, 1863); District of Hilton Head (December 6-February 5, 1864); and the District of Florida (February 16-March 24, 1864). Returning to Virginia he commanded: 2nd Brigade, 3rd Division, 6th Corps, Army of the Potomac (May 5-6, 1864); and 3rd Division, 6th Corps, in the Army of the Shenandoah (October 19-December 6, 1864) and in the Army of the Potomac (December 6, 1864-April 16, 1865). Seymour saw action in the Seven Days, at 2nd Bull Run, South Mountain, and Antietam before being sent to South Carolina where he led an attack on Battery Wagner. He then led an invasion of northern Florida but was defeated at Olustee in February 1864. Returning to Virginia he was captured on the second day at the Wilderness and was imprisoned in Charleston under the fire of the Union besiegers. Exchanged in August 1864, he rejoined the forces in the field at the end of Sheridan's victories in the Shenandoah Valley. Returning to the Army of the Potomac, he took part in the remainder of the Petersburg siege and the Appomattox Campaign. He received regular army brevets up to major general for South Mountain, Antietam, Petersburg, and the war. He was also brevetted major general of volunteers. Resigning from the army in 1876, he lived the rest of his life in Florence, Italy.

SHACKELFORD, James Murrell (1827-1909)

The loss of a spouse cost the Union army the services of one of its generals, James M. Shackelford. The Kentucky native had served as a lieutenant of the 4th Kentucky during the Mexican War and then entered upon the practice of law. Remaining loyal to the Union, he enlisted at the beginning of 1862 and his assignments included: colonel, 25th Kentucky (January 1, 1862); colonel, 8th Kentucky Cavalry (September 13, 1862); brigadier general, USV (March 2, 1863); and commanding in the Army of the Ohio: 1st Brigade, 2nd Division, 23rd Corps (June 24-August 6, 1863); 3rd Brigade, 4th Division, 23rd Corps (August 6-September 10, 1863); the division (September 10-November 3, 1863); and Cavalry Corps (November 1863-January 1864). As commander of an infantry regiment, he fought at Fort Donelson, but ill health forced his resignation the next month on March 24, 1862. Having recovered, he was recommissioned in September as the colonel of a mounted regiment. Advanced to brigadier general, he took part in the pursuit of John Hunt Morgan's raiders and actually received Hunt's surrender in Ohio. He suffered a slight foot wound in the September 3, 1863, action at Geiger's Lake, Kentucky. After commanding the mounted arm in the defense of Knoxville he resigned effective January 18, 1864, citing the loss of his wife. He then resumed his practice and for a time was a judge. He also represented the Choctaw Indians in their dealings with the U.S. government.

SHADOW

See: *Linebaugh, John H.*

SHAKOPEE (?-1864)

Along with fellow Santee Sioux subchieftain Medicine Bottle, Shakopee (or Little Six) was spirited out of Canada to face a farcical trial and execution in Minnesota for his role in the 1862 Sioux uprising there. The tribes had not been provided with the food promised under treaty obligations, due to the corruption of the Indian agent, and four angry braves massacred five whites in retaliation. Shakopee then felt that the Santee had no choice but war and joined with Little Crow in the attacks on New Ulm and Fort Ridgely. Once the uprising had spent its force he fled to Canada. Thinking himself safe, he fell into a trap set up by an American citizen, two Canadians, and a U.S. Army lieutenant. The foursome drugged their "friends" on spiked alcohol and dog-sledded them back to Minnesota for an eventual hanging at Fort Snelling. (Brown, Dee, *Bury My Heart At Wounded Knee*)

SHALER, Alexander (1827-1911)

In the case of Union General Alexander Shaler, the Confederates got a measure of revenge against at least one commander of a prisoner of war camp. Born in Connecticut, Shaler had been raised in New York City and appears to have been independently wealthy since he was able to contribute so much time to the state militia. His assignments included: major, 7th New York Militia (prewar-1861); lieutenant colonel, 65th New York (June 11, 1861); colonel, 65th New York (June 17, 1862); commanding 1st Brigade, 3rd Division, 6th Corps, Army of the Potomac (March-May 1863 and June-December 30, 1863); brigadier general, USV (May 26, 1863); commanding prisoner of war camp, Johnson's Island, Ohio (early 1864); commanding 4th Brigade, 1st Division, 6th Corps, Army of the Potomac (April 18-May 6, 1864); commanding 3rd Brigade, 2nd Division, 19th Corps, Department of the Gulf (November 3-December 5, 1864); and commanding 2nd Division, 7th Corps, Department of Arkansas (December 28, 1864-August 1, 1865). Accompanying the famed 7th New York Militia, he was one of the first volunteers from the North to reach Washington at the outbreak of the war. He then joined a volunteer regiment as second in command. He served at Yorktown and was in command at Williamsburg. After fighting at Seven Pines he was made colonel shortly before the beginning of the Seven Days. His regiment—which was also known as the 1st U.S. Chasseurs—was too far in the rear with its division at Antietam to be engaged. However, at Chancellorsville Shaler fought on Marye's Heights and at Salem Church in command of the brigade. Promotion to brigadier general followed later that month. And in 1893 he was awarded the Congressional Medal of Honor for the storming of Marye's Heights. In reserve at Gettysburg, he led his men through the Bristoe and Mine Run campaigns. During the early part of 1864 he commanded the prisoner of war camp at Johnson's Island, Ohio. Within a month of his return to the Army of the Potomac he was captured, on the second day of the Wilderness. In retaliation for the treatment of some Confederate prisoners in Charleston Harbor the Richmond authorities dispatched Shaler and four other Union generals to that city for confinement. However, the five generals wrote to Washington to deny that they were placed in unnecessary danger. An exchange of prisoners was soon arranged. Shaler was then assigned to duty along the Gulf coast and finished the war in Arkansas. In July of 1865 he was brevetted major general and was mustered out on August 24. After the war he was involved in civic and veterans' affairs.

SHANKS, John T. (1832-?)

Fighting in Arkansas and Tennessee and rising from private to captain, Texas-born bookkeeper John Shanks lost his company when it was consolidated with another. Joining John Hunt Morgan's Confederate cavalry as a scout in 1863, Shanks was captured at Buffington Island, Ohio, on July 19, 1863, during Morgan's famous Indiana and Ohio raid. Confined at Camp Douglas, Shanks became a spokesman for the enlisted prisoners and, because of his clerical abilities, became a clerk in the office of the commandant, Colonel Benjamin J. Sweet. Shanks' ingratiation with the commandant made him the natural choice to work under cover when word was received that rebel agents planned to attack the camp on November 8, 1864, free the prisoners, and capture Chicago. After a staged escape, Shanks was to contact the conspirators and identify them to Sweet. Not totally trusted, he was followed everywhere. With the conspiracy broken up, Shanks was the key witness in convicting one of the conspirators, Colonel George St. Leger Grenfell, a British soldier-of-fortune. After the trial, Shanks received a commission on April 6, 1865, as captain, Company I, 6th United States Volunteers, a regiment composed of ex-prisoners, which he commanded on the plains until October 11, 1866. (Brown, D. Alexander, *Galvanized Yankees*)

SHANNON, Alexander May (?-?)

When John Bell Hood moved the Army of Tennessee off to middle Tennessee in late 1864 and let Sherman's army march through Georgia, there was not much to stop the enemy. But one force, under Alexander M. Shannon, was active on the fringes of Sherman's army. Shannon was the captain of Company C, 8th Texas Cavalry. While his regiment had participated in such battles as Shiloh, Perryville, Murfreesboro, Chickamauga, and Atlanta, he had become known for his activities behind enemy lines, often in Union uniform. During the March to the

Sea he led a detachment of 30 men in gathering information on troop movements. However, they also became involved in attacks on stragglers and foraging parties. Following the fall of Savannah Shannon served through the Carolinas Campaign, reporting to Joe Wheeler. After the war he was a business partner of John B. Hood.

SHARP, Jacob Hunter (1833-1907)

Succeeding the wounded William F. Tucker in command of a brigade during the Atlanta Campaign, Alabamian lawyer Jacob H. Sharp was promoted to brigadier general and commanded the unit for the balance of the war. His assignments included: private, 1st (Blythe's) Mississippi Battalion (early 1861); captain, 44th (Blythe's) Mississippi (1861); colonel, 44th Mississippi (1863); commanding Anderson's Brigade, Hindman's Division, Polk's Corps, Army of Tennessee (September 20, 1863); commanding Tucker's (old) Brigade, Hindman's-Johnson's Division, Hood's-Lee's Corps, Army of Tennessee (May 14, 1864-March 1865); brigadier general, CSA (July 26, 1864); and commanding brigade, Hill's Division, Lee's Corps, Army of Tennessee (April 9-26, 1865). He fought as a company commander at Shiloh and in the campaigns of Perryville, Murfreesboro, and Tullahoma. Promoted to colonel, he took command of the brigade when J. Patton Anderson took over the division upon the wounding of Thomas C. Hindman at Chickamauga. His regiment fought at Chattanooga and then embarked upon the Atlanta Campaign. When Tucker was wounded at Resaca, Sharp took command of the brigade and was promoted to brigadier general and its permanent command two months later. Accompanying Hood into middle Tennessee, he fought at Franklin and Nashville. He later commanded a brigade during parts of the Carolinas Campaign. Resuming his law practice, he was active in restoring white government to Mississippi and engaged in journalism.

SHAW, Robert Gould (1837-1863)

Son of a prominent Boston abolitionist family, Robert Shaw was serving as a captain in the 2nd Massachusetts when he was tapped by Massachusetts Governor John Andrew for a special assignment. Shaw was to raise and command the first regiment of black troops organized in a Northern state. All the previous "colored" regiments had been raised principally from freed slaves in occupied areas. Shaw went about the organization of his command, recruiting free blacks from all over New England and some from beyond. The regiment was mustered into service on May 13, 1863, with Shaw as its colonel, and was sent to the South Carolina coast to take part in the operations against the cradle of secession, Charleston. After leading the regiment in smaller actions on James Island, at Legaresville on July 13, and Secessionville on July 16, Shaw moved the regiment over to Morris Island. On July 18, 1863, he led the 54th, in conjunction with two brigades of white troops, in an assault on Confederate Battery Wagner. In the unsuccessful charge, the black troops proved themselves to be fully capable of standing up to enemy fire but lost about one quarter of their men, including Colonel Shaw. The rebels in the battery were so outraged by the Union commanders arming blacks that they decided to insult the white officer by burying him in a common grave with his black enlisted men. But Shaw's parents, when they heard of it, were pleased and believed that was the way their son would have wanted it. (Burchard, Peter, *One Gallant Rush: Robert Gould Shaw and His Brave Black Regiment*)

SHEADS, Carrie (?-?)

When the great Civil War armies invaded the peaceful Adams County countryside in the summer of 1863 the principal of the young ladies' Oakridge Seminary, Carrie Sheads, found herself at the head of a corps of nurses. During the first day of the battle of Gettysburg the school was taken over by the Union forces as a field hospital. The principal, staff, and students were soon at work tending the wounded, but the Union forces were quickly forced to fall back to the south and east of town. The occupying Confederate troops allowed the nurses' operations to continue until the close of the battle, and the Southern withdrawal allowed the Union army to retake control. Shortly after the battle the care of the wounded was transferred to the appropriate authorities and the school began to pick up the pieces.

SHEATS, Charles Christopher (1839-1904)

The idea of secession was not at all popular in some of the mountainous regions of the Confederacy, and in one such area, the county of Winston in Alabama, the opposition, under the leadership of Charles Sheats, was especially vehement. Sheats, a school teacher before the war, had been elected as a "cooperationist," or Unionist, delegate to the state secession convention. Refusing all attempts at coercion in Montgomery, he and two other delegates refused to sign the Ordinance of Secession. He was promptly seized by an angered mob and thrown in jail, where he remained until the close of the convention. Returning home, he was greeted as a hero and that summer was elected to the state legislature where he voted against war measures and tried to concentrate on financial affairs, realizing that he alone could not stop the war. Then in early April 1862 he was the principal organzier of a Unionist gathering of mountaineers at Bill Looney's Tavern back in Winston. Over 2,500 were present, including some from other states. Although the county did not actually secede from the state, it did reserve that right—since Alabama felt it could secede from the Union. The county was dubbed "The Free State of Winston" by one secessionist. Many Winston men went to the Union Army and others resisted officers who tried to enforce the Confederate draft. In September the area was occupied by Southern troops, and Sheats was ordered to Montgomery where he was imprisoned until sent into the Union lines in 1864. During this time the area became a haven for rebel deserters, and Winston had a vicious civil war of its own. After the war Sheats was a delegate to the 1865 state constitutional convention, editor of *The North Alabamian*, a presidential elector for Grant, U.S. consul in Denmark, one-term U.S. congressman, and federal appointee.

SHEFFIELD, James Lawrence (1819-1892)

While many Confederate officers sacrificed their blood for the infant nation, James L. Sheffield also donated a sizable fortune to the cause. A sheriff and state legislator in his native Alabama before the war, he had served in the secession convention. Deciding to take the field, he raised the 48th Alabama, equipping it himself at a cost of $60,000. He was commissioned colonel on May 13, 1862. During the war he held the following brigade commands: Taliaferro's Brigade, Jackson's (old) Division, Jackson's Command, Army of Northern Virginia (September 17, 1862); Law's Brigade, Hood's Division, 1st Corps, Army of Northern Virginia (July 2-September 1863); and Law's Brigade, Hood's Division, Longstreet's Corps, Army of Tennessee (September 20-October 1863). In his first action at Cedar Mountain he was wounded. He recovered in time to fight later that month at 2nd Bull Run. At Antietam he succeeded to brigade command and held it until the end of the battle. After serving with Longstreet in southeastern Virginia, he fought at Gettysburg on Little Round Top, again taking over command of the brigade. Accompanying Longstreet's Corps to the West, he fought at Chickamauga and Knoxville. At the former he was for the last time in brigade command. Missing the battle of the Wilderness, he resigned his commission on May 31, 1864.

SHELBY, Joseph Orville (1830-1897)

One of the Confederacy's most effective cavalry leaders, Joseph O. Shelby served entirely in the Trans-Mississippi West. A planter and rope manufacturer, he had had investments in both his native Kentucky and Missouri. During the Bleeding Kansas episode he led a company of Kentuckians on the slavery side. Early in the Civil War he entered the Missouri State Guard and his assignments included: captain, Shelby's Ranger Company, Missouri State Guard (spring 1861); colonel, 5th Missouri Cavalry (1862); commanding brigade, Marmaduke's Cavalry Division, 1st Corps, Trans-Mississippi Department (summer-December 1862); commanding brigade, Marmaduke's Cavalry Division, District of Arkansas, Trans-Mississippi Department (January-July 4, 1863 and late 1863-September 1864); brigadier general, CSA (December 15, 1863); commanding division, Army of Missouri, Trans-Mississippi Department (September 18-September 1864); and commanding 1st (Missouri) Cavalry Brigade, 1st (Missouri) Cavalry Division, Cavalry Corps, Trans-Mississippi Department (September 1864-May 26, 1865). As a company commander he fought at Carthage, Wilson's Creek, and Pea Ridge before being sent back to Missouri to raise a regiment. As a colonel in charge of a brigade in John S. Marmaduke's mounted division, he fought at Prairie Grove and was wounded at Helena. Upon his recovery he was promoted to brigadier general and led a brigade at Jenkins' Ferry. During Price's invasion of Missouri in the late summer and fall of 1864 he led a cavalry division. When the Confederacy's collapse came he refused to surrender and led part of his force to Mexico where they unsuccessfully offered their services to either side. He then returned to his business interests in Missouri. (O'Flaherty, Daniel, *General Jo Shelby, Undefeated Rebel*)

SHELDON, Lionel Allen (1831-1917)

A New York-born Ohio lawyer and judge, Lionel A. Sheldon had served for a year in the militia before entering the field. His assignments included: brigadier general, Ohio Militia (1860); lieutenant colonel, 42nd Ohio (November 27, 1861); colonel, 42nd Ohio (March 14, 1862); commanding 1st Brigade, 9th Division, Right Wing, 13th Corps, Department of the Tennessee (November-December 18, 1862); commanding 1st Brigade, 3rd Division, Yazoo Expedition, Department of the Tennessee (December 18, 1862-January 4, 1863); commanding 2nd Brigade, 9th Division, 13th Corps, Army of the Tennessee (February 9-May 1, 1863); commanding 3rd Brigade, 1st Division, 13th Corps, Department of the Gulf (October 19-26, 1863); commanding 2nd Brigade, 1st Division, 13th Corps, Department of the Gulf (April 27-May 9, 1864); and commanding 1st Brigade, 3rd Division, 19th Corps, Department of the Gulf (August 16-September 11, 1864). His regiment initially served in western Virginia, eastern Kentucky, and East Tennessee—taking part in the capture of Cumberland Gap—before being ordered to Memphis for operations along the Mississippi. Frequently in brigade command, Sheldon fought at Chickasaw Bluffs, Arkansas Post and Vicksburg. Transferred to the Gulf coast with the 13th Corps, he campaigned in both eastern and western Louisiana and performed post duty at Baton Rouge. Mustered out with his regiment on December 2, 1864, he was brevetted brigadier a few months later. After the war he was a lawyer in New Orleans and California, active in railroading, a Louisiana congressman, and governor of New Mexico.

SHELLEY, Charles Miller (1833-1907)

Distinguishing himself in one of the first actions of the Civil War—Blackburn's Ford—Tennessee-born Alabama architect Charles M. Shelley rose to become a Confederate brigadier general. His assignments included: lieutenant, Alabama Militia Artillery (February 1861); captain, 1st Company E, 5th Alabama (May 11, 1861); colonel, 30th Alabama (January 31, 1862); commanding Cumming's (old) Brigade, Stevenson's Divison, Hood's-Lee's Corps, Army of Tennessee (August 31-October 2, 1864); brigadier general, CSA (September 17, 1864); commanding Cantey's Brigade, Walthall's Division, Stewart's Corps, Army of Tennessee (October 2, 1864-April 9, 1865); and commanding brigade, Loring's Division, Stewart's Corps, Army of Tennessee (April 9-26, 1865). After serving in the defenses of Mobile, his company was converted to infantry and dispatched to Virginia. As a captain he was highly commended for his role in repulsing the Union forces at Blackburn's Ford along Bull Run a few days before the main battle. His regiment then fought at 1st Bull Run and Shelley subsequently raised a new regiment which he led in the western theater. He served in the Kentucky Campaign and was captured at Port Gibson at the beginning of the Vicksburg Campaign. Exchanged, he again led his men at Chattanooga and during the Atlanta Campaign, succeeding to command of a brigade at Jonesboro. He led a different brigade as a brigadier general at

Franklin and Nashville and in the Carolinas. Following the surrender he was a sheriff, congressman, and treasury official.

SHELTON, Mary E. (?-?)

An Iowa resident, Mrs. Mary E. Shelton was a field agent for the United States Sanitary Commission and, as well, a campaigner for the support of her fellow Iowans for the work of the commission. Her first field work came at Helena, Arkansas, in late 1863, and she later moved on to Vicksburg and Jackson. She often served as a hospital dietitian and sought the aid of the Iowa Ladies' Aid Society, under Anne Whittenmeyer, in the work of the commission. She was active throughout the conflict.

SHEPARD, Isaac Fitzgerald (1816-1889)

A Massachusetts educator, journalist, and legislator, Isaac F. Shepard headed to Missouri early in the Civil War to support his abolitionist views. The Harvard graduate then entered the state militia to back up his beliefs with action. His assignments included: major and assistant adjutant general, Missouri Militia (June 18, 1861); lieutenant colonel, 19th Missouri (August 30, 1861); colonel, 3rd Missouri (January 18, 1862); colonel, 1st Mississippi African Descent (May 9, 1863); commanding African Brigade, District of Northeastern Louisiana, Army of the Tennessee (May-July 31, 1863); commanding the district (July 31-August 1863); brigadier general, USV (November 17, 1863, to rank from October 27); and commanding 1st Brigade, 1st Division, U.S. Colored Troops, District of Vicksburg, Department of the Tennessee (March-ca. July 1864). He served on Nathaniel Lyon's staff at Wilson's Creek and then became lieutenant colonel of a regiment in the process of organization. Never completing its organization the unit was merged into the 3rd Missouri of which Shepard became colonel early in 1862. This command he led at the capture of Arkansas Post and then, given his New England upbringing, accepted command of a regiment of black troops recently freed from slavery. As a brigade and district commander, he served mostly in northeastern Louisiana—including during the Vicksburg Campaign—and at Vicksburg as part of the garrison. Appointed a brigadier general in the fall of 1863, he left the service when his commission expired on July 4, 1864, when the Senate failed to confirm the appointment. Active in Republican circles after the war, he also was a diplomat to China, an official of the Grand Army of the Republic, Missouri's adjutant general, and a journalist. He finally retired back to Massachusetts.

SHEPHERD, Haywood (?-1859)

It is certainly ironic that in John Brown's famous raid upon Harpers Ferry, Virginia—to initiate an uprising among Virginia's slave population and put an end to the "peculiar institution" of the South—the first fatality was a free black, Haywood Shepherd. The stationmaster for the Baltimore and Ohio Railroad, he had gone to investigate the gunfire coming from the armory and was cut down in a fusillade of bullets. He died several hours later from his wounds, probably unaware of the cause in which he died.

SHEPHERD, Russell Benjamin (?-?)

After over 20 months serving with heavy artillery in the Washington defenses, Russell Shepherd moved into the field for 10 bloody months with his unit which set two records for battle losses. Mustered in as first lieutenant and adjutant of the 18th Maine on August 21, 1862, Shepherd's later assignments included: major, 18th Maine, soon redesignated 1st Maine Heavy Artillery (January 1, 1863); lieutenant colonel, 1st Maine Heavy Artillery (September 24, 1864); colonel, 1st Maine Heavy Artillery (October 21, 1864); commanding 1st Brigade, 3rd Division, 2nd Corps, Army of the Potomac (April 6-May 16, 1865); and commanding 3rd Brigade, Defenses North of the Potomac, 22nd Corps, Department of Washington (June 5-August 1, 1865). Sent into the field with the Army of the Potomac as replacements for Grant's heavy losses, the 1st served as infantry. The regiment suffered heavy losses at Spotsylvania, its first action, and later fought at North Anna, Totopotomoy, and Cold Harbor. During the June 18, 1864, assault on Petersburg, the regiment, part of the time under Shepherd's command, suffered 632 casualties, the largest numerical loss in a single engagement of any Union regiment in the war. The heavy losses among officers caused Shepherd to become the regiment's permanent commander. Continuing in service through the Petersburg and Appomattox Campaigns, the 1st lost 1,283 of its 2,202 men. This was a record for total battle casualties. Shepherd did not become one of the statistics, however, and was mustered out as a brevet brigadier general of volunteers on September 11, 1865. (Shaw, Horace H., *The First Maine Heavy Artillery, 1862-1865*)

SHEPLEY, George Foster (1819-1878)

A political friend of Benjamin F. Butler, George F. Shepley became his right-hand man during the occupation of New Orleans. A Maine lawyer, he had been serving as a U.S. district attorney at the outbreak of the Civil War when he entered the army. His assignments included: colonel, 12th Maine (November 16, 1861); commanding 3rd Brigade, New Orleans Expedition, Department of the Gulf (March-September 1862); military governor of Louisiana (June 2, 1862-March 4, 1864); brigadier general, USV (July 18, 1862); commanding District of Eastern Virginia, Department of Virginia and North Carolina (spring-ca. July 1864); chief of staff, 25th Corps, Army of the James (early 1865); and military governor of Richmond (April 3-July 1, 1865). Although most of his brigade was not present at the fall of New Orleans, he was given command of the post and soon was made military governor of the state. During the almost two years that he held this position—having power only in Union-occupied areas—he was in fact responsible for many of the excesses which were blamed on Butler. Through a blanket pardon he virtually emptied the state prisons of dangerous criminals. With the formation of a Unionist state government, Michael Hahn was elected Union governor, and Shepley left office upon his inauguration. He then commanded a district in Virginia and in the final months of the war was Godfrey Weitzel's staff chief. Following the fall of Richmond he again

George F. Shepley, a Butler friend. (*Leslie's*)

became a military governor. Resigning on July 1, 1865, he returned to the practice of law and later became a judge.

SHEPPARD, William Ludwell (1833-1912)

Serving in the Confederate artillery, William Sheppard had ample opportunity to produce his sketches of army life. Born in Richmond, Sheppard displayed an early aptitude for art but at first was unable to make it his career. As a sideline to his mercantile business, he designed labels for tobacco products. His talent discovered, he went to New York for artistic training. With the outbreak of the war, he became a second lieutenant in the Richmond Howitzers. His unit fought through all the campaigns of the Army of Northern Virginia, and he depicted life in camp and battle. After the war his sketches appeared in several magazines and he provided illustrations for numerous books. But he considered his masterpiece to be the sculpting of the monument to the Richmond Howitzers which stands in the Confederacy's former capital. In the postwar period he studied in London and Paris and was active in the Richmond Art Club. He was also a landscape artist and portrait painter. Sheppard remained active in artistic pursuits until the final long illness that claimed his life in 1912.

SHERIDAN, Philip Henry (1831-1888)

While on his meteoric rise in the Union army, Philip H. Sheridan earned the enmity of many Virginians for laying waste to the Shenandoah Valley. His date and place of birth is uncertain, but he himself claimed to have been born in New York in 1831. Although he was destined to come out of the Civil War with the third greatest reputation among the victors, his military career had not begun auspiciously. It took him five years to graduate from West Point (1853) because of an altercation with fellow cadet and future Union general, William R. Terrill. Posted to the infantry, he was still a second lieutenant at the outbreak of the Civil War. His assignments included: second lieutenant, 4th Infantry (since November 22, 1854); first lieutenant, 4th Infantry (March 1, 1861); captain, 13th Infantry (May 14, 1861); chief quartermaster and chief commissary of Subsistence, Army of Southwest Missouri, Department of the Missouri (ca. December 25, 1861-early 1862); colonel, 2nd Michigan Cavalry (May 25, 1862); commanding 2nd Brigade, Cavalry Division, Army of the Mississippi (June 1-September 4, 1862); brigadier general, USV (July 1, 1862); commanding 11th Division, Army of the Ohio (September-September 29, 1862); commanding 11th Division, 3rd Corps, Army of the Ohio (September 29-November 5, 1862); commanding 3rd Division, Right Wing, 14th Corps, Army of the Cumberland (November 5, 1862-January 9, 1863); major general, USV (December 31, 1862); commanding 3rd Division, 20th Corps, Army of the Cumberland (January 9-October 9, 1863); commanding 2nd Division, 4th Corps, Army of the Cumberland (October 10, 1863-February 17, 1864 and February 27-April 1864); commanding Cavalry Corps, Army of the Potomac (April 4-August 2, 1864); commanding Army of the Shenandoah (August 6-October 16, 1864 and October 19, 1864-February 28, 1865); also commanding Middle Military Division (August 6, 1864-February 27, 1865); brigadier general, USA (September 20, 1864); major general, USA (November 8, 1864); and commanding Sheridan's Cavalry Command (March-April 1865). After serving in a staff position during the early part of the war he was recommended for the command of a cavalry regiment by Gordon Granger. Within days of taking command he was in charge of the brigade with which he earned his first star at Booneville in northern Mississippi. In the late summer of 1862 he was given a division in Kentucky and middle Tennessee. He fought well at Perryville and Murfreesboro and was given a second star in the volunteers to date from the latter. At Chickamauga his division, along with almost two-thirds of the army, was swept from the field. However, at Chattanooga he regained his somewhat tarnished reputation when his division broke through the Rebel lines atop Missionary Ridge. There was some question of who, if anyone, had ordered the troops all the way up to the crest. His division made a limited pursuit. When Grant went to the East, he placed Sheridan in command of the Army of the Potomac's mounted arm. Against Jeb Stuart's depleted horsemen Sheridan met with mixed success in the Overland Campaign but did manage to mortally wound the Confederate cavalryman at Yellow Tavern. His purposes were thwarted at Haws' Shop and Trevilian Station. His Irish temperament brought him into conflict with Generals Meade and Warren and Duffié and Stevenson. Following Early's threat to Washington, Grant tapped Sheridan to command a new military division, comprised of three departments, and charged him with clearing out

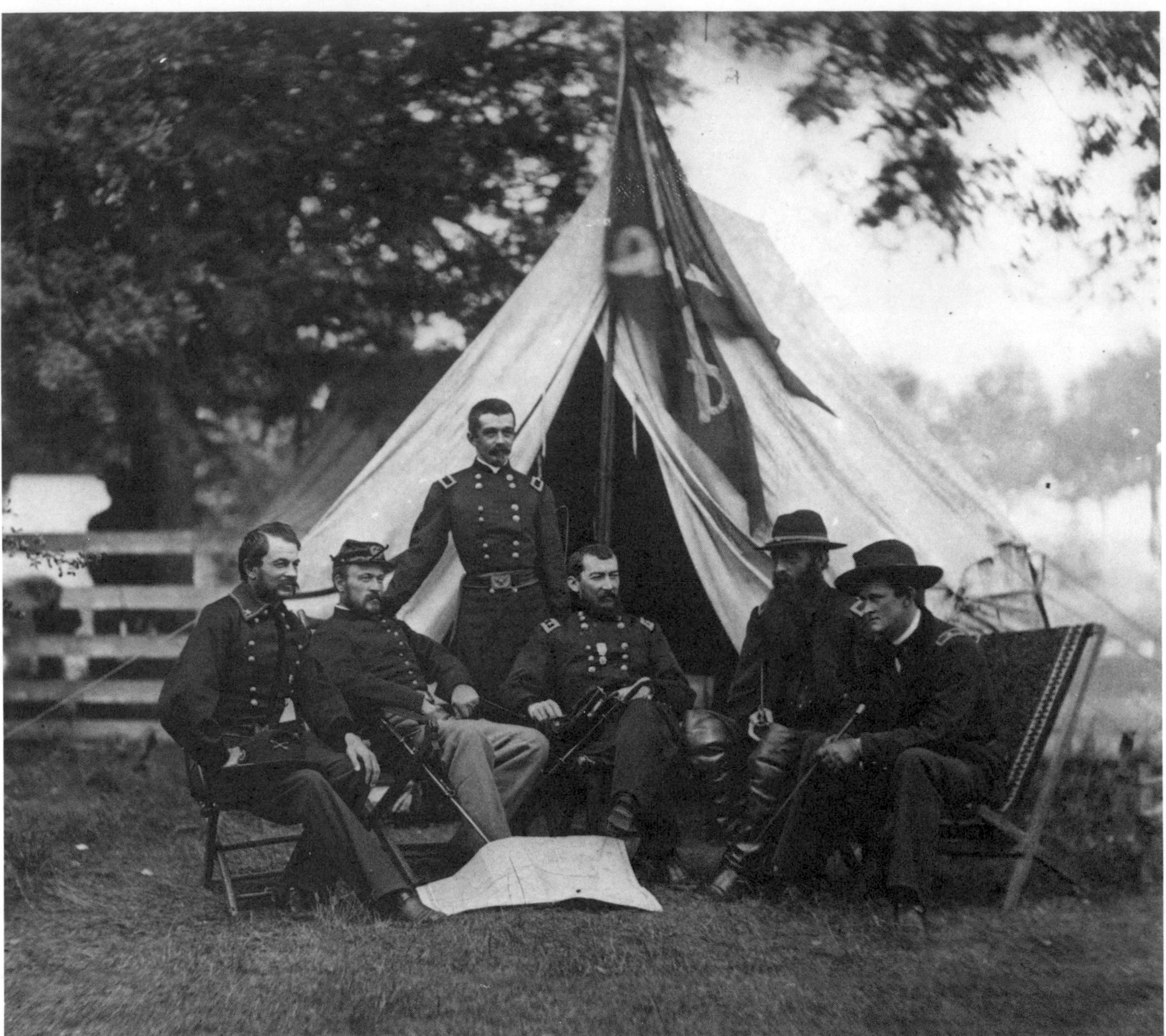

Philip Henry Sheridan and his generals. Left to right: Alfred T.A. Torbert, James H. Wilson, Henry E. Davies, Sheridan, David M. Gregg, and Wesley Merritt. (NA)

the Shenandoah Valley. Despite being plagued by irregulars along his supply lines, he managed to worst Early at 3rd Winchester, Fisher's Hill, and Cedar Creek. At the outbreak of the latter battle he was returning from a meeting with Grant and rode at a gallop from Winchester to the scene of the early morning reverse. Reforming his men, he drove the enemy—who had lost all sense of order while plundering the camps—from the field, taking many prisoners. For this campaign he was named brigadier and major general in the regular army, vacating his volunteer commission, and received the Thanks of Congress. He also burned his way through the Valley, preventing future Confederate use of its grain and other stores. The next March he destroyed Early's remaining forces at Waynesboro and then went on a raid, threatening Lynchburg. Rejoining Grant, he smashed through the Confederate lines at Five Forks, necessitating the evacuation of both Petersburg and Richmond. During the action he unfairly removed Warren for slowness. It was his cavalry command, backed by infantry, which finally blocked Lee's escape at Appomattox. His role in the final campaign even eclipsed that of army commander Meade. After a postwar show of force against Maximilian in Mexico, he headed the Reconstruction government of Texas and Louisiana. His severity forced his removal within half a year. Remaining in the regular army, he died as a full general in 1888, having been the commander-in-chief since 1884. In the meantime he had commanded the Division of the Missouri, observed the Franco-Prussian War, and worked for the creation of Yellowstone National Park and its preservation. By the use of troops to protect the park he may have been trying to salve his conscience for the destruction in the Shenandoah. (O'Connor, Richard, *Sheridan the Inevitable* and Sheridan, Philip H., *Personal Memoirs*)

SHERMAN, Francis Trowbridge (1825-1905)

It was not until after the close of hostilities that Francis T. Sherman received his commission as a Union brigadier general. Born in Connecticut, he had grown up in the booming environment of Chicago. In the middle of a varied career he had participated in the California Gold Rush. His wartime assignments included: lieutenant colonel, 56th Illinois (October 31, 1861); major, 12th Illinois Cavalry (March 8, 1862); colonel 88th Illinois (September 4, 1862); commanding 1st Brigade, 3rd Division, 20th Corps, Army of the Cumberland (February 13-April 12 and September 28-October 9, 1863); commanding 1st Brigade, 2nd Division, 4th Corps, Army of the Cumberland (October 18, 1863-March 4, 1864 and April 6-May 22, 1864); chief of staff, 4th Corps, Army of the Cumberland (May 22-July 7, 1864); acting inspector general, Army of the Shenandoah and Middle Military Division (fall 1864-March 1865); acting inspector general, Cavalry Corps, Army of the Potomac (March-May 1865); acting provost marshal, Military Division of the Gulf (summer 1865); brigadier general, USV (July 21, 1865). Originally commissioned as second in command of a volunteer regiment, he was mustered out with it on February 5, 1862, the unit apparently not having completed its organization. The next month he became a battalion commander in a mounted regiment which served in the lower Shenandoah Valley. Again transferring to the infantry, he was given the eagles of a colonel, and he led his regiment at Murfreesboro and during the Tullahoma Campaign. Having missed Chickamauga, he led a brigade at Chattanooga. In the course of the Atlanta Campaign he gave up his command to become chief of staff to Oliver O. Howard. He was captured on July 7, 1864, while scouting and was not exchanged for three months. He then joined Philip Sheridan's staff in the Shenandoah Valley as his inspector. Present at the fight at Waynesboro when the remainder of Early's army was scattered, he accompanied Sheridan to the Petersburg front and took part in the actions at Five Forks, Sayler's Creek, and Appomattox. Following the surrender of Lee's army, Sherman was sent to Washington with the flags captured by Sheridan's cavalry. Brevetted for the war, he received the full rank of brigadier general that summer while serving as provost marshal of Sheridan's forces in Louisiana and Texas. Mustered out on January 15, 1866, he was a manufacturer, postmaster, and legislator in the postwar years.

SHERMAN, John (1823-1900)

The brother of William Tecumseh Sherman, John Sherman had a highly distinguished political career, and his antitrust legislation is still felt today. The native of Ohio had been admitted to the bar in 1844 and was a delegate to the Whig national conventions of 1848 and 1852. During the latter he was the meeting's secretary. With the breakup of his old party, Sherman became one of the organizers of the Republican Party. In 1855 he presided over the first Ohio state convention of the party and took a seat in Congress the same year. As a Republican, he was repeatedly reelected. On March 21, 1861, he resigned his House seat in order to replace Salmon P. Chase—who had resigned to become Lincoln's secretary of the treasury—in the Senate. During his tenure he was noted for being a moderate and backed Andrew Johnson during the impeachment crisis. Twice reelected, Sherman resigned on March 8, 1877, in order to become Rutherford B. Hayes' treasury secretary. At the end of Hayes' term, Sherman was elected to the Senate again in place of the incoming president, James A. Garfield. Again reelected twice, Sherman resigned in 1897 to become secretary of state under William McKinley. After a year in office he retired to private life. His longest-lasting legislation was the Sherman Anti-Trust Act, but the Sherman Silver Purchase Act was also very important in its day.

SHERMAN, Thomas West (1813-1879)

Following a rather active prewar regular army career, Thomas W. Sherman won the brevets of major general in both the regulars and the volunteers. The native Rhode Islander and West Pointer (1836) had been posted to the artillery. He had seen service in the Trail of Tears incident, the Seminole and Mexican wars, on the Minnesota and Dakota frontiers, and during the disturbances in Kansas. He had won a brevet in Mexico. His Civil War assignments included: captain, 3rd Artillery (since May 28, 1846); major, 3rd Artillery (April 27, 1861); lieutenant colonel, 5th Artillery (May 14, 1861); brigadier general, USV (August 6, 1861, to rank from May 17); commanding South Carolina Expedition (September 19, 1861-March 15, 1862); commanding Department of the South (March 15-31, 1862); commanding 6th Division, Army of the Tennessee (April 30-June 10, 1862); commanding division, U.S. Forces Carrollton, La., 19th Corps, Department of the Gulf (September 18, 1862-January 9, 1863); commanding Defenses of New Orleans, 19th Corps, Department of the Gulf (January 9-May 21, 1863 and June 18-November 7, 1864); also commanding 2nd Division, 19th Corps, Department of the Gulf (January 13-May 27, 1863); colonel, 3rd Artillery (June 1, 1863); and commanding Defenses of New Orleans, Department of the Gulf (November 7, 1864-February 9, 1865). In conjunction with the navy, he commanded the troops which captured Port Royal on the South Carolina coast. He then briefly commanded the department before being made a division commander in the forces under Halleck for the advance on Corinth, Mississippi. However, he got into trouble with his superiors and was relieved on June 10, 1862. Three months later he was given command of a division in Louisiana and early in 1863 was assigned to New Orleans. Taking part in the assaults on Port Hudson, he was severely wounded on May 27, 1863. Having lost his left leg, he was brevetted brigadier general in the regular establishment. Out of action for almost a year, he commanded the New Orleans defenses for the balance of the war. With the two brevets as major general for the war, he was mustered out of the volunteers on April 30, 1866. In the regular army he commanded along the East coast until his retirement in 1870 with the advanced grade of major general for pension purposes.

SHERMAN, William Tecumseh (1820-1891)

He never commanded in a major Union victory and his military career had repeated ups and downs, but William T. Sherman is the second best known of Northern commanders. His father had died when he was nine years old, and Sherman was raised by Senator Thomas Ewing and eventually married into the family. Through the influence of his patron, he obtained an appointment to West Point. Only five cadets of the class of 1840 graduated ahead of him, and he was appointed to the artillery. He received a brevet for his services in California during the Mexican War but resigned in 1853 as a captain and commissary officer. The years until the Civil War were not filled with success. Living in California and Kansas, he failed in banking and the law. In 1859 he seemed to have found his niche as the superintendent of a military academy which is now Louisiana State University. However, he resigned this post upon the secession of the state and went to St. Louis as head of a streetcar company and then volunteered for the Union army. His assignments included: colonel, 13th Infantry (May 14, 1861); commanding 3rd Brigade, 1st Division, Army of Northeastern Virginia (June-August 17, 1861); brigadier general, USV (August 7, 1861, to rank from May 17); commanding brigade, Division of the Potomac (August 17-28, 1861); second-in-command, Department of the Cumberland (August 28-October 8, 1861); commanding the department (October 8-November 9, 1861); commanding District of Cairo, Department of the Missouri (February 14-March 1, 1862); commanding 5th Division, Army of the Tennessee (March 1-July 21, 1862); major general, USV (May 1, 1862); commanding 5th Division, District of Memphis, Army of the Tennessee (July 21-September 24, 1862); commanding 1st Division, District of Memphis, Army of the Tennessee (September 24-October 26, 1862); also commanding the district (July 21-October 26, 1862); commanding District of Memphis, 13th Corps, Army of the Tennessee (October 24-November 25, 1862); commanding

William T. Sherman (arm on cannon's breech) and staff before Atlanta. (AC)

Yazoo Expedition, Army of the Tennessee (December 18, 1862-January 4, 1863); commanding 2nd Corps, Army of the Mississippi (January 4-12, 1863); commanding 15th Corps, Army of the Tennessee (January 12-October 29, 1863); brigadier general, USA (July 4, 1863); commanding Army and Department of the Tennessee (October 24, 1863-March 26, 1864); commanding Military Division of the Mississippi (March 18, 1864-June 27, 1865); major general, USA (August 12, 1864); lieutenant general, USA (July 25, 1866); general, USA (March 4, 1869); and commander-in-chief, USA (March 8, 1869-November 1, 1883). Appointed to the colonelcy of one of the regular army's newly authorized infantry regiments, he led the brigade of volunteers of the 1st Division which crossed Bull Run to aid the 2nd and 3rd divisions after the attack on the enemy left had begun. Despite being caught up in the rout—he already had a low opinion of volunteers—he was named a brigadier general the next month. Briefly commanding a brigade around Washington, he was then sent to Kentucky as deputy to Robert Anderson. He soon succeeded the hero of Fort Sumter in command of the department but got into trouble over his overestimates of the enemy strength. The newspapers actually reported him as being insane. Removed from command, he was given another chance by his friend Henry W. Halleck in Missouri. But again, while inspecting troops in the central part of the state, he allowed his overactive imagination to run away with him. During the campaign against Forts Henry and Donelson he was stationed at Paducah, Kentucky and charged with forwarding reinforcements to Grant. Forming a good working relationship with the future commander-in-chief, Sherman offered to waive his seniority rights and take a command under him. Commanding a division, he was largely responsible for the poor state of preparedness at Shiloh but redeemed himself during the defensive fighting of the first day and was wounded. The next day his command played only a minor role. Praised by Grant, he was soon made a major general of volunteers. He was instrumental in persuading Grant to remain in the army during his difficulties with Halleck during the advance on Corinth, Mississippi. During the early operations against Vicksburg he ordered a doomed assault at Chickasaw Bluffs and a few days later was superseded by John A. McClernand who accepted Sherman's proposal to attack Arkansas Post. Grant initially criticized this movement as unnecessary but declared it an important achievement when it succeeded and he learned that Sherman had suggested it. Sherman's corps did little fighting in the advance on Vicksburg in May until the disastrous assaults were made. Following the fall of the river city he was named a brigadier general in the regular army and led an expedition against Jackson. That fall he went to the relief of Chattanooga where he failed to achieve his objectives in the assault against Tunnel Hill at the end of Missionary Ridge. Nonetheless, he was highly praised by Grant who then sent him to relieve the pressure on Burnside at Knoxville. Back in Mississippi, he led the Meridian expedition and then succeeded Grant in overall command in the West. Facing Joseph E. Johnston's army, he forced it all the way back to Atlanta where the Confederate was replaced by John B. Hood who launched three disastrous attacks against the Union troops near the city. Eventually taking possession of Atlanta, Sherman ordered the population evacuated and the military value of the city destroyed. Sending George H. Thomas back to Middle Tennessee to deal with Hood, he embarked on his March to the Sea. Taking Savannah, he announced the city as a Christmas gift to the president and the country. Marching north to aid Grant in the final drive against Richmond, he drove through the Carolinas and accepted Johnston's surrender at Durham Station. His terms were considered too liberal and touching upon political matters and they were disapproved by Secretary of War Stanton. This led to a long-running feud between the two. Terms were finally arranged on the basis of the Appomattox surrender. During the last two campaigns Sherman had earned a reputation for destruction and for the lack of discipline of his troops—his marauding stragglers being known as "Sherman's bummers." Especially resented by Southerners was the burning of Columbia, South Carolina. But there are indications that the fires had spread from cotton set ablaze by the retreating Confederates under Wade Hampton. On August 12, 1864, Sherman had been promoted to major general in the regular army, and he vacated his volunteer commission. Also, he was the only man to twice receive the Thanks of Congress during the Civil War—first for Chattanooga and second for Atlanta and Savannah. After the war he remained in the service, replacing Grant as commander-in-chief and retiring in 1884. He was noted for his absolute refusal to be drawn into politics. (Hart, B.H. Liddell, *Sherman: Soldier, Realist, American* and Lewis, Lloyd, *Sherman: Fighting Prophet*)

SHERRILL, Eliakim (1813-1863)

At the battle of Gettysburg, former Congressman Eliakim Sherrill became the second commander of his brigade to be fatally struck in two days. The native New York farmer and tanner had been a member of the state senate and the national legislature as well as being active in the militia. His military assignments included: colonel, 126th New York (ca. August 22, 1862); and commanding 3rd Brigade, 3rd Division, 2nd Corps, Army of the Potomac (July 2-3, 1863). When in the service less than a month, he found himself wounded and a prisoner in the fall of Harpers Ferry. Paroled and eventually exchanged, he served in the Washington fortifications until the Gettysburg Campaign. Joining the Army of the Potomac with his regiment on June 25, 1863, he succeeded to brigade command upon the death of Colonel George L. Willard on the second day of the fight. The next day, during the repulse of Pickett's Charge, he himself fell mortally wounded. He died the following day.

SHIELDS, James (1810-1879)

One of numerous Union generals sent after the elusive "Stonewall" Jackson in the Shenandoah during 1862, James Shields proved singularly unsuccessful. The native of County Tyrone, Ireland, had immigrated to the United States in about 1826 and settled in Illinois. A lawyer and Democratic politician, he had sat on the state supreme court and been a land office commissioner before the Mexican War. During that conflict he served as a brigadier general of volunteers and won the brevet of major general for his role at the battle of Cerro Gordo. Failing to gain reelection to the U.S. Senate from Illinois in 1855, he moved to Minnesota and was soon back in Washington for a special one-year Senate term. Named to his old volunteer rank upon the outbreak of the Civil War, his assignments included: brigadier general, USV (August 19, 1861); commanding Lander's (old) Division, Department of Western Virginia (March 6-13, 1862); commanding 2nd Division, 5th Corps, Army of the Potomac (March 13-April 4, 1862); commanding 2nd Division, Department of the Shenandoah (April 4-May 10, 1862); and commanding division, Department of the Rappahannock (May 10-June 26, 1862). Assigned in May 1862 to work in conjunction with John C. Frémont for the destruction of Jackson's troublesome force in the Valley, he failed the next month when Frémont was held up at Cross Keys and Shields was eventually defeated at Port Republic. After this debacle it appears that Shields was awaiting orders until his March 28, 1863 resignation. He then lived briefly in San Francisco before settling in Missouri, which became the third state he represented in the U.S. Senate. (Condon, William Henry, *Life of Major General James Shields, Hero of Three Wars and Senator From Three States*)

SHIPP, Scott (1839-1917)

An 1859 graduate of the Virginia Military Institute, Scott Shipp served as the commandant of cadets at his alma mater during the latter part of the Civil War and as such led the cadet battalion in the field when called. With the outbreak of hostilities he had left his position on the faculty and joined the Confederate army as major, 21st Virginia, in June 1861. With this unit he took part in early operations in western Virginia. On January 20, 1862, he was detached from his regiment and assigned to duty at VMI with the rank of lieutenant colonel. In this position he led the cadet battalion in the field during part of the Shenandoah Valley Campaign of 1862, but they saw no action. During the summer of 1863, while the school was out of session he served as a private in Company H, 4th Virginia Cavalry. Resuming his duties at the academy, he again led the cadet battalion at the battle of New Market where they suffered heavy casualties. For the remainder of the war the cadets divided their time between their studies and service in the field. Shipp was in the field and in the trenches around Petersburg and Richmond and also tried to intercept Union cavalry raids in the Shenandoah region. At the time of the fall of Richmond, Shipp was commanding a mixed force of cadets, regular troops, and convalescents. On April 3, 1865, the battalion was disbanded. With the reopening of the school Shipp resumed his duties and became a lawyer. Late in the century he became superintendent of the institute. (Wise, Jennings C., *The Military History of the Virginia Military Institute from 1839 to 1865*)

James Shields, Stonewall Jackson victim. (*Leslie's*)

SHIRAS, Alexander Eakin (ca. 1812-1875)

Serving in the commissary department throughout the Civil War, Alexander E. Shiras was made the assistant commissary general of subsistence halfway through the conflict. The Pennsylvania-born officer had received his appointment to West Point from New Jersey and upon his 1833 graduation was posted to the artillery. Transferred to the subsistence department in the 1840s, his Civil War-era assignments included: captain and commissary of Subsistence (since March 3, 1847); major and commissary of Subsistence (May 11, 1861); and colonel and assistant commissary general of Subsistence (February 9, 1863). Stationed in Washington, he also worked as a member of the United States Sanitary Commission. Brevetted brigadier and major general for his war service, he continued in the regular army until his death while on active duty as the commissary general of subsistence, with the staff rank of brigadier general.

SHIRK, James W. (?-?)

A lieutenant commander in the Union navy, James W. Shirk led the gunboat *Lexington* in the western waters until named to command an ironclad. His first vessel, armed with two 32-pounders and four eight-inchers, fought at Fort Henry, Shiloh, St. Charles, on the Yazoo River in December 1862, and at Arkansas Post. Transferred to command of the river ironclad *Tuscumbia*, five guns, he fought at Vicksburg and Grand Gulf.

SHORTER, John Gill (1818-1872)

At first extremely popular as governor of Alabama, John G. Shorter fell in the public esteem along with the Davis administration with which he was closely associated. Born in

Georgia, he had taken up the practice of law in Alabama in 1838, sat in the state legislature, and served as a judge. Giving up his judgeship in early 1861, he became a commissioner from Alabama to the Georgia secession convention. He was then named to the Provisional Confederate Congress where he was appointed chairman of the Committee on Engrossment. He also sat on the committees on Buildings; Executive Departments; and Flag and Seal. Elected governor in August 1861, he resigned his congressional seat in November. Sworn in on December 2, 1861, he was active in preparing the state, especially Mobile, for defense and organizing troops for the field armies. However, his pro-Davis stance rapidly made him unpopular and he was handily beaten by Thomas H. Watts in 1863. Dropping out of politics, he resumed the practice of law. (Denman, Clarence P., *The Secession Movement in Alabama*)

SHOUP, Francis Asbury (1834-1896)

When John B. Hood relieved Joseph E. Johnston of command of the Army of Tennessee before Atlanta, Francis A. Shoup became the army's chief of staff. The native Indianan West Pointer (1855) had become a career artillerist, seeing action against the Seminoles before resigning as a first lieutenant in the 1st Artillery on January 10, 1860. He took up the practice of law in Florida and despite his northern birth joined the Confederacy. His assignments included: major, Artillery (October 1861); lieutenant colonel, Artillery (1861); brigadier general, CSA (September 12, 1862); commanding 3rd Brigade, Smith's Division, Department of Mississippi and East Louisiana (May-July 4, 1863); chief of artillery, Army of Tennessee (early 1864-July 24, 1864); and chief of staff, Army of Tennessee (July 24-ca. December 1864). During the Battle of Shiloh he served as chief artillerist with William J. Hardee's 3rd Corps and then fought at Prairie Grove as adjutant to Thomas C. Hindman. During the siege of Vicksburg he directed a brigade and was paroled with the garrison on July 4, 1863. Exchanged a few months later, he joined Johnston for the Atlanta Campaign as chief artillerist and then became Hood's staff chief until the latter's resignation after the disastrous battles at Franklin and Nashville. Thereafter he was involved in education and the Episcopal ministry.

SIBLEY, Henry Hastings (1811-1891)

Although he was a Union brigadier general, Henry H. Sibley never saw a Confederate unit except as prisoners of war. The Michigan-born fur trader had been one of the early settlers in what later became Minnesota. He sat in its territorial legislature and was the state's first governor. He entered the service during the uprising of the Sioux in 1862 and his assignments included: brigadier general, USV (September 29, 1862); and brigadier general, USV (reappointed March 20, 1863). Following a successful campaign against the Indians he tried by court-martial hundreds of his captives. The death sentences were reviewed in Washington and most were set aside. But on December 26, 1862, 38 were hanged on a massive scaffold. While his first appointment as a brigadier general was not ratified by the Senate and expired on March 4, 1863, he was reappointed a few day later. In the later stages of his service he was engaged in negotiating peace treaties with various tribes. Brevetted major general on November 29, 1865, for his service, he was mustered out on April 30, 1866. Thereafter he was involved in insurance, banking, and gas and also sat in the state legislature. He was also involved in historical circles. NOTE: He is not to be confused with Confederate General Henry Hopkins Sibley.

SIBLEY, Henry Hopkins (1816-1886)

Although he designed the conical Sibley field tent, used by both armies during the Civil War, Henry Hopkins Sibley suffered from an excessive fondness for the bottle which to a large extent denied the Confederacy the full advantages of his West Point (1838) training. The native Louisianian had been posted to the dragoons and won a brevet during the Mexican War. On May 13, 1861, the same date as his commission as major, 1st Dragoons, he resigned from the regular army to join the South. His Confederate assignments included: colonel, Cavalry (May 16, 1861); brigadier general, CSA (June 17, 1861); and commanding Army of New Mexico (December 14, 1861-December 1, 1862). In the summer of 1861 he was sent to Texas to take command of the forces operating on the upper Rio Grande. Invading what is now New Mexico, he commanded during the campaign and was in command at the Confederate victory at Valverde. However, the next month a portion of his forces, under William R. Scurry, was forced to break off an action at Pigeon's Ranch in Glorieta Pass when a force under John M. Chivington, then a major, destroyed virtually its entire supply train and herd of horses and mules. This soon committed Sibley to evacuate Santa Fe and fall back into Texas. For the balance of the war—during which time it was common knowledge that he was a heavy drinker—he served in the Trans-Mississippi Department but was often without a command. He later spent four years as an Egyptian artillery general and upon his return to the United States joined the lecture circuit, which did not provide him with a large income.

SICKEL, Horatio Gates (1817-1890)

Although he spent much of the Civil War in the defenses of the Union capital, Horatio G. Sickel served with the prestigious Pennsylvania Reserve Corps. The Pennsylvania-born coachmaker's assignments included: captain, 3rd Pennsylvania Reserves (May 27, 1861); colonel, 3rd Pennsylvania Reserves (July 28, 1861); commanding 3rd Division, 1st Corps, Army of the Potomac (December 25, 1862-January 11, 1863); commanding Pennsylvania Reserves Division, 22nd Corps, Department of Washington (February 6-April 12, 1863); commanding 2nd Brigade, Pennsylvania Reserves Division, 22nd Corps, Department of Washington (April 12-15, 1863); commanding 2nd Brigade, Pennsylvania Reserves Division, District of Alexandria, 22nd Corps, Department of Washington (April 15-September 1863 and October 1863-April 1864); commanding 3rd Brigade, 2nd Infantry Division, Department of West Virginia (April-June 9, 1864); colonel, 198th Pennsylvania (September 15, 1864); and commanding 1st Brigade, 1st Division, 5th Corps, Army of the Potomac (September 24-November 7, 1864 and January 5-February 27, 1865). Following initial service in northern Virginia he took his regiment to the Peninsula and fought in the Seven Days. Heading north again he fought at 2nd Bull Run and Fredericksburg before the depleted division was transferred to the Washington area. During the Gettysburg Campaign he commanded the one brigade that did not rejoin the Army of the Potomac and then served at Alexandria. He took the field again under David Hunter for part of the Lynchburg expedition before being mustered out with the regiment on June 17, 1864. Named colonel of a regiment composed of reenlisting members of the division that summer, he served at Petersburg and Appomattox. Thrice wounded, he was named brevet brigadier general of volunteers on October 21, 1864, and major general for the war. Mustered out with his regiment on June 4, 1865, he was later active in banking, railroading, and public affairs.

SICKLES, Daniel Edgar (1819-1914)

In his pre- and post-Civil War careers, as well as during the conflict, Daniel E. Sickles proved to be one of the most controversial of Union corps commanders. Prewar, the New York City native had already become the first man acquitted of a murder charge on the grounds of temporary insanity. Sickles, a congressman, shot down Philip Barton Key—the son of the composer of the "Star Spangled Banner"—in LaFayette Park, across the street from both Sickles' home and the White House. Key had been having an affair with Sickles' wife, whom Sickles had married while serving as secretary of the U.S. legation in London. Defense attorney Edwin M. Stanton gained the innovative verdict. Sickles then publicly forgave his wife, outraging the public, which had applauded his role in the shooting, and apparently ending his political career. Just then the Civil War broke out and he saw his chance to get a new start. Offering his services, his assignments included: colonel, 70th New York (June 20, 1861); brigadier general, USV (September 3, 1861); commanding 2nd ("Excelsior") Brigade, Hooker's Division, Army of the Potomac (October 3, 1861-March 13, 1862); commanding 2nd ("Excelsior") Brigade, 2nd Division, 3rd Corps, Army of the Potomac (May 24-July 16, 1862); commanding the division (September 5, 1862-January 12, 1863); major general, USV (November 29, 1862); and commanding the corps (February 5-May 29 and June 3-July 2, 1863). When authorized to raise a regiment he proceeded to recruit enough men for a brigade and was soon rewarded with a brigadier's star. Frequently absent from his command seeking advancement in Washington, he nonetheless commanded his brigade at Seven Pines and during the Seven Days. In charge of the division, he fought at Fredericksburg and received the regular army brevet of brigadier general in 1867. His prewar reputation as a womanizer and heavy drinker returned to him during his career as a brigade and division commander, and his brigade was considered a rowdy bunch. But his heyday came when Joseph Hooker took command of the army. Many officers complained that Hooker, Sickles, and Daniel Butterfield had converted the army headquarters into a combination of bar and brothel. Sickles' own headquarters were considered to be even worse. After fighting at Chancellorsville, Sickles retained charge of the 3rd Corps even after Hooker's removal. Then on the second day of Gettysburg he did not like the sector assigned to his men along Cemetery Ridge. It was too long and low to his liking and he unilaterally decided to advance to the Peach Orchard. If he had survived the battle unscathed he probably would have been court-martialed. But some claim that his advanced position absorbed the shock of Longstreet's assault before it could reach the ridge. This theory claims that if the assault had hit the ridge in full strength it would have broken the Union line. This is, however, highly debatable since his movement put the left flank of the 2nd Corps in the air as well as both of his own. Always courageous on the field of battle, he was struck in the leg by a shell as his command was beginning its withdrawal. The leg was amputated within half an hour. In 1867 he was brevetted regular army major general for his role in the battle and three decades later was awarded the Congressional Medal of Honor. He donated his leg to an army medical museum and in later years is said to have visited it. During his recovery he engaged in a feud with Meade over his generalship and who had won the battle. As a result he was denied further field command and was assigned a series of special missions by the War Department. Made colonel, 42nd Infantry, in the 1866 regular army reorganization, he was mustered out of the volunteer service as a major general (since late 1862) on January 1, 1868. The next year, he was retired with the advanced rank of major general in

Ever-controversial Daniel E. Sickles. (*Leslie's*)

the regular establishment. Appointed U.S. minister to Spain by Grant, he furthered his reputation as a ladies' man. In the 1890s he served a term in Congress. For 26 years—until forced out in a financial scandal—he chaired the New York State Monuments Commission. (Pinchon, Edgcumb, *Dan Sickles: Hero of Gettysburg and "Yankee King of Spain"* and Swanberg, W.A., *Sickles the Incredible*)

SIDMAN, George Dallas (1844-?)

Enlisting on August 1, 1861, as a musician in Company C, 16th Michigan, George D. Sidman had a distinguished career despite washing out as a drummer. The New York native was allowed to carry a musket when it was discovered that the unit had too many musicians. In the battle of Gaines' Mill, during the Seven Days, he earned a Congressional Medal of Honor for leading a charge and being severely wounded in the hip. Destroying his musket to keep it out of enemy hands, he succeeded in dragging himself off the field. He was captured a few days later in a field hospital after the further Union defeat at Savage Station. Exchanged on August 18, 1862, following confinement in Libby Prison, Castle Thunder, and Belle Island, he escaped from a Union hospital and repeatedly tried to rejoin his unit with his still-open wound. He reached Antietam on a captured stray horse. He was again wounded at Fredericksburg while carrying the brigade flag in the assault on Marye's Heights. Later he dodged enemy fire to bring water to wounded comrades. Promoted to corporal, he was in the color guard at Chancellorsville, Kelly's Ford, and Middleburg. In the last he received a third wound and, although he did rejoin the regiment, was incapable of further field duty. Transferred to the Invalid Corps in February 1864, he served in Washington, was present at the trial of the Lincoln conspirators, and witnessed their hangings and that of Henry Wirz. After the war he was a tax assessor and a diplomat to Germany and spent several years in South Africa, even offering his services to the British during the Zulu War. In the 1880s and 1890s he was employed by the Pension Bureau. (Mitchell, Joseph B., *The Badge of Gallantry*)

SIGEL, Franz (1824-1902)

One of the failures of Lincoln's policy of naming leaders of the various foreign-born communities to high military posts was that of the German, Franz Sigel. A native of the Grand Duchy of Baden, he had received his military education at an academy in Karlsruhe and served in the duke's armed forces as a lieutenant. A major figure in the 1848 revolutions, he was forced to flee to Switzerland when the movement was crushed by the Prussians. He eventually moved via England and New York to St. Louis where he became a teacher. Having served in the New York militia, he volunteered his services at the outbreak of the Civil War. His assignments included: colonel, 3rd Missouri (May 4, 1861); commanding 4th Brigade, Army of Southwest Missouri, Western Department (summer-November 1861); brigadier general, USV (August 7, 1861, to date from May 17); commanding 4th Brigade, Army of Southwest Missouri, Department of the Missouri (November 1861-February 1862); commanding 1st Division, Army of Southwest Missouri, Department of the Missouri (February-May 9, 1862); major general, USV (March 21, 1862); commanding division, Department of the Shenandoah (June 4-26, 1862); commanding 1st Corps, Army of Virginia (June 30-July 7 and July 12-September 12, 1862); commanding 11th Corps, Army of the Potomac (September 12, 1862-January 10, 1863 and February 5-22, 1863); commanding Department of West Virginia (March 10-May 21, 1864); and commanding Reserve Division, Department of West Virginia (May 24-July 8, 1864). Under Nathaniel Lyon, he took part in the capture of Camp Jackson and at Wilson's Creek led the larger portion of the army from the field following his chief's death. By now a brigadier general, he led two divisions at Pea Ridge and was rewarded with a second star. Moving east, he commanded a division in the Shenandoah Valley and succeeded John C. Frémont in corps command when that officer refused to serve under John Pope. After fighting at 2nd Bull Run his corps became part of the Army of the Potomac, and he led it in the Washington vicinity and northern Virginia during the Maryland and Fredericksburg campaigns. Ill health forced him to relinquish command early in 1863. The next year he took charge of the Department of West Virginia and led an expedition in the Shenandoah which was thoroughly defeated at New Market by John C. Breckinridge. Since Sigel had had a superior force he was quickly removed and assigned to a quieter sector. For the last 10 months of his career he held no commands and he resigned on May 4, 1865. He subsequently served as a pension agent and was a candidate for elective office.

Franz Sigel, loser at New Market. (*Leslie's*)

SILL, Joshua Woodrow (1831-1862)

Ohio-born West Pointer (1853) Joshua Sill had served as an ordnance officer until resigning in 1861, when his services were on the verge of becoming much more important to the government. However, with the outbreak of actual war, Sill left his position as an engineering and mathematics professor in Brooklyn and tendered his services to his native state. After serving in staff positions, he was, on August 27, 1861, appointed colonel, 33rd Ohio. His later assignments included: commanding 9th Brigade, Army of the Ohio (November 30-December 2, 1862); commanding 9th Brigade, 3rd Division, Army of the Ohio (December 2, 1861-August 10, 1862); brigadier general, USV (July 16, 1862); commanding 4th Brigade, 2nd Division, Army of the Ohio (August-September 1862); commanding 2nd Division, 1st Corps, Army of the Ohio (September 29-November 5, 1862); commanding 2nd Division, Right Wing, 14th Corps, Army of the Cumberland (November 5-late December 1862); and commanding 1st Brigade, 3rd Division, Right Wing, Army of the Cumberland (to December 31, 1862). After leading his regiment in Kentucky, seeing action in skirmishes in October and November 1861 at Clay Village, Dry Ridge, Ivy Mountain, and Piketon, Sill was given command of a brigade. His brigade saw action at Paint Rock Bridge, Alabama, on April 28, 1862. It was men from Sill's command who made the daring raid which captured a rebel train, only to be caught after destroying miles of railroad bridges and equipment. With Bragg's invasion of Kentucky, Sill returned to that state and commanded a division. But, being sent off to Frankfort, he missed the battle of Perryville. However, commanding a brigade at Stones River, Sill was instantly killed while holding off a Confederate assault on the Union right center on the last day of 1862.

SIMMONS, James Fowler (1795-1864)

In the midst of the Civil War Rhode Island Senator James F. Simmons resigned. The native of the Ocean State had engaged in manufacturing and farming before taking a seat in the state legislature in 1828. He served until 1841 when he became a Whig senator in Washington. However, he failed to gain reelection at the end of his six-year term. In 1850 he lost another bid for the state's other seat and resumed manufacturing and farming. After a lapse of 10 years he returned to the Senate on March 4, 1857, but on August 15, 1862, he resigned and returned to his own business. He died within two years, on July 10, 1864.

SIMMS, James Phillip (1837-1887)

A Georgia lawyer, James P. Simms does not appear to have entered the Confederate army until a year after Fort Sumter. His assignments included: major, 53rd Georgia (September 24, 1862); colonel, 53rd Georgia (October 8, 1862); commanding Bryan's (old) Brigade, Kershaw's Division, 1st Corps, Army of Northern Virginia (June 2, 1864-April 6, 1865, except for the early part of 1865); and brigadier general, CSA (December 8, 1864). After indicating service in the Seven Days Battles, the records are silent on whether he took part in the Maryland and Fredericksburg campaigns. He was however present for the fighting at Salem Church in the battle of Chancellorsville and in the heavy fighting on the second day at Gettysburg. Going to the West with Longstreet, the brigade arrived too late for Chickamauga, but Simms led the regiment at Knoxville and back in Virginia at the Wilderness, Spotsylvania, and Cold Harbor. During the latter action he assumed command of the brigade when General Goode Bryan relinquished it. He led the brigade at Petersburg and then went with the division to reinforce Early in the Shenandoah, seeing action at Cedar Creek. Returning to the trenches around Richmond and Petersburg, he led the brigade in the retreat toward Appomattox but was captured in the debacle at Sayler's Creek on April 6, 1865.

SIMMS, William Elliott (1822-1898)

Despite the fact that his state never seceded from the Union, William E. Simms represented Kentucky as a senator in both of the Regular Confederate congresses. A Mexican War veteran, he had served in the state legislature, practiced law, and edited the *Kentucky State Flag*. A Democrat in the U.S. Congress, he condemned the Republicans and became known as an extreme states' righter—for Kentucky. At the outbreak of the Civil War he joined the Confederacy and as lieutenant colonel, 1st Kentucky Cavalry Battalion, he served with General Humphrey Marshall in Kentucky and western Virginia in the first months of the war. In November of the first year of the war he was appointed a commissioner of the provisional government of the state in order to treat with the Confederate government in Richmond. There he was appointed one of the state's senators in the First, and later the Second, Regular Confederate Congress. He sat on the committees on: Accounts; Foreign Affairs (Second Congress); Indian Affairs (First Congress); Naval Affairs; and Public Buildings (Second Congress). On the floor itself he appears to have been a proponent of total war and favored the idea that Jefferson Davis himself command the armies in the field. With the failing of the war effort, he supported major command changes. After a year's exile he returned to his Kentucky agricultural pursuits and gave up politics.

SINCLAIR, James (ca. 1823-1877)

Late in the war desertion was a major problem for the Confederate armies, requiring the detachment of line troops to round up deserters. The case of James Sinclair indicates that the problem was limited to neither the latter part of the war nor to the enlisted ranks. A clergyman in the Presbyterian church in North Carolina he had entered the Confederate army. His assignments were: chaplain, 5th North Carolina (May 15, 1861); and colonel, 35th North Carolina (November 8, 1861). Taking part in the March 1862 battle of New Bern in command of his regiment, he ordered it back before it had suffered any casualties. The next month he was replaced by a new colonel in the reorganization. Going over to the enemy, he served as a chaplain for the Union army. A scalawag after the war, he was a Republican member of the state legislature during Reconstruction.

SINGLETON, Otho Robards (1814-1889)

Elected to both of the Confederate regular congresses from his central Mississippi 5th District, Otho Robards Singleton failed to attend the second, and final, session of the Second Congress, having become disenchanted with the war. Born in Kentucky, he had taken up the practice of law in Canton, Mississippi. He served in both houses of the state legislature and withdrew from the U.S. Congress with the rest of the Mississippi delegation during the secession winter. As a private in the army, he ran for the Confederate Congress and won. He chaired the Committee on Indian Affairs in both congresses and sat on that on Pay and Mileage in the First Congress. He was a solid supporter of a strong central government to win the war and believed in the use of force to keep the states in line. He was also opposed to the use of substitutes for military service. On leave after the first session of the Second Congress, he was active in reestablishing conservative rule in the state in the latter stages of Reconstruction and served six terms in the U.S. Congress.

Otho R. Singleton, Confederate administration supporter. (*Harper's*)

SLACK, James Richard (1818-1881)

Serving entirely in the western theater, Indiana lawyer and legislator James R. Slack rose to the rank of brevet major general in the Union army. The Pennsylvania native's assignments included: colonel, 47th Indiana (December 13, 1861); commanding 1st Brigade, 2nd Division, Army of the Mississippi (February 23-March 4, 1862); commanding 1st Brigade, 3rd Division, Army of the Mississippi (March 4-April 24, 1862); commanding 1st Brigade, 2nd Division, District of Eastern Arkansas, Army of the Tennessee (December 1862); commanding 1st Brigade, 12th Division, 13th Corps, Army of the Tennessee (February 8-20, 1863); commanding 2nd Brigade, 12th Division, 13th Corps, Army of the Tennessee (April 9-July 28, 1863); commanding 2nd Brigade, 3rd Division, 13th Corps, Army of the Tennessee (July 28-August 7, 1863); commanding 2nd Brigade, 3rd Division, 13th Corps, Department of the Gulf (August 7-November 21, 1863 and April 8-June 11, 1864); commanding 2nd Brigade, 2nd Division, 19th Corps, Department of the Gulf (August 18-November 2, 1864); brigadier general, USV (November 10, 1864); and commanding 1st Brigade, 1st Division, 13th Corps, Department of the Gulf (February 24-May 7 and May 26-July 20, 1865). As a brigade commander he fought at Island #10 and then served in garrison in Arkansas until taking part in the operations against Vicksburg. Following its capture he went on the expedition to Jackson. Transferred to the Gulf, he played a minor role in the Red River Campaign and a major one in the capture of Mobile. Brevetted major general, he was mustered out on January 15, 1866, and returned to his practice. In the 1870s he sat as a circuit judge.

SLACK, William Yarnel (1816-1862)

Lawyer and Mexican War captain, William Slack was made a brigadier general in the Missouri State Guard, the pro-Southern state forces serving under Sterling Price. On July 4, 1861, General Slack was directed to assemble the units of the 5th District of Missouri together and a week later the command was designated the 4th Division, Missouri State Guard. Actually a brigade, Slack's command took part in the fighting at Carthage and Wilson's Creek where he was severely wounded in the hip. Considered to be Price's best brigadier, Slack was given command of the 2nd Brigade, Confederate Volunteers, of the Missouri State Guard on January 23, 1862. This command was composed of those members of the organization who had decided to enlist in Confederate service while others remained in state ranks. At the battle of Pea Ridge, on March 7, Slack was again wounded. Moved to avoid capture, he died exactly two weeks later. Possibly without knowing of his demise, the Richmond authorities appointed him a brigadier in the Confederate army on April 17, to rank from April 12.

SLAUGHTER, James Edwin (1827-1901)

Although he spent most of his Confederate career in staff positions, General James E. Slaughter commanded the troops engaged in the last land engagement of the Civil War. The native Virginian had been commissioned directly into the regular army during the Mexican War. Initially posted to the infantry, he then served with the Regiment of Voltigeurs and Foot Riflemen until that unit was discontinued at the close of the war. Transferred to the artillery, he was dismissed as a first lieutenant in the 1st Artillery on May 14, 1861. His Southern assignments included: captain, Artillery (spring 1861); major, Artillery (November 1861); brigadier general, CSA (March 8, 1862); commanding brigade, District of the Gulf, Department #2 (1862-63); and commanding in the Trans-Mississippi Department: division, District of Texas, New Mexico and Arizona (December 15, 1863-January 1864); Eastern Sub-District, District of Texas, New Mexico and Arizona (January 1864); 7th (Texas) Cavalry Brigade, 3rd (Texas) Cavalry Division, 3rd Corps (September 1864-May 26, 1865); and also Western Sub-District, District of Texas, New Mexico and Arizona (October 1864-May 26, 1865). He was on Bragg's staff at Pensacola and fought at Shiloh as an inspector with Albert S. Johnston. He held the same post with Beauregard during the Corinth siege and with Bragg during the Kentucky Campaign. In the spring of 1863 he became Magruder's chief artillerist at Galveston. Remaining in Texas for the balance of the war, he was mostly engaged in district commands but also led a mounted brigade. Ironically, his Confederates won the last battle of the war, on May 12, 1865, at Brownsville. For a time after the war he lived in Mexico and upon his return he was a civil engineer and postmaster.

SLEMMER, Adam Jacoby (1829-1868)

The man most responsible for keeping Fort Pickens in Pensacola Harbor in Union hands, Adam J. Slemmer, survived a crippling Civil War wound only to die of heart disease at the age of 39. The Pennsylvania native had been posted to the artillery following his 1850 graduation from West Point, and he served against the Seminoles (in Florida) and in California. He also spent four years teaching at his alma mater. He was commanding at Pensacola, Florida, when the state seceded. Moving his command to Fort Pickens, he held it during the first months of the war despite repeated bombardment and summonses to surrender. His wartime assignments included: first lieutenant, 1st Artillery (since April 30, 1854); major, 16th Infantry (May 14, 1861); acting assistant inspector general, Army of the Ohio (1861-November 1862); brigadier general, USV (from November 29, 1862); and lieutenant colonel, 4th Infantry (February 8, 1864). Given a field commission in one of the newly authorized regular army infantry regiments, he was soon assigned to duty as a staff officer in Kentucky. Serving under Don C. Buell, he took part in the painfully slow advance upon Corinth, Mississippi, and the Perryville Campaign. At Murfreesboro he led a battalion and one company of his regiment and fell severely wounded, ending his active military career. Soon thereafter named a brigadier general of volunteers, to date from November 29, 1862, he held administrative assignments for the balance of the war. Mustered out of the volunteers on August 24, 1865, he died while commanding Fort Laramie, Dakota Territory. He had been brevetted a regular army brigadier general for his war service.

SLIDELL, John (1793-1871)

His capture aboard the British mail steamer *Trent* did the cause of Confederate diplomacy more good than all of John Slidell's years of subsequent effort in Paris. A New York-born lawyer and merchant, he had been ruined by the War of 1812 and relocated to New Orleans following a duel. There he practiced commercial law and served in the state legislature, losing several races for both houses of the U.S. Congress. He finally took a seat in the House of Representatives in 1843, for one term as a Democrat. Ten years later he was admitted to the Senate, where he sat until 1861. Having become a proponent of slavery, he backed the Lecompton Constitution for Kansas and opposed Stephen A. Douglas. Appointed ambassador to France from the Confederacy shortly after the outset of the war, he was seized along with James M. Mason, the minister to England, in November 1861 by Captain Charles Wilkes of the USS *San Jacinto*. Questionable under international law, this capture aroused great resentment in Britain and brought the two countries to the verge of armed conflict. Fortunately the Washington authorities backed down and released the captives on January 1, 1862. Slidell eventually arrived in Paris but was unable to gain the active support, let alone the recognition, of Napoleon III. He did play a major role in the negotiation of the disastrous Erlanger cotton loan. After the war he never returned to the United States, remaining in France until the fall of Napoleon III, and he died under the British crown. (Sears, Louis Martin, *John Slidell* and Willson, B., *John Slidell and the Confederates in Paris*)

SLOCUM, Henry Warner (1826-1894)

A former regular army officer, New Yorker Henry W. Slocum rose in the Civil War volunteers to become, within a little over a year, the second youngest major general at the time of his appointment. Graduating from West Point in 1852 he had served four years in the artillery before resigning to become a Syracuse lawyer. With the coming of the war he kept up his interest in military affairs and his assignments included: colonel of Artillery, New York Militia (since 1859); colonel, 27th New York (May 21, 1861); brigadier general, USV (August 9, 1861); commanding 2nd Brigade, Franklin's Division, Army of the Potomac (October 3, 1861-March 13, 1862); commanding 2nd Brigade, 1st Division, 1st Corps, Army of the Potomac (March 13-April 4, 1862); commanding 2nd Brigade, 1st Division, Department of the Rappahannock (April 4-May 18, 1862); commanding 1st Division, 6th Corps, Army of the Potomac (May 18-October 15, 1862); major general, USV (July 4, 1862); commanding 12th Corps, Army of the Potomac (October 20, 1862-July 1, 1863, July 4-August 31, and September 13-25, 1863); temporarily commanding Right Wing (5th, 11th, and 12th corps), Army of the Potomac (April 28-30, 1863); commanding Right Wing, Army of the Potomac (July 1-4, 1863); commanding 12th Corps, Army of the Cumberland (September 25, 1863-April 18, 1864); commanding District of Vicksburg, Department of the Tennessee (April 20-August 14, 1864); commanding 20th Corps, Army of the Cumberland (August 27-November 11, 1864); commanding Left Wing or Army of Georgia (not officially designated as such until March 28, 1865), Military Division of the Mississippi (November 11, 1864-June 1, 1865); and commanding District of Vicksburg, Department of Mississippi and the department (June 24-27, 1865). Severely wounded in the thigh at 1st Bull Run, he was promoted to brigadier general during his recovery. He served in brigade command at Yorktown and West Point and led a division during the Seven Days. Given his second star a few days later, he fought at 2nd Bull Run, South Mountain, and Antietam. Taking over Mansfield's 12th Corps after the latter battle, his corps was on its way to Fredericksburg at the time of the Union defeat. In the early stages of the Chancellorsville Campaign, Slocum directed three corps. After the defeat there, he was highly critical of General Joseph Hooker for his timidity. At Gettysburg he commanded the right wing in the fighting on Culp's Hill. After the Union loss at Chickamauga it was determined to send the 11th and 12th corps under Hooker to the aid of the Army of the Cumberland at Chattanooga. To avoid conflict with Hooker, Slocum was left with one of his two divisions guarding rail lines in the rear. Thus he missed the battle of Chattanooga. When Sherman took the field in the Atlanta Campaign, Slocum was sent to Vicksburg after his resignation—he still refused to serve under Hooker—was rejected. He was recalled to Georgia in August 1864 after Hooker had left the army, feeling he had been cheated out of the command of the Army of the Tennessee when it was given to his junior, Oliver O. Howard. Commanding the 20th Corps—the old 11th and 12th combined—Slocum took part in the final stages of the Atlanta Siege and was one of the first to enter the city. While Sherman chased Hood in northern Georgia, Slocum continued as military governor of the city. During the March to the Sea he commanded Sherman's left wing and took part in the capture of Savannah. During the Carolinas Campaign he fought at Averysboro and Bentonville. In the final months his command was officially recognized by its previously informal title of the Army of Georgia. Following Johnston's surrender he was sent back to Mississippi. Resigning on September 28, 1865, he converted to the Democratic Party, losing much of his political advantage as a war hero. He sat for six years in Congress and was active in the efforts to clear Fitz-John Porter of the stigma stemming from 2nd Bull Run. (Slocum, Charles Elihu, *The Life and Services of Major General Henry Warner Slocum*)

SLOUGH, John Potts (1829-1867)

Something of a troublemaker in both his prewar and Civil War careers, John P. Slough lost his life in a postwar personal encounter. The Ohio native had been a member of the state legislature until expelled over some political fisticuffs with a fellow member. Settling briefly in Kansas, he was in Colorado when he volunteered for the Union army. His assignments included: captain, 1st Colorado (June 24, 1861); colonel, 1st Colorado (August 26, 1861); commanding brigade, Harpers Ferry, Department of the Shenandoah (May-June 1862); commanding 2nd Brigade, Sigel's Division, Department of the Shenandoah (June 4-26, 1862); commanding 2nd Brigade, 2nd Division, 2nd Corps, Army of Virginia (June 26-July 1, 1862); brigadier general, USV (August 25, 1862); commanding District of Alexandria, Military District of Washington, Army of the Potomac (October 1862-February 2, 1863); and commanding District of Alexandria, 22nd Corps, Department of Washington (February 2, 1863-November 5, 1864, December 5, 1864-April 26, 1865, and June 5-July 20, 1865). Despite orders to the contrary from Edward R.S. Canby, he won a significant fight at Glorieta Pass which was instrumental in forcing Henry H. Sibley's Confederates from New Mexico. Chafing under Canby's timidity, Slough went to Washington and was commanding a brigade as an acting brigadier in the spring and early summer of 1862. He helped defend Harpers Ferry during the Shenandoah Valley Campaign and briefly served under John Pope but apparently lost his command because he had not been formally appointed. This was rectified in August and for the balance of the conflict he was in charge at Alexandria, Virginia. There he frequently came into conflict with the commanders of the Army of the Potomac. Hooker wanted to relieve Slough shortly before his own removal. Mustered out on August 24, 1865, he settled in the New Mexico Territory and became the chief justice of its supreme court. He was highly unpopular, and there was a legislative move to displace him. On December 15, 1867, in a Santa Fe poolroom, he accosted one of his sharpest legislative critics and was wounded in a scuffle. Two days later he was dead.

SMALL, Robert (1839-1915)

In one of the more sensational escapes from slavery, Robert Small and 16 others sailed out to the Union blockading squadron and provided much intelligence of value to the Northern war effort. A Beaufort, South Carolina, native, he had been hired out by his master and was serving as a pilot aboard the *Planter*, which was engaged in the transport of army supplies including heavy armament. On the night of May 13, 1862, while the captain was ashore, Small set off with his band—including five women and three children—saluting the Confederate forts as he steamed out of the harbor of Charleston. He then lowered his colors before the blockading squadron and turned over the vessel. It contained two guns as armament and four as cargo. He was also able to provide the Union authorities with much information of value about the numerous inlets in the area, enabling them to launch operations against the Charleston defenses. For the rest of the war he served as a pilot aboard Union vessels, and during Reconstruction the hero was a representative in both the state legislature and the U.S. Congress. (Uya, Okon Edet, *From Slavery to Public Service—Robert Small 1839-1915*)

SMALLEY, George Washburn (1833-1916)

As a war correspondent for the *New York Tribune*, Massachusetts-born George W. Smalley proved to be an exceptional and inventive journalist. A student at both Yale and Harvard Law School, he was a prominent Boston lawyer until the outbreak of the Civil War. He was also an abolitionist and disciple of Wendell Phillips whose adopted daughter he married. Through Phillips he received an assignment from the *Tribune* to cover the life of Southern blacks. From November 1861 he served as a war correspondent during the Shenandoah Valley Campaign, Pope's campaign in northern Virginia, and during the invasion of Maryland. During the battle of Antietam he served as an impromptu aide to General Hooker and narrowly missed being hurt when the general was wounded. When his preliminary account of the fight was rerouted to Washington—instead of to the *Tribune*—he caught a train for New York, writing his report more fully on board. It was considered accurate and concise and was a scoop for the paper. Shortly afterwards he was forced by illhealth to take a desk job in New York. During the Draft Riots he aided in the armed defense of the journal's building. After the conflict he covered the Austro-Prussian War—perhaps as the first man to dispatch a cabled international news report—and organized the *Tribune*'s foreign office for the Franco-Prussian War. He remained in Europe until 1895 when sent by the *London Times* to cover the United States. Ten years later he returned to London in semi-retirement and died there in 1916.

SMITH, Andrew Jackson (1815-1897)

Extremely capable as a high-level commander in the Union army, Andrew J. Smith scored his greatest success when he worsted Nathan Bedford Forrest at Tupelo—no easy accomplishment. The native Pennsylvanian and West Pointer (1838) had spent nearly a quarter of a century as an officer of the 1st Dragoons, seeing action on the frontier and in Mexico. His Civil War assignments included: captain, 1st Dragoons (since February 16, 1847); major, 1st Dragoons (May 13, 1861); major, 1st Cavalry (designation change August 3, 1861); colonel, 2nd California Cavalry (October 2, 1861); chief of Cavalry, Department of the Missouri (February 11-March 15, 1862); chief of Cavalry, Department of the Mississippi (March 15-July 11, 1862); brigadier general, USV (March 20, 1862, to rank from March 17); commanding 1st Division, Army of Kentucky, Department of the Ohio (October-November 13, 1862); commanding 10th Division, Right Wing, 13th Corps, Army of the Tennessee (November 13-December 18, 1862); commanding 1st Division, Yazoo Expedition, Army of the Tennessee (December 18, 1862-January 4, 1863); commanding 1st Division 1st Corps, Army of the Mississippi (January 4-12, 1863); commanding 10th Division, 13th Corps, Army of the Tennessee (January 12-August 7, 1863); commanding 6th Division, 16th Corps, Army of the Tennessee (August 5, 1863-January 25, 1864); commanding 3rd Division, 16th Corps, Army of the Tennessee (January 24-March 7, 1864); commanding Right Wing, 16th Corps, Army of the Tennessee (March 1864 and June-December 5, 1864); commanding Detachment Army of the Tennessee, Department of the Gulf (March-June 1864); lieutenant colonel, 5th Cavalry (May 9, 1864); major general, USV (May 14, 1864); commanding Detachment Army of the Tennessee, Department of the Cumberland (December 5, 1864-February 18, 1865); and commanding 16th Corps, Department of the Gulf (February 18-July 20, 1865). Serving on the West Coast at the beginning of the war, he accepted the colonelcy of a California mounted volunteer regiment but resigned a month later on November 3, 1861, and headed east. He became Henry W. Halleck's cavalry chief and as such served in the advance on Corinth, Mississippi. Named a brigadier general of volunteers, he commanded a division in Kentucky and Tennessee before leading it at Chickasaw Bluffs in Sherman's repulse there. Then, under John A. McClernand he participated in the capture of Arkansas Post. Back in front of Vicksburg, he directed a division of the 13th Corps and then commanded in western Tennessee and northern Mississippi. However, during this time he did lead that portion of the Army of the Tennessee which joined Nathaniel P. Banks for the disastrous Red River Campaign, during which he won a brevet for Pleasant Hill. For his victory over the Confederate cavalry at Tupelo he was brevetted brigadier general in the regular establishment. He was brevetted major general for Nashville where he directed the detachment of the army that joined Thomas' Department of the Cumberland. This force was reorganized into the new 16th Corps and sent to the Gulf coast where he took part in the operations against Mobile. Mustered out of the volunteers on January 15, 1866, he reverted to his regular army rank of lieutenant colonel but was soon promoted to the colonelcy of the new 7th Cavalry. In order to accept a postmastership in St. Louis, he resigned in 1869. Twenty years later he was placed on the retired list as a colonel. In the meantime he had served as city auditor and as a general of militia during the suppression of the 1877 labor strikes.

SMITH, Caleb Blood (1808-1864)

Illhealth forced the resignation of Lincoln's first interior secretary, Caleb B. Smith of Indiana. The Boston native had become a lawyer and state legislator in Indiana. As a Whig, he sat in the U.S. House of Representatives from 1843 to 1849. An opponent of the extension of slavery, he voted against both the annexation of Texas and the Mexican War. An early member of Indiana's Republican Party, he attended the 1860 national convention in Chicago and seconded Lincoln's nomination. In return, he was named to the Interior cabinet post when Lincoln was sworn in. He opposed the reinforcement of Fort Sumter and favored the evacuation of its garrison to avoid hostilities but was overridden. After almost two years of service he resigned for health reasons on January 8, 1863, and was succeeded by John P. Usher. Becoming a district judge back in Indiana, he died on January 7, 1864.

SMITH, Caraway (?-?)

As a part of the relatively small Confederate forces left in Florida, Caraway Smith was usually involved in small-unit actions rather than the larger fights common in the Virginia and western theaters. His assignments included: captain, Ancilla Troop Florida Cavalry (early 1862); colonel, 2nd Florida Cavalry (December 4, 1862); commanding sub-district, District of Middle Florida, Department of South Carolina, Georgia and Florida (December 1863); and commanding Cavalry, District of East Florida, Department of South Carolina, Georgia and Florida (February 1864). Serving the entire war in his home state, he was often in command of a geographical area, directing the operations of semi-independent companies of cavalry, partisan rangers, and infantry. One exception was the fight at Olustee when forces from all over the state and from Georgia concentrated to defeat a Union expedition. He commanded the equivalent of a brigade of cavalry in this Confederate victory. Small-scale operations continued until the district was surrendered on May 17, 1865.

SMITH, Charles Ferguson (1807-1862)

Due to an unfortunate accident Union General Charles F. Smith was unable to display the same capabilities in the Civil War which he had shown in the Mexican War, when he had earned three brevets. A West Pointer (1825), he had served in the infantry and artillery and as the commandant of cadets at his alma mater. The Pennsylvanian's Civil War-era assignments included: lieutenant colonel, 10th Infantry (since March 3, 1855); commanding Department of Utah (February 1860-February 1861); commanding Department of Washington (April 10-28, 1862); brigadier general, USV (August 31, 1861); commanding District of Western Kentucky, Western Department (September 8-November 9, 1861); colonel, 3rd Infantry (September 9, 1861); commanding District of Western Kentucky, Department of the Missouri (November 9, 1861-January 31, 1862); commanding 2nd Division, Military District of Cairo, Department of the Missouri (February 1-17, 1862); commanding 2nd Division, Army of the Tennessee (February 17-April 2, 1862); and major general, USV (March 21, 1862). Recalled from the West in early 1861, he commanded in the nation's capital for about two weeks before being assigned to recruiting duty in the North. Made a brigadier of volunteers, he served in western Kentucky and took part in the Henry-Donelson Campaign. Rewarded with a promotion to major general, he was given charge of the advance up the Tennessee River in the beginning stages of the Shiloh Campaign while Grant was left at Fort Henry per Halleck's orders. Finally, on April 2, 1862, he was forced to relinquish command to his former student when an injury to his leg—suffered while boarding a small boat—became infected. He died on April 25, 1862, leaving unfulfilled the great hopes that had been held for him in the war.

SMITH, Charles Henry (1826-1903)

A Georgia lawyer and Confederate staff officer, Charles H. Smith wrote a series of four satirical letters to "Mr. Lincoln, sir," which appeared, during 1861 and 1862, in the Rome (Ga.) *Southern Confederacy*. Signing as "Bill Arp," Smith utilized satire, and good-natured humor to ridicule the Lincoln administration and the entire North. Complaining that "It is utterly impossible for us to disperse in twenty days" in compliance with a Lincoln proclamation, Bill Arp asked for an extension of time. Using his quaint dialect he explained that, "I tried my darn'dst yesterday to disperse and retire, but it was no go." Smith trumpeted the Confederate fighting ability in a later letter: "The Lee side of any shore is unhealthy to your population; keep away from those Virginia watercourses, go around them or under them, but for the sake of economy don't try to cross them. It is too hard upon your burial squads and ambulance horses." Following the war, Smith returned to the practice of law, dabbled in politics, and took up farming.

SMITH, Edmund Kirby (1824-1893)

Following the fall of Vicksburg and Port Hudson and the closing of the Mississippi, Confederate General E. Kirby Smith was confronted with the command of a virtually independent area of the Confederacy and with all of its inherent administrative problems. The Floridian West Pointer (1845)—nicknamed "Seminole" at the academy—had been posted to the infantry upon his graduation and won two brevets in the Mexican War. In 1855 he transferred to the cavalry and served until his resignation as major in the 2nd Cavalry on April 6, 1861. In the meantime he had taught mathematics at his alma mater and been wounded in 1859 fighting Indians in the Nescutunga Valley of Texas. When Texas seceded, Smith refused to surrender his command to the state forces under Ben McCulloch. Joining the Confederacy, his assignments included: lieutenant colonel, Cavalry (spring 1861); chief of staff, Army of the Shenandoah (spring-summer 1861); brigadier general, CSA (June 17, 1861); commanding 4th Brigade, Army of the Shenandoah (ca. June-July 20, 1861); commanding 4th Brigade, 2nd Corps, Army of the Potomac (July 20-21, 1861); major general, CSA (October 11, 1861); commanding 4th Division, Potomac District, Department of Northern Virginia (October 22, 1861-February 21, 1862); commanding Department of East Tennessee (March 8-August 25, ca. October 31-December 1862, and December 23, 1862-January 1863); commanding Army of Kentucky, Department #2 (August 25-November 20, 1862); lieutenant general, CSA (October 9, 1862); also commanding corps, Army of Tennessee (November 20-December 1862); commanding Southwestern Army (January 14-March 7, 1863); commanding Trans-Mississippi Department (March 7, 1863-April 19, 1865 and April 22-May 26, 1865); and general, PACS (February 19, 1864). After serving as Joseph E. Johnston's staff head in the Shenandoah Valley he was promoted to brigadier general and given command of a brigade which he led at 1st Bull Run. Wounded severely in that action, he returned to duty as a major general and division commander in northern Virginia. Early in 1862 he was dispatched to command in East Tennessee. Cooperating with Braxton Bragg in the invasion of Kentucky, he scored a victory at Richmond and was soon named to the newly created grade of lieutenant general. Early in 1863 he was transferred to the Trans-Mississippi West where he remained for the balance of the war. With the fall of the Mississippi River to the Union Forces he was virtually cut off from Richmond. He was forced to deal himself with such matters as impressment of supplies, destruction of cotton to prevent capture, and blockade-running through Mexico, in addition to his normal military duties. He also, in an irregular fashion, promoted officers to general's rank, sometimes making his actions subject to the president's approval and sometimes not. Davis approved some and never acted on others. Smith could be forgiven for exceeding his authority in such matters due to the situation of his command as an almost separate country. In the spring of 1864 he soundly defeated Nathanial P. Banks' Red River Campaign and then dispatched reinforcements northward to defeat Steele's cooperating column in Arkansas. With the pressure relieved,

Smith attempted to send reinforcements east of the Mississippi but, as in the case of his earlier attempts to relieve Vicksburg, it proved impracticable due to Union naval control of the river. Instead he dispatched Sterling Price, with all available cavalry, on an unsuccessful invasion of Missouri. Thereafter the war west of the river was principally one of small raids and guerrilla activity. By now a full general, he surrendered his department—the only significant Confederate army left—on May 26, 1865. After the war he was active in the telegraph business and education. At the time of his death he was the last of the full Confederate ex-generals. (Parkes, Joseph H., *General Kirby Smith C.S.A.*)

SMITH, Gerrit (1797-1874)

Although for the rest of his life Gerrit Smith denied vigorously any foreknowledge of John Brown's raid on Harpers Ferry, the evidence is now quite clear that he was involved. A wealthy New Yorker, he had been well known for his interest in charities, making large contributions. Involved in many of the reform movements of the day, he concentrated upon the antislavery issue. He aided runaways and was a member of the Kansas Aid Society and was also connected with the New England Emigrant Aid Company. John Brown visited his home in early 1858, with his plan for freeing Virginia's slaves, and sought financial as well as moral support. Both were given, it now appears, after a second visit in early 1859. Following the disaster at Harpers Ferry, Smith went into a state of temporary insanity. A believer in political action, he was closely linked with the Liberty party and was its candidate for a number of offices. As an independent he did sit in Congress and during the Civil War he worked hard for the war effort, becoming a Republican. A moderate on Reconstruction, he signed the papers which freed Jefferson Davis. (Hammond, C.A., *Gerrit Smith*)

SMITH, Giles Alexander (1829-1876)

Based on seniority Giles A. Smith was the last major general of volunteers appointed in the Civil War era. The brother of Morgan L. Smith had been a hotelier at the beginning of the Civil War when he enlisted in his brother's regiment. His assignments included: captain 8th Missouri (June 14, 1861); lieutenant colonel, 8th Missouri (June 12, 1862); colonel, 8th Missouri (June 30, 1862); commanding 1st Brigade, 2nd Division, District of Memphis, 13th Corps, Army of the Tennessee (November 12-December 18, 1862); commanding 1st Brigade, 2nd Division, Yazoo Expedition, Army of the Tennessee (December 18, 1862-January 4, 1863); commanding 1st Brigade, 2nd Division, 2nd Corps, Army of the Mississippi (January 4-12, 1863); commanding 1st Brigade, 2nd Division, 15th Corps, Army of the Tennessee (January 12-July 20, October 19-November 24, 1863, and February 21-July 20, 1864); brigadier general, USV (August 4, 1863); commanding the division (September 10-October 6, 1863); commanding 4th Division, 17th Corps, Army of the Tennessee (July 21-September 20, 1864 and October 31, 1864-June 1, 1865); commanding 1st Division, 25th Corps, Department of Texas (May 29-December 28, 1865); and major general, USV (November 24, 1865). The New York-born Illinois resident fought as a company commander at Fort Donelson and Shiloh and as a field officer took part in the advance on Corinth, Mississippi. Succeeding his brother as colonel, he directed a brigade at Chickasaw Bayou, Arkansas Post, and Vicksburg. Moving to the relief of Chattanooga as a brigadier general, he was severely wounded in the fighting near Tunnel Hill but returned to duty early the next year. Leading a brigade and then a division, he fought through the Atlanta Campaign and was particularly distinguished in the fighting at the battle of Atlanta proper. For the campaign he was later brevetted major general. He then took part in the March to the Sea and the Carolinas Campaign. With the rebellion crushed, he was given command of the all-black 25th Corps and sent to the Texas-Mexico border to serve under Sheridan in any operations against the Imperialists and the French. Although two other officers, Benjamin H. Grierson and Wager Swayne, were named major generals in 1866, their commissions were backdated prior to Smith's. Finally mustered out on February 1, 1866, he was briefly a postal official under Grant.

SMITH, Green Clay (1826-1895)

Although he was involved in an early success against Confederate raider John Hunt Morgan, Union General Green C. Smith was considered a failure in later operations against the cavalryman. The Kentucky native had been a lawyer and state legislator and served in the Mexican War as a second lieutenant in the 1st Kentucky. A Unionist, he joined the army again in 1862 and his assignments included: colonel, 4th Kentucky Cavalry (March 15, 1862); brigadier general, USV (June 11, 1862); commanding 2nd Division, Army of Kentucky, Department of the Ohio (August 25-October 14, 1862); and commanding 1st Brigade, 2nd Division, Army of Kentucky, Department of the Ohio (October 14, 1862-January 1863). His command was part of the force which defeated Morgan at Lebanon, Tennessee, on May 5, 1862, and he was promoted to brigadier general the following month. But he didn't live up to his promise, and his commanders wanted to get rid of him. Having been elected to Congress, he resigned from the army on December 1, 1863, and took his seat six days later, at the beginning of the first session of the 38th Congress. In the midst of his second term he was named Montana's territorial governor. Brevetted major general for the war in 1865, he became a Baptist preacher and was active in the prohibition movement.

SMITH, Gustavus Adolphus (1820-1885)

Unable to serve in the field due to his wounds, Gustavus A. Smith had his brigadier general's commission expire on March 4, 1863, when the U.S. Senate failed to ratify it. The Philadelphia native had been engaged in the carriage-making business in 1861 when he volunteered his services. After duty as a drillmaster his assignments included: colonel, 35th Illinois (September 1, 1861); brigadier general, USV (September 19, 1862); colonel, 35th Illinois (reverted March 4, 1863); and colonel, 155th Illinois (February 28, 1865). In his first major battle, Pea Ridge, he was severely wounded in the head and shoulder. Promoted to brigadier general, he was assigned to recruiting duty but reverted to his colonelcy when his commission expired. Six months later he was discharged for fraudulent recruiting practices, on September 22, 1863. Near the end of the war he was placed in command of a new regiment with which he performed guard duty along the Nashville and Chattanooga Railroad. Brevetted brigadier general for the war, he was mustered out with his regiment on December 14, 1865, and later became a tax official in New Mexico.

SMITH, Gustavus Woodson (1821-1896)

Considerations of rank prompted a senior Confederate major general, Gustavus W. Smith, to resign his commission. The Kentucky-born West Pointer (1842) had served with the engineers in Mexico, winning two brevets, and taught at his alma mater before resigning as a first lieutenant in 1854. As a civil engineer he became New York City's street commissioner. Joining the Confederacy, his assignments included: major general, CSA (September 19, 1861); commanding 2nd Corps, Army of the Potomac (September-October 22, 1861); commanding 2nd Division, Potomac District, Department of Northern Virginia (October 22, 1861-March 23 1862); commanding Aquia District, Department of Northern Virginia (March 23-April 18, 1862); commanding Reserve, Department of Northern Virginia (April 18-early May 1862); commanding 1st Division, Department of Northern Virginia (early May-May 31 and June 1-2, 1862); commanding the department (May 31-June 1, 1862); commanding Department of North Carolina and Southern Virginia (September 19, 1862-February 17, 1863); acting secretary of war (November 17-21, 1862); major general, Georgia Militia (June 1864); commanding 1st Division, Georgia Militia, Army of Tennessee (June-October 1864); and commanding 1st Division, Georgia Militia, Department of South Carolina, Georgia and Florida (October 1864-April 20, 1865). In the first fall and winter of the war he was the senior major general operating in northern Virginia and, going to the Peninsula, commanded the reserves at Yorktown. At Seven Pines he led a division until the wounding of Joseph E. Johnston put him in charge of the army. Within a few hours, however, he was relieved by Robert E. Lee. Smith then suffered an attack of paralysis which made him miss the rest of the Peninsula Campaign. Upon his recovery, he was assigned to command all forces operating to the South of Lee's army. However, in the fall of 1862 the new grade of lieutenant general was created; and while Smith did not gain one of the promotions, several major generals junior to him did. Smith resigned his Confederate commission on February 17, 1863, having served four days as the acting head of the War Department. The next year he was appointed to the same rank in the Georgia militia by Governor Joseph E. Brown. During the Atlanta and Savannah campaigns Smith led a division of these troops with the Army of Tennessee and the forces along the coast. He commanded during the largest action of the March to the Sea—Griswoldville. After surrendering on April 20, 1865, at Macon, he was engaged in the iron and insurance businesses. Active in historical writing, he wrote a work on the controversial and confused battle at Seven Pines, *The Battle of Seven Pines*. He also wrote on other aspects of the Civil War as well as the Mexican War.

SMITH, Hiram (?-1862)

Missouri resident Hiram Smith was told at 11:00 A.M. that he was to die at 1:00 P.M. for the disappearance of Andrew Allsman. The story began when Andrew Allsman, a resident of the strongly pro-Southern town of Palmyra, Missouri, vanished after having been paroled by Confederate troops. He had served in the 3rd Missouri Cavalry in the Union army until discharged on account of his advanced age. Unpopular at home, he was accused of spying on his neighbors for the Union. Captured when the Confederates raided the town, he was sentenced to death but then paroled. His body was never found. John McNeil, a Union general, then declared that 10 men would die if Allsman was not returned. One of the doomed men was William T. Humphrey, whose wife pleaded for his release. Since there was evidence that Humphrey had not belonged to a Confederate band, he was spared and Hiram Smith was the substitute victim. He died with the other nine men on October 18, 1862.

SMITH, James (ca. 1826-1881)

It took more than 100 years for the remains of Medal of Honor winner James Smith to be exhumed from a pauper's grave and transferred to Arlington National Cemetery. The British native had deserted the Royal Navy in the 1850s in Canada. Sometime in early 1864 he joined the U.S. Navy and was assigned to the USS *Richmond*. In the battle of Mobile Bay on August 5, 1864, he was a member of the bow gun crew. When all the others were placed hors de combat, Smith continued to man the gun on his own. For this action he was awarded the coveted medal. Following the war he was in the shipping business and married into a socially prominent family who disapproved of the match. It was apparently for this reason that he was buried in a pauper's grave in New York City. He was subsequently buried under three other unknown persons before he was found in 1985 and plans were made for reburial in Arlington.

SMITH, James Argyle (1831-1901)

Transferring from the staff to the line, the Tennessee West Pointer (1853) James A. Smith rose to the rank of brigadier general in the Confederate service while serving in the western theater. Posted to the infantry upon his graduation, he had resigned as a first lieutenant in the 6th Infantry on May 9, 1861, following frontier duty. His Southern assignments included: captain, Infantry (spring (1861); major and assistant adjutant general (March 1862); lieutenant colonel, 2nd Tennessee (spring 1862); colonel, 5th (AKA 9th) Confederate (July 21, 1862); brigadier general, CSA (September 30, 1863); and commanding in the Army of Tennessee: brigade Cleburne's Division, Hill's-Breckinridge's Corps (ca. October-November 30, 1863); brigade, Cleburne's Division, Hardee's Corps (November 30, 1863-spring 1864 and June-July 22, 1864); Mercer's (old) Brigade, Cleburne's Division, Hardee's-Cheatham's Corps (fall-

November 30, 1864); the division (November 30, 1864-April 9, 1865); and brigade, Brown's Division, Hardee's Corps (April 9-26, 1865). After serving as Leonidas Polk's adjutant he took command of a Tennessee regiment shortly before Shiloh and later led a unit designated as a "Confederate" unit at Perryville and Murfreesboro and in the Tullahoma Campaign. At Chickamauga he commanded the 3rd and 5th Confederate. Promoted to brigadier general later that month, he fought through the Atlanta Campaign until wounded at the battle of Atlanta proper. Returning to duty, he led another brigade in the invasion of middle Tennessee. Guarding the trains during the fight at Franklin, he then succeeded Patrick R. Cleburne in division command. He fought at Nashville and in the Carolinas. In the final reorganization of the Army of Tennessee, he was reduced to command of a brigade with which he surrendered at Durham Station. He was subsequently a farmer and engaged as an education official in Mississippi.

SMITH, James Youngs (1809-1876)

While other states were resorting to the use of conscription to meet their quotas for troops, Rhode Island's Governor James Y. Smith used large bounties and recruiting agents to gain volunteers and avoid the draft. A native of Connecticut, he had become a wealthy man from his lumber and clothing interests by the time the Civil War broke out. His business had expanded into Rhode Island, and he was Providence's mayor in the mid-1850s and sat in the state legislature. Defeated for the governorship in 1861 by William Sprague, he won on the same Republican ticket two years later. In that race he defeated the interim governor, William C. Cozzens. In each of the next two years he was reelected but refused to serve a fourth term, leaving office in 1866. His last victory was overwhelming, perhaps due to his popularity for not implementing the draft. After his term was up he served on boards and commissions dealing with education and charities.

SMITH, Jesse C. (?-?)

Due to the emergency posed by Lee's 1863 invasion of Maryland and Pennsylvania the War Department bypassed its standing policy of not accepting state general officers into the volunteer service. Thus on June 18, 1863, New Yorker Jesse C. Smith—of that state's National Guard—was mustered in. Commanding three state regiments, his brigade was designated the 3rd Brigade, 1st (Smith's) Division, Department of the Susquehanna. This force was a constant threat to the flanks of Lee's columns although it was not engaged in the battle of Gettysburg. With the emergency gone Smith and his command were mustered out on July 24, 1863.

SMITH, John Eugene (1816-1897)

The only Union general born in Switzerland, John E. Smith served throughout the Civil War with the Army of the Tennessee and was brevetted major general on January 12, 1865, for gallantry in action throughout the war. The son of a Napoleonic officer, he was born in the canton of Bern and was brought to America in early childhood. Raised in Philadelphia he was a jeweler before moving to Galena, Illinois, where he held minor elective office. Enlisting in the first summer of the war, his assignments included: colonel, 45th Illinois (July 23, 1861); brigadier general, USV (November 29, 1862); and commanding in the Army of the Tennessee: 1st Brigade, 3rd Division, Right Wing, 13th Corps (December-December 18, 1862); 8th Division, 16th Corps (December 26, 1862-April 3, 1863); 1st Brigade, 3rd Division, 17th Corps (April 23-June 3, 1863); 7th Division, 17th Corps (June 3-September 14, 1863); also 3rd Division, 17th Corps (July 20-22, 1863); 2nd Division, 17th Corps (September 14-December 20, 1863); and 3rd Division, 15th Corps (December 20, 1863-April 26, 1865). He led his regiment at Fort Donelson, Shiloh, and the Corinth siege before being named a brigadier general. He took part in the operations against Vicksburg and advanced to divisional command during the siege. He directed the only division of the corps present at Chattanooga and was left to guard the rear during the Atlanta Campaign. With the main army, he took part in the March to the Sea and the Carolinas Campaign. Before being mustered out on April 30, 1866, he served in western Tennessee. Within months he was back in uniform as a colonel of regular infantry. In 1867 he was brevetted brigadier and major general of regulars for Vicksburg and the capture of Savannah. He retired from the army in 1881 as colonel, 14th Infantry, and settled in Chicago.

SMITH, John Gregory (1818-1891)

The last Vermont war governor, John G. Smith's call to organize the militia could not be acted upon in time to prevent the raid on his birthplace—St. Albans, Vermont. A lawyer, he also had banking and railroad interests. A Republican, he served in both houses of the state legislature and was the speaker of the lower chamber during the first two years of the Civil War. Nominated for governor, he was elected in 1863 and reelected the following year. Under groundwork laid by his predecessor, Frederick Holbrook, he made Vermont the premier state in the field of providing hospital care for its volunteers. He also pushed through the bill granting soldiers the absentee ballot in the field. After the war's close in 1865 he retired from office but attended three later national conventions.

SMITH, Joseph (1790-1877)

The most important contribution to the Union war effort made by Joseph Smith, a naval veteran of 52 years' service, was his presiding over the board which gave the green light to the construction of the revolutionary vessel *Monitor.* After entering the navy in 1809, the Massachusetts native served in the War of 1812 and against the Barbary Coast pirates. He spent over two decades, from the 1840s through the 1860s, as chief of the Bureau of Navy Yards and Docks. The same year that the *Monitor* won its victory over the *Virginia*—1862—he was placed on the retired list with the rank of rear admiral. However, he continued in his bureau assignment until 1869.

SMITH, Martin Luther (1819-1866)

Although an engineer by training, New Yorker Martin L. Smith did command Confederate line troops in battle. The West Pointer (1842) had served his entire tour in the old army with the topographical engineers. Service in the South led to his resignation, as a captain, on April 1, 1861, and his joining the Confederacy. His assignments included: major, Engineers (March 16, 1861); colonel, 21st Louisiana (February 1862); brigadier general, CSA (April 11, 1862); commanding 3rd District, Department of Southern Mississippi and East Louisiana (June 26-ca. October 1862); commanding 2nd Military District, Department of Mississippi and East Louisiana (October 21-late December 1862); major general, CSA (November 4, 1862); commanding division, 2nd Military District, Department of Mississippi and East Louisiana (late December 1862-April 1863); commanding division, Department of Mississippi and East Louisiana (April-July 4, 1863); chief engineer, Army of Northern Virginia (April-July 1864); chief engineer, Army of Tennessee (July 20-October 1864); and chief engineer, Military Division of the West (October 1864-early 1865). Despite the fact that he was given charge of a volunteer regiment of infantry, he worked early in the war on the defenses of New Orleans and Vicksburg. At Chickasaw Bayou he led a division in the repulse of Sherman and was later captured at Vicksburg. Although paroled on July 4, 1863, he was not exchanged until about February 1864. He then served successively as the chief engineer to Robert E. Lee, John B. Hood, and Pierre G.T. Beauregard. During the later period he worked on the defenses at Mobile. He died a little more than a year after the fall of the Confederacy.

SMITH, Maurice Thompson (1828-1863)

A graduate of the University of North Carolina, Maurice Smith entered Confederate service and proved to be an example of the changing values of the "Old South." Smith left his planting and became captain, Company K, 55th North Carolina, on May 30, 1862. Early the next year he was promoted to lieutenant colonel. In the action at Fort Huger on April 19, 1863, during Longstreet's siege of Suffolk, the 55th and other units were surprised by a Union force and five guns and over 130 men were captured. There were recriminations between the North Carolinians and the Alabamians supporting them, with each blaming the other for the debacle. A report by Captains Terrell and Cussons of the staff of the Alabamians' commander, General Law, outraged the officers of the 55th. The regimental commander, Colonel Connally, resenting the charge of cowardice and having determined who the originators of the charge were, suggested that officers of the regiment challenge the two staff officers to duels with all field and company officers taking part until each was killed or satisfaction had been given. Smith, the second in command, was the only man to declare that he was morally opposed to the "code duello" and would not participate. The proceedings continued without him. A little over two months later Lieutenant Colonel Smith was mortally wounded on the first day at Gettysburg and called "a gallant and efficient officer" by his brigade commander, General Davis, proving that he had made his earlier decision on moral grounds. (Freeman, Douglas S., *Lee's Lieutenants*)

SMITH, Melancton (1810-1893)

Rising to the rank of captain in the U.S. navy, New York-born Melancton Smith had a very active career in the Civil War. Having entered the service at the age of 15, he had served in the Pacific, West Indies, and Mediterranean and seen action in the Seminole War. During the Mexican War he was executive officer at the Pensacola navy yard. By the outbreak of the Civil War he was a commander and, in command of the *Massachusetts*, he fought against Confederate positions on Ship Island on July 9, 1861, and against the *Florida* on October 19. Placed in charge of the *Mississippi* for the New Orleans expedition, he distinguished himself under Farragut. Promoted to captain in 1862, he was forced to fire and abandon his vessel on the night of March 14, 1863, when he failed in an attempt to slip by the enemy guns at Port Hudson. Briefly in command of the *Monongahela* he was soon ordered back North and given command of the monitor *Onondaga* in the James River, commanding several other vessels as well. In May 1864 he was commanding a wooden flotilla in Albemarle Sound when attacked by the armored ram *Albemarle*. Although forced to retreat he was praised for his actions in the unequal fight. His last wartime combat came in the two bombardments of Fort Fisher, in December 1864 and January 1865. During these actions he commanded the *Wabash*. He continued in the navy after the war and retired as a rear admiral in 1871; he served for a time as governor of the Philadelphia Naval Asylum.

SMITH, Morgan Lewis (1821-1874)

Having earlier served a term of five years as an enlisted man, under the assumed name of Martin L. Sanford, Morgan L. Smith raised a regiment of Missourians for the Union army and eventually became a brigadier general. The New York native had taught school and was a riverboatman in 1861. He recruited his command from the tough neighborhoods along the St. Louis shoreline. His assignments included: colonel, 8th Missouri (July 4, 1861); commanding 5th Brigade, 2nd Division, District of Cairo, Department of the Missouri (February 1-17, 1862); commanding 1st Brigade, 3rd Division, Army of the Tennessee (February 17-May 12, 1862); commanding 1st Brigade, 5th Division, Army of the Tennessee (May 12-July 21, 1862); brigadier general, USV (July 16, 1862); commanding 1st Brigade, 5th Division, District of Memphis, Army of the Tennessee (July 21-September 24, 1862); commanding 1st Brigade, 1st Division, District of Memphis, Army of the Tennessee (September 24-October 26, 1862); commanding 1st Brigade, District of Memphis, 13th Corps, Army of the Tennessee (October 25-November 12, 1862); commanding 2nd Division, District of Memphis, 13th Corps, Army of the Tennessee (November 12-December 18, 1862); commanding 2nd Division, Yazoo Expedition, Army of the Tennessee (December 18-28, 1862); commanding 2nd Division, 15th Corps, Army of the Tennessee (October 6, 1863-July 22, 1864 and July 27-August 5, 1864); commanding the corps (July 22-27, 1864); commanding Post of Vicksburg, District of Vicksburg, Department of the Tennessee, (September 27-November 28, 1864); and commanding Post of Vicksburg, District of Vicksburg Department of Mississippi (November 28, 1864-June 22, 1865). He led his relatively well-disciplined rowdies at Fort Donelson, but as a brigade commander in Lew Wallace's division arrived too late on the first day of Shiloh to play a role in it. However he fought well on the second and after the advance on Corinth, Mississippi, was made a brigadier general. Serving under Sherman, he was severely wounded at Chickasaw Bayou and was not able to take the field again until the following fall. He led a division at Chattanooga and in the Atlanta Campaign. When James B. McPherson was killed at the battle of Atlanta and John A. Logan took over the army, Smith moved up to command the corps for five days. Resuming charge of his division, he was relieved after about a week. Since at the war's close he was not given the usual brevet as major general it can be assumed that he had somehow displeased his superiors. In any event he finished out the war in charge of the post at Vicksburg and resigned on July 12, 1865. After the war he was Johnson's diplomatic representative in Hawaii and thereafter engaged in various business enterprises.

SMITH, Orland (?-?)

More than a year prior to his receiving a brigadier generalship by brevet, Orland Smith had already resigned his colonelcy. A Maine native, he had entered the Union army from Ohio. His assignments included: lieutenant colonel, 73rd Ohio (November 26, 1861); colonel, 73rd Ohio (December 30, 1861); commanding 2nd Brigade, 2nd Division, 11th Corps, Army of the Potomac (October 25, 1862-April 17, 1863 and May 24-September 25, 1863); and commanding 2nd Brigade, 2nd Division, 11th Corps, Army of the Potomac (September 25, 1863-January 3, 1864). He served in western Virginia and fought at McDowell and, during the Shenandoah Valley Campaign, at Cross Keys. After fighting at 2nd Bull Run, he served in the Washington defenses, sometimes in command of a brigade. He led a brigade on the infamous Mud March and was caught up in the rout of the 11th Corps at Chancellorsville. But when a similar fate befell the corps at Gettysburg on the first day, he and his brigade were in the rear, holding Cemetery Hill to which the routed troops retired. He was transferred along with most of the 11th and 12th corps to Chattanooga and took part in the battles around that city and in the relief expedition to Knoxville. Early the next year he was reduced to the command of just his regiment and a few weeks later, on February 17, 1864, resigned. In March 1865 he was given a brevet for his services. Thereafter he was involved in railroading.

SMITH, Preston (1823-1863)

Native Tennessee lawyer Preston Smith gave his life to the Confederacy—not leading his men but, rather, when he accidentally rode into the enemy lines. The Memphis resident's Confederate assignments included: colonel, 154th Tennessee Senior (May 14, 1861); commanding 1st Brigade, 2nd Division, 1st Geographical Division, Department #2 (October 24, 1861-March 5, 1862); commanding 1st Brigade, 1st Grand Division, Army of the Mississippi (March 5-12, 1862); commanding 1st Brigade, 2nd Division, 1st Grand Division, Army of the Mississippi (March 12-mid-March 1862); commanding 1st (Johnson's) Brigade, 2nd Division, 1st Corps, Army of the Mississippi (April 6-7, 1862); commanding brigade, Cheatham's Division, Army of the Mississippi (July 2-August 15, 1862); commanding brigade, Cheatham's Division, Right Wing, Army of the Mississippi (August 15-late August 1862 and October-November 20, 1862); commanding brigade, Cleburne's Division, Left Wing, Army of the Mississippi (August-October 1862); brigadier general, CSA (October 27, 1862); and commanding brigade, Cheatham's Division, Polk's Corps, Army of Tennessee (November 20-December 1862 and January-September 19, 1863). His regiment kept its old militia numerical designation but was authorized to append the word "Senior" to its title in order to indicate its seniority to other Tennessee regiments. During the battle of Belmont, Smith commanded a brigade which was part of the reinforcements sent from Columbus, Kentucky, to the Missouri side of the Mississippi River. On the first day at Shiloh he succeeded the wounded Bushrod R. Johnson in brigade command but himself fell wounded the next day. He recovered to take part in the Tullahoma Campaign and was also in the Kentucky and Murfreesboro campaigns but not in the main battles. He went on to Chickamauga, and while reconnoitering on the evening of the first day at that battle and planning an attack, he rode into the enemy and was mortally wounded. Within the hour he was dead.

SMITH, Robert Benjamin

See: *Hilton, Robert Benjamin*

SMITH, Robert Frederick (?-1893)

Pennsylvania-born Robert F. Smith served for almost four years as a colonel before being brevetted brigadier general of Union volunteers in the final months of the war. His assignments included: colonel, 16th Illinois (May 24, 1861); commanding 2nd Brigade, 1st Division, Army of the Mississippi (July 17-August 15, 1862); and commanding in the Army of the Cumberland: 1st Brigade, 4th Division, 14th Corps (January 9-May 5, 1863); the division (May 5-June 8, 1863); 1st Brigade, 2nd Division, Reserve Corps (June 8-August 3, 1863); and 1st Brigade, 2nd Division, 14th Corps (October 10-November 12, 1863 and October 15, 1864-January 18, 1865). He led his regiment at Island #10 and during the advance on Corinth. During the Tullahoma Campaign he led a brigade but missed Chickamauga and Chattanooga. He again led his regiment during the Atlanta Campaign and took charge of a brigade for the March to the Sea. Brevetted for the war, he was mustered out with his regiment on July 8, 1865.

SMITH, Thomas Benton (1838-1923)

As with any war, the Civil War had its cases of cruelty against prisoners of war. Tennessee native Thomas B. Smith was one of those cases. Educated at the Nashville Military Institute, he had been a railroad employee at the outbreak of the Civil War. Joining the Confederacy, his assignments included: second lieutenant, Company C (later B), 20th Tennessee (June 12, 1861); captain, Company B, 20th Tennessee (1861); colonel, 20th Tennessee (May 8, 1862); commanding 4th Brigade, 1st (Clark's) Division, Breckinridge's Command, District of the Mississippi, Department #2 (August-August 5, 1862); commanding the division (August 5, 1862); commanding Tyler's (old) Brigade, Bate's Division, Hardee's-Cheatham's Corps, Army of Tennessee (early 1864-December 16, 1864); and brigadier general, CSA (July 29, 1864). As a company officer he fought at Mill Springs and Shiloh and then at the reorganization of the regiment was elected colonel. Due to illness within his regiment, it was consolidated with three others into a depleted battalion. Smith himself was given charge of the brigade and at Baton Rouge succeeded Charles Clark, Jr., in command of the division when the latter was wounded and captured. Rejoining the main army, Smith was wounded at Murfreesboro but recovered in time to be again wounded at Chickamauga. Missing Chattanooga, he fought through the Atlanta Campaign as a brigade commander and in the course of it was promoted to brigadier general. He fought at Franklin and was taken prisoner at Nashville. While a prisoner and being herded to the rear with much of his command, he was repeatedly struck by Colonel William L. McMillan around the head with a sword. The injuries were so serious that Smith was expected to die but he survived—with permanent damage—and returned to railroad work. However, he was forced by his injuries to enter the asylum at Nashville in 1876. He died there nearly half a century later.

SMITH, Thomas Church Haskell (1819-1897)

A partisan of John Pope, Thomas C.H. Smith was a key witness in the court-martial of Fitz-John Porter, and his subsequent career fared accordingly. The Massachusetts-born attorney had been engaged in the telegraph business at the outbreak of the Civil War. He enlisted and his assignments included: lieutenant colonel, 1st Ohio Cavalry (September 5, 1861); brigadier general, USV (March 16, 1863, to rank from November 29, 1862); and commanding District of Wisconsin, Department of the Northwest (1863). He served on Pope's staff during the slow advance on Corinth, Mississippi, and was formally named his aide-de-camp in July 1862. When Pope went east to head the new Army of Virginia, Smith went along and became embroiled in the Porter controversy. Promoted to brigadier general the next year, he again accompanied Pope, this time to the Northwest, and was placed in charge of the District of Wisconsin where he was responsible for putting down draft riots. He then went to Missouri as Pope's inspector general before being mustered out on January 15, 1866. He was in the livestock business until the great Chicago fire wiped him out. After working for the Treasury Department he put in a five-year, 1878-1883, stint as a regular army paymaster.

SMITH, Thomas Kilby (1820-1887)

Massachusetts-born attorney T. Kilby Smith had practiced his profession in Ohio, under future Secretary of the Treasury and Chief Justice of the Supreme Court Salmon P. Chase. He had also served as a U.S. marshal before the Civil War, in which his military assignments included: lieutenant colonel, 54th Ohio (September 9, 1816); colonel, 54th Ohio (October 31, 1861); commanding 2nd Brigade, 5th Division, Army of the Tennessee (April 6-May 12, 1862); commanding 2nd (sometimes styled 4th) Brigade, 2nd Division, Yazoo Expedition, Army of the Tennessee (December 28, 1862-January 4, 1863); commanding 2nd Brigade, 2nd Division, 2nd Corps, Army of the Mississippi (January 4-12, 1863); commanding 2nd Brigade, 2nd Division, 15th Corps, Army of the Tennessee (January 12-May 23, 1863); acting aide-de-camp, Army of the Tennessee (May-September 1863); brigadier general, USV (August 11, 1863), commanding 2nd Brigade, 1st Division, 17th Corps, Army of the Tennessee (September 14-October 29, 1863); commanding 1st Brigade, 4th Division, 17th Corps, Army of the Tennessee (October 24, 1863-February 28, 1864); commanding Provisional Division ("Red River Division"), 17th Corps, Department of the Gulf (March-June 1864); and commanding 3rd Division, Detachment Army of the Tennessee, Army of the Cumberland (January 4-17, 1865). At Shiloh he succeeded the wounded David Stuart in brigade command and led it during part of the advance on Corinth. He again took over a brigade at Chickasaw Bayou during Sherman's assaults there. This he directed in the capture of Fort Hindman or Arkansas Post before returning to the operations against Vicksburg proper. Early in the siege he joined the staff of General Grant as an aide until named a brigadier general and given a brigade. The next spring he led that portion of the 17th Corps which participated in the Red River Campaign and was later transferred to Tennessee. Brevetted major general for the war, he was mustered out on January 15, 1866, and was briefly a diplomat to Panama. His final years were spent in New York in the business end of the journalism profession. (Smith, Walter George, *Life and Letters of Thomas Kilby Smith, Brevet Major General, USV, 1820-1887*)

SMITH, Walter W. (?-?)

In the early months of the Civil War there were many questions concerning the legality of the use of privateers. Walter W. Smith got caught up in the dispute. The Confederate sailor was a member of the crew of the *Jeff Davis*, which had been fitted out at Charleston on June 28, 1861. On July 16 the privateer captured the schooner *Enchantress*, and Smith was made the head of the prize crew sent to take the vessel into port. Six days later the prize was retaken by the Union fleet and Smith was charged with piracy. Convicted in October, he faced the hangman's noose. But the Confederate government retaliated by the selection of Colonel Michael Corcoran as a hostage. Soon 13 more hostages were selected to guarantee the treatment of additional captured privateers as prisoners of war. The crisis was resolved when the courts ruled that the men were in fact not pirates but regularly enlisted soldiers. From then on Smith was treated as a prisoner of war. His case is treated in detail in the *Official Records*, Series II, Volume III.

SMITH, William (1796-1887)

With no militia experience, ex-Virginia governor William Smith was one of the oldest men to seek an active field commission, and he became one of the more colorful officers of Lee's army. He had earned the nickname "Extra Billy" for some questionable charges made while running a postal route. Returning from a brief residence in California, Smith was serving out a fourth term in the U.S. Congress when the war began. Happening to be at Fairfax Court House when a detachment of regular cavalry charged through the town, killing the Confederate commander, Captain J.Q. Marr, Smith directed the defense. After this first blood the 64-year-old politician sought and received the colonelcy of the 49th Virginia. His later assignments included: commanding Early's Brigade, Ewell's-Early's Division, 2nd Corps, Army of Northern Virginia (September 17, 1862 and ca. April 4-July 10, 1863); brigadier general, CSA (April 23, to rank from January 31, 1863); and major general, CSA (August 12, 1863). He fought at 1st Bull Run and in November 1861 was elected to the First Regular Congress where he sat on the committee on Claims and Naval Affairs. Returning to the field when action was imminent, he fought at Williamsburg and was wounded at Seven Pines. He returned to fight during the Seven Days and the 2nd Bull Run Campaign in which he was teased for carrying an umbrella during the rainstorm at Chantilly. He had gained a reputation for despising West Point and its tactics, finding that neither he nor his men understood them and that common sense was more useful in battle. At Antietam he took over the brigade and suffered three wounds. However, he remained in control until the action was over. After recovering and receiving a generalship, he resigned his congressional seat and returned to the field in time for Chancellorsville. Although elected to another term as governor he participated in the invasion of Pennsylvania and fought at Gettysburg. A few days later he left the field and then received a second promotion, being assigned to duty encouraging recruiting in Virginia. He was inaugurated on January 1, 1864, and served until the war's close. Remaining active in Virginia politics, Smith sat in the legislature into his 80s. (Freeman, Douglas S., *Lee's Lieutenants*)

SMITH, William Duncan (1825-1862)

Yellow fever cut short the promising career of Confederate Brigadier General William D. Smith. The native Georgian West Pointer (1846) had been wounded at Molino del Rey during the Mexican War while serving with the 2nd Dragoons. Resigning as a captain on January 28, 1861, he offered his services to the Confederacy. His assignments included: captain, Cavalry (March 16, 1861); colonel, 20th Georgia (July 14, 1861); brigadier general, CSA (March 14, 1862, to rank from the 7th); and commanding 1st Military District of South Carolina, Department of South Carolina, Georgia and Florida (July 8-October 4, 1862). Taking charge of a volunteer regiment, he led it in northern Virginia until promoted to brigadier general and ordered to South Carolina. There he fought at Secessionville and commanded a district until his death. Highly respected, he was repeatedly recommended for promotion and a larger command. His death came on October 4, 1862.

SMITH, William Farrar (1824-1903)

Known as "Baldy" since his West Point (1845) days—his hair was thin then but fuller than most of his peers by the time of the Civil War—William F. Smith was one of the more troublesome Union generals. The Vermonter had been posted to the Topographical Engineers upon graduation and served on survey duty and as an instructor at the academy. His Civil War assignments included: captain, Topographical Engineers (since July 1, 1859); colonel, 3rd Vermont (July 16, 1861); brigadier general, USV (August 13, 1861); commanding brigade, Division of the Potomac (August-October 3, 1861); commanding division, Army of the Potomac (October 3, 1861-March 13, 1862); commanding 2nd Division, 4th Corps, Army of the Potomac (March 13-May 18, 1862); commanding 2nd Division, 6th Corps, Army of the Potomac, (May 18-November 16, 1862); major general, USV (July 4, 1862); commanding the corps (November 16, 1862-February 4, 1863); commanding 9th Corps, Army of the Potomac (February 5-March 17, 1863); major, Engineers (March 3, 1863); commanding 1st Division, Department of the Susquehanna (June 17-August 3, 1863); chief engineer, Army of the Cumberland (late summer-October 18, 1863); chief engineer, Military Division of the Mississippi (October 18, 1863-early 1864); major general, USV (reappointed March 9, 1864); and commanding 18th Corps, Army of the James (May 2-July 10, 1864). At 1st Bull Run he served as a staff officer to Union commander Irwin McDowell and that August was made a brigadier and assigned a brigade. Two months later he was in charge of a division which was later assigned to the 4th and finally the 6th Corps. This command he led at Yorktown, Williamsburg, the Seven Days—where he earned a brevet for White Oak Swamp—South Mountain, and Antietam. At Fredericksburg he commanded the corps, which was not fully committed to action. A week after the battle he coauthored, with William B. Franklin, a letter to Washington criticizing the current army commander, Burnside, and outlining the pair's own plans for an advance to Richmond. This outraged Burnside and many in Congress. After a brief stint in command of the 9th Corps Smith was removed when the Senate refused to confirm his previous appointment as a major general and his commission expired on March 4, 1863. Reverting to the rank of brigadier general, he commanded a division of militia in Pennsylvania during Lee's invasion and faced Jeb Stuart at Carlisle. He then went West to serve as chief engineer at Chattanooga where he designed the famous "cracker line" which relieved the siege conditions prevailing in the city. Grant's friendship with Smith prompted the latter's reappointment as a major general and assignment to one of Butler's corps in Virginia. He took part in the Bermuda Hundred operations before being sent to reinforce the Army of the Potomac at Cold Harbor. Arriving late, he still took part in the bloody repulse on

June 3. Before returning to Butler's command he became embroiled in a dispute with Meade over Cold Harbor. At the initial assaults on Petersburg—which, if properly pressed, could have ended the war in a matter of days—he showed an excessive amount of caution and botched the opportunity, leading to a dispute with Winfield S. Hancock who arrived on the field late in the day. A month later he was removed from command. Malaria, contracted in Florida, may have been a contributing cause for his poor performance, but his friendship with Democratic presidential candidate McClellan did not endear him to Congress or help play down his cantankerous nature. He resigned his volunteer commission on November 4, 1865, and his regular one on March 21, 1867. He was a civil engineer afterwards and held numerous government appointments. *Battles and Leaders* contains a number of his contributions. (Wilson, James Harrison, *Life and Services of William Farrar Smith, Major General, United States Volunteers in the Civil War*)

SMITH, William Nathan Harrell (1812-1889)

For the entire time that North Carolina was represented in the Confederate Congress, William N.H. Smith was there for the northeastern 1st District. He proved to be a loyal supporter of the war effort despite being a former Unionist and coming from an often troublesome state. A native of North Carolina, he had practiced law and become a Whig politician in the state legislature. As a Democrat, he sat in the 36th Congress and narrowly missed being elected its speaker of the house. He left office on March 3, 1861, and was still a Unionist until Lincoln called for 75,000 volunteers after the surrender of Fort Sumter. Taking his seat in the Provisional Confederate Congress on July 20, 1861, he held no committee assignments in that body. In the First Regular Congress he chaired the Committee on Elections and sat on those on: the Medical Department; and Rules and Officers. In the Second Congress he chaired the Committee on Claims and remained on the Committee on Rules and Officers. Granting the central government broad powers for the war effort—over volunteers, transportation, and commerce—he was also a protector of local and states' rights and wanted the Confederacy to pay claims against it quickly. In the postwar years he backed Andrew Johnson and was a leader in the restoration of a conservative state government. For the final 11 years of his life he was the state supreme court's presiding judge.

SMITH, William Sooy (1830-1916)

On July 15, 1864, a few months after being worsted at the hands of Nathan Bedford Forrest, Union cavalryman William Sooy Smith resigned, citing ill health. A native Ohio West Pointer (1856), he had been posted to the artillery. The next year he resigned in order to enter railroad engineering and, later, general civil engineering. Reentering the military at the outbreak of the Civil War, his assignments included: colonel, 13th Ohio (June 26, 1861); commanding 14th Brigade, 5th Division, Army of the Ohio (December 2, 1861-July 2, 1862); brigadier general, USV (April 15, 1862); commanding 3rd Division, Army of the Ohio (July 2-11, 1862); commanding 17th Brigade, 3rd Division, Army of the Ohio (August 19-23, 1862); commanding 4th Division, Army of the Ohio (August 23-September 29, 1862); commanding 4th Division, 2nd Corps, Army of the Ohio (September 29-November 5, 1862); commanding 2nd Division, Left Wing, 14th Corps, Army of the Cumberland (November 5-December 10, 1862); commanding 1st Division, 16th Corps, Army of the Tennessee (March 22-July 20, 1863); chief of Cavalry, Army of the Tennessee (1863); and chief of Cavalry, Military Division of the Mississippi (November 11, 1863-1864). After commanding his regiment in operations in western Virginia, including Carnifax's Ferry, he led one of Buell's brigades at Shiloh. Along with most of the corps, his division was not engaged at Perryville, and he had relinquished command three weeks before Murfreesboro. Commanding a division in the Army of the Tennessee, he joined the siege operations at Vicksburg on June 12, 1863, and served until after the fall of the city and the capture of Jackson. He then became Grant's cavalry chief, directing operations for the relief of Chattanooga and Knoxville. When Sherman launched his Meridian Campaign in early 1864 it was agreed that Smith would lead a mounted column from Memphis to join forces with his chief. However, his superiority in numbers did not do him much good in dealing with Forrest. Smith was driven back from West Point in a series of debacles and was unable to reinforce Sherman. Returning to engineering after his resignation, he proved to be rather revolutionary in his techniques for bridge supports and the foundations of skyscrapers in Chicago.

SMYTH, Thomas Alfred (1832-1865)

The unenviable distinction of being the last Union general to die from Civil War wounds went to Irishman Thomas A. Smyth. He had emigrated from the family farm in County Cork and settled in Philadelphia where he worked as a carver until departing to take part in William Walker's filibustering expedition to Nicaragua. Upon his return he was a coachmaker in Delaware. His military assignments included: major, 1st Delaware (October 17, 1861); lieutenant colonel, 1st Delaware (December 30, 1862); colonel, 1st Delaware (February 7, 1863); commanding 2nd Brigade, 3rd Division, 2nd Corps, Army of the Potomac (May 16-July 3, July 4-August 14, and September 3-December 28, 1863, and February 13-March 25, 1864); commanding 2nd "Irish" Brigade, 1st Division, 2nd Corps, Army of the Potomac (March 25-May 17, 1864); commanding 3rd Brigade, 2nd Division, 2nd Corps, Army of the Potomac (May 17-July 31, August 23-November 5, and November 15-December 22, 1864, and February 28-April 7, 1865); brigadier general, USV (October 1, 1864); and commanding the division (July 31-August 22, 1864 and December 23, 1864-February 25, 1865). After initial service in southeastern Virginia the regiment fought at Antietam and Smyth commanded it at Fredericksburg and Chancellorsville. He commanded a brigade at Gettysburg until wounded on the third day. Returning to duty the next day, he served through the Bristoe and Mine Run campaigns. In the early part of the Overland Campaign he directed the Irish Brigade. Through the remainder of the campaign he commanded a different brigade and at times during the Petersburg siege he commanded the division. During the final operations against Lee's army he led his brigade until mortally wounded through the mouth at Farmville. Two days later, the same day that Lee surrendered, he succumbed to his wounds. (Conyngham, David Powers, *The Irish Brigade and Its Campaigns* and Maull, D.W., *The Life and Military Services of the Late Brigadier General Thomas A. Smyth*)

SNEAD, Thomas Lowndes (1828-1890)

While serving as a staff officer, Thomas L. Snead was elected to the Second Confederate Congress from Missouri's 1st District (St. Louis) by the soldier vote. A native of Virginia, he had practiced law there before moving to St. Louis where he also published the *St. Louis Bulletin*. While the Union was being disrupted, he was serving as aide-de-camp and military secretary to Missouri's secessionist governor, Claiborne F. Jackson. Joining the army, his assignments included: colonel and adjutant general, Missouri State Guard (1861); and major and assistant adjutant general, CSA (1862). On the staff of General Sterling Price, he fought at Booneville, Carthage, Wilson's Creek, and Lexington and later accompanied Price to Mississippi with the Army of the West. In a May 1864 special election in which only soldiers and refugees could vote, since St. Louis was behind Union lines, he was elected to the Second Confederate Congress. Resigning his commission in the army, he was seated at the beginning of the second session on November 7, 1864. With his district occupied and his being a soldier, he voted for a vigorous prosecution of the war but was wary of Jefferson Davis' leadership. Moving to New York after the war—the atmosphere in St. Louis was strongly anti-Confederate—he edited the *New York Daily News* and practiced law. He wrote *The Fight for Missouri* and numerous articles for *Battles and Leaders of the Civil War*.

SNYDER, George W. (ca. 1833-1861)

At the outbreak of the Civil War, West Pointer George Snyder, class of 1856, was a first lieutenant of engineers, assisting in the construction of the soon-to-be-famous Fort Sumter in Charleston Harbor, South Carolina. During the bombardment of the fort, Snyder, in his first combat, was part of the group that assisted in the reraising of the flag after it had been shot down; during the night of the attack, Lieutenant Snyder had gone outside the fort's walls to examine the damage wrought by the hostile shells. After the fall of the fort, the young lieutenant was brevetted captain for his actions. He was present at the battle of 1st Bull Run, as an engineer on Colonel Heintzelman's staff, and earned another brevet, as major. While engaged in the construction of the defensive works on the south side of the Potomac at Washington he died on November 17, 1861, from, as the chief engineer, General J.G. Barnard put it, "overzealousness in discharge of his duties while in impaired health from his services at Charleston Harbor and Fort Sumter." (Swanberg, W.A., *First Blood*)

SORREL, Gilbert Moxley (1838-1901)

Although he served through most of the war on the staff of James Longstreet, G. Moxley Sorrel did hold a field command for about four months late in the conflict. A clerk and militia private before the war in Savannah, he participated in the capture of Fort Pulaski and was an observer at the bombardment in Charleston Harbor. Going to Virginia he served as a volunteer aide-de-camp to Longstreet at 1st Bull Run. He remained with the South Carolinian through the general's wounding at the Wilderness. He participated in all of "Old Pete's" campaigns, gaining advancement from captain to lieutenant colonel as his chief received his own promotions. Sorrel directed a flanking movement in the Wilderness which marked him for higher responsibilities. During the Petersburg fighting he was wounded in the leg. Then he was appointed brigadier general, CSA (October 27, 1864) and commanded Wright's (old) Brigade, Mahone's Division, 3rd Corps, Army of Northern Virginia (October 31, 1864-February 7, 1865). Suffering a severe chest wound on the latter date, he was returning to duty when the army surrendered. A Savannah merchant in his postwar years, he also wrote *Recollections of a Confederate Officer*.

SOULÉ, Pierre (1801-1870)

Exiled from his native France, Pierre Soulé always managed to keep in the middle of trouble. Fleeing by a circuitous route to New Orleans, he eventually became a lawyer and rose to represent Louisiana in the Senate. While serving as minister to Spain he became involved with the Ostend Manifesto calling for the annexation of Cuba, with or without Spain's consent. When this was rejected, he resigned. In the intervening years until the Civil War he practiced law. Although opposed to secession he backed Louisiana's decision and once the Crescent City was captured earned the wrath of Union General Benjamin F. Butler. In June 1862 he was arrested and confined in Fort Lafayette until he fled while on parole in Boston. Running the blockade into the Confederacy, he became part of the Beauregard bloc and for a time served on his staff as an honorary brigadier. Since Jefferson Davis was a foe of Beauregard, there was no action to make his position official. Again running the blockade in 1864, he attempted to raise a foreign legion to fill the Confederate ranks. After the war he was busy with efforts to establish a Confederate veterans' colony in Sonora.

SPANGLER, Edward (?-1875)

A scene shifter in Ford's Theater, Edward (sometimes Edmund or Edman) Spangler was befriended by the actor John Wilkes Booth and as a result was sentenced to six years imprisonment. The Maryland native was arrested with the other conspirators and was accused of having built the stables where Booth kept his horse behind the theater and of holding his horse while the assassination was under way. For his role he was sent to Dry Tortugas and, having survived a yellow fever epidemic there, was released in 1869 after serving only two-thirds of his sentence.

SPARROW, Edward (1810-1882)

As the Confederate Senate's chairman of the Committee on Military Affairs, Louisiana's Edward Sparrow believed that the unlimited war powers rested in the hands of Congress. A Dublin, Ireland, native, he had been raised in Ohio before he took up law in Louisiana. He was a court clerk and sheriff before becoming a planter. Favoring the immediate disruption of the Union, he attended the secession convention. Named to the Provisional Confederate Congress—he was to serve throughout the war—he sat on the committees on: Flag and Seal; Indian Affairs; and Military Affairs. Elected to the Senate in November 1861, he chaired the Committee on Military Affairs for the rest of the conflict. His one reluctance in granting the central government adequate warmaking powers came on the matter of exemptions from military service. He felt this should be left in the hands of the several states. Part of the anti-Bragg faction, he supported both Joseph E. Johnston and P.G.T. Beauregard. He returned to his relatively untouched plantation at the close of the war.

SPEAR, Ellis (1834-1917)

When Maine schoolmaster Ellis Spear entered the Union army in the summer of 1862, the frail man was not expected to withstand the rigors of army life. Nonetheless, he rose to the rank of brevet brigadier. His assignments included: captain, Company G, 20th Maine (August 29, 1862); major, 20th Maine (August 28, 1863); and colonel, 20th Maine (May 29, 1865). His regiment was in reserve at Antietam but later fought at Fredericksburg, Chancellorsville, and Gettysburg. In the Overland Campaign it fought at the Wilderness, Spotsylvania, theNorth Anna, and Cold Harbor. During the Petersburg operations, Spear earned brevets for Peebles' Farm and Lewis' Farm. Present at the final defeat of the Army of Northern Virginia, he was brevetted brigadier general for Appomattox before being mustered out with the full rank of colonel on July 16, 1865. After the war he was a lawyer, banker, and educator. (Pullen, John J., *The 20th Maine*)

Edward Spangler, Booth horse holder. (NA)

SPEAR, Samuel Perkins (1815-1875)

As an enlisted man, Samuel P. Spear was a veteran of the Seminole and Mexican Wars and Indian fighting on the frontier when he transferred to the volunteer service and rose to the rank of brevet brigadier general. A native of Massachusetts he had enlisted in the regular army from Pennsylvania and served in the dragoons and the ordnance department; he was wounded at Cerro Gordo. His Civil War-era assignments included: private, Company F, 2nd Cavalry (since March 2, 1860); corporal, Company F, 2nd Cavalry (1860 or 1861); sergeant, Company F, 2nd Cavalry (1860 or 1861); first sergeant, Company F, 2nd Cavalry (1860 or 1861); first sergeant, Company F, 5th Cavalry (change of designation August 3, 1861); lieutenant colonel, 11th Pennsylvania Cavalry (October 5, 1861); colonel, 11th Pennsylvania Cavalry (August 20, 1862); commanding Cavalry Brigade, U.S. Forces at Yorktown, 18th Corps, Department of Virginia and North Carolina (January 25-April 28, 1864); and commanding 2nd Brigade, Cavalry Division, Army of the James (April 28, 1864-May 9, 1865). As a volunteer officer, he served in southeastern Virginia and North Carolina. His exploits included the capture of Robert E. Lee's son, "Rooney" Lee. In the operations against Richmond and Petersburg he was in command of a brigade and took part in raids under August V. Kautz and James H. Wilson. In the war's last months he was brevetted a brigadier general for his role in the fighting on the Darbytown Road. He resigned his commission on May 9, 1865, a month after Lee's surrender, and died a decade later.

SPEARS, James Gallant (1816-1869)

As far as James G. Spears was concerned, he was all for preserving the Union but not for abolishing slavery, and he made no bones about letting his position be known beyond a shadow of a doubt. This resulted in his dismissal as a Union brigadier general. A native Tennessean lawyer and planter he had been a Douglas Democrat in 1860, with strong Unionist sentiments. Fleeing from impending arrest by Confederate authorities, he entered the Union army in Kentucky. His assignments included: lieutenant colonel, 1st Tennessee (September 1, 1861); brigadier general, USV (March 5, 1862); commanding 25th Brigade, 7th Division, Army of the Ohio (March 26-October 10, 1862); commanding 1st Brigade, Cumberland Division, Department of the Ohio (October-November 1862); commanding 1st Brigade, 2nd Division, Center, 14th Corps, Army of the Cumberland (November 12, 1862-April 17, 1863); commanding East Tennessee Brigade, District of Central Kentucky, Department of the Ohio (April-June 1863); commanding 3rd Brigade, 3rd Division, Reserve Corps, Army of the Cumberland (August 30-October 9, 1862); commanding brigade, Post of Chattanooga, Army of the Cumberland (November-December 1863); commanding 1st East Tennessee Brigade, 2nd Division, 23rd Corps, Department of the Ohio (December 1863-January 2, 1864); and commanding 3rd Brigade, 3rd Division, 12th Corps, Army of the Cumberland (January 2-February 6, 1864). Before being named a brigadier general he fought at Wild Cat Mountain and Mill Springs. Commanding a brigade he took part in the occupation of Cumberland Gap and then joined the main army for the fight at Murfreesboro. After taking part in the relief of Knoxville he briefly directed a 12th Corps brigade, but on February 6, 1864, he was arrested following an investigation ordered by Lincoln himself. It seems that he was so outspoken in regard to the Emancipation Proclamation—which he felt had stolen his slave property from him—that word had spread widely. Allowed to resign, he refused and was accordingly dismissed. He then retired to private life.

SPEED, James (1812-1887)

A longtime, close advisor to Abraham Lincoln on border state matters pertaining to his native Kentucky, James Speed was rewarded with the cabinet post of attorney general late in the war. In the prewar years Speed had practiced law and sat in the state legislature. He was noted for his extreme Unionist views in his divided state and worked hard to keep it in the Union when secession became the rage throughout the South. Having succeeded in this, he continued to work closely with the Lincoln administration and was named attorney general on December 1, 1864, to replace Edward Bates who had resigned the previous month. During his tenure in the Lincoln cabinet he maintained a moderate stance on the treatment of the secessionists. But once Lincoln was assassinated, and Speed remained on, in Andrew Johnson's cabinet, he became much more radical. He supported the idea of a military commission to try the murder conspirators and favored the granting of the right to vote to blacks. His belief in harsh treatment of the former rebels brought him into conflict with the new president and, in 1866, he resigned in protest. He was later a law professor in Louisville.

James Speed, Lincoln's last attorney general. (NA)

SPENCER, Christopher Miner (1833-1922)

As the inventor of the first successful breech-loading rifled carbine, Christopher M. Spencer saw his weapon become the standard arm for the Union cavalry in the latter stages of the Civil War. During his career as a mechanic, in many different fields, the Connecticut native had become interested in firearms. In 1860 he patented a repeating rifle and founded the Spencer Repeating Rifle Company which provided the Union armies with some 200,000 guns. During the course of the war he continued to invent new systems. The most important of these was his seven-shot carbine, also a breech-loader, which became the backbone of the Union cavalry and was also used by the infantry. Following the war he continued to invent in the field of weaponry as well as in other fields. (Buckeridge, J.O., *Lincoln's Choice*)

SPENCER, George Eliphaz (1836-1893)

An Iowa attorney who had represented Alabama in the U.S. Senate before the Civil War, George E. Spencer won the brevet of brigadier general while commanding a regiment of loyal Alabamians. The New York native's assignments included: captain and assistant adjutant general, USV (October 24, 1862); colonel, 1st Alabama Cavalry (September 11, 1863); and commanding 3rd Brigade, 3rd Division, Cavalry Corps, Military Division of the Mississippi (January-April 1865). During the fighting at Shiloh he served as a volunteer aide on the staff of John M. Thayer and six months later received a formal appointment as an assistant adjutant general to Grenville M. Dodge in western Tennessee and northern Mississippi. After almost a year he took charge of the regiment of loyal Southerners with which he saw action in the Atlanta Campaign (as the headquarters guard of the 16th Corps), the March to the Sea, and the Carolinas Campaign. In the latter he had command of a brigade. For the last two campaigns he was brevetted; on July 22, 1865, his resignation was accepted. In the postwar years the Republican politician was active in railroading, ranching, and minerals.

SPINOLA, Francis Barretto (1821-1891)

New York politician Francis B. Spinola was made a brigadier general of volunteers for his ability to raise troops but proved to be a poor field leader and was forced to resign from the army because of his dealings with draft brokers. The lawyer and Democratic politico had held numerous state elective offices and attended the 1860 convention in Charleston. He raised four regiments for the Union army and was rewarded with a brigadier general's star. His assignments included: brigadier general, USV (October 1, 1862); commanding Empire Brigade, Division at Suffolk, 7th Corps, Department of Virginia (October 1-December 28, 1862); commanding 1st Brigade, 5th Division, 18th Corps, Department of North Carolina (January 11-April 22, 1863); commanding Keystone Brigade, District of Pamlico, 18th Corps, Department of North Carolina (April 22-May 9 and May 29-June 26, 1863); and commanding Spinola's Independent Brigade, 7th Corps, Department of Virginia (June 26-July 1863). He led a brigade in southeastern Virginia and North Carolina before being sent to back up the Army of the Potomac following the Gettysburg victory. In the subsequent operations he was wounded at Manassas Gap. Relieved from duty in the spring 1864 reorganization, he was assigned to recruiting duty but became involved in a scandal relating to the swindling of recruits out of their bounty money by brokers. Convicted by a court-martial, he was allowed to resign on June 8, 1865, rather than be dismissed. He died while serving his third term in Congress. In the meantime he had been in the insurance and banking businesses.

SPRAGUE, John Wilson (1817-1893)

For a rear area action at Decatur, Alabama, on July 22, 1864—the date of the battle of Atlanta—John W. Sprague won the Congressional Medal of Honor. Born in New York, he had been a businessman and public official before his enlistment in Ohio. His assignments included: captain, 7th Ohio (April 25, 1861); colonel, 63rd Ohio (January 23, 1862); commanding 3rd Brigade, 5th Division, District of Memphis, 16th Corps, Army of the Tennessee (July 25-August 25, 1863); commanding 2nd Brigade, 4th Division, 16th Corps, Army of the Tennessee (March 10-September 18, 1864); brigadier general, USV (July 30, 1864); commanding 1st Division, 17th Corps, Army of the Tennessee (October 23-31, 1864); and commanding 2nd Brigade, 1st Division, 17th Corps, Army of the Tennessee (November 1, 1864-January 29, 1865 and March 28-May 20, 1865). As a company commander, he served in western Virginia until promoted to the colonelcy of a new regiment. This he led at Island #10, in the advance to Corinth, Mississippi, and at Iuka and Corinth. Assigned to garrison duty in western Tennessee, he did not rejoin the main army until the Atlanta Campaign when he saved the corps' trains at Decatur. He received his medal in 1894, posthumously. He led his brigade, and briefly the division, in the Savannah and Carolinas campaigns. Brevetted major general for his war service, he was mustered out on September 1, 1866, and went into railroading.

SPRAGUE, Kate Chase (1840-1899)

As the daughter of Lincoln's ambitious secretary of the Treasury, Kate Chase was not only one of the reigning belles of Washington but also an active campaigner for her father's political career. Her father being a widower she took over the responsibilities of being a Washington hostess and met many of the country's leading politicians. Her November 12, 1863, marriage to former Rhode Island governor and then-senator William Sprague was a high-point of the dismal winter. For the remainder of the war they were at the top of the capital's social circle. She tried to further her father's presidential aspirations in 1868. By 1873 her marriage was already falling apart; he was drinking heavily and she was allegedly too intimate with another senator. Then her husband's fortune was wiped out, her father died, and their fourth child was born with a mental disorder. Separated shortly thereafter, the couple divorced in 1882. She ended her life barely eking out a living by running a small dairy and poultry farm. (Phelps, Mary Merwin, *Kate Chase: Dominant Daughter*)

SPRAGUE, William (1830-1915)

Today, it would be rather unusual for the governor of a state to accompany the troops onto the field of battle, but that is exactly what Rhode Island's Governor William Sprague did during the Civil War. And it was not an extraordinary event, although to the army Sprague was one of the most meddlesome of governors. By 1860 when he was first elected governor he had been active in manufacturing and was a colonel of the state militia. Taking office just before the Civil War, he actively prepared the state. He was instrumental in the early raising of volunteers. Accompanying the 2nd Rhode Island, he was present at 1st Bull Run where he had a horse shot out from under him. It also appears that he roamed the field, issuing questionable orders and adding to the confusion of the green troops. Many months later he led an expedition back to the battlefield to recover the remains of some of the regiment's officers. Allegedly he was offered a brigadier's star but declined rather than give up his office. He was frequently in the field, however, during the Peninsula Campaign. After attending the governor's conference at Altoona, he took a seat in the U.S. Senate on March 4, 1863. A Democrat, he generally supported Lincoln. He was chairman of the Committee on Manufacturers and also served on the military committee. On November 12, 1863, he married Kate Chase, the daughter of Lincoln's ambitious secretary of the treasury. It was destined to be an unhappy marriage, but for a while they were high in the capital's social circles. He remained in the Senate for two terms, becoming more and more critical of the Radical Republicans. When he died in Paris, he was the last of the Union's war governors. (Shoemaker, Henry W., *The Last of the War Governors: A Biographical Appreciation of Colonel William Sprague*)

SQUIER

See: *Bras Coupe*

STAFFORD, Leroy Augustus (1822-1864)

A successful Louisiana planter, Leroy A. Stafford had started his military career in the Mexican War as an enlisted man and in the Civil War rose to be a Confederate brigadier. His assignments included: captain, Company B, 9th Louisiana (July 1861), and lieutenant colonel, 9th Louisiana (late 1861); colonel, 9th Louisiana (April 24, 1862); commanding 1st Louisiana Brigade, Ewell's Division, Jackson's Command, Army of Northern Virginia (June 27-July 1862); commanding 2nd Louisiana Brigade, McLaws Division, 1st Corps, same army (July 26-27, 1862); commanding 2nd Louisiana Brigade, Jackson's-Johnson's Division, 2nd Corps, same army (July 27-mid-August, August 28-September 7, September 17, 1862, and October 1863-May 5, 1864); and brigadier general, CSA (October 8, 1863). After serving in the Shenandoah Valley Campaign, Stafford led the brigade in the latter part of the Seven Days Battles and a newly created brigade at Cedar Mountain. He resumed command at 2nd Bull Run when his successor was hit. Again at Antietam he succeeded to brigade command only to be wounded in the foot. Returning to duty, he led his regiment at Gettysburg and was promoted to general that fall. He directed his brigade at Mine Run and on the first day of the Wilderness he was mortally wounded. Three days later, on May 8, he was dead. (Freeman, Douglas S., *Lee's Lieutenants*)

STAGER, Anson (1825-1885)

At the beginning of the Civil War Anson Stager was the general superintendent of Western Union, and it was soon realized that he would be of great value to the military. Accordingly, he was appointed a captain in the Quartermaster General's Department, which was responsible for maintaining telegraphic communications. His appointment, dated November 11, 1861, put him on the road to conflict with another branch of the army, the Signal Corps. This corps, under A.J. Myer, was also experimenting with telegraphic communications in the field. On February 26, 1862, Stager was named colonel and additional aide-de-camp and named to head the U.S. Military Telegraph Corps, which had been created the previous day and given control of all the nation's telegraph offices and lines. This new organization, part military and part civilian, became almost independent of the Quartermaster General's Department. Using Morse-type equipment, while the Signal Corps used the less-efficient Beardslee system, the Military Telegraph Corps was given full control over telegraph operations on November 10, 1863, when, after a heated exchange between Myer and Secretary of War Stanton, the former was removed as head of the Signal Corps and it was limited to visual communications. Stager was brevetted brigadier general of volunteers and was mustered out in 1866, returning to Western Union.

STAGG, Peter (?-1884)

Serving during much of the Civil War in George A. Custer's famous brigade of Michigan cavalry, Peter Stagg was brevetted brigadier general for his war services. The New Jersey native had entered the Union army in Michigan. His assignments included: second lieutenant, 1st Michigan Cavalry (August 22, 1861); major, 1st Michigan Cavalry (November 12, 1862); lieutenant colonel, 1st Michigan Cavalry (December 7, 1862); colonel, 1st Michigan Cavalry (August 17, 1864); commanding 1st Brigade, 1st Division, Cavalry Corps, Army of the Shenandoah (October 26, 1864-March 25, 1865); also commanding the division (January 31-February 3, 1865); and commanding 1st Brigade, 1st Division, Cavalry Corps, Army of the Potomac (March 25-June 1, 1865). His regiment fought in the Shenandoah and at Cedar Mountain and 2nd Bull Run. Assigned to the vicinity of Washington, it was active in operations against Confederate guerrillas and then joined Custer's command just before Gettysburg. He was wounded the day after the close of the battle while pursuing the retreating Confederates. He took part in the Bristoe Campaign, and the regiment was on its veteran furlough from December 1863 to March 1864. He commanded the regiment at the Wilderness and the brigade back in the Shenandoah Valley. Back on the Petersburg lines, he led the Michigan brigade at Five Forks and in the pursuit to Appomattox. His regiment was one of those retained after the peace and he served in the Department of the Missouri, District of the Plains, District of Dakota, and the District of Utah until the regiment was mustered out on March 10, 1866.

STAHEL, Julius (1825-1912)

One of the numerous emigrés to the United States from the revolutions in Europe during the late 1840s, Julius Stahel became a Union major general and earned the Congressional Medal of Honor. His Hungarian name was Számvald and he had risen from private to lieutenant in the Austrian army. However, he was forced to flee when the revolutionaries he had joined were crushed in 1849. For the next decade he was a journalist and educator in England and Germany. Entering the United States in 1859, he was a journalist in New York City for the German-speaking community. Upon the outbreak of the Civil War he was one of the organizers of the "1st German Rifles." His assignments included: lieutenant colonel, 8th New York (ca. April 23, 1861); colonel, 8th New York (August 11, 1861); brigadier general, USV (November 12, 1861); commanding 1st Brigade, Blenker's Division, Army of the Potomac (December 1861-March 13, 1862); commanding 1st Brigade, Blenker's Division, 2nd Corps, Army of the Potomac (March 13-31, 1862); commanding 1st Brigade, Blenker's Division, Mountain Department (April 1-June 26, 1862); commanding 1st Brigade, 1st Division, 1st Corps, Army of Virginia (June 26-August 30, 1862); commanding the division (August 30-September 12, 1862); commanding 1st Division, 11th Corps, Army of the Potomac (September 12, 1862-January 10, 1863); commanding the corps (January 10-19, 1863); commanding Cavalry Division, 22nd Corps, Department of Washington (February 2-June 26, 1863); major general, USV (March 14, 1863); and commanding 1st Cavalry Division, Department of West Virginia (April-June 9, 1864). At 1st Bull Run he commanded the regiment in reserve near Centerville while Louis Blenker led the brigade. He was rapidly promoted colonel and brigadier general and assigned to command of a brigade that was eventually transferred to John C. Frémont's command in western Virginia. He fought against Stonewall Jackson in the Shenandoah and then joined John Pope for the campaign in northern Virginia. At 2nd Bull Run he rose to command of the division when Robert C. Schenck was wounded. When the Army of Virginia was merged into that of the Potomac, Stahel commanded a division of the 11th Corps—and briefly the corps itself—in the vicinity of Washington and the Loudoun Valley during the Antietam and Fredericksburg campaigns. He then directed the mounted arm in the Washington fortifications but found himself without a command when his division was transferred to the Army of the Potomac. He again held a cavalry command under David Hunter. Taking part in the early stages of the Lynchburg expedition, his reputation was tarnished by the poor showing of the Union forces in that campaign. In 1893 however he was rewarded with the Congressional Medal of Honor for the battle of Piedmont where he was severely wounded. By now a major general, he was forced to give up field duty and, until he resigned on February 8, 1865, he was confined to administrative duties and sat as a member of courts-martial. He was subsequently a diplomat to Japan and China and then was engaged in the insurance business.

STANFORD, Amasa Leland (1824-1893)

Besides keeping the state of California in the Union, the main service of Governor Amasa L. Stanford was in aiding the construction of the Central Pacific Railroad. A native of New York, he had practiced law in Wisconsin before settling in California in 1852 where he ran a general store, served as justice of the peace, and was an unsuccessful candidate for state treasurer and governor. He was named a delegate to the Republican National Convention in 1860 but did not attend. The next year he became the president of the Central Pacific and assured Lincoln of the loyalty of his state. That summer he was elected governor and took his seat on January 10, 1862. In this post he furthered the railroad project through the fostering of stock and bond issues. He left office on December 10, 1863, when the state changed from two- to four-year gubernatorial terms; he had not been renominated by his party. In the postwar years he served as president of both the Central Pacific and the Southern Pacific railroads and founded what is now Stanford University in honor of his son. (Hittell, Theodore H., *History of California*)

STANLEY, David Sloane (1828-1902)

As far as William T. Sherman was concerned David S. Stanley did not measure up as a major general and corps commander in an active campaign. The Ohio native had graduated from West Point in 1852 and been posted to the dragoons, with which he saw extensive service on the Indian frontier. He also took part in the Kansas disturbances in the late 1850s and turned down a Confederate colonelcy in 1861. Remaining loyal, his assignments included: 1st lieutenant, 1st Cavalry (since March 27, 1855); captain, 1st Cavalry (March 16, 1861); captain, 4th Cavalry (designation change August 3, 1861); brigadier general, USV (September 28, 1861); commanding 1st Division, Army of the Mississippi (March 4-April 24, 1862); commanding 2nd Division, Army of the Mississippi (April 24-October 26, 1862); commanding 8th Division, Left Wing, 13th Corps, Army of the Tennessee (November 1-11, 1862); chief of Cavalry, Army of the Cumberland (November 1862-January 9, 1863); major general, USV (November 29, 1862); commanding Cavalry Division, Army of the Cumberland (January 9-March 1863); commanding Cavalry Corps, Army of the Cumberland (March-September 9 and November 9-20, 1863); commanding 1st Division, 4th Corps, Army of the Cumberland (November 21, 1863-February 13, 1864 and March 14-July 27, 1864); major, 5th Cavalry (December 1, 1863); and commanding the corps (July 27-December 1, 1864 and January 31-August 1, 1865). As a company commander, he fought at Wilson's Creek and in other engagements in Missouri before transferring to the volunteer service as a brigadier general. But from November 1861 until January 1862 he was out of action due to the accidental breaking of his leg. He then led a division of the Army of the Mississippi—Pope's and later Rosecrans'—at Island #10, during the advance on Corinth, and at the battles of Iuka and Corinth. Promoted to major general, he was placed in charge of the Army of the Cumberland's mounted arm and won a regular army brevet for Murfreesboro. As cavalry chief, he rode through the Tullahoma Campaign but was absent and ill at the time of Chickamauga. He commanded an infantry division during the early part of the Atlanta Campaign and won another brevet at Resaca. Rising to corps command he disappointed Sherman at Jonesboro, and this may have resulted in Stanley's 4th Corps being the one corps of the Army of the Cumberland to be sent back into Tennessee when Sherman was paring down his forces for the March to the Sea. Ironically Stanley won the Congressional Medal of Honor in 1893 for the battle of Franklin in which he was wounded. Having been brevetted brigadier general in the regular establishment for an affair at Ruff's Station the month before, he was brevetted major general for Franklin. Returning to duty in early 1865, Stanley was stationed in Tennessee for the balance of the war and was mustered out of the volunteers on February 1, 1866. Remaining in the army, much of the time on the frontier, he retired in 1892, having been a brigadier general for eight years. (Stanley, David Sloane, *Personal Memoirs of Major General D.S. Stanley, U.S.A.*)

STANLEY, Henry Morton (1841-1904)

John Rowlands renamed himself Henry Morton Stanley after leaving Wales at age 15 as a cabin boy enroute to New Orleans. There he jumped ship and embarked on a most extraordinary career in the Civil War and beyond. Having adopted the name of his New Orleans benefactor, young Stanley was sent to study plantation management in Arkansas, but in July 1861 he ran off and joined the "Dixie Grays," later Company E, 6th Arkansas. Taking part in the rebel attack on the first day at Shiloh, his unit was at a disadvantage, being armed with outmoded steel flintlock muskets. Captured on the second day and confined at Camp Douglas, Chicago, Stanley accepted the unauthorized offer of the commandant, Colonel James A. Mulligan, to take the oath of allegiance and join the Union army. Assigned to an artillery unit he was sent to Harpers Ferry where he promptly fell ill and, on June 22, 1862, was discharged. Stanley went to Cuba in search of his benefactor, discovered he had died, and returned to New York where he enlisted in the Union navy. Serving aboard the USS *Minnesota* he took part in both attacks on Fort Fisher, North Carolina. On February 10, 1865, Stanley, probably the only man to serve in the Union and Confederate armies and the Union navy, ended his military career by deserting in Portsmouth, New Hampshire. Stanley went on to more adventures as a noted journalist and explorer, famed for his Lake Tanganyika greeting "Dr. Livingstone, I presume." (Stanley, Henry Morton, *Autobiography*)

STANLEY, Timothy Robbins (?-1874)

Four months after mustering out with his regiment on November 9, 1864, Connecticut native Timothy R. Stanley was brevetted brigadier general of volunteers for the war. The Ohio lawyer's assignments included: colonel, 18th Ohio (May 29, 1861; three-months unit); colonel, 18th Ohio (August 6, 1861; three-years unit); commanding 29th Brigade, 8th Division, Army of the Ohio (September 14-November 5, 1862); and commanding in the Department and Army of the Cumberland: 2nd Brigade, 2nd Division, Center, 14th Corps (November 5, 1862-January 9, 1863); 2nd Brigade, 2nd Division, 14th Corps (March 5-June 23 and July 23-September 20, 1863); Engineer Brigade (November 1863-April 1864); 1st Separate Brigade, Post of Chattanooga (April-November 1864); and also the post (May-October 17, 1864). For a time he served guarding the Baltimore and Ohio Railroad before reorganizing his three-months unit for a term of three years in advance of its being mustered out in August 1861. Sent into Kentucky, he led his command into middle Tennessee and northern Alabama. He commanded a brigade at Murfreesboro but was on leave at the time of the Tullahoma Campaign. Returning to duty, he was wounded on the second day at Chickamauga. Recovering, he took over the Army of the Cumberland's engineering brigade in time for the breakout from Chattanooga, and he remained on post duty in the city until his unit was finally mustered out. Both before and after the war he was active in Republican politics.

STANNARD, George Jerrison (1820-1886)

The high point of George J. Stannard's distinguished Civil War career came on the third day at Gettysburg while in command of a regiment of green Vermonters. The native Vermonter had been a St. Albans foundry operator and active in the state militia before Fort Sumter was fired upon. Enlisting, his assignments included: colonel, 4th Vermont Militia (prewar); lieutenant colonel, 2nd Vermont (June 20, 1861); colonel, 9th Vermont (July 9, 1862); brigadier general, USV (March 11, 1863); commanding 2nd Brigade, Abercrombie's Division, 22nd Corps, Department of Washington (April 17-June 26, 1863); commanding 3rd Brigade, 3rd Division, 1st Corps, Army of the Potomac (June 26-July 3, 1863); commanding 1st Brigade, 2nd Division, 18th Corps, Army of the James (May 16-June 20, 1864); and commanding 1st Division, 18th Corps, Army of the James (June 20-July 31 and September 15-29, 1864). As a militia officer he was involved in recruiting and organizational work before being himself mustered into the volunteer service. He fought at 1st Bull Run and on the Peninsula. Just after the close of the Seven Days he was named to head a new regiment with which he was captured at Harpers Ferry two months later. Upon his exchange he was given a brigadier's star and placed in charge of a brigade of nine-months regiments from his native state and posted in the defenses of Washington. With Lee's invasion of Maryland and Pennsylvania, his command was ordered to join the Army of the Potomac but missed the fighting of its corps on the first day at Gettysburg. During Pickett's Charge on the third day a gap developed in the Confederate lines and Stannard ordered his men into the gap, firing into both exposed flanks. In the action he was severely wounded by a shell. Returning to duty, he was assigned to the command of a brigade in the army under Benjamin F. Butler. He took part in the operations at Bermuda Hundred and when his corps joined the Army of the Potomac at Cold Harbor suffered a second wound. In the early stages of the Petersburg operations he was again wounded. While in command of a division along the Richmond lines he was wounded at Fort Harrison, losing an arm. He was brevetted major general for this battle. Assigned to the Department of the East upon his recovery, he performed guard and garrison duty along Vermont's border with Canada following the Confederate raid on his hometown. After duty with the Freedmen's Bureau in Baltimore he resigned on June 28, 1866, and was later a customs official and the doorkeeper of the U.S. House of Representatives.

STANTON, Edwin McMasters (1814-1869)

As the most controversial member of Lincoln's cabinet, Edwin M. Stanton nevertheless proved to be a highly capable administrator as the head of the War Department. Born in Ohio, he had proved to be a highly effective attorney in Pittsburgh and Washington. He was a special counsel in the 1856 California fraudulent lands cases and on December 20, 1860, was rewarded with the office of attorney general in the final days of the Buchanan administration. Opposed to slavery, he nonetheless felt that the South's rights had to be protected in order to save the Union. Thus he accepted the Dred Scott decision, supported the Buchanan programs, and backed John C. Breckinridge in the 1860 presidential race. Nominally a Democrat, he had taken little active part in politics until just prior to the Civil War. When the Lincoln administration took office in March 1861 Stanton retired to private life. During this period he was a harsh critic of the Lincoln policies but was nonetheless named to succeed Simon Cameron as secretary of war, in a Republican administration, on January 15, 1862. With no military experience, he moved into the office with zeal, fighting fraud and waste in the rapidly enlarged military. A capable organizer, he brought order out of chaos. He worked well with congressional leaders and his generals in the field. When one, George B. McClellan, a personal friend, failed to perform adequately Stanton was one of the leading forces pushing for his removal. His manner and his restrictions on the press earned him few friends and later led to some apparently unfounded charges that he was behind the assassination of Lincoln. After the end of the war he worked with the Radical

Republicans in their efforts to secure harsher treatment for the South. This brought him into conflict with his new president, Andrew Johnson. Matters came to a head in 1868 when the president sought to remove Stanton from office. Congress reinstated him under the Tenure of Office Act but Johnson persisted. At that point Stanton refused to leave his office until removed by force. He finally quit on May 26, 1868, when it became apparent that Johnson would win out. He resumed his legal practice and in December 1869 was named to the Supreme Court by Grant but died before he could be sworn in. (Thomas, Benjamin P. and Hyman, Harold, *Stanton, the Life and Times of Lincoln's Secretary of War*)

Edwin M. Stanton, controversial secretary of war. (NA)

STAPLES, John Summerfield (ca. 1844-1888)

The draft laws in the North during the Civil War allowed persons drafted but not willing to serve to hire the services of a substitute. Although exempt, because of his position, Abraham Lincoln did not feel it was proper for him to do nothing, so on September 30, 1864, he instructed Provost Marshal General James B. Fry to locate a "representative recruit." The next day there appeared in the president's office one John Staples. Staples, a Pennsylvanian, had agreed to become Lincoln's substitute. He had previously served in a Pennsylvania unit on the North Carolina coast but had been discharged after a four-month bout with typhoid. He was working as a carpenter in the capital and was willing to return to the service. Lincoln paid $500, the previous year the going rate was $300, and wished Staples well. Serving with the 2nd District of Columbia, Staples saw duty as a clerk in Alexandria, Virginia, at Camp Sedgewick, and at the regimental hospital. With the war's end, he was mustered out on September 12, 1865. Subsequently he was a wheelwright in Stroudsburg, Pennsylvania, and Waterloo, New York. He was denied a disability pension because his illness was not considered service related.

STARK, Benjamin (1820-1898)

When President Lincoln's close friend Edward D. Baker was killed in the battle of Ball's Bluff, Benjamin Stark was named to succeed him in the U.S. Senate from Oregon. Born in Louisiana and Connecticut-educated, he had been a merchant in New York City for 13 years before moving his business to San Francisco in 1849. The next year he moved to Oregon and took up the practice of law. He sat in the territorial legislature in 1852 and was a colonel of volunteers in the Indian fighting of 1853. He was in the state legislature in 1860 and took his seat as a Democrat in the Senate on October 29, 1861. Benjamin F. Harding was then elected to permanently fill the seat—Stark was not a candidate for the post—and Stark relinquished his seat on September 12, 1862, and resumed the practice of law. Keeping an active interest in politics, he was a delegate to the Democratic national convention of 1864. Moving back to Connecticut, he sat in that state's legislature and on the board of prison commissioners.

STARKE, Peter Burwell (1815-1888)

Leaving the Mississippi Senate in 1862, Virginia native Peter B. Starke rose to the rank of brigadier general with the cavalry under Nathan Bedford Forrest. His Confederate assignments included: colonel, 28th Mississippi Cavalry (February 24, 1862); brigadier general, CSA (November 4, 1864); commanding brigade, Jackson's Cavalry Division, Army of Tennessee (ca. November 4, 1864-February 18, 1865); and commanding brigade, Chalmers' Division, Forrest's Cavalry Corps, Department of Alabama, Mississippi and East Louisiana (February 18-May 4, 1865). Commanding his mounted regiment he served in the vicinity of Vicksburg until its fall, at which time he was with the forces under Joseph E. Johnston trying to relieve the city. He then took part in the unsuccessful defense of Jackson, Mississippi, against Sherman. Joining the Army of Tennessee in Georgia in the spring of 1864, he fought through the Atlanta Campaign and was promoted to brigadier general during the Franklin-Nashville Campaign. Joining Forrest, he opposed Wilson's raid through Alabama and Georgia. He held several minor offices in Mississippi before returning to Virginia for his remaining years.

STARKE, William Edwin (1814-1862)

When a second brigade of Louisiana troops in Lee's army was formed in the summer of 1862, Virginian William E. Starke was considered a good choice for its brigadier since he had lived in New Orleans for a number of years. Giving up his cotton broker business he entered the military as a colonel and served as an aide-de-camp to General R.S. Garnett until that general's death. His later assignments included: colonel, 60th Virginia (1861); brigadier general, CSA (August 6, 1862); commanding 2nd Louisiana Brigade, Jackson's (old) Division, 2nd Corps, Army of Northern Virginia (mid-August-August 28 and September 7-17, 1862); and commanding the division (August 28-September 7 and September 17, 1862). After serving in western Virginia and North Carolina, Starke joined what was to become the Army of Northern Virginia as a part of A.P. Hill's Division. In the first action of the Seven Days Battles, Mechanicsville, he received a severe wound but insisted upon resuming command for the fighting three days later at Frayser's Farm. A month after the close of the fighting he was promoted and transferred to command the Louisianans assigned to Jackson's former division. Fighting at 2nd Bull Run, he succeeded to command of the division and led it creditably. The same thing happened three weeks later at Antietam but this time General Starke was killed. (Freeman, Douglas S., *Lee's Lieutenants*)

STARKWEATHER, John Converse (1830-1890)

Another of the many careers victimized by Nathan Bedford Forrest was that of John C. Starkweather. The native New Yorker had been practicing law in Wisconsin at the outbreak of the Civil War and he promptly volunteered. His assignments included: colonel, 1st Wisconsin (May 17, 1861); colonel, 1st Wisconsin (three-years unit October 8, 1861); commanding 28th Brigade, 3rd Division, Army of the Ohio (August-September 29, 1862); commanding 28th Brigade, 3rd Division, 1st Corps, Army of the Ohio (September 29-November 5, 1862); commanding 3rd Brigade, 1st Division, Center, 14th Corps, Army of the Cumberland (December 20, 1862-January 9, 1863); commanding 3rd Brigade, 1st Division, 14th Corps, Army of the Cumberland (January 9-March 9 and fall-winter 1863); commanding 2nd Brigade, 1st Division, 14th Corps, Army of the Cumberland (April 21-June 15 and July 30-September 28, 1863); and brigadier general, USV (July 17, 1863). At the head of his three-months regiment, he fought at Falling Waters and Edwards' Ferry, under Robert Patterson, before being mustered out on August 21, 1861. Reenlisting his regiment, he led a brigade at Perryville, Murfreesboro, Chickamauga, and Chattanooga. During the early stages of the Atlanta Campaign he was sent back to command at Pulaski, Tennessee. It was here that Forrest routed his forces and shattered his career in September 1864. He then served on the William A. Hammond court-martial and spent the balance of the war awaiting orders which never came. Philip H. Sheridan absolutely refused to have Starkweather under his command. Resigning on May 11, 1865, he practiced law for the balance of his life, mostly in the nation's capital.

STARR, Ebenezer Townsend (1816-?)

The grandson of an armorer in the Revolution, Ebenezer Starr entered the family firearms business and during the Civil War became the third largest supplier of revolvers to the Union armies. Despite the fact that the family business went under in 1845, Starr continued to tinker and, beginning in 1856, he received 11 patents for firearms. His new Starr Arms Company, of which he served as vice president for mechanical matters, was headquartered in New York City and produced a Model 1858 Percussion Army Revolver. The double-action .44-caliber piece was widely used in the western campaigns of the Civil War. Including an 1863 single-action model, also .44-caliber, and a .36-caliber Navy model, the Starr Arms Company provided 47,952 revolvers to the war effort, placing it just behind Colt and Remington. Due to competition the unit price dropped from $25 to $12. Before the close of hostilities, Starr left the company and faded into obscurity and the firm closed its doors in 1867.

STEARNS, George Luther (1809-1867)

A longtime abolitionist, George Stearns was instrumental in the recruiting of blacks for the Union army. A Massachusetts businessman, Stearns had been an opponent of the Fugitive Slave Law, arming himself to protect any runaway seeking his protection from Federal authorities. He was chairman of the Massachusetts Committee for Kansas which provided arms and other supplies to the anti-slavery elements. He was a financial backer of John Brown's activities and fled to Canada after the Harpers Ferry Raid. Returning shortly, he testified before a Congressional committee that it was among the "greatest events of this age." Following the election of Lincoln, which he had supported, in December 1861 he became the treasurer of the Emancipation League, which tried to influence the administration to make emancipation a war aim. Following the Emancipation Proclamation, he approached Massachusetts Governor John Andrew with a plan to raise a black regiment. Given permission, he recruited the 54th Massachusetts and, without first seeking permission, started raising the 55th. Offering his recruiting organization to the War Department, he was appointed a major and assistant adjutant general and assigned to duty. After raising troops in Pennsylvania, he was sent to Tennessee where he raised six regiments in three months. He also made arrangements for the families of his enlistees. In December 1863 he went on leave and after a dispute with Stanton on his return he resigned. He had been upset about lower pay and more fatigue duty for black soldiers. He initially supported John C. Frémont as a rival to Lincoln in 1864 and then supported the Radical Republicans. After the war he was involved in a number of publications urging better treatment of blacks. (Stearns, Frank P., *Life and Public Services of George Luther Stearns*)

STEDMAN, Edmund Clarence (1833-1908)

A native of Connecticut, poet Edmund C. Stedman had been working for the *New York World* for less than a year when the

Civil War broke out. He was sent to the Virginia front during the first year of the war, but during 1862 and 1863 he left journalism to work in the attorney general's department and the next year became a Wall Street broker. Continuing to write poetry, he became known as "The Bard of Wall Street." During the secession crisis he had written a poem entitled "John Brown's Invasion," and a campaign song, "Honest Abe of the West."

STEEDMAN, James Blair (1817-1883)

Next to George H. Thomas, James B. Steedman was the greatest Union hero to emerge from the defeat at Chickamauga. A printer by trade, he had been born in Pennsylvania and served in the Texan army before sitting in the Ohio legislature. He went to California in search of gold and was publisher of a Douglas Democratic newspaper. Without real combat experience, he was nevertheless helped by his large frame in projecting a sense of authority, and he joined the Union army the same month as the firing on Fort Sumter. His assignments included: colonel, 14th Ohio (April 27, 1861); colonel, 14th Ohio (reorganized September 1, 1861); brigadier general, USV (July 17, 1862); commanding 3rd Brigade, 1st Division, 3rd Corps, Army of the Ohio (September 29-November 5, 1862); commanding 3rd Brigade, 3rd Division, Center, 14th Corps, Army of the Cumberland (November 5, 1862-January 9, 1863); commanding 3rd Brigade, 3rd Division, 14th Corps, Army of the Cumberland (January 9-28, 1863); also commanding the division (January 9-April 17, 1863); commanding 2nd Brigade, 3rd Division, 14th Corps, Army of the Cumberland (April 27-August 15, 1863); commanding 1st Division, Reserve Corps, Army of the Cumberland (August 15-October 9, 1863); commanding 1st Brigade, 2nd Division, 4th Corps, Army of the Cumberland (October 10-18, 1863); commanding Post of Chattanooga, Army of the Cumberland (October 1863-May 1864); major general, USV (April 20, 1864); and commanding District of the Etowah, Department of the Cumberland (November 12, 1864-May 1865). After fighting at Philippi he managed to reenlist most of his men after they had been mustered out on August 13, 1861. Six months after the fighting at Mill Springs he was made a brigadier general and as such he commanded a brigade at Perryville, Murfreesboro, and in the Tullahoma Campaign. At Chickamauga he led his troops through heavy enemy fire to join Thomas' beleaguered command on the second day. For his efforts he was given a second star the next spring. In the meantime he was assigned to post duty at Chattanooga and spent most of the rest of the war in the rear. But during Hood's invasion of Tennessee he commanded a provisional detachment of troops at Nashville. Resigning on August 18, 1866, he became a state legislator and appointive office holder and also returned to journalism.

STEELE, Frederick (1819-1868)

As a Union major general, Frederick Steele led some of the lesser known, but important, operations that occurred west of the Mississippi. The native New Yorker and West Pointer (1843) had been posted to the infantry with which he won two brevets in the Mexican War. The interwar years were filled with routine garrison duties and the ever-slow rate of promotions. His Civil War assignments included: captain, 2nd Infantry (since February 5, 1855); major, 11th Infantry (May 14, 1861); colonel, 8th Iowa (September 23, 1861); brigadier general, USV (January 29, 1862); commanding the army (August 29-October 7, 1862); commanding 1st Division, Army of Southwest Missouri, Department of the Missouri (May 9-August 29, 1862); commanding 1st Division, District of Eastern Arkansas, Department of the Missouri (December 1862); commanding 11th Division, 13th Corps, Army of the Tennessee (December 1862); commanding 4th Division, Yazoo Expedition, Army of the Tennessee (December 18, 1862-January 4, 1863); commanding 1st Division, 2nd Corps, Army of the Mississippi (January 4-12, 1863); commanding 1st Division, 15th Corps, Army of the Tennessee (January 12-July 27, 1863); major general, USV (March 17, 1863, to rank from November 29, 1862); also commanding the corps (July 1863); commanding Arkansas Expedition, Army of the Tennessee (August 10, 1863-January 6, 1864); lieutenant colonel, 13th Infantry (August 26, 1863); commanding 7th Corps, Department of Arkansas (January 6-December 22, 1864); also commanding the department (January 30-December 22, 1864); commanding 1st Division, Reserve Corps, Department of the Gulf (February 3-8, 1865); commanding District of West Florida, Department of the Gulf (ca. March-ca. June 1865); and colonel, 20th Infantry (July 28, 1866). He fought at Dug Springs and then, in command of four companies of regulars, at Wilson's Creek. In the preliminary operations against Vicksburg, he took part in the occupation of Helena, Arkansas. Moving to the eastern side of the Mississippi, he fought under Sherman in the disastrous repulse at Chickasaw Bayou. He then commanded a division under John A. McClernand in the movement up the Arkansas River and the capture of Arkansas Post. The command was later recalled to the main army, and Steele earned a brevet in the operations that led to the fall of Vicksburg. After participating in the Siege of Jackson, Mississippi, he was placed in charge of an expedition which eventually captured Little Rock and for which he was brevetted a regular army brigadier general—by this time he was a full major general of volunteers. In the spring of 1864 it was determined that Steele should launch an expedition southward to cooperate with Banks' command along the Red River line. Steele's so-called Camden expedition failed when Banks was forced to withdraw. His final wartime services came in the operations against Mobile. Brevetted major general in the regular service for the war, he was not mustered out of the volunteers until January 1, 1867. While commanding the Department of the Columbia he suffered fatal injuries when he fell from a carriage during an apoplectic attack.

STEELE, William (1819-1885)

Marriage into a Texas family explains why native New Yorker William Steele became a Confederate brigadier general. A West Pointer (1840), he had been posted to the dragoons, then fought the Seminoles and won a brevet in Mexico. Most of his remaining old army service—until his May 30, 1861, resignation as a captain in the 2nd Dragoons—was spent on the Texas frontier. His Southern assignments included: colonel, 7th Texas Cavalry (1861); brigadier general, CSA (September 12, 1862); and commanding the Trans-Mississippi Department: division, District of Arkansas (spring 1863); Indian Territory (ca. October 3-December 11, 1863); cavalry division, District of West Louisiana (April 12-21, 1864); division, Wharton's Cavalry Corps (April-June 1864); cavalry brigade, District of Texas, New Mexico and Arizona (June-summer 1864); 1st (Texas) Cavalry Brigade, 1st (Texas) Cavalry Division, 2nd Corps (September 1864-March 1865); and division, Wharton's Cavalry Corps (March-May 26, 1865). He took part in Henry H. Sibley's campaign in New Mexico before becoming a brigadier general. Thereafter he led various mounted brigades and divisions in Texas, Louisiana, and Arkansas. In 1863 he commanded in the Indian Territory—now Oklahoma—and later at Galveston. In the Red River Campaign he succeeded Thomas Green in command of the cavalry division. After the Confederacy's collapse he was a commission merchant and adjutant general of Texas.

STEEN, Alexander Early (?-1862)

A brigadier general in the Missouri State Guard, Alexander E. Steen is frequently and erroneously listed as a general in the Confederate army. His actual assignments for the South included: brigadier general, Missouri State Guard (early 1861); commanding 5th Military District, Missouri State Guard (to July 11, 1861); commanding 5th Division, Missouri State Guard (July 11, 1861-March 1862); commanding 3rd Brigade, 1st Division, Army of the West, Department No. 2 (March 1862); and colonel, 10th Missouri (November 10, 1862). He had served in the regular army during the Mexican War in one of the infantry regiments raised for the duration of that conflict and again during the period 1852 to 1861. During this time he had suffered a wound in 1857 on the Gila River in what is now New Mexico. He resigned as first lieutenant, 3rd Infantry, on May 10, 1861. Commanding his division of the state forces, the native Missourian took part in the final stages of the Lexington Siege. In the spring of 1862 he was transferred with the Guard to the east side of the Mississippi. Returning to Missouri he raised a regiment for Confederate service, which was designated the 10th Missouri after his death, and was commissioned its colonel. In the battle of Prairie Grove he was shot in the head and killed while leading his regiment.

STEMBEL, Roger N. (?-?)

Until wounded at Fort Pillow, Union naval officer Roger N. Stembel commanded vessels in some of the more important actions on the western rivers early in the war. With the rank of commander, he directed the USS *Lexington*—one of only two gunboats present—during Grant's fight at Belmont and helped to cover the withdrawal of the Union troops. Again accompanying Grant's army, he took part in the advance up the Tennessee River against Fort Henry. In this action, in which the army played a virtually nonexistent role, Stembel was in command of Foote's flagship *Cincinnati*. In this fight, in which the vessel was armed with six 32-pounders, three eight-inchers, four 42-pounder army rifles, and one 12-pounder boat howitzer, the *Cincinnati* lost one man killed and nine wounded. Stembel went on to command the same craft—having missed the fight at Fort Donelson—at Island #10 and Fort Pillow. At the latter he was severely wounded.

STEPHENS, Alexander Hamilton (1812-1883)

Although he had been a strong unionist until the last moment, Alexander Stephens, called "Little Ellick" in reference to his 90 pounds, became the Confederacy's vice president and a thorn in the side of President Davis. A Georgia lawyer, Stephens served in the state legislature and, from 1843 to 1859, in the U.S. House of Representatives where he quickly became a leader of the Whigs. Despite his strong belief in states' rights he remained a firm believer in the Union and supported Stephen Douglas in 1860. With the defection of other Georgia unionists, he followed his state in secession, attending the secession convention as a unionist delegate but signing the resulting secession document. In February 1861 he took his seat in the Provisional Congress in Montgomery, Alabama, where he chaired the Rules Committee and the Committee on the Executive Departments. His hopes to become provisional president were dashed and he accepted the vice presidency. Under the provisional government this office held no specific responsibilities, so he retained his seat in Congress until the implementation of the permanent Confederate Constitution in February 1862. Almost immediately there was friction between the chief executive and his deputy. Stephens, finding his advice often ignored, became an obstructionist when faced with the president's proposals. After refusing to go on a couple of earlier missions, he had to be ordered to proceed to Virginia as the Confederacy's commissioner to the then-independent state. He soon joined forces with three other Georgians: his brother Linton, Robert Toombs, and Governor Joe Brown. Davis' support for the draft and the right to suspend the writ of habeas corpus provided the malcontents with ammunition in their defense of state sovereignty. Stephens was delighted with the governor's efforts to scuttle conscription by exempting large number of Georgians as being vital to the operation of state government or by placing them in the state militia, which was dubbed "Joe Brown's pets." The vice president was an outspoken proponent of a negotiated peace. It was this position which gave Davis an opportunity to defuse the vice president's attacks. He summoned Stephens from his Liberty Hall estate, to which he retired, often for months at a time, to sulk about the political situation, and assigned him a mission to Washington to deal in public on an exchange of prisoners but also, if the opportunity arose, to discuss a peaceful settlement of the war. Although originally his own idea, Stephens became lukewarm when the mission was set to coincide with the Gettysburg Campaign. The Lincoln administration refused to receive Stephens on the grounds that there were military channels to discuss exchanges. Stephens returned to his sulking and a long

Alexander H. Stephens, troublesome vice president of the Confederacy. (NA)

and heated correspondence with the president. Again, in February 1865, Davis sent Stephens, along with Senator Robert Hunter and Judge John A. Campbell, to meet with Lincoln. This time, on the 3rd, the meeting took place, on the *River Queen* in Hampton Roads, but was a complete failure. Stephens realized that Davis had outsmarted him, knowing the conference was doomed, and was forced to make a formal report to Congress acknowledging the disaster and thus refuting his previous claims of a possible settlement. Returning to Georgia, he saw Davis when they were both captives of the Federal authorities. They never met again. After five months imprisonment in Boston's Fort Warren, Stephens was released, but the next year he was denied the right to sit in the Senate seat to which he had been elected. In 1871 he purchased the *Atlanta Southern Sun*. His publication of *A Constitutional View of the Late War Between the States* was financially highly successful. He returned to the U.S. House of Representatives from 1873 to 1882 before being elected governor of Georgia. He died a few months after taking office. (Von Abele, Rudolph Radama, *Alexander H. Stephens, A Biography*)

STEPHENS, Linton (1823-1872)

Half-brother of the Confederate vice president, Linton Stephens was part of the group of Georgia politicians who were constantly on the alert to protect their native state from the encroachment upon its sovereignty represented by Jefferson Davis. Admitted to the bar, he had served in the state legislature from 1849 to 1855, was an unsuccessful congressional candidate in 1855 and 1857, and was appointed to the state supreme court in 1859. While his half-brother, Alexander, was serving in Washington, Linton served as his Georgia spokesman and shared his views opposing secession. With the outbreak of the war, however, he became the lieutenant colonel of the 15th Georgia, on July 15, 1861. He was forced to resign due to ill health on December 19, 1861. Reelected the same year to the legislature, he served there for the rest of the war as an advocate of a peace settlement and, along with Governor Joe Brown, Robert Toombs, and his half-brother, he was opposed to the policies of the Davis administration and tried to throw numerous obstacles in its path. His home often served as the locale for the group's strategy sessions. Opposed to the central government's direct conscription of troops, he favored the recruitment of troops by the states and supported the governor's policy of granting mass exemptions to the state militia and the padded state payrolls. He even commanded the 7th Georgia State Guard Cavalry Battalion subject to the governor's orders. Following the Confederacy's fall he resumed the practice of law. (Waddell, James D., *Biographical Sketch of Linton Stephens*)

STEPHENS, William H. (?-?)

Entering the Confederate service at the head of the "Jackson Grays," William H. Stephens rose from captain to colonel on May 23, 1861, when the company became Company G, 6th Tennessee. His commands in Department No. 2 included: 4th Brigade, 1st Geographical Division (September 7-October 24, 1861); 2nd Brigade, 2nd Division, 1st Geographical Division (October 24, 1861-March 5, 1862); 2nd Brigade, 1st Grand Division, Army of the Mississippi (March 5-29, 1862); and 2nd Brigade, 2nd Division, 1st Corps, Army of the Mississippi (March 29-April 6, 1862). After transferring from state to Confederate service on August 12, 1861, he was soon given command of a brigade which he commanded at Columbus, Kentucky, during the battle of Belmont across the Mississippi River. He commanded the brigade during the first half of the first day at Shiloh until relieved by Colonel George Maney. Stephens led the regiment during the remainder of the fight but a month later he failed to gain reelection to the colonelcy upon the May 8, 1862, reorganization of the regiment, and his military career ended.

STEUART, George Hume (1828-1903)

Although their state did not secede, a number of Maryland West Pointers joined the Confederacy, among them George H. Steuart of the class of 1848. A veteran of 13 years in the mounted service, he resigned his captaincy on April 22, 1861. His assignments for the Confederacy included: captain, Cavalry (early 1861); lieutenant colonel, 1st Maryland (ca. May 1861); colonel, 1st Maryland (July 21, 1861); brigadier general, CSA (March 6, 1862); commanding in Ewell's Division, Valley District, Department of Northern Virginia: Maryland Line (ca. April-May 24, 1862), Cavalry (May 24-June 2, 1862), and 2nd Brigade (June 4-8, 1862); commanding brigade, Johnson's

Division, 2nd Corps, Army of Northern Virginia (May 28, 1863-May 12, 1864); and commanding Barton's (old) Brigade, Pickett's Division, 1st Corps, Army of Northern Virginia (September 1864-April 9, 1865). Distinguished at 1st Bull Run, he succeeded to regimental command there. He held a series of commands in the Shenandoah Valley Campaign of 1862 until wounded at Cross Keys. After a long recovery he was given command of a brigade which he led at Culp's Hill at Gettysburg. He led it in the fall campaigns of 1863 and at the Wilderness. During the massive Union assault at Spotsylvania's Bloody Angle he was captured along with much of his unit. Exchanged that summer, he commanded a brigade in Pickett's Division for the war's final campaigns. He saw action during the Petersburg fighting and at Five Forks and Sayler's Creek before surrendering at Appomattox. Known as "Maryland" Steuart to distinguish him from the more famous cavalryman, he returned home as a farmer and was active in veterans' organizations. (Freeman, Douglas S., *Lee's Lieutenants*)

STEVENS, Clement Hoffman (1821-1864)

A volunteer aide at the beginning of the Civil War, Connecticut-born Clement H. Stevens rose to the rank of brigadier general in the Confederate service before giving up his life. After serving as a secretary at sea, he had been a South Carolina banker at the outbreak of the Civil War. His Confederate assignments included: volunteer aide-de-camp (summer 1861); colonel, 24th South Carolina (ca. April 1, 1862); brigadier general, CSA (January 20, 1864); and commanding Wilson's (old) Brigade, Walker's Division, Hardee's Corps, Army of Tennessee (ca. February 20-July 20, 1864). During the encirclement of Fort Sumter in Charleston Harbor, Stevens designed an ironclad battery which played a leading role in the reduction of the Federal fort, and the idea was later adapted to the CSS *Virginia*. He then served as a volunteer aide to Bernard E. Bee who was killed at 1st Bull Run. Commissioned colonel of a new regiment, Stevens commanded it at Secessionville and was then sent to Mississippi to aide Joseph E. Johnston in his unsuccessful attempt to lift the siege of Vicksburg. Thereafter he served in the Army of Tennessee. Under Bragg, he fought at Chickamauga and Chattanooga. Wounded at the former, he was named a brigadier general early the next year. Nicknamed "Rock" for his performance at Chickamauga, he led his brigade through the Atlanta Campaign until mortally wounded in the battle of Peach Tree Creek on July 20, 1864. He died on the 25th, in the beleaguered city.

STEVENS, Isaac Ingalls (1818-1862)

Graduating first in his 1839 class at West Point, Isaac Stevens had a distinguished career, in and out of the military, before becoming a general officer in the volunteers during the Civil War. Assigned to the engineers, he had served as a first lieutenant in the Mexican War, being wounded at brevetted captain and major. Resigning in 1853 to become territorial governor of Washington, he made railroad surveys and treaties with the Indians. He served two terms as territorial delegate to Congress and was campaign chairman of the Breckinridge ticket in 1860, for which he lost his seat. Offering his services to the military, Stevens' assignments included: colonel, 79th New York (July 30, 1861); brigadier general, USV (September 28, 1861); commanding 2nd Brigade, W.F. Smith's Division, Army of the Potomac (October 3-26, 1861); commanding 2nd Brigade, in the South Carolina Expeditionary Corps (October 1861-March 15, 1862) and in the Department of the South (March 15-April 1862); commanding 2nd Division, Department of the South (April-July 22, 1862); major general, USV (July 4, 1862); and commanding 1st Division, 9th Corps, Army of the Potomac (July 22-September 1, 1862). Given command of the New York "Highlanders," he brought the demoralized regiment, which had lost its commander at 1st Bull Run, into fighting trim. In the expedition along the South Carolina coast he fought at Port Royal, Coosa River, Stono River, and Secessionville. Made the first commander of the newly organized 9th Corps' 1st Division, he was transferred to Virginia where he led it in the attacks on Jackson's left flank at 2nd Bull Run. On September 1, 1862, at the battle of Chantilly, in reality the last fight of the 2nd Bull Run Campaign, he was instantly killed by a bullet. (Stevens, Hazard, *The Life of Isaac Ingalls Stevens*)

STEVENS, Thaddeus (1792-1868)

Known primarily as an extreme Radical Republican, Thaddeus Stevens was in fact a champion of the equality of man—rich and poor, black and white. Born into a poor Vermont family, Stevens was put through school by his widowed mother. Graduating from Dartmouth, he moved in 1815 to Pennsylvania. Studying law, he later set up his practice in Gettysburg where he became known for defending runaway slaves gratis. His reputation grew for his use of the insanity defense in a murder case, a novelty at the time. Eventually he acquired a great deal of land in the area and went into the iron business. Although one of his forges was a frequent money loser, he kept it going rather than displace his employees. In politics he moved from Federalist to Anti-Mason, to Whig, and finally to Republican. He served in the state legislature from 1833 until 1842, where he is most remembered for his defense of free public schools. He was a master at the distribution of patronage, especially on the unnecessary Gettysburg railroad. In 1842 he returned to the management of his personal affairs, including the donation of land to what is now Gettysburg College. Elected to Congress as a Whig in 1848, he was a constant opponent of extending slavery or appeasing the South in any way. During the Civil War he wielded great influence as head of the House Ways and Means Committee. Although he had supported Lincoln in 1860, he was a constant critic of his moderate actions against the South, favoring instead a war of extermination and recolonization of the South, abolishing the old state lines. With his control of the Congress' purse, he became a leader of the Radical Republicans. The Confederates, however, got even with him for his harsh rhetoric by burning his Caledonia ironworks during the Gettysburg Campaign. Stevens provided for the support of some of the families, who were unemployed by this action, for as long as three years. As chairman of the Committee on Reconstruction, he became an opponent of the Lincoln-Johnson policy as too lenient. It was Stevens who was the prime instigator of the impeachment proceedings against Johnson. He died a few months after the acquittal. In a final declaration for equality, he arranged to be buried in a remote cemetery since it did not have racial barriers. (McCall, Samuel W., *Thaddeus Stevens*)

STEVENS, Walter Husted (1827-1867)

Despite his New York birth and appointment to West Point, Walter H. Stevens developed an attachment to the South through his service there and his marriage into a Louisiana family and so joined the Confederate army, rising to brigadier general. Graduating from the U.S. Military Academy in 1848, he had been posted to the engineers and served with that branch until he was dismissed on May 2, 1861, as a first lieutenant. In fairness to him it must be stated that his resignation had been refused by the War Department, and he was then ousted. His Confederate assignments included: captain, Engineers, (spring 1861); major, Engineers (1861); colonel, Engineers (1862); commanding Richmond Defenses, Department of Richmond (fall 1863-July 1864); chief engineer, Army of Northern Virginia (July 1864-April 9, 1865); and brigadier general, CSA (August 28, 1864). At 1st Bull Run he served as an engineer on the staff of Pierre G.T. Beauregard and then with Joseph E. Johnston in northern Virginia and at Seven Pines. He was then assigned to the construction and command of the defenses of the Confederate capital. Rejoining the main army in Virginia in the summer of 1864, he became its chief engineer and after serving in the Petersburg and Appomattox campaigns was surrendered at the latter place. While working in Mexico on a railroad organized by Emperor Maximilian he died of disease.

STEVENSON, Carter Littlepage (1817-1888)

A veteran of much hard campaigning in the old army, Virginian West Pointer (1838) Carter L. Stevenson became one of the fighting division commanders of the Confederate army of the West. Posted to the infantry, he had fought in the Second Seminole War and in the Mexican War. In the interwar years he campaigned against the Indians on the frontier and participated in the campaign against the Mormons in Utah. When his June 6, 1861, resignation was not forwarded by his superiors, he was dismissed from the regular army as a captain in the 5th Infantry on June 25, 1861. He was charged with having "expressed treasonable designs against" the United States. Joining the Confederacy, his assignments included: major, Infantry (spring 1861); colonel, 53rd Virginia (July 1861); brigadier general, CSA (March 6, 1862, to rank from February 27); commanding 2nd Brigade, Department of East Tennessee (spring-June 1862); commanding 1st Division, Department of East Tennessee (mid-June-December 18, 1862); major general, CSA (October 13, 1862, to rank from the 10th); commanding Defenses of Vicksburg, Department of Mississippi and East Louisiana (December 1862-January 1863); commanding division, 2nd Military District, Department of Mississippi and East Louisiana (January-April 1863); also commanding the district (January-April 1863); commanding division, Department of Mississippi and East Louisiana (April-July 4, 1863); and commanding in the Army of Tennessee: division (early October 1863); division, Hill's-Breckinridge's Corps (October 18-November 1863); division, Hardee's Corps (November 1863-February 20, 1864); division, Hood's-Lee's Corps (February 20, 1864-April 26, 1865); and also the corps (July 18-19, 1864). As a regimental commander, he served in western Virginia. Promoted to brigadier general, he served at Cumberland Gap and in the Kentucky Campaign. Transferred at the end of 1862 to Mississippi, he fought at Chickasaw Bayou and in the defense of Vicksburg. Captured upon the fall of the city, he and his division were exchanged in time to fight at Chattanooga. Long a major general, he led his division in the Atlanta Campaign and then embarked on Hood's invasion of middle Tennessee. At the time of the fight at Franklin his division was still on the south side of Duck River. He did however fight at Nashville and then went on to the Carolinas. Following Joseph E. Johnston's surrender, he was a civil engineer in his native state.

STEVENSON, John Dunlap (1821-1897)

Based upon his record with the volunteers in both the Mexican and Civil wars, John D. Stevenson appears to have earned himself an unusually high position in the enlarged 1866 regular army. A native of the Shenandoah Valley in Virginia, he had taken up the practice of law in Missouri prior to the Mexican war. During that conflict he served as a captain of Missouri cavalry in the Southwest. Between the wars he served as a state legislator before returning to the military. His Civil War assignments included: colonel, 7th Missouri (June 1, 1861); commanding 4th Brigade, 3rd Division, Right Wing, 13th Corps, Army of the Tennessee (November 1-December 18, 1862); brigadier general, USV (November 29, 1862); commanding 3rd Brigade, 3rd Division, 17th Corps, Army of the Tennessee (December 18, 1862-July 20, 1863); commanding the division (July 22-September 1863); commanding District of Corinth, 16th Corps, Army of the Tennessee (December 12, 1863-January 25, 1864); brigadier general, USV (reappointed August 7, 1864, to rank from November 29, 1862); commanding Reserve Division, Department of West Virginia (August 15, 1864-February 21, 1865 and February 27-ca. June 1865); also commanding 3rd Infantry Division, Department of West Virginia (January-April 1865); and commanding the department (February 22-27, 1865). After initial service in Missouri he was transferred with his regiment to western Tennessee and northern Mississippi. Promoted to brigadier, he led a brigade through the entire campaign for Vicksburg. Later that summer he led an expedition into northern Louisiana and was assigned to guard the railroad in preparation for the Atlanta Campaign. However, he resigned on April 22, 1864, and was relieved of duty on May 12. But by midsummer he had accepted reappointment—with rank from his original commission—and was assigned to duty at Harpers Ferry. Here he greatly annoyed his superior, Sheridan, with constant suggestions on how to deal with the pesky partisan rangers. However, some of the Valley native's advice was acted upon—without credit. At the end of the war he was brevetted major general and mustered out on January 15, 1866. Later that year he was named a colonel in the expanded regular establishment. After a year without an assignment in 1869 and 1870, he was named to command the 25th Infantry, a colored unit. Sixteen days later he was discharged at his own request. Reurning to St. Louis, he practiced law.

STEVENSON, Thomas Greely (1836-1864)

A militia major before the Civil War, Boston native Thomas G. Stevenson was twice appointed a brigadier general before being killed at Spotsylvania. His assignments included: major, 4th Massachusetts Militia Battalion (prewar); colonel, 24th Massachusetts (December 3, 1861); brigadier general, USV (December 24, 1862); commanding 2nd Brigade, 1st Division, Department of North Carolina (April 2, 1862-January 2, 1863); commanding 2nd Brigade, 4th Division, 18th Corps, Department of North Carolina (January 2-February 1863); commanding 1st Brigade, 2nd Division, 18th Corps, Department of North Carolina (March 6-April 16, 1863); also commanding 1st Brigade, 1st Division, (detachment 18th Corps), St. Helena Island, 10th Corps, Department of the South (March 6-April 17, 1863); reappointed brigadier general, USV (April 9, 1863, to rank from March 14); commanding brigade, U.S. Forces Seabrook Island, 10th Corps, Department of the South (April 16-May 11, 1863); commanding the island (May 11-July 6, 1863); commanding 1st Brigade, 1st Division 10th Corps, Department of the South (July 6-19, 1863); commanding 3rd Brigade, Morris Island, 10th Corps, Department of the South (July 19-September 19 and October 19-November 23, 1863); commanding 1st Brigade, Morris Island, 10th Corps, Department of the South (November 23, 1863-January 15, 1864); and commanding 1st Division, 9th Corps, Army of the Potomac (April 19-May 10, 1864). On the North Carolina coast his command took part in the operations against Roanoke Island and New Bern. Promoted to brigadier general in late 1862, his commission was allowed to expire by the Senate on March 4, 1863. Reappointed the next month, he spent most of the next year operating against Charleston. After a bout with malaria in early 1864 he rejoined Ambrose E. Burnside as a division leader in the 9th Corps, which was to accompany the Army of the Potomac in Grant's Overland Campaign. He served in the Wilderness and went on to Spotsylvania where he was killed on May 10, 1864.

STEWART, Alexander Peter (1821-1908)

Known to his men as "Old Straight," Alexander P. Stewart rose to the temporary command of the infantry and artillery of the Army of Tennessee in the final stages of the Civil War. The Tennessean West Pointer (1842) had served in the artillery until his 1845 resignation as a second lieutenant in the 3rd Artillery. For the next decade and a half he was a professor at Cumberland University in his native state. Upon the outbreak of the Civil War he joined the Confederacy, where his assignments included: major, Artillery (1861); brigadier general, CSA (November 8, 1861); commanding brigade, 1st Geographical Division, Department #2 (December 1861-February 1862); commanding brigade, McCowan's Command, 1st Geographical Division, Department #2 (February-April 1862); commanding 2nd Brigade, 1st (Clark's) Division, 1st Corps, Army of the Mississippi (early April-April 6 and April 14-July 2, 1862); commanding the division (April 6-14, 1862); commanding 2nd Brigade, 1st (Cheatham's) Division, Army of the Mississippi (July 2-August 1862); commanding 2nd Brigade, Cheatham's Division, Right Wing, Army of the Mississippi (August-November 20, 1862); commanding 2nd Brigade, Cheatham's Division, Polk's Corps, Army of Tennessee (November 20, 1862-February 27, 1863); commanding McCown's (old) Division, Polk's Corps, Army of Tennessee (February 27-June 6, 1863); major general, CSA (June 5, 1863); commanding division, Hardee's-Hill's-Breckinridge's-Hindman's-Hood's Corps, Army of Tennessee (June 6-September 1, 1863 and October 1, 1863-July 7, 1864); commanding division, Buckner's Corps, Army of Tennessee (September 1-October 1, 1863); lieutenant general, CSA (June 23, 1864); commanding army of Mississippi (Polk's Corps), Army of Tennessee (July 7-26, 1864); commanding corps, Army of Tennessee (July 26-29, 1864, August 1864-March 1865, and April 9-26, 1865); and commanding the army (March-April 9, 1865). As an artillery officer, he commanded the guns stationed at Columbus, Kentucky, and thus witnessed the fight across the river at Belmont. The next day he was named a brigadier general and he led his brigade at Island #10. At Shiloh he succeeded to command of the division when Charles Clark was wounded. Again in charge of a brigade he participated in the defense of Corinth, Mississippi, and fought at Perryville and Murfreesboro. He led a division as a major general, in the Tullahoma Campaign and at Chickamauga and Chattanooga. During the Atlanta Campaign he was promoted to lieutenant general and assigned to replace Leonidas Polk in command of what was still styled the "Army of Mississippi" but was in actuality a corps of the Army of Tennessee. Wounded at Ezra Church, he recovered to take part in the final stages of the Atlanta fighting and then went on Hood's ill-fated expedition into middle Tennessee. There he fought at Franklin and Nashville before moving into the Carolinas. When Joseph E. Johnston took charge of the varied forces in North Carolina, Stewart took command of the infantry and artillery of the Army of Tennessee proper until the final reorganization on April 9, 1865. From then until the end he was again in corps command. He was later an educator, businessman, and commissioner of the Chickamauga and Chattanooga National Military Park. (Wingfield, Marshall, *General A.P. Stewart, His Life and Letters*)

STEWART, Joseph B. (?-?)

One of the few people who apparently kept their cool when Lincoln was shot in Ford's Theater was Joseph B. Stewart. Seated in the front row, he immediately recognized the assassin as John Wilkes Booth when he landed on the stage. Stewart himself then sprang on stage and began to give chase, yelling "Stop that man!" Slowed by someone slamming the exit door—he testified that it was probably Edmund Spangler—he caught up with Booth when the killer had already mounted and was taking off. He was unsuccessful in his attempts to grab hold of the reins. During the trial he testified that Spangler appeared to be in perfect control of the situation and could have blocked Booth's escape route but made no effort to do so.

STEWART, Richard H. (?-?)

John Wilkes Booth was so outraged by the treatment he had received at the farm of Dr. Richard H. Stewart that he sent back a highly insulting note and $2.50 as a further insult for the food that he and David Herold had received. Stewart was the richest man in Virginia's King George County and was a staunch Confederate. His place was the first stopping point for the fugitives since crossing the Potomac, but the doctor was outraged to find the assassin of Lincoln at his door. Not inviting the pair into the house—it was full of relatives and others returning from the war—he made them stay outside. He did, however, provide them with food. Whether or not it was by Stewart's arrangement, the fleeing men were able to get a wagon and team driven by William Lucas, a black living on the farm, to take them to Port Conway on the Rappahannock River. When detectives came to question him later, Dr. Stewart readily admitted that two men had come to his door and that one was lame. Explaining that he was not a surgeon, he declared that he had not provided medical treatment. Despite seeing the insulting note from Booth, the detectives were skeptical and took him into custody. He was later freed.

STEWART, William Morris (1827-1909)

When Nevada was admitted to the Union in 1864, William M. Stewart became its first senator. Born in New York, he had moved with his parents to Ohio where he eventually taught school before going to San Francisco where he engaged in mining. In 1850, two years after his arrival, he was admitted to the bar and later served as a district attorney. In 1854 he was the state's attorney general. Six years later he settled in Nevada and again engaged in mining operations. The next year he served on the territorial council and in 1863 was a member of the state constitutional convention. With statehood, he became, as a Republican, Nevada's senior senator. He took his seat on December 15, 1864, and by lot it was determined that his term would expire in 1869. Reelected, he remained in Washington until 1875 and then resumed the practice of law. He served three more terms in the Senate, from 1887 to 1905, but did not seek a fourth consecutive term, instead retiring in the nation's capital. (Brown, George R., ed., *Reminiscences of Senator William Morris Stewart*)

STILLSON, Jerome Bonaparte (1841-1880)

The highly successful journalism career of Jerome B. Stillson may have gotten off to a slow start in the Civil War, but he was well on the way to the top of his profession when he died at the age of 39. A native New Yorker, his performance during Grant's Overland Campaign had been disappointing. He redeemed himself covering Philip H. Sheridan's campaign in the Shenandoah Valley in the fall of 1864, as a reporter for the *New York World*. After the war he served in editorial positions before returning to reporting. Following the 1876 battle of the Little Big Horn—Custer's swan song—Stillson was granted an interview with Sitting Bull. (Starr, Louis M., *Bohemian Brigade*)

STIMERS, Alban C. (1827-1876)

A hero of the clash between the *Monitor* and the *Merrimac*, Alban C. Stimers was subsequently forced out of the U.S. Navy. The New York-born Stimers had entered the navy in 1849 as a third assistant engineer. By the outbreak of the Civil War he had risen to the rank of chief engineer aboard the USS *Roanoke* and was part of the commission which recommended against the government's purchase of the Stevens Battery. On November 5, 1861, he was assigned to assist Swedish-born engineer John Ericsson, then working in New York on the construction of the Union's first successful ironclad as a counter to the threat posed by the Confederate ironclad *Virginia*, which was being constructed from the remains of the scuttled USS *Merrimac*. Ironically, before the war Stimers had served aboard this reconstructed ship. Working 16 hours a day, he was responsible for keeping construction as close to schedule as possible. Since the *Monitor* was only rated for an assistant engineer, Stimers went along as a "technical passenger" on its cruise to Hampton Roads. During the voyage the vessel nearly foundered, and it was Stimers who got the blowers and boilers working again, after the rest of the crew in the boiler room had passed out from carbon monoxide. During the battle with the *Virginia* he worked the mechanism for rotating the turret and later assumed command of one of the gun crews. Shortly afterwards, he rejoined Ericsson in New York for work on the 10-member *Passaic* class of monitors. Stimers was present during Du Pont's attack on Charleston Harbor, with mechanics who repaired the damaged monitors for the resumption of the engagement which never came. In order to diffuse criticism of himself for the action, Du Pont pressed charges against Stimers. The charges were dismissed as spurious. Although no longer on good terms with Ericsson, Stimers was given charge by the Navy Department of the 20-member *Casco* class. Due to a series of change orders and supply problems, the vessels were found to draw too much water for their designed purpose. A congressional investigation found him guilty of a professional error, and he was thereafter assigned to relatively unattractive duty until he resigned on August 3, 1865. He died in 1876 following a civilian career in steam engineering.

STOKES, James Hughes (1815-1890)

It was not until well after the fighting had ended that Captain James H. Stokes was promoted to brigadier general in the Union army. The native Marylander and West Pointer (1835) had served with the artillery and then in the quartermaster's department until his 1843 resignation as a captain. In the meantime he fought the Seminoles in Florida and took part in the Trail of Tears incident. He was in railroading in Illinois until the Civil War. His assignments in that conflict included:

captain, Chicago (Ill.) Board of Trade Battery (July 31, 1862); lieutenant colonel and quartermaster (February 10-August 22, 1864); captain and assistant adjutant general, USV (August 22, 1864); and brigadier general, USV (July 20, 1865). With neighboring Missouri on the brink of secession, Stokes managed to spirit away 20,000 firearms from the St. Louis arsenal to Illinois. For the next year he engaged in the acquisition of arms for his adopted state and then recruited a battery. With this battery, he served at Murfreesboro with the Pioneer Brigade and later in the Tullahoma and Chickamauga campaigns with the Army of the Cumberland's Cavalry Corps. At Chattanooga he was in charge of a division of reserve artillery. Early in 1864 he was assigned to duty as an inspector of the quartermaster service. However, on August 22, 1864, he was mustered out of this position and was recommissioned, again as a captain, in the adjutant's branch. In this capacity, he served in the capital's defenses until promoted to brigadier general. Mustered out on August 24, 1865, he fought off growing blindness, stemming from his Florida service, and engaged in the Chicago real estate business.

STOLBRAND, Charles John (1821-1894)

Charles Stolbrand was the only Swedish-born general officer in the Union army. An artilleryman in the Schleswig-Holstein War of 1848 to 1850, Stolbrand came to settle in Chicago. He raised Battery G, 2nd Illinois Light Artillery, and was made its captain on October 5, 1861. His later assignments included: major, 2nd Illinois Light Artillery (December 3, 1861); brigadier general, USV (February 18, 1865); and commanding 2nd Brigade, 4th Division, 17th Corps, Army of the Tennessee (April 28-June 15, 1865). As an artillery major, Stolbrand took part in the capture of Island #10 in the Mississippi and was General Logan's artillery chief from the fall of 1862 through January 1865. He served in charge of the division's artillery at Port Gibson, Raymond, Champion Hill, and during the Vicksburg siege. During the Atlanta Campaign he was chief of artillery for Logan's 15th Corps, Army of the Tennessee. He was captured on May 19, 1864, while making a reconnaissance near Kingston. Escaping five months later he rejoined the corps for the Savannah Campaign. Due to the slow promotions in the artillery service, Stolbrand, still a major, decided to resign in January 1865. General Sherman sent him "home" via the White House to deliver some dispatches. In fact they were a strong recommendation from the general, and Lincoln immediately appointed Stolbrand a brigadier and returned him to Sherman. In the final days of the war a brigade was organized for him, and in June, after war's end, he was dispatched with the brigade to the District of Kansas. After serving on the plains he was mustered out on January 15, 1866, and settled in Charleston, South Carolina, where he became a Republican politician and served in several government offices.

STONE, Charles Pomeroy (1824-1887)

Ironically, the man who would later lay the foundation for the Statue of Liberty in New York Harbor, Charles P. Stone, had been confined, without charges, for 189 days in the same harbor during the Civil War. A Massachusetts native and West Pointer (1845), he had served in the ordnance branch, earning two brevets in Mexico, before resigning in 1856 to enter private business. An exploration of Mexico led to his publication of *Notes on the State of Sonora*. Donning his uniform again at the outbreak of the Civil War, his assignments included: colonel and inspector general, District of Columbia Volunteers (April 16, 1861); commanding District of Columbia Volunteers (April 16-July 23, 1861); colonel, 14th Infantry (to rank from May 14, 1861); brigadier general, USV (to rank from May 17, 1861); commanding 7th Brigade, 3rd Division, Department of Pennsylvania (July 1861); commanding 3rd Brigade, Department of the Shenandoah (July 25-August 8, 1861); commanding brigade, Division of the Potomac (August-October 3, 1861) commanding division, Army of the Potomac (October 3, 1861-February 8, 1862); chief of staff, Department of the Gulf (July 25, 1863-April 16, 1864); and commanding 1st Brigade, 2nd Division, 5th Corps, Army of the Potomac (August 21-September 10, 1864). He played a key role in maintaining order during Lincoln's inauguration, while heading the forces in the capital, and was soon appointed commander of one of the new regular army infantry regiments and a brigadier of volunteers. He served with Patterson and in the Shenandoah Valley. While Stone was commanding a division along the Potomac, one of his subordinates, Edward Baker, exceeded orders and crossed his entire brigade over the river. Baker, a personal friend of Lincoln, was killed in the resultant debacle at Ball's Bluff. A scapegoat was needed and Stone seemed to fit the bill. He appeared several times before the Joint Committee on the Conduct of the War where he was accused of being too friendly with secessionists and enemy commanders, even of having gone so far as to return an escaped slave to his master. Late on the night of February 8, 1862, Stone was arrested without charges and whisked away to Fort Lafayette in New York Harbor. Held incommunicado, he was eventually transferred to solitary confinement in Fort Hamilton. His requests for a court of inquiry were rejected. Finally, after 189 days he was reluctantly freed—without charges ever having been placed against him. For nine months after his August 6, 1862 release he was unassigned. During the operations against Port Hudson he was present and was later Banks' chief of staff. By order of the War Department he was mustered out of his volunteer commission on April 4, 1864, and spent another period unemployed. Using his regular rank, he commanded a brigade in the Army of the Potomac during part of the Petersburg operations. Possibly due to constant surveillance, he resigned that commission also on September 13, 1864. Never charged and never cleared, he nonetheless prospered in civil life as an engineer. He served in Egypt for 13 years, becoming a lieutenant general and chief of staff in the service of the Khedive. In the last year of his life he constructed the pedestal for France's gift to the United States. (Johnson, Robert U. and Buel, Clarence C., eds., *Battles and Leaders of the Civil War*)

STONE, Lucy (1818-1893)

Married to a fellow reformer Henry Blackwell, Lucy Stone continued to use her maiden name, with her husband's blessing, starting a tradition in emancipated marriages. She revolted against her traditional family upbringing and demanded equal treatment for women. After graduating from Oberlin College, the only higher institution then admitting women, she became a lecturer for the Massachusetts Anti-Slavery Society. Although she had resolved not to marry, she finally consented when pursued persistently by fellow reformer Blackwell in 1855. The pair had a truly liberated marriage, often sharing the same platform, as individuals, in the causes of abolition and women's rights. Their marriage ceremony, performed by Thomas Wentworth Higginson, an abolitionist preacher, was preceded by a joint statement protesting the standard matrimonial laws. However, the birth of a child soon placed her in semi-retirement. In 1867 she resumed her career, working for equal suffrage for both blacks and women. She was active in the field almost until the time of her death from cancer. One of her more controversial actions was a refusal to pay her property taxes since she was denied representation. (Wheeler, Leslie, *Loving Warriors*)

STONE, Robert King (?-?)

Lincoln's personal surgeon, Robert K. Stone, did not reach the mortally wounded president's side until after he had been moved across the street to the Petersen House from Ford's Theater. By that time Lincoln's pulse had been restarted by the first two doctors to reach his side, Charles A. Leale and Charles Taft. It was at the special request of Mary Lincoln that Stone was summoned to take charge of the case. He quickly realized that there was no hope and so informed Robert Lincoln. Stone remained at the house until the next morning when Lincoln died. At noon he took part in the autopsy.

STONE, Roy (?-1901)

Although brevetted brigadier general, Roy Stone did not achieve the full grade until the Spanish-American War. His Civil War assignments included: major, 13th Pennsylvania Reserves (June 21, 1861); colonel, 149th Pennsylvania (August 30, 1862); commanding 2nd Brigade, 3rd Division, 1st Corps, Army of the Potomac (February 16-July 1, 1863); and commanding 3rd Brigade, 4th Division, 5th Corps, Army of the Potomac (March 25-May 6, 1864). As a major he led his first regiment in the battles of the Seven Days before being given a regiment of his own. Serving in the Washington defenses until December 1862, the regiment saw no action. Soon given a brigade, Stone led it at Chancellorsville and on the first day at Gettysburg where he fell wounded in the fighting near the McPherson Barn. Captured and paroled by the Confederates, he returned to duty in time to command the brigade at the Wilderness where he was injured when his horse fell on him on the second day. He commanded the volunteer depot at Camp Curtin, near Harrisburg, Pennsylvania, from September 7 until December 15, 1864, when ordered to take command of the prison at Alton, Illinois. Tendering his resignation on January 27, 1865, he was not relieved until March 6. He received a brevet as brigadier general of volunteers for Gettysburg and was commissioned brigadier general, USV, during the war with Spain.

STONE, William Milo (1827-1893)

A founder of the Iowa Republican Party, William M. Stone resigned a colonelcy to run for the governorship in 1863. The native New Yorker had practiced law in Ohio before moving to Iowa in 1854. There he practiced law and edited the *Knoxville Journal*. He also served as a judge in the late 1850s. He entered the army in 1861 and his assignments included: captain, Company B, 3rd Iowa (June 8, 1861); major, 3rd Iowa (June 26, 1861); colonel, 22nd Iowa (September 9, 1862); commanding District of Rolla, Department of the Missouri (temporarily in December 1862); commanding 2nd Brigade, 1st Division, 13th Corps, Army of the Tennessee (July 28-August 7, 1863); and commanding 2nd Brigade, 1st Division, 13th Corps, Department of the Gulf (August 7-15, 1863). On September 17, 1861, he was wounded at Blue Mills in Missouri and the next spring was captured at Shiloh. Exchanged he was given the colonelcy of a new regiment which he led in the Vicksburg Campaign, sustaining another wound. He served through the operations against Jackson, Mississippi, commanding a brigade part of the time. His corps was then transferred to the Department of the Gulf, but he resigned on August 13, 1863, to accept the Iowa gubernatorial nomination. The Republican was elected and took his seat on January 14, 1864. During his two terms relief for soldiers' families was voted in and the militia was organized. Also, the antislavery constitutional amendment was approved. Later, he was a land office commissioner.

STONEMAN, George (1822-1894)

Somehow the cavalry raids of George Stoneman never seemed to achieve the results hoped for by the Union authorities. The native New Yorker and West Pointer (1846) had been posted to the dragoons and then the cavalry before the Civil War. During the Mexican War he had served in California and later on the Indian frontier. His Civil War assignments included: captain, 2nd Cavalry (since March 3, 1855); major, 1st Cavalry (May 9, 1861); major, 4th Cavalry (designation change August 3, 1861); brigadier general, USV (August 13, 1861); commanding Cavalry Division, Reserve, Army of the Potomac (August 14-October 1861); commanding Stoneman's Cavalry Command, Army of the Potomac (October 1861-January 1862); commanding Stoneman's Command, Army of the Potomac (June-July 1862); commanding 1st Division, 2nd Corps, Army of the Potomac (July 17-August 15, 1862); commanding Cavalry Division, Army of the Potomac (August-September 1862); commanding 1st Division, 3rd Corps, Army of the Potomac (September 13-October 30, 1862); commanding the corps (October 30, 1862-February 5, 1863); major general, USV (November 29, 1862); commanding Cavalry Corps, Army of the Potomac (February 12-May 22, 1863); chief of Cavalry Bureau (1863); lieutenant colonel, 3rd Cavalry (March 30, 1864); commanding 23rd Corps, Army of the Ohio (February 10-April 4, 1864); commanding Cavalry Division, 23rd Corps, Army of the Ohio (April 10-July 31, 1864); commanding the army (November 17, 1864-January 17, 1865); and commanding District of East Tennessee, Department of the Cumberland (March 9-June 27, 1865). He led a mixed force on the Peninsula

George Stoneman, unsuccessful Union cavalry raider. (*Leslie's*)

during the Seven Days. In the summer of 1862 he commanded the Army of the Potomac's cavalry and then was assigned to the 3rd Corps at Washington during the Maryland Campaign. He led the corps at Fredericksburg where he won a regular army brevet. During the Chancellorsville Campaign he led a raid toward Richmond that did little more than leave Joseph Hooker with virtually no cavalry. Sent to head the cavalry bureau he returned to the field the next year in East Tennessee and took part in the Atlanta Campaign. When that city was invested Stoneman and Edward M. McCook were dispatched to wreck the railroad to the south in an effort to dislodge Hood's army. Stoneman also received permission to attempt to effect the release of the Union prisoners at Andersonville. It turned into a debacle when Stoneman was captured himself near Macon on July 31, 1864, by Wheeler's cavalry. Exchanged in October, he led a raid against the Confederate salt works and lead mines in southwestern Virginia during the last month of the year. His final raid of the war, into North Carolina, was launched too late to be of much assistance to Sherman's army. He was, however, brevetted brigadier general of regulars for the capture of Salisbury, North Carolina. Also brevetted major general for the war, he was mustered out of the volunteer service on September 1, 1866, and reverted to his regular army rank. He served in the Southwest until his 1871 retirement as colonel, 21st Infantry. Settling in California, he was in railroading and served a term as governor. (Van Nappen, Ina Woestemeyer, *Stoneman's Last Raid*)

STOREY, Wilbur Fisk (1819-1884)

With his sharp editorial criticism of the administration's war aims, Wilbur Storey managed to bring down the wrath of the Union army on his newspaper. At the outbreak of the Civil War, Vermont-born Storey was the publisher of the *Detroit Free Press*, one of the leading Democratic organs in the West. During the first year of the conflict, Storey purchased the *Chicago Times* from Cyrus McCormick and continued to support the prosecution of the war until Lincoln issued the Emancipation Proclamation in September 1862. He felt that the administration had deceived the country as to its goals for the war. He launched blistering attacks on the government and the *Times* became a copperhead paper. Describing Storey's attacks as "incendiary," the commander of the Department of the Ohio, General Ambrose Burnside, ordered the suppression of the *Times* on June 3, 1863. The army's occupation of the premises brought angry mobs into the streets of Chicago as Peace Democrats and Republicans faced each other. The Copperheads threatened to burn the plant of the pro-Union *Tribune* in retaliation for the closure. To prevent rioting, Lincoln was wired to revoke the general's order. It was revoked the next day. The *Times* resumed its attacks but with a bit less venom. Following the war, Storey continued with his view of journalism as "raising hell" by campaigning against political corruption. He continued his crusading journalism until he suffered a stroke in 1878.

STOUGHTON, Edwin Henry (1838-1868)

When Edwin H. Stoughton was captured by John S. Mosby, Lincoln was far more upset by the loss of horses in the raid, explaining, "I can make new brigadier generals, but I can't make horses." The native Vermonter had graduated from the five-year class of 1859 at West Point and been posted to the infantry. His Civil War assignments included: second lieutenant, 6th Infantry (since September 5, 1859); colonel, 4th Vermont (September 21, 1861); commanding 3rd Brigade, 1st Division, 6th Corps, Army of the Potomac (October-early November 1862); brigadier general, USV (November 5, 1862); commanding 2nd Brigade, Casey's Division, Military District of Washington, Department of the Potomac (November 5, 1862-February 2, 1863); and commanding 2nd Brigade, Casey's Division, 22nd Corps, Department of Washington (February 2-March 8, 1863). Resigning his regular commission on March 4, 1861—the date of Lincoln's inauguration—he received a colonelcy in the volunteers the next fall. Commanding his regiment, he fought at Yorktown, Williamsburg, and the Seven Days. Following a three-month leave he returned to command the brigade briefly before being named a brigadier and assigned to the capital's defenses. Making his headquarters at Fairfax Court House, at some distance from his men, he quickly gained a reputation for his fondness for liquor and women. Following a party he retired to bed on March 8, 1863, only to be awakened by a man who inquired if he knew of Mosby. Stoughton roused himself, thinking someone had caught the guerrilla only to find that it was Mosby in person, and Stoughton was a captive. Having failed to gain Senate approval, his brigadier's commission had expired four days earlier and was not renewed following his May release from Libby Prison where Mosby's daring raid—with only 29 men—had landed him. He entered upon the practice of law in New York until his death. (Jones, Virgil Carrington, *Gray Ghosts and Rebel Raiders*)

STOVALL, Marcellus Augustus (1818-1895)

After fighting the Seminoles in Florida, Georgia native Marcellus A. Stovall studied for a year at West Point before resigning due to ill health in 1837, but he went on to become a Confederate brigadier general. His assignments included: captain, Cherokee (Ga.) Artillery (1861); colonel, Georgia Artillery (1861); lieutenant colonel, 3rd Georgia Battalion (October 8, 1861); brigadier general, CSA (January 20, 1863); commanding brigade, Breckinridge's Division, Department of the West (June 6-August 25, 1863); commanding brigade, Breckinridge's Division, Hill's-Breckinridge's Corps, Army of Tennessee (August 28-November 12, 1863); and commanding brigade, Stewart's-Clayton's Division, Breckinridge's-Hindman's-Hood's-Lee's Corps, Army of Tennessee (November 12, 1863-early 1865). His initial service came in East Tennessee and during the Kentucky Campaign. He commanded his battalion at Murfreesboro before being named a brigadier general. He led a brigade under Joseph E. Johnston trying to relieve the Vicksburg garrison. He later fought at Chickamauga, Chattanooga, during the Atlanta Campaign, and at Franklin and Nashville. His final service came in the Carolinas Campaign in which he served in the early stages. After the war he engaged in the cotton, fertilizer, and chemical businesses.

STOWE, Harriet Beecher (1811-1896)

The sister of Henry Ward Beecher, Harriet Beecher Stowe was able to focus public attention upon the slavery question through the publication of her novel *Uncle Tom's Cabin*. A native of Connecticut, she had briefly visited Kentucky where she was able to view slavery firsthand and gain material for her later writings. Accompanying her husband to Bowdoin College in Maine, she, with his encouragement, finally decided to write about her observations in the earlier Kentucky visit. The novel was serialized in the abolitionist *National Era* in 1851 and 1852, then, in 1852 appeared in book form and sold 10,000 copies the first week and 300,000 in 10 months. Another 150,000 were sold in Great Britain and by the outbreak of the Civil War over a million had been sold, including pirated editions. Condemned for alleged distortions by Southerners, she received much hate mail, including a severed black ear. While the book was not a literary masterpiece, it did have a great impact upon the political scene of the day. She continued to write for many years but never again achieved the same level of success. (Gilbertson, Catherine, *Harriet Beecher Stowe* and Wilson, Robert Forrest, *Crusader in Crinoline, the Life of Harriet Beecher Stowe*)

STRAHL, Otho French (1831-1864)

At the age of 34, Ohio native Otho F. Strahl became one of six Confederate generals to be killed at Franklin. The Tennessee lawyer's assignments included: captain, 4th Tennessee (May 1861); lieutenant colonel, 4th Tennessee (May 15, 1861); colonel, 4th Tennessee (ca. May 1862); commanding Stewart's (old) Brigade, Cheatham's Division, Polk's Corps, Army of Tennessee (July-November 1863); brigadier general, CSA (July 28, 1863); commanding brigade, Stewart's Division, Breckinridge's-Hindman's Corps, Army of Tennessee (November 1863-February 20, 1864); and commanding brigade, Cheatham's-Brown's Division, Hardee's-Cheatham's Corps Army of Tennessee (February 20-November 30, 1864). At Shiloh he succeeded to command of the regiment and was soon promoted to colonel. He then served in the Corinth siege and fought at Perryville. At Murfreesboro he commanded the consolidated 4th and 5th Tennessee. After serving in the Tullahoma Campaign he was promoted to brigadier general, and he led a brigade at Chickamauga, Chattanooga, and during the Atlanta Campaign. Accompanying John B. Hood into middle Tennessee, he died in front of the Union works at Franklin during the suicidal attack ordered by Hood.

Harriet Beecher Stowe of *Uncle Tom's Cabin* fame. (NA)

STREIGHT, Abel D. (?-1892)

Launching his raid into the Deep South at approximately the same time as Grierson's raid, Abel D. Streight was not as fortunate. Born in New York, he had entered the Union army from Indiana and his assignments included: colonel, 51st Indiana (December 12, 1861); commanding Provisional Brigade, 14th Corps, Army of the Cumberland (April-May 3, 1863); and commanding 1st Brigade, 3rd Division, 4th Corps, Army of the Cumberland (November 17, 1864-March 15, 1865). Arriving too late for the fighting at Shiloh, he took part in the siege operations against Corinth and was in reserve at Perryville. After fighting at Murfreesboro he proposed a mounted raid from Nashville into Alabama and Georgia to destroy railroads and hopefully force Bragg's Army of Tennessee out of middle Tennessee. Setting out on April 11, 1863, with about 1,700 men mounted mostly on mules—but with many on foot, waiting to mount captured horses and mules—he soon ran into delays. With Forrest's cavalry hot on his tail, he fought delaying actions, principally at Sand Mountain and Hog Mountain on the last day of April. Finally, on May 3, 1863, he surrendered his command to about 400 men under Forrest who had bluffed him into believing that there were more Confederates by marching them in circles. Confined in Libby Prison in Richmond, he made his escape on February 9, 1864, in the tunnel engineered by Colonel Thomas E. Rose. Rejoining his regiment, which had been exchanged the previous November, he guarded rail lines until given a brigade in late 1864. He then fought at Franklin and Nashville. Three days after being brevetted brigadier for his war service he resigned on March 16, 1865. (Hartpence, William R., *History of the 51st Indiana*)

Silas H. Stringham, Union naval commander at Hatteras. (*Leslie's*)

STRINGHAM, Silas Horton (1798-1876)

By the outbreak of the Civil War many of the senior officers of the regular navy were so advanced in years that they were soon incapable of commanding at sea. Such was the case of Silas H. Stringham, a veteran of the War of 1812, the Algerine War, and the Mexican War. A midshipman in 1809, the native New Yorker was a commodore at the start of the conflict. At the very outset he was called to Washington to assist in planning but turned down command of a proposed Fort Sumter relief expedition. Given command of the blockading squadron, he led the naval portion of the movement against Hatteras Inlet. Both Forts Clark and Hatteras fell quickly. Returning to Washington he soon became embroiled in a feud with Assistant Secretary of the Navy Fox which was a common occurrence for older officers. This led to his resignation on December 21, 1861. The next year he was promoted to rear admiral on the retired list.

STRONG, George Crockett (1832-1863)

George C. Strong, killed at Battery Wagner. (*Leslie's*)

A relatively recent graduate of West Point (1857), Vermont native George C. Strong had been acting in his new capacity of brigadier general of volunteers for a little more than a month when he was mortally wounded in the bloody assault on Battery Wagner on July 18, 1863. Appointed to the military academy from Massachusetts, he had been posted to the ordnance branch upon his graduation. His Civil War assignments included: second lieutenant, Ordnance (since July 31, 1859); first lieutenant, Ordnance (January 25, 1861); major and assistant adjutant general, USV (October 1, 1861); captain, Ordnance (March 3, 1863); brigadier general, USV (March 23, 1863, to rank from November 29, 1862); commanding U.S. Forces St. Helena Island, 10th Corps, Department of the South (June 13-July 5, 1863); commanding 2nd Brigade, 2nd Division, 10th Corps, Department of the South (July 5-18, 1863); and major general, USV (July 31, 1863, to rank from the 18th). At 1st Bull Run he served as Irvin McDowell's chief ordnance officer and was subsequently an assistant ordnance officer on McClellan's staff. Late in 1861 he joined Benjamin F. Butler's staff as adjutant and was active in organizing the expedition against New Orleans. He eventually became Butler's chief of staff then, in June 1863, was appointed a brigadier general and proceeded to the South Carolina coast. Commanding a brigade in the bloody repulse at Battery Wagner, he received a mortal wound in the thigh. The other brigade commander in the assault was killed and five of the six regimental leaders in Strong's brigade also fell. Dying on July 30, he was posthumously appointed a major general the next day, to date from his wounding.

STRONG, Henry B. (ca. 1821-1862)

After having been in temporary command of the brigade, Henry B. Strong had only resumed command of his regiment that morning when he was struck down at the battle of Antietam. He had been an Irish-born clerk working in New Orleans when the Civil War began. Joining the army, his assignments included: captain, Company B, 6th Louisiana (June 5, 1861); lieutenant colonel, 6th Louisiana (May 9, 1862); colonel, 6th Louisiana (ca. June 27, 1862); and commanding Taylor's (old) Brigade, Ewell's Division, Jackson's Corps, Army of Northern Virginia (August 29-September 17, 1862). He served in action at 1st Bull Run, in the Shenandoah Valley Campaign and at Cedar Mountain before assuming command of the brigade when Colonel Henry Forno was wounded at 2nd Bull Run. He led the brigade through the capture of Harpers Ferry and on the morning of the battle of Antietam he was relieved by General Harry T. Hays and resumed command of the 6th. In the fighting near the Dunkard Church he was fatally shot.

STRONG, William Kerley (1805-1867)

Retired New York merchant William K. Strong was named a brigadier general of volunteers for largely political reasons and never commanded in the field. Touring Egypt at the outbreak of the Civil War, he headed back to the United States via France where he arranged for the purchase of arms for the Union war effort. Since he was a well known War Democrat, Lincoln appointed him a brigadier general in the first fall of the war. His assignments included: brigadier general, USV (September 28, 1861); commanding District of Cairo, Department of the Tennessee (July-August 12, 1862); and commanding District of St. Louis, Department of the Missouri (June 6-November 30, 1863). At first assigned to command St. Louis' Benton Barracks, he briefly commanded the District of Cairo. Following a stint in New York he was named head of a commission investigating military affairs in Missouri. Until his resignation was accepted, effective October 20, 1863, he directed the District of St. Louis. Paralyzed in a Central Park carriage accident before the end of the Civil War, he died two years after its close.

STUART, David (1816-1868)

After compiling a record of gallant service to his country, David Stuart suffered disappointment as the U.S. Senate rejected his appointment as a brigadier of volunteers. A lawyer and politician, and having served in the Congress, Stuart had entered the federal service as lieutenant colonel, 42nd Illinois, on July 22, 1861. His later assignments included: lieutenant colonel, 55th Illinois (October 31, 1861); commanding 2nd Brigade, 5th Division, Army of the Tennessee (March 1-April 6, 1862); commanding 4th Brigade, District of Memphis, 13th Corps, Army of the Tennessee (October 26-November 12, 1862); commanding 2nd Brigade, 2nd Division, District of Memphis, 13th Corps, Army of the Tennessee (November 11-December 18, 1862); brigadier general, USV (November 29, 1862); commanding 2nd Brigade, 2nd Division, Yazoo Expedition, Army of the Tennessee (December 18-28, 1862); commanding the division (December 28, 1862-January 4, 1863); and commanding 2nd Division, 15th Corps, Army of the Tennessee (January 4-April 4, 1863). Leading a brigade, detached from Sherman's Division, Stuart held the extreme left on the first day at Shiloh and while valiantly holding off the rebel attacks he was wounded. Returning to duty, he took part in the capture of Corinth, the attack on Chickasaw Bluffs in the Yazoo Expedition during which he succeeded to division command, and the taking of Arkansas Post. With his rejection by the Senate (on March 11, 1863), he was reluctantly relieved from command on April 4 by Sherman who wrote that Stuart gave "energetic, patriotic, and successful services. Ever present, ever active, and by a high-toned spirit of honor and dignity imparting to his troops a similar tone." He resigned and returned to the law.

STUART, James Ewell Brown (1833-1864)

Known as "Jeb," Stuart was probably the most famous cavalryman of the Civil War. A Virginia-born West Pointer (1854), Stuart was already a veteran of Indian fighting on the plains and of Bleeding Kansas when, as a first lieutenant in the 1st Cavalry, he carried orders for Robert E. Lee to proceed to Harpers Ferry to crush John Brown's raid. Stuart, volunteering as aide-de-camp, went along and read the ultimatum to Brown before the assault in which he distinguished himself. Promoted to captain on April 22, 1861, Stuart resigned on May 14, 1861, having arrived on the 6th in Richmond and been made a lieutenant colonel of Virginia infantry. His later appointments included: captain of Cavalry, CSA (May 24, 1861); colonel, 1st Virginia Cavalry (July 16, 1861); brigadier general, CSA (September 24, 1861); and major general, CSA (July 25, 1862). His commands in the Army of Northern Virginia included: Cavalry Brigade (October 22, 1861-July 28, 1862); Cavalry

Division (July 28, 1862-September 9, 1863); temporarily Jackson's 2nd Corps (May 3-6, 1863); and Cavalry Corps (September 9, 1863-May 11, 1864). After early service in the Shenandoah Valley, Stuart led his regiment in the battle of 1st Bull Run and participated in the pursuit of the routed Federals. He then directed the army's outposts until given command of the cavalry brigade. Besides leading the cavalry in the Army of Northern Virginia's fights at the Seven Days, 2nd Bull Run, Antietam, Fredericksburg, Chancellorsville, Gettysburg, and the Wilderness, Stuart was also a raider. Twice he led his command around McClellan's army, once in the Peninsula Campaign and once after the battle of Antietam. While these exploits were not that important militarily, they provided a boost to the Southern morale. During the 2nd Bull Run Campaign, he lost his famed plumed hat and cloak to pursuing Federals. In a later Confederate raid, Stuart managed to overrun Union army commander Pope's headquarters and capture his full uniform and orders that provided Lee with much valuable intelligence. At the end of 1862, Stuart led a raid north of the Rappahannock River, inflicting some 230 casualties while losing only 27 of his own men. At Chancellorsville he took over command of his friend Stonewall Jackson's Corps after that officer had been mortally wounded by his own men. Returning to the cavalry shortly after, he commanded the Southern horsemen in the largest cavalry engagement ever fought on the American continent, Brandy Station, on June 9, 1863. Although the battle was a draw, the Confederates did hold the field. However, the fight represented the rise of the Union cavalry and foreshadowed the decline of the formerly invincible Southern mounted arm. During the Gettysburg Campaign, Stuart, acting under ambiguous orders, again circled the Union army, but in the process deprived Lee of his eyes and ears while in enemy territory. Arriving late on the second day of the battle, Stuart failed the next day to get into the enemy's rear flank, being defeated by Generals Gregg and Custer. During Grant's drive on Richmond in the spring of 1864, Stuart halted Sheridan's cavalry at Yellow Tavern on the outskirts of Richmond on May 11. In the fight he was mortally wounded and died the next day in the rebel capital. (Davis, Burke, *Jeb Stuart: The Last Cavalier*)

STUMBAUGH, Frederick Shearer (1817-1897)

The records are strangely silent on the reasoning behind the revocation of Frederick S. Stumbaugh's appointment as a brigadier general. The native Pennsylvanian lawyer had been active in the state militia and enlisted a large portion of it into his first regiment, a three-months unit. His assignments included: colonel, 2nd Pennsylvania (April 20, 1861); colonel, 77th Pennsylvania (October 26, 1861); and brigadier general, USV (November 29, 1862). With his first unit he served under Patterson in the lower end of the Shenandoah Valley until he was mustered out on July 27, 1861, at the expiration of the regiment's enlistment. Raising a new regiment, he fought on the second day at Shiloh as part of the forces under Buell and participated in the advance on Corinth, Mississippi. His command was too far to the rear to fight at Perryville and, having been named a brigadier general, he was absent at Murfreesboro. On January 22, 1863, his commission was revoked and he reverted to his colonelcy. However, he was discharged at his own request on May 13, 1863, and resumed the practice of law.

STUMBLING BEAR (fl. 1850s-1870s)

A proven fighter since the 1850s, Kiowa leader Stumbling Bear was still fighting well into the Civil War. In 1864, when the 1st New Mexico under Colonel Kit Carson attacked his Kiowa village at Adobe Wells in Texas, he proved again his fighting prowess. If he had displayed such gallantry in the Union army he probably would have been brevetted. Instead, Carson won a brevet for his campaigns. In 1865 Stumbling Bear signed the Treaty of Little Arkansas and, two years later, that of Medicine Lodge. By the time he visited Washington in 1872, with other Kiowas and Comanches, he was a proponent of following the white man's ways and giving up the traditional buffalo hunt.

STURGIS, Samuel Davis (1822-1889)

The Civil War field career of Samuel D. Sturgis fell victim to Confederate cavalryman Nathan Bedford Forrest. The native Pennsylvanian and West Pointer (1846) had been posted to the dragoons with which he served in Mexico; he was captured near Buena Vista and was held for eight days. Transferred to the cavalry in the 1855 enlargement of the army, he was stationed at Fort Smith, Arkansas, upon the outbreak of the Civil War. He managed to march his threatened command to Kansas during the secession crisis. His assignments included: captain, 1st Cavalry (since March 3, 1855); major, 1st Cavalry (May 3, 1861); commanding 1st Brigade, District of Southwest Missouri, Western Department (July-August 10, 1861); major, 4th Cavalry (change of designation August 3, 1861); temporarily commanding the district (August 10, 1861); brigadier general, USV (August 10, 1861); chief of staff, Western Department (November 1861); commanding brigade, Military District of Washington, Department of the Potomac (May-August 1862); commanding Reserve Corps, Army of Virginia (August-September 1862); commanding 1nd Division, 9th Corps, Army of the Potomac (September 3, 1862-February 7, 1863 and March 6-19, 1863); commanding 2nd Division, 9th Corps, Department of the Ohio (March 19-May 21, 1863); commanding District of Central Kentucky, Department of the Ohio (June 4-24, 1863); commanding 1st Division, 23rd Corps, Department of the Ohio (June 24-July 10, 1863); chief of Cavalry, Department of the Ohio (July 8-November 3, 1863); lieutenant colonel, 6th Cavalry (October 27, 1863); commanding Cavalry Corps, Department of the Ohio (November 3, 1863-April 10, 1864); and commanding Expeditionary Force, District of West Tennessee, Department of the Tennessee (June 1864). At Wilson's Creek he won a brevet for his role in assuming command of the army after the death of Nathaniel Lyon and leading one wing of the force from the field. From the date of this action he was appointed a brigadier general of volunteers and served briefly as David Hunter's staff chief in St. Louis. Transferred to the East, he commanded a brigade in

Samuel D. Sturgis, Forrest victim. (*Leslie's*)

the capital's fortifications and during the 2nd Bull Run Campaign organized a provisional force to go to the relief of Pope's Army of Virginia. While waiting to entrain his "corps," he became involved in a dispute over transportation priorities and declared, "I don't care for John Pope one pinch of owl dung." He was a McClellan man. After leading his scratch force at 2nd Bull Run he took charge of a 9th Corps division. Brevetted for that battle, he fought at South Mountain—earning the brevet of brigadier general, in 1865—and Antietam. Back in Virginia, he won an 1865 brevet as major general in the regular service for Fredericksburg during which his command unsuccessfully stormed Marye's Heights. Early in 1863 the corps was transferred to the Ohio Valley, and he eventually became the department's chief cavalryman. Having proved moderately successful in mounted operations in East Tennessee, he was given the difficult task of dealing with the troublesome Forrest. He failed dismally at Brice's Crossroads. An inquiry was called for and he spent the balance of the war awaiting an assignment which never came. Mustered out of the volunteers on August 24, 1865, he remained in the service until his retirement in 1888 as Colonel, 7th Cavalry—George Custer's regiment. (Bearss, Edwin C., *Forrest at Brice's Cross Roads*)

SULLIVAN, Cary (?-1864)

There is some confusion as to his true identity, but to his fellow inmates at Andersonville, whom he terrorized, he was known as Cary Sullivan of the 72nd New York and, more importantly, as one of the most notorious members of the cutthroat gangs, known as "Raiders." At the end of June 1864 it was agreed between the prisoners and the camp's commandant, Major Henry Wirz, that the depredations should be brought to an end. Some 125 raiders were removed from the compound. A prisoners' court was convened and the suspects tried. Six men, including Sullivan, received the death penalty. Sullivan met his fate on July 11, 1864, without availing himself of the traditional right to say a few final words. For some reason his grave in the National Cemetery at Andersonville is marked "W. Rickson, U.S.N." (McElroy, John, *Andersonville: A Story of Rebel Military Prisons*)

SULLIVAN, Jeremiah Cutler (1830-1890)

Generals Philip H. Sheridan and Winfield S. Hancock felt that former U.S. Navy officer Jeremiah C. Sullivan did not measure up as an infantry division commander. An Indiana native, Sullivan had served as a midshipman aboard the *Savannah, Vincennes, Constitution,* and *San Jacinto* from 1848 to 1854. He resigned while serving at Annapolis to study and practice law. The firing on Fort Sumter prompted him to join the army. His assignments included: captain, 6th Indiana (April 18, 1861); colonel, 13th Indiana (June 19, 1861); commanding 2nd Brigade, Landers' Division, Department of West Virginia (January-March 13, 1862); commanding 2nd Brigade, 2nd Division, 5th Corps, Army of the Potomac (March 13-April 4, 1862); commanding 2nd Brigade, 2nd Division, Department of the Shenandoah (April 4-May 1, 1862); brigadier general, USV (April 28, 1862); commanding 2nd Brigade, 3rd Division, Army of the Mississippi (June 20-October 3, 1862); commanding District of Jackson, 13th Corps, Army of the Tennessee (November 19-December 18, 1862); commanding District of Jackson, 16th Corps, Army of the Tennessee (December 18-22, 1862); commanding District of Jackson, Left Wing, 16th Corps, Army of the Tennessee (December 22, 1862-March 18, 1863); acting assistant adjutant general, Army of the Tennessee (spring 1863); chief of staff, 15th Corps, Army of the Tennessee (summer 1863); commanding Maryland Heights Division, Department of West Virginia (September 18-December 1863); commanding 1st Division, Department of West Virginia (December 1863-April 1864); commanding 1st Infantry Division, Department of West Virginia (April-July 3, 1864); and commanding 1st Separate Brigade, District of the Kanawha, Department of West Virginia (August 6-October 9, 1864). As a company commander in a three-months regiment, he fought at Philippi before taking charge of a three-years regiment as colonel. As such he fought at Rich and Cheat Mountains. He was a brigade commander at Kernstown before being appointed a brigadier general and transferred to the West. As a brigade commander, he fought at Iuka and Corinth but at the latter relinquished command for some unknown reason. He was then in district command until he participated in the early stages of the Vicksburg Campaign as an acting inspector general under Grant. That summer he was James B. McPherson's staff chief. Transferred back to the East, he fought in the Union disaster at New Market, as a division commander, and took part in the equally disastrous Lynchburg expedition. With these two debacles he was assigned to a relatively quiet sector in West Virginia, and no commander seemed willing to have Sullivan serve under him. Without a command, he resigned on May 11, 1865, and held clerical positions in the postwar years.

SULLY, Alfred (1821-1879)

Philadelphia native Alfred Sully spent more of his Civil War career fighting Indians than Confederates. The West Pointer (1841) had been posted to the infantry with which he took part in actions against the Seminoles in Florida. He fought in Mexico and was then on the frontier fighting the Cheyenne at the outbreak of the Civil War. His assignments in that conflict included: captain, 2nd Infantry (since February 23, 1852); colonel, 1st Minnesota (March 4, 1862); major, 8th Infantry (March 15, 1862); commanding 1st Brigade, 2nd Division, 2nd Corps, Army of the Potomac (June-July, October 29-December 19, 1862, and March 10-May 1, 1863); brigadier general, USV (September 26, 1862); commanding 3rd Division, 2nd Corps, Army of the Potomac (December 20, 1862-January 10, 1863); commanding District of Dakota, Department of the Northwest (May-December 4, 1863); commanding District of Iowa (included Dakota Territory), Department of the Northwest (December 4, 1863-June 27, 1865); and temporarily commanding the department (November 24-December 1864). Initially he served in his regular army capacity in northern Missouri and the Washington defenses before being named commander of a volunteer regiment. This he led to the Peninsula where he fought at Yorktown and was brevetted for Seven Pines. While commanding the brigade during the Seven Days he was brevetted for Malvern Hill. He led his regiment at Antietam and was shortly thereafter awarded a brigadier's star. He took part in the assaults at Fredericksburg and was preparing to move his brigade for the Chancellorsville Campaign when he was relieved by his division commander, John Gibbon. The problem stemmed from the refusal of the 34th New York to perform its duty. Apparently Sully was unsure of his right to use the amount of force called for by regular army regulations against volunteers. Following his removal he asked for a court of inquiry. That panel cleared him of the charges on May 16, 1863, but he was nonetheless shunted off to the Northwest. For his campaigns against the Sioux during the war he was brevetted brigadier general in the regular army and was also brevetted major general of volunteers. Mustered out of the latter on April 30, 1866, he remained in the army and saw extensive frontier service. He died as colonel, 21st Infantry, while commanding Fort Vancouver, Washington Territory. (Sully, Langdon, *No Tears for the General: The Life of Alfred Sully, 1821-1879*)

SUMNER, Charles (1811-1874)

An abolitionist Republican senator from Massachusetts, Charles Sumner, became one of the most hated men in the South. In 1856 he was actually assaulted by a cane-wielding South Carolina congressman. A lawyer and professor, Sumner had vehemently opposed the war with Mexico and the resultant expansion of slavery before being sent to the Senate in 1851. He quickly became known for his extreme rhetoric against the South and her representatives. One particularly strong attack, on May 19 and 20, 1856, against South Carolina Senator Andrew P. Butler, resulted two days later in a severe caning at the hands of Representative Preston Brooks. Temporarily blinded at the first blow, he was driven under his desk while the blows kept coming. In an effort to rise, Sumner actually ripped the desk from the floor. The attack was finally broken up by other congressmen, and Sumner was taken from the chamber, bleeding. Brooks' cane was also shattered. Sumner's condition was a matter of dispute for years, and the true extent of his injuries will never be known. Southerners believed they were exaggerated by the North for political advantage. But the fact remains that, despite short periods at the Capitol, he sought treatment at home and abroad and did not return to the Senate on a regular basis until December 1859. During his absence he had been reelected without campaigning. He blocked efforts to negotiate following the secession of the Southern states and became a Lincoln supporter but opposed his lenient plans for reconstruction. He remained in the Senate during the war, as chairman of the Foreign Relations Committee, and a radical Republican until his death. (Donald, David, *Charles Sumner and the Coming of the Civil War* and *Charles Sumner and the Rights of Man*)

SUMNER, Edwin Vose (1797-1863)

Known as "Bull" or "Bull Head" Sumner, Edwin V. Sumner was at age 65 the oldest Union corps commander in the primary fields of military operation. The Massachusetts native had been appointed a lieutenant in the regular army in 1819 and served, successively, in the infantry, dragoons, and cavalry. Wounded at Cerro Gordo, he earned two brevets in Mexico and was in charge of Fort Leavenworth during the period of Bleeding Kansas. His Civil War-era assignments included: colonel, 1st Cavalry (since March 3, 1855); brigadier general, USA (March 16, 1861); commanding Department of the Pacific (April 25-October 20, 1861); commanding division, Army of the Potomac (November 25, 1861-March 13, 1862); commanding 2nd Corps, Army of the Potomac (March 13-October 7, 1862); major general, USV (July 4, 1862); and commanding Right Grand Division, Army of the Potomac (November 14, 1862-January 25, 1863). Named one of the regular army's general officers in place of David E. Twiggs, he commanded on the West Coast during the first months of the war before being called to Washington to command a division under McClellan. By the time of the movement to the Peninsula he was in charge of a corps. After serving in the Yorktown operations he acted as second-in-command to McClellan at Williamsburg, although his own corps was not on the field. Distinguished at Seven Pines—he was brevetted regular army major general—he went on to fight in the Seven Days. His corps covered the withdrawal of Pope's Army of Virginia after 2nd Bull Run and attacked the Confederate center at Antietam in a piecemeal fashion. Under Burnside, he led the Right Grand Division—2nd and 9th corps—at Fredericksburg. It was his command which made

"Bull Head" Edwin V. Sumner. (*Leslie's*)

most of the futile assaults against Marye's Heights. Upon the relief of Burnside after the infamous Mud March, Sumner requested other duty. He died in New York State on the way to his new command in the Department of the Missouri. (Stanley, F., *E.V. Sumner, Major General United States Army (1797-1863)*)

SURRATT, John Harrison (1844-1916)

The one member of the Lincoln conspirators to escape punishment was the former Confederate courier John H. Surratt. The Maryland native had been involved with the early plots to kidnap the president and carry him off to Richmond. There is much controversy as to whether or not he was involved in the assassination plot. He later claimed that he had been in Canada on the day of the murder and could not have been involved. However, there was testimony that it was he who had prepared the hole in the president's box door and arranged the wooden obstruction to prevent John Wilkes Booth from being interrupted in his preparations for the killing. Union soldiers later claimed that it was Surratt who repeatedly announced the time in front of Ford's Theater in order to alert the other conspirators that the moment was close at hand. Some claim that Booth assigned Surratt to the killing of General Grant. While his friends were being rounded up, Surratt showed up in Canada and remained there until September 1865 when he sailed for Europe, eventually joining the guards at the Vatican. Spotted by an old schoolmate, he fled to Egypt where he was finally apprehended. A trial was held in 1867, but the jury could not come to a decision and he was released. This may have been out of a sense of guilt over Mary Surratt's execution. His remaining years were spent as a clerk and on the lecture circuit. (Campbell, Helen Jones, *Confederate Courier*)

SURRATT, Mary E. (1820-1865)

To this day the guilt or innocence of Mary E. Surratt in the Lincoln assassination conspiracy is a matter of intense debate. The Maryland widow had leased out her tavern in Surrattsville to a John M. Lloyd, who was destined to be a star witness against her. In the meantime Mrs. Surratt ran a boarding house on Washington's H Street. Her son, John H. Surratt, was an active member in the plots of John Wilkes Booth to kidnap Lincoln and hustle him off to the South. And it was in her boarding house that much of the planning was done. Whether she knew it or not is an open question. Shortly after the assassination she was arrested and was put on trial with the other conspirators—John Surratt had escaped to Canada—and was given little resembling a fair trial by the military commission. Along with three others she was sentenced to hang. Many believed that she would not actually go to the gallows, and

Mary E. Surratt went to the gallows, but her guilt is still questioned today. (LC)

General Winfield S. Hancock, the military commander in the capital, set up a relay of horses to carry any reprieve order from the White House to the arsenal grounds where the execution was to take place. On July 7, 1865, she was hanged.

SWANN, Oswald (?-?)

Although Oswald Swann had aided in the flight of John Wilkes Booth and David Herold, he provided vital information to detectives which kept them on the trail of the assassination conspirators. After leaving the home of Dr. Samuel A. Mudd, Booth and Herold found themselves lost when they emerged from the Zekiah Swamp near Brice's Chapel, Maryland. Herold then located Swann, a black, who agreed to lead them to their next stopping place, the home of a "Captain" Samuel Cox. Having completed his mission, Swann later told the authorities that he had noticed a whispered conversation before the pair had been ordered from the house. He further reported that he then saw them returning to the Cox place.

SWAYNE, Noah Haynes (1804-1884)

The death of Supreme Court Justice John McLean opened the way for Noah H. Swayne to become the first of five Lincoln appointments to the highest court, despite the fact that he had no judicial experience. Born in Virginia to an antislavery family, he had moved to Ohio where he practiced law and defended escaped slaves, at least partially due to his revulsion at the institution of slavery. He was a government attorney and sat in the state legislature. Joining the Republicans in the 1850s, he was named to the Supreme Court on January 21, 1862, and was confirmed with only one dissenting vote three days later. He staunchly supported the Union's war effort, most notably in the *Prize Cases*. He was highly influential in securing Ohio's ratification of the 15th Amendment and twice, in 1864 and 1873, maneuvered for the chief justiceship. He resigned on account of age in 1881, ending 28 years on the bench. (Pfeffer, Leo, *This Honorable Court*)

SWAYNE, Wager (1834-1902)

Like his father—Noah H. Swayne, appointed to the U.S. Supreme Court during the Civil War—Wager Swayne had been a lawyer at the outbreak of the war. He became the last major general of volunteers appointed and earned the Congressional Medal of Honor. The Ohio native's assignments included: major, 43rd Ohio (August 31, 1861); lieutenant colonel, 43rd Ohio (December 14, 1861); colonel, 43rd Ohio (October 18, 1862); commanding 2nd Brigade, 4th Division, 16th Corps, Army of the Tennessee (September 18-23, 1864); commanding 2nd Brigade, 1st Division, 17th Corps, Army of the Tennessee (September 22-November 1, 1864); brigadier general, USV (March 8, 1865); and major general, USV (May 1, 1866, to rank from June 20, 1865). He led his regiment at Island #10 and it served in the Corinth siege and at Iuka. Again in charge of the regiment, he fought at Corinth and was then assigned to garrison duty until the commencement of the Atlanta Campaign. He commanded a brigade during part of the March to the Sea, and leading his regiment on February 2, 1865, in the Carolinas Campaign, he was wounded at the crossing of the Salkehatchie River at River's Bridge in South Carolina. This resulted in the loss of his right leg. Brevetted brigadier general three days later, he was given the full rank in March. Placed in charge of the Freedmen's Bureau in Alabama, he was named a major general and served until mustered out on September 1, 1867. In the meantime he was commissioned a colonel in the regular army and was brevetted brigadier general for his wounding and major general for the war in 1867. Retired in 1870, he resumed the practice of law. His gallantry at Corinth in 1862 won him the coveted medal in 1893.

SWEENY, Thomas William (1820-1892)

Losing an arm at Churubusco during the Mexican War did not affect the drive of Thomas W. Sweeny for combat with the enemy, or fellow officers, and it eventually cost him his command. The Irish native had emmigrated to the United States in 1832 and been employed by a publishing firm before his militia activity drew him into a military career. He served in the New York volunteers in Mexico but soon transferred to the regulars. A first lieutenant since 1851, his Civil War assignments included: captain, 2nd Infantry (January 19, 1861); brigadier general, Missouri Volunteers (May 20, 1861); colonel, 52nd Illinois (January 21, 1862); commanding 3rd Brigade, 2nd Division, Army of the Tennessee (March 29-April 7, 1862); commanding 1st Brigade, 2nd Division, District of Corinth, same army (August 12-September 1 and October 3-November 1, 1862); commanding 1st Brigade, District of Corinth, 13th Corps (October 24-December 18, 1862), 17th Corps (December 18, 1862-January 20, 1863), and 16th Corps (January 20-March 20, 1863), Army of the Tennessee; brigadier general, USV (March 16, 1863, to rank from November 29, 1862); commanding 1st Brigade, 2nd Division, 16th Corps, Army of the Tennessee (March 18-July 20, 1863); commanding the division (September 12, 1863-July 25, 1864); and major, 16th Infantry (October 20, 1863). His early experience with the Missouri troops included the surrender of Camp Jackson and the fighting at Wilson's Creek where he was severely wounded before being mustered out on August 14, 1861. Commanding a regiment of Illinois troops, he fought at Fort Donelson and in command of a brigade at Shiloh until wounded on the second day. When he returned to duty, in the District of Corinth, his problems with General Grenville M. Dodge began. Sweeny, a regular, resented the political appointees and especially Dodge, all the more because the latter was more than a decade his junior. Sweeny was a stickler for the regulations and resented the lax attitudes of the volunteers. The strains in garrison duty during 1862 and 1863 were exacerbated in the Chattanooga and Atlanta Campaigns. Unfortunately, the requirements of the service kept throwing the two officers together. Sweeny soon became involved in a quarrel with the corps surgeon over the issuance of orders without following proper military channels, even challenging him to a duel which was declined. Then came the battle of Atlanta in which Sweeny deeply resented the actions of Dodge in directing his regiments without reference to

Sweeny. On July 25, 1864, the matter came to a head when Generals Dodge and Fuller were treated to a tirade against the volunteer officers in Sweeny's tent. Several fistfights were started by the Irishman as were demands for duels. In the end he was placed under arrest but was finally acquitted in January 1865—a case of the regular army protecting one of its own. However, General Howard, the army commander, refused to have Sweeny reinstated, and he held no further commands during the war. After the war he was arrested in the Fenian plot against Canada but was soon back in the army, where he stayed until his retirement in 1870 as a brigadier general.

SWEET, Benjamin Jeffery (1832-1874)

Although a brevet brigadier, Benjamin Sweet, a former Wisconsin state senator, performed his most important Civil War service off the battlefield. Appointed major, 6th Wisconsin, July 16, 1861, Sweet's later assignments included: lieutenant colonel, 6th Wisconsin (September 17, 1861); colonel, 21st Wisconsin (September 5, 1862); colonel, 8th United States Veteran Reserve Corps (September 25, 1863); and brevet brigadier general, USV (December 20, 1864). Serving in the East in the early part of the war, he returned to Wisconsin and raised a new regiment; although suffering from malaria, he led it in its first battle at Perryville on October 8, 1862, where he was severely wounded. Limited to post duty by his wound, he was commanding at Fort Thomas at Gallatin, Tennessee, when, on April 27, 1863, he was praised for his actions in a skirmish at Negro Head Cut near Woodburn, Kentucky. Transferred to the Veteran Reserve Corps, following his resignation from line duty on September 8, 1863, he was assigned to duty at Camp Douglas prison camp in Chicago. He assumed command of the post on May 2, 1864, and in November he efficiently broke up a conspiracy to free the prisoners and burn the city. Faking the escape of John Shanks, one of his prisoners turned spy, he was able to learn the identities of the rebel agents, and as a result earned his brevet. Resigning on September 19, 1865, he resumed the practice of law and became a federal bureaucrat. (Bross, William, *Biographical Sketch of the Late General B.J. Sweet*)

SWEITZER, Jacob Bowman (?-1888)

Even though he had been mustered out with his regiment the previous summer, Jacob B. Sweitzer received a brevet as brigadier general for his war service in the omnibus brevet bill of March 13, 1865. The native Pennsylvanian's assignments had included: major, 33rd Pennsylvania (July 4, 1861); lieutenant colonel, 33rd Pennsylvania (November 17, 1861); lieutenant colonel, 62nd Pennsylvania (change of designation November 18, 1861); colonel, 62nd Pennsylvania (June 27, 1862); commanding 2nd Brigade, 1st Division, 5th Corps, Army of the Potomac (October 30-November 1, 1862, November 16, 1862-March 12, 1863, April 12-October 24, November 16-December 18, 1863, and February 3-July 3, 1864); and commanding the division (October 24-November 6, 1863 and December 31, 1863-February 3, 1864). Enlisting on the divided nation's first civil war Independence Day, he fought at Yorktown and was wounded and captured during the Seven Days. Declared exchanged on August 27, 1862, he commanded his regiment in reserve at Antietam and the brigade at Fredericksburg, Chancellorsville, and Gettysburg. During the latter part of the year he commanded the division at times and took part in the Bristoe and Mine Run campaigns. He led the brigade again through the Overland Campaign, until his regiment was relieved from the lines at Petersburg for mustering out. He was mustered out with it on July 13, 1864.

SWIFT, Delia

See: *Fury, Bridget*

SWIFT, Henry Adoniram (1823-1869)

With the resignations of both the governor and lieutenant governor to take seats in Congress, Henry A. Swift succeeded to the Minnesota gubernatorial chair on July 10, 1863. A native of Ohio, he had practiced law before moving to Minnesota in 1853 and becoming a real estate and insurance agent. A Republican, he worked for the admission of the state and failed in a bid for a congressional seat. In 1861 he won a seat in the upper state house and two years later, as president of the senate, succeeded Alexander Ramsey in the governorship. Much of his time was spent in dealing with the Indians, but he did help arrange for the purchase of parts of the Gettysburg battlefield. Not seeking reelection, he left office on January 11, 1864, and returned to the legislature. (Blegen, Theodore C., *Minnesota: A History of the State*)

SWINTON, John (1829-1901)

The managing editor of the *New York Times* during the Civil War, John Swinton later became a crusading journalist in the movement for social and labor reform. Scottish-born, he had learned typesetting in Canada before relocating to the United States. During the trouble in Kansas he was active in the free-soil movement and headed the *Lawrence Republican*. Moving back to New York he wrote an occasional piece for the *Times* and was hired on a regular basis in 1860 as head of the editorial staff. After holding this position throughout the war, he left the paper in 1870 and became active in the labor struggles of the day. He later served eight years in the same position on the *New York Sun* and published a weekly labor sheet, *John Swinton's Paper*.

SWINTON, William (1833-1892)

Unlike his brother John, William Swinton worked for the *New York Times* in the field, as a war correspondent, until expelled from the army's lines in 1864. A Scottish-born former student for the ministry and a teacher, he had joined the *Times* in 1858 and four years later was covering the Army of the Potomac. Knowledgeable on military matters, he was often highly critical of military leaders and often gathered his information by what was considered, by the authorities, to be questionable means. On the first night of the battle of the Wilderness, he was caught overhearing a Grant-Meade conversation. A few weeks later he angered Burnside with an unfavorable report. Then on July 1, 1864, the War Department stripped him of his credentials and ordered him expelled from the camps of the Army of the Potomac. He then wrote *The Times Review of McClellan; His Military Career Reviewed and Exposed* and, after the war, *Campaigns of the Army of the Potomac* as well as a regimental history of the 7th New York and an account of 12 important battles. He subsequently was a professor and textbook writer.

SYKES, George (1822-1880)

Known in the regular army as "Tardy George," George Sykes was removed from a corps command in the Army of the Potomac's spring 1864 reorganization; Grant had made his headquarters with that force and determined that Sykes was not the man he wanted for the offensive operations he planned. A Delaware native and West Pointer (1842), Sykes was a veteran of infantry service in both the Seminole and Mexican wars, earning a brevet in the latter. The regular's service in the Civil War included: captain, 3rd Infantry (since September 30, 1855); major, 14th Infantry (May 14, 1861); commanding Reserve Infantry Brigade, Army of the Potomac (August 1861-March 13, 1862); brigadier general, USV (September 28, 1861); commanding Infantry Reserve, Army of the Potomac (March 13-May 1862); commanding 2nd Division, 5th Corps, Army of the Potomac (March 18-December 1862 and January-June 28, 1863); major general, USV (November 29, 1862); commanding the corps (February 1-5, 16-23, and June 28-October 7, 1863 and October 15, 1863-March 23, 1865); lieutenant colonel, 5th Infantry (October 16, 1863); and commanding District of South Kansas, Department of Kansas (September 1-October 10, 1864). At 1st Bull Run he commanded the only regular army infantry on the field—an eight-company battalion from various regiments—and was highly effective in slowing the rout of the volunteers. He then commanded the regulars near Washington and in the midst of the Peninsula Campaign was given charge of a division composed mostly of regular army units. He had already fought at Yorktown and in divisional command participated in the Seven Days fighting. He was at 2nd Bull Run and in reserve at Antietam. Given a second star in the volunteer service, he fought at Fredericksburg and Chancellorsville before taking charge of the 5th Corps upon George G. Meade's assumption of army command just prior to Gettysburg. There he fought in support of the hard-pressed 3rd Corps on the second day. That fall, in the Bristoe and Mine Run campaigns, he behaved true to his nickname and was found lacking by Meade. Prior to the Wilderness Campaign, Meade and Grant agreed upon his replacement and Sykes finished the war in Kansas. Mustered out of the volunteer service on January 15, 1866, he reverted to his regular army rank and died on active duty in Texas as colonel, 20th Infantry, and brevet major general for the war.

"Tardy George" Sykes. (*Leslie's*)

SZÁMVALD, Julius

See: *Stahel, Julius*

T

TAFT, Charles Sabin (?-?)

Seated in the orchestra section of Ford's Theater on the night of the Lincoln assassination, Dr. Charles Taft was boosted up into the presidential box by the crowd and became the second medical man to reach Lincoln. Joining Army Assistant Surgeon Charles A. Leale, he worked to revive the President and then assisted in the direction of the wounded man to the Petersen House across the street. He remained through the night and was surprised by how long the president lived, considering the extent of the wounds. The next day he was present for the autopsy.

TALBOT, Theodore (1825-1862)

Born in the District of Columbia, Theodore Talbot served in the California volunteers before being commissioned directly into the 1st Artillery as a second lieutenant during the Mexican War. He was serving with his company as part of the garrison of Fort Moultrie when South Carolina seceded. A few days later the two artillery companies comprising the garrison were surreptitiously transferred to Fort Sumter in the middle of Charleston Harbor. Following the firing upon the *Star of the West* by the state forces on January 9, 1861, Talbot, a first lieutenant since 1848, was sent to see Governor Pickens and was given a safe conduct to Washington in order to obtain instructions from the national government. On January 19 Talbot returned from the seat of government with instructions for Major Anderson that in effect left the decision on war or peace to the fort commander. He also brought with him the ridiculous story of how, when ushered in to see the president, Talbot was asked by Buchanan what the administration should do. Since March 16 a captain in the Adjutant General's Department, Talbot was allowed to leave Charleston after an interview with Governor Pickens on April 4. On August 3, 1861, he was again promoted, to major and assistant adjutant general, in which grade he served until his death on April 22, 1862. His principal assignment during this period was as assistant adjutant general of the Department of Washington. (Swanberg, W.A. *First Blood*)

TALCOTT, Thomas Mann Randolph (1838-1920)

It was not until the final full year of war that the Confederate War Department completed the formal organization of engineer regiments. To the command of the first of these was appointed Thomas M.R. Talcott, a civil engineer and the son of an old army friend of Robert E. Lee. His Confederate assignments included: captain, Engineers (1861); major, Engineers (April 26, 1862); lieutenant colonel, Engineers, (July 25, 1863); and colonel, 1st Confederate Engineers (April 1, 1864). After general engineering duties he was assigned as an aide to General Lee when that officer was serving as an advisor to the president in the spring of 1862. Becoming part of Lee's personal staff with the Army of Northern Virginia, he was generally assigned to engineering projects. In the winter of 1863-64 he was detailed to begin organization of an engineer regiment and was made its commander upon its completion. He served through the surrender at Appomattox and returned to civil engineering in Richmond. (Freeman, Douglas S., *R.E. Lee*)

TALIAFERRO, Alexander Galt (1808-1884)

As a regimental, and briefly as a brigade, commander, Alexander G. Taliaferro fought through much of the heavy campaigning of Jackson's command in 1862, until he was disabled for further field service. A lawyer in his native Virginia, he had also been a field-grade officer in the state militia at the beginning of hostilities. Volunteering for active service, his assignments included: captain, Company G, 13th Virginia (May 28, 1861); lieutenant colonel, 23rd Virginia (September 12, 1861); colonel, 23rd Virginia (April 15, 1862); commanding 3rd Brigade, Jackson's (old) Division, Jackson's Corps, Army of Northern Virginia (August 9-ca. 28, 1862); and commanding post at Charlottesville (September 1863-March 18, 1865). During the battle of 1st Bull Run his regiment was left behind to guard Manassas Junction. Transferring to another regiment, he saw action at Cheat Mountain, in the Romney

Campaign, and in command of the regiment at Kernstown, McDowell, in the Shenandoah Valley Campaign, and at Cedar Mountain. He was wounded at both Kernstown and Port Republic during the Shenandoah Valley Campaign. At Cedar Mountain he succeeded to brigade command when General William B. Taliaferro took over the division. He led the brigade at 2nd Bull Run until he was again wounded. Unfit to rejoin his unit, he was assigned to post duty until his resignation for health reasons on March 18, 1865.

TALIAFERRO, William Booth (1822-1898)

Stonewall Jackson never forgot that William B. Taliaferro had sided with General Loring in the feud over the Romney Campaign. A Virginia lawyer and politician, Taliaferro had served as a captain and major in two of the regular army regiments raised for the Mexican War. As a major general of militia he was present during a part of the John Brown crisis at Harpers Ferry. As a militia officer he was assigned to duty in the Norfolk area and later to volunteer service on the Peninsula. His later assignments included: colonel, 23rd Virginia (spring 1861); commanding brigade, Army of the Northwest (summer 1861-ca. March 1862); brigadier general, CSA (March 4, 1862); commanding brigade, Valley District, Department of Northern Virginia (March 1862); commanding brigade, Jackson's Division, same district and department (May and June 1862); commanding brigade, Jackson's Division, 2nd Corps, Army of Northern Virginia (July-August 9, 1862); commanding the division (August 9-28 and fall 1862-February 20, 1863); commanding brigade, District of Georgia, Department of South Carolina, Georgia and Florida (March 6-July 1863); commanding 1st Subdivision, 1st Military District of South Carolina, same department (July-October 22, 1863); commanding 7th Military District of South Carolina, same department (October 22, 1863-October 17, 1864); commanding 3rd Sub-district of South Carolina, District of South Carolina, same department (from October 17, 1864); and also commanding brigade (after December 28 a division), same department or (from March) Hardee's Corps (July 1864-April 9, 1865). Sent to western Virginia, he participated in the Romney Campaign and fought at McDowell and in the Valley Campaign. He took command of Jackson's Division, over Stonewall's protest, at Cedar Mountain and was wounded at Groveton. After Fredericksburg he was shunted off to the coast where he served in the defense of Charleston. He commanded a division of coast defenders in opposing Sherman's march through the Carolinas and saw action at Bentonville. In the April 9, 1865, reorganization of Johnston's forces it appears that Taliaferro lost his position, but he was still paroled with that army. He was a legislator and judge back in Virginia after the war. (Robertson, James I., Jr., *The Stonewall Brigade*)

TANEY, Roger Brooke (1777-1864)

When Supreme Court Chief Justice Roger B. Taney died on October 12, 1864, some of the comments included: "The Hon. old Roger B. Taney has earned the gratitude of the country by dying at last," "Providence has given us a victory," and "Better late than never." The Maryland native had practiced law, sat in the state legislature, and served as state attorney general, U.S. attorney general, acting secretary of war, and secretary of the treasury. During this period he supported the War of 1812 and opposed the second national bank. As a reward for his political support, Andrew Jackson appointed him as an associate justice of the Supreme Court, but Senate confirmation was postponed. In the meantime Chief Justice John Marshall died and Jackson named Taney to the post on December 28, 1835. he was finally confirmed on March 15, 1836, and began his highly controversial 28 years as presiding judge. His ruling in the *Dred Scott* case ignited outrage throughout large sectors of the country. He held that since the slave had returned to slave territory he was still a slave and therefore could not sue. Additionally, he declared that even if a black were not a slave he was still not a citizen and therefore was to be denied the right to appeal to the courts. Early in the Civil War he clashed with Lincoln over the presidential right to suspend *habeas corpus* without the consent of Congress. In 1863 he also voted, in the minority, against the president's right to declare a blockade without a declaration of war or authorization by Congress. Many Unionists were greatly encouraged in the cause when he died. (Swisher, Carl B., *Roger B. Taney*)

Roger B. Taney of Maryland, chief justice of the Supreme Court at the time of the *Dred Scott* decision. (NA)

TAPPAN, Arthur (1786-1865)

As with any reform movement there were splits in the abolitionist ranks over tactics. In one such dispute—over linkage with other movements—Arthur Tappan broke with William Lloyd Garrison and the American Anti-Slavery Society in 1840 and helped establish the American and Foreign Anti-Slavery Society and its publication, the *American and Foreign Anti-Slavery Reporter*. Tappan had been connected with Garrison and the *Liberator* since 1830 when Tappan paid Garrison's fine, releasing him from a Baltimore jail. After the split with the Garrisonians he backed the Liberty Party, cofounded the antislavery *National Era*, and founded the American Missionary Association to pressure missionary groups to take abolitionist stands. The Fugitive Slave Law did nothing to slow his activities in helping escaping slaves avoid recapture. As early as the 1830s he was active in unsuccessful attempts to establish schools for blacks against local opposition. He died at the same time that slavery was being extinguished. (Tappan, Lewis, *The Life of Arthur Tappan*)

TAPPAN, Benjamin (1773-1857)

The Ohio law partner of Edwin M. Stanton, Massachusetts-born Benjamin Tappan was a leader of the moderate antislavery faction in the U.S. Senate in the pre-Civil War years. Entering politics early in the century, he served in the state legislature and as a judge, with time out for a stint as a staff officer in the War of 1812. In 1838 he became the compromise candidate for senator based upon his antislavery and anti-abolitionist position. Although he did not present abolitionist petitions and did support the annexation of Texas, he was active in free-soil circles and voted for Frémont the year before his death.

TAPPAN, James Camp (1825-1906)

Arkansas lawyer and judge James C. Tappan served the Confederacy on both sides of the Mississippi River and rose to the rank of brigadier general. Born of northern stock in Tennessee, he practiced his profession in Mississippi before settling in Arkansas. His military assignments included: colonel, 13th Arkansas (May 11, 1861); brigadier general, CSA (November 5, 1862); and commanding in the Trans-Mississippi Department: brigade, Price's Division, District of Arkansas (spring 1863-March 24, 1864); Churchill's (Arkansas) Division, Detachment District of Arkansas, District of West Louisiana (March 24-April 1864); brigade, Churchill's (Arkansas) Division, District of Arkansas (April-ca. August 1864); the division (ca. August-September 1864); and 3rd (Arkansas) Brigade, 1st (Arkansas) Division, 2nd Corps (September 1864-May 26, 1865). His regiment was part of the Confederate force already on the west bank of the Mississippi when Grant attacked at Belmont, and Tappan was praised for his handling of his unit. Transferred to the east side of the river, he fought at Shiloh, in the Corinth siege, and at Richmond and Perryville. Promoted to brigadier general shortly thereafter, he was transferred to the Trans-Mississippi Department. He led a brigade in the unsuccessful defense of Little Rock and a division during the repulse of Banks' Red River Campaign. Heading north, he was again in charge of his brigade at Jenkins' Ferry. After the war—he saw little action after the repulse of Frederick Steele's column—he resumed his practice and returned to the state legislature.

TAPPAN, Lewis (1788-1873)

Like his brother Arthur but unlike his brother Benjamin, Lewis Tappan became an abolitionist crusader. A native of Massachusetts, he had been active in religious circles and through his connections became associated with the movement to free the slaves. In 1833 he helped found the New York Anti-Slavery Society and the American Anti-Slavery Society. The next year his home was sacked by a mob in retaliation. Upset with the Garrisonian plan to link other reform movements to the cause, he helped establish, with Arthur, the American and Foreign Anti-Slavery Society in 1840 and the American Missionary Association in 1846. He backed the operations of the Underground Railroad after the enactment of the Fugitive Slave Act in 1850. Undergoing more of a radical reformation than his brother, he left the American and Foreign Anti-Slavery Society in 1855 to become an officer of the Abolition Society. He was also active in providing for the freed blacks. (Bowen, C.W., *Arthur and Lewis Tappan*)

TATTNALL, Josiah (1795-1871)

A veteran of the War of 1812, the campaign against the Barbary pirates, and the Mexican War, Josiah Tattnall was eventually found by the Confederacy to be too old for service afloat. The Georgia-born, English-educated Tattnall had been in the U.S. Navy since 1812, but, although he was not a secessionist, he resigned his commission as a captain on February 20, 1861. Eight days later he was named Georgia's senior naval officer. The next month he was appointed captain, CSN, and assigned to command of the naval defenses of Georgia and South Carolina. He led his vessels in an attack upon the Union fleet at Port Royal in November 1861. The following March, Tattnall was ordered to Virginia to replace the wounded Buchanan in command of the defenses there. In this position he made the decision to scuttle the ironclad *Virginia* when the army evacuated Norfolk. Censured by a court of inquiry, Tattnall requested a court-martial which cleared him of blame. In July 1862 he returned to duty on the Georgia coast but on April 2, 1863, he was relieved as too old for sea duty and assigned to shore duty in Savannah. For the remainder of the war, he busied himself with construction and supply matters. After surrendering with Johnston's command, he moved to Nova Scotia before returning, broke, to Savannah in 1870. The post of Inspector of the Port was created for him by a grateful city. (Jones, Charles C., *Life and Services of Commodore Josiah Tattnall*)

TAYLOR, Benjamin Franklin (1819-1887)

As a war correspondent for the *Chicago Daily Journal* Benjamin F. Taylor managed to get on the wrong side of General William T. Sherman—a common fate for journalists. A native of New York, Taylor had tried teaching before moving to Chicago and joining the paper in the 1840s. During the latter half of the Civil War he gave up his position as literary editor to cover the fighting. He covered the fighting at Chattanooga and his reports were published after the war as a collection entitled *Mission Ridge and Lookout Mountain, with Pictures of Life in Camp and Field*. Threatened with arrest by Sherman in May 1864—for revealing too much military information—he fled to Virginia where he covered the fighting in the Shenandoah Valley. After the war he was a free-lance writer and poet.

TAYLOR, Ezra (?-1885)

Near the end of the Civil War native Irishman Ezra Taylor received the brevet of brigadier general of volunteers for his three years of service with the Union artillery. His assignments included: captain, Battery B, 1st Illinois Light Artillery (1861); major, 1st Illinois Light Artillery (October 23, 1861); commanding Artillery, 5th Division, Army of the Tennessee (April 1862); chief of Artillery 15th Corps, Army of the Tennessee (1863); colonel, 1st Illinois Light Artillery (October 27, 1863); and chief of Artillery, Army of the Tennessee (1863-64). He commanded his battery of six six-pounder smoothbores at Belmont and Fort Donelson and directed Sherman's guns at Shiloh. He served in the advance on Corinth, Mississippi, and was again Sherman's chief artillerist during the Vicksburg, Chattanooga, and Atlanta campaigns. In the midst of the siege of the latter city his resignation was accepted effective August 20, 1864. He received his brevet the following March.

TAYLOR, George William (1808-1862)

A veteran of both the regular army and navy, George Taylor led his brigade to meet a Confederate raiding party only to find out that he had attacked Stonewall Jackson's command. The iron manufacturer and veteran of the Mexican War had been named colonel of the 3rd New Jersey on June 4, 1861. Serving in the Washington defenses and along the Rappahannock River, Taylor's command did not see its first real action until it moved to the Peninsula. There Taylor was promoted brigadier general, USV, on May 9, 1862, and nine days later he assumed command of the New Jersey Brigade which was officially designated the 1st Brigade, 1st Division, 6th Corps, Army of the Potomac. During the Seven Days he commanded the brigade at Gaines' Mill and Frayser's Farm. With the defeat of McClellan's drive on Richmond, the brigade was transferred back to Washington, and when the telegraph to Pope's Army of Virginia supply base at Manassas went dead, the brigade was sent out the Orange and Alexandria Railroad to deal with the rebel "raiders." Dismounting from the cars short of the station, Taylor formed his men and advanced on the junction. Instead of cavalry raiders, A.P. Hill's famed Light Division came out to meet him. The battle turned into a slaughter, with 339 Union casualties. In this action, on August 27, 1862, Taylor was wounded. He died four days later, back in Alexandria.

TAYLOR, James Edward (?-?)

A young artist from Ohio, James Taylor, interrupted his artistic education in New York to join the Union army and in the process discovered his calling, military art. Enlisting in the 10th New York, he served for two years, rising to the rank of sergeant. His unit served in the fights on the Peninsula, 2nd Bull Run, Antietam, Fredericksburg, and Chancellorsville. Mustered out in 1863, he returned to the brush. With his interest in military subjects he applied for and got a position as a special artist with *Frank Leslie's Weekly*. His principal assignment was covering the 1864 campaign of General Sheridan in the Shenandoah Valley. Following the Union victories in that sector, Taylor continued to send illustrations to the journal from the Richmond front. During the war 61 of these appeared in *Leslie's*. He remained with the weekly until 1883 and then set up a studio in New York. He also compiled and published the massive *With Sheridan up the Shenandoah Valley in 1864: Leaves from a Special Artist's Sketch Book and Diary*)

TAYLOR, John P. (?-?)

Attrition in his regiment cost native Pennsylvanian John P. Taylor his commission on September 9, 1864, but he was rewarded with the brevet of brigadier general of volunteers on August 4, 1865. His assignments included: captain, 1st Pennsylvania Cavalry (August 10, 1861); lieutenant colonel, 1st Pennsylvania Cavalry (September 5, 1862); colonel, 1st Pennsylvania Cavalry (March 2, 1863); commanding 1st Brigade, 2nd Division, Cavalry Corps, Army of the Potomac (October 1-December 25, 1863 and January 5-February 3, 1864); and commanding the division (December 25, 1863-January 5, 1864 and January 22-February 10, 1864). His regiment fought in the Shenandoah Valley and at 2nd Bull Run and Fredericksburg before he became its commanding officer. He led the regiment in Stoneman's raid during the Chancellorsville Campaign and at Gettysburg and then advanced to brigade command for the Bristoe and Mine Run operations. Again in regimental command he served through the Overland and part of the Petersburg campaigns. Then his regiment was reduced to a battalion of five companies due to battle and other casualties, and he was mustered out with the non-reenlisting members of the unit.

TAYLOR, Joseph Pannel (1796-1864)

Although a brother of President Zachary Taylor, Joseph Taylor is one of the lesser known Union generals, having served in the thankless job of commissary of subsistence. Born in Kentucky, Taylor had served as an enlisted man and subaltern in the War of 1812. Serving in the artillery after that war, he rose to a captaincy before being assigned to commissary duties in 1829. For two decades before the Civil War, including service in the field in Mexico, Taylor had been a lieutenant colonel and assistant commissary general of subsistence. He succeeded his predecessor as commissary general, with the rank of colonel, on September 29, 1861, upon the latter's death. He was promoted brigadier general, USA, on February 9, 1863. He died in that office on June 29, 1864.

TAYLOR, Nelson (1821-1894)

A veteran of the Mexican War, Nelson Taylor served four months as a general officer in the Civil War. Taylor had been a company commander in the New York volunteers during the war with Mexico and then settled for a few years in California where he held several offices. Returning to the East he graduated from Harvard Law School in 1860 and went into practice in New York. That year he was a Democratic candidate for Congress but was defeated in the election, which saw Lincoln win the top office. With the beginning of the war he became the first colonel of the 72nd New York, part of Dan Sickles' Excelsior Brigade, on July 23, 1861. His later assignments included: commanding 2nd Brigade, 2nd Division, 3rd Corps, Army of the Potomac (March 13-May 11 and July 16-September 5, 1862); brigadier general, USV (September 7, 1862); commanding 3rd Brigade, 2nd Division, 1st Corps, Army of the Potomac (October 4-December 13, 1862 and December 20, 1862-January 23, 1863); and also commanding the division (October 4-November 5 and December 13-20, 1862). After service in the Washington area, Taylor led the Excelsior Brigade at Yorktown and Williamsburg. During the battles of Seven Pines and the Seven Days he commanded the regiment. At 2nd Bull Run, Taylor, again commanding the brigade, led attacks on Stonewall Jackson's left along the unfinished railroad line where the 2nd lost heavily. Taylor was in the Washington defenses at the time of Antietam but rejoined the army in command of a different brigade at Fredericksburg. Here again he attacked Jackson's line and succeeded to command of the division when General Gibbon was wounded. His resignation, for unexplained reasons, was accepted on January 19, 1863, and he returned to the practice of law. He served an 1865 to 1867 term in Congress. In 1869 he returned to his native Connecticut and practiced law there.

TAYLOR, Richard (1826-1879)

Brother-in-law of Jefferson Davis and son of President Zachary Taylor, Richard Taylor served as a Confederate lieutenant general and department commander. Born in Kentucky and educated at Harvard and Yale, he had served as his father's military secretary during the Mexican War. A Louisiana plantation owner, he was active in state politics and supported secession at the convention. His military assignments included: colonel, 9th Louisiana (July 7, 1861); brigadier general, CSA (October 21, 1861); commanding 1st Louisiana Brigade, E.K. Smith's-Ewell's Division, Potomac District (Valley District from April), Department of Northern Virginia (October 22, 1861-June 26, 1862); commanding same brigade, Ewell's Division, Jackson's Corps, Army of Northern Virginia (June 26 and July 1862); major general, CSA (July 28, 1862); commanding District of West Louisiana, Trans-Mississippi Department (August 20, 1862-June 10, 1864); lieutenant general, CSA (May 16, to rank from April 8, 1864); commanding Department of Alabama, Mississippi and East Louisiana (September 23-November 22, 1864 and December 12, 1864-May 4, 1865); and also commanding Army of Tennessee (January 23-February 22, 1865). Too late for the fighting at 1st Bull Run, he commanded a brigade in the Shenandoah Valley Campaign and, until taken ill, in the Seven Days. Transferred west of the Mississippi he commanded in western Louisiana and directed the forces which defeated Banks at Mansfield and Pleasant Hill. Critical of department commander E.K. Smith for not letting him follow up the victories, he was relieved at his own request. Promoted, he was given command in the Deep South and was in overall control of the forces defeated at Mobile and Selma. He surrendered the last major force east of the Mississippi. After the war he was active in trying to alleviate the effects of Reconstruction upon the South. (Taylor, Richard, *Destruction and Reconstruction*)

TAYLOR, Thomas Hart (1825-1901)

A veteran of the Mexican War as a first lieutenant of the 3rd Kentucky, businessman Thomas H. Taylor joined the Confederate service and rose to the rank of brigadier general. The native Kentuckian's assignments included: captain, Infantry (1861); lieutenant colonel, 1st Kentucky (summer 1861); colonel, 1st Kentucky (October 14, 1861); commanding 1st Brigade, Department of East Tennessee (ca. June-July 1862); commanding brigade, 1st (Stevenson's) Division, Department of East Tennessee (early July-December 18, 1862); brigadier general, CSA (November 4, 1862); commanding brigade, Stevenson's Division, 2nd Military District, Department of Mississippi and East Louisiana (January-April 1863); provost marshal general, Department of Mississippi and East Louisiana (April-July 4, 1863); commanding District of Southern Mississippi and East Louisiana, Department of Alabama, Mississippi and East Louisiana (March 5-April 5, 1864); provost marshal general, Department of Alabama, Mississippi and East Louisiana (mid-1864); and commanding Taylor's Command (Post of Mobile), District of the Gulf, Department of Alabama, Mississippi and East Louisiana (fall 1864-April 12, 1865). He served in northern Virginia and on the Peninsula with a 12-months regiment which was mustered out in May 1862. He was then assigned to East Tennessee where he commanded a brigade and took part in the Kentucky Campaign of the summer and fall of 1862. Transferred to Mississippi, he was the provost marshal during the Vicksburg siege and was paroled upon the capture of the city. He then performed district and provost marshal duty (as a brigadier general since the fall of 1862). However, his appointment was never forwarded to the Senate for confirmation and he reverted to his rank of colonel. During the final winter and spring of the war he was in charge of the Post of Mobile until its evacuation. After engaging in business in Mobile, he became a law officer in his native state.

TAYLOR, Walter H. (ca. 1838-?)

The youngest member of Robert E. Lee's personal staff was Walter H. Taylor who served the entire war with Lee. He had attended the Virginia Military institute in the mid 1850s and was in banking when the secession crisis broke. Offering his services, they included: lieutenant, Virginia Militia (early 1861); lieutenant colonel, Virginia Forces (May 1861); captain and aide-de-camp, CSA (November 8, 1861); major and aide-de-camp, CSA (March 27, 1862); and lieutenant colonel and assistant adjutant General, CSA (November 4, 1864). Joining Lee's staff in May 1861, he assisted in the organization of the Virginia forces and their transfer to the Confederacy. He was one of only two staff officers, and the only one to survive, who accompanied his chief to western Virginia. He served with Lee on the South Carolina coast before the general was made the personal advisor of the president. Here Taylor's position was upgraded to that of a major and he was promoted. In June of 1862 he began his connection with the Army of Northern Virginia which was destined to last until Appomattox. A young man wishing for action, Taylor on at least three occasions joined in the fighting. Upset by the idea of surrender, he was not present during Lee's meeting with Grant in the McLean House. After the war he wrote two works based upon his experiences, *Four Years with General Lee* and *General Lee.* (Freeman, Douglas S., *R.E. Lee*)

TEBE, Marie (?-?)

Attaching herself to the Collis Zouaves (officially the 114th Pennsylvania) as a vivandière, Marie Tebe earned the Kearney Cross issued by General David B. Birney but refused to wear it. Her duties were as a combination of laundress, nurse, and cook. In action she frequently carried canteens to the wounded. At Chancellorsville her clothes were pierced on numerous occasions while on these missions of mercy. Thereafter she was warned to stay behind the firing line.

TERRELL, Alexander Watkins (1827-1912)

Serving in the cut-off Trans-Mississippi Department, Alexander W. Terrell was promoted extralegally by General E. Kirby Smith when the collapse of the Confederacy was already nearly complete. His assignments included: major, 1st Texas Cavalry, Arizona Brigade (1861); captain and volunteer aide-de-camp (June 12, 1862); lieutenant colonel, Terrell's (Tex.) Cavalry Battalion; colonel, Terrell's (Tex.) Cavalry Regiment (1863); commanding 4th Texas Cavalry Brigade, 4th Texas Cavalry Division, 1st Corps, Trans-Mississippi Department (September and November 1864 and early 1865); and brigadier general, CSA, by Smith (May 16, 1865). After initially serving in the District of Texas, New Mexico and Arizona, Terrell and his regiment were part of the force sent to the District of West Louisiana to help defeat Banks' Red River Campaign in the spring of 1864. He continued to serve in the western portion of Louisiana for the remainder of the war, much of the time in command of a cavalry brigade. In recognition of this fact, Smith promoted him to brigadier in orders 10 days before the department was surrendered. After the collapse Terrell went to Mexico with other ex-Confederates. (Spencer, John, *Terrell's Texas Cavalry*)

TERRELL, Leigh Richmond (1835-1864)

Early in the war Leigh Terrell was made a lieutenant in the 4th Alabama, and when the regimental commander, Colonel E.M. Law, was given command of Whiting's Brigade, Terrell was assigned to his staff as assistant adjutant general. As such he saw action and was commended for his part in the battles of 2nd Bull Run and Antietam. Promoted to captain in the adjutant general's department, he saw further action at Fredericksburg. In April 1863, still on Law's staff, he filed a report on the fall of Fort Huger—on the 19th during Longstreet's siege of Suffolk—that was not flattering of the role of the 55th North Carolina. That regiment's commander, Colonel John K. Connally, and Major Alfred H. Belo demanded satisfaction from Terrell and Captain John Cussons, another officer on the staff. When this was not forthcoming they challenged the two captains to a pair of duels. While Cussons and Belo fired two rounds at each other in a display of rather poor marksmanship, Terrell and Connally resolved the matter verbally. Everyone agreed to go back to killing Yankees. Captain Terrell continued on Law's staff, seeing action at Wauhatchie, the Wilderness, Spotsylvania, and Cold Harbor, until promoted to lieutenant colonel and assigned to the 47th Alabama on June 15, 1864. Three days later he was wounded in the shoulder and on October 13 he was mortally wounded in the siege lines around Richmond and Petersburg. He died nine days later. (Freeman, Douglas S., *Lee's Lieutenants*)

TERRILL, James Barbour (1838-1864)

Both James and his brother William Barbour died in the Civil War, but they fought on opposite sides. An 1858 graduate of the Virginia Military Academy, James Terrill was practicing law in Warm Springs, Virginia, at the time of the firing on Fort Sumter. Unlike his brother, James decided to go with his native state and became the major in A.P. Hill's 13th Virginia in May 1861. His later assignments included: lieutenant colonel, 13th Virginia (ca. October 30, 1862); colonel, 13th Virginia (May 15, 1863); and brigadier general, CSA (May 31, 1864). Terrill's regiment was left behind at Manassas Junction when the brigade went forward into the battle of 1st Bull Run and did not participate in the fight. However, in September 1861 Terrill led the infantry under Colonel Jeb Stuart in the skirmish at Lewinsville, Virginia. Terrill's later battles included the Shenandoah Valley Campaign, Gaines' Mill, White Oak Swamp, Malvern Hill, Cedar Mountain, and, in command of the regiment, Fredericksburg. During the Gettysburg Campaign, the regiment was left behind in Winchester. He then led the regiment in the fighting at the Wilderness and Spotsylvania, and on May 30, 1864, he was nominated by Davis to the Senate as a temporary brigadier to take over the command of the wounded General Pegram. But on the same day, at Bethesda Church, he was killed in action and his body was left to the enemy. His appointment was confirmed the next day. (Freeman, Douglas S., *Lee's Lieutenants*)

TERRILL, William Rufus (1834-1862)

William Terrill managed to rise to the rank of brigadier general before being killed in Kentucky. A Virginia-born West Pointer (1853) and artillery officer, Terrill was reluctant to fight in Virginia but continued in the regular army, as a first lieutenant in the 4th Artillery. On May 14, 1861, he was appointed captain of the newly authorized Battery H, 5th Artillery, and he spent the next few months organizing his command. His later assignments included: brigadier general, USV (September 9, 1862); commanding 33rd Brigade, 10th Division, Army of the Ohio (mid-September-September 29, 1862); and commanding

33rd Brigade, 10th Division, 1st Corps, Army of the Ohio (September 29-October 8, 1862). Moving his company to Kentucky late in 1861, Terrill led it in the campaign through middle Tennessee the next spring and, as a part of McCook's Division of Buell's Army of the Ohio, arrived to reinforce Grant's command at Shiloh. On the second day of that fight, Terrill and his battery distinguished themselves. He then participated in the siege of Corinth, before being sent back to Kentucky to face Bragg's invasion. Promoted to brigadier and given command of a newly organized brigade, he led it in the battle of Perryville on October 8, 1862. The division was heavily engaged and the division and both brigade commanders were killed. Terrill himself was struck by a piece of shell late in the day and died that night.

TERRY, Alfred Howe (1827-1890)

A militia officer at the outbreak of the Civil War, Connecticut native Alfred H. Terry received the Thanks of Congress for his capture of Fort Fisher and then remained in the regular army and died as a major general. A lawyer and court clerk, he capitalized on his militia experience to lead a regiment to Washington early in the war. His assignments included: colonel, 2nd Connecticut (May 7, 1861); colonel, 7th Connecticut (September 17, 1861); brigadier general, USV (April 25, 1862); commanding District of Hilton Head, Department of the South (August 12-September 3, 1862); commanding U.S. Forces, Hilton Head, 10th Corps, Department of the South (October 20, 1862-May 12, 1863); commanding 1st Division, 10th Corps, Department of the South (July 6-19, 1863); commanding U.S. Forces, Morris Island, 10th Corps, Department of the South (July 19-October 18, 1863); commanding Northern District, 10th Corps, Department of the South (January 17-February 1864 and March-April 25, 1864); commanding 10th Corps, Army of the James (April 28-May 4, June 14-21, July 18-23, October 10-November 4, and November 18-December 3, 1864); commanding 1st Division, 10th Corps, Army of the James (May 4-June 11, June 21-July 18, and July 23-October 10, 1864); commanding 1st Division, 24th Corps, Army of the James (December 3-6, 1864); commanding the corps (December 6, 1864-January 2, 1865), commanding Terry's Provisional Corps, Department of North Carolina (January 6-March 27, 1865); major general, USV (provisionally January 15, 1865); brigadier general, USA (January 15, 1865); commanding 10th Corps, Department of North Carolina (March 27-May 13, 1865); major general, USV (commissioned April 20, 1865);

Captor of Fort Fisher Alfred H. Terry (seated, hatless) and staff. (NA)

and commanding Department of Virginia and the Army of the James (May-June 27, 1865). In command of his three-months regiment he fought under Daniel Tyler at 1st Bull Run. Within a little over a month after being mustered out on August 7, 1861, he was commissioned colonel of a newly organized three-years regiment. As such he fought at the occupation of Port Royal and the capture of Fort Pulaski. Named a brigadier general, he served in the operations against Charleston and later accompanied the corps in its move to join Benjamin F. Butler in the spring of 1864. He fought at Bermuda Hundred and Petersburg in divisional and corps command. He was also active in moves north of the James River against Richmond. After Butler's failure to take Fort Fisher—guarding Wilmington, North Carolina, and the last major open port for blockade runners—he was tapped to make a second attempt. In a two-day bombardment and assault he captured the work and soon took the city. For this he was awarded the Thanks of Congress on January 24, 1865, and was provisionally commissioned a major general of volunteers. In an extraordinary move, he was also appointed a brigadier general in the regular army without ever having served in that body. Still in North Carolina, his corps became a part of the Army of the Ohio under John M. Schofield and linked up with Sherman during his march through the state. On April 20 his commission as major general of volunteers was formalized; he had been named to that grade by brevet on August 26, 1864, for his services to that point. Mustered out of the volunteers on September 1, 1866, he served on the frontier and was George A. Custer's superior when the latter was killed at the Little Big Horn, apparently while exceeding orders. Made a major general in 1886, Terry was placed on the retired list two years later.

TERRY, Henry Dwight (1812-1869)

Michigan lawyer Henry D. Terry appears to have been one of those general officer who failed to make the grade. Born in Connecticut, he had taken time out from his law practice to be active in the militia in Detroit. Upon the outbreak of the Civil War he raised a volunteer regiment. His assignments included: colonel, 5th Michigan (June 10, 1861); brigadier general, USV (July 17, 1862); commanding 2nd Provisional Brigade, Division at Suffolk, 7th Corps, Department of Virginia (January 21-April 9, 1863); commanding 1st Brigade, 1st Division, 7th Corps, Department of Virginia (April 9-July 11, 1863); commanding 3rd Division, 6th Corps, Army of the Potomac (August 4, 1863-January 10, 1864); and commanding Sandusky and Johnson Island prison camp (January 14-May 11, 1864). He led his regiment to the Peninsula and saw action at Yorktown, Williamsburg, and Seven Pines. He was then absent until ordered to report at Fortress Monroe, as a brigadier general, in December 1862. He fought against Longstreet at Suffolk and transferred to the Army of the Potomac after Gettysburg. As a division commander he took part in the Bristoe and Mine Run operations. Early in 1864 his unit was assigned to guard the prisoners of war at Johnson's Island, Ohio. Relieved in May 1864, it appears he held no further commands before his February 7, 1865, resignation. He then took up a new practice in the nation's capital.

TERRY, William (1824-1888)

The least-known commander in the Stonewall Brigade, William Terry did not take it over until it had ceased to exist officially as a unit. A lawyer and journalist in the Upper Shenandoah Valley, he had been an officer in the militia for a number of years before the Civil War and was present for part of the John Brown crisis at Harpers Ferry. Upon the outbreak of the war he went with his company back to the ferry, where the company became part of what was to be the Stonewall Brigade. His assignments included: first lieutenant, Company A, 4th Virginia (ca. May 1861); major, 4th Virginia (April 23, 1862); colonel, 4th Virginia (September 11, 1863); brigadier general, CSA (May 19, 1864); commanding brigade, Johnson's-Gordon's Division, 2nd Corps, Army of Northern Virginia (May 14-June 13 and December 1864-March 25, 1865); and commanding brigade, Gordon's Division, Valley District, Department of Northern Virginia (June 13-December 1864). He fought at 1st Bull Run as a company officer before being elected to field grade upon the reorganization of the regiment. He fought in the Shenandoah, the Seven Days, and at 2nd Bull Run where he was wounded. He returned in time to fight at Fredericksburg where he succeeded to regimental command. He was at the regiment's head at Chancellorsville, Gettysburg, the Wilderness, and at Spotsylvania when the greater part of Johnson's Division was captured. Two days later, 14 Virginia regiments, five from the Stonewall Brigade, were consolidated into one brigade, and Terry was soon promoted to brigadier and given command. He then fought at Cold Harbor, 3rd Winchester, where he was again wounded, Fisher's Hill, and Cedar Creek. Taking up position in the Petersburg trenches, he was wounded in the assault on Fort Stedman on March 25, 1865, and was put out of the war. After the war he resumed the practice of law and served as a U.S. congressman. He drowned during a storm. (Robertson, James I., Jr., *The Stonewall Brigade*)

TERRY, William Richard (1827-1897)

It is claimed that William R. Terry suffered seven wounds during the Civil War. A graduate of the Virginia Military Institute, he had been a merchant in 1861. He raised a cavalry company in his home county, Bedford, and joined the Confederate army where his assignments included: captain, Company A, 2nd Virginia Cavalry (spring 1861); colonel, 24th Virginia (September 1861); commanding Kemper's Brigade, Kemper's Division, 1st Corps, Army of Northern Virginia (August 30-September 1862); commanding Kemper's Brigade, Department of Richmond (September 1863-January 1864); commanding Kemper's Brigade, Department of North Carolina (January-May 1864); commanding Kemper's Brigade, Ransom's Division, Department of Richmond (May 1864); commanding Kemper's (old) Brigade, Pickett's Division, 1st Corps, Army of Northern Virginia (May 1864-March 31, 1865); and brigadier general, CSA (May 30, 1864). After leading his cavalry at 1st Bull Run, he was rewarded by being promoted to colonel and assigned to the 24th Virginia. Leading a charge at Williamsburg, he was wounded but returned to duty in time for 2nd Bull Run. Here he relieved the wounded Colonel Corse in command of the brigade. At the head of the 24th, he fought at Antietam before serving in southeastern Virginia with Longstreet early the next year. Rejoining Lee's army, he was wounded in Pickett's Charge at Gettysburg. With the division again detached he served in Richmond and North Carolina, with fighting at New Bern and Drewry's Bluff. Back with Lee, he was promoted to brigadier and saw more action at Cold Harbor and Petersburg. On March 31, 1865, he received his final wound, at Dinwiddie Court House in a minor Confederate triumph the day before the Five Forks disaster which necessitated the evacuation of the Richmond and Petersburg lines. After the war he served as a state legislator, prison superintendent, and in charge of a soldiers' home. He is often confused with Brigadier General William Terry, also of Virginia.

TEW, Charles Courtenay (1827-1862)

Well qualified for military service, Charles Tew did not live long enough to become a brigadier general in the Confederacy. In 1846 Tew had graduated at the head of his class at the South Carolina Military Academy, or the Citadel. After serving for over a decade as an instructor at his alma mater, Tew moved to North Carolina and founded the Hillsboro Military Academy in 1858. With the outbreak of the Civil War, Tew was assigned to duty drilling troops and commanding Fort Macon. On June 5, 1861, he succeeded General T.H. Holmes in command of the Southern Department Coast Defenses of North Carolina. Having been appointed colonel, 2nd North Carolina State Troops, on May 8, 1861, Tew assumed command of his regiment on June 20. After service in Virginia's Aquia District and back in North Carolina, the 2nd moved to the Peninsula of Virginia in time to participate in the Seven Days Battles where Tew saw action at Gaines' Mill and Malvern Hill. Taking part in the Maryland invasion, Tew saw action at Fox's Gap on South Mountain, and at Antietam he assumed command of the brigade after the mortal wounding of General G.B. Anderson and was himself killed shortly thereafter while fighting in the Bloody Lane. Tew's division commander, General D.H. Hill, described him as "one of the most finished scholars on the continent, and [Tew] had no superior as a soldier on the field." Had Tew survived the Maryland Campaign he probably would have been promoted to permanent command of Anderson's Brigade. (Freeman, Douglas S., *Lee's Lieutenants*)

THAYER, Eli (1819-1899)

Massachusetts Free-Soiler Eli Thayer was always bitter about the deception John Brown played upon him in obtaining arms for the Harpers Ferry raid by claiming that they were for the use of Kansas free-staters. Already noted as a pioneer in collegiate education for women, he had originated the Emigrant Aid Company in 1854 to bring Kansas into the Union as a slave-free state. From 1857 to 1861 he served as a Republican congressman, but was defeated in 1860, in part due to his support of Lincoln over Seward for the presidential nomination. The previous year he had provided Brown with weapons only to find them being used in the Harpers Ferry insurrection. During the Civil War he served as a treasury agent and subsequently ran twice, unsuccessfully, as a Democrat for Congress. He also came into conflict with the Garrisonian abolitionists over their "disunionist" sentiments. In 1887 he praised his own role in the struggle over slavery in his *The New England Emigrant Aid Company, and Its Influence, through the Kansas Contest, upon National History* and two years later in *A History of the Kansas Crusade, Its Friends and Its Foes*)

THAYER, John Milton (1820-1906)

The first appointment of John M. Thayer as a Union brigadier general was not confirmed by the Senate, but he was almost immediately reappointed and confirmed. The Massachusetts native had been active in that state's militia while practicing law before he moved to Nebraska. While farming he was also a brigadier general in the territorial militia during fighting with the Pawnees. His Civil War assignments included: colonel, 1st Nebraska (July 21, 1861); commanding 3rd Brigade, 3rd Division, District of Cairo, Department of the Missouri (February 14-17, 1862); commanding 2nd Brigade, 3rd Division, Army of the Tennessee (February 17-June 1862); brigadier general, USV (October 4, 1862); commanding 2nd Brigade, 1st Division, District of Eastern Arkansas, Department of the Missouri (December 1862); commanding 3rd Brigade, 11th Division, 13th Corps, Army of the Tennessee (December-December 18, 1862); commanding 3rd Brigade, 4th Division, Yazoo Expedition, Army of the Tennessee (December 18, 1862-January 4, 1863); commanding 3rd Brigade, 1st Division, 2nd Corps, Army of the Mississippi (January 4-12, 1863); commanding 3rd Brigade, 1st Division, 15th Corps, Army of the Tennessee (January 12-August 1, 1863); reappointed brigadier general, USV (March 13, 1863); also commanding the division (July 27-28, 1863); commanding District of the Frontier, 7th Corps, Department of Arkansas (February 23-March 24, May 19-December 3, 1864, and January 5-February 1, 1865); and commanding District of Eastern Arkansas, 7th Corps, Department of Arkansas (May 25-June 12, 1865). Arriving during the siege at Fort Donelson, he was given charge of a brigade in Lew Wallace's newly created division and fought under him again on the second day at Shiloh. He took part the advance on Corinth and the following fall was made a brigadier general. After taking part in Sherman's disastrous operations at Chickasaw Bayou, he accompanied John A. McClernand up the Arkansas River and helped capture Arkansas Post. Leading his brigade, he fought at Vicksburg and in the second capture of Jackson, where he was briefly in command of the division. Transferred to the western side of the Mississippi, he took part in Steele's unsuccessful Camden expedition in support of the equally unfortunate Red River operations of Banks. Thayer finished out the war in Arkansas and was brevetted major general for his services. Resigning on July 19, 1865, he subsequently became one of Nebraska's first two U.S. senators, governor of the Wyoming Territory, and governor of Nebraska.

THAYER, Sylvanus (1785-1872)

One man—Sylvanus Thayer—had a tremendous impact on most of the top military leaders on both sides during the Civil

War. The Massachusetts native had graduated from West Point in 1808 at a time when there were no official class standings. But since he was the third graduate of his class to receive his commission, and that in the engineers, it is apparent that he stood close to the top. Except for a brief period in the ordnance branch, all of his service was with the engineers. After fighting in the War of 1812, in which he earned one brevet, he returned to the academy in 1817 as its superintendent. From then until 1833 he left his imprint on that institution. The reforms in the course of instruction that he implemented remained in force for well over a century. Following his departure from the academy he was engaged in the construction of fortifications along the New England coast, principally in Boston Harbor. Having been a lieutenant colonel since 1838, he was advanced to colonel on March 3, 1863. For his long and distinguished career he was brevetted brigadier general on May 31, 1863, and the next day he was retired. He later founded Dartmouth's Thayer School of Engineering.

THOBURN, Joseph (?-1864)

Most of the Civil War service of Joseph Thoburn was spent in the Shenandoah Valley and in western Virginia and he was destined to die in the Valley. His assignments included: colonel, 1st West Virginia (ca. October 30, 1861); commanding 2nd Brigade, 2nd Division, Department of West Virginia (December 1863-April 1864); commanding 2nd Brigade, 1st Infantry Division, Department of West Virginia (April-July 22, 1864); and commanding the division (July 22-October 19, 1864). He led his regiment at Port Republic and Cedar Mountain but missed 2nd Bull Run. Upon his return to duty he served in western Virginia, fending off the various Confederate raids in the region. Reentering the Valley, he fought in the Union defeat at New Market as a brigade commander. In the same capacity, he participated in the drive on Lynchburg. As a division commander under Philip H. Sheridan, he fought at 3rd Winchester and Fisher's Hill. The next month he was killed during the surprise attack of Jubal Early's forces at Cedar Creek, commanding the division while still only a colonel.

THOMAS, Allen (1830-1907)

Captured at the fall of Vicksburg, Maryland-born Louisiana planter Allen Thomas was exchanged and transferred to the Trans-Mississippi Department where he was assigned to reorganizing the paroled and exchanged prisoners and became a brigadier general. The former attorney's Confederate assignments included: major, Thomas' Louisiana Battalion (1861); colonel, 29th (also known as 28th) Louisiana (October 1862, to rank from May 3); commanding brigade, Provisional Division, Department of Mississippi and East Louisiana (December 1862-January 1863); brigadier general, CSA (February 4, 1864); commanding 1st (Louisiana) Brigade, Polignac's Division, 1st Corps (or District of West Louisiana), Trans-Mississippi Department (September 1864-February 1865); and commanding the division (February-May 26, 1865). Serving in defense of Vicksburg, he was in charge of a brigade at Chickasaw Bayou and his regiment in the siege proper. Taken prisoner, he was exchanged and sent into western Louisiana where he came under the command of his brother-in-law, Richard Taylor. About this time he carried John C. Pemberton's report of the campaign to the authorities in Richmond. Late in 1864 he took charge of a brigade of Louisianans in the division of Prince Polignac. When that officer sailed for Europe on a diplomatic mission, Thomas succeeded him in divisional command. After the Confederacy's fall General Thomas was a planter, politician, educator, diplomat, and public official.

THOMAS, Bryan Morel (1836-1905)

Beginning the war as a staff officer, recent graduate of West Point (1858) Bryan M. Thomas rose to the rank of brigadier general and command of a brigade in the later stages of the conflict. The Georgia native had resigned his first lieutenant's commission in the infantry on April 6, 1861, and offered his services to the Confederacy. The veteran of Indian fighting and the Utah expedition saw the following assignments: lieutenant, Infantry (spring 1861); major, Infantry (late 1861); colonel, Thomas' Alabama Reserves Cavalry Regiment (1864); brigadier general, CSA (August 4, 1864); and commanding brigade, District of the Gulf, Department of Alabama, Mississippi and East Louisiana (August 1864-April 9, 1865). At Shiloh, Perryville, and Murfreesboro he served as Jones M. Withers' ordnance and artillery chief. Named to organized Alabama reserve units, he took command of a mounted regiment and in the summer of 1864 was appointed a brigadier general. The balance of his service was spent in the defenses of Mobile where he commanded a brigade. Captured at the fall of Fort Blakely on April 9, 1865, he was a planter, law officer, and educator after the war.

THOMAS, Charles (?-1878)

A veteran ordnance and artillery officer, Charles Thomas had served in the Quartermaster General's Department from 1838 until the outbreak of the Civil War, when he was a colonel and assistant quartermaster general. He was assigned to purchasing duty in England from October 1861 to May 1862. Returning to this country, he served at the department headquarters and in the field on inspection duty. When Quartermaster General Montgomery Meigs went on an extended inspection tour in August 1863, Thomas took over his job in an acting capacity, until January 9, 1864, when he resumed his number two position. Serving through the rest of the war, Thomas retired in 1866 after 47 years of service. He was brevetted brigadier and major general in the regular army during the war.

THOMAS, Edward Lloyd (1825-1898)

Capitalizing upon his Mexican War experience, as a lieutenant of Georgia cavalry, plantation owner Edward L. Thomas was granted permission to raise a regiment for the Confederacy. His assignments included: colonel, 35th Georgia (October 15, 1861); commanding Pettigrew's Brigade, G.W. Smith's-Whiting's Division, Department of Northern Virginia (May 31-June 1862); commanding J.R. Anderson's Brigade, A.P.

Nashville victor George H. Thomas (pen in hand) and other officers. (NA)

Hill's Division (in 1st Corps from June 29 and in 2nd Corps from July 27), Army of Northern Virginia (June 30, 1862-May 30, 1863); brigadier general, CSA (November 1, 1862); and commanding brigade, Pender's-Wilcox's Division, 3rd Corps, same army (May 30, 1863-January 1865 and February-April 9, 1865). Sent to the Peninsula in Virginia, Thomas was involved in the Yorktown operations and at the battle of Seven Pines succeeded to the brigade command of the wounded and captured Pettigrew. He reverted to regimental leadership when the brigade was broken up in June. The 35th was assigned to J.R. Anderson's Brigade, and when this officer was wounded at Glendale, Thomas was in charge of the brigade that he would direct until Appomattox. His wound, received a few days earlier at Mechanicsville, did not alter this. He led his fellow Georgians at Cedar Mountain, 2nd Bull Run, and Harpers Ferry but was still paroling the prisoners when the fight at Antietam occurred. Promoted six weeks later, he went on to fight at Fredericksburg, Chancellorsville, Gettysburg, and in the Overland, Petersburg, and Appamattox campaigns. After the surrender he went back to his land and held a number of government appointments. (Freeman, Douglas S., *Lee's Lieutenants*)

THOMAS, George Henry (1816-1870)

Unlike his fellow Virginian Robert E. Lee, George Thomas remained loyal to the Union. During Nat Turner's bloody slave revolt, Thomas had led his family to safety and subsequently attended West Point (1840). A veteran of the Seminole and Mexican wars and an artillery and cavalry instructor at the academy, he was a major in the 2nd, soon to be the 5th Cavalry at the time of the secession crisis. His war assignments included: lieutenant colonel, 2nd Cavalry (April 25, 1861); colonel, 2nd Cavalry (May 3, 1861); commanding 1st Brigade, in the 1st Division, Department of Pennsylvania (June-July 25,

1861), in the Department of the Shenandoah (July 25-August 17, 1861), and in Banks' Division, Army of the Potomac (August 17-28, 1861); brigadier general, USV (August 3, 1861); commanding Camp Dick Robinson, Ken., Department of the Ohio (October-December 2, 1861); commanding 1st Division, Army of the Ohio (December 2, 1861-April 30, 1862 and June 10-September 29, 1862); major general, USV (April 25, 1862); commanding Army of the Tennessee (April 30-June 10, 1862); second in command of the Army of the Ohio (September 29-October 24, 1862); commanding Centre, 14th Corps, Army of the Cumberland (November 5, 1862-January 9, 1863); commanding the corps (January 9-October 28, 1863); brigadier general, USA (October 27, 1863); commanding the army (October 28, 1863-September 26, 1864); commanding Department of the Cumberland (October 28, 1863-June 27, 1865); and major general, USA (December 15, 1864). After brief service in the East, Thomas was sent to Kentucky and commanded at Mill Springs. After arriving too late for the fighting at Shiloh, he commanded the Army of the Tennessee, replacing Grant who was shelved by being made second in command to Halleck. After participating in the slow drive on Corinth, Thomas returned to Kentucky and fought at Perryville and later at Stones River and in the Tullahoma Campaign. At Chickamauga, after most of the army had fled the field, Thomas stubbornly held out on the second day at Snodgrass Hill, earning the nickname "The Rock of Chickamauga." After the defeat the army was besieged at Chattanooga, and Grant was promoted to overall command in the West and sent with reinforcements. He was given duplicate orders, one leaving General Rosecrans in command of the Army of the Cumberland and the other giving Thomas the post. Grant chose the latter although he resented Thomas for being replaced after Shiloh. Thomas' men broke through the Confederate lines at Missionary Ridge and later took part in the capture of Atlanta. With Hood's Army of Tennessee threatening Tennessee, in Sherman's rear, Thomas was detached with two corps to deal with him. This was effectively the end of the Army of the Cumberland. After being briefly besieged at Nashville, Thomas, who was about to be removed for being too slow, attacked and routed the rebels. For this, one of the most decisive battles of the war, Thomas became one of 13 officers to receive the Thanks of Congress. Hood's command was no longer a real threat to anyone. With most of his forces sent to other theaters of operations, Thomas remained in command in Tennessee until 1867, when he was assigned to command on the Pacific coast until his death in 1870. (McKinney, Francis F., *Education in Violence: The Life of George H. Thomas and the History of the Army of the Cumberland*)

THOMAS, Henry Goddard (1837-1897)

It is claimed that Henry G. Thomas was the first regular army officer to accept a colonelcy in a black regiment. In any case, his work in the recruitment and training of black troops was highly important to the Union war effort. A Maine attorney he had enlisted at the outbreak of the Civil War and his assignments included: captain, 5th Maine (June 24, 1861); captain, 11th Infantry (August 5, 1861); colonel, 1st Kansas Colored Infantry (March 20, 1863); colonel, 19th United States Colored Troops (January 16, 1864); commanding 2nd Brigade, 4th Division, 9th Corps, Army of the Potomac (May 4-September 7, 1864); commanding 2nd Brigade, 3rd Division, 9th Corps, Army of the Potomac (October-November 26, 1864); brigadier general, USV (November 30, 1864); commanding 3rd Brigade, 3rd Division, 25th Corps, Army of the James (December 15-31, 1864); and commanding 3rd Brigade, 1st Division, 25th Corps, Army of the James (December 31, 1864-April 27, 1865). After fighting at 1st Bull Run as a volunteer officer he entered the regular army as a captain. On recruiting duty until the fall of 1862, he missed the early battles of his regiment, and the next winter he took charge of a black regiment. Mustered out of this regiment on July 11, 1863, he continued with the recruiting of black regiments and six months later again took command of one. He led a brigade of black troops through the Overland Campaign—earning a brevet for Spotsylvania—and in the Petersburg siege. For the latter he won another brevet in the regular service for the fight at the Crater. Promoted to brigadier general, he was transferred to the Army of the James and fought through to Appomattox. For his war service he was brevetted through brigadier general of regulars and major general of volunteers. Mustered out on January 15, 1866, he reverted to his regular army rank of captain. He retired as a major in the pay department in 1891.

THOMAS, Lorenzo (1804-1875)

Although he held the position of adjutant general of the U.S. Army, Lorenzo Thomas provided his most important service in the raising of the United States Colored Troops. Graduating from West Point in 1823, Thomas had served in the Seminole and Mexican Wars, earning a brevet in the latter. A lieutenant colonel in the Adjutant General's Department at the outbreak of the war, he was promoted to full colonel and named to replace General Samuel Cooper, who had gone over to the Confederacy, on March 7, 1861. On August 3, 1861, his post was rated for a brigadier general and he was accordingly promoted. His office was responsible for the massive paperwork of the army. President Lincoln assigned him to investigate the activities of General John C. Frémont in Missouri in the latter part of 1861. His report led to Frémont's removal from command and earned for Thomas the enmity of the Radical Republicans, and especially of future Secretary of War Edwin M. Stanton. Long protected from Stanton by Lincoln, on March 13, 1863, Thomas was finally assigned by Stanton to duty in the West raising black troops. Thomas was successfully engaged in this until the war closed, and for his services he was brevetted major general. In the incident for which Andrew Johnson faced impeachment, Thomas was named as acting secretary of war by Johnson to replace Stanton (who refused to give up his office). Thomas continued as adjutant general until he retired in 1869.

THOMAS, Stephen (1809-1903)

This native Vermont legislator and judge won the Congressional Medal of Honor for hand-to-hand fighting at Cedar Creek, on his way to becoming a Union brigadier general. Thomas' assignments included: colonel, 8th Vermont (February 18, 1862); commanding 2nd Brigade, 1st Division, 19th Corps, Department of the Gulf (May 14-July 11, 1863); commanding 2nd Brigade, 1st Division, 19th Corps, Army of the Shenandoah (October 15-24 and November 1-December 3, 1864); and brigadier general, USV (April 21, 1865, to rank from February 1). Assigned with his regiment to the expedition against New Orleans, he was not however present at the capture. During the operations against Port Hudson he succeeded to brigade command and was wounded. He then took part in the Sabine Pass expedition. In the summer of 1864 the regiment, along with much of the 19th Corps, was transferred to Virginia. Sent into the Shenandoah Valley, he fought at 3rd Winchester and Fisher's Hill. Cedar Creek became the high point of his military career when he held his brigade position in hand-to-hand combat during the early stages of the Confederate surprise attack. He received his medal in 1892. Mustered out on January 25, 1865, he was remustered as a brigadier general after Lee's surrender. Mustered out a second time, on August 24, 1865, he entered politics and served a term as lieutenant governor. For a time he was a pension agent and subsequently engaged in agricultural pursuits.

THOMAS, William Holland (1805-1893)

One of the unique units of the Civil War was a legion of Cherokees and white North Carolinian mountain men commanded by William H. Thomas. A friend of the Indians in western North Carolina, Thomas gained the permission of Andrew Jackson for a number of them to remain in the area—while the majority was deported west of the Mississippi in 1838—and was made one of their chiefs. The state legislator determined to raise an Indian company for the local defense of their area at the outbreak of the war. His assignments included: captain, North Carolina Cherokee company (April 9, 1862); major, Cherokee battalion (July 19, 1862); and colonel, Thomas' (N.C.) Legion (September 27, 1862). With the success of his recruiting activities he kept enlarging his force until it was composed of infantry, cavalry, artillery, and sappers and organized into a regiment and a battalion. His force was used in the mountains of western North Carolina and East Tennessee. However, he was eventually detached from his command—with his two Cherokee companies—after a feud with his brigade commander, Brigadier General Alfred E. Jackson, and sent to round up deserters in their home district. The white portion of the unit fought in East Tennessee and the Shenandoah Valley under Early before rejoining Thomas. By the time that they returned the war was almost over. However, a company of the legion fired the last shot of the war in North Carolina on May 9, 1865, near Waynesville. The next day they surrendered, but the Union commander was so intimidated by the Cherokees that he allowed them to keep their arms and to leave the area. This "surrender" marked the end of Thomas' Legion. Thomas himself had surrendered two days earlier. (Crow, Vernon, *Storm in the Mountains: Thomas' Confederate Legion of Cherokee Indians and Mountaineers*)

THOMPSON, Albert P. (?-1864)

In the same month that he joined Forrest's cavalry, Kentuckian Albert P. Thompson died within sight of his home in one of the great cavalryman's raids. His Confederate assignments included: lieutenant colonel, 3rd Kentucky (July 5, 1861); colonel, 3rd Kentucky (October 25, 1861); commanding 1st Brigade, 2nd Division, Breckinridge's Command, District of the Mississippi, Department No. 2 (July 28-August 5, 1862); and commanding 3rd Brigade, 2nd Division, Forrest's Cavalry Corps, Department of Alabama, Mississippi and East Louisiana (March 7-25, 1864). After service in central Kentucky and northern Mississippi, he led a brigade until wounded in the failed Confederate attack on Baton Rouge. Returning to duty, he served in Buford's Brigade at Jackson, Mississippi and Port Hudson, Louisiana. Ordered to Middle Tennessee, the brigade had its orders changed so that it could face Grierson's raid through Mississippi in April 1863. Then, with Grant's army threatening Vicksburg, Thompson and the brigade fought at Champion Hill where, with the rest of Loring's Division, they were cut off from Pemberton's army and subsequently joined Joe Johnston. During this campaign, Thompson was detached with six of his companies to serve as mounted infantry. With the fall of the river fortress, Thompson continued to serve in the Mississippi area until March 1864 when his regiment was mounted and he was given command of a brigade of cavalry under Forrest. A few weeks later, on Forrest's raid to the Ohio River, he was killed in the attack on Paducah, Kentucky.

THOMPSON, Allen and James

The Thompson brothers from New York are the only case of two brothers receiving the Congressional Medal of Honor. They belonged to Company K, 4th New York Heavy Artillery, which had originally been organized in June 1863 as part of the 11th New York Heavy Artillery—which only lasted a month. The unit served in the defenses of Washington until the spring of 1864 when it joined the Army of the Potomac for the Overland Campaign. At the tail end of the Petersburg siege, at Five Forks, the pair earned their medals. The citation reads as follows: "Made a hazardous reconnaissance through timber and slashings, preceding the Union line of battle, signaling the troops and leading them through the obstructions." (Mitchell, Joseph B., *The Badge of Gallantry*)

THOMPSON, Franklin

See: *Edmonds, Sarah Emma*

THOMPSON, Jacob (1810-1885)

Involved in the Confederacy's activities in Canada, Jacob Thompson managed to get himself indicted in the investigation of the Lincoln assassination. When he fled to Europe, it now appears from recently uncovered evidence, he converted a Confederate fortune to his personal use. Born in North Carolina, he had practiced law before moving to Mississippi. He served in the House of Representatives for over a decade and in 1857 he became secretary of the interior under Buchanan. Charged in the embezzlement of funds from the Indian Trust Fund, he was later cleared. A firm believer in secession, he left the cabinet in protest against the Fort Sumter relief expedition by the *Star of the West* but not until after he had notified the South Carolina authorities of her coming. He served as a lieutenant colonel on the staffs of Beauregard and Pemberton before entering the state legislature in 1863. The next year Jefferson Davis sent him to Canada as a commissioner. He was given large sums of money, for which, given the nature of his service, he was not required to fully account. He was involved in the Northwest Conspiracy to free rebel prisoners and stage a general uprising. He also spent money to gain political and journalistic support for the South and in an attempt to cause a financial panic by speculating in gold. To a lesser extent he was involved in the St. Albans Raid and the plot to burn New York. Although he had known John Wilkes Booth in Canada, he was acquitted for complicity in the assassination but by then had already fled to Europe. Unlike other agents in exile he failed to account for his funds to top ex-Confederate officials in Europe and was investigated by ex-Secretary of War Breckinridge and ex-Secretary of State Benjamin. Failing to account for £35,000, Thompson agreed to a compromise: he paid £12,000 to the former Confederates and the rest was forgotten about. Benjamin agreed to this because he feared a scandal and knew he could not press the claim legally since the Confederacy was defunct. During the next few years, Thompson lived the high-life in Europe, making extensive tours. His windfall of £23,000, or US$113,780, offset much of the wartime losses to his extensive holdings. However, other ex-Confederates charged that his total haul exceeded $300,000, and events show this to be quite likely. Returning to the United States in 1869, he parlayed his holdings into an estate estimated at $500,000 by the time of his death. Thompson had proved that crime against a defunct government does pay. (Davis, WIlliam C., "The Conduct of 'Mr. Thompson,'" *CWTI*, May 1970)

THOMPSON, John Reuben (1823-1873)

A staunch secessionist, Virginian John R. Thompson supported the movement and the Confederacy through his editing, poems, and propaganda abroad. After briefly practicing law his father bought him the *Southern Literary Messenger*, with which he was connected through 1860. His publication was the literary periodical of the South in the pre-secession days. During the Civil War he served as assistant secretary to Virginia governor John Letcher and was an editor for the *Richmond Record* and *The Southern Illustrated News*. In July 1864, due to ill-health he went to England where he wrote for the *Index*, a pro-Confederate organ for which he had already contributed from Richmond. His wartime poems included: "Music in Camp," "The Burial of Latané," "Lee to the Rear," and "Ashby." After the war he worked for the *London Standard* and *New York Evening Post*." He also assisted in the writing of Heros von Borcke's *Memoirs of the Confederate War for Independence*.

THOMPSON, Meriwether Jefferson (1826-1876)

Better known as M. Jeff. Thompson, the Virginia-born former mayor of St. Joseph, Missouri, was one of the more shadowy characters of the Civil War. Highly successful in just about everything he attempted, he was known for his penchant for weapons. With the secession crisis in Missouri, the professional engineer entered the service of his adopted state and became lieutenant colonel, 3rd Infantry, 1st Division, Missouri State Guard. By the fall of Fort Sumter he was a colonel and inspector in the Guard's 4th Military District and on April 15, 1861, he wrote offering his services to Jefferson Davis. By that summer he was brigadier general in the Guard, but, although he often served in command of Confederate troops, he was never mustered into that service. His small force was active in raiding in southeastern Missouri during the war's first season, but in December his force was disbanded preparatory to reorganizing for Confederate service. In the spring of 1862 he was assigned to duty with several of his new volunteer companies, to serve as gunners and marines aboard J.E. Montgomery's River Defense Fleet. However, there was much ill blood between Thompson's men and Montgomery's river steamboatmen and Thompson had to request a transfer of his command. That summer he served with Confederate troops in the vicinity of Lake Pontchartrain, threatening New Orleans. The next summer, 1863, he was serving back in his old haunts, where his men had become known as the "Swamp Rats," in northeastern Arkansas and southeastern Missouri. On August 22, 1863, he was captured in Randolph County, Arkansas, and confined at Johnson's Island and Fort Delaware. "Beast" Butler of New Orleans ill-fame, had developed a great deal of respect for Thompson due to the latter's kind treatment of prisoners and requested that Thompson be released on his parole. This, for Butler, unusual request was denied by the U.S. War Department because of the Sawyer-Flinn dispute. In about August 1864 he was exchanged after having been sent to Charleston Harbor to be placed under Confederate fire—although this was, according to Thompson, never done. On August 9 he was ordered to report to the Trans-Mississippi Department. During part of Price's invasion of Missouri, he commanded Shelby's Brigade, Shelby's Division, Army of Missouri, Trans-Mississippi Department (October 7-December 1864) and the division (December 1864). Falling back into Arkansas, he surrendered the Northern Sub-District of Arkansas, District of Arkansas and West Louisiana, Trans-Mississippi Department, on May 11, 1865. (Monaghan, James, *Swamp Fox of the Confederacy; the Life and Military Services of M. Jeff. Thompson*)

THOMSON, John Renshaw (1800-1862)

New Jersey's senior senator, John R. Thomson, died when the outcome of the Civil War was still in considerable doubt. Born in Pennsylvania, he had been a merchant in the United States and at Canton, China. From 1823 to 1825 he was the U.S. consul at Canton before returning to New Jersey, where he was involved in canals and railroads. An unsuccessful gubernatorial candidate in 1844, he was named to fill a vacancy in the U.S. Senate and took his seat in 1853 as a Democrat. He was reelected four years later and served until his death on September 12, 1862, at a time when the Confederate army was in Maryland and threatening Pennsylvania.

THOUVENEL, Édouard (?-?)

Although French Emperor Napoleon III was strongly in favor of an interventionist course in the American Civil War, his foreign minister during the early part of that conflict, Édouard Thouvenel, was not convinced that such would be the wisest path for France to follow. Many claim that this led to his forced resignation from the government on October 15, 1862. News of the seizure of two Confederate commissioners, Mason and Slidell, from on board the British vessel *Trent* by the U.S. Navy, had much of Europe in a state of outrage when Thouvenel was approached by American diplomats. They sought his views on the situation. True to his abstentionist views, he declared that France considered the action to be a gross violation of international law. But when questioned upon the course France would follow in the dispute, he stated that France would place the moral force of its opinion behind the British, but he seemed to rule out any military action. The minister was worried about the growth of German power at a time when France was preoccupied with events in Mexico and Italy. Earning the displeasure of his sovereign, Thouvenel was forced out in favor of Édouard Drouyn de L'Huys.

THRUSTON, Charles Mynn (1798-1873)

At the age of 64, War of 1812 veteran and Union Brigadier General Charles M. Thruston felt that he was too old for the important command along the Baltimore and Ohio Railroad. A native of Kentucky, he received his West Point appointment from the District of Columbia and graduated in 1814. Posted to the artillery, he served in the second war with Great Britain and the Seminole War. Resigning as captain, 3rd Artillery, in 1836, he entered farming in western Maryland. He also engaged in banking and was Cumberland's mayor during the early months of the Civil War. Appointed to a brigadier generalship of volunteers on September 7, 1861, he was charged with protecting the vital rail line. His efforts proved ineffective and he resigned on April 17, 1862. He then returned to his agricultural pursuits.

THRUSTON, Henry C. (?-1909)

Towering over the Union's biggest Yankee—David Van Buskirk at 6 feet 10 1/2 inches—the Confederacy's was Henry C. Thruston. He enlisted with four of his brothers, all 6 1/2 feet or taller, in the Morgan County (Texas) Rangers. At mustering in he measured 7 feet 7 1/2 inches. He fought at Pea Ridge and then transferred to Company I, 4th Missouri Cavalry. Serving under Earl Van Dorn and Sterling Price, he fought in Arkansas and Missouri. In the spring of 1864 he was wounded at Poison Springs, Arkansas. In the invasion of Missouri later that year he was lightly wounded in the top of the head. A smaller man would have been spared. Surrendered and paroled on June 7, 1865, he settled in Texas for his remaining years.

THULSTRUP, Bror Thure (1848-1930)

A graduate of the National Military Academy in his native Sweden and a veteran of the French Foreign Legion, including service in the Franco-Prussian War, Bror T. Thulstrup—known in the United States as Thure de Thulstrup—naturally turned to military subjects when he decided to enter the field of creative art. His interest in topographical engineering led him into drawing and eventually he moved toward paint and canvas. Pursuing this field he moved to Canada and then the United States. Studying in the post-Civil War years, he was naturally drawn to the subject, and one of his more famous works is of Pickett's Charge at Gettysburg. A military man himself, he was strict in his devotion to accuracy in uniforms and equipment. As a free lance artist he worked for both *Harper's Weekly* and *Frank Leslie's Illustrated Newspaper*. A collection of his work was published in 1898 as *Drawings by Thulstrup and Others*.

TIBBITS, William Badger (1837-1880)

The Civil War had been over for nearly half a year when native New York manufacturer and lawyer William B. Tibbits was commissioned a brigadier general of volunteers. His assignments included: captain, 2nd New York (May 14, 1861); major, 2nd New York (October 13, 1862); colonel, 21st New York Cavalry (February 5, 1864); commanding 1st Brigade, 1st Cavalry Division, Department of West Virginia (April-June and July-August 1864); commanding 1st Brigade, 2nd Cavalry Division, Department of West Virginia (November 10, 1864-February 1865); also commanding 2nd Brigade, 2nd Cavalry Division, Department of West Virginia (December 28, 1864-January 13, 1865); commanding the division (February-April 1865); and brigadier general, USV (October 18, 1865). Sent to Fortress Monroe, his first regiment took part in the defeat at Big Bethel and then joined the Army of the Potomac for the Seven Days. Moving into northern Virginia, he fought at Bristoe Station and 2nd Bull Run but was in the vicinity of Washington at the time of Antietam. At the end of 1862 he participated in the battle of Fredericksburg. After fighting at Chancellorsville, he was mustered out with his two-years regiment on May 26, 1863. Early the next year he again took the field, this time at the head of a mounted regiment. He then led a brigade at New Market, Piedmont, and in the Lynchburg expedition. He finished out the war in the Shenandoah Valley and western Virginia. Brevetted brigadier general for the war on October 21, 1864, he was advanced to the full grade a year later. Brevetted major general for the war, he was mustered out on January 15, 1866.

TIDBALL, John Coldwell (ca. 1825-1906)

During the course of the Civil War, Virginia native and West Pointer (1848) John C. Tidball rose from a first lieutenancy to the brevet rank of major general. Posted to the artillery, he had served against the Seminoles and in suppressing John Brown's raid on Harpers Ferry. Having received his appointment from Ohio, he remained loyal to the Union and his assignments included: first lieutenant, 2nd Artillery (since March 31, 1853); captain, 2nd Artillery (May 14, 1861); commanding 2nd Horse Artillery Brigade, Cavalry Corps, Army of the Potomac (June-August 1863); colonel, 4th New York Heavy Artillery (August 28, 1863); commanding 4th Brigade, Defenses South of the Potomac, 22nd Corps, Department of Washington (September 2-November 5, 1863); commanding 3rd Brigade, Defenses South of the Potomac, 22nd Corps, Department of Washington (November 5, 1863-March 26, 1864); commanding Artillery Brigade, 2nd Corps, Army of the Potomac (March 29-ca. July 10, 1864); Commandant of Cadets, U.S. Military Academy (July 10-September 22, 1864); commanding Artillery Brigade, 9th Corps, Army of the Potomac (ca. September 1864-June 1865); and again commanding 3rd Brigade, Defenses South of the Potomac, 22nd Corps, Department of Washington (June 30-August 20, 1865). After serving at Fort Pickens he led Battery K, 3rd Artillery to the Peninsula and commanded its four 10-pound Parrotts at Yorktown and Williamsburg. Returning to his own regiment, he commanded Battery A's six three-inch Rifles during the Seven Days, earning a brevet for Gaines' Mill. He led his battery at Antietam, Fredericksburg, and in Stoneman's raid during the Chancellorsville Campaign. He earned another brevet for the former. In charge of a brigade of horse artillery, he fought at Aldie, Upperville, and Gettysburg, before being named to command a regiment of volunteer heavy artillery and a brigade in the defenses of the capital. Joining Grant's forces for the Overland Campaign, he fought at the Wilderness in command of the 2nd Corps' guns. On August 1, 1864, he was brevetted major general of regulars for the actions at Po River, Spotsylvania, and Petersburg. In the same period he also fought at the North Anna, Totopotomoy, and Cold Harbor. After a stint back at West Point he took command of the 9th Corps' batteries and was brevetted major general of volunteers for his role in the repulse of the Confederate assault on Fort Stedman in the latter part of the Petersburg siege. He had been brevetted brigadier in the same service on March 13, 1865. At the close of the war he briefly commanded a brigade back in the Washington fortifications and was mustered out of the volunteer service on September 26, 1865. Remaining in the regular army, he served until his 1889 retirement as colonel, 1st Artillery.

TILDEN, Samuel Jones (1814-1886)

Despite being the first post-Civil War presidential candidate who had not supported the war, Samuel J. Tilden came close to winning the 1876 race. Born in New York, he had practiced law and for a time been a leader in the free-soil faction of the Democratic Party. His practice and mining investments earned him a huge fortune which he would later leave to the New York Public Library. An opponent of Lincoln in 1860 and an opponent of the war that followed, he also fought to restrain the growth in federal powers caused by the war. During Reconstruction he favored a moderate approach and was a supporter of Johnson's policies. As head of the party organization in New York he broke up the Tweed Ring and as governor crushed the Canal Ring. These reforms increased his national reputation, and he became the Democratic nominee for president in 1876. In the popular vote he beat Rutherford B. Hayes by 4,284,757 to 4,033,950. But a snag developed in the Electoral College where the electoral votes of Florida, Louisiana, Oregon, and South Carolina were also claimed by the Republicans. In a partisan line vote a special commission ruled in favor of Hayes by one vote, giving Hayes 185 electoral votes to 184 for Tilden. This was confirmed by Congress only two days before the scheduled inauguration. Reluctantly Tilden accepted the results and remained active in state politics.

TILGHMAN, Lloyd (1816-1863)

In two separate efforts to keep Southern rivers blocked to the Union forces, Maryland West Pointer (1836) Lloyd Tilghman was captured in the first and later in the second, killed. He had resigned his commission as a second lieutenant in the 1st Dragoons less than three months after his graduation, then engaged in railroad engineering until the outbreak of the Civil War, except for reentering the service as an artillery captain with the Maryland and District of Columbia volunteers during the Mexican War. Residing in Kentucky when Fort Sumter was fired upon, he offered his services to the Confederacy and his assignments included: brigadier general, CSA (October 18, 1861); commanding Fort Henry, Department #2 (January-February 6, 1862); commanding brigade, Lovell's Division, District of the Mississippi, Army of West Tennessee (October 6-16, 1862); commanding brigade, Lovell's Corps, Army of West Tennessee (October 16-December 7, 1862); commanding brigade, 1st Corps, Department of Mississippi and East Louisiana (December 7, 1862-January 2, 1863); commanding brigade, 1st Loring's Division, 2nd Military District, Department of Mississippi and East Louisiana (January 2-April 1863); and commanding brigade, Loring's Division, 2nd Military District, Department of Mississippi and East Louisiana (January 2-April 1863); and commanding brigade, Loring's Division, Department of Mississippi and East Louisiana (April-May 16, 1863). Inspecting the forts on the Tennessee and Cumberland rivers, he felt that the positioning of Fort Henry on the former was highly defective. Nonetheless he did make a brave stand with a handful of men against the Union gunboats, having dispatched the greater part of his command to Fort Donelson. Forced to capitulate, he was not exchanged until August 27, 1862, for John F. Reynolds. Assigned to command of a brigade, he spent the balance of his life in the defense of Vicksburg. Initially, he was in charge of the camp of paroled and exchanged prisoners at the river city. When Grant crossed the river south of the city Tilghman's brigade served as a part of John C. Pemberton's field force. On May 16, 1863, he was killed by a shell while supervising his own artillery.

TILLSON, Davis (1830-1895)

Unable to complete his studies at West Point, Maine native Davis Tillson nonetheless became a Union general. He had begun his studies in 1849 but was forced to resign two years later when he suffered an accidental injury which resulted in the amputation of his leg. In 1861 he gave up a seat in the state legislature in order to volunteer. His assignments included: captain, 2nd Maine Battery (November 30, 1861); major, 1st Maine Light Artillery Battalion (May 22, 1862); chief of artillery, 3rd Corps, Army of Virginia (ca. June-ca. September 12, 1862); lieutenant colonel, 1st Maine Light Artillery Battalion (December 24, 1862); brigadier general, USV (March 21, 1863, to rank from November 29, 1862); inspector of Artillery, Army of the Potomac (March-April 1863); chief of Artillery, Department of the Ohio (ca. April 1863-April 1864); commanding 2nd Brigade, 4th Division, 23rd Corps, Army of the Ohio (April 10, 1864-January 28, 1865); commanding the division (January 14-February 10, 1865); commanding 4th Division, District of East Tennessee, Department of the Cumberland (February 10-May 17, 1865); and also commanding the district (February 10-March 9, 1865). As an artillery field officer, he fought at Cedar Mountain and 2nd Bull Run. Promoted to brigadier general, he served briefly as an inspector of artillery and then went to head the long arm in the Department of the Ohio. He then transferred to the infantry and spent most of the rest of the war in East Tennessee. Brevetted major general for the war, he was mustered out on December 1, 1866, after having worked for the Freedmen's Bureau in Tennessee and Georgia. After a year growing Georgia cotton he returned to Maine and engaged in the granite and lime business.

TILLSON, John (?-1892)

Serving throughout the war in the western theater, this Illinois native won the brevet of brigadier general of volunteers and two regular army brevets for his wartime service. His assignments included: captain, 10th Illinois (April 29, 1861); major, 10th Illinois (May 27, 1861); lieutenant colonel, 10th Illinois (September 9, 1861); captain, 19th Infantry (October 26, 1861); colonel, 10th Illinois (July 17, 1862); commanding 1st Brigade, 2nd Division, Reserve Corps, Army of the Cumberland (August 3-October 10, 1863); commanding 3rd Brigade, 4th Division, 16th Corps, Army of the Tennessee (August 20-September 23, 1864); and commanding 3rd Brigade, 1st Division, 17th Corps, Army of the Tennessee (September 22, 1864-March 26, 1865 and April 12-July 4, 1865). While his regiment was stationed at Cairo, Illinois, he was mustered out with it on July 29, 1861, upon the expiration of its three-months term of enlistment. Six weeks later he was recommissioned in the three-years unit with an advance in grade. He commanded the regiment at Island #10 and served during the advance on Corinth, Mississippi. The next year was spent primarily in dealing with enemy raids, especially those of John Hunt Morgan and Joseph Wheeler. Rejoining the main army in the West, he fought at Chattanooga, and during the Atlanta Campaign he took over charge of a brigade. He led this on the March to the Sea and in the Carolinas. Mustered out of the volunteers with his regiment on July 4, 1865, he resigned from the regular army early the next year.

TILTON, William Stowell (?-1889)

One month after receiving his brevet as a brigadier general of volunteers William S. Tilton was mustered out with his regiment at the expiration of its term. The Massachusetts native's assignments included: first lieutenant and adjutant, 22nd Massachusetts (September 12, 1861); major, 22nd Massachusetts (October 2, 1861); lieutenant colonel, 22nd Massachusetts (June 28, 1862); colonel, 22nd Massachusetts (October 17, 1862); and commanding 1st Brigade, 1st Division, 5th Corps, Army of the Potomac (May 5-August 18, 1863, November 19, 1863-March 25, 1864, and June 18-August 22, 1864). Entering the service as the adjutant of a new regiment, he was made a field officer in a few weeks, and as such he served at Yorktown. The day after being wounded and captured at Gaines' Mill—during the Seven Days—he was named a lieutenant colonel. Declared exchanged on August 27, 1862, he directed the regiment at Antietam and a month later was named to its permanent command. He fought at Fredericksburg and Chancellorsville. At Gettysburg and in the Mine Run Campaign he directed the brigade but lost it in the spring 1864 reorganization. Back in charge of his regiment he fought throughout the Overland Campaign and was for a time in charge of a brigade at Petersburg. For his war service to date he was brevetted on September 9, 1864, and he was mustered out on October 17, 1864.

TIMROD, Henry (1828-1867)

A college dropout, a failure as a law student, Henry Timrod throughout his life turned to the meager income that his poetry could provide him. His verse was published by the *Southern Literary Messenger* and in an 1859 collection, and his reputation grew beyond his native Charleston. A southern patriot, he celebrated the formation of the Confederacy with "Ethnogenesis" and predicted a stout defense if invaded. His poems show a rise and fall of optimism which matches the military fortunes of the Confederacy. In the winter of 1861-62, Timrod served as a private in the 13th South Carolina. In the spring he became secretary to Colonel Keitt of the 20th South Carolina. He shortly thereafter went west to cover General Beauregard's army in Northern Mississippi for the *Charleston Mercury*. Because journalists were expelled from the army's lines (prior to the retreat from Corinth), Timrod returned to his regiment in South Carolina. Discharged due to tuberculosis in December 1862 he continued to praise in verse the defenders of Charleston, General Ripley, and, in "Carmen Triumphale," victory at Chancellorsville. As associate editor of the *South Carolinian* in 1864 his prospects improved. However, illness curtailed his writing. In late 1866, he wrote his most famous piece, "Ode," mourning the lost cause of the Confederacy. He died the next year. (Parks, Edd W., *Henry Timrod*)

TOD, David (1805-1868)

Although a Democrat, Ohio's David Tod became an ardent supporter of the Lincoln war effort and became the Union Party's gubernatorial candidate in 1861. A lawyer, postmaster, and state legislator, he was also involved in railroading, coal, and iron. Twice defeated for the governorship in the 1840s, he was named minister to Brazil and served from 1847 to 1857. A year after his return he was defeated in a bid for Congress, then chaired the party's national convention in 1860. Elected governor in 1861, he took up his duties in 1862. He worked against the peace movement and draft resistance. He was a moving force in protecting the state's southern border from enemy raids. His weak support of the Emancipation Proclamation cost him renomination for a second term by the Union ticket and he left office in 1864. Offered the treasury portfolio in Lincoln's cabinet, he refused for health and business reasons. However, he continued in the Republican Party after the war. (Wright, G.B., *Honorable David Tod*)

TODD, George (?-1864)

One of bushwhacker William C. Quantrill's principal deputies, George Todd, succeeded to the command of most of the cutthroat's band after embarrassing Quantrill in front of the rest of the men. Todd had long ridden with Quantrill, and when the latter had been named a captain, Todd was made a lieutenant. Participating in most of the bloody guerrilla actions in Missouri, Todd and Quantrill eventually came into conflict—at one point they even exchanged shots—until Todd placed a gun in Quantrill's face and forced him to back down. Quantrill rode off with a few of his men. Todd, now called captain since Quantrill had styled himself a colonel, was left in charge. He led his men in the Centralia massacre and had a running feud with another former Quantrill lieutenant, Bloody Bill Anderson. Finally, in late October 1864 he was killed outside Independence, Missouri, while scouting for Price's army.

TODD, John Blair Smith (1814-1872)

When the Senate failed to confirm his appointment as a brigadier general of volunteers Kentucky-born John B.S. Todd returned to Congress as the delegate from the Dakota Territory. He had received his appointment to West Point from Illinois and, upon his 1837 graduation, been posted to the Infantry with which he served in the Seminole and Mexican wars and on the frontier. Resigning as captain, 6th Infantry, in 1856, he set himself up as a lawyer in Dakota. When the territory was formed he was sent to Washington as its first delegate and took his seat on December 9, 1861. His military assignments included: brigadier general, USV (September 19, 1861); commanding District of North Missouri, Department of the Missouri (October 15-December 1, 1861); and commanding 6th Division, Army of the Tennessee (June 15-July 16, 1862). He served in Missouri and then attended the 37th Congress' second session. He briefly commanded a division under Grant but relinquished it when his commission expired on July 17, 1862. He then attended the third session but was defeated for reelection by William Jayne. Contesting the result, Todd won and was seated on June 17, 1864. Losing another reelection bid for the next full term that year, he returned to Dakota and sat in the territorial legislature.

TOMPKINS, Charles H. (1830-?)

After having dropped out of West Point in 1849—following two years of study—Charles H. Tompkins had been serving as an enlisted man since 1856 when the war in which he was to earn a brevet generalship and a Congressional Medal of Honor began. His Civil War assignments included: sergeant, Company F, 1st Dragoons (by January 10, 1861); second lieutenant, 2nd Cavalry (March 23, 1861); first lieutenant, 2nd Cavalry (April 30, 1861); first lieutenant, 5th Cavalry (change of designation August 3, 1861); first lieutenant and regimental quartermaster, 5th Cavalry (August 28, 1861); captain and assistant quartermaster (November 13, 1861); and colonel, 1st Vermont Cavalry (April 24, 1862). On June 1, 1861, he led a small force of cavalry from the lines around Washington to Fairfax Court House where they met the enemy. In this action the first Confederate soldier was killed, and Tompkins earned his first brevet and—in 1893—the Congressional Medal of Honor. Later brevets followed for his service as the commander of a volunteer regiment in the campaigns in northern Virginia and in the Quartermaster's Department following his resignation from the volunteers on September 9, 1862. He ended the war as a quartermaster captain and brevet brigadier for the war. Continuing in the regular establishment, he retired in 1894 as a colonel and assistant quartermaster general.

TOMPKINS, Charles Henry (?-1895)

A New York-born Rhode Island resident, Charles H. Tompkins raised and commanded the first artillery battery from his state and rose to be the chief artillerist of a Union corps, earning the brevet of brigadier on the way. His assignments included: captain, 1st Rhode Island Battery (May 2, 1861); major, 1st Rhode Island Light Artillery (August 1, 1861); colonel, 1st Rhode Island Light Artillery (September 13, 1861); chief of Artillery, 1st Division, 6th Corps, Army of the Potomac (spring 1863); and chief of Artillery, 6th Corps, Army of the Potomac and of the Shenandoah (spring 1863-early 1865). With his initial battery he served in Patterson's campaign in the Shenandoah Valley before becoming a field officer in his state's light artillery regiment. After holding a number of staff and field assignments he became a divisional artillery chief in time for the fighting at Chancellorsville. When the artillery of the army was divided into brigades attached to each corps in the spring of 1863, he was given charge of the artillery brigade assigned to the 6th Corps and directed the guns at Gettysburg, the Wilderness, Spotsylvania, Cold Harbor, Petersburg, and in the Shenandoah Valley Campaign of 1864. For the last series of operations he received his brevet as a brigadier. Absent from the final surrender at Appomattox, he was mustered out on April 21, 1865.

TOMPKINS, Sally Louisa (1833-1916)

In order to retain her services to the Confederacy when all military hospitals were put under military control, Jefferson Davis had Sally L. Tompkins commissioned a captain of cavalry on September 9, 1861. She was thus the only woman to officially become an officer in the armies of the Confederacy. A resident of Richmond, she had long been active in charity work, and when the call went out after 1st Bull Run for Richmonders to open their homes for the wounded and sick, she used the home of Judge John Robertson as a hospital. Despite being sent some of the most serious cases, her Robertson Hospital maintained an enviable record. From August 1, 1861, to April 2, 1865, there occurred only 73 deaths out of 1,333 admissions. Refusing to accept any pay for her work, she made good use of her rank in running her operations. Her hospital was in operation until June 13, 1865, under the Union occupation. After the war she was active in philanthropic work through the Protestant Episcopal Church. She was buried with military honors, and two chapters of the United Daughters of the Confederacy were named for her.

TOOMBS, Robert Augustus (1810-1885)

During his career as a lawyer and politician, serving in both houses in his native Georgia and in the U.S. Senate, Robert A. Toombs gradually became a secessionist. After attending the state's secession convention, he was named to the Provisional Confederate Congress where he served on the Committee on Finance. An aspirant for the presidency, he instead became the first secretary of state on February 21, 1861. Bored, he stepped down in July and, capitalizing upon his experience as a captain of volunteers during the Creek War, entered the military service. His assignments included: brigadier general, CSA (July 19, 1861); commanding brigade, 2nd Corps, Army of the Potomac (summer-October 22, 1861); commanding brigade, G.W. Smith's Division, (in Potomac District until March), Department of Northern Virginia (October 22, 1861-April 1862); commanding brigade, D.R. Jones' Division, Magruder's Command, same department (April-July 3, 1862); temporarily commanding the division (April 1862); and commanding brigade, Jones' Division, 1st Corps, Army of Northern Virginia (July and August 30-September 17, 1862). Seeing action in the Seven Days, he was criticized by D.H. Hill for the behavior of his brigade at Malvern Hill. His demand for satisfaction went unanswered. Still retaining a seat in congress, he was absent for part of the summer but rejoined his command at 2nd Bull Run. At Antietam his brigade performed creditably and he suffered a hand wound. At about the time that congress adjourned he submitted his resignation, which took effect on March 4, 1863. He was disgruntled about being passed over for promotion. He lost a race for the Senate but was named adjutant and inspector general for the Georgia Militia in the Atlanta Campaign. Fleeing the country to avoid arrest at the war's close, he returned and resumed his law practice. Late in life he suffered from blindness and alcoholism. (Thompson, William Y., *Robert Toombs of Georgia*)

Robert A. Toombs, Confederate congressman and general. (*Harper's*)

TOON, Thomas Fentress (1840-1902)

A Wake Forest College student at the outbreak of the war, Thomas F. Toon enlisted on April 24, 1861, but then returned to complete his studies. Once finished he rejoined his company in time for mustering in. His assignments included: first lieutenant, Company K, 20th North Carolina (June 18, 1861); captain, Company K, 20th North Carolina (July 19, 1861); colonel, 20th North Carolina (February 26, 1863); commanding Johnston's Brigade, Ramseur's Division, 2nd Corps, Army of Northern Virginia (May 12-June 13, 1864); temporary brigadier general, CSA (May 31, 1864); and commanding Johnston's Brigade, Ramseur's Division, Valley District, Department of Northern Virginia (June 13-August 1864). As a company officer, he was so distinguished at Seven Pines, the Seven Days, South Mountain, and Fredericksburg that the following winter he was promoted three grades to command the regiment. He returned in time to fight at Mine Run, the Wilderness, and Spotsylvania. With General Johnston wounded in the latter, Toon took over the brigade and was appointed a temporary brigadier. As such he served in Early's campaign to the outskirts of Washington, including fighting at Monocacy. In August Johnston resumed command, and Toon reverted to colonel in charge of the 20th. Toon then fought at 3rd Winchester, Fisher's Hill, and Cedar Creek. Moving to the Petersburg trenches, he was severely wounded in the Confederate assault on Fort Stedman. He served in education and railroading after the war and also sat in the legislature.

TORBERT, Alfred Thomas Archimedes (1833-1880)

Despite considering the Confederacy, Alfred T.A. Torbert stayed put and rose in the Union ranks to become the temporary commander of a military division. The Delaware West Pointer (1855) had been posted to the infantry and seen service against the Seminoles, on the frontier, and in the anti-Mormon campaign. His Civil War-era assignments included: second lieutenant, 5th Infantry (since July 19, 1855); first lieutenant, 5th Infantry (February 25, 1861); first lieutenant, Artillery, CSA (March 16, 1861); colonel, 1st New Jersey (September 16, 1861); captain, 5th Infantry (September 25, 1861); commanding 1st Brigade, 1st Division, 6th Corps, Army of the Potomac (August 29-December 24, 1862, February 8-April 10, 1863, and June 27, 1863-March 25, 1864); brigadier general, USV (November 29, 1862); commanding the division (March 25-April 23, 1864); commanding 1st Division, Cavalry Corps, Army of the Potomac (April 10-May 7 and May 25-August 6, 1864); commanding Cavalry Corps, Army of the Shenandoah (August 6, 1864-January 26, 1865); commanding the army (February 28-June 27, 1865); and also commanding Middle Military Division (February 28-March 7, 1865). On leave during the final stages of the secession crisis, he was appointed to an artillery lieutenancy in the Confederate forces but never accepted the commission. Returning to duty on April 17, 1861, he was assigned to recruiting in New Jersey, and five months later he became colonel of a volunteer regiment which was already serving near Washington. He led his veterans of the 1st Bull Run campaign to the Peninsula and saw action at Yorktown and during the Seven Days. Moving back north, he led the brigade in a supporting position during the latter part of the battle of 2nd Bull Run. Wounded at South Mountain, he went on to fight at Antietam, Fredericksburg, and Gettysburg. In the latter his brigade lost only 11 men wounded, but he was still brevetted for the battle. He then served in the Bristoe and Mine Run operations before being assigned to the command of a mounted division for the Overland Campaign. He fell ill during the Wilderness fighting but returned to duty in time to win another brevet at Haw's Shop. He served in the beginning of the Petersburg operations but was dispatched to command the cavalry under Sheridan in the Shenandoah. Brevetted for 3rd Winchester, he administered a crushing defeat on the enemy cavalry at Tom's Brook in October 1864. Later that month he won the regular army brevet of brigadier general at Cedar Creek. As of September 9, 1864, he had been brevetted major general of volunteers for the war to date. When Sheridan moved to Petersburg, Torbert took over the army, much reduced in strength, and finished the war in the Valley. Brevetted major general of regulars for the war, he was mustered out of the volunteers on January 15, 1866. He did not receive a regular army promotion from captain in the expansion of the army later that year, so resigned on October 31. From 1869 to 1878 he was a diplomat in Latin America and France. In 1880 he drowned in a shipwreck off Florida while on a business trip to Mexico.

TOTTEN, James (ca. 1818-1871)

A meritorious career in the Civil War was destroyed when James Totten was dismissed from the regular army five years later. The Pennsylvania native had received his West Point appointment from Virginia and had been posted to the artillery following his 1837 graduation. He served in Mexico, Florida, and Kansas before the Civil War. His later assignments included: captain, 2nd Artillery (since October 20, 1855); major, 1st Missouri Light Artillery (August 19, 1861); chief of artillery, Western Department (summer 1861-November 2, 1861); lieutenant colonel, 1st Missouri Light Artillery (September 1, 1861); chief of Artillery, Department of the Missouri (November 2, 1861-February 19, 1862); major and assistant inspector general (November 12, 1861); brigadier general, Missouri Militia (February 20, 1862); commanding District of Central Missouri, Department of the Missouri (March 11-October 12, 1862); commanding 2nd Division, Army of the Frontier, Department of the Missouri (October 12-December 1862); inspector general, Department of the Missouri (1863-August 6, 1864); chief of Artillery and chief of Ordnance, Military Division of the Mississippi (August 6, 1864-spring 1865); and lieutenant colonel and assistant inspector general (June 13, 1867). For commanding the six guns of Battery F, 2nd Artillery, at Booneville and Wilson's Creek, he won two regular army brevets before entering the volunteers. For the balance of the war he held a series of field and staff assignments in the western theater as an officer of U.S. volunteers, Missouri militia, and the regular army. Brevetted for his role in the capture of Mobile,

Artillerist James Totten. (*Leslie's*)

he also received the regular army brevet of brigadier general for the war. He was mustered out of the Missouri militia on June 15, 1865, and reverted to his regular army grade as a staff major. Two years later this was increased to a lieutenant colonelcy. However, in 1870 he was dismissed for "conduct to the prejudice of good order and military discipline," disobedience, and neglect. He died the next year.

TOTTEN, Joseph Gilbert (1788-1864)

The chief engineer of the U.S. Army at the beginning of the Civil War, Joseph Totten, had held that office since 1838. An early graduate of West Point (1805), Totten was a veteran of both the War of 1812 and the Mexican War. Serving entirely in the engineers, he had risen to the rank of colonel by 1861. He had also earned brevets, two for the war with Great Britain and one for his service with Winfield Scott in Mexico, especially at the siege of Vera Cruz. During the Civil War, in addition to his regular duties of maintaining harbor channels and defenses and lighthouses, he was responsible for providing engineering officers to the armies in the field and providing special supervision for such projects as the massive defensive ring around the nation's capital which was never really challenged by the rebels because of its strength. On March 3, 1863, the Corps of Topographical Engineers was merged into the Corps of Engineers, and Totten was promoted to brigadier general, USA, in recognition of his heightened responsibilities. While still serving in this office, Totten died suddenly, on April 22, 1864 of pneumonia. He was subsequently brevetted major general in the regular army for eminent service, to rank from the day preceding his death. (Barnard, John G., *Eulogy on the Late Brevet Major General Joseph G. Totten*)

TOWER, Zealous Bates (1819-1900)

A number one graduate from West Point (1841), Massachusetts native Zealous B. Tower emerged from the Civil War with all the brevets which he could earn. In consideration of his class standing he had been posted to the engineers and in the Mexican war served on Winfield Scott's staff. Wounded at Chapultepec, he earned three brevets south of the border and went on to routine engineering duties on both coasts during the interwar years. Before fighting had begun in 1861 he was sent to Fort Pickens, Florida, as a member of the secret relief expedition. From February to May he served in maintaining Union possession of that important work. Brevetted for his role there, he was recalled to the North and soon was promoted to major. His Civil War assignments included: captain, Engineers (since July 1, 1855); major, Engineers (August 6, 1861); commanding 2nd Brigade, Ord's Division, Department of the Rappahannock (June 10-26, 1862); brigadier general, USV (June 12, 1862, to rank from November 23, 1861); commanding 2nd Brigade, 2nd Division, 3rd Corps, Army of Virginia (June 28-August 30, 1862); superintendent, U.S. Military Academy (July 8-September 8, 1864); and inspector general of Fortifications, Military Division of the Mississippi (October 20, 1864-July 1865). Awarded a brigadier's star, he was given a brigade in northern Virginia and earned a brevet at Cedar Mountain. On August 30, 1862, he was so severely wounded at 2nd Bull Run that he did not again serve in a field command. Incapable of performing any duties until July 1864, he was then named to head his old alma mater. Three months later he became Sherman's inspector for western fortifications. He spent most of his time at Nashville and was present during the battle. In March 1865 he was brevetted brigadier—for 2nd Bull Run—and major general for the war. Three months later he was brevetted major general in the volunteers for his wartime services. Mustered out of the volunteers on January 15, 1866, he rose to colonel in the regular engineers by the time of his 1883 retirement.

TOWNSEND, Edward Davis (1817-1893)

A West Pointer (1837), Edward Townsend served throughout the Civil War in the Adjutant General's Department. Upon graduation he had been assigned to an artillery regiment, of which he soon became the adjutant and with which he fought in the Seminole War. Assigned to the Adjutant General's Department in 1846 he rose to lieutenant colonel by the time of Fort Sumter. He was promoted to colonel on August 3, 1861, while serving as General Winfield Scott's chief of staff. On November 1, 1861, he was assigned to the department's headquarters in Washington. On March 23, 1863, the adjutant general, Lorenzo Thomas, was assigned to special duty, and Townsend became the acting head of the department for the duration of the war. Remaining in the army after the war, for which war he was brevetted brigadier and major general, he was promoted to brigadier general, USA, and permanently succeeded General Thomas on February 22, 1869. He held this post until his retirement in 1880. At the close of hostilities, Townsend supervised the demobilization of the volunteer armies.

TOWNSEND, George Alfred (1841-1914)

On the battlefield of South Mountain there is a memorial arch, dedicated not to the soldiers who fought there but rather to the journalists who covered the war. The driving force behind the arch was George Townsend. Born in Delaware, he had been in the profession for less than a year when the war began. After working for two Philadelphia papers, the *Inquirer* and the *Press*, he covered the Peninsula Campaign and the battle of Cedar Mountain for the *New York Herald*. He became a syndicated columnist, using the pen name "Gath," and made an extensive European tour, lecturing part of the time, before returning to cover the final Union triumph in Virginia. After the war he branched out into fiction and feature writing from Washington and bought an estate, Gapland, on South Mountain. Following an 1895 visit to Antietam, Townsend thought it fitting to erect a monument to the journalists of the war. Choosing his estate as the site, he sought financial support from leading businessmen and newspapers. Dedicated the following year, the $5,000 arch, like many of the estate's bizarre structures, incorporated several architectural styles. Bearing the names of 151 correspondents and artists, only nine being Southern, the memorial is is part Norman, Moorish, and

Roman. Spending most of his subsequent time in Washington, Townsend died in New York while visiting his daughter. (Hindes, Ruthanna, *George Alfred Townsend*)

TRACY, Benjamin Franklin (1830-1915)

A brevet brigadier general of volunteers and winner of the Congressional Medal of Honor in the Civil War, Benjamin F. Tracy went on to become a founder of a modernized and expanded navy as Benjamin Harrison's secretary of the navy. The New York attorney's wartime assignments included: colonel, 109th New York (August 28, 1862); and colonel, 127th United States Colored Troops (September 10, 1864). While his regiment was assigned to the Annapolis area, Tracy was in command of the prison camp at Elmira, New York, and was also engaged in recruiting activities. When his regiment took the field for Grant's Overland Campaign he rejoined it, and at the Wilderness he won the coveted medal for having carried the unit's colors on the second day of the fight. The medal was awarded in 1895. He was honorably discharged only a few days later, on May 17, 1864, but again took the field as commander of a black regiment. This he led at Petersburg and Appomattox. He was again honorably discharged on June 13, 1865. He served as a district attorney and judge before becoming secretary of the navy in 1889. He left that office in 1893. In the adultery trial of Henry Ward Beecher he served as the defendant's attorney.

TRACY, Edward Dorr (1833-1863)

Georgia-born Alabama lawyer Edward D. Tracy gave his life for the Confederacy in the first stages of Grant's final drive against Vicksburg. His assignments included: captain, Company I, 4th Alabama (May 7, 1861); major, 4th Alabama (July 25, 1861); lieutenant colonel, 19th Alabama (October 12, 1861); brigadier general, CSA (August 16, 1862); commanding brigade, McCown's Division, Department of East Tennessee (October 31-December 1862); commanding brigade, Stevenson's Division, 2nd Military District, Department of Mississippi and East Louisiana (January-April 1863); and commanding brigade, Stevenson's Division, Department of Mississippi and East Louisiana (April-May 1, 1863). He commanded his company at 1st Bull Run and was shortly afterwards made a field officer. That fall he was named second in command of another regiment in the western theater, and he had a horse killed under him at Shiloh. He then served in East Tennessee. Promoted to brigadier general, he and his brigade were transferred to Stevenson's division and ordered to Mississippi. After Grant had crossed the Mississippi the first significant action came at Port Gibson on May 1, 1863. It was in this fight that Tracy fell.

TRAPIER, James Heyward (1815-1865)

Despite his West Point (1838) education, South Carolinian James H. Trapier was found wanting as a field commander and was relegated to district command in his native state for the balance of the war. He had served a week in the artillery after his graduation before being assigned to the engineers. In 1848 he resigned as a first lieutenant to return to his plantation. Also active in the militia, he offered his services to his state in 1861 and his assignments included: captain, South Carolina Engineers (early 1861); major, South Carolina Engineers (spring 1861); brigadier general, CSA (October 21, 1861); commanding Department of Middle and Eastern Florida (October 22, 1861-early 1862 and March 14-19, 1862); commanding brigade, Withers' Division, 2nd Corps, Army of the Mississippi (late April-June 1862); commanding 4th Military District of South Carolina, Department of South Carolina, Georgia and Florida (November 6, 1862-March 14, 1863 and June 16, 1863-October 17, 1864); commanding Sub-District #2, 1st Military District of South Carolina, Department of South Carolina, Georgia and Florida (March 14-May 10, 1863); commanding 2nd Military District of South Carolina, Department of South Carolina, Georgia and Florida (May 10-28, 1863); commanding 1st Sub-District of South Carolina, Department of South Carolina, Georgia and Florida (October 17, 1864-ca. April 1865); and also commanding brigade, Department of South Carolina, Georgia and Florida (October 17, 1864-ca. April 1865). During the bombardment of Fort Sumter he was present as an engineering officer. Promoted to brigadier general, he commanded in Florida and was then sent to Beauregard's army in Mississippi. Failing to make the grade, he was returned to district command in South Carolina after participating in the Corinth siege. During the Carolinas Campaign his sub-district, now styled a brigade, was not part of Hardee's Corps of Joseph E. Johnston's army but was presumably included in the surrender of April 26, 1865. He died on December 21st of the same year.

TREMAIN, Henry Edwin (1840-1910)

During the battle of Resaca Henry E. Tremain, a staff officer, won the Congressional Medal of Honor for riding between two Union brigades which were accidentally firing upon one another to stop them. The New Yorker's assignments included: first lieutenant, 73rd New York (August 14, 1861); captain, 73rd New York (November 1, 1862); and major and aide-de-camp, USV (April 25, 1863). Enlisting in the Excelsior Brigade, he accompanied his unit to the Peninsula where it fought during the Seven Days. At 2nd Bull Run, while serving as an acting aide to brigade commander Daniel E. Sickles, he was captured and sent to Libby Prison in Richmond. Exchanged on September 21, 1862, he soon received a formal staff appointment and joined the staff of Joseph Hooker. It was under the latter that he and Paul A. Oliver won their medals at Resaca during the Atlanta Campaign. Tremain's medal was issued in 1892. Mustered out of the service on April 20, 1866, with the brevet of brigadier general for the war from November 30, 1865, he entered upon the practice of law and was active in Republican Party affairs.

TRENHOLM, George Alfred (1807-1876)

The Confederacy's last secretary of the treasury, George Trenholm, presided over the dwindling of his nation's resources and of his own personal fortune. A highly successful businessman in foreign trade, Trenholm had served four years in the South Carolina legislature before retiring from politics in 1856. Having supported the principle of nullification as propounded by Calhoun, he was an early secessionist. Throwing himself fully behind the new Confederacy, he ran a successful fleet of blockade runners early in the war. He maintained branches of his company in Liverpool, Nassau, and Bermuda. The English office served as the headquarters for the Confederate purchasing agents, Caleb Huse and James Bulloch, as well as a depository for Confederate funds. His firm was also involved in the securing of the Erlanger loan for the Confederacy. He served as an advisor to his predecessor in the treasury post, Christopher Memminger, until the latter's resignation. On July 18, 1864, he succeeded to the cabinet position. To the regret of the Confederate Congress, he continued Memminger's policies and called on the legislators to crack down on inflation by imposing heavy taxes rather than just issuing more notes. By the time Congress acted the war was just about over. In the retreat of the rebel cabinet, Trenholm had to be left behind because of ill health and Postmaster General John Reagan took over his duties on a temporary basis. The war cost Trenholm most of his fortune and he spent several months in jail. The Federal authorities sold his company's assets to retrieve duties which had not been collected on imports it had made during the war. With a small amount of money saved from the debacle he recouped a portion of his former wealth and served his last two years back in the state legislature. (Nepveux, Ethel S., *George Alfred Trenholm and the Company That Went to War 1861-1865*)

TRIGG, Robert Craig (1830-1872)

A lawyer and graduate of the Virginia Military Institute, Robert C. Trigg commanded one of the handful of Virginia units to serve in the western theater. Entering the army, he was commissioned colonel, 54th Virginia, on September 4, 1861. His other assignments included: commanding brigade, Department of East Tennessee (summer-August 6, 1863); commanding brigade, Preston's Division, Buckner's Corps, Army of Tennessee (August 6-September 1863); commanding brigade, Buckner's Corps, Army of Tennessee (August 6-September 1863); commanding brigade, Buckner's Division, 1st Corps, Army of Tennessee (September-November 1863); and commanding Reynolds' Brigade, Stevenson's Division, 2nd Corps, Army of Tennessee (May 27-June 1864). After initial service in western Virginia, eastern Kentucky, and East Tennessee, his command became part of Bragg's army and he led a brigade at Chickamauga. Taking part in the Atlanta Campaign, he succeeded to brigade command upon the wounding of General A.W. Reynolds at New Hope Church. But with the heavy losses suffered in that campaign, the brigade was consolidated with another and Trigg was no longer a brigade commander. He spent the latter part of the war rounding up deserters. His detachment was in Virginia when the regiment surrendered in North Carolina. Trigg disbanded his men at that time.

TRIMBLE, Isaac Ridgeway (1802-1888)

A West Pointer (1822) and veteran of 10 years' artillery service, Isaac R. Trimble left railroad engineering to aid the Confederacy. He started by burning railroad bridges north of Baltimore. After obstructing the route for Washington-bound troops, he left his adopted state, Maryland, and went to the state of his birth, Virginia, to offer his services in a more orthodox manner. His assignments included: colonel, Virginia Engineers (May 1861); brigadier general, CSA (August 9, 1861); commanding Crittenden's (old) Brigade, E.K. Smith's-Ewell's Division, Potomac District (Valley District after April), Department of Northern Virginia (November 22, 1861-June 26, 1862); commanding brigade, Ewell's Division, 2nd Corps, Army of Northern Virginia (June 26-August 29, 1862); major general, CSA (April 23, to date from January 17, 1863); commanding Valley District, Department of Northern Virginia (May 28-late June 1863); and commanding Pender's Division, 3rd Corps, Army of Northern Virginia (July 3, 1863). After constructing batteries along the Potomac at Evansport, in the Department of Fredericksburg, and later in the Aquia District, he was given a brigade in what became Ewell's Division. He fought under Jackson in the Shenandoah and in the Seven Days. Moving north, his actions included Cedar Mountain, Hazel Run, Manassas Junction, and 2nd Bull Run where he was severely wounded. In early 1863 he was promoted with the expectation that he would command Jackson's former division but was found too feeble. Instead he was given charge of the Valley District, an assignment of which he soon tired. He accompanied the army into Pennsylvania without a command, serving as a volunteer aide to Ewell. On July 3 he took over command of the wounded Pender's Division for Pickett's Charge. Wounded, he lost a leg and was captured. Exchanged in February 1865, he was unable to rejoin Lee before Appomattox. He returned to Baltimore as an engineer. (Freeman, Douglas S., *Lee's Lieutenants*)

TRIPLER, Charles Stuart (?-1866)

A veteran of three decades of medical service in the regular army, Charles S. Tripler was the first medical director of the Army of the Potomac. A native New Yorker, he had become an assistant surgeon in 1830, and his Civil War assignments included: major and surgeon, USA (since July 7, 1838); medical director, Department of Pennsylvania (April-August 1861); medical director, Army of the Potomac (August-October 3, 1861); medical director, Army of the Potomac (October 3, 1861-July 1862); and medical director, Northern Department (March 1864-October 20, 1866). The veteran of the Seminole and Mexican wars served under Patterson and then McClellan. Relieved of field service, he served in administrative positions, mostly on boards and commissions. He then served until his death in the Northwest. He received regular army brevets through that of brigadier general for the war.

TRUMBULL, Lyman (1813-1896)

A senator from Lincoln's home state, Lyman Trumbull was one of those who visited the president on October 26, 1861, to pressure him into forcing McClellan into a battle. Born in Connecticut, he had practiced law in Georgia and Illinois before entering politics. He was a state legislator, state secretary of state, and an associate judge on the state supreme court. In 1854 he was elected as a Republican to the U.S. House of Representatives, but before he could take his seat he was named to the Senate. He served there from 1855 to 1873. John Hay called the three senatorial visitors—Trumbull, Benjamin F. Wade, and Zachariah Chandler—the "Jacobin Club." After three terms in the Senate, Trumbull resumed his law practice in Chicago and lost a bid, as a Democrat, for the gubernatorial chair in 1880. (White, Horace, *The Life of Lyman Trumbull*)

TRUMBULL, Thomas S. (?-?)

In some of the major battles of the Army of the Potomac, Thomas S. Trumbull was in charge of the heavy artillery. The Connecticut soldier's assignments included: major, 1st Connecticut Heavy Artillery (early 1862); and lieutenant colonel, 1st Connecticut Heavy Artillery (1864). He accompanied McClellan's army to the Peninsula and took a leading role in the siege operations at Yorktown. At Fredericksburg he directed a battalion of seven heavy guns, from two companies of his regiment, in the bombardment of the city and the enemy works. After a stint in the defenses of the nation's capital he took part in the bombardment of the Petersburg and Richmond trenches.

TUBMAN, Harriet (ca. 1821-1913)

Herself an escaped slave, Harriet Tubman is credited with having guided at least 300 additional people, including her own parents, to freedom. Born into a Maryland slave family, she made her escape in 1849 after an unsuccessful arranged slave marriage. Her original slave name had been Araminta, but she soon changed it to Harriet. Once established in the North she made repeated trips to the South, risking recapture, to liberate others. She soon became closely associated with prominant abolitionists, throughout the North, who were in the underground railroad. Although illiterate, she proved highly resourceful and volunteered as a cook, nurse, and laundress to the Union forces operating on the South Carolina coast. It is alleged that she was also resourceful as a spy behind Confederate lines. After emancipation she was active in education and charity work for her fellow freedmen.

TUCKER, John Randolph (1812-1883)

With the secession of his native Virginia, John R. Tucker resigned his commodore's commission in the U.S. Navy in order to join the second of three navies he was to serve—the Confederacy's. A veteran of 35 years at sea and of the Mexican War, Tucker was appointed a commander in the Southern fleet. After briefly commanding the *Yorktown*, he was given command of the *Patrick Henry* with which he took part in the famous action in Hampton Roads, including the duel between the *Monitor* and the *Merrimac*. At the battle of Drewry's Bluff, his crew and guns, mounted on the bluff, played a prominent role in the repulse of the Union naval expedition up the James River against Richmond. Promoted to captain he was transferred to Charleston, where he was placed in charge of all naval forces. With the fall of that city in early 1865, Tucker returned to Drewry's Bluff and joined in the retreat from the Richmond-Petersburg lines. In the rearguard action at Sayler's Creek on April 6, 1865, he was captured along with most of his command. As a rear admiral in the Peruvian navy, Tucker commanded the joint Peruvian-Chilean fleets in the 1866 war with Spain. As president of the Peruvian Hydrographic Commission he led a surveying expedition to the upper Amazon. Returning to Virginia, he died there in 1883. (Scharf, J. Thomas, *History of the Confederate States Navy*)

TUCKER, Julius G. (?-?)

As the Confederacy grew ever poorer in manpower, the War Department began authorizing officers to recruit and organize prisoners of war for the Confederate army. One of these officers was Julius G. Tucker. His Confederate assignments included: lieutenant, Cavalry (1861); captain, 13th Virginia Cavalry (1862); lieutenant colonel, 1st Confederate Foreign Battalion (October 16, 1864); and colonel, Tucker's Regiment Confederate Infantry (February 25, 1865). As a cavalry officer he served through most of the campaigns of the Army of Northern Virginia, while some of the time his company was detached from the regiment to serve as part of the provost guard for the Second Corps. Here he gained some experience in dealing with prisoners of war. In the fall of 1864 he went to work recruiting foreign-born Union prisoners at the prison camps in Richmond, Salisbury, and Florence. He got into a feud with General York over who would get the lion's share of the recruits, and the War Department decided in favor of Tucker. With his battalion organized, he took command and eventually raised it to a regiment following the spring. The unit was assigned to duty with the remnants of the Army of Tennessee in North Carolina. Serving as pioneer [engineer] troops, Tucker and his command surrendered along with Johnston's army.

TUCKER, William Feimster (1827-1881)

Surviving the Civil War, Confederate General William F. Tucker was assassinated by hired gunmen a decade and a half after the close of the conflict. The North Carolinian had been a judge and lawyer in Mississippi before the secession crisis. His military assignments included: captain, Company K, 11th Mississippi (May 1861); colonel, 41st Mississippi (May 8, 1862); commanding Anderson's Brigade, Hindman's Division, Breckinridge's Corps, Army of Tennessee (November 1863); brigadier general, CSA (March 1, 1864); commanding Anderson's (old) Brigade, Hindman's Division, Hood's Corps, Army of Tennessee (March-May 14, 1864); and commanding District of South Mississippi and East Louisiana, Department of Alabama, Mississippi and East Louisiana (ca. April-May 1865). As a company commander he fought at 1st Bull Run and continued to serve in northern Virginia until his company was ordered back to Mississippi to become part of a new regiment of which Tucker became colonel. This unit he commanded at Perryville, Murfreesboro, during the Tullahoma Campaign, at Chickamauga, and Chattanooga. Shortly before the beginning of the Atlanta Campaign he was advanced to brigadier general and given charge of a brigade. This he led in the campaign until severely wounded at Resaca. Incapacitated for further field duty, he was in district command in Mississippi and Louisiana during the last days of the Confederacy. A lawyer and state legislator after the war, he was shot apparently as a result of a fraud case he was prosecuting.

TURCHIN, John Basil (1822-1901)

A graduate of the Imperial Military School in St. Petersburg, John B. Turchin immigrated to the United States in 1856 and upon the outbreak of the Civil War joined the Union army. Born Ivan Vasilovitch Turchinoff, he had risen to the rank of colonel and served on the personal staff of the future Czar Alexander II. He had seen service in Hungary, Finland, and the Crimea before settling in the United States as an engineer with the Illinois Central Railroad. Enlisting early in the Civil War, his assignments included: colonel, 19th Illinois (June 17, 1861); commanding 8th Brigade, Army of the Ohio (November-December 2, 1861); commanding 8th Brigade, 3rd Division, Army of the Ohio (December 2, 1861-July 2, 1862); brigadier general, USV (August 6, to rank from July 17, 1862); commanding 2nd Division, Cavalry Corps, Army of the Cumberland (March-July 28, 1863); commanding 3rd Brigade, 4th Division, 14th Corps, Army of the Cumberland (July 28-October 9, 1863); and commanding 1st Brigade, 3rd Division, 14th Corps, Army of the Cumberland (October 9, 1863 July 15, 1864). A strict disciplinarian in camp, he was noted for his Old World ways of dealing with occupied areas, and this soon got him in trouble with his superiors. His brigade occupied Huntsville and Athens, Alabama, and in the latter place he let his troops run wild, since his advance had been fired upon, apparently by civilians of the town. Another irritant to General Buell was the presence of Mrs. Turchin with the command in the field in violation of orders. She allegedly commanded the regiment in a minor action in 1862 in Tennessee when the colonel was ill. Finally, Buell relieved Turchin on July 2, 1862, and had him court-martialed on the two charges. Mrs. Turchin then journeyed to Washington and persuaded Lincoln to set aside the verdict and restore her husband to duty. Not only did she achieve this but she also gained him a brigadier general's star. Returning to duty, he commanded a mounted division in the Tullahoma Campaign and won the sobriquet, "The Russian Thunderbolt," at Chickamauga for his effective charges. At Chattanooga one of his regiments claimed to be the first regiment to enter the enemy works on Missionary Ridge. The next spring he took part in the Atlanta Campaign until forced by ill-health to relinquish command in mid-July 1864. Not returning to duty, he resigned on October 4, 1864. He subsequently wrote a revealing account of one of his many battles, *Chickamauga*, in which he was harshly critical of many of his fellow commanders. He also worked as an engineer. His mind weakened, he died in an insane asylum in Illinois.

TURCHIN, Mrs. John Basil (?-?)

The wife of a Russian-born Union officer served as a nurse with his regiment, actually commanded it for 10 days, and salvaged his career when he got into hot water with his superiors. Also born in Russia, Mrs. John B. Turchin had been the daughter of the commander of Turchin's regiment in the Czar's army and eventually married him. She followed him on numerous campaigns and also in 1856, when the couple moved to the United States and settled in Illinois. When he became colonel of the 19th Illinois she went along as an unofficial nurse. When her husband was ill, while the regiment was serving in Tennessee, she took over command of the unit for 10 days and allegedly commanded it in a minor skirmish. Because of her husband's lax policy on unrestricted foraging and harsh treatment of enemy civilians, he was court-martialed. But Mrs. Turchin gained a private interview with Lincoln and got the verdict set aside, with a promise of a commission as brigadier general. She had saved the career of the only Russian to become a Union general officer.

TURCHINOFF, Ivan Vasilovitch

See: *Turchin, John Basil*

TURNER, John Wesley (1833-1899)

Although most of the Civil War service of Union General John W. Turner was spent in staff positions, he was nevertheless rewarded with all the brevets he could receive. The New York native had taken his West Point appointment from Illinois and graduated in 1855. Posted to the artillery, he served in Florida and on the frontier. His wartime assignments included: second lieutenant, 1st Artillery (since November 18, 1855); first lieutenant, 1st Artillery (April 21, 1861); captain and commissary of Subsistence (August 3, 1861); chief commissary of Subsistence, Army of Southwestern Missouri, Western Department (October-November 1861); chief commissary of Subsistence, Department of Kansas (November 9, 1861-March 11, 1862); chief commissary of Subsistence, Department of the South (March 31-April 19, 1862); colonel and additional aide-de-camp (May 3, 1862); chief commissary of Subsistence, Department of the Gulf (May 22-December 23, 1862); chief of staff, Department of the South (June 13, 1863-May 4, 1864); brigadier general, USV (September 7, 1863); commanding 2nd Division, 10th Corps, Army of the James (June 22-August 23, 1864); chief of staff, Army of the James (November 20, 1864-March 20, 1865); commanding Independent Division, 24th Corps, Army of the James (March 25-April 27, 1865); and commanding the corps (April 27-May 17 and July 8-August 1, 1865). He served as David Hunter's commissary chief in Missouri, Kansas, and along the South Carolina coast. He then held the same position with Butler in the Department of the Gulf before rejoining Hunter. He then became Quincy A. Gillmore's staff chief during the operations against Charleston. Made a brigadier general of volunteers, he was in charge of a division in the operations against Petersburg and then served as chief of staff in the Army of the James. Again in divisional command for the final campaign, he fought at Fort Gregg and Appomattox. Brevetted major general of volunteers for the campaign to date on October 1, 1864, he received regular army brevets for Battery Wagner, the Petersburg mine, and Fort Gregg. Brevetted major general in the regular establishment for the war, he was mustered out of the volunteers on September 1, 1866. Afterwards he continued in the commissary department until he resigned in 1871. In civil life he was a highly successful businessman.

TURNER, Joseph Addison (1826-1868)

As a Georgia journalist, Joseph A. Turner was a supporter of the national ideas of Jefferson Davis and an opponent of Governor Joseph Brown and his states' rights philosophy. A native of the state, he had been a teacher and lawyer before entering the journalistic profession. He met with mixed success in this field and that of politics. A state senator before he Civil War, he was not an out-and-out secessionist, but neither did he wish to bow down to the Washington authorities. Once the Confederacy was established he began publication of *The Countryman*, which was pro-Davis and anti-Brown and was well received by the troops in the field. In return Governor Brown accused him of being a war profiteer—he was engaged in the sale of hats to the army. At the war's close his paper was suppressed by the occupation forces, and he was, as a result, financially ruined. He then wrote his *Autobiography of "The Countryman."* Two years after an unsuccessful bid for a judgeship he died. (Andrews, J. Cutler, *The South Reports the Civil War*)

TURNER, Nat (1800-1831)

A religious and literate slave foreman in Southampton County, Virginia, Nat Turner had not shown any predilection for revenge, yet he became the leader of the bloodiest slave insurrection in U.S. history. Turner had considered his master kind and was even allowed to serve as a preacher for the slave community on the plantation. The revolt against slavery in general had originally been planned for the Fourth of July, 1831, but had to be postponed due to Turner's illness. On the night of August 21-22, Nat Turner and six fellow slaves launched the attack by entering the bedroom of his owners, Mr. and Mrs. Joseph Travis. Turner failed in his attempt to kill his master; one of the others did it for him. In fact, Turner himself only killed one of the 57 victims of the insurrection, Mrs. Margaret Whitehead, whom he finally killed with a blow to her head with a fence post after repeatedly striking her with a dull sword. For 48 hours the bloodletting continued, with the rebels numbering between 60 and 80, some mounted and serving as cavalry to prevent the inhabitants of the plantations from escaping and warning others. Moving on the town of Jerusalem, the marauding band was met by 18 whites, and the slaves drove them back until more whites appeared. The rebellious slaves then withdrew. There followed a reign of terror as 2,800 militia and federal troops swept through the county, killing an estimated 100 to 200 blacks. Some two months later Turner was captured by a single white man and was subsequently hanged along with 16 others. The bloody revolt influenced the South to adopt a policy of not questioning the system of slavery since it feared such a discussion would encourage further revolts. (Johnson, F. Roy, *The Nat Turner Slave Insurrection*)

TURPIE, David (1828-1909)

The expulsion of Southern-leaning Indiana Senator Jesse D. Bright caused David Turpie to serve seven weeks in Washington in early 1863. Turpie had been born in Ohio and taken up the practice of law in Indiana in 1849. Three years later he served a term in the state legislature. From 1854 to 1856 he was a judge, and he again sat in the legislature in 1858. He was elected as a Democrat to take over Bright's seat and was seated on January 14, 1863, relieving Joseph A. Wright who had been appointed to the position when the legislature was not in session. However, there was little time to the term, and Turpie returned to his practice after the March 3, 1863, expiration. He later served in the state legislature and as a district attorney. From 1887 to 1899 he was again a Democratic senator but lost a bid for a third complete term, at which point he retired from politics.

TUTTLE, James Madison (1823-1892)

There are hints that corruption led to the end of the military career of Union General James M. Tuttle. Born in Ohio, he had settled in Iowa as a farmer and shopkeeper who also held various local offices. He entered the service as the second-in-command of a volunteer regiment in 1861 and his assignments included: lieutenant colonel, 2nd Iowa (May 31, 1861); colonel, 2nd Iowa (September 6, 1861); commanding 1st Brigade, 2nd Division, Army of the Tennessee (April 5-6 and April 9-July 1862); commanding the division (April 6-9, 1862); brigadier general, USV (June 9, 1862); and commanding in the Army of the Tennessee: 1st Brigade, 2nd Division, District of Corinth (July-August 12, 1862); District of Corinth (July-August 12, 1862); District of Cairo (August 12-November 17, 1862); 3rd Division, 15th Corps (April 3-August 9 and September 21-December 20, 1863); also Post of Natchez, District of Vicksburg (August 1863-July 1864); and 1st Division, 16th Corps (December 20, 1863-March 7, 1864). He led his regiment at Fort Donelson and was wounded on the 15th. Taking charge of a brigade the day before the battle of Shiloh, he fought well at the Hornet's Nest and succeeded the mortally wounded William H.L. Wallace in command of the division. As a brigade leader, he took part in the slow advance on Corinth, Mississippi. That summer and fall he commanded at Cairo, Illinois, but rejoined the army for the Vicksburg Campaign. After that city's fall he took part in the siege of Jackson. During the time that much of the corps was fighting at Chattanooga and on the road to Atlanta he was in post command at Natchez. His resignation, under questionable circumstances, was accepted by the War Department on June 14, 1864. In the meantime he had twice been defeated as a Democratic candidate for governor. In the postwar years he sat in the state legislature and engaged in farming, meat-packing, real estate, and mining.

TWAIN, Mark

See: *Clemens, Samuel Langhorne*

TWIGGS, David Emanuel (1790-1862)

Of all the officers of the Old Army who went over to the Confederacy, only one, Brevet Major General David E. Twiggs, committed an act of treason at the time. He was a veteran of virtually half a century of service, including action in the War of 1812 and the Black Hawk, Seminole, and Mexican wars. Having risen to the rank of brigadier general, he was commanding the Department of Texas during the secession crisis. Most departing officers submitted their resignations, and many of the commanders among them actually waited for the arrival of their successors before leaving their stations. Twiggs instead surrendered his trust to Colonel Ben McCulloch of the state forces on February 18, 1861. On March 1 he was dismissed from the army. His Confederate assignments included: major general, CSA (March 22, 1861); commanding Military District of Louisiana (April 17-May 27, 1861); and commanding Department No. 1 (May 27-October 18, 1861). His command comprised Louisiana, southern Mississippi, and southern Alabama, but he was no longer fit for active duty and retired. He died the following July, having provided the Confederacy his greatest service while still wearing a blue uniform.

TYLER, Daniel (1799-1882)

As a state brigadier general at 1st Bull Run, Daniel Tyler was not particularly distinguished in the battle but was nonetheless named to the same rank in the national service the next year. The Connecticut native was a West Pointer (1819) and had also studied at the French military school in Metz. Although he briefly served in the infantry, his specialty was artillery and ordnance. In charge of investigations of military contractors, he raised their ire by his honesty and was still a first lieutenant when he resigned in 1834 to enter business. He was highly successful in canal and railroad companies. At the outbreak of the Civil War he reentered the service at the head of a 90-day volunteer unit. His assignments included: colonel, 1st Connecticut (April 23, 1861); brigadier general, Connecticut Volunteers (May 10, 1861); commanding 1st Division, Army of Northeastern Virginia (June-August 1861); brigadier general, USV (March 13, 1862); commanding 2nd Brigade, 1st Division, Army of the Mississippi (May-June 26, 1862); and commanding District of Delaware, 8th Corps, Middle Department (July 3, 1863-January 19, 1864). In the first major campaign in Virginia he fought at Blackburn's Ford and in the main battle at 1st Bull Run. There he held the front along Bull Run and at the Stone Bridge. Mustered out on August 11, 1861, he received the star of a national brigadier the next March and was dispatched to the West where he commanded a brigade in the painfully slow advance on Corinth. He then sat on a commission investigating Don C. Buell's Perryville Campaign. His last six months of military service were spent in charge of the forces in Delaware. Having passed his 65th birthday, he resigned on April 6, 1864, and then travelled widely before founding the town of Anniston, Alabama, and reentering the iron and railroad businesses. (Mitchell, Donald Grant, ed., *Daniel Tyler: A Memorial Volume Containing His Autobiography and War Record*)

TYLER, Erastus Barnard (1822-1891)

New York-born and Ohio-raised trapper and fur merchant Erastus B. Tyler entered the Union army as a colonel and finished the war as a brevet major general. His assignments included: colonel, 7th Ohio (April 25, 1861); commanding 3rd Brigade, Lander's Division, Department of West Virginia (January 5-March 13, 1862); commanding 3rd Brigade, 2nd Division, 5th Corps, Army of the Potomac (March 13-April 4, 1862); commanding 3rd Brigade, 2nd Division, Department of the Shenandoah (April 4-May 10, 1862); commanding 3rd Brigade, Shields' Division, Department of the Rappahannock (May 10-June 26, 1862); brigadier general, USV (May 14, 1862); commanding 1st Brigade, 3rd Division, 5th Corps, Army of the Potomac (September 12, 1862-January 1863 and March 28-May 25, 1863); commanding Defenses of Baltimore, 8th Corps, Middle Department (June 29-October 1, 1863);

Union district commander Daniel Tyler. (*Leslie's*)

commanding the corps and the department (September 28-October 10, 1863); commanding 3rd Separate Brigade, 8th Corps, Middle Department (October 1-December 18, 1863); and commanding 1st Separate Brigade, 8th Corps, Middle Department (December 18, 1863-March 12, 1864, March 24-November 18, 1864, and December 20, 1864-June 5, 1865). His first action came when his regiment was surprised in camp by John B. Floyd's Confederate command on August 28, 1861, at Cross Lanes in western Virginia. He then served along the upper Potomac and in the lower Shenandoah Valley. He fought at Kernstown and in the Shenandoah Valley Campaign, seeing action at Port Republic. Promoted to brigadier general he was given charge of a brigade of nine-months Pennsylvania troops and was in reserve at Antietam. He took part in the assaults on Marye's Heights at Fredericksburg. After fighting at Chancellorsville his men were mustered out and he was assigned to the Baltimore command. For the balance of the war he remained in this vicinity but did take his brigade to the aid of Lew Wallace at Monocacy during Early's raid against Washington. Brevetted major general of volunteers on March 13, 1865, he was mustered out on August 24, 1865. Settling in Baltimore, he served as the city's postmaster and was engaged in Masonic and veterans' affairs.

TYLER, John (1790-1862)

Of the five ex-presidents alive at the start of the Civil War only one, John Tyler, was from a Southern state, Virginia, and thus the only one to join the Confederacy. The first vice president to succeed to the presidency upon the death of his predecessor—and sometimes called "His Accidency"—he considered the annexation of Texas to be his most important accomplishment during his 1841 to 1845 term. Throughout a career as National Republican, Democrat, Whig, and Democrat again, he stuck to his belief in a strict interpretation of the constitution. Before his presidency he had served as governor, congressman, senator, and state legislator, and afterwards he went into retirement but became involved in the secession crisis. He had always believed in the right of a state to secede but rightly predicted that war would follow and the North would win. Trying to find a peaceful formula for the crisis, he attended the Washington Peace Conference of which he was elected president. After its collapse he attended the state secession convention as an advocate of secession. On August 1, 1861, he was admitted to the Provisional Confederate Congress where he was a relatively inactive legislator although he did tend to support Davis. Elected to a seat in the First Regular Congress, he died on January 18, 1862, before he could take his seat. (Seager, Robert, *And Tyler Too* and Morgan, Robert, *A Whig Embattled: The Presidency Under John Tyler*)

TYLER, Robert Charles (ca. 1833-1865)

Little is known of the prewar career of one of the Confederacy's most obscure general officers, Robert C. Tyler. Apparently born and raised in Baltimore, he appears to have served as a first lieutenant in the 1856 filibustering expedition of William Walker to Nicaragua. Returning to Baltimore, he eventually moved to Memphis where he joined the Confederate army. His assignments included: private, Company D, 15th Tennessee (April 18, 1861); captain and quartermaster, 15th Tennessee (1861); lieutenant colonel, 15th Tennessee (December 26, 1861); colonel, 15th Tennessee (May 1862); commanding brigade, Breckinridge's Division, Breckinridge's Corps, Army of Tennessee (November-November 25, 1863); and brigadier general, CSA (February 23, 1864). As a supply officer, he was present at Belmont. Promoted to lieutenant colonel, he commanded his unit at Shiloh where he was wounded. Assigned to provost duty, he served in the Kentucky Campaign but took charge of the regiment again in time for Perryville. Following the Tullahoma Campaign he led the regiment—he had become its colonel at the spring 1862 reorganization—at Chickamauga and was again wounded. Returning to duty, he led a brigade at Chattanooga where he lost a leg on Missionary Ridge. Promoted to brigadier general early the next year, he never rejoined the main army and appears to have spent the next year and a half in the hospital at West Point, Georgia. He may have engaged in some light duty there, as a local fortification was named for him. It was at Fort Tyler that he was killed on April 16, 1865, while trying to defend it against James H. Wilson's Union raiders.

TYLER, Robert Ogden (1831-1874)

A career artillerist, West Pointer (1853) Robert Tyler spent most of the war directing heavy guns. A first lieutenant in the 3rd Artillery, Tyler had served as a captain and assistant quartermaster from May 17, 1861, until assigned to the 4th Connecticut as colonel on August 29. He was largely responsible for converting this regiment into the 1st Connecticut Heavy Artillery the following winter. His later assignments included: commanding Artillery, District of Alexandria, Military District of Washington (October 1862-February 2, 1862, except when in the field); brigadier general , USV (November 29, 1862); commanding Artillery Defenses of Alexandria (February 2-April 15, 1863) and Defenses South of the Potomac (April 15-26, 1863), 22nd Corps, Department of Washington; commanding Artillery Reserve, Army of the Potomac (May-December 23, 1863); commanding a division, 22nd Corps, Department of Washington (January-May 1864); commanding 4th Division, 2nd Corps, Army of the Potomac (May 18-29, 1864); and commanding 4th Brigade, 2nd Division, 2nd Corps, Army of the Potomac (May 29-June 7, 1864). In charge of the siege train during McClellan's disastrous Peninsula Campaign, Tyler managed to save all but one gun. After serving in the Washington defenses, he commanded some of the artillery on Stafford Heights opposite Fredericksburg. At Chancellorsville and Gettysburg and in the Bristoe and Mine Run campaigns Tyler was responsible for farming out his batteries to the most-needed places. Again called into the field, he brought a division of unbloodied heavy artillery regiments into the fighting at Spotsylvania and Cold Harbor where he was wounded out of action. Brevetted to major general in both the regulars and volunteers he was deputy quartermaster general after the war and until his death. (Taylor, John E., *History of the First Connecticut Artillery and of the Siege Trains of the Armies Operating Against Richmond*)

TYNDALE, Hector (1821-1880)

Although, at the request of his mother, he turned down a West Point appointment and instead became a ceramics expert, Hector Tyndale nonetheless became a brevet major general in the Union army. Linked to the abolitionist cause, the Philadelphia native accompanied John Brown's wife to Virginia just before the hanging. Returning from a business trip to Paris, he volunteered for the Union service and his assignments included: major, 28th Pennsylvania (June 28, 1861); lieutenant colonel, 28th Pennsylvania (April 25, 1862); commanding 1st Brigade, 2nd Division, 12th Corps, Army of the Potomac (September 17, 1862); brigadier general, USV (April 9, 1863, to rank from November 29, 1862); commanding 1st Brigade, 3rd Division, 11th Corps, Army of the Potomac (July 13-September 19, 1863); commanding 1st Brigade, 3rd Division, 11th Corps, Army of the Cumberland (late 1863-early 1864); commanding the division (February 15-April 16, 1864); and commanding 3rd Brigade, 1st Division, 20th Corps, Army of the Cumberland (April 14-May 2, 1864). As a field officer, he served in the Shenandoah Valley Campaign and commanded the regiment at Cedar Mountain, but it was not engaged, being on a reconnaissance. The regiment then fought at 2nd Bull Run. In Maryland Tyndale commanded a brigade at Antietam, displaying marked ability, and lost three horses and was twice wounded. For this he was jumped two grades to brigadier general. When he returned to duty he was assigned to a brigade in the 11th Corps, which he took to the relief of Chattanooga, fighting at Wauhatchie and Chattanooga. That winter he commanded the division for a time but was reduced to a brigade upon the consolidation of the 11th and 12th corps. Just before the Atlanta Campaign got under way he went on leave and resigned his commission for health reasons on August 26, 1864. He was apparently assigned to command of the 1st Brigade, 1st Division, 4th Corps, Army of the Cumberland, but never reported. Brevetted major general the next year for the war, he returned to Philadelphia where he rebuilt his business and was active in charitable causes. (McLaughlin, John, *A Memoir of Hector Tyndale*)

U

ULLMANN, Daniel (1810-1892)

A New York City lawyer and Know-Nothing politician, Daniel Ullmann spent most of the war organizing and commanding black troops. On April 28, 1862, Ullmann was made colonel, 78th New York, and on January 13, 1863, brigadier general, USV. His commands included: 2nd Brigade, 2nd Division, 2nd Corps, Army of Virginia (July 10-16, 1862); and the following in the Department of the Gulf: Ullmann's Brigade, Corps d'Afrique (July-September 22, 1863); Corps d'Afrique (September 22, 1863-April 23, 1864); District of Port Hudson (April 23-June 9, 1864); and District of Morganza (November 23, 1864-February 26, 1865). After service in the Shenandoah Valley, Ullmann served in Pope's campaign in Virginia, but was struck by typhoid and missed the fighting at Cedar Mountain. However, in the retreat from that defeat he was captured and confined in Libby Prison until paroled in October 1862. Promoted to brigadier he was sent to New Orleans to raise black troops which were initially known as the Corps d'Afrique and subsequently designated U.S. Colored Troops. With a portion of his command Ullmann participated in the siege of Port Hudson and he subsequently complained that his men were treated more as laborers than as soldiers and supplied with "arms almost entirely unserviceable." Having faith in his men, he continued to lobby for them. Serving part of the time until November 1864 as post and district commander at Port Hudson, and then at the District of Morganza, Ullmann usually had at least part of his black troops under his command. He was relieved from duty on February 26, 1865, being incapacitated, possibly by typhoid once again. He did not return to service but was brevetted major general. After the war he retired in New York State to enjoy literary and scientific pursuits.

UNCLE TOM

See: *Henson, Josiah*

UNDERWOOD, Adin Ballou (1828-1888)

By the time that Massachusetts native Adin B. Underwood received his commission as a brigadier general in the Union army he had already been invalided out of active service. A Harvard-educated lawyer, he was practicing law when he began recruiting for the Union army. His assignments included: captain, 2nd Massachusetts (May 25, 1861); lieutenant colonel, 33rd Massachusetts (August 13, 1862); colonel, 33rd Massachusetts (April 3, 1863); and brigadier general, USV (November 19, 1863, to rank from November 6). As a company commander, he served in the Shenandoah Valley before becoming second-in-command of a new regiment. He was its colonel by the time of Chancellorsville and commanded it when the 11th Corps was routed by Stonewall Jackson. He fought at Gettysburg and was transferred, with the corps, to the West after the disaster there at Chickamauga. In the fighting at Wauhatchie—a move to relieve the pressure on Chattanooga—he was severely wounded. His leg was shattered, but the normal amputation was not performed and the bones rejoined, leaving the one leg four inches (10 cm.) shorter than the other. Although he saw no further action he was named a brigadier general and brevetted major general for the war at its close. Mustered out on August 24, 1865, he was subsequently Boston's port surveyor.

UNKNOWN

The death of a young Georgia soldier early in the Civil War illustrates many of the ironies of that conflict. Serving in the campaign in western Virginia during the first spring of the Civil War, he was probably a member of the 1st Georgia. Confederate forces under Brigadier General Robert S. Garnett were forced from their positions on Laurel Hill. The command made a fighting retirement in the face of the rapid Union pursuit. Garnett leapfrogged his regiments in the retreat, with each taking its turn as the rear guard. Finally, at Carrick's Ford, Garnett remained behind with 10 men from a Virginia regiment. Why the Georgian was there is unknown. Then Garnett sent away the Virginians and was about to leave when he was struck and killed. At the same instant the Georgia private reeled and fell next to his general. Many Union soldiers had witnessed his bravery, and this early in the war could afford an unusual concern. They knew that Garnett's body—he was the first general to die in the Civil War—would be returned to his family for burial. But what would be the fate of his brave companion? They formally buried their late opponent and inscribed on the marker, "Name Unknown. A brave fellow, who shared his general's fate, and fell fighting at his side, while his companions fled." (Jones, Virgil Carrington, *Gray Ghosts and Rebel Raiders*)

UPTON, Emory (1839-1881)

Graduating from West Point after the firing on Fort Sumter, Emory Upton rose to the rank of brevet major general of volunteers and of regulars. Eighth in his class, he was posted to the artillery and assigned to duty organizing volunteers. The New York native's assignments included: second lieutenant, 4th Artillery (May 6, 1861); first lieutenant, 5th Artillery (May 14, 1861); commanding Artillery, 1st Division, 6th Corps, Army of the Potomac (September-October 1862); colonel, 121st New York (October 23, 1862); commanding 2nd Brigade, 1st Division, 6th Corps, Army of the Potomac (July 1-2, July 4-August 5, 1863, and November 6, 1863-July 8, 1864); brigadier general, USV (May 12, 1864); commanding 2nd Brigade, 1st Division, 6th Corps, Army of the Shenandoah (August 6-September 19, 1864); commanding 4th Division, 6th Corps, Army of the Shenandoah (August 6-September 19, 1864); commanding the division (September 19, 1864); commanding 4th Division, Cavalry Corps, Military Division of the Mississippi (December 13, 1864-June 26, 1865); captain, 5th Artillery (February 22, 1865); and commanding Cavalry Brigade, District of East Tennessee, Department of the Cumberland (July-November 1865). While serving on Daniel Tyler's divisional staff at 1st Bull Run, Upton was wounded. Returning to duty he directed the six 12-pounder Napoleons of Battery D, 2nd Artillery, on the Peninsula. He was a divisional artillery chief at South Mountain and Antietam before becoming the colonel of a volunteer infantry regiment. This he led at Fredericksburg, Chancellorsville, and Gettysburg. At the latter he was briefly in charge of the brigade. That fall he was given a regular army brevet for Rappahannock Station. Leading his brigade in the Overland Campaign, his greatest moment came at Spotsylvania. Here he suggested a surprise assault on the enemy's earthworks and was given permission to try it. He led his 12 regiments into the Confederate lines, and his penetration would have been wider if Gershom Mott's division had supported him properly. The lessons of the May 10, 1864, assault were not lost on the senior Union officers, and a larger and more successful attack was made two days later. Upton was made a brigadier general from the date of this second assault. He then fought at Cold Harbor and Petersburg before going with the 6th Corps to the Shenandoah Valley. There he succeeded the mortally wounded David A. Russell in charge of the division at 3rd Winchester but soon fell wounded himself. Recovering, he was assigned to command a division of cavalry under James H. Wilson. He had now commanded, successively, artillery, infantry, and cavalry in the war. Having received one brevet for Spotsylvania and two for 3rd Winchester, he was made a brevet brigadier general in the regular army for the capture of Selma, Alabama. Brevetted major general of regulars for the war—he already held that grade in the volunteer service—he remained in the army after his April 30, 1866, muster out of the volunteers. With frequent interruptions of his career for medical reasons, he served at West Point and on the West Coast until he committed suicide while commanding San Francisco's Presidio as colonel, 4th Artillery. (Michie, Peter S., *The Life and Letters of Emory Upton*)

USHER, John Palmer (1816-1889)

When fellow Indiana lawyer Caleb B. Smith gave up his cabinet portfolio as secretary of the interior under Lincoln, John P. Usher moved up to the cabinet-level post. A longtime Republican Party organizer, he had been rewarded by Smith with an appointment as assistant interior secretary in early 1862. Then on January 8, 1863, the New York native took over as head of the Interior Department. On March 9, 1865, he submitted his resignation to take effect on May 15 and it was accepted by Lincoln. For the balance of his years he was a railroad attorney. (Richardson, Elmo R., *John Palmer Usher, Lincoln's Secretary of the Interior*)

John P. Usher, Lincoln's last interior secretary. (NA)

V

VALLANDIGHAM, Clement Laird (1820-1871)

The unofficial leader of the Copperheads, the Northern peace movement, Clement Vallandigham was unable to find a home in either the North or the South during the war. Vallandigham had been a prominent Democratic politician in Ohio, having served for a number of years in the legislature, and at the outbreak of the war was a member of Congress. During the 1860 election he had supported the candidacy of Stephen Douglas, wishing that the extremists, Lincoln and Breckinridge, would drop out so that the two sections could become reconciled. Lincoln being elected, he criticized the prosecution of the war and opposed all war measures. Losing popularity at home, he was defeated for reelection in 1862. Launching a campaign for the Democratic nomination for governor, he attacked the administration so vehemently that General Burnside, commanding the Department of the Ohio, ordered his arrest on May 5, 1863. Convicted by a military court, which he protested had no authority over him, he was sentenced to imprisonment for the duration. Lincoln, under pressure, commuted this to expulsion to the Confederate lines. Untrusted in the South, he was in Canada by July where he received word of his gubernatorial nomination. From his Canadian platform, he continued to attack the national Republicans, more strongly than he attacked his opponent, John Brough. Vallandigham was soundly beaten, especially by the army vote, and in June 1864 slipped back into Ohio where the authorities watched but tolerated the uncowed man. But with the war coming to a successful conclusion, his time was past. Failing in politics after the war, he resumed his law practice and, in demonstrating how an alleged murder victim could have shot himself, he fatally wounded himself with the wrong gun. He won the case. (Klement, Frank L., *The Limits of Dissent: Clement L. Vallandigham and the Civil War*)

VAN ALEN, James Henry (1819-1889)

Having raised and equipped a volunteer cavalry regiment at his own expense, James H. Van Alen—of a wealthy family—failed to find much combat in the Civil War. The native New Yorker's assignments included: colonel, 3rd New York Cavalry (August 28, 1861); brigadier general, USV (April 15, 1862); and aide-de-camp, Army of the Potomac (May 1863). His regiment had initially been posted to the Washington vicinity, and about the time that it was transferred to the North Carolina coast he was appointed a brigadier general. After the fall of Yorktown and Gloucester Point in May 1862, he was assigned to command those points which were soon well to the rear of the front. He held the post until October 1862 and the next month he was assigned to the court of inquiry investigating the causes of the Union defeat at 2nd Bull Run, and especially Irvin McDowell's role in it. This lasted into early 1863, and he was then assigned as Hooker's aide at Chancellorsville but was soon sent to the rear to direct operations at the Aquia Creek supply base and along the Richmond, Fredericksburg and Potomac Railroad. He resigned on July 14, 1863. He traveled extensively until he drowned when he fell or jumped from a transatlantic liner.

VAN BUREN, Martin (1782-1862)

The oldest of the five living ex-presidents in 1861, Martin Van Buren was also the only one to give the Union his unqualified support. Retired in New York, he had opposed a Republican victory in 1860, but once Fort Sumter had been fired upon he publicly endorsed the war effort. On July 24, 1862, the country's eighth president died at his home while the fate of the nation was still in serious doubt. (Niven, John, *Martin Van Buren and the Romantic Age of American Politics*)

VAN BUSKIRK, David (1826-1886)

Wars generally have their odd anecdotes, and the Civil War was no exception, with its "Monroe County Grenadiers," a company of six-footers, and one of their officers, David Van Buskirk, the tallest Union soldier. An Indiana farmer, Van Buskirk had been a delegate to the 1860 Republican convention. In June 1861 he joined forces with another six-footer, Bloomington cobbler Peter Kopp, who was a veteran of the French army, to organize a company of men of 5 feet 10 inches and taller. On September 12, the unit was mustered into Federal service as Company F, 27th Indiana, with Van Buskirk as its second lieutenant. He saw action at Smithfield, Buckton Station, Middleton, and Newton, Virginia, before being taken prisoner by Stonewall Jackson's troops at Winchester on May 25, 1862, during the Shenandoah Valley Campaign. Confined in Libby Prison, he became an object of much curiosity and was soon made part of a freak show. In this capacity, he received all he could eat, which was much more than his fellow prisoners got. He was even visited by a curious Jefferson Davis while in Libby. Finally in September the 380-pound, 6-feet-10 1/2-inch-tall prisoner was exchanged. He rejoined his unit, now as its captain, having been twice promoted during his captivity. He fought at Fredericksburg, Chancellorsville, and Gettysburg before the unit went to New York to prevent further draft riots. Sent west, the regiment took part in the Chattanooga Campaign but not in the battle. On April 26, 1864, Van Buskirk, suffering from rheumatism, resigned and returned to his farming. He was subsequently a minor Republican officer holder and turned down an offer from P.T. Barnum, having had enough of being an exhibit.

VANCE, Robert Frank (1828-1899)

North Carolinian Robert B. Vance spent the last year of the Civil War as a prisoner. The brother of the state governor, Zebulon Vance, this court clerk had raised a company for the Confederacy, and his later assignments included: colonel, 29th North Carolina (September 11, 1861); commanding 2nd (Rains' old) Brigade, McCown's Division, Hardee's Corps, Army of Tennessee (December 31, 1862-ca. February 1863); brigadier general, CSA (March 16, 1863); and commanding Western District of North Carolina, Department of East Tennessee (September 16-November 18, 1863 and December 4, 1863-January 14, 1864). As a regimental commander, he served at Cumberland Gap in East Tennessee and succeeded to command of a brigade at Murfreesboro. Forced from the field by a bout with typhoid fever, he was nonetheless promoted to brigadier general. Upon his return to duty he was assigned to command in the mountains of western Virginia where he had to deal with deserters and draft resisters as well as the Union troops. In a minor action at Cosby Creek, across the border in Tennessee, he was captured on January 14, 1864. It was not until March 10, 1865, that his confinement in Fort Delaware came to an end. By then the war was all but over, and he does not appear to have held any further commands. After the war he served in both the state and national legislatures and as an assistant patent commissioner.

VANCE, Zebulon Baird (1830-1894)

As the governor of a state which had already provided so many troops to the Confederate cause, North Carolinian Zebulon B. Vance came into conflict with Jefferson Davis' ideas over conscription. A lawyer by training, he sat in the state and national legislatures and was a Unionist supporting John Bell for the presidency in 1860. Nevertheless he joined the Confederate army where his assignments included: captain, Company F, 4th North Carolina Volunteers (May 3, 1861); and colonel, 26th North Carolina (August 27, 1861). He fought at New Bern and during the Seven Days on the Peninsula. Elected governor, he resigned his commission on August 12, 1862. This was accepted on August 29th and he was sworn in at the state capitol on September 8th. As governor he engaged the state in blockade-running and pardoned the state's deserters. An opponent of a separate surrender by the state, he won reelection in 1864 and was arrested on May 13, 1865, by the Union authorities. Released on July 6, 1865, he resumed his practice and was again governor in the late 1870s. (Tucker, Glenn, *Zeb Vance: Champion of Personal Freedom*)

VAN CLEVE, Horatio Phillips (1809-1891)

Being caught up in the rout of two-thirds of the Union army at Chickamauga effectively ended the active field career of Horatio P. Van Cleve. The New Jersey-born West Pointer (1831) had been posted to the infantry and performed routine garrison duty until his 1836 resignation as a second lieutenant. In the quarter century before the outbreak of the Civil War he was a farmer, teacher, civil engineer, and surveyor in Michigan and Minnesota. Volunteering for the Union army, he was given charge of a regiment of volunteers and his assignments included: colonel, 2nd Minnesota (July 22, 1861); brigadier general, USV (March 21, 1862); commanding 14th Brigade, 5th Division, Army of the Ohio (July 2-September 29, 1862); commanding 5th Division 2nd Corps, Army of the Ohio (September 29-November 5, 1862); commanding 3rd Division, Left Wing, 14th Corps, Army of the Cumberland (November 5-December 31, 1862); commanding 3rd Division, 21st Corps, Army of the Cumberland (March 13-October 9, 1863); commanding Post of Murfreesboro, Army of the Cumberland (November 27, 1863-January 1864); commanding 2nd Brigade, Post of Nashville, District of Nashville, Army of the Cumberland (January-ca. July 1864); also commanding 2nd Brigade, 3rd Division, 12th Corps, Army of the Cumberland (January 2-April 14, 1864); commanding 1st Brigade, Defenses of the Nashville and Chattanooga Railroad, Department of the Cumberland (July 1864-April 1865); and commanding 1st Brigade, 1st Sub-District, District of Middle Tennessee, Army of the Cumberland (March-August 21, 1865). He led his regiment at Mill Springs and in Halleck's advance on Corinth, Mississippi, following the battle of Shiloh. Promoted to brigadier general, he was given a brigade but did not get into the fight at Perryville. On the last day of the year he fell wounded at Murfreesboro while at the head of a division. He recovered in time to lead it in the Tullahoma Campaign and in the disaster at Chickamauga. With the old 20th and 21st corps merged into the new 4th, he was relegated to post duty at Murfreesboro, Nashville, and along the Nashville and Chattanooga Railroad. Brevetted major general for the war, he was mustered out on August 24, 1865, and was later a postmaster and state adjutant general.

VANDERBILT, Cornelius (1794-1877)

The connection of shipping magnate Cornelius Vanderbilt with the Civil War was not a highly creditable one. A native of New York, he had entered the shipping business at the age of 16 and during the War of 1812 transported supplies to the troops in the New York area. Building his empire, he became known as "Commodore" Vanderbilt, expanding from the New York area to New England, via Nicaragua to California, and finally across the Atlantic to Le Havre. Upon the outbreak of the Civil War he sold two of his three transatlantic vessels but fitted out his best craft, the *Vanderbilt*, as a warship. Some say he only loaned it to the government, but it was accepted as a gift and its service included the pursuit of the Confederate raider *Alabama* and blockading duty that included the capture of the British *Peterhoff*. He later made a large profit by buying decrepit craft for blockading duty. Many of these vessels took part in the New Orleans expedition and were found to be unseaworthy. However, probably due to his influence, he was able to keep his name out of the censorious congressional report. Since 1862 he had been shifting his interests into railroading, and by the time of his death he had established an empire on land which included the first continuous service from New York to Chicago. In his final years he belatedly became something of a philanthropist especially towards what became Vanderbilt University.

VAN DERVEER, Ferdinand (1823-1892)

Once mustered out of the service with his regiment, Ohio lawyer and former sheriff Ferdinand Van Derveer was recommissioned in the army as a brigadier general of volunteers but never saw major action at this grade. During the Mexican War he had risen from first sergeant to first lieutenant and adjutant, then to captain in the 1st Ohio and had been particularly distinguished at Monterrey. His Civil War assignments included: colonel, 35th Ohio (September 24, 1861); commanding 3rd Brigade, 1st Division, Army of the Ohio (August 6-September 29, 1862); commanding 3rd Brigade, 3rd Division, 14th Corps, Army of the Cumberland (January 28-October 10, 1863); commanding 2nd Brigade, 3rd Division, 14th Corps, Army of the Cumberland (November 1863-January 14, 1864 and February 16-June 27, 1864); brigadier general, USV (October 4, 1864); and commanding 2nd Brigade, 2nd Division, 4th Corps, Army of the Cumberland (February 8-June 5, 1865). Having led his regiment at Perryville, he missed Murfreesboro, guarding the Cumberland River fords at the time, but led a brigade at Chickamauga and Chattanooga. At the latter his command was one of the first to reach the crest of Missionary Ridge. During the Atlanta Campaign he led his command to the very outskirts of the city but became ill and was forced to relinquish command. Mustered out with his regiment on August 26, 1864, he was recalled into the service as a brigadier general and when fit for duty joined the 4th Corps in northern Alabama in the final months of the war. With the reduction of the volunteer establishment, he found himself without a command and resigned on June 15, 1865. He resumed his practice and eventually became a judge.

VANDEVER, William (1817-1893)

Because he had entered the Union army, Republican Congressman William Vandever lost his seat. The Maryland-born Iowa lawyer had first been elected to Congress in 1858 and won reelection two years later. Entering the service, his assignments included: colonel, 9th Iowa (September 24, 1861); commanding 2nd Brigade, 4th Division, Army of Southwest Missouri, Department of the Missouri (February-May 1862); brigadier general, USV (November 29, 1862); commanding 1st Brigade, 9th Division, 13th Corps, Army of the Tennessee (January 4-February 4, 1863); commanding 2nd Division, Army of the Frontier, Department of the Missouri (May 23-June 5, 1863); commanding 1st Brigade, Herron's Division, Army of the Tennessee (June 11-July 28, 1863); commanding 1st Brigade, 2nd Division, 13th Corps, Army of the Tennessee (July 28-August 7, 1863); commanding 1st Brigade, 2nd Division, 13th Corps, Department of the Gulf (August 7-25 and October 6-November 11, 1863); commanding 3rd Brigade, 2nd Division, 16th Corps, Army of the Tennessee (June 20-August 2, 1864); commanding 1st Brigade, 2nd Division, 14th Corps, Army of the Cumberland (January 18-June 23, 1865); and commanding the division (June 23-July 18, 1865). Having taken his seat in Congress on July 4, 1861, he attended the first session before being commissioned. However, the seat was contested and in January 1863 it was ruled that Vandever was not entitled to a seat, having gone off to the army. The contestant, however, was also not seated. Meanwhile, Vandever had commanded his regiment at Pea Ridge and been promoted to brigadier general. Following service in Missouri and Arkansas, he led his brigade to Vicksburg and joined the besiegers on June 11, 1863. After the city's fall he was transferred, as a part of the 13th Corps, to the Gulf. During the course of the Atlanta Campaign he was transferred to Georgia and given charge of a brigade which had been left behind at Rome by the main army. After a few weeks, he was assigned on August 2, 1864, to command the post and hospitals at Marietta. The following November he was assigned to court-martial duty, principally the case against Thomas W. Sweeny. In the final months of the war he directed a brigade in the march through the Carolinas. Brevetted major general on June 7, 1865, for the war, he was mustered out on August 24, 1865. Resuming his law practice, he was also an Indian commissioner and served two more congressional terms, this time from California.

VAN DORN, Earl (1820-1863)

One of the Confederacy's most promising general officers early in the Civil War, Mississippian West Pointer (1842) Earl Van Dorn proved to be a disappointment and died, not at the hands of the enemy but at those of a jealous husband. Posted to the infantry, he had won two brevets in the Mexican War, being wounded at the City of Mexico. Transferring to the cavalry in 1855, he was wounded in Indian fighting in 1858 near Wichita Village, Indian Territory (now Oklahoma). Resigning as a major in the 2nd Cavalry on January 31, 1861, he offered his services to his native state. His assignments included: brigadier general, Mississippi State Troops (ca. January 1861); major general, Mississippi State Troops (ca. February 1861); colonel, Cavalry (March 16, 1861); commanding Department of Texas (April 21-September 4, 1861); brigadier general, CSA (June 5, 1861); major general, CSA (September 19, 1861); commanding division, 1st Corps, Army of the Potomac (October 4-22, 1861); commanding 1st Division, Potomac District, Department of Northern Virginia (October 22, 1861-January 10, 1862); commanding Trans-Mississippi District, Department #2 (March 4-June 20, 1862); commanding Department of Southern Mississippi and East Louisiana (June 20-July 2, 1862); commanding District of the Mississippi, Department #2 (July 2-October 1, 1862); commanding Army of West Tennessee, Department of Mississippi and East Louisiana (October 1862); commanding 1st Corps, Army of the Department of Mississippi and East Louisiana (December 1862); commanding cavalry division, Army of the Department of Mississippi and East Louisiana (January 13-20, 1863); commanding Cavalry Corps, Department of Mississippi and East Louisiana (January 20-February 1863); and commanding cavalry division, Army of Tennessee (February 25-May 7, 1863). Early in the war he commanded in Texas where he seized U.S. property and received the surrender of regular army detachments. Promoted rapidly to brigadier and major general, he was ordered to Virginia where he led a division near Manassas. Early in 1862 he was sent to command in Arkansas in order to get Ben McCulloch and Sterling Price to cooperate. Launching an attack at Pea Ridge, he was repulsed after two days of fighting. Ordered east of the Mississippi, he arrived too late to take part in the fighting at Shiloh but participated in the unsuccessful defense of Corinth, Mississippi. In the summer of 1862 he successfully defended Vicksburg but failed in his designs on Baton Rouge when the attack under John C. Breckinridge failed. Another failure occurred when he attempted to retake Corinth in October 1862. By this time many Southerners were disenchanted with him, and he was placed in charge of the mounted troops under Pemberton. His raid on Holly Springs, Mississippi, was a major factor in ending Grant's campaign in central Mississippi. Moving his division into middle Tennessee, he was killed on May 7, 1863, by Dr. George B. Peters for attentions paid by the general upon the physician's wife in Spring Hill. (Hartje, Robert G., *Van Dorn, The Life and Times of a Confederate General*)

Earl Van Dorn, victim of a personal dispute. (AC)

VAN LEW, Elizabeth (fl. 1861-1865)

Utilizing a carefully nurtured reputation as a harmless eccentric, Richmond Unionist Elizabeth Van Lew proved to be one of the most effective spies in the Confederate capital. Her neighbors just nicknamed her "Crazy Bet" or more politely "Miss Lizzie" when she started setting up a bedroom for George B. McClellan when it looked like his Peninsula Campaign would result in the city's fall. No one would dare do such a thing if they were really involved in undercover activities—at least so thought the neighbors. In fact, Van Lew was working hard to get information on the capital's defenses and manpower through to McClellan. Later in the war she broadened the scope of her activities by providing refuge and aid to fleeing Union prisoners of war. She often used them to deliver messages to the Washington authorities. It was her information smuggled out of Richmond that revealed the weakness of the Richmond defenses in early 1864 which resulted in the unsuccessful Kilpatrick-Dahlgren raid. At the end of the war the Union authorities gave her high marks for her work.

VAN VLIET, Stewart (1815-1901)

Coming into conflict with the navy, and especially L.M. Goldsborough, the Army of the Potomac's chief quartermaster, Stewart Van Vliet asked to be relieved from his post and spent the balance of the Civil War serving his department in New York. The Vermont native had received his appointment to West Point from New York and upon his 1840 graduation was posted to the artillery. He saw service in Florida and then transferred to the supply service in 1847. Serving in Mexico, on the frontier, and in preparation for the Utah expedition of 1857 and 1858, he was a captain at the outbreak of the Civil War. His assignments included: captain and assistant quartermaster (since June 4, 1847); major and quartermaster (August 3, 1861); chief quartermaster, Army of the Potomac (August 20, 1861-July 10, 1862); brigadier general, USV (September 23, 1861); and brigadier general, USV (reappointed November 23, 1865, to date from March 13, 1865). In the first summer of the war he became McClellan's supply chief and directed the department's operations during the Peninsula Campaign. Since the army's supply lines reached it by sea, he had many dealings with the navy but unfortunately seems to have considered it part of the army and subordinate to him. Finally he asked for relief, which was granted on July 10, 1862, and exactly a week later his volunteer commission lapsed due to nonconfirmation by the Senate. He spent the balance of the conflict obtaining supplies at New York and forwarding them and troops to the field. He was brevetted brigadier general for the war and major general for his service in the department. He was recommissioned a brigadier general of volunteers after the close of hostilities and brevetted major general. He was mustered out of the volunteers on September 1, 1866, but remained in the regular establishment until his 1881 retirement as assistant quartermaster with the rank of colonel.

VAN WINKLE, Peter Godwin (1808-?)

When the secession of western Virginia from secessionist Virginia was recognized by the granting of statehood, Peter G. Van Winkle became West Virginia's first senator. Born in New York, he had taken up the practice of law in that part of Virginia which was to become West Virginia in 1835. Active also in railroading, he became a company president. He was a member of the Wheeling convention of 1861 which rejected secession and began laying the groundwork for the new state. He was also a delegate to the constitutional convention for West Virginia. With the state organization completed, he took a seat in the lower house of the state legislature but was soon thereafter named as a Unionist to the Senate. He was seated on August 4, 1863, and held it until the expiration of the term in 1869. He then retired from public life.

VAN WYCK, Charles Henry (1824-1895)

A Democrat turned Republican, Charles H. Van Wyck served in Congress at the beginning of the war and then raised a regiment and became one of the last batch of brigadier generals to be appointed in the volunteer service. His military assignments included: colonel, 56th New York (September 4, 1861); and brigadier general, USV (September 27, 1865). During the early part of the war, he was often absent from his command, being a New York congressman since 1859. During 1862 the lawyer-congressman chaired the subcommittee which investigated the corrupt affairs of General Justus McKinstry in the Department of the West. Van Wyck joined his regiment for the Seven Days but the unit was not engaged. Remaining on the Peninsula until the end of 1862, he was engaged in some minor operations before moving to North Carolina and then South Carolina. His congressional term having expired in March 1863, he served through the operations against Charleston. In the final months of the war he was in charge of an informal brigade and was brevetted brigadier for his war service; shortly before being mustered out, he was given the full rank. After the war he again sat as a congressman from New York and later as a senator from Nebraska, where he became a Populist advocating the direct popular election of senators, an action which caused an angered legislature to decline to reelect him. His later campaigns for state office were also unsuccessful.

VAUGHAN, Alfred Jefferson, Jr. (1830-1899)

Virginia Military Institute graduate Alfred J. Vaughan, Jr., rose to the rank of brigadier general in the Confederate army while fighting in most of the major actions in the western theater until wounded during the Atlanta Campaign. The Virginia-born civil engineer and farmer had entered the Confederate service from Tennessee. His assignments included: captain, Company F, 13th Tennessee (spring 1861); lieutenant colonel, 13th Tennessee (June 4, 1861); colonel, 13th Tennessee (ca. November 1861); commanding Preston Smith's Brigade, Cleburne's Divison, Left Wing, Army of the Mississippi (August 30-September 1862); commanding Smith's Brigade, Cheatham's Division, Polk's Corps, Army of Tennessee (December 1862-ca. January 1863 and September 19-November 1863); colonel, 13th and 154th Senior Tennessee Consolidated (March 1863); brigadier general, CSA (November 18, 1863); commanding brigade, Hindman's Division, Breckinridge's-Hindman's Corps, Army of Tennessee (November 1863-February 20, 1864); and commanding brigade, Cheatham's Division, Hardee's Corps, Army of Tennessee (February 20-July 4, 1864). After briefly commanding the Dixie Rifles he was named a field officer and as a colonel led his regiment across the Mississippi during the fight at Belmont. He was at its head at Shiloh and during the operations around Corinth. During the Kentucky Campaign he succeeded to the command of the brigade at Richmond and led it again at Murfreesboro. After serving in the Tullahoma Campaign he took command of the brigade when Preston Smith was killed. Named a brigadier general, he fought at Chattanooga and then during the Atlanta Campaign. In a small action at Vining's Station his leg was torn off by a shell on July 4, 1864. This effectively ended his field career. Active in veterans' organizations after the war, he was a farmer and political activist in Mississippi. He was subsequently a court clerk in Memphis.

VAUGHN, John Crawford (1824-1875)

Although at one point his command was deemed little more than a band of marauders, Tennesseean John C. Vaughn led his brigade as part of the escort for Jefferson Davis during the president's flight. A merchant by profession, he had served as a company commander in the 5th Tennessee during the Mexican War. After witnessing the firing on Fort Sumter he returned home and raised a regiment for the Confederacy. His assignments included: colonel, 3rd Tennessee PACS (June 6, 1861); brigadier general, CSA (September 22, 1862); commanding brigade, Defenses of Vicksburg, Department of Mississippi and East Louisiana (December 1862-January 1863); commanding brigade, Smith's Division, 2nd Military District, Department of Mississippi and East Louisiana (January-April 1863); commanding brigade, Smith's Division, Department of Mississippi and East Louisiana (April-July 4, 1863); commanding brigade, Stevenson's Division, Hill's-Breckinridge's Corps, Army of Tennessee (fall 1863); commanding brigade, Buckner's Division, Department of East Tennessee (November 1863-

January 1864); commanding cavalry brigade, Department of East Tennessee (January-March and April-June 1864); commanding division, Cavalry Corps, Department of East Tennessee (March-April 1864); commanding cavalry brigade, Valley District, Army of Northern Virginia (June-summer 1864); and commanding cavalry brigade, Department of Western Virginia and East Tennessee (fall 1864-April 1865). He led his regiment in western Virginia and at 1st Bull Run before being ordered to East Tennessee. Promoted to brigadier general, he was ordered to the Vicksburg area and commanded a brigade at Chickasaw Bayou. Captured upon the fall of Vicksburg, he was exchanged on September 12, 1863, and then managed to have his command converted into mounted infantry. As such it served under James Longstreet in East Tennessee and then moved into Virginia. He fought at Piedmont and in the defense of Lynchburg. Accompanying Jubal A. Early northward he was wounded at Martinsburg, West Virginia. Upon his recovery, he resumed command of his brigade and led it until after the fall of Richmond when he joined the fleeing government officials. He surrendered in Georgia and later served in the Tennessee legislature.

VEATCH, James Clifford (1819-1895)

Indiana lawyer James C. Veatch was sitting in the state legislature when he volunteered for the Union army. The Indianan's assignments included: colonel, 25th Indiana (August 19, 1861); commanding 2nd Brigade, 4th Division, Army of the Tennessee (February 17-July 1862); brigadier general, USV (April 28, 1862); commanding 4th Division, District of Memphis, Army of the Tennessee (July-September 24, 1862); commanding 2nd Brigade, 4th Division, District of Jackson, Army of the Tennessee (September 24-October 26, 1862); commanding District of Memphis, 16th Corps, Army of the Tennessee (January 5-25, 1863); commanding 5th Division, 16th Corps, Army of the Tennessee (March 31, 1863-January 25, 1864); commanding 4th Division, 16th Corps, Army of the Tennessee (January 24-July 17, 1864); commanding 1st Division, Reserve Corps, Department of the Gulf (February 8-18, 1865); and commanding 1st Division, 13th Corps, Department of the Gulf (February 18-May 25, 1865). He led his regiment at Fort Donelson and a brigade at Shiloh. Following the siege of Corinth he was assigned to Memphis as a brigadier general for some time but did see action at the Hatchie River in October 1862. Back in the major theater of operations, he led a division in the Georgia campaign to the outskirts of Atlanta but was forced by illness to relinquish command just before the major battles of the campaign. Having apparently raised the ire of his army commander, Oliver O. Howard, he was not welcome back with that army and instead was shunted off to the Gulf coast where he won a brevet as major general for Mobile. Mustered out on August 24, 1865, he was a tax official and his state's adjutant general.

VELAZQUEZ, Loreta Janeta (1838-?)

If there has ever been a case of exaggeration with a hidden element of truth, it is likely to be in the claims put forward by Loreta J. Velazquez in her book, *The Woman in Battle: A Narrative of the Exploits, Adventures, and Travels of Madame Loreta Janeta Velazquez, Otherwise Known as Lieutenant Harry T. Buford, Confederate States Army.* In this work published in 1876, she claims to have fought at 1st Bull Run, Fort Donelson, and Shiloh—being wounded at the latter two—to have been a blockade runner and spy, and to have had several wartime marriages and access to the presidents and secretaries of war of both the United and Confederate States, as well as to high-ranking generals on both sides, while passing as a man. Little in her work can be even circumstantially supported. Yet there may be an element of truth. She may have done some of the things she claimed, but this will never be definitely known due to her penchant for exaggeration. It must be realized that she may have written the work solely to provide an income for herself and her infant daughter. One of her harshest critics was none other than ex-Confederate General Jubal A. Early.

VENABLE, Charles Scott (1827-1900)

As an aide-de-camp to General Lee, Charles Venable served throughout the campaigns of the Army of Northern Virginia. Born in Virginia, he graduated from Hampden-Sidney College at the age of 15 and was, for several years, a tutor in mathematics at the school. Receiving further education at the University of Virginia and in Berlin and Bonn, he became a mathematics professor at various schools in Virginia and South Carolina as well as an astronomer. He served as a lieutenant during the firing on Fort Sumter and later fought at 1st Bull Run as a private in Company A, 2nd South Carolina. He joined Lee's staff as a major, when that general was the military advisor to Jefferson Davis. When Lee was given command of the Department, soon to be the Army, of Northern Virginia, Venable continued as his aide-de-camp. Serving from the Peninsula Campaign to Appomattox, he was promoted to lieutenant colonel. Following the surrender, he resumed his career as an educator. During a visit to Prussia, he was received at the castle of General Stuart's former aide-de-camp, Heros von Borcke, with Prussian and Confederate flags flying.

VESEY, Denmark (1767-1822)

At the turn of the century, after purchasing his freedom from his master with $600 he had won in a lottery, Denmark Vesey, a free black carpenter, began plotting with other blacks for an uprising of the slaves in Charleston, South Carolina. But the group of conspirators grew very large, and it was impossible to keep the plan a secret. Word leaked out a month before the planned July 2, 1822, revolt, and Vesey and coconspirator Peter Poyas were arrested. They denied everything and were eventually released. With the date of the uprising moved up to June 16, excessive black activity the night before led the authorities to believe that a revolt was imminent and they rearrested Vesey, Poyas, and many slaves. Thirty-five blacks, including the two free blacks, were hanged for their part in the threatened insurrection, and an additional 43 slaves were banished. The fear of such a plot to kill slaveholders was to remain a part of southern life until the Civil War, almost four decades later. (Lofton, John, *Denmark Vesey's Revolt)*

VEST, George Graham (1830-1904)

The record is unclear, but for either a public or private matter—whether from a bill requesting the ages of government clerks or an affair of the heart—Missouri's George G. Vest was the only Confederate congressman to be publicly whipped (by a woman in an impromptu punishment). Appointed to the Provisional Confederate Congress, the Kentucky-born Democratic lawyer automatically became a member of the First Regular Congress, since no elections could be held in his occupied 5th District. In the Provisional Congress he sat on the Committee on the Judiciary and in the First Congress on the Committee on Elections. He supported the government's war policies in the hope that there would be a reconquest of his constituency in central Missouri. Nonetheless, by the war's end he was highly critical of the Davis administration and supported calls for its reorganization, both in the cabinet and in the field. As an administration supporter he had been reelected by the soldier and refugee vote in a special election organized by the Congress. In the Second Congress he sat on the Committee on the Judiciary before being named to the Senate on January 12, 1865, where he held no committee assignments. Returning to the legal profession at the war's close—and after submitting to Missouri's test oath—he later served four terms in the U.S. Senate. He was always considered an effective legislator, even gaining the respect of opposing Republican newspapers. (French, Edwin Malcolm Chase, *Senator George G. Vest)*

VICTORIA, Queen (1819-1901)

The United Kingdom of Great Britain and Ireland was ruled during the Civil War years by Queen Victoria. Raised for the throne, she acceded to it at age 18. With internal warfare breaking out in the United States, she issued a proclamation of neutrality on May 13, 1861. This policy, which granted the Confederacy belligerent's status, was unsatisfactory to both sides. Outraged by the United States' seizure of Confederate commissioners Mason and Slidell from the British mail steamer *Trent*, she did allow her husband, Prince Albert, to modify the foreign secretary's ultimatum to Washington. This, together with the eventual release of the prisoners, alleviated the crisis. On December 4, 1861, she banned all munitions exports to either side but lifted the ban the next February. Even after the December 1861 death of her husband, she fought against any effort to bring her country into the conflict. The prime minister, Lord Palmerston, was openly sympathetic to the South. Neutrality irritated many Northerners since they expected Britain, which had recently abolished slavery throughout its empire, to back the Union's war against slavery. The Confederacy, on the other hand, thought that Britain, in need of cotton, would come to her assistance. Both were wrong and both were unhappy with the situation. Queen Victoria ruled into the next century. (Warren, Gordon H., *Fountain of Discontent: The Trent Affair and Freedom of the Seas*)

VIELE, Egbert Ludovicus (1825-1902)

The Civil War services of General Egbert L. Viele are overshadowed by his topographical and engineering work which to a large degree made possible the construction of New York City's modern skyline. The native New Yorker and West Pointer (1847) had been posted to the infantry and took part in the occupation of Mexico. After routine interwar duty he resigned as a first lieutenant in 1853 and engaged in engineering assignments in New Jersey until the Civil War. His assignments included: captain of Engineers, 7th New York Militia (April 19-30, 1861); brigadier general, USV (August 17, 1861); commanding 1st Brigade, South Carolina Expeditionary Corps (September 19, 1861-March 15, 1862); commanding brigade, Department of Virginia (May 8-June 1, 1862); and commanding Norfolk, 7th Corps, Department of Virginia (July 22, 1862-August 1, 1863). Early in the war he published his *Handbook for Active Service* which found wide acceptance among both the Northern and Southern volunteers. He served as an engineering officer with the famous 7th New York Militia in the Washington defenses shortly after the firing on Fort Sumter. As a brigadier, he led his men in the South Carolina coastal operations and was involved in the reduction of Fort Pulaski near Savannah. Sent to Virginia, he acted as military governor at Norfolk and completed his military service by supervising the draft in northern Ohio. Resigning on October 20, 1863, he later became park commissioner for New York City and sat in Congress.

VILLARD, Henry (1835-1900)

Emigrating from his native Bavaria in 1853, Ferdinand Heinrich Gustav Hilgard changed his name to Henry Villard and, after mastering the new tongue, became a leading journalist. Headquartering himself in Washington early in the war, he worked as a correspondent for numerous papers, including the *Cincinnati Commercial, New York Herald*, and *New York Tribune*. He was frequently at the front and reported on the Army of the Potomac's campaigns. He covered the 1st Bull Run Campaign and later the Fredericksburg fight. His coverage of the latter battle was not carried right away by the *Tribune* because they did not want to publish such disastrous news without verification. This was a bitter pill for Villard to swallow since he had had to send his dispatch by messenger after the military-controlled telegraph refused to transmit it. After recounting at the Willard Hotel how General Burnside had slaughtered his army, Villard was escorted to give the news to Lincoln, which he did with full frankness. Villard was also a critic of Mrs. Lincoln's vanity. Despite trouble with the *Tribune*'s editor Horace Greeley, Villard continued with the paper, with only a short intermission, until the close of the war. After a short stint as an American correspondent in Europe, Villard returned and became a financier of railroads and newspapers. (Villard, Henry, *Memoirs of Henry Villard*)

VILLEPIGUE, John Bordenave (1830-1862)

The death from fever of talented General John B. Villepigue was a severe blow to the Confederate cause. The South Carolinian

West Pointer (1854) had served on the frontier with the 2nd Dragoons before resigning as a first lieutenant on March 31, 1861. Joining the Confederacy, his assignments included: captain, Artillery (spring 1861); colonel, 36th Georgia (1861); commanding Army of Mobile, Department of Alabama and West Florida (February 28-March 15, 1862); brigadier general, CSA (March 13, 1862); commanding Fort Pillow, Department #2 (April-June 4, 1862); commanding brigade at Grenada, Miss., Department #2 (June 4-July 1862); commanding 3rd Sub-District, District of the Mississippi, Department #2 (July-ca. August 1862); and commanding brigade, 1st Division, District of the Mississippi, Department #2 (October 1862). Wounded at Fort McRee in Pensacola Harbor on November 22, 1861, he later commanded the forces at Mobile and was promoted to brigadier general. He then served as Braxton Bragg's artillery and engineering chief. Placed in charge of Fort Pillow on the Mississippi River, he ably defended it against Union gunboats. Ordered to withdraw, he destroyed his works and moved his command to Grenada, Mississippi. He then led his men around Vicksburg and led a brigade at Corinth. However, the next month he died of fever, on November 9, 1862, and Port Hudson.

VILLERÉ, Charles Jacques (ca. 1828-1899)

Although a supporter of a strong central government for the Confederacy, Congressman—and brother-in-law of General P.G.T. Beauregard—Charles J. Villeré was an opponent of the Davis administration. Born on the battlefield of New Orleans, he became a Louisiana lawyer and planter. A Democrat and secessionist, he was defeated for the U.S. Congress in 1860. Before the cavalry company which he organized at the outbreak of the war could get into action he was elected to represent the state's 1st District in the First Regular Confederate Congress, where he sat on the committees on: Claims; Commerce; and Military Affairs. In the Second Congress he was only a member of the Committee on Military Affairs. He used this latter post for his attacks on Davis and his defense of Beauregard. Following the war he went into retirement but supervised the Louisiana Lottery in the 1890s.

VINCENT, Strong (1837-1863)

A Pennsylvania lawyer, Strong Vincent entered the army in the Civil War and earned his general's star by giving up his life on Little Round Top. After serving as first lieutenant and adjutant of a militia regiment from April 21 to July 25 1861, Vincent became lieutenant colonel, 83rd Pennsylvania, on September 14, 1861. His later assignments included: colonel, 83rd Pennsylvania (June 27, 1862); commanding 3rd Brigade, 1st Division, 5th Corps, Army of the Potomac (May 20-July 2, 1863); and brigadier general, USV (July 3, 1863). He served at the siege of Yorktown and Hanover Court House before being stricken down by malaria. Returning to the field, he led his regiment at Fredericksburg and Chancellorsville before taking over command of the brigade. On the second day at Gettysburg, Vincent followed the orders of his corps commander, General Sykes, without waiting for the approval of his division leader, General Barnes. Taking his command onto the exposed position atop Little Round Top, his four regiments became the left of the entire army with the 20th Maine holding the left flank. When his right regiment, the 16th Michigan, began to falter, Vincent raced over to reform it and fell mortally wounded. By some mistake his brigadier's commission was dated the 3rd instead of July 2, as was the custom. Vincent died four days after being wounded. (Judson, A.M., *History of the Eighty-third Regiment Pennsylvania Volunteers*)

VINTON, Francis Laurens (1835-1879)

Without even waiting for the end of his graduation leave, Francis L. Vinton resigned from the U.S. Army in order to attend Paris' École des Mines. The West Pointer (1856) had been posted to the cavalry before his resignation and was an educator in his field of engineering in New York at the outbreak of the Civil War. The Maine native was recommissioned in the regular army and his assignments included: captain, 16th Infantry (August 5, 1861); colonel, 43rd New York (October 31, 1861); brigadier general, USV (September 19, 1862); commanding 3rd Brigade, 2nd Division, 6th Corps, Army of the Potomac (September 25-December 13, 1862); and brigadier general, USV (reappointed April 9, 1863, to rank from March 13). Soon after being named a company commander of one of the new regular army infantry regiments he received the colonelcy of a New York volunteer regiment which he led to the Peninsula, seeing action at Yorktown, Williamsburg, and in the Seven Days. Having missed the fight at Antietam, he was named a brigadier general two days later, and while leading his brigade at Fredericksburg he fell severely wounded. This wound ended his military career. His first brigadier general's commission was not confirmed, but he was reappointed and confirmed. However, he shortly thereafter submitted his resignation which was accepted effective May 3, 1863, from both the regulars and volunteers. Subsequently he taught engineering in New York and was a mining engineer in Colorado.

VOGDES, Israel (1816-1889)

A brigadier general of volunteers during the Civil War, Israel Vogdes is largely forgotten since he served, albeit creditably, in the lesser theaters of the war. The Pennsylvania native was a West Pointer (1837) and had been posted to the artillery. He spent a dozen years as an instructor at the academy and saw limited service against the Seminoles in Florida. His Civil War-era assignments included: captain, 1st Artillery (since August 20, 1847); major, 1st Artillery (May 14, 1861); brigadier general, USV (November 29, 1862); commanding U.S. Forces Folly Island, 10th Corps, Department of the South (April 8-July 19, 1863); lieutenant colonel, 5th Artillery (June 1, 1863); also commanding 1st Brigade, 2nd Division, 10th Corps, Department of the South (July 6-19, 1863); commanding 1st Brigade, U.S. Forces Morris Island, 10th Corps, Department of the South (July 19-August 1, 1863); colonel, 1st Artillery (August 1, 1863); commanding U.S. Forces North End Folly Island, 10th Corps, Department of the South (August 16-December 16, 1863); commanding 2nd Division, District of Florida, Department of the South (February 25-28, 1864); commanding Defenses of Norfolk and Portsmouth, District of Eastern Virginia, Department of Virginia and North Carolina (May 1864-April 1865); and commanding 4th Separate Brigade, District of Florida, Department of the South (April 19-July 10, 1865). Prominently engaged in the defense of Fort Pickens in Florida's Pensacola Harbor, he was captured in the repulse of the Confederate assault on Santa Rosa Island on October 9, 1861. Not declared exchanged until August 27, 1862, he was shortly thereafter named a brigadier general of volunteers. His subsequent services were geared principally toward the capture of Charleston. At times he also served in Florida. Brevetted brigadier in the regular establishment, he was mustered out of the volunteers on January 15, 1866, and spent the rest of his career in garrison duty. He retired in 1881 and settled in New York City.

VON BORCKE, Heros (ca. 1836-1895)

The American Civil War attracted many European military men as observers and participants to both sides. One of the latter, for the South, was a Prussian lieutenant, Heros Von Borcke. Taking a leave of absence from Prussia and barely avoiding capture on a blockade runner, he arrived in the Confederacy in the spring of 1862. With a letter of introduction to the secretary of war from the German consul in Charleston, von Borcke obtained a commission as a lieutenant and assignment to the staff of General J.E.B. Stuart. Quickly becoming a favorite of the rebel cavalry leader, he was rapidly promoted to major. He participated in the battles of Seven Pines, the Seven Days, Verdiersville, Fredericksburg, Chancellorsville, and Brandy Station. He was chosen to present the fancy gift uniform from Stuart to Stonewall Jackson. In the early stages of the Gettysburg Campaign von Borcke was wounded in a fight at Middleburg, Virginia. Narrowly avoiding capture while recovering, he found his Confederate military career was over. Given the Thanks of the Confederate Congress, he was sent on a diplomatic mission to Britain with the new rank of lieutenant colonel. He returned in time to rush to the bedside of his beloved, dying commander, Stuart. When the Confederacy fell, he was again on a foreign mission. Von Borcke distinguished himself in the Franco-Prussian War but never forgot the Confederacy. When Lee's former aide-de-camp, Charles Venable, visited Prussia, both the Prussian and Confederate flags flew over his castle. He visited the Virginia battlefields in 1884 and was feted by his former comrades. He also wrote *Memoirs of the Confederate War for Independence* and *Die grosse Reiterschlacht bei Brandy Station*)

VON CLAUSEWITZ, Karl

See: *Clausewitz, Karl von*

VON GILSA, Leopold (?-?)

At the head of one of New York's numerous German regiments marched Leopold von Gilsa. His assignments included: colonel, 41st New York (ca. June 10, 1861); commanding 1st Brigade, 1st Division, 11th Corps, Army of the Potomac (September 12, 1862-January 12, 1863, February 2-May 25, and June 5-July 17, 1863); commanding 1st Brigade, South End Folly Island, 10th Corps, Department of the South (October 24-November 28, 1863 and January 13-15, 1864); commanding 1st Brigade, Gordon's-Ames'-Schimmelfennig's Division, 10th Corps, Department of the South (January 15-April 25, 1864); and commanding Folly Island, Northern District, Department of the South (April 25-October 26, 1864). His regiment was also called the 2nd Yaeger Regiment and the De Kalb Regiment. During the fighting at 1st Bull Run it was in reserve at Arlington Heights and Fairfax Court House. Transferred to the Shenandoah Valley, he was wounded at Cross Keys. Returning to duty he commanded a brigade in the Washington fortifications and in operations near Snicker's Gap. His regiment served on the infamous Mud March in January 1863, and he commanded a brigade when the corps was surprised and routed at Chancellorsville by Stonewall Jackson. A similar fate befell von Gilsa at Gettysburg on the first day, and the division commander, wishing to get out of the roundly criticized corps, managed to get the division transferred to the South Carolina coast two weeks later. Von Gilsa went along and held several commands there in the operations against Charleston. His regiment later served in the Washington defenses, and von Gilsa was probably mustered out with it on December 9, 1865.

VON SCHACK, George (?-1887)

German native George Von Schack won the brevet of brigadier general of volunteers in the Union army during the Civil War. Enlisting in the "Steuben Rifles," his assignments included: major, 7th New York (July 31, 1861); colonel, 7th New York (February 8, 1862); commanding 1st Brigade, 1st Division, 2nd Corps, Army of the Potomac (December 13, 1862-February 14, 1863); lieutenant colonel, 7th New York Veteran (July 15, 1864); colonel, 7th New York Veteran (November 2, 1864); and commanding 3rd Brigade, 1st Division, 2nd Corps, Army of the Potomac (January 28-February 22, 1865). His unit should not be confused with the famous militia outfit with the same numerical designation. His unit fought at Big Bethel, and Von Schack commanded it at the Seven Days on the Peninsula. At Fredericksburg he succeeded to brigade command before the unit was mustered out at the expiration of its two-year tour of duty on May 8, 1863. When a regiment of veterans was formed the next years, Von Schack became its second in command and eventually its commander. This regiment he led at Petersburg and for a time he was again in charge of a brigade. Mustered out a second time with his new regiment on August 4, 1865, he was brevetted for his role on the Peninsula back in 1862. The Prussian army veteran then decided to remain in the United States.

VON STEINWEHR, Adolph Wilhelm August Friedrich, Baron (1822-1877)

Coming from an Old World military family, Baron Adolph von Steinwehr effectively ended his American military career by turning down a brigade command as beneath a man who had long directed a division and even a corps briefly. Born in the Duchy of Brunswick, his ancestors had fought for the duke and in the Prussian army. He himself had been a lieutenant in the duke's employ when he took a leave to visit America. He failed to gain a regular army commission for the Mexican War but returned home with an Alabamian wife. Within five years they were back in the United States and he became a Connecticut farmer. With the outbreak of the Civil War he finally got his chance to serve in the American forces. His assignments included: colonel, 29th New York (June 6, 1861); brigadier general, USV (October 12, 1861); commanding 2nd Brigade, Blenker's Division, Army of the Potomac (December 1861-March 13, 1862); commanding 2nd Brigade, Blenker's Division, 2nd Corps, Army of the Potomac (March 13-31, 1862); commanding 2nd Brigade, Blenker's Division, Mountain Department (April 1-June 26, 1862); commanding 2nd Division, 1st Corps, Army of Virginia (June 26-September 12, 1862); commanding 2nd Division, 11th Corps, Army of the Potomac (September 12, 1862-February 22, 1863, March 5-28, and April 12-September 25, 1863); commanding the corps (February 22-March 5, 1863); and commanding 2nd Division, 11th Corps, Army of the Cumberland (September 25-November 28, 1863 and March 3-April 16, 1864). His regiment was in reserve at Centerville during the battle of 1st Bull Run but helped to stem the Union rout. Given a general's star, he served in the Shenandoah Valley but for some undetermined reason missed the battle of Cross Keys. By the battle of 2nd Bull Run he was in charge of a division and held the same post in the Washington area during the Maryland Campaign. At Chancellorsville his two brigades were caught up in the rout of the corps, but on the first day at Gettysburg his division was left south of town to guard Cemetery Hill. Only one of his brigades—Charles R. Coster's—was caught up in the defeat when it was sent north of the town to relieve the pressure. Transferred with the corps to Chattanooga, he led his division at Chattanooga and in the Knoxville relief expedition. The next year the 11th and 12th corps were consolidated into the new 20th Corps. In the shake-up von Steinwehr was reduced to a brigade command in the 14th Corps while officers junior in rank were given divisions in the new formation. He rejected the post and appears to have been unemployed for the remainder of the war. Resigning on July 3, 1865, he became a government engineer, taught at Yale, and was a topographical engineer and geographer.

VON WEBER, Max

See: *Weber, Max*

VON WILLICH, August

See: *Willich, August*

WADDELL, James Iredell (1824-1886)

The time it took for James I. Waddell to finally join the Confederate cause may well have been a record, but he made up for it by surrendering the last Confederate fighting command—almost seven months after Lee's surrender. At the outbreak of the Civil War Waddell, after decades in the navy, had been a lieutenant serving in the East Indies Squadron. Being a North Carolinian, he resigned his commission, explaining that he did not wish to fight against the home of his father and relatives and only wished he could fight for the United States against a foreign foe. He had no hostility toward the U.S. Constitution. In December 1861 he married into a secessionist family, and the Navy Department acted upon his letter of resignation by dismissing him. So in February 1862 he slipped into the Confederacy and was commissioned a first lieutenant on March 27, 1862. After duty at Drewry's Bluff and in Charleston Harbor, he was assigned to "special service." He was next ordered to run the blockade and convert the *Sea King* into the last of the Confederate cruisers, the *Shenandoah*. Waddell commissioned the vessel in the Confederate navy on October 19, 1864. On a cruise to Australia, he began the capture of an eventual total of 36 prizes. After repairing in Melbourne in January and February 1865, Waddell sailed through the Pacific, rounding up more prizes, and moved on to the American whaling fleet in the Bering Sea and the Arctic Ocean. Virtually destroying the fleet, he scored his last victories on June 28 against 11 whalers. On August 2, 1865, it was finally learned from a British vessel that the war was over. Dismounting his guns, Waddell decided the best thing to do was to turn over the vessel to the British authorities at Liverpool where the *Sea King* had been constructed. The *Shenandoah* finally lowered its flag, the last to fly over a Confederate combat unit, on November 6, 1865. (Waddell, James T., *C.S.S. Shenandoah: The Memoirs of Lieutenant Commanding James I. Waddell*)

WADE, Benjamin Franklin (1800-1878)

As one of the most powerful leaders of the Radical Republicans in Congress, Benjamin F. Wade made no end of trouble for the with his parents to Ohio where he entered upon the practice of law and became an antislavery politician. He served in the state legislature's upper house and at the time of his appointment to the U.S. Senate was serving as a judge. During his tenure in the Senate he joined the Republicans when his own Whig Party broke up. He took his seat on March 15, 1851, and held it until 1869, having been defeated the year before. In his final two years he was the president pro tempore. Early in the Civil War he visited Lincoln, on October 26, 1861, as a member (with Zachariah Chandler and Lyman Trumbull) of what John Hay called the "Jacobin Club." After the defeats at 1st Bull Run and Ball's Bluff they wanted to know why McClellan's huge army had not begun an offensive. The pressure did not work as the Army of the Potomac did not move until the next spring. Named to the chairmanship of the Joint Committee on the Conduct of the War, Wade had a forum for launching his attacks on the administration and its military leaders. Many officers' reputations were ruined by their appearances before the panel. Wade frequently was the only member present to ask questions since there was no requirement for a quorum. In response to Lincoln's moderate plan for Reconstruction, he joined with Henry W. Davis to introduce the Wade-Davis Bill in 1864. This bill called for a harsher treatment of the yet-to-be-conquered South, including a delay in the restoration of civil government and heavy restrictions on ex-Confederate officers and volunteers. The bill was passed on July 2, 1864, but was pocket-vetoed by the president. Wade and Davis replied with their denunciatory Manifesto against the president's policies. In his final years in the Senate, Wade fought the moderate Reconstruction policies of Andrew Johnson. For his remaining years he resumed his practice but remained active in politics. (Trefousse, Hans Louis, *Benjamin Franklin Wade, Radical Republican from Ohio*)

WADE, Jennie (Mary Virginia) (1843-1863)

Known to history as Jennie, Gettysburg native Mary Virginia Wade had moved in with her sister Mrs. McClellan to help with her newborn infant when the battle surrounded the Baltimore

Street house. The family took shelter in the cellar. However, Jennie went up to the kitchen on the third day of the battle to bake more bread for the family and the nearby Union soldiers. While she was baking, a stray bullet, probably from a Confederate skirmisher, passed through two wooden doors and struck Jennie in the back. She died instantly. She thus became the only Gettysburg civilian to have been killed in the battle. She never received the message that her fiancé, Corporal Johnston Skelly, had been mortally wounded about two weeks earlier at the second battle of Winchester.

WADE, Melancthon Smith (1802-1868)

A retired Ohio businessman for over twenty years, Melancthon Wade was involved in organizing Ohio regiments for the field early in the Civil War. A longtime officer of the state militia, having risen to brigadier general by the outbreak of the war, Wade was a natural choice for the assignment. Given command of the state's principal recruiting depot, Camp Dennison near Cincinnati, he was appointed brigadier general, USV, on October 1, 1861. During his period as the camp's first commandant, he supervised the raising of the equivalent of at least 23 regiments for the Union service. However, ill health forced his resignation on March 18, 1862. Until his death in 1868, he was a horticulturalist.

WADLEY, William Morrill (1812-1882)

With the Confederacy founded on the basis of states' rights and the free enterprise of the capitalistic system, it was inevitable that the appointment of William M. Wadley to oversee the South's railroads in a military capacity would run into trouble with the Congress. A native of New Hampshire, he had began working for Georgia railroads in 1835 and became one of the leading managers of transportation in the South. A secessionist, he was a quartermaster at the outbreak of the war and in 1862 he was appointed the military superintendent of Confederate rail operations. Favoring a form of nationalization, he was rejected by the legislative branch and served the rest of the war as a member of the iron commission. He then retired to New Orleans. (Catherwood, T.B., ed., *Life of William M. Wadley*)

WADSWORTH, James Samuel 1807-1864)

In the spring 1864 reorganization of the Army of the Potomac many officers were shelved or given smaller commands. It is thus surprising that wealthy New Yorker James S. Wadsworth, with no military service prior to the Civil War, was retained in division command. A non-practicing attorney, he had been active in Democratic, free-soil, and, finally, Republican politics and was a member of the Washington Peace Convention in 1861. Volunteering his services without pay, he was initially on the staff of Irvin McDowell. His assignments included: volunteer aide-de-camp (July 8, 1861); volunteer aide-de-camp, Army of Northeastern Virginia (July-August 1861); brigadier general, USV (August 9, 1861); commanding 2nd Brigade, McDowell's Division, Army of the Potomac (October 3, 1861-March 13, 1862); commanding 2nd Brigade, 3rd Division, 1st Corps, Army of the Potomac (March 13-17,

James S. Wadsworth (seated right) and staff. (NA)

1862); commanding Military District of Washington, Department of the Potomac (March 17-September 7, 1862); commanding 1st Division, 1st Corps, Army of the Potomac (December 27, 1862-January 2, 1863, January 4-February 27, and March 9-July 15, 1863) commanding the corps (January 2-4 and March 1-9, 1863); and commanding 4th Division, 5th Corps, Army of the Potomac (March 25-May 6, 1864). After service on McDowell's staff at 1st Bull Run he was rewarded with a brigadier's star and led a brigade near Washington until he was named to command the Military District of Washington. In the fall of 1862, he was defeated for the New York governorship on the Republican ticket in an off-year election. Returning to duty, he was given a division in the 1st Corps which was only lightly engaged at Chancellorsville. However, on the first day at Gettysburg his division was the first infantry on the field and fought well before being forced to fall back. He left his command within two weeks but returned to command a division—composed of 1st Corps troops transferred to the 5th Corps—in the Overland Campaign. In the confused fighting of the second day in the Wilderness he fell with a head wound. The bullet entered the brain, and he died on May 8, 1864, in an enemy field hospital. (Pearson, Henry Greenleaf, *James S. Wadsworth of Geneseo, Brevet Major General of United States Volunteers*)

WAGNER, George Day (1829-1869)

For disobedience of orders at Franklin, George D. Wagner was relieved of division command and relegated to district command in Missouri. Born in Ohio and raised in Indiana, he had been a Republican member of the state legislature in 1861. Joining the volunteers, his assignments included: colonel, 15th Indiana (June 14, 1861); commanding 21st Brigade, 6th Division, Army of the Ohio (February 11-September 29, 1862); commanding 21st Brigade, 6th Division, 2nd Corps, Army of the Ohio (September 29-November 5, 1862); commanding 2nd Brigade, 1st Division, Left Wing, 14th Corps, Army of the Cumberland (November 5, 1862-January 9, 1863); commanding 2nd Brigade, 1st Division, 21st Corps, Army of the Cumberland (January 9-20 and April 13-October 9, 1863); commanding the division (February 19-April 13, 1863); brigadier general, USV (April 4, 1863, to rank from November 29, 1862); commanding 2nd Brigade, 2nd Division, 4th Corps, Army of the Cumberland (October 10, 1863-January 12, 1864, April 21-July 10, and July 25-September 30, 1864); commanding the division (February 17-27 and September 30-December 2, 1864); and commanding District of St. Louis, Department of the Missouri (April 8-July 20, 1865). Following service in western Virginia, he led one of Buell's brigades on the second day at Shiloh. At Perryville his command was the only brigade engaged out of the entire 2nd Corps. He went on to serve at Murfreesboro, through the Tullahoma Campaign, Chickamauga, and Chattanooga. There followed the Atlanta Campaign during which he led his brigade most of the time, although he missed some of the major battles before the city itself. Taking over the division, he accompanied the balance of the corps back to face Hood in Tennessee. At Franklin his division was placed in advance of the main Union works with orders to withdraw into the main line when it appeared that Hood was about to launch a major infantry assault. When Hood did, Wagner decided to stay and fight. Heavily outnumbered, the two brigades in the forward position were faced with annihilation and fled. The Confederates followed so closely upon their heels that the main line could not open fire. Some enemy troops penetrated the main line but fortunately there were reserves ready to handle them. For being the cause of a near disaster, Wagner was relieved two days afterwards and a week later was sent home for orders. His only remaining duty came in St. Louis near the close of hostilities. Mustered out on August 24, 1865—the date the first batch of volunteer general officers were discharged—he did not receive the customary brevet as a major general. Becoming a lawyer, he was also involved in agricultural organizations.

WAINWRIGHT, Charles Shiels (1826-1907)

A wealthy farmer who had traveled through Europe and studied artillery there, Charles S. Wainwright put his knowledge to good use during the Civil War. The New Yorker's assignments included: major, 1st New York Light Artillery (October 17, 1861); chief of Artillery, Hooker's Division, Army of the Potomac (January 31-March 13, 1862); chief of Artillery, 2nd Division, 3rd Corps, Army of the Potomac (March 13-September 7, 1862); lieutenant colonel, 1st New York Light Artillery (April 30, 1862); colonel, 1st New York Light Artillery (June 1, 1862); chief of Artillery, 3rd Corps, Army of Virginia (September 7-12, 1862); chief of Artillery, 1st Corps, Army of the Potomac (September 12, 1862-March 24, 1864); and chief of Artillery, 5th Corps, Army of the Potomac (March 24, 1864-June 21, 1865). He spent the beginning of the war drilling his batteries and on a board weeding out incompetent artillery officers. Taking part in the Peninsula Campaign he was promoted to commmand the regiment after the death of Colonel Guilford Bailey at Seven Pines. On leave at the time, he missed the Seven Days but served creditably at Antietam, Fredericksburg, Chancellorsville, Gettysburg, the Wilderness, Spotsylvania, Cold Harbor, Petersburg, and Appomattox. He had already received a brevet brigadier generalship in 1864 for the campaign to that point when he was mustered out on June 21, 1865. He returned to his New York farm and died in Washington. (Nevins, Allan, ed., *A Diary of Battle: The Personal Journals of Colonel Charles S. Wainwright 1861-1865*)

WALCUTT, Charles Carroll (1838-1898)

Although at first his company of volunteers was not accepted by the state, which had already fulfilled its quota, Ohio surveyor Charles C. Walcutt persisted and eventually rose to the rank of brevet major general. The Ohio native's assignments included: major, 46th Ohio (October 1, 1861); lieutenant colonel, 46th Ohio (January 30, 1862); colonel, 46th Ohio (October 16, 1862); commanding 1st Brigade, 1st Division, 16th Corps, Army of the Tennessee (January 20-March 22, 1863); commanding 2nd Brigade, 4th Division, 15th Corps, Army of the

Tennessee (November 25, 1863-March 12, 1864 and April 15-September 14, 1864); brigadier general, USV (July 30, 1864); commanding 2nd Brigade, 1st Division, 15th Corps, Army of the Tennessee (September 25-November 22, 1864 and March 28-April 4, 1865); and commanding 1st Division, 14th Corps, Army of the Cumberland (April 4-June 17 and June 27-July 18, 1865). In his first major battle, Shiloh, he was severely wounded in the shoulder and the bullet was never removed. His regiment then went on to the advance on Corinth, Mississippi. As colonel, he led his men in the siege operations at Vicksburg from June 12, 1863, until the city's fall. He took part in the recapture of Jackson, and at Chattanooga succeeded to brigade command. He led a brigade throughout the Atlanta Campaign and while before the city itself was named a brigadier general. On the famous March to the Sea he was again wounded at Griswoldville. Brevetted major general for this fight, he did not return to duty until the next spring. He led a brigade and then a division in the later stages of the Carolinas Campaign. Mustered out on January 15, 1866, he was named lieutenant colonel of the newly authorized 10th Cavalry (a black unit), but resigned later that same year. He was then a prison warden, tax official, and mayor of Columbus. He was also active in Republican and veterans' circles.

WALKE, Henry (1808-1896)

Serving on the Western rivers, Henry Walke gained a reputation as a daring and effective gunboat commander. Having entered the navy as a midshipman in 1827, he had sailed around the world and fought in the Mexican War. His assignments included: lieutenant, USN (since 1839); commanding *Tyler* (November 1861); commander, USN (late 1861 or early 1862); commanding *Carondelet* (February-April 1862); commanding *Lafayette* (1862); and commanding *Sacramento* (1863-65). In command of the *Tyler* he covered the Union forces in their withdrawal after the fight at Belmont. In his next command he took part in the reduction of Fort Henry and a few days later maintained a bombardment, virtually unaided, of several hours' duration at Fort Donelson. He later ran the Confederate batteries at Island #10 and Vicksburg. In 1863 he took part in the bombardment of Grand Gulf below the river city. The year after the war ended he was named commodore and retired in 1871 as a rear admiral. Six years later he published *Naval Scenes and Reminiscences of the Civil War*.

WALKER, Francis Amasa (1840-1897)

From his position on the staff of a Union corps commander Francis A. Walker was able to gather the information which he later used to write histories of his corps and its most famous leader. His wartime services included: private, 15th Massachusetts (August 1, 1861); sergeant major, 15th Massachusetts (1861); captain and assistant adjutant general, USV (September 14, 1861); major and assistant adjutant general, USV (August 11, 1862); and lieutenant colonel and assistant adjutant general, USV (January 1, 1863). After initial service in the ranks he received a staff appointment with General Winfield S. Hancock as his adjutant. Serving through most of that officer's campaigns he was wounded and captured at Chancellorsville. Returning to duty following his release, he was with the 2nd Corps until his resignation on January 9, 1865, and was brevetted brigadier. After the war he was an economics professor and writer, but for Civil War history purposes his most important postwar work was his historical writing. In 1887 he published *History of the Second Army Corps* and in 1895 *General Hancock*.

WALKER, Francis Marion (?-1864)

A veteran of the Mexican War, as a second lieutenant in the 5th Tennessee, Francis Marion Walker entered the Confederate service at the head of the "Marsh Blues" in the spring of 1861. His assignments included: captain, Company A, 19th Tennessee (June 1861); lieutenant colonel, 19th Tennessee (June 11, 1861); colonel, 19th Tennessee (May 8, 1862); commanding brigade, District of the Mississippi, Department No. 2 (September 1862); commanding 3rd Brigade, Breckinridge's Division, 1st Corps, Army of Tennessee (November 20-December 19, 1862); and commanding Maney's Brigade, Cheatham's Division, 1st Corps, Army of Tennessee (June-July 22, 1864). In his first significant action, Mill Springs in early 1862, he succeeded to regimental command when the colonel took over the brigade following the death of General Zollicoffer. Following the battle of Shiloh, he was elected to command the regiment upon its reorganization. He led a brigade in the fall of 1862 when it was transferred from the District of the Mississippi to Bragg's army in Tennessee. But he was only in command of his regiment at Murfreesboro. He led the 19th at Chickamauga and Chattanooga. Taking part in the Atlanta Campaign, he distinguished himself at Kennesaw Mountain in June and was given command of a brigade. He insisted that the 19th be transferred to his new brigade. He was killed on July 22, 1864, during Hood's attack at the battle of Atlanta.

WALKER, Henry Harrison (1832-1912)

A veteran of "Bleeding Kansas," West Pointer (1853) Henry Walker resigned his commission as a first lieutenant in the regular army on May 3, 1861. He was shortly appointed an infantry captain in Confederate service. His later assignments included: lieutenant colonel, 40th Virginia (spring 1861); brigadier general, CSA (July 1, 1863); and commanding Field's-Heth's old Brigade, Heth's Division, A.P. Hill's Corps, Army of Northern Virginia (July 19, 1863-May 10, 1864); also commanding Archer's Brigade, same division (July 1863-early 1864). During the Seven Days, Walker was twice wounded at Gaines' Mill. He was described by his brigade commander Charles W. Field as a "most gallant and meritorious officer." Following a slow recovery he commanded a battalion of guard forces in Richmond and while that city was relatively unprotected during the Gettysburg Campaign he armed several hundred convalescents in the Department of Henrico. Promoted to a general's wreath he was given a Virginia brigade in Lee's army. Leading his own and Archer's brigades he was engaged in the battle of Bristoe Station and the Mine Run Campaign. During the winter of 1863-64 his command served in the Valley District. Returning to the main army he took part in the battle of the Wilderness and was severely wounded at Spotsylvania where he lost a foot. He subsequently served on court-martial duty and in guarding the line of the Richmond and Danville Railroad. Following Lee's surrender, he failed to join Johnston's army in time and was paroled on May 7, 1865, in Richmond. After the war he was a New Jersey broker. (Freeman, Douglas S., *Lee's Lieutenants*)

WALKER, James Alexander (1832-1901)

Before the war, Virginian James A. Walker had been expelled from the Virginia Military Institute upon the recommendation of Thomas J. Jackson and had challenged him to a duel, but during the war, Walker earned Jackson's respect in the field. Following his expulsion, Walker had worked for a railroad and then studied law. Raising the Pulaski Guard he joined Jackson's command at Harpers Ferry. His assignments included: captain, Company C, 4th Virginia (April 1861); lieutenant colonel, 13th Virginia (June 1861); colonel, 13th Virginia (February 26, 1862); commanding Elzey's Brigade, Ewell's Division, in the Valley District, Department of Northern Virginia (June 8-mid-June 1862) and in Jackson's Command, Army of Northern Virginia (June 27-July 1, 1862); commanding Trimble's Brigade (early September-September 17, 1862) and Early's Brigade (fall 1862-ca. April 4, 1863), Ewell's-Early's Division, 2nd Corps, Army of Northern Virginia; brigadier general, CSA (May 15, 1863); commanding Stonewall Brigade, Johnson's Division, same corps and army (May 19, 1863-May 12, 1864); and commanding Ramseur's-Pegram's (old) Division, same corps and army (February-April 9, 1865). After serving briefly in what was to become the Stonewall Brigade, Walker transferred to A.P. Hill's regiment and succeeded him in its command. He fought in the Shenandoah and during the Seven Days in which he commanded the brigade for a while. At Cedar Mountain and 2nd Bull Run he led the 13th and was again in command of a brigade, Trimble's, at Antietam until wounded. Returning in time for Fredericksburg, he directed Early's Brigade there. After Chancellorsville he was promoted to brigadier, upon the recommendation of his former enemy Jackson, and assigned to command the famed Stonewall Brigade. He led it at Gettysburg and the Wilderness until severely wounded at Spotsylvania's Bloody Angle where the command ceased to exist. Although still suffering from his wound, he returned to command a division in February 1865 and surrendered at Appomattox. After the war he was active in politics until he was wounded in a duel with the lawyer for a victorious opponent. (Robertson, James I., Jr., *The Stonewall Brigade*)

WALKER, John George (1822-1893)

Following service in Virginia and North Carolina, Missouri veteran of the regular army John G. Walker was transferred west and finished out his service as a Confederate general in the Trans-Mississippi Department. He had been commissioned directly as a first lieutenant in the Regiment of Mounted Riflemen at the outbreak of the Mexican War. During that conflict he won a brevet and was wounded at Molino del Rey. Resigning as a captain on July 31, 1861, he joined the Confederacy. There his assignments included: major, Cavalry (December 21, 1861, to rank from March 16); lieutenant colonel, 8th Texas Cavalry (1861); brigadier general, CSA (January 9, 1862); commanding 4th Brigade, Department of North Carolina (early 1862-June 1862); commanding 4th Brigade, Holmes' Division, Army of Northern Virginia (June-August 1862); commanding division, 1st Corps, Army of Northern Virginia (August-November 7, 1862); major general, CSA (November 8, 1862); commanding division, District of West Louisiana, Trans-Mississippi Department (November 1863-June 10, 1864); commanding the district (June 10-August 4, 1864); commanding district of Texas, New Mexico and Arizona, Trans-Mississippi Department (August 4, 1864-March 31, 1865); and also commanding 3rd Corps, Trans-Mississippi Department (September 1864-March 31, 1865). He led a brigade in North Carolina and then accompanied Theophilus H. Holmes to the Peninsula in Virginia where he played a minor role in the Seven Days. Left in southeastern Virginia during the 2nd Bull Run Campaign, he rejoined Lee as commander of a small division for the invasion of Maryland. He led one of the three columns under Stonewall Jackson which converged on the garrison of Harpers Ferry and then fought at Antietam. Promoted to major general, he was transferred to Louisiana where he eventually led a division. After fighting in the Red River Campaign, he commanded the western part of the state for a while and then took command of the Confederates in Texas and farther west. Fleeing to Mexico upon the Confederacy's collapse, he returned to become a U.S. diplomat in Colombia. (Freeman, Douglas S., *Lee's Lieutenants*)

WALKER, Joseph (1835-1902)

A South Carolina merchant, Joseph Walker entered the Confederate service on the day Fort Sumter surrendered. His assignments included: captain, Company K, 5th South Carolina (April 13, 1861); lieutenant colonel, Palmetto (S.C.) Sharpshooters (April 15, 1862); colonel, Palmetto (S.C.) Sharpshooters (July 22, 1862); and commanding Jenkins' Brigade, Jones' Division, Longstreet's Command, Army of Northern Virginia (August 30-fall 1862). With his company soon ordered to Virginia, he served at 1st Bull Run and on the Manassas and Yorktown lines. When a new regiment, the Palmetto Sharpshooters, was formed from the 5th and other units, Walker became its second in command. As such he directed the regiment at Williamsburg and during a part of the Seven Days Battles while Colonel Michah Jenkins exercised brigade command. After being promoted, he took over the brigade at 2nd Bull Run when the new General Jenkins was wounded. The brigade was under his leadership at South Mountain and Antietam. The unit served at Fredericksburg, in southeastern Virginia, and the Department of Richmond before accompanying Longstreet to the West. There Walker led the regiment at Chickamauga and Knoxville. He served in the Wilderness Campaign and then took a seat in the state legislature. It is unclear whether he subsequently served with the regiment.

WALKER, Joseph Knox (1818-1863)

Devastated by the fighting at Shiloh, the 2nd Tennessee was consolidated into four companies the next month and three days later its colonel, J. Knox Walker, resigned. He had been commissioned on May 11, 1861, and commanded the 1st Brigade, 1st Division, 1st Geographical Division, Department No. 2 (October 24, 1861-March 5, 1862). He led the brigade across the Mississippi River during the battle of Belmont and played a key role in Grant's defeat. Joining the Army of the Mississippi early in 1862, he led the regiment at Shiloh where it suffered heavily. When the regiment was reorganized as a battalion he gave up his commission on May 14. He died the next year.

WALKER, Leroy Pope (1817-1884)

Following his resignation as the Confederacy's first war secretary, Alabamian Leroy P. Walker served briefly as a general officer. Admitted to the bar in 1837, he had entered politics and become a state legislator and judge. Attending the Nashville Southern convention of 1850 and both Democratic conventions in 1860, he became known for his support of the rights of his region. Tapped by Jefferson Davis, he took charge of the War Department on February 21, 1861, and held it until he resigned, in part due to his weakened health, on September 16, 1861. His tenure was not a sparkling success. His post was somewhat perfunctory since the military-minded Davis directed much of the department's operations himself. The day after his resignation the president named him a brigadier general, and he was assigned to the Department of Alabama and West Florida. Disgusted at not getting a more active command, he resigned his commission on March 31, 1862. On April 6, 1864, he was commissioned a colonel and was assigned to court-martial duty in Alabama. After the war he returned to his practice and remained active in political matters. (Harris, William Charles, *Leroy Pope Walker: Confederate Secretary of War*)

WALKER, Lucius Marshall (1829-1863)

Confederate Brigadier General Lucius M. Walker lost his life during the war, not facing the enemy but in a duel with a fellow division commander. The Tennessee native and West Pointer (1850) had resigned as a second lieutenant of dragoons in 1852 to become a Memphis merchant. His Confederate assignments included: lieutenant colonel, 40th Tennessee (October 5, 1861); commanding Post of Memphis, 1st Geographical Division, Department #2 (October-November 1861); colonel, 40th Tennessee (November 11, 1861); brigadier general, CSA (March 11, 1862); commanding brigade, McCown's Command, Department #2 (March-April 1862); commanding 3rd Brigade, 2nd (Anderson's) Division, 2nd Corps, Army of the Mississippi (June-July 2, 1862); commanding brigade, Jones'-Anderson's Division, Army of the Mississippi (July 2-August 15, 1862); commanding brigade, Anderson's Division, Left Wing, Army of the Mississippi (August 15-fall 1862); and commanding cavalry division, District of Arkansas, Trans-Mississippi Department (ca. March-September 6, 1863). He became the commander of a regiment which, although designated as a Tennessee unit, was really composed of companies from Alabama, Arkansas, Florida, and Kentucky. In order to solve the confusion it had wrought, the Confederate War Department decided to name it the 5th Confederate. But this only made matters worse since there already was a unit of this name under James A. Smith. Walker, however, was promoted to brigadier general in early 1862 and commanded a brigade at New Madrid and Island #10. Being ill, he missed the fight at Shiloh but commanded a brigade during the Corinth siege. That spring and summer, he aroused the displeasure of Braxton Bragg who declared him to be unfit for any command and was more than happy to approve his transfer west of the Mississippi. There Walker commanded a cavalry division in Arkansas and saw action at Helena and in the Little Rock vicinity. During the operations in that area fellow cavalry division commander John S. Marmaduke impugned his courage and a duel resulted, on September 6, 1863, in which Walker fell mortally wounded. He died the next day.

WALKER, Mary Edwards (1831-1919)

One of the most controversial Congressional Medal of Honor winners, Doctor Mary Walker was an unyielding champion of women's rights, antagonizing many during the postwar years. In 1855 she had graduated, the only female in her class, from a

Female Medal of Honor winner Dr. Mary E. Edwards. (NA)

New York medical school. Her gender, and a subsequent divorce, limited the success of her private practice. With the outbreak of the Civil War she closed her practice and, being refused an appointment as an army surgeon, volunteered at the Patent Office Hospital in Washington. Walker finally was appointed assistant surgeon, 52nd Ohio, by General George Thomas in September 1863. Captured while attending civilians away from her unit, she was confined in Castle Thunder in Richmond until exchanged on August 12, 1864, after four months captivity. She resumed her medical activities in Kentucky and Tennessee but, despite repeated requests, she was not again sent into the field. Mustered out in June 1865, she was awarded the Medal of Honor a few months later. With the coming of peace she took up writing and resumed her crusade for women's rights. Having been a "Bloomer girl" since the early 1850s, Walker adopted male attire in the 1870s. Lecturing for dress reform and suffrage provided her with her living but a break with others in the movement over tactics brought such income to an end. She was later fired from a job with the Pension Office for insubordination but subsequently obtained a $20 per month pension for her military service. In 1917 her Medal of Honor was revoked on the grounds that her meritorious service was not combat-related, a new policy. However, she refused to return the decoration. She died at the age of 87, with her reputation diminished due to her appearances in sideshows and constant scheming against friends and family. (McCool, Charles, *Dr. Mary Walker: The Little Lady in Pants*)

WALKER, Reuben Lindsay (1827-1890)

Free of a single wound from his four years with the artillery in Virginia, Brigadier General R. Lindsay Walker felt that he had to apologize for his invulnerability and deny being at fault. A Virginia engineer, he had drawn upon his education at the Virginia Military Institute to organize an artillery battery for the Confederacy and become its commander. His assignments included: captain, Richmond Purcell Artillery (spring 1861); major, Artillery (March 31, 1862); commanding Artillery Battalion, A.P. Hill's Division (in 1st Corps from June 29 and in 2nd Corps from July 27), Army of Northern Virginia (May-June and July 1862-May 30, 1863); lieutenant colonel, Artillery (ca. July 1862); colonel, Artillery (early 1863); commanding Artillery, 3rd Corps, Army of Northern Virginia (June 4 1863-April 1865); and brigadier general, CSA (February 18, 1865). Serving initially in the Fredericksburg area with his battery, he was detached briefly to fight at 1st Bull Run. The next spring he was named as A.P. Hill's artillery chief and held that position until after the latter's death. Walker missed only the Seven Days Battles, because of illness, and was in all the rest of the actions of the division and later of the corps. Two months before the surrender he was promoted to be a brigadier. The other two corps artillery chiefs had held that rank for some time. During the retreat to Appomattox, he was detached with the excess artillery and was attacked by Custer's cavalry. He engaged in farming and engineering after the war. (Wise, Jennings C., *The Long Arm of Lee*)

WALKER, Richard Wilde (1823-1874)

The man who administered the oath of office to Jefferson Davis, Richard W. Walker, later turned against him as a senator in the Second Confederate Congress. An Alabama-born lawyer, he was the brother of the Confederacy's first secretary of war. After having served as the speaker of the state legislature, he was serving on the state supreme court at the outset of the war. Elected to the Provisional Confederate Congress, he took part in the drafting of both the provisional and regular constitutions and served on the Committee on Foreign Affairs. An administration supporter during this term, he did not seek reelection. It was not until the Second Congress that he returned to Richmond, as a senator. There he served on the committees on: Commerce; Engrossment and Enrollment; the Judiciary; Post Offices and Post Roads; and Public Buildings. By this time he was concerned over the growth of the central government and favored limitations. He supported strong measures for manning and supplying the field armies and endorsed the freedom of slaves in return for military service. Retiring from politics at the war's close, he returned to the private practice of law.

WALKER, William (1824-1860)

The epitome of the filibustering era was Nashville native William Walker, who was executed some three months before South Carolina's secession. He had studied medicine and law but was unsuccessful in the latter as well as in journalism. In 1853 he led a filibustering expedition in Mexico. In 1855 he installed himself as leader of the government in Nicaragua but was forced out in 1857. His efforts to reintroduce slavery in Central America continued later in the year when he attempted to reenter Nicaragua but was arrested by U.S. naval forces under Commodore Hiram Paulding. In 1860 he attempted to enter Honduras but was caught by the British who handed him over to the local authorities by whom he was tried and shot on September 12, 1860. His nickname, which became something of a title, was "The Grey-Eyed Man of Destiny."

WALKER, William Henry Talbot (1816-1864)

Along with Patrick R. Cleburne, William H.T. Walker proposed the arming and freeing of the slaves in an effort to achieve the South's independence; but within the year both generals would be dead, as would the Confederacy, before the plan could be effectively implemented. The native Georgian West Pointer (1837) had resigned from the army as a first lieutenant in the 6th Infantry in 1838 after being wounded and brevetted during Seminole fighting in Florida. Reinstated two years later, he was again wounded at Molino del Rey during the Mexican War. During that conflict he was twice brevetted. With the secession crisis reaching its peak, he again resigned, on December 20, 1860, with the rank of captain, 6th Infantry. His Southern assignments included: major general, Georgia Volunteers (April 25, 1861); brigadier general, CSA (May 25, 1861); assigned to command 1st Brigade, 4th Division, Potomac District, Department of Northern Virginia (October 22-29, 1861); major general, Georgia State Troops (December

1861); brigadier general, CSA (February 9, 1863) commanding brigade, Department of the West (May-June 1863); major general, CSA (May 23, 1863); commanding division, Department of the West (June-July 1863); commanding division, Department of the West (June-July 1863); commanding division, Hill's Corps, Army of Tennessee (August 25-September 1863); commanding Reserve Corps, Army of Tennessee (September 1863); commanding division, Polk's Corps, Army of Tennessee (September-September 26, 1863); commanding division, Longstreet's Corps, Army of Tennessee (September 26-November 12, 1863); and commanding division, Hardee's Corps, Army of Tennessee (November 12-November 1863 and December 1863-July 22, 1864). As a brigadier general in the Confederate army, he served in northern Virginia until his resignation on October 29, 1861. Within two months he was a major general of state troops and served as such for over a year. Reappointed in the Confederate service early in 1863, he was assigned to the forces under Joseph E. Johnston attempting to relieve the pressure on Vicksburg. Promoted to major general during that campaign, he fought twice at Jackson and then commanded the Reserve Corps at Chickamauga. Missing the battle of Chattanooga, he then engaged in the movement with Cleburne for the recruiting of black troops. On January 1, 1864, the plan was approved by the Army of Tennessee's corps and division commanders. Forwarded to the authorities it was not acted upon until it was too late. Walker then commanded his division through the Atlanta Campaign until killed in the battle of Atlanta proper on July 22, 1864.

WALKER, William Stephen (1822-1899)

Having served most of the Civil War on the Atlantic seaboard, Confederate General William S. Walker was wounded and captured in his first major action. The Pittsburgh native joined the regular army during the Mexican War as the first lieutenant and adjutant of the Regiment of Voltiguers and Foot Riflemen. Winning a brevet he was mustered out in 1848. With the enlargement of the regular establishment in 1855, he was recommissioned as a company commander in the 1st Cavalry. Raised in Mississippi, he resigned on May 1, 1861, to join the Confederacy. His assignments included: captain, Infantry (from March 16, 1861); colonel and assistant inspector general (1862); assistant inspector general, Department of South Carolina and Georgia (1862); brigadier general, CSA (October 30, 1862); commanding 4th and 5th Military Districts of South Carolina, Department of South Carolina, Georgia and Florida (May 6-28, 1862); and commanding 3rd Military District of South Carolina, Department of South Carolina, Georgia and Florida (May 28, 1862-May 1864). Assigned initially to mustering duty, he served as a staff officer on the South Carolina coast during 1862 and then transferred to the line, commanding a number of districts and being promoted to brigadier general. In the spring of 1864 he was ordered to reinforce Beauregard in southern Virginia and was engaged in the defense of Petersburg when wounded and captured on May 20. He was exchanged that fall, having lost a foot, and was assigned to post duty for the balance of the war. He then retired in Georgia.

WALLACE, Lewis (1827-1905)

Although he would have much preferred to be remembered as a highly successful military hero, Lew Wallace has been thwarted in this ambition and is best known as an author. Born in Indiana, he had worked as a clerk and early displayed a fascination for Mexico which would affect him in later years. During the Mexican War he served as a second lieutenant in the 1st Indiana but saw only minor action. In 1849 he was admitted to the bar in his native state and seven years later entered the state senate. With the outbreak of the Civil War he offered his services, and his assignments included: adjutant general of Indiana (April 1861); colonel, 11th Indiana (April 25, 1861); colonel, 11th Indiana (reorganized August 31, 1861); brigadier general, USV (September 3, 1861); commanding 3rd Division, District of Cairo, Department of the Missouri (February 14-17, 1862); major general, USV (March 21, 1862); commanding 3rd Division, Army of the Tennessee (February 17-June 1862), commanding 8th Corps, Middle Department (March 22, 1864-February 1, 1865 and April 19-August 1, 1865); and also commanding the department (March 22, 1864-February 1, 1865 and April 19-June 27, 1865). His career got off to a promising start when he routed an inferior Confederate force at Romney, Virginia. Promoted to brigadier general, he was given charge of a newly organized division in the midst of the operations against Fort Donelson and was soon rewarded with a second star. However, that spring his reputation plummeted after the battle of Shiloh. On the first day his division was stationed north of the main army at Crump's Landing, and a series of contradictory

Lew Wallace, *Ben Hur* author and Union general. (NA)

orders from Grant forced him to countermarch his command and delayed his arrival on the main battlefield until the fighting was nearly over. He redeemed himself on the second day, but a scapegoat was needed for the near disaster the day before and this was Wallace. Sent home to await further orders, he offered his services to Indiana Governor Oliver P. Morton and, despite his high rank, took temporary command of a regiment during the emergency posed by Kirby Smith's invasion of Kentucky. With Cincinnati threatened, Wallace was placed in charge of a mostly civilian defense force. Through a show of tremendous energy he was able to save the city without a major fight. He was then head of the commission which examined Buell's handling of the invasion and other boards until placed in charge in Maryland in early 1864. There he bought valuable time for the defenders of Washington during Early's drive into the state when he made a stand at Monocacy with an inferior scratch force. At the close of the war he sat on the court-martial which tried the Lincoln conspirators and presided over that which sent Andersonville chief Henry Wirz to the gallows. He then joined a movement to aid the Juárez forces against Maximilian in Mexico. He tried to raise money and troops and even accepted the title of major general from the Juárez group. On November 30, 1865, he resigned from the U.S. service, but his Mexican venture collapsed and he realized little of the money which he had hoped to gain from it. In later years he was governor of the New Mexico Territory and a diplomat to Turkey. As a prolific writer, who often drew upon his own experiences, he is best remembered for *Ben Hur: A Tale of the Christ*, one of the most popular novels of the nineteenth century. (McKee, Irving, *"Ben Hur" Wallace, the Life of General Lew Wallace)*

WALLACE, William Harvey Lamb (1821-1862)

After gaining six hours of valuable time for Grant's army at Shiloh, William H.L. Wallace was mortally wounded as he withdrew his division from its positions in the Hornet's Nest. An Illinois lawyer—born in Ohio—he had served in the Mexican War as an adjutant with the 1st Illinois before returning to his practice. At the outbreak of the Civil War he raised a 90-day regiment and later reenlisted it for the war. His assignments included: colonel, 11th Illinois (May 1, 1861); commanding 3rd Brigade, Military District of Cairo, Department of the Missouri (October 14, 1861-February 1, 1862); commanding 2nd Brigade, 1st Division, Military District of Cairo, Department of the Missouri (February 1-17, 1862); commanding 2nd Brigade, 1st Division, Army of the Tennessee (February 17-March 29, 1862); brigadier general, USV (March 21, 1862); and commanding 2nd Division, Army of the Tennessee (April 2-6, 1862). The army having arrived too late to assist the navy in the capture of Fort Henry, Wallace moved on to Fort Donelson where he played a key role in thwarting the Confederate breakout attempt. Promoted to brigadier, he was soon given command of Charles F. Smith's old division when that officer suffered an accident which later proved fatal. On the first day at Shiloh he brought up his division to the support of the units which had faced the first surprise onslaught and held his position along a partially sunken road for six hours, allowing the situation to stabilize. While withdrawing his men, he was shot through the temple and eye. Left for dead, he was recovered the next morning, still breathing. For the next three days he was nursed by his wife who had arrived during the fight. Nonetheless, he died on April 10, 1862. (Wallace, Isabel, *Life and Letters of General W.H.L. Wallace*)

WALLACE, William Henry (1827-1905)

Appointed as a temporary brigadier, William Henry Wallace finished the war before the regular brigade commander was able to return. A South Carolina planter, he had tinkered in journalism, the law, and politics. As a state legislator in 1860 he voted for the calling of a convention to decide on the issue of secession. Instead of seeking reelection he enlisted in the Confederate service. His assignments included: private, Company A, 18th South Carolina (ca. November 18, 1861); first lieutenant and adjutant, 18th South Carolina (ca. January 2, 1862); lieutenant colonel, 18th South Carolina (May 1862); colonel, 18th South Carolina (August 30, 1862); brigadier general, CSA (September 20, 1864); commanding Elliott's Brigade, Johnson's Division, Department of North Carolina and Southern Virginia (September-October 19, 1864); and commanding Elliott's Brigade, Johnson's Division, Anderson's Corps, Army of Northern Virginia (October 19, 1864-April 9, 1865). In the spring 1862 reorganization he became a field officer and as a part of Evans' Brigade went to Virginia. Under Lee he fought at 2nd Bull Run where he assumed command of the regiment and in Maryland at South Mountain and Antietam before returning to his native state with the brigade. After over a year in the Charleston vicinity, Wallace again went to Virginia and took a position in the Petersburg lines. On July 30, 1864, four of his companies were blown up in the mine explosion and the brigade commander was wounded preparing a counterstroke. Shortly thereafter Wallace took over and led the brigade through to Appomattox. Following the same civilian pursuits after the war, he also became a judge. (Freeman, Douglas S., *Lee's Lieutenants*)

WALLACE, William W. (?-?)

One of the more unique units organized for the Civil War was the "Bible Company," from Huntington County, Pennsylvania. Its organizer and commander was a Scotch Presbyterian coal mine operator named William Wallace. Following the Union defeats in the spring and early summer of 1862, President Lincoln called for an additional 300,000 men for nine months' service. Wallace, aided by a divinity student and a law student, began organizing a company in the name of God and religion, with each man taking a musket and his Bible to face the foe. In August 1862 the Huntington Bible Company became Company C, 125th Pennsylvania, and was given the honor of serving as the color unit. Wallace suggested that morning roll calls be followed by a religious meeting. The company adopted the slogan "In God We Trust," and there is some speculation that it provided the inspiration for placing the motto on U.S. coins (starting two years later). Captain Wallace converted the motto into a battle cry at the battle of Antietam when directed to lead his company into some woods. When the color bearer was hit, Wallace took the regimental standard and held it during a Rebel counterattack. A Confederate veteran later told him that 100 men had fired on him. After serving in the battle of Chancellorsville, Wallace and his company were mustered out on May 18, 1863, at the expiration of their term. The next month Wallace was again briefly in the service opposing Lee's invasion of Pennsylvania as part of the state's Emergency Militia.

WALTHALL, Edward Cary (1831-1898)

Entering the Confederate service as a lieutenant in the Yalobusha Rifles, Virginia-born and Mississippi-raised lawyer and district attorney Edward C. Walthall rose to the rank of major general. His assignments included: first lieutenant, Company H., 15th Mississippi (1861); lieutenant colonel, 15th Mississippi (1861); colonel, 29th Mississippi (April 11, 1862); brigadier general, CSA (December 13, 1862); commanding brigade, Withers'-Hindman's Division, Polk's-Cheatham's-Hardee's Corps, Army of Tennessee (June 2-August 21 and September 22-November 1863); commanding brigade, Liddell's Division, Reserve Corps, Army of Tennessee (August 21-September 22, 1863); commanding brigade, Cheatham's Division, Hardee's Corps, Army of Tennessee (November-November 25, 1863 and early 1864-February 20, 1864); commanding brigade, Hindman's Division, Hindman's-Hood's Corps, Army of Tennessee (February 20-ca. July 6, 1864); major general, CSA (July 6, 1864); and commanding in the Army of Tennessee: Cantey's (old) Division, Polk's (Army of Mississippi)-Stewart's Corps (ca. July 6, 1864-March 1865); the corps (March-April 9, 1865); and McLaws' Division, Stewart's Corps (April 9-26, 1865). Almost immediately named a field officer, he fought at Mill Springs and was then made colonel of another regiment. This he led in the defense of Corinth and in the Kentucky Campaign. He led a brigade in the Tullahoma Campaign and at Chickamauga. At Chattanooga he defended Lookout Mountain and was wounded the next day on Missionary Ridge. Recovering, he led his brigade in the Atlanta Campaign until tapped to command a division, with the appropriate advancement to major general. He led his division at Franklin and was in charge of covering the retreat after the defeat at Nashville. During the Carolinas Campaign he commanded the corps for a time while Alexander P. Stewart led the infantry and artillery of the Army of Tennessee. In the final reorganization and consolidation of the forces in North Carolina, Walthall was placed in charge of a division of troops formerly assigned to guarding the Atlantic seaboard. Surrendered with Joseph E. Johnston, he returned to his practice, entered politics, and eventually sat in the U.S. Senate.

WALTON, James Burdge (1813-1885)

Although he had served for over two decades in the famed Washington Artillery of New Orleans, James B. Walton was gradually eased out of his position as commander of the First Corps' artillery. A prominent New Orleans merchant, the New Jersey-born Walton had joined the Washington Artillery as adjutant upon its organization in 1839. In the Mexican War he commanded the 1st Louisiana and had risen to command of the battery by the outbreak of the Civil War, when the unit offered its services to the Confederacy. It sent four batteries to Virginia and one was organized later, serving in the West. Walton's assignments included: major, Washington Artillery Battalion (May 26, 1861); colonel, Washington Artillery Battalion (March 26, 1862); and nominal chief of Artillery, 1st Corps, Army of Northern Virginia (June 4-early September 1863). After serving at 1st Bull Run, Walton and his command were assigned to Longstreet's forces and served in the Seven Days, 2nd Bull Run, and Antietam. At both Fredericksburg and Chancellorsville, Walton directed his guns on Marye's Heights, earning much distinction. In the battle of Gettysburg, he was humiliated by, in effect, being superseded by one of his subordinates, E. Porter Alexander. When the First Corps was sent to Georgia only part of the artillery went along, and Walton held various commands in southern Virginia. When the battalion was ordered back to the First Corps, Walton resigned on July 18, 1864, rather than serve under Alexander who was now officially the corps' artillery chief. There had been an effort to ease Walton out the previous month by assigning him to inspection duties. He returned to his business interests. (Owen, William M., *In Camp and Battle With the Washington Artillery of New Orleans*)

WANGELIN, Hugo (?-?)

Half a year after being mustered out of the volunteer service, Hugo Wangelin finally received his brevet as brigadier general for his war service in the western theater. The German native had received some military training in Europe before coming to the United States, then returning to serve a year in the Prussian army before settling in Missouri. His assignments included: major, 12th Missouri (December 19, 1861); colonel, 12th Missouri (July 20, 1862); commanding 2nd Brigade, 1st Division, 15th Corps, Army of the Tennessee (July 30-August 24, 1863); and commanding 3rd Brigade, 1st Division, 15th Corps, Army of the Tennessee (March 8-September 25, 1864). After service in Missouri and Arkansas he commanded the regiment at Pea Ridge, Chickasaw Bayou, and Arkansas Post. In the latter the unit was not engaged. He went on to fight at Vicksburg and during the recapture of Jackson, Mississippi. He was wounded at Chattanooga but recovered only to suffer the same fate at the battle of Atlanta. He was then mustered out with part of his regiment on October 17, 1864, and spent the balance of the war as a postmaster in Illinois.

WARD, Artemas

See: *Browne, Charles Farrar*

WARD, George Taliaferro (1810-1862)

A Transylvania University graduate, wealthy planter and banker, George Ward was one of those early, promising Confederate officers who didn't live long enough to earn a general's wreath. Ward had long been involved in politics when the secession crisis came to his native Florida. In the state convention, Ward tried to delay the rush to independence. However, with the action taken, he was appointed to the Provisional Confederate Congress on May 2, 1861, where he served on the Claims, Military Affairs, and Public Lands committees. On July 13 he was appointed colonel of the 2nd Florida, the first regiment from the state sent to Virginia. That fall the regiment joined Magruder's army on the Peninsula. He resigned from Congress on February 5, 1862. In the spring of 1862, Ward was commanding a demi-brigade composed of his own regiment and the 2nd Mississippi Battalion, in D.H. Hill's Division. During the siege at Yorktown, Ward's command made a charge upon some Union sharpshooters near Fort Magruder, a charge which General Magruder described as "quick and reckless." At the battle of Williamsburg, a short time later, Colonel Ward was killed, a fact much lamented as a tragedy for the fledgling nation. (Evans, Clement A., ed., *Confederate Military History*)

WARD, James Harmon (1806-1861)

In an effort to keep the lower Potomac River open and the capital's supply lines secure, Commander James Ward became the first Union naval officer to sacrifice his life. Having served in the navy since 1823, the Connecticut-born Ward had been the captain of the USS *North Carolina* at the start of the Civil War. The Navy Department, in order to keep Washington's communications open, created the Potomac Flotilla in May 1862 and appointed Ward as its first head. On May 31 and June 1, his new command pounded the Confederate shore battery at Aquia Creek. Fearing that a more effective rebel battery would be established at Mathias Point, he dispatched a landing party to secure the threatening position. With their day's work at an end, the shore party was about to reembark for the night when they were attacked by Colonel John M. Brockenbrough's 40th Virginia. While sighting a gun on board his flagship, the *Thomas Freeborn*, a converted New York ferry boat, Ward was struck by a bullet. He died an hour later, the only fatality of the expedition.

WARD, John Henry Hobart (1823-1903)

Drinking on the job cost Union Brigadier General John H.H. Ward his commission. The New York City native had been an enlisted man in the regular army's 7th Infantry during the Mexican War, and was wounded at Monterrey. Following his discharge in 1847 he was involved in his state's military affairs and later entered the Union army for the Civil War. His assignments included: colonel, 38th New York (June 8, 1861); commanding 2nd Brigade, 3rd Division, Army of Northeastern

Naval action at Aquia Creek in which Commander James H. Ward was killed. (*Leslie's*)

Virginia (July 21-August 17, 1861); commanding 2nd Brigade, 3rd Division, 2nd Corps, Army of the Potomac (May 30-June 9, 1862); commanding 2nd Brigade, 1st Division, 3rd Corps, Army of the Potomac (September 1-13, 1862, October 30, 1862-January 26, 1863, February 15-March, April-May 29, June 3-July 2, July 7-August, and September-December 29, 1863, January 17-28 and February 17-March 24, 1864); brigadier general, USV (October 4, 1862); commanding the division (May 29-June 3, July 2-7, 1863, and January 28-February 17, 1864); and commanding 1st Brigade, 3rd Division, 2nd Corps, Army commanding 1st Brigade, 2nd Division, 6th Corps, Army of the Shenandoah (September 21-December 6, 1864); captain, 8th Infantry (October 8, 1864); of the Potomac (April 20-May 12, 1864). He fought at 1st Bull Run where he succeeded to command of the brigade. On the Peninsula, he was at Yorktown and Williamsburg and again took charge of a brigade at Seven Pines. He led the regiment at the Seven Days and then took over the brigade at Chantilly. He directed a brigade at Fredericksburg and Chancellorsville and took over the division when Sickles' line was broken at Gettysburg on the second day. A brigadier since the fall of 1862, he retained a brigade level command after the consolidations of March 1864. He fought at the Wilderness but was drunk and apparently ran away from the action. In the midst of the fighting at Spotsylvania he was relieved of command on May 12, 1864, and soon placed under arrest. Without the benefit of a court-martial, he was mustered out of the service on July 18, 1864. Efforts by friends to gain a hearing failed, and he was employed for many years as a court clerk. In 1903 he was struck and killed by a train.

Drunken General John H.H. Ward. (*Leslie's*)

WARD, William Thomas (1808-1878)

Although he spent most of the early part of the Civil War in garrison commands, Virginia-born Kentuckian William T. Ward won the brevet of major general in more active theaters by war's end. The lawyer had served in the Mexican War as a major of volunteers and sat in the state legislature and the U.S. Congress. His Civil War assignments included: brigadier general, USV (September 18, 1861); commanding 16th Brigade, Army of the Ohio (November 1861-March 1862); commanding brigade, 12th Division, Army of the Ohio (September-November 5, 1862); and commanding in the Army or Department of the Cumberland: brigade, Post of Gallatin (November 24, 1862-May 14, 1863); 2nd Brigade, 3rd Division, Reserve Corps (June 8-August 5, 1863); brigade, Post of Nashville, District of Nashville (October 1863-January 1864); 1st Division, 11th Corps (January 12-April 16, 1864); 1st Brigade, 3rd Division, 20th Corps (April 14-May 15 and May 15-June 29, 1864); and the division (June 29-September 23, 1864 and October 23, 1864-June 1, 1865). For apparently political reasons the loyal border-stater was commissioned brigadier general and at first served mostly in Kentucky and Tennessee. He dealt ineffectively with the raid of John Hunt Morgan in 1862 and continued on post duty until early 1864. After briefly commanding a division he led a brigade in the Atlanta Campaign. Struck twice in the battle of Resaca, he remained with his men and only briefly relinquished actual command. Succeeding to command of Daniel Butterfield's division late the next month, Ward led it through the balance of the operations against Atlanta. He subsequently served through the March to the Sea and the Carolinas Campaign. Brevetted major general on February 24, 1865, he was mustered out on August 24, 1865, and resumed his legal practice.

WARNER, James Meech (1836-1897)

Although he had been with an active field army only during the last year of the Civil War, James M. Warner emerged as a brigadier general of volunteers and, by brevet, of the regular army. The native Vermonter had graduated from his 1860 West Point class with only one cadet standing below him; he was posted to the infantry. From that time until the middle of 1862 he was stationed at Fort Wise, Colorado. His wartime assignments included: brevet second lieutenant, 10th Infantry (July 1, 1860); second lieutenant, 8th Infantry (February 28, 1861); first lieutenant, 8th Infantry (May 30, 1861); colonel, 11th Vermont (September 1, 1862); colonel, 1st Vermont Heavy Artillery (designation change December 10, 1862); commanding 1st Brigade, Defenses North of the Potomac, 22nd Corps, Department of Washington (March 26-May 12, 1864); commanding 2nd Brigade, 2nd Division, 6th Corps, Army of the Shenandoah (September 18-21, 1864); commanding 1st Brigade, 2nd Division, 6th Corps, Army of the Shenandoah (September 21-December 6, 1864); captain, 8th Infantry (October 8, 1864); commanding 1st Brigade, 2nd Division, 6th Corps, Army of the Potomac (December 6, 1864-April 22, 1865 and May 2-June 28, 1865); and brigadier general, USV (May 8, 1865). Ordered east, he was given command of a volunteer regiment which was soon converted to heavy artillery and assigned to the capital's fortifications. With the artillerists ordered to join Grant as infantry, Warner was wounded almost immediately upon his arrival at Spotsylvania. Recovered, he took part in the repulse of Early at Washington and then commanded a brigade at 3rd Winchester, Fisher's Hill, and Cedar Creek in the Shenandoah. For these three actions and Spotsylvania, he was brevetted brigadier general of volunteers to date from August 1, 1864. He rejoined the Army of the Potomac, then besieging Petersburg, and took part in the final assaults on the enemy works there. After Appomattox, from which date he was brevetted brigadier general in the regular army, he was named a full brigadier in the volunteer service. He was mustered out of the volunteers on January 15, 1866, and resigned from the regular army on February 13, 1866. He entered business, received a patronage position, and was an unsuccessful mayoral candidate in Albany, New York.

WARREN, Edward (1828-1893)

A North Carolina native, Edward Warren had been active in the medical profession in Maryland when he joined the Confederacy and wrote one of the leading medical manuals for that service. He received his training both in Pennsylvania and France and upon the outbreak of the Civil War was a professor at the University of Maryland and the editor of the *Baltimore Journal of Medicine*. Returning to North Carolina, he became its surgeon general and also an inspector in the Confederate medical service. A member of the medical examining board, he favored tough standards and an increase in the department's manpower. In 1863 his *An Epitome of Practical Surgery for Field and Hospital* was published. After the war he was active in the medical field in the United States, Europe, and the Middle East. He wrote *A Doctor's Experiences in Three Continents* and died in Paris. (Cunningham, Horace Herndon, *Doctors in Gray*)

WARREN, Edward Tiffin Harrison (1829-1864)

When Edward T.H. Warren was killed at the battle of the Wilderness, it was found unnecessary to secure a replacement for his as colonel of his regiment—since most of the command was captured a few days later at Spotsylvania. A native Virginia, he had been practicing law in Harrisonburg at the outbreak of the Civil War. His assignments included: lieutenant colonel, 10th Virginia (July 1, 1861); colonel, 10th Virginia (August 16, 1862); and commanding 3rd Brigade, Jackson's (old) Division, Jackson's Corps, Army of Northern Virginia (June 27-28, ca. September 5-17, and fall 1862-May 2, 1863). After serving in northern Virginia, including action at 1st Bull Run, Warren and his regiment were transferred to the Shenandoah Valley. At the battle of McDowell he succeeded to command of the regiment upon the death of the colonel. He fought through the rest of the Valley Campaign and the Seven Days, where he briefly commanded the brigade. He was again in charge of the brigade at Harpers Ferry, Antietam, Fredericksburg, and Chancellorsville. Wounded in the latter, he returned in time for Gettysburg but commanded only the 10th. Serving through the Bristoe and Mine Run campaigns, he was killed the following May in the battle of the Wilderness.

WARREN, Fitz-Henry (1816-1878)

It seems to have been an afterthought to award Brigadier General Fitz-Henry Warren the brevet of major general on the very day of his mustering out rather than in the general appointments of March 1865. Born in Massachusetts, he had settled in Iowa where he engaged in journalism and politics and was a postal official. His military assignments included: colonel, 1st Iowa Cavalry (June 13, 1861); brigadier general, USV (July 16, 1862); commanding 2nd Brigade, 2nd Division, Army of Southeast Missouri, Department of the Missouri (February-March 1863); and commanding in the Department of the Gulf: 1st Brigade, 1st Division, 13th Corps (December 12, 1863-January 28, 1864, January 30-February 8, and March 11-April 3, 1864); the division (February 8-March 11 and April 3-May 23, 1864); District of Baton Rouge (May 31-June 13, 1864); and U.S. Forces Texas (June 9-August 1, 1864). His early service came in the irregular campaigning in Missouri. During the Gettysburg Campaign he was ordered to report to General Darius N. Couch commanding the Department of the Susquehanna. Later that year he was assigned to the Department of the Gulf and held various commands there until he was forced by ill-health to relinquish command the following summer. Following limited duty in the Department of the East he was brevetted major general for the war and mustered out on August 24, 1865. After a term in the state legislature he was an American diplomat in Guatemala and then engaged in journalism in New York City.

WARREN, Gouverneur Kemble (1830-1882)

The "Savior of Little Round Top," Gouverneur K. Warren had barely been removed from corps command when the Civil War ended. He spent the rest of his life trying to correct the injustice. After graduating from West Point, second in his class of 1850, the native New Yorker had been posted to the topographical engineers with which he served until the early part of the war, working on river, canal, and railroad projects. He also was a professor of mathematics back at the academy. Seeking advancement he joined the volunteers and his wartime assignments included: first lieutenant, Topographical Engineers (since July 1, 1856); lieutenant colonel, 5th New York (May 14, 1861); captain, Topographical Engineers (September 9, 1861); colonel, 5th New York (September 11, 1861); commanding 3rd Brigade, 2nd Division, 5th Corps, Army of the Potomac (May 18-late December 1862 and January-February 5, 1863); brigadier general, USV (September 26, 1862); commanding 2nd Division, 5th Corps, Army of the Potomac (late December 1862-January 1863); chief topographical engineer, Army of the Potomac (February 2-March 3, 1863); captain, Engineers (March 3, 1863); chief engineer, Army of the Potomac (March 3-August 12, 1863); major general, USV (May 3, 1863); commanding 2nd Corps, Army of the Potomac (August 16-26 and September 2-

December 16, 1863, December 29, 1863-January 9, 1864, and January 15-March 24, 1864); commanding 5th Corps, Army of the Potomac (March 24, 1864-January 2, 1865 and January 27-April 1, 1865); major, Engineers (June 25, 1864); and commanding District of Vicksburg, Department of Mississippi and the department (May 14-June 24, 1865). As second in command of his regiment he fought in the first land engagement of the war, Big Bethel. promoted to colonel he led the regiment to the Peninsula where, during the Seven Days, he was wounded at Gaines' Mill. Returning to duty in time for 2nd Bull Run, he directed his brigade at Antietam and at Fredericksburg he joined the staff of General Hooker as chief topographical engineer. In March 1863 he became chief engineer upon the merger of the engineers and the topographical engineers. At Chancellorsville he called for aggressive action and became disenchanted with the high command. Continuing on the staff of General Meade, he had his greatest day at Gettysburg. He had been dispatched to the field on the first day and had assisted in placing the army into position along Cemetery Ridge. The next afternoon he ascended Little Round Top and to his amazement found only a signal station, packing to leave. The key to the Union army's position was undefended. Racing down the hill, he gathered troops and a battery which reached the crest in the nick of time to save the position and the army's left flank. A statue to Warren now stands on the spot. Here he suffered his second wound of the war. Temporarily replacing the wounded Hancock in command of the 2nd Corps, he scored a major success at Bristoe Station but earned the displeasure of Meade for unilaterally aborting an attack at Mine Run. Although Meade had to admit that Warren was justified, a rift had begun to develop. While he commanded the 5th Corps in the Overland Campaign, the gulf widened, and new ones developed with Commander in Chief Grant and cavalrymen Philip H. Sheridan and James H. Wilson. Nonetheless, he fought at the Wilderness, Spotsylvania, North Anna, and Cold Harbor. During the Petersburg siege he was accused of failing to hold the enemy opposite his positions in place, contributing to the repulse at the Crater. He fought creditably, however, during the siege along the Weldon Railroad. When the final campaign in Virginia got under way in late March 1865, Warren's corps was placed under Sheridan's direction, and the latter was given discretionary power to remove the corps commander. Sheridan's anger was aroused when Warren arrived with his men several hours later than expected. Then in the attack on Five Forks the cavalryman was further enraged by the poorly organized attack of Warren's 5th Corps. Actually, this was due to faulty information provided by Sheridan. Warren went forward to coordinate the attack for the final success. But when Sheridan couldn't find him at a convenient place the hot-tempered cavalryman removed Warren from command. Following brief duty in Mississippi Warren resigned his volunteer commission on May 27, 1865, but remained in the regular army. He repeatedly asked for a court of inquiry which was not granted until 1879. Sitting for three years, the court ruled that he might have been slow arriving, but that his efforts had greatly contributed to the crushing victory. There were hints of criticism of the manner of the removal. But Warren had died a few months earlier, leaving instructions that he not be buried in his uniform—that of a lieutenant colonel of engineers—and that there be no patriotic emblems present at the funeral. Thus, bitterly, died the victim of one of the greatest injustices of the Civil War. (Taylor, Emerson Clifford, *Gouverneur Kemble Warren: The Life and Letters of an American Soldier, 1830-1882*)

Gouverneur K. Warren, victim of Sheridan's wrath. (*Leslie's*)

WASHBURN, Cadwallader Colden (1818-1882)

While he was a capable officer, Cadwallader C. Washburn may also have benefited from political connections during his military career. The Maine native had engaged in business and the practice of law in Wisconsin before becoming a Republican congressman in 1854. After trying to avoid a conflict—he attended the Washington Peace Convention in early 1861—he entered the Union army at the beginning of the second year of the war. His assignments included: colonel, 2nd Wisconsin Cavalry (February 6, 1862); brigadier general, USV (July 19, 1862); commanding 3rd (Cavalry) Division, District of Eastern Arkansas (December 1862); commanding 2nd Cavalry Division, 13th Corps, Army of the Tennessee (February 8-April 3, 1863); major general, USV (March 13, 1863, to rank from November 29, 1862); commanding District of Eastern Arkansas, Army of the Tennessee (April 3-June 1863); also commanding 1st Cavalry Division, 16th Corps, Army of the Tennessee (March 31-June 9, 1863); also commanding Cavalry Division, District of Eastern Arkansas, Army of the Tennessee (May-June 1863); commanding Detachment 16th Corps, Army of the Tennessee (June-July 1863); commanding 13th Corps, Army of the Tennessee (July 28-August 7, 1863); commanding 13th Corps, Department of the Gulf (August 7-September 15 and October 19-25, 1863); commanding 1st Division, 13th Corps, Department of the Gulf (September 15-October 19 and

October 26-November 25, 1863); and commanding District of West Tennessee, Army of the Tennessee (April 17, 1864-February 3, 1865 and March 4-May 29, 1865). After service in Missouri he was made a brigadier general and then a major general of volunteers. He commanded the expedition against Vicksburg through Yazoo Pass. This was halted at Fort Pemberton. During the final drive against Vicksburg he brought a detachment of the 16th Corps to reinforce the besiegers. After the fall of the city he was given charge of the 13th Corps which was soon transferred to the Department of the Gulf. He was then tapped to command the oft troublesome District of West Tennessee, where he was responsible for protecting rail lines and protecting the area generally from the frequent raids of Nathan Bedford Forrest. He often dispatched expeditions to deal with the pesky cavalryman, usually with poor results. With the war over he resigned, effective May 25, 1865. His military career may have been furthered by the fact that his brother, Congressman Elihu B. Washburne, was close to both Lincoln and Grant. Resuming his political career, he served two terms as a congressman and one as governor. He also amassed a large fortune in business, especially as one of the founders of what was to become the General Mills corporation. (Hunt, Gaillard, *Israel, Elihu and Cadwallader Washburn*)

WASHBURN, Francis (?-1865)

In the last days of the Civil War in Virginia, Union officer Francis Washburn won the brevet of brigadier general of volunteers but lost his life in the effort. The Massachusetts native had forsaken his studies in Europe to join the army, and his assignments included: second lieutenant, 1st Massachusetts Cavalry (December 26, 1861); first lieutenant, 1st Massachusetts Cavalry (March 7, 1862); captain, 2nd Massachusetts Cavalry (January 26, 1863); lieutenant colonel, 4th Massachusetts Cavalry (February 4, 1864); and colonel, 4th Massachusetts Cavalry (February 25, 1865). With his first unit he served as a subaltern in South Carolina and during the Maryland Campaign, before gaining a captaincy in another regiment. With this he served in the vicinity of Washington and a year later became a field officer in yet another unit. With this unit he served at Olustee, Bermuda Hundred, and in front of Richmond and Petersburg. Taking part in the pursuit of Lee's army, he was mortally wounded on April 6, 1865, while attempting to burn the High Bridge, one of the escape routes. Brevetted from that date, he died on the 22nd.

WASHBURN, Israel (1813-1883)

The brother of Union General Cadwallader C. Washburn and Congressman Elihu Washburne, Israel Washburn served as Maine's governor during the first years of the Civil War. A Whig lawyer and state representative, he became a Republican while serving in Congress from 1851 to 1861. Elected governor on September 10, 1860, the Maine native resigned his congressional seat to take up his duties on January 1, 1861. He was sworn in the next day and during his two terms his administration provided for the raising of volunteers, the organization of a militia and coast guard, and the construction of coastal defenses. Refusing a third term, he left office on January 7, 1863 and later that year became the customs collector at Portland. He held that post until 1877. He was also involved in education and railroading. (Hunt, Gaillard, *Israel, Elihu and Cadwallader Washburn*)

WASHBURNE, Elihu Benjamin (1816-1887)

Once Ulysses S. Grant had reached the pinnacle of success there were many who claimed to have furthered his career, but most of the credit belongs to his neighbor and Galena, Illinois, congressman, Elihu B. Washburne. The brother of Israel and Cadwallader Washburn—Elihu added the "e" to the family name—had been born in Maine and received his legal education at Harvard. Moving to Galena, he ran as a Whig for Congress in 1848 but lost. Two years later he won his first of nine successive congressional races. During the Civil War he took Grant to the office of the governor—Washburne's political foe—and the result was that Grant gained the colonelcy of the 21st Illinois. Throughout Grant's career Washburne furthered his cause. He used his influence with fellow Republican Abraham Lincoln to gain a brigadier's star for his neighbor. Washburne was also influential in smoothing over the difficulties between Grant and Halleck. It was Washburne who introduced the legislation that re-created the post of lieutenant general, which was immediately given to Grant. When Grant became president he rewarded his benefactor with the post of secretary of state. Resigning from Congress on March 6, 1869, to join the cabinet, he was apparently unqualified for the post and resigned within a few days to become the U.S. minister in Paris. During the Franco-Prussian War and the subsequent chaos of the Commune he remained in Paris, at first protecting the German legations with the American flag during the war and later, during the Commune, protecting all foreigners in the city. Returning to the United States in 1877, he ran for the Republican presidential nomination in 1880 and caused a rift with his old friend, who felt that the votes Washburne received had prevented Grant's nomination to a third, nonconsecutive term. He was later the president of the Chicago Historical Society. (Hunt, Gaillard, *Israel, Elihu and Cadwallader Washburn*)

WASHINGTON, Edward Crawford (?-1863)

Commissioned directly into the regular army—as captain, 13th Infantry (May 14, 1861)—Edward C. Washington gave his life in the charge that entitled his battalion to inscribe on its colors the phrase, "First at Vicksburg." After commanding the prisoner of war camp at Alton, Illinois, in 1862, the Virginia-born and Pennsylvania-raised soldier took command of his company, in the regiment's 1st Battalion, for the operations against Vicksburg. He led his men in Steele's Bayou Campaign early in 1863 and as commander of the battalion took part in Grant's successful swing to the south and east of the river fortress. When the Union troops reached the lines around the city itself, it was determined to attempt to take the place by storm. In the May 19, 1863, assault the regular battalion was the first to plant its colors upon the enemy's works but was soon forced to retire. Washington had been mortally wounded, and he died the next day. From the date of his death he was brevetted major.

WASHINGTON, John A. (?-1861)

The custodian of Mount Vernon, John A. Washington was the first member of Robert E. Lee's military family to die in the conflict. On May 13, 1861, Washington was appointed aide-de-camp to General Lee, with the rank of lieutenant colonel in the Virginia volunteers. At this time Lee was serving as the commander of the Virginia forces and arranging for their transfer into Confederate service. Serving on the undermanned staff, Washington soon became an acting assistant adjutant general and was subsequently promoted to colonel. On July 28 Lee, Washington, and Lieutenant Colonel W.H. Taylor, another staff officer, left Richmond for western Virginia in an effort to recover the sagging fortunes of the Confederacy in that area. With the failure of Lee's overcomplicated plan of attack at Cheat Mountain the previous day, Washington begged for permission to accompany Lee's son, W.H.F. Lee, and his cavalry in a reconnaissance expedition to see if the plan could be revived. The patrol ran into Union pickets and Washington was left dead on the field. (Freeman, Douglas S., *R.E. Lee*)

WASHINGTON, Thornton Augustin (?-1894)

West Pointer (1849) Thornton A. Washington resigned his commission as first lieutenant, 1st Infantry, on April 8, 1861. His experience had included service as regimental adjutant and quartermaster, so he requested appointment in one of those departments in the Confederate service. On November 8, 1861, already a captain in the Adjutant General's Department, he was assigned as assistant adjutant general to Robert E. Lee on the coast of South Carolina. After the general was transferred to Richmond as an advisor to the president, Lee decided that he needed the services of his fellow Virginian, by now a major, and had him assigned again to his staff, in March 1862. Washington left this assignment in the latter part of April and the next year was serving as a quartermaster in charge of all departmental purchasing in Texas, with headquarters at San Antonio.

WATERHOUSE, Richard (1832-1876)

Serving in the Trans-Mississippi West, Richard Waterhouse was one of several Confederate officers promoted to general by E. Kirby Smith in an extralegal fashion—but his promotion was finally sanctioned by Jefferson Davis, nearly a year later. As a youth he had fought in the Mexican War and then moved with his family from his native Tennessee to Texas. Engaged in trade before the war, he threw in his lot with the Confederacy. His assignments included: colonel, 19th Texas (May 13, 1862); brigadier general, CSA (per Edmund Kirby Smith, May 13, 1864, to rank from April 30); commanding 2nd (Texas) Brigade, 1st (Texas) Division, 1st Corps (or District of West Louisiana), Trans-Mississippi Department (September 1864-May 26, 1865); and brigadier general, CSA (per Jefferson Davis, March 17, 1865). Serving entirely west of the Mississippi River, he fought in Arkansas and at Milliken's Bend in Louisiana during the Vicksburg Campaign. For his abilities in leading his regiment at Mansfield and Pleasant Hill during the Red River Campaign, he was named a brigadier general, but by his department commander because the area was cut off from the authorities in Richmond. After Waterhouse had commanded a brigade for several months, Davis made the appointment legal. Until his death in an accident, he was a land speculator.

WATIE, Stand (1806-1871)

The highest-ranking Indian in the Confederate army was a three-quarter Cherokee named Degataga, better known as Brigadier General Stand Watie. He was in large part responsible for swinging the Cherokee from a neutralist position into an alliance with the Confederacy. Connecticut-educated, he was part of the pro-treaty faction which had accepted the tribe's eviction to Indian Territory. He became a leading planter and journalist among his people and fought at Wilson's Creek in command of a company. His later assignments included: colonel, 1st Cherokee Mounted Volunteers or 2nd Mounted Rifles (July 12, 1861); brigadier general, CSA (May 6, 1864); and commanding 1st Brigade, Cooper's Indian Division, Cavalry Corps, Trans-Mississippi Department (fall 1864-May 1865). In the pursuit of the fleeing band of Upper Creeks under Opothleyohola, which included some Cherokees and Seminoles as well, Watie's staunch Confederate Indians did not suffer from

Stand Watie, highest ranking Confederate Indian. (NA)

the same qualms as Colonel John Drew's Cherokee regiment over killing fellow Cherokees. After fighting at Pea Ridge he fought mostly in the Indian Territory but did take part in Price's invasion of Missouri in 1864. He did not surrender his command until June 23, 1865. After that he was a planter and businessman in what is now Oklahoma. (Franks, Kenny A., *Stand Watie and the Agony of the Cherokee Nation*)

WATKINS, Louis Douglass (1833-1868)

Long active in the militia of the District of Columbia, Florida-born Louis D. Watkins transferred to the district's volunteers in 1861 when it appeared that his unit was pro-Southern. His assignments included: private, Company A, 3rd District of Columbia Battalion (April 15, 1861); first lieutenant, 14th Infantry (May 14, 1861); first lieutenant, 2nd Cavalry (June 22, 1861); first lieutenant, 5th Cavalry (designation change August 3, 1861); captain, 5th Cavalry (July 17, 1862); chief of Cavalry, Army of Kentucky, Department of the Ohio (December 1862-January 1863); colonel, 6th Kentucky Cavalry (February 1, 1863); commanding 3rd Brigade, 1st Division, Cavalry Corps, Army of the Cumberland (July 8, 1863-July 5, 1864 and August 10-October 29, 1864); commanding 3rd Brigade, 1st Division, Cavalry Corps, Military Division of the Mississippi (October 29, 1864-January 23, 1865); and brigadier general, USV (September 25, 1865). After brief service as an enlisted man in the volunteers he was commissioned directly into one of the new regular army infantry regiments and then secured a transfer to the cavalry. Fighting with his regiment on the Peninsula, he was severely wounded at Gaines' Mill during the Seven Days. Recovering, he became an aide to General Andrew J. Smith and was then named to direct the cavalry of the Army of the Ohio. He won a brevet for Samuel P. Carter's raid into East Tennessee during the winter of 1862-63. Commissioned colonel of a mounted Kentucky regiment, he won further brevets for Thompson's Station, Tennessee, Lafayette, Georgia, and the defense of Resaca. These brought him to the grade of brevet brigadier general in both the regulars and the volunteers. He took part in the Atlanta and Franklin-Nashville campaigns as a brigade commander. With his brigade divided among the other brigades of the division early in 1865, he finished the war in Louisville. Promoted to brigadier general of volunteers long after the close of hostilities, he was mustered out of that service on September 1, 1866. By that time, however, he had been advanced to lieutenant colonel, 20th Infantry. He served in the postwar years in Virginia and Louisiana until his death in New Orleans while on active duty.

WATSON, John William Clark (1808-1890)

A former Whig and an opponent of secession, John W.C. Watson reluctantly went along with his state and was elected to the Confederate Senate in the Second Regular Congress. A Virginia-born lawyer, he had moved to Mississippi in 1845. He failed in a bid to sit in the state convention which eventually took the state out of the Union. Elected in 1863, he sat on the committees on: Claims; Engrossment and Enrollment; the Judiciary; and Printing. He felt that the conscription laws were adequate if properly enforced and wanted a reorganization of the army's high command as well as Davis' cabinet. But for the prosecution of the war he favored the suspension of the writ of habeas corpus and the use of black troops. He also urged the opening of peace negotiations. Willing to cooperate with the victorious Union forces at the war's close, he refused to aid in the defense of Jefferson Davis. Nonetheless he was active in the redemption of the state government from black and Republican control. After the war he served six years as a judge and was active in the prohibitionist movement.

WATTERSON, Henry (1840-1921)

It was his violent antipathy for Confederate General Braxton Bragg which cost Henry Watterson his editorship of the *Chattanooga Daily Rebel*. A native of Washington, D.C., he had worked on the family plantation in Tennessee until joining the reportorial staff of the *New York Times* in 1858. Although initially opposed to secession, he was serving on the staff of Rebel cavalryman Nathan Bedford Forrest when called upon to rejoin the journalistic profession late in 1862. He immediately gained a reputation for his harsh criticism of Bragg's failures—and the enmity of the general. The failures at Murfreesboro added fuel to the fire. During the dismal Tullahoma Campaign Bragg banned the *Rebel* from his army's lines but Watterson had this ban lifted by allowing the army's intelligence network to plant false stories in his paper to fool the enemy. At a party shortly thereafter he was strongly critical of Bragg in a discussion with a Rebel officer who turned out to be the general himself. Watterson kept the paper running until the fall of Chattanooga. Chickamauga launched the editor on another tirade against Bragg who again ordered a ban upon the paper's circulation. The paper's publisher, Franc M. Paul, was forced to accept Watterson's resignation in order to rebuild his circulation. Watterson then joined the *Atlanta Southern Confederacy* and later the *Montgomery Mail*. After a stint as a prisoner, he worked for a paper in Ohio before becoming the editor of the *Louisville Courier-Journal* for half a century. He served a term in Congress and was in the Wilson administration. (Wall, Joseph Frazier, *Henry Watterson, Reconstructed Rebel*)

WATTS, Thomas Hill (1819-1892)

In a varied Confederate career, Thomas H. Watts served as a member of the Alabama secession convention, colonel of infantry, attorney general, and governor. Born when his state was still a territory, he became a lawyer in 1841 and later served in both houses of the state legislature but failed in a bid for a seat in Congress. A Unionist, he supported Bell's Constitutional Union ticket in 1860 but, following Lincoln's election, came around to the secessionist cause. In August 1861 he was defeated by John G. Shorter for the governorship and shortly afterwards raised and was commissioned colonel of the 17th Alabama. He served at Pensacola and Corinth before being named Davis' attorney general on March 18, 1862. Then in an August 1863 rematch with Shorter he was elected governor. He continued as attorney general until October 1, 1863. He took office in the state capital in December 1863 and was engaged in a futile attempt to promote resistance to the Federal invasion. He was removed from office by the Federal military in April 1865 and subsequently arrested. Resuming his law practice after his release, he joined the Democratic Party, served again as a state legislator, and was president of the state bar association. (Denman, Clarence P., *The Secession Movement in Alabama*)

WAUD, Alfred R. (1828-1891)

Probably the most prolific special artist of the Civil War was Alfred R. Waud who covered the campaigns of the Army of the Potomac throughout the conflict. Born in England, he had been educated in his craft at the Royal Academy's School of Design. Having come to the United States in 1850, he was working for the *New York Illustrated News* at the start of hostilities. His field sketches (he rarely ventured into painting) started with a Maryland scene the day before the firing on Fort Sumter and continued through Lee's surrender at Appomattox. Waud transferred to *Harper's Weekly* in February 1862, a relationship which lasted until his death. From this point on his sketches regularly appeared and were generally well received by the soldiers in the field, the sharpest critics of the art. Waud was noted for going under fire to obtain better views of the action and was usually armed. Many of Waud's works appeared with the *Century Magazine's* extensive series of articles on the war. They were later included in the book version, *Battles and Leaders of the Civil War*. For the rest of his life, Waud continued to work for *Harper's*, depicting scenes in the South and West. The Library of Congress maintains a collection of some 2,300 sketches by Waud and his brother, William. (Ray, Frederic E., *Alfred R. Waud, Civil War Artist*)

WAUD, William (?-?)

Although overshadowed by his brother Alfred, William Waud also covered most of the war for the illustrated weeklies as a special artist. Together the two brothers are responsible for the Library of Congress' collection of 2,300 original sketches. Born in England, Waud began his Civil War career by covering the firing on Fort Sumter for *Frank Leslie's Illustrated*. Later he covered the Union navy's seizure of New Orleans. Temporarily put out of action by illness, he joined *Harper's Weekly*, and his brother, in covering the war in Virginia. Following the close of the war *Harper's* could not help editorializing its "special pride" for the Wauds and their colleagues. The editors wrote,

Buford's cavalry in action, by Alfred R. Waud. (AC)

"They have shared the soldiers' fare; they have ridden and waded, and climbed and floundered, always trusting in lead pencils and keeping their paper dry." (Ray, Frederic E., *Alfred R. Waud, Civil War Artist*)

WAUL, Thomas Neville (1813-1903)

Having lost a bid for reelection to the Provisional Confederate Congress, this Texas planter and lawyer returned home, raised a legion for the Confederate army, and rose to the rank of brigadier general. The South Carolina native served in the Congress from February 4, 1861, to February 17, 1862 (the end of the provisional government), and sat on the committees on Commercial Affairs and Indian Affairs. His military assignments following his November 1861 election loss included: colonel, Waul's Texas Legion (May 17, 1862); brigadier general, CSA (September 18, 1863); commanding brigade, Walker's Division, District of West Tennessee, Trans-Mississippi Department (February-April and May-summer 1864); commanding brigade, Walker's Division, District of Arkansas, Trans-Mississippi Department (April-May 1864); and commanding 1st (Texas) Brigade, 1st (Texas) Division, 1st Corps (or District of West Louisiana), Trans-Mississippi Department (summer 1864-May 26, 1865). Captured at Vicksburg, he was transferred to the west side of the Mississippi and promoted to brigadier general upon his exchange. After serving in various minor posts in Texas he was ordered to Arkansas and West Louisiana where he fought at Mansfield and Pleasant Hill during the Red River Campaign. Moving north to intercept Steele's expedition against Camden, Arkansas, he fought at Jenkins' Ferry. Following the surrender of E. Kirby Smith's department he resumed his legal practice and was active in reconstruction politics.

WAYNE, Henry Constantine (1815-1883)

One of the briefest careers of a Confederate general was that of Georgian Henry C. Wayne. The West Pointer (1838) had served in the quartermaster's department. He served in Mexico and earned a brevet to major. In 1855 he was involved in the army's experiment in using camels to transport supplies in the West. He resigned his commission on December 31, 1860, to go with his state. Governor Brown named him adjutant and inspector general of the state forces. As such he played a leading role in raising troops. He became brigadier general, CSA, on December 16, 1861, but resigned on January 11, 1862, four days after being assigned to duty in northern Virginia. Again working under the governor's authority he was responsible for the state's militia which governor Joseph Brown kept jealously from Confederate control. After the fall of the South he was in the lumber business in Savannah.

WAYNE, James Moore (ca. 1790-1867)

When his state seceded, Georgian James M. Wayne elected to retain his seat on the U.S. Supreme Court. He was considered a traitor by many in the South. Born in Savannah, he had fought as an officer of the Chatham Light Dragoons during the War of 1812 and then entered the state legislature. He later served as his hometown's mayor and a judge on local and state courts. At the time of his appointment by Andrew Jackson to the high bench on January 7, 1835, he was the chairman of the Committee on Foreign Relations in the U.S. House of Representatives. He was confirmed by a voice vote two days later. In the infamous *Dred Scott* decision Wayne held that Dred Scott was still a slave, and even if he were not a slave a black could never be a citizen and be entitled to sue in state or federal courts. This view was shared by the chief justice, Roger B. Taney. During the Civil War he was a strong backer of the Union cause and was described as an enemy alien in the South. During Reconstruction he favored a moderate approach and refused to perform his circuit duties in states that were under military rule. (Lawrence, Alexander A., *James Moore Wayne, Southern Unionist*)

WEBB, Alexander Stewart (1835-1911)

Ten days after being promoted to brigadier general, Alexander S. Webb earned the Congressional Medal of Honor for his leadership of the Philadelphia Brigade in the face of Pickett's Charge. The New York City native and West Pointer (1855) had been posted to the artillery where he participated in the Seminole War. He had also lectured at the academy before the Civil War. His wartime assignments included: second lieutenant, 2nd Artillery (since October 20, 1855); first lieutenant, 2nd Artillery (April 28, 1861); captain, 11th Infantry (from May 14, 1861); assistant inspector general, Artillery, Army of the Potomac (ca. August 15, 1861-summer 1862); major, 1st Rhode Island Light Artillery (September 14, 1861); lieutenant colonel and assistant adjutant general (August 20, 1862-June 28, 1863); assistant inspector general and chief of staff, 5th Corps, Army of the Potomac (September-November 1862); assistant inspector general, Camp Barry, 22nd Corps, Department of Washington (November 1862-January 1863); assistant inspector general, 5th Corps, Army of the Potomac (January 7-June 28, 1863); brigadier general, USV (June 23, 1863); commanding 2nd ("Philadelphia") Brigade, 2nd Division, 2nd Corps, Army of the Potomac (June 28-August 15, 1863); commanding the division (August 15-December 10, 1863); commanding 1st Brigade, 2nd Division, 2nd Corps, Army of the Potomac) (March 25-May 12, 1864); chief of staff, Army of the Potomac (January 11-June 28, 1865); and assistant inspector general, Military Division of the Atlantic (July 1, 1865-February 21, 1866). After serving at Fort Pickens, he and his battery were held in reserve at 1st Bull Run. The next month he took a staff position with the Army of the Potomac's chief artillerist, William F. Barry. As such he served through the Peninsula Campaign. He then held staff positions with the 5th Corps and in the Washington defenses until named brigadier general and assigned to command of the sometimes troublesome Philadelphia Brigade. In his staff assignments he had distinguished himself at Antietam and Chancellorsville. But it was after his promotion that his greatest hour came, on the third day at Gettysburg, when his brigade was the focal point of the Confederate assault. In 1891 he

Alexander S. Webb, defender against Pickett's Charge. (*Leslie's*)

received his medal for the battle in which he was wounded and also earned a regular army brevet. While in command of the division, he won another brevet at Bristoe Station and participated in the Mine Run operations. Participating in the Overland Campaign, he fought in the Wilderness and fell severely wounded in the fighting at the "Bloody Angle" of Spotsylvania on May 12, 1864. Not returning to duty until the following year, he was Meade's staff chief during the final months of the war, seeing action in the Petersburg and Appomattox campaign and major general for the war. In the volunteer forces he was advanced to major general by brevet for Gettysburg, Bristoe Station, the Wilderness, and Spotsylvania. Mustered out of the volunteers on January 15, 1866, he remained in the regular establishment until his honorable discharge in 1870 as lieutenant colonel, 5th Infantry. He spent nearly a third of a century as the president of the City College of New York. (Banes, Charles H., *History of the Philadelphia Brigade*)

WEBB, William A. (?-?)

By early 1863 the Confederate Navy Department realized that it needed to shake up its officer corps and bring the more daring younger officers to important commands. In its choice of William A. Webb for the command of the Savannah Squadron it got more than it had bargained for—recklessness. As a lieutenant, Webb had commanded the one-gun *Teaser*, and as a

William A. Webb's former command, the ironclad *Atlanta*, as a Union blockader on the James River. (NA)

consort to the CSS *Virginia* he had thrown his wooden vessel into action against the wooden blockading fleet in Hampton Roads. Next, Webb organized a fleet of torpedo boats, of various types of craft, equipped with 20-foot poles mounting 60-pound explosive charges. Before he could place them into action, he was promoted to commander in the provisional navy and assigned to command the squadron at Savannah, including the ironclad *Atlanta*, formerly the blockade runner *Fingal*. His assignment was to take some action with what was believed to be the most powerful vessel afloat. Delayed by mechanical problems and betrayed by deserters from his crew, Webb was forced to alter his well-laid plans. His new plan called for an attack on the two Union ironclads guarding his escape route to the sea. It would have been much better to have tried to slip by the formidable vessels in order to wreak havoc among the wooden blockaders on the South Atlantic coast. As it turned out, Webb attacked the *Weehawken* and *Nahant* on June 17, 1863. After only 35 minutes, and without the *Nahant* really getting into the fray, Webb surrendered his craft. He and his officers were vilified by the Southern public for the loss of the vessel upon which so much hope had been placed. Webb's naval career had ended. (Scharf, J. Thomas, *History of the Confederate States Navy*)

WEBER, Max (1824-1901)

A fellow graduate of Franz Sigel, from the military academy at Karlsruhe, Max Weber also became a political refugee and joined the Union army but saw only limited action. The German officer had fled his native Baden when the Prussians crushed the 1848 revolution. Settling in New York City, he operated a hotel which became a meeting place for German immigrants. Capitalizing on his lieutenancy in the duke's service, he raised the United Turner Rifles upon the outbreak of the Civil War. His assignments included: colonel, 20th New York (May 9, 1861); brigadier general, USV (April 28, 1862); commanding brigade, Department of Virginia (May 8-July 22, 1862); commanding brigade, Division at Suffolk, 7th Corps, Department of Virginia (July 22-September 8, 1862); commanding 3rd Brigade, 3rd Division, 2nd Corps, Army of the Potomac (September 12-17, 1862); commanding 1st Separate Brigade, Department of West Virginia (April 19-26, 1864); commanding Reserve Division, Department of West Virginia (spring 1864); commanding Harpers Ferry and Defenses, District of Harpers Ferry, Department of West Virginia (summer 1864); again commanding Reserve Division, Department of West Virginia (August 6-15, 1864); and commanding Monocacy to Sleepy Hollow, Reserve Division, Department of West Virginia (August 15-October 20, 1864). His early service was in the vicinity of Fortress Monroe and along the North Carolina coast. Made a brigadier general, he was transferred with his brigade to the Army of the Potomac during the Maryland Campaign. At Antietam his right arm was crippled in the disaster which befell John Sedgwick's division. Returning to limited duty late in 1863, he was at the general headquarters of the Department of Washington until assigned to duty at Harpers Ferry in April 1864. He was forced to leave his post and move to Maryland Heights when Jubal Early invaded Maryland. Within a few days he was back at his headquarters and remained there until relieved on October 20. For the balance of the war he was unassigned and he resigned on May 13, 1865. Subsequently he was an American diplomat at Nantes, France, and a tax official.

WEBSTER, Daniel (1782-1852)

A decade before the secession crisis came to a head, Senator Daniel Webster proved to be one of the leading forces for compromise. The New Hampshire native had served two terms in Congress (from 1813 to 1817) after launching a highly successful legal practice and becoming noted for his oratorical skills. An opponent of the War of 1812, he even dabbled in the idea of secession for the New England states. This idea would haunt him in the future. At the end of his second term he set up his practice in Boston and did not return to Congress until 1823. Named to the Senate in 1827, in January 1830 he engaged in his most famous debate, with South Carolina's Senator Robert Hayne, in which he dealt with the touchy questions of western expansion, the protective tariff, and slavery. But the most important feature of his speech was the defense of a consolidated national government to preserve the Union. Although an opponent of the Mexican War, he did favor funding it as long as there was no seizure of territory which could be used for the expansion of slavery. He was a staunch supporter of the Wilmot Proviso. In the debates of 1850 over the occupied territories, Webster displayed an irritation with the abolitionists and declared in favor of Henry Clay's compromise that year. He explained that the Union was foremost and that the North would have to accept slavery in order to ensure its preservation. In 1852 he lost a bid for the Whig presidential nomination to Winfield Scott. Webster died before the election was held, having predicted the collapse of his party over the slavery issue. (Bartlett, Irving, *Daniel Webster*)

WEBSTER, Fletcher (?-1862)

The son of Daniel Webster, Fletcher Webster raised a Massachusetts infantry regiment and lost his life at 2nd Bull Run. He had been commissioned colonel, 12th Massachusetts, on about June 26, 1861, and had previously led his men at Cedar Mountain. With the Union army being forced from the field at 2nd Bull Run on August 30, 1862, he placed his men in line on Chinn Ridge in an attempt to stem the tide of defeat but soon received a fatal bullet.

WEBSTER, George (?-1862)

In answer to Lincoln's call for more troops in mid-1862, George Webster, a combat veteran, was given command of a new regiment, only to fall in its first battle. In the first year of the war Webster became a major in the 25th Ohio. After commanding the Union forces in a skirmish at Huntersville, West Virginia, on January 3, 1862, he became the regiment's lieutenant colonel. The 25th Ohio then participated in the campaign against Stonewall Jackson's command in the Shenandoah

Valley. On August 20, 1862, Webster became Colonel, 98th Ohio. His later commands included the 34th Brigade, 10th Division, Army of the Ohio (mid-September 1862-September 29, 1862) and 34th Brigade, 10th Division, 1st Corps, Army of the Ohio (September 29-October 8, 1862). Holding the left of the Union line at the battle of Perryville, the division suffered heavily. The 34th Brigade suffered the highest casualties, 579 killed, wounded, and missing, of any brigade in the battle. Among the killed was the brigade commander, George Webster, who fell late in the battle. (Culp, Edward C., *The Twenty-fifth Ohio Veteran Volunteer Infantry in the War for the Union*)

WEBSTER, Joseph Dana (1811-1876)

Born in New Hampshire, Joseph Webster had served for 16 years in the regular army with the topographical engineers before resigning and moving to his wife's hometown in Chicago. With the outbreak of the Civil War Webster was made chief engineer of the state of Illinois by the governor and was working at Cairo when he was appointed major and additional paymaster, USV, on June 1, 1861. Although in a new department, he continued his engineering duties. His later appointments included: colonel, 1st Illinois Light Artillery (February 1, 1862) and brigadier general, USV (November 29, 1862). Although appointed colonel of the artillery regiment, he continued to serve in staff assignments since in most cases the field and staff of an artillery regiment did not serve with their unit because the batteries were assigned independently. He was chief engineer and chief of staff to General Grant at the battles of Belmont, Forts Henry and Donelson, and Shiloh. Late on the first day of the latter battle he assembled more than 50 guns above Pittsburg Landing, when it appeared that the Confederate army would drive the disorganized Union troops back into the Tennessee River; he stabilized the line. He was subsequently promoted and assigned to superintend the railroads supplying Grant's drive on Vicksburg. After the fall of that city he served as chief of staff to General Sherman and again during the Atlanta Campaign he was in the rear providing logistical support to the advancing army. During the Franklin-Nashville Campaign he was chief of staff to General G.H. Thomas. Brevetted major general, USV, for his war services he resigned November 6, 1865, and became a tax official in Chicago. (Catton, Bruce, *Grant Moves South*)

WEBSTER, Timothy (1821-1862)

An English-born New Jersey mechanic, Timothy Webster grew bored with his job and became a guard, the first step on the way to employment with the Pinkerton Agency—and execution as a spy during the Civil War. Having joined Pinkerton in the 1850s, Webster was sent by him to offer the services of the agency to President Lincoln. The team went into the pay of General George McClellan, then commanding the Department of the Ohio, and Webster began his first expedition in May 1861. It took him to Louisville and Bowling Green, in Kentucky, and Clarksville, Memphis, Chattanooga, Grand Junction, Jackson and Humboldt, Tennessee. Throughout the adventure he befriended secessionists and gathered military information. He next operated in the Baltimore-Washington-Richmond area. With quick thinking, he was able to avoid detection, once punching out an accuser and pretending to be enraged by the charge. He managed to infiltrate the Knights of Liberty, a secret secession organization. He became a messenger for the *Richmond Examiner* to cover his Richmond comings and goings. His connections allowed him to visit rebel fortifications and war industries and even gained him an audience with Secretary of War Benjamin. Supplies about to run the blockade were seized in Baltimore based on his information. Once arrested as a Confederate spy, a phony escape had to be arranged. Then in the company of Hattie Lawton, a female Pinkerton agent, he became ill in Richmond and was eventually exposed by two other agents who were sent after them and themselves were captured. Sentenced to hang, his request for a firing squad was refused. He was hanged on April 24, 1862.

WEED, Stephen Hinsdale (1831-1863)

Desiring further advancement, Stephen Weed was one of many regular army artillery officers who transferred out of the slow-moving promotion lists to the volunteers. He did become a general, but fell less than a month later. The West Pointer (1854), having served in the Seminole fighting and against the Mormons as an artillery lieutenant, was promoted to captain in the newly raised 5th Artillery and assigned to command Battery I on May 14, 1861. Over the next two years he did not receive a promotion, as slow advancement was common in the artillery. During this time he saw action in the Seven Days, 2nd Bull Run as divisional artillery chief, Antietam, and at Fredericksburg and Chancellorsville as chief of artillery for the 5th Corps. On June 6, 1863, he received his volunteer commission as a brigadier general and was given command of the 3rd Brigade, 2nd Division, 5th Corps, Army of the Potomac. His brigade was the only volunteer unit in a division composed of regular army troops. In his first action wearing a general's star, on the second day at Gettysburg, Weed was on his way to reinforce Sickles' 3rd Corps in the Peach Orchard when he was redirected to the crest of Little Round Top by his corps commander. During the fighting on the hilltop Weed was struck by a rebel sharpshooter firing from Devil's Den. He died a few hours later but his actions in bringing up an artillery battery helped save the Union left flank.

WEED, Thurlow (1797-1882)

As a New York state legislator and, for over three decades, the editor of the *Albany Evening Journal*, Thurlow Weed was a major power in the state's Whig and, later, Republican parties. He had early learned the printing trade and had a brief experience in the militia during the War of 1812. After working on several papers he was named editor of the *Journal* by the Anti-Masons in 1830. Becoming a Seward partisan, he was a leading force in the Whig Party. However, he scorned the idea of a separate party for the abolitionists. He did support the Wilmot Proviso. With the decline of his party he eventually drifted into the Republican Party. He backed Seward for the

1860 presidential nomination, but this may have backfired with the former Democrats in the new party. During the campaign he was an advisor to Lincoln and the next year he went to Europe to smooth over the ill feelings over the *Trent* Affair. In 1863 he gave up the *Journal* but remained active in politics, opposing the influence of Radical Republicans on Lincoln. Although he probably would have supported a War Democrat he couldn't accept McClellan's running on a peace plank. But by this time his influence in the party was failing. After the war he briefly returned to active journalism but soon retired, only submitting an occasional political article for publication. (Barnes, T.W., *Life of Thurlow Weed* and Van Deusen, Glyndon Garlock, *Thurlow Weed, Wizard of the Lobby*)

WEICHMANN, Louis J. (1842-1902)

A boarder at the Washington boardinghouse of Mrs. Mary E. Surratt, Louis J. Weichmann was arrested the morning after the assassination of Lincoln but instead became a star witness in the trial of the conspirators. Of German heritage, he had been born in Baltimore and raised in Washington and Philadelphia. Having flunked out when preparing for the Catholic priesthood, he worked during the Civil War in a clerical position in the War Department. He resided in the boardinghouse of the mother of a former classmate, John H. Surratt. This was where much of the planning was done to kidnap Lincoln and spirit him off to Richmond. There have been charges that Weichmann may actually have been a member of the group but, following his release, he provided extensive testimony against the members of the conspiracy, all of whom he knew to one degree or another. His testimony, and that of John M. Lloyd, is credited with having sent Mrs. Surratt to the gallows. Following her execution—many had thought that it would not be carried out—large segments of the public blamed Weichmann, and he spent much of the rest of his life defending his testimony. When John H. Surratt was finally apprehended, Weichmann was again in the witness box but this time the trial ended in a deadlocked jury. To defend himself against the charges of the younger Surratt and the public at large, he wrote his own account of the tragedy but it was not published until seven decades after his death. (Weichmann, Louis J., ed. by Floyd E. Risvold, *A True History of the Assassination of Abraham Lincoln and of the Conspiracy of 1865*)

WEIGHTMAN, Richard Hanson (?-1861)

When Confederate Brigadier General Ben McCulloch took over control of the mixed forces in southwestern Missouri in the summer of 1861 he had nothing but contempt for the Missouri State Guard and its officers. There was, however, one exception—Richard H. Weightman. A former cadet at West Point, although he had never graduated, and a veteran of the Mexican War as a captain of Missouri volunteers, Weightman promptly reentered the state's service at the outbreak of the Civil War. Appointed colonel, 1st Cavalry, Missouri State Guard, he succeeded to the command of the 1st Brigade, 2nd Division, Missouri State Guard, upon the death of his predecessor in a small skirmish in June 1861. He distinguished himself in both this action and at Carthage the next month. On August 10, he was struck down by three bullets at Wilson's Creek and died while listening to the victory cheers of his men.

Richard H. Weightman, victim of Wilson's Creek. (NA)

WEISIGER, David Addison (1818-1899)

The friction between Confederate brigadier David A. Weisiger and his division commander, William Mahone, did not affect their ability to work together in the last year of the war during which their division was considered by many to be the best in Lee's army. A Petersburg businessman and veteran of the Mexican War, as a second lieutenant in the 1st Virginia, Weisiger had been active in the militia. As a captain he was present at the John Brown hanging and took the field at the head of the 4th Militia Battalion in April 1861. His later assignments included: colonel, 12th Virginia (May 9, 1861); commanding Mahone's Brigade, Anderson's-Mahone's Division, 1st (3rd after May 30, 1863) Corps, Army of Northern Virginia (August 30, 1862 and May 7, 1864-April 9, 1865); and brigadier general, CSA (November 1, to rank from July 30, 1864). After occupying Norfolk in the first months of the conflict, he moved with his regiment to the Peninsula and battled at Seven Pines and the Seven Days. Succeeding to command of the brigade when Mahone was wounded in Longstreet's assault at 2nd Bull Run, Weisiger was also hit. Unable to return to duty until mid-1863, he fought at Gettysburg and in the fall campaigns. The day after the Wilderness he again took over brigade leadership and held it for the balance of the conflict.

After Spotsylvania and Cold Harbor the brigade took up its duties in the Petersburg trenches. It was one of Mahone's two brigades which played the key role at the Crater on July 30. Two months later, Weisiger was promoted to brigadier to rank from the date of this victory. After the city's fall he surrendered at Appomattox and was a banker and businessman for the remainder of his life. (Freeman, Douglas S., *Lee's Lieutenants*)

WEITZEL, Godfrey (1835-1884)

Despite having operated against Richmond for only a year, Godfrey Weitzel had the honor to command the troops which first entered the Confederate capital. The Ohio native had graduated second in his 1855 West Point class and been posted to the engineers. In the prewar years he taught at the academy and worked on the fortifications near New Orleans. His wartime assignments included: first lieutenant, Engineers (since July 1, 1860); chief engineer, Military District of Washington, Department of the Potomac (ca. December 9, 1861-February 22, 1862); chief engineer, Department of the Gulf (early 1862-August 29, 1862); brigadier general, USV (August 29, 1862); commanding Reserve Brigade, Department of the Gulf (September 22, 1862-January 3, 1863); commanding 2nd Brigade, 1st Division, 19th Corps, Department of the Gulf (January 12-May 14, 1863); captain, Engineers (March 3, 1863); commanding the division (July 15-28 and September 1-December 13, 1863); commanding 2nd Division, 18th Corps, Army of the James (May 7-20, 1864); chief engineer, Army of the James (spring-September 30, 1864); commanding 18th Corps, Army of the James (October 1-December 3, 1864); major general, USV (November 17, 1864); commanding 25th Corps, Army of the James (December 3, 1864-January 1, 1865 and February 2-May 1865); and commanding 25th Corps, Department of Texas (May 1865-January 8, 1866). Early in the war he served in engineering duties at Fort Pickens, Cincinnati, Washington, and New Orleans. Named a brigadier general of volunteers in the summer of 1862, he led a division at Port Hudson and was brevetted for it. In the spring of 1864 he joined Butler's Army of the James for the final year's operations against Richmond and Petersburg. He fought at Bermuda Hundred in divisional command and then served about half a year as the army's engineering head. Placed in charge of the 18th Corps, he was brevetted for Fort Harrison and shortly thereafter was given his second star; he had already achieved that grade by brevet on August 26, 1864, for the war to date. In December 1864 he was given charge of the newly created 25th Corps, the only all-black corps in the history of the American army. He was involved in Butler's fiasco during the first attack on Fort Fisher. He was brevetted brigadier general in the regular army for the fall of Richmond and major general for the war. Mustered out of the volunteer service on March 1, 1866, having served along the Texas-Mexico border under Sheridan, he returned to his engineering duties until his death while still serving as a lieutenant colonel. He was noted for his canal and lighthouse work.

Union corps commander Godfrey Weitzel. (*Leslie's*)

WELD, Theodore Dwight (1803-1895)

Probably the greatest of the early abolitionists, Theodore D. Weld is little remembered in history because of his own quest for anonymity by preaching only in the country; he believed that towns must follow the views of the countryside. A Connecticut-born New York revivalist minister, he had been an early temperance advocate. Influenced by the activities of the British Anti-Slavery Society, he was converted to that cause by 1830 and worked with the American organization of the same name. Working at Lane Seminary in Ohio, he influenced many of the later converts, including the Beechers, the Grimké sisters (one of whom he later married), and Edwin Stanton. Fired from his teaching job, he and many of his students took to the speaking circuit, where Weld seriously damaged his voice. He was editor of the *Emancipator*, writing most of the articles under other names or anonymously. He also wrote several books, including the damning *American Slavery As It Is*. In the 1840s he ran a school in New Jersey and was semi-retired from the movement. During the Civil War he backed the Union tickets. He refused to allow others to write about his activities. Thus he has remained in the background of history. (Thomas, Benjamin, *Theodore Weld: Crusader for Freedom*)

WELLES, Gideon (1802-1878)

As one of only two cabinet members to serve throughout Lincoln's presidency—the other was William H. Seward—Secretary of the Navy Gideon Welles oversaw the increasingly effective blockade of the Confederacy's coastline. The Connecticut native had been a well-known journalist before the Civil War and was also an activist state legislator. Switching from the Democrats to the Republicans in the 1850s, he was called into the cabinet as secretary of the navy at the beginning of Abraham Lincoln's first term—he had been a bureau chief in the department in the late 1840s. He was soon thrust into the conversion of an outmoded peacetime navy into a modern wartime force. During his tenure many innovations in armament and armor were made that forever altered the face of naval warfare. He tended to be a moderating influence in the cabinet, at times counterbalancing the views of Edwin M. Stanton, Salmon P. Chase, and William H. Seward. Following Lincoln's assassination he remained in the cabinet to serve Andrew Johnson and did not leave office until Grant was inaugurated in 1869. In 1874 he published his *Lincoln and Seward*, among other historical writings. (Welles, Gideon, *Diary of Gideon Welles: Secretary of the Navy Under Lincoln and Johnson*; West, Richard S., Jr., *Gideon Welles, Lincoln's Navy Department*; and Niven, John, *Gideon Welles: Lincoln's Secretary of the Navy*)

U.S. Navy Secretary Gideon Welles. (NA)

WELLS, James Madison (1808-1899)

Condemned by his family and friends for his opposition to secession, Louisiana native James M. Wells became the Unionist governor of the state upon the resignation of Michael Hahn on March 4, 1865. He had studied law, run a plantation, and served as a sheriff before the Civil War. In February 1864 he was elected lieutenant governor, under Hahn, and took up his duties the next month. Upon the governor's resignation to claim a U.S. Senate seat, Wells was inaugurated in his place. Elected himself in November 1865 on the Citizen Party ticket, he served until removed on June 3, 1867, following a long feud with General Philip H. Sheridan over politics. Wells had favored the granting of suffrage to blacks. He retired to his plantation but held a number of government appointments. (Fortier, Alcee, *A History of Louisiana*)

WELLS, William (1837-1892)

In one of the more outstanding cases of advancement during the Civil War William Wells rose from private to brevet major general. The Vermont merchant had enlisted in the state's only mounted regiment early in the war. His assignments included: private, 1st Vermont Cavalry (September 9, 1861); first lieutenant, 1st Vermont Cavalry (October 14, 1861); captain, 1st Vermont Cavalry (November 19, 1861); major, 1st Vermont Cavalry (December 30, 1862); colonel, 1st Vermont Cavalry (July 2, 1864); commanding 2nd Brigade, 3rd Division, Cavalry Corps, Army of the Shenandoah (September 19-October 22, 1864 and November 10, 1864-March 25, 1865); commanding 2nd Brigade, 3rd Division, Cavalry Corps, Army of the Potomac (March 25-May 22, 1865); brigadier general, USV (May 19, 1865); commanding the division (May 22-June 1, 1865); commanding the corps (June 1-24, 1865); and commanding 1st Separate Brigade, 22nd Corps, Department of Washington (June 22-July 7, 1865). His company fought in the Shenandoah and at 2nd Bull Run. After duty in the Washington area Wells fought as a major at Gettysburg on the far southern flank of the Union army. His regiment took part in the Bristoe and Mine Run operations and the Kilpatrick-Dahlgren raid. In the course of the Overland Campaign he became the regiment's colonel and, in the Shenandoah Valley, took command of the brigade at Fisher's Hill. In this position he fought at Cedar Creek and back near Petersburg at Five Forks and then Appomattox. Brevetted major general for his war service, he was in temporary command of the corps after hostilities had ended and then held a command at Washington. Mustered out on January 15, 1866, he was state adjutant general, a tax official, and a state senator.

WELSH, Thomas (1824-1863)

Like so many enlisted men, Union General Thomas Welsh survived bullets on the battlefield but succumbed to disease. The Pennsylvania native had been engaged in the lumber business when he first answered his country's call. While serving as a private in a Kentucky volunteer unit he was wounded at Buena Vista in Mexico. After being mustered out, he was appointed to a second lieutenancy in one of the extra regular army regiments raised especially for that war. Again mustered out, he returned to his business interests until the Civil War. His assignments in that conflict included: captain, 2nd Pennsylvania (April 20, 1861); lieutenant colonel, 2nd Pennsylvania (April 20, 1861);

colonel, 45th Pennsylvania (October 21, 1861); commanding 2nd Brigade, 1st Division, Department of the South (April-July 1862); commanding 2nd Brigade, 1st Division, 9th Corps, Army of the Potomac (August 3-September 24, 1862); commanding 3rd Brigade, 1st Division, 9th Corps, Army of the Potomac (September 26-October 22, 1862 and January 27-February 7, 1863); brigadier general, USV (November 29, 1862); brigadier general, USV (reappointed March 23, 1863, to rank from March 13); commanding 1st Division, 9th Corps, Army of the Ohio (April 13-June 14, 1863); and commanding 1st Division, 9th Corps, Army of the Tennessee (June 14-August 1863). With his initial command, he served under Patterson in the Shenandoah Valley before being mustered out on July 26, 1861, at the expiration of its term of service. In command of a new regiment, he was placed in charge of a brigade on the South Carolina coast. Joining the 9th Corps in Virginia, he again commanded a brigade and led it at South Mountain and Antietam. Not having received notice of his appointment as a brigadier general, he was again in command of only his own regiment at Fredericksburg. Following that defeat the corps was transferred to the Department of the Ohio, and he was soon in charge of a division which he took to aid in the operations against Vicksburg. He served through the balance of the siege and then took part in the capture of Jackson, Mississippi. At some time after this he contracted malaria and on August 14, 1863, he died in Cincinnati.

WESSELLS, Henry Walton (1809-1889)

The surrender of Plymouth, North Carolina, effectively ended the active field career of Henry W. Wessells. The Connecticut West Pointer (1833) had been posted to the infantry and fought the Seminoles. During the Mexican War he was wounded at Churubusco and received a brevet promotion. The interwar years saw him performing routine duty on the frontier and West Coast. His Civil War-era assignments included: captain, 2nd Infantry (since February 16, 1847); major, 6th Infantry (June 6, 1861); colonel, 8th Kansas (September 29, 1861); brigadier general, USV (April 25, 1862); commanding 2nd Brigade, 1st Division, 4th Corps, Army of the Potomac (May 19-24, 1862); commanding 2nd Brigade, 2nd Division, 4th Corps, Army of the Potomac (June 7-September 26, 1862); commanding brigade, Division at Suffolk, 7th Corps, Department of Virginia (September 26-December 24, 1862); commanding 1st Division, Department of North Carolina (December 28, 1862-January 2, 1863); commanding 4th Division, 18th Corps, Department of North Carolina (January 2-March 14 and April 14-May 3, 1863); commanding District of the Albermarle, 18th Corps, Department of North Carolina (May 3-August 1, 1863); commanding Sub-District of the Albemarle, District of North Carolina (August 1, 1863-April 20, 1864); and lieutenant colonel, 18th Infantry (February 16, 1865). His initial service was on the troublesome Kansas-Missouri border. Resigning the colonelcy of a Kansas volunteer regiment on February 7, 1862, he became a brigadier general of volunteers two months later. Commanding his brigade on the Peninsula, he was wounded at Seven Pines. The wound proved to be slight and he was soon back on duty. Remaining in southeastern Virginia when the Army of the Potomac moved north, he eventually took command in northeastern North Carolina. On April 20, 1864, he was forced to surrender to Confederate forces under Robert F. Hoke at Plymouth. He was later brevetted for the unsuccessful defense. As a prisoner of war, he was placed under the Union guns firing on Charleston. Exchanged in August 1864, he was relegated to administrative works. He was commissary of prisoners and headed a draft center. Mustered out of the volunteers on January 15, 1866, he was brevetted brigadier general in the regulars for the war. Serving on the frontier, he remained in the regular establishment until his 1871 retirement as a lieutenant colonel.

WEST, Joseph Rodman (1812-1898)

The only Union general officer to be born in Louisiana, Joseph R. West spent much of the Civil War dealing with the Indians. Raised in Philadelphia the New Orleans native had served in the Mexican War as a captain of volunteers. Settling in California in 1849 he published the *San Francisco Price Current* until the outbreak of the Civil War when he again volunteered. This time his assignments included: lieutenant colonel, 1st California (August 5, 1861); colonel, 1st California (June 1, 1862); brigadier general, USV (October 25, 1862); commanding 2nd Division, 7th Corps, Department of Arkansas (April 25-June 16, 1864); commanding Cavalry Division, 7th Corps, Department of Arkansas (September 15, 1864-March 18, 1865); commanding 1st Brigade, 1st Division, Cavalry Corps, Military Division of West Mississippi (April 14-May 15, 1865); and commanding 2nd Division, Cavalry Corps, Department of the Gulf (May 15-June 12, 1865). He was part of the California Column, which drove the Confederates out of the Southwest, and then succeeded James H. Carleton in command of the regiment. As a brigadier general, he led a January 1863 expedition which, by treachery, captured the noted Apache chief Mangas Coloradas. The Indian did not survive the night and the official report stated that he was shot trying to escape. However, there is overwhelming evidence that he was being tortured by his guards, who killed him when he protested; a witness also claimed that West himself had instructed the guards that he did not want the Apache alive in the morning. He continued to serve in Arizona until the spring of 1864 when he was transferred to Arkansas. He took part in the repulse of Sterling Price's invasion of Missouri and then commanded the cavalry of the Department of the Gulf at the end of the war. Mustered out on January 4, 1866, he was brevetted major general the same day. Returning to the city of his birth he was a marshal, customs official, and Republican senator. Remaining in the nation's capital at the end of his term, he was a city official.

WEST, Robert Mayhew (1834-1869)

Problems with alcohol and George A. Custer brought the highly creditable military career of Robert M. West to an unhappy conclusion. The New Jersey native had entered the regular army as an enlisted man in 1856 from Pennsylvania. His Civil War assignments included: private, Company F, Regiment of

Mounted Riflemen (since April 12, 1856); captain, Company G, 1st Pennsylvania Light Artillery (July 25, 1861); major, 1st Pennsylvania Light Artillery (September 13, 1861); chief of Artillery, 1st Division, 4th Corps, Army of the Potomac (early 1862-June 1862); commanding Reserve Artillery, 4th Corps, Army of the Potomac (June-ca. September 1862); colonel, 1st Pennsylvania Light Artillery (July 28, 1862); commanding Advance Brigade, 7th Corps, Department of Virginia (April 12-May 4, 1862); commanding Advance Brigade, 4th Corps, Department of Virginia (May 4-July 15, 1863); commanding U.S. Forces Yorktown, Department of Virginia and North Carolina (December 22, 1863-January 22, 1864 and February 16-March 8, 1864); commanding 1st Brigade, U.S. Forces Yorktown, Department of Virginia and North Carolina (January 22-February 16, 1864); colonel, 5th Pennsylvania Cavalry (April 29, 1864); commanding 1st Brigade, Cavalry Division, Army of the James (June 15-October 23, 1864, November 5, 1864-March 11, 1865, and March 20-May 1865); and commanding the division (October 23-November 5, 1864 and March 11-20, 1865). Serving as an artillery commander, he went to the Peninsula where he fought at Yorktown, Williamsburg, Seven Pines, and during the Seven Days. When the Army of the Potomac left the Peninsula in the summer of 1862 West and the 4th Corps remained. During the minor operations in that area, he earned an 1867 brevet for a fight at Charles City Court House. Transferring to the mounted arm in the spring of 1864, he took part in operations against Richmond and Petersburg. There he won 1867 brevets for New Market Heights and Five Forks. For the latter he was also brevetted brigadier general of volunteers. After participating in the Appomattox Campaign he was mustered out with his regiment on August 7, 1865. The next year he was named captain of Company K of the newly formed 7th Cavalry. Serving on the frontier, he took up drinking and came into conflict with Custer over the shooting of deserters. He pressed charges against Custer and in return was charged by him with drunkenness. He was suspended from rank for two months. Obtaining a sutlership, he resigned in 1869 but died six months later.

WHARTON, A.D. (?-?)

When Tennesseean A.D. Wharton's vessel returned to the United States at the outbreak of the Civil War, the veteran of over four years in the old navy tendered his resignation. Since it was realized that he planned to join the Confederate forces, he was imprisoned at Forts Lafayette and Warren. Exchanged early in 1862, he became a lieutenant in the Southern navy on February 8, 1862. Assigned to the CSS *Arkansas*, he commanded two of that ship's guns during its run down the Mississippi to Vicksburg. Before the *Arkansas* was scuttled near Baton Rouge in August, Wharton had been transferred to the *Harriet Lane* which had recently been captured. It was hoped to turn her into a cruiser. This being found impracticable, he spent the year 1863 in command of the *Webb* while awaiting the completion of the *Missouri*. At the end of the year he suggested using the *Webb* for running the blockade. However, before receiving approval he was assigned to the ironclad *Tennessee* at Mobile. On August 5, 1864, in the famous battle of Mobile Bay, Wharton commanded the ironclad's forward gun division and personally fired a shot which nearly sank Farragut's flagship, the *Hartford*. He later lamented not having ricocheted the shot to strike along the water line. In the end the *Tennessee* was forced to surrender and Lieutenant Wharton again became a prisoner. Shortly exchanged, he was named executive officer aboard the ironclad *Richmond* in the James River Squadron. In January 1865 he led an expedition of his own design to destroy the bridges on the Tennessee River in East Tennessee. The mission was a failure and Wharton became a prisoner for the third and final time. Released at the close of the war, he became an official in the Nashville school system and a member of the Board of Visitors at Annapolis. (Scharf, J. Thomas, *History of the Confederate States Navy*)

WHARTON, Gabriel Colvin (1824-1906)

Escaping from surrounded Fort Donelson with John B. Floyd, Virginian Gabriel C. Wharton returned to western Virginia where he rose to the rank of brigadier general in the Confederate service. A graduate of the Virginia Military Institute, he had been a civil engineer when Fort Sumter was fired upon. His Confederate assignments included: major, 45th Virginia (ca. June 17, 1861); colonel, 51st Virginia (ca. July 17, 1861); commanding 1st Brigade, Floyd's Division, Central Army of Kentucky, Department #2 (February 9-16, 1862); commanding 3rd Brigade, Department of Western Virginia (early 1863-July 1863); brigadier general, CSA (September 25, 1863, to rank from July 8); commanding Valley District, Department of Northern Virginia (July 1863); commanding brigade, Ransom's Division, Department of Southwestern Virginia and East Tennessee (fall 1863-January 1864); commanding brigade, Department of Southwestern Virginia and East Tennessee (January 1864); commanding Ransom's Division, Department of East Tennessee (January-February 1864); commanding brigade, Department of East Tennessee (February-March 1864); commanding brigade, Department of Western Virginia (April-May 1864); commanding brigade, Breckinridge's Division, Valley District, Department of Northern Virginia (May-June and June-summer 1864); commanding brigade, Breckinridge's Division, Army of Northern Virginia (June 1864); and commanding division, Valley District, Department of Northern Virginia (summer 1864-March 2, 1865). Following the confused campaigning in western Virginia during the first part of the war, Wharton and his regiment were ordered to the West where they took part in the defense of Fort Donelson. When surrender became imminent Wharton escaped with most of the division. For the next two years he served in southwestern Virginia and East Tennessee and received promotion to brigadier general. He commanded a brigade in the victory at New Market against Franz Sigel and then joined Lee's army at Cold Harbor. His brigade was part of the relief force that arrived in time to save Lynchburg. Returning to the Shenandoah Valley, he advanced into Maryland with Jubal A. Early and fought at Monocacy and on the outskirts of Washington. He led a division at 3rd Winchester, Fisher's Hill, and Cedar Creek. In Early's final disaster at Waynesboro, Wharton's division disintegrated. In the postwar years he was active in mining and served in the state legislature. (Freeman, Douglas S., *Lee's Lieutenants*)

WHARTON, John Austin (1828-1865)

Having survived one wound and fought through the entire war, John A. Wharton was destined to die in a personal altercation—three days before Lee surrendered. Tennessee-born and Texas-educated, he had become a lawyer by the time of the secession crisis during which he attended the convention that took the state out of the Union. After falling ill on the way to fight at 1st Bull Run as an independent volunteer, he returned to Texas and formally joined the Confederate army. His assignments included: captain, 8th Texas Cavalry (mid 1861); colonel, 8th Texas Cavalry (early 1862); commanding Cavalry Brigade, Right Wing, Army of the Mississippi (September 27-November 20, 1862); brigadier general, CSA (November 18, 1862); commanding Cavalry Brigade, Polk's Corps, Army of Tennessee (November 22-ca. December 28, 1862); commanding brigade, Wheeler's Cavalry Division, Army of Tennessee (ca. December 28, 1862-January 22, 1863); commanding division, Wheeler's Cavalry Corps, Army of Tennessee (January 22-April 1864); major general, CSA (November 10, 1863); commanding Cavalry Division, District of West Louisiana, Trans-Mississippi Department (from April 21, 1864); commanding Cavalry Division, District of Arkansas, Trans-Mississippi Department (fall 1864); and commanding Cavalry Corps, Trans-Mississippi Department (various times from the spring of 1864 to April 1865). In command of his regiment he was wounded at Shiloh but returned to lead a brigade at Perryville and Murfreesboro. He took over the division and led it at Chickamauga and in Wheeler's Raid during the Chattanooga Campaign. In the spring of 1864 he was granted leave to visit Texas for reasons of health. However, upon crossing the Mississippi, he joined Taylor's troops fighting Banks' Red River Campaign and commanded the cavalry. With frequent leaves he continued to serve in the Trans-Mississippi Department until April 6, 1865, when he was shot and killed by a former subordinate, George W. Baylor, apparently in a dispute over the junior's failure to gain promotion. During the war, Wharton's mother, proud of her son's distinguished combat record, refused to allow his friends to run him for a seat in the Confederate Congress.

WHEAT, Chatham Roberdeau (1826-1862)

An adventurer, Chatham Roberdeau Wheat, was found to be the only officer capable of keeping his battalion of New Orleans toughs under any sort of discipline. The Virginia-born Wheat had become a New Orleans lawyer and served as a state legislator. But he was also a military adventurer, having served in Latin America with Lopez, Caravajal, Walker, and Alvarez, and in Italy with Garibaldi. Returning home at the outbreak of the Civil War, he was commissioned major, 1st Louisiana Special Battalion. One of the unit's companies had given its nickname, "Tigers," to the entire battalion. Wheat needed every inch of his 6-foot-4-inch frame to keep the rowdy toughs from the city's wharves and alleys in line. Moving to Virginia, Wheat led his men at the battle of 1st Bull Run where they were one of the first two units to face the Union flank attack. In the defense Wheat was wounded through both lungs. He defied the medical experts and recovered. The next summer, after taking part in the Shenandoah Valley Campaign, he was killed at the battle of Gaines' Mill during the Seven Days. The Tigers proved to be too unruly without him and were shortly thereafter broken up. (Dufour, Charles L., *Gentle Tiger, The Gallant Life of Roberdeau Wheat*)

WHEATON, Frank (1833-1903)

Having received a direct appointment in the regular army upon its 1855 expansion, Frank Wheaton emerged from the Civil War with all the brevets he could earn and eventually retired as a full major general in the regular establishment. For the five years prior to his appointment the Rhode Island native had worked on surveys of the Mexican-U.S. boundary. His prewar service was mostly on the frontier and his wartime assignments included: first lieutenant, 1st Cavalry (since March 3, 1855); captain, 1st Cavalry (March 1, 1861); lieutenant colonel, 2nd Rhode Island (July 10, 1861); colonel, 2nd Rhode Island (July 21, 1861); captain, 4th Cavalry (change of designation August 3, 1861); brigadier general, USV (November 29, 1862); commanding 3rd Brigade, 3rd Division, 6th Corps, Army of the Potomac (December 15, 1862-January 1863, February-July 1, 1863, and July 4, 1863-January 1864); commanding the division (July 1-4, 1863); major, 2nd Cavalry (November 5, 1863); commanding 1st Brigade, 2nd Division, 6th Corps, Army of the Potomac (March 24-May 6, May 7-June 21, and June 28-July 8, 1864); commanding the division (May 6-7 and June 21-28, 1864); commanding 1st Brigade, 2nd Division, 6th Corps, Army of the Shenandoah (August 6-September 21, 1864); commanding 1st Division, 6th Corps, Army of the Shenandoah (September 21-December 6, 1864); and commanding 1st Division, 6th Corps, Army of the Potomac (December 6, 1864-June 28, 1865). Only a few days after he entered the volunteer service his regiment was heavily engaged at 1st Bull Run, losing its colonel and major. Having taken over command of the unit during the fight, Wheaton was made its permanent colonel to rank from the day of the battle. Following a winter in the Washington area, he led his regiment to the Peninsula where he fought at Yorktown, Williamsburg, and in the Seven Days. At Antietam the division was too far in the rear to participate. He was then awarded the star of a brigadier to rank from November 29, 1862, but he apparently did not receive it until December 15, 1862, when he took charge of another brigade. In the meantime he had commanded the Rhode Islanders in the battle of Fredericksburg. He fought at Marye's Heights and Salem Church during the Chancellorsville fighting. Although in reserve at Gettysburg he took temporary command of the division when John Newton was assigned to command the 1st Corps. Within a few hours after the battle he was back in brigade command and as such served in the Bristoe and Mine Run operations. In the Overland Campaign he was in temporary command of the division during a part of the Wilderness fighting—also earning a brevet—and then fought at Spotsylvania and Cold Harbor. During the early operations against Petersburg he again commanded the division for a week. After aiding in the defense of Washington in the face of Early's threat he won the brevet of major general of volunteers for the Shenandoah Valley Campaign where he fought at 3rd Winchester, Fisher's Hill, and Cedar Creek. At the latter two he succeeded to command of the division and held that post until the end of the war. Returning to the Petersburg lines, he was brevetted brigadier general of regulars and took part in the Appomattox Campaign. He was brevetted major general of regulars for his war service in the final month of the war. Mustered out of the volunteers on April 30, 1866, he remained in the army until his 1897 retirement. In the meantime he commanded the principal expedition in the 1873 Modoc War and served in Texas.

WHEELER, Joseph (1836-1906)

One of only a handful of Confederates to be buried in Arlington National Cemetary, Joseph Wheeler qualified on the basis of his later service as a major general of volunteers in the Spanish-American War. The Georgia-born West Pointer (1859) had resigned his commission as a second lieutenant in the Regiment of Mounted Riflemen—he had briefly been posted to the dragoons in 1859—and, joining the South, had a meteoric rise. The cavalryman's assignments included: first lieutenant, Artillery (1861); colonel, 19th Alabama (September 4, 1861); commanding Cavalry Brigade, Left Wing, Army of the Mississippi (September 14-November 20, 1862); brigadier general, CSA (October 30, 1862); commanding Cavalry Brigade, Polk's Corps, Army of Tennessee (November 20-22, 1862); commanding Cavalry Brigade, Hardee's Corps, Army of Tennessee (November 22-December 1862); commanding cavalry division, Army of Tennessee (December 1862-March 16, 1863); major general, CSA (January 30, 1863); commanding cavalry corps, Army of Tennessee (March 16, 1863-fall 1864); commanding Cavalry Corps, Department of South Carolina, Georgia and Florida (fall 1864-March 1865); lieutenant general, CSA (February 28, 1865); and commanding corps, Hampton's Cavalry Command, Army of Tennessee (March-April 26, 1865). He led an infantry regiment at Shiloh and during the operations around Corinth, Mississippi, but was then assigned in the summer of 1862 to be chief of cavalry for Bragg's Army of the Mississippi. He led a mounted brigade at Perryville and a division at Murfreesboro. Given command of a corps of mounted troopers, he led it in the Tullahoma Campaign and at Chickamauga was in charge of one of the two cavalry corps (the other was under Nathan Bedford Forrest). However, soon after the battle conflicts between Forrest and Wheeler and Forrest and Bragg led to the reassignment of Forrest. Thus Wheeler was again in charge of all the mounted troops with the Army of Tennessee. He fought thus at Chattanooga and led his men in the Atlanta Campaign. During these last two campaigns he was noted for his raids on the Union supply lines. Following the fall of Atlanta, Wheeler's corps was left behind to deal with Sherman while Hood launched his invasion of middle Tennessee. With the small force at hand Wheeler proved unsuccessful in hindering Sherman's March to the Sea. During the course of the campaign in the Carolinas, Wheeler was placed under the orders of Wade Hampton who had been transferred from Virginia. Taken prisoner in Georgia in May 1865, Wheeler was held at Fort Delaware until June 8th. A longtime congressman from Alabama in the postwar years, he donned the blue as a major general of volunteers in the war with Spain. In 1900 he was retired with the regular army rank of brigadier general. His Confederate career had earned him the sobriquet "Fightin' Joe." (Dyer, John Percy, *"Fightin' Joe" Wheeler* and *From Shiloh to San Juan*)

WHIPPLE, Amiel Weeks (1816-1863)

Massachusetts native Amiel W. Whipple received his second star posthumously. A West Pointer (1841), he had been posted briefly to the artillery before being transferred to the topographical engineers. His prewar assignments included surveying both the northern and southern boundaries of the United States, railroad planning, and river and lake clearing. His Civil War assignments included: captain, Topographical Engineers (since July 1, 1855); chief topographical engineer, Army of Northeastern Virginia (July-August 1861); major, Topographical Engineers (September 9, 1861); chief topographical engineer, McDowell's Division, Army of the Potomac (October 3, 1861-March 13, 1862); chief topographical engineer, 1st Corps, Army of the Potomac (March 13-April 2, 1862); brigadier general, USV (April 14, 1862); commanding brigade, Military District of Washington, Department of the Potomac (May-August 1862); commanding division, same district and department (August-November 8, 1862); commanding 3rd Division, 3rd Corps, Army of the Potomac (November 8, 1862-May 3, 1863); major, Engineers (merger of two branches March 3, 1863); and major general, USV (May 6, 1863). Winning a brevet for 1st Bull Run where he was on McDowell's staff, he remained with his chief until the spring of 1862 when he was named a brigadier general of volunteers and was assigned to a brigade—later a division—in the Washington defenses. Taking the field late that year with his division, he won another brevet for Fredericksburg. Then on May 3, 1863, he was mortally wounded while directing his division at Chancellorsville. He died on the 7th and was posthumously brevetted a regular army brigadier general for the fight.

WHIPPLE, William Denison (1826-1902)

The entire Civil War career of William D. Whipple—for which he was brevetted major general in the regular army—was spent in staff assignments. The native New Yorker and West Pointer (1851) had been posted to the infantry and served on the frontier. Escaping from the Texans upon their secession, he reported in the East where his assignments included: first lieutenant, 3rd Infantry (since December 31, 1856); brevet captain and assistant adjutant general (May 11, 1861); assistant adjutant general, 2nd Division, Army of Northeastern Virginia (July 1861); captain and assistant adjutant general (August 3,

1861); lieutenant colonel and additional aide-de-camp (February 10, 1862); major and assistant adjutant general (July 17, 1862); brigadier general, USV (July 17, 1863); assistant adjutant general, Army of the Cumberland (November 12-December 1863); chief of staff, Army of the Cumberland (December 1863-spring 1865); and reappointed brigadier general, USV (September 6, 1864). At 1st Bull Run he was David Hunter's adjutant and later held similar posts in the Departments of Pennsylvania and Virginia and the Middle Department. Made a brigadier general of volunteers, he became Thomas' staff chief and fought at Chattanooga. His commission was not confirmed by the Senate and expired on July 4, 1864. Reappointed two months later, he was brevetted for Atlanta and Nashville. Mustered out of he volunteers on January 15, 1866, he remained in the regular army until his 1890 retirement as a staff colonel, having meanwhile served as Sherman's aide.

WHITAKER, Walter Chiles (1823-1887)

Kentucky lawyer, planter, and politician Walter C. Whitaker played a leading role in bringing his state back into the Union fold after a period of "neutrality." A lieutenant during the Mexican War, he had again enlisted in 1861. His assignments included: colonel, 6th Kentucky (December 24, 1861); brigadier general, USV (June 25, 1863); commanding 1st Division, Reserve Corps, Army of the Cumberland (August 11-15, 1863); commanding 1st Brigade, 1st Division, Reserve Corps, Army of the Cumberland (August 15-October 9, 1863); commanding 2nd Brigade, 1st Division, 4th Corps, Army of the Cumberland (October 10-December 8, 1863, March 15-June 30, and November 28-December 23, 1864); and commanding the division (September 19-November 28, 1864). Under Buell he served on the second day at Shiloh but was not engaged at Perryville. His regiment fought at Murfreesboro and the next summer he was named a brigadier general. His most important service came on the second day at Chickamauga when, serving under James B. Steedman, his brigade came to the support of George H. Thomas on Horseshoe Ridge after most of the Union army had been driven from the field. He then fought at Chattanooga and won the brevet of major general during the Atlanta Campaign. Following the fall of that city the 4th Corps was sent back to Tennessee to deal with Hood, and Whitaker commanded his brigade at Franklin and Nashville. Mustered out on August 24, 1865, he returned to the law but drinking—which dated back to his army days—contributed to a deteriorating mental condition which denied him much success in private life.

WHITE, Elijah Viers (1832-1907)

A hard fighter, Elijah V. White was nonetheless a problem for his superiors. A Maryland native and veteran of the Kansas troubles, he had been farming in Loudoun County, Virginia, at the outbreak of the Civil War. Since John Brown's raid he had been a member of the Loudoun Cavalry. His later assignments included: private, Company G, 7th Virginia Cavalry (early 1861); captain, White's (Va.) Rebels (January 11, 1862); lieutenant colonel, 35th Virginia Cavalry Battalion (February 4, 1863); and commanding Dearing's Brigade, Rosser's Division, Cavalry Corps, Army of Northern Virginia (April 7-8, 1865). After distinguishing himself at Ball's Bluff as a volunteer aide, he was authorized to raise an independent company for border service. Assigned to Ewell's divisional headquarters, White and his men fought in the Valley Campaign, the Seven Days, and at Cedar Mountain; White was wounded in the Valley. Finally returning to Loudoun County during the 2nd Bull Run campaign, his unit was highly successful. The command joined the Maryland invasion but was ordered back to Virginia by Jeb Stuart when he became displeased with its lack of discipline. This was not one of White's strong points; lax in filing reports, he was notorious for disliking drill and saber-grinding. White was again wounded in a fight at Leesburg. In October 1862 his command was increased to a battalion, which nearly mutinied upon assignment to a regular cavalry brigade. The command, by now nicknamed "The Comanches," was given frequent opportunity for separate forays, but did fight in regular service at Brandy Station, Gettysburg, Mine Run, the Wilderness, Trevilian Station, in the Shenandoah Valley, and Petersburg. White briefly took over brigade command upon the death of General Dearing at High Bridge. White and many of his men slipped out of the trap at Appomattox only to surrender later. After the war White resumed farming and served as a banker and sheriff. (Myers, Frank M., *The Comanches: A History of White's Battalion, Virginia Cavalry, Laurel Brigade, Hampton Division, ANVa., C.S.A.*)

WHITE, Harry (1834-1920)

When the Confederates passed through the Shenandoah Valley on their way to Gettysburg, they scored a sizable victory at 2nd Winchester, taking many prisoners. One of them, Harry White, proved so politically valuable that they tried to keep him incommunicado. A native Pennsylvanian, he had been commissioned major, 67th Pennsylvania, on December 13, 1861. The regiment's early history had been one of guard duty until a large portion of it was captured in June 1863. Sent to Libby Prison, White was not allowed to communicate with the outside world. The reason: He had recently been elected, as a Republican, to the Pennsylvania senate, a body that was evenly divided between pro- and antiwar factions. White's absence prevented the legislature from following an effective war program, and his seat could not be declared vacant until his formal resignation was received. That is what the Richmond authorities wanted to avoid. However, when a fellow prisoner was exchanged, White wrote out a letter, resigning from the legislature, on a piece of toilet paper and it was substituted for the stuffing in a button on the other man's uniform. With this paper in the governor's hands a special election was called, ending the deadlock. Eventually, White was exchanged and mustered out on February 22, 1865. He was also brevetted brigadier of volunteers for his war service. Resuming his political career he sat in the U.S. Congress. (Tucker, Glenn, *Chickamauga: Bloody Battle in the West*)

WHITE HORSE (fl. 1850s-1870s)

One of the Southern Cheyenne Dog Soldier chiefs, White Horse had a reputation dating back to the 1850s. Following the massacre at Sand Creek he went on the war path but was convinced to sign the Treaty of Medicine Lodge in 1867. However, when the United States reneged on the provisions—Congress had not yet ratified the document—White Horse and the other Dog Soldier chiefs were unable to restrain their young braves and finally joined in the 1868-69 war. White Horse fought at Beecher's Island. After the war he remained off the reservation for a time but eventually returned. Again in 1874 and 1875 there was war (the Red River War), and White Horse went on the warpath, fighting at Palo Duro Canyon before surrendering in early 1875. (Brown, Dee, *Bury My Heart At Wounded Knee*)

WHITE, Julius (1816-1890)

Waiving his right to command at Harpers Ferry—due to his lack of knowledge of the terrain—Julius White was arrested for faults of his subordinate. A New York-born Illinois businessman, he had served in the state legislature and as a customs official before joining the Union Army. His assignments included: colonel, 37th Illinois (September 18, 1861); commanding 2nd Brigade, 3rd Division, Army of Southwestern Missouri, Department of Missouri (February-May 1862); brigadier general, USV (June 9, 1862); commanding Railroad Brigade, 8th Corps, Middle Department (mid-September 1862; but relinquished); commanding 4th Division, 23rd Corps, Department of the Ohio (June 24-August 6, 1863); commanding 1st Brigade, 4th Division, 23rd Corps, Department of the Ohio (August 6-21, 1863); commanding 2nd Division, 23rd Corps, Department of the Ohio (August 21-December 24, 1863); chief of staff, 9th Corps, Army of the Potomac (spring-ca. August 6, 1864); and commanding 1st Division, 9th Corps, Army of the Potomac (August 6-28, 1864). Assigned to southwestern Missouri, he rose to brigade command and fought at Pea Ridge. Promoted to brigadier, he was assigned to command Harpers Ferry in the late summer of 1862. But with the approach of the enemy he felt it inappropriate to actually assume command, preferring to leave Colonel Dixon S. Miles in charge. Miles made faulty dispositions and determined to surrender but was accidently killed during the truce. White then had no choice other than capitulation, but the War Department placed him under arrest anyway. Eventually cleared, he was sent to the Department of the Ohio and took part in the Knoxville Campaign. During the Overland and the beginning of the Petersburg campaigns he was Burnside's chief of staff. With his chief's removal he was given a division which was soon broken up. White then went on an indefinite sick leave and resigned on November 19, 1864. Returning to his business interests, he was active in veterans' affairs. Near the close of the war he was brevetted major general of volunteers.

WHITEAKER, John (1820-1902)

Oregon's first state governor, John Whiteaker, wasn't even nominated for reelection during the Civil War, due to his proslavery views. Born in Indiana, he had gone West in the California Gold Rush before settling in the Oregon Territory. As a Democrat, he was elected to a judgeship and to the territorial legislature. In June 1858 he was elected and on July 8, 1858, was sworn in as governor in advance of the admission of the state to the Union. Concentrating on internal concerns in the state, he was nonetheless considered a traitor by many on the national issue of slavery; he was not nominated for a second term and left office on September 10, 1862. After the war he served in both state houses and the U.S. Congress. In the latter he favored the removal of the Indians from his state. (Turnbull, George S., *Governors of Oregon*)

WHITFIELD, John Wilkins (1818-1879)

Within a period of only a few months after receiving his commission as a Confederate brigadier general, John W. Whitfield appears to have lost his command. The Tennessee native had been an Indian agent, territorial delegate from Kansas to the U.S. Congress, and land office official before settling in Texas. His Confederate assignments included: major, 4th Texas Cavalry Battalion (1861); colonel, 27th Texas Cavalry (spring 1862); brigadier general, CSA (May 9, 1863); commanding brigade, Jackson's Cavalry Division, Department of the West (June 9-July 1863); and commanding brigade, Jackson's Cavalry Division, Department of Mississippi and East Louisiana (July-fall 1863). Considering his Mexican War service—he had been a captain in the 1st Tennessee and lieutenant colonel of the 2nd Tennessee—he took a step down when he took command of the battalion. He served in the Indian Territory early in the war and then led his battalion at Pea Ridge and across the Mississippi. At about this time his unit was increased to a regiment which was often styled "Whitfield's Legion." Leading this he was severely wounded at Iuka. Returning to duty the following spring, he was commissioned a brigadier general and assigned to a brigade which he led during the siege of Jackson. That fall he disappears from the extant records, until he was paroled back in Texas on June 29, 1865. After the war he was a state legislator.

WHITING, Charles Jarvis (?-1890)

In one of those desperation movements of a war, Captain Charles J. Whiting led his regular cavalry regiment in a suicidal charge to stabilize the Union line following a Confederate breakthrough at Gaines' Mill. He lost all but one of his officers. A native of Massachusetts, he had been appointed to West Point from Maine and upon his 1835 graduation was posted to the artillery. He resigned the next year while still a second lieutenant. He reentered the service upon the enlargement of the army in 1855. His assignments included: captain, 2nd Cavalry (since March 3, 1855); captain, 5th Cavalry (change of designation August 3, 1861); major, 2nd Cavalry (July 17, 1862); commanding 1st Brigade, Pleasonton's Cavalry Division, Army of the Potomac (September-November 1862); and commanding Reserve Brigade (attached to 1st Division from June 6), Cavalry Corps, Army of the Potomac (May 22-June 9, 1863). Following the breakthrough of Hood's Texans at Gaines' Mill on the Peninsula, Whiting led his futile charge. He fell wounded into the enemy's hands. Exchanged and recovered, he was promoted to major and commanded a brigade at Antietam. At Fredericksburg he served in the provost guard and fought at Chancellorsville. Again in brigade command he fought at Brandy Station but appears to have been relieved shortly thereafter. He was dismissed from the service on November 5, 1863. Reinstated in 1866, he was a lieutenant colonel, 6th Cavalry, but was mustered out as a supernumerary five years later.

WHITING, William Henry Chase (1824-1865)

One of the generals who failed to make the grade while serving under Lee, William H.C. Whiting was quietly moved aside to make room for the promotion of John Bell Hood. Having graduated at the top of the 1845 West Point class, Whiting had served in the engineers until he resigned as a captain on February 20, 1861. The native Mississippian held the following assignments in Confederate service: major, Engineers (early 1861); brigadier general, CSA (August 28, 1861); commanding division (known as Forces near Dumfries and in the Potomac District until March), Department of Northern Virginia (late 1861-June 1862); commanding division, Valley District, same department (June 1862); commanding division, in 2nd Corps (June 26-July 1862) and in 1st Corps (July 1862), Army of Northern Virginia; commanding District of the Cape Fear (an independent department September 26, 1863-April 18, 1864), Department of North Carolina (November 8, 1862-July 14, 1863 and September 26, 1863-January 15, 1865); and commanding the Department (July 14-September 26, 1863). As Joe Johnston's engineering officer, he served in the Shenandoah and at 1st Bull Run where he so impressed Jefferson Davis that he was promised promotion three grades to brigadier. He commanded what was in effect a division on the Manassas lines and was the center of a controversy between Johnston and Davis, who wanted Whiting to command a brigade of Mississippi troops. Johnston felt that to move troops many miles in the face of the enemy was suicidal. Whiting served through the Peninsula Campaign, seeing action at Yorktown, Seven Pines, and in the Seven Days. During this time he moved to reinforce Jackson to fool the Union. Ill for several months, he was supplanted by Hood and sent to North Carolina, where his engineering skills could be used to advantage. With the exception of a brief time in command of the department and in command of a field division in May 1864 around Petersburg, he served in the Cape Fear area until his capture. When Fort Fisher was threatened by a joint navy-army Union attack he moved into the fort where he was mortally wounded and captured on January 15, 1865. He died in New York, a prisoner, on March 10.

WHITMAN, Walt (1819-1892)

Already a widely distributed poet, Walt Whitman mined new material from the Civil War—fortuitously, because many of the native New Yorker's works had been financial failures. At the end of 1862 he visited the Washington hospitals in search of his wounded brother who had already recovered and returned to duty. Whitman's visit, however, prompted him to obtain a government clerkship in order to remain in the capital. In addition, he worked on his own hook in the hospitals, tending to the needs of the sick and wounded. His experience provided the material for his collection of works entitled *Drum Taps* which in its later editions included "When Lilacs Last in the Dooryard Bloom'd"—in response to the assassination of Abraham Lincoln. Many consider this to have been his masterpiece. In his later years he continued to write but with less frequency.

WHITTENMEYER, Anne (?-?)

During the Civil War many organizations were set up to provide aid for the soldiers in the field, principally with items not provided for by the federal government. Many of these groups were national but most were local, such as the Iowa Ladies' Aid Society under the presidency of Mrs. Anne Whittenmeyer. In cooperation with her secretary, Mrs. Mary E. Shelton, also a member of the United States Sanitary Commission, the efforts of the two groups were complementary.

WHITTIER, John Greenleaf (1807-1892)

A Massachusetts abolitionist poet, John G. Whittier gave us one of the great myths of the Civil War—Barbara Fritchie's flag waving. Three decades before the war he had become dedicated to the cause of freedom and had written many poems and editorials in its behalf as well as provided political advice to many politicians. He was the editor of numerous publications, but ill-health frequently caused him to cut back on these activities and his lecturing. When he heard indirectly of the Fritchie incident he wrote his poem, "Barbara Frietchie," which credited her with having waved a U.S. flag in the face of Stonewall Jackson, crying, "Shoot if you must this old gray head, but spare your country's flag." Fritchie did wave a flag a few days later, but at passing Union troops. There is now plenty of firsthand information that Whittier's incident never occurred. As late as 1888 Whittier was defending his poem. In fact, there was a flag-waving incident in Frederick, involving a Mrs. Mary A. Quantrill. Whittier continued to write after the war and gave advice to Republicans. (Kennedy, W.S., *John G. Whittier, the Poet of Freedom*)

WICKHAM, Williams Carter (1820-1888)

Despite the fact that he had opposed secession, Virginia planter, lawyer, and state legislator Williams C. Wickham served in either the cavalry or the Confederate Congress throughout the war. His military assignments included: captain, Hanover (Va.) Dragoons (ca. April 1861); lieutenant colonel, 4th Virginia Cavalry (September 1861); colonel, 4th Virginia Cavalry (August 1862); brigadier general, CSA (September 1, 1863); commanding brigade, F. Lee's Division, Cavalry Corps, Army of Northern Virginia (September 9, 1863-August 1864); commanding brigade, F. Lee's Cavalry Division, Valley District, Department of Northern Virginia (August-September 19, 1864); and commanding the division (September 1864). He

Confederate cavalryman Williams C. Wickham. (NA)

fought at 1st Bull Run and was wounded at Williamsburg. While recuperating at home he was captured and not exchanged until August 1862. Promoted to colonel, he led the regiment at 2nd Bull Run, South Mountain, and Antietam. That fall he suffered another wound but was back on duty in time for Fredericksburg. He then fought at Chancellorsville, Gettysburg, and in the Mine Run operations. He opposed Kilpatrick's raid on Richmond in February 1864. After serving through the Overland and part of the Petersburg Campaign he was sent with the division to the Shenandoah to reinforce Early. At 3rd Winchester he succeeded the wounded Fitz Lee in command of the division but soon resigned to take his seat in the Second Confederate Congress. He had been elected the previous year but had missed the first session due to his active campaigning in the field. He was admitted on the opening day of the second session, November 7, and his resignation from the army was accepted two days later. Sitting on the Committee on Military Affairs, he soon became known as a friend of the military and an opponent of the president. He supported the Hampton Roads Peace Conference which ended in failure. Almost immediately after Lee's Appomattox surrender, Wickham embraced the Republican Party, being much reviled for it. He was on his county board and active in railroading before sitting in the state legislature. (Freeman, Douglas S., *Lee's Lieutenants*)

WIECHMANN, Louis J.

See: *Weichmann, Louis J.*

WIGFALL, Louis Trezevant (1816-1874)

Although also a brigadier, Louis T. Wigfall gave his principal service, if such it can be called, in the Confederate Senate. Born in South Carolina, he had been an early secessionist there and in Texas which he represented in the U.S. Senate. He was admitted to the Provisional Confederate Congress on April 29, 1861, where he served on the Committee on Foreign Affairs. Earlier that month he had played a leading role in arranging Fort Sumter's surrender, and he soon decided to return to the military. His brief service was limited to northern Virginia where his assignments included: colonel, 1st Texas (August 28, 1861); brigadier general, CSA (October 21, 1861); and commanding Texas Brigade, Forces Near Dumfries, Potomac District, Department of Northern Virginia (November 12, 1861-February 20, 1862). Resigning on the latter date, he took a seat in the First Regular Congress and served throughout the war. He sat on the committees on: Foreign Affairs; Military Affairs; Territories; and Flag and Seal. A cantankerous soul who had fought two prewar duels, Wigfall soon came into conflict with President Davis. After the chief executive vetoed Wigfall's bill to upgrade staff positions in the army and limit presidential selections, the Texan carried his fight into social circles, refusing to stand when Davis entered. A friend of the military and the generals, he was especially supportive of Joe Johnston and Beauregard. However, he was also an obstructionist in opposing Davis' nominations. He spent six years in self-imposed exile in England before returning via Baltimore to Texas, never adjusting to defeat. (King, A.L., *Louis Wigfall: Southern Fire-Eater*)

WILCOX, Cadmus Marcellus (1824-1890)

An experienced officer, West Pointer (1846), Mexican War brevet winner, and author of a rifle manual, Cadmus M. Wilcox proved to be a steady and competent divisional leader in the Army of Northern Virginia. He resigned his infantry captain's commission on June 8, 1861, to cast his lot with his native South. The North Carolina-born and Tennessee-raised officer entered the Confederate service in an Alabama unit. His assignments included: colonel, 9th Alabama (May 1861); brigadier general, CSA (October 21, 1861); commanding brigade, G.W. Smith's Division (in the Potomac District until March), Department of Northern Virginia (October 22, 1861-ca. March 1862); commanding brigade, Longstreet's Division (in 1st Corps from July), Army of Northern Virginia (ca. March-August 1862); commanding brigade and division, 1st Corps, same army (August-September 1862); commanding Anderson's Division, same corps and army (September-November 1862); commanding brigade, same division, corps and army (December 1862-May 30, 1862); commanding brigade, Anderson's Division, 3rd Corps, Army of Northern Virginia (May 30-August 1863); major general, CSA (to rank from August 3, 1863); and commanding the division (August 1863-February 1865 and March-April 9, 1865). After serving in the Shenandoah and northern Virginia, he led his brigade on the Peninsula, including fighting at Williamsburg, Seven

Pines, and the Seven Days. At 2nd Bull Run he was in charge of a provisional division composed of three brigades from Longstreet's former command. This force was later assigned to Anderson's Division, and Wilcox was in temporary command of the division after Antietam. He led his brigade at Fredericksburg and made crucial independent decisions that aided in the victory. After fighting at Gettysburg he was promoted to major general and transferred to command Pender's former division. In this position he served out the war fighting at the Wilderness, Spotsylvania, Cold Harbor, and Petersburg and surrendered at Appomattox. When the lines around Petersburg were crumbling, it was his men who held firm and allowed sufficient time for the evacuation. Settling in the reunited nation's capital, he held a number of government appointments. His eight pallbearers were a bi-partisan group of generals. (Freeman, Douglas S., *Lee's Lieutenants*)

WILCOX, John Allen (1819-1864)

When Confederate Congressman John A. Wilcox died of apoplexy on February 7, 1864, the Davis administration lost an unwavering friend in the legislative branch. A native of North Carolina, he was the brother of Confederate General Cadmus M. Wilcox. Raised apparently in Tennessee, he had practiced law in Mississippi and served as the lieutenant colonel of the 2nd Mississippi during the Mexican War. Defeated in a bid for a second U.S. congressional term, he moved to Texas. His political career had spanned the Whig, Know-Nothing, and Democratic parties. He helped draft the Texas secession ordinance and was elected to the First Regular Confederate Congress that November. There he sat on the committees on: Enrolled Bills; Military Affairs; and Territories and Public Lands; he chaired the latter. Deferring to executive authority during the emergency posed by the war, he never introduced a bill which did not have administration backing and always voted for the president's program. In between the sessions in Richmond he returned to Texas where he served on the staff of General John B. Magruder as a volunteer aide with the honorary rank of colonel. In late 1863 he was reelected by his southernmost, 1st District constituents, but he died before the expiration of the First Congress.

WILD, Edward Augustus (1825-1891)

Always ready to fight for a cause in which he believed, medical doctor and Union General Edward A. Wild was frequently in hot water with his Civil War superiors. A graduate of both Harvard and the Jefferson Medical College in Philadelphia, the Massachusetts native had gone to Paris to further his studies and while there become a partisan of Garibaldi. After practicing for a time in the United States he served as a surgeon with the Turkish Army in the Crimean War. Long an abolitionist and believer in the equality of the races, he was one of the first men to offer their services to Governor John A. Andrew. His assignments included: captain, Company A, 1st Massachusetts (May 23, 1861); colonel, 35th Massachusetts (August 21, 1862); brigadier general, USV (April 24, 1863); commanding 3rd or African Brigade, North End Folly Island, 10th Corps, Department of the South (August 16-October 2, 1863); commanding African Brigade, Norfolk, Department of Virginia and North Carolina (November 2, 1863-January 19, 1864); commanding U.S. Forces Norfolk and Portsmouth, 18th Corps, Department of Virginia and North Carolina (January 8-April 28, 1864); commanding 1st Brigade, Hinks' U.S. Colored Troop Division, Army of the James (April 20-June 19, 1864); commanding 3rd Division, 25th Corps, Army of the James (December 30-31, 1864); commanding 1st Division, 25th Corps, Army of the James (December 31, 1864-March 27, 1865); and commanding 2nd Brigade, 1st Division, 25th Corps, Army of the James (March 28-April 18, 1865). He led his company at 1st Bull Run and the next spring led it to the Peninsula where it served in the Yorktown siege operations. At Seven Pines he was severely wounded in the right hand. While recovering, he raised a new regiment and again took the field as its colonel. At South Mountain he was severely wounded in the left arm but refused to leave the field until his command was safe. Utilizing his medical knowledge, he directed the surgeons to amputate. While recuperating he was active in recruiting black soldiers in Massachusetts and was then appointed a brigadier general and assigned to similar recruiting in North Carolina. He then led a brigade of black troops in the operations against Charleston. Back in North Carolina, he led a raid into the Northeastern part of the state that was noted for its destructiveness. He captured an alleged guerrilla, Daniel Bright, and promptly tried and hanged him. This led to a long series of communications between the Union and Confederate commanders and to a number of hostage-taking incidents. Wild was defended by Benjamin F. Butler and transferred to the Norfolk area. He then did well in the Bermuda Hundred operations, but excessive methods in dealing with rebel sympathizers led to his arrest on June 19, 1864, by his division commander, Edward W. Hinks. Convicted of insubordination, he was freed by Butler on a technicality—the prejudice against commanders of black troops was so great that regulations called for their trial only by similar officers. After a period of recruiting duty, he returned to field command but was soon under charges again at the insistence of one of his brigade commanders. Acquitted, he was nonetheless reduced to brigade command and was left behind during the final operations against Petersburg and Richmond, which resulted in his men being among the first Union troops to enter Richmond. This upset his superiors. With the war virtually over he engaged in a feud with Edward O.C. Ord, the army commander, then was assigned to the Freedmen's Bureau in Georgia. Mustered out on January 15, 1866, he was incapacitated for further medical practice, and he entered the mining business in the West and South America. He died in Colombia. His biggest problem in the army may have stemmed from his honest belief that blacks were the equals of whites as soldiers and citizens—an idea inimical to most officers of the day. (Kennard, Martin, *Memorial Portrait of the Late Brig. Gen. Edward Augustus Wild*)

WILDER, John Thomas (1830-1917)

The moving force behind converting one Union infantry brigade into mounted infantry and arming it with Spencer repeating carbines was its commander, John T. Wilder. The New York native's assignments included: lieutenant colonel, 17th Indiana (June 4, 1861); colonel, 17th Indiana (April 25, 1862); commanding 1st Brigade, 5th Division, 14th Corps, Army of the Cumberland (January 9-June 8, 1863); commanding 1st Brigade, 4th Division, 14th Corps, Army of the Cumberland (June 8-July 10 and August 10-October 9, 1863); commanding Wilder's Mounted Brigade, Cavalry Corps, Army of the Cumberland (October 16-November 8, 1863); and commanding 3rd Brigade, 2nd Division, Cavalry Corps, Army of the Cumberland (November 8-December 25 1863 and February 20-June 14, 1864). The unit's early career came in western Virginia and then in the advance on Corinth, Mississippi. Reequipped as mounted infantry—Wilder's own regiment had mounted on February 12, 1863—the brigade debuted in its new role during the Tullahoma Campaign with a startling performance at Hoover's Gap. Wilder again gained his command a name in history when it served on the front and flanks at Chickamauga. He led the brigade during parts of the Atlanta Campaign, and on August 7, 1864, he was brevetted brigadier general for the war to date. But on October 4, 1864, he resigned from the army and became a leading Tennessee industrialist with interests in railroading and mining. (Williams, Samuel C., *General John T. Wilder, Commander of the Lightning Brigade* and Sunderland, Glenn W., *Lightning At Hoover's Gap: Wilder's Brigade in the Civil War*)

WILDES, Thomas Francis (1834-1883)

Canadian-born editor and teacher Thomas Wildes was honored by a Virginia town for saving it from the torch of General Sheridan. Wildes had been named lieutenant colonel of the 116th Ohio upon its organization on August 18, 1862. His later military assignments included: commanding 1st Brigade, 1st Infantry Division, Army of West Virginia (October 19-December 24, 1864); commanding 1st Brigade, Independent Division, 24th Corps, Army of the James (December 24, 1864-February 3, 1865); and colonel, 186th Ohio (February 28, 1865). He served in West Virginia and in the Shenandoah Valley from 1862 to 1864. At the battle of Piedmont he was wounded by the concussion from a shell and in the 3rd Battle of Winchester he was thrown from his horse. On October 3, 1864, Lieutenant John R. Meigs, the only son of the Union Quartermaster General, was killed in a controversial encounter with some rebel scouts. In retaliation, General Sheridan ordered the nearby town of Dayton put to the torch. Seeing the distress of the townspeople, Wildes dissuaded the general from destroying the town and only a few scattered buildings outside of town were burned. After the war the townspeople erected a tablet in Wildes' honor. At the battle of Cedar Creek, Wildes succeeded to the command of the brigade upon the death of Colonel George D. Wells and led it through the rest of the Valley Campaign of 1864, then joined the forces facing Petersburg and Richmond at the end of the year. Given command of a new regiment in March 1865, he commanded it in garrison duty in Tennessee until the end of the war. He was brevetted brigadier general of volunteers the next month and after the war he studied and practiced law. (Wildes, Thomas F., *Record of the One Hundred and Sixteenth Regiment, Ohio Infantry Volunteers*)

WILKES, Charles (1798-1877)

During the 19th century naval commanders on the high seas had a far greater degree of independence than is the case today. This was due to the lack of rapid communications. One of these officers was destined to commit an act that brought international law into question and caused grave diplomatic problems for the United States. Charles Wilkes had entered the navy as a midshipman in 1818 and acquired a reputation for violating orders. Unpopular with his subordinate officers, he was much harsher with the enlisted men and was once publicly reprimanded for illegally punishing a seaman. At the beginning of hostilities he was a captain, in command of the *San Jacinto*. With this vessel he stopped the British mail steamer *Trent*, seizing two of its passengers, Confederate commissioners James M. Mason and John Slidell. For this action he was feted in the North and reviled in the South. In the end, however, the captives had to be freed. While commanding the West India Squadron in early 1863 he seized another British vessel, the *Peterhoff*, bound for Mexico, on the grounds that much of its cargo was destined for transfer to the Confederacy. The courts later ruled against his interpretation. He had been promoted to commodore on July 16, 1862, while commanding the James River Flotilla and on June 25, 1864, was retired. Two years later he was promoted on the retired list to rear admiral. (Warren, Gordon H., *Fountain of Discontent: The* Trent *Affair and Freedom of the Seas*)

WILKESON, Bayard (ca. 1843-1863)

New Yorker Bayard Wilkeson was commissioned directly into the regular army as a second lieutenant on October 22, 1861,

Charles Wilkes of the *Trent* affair. (*Leslie's*)

and assigned to the newly organized Battery G, 4th United States Artillery, with which he became one of the artillery heroes of Gettysburg. Serving in West Virginia and during the Peninsula Campaign, Wilkeson distinguished himself at Deserted House on January 30, 1863, and at Fredericksburg during the battle of Chancellorsville. Having commanded his battery at the latter battle, Wilkeson, a first lieutenant since August 14, 1862, again led it during the first day at Gettysburg. His command went into position on a small hill now known as Barlow's Knoll, north of town. Here Wilkeson supported the right of the Union line. His fire was so effective against Gordon's Georgia Brigade, that Gordon ordered two Confederate batteries to fire on the mounted battery commander. Eventually Wilkeson was struck down by an artillery round which nearly severed his leg. The young lieutenant completed the shell's work by amputating the limb with a common knife. That night after the Federal forces had abandoned the area north of town, Wilkeson died in the Alms House. He was posthumously brevetted captain, major, and lieutenant colonel for Deserted House, Fredericksburg, and Gettysburg.

WILKESON, Samuel (1817-1889)

Probably the saddest journalistic assignment Samuel Wilkeson ever had was covering the Gettysburg Campaign, where his son Bayard was killed in battle. A native of New York, he had studied law before turning to writing. He eventually became a correspondent for the *New York Tribune* and for a time during the Civil War headed its Washington bureau and worked in the field. Following the war he worked for Jay Cooke and Company and then went into railroading, becoming the president of the Northern Pacific Railroad. (Starr, Louis M., *Bohemian Brigade*)

Samuel Wilkeson of the *New York Tribune*. (NA)

WILKIE, Franc Bangs (1832-1892)

Covering the campaigns of Lyon, Frémont, and Grant, Franc B. Wilkie was considered one of the best war correspondents in the western theater. After a series of odd jobs he had been serving as city editor on the *Dubuque Daily Herald* when he went to the front with the 1st Iowa in 1861. His reporting soon gained him the position of chief western war correspondent for the *New York Times*. Signing his reports as "Galway," he covered the Henry-Donelson and Vicksburg campaigns. In September 1863 he left the field to become a member of the editorial board at the *Chicago Times*. Following the war he continued with his paper for a quarter century and was briefly a war correspondent in Europe. In 1888 he published his highly autobiographical *Pen and Powder*.

WILKINSON, John (1821-1891)

One of the lesser known Confederate naval leaders, John Wilkinson had one of the most varied of oceangoing careers. A veteran of two dozen years in the old navy, with more than the usual amount of sea duty, Wilkinson resigned his commission on April 6, 1861, and offered his services to his native state of Virginia. Appointed a lieutenant in the Virginia navy, he served at Fort Powhatan and on Aquia Creek. Transferred to the Confederate navy on June 10, he was subsequently sent to the Mississippi where he briefly commanded the *Jackson* before being named executive officer of the *Louisiana*. Assuming command during the Union capture of New Orleans, Wilkinson was forced to destroy his craft. Captured shortly thereafter, he was exchanged and sent to England where he bought a ship, which was renamed *R.E. Lee*, and ran the blockade. After directing the failed conspiracy to free the prisoners at Johnson's Island, he returned to Bermuda and took command of the blockade runner *Whisper*. After briefly commanding the ironclad *Roanoke*, he was for a time involved in another plot to free Confederate prisoners—this time at Point Lookout. Then he directed blockade-running operations at Wilmington, North Carolina. Given command of the raider *Chickamauga*, he made a short but successful cruise along the Atlantic coast before anchoring under Fort Fisher. After participating in the defense of that fort, he took command of another blockade runner, the *Chameleon*, which failed in several attempts to make its return voyage to Wilmington. With the Confederacy collapsing, he went to Liverpool and turned over his government funds to Captain Bulloch. He was engaged in business in Nova Scotia before returning to Virginia in 1874. (Wilkinson, John, *Narrative of a Blockade Runner*)

WILKINSON, Morton Smith (1819-1894)

An early settler of the Minnesota Territory, Morton S. Wilkinson represented the state in the U.S. Senate during most of the Civil War. Born in New York, he had moved to Illinois in 1837 and engaged in railroad work. Returning to New York in 1840, he studied law and was admitted to the bar two years later. The following year he took up practice in Michigan. After four years there he moved on to Minnesota in 1847. He was in the territorial legislature within two years and held various offices during the 1850s. In 1859 he became a Republican senator but failed to gain reelection to a second term. In the meantime he had attended the Republican national convention of 1864. Leaving the Senate on March 3, 1865, he returned to Washington as a one-term congressman in 1869 but lost a bid for reelection in 1870. He subsequently sat in the state senate, was a prosecuting attorney, and engaged in private practice.

WILLARD, George Lamb (1827-1863)

Having enlisted in the regular army during the Mexican War, New Yorker George L. Willard soon became an officer an later rose to be a colonel before his death at Gettysburg. His Civil War-era assignments included: first lieutenant, 8th Infantry (since December 31, 1853); captain, 8th Infantry (April 27, 1861); Major, 19th Infantry (February 19, 1862); colonel, 125th New York (August 27, 1862); commanding 3rd Brigade, Abercrombie's Division, 22nd Corps, Department of Washington (April 26-May 6, 1863); and commanding 3rd Brigade, 3rd Division, 2nd Corps, Army of the Potomac (June 28-July 2, 1863). Fighting with the regulars he earned the brevet of lieutenant colonel for the Peninsula Campaign before transferring to the volunteers. He had been in command of his regiment for less than a month when he was captured in the fall of Harpers Ferry. Paroled and exchanged, he found himself in charge of a brigade in the capital's fortifications. With Lee's invasion of the North, he was sent to the Army of the Potomac and was directing a 2nd Corps brigade when he was struck and killed on the second day at Gettysburg. He was posthumously brevetted colonel of regulars.

WILLCOX, Orlando Bolivar (1823-1907)

Former regular army officer Orlando B. Willcox served in both the eastern and western theaters of war and earned the brevet of major general of volunteers and the Congressional Medal of Honor. The Michigan native had been posted to the artillery following his 1847 graduation from West Point. Following service in the Mexican and Seminole wars he resigned as a first lieutenant in 1857. He gave up his Detroit law practice upon the outbreak of the Civil War and his assignments included: colonel, 1st Michigan (May 1, 1861); commanding 2nd Brigade, 3rd Division, Army of Northeastern Virginia (June-July 21, 1861); commanding 1st Division, 9th Corps, Army of the Potomac (September 8-October 8, 1862 and February 7-April 4, 1863); commanding the corps (October 8, 1862-January 16, 1863); commanding 1st Division, 9th Corps, Department of the Ohio (March 19-April 13, 1863); also commanding District of Central Kentucky, Department of the Ohio (April 10-June 4, 1863); commanding 9th Corps, Department of the Ohio (April 11-June 5, 1863, January 17-26, and March 16-April 13, 1864); commanding Left Wing, Forces in East Tennessee, Department of the Ohio (September 1863-January 11, 1864); commanding 2nd Division, 9th Corps, Department of the Ohio (January 26-March 16, 1864); commanding 3rd Division, 9th Corps, Army of the Potomac (April 19-September 2, 1864); again commanding 1st Division, 9th Corps, Army of the Potomac (September 13-December 30, 1864, February 2-25, and March 7-June 17, 1865); again commanding the corps (December 31, 1864-January 12, 1865, January 24-February 2, and June 17-July 2, 1865); and also commanding District of Washington, 22nd Corps, Department of Washington (April 26-August 2, 1865). As a part of Samuel P. Heintzelman's division, Willcox led his brigade in the wide circuit around the Confederate left at 1st Bull Run. In the fighting in that sector he fell wounded and was captured. While a prisoner he became one of the hostages held by the Richmond authorities to guarantee the well-being of captured Confederate privateers (See: Walter W. Smith). Exchanged on August 19, 1862, he was named a brigadier general of volunteers to rank from the date of his capture. With the 9th Corps, he fought at Antietam and Fredericksburg before going with Burnside to the West. He held various commands in Kentucky and Tennessee. Returning to the Army of the Potomac, he fought at the Wilderness and was brevetted for Spotsylvania in 1867. During the Petersburg Campaign he commanded a division, at times the corps, and was brevetted in 1867 for the final assault on the city. Also during the Overland-Petersburg Campaign he was brevetted major general of volunteers on August 1, 1864. Mustered out of the volunteers on January 15, 1866, he was named colonel, 29th Infantry, that summer. Two decades later he became a brigadier general and retired in 1887. For 1st Bull Run he was awarded the Congressional Medal of Honor in 1895. He died in Canada where he had settled in 1905.

WILLEY, Waitman Thomas (1811-1900)

Coming from that part of Virginia destined to become West Virginia, Waitman T. Willey was chosen to replace the retired James M. Mason in the U.S. Senate at the outbreak of the Civil War. He had entered upon the practice of law in 1833 and served throughout the 1840s and into the 1850s as a court clerk. A Southern Unionist, he was a delegate to the Constitutional Union convention of 1860 which put forward the Bell-Everett ticket. Representing Virginia, he took over Mason's seat on July 9, 1861, and held it until the end of the term, on March 3, 1863. With the creation of the new state of West Virginia and its admission to the Union that same year, he was named as one of its two senators. Taking his seat on August 4, 1863, he was reelected two years later. Not a candidate for reelection, he left office in 1871. He again became a court clerk in 1882 and held the post until his 1896 retirement.

WILLIAMS, Alpheus Starkey (1810-1878)

Mexican War veteran Alpheus S. Williams served throughout the Civil War and on January 12, 1865, was brevetted major general of volunteers, with the unusual notation for "marked ability and energy." The native of Connecticut had graduated from Yale and eventually entered the practice of law in Detroit. He was widely travelled before the Mexican War in which he served as a lieutenant colonel in the 1st Michigan. In charge of the state's military preparations in 1861, his assignments included: brigadier general, Michigan Volunteers (April 24, 1861); commanding 3rd Brigade, 1st Division, Department of Pennsylvania (June-July 25, 1861); brigadier general, USV (August 9, 1861, to rank from May 17); commanding 1st Brigade, Banks' Division, Army of the Potomac (October 18, 1861-March 13, 1862); commanding 1st Division, 5th Corps, Army of the Potomac (March 13-April 4, 1862); commanding 1st Division, Department of the Shenandoah (April 4-June 26, 1862); commanding 1st Division, 2nd Corps, Army of Virginia (June 26-September 4, 1862); commanding the corps (September 4-12, 1862); commanding 1st Division, 12th Corps, Army of the Potomac (September 12-17, 1862, October 20, 1862-July 1, 1863, July 4-August 31, and September 13-25, 1863); commanding the corps (September 17-October 20, 1862, July 1-4, and August 31-September 13, 1863), commanding 1st Division, 12th Corps, Army of the Cumberland (September 25-December 22, 1863 and January 30-April 14, 1864); commanding 1st Division, 20th Corps, Army of the Cumberland (April 14-July 28, August 27-November 11, 1864, and April 2-June 4, 1865); and commanding the corps (July 28-August 27, 1864 and November 11, 1864-April 2, 1865). While still a state general he served under Patterson. As a national volunteer officer, he served under Banks around Washington and in the Shenandoah Valley. With the command merged into Pope's Army of Virginia, he fought at Cedar Mountain but was not fully engaged at 2nd Bull Run. Briefly in corps command at the outset of the Maryland Campaign, he succeeded to direction of the 12th Corps upon the death of Joseph K.F. Mansfield at Antietam. In charge of his division he fought at Chancellorsville and succeeded Henry W. Slocum in charge of the corps at Gettysburg while the latter exercised command of the right wing. Sent west in the fall of 1863, Williams' division was guarding the supply lines during the battle of Chattanooga, due to Slocum's refusal to serve under Hooker. When the 11th and 12th corps were merged prior to the Atlanta Campaign, Williams retained his division in the new 20th Corps. Fighting throughout that campaign, he succeeded Hooker in corps command in front of the city. In both division and corps command, at different times, he served through the Savannah and Carolinas campaigns. Mustered out on January 15, 1866, he was an American diplomat in El Salvador until 1869. Entering politics, he was defeated for governor the next year. He died in the nation's capital during his second term in Congress. (Quaife, M.M., *From the Cannon's Mouth: The Civil War Letters of General Alpheus S. Williams*)

WILLIAMS, David Henry (1819-1891)

In many cases, where a general's commission expired due to a lack of confirmation by the U.S. Senate, the general was reappointed within a matter of days. But this was not the case with David H. Williams, who simply went home when his appointment expired on March 4, 1863. The New York-born Pittsburgh engineer had served in the Mexican War, apparently as an enlisted man, and kept up his military interest through the state militia. His Civil War assignments included: colonel, 31st Pennsylvania (July 23, 1861); colonel, 82nd Pennsylvania (change of designation summer 1862); and brigadier general, USV (November 29, 1862). After service in and around Washington, he took his regiment to the Peninsula and saw action at Yorktown, Williamsburg, Seven Pines, and during the Seven Days. The division was too far to the rear during the battle of Antietam to have taken a part in it. He was still in charge of his regiment at Fredericksburg but was only slightly engaged. Sometime after that he received his star but lost it when the Senate failed to act upon his nomination. He resumed his engineering pursuits and then turned to writing, until poor health overtook him.

WILLIAMS, James (1796-1869)

While a U.S. diplomat, James Williams was opposed to secession, but once it became an established fact he readily joined the Confederacy. A Tennessee native, he had been active in journalism, riverboats, railroads, mining, and manufacturing before being appointed a minister to Turkey in 1857. He had also been elected to the state legislature as a Whig for one term. By the time of the Civil War, he was a Democrat and returned to the United States as a Unionist, but soon changed his colors. Sent as an agent to Great Britain, he wrote propagandistic articles for the *London Times* and the *Index*, a Confederate organ. He also wrote *Letters on Slavery from the Old World, The South Vindicated*, and *The Rise and Fall of the Model Republic*. He was instrumental in opening diplomatic channels with Mexico in 1863 but was a failure in attempts to gain recognition from France and Germany. Remaining in Europe after the war, he died in Graz, Austria. (Cullop, Charles P., *Confederate Propaganda in Europe*)

WILLIAMS, Jesse Milton (1831-1864)

Although he led his brigade in several major battles of the Army of Northern Virginia, Jesse M. Williams never received the right to wear the wreathed stars of a general officer. He had enlisted early in the war and his assignments included: captain, Company D, 2nd Louisiana (May 11, 1861); colonel, 2nd Louisiana (ca. July 1, 1862); and commanding Starke's-Nicholls' Brigade, Jackson's-Trimble's-Johnson's Division, 2nd Corps, Army of Northern Virginia (September 17, 1862 and May 2-July 19, 1863). As a company officer, he fought at Yorktown and in the Seven Days Battles. In the summer of 1862 he was promoted to regimental command, and he led the 2nd at Cedar Mountain and 2nd Bull Run. At Antietam he took over command of the brigade until he was wounded out of action. At Chancellorsville he again succeeded to brigade command and led it through the rest of the battle and in the Gettysburg Campaign. Returning to the direction of the 2nd, he served through the Bristoe and Mine Run campaigns and fought at the Wilderness. On May 12, 1864, in the heavy fighting at Spotsylvania's "Bloody Angle," he was killed.

WILLIAMS, John J. (?-1865)

More than a month after Lee's surrender at Appomattox, Private John J. Williams became the last Union combat fatality. He had belonged to the 34th Indiana, a unit which had served throughout the campaigns to open the Mississippi River that culminated in the capture of Vicksburg. The regiment was then transferred to New Orleans for service along the Gulf Coast of Texas. There, in the last land fight of the Civil War, on May 13, 1865, Williams was killed in the Confederate victory at Palmito Ranch. To the East, the war had already been decided.

WILLIAMS, John Stuart (1818-1898)

Despite his opposition to the idea of secession, native Kentuckian John S. Williams joined the Confederacy and became a brigadier general. The lawyer and state legislator had served in the Mexican War as captain of an independent Kentucky company and later as colonel of the 4th Kentucky. In one of his political races he was derisively dubbed "Cerro Gordo" Williams by his opponent, Roger W. Hanson, over Williams' disputed actions in that Mexican War battle. Williams won the election and retained the nickname as a mark of honor. Reluctantly, he finally entered the Confederate army where his assignments included: colonel, 5th Kentucky (November 16, 1861); brigadier general, CSA (April 16, 1862); commanding Department of Southwestern Virginia (November 19-25, 1862); commanding Department of Western Virginia (November 25-December 10, 1862); commanding 2nd Brigade, Department of Western Virginia (ca. December 10, 1862-mid 1863); commanding cavalry brigade, Department of Western Virginia and East Tennessee (fall 1863-ca. December 1863); commanding Kentucky Brigade, Humes' Division, Wheeler's Cavalry Corps, Army of Tennessee (ca. June-July 1864); and commanding Kentucky Brigade, Kelly's Division, Wheeler's Cavalry Corps, Army of Tennessee (July-September 1864). Early in the war he commanded his regiment in the Kentucky-Virginia border area, under Humphrey Marshall, and was for a time in departmental command. He won a battle for the defense of the Abingdon, Virginia, salt works while in command of a brigade. During the Atlanta Campaign he was assigned to command a Kentucky brigade under Wheeler but became separated on a raid into Tennessee, for which he was roundly criticized by the famed cavalryman. He finished out the war in the mountains of southwestern Virginia and was a farmer and state national legislator after the war.

WILLIAMS, Lawrence Orton

See: *Williams, William Orton*

WILLIAMS, Nelson Grosvenor (1823-1897)

Because he had already left the service, two days before his commission as a brigadier general of volunteers took effect, the U.S. Senate later negated his appointment, on March 9, 1863. The New York native had dropped out of West Point after one year in 1840 due to poor grades. Moving to Iowa in 1855, he was a merchant and farmer until the outbreak of the Civil War when he enlisted. His assignments included: colonel, 3rd Iowa (June 26, 1861); commanding 1st Brigade, 4th Division, Army of the Tennessee (March-April 6, 1862); and brigadier general, USV (November 29, 1862). After initial service in Missouri, he took charge of a brigade at Pittsburg Landing on the Tennessee River. On the first day at Shiloh he was severely injured when his horse was shot out from under him. Never recovering adequately for active field service, he resigned on November 27, 1862. Returning home, he received his commission shortly thereafter, but it was rejected by the Senate when it was obvious that he could not take the field. He finished out his years, from 1869, as a customs official in New York City.

WILLIAMS, R.S. (?-?)

The inventor of the first Confederate machine gun to actually be fired in combat was Kentuckian R.S. Williams. At the beginning of the war he offered his creation to the Confederate War Department whose Bureau of Ordnance secretly adopted it. It was capable of firing 65 rounds a minute from its single 1.57-caliber barrel while being crank-operated. One battery of these novel weapons saw action at Seven Pines, and on January 14, 1863, Williams was given the authority to raise a battery of Kentuckians to be equipped with his invention. Apparently, this unit saw some action with Williams as its captain.

WILLIAMS, Seth (1822-1866)

Career army staff officer Seth Williams served throughout the Civil War in top staff assignments with the armies in Virginia. A West Pointer (1842) from Maine, he had originally been posted to the artillery. As a staff aide in Mexico, he earned a brevet and in 1853 he formally transferred to the adjutant general's office. In fact, he had already been serving, for three years, as the post adjutant at his alma mater. His Civil War-era assignments included: brevet captain and assistant adjutant general (since August 16, 1853); brevet major and assistant adjutant general (May 11, 1861); major and assistant adjutant general (August 3, 1861); brigadier general, USV (September 23, 1861); assistant adjutant general, Army of the Potomac (ca. September 23, 1861-March 1864); lieutenant colonel and assistant adjutant general (July 17, 1862); and inspector general, Grant's staff (March 1864-February 9, 1866). He served with the Army of the Potomac throughout its campaigns and under its successive commanders: McClellan, Burnside, Hooker, and Meade. With Grant's promotion to overall command, Williams became the inspector for all the armies operating against Richmond. He received brevets through major general in both the volunteer and regular services. Still holding commissions in both services, he had just been assigned to duty as the adjutant for the Military Division of the Atlantic when he was taken ill. He died on March 23, 1866.

WILLIAMS, Thomas (1815-1862)

A strict disciplinarian, Thomas Williams was never able to effectively handle his volunteers, and when he was killed in action there were wild rumors that he had been held in front of a cannon by his own men. Born in New York, he had moved to his father's former Michigan home soon after the close of the War of 1812. Before being appointed to West Point he served as a trumpeter in a militia company during the Black Hawk War. Graduating in 1837, he was posted to the artillery and fought in the Seminole and Mexican wars, earning two brevets in the latter. His Civil War-era assignments included: captain, 4th Artillery (since September 12, 1850); major, 5th Artillery (May 14, 1861); inspector general, Department of Virginia (1861); brigadier general, USV (September 28, 1861); commanding Hatteras Inlet, N.C., Department of Virginia (October 13-December 1861); commanding 4th Brigade, North Carolina Expeditionary Corps (December 1861-February 1862); and commanding 2nd Brigade, New Orleans Expeditionary Corps, Department of the Gulf (March-August 5, 1862). After recruiting and staff assignments he was given charge of the land forces operating in Hatteras Inlet where he soon ran into problems with his volunteers. His harsh discipline and rigorous schedule brought him into conflict with many of his officers, especially his predecessor, Colonel Rush C. Hawkins. His overworked soldiers even dug pitfalls for him. When climbing out of one he fell immediately into a second—to the pleasure of the troops. Instead of taking part in Burnside's expedition he was assigned to Butler for the operations against New Orleans. Again, on Ship Island, he came into conflict with his volunteers over his regime. After New Orleans fell he was sent to Baton Rouge and later took part in early operations against Vicksburg, including work on a canal to isolate the river city. Failing in this, he returned to Baton Rouge where he arrested several of his officers for refusing to return fugitive slaves. In return, charges were laid against him for his behavior and his failure to react effectively when his transports were shelled by a Rebel battery. Accounts of his defense of Baton Rouge on August 5, 1862, vary; some claim he had no defensive plan. During the fight he was killed. Official accounts say he was shot in the heart, but Butler's unofficial account states that he was decapitated by a cannonball. The vessel carrying his coffin to New Orleans sank in a collision. All of the charges were dropped at that time.

WILLIAMS, Thomas Henry (1822-1904)

In order to improve the medical treatment of wounded Confederate soldiers, Thomas H. Williams made the sensible, but not always practical, request that there be more coordination between the medical department and the high command in regard to troop movements. The native Marylander had received his medical education in that state and in 1849 joined the regular army as an assistant surgeon. Resigning on June 1, 1861, he offered his services to the South and was appointed a full surgeon. He was a director and inspector during the first year of the war in Virginia and served as an assistant to the surgeon general. As such he was responsible for many of the hospitals and the medical staffs themselves in their organization. In 1863 he served for a time as the medical director of the Army of Northern Virginia, where he found that even the high command did not always have an early enough warning of impending battles to alert the surgeons and so facilitate the accumulation and transport of medical equipment and supplies. After the war he retired to private practice in Virginia and then Maryland. (Cunningham, Horace Herndon, *Doctors in Gray*)

WILLIAMS, William Orton (?-1863)

One of the mysteries of the Civil War is what was William Orton Williams up to when he was captured and executed as a spy by the Union authorities. Born in New York, the son of a Virginian army officer who was killed in the war with Mexico, William Orton Williams had been a lieutenant in the 2nd Cavalry when the Civil War began. When Virginia seceded, he resigned his position on the staff of General Scott and offered his services to the Confederacy. As a lieutenant he served on the staff of General Leonidas Polk in western Tennessee. At the battle of Shiloh and in the subsequent siege at Corinth he was assistant artillery chief to General Braxton Bragg, with the rank of captain. On April 2, 1863, he was appointed a colonel, under the assumed name Lawrence W. Orton, and ordered to report to General Joseph Wheeler. Then, on June 8, 1863, he and a cousin, Walter G. Peter, went behind Union lines posing as Union inspectors. Posing as "Colonel Lawrence W. Auton" and "Major George Dunlop," they visited Fort Granger, told their story, and even borrowed $50 from the commander before going on their way. However, suspicions were aroused and they were brought back for further questioning. Their identities revealed, they were tried as spies at three in the morning and hanged a few hours later. Williams, sometimes identified as Lawrence Orton Williams, is now believed to have been on his way to Canada to take ship for Europe on a diplomatic or ordnance purchasing mission. After the war, Robert E. Lee, whose wife was related to Williams, was still outraged by the hanging. (Freeman, Douglas S., *R.E. Lee*)

WILLIAMSON, James Alexander (1829-1902)

Although a novice in military matters, James A. Williamson rose rapidly to the rank of brevet major general, winning the Congressional Medal of Honor on the way. The native Kentuckian had been raised in Indiana and Iowa where he became a lawyer and Democratic politician. His military assignments included: first lieutenant and adjutant, 4th Iowa (August 8, 1861); lieutenant colonel, 4th Iowa (April 4, 1862); colonel, 4th Iowa (July 21, 1862); commanding 3rd Brigade, 1st Division, 15th Corps, Army of the Tennessee (August 1-September 15, 1863, November 1-December 28, 1864, and December 31, 1864-January 15, 1865); commanding 2nd Brigade, 1st Division, 15th Corps, Army of the Tennessee (September 1-December 28, 1863 and May 5-September 25, 1864); brigadier general, USV (April 1, 1865, to rank from January 13, 1865); and commanding District of St. Louis, Department of the Missouri (June 20-July 21, 1865). He fought as the regimental adjutant at Pea Ridge and the next month became a field officer. While still serving in Arkansas he was advanced to colonel and then led the unit east of the Mississippi. There he gallantly directed the charge of his regiment at Chickasaw Bayou and then held on to his position after the supporting troops were withdrawn. For this the regiment was authorized by Grant to inscribe "First at Chickasaw Bayou" on its colors. Williamson himself received the nation's highest medal for this battle in 1895. He then took part in the seizure of Fort Hindman, or Arkansas Post. Ill-health forced him to relinquish command of his regiment during the Vicksburg siege, but he returned to duty in time to command a brigade in the relief of Chattanooga. He continued in this higher position during the Atlanta and Savannah campaigns. For the latter three operations he was brevetted brigadier general on December 19, 1864, and the next spring was given the full rank. After some months of leave at home, he commanded at St. Louis and then served on the Plains. Brevetted major general for the war, he was mustered out on August 24, 1865, and resumed his political activities—this time as a Republican. He was also active in railroading and served as a land commissioner.

WILLICH, August (1810-1878)

Drawing upon his service in the Prussian army, August Willich directed his regiment—both on the parade ground and the battlefield—by Prussian bugle calls, a unique system for the Union army. Born in Braunsberg, Prussia, he had graduated from the military academy in 1825. A social reformer, he turned communist and in 1846 resigned with other officers. However, their letters of resignation were so revolutionary in tone that they were hauled before a court-martial before being permitted to resign. He fought with the revolutionaries in Baden in 1848 and then fled to the United States. Settling in New York for a time, he worked as a carpenter before moving to Cincinnati where he became a leader of the refugee 48ers. The editorial slant of the newspaper he founded for the German-speaking community there earned him the nickname "Reddest of the Red." In a matter of 24 hours he and other 48ers managed to raise the 9th Ohio from the German community for the Union army. His assignments included: first lieutenant and adjutant, 9th Ohio (May 8, 1861); major, 9th Ohio (June 13, 1861); colonel, 32nd Indiana (August 24, 1861); brigadier general, USV (July 17, 1862); commanding 6th Brigade, 2nd Division, Army of the Ohio (August 10-September 29, 1862); and commanding in the Army of the Cumberland: 1st Brigade, 2nd Division, Right Wing, 14th Corps (November 5-December 31, 1862); 1st Brigade, 2nd Division, 20th Corps (May 28-September 19, 1863); the division (September 19-October 9, 1863); 1st Brigade, 3rd Division, 4th Corps (October 10, 1863-January 8, 1864); the division (January 8-February 12, 1864); and again 1st Brigade, 3rd Division, 4th Corps (May 3-15, 1864 and June 2-August 1, 1865). He distinguished himself with the Ohio regiment in western Virginia at Rich Mountain and Carnifax Ferry. Promoted to the colonelcy of an Indiana German regiment, he defeated Terry's Texas Rangers in November 1861. As part of Buell's reinforcing army, he fought at Shiloh on the second day. After serving in the advance on Corinth, he was named brigadier general. His regiment returned to Kentucky, but Willich was not present at Perryville. On the first day at Murfreesboro, while commanding a brigade, he had his horse shot from under him and was taken prisoner. Not exchanged until May 1863, he led the brigade in the Tullahoma Campaign and took over the division at Chickamauga. Again at the head of the brigade, he fought at Chattanooga. In the Atlanta Campaign he was so severely wounded in the shoulder at Resaca that he was forced to give up field duty. Stationed at Cincinnati for the balance of the war, he again commanded his brigade after the close of hostilities and was sent to Texas. Brevetted major general for the war on October 21, 1865, he was mustered out the following January 15. After a few years as a public official he returned to Europe during the Franco-Prussian War and had his services rejected on account of age by the same monarch, Wilhelm I, whom he had earlier tried to dethrone. After studying under Karl Marx he returned to the United States.

WILLIS, Edward S. (1840-1864)

When Grant began his relentless drive on Richmond in May 1864, the effect on the Confederate general officers' corps was devastating. This opened the way for the promotion of younger officers, such as Edward S. Willis, many of whom did not last long enough in their new positions to actually receive their new commissions. A native of Georgia, Willis had been attending classes at West Point when the war began. He promptly resigned his commission and offered his services to the Confederacy. His assignments included: first lieutenant and adjutant, 12th Georgia (July 5, 1861); lieutenant colonel, 12th Georgia (December 13, 1862); colonel, 12th Georgia (January 22, 1863); and commanding Pegram's Brigade, Early's-Gordon's Division, 2nd Corps, Army of Northern Virginia (ca. May 5-30, 1864). After serving in western Virginia, including actions at Greenbrier and Alleghany, he was detailed to Stonewall Jackson's staff, part of the time serving as assistant chief of artillery. During the Shenandoah Valley Campaign he was briefly captured at Port Republic while trying to rally a Union cavalry unit he mistook for Confederates. Feigning illness, he later made good his escape. Serving with Jackson, he participated in the Seven Days Battles, Cedar Mountain, and 2nd Bull Run. With the death of the 12th's lieutenant colonel at Fredericksburg and the resignation of its colonel the next month, Willis became a colonel. He distinguished himself at Chancellorsville and was heavily engaged on the first day at Gettysburg. After a stint of detached service with his regiment in the Valley in the winter of 1863-64, he rejoined Lee to face Grant in the spring. After General John Pegram was wounded at the Wilderness, Willis was transferred to temporary command of the Virginia brigade. He saw action at Spotsylvania and the North Anna. On May 30, 1864, in a futile charge at Bethesda Church, he fell mortally wounded. He died the next day after having been visited by men from his old command. (Thomas, Henry W., *The History of the Doles-Cook Brigade, Army of Northern Virginia, 1861-1865*)

WILLISTON, Edward Bancroft (1837-1920)

By the use of some daring artillery tactics Vermonter Edward B. Williston earned himself a Congressional Medal of Honor. He had been living in San Francisco at the outbreak of the Civil War when he received a commission in the regular army. His assignments included: second lieutenant, Battery D, 2nd Artillery (August 5, 1861); first lieutenant, Battery D, 2nd Artillery (September 27, 1861); and captain, Battery D, 2nd Artillery (March 8, 1865). He served with his guns at 1st Bull Run, the Seven Days, South Mountain, Antietam, and Fredericksburg. Earning brevets for Chancellorsville and Gettysburg, he went on to participate in Grant's Overland Campaign, with his battery converted to horse artillery. Then during Sheridan's raid Williston distinguished himself and earned his medal in the fighting at Trevilian Station, where he brought up his battery at a critical moment and personally took one piece onto the skirmish line, an unusual use of artillery in the Civil War. He later fought in the Shenandoah Valley and earned another brevet for 3rd Winchester. Near the close of the war he received a fourth brevet, to colonel, for his war services. Remaining in the regular army after the war, he retired in 1900 as a full colonel of artillery, having served as a brigadier general of volunteers in the Spanish-American War. (Mitchell, Joseph B., *The Badge of Gallantry*)

WILMOT, David (1814-1868)

Pennsylvania Congressman David Wilmot's most important contribution to the sectional conflict over slavery was his proposal of the so-called "Wilmot Proviso" during the Mexican War. Having taken up the practice of law in 1834, the native Pennsylvanian became a Jacksonian Democrat. He favored labor organization and hard money and opposed debtor's imprisonment. He served three terms in the U.S. House of Representatives, from 1845 to 1851, but did not seek reelection in 1850. In 1846 he had proposed an amendment to an appropriations bill that would eliminate slavery from any lands gained in the war with Mexico. Cheered in the North, he was roundly condemned in the South. The amendment failed but it quickly became a cause celebre. In 1847 and 1848 he attended the conventions of the free-soil Democrats. In 1853 he became a judge and held the post until the beginning of the Civil War. In the meantime he had been one of the organizers of the new Republican Party and had drafted its 1856 platform. In 1857 he lost a gubernatorial bid. Three years later he was a delegate and the temporary chairman of the Republican national convention which nominated Lincoln. When Simon Cameron became Lincoln's secretary of war, Wilmot took over Cameron's senatorial seat, on March 14, 1861, and held it until the expiration of the term on March 3, 1863. He had been a member of the Washington Peace Conference in early 1861 and backed the war effort during his tenure. For the final five years of his life he was a claims judge.

WILSON, Claudius Charles (1831-1863)

Native Georgia lawyer Claudius C. Wilson served only 11 days as a Confederate brigadier general before succumbing to disease. His assignments included: captain, Company I, 25th Georgia (summer 1861); colonel, 25th Georgia (September 2, 1861); commanding brigade, Walker's Division, Department of the West (June-July 1863); commanding brigade, Walker's Division, Department of Mississippi and East Louisiana (July-August 23, 1863); commanding brigade, Walker's Division, Hill's Corps, Army of Tennessee (August 25-September 1863); commanding brigade, Walker's Division, Reserve Corps, Army of Tennessee (September 1863); commanding brigade, Walker's Division, Longstreet's Corps, Army of Tennessee (September 26-November 12, 1863); commanding brigade, Walker's Division, Hardee's Corps, Army of Tennessee (November 12-27, 1863); and brigadier general, CSA (November 16, 1863). Elected colonel of his regiment upon its organization, he served on the Georgia and South Carolina coasts until ordered to join Joseph E. Johnston in his efforts to relieve the pressure on Vicksburg in the spring and summer of 1863. In Mississippi he led a brigade during these operations and the subsequent defense of Jackson. Joining the Army of Tennessee, he fought at Chickamauga. Promoted to brigadier general, he fought at Chattanooga but died a couple of days later, on November 27, of camp fever.

WILSON, George D. (?-1862)

When seven of the Andrews' Raiders were executed on June 18, 1862, George Wilson, one of the condemned, made a brief address to the bloodthirsty crowd of onlookers. While serving as a private in Company B, 2nd Ohio, Wilson had been tapped to take part in the raid under the command of a civilian, James J. Andrews. With the failed raid coming to an end after an 87-mile chase, the raiders abandoned the stolen locomotive, *The General*, and tried to return to the Union lines. Wilson and three others tried to make it out of Georgia as a group but were tracked down with dogs and caught in less than a day. Twelve of the 22 captives confined at Chattanooga were chosen at random to be sent to Knoxville to stand trial as train thieves and, since they were in civilian clothes, as spies. Seven were tried and sentenced to hang before Union activity in the area caused the prisoners to be sent to Atlanta. Here, at 4:30 P.M. on June 18 they were taken to the gallows. Mounting the scaffold, Wilson warned the spectators that since they were Union soldiers on a military mission, the Federal government would be forced to execute prisoners in retaliation. He also assured them that the Union would be restored. Then the seven were promptly hanged. The raiders were later given the Congressional Medal of Honor for their sacrifice. (O'Neill, Charles, *Wild Train: The Story of the Andrews Raiders*)

WILSON, Henry (1812-1875)

A longtime abolitionist and organizer of the Republican Party, Henry Wilson served as the chairman of the Senate's Committee on Military Affairs throughout the Civil War. Born Jeremiah Jones Colbaith in New Hampshire, he had his name changed to Henry Wilson in 1833 when he moved to Massachusetts and became a shoemaker. His 1836 travels through the South influenced him greatly in his antislavery views. Upon his return he resumed his trade and taught school. As an early abolitionist he faced much criticism, even in the North, at a time when the movement was not yet popular. He served in the state legislature in 1841 and 1842. He was in the state senate from 1844 to 1846 and 1850 to 1852. In the last two years he was that body's president. In 1848 he had been a delegate to the Whig national convention but withdrew when that body failed to adopt an antislavery plank in its platform. That same year he became the owner/editor of the *Boston Republican* and continued publishing it until 1851. He was president of the free-soil convention of 1852. That year he lost a congressional bid as a Free-Soiler and the next one for the governorship. When Edward Everett resigned from the U.S. Senate, Wilson was selected by a coalition of antislavery elements to replace him. Repeatedly reelected, he held the office until his resignation on March 3, 1873, in order to become Grant's second vice president the next day. During his senatorial tenure he was active in the issues involved in the sectional conflict, and in 1861 he became chairman of the military committee. His friendship with Rose O'Neal Greenhow, who turned out to be a Confederate spy, may have cost the Union many military secrets. Early in the war he raised, and briefly commanded as a colonel, the 22nd Massachusetts. A staunch supporter of the war effort, he continued in the committee chairmanship until his resignation from the Senate. He died while serving as Grant's vice president. In his final years he compiled the information for his massive *History of the Rise and Fall of the Slave Power in America*. This work drew upon his intimate knowledge of the long struggle to abolish the "peculiar institution."

WILSON, James Harrison (1837-1925)

Transferring from staff duties to field command late in the war, James H. Wilson led one of the most celebrated raids of the Civil War and defeated Nathan Bedford Forrest. The Illinois native had graduated sixth in his 1860 West Point class and, as a topographical engineer, served on the West Coast until the outbreak of hostilities. His later assignments included: brevet second lieutenant, Topographical Engineers (since July 1, 1860); second lieutenant, Topographical Engineers (June 10, 1861); first lieutenant, Topographical Engineers (September 9, 1861); chief topographical engineer, South Carolina Expeditionary Corps (1861-March 15, 1862); chief topographical engineer, Department of the South (March 15-mid-1862); volunteer aide-de-camp, Army of the Potomac (September 1862); chief topographical engineer, Army of the Tennessee (October 17, 1862-March 3, 1863); lieutenant colonel and assistant inspector general (November 8, 1862-November 17, 1863); first lieutenant, Engineers (merger of the two branches March 3, 1863); assistant engineer and inspector general, Army of the Tennessee (March 3-October 31, 1863); captain, Engineers (May 7, 1863); brigadier general, USV (October 30, 1863); chief of Cavalry Bureau (February 17-April 7, 1864); commanding 3rd Division, Cavalry Corps, Army of the Potomac (April 13-August 6, 1864); commanding 3rd Division, Cavalry Corps, Army of the Shenandoah (August 6-September 30, 1864); commanding Cavalry Corps, Military Division of the Mississippi (October 29, 1864-June 26, 1865); and major general, USV (June 21, to date from May 6, 1865). Serving as the chief topographer of the expedition against the South Carolina coast, he took part in the capture of Port Royal and then, in the same position for the Department of the South, he was brevetted for the reduction of Fort Pulaski at the mouth of the Savannah River. As a volunteer aide to McClellan he took part in the fighting at South Mountain and Antietam before joining Grant for the Vicksburg Campaign. He won another brevet for Chattanooga and took part in Sherman's relief expedition to Knoxville. After brief service as head of the Cavalry Bureau in Washington with the rank of brigadier general of volunteers—during which time he did much to revitalize that branch—he took charge of a mounted division for the Overland Campaign. He was brevetted for the Wilderness and remained in the saddle until his command was transferred from the Petersburg front to the Shenandoah. He fought at 3rd Winchester before being tapped to lead the mounted troops in the West. At the head of his corps he played a leading role in the virtual annihilation and vigorous pursuit of the Army of Tennessee at Nashville. Brevetted brigadier general in the regular establishment for this—he had already been made a major general by brevet in the volunteers, on October 5, 1864—he led his troopers through Alabama. He was brevetted major general for the capture of Selma and part of his command captured Jefferson Davis. Following the close of hostilities he was awarded a second star. Mustered out of the volunteers on January 8, 1866, he continued to perform engineering duties despite having been named lieutenant colonel of the 35th Infantry in the expansion of the military later that year. At his own request he left the army in 1870 to enter the railroad business. During this time he was active in the field of historical writing and compiled biographies of many of his fellow officers. He again served as a general officer of volunteers during the Spanish-American War and the Boxer Rebellion. He was retired as a brigadier general in the regular army in 1901 and attended the coronation of Edward VII as the representative of Theodore Roosevelt. (Longacre, Edward G., *From Union Stars to Top Hat: A Biography of the Extraordinary General James Harrison Wilson*)

WILSON, Robert (1803-1870)

As acting president of the Missouri secession convention, Robert Wilson did much to retain the state for the Union. Born in Virginia, he had moved to Missouri in 1820 and become a teacher. In 1825 he became a probate judge and four years later began an 11-year stint as a court clerk. In 1837 he served as a brigadier general of state troops in the Mormon War in Utah. Admitted to the bar in 1840, he took up private practice and four years later took a seat in the legislature. In 1854 he sat as a state senator. A Unionist delegate to the convention, called to determine the relationship between the state and the national government, he was elected its vice president. In its later stages he was the acting presiding officer. With the expulsion of Senator Waldo P. Johnson, Wilson was named as a Unionist to succeed him and took his seat on January 17, 1862. He relinquished his seat when a permanent successor, B. Gratz Brown, was admitted on November 13, 1863. Wilson then took up farming.

WINCHESTER, Oliver Fisher (1810-1880)

Although his Winchester Rifle, of Wild West fame, was not developed until a year after the close of the Civil War, Oliver F. Winchester still had a substantial impact on the firearms used in that conflict. A native of Massachusetts, he had been engaged in the manufacture of men's clothing before becoming president of the reorganized New Haven Arms Company in 1857. Although mainly producing sporting weapons, he gave his superintendent, Tyler Henry, free reign in experimentation on improved models. The resulting Henry Rifle was a repeater with rim-fire copper cartridges. While the War Department considered the piece too fragile for army use, many units equipped themselves with it at their own expense. It was also popular with citizens and militia in areas threatened by Confederate raids. After the war Winchester obtained the rights to a method allowing loading through the frame gate. Merging this with the Henry Rifle, he developed the Winchester. As head of the Winchester Repeating Arms Company he remained in business until the time of his death.

WINDER, Charles Sidney (1829-1862)

A harsh disciplinarian, Charles S. Winder was not one of the more popular commanders of the Stonewall Brigade. Winder was a West Pointer (1850) from Maryland who had served in the artillery until his April 1, 1861, resignation. His assignments for the South included: major, Artillery (to rank from March 16, 1861); colonel, 6th South Carolina (July 8, 1861); brigadier general, CSA (March 1, 1862); commanding G.B. Anderson's (old) Brigade (the old garrison at Manassas), D.H. Hill's Division, Department of Northern Virginia (March 25-April 2, 1862); commanding Stonewall Brigade (in Jackson's Division from May), Valley District, same department (April 2-June 26, 1862); commanding Stonewall Brigade, Jackson's Division, 2nd Corps, Army of Northern Virginia (June 26-August 9, 1862); and commanding the division (August 9, 1862). He held a staff position during the bombardment of Fort Sumter and then headed the 6th South Carolina on the Manassas lines. He held a brigade command there for a few days before being sent to the Valley. Unpopular as an outsider with the brigade, his regular army ways offended even Jackson when he had 30 men bucked and gagged; a very cruel but common punishment. Some men promised that Winder would not survive his next battle. Winder proved a mediator in the problems between Jackson and Turner Ashby. He fought throughout the Valley Campaign and with Lee during the Seven Days. At Cedar Mountain he led the division when the senior brigadier A.R. Lawton, had conveniently been left behind to guard the wagon trains. The Confederacy lost his services when he was mortally wounded by a shell that day. (Robertson, James I., Jr., *The Stonewall Brigade*)

WINDER, John Henry (1800-1865)

If Marylander John H. Winder had survived the Civil War, he, rather than Henry Wirz, would probably have been hanged for the treatment of Union prisoners of war. The West Pointer (1820) had served with the artillery and riflemen before resigning as a second lieutenant in 1823. Four years later he was reinstated with his previous rank. During the Mexican War he won two brevets, and during times of peace he was a professor of tactics at his alma mater. Resigning as a major in the 3rd Artillery on April 27, 1861, he joined the Confederacy. His Southern assignments included: brigadier general, CSA (June 21, 1861); commanding Department of Henrico (October 21, 1861-May 5, 1864); and commanding 2nd Military District, Department of North Carolina and Southern Virginia (May 25-June 9, 1864). Assigned to duty as provost marshal in Richmond, his duties included guarding prisoners of war on Belle Isle and at Libby Prison. Eventually placed in military command of the capital's vicinity, his powers over the lives of the inhabitants were expanded, with the normal resentment developing. In the spring of 1864 he took command in the area around Goldsboro, North Carolina, but in June was assigned to command the prisoner of war camp at Andersonville. A month later his powers were expanded over all such camps in Alabama as well as Georgia. On November 21, 1864, he was placed in charge of all camps east of the Mississippi. Already despised in the South, he now aroused a similar feeling in the North. There were accusations that he was deliberately attempting to starve the Union captives, but in actuality it was the extreme shortage of supplies and the lack of an effective distribution network that was responsible. The strenuous nature of his work proved too much for him and he died at Florence, South Carolina, on February 7, 1865.

WING, Henry E. (ca. 1839-19 ?)

The Civil War correspondent's job was just beginning when a battle ended. Getting the story to the editor was often a frustrating and dangerous enterprise. Henry Wing, carrying the story of the first day's battle in the Wilderness, managed to be escorted by Mosby's guerrillas, then pursued by them, fed by New York Cavalry, detained by rebel cavalry, and ordered arrested as a spy by Secretary of War Stanton. Graduating from law school, Wing had enlisted in the 27th Connecticut in September 1862 and become a color corporal. While in camp he wrote for the *New Haven Palladium*. Being wounded out of the army at Fredericksburg, he became a reporter for the *Norwich Bulletin* before being picked up by the *New York Tribune*. Eventually growing bored with covering the Senate, he was assigned as a courier for the *Tribune*'s reporters with the Army of the Potomac. He was almost immediately promoted to reporter. After covering the 2nd Corps in the first day at the Wilderness, he, as junior reporter, volunteered for the hazardous journey through Mosby country to deliver the pooled reports. After a series of adventures he reached a Union camp equipped with a telegraph—restricted to military use. When Stanton asked for his report, Wing demanded to be able to send it on to his paper as well. Stanton ordered his arrest, but Lincoln shortly agreed to the report being sent to the journal and then sent a train for Wing. Giving a fuller report in a 2 A.M. meeting at the White House, Wing was kissed by the president when he gave Grant's personal message that there would be no turning back under any circumstances. Wing's scoop, which at Lincoln's request was shared with the Associated Press, was the only news of the fighting that the government received that day. The next day Lincoln provided Wing with a cavalry and artillery escort to retrieve his horse which he had secreted in a thicket when chased by Mosby's men. Returning to the front, he covered the rest of the war but now with a special government contact, the president. Immediately after Appomattox, he took over as co-publisher of the *Litchfield Enquirer*, just in time to report his friend Lincoln's death in his first issue. After the war he continued in journalism and then moved into advertising and the law before entering the ministry. (Starr, Louis M., *Bohemian Brigade*)

WINKLER, William M. (1831-1890)

The Civil War was a period during which most of the Congressional Medals of Honor were awarded for actions involving battle flags, either carrying one's own or capturing the enemy's. Many other courageous acts were neglected—like that of William Winkler at Fair Garden, Tennessee, on January 26, 1864. Winkler had been a Polish officer in the Prussian army before immigrating to the United States in 1849. A prewar railroad surveyor and farmer, he became the first sergeant in Company L, 4th Indiana Cavalry. This unit served in actions in Kentucky, Tennessee, and Georgia. Then at Fair Garden, during the East Tennessee Campaign, Winkler, with only four men, came upon a retreating rebel artillery section. They charged and Winkler himself sabered the enemy lieutenant, killed another man, and wounded four more. Wounding a horse, he brought the two enemy guns to a bloody halt. His four companions, who had fallen behind, came up and captured the remaining rebels. The only recognition Winkler received for this action was to be cited briefly in brigade and division reports for gallantry, without a description of the affair. He subsequently served in the Atlanta Campaign and in Wilson's raid before returning to civil life at the end of the war. After the war he was a bookkeeper, surveyor, real estate and loan broker, and also served as postmaster in Columbus, Indiana. (Rowell, John W., *Yankee Artillerymen: Through the Civil War With Eli Lilly's Indiana Battery*)

WINSLOW, Edward Francis (1837-1914)

Maine-born Iowa businessman Edward F. Winslow became one of the leading cavalry officers in the Mississippi Valley although he never received a full promotion above the grade of colonel. His assignments included: captain, Company F, 4th Iowa Cavalry (November 23, 1861); major, 4th Iowa Cavalry (February 6, 1863); colonel, 4th Iowa Cavalry (July 4, 1863); commanding Cavalry Brigade, 15th Corps, Army of the Tennessee (August 8-December 1863); commanding Cavalry Brigade, 17th Corps, Army of the Tennessee (December 1863-April 1864); commanding 2nd Brigade, 1st Cavalry Division, 16th Corps, Army of the Tennessee (April-June 20, 1864); commanding 2nd Division, Cavalry Corps, District of West Tennessee, Army of the Tennessee (June-October 1864); commanding 1st Brigade, 4th Division, Cavalry Corps, Military Division of the Mississippi (November 9, 1864-June 26, 1865); also commanding 2nd Brigade, Cavalry Division, District of West Tennessee, Army of the Tennessee (December 1864-February 1865); and also commanding 4th Division, Cavalry Corps, Military Division of the Mississippi (April 20-June 26, 1865). As a company commander he served in Missouri and Arkansas and was stationed at Helena until April 1863, by which time he had become a field officer. During the Vicksburg Campaign, he was wounded at Mechanicsburg on May 29, 1863. He recovered to take part in the Canton expedition later in the year and the Meridian Campaign early the next. Serving in the District of West Tennessee—with headquarters in Memphis—he took part in the operations against Nathan Bedford Forrest, including Brice's Crossroads, Tupelo, and under Andrew J. Smith in August 1864. In the final stages of the war he succeeded to division command during Wilson's raid in Alabama and Georgia. Mustered out with his regiment on August 10, 1865—with the brevet of brigadier general from December 12, 1864—he was active in railroads across the country after the war.

WINSLOW, John Ancrum (1811-1873)

Union naval officer John A. Winslow spent much of his Civil War career chasing after Raphael Semmes and his Confederate raider *Alabama*. Winslow had entered the navy in 1827 and by the time of the firing on Fort Sumter was a lieutenant. Promoted to captain on July 16, 1862, he commanded the USS *Kearsarge* for much of the war. He finally caught up with his quest in June of 1864 outside of Cherbourg Harbor in France. The raider had taken sanctuary there for some repair work and refueling. Setting up a blockade of the port, Winslow soon learned that Semmes planned to come out and fight him. The battle took place on June 19 after Winslow had made sure that they were outside French territorial waters. In 80 minutes the *Alabama* was forced to strike her colors. Winslow was outraged when Semmes made his own escape aboard a British yacht. The *Alabama* soon sank and Winslow became a hero. (Ellicott, John M., *The Life of John Ancrum Winslow*)

WINTHROP, Theodore (1828-1861)

A Yale graduate, Theodore Winthrop had been a writer of some promise when his life was cut short by the Civil War. Serving in the 7th New York Militia, he went to the defense of Washington in April 1861 and did not return to New York when the regiment was mustered out in early June. Instead, he joined the staff of General Benjamin F. Butler as a major. On the 10th of that month he accompanied the expedition to Big Bethel. In the battle there he was killed while standing on a fence waving on the attacking Union forces with his sword. (Johnson, Laura W., *The Life and Poems of Theodore Winthrop*)

Captain John A. Winslow (3rd from left) and officers of the *Kearsarge*, victors over the CSS *Alabama*. (NA)

WIRZ, Henry (1823-1865)

If Confederate General John H. Winder, had not died in February 1865, the victorious Union would probably have hanged him instead of Andersonville commandant Henry Wirz, and would probably have granted Wirz's request to return to his native Zürich, Switzerland. But the North needed a scapegoat. Educated in Zürich, Paris, and Berlin, Wirz had immigrated to Kentucky in 1849 and was practicing medicine in Louisiana at the outbreak of the Civil War. His Confederate assignments included: private, Company D, 4th Louisiana Battalion (June 16, 1861); lieutenant, 4th Louisiana Battalion (1861); captain and assistant adjutant general (August 1862); and major and assistant adjutant general (ca. 1863). Severely wounded at Seven Pines, his right arm was virtually paralyzed for life. Named as a staff officer, he was assigned to duty at the Tuscaloosa military prison in Alabama but was granted leave to visit Europe. Upon his return he served as a dispatch bearer until ordered to direct the interior of the Andersonville prison. He took command in March 1864 and held it until the end of the war. After awaiting capture at the camp, he was at first given a safe-conduct but was then sent to Washington for trial by a military tribunal. All his objections were overruled, and the trial proceeded with contradictory evidence of his having taken part in the killing of prisoners. It was clear, however, that he had felt no need to exceed his orders in order to improve conditions. Convicted, he was sentenced to hang. With four companies chanting "Remember Andersonville," and 250 other curiosity seekers, the sentence was carried out in a bungled manner. (McElroy, John, *Andersonville: A Story of Rebel Military Prisons*)

WISE, Henry Alexander (1806-1876)

Virginia governor at the time that John Brown went to the gallows, Henry A. Wise had no military experience but became one of the more colorful brigadiers in Lee's army. His prewar career had included the practice of law in Tennessee and Virginia, sitting as a states' rights member of congress, a post as diplomatic representative to Brazil, as well as chief executive of the Old Dominion. Entering the Confederate military, he held the following assignments: brigadier general, CSA (June 5, 1861); commanding District of the Albemarle, Department of Norfolk (December 21, 1861-February 23, 1862); commanding Wise's Command, Army of Northern Virginia (June-July 1862); commanding brigade, D.H. Hill's Division, Army of Northern Virginia (July 1862); commanding brigade, Department of Virginia and North Carolina (August-December 1862); commanding brigade, Elzey's Command, same department (December 1862-April 1, 1863); commanding brigade,

Henry Wirz's domain: the prison at Andersonville. (AC)

Department of Richmond (April 1-September 1863); commanding 6th Military District of South Carolina, Department of South Carolina, Georgia and Florida (October 22, 1863-May 1864); commanding brigade, Whiting's Division, Department of North Carolina and Southern Virginia (mid-May 1864); commanding brigade, Johnson's Division, same department (May-June 1, 1864); commanding 1st Military District, same department (June 1-December 1864); and commanding brigade, Johnson's Division, Anderson's Corps, Army of Northern Virginia (December 1864-April 9, 1865). After service at the head of the Wise Legion in the Kanawha Valley of western Virginia, he was transferred to eastern North Carolina because of difficulties with another commander in the region, John B. Floyd. He was in command when Union General Burnside captured Roanoke Island in February 1862. His son was mortally wounded in this action. Subsequently he served in the Seven Days and for about a year in the Richmond Defenses. Once requested to report at his commander's headquarters as early in the morning as possible, he showed up before six. In the fall of 1863 he was transferred to South Carolina and remained there until the following spring. He fought at Drewry's Bluff and then commanded a district in the Petersburg area during the siege. In the retreat to Appomattox, he proved that he had learned something of the art of war by keeping his command together and bringing it out of the debacle at Sayler's Creek as a unit. In the last days before Appomattox he wore what looked like war paint. Actually, he had washed in a muddy stream and his face was streaked. He died without ever accepting amnesty. (Wise, Barton H., *The Life of Henry A. Wise of Virginia*)

WISE, John (1808-?1879)

The premier balloonist in the United States, John Wise, initially entered his country's service in the infantry and may well have wished that he had remained there. Instead, the Pennsylvania veteran of 26 years in the air, who had offered to bomb Vera Cruz during the Mexican War, was asked to construct and direct a balloon to accompany the Union army in the field. Agreeing to do so without pay, in July 1861 he raced to join McDowell's army in time for the battle of 1st Bull Run. When the military leader of the detail manning the inflated balloon, Chief Signal Officer Albert J. Myer, attached a horsedrawn wagon to the balloon to achieve more speed, it became entangled in some trees and deflated. This had been done over Wise's protest, but he had no official status. Returning to the capital, Wise made a successful ascent and observed the enemy movements from Arlington Heights. Again ordered closer to the front, Wise was frustrated when the tow ropes were severed by telegraph lines. Wise ordered the runaway craft shot down to prevent its falling into enemy hands. Leaving Washington after this failure, he raised a cavalry company. After the war, he was a librarian before resuming ballooning. In 1879 Wise and his passengers were lost when their balloon vanished over Lake Michigan.

WISTAR, Isaac Jones (1827-1905)

One of the numerous, able regimental commanders who failed to measure up as general officers was Philadelphia native Isaac J. Wistar. A lawyer by profession, he had raised a company at the outbreak of the war and his assignments included: captain, 71st Pennsylvania (June 1861); lieutenant colonel, 71st Pennsylvania (June 28, 1861); colonel, 71st Pennsylvania (November 11, 1861); brigadier general, USV (March 16, 1863, to rank from November 29, 1862); commanding Reserve Brigade, 7th Corps, Department of Virginia (May 13-June 1863); commanding Wistar's Independent Brigade, 7th Corps, Department of Virginia (June-July 1863); commanding U.S. Forces Yorktown (in District of Virginia August 12-September 23), 18th Corps, Department of Virginia and North Carolina (August 1-December 22, 1863, January 22-February 16, and March 8-April 28, 1864); commanding 2nd Division, 18th Corps, Army of the James (April 22-May 7, 1864); and commanding 2nd Brigade, 2nd Division, 18th Corps, Army of the James (May 7-18, 1864). After being wounded at Ball's Bluff, he succeeded Edward D. Baker as colonel of the regiment, which was also known as the 1st California. Apparently missing the Peninsula Campaign, he was again wounded at Antietam. Upon his recovery he was promoted to brigadier general and assigned to duty in southeastern Virginia. His next major action came in the operations of Butler at Bermuda Hundred. Apparently he was largely responsible for the Union defeat at Drewry's Bluff on May 16, 1864, in which fellow brigade commander Charles A. Heckman was captured. Two days later, he was relieved of command and on September 15, 1864, he resigned. He resumed his law practice and made several studies of the penal system. He was also in the coal business. (Wistar, Isaac Jones, *Autobiography of Isaac Jones Wistar, 1827-1905*)

WITHERS, Jones Mitchell (1814-1890)

Having twice resigned from the old army, native Alabamian West Pointer (1835) Jones M. Withers rose to the rank of major general in the Confederate service. Posted to the 1st Dragoons, he had resigned as a brevet second lieutenant the very year of his graduation. The Mexican War brought him a commission as lieutenant colonel in the specially authorized 13th Infantry; this he resigned in 1848. A merchant and state legislator in Mobile, he was that city's mayor in the immediate pre-Civil War years. Offering his military talents to the South, his assignments included: colonel, 3rd Alabama (April 28, 1861); brigadier general, CSA (July 10, 1861); commanding District of Alabama, Department of Alabama and West Florida (October 14, 1861-January 27, 1862); commanding Army of Mobile (January 27-February 28, 1862); commanding division, 2nd Corps, Army of the Mississippi (ca. March 29-June 1862); commanding Reserve Corps, Army of the Mississippi (June-July 2, 1862); commanding Reserve Division, Army of the Mississippi (July 2-August 15, 1862); commanding division, Right Wing, Army of the Mississippi (August 15-November 20, 1862); major general, CSA (August 16, 1862, to rank from April 6); commanding division, Polk's Corps, Army of Tennessee (November 20, 1862-August 13, 1863); commanding District of Northern Alabama, Department of Alabama, Mississippi and East Florida (February 6-July 27, 1864); and commanding Alabama Reserve Forces (July 27, 1864-May 1865). Promoted to brigadier general early in the war, he commanded in the vicinity of his hometown. Given command of a division under Albert S. Johnston, he fought at Shiloh and during the Union advance on Corinth, Mississippi. Named a major general, he served in the Perryville and Tullahoma campaigns before being succeeded by Thomas C. Hindman. For the balance of the war he was stationed in Alabama either in district or reserve commands. A postwar merchant and journalist, he again served as mayor and was a federal official.

WOFFORD, William Tatum (1824-1884)

A Georgia lawyer, state legislator, and editor, William T. Wofford voted against secession but nonetheless entered the Confederate army and became a department commander in the final months of the war. He had been a captain in the Mexican War. His assignments included: colonel, 18th Georgia (early 1861); commanding Texas Brigade, Hood's Division, 1st Corps, Army of Northern Virginia (September 1862); brigadier general, CSA (April 23, to date from January 17, 1863); commanding Cobb's (old) Brigade, McLaw's-Kershaw's Division, 1st Corps, same army (ca. January-September 1863 and spring-summer 1864); commanding brigade, McLaw's Division, Longstreet's Corps, Army of Tennessee (fall 1863); and commanding Department of Northern Georgia (January 23-May 2, 1865). After serving in North Carolina and northern Virginia, Wofford joined Hood's Texas Brigade and saw action at Yorktown, West Point, Seven Pines, 2nd Bull Run and Antietam. In the latter action he commanded a brigade. Given charge of Cobb's former command, he led it at Chancellorsville and Gettysburg but arrived too late to participate in the victory at Chickamauga. Apparently not present for the Knoxville Campaign, he next fought at the Wilderness and Spotsylvania. His brigade later served around Richmond and Petersburg and in the Shenandoah, but he was apparently absent. For the last few months of the war he was in command in northern Georgia, principally charged with rounding up deserters and conscripts. After the surrender he was active in railroading, politics, and education. (Freeman, Douglas S., *Lee's Lieutenants*)

WOOD

See: *Powell, Lewis Thornton*

WOOD, Benjamin (1820-1900)

The editor-publisher of the *New York Daily News*, Benjamin Wood served as a Democratic congressman through most of the Civil War. Born in Kentucky, he had moved to New York City with his parents and eventually entered the shipping business with his brother, Fernando Wood. In 1860 he purchased the *News* and directed it until his death four decades later. That same year he was elected to Congress and sat in the House, from

March 4, 1861, to March 3, 1865, when he left office after being defeated for reelection. Throughout his term he proved to be a thorn in the side of Lincoln and the war effort. An associate of Clement Vallandigham, he opposed the firing upon draft rioters by U.S. troops and generally favored an immediate peace. In 1866 and 1867 he sat in the state senate. He again sat in Congress from 1881 to 1883.

WOOD, Fernando (1812-1881)

Like his younger brother Benjamin, Fernando Wood was a harsh critic of the Lincoln administration and the war effort. Born in Philadelphia, he had moved to New York City with his father in 1820 and was engaged in the shipping business from 1831 to 1850. A leader of the Tammany Hall faction of the city's Democratic Party, he was elected to the House of Representatives in 1840 but lost the election two years later. He then became the State Department's dispatch agent for the city, until 1847. After losing an 1850 bid for mayor, he was later successful and headed the city government from 1855 to 1858 and in 1861 and 1862. In 1859 he wrote to Governor Wise of Virginia recommending that John Brown not be hanged as there was too much sympathy for him in the North; Wood feared that it would hurt the South in the long run. At the 1860 Democratic convention in Charleston he headed an anti-Douglas New York delegation which was unseated on a technicality. During the peak of the secession crisis he suggested that New York City leave both the state and the Union and become independent. In 1862 he was elected to Congress again and served from March 4, 1863, to March 3, 1865, once again losing a bid for reelection. He returned to Congress in 1867 and served until his death. (Pleasants, Samuel Augustus, *Fernando Wood of New York*)

Fernando Wood, New York mayor and Lincoln critic. (NA)

WOOD, John (1798-1880)

Leaving office as the governor of Illinois at the beginning of the Civil War, John Wood entered the Union army. An early Illinois settler, from New York, he had opposed the recognition of slavery in a new state constitution and served in the Black Hawk War. He was also mayor of Quincy and served in the state senate before being elected lieutenant governor in 1856. Upon his predecessor's death he moved up to the chief executive's post on March 21, 1860. His term expired on January 14, 1861, in the midst of the secession crisis. He was appointed major of the 65th Illinois, apparently upon its organization on June 5, 1864. This unit was captured at Harpers Ferry and not declared exchanged until April 1863. His later military assignments included: colonel, 137th Illinois (ca. June 5, 1864) and commanding 3rd Brigade, District of Memphis, District of West Tennessee, Department of the Tennessee (June-September 1864). He commanded his brigade in A.J. Smith's August 1864 invasion of Mississippi to find Forrest. The next month, on the 4th, he mustered out with his 100-days unit. He returned home to his business interests. (Davidson, Alexander and Stuve, Bernard, *A Complete History of Illinois from 1673 to 1873*)

WOOD, John Taylor (1830-1904)

Perhaps the most unorthodox of Confederate naval commanders was the grandson of President Zachary Taylor, John Taylor Wood. The Louisiana veteran of the Mexican War had been serving as an assistant professor of seamanship and gunnery at the Naval Academy when he resigned on April 21, 1861, to offer his services to the South. Serving at first with the Virginia forces, he took part in the blockading of the Potomac River. Commissioned a lieutenant in the Confederate Navy on October 4, 1861, he was assigned to the CSS *Virginia* at the beginning of the next year. During the fight with the *Monitor* he commanded the aft gun. After the scuttling of his vessel, Wood took command of a company of sharpshooters which fought at Drewry's Bluff. Given the rank of colonel of cavalry, he was assigned to Jefferson Davis' staff as an aide-de-camp. Chaffing for action, he frequently received permission to launch commando-style raids against the Union fleet. His small boat expeditions had by early 1864 captured two Union gunboats and five other vessels. Then on February 2, during a raid in conjunction with an advance by General Pickett on New Bern, North Carolina, Wood captured the gunboat *Underwriter*. However, he was forced to destroy the prize. By August he was a commander and was given command of the raider *Tallahassee* with which, in less than a month before docking at Fort Fisher, he captured 31 prizes. He declined command of the James River Squadron during the last winter of the war and notified President Davis of Lee's plans to abandon Richmond and

Petersburg. Accompanying the fleeing government, he was briefly captured with Davis in Georgia before making his escape to Cuba. he settled in Nova Scotia and was engaged in the insurance business. (Shingleton, Royce Gordon, *John Taylor Wood: Sea Ghost of the Confederacy*)

WOOD, Sterling Alexander Martin (1823-1891)

There is only a hint of military failure to explain the resignation of Alabamian Sterling A.M. Wood as a Confederate brigadier general. A lawyer, state legislator, and journalist before the Civil War, he was a supporter of the secession movement and the candidacy of John C. Breckinridge for president in 1860. Entering the Confederate army, his assignments included: colonel, 7th Alabama (May 18, 1861); brigadier general, CSA (January 7, 1862); commanding 3rd Brigade, 3rd Corps, Army of the Mississippi (spring-April 6 and April 6-July 2, 1862); commanding brigade, Buckner's Division, Army of the Mississippi (July 2-August 15, 1862); commanding brigade, Buckner's Division, Left Wing, Army of the Mississippi (August 15-October 8 and fall-November 20, 1862); and commanding brigade, Buckner's-Cleburne's Division, Hardee's-Hill's-Breckinridge's Corps, Army of Tennessee (November 20, 1862-October 17, 1863). Initially stationed at Pensacola, he was promoted to brigadier general and became part of the Confederate buildup at Corinth, Mississippi, just prior to Shiloh. There he ably led his brigade and was temporarily disabled by the fall of his mount. Following the defense of Corinth, he embarked upon Bragg's invasion of Kentucky and was severely wounded by a shell at Perryville. He recovered in time to fight at Murfreesboro and then went on to serve in the Tullahoma Campaign. The battle of Chickamauga proved to be his last. His division commander, Patrick R. Cleburne, failed to praise him in his battle report. Less than a month later he resigned, on October 17, 1863. He resumed his law practice and in the 1880s sat in the state legislature again.

WOOD, Thomas John (1823-1906)

It is somewhat ironic that the alacrity with which Thomas J. Wood obeyed an order on the second day at Chickamauga caused a rift between him and his commander, William S. Rosecrans. The career soldier was a native of Kentucky and a West Pointer (1845). Posted initially to the topographical engineers, he had transferred to the dragoons the next year. In addition to Indian fighting, he won a brevet in Mexico and served during the Kansas troubles and on the Mormon expedition. His Civil War-era assignments included: captain, 1st Cavalry (since March 3, 1855); major, 1st Cavalry (March 16, 1861); lieutenant colonel, 1st Cavalry (May 9, 1861); lieutenant colonel, 4th Cavalry (designation change August 3, 1861); brigadier general, USV (October 11, 1861); commanding 2nd Brigade, McCook's Command, Department of the Cumberland (October-November 9, 1861); commanding 5th Brigade, Army of the Ohio (November 9-December 2, 1861); colonel, 2nd Cavalry (November 12, 1861); commanding 5th Brigade, 2nd Division, Army of the Ohio (December 2, 1861-January 8, 1862); commanding 6th Division, Army of the Ohio (February 11-September 29, 1862); commanding 6th Division, 2nd Corps, Army of the Ohio (September 29-November 5, 1862); commanding 1st Division, Left Wing, 14th Corps, Army of the Cumberland (November 5-December 31, 1862); commanding 21st Corps, Army of the Cumberland (February 19-March 19, 1863); commanding 1st Division, 21st Corps, Army of the Cumberland (May 10-October 9, 1863); commanding 3rd Division, 4th Corps, Army of the Cumberland (October 10, 1863-January 8, 1864, February 12-September 2, September 6-December 2, 1864, January 31-February 7, and March 20-August 1, 1865); commanding the corps (December 1, 1864-January 31, 1865); and major general, USV (February 22, 1865, to rank from January 27, 1865). Because so many officers of the mounted branch resigned to join the Confederacy, Wood rose rapidly during the first months of the war. By the first fall of the conflict he was a brigadier general of volunteers and was assigned to duty in Kentucky. As a part of Buell's relief force, he fought at Shiloh, but only one of his brigades was actively engaged at Perryville. Wounded on the first day at Murfreesboro, he remained on the field until nightfall. Returning to duty, he led a division in the Tullahoma Campaign and went on to Chickamauga. There on the second day he received an order from Rosecrans' headquarters directing him to move his division to the left in order to fill a gap which he knew did not exist. His movement created a real quarter-mile gap through which James Longstreet's Confederates almost immediately poured. This sent nearly two-thirds of the Union army fleeing toward Chattanooga. Rosecrans was outraged that Wood had not challenged the order, but it must be remembered that he had been criticized by his commander shortly before for not complying promptly enough to a previous order. Ironically, Wood received a regular army brevet of brigadier general for the battle and Rosecrans was soon removed from command. Making up for his showing, men from Wood's division were among the first to reach the crest of Missionary Ridge at Chattanooga. He was again distinguished during the Atlanta Campaign during which he remained on the field at Lovejoy's Station despite a severe leg wound. He returned to duty four days later and was sent back to Tennessee with the rest of the 4th Corps to face Hood's invasion. He commanded his division in the repulse of the Confederates at Franklin and ably directed the corps at Nashville, for which he was brevetted major general in the regular army. Early the next year he won that full rank in the volunteers and was assigned to occupation duty in Mississippi. Mustered out of the volunteers on September 1, 1866, he reverted to his colonelcy. On account of his wounds, he was placed on the retired list as a major general in 1868, but this was reduced to brigadier general seven years later.

WOODBURY, Daniel Phineas (1812-1864)

Despite having married into a Southern family, New Hampshire native Daniel P. Woodbury remained loyal to the Union and was one of its leading engineering officers until his death from yellow fever on August 15, 1864. A West Pointer (1836), he had served at various times with both the artillery and the engineers. With the latter he was connected with the construction of fortifications on the coast and frontier and of the Cumberland Road. His Civil War-era assignments included: captain, Engineers (since March 3, 1853); major, Engineers (August 6, 1861); lieutenant colonel and additional aide-de-camp (September 28, 1861); brigadier general, USV (March 19, 1862); commanding Volunteer Engineer Brigade, Army of the Potomac (March 1862-March 20, 1863); commanding District of Key West and Tortugas, Department of the Gulf (March 1863-August 15, 1864); and lieutenant colonel, Engineers (June 1, 1863). As an engineering officer on the divisional staff of David Hunter at 1st Bull Run, he found the route via Sudley Spring Ford which Hunter and Samuel P. Heintzelman's divisions used to turn the Confederate left. Involved in the construction of the Washington defenses, he was made a brigadier general and placed in charge of the volunteer engineers for the Peninsula Campaign. He was in charge of the siege operations at Yorktown and aided on the advance toward Richmond. For the campaign he was brevetted colonel in the regular army. It was his command which threw the pontoon bridges across the Rappahannock at Fredericksburg in December 1862. Four months later he was transferred to a district command on the Gulf coast. It was a fitting assignment since he had been involved in the construction, before the war, of Fort Taylor at Key West and Fort Jefferson at Dry Tortugas. It was while in this command that he died of yellow fever.

WOODRUFF, James (1821-?)

One species of artillery piece, that invented by James Woodruff, has been treated by history as an "eccentric weapon." This is not totally fair. During the first year of the Civil War, carriagemaker Woodruff developed a small field artillery piece designed for service with either infantry or mounted troops. Weighing only 256 pounds, the two-pounder smoothbore gun was very mobile. After much difficulty, and a couple of visits to the President to lobby for his weapon, and the arming and acceptance of the 6th Illinois Cavalry, he received an order on November 15, 1861. The price was $285.00 for each of 30 guns. This was apparently the only federal order. Many of these guns did not see any action, but some did in the West. Battery K, 1st Illinois Light Artillery, used them to good effect on Grierson's famous raid through Mississippi in 1863. At least five of the guns were captured by Confederates in Missouri and Mississippi, but there is no known record of Rebel use of the prizes. With the troops themselves, the gun received mixed reviews, praised by some and ridiculed by others. After providing the 30 guns, and six for the city of Quincy, Illinois, in February 1862, Woodruff returned to the manufacture of knapsacks, haversacks, and ambulances. On October 30, 1862, he was appointed a captain and assistant provost marshal and on May 7, 1863, he was promoted to major and provost marshal. He resigned the following year.

WOODS, Charles Robert (1827-1885)

As a first lieutenant in the 9th United States Infantry, West Pointer (1852) Charles Woods began his own Civil War record as commander of the troops aboard the *Star of the West* in its ill-fated attempt to reinforce the beleaguered garrison of Fort Sumter. Shots fired across her bow on January 9, 1861, caused the ship to abandon the effort. Woods' later duties included: captain, 9th Infantry (April 1, 1861); colonel, 76th Ohio (October 13, 1861); commanding 2nd Brigade, 1st Division, 15th Corps, Army of the Tennessee (May 22-July 30 and August 24-September 1, 1863); brigadier general, USV (August 4, 1863); commanding 1st Brigade, 1st Division, 15th Corps, Army of the Tennessee (September 13-December 12, 1863, February 6-July 15, and August 19-22, 1864); major, 18th U.S. Infantry (April 20, 1864); commanding 1st Division, 15th Corps, Army of the Tennessee (January 13-February 6 and July 15-August 19, 1864, September 23, 1864-April 2, 1865, and April 5-August 1, 1865); and commanding 3rd Division, 17th Corps, Army of the Tennessee (August 23-September 22, 1864). Transferring to the volunteers, Woods commanded his regiment in West Virginia and at Fort Donelson, Shiloh, Chickasaw Bayou, and Arkansas Post. He commanded his brigade during the siege of Vicksburg and at Chattanooga and Ringgold. During the Atlanta Campaign he led the brigade at Resaca, New Hope Church, and Kennesaw Mountain and in the battles for Atlanta proper he commanded divisions in the 15th and 17th Corps. On the March to the Sea, his division saw action at Griswoldville and in the Carolinas Campaign at Bentonville. Mustered out of the volunteer service he continued in the regular army until his retirement as colonel, 2nd Infantry, in 1874. During the war he earned regular army brevets as: lieutenant colonel for Vicksburg, colonel for Chattanooga, brigadier general for Atlanta, and major general for Bentonville. He was also named brevet major general, USV, for Griswoldville.

WOODS, Edward McPherson (1859-1863)

Although indirectly, young Edward Woods was the youngest fatality of the battle of Gettysburg. After the departure of the armies, the battlefield became an attraction for the local populace. Even though it was strictly prohibited by the provost marshal's office in town, many persons collected souvenirs of the battle, principally rifles. Many children were roaming the field, including Edward Woods and his older brother. The elder child picked up a gun, still loaded, and it discharged. The Sunday July 5 excursion to the field ended in the death of three-year-old Edward Woods.

WOODS, William Burnham (1824-1887)

The Civil War career of William B. Woods closely followed that of his younger brother, Charles R. Woods. An Ohio lawyer and Democratic politician, he became a Republican during the Civil War. His assignments included: lieutenant colonel, 76th Ohio (February 6, 1862); colonel, 76th Ohio (September 10, 1863); commanding 1st Brigade, 1st Division, 15th Corps, Army of the Tennessee (January 21-June 16, 1865); also commanding the division (April 2-5, 1865); and brigadier general, USV (May 31, 1865). He became his brother's second-in-command shortly before the capture of Fort Donelson and the regiment fought at Shiloh, in the advance on Corinth, and at Chickasaw Bayou. In the assault on Fort Hindman at Arkansas Post, Woods fell lightly wounded. During the Vicksburg Campaign and the recapture of Jackson, he led the regiment while his brother was at the head of the brigade. Succeeding his brother as colonel, he won the brevet of brigadier general for the Atlanta and Savannah campaigns. During the drive through the Carolinas he commanded a brigade in his brother's division and for a few days the division itself. After the close of hostilities he was made a brigadier general. Brevetted major general for the war, he was mustered out on February 17, 1866. Settling in Alabama and then Georgia, he was named a federal judge by Grant and was noted for his moderation. He often ruled against the rights of the ex-slaves.

WOOL, John Ellis (1784-1869)

Veteran of both the War of 1812 and the Mexican War, John E. Wool was the fourth-ranking general in the regular establishment when he retired on August 1, 1863. Entering the army in the earlier war as a captain of infantry, the native New Yorker had emerged as a major and soon became the army's inspector general with the staff rank of colonel. During the course of that war he was wounded at Queenston Heights in the American land grab at Canada and earned a brevet. Sent abroad as a military observer, he returned to take part in the Trail of Tears incident. Particularly distinguished at Buena Vista in Mexico, he was awarded the Thanks of Congress, a sword, and another brevet. In the interwar years he was in departmental command. His Civil War assignments included: brigadier general, USA (since June 25, 1841); commanding Department of the East (prewar-August 17, 1861); commanding Department of Virginia (August 17, 1861-June 2, 1862); major general, USA (May 16, 1862); commanding Middle Department (June 9-December 22, 1862); also commanding 8th Corps, Middle Department (July 22-December 22, 1862); and again commanding Department of the East (January 12-July 18, 1863). Taking command early in the war at Fortress Monroe at the eastern end of the Peninsula, he preserved it as a Union base for further operations against Richmond. Returning to the Department of the East, he was involved in restoring calm after the New York draft riots. On August 1, 1863, only weeks later, he was retired after a half a century of service.

WOOLSON, Albert (1847-1956)

The last Union veteran of the Civil War was Minnesotan Albert Woolson who died at the age of 109. Born in Watertown, New York, he was only 14 when the war began. He enlisted in the 1st Minnesota Heavy Artillery in the latter stages of the conflict, and he served in Companies C and D from the organization of the unit in the fall of 1864 until the close of the war. Throughout his term of service his regiment was assigned to garrison duty at Chattanooga, and the only deaths suffered by it were from disease. On August 2, 1956, the Union armies passed into history with Woolson's death.

WORDEN, John Lorimer (1818-1897)

During the Civil War John L. Worden enjoyed a varied and successful career in the U.S. Navy, but is best remembered for his service in command of the first ironclad in the Union, the USS *Monitor*. After 16 years in the navy, Worden had been a lieutenant at the war's beginning. In March 1861, before Fort Sumter had been fired upon, he was sent to Fort Pickens in Pensacola Harbor, Florida, with verbal orders for the commander not to surrender to the secessionists. On his return journey by train, he was seized and held for seven months by the Confederates. Exchanged in October, he was soon offered command of John Ericsson's experimental craft, the *Monitor*. Assuming command on January 16, 1862, he got his vessel ready despite numerous accidents and problems with the revolutionary machinery. Leaving New York on March 6, the *Monitor* was too late in arriving at Hampton Roads to prevent the disaster to the *Cumberland* and *Congress* on the 8th. The following day Worden moved his craft out to challenge the *Virginia* and to protect the rest of the Union's wooden fleet. After about four hours of directing the fight from the exposed pilot house, Worden was wounded in the face when a rebel shell exploded right against the slit through which he was looking. He relinquished command, and his vessel pulled briefly out of the fight, but before it could return the *Virginia* had left the scene. Each thought, incorrectly, that it had inflicted a mortal blow on the other. The victory has been given to the *Monitor* since it fulfilled its mission of defending the blockading fleet. Honors soon followed for Worden. He was given the Thanks of Congress and was promoted commander, USN (July 12, 1862) and captain, USN (February 3, 1863). On February 28, 1863, Worden, now commanding the USS *Montauk* and serving in the South Atlantic Blockading Squadron, destroyed the rebel steamer *Nashville* in the Ogeechee River in Georgia. In June, he left the *Montauk* and returned to New York to help supervise the construction of more advanced monitors. Performing this duty until the end of the war, he was eventually promoted to rear admiral, USN, before retiring in 1886. (MacCartney, Clarence Edward, *Mr. Lincoln's Admirals*)

WORK, Henry Clay (1832-1884)

With his father once imprisoned for his work aiding escaped slaves on the underground railroad, Henry Clay Work was well inclined to write pro-Union songs during the Civil War. A native of Connecticut, he had been raised there and in Illinois. Trained as a printer, he relocated to Chicago to accept employment in the field but continued to write songs as a sideline, a hobby he had long pursued. With the coming of the Civil War his employer, George F. Root, urged him into patriotic songwriting. His songs included: "Kingdom Coming," "Babylon is Fallen!" "Wake Nicodemus," and "Marching Through Georgia." The latter, although it did not appear until the final months of the war, has earned the most lasting fame. After the war he continued his writing in Illinois and New Jersey, and, by one count, is credited with 73 works.

WORK, Phillip Alexander (1832-1911)

Surviving the slaughter of 82 percent of his regiment in the infamous Cornfield at Antietam, Phillip Work was forced out of the Confederate army by a different kind of wound—syphilis. A member of the Texas convention that removed the state from the Union, Work had been appointed captain, Company F, 1st Texas, on May 28, 1861, and sent to Virginia. He became a lieutenant colonel on May 19, 1862. After serving through the Peninsular Campaign, Work took command of the regiment for the battles of Groveton, 2nd Bull Run, and Antietam, where it was mowed down. He was not present at Fredericksburg but again commanded the regiment at Gettysburg. His resignation for medical reasons was accepted effective from January 5, 1864. Back in Texas he raised a company and became its captain, and they served together in the District of Texas, New Mexico and Arizona, Trans-Mississippi Department, until the close of the war.

WRIGHT, Ambrose Ransom (1826-1872)

A Georgia lawyer and frequently unsuccessful political aspirant, "Rans" Wright was a hard-fighting brigadier under Lee for much of the war. His assignments included: colonel, 3rd Georgia (May 8, 1861); brigadier general, CSA (June 3, 1862); commanding Blanchard's (old) Brigade, Huger's Division, Army of Northern Virginia (June-July 1862); commanding brigade, Anderson's-Mahone's Division, 1st (3rd after May 30, 1863) Corps, same army (July-September 17 and fall 1862-July 1, and July 2, 1863-August 1864); major general, CSA (November 26, 1864); and commanding division, Department of South Carolina, Georgia and Florida (November 1864-February 1865). After service in the Norfolk area, including action at South Mills, North Carolina, he led his regiment to the Peninsula. Following Seven Pines he was given charge of the brigade, supervising its movements through the Seven Days, 2nd Bull Run, and Antietam. Wounded in the latter, he returned to fight at Fredericksburg, Chancellorsville, and Gettysburg where he temporarily relinquished command due to illness. He fought through the Overland Campaign and at the Crater. Ordered to the Army of Tennessee in August 1864, he does not appear to have joined, possibly because of illness and perhaps for political reasons—he had been elected president of the Georgia senate the previous year. Promoted to major general, he served in the Savannah and Carolinas campaigns. He was a lawyer, journalist, and politician postwar and died before he could be sworn in as a congressman. (Freeman, Douglas S., *Lee's Lieutenants*)

WRIGHT, George (1801-1865)

A longtime regular army officer, George Wright spent the entire war on the West Coast, fighting Indians and Southern sympathizers only to die in an accident shortly after war's end. A West Pointer (1822) from Vermont, Wright, a veteran infantryman of the Seminole and Mexican wars, had risen to the rank of colonel, 9th Infantry, by the outbreak of hostilities and was commanding the District of Oregon, Department of the Pacific (to September 13, 1861). His later commands in the Department of the Pacific included: commanding District of Southern California (September 14-October 14, 1861); brigadier general, USV (September 28, 1861); commanding the department (October 20-July 1, 1864); and commanding District of California (July 1, 1864-July 27, 1865). In a region virtually denuded of troops, Wright was responsible for taking over the role of the regular army. Early in the war his principal duty was to prevent Confederate sympathizers from heading east to join in the fighting and to foil plots to break away southern California to join the Confederacy. His methods, while not always constitutional, received the approval of the military authorities in Washington. In 1864 he was charged with protecting northern California and Oregon during Indian troubles sparked by the absence of troops. He received a regular army brevet to brigadier general on December 29, 1864, for his long service. On his way to assume command of the newly formed Department of the Columbia, Wright was drowned in the wreck of the *Brother Jonathan*.

WRIGHT, Horatio Gouverneur (1820-1899)

An engineer officer by training and experience, Horatio G. Wright was able to make the jump to being an able division and corps leader but not to being an army leader. The Connecticut native had graduated second in his 1841 class at West Point and accordingly had been assigned to the engineering branch. Before the Civil War he taught at his alma mater and was involved in the construction of fortifications in Florida. When Virginia seceded he was the engineering officer in the expedition to evacuate and destroy the Norfolk Navy Yard. In an unsuccessful attempt to demolish the dry dock he was captured. Released, he was a volunteer aide on Samuel P. Heintzelman's staff during the seizure of Arlington Heights. His assignments included: captain, Engineers (since July 1, 1855); aide-de-camp, 3rd Division, Department of Northeastern Virginia (June-July 15, 1861); chief engineer, 3rd Division, Department of Northeastern Virginia (July 15-August 1861); major, Engineers (August 6, 1861); chief engineer, South Carolina Expedition (September-October 1861); brigadier general, USV (September 14, 1861); commanding 3rd Brigade, South Carolina Expedition (October 1861-April 1862); commanding 1st Division, Department of the South (April-July 1862); major general, USV (July 18, 1862); commanding Department of the Ohio (August 25, 1862-March 25, 1863); reappointed brigadier general, USV (March 24, 1863); commanding District of Western Kentucky, Department of the Ohio (March 25-April 4, 1864); commanding 1st Division, 6th Corps, Army of the Potomac (May 23-December 16, 1863 and April 23-May 9, 1864); commanding the corps (May 9-July 8, 1864, December 6, 1864-January 16, 1865, and February 11-June 28, 1865); reappointed major general, USV (May 12, 1864); commanding 6th Corps, Army of the Shenandoah (August 6-October 16 and October 19-December 6, 1864); commanding the army (October 16-19, 1864); and lieutenant colonel, Engineers (November 23, 1865). At 1st Bull Run he was the chief engineering officer with Heintzelman. He then assisted in organizing the Port Royal Expedition. Promoted to brigadier general he was given one of its brigades when it sailed. He remained on the South Carolina coast after Port Royal's fall and led a division in the failed Union assault at Secessionville. Given a second star, he was assigned to command the Department of the Ohio but lost it when the Senate rejected his nomination on March 24, 1863. He was immediately recommissioned as a brigadier general and given a district command until assigned to the Army of the Potomac. His division was in reserve at Gettysburg, but he later took part in the Bristoe and Mine Run campaigns, earning a brevet for Rappahannock Station. In the Overland Campaign he fought at the Wilderness, earned a brevet for Spotsylvania, and was brevetted brigadier general in the regular army for Cold Harbor. Having succeeded the deceased John Sedgwick in corps command at Spotsylvania, he was again made a major general. After leading the 6th Corps to Petersburg, he took it to the rescue of Washington from the threat posed by Jubal Early. As part of Sheridan's army he fought at 3rd Winchester and Fisher's Hill and was in temporary command of the army when surprised at Cedar Creek. He failed to stabilize the situation, and it was not until Sheridan returned that a victory was gained. Returning to the Army of the Potomac two months later, he was brevetted regular army major general for his role in the final assault on Petersburg. He then took part in the pursuit to Appomattox. Mustered out of the volunteer service on September 1, 1866, he returned to his engineering duties until his retirement in 1884 as chief engineer of the army with the rank of brigadier general. Among his duties had been the completion of the long-delayed Washington Monument. Somewhat appropriately he was buried in front of the Lee home on Arlington Heights which he had helped to seize decades earlier.

WRIGHT, Joseph Albert (1810-1867)

When Senator Andrew Johnson was named military governor of Tennessee, Joseph A. Wright succeeded him on the Joint Committee on the Conduct of the War. The Pennsylvania native had moved to Indiana at about 10 years of age and was admitted to the bar in 1829. He then entered politics, serving in both houses of the state legislature. As a Democrat, he served one term in Congress during the mid-1840s but was defeated in an attempt at reelection. He was the state's governor from 1849 to 1857 and then was a diplomat to Prussia until July 1, 1861. On February 24, 1862, he was named to replace Jesse D. Bright who had been expelled from the Senate. He held the seat until January 14, 1863, when he became the commissioner to the Hamburg Exhibition of that year. During the final part of his senatorial term he joined the infamous committee which was controlled by the Radical Republicans and headed by Benjamin F. Wade, but he did not take an active role in its affairs. On June 30, 1865, he was renamed to his old post in Berlin and died there.

WRIGHT, Marcus Joseph (1831-1922)

Civil War historians would rate Marcus J. Wright's postwar, yeoman service in the compilation of the *Official Records* as more important than his services in the field as a Confederate brigadier general. The Tennessee native had been a lawyer and court clerk prior to the secession of his state and was also active in the militia. When his regiment joined the Southern cause he went with it as second in command. His assignments included: lieutenant colonel, 154th Tennessee Senior (May 14, 1861); brigadier general, CSA (December 20, 1862, to rank from the 13th); commanding brigade, Cheatham's Division, Polk's-Hardee's Corps, Army of Tennessee (early 1863-early 1864); and commanding District of North Mississippi and West Tennessee, Department of Alabama, Mississippi and East Louisiana (February 3-May 1865). Keeping its old regimental number, his regiment was specially authorized to attach the word "Senior" to its designation. Wright commanded the regiment at Belmont and again succeeded to that position at Shiloh where he was severely wounded. Recovering, he was at Perryville on Benjamin F. Cheatham's staff. Promoted to brigadier general, he led a Tennessee brigade during the Tullahoma, Chickamauga, and Chattanooga campaigns. During the Atlanta Campaign he was in post command in Georgia and in the final months of the war led a district in northern Mississippi. A lawyer and naval official after the surrender, he was chosen by the War Department to supervise the collection of Confederate records in 1878. Given the widely scattered collections and the reluctance of many ex-Confederates to cooperate with a project they thought would be a vindication of the Northern cause, his was a difficult task. Nonetheless he was able to prove to many that the work would be an unbiased historical record and was successful in gaining access to some large and valuable stores of papers. Wright also engaged in historical writing of his own.

WRIGHT, William (1790-1866)

In the midst of the Civil War former senator William Wright was reelected to the national legislature. Born in New York, he had served as a volunteer in the War of 1812 and then taken up the saddler's trade in Connecticut. Moving to New Jersey in 1821, he was the mayor of Newark from 1840 to 1843. He then sat for two terms in Congress as a Whig and supporter of Clay. In 1847 he lost a bid for the governorship. A delegate to the Whig convention of 1848, he nonetheless switched his allegiance to the Democrats two years later. As such he sat in the U.S. Senate from 1853 to 1859 but then lost a bid for reelection. However, he won an election for the state's other senate seat four years later and served from March 4, 1863, until his death.

WYATT, Henry L. (?-1861)

Although John Q. Marr, a Virginia volunteer, had been killed in action nine days previously, Henry L. Wyatt became the first Confederate soldier to die in action—since Marr was not in Confederate service. At the war's outbreak Wyatt had enlisted as a private in the Southern Stars, which became Company K, 1st North Carolina, and was mustered into service on May 13, 1861. Less than a month later, on June 10, at the battle of Big Bethel, Wyatt and four others volunteered to advance beyond the Confederate lines to burn a house that was a potential haven for enemy sharpshooters. A bullet in the forehead made him the first non-Virginian to be killed in the Old Dominion.

WYNDHAM, Percy (?-?)

Soldier of fortune Sir Percy Wyndham had the distinct embarrassment of being captured by the Confederate cavalry leader whom he himself had boasted would become his captive. The Englishman had served with Garibaldi's forces in Italy before coming to America to fight in the Civil War. By special permission of the War Department, he was allowed to raise a cavalry regiment which was later accredited to the state of New Jersey. His assignments included: colonel, Halsted's Horse (October 18, 1861); colonel, 1st New Jersey Cavalry (change of designation February 19, 1862); and commanding 2nd Brigade, 3rd Division, Cavalry Corps, Army of the Potomac (February 16-June 9, 1863). Completing his regiment's training he joined the forces operating against Stonewall Jackson in the Shenandoah Valley and bragged that he would sweep up Turner Ashby and his men. Instead, he was captured near Harrisonburg in a fight with the gray-clad horsemen. Exchanged on September 21, 1862, he took charge of a brigade for Stoneman's raid during the Chancellorsville Campaign and fell wounded at Brandy Station. Recovering, he led his regiment in the Bristoe and Mine Run campaigns. His last appearance in the *Official Records* is just prior to the beginning of the Overland Campaign. His regiment was mustered out on July 24, 1865.

Percy Wyndham, flamboyant Union horse soldier. (NA)

WYNKOOP, Edward W. (1836-1891)

Sympathy for the Indians brought Edward W. Wynkoop into conflict with his commander, the notorious John M. Chivington. Born in Philadelphia, he had settled in Kansas in the mid-1850s and gone to Colorado in search of gold in 1858. One of the first settlers of Denver, he enlisted in the Union army early in the Civil War. His assignments included: captain, 1st Colorado (1861); captain, 1st Colorado Cavalry (designation change November 1, 1862); and major, 1st Colorado Cavalry (by early 1864). He fought at Apache Canyon and Glorieta Pass against the invading Confederates. In command at Fort Lyon in 1864 he began to understand the problems of the Indians but could not convince his fellow whites of this. Chivington simply wanted to exterminate them and did his best at Sand Creek. Leaving the army, Wynkoop became an Indian agent for the Cheyennes and Arapahos. Frustrated in his attempts to maintain the peace, he resigned in 1868. He was also highly critical of Custer's so-called battle of the Washita and said it was no better than Chivington at Sand Creek. He was subsequently in the iron business and held various official positions. (Brown, Dee, *Bury My Heart at Wounded Knee*)

WYNKOOP, George Campbell (?-1882)

Generally, state officers above the grade of colonel were not accepted into the national volunteers except at the outbreak of the Civil War. George C. Wynkoop served the Federal government briefly as a Pennsylvania brigadier general and then became the colonel of a mounted volunteer regiment. His assignments included: brigadier general, Pennsylvania Volunteers (April 20, 1861); commanding 2nd Brigade, 2nd Division, Department of Pennsylvania (June-July 25, 1861); and colonel, 7th Pennsylvania Cavalry (August 21, 1861). Serving under Robert Patterson, he was part of the force which was unsuccessful in pinning Joseph E. Johnston down in the Shenandoah Valley during the 1st Bull Run Campaign. Mustered out on August 1, 1861, he became head of a new regiment at the end of the month and led it to the western theater. Serving in Tennessee and Kentucky, he was engaged in operations against John Hunt Morgan. Illness was the probable cause of his June 25, 1863, honorable discharge.

X

See: *Mason, Charles*

YANCEY, William Lowndes (1814-1863)

One of the most extreme of states' righters, William L. Yancey wrote the Alabama secession ordinance and even feuded with Jefferson Davis when he persisted in views in favor of local rights during his tenure in the Confederate Senate. In the 1830s he had edited the Unionist *Greenville* (S.C.) *Mountaineer* and practiced law. In 1836 he moved to Alabama and rented a plantation. He also edited the *Cahaba Democrat* and the *Cahaba Gazette*. He served in the state legislature in the early 1840s and sat in the U.S. Congress until his first debate—which resulted in a duel with future Confederate General Thomas L. Clingman—prompted him to resign. Over the years his belief in the inalienable rights of the states grew. He proposed a Southern confederacy as early as 1858 and was a leading figure in the splitting of the Democratic Party in 1860. Following his work at the Alabama secession convention he was sent to England and France by Jefferson Davis to seek recognition for the fledgling country. While abroad he was elected to the Confederate Senate, and he returned to take his seat on March 27, 1862. He served on the committees on: Foreign Affairs; Naval Affairs; Public Lands; and Territories. Remembering his states' rights views, it is easy to see how he came into conflict with Davis' idea of a strong central government. He constantly wanted to limit the president's powers, especially in the field of appointments, and wanted to require the payment of market prices for impressed goods. Between congressional sessions he died at his home on July 23, 1863. (DuBose, John Witherspoon, *The Life and Times of William Lowndes Yancey*)

YANDELL, David Wendel (1826-1898)

Although only a medical officer, David W. Yandell became involved in the intricate politics of the Confederacy's Western command. A Tennessee native, he had received his medical training in Kentucky, England, Ireland, and France. By the outbreak of the Civil War he was a professor of medicine in Kentucky. He joined the Confederate medical service, and as a military medical officer, his assignments included: medical director, Central Geographical Division of Kentucky, Department No. 2 (September-October 1861); Medical Director, Central Army of Kentucky, Department No. 2 (October 1861-March 1862); medical director, Department No. 2 (March 1862-July 1863); and medical director, Army of Tennessee (July 1863-April 1865). He served under Generals Simon B Buckner, Albert Sidney Johnston, Braxton Bragg, and Joseph E. Johnston and became part of the anti-Bragg faction and a staunch supporter of Joe Johnston. After the surrender in North Carolina—he had been present at such battles as Shiloh, Murfreesboro, and Chickamauga—he returned to medical education and was surgeon general for the Kentucky militia. (Cunningham, Horace Herndon, *Doctors in Gray*)

YATES, Charles (?-1870)

Except in the initial period of the Civil War it was not the practice of the Federal government to accept into the volunteer service officers with a rank above that of colonel. However, in the emergency caused by the Confederate invasion of Maryland and Pennsylvania in the spring and summer of 1863 exceptions were made. Such was the case of Charles Yates. The native New Yorker was accepted into national service on June 19, 1863, along with the two regiments of New York National Guard troops under his command. For a time he commanded the post at Fenwick, Pennsylvania, in the Department of the Susquehanna. With the battle of Gettysburg won and the emergency past, he was mustered out on July 20, 1863.

YATES, Richard (1818-1873)

As the staunchly Republican governor of Illinois for most of the Civil War, Richard Yates was one of Lincoln's most loyal Northern state executives. Born in Kentucky, he had taken up the practice of law in Illinois and was soon engaged in politics, serving in the state legislature and the U.S. Congress. He was a delegate to the Republican National Convention of 1860 and that fall won election as governor. Taking up his duties on January 14, 1861, he threw himself into the raising of troops and greatly exceeded the state's quota. When in 1863 the state legislature suggested compromise with the Southern states, he prorogued that body and governed without it for the next year. Ineligible for reelection, he left office on January 16, 1865, but on March 4 he took a seat in the U.S. Senate. Serving until 1871, he was later a government appointee. (State Centennial Commission, *Centennial History of Illinois*)

YORK, Zebulon (1819-1900)

A transplanted Maine Yankee, Zebulon York lost an arm and the co-ownership of some 1,700 slaves during the Civil War. A Louisiana attorney, he had been the state's largest realty tax payer at the outbreak of hostilities, sharing ownership of six cotton plantations. He organized a company for Confederate service and his later assignments included: major and lieutenant colonel, 14th Louisiana (1861); colonel, 14th Louisiana (spring 1862); brigadier general, CSA (May 31, 1864); and commanding Consolidated Louisiana Brigade, Gordon's Division, 2nd Corps (Valley District after June 13), Army of Northern Virginia (June 4-September 19, 1864). Distinguishing himself in the battle of Williamsburg, he went on to command the regiment in the Seven Days. In the summer of 1862 he was sent with General Richard Taylor to Louisiana to gather recruits for the two Louisiana brigades in Virginia. He was on this duty into 1864, and following the disaster at Spotsylvania he was given command of the consolidated Louisiana brigades. Sent to the Shenandoah Valley, he led this unit at Lynchburg, Monocacy, and on the outskirts of Washington. At 3rd Winchester he was wounded by a shell, costing him an arm. Upon his recovery he was again assigned to duty recruiting for the Louisiana troops, this time in North Carolina from among foreign-born Union prisoners. The war ended before he could rejoin the army in the field. Ruined by the war, he ran a hotel in Mississippi. (Freeman, Douglas S., *Lee's Lieutenants*)

YOUNG, Bennett H. (1843-1919)

The raid of Lieutenant Bennett H. Young on St. Albans, Vermont, led to a major international incident with Great Britain. The Kentucky-born Confederate officer had been authorized on June 16, 1864, to recruit a force of no more than 20 men from escaped Confederate prisoners in Canada. The so-styled 5th Company, Confederate States Retributors, was intended to launch raids against prisoner of war camps near the border. Having himself escaped from Camp Douglas near Chicago—where he had been confined after raiding with John

Richard Yates, Illinois' war governor. (NA)

Hunt Morgan in Ohio—Young planned to hit the prison on Johnson's Island, Ohio. Forced to change his plans due to a leak, he led his 20 men on a raid against St. Albans. With perfect planning they looted three banks of a total of $201,522, while others gathered up any stray passers-by to prevent an alarm. However, a Union officer on leave managed to alert the town. In the action that followed one civilian and one raider were killed. In addition another four raiders were wounded; the balance then raced for the Canadian line with the citizens in hot pursuit. Violating international law, the posse crossed onto foreign soil and arrested the Confederate unit. On their return they were stopped by the Canadian authorities and forced to relinquish their 14 prisoners, including Young. Following two trials the Confederates were ruled to be belligerents engaged in legal military operations and released. This raised a howl of protest, especially since only $86,000 from the October 19, 1864 raid had been recovered. Young subsequently returned to Kentucky and took up the practice of law.

YOUNG, Henry H. (ca. 1840-1866)

As unofficial chief of scouts to Philip H. Sheridan, Henry H. Young survived some daring adventures during the Civil War but died shortly thereafter on the Mexican border. His military assignments included: second lieutenant, Company B, 2nd Rhode Island (June 6, 1861); first lieutenant, Company B, 2nd Rhode Island (summer 1861); captain, Company B, 2nd Rhode Island (November 1861); and major, 2nd Rhode Island (1864). He led his company at 1st Bull Run and served with it until April 30, 1863, when he was named brigade inspector. While on the staff of Colonel Oliver Edwards he attracted the attention of Sheridan and in 1864 joined his staff as an aide-de-camp but was assigned to scouting duties. He organized a force of 58 men who frequently wore Confederate uniforms in their forays. In February 1865 Major Young scored a coup when he captured his old rival, Harry Gilmore, in bed. During the Appomattox retreat Young's men were responsible for the rerouting of supply trains bound for Lee's starving army. With the war over he accompanied Sheridan to Texas for possible action against the Imperial forces in Mexico. In a secret operation to help the Liberals Young was killed in an ambush along the Rio Grande. Sheridan mourned his loss.

YOUNG, John Russell (1840-1899)

One of the first correspondents to write an account of the Union disaster at 1st Bull Run, John R. Young became the managing editor of the *Philadelphia Press* the following year. A native of Ireland, he had come to America as an infant and in 1857 became a copy boy for the *Press*. His early war reporting gained him the editorial position which he held throughout the war. He was a cofounder of the Union League of Philadelphia and in the final months of the war worked on publicity for the national loan being managed by Jay Cooke. After some confidential European missions for various cabinet officials, Young became a foreign correspondent and editor for the *New York Herald* in 1872. While in London in 1877 former President Grant asked Young to accompany him on his round the world tour. This resulted in a close friendship with the ex-president and an introduction to the Far East. Young's account of the trip appeared as *Around the World with General Grant* in 1879. Three years later, at Grant's urging, Young was named minister to China and was highly successful in the difficult post. He later returned to the *Herald* and for the last two years of his life he was the librarian of Congress. (Young, John Russell, *Men and Memories*)

YOUNG, Pierce Manning Butler (1836-1896)

Resigning his cadetship at West Point in March 1861, three months before his scheduled graduation, P.M.B. Young joined the Confederacy and rose to be a major general. His services included: second lieutenant, Artillery (March 16, 1861); first lieutenant and aide-de-camp (July 1861); first lieutenant and adjutant, Cobb's (Ga.) Legion (July 1861), lieutenant colonel, Cobb's Legion (November 1861); colonel, Cobb's Legion (November 1, 1862); brigadier general, CSA (September 28, 1863); commanding Butler's (old) Brigade, Hampton's-Butler's Division, Cavalry Corps, Army of Northern Virginia (October 1863-November 1864); major general, CSA (December 30, 1864); commanding Iverson's (old) Division, Hampton's Cavalry Command, Department of South Carolina, Georgia and Florida (February 1865); and commanding Military District of Georgia and South Carolina, same department (March-April 1865). After service at Pensacola and on W.H.T. Walker's staff, the South Carolina-born and Georgia-raised Young went to Virginia with the legion, eventually commanding the cavalry of the mixed branch unit. He fought at the Seven Days and was wounded at South Mountain. Recovering, he was at Fredericksburg, Brandy Station, and Gettysburg before being given a brigade. This he directed through the Overland and half of the Petersburg campaigns. Sent in November 1864 to secure remounts for his command, he was active against Sherman in the Augusta-Savannah area. After the war he was a planter, congressman, and diplomatic representative to Russia, Guatemala, and Honduras. (Freeman, Douglas S., *Lee's Lieutenants*)

YOUNG, William Hugh (1838-1901)

Less than two months after being named a brigadier general William H. Young's Confederate career came to an end when he was wounded and captured at Allatoona. Missouri-born and Texas-raised, he had been a student at the University of Virginia when the Civil War broke out. Recruiting a company, his later assignments included: captain, 9th Texas (September 1861); colonel, 9th Texas (ca. May 1862); commanding Ector's (old) Brigade, French's Division, Polk's-Stewart's Corps, Army of Tennessee (July-October 5, 1864); and brigadier general, CSA (August 15, 1864). He led his company at Shiloh and in the reorganization that spring he became the regiment's colonel. As such he served in the defense of Corinth, Mississippi, and in the Kentucky Campaign. Wounded at Murfreesboro, he recovered in time to lead his regiment under Joseph E. Johnston in the unsuccessful efforts to relieve the pressure on Vicksburg. He was again wounded at Jackson and at Chickamauga. Leading his regiment in the Atlanta Campaign, he was twice wounded at Kenesaw Mountain. Remaining in the field, he took over command of the brigade in July and the next month was named a brigadier general. In Hood's raids against Sherman's supply lines, Young was wounded and captured on October 5, 1864, at Allatoona, Georgia. He was confined on Johnson's Island, Ohio, until July 24, 1865. Thereafter he engaged in the practice of law and the real estate business.

YOUNGER, Cole (1844-1916)

Many of the famed outlaws of the Wild West were spawned in the sectional fighting of the Civil War. The Younger Brothers, of whom Cole was the eldest, were a case in point. Already a Southern partisan, he had joined with the brutal Missouri guerrilla William C. Quantrill in 1862 following the murder of his father by Unionists. He was with Quantrill at the massacre at Lawrence and Baxter Springs, but by March 1864 he had drifted out of the group. During that time he had ridden with Frank James and the year after the Civil War ended met Jesse James. This was the beginning of the James-Younger gang that rode until the disastrous Northfield, Minnesota, bank raid. Here Cole Younger was wounded and two weeks later captured, having suffered another 11 wounds. Sentenced to life, he was freed in 1901 and went into the tombstone business. Later he appeared in a Wild West extravaganza with Frank James. (Younger, Cole, *The Story of Cole Younger*)

Three of the notorious Younger brothers, with sister Rhetta. Left to right: James, Robert, and Cole. (NA)

YOUNGER, James (1848-1902)

Part of the famed James-Younger gang in the Wild West, Jim Younger and his brothers had received their education in crime as members of Quantrill's guerrillas in Missouri during the Civil War. When their father was killed by Missouri Unionists in 1862 four of the eight sons joined up with the brutal killer and took part in the sacking of Lawrence, Kansas, and the massacre at Baxter Springs. Meeting Frank James in this service—and his brother Jesse just after the war—the four Youngers became part of the infamous James-Younger gang of train, stage, and bank robbers. Jim took part in the crimes, killing a number of persons, including lawmen, until the 1876 raid on the Northfield, Minnesota, bank. Here Jim was severely wounded. In the getaway the Jameses wanted to put him out of his misery so they could travel faster. Faced down by two of Younger's brothers, the Jameses rode off. Two weeks later the Youngers were badly shot up and captured. Serving a life sentence, James was freed in 1901 but committed suicide the next year.

YOUNGER, John (1851-1874)

Only 10 years old when he launched his career of killing in the Civil War, John Younger went into the business fulltime when his father was killed by Unionist irregulars. He and his elder brother James killed four Union soldiers early in the war and later joined up with the notorious guerrilla William C. Quantrill, in 1862. In all, four of the eight Younger Brothers took part in the slaughter at Lawrence, Kansas, and later at Baxter Springs. Having in this service met Frank James—and after the war his brother Jesse—the four Youngers became part of the James-Younger train, bank, and stage robbing team in 1866. They were a terror to banks and transport companies throughout Missouri and the surrounding area. Then in 1874 Jim and John ran into three lawmen—two of whom they killed—but Jim was wounded and John was dead.

YOUNGER, Robert (1853-1889)

The youngest of the criminal Younger Brothers, Bob Younger was only 12 when he served under the brutal guerrilla William C. Quantrill in the raid on Lawrence, Kansas. The death of his father in 1862 at the hands of Missouri Unionists had launched four of the eight brothers into a life of crime. In 1866 they joined up with the Jameses—they had met Frank James in Quantrill's band—and they terrorized railroads and banks in the Missouri area for the next 10 years. In the 1876 raid on a bank in Northfield, Minnesota, Bob received two wounds. Two weeks later he was further shot up when the three surviving brothers were captured. Given a life sentence, he died in prison of tuberculosis.

Z

ZEILIN, Jacob (1806-1880)

Commandant of the United States Marine Corps at the close of the Civil War, Jacob Zeilin went on to become the first brigadier general in that service. A native Philadelphian, he had attended West Point for a while but subsequently entered the Marine Corps as a second lieutenant in 1831. His prewar career included sea duty in the Mediterranean, off Brazil, and in the East Indies. During the Mexican War he was a first lieutenant aboard the *Congress* along the California and Mexican coasts. He earned a brevet as major during that war. He later commanded a battalion during the operations to open up Japan. By the time of the Civil War he was a captain and commanded a company of the marine battalion at 1st Bull Run. He was wounded and the battalion, for the first time in the corps' history, had to retreat. In the summer of 1863 he took part in the naval operations against Charleston and then on June 10, 1864, he was promoted colonel and made the corps' commandant. There were several more senior officers but Secretary of the Navy Gideon Welles handpicked Zeilin, ordering all those senior to him to be retired on account of age. He commanded the corps until his retirement in 1876, after being appointed brigadier in 1867. (Pierce, Philip, *The Compact History of the United States Marine Corps*)

ZEPPELIN, Ferdinand von (ca. 1839-1917)

While visiting the United States as a military observer, Count Ferdinand von Zeppelin the future founder of commercial aviation—and bombing from the air—experienced his first flight in a balloon. A lieutenant in the Württemburg army studying in England, Zeppelin had decided, in 1863, to observe the American Civil War in order to answer his own doubts about his ability, as a Christian, to take part in a war. Arriving in Washington, the Prussian Ambassador Rudolf von Schleiden arranged an interview with President Lincoln who approved Zeppelin's status as an observer. He was given a pass to travel freely in the Union army. Joining the Army of the Potomac after the defeat at Chancellorsville, Zeppelin became acquainted with General Carl Schurz, a fellow German, whom he regarded as less than a military genius. Attaching himself to the staff of Union cavalry commander General Alfred Pleasonton, he was present for one of the cavalry battles leading up to the battle of Gettysburg. Breaking with neutrality, he offered to make a reconnaissance and was urged by Pleasonton to join the Union army. He declined the invitation and soon left the army, but minus his English-made barometer which General Daniel Butterfield had purloined. Traveling from Niagara Falls to the upper Mississippi, he had the opportunity to ascend in a balloon at St. Paul on August 17, 1863. Returning shortly to Wurttemburg, he had a distinguished career in the Franco-Prussian War and later developed the dirigible and the technique of aerial bombardment. With the prospect of war between the United States and Germany, he refused, when asked by a journalist, to consider the possibility of bombing his friends with the reply, "Never! Never!" He died a month before war was declared.

ZOGBAUM, Rufus Fairchild (1849-1925)

Although too young to have participated in the Civil War, Rufus F. Zogbaum painted many scenes of that and other conflicts in the latter part of the 19th and the early part of the 20th century. Born in Charleston, he and his family had moved to New York around the beginning of the war. He gained his art education at Heidelberg, New York, and Paris and then launched his career in the United States, depicting historic action scenes both on land and sea. His Civil War subjects included the fighting at Hampton Roads, Lee's Surrender, and the "First Minnesota Regiment at the Battle of Gettysburg." Covering other historic events, he benefited from first-hand observation of many Spanish-American War actions. His art publications included: *Horse, Foot, and Dragoons*; *"All Hands"*; and *The Junior Officer of the Watch*. He died in New York after almost a half a century of work.

ZOLLICOFFER, Felix Kirk (1812-1862)

A veteran of the Seminole War as a first lieutenant, then a newspaperman and Whig Congressman, Felix Zollicoffer was made a brigadier general in the Tennessee state forces following the fall of Fort Sumter. He was transferred into Confederate service, with the same rank, on July 9, 1861, and given command of the District of East Tennessee, Department Number 2, on August 1, with the assignment to "preserve peace, protect the railroad, and repel invasion." This was a difficult task since eastern Tennessee was generally not aslaveholding area and was unsympathetic to the Confederate cause. Zollicoffer moved his forces into southeastern Kentucky in late 1861 before being superseded by General G.B. Crittenden on December 8. Zollicoffer was then given command of the 1st Brigade of the district. His rash move across the Cumberland River forced the rebels to give battle, at a disadvantage, at Mill Springs on January 18, 1862. While studying the field he came across another officer on the same mission. He told that officer not to fire on his own men. But the other man was Colonel Speed S. Fry of the 4th Kentucky, a Union regiment. After riding away and being fired upon, Fry, realizing his mistake, turned and shot the Confederate. Also fired upon by some other Federals, Zollicoffer fell dead. (Myers, Raymond E., *The Zollie Tree*)

Blundering Confederate General Felix K. Zollicoffer dies at Mill Springs. (*Leslie's*)

ZOOK, Samuel Kosciuszko (1821-1863)

Having grown up on the site of the Revolutionary War encampment at Valley Forge, Pennsylvania, it was perhaps appropriate that Samuel Zook should end his life in the battle of Gettysburg. An interest in electricity had eventually led Zook to become the superintendent of the Washington and New York Telegraph Company, with headquarters in New York where he continued his interest in things military by entering the militia. On July 7, 1861, Zook was made a lieutenant colonel and sent to the 6th New York Militia which was in Federal service for three months. After serving as military governor in Annapolis during the campaign of 1st Bull Run, he was mustered out at the expiration of the regiment's term on July 31. His later assignments included: colonel, 57th New York (October 19, 1861); commanding 3rd Brigade, 1st Division, 2nd Corps, Army of the Potomac (October 8, 1862-January 24, 1863, March 24-May 15, and May 25-July 2, 1863); brigadier general, USV (November 29, 1862); and commanding 1st Division, 2nd Corps, Army of the Potomac (January 24-February 20, 1863). Zook participated in the Peninsular Campaign and commanded a brigade in the attacks on Marye's Heights at Fredericksburg where he had a horse shot out from under him and was praised by division commander General Hancock for the "spirit" with which he led his men. Promoted to a general's star, Zook led the brigade at Chancellorsville and at Gettysburg where, while going to the aid of the 3rd Corps, he was mortally wounded on the edge of the Wheatfield on the second day. He died the next day and was posthumously brevetted major general for Gettysburg. (*Memorial to Samuel K. Zook, Bvt. Major General United States Volunteers*)

APPENDIX A
CHRONOLOGY

NOVEMBER 1860
6—Lincoln elected.

DECEMBER 1860
20—South Carolina secedes.
26—Garrison transferred from Fort Moultrie to Fort Sumter.

JANUARY 1861
9—Mississippi secedes; *Star of the West* fired upon.
10—Florida secedes.
11—Alabama secedes.
19—Georgia secedes.
21—Withdrawal of five Southern members of the U.S. Senate: Yulee and Mallory of Florida, Clay and Fitzpatrick of Alabama, and Davis of Mississippi.
26—Louisiana secedes.
29—Kansas admitted to the Union as a free state.

FEBRUARY 1861
1—Texas convention votes for secession.
4—1st Session, Provisional Confederate Congress, convenes as a convention.
9—Jefferson Davis elected provisional Confederate president.
18—Jefferson Davis inaugurated.
23—Texas voters approve secession.

MARCH 1861
4—Lincoln inaugurated; Special Senate Session of 37th Congress convenes.
16—1st Session, Provisional Confederate Congress, adjourns.
28—Special Senate Session of 37th Congress adjourns.

APRIL 1861
12—Bombardment of Fort Sumter begins.
13—Fort Sumter surrenders to Southern forces.
17—Virginia secedes.
19—6th Massachusetts attacked by Baltimore mob; Lincoln declares blockade of Southern coast.
20—Norfolk, Virginia, Navy Yard evacuated.
29—2nd Session, Provisional Confederate Congress, convenes; Maryland rejects secession.

MAY 1861
6—Arkansas secedes; Tennessee legislature calls for popular vote on secession.
10—Union forces capture Camp Jackson, and a riot follows in St. Louis.
13—Baltimore occupied by U.S. troops.
20—North Carolina secedes.
21—2nd Session, Provisional Confederate Congress, adjourns.
23—Virginia voters approve secession.
24—Union troops sieze Alexandria, Virginia.

JUNE 1861
1—Skirmish at Fairfax Courthouse, Virginia.
3—Battle of Philippi (western Virginia).
8—Tennessee voters approve secession.
10—Battle of Big Bethel (Virginia).
17—Battle of Booneville (Missouri).

JULY 1861
4—1st Session, 37th Congress, convenes.
5—Battle of Carthage (Missouri).
11—Battle of Rich Mountain (western Virginia).
13—Battle of Carrick's Ford (western Virginia).
18—Battle of Blackburn's Ford (Virginia).
20—3rd Session, Provincial Confederate Congress, convenes.
21—Battle of 1st Bull Run (Virginia).

AUGUST 1861
6—1st Session, 37th Congress adjourns.
10—Battle of Wilson's Creek.
27—Fort Clark, North Carolina, captured by Union.

28—Fort Hatteras, North Carolina, surrenders to Union.
31—3rd Session, Provisional Confederate Congress, adjourns.

SEPTEMBER 1861

3—4th (called) Session, Provisional Confederate Congress, convenes and adjourns; Confederate troops enter Kentucky, ending the state's neutrality.
6—Union troops capture Paducah, Kentucky.
10—Battle of Carnifax Ferry (Virginia).
11—Cheat Mountain Campaign (to the 15th).
12—Siege of Lexington, Missouri (to the 20th).
20—Lexington, Missouri, surrenders to Confederates.

OCTOBER 1861

21—Battle of Ball's Bluff (Virginia).

NOVEMBER 1861

6—Jefferson Davis elected regular president of the Confederacy.
7—Belmont, Missouri, and Port Royal, South Carolina, fall to Union.
8—Seizure of Confederates Mason and Slidell from aboard the British *Trent* by the USS *San Jacinto*.
18—5th Session, Provisional Confederate Congress, convenes.
28—Missouri admitted to Confederacy despite its not having seceded.

DECEMBER 1861

2—2nd Session, 37th Congress, convenes.
13—Battle of Camp Alleghany (western Virginia).
20—Battle of Dranesville (Virginia).

JANUARY 1862

19—Battle of Mill Springs (or Fishing Creek, Logan's Crossroads) (Kentucky).

FEBRUARY 1862

6—Battle of Fort Henry (Tennessee).
8—Battle of Roanoke Island (North Carolina).
12—Battle of Fort Donelson (Tennessee) (to the 16th).
16—Fort Donelson surrenders to Union.
17—5th (final) Session, Provisional Confederate Congress, adjourns.
18—1st Session, 1st Confederate Congress, convenes.
21—Battle of Valverde (New Mexico Territory).
22—Jefferson Davis inaugurated as regular president.

MARCH 1862

6—Battle of Pea Ridge (Arkansas) (to the 8th).
8—Hampton Roads Naval Actions (Virginia) (to the 9th).
9—*Monitor* vs. *Virginia* at Hampton Roads.
14—Capture of New Madrid, Missouri, and New Bern, North Carolina, by Union.
23—Battle of Kernstown (Virginia).
26—Battle of Apache Canyon (New Mexico Territory).
28—Battle of Glorieta (or Pigeon's Ranch) (New Mexico Territory).

APRIL 1862

5—Siege of Yorktown, Virginia (to May 4).
6—Battle of Shiloh (Tennessee) (to the 7th).
7—Island # 10 (Missouri) falls to Union.
11—Fort Pulaski (Georgia) captured by Union.
18—Bombardment of Forts Jackson and St. Philip, Louisiana (to the 24th).
21—1st Session, 1st Confederate Congress, adjourns.
24—Federal naval forces pass Forts Jackson and St. Philip below New Orleans.
25—Fort Macon, North Carolina, captured and New Orleans falls to Union.

MAY 1862

4—Yorktown, Virginia, occupied by Union.
5—Battle of Williamsburg (Virginia).
8—Battle of McDowell (West Virginia).
10—Norfolk, Virginia, occupied by Union; battle of Plum Bend (Tennessee).
15—Battle of Drewry's Bluff (Virginia).
23—Battle of Front Royal (Virginia).
25—Battle of 1st Winchester (Virginia).
30—Corinth, Mississippi, taken by Union.
31—Battle of Seven Pines or Fair Oaks (Virginia) (to June 1st).

JUNE 1862

5—Fort Pillow, Tennessee, abandoned by Confederates.
6—Battle of Memphis (Tennessee).
8—Battle of Cross Keys (Virginia).
9—Battle of Port Republic (Virginia).
16—Battle of Secessionville (South Carolina).
25—Battles of the Seven Days (Virginia) (to July 1; includes those marked with *).
26—Beaver Dam Creek*.
27—Gaines' Mill*.
29—Savage Station*.
30—Frayser's Farm*; White Oak Swamp*.

JULY 1862

1—Malvern Hill*.
17—2nd Session, 37th Congress, adjourns.

AUGUST 1862

5—Battle of Baton Rouge (Louisiana).
9—Battle of Cedar (or Slaughter) Mountain (Virginia).
17—Sioux uprising (to September 23) in Minnesota.
18—2nd Session, 1st Confederate Congress, convenes.
28—Battle of 2nd Bull Run (Virginia) (to the 30th).
30—Battle of Richmond (Kentucky).

SEPTEMBER 1862

1—Battle of Chantilly (Virginia).
14—Battles of South Mountain (Maryland) and Crampton's Gap (Maryland).
15—Fall of Harpers Ferry, West Virginia, to Confederates.
17—Battles of Antietam (Maryland) and Munfordville (Kentucky).

19—Battle of Iuka (Mississippi).
22—Emancipation Proclamation issued.

OCTOBER 1862

3—Battle of Corinth (Mississippi) (to the 4th).
8—Battle of Perryville (Kentucky).
13—2nd Session, 1st Confederate Congress, convenes.

DECEMBER 1862

1—3rd Session, 37th Congress, convenes.
7—Battle of Prairie Grove (Arkansas).
13—Battle of Fredericksburg (Virginia).
20—Holly Springs, Mississippi, raided by Southerners.
29—Battle of Chickasaw Bayou (Mississippi).
31—Battle of Murfreesboro (Tennessee) (to January 2, 1863).

JANUARY 1863

1—Emancipation Proclamation takes effect; battle of Galveston Harbor (Texas).
11—Arkansas Post, Arkansas, captured by Union forces.
12—3rd Session, 1st Confederate Congress, convenes.
19—"Mud March" (to the 22nd) by Army of the Potomac from Rappahannock River.
31—Charleston blockade disrupted (South Carolina).

MARCH 1863

3—3rd (final) Session, 37th Congress, adjourns.
4—Special Senate Session, 38th Congress, convenes.
11—Yazoo Pass Expedition blocked at Fort Pemberton, Mississippi.
14—Special Senate Session, 38th Congress, adjourns.
17—Battle of Kelly's Ford (Virginia).

APRIL 1863

7—Charleston naval attack by Union ironclads.
17—Grierson's Raid begins from La Grange, Tennessee.

MAY 1863

1—3rd Session, 1st Confederate Congress, adjourns; battle of Port Gibson (Mississippi) (Vicksburg Campaign); battle of Chancellorsville (Virginia) (to the 4th).
12—Battle of Raymond (Mississippi) (Vicksburg Campaign).
14—Battle of Jackson (Mississippi) (Vicksburg Campaign).
16—Battle of Champion Hill (Mississippi) (Vicksburg Campaign).
17—Battle of Big Black River Bridge (Mississippi) (Vicksburg Campaign).
18—Vicksburg, Mississippi, siege begins (to July 4).
19—1st Vicksburg assault by Union.
21—Port Hudson, Louisiana, siege begins (to July 8).
22—2nd Union assault at Vicksburg, Mississippi.
27—1st Union assault at Port Hudson, Louisiana.

JUNE 1863

7—Battle of Milliken's Bend (Louisiana).
9—Battle of Brandy Station (Virginia).
14—2nd Union assault at Port Hudson; battle of 2nd Winchester (Virginia).
15—Stephenson's Depot (Virginia).
23—Tullahoma Campaign begun by Union (Tennessee) (to July 7).

JULY 1863

1—Battle of Gettysburg (Pennsylvania) (to the 3rd).
4—Vicksburg, Mississippi, surrenders to Union.
8—Port Hudson, Louisiana, surrenders to Union; Morgan's raid north of the Ohio begins in Indiana (to the 26th).
10—Union siege of Battery Wagner in Charleston Harbor, South Carolina, begins (to September 6).
11—1st Union assault on Battery Wagner in Charleston Harbor.
13—New York City draft riots begin (to the 15th).
18—2nd Union assault on Battery Wagner in Charleston Harbor.
26—John Hunt Morgan captured at New Lisbon, Ohio.

AUGUST 1863

17—Fort Sumter, South Carolina, bombarded by Union.
21—Lawrence, Kansas, sacked by Quantrill's Confederate raiders.

SEPTEMBER 1863

6—Battery Wagner in Charleston Harbor abandoned by Confederates.
10—Little Rock, Arkansas, captured by Union.
19—Battle of Chickamauga (Georgia) (to the 20th).

OCTOBER 1863

9—Bristoe Campaign begins in Virginia (to the 22nd).
14—Battle of Bristoe Station (Virginia).

NOVEMBER 1863

7—Battle of Rappahannock Station (Virginia).
23—Battle of Chattanooga (Tennessee) (to the 25th).
26—Mine Run Campaign begins in Virginia (to December 2).
29—Battle of Fort Sanders (Knoxville, Tennessee).

DECEMBER 1863

7—4th Session, 1st Confederate Congress, convenes; 1st Session, 38th Congress, convenes.

FEBRUARY 1864

3—Meridian Campaign begins in Mississippi (to the 14th).
17—4th (final) Session, 1st Confederate Congress, adjourns.
20—Battle of Olustee (Florida).
22—Battle of Okolona (Mississippi).

MARCH 1864

12—Red River Campaign begins (Louisiana).

APRIL 1864

8—Battle of Mansfield (Louisiana).
9—Battle of Pleasant Hill (Louisiana).

12—Fort Pillow, Tennessee, massacre; battle of Blair's Landing (Louisiana) (to the 13th).
17—Battle of Plymouth (North Carolina) (to the 20th).
30—Battle of Jenkins' Ferry (Arkansas).

MAY 1864

2—1st Session, 2nd Confederate Congress, convenes.
5—Battle of the Wilderness (Virginia) (to the 6th).
6—Battle of Port Walthall Junction (Virginia) (to the 7th).
7—Atlanta Campaign (to September 2) begins from Chattanooga, Tennessee.
8—Battle of Spotsylvania (Virginia) (to the 21st).
9—Battles of Snake Creek Gap and Dalton (Georgia) (latter to the 13th).
11—Battle of Yellow Tavern (Virginia).
14—Battle of Resaca (Georgia) to the 15th.
15—Battle of New Market (Virginia).
16—Battle of Drewry's Bluff (Virginia).
23—Battle of the North Anna (Virginia) (to the 26th).
25—Battle of New Hope Church (Georgia) (to June 4).
30—Bethesda Church (Virginia) (to June 3).

JUNE 1864

1—Battle of Cold Harbor (Virginia) (to the 3rd).
10—Battle of Brice's Crossroads (Mississippi).
11—Battle of Trevilian Station (Virginia).
14—1st Session, 2nd Confederate Congress, adjourns; battle of Pine Mountain (Georgia).
15—Petersburg, Virginia, assaults (to the 18th) by Union.
18—Petersburg, Virginia, siege begun by Union (to April 2, 1865).
27—Battle of Kennesaw Mountain (Georgia).

JULY 1864

4—1st Session, 38th Congress, adjourns.
9—Battle of Monocacy (Maryland).
11—Battle of Fort Stevens (Maryland).
14—Battle of Tupelo (Mississippi).
20—Battle of Peachtree Creek (Georgia).
22—Battle of Atlanta (Georgia).
28—Battle of Ezra Church (Georgia).
30—Petersburg Mine exploded by Union sappers and battle of the Crater follows (Virginia).

AUGUST 1864

5—Battle of Mobile Bay (Alabama).
18—Battle of the Weldon Railroad (Virginia) (to the 19th).
25—Battle of Reams' Station (Virginia).
31—Battle of Jonesboro (Georgia) (to September 1).

SEPTEMBER 1864

2—Atlanta occupied by Union troops (Georgia).
19—3rd Battle of Winchester (Virginia).
22—Battle of Fisher's Hill (Virginia).
29—Battle of Peebles' Farm (to October 2) and Chaffin's Farm/Fort Harrison (to October 1) (Virginia).

OCTOBER 1864

5—Battle of Allatoona (Georgia).
9—Battle of Tom's Brook (Virginia).
19—Battle of Cedar Creek (Virginia).
23—Battle of Westport (Missouri).
27—Battle of Burgess' Mill/Boydton Plank Road (Virginia).

NOVEMBER 1864

7—2nd Session, 2nd Confederate Congress, convenes.
8—Lincoln reelected.
16—March to the Sea (to December 21) begins from Atlanta, Georgia.
29—Battles of Spring Hill (Tennessee) and Sand Creek (Colorado Territory).
30—Battle of Franklin (Tennessee).

DECEMBER 1864

5—2nd Session, 38th Congress, convenes.
15—Battle of Nashville (Tennessee) (to the 16th).
21—Savannah, Georgia, occupied by Union.
24—1st Union attack on Fort Fisher, North Carolina (to the 25th).

JANUARY 1865

13—2nd Union attack on Fort Fisher (to the 15th).
15—Fort Fisher, North Carolina, falls to Union naval and land forces.
19—Carolinas Campaign begins at Savannah, Georgia (to April 26).

FEBRUARY 1865

5—Battle of Hatcher's Run (Virginia) (to the 7th).

MARCH 1865

2—Battle of Waynesboro (Virginia).
3—2nd (final) Session, 38th Congress, adjourns.
4—Lincoln reinaugurated.
8—Battle of Kinston (North Carolina) (to the 10th).
16—Battle of Averysboro (North Carolina).
18—2nd (final) Session 2nd Confederate Congress, adjourns.
19—Battle of Bentonville (North Carolina) (to the 21st).
22—Wilson's raid (to April 24) south into Alabama.
25—Battle of Fort Stedman (Virginia); siege of Mobile, Alabama (to April 12).
31—Battle of Dinwiddie Court House (Virginia).

APRIL 1865

1—Battle of Five Forks (Virginia).
2—Selma, Alabama, falls; final Union assault on Petersburg, Virginia.
3—Richmond and Petersburg occupied by Union forces.
6—Battle of Sayler's Creek (Virginia).
7—Battle of High Bridge (Virginia).
9—Battles of Appomattox (Virginia) and Fort Blakely (Alabama); Lee surrenders at Appomattox.

12—Mobile, Alabama, surrenders to Union forces.
14—Lincoln shot by John Wilkes Booth.
15—Lincoln dies.
26—Johnston surrenders to Sherman in North Carolina.

MAY 1865

4—Taylor surrenders to Canby in Alabama.
26—Smith surrenders to Canby in Trans—Mississippi.

JUNE 1865

28—CSS *Shenandoah* ends operations in Bering Sea, having taken 11 whalers that day.

AUGUST 1865

2—CSS *Shenandoah* learns of end of the war.

NOVEMBER 1865

6—CSS *Shenandoah* surrenders to British at Liverpool.

APPENDIX B

OFFICERS RECEIVING THE THANKS OF THE U.S. CONGRESS

Name	For
Bailey, Joseph	Rescue of gunboats during Red River Campaign
Banks, Nathaniel P.	Capture of Port Hudson
Burnside, Ambrose E.	Defense of Knoxville
Grant, Ulysses S.	War to date, December 17, 1863
Hancock, Winfield S.	Gettysburg
Hooker, Joseph	Early part of Gettysburg Campaign
Howard, Oliver O.	Gettysburg
Lyon, Nathaniel	Wilson's Creek
Meade, George Gordon	Gettysburg
Rosecrans, William S.	Murfreesboro
Sheridan, Philip H.	Cedar Creek
Sherman, William T.	Relief of Chattanooga
Sherman, William T.	Atlanta Campaign and March to the Sea
Terry, Alfred H.	Capture of Fort Fisher
Thomas, George H.	Nashville

SELECTED BIBLIOGRAPHY

Amann, William. *Personnel of the Civil War*. Thomas Yoseloff: New York, 1961. Provides valuable information on local unit designations, general officer assignments, and organizational data on geographical commands.

Boatner, Mark Mayo III. *The Civil War Dictionary*. David McKay Company: New York, 1959. Provides thumbnail sketches of leaders, battles, campaigns, events, units, weapons, etc. While generally an excellent work, there is a lack of coverage of naval figures and of Confederates below the rank of general. Also, for some of the Union officers, included because of their brevets to the rank of brigadier general, there is little indication of what they did to earn them. There is also little coverage of congressmen. Some of author's statements as to the presence of certain officers at certain battles can be contradicted in the *Official Records*.

Bowman, John S., ed. *The Civil War Almanac*. Facts On File, Inc: New York, 1982. Basically a chronology of events, it is also valuable for its sections on naval matters and weapons and its approximately 130 biographical sketches of civilian and military personalities.

Cullum, George W. *Biographical Register of the Officers and Graduates of the United States Military Academy*, 2 vols. J.F. Throw: New York, 1891. Especially valuable for providing information upon the stations of officers in the pre- and postwar years.

Cyclopedia of American Bibliography, 7 vols. Appleton & Co.: New York, 1891. A general biographical work that provides some information, albeit limited, on the Civil War careers of those covered in its seven volumes.

Dictionary of American Biography, 20 vols. Charles Scribner's Sons: New York, 1928. Being a more general work, it provides only limited information on the Civil War careers of the personalities which it covers. However, it is a starting point.

Dyer, Frederick H. *A Compendium of the War of the Rebellion*, 3 vols. Dyer Publishing Co.: Des Moines, 1908; National Historical Society: Dayton, 1979 (reprints in 2 vols). Provides histories of all Union regiments and smaller units, indexes of battles by state, and tables of organization for larger units, including the dates for their commanders.

Evans, Clement A., ed. *Confederate Military History*, 13 vols. Confederate Publishing Co.: Atlanta, 1899. The volumes of this work are primarily concerned with providing histories of one or two states in each book. Each state military account was written by a different participant in the war, and they vary in quality. All accounts, however, include biographies of the generals from their state. The Alabama chapter, by Joseph Wheeler, also has histories of the state's regiments. There are also volumes on secession, naval matters, and reconstruction. The major drawback is the lack of a comprehensive index.

Freeman, Douglas Southall. *Lee's Lieutenants: A Study in Command*, 3 vols. Charles Scribner's Sons: New York, 1941-1946. An excellent narrative history of the command structure of the Army of Northern Virginia. The author's *R.E. Lee: A Biography* also proved highly valuable.

Heitman, Francis B. *Historical Register and Dictionary of the United States Army From Its Organization, September 29, 1789, to March 2, 1903*, 2 vols. Government Printing Office: Washington, 1903. For my purposes, the most important of the compilations in this work was that listing the enlistment, assignments, and separation of all regular army officers plus those Civil War volunteers who achieved the grade of general, whether by full grade or brevet. These entries provide information on brevets. Other useful, but briefer, lists cover: wounds suffered by regular army officers, Mexican War volunteer officers, and field-grade volunteer officers in the Civil War.

Henry, Guy V. *Military Record of Civilian Appointments in the United States Army*, 2 vols. Carleton: New York, 1869. Similar to Cullum's work, it proved valuable in determining the careers of the officers appointed from civil life when the regular army was expanded under Lincoln's orders in May 1861.

Johnson, Robert Underwood and Buel, Clarence Clough, eds. *Battles and Leaders of the Civil War*, 4 vols. The Century

Co: New York, 1887. Reprint 1956. Exceptionally valuable for its tables of organization for major battles as well as for its first-person accounts.

Krick, Robert K. *Lee's Colonel's: A Biographical Register of the Field Officers of the Army of Northern Virginia*, 2nd ed. Press of Morningside Bookshop: Dayton, 1984. Brief sketches of the 1,965 field-grade officers who at one time or another served with the Army of Northern Virginia but never achieved the rank of brigadier general. Sketches include, as available, dates and places of birth and death, pre- and postwar careers, height, unit, promotions, wounds, and end of military service. Also included in the 2nd edition is a listing by name and unit of those field-grade officers who never served with Lee.

Long, E.B. and Barbara. *The Civil War Day By Day: An Almanac 1861-1865*. Doubleday: Garden City, 1971. An excellent chronology of the conflict, with much information on organizational changes and assignments of commanders.

Lonn, Ella. *Foreigners in the Confederacy*. University of North Carolina Press: Chapel Hill, 1940; and *Foreigners in the Union Army and Navy*. Louisiana State University Press: Baton Rouge, 1951. Accounts of the foreign-born contribution to the Civil War.

Scharf, J. Thomas. *History of the Confederate States Navy: From Its Organization to the Surrender of Its Last Vessels*. Joseph McDonough: Albany, 1887. A rather disjointed narrative of Confederate naval operations, but it does provide thumbnail sketches of some officers. The prime defect of this book, as with most from its period, is the lack of an adequate index. It was written by an ex-Confederate midshipman.

Sifakis, Carl. *The Dictionary of Historical Nicknames: A Treasury of More than 7,500 Famous and Infamous Nicknames From World History*. Facts On File: New York, 1984. Provides the origins of nicknames of Civil War personalities.

U.S. Navy Department. *Official Records of the Union and Confederate Navies in the War of Rebellion*, 31 vols. Government Printing Office: Washington, 1894-1927. U.S. War Department. *The War of Rebellion: A Compilation of the Official Records of the Union and Confederate Armies*, 70 vols. in 128 books divided into four series, plus Atlas. Government Printing Office: Washington, 1881-1901. The two most important of primary sources on the military aspects of the Civil War. While difficult to use they provide a goldmine of information. Organized by campaigns in specified geographic regions, they are subdivided into post-action reports and correspondence. In the War Department series special volumes deal with prisoners of war and correspondence between the two governments. For my book's purpose the information contained in the hundreds of organizational tables and the orders assigning officers to duty proved exceedingly valuable.

Wakelyn, Jon L. *Biographical Dictionary of the Confederacy*. Greenwood Press: Westport, Connecticut, 1977. Short biographies of 651 leaders of the Confederacy, including congressmen, cabinet members, governors, bureaucrats, clergy, surgeons, and military leaders. However, the selection criteria in the latter category is somewhat confusing.

Warner, Ezra. *Generals in Gray: Lives of the Confederate Commanders*. Louisiana State University Press: Baton Rouge, 1959; and *Generals in Blue: Lives of the Union Commanders*. Louisiana State University Press: Baton Rouge, 1964. Sketches of the 583 Union and 425 Southern generals. Good coverage of pre- and postwar careers. The wartime portion of the entries tends to be far more complete for the Northern generals.

Warner, Ezra J. and Yearns, W. Buck. *Biographical Register of the Confederate Congress*. Louisiana State University Press: Baton Rouge, 1975. Biographical sketches of the 267 Southern congressmen, providing coverage of pre- and postwar careers, committee assignments, policy concerns, and electoral opponents. Maps of the congressional districts are also included.

Wise, Jennings Cropper. *The Long Arm of Lee: The History of the Artillery of the Army of Northern Virginia*. J.P. Bell Co.: Lynchburg, Virginia, 1915 (reprint 1959). An excellent study of Lee's artillery, providing valuable information on the artillery commanders.

Wright, Marcus J. *General Officers of the Confederate Army*. Neale Publishing Co.: New York, 1911. Long the definitive work on the Southern command structure, it was superseded by Ezra J. Warner's work.

PERIODICALS

Civil War Times Illustrated, its predecessor *Civil War Times*, *American History Illustrated*, and *Civil War History* all provide articles on Civil War personalities. In addition, the *Southern Historical Society Papers* (47 vols., 1876-1930) are a goldmine of information on Confederate units and leaders.

INDEX